KU-439-076

IMMIGRATION LAW HANDBOOK

Ninth Edition

MARGARET PHELAN

AND

JAMES GILLESPIE

Barrister (retired)

OXFORD
UNIVERSITY PRESS

OXFORD
UNIVERSITY PRESS

Great Clarendon Street, Oxford, OX2 6DP,
United Kingdom

Oxford University Press is a department of the University of Oxford.
It furthers the University's objective of excellence in research, scholarship,
and education by publishing worldwide. Oxford is a registered trade mark of
Oxford University Press in the UK and in certain other countries

© Margaret Phelan and James Gillespie, 2015

The moral rights of the authors have been asserted

First Edition published in 1997
Ninth Edition published in 2015

Impression: 2

All rights reserved. No part of this publication may be reproduced, stored in
a retrieval system, or transmitted, in any form or by any means, without the
prior permission in writing of Oxford University Press, or as expressly permitted
by law, by licence or under terms agreed with the appropriate reprographics
rights organization. Enquiries concerning reproduction outside the scope of the
above should be sent to the Rights Department, Oxford University Press, at the
address above

You must not circulate this work in any other form
and you must impose this same condition on any acquirer

Crown copyright material is reproduced under Class Licence
Number C01P0000148 with the permission of OPSI
and the Queen's Printer for Scotland

Published in the United States of America by Oxford University Press
198 Madison Avenue, New York, NY 10016, United States of America

British Library Cataloguing in Publication Data
Data available

Library of Congress Control Number: 2014950231

ISBN 978–0–19–872408–7

Printed in Great Britain by
Ashford Colour Press Ltd, Gosport, Hampshire

Links to third party websites are provided by Oxford in good faith and
for information only. Oxford disclaims any responsibility for the materials
contained in any third party website referenced in this work.

CONTENTS

EUROPEAN MATERIALS

INTERNATIONAL MATERIALS

PREFACE

In 2010 Lord Neuberger MR (as he then was) observed that "immigration and asylum law have been the subject of a large and increasing, almost bewildering volume of legislation..." (*ZA (Nigeria) v SSHD*). The sense of bewilderment has been added to in the two years since the last edition with considerable changes both to statutes and Immigration Rules. The Statutes section of the 9th edition has been substantially amended to include the Immigration Act 2014, which introduces new restrictions on access to housing and other facilities and services as well as making significant changes to existing law affecting detention, enforcement, marriage, deprivation of citizenship and other areas. These changes are incorporated in the text of the affected legislation. As with previous editions, amendments to the text of statutory provisions include changes that have not yet come into force. The text of the materials in the Statutes and Statutory Instruments section reflects legislation passed or made up to 20 October 2014.

There have been some 21 Statements of Changes to the Immigration Rules since the last edition. As Lord Justice Aikens said in *MM* [2014] EWCA Civ 985: "The IRs are voluminous and they change with dizzying frequency". The text of the Immigration Rules included in this edition reflects all changes up to and including those in HC 693 published on 16 October 2014. To date there have been no further changes. The annotations to the Immigration Rules identify those changes that have been made to the Rules since the last edition. As with the statutes the text of the Immigration Rules includes published changes that have not yet come into force; where this is the case the annotations state the date when the change will come into effect. In view of the frequency of rule changes, users of the Handbook are reminded of the importance of checking online for any new published changes: www.gov.uk/government/collections/immigration-rules-statement-of-changes.

Other significant new material in this edition includes the new rules of procedure for the First-tier Tribunal and, in the European section, the new Dublin III Regulation governing responsibility for asylum claims in the EU. The international materials have been expanded to include recent Guidelines issued by UNHCR supplementing the Handbook. The UNHCR Handbook and Guidelines are reproduced with the kind permission of UNHCR.

Margaret Phelan
James Gillespie
25 November 2014

STATUTES

Immigration Act 1971
(1971, c. 77)

Arrangement of Sections

Part I. Regulation of Entry into and Stay in United Kingdom

Part II. Appeals

. . .

Part III. Criminal Proceedings

An Act to amend and replace the present immigration laws, to make certain related changes in the citizenship law and enable help to be given to those wishing to return abroad, and for purposes connected therewith. [28 October 1971]

PART I

REGULATION OF ENTRY INTO AND STAY IN UNITED KINGDOM

1. General principles

(1) All those who are in this Act expressed to have the right of abode in the United Kingdom shall be free to live in and to come and go into and from, the United Kingdom

without let or hindrance except such as may be required under and in accordance with this Act to enable their right to be established or as may be otherwise lawfully imposed on any person.

(2) Those not having that right may live, work and settle in the United Kingdom by permission and subject to such regulation and control of their entry into, stay in and departure from the United Kingdom as is imposed by this Act; and indefinite leave to enter or remain in the United Kingdom shall, by virtue of this provision, be treated as having been given under this Act to those in the United Kingdom at its coming into force, if they are then settled there (and not exempt under this Act from the provisions relating to leave to enter or remain).

(3) Arrival in and departure from the United Kingdom on a local journey from or to any of the Islands (that is to say, the Channel Islands and Isle of Man) or the Republic of Ireland shall not be subject to control under this Act, nor shall a person require leave to enter the United Kingdom on so arriving, except in so far as any of those places is for any purpose excluded from this subsection under the powers conferred by this Act; and in this Act the United Kingdom and those places, or such of them as are not so excluded, are collectively referred to as 'the common travel area'.

(4) The rules laid down by the Secretary of State as to the practice to be followed in the administration of this Act for regulating the entry into and stay in the United Kingdom of persons not having the right of abode shall include provision for admitting (in such cases and subject to such restrictions as may be provided by the rules, and subject or not to conditions as to length of stay or otherwise) persons coming for the purpose of taking employment, or for purposes of study, or as visitors, or as dependants of persons lawfully in or entering the United Kingdom.

(5) . . .

Note: Section 1(5) repealed by Immigration Act 1988, s 1.

[2. Statement of right of abode in United Kingdom

(1) A person is under this Act to have the right of abode in the United Kingdom if—

(a) he is a British citizen; or

(b) he is a Commonwealth citizen who—

(i) immediately before the commencement of the British Nationality Act 1981 was a Commonwealth citizen having the right of abode in the United Kingdom by virtue of section 2(1)(d) or section 2(2) of this Act as then in force; and

(ii) has not ceased to be a Commonwealth citizen in the meanwhile.

(2) In relation to Commonwealth citizens who have the right of abode in the United Kingdom by virtue of subsection (1)(b) above, this Act, except this section and [section 5(2)], shall apply as if they were British citizens; and in this Act (except as aforesaid) 'British citizen' shall be construed accordingly.]

Note: Section 2 substituted by British Nationality Act 1981, s 39(2). Words in square brackets in s 2(2) substituted by the Immigration Act 1988, s 3(3).

[2A. Deprivation of right of abode

(1) The Secretary of State may by order remove from a specified person a right of abode in the United Kingdom which he has under section 2(1)(b).

(2) The Secretary of State may make an order under subsection (1) in respect of a person only if the Secretary of State thinks that it would be conducive to the public good for the person to be excluded or removed from the United Kingdom.

(3) An order under subsection (1) may be revoked by order of the Secretary of State.

(4) While an order under subsection (1) has effect in relation to a person—

(a) section 2(2) shall not apply to him, and

(b) any certificate of entitlement granted to him shall have no effect.]

Note: Section 2A inserted by Immigration, Asylum and Nationality Act 2006, s 57(1) from 16 June 2006 (SI 2006/1497).

3. General provisions for regulation and control

(1) Except as otherwise provided by or under this Act, where a person is not [a British citizen]—

(a) he shall not enter the United Kingdom unless given leave to do so in accordance with [the provisions of, or made under,] this Act;

(b) he may be given leave to enter the United Kingdom (or, when already there, leave to remain in the United Kingdom) either for a limited or for an indefinite period);

[(c) if he is given limited leave to enter or remain in the United Kingdom, it may be given subject to all or any of the following conditions, namely—

(i) a condition restricting his employment or occupation in the United Kingdom;

[(ia) a condition restricting his studies in the United Kingdom;]

(ii) a condition requiring him to maintain and accommodate himself, and any dependants of his, without recourse to public funds;. . .

(iii) a condition requiring him to register with the police.

{(iv) a condition requiring him to report to an immigration officer or the Secretary of State; and

(v) a condition about residence.}]

(2) The Secretary of State shall from time to time (and as soon as may be) lay before Parliament statements of the rules, or of any changes in the rules, laid down by him as to the practice to be followed in the administration of this Act for regulating the entry into and stay in the United Kingdom of persons required by this Act to have leave to enter, including any rules as to the period for which leave is to be given and the conditions to be attached in different circumstances; and section 1(4) above shall not be taken to require uniform provision to be made by the rules as regards admission of persons for a purpose or in a capacity specified in section 1(4) (and in particular, for this as well as other purposes of this Act, account may be taken of citizenship or nationality).

If a statement laid before either House of Parliament under this subsection is disapproved by a resolution of that House passed within the period of forty days beginning with the date of laying (and exclusive of any period during which Parliament is dissolved or prorogued or during which both Houses are adjourned for more than four days), then the Secretary of State shall as soon as may be make such changes or further changes in the rules as appear to him to be required in the circumstances, so that the statement of those changes be laid before Parliament at latest by the end of the period of forty days beginning with the date of the resolution (but exclusive as aforesaid).

(3) In the case of a limited leave to enter or remain in the United Kingdom,—

(a) a person's leave may be varied, whether by restricting, enlarging or removing the limit on its duration, or by adding, varying or revoking conditions, but if the limit on its duration is removed, any conditions attached to the leave shall cease to apply; and

(b) the limitation on and any conditions attached to a person's leave [(whether imposed originally or on a variation) shall], if not superseded, apply also to any subsequent leave he may obtain after an absence from the United Kingdom within the period limited for the duration of the earlier leave.

(4) A person's leave to enter or remain in the United Kingdom shall lapse on his going to a country or territory outside the common travel area (whether or not he lands there), unless within the period for which he had leave he returns to the United Kingdom in circumstances in which he is not required to obtain leave to enter; but, if he does so return, his previous leave (and any limitation on it or conditions attached to it) shall continue to apply.

[(5) A person who is not a British citizen is liable to deportation from the United Kingdom if—

(a) the Secretary of State deems his deportation to be conducive to the public good; or

(b) another person to whose family he belongs is or has been ordered to be deported.]

(6) Without prejudice to the operation of subsection (5) above, a person who is not [a British citizen] shall also be liable to deportation from the United Kingdom if, after he has attained the age of seventeen, he is convicted of an offence for which he is punishable with imprisonment and on his conviction is recommended for deportation by a court empowered by this Act to do so.

(7) Where it appears to Her Majesty proper so to do by reason of restrictions or conditions imposed on [British citizens, British Dependent Territories citizens or British Overseas citizens] when leaving or seeking to leave any country or the territory subject to the government of any country, Her Majesty may by Order in Council make provision for prohibiting persons who are nationals or citizens of that country and are not [British citizens] from embarking in the United Kingdom, or from doing so elsewhere than at a port of exit, or for imposing restrictions or conditions on them when embarking or about to embark in the United Kingdom; and Her Majesty may also make provision by Order in Council to enable those who are not [British citizens] to be, in such cases as may be prescribed by the Order, prohibited in the interests of safety from so embarking on a ship or aircraft specified or indicated in the prohibition.

Any Order in Council under this subsection shall be subject to annulment in pursuance of a resolution of either House of Parliament.

(8) When any question arises under this Act whether or not a person is [a British citizen], or is entitled to any exemption under this Act, it shall lie on the person asserting it to prove that he is.

[(9) A person seeking to enter the United Kingdom and claiming to have the right of abode there shall prove it by means of—

(a) a United Kingdom passport describing him as a British citizen,

(b) a United Kingdom passport describing him as a British subject with the right of abode in the United Kingdom, {or}

(c) . . .

(d) . . .

(e) a certificate of entitlement.]

Note: Section 3(1)(c) substituted by Asylum and Immigration Act 1996 from 1 November 1996. Words in square brackets in s 3(6)–(8) and first square brackets in s 3(1) substituted by British Nationality Act 1981. Words in square brackets in s 3(3) substituted by Immigration Act 1988. Words in square brackets in s 3(1)(a) inserted by Immigration and Asylum Act 1999 from 14 February 2000. Section 3(5) substituted by Immigration and Asylum Act 1999 from 2 October 2000. Section 3(9) substituted by Immigration, Asylum and Nationality Act 2006, s 30 from 16 June 2006 (SI 2006/1497). Subsection (1)(c)(iv) and (v) inserted by UK Borders Act 2007, s 16 from 31 January 2008 (SI 2008/99). Subsection (1)(c)(ia) inserted by Borders, Citizenship and Immigration Act 2009, s 50(1) from 21 July 2009. Subsections (9)(c) and (d) omitted by Identity Documents Act 2010, Schedule, paragraph 1 from 21 January 2011 (s 14). Section 3 has effect in a form modified by and in circumstances specified by the Channel Tunnel (International Arrangements) Order (SI 1993/1813) as amended by SIs 1994/1405, 2000/913, 2001/178, 2001/3707, 2006/1003 and 2007/3759.

[3A. Further provision as to leave to enter

(1) The Secretary of State may by order make further provision with respect to the giving, refusing or varying of leave to enter the United Kingdom.

(2) An order under subsection (1) may, in particular, provide for—

(a) leave to be given or refused before the person concerned arrives in the United Kingdom;

(b) the form or manner in which leave may be given, refused or varied;

(c) the imposition of conditions;

(d) a person's leave to enter not to lapse on his leaving the common travel area.

(3) The Secretary of State may by order provide that, in such circumstances as may be prescribed—

(a) an entry visa, or

(b) such other form of entry clearance as may be prescribed, is to have effect as leave to enter the United Kingdom.

(4) An order under subsection (3) may, in particular—

(a) provide for a clearance to have effect as leave to enter—

(i) on a prescribed number of occasions during the period for which the clearance has effect;

(ii) on an unlimited number of occasions during that period;

(iii) subject to prescribed conditions; and

(b) provide for a clearance which has the effect referred to in paragraph (a)(i) or (ii) to be varied by the Secretary of State or an immigration officer so that it ceases to have that effect.

(5) Only conditions of a kind that could be imposed on leave to enter given under section 3 may be prescribed.

(6) In subsections (3), (4) and (5) 'prescribed' means prescribed in an order made under subsection (3).

(7) The Secretary of State may, in such circumstances as may be prescribed in an order made by him, give or refuse leave to enter the United Kingdom.

(8) An order under subsection (7) may provide that, in such circumstances as may be prescribed by the order, paragraphs 2, 4, 6, 7, 8, 9 and 21 of Part I of Schedule 2 to this Act are to be read, in relation to the exercise by the Secretary of State of functions which he has as a result of the order, as if references to an immigration officer included references to the Secretary of State.

(9) Subsection (8) is not to be read as affecting any power conferred by subsection (10).

(10) An order under this section may—

(a) contain such incidental, supplemental, consequential and transitional provision as the Secretary of State considers appropriate; and

(b) make different provision for different cases.

(11) This Act and any provision made under it has effect subject to any order made under this section.

(12) An order under this section must be made by statutory instrument.

(13) But no such order is to be made unless a draft of the order has been laid before Parliament and approved by a resolution of each House.]

Note: Section 3A inserted by Immigration and Asylum Act 1999 from 14 February 2000.

[3B. Further provision as to leave to remain

(1) The Secretary of State may by order make further provision with respect to the giving, refusing or varying of leave to remain in the United Kingdom.

(2) An order under subsection (1) may, in particular, provide for—

(a) the form or manner in which leave may be given, refused or varied;

(b) the imposition of conditions;

(c) a person's leave to remain in the United Kingdom not to lapse on his leaving the common travel area.

(3) An order under this section may—

(a) contain such incidental, supplemental, consequential and transitional provision as the Secretary of State considers appropriate; and

(b) make different provision for different cases.

(4) This Act and any provision made under it has effect subject to any order made under this section.

(5) An order under this section must be made by statutory instrument.

(6) But no such order is to be made unless a draft of the order has been laid before Parliament and approved by a resolution of each House.]

Note: Section 3B inserted by Immigration and Asylum Act 1999 from 14 February 2000.

[3C. Continuation of leave pending variation decision

(1) This section applies if—

(a) a person who has limited leave to enter or remain in the United Kingdom applies to the Secretary of State for variation of the leave,

(b) the application for variation is made before the leave expires, and

(c) the leave expires without the application for variation having been decided.

(2) The leave is extended by virtue of this section during any period when—

(a) the application for variation is neither decided nor withdrawn,

(b) an appeal under section 82(1) of the Nationality, Asylum and Immigration Act 2002 could be brought [, while the appellant is in the United Kingdom] against the decision on the application for variation (ignoring any possibility of an appeal out of time with permission),

(c) an appeal under that section against that decision [, brought while the appellant is in the United Kingdom,] is pending (within the meaning of section 104 of that Act)[, or

(d) an administrative review of the decision on the application for variation—

(i) could be sought, or

(ii) is pending]

(3) Leave extended by virtue of this section shall lapse if the applicant leaves the United Kingdom.

(4) A person may not make an application for variation of his leave to enter or remain in the United Kingdom while that leave is extended by virtue of this section.

(5) But subsection (4) does not prevent the variation of the application mentioned in subsection (1)(a).

[(6) The Secretary of State may make regulations determining when an application is decided for the purposes of this section; and the regulations—

(a) may make provision by reference to receipt of a notice,

(b) may provide for a notice to be treated as having been received in specified circumstances,

(c) may make different provision for different purposes or circumstances,

(d) shall be made by statutory instrument, and

(e) shall be subject to annulment in pursuance of a resolution of either House of Parliament.]]

[(7) In this section—

"administrative review" means a review conducted under the immigration rules; the question of whether an administrative review is pending is to be determined in accordance with the immigration rules.]

Note: Section 3C substituted by Nationality, Immigration and Asylum Act 2002, s 118 from 1 April 2003 (SI 2003/754). Transitional provisions set out in SI 2003/754. Subsection (2)(d) and (7) inserted by Sch 9 Immigration Act 2014 from 20 October 2014 with savings set out in articles 9-11 SI 2014/2771. Other words added to subsection (2)(b) and (c) and subsection (6) substituted by Immigration, Nationality and Asylum Act 2006, s 11 from 31 August 2006 (SI 2006/2226), applying to applications made before that date in respect of which no decision has been made, as it applies to applications made on or after that date.

[3D. Continuation of leave following revocation

(1) This section applies if a person's leave to enter or remain in the United Kingdom—

(a) is varied with the result that he has no leave to enter or remain in the United Kingdom, or

(b) is revoked.

(2) The person's leave is extended by virtue of this section during any period when—

(a) an appeal under section 82(1) of the Nationality, Immigration and Asylum Act 2002 could be brought, while the person is in the United Kingdom, against the variation or revocation (ignoring any possibility of an appeal out of time with permission),

(b) an appeal under that section against the variation or revocation, brought while the appellant is in the United Kingdom, is pending (within the meaning of section 104 of that Act)[, or

(c) an administrative review of the variation or revocation—

(i) could be sought, or

(ii) is pending]

(3) A person's leave as extended by virtue of this section shall lapse if he leaves the United Kingdom.

(4) A person may not make an application for variation of his leave to enter or remain in the United Kingdom while that leave is extended by virtue of this section.]

[(5) In this section—

"administrative review" means a review conducted under the immigration rules;

the question of whether an administrative review is pending is to be determined in accordance with the immigration rules.]

Note: Section 3D inserted by Immigration, Asylum and Nationality Act 2006, s 11 from 31 August 2006 (SI 2006/2226), only in relation to a decision made on or after that date. Subsection (2)(c) and (5) inserted by Immigration Act 2014 Sch 9 from 20 October 2014 with savings set out in articles 9-11 SI 2014/2771.

4. Administration of control

(1) The power under this Act to give or refuse leave to enter the United Kingdom shall be exercised by immigration officers, and the power to give leave to remain in the United Kingdom, or to vary any leave under section 3(3)(a) (whether as regards duration or conditions), shall be exercised by the Secretary of State; and, unless otherwise [allowed by or under] this Act, those powers shall be exercised by notice in writing given to the person affected, except that the powers under section 3(3)(a) may be exercised generally in respect of any class of persons by order made by statutory instrument.

(2) The provisions of Schedule 2 to this Act shall have effect with respect to—

(a) the appointment and powers of immigration officers and medical inspectors for purposes of this Act;

(b) the examination of persons arriving in or leaving the United Kingdom by ship or aircraft, and the special powers exercisable in the case of those who arrive as, or with a view to becoming, members of the crews of ships and aircraft; and

(c) the exercise by immigration officers of their powers in relation to entry into the United Kingdom, and the removal from the United Kingdom of persons refused leave to enter or entering or remaining unlawfully; and

(d) the detention of persons pending examination or pending removal from the United Kingdom;

and for other purposes supplementary to the foregoing provisions of this Act.

(3) The Secretary of State may by regulations made by statutory instrument, which shall be subject to annulment in pursuance of a resolution of either House of Parliament, make provision as to the effect of a condition under this Act requiring a person to register with the police; and the regulations may include provision—

(a) as to the officers of police by whom registers are to be maintained, and as to the form and content of the registers;

(b) as to the place and manner in which anyone is to register and as to the documents and information to be furnished by him, whether on registration or on any change of circumstances;

(c) as to the issue of certificates of registration and as to the payment of fees for certificates of registration;

and the regulations may require anyone who is for the time being subject to such a condition to produce a certificate of registration to such persons and in such circumstances as may be prescribed by the regulations.

(4) The Secretary of State may by order made by statutory instrument, which shall be subject to annulment in pursuance of a resolution of either House of Parliament, make

such provision as appears to him to be expedient in connection with this Act for records to be made and kept of persons staying at hotels and other premises where lodging or sleeping accommodation is provided, and for persons (whether [British citizens] or not) who stay at any such premises to supply the necessary information.

Note: Words in square brackets in s 4(4) substituted by British Nationality Act 1981, s 39(6). Words in square brackets in s 4(1) substituted by Immigration and Asylum Act 1999 from 14 February 2000. Section 4 has effect in a form modified by and in circumstances specified by the Channel Tunnel (International Arrangements) Order (SI 1993/1813) as amended by SIs 1994/1405, 2000/913, 2001/178, 2001/3707, 2006/1003 and 2007/3759.

5. Procedure for, and further provisions as to, deportation

(1) Where a person is under section 3(5) or (6) above liable to deportation, then subject to the following provisions of this Act the Secretary of State may make a deportation order against him, that is to say an order requiring him to leave and prohibiting him from entering the United Kingdom; and a deportation order against a person shall invalidate any leave to enter or remain in the United Kingdom given him before the order is made or while it is in force.

(2) A deportation order against a person may at any time be revoked by a further order of the Secretary of State, and shall cease to have effect if he becomes [a British citizen].

(3) A deportation order shall not be made against a person as belonging to the family of another person if more than eight weeks have elapsed since the other person left the United Kingdom after the making of the deportation order against him; and a deportation order made against a person on that ground shall cease to have effect if he ceases to belong to the family of the other person, or if the deportation order made against the other person ceases to have effect.

(4) For purposes of deportation the following shall be those who are regarded as belonging to another person's family—

(a) where that other person is a man, his wife [or civil partner,] and his or her children under the age of eighteen; and

[(b) where that other person is a woman, her husband [or civil partner,] and her or his children under the age of eighteen;]

and for purposes of this subsection an adopted child, whether legally adopted or not, may be treated as the child of the adopter and, if legally adopted, shall be regarded as the child only of the adopter; an illegitimate child (subject to the foregoing rule as to adoptions) shall be regarded as the child of the mother; and 'wife' includes each of two or more wives.

(5) The provisions of Schedule 3 to this Act shall have effect with respect to the removal from the United Kingdom of persons against whom deportation orders are in force and with respect to the detention or control of persons in connection with deportation.

(6) Where a person is liable to deportation under section [3(5)] or (6) above but, without a deportation order being made against him, leaves the United Kingdom to live permanently abroad, the Secretary of State may make payments of such amounts as he may determine to meet that person's expenses in so leaving the United Kingdom, including travelling expenses for members of his family or household.

Note: Words in square brackets in s 5(2) substituted by British Nationality Act 1981, s 39(6). Figures in square brackets in s 5(6) substituted by Immigration Act 1988, s 10. Section 5(4)(b) substituted by Asylum and Immigration Act 1996 from 1 October 1996. Transitional provisions set out in SI 2003/754. Words in square brackets in subsection (4) inserted by Sch 27 Civil Partnership Act 2004 from 5 December 2005 (SI 2005/3175).

6. Recommendations by court for deportation

(1) Where under section 3(6) above a person convicted of an offence is liable to deportation on the recommendation of a court, he may be recommended for deportation by any court having power to sentence him for the offence unless the court commits him to be sentenced or further dealt with for that offence by another court:

Provided that in Scotland the power to recommend a person for deportation shall be exercisable only by the sheriff or the High Court of Justiciary, and shall not be exercisable by the latter on an appeal unless the appeal is against a conviction on indictment or against a sentence upon such a conviction.

(2) A court shall not recommend a person for deportation unless he has been given not less than seven days notice in writing stating that a person is not liable to deportation if he is [a British citizen] describing the persons who are [British citizens] and stating (so far as material) the effect of section 3(8) above and section 7 below; but the powers of adjournment conferred by [section 10(3) of the Magistrates' Courts Act 1980], [section 179 or 380 of the Criminal Procedure (Scotland) Act 1975] or any corresponding enactment for the time being in force in Northern Ireland shall include power to adjourn, after convicting an offender, for the purpose of enabling a notice to be given to him under this subsection or, if a notice was so given to him less than seven days previously, for the purpose of enabling the necessary seven days to elapse.

(3) For purposes of section 3(6) above—

(a) a person shall be deemed to have attained the age of seventeen at the time of his conviction if, on consideration of any available evidence, he appears to have done so to the court making or considering a recommendation for deportation; and

(b) the question whether an offence is one for which a person is punishable with imprisonment shall be determined without regard to any enactment restricting the imprisonment of young offenders or [persons who have not previously been sentenced to imprisonment]; and for purposes of deportation a person who on being charged with an offence is found to have committed it shall, notwithstanding any enactment to the contrary and notwithstanding that the court does not proceed to conviction, be regarded as a person convicted of the offence, and references to conviction shall be construed accordingly.

(4) Notwithstanding any rule of practice restricting the matters which ought to be taken into account in dealing with an offender who is sentenced to imprisonment, a recommendation for deportation may be made in respect of an offender who is sentenced to imprisonment for life.

(5) Where a court recommends or purports to recommend a person for deportation, the validity of the recommendation shall not be called in question except on an appeal against the recommendation or against the conviction on which it is made; but—

(a) the recommendation shall be treated as a sentence for the purpose of any enactment providing an appeal against sentence;

(b) . . .

(6) A deportation order shall not be made on the recommendation of a court so long as an appeal or further appeal is pending against the recommendation or against the conviction on which it was made; and for this purpose an appeal or further appeal shall be treated as pending (where one is competent but has not been brought) until the expiration of the time for bringing that appeal or, in Scotland, until the expiration of twenty-eight days from the date of the recommendation.

(7) For the purpose of giving effect to any of the provisions of this section in its application to Scotland, the High Court of Justiciary shall have power to make rules by act of adjournal.

Note: Words in first and second square brackets in s 6(2) substituted by British Nationality Act 1981, s 39(6). Words in third square brackets in s 6(2) substituted by Magistrates' Courts Act 1980, s 154. Words in fourth square brackets in s 6(2) substituted by Criminal Procedure (Scotland) Act 1975, s 461. Words in square brackets in s 6(3)(b) substituted (E.W.) by Criminal Justice Act 1972, s 64(1). Words omitted from s 6(5) repealed by Criminal Justice (Scotland) Act 1980, s 83(3) and Criminal Justice Act 1982, ss 77, 78.

7. Exemption from deportation for certain existing residents

(1) Notwithstanding anything in section 3(5) or (6) above but subject to the provisions of this section, a Commonwealth citizen or citizen of the Republic of Ireland who was such a citizen at the coming into force of this Act and was then ordinarily resident in the United Kingdom—

(a) . . .

[(b) shall not be liable to deportation under section 3(5) if at the time of the Secretary of State's decision he had for the last five years been ordinarily resident in the United Kingdom and Islands;] and

(c) shall not on conviction of an offence be recommended for deportation under section 3(6) if at the time of the conviction he had for the last five years been ordinarily resident in the United Kingdom and Islands.

(2) A person who has at any time become ordinarily resident in the United Kingdom or in any of the Islands shall not be treated for the purposes of this section as having ceased to be so by reason only of his having remained there in breach of the immigration laws.

(3) The 'last five years' before the material time under subsection (1)(b) or (c) above is to be taken as a period amounting in total to five years exclusive of any time during which the person claiming exemption under this section was undergoing imprisonment or detention by virtue of a sentence passed for an offence on a conviction in the United Kingdom and Islands, and the period for which he was imprisoned or detained by virtue of the sentence amounted to six months or more.

(4) For purposes of subsection (3) above—

(a) 'sentence' includes any order made on conviction of an offence; and

(b) two or more sentences for consecutive (or partly consecutive) terms shall be treated as a single sentence; and

(c) a person shall be deemed to be detained by virtue of a sentence—

(i) at any time when he is liable to imprisonment or detention by virtue of the sentence, but is unlawfully at large; and

(ii) (unless the sentence is passed after the material time) during any period of custody by which under any relevant enactment the term to be served under the sentence is reduced.

In paragraph (c)(ii) above 'relevant enactment' means [section 240{, 240ZA or 240A} of the Criminal Justice Act 2003] (or, before that section operated, section 17(2) of the Criminal Justice Administration Act 1962) and any similar enactment which is for the time being or has (before or after the passing of this Act) been in force in any part of the United Kingdom and Islands.

(5) Nothing in this section shall be taken to exclude the operation of section 3(8) above in relation to an exemption under this section.

Note: Subsection (1)(a) repealed by Nationality, Immigration and Asylum Act 2002, s 75 from 10 February 2003 (SI 2003/1). Subsection (1)(b) substituted by Nationality, Immigration and Asylum Act 2003, s 75 from 10 February 2003 (SI 2003/1). Words in square brackets in subsection 4 substituted by Sch 32 Criminal Justice Act 2003 from 4 April 2005 (SI 2005/950). Words in curly brackets in subsection 4 inserted by Legal Aid, Sentencing and Punishment of Offenders Act 2012, Sch 13, paragraph 7, from 3 December 2012 (SI 2012/2906).

8. Exceptions for seamen, aircrews and other special cases

(1) Where a person arrives at a place in the United Kingdom as a member of the crew of a ship or aircraft under an engagement requiring him to leave on that ship as a member of the crew, or to leave within seven days on that or another aircraft as a member of its crew, then unless either—

(a) there is in force a deportation order made against him; or

(b) he has at any time been refused leave to enter the United Kingdom and has not since then been given leave to enter or remain in the United Kingdom; or

(c) an immigration officer requires him to submit to examination in accordance with Schedule 2 to this Act;

he may without leave enter the United Kingdom at that place and remain until the departure of the ship or aircraft on which he is required by his engagement to leave.

(2) The Secretary of State may by order exempt any person or class of persons, either unconditionally or subject to such conditions as may be imposed by or under the order, from all or any of the provisions of this Act relating to those who are not [British citizens].

An order under this subsection, if made with respect to a class of persons, shall be made by statutory instrument, which shall be subject to annulment in pursuance of a resolution of either House of Parliament.

(3) [Subject to subsection 3A below,] the provisions of this Act relating to those who are not [British citizens] shall not apply to any person so long as he is a member of a mission (within the meaning of the Diplomatic Privileges Act 1964), a person who is a member of the family and forms part of the household of such a member, or a person otherwise entitled to the like immunity from jurisdiction as is conferred by that Act on a diplomatic agent.

[(3A) For the purposes of subsection (3), a member of a mission other than diplomatic agent (as defined by the 1964 Act) is not to count as a member of a mission unless—

(a) he was resident outside the United Kingdom, and was not in the United Kingdom, when he was offered a post as such a member; and

(b) he has not ceased to be such a member after having taken up the post.]

(4) The provisions of this Act relating to those who are not [British citizens], other than the provisions relating to deportation, shall also not apply to any person so long as either—

(a) he is subject, as a member of the home forces, to service law; or

(b) being a member of a Commonwealth force or of a force raised under the law of any . . . , colony, protectorate or protected state, is undergoing or about to undergo training in the United Kingdom with any body, contingent or detachment of the home forces; or

(c) he is serving or posted for service in the United Kingdom as a member of a visiting force or of any force raised as aforesaid or as a member of an international headquarters or defence organisation designated for the time being by an Order in Council under section 1 of the International Headquarters and Defence Organisations Act 1964.

(5) Where a person having a limited leave to enter or remain in the United Kingdom becomes entitled to an exemption under this section, that leave shall continue to apply after he ceases to be entitled to the exemption, unless it has by then expired; and a person is not to be regarded for purposes of this Act as having been [settled in the United Kingdom at any time when he was entitled under the former immigration laws to any exemption corresponding to any of those afforded by subsection (3) or (4)(b) or (c) above or by any order under subsection (2) above].

[(5A) An order under subsection (2) above may, as regards any person or class of persons to whom it applies, provide for that person or class to be in specified circumstances regarded (notwithstanding the order) as settled in the United Kingdom for the purposes of section 1(1) of the British Nationality Act 1981.]

(6) In this section 'the home forces' means any of Her Majesty's forces other than a Commonwealth force or a force raised under the law of any associated state, colony, protectorate or protected state; 'Commonwealth force' means a force of any country to which provisions of the Visiting Forces Act 1952 apply without an Order in Council under section 1 of the Act; and 'visiting force' means a body, contingent or detachment of the forces of a country to which any of those provisions apply, being a body, contingent or detachment for the time being present in the United Kingdom on the invitation of Her Majesty's Government in the United Kingdom.

Note: Section 8(3A) inserted by Immigration and Asylum Act 1999 from 1 March 2000. First words in square brackets in s 8(3) inserted by Immigration Act 1988. Other words in square brackets in s 8(2), (3), (4) and (5) substituted and s 8(5A) inserted by British Nationality Act 1981. Section 8(3A) substituted by Immigration and Asylum Act 1999 from 1 March 2000. Section 8 has effect in a form modified by and in circumstances specified by the Channel Tunnel (International Arrangements) Order (SI 1993/1813) as amended by SIs 1994/1405, 2000/913, 2001/178, 2001/3707, 2006/1003 and 2007/3759.

[8A. Persons ceasing to be exempt

(1) A person is exempt for the purposes of this section if he is exempt from provisions of this Act as a result of section 8(2) or (3).

(2) If a person who is exempt—

(a) ceases to be exempt, and

(b) requires leave to enter or remain in the United Kingdom as a result, he is to be treated as if he had been given leave to remain in the United Kingdom for a period of 90 days beginning on the day on which he ceased to be exempt.

(3) If—

(a) a person who is exempt ceases to be exempt, and

(b) there is in force in respect of him leave for him to enter or remain in the United Kingdom which expires before the end of the period mentioned in subsection (2), his leave is to be treated as expiring at the end of that period.]

Note: Section 8A inserted by Immigration and Asylum Act 1999 from 1 March 2000.

[8B. Persons excluded from the United Kingdom under international obligations

(1) An excluded person must be refused—

(a) leave to enter the United Kingdom;

(b) leave to remain in the United Kingdom.

(2) A person's leave to enter or remain in the United Kingdom is cancelled on his becoming an excluded person.

(3) A person's exemption from the provisions of this Act as a result of section 8(1), (2) or (3) ceases on his becoming an excluded person.

(4) 'Excluded person' means a person—

(a) named by or under, or

(b) of a description specified in, a designated instrument.

(5) The Secretary of State may by order designate an instrument if it is a resolution of the Security Council of the United Nations or an instrument made by the Council of the European Union and it—

(a) requires that a person is not to be admitted to the United Kingdom (however that requirement is expressed); or

(b) recommends that a person should not be admitted to the United Kingdom (however that recommendation is expressed).

(6) Subsections (1) to (3) are subject to such exceptions (if any) as may be specified in the order designating the instrument in question.

(7) An order under this section must be made by statutory instrument.

(8) Such a statutory instrument shall be laid before Parliament without delay.]

Note: Section 8B inserted by Immigration and Asylum Act 1999 from 1 March 2000.

9. Further provisions as to common travel area

(1) Subject to subsection (5) below, the provisions of Schedule 4 to this Act shall have effect for the purpose of taking account in the United Kingdom of the operation in any of the Islands of the immigration laws there.

(2) Persons who lawfully enter the United Kingdom on a local journey from a place in the common travel area after having either—

(a) entered any of the Islands or the Republic of Ireland on coming from a place outside the common travel area; or

(b) left the United Kingdom while having a limited leave to enter or remain which has since expired;

if they are not [British citizens] (and are not to be regarded under Schedule 4 to this Act as having leave to enter the United Kingdom), shall be subject in the United Kingdom to such restrictions on the period for which they may remain, and such conditions restricting their employment or occupation or requiring them to register with the police or both, as may be imposed by an order of the Secretary of State and may be applicable to them.

(3) Any provision of this Act applying to a limited leave or to conditions attached to a limited leave shall, unless otherwise provided, have effect in relation to a person subject to any restriction or condition by virtue of an order under subsection (2) above as if the provisions of the order applicable to him were terms on which he had been given leave under this Act to enter the United Kingdom.

(4) Section 1(3) above shall not be taken to affect the operation of a deportation order; and, subject to Schedule 4 to this Act, a person who is not [a British citizen] may not by virtue of section 1(3) enter the United Kingdom without leave on a local journey from a place in the common travel area if either—

(a) he is on arrival in the United Kingdom given written notice by an immigration officer stating that, the Secretary of State having issued directions for him not to be given entry to the United Kingdom on the ground that his exclusion is conducive to the public good as being in the interests of national security, he is accordingly refused leave to enter the United Kingdom; or

(b) he has at any time been refused leave to enter the United Kingdom and has not since then been given leave to enter or remain in the United Kingdom.

(5) If it appears to the Secretary of State necessary so to do by reason of differences between the immigration laws of the United Kingdom and any of the Islands, he may by order exclude that island from section 1(3) above for such purposes as may be specified in the order, and references in this Act to the Islands. . .shall apply to an island so excluded so far only as may be provided by order of the Secretary of State.

(6) The Secretary of State shall also have power by order to exclude the Republic of Ireland from section 1(3) for such purposes as may be specified in the order.

(7) An order of the Secretary of State under this section shall be made by statutory instrument, which shall be subject to annulment in pursuance of a resolution of either House of Parliament.

Note: Words in square brackets in s 9(2) and (4) substituted by British Nationality Act 1981, s 39(6). Words omitted from s 9(5) repealed by British Nationality Act 1981, s 52(8).

10. Entry otherwise than by sea or air

(1) Her Majesty may by Order in Council direct that any of the provisions of this Act shall have effect in relation to persons entering or seeking to enter the United Kingdom on arrival otherwise than by ship or aircraft as they have effect in the case of a person arriving by ship or aircraft;. . .

[(1A) Her Majesty may by Order in Council direct that paragraph 27B or 27C of Schedule 2 shall have effect in relation to trains or vehicles as it has effect in relation to ships or aircraft.

(1B) Any Order in Council under this section may make—

(a) such adaptations or modifications of the provisions concerned, and

(b) such supplementary provisions,

as appear to Her Majesty to be necessary or expedient for the purposes of the Order.]

(2) The provision made by an Order in Council under [subsection (1)] may include provision for excluding the Republic of Ireland from section 1(3) of this Act either generally or for any specified purposes.

(3) No recommendation shall be made to Her Majesty to make an Order in Council under this section unless a draft of the Order has been laid before Parliament and approved by a resolution of each House of Parliament.

Note: Words omitted from s 10(1), s 10(1A), s 10(1B) and words in square brackets in s 10(2) substituted by Immigration and Asylum Act 1999, Sch 14 from 3 December 2012 (SI 2012/2906).

11. Construction of references to entry and other phrases relating to travel

(1) A person arriving in the United Kingdom by ship or aircraft shall for purposes of this Act be deemed not to enter the United Kingdom unless and until he disembarks, and on disembarkation at a port shall further be deemed not to enter the United Kingdom so long as he remains in such area (if any) at the port as may be approved for this purpose by an immigration officer; and a person who has not otherwise entered the United Kingdom shall be deemed not to do so as long as he is detained, or temporarily admitted or released while liable to detention, under the powers conferred by Schedule 2 to this Act [or by Part III of the Immigration and Asylum Act 1999] [or section 62 of the Nationality, Immigration and Asylum Act 2002] [or by section 68 of the Nationality, Immigration and Asylum Act 2002].

[**1A** . . .]

(2) In this Act 'disembark' means disembark from a ship or aircraft, and 'embark' means embark in a ship or aircraft; and, except in subsection (1) above,—

(a) references to disembarking in the United Kingdom do not apply to disembarking after a local journey from a place in the United Kingdom or elsewhere in the common travel area; and

(b) references to embarking in the United Kingdom do not apply to embarking for a local journey to a place in the United Kingdom or elsewhere in the common travel area.

(3) Except in so far as the context otherwise requires, references in this Act to arriving in the United Kingdom by ship shall extend to arrival by any floating structure, and 'disembark' shall be construed accordingly; but the provisions of this Act specially relating to members of the crew of a ship shall not by virtue of this provision apply in relation to any floating structure not being a ship.

(4) For purposes of this Act 'common travel area' has the meaning given by section 1(3), and a journey is, in relation to the common travel area, a local journey if but only if it begins and ends in the common travel area and is not made by a ship or aircraft which—

(a) in the case of a journey to a place in the United Kingdom, began its voyage from, or has during its voyage called at, a place not in the common travel area; or

(b) in the case of a journey from a place in the United Kingdom, is due to end its voyage in, or call in the course of its voyage at, a place not in the common travel area.

(5) A person who enters the United Kingdom lawfully by virtue of section 8(1) above, and seeks to remain beyond the time limited by section 8(1), shall be treated for purposes of this Act as seeking to enter the United Kingdom.

Note: Words in first square brackets in subsection (1) inserted by Immigration and Asylum Act 1999, Sch 14, paragraph 48 from a date to be appointed. Words in second square brackets in subsection (1) inserted by Nationality, Immigration and Asylum Act 2002, s 62 from 10 February 2003 (SI 2003/1). Words in third square brackets inserted by SI 2003/1016 from 4 April 2003. Subsection (1A) repealed from 2 August 1993 (SI 1993/1813). Section 11 has effect in a form modified by and in circumstances specified by the Channel Tunnel (International Arrangements) Order (SI 1993/1813) as amended by SIs 1994/1405, 2000/913, 2001/178, 2001/3707, 2006/1003 and 2007/3759. Subsection (1A) deleted from 5 November 1993 (SI 1993/1813).

PART II

APPEALS

. . .

Note: Part II repealed by Immigration and Asylum Act 1999 from 2 October 2000 (SI 2000/2444). Transitional provisions set out in SI 2003/754.

Part III

Criminal Proceedings

24. Illegal entry and similar offences

(1) A person who is not [a British citizen] shall be guilty of an offence punishable on summary conviction with a fine of not more than [level 5] on the standard scale or with imprisonment for not more than six months, or with both, in any of the following cases:—

(a) if contrary to this Act he knowingly enters the United Kingdom in breach of a deportation order or without leave;

(aa) . . .

(b) if, having only a limited leave to enter or remain in the United Kingdom, he knowingly either—

(i) remains beyond the time limited by the leave; or

(ii) fails to observe a condition of the leave;

(c) if, having lawfully entered the United Kingdom without leave by virtue of section 8(1) above, he remains without leave beyond the time allowed by section 8(1);

(d) if, without reasonable excuse, he fails to comply with any requirement imposed on him under Schedule 2 to this Act to report to a medical officer of health, or to attend, or submit to a test or examination, as required by such an officer;

(e) if, without reasonable excuse, he fails to observe any restriction imposed on him under Schedule 2 or 3 to this Act as to residence, [as to his employment or occupation] or as to reporting to the police [, to an immigration officer or to the Secretary of State];

(f) if he disembarks in the United Kingdom from a ship or aircraft after being placed on board under Schedule 2 or 3 to this Act with a view to his removal from the United Kingdom;

(g) if he embarks in contravention of a restriction imposed by or under an Order in Council under section 3(7) of this Act.

[(**1A**) A person commits an offence under subsection (1)(b)(i) above on the day when he first knows that the time limited by his leave has expired and continues to commit it throughout any period during which he is in the United Kingdom thereafter; but a person shall not be prosecuted under that provision more than once in respect of the same limited leave.]

(2) . . .

(3) The extended time limit for prosecutions which is provided for by section 28 below shall apply to offences under [subsection (1)(a) and (c)] above.

(4) In proceedings for an offence against subsection (1)(a) above of entering the United Kingdom without leave,—

(a) any stamp purporting to have been imprinted on a passport or other travel document by an immigration officer on a particular date for the purpose of giving leave shall be presumed to have been duly so imprinted, unless the contrary is proved;

(b) proof that a person had leave to enter the United Kingdom shall lie on the defence if, but only if, he is shown to have entered within six months before the date when the proceedings were commenced.

Note: Words in first square brackets in s 24(1) substituted by British Nationality Act 1981. Words in second square brackets in s 24(1) substituted by Asylum and Immigration Act 1996 from 1 October 1996. Words in first square brackets in s 24(1)(e) added by and words in square brackets in s 24(3) substituted by Immigration Act 1988. Words in second square brackets in subsection 24(1)(e) substituted by Nationality, Immigration and Asylum Act 2002, s 62, from 10 February 2003 (SI 2003/1). Section 24(1A) added by Immigration Act 1988, s 6, except in relation to persons whose leave had expired before 10 July 1988. Sections 24(1)(aa) and 24(2) omitted by Immigration and Asylum Act 1999 from 14 February 2000. Subsection (1)(d) applies in Scotland in modified form (1972 c 58, Sch 6). Section 24 has effect in a form modified by and in circumstances specified by the Channel Tunnel (International Arrangements) Order (SI 1993/1813) as amended by SIs 1994/1405, 2000/913, 2001/178, 2001/3707, 2006/1003 and 2007/3759.

[24A. Deception

(1) A person who is not a British citizen is guilty of an offence if, by means which include deception by him—

(a) he obtains or seeks to obtain leave to enter or remain in the United Kingdom; or

(b) he secures or seeks to secure the avoidance, postponement or revocation of enforcement action against him.

(2) 'Enforcement action', in relation to a person, means—

(a) the giving of directions for his removal from the United Kingdom ('directions') under Schedule 2 to this Act or section 10 of the Immigration and Asylum Act 1999;

(b) the making of a deportation order against him under section 5 of this Act; or

(c) his removal from the United Kingdom in consequence of directions or a deportation order.

(3) A person guilty of an offence under this section is liable—

(a) on summary conviction, to imprisonment for a term not exceeding six months or to a fine not exceeding the statutory maximum, or to both; or

(b) on conviction on indictment, to imprisonment for a term not exceeding two years or to a fine, or to both.

(4) . . .]

Note: Section 24A inserted by Immigration and Asylum Act 1999 from 14 February 2000. Section 24A(4) repealed by Nationality, Immigration and Asylum Act 2002, s 156 from 10 February 2003 (SI 2003/1).

[25. Assisting unlawful immigration to Member State

(1) A person commits an offence if he—

(a) does an act which facilitates the commission of a breach of immigration law by an individual who is not a citizen of the European Union,

(b) knows or has reasonable cause for believing that the act facilitates the commission of a breach of immigration law by the individual, and

(c) knows or has reasonable cause for believing that the individual is not a citizen of the European Union.

(2) In subsection (1) 'immigration law' means a law which has effect in a member State and which controls, in respect of some or all persons who are not nationals of the State, entitlement to—

(a) enter the State,

(b) transit across the State, or

(c) be in the State.

(3) A document issued by the government of a member State certifying a matter of law in that State—

(a) shall be admissible in proceedings for an offence under this section, and

(b) shall be conclusive as to the matter certified.

[(4) Subsection (1) applies to things done whether inside or outside the United Kingdom.]

(5) . . .

(6) A person guilty of an offence under this section shall be liable—

(a) on conviction on indictment, to imprisonment for a term not exceeding 14 years, to a fine or to both, or

(b) on summary conviction, to imprisonment for a term not exceeding six months, to a fine not exceeding the statutory maximum or to both.

[(7) In this section—

(a) a reference to a member State includes a reference to a State on a list prescribed for the purposes of this section by order of the Secretary of State (to be known as the 'Section 25 List of Schengen Acquis States'), and

(b) a reference to a citizen of the European Union includes a reference to a person who is a national of a State on that list.

(8) An order under subsection (7)(a)—

(a) may be made only if the Secretary of State thinks it necessary for the purpose of complying with the United Kingdom's obligations under the {EU} Treaties,

(b) may include transitional, consequential or incidental provision,

(c) shall be made by statutory instrument, and

(d) shall be subject to annulment in pursuance of a resolution of either House of Parliament.]

Note: Section 25 substituted by Nationality, Immigration and Asylum Act 2002, s 143, from 10 February 2003 (SI 2003/1). Subsections (7) and (8) inserted by Asylum and Immigration Act 2004, s 1 from 1 October 2004. Subsection (4) substituted and subsection (5) deleted by UK Borders Act 2007 (s 30) from 31 January 2008 (SI 2008/99). The term 'EU' substituted from 22 April 2011 (SI 2011/1043). Section 25 has effect in a form modified by and in circumstances specified by the Channel Tunnel (International Arrangements) Order (SI 1993/1813) as amended by SIs 1994/1405, 2000/913, 2001/178, 2001/3707, 2006/1003 and 2007/3759.

[25A. Helping asylum-seeker to enter United Kingdom

(1) A person commits an offence if—

(a) he knowingly and for gain facilitates the arrival in [, or the entry into,] the United Kingdom of an individual, and

(b) he knows or has reasonable cause to believe that the individual is an asylum-seeker.

(2) In this section 'asylum-seeker' means a person who intends to claim that to remove him from or require him to leave the United Kingdom would be contrary to the United Kingdom's obligations under—

(a) the Refugee Convention (within the meaning given by section 167(1) of the Immigration and Asylum Act 1999 (c. 33) (interpretation)), or

(b) the Human Rights Convention (within the meaning given by that section).

(3) Subsection (1) does not apply to anything done by a person acting on behalf of an organisation which—

(a) aims to assist asylum-seekers, and

(b) does not charge for its services.

(4) [Subsections (4) and (6)] of section 25 apply for the purpose of the offence in subsection (1) of this section as they apply for the purpose of the offence in subsection (1) of that section.]

Note: Section 25A inserted by Nationality, Immigration and Asylum Act 2002, s 143 from 10 February 2003 (SI 2003/1). Words in square brackets in subsections (1)(a) and (4) inserted by UK Borders Act 2007, ss 29–30 from 31 January 2008 (SI 2008/99).

[25B. Assisting entry to United Kingdom in breach of deportation or exclusion order

(1) A person commits an offence if he—

(a) does an act which facilitates a breach of a deportation order in force against an individual who is a citizen of the European Union, and

(b) knows or has reasonable cause for believing that the act facilitates a breach of the deportation order.

(2) Subsection (3) applies where the Secretary of State personally directs that the exclusion from the United Kingdom of an individual who is a citizen of the European Union is conducive to the public good.

(3) A person commits an offence if he—

(a) does an act which assists the individual to arrive in, enter or remain in the United Kingdom,

(b) knows or has reasonable cause for believing that the act assists the individual to arrive in, enter or remain in the United Kingdom, and

(c) knows or has reasonable cause for believing that the Secretary of State has personally directed that the individual's exclusion from the United Kingdom is conducive to the public good.

(4) [Subsections (4) and (6)] of section 25 apply for the purpose of an offence under this section as they apply for the purpose of an offence under that section.]

Note: Section 25B inserted by Nationality, Immigration and Asylum Act 2002, s 143 from 10 February 2003 (SI 2003/1). Words in square brackets in subsection (4) substituted by UK Borders Act 2007, s 30 from 31 January 2008 (SI 2008/99).

[25C. Forfeiture of vehicle, ship or aircraft

(1) This section applies where a person is convicted on indictment of an offence under section 25, 25A or 25B.

(2) The court may order the forfeiture of a vehicle used or intended to be used in connection with the offence if the convicted person—

(a) owned the vehicle at the time the offence was committed,

(b) was at that time a director, secretary or manager of a company which owned the vehicle,

(c) was at that time in possession of the vehicle under a hire-purchase agreement,

(d) was at that time a director, secretary or manager of a company which was in possession of the vehicle under a hire-purchase agreement, or

(e) was driving the vehicle in the course of the commission of the offence.

(3) The court may order the forfeiture of a ship or aircraft used or intended to be used in connection with the offence if the convicted person—

(a) owned the ship or aircraft at the time the offence was committed,

(b) was at that time a director, secretary or manager of a company which owned the ship or aircraft,

(c) was at that time in possession of the ship or aircraft under a hire-purchase agreement,

(d) was at that time a director, secretary or manager of a company which was in possession of the ship or aircraft under a hire-purchase agreement,

(e) was at that time a charterer of the ship or aircraft, or

(f) committed the offence while acting as captain of the ship or aircraft.

(4) But in a case to which subsection (3)(a) or (b) does not apply, forfeiture may be ordered only—

(a) in the case of a ship, if subsection (5) or (6) applies;

(b) in the case of an aircraft, if subsection (5) or (7) applies.

(5) This subsection applies where—

(a) in the course of the commission of the offence, the ship or aircraft carried more than 20 illegal entrants, and

(b) a person who, at the time the offence was committed, owned the ship or aircraft or was a director, secretary or manager of a company which owned it, knew or ought to have known of the intention to use it in the course of the commission of an offence under section 25, 25A or 25B.

(6) This subsection applies where a ship's gross tonnage is less than 500 tons.

(7) This subsection applies where the maximum weight at which an aircraft (which is not a hovercraft) may take off in accordance with its certificate of airworthiness is less than 5,700 kilogrammes.

(8) Where a person who claims to have an interest in a vehicle, ship or aircraft applies to a court to make representations on the question of forfeiture, the court may not make an order under this section in respect of the ship, aircraft or vehicle unless the person has been given an opportunity to make representations.

(9) In the case of an offence under section 25, the reference in subsection (5)(a) to an illegal entrant shall be taken to include a reference to—

(a) an individual who seeks to enter a member State in breach of immigration law [(for which purpose 'member State' and 'immigration law' have the meanings given by section 25(2) and (7))] and

(b) an individual who is a passenger for the purpose of section 145 of the Nationality, Immigration and Asylum Act 2002 (traffic in prostitution) [or section 4 of the Asylum and Immigration (Treatment of Claimants, etc.) Act 2004 (trafficking people for exploitation)].

(10) In the case of an offence under section 25A, the reference in subsection (5)(a) to an illegal entrant shall be taken to include a reference to—

(a) an asylum-seeker (within the meaning of that section), and

(b) an individual who is a passenger for the purpose of section 145(1) of the Nationality, Immigration and Asylum Act 2002 [or section 4 of the Asylum and Immigration (Treatment of Claimants, etc.) Act 2004 (trafficking people for exploitation)].

(11) In the case of an offence under section 25B, the reference in subsection (5)(a) to an illegal entrant shall be taken to include a reference to an individual who is a passenger

for the purpose of section 145(1) of the Nationality, Immigration and Asylum Act 2002 [or section 4 of the Asylum and Immigration (Treatment of Claimants, etc.) Act 2004 (trafficking people for exploitation)].

Note: Section 25C inserted by Nationality, Immigration and Asylum Act 2002, s 143 from 10 February 2003 (SI 2003/1). Words in square brackets in subsection 9(a) substituted by Asylum and Immigration (Treatment of Claimants etc.) Act 2004, s 1 from 1 October 2004. Other words in square brackets inserted by Asylum and Immigration (Treatment of Claimants etc.) Act 2004, s 5 from 1 December 2004 (SI 2004/2999; SSI 2004/494).

[25D. Detention of ship, aircraft or vehicle

(1) If a person has been arrested for an offence under section 25[, 25A or 25B], a senior officer or a constable may detain a relevant ship, aircraft or vehicle—

(a) until a decision is taken as to whether or not to charge the arrested person with that offence; or

(b) if the arrested person has been charged—

(i) until he is acquitted, the charge against him is dismissed or the proceedings are discontinued; or

(ii) if he has been convicted, until the court decides whether or not to order forfeiture of the ship, aircraft or vehicle.

(2) A ship, aircraft or vehicle is a relevant ship, aircraft or vehicle, in relation to an arrested person, if it is one which the officer or constable concerned has reasonable grounds for believing could, on conviction of the arrested person for the offence for which he was arrested, be the subject of an order for forfeiture made under [section 25C].

(3) [A person (other than the arrested person) may apply to the court for the release of a ship, aircraft or vehicle on the grounds that—

(a) he owns the ship, aircraft or vehicle,

(b) he was, immediately before the detention of the ship, aircraft or vehicle, in possession of it under a hire-purchase agreement, or

(c) he is a charterer of the ship or aircraft.]

(4) The court to which an application is made under subsection (3) may, on such security or surety being tendered as it considers satisfactory, release the ship, aircraft or vehicle on condition that it is made available to the court if—

(a) the arrested person is convicted; and

(b) an order for its forfeiture is made under [section 25C].

(5) In the application to Scotland of subsection (1), for paragraphs (a) and (b) substitute—

'(a) until a decision is taken as to whether or not to institute criminal proceedings against the arrested person for that offence; or

(b) if criminal proceedings have been instituted against the arrested person—

(i) until he is acquitted or, under section 65 or 147 of the Criminal Procedure (Scotland) Act 1995, discharged or liberated or the trial diet is deserted simpliciter;

(ii) if he has been convicted, until the court decides whether or not to order forfeiture of the ship, aircraft or vehicle, and for the purposes of this subsection, criminal proceedings are instituted against a person at whichever is the earliest of his first appearance before the sheriff on petition, or the service on him of an indictment or complaint.'

(6) 'Court' means—

(a) in England and Wales—

[(ia) if the arrested person has not been charged, or he has been charged but proceedings for the offence have not begun to be heard, a magistrates' court;]

(iii) if he has been charged and proceedings for the offence are being heard, the court hearing the proceedings;

(b) in Scotland, the sheriff; and

(c) in Northern Ireland—

(i) if the arrested person has not been charged, the magistrates' court for the county court division in which he was arrested;

(ii) if he has been charged but proceedings for the offence have not begun to be heard, the magistrates' court for the county court division in which he was charged;

(iii) if he has been charged and proceedings for the offence are being heard, the court hearing the proceedings.

(7) . . .

(8) 'Senior officer' means an immigration officer not below the rank of chief immigration officer.]

Note: Section 25D (previously s 25A) renumbered by Nationality, Immigration and Asylum Act 2002 from 10 February 2003 (SI 2003/1) and inserted by Immigration and Asylum Act 1999 from 2 October 2000. Words in square brackets in subsection (2) substituted by and subsection (3) substituted by Nationality, Immigration and Asylum Act 2002, s 144 from 10 February 2003 (SI 2003/1). Words in square brackets in subsection (4)(b) substituted by and subsection (7) omitted by Nationality, Immigration and Asylum Act 2002, s 144 from 10 February 2003 (SI 2003/1). Words in square brackets in subsection (6)(a)(ia) substituted for original (6)(a) (i) and (ii) by Sch 8 Courts Act 2003 from 1 April 2005 (SI 2005/190).

26. General offences in connection with administration of Act

(1) A person shall be guilty of an offence punishable on summary conviction with a fine of not more than [level 5 on the standard scale] or with imprisonment for not more than six months, or with both, in any of the following cases—

(a) if, without reasonable excuse, he refuses or fails to submit to examination under Schedule 2 of this Act;

(b) if, without reasonable excuse, he refuses or fails to furnish or produce any information in his possession, or any documents in his possession or control, which he is on an examination under that Schedule required to furnish or produce;

(c) if on any such examination or otherwise he makes or causes to be made to an immigration officer or other person lawfully acting in the execution of [a relevant enactment] a return, statement or representation which he knows to be false or does not believe to be true;

(d) if, without lawful authority, he alters any [certificate of entitlement], entry clearance, work permit or other document issued or made under or for the purposes of this Act, or uses for the purposes of this Act, or has in his possession for such use, any passport, [certificate of entitlement], entry clearance, work permit or other document which he knows or has reasonable cause to believe to be false;

(e) if, without reasonable excuse, he fails to complete and produce a landing or embarkation card in accordance with any order under Schedule 2 of this Act;

(f) if, without reasonable excuse, he fails to comply with any requirement of regulations under section 4(3) or of an order under section 4(4) above;

(g) if, without reasonable excuse, he obstructs an immigration officer or other person lawfully acting in the execution of this Act.

(2) The extended time limit for prosecutions which is provided for by section 28 below shall apply to offences under subsection (1)(c) and (d) above.

[(3) 'Relevant enactment' means—

(a) this Act;

(b) the Immigration Act 1988;

(c) the Asylum and Immigration Appeals Act 1993 (apart from section 4 or 5); . . .

(d) the Immigration and Asylum Act 1999 (apart from Part VI)]; [or

(e) the Nationality, Immigration and Asylum Act 2002 (apart from Part 5).]

Note: Words in first square brackets in s 26(1) substituted by virtue of Criminal Justice Act 1982, and amended by Asylum and Immigration Act 1996 from 1 October 1996. Words in square brackets in s 26(1)(d) substituted by British Nationality Act 1981, s 39(6). Words in square brackets in s 26(1)(c) and subsection (3) inserted by Immigration and Asylum Act 1999 from 14 February 2000. Subsection 3(e) inserted by and words in subsection 3(c) omitted by Nationality, Immigration and Asylum Act 2002, s 151 from 10 February 2003 (SI 2003/1).

[26A. Registration card

(1) In this section 'registration card' means a document which—

(a) carries information about a person (whether or not wholly or partly electronically), and

[(b) is issued by the Secretary of State to the person wholly or partly in connection with—

(i) a claim for asylum (whether or not made by that person), or

(ii) a claim for support under section 4 of the Immigration and Asylum Act 1999 (whether or not made by that person).]

(2) In subsection (1) 'claim for asylum' has the meaning given by section 18 of the Nationality, Immigration and Asylum Act 2002.

(3) A person commits an offence if he—

(a) makes a false registration card,

(b) alters a registration card with intent to deceive or to enable another to deceive,

(c) has a false or altered registration card in his possession without reasonable excuse,

(d) uses or attempts to use a false registration card for a purpose for which a registration card is issued,

(e) uses or attempts to use an altered registration card with intent to deceive,

(f) makes an article designed to be used in making a false registration card,

(g) makes an article designed to be used in altering a registration card with intent to deceive or to enable another to deceive, or

(h) has an article within paragraph (f) or (g) in his possession without reasonable excuse.

(4) In subsection (3) 'false registration card' means a document which is designed to appear to be a registration card.

(5) A person who is guilty of an offence under subsection (3)(a), (b), (d), (e), (f) or (g) shall be liable—

(a) on conviction on indictment, to imprisonment for a term not exceeding ten years, to a fine or to both, or

(b) on summary conviction, to imprisonment for a term not exceeding six months, to a fine not exceeding the statutory maximum or to both.

(6) A person who is guilty of an offence under subsection (3)(c) or (h) shall be liable—

(a) on conviction on indictment, to imprisonment for a term not exceeding two years, to a fine or to both, or

(b) on summary conviction, to imprisonment for a term not exceeding six months, to a fine not exceeding the statutory maximum or to both.

(7) The Secretary of State may by order—

(a) amend the definition of 'registration card' in subsection (1);

(b) make consequential amendment of this section.

(8) An order under subsection (7)—

(a) must be made by statutory instrument, and

(b) may not be made unless a draft has been laid before and approved by resolution of each House of Parliament.]

Note: Section 26A inserted by Nationality, Immigration and Asylum Act 2002, s 148 from 10 February 2003 (SI 2003/1). Subsection (1)(b) substituted by The Immigration (Registration Card) Order 2008 (SI 2008/1693) from 27 June 2008.

[26B. Possession of immigration stamp

(1) A person commits an offence if he has an immigration stamp in his possession without reasonable excuse.

(2) A person commits an offence if he has a replica immigration stamp in his possession without reasonable excuse.

(3) In this section—

(a) 'immigration stamp' means a device which is designed for the purpose of stamping documents in the exercise of an immigration function,

(b) 'replica immigration stamp' means a device which is designed for the purpose of stamping a document so that it appears to have been stamped in the exercise of an immigration function, and

(c) 'immigration function' means a function of an immigration officer or the Secretary of State under the Immigration Acts.

(4) A person who is guilty of an offence under this section shall be liable—

(a) on conviction on indictment, to imprisonment for a term not exceeding two years, to a fine or to both, or

(b) on summary conviction, to imprisonment for a term not exceeding six months, to a fine not exceeding the statutory maximum or to both.]

Note: Section 26B inserted by Nationality, Immigration and Asylum Act 2002, s 148 from 10 February 2003 (SI 2003/1).

27. Offences by persons connected with ships or aircraft or with ports

A person shall be guilty of an offence punishable on summary conviction with a fine of not more than [level 5 on the standard scale] or with imprisonment for not more than six months, or with both, in any of the following cases—

(a) if, being the captain of a ship or aircraft,—

(i) he knowingly permits a person to disembark in the United Kingdom when required under Schedule 2 or 3 to this Act to prevent it, or fails without reasonable excuse to take any steps he is required by or under Schedule 2 to take in connection with the disembarkation or examination of passengers or for furnishing a passenger list or particulars of members of the crew; or

(ii) he fails, without reasonable excuse, to comply with any directions given him under Schedule 2 or 3 [or under the Immigration and Asylum Act 1999] with respect to the removal of a person from the United Kingdom;

(b) if, as owner or agent of a ship or aircraft,—

(i) he arranges, or is knowingly concerned in any arrangements, for the ship or aircraft to call at a port other than a port of entry contrary to any provision of Schedule 2 to this Act; or

(ii) he fails, with reasonable excuse, to take any steps required by an order under Schedule 2 for the supply to passengers of landing or embarkation cards; or

(iii) he fails, without reasonable excuse, to make arrangements for [or in connection with] the removal of a person from the United Kingdom when required to do so by directions given under Schedule 2 or 3 to this Act [or under the Immigration and Asylum Act 1999]; or

[(iiia) he fails, without reasonable excuse, to comply with a direction under paragraph 5B of Schedule 2; or]

(iv) he fails, without reasonable excuse, to comply with [[any other requirement] imposed by or under Schedule 2]

(c) if, as a person concerned in the management of a port, he fails, without reasonable excuse, to take any steps required by Schedule 2 in relation to the embarkation or disembarkation of passengers where a control area is designated.

[(ca) if as a person concerned in the management of a port he fails, without reasonable excuse, to comply with a direction under paragraph 5B of Schedule 2.]

Note: Words in first square brackets in s 27 substituted by virtue of Criminal Justice Act 1982, and amended by Asylum and Immigration Act 1996 from 1 October 1996. Words in square brackets in subsection (b)(iv) substituted and words omitted from subsection (c) by Immigration, Asylum and Nationality Act 2006, s 31 from 1 March 2008 (SI 2007/3138 as amended by SI 2007/3580). Subsections (b)(iiia) and (ca) inserted and words in first square brackets in subsection (iv) substituted by Sch 8 Immigration Act 2014 from 28 July 2014 (SI 2014/1820). Other words in square brackets inserted by Immigration and Asylum Act 1999 from 2 October 2000. Section 27 has effect in a form modified by and in circumstances specified by the Channel Tunnel (International Arrangements) Order (SI 1993/1813) as amended by SIs 1994/1405, 2000/913, 2001/178, 2001/3707, 2006/1003 and 2007/3759.

28. Proceedings

(1) Where the offence is one to which, under section 24, [. . .] or 26 above, an extended time limit for prosecutions is to apply, then—

(a) an information relating to the offence may in England and Wales be tried by a magistrates' court if it is laid within six months after the commission of the offence, or if it is laid within three years after the commission of the offence and not more than two months after the date certified by [an officer of police above the rank of chief superintendent] to be the date on which evidence sufficient to justify proceedings came to the notice of an officer of [the police force to which he belongs] and;

(b) summary proceedings for the offence may in Scotland be commenced within six months after the commission of the offence, or within three years after the commission of the offence and not more than two months after the date on which evidence sufficient in the opinion of the Lord Advocate to justify proceedings came to his knowledge; and

(c) a complaint charging the commission of the offence may in Northern Ireland be heard and determined by a magistrates' court if it is made within six months after the commission of the offence, or if it is made within three years after the commission of the offence and not more than two months after the date certified by an officer of police not below the rank of assistant chief constable to be the date on which evidence sufficient to justify the proceedings came to the notice of the police in Northern Ireland.

(2) For purposes of subsection (1)(b) above proceedings shall be deemed to be commenced on the date on which a warrant to apprehend or to cite the accused is granted, if such warrant is executed without undue delay; and a certificate of the Lord Advocate as to the date on which such evidence as is mentioned in subsection (1)(b) came to his knowledge shall be conclusive evidence.

(3) For the purposes of the trial of a person for an offence under this Part of this Act, the offence shall be deemed to have been committed either at the place at which it actually was committed or at any place at which he may be.

(4) Any powers exercisable under this Act in the case of any person may be exercised notwithstanding that proceedings for an offence under this Part of this Act have been taken against him.

Note: Words omitted from subsection (1) by Nationality, Immigration and Asylum Act 2002, s 156 from 10 February 2003 (SI 2003/1). Words in square brackets in s 28(1)(a) substituted by Immigration Act 1988.

[28A. Arrest without warrant

(1) [An] immigration officer may arrest without warrant a person—

(a) who has committed or attempted to commit an offence under section 24 or 24A; or

(b) whom he has reasonable grounds for suspecting has committed or attempted to commit such an offence.

(2) But subsection (1) does not apply in relation to an offence under section 24(1)(d).

(3) An immigration officer may arrest without warrant a person—

(a) who has committed an offence under section [25, 25A or 25B]; or

(b) whom he has reasonable grounds for suspecting has committed that offence.

(4) . . .

(5) An immigration officer may arrest without warrant a person ('the suspect') who, or whom he has reasonable grounds for suspecting—

(a) has committed or attempted to commit an offence under section 26(1)(g); or

(b) is committing or attempting to commit that offence.

(6) The power conferred by subsection (5) is exercisable only if either the first or the second condition is satisfied.

(7) The first condition is that it appears to the officer that service of a summons (or, in Scotland, a copy complaint) is impracticable or inappropriate because—

(a) he does not know, and cannot readily discover, the suspect's name;

(b) he has reasonable grounds for doubting whether a name given by the suspect as his name is his real name;

(c) the suspect has failed to give him a satisfactory address for service; or

(d) he has reasonable grounds for doubting whether an address given by the suspect is a satisfactory address for service.

(8) The second condition is that the officer has reasonable grounds for believing that arrest is necessary to prevent the suspect—

(a) causing physical injury to himself or another person;

(b) suffering physical injury; or

(c) causing loss of or damage to property.

(9) For the purposes of subsection (7), an address is a satisfactory address for service if it appears to the officer—

(a) that the suspect will be at that address for a sufficiently long period for it to be possible to serve him with a summons (or copy complaint); or

(b) that some other person specified by the suspect will accept service of a summons (or copy complaint) for the suspect at that address.

[(9A) [An] immigration officer may arrest without warrant a person—

(a) who has committed an offence under section 26A or 26B; or

(b) who he has reasonable grounds for suspecting has committed an offence under section 26A or 26B.]

(10) In relation to the exercise of the powers conferred by subsections (3)(b) . . . and (5), it is immaterial that no offence has been committed.

(11) In Scotland the powers conferred by subsections (3) . . . and (5) may also be exercised by a constable.]

Note: Section 28A inserted by Immigration and Asylum Act 1999 from 14 February 2000. Words in square brackets in subsection (3)(a) substituted by and subsection (4) omitted by Nationality, Immigration and Asylum Act 2002, s 144 from 10 February 2003 (SI 2003/1). Subsection (9A) inserted by Nationality, Immigration and Asylum Act 2002, s 150 from 10 February 2003 (SI 2003/1). Words omitted from subsections (10) and (11) by Nationality, Immigration and Asylum Act 2002, s 144 from 10 February 2003 (SI 2003/1). Words in square brackets in subsections (1) and (9A) substituted (England and Wales) by Serious Organised Crime and Police Act 2005, Schedule 7 paragraph 53 from 1 April 2006 (SI 2006/378).

[28AA. Arrest with warrant

(1) This section applies if on an application by an immigration officer a justice of the peace is satisfied that there are reasonable grounds for suspecting that a person has committed an offence under—

(a) section 24(1)(d), or

[(b) section 21(1) of the Immigration, Asylum and Nationality Act 2006.]

(2) The justice of the peace may grant a warrant authorising any immigration officer to arrest the person.

(3) In the application of this section to Scotland a reference to a justice of the peace shall be treated as a reference to the sheriff or a justice of the peace.]

Note: Section 28AA inserted by Nationality, Immigration and Asylum Act 2002, s 152 from 10 February 2003 (SI 2003/1). Subsection (1)(b) substituted by UK Borders Act 2007, s 27 from 29 February 2008 (SI 2008/309).

[28B. Search and arrest by warrant

(1) Subsection (2) applies if a justice of the peace is, by written information on oath, satisfied that there are reasonable grounds for suspecting that a person ('the suspect') who is liable to be arrested for a relevant offence is to be found on any premises.

(2) The justice may grant a warrant authorising any immigration officer or constable to enter, if need be by force, the premises named in the warrant for the purpose of searching for and arresting the suspect.

(3) Subsection (4) applies if in Scotland the sheriff or a justice of the peace is by evidence on oath satisfied as mentioned in subsection (1).

(4) The sheriff or justice may grant a warrant authorising any immigration officer or constable to enter, if need be by force, the premises named in the warrant for the purpose of searching for and arresting the suspect.

(5) 'Relevant offence' means an offence under section 24(1)(a), (b), (c), (d), (e) or (f), [24A, 26A or 26B].]

Note: Section 28B inserted by Immigration and Asylum Act 1999 from 14 February 2000. Words in square brackets in subsection (5) substituted by Nationality, Immigration and Asylum Act 2002, ss 144, 150 from 10 February 2003 (SI 2003/1).

[28C. Search and arrest without warrant

(1) An immigration officer may enter and search any premises for the purpose of arresting a person for an offence under [section 25, 25A or 25B].

(2) The power may be exercised—

(a) only to the extent that it is reasonably required for that purpose; and

(b) only if the officer has reasonable grounds for believing that the person whom he is seeking is on the premises.

(3) In relation to premises consisting of two or more separate dwellings, the power is limited to entering and searching—

(a) any parts of the premises which the occupiers of any dwelling comprised in the premises use in common with the occupiers of any such other dwelling; and

(b) any such dwelling in which the officer has reasonable grounds for believing that the person whom he is seeking may be.

(4) The power may be exercised only if the officer produces identification showing that he is an immigration officer (whether or not he is asked to do so).]

Note: Section 28C inserted by Immigration and Asylum Act 1999 from 14 February 2000. Words in square brackets in subsection (1) substituted by Nationality, Immigration and Asylum Act 2002, s 144 from 10 February 2003 (SI 2003/1).

[28CA. Business premises: entry to arrest

(1) A constable or immigration officer may enter and search any business premises for the purpose of arresting a person—

(a) for an offence under section 24,

(b) for an offence under section 24A, or

(c) under paragraph 17 of Schedule 2.

(2) The power under subsection (1) may be exercised only—

(a) to the extent that it is reasonably required for a purpose specified in subsection (1),

(b) if the constable or immigration officer has reasonable grounds for believing that the person whom he is seeking is on the premises,

(c) with the authority of the Secretary of State (in the case of an immigration officer) or a Chief Superintendent (in the case of a constable), and

(d) if the constable or immigration officer produces identification showing his status.

(3) Authority for the purposes of subsection (2)(c)—

(a) may be given on behalf of the Secretary of State only by a civil servant of the rank of at least Assistant Director, and

(b) shall expire at the end of the period of seven days beginning with the day on which it is given.

(4) Subsection (2)(d) applies—

(a) whether or not a constable or immigration officer is asked to produce identification, but

(b) only where premises are occupied.

(5) Subsection (6) applies where a constable or immigration officer—

(a) enters premises in reliance on this section, and

(b) detains a person on the premises.

(6) A detainee custody officer may enter the premises for the purpose of carrying out a search.

(7) In subsection (6)—

'detainee custody officer' means a person in respect of whom a certificate of authorisation is in force under section 154 of the Immigration and Asylum Act 1999 (c. 33) (detained persons: escort and custody), and

'search' means a search under paragraph 2(1)(a) of Schedule 13 to that Act (escort arrangements: power to search detained person).]

Note: Section 28CA inserted by Nationality, Immigration and Asylum Act 2002, s 153 from 10 February 2003 (SI 2003/1).

[28D. Entry and search of premises

(1) If, on an application made by an immigration officer, a justice of the peace is satisfied that there are reasonable grounds for believing that—

(a) a relevant offence has been committed,

(b) there is material on premises specified in the application which is likely to be of substantial value (whether by itself or together with other material) to the investigation of the offence,

(c) the material is likely to be relevant evidence,

(d) the material does not consist of or include items subject to legal privilege, excluded material or special procedure material, and

(e) any of the conditions specified in subsection (2) applies, he may issue a warrant authorising an immigration officer to enter and search the premises.

(2) The conditions are that—

(a) it is not practicable to communicate with any person entitled to grant entry to the premises;

(b) it is practicable to communicate with a person entitled to grant entry to the premises but it is not practicable to communicate with any person entitled to grant access to the evidence;

(c) entry to the premises will not be granted unless a warrant is produced;

(d) the purpose of a search may be frustrated or seriously prejudiced unless an immigration officer arriving at the premises can secure immediate entry to them.

(3) An immigration officer may seize and retain anything for which a search has been authorised under subsection (1).

(4) 'Relevant offence' means an offence under section 24(1)(a), (b), (c), (d), (e) or (f), [24A, 25, 25A, 25B, 26A or 26B].

(5) In relation to England and Wales, expressions which are given a meaning by the Police and Criminal Evidence Act 1984 have the same meaning when used in this section.

(6) In relation to Northern Ireland, expressions which are given a meaning by the Police and Criminal Evidence (Northern Ireland) Order 1989 have the same meaning when used in this section.

(7) In the application of subsection (1) to Scotland—

(a) read the reference to a justice of the peace as a reference to the sheriff or a justice of the peace; and

(b) in paragraph (d), omit the reference to excluded material and special procedure material.]

Note: Section 28D inserted by Immigration and Asylum Act 1999 from 14 February 2000. Words in square brackets in subsection (4) substituted by Nationality, Immigration and Asylum Act 2002, ss 144, 150 from 10 February 2003 (SI 2003/1).

[28E. Entry and search of premises following arrest

(1) This section applies if a person is arrested for an offence under this Part at a place other than a police station.

(2) An immigration officer may enter and search any premises—

(a) in which the person was when arrested, or

(b) in which he was immediately before he was arrested, for evidence relating to the offence for which the arrest was made ('relevant evidence').

(3) The power may be exercised—

(a) only if the officer has reasonable grounds for believing that there is relevant evidence on the premises; and

(b) only to the extent that it is reasonably required for the purpose of discovering relevant evidence.

(4) In relation to premises consisting of two or more separate dwellings, the power is limited to entering and searching—

(a) any dwelling in which the arrest took place or in which the arrested person was immediately before his arrest; and

(b) any parts of the premises which the occupier of any such dwelling uses in common with the occupiers of any other dwellings comprised in the premises.

(5) An officer searching premises under subsection (2) may seize and retain anything he finds which he has reasonable grounds for believing is relevant evidence.

(6) Subsection (5) does not apply to items which the officer has reasonable grounds for believing are items subject to legal privilege.]

Note: Section 28E inserted by Immigration and Asylum Act 1999 from 14 February 2000.

[28F. Entry and search of premises following arrest under section 25, 25A or 25B

(1) An immigration officer may enter and search any premises occupied or controlled by a person arrested for an offence under [section 25, 25A, 25B.]

(2) The power may be exercised—

(a) only if the officer has reasonable grounds for suspecting that there is relevant evidence on the premises;

(b) only to the extent that it is reasonably required for the purpose of discovering relevant evidence; and

(c) subject to subsection (3), only if a senior officer has authorised it in writing.

(3) The power may be exercised—

(a) before taking the arrested person to a place where he is to be detained; and

(b) without obtaining an authorisation under subsection (2)(c), if the presence of that person at a place other than one where he is to be detained is necessary for the effective investigation of the offence.

(4) An officer who has relied on subsection (3) must inform a senior officer as soon as is practicable.

(5) The officer authorising a search, or who is informed of one under subsection (4), must make a record in writing of—

(a) the grounds for the search; and

(b) the nature of the evidence that was sought.

(6) An officer searching premises under this section may seize and retain anything he finds which he has reasonable grounds for suspecting is relevant evidence.

(7) 'Relevant evidence' means evidence, other than items subject to legal privilege, that relates to the offence in question.

(8) 'Senior officer' means an immigration officer not below the rank of chief immigration officer.]

Note: Section 28F inserted by Immigration and Asylum Act 1999 from 14 February 2000. Words in square brackets in subsection (1) substituted by Nationality, Immigration and Asylum Act 2002, s 144 from 10 February 2003 (SI 2003/1).

[28FA. Search for personnel records: warrant unnecessary

(1) This section applies where—

(a) a person has been arrested for an offence under section 24(1) or 24A(1),

(b) a person has been arrested under paragraph 17 of Schedule 2,

(c) a constable or immigration officer reasonably believes that a person is liable to arrest for an offence under section 24(1) or 24A(1), or

(d) a constable or immigration officer reasonably believes that a person is liable to arrest under paragraph 17 of Schedule 2.

(2) A constable or immigration officer may search business premises where the arrest was made or where the person liable to arrest is if the constable or immigration officer reasonably believes—

(a) that a person has committed an immigration employment offence in relation to the person arrested or liable to arrest, and

(b) that employee records, other than items subject to legal privilege, will be found on the premises and will be of substantial value (whether on their own or together with other material) in the investigation of the immigration employment offence.

(3) A constable or officer searching premises under subsection (2) may seize and retain employee records, other than items subject to legal privilege, which he reasonably suspects will be of substantial value (whether on their own or together with other material) in the investigation of—

(a) an immigration employment offence, or

(b) an offence under section 105 or 106 of the Immigration and Asylum Act 1999 (c. 33) (support for asylum-seeker: fraud).

(4) The power under subsection (2) may be exercised only—

(a) to the extent that it is reasonably required for the purpose of discovering employee records other than items subject to legal privilege,

(b) if the constable or immigration officer produces identification showing his status, and

(c) if the constable or immigration officer reasonably believes that at least one of the conditions in subsection (5) applies.

(5) Those conditions are—

(a) that it is not practicable to communicate with a person entitled to grant access to the records,

(b) that permission to search has been refused,

(c) that permission to search would be refused if requested, and

(d) that the purpose of a search may be frustrated or seriously prejudiced if it is not carried out in reliance on subsection (2).

(6) Subsection (4)(b) applies—

(a) whether or not a constable or immigration officer is asked to produce identification, but

(b) only where premises are occupied.

(7) In this section 'immigration employment offence' means [an offence under section 21 of the Immigration, Asylum and Nationality Act 2006] (employment).]

Note: Section 28FA inserted by Nationality, Immigration and Asylum Act 2002, s 154 from 10 February 2003 (SI 2003/1). Words in square brackets in subsection (7) substituted by UK Borders Act 2007, s 28 from 29 February 2008 (SI 2008/309).

[28FB. Search for personnel records: with warrant

(1) This section applies where on an application made by an immigration officer in respect of business premises a justice of the peace is satisfied that there are reasonable grounds for believing—

(a) that an employer has provided inaccurate or incomplete information under section 134 of the Nationality, Immigration and Asylum Act 2002 (compulsory disclosure by employer),

(b) that employee records, other than items subject to legal privilege, will be found on the premises and will enable deduction of some or all of the information which the employer was required to provide, and

(c) that at least one of the conditions in subsection (2) is satisfied.

(2) Those conditions are—

(a) that it is not practicable to communicate with a person entitled to grant access to the premises,

(b) that it is not practicable to communicate with a person entitled to grant access to the records,

(c) that entry to the premises or access to the records will not be granted unless a warrant is produced, and

(d) that the purpose of a search may be frustrated or seriously prejudiced unless an immigration officer arriving at the premises can secure immediate entry.

(3) The justice of the peace may issue a warrant authorising an immigration officer to enter and search the premises.

(4) Subsection (7)(a) of section 28D shall have effect for the purposes of this section as it has effect for the purposes of that section.

(5) An immigration officer searching premises under a warrant issued under this section may seize and retain employee records, other than items subject to legal privilege, which he reasonably suspects will be of substantial value (whether on their own or together with other material) in the investigation of—

(a) an offence under section 137 of the Nationality, Immigration and Asylum Act 2002 (disclosure of information: offences) in respect of a requirement under section 134 of that Act, or

(b) an offence under section 105 or 106 of the Immigration and Asylum Act 1999 (c. 33) (support for asylum-seeker: fraud).]

Note: Section 28FB inserted by Nationality, Immigration and Asylum Act 2002, s 154 from 10 February 2003 (SI 2003/1).

[28G. Searching arrested persons

(1) This section applies if a person is arrested for an offence under this Part at a place other than a police station.

(2) An immigration officer may search the arrested person if he has reasonable grounds for believing that the arrested person may present a danger to himself or others.

(3) The officer may search the arrested person for—

(a) anything which he might use to assist his escape from lawful custody; or

(b) anything which might be evidence relating to the offence for which he has been arrested.

(4) The power conferred by subsection (3) may be exercised—

(a) only if the officer has reasonable grounds for believing that the arrested person may have concealed on him anything of a kind mentioned in that subsection; and

(b) only to the extent that it is reasonably required for the purpose of discovering any such thing.

(5) A power conferred by this section to search a person is not to be read as authorising an officer to require a person to remove any of his clothing in public other than an outer coat, jacket or glove; but it does authorise the search of a person's mouth.

(6) An officer searching a person under subsection (2) may seize and retain anything he finds, if he has reasonable grounds for believing that that person might use it to cause physical injury to himself or to another person.

(7) An officer searching a person under subsection (3) may seize and retain anything he finds, if he has reasonable grounds for believing—

(a) that that person might use it to assist his escape from lawful custody; or

(b) that it is evidence which relates to the offence in question.

(8) Subsection (7)(b) does not apply to an item subject to legal privilege.]

Note: Section 28G inserted by Immigration and Asylum Act 1999 from 14 February 2000.

[28H. Searching persons in police custody

(1) This section applies if a person—

(a) has been arrested for an offence under this Part; and

(b) is in custody at a police station or in police detention at a place other than a police station.

(2) An immigration officer may at any time, search the arrested person in order to see whether he has with him anything—

(a) which he might use to—

(i) cause physical injury to himself or others;

(ii) damage property;

(iii) interfere with evidence; or

(iv) assist his escape; or

(b) which the officer has reasonable grounds for believing is evidence relating to the offence in question.

(3) The power may be exercised only to the extent that the custody officer concerned considers it to be necessary for the purpose of discovering anything of a kind mentioned in subsection (2).

(4) An officer searching a person under this section may seize anything he finds, if he has reasonable grounds for believing that—

(a) that person might use it for one or more of the purposes mentioned in subsection (2)(a); or

(b) it is evidence relating to the offence in question.

(5) Anything seized under subsection (4)(a) may be retained by the police.

(6) Anything seized under subsection (4)(b) may be retained by an immigration officer.

(7) The person from whom something is seized must be told the reason for the seizure unless he is—

(a) violent or appears likely to become violent; or

(b) incapable of understanding what is said to him.

(8) An intimate search may not be conducted under this section.

(9) The person carrying out a search under this section must be of the same sex as the person searched.

(10) 'Custody officer'—

(a) in relation to England and Wales, has the same meaning as in the Police and Criminal Evidence Act 1984;

(b) in relation to Scotland, means the officer in charge of a police station; and

(c) in relation to Northern Ireland, has the same meaning as in the Police and Criminal Evidence (Northern Ireland) Order 1989.

(11) 'Intimate search'—

(a) in relation to England and Wales, has the meaning given by section 65 of the Act of 1984;

(b) in relation to Scotland, means a search which consists of the physical examination of a person's body orifices other than the mouth; and

(c) in relation to Northern Ireland, has the same meaning as in the 1989 Order.

(12) 'Police detention'—

(a) in relation to England and Wales, has the meaning given by section 118(2) of the 1984 Act; and

(b) in relation to Northern Ireland, has the meaning given by Article 2 of the 1989 Order.

(13) In relation to Scotland, a person is in police detention if—

(a) he has been taken to a police station after being arrested for an offence; or

(b) he is arrested at a police station after attending voluntarily at the station, accompanying a constable to it or being detained under section 14 of the Criminal Procedure (Scotland) Act 1995, and is detained there or is detained elsewhere in the charge of a constable, but is not in police detention if he is in court after being charged.]

Note: Section 28H inserted by Immigration and Asylum Act 1999 from 14 February 2000.

[28I. Seized material: access and copying

(1) If a person showing himself—

(a) to be the occupier of the premises on which seized material was seized, or

(b) to have had custody or control of the material immediately before it was seized,

asks the immigration officer who seized the material for a record of what he seized, the officer must provide the record to that person within a reasonable time.

(2) If a relevant person asks an immigration officer for permission to be granted access to seized material, the officer must arrange for him to have access to the material under the supervision—

(a) in the case of seized material within subsection (8)(a), of an immigration officer;

(b) in the case of seized material within subsection (8)(b), of a constable.

(3) An immigration officer may photograph or copy, or have photographed or copied, seized material.

(4) If a relevant person asks an immigration officer for a photograph or copy of seized material, the officer must arrange for—

(a) that person to have access to the material for the purpose of photographing or copying it under the supervision—

(i) in the case of seized material within subsection (8)(a), of an immigration officer;

(ii) in the case of seized material within subsection (8)(b), of a constable; or

(b) the material to be photographed or copied.

(5) A photograph or copy made under subsection (4)(b) must be supplied within a reasonable time.

(6) There is no duty under this section to arrange for access to, or the supply of a photograph or copy of, any material if there are reasonable grounds for believing that to do so would prejudice—

(a) the exercise of any functions in connection with which the material was seized; or

(b) an investigation which is being conducted under this Act, or any criminal proceedings which may be brought as a result.

(7) 'Relevant person' means—

(a) a person who had custody or control of seized material immediately before it was seized, or

(b) someone acting on behalf of such a person.

(8) 'Seized material' means anything—

(a) seized and retained by an immigration officer, or

(b) seized by an immigration officer and retained by the police, under this Part.]

Note: Section 28I inserted by Immigration and Asylum Act 1999 from 14 February 2000.

[28J. Search warrants: safeguards

(1) The entry or search of premises under a warrant is unlawful unless it complies with this section and section 28K.

(2) If an immigration officer applies for a warrant, he must—

(a) state the ground on which he makes the application and the provision of this Act under which the warrant would be issued;

(b) specify the premises which it is desired to enter and search; and

(c) identify, so far as is practicable, the persons or articles to be sought.

(3) In Northern Ireland, an application for a warrant is to be supported by a complaint in writing and substantiated on oath.

(4) Otherwise, an application for a warrant is to be made ex parte and supported by an information in writing or, in Scotland, evidence on oath.

(5) The officer must answer on oath any question that the justice of the peace or sheriff hearing the application asks him.

(6) A warrant shall authorise an entry on one occasion only.

(7) A warrant must specify—

(a) the name of the person applying for it;

(b) the date on which it is issued;

(c) the premises to be searched; and

(d) the provision of this Act under which it is issued.

(8) A warrant must identify, so far as is practicable, the persons or articles to be sought.

(9) Two copies of a warrant must be made.

(10) The copies must be clearly certified as copies.

(11) 'Warrant' means a warrant to enter and search premises issued to an immigration officer under this Part or under paragraph 17(2) [or 25A(6A)] of Schedule 2.]

Note: Section 28J inserted by Immigration and Asylum Act 1999 from 14 February 2000. Words in square brackets in subsection (11) inserted by Immigration Act 2014 Sch 1 from 28 July 2014 (SI 2014/1820).

[28K. Execution of warrants

(1) A warrant may be executed by any immigration officer.

(2) A warrant may authorise persons to accompany the officer executing it.

(3) Entry and search under a warrant must be—

(a) within one month from the date of its issue; and

(b) at a reasonable hour, unless it appears to the officer executing it that the purpose of a search might be frustrated.

(4) If the occupier of premises which are to be entered and searched is present at the time when an immigration officer seeks to execute a warrant, the officer must—

(a) identify himself to the occupier and produce identification showing that he is an immigration officer;

(b) show the occupier the warrant; and

(c) supply him with a copy of it.

(5) If—

(a) the occupier is not present, but

(b) some other person who appears to the officer to be in charge of the premises is present,

subsection (4) has effect as if each reference to the occupier were a reference to that other person.

(6) If there is no person present who appears to the officer to be in charge of the premises, the officer must leave a copy of the warrant in a prominent place on the premises.

(7) A search under a warrant may only be a search to the extent required for the purpose for which the warrant was issued.

(8) An officer executing a warrant must make an endorsement on it stating—

(a) whether the persons or articles sought were found; and

(b) whether any articles, other than articles which were sought, were seized.

(9) A warrant which has been executed, or has not been executed within the time authorised for its execution, must be returned—

[(a) if issued by a justice of the peace in England and Wales, to the designated officer for the local justice area in which the justice was acting when he issued the warrant;]

(b) if issued by a justice of the peace in Northern Ireland, to the clerk of petty sessions for the petty sessions district in which the premises are situated;

(c) if issued by a justice of the peace in Scotland, to the clerk of the district court for the commission area for which the justice of the peace was appointed;

(d) if issued by the sheriff, to the sheriff clerk.

(10) A warrant returned under subsection (9)(a) must be retained for 12 months by the [designated officer].

(11) A warrant issued under subsection (9)(b) or (c) must be retained for 12 months by the clerk.

(12) A warrant returned under subsection (9)(d) must be retained for 12 months by the sheriff clerk.

(13) If during that 12-month period the occupier of the premises to which it relates asks to inspect it, he must be allowed to do so.

(14) 'Warrant' means a warrant to enter and search premises issued to an immigration officer under this Part or under paragraph 17(2) [or 25A(6A)] of Schedule 2.]

Note: Section 28K inserted by Immigration and Asylum Act 1999 from 14 February 2000. Words in square brackets in subsections (9) and (10) substituted by Sch 8 Courts Act 2003 from 1 April 2005 (SI 2005/910). Words in square brackets in subsection (14) inserted by Immigration Act 2014 Sch 1 from 28 July 2014 (SI 2014/1820).

[28L. Interpretation of Part III

[(1)] In this Part, 'premises' and 'items subject to legal privilege' have the same meaning—

(a) in relation to England and Wales, as in the Police and Criminal Evidence Act 1984;

(b) in relation to Northern Ireland, as in the Police and Criminal Evidence (Northern Ireland) Order 1989; and

(c) in relation to Scotland, as in {section 412 of the Proceeds of Crime Act 2002}.

[(2) In this Part, 'business premises' means premises (or any part of premises) not used as a dwelling.

(3) In this Part, 'employee records' means records which show an employee's—

(a) name,

(b) date of birth,

(c) address,

(d) length of service,

(e) rate of pay, or

(f) nationality or citizenship.

(4) The Secretary of State may by order amend section 28CA(3)(a) to reflect a change in nomenclature.

(5) An order under subsection (4)—

(a) must be made by statutory instrument, and

(b) shall be subject to annulment in pursuance of a resolution of either House of Parliament.]

Note: Section 28L inserted by Immigration and Asylum Act 1999 from 14 February 2000. Words in curly brackets in subsection (1) substituted from 24 February 2003 by Proceeds of Crime Act 2002 Sch 11. Subsections (2)–(5) inserted by Nationality, Immigration and Asylum Act 2002, s 155 from 10 February 2003 (SI 2003/1).

PART IV

SUPPLEMENTARY

29. . . .

Note: Repealed by Nationality, Immigration and Asylum Act 2002, s 58 and Sch 9 from 1 April 2003 (SI 2003/754).

30. . . .

Note: Repealed by British Nationality Act 1981, s 52(8) and Mental Health (Scotland) Act 1984, s 127(2).

31. Expenses

There shall be defrayed out of moneys provided by Parliament any expenses incurred [by the Lord Chancellor under Schedule 5 to this Act or] by a Secretary of State under or by virtue of this Act—

(a) by way of administrative expenses . . .; or

(b) in connection with the removal of any person from the United Kingdom under Schedule 2 or 3 to this Act or the departure with him of his dependants, or his or their maintenance pending departure; or

(c) . . .

(d) . . .

Note: Words in square brackets in s 31 inserted and s 31(c) repealed by SI 1987/465. Words omitted from s 31(a) repealed by British Nationality Act 1981, s 52(8). Section 31(d) repealed by Nationality, Immigration and Asylum Act 2002, s 58 and Sch 9 from 1 April 2003 (SI 2003/754).

[31A. Procedural requirements as to applications

. . .]

Note: Section 31A repealed by Immigration, Asylum and Nationality Act 2006, s 50 from 29 February 2008 (SI 2008/310).

32. General provisions as to Orders in Council, etc.

(1) Any power conferred by Part I of this Act to make an Order in Council or order (other than a deportation order) or to give any directions includes power to revoke or vary the Order in Council, order or directions.

(2) Any document purporting to be an order, notice or direction made or given by the Secretary of State for the purposes of [the Immigration Acts] and to be signed by him or on his behalf, and any document purporting to be a certificate of the Secretary of State so given and to be signed by him [or on his behalf] shall be received in evidence, and shall, until the contrary is proved, be deemed to be made or issued by him.

(3) Prima facie evidence of any such order, notice, direction or certificate as aforesaid may, in any legal proceedings or [other proceedings under the Immigration Acts], be given

by the production of a document bearing a certificate purporting to be signed by or on behalf of the Secretary of State and stating that the document is a true copy of the order, notice, direction or certificate.

(4) Where an order under section 8(2) above applies to persons specified in a schedule to the order, or any directions of the Secretary of State given for the purposes of [the Immigration Acts] apply to persons specified in a schedule to the directions, prima facie evidence of the provisions of the order or directions other than the schedule and of any entry contained in the schedule may, in any legal proceedings or [other proceedings under the Immigration Acts], be given by the production of a document purporting to be signed by or on behalf of the Secretary of State and stating that the document is a true copy of the said provisions and of the relevant entry.

(5) . . .

Note: Words in square brackets in subsections (2), (3) and (4) inserted by Immigration and Asylum Act 1999 from 6 December 1999. Subsection (5) substituted by Nationality, Immigration and Asylum Act 2002, s 158 from 10 February 2003 (SI 2003/1). Subsection (5) ceased to have effect by Immigration, Asylum and Nationality Act 2006, s 61 and Sch 3 from 30 March 2006 (Royal Assent).

33. Interpretation

(1) For purposes of this Act, except in so far as the context otherwise requires—

'aircraft' includes hovercraft, 'airport' includes hoverport and 'port' includes airport;

'captain' means master (of a ship) or commander (of an aircraft);

['certificate of entitlement' means a certificate under section 10 of the Nationality, Immigration and Asylum Act 2002 that a person has the right of abode in the United Kingdom];

['Convention adoption' has the same meaning as in the Adoption Act 1976 and {the Adoption and Children (Scotland) Act 2007}{or in the Adoption and Children Act 2002};]

'crew', in relation to a ship or aircraft, means all persons actually employed in the working or service of the ship or aircraft, including the captain, and 'member of the crew' shall be construed accordingly;

['entrant' means a person entering or seeking to enter the United Kingdom and 'illegal entrant' means a person—

(a) unlawfully entering or seeking to enter in breach of a deportation order or of the immigration laws, or

(b) entering or seeking to enter by means which include deception by another person, and includes also a person who has entered as mentioned in paragraph (a) or (b) above;]

'entry clearance' means a visa, entry certificate or other document which, in accordance with the immigration rules, is to be taken as evidence [or the requisite evidence] of a person's eligibility, though not [a British citizen], for entry into the United Kingdom (but does not include a work permit);

'immigration laws' means this Act and any law for purposes similar to this Act which is for the time being or has (before or after the passing of this Act) been in force in any part of the United Kingdom and Islands;

'immigration rules' means the rules for the time being laid down as mentioned in section 3(2) above;

'the Islands' means the Channel Islands and the Isle of Man, and 'the United Kingdom and Islands' means the United Kingdom and the Islands taken together;

'legally adopted' means adopted in pursuance of an order made by any court in the United Kingdom and Islands [under a Convention adoption] or by any adoption specified as an overseas adoption by order of the Secretary of State under [section 72(2) the Adoption Act 1976] {or by regulations made by the Scottish Ministers under section 67(1) of the Adoption and Children (Scotland) Act 2007};

'limited leave' and 'indefinite leave' mean respectively leave under this Act to enter or remain in the United Kingdom which is, and one which is not, limited as to duration;

'settled' shall be construed in accordance with [subsection (2A) below];

'ship' includes every description of vessel used in navigation;

['United Kingdom passport' means a current passport issued by the Government of the United Kingdom, or by the Lieutenant-Governor of any of the Islands or by the Government of any territory which is for the time being a dependent territory within the meaning of the British Nationality Act 1981;]

'work permit' means a permit indicating, in accordance with the immigration rules, that a person named in it is eligible, though not [a British citizen], for entry into the United Kingdom for the purpose of taking employment.

(1A) A reference to being the owner of a vehicle, ship or aircraft includes a reference to being any of a number of persons who jointly own it.

(2) It is hereby declared that, except as otherwise provided in this Act, a person is not to be treated for the purposes of any provision of this Act as ordinarily resident in the United Kingdom or in any of the Islands at a time when he is there in breach of the immigration laws.

(2A) Subject to section 8(5) above, references to a person being settled in the United Kingdom are references to his being ordinarily resident there without being subject under the immigration laws to any restriction on the period for which he may remain.]

(3) The ports of entry for purposes of this Act, and the ports of exit for purposes of any Order in Council under section 3(7) above, shall be such ports as may from time to time be designated for the purpose by order of the Secretary of State made by statutory instrument.

[(4) For the purposes of this Act, the question of whether an appeal is pending shall be determined {in accordance with section 104 of the Nationality, Immigration and Asylum Act 2002 (pending appeals)}.]

(5) This Act shall not be taken to supersede or impair any power exercisable by Her Majesty in relation to aliens by virtue of Her prerogative.

Note: Definition of certificate of entitlement in s 33(1) substituted by Nationality, Immigration and Asylum Act 2002, s 10 from 21 December 2006 (SI 2006/3144). Definition of 'Convention adoption' and amendment to definition of 'legally adopted' inserted by Adoption (Intercountry Aspects) Act 1999, Sch 2 from 1 June 2003 (SI 2003/362) and amended by Adoption and Children Act 2002 and further amended from 14 July 2011 by the Adoption and Children (Scotland) Act 2007 (Consequential Modifications) Order 2007 (SI 2011/1740). Definition of 'entrant' in s 33(1) substituted by Asylum and Immigration Act 1996 from 1 October 1996. Words in fifth square brackets in s 33(1) substituted by Adoption Act 1976. Other words in square brackets in s 33(1) substituted by British Nationality Act 1981. Subsection (1A) inserted by Nationality, Immigration and Asylum Act 2002, s 144 from 10 February 2003 (SI 2003/1). Subsection (2A) inserted by British Nationality Act 1981. Subsection (4) substituted by Immigration and Asylum Act 1999 from 2 October 2000. Words in curly brackets in subsection (4) substituted by Sch 7 Nationality,

Immigration and Asylum Act 2002 from 1 April 2003 (SI 2003/754). Section 33 has effect in a form modified by and in circumstances specified by the Channel Tunnel (International Arrangements) Order (SI 1993/1813) as amended by SIs 1994/1405, 2000/913, 2001/178, 2001/3707, 2006/1003 and 2007/3759.

34. Repeal, transitional and temporary

(1) Subject to the following provisions of this section, the enactments mentioned in Schedule 6 to this Act are hereby repealed, as from the coming into force of this Act, to the extent mentioned in column 3 of the Schedule; and—

(a) this Act, as from its coming into force, shall apply in relation to entrants or others arriving in the United Kingdom at whatever date before or after it comes into force; and

(b) after this Act comes into force anything done under or for the purposes of the former immigration laws shall have effect, in so far as any corresponding action could be taken under or for the purposes of this Act, as if done by way of action so taken, and in relation to anything so done this Act shall apply accordingly.

(2) Without prejudice to the generality of subsection (1)(a) and (b) above, a person refused leave to land by virtue of the Aliens Restriction Act 1914 shall be treated as having been refused leave to enter under this Act, and a person given leave to land by virtue of that Act shall be treated as having been given leave to enter under this Act; and similarly with the Commonwealth Immigrants Acts 1962 and 1968.

(3) A person treated in accordance with subsection (2) above as having leave to enter the United Kingdom—

(a) shall be treated as having an indefinite leave, if he is not at the coming in to force of this Act subject to a condition limiting his stay in the United Kingdom; and

(b) shall be treated, if he is then subject to such a condition, as having a limited leave of such duration, and subject to such conditions (capable of being attached to leave under this Act), as correspond to the conditions to which he is then subject, but not to conditions not capable of being so attached.

This subsection shall have effect in relation to any restriction or requirement imposed by Order in Council under the Aliens Restriction Act 1914 as if it had been imposed by way of a landing condition.

(4) Notwithstanding anything in the foregoing provisions of this Act, the former immigration laws shall continue to apply, and this Act shall not apply,—

(a) in relation to the making of deportation orders and matters connected therewith in any case where a decision to make the order has been notified to the person concerned before the coming into force of this Act;

(b) in relation to removal from the United Kingdom and matters connected therewith (including detention pending removal or pending the giving of directions for removal) in any case where a person is to be removed in pursuance of a decision taken before the coming into force of this Act or in pursuance of a deportation order to the making of which paragraph (a) above applies;

(c) in relation to appeals against any decision taken or other thing done under the former immigration laws, whether taken or done before the coming into force of this Act or by virtue of this subsection.

(5) Subsection (1) above shall not be taken as empowering a court on appeal to recommend for deportation a person whom the court below could not recommend for

deportation, or as affecting any right of appeal in respect of a recommendation for deportation made before this Act comes into force, or as enabling a notice given before this Act comes into force and not complying with section 6(2) to take the place of the notice required by section 6(2) to be given before a person is recommended for deportation.

(6) . . .

Note: Section 34(6) repealed by Statute Law (Repeals) Act 1993, s 1.

35. Commencement, and interim provisions

(1) Except as otherwise provided by this Act, Parts I to III of this Act shall come into force on such day as the Secretary of State may appoint by order made by statutory instrument; and references to the coming into force of this Act shall be construed as references to the beginning of the day so appointed.

(2) Section 25 above, except section 25(2), and section 28 in its application to offences under section 25(1) shall come into force at the end of one month beginning with the date this Act is passed.

(3) . . .

(4) . . .

(5) . . .

Note: Section 35(3)–(5) repealed by Statute Law (Repeals) Act 1986.

36. Power to extend to Islands

Her Majesty may by Order in Council direct that any of the provisions of this Act shall extend, with such exceptions, adaptations and modifications, if any, as may be specified in the Order, to any of the Islands; and any Order in Council under this subsection may be varied or revoked by a further Order in Council.

Note: Part 1, Part 3 and Part 4 (except for ss 29–30, 34–36) extended to the Isle of Man with modifications: see SI 2008/680 as amended by SI 2011/1408.

37. Short title and extent

(1) This Act may be cited as the Immigration Act 1971.

(2) It is hereby declared that this Act extends to Northern Ireland, and (without prejudice to any provision of Schedule 1 to this Act as to the extent of that Schedule) where an enactment repealed by this Act extends outside the United Kingdom, the repeal shall be of like extent.

Schedules

Schedule 1

Note: Repealed by British Nationality Act 1981, s 52(8).

Section 4

Schedule 2

Administrative Provisions as to Control on Entry etc.

Part I General Provisions

Immigration officers and medical inspectors

1.—(1) Immigration officers for the purposes of this Act shall be appointed by the Secretary of State, and he may arrange with the Commissioners of Customs and Excise for the employment of officers of customs and excise as immigration officers under this Act.

(2) Medical inspectors for the purposes of this Act may be appointed by the Secretary of State or, in Northern Ireland, by the Minister of Health and Social Services or other appropriate Minister of the Government of Northern Ireland in pursuance of arrangements made between that Minister and the Secretary of State, and shall be fully qualified medical practitioners.

[(2A) The Secretary of State may direct that his function of appointing medical inspectors under sub-paragraph (2) is also to be exercisable by such persons specified in the direction who exercise functions relating to health in England or Wales.]

(3) In the exercise of their functions under this Act immigration officers shall act in accordance with such instructions (not inconsistent with the immigration rules) as may be given them by the Secretary of State, and medical inspectors shall act in accordance with such instructions as may be given them by the Secretary of State or, in Northern Ireland, as may be given in pursuance of the arrangements mentioned in sub-paragraph (2) above by the Minister making appointments of medical inspectors in Northern Ireland.

(4) An immigration officer or medical inspector may board any ship [or aircraft] for the purpose of exercising his functions under this Act.

(5) An immigration officer, for the purpose of satisfying himself whether there are persons he may wish to examine under paragraph 2 below, may search any ship [or aircraft] and anything on board it, or any vehicle taken off a ship or aircraft on which it has been brought to the United Kingdom.

Note: Words in square brackets in subparagraphs (4) and (5) substituted by SI 1993/1813. Subparagraph (2A) inserted by Health Protection Agency Act 2004, s 12(3) and Sch 3 from 22 September 2004. Paragraph 1 has effect in a form modified by and in circumstances specified by the Channel Tunnel (International Arrangements) Order (SI 1993/1813) as amended by SIs 1994/1405, 2000/913, 2001/178, 2001/3707, 2006/1003 and 2007/3759.

Examination by immigration officers, and medical examination

2.—(1) An immigration officer may examine any persons who have arrived in the United Kingdom by ship [or aircraft] (including transit passengers, members of the crew and others not seeking to enter the United Kingdom) for the purpose of determining—

(a) whether any of them is or is not [a British citizen]; and

(b) whether, if he is not, he may or may not enter the United Kingdom without leave; and

[(c) whether, if he may not—

(i) he has been given leave which is still in force,

(ii) he should be given leave and for what period or on what conditions (if any), or

(iii) he should be refused leave.]

(2) Any such person, if he is seeking to enter the United Kingdom, may be examined also by a medical inspector or by any qualified person carrying out a test or examination required by a medical inspector.

(3) A person, on being examined under this paragraph by an immigration officer or medical inspector, may be required in writing by him to submit to further examination; but a requirement under this sub-paragraph shall not prevent a person who arrives as a transit passenger, or as a member of the crew of a ship or aircraft, or for the purpose of joining a ship or aircraft as a member of the crew, from leaving by his intended ship or aircraft.

Note: Words in first square brackets substituted by SI 1993/1813. Words in square brackets in subparagraph (1)(a) substituted by British Nationality Act 1981, s 39(6). Subparagraph (1)(c) substituted by Immigration and Asylum Act 1999 from 14 February 2000. Paragraph 2 has effect in a form modified by and in circumstances specified by the Channel Tunnel (International Arrangements) Order (SI 1993/1813) as amended by SIs 1994/1405, 2000/913, 2001/178, 2001/3707, 2006/1003 and 2007/3759.

[Examination of persons who arrive with continuing leave

2A.—(1) This paragraph applies to a person who has arrived in the United Kingdom with leave to enter which is in force but which was given to him before his arrival.

(2) He may be examined by an immigration officer for the purpose of establishing—

(a) whether there has been such a change in the circumstances of his case, since that leave was given, that it should be cancelled;

(b) whether that leave was obtained as a result of false information given by him or his failure to disclose material facts; or

(c) whether there are medical grounds on which that leave should be cancelled.

[(2A) Where the person's leave to enter derives, by virtue of section 3A(3), from an entry clearance, he may also be examined by an immigration officer for the purpose of establishing whether the leave should be cancelled on the grounds that the person's purpose in arriving in the United Kingdom is different from the purpose specified in the entry clearance.]

(3) He may also be examined by an immigration officer for the purpose of determining whether it would be conducive to the public good for that leave to be cancelled.

(4) He may also be examined by a medical inspector or by any qualified person carrying out a test or examination required by a medical inspector.

(5) A person examined under this paragraph may be required by the officer or inspector to submit to further examination.

(6) A requirement under sub-paragraph (5) does not prevent a person who arrives—

(a) as a transit passenger,

(b) as a member of the crew of a ship or aircraft, or

(c) for the purpose of joining a ship or aircraft as a member of the crew, from leaving by his intended ship or aircraft.

(7) An immigration officer examining a person under this paragraph may by notice suspend his leave to enter until the examination is completed.

(8) An immigration officer may, on the completion of any examination of a person under this paragraph, cancel his leave to enter.

(9) Cancellation of a person's leave under sub-paragraph (8) is to be treated for the purposes of this Act and [Part 5 of the Nationality, Immigration and Asylum Act 2002 [(appeals in respect of protection and human rights claims)]] as if he had been refused leave to enter at a time when he had a current entry clearance.

(10) A requirement imposed under sub-paragraph (5) and a notice given under sub-paragraph (7) must be in writing.]

Note: Paragraph 2A inserted by Immigration and Asylum Act 1999 from 14 February 2000. Words in first square brackets in paragraph 2A(9) substituted by Sch 7 Nationality, Immigration and Asylum Act 2002 from 1 April 2003 (SI 2003/754). Words in second square brackets in paragraph 2A(9) substituted by Sch 9 Immigration Act 2014 from 20 October 2014 with savings set out in articles 9-11 SI 2014/2771. Subparagraph (2A) inserted by Asylum and Immigration Act 2004, s 18 from 1 October 2004 (SI 2004/2523).

3.—(1) An immigration officer [or designated person] may examine any person who is embarking or seeking to embark in the United Kingdom for the purpose of determining whether he is [a British citizen] [and, if he is not a British citizen, for the purpose of establishing—

(a) his identity;

(b) whether he entered the United Kingdom lawfully;

(c) whether he has complied with any conditions of leave to enter or remain in the United Kingdom;

(d) whether his return to the United Kingdom is prohibited or restricted.

[(1A) If a person is examined under sub-paragraph (1) (whether by an immigration officer or designated person), an immigration officer may require the person, by notice in writing, to submit to further examination by the immigration officer for a purpose specified in that sub-paragraph.]]

(2) So long as any Order in Council is in force under section 3(7) of this Act, an immigration officer may examine any person who is embarking or seeking to embark in the United Kingdom for the purpose of determining—

(a) whether any of the provisions of the Order apply to him; and

(b) whether, if so, any power conferred by the Order should be exercised in relation to him and in what way.

Note: Words in first square brackets in subparagraph (1) inserted and subparagraph (1A) substituted by Sch 8 Immigration Act 2014 from 28 July 2014 (SI 2014/1820). Words in second square brackets in subparagraph (1) substituted by British Nationality Act 1981. Other words in square brackets substituted by Immigration, Asylum and Nationality Act 2006, s 42 from 31 August 2006 (SI 2006/2226). Paragraph 3 has effect in a form modified by and in circumstances specified by the Channel Tunnel (International Arrangements) Order (SI 1993/1813) as amended by SIs 1994/1405, 2000/913, 2001/178, 2001/3707, 2006/1003 and 2007/3759.

Information and documents

4.—(1) It shall be the duty of any person examined under paragraph 2, [2A] or 3 above to furnish to the person carrying out the examination all such information in his possession as that person may require for the purpose of [that or any other person's functions] under that paragraph.

(2) A person on his examination under paragraph 2, [2A] or 3 above by an immigration officer [, or on his examination under paragraph 3 above by a designated person, shall, if so required by an immigration officer or designated person];—

(a) produce either a valid passport with photograph or some other document satisfactorily establishing his identity and nationality or citizenship; and

(b) declare whether or not he is carrying or conveying [, or has carried or conveyed] documents of any relevant description specified by [the immigration officer or designated person], and produce any documents of that description which he is carrying or conveying.

In paragraph (b), 'relevant description' means any description appearing to [the immigration officer or designated person] to be relevant for the purposes of the examination.

(3) Where under sub-paragraph (2)(b) above a person has been required to declare whether or not he is carrying or conveying [or has carried or conveyed,] documents of any description,

[(a) he and any baggage or vehicle belonging to him or under his control; and

(b) any ship, aircraft or vehicle in which he arrived in the United Kingdom,];

may be searched with a view to ascertaining whether he is doing, [or, as the case may be, has done], so by [an immigration officer or a person acting under the directions of an immigration officer]:

Provided that no woman or girl shall be searched except by a woman.

[(4) Where a passport or other document is [produced to or found by an immigration officer] in accordance with this paragraph [the] immigration officer may examine it and detain it—

(a) for the purpose of examining it, for a period not exceeding 7 days;

(b) for any purpose, until the person to whom the document relates is given leave to enter the United Kingdom or is about to depart or be removed following refusal of leave or until it is decided that the person does not require leave to enter;

(c) after a time described in paragraph (b), while the immigration officer thinks that the document may be required in connection with proceedings in respect of an appeal under the Immigration Acts or in respect of an offence.

[(4A) Where a passport or other document is produced to a designated person in accordance with this paragraph, the designated person—

(a) may examine it and detain it; and

(b) must deliver any detained passport or document to an immigration officer as soon as reasonably practicable.

(4B) If a passport or document is delivered to an immigration officer in accordance with sub-paragraph (4A)(b), sub-paragraph (4) applies as if the immigration officer had detained the document (and, accordingly, the immigration officer may continue to detain it in accordance with sub-paragraph (4)(a), (b) or (c)).]

(5) For the purpose of ascertaining that a passport or other document produced or found in accordance with this paragraph relates to a person examined under paragraph 2, 2A or 3 above, the person carrying out the examination may require the person being examined to provide [biometric] information (whether or not by submitting to a process by means of which information is obtained or recorded)[. . .]

[(6) "Biometric information" has the meaning given by section 15 of the UK Borders Act 2007.]

[(7) A person ("P") who is under 16 may not be required to provide biometric information under sub-paragraph (5) unless—

(a) the decision to require P to provide the information has been confirmed by a chief immigration officer, and

(b) the information is provided in the presence of a person of full age who is—

(i) P's parent or guardian, or

(ii) a person who for the time being takes responsibility for P.

(8) The person mentioned in sub-paragraph (7)(b)(ii) may not be—

(a) a person who is entitled to require the provision of information under sub-paragraph (5) (an "authorised person"), or

(b) an officer of the Secretary of State who is not such a person.

(9) Sub-paragraph (7) does not prevent an authorised person requiring the provision of biometric information by a person the authorised person reasonably believes to be 16 or over.]

Note: Words in first square brackets in paragraph 4(1) and first and third square brackets in paragraph 4(2) inserted by Immigration and Asylum Act 1999 from 14 February 2000. Subparagraph (2A) ceased to have effect and subparagraph 4 substituted by Immigration, Asylum and Nationality Act 2006, s 27 from 31 August 2006 (SI 2006/2226). Where, immediately before that date, a passport or other document produced or found in accordance with paragraph 4 is being examined or detained by an immigration officer under paragraph 4(2A) or paragraph 4(4), paragraph 4(4) shall apply to the examination or detention of those documents on or after 31 August 2006 as if it had been in force on the date on which the passport or other document was produced or found, and paragraph 4(2A) shall cease to have effect. Paragraph 4(5) shall apply only where the examination under paragraph 2, 2A or 3 of that Schedule begins on or after 31 August 2006. Other words in square brackets in subparagraphs (1), (2), (3) and (4) substituted and subparagraphs (4A) and (4B) inserted by Sch 8 Immigration Act 2014 from 28 July 2014 (SI 2014/1820). Word in square brackets inserted and other words omitted from subparagraph (5) and subparagraph (6) inserted by Sch 2 Immigration Act 2014 from 28 July 2014 (SI 2014/1820. Subparagraphs (7)–(9) inserted by s 13 Immigration Act 2014 from 28 July 2014 (SI 2014/1820).

5. The Secretary of State may by order made by statutory instrument make provision for [requiring (a) passengers] disembarking or embarking in the United Kingdom, or any class of such passengers, to produce to an immigration officer, if so required, landing or embarkation [cards, and (b) passengers embarking in the United Kingdom, or any class of such passengers, to produce to a designated person, if so required, embarkations cards, in such form] as the Secretary of State may direct, and for requiring the owners or agents of ships and aircraft to supply such cards to those passengers.

Note: Paragraph 5 has effect in a form modified by and in circumstances specified by the Channel Tunnel (International Arrangements) Order (SI 1993/1813) as amended by SIs 1994/1405, 2000/913, 2001/178, 2001/3707, 2006/1003 and 2007/3759. Words in square brackets substituted by Schedule 8 Immigration Act 2014 from 28 July 2014 (SI 2014/1820).

[Designated persons

5A.—(1) In this Schedule "designated person" means a person designated by the Secretary of State for the purposes of this Schedule.

(2) A designation under this paragraph is subject to such limitations as may be specified in the designation.

(3) A limitation under sub-paragraph (2) may, in particular, relate to the functions that are exercisable by virtue of the designation (and, accordingly, the exercise of functions under this Schedule by a designated person is subject to any such limitations specified in the person's designation).

(4) A designation under this paragraph—
   (a) may be permanent or for a specified period,
   (b) may (in either case) be withdrawn, and
   (c) may be varied.

(5) The power to designate, or to withdraw or vary a designation, is exercised by the Secretary of State giving notice to the person in question.

(6) The Secretary of State may designate a person under this paragraph only if the Secretary of State is satisfied that the person—
   (a) is capable of effectively carrying out the functions that are exercisable by virtue of the designation,
   (b) has received adequate training in respect of the exercise of those functions, and
   (c) is otherwise a suitable person to exercise those functions.]

Note: Paragraph 5A inserted by Sch 8 Immigration Act 2014 from 28 July 2014 (SI 2014/1820).

[Directions to carriers and operators of ports etc

5B.—(1) The Secretary of State may direct—

(a) an owner or agent of a ship or aircraft, or

(b) a person concerned in the management of a port,

to make arrangements for designated persons to exercise a specified function, or a function of a specified description, in relation to persons of a specified description.

(2) A direction under this paragraph must specify—

(a) the port where, and

(b) the date (or dates) and time (or times) when,

a function is to be exercised under the arrangements.

(3) A direction under this paragraph must be in writing.

(4) A direction under this paragraph may specify a description of persons by reference, in particular, to—

(a) the destination to which persons are travelling;

(b) the route by which persons are travelling;

(c) the date and time when the persons are travelling.

(5) In this paragraph—

"function" means a function under this Schedule;

"specified" means specified in a direction under this paragraph.]

Note: Paragraph 5B inserted by Sch 8 Immigration Act 2014 from 28 July 2014 (SI 2014/1820).

Notice of leave to enter or of refusal of leave

6.—(1) Subject to sub-paragraph (3) below, where a person examined by an immigration officer under paragraph 2 above is to be given a limited leave to enter the United Kingdom or is to be refused leave, the notice giving or refusing leave shall be given not later than [twenty four] hours after the conclusion of his examination (including any further examination) in pursuance of that paragraph; and if notice giving or refusing leave is not given him before the end of those [twenty four] hours, he shall (if not [a British citizen]) be deemed to have been given [leave to enter the United Kingdom for a period of six months subject to a condition prohibiting his taking employment] and the immigration officer shall as soon as may be given him written notice of that leave.

(2) Where on a person's examination under paragraph 2 above he is given notice of leave to enter the United Kingdom, then at any time before the end of [twenty four hours] from the conclusion of the examination he may be given a further notice in writing by an immigration officer cancelling the earlier notice and refusing him leave to enter.

(3) Where in accordance with this paragraph a person is given notice refusing him leave to enter the United Kingdom, that notice may at any time be cancelled by notice in writing given him by an immigration officer; and where a person is given a notice of cancellation under this sub-paragraph, [and the immigration officer does not at the same time give him indefinite or limited leave to enter {or require him to submit to further examination}, he shall be deemed to have been given leave to enter for a period of six months subject to a condition prohibiting his taking employment and the immigration officer shall as soon as may be give him written notice of that leave.]

(4) Where an entrant is a member of a party in charge of a person appearing to the immigration officer to be a responsible person, any notice to be given in relation to that entrant in accordance with this paragraph shall be duly given if delivered to the person in charge of the party.

Note: Words in third square brackets substituted by British Nationality Act 1981, s 39(6); other words in square brackets substituted by Immigration Act 1988, s 10. Words in curly brackets in paragraph 6(3) inserted by Nationality, Immigration and Asylum Act 2002, s 119 from 8 January 2003 (SI 2002/2811).

[Power to require medical examination after entry

7.—(1) This paragraph applies if an immigration officer examining a person under paragraph 2 decides—
(a) that he may be given leave to enter the United Kingdom; but
(b) that a further medical test or examination may be required in the interests of public health.

(2) This paragraph also applies if an immigration officer examining a person under paragraph 2A decides—
(a) that his leave to enter the United Kingdom should not be cancelled; but
(b) that a further medical test or examination may be required in the interests of public health.

(3) The immigration officer may give the person concerned notice in writing requiring him—
(a) to report his arrival to such medical officer of health as may be specified in the notice; and
(b) to attend at such place and time and submit to such test or examination (if any), as that medical officer of health may require.

(4) In reaching a decision under paragraph (b) of sub-paragraph (1) or (2), the immigration officer must act on the advice of—
(a) a medical inspector; or
(b) if no medical inspector is available, a fully qualified medical practitioner.]

Note: Paragraph 7 substituted by Immigration and Asylum Act 1999 from 14 February 2000.

Removal of persons refused leave to enter and illegal entrants

8.—(1) Where a person arriving in the United Kingdom is refused leave to enter, an immigration officer may, subject to sub-paragraph (2) below—
(a) give the captain of the ship or aircraft in which he arrives directions requiring the captain to remove him from the United Kingdom in that ship or aircraft; or
(b) give the owners or agents of that ship or aircraft directions requiring them to remove him from the United Kingdom in any ship or aircraft specified or indicated in the directions, being a ship or aircraft of which they are the owners or agents; or
(c) give those owners or agents directions requiring them to make arrangements for his removal from the United Kingdom in any ship or aircraft specified or indicated in the directions to a country or territory so specified, being either—
(i) a country of which he is a national or citizen; or
(ii) a country or territory in which he has obtained a passport or other document of identity; or
(iii) a country or territory in which he embarked for the United Kingdom; or
(iv) a country or territory to which there is reason to believe that he will be admitted.

(2) No directions shall be given under this paragraph in respect of anyone after the expiration of two months beginning with the date on which he was refused leave to enter the United Kingdom [(ignoring any period during which an appeal by him under the Immigration Acts is pending)] [except that directions may be given under sub-paragraph (1)(b) or (c) after the end of that period if the immigration officer has within that period given written notice to the owners or agents in question of his intention to give directions to them in respect of that person].

Note: Words in first square brackets in subparagraph (2) inserted by Sch 7 Nationality, Immigration and Asylum Act 2002 from 1 April 2003 (SI 2003/754). Words in second square brackets in subparagraph (2) added by Immigration Act 1988, s 10. Paragraph 8 modified in relation to certain persons entering or seeking to enter through Republic of Ireland with effect from 17 July 2002: see the Immigration (Entry otherwise than by Sea or Air) Order 2002 (SI 2002/1832). Paragraph 8 has effect in a form modified by and in circumstances specified by the Channel Tunnel (International Arrangements) Order (SI 1993/1813) as amended by SIs 1994/1405, 2000/913, 2001/178, 2001/3707, 2006/1003 and 2007/3759.

9.—(1) Where an illegal entrant is not given leave to enter or remain in the United Kingdom, an immigration officer may give any such directions in respect of him as in a case within paragraph 8 above are authorised by paragraph 8(1).

[(2) Any leave to enter the United Kingdom which is obtained by deception shall be disregarded for the purposes of this paragraph.]

Note: Paragraph 9(2) added by Asylum and Immigration Act 1996 from 1 October 1996. Subparagraph (1) modified in relation to certain persons entering or seeking to enter through Republic of Ireland with effect from 17 July 2002: see the Immigration (Entry otherwise than by Sea or Air) Order 2002 (SI 2002/1832). Paragraph 9 has effect in a form modified by and in circumstances specified by the Channel Tunnel (International Arrangements) Order (SI 1993/1813) as amended by SIs 1994/1405, 2000/913, 2001/178, 2001/3707, 2006/1003 and 2007/3759.

10.—(1) Where it appears to the Secretary of State either—

(a) that directions might be given in respect of a person under paragraph 8 or 9 above, but that it is not practicable for them to be given or that, if given, they would be ineffective; or

(b) that directions might have been given in respect of a person under paragraph 8 above [but that the requirements of paragraph 8(2) have not been complied with];

then the Secretary of State may give to the owners or agents of any ship or aircraft any such directions in respect of that person as are authorised by paragraph 8(1)(c).

(2) Where the Secretary of State may give directions for a person's removal in accordance with sub-paragraph (1) above, he may instead give directions for his removal in accordance with arrangements to be made by the Secretary of State to any country or territory to which he could be removed under sub-paragraph (1).

(3) The costs of complying with any directions given under this paragraph shall be defrayed by the Secretary of State.

Note: Paragraph 10 has effect in a form modified by and in circumstances specified by the Channel Tunnel (International Arrangements) Order (SI 1993/1813) as amended by SIs 1994/1405, 2000/913, 2001/178, 2001/3707, 2006/1003 and 2007/3759.

[**10A** Where directions are given in respect of a person under any of paragraphs 8 to 10 above, directions to the same effect may be given under that paragraph in respect of a member of the person's family].

Note: Paragraph 10A inserted by Nationality, Immigration and Asylum Act 2002 from 10 February 2003 (SI 2003/1).

11. A person in respect of whom directions are given under any of paragraphs 8 to 10 above may be placed, under the authority of an immigration officer [or the Secretary of State], on board any ship or aircraft in which he is to be removed in accordance with the directions.

Note: Paragraph 11 modified in relation to certain persons entering or seeking to enter through Republic of Ireland with effect from 17 July 2002: see the Immigration (Entry otherwise than by Sea or Air) Order 2002 (SI 2002/1832). Paragraph 11 has effect in a form modified by and in circumstances specified by the Channel Tunnel (International Arrangements) Order (SI 1993/1813) as amended by SIs 1994/1405, 2000/913, 2001/178, 2001/3707, 2006/1003 and 2007/3759. Words in square brackets inserted by Sch 9 Immigration Act 2014 from 20 October 2014 with saving set out in SI 2014/2771 articles 9-11.

Seamen and aircrews

12.—(1) If, on a person's examination by an immigration officer under paragraph 2 above, the immigration officer is satisfied that he has come to the United Kingdom for the purpose of joining a ship or aircraft as a member of the crew, then the immigration officer may limit the duration of any leave he gives that person to enter the United Kingdom by requiring him to leave the United Kingdom in a ship or aircraft specified or indicated by the notice giving leave.

(2) Where a person (not being [a British citizen]) arrives in the United Kingdom for the purpose of joining a ship or aircraft as a member of the crew and, having been given leave to enter as mentioned in sub-paragraph (1) above, remains beyond the time limited by that leave, or is reasonably suspected by an immigration officer of intending to do so, an immigration officer may—

(a) give the captain of that ship or aircraft directions requiring the captain to remove him from the United Kingdom in that ship or aircraft; or

(b) give the owners or agents of that ship or aircraft directions requiring them to remove him from the United Kingdom in any ship or aircraft specified or indicated in the directions, being a ship or aircraft of which they are the owners or agents; or

(c) give those owners or agents directions requiring them to make arrangements for his removal from the United Kingdom in any ship or aircraft specified or indicated in the directions to a country or territory so specified, being either—

(i) a country of which he is a national or citizen; or

(ii) a country or territory in which he has obtained a passport or other document of identity; or

(iii) a country or territory in which he embarked for the United Kingdom; or

(iv) a country or territory where he was engaged as a member of the crew of the ship or aircraft which he arrived in the United Kingdom to join; or

(v) a country or territory to which there is reason to believe that he will be admitted.

Note: Words in square brackets substituted by British Nationality Act 1981, s 39(6).

13.—(1) Where a person being a member of the crew of a ship or aircraft is examined by an immigration officer under paragraph 2 above, the immigration officer may limit the duration of any leave he gives that person to enter the United Kingdom—

(a) in the manner authorised by paragraph 12(1) above; or

(b) if that person is to be allowed to enter the United Kingdom in order to receive hospital treatment, by requiring him, on completion of that treatment, to leave the United Kingdom in accordance with arrangements to be made for his repatriation; or

(c) by requiring him to leave the United Kingdom within a specified period in accordance with arrangements to be made for his repatriation.

(2) Where a person (not being [a British citizen]) arrives in the United Kingdom as a member of the crew of a ship or aircraft, and either—

(A) having lawfully entered the United Kingdom without leave by virtue of section 8(1) of this Act, he remains without leave beyond the time allowed by section 8(1), or is reasonably suspected by an immigration officer of intending to do so; or

(B) having been given leave limited as mentioned in sub-paragraph (1) above, he remains beyond the time limited by that leave, or is reasonably suspected by an immigration officer of intending to do so;

an immigration officer may—

(a) give the captain of the ship or aircraft in which he arrived directions requiring the captain to remove him from the United Kingdom in that ship or aircraft; or

(b) give the owners or agents of that ship or aircraft directions requiring them to remove him from the United Kingdom in any ship or aircraft specified or indicated in the directions, being a ship or aircraft of which they are the owners or agents; or

(c) give those owners or agents directions requiring them to make arrangements for his removal from the United Kingdom in any ship or aircraft specified or indicated in the directions to a country or territory so specified, being either—

(i) a country of which he is a national or citizen; or

(ii) a country or territory in which he has obtained a passport or other document of identity; or

(iii) a country in which he embarked for the United Kingdom; or

(iv) a country or territory in which he was engaged as a member of the crew of the ship or aircraft in which he arrived in the United Kingdom; or

(v) a country or territory to which there is reason to believe that he will be admitted.

Note: Words in square brackets substituted by British Nationality Act 1981, s 39(6). Paragraph 13 has effect in a form modified by and in circumstances specified by the Channel Tunnel (International Arrangements) Order (SI 1993/1813) as amended by SIs 1994/1405, 2000/913, 2001/178, 2001/3707, 2006/1003 and 2007/3759.

14.—(1) Where it appears to the Secretary of State that directions might be given in respect of a person under paragraph 12 or 13 above, but that it is not practicable for them to be given or that, if given, they would be ineffective, then the Secretary of State may give to the owners or agents of any ship or aircraft any such directions in respect of that person as are authorised by paragraph 12(2)(c) or 13(2)(c).

(2) Where the Secretary of State may give directions for a person's removal in accordance with sub-paragraph (1) above, he may instead give directions for his removal in accordance with arrangements to be made by the Secretary of State to any country or territory to which he could be removed under sub-paragraph (1).

(3) The costs of complying with any directions given under this paragraph shall be defrayed by the Secretary of State.

15. A person in respect of whom directions are given under any of paragraphs 12 to 14 above may be placed, under the authority of an immigration officer, on board any ship or aircraft in which he is to be removed in accordance with the directions.

Note: Paragraph 15 has effect in a form modified by and in circumstances specified by the Channel Tunnel (International Arrangements) Order (SI 1993/1813) as amended by SIs 1994/1405, 2000/913, 2001/178, 2001/3707, 2006/1003 and 2007/3759.

Detention of persons liable to examination or removal

16.—(1) A person who may be required to submit to examination under paragraph 2 above may be detained under the authority of an immigration officer pending his examination and pending a decision to give or refuse him leave to enter.

[(**1A**) A person whose leave to enter has been suspended under paragraph 2A may be detained under the authority of an immigration officer pending—

(a) completion of his examination under that paragraph; and

(b) a decision on whether to cancel his leave to enter.]

[(**1B**) A person who has been required to submit to further examination under paragraph 3(1A) may be detained under the authority of an immigration officer, for a period not exceeding 12 hours, pending the completion of the examination.]

[(2) If there are reasonable grounds for suspecting that a person is someone in respect of whom directions may be given under any of paragraphs [8 to 10A] or 12 to 14, that person may be detained under the authority of an immigration officer pending—

(a) a decision whether or not to give such directions;

(b) his removal in pursuance of such directions.]

[(**2A**) But the detention of an unaccompanied child under sub-paragraph (2) is subject to paragraph 18B]

(3) A person on board a ship or aircraft may, under the authority of an immigration officer, be removed from the ship or aircraft for detention under this paragraph; but if an immigration officer so requires the captain of a ship or aircraft shall prevent from disembarking in the United Kingdom any person who has arrived in the United Kingdom in the ship or aircraft and been refused leave to enter, and the captain may for that purpose detain him in custody on board the ship or aircraft.

(4) The captain of a ship or aircraft, if so required by an immigration officer, shall prevent from disembarking in the United Kingdom or before the directions for his removal have been fulfilled any person placed on board the ship or aircraft under paragraph 11 or 15 above, and the captain may for that purpose detain him in custody on board the ship or aircraft.

Note: Subparagraph (1A) inserted by Immigration and Asylum Act 1999 from 14 February 2000, subparagraph (2) substituted by Immigration and Asylum Act 1999. Words in square brackets substituted by Nationality, Immigration and Asylum Act 2002 from 10 February 2003 (SI 2003/1). Subparagraph (1B) inserted by Immigration, Asylum and Nationality Act 2006, s 42 from 31 August 2006 (SI 2006/2226). Paragraph 16 has effect in a form modified by and in circumstances specified by the Channel Tunnel (International Arrangements) Order (SI 1993/1813) as amended by SIs 1994/1405, 2000/913, 2001/178, 2001/3707, 2006/1003 and 2007/3759. Subparagraph (2A) inserted by s 5 Immigration Act 2014 from 28 July 2014 (SI 2014/1820).

17.—(1) A person liable to be detained under paragraph 16 above may be arrested without warrant by a constable or by an immigration officer.

(2) If—

(a) a justice of the peace is by written information on oath satisfied that there is reasonable ground for suspecting that a person liable to be arrested under this paragraph is to be found on any premises; or

(b) in Scotland, a sheriff, or a . . . justice of the peace, having jurisdiction in the place where the premises are situated is by evidence on oath so satisfied; he may grant a warrant [authorising any immigration officer or constable to enter], [if need be by reasonable force], the premises named in the warrant for the purpose of searching for and arresting that person.

[(3) Sub-paragraph (4) applies where an immigration officer or constable—

(a) enters premises in reliance on a warrant under sub-paragraph (2), and

(b) detains a person on the premises.

(4) A detainee custody officer may enter the premises, if need be by reasonable force, for the purpose of carrying out a search.

(5) In sub-paragraph (4)—

'detainee custody officer' means a person in respect of whom a certificate of authorisation is in force under section 154 of the Immigration and Asylum Act 1999 (c. 33) (detained persons: escort and custody), and

'search' means a search under paragraph 2(1)(a) of Schedule 13 to that Act (escort arrangements: power to search detained person).]

Note: Words omitted from (2)(b) repealed by Asylum and Immigration Act 1996 from 1 October 1996; other words omitted by Police and Criminal Evidence Act 1984, s 119(2). Words in first square brackets in (2)(b) substituted by Immigration and Asylum Act 1999, s 140(2); words in second square brackets substituted by Nationality, Immigration and Asylum Act 2002 from 10 February 2003 (SI 2003/1).

18.—(1) Persons may be detained under paragraph 16 above in such places as the Secretary of State may direct (when not detained in accordance with paragraph 16 on board a ship or aircraft).

[(**1A**) But the detention of an unaccompanied child under paragraph 16(2) is subject to paragraph 18B].

(2) Where a person is detained [or liable to be detained] under paragraph 16, any immigration officer, constable or prison officer, or any other person authorised by the Secretary of State, may take all such steps as may be reasonably necessary for photographing, measuring or otherwise identifying him.

[(**2A**) The power conferred by sub-paragraph (2) includes power to take [biometric information (within the meaning given by section 15 of the UK Borders Act 2007)]]

[(**2B**) Paragraph 4(7) to (9) applies to sub-paragraph (2) as it applies to paragraph 4(5).]

(3) Any person detained under paragraph 16 may be taken in the custody of a constable, [an immigration officer or] any person acting under the authority of an immigration officer, to and from any place where his attendance is required for the purpose of ascertaining his citizenship or nationality or of making arrangements for his admission to a country or territory other than the United Kingdom, or where he is required to be for any other purpose connected with the operation of this Act.

(4) A person shall be deemed to be in legal custody at any time when he is detained under paragraph 16 or is being removed in pursuance of sub-paragraph (3) above.

Note: Subparagraph (2A) inserted by Immigration and Asylum Act 1999 from 11 December 1999 (SI 2000/3099). Subparagraph (1A) inserted by s 5 Immigration Act 2014 words in square brackets in subparagraph (2) inserted by s 2 that Act, words in square brackets in subparagraph (2A) substituted by Sch 2 that Act, subparagraph (2B) inserted by s 13 that Act, words in square brackets in subparagraph (3) substituted by Sch 1 of that Act from 28 July 2014 (SI 2014/1820).

[18A.—(1) An immigration officer or constable may search a person ("P") who is detained under paragraph 16 for anything which P might use—

(a) to cause physical injury to P or others, or

(b) to assist P's escape from legal custody.

(2) The power to search P—

(a) unless sub-paragraph (3) applies, does not include power to require P to remove any clothing other than an outer coat, jacket or glove, but

(b) includes power to require P to open P's mouth.

(3) This sub-paragraph applies if an immigration officer or constable has reasonable grounds to believe that there is concealed on P anything which P might use as mentioned in sub-paragraph (1).

(4) The power to search P may be exercised only to the extent reasonably required for the purpose of discovering anything which P might use as mentioned in sub-paragraph (1).

(5) An intimate search (as defined in section 28H(11)) may not be conducted under this paragraph.

(6) An immigration officer or constable may seize and retain anything found on a search of P if the officer or constable has reasonable grounds to believe P might use it as mentioned in sub-paragraph (1).

(7) Nothing seized under sub-paragraph (6) may be retained when P is released from detention under paragraph 16.]

Note: Paragraph 18A inserted by Schedule 1 Immigration Act 2014 from 28 July 2014 (SI 2014/1820).

[18B.—(1) Where a person detained under paragraph 16(2) is an unaccompanied child, the only place where the child may be detained is a short-term holding facility, except where—

(a) the child is being transferred to or from a short-term holding facility, or

(b) sub-paragraph (3) of paragraph 18 applies.

(2) An unaccompanied child may be detained under paragraph 16(2) in a short-term holding facility for a maximum period of 24 hours, and only for so long as the following two conditions are met.

(3) The first condition is that—

(a) directions are in force that require the child to be removed from the short-term holding facility within the relevant 24 hour period, or

(b) a decision on whether or not to give directions is likely to result in such directions.

(4) The second condition is that the immigration officer under whose authority the child is being detained reasonably believes that the child will be removed from the short-term holding facility within the relevant 24 hour period in accordance with those directions.

(5) An unaccompanied child detained under paragraph 16(2) who has been removed from a short-term holding facility and detained elsewhere may be detained again in a short-term holding facility but only if, and for as long as, the relevant 24 hour period has not ended.

(6) An unaccompanied child who has been released following detention under paragraph 16(2) may be detained again in a short-term holding facility in accordance with this paragraph.

(7) In this paragraph—

"relevant 24 hour period", in relation to the detention of a child in a short-term holding facility, means the period of 24 hours starting when the child was detained (or, in a case falling within sub-paragraph (5), first detained) in a short-term holding facility;

"short-term holding facility" has the same meaning as in Part 8 of the Immigration and Asylum Act 1999;

"unaccompanied child" means a person—

(a) who is under the age of 18, and

(b) who is not accompanied (whilst in detention) by his or her parent or another individual who has care of him or her.]

Note: Paragraph 18B inserted by s 5 Immigration Act 2014 fron 28 July 2014 (SI 2014/1820).

19.—(1) Where a person is refused leave to enter the United Kingdom and directions are given in respect of him under paragraph 8 or 10 above, then subject to the provisions of this paragraph the owners or agents of the ship or aircraft in which he arrived shall be liable to pay the Secretary of State on demand any expenses incurred by the latter in respect of the custody, accommodation or maintenance of that person [for any period (not exceeding 14 days)] after his arrival while he was detained or liable to be detained under paragraph 16 above.

(2) Sub-paragraph (1) above shall not apply to expenses in respect of a person who, when he arrived in the United Kingdom, held a [certificate of entitlement] or a current entry clearance or was the person named in a current work permit; and for this purpose a document purporting to be a [certificate of entitlement], entry clearance or work permit is to be regarded as being one unless its falsity is reasonably apparent.

(3) If, before the directions for a person's removal under paragraph 8 or 10 above have been carried out, he is given leave to enter the United Kingdom, or if he is afterwards given that leave in consequence of the determination in his favour of an appeal under this Act (being an appeal against a refusal of leave to enter by virtue of which the directions were given), or it is determined on an appeal under this Act that he does not require leave to enter (being an appeal occasioned by such a refusal), no sum shall be demanded under sub-paragraph (1) above for expenses incurred in respect of that person and any sum already demanded and paid shall be refunded.

(4) Sub-paragraph (1) above shall not have effect in relation to directions which in consequence of an appeal under this Act, have ceased to have effect or are for the time being of no effect; and the expenses to which that sub-paragraph applies include expenses in conveying the person in question to and from the place where he is detained or accommodated unless the journey is made for the purpose of attending an appeal by him under this Act.

Note: Words in square brackets in subparagraph (1) substituted by Asylum and Immigration Act 1996 from 1 October 1996. Words in square brackets in subparagraph (2) substituted by British Nationality Act 1981, s 39(6). Paragraph 19 has effect in a form modified by and in circumstances specified by the Channel Tunnel (International Arrangements) Order (SI 1993/1813) as amended by SIs 1994/1405, 2000/913, 2001/178, 2001/3707, 2006/1003 and 2007/3759.

20.—(1) Subject to the provisions of this paragraph, in either of the following cases, that is to say,—

(a) where directions are given in respect of an illegal entrant under paragraph 9 or 10 above; and

(b) where a person has lawfully entered the United Kingdom without leave by virtue of section 8(1) of this Act, but directions are given in respect of him under paragraph 13(2)(A) above or, in a case within paragraph 13(2)(A), under paragraph 14; the owners or agents of the ship or aircraft in which he arrived in the United Kingdom shall be liable to pay the Secretary of State on demand any expenses incurred by the latter in respect of the custody, accommodation or maintenance of that person [for any period (not exceeding 14 days)] after his arrival while he was detained or liable to be detained under paragraph 16 above.

[(**1A**) Sub-paragraph (1) above shall not apply to expenses in respect of an illegal entrant if he obtained leave to enter by deception and the leave has not been cancelled under paragraph 6(2) above.]

(2) If, before the directions for a person's removal from the United Kingdom have been carried out, he is given leave to remain in the United Kingdom, no sum shall be demanded under sub-paragraph (1) above for expenses incurred in respect of that person and any sum already demanded and paid shall be refunded.

(3) Sub-paragraph (1) above shall not have effect in relation to directions which, in consequence of an appeal under this Act, are for the time being of no effect; and the expenses to which that sub-paragraph applies include expenses in conveying the person in question to and from the place where he is detained or accommodated unless the journey is made for the purpose of attending an appeal by him under this Act.

Note: Words in square brackets substituted and (1A) inserted by Asylum and Immigration Act 1996 from 1 October 1996. Paragraph 20 has effect in a form modified by and in circumstances specified by the Channel Tunnel (International Arrangements) Order (SI 1993/1813) as amended by SIs 1994/1405, 2000/913, 2001/178, 2001/3707, 2006/1003 and 2007/3759.

Temporary admission of persons liable to detention

21.—(1) A person liable to detention or detained under paragraph 16 [(1), (1A) or (2)] above may, under the written authority of an immigration officer, be temporarily admitted to the United Kingdom without being detained or be released from detention; but this shall not prejudice a later exercise of the power to detain him.

(2) So long as a person is at large in the United Kingdom by virtue of this paragraph, he shall be subject to such restrictions as to residence [, as to his employment or occupation] and as to reporting to the police or an immigration officer as may from time to time be notified to him in writing by an immigration officer.

[(**2A**) The provisions that may be included in restrictions as to residence imposed under sub-paragraph (2) include provisions of such a description as may be prescribed by regulations made by the Secretary of State.

(**2B**) The regulations may, among other things, provide for the inclusion of provisions—

(a) prohibiting residence in one or more particular areas;

(b) requiring the person concerned to reside in accommodation provided under section 4 of the Immigration and Asylum Act 1999 and prohibiting him from being absent from that accommodation except in accordance with the restrictions imposed on him.

(**2C**) The regulations may provide that a particular description of provision may be imposed only for prescribed purposes.

(**2D**) The power to make regulations conferred by this paragraph is exercisable by statutory instrument and includes a power to make different provision for different cases.

(**2E**) But no regulations under this paragraph are to be made unless a draft of the regulations has been laid before Parliament and approved by a resolution of each House.]

[(3) Sub-paragraph (4) below applies where a person who is at large in the United Kingdom by virtue of this paragraph is subject to a restriction as to reporting to an immigration officer with a view to the conclusion of his examination under paragraph 2 [or 2A] above.

(4) If the person fails at any time to comply with that restriction—
 (a) an immigration officer may direct that the person's examination shall be treated as concluded at that time; but
 (b) nothing in paragraph 6 above shall require the notice giving or refusing him leave to enter the United Kingdom to be given within twenty-four hours after that time.]

Note: Words in square brackets in subparagraph (1) inserted by Immigration, Asylum and Nationality Act 2006, s 42 from 31 August 2006 (SI 2006/2226). Words in square brackets in subparagraph (2) inserted by Immigration Act 1988, s 10; subparagraphs (3) and (4) inserted by Asylum and Immigration Act 1996 from 1 October 1996. Subparagraphs (2A), (2B), (2C), (2D) and (2E) inserted by Immigration and Asylum Act 1999 from 11 November 1999, other words in square brackets inserted and words in subparagraph (4)(a) omitted by Immigration and Asylum Act 1999 from 14 February 2000.

Temporary release of persons liable to detention

22.—[(1) The following, namely—
 (a) a person detained under paragraph 16(1) above pending examination;
 [(aa) a person detained under paragraph 16(1A) above pending completion of his examination or a decision on whether to cancel his leave to enter;] and
 (b) a person detained under paragraph 16(2) above pending the giving of directions,

may be released on bail in accordance with this paragraph.

(1A) An immigration officer not below the rank of chief immigration officer or [the First-tier Tribunal] may release a person so detained on his entering into a recognizance or, in Scotland, bail bond conditioned for his appearance before an immigration officer at a time and place named in the recognizance or bail bond or at such other time and place as may in the meantime be notified to him in writing by an immigration officer.

(1B) Sub-paragraph (1)(a) above shall not apply unless seven days have elapsed since the date of the person's arrival in the United Kingdom.]

(2) The conditions of a recognizance or bail bond taken under this paragraph may include conditions appearing to the [immigration officer or [the First-tier Tribunal]] to be likely to result in the appearance of the person bailed at the required time and place; and any recognizance shall be with or without sureties as the [officer or [the First-tier Tribunal]] may determine.

(3) In any case in which an [immigration officer or [the First-tier Tribunal]] has power under this paragraph to release a person on bail, the [officer or [the First-tier Tribunal]] may, instead of taking the bail, fix the amount and conditions of the bail (including the amount in which any sureties are to be bound) with a view to its being taken subsequently by any such person as may be specified by the [officer or [the First-tier Tribunal]]; and on the recognizance or bail bond being so taken the person to be bailed shall be released.

[(4) A person must not be released on bail in accordance with this paragraph without the consent of the Secretary of State if—
 (a) directions for the removal of the person from the United Kingdom are for the time being in force, and
 (b) the directions require the person to be removed from the United Kingdom within the period of 14 days starting with the date of the decision on whether the person should be released on bail.]

Note: Subparagraphs (1)–(1B) substituted by Asylum and Immigration Act 1996 from 1 October 1996 and subparagraphs (2) and (3) amended by the same Act from 1 September 1996 (SI 1996/2053). Subparagraph (1)(aa) inserted by Immigration and Asylum Act 1999 from 14 February 2000. Words 'the First-tier Tribunal' substituted from 15 February 2010 (SI 2010/21). Subparagraph (4) inserted by s 7 Immigration Act 2014 from 28 July 2014 (SI 2014/1820).

23.—(1) Where a recognizance entered into under paragraph 22 above appears to [the First-tier Tribunal] to be forfeited, [the First-tier Tribunal] may by order declare it to be forfeited and adjudge the persons bound thereby, whether as principal or sureties, or any of them, to pay the sum in which they are respectively bound or such part of it, if any, as [the First-tier Tribunal] thinks fit; and an order under this sub-paragraph shall specify a magistrates' court or, in Northern Ireland, court of summary jurisdiction, and—

(a) the recognizance shall be treated for the purposes of collection, enforcement and remission of the sum forfeited as having been forfeited by the court so specified; and

(b) [the First-tier Tribunal] shall, as soon as practicable, give particulars of the recognizance to the [proper officer] of that court.

[(**1A**) In sub-paragraph (3) "proper officer" means—

(a) in relation to a magistrates' court in England and Wales, the [designated officer] for the court; and

(b) in relation to a court of summary jurisdiction in Northern Ireland, the clerk of the court.]

(2) Where a person released on bail under paragraph 22 above as it applies in Scotland fails to comply with the terms of his bail bond, [the First-tier Tribunal] may declare the bail to be forefeited, and any bail so forfeited shall be transmitted by [the First-tier Tribunal] to the sheriff court having jurisdiction in the area where the proceedings took place, and shall be treated as having been forfeited by that court.

(3) Any sum the payment of which is enforceable by a magistrates' court in England or Wales by virtue of this paragraph shall be treated for the [purposes of section 38 of the Courts Act 2003 (application of receipts of designated officers) as being] due under a recognizance forfeited by such a court. . .

(4) Any sum the payment of which is enforceable by virtue of this paragraph by a court of summary jurisdiction in Northern Ireland shall, for the purposes of section 20(5) of the Administration of Justice Act (Northern Ireland) 1954, be treated as a forfeited recognizance.

Note: Words in square brackets in subparagraph 3 substituted by Justices of the Peace Act 1979; words omitted repealed by Criminal Justice Act 1972. Subparagraph (1A) inserted by and words in brackets in subparagraph (1) substituted by Access to Justice Act 1999, Sch 13 paragraph 70 from 1 April 2001 (SI 2001/916). Words in square brackets in subparagraph (1A)((a) and subparagraph (3) substituted by Sch 8 Courts Act 2003 from 1 April 2005 (SI 2005/910).). Words 'the First-tier Tribunal' substituted from 15 February 2010 (SI 2010/21). Other words in square brackets substituted by Sch 2 Asylum and Immigration (Treatment of Claimants etc.) Act 2004 from 4 April 2005 (SI 2005/565).

24.—(1) An immigration officer or constable may arrest without warrant a person who has been released by virtue of paragraph 22 above—

(a) if he has reasonable grounds for believing that that person is likely to break the condition of his recognizance or bail bond that he will appear at the time and place required or to break any other condition of it, or has reasonable ground to suspect that the person is breaking or has broken any such other condition; or

(b) if, a recognizance with sureties having been taken, he is notified in writing by any surety of the surety's belief that that person is likely to break the first-mentioned condition, and of the surety's wish for that reason to be relieved of his obligations as a surety; and paragraph 17(2) above shall apply for the arrest of a person under this paragraph as it applies for the arrest of a person under paragraph 17.

(2) A person arrested under this paragraph—

(a) if not required by a condition on which he was released to appear before an immigration officer within twenty-four hours after the time of his arrest, shall as soon as practicable be brought before [the First-tier Tribunal] or, if that is not practicable within those twenty-four hours, before {in England and Wales, a justice of the peace, in Northern Ireland,} a justice of the peace acting for the petty sessions area in which he is arrested or, in Scotland, the sheriff; and

(b) if required by such a condition to appear within those twenty-four hours before an immigration officer, shall be brought before that officer.

(3) [Where a person is brought before the First-tier Tribunal, a justice of the peace or the sheriff by virtue of sub-paragraph (2)(a), the Tribunal, justice of the peace or sheriff]—

(a) if of the opinion that that person has broken or is likely to break any condition on which he was released, may either—

(i) direct that he be detained under the authority of the person by whom he was arrested; or

(ii) release him, on his original recognizance or on a new recognizance, with or without sureties, or, in Scotland, on his original bail or on new bail; and

(b) if not of that opinion, shall release him on his original recognizance or bail.

Note: Words in square brackets substituted by Sch 2 Asylum and Immigration (Treatment of Claimants etc.) Act 2004 from 4 April 2005 (SI 2005/565). Words in curly brackets in subparagraph (2) inserted by Courts Act 2003 from 1 April 2005. Words 'the First-tier Tribunal' substituted from 15 February 2010 (SI 2010/21).

[25.—(1) Tribunal Procedure Rules [must] make provision with respect to applications to the First-tier Tribunal under paragraphs 22 to 24 and matters arising out of such applications.]

[(2) Tribunal Procedure Rules must secure that, where the First-tier Tribunal has decided not to release a person on bail under paragraph 22, the Tribunal is required to dismiss without a hearing any further application by the person for release on bail (whether under paragraph 22 or otherwise) that is made during the period of 28 days starting with the date of the Tribunal's decision, unless the person demonstrates to the Tribunal that there has been a material change in circumstances.]

Note: Paragraph 25 substituted by SI 2010/21 from 15 February 2010. Subparagraph (1) renumbered and word in square bracket substituted, subparagraph (2) inserted by s 7 Immigration Act 2014 from 20 October 2014 (SI 2014/2771).

[Entry and search of premises

25A.—(1) This paragraph applies if—

(a) a person is arrested under this Schedule; or

(b) a person who was arrested [other than under this Schedule] is detained by an immigration officer under this Schedule.

(2) An immigration officer may enter and search any premises—

(a) occupied or controlled by the arrested person, or

(b) in which that person was when he was arrested, or immediately before he was arrested, for relevant documents.

(3) The power may be exercised—

(a) only if the officer has reasonable grounds for believing that there are relevant documents on the premises;

(b) only to the extent that it is reasonably required for the purpose of discovering relevant documents; and

(c) subject to sub-paragraph (4), only if a senior officer has authorised its exercise in writing.

(4) An immigration officer may conduct a search under sub-paragraph (2)—

(a) before taking the arrested person to a place where he is to be detained; and

(b) without obtaining an authorisation under sub-paragraph (3)(c), if the presence of that person at a place other than one where he is to be detained is necessary to make an effective search for any relevant documents.

(5) An officer who has conducted a search under sub-paragraph (4) must inform a senior officer as soon as is practicable.

(6) The officer authorising a search, or who is informed of one under sub-paragraph (5), must make a record in writing of—
 (a) the grounds for the search; and
 (b) the nature of the documents that were sought.

[(6A) If, on an application made by an immigration officer, a justice of the peace is satisfied that—
 (a) there are reasonable grounds for believing that relevant documents may be found on premises not within sub-paragraph (2) which are specified in the application, and
 (b) any of the conditions in sub-paragraph (6B) is met,

the justice of the peace may issue a warrant authorising an immigration officer to enter and search the premises.

(6B) The conditions are that—
 (a) it is not practicable to communicate with any person entitled to grant entry to the premises;
 (b) it is practicable to communicate with a person entitled to grant entry to the premises but it is not practicable to communicate with any person entitled to grant access to the relevant documents;
 (c) entry to the premises will not be granted unless a warrant is produced;
 (d) the purpose of a search may be frustrated or seriously prejudiced unless an immigration officer arriving at the premises can secure immediate entry.

(6C) In the application of sub-paragraph (6A) to Scotland, references to a justice of the peace are to be treated as references to the sheriff or a justice of the peace.]

(7) An officer searching premises under [this paragraph]—
 (a) may seize . . . any documents he finds which he has reasonable grounds for believing are relevant documents;

. . .

(8) But sub-paragraph (7)(a) does not apply to documents which the officer has reasonable grounds for believing are items subject to legal privilege.

[(8A) An immigration officer may retain a document seized under sub-paragraph (7) while the officer has reasonable grounds for believing that—
 (a) the arrested person may be liable to removal from the United Kingdom in accordance with a provision of the Immigration Acts, and
 (b) retention of the document may facilitate the person's removal.]

(9) 'Relevant documents' means any documents which might—
 (a) establish the arrested person's identity, nationality or citizenship; or
 (b) indicate the place from which he has travelled to the United Kingdom or to which he is proposing to go.

(10) 'Senior officer' means an immigration officer not below the rank of chief immigration officer.]

Note: Paragraph 25A inserted by Immigration and Asylum Act 1999 from 14 February 2000. Subparagraphs (6A), (6B), (6C) and (8A) inserted, words in square brackets substituted and words omitted from subparagraph (7) by Sch 1 Immigration Act 2014 from 28 July 2014 (SI 2014/1820).

[Searching persons arrested by immigration officers

25B.—(1) This paragraph applies if a person is arrested under this Schedule.

(2) An immigration officer may search the arrested person if he has reasonable grounds for believing that the arrested person may present a danger to himself or others.

(3) The officer may search the arrested person for—
 (a) anything which he might use to assist his escape from lawful custody; or
 (b) any document which might—
  (i) establish his identity, nationality or citizenship; or
  (ii) indicate the place from which he has travelled to the United Kingdom or to which he is proposing to go.

(4) The power conferred by sub-paragraph (3) may be exercised—
  (a) only if the officer has reasonable grounds for believing that the arrested person may have concealed on him anything of a kind mentioned in that sub-paragraph; and
  (b) only to the extent that it is reasonably required for the purpose of discovering any such thing.

(5) A power conferred by this paragraph to search a person is not to be read as authorising an officer to require a person to remove any of his clothing in public other than an outer coat, jacket or glove; but it does authorise the search of a person's mouth.

(6) An officer searching a person under sub-paragraph (2) may seize and retain anything he finds, if he has reasonable grounds for believing that the person searched might use it to cause physical injury to himself or to another person.

(7) An officer searching a person under sub-paragraph (3)(a) may seize and retain anything he finds, if he has reasonable grounds for believing that he might use it to assist his escape from lawful custody.

(8) An officer searching a person under sub-paragraph (3)(b) may seize and retain anything he finds, other than an item subject to legal privilege, if he has reasonable grounds for believing that it might be a document falling within that sub-paragraph.

(9) Nothing seized under sub-paragraph (6) or (7) may be retained when the person from whom it was seized—
  (a) is no longer in custody, or
  (b) is in the custody of a court but has been released on bail.]

Note: Paragraph 25B inserted by Immigration and Asylum Act 1999 from 14 February 2000.

[Searching persons in police custody

25C.—(1) This paragraph applies if a person—
  (a) has been arrested under this Schedule; and
  (b) is in custody at a police station.

(2) An immigration officer may, at any time, search the arrested person in order to ascertain whether he has with him—
  (a) anything which he might use to—
    (i) cause physical injury to himself or others;
    (ii) damage property;
    (iii) interfere with evidence; or
    (iv) assist his escape; or
  (b) any document which might—
    (i) establish his identity, nationality or citizenship; or
    (ii) indicate the place from which he has travelled to the United Kingdom or to which he is proposing to go.

(3) The power may be exercised only to the extent that the officer considers it to be necessary for the purpose of discovering anything of a kind mentioned in sub-paragraph (2).

(4) An officer searching a person under this paragraph may seize and retain anything he finds, if he has reasonable grounds for believing that—
  (a) that person might use it for one or more of the purposes mentioned in sub-paragraph (2)(a); or
  (b) it might be a document falling within sub-paragraph (2)(b).

(5) But the officer may not retain anything seized under sub-paragraph (2)(a)—
  (a) for longer than is necessary in view of the purpose for which the search was carried out; or
  (b) when the person from whom it was seized is no longer in custody or is in the custody of a court but has been released on bail.

(6) The person from whom something is seized must be told the reason for the seizure unless he is—
(a) violent or appears likely to become violent; or
(b) incapable of understanding what is said to him.

(7) An intimate search may not be conducted under this paragraph.

(8) The person carrying out a search under this paragraph must be of the same sex as the person searched.

(9) 'Intimate search' has the same meaning as in section 28H(11).]

Note: Paragraph 25C inserted by Immigration and Asylum Act 1999 from 14 February 2000.

[Access and copying

25D.—(1) If a person showing himself—
(a) to be the occupier of the premises on which seized material was seized, or
(b) to have had custody or control of the material immediately before it was seized, asks the immigration officer who seized the material for a record of what he seized, the officer must provide the record to that person within a reasonable time.

(2) If a relevant person asks an immigration officer for permission to be granted access to seized material, the officer must arrange for that person to have access to the material under the supervision of an immigration officer.

(3) An immigration officer may photograph or copy, or have photographed or copied, seized material.

(4) If a relevant person asks an immigration officer for a photograph or copy of seized material, the officer must arrange for—
(a) that person to have access to the material under the supervision of an immigration officer for the purpose of photographing or copying it; or
(b) the material to be photographed or copied.

(5) A photograph or copy made under sub-paragraph (4)(b) must be supplied within a reasonable time.

(6) There is no duty under this paragraph to arrange for access to, or the supply of a photograph or copy of, any material if there are reasonable grounds for believing that to do so would prejudice—
(a) the exercise of any functions in connection with which the material was seized; or
(b) an investigation which is being conducted under this Act, or any criminal proceedings which may be brought as a result.

(7) 'Relevant person' means—
(a) a person who had custody or control of seized material immediately before it was seized, or
(b) someone acting on behalf of such a person.

(8) 'Seized material' means anything which has been seized and retained under this Schedule.]

Note: Paragraph 25D inserted by Immigration and Asylum Act 1999 from 14 February 2000.

[**25E.** Section 28L applies for the purposes of this Schedule as it applies for the purposes of Part III.]

Note: Paragraph 25E inserted by Immigration and Asylum Act 1999 from 14 February 2000.

Supplementary duties of those connected with ships or aircraft or with ports

26.—(1) The owners or agents of a ship or aircraft employed to carry passengers for reward shall not, without the approval of the Secretary of State, arrange for the ship or aircraft to call at a port in the United Kingdom other than a port of entry for the purpose of disembarking passengers, if any of the passengers on board may not enter the United Kingdom without leave, or for the purpose of embarking passengers unless the owners or agents have reasonable cause to believe all of them to be [British citizens].

[(1A) Sub-paragraph (1) does not apply in such circumstances, if any, as the Secretary of State may by order prescribe.]

(2) The Secretary of State may from time to time give written notice to the owners or agents of any ships or aircraft designating control areas for the embarkation or disembarkation of passengers in any port in the United Kingdom, and specifying the conditions and restrictions (if any) to be observed in any control area; and where by notice given to any owners or agents a control area is for the time being designated for the embarkation or disembarkation of passengers at any port, the owners or agents shall take all reasonable steps to secure that, in the case of their ships or aircraft, passengers do not embark or disembark, as the case may be, at the port outside the control area and that any conditions or restrictions notified to them are observed.

(3) The Secretary of State may also from time to time give to any persons concerned with the management of a port in the United Kingdom written notice designating control areas in the port and specifying conditions or restrictions to be observed in any control area; and any such person shall take all reasonable steps to secure that any conditions or restrictions as notified to him are observed.

[(3A) The power conferred by sub-paragraph (1A) is exercisable by statutory instrument; and any such instrument shall be subject to annulment by a resolution of either House of Parliament.]

Note: Words in square brackets substituted by British Nationality Act 1981. Words omitted from paragraph 26(1) and paragraphs 26(1A) and 26(3A) inserted by Immigration and Asylum Act 1999 from 14 February 2000. Paragraph 26 has effect in a form modified by and in circumstances specified by the Channel Tunnel (International Arrangements) Order (SI 1993/1813) as amended by SIs 1994/1405, 2000/913, 2001/178, 2001/3707, 2006/1003 and 2007/3759.

27.—(1) The captain of a ship or aircraft arriving in the United Kingdom—

(a) shall take such steps as may be necessary to secure that persons on board do not disembark there unless either they have been examined by an immigration officer, or they disembark in accordance with arrangements approved by an immigration officer, or they are members of the crew who may lawfully enter the United Kingdom without leave by virtue of section 8(1) of this Act; and

(b) where the examination of persons on board is to be carried out on the ship or aircraft, shall take such steps as may be necessary to secure that those to be examined are presented for the purpose in an orderly manner.

[(2) The Secretary of State may by order require, or enable an immigration officer to require, a responsible person in respect of a ship or aircraft to supply—

(a) a passenger list showing the names and nationality or citizenship of passengers arriving or leaving on board the ship or aircraft;

(b) particulars of members of the crew of the ship or aircraft.

(3) An order under sub-paragraph (2) may relate—

(a) to all ships or aircraft arriving or expected to arrive in the United Kingdom;

(b) to all ships or aircraft leaving or expected to leave the United Kingdom;

(c) to ships or aircraft arriving or expected to arrive in the United Kingdom from or by way of a specified country;

(d) to ships or aircraft leaving or expected to leave the United Kingdom to travel to or by way of a specified country;

(e) to specified ships or specified aircraft.

(4) For the purposes of sub-paragraph (2) the following are responsible persons in respect of a ship or aircraft—
 (a) the owner or agent, and
 (b) the captain.

(5) An order under sub-paragraph (2)—
 (a) may specify the time at which or period during which information is to be provided,
 (b) may specify the form and manner in which information is to be provided,
 (c) shall be made by statutory instrument, and
 (d) shall be subject to annulment in pursuance of a resolution of either House of Parliament.]

Note: Subparagraph (2) substituted (from 5 November 2007 (SI 2007/3138)) and subparagraphs (3)–(5) inserted (from 1 March 2008 (SI 2007/3138 as amended by SI 2007/3580)) by Immigration, Asylum and Nationality Act 2006, s 31. Paragraph 27 has effect in a form modified by and in circumstances specified by the Channel Tunnel (International Arrangements) Order (SI 1993/1813) as amended by SIs 1994/1405, 2000/913, 2001/178, 2001/3707, 2006/1003 and 2007/3759.

27A. . . .

[Passenger information

27B.—(1) This paragraph applies to ships or aircraft—
 (a) which have arrived, or are expected to arrive, in the United Kingdom; or
 (b) which have left, or are expected to leave, the United Kingdom.

(2) If an immigration officer asks the owner or agent ('the carrier') of a ship or aircraft for passenger information [or service information], the carrier must provide that information to the officer.

(3) The officer may ask for passenger information [or service information] relating to—
 (a) a particular ship or particular aircraft of the carrier;
 (b) particular ships or aircraft (however described) of the carrier; or
 (c) all of the carrier's ships or aircraft.

(4) The officer may ask for—
 (a) all passenger information [or service information] in relation to the ship or aircraft concerned; or
 (b) particular passenger information [or service information] in relation to that ship or aircraft.

[(4A) The officer may ask the carrier to provide a copy of all or part of a document that relates to a passenger and contains passenger information [or service information].]

(5) A request under sub-paragraph (2)—
 (a) must be in writing;
 (b) must state the date on which it ceases to have effect; and
 (c) continues in force until that date, unless withdrawn earlier by written notice by an immigration officer.

(6) The date may not be later than six months after the request is made.

(7) The fact that a request under sub-paragraph (2) has ceased to have effect as a result of sub-paragraph (5) does not prevent the request from being renewed.

(8) The information must be provided—
 (a) in such form and manner as the Secretary of State may direct; and
 (b) at such time as may be stated in the request.

(9) 'Passenger information' [or service information] means such information relating to the passengers carried, or expected to be carried, by the ship or aircraft as may be specified.

[(9A) 'Service information' means such information relating to the voyage or flight undertaken by the ship or aircraft as may be specified.]

(10) 'Specified' means specified in an order made by statutory instrument by the Secretary of State.

(11) Such an instrument shall be subject to annulment in pursuance of a resolution of either House of Parliament.]

Note: Paragraph 27B inserted by Immigration and Asylum Act 1999 from 3 April 2000. Subparagraph 4A inserted by Asylum and Immigration (Treatment of Claimants etc.) Act 2004, s 16 from a date to be appointed. Words in square brackets and subparagraph (9A) inserted by Immigration, Asylum and Nationality Act 2006, s 31 from 5 November 2007 (SI 2007/3138). Paragraph 27(B2) modified in its extension to Guernsey by Art 6, Sch 3, SI 2011/2444.

[Notification of non-EEA arrivals

27C.—(1) If a senior officer, or an immigration officer authorised by a senior officer, gives written notice to the owner or agent ('the carrier') of a ship or aircraft, the carrier must inform a relevant officer of the expected arrival in the United Kingdom of any ship or aircraft—

(a) of which he is the owner or agent; and

(b) which he expects to carry a person who is not an EEA national.

(2) The notice may relate to—

(a) a particular ship or particular aircraft of the carrier;

(b) particular ships or aircraft (however described) of the carrier; or

(c) all of the carrier's ships or aircraft.

(3) The notice—

(a) must state the date on which it ceases to have effect; and

(b) continues in force until that date, unless withdrawn earlier by written notice given by a senior officer.

(4) The date may not be later than six months after the notice is given.

(5) The fact that a notice under sub-paragraph (1) has ceased to have effect as a result of sub-paragraph (3) does not prevent the notice from being renewed.

(6) The information must be provided—

(a) in such form and manner as the notice may require; and

(b) before the ship or aircraft concerned departs for the United Kingdom.

(7) If a ship or aircraft travelling to the United Kingdom stops at one or more places before arriving in the United Kingdom, it is to be treated as departing for the United Kingdom when it leaves the last of those places.

(8) 'Senior officer' means an immigration officer not below the rank of chief immigration officer.

(9) 'Relevant officer' means—

(a) the officer who gave the notice under sub-paragraph (1); or

(b) any immigration officer at the port at which the ship or aircraft concerned is expected to arrive.

(10) 'EEA national' means a national of a State which is a Contracting Party to the Agreement on the European Economic Area signed at Oporto on 2nd May 1992 as it has effect for the time being.]

Note: Paragraph 27C inserted by Immigration and Asylum Act 1999 from 3 April 2000.

Part II

Effect of Appeals

Stay on directions for removal

28. . . .

Note: Paragraph 28 omitted by Immigration and Asylum Act 1999 from 2 October 2000. Transitional provisions set out in SI 2003/754.

Grant of bail pending appeal

29.—(1) Where a person (in the following provisions of this Schedule referred to as 'an appellant') has an appeal pending under [Part 5 of the Nationality, Immigration and Asylum Act 2002] and is for the time being detained under Part I of this Schedule, he may be released on bail in accordance with this paragraph [and paragraph 22 does not apply].

(2) An immigration officer not below the rank of chief immigration officer or a police officer not below the rank of inspector may release an appellant on his entering into a recognizance or, in Scotland, bail bond conditioned for his appearance before [the First-tier Tribunal] at a time and place named in the recognizance or bail bond.

(3) [the First-tier Tribunal] may release an appellant on his entering into a recognizance or, in Scotland, bail bond conditioned for his appearance before [the Tribunal] at a time and place named in the recognizance or bail bond; . . .

(4) . . .

(5) The conditions of a recognizance or bail bond taken under this paragraph may include conditions appearing to the person fixing the bail to be likely to result in the appearance of the appellant at the time and place named; and any recognizance shall be with or without sureties as that person may determine.

(6) In any case in which [the First-tier Tribunal] has power or is required by this paragraph to release an appellant on bail, [the Tribunal] may, instead of taking the bail, fix the amount and conditions of the bail (including the amount in which any sureties are to be bound) with a view to its being taken subsequently by any such person as may be specified by [the Tribunal]; and on the recognizance or bail bond being so taken the appellant shall be released.

Note: Words in first square brackets substituted by Sch 7 Nationality, Immigration and Asylum Act 2002 from 1 April 2003 (SI 2003/754). Transitional provisions regarding subparagraph (1) set out in SI 2003/754. Words 'the First-tier Tribunal' substituted from 15 February 2010 (SI 2010/21). Words in second square brackets in subparagraph (1) inserted by s 7 Immigration Act 2014 from 20 October 2014 (SI 2014/2771). Other words in square brackets substituted by and words omitted by Sch 2 Asylum and Immigration (Treatment of Claimants etc.) Act 2004 from 4 April 2005 (SI 2005/565).

Restrictions on grant of bail

30.—(1) An appellant shall not be released under paragraph 29 above without the consent of the Secretary of State if [-

(a)] directions for the removal of the appellant from the United Kingdom are for the time being in force, [and

(b) the directions require the person to be removed from the United Kingdom within the period of 14 days starting with the date of the decision on whether the person should be released on bail.]

or the power to give such directions is for the time being exercisable.

(2) Notwithstanding paragraph 29(3) or (4) above, [the Tribunal] shall not be obliged to release an appellant unless the appellant enters into a proper recognizance, with sufficient and satisfactory sureties if required, or in Scotland sufficient and satisfactory bail is found if so required; and [the Tribunal] shall not be obliged to release an appellant if it appears to [the Tribunal]—
   (a) that the appellant, having on any previous occasion been released on bail (whether under paragraph 24 or under any other provision), has failed to comply with the conditions of any recognizance or bail bond entered into by him on that occasion;
   (b) that the appellant is likely to commit an offence unless he is retained in detention;
   (c) that the release of the appellant is likely to cause danger to public health;
   (d) that the appellant is suffering from mental disorder and that his continued detention is necessary in his own interests or for the protection of any other person; or
   (e) that the appellant is under the age of seventeen, that arrangements ought to be made for his care in the event of his release and that no satisfactory arrangements for that purpose have been made.

Note: Subparagraph (1)(b) renumbered and substituted by s 7 Immigration Act 2014 from 28 July 2014 (SI 2014/18200). Words in other square brackets substituted by Sch 2 Asylum and Immigration Act 2004 from 4 April 2005 (SI 2005/565).

Forfeiture of recognizances

31.—(1) Where under paragraph 29 above (as it applies in England and Wales or in Northern Ireland) a recognizance is entered into conditioned for the appearance of an appellant, [before the Tribunal], and it appears to [the Tribunal] to be forfeited, [the Tribunal] may by order declare it to be forfeited and adjudge the persons bound thereby, whether as principal or sureties, or any of them, to pay the sum in which they are respectively bound or such part of it, if any, as [the Tribunal] thinks fit.

(2) An order under this paragraph shall, for the purposes of this sub-paragraph, specify a magistrates' court or, in Northern Ireland, court of summary jurisdiction; and the recognizance shall be treated for the purposes of collection, enforcement and remission of the sum forfeited as having been forfeited by the court so specified.

(3) Where [the Tribunal] makes an order under this paragraph [the Tribunal] shall, as soon as practicable, give particulars of the recognizance to the [proper officer] of the court specified in the order in pursuance of sub-paragraph (2) above.

[(3A) In sub-paragraph (3) "proper officer" means—
   (a) in relation to a magistrates' court in England and Wales, the {designated officer} for the court; and
   (b) in relation to a court of summary jurisdiction in Northern Ireland, the clerk of the court.]

(4) Any sum the payment of which is enforceable by a magistrates' court in England or Wales by virtue of this paragraph shall be treated for the purposes of the [Justices of the Peace Act 1979 and, in particular, section 61 thereof] as being due under a recognizance forfeited by such a court. . .

(5) Any sum the payment of which is enforceable by virtue of this paragraph by a court of summary jurisdiction in Northern Ireland shall, for the purposes of section 20(5) of the Administration of Justice Act (Northern Ireland) 1954, be treated as a forfeited recognizance.

Note: Words in square brackets in subparagraph (4) substituted by Justices of the Peace Act 1979, s 71; words omitted by Criminal Justice Act 1972, s 64a. Other words in square brackets substituted by Sch 2 Asylum and Immigration Act 2004 from 4 April 2005, (SI 2005/565). Subparagraph (3A) inserted by and words in brackets in subparagraph (3) substituted by Access to Justice Act 1999, Sch 13 paragraph 70 from 1 April 2001 (SI 2001/916). Words substituted in subparagraph (3A)(a) by Courts Act 2003 from 1 April 2005.

32. Where under paragraph 29 above (as it applies in Scotland) a person released on bail fails to comply with the terms of a bail bond conditioned for his appearance [before the Tribunal], [the Tribunal] may declare the bail to be forfeited, and any bail so forfeited shall be transmitted by

[the Tribunal] to the sheriff court having jurisdiction in the area where the proceedings took place, and shall be treated as having been forfeited by that court.

Note: Words in square brackets substituted by Sch 2 Asylum and Immigration Act 2004 from 4 April 2005 (SI 2005/565).

Arrest of appellants released on bail

33.—(1) An immigration officer or constable may arrest without warrant a person who has been released by virtue of this Part of this Schedule—

(a) if he has reasonable grounds for believing that that person is likely to break the condition of his recognizance or bail bond that he will appear at the time and place required or to break any other condition of it, or has reasonable ground to suspect that that person is breaking or has broken any such other condition; or

(b) if, a recognizance with sureties having been taken, he is notified in writing by any surety of the surety's belief that that person is likely to break the first-mentioned condition, and of the surety's wish for that reason to be relieved of his obligations as a surety; and paragraph 17(2) above shall apply for the arrest of a person under this paragraph as it applies for the arrest of a person under paragraph 17.

(2) A person arrested under this paragraph—

(a) if not required by a condition on which he was released to appear [before the Tribunal] within twenty-four hours after the time of his arrest, shall as soon as practicable be brought [before the Tribunal], or, if that is not practicable within those twenty-four hours, before {in England and Wales, a justice of the peace, in Northern Ireland,} a justice of the peace acting for the petty sessions area in which he is arrested or, in Scotland, the sheriff; and

(b) if required by such a condition to appear within those twenty-four hours [before the Tribunal] shall be brought [before it].

(3) [Where a person is brought before the First-tier Tribunal, a justice of the peace or the sheriff by virtue of sub-paragraph (2)(a), the Tribunal, justice of the peace or sheriff—]

(a) if of the opinion that that person has broken or is likely to break any condition on which he was released, may either—

(i) direct that he be detained under the authority of the person by whom he was arrested; or

(ii) release him on his original recognizance or on a new recognizance, with or without sureties, or, in Scotland, on his original bail or on new bail; and

(b) if not of that opinion, shall release him on his original recognizance or bail.

Note: Words in square brackets substituted by Sch 2 Asylum and Immigration Act 2004 from 4 April 2005 (SI 2005/565). Words inserted in subparagraph (2)(a) by Courts Act 2003 from 1 April 2005. Words 'the First-tier Tribunal' substituted from 15 February 2010 (SI 2010/21).

[33A.—(1) Tribunal Procedure Rules must make provision with respect to applications to the First-tier Tribunal under paragraphs 29 to 33 and matters arising out of such applications.

(2) Tribunal Procedure Rules must secure that, where the First-tier Tribunal has decided not to release a person on bail under paragraph 29, the Tribunal is required to dismiss without a hearing any further application by the person for release on bail (whether under paragraph 29 or otherwise) that is made during the period of 28 days starting with the date of the Tribunal's decision, unless the person demonstrates to the Tribunal that there has been a material change in circumstances.]

Note: Paragraph 33A inserted by s 7 Immigration Act 2014 from 20 October 2014 (SI 2014/2771).

Grant of bail pending removal

[34.—(1) Paragraph 22 above shall apply in relation to a person—

(a) directions for whose removal from the United Kingdom are for the time being in force; and

(b) who is for the time being detained under Part I of this Schedule, as it applies in relation to a person detained under paragraph 16(1) above pending examination [, detained under paragraph 16(1A) above pending completion of his examination or a decision on whether to cancel his leave to enter] or detained under paragraph 16(2) above pending the giving of directions.

(2) Paragraphs 23 to 25 above shall apply as if any reference to paragraph 22 above included a reference to that paragraph as it applies by virtue of this paragraph.]

Note: Paragraph 34 inserted by Asylum and Immigration Act 1996 from 1 October 1996. Words in square brackets inserted by Immigration and Asylum Act 1999 from 2 October 2000.

Section 5

SCHEDULE 3

SUPPLEMENTARY PROVISIONS AS TO DEPORTATION

Removal of persons liable to deportation

1.—(1) Where a deportation order is in force against any person, the Secretary of State may give directions for his removal to a country or territory specified in the directions being either—

(a) a country of which he is a national or citizen; or

(b) a country or territory to which there is reason to believe that he will be admitted.

(2) The directions under sub-paragraph (1) above may be either—

(a) directions given to the captain of a ship or aircraft about to leave the United Kingdom requiring him to remove the person in question in that ship or aircraft; or

(b) directions given to the owners or agents of any ship or aircraft requiring them to make arrangements for his removal in a ship or aircraft specified or indicated in the directions; or

(c) directions for his removal in accordance with arrangements to be made by the Secretary of State.

(3) In relation to directions given under this paragraph, paragraphs 11 and 16(4) of Schedule 2 to this Act shall apply, with the substitution of references to the Secretary of State for references to an immigration officer, as they apply in relation to directions for removal given under paragraph 8 of that Schedule.

(4) The Secretary of State, if he thinks fit, may apply in or towards payment of the expenses of or incidental to the voyage from the United Kingdom of a person against whom a deportation order is in force, or the maintenance until departure of such a person and his dependants, if any, any money belonging to that person; and except so far as they are paid as aforesaid, those expenses shall be defrayed by the Secretary of State.

Detention or control pending deportation

2.—(1) Where a recommendation for deportation made by a court is in force in respect of any person, [and that person is not detained in pursuance of the sentence or order of any court] he shall, unless the court by which the recommendation is made otherwise directs, [or a direction is given under sub-paragraph (1A) below,] be detained pending the making of a deportation order in pursuance of the recommendation, unless the Secretary of State directs him to be released pending further consideration of his case [or he is released on bail].

[(1A) Where—

(a) a recommendation for deportation made by a court on a conviction of a person is in force in respect of him; and

(b) he appeals against his conviction or against that recommendation, the powers that the court determining the appeal may exercise include power to direct him to be released without setting aside the recommendation.]

(2) Where notice has been given to a person in accordance with regulations under [section 105 of the Nationality, Immigration and Asylum Act 2002 (notice of decision)] of a decision to make a

deportation order against him, [and he is not detained in pursuance of the sentence or order of a court], he may be detained under the authority of the Secretary of State pending the making of the deportation order.

(3) Where a deportation order is in force against any person, he may be detained under the authority of the Secretary of State pending his removal or departure from the United Kingdom (and if already detained by virtue of sub-paragraph (1) or (2) above when the order is made, shall continue to be detained unless [he is released on bail or] the Secretary of State directs otherwise).

(4) In relation to detention under sub-paragraph (2) or (3) above, paragraphs 17 [,[to 18A] and 25A to 25E] of Schedule 2 to this Act shall apply as they apply in relation to detention under paragraph 16 of that Schedule [; and for that purpose the reference in paragraph 17(1) to a person liable to detention includes a reference to a person who would be liable to detention upon receipt of a notice which is ready to be given to him.]

[(4A) Paragraphs 22 to 25 of Schedule 2 to this Act apply in relation to a person detained under sub-paragraph (1), (2) or (3) as they apply in relation to a person detained under paragraph 16 of that Schedule.]

[(5) A person to whom this sub-paragraph applies shall be subject to such restrictions as to residence, [as to his employment or occupation] and as to reporting to the police [or an immigration officer] as may from time to time be notified to him in writing by the Secretary of State.

(6) The persons to whom sub-paragraph (5) above applies are—

(a) a person liable to be detained under sub-paragraph (1) above, while by virtue of a direction of the Secretary of State he is not so detained; and

(b) a person liable to be detained under sub-paragraph (2) or (3) above, while he is not so detained.]

Effect of appeals

[3. So far as they relate to an appeal under section 82(1) of the Nationality, Immigration and Asylum Act 2002 against a decision [that relates to a deportation order] and refusal to revoke deportation order, paragraphs 29 to [33A] to this Act shall apply for the purposes of this schedule as if the reference in paragraph 29(1) to Part 1 of that Schedule were a reference to this Schedule.]

[Powers of courts pending deportation

4. Where the release of a person recommended for deportation is directed by a court, he shall be subject to such restrictions as to residence [as to his employment or occupation] and as to reporting to the police as the court may direct.

5.—(1) On an application made—

(a) by or on behalf of a person recommended for deportation whose release was so directed; or

(b) by a constable; or

(c) by an Immigration Officer,

the appropriate court shall have the powers specified in sub-paragraph (2) below.

(2) The powers mentioned in sub-paragraph (1) above are—

(a) if the person to whom the application relates is not subject to any such restrictions imposed by a court as are mentioned in paragraph 4 above, to order that he shall be subject to any such restrictions as the court may direct; and

(b) if he is subject to restrictions imposed by a court by virtue of that paragraph or this paragraph—

(i) to direct that any of them shall be varied or shall cease to have effect; or

(ii) to give further directions as to his residence and reporting.

6.—(1) In this Schedule 'the appropriate court' means, except in a case to which sub-paragraph (2) below applies, the court which directed release.

(2) This sub-paragraph applies where the court which directed release was—

(a) the Crown Court;

(b) the Court of Appeal;

(c) the High Court of Justiciary;

(d) the Crown Court in Northern Ireland; or

(e) the Court of Appeal in Northern Ireland.

[(2A) Where the Crown Court directed release, the appropriate court is that court or a magistrates' court]

(3) Where . . . the Crown Court or the Crown Court in Northern Ireland directed release, the appropriate court is—

(a) the court that directed release; or

(b) a magistrates' court acting for the . . . county court division where the person to whom the application relates resides.

(4) Where the Court of Appeal or the Court of Appeal in Northern Ireland gave the direction, the appropriate court is the Crown Court or the Crown Court in Northern Ireland, as the case may be.

(5) Where the High Court of Justiciary directed release, the appropriate court is—

(a) that court; or

(b) in a case where release was directed by that court on appeal, the court from which the appeal was made.

7.—(1) A constable or immigration officer may arrest without warrant any person who is subject to restrictions imposed by a court under this Schedule and who at the time of the arrest is in the relevant part of the United Kingdom—

(a) if he has reasonable grounds to suspect that that person is contravening or has contravened any of those restrictions; or

(b) if he has reasonable grounds for believing that that person is likely to contravene any of them.

(2) In sub-paragraph (2) above 'the relevant part of the United Kingdom' means—

(a) England and Wales, in a case where a court with jurisdiction in England or Wales imposed the restrictions;

(b) Scotland, in a case where a court with jurisdiction in Scotland imposed them; and

(c) Northern Ireland, in a case where a court in Northern Ireland imposed them.

8.—(1) A person arrested in [England or Wales in pursuance of paragraph 7 above shall be brought as soon as practicable and in any event within twenty-four hours after his arrest before a justice of the peace in England or Wales, and a person arrested in] Northern Ireland in pursuance of paragraph 7 above shall be brought as soon as practicable and in any event within 24 hours after his arrest before a justice of the peace for the petty sessions. . . district in which he was arrested.

(2) In reckoning for the purposes of this paragraph any period of 24 hours, no account shall be taken of Christmas Day, Good Friday or any Sunday.

9.—(1) A person arrested in Scotland in pursuance of paragraph 7 above shall wherever practicable be brought before the appropriate court not later than in the course of the first day after his arrest, such day not being a Saturday, a Sunday or a court holiday prescribed for that court under section 10 of the Bail etc. (Scotland) Act 1980.

(2) Nothing in this paragraph shall prevent a person arrested in Scotland being brought before a court on a Saturday, a Sunday or such a court holiday as is mentioned in sub-paragraph (1) above where the court is, in pursuance of section 10 of the said Act of 1980, sitting on such day for the disposal of criminal business.

10. Any justice of the peace or court before whom a person is brought by virtue of paragraph 8 or 9 above—
   (a) if of the opinion that that person is contravening, has contravened or is likely to contravene any restriction imposed on him by a court under this Schedule, may direct—
      (i) that he be detained; or
      (ii) that he be released subject to such restrictions as to his residence and reporting to the police as the court may direct; and
   (b) if not of that opinion, shall release him without altering the restrictions as to his residence and his reporting to the police.]

Note: Paragraph 1: has effect in a form modified by and in circumstances specified by the Channel Tunnel (International Arrangements) Order (SI 1993/1813) as amended by SIs 1994/1405, 2000/913, 2001/178, 2001/3707, 2006/1003 and 2007/3759. Paragraph 2: words in second square brackets in paragraph 2(1) and paragraphs 2(1A), (5) and (6) added by Criminal Justice Act 1982. Words in first square brackets in paragraph 2(2) substituted by Sch 7 Nationality, Immigration and Asylum Act 2002 from 1 April 2003 (SI 2003/754). Other words in square brackets in paragraphs 2(1) and (2) substituted by Sch 2 Asylum and Immigration (Treatment of Claimants, etc.) Act 2004 from 4 April 2005 (SI 2005/565). Other words in square brackets in paragraph 2(2) and paragraph 2(4A) inserted by Immigration and Asylum Act 1999, s 54 from 10 February 2003 (SI 2003/2). Words in first square brackets in paragraph 2(4) substituted by Sch 2 Immigration Act 2014 from 28 July 2014 (SI 2014/1820). Words in first square brackets in paragraph 2(5) added by Immigration Act 1988, s 10, other words in square brackets inserted by Asylum and Immigration Act 1996 from 1 October 1996. Words in last square brackets in paragraph 2(4) inserted by Immigration, Asylum and Nationality Act 2006 from 31 August 2006 (SI 2006/2226). Paragraph 3 substituted by Sch 7 Nationality, Immigration and Asylum Act 2002 from 1 April 2003 (SI 2003/754, which sets out transitional provisions). Words in square brackets in paragraph 3 substituted by Sch 9 Immigration Act 2014 from 20 October 2014 with savings set out in articles 9-11 SI 2014/2771. Paragraphs 4–10: added by Criminal Justice Act 1982. Paragraph 4: words in square brackets added by Immigration Act 1988, s 10. Paragraph 6: subparagraph (2A) inserted and words omitted from subparagraph (3) by Courts Act 2003, Sch 8 paragraph 150 from 1 April 2005 (SI 2005/910). Paragraph 8: words substituted in and omitted from subparagraph (1) by Courts Act 2003, Sch paragraph 150 from 1 April 2005 (SI 2005/910).

Section 9

Schedule 4

Integration with United Kingdom Law of Immigration Law of Islands

Leave to enter

1.—(1) Where under the immigration laws of any of the Islands a person is or has been given leave to enter or remain in the island, or is or has been refused leave, this Act shall have effect in relation to him, if he is not [a British citizen], as if the leave were leave (of like duration) given under this Act to enter or remain in the United Kingdom, or, as the case may be, as if he had under this Act been refused leave to enter the United Kingdom.

(2) Where under the immigration laws of any of the Islands a person has a limited leave to enter or remain in the island subject to any such conditions as are authorised in the United Kingdom by section 3(1) of this Act (being conditions imposed by notice given to him, whether the notice of leave or a subsequent notice), then on his coming to the United Kingdom this Act shall apply, if he is not [a British citizen], as if those conditions related to his stay in the United Kingdom and had been imposed by notice under this Act.

(3) Without prejudice to the generality of sub-paragraphs (1) and (2) above, anything having effect in the United Kingdom by virtue of either of those sub-paragraphs may in relation to the United Kingdom be varied or revoked under this Act in like manner, and subject to the like appeal (if any), as if it had originated under this Act as mentioned in that sub-paragraph.

(4) Where anything having effect in the United Kingdom by virtue of sub-paragraph (1) or (2) above ceases to have effect or is altered in effect as mentioned in sub-paragraph (3) or otherwise by anything done under this Act, sub-paragraph (1) or (2) shall not thereafter apply to it or, as the case may be, shall apply to it as so altered in effect.

(5) Nothing in this paragraph shall be taken as conferring on a person a right of appeal under this Act against any decision or action taken in any of the Islands.

2. Notwithstanding section 3(4) of this Act, leave given to a person under this Act to enter or remain in the United Kingdom shall not continue to apply on his return to the United Kingdom after an absence if he has during that absence entered any of the Islands in circumstances in which he is required under the immigration laws of that island to obtain leave to enter.

Deportation

[3.—(1) This Act has effect in relation to a person who is subject to an Islands deportation order as if the order were a deportation order made against him under this Act.

(2) Sub-paragraph (1) does not apply if the person concerned is—

(a) a British citizen;

(b) an EEA national;

(c) a member of the family of an EEA national; or

(d) a member of the family of a British citizen who is neither such a citizen nor an EEA national.

(3) The Secretary of State does not, as a result of sub-paragraph (1), have power to revoke an Islands deportation order.

(4) In any particular case, the Secretary of State may direct that paragraph (b), (c) or (d) of sub-paragraph (2) is not to apply in relation to the Islands deportation order.

(5) Nothing in this paragraph makes it unlawful for a person in respect of whom an Islands deportation order is in force in any of the Islands to enter the United Kingdom on his way from that island to a place outside the United Kingdom.

(6) 'Islands deportation order' means an order made under the immigration laws of any of the Islands under which a person is, or has been, ordered to leave the island and forbidden to return.

(7) Subsections (10) and (12) to (14) of section 80 of the Immigration and Asylum Act 1999 apply for the purposes of this section as they apply for the purposes of that section.]

Illegal entrants

4. Notwithstanding anything in section 1(3) of this Act, it shall not be lawful for a person who is not [a British citizen] to enter the United Kingdom from any of the Islands where his presence was unlawful under the immigration laws of that island, unless he is given leave to enter.

Note: Words in square brackets substituted by British Nationality Act 1981, s 39(6). Paragraph 3 substituted by Immigration and Asylum Act 1999 from 2 October 2000.

Schedule 5

Note: Schedule 5 repealed by Immigration and Asylum Act 1999 from 14 February 2000.

Section 34

Schedule 6

. . .

Repeals

British Nationality Act 1981
(1981, c. 61)

Arrangement of Sections

Part I. British Citizenship

Acquisition after commencement

Acquisition after commencement: special cases

Acquisition at commencement

Renunciation and resumption

Supplementary

SCHEDULES

An Act to make fresh provision about citizenship and nationality, and to amend the Immigration Act 1971 as regards the right of abode in the United Kingdom.

[30 October 1981]

PART I

BRITISH CITIZENSHIP

Acquisition after commencement

1. Acquisition by birth or adoption

(1) A person born in the United Kingdom after commencement [, or in a qualifying territory on or after the appointed day,] shall be a British citizen if at the time of the birth his father or mother is—

(a) a British citizen; or
(b) settled in the United Kingdom [or that territory].

[(1A) A person born in the United Kingdom or a qualifying territory on or after the relevant day shall be a British citizen if at the time of the birth his father or mother is a member of the armed forces.]

(2) A new-born infant who, after commencement, is found abandoned in the United Kingdom [, or on or after the appointed day is found abandoned in a qualifying territory,] shall, unless the contrary is shown, be deemed for the purposes of subsection (1)—

(a) to have been born in the United Kingdom after commencement; [or in that territory on or after the appointed day] and

(b) to have been born to a parent who at the time of the birth was a British citizen or settled in the United Kingdom [or that territory].

(3) A person born in the United Kingdom after commencement who is not a British citizen by virtue of subsection (1)[, (1A)] or (2) shall be entitled to be registered as a British citizen if, while he is a minor—

(a) his father or mother becomes a British citizen or becomes settled in the United Kingdom; and

(b) an application is made for his registration as a British citizen.

[(3A) A person born in the United Kingdom on or after the relevant day who is not a British citizen by virtue of subsection (1), (1A) or (2) shall be entitled to be registered as a British citizen if, while he is a minor—

(a) his father or mother becomes a member of the armed forces; and

(b) an application is made for his registration as a British citizen.]

(4) A person born in the United Kingdom after commencement who is not a British citizen by virtue of subsection (1) [,(1A)] or (2) shall be entitled, on an application for his registration as a British citizen made at any time after he has attained the age of ten years, to be registered as such a citizen if, as regards each of the first ten years of that person's life, the number of days on which he was absent from the United Kingdom in that year does not exceed 90.

[(5) Where—

(a) any court in the United Kingdom [or, on or after the appointed day, any court in a qualifying territory] makes an order authorising the adoption of a minor who is not a British citizen; or

(b) a minor who is not a British citizen is adopted under a Convention adoption, that minor shall, if the requirements of subsection (5A) are met, be a British citizen as from the date on which the order is made or the Convention adoption is effected, as the case may be {effected under the law of a country or territory outside the United Kingdom}.

(5A) Those requirements are that on the date on which the order is made or the Convention adoption is effected (as the case may be)—

(a) the adopter or, in the case of a joint adoption, one of the adopters is a British citizen; and

(b) in a case within subsection (5)(b), the adopter or, in the case of a joint adoption, both of the adopters are habitually resident in the United Kingdom {or in a designated territory}.]

(6) Where an order [or a Convention adoption] in consequence of which any person became a British citizen by virtue of subsection (5) ceases to have effect, whether on annulment or otherwise, the cesser shall not effect the status of that person as a British citizen.

(7) If in the special circumstances of any particular case the Secretary of State thinks fit, he may for the purposes of subsection (4) treat the person to whom the application relates as fulfilling the requirement specified in that subsection although, as regards any one or more of the first ten years of that person's life, the number of days on which he was absent from the United Kingdom in that year or each of the years in question exceeds 90.

(8) In this section and elsewhere in this Act 'settled' has the meaning given by section 50. . .

[(9) The relevant day for the purposes of subsection (1A) or (3A) is the day appointed for the commencement of section 42 of the Borders, Citizenship and Immigration Act 2009 (which inserted those subsections)].

Note: Subsection (5) substituted and words in square brackets in subsection (6) inserted by Adoption (Intercountry Aspects) Act 1999, s 7 from 1 June 2003 (SI 2003/362). Subsections (1A), (3A) and (9) and words in square brackets in subsections (3)–(4) inserted by s 42 Borders Citizenship and Immigration Act 2009 from 13 January 2010 (SI 2009/2731). Other words in square brackets inserted by Sch 1 British Overseas Territories Act 2002, from 21 May 2002 (SI 2002/1252). The reference in subsection (5)(a) to an order authorising the adoption of a minor is to be read as including a reference to a parental order in respect of a minor and the reference in subsection (5A)(a) to the adopter or, in the case of a joint adoption, one of the adopters is to be read as including a reference to one of the persons who obtained the parental order (SI 2010/985). Words in curly brackets inserted and words omitted from subsection (8) by Adoption and Children Act 2002 from 30 December 2005.

2. Acquisition by descent

(1) A person born outside the United Kingdom [and the qualifying territories] after commencement shall be a British citizen if at the time of the birth his father or mother—

(a) is a British citizen otherwise than by descent; or

(b) is a British citizen and is serving outside the United Kingdom [and the qualifying territories] in service to which this paragraph applies, his or her recruitment for that service having taken place in the United Kingdom [or a qualifying territory]; or

(c) is a British citizen and is serving outside the United Kingdom [and the qualifying territories] in service under a {EU} institution, his or her recruitment for that service having taken place in a country which at the time of the recruitment was a member of the {European Union}.

(2) Paragraph (b) of subsection (1) applies to—

(a) Crown service under the government of the United Kingdom [or of a qualifying territory]; and

(b) service of any description for the time being designated under subsection (3).

(3) For the purposes of this section the Secretary of State may by order made by statutory instrument designate any description of service which he considers to be closely associated with the activities outside the United Kingdom [and the qualifying territories] of Her Majesty's government in the United Kingdom [or in a qualifying territory].

(4) Any order made under subsection (3) shall be subject to annulment in pursuance of a resolution of either House of Parliament.

Note: Words in square brackets inserted by Sch 1 British Overseas Territories Act 2002 from 21 May 2002 (SI 2002/1252), but without effect to the operation of this section in relation to persons born before that date.

3. Acquisition by registration: minors

(1) If while a person is a minor an application is made for his registration as a British citizen, the Secretary of State may, if he thinks fit, cause him to be registered as such a citizen.

(2) A person born outside the United Kingdom [and the qualifying territories] shall be entitled, on an application for his registration as a British citizen made [while he is a minor], to be registered as such a citizen if the requirements specified in subsection (3) or, in the case of a person born stateless, the requirements specified in paragraphs (a) and (b) of that subsection, are fulfilled in the case of either that person's father or his mother ('the parent in question').

(3) The requirements referred to in subsection (2) are—

(a) that the parent in question was a British citizen by descent at the time of the birth; and

(b) that the father or mother of the parent in question—

(i) was a British citizen otherwise than by descent at the time of the birth of the parent in question; or

(ii) became a British citizen otherwise than by descent at commencement, or would have become such a citizen otherwise than by descent at commencement but for his or her death; and

(c) that, as regards some period of three years ending with a date not later than the date of the birth—

(i) the parent in question was in the United Kingdom [or a qualifying territory] at the beginning of that period; and

(ii) the number of days on which the parent in question was absent from the United Kingdom [and the qualifying territories] in that period does not exceed 270.

(4) . . .

(5) A person born outside the United Kingdom [and the qualifying territories] shall be entitled, on an application for his registration as a British citizen made while he is a minor, to be registered as such a citizen if the following requirements are satisfied, namely—

(a) that at the time of that person's birth his father or mother was a British citizen by descent; and

(b) subject to subsection (6), that that person and his father and mother were in the United Kingdom [or a qualifying territory] at the beginning of the period of three years ending with the date of the application and that, in the case of each of them, the number of days on which the person in question was absent from the United Kingdom [and the qualifying territories] in that period does not exceed 270; and

(c) subject to subsection (6), that the consent of his father and mother to the registration has been signified in the prescribed manner.

(6) In the case of an application under subsection (5) for the registration of a person as a British citizen—

(a) if his father or mother died, or their marriage [or civil partnership] was terminated, on or before the date of the application, or his father and mother were legally separated on that date, the references to his father and mother in paragraph (b) of that subsection shall be read either as references to his father or as references to his mother; [and]

(b) if his father or mother died on or before that date, the reference to his father and mother in paragraph (c) of that subsection shall be read as a reference to either of them; [. . .]

(c) [. . .]

Note: Last word in square brackets in subsection (6)(a) inserted and words deleted from subsections (6)(b) and (c) by, Nationality, Immigration and Asylum Act 2002, s 9 from 7 November 2002, with effect in relation to children born on or after a date to be appointed. Other words in square brackets inserted by Sch 1 British Overseas Territories Act 2002, from 21 May 2002 (SI 2002/1252) but without effect to the operation of this section in relation to persons born before that date. Words in first square brackets in subsection (6)(a) inserted by Sch 27 Civil Partnership Act 2004 from 5 December 2005 (SI 2005/3175). Words in second square brackets in subsection (2) substituted and subsection (4) revoked by s 43 Borders, Citizenship and Immigration Act 2009 from 13 January 2010 (SI 2009/2731).

4. Acquisition by registration: [British overseas territories] citizens etc.

(1) This section applies to any person who is a [British overseas territories] citizen, [a British National (Overseas)] a British Overseas citizen, a British subject under this Act or a British protected person.

(2) A person to whom this section applies shall be entitled, on an application for his registration as a British citizen, to be registered as such a citizen if the following requirements are satisfied in the case of that person, namely—

(a) subject to subsection (3), that he was in the United Kingdom at the beginning of the period of five years ending with the date of the application and that the number of days on which he was absent from the United Kingdom in that period does not exceed 450; and

(b) that the number of days on which he was absent from the United Kingdom in the period of twelve months so ending does not exceed 90; and

(c) that he was not at any time in the period of twelve months so ending subject under the immigration law to any restriction on the period for which he might remain in the United Kingdom; and

(d) that he was not at any time in the period of five years so ending in the United Kingdom in breach of the immigration laws.

(3) So much of subsection (2)(a) as requires the person in question to have been in the United Kingdom at the beginning of the period there mentioned shall not apply in relation to a person who was settled in the United Kingdom immediately before commencement.

(4) If in the special circumstances of any particular case the Secretary of State thinks fit, he may for the purposes of subsection (2) do all or any of the following things, namely—

(a) treat the person to whom the application relates as fulfilling the requirement specified in subsection (2)(a) or subsection (2)(b), or both, although the number of days on which he was absent from the United Kingdom in the period there mentioned exceeds the number there mentioned;

(b) disregard any such restriction as is mentioned in subsection (2)(c), not being a restriction to which that person was subject on the date of the application;

(c) treat that person as fulfilling the requirement specified in subsection (2)(d) although he was in the United Kingdom in breach of the immigration laws in the period there mentioned.

(5) If, on an application for registration as a British citizen made by a person to whom this section applies, the Secretary of State is satisfied that the applicant has at any time served in service to which this subsection applies, he may, if he thinks fit in the special circumstances of the applicant's case, cause him to be registered as such a citizen.

(6) Subsection (5) applies to—

(a) Crown service under the government of a [British overseas territory]; and

(b) paid or unpaid service (not falling within paragraph (a)) as a member of any body established by law in a [British overseas territory] members of which are appointed by or on behalf of the Crown.

Note: Words in second square brackets in s 4(1) inserted by SI 1986/948. Dependent territories became British overseas territories from 26 February 2002, British Overseas Territories Act 2002, s 1.

[4A. Acquisition by registration: further provision for British overseas territories citizens

(1) If an application is made to register as a British citizen a person who is a British overseas territories citizen, the Secretary of State may if he thinks fit cause the person to be so registered.

(2) Subsection (1) does not apply in the case of a British overseas territories citizen who—

(a) is such a citizen by virtue only of a connection with the Sovereign Base Areas of Akrotiri and Dhekelia; or

(b) has ceased to be a British citizen as a result of a declaration of renunciation.]

Note: Section 4A inserted by British Overseas Territories Act, s 4 from 21 May 2002 (SI 2002/1252).

[4B. Acquisition by registration: certain persons without other citizenship

(1) This section applies to a person who has the status of—

(a) British Overseas citizen,

(b) British subject under this Act, . . .

(c) British protected person [, or

(d) British National (Overseas).]

(2) A person to whom this section applies shall be entitled to be registered as a British citizen if—

(a) he applies for registration under this section,

(b) the Secretary of State is satisfied that the person does not have, apart from the status mentioned in subsection (1), any citizenship or nationality, and

(c) the Secretary of State is satisfied that the person has not after [the relevant day] renounced, voluntarily relinquished or lost through action or inaction any citizenship or nationality.]

[(3) For the purposes of subsection (2)(c), the "relevant day" means—

(a) in the case of a person to whom this section applies by virtue of subsection (1)(d) only, 19 March 2009, and

(b) in any other case, 4 July 2002.]

Note: Section 4B inserted by Nationality, Immigration and Asylum Act 2002, s 12 from 30 April 2003 (SI 2003/754). Subsections (1)(d) and (3) inserted and words in square brackets in subsection (2)(c) substituted by s 44 Borders, Citizenship and Immigration Act 2009 from 13 January 2010 (SI 2009/2731).

[4C. Acquisition by registration: certain persons born between 1961 and 1983

(1) A person is entitled to be registered as a British citizen if—

(a) he applies for registration under this section, and

(b) he satisfies each of the following conditions.

(2) The first condition is that the applicant was born [. . .] before 1 January 1983.

[(3) The second condition is that the applicant would at some time before 1 January 1983 have become a citizen of the United Kingdom and Colonies—

(a) under section 5 of, or paragraph 3 of Schedule 3 to, the 1948 Act if assumption A had applied,

(b) under section 12(3), (4) or (5) of that Act if assumption B had applied and as a result of its application the applicant would have been a British subject immediately before 1st January 1949, or

(c) under section 12(2) of that Act if one or both of the following had applied—

(i) assumption A had applied;

(ii) assumption B had applied and as a result of its application the applicant would have been a British subject immediately before 1st January 1949.

(3A) Assumption A is that—

(a) section 5 or 12(2) of, or paragraph 3 of Schedule 3 to, the 1948 Act (as the case may be) provided for citizenship by descent from a mother in the same terms as it provided for citizenship by descent from a father, and

(b) references in that provision to a father were references to the applicant's mother.

(3B) Assumption B is that—

(a) a provision of the law at some time before 1st January 1949 which provided for a nationality status to be acquired by descent from a father provided in the same terms for its acquisition by descent from a mother, and

(b) references in that provision to a father were references to the applicant's mother.

(3C) For the purposes of subsection (3B), a nationality status is acquired by a person ("P") by descent where its acquisition—

(a) depends, amongst other things, on the nationality status of one or both of P's parents, and

(b) does not depend upon an application being made for P's registration as a person who has the status in question.

(3D) For the purposes of subsection (3), it is not to be assumed that any registration or other requirements of the provisions mentioned in that subsection or in subsection (3B) were met.]

(4) The third condition is that immediately before 1st January 1983 the applicant would have had the right of abode in the United Kingdom by virtue of section 2 of the Immigration Act 1971 (c. 77) had he become a citizen of the United Kingdom and Colonies as described in subsection (3) above.

[(5) For the purposes of the interpretation of section 5 of the 1948 Act in its application in the case of assumption A to a case of descent from a mother, the reference in the proviso to subsection (1) of that section to "a citizen of the United Kingdom and Colonies by descent only" includes a reference to a female person who became a citizen of the United Kingdom and Colonies by virtue of—

(a) section 12(2), (4) or (6) only of the 1948 Act,

(b) section 13(2) of that Act,

(c) paragraph 3 of Schedule 3 to that Act, or

(d) section 1(1)(a) or (c) of the British Nationality (No. 2) Act 1964.]

Note: Section 4C inserted by Nationality, Immigration and Asylum Act 2002, s 13 from 30 April 2003 (SI 2003/754). Words omitted in subsections (2), subsections (3) substituted and subsections (5) inserted by s 45 Borders, Citizenship and Immigration Act 2009 from 13 January 2010 (SI 2009/2731).

[4D. Acquisition by registration: children of members of the armed forces

(1) A person ("P") born outside the United Kingdom and the qualifying territories on or after the relevant day is entitled to be registered as a British citizen if—

(a) an application is made for P's registration under this section; and

(b) each of the following conditions is satisfied.

(2) The first condition is that, at the time of P's birth, P's father or mother was—

(a) a member of the armed forces; and

(b) serving outside the United Kingdom and the qualifying territories.

(3) The second condition is that, if P is a minor on the date of the application, the consent of P's father and mother to P's registration as a British citizen has been signified in the prescribed manner.

(4) But if P's father or mother has died on or before the date of the application, the reference in subsection (3) to P's father and mother is to be read as a reference to either of them.

(5) The Secretary of State may, in the special circumstances of a particular case, waive the need for the second condition to be satisfied.

(6) The relevant day for the purposes of this section is the day appointed for the commencement of section 46 of the Borders, Citizenship and Immigration Act 2009 (which inserted this section).]

Note: Section 4D inserted by s 46 Borders, Citizenship and Immigration Act 2009 from 13 January 2010 (SI 2009/2731).

[4E. The general conditions

For the purposes of sections 4F to 4I, a person ("P") meets the general conditions if—

(a) P was born before 1 July 2006;

(b) at the time of P's birth, P's mother—

(i) was not married, or

(ii) was married to a person other than P's natural father;

(c) no person is treated as the father of P under section 28 of the Human Fertilisation and Embryology Act 1990; and

(d) P has never been a British citizen.]

Note: Section 4E inserted by s 65 Immigation Act 2014 from a date to be appointed.

[4F. Person unable to be registered under other provisions of this Act

(1) A person ("P") is entitled to be registered as a British citizen on an application made under this section if—

(a) P meets the general conditions; and

(b) P would be entitled to be registered as a British citizen under—

(i) section 1(3),
(ii) section 3(2),
(iii) section 3(5),
(iv) paragraph 4 of Schedule 2, or
(v) paragraph 5 of Schedule 2,

had P's mother been married to P's natural father at the time of P's birth.

(2) In the following provisions of this section "relevant registration provision" means the provision under which P would be entitled to be registered as a British citizen (as mentioned in subsection (1)(b)).

(3) If the relevant registration provision is section 3(2), a person who is registered as a British citizen under this section is a British citizen by descent.

(4) If the relevant registration provision is section 3(5), the Secretary of State may, in the special circumstances of the particular case, waive the need for any or all of the parental consents to be given.

(5) For that purpose, the "parental consents" are—

(a) the consent of P's natural father, and
(b) the consent of P's mother,

insofar as they would be required by section 3(5)(c) (as read with section 3(6)(b)), had P's mother been married to P's natural father at the time of P's birth.]

Note: Section 4F inserted by s 65 Immigration Act 2014 from a date to be appointed.

[4G. Person unable to become citizen automatically after commencement

(1) A person ("P") is entitled to be registered as a British citizen on an application made under this section if—

(a) P meets the general conditions; and

(b) at any time in the period after commencement, P would have automatically become a British citizen at birth by the operation of any provision of this Act or the British Nationality (Falkland Islands) Act 1983, had P's mother been married to P's natural father at the time of P's birth.

(2) A person who is registered as a British citizen under this section is a British citizen by descent if the British citizenship which the person would have acquired at birth (as mentioned in subsection (1)(b)) would (by virtue of section 14) have been British citizenship by descent.

(3) If P is under the age of 18, no application may be made unless the consent of P's natural father and mother to the registration has been signified in the prescribed manner.

(4) But if P's natural father or mother has died on or before the date of the application, the reference in subsection (3) to P's natural father and mother is to be read as a reference to either of them.

(5) The Secretary of State may, in the special circumstances of a particular case, waive the need for any or all of the consents required by subsection (3) (as read with subsection (4)) to be given.

(6) The reference in this section to the period after commencement does not include the time of commencement (and, accordingly, this section does not apply to any case in which a person was unable to become a British citizen at commencement).]

Note: Section 4G inserted by s 65 Immigration Act 2014 from a date to be appointed.

[4H. Citizen of UK and colonies unable to become citizen at commencement

(1) A person ("P") is entitled to be registered as a British citizen on an application made under this section if—

(a) P meets the general conditions;

(b) P was a citizen of the United Kingdom and Colonies immediately before commencement; and

(c) P would have automatically become a British citizen at commencement, by the operation of any provision of this Act, had P's mother been married to P's natural father at the time of P's birth.

(2) A person who is registered as a British citizen under this section is a British citizen by descent if the British citizenship which the person would have acquired at commencement (as mentioned in subsection (1)(c)) would (by virtue of section 14) have been British citizenship by descent.]

Note: Section 4H inserted by s 65 Immigration Act 2014 from a date to be appointed.

[4I. Other person unable to become citizen at commencement

(1) A person ("P") is entitled to be registered as a British citizen on an application made under this section if—

(a) P meets the general conditions;

(b) P is either—

(i) an eligible former British national, or

(ii) an eligible non-British national; and

(c) had P's mother been married to P's natural father at the time of P's birth, P—

(i) would have been a citizen of the United Kingdom and Colonies immediately before commencement, and

(ii) would have automatically become a British citizen at commencement by the operation of any provision of this Act.

(2) P is an "eligible former British national" if P was not a citizen of the United Kingdom and Colonies immediately before commencement and either—

(a) P ceased to be a British subject or a citizen of the United Kingdom and Colonies by virtue of the commencement of any independence legislation, but would not have done so had P's mother been married to P's natural father at the time of P's birth, or

(b) P was a British subject who did not automatically become a citizen of the United Kingdom and Colonies at commencement of the British Nationality Act 1948 by the operation of any provision of it, but would have done so had P's mother been married to P's natural father at the time of P's birth.

(3) P is an "eligible non-British national" if—

(a) P was never a British subject or citizen of the United Kingdom and Colonies; and

(b) had P's mother been married to P's natural father at the time of P's birth, P would have automatically become a British subject or citizen of the United Kingdom and Colonies—

(i) at birth, or

(ii) by virtue of paragraph 3 of Schedule 3 to the British Nationality Act 1948 (child of male British subject to become citizen of the United Kingdom and Colonies if the father becomes such a citizen).

(4) A person who is registered as a British citizen under this section is a British citizen by descent if the British citizenship which the person would have acquired at commencement (as mentioned in subsection (1)(c)(ii)) would (by virtue of section 14) have been British citizenship by descent.

(5) In determining for the purposes of subsection (1)(c)(i) whether P would have been a citizen of the United Kingdom and Colonies immediately before commencement, it must be assumed that P would not have—

(a) renounced or been deprived of any notional British nationality, or

(b) lost any notional British nationality by virtue of P acquiring the nationality of a country or territory outside the United Kingdom.

(6) A "notional British nationality" is—

(a) in a case where P is an eligible former British national, any status as a British subject or a citizen of the United Kingdom and Colonies which P would have held at any time after P's nationality loss (had that loss not occurred and had P's mother had been married to P's natural father at the time of P's birth);

(b) in a case where P is an eligible non-British national—

(i) P's status as a British subject or citizen of the United Kingdom and Colonies mentioned in subsection (3)(b), and

(ii) any other status as a British subject or citizen of the United Kingdom and Colonies which P would have held at any time afterwards (had P's mother been married to P's natural father at the time of P's birth).

(7) In this section—

"British subject" has any meaning which it had for the purposes of the British Nationality and Status of Aliens Act 1914;

"independence legislation" means an Act of Parliament or any subordinate legislation (within the meaning of the Interpretation Act 1978) forming part of the law in the United Kingdom (whenever passed or made, and whether or not still in force)—

(a) providing for a country or territory to become independent from the United Kingdom, or

(b) dealing with nationality, or any other ancillary matters, in connection with a country or territory becoming independent from the United Kingdom;

"P's nationality loss" means P's—

(a) ceasing to be a British subject or citizen of the United Kingdom and Colonies (as mentioned in subsection (2)(a)), or

(b) not becoming a citizen of the United Kingdom and Colonies (as mentioned in subsection (2)(b)).]

Note: Section 4I inserted by s 65 Immigration Act 2014 from a date to be appointed.

[4J. Sections 4E to 4I: supplementary provision

(1) In sections 4E to 4I and this section, a person's "natural father" is a person who satisfies the requirements as to proof of paternity that are prescribed in regulations under section 50(9B).

(2) The power under section 50(9B) to make different provision for different circumstances includes power to make provision for the purposes of any provision of sections 4E to 4I which is different from other provision made under section 50(9B).

(3) The following provisions apply for the purposes of sections 4E to 4I.

(4) A reference to a person automatically becoming a British citizen, or a citizen of the United Kingdom and Colonies, is a reference to the person becoming such a citizen without the need for—

(a) the person to be registered as such a citizen by the Secretary of State or any other minister of the Crown;

(b) the birth of the person to be registered by a diplomatic or consular representative of the United Kingdom; or

(c) the person to be naturalised as such a citizen.

(5) If the mother of a person could not actually have been married to the person's natural father at the time of the person's birth (for whatever reason), that fact does not prevent an assumption being made that the couple were married at the time of the birth.]

Note: Section 4J inserted by s 65 Immigration Act 2014 from a date to be appointed.

5. Acquisition by registration: nationals for purposes of the [EU] Treaties

A [British overseas territories] citizen who falls to be treated as a national of the United Kingdom for the purposes of the [EU] Treaties shall be entitled to be registered as a British citizen if an application is made for his registration as such a citizen.

Note: British dependent territories became British overseas territories from 26 February 2002, British Overseas Territories Act 2002, s 1.

6. Acquisition by naturalisation

(1) If, on an application for naturalisation as a British citizen made by a person of full age and capacity, the Secretary of State is satisfied that the applicant fulfils the requirements of Schedule 1 for naturalisation as such a citizen under this subsection, he may, if he thinks fit, grant to him a certificate of naturalisation as such a citizen.

(2) If, on an application for naturalisation as a British citizen made by a person of full age and capacity who on the date of the application [has a relevant family association], the Secretary of State is satisfied that the applicant fulfils the requirements of Schedule 1 for naturalisation as such a citizen under this subsection, he may, if he thinks fit, grant to him a certificate of naturalisation as such a citizen.

[(3) For the purposes of this section and Schedule 1, a person ("A") has a relevant family association if A has a connection of a prescribed description to a person of a prescribed description.

(4) If in the special circumstances of any particular case the Secretary of State thinks fit, the Secretary of State may for the purposes of subsection (3) treat A as having a relevant family association on the date of the application although the relevant family association ceased to exist before that date.]

Note: Words in square brackets substituted and subsections (3)–(4) inserted by s 40 Borders, Citizenship and Immigration Act 2009 from a date to be appointed.

Acquisition after commencement: special cases

7. . . .

Note: Section 7 repealed by Sch 2 of Nationality, Immigration and Asylum Act 2002 from 1 April 2003 (SI 2003/754).

8. . . .

Note: Section 8 repealed by Sch 2 of Nationality, Immigration and Asylum Act 2002 from 1 April 2003 (SI 2003/754).

9. . . .

Note: Section 9 repealed by Sch 2 of Nationality, Immigration and Asylum Act 2002 from 1 April 2003 (SI 2003/754).

10. Registration following renunciation of citizenship of UK and Colonies

(1) Subject to subsection (3), a person shall be entitled, on an application for his registration as a British citizen, to be registered as such a citizen if immediately before commencement he would (had he applied for it) have been entitled under section 1(1) of the British Nationality Act 1964 (resumption of citizenship) to be registered as a citizen of the United Kingdom and Colonies by virtue of having an appropriate qualifying connection with the United Kingdom or, [. . .] by virtue of having been married before commencement to a person who has, or would if living have, such a connection.

(2) On an application for his registration as a British citizen made by a person of full capacity who had before commencement ceased to be a citizen of the United Kingdom and Colonies as a result of a declaration of renunciation, the Secretary of State may, if he thinks fit, cause that person to be registered as a British citizen if that person—

(a) has an appropriate qualifying connection with the United Kingdom; or

(b) [. . .] has been married to [, or has been the civil partner of,] a person who has, or would if living have, such a connection.

(3) A person shall not be entitled to registration under subsection (1) on more than one occasion.

(4) For the purposes of this section a person shall be taken to have an appropriate qualifying connection with the United Kingdom if he, his father or his father's father—

(a) was born in the United Kingdom; or

(b) is or was a person naturalised in the United Kingdom; or

(c) was registered as a citizen of the United Kingdom and Colonies in the United Kingdom or in a country which at the time was mentioned in section 1(3) of the 1948 Act.

Note: The words deleted from subsections (1) and (2) repealed by Nationality, Immigration and Asylum Act 2002, s 5 from 7 November 2002 in relation to applications made after that date or not yet decided before that date (s 162(3)). Words in square brackets in subsection (2) inserted by Sch 27 Civil Partnership Act 2004 from 5 December 2005 (SI 2005/3175).

Acquisition at commencement

11. Citizens of UK and Colonies who are to become British citizens at commencement

(1) Subject to subsection (2), a person who immediately before commencement—

(a) was a citizen of the United Kingdom and Colonies; and

(b) had the right of abode in the United Kingdom under the Immigration Act 1971 as then in force,

shall at commencement become a British citizen.

(2) A person who was registered as a citizen of the United Kingdom and Colonies under section 1 of the British Nationality (No. 2) Act 1964 (stateless persons) on the ground mentioned in subsection (1)(a) of that section (namely that his mother was a citizen of the United Kingdom and Colonies at the time when he was born) shall not become a British citizen under subsection (1) unless—

(a) his mother becomes a British citizen under subsection (1) or would have done so but for her death; or

(b) immediately before commencement he had the right of abode in the United Kingdom by virtue of section 2(1)(c) of the Immigration Act 1971 as then in force (settlement in United Kingdom, combined with five or more years' ordinary residence there as a citizen of the United Kingdom and Colonies).

(3) A person who—

(a) immediately before commencement was a citizen of the United Kingdom and Colonies by virtue of having been registered under subsection (6) of section 12 of the 1948 Act (British subjects before commencement of 1948 Act becoming citizens of United Kingdom and Colonies) under arrangements made by virtue of subsection (7) of that section (registration in independent Commonwealth country by United Kingdom High Commissioner); and

(b) was so registered on an application under the said subsection (6) based on the applicant's descent in the male line from a person ('the relevant person') possessing one of the qualifications specified in subsection (1)(a) and (b) of that section (birth or naturalisation in the United Kingdom and Colonies),

shall at commencement become a British citizen if the relevant person was born or naturalised in the United Kingdom.

Renunciation and resumption

12. Renunciation

(1) If any British citizen of full age and capacity makes in the prescribed manner a declaration of renunciation of British citizenship, then, subject to subsections (3) and (4), the Secretary of State shall cause the declaration to be registered.

(2) On the registration of a declaration made in pursuance of this section the person who made it shall cease to be a British citizen.

(3) A declaration made by a person in pursuance of this section shall not be registered unless the Secretary of State is satisfied that the person who made it will after the registration have or acquire some citizenship or nationality other than British citizenship; and if that person does not have any such citizenship or nationality on the date of registration

and does not acquire some such citizenship or nationality within six months from that date, he shall be, and be deemed to have remained, a British citizen notwithstanding the registration.

(4) The Secretary of State may withhold registration of any declaration made in pursuance of this section if it is made during any war in which Her Majesty may be engaged in right of Her Majesty's government in the United Kingdom.

(5) For the purposes of this section any person who has been married [or has formed a civil partnership] shall be deemed to be of full age.

Note: Words in square brackets in subsection (5) inserted by Sch 27 Civil Partnership Act 2004 from 5 December 2005 (SI 2005/3175).

13. Resumption

(1) Subject to subsection (2), a person who has ceased to be a British citizen as a result of a declaration of renunciation shall be entitled, on an application for his registration as a British citizen, to be registered as such a citizen if—

(a) he is of full capacity; and

(b) his renunciation of British citizenship was necessary to enable him to retain or acquire some other citizenship or nationality.

(2) A person shall not be entitled to registration under subsection (1) on more than one occasion.

(3) If a person of full capacity who has ceased to be a British citizen as a result of a declaration of renunciation (for whatever reason made) makes an application for his registration as such a citizen, the Secretary of State may, if he thinks fit, cause him to be registered as such a citizen.

Supplementary

14. Meaning of British citizen 'by descent'

(1) For the purposes of this Act a British citizen is a British citizen 'by descent' if and only if—

(a) he is a person born outside the United Kingdom after commencement who is a British citizen by virtue of section 2(1)(a) only or by virtue of registration under section 3(2) or 9; or

(b) subject to subsection (2), he is a person born outside the United Kingdom before commencement who became a British citizen at commencement and immediately before commencement—

(i) was a citizen of the United Kingdom and Colonies by virtue of section 5 of the 1948 Act (citizenship by descent); or

(ii) was a person who, under any provision of the British Nationality Acts 1948 to 1965, was deemed for the purposes of the proviso to section 5(1) of the 1948 Act to be a citizen of the United Kingdom and Colonies by descent only, or would have been so deemed if male; or

(iii) had the right of abode in the United Kingdom by virtue only of paragraph (b) of subsection (1) of section 2 of the Immigration Act 1971 as then in force (connection with United Kingdom through parent or grandparent), or by virtue only of that paragraph and paragraph (c) of that subsection (settlement in United Kingdom with five years' ordinary residence there), or by virtue only of being or having been the wife of a person who immediately before commencement had that right by virtue only of the said paragraph (b) or the said paragraphs (b) and (c); or

(iv) being a woman, was a citizen of the United Kingdom and Colonies as a result of her registration as such a citizen under section 6(2) of the 1948 Act by virtue of having been married to a man who at commencement became a British citizen by descent or would have done so but for his having died or ceased to be a citizen of the United Kingdom and Colonies as a result of a declaration of renunciation; or

(c) he is a British citizen by virtue of registration under section 3(1) and either—

(i) his father or mother was a British citizen at the time of the birth; or

(ii) his father or mother was a citizen of the United Kingdom and Colonies at that time and became a British citizen at commencement, or would have done so but for his or her death; or

(d) he is a British citizen by virtue of registration under [section 4B [4C] or 5]; or

[(da) the person is a British citizen by descent by virtue of section 4F(3), 4G(2), 4H(2) or 4I(4); or]

(e) subject to subsection (2), being a woman born outside the United Kingdom before commencement, she is a British citizen as a result of her registration as such a citizen under section 8 by virtue of being or having been married to a man who at commencement became a British citizen by descent or would have done so but for his having died or ceased to be a citizen of the United Kingdom and Colonies as a result of a declaration of renunciation; or

(f) he is a British citizen by virtue of registration under section 10 who, having before commencement ceased to be a citizen of the United Kingdom and Colonies as a result of a declaration of renunciation, would, if he had not so ceased, have at commencement become a British citizen by descent by virtue of paragraph (b); or

(g) he is a British citizen by virtue of registration under section 13 who, immediately before he ceased to be a British citizen as a result of a declaration of renunciation, was such a citizen by descent; or

(h) he is a person born in a [British overseas territory] after commencement who is a British citizen by virtue of paragraph 2 of Schedule 2.

(2) A person born outside the United Kingdom before commencement is not a British citizen 'by descent' by virtue of subsection (1)(b) or (e) if his father was at the time of his birth serving outside the United Kingdom—

(a) in service of a description mentioned in subsection (3), his recruitment for the service in question having taken place in the United Kingdom; or

(b) in service under a [EU] institution, his recruitment for that service having taken place in a country which at the time of the recruitment was a member of the [European Union].

(3) The descriptions of service referred to in subsection (2) are—

(a) Crown service under the government of the United Kingdom; and

(b) service of any description at any time designated under section 2(3).

Note: First words in square brackets in subsection (1)(d) substituted by Nationality, Immigration and Asylum Act 2002, s 12 from 30 April 2003 (SI 2003/754). Second words in square brackets in subsection (1)(d) inserted by Nationality, Immigration and Asylum Act 2002, s 13 from 30 April

2003 (SI 2003/754). Subsection (1)(da) inserted by Sch 9 Immigration Act 2014 from a date to be appointed. British dependent territories became British overseas territories from 26 February 2002, British Overseas Territories Act 2002, s 1.

PART II

[BRITISH OVERSEAS TERRITORIES] CITIZENSHIP

Acquisition after commencement

15. Acquisition by birth or adoption

(1) A person born in a [British overseas territory] after commencement shall be a [British overseas territories] citizen if at the time of the birth his father or mother is—

(a) a [British overseas territories] citizen; or

(b) settled in a [British overseas territory].

(2) A new-born infant who, after commencement, is found abandoned in a [British overseas territory] shall, unless the contrary is shown, be deemed for the purposes of subsection (1)—

(a) to have been born in that territory after commencement; and

(b) to have been born to a parent who at the time of the birth was a [British over-seas territories] citizen or settled in a [British overseas territory].

(3) A person born in a [British overseas territory] after commencement who is not a [British overseas territories] citizen by virtue of subsection (1) or (2) shall be entitled to be registered as such a citizen if, while he is a minor—

(a) his father or mother becomes such a citizen or becomes settled in a [British overseas territory]; and

(b) an application is made for his registration as such a citizen.

(4) A person born in a [British overseas territory] after commencement who is not a [British overseas territories] citizen by virtue of subsection (1) or (2) shall be entitled, on an application for his registration as a [British overseas territories] citizen made at any time after he has attained the age of ten years, to be registered as such a citizen if, as regards each of the first ten years of that person's life, the number of days on which he was absent from that territory in that year does not exceed 90.

(5) Where after commencement an order authorising the adoption of a minor who is not a [British overseas territories] citizen is made by a court in any [British overseas territory], he shall be a [British overseas territories] citizen as from the date on which the order is made if the adopter or, in the case of a joint adoption, one of the adopters, is a [British overseas territories] citizen on that date.

[(**5A**) Where—

(a) a minor who is not a British overseas territories citizen is adopted under a Convention adoption,

(b) on the date on which the adoption is effected—

(i) the adopter or, in the case of a joint adoption, one of the adopters is a British overseas territories citizen, and

(ii) the adopter or, in the case of a joint adoption, both of the adopters are habitually resident in a designated territory, and

(c) the Convention adoption is effected under the law of a country or territory outside the designated territory,

the minor shall be a British overseas territories citizen as from that date.]

(6) Where an order [or a Convention adoption] in consequence of which any person became a [British overseas territories] citizen by virtue of subsection (5) ceases to have effect, whether on annulment or otherwise, the cesser shall not affect the status of that person as such a citizen.

(7) If in the special circumstances of any particular case the Secretary of State thinks fit, he may for the purposes of subsection (4) treat the person to whom the application relates as fulfilling the requirements specified in that subsection although, as regards any one or more of the first ten years of that person's life, the number of days on which he was absent from the [British overseas territory] there mentioned in that year or each of the years in question exceeds 90.

Note: British dependent territories became British overseas territories from 26 February 2002, British Overseas Territories Act 2002, s 1. Subsection (5A) and words in subsection (6) inserted from 30 December 2005 by Adoption and Children Act 2002.

16. Acquisition by descent

(1) A person born outside the [British overseas territories] after commencement shall be a [British overseas territories] citizen if at the time of the birth his father or mother—

(a) is such a citizen otherwise than by descent; or

(b) is such a citizen and is serving outside the [British overseas territories] in service to which this paragraph applies, his or her recruitment for that service having taken place in a [British overseas territory].

(2) Paragraph (b) of subsection (1) applies to—

(a) Crown service under the government of a [British overseas territory]; and

(b) service of any description for the time being designated under subsection (3).

(3) For the purposes of this section the Secretary of State may by order made by statutory instrument designate any description of service which he considers to be closely associated with the activities outside the [British overseas territories] of the government of any [British overseas territory].

(4) Any order made under subsection (3) shall be subject to annulment in pursuance of a resolution of either House of Parliament.

Note: British dependent territories became British overseas territories from 26 February 2002, British Overseas Territories Act 2002, s 1.

17. Acquisition by registration: minors

(1) If while a person is a minor an application is made for his registration as a [British overseas territories] citizen the Secretary of State may, if he thinks fit, cause him to be registered as such a citizen.

(2) A person born outside the [British overseas territories] shall be entitled, on an application for his registration as a [British overseas territories] citizen made within the period of twelve months from the date of the birth, to be registered as such a citizen if the requirements specified in subsection (3) or, in the case of a person born stateless, the

requirements specified in paragraphs (a) and (b) of that subsection, are fulfilled in the case of either that person's father or his mother ('the parent in question').

(3) The requirements referred to in subsection (2) are—

(a) that the parent in question was a [British overseas territories] citizen by descent at the time of the birth; and

(b) that the father or mother of the parent in question—

(i) was a [British overseas territories] citizen otherwise than by descent at the time of the birth of the parent in question; or

(ii) became a [British overseas territories] citizen otherwise than by descent at commencement, or would have become such a citizen otherwise than by descent at commencement but for his or her death; and

(c) that, as regards some period of three years ending with a date not later than the date of the birth—

(i) the parent in question was in a [British overseas territory] at the beginning of that period; and

(ii) the number of days on which the parent in question was absent from that territory in that period does not exceed 270.

(4) If in the special circumstances of any particular case the Secretary of State thinks fit, he may treat subsection (2) as if the reference to twelve months were a reference to six years.

(5) A person born outside the [British overseas territories] shall be entitled, on an application for his registration as a [British overseas territories citizen] made while he is a minor, to be registered as such a citizen if the following requirements are satisfied, namely—

(a) that at the time of that person's birth his father or mother was a [British overseas territories] citizen by descent; and

(b) subject to subsection (6), that that person and his father and mother were in one and the same [British overseas territory] (no matter which) at the beginning of the period of three years ending with the date of the application and that, in the case of each of them, the number of days on which the person in question was absent from the last-mentioned territory in that period does not exceed 270; and

(c) subject to subsection (6), that the consent of his father and mother to the registration has been signified in the prescribed manner.

(6) In the case of an application under subsection (5) for the registration of a person as a [British overseas territories] citizen—

(a) if his father or mother died, or their marriage [or civil partnership] was terminated, on or before the date of the application, or his father and mother were legally separated on that date, the references to his father and mother in paragraph (b) of that subsection shall be read either as references to his father or as references to his mother; [and]

(b) if his father or mother died on or before that date, the reference to his father and mother in paragraph (c) of that subsection shall be read as a reference to either of them; [. . .

(c) . . .]

Note: Last word in square brackets in subsection (6)(a) inserted, and words deleted from subsections (6)(b) and (c) by Nationality, Immigration and Asylum Act 2002, s 9 from 7 November 2002, in relation to children born on or after a date to be appointed. British dependent territories became British overseas territories from 26 February 2002, British Overseas Territories Act 2002, s 1. Words in first square brackets in subsection (6)(a) inserted by Sch 27 Civil Partnership Act 2004 from 5 December 2005 (SI 2005/3175).

18. Acquisition by naturalisation

(1) If, on an application for naturalisation as a [British overseas territories] citizen made by a person of full age and capacity, the Secretary of State is satisfied that the applicant fulfils the requirements of Schedule 1 for naturalisation as such a citizen under this subsection, he may, if he thinks fit, grant to him a certificate of naturalisation as such a citizen.

(2) If, on an application for naturalisation as a [British overseas territories] citizen made by a person of full age and capacity who on the date of the application is married to such a citizen [or is the civil partner of such a citizen] the Secretary of State is satisfied that the applicant fulfils the requirements of Schedule 1 for naturalisation as such a citizen under this subsection, he may, if he thinks fit, grant to him a certificate of naturalisation as such a citizen.

(3) Every application under this section shall specify the [British overseas territory] which is to be treated as the relevant territory for the purposes of that application; and, in relation to any such application, references in Schedule 1 to the relevant territory shall be construed accordingly.

Note: British dependent territories became British overseas territories from 26 February 2002, British Overseas Territories Act 2002, s 1. Words in square brackets in subsection (2) inserted by Sch 27 Civil Partnership Act 2004 from 5 December 2005 (SI 2005/3175).

Acquisition after commencement: special cases

19. . . .

Note: Section 19 repealed by Sch 2 Nationality, Immigration and Asylum Act 2002 from 1 April 2003 (SI 2003/754).

20. . . .

Note: Section 20 repealed by Sch 2 Nationality, Immigration and Asylum Act 2002 from 1 April 2003 (SI 2003/754).

21. . . .

Note: Section 21 repealed by Sch 2 Nationality, Immigration and Asylum Act 2002 from 1 April 2003 (SI 2003/754).

22. Right to registration replacing right to resume citizenship of UK and Colonies

(1) Subject to subsection (3), a person shall be entitled, on an application for his registration as a [British overseas territories] citizen, to be registered as such a citizen if immediately before commencement he would (had he applied for it) have been entitled under section 1(1) of the British Nationality Act 1964 (resumption of citizenship) to be registered as a citizen of the United Kingdom and Colonies by virtue of having an appropriate qualifying connection with a [British overseas territory] or, [. . .,] by virtue of having been married before commencement to a person who has, or would if living have, such a connection.

(2) On an application for his registration as a [British overseas territories] citizen made by a person of full capacity who had before commencement ceased to be a citizen of the United Kingdom and Colonies as a result of a declaration of renunciation, the Secretary

of State may, if he thinks fit, cause that person to be registered as a [British overseas territories] citizen if that person—

(a) has an appropriate qualifying connection with a [British overseas territory]; or

(b) [. . .] has been married to [or has been the civil partner of,] a person who has, or would if living have, such a connection.

(3) A person shall not be entitled to registration under subsection (1) on more than one occasion.

(4) For the purposes of this section a person shall be taken to have an appropriate qualifying connection with a [British overseas territory] if he, his father or his father's father—

(a) was born in that territory; or

(b) is or was a person naturalised in that territory; or

(c) was registered as a citizen of the United Kingdom and Colonies in that territory; or

(d) became a British subject by reason of the annexation of any territory included in that territory.

Note: The words deleted from subsections (1) and (2) cease to have effect with regard to applications made after 7 November 2002, or applications not determined before that date: Nationality, Immigration and Asylum Act 2002, s 5. British dependent territories became British overseas territories from 26 February 2002, British Overseas Territories Act 2002, s 1. Words in square brackets in subsection (2)(b) inserted by Sch 27 Civil Partnership Act 2004 from 5 December 2005 (SI 2005/3175).

Acquisition at commencement

23. Citizens of UK and Colonies who are to become [British overseas territories] citizens at commencement

(1) A person shall at commencement become a [British overseas territories] citizen if—

(a) immediately before commencement he was a citizen of the United Kingdom and Colonies who had that citizenship by his birth, naturalisation or registration in a [British overseas territory]; or

(b) he was immediately before commencement a citizen of the United Kingdom and Colonies, and was born to a parent—

(i) who at the time of the birth ('the material time') was a citizen of the United Kingdom and Colonies; and

(ii) who either had that citizenship at the material time by his birth, naturalisation or registration in a [British overseas territory] or was himself born to a parent who at the time of that birth so had that citizenship; or

(c) being a woman, she was immediately before commencement a citizen of the United Kingdom and Colonies and either was then, or had at any time been, the wife of a man who under paragraph (a) or (b) becomes a [British overseas territories] citizen at commencement or would have done so but for his death.

(2) A person shall at commencement become a [British overseas territories] citizen if—

(a) immediately before commencement he was a citizen of the United Kingdom and Colonies by virtue of registration under section 7 of the 1948 Act (minor children) or section 1 of the British Nationality (No. 2) Act 1964 (stateless persons); and

(b) he was so registered otherwise than in a [British overseas territory]; and

(c) his father or mother (in the case of a person registered under the said section 7) or his mother (in the case of a person registered under the said section 1)—

(i) was a citizen of the United Kingdom and Colonies at the time of the registration or would have been such a citizen at that time but for his or her death; and

(ii) becomes a [British overseas territories] citizen at commencement or would have done so but for his or her death.

(3) A person who—

(a) immediately before commencement was a citizen of the United Kingdom and Colonies by virtue of having been registered under subsection (6) of section 12 of the 1948 Act (British subjects before commencement of 1948 Act becoming citizens of United Kingdom and Colonies) otherwise than in a [British overseas territory]; and

(b) was so registered on an application under that subsection based on the applicant's descent in the male line from a person ('the relevant person') possessing one of the qualifications specified in subsection (1) of that section (birth or naturalisation in the United Kingdom and Colonies, or acquisition of the status of British subject by reason of annexation of territory),

shall at commencement become a [British overseas territories] citizen if the relevant person—

(i) was born or naturalised in a [British overseas territory]; or

(ii) became a British subject by reason of the annexation of any territory included in a [British overseas territory].

(4) A person who—

(a) immediately before commencement was a citizen of the United Kingdom and Colonies by virtue of registration under section 1 of the British Nationality Act 1964 (resumption of citizenship); and

(b) was so registered otherwise than in a [British overseas territory]; and

(c) was so registered by virtue of having an appropriate qualifying connection with a [British overseas territory] or, if a woman, by virtue of having been married to a person who at the time of the registration had or would, if then living, have had such a connection,

shall at commencement become a [British overseas territories] citizen.

(5) For the purposes of subsection (4) a person shall be taken to have an appropriate qualifying connection with a [British overseas territory] if he, his father or his father's father—

(a) was born in a [British overseas territory]; or

(b) is or was a person naturalised in a [British overseas territory]; or

(c) was registered as a citizen of the United Kingdom and Colonies in a [British overseas territory]; or

(d) became a British subject by reason of the annexation of any territory included in a [British overseas territory].

(6) For the purposes of subsection (1)(b) references to citizenship of the United Kingdom and Colonies shall, in relation to a time before the year 1949, be construed as references to British nationality.

Note: British dependent territories became British overseas territories from 26 February 2002, British Overseas Territories Act 2002, s 1.

Renunciation and resumption

24. Renunciation and resumption

The provisions of sections 12 and 13 shall apply in relation to [British overseas territories] citizens and [British Overseas Territories] citizenship as they apply in relation to British citizens and British citizenship.

Note: British dependent territories became British overseas territories from 26 February 2002, British Overseas Territories Act 2002, s 1.

Supplementary

25. Meaning of [British overseas territories] citizen 'by descent'

(1) For the purposes of this Act a [British overseas territories] citizen is such a citizen 'by descent' if and only if—

(a) he is a person born outside the [British overseas territories] after commencement who is a [British overseas territories] citizen by virtue of section 16(1)(a) only or by virtue of registration under section 17(2) or 21; or

(b) subject to subsection (2), he is a person born outside the [British overseas territories] before commencement who became a [British overseas territories] citizen at commencement and immediately before commencement—

(i) was a citizen of the United Kingdom and Colonies by virtue of section 5 of the 1948 Act (citizenship by descent); or

(ii) was a person who, under any provision of the British Nationality Acts 1948 to 1965, was deemed for the purposes of the proviso to section 5(1) of the 1948 Act to be a citizen of the United Kingdom and Colonies by descent only, or would have been so deemed if male; or

(c) he is a [British overseas territories] citizen by virtue of registration under section 17(1) and either—

(i) his father or mother was a [British overseas territories] citizen at the time of the birth; or

(ii) his father or mother was a citizen of the United Kingdom and Colonies at that time and became a [British overseas territories] citizen at commencement, or would have done so but for his or her death; or

(d) subject to subsection (2), he is a person born outside the [British overseas territories] before commencement who became a [British overseas territories] citizen at commencement under section 23(1)(b) only; or

(e) subject to subsection (2), being a woman, she became a [British overseas territories] citizen at commencement under section 23(1)(c) only, and did so only by virtue of having been, immediately before commencement or earlier, the wife of a man who immediately after commencement was, or would but for his death have been, a [British overseas territories] citizen by descent by virtue of paragraph (b) or (d) of this subsection; or

(f) subject to subsection (2), being a woman born outside the [British overseas territories] before commencement, she is a [British overseas territories] citizen as a result of her registration as such a citizen under section 20 by virtue of being or having been married to a man who at commencement became such a citizen by descent or would have done so but for his having died or ceased to be a citizen of the United Kingdom and Colonies as a result of a declaration of renunciation; or

(g) he is a [British overseas territories] citizen by virtue of registration under section 22 who, having before commencement ceased to be a citizen of the United Kingdom and Colonies as a result of a declaration of renunciation, would, if he had not so ceased, have at commencement become a [British overseas territories] citizen by descent by virtue of paragraph (b), (d) or (e);

(h) he is a [British overseas territories] citizen by virtue of registration under section 13 (as applied by section 24) who, immediately before he ceased to be a [British overseas territories] citizen as a result of a declaration of renunciation, was such a citizen by descent; or

(i) he is a person born in the United Kingdom after commencement who is a [British overseas territories] citizen by virtue of paragraph 1 of Schedule 2.

(2) A person born outside the [British overseas territories] before commencement is not a [British overseas territories] citizen 'by descent' by virtue of subsection (1)(b), (d), (e) or (f) if his father was at the time of his birth serving outside the [British overseas territories] in service of a description mentioned in subsection (3), his recruitment for the service in question having taken place in a [British overseas territory].

(3) The descriptions of service referred to in subsection (2) are—

(a) Crown service under the government of a [British overseas territory]; and

(b) service of any description at any time designated under section 16(3).

Note: British dependent territories became British overseas territories from 26 February 2002, British Overseas Territories Act 2002, s 1.

Part III

British Overseas Citizenship

26. Citizens of UK and Colonies who are to become British Overseas citizens at commencement

Any person who was a citizen of the United Kingdom and Colonies immediately before commencement and who does not at commencement become either a British citizen or a [British overseas territories] citizen shall at commencement become a British Overseas citizen.

Note: British dependent territories became British overseas territories from 26 February 2002, British Overseas Territories Act 2002, s 1.

27. Registration of minors

(1) If while a person is a minor an application is made for his registration as a British Overseas citizen, the Secretary of State may, if he thinks fit, cause him to be registered as such a citizen.

(2) . . .

Note: Section 27(2) repealed by Sch 2 Nationality, Immigration and Asylum Act 2002 from 1 April 2003 (SI 2003/754).

28. . . .

Note: Section 28 repealed by Sch 2 Nationality, Immigration and Asylum Act 2002 from 1 April 2003 (SI 2003/754).

29. Renunciation

The provisions of section 12 shall apply in relation to British Overseas citizens and British Overseas citizenship as they apply in relation to British citizens and British citizenship.

PART IV
BRITISH SUBJECTS

30. Continuance as British subjects of existing British subjects of certain descriptions

A person who immediately before commencement was—

(a) a British subject without citizenship by virtue of section 13 or 16 of the 1948 Act; or

(b) a British subject by virtue of section 1 of the British Nationality Act 1965 (registration of alien women who have been married to British subjects of certain descriptions),

shall as from commencement be a British subject by virtue of this section.

31. Continuance as British subjects of certain former citizens of Eire

(1) A person is within this subsection if immediately before 1st January 1949 he was both a citizen of Eire and a British subject.

(2) A person within subsections (1) who immediately before commencement was a British subject by virtue of section 2 of the 1948 Act (continuance of certain citizens of Eire as British subjects) shall as from commencement be a British subject by virtue of this subsection.

(3) If at any time after commencement a citizen of the Republic of Ireland who is within subsection (1) but is not a British subject by virtue of subsection (2) gives notice in writing to the Secretary of State claiming to remain a British subject on either or both of the following grounds, namely—

(a) that he is or has been in Crown Service under the government of the United Kingdom; and

(b) that he has associations by way of descent, residence or otherwise with the United Kingdom or with any [British overseas territory], he shall as from that time be a British subject by virtue of this subsection.

(4) A person who is a British subject by virtue of subsection (2) or (3) shall be deemed to have remained a British subject from 1 January 1949 to the time when (whether already a British subject by virtue of the said section 2 or not) he became a British subject by virtue of that subsection.

Note: British dependent territories became British overseas territories from 26 February 2002, British Overseas Territories Act 2002, s 1.

32. Registration of minors

If while a person is a minor an application is made for his registration as a British subject, the Secretary of State may, if he thinks fit, cause him to be registered as a British subject.

33. . . .

Note: Section 33 repealed by Sch 2 Nationality, Immigration and Asylum Act 2002 from 1 April 2003 (SI 2003/754).

34. Renunciation

The provisions of section 12 shall apply in relation to British subjects and the status of a British subject as they apply in relation to British citizens and British citizenship.

35. Circumstances in which British subjects are to lose that status

A person who under this Act is a British subject otherwise than by virtue of section 31 shall cease to be such a subject if, in whatever circumstances and whether under this Act or otherwise, he acquires any other citizenship or nationality whatever.

Part V

Miscellaneous and Supplementary

36. Provisions for reducing statelessness

The provisions of Schedule 2 shall have effect for the purpose of reducing statelessness.

37. Commonwealth citizenship

(1) Every person who—

(a) under [the British Nationality Acts 1981 and 1983] [or the British Overseas Territories Act 2002] is a British citizen, a [British overseas territories] citizen, [a British National (Overseas),] a British Overseas citizen or a British subject; or

(b) under any enactment for the time being in force in any country mentioned in Schedule 3 is a citizen of that country,

shall have the status of a Commonwealth citizen.

(2) Her Majesty may by Order in Council amend Schedule 3 by the alteration of any entry, the removal of any entry, or the insertion of any additional entry.

(3) Any Order in Council made under this section shall be subject to annulment in pursuance of a resolution of either House of Parliament.

(4) After commencement no person shall have the status of a Commonwealth citizen or the status of a British subject otherwise than under this Act.

Note: Words in first square brackets in subsection (1) substituted by British Nationality (Falkland Islands) Act 1983. Words in second square brackets inserted by Sch 1 British Overseas Territories Act 2002 from 21 May 2002 (SI 2002/1252). Words in fourth square brackets in subsection (1) inserted by SI 1986/948. British dependent territories became British overseas territories from 26 February 2002, British Overseas Territories Act 2002, s 1.

38. British protected persons

(1) Her Majesty may by Order in Council made in relation to any territory which was at any time before commencement—

(a) a protectorate or protected state for the purposes of the 1948 Act; or

(b) a United Kingdom trust territory within the meaning of that Act,

declare to be British protected persons for the purposes of this Act any class of persons who are connected with that territory and are not citizens of any country mentioned in Schedule 3 which consists of or includes that territory.

(2) Any Order in Council made under this section shall be subject to annulment in pursuance of a resolution of either House of Parliament.

39. Amendment of Immigration Act 1971

(1) . . .

(2) . . .

(3) . . .

(4) . . .

(5) . . .

(6) . . .

(7) . . .

(8) A certificate of patriality issued under the Immigration Act 1971 and in force immediately before commencement shall have effect after commencement as if it were a certificate of entitlement issued under that Act [as in force after commencement] unless at commencement the holder ceases to have the right of abode in the United Kingdom.

Note: Section 39(1), (2), (4), (6) amend Immigration Act 1971. Section 39(3), (5) repealed, and words in square brackets in subsection (8) substituted by Immigration Act 1988, s 3. Section 39(7) amended Mental Health Act 1959, Mental Health (Scotland) Act 1960.

[40. Deprivation of citizenship

(1) In this section a reference to a person's 'citizenship status' is a reference to his status as—

(a) a British citizen,

(b) a British overseas territories citizen,

(c) a British Overseas citizen,

(d) a British National (Overseas),

(e) a British protected person, or

(f) a British subject.

[(2) The Secretary of State may by order deprive a person of a citizenship status if the Secretary of State is satisfied that deprivation is conducive to the public good.]

(3) The Secretary of State may by order deprive a person of a citizenship status which results from his registration or naturalisation if the Secretary of State is satisfied that the registration or naturalisation was obtained by means of—

(a) fraud,

(b) false representation, or

(c) concealment of a material fact.

(4) The Secretary of State may not make an order under subsection (2) if he is satisfied that the order would make a person stateless.

[(4A) But that does not prevent the Secretary of State from making an order under subsection (2) to deprive a person of a citizenship status if—

(a) the citizenship status results from the person's naturalisation,

(b) the Secretary of State is satisfied that the deprivation is conducive to the public good because the person, while having that citizenship status, has conducted him or herself in a manner which is seriously prejudicial to the vital interests of the United Kingdom, any of the Islands, or any British overseas territory, and

(c) the Secretary of State has reasonable grounds for believing that the person is able, under the law of a country or territory outside the United Kingdom, to become a national of such a country or territory.]

(5) Before making an order under this section in respect of a person the Secretary of State must give the person written notice specifying—

(a) that the Secretary of State has decided to make an order,

(b) the reasons for the order, and

(c) the person's right of appeal under section 40A(1) or under section 2B of the Special Immigration Appeals Commission Act 1997 (c. 68).

(6) Where a person acquired a citizenship status by the operation of a law which applied to him because of his registration or naturalisation under an enactment having effect before commencement, the Secretary of State may by order deprive the person of the citizenship status if the Secretary of State is satisfied that the registration or naturalisation was obtained by means of—

(a) fraud,

(b) false representation, or

(c) concealment of a material fact.]

Note: Section 40 substituted by Nationality, Immigration and Asylum Act 2002, s 4 from 1 April 2003 (SI 2003/754). Subsection (2) substituted by Immigration, Asylum and Nationality Act 2006, s 56 from 16 June 2006 (SI 2006/1498). Subsection (4A) inserted by s 66 Immigration Act 2014 from 28 July 2014 (SI 2014/1820).

[40A. Deprivation of citizenship: appeal

(1) A person who is given notice under section 40(5) of a decision to make an order in respect of him under section 40 may appeal against the decision to [the First-tier Tribunal].

(2) Subsection (1) shall not apply to a decision if the Secretary of State certifies that it was taken wholly or partly in reliance on information which in his opinion should not be made public—

(a) in the interests of national security,

(b) in the interests of the relationship between the United Kingdom and another country, or

(c) otherwise in the public interest.

[(3) The following provisions of the Nationality, Immigration and Asylum Act 2002 (c. 41) shall apply in relation to an appeal under this section as they apply in relation to an appeal under section 82 [. . .] of that Act—

(a) . . .

(b) section 106 (rules),

(c) section 107 (practice directions)] [, and

(d) section 108 (forged document: proceedings in private).]

(6). . .

(7). . .

(8). . .]

Note: Section 40A inserted by Nationality, Immigration and Asylum Act 2002, s 4 from 1 April 2003 (SI 2003/754). Words in first square brackets substituted and subsections (3)(b) revoked from

15 February 2010 (SI 2010/21). Words in other square brackets substituted by and subsections (6)–(8) omitted by Sch 2 Asylum and Immigration (Treatment of Claimants etc.) Act 2004 from 4 April 2005 (SI 2005/565). Words in square brackets in subsection (3) and subsection (3)(e) inserted by Immigration, Asylum and Nationality Act 2006, s 56 from 16 June 2006 (SI 2006/1498). Numbers in subsection (3) and subsection (3)(a) omitted by Sch 9 Immigration Act 2014 from 20 October 2014 with savings set out in SI 2014/2771 articles 9-11.

[40B. Review of power under section 40(4A)

(1) The Secretary of State must arrange for a review of the operation of the relevant deprivation power to be carried out in relation to each of the following periods—

(a) the initial one year period;

(b) each subsequent three year period.

(2) The "relevant deprivation power" is the power to make orders under section 40(2) to deprive persons of a citizenship status in the circumstances set out in section 40(4A).

(3) A review must be completed as soon as practicable after the end of the period to which the review relates.

(4) As soon as practicable after a person has carried out a review in relation to a particular period, the person must—

(a) produce a report of the outcome of the review, and

(b) send a copy of the report to the Secretary of State.

(5) The Secretary of State must lay before each House of Parliament a copy of each report sent under subsection (4)(b).

(6) The Secretary of State may, after consultation with the person who produced the report, exclude a part of the report from the copy laid before Parliament if the Secretary of State is of the opinion that it would be contrary to the public interest or prejudicial to national security for that part of the report to be made public.

(7) The Secretary of State may—

(a) make such payments as the Secretary of State thinks appropriate in connection with the carrying out of a review, and

(b) make such other arrangements as the Secretary of State thinks appropriate in connection with the carrying out of a review (including arrangements for the provision of staff, other resources and facilities).

(8) In this section—

"initial one year period" means the period of one year beginning with the day when section 40(4A) comes into force;

"subsequent three year period" means a period of three years beginning with the first day after the most recent of—

(a) the initial one year period, or

(b) the most recent subsequent three year period.]

Note: Section 40B inserted by s 66 Immigration Act 2014 from 28 July 2014 (SI 2014/1820).

41. Regulations and Orders in Council

(1) The Secretary of State may by regulations make provision generally for carrying into effect the purposes of this Act, and in particular provision—

(a) for prescribing anything which under this Act is to be prescribed;

(b) for prescribing the manner in which, and the persons to and by whom, applications for registration or naturalisation under any provision of this Act may or must be made;

[(bza) requiring an application for registration or naturalisation of a person as a British citizen to be accompanied by biometric information, or enabling an authorised person to require an individual to whom such an application relates to provide biometric information;]

[(ba) for determining whether a person has sufficient knowledge of a language for the purpose of an application for naturalisation;

(bb) for determining whether a person has sufficient knowledge about life in the United Kingdom for the purpose of an application for naturalisation;]

[(bc) for amending paragraph 4B(3)(a) or (b) or (4)(a) or (b) of Schedule 1 to substitute a different number for the number for the time being specified there;

(bd) for determining whether a person has, for the purposes of an application for naturalisation under section 6, participated in activities prescribed for the purposes of paragraph 4B(5)(a) of Schedule 1;

(be) for determining whether a person is to be treated for the purposes of such an application as having so participated;]

(c) for the registration of anything required or authorised by or under this Act to be registered;

[(d) for the time within which an obligation to make a citizenship oath and pledge at a citizenship ceremony must be satisfied;

(da) for the time within which an obligation to make a citizenship oath or pledge must be satisfied;

(db) for the content and conduct of a citizenship ceremony;

(dc) for the administration and making of a citizenship oath or pledge;

(dd) for the registration and certification of the making of a citizenship oath or pledge;

(de) for the completion and grant of a certificate of registration or naturalisation;]

(e) for the giving of any notice required or authorised to be given to any person under this Act;

(f) for the cancellation of the registration of, and the cancellation and amendment of certificates of naturalisation relating to, persons deprived of citizenship [or of the status of a British National (overseas)] under this Act, and for requiring such certificates to be delivered up for those purposes;

(g) for the births and deaths of persons of any class or description born or dying in a country mentioned in Schedule 3 to be registered there by the High Commissioner for Her Majesty's government in the United Kingdom or by members of his official staff;

(h) for the births and deaths of persons of any class or description born or dying in a foreign country to be registered there by consular officers or other officers in the service of Her Majesty's government in the United Kingdom;

(i) for enabling the births and deaths of British citizens, [British overseas territories citizens], [British Nationals (Overseas),] British Overseas citizens, British subjects and British protected persons born or dying in any country in which Her Majesty's government in the United Kingdom has for the time being no diplomatic or consular representatives to be registered—

(i) by persons serving in the diplomatic, consular or other foreign service of any country which, by arrangement with Her Majesty's government in the United Kingdom, has undertaken to represent that government's interest in that country, or

(ii) by a person authorised in that behalf by the Secretary of State.

[(j) as to the consequences of failure to comply with provision made under any of paragraphs (a) to (i).]

[(**1ZA**) In subsection (1)(bza) "authorised person" and "biometric information" have the same meaning as in section 126 of the Nationality, Immigration and Asylum Act 2002.

(**1ZB**) Section 126(4) to (7) of that Act applies to regulations under subsection (1)(bza) as it applies to regulations under section 126(1) of that Act.

(**1ZC**) Section 8 of the UK Borders Act 2007 (power to make regulations about use and retention of biometric information) applies to biometric information provided in accordance with regulations under subsection (1)(bza) as it applies to biometric information provided in accordance with regulations under section 5(1) of that Act.

(**1ZD**) But (despite section 8(5)(b) of that Act) regulations made by virtue of subsection (1ZC) may provide for photographs of a person who is registered or naturalised as a British citizen to be retained until the person is issued with a United Kingdom passport describing the person as a British citizen.]

[(**1A**) Regulations under subsection (1)(ba) or (bb) may, in particular—

(a) make provision by reference to possession of a specified qualification;

(b) make provision by reference to possession of a qualification of a specified kind;

(c) make provision by reference to attendance on a specified course;

(d) make provision by reference to attendance on a course of a specified kind;

(e) make provision by reference to a specified level of achievement;

(f) enable a person designated by the Secretary of State to determine sufficiency of knowledge in specified circumstances;

(g) enable the Secretary of State to accept a qualification of a specified kind as evidence of sufficient knowledge of a language].

[(**1B**) Regulations under subsection (1)(bc) may make provision so that—

(a) the number specified in sub-paragraph (3)(a) of paragraph 4B of Schedule 1 is the same as the number specified in sub-paragraph (4)(a) of that paragraph;

(b) the number specified in sub-paragraph (3)(b) of that paragraph is the same as the number specified in sub-paragraph (4)(b) of that paragraph.

(**1C**) Regulations under subsection (1)(bd) or (be)—

(a) may make provision that applies in relation to time before the commencement of section 41 of the Borders, Citizenship and Immigration Act 2009;

(b) may enable the Secretary of State to make arrangements for such persons as the Secretary of State thinks appropriate to determine whether, in accordance with those regulations, a person has, or (as the case may be) is to be treated as having, participated in an activity.]

(2) . . .

(3) Regulations under subsection (1) . . . may make different provision for different circumstances; and—

(a) regulations under subsection (1) may provide for the extension of any time-limit for the [making of oaths and pledges of citizenship]; and

. . .

[(**3A**) Regulations under subsection (1)(d) to (de) may, in particular—

(a) enable the Secretary of State to designate or authorise a person to exercise a function (which may include a discretion) in connection with a citizenship ceremony or a citizenship oath or pledge;

(b) require, or enable the Secretary of State to require, a local authority to provide specified facilities and to make specified arrangements in connection with citizenship ceremonies;

(c) impose, or enable the Secretary of State to impose, a function (which may include a discretion) on a local authority or on a registrar.

[(**3B**) In subsection (3A)—

'local authority' means—

(a) in relation to England and Wales, a county council, a county borough council, a metropolitan district council, a London Borough Council and the Common Council of the City of London, and

(b) in relation to Scotland, a council constituted under section 2 of the Local Government etc. (Scotland) Act 1994 (c. 39), and

'registrar' means—

(a) in relation to England and Wales, a superintendent registrar of births, deaths and marriages (or, in accordance with section 8 of the Registration Service Act 1953 (c. 37), a deputy superintendent registrar), and

(b) in relation to Scotland, a district registrar within the meaning of section 7(12) of the Registration of Births, Deaths and Marriages (Scotland) Act 1965 (c. 49).]

(**4**) Her Majesty may by Order in Council provide for any Act or Northern Ireland legislation to which this subsection applies to apply, with such adaptations and modifications as appear to Her necessary, to births and deaths registered—

(a) in accordance with regulations made in pursuance of subsection (1)(g) to (i) of this section or subsection (1)(f) and (g) of section 29 of the 1948 Act; or

(b) at a consulate of Her Majesty in accordance with regulations made under the British Nationality and Status of Aliens Acts 1914 to 1943 or in accordance with instructions of the Secretary of State; or

(c) by a High Commissioner for Her Majesty's government in the United Kingdom or members of his official staff in accordance with instructions of the Secretary of State;

and an Order in Council under this subsection may exclude, in relation to births and deaths so registered, any of the provisions of section 45.

(**5**) Subsection (4) applies to—

(a) the Births and Deaths Registration Act 1953, the Registration Service Act 1953 and the Registration of Births, Deaths and Marriages (Scotland) Act 1965; and

(b) so much of any Northern Ireland legislation for the time being in force (whether passed or made before or after commencement) as relates to the registration of births and deaths.

(**6**) The power to make regulations under subsection (1) or (2) shall be exercisable by statutory instrument.

(**7**) Any regulations or Order in Council made under this section [(other than regulations referred to in subsection (8))] shall be subject to annulment in pursuance of a resolution of either House of Parliament.

[(**8**) Any regulations (whether alone or with other provision)—

(a) under subsection (1)(a) for prescribing activities for the purposes of paragraph 4B(5)(a) of Schedule 1; or

(b) under subsection [(1)(bza), (bc)], (bd) or (be), may not be made unless a draft has been laid before and approved by a resolution of each House of Parliament.]

Note: Words in square brackets in subsections (1)(f), (1)(i), inserted by SI 1986/948. Subsections (1)(ba), (bb) inserted by Nationality, Immigration and Asylum Act 2002, s 1 from 6 July 2004 (SI 2004/1707) and s 1A inserted by s 1 of that Act from 1 November 2005 (SI 2005/2782). Section 41(1)(d) substituted by paragraph 4, Sch 1 Nationality, Immigration and Asylum Act 2002 from 1 January 2004 (SI 2003/3156). Words in square brackets in subsections (3)(a) substituted by paragraph 5, Sch 1 of the Nationality, Immigration and Asylum Act 2002 from 1 January 2004 (SI 2003/3156). Subsections (3A) and (3B) inserted by paragraph 7, Sch 1, Nationality, Immigration and Asylum Act 2002 from 1 January 2004 (SI 2003/3156). British dependent territories became British overseas territories from 26 February 2002, British Overseas Territories Act 2002, s 1. Subsection (1)(j) inserted and subsections (2), (3)(b) and words in (3)(a) omitted by Sch 2 Immigration, Asylum and Nationality Act 2006 from 1 April 2003 (SI 2003/754). Subsections (1)(bc)–(be), (1B)–(1C), (8) and words in square brackets in subsection (7) inserted by s 41 Borders, Citizenship and Immigration Act 2009 from a date to be appointed. Words omitted from subsections (1)(g), (h) and (i) and words substituted in subsection (4) by SI 2014/542 from a date to be appointed. Subsections (1)(bza), (1ZA)–(1ZD) inserted and letters in square brackets in subsection (8)(b) substituted by s 10 Immigration Act 2014 from a date to be appointed.

[41A. Registration: requirement to be of good character

(1) An application for registration of an adult or young person as a British citizen under section 1(3), (3A) or (4), 3(1), (2) or (5), 4(2) or (5), 4A, 4C, 4D, [4F, 4G, 4H, 4I], 5, 10(1) or (2) or 13(1) or (3) must not be granted unless the Secretary of State is satisfied that the adult or young person is of good character.

(2) An application for registration of an adult or young person as a British overseas territories citizen under section 15(3) or (4), 17(1) or (5), 22(1) or (2) or 24 must not be granted unless the Secretary of State is satisfied that the adult or young person is of good character.

(3) An application for registration of an adult or young person as a British Overseas citizen under section 27(1) must not be granted unless the Secretary of State is satisfied that the adult or young person is of good character.

(4) An application for registration of an adult or young person as a British subject under section 32 must not be granted unless the Secretary of State is satisfied that the adult or young person is of good character.

(5) In this section, “adult or young person” means a person who has attained the age of 10 years at the time when the application is made.]

Note: Section 41A inserted by s 47 Borders, Citizenship and Immigration Act 2009 from 13 January 2010 (SI 2001/2731). Words in square brackets in subs-s (1) substituted by Sch 9 Immigration Act 2014 from a date to be appointed.

[42. Registration and naturalisation: citizenship ceremony, oath and pledge

(1) A person of full age shall not be registered under this Act as a British citizen unless he has made the relevant citizenship oath and pledge specified in Schedule 5 at a citizenship ceremony.

(2) A certificate of naturalisation as a British citizen shall not be granted under this Act to a person of full age unless he has made the relevant citizenship oath and pledge specified in Schedule 5 at a citizenship ceremony.

(3) A person of full age shall not be registered under this Act as a British overseas territories citizen unless he has made the relevant citizenship oath and pledge specified in Schedule 5.

(4) A certificate of naturalisation as a British overseas territories citizen shall not be granted under this Act to a person of full age unless he has made the relevant citizenship oath and pledge specified in Schedule 5.

(5) A person of full age shall not be registered under this Act as a British Overseas citizen or a British subject unless he has made the relevant citizenship oath specified in Schedule 5.

(6) Where the Secretary of State thinks it appropriate because of the special circumstances of a case he may—

(a) disapply any of subsections (1) to (5), or

(b) modify the effect of any of those subsections.

(7) Sections 5 and 6 of the Oaths Act 1978 (c. 19) (affirmation) apply to a citizenship oath; and a reference in this Act to a citizenship oath includes a reference to a citizenship affirmation.]

Note: Section 42 substituted by paragraph 1, Sch 1 Nationality, Immigration and Asylum Act 2002 from 1 January 2004 (SI 2003/3156).

[42A. . . .]

Note: Section 42A inserted by paragraph 1, Sch 1 Nationality, Immigration and Asylum Act 2002 from 1 January 2004 (SI 2003/3156). Ceases to have effect from 2 April 2007, Sch 3 Immigration, Asylum and Nationality Act 2006 (SI 2007/1109).

[42B. Registration and naturalisation: timing

(1) A person who is registered under this Act as a citizen of any description or as a British subject shall be treated as having become a citizen or subject—

(a) immediately on making the required citizenship oath and pledge in accordance with section 42, or

(b) where the requirement for an oath and pledge is disapplied, immediately on registration.

(2) A person granted a certificate of naturalisation under this Act as a citizen of any description shall be treated as having become a citizen—

(a) immediately on making the required citizenship oath and pledge in accordance with section 42, or

(b) where the requirement for an oath and pledge is disapplied, immediately on the grant of the certificate.

(3) In the application of subsection (1) to registration as a British Overseas citizen or as a British subject the reference to the citizenship oath and pledge shall be taken as a reference to the citizenship oath.]

Note: Section 42B inserted by paragraph 1, Sch 1 Nationality, Immigration and Asylum Act 2002 from January 2004 (SI 2003/3156).

43. Exercise of functions of Secretary of State by Governors and others

(1) Subject to subsection (3), the Secretary of State may in the case of any of his functions under this Act with respect to any of the matters mentioned in subsection (2), make arrangements for that function to be exercised—

(a) in any of the Islands, by the Lieutenant-Governor in cases concerning British citizens or British citizenship;

(b) in any [British overseas territory] [. . .], by the Governor in cases concerning [British overseas territories] citizens or [British overseas territories] citizenship [and in cases concerning British National (Overseas) or the status of a British National (Overseas)];

(2) The said matters are—

(a) registration and naturalisation; and

(b) renunciation, resumption and deprivation of British citizenship or [British overseas territories] citizenship.

[(c) renunciation and deprivation of the status of a British National (Overseas).]

(3) Nothing in this section applies in the case of any power to make regulations or rules conferred on the Secretary of State by this Act.

(4) Arrangements under subsection (1) may provide for any such function as is there mentioned to be exercisable only with the approval of the Secretary of State.

Note: Words in fifth square brackets in subsection (1)(b) and subsection (2)(c) added by SI 1986/948. British dependent territories became British overseas territories from 26 February 2002, British Overseas Territories Act 2002, s 1.

44. Decisions involving exercise of discretion

(1) Any discretion vested by or under this Act in the Secretary of State, a Governor or a Lieutenant-Governor shall be exercised without regard to the race, colour or religion of any person who may be affected by its exercise.

(2) . . .

(3) . . .

Note: Subsections (2) and (3) cease to have effect from 7 November 2002, Nationality, Immigration and Asylum Act 2002, s 7.

[44A. Waiver of requirement for full capacity

Where a provision of this Act requires an applicant to be of full capacity, the Secretary of State may waive the requirement in respect of a specified applicant if he thinks it in the applicant's best interests.]

Note: Section 44A inserted by Immigration, Asylum and Nationality Act 2006, s 49 from 31 August 2006 (SI 2006/2226, which contains transitional provisions).

45. Evidence

(1) Every document purporting to be a notice, certificate, order or declaration, or an entry in a register, or a subscription of an oath of allegiance, given, granted or made under this Act or any of the former nationality Acts shall be received in evidence and shall, unless the contrary is proved, be deemed to have been given, granted or made by or on behalf of the person by whom or on whose behalf it purports to have been given, granted or made.

(2) Prima facie evidence of any such document may be given by the production of a document purporting to be certified as a true copy of it by such person and in such manner as may be prescribed.

(3) Any entry in a register made under this Act or any of the former nationality Acts shall be received as evidence (and in Scotland as sufficient evidence) of the matters stated in the entry.

(4) A certificate given by or on behalf of the Secretary of State that a person was at any time in Crown service under the government of the United Kingdom or that a person's recruitment for such service took place in the United Kingdom shall, for the purposes of this Act, be conclusive evidence of that fact.

46. Offences and proceedings

(1) Any person who for the purpose of procuring anything to be done or not to be done under this Act—

(a) makes any statement which he knows to be false in a material particular; or

(b) recklessly makes any statement which is false in a material particular, shall be liable on summary conviction in the United Kingdom to imprisonment for a term not exceeding three months or to a fine not exceeding [level 5 on the standard scale], or both.

(2) Any person who without reasonable excuse fails to comply with any requirement imposed on him by regulations made under this Act with respect to the delivering up of certificates of naturalisation shall be liable on summary conviction in the United Kingdom to a fine not exceeding [level 4 on the standard scale].

(3) In the case of an offence under subsection (1)—

(a) any information relating to the offence may in England and Wales be tried by a magistrates' court if it is laid within six months after the commission of the offence, or if it is laid within three years after the commission of the offence and not more than two months after the date certified by a chief officer of police to be the date on which evidence sufficient to justify proceedings came to the notice of an officer of his police force; and

(b) summary proceedings for the offence may in Scotland be commenced within six months after the commission of the offence, or within three years after the commission of the offence and not more than two months after the date on which evidence sufficient in the opinion of the Lord Advocate to justify proceedings came to his knowledge; and

(c) a complaint charging the commission of the offence may in Northern Ireland be heard and determined by a magistrates' court if it is made within six months after the commission of the offence, or if it is made within three years after the commission of the offence and not more than two months after the date certified by an officer of police not below the rank of assistant chief constable to be the date on which evidence sufficient to justify the proceedings came to the notice of the police in Northern Ireland.

(4) For the purposes of subsection (3)(b) proceedings shall be deemed to be commenced on the date on which a warrant to apprehend or to cite the accused is granted, if such warrant is executed without undue delay; and a certificate of the Lord Advocate as to the date on which such evidence as is mentioned in subsection (3)(b) came to his knowledge shall be conclusive evidence.

(5) For the purposes of the trial of a person for an offence under subsection (1) or (2), the offence shall be deemed to have been committed either at the place at which it actually was committed or at any place at which he may be.

(6) In their application to the Bailiwick of Jersey subsections (1) and (2) shall have effect with the omission of the words 'on summary conviction'.

Note: Words in square brackets in s 46(1), (2), substituted by virtue of Criminal Justice Act 1982, s 46.

47. . . .

Note: Section 47 ceases to have effect in relation to a child born on or after 1 July 2006, Nationality, Immigration and Asylum Act 2002, s 9(SI 2006/1498).

48. Posthumous children

Any reference in this Act to the status of description of the father or mother of a person at the time of that person's birth shall, in relation to a person born after the death of his father or mother, be construed as a reference to the status or description of the parent in question at the time of that parent's death; and where that death occurred before, and the birth occurs after, commencement, the status or description which would have been applicable to the father or mother had he or she died after commencement shall be deemed to be the status or description applicable to him or her at the time of his or her death.

49. Registration and naturalisation under British Nationality Acts 1948 to 1965

. . .

Note: Section 49 repealed by s 52(8) and Sch 9 of this Act.

50. Interpretation

(1) In this Act, unless the context otherwise requires—

'the 1948 Act' means the British Nationality Act 1948;

'alien' means a person who is neither a Commonwealth citizen nor a British protected person nor a citizen of the Republic of Ireland;

['appointed day' means the day appointed by the Secretary of State under section 8 of the British Overseas Territories Act 2002 for the commencement of Schedule 1 to that Act;]

'association' means an unincorporated body of persons;

['British National (Overseas)' means a person who is a British National (Overseas) under the Hong Kong (British Nationality) Order 1986, and 'status of a British National (Overseas)' shall be construed accordingly;

'British Overseas citizen' includes a person who is a British Overseas citizen under the Hong Kong (British Nationality) Order 1986.]

['British overseas territory' means a territory mentioned in Schedule 6;

'British protected person' means a person who is a member of any class of persons declared to be British protected persons by an Order in Council for the time being in force under section 38 or is a British protected person by virtue of the Solomon Islands Act 1978;

'commencement', without more, means the commencement of this Act;

'Commonwealth citizen' means a person who has the status of a Commonwealth citizen under this Act;

'company' means a body corporate;

['Convention adoption' means an adoption effected under the law of a country or territory in which the Convention is in force, and certified in pursuance of Article 23(1) of the Convention;]

'Crown service' means the service of the Crown, whether within Her Majesty's dominions or elsewhere;

'Crown service under the government of the United Kingdom' means Crown service under Her Majesty's government in the United Kingdom or under Her Majesty's government in Northern Ireland [or under the Scottish Administration] [or under the Welsh Assembly Government];

['designated territory' means a qualifying territory, or the Sovereign Base Areas of Akrotiri and Dhekelia, which is designated by Her Majesty by Order in Council under subsection (14)]

[. . .]

'enactment' includes an enactment comprised in Northern Ireland legislation;

'foreign country' means a country other than the United Kingdom, a [British overseas territory], a country mentioned in Schedule 3 and the Republic of Ireland;

'the former nationality Acts' means—

(a) the British Nationality Acts 1948 to 1965;

(b) the British Nationality and Status of Aliens Acts 1914 to 1943; and

(c) any Act repealed by the said Acts of 1914 to 1943 or by the Naturalization Act 1870;

'Governor', in relation to a [British overseas territory], includes the officer for the time being administering the government of that territory;

'High Commissioner' includes an acting High Commissioner;

'immigration laws'—

(a) in relation to the United Kingdom, means the Immigration Act 1971 and any law for purposes similar to that Act which is for the time being or has at any time been in force in any part of the United Kingdom;

(b) in relation to a [British overseas territory], means any law for purposes similar to the Immigration Act 1971 which is for the time being or has at any time been in force in that territory;

'the Islands' means the Channel Islands and the Isle of Man;

'minor' means a person who has not attained the age of eighteen years;

'prescribed' means prescribed by regulations made under section 41;

['qualifying territory' means a British overseas territory other than the Sovereign Base Areas of Akrotiri and Dhekelia;]

'settled' shall be construed in accordance with subsections (2) to (4);

'ship' includes a hovercraft;

'statutory provision' means any enactment or any provision contained in—

(a) subordinate legislation (as defined in section 21(1) of the Interpretation Act 1978); or

(b) any instrument of a legislative character made under any Northern Ireland legislation;

'the United Kingdom' means Great Britain, Northern Ireland and the Islands, taken together;

'United Kingdom consulate' means the office of a consular officer of Her Majesty's government in the United Kingdom where a register of births is kept or, where there is no such office, such office as may be prescribed.

[(**1A**) Subject to subsection (1B), references in this Act to being a member of the armed forces are references to being—

(a) a member of the regular forces within the meaning of the Armed Forces Act 2006, or

(b) a member of the reserve forces within the meaning of that Act subject to service law by virtue of paragraph (a), (b) or (c) of section 367(2) of that Act.

(**1B**) A person is not to be regarded as a member of the armed forces by virtue of subsection (1A) if the person is treated as a member of a regular or reserve force by virtue of—

(a) section 369 of the Armed Forces Act 2006, or

(b) section 4(3) of the Visiting Forces (British Commonwealth) Act 1933.]

(**2**) Subject to subsection (3), references in this Act to a person being settled in the United Kingdom or in a [British overseas territory] are references to his being ordinarily resident in the United Kingdom or, as the case may be, in that territory without being subject under the immigration laws to any restriction on the period for which he may remain.

(**3**) Subject to subsection (4), a person is not to be regarded for the purposes of this Act—

(a) as having been settled in the United Kingdom at any time when he was entitled to an exception under section 8(3) or (4)(b) or (c) of the Immigration Act 1971 or, unless the order under section 8(2) of that Act conferring the exemption in question provides otherwise, to an exemption under the said section 8(2), or to any corresponding exemption under the former immigration laws; or

(b) as having been settled in a [British overseas territory] at any time when he was under the immigration laws entitled to any exemption corresponding to any such exemption as is mentioned in paragraph (a) (that paragraph being for the purposes of this paragraph read as if the words from 'unless' to 'otherwise' were omitted).

(**4**) A person to whom a child is born in the United Kingdom after commencement is to be regarded for the purposes of section 1(1) as being settled in the United Kingdom at the time of the birth if—

(a) he would fall to be so regarded but for his being at that time entitled to an exemption under section 8(3) of the Immigration Act 1971; and

(b) immediately before he became entitled to that exemption he was settled in the United Kingdom; and

(c) he was ordinarily resident in the United Kingdom from the time when he became entitled to that exemption to the time of the birth;

but this subsection shall not apply if at the time of the birth the child's father or mother is a person on whom any immunity from jurisdiction is conferred by or under the Diplomatic Privileges Act 1964.

(**5**) It is hereby declared that a person is not to be treated for the purpose of any provision of this Act as ordinarily resident in the United Kingdom or in a [British overseas territory] at a time when he is in the United Kingdom or, as the case may be, in that territory in breach of the immigration laws.

(**6**) For the purposes of this Act—

(a) a person shall be taken to have been naturalised in the United Kingdom if, but only if, he is—

(i) a person to whom a certificate of naturalisation was granted under any of the former nationality Acts by the Secretary of State or, in any of the Islands, by the Lieutenant-Governor; or

(ii) a person who by virtue of section 27(2) of the British Nationality and Status of Aliens Act 1914 was deemed to be a person to whom a certificate of naturalisation was granted, if the certificate of naturalisation in which his name was included was granted by the Secretary of State; or

(iii) a person who by virtue of section 10(5) of the Naturalisation Act 1870 was deemed to be a naturalised British subject by reason of his residence with his father or mother;

(b) a person shall be taken to have been naturalised in a [British overseas territory] if, but only if, he is—

(i) a person to whom a certificate of naturalisation was granted under any of the former nationality Acts by the Governor of that territory or by a person for the time being specified in a direction given in relation to that territory under paragraph 4 of Schedule 3 to the West Indies Act 1967 or for the time being holding an office so specified; or

(ii) a person who by virtue of the said section 27(2) was deemed to be a person to whom a certificate of naturalisation was granted, if the certificate of naturalisation in which his name was included was granted by the Governor of that territory; or

(iii) a person who by the law in force in that territory enjoyed the privileges of naturalisation within that territory only;

and references in this Act to naturalisation in the United Kingdom or in a [British overseas territory] shall be construed accordingly.

(7) For the purposes of this Act a person born outside the United Kingdom aboard a ship or aircraft—

(a) shall be deemed to have been born in the United Kingdom if—

(i) at the time of the birth his father or mother was a British citizen; or

(ii) he would, but for this subsection, have been born stateless,

and (in either case) at the time of the birth the ship or aircraft was registered in the United Kingdom or was an unregistered ship or aircraft of the government of the United Kingdom; but

(b) subject to paragraph (a), is to be regarded as born outside the United Kingdom, whoever was the owner of the ship or aircraft at that time, and irrespective of whether or where it was then registered.

[(7A) For the purposes of this Act a person born outside a qualifying territory aboard a ship or aircraft—

(a) shall be deemed to have been born in that territory if—

(i) at the time of the birth his father or mother was a British citizen or a British overseas territories citizen; or

(ii) he would, but for this subsection, have been born stateless,

and (in either case) at the time of the birth the ship or aircraft was registered in that territory or was an unregistered ship or aircraft of the government of that territory; but

(b) subject to paragraph (a), is to be regarded as born outside that territory, whoever was the owner of the ship or aircraft at the time, and irrespective of whether or where it was then registered.

(7B) For the purposes of this Act a person born outside a British overseas territory, other than a qualifying territory, aboard a ship or aircraft—

(a) shall be deemed to have been born in that territory if—

(i) at the time of the birth his father or mother was a British overseas territories citizen; or

(ii) he would, but for this subsection, have been born stateless,

and (in either case) at the time of the birth the ship or aircraft was registered in that territory or was an unregistered ship or aircraft of the government of that territory; but

(b) subject to paragraph (a), is to be regarded as born outside that territory, whoever was the owner of the ship or aircraft at the time, and irrespective of whether or where it was then registered.]

(8) For the purposes of this Act an application under any provision thereof shall be taken to have been made at the time of its receipt by a person authorised to receive it on behalf of the person to whom it is made; and references in this Act to the date of such an application are references to the date of its receipt by a person so authorised.

[(9) For the purposes of this Act a child's mother is the woman who gives birth to the child.

(9A) For the purposes of this Act a child's father is—

(a) the husband, at the time of the child's birth, of the woman who gives birth to the child, or

[(b) where a person is treated as the father of the child under section 28 of the Human Fertilisation and Embryology Act 1990 or section 35 or 36 of the Human Fertilisation and Embryology Act 2008, that person, or

(ba) where a person is treated as a parent of the child under section 42 or 43 of the Human Fertilisation and Embryology Act 2008, that person, or

(c) where none of paragraphs (a) to (ba) applies, a person who satisfies prescribed requirements as to proof of paternity.]

(b) where a person is treated as the father of the child under section 28 of the Human Fertilisation and Embryology Act 1990 (c. 37) (father), that person, or

(c) where neither paragraph (a) nor paragraph (b) applies, any person who satisfies prescribed requirements as to proof of paternity.

(9B) In subsection (9A)(c) 'prescribed' means prescribed by regulations of the Secretary of State; and the regulations—

(a) may confer a function (which may be a discretionary function) on the Secretary of State or another person,

(b) may make provision which applies generally or only in specified circumstances,

(c) may make different provision for different circumstances,

(d) must be made by statutory instrument, and

(e) shall be subject to annulment in pursuance of a resolution of either House of Parliament.

(9C) The expressions 'parent', 'child' and 'descended' shall be construed in accordance with subsections (9) and (9A).]

(10) For the purposes of this Act—

(a) a period 'from' or 'to' a specified date includes that date; and

(b) any reference to a day on which a person was absent from the United Kingdom or from a [British overseas territory] or from the [British overseas] territories is a reference to a day for the whole of which he was so absent.

(11) For the purposes of this Act—

(a) a person is of full age if he has attained the age of eighteen years, and of full capacity if he is not of unsound mind; and

(b) a person attains any particular age at the beginning of the relevant anniversary of the date of his birth.

(12) References in this Act to any country mentioned in Schedule 3 include references to the dependencies of that country.

(13) Her Majesty may by Order in Council subject to annulment in pursuance of a resolution of either House of Parliament amend Schedule 6 in any of the following circumstances, namely—

(a) where the name of any territory mentioned in it is altered; or

(b) where any territory mentioned in it is divided into two or more territories.

(14) For the purposes of the definition of "designated territory" in subsection (1), an Order in Council may—

(a) designate any qualifying territory, or the Sovereign Base Areas of Akrotiri and Dhekelia, if the Convention is in force there, and

(b) make different designations for the purposes of section 1 and section 15; and, for the purposes of this subsection and the definition of "Convention adoption" in subsection (1), "the Convention" means the Convention on the Protection of Children and Co-operation in respect of Intercountry Adoption, concluded at the Hague on 29th May 1993.

An Order in Council under this subsection shall be subject to annulment in pursuance of a resolution of either House of Parliament.]

Note: Words in second square brackets in s 50(1) inserted by SI 1986/948. 'Scottish Administration' inserted from 6 May 1999 (SI 1999/1042). 'Welsh Assembly' inserted from 6 November 2009 (SI 2009/2958). Other words in square brackets inserted in subsection 1 and subsections (7A) and (7B) substituted by Sch 1 British Overseas Territories Act from 21 May 2002 (SI 2002/1252). Subsection (9) substituted by Nationality, Immigration and Asylum Act 2002, s 9, from 7 November 2002, with effect in relation to children born on or after 1 July 2006 (SI 2006/1498). British dependent territories became British overseas territories from 26 February 2002, British Overseas Territories Act 2002, s 1. Definitions of 'Convention adoption' and 'designated territory inserted and subsection (14) inserted by Adoption and Children Act 2002, s 137 and Schedule 4 from 30 December 2005 (SI 2005/2213). Subsection (1A)–(1B) inserted by s 59 Borders, Citizenship and Immigration Act 2009 from 13 January 2010 (SI 2009/2731). Subsections 9A(b)–(c) substituted by Sch 6 Human Fertilisation and Embryology Act 2008 from 6 April 2010 (SI 2010/987).

[50A. Meaning of references to being in breach of immigration laws

(1) This section applies for the construction of a reference to being in the United Kingdom "in breach of the immigration laws" in—

(a) section 4(2) or (4);

(b) section 50(5); or

(c) Schedule 1.

(2) It applies only for the purpose of determining on or after the relevant day—

(a) whether a person born on or after the relevant day is a British citizen under section 1(1),

(b) whether, on an application under section 1(3) or 4(2) made on or after the relevant day, a person is entitled to be registered as a British citizen, or

(c) whether, on an application under section 6(1) or (2) made on or after the relevant day, the applicant fulfils the requirements of Schedule 1 for naturalisation as a British citizen under section 6(1) or (2).

(3) But that is subject to section 48(3)(d) and (4) of the Borders, Citizenship and Immigration Act 2009 (saving in relation to section 11 of the Nationality, Immigration and Asylum Act 2002).

(4) A person is in the United Kingdom in breach of the immigration laws if (and only if) the person—

(a) is in the United Kingdom;

(b) does not have the right of abode in the United Kingdom within the meaning of section 2 of the Immigration Act 1971;

(c) does not have leave to enter or remain in the United Kingdom (whether or not the person previously had leave);

(d) does not have a qualifying CTA entitlement;

(e) is not entitled to reside in the United Kingdom by virtue of any provision made under section 2(2) of the European Communities Act 1972 (whether or not the person was previously entitled);

(f) is not entitled to enter and remain in the United Kingdom by virtue of section 8(1) of the Immigration Act 1971 (crew) (whether or not the person was previously entitled); and

(g) does not have the benefit of an exemption under section 8(2) to (4) of that Act (diplomats, soldiers and other special cases) (whether or not the person previously had the benefit of an exemption).

(5) For the purposes of subsection (4)(d), a person has a qualifying CTA entitlement if the person—

(a) is a citizen of the Republic of Ireland,

(b) last arrived in the United Kingdom on a local journey (within the meaning of the Immigration Act 1971) from the Republic of Ireland, and

(c) on that arrival, was a citizen of the Republic of Ireland and was entitled to enter without leave by virtue of section 1(3) of the Immigration Act 1971 (entry from the common travel area).

(6) Section 11(1) of the Immigration Act 1971 (person deemed not to be in the United Kingdom before disembarkation, while in controlled area or while under immigration control) applies for the purposes of this section as it applies for the purposes of that Act.

(7) This section is without prejudice to the generality of—

(a) a reference to being in a place outside the United Kingdom in breach of immigration laws, and

(b) a reference in a provision other than one specified in subsection (1) to being in the United Kingdom in breach of immigration laws.

(8) The relevant day for the purposes of subsection (2) is the day appointed for the commencement of section 48 of the Borders, Citizenship and Immigration Act 2009 (which inserted this section).]

Note: Section 50A inserted by s 48 Borders, Citizenship and Immigration Act 2009 from 13 January 2010 (SI 2009/2731).

51. Meaning of certain expressions relating to nationality to other Acts and instruments

(1) Without prejudice to subsection (3)(c), in any enactment or instrument whatever passed or made before commencement 'British subject' and 'Commonwealth citizen' have the same meaning, that is—

(a) in relation to any time before commencement—

(i) a person who under the 1948 Act was at that time a citizen of the United Kingdom and Colonies or who, under any enactment then in force in a country mentioned in section 1(3) of that Act as then in force, was at that time a citizen of that country; and

(ii) any other person who had at that time the status of a British subject under that Act or any other enactment then in force;

(b) in relation to any time after commencement, a person who has the status of a Commonwealth citizen under this Act.

(2) In any enactment or instrument whatever passed or made after commencement—

'British subject' means a person who has the status of a British subject under this Act;

'Commonwealth citizen' means a person who has the status of a Commonwealth citizen under this Act.

(3) In any enactment or instrument whatever passed or made before commencement—

(a) 'citizen of the United Kingdom and Colonies'—

(i) in relation to any time before commencement, means a person who under the 1948 Act was at that time a citizen of the United Kingdom and Colonies;

(ii) in relation to any time after commencement, means a person who under [the British Nationality Acts 1981 and 1983] [or the British Overseas Territories Act 2002] is a British citizen, a [British overseas territories] citizen or a British Overseas citizen [or who under the Hong Kong (British Nationality) Order 1986 is a British National (Overseas)];

(b) any reference to ceasing to be a citizen of the United Kingdom and Colonies shall, in relation to any time after commencement, be construed as a reference to becoming a person who is neither a British citizen nor a [British overseas territories] citizen [nor a British National (Overseas)] nor a British Overseas citizen;

(c) any reference to a person who is a British subject (or a British subject without citizenship) by virtue of section 2, 13, or 16 of the 1948 Act or by virtue of, or of section 1 of, the British Nationality Act 1965 shall, in relation to any time after commencement, be construed as a reference to a person who under this Act is a British subject.

(4) In any statutory provision, whether passed or made before or after commencement, and in any other instrument whatever made after commencement 'alien', in relation to any time after commencement, means a person who is neither a Commonwealth citizen nor a British protected person nor a citizen of the Republic of Ireland.

(5) The preceding provisions of this section—

(a) shall not apply in cases where the context otherwise requires; and

(b) shall not apply to this Act or to any instrument made under this Act.

Note: Words in first square brackets in s 51(3) substituted by British Nationality (Falkland Islands) Act 1983. Words in second square brackets inserted by Sch 1 British Overseas Territories Act 2002 from 21 May 2002 (SI 2002/1252). Words at end of subsection (3)(a)(ii) and in second square brackets in subsection (3)(b) inserted by SI 1986/948. British dependent territories became British overseas territories from 26 February 2002, British Overseas Territories Act 2002, s 1.

52. Consequential amendments, transitional provisions, repeals and savings

(1) In any enactment or instrument whatever passed or made before commencement, for any reference to section 1(3) of the 1948 Act (list of countries whose citizens are Commonwealth citizens under that Act) there shall be substituted a reference to Schedule 3 to this Act, unless the context makes that substitution inappropriate.

(2) Subject to subsection (3), Her Majesty may by Order in Council make such consequential modifications of—

(a) any enactment of the Parliament of the United Kingdom passed before commencement;

(b) any provision contained in any Northern Ireland legislation passed or made before commencement; or

(c) any instrument made before commencement under any such enactment or provision, as appear to Her necessary or expedient for preserving after commencement the substantive effect of that enactment, provision or instrument.

(3) Subsection (2) shall not apply in relation to—

(a) the Immigration Act 1971; or

(b) any provision of this Act not contained in Schedule 7.

(4) Any Order in Council made under subsection (2) shall be subject to annulment in pursuance of a resolution of either House of Parliament.

(5) Any provision made by Order in Council under subsection (2) after commencement may be made with retrospective effect as from commencement or any later date.

(6) The enactments specified in Schedule 7 shall have effect subject to the amendments there specified, being amendments consequential on the provisions of this Act.

(7) This Act shall have effect subject to the transitional provisions contained in Schedule 8.

(8) The enactments mentioned in Schedule 9 are hereby repealed to the extent specified in the third column of that Schedule.

(9) Without prejudice to section 51, nothing in this Act affects the operation, in relation to any time before commencement, of any statutory provision passed or made before commencement.

(10) Nothing in this Act shall be taken as prejudicing the operation of sections 16 and 17 of the Interpretation Act 1978 (which relate to the effect of repeals).

(11) In this section 'modifications' includes additions, omissions and alterations.

53. Citation, commencement and extent

(1) This Act may be cited as the British Nationality Act 1981.

(2) This Act, except the provisions mentioned in subsection (3), shall come into force on such day as the Secretary of State may by order made by statutory instrument appoint; and references to the commencement of this Act shall be construed as references to the beginning of that day.

(3) Section 49 and this section shall come into force on the passing of this Act.

(4) This Act extends to Northern Ireland.

(5) The provisions of this Act, except those mentioned in subsection (7), extend to the Islands and all [British overseas territories]; and section 36 of the Immigration Act 1971 (power to extend provisions of that Act to Islands) shall apply to the said excepted provisions as if they were provisions of that Act.

(6) . . .

(7) The provisions referred to in subsections (5) . . . are—

(a) section 39 and Schedule 4;

(b) section 52(7) and Schedule 8 so far as they relate to the Immigration Act 1971; and

(c) section 52(8) and Schedule 9 so far as they relate to provisions of the Immigration Act 1971 other than Schedule 1.

Note: Subsection (6) and words in subsection 7 repealed by Statute Law Repeals Act 1995 Schedule 1, Pt. II. British dependent territories became British overseas territories from 26 February 2002, British Overseas Territories Act 2002, s 1.

SCHEDULES

Sections 6 and 18

SCHEDULE 1

REQUIREMENTS FOR NATURALISATION

Naturalisation as a British citizen under section 6(1)

1.—(1) Subject to paragraph 2, the requirements for naturalisation as a British citizen under section 6(1) are, in the case of any person who applies for it—

(a) the requirements specified in sub-paragraph (2) of this paragraph, [. . .]; and

(b) that he is of good character; and

(c) that he has a sufficient knowledge of the English, Welsh or Scottish Gaelic language; and

[(ca)that he has sufficient knowledge about life in the United Kingdom; and]

(d) that either—

(i) his intentions are such that, in the event of a certificate of naturalisation as a British citizen being granted to him, his home or (if he has more than one) his principal home will be in the United Kingdom; or

(ii) he intends, in the event of such a certificate being granted to him, to enter into, or continue in, Crown service under the government of the United Kingdom, or service under an international organisation of which the United Kingdom or Her Majesty's government therein is a member, or service in the employment of a company or association established in the United Kingdom.

[(2) The requirements referred to in sub-paragraph (1)(a) of this paragraph are—

(a) that the applicant ("A") was in the United Kingdom at the beginning of the qualifying period;

(b) that the number of days on which A was absent from the United Kingdom in each year of the qualifying period does not exceed 90;

(c) that A had a qualifying immigration status for the whole of the qualifying period;

(d) that on the date of the application A has probationary citizenship leave, permanent residence leave, a qualifying CTA entitlement, a Commonwealth right of abode or a permanent EEA entitlement;

(e) that, where on the date of the application A has probationary citizenship leave granted for the purpose of taking employment in the United Kingdom, A has been in continuous employment since the date of the grant of that leave; and

(f) that A was not at any time in the qualifying period in the United Kingdom in breach of the immigration laws.]

(3) . . .

Note: Words omitted from subparagraph (1)(a), subparagraph (2) substituted and subparagraph (3) revoked by s 39 Borders, Citizenship and Immigration Act 2009 from a date to be appointed. Subparagraph (1)(ca) inserted by s 1 Nationality, Immigration and Asylum Act 2002, from 1 November 2005 (SI 2005/2782).

2.—[(1)] If in the special circumstances of any particular case the Secretary of State thinks fit, he may for the purposes of paragraph 1 do all or any of the following things, namely—

[(a) treat the applicant as fulfilling the requirement specified in paragraph 1(2)(b) although the number of days on which the applicant was absent from the United Kingdom in a year of the qualifying period exceeds 90;]

(b) treat the applicant as having been in the United Kingdom for the whole or any part of any period during which he would otherwise fall to be treated under paragraph 9(1) as having been absent;

[(ba) treat the applicant as fulfilling the requirement specified in paragraph 1(2)(c) where the applicant has had a qualifying immigration status for only part of the qualifying period;

(bb) treat the applicant as fulfilling the requirement specified in paragraph 1(2)(d) where the applicant has had probationary citizenship leave but it expired in the qualifying period;]

(c) . . .

[(ca) treat the applicant as fulfilling the requirement specified in paragraph 1(2)(e) although the applicant has not been in continuous employment since the date of the grant mentioned there;]

(d) treat the applicant as fulfilling the requirement specified in paragraph [1(2)(f)] although he was in the United Kingdom in breach of the immigration laws in the [qualifying period] there mentioned;

(e) waive the need to fulfil [either or both of the requirements specified in paragraph 1(1)(c) and (ca)] if he considers that because of the applicant's age or physical or mental condition it would be unreasonable to [expect him to fulfil that requirement or those requirements].

[(2) If in the special circumstances of a particular case that is an armed forces case or an exceptional Crown service case the Secretary of State thinks fit, the Secretary of State may for the purposes of paragraph 1 waive the need to fulfil all or any of the requirements specified in paragraph 1(2).

(3) An armed forces case is a case where, on the date of the application, the applicant is or has been a member of the armed forces.

(4) An exceptional Crown service case is a case where—

(a) the applicant is, on the date of the application, serving outside the United Kingdom in Crown service under the government of the United Kingdom; and

(b) the Secretary of State considers the applicant's performance in the service to be exceptional.]

[(5) In paragraph 1(2)(e) and sub-paragraph (1)(ca) of this paragraph, "employment" includes self-employment.]

[(2) Sub-paragraph (3) applies in a case where, on the date of the application, the applicant is or has been a member of the armed forces.

(3) If in the special circumstances of the particular case the Secretary of State thinks fit, he may for the purposes of paragraph 1 treat the applicant as fulfilling the requirement specified in paragraph 1(2)(a) although the applicant was not in the United Kingdom at the beginning of the period there mentioned.]

Note: Subparagraph (1)(a) and words in square brackets in subparagraph (1)(d) substituted, subparagraph (1)(c) revoked and subparagraphs (1)(ba)–(bb), (ca), (2)–(5) inserted by s 39 Borders, Citizenship and Immigration Act 2009 from a date to be appointed. Words in square brackets in paragraph 2(e) substituted by s 1 Nationality, Immigration and Asylum Act 2002, from 1 November 2005 (SI 2005/2782). Paragraph 2 becomes paragraph 2(1) and subparagraphs (2) and (3) inserted by s 1 Citizenship (Armed Forces) Act 2014 from 13 May 2014.

[**2A.**—(1) A person has a qualifying immigration status for the purposes of paragraph 1(2) if the person has—

(a) qualifying temporary residence leave;

(b) probationary citizenship leave;

(c) permanent residence leave;

(d) a qualifying CTA entitlement;

(e) a Commonwealth right of abode; or

(f) a temporary or permanent EEA entitlement.

(2) A person who is required for those purposes to have a qualifying immigration status for the whole of the qualifying period need not have the same qualifying immigration status for the whole of that period.]

Note: Paragraph 2A inserted by s 39 Borders, Citizenship and Immigration Act 2009 from a date to be appointed.

Naturalisation as a British citizen under section 6(2)

[3(1) Subject to paragraph 4, the requirements for naturalisation as a British citizen under section 6(2) are, in the case of any person ("A") who applies for it—
(a) the requirements specified in sub-paragraph (2) of this paragraph;
(b) the requirement specified in sub-paragraph (3) of this paragraph;
(c) that A is of good character;
(d) that A has a sufficient knowledge of the English, Welsh or Scottish Gaelic language; and
(e) that A has sufficient knowledge about life in the United Kingdom.

(2) The requirements referred to in sub-paragraph (1)(a) are—
(a) that A was in the United Kingdom at the beginning of the qualifying period;
(b) that the number of days on which A was absent from the United Kingdom in each year of the qualifying period does not exceed 90;
(c) that, subject to sub-paragraph (5)—
(i) A had a relevant family association for the whole of the qualifying period, and
(ii) A had a qualifying immigration status for the whole of that period;
(d) that on the date of the application—
(i) A has probationary citizenship leave, or permanent residence leave, based on A's having the relevant family association referred to in section 6(2), or
(ii) A has a qualifying CTA entitlement or a Commonwealth right of abode; and
(e) that A was not at any time in the qualifying period in the United Kingdom in breach of the immigration laws.

(3) The requirement referred to in sub-paragraph (1)(b) is—
(a) that A's intentions are such that, in the event of a certificate of naturalisation as a British citizen being granted to A, A's home or (if A has more than one) A's principal home will be in the United Kingdom;
(b) that A intends, in the event of such a certificate being granted to A, to enter into, or continue in, service of a description mentioned in sub-paragraph (4); or
(c) that, in the event of such a certificate being granted to A—
(i) the person with whom A has the relevant family association referred to in section 6(2) ("B") intends to enter into, or continue in, service of a description mentioned in sub-paragraph (4); and
(ii) A intends to reside with B for the period during which B is in the service in question.

(4) The descriptions of service referred to in sub-paragraph (3) are—
(a) Crown service under the government of the United Kingdom;
(b) service under an international organisation of which the United Kingdom, or Her Majesty's government in the United Kingdom, is a member; or
(c) service in the employment of a company or association established in the United Kingdom.

(5) Where the relevant family association referred to in section 6(2) is (in accordance with regulations under section 41(1)(a)) that A is the partner of a person who is a British citizen or who has permanent residence leave—
(a) the requirement specified in sub-paragraph (2)(c)(i) is fulfilled only if A was that person's partner for the whole of the qualifying period, and
(b) for the purposes of sub-paragraph (2)(c)(ii), A can rely upon having a qualifying immigration status falling within paragraph 4A(1)(a), (b) or (c) only if that partnership is the relevant family association upon which the leave to which the status relates is based.

(6) For the purposes of sub-paragraph (5), A is a person's partner if—
(a) that person is A's spouse or civil partner or is in a relationship with A that is of a description that the regulations referred to in that sub-paragraph specify, and
(b) the marriage, civil partnership or other relationship satisfies the conditions (if any) that those regulations specify.

(7) For the purposes of sub-paragraph (5), the relationship by reference to which A and the other person are partners need not be of the same description for the whole of the qualifying period.]

Note: Paragraph 3 substituted by s 40 Borders, Citizenship and Immigration Act 2009 from a date to be appointed.

[**4.** If in the special circumstances of any particular case the Secretary of State thinks fit, the Secretary of State may for the purposes of paragraph 3 do all or any of the following, namely—
(a) treat A as fulfilling the requirement specified in paragraph 3(2)(b), although the number of days on which A was absent from the United Kingdom in a year of the qualifying period exceeds 90;
(b) treat A as having been in the United Kingdom for the whole or any part of any period during which A would otherwise fall to be treated under paragraph 9(1) as having been absent;
(c) treat A as fulfilling the requirement specified in paragraph 3(2)(c)(i) (including where it can be fulfilled only as set out in paragraph 3(5)) where a relevant family association of A's has ceased to exist;
(d) treat A as fulfilling the requirement specified in paragraph 3(2)(c)(ii) (including where it can be fulfilled only as set out in paragraph 3(5)) where A has had a qualifying immigration status for only part of the qualifying period;
(e) treat A as fulfilling the requirement specified in paragraph 3(2)(d) where A has had probationary citizenship leave but it expired in the qualifying period;
(f) treat A as fulfilling the requirement specified in paragraph 3(2)(e) although A was in the United Kingdom in breach of the immigration laws in the qualifying period;
(g) waive the need to fulfil either or both of the requirements specified in paragraph 3(1)(d) and (e) if the Secretary of State considers that because of A's age or physical or mental condition it would be unreasonable to expect A to fulfil that requirement or those requirements;
(h) waive the need to fulfil all or any of the requirements specified in paragraph 3(2)(a), (b), (c) or (d) (including where paragraph 3(2)(c) can be fulfilled only as set out in paragraph 3(5)) if—
(i) on the date of the application, the person with whom A has the relevant family association referred to in section 6(2) is serving in service to which section 2(1)(b) applies, and
(ii) that person's recruitment for that service took place in the United Kingdom.]

Note: Paragraph 4 substituted by s 40 Borders, Citizenship and Immigration Act 2009 from a date to be appointed.

[**4A.**—(1) Subject to paragraph 3(5), a person has a qualifying immigration status for the purposes of paragraph 3 if the person has—
(a) qualifying temporary residence leave based on a relevant family association;
(b) probationary citizenship leave based on a relevant family association;
(c) permanent residence leave based on a relevant family association;
(d) a qualifying CTA entitlement; or
(e) a Commonwealth right of abode.

(2) For the purposes of paragraph 3 and this paragraph, the leave mentioned in sub-paragraph (1)(a), (b) or (c) is based on a relevant family association if it was granted on the basis of the person having a relevant family association.

(3) A person who is required for the purposes of paragraph 3 to have, for the whole of the qualifying period, a qualifying immigration status and a relevant family association need not, for the whole of that period—
(a) have the same qualifying immigration status; or
(b) (subject to paragraph 3(5)) have the same relevant family association.

(4) Where, by virtue of sub-paragraph (3)(a), a person relies upon having more than one qualifying immigration status falling within sub-paragraph (1)(a), (b) or (c)—
- (a) subject to paragraph 3(5), it is not necessary that the leave to which each status relates is based on the same relevant family association, and
- (b) in a case where paragraph 3(5) applies, the relationship by reference to which the persons referred to in paragraph 3(5) are partners need not be of the same description in respect of each grant of leave.]

Note: Paragraph 4A inserted by s 40 Borders, Citizenship and Immigration Act 2009 from a date to be appointed.

[The qualifying period for naturalisation as a British citizen under section 6

4B.—(1) The qualifying period for the purposes of paragraph 1 or 3 is a period of years which ends with the date of the application in question.

(2) The length of the period is determined in accordance with the following provisions of this paragraph.

(3) In the case of an applicant who does not meet the activity condition, the number of years in the period is—
- (a) 8, in a case within paragraph 1;
- (b) 5, in a case within paragraph 3.

(4) In the case of an applicant who meets the activity condition, the number of years in the period is—
- (a) 6, in a case within paragraph 1;
- (b) 3, in a case within paragraph 3.

(5) The applicant meets the activity condition if the Secretary of State is satisfied that the applicant—
- (a) has participated otherwise than for payment in prescribed activities; or
- (b) is to be treated as having so participated.]

Note: Paragraph 4B inserted by s 41 Borders, Citizenship and Immigration Act 2009 from a date to be appointed.

Naturalisation as a [British overseas territories] citizen under section 18(1)

5.—(1) Subject to paragraph 6, the requirements for naturalisation as a [British overseas territories] citizen under section 18(1) are, in the case of any person who applies for it—
- (a) the requirements specified in sub-paragraph (2) of this paragraph, or the alternative requirement specified in sub-paragraph (3) of this paragraph; and
- (b) that he is of good character; and
- (c) that he has a sufficient knowledge of the English language or any other language recognised for official purposes in the relevant territory; and
- (d) that either—
  - (i) his intentions are such that, in the event of a certificate of naturalisation as a [British overseas territories] citizen being granted to him, his home or (if he has more than one) his principal home will be in the relevant territory; or
  - (ii) he intends, in the event of such a certificate being granted to him, to enter into, or continue in, Crown service under the government of that territory, or service under an international organisation of which that territory or the government of that territory is a member, or service in the employment of a company or association established in that territory.

(2) The requirements referred to in sub-paragraph (1)(a) of this paragraph are—
- (a) that he was in the relevant territory at the beginning of the period of five years ending with the date of the application, and that the number of days on which he was absent from that territory in that period does not exceed 450; and

(b) that the number of days on which he was absent from that territory in the period of twelve months so ending does not exceed 90; and
(c) that he was not at any time in the period of twelve months so ending subject under the immigration laws to any restriction on the period for which he might remain in that territory; and
(d) that he was not at any time in the period of five years so ending in that territory in breach of the immigration laws.

(3) The alternative requirement referred to in sub-paragraph (1)(a) of this paragraph is that on the date of the application he is serving outside the relevant territory in Crown service under the government of that territory.

Note: Words in square brackets substituted by s 2 British Overseas Territories Act 2002 from 26 February 2002.

6. If in the special circumstances of any particular case the Secretary of State thinks fit, he may for the purposes of paragraph 5 do all or any of the following things, namely—
(a) treat the applicant as fulfilling the requirement specified in paragraph 5(2)(a) or paragraph 5(2)(b), or both, although the number of days on which he was absent from the relevant territory in the period there mentioned exceeds the number there mentioned;
(b) treat the applicant as having been in the relevant territory for the whole or any part of any period during which he would otherwise fall to be treated under paragraph 9(2) as having been absent;
(c) disregard any such restriction as is mentioned in paragraph 5(2)(c), not being a restriction to which the applicant was subject on the date of the application;
(d) treat the applicant as fulfilling the requirement specified in paragraph 5(2)(d) although he was in the relevant territory in breach of the immigration laws in the period there mentioned;
(e) waive the need to fulfil the requirement specified in paragraph 5(1)(c) if he considers that because of the applicant's age or physical or mental condition it would be unreasonable to expect him to fulfil it.

Naturalisation as a [British overseas territories] citizen under section 18(2)

7. Subject to paragraph 8, the requirements for naturalisation as a [British overseas territories] citizen under section 18(2) are, in the case of any person who applies for it—
(a) that he was in the relevant territory at the beginning of the period of three years ending with the date of the application, and that the number of days on which he was absent from that territory in that period does not exceed 270; and
(b) that the number of days on which he was absent from that territory in the period of twelve months so ending does not exceed 90; and
(c) that on the date of the application he was not subject under the immigration laws to any restriction on the period for which he might remain in that territory; and
(d) that he was not at any time in the period of three years ending with the date of the application in that territory in breach of the immigration laws; and
(e) the [requirements specified in paragraph 5(1)(b) and (c)].

Note: Words in square brackets in subparagraph (e) substituted by s 2 of Nationality, Immigration and Asylum Act 2002, from 1 November 2005 (SI 2005/2782).

8. Paragraph 6 shall apply in relation to paragraph 7 with the following modifications, namely—
(a) the reference to the purposes of paragraph 5 shall be read as a reference to the purposes of paragraph 7;
(b) the references to paragraphs 5(2)(a), 5(2)(b) and 5(2)(d) shall be read as references to paragraphs 7(a), 7(b) and 7(d) respectively;
(c) paragraph 6(c) [. . .] shall be omitted; and

(d) after paragraph (e) there shall be added—

'(f) waive the need to fulfil all or any of the requirements specified in paragraph 7(a) and (b) if on the date of the application the person to whom the applicant is married [, or of whom the applicant is the civil partner,] is serving in service to which section 16(1)(b) applies, that person's recruitment for that service having taken place in a [British overseas territory]'.

Note: Words in square brackets in paragraph 8(c) omitted by Nationality, Immigration and Asylum Act 2002, s 2 from 1 November 2005 (SI 2005/2782). Words in square brackets in subparagraph 8(d) inserted by Sch 27 Civil Partnerships Act 2004 from 5 December 2005 (SI 2005/3175).

Periods to be treated as periods of absence from UK or a [British overseas territory]

9.—(1) For the purposes of this Schedule a person shall (subject to [paragraph 2(1)(b) or 4(b)]) be treated as having been absent from the United Kingdom during any of the following periods, that is to say—

(a) any period when he was in the United Kingdom and either was entitled to an exemption under section 8(3) or (4) of the Immigration Act 1971 (exemptions for diplomatic agents etc. and members of the forces) or was a member of the family and formed part of the household of a person so entitled;

(b) any period when he was detained—

(i) in any place of detention in the United Kingdom in pursuance of a sentence passed on him by a court in the United Kingdom or elsewhere for any offence;

(ii) in any hospital in the United Kingdom under a hospital order made under [Part III of the Mental Health Act 1983] or section 175 or 376 of the Criminal Procedure (Scotland) Act 1975 or Part III of the Mental Health [(Northern Ireland) Order 1986], being an order made in connection with his conviction of an offence; or

(iii) under any power of detention conferred by the immigration laws of the United Kingdom;

(c) any period when, being liable to be detained as mentioned in paragraph (b)(i) or (ii) of this sub-paragraph, he was unlawfully at large or absent without leave and for that reason liable to be arrested or taken into custody;

(d) any period when, his actual detention under any such power as is mentioned in paragraph (b)(iii) of this sub-paragraph being required or specifically authorised, he was unlawfully at large and for that reason liable to be arrested.

(2) For the purposes of this Schedule a person shall (subject to paragraph 6(b)) be treated as having been absent from any particular [British overseas territory] during any of the following periods, that is to say—

(a) any period when he was in that territory and either was entitled to an exemption under the immigration laws of that territory corresponding to any such exemption as is mentioned in sub-paragraph (1)(a) or was a member of the family and formed part of the household of a person so entitled;

(b) any period when he was detained—

(i) in any place of detention in the relevant territory in pursuance of a sentence passed on him by a court in that territory or elsewhere for any offence;

(ii) in any hospital in that territory under a direction (however described) made under any law for purposes similar to [Part III of the Mental Health Act 1983] which was for the time being in force in that territory, being a direction made in connection with his conviction of an offence and corresponding to a hospital order under that Part; or

(iii) under any power of detention conferred by the immigration laws of that territory;

(c) any period when, being liable to be detained as mentioned in paragraph (b)(i) or (ii) of this sub-paragraph, he was unlawfully at large or absent without leave and for that reason liable to be arrested or taken into custody;

(d) any period when, his actual detention under any such power as is mentioned in paragraph (b)(iii) of this sub-paragraph being required or specifically authorised, he was unlawfully at large and for that reason liable to be arrested.

Note: Words in first square brackets in subparagraphs (1)(b) and 9(2)(b) substituted by Mental Health Act 1983, s 148. Words in second square brackets in subparagraph (1)(b) substituted by SI 1956/596. Words in first square brackets in paragraph 9 substituted by s 49 Borders, Citizenship and Immigration Act 2009 from 13 January 2010 (SI 2009/2731).

Interpretation

10. In this Schedule 'the relevant territory' has the meaning given by section 18(3).

[11.—(1) This paragraph applies for the purposes of this Schedule.

(2) A person has qualifying temporary residence leave if—
- (a) the person has limited leave to enter or remain in the United Kingdom, and
- (b) the leave is granted for a purpose by reference to which a grant of probationary citizenship leave may be made.

(3) A person has probationary citizenship leave if—
- (a) the person has limited leave to enter or remain in the United Kingdom, and
- (b) the leave is of a description identified in rules under section 3 of the Immigration Act 1971 as "probationary citizenship leave", and the reference in sub-paragraph (2) to a grant of probationary citizenship leave is to be construed accordingly.

(4) A person has permanent residence leave if the person has indefinite leave to enter or remain in the United Kingdom.

(5) A person has a qualifying CTA entitlement if the person—
- (a) is a citizen of the Republic of Ireland,
- (b) last arrived in the United Kingdom on a local journey (within the meaning of the Immigration Act 1971) from the Republic of Ireland, and
- (c) on that arrival, was a citizen of the Republic of Ireland and was entitled to enter without leave by virtue of section 1(3) of the Immigration Act 1971 (entry from the common travel area).

(6) A person has a Commonwealth right of abode if the person has the right of abode in the United Kingdom by virtue of section 2(1)(b) of the Immigration Act 1971.

(7) A person has a permanent EEA entitlement if the person is entitled to reside in the United Kingdom permanently by virtue of any provision made under section 2(2) of the European Communities Act 1972.

(8) A person has a temporary EEA entitlement if the person does not have a permanent EEA entitlement but is entitled to reside in the United Kingdom by virtue of any provision made under section 2(2) of the European Communities Act 1972.

(9) A reference in this paragraph to having leave to enter or remain in the United Kingdom is to be construed in accordance with the Immigration Act 1971.]

Note: Paragraph 11 inserted by s 49 Borders, Citizenship and Immigration Act 2009 from 13 January 2010 (SI 2009/2731).

Section 36

SCHEDULE 2

PROVISIONS FOR REDUCING STATELESSNESS

Persons born in the United Kingdom after commencement

1.—(1) Where a person born in the United Kingdom after commencement would, but for this paragraph, be born stateless, then, subject to sub-paragraph (3)—
- (a) if at the time of the birth his father or mother is a citizen or subject of a description mentioned in sub-paragraph (2), he shall be a citizen or subject of that description; and accordingly

(b) [. . .] at the time of the birth each of his parents is a citizen or subject of a different description so mentioned, he shall be a citizen or subject of the same description so mentioned as each of them is respectively at that time.

(2) The descriptions referred to in sub-paragraph (1) are a [British overseas territories] citizen, a British Overseas citizen and a British subject under this Act.

(3) A person shall not be a British subject by virtue of this paragraph if by virtue of it he is a citizen of a description mentioned in sub-paragraph (2).

Note: British dependent territories became British overseas territories from 26 February 2002, British Overseas Territories Act 2002, s 1. Words deleted from paragraphs 1(1)(b) cease to have effect in relation to children born on or after 1 July 2006 (SI 2006/1498).

Persons born in a [British overseas territory] after commencement

2.—(1) Where a person born in a [British overseas territory] after commencement would, but for this paragraph, be born stateless, then, subject to sub-paragraph (3)—

(a) if at the time of the birth his father or mother is a citizen or subject of a description mentioned in sub-paragraph (2), he shall be a citizen or subject of that description; and accordingly

(b) [. . .] at the time of the birth each of his parents is a citizen or subject of a different description so mentioned, he shall be a citizen or subject of the same description so mentioned as each of them is respectively at that time.

(2) The descriptions referred to in sub-paragraph (1) are a British citizen, a British Overseas citizen and a British subject under this Act.

(3) A person shall not be a British subject by virtue of this paragraph if by virtue of it he is a citizen of a description mentioned in sub-paragraph (2).

Note: British dependent territories became British overseas territories from 26 February 2002, British Overseas Territories Act 2002, s 1. Words deleted from paragraph 2(1)(b) cease to have effect in relation to children born on or after 1 July 2006 (SI 2006/1498).

Persons born in the United Kingdom or a [British overseas territory] after commencement

3.—(1) A person born in the United Kingdom or a [British overseas territory] after commencement shall be entitled, on an application for his registration under this paragraph, to be so registered if the following requirements are satisfied in his case, namely—

(a) that he is and always has been stateless; and

(b) that on the date of the application he [. . .] was under the age of twenty-two; and

(c) that he was in the United Kingdom or a [British overseas territory] (no matter which) at the beginning of the period of five years ending with that date and that (subject to paragraph 6) the number of days on which he was absent from both the United Kingdom and the [British overseas territories] in that period does not exceed 450.

(2) A person entitled to registration under this paragraph—

(a) shall be registered under it as a British citizen if, in the period of five years mentioned in sub-paragraph (1), the number of days wholly or partly spent by him in the United Kingdom exceeds the number of days wholly or partly spent by him in the [British overseas territories];

(b) in any other case, shall be registered under it as a [British overseas territories] citizen.

Note: British dependent territories became British overseas territories from 26 February 2002, British Overseas Territories Act 2002, s 1. Words deleted from paragraph 3(1)(b) cease to have effect in relation to an application made on or after 1 April 2003 or an application not determined by that date, Nationality, Immigration and Asylum Act 2002, s 8 and SI 2003/754.

Persons born outside the United Kingdom and the [British Overseas Territories] after commencement

4.—(1) A person born outside the United Kingdom and the [British overseas territories] after commencement shall be entitled, on an application for his registration under this paragraph, to be so registered if the following requirements are satisfied, namely—

(a) that that person is and always has been stateless; and

(b) that at the time of that person's birth his father or mother was a citizen or subject of a description mentioned in sub-paragraph (4); and

(c) that that person was in the United Kingdom or a [British overseas territory] (no matter which) at the beginning of the period of three years ending with the date of the application and that (subject to paragraph 6) the number of days on which he was absent from both the United Kingdom and the [British overseas territories] in that period does not exceed 270.

(2) A person entitled to registration under this paragraph—

(a) shall be registered under it as a citizen or subject of a description available to him in accordance with sub-paragraph (3); and

(b) if more than one description is so available to him, shall be registered under this paragraph as a citizen of whichever one or more of the descriptions so available to him is or are stated in the application under this paragraph to be wanted.

(3) For the purposes of this paragraph the descriptions of citizen or subject available to a person entitled to registration under this paragraph are—

(a) in the case of a person whose father or mother was at the time of that person's birth a citizen of a description mentioned in sub-paragraph (4), any description of citizen so mentioned which applied to his father or mother at that time;

(b) in any case, a British subject under this Act.

(4) The description referred to in sub-paragraphs (1) to (3) are a British citizen, a [British overseas territories] citizen, a British Overseas citizen and a British subject under this Act.

Note: British dependent territories became British overseas territories from 26 February 2002, British Overseas Territories Act 2002, s 1.

Persons born stateless before commencement

5.—(1) A person born before commencement shall be entitled, on an application for his registration under this paragraph, to be so registered if the circumstances are such that, if—

(a) this Act had not been passed, and the enactments repealed or amended by this Act had continued in force accordingly; and

(b) an application for the registration of that person under section 1 of the British Nationality (No. 2) Act 1964 (stateless persons) as a citizen of the United Kingdom and Colonies had been made on the date of the application under this paragraph, that person would have been entitled under that section to be registered as such a citizen.

(2) A person entitled to registration under this paragraph shall be registered under it as such a citizen as he would have become at commencement if, immediately before commencement, he had been registered as a citizen of the United Kingdom and Colonies under section 1 of the British Nationality (No. 2) Act 1964 on whichever of the grounds mentioned in subsection (1)(a) to (c) of that section he would have been entitled to be so registered on in the circumstances described in sub-paragraph (1)(a) and (b) of this paragraph.

Supplementary

6. If in the special circumstances of any particular case the Secretary of State thinks fit, he may for the purposes of paragraph 3 or 4 treat the person who is the subject of the application as fulfilling the requirement specified in sub-paragraph (1)(c) of that paragraph although

the number of days on which he was absent from both the United Kingdom and the [British overseas territories] in the period there mentioned exceeds the number there mentioned.

Note: British dependent territories became British overseas territories from 26 February 2002, British Overseas Territories Act 2002, s 1.

Section 37

Schedule 3

Countries Whose Citizens Are Commonwealth Citizens

Antigua and Barbuda
Australia
The Bahamas
Bangladesh
Barbados
Belize
Botswana
[Brunei]
[Cameroon]
Canada
Kenya
Kiribati
Lesotho
Malawi
Malaysia
[Maldives]
Malta
Mauritius
[Mozambique]
Nauru
New Zealand
Nigeria
[Pakistan]
[Rwanda]
Uganda
Vanuatu
Western Samoa
Papua New Guinea
[Saint Christopher and Nevis]
Saint Lucia
Saint Vincent and the Grenadines
Republic of Cyprus
Dominica
Fiji
The Gambia
Ghana
Grenada
Guyana
India
Jamaica
Seychelles
Sierra Leone
Singapore
Solomon Islands
Sri Lanka
Swaziland
Tanzania
Tonga
Trinidad and Tobago
Tuvalu
Zambia
Zimbabwe
[Namibia]

Note: 'Brunei' inserted by SI 1983/1699; 'Maldives' inserted by Brunei and Maldives Act 1985; 'Pakistan' inserted by SI 1989/1331; 'Saint Christopher and Nevis' inserted by SI 1983/882; 'Namibia' inserted by SI 1990/1502. 'Cameroon' and 'Mozambique' inserted by SI 1998/3161 from 25 January 1999. 'Rwanda' inserted from 10 March 2010 (SI 2010/246).

Schedule 4

Note: Schedule 4 amends Immigration Act 1971, ss 3–6, 8, 9, 13, 14, 22, 24–26, 29, 33, Schs 2, 4.

. . .

Section 42(1)

[SCHEDULE 5

CITIZENSHIP OATH AND PLEDGE

1. The form of citizenship oath and pledge is as follows for registration of or naturalisation as a British citizen—

OATH

'I, [name], swear by Almighty God that, on becoming a British citizen, I will be faithful and bear true allegiance to Her Majesty Queen Elizabeth the Second, Her Heirs and Successors according to law.'

PLEDGE

'I will give my loyalty to the United Kingdom and respect its rights and freedoms. I will uphold its democratic values. I will observe its laws faithfully and fulfil my duties and obligations as a British citizen.'

2. The form of citizenship oath and pledge is as follows for registration of or naturalisation as a British overseas territories citizen—

OATH

'I, [name], swear by Almighty God that, on becoming a British overseas territories citizen, I will be faithful and bear true allegiance to Her Majesty Queen Elizabeth the Second, Her Heirs and Successors according to law.'

PLEDGE

'I will give my loyalty to [name of territory] and respect its rights and freedoms. I will uphold its democratic values. I will observe its laws faithfully and fulfil my duties and obligations as a British overseas territories citizen.'

3. The form of citizenship oath is as follows for registration of a British Overseas citizen—
'I, [name], swear by Almighty God that, on becoming a British Overseas citizen, I will be faithful and bear true allegiance to Her Majesty Queen Elizabeth the Second, Her Heirs and Successors according to law.'

4. The form of citizenship oath is as follows for registration of a British subject—
'I, [name], swear by Almighty God that, on becoming a British subject, I will be faithful and bear true allegiance to Her Majesty Queen Elizabeth the Second, Her Heirs and Successors according to law.']

Note: Schedule 5 substituted by Nationality, Immigration and Asylum Act 2002, Sch 1, paragraph 2, from 1 January 2004 (SI 2003/3156).

Section 50(1)

SCHEDULE 6

[BRITISH OVERSEAS TERRITORIES]

Anguilla
Bermuda
British Antarctic Territory

British Indian Ocean Territory
Cayman Islands
Falkland Islands [. . .]
Gibraltar
. . .
Montserrat
Pitcairn, Henderson, Ducie and Oeno Islands
. . .
[St Helena, Ascension and Tristan da Cunha]
[South Georgia and the South Sandwich Islands]
The Sovereign Base Areas of Akrotiri and Dhekelia (that is to say the areas mentioned in section 2(1) of the Cyprus Act 1960)
Turks and Caicos Islands
Virgin Islands

Note: British dependent territories became British overseas territories from 26 February 2002, British Overseas Territories Act 2002, s 1. First words omitted in Sch 6 repealed by SI 2002/3497. Second words omitted repealed by SI 1986/948. Third words omitted repealed by SI 1983/893. Words in first square brackets substituted from 14 November 2009 (SI 2009/2744), words in second square brackets inserted by SI 2001/3497 from 4 December 2001.

Senior Courts Act

(1981, c. 54)

Note: Citation of Act altered to Senior Courts Act (formerly Supreme Court Act) by Constitutional Reform Act 2005 Schedule 11 from 1 October 2009 (SI 2009/1604).

31A. Transfer of judicial review applications to Upper Tribunal

(1) This section applies where an application is made to the High Court—
(a) for judicial review, or
(b) for permission to apply for judicial review.

(2) If Conditions 1, 2 and 3 are met, the High Court must by order transfer the application to the Upper Tribunal.

[(2A) . . .]

(3) If Conditions 1 [and 2] are met, but Condition 3 is not, the High Court may by order transfer the application to the Upper Tribunal if it appears to the High Court to be just and convenient to do so.

(4) Condition 1 is that the application does not seek anything other than—
(a) relief under section 31(1)(a) and (b);
(b) permission to apply for relief under section 31(1)(a) and (b);
(c) an award under section 31(4);
(d) interest;
(e) costs.

(5) Condition 2 is that the application does not call into question anything done by the Crown Court.

(6) Condition 3 is that the application falls within a class specified under section 18(6) of the Tribunals, Courts and Enforcement Act 2007.

(7) . . .
[(8) . . .]

Note: Section 31A inserted by Tribunal, Courts and Enforcement Act 2007, s 19 from 3 November 2008 (SI 2008/2696). Subsections (2A) and (8) inserted by Borders, Citizenship and Immigration Act 2009, s 53 from 8 August 2011 (SI 2011/1741). Subsections (2A), (7) and (8) omitted and numbers in square brackets in subsection (2)-(3) substituted from 1 November 2013 by section 22 Crime and Courts Act 2013.

Immigration Act 1988
(1988, c. 14)

An Act to make further provision for the regulation of immigration into the United Kingdom; and for connected purposes. [10 May 1988]

1. Termination of saving in respect of Commonwealth citizens settled before 1973

. . .

Note: Section 1 repeals Immigration Act 1971, s 1(5).

2. Restriction on exercise of right of abode in cases of polygamy

(1) this section applies to any woman who—

(a) has the right of abode in the United Kingdom under section 2(1)(b) of the principal Act as, or as having been, the wife of a man ('the husband')—

(i) to whom she is or was polygamously married; and

(ii) who is or was such a citizen of the United Kingdom and Colonies, Commonwealth citizen or British subject as is mentioned in section 2(2)(a) or (b) of that Act as in force immediately before the commencement of the British Nationality Act 1981; and

(b) has not before the coming into force of this section and since her marriage to the husband been in the United Kingdom.

(2) A woman to whom this section applies shall not be entitled to enter the United Kingdom in the exercise of the right of abode mentioned in subsection (1)(a) above or to be granted a certificate of entitlement in respect of that right if there is another woman living (whether or not one to whom this section applies) who is the wife or widow of the husband and who—

(a) is, or at any time since her marriage to the husband has been, in the United Kingdom; or

(b) has been granted a certificate of entitlement in respect of the right of abode mentioned in subsection (1)(a) above or an entry clearance to enter the United Kingdom as the wife of the husband.

(3) So long as a woman is precluded by subsection (2) above from entering the United Kingdom in the exercise of her right of abode or being granted a certificate of entitlement in respect of that right the principal Act shall apply to her as it applies to a person not having a right of abode.

(4) Subsection (2) above shall not preclude a woman from re-entering the United Kingdom if since her marriage to the husband she has at any time previously been in the United Kingdom and there was at that time no such other woman living as is mentioned in that subsection.

(5) Where a woman claims that this section does not apply to her because she had been in the United Kingdom before the coming into force of this section and since her marriage to the husband it shall be for her to prove that fact.

(6) For the purposes of this section a marriage may be polygamous although at its inception neither party has any spouse additional to the other.

(7) For the purposes of subsection (1)(b), (2)(a), (4) and (5) above there shall be disregarded presence in the United Kingdom as a visitor or an illegal entrant and presence in circumstances in which a person is deemed by section 11(1) of the principal Act not to have entered the United Kingdom.

(8) In subsection (2)(b) above the reference to a certificate of entitlement includes a reference to a certificate treated as such a certificate by virtue of section 39(8) of the British Nationality Act 1981.

(9) No application by a woman for a certificate of entitlement in respect of such a right of abode as is mentioned in subsection (1)(a) above or for an entry clearance shall be granted if another application for such a certificate or clearance is pending and that application is made by a woman as the wife or widow of the same husband.

(10) For the purposes of subsection (9) above an application shall be regarded as pending so long as it and any appeal proceedings relating to it have not been finally determined.

3. Proof of right of abode

. . .

Note: Amends Immigration Act 1971, ss 3(9), 13(3), 2(2); British Nationality Act 1981, s 39.

4. Members of diplomatic missions

. . .

Note: Amends Immigration Act 1971, s 8.

5. . . .

Note: Section 5 repealed by Immigration and Asylum Act 1999 from 2 October 2000, transitional provisions set out in SI 2003/754.

6. Knowingly overstaying limited leave

(1) . . .

(2) . . .

(3) These amendments do not apply in relation to a person whose leave has expired before the coming into force of this section.

Note: Section 6(1) and (2) amend Immigration Act 1971, s 24.

7. Persons exercising Community rights and nationals of member States

(1) A person shall not under the principal Act require leave to enter or remain in the United Kingdom in any case in which he is entitled to do so by virtue of an enforceable [EU] right or of any provision made under section 2(2) of the European Communities Act 1972.

(2) The Secretary of State may by order made by statutory instrument give leave to enter the United Kingdom for a limited period to any class of persons who are nationals of member States but who are not entitled to enter the United Kingdom as mentioned in subsection (1) above; and any such order may give leave subject to such conditions as may be imposed by the order.

(3) References in the principal Act to limited leave shall include references to leave given by an order under subsection (2) above and a person having leave by virtue of such an order shall be treated as having been given that leave by a notice given to him by an immigration officer within the period specified in paragraph 6(1) of Schedule 2 to that Act.

Note: 'EU' substituted from 22 April 2011 (SI 2011/1043).

8. . . .

Note: Section 8 repealed by Sch 14 Immigration and Asylum Act 1999 from a date to be notified.

9. . . .

Note: Section 9 repealed by Sch 14 Immigration and Asylum Act 1999 from 30 June 2003, (SI 2003/1469).

10. Miscellaneous minor amendments

The principal Act shall have effect with the amendments specified in the Schedule to this Act.

11. Expenses and receipts

(1) There shall be paid out of money provided by Parliament any expenses incurred by the Secretary of State in consequences of this Act.

(2) Any sums received by the Secretary of State by virtue of this Act shall be paid into the Consolidated Fund.

12. Short title, interpretation, commencement and extent

(1) This Act may be cited as the Immigration Act 1988.

(2) In this Act 'the principal Act' means the Immigration Act 1971 and any expression which is also used in that Act has the same meaning as in that Act.

(3) Except as provided in subsection (4) below this Act shall come into force at the end of the period of two months beginning with the day on which it is passed.

(4) Sections 1, 2, 3, 4, 5 and 7(1) and paragraph 1 of the Schedule shall come into force on such day as may be appointed by the Secretary of State by an order made by statutory instrument; and such an order may appoint different days for different provisions and contain such transitional provisions and savings as the Secretary of State thinks necessary or expedient in connection with any provision brought into force.

(5) This Act extends to Northern Ireland and section 36 of the principal Act (power to extend any of its provisions to the Channel Islands or the Isle of Man) shall apply also to the provisions of this Act.

Section 10

Schedule

Minor Amendments

. . .

Asylum and Immigration Appeals Act 1993
(1993, c. 23)

An Act to make provision about persons who claim asylum in the United Kingdom and their dependants; to amend the law with respect to certain rights of appeal under the Immigration Act 1971; and to extend the provisions of the Immigration (Carriers' Liability) Act 1987 to transit passengers. [1 July 1993]

Introductory

1. Interpretation

In this Act—

'the 1971 Act' means the Immigration Act 1971;

'claim for asylum' means a claim made by a person (whether before or after the coming into force of this section) that it would be contrary to the United Kingdom's obligations under the Convention for him to be removed from, or required to leave, the United Kingdom; and

'the Convention' means the Convention relating to the Status of Refugees done at Geneva on 28 July 1951 and the Protocol to that Convention.

2. Primacy of Convention

Nothing in the immigration rules (within the meaning of the 1971 Act) shall lay down any practice which would be contrary to the Convention.

Treatment of persons who claim asylum

3. . . .

Note: Section 3 repealed by Immigration and Asylum Act 1999 from 11 December 2000.

4. . . .

Note: Section 4 repealed by Immigration and Asylum Act 1999 from 3 April 2000.

5. . . .

Note: Section 5 repealed by Immigration and Asylum Act 1999 from 3 April 2000.

6. . . .

Note: Section 6 repealed by Immigration and Asylum Act 1999 from 11 November 1999, with effect from 26 July 1993.

7. . . .

Note: Section 7 repealed by Immigration and Asylum Act 1999 from 2 October 2000.

8. . . .

Note: Section 8 repealed by Immigration and Asylum Act 1999 from 2 October 2000, transitional provisions set out in SI 2003/754.

9. . . .

Note: Section 9 repealed by Immigration and Asylum Act 1999 from 2 October 2000.

[9A. . . .

Note: Section 9A repealed by Sch 2 Asylum and Immigration Act 2004 from 4 April 2005 (SI 2005/565).

10. Visitors, short-term and prospective students and their dependants

. . .

Note: Section 10 repealed by Immigration and Asylum Act 1999 from 2 October 2000.

11. Refusals which are mandatory under immigration rules

. . .

Note: Section 11 repealed by Immigration and Asylum Act 1999 from 2 October 2000.

12. . . .

Note: Section 12 repealed by Immigration and Asylum Act 1999.

Supplementary

13. Financial provision

(1) There shall be paid out of money provided by Parliament—

(a) any expenditure incurred by the Secretary of State under this Act; and

(b) any increase attributable to this Act in the sums payable out of such money under any other enactment.

(2) Any sums received by the Secretary of State by virtue of this Act shall be paid into the Consolidated Fund.

14. Commencement

(1) Sections 4 to 11 above (and section 1 above so far as it relates to those sections) shall not come into force until such day as the Secretary of State may by order appoint, and different days may be appointed for provisions or for different purposes.

(2) An order under subsection (1) above—

(a) shall be made by statutory instrument; and

(b) may contain such transitional and supplemental provisions as the Secretary of State thinks necessary or expedient.

(3) Without prejudice to the generality of subsections (1) and (2) above, with respect to any provision of section 4 above an order under subsection (1) above may appoint different days in relation to different descriptions of asylum-seekers and dependants of asylum-seekers; and any such descriptions may be framed by reference to nationality, citizenship, origin or other connection with any particular country or territory, but not by reference to race, colour or religion.

15. Extent

(1) Her Majesty may by Order in Council direct that any of the provisions of this Act shall extend, with such modifications as appear to Her Majesty to be appropriate, to any of the Channel Islands or the Isle of Man.

(2) This Act extends to Northern Ireland.

16. Short title

This Act may be cited as the Asylum and Immigration Appeals Act 1993.

SCHEDULES

SCHEDULE 1

. . .

Note: Schedule 1 repealed by Immigration and Asylum Act 1999 from 3 April 2000.

Section 8(6)

SCHEDULE 2

Note: Schedule 2 repealed by Immigration and Asylum Act 1999 from 2 October 2000.

Special Immigration Appeals Commission Act 1997
(1997, c. 68)

An Act to establish the Special Immigration Appeals Commission; to make provision with respect to its jurisdiction; and for connected purposes [17 December 1997]

1. Establishment of the commission

(1) There shall be a commission, known as the Special Immigration Appeals Commission, for the purpose of exercising the jurisdiction conferred by this Act.

(2) Schedule 1 to this Act shall have effect in relation to the Commission.

[(3) The Commission shall be a superior court of record.

(4) A decision of the Commission shall be questioned in legal proceedings only in accordance with—

(a) section 7, or

(b) . . .]

Note: Words in square brackets inserted by Anti-terrorism, Crime and Security Act 2001, s 35 from 13 December 2001. Subsection 4(b) repealed by Prevention of Terrorism Act 2005, s 16 from 14 March 2005.

[2. Jurisdiction: appeals

(1) A person may appeal to the Special Immigration Appeals Commission against a decision if—

(a) he would be able to appeal against the decision under section 82(1) [. . .] of the Nationality, Immigration and Asylum Act 2002 but for a certificate of the Secretary of State under section 97 of that Act (national security &c.), or

(b) an appeal against the decision under section 82(1) [. . .] of that Act lapsed under section 99 of that Act by virtue of a certificate of the Secretary of State under section 97 of that Act.

(2) The following provisions shall apply, with any necessary modifications, in relation to an appeal against an immigration decision under this section as they apply in relation to an appeal under section 82(1) of the Nationality, Immigration and Asylum Act 2002—

(a) section 3C [or 3D] of the Immigration Act 1971 (c. 77) [continuation of leave],

(b) section 78 of the Nationality, Immigration and Asylum Act 2002 (no removal while appeal pending),

(c) section 79 of that Act (deportation order: appeal),

[(ca) section 78A of that Act (restriction on removal of children and their parents),]

(d) . . .

(e) section 84 of that Act (grounds of appeal),

(f) section 85 of that Act (matters to be considered),

(g) section 86 of that Act (determination of appeal),

(h) . . .

(i) section 96 of that Act (earlier right of appeal),

(j) section 104 of that Act (pending appeal),

(k) section 105 of that Act (notice of immigration decision), and

(l) . . .

(3) . . .

(4) . . .

(5) A person may bring or continue an appeal [. . .] under this section while he is in the United Kingdom only if he would be able to bring or continue the appeal while he was in the United Kingdom if it were an appeal under section 82(1) of that Act.

(6) . . .

[**2A.** . . .]

Note: Section 2 substituted and s 2A ceased to have effect by Sch 7 Nationality, Immigration and Asylum Act 2002 from 1 April 2003 (SI 2003/754). Words in square brackets in s 2 inserted or substituted by Sch 1 Immigration, Asylum and Nationality Act 2006 from 31 August 2006 (SI 2006/2226). Subsections (2)(d), (h), (l), (3), (4) and (6) omitted and words omitted from subsection (1) and (5) by Sch 9 Immigration Act 2014 from a date to be appointed. Subsection (2)(ca) inserted by Sch 9 Immigration Act 2014 from 28 July 2014 (SI 2014/1820).

[**2B.** A person may appeal to the Special Immigration Appeals Commission against a decision to make an order under section 40 of the British Nationality Act 1981 (c. 61) (deprivation of citizenship) if he is not entitled to appeal under section 40A(1) of that Act because of a certificate under section 40A(2)] [. . .]

Note: Section 2B inserted by Nationality, Immigration and Asylum Act 2002, s 4 from 1 April 2003 (SI 2003/754). Transitional provisions set out in SI 2003/754. Words in second square brackets in s 2B inserted by Sch 2 Asylum and Immigration Act 2004 from 4 April 2004 (SI 2005/565) and omitted by Sch 9 Immigration Act 2014 from a date to be appointed.

[2C. Jurisdiction: review of certain exclusion decisions

(1) Subsection (2) applies in relation to any direction about the exclusion of a non-EEA national from the United Kingdom which—

(a) is made by the Secretary of State wholly or partly on the ground that the exclusion from the United Kingdom of the non-EEA national is conducive to the public good,

(b) is not subject to a right of appeal, and

(c) is certified by the Secretary of State as a direction that was made wholly or partly in reliance on information which, in the opinion of the Secretary of State, should not be made public—

(i) in the interests of national security,

(ii) in the interests of the relationship between the United Kingdom and another country, or

(iii) otherwise in the public interest.

(2) The non-EEA national to whom the direction relates may apply to the Special Immigration Appeals Commission to set aside the direction.

(3) In determining whether the direction should be set aside, the Commission must apply the principles which would be applied in judicial review proceedings.

(4) If the Commission decides that the direction should be set aside, it may make any such order, or give any such relief, as may be made or given in judicial review proceedings.

(5) In this section—

"non-EEA national" means any person who is not a national of an EEA state, and references in this section to the Secretary of State are to the Secretary of State acting in person.]

Note: Section 2C inserted by s 15 Justice and Security Act 2013 from 25/4/2013.

[2D. Jurisdiction: review of certain naturalisation and citizenship decisions

(1) Subsection (2) applies in relation to any decision of the Secretary of State which—

(a) is either—

(i) a refusal to issue a certificate of naturalisation under section 6 of the British Nationality Act 1981 to an applicant under that section, or

(ii) a refusal to grant an application of the kind mentioned in section 41A of that Act (applications to register an adult or young person as a British citizen etc.), and

(b) is certified by the Secretary of State as a decision that was made wholly or partly in reliance on information which, in the opinion of the Secretary of State, should not be made public—

(i) in the interests of national security,

(ii) in the interests of the relationship between the United Kingdom and another country, or

(iii) otherwise in the public interest.

(2) The applicant to whom the decision relates may apply to the Special Immigration Appeals Commission to set aside the decision.

(3) In determining whether the decision should be set aside, the Commission must apply the principles which would be applied in judicial review proceedings.

(4) If the Commission decides that the decision should be set aside, it may make any such order, or give any such relief, as may be made or given in judicial review proceedings.]

Note: Section 2D inserted by s 15 Justice and Security Act 2013 from 25/4/2013.

[2E. Jurisdiction: review of certain deportation decisions

(1) Subsection (2) applies in relation to a relevant deportation decision which has been certified under section 97 or 97A(1) of the Nationality, Immigration and Asylum Act 2002 (certification on grounds of national security etc).

(2) The person to whom the decision relates may apply to the Special Immigration Appeals Commission to set aside the decision.

(3) In determining whether the decision should be set aside, the Commission must apply the principles which would be applied in judicial review proceedings.

(4) If the Commission decides that the decision should be set aside, it may make any such order, or give any such relief, as may be made or given in judicial review proceedings.

(5) In this section "relevant deportation decision" means a decision of the Secretary of State about the deportation of a person from the United Kingdom, if and to the extent that—

(a) the decision is not subject to a right of appeal, or

(b) the decision (being subject to a right of appeal) gives rise to issues which may not be raised on such an appeal.]

Note: Section 2E inserted by s 18 Immigration Act 2014 from a date to be appointed.

3. Jurisdiction: bail

(1) In the case of a person to whom subsection (2) below applies, the provisions of Schedule 2 to the Immigration Act 1971 specified in Schedule 3 to this Act shall have effect with the modifications set out there.

(2) This subsection applies to a person who is detained under the Immigration Act 1971 [or the Nationality, Immigration and Asylum Act 2002] if—

(a) the Secretary of State certifies that his detention is necessary in the interests of national security,

(b) he is detained following a decision to refuse him leave to enter the United Kingdom on the ground that his exclusion is in the interests of national security, or

(c) he is detained following a decision to make a deportation order against him on the ground that his deportation is in the interests of national security.

Note: Words in square brackets inserted from 4 April 2003 (SI 2003/1016).

4. . . .

Note: Section 4 ceased to have effect from 1 April 2003 (SI 2003/754), Sch 7 Nationality, Immigration and Asylum Act 2002. Transitional provisions set out in SI 2003/754.

5. Procedure in relation to jurisdiction under sections 2 and 3

(1) The Lord Chancellor may make rules—

(a) for regulating the exercise of the rights of appeal conferred by section 2 [or 2B] . . . above,

(b) for prescribing the practice and procedure to be followed on or in connection with appeals under [section 2 [or 2B]. . .] above, including the mode and burden of proof and admissibility of evidence on such appeals, and

(c) for other matters preliminary or incidental to or arising out of such appeals, including proof of the decisions of the Special Immigration Appeals Commission.

(2) Rules under this section shall provide that an appellant has the right to be legally represented in any proceedings before the Commission on an appeal under section 2 [or 2B] [. . .] above, subject to any power conferred on the Commission by such rules.

[(2A) Rules under this section may, in particular, do anything which may be done by [Tribunal Procedure Rules].

(3) Rules under this section may, in particular—

(a) make provision enabling proceedings before the Commission to take place without the appellant being given full particulars of the reasons for the decision which is the subject of the appeal,

(b) make provision enabling the Commission to hold proceedings in the absence of any person, including the appellant and any legal representative appointed by him,

(c) make provision about the functions in proceedings before the Commission of persons appointed under section 6 below, and

(d) make provision enabling the Commission to give the appellant a summary of any evidence taken in his absence.

(4) Rules under this section may also include provision—

(a) enabling any functions of the Commission which relate to matters preliminary or incidental to an appeal, or which are conferred by Part II of Schedule 2 to the Immigration Act 1971, to be performed by a single member of the Commission, or

(b) conferring on the Commission such ancillary powers as the Lord Chancellor thinks necessary for the purposes of the exercise of its functions.

(5) The power to make rules under this section shall include power to make rules with respect to applications to the Commission under paragraphs 22 to 24 of Schedule 2 to the Immigration Act 1971 and matters arising out of such applications.

[(5A) Rules under this section must secure that, where the Commission has decided not to release a person on bail under paragraph 22 or 29 of Schedule 2 to the Immigration Act 1971, the Commission is required to dismiss any further application by the person for release on bail that is made during the period of 28 days starting with the date of the Commission's decision, unless there has been a material change in circumstances.]

(6) In making rules under this section, the Lord Chancellor shall have regard, in particular, to—

(a) the need to secure that decisions which are the subject of appeals are properly reviewed, and

(b) the need to secure that information is not disclosed contrary to the public interest.

(7) . . .

(8) The power to make rules under this section shall be exercisable by statutory instrument.

(9) No rules shall be made under this section unless a draft of them has been laid before and approved by resolution of each House of Parliament.

Note: Subsection (7) omitted by Sch 5 Regulation of Investigatory Powers Act 2000 from 2 October 2002 (SI 2000/2543). Words deleted from and words in square brackets in subsections 5(1) and 5(2), and subsection 5(2A) inserted by Sch 7 Nationality, Immigration and Asylum Act 2002 from 1 April 2003 (SI 2003/754, which sets out transitional provisions). Words in square brackets in subsection (2A) substituted from 15 February 2010 (SI 2010/21). Subsection (5A) inserted by Sch 9 Immigration Act 2014 from 20 October 2014 with savings, SI 2014/2771 articles 9-11.

6. Appointment of person to represent the appellant's interests

(1) The relevant law officer may appoint a person to represent the interests of an appellant in any proceedings before the Special Immigration Appeals Commission from which the appellant and any legal representative of his are excluded.

(2) For the purposes of subsection (1) above, the relevant law officer is—

(a) in relation to proceedings before the Commission in England and Wales, the Attorney General,

(b) in relation to proceedings before the Commission in Scotland, the Lord Advocate, and

(c) in relation to proceedings before the Commission in Northern Ireland, the Attorney General for Northern Ireland.

(3) A person appointed under subsection (1) above—

(a) if appointed for the purposes of proceedings in England and Wales, shall have a general qualification for the purposes of section 71 of the Courts and Legal Services Act 1990,

(b) if appointed for the purposes of proceedings in Scotland, shall be—

(i) an advocate, or

(ii) a solicitor who has by virtue of section 25A of the Solicitors (Scotland) Act 1980 rights of audience in the Court of Session and the High Court of Justiciary, and

(c) if appointed for the purposes of proceedings in Northern Ireland, shall be a member of the Bar of Northern Ireland.

(4) A person appointed under subsection (1) above shall not be responsible to the person whose interests he is appointed to represent.

[6A. Procedure in relation to jurisdiction under sections 2C [to 2E]

(1) Sections 5 and 6 apply in relation to reviews under section 2C [, 2D or 2E] as they apply in relation to appeals under section 2 or 2B.

(2) Accordingly—

(a) references to appeals are to be read as references to reviews (and references to appeals under section 2 or 2B are to be read as references to reviews under section 2C [, 2D or 2E]), and

(b) references to an appellant are to be read as references to an applicant under section 2C(2) [, 2D(2) or (as the case may be) 2E(2).]]

Note: Section 6A inserted by Sch 2 Justice and Security Act 2013 from 26 June 2013 (SI 2013/1482). Words in square brackets substituted by Sch 9 Immigration Act 2014 from 20 October 2014 with savings set out in articles 9-11 SI 2014/2771.

7. Appeals from the Commission

(1) Where the Special Immigration Appeals Commission has made a final determination of an appeal, any party to the appeal may bring a further appeal to the appropriate appeal court on any question of law material to that determination.

[(1A) Where the Commission has made a final determination of a review under section 2C [, 2D or 2E(2)], any party to the review may bring an appeal against that determination to the appropriate appeal court.]

(2) An appeal under this section may be brought only with the leave of the Commission or, if such leave is refused, with the leave of the appropriate appeal court.

(3) In this section 'the appropriate appeal court' means—

(a) in relation to a determination made by the Commission in England and Wales, the Court of Appeal,

(b) in relation to a determination made by the Commission in Scotland, the Court of Session, and

(c) in relation to a determination made by the Commission in Northern Ireland, the Court of Appeal in Northern Ireland.

(4) . . .

[7A. . . .]

Note: Section 7(4) omitted and s 7A inserted by Immigration and Asylum Act 1999 from 2 October 2000. Section 7A ceased to have effect from 1 April 2003 (SI 2003/754), Sch 7 Nationality, Immigration and Asylum Act 2002. SI 2003/754 sets out transitional provisions. Subsection (1A) inserted by Sch 2 Justice and Security Act 2013 from 26 June 2013 (SI 2013/1482). Words in square brackets in subsection (1A) substituted by Sch 9 Immigration Act 2014 from a date to be appointed.

8. Procedure on applications to the Commission for leave to appeal

(1) The Lord Chancellor may make rules regulating, and prescribing the procedure to be followed on, applications to the Special Immigration Appeals Commission for leave to appeal under section 7 above.

(2) Rules under this section may include provision enabling an application for leave to appeal to be heard by a single member of the Commission.

(3) The power to make rules under this section shall be exercisable by statutory instrument.

(4) No rules shall be made under this section unless a draft of them has been laid before and approved by resolution of each House of Parliament.

9. Short title, commencement and extent

(1) This Act may be cited as the Special Immigration Appeals Commission Act 1997.

(2) This Act, except for this section, shall come into force on such day as the Secretary of State may by order made by statutory instrument appoint; and different days may be so appointed for different purposes.

(3) Her Majesty may by Order in Council direct that any of the provisions of this Act shall extend, with such modifications as appear to Her Majesty to be appropriate, to any of the Channel Islands or the Isle of Man.

(4) This Act extends to Northern Ireland.

Note: Commencement: s 9 on 17 December 1997, ss 5 and 8 on 11 June 1998, remainder of Act on 3 August 1998.

SCHEDULES

Section 1

SCHEDULE 1
THE COMMISSION

Members

1.—(1) The Special Immigration Appeals Commission shall consist of such number of members appointed by the Lord Chancellor as he may determine.

(2) A member of the Commission shall hold and vacate office in accordance with the terms of his appointment and shall, on ceasing to hold office, be eligible for reappointment.

(3) A member of the Commission may resign his office at any time by notice in writing to the Lord Chancellor.

Chairman

2. The Lord Chancellor shall appoint one of the members of the Commission to be its chairman.

Payments to members

3.—(1) The Lord Chancellor may pay to the members of the Commission such remuneration and allowances as he may determine.

(2) The Lord Chancellor may, if he thinks fit in the case of any member of the Commission, pay such pension, allowance or gratuity to or in respect of the member, or such sums towards the provision of such pension, allowance or gratuity, as he may determine.

(3) If a person ceases to be a member of the Commission and it appears to the Lord Chancellor that there are special circumstances which make it right that the person should receive compensation, he may pay to that person a sum of such amount as he may determine.

Proceedings

4. The Commission shall sit at such times and in such places as the Lord Chancellor may direct and may sit in two or more divisions.

5. The Commission shall be deemed to be duly constituted if it consists of three members of whom—
   (a) at least one holds or has held high judicial office (within the meaning of [Part 3 of the Constitutional Reform Act 2005) or is or has been a member of the Judicial Committee of the Privy Council]), and
   [(b) at least one is or has been [a judge of the First-tier Tribunal, or of the Upper Tribunal, who is assigned to a chamber with responsibility for immigration and asylum matters].

Note: Paragraph 5(b) substituted by Sch 2 Asylum and Immigration Act 2004 from 4 April 2005 (SI 2005/565). Words in first square brackets substituted from 1 October 2009 by Schedule 17 Constitutional Reform Act 2005. Words in second square brackets substituted from 15 February 2010 (SI 2010/21).

6. The chairman or, in his absence, such other member of the Commission as he may nominate, shall preside at sittings of the Commission and report its decisions.

Staff

7. The Lord Chancellor may appoint such officers and servants for the Commission as he thinks fit.

Expenses

8. The Lord Chancellor shall defray the remuneration of persons appointed under paragraph 7 above and such expenses of the Commission as he thinks fit.

Section 2

SCHEDULE 2

APPEALS: SUPPLEMENTARY

. . .

Note: Schedule 2 ceased to have effect from 1 April 2003 (SI 2003/754), Sch 7 Nationality, Immigration and Asylum Act 2002. SI 2003/754 sets out transitional provisions.

Section 3

SCHEDULE 3

BAIL: MODIFICATIONS OF SCHEDULE 2 TO THE IMMIGRATION ACT 1971

1.—(1) Paragraph 22 shall be amended as follows.

(2) In sub-paragraph (1A), for the words from the beginning to ['Tribunal'] there shall be substituted 'The Special Immigration Appeals Commission'.

(3) In sub-paragraph (2)—
   (a) for the words 'immigration officer or [the First-tier Tribunal] there shall be substituted 'Special Immigration Appeals Commission', and
   (b) for the words 'officer or [the First-tier Tribunal]' there shall be substituted 'Commission'.

(4) In sub-paragraph (3)—
   (a) for 'an immigration officer or [the First-tier Tribunal] there shall be substituted 'the Special Immigration Appeals Commission', and
   (b) for 'officer or [the First-tier Tribunal]', in both places, there shall be substituted 'Commission'.

Note: Words in first square brackets substituted by Sch 2 Asylum and Immigration Act 2004 from 4 April 2005 (SI 2005/565). Words in other square brackets substituted from 15 February 2010 (SI 2010/21).

2.—(1) Paragraph 23 shall be amended as follows.

(2) In sub-paragraph (1)—

(a) for ['the First-tier Tribunal'] there shall be substituted 'the Special Immigration Appeals Commission', and

(b) for ['the First-tier Tribunal'], in each place, there shall be substituted 'the Commission'.

(3) In sub-paragraph (2)—

(a) for ['the First-tier Tribunal'] there shall be substituted 'the Special Immigration Appeals Commission', and

(b) for ['the First-tier Tribunal'] there shall be substituted 'the Commission'.

Note: Words in square brackets substituted from 15 February 2010 (SI 2010/21).

3.—(1) Paragraph 24 shall be amended as follows.

(2) For sub-paragraph (2), there shall be substituted—

'(2) A person arrested under this paragraph shall be brought before the Special Immigration Appeals Commission within twenty-four hours.'

(3) In sub-paragraph (3), for the words from the beginning to 'above' there shall be substituted 'Where a person is brought before the Special Immigration Appeals Commission by virtue of sub-paragraph (2) above, the Commission—'.

4.—(1) Paragraph 29 shall be amended as follows.

[(**1A**) In sub-paragraph (1) after "2002" there shall be inserted "or section 2 of the Special Immigration Appeals Commission Act 1997 or a review pending under section 2E of that Act".]

(2) For sub-paragraphs (2) to (4) there shall be substituted—

'(2) The Special Immigration Appeals Commission may release an appellant on his entering into a recognizance or, in Scotland, bail bond conditioned for his appearance before the Commission at a time and place named in the recognizance or bail bond.'

(3) For sub-paragraph (6) there shall be substituted—

'(6) In any case in which the Special Immigration Appeals Commission has power to release an appellant on bail, the Commission may, instead of taking the bail, fix the amount and conditions of the bail (including the amount in which any sureties are to be bound) with a view to its being taken subsequently by any such person as may be specified by the Commission; and on the recognizance or bail bond being so taken the appellant shall be released.'

Note: Subsection 4(1A) inserted by Sch 9 Immigration Act 2014 from 28 July 2014 (SI 2014/1820).

5. Paragraph 30(2) shall be omitted.

6.—(1) Paragraph 31 shall be amended as follows.

(2) In sub-paragraph (1)—

(a) for ['the Tribunal'] there shall be substituted 'the Special Immigration Appeals Commission',

(b) for ['the Tribunal'] there shall be substituted 'the Commission', and

(c) for ['the Tribunal'], in both places, there shall be substituted 'the Commission'.

(3) In sub-paragraph (3)—

(a) for ['the Tribunal'] there shall be substituted 'the Special Immigration Appeals Commission', and

(b) for ['the Tribunal'] there shall be substituted 'it'.

7. Paragraph 32 shall be amended as follows—

(a) for ['the Tribunal'] there shall be substituted 'the Special Immigration Appeals Commission',

(b) for ['the Tribunal'] there shall be substituted 'the Commission', and
(c) for ['the Tribunal'] there shall be substituted 'the Commission'.

Note: Words in square brackets substituted by Sch 2 Asylum and Immigration Act 2004 from 4 April 2005 (SI 2005/565).

8.—(1) Paragraph 33 shall be amended as follows.

(2) For sub-paragraph (2), there shall be substituted—

'(2) A person arrested under this paragraph shall be brought before the Special Immigration Appeals Commission within twenty-four hours.'

(3) In sub-paragraph (3), for the words from the beginning to 'above' there shall be substituted 'Where a person is brought before the Special Immigration Appeals Commission by virtue of sub-paragraph (2) above, the Commission—'.

Note: Extends jurisdiction of Tribunal to Special Immigration Appeals Commission in paragraphs 22–24, 29, 31–33.

Crime (Sentences) Act 1997

(1997, c. 43)

32A. Removal of prisoners liable to removal from United Kingdom

(1) Where P—

(a) is a life prisoner in respect of whom a minimum term order has been made, and

(b) is liable to removal from the United Kingdom,

the Secretary of State may remove P from prison under this section at any time after P has served the relevant part of the sentence (whether or not the Parole Board has directed P's release under section 28).

(2) But if P is serving two or more life sentences—

(a) this section does not apply to P unless a minimum term order has been made in respect of each of those sentences; and

(b) the Secretary of State may not remove P from prison under this section until P has served the relevant part of each of them.

(3) If P is removed from prison under this section—

(a) P is so removed only for the purpose of enabling the Secretary of State to remove P from the United Kingdom under powers conferred by—

(i) Schedule 2 or 3 to the Immigration Act 1971, or

(ii) section 10 of the Immigration and Asylum Act 1999, and

(b) so long as remaining in the United Kingdom, P remains liable to be detained in pursuance of the sentence.

(4) So long as P, having been removed from prison under this section, remains in the United Kingdom but has not been returned to prison, any duty or power of the Secretary of State under section 28 or 30 is exercisable in relation to P as if P were in prison.

(5) In this section—

'liable to removal from the United Kingdom' has the meaning given by section 259 of the Criminal Justice Act 2003;

'the relevant part' has the meaning given by section 28.

Note: Sections 32A and 32B inserted from 1 May 2012 by the Legal Aid, Sentencing and Punishment of Offenders Act 2012, s 119.

32B. Re-entry into United Kingdom of offender removed from prison

(1) This section applies if P, having been removed from prison under section 32A, is removed from the United Kingdom.

(2) If P enters the United Kingdom—

(a) P is liable to be detained in pursuance of the sentence from the time of P's entry into the United Kingdom;

(b) if no direction was given by the Parole Board under subsection (5) of section 28 before P's removal from prison, that section applies to P;

(c) if such a direction was given before that removal, P is to be treated as if P had been recalled to prison under section 32.

(3) A person who is liable to be detained by virtue of subsection (2)(a) is, if at large, to be taken for the purposes of section 49 of the Prison Act 1952 (persons unlawfully at large) to be unlawfully at large.

(4) Subsection (2)(a) does not prevent P's further removal from the United Kingdom.

Note: Sections 32A and 32B inserted from 1 May 2012 by the Legal Aid, Sentencing and Punishment of Offenders Act 2012, s 119.

Human Rights Act 1998
(1998, c. 42)

Arrangement of Sections

An Act to give further effect to rights and freedoms guaranteed under the European Convention on Human Rights; to make provision with respect to holders of certain judicial offices who become judges of the European Court of Human Rights; and for connected purposes. [9 November 1998]

Introduction

1. The Convention Rights

(1) In this Act 'the Convention rights' means the rights and fundamental freedoms set out in—

(a) Articles 2 to 12 and 14 of the Convention,

(b) Articles 1 to 3 of the First Protocol, and

(c) [Article 1 of the Thirteenth Protocol] as read with Articles 16 to 18 of the Convention.

(2) Those Articles are to have effect for the purposes of this Act subject to any designated derogation or reservation (as to which see sections 14 and 15).

(3) The Articles are set out in Schedule 1.

(4) The [Secretary of State] may by order make such amendments to this Act as he considers appropriate to reflect the effect, in relation to the United Kingdom, of a protocol.

(5) In subsection (4) 'protocol' means a protocol to the Convention—

(a) which the United Kingdom has ratified; or

(b) which the United Kingdom has signed with a view to ratification.

(6) No amendment may be made by an order under subsection (4) so as to come into force before the protocol concerned is in force in relation to the United Kingdom.

Note: Commencement 2 October 2000. Words in square brackets in subsection (1)(c) substituted from 22 June 2004 (SI 2004/1574). Words in square brackets in subsection (4) substituted from 19 August 2003 (SI 2003/1887).

2. Interpretation of Convention Rights

(1) A court or tribunal determining a question which has arisen in connection with a Convention right must take into account any—

(a) judgment, decision, declaration or advisory opinion of the European Court of Human Rights,

(b) opinion of the Commission given in a report adopted under Article 31 of the Convention,

(c) decision of the Commission in connection with Article 26 or 27(2) of the Convention, or

(d) decision of the Committee of Ministers taken under Article 46 of the Convention,

whenever made or given, so far as, in the opinion of the court or tribunal, it is relevant to the proceedings in which that question has arisen.

(2) Evidence of any judgment, decision, declaration or opinion of which account may have to be taken under this section is to be given in proceedings before any court or tribunal in such manner as may be provided by rules.

(3) In this section 'rules' means rules of court or, in the case of proceedings before a tribunal, rules made for the purposes of this section—

(a) by [the Lord Chancellor or] the Secretary of State, in relation to any proceedings outside Scotland;

(b) by the Secretary of State, in relation to proceedings in Scotland; or

(c) by a Northern Ireland department, in relation to proceedings before a tribunal in Northern Ireland—

(i) which deals with transferred matters; and

(ii) for which no rules made under paragraph (a) are in force.

Note: Commencement 2 October 2000. Words in square brackets in subsection (3)(a) omitted from 19 August 2003 (SI 2003/1887), re-inserted from 12 January 2006 (SI 2005/3429).

Legislation

3. Interpretation of legislation

(1) So far as it is possible to do so, primary legislation and subordinate legislation must be read and given effect in a way which is compatible with the Convention rights.

(2) This section—

(a) applies to primary legislation and subordinate legislation whenever enacted;

(b) does not affect the validity, continuing operation or enforcement of any incompatible primary legislation; and

(c) does not affect the validity, continuing operation or enforcement of any incompatible subordinate legislation if (disregarding any possibility of revocation) primary legislation prevents removal of the incompatibility.

Note: Commencement 2 October 2000.

4. Declaration of incompatibility

(1) Subsection (2) applies in any proceedings in which a court determines whether a provision of primary legislation is compatible with a Convention right.

(2) If the court is satisfied that the provision is incompatible with a Convention right, it may make a declaration of that incompatibility.

(3) Subsection (4) applies in any proceedings in which a court determines whether a provision of subordinate legislation, made in the exercise of a power conferred by primary legislation, is compatible with a Convention right.

(4) If the court is satisfied—

(a) that the provision is incompatible with a Convention right, and

(b) that (disregarding any possibility of revocation) the primary legislation concerned prevents removal of the incompatibility, it may make a declaration of that incompatibility.

(5) In this section 'court' means—

[(a) the Supreme Court;]

(b) the Judicial Committee of the Privy Council;

(c) the [Court Martial Appeal Court];

(d) in Scotland, the High Court of Justiciary sitting otherwise than as a trial court or the Court of Session;

(e) in England and Wales or Northern Ireland, the High Court or the Court of Appeal.

[(f) the Court of Protection, in any matter being dealt with by the President of the Family Division, the Vice-Chancellor or a puisne judge of the High Court.]

(6) A declaration under this section ('a declaration of incompatibility')—

(a) does not affect the validity, continuing operation or enforcement of the provision in respect of which it is given; and

(b) is not binding on the parties to the proceedings in which it is made.

Note: Commencement 2 October 2000. Subsection (5)(a) substituted by the Constitutional Reform Act 2005 Sch 9 from 1 October 2009 (SI 2009/1604). Words substituted in subsection (5)(c) by Armed Forces Act 2006 Sch 16 from 28 March 2009 (for certain purposes) (SI 2009/812) and from 31 October 2009 otherwise (SI 2009/1167). Subsection (5)(f) inserted by Mental Capacity Act 2005 Sch 6 from 1 October 2007 (SI 2007/1897).

5. Right of Crown to intervene

(1) Where a court is considering whether to make a declaration of incompatibility, the Crown is entitled to notice in accordance with rules of court.

(2) In any case to which subsection (1) applies—

(a) a Minister of the Crown (or a person nominated by him),

(b) a member of the Scottish Executive,

(c) a Northern Ireland Minister,

(d) a Northern Ireland department, is entitled, on giving notice in accordance with rules of court, to be joined as a party to the proceedings.

(3) Notice under subsection (2) may be given at any time during the proceedings.

(4) A person who has been made a party to criminal proceedings (other than in Scotland) as the result of a notice under subsection (2) may, with leave, appeal to [the Supreme Court] against any declaration of incompatibility made in the proceedings.

(5) In subsection (4)—

'criminal proceedings' includes all proceedings before the [Court-Martial Appeal Court]; and 'leave' means leave granted by the court making the declaration of incompatibility or by [the Supreme Court].

Note: Commencement 2 October 2000. Words 'the Supreme Court' substituted by the Constitutional Reform Act 2005 Sch 9 from 1 October 2009 (SI 2009/1604). Words 'Court Martial Appeal Court' substituted by Armed Forces Act 2006 Sch 16 from 28 March 2009 (for certain purposes) (SI 2009/812) and from 31 October 2009 otherwise (SI 2009/1167).

Public authorities

6. Acts of public authorities

(1) It is unlawful for a public authority to act in a way which is incompatible with a Convention right.

(2) Subsection (1) does not apply to an act if—

(a) as the result of one or more provisions of primary legislation, the authority could not have acted differently; or

(b) in the case of one or more provisions of, or made under, primary legislation which cannot be read or given effect in a way which is compatible with the Convention rights, the authority was acting so as to give effect to or enforce those provisions.

(3) In this section 'public authority' includes—

(a) a court or tribunal, and

(b) any person certain of whose functions are functions of a public nature, but does not include either House of Parliament or a person exercising functions in connection with proceedings in Parliament.

(4) . . .

(5) In relation to a particular act, a person is not a public authority by virtue only of subsection (3)(b) if the nature of the act is private.

(6) 'An act' includes a failure to act but does not include a failure to—

(a) introduce in, or lay before, Parliament a proposal for legislation; or

(b) make any primary legislation or remedial order.

Note: Commencement 2 October 2000. Sub-section (4) deleted by the Constitutional Reform Act 2005 Sch 9 from 1 October 2009 (SI 2009/1604).

7. Proceedings

(1) A person who claims that a public authority has acted (or proposes to act) in a way which is made unlawful by section 6(1) may—

(a) bring proceedings against the authority under this Act in the appropriate court or tribunal, or

(b) rely on the Convention right or rights concerned in any legal proceedings, but only if he is (or would be) a victim of the unlawful act.

(2) In subsection (1)(a) 'appropriate court or tribunal' means such court or tribunal as may be determined in accordance with rules; and proceedings against an authority include a counterclaim or similar proceeding.

(3) If the proceedings are brought on an application for judicial review, the applicant is to be taken to have a sufficient interest in relation to the unlawful act only if he is, or would be, a victim of that act.

(4) If the proceedings are made by way of a petition for judicial review in Scotland, the applicant shall be taken to have title and interest to sue in relation to the unlawful act only if he is, or would be, a victim of that act.

(5) Proceedings under subsection (1)(a) must be brought before the end of—

(a) the period of one year beginning with the date on which the act complained of took place; or

(b) such longer period as the court or tribunal considers equitable having regard to all the circumstances, but that is subject to any rule imposing a stricter time limit in relation to the procedure in question.

(6) In subsection (1)(b) 'legal proceedings' includes—

(a) proceedings brought by or at the instigation of a public authority; and

(b) an appeal against the decision of a court or tribunal.

(7) For the purposes of this section, a person is a victim of an unlawful act only if he would be a victim for the purposes of Article 34 of the Convention if proceedings were brought in the European Court of Human Rights in respect of that act.

(8) Nothing in this Act creates a criminal offence.

(9) In this section 'rules' means—

(a) in relation to proceedings before a court or tribunal outside Scotland, rules made by [the Lord Chancellor or] the Secretary of State for the purposes of this section or rules of court,

(b) in relation to proceedings before a court or tribunal in Scotland, rules made by the Secretary of State for those purposes,

(c) in relation to proceedings before a tribunal in Northern Ireland—

(i) which deals with transferred matters; and

(ii) for which no rules made under paragraph (a) are in force, rules made by a Northern Ireland department for those purposes, and includes provision made by order under section 1 of the Courts and Legal Services Act 1990.

(10) In making rules, regard must be had to section 9.

(11) The Minister who has power to make rules in relation to a particular tribunal may, to the extent he considers it necessary to ensure that the tribunal can provide an appropriate remedy in relation to an act (or proposed act) of a public authority which is (or would be) unlawful as a result of section 6(1), by order add to—

(a) the relief or remedies which the tribunal may grant; or

(b) the grounds on which it may grant any of them.

(12) An order made under subsection (11) may contain such incidental, supplemental, consequential or transitional provision as the Minister making it considers appropriate.

(13) 'The Minister' includes the Northern Ireland department concerned.

Note: Commencement 2 October 2000. Words in square brackets in subsection (9)(a) omitted from 19 August 2003 (SI 2003/1887), re-inserted from 12 January 2006 (SI 2005/3429).

8. Judicial remedies

(1) In relation to any act (or proposed act) of a public authority which the court finds is (or would be) unlawful, it may grant such relief or remedy, or make such order, within its powers as it considers just and appropriate.

(2) But damages may be awarded only by a court which has power to award damages, or to order the payment of compensation, in civil proceedings.

(3) No award of damages is to be made unless, taking account of all the circumstances of the case, including—

(a) any other relief or remedy granted, or order made, in relation to the act in question (by that or any other court), and

(b) the consequences of any decision (of that or any other court) in respect of that act, the court is satisfied that the award is necessary to afford just satisfaction to the person in whose favour it is made.

(4) In determining—

(a) whether to award damages, or

(b) the amount of an award, the court must take into account the principles applied by the European Court of Human Rights in relation to the award of compensation under Article 41 of the Convention.

(5) A public authority against which damages are awarded is to be treated—

(a) in Scotland, for the purposes of section 3 of the Law Reform (Miscellaneous Provisions) (Scotland) Act 1940 as if the award were made in an action of damages in which the authority has been found liable in respect of loss or damage to the person to whom the award is made;

(b) for the purposes of the Civil Liability (Contribution) Act 1978 as liable in respect of damage suffered by the person to whom the award is made.

(6) In this section—

'court' includes a tribunal;

'damages' means damages for an unlawful act of a public authority; and

'unlawful' means unlawful under section 6(1).

Note: Commencement 2 October 2000.

9. Judicial acts

(1) Proceedings under section 7(1)(a) in respect of a judicial act may be brought only—

(a) by exercising a right of appeal;

(b) on an application (in Scotland a petition) for judicial review; or

(c) in such other forum as may be prescribed by rules.

(2) That does not affect any rule of law which prevents a court from being the subject of judicial review.

(3) In proceedings under this Act in respect of a judicial act done in good faith, damages may not be awarded otherwise than to compensate a person to the extent required by Article 5(5) of the Convention.

(4) An award of damages permitted by subsection (3) is to be made against the Crown; but no award may be made unless the appropriate person, if not a party to the proceedings, is joined.

(5) In this section—

'appropriate person' means the Minister responsible for the court concerned, or a person or government department nominated by him;

'court' includes a tribunal;

'judge' includes a member of a tribunal, a justice of the peace [(or, in Northern Ireland, a lay magistrate)] and a clerk or other officer entitled to exercise the jurisdiction of a court;

'judicial act' means a judicial act of a court and includes an act done on the instructions, or on behalf, of a judge; and

'rules' has the same meaning as in section 7(9).

Note: Commencement 2 October 2000. Words in square brackets in subsection (5) inserted (NI) by Justice (Northern Ireland) Act 2002 Sch 4 from 1 April 2005 (SR 2005/109).

Remedial action

10. Power to take remedial action

(1) This section applies if—

(a) a provision of legislation has been declared under section 4 to be incompatible with a Convention right and, if an appeal lies—

(i) all persons who may appeal have stated in writing that they do not intend to do so;

(ii) the time for bringing an appeal has expired and no appeal has been brought within that time; or

(iii) an appeal brought within that time has been determined or abandoned; or

(b) it appears to a Minister of the Crown or Her Majesty in Council that, having regard to a finding of the European Court of Human Rights made after the coming into force of this section in proceedings against the United Kingdom, a provision of legislation is incompatible with an obligation of the United Kingdom arising from the Convention.

(2) If a Minister of the Crown considers that there are compelling reasons for proceeding under this section, he may by order make such amendments to the legislation as he considers necessary to remove the incompatibility.

(3) If, in the case of subordinate legislation, a Minister of the Crown considers—

(a) that it is necessary to amend the primary legislation under which the subordinate legislation in question was made, in order to enable the incompatibility to be removed, and

(b) that there are compelling reasons for proceeding under this section, he may by order make such amendments to the primary legislation as he considers necessary.

(4) This section also applies where the provision in question is in subordinate legislation and has been quashed, or declared invalid, by reason of incompatibility with a Convention right and the Minister proposes to proceed under paragraph 2(b) of Schedule 2.

(5) If the legislation is an Order in Council, the power conferred by subsection (2) or (3) is exercisable by Her Majesty in Council.

(6) In this section 'legislation' does not include a Measure of the Church Assembly or of the General Synod of the Church of England.

(7) Schedule 2 makes further provision about remedial orders.

Note: Commencement 2 October 2000.

Other rights and proceedings

11. Safeguard for existing human rights

A person's reliance on a Convention right does not restrict—

(a) any other right or freedom conferred on him by or under any law having effect in any part of the United Kingdom; or

(b) his right to make any claim or bring any proceedings which he could make or bring apart from sections 7 to 9.

Note: Commencement 2 October 2000.

12. Freedom of expression

(1) This section applies if a court is considering whether to grant any relief which, if granted, might affect the exercise of the Convention right to freedom of expression.

(2) If the person against whom the application for relief is made ('the respondent') is neither present nor represented, no such relief is to be granted unless the court is satisfied—

(a) that the applicant has taken all practicable steps to notify the respondent; or

(b) that there are compelling reasons why the respondent should not be notified.

(3) No such relief is to be granted so as to restrain publication before trial unless the court is satisfied that the applicant is likely to establish that publication should not be allowed.

(4) The court must have particular regard to the importance of the Convention right to freedom of expression and, where the proceedings relate to material which the respondent claims, or which appears to the court, to be journalistic, literary or artistic material (or to conduct connected with such material), to—

(a) the extent to which—

(i) the material has, or is about to, become available to the public; or

(ii) it is, or would be, in the public interest for the material to be published;

(b) any relevant privacy code.

(5) In this section—

'court' includes a tribunal; and

'relief' includes any remedy or order (other than in criminal proceedings).

Note: Commencement 2 October 2000.

13. Freedom of thought, conscience and religion

(1) If a court's determination of any question arising under this Act might affect the exercise by a religious organisation (itself or its members collectively) of the Convention right to freedom of thought, conscience and religion, it must have particular regard to the importance of that right.

(2) In this section 'court' includes a tribunal.

Note: Commencement 2 October 2000.

Derogations and reservations

14. Derogations

(1) In this Act 'designated derogation' means [. . .] any derogation by the United Kingdom from an Article of the Convention, or of any protocol to the Convention, which is designated for the purposes of this Act in an order made by the [Secretary of State].

(2) . . .

(3) If a designated derogation is amended or replaced it ceases to be a designated derogation.

(4) But subsection (3) does not prevent the Secretary of State from exercising his power under subsection (1)[. . .] to make a fresh designation order in respect of the Article concerned.

(5) The Secretary of State must by order make such amendments to Schedule 3 as he considers appropriate to reflect—

(a) any designation order; or

(b) the effect of subsection (3).

(6) A designation order may be made in anticipation of the making by the United Kingdom of a proposed derogation.

Note: Commencement 2 October 2000. Words omitted from 1 April 2001 (SI 2001/1216). Words in square brackets in subsection (4) substituted from 19 August 2003 (SI 2003/1887).

15. Reservations

(1) In this Act 'designated reservation' means—

(a) the United Kingdom's reservation to Article 2 of the First Protocol to the Convention; and

(b) any other reservation by the United Kingdom to an Article of the Convention, or of any protocol to the Convention, which is designated for the purposes of this Act in an order made by the [Secretary of State].

(2) The text of the reservation referred to in subsection (1)(a) is set out in Part II of Schedule 3.

(3) If a designated reservation is withdrawn wholly or in part it ceases to be a designated reservation.

(4) But subsection (3) does not prevent the [Secretary of State] from exercising his power under subsection (1)(b) to make a fresh designation order in respect of the Article concerned.

(5) The [Secretary of State] must by order make such amendments to this Act as he considers appropriate to reflect—

(a) any designation order; or

(b) the effect of subsection (3).

Note: Commencement 2 October 2000. Words in square brackets substituted from 19 August 2003 (SI 2003/1887).

16. Period for which designated derogations have effect

(1) If it has not already been withdrawn by the United Kingdom, a designated derogation ceases to have effect for the purposes of this Act—

[. . .] at the end of the period of five years beginning with the date on which the order designation was made.

(2) At any time before the period—

(a) fixed by subsection (1) . . ., or

(b) extended by an order under this subsection, comes to an end, the [Secretary of State] may by order extend it by a further period of five years.

(3) An order under section 14(1) . . . ceases to have effect at the end of the period for consideration, unless a resolution has been passed by each House approving the order.

(4) Subsection (3) does not affect—

(a) anything done in reliance on the order; or

(b) the power to make a fresh order under section 14(1)[. . .].

(5) In subsection (3) 'period for consideration' means the period of forty days beginning with the day on which the order was made.

(6) In calculating the period for consideration, no account is to be taken of any time during which—

(a) Parliament is dissolved or prorogued; or

(b) both Houses are adjourned for more than four days.

(7) If a designated derogation is withdrawn by the United Kingdom, the [Secretary of State] must by order make such amendments to this Act as he considers are required to reflect that withdrawal.

Note: Commencement 2 October 2000. Words omitted from 1 April 2001 (SI 2001/1216). Words in square brackets substituted from 19 August 2003 (SI 2003/1887).

17. Periodic review of designated reservations

(1) The appropriate Minister must review the designated reservation referred to in section 15(1)(a)—

(a) before the end of the period of five years beginning with the date on which section 1(2) came into force; and

(b) if that designation is still in force, before the end of the period of five years beginning with the date on which the last report relating to it was laid under subsection (3).

(2) The appropriate Minister must review each of the other designated reservations (if any)—

(a) before the end of the period of five years beginning with the date on which the order designating the reservation first came into force; and

(b) if the designation is still in force, before the end of the period of five years beginning with the date on which the last report relating to it was laid under subsection (3).

(3) The Minister conducting a review under this section must prepare a report on the result of the review and lay a copy of it before each House of Parliament.

Note: Commencement 2 October 2000.

Judges of the European Court of Human Rights

18. Appointment to European Court of Human Rights

(1) In this section 'judicial office' means the office of—

(a) Lord Justice of Appeal, Justice of the High Court or Circuit judge, in England and Wales;

(b) judge of the Court of Session or sheriff, in Scotland;

(c) Lord Justice of Appeal, judge of the High Court or county court judge, in Northern Ireland.

(2) The holder of a judicial office may become a judge of the European Court of Human Rights ('the Court') without being required to relinquish his office.

(3) But he is not required to perform the duties of his judicial office while he is a judge of the Court.

(4) In respect of any period during which he is a judge of the Court—

(a) a Lord Justice of Appeal or Justice of the High Court is not to count as a judge of the relevant court for the purposes of section 2(1) or 4(1) of the [the Senior Courts Act 1981] (maximum number of judges) nor as a judge of the [Senior Courts] for the purposes of section 12(1) to (6) of that Act (salaries etc.);

(b) a judge of the Court of Session is not to count as a judge of that court for the purposes of section 1(1) of the Court of Session Act 1988 (maximum number of judges) or of section 9(1)(c) of the Administration of Justice Act 1973 ('the 1973 Act') (salaries etc.);

(c) a Lord Justice of Appeal or judge of the High Court in Northern Ireland is not to count as a judge of the relevant court for the purposes of section 2(1) or 3(1) of the Judicature (Northern Ireland) Act 1978 (maximum number of judges) nor as a judge of the [Court of Judicature] of Northern Ireland for the purposes of section 9(1)(d) of the 1973 Act (salaries etc.);

(d) a Circuit judge is not to count as such for the purposes of section 18 of the Court Act 1971 (salaries etc.);

(e) a sheriff is not to count as such for the purposes of section 14 of the Sheriff Courts (Scotland) Act 1907 (salaries etc.);

(f) a county court judge of Northern Ireland is not to count as such for the purposes of section 106 of the County Courts Act (Northern Ireland) 1959 (salaries etc.).

(5) If a sheriff principal is appointed a judge of the Court, section 11(1) of the Sheriff Courts (Scotland) Act 1971 (temporary appointment of sheriff principal) applies, while he holds that appointment, as if his office is vacant.

(6) Schedule 4 makes provision about judicial pensions in relation to the holder of a judicial office who serves as a judge of the Court.

(7) The Lord Chancellor or the Secretary of State may by order make such transitional provision (including, in particular, provision for a temporary increase in the maximum number of judges) as he considers appropriate in relation to any holder of a judicial office who has completed his service as a judge of the Court.

[(7A) The following paragraphs apply to the making of an order under subsection (7) in relation to any holder of a judicial office listed in subsection (1)(a)—

(a) before deciding what transitional provision it is appropriate to make, the person making the order must consult the Lord Chief Justice of England and Wales;

(b) before making the order, that person must consult the Lord Chief Justice of England and Wales.

(7B) The following paragraphs apply to the making of an order under subsection (7) in relation to any holder of a judicial office listed in subsection (1)(c)—

(a) before deciding what transitional provision it is appropriate to make, the person making the order must consult the Lord Chief Justice of Northern Ireland;

(b) before making the order, that person must consult the Lord Chief Justice of Northern Ireland.

(7C) The Lord Chief Justice of England and Wales may nominate a judicial office holder (within the meaning of section 109(4) of the Constitutional Reform Act 2005) to exercise his functions under this section.

(7D) The Lord Chief Justice of Northern Ireland may nominate any of the following to exercise his functions under this section—

(a) the holder of one of the offices listed in Schedule 1 to the Justice (Northern Ireland) Act 2002;

(b) a Lord Justice of Appeal (as defined in section 88 of that Act).]

Note: Commencement 9 November 1998. Subsections (7A)-(7D) inserted by Sch 4 Constitutional Reform Act from 3 April 2006 (SI 2006/1014). Words in sub-section (4) substituted by Constitutional Reform Act 2005 Sch 11 from 1 October 2009 (SI 2009/1604).

Parliamentary procedure

19. Statements of compatibility

(1) A Minister of the Crown in charge of a Bill in either House of Parliament must, before Second Reading of the Bill—

(a) make a statement to the effect that in his view the provisions of the Bill are compatible with the Convention rights ('a statement of compatibility'); or

(b) make a statement to the effect that although he is unable to make a statement of compatibility the government nevertheless wishes the House to proceed with the Bill.

(2) The statement must be in writing and be published in such manner as the Minister making it considers appropriate.

Note: Commencement 24 November 1998.

Supplemental

20. Orders etc. under this Act

(1) Any power of a Minister of the Crown to make an order under this Act is exercisable by statutory instrument.

(2) The power of [the Lord Chancellor or] the Secretary of State to make rules (other than rules of court) under section 2(3) or 7(9) is exercisable by statutory instrument.

(3) Any statutory instrument made under section 14, 15 or 16(7) must be laid before Parliament.

(4) No order may be made by [the Lord Chancellor or] the Secretary of State under section 1(4), 7(11) or 16(2) unless a draft of the order has been laid before, and approved by, each House of Parliament.

(5) Any statutory instrument made under section 18(7) or Schedule 4, or to which subsection (2) applies, shall be subject to annulment in pursuance of a resolution of either House of Parliament.

(6) The power of a Northern Ireland department to make—

(a) rules under section 2(3)(c) or 7(9)(c), or

(b) an order under section 7(11), is exercisable by statutory rule for the purposes of the Statutory Rules (Northern Ireland) Order 1979.

(7) Any rules made under section 2(3)(c) or 7(9)(c) shall be subject to negative resolution; and section 41(6) of the Interpretation Act (Northern Ireland) 1954 (meaning of

'subject to negative resolution') shall apply as if the power to make the rules were conferred by an Act of the Northern Ireland Assembly.

(8) No order may be made by a Northern Ireland department under section 7(11) unless a draft of the order has been laid before, and approved by, the Northern Ireland Assembly.

Note: Commencement 9 November 1998. Words in square brackets omitted from 19 August 2003 (SI 2003/1887), re-inserted from 12 January 2006 (SI 2005/3429).

21. Interpretation, etc.

(1) In this Act—

'amend' includes repeal and apply (with or without modifications);

'the appropriate Minister' means the Minister of the Crown having charge of the appropriate authorised government department (within the meaning of the Crown Proceedings Act 1947);

'the Commission' means the European Commission of Human Rights;

'the Convention' means the Convention for the Protection of Human Rights and Fundamental Freedoms, agreed by the Council of Europe at Rome on 4 November 1950 as it has effect for the time being in relation to the United Kingdom;

'declaration of incompatibility' means a declaration under section 4;

'Minister of the Crown' has the same meaning as in the Ministers of the Crown Act 1975;

'Northern Ireland Minister' includes the First Minister and the deputy First Minister in Northern Ireland;

'primary legislation' means any—

(a) public general Act;

(b) local and personal Act;

(c) private Act;

(d) Measure of the Church Assembly;

(e) Measure of the General Synod of the Church of England;

(f) Order in Council—

(i) made in exercise of Her Majesty's Royal Prerogative;

(ii) made under section 38(1)(a) of the Northern Ireland Constitution Act 1973 or the corresponding provision of the Northern Ireland Act 1998; or

(iii) amending an Act of a kind mentioned in paragraph (a), (b) or (c);

and includes an order or other instrument made under primary legislation (otherwise than by the [Welsh Ministers, the First Minister for Wales, the Counsel General to the Welsh Assembly Government,] a member of the Scottish Executive, a Northern Ireland Minister or a Northern Ireland department) to the extent to which it operates to bring one or more provisions of that legislation into force or amends any primary legislation;

'the First Protocol' means the protocol to the Convention agreed at Paris on 20 March 1952;

. . .

'the Eleventh Protocol' means the protocol to the Convention (restructuring the control machinery established by the Convention) agreed at Strasbourg on 11 May 1994;

['the Thirteenth Protocol' means the protocol to the Convention (concerning the abolition of the death penalty in all circumstances) agreed at Vilnius on 3 May 2002;]

'remedial order' means an order under section 10;

'subordinate legislation' means any—

(a) Order in Council other than one—

(i) made in exercise of Her Majesty's Royal Prerogative;

(ii) made under section 38(1)(a) of the Northern Ireland Constitution Act 1973 or the corresponding provision of the Northern Ireland Act 1998; or

(iii) amending an Act of a kind mentioned in the definition of primary legislation;

(b) Act of the Scottish Parliament;

[(ba) Measure of the National Assembly for Wales;

(bb) Act of the National Assembly for Wales;]

(c) Act of the Parliament of Northern Ireland;

(d) Measure of the Assembly established under section 1 of the Northern Ireland Assembly Act 1973;

(e) Act of the Northern Ireland Assembly;

(f) order, rules, regulations, scheme, warrant, byelaw or other instrument made under primary legislation (except to the extent to which it operates to bring one or more provisions of that legislation into force or amends any primary legislation);

(g) order, rules, regulations, scheme, warrant, byelaw or other instrument made under legislation mentioned in paragraph (b), (c), (d) or (e) or made under an Order in Council applying only to Northern Ireland;

(h) order, rules, regulations, scheme, warrant, byelaw or other instrument made by a member of the Scottish Executive, [Welsh Ministers, the First Minister for Wales, the Counsel General to the Welsh Assembly Government,] a Northern Ireland Minister or a Northern Ireland department in exercise of prerogative or other executive functions of Her Majesty which are exercisable by such a person on behalf of Her Majesty;

'transferred matters' has the same meaning as in the Northern Ireland Act 1998; and

'tribunal' means any tribunal in which legal proceedings may be brought.

(2) The references in paragraphs (b) and (c) of section 2(1) to Articles are to Articles of the Convention as they had effect immediately before the coming into force of the Eleventh Protocol.

(3) The reference in paragraph (d) of section 2(1) to Article 46 includes a reference to Articles 32 and 54 of the Convention as they had effect immediately before the coming into force of the Eleventh Protocol.

(4) The references in section 2(1) to a report or decision of the Commission or a decision of the Committee of Ministers include references to a report or decision made as provided by paragraphs 3, 4 and 6 of Article 5 of the Eleventh Protocol (transitional provisions).

(5) . . .

Note: Commencement of s 21(5) on 9 November 1998, remainder of s 21 on 2 October 2000. Words omitted and second words in square brackets in subsection (1) substituted by SI 2004/1574 from 22 June 2004. Other words in square brackets substituted from 4 May 2007, Government of Wales Act 2006, s 160. Subsection (5) omitted from 31 October 2009 by Sch 17 Armed Forces Act 2006.

22. Short title, commencement, application and extent

(1) This Act may be cited as the Human Rights Act 1998.

(2) Sections 18, 20 and 21(5) and this section come into force on the passing of this Act.

(3) The other provisions of this Act come into force on such day as the Secretary of State may by order appoint; and different days may be appointed for different purposes.

(4) Paragraph (b) of subsection (1) of section 7 applies to proceedings brought by or at the instigation of a public authority whenever the act in question took place; but otherwise that subsection does not apply to an act taking place before the coming into force of that section.

(5) This Act binds the Crown.

(6) This Act extends to Northern Ireland.

(7) . . .

Note: Commencement 9 November 1998. Sub-section (7) deleted by Armed Forces Act 2006 Sch 17 from 28 March 2009 (for certain purposes) (SI 2009/812) and from 31 October 2009 otherwise (SI 2009/1167).

Schedules

Section 1(3)

Schedule 1

The Articles

Part I

The Convention Rights and Freedoms

Article 2 — *Right to life*

1. Everyone's right to life shall be protected by law. No one shall be deprived of his life intentionally save in the execution of a sentence of a court following his conviction of a crime for which this penalty is provided by law.
2. Deprivation of life shall not be regarded as inflicted in contravention of this Article when it results from the use of force which is no more than absolutely necessary:
   (a) in defence of any person from unlawful violence;
   (b) in order to effect a lawful arrest or to prevent the escape of a person lawfully detained;
   (c) in action lawfully taken for the purpose of quelling a riot or insurrection.

Article 3 — *Prohibition of torture*

No one shall be subjected to torture or to inhuman or degrading treatment or punishment.

Article 4 — *Prohibition of slavery and forced labour*

1. No one shall be held in slavery or servitude.
2. No one shall be required to perform forced or compulsory labour.
3. For the purpose of this Article the term 'forced or compulsory labour' shall not include:
   (a) any work required to be done in the ordinary course of detention imposed according to the provisions of Article 5 of this Convention or during conditional release from such detention;
   (b) any service of a military character or, in case of conscientious objectors in countries where they are recognised, service exacted instead of compulsory military service;

(c) any service exacted in case of an emergency or calamity threatening the life or well-being of the community;
(d) any work or service which forms part of normal civic obligations.

Article 5 *Right to liberty and security*

1. Everyone has the right to liberty and security of person. No one shall be deprived of his liberty save in the following cases and in accordance with a procedure prescribed by law:
   (a) the lawful detention of a person after conviction by a competent court;
   (b) the lawful arrest or detention of a person for non-compliance with the lawful order of a court or in order to secure the fulfilment of any obligation prescribed by law;
   (c) the lawful arrest or detention of a person effected for the purpose of bringing him before the competent legal authority on reasonable suspicion of having committed an offence or when it is reasonably considered necessary to prevent his committing an offence or fleeing after having done so;
   (d) the detention of a minor by lawful order for the purpose of educational supervision or his lawful detention for the purpose of bringing him before the competent legal authority;
   (e) the lawful detention of persons for the prevention of the spreading of infectious diseases, of persons of unsound mind, alcoholics or drug addicts or vagrants;
   (f) the lawful arrest or detention of a person to prevent his effecting an unauthorised entry into the country or of a person against whom action is being taken with a view to deportation or extradition.
2. Everyone who is arrested shall be informed promptly, in a language which he understands, of the reasons for his arrest and of any charge against him.
3. Everyone arrested or detained in accordance with the provisions of paragraph 1(c) of this Article shall be brought promptly before a judge or other officer authorised by law to exercise judicial power and shall be entitled to trial within a reasonable time or to release pending trial. Release may be conditioned by guarantees to appear for trial.
4. Everyone who is deprived of his liberty by arrest or detention shall be entitled to take proceedings by which the lawfulness of his detention shall be decided speedily by a court and his release ordered if the detention is not lawful.
5. Everyone who has been the victim of arrest or detention in contravention of the provisions of this Article shall have an enforceable right to compensation.

Article 6 *Right to a fair trial*

1. In the determination of his civil rights and obligations or of any criminal charge against him, everyone is entitled to a fair and public hearing within a reasonable time by an independent and impartial tribunal established by law. Judgment shall be pronounced publicly but the press and public may be excluded from all or part of the trial in the interest of morals, public order or national security in a democratic society, where the interests of juveniles or the protection of the private life of the parties so require, or to the extent strictly necessary in the opinion of the court in special circumstances where publicity would prejudice the interests of justice.
2. Everyone charged with a criminal offence shall be presumed innocent until proved guilty according to law.
3. Everyone charged with a criminal offence has the following minimum rights:
   (a) to be informed promptly, in a language which he understands and in detail, of the nature and cause of the accusation against him;
   (b) to have adequate time and facilities for the preparation of his defence;
   (c) to defend himself in person or through legal assistance of his own choosing or, if he has not sufficient means to pay for legal assistance, to be given it free when the interests of justice so require;

(d) to examine or have examined witnesses against him and to obtain the attendance and examination of witnesses on his behalf under the same conditions as witnesses against him;
(e) to have the free assistance of an interpreter if he cannot understand or speak the language used in court.

Article 7 *No punishment without law*

1. No one shall be held guilty of any criminal offence on account of any act or omission which did not constitute a criminal offence under national or international law at the time when it was committed. Nor shall a heavier penalty be imposed than the one that was applicable at the time the criminal offence was committed.
2. This Article shall not prejudice the trial and punishment of any person for any act or omission which, at the time when it was committed, was criminal according to the general principles of law recognised by civilised nations.

Article 8 *Right to respect for private and family life*

1. Everyone has the right to respect for his private and family life, his home and his correspondence.
2. There shall be no interference by a public authority with the exercise of this right except such as is in accordance with the law and is necessary in a democratic society in the interests of national security, public safety or the economic well being of the country, for the prevention of disorder or crime, for the protection of health or morals, or for the protection of the rights and freedoms of others.

Article 9 *Freedom of thought, conscience and religion*

1. Everyone has the right to freedom of thought, conscience and religion; this right includes freedom to change his religion or belief and freedom, either alone or in community with others and in public or private, to manifest his religion or belief, in worship, teaching, practice and observance.
2. Freedom to manifest one's religion or beliefs shall be subject only to such limitations as are prescribed by law and are necessary in a democratic society in the interests of public safety, for the protection of public order, health or morals, or for the protection of the rights and freedoms of others.

Article 10 *Freedom of expression*

1. Everyone has the right to freedom of expression. This right shall include freedom to hold opinions and to receive and impart information and ideas without interference by public authority and regardless of frontiers. This Article shall not prevent States from requiring the licensing of broadcasting, television or cinema enterprises.
2. The exercise of these freedoms, since it carries with it duties and responsibilities, may be subject to such formalities, conditions, restrictions or penalties as are prescribed by law and are necessary in a democratic society, in the interests of national security, territorial integrity or public safety, for the prevention of disorder or crime, for the protection of health or morals, for the protection of the reputation or rights of others, for preventing the disclosure of information received in confidence, or for maintaining the authority and impartiality of the judiciary.

Article 11 *Freedom of assembly and association*

1. Everyone has the right to freedom of peaceful assembly and to freedom of association with others, including the right to form and to join trade unions for the protection of his interests.

2. No restrictions shall be placed on the exercise of these rights other than such as are prescribed by law and are necessary in a democratic society in the interests of national security or public safety, for the prevention of disorder or crime, for the protection of health or morals or for the protection of the rights and freedoms of others. This Article shall not prevent the imposition of lawful restrictions on the exercise of these rights by members of the armed forces, of the police or of the administration of the State.

Article 12 *Right to marry*

Men and women of marriageable age have the right to marry and to found a family, according to the national laws governing the exercise of this right.

Article 14 *Prohibition of discrimination*

The enjoyment of the rights and freedoms set forth in this Convention shall be secured without discrimination on any ground such as sex, race, colour, language, religion, political or other opinion, national or social origin, association with a national minority, property, birth or other status.

Article 16 *Restrictions on political activity of aliens*

Nothing in Articles 10, 11 and 14 shall be regarded as preventing the High Contracting Parties from imposing restrictions on the political activity of aliens.

Article 17 *Prohibition of abuse of rights*

Nothing in this Convention may be interpreted as implying for any State, group or person any right to engage in any activity or perform any act aimed at the destruction of any of the rights and freedoms set forth herein or at their limitation to a greater extent than is provided for in the Convention.

Article 18 *Limitation on use of restrictions on rights*

The restrictions permitted under this Convention to the said rights and freedoms shall not be applied for any purpose other than those for which they have been prescribed.

Part II
The First Protocol

Article 1 *Protection of property*

Every natural or legal person is entitled to the peaceful enjoyment of his possessions. No one shall be deprived of his possessions except in the public interest and subject to the conditions provided for by law and by the general principles of international law.

The preceding provisions shall not, however, in any way impair the right of a State to enforce such laws as it deems necessary to control the use of property in accordance with the general interest or to secure the payment of taxes or other contributions or penalties.

Article 2 *Right to education*

No person shall be denied the right to education. In the exercise of any functions which it assumes in relation to education and to teaching, the State shall respect the right of parents to ensure such education and teaching in conformity with their own religious and philosophical convictions.

Article 3 *Right to free elections*

The High Contracting Parties undertake to hold free elections at reasonable intervals by secret ballot, under conditions which will ensure the free expression of the opinion of the people in the choice of the legislature.

[PART III

ARTICLE 1 OF THE THIRTEENTH PROTOCOL

Abolition of the death penalty

The death penalty shall be abolished. No one shall be condemned to such penalty or executed.]

Note: Part 3 substituted from 22 June 2004 (SI 2004/1574).

Section 10

SCHEDULE 2

REMEDIAL ORDERS

Orders

1.—(1) A remedial order may—
- (a) contain such incidental, supplemental, consequential or transitional provision as the person making it considers appropriate;
- (b) be made so as to have effect from a date earlier than that on which it is made;
- (c) make provision for the delegation of specific functions;
- (d) make different provision for different cases.

(2) The power conferred by sub-paragraph (1)(a) includes—
- (a) power to amend primary legislation (including primary legislation other than that which contains the incompatible provision); and
- (b) power to amend or revoke subordinate legislation (including subordinate legislation other than that which contains the incompatible provision).

(3) A remedial order may be made so as to have the same extent as the legislation which it affects.

(4) No person is to be guilty of an offence solely as a result of the retrospective effect of a remedial order.

Procedure

2. No remedial order may be made unless—
- (a) a draft of the order has been approved by a resolution of each House of Parliament made after the end of the period of 60 days beginning with the day on which the draft was laid; or
- (b) it is declared in the order that it appears to the person making it that, because of the urgency of the matter, it is necessary to make the order without a draft being so approved.

Orders laid in draft

3.—(1) No draft may be laid under paragraph 2(a) unless—
- (a) the person proposing to make the order has laid before Parliament a document which contains a draft of the proposed order and the required information; and

(b) the period of 60 days, beginning with the day on which the document required by this sub-paragraph was laid, has ended.

(2) If representations have been made during that period, the draft laid under paragraph 2(a) must be accompanied by a statement containing—

(a) a summary of the representations; and

(b) if, as a result of the representations, the proposed order has been changed, details of the changes.

Urgent cases

4.—(1) If a remedial order ('the original order') is made without being approved in draft, the person making it must lay it before Parliament, accompanied by the required information, after it is made.

(2) If representations have been made during the period of 60 days beginning with the day on which the original order was made, the person making it must (after the end of that period) lay before Parliament a statement containing—

(a) a summary of the representations; and

(b) if, as a result of the representations, he considers it appropriate to make changes to the original order, details of the changes.

(3) If sub-paragraph (2)(b) applies, the person making the statement must—

(a) make a further remedial order replacing the original order; and

(b) lay the replacement order before Parliament.

(4) If, at the end of the period of 120 days beginning with the day on which the original order was made, a resolution has not been passed by each House approving the original or replacement order, the order ceases to have effect (but without that affecting anything previously done under either order or the power to make a fresh remedial order).

Definitions

5. In this Schedule—

'representations' means representations about a remedial order (or proposed remedial order) made to the person making (or proposing to make) it and includes any relevant Parliamentary report or resolution; and

'required information' means—

(a) an explanation of the incompatibility which the order (or proposed order) seeks to remove, including particulars of the relevant declaration, finding or order; and

(b) a statement of the reasons for proceeding under section 10 and for making an order in those terms.

Calculating periods

6. In calculating any period for the purposes of this Schedule, no account is to be taken of any time during which—

(a) Parliament is dissolved or prorogued; or

(b) both Houses are adjourned for more than four days.

[7. —(1) This paragraph applies in relation to–

(a) any remedial order made, and any draft of such an order proposed to be made,

(i) by the Scottish Ministers; or

(ii) within devolved competence (within the meaning of the Scotland Act 1998) by Her Majesty in Council; and

(b) any document or statement to be laid in connection with such an order (or proposed order).

(2) This Schedule has effect in relation to any such order (or proposed order), document or statement subject to the following modifications.

(3) Any reference to Parliament, each House of Parliament or both Houses of Parliament shall be construed as a reference to the Scottish Parliament.

(4) Paragraph 6 does not apply and instead, in calculating any period for the purposes of this Schedule, no account is to be taken of any time during which the Scottish Parliament is dissolved or is in recess for more than four days.]

Note: Paragraph (7) inserted from 27 July 2000 (SI 2000/2040).

Section 14 and 15

Schedule 3

Derogation and Reservation

Part II

Reservation

At the time of signing the present (First) Protocol, I declare that, in view of certain provisions of the Education Acts in the United Kingdom, the principle affirmed in the second sentence of Article 2 is accepted by the United Kingdom only so far as it is compatible with the provision of efficient instruction and training, and the avoidance of unreasonable public expenditure.

Dated 20 March 1952. Made by the United Kingdom Permanent Representative to the Council of Europe.

Note: Part 1 repealed from 1 April 2001 (SI 2001/1216), new Part 1 inserted from 20 December 2001 (SI 2001/4032), and repealed from 8 April 2005 (SI 2005/1071).

Section 18(6)

Schedule 4

Judicial Pensions

. . .

Immigration and Asylum Act 1999
(1999, c. 33)

Arrangement of Sections

Part I. Immigration: General

Leave to enter, or remain in, the United Kingdom

Exemption from immigration control

Removal from the United Kingdom

Provision of financial security

Information

Employment: code of practice

Monitoring entry clearance

Support and assistance by local authorities etc.

99. Provision of support by local authorities
100. Local authority and other assistance for Secretary of State
101. Reception zones

Appeals

102. . . .
103. Appeals: general
103A. Appeals: location of support under [section 4 or 95]
103B. Appeals: travelling expenses
104. . . .

Offences

105. False representations
106. Dishonest representations
107. Delay or obstruction
108. Failure of sponsor to maintain
109. Supplemental
109A. Arrest
109B. Entry, search and seizure

Expenditure

110. Payments to local authorities
111. Grants to voluntary organisations
112. Recovery of expenditure on support: misrepresentation etc.
113. Recovery of expenditure on support from sponsor
114. Overpayments

Exclusions

115. Exclusion from benefits
116. . . .
117. . . .
118. Housing authority accommodation
119. Homelessness: Scotland and Northern Ireland
120. . . .
121. . . .
122. Family with children
123. Back-dating of benefits where person recorded as refugee

Miscellaneous

124. Secretary of State to be corporation sole for purposes of Part VI
125. Entry of premises
126. Information from property owners
127. Requirement to supply information about redirection of post

PART VII. POWER TO ARREST, SEARCH AND FINGERPRINT

128.–140. . . .

SCHEDULES

An Act to make provision about immigration and asylum; provision about procedures in connection with marriage on superintendent registrar's certificate; and for connected purposes. [11 November 1999]

PART I

IMMIGRATION: GENERAL

Leave to enter, or remain in, the United Kingdom

1. . . .

Note: Amends Immigration Act 1971, s 3A.

2. . . .

Note: Amends Immigration Act 1971, s 3B.

3. . . .

Note: Amends Immigration Act 1971, s 3C.

4. Accommodation

(1) The Secretary of State may provide, or arrange for the provision of, facilities for the accommodation of persons—

(a) temporarily admitted to the United Kingdom under paragraph 21 of Schedule 2 to the 1971 Act;

(b) released from detention under that paragraph; or

(c) released on bail from detention under any provision of the Immigration Acts.

[(2) The Secretary of State may provide, or arrange for the provision of, facilities for the accommodation of a person if—

(a) he was (but is no longer) an asylum-seeker, and

(b) his claim for asylum was rejected.

(3) The Secretary of State may provide, or arrange for the provision of, facilities for the accommodation of a dependant of a person for whom facilities may be provided under subsection (2).

(4) The following expressions have the same meaning in this section as in Part VI of this Act (as defined in section 94)—

(a) asylum-seeker,

(b) claim for asylum, and

(c) dependant.]

[(5) The Secretary of State may make regulations specifying criteria to be used in determining—

(a) whether or not to provide accommodation, or arrange for the provision of accommodation, for a person under this section;

(b) whether or not to continue to provide accommodation, or arrange for the provision of accommodation, for a person under this section.

(6) The regulations may, in particular—

(a) provide for the continuation of the provision of accommodation for a person to be conditional upon his performance of or participation in community activities in accordance with arrangements made by the Secretary of State;

(b) provide for the continuation of the provision of accommodation to be subject to other conditions;

(c) provide for the provision of accommodation (or the continuation of the provision of accommodation) to be a matter for the Secretary of State's discretion to a specified extent or in a specified class of case.

(7) For the purposes of subsection (6)(a)—

(a) 'community activities' means activities that appear to the Secretary of State to be beneficial to the public or a section of the public, and

(b) the Secretary of State may, in particular—

(i) appoint one person to supervise or manage the performance of or participation in activities by another person;

(ii) enter into a contract (with a local authority or any other person) for the provision of services by way of making arrangements for community activities in accordance with this section;

(iii) pay, or arrange for the payment of, allowances to a person performing or participating in community activities in accordance with arrangements under this section.

(8) Regulations by virtue of subsection (6)(a) may, in particular, provide for a condition requiring the performance of or participation in community activities to apply to a person only if the Secretary of State has made arrangements for community activities in an area that includes the place where accommodation is provided for the person.

(9) A local authority or other person may undertake to manage or participate in arrangements for community activities in accordance with this section.]

[(10) The Secretary of State may make regulations permitting a person who is provided with accommodation under this section to be supplied also with services or facilities of a specified kind.

(11) Regulations under subsection (10)—

(a) may, in particular, permit a person to be supplied with a voucher which may be exchanged for goods or services,

(b) may not permit a person to be supplied with money,

(c) may restrict the extent or value of services or facilities to be provided, and

(d) may confer a discretion.]

Note: Commencement 11 November 1999. Heading substituted and subsection (2) inserted by Nationality, Immigration and Asylum Act 2002, s 49 from 7 November 2002. Subsections (5)–(9) inserted by Asylum and Immigration Act 2004, s 10 from 1 December 2004 (SI 2004/2999). Subsections (10)–(11) inserted by Immigration, Asylum and Nationality Act 2006, s 43 from 16 June 2006 (SI 2006/1497).

5. . . .

Note: Ceased to have effect from 2 April 2007, Sch 2 Immigration, Asylum and Nationality Act 2006 (SI 2007/1109).

Exemption from immigration control

6. . . .

Note: Amends Immigration Act 1971, s 8.

7. . . .

Note: Amends Immigration Act 1971, s 8.

8. . . .

Note: Amends Immigration Act 1971, s 8.

Removal from the United Kingdom

9. Treatment of certain overstayers

(1) During the regularisation period overstayers may apply, in the prescribed manner, for leave to remain in the United Kingdom.

(2) The regularisation period begins on the day prescribed for the purposes of this subsection and is not to be less than three months.

(3) The regularisation period ends—

(a) on the day prescribed for the purposes of this subsection; or

(b) if later, on the day before that on which section 65 comes into force.

(4) Section 10 and paragraph 12 of Schedule 15 come into force on the day after that on which the regularisation period ends.

(5) The Secretary of State must publicise the effect of this section in the way appearing to him to be best calculated to bring it to the attention of those affected.

(6) 'Overstayer' means a person who, having only limited leave to enter or remain in the United Kingdom, remains beyond the time limited by the leave.

Note: Commencement 11 November 1999, s 170.

[10 Removal of certain persons unlawfully in the United Kingdom

(1) A person may be removed from the United Kingdom under the authority of the Secretary of State or an immigration officer if the person requires leave to enter or remain in the United Kingdom but does not have it.

(2) Where a person ("P") is liable to be or has been removed from the United Kingdom under subsection (1), a member of P's family who meets the following three conditions may also be removed from the United Kingdom under the authority of the Secretary of State or an immigration officer, provided that the Secretary of State or immigration officer has given the family member written notice of the intention to remove him or her.

(3) The first condition is that the family member is—

(a) P's partner,

(b) P's child, or a child living in the same household as P in circumstances where P has care of the child,

(c) in a case where P is a child, P's parent, or

(d) an adult dependent relative of P.

(4) The second condition is that—

(a) in a case where the family member has leave to enter or remain in the United Kingdom, that leave was granted on the basis of his or her family life with P;

(b) in a case where the family member does not have leave to enter or remain in the United Kingdom, in the opinion of the Secretary of State or immigration officer the family member—

(i) would not, on making an application for such leave, be granted leave in his or her own right, but

(ii) would be granted leave on the basis of his or her family life with P, if P had leave to enter or remain.

(5) The third condition is that the family member is neither a British citizen, nor is he or she entitled to enter or remain in the United Kingdom by virtue of an enforceable EU right or of any provision made under section 2(2) of the European Communities Act 1972.

(6) A notice given to a family member under subsection (2) invalidates any leave to enter or remain in the United Kingdom previously given to the family member.

(7) For the purposes of removing a person from the United Kingdom under subsection (1) or (2), the Secretary of State or an immigration officer may give any such direction for the removal of the person as may be given under paragraphs 8 to 10 of Schedule 2 to the 1971 Act.

(8) But subsection (7) does not apply where a deportation order is in force against a person (and any directions for such a person's removal must be given under Schedule 3 to the 1971 Act).

(9) The following paragraphs of Schedule 2 to the 1971 Act apply in relation to directions under subsection (7) (and the persons subject to those directions) as they apply in

relation to directions under paragraphs 8 to 10 of Schedule 2 (and the persons subject to those directions)—

(a) paragraph 11 (placing of person on board ship or aircraft);

(b) paragraph 16(2) to (4) (detention of person where reasonable grounds for suspecting removal directions may be given or pending removal in pursuance of directions);

(c) paragraph 17 (arrest of person liable to be detained and search of premises for person liable to arrest);

(d) paragraph 18 (supplementary provisions on detention);

(e) paragraph 18A (search of detained person);

(f) paragraph 18B (detention of unaccompanied children);

(g) paragraphs 19 and 20 (payment of expenses of custody etc);

(h) paragraph 21 (temporary admission to UK of person liable to detention);

(i) paragraphs 22 to 25 (bail);

(j) paragraphs 25A to 25E (searches etc).

(10) The Secretary of State may by regulations make further provision about—

(a) the time period during which a family member may be removed under subsection (2);

(b) the service of a notice under subsection (2).

(11) In this section "child" means a person who is under the age of 18.]

Note: Section 10 substituted by s 1 Immigration Act 2014 from 20 October 2014 with savings set out in articles 9-11, 14-15 of SI 2014/2771, and transitional provisions in SI 2014/1820.

11. . . .

Note: Section 11 ceased to have effect from 1 October 2004, Asylum and Immigration Act 2004, s 33 (SI 2004/2523).

12. . . .

Note: Section 12 ceased to have effect from 1 October 2004, Asylum and Immigration Act 2004, s 33 (SI 2004/2523).

13. Proof of identity of persons to be removed or deported

(1) This section applies if a person—

(a) is to be removed from the United Kingdom to a country of which he is a national or citizen; but

(b) does not have a valid passport or other document establishing his identity and nationality or citizenship and permitting him to travel.

(2) If the country to which the person is to be removed indicates that he will not be admitted to it unless identification data relating to him are provided by the Secretary of State, he may provide them with such data.

(3) In providing identification data, the Secretary of State must not disclose whether the person concerned has made a claim for asylum.

(4) For the purposes of paragraph 4(1) of Schedule 4 to the Data Protection Act 1998, the provision under this section of identification data is a transfer of personal data which is necessary for reasons of substantial public interest.

(5) 'Identification data' means—

(a) fingerprints taken under section 141; or

(b) data collected in accordance with regulations made under section 144.

(6) 'Removed' means removed as a result of directions given under section 10 or under Schedule 2 or 3 to the 1971 Act.

Note: Commenced 11 December 2000, SI 2000/3099.

14. Escorts for persons removed from the United Kingdom under directions

(1) Directions for, or requiring arrangements to be made for, the removal of a person from the United Kingdom may include or be amended to include provision for the person who is to be removed to be accompanied by an escort consisting of one or more persons specified in the directions.

(2) The Secretary of State may by regulations make further provision supplementing subsection (1).

(3) The regulations may, in particular, include provision—

(a) requiring the person to whom the directions are given to provide for the return of the escort to the United Kingdom;

(b) requiring him to bear such costs in connection with the escort (including, in particular, remuneration) as may be prescribed;

(c) as to the cases in which the Secretary of State is to bear those costs;

(d) prescribing the kinds of expenditure which are to count in calculating the costs incurred in connection with escorts.

Note: Commencement 1 March 2000 (SI 2000/168).

15. . . .

Note: Section 15 repealed by Nationality, Immigration and Asylum Act 2002, s 77 from 1 April 2003 (SI 2003/754).

Provision of financial security

16. Security on grant of entry clearance

(1) In such circumstances as may be specified, the Secretary of State may require security to be given, with respect to a person applying for entry clearance, before clearance is given.

(2) In such circumstances as may be specified—

(a) the Secretary of State may accept security with respect to a person who is applying for entry clearance but for whom security is not required; and

(b) in determining whether to give clearance, account may be taken of any security so provided.

(3) 'Security' means—

(a) the deposit of a sum of money by the applicant, his agent or any other person, or

(b) the provision by the applicant, his agent or any other person of a financial guarantee of a specified kind, with a view to securing that the applicant will, if given leave to enter the United Kingdom for a limited period, leave the United Kingdom at the end of that period.

(4) Immigration rules must make provision as to the circumstances in which a security provided under this section—

(a) is to be repaid, released or otherwise cancelled; or

(b) is to be forfeited or otherwise realised by the Secretary of State.

(5) No security provided under this section may be forfeited or otherwise realised unless the person providing it has been given an opportunity, in accordance with immigration rules, to make representations to the Secretary of State.

(6) Immigration rules may, in particular—

(a) fix the maximum amount that may be required, or accepted, by way of security provided under this section;

(b) specify the form and manner in which such a security is to be given or may be accepted;

(c) make provision, where such a security has been forfeited or otherwise realised, for the person providing it to be reimbursed in such circumstances as may be specified;

(d) make different provision for different cases or descriptions of case.

(7) 'Specified' means specified by immigration rules.

(8) Any security forfeited or otherwise realised by the Secretary of State under this section must be paid into the Consolidated Fund.

Note: Commencement on a date to be appointed.

17. Provision of further security on extension of leave

(1) This section applies if security has been provided under section 16(1) or (2) with respect to a person who, having entered the United Kingdom (with leave to do so), applies—

(a) to extend his leave to enter the United Kingdom; or

(b) for leave to remain in the United Kingdom for a limited period.

(2) The Secretary of State may refuse the application if security of such kind as the Secretary of State considers appropriate is not provided, or continued, with respect to the applicant.

(3) Immigration rules must make provision as to the circumstances in which a security provided under this section—

(a) is to be repaid, released or otherwise cancelled; or

(b) is to be forfeited or otherwise realised by the Secretary of State.

(4) No security provided under this section may be forfeited or otherwise realised unless the person providing it has been given an opportunity, in accordance with immigration rules, to make representations to the Secretary of State.

(5) Subsection (7) of section 16 applies in relation to this section as it applies in relation to that section.

(6) Any security forfeited or otherwise realised by the Secretary of State under this section must be paid into the Consolidated Fund.

Note: Commencement on a date to be appointed.

Information

18. . . .

Note: Amends paragraph 27B, Sch 2 Immigration Act 1971.

19. . . .

Note: Amends paragraph 27C, Sch 2 Immigration Act 1971.

20. Supply of information to Secretary of State

(1) This section applies to information held by—

(a) a chief officer of police;

[(b) [the National Crime Agency;]]

(c) . . .

(d) . . .

(e) a person with whom the Secretary of State has made a contract or other arrangements under section 95 or 98 or a sub-contractor of such a person; or

(f) any specified person, for purposes specified in relation to that person.

[(1A) This section also applies to a document or article which—

(a) comes into the possession of a person listed in subsection (1) or someone acting on his behalf, or

(b) is discovered by a person listed in subsection (1) or someone acting on his behalf.]

(2) The information [, document or article] may be supplied to the Secretary of State for use for immigration purposes.

[(2A) The Secretary of State may—

(a) retain for immigration purposes a document or article supplied to him under subsection (2), and

(b) dispose of a document or article supplied to him under subsection (2) in such manner as he thinks appropriate (and the reference to use in subsection (2) includes a reference to disposal).]

(3) 'Immigration purposes' means any of the following—

(a) the administration of immigration control under the Immigration Acts;

(b) the prevention, detection, investigation or prosecution of criminal offences under those Acts;

(c) the imposition of penalties or charges under Part II;

(d) the provision of support for asylum-seekers and their dependants under Part VI;

(e) such other purposes as may be specified.

(4) 'Chief officer of police' means—

(a) the chief officer of police for a police area in England and Wales;

[(b) the chief constable of the Police Service of Scotland;]

(c) the [Chief Constable of the Police Service of Northern Ireland].

(5) 'Specified' means specified in an order made by the Secretary of State.

(6) This section does not limit the circumstances in which information [, documents or articles] may be supplied apart from this section.

Note: Commencement 1 January 2000 (SI 1999/3190). Subsection (1)(b) substituted by Sch 4 Serious Organised Crime and Police Act 2005 from 1 April 2006 (SI 2006/378), and words in square brackets in subs-s (1)(b) substituted by Crime and Courts Act 2013 Sch 8 from 7 October 2013 (SI 2013/1682). Subsection (1)(d) omitted from 31 January 2008 (Schedule, UK Borders Act 2007). Subsection (1A) and subsection (2A) inserted by s 132 Nationality, Immigration and Asylum Act 2002 from 10 February 2003 (SI 2003/1). Words in square brackets in subsections (2) and (6) inserted by s 132 Nationality, Immigration and Asylum Act 2002 from 10 February 2003 (SI 2003/1). Words in square brackets in subsection (4)(c) substituted from 4 November 2001 by s 78 Police (Northern Ireland) Act 2000 (SR 2001/396). Subsection (2)(b) substituted by Sch 8 Crime and Courts Act 2013 from 7 October 2013 (SI 2013/1682). Subsection (4)(b) substituted from 1 April 2013 (SI 2013/602).

21. Supply of information by Secretary of State

(1) This section applies to information held by the Secretary of State in connection with the exercise of functions under any of the Immigration Acts.

(2) The information may be supplied to—

(a) a chief officer of police, for use for police purposes;

[(b) the National Crime Agency, for use in connection with the discharge of any function of that Agency;]

(c) . . .

(d) the Commissioners of Customs and Excise, or a person providing services to them, for use for customs purposes; or

(e) any specified person, for use for purposes specified in relation to that person.

(3) 'Police purposes' means any of the following—

(a) the prevention, detection, investigation or prosecution of criminal offences;

(b) safeguarding national security;

(c) such other purposes as may be specified.

[(4) . . .

(6) 'Customs purposes' means any of the Commissioners' functions in relation to—

(a) the prevention, detection, investigation or prosecution of criminal offences;

(b) the prevention, detection or investigation of conduct in respect of which penalties which are not criminal penalties are provided for by or under any enactment;

(c) the assessment or determination of penalties which are not criminal penalties;

(d) checking the accuracy of information relating to, or provided for purposes connected with, any matter under the care and management of the Commissioners or any assigned matter (as defined by section 1(1) of the Customs and Excise Management Act 1979);

(e) amending or supplementing any such information (where appropriate);

(f) legal or other proceedings relating to anything mentioned in paragraphs (a) to (e);

(g) safeguarding national security; and

(h) such other purposes as may be specified.

(7) 'Chief officer of police' and 'specified' have the same meaning as in section 20.

(8) This section does not limit the circumstances in which information may be supplied apart from this section.

Note: Commencement 1 January 2000 (SI 1999/3190). Subsection (2)(b) substituted and subsection (4) omitted by Sch 8 Crime and Courts Act 2013 from 7 October 2013 (SI 2013/1682).

Employment: code of practice

22. . . .

Note: Amends Asylum and Immigration Act 1996, s 8A.

Monitoring entry clearance

23. . . .

Note: Repealed by Sch 9 Immigration Act 2014 from 20 October 2014 with savings set out in articles 9-11 SI 2014/2771.

Reporting suspicious marriages

24. Duty to report suspicious marriages

(1) Subsection (3) applies if—

(a) a superintendent registrar to whom a notice of marriage has been given under section 27 of the Marriage Act 1949,

[(aa) a superintendent registrar, or registrar of births, deaths and marriages, who receives information in advance of a person giving such a notice,]

(b) any other person who, under section 28(2) of that Act, has attested a declaration accompanying such a notice,

(c) a district registrar to whom a marriage notice or an approved certificate has been submitted under section 3 of the Marriage (Scotland) Act 1977, [..]

[(ca) a district registrar who receives information in advance of a person submitting such a notice or certificate,]

(d) a registrar or deputy registrar to whom notice has been given under section 13 of the Marriages (Ireland) Act 1844 or section 4 of the Marriage Law (Ireland) Amendment Act 1863,

(da) a registrar or deputy registrar who receives information in advance of a person giving such a notice,] has reasonable grounds for suspecting that the marriage will be a sham marriage.

(2) Subsection (3) also applies if—

(a) a marriage is solemnized in the presence of a registrar of marriages or, in relation to Scotland, an authorised registrar (within the meaning of the Act of 1977); and

(b) before, during or immediately after solemnization of the marriage, the registrar has reasonable grounds for suspecting that the marriage will be, or is, a sham marriage.

(3) The person concerned must report his suspicion to the Secretary of State without delay and in such form and manner as may be prescribed by regulations.

(4) The regulations are to be made—

(a) in relation to England and Wales, by the Registrar General for England and Wales with the approval of [the Secretary of State];

(b) in relation to Scotland, by the Secretary of State after consulting the Registrar General of Births, Deaths and Marriages for Scotland;

(c) in relation to Northern Ireland, by the Secretary of State after consulting the Registrar General in Northern Ireland.

[(5) A marriage (whether or not it is void) is a "sham marriage" if—

(a) either, or both, of the parties to the marriage is not a relevant national,

(b) there is no genuine relationship between the parties to the marriage, and

(c) either, or both, of the parties to the marriage enter into the marriage for one or more of these purposes—

(i) avoiding the effect of one or more provisions of United Kingdom immigration law or the immigration rules;

(ii) enabling a party to the marriage to obtain a right conferred by that law or those rules to reside in the United Kingdom.

(6) In subsection (5)—

"relevant national" means—

(a) a British citizen,

(b) a national of an EEA State other than the United Kingdom, or

(c) a national of Switzerland;

"United Kingdom immigration law" includes any subordinate legislation concerning the right of relevant nationals to move between and reside in member States.]

Note: Commencement 1 January 2001 (SI 2000/2698). Words in square brackets in sub-section (4)(a) substituted by SI 2008/678 from 3 April 2008. Subsections (1)(aa), (ca) and (da) inserted by s 56 Immigration Act 2014 from 14 July 2014 (SI 2014/1820). Subsection (5) substituted by s 55 Immigration Act 2014 from a date to be appointed.

[24A. Duty to report suspicious civil partnerships

(1) Subsection (3) applies if—

(a) a registration authority to whom a notice of proposed civil partnership has been given under section 8 of the Civil Partnership Act 2004,

[(aa) a registration authority that receives information in advance of a person giving such a notice,]

(b) any person who, under section 8 of the 2004 Act, has attested a declaration accompanying such a notice,

(c) a district registrar to whom a notice of proposed civil partnership has been given under section 88 of the 2004 Act,

[(ca) a district registrar who receives information in advance of a person giving such a notice,]

(d) a registrar to whom a civil partnership notice has been given under section 139 of the 2004 Act, [or

[(da) a registrar who receives information in advance of a person giving such a notice,]
has reasonable grounds for suspecting that the civil partnership will be a sham civil partnership.

(2) Subsection (3) also applies if—

(a) two people register as civil partners of each other under Part 2, 3 or 4 of the 2004 Act in the presence of the registrar, and

(b) before, during or immediately after they do so, the registrar has reasonable grounds for suspecting that the civil partnership will be, or is, a sham civil partnership.

(3) The person concerned must report his suspicion to the Secretary of State without delay and in such form and manner as may be prescribed by regulations.

(4) The regulations are to be made—

(a) in relation to England and Wales, by the Registrar General for England and Wales with the approval of [the Secretary of State];

(b) in relation to Scotland, by the Secretary of State after consulting the Registrar General of Births, Deaths and Marriages for Scotland;

(c) in relation to Northern Ireland, by the Secretary of State after consulting the Registrar General in Northern Ireland.

[(**5**) A civil partnership (whether or not it is void) is a "sham civil partnership" if—

(a) either, or both, of the parties to the civil partnership is not a relevant national,

(b) there is no genuine relationship between the parties to the civil partnership, and

(c) either, or both, of the parties to the civil partnership enter into the civil partnership for one or more of these purposes—

(i) avoiding the effect of one or more provisions of United Kingdom immigration law or the immigration rules;

(ii) enabling a party to the civil partnership to obtain a right conferred by that law or those rules to reside in the United Kingdom.

(**5A**) In subsection (5)—

"relevant national" means—

(a) a British citizen,

(b) a national of an EEA State other than the United Kingdom, or

(c) a national of Switzerland;

"United Kingdom immigration law" includes any subordinate legislation concerning the right of relevant nationals to move between and reside in member States.]

(**6**) 'The registrar' means—

(a) in relation to England and Wales, the civil partnership registrar acting under Part 2 of the 2004 Act;

(b) in relation to Scotland, the authorised registrar acting under Part 3 of the 2004 Act;

(c) in relation to Northern Ireland, the registrar acting under Part 4 of the 2004 Act.]

Note: Section 24A inserted by Sch 27 Civil Partnership Act 2004 from 15 April 2004 for the purposes of making regulations (SI 2005/1112), remainder 5 December 2005 (SI 2005/3175). Words in square brackets in sub-section (4)(a) substituted by SI 2008/678 from 3 April 2008. Subsections (1)(aa),(ca) and (da) inserted by s 56 Immigration Act 2014 from 14 July 2014 (SI 2014/1820). Subsection (5) substituted by s 55 Immigration Act 2014 from a date to be appointed.

Immigration control: facilities and charges

25. Provision of facilities for immigration control at ports

(1) The person responsible for the management of a control port ('the manager') must provide the Secretary of State free of charge with such facilities at the port as the Secretary of State may direct as being reasonably necessary for, or in connection with, the operation of immigration control there.

(2) Before giving such a direction, the Secretary of State must consult such persons likely to be affected by it as he considers appropriate.

(3) If the Secretary of State gives such a direction, he must send a copy of it to the person appearing to him to be the manager.

(4) If the manager persistently fails to comply with the direction (or part of it), the Secretary of State may—

(a) in the case of a control port which is not a port of entry, revoke any approval in relation to the port given under paragraph 26(1) of Schedule 2 to the 1971 Act;

(b) in the case of a control port which is a port of entry, by order revoke its designation as a port of entry.

(5) A direction under this section is enforceable, on the application of the Secretary of State—

(a) by injunction granted [in England and Wales by the county court or in Northern Ireland] by a county court; or

(b) in Scotland, by an order under section 45 of the Court of Session Act 1988.

(6) 'Control port' means a port in which a control area is designated under paragraph 26(3) of Schedule 2 to the 1971 Act.

(7) 'Facilities' means accommodation, facilities, equipment and services of a class or description specified in an order made by the Secretary of State.

Note: Commenced on 17 February 2003 for the purpose of enabling the Secretary of State to exercise power to make subordinate legislation; otherwise commenced on 1 April 2003 (SI 2003/2). Words inserted in subsection (5)(a) by Sch 9 Crime and Courts Act 2013 from a date to be appointed.

26. Charges: immigration control

(1) The Secretary of State may, at the request of any person and in consideration of such charges as he may determine, make arrangements—

(a) for the provision at any control port of immigration officers or facilities in addition to those (if any) needed to provide a basic service at the port;

(b) for the provision of immigration officers or facilities for dealing with passengers of a particular description or in particular circumstances.

(2) 'Control port' has the same meaning as in section 25.

(3) 'Facilities' includes equipment.

(4) 'Basic service' has such meaning as may be prescribed.

Note: Commenced on 5 June 2003 for purpose of enabling Secretary of State to make subordinate legislation; remainder commenced on 30 June 2003 (SI 2003/1469).

Charges: travel documents

27. . . .

Note: Repealed 2 April 2007 Sch 2 Immigration, Asylum and Nationality Act 2006 (SI 2007/1109).

Offences

28. . . .

Note: Amends Immigration Act 1971, s 24A.

29. . . .

Note: Repealed by Sch 9 Nationality, Immigration and Asylum Act 2002 from 1 April 2003 (SI 2003/754).

30. . . .

Note: Amends Immigration Act 1971, s 26.

31. Defences based on Article 31(1) of the Refugee Convention

(1) It is a defence for a refugee charged with an offence to which this section applies to show that, having come to the United Kingdom directly from a country where his life or freedom was threatened (within the meaning of the Refugee Convention), he—

(a) presented himself to the authorities in the United Kingdom without delay;

(b) showed good cause for his illegal entry or presence; and

(c) made a claim for asylum as soon as was reasonably practicable after his arrival in the United Kingdom.

(2) If, in coming from the country where his life or freedom was threatened, the refugee stopped in another country outside the United Kingdom, subsection (1) applies only if he shows that he could not reasonably have expected to be given protection under the Refugee Convention in that other country.

(3) In England and Wales and Northern Ireland the offences to which this section applies are any offence, and any attempt to commit an offence, under—

(a) Part I of the Forgery and Counterfeiting Act 1981 (forgery and connected offences);

[(aa) section 4 or 6 of the Identity Documents Act 2010;]

(b) section 24A of the 1971 Act (deception); or

(c) section 26(1)(d) of the 1971 Act (falsification of documents).

(4) In Scotland, the offences to which this section applies are those—

(a) of fraud,

(b) of uttering a forged document,

[(ba) under section 4 or 6 of the Identity Documents Act 2010;]

(c) under section 24A of the 1971 Act (deception), or

(d) under section 26(1)(d) of the 1971 Act (falsification of documents), and any attempt to commit any of those offences.

(5) A refugee who has made a claim for asylum is not entitled to the defence provided by subsection (1) in relation to any offence committed by him after making that claim.

(6) 'Refugee' has the same meaning as it has for the purposes of the Refugee Convention.

(7) If the Secretary of State has refused to grant a claim for asylum made by a person who claims that he has a defence under subsection (1), that person is to be taken not to be a refugee unless he shows that he is.

(8) A person who—

(a) was convicted in England and Wales or Northern Ireland of an offence to which this section applies before the commencement of this section, but

(b) at no time during the proceedings for that offence argued that he had a defence based on Article 31(1), may apply to the Criminal Cases Review Commission with a view to his case being referred to the Court of Appeal by the Commission on the ground that he would have had a defence under this section had it been in force at the material time.

(9) A person who—

(a) was convicted in Scotland of an offence to which this section applies before the commencement of this section, but

(b) at no time during the proceedings for that offence argued that he had a defence based on Article 31(1), may apply to the Scottish Criminal Cases Review Commission with a view to his case being referred to the High Court of Justiciary by the Commission on the ground that he would have had a defence under this section had it been in force at the material time.

(10) The Secretary of State may by order amend—

(a) subsection (3), or

(b) subsection (4), by adding offences to those for the time being listed there.

(11) Before making an order under subsection (10)(b), the Secretary of State must consult the Scottish Ministers.

Note: Commencement 11 November 1999, s 170. Subsections (3)(aa) and (4)(ba) substituted by Identity Documents Act 2010, Schedule, paragraph 10 from 21 January 2011 (s 14).

Part II

Carriers' Liability

Clandestine entrants

32. Penalty for carrying clandestine entrants

(1) A person is a clandestine entrant if—

(a) he arrives in the United Kingdom concealed in a vehicle, ship or aircraft,

[(aa) he arrives in the United Kingdom concealed in a rail freight wagon,]

(b) he passes, or attempts to pass, through immigration control concealed in a vehicle, or

(c) he arrives in the United Kingdom on a ship or aircraft, having embarked—

(i) concealed in a vehicle; and

(ii) at a time when the ship or aircraft was outside the United Kingdom, and claims, or indicates that he intends to seek, asylum in the United Kingdom or evades, or attempts to evade, immigration control.

[(2) The Secretary of State may require a person who is responsible for a clandestine entrant to pay—

(a) a penalty in respect of the clandestine entrant;

(b) a penalty in respect of any person who was concealed with the clandestine entrant in the same transporter.]

[(2A) In imposing a penalty under subsection (2) the Secretary of State—

(a) must specify an amount which does not exceed the maximum prescribed for the purpose of this paragraph,

(b) may, in respect of a clandestine entrant or a concealed person, impose separate penalties on more than one of the persons responsible for the clandestine entrant, and

(c) may not impose penalties in respect of a clandestine entrant or a concealed person which amount in aggregate to more than the maximum prescribed for the purpose of this paragraph.]

(3) A penalty imposed under this section must be paid to the Secretary of State before the end of the prescribed period.

[(4) Where a penalty is imposed under subsection (2) on the driver of a vehicle who is an employee of the vehicle's owner or hirer—

(a) the employee and the employer shall be jointly and severally liable for the penalty imposed on the driver (irrespective of whether a penalty is also imposed on the employer), and

(b) a provision of this Part about notification, objection or appeal shall have effect as if the penalty imposed on the driver were also imposed on the employer (irrespective of whether a penalty is also imposed on the employer in his capacity as the owner or hirer of the vehicle).]

[(**4A**) In the case of a detached trailer, subsection (4) shall have effect as if a reference to the driver were a reference to the operator.]

(**5**) In the case of a clandestine entrant to whom subsection (1)(a) applies, each of the following is a responsible person—

(a) if the transporter is a ship or aircraft, the owner [and] captain;

(b) if it is a vehicle (but not a detached trailer), the owner, hirer [and] driver of the vehicle;

(c) if it is a detached trailer, the owner, hirer [and] operator of the trailer.

[(**5A**) In the case of a clandestine entrant to whom subsection (1)(aa) applies, the responsible person is—

(a) where the entrant arrived concealed in a freight train, the train operator who, at the train's last scheduled stop before arrival in the United Kingdom, was responsible for certifying it as fit to travel to the United Kingdom, or

(b) where the entrant arrived concealed in a freight shuttle wagon, the operator of the shuttle-train of which the wagon formed part.]

(**6**) In the case of a clandestine entrant to whom subsection (1)(b) or (c) applies, each of the following is a responsible person—

(a) if the transporter is a detached trailer, the owner, hirer [and] operator of the trailer;

(b) if it is not, the owner, hirer [and] driver of the vehicle.

[(**6A**) Where a person falls within the definition of responsible person in more than one capacity, a separate penalty may be imposed on him under subsection (2) in respect of each capacity.]

(**7**) Subject to any defence provided by section 34, it is immaterial whether a responsible person knew or suspected—

(a) that the clandestine entrant was concealed in the transporter; or

(b) that there were one or more other persons concealed with the clandestine entrant in the same transporter.

(**8**) Subsection (9) applies if a transporter ('the carried transporter') is itself being carried in or on another transporter.

(**9**) If a person is concealed in the carried transporter, the question whether any other person is concealed with that person in the same transporter is to be determined by reference to the carried transporter and not by reference to the transporter in or on which it is carried.

(**10**) 'Immigration control' means United Kingdom immigration control and includes any United Kingdom immigration control operated in a prescribed control zone outside the United Kingdom.

Note: Sections 32(2)(a), 32(3) and 32(10) commenced 6 December 1999 (SI 1999/3190), remainder on 3 April 2000 (SI 2000/464). Subsections (1)(aa), (2A), (4A), (5A) and (6A) inserted and subsections (2) and (4) substituted by and words in square brackets in subsections (5) and (6) inserted by Sch 8 Nationality, Immigration and Asylum Act 2002 from 8 December 2002 (SI 2002/2811) for certain purposes; from 11 May 2012 for other purposes (SI 2012/1263).

[32A. Level of penalty: code of practice

(1) The Secretary of State shall issue a code of practice specifying matters to be considered in determining the amount of a penalty under section 32.

(2) The Secretary of State shall have regard to the code (in addition to any other matters he thinks relevant)—

(a) when imposing a penalty under section 32, and

(b) when considering a notice of objection under section 35(4).

(3) Before issuing the code the Secretary of State shall lay a draft before Parliament.

(4) After laying the draft code before Parliament the Secretary of State may bring the code into operation by order.

(5) The Secretary of State may from time to time revise the whole or any part of the code and issue the code as revised.

(6) Subsections (3) and (4) also apply to a revision or proposed revision of the code.]

Note: Section 32A inserted by Sch 8 Nationality, Immigration and Asylum Act 2002 from 14 November 2002 for the purpose of enabling the Secretary of State to exercise the power under s 32A(1), (3) and (4); otherwise takes effect from 8 December 2002 (SI 2002/2811) for certain purposes and from 11 May 2012 for other purposes (SI 2012/1263).

33. [Prevention of clandestine entrants: code of practice]

(1) The Secretary of State must issue a code of practice to be followed by any person operating a system for preventing the carriage of clandestine entrants.

(2) Before issuing the code, the Secretary of State must—

(a) consult such persons as he considers appropriate; and

(b) lay a draft before . . . Parliament.

(3) The requirement of subsection (2)(a) may be satisfied by consultation before the passing of this Act.

(4) After laying the draft code before Parliament, the Secretary of State may bring the code into operation by an order.

(5) The Secretary of State may from time to time revise the whole or any part of the code and issue the code as revised.

(6) Subsections (2) and (4) also apply to any revision, or proposed revision, of the code.

Note: Commenced 6 December 1999 (SI 1999/3190). Heading substituted and words omitted from subsection (2)(b) by Sch 8 Nationality, Immigration and Asylum Act 2002 from 8 December 2002 (SI 2002/2811) for certain purposes and for other purposes from 11 May 2012 (SI 2012/1263).

34. Defences to claim that penalty is due under section 32

[(1) A person ('the carrier') shall not be liable to the imposition of a penalty under section 32(2) if he has a defence under this section.]

(2) It is a defence for the carrier to show that he, or an employee of his who was directly responsible for allowing the clandestine entrant to be concealed, was acting under duress.

(3) It is also a defence for the carrier to show that—

(a) he did not know, and had no reasonable grounds for suspecting, that a clandestine entrant was, or might be, concealed in the transporter;

(b) an effective system for preventing the carriage of clandestine entrants was in operation in relation to the transporter; and

(c) . . . on the occasion in question the person or persons responsible for operating that system did so properly.

[(3A) It is also a defence for the carrier to show that—

(a) he knew or suspected that a clandestine entrant was or might be concealed in a rail freight wagon, having boarded after the wagon began its journey to the United Kingdom;

(b) he could not stop the train or shuttle-train of which the wagon formed part without endangering safety;

(c) an effective system for preventing the carriage of clandestine entrants was in operation in relation to the train or shuttle-train; and

(d) on the occasion in question the person or persons responsible for operating the system did so properly.]

(4) In determining, for the purposes of this section, whether a particular system is effective, regard is to be had to the code of practice issued by the Secretary of State under section 33.

(5) . . .

[(6) Where a person has a defence under subsection (2) in respect of a clandestine entrant, every other responsible person in respect of the clandestine entrant is also entitled to the benefit of the defence.]

Note: Commencement 3 April 2000 (SI 2000/464). Subsections (1) and (6) substituted by and subsection (3A) inserted by and words in subsection (3)(c) omitted by and subsection (5) omitted by Sch 8 Nationality, Immigration and Asylum Act 2002 from 8 December 2002 (SI 2002/2811) for certain purposes and from 11 May 2012 for other purposes (SI 2012/1263).

35. Procedure

(1) If the Secretary of State decides that a person ('P') is liable to one or more penalties under section 32, he must notify P of his decision.

(2) A notice under subsection (1) (a 'penalty notice') must—

(a) state the Secretary of State's reasons for deciding that P is liable to the penalty (or penalties);

(b) state the amount of the penalty (or penalties) to which P is liable;

(c) specify the date before which, and the manner in which, the penalty (or penalties) must be paid; and

(d) include an explanation of the steps—

(i) that P [may] take if he objects to the penalty;

(ii) that the Secretary of State may take under this Part to recover any unpaid penalty.

[(3) Subsection (4) applies where a person to whom a penalty notice is issued objects on the ground that—

(a) he is not liable to the imposition of a penalty, or

(b) the amount of the penalty is too high.

(4) The person may give a notice of objection to the Secretary of State.

(5) A notice of objection must—

(a) be in writing,

(b) give the objector's reasons, and

(c) be given before the end of such period as may be prescribed.

(6) Where the Secretary of State receives a notice of objection to a penalty in accordance with this section he shall consider it and—

(a) cancel the penalty,

(b) reduce the penalty,

(c) increase the penalty, or

(d) determine to take no action under paragraphs (a) to (c).

(7) Where the Secretary of State considers a notice of objection under subsection (6) he shall—

(a) inform the objector of his decision before the end of such period as may be prescribed or such longer period as he may agree with the objector,

(b) if he increases the penalty, issue a new penalty notice under subsection (1), and

(c) if he reduces the penalty, notify the objector of the reduced amount.]

(8) . . .

(9) The Secretary of State may by regulations provide, in relation to detached trailers, for a penalty notice which is [issued] in such manner as may be prescribed to have effect as a penalty notice properly [issued to] the responsible person or persons concerned under this section.

(10) Any sum payable to the Secretary of State as a penalty under section 32 may be recovered by the Secretary of State as a debt due to him.

[(11) In proceedings for enforcement of a penalty under subsection (10) no question may be raised as to—

(a) liability to the imposition of the penalty, or

(b) its amount.

(12) A document which is to be issued to or served on a person outside the United Kingdom for the purpose of subsection (1) or (7) or in the course of proceedings under subsection (10) may be issued or served—

(a) in person,

(b) by post,

(c) by facsimile transmission, or

(d) in another prescribed manner.

(13) The Secretary of State may by regulations provide that a document issued or served in a manner listed in subsection (12) in accordance with the regulations is to be taken to have been received at a time specified by or determined in accordance with the regulations.]

Note: Section 35(7)–(9) commenced 6 December 1999 (SI 1999/3190), remainder 3 April 2000 (SI 2000/464). Subsections (3)–(7) substituted by and subsection (8) omitted by and subsections (11)–(13) inserted by and words in square brackets in subsection (2) and (9) substituted by Sch 8 Nationality, Immigration and Asylum Act 2002 from 8 December 2002 (SI 2002/2811) for certain purposes and from 11 May 2012 for other purposes (SI 2012/1263).

[35A. Appeal

(1) A person may appeal to the court against a penalty imposed on him under section 32 on the ground that—

(a) he is not liable to the imposition of a penalty, or

(b) the amount of the penalty is too high.

(2) On an appeal under this section the court may—

(a) allow the appeal and cancel the penalty,

(b) allow the appeal and reduce the penalty, or

(c) dismiss the appeal.

(3) An appeal under this section shall be a re-hearing of the Secretary of State's decision to impose a penalty and shall be determined having regard to—

(a) any code of practice under section 32A which has effect at the time of the appeal,

(b) the code of practice under section 33 which had effect at the time of the events to which the penalty relates, and

(c) any other matters which the court thinks relevant (which may include matters of which the Secretary of State was unaware).

(4) Subsection (3) has effect despite any provision of Civil Procedure Rules.

(5) An appeal may be brought by a person under this section against a penalty whether or not—

(a) he has given notice of objection under section 35(4);

(b) the penalty has been increased or reduced under section 35(6).]

Note: Section 35A inserted by Sch 8 Nationality, Immigration and Asylum Act 2002 from 8 December 2002 (SI 2002/2811) for certain purposes and from 11 May 2012 for other purposes (SI 2012/1263).

36. Power to detain vehicles etc. in connection with penalties under section 32

(1) If a penalty notice has been [issued] under section 35, a senior officer may detain any relevant—

(a) vehicle,

(b) small ship, . . .

(c) small aircraft, . . . [or

(d) rail freight wagon,] until all penalties to which the notice relates, and any expenses reasonably incurred by the Secretary of State in connection with the detention, have been paid.

(2) That power—

(a) may be exercised only if, in the opinion of the senior officer concerned, there is a significant risk that the penalty (or one or more of the penalties) will not be paid before the end of the prescribed period if the transporter is not detained; and

(b) may not be exercised if alternative security which the Secretary of State considers is satisfactory, has been given.

[(2A) A vehicle may be detained under subsection (1) only if—

(a) the driver of the vehicle is an employee of its owner or hirer,

(b) the driver of the vehicle is its owner or hirer, or

(c) a penalty notice is issued to the owner or hirer of the vehicle.

(2B) A senior officer may detain a relevant vehicle, small ship, small aircraft or rail freight wagon pending—

(a) a decision whether to issue a penalty notice,

(b) the issue of a penalty notice, or

(c) a decision whether to detain under subsection (1).

(2C) That power may not be exercised in any case—

(a) for longer than is necessary in the circumstances of the case, or

(b) after the expiry of the period of 24 hours beginning with the conclusion of the first search of the vehicle, ship, aircraft or wagon by an immigration officer after it arrived in the United Kingdom.]

(3) If a transporter is detained under this section, the owner, consignor or any other person who has an interest in any freight or other thing carried in or on the transporter may remove it, or arrange for it to be removed, at such time and in such way as is reasonable.

(4) The detention of a transporter under this section is lawful even though it is subsequently established that the penalty notice on which the detention was based was ill-founded in respect of all or any of the penalties to which it related.

(5) But subsection (4) does not apply if the Secretary of State was acting unreasonably in issuing the penalty notice.

Note: Section 36(2)(a) commenced 6 December 1999 (SI 1999/3190), remainder 3 April 2000 (SI 2000/464). Subsections (2A), (2B) and (2C) inserted by and words in square brackets in subsection (1) substituted by Sch 8 Nationality Immigration and Asylum Act 2002 from 8 December 2002 (SI 2002/2811) for certain purposes and from 11 May 2012 for other purposes (SI 2012/1263).

[36A. Detention in default of payment

(1) This section applies where a person to whom a penalty notice has been issued under section 35 fails to pay the penalty before the date specified in accordance with section 35(2)(c).

(2) The Secretary of State may make arrangements for the detention of any vehicle, small ship, small aircraft or rail freight wagon which the person to whom the penalty notice was issued uses in the course of a business.

(3) A vehicle, ship, aircraft or wagon may be detained under subsection (2) whether or not the person to whom the penalty notice was issued owns it.

(4) But a vehicle may be detained under subsection (2) only if the person to whom the penalty notice was issued—

(a) is the owner or hirer of the vehicle, or

(b) was an employee of the owner or hirer of the vehicle when the penalty notice was issued.

(5) The power under subsection (2) may not be exercised while an appeal against the penalty under section 35A is pending or could be brought (ignoring the possibility of an appeal out of time with permission).

(6) The Secretary of State shall arrange for the release of a vehicle, ship, aircraft or wagon detained under this section if the person to whom the penalty notice was issued pays—

(a) the penalty, and

(b) expenses reasonably incurred in connection with the detention.]

Note: Section 36A inserted by Sch 8 Nationality, Immigration and Asylum Act 2002 from 8 December 2002 (SI 2002/2811) for certain purposes and from 11 May 2012 for other purposes (SI 2012/1263).

37. Effect of detention

(1) This section applies if a transporter is detained under [section 36(1)].

(2) The person to whom the penalty notice was addressed, or the owner or any other person [whose interests may be affected by detention of the transporter], may apply to the court for the transporter to be released.

(3) The court may release the transporter if it considers that—

(a) satisfactory security has been tendered in place of the transporter for the payment of the penalty alleged to be due and connected expenses;

(b) there is no significant risk that the penalty (or one or more of the penalties) and any connected expenses will not be paid; or

(c) there is a significant doubt as to whether the penalty is payable. . . .

[(**3A**) The court may also release the transporter on the application of the owner of the transporter under subsection (2) if—

(a) a penalty notice was not issued to the owner or an employee of his, and

(b) the court considers it right to release the transporter.

(**3B**) In determining whether to release a transporter under subsection (3A) the court shall consider—

(a) the extent of any hardship caused by detention,

(b) the extent (if any) to which the owner is responsible for the matters in respect of which the penalty notice was issued, and

(c) any other matter which appears to the court to be relevant (whether specific to the circumstances of the case or of a general nature).]

(4) If the court has not ordered the release of the transporter, the Secretary of State may sell it if the penalty in question and connected expenses are not paid before the end of the period of 84 days beginning with the date on which the detention began.

(5) 'Connected expenses' means expenses reasonably incurred by the Secretary of State in connection with the detention.

[(**5A**) The power of sale under subsection (4) may be exercised only when no appeal against the imposition of the penalty is pending or can be brought (ignoring the possibility of an appeal out of time with permission).

(**5B**) The power of sale under subsection (4) shall lapse if not exercised within a prescribed period.]

(6) Schedule 1 applies to the sale of transporters under this section.

[(7) This section applies to a transporter detained under section 36A as it applies to a transporter detained under section 36(1); but for that purpose—

(a) the court may release the transporter only if the court considers that the detention was unlawful or under subsection (3A) (and subsection (3) shall not apply), and

(b) the reference in subsection (4) to the period of 84 days shall be taken as a reference to a period prescribed for the purpose of this paragraph.]

Note: Section 37(6) commenced 6 December 1999 (SI 1999/3190), remainder 3 April 2000 (SI 2000/464). Subsections (3A)–(3B), (5A)–(5B) and (7) inserted by Sch 8 Nationality, Immigration and Asylum Act 2002 from 8 December 2002 (SI 2002/2811). Words in square brackets in subsections (1) and (2) and words in subsection (3)(c) omitted by Sch 8 Nationality, Immigration and Asylum Act 2002 from 8 December 2002 (SI 2002/2811) for certain purposes and from 11 May 2012 for other purposes (SI 2012/1263).

38. Assisting illegal entry and harbouring

. . .

Note: Inserts s 25A of Immigration Act 1971 from 3 April 2000. Subsections (1) and (3) repealed by Sch 9 Nationality, Immigration and Asylum Act 2002 from a date to be appointed.

39. . . .

Note: Section 39 repealed by Sch 8 Nationality, Immigration and Asylum Act 2002 from 8 December 2002 (SI 2002/2811).

Passengers without proper documents

[40. Charges in respect of passenger without proper documents

(1) This section applies if an individual requiring leave to enter the United Kingdom arrives in the United Kingdom by ship or aircraft and, on being required to do so by an immigration officer, fails to produce—

(a) an immigration document which is in force and which satisfactorily establishes his identity and his nationality or citizenship, and

(b) if the individual requires a visa, a visa of the required kind.

(2) The Secretary of State may charge the owner of the ship or aircraft; in respect of the individual, the sum of £2,000.

(3) The charge shall be payable to the Secretary of State on demand.

(4) No charge shall be payable in respect of any individual who is shown by the owner to have produced the required document or documents to the owner or his employee or agent when embarking on the ship or aircraft for the voyage or flight to the United Kingdom.

(5) For the purpose of subsection (4) an owner shall be entitled to regard a document as—

(a) being what it purports to be unless its falsity is reasonably apparent, and

(b) relating to the individual producing it unless it is reasonably apparent that it does not relate to him.

(6) For the purposes of this section an individual requires a visa if—

(a) under the immigration rules he requires a visa for entry into the United Kingdom, or

(b) as a result of section 41 he requires a visa for passing through the United Kingdom.

(7) The Secretary of State may by order amend this section for the purpose of applying it in relation to an individual who—

(a) requires leave to enter the United Kingdom, and

(b) arrives in the United Kingdom by train.

(8) An order under subsection (7) may provide for the application of this section—

(a) except in cases of a specified kind;

(b) subject to a specified defence.

(9) In this section 'immigration document' means—

(a) a passport, and

(b) a document which relates to a national of a country other than the United Kingdom and which is designed to serve the same purpose as a passport.

(10) The Secretary of State may by order substitute a sum for the sum in subsection (2).]

Note: Section 40 substituted by Sch 8 Nationality, Immigration and Asylum Act 2002 from 8 December 2002 (SI 2003/2811).

40A. Notification and objection

(1) If the Secretary of State decides to charge a person under section 40, the Secretary of State must notify the person of his decision.

(2) A notice under subsection (1) (a 'charge notice') must—

(a) state the Secretary of State's reasons for deciding to charge the person,

(b) state the amount of the charge,

(c) specify the date before which, and the manner in which, the charge must be paid,

(d) include an explanation of the steps that the person may take if he objects to the charge, and

(e) include an explanation of the steps that the Secretary of State may take under this Part to recover any unpaid charge.

(3) Where a person on whom a charge notice is served objects to the imposition of the charge on him, he may give a notice of objection to the Secretary of State.

(4) A notice of objection must—

(a) be in writing,

(b) give the objector's reasons, and

(c) be given before the end of such period as may be prescribed.

(5) Where the Secretary of State receives a notice of objection to a charge in accordance with this section, he shall—

(a) consider it, and

(b) determine whether or not to cancel the charge.

(6) Where the Secretary of State considers a notice of objection, he shall inform the objector of his decision before the end of—

(a) such period as may be prescribed, or

(b) such longer period as he may agree with the objector.

(7) Any sum payable to the Secretary of State as a charge under section 40 may be recovered by the Secretary of State as a debt due to him.

(8) In proceedings for enforcement of a charge under subsection (7) no question may be raised as to the validity of the charge.

(9) Subsections (12) and (13) of section 35 shall have effect for the purpose of this section as they have effect for the purpose of section 35(1), (7) and (10).]

Note: Section 40A inserted by Sch 8 Nationality, Immigration and Asylum Act 2002 from 8 December 2002 (SI 2002/2811).

40B. Appeal

(1) A person may appeal to the court against a decision to charge him under section 40.

(2) On an appeal under this section the court may—

(a) allow the appeal and cancel the charge, or

(b) dismiss the appeal.

(3) An appeal under this section—

(a) shall be a re-hearing of the Secretary of State's decision to impose a charge, and

(b) may be determined having regard to matters of which the Secretary of State was unaware.

(4) Subsection (3)(a) has effect despite any provision of Civil Procedure Rules.

(5) An appeal may be brought by a person under this section against a decision to charge him whether or not he has given notice of objection under section 40A(3).

Note: Section 40B inserted by Sch 8 Nationality, Immigration and Asylum Act 2002 from 8 December 2002 (SI 2002/2811).

41. Visas for transit passengers

(1) The Secretary of State may by order require transit passengers to hold a transit visa.

(2) 'Transit passengers' means persons of any description specified in the order who on arrival in the United Kingdom pass through to another country without entering the United Kingdom; and 'transit visa' means a visa for that purpose.

(3) The order—

(a) may specify a description of persons by reference to nationality, citizenship, origin or other connection with any particular country but not by reference to race, colour or religion;

(b) may not provide for the requirement imposed by the order to apply to any person who under the 1971 Act has the right of abode in the United Kingdom;

(c) may provide for any category of persons of a description specified in the order to be exempt from the requirement imposed by the order;

(d) may make provision about the method of application for visas required by the order.

Note: Commenced 8 December 2002 (SI 2002/2815).

42. . . .

Note: Section 42 repealed by Sch 8 Nationality, Immigration and Asylum Act from 8 December 2002 (SI 2002/2811).

Interpretation

43. Interpretation of Part II

[(1)] In this Part—

'aircraft' includes hovercraft;

'captain' means the master of a ship or commander of an aircraft;

'concealed' includes being concealed in any freight, stores or other thing carried in or on the vehicle, ship [, aircraft or rail freight wagon] concerned;

. . .

'detached trailer' means a trailer, semi-trailer, caravan or any other thing which is designed or adapted for towing by a vehicle but which has been detached for transport—

(a) in or on the vehicle concerned; or

(b) in the ship or aircraft concerned (whether separately or in or on a vehicle);

'equipment', in relation to an aircraft, includes—

(a) any certificate of registration, maintenance or airworthiness of the aircraft;

(b) any log book relating to the use of the aircraft; and

(c) any similar document;

['freight shuttle wagon' means a wagon which—

(a) forms part of a shuttle-train, and

(b) is designed to carry commercial goods vehicles;

'freight train' means any train other than—

(a) a train engaged on a service for the carriage of passengers, or

(b) a shuttle-train;]

'hirer', in relation to a vehicle, means any person who has hired the vehicle from another person;

'operating weight', in relation to an aircraft, means the maximum total weight of the aircraft and its contents at which the aircraft may take off anywhere in the world, in the most favourable circumstances, in accordance with the certificate of airworthiness in force in respect of the aircraft;

'owner' includes—

(a) in relation to a ship or aircraft, the agent or operator of the ship or aircraft;

. . .

(b) . . . and in relation to a transporter which is the subject of a hire-purchase agreement, includes the person in possession of it under that agreement;

'penalty notice' has the meaning given in section 35(2);

['rail freight wagon' means—

(a) any rolling stock, other than a locomotive, which forms part of a freight train, or

(b) a freight shuttle wagon, and for the purpose of this definition, 'rolling stock' and 'locomotive' have the meanings given by section 83 of the Railways Act 1993 (c. 43);]

'senior officer' means an immigration officer not below the rank of chief immigration officer;

'ship' includes every description of vessel used in navigation;

['shuttle-train' has the meaning given by section 1(9) of the Channel Tunnel Act 1987 (c. 53);]

'small aircraft' means an aircraft which has an operating weight of less than 5,700 kilogrammes;

'small ship' means a ship which has a gross tonnage of less than 500 tonnes;

'train' means a train which—

(a) is engaged on an international service as defined by section 13(6) of the Channel Tunnel Act 1987; but

(b) is not a shuttle train as defined by section 1(9) of that Act;

'train operator', in relation to a person arriving in the United Kingdom on a train, means the operator of trains who embarked that person on that train for the journey to the United Kingdom;

'transporter' means a vehicle, ship, [aircraft or rail freight wagon] together with—

(a) its equipment; and

(b) any stores for use in connection with its operation;

'vehicle' includes a trailer, semi-trailer, caravan or other thing which is designed or adapted to be towed by another vehicle.

[(2) A reference in this Part to 'the court' is a reference—

(a) in England and Wales, to [the county court],

(b) in Scotland, to the sheriff, and

(c) in Northern Ireland, to a county court.

(3) But—

(a) a county court [in Northern Ireland, or the county court in England and Wales,] may transfer proceedings under this Part to the High Court, and

(b) the sheriff may transfer proceedings under this Part to the Court of Session.]

Note: Commenced 6 December 1999 (SI 1999/3190). Subsections (2) and (3) and words in square brackets in subsection (1) inserted by and words in subsection (1) omitted by Sch 8 Nationality, Immigration and Asylum Act from 8 December 2002 (SI 2002/2811). Words in square brackets in subsection (2)(a) substituted and in square brackets in subsection (3)(a) inserted by Sch 9 Crime and Courts Act 2013 from a date to be appointed.

Part III

Bail

Routine bail hearings

. . .

44–52. . . .

Note: Sections 44 to 52 repealed by the Nationality, Immigration and Asylum Act 2002, s 68 from 10 February 2003 (SI 2003/1).

Bail hearings under other enactments

53. Applications for bail in immigration cases

(1) The Secretary of State may by regulations make new provision in relation to applications for bail by persons detained under the 1971 Act [or under section 62 of the Nationality, Immigration and Asylum Act 2002].

(2) The regulations may confer a right to be released on bail in prescribed circumstances.

(3) The regulations may, in particular, make provision—

(a) creating or transferring jurisdiction to hear an application for bail by a person detained under the 1971 Act [or under section 62 of the Nationality, Immigration and Asylum Act 2002];

(b) as to the places in which such an application may be held;

(c) as to the procedure to be followed on, or in connection with, such an application;

(d) as to circumstances in which, and conditions (including financial conditions) on which, an applicant may be released on bail;

(e) amending or repealing any enactment so far as it relates to such an application.

(4) The regulations must include provision for securing that an application for bail made by a person who has brought an appeal under any provision of [the Nationality, Immigration and Asylum Act 2002] or the Special Immigration Appeals Commission Act 1997 is heard by the appellate authority hearing that appeal.

(5) . . .

(6) Regulations under this section require the approval of the Lord Chancellor.

[(6A) In so far as regulations under this section relate to England and Wales, the Lord Chancellor must consult the Lord Chief Justice of England and Wales before giving his approval.

(6B) In so far as regulations under this section relate to Northern Ireland, the Lord Chancellor must consult the Lord Chief Justice of Northern Ireland before giving his approval.]

(7) In so far as regulations under this section relate to the sheriff or the Court of Session, the Lord Chancellor must obtain the consent of the Scottish Ministers before giving his approval.

[(8) The Lord Chief Justice of England and Wales may nominate a judicial office holder (as defined in section 109(4) of the Constitutional Reform Act 2005) to exercise his functions under this section.

(9) The Lord Chief Justice of Northern Ireland may nominate any of the following to exercise his functions under this section—

(a) the holder of one of the offices listed in Schedule 1 to the Justice (Northern Ireland) Act 2002;

(b) a Lord Justice of Appeal (as defined in section 88 of that Act).]

Note: Section 53 commenced 10 February 2003 (SI 2003/2). Words in square brackets in subsections (1) and (3) inserted by and subsection (5) omitted by Nationality, Immigration and Asylum Act 2002, ss 62, 68 from 10 February 2003 (SI 2003/1). Words in square brackets in subsection (4) substituted by Sch 7 Nationality, Immigration and Asylum Act 2002 from 1 April 2003 (SI 2003/754). Subsections (6A), (8)–(9) inserted by Sch 4 Constitutional Reform Act 2005 from 3 April 2006 (SI 2006/1014). Any function of the Lord Chancellor under subsection (6) to become a protected function from a date to be appointed, Sch 7 Constitutional Reform Act 2005.

54. Extension of right to apply for bail in deportation cases

Note: Amends paragraph 2, Sch 3 Immigration Act 1971.

Grants

55. . . .

Note: Section 55 ceased to have effect from 10 February 2003, Nationality, Immigration and Asylum Act 2002, s 68.

Part IV

Appeals

. . .

Note: Part IV repealed by the Nationality, Immigration and Asylum Act 2002, s 114 and Sch 9 from 1 April 2003 (SI 2003/754, which sets out transitional provisions).

Part V

Immigration Advisers and Immigration Service Providers

Interpretation

82. Interpretation of Part V

(1) In this Part—

'claim for asylum' means a claim that it would be contrary to the United Kingdom's obligations under—

(a) the Refugee Convention, or

(b) Article 3 of the Human Rights Convention, for the claimant to be removed from, or required to leave, the United Kingdom;

'the Commissioner' means the Immigration Services Commissioner;

'the complaints scheme' means the scheme established under paragraph 5(1) of Schedule 5;

'designated judge' has the same meaning as in section 119(1) of the Courts and Legal Services Act 1990;

'designated professional body' has the meaning given by section 86;

['designated qualifying regulator' has the meaning given by section 86A;]

'immigration advice' means advice which—

(a) relates to a particular individual;

(b) is given in connection with one or more relevant matters;

(c) is given by a person who knows that he is giving it in relation to a particular individual and in connection with one or more relevant matters; and

(d) is not given in connection with representing an individual before a court in criminal proceedings or matters ancillary to criminal proceedings;

'immigration services' means the making of representations on behalf of a particular individual—

(a) in civil proceedings before a court, tribunal or adjudicator in the United Kingdom, or

(b) in correspondence with a Minister of the Crown or government department, in connection with one or more relevant matters;

'Minister of the Crown' has the same meaning as in the Ministers of the Crown Act 1975;

'qualified person' means a person who is qualified for the purposes of section 84;

'registered person' means a person who is registered with the Commissioner under section 85;

'relevant matters' means any of the following—

(a) a claim for asylum;

(b) an application for, or for the variation of, entry clearance or leave to enter or remain in the United Kingdom;

[(ba) an application for an immigration employment document;]

(c) unlawful entry into the United Kingdom;

(d) nationality and citizenship under the law of the United Kingdom;

(e) citizenship of the European Union;

(f) admission to Member States under [EU] law;

(g) residence in a Member State in accordance with rights conferred by or under [EU] law;

(h) removal or deportation from the United Kingdom;

(i) an application for bail under the Immigration Acts or under the Special Immigration Appeals Commission Act 1997;

(j) an appeal against, or an application for judicial review in relation to, any decision taken in connection with a matter referred to in paragraphs (a) to (i).

[. . .]

(2) In this Part, references to the provision of immigration advice or immigration services are to the provision of such advice or services by a person—

(a) in the United Kingdom (regardless of whether the persons to whom they are provided are in the United Kingdom or elsewhere); and

(b) in the course of a business carried on (whether or not for profit) by him or by another person.

[(3) In the definition of 'relevant matters' in subsection (1) 'immigration employment document' means—

(a) a work permit (within the meaning of section 33(1) of the Immigration Act 1971 (interpretation)), and

(b) any other document which relates to employment and is issued for a purpose of immigration rules or in connection with leave to enter or remain in the United Kingdom.]

Note: Commenced 22 May 2000 (SI 2000/1282). First words in square brackets in subsection (1) inserted Sch 18 Legal Services Act 2007 from 1 April 2011 (SI 2011/720). Second words in square brackets in subsection (1) and subsection (3) inserted by Nationality, Immigration and Asylum Act 2002, s 123 from 1 April 2004 (SI 2003/2993). Words omitted from subsection (1) from 18 January 2010 (SI 2010/22).

The Immigration Services Commissioner

83. The Commissioner

(1) There is to be an Immigration Services Commissioner (referred to in this Part as 'the Commissioner').

(2) The Commissioner is to be appointed by the Secretary of State after consulting the Lord Chancellor and the Scottish Ministers.

(3) It is to be the general duty of the Commissioner to promote good practice by those who provide immigration advice or immigration services.

(4) In addition to any other functions conferred on him by this Part, the Commissioner is to have the regulatory functions set out in Part I of Schedule 5.

(5) The Commissioner must exercise his functions so as to secure, so far as is reasonably practicable, that those who provide immigration advice or immigration services—

(a) are fit and competent to do so;

(b) act in the best interests of their clients;

(c) do not knowingly mislead any court, tribunal or adjudicator in the United Kingdom;

(d) do not seek to abuse any procedure operating in the United Kingdom in connection with immigration or asylum (including any appellate or other judicial procedure);

(e) do not advise any person to do something which would amount to such an abuse.

(6) The Commissioner—

(a) must arrange for the publication, in such form and manner and to such extent as he considers appropriate, of information about his functions and about matters falling within the scope of his functions; and

(b) may give advice about his functions and about such matters.

[(**6A**) The duties imposed on the Commissioner by subsections (3) and (5) apply in relation to persons within section 84(2)(ba) only to the extent that those duties have effect in relation to the Commissioner's functions under section 92 or 92A.]

(7) Part II of Schedule 5 makes further provision with respect to the Commissioner.

Note: Section 83(4) and (5) commenced 22 May 2000 for the purposes of Sch 5, and 30 October 2000 (SI 2000/1985). Subsection (6A) inserted by Sch 18 Legal Services Act 2007 from 1 April 2011 (SI 2011/720).

The general prohibition

84. Provision of immigration services

(1) No person may provide immigration advice or immigration services unless he is a qualified person.

[(2) A person is a qualified person if he is—

(a) a registered person,

(b) authorised by a designated professional body to practise as a member of the profession whose members the body regulates,

[(ba) a person authorised to provide immigration advice or immigration services by a designated qualifying regulator,]

(c) the equivalent in an EEA State of—

(i) a registered person, or

(ii) a person within paragraph (b) [or (ba)],

(d) a person permitted, by virtue of exemption from a prohibition, to provide in an EEA State advice or services equivalent to immigration advice or services, or

(e) acting on behalf of, and under the supervision of, a person within any of paragraphs (a) to (d) (whether or not under a contract of employment).

(3) Subsection (2)(a) and (e) are subject to

[(a)] any limitation on the effect of a person's registration imposed under paragraph 2(2) of Schedule 6.]

[(b) paragraph 4B(5) of that Schedule (effect of suspension of registration).]

[(3A) A person's entitlement to provide immigration advice or immigration services by virtue of subsection (2)(ba)—

(a) is subject to any limitation on that person's authorisation imposed by the regulatory arrangements of the designated qualifying regulator in question, and

(b) does not extend to the provision of such advice or services by the person other than in England and Wales (regardless of whether the persons to whom they are provided are in England and Wales or elsewhere).

(3B) In subsection (3A) 'regulatory arrangements' has the same meaning as in the Legal Services Act 2007 (see section 21 of that Act).]

(4) Subsection (1) does not apply to a person who—

(a) . . .

(b) . . .

(c) . . .

(d) . . . falls within a category of person specified in an order made by the Secretary of State for the purposes of this subsection.

(5) . . .

(6) Subsection (1) does not apply to a person—

(a) holding an office under the Crown, when acting in that capacity;

(b) employed by, or for the purposes of, a government department, when acting in that capacity;

(c) acting under the control of a government department; or

(d) otherwise exercising functions on behalf of the Crown.

(7) . . .

Note: Subsections (4)(a) and (d), (5) and (7) commenced 30 October 2000 (SI 2000/1985), remainder on 30 April 2001 (SI 2001/1394). Subsections (2) and (3) substituted by Asylum and

Immigration (Treatment of Claimants etc.) Act 2004, s 37 from 1 October 2004 (SI 2004/2523). Subsections (2)(ba), (3A) and (3B) and words in square brackets in subsection (2)(c)(ii) inserted by Sch 18 Legal Services Act 2007 from 1 April 2011 (SI 2011/720). Words omitted from subs-s (4) and subs-ss (5) and (7) omitted; subs-s (3)(b) inserted by Sch 7 Immigration Act 2014 from 17 November 2014 (SI 2014/2771).

85. Registration and exemption by the Commissioner

(1) The Commissioner must prepare and maintain a register for the purposes of section 84(2)(a) . . .

(2) . . .

(3) Schedule 6 makes further provision with respect to registration.

Note: Subsection (3) commenced 1 August 2000, remainder 30 October 2000 (SI 2000/1985). Words omitted from subsection (1) by Asylum and Immigration (Treatment of Claimants etc.) Act 2004, s 37 from 1 October 2004 (SI 2004/2523). Subsection (2) omitted by Sch 7 Immigration Act 2014 from a date to be appointed.

86. Designated professional bodies

(1) 'Designated professional body' means—

(a) The Law Society;

(b) The Law Society of Scotland;

(c) The Law Society of Northern Ireland;

(d) . . .

(e) . . .

(f) The Faculty of Advocates; or

(g) The General Council of the Bar of Northern Ireland.

[(2) The Secretary of State may by order remove a body from the list in subsection (1) if he considers that the body—

(a) has failed to provide effective regulation of its members in their provision of immigration advice or immigration services, or

(b) has failed to comply with a request of the Commissioner for the provision of information (whether general or in relation to a particular case or matter).]

(3) If a designated professional body asks the Secretary of State to amend subsection (1) so as to remove its name, the Secretary of State may by order do so.

(4) If the Secretary of State is proposing to act under subsection (2) he must, before doing so—

(a) consult the Commissioner;

(b) . . .

(c) consult the [Scottish Legal Complaints Commission], if the proposed order would affect a designated professional body in Scotland;

(d) consult the lay observers appointed under Article 42 of the Solicitors (Northern Ireland) Order 1976, if the proposed order would affect a designated professional body in Northern Ireland;

(e) notify the body concerned of his proposal and give it a reasonable period within which to make representations; and

(f) consider any representations so made.

(5) An order under subsection (2) requires the approval of—

(a) the Lord Chancellor, if it affects a designated professional body in . . . Northern Ireland;

(b) the Scottish Ministers, if it affects a designated professional body in Scotland.

(6) Before deciding whether or not to give his approval under subsection (5)(a), the Lord Chancellor must consult—

(a) . . .

(b) the Lord Chief Justice of Northern Ireland, if [the order] affects a designated professional body in Northern Ireland.

(7) Before deciding whether or not to give their approval under subsection (5)(b), the Scottish Ministers must consult the Lord President of the Court of Session.

(8) If the Secretary of State considers that a body [(other than a body in England and Wales)] which—

(a) is concerned (whether wholly or in part) with regulating the legal profession, or a branch of it, in an EEA State,

(b) is not a designated professional body, and

(c) is capable of providing effective regulation of its members in their provision of immigration advice or immigration services, ought to be designated, he may by order amend subsection (1) to include the name of that body.

(9) The Commissioner must—

(a) keep under review the list of designated professional bodies set out in subsection (1); and

[(b) report to the Secretary of State if the Commissioner considers that a designated professional body—

(i) is failing to provide effective regulation of its members in their provision of immigration advice or immigration services, or

(ii) has failed to comply with a request of the Commissioner for the provision of information (whether general or in relation to a particular case or matter).]

[(9A) A designated professional body shall comply with a request of the Commissioner for the provision of information (whether general or in relation to a specified case or matter).]

(10) For the purpose of meeting the costs incurred by the Commissioner in discharging his functions under this Part, each designated professional body must pay to the Commissioner, in each year and on such date as may be specified, such fee as may be specified.

(11) Any unpaid fee for which a designated professional body is liable under subsection (10) may be recovered from that body as a debt due to the Commissioner.

(12) 'Specified' means specified by an order made by the Secretary of State.

Note: Subsections (1)–(9) commenced 22 May 2000 (SI 2000/1282), remainder 30 October 2000 (SI 2000/1985). Words in square brackets substituted by Asylum and Immigration (Treatment of Claimants etc.) Act 2004, s 41 from 1 October 2004 (SI 2004/2523). Words in square brackets in subsection (4)(c) substituted by s 196 Legal Services Act 2007 from 1 October 2008 (SI 2008/1436). Subsections (1)(a), (d) and (e), (4)(b) and (6)(a) omitted and words in subsection (5)(a) omitted and words in subsection (6)(b) substituted by Schs 18 and 23 Legal Services Act 2007 from 1 April 2011 (SI 2011/720).

[86A. Designated qualifying regulators

(1) 'Designated qualifying regulator' means a body which is a qualifying regulator and is listed in subsection (2).

(2) The listed bodies are—

(a) the Law Society;

(b) the Institute of Legal Executives;

(c) the General Council of the Bar.

(3) The Secretary of State may by order remove a body from the list in subsection (2) if the Secretary of State considers that the body has failed to provide effective regulation of relevant authorised persons in their provision of immigration advice or immigration services.

(4) If a designated qualifying regulator asks the Secretary of State to amend subsection (2) so as to remove its name, the Secretary of State may by order do so.

(5) Where, at a time when a body is listed in subsection (2), the body ceases to be a qualifying regulator by virtue of paragraph 8(1)(a) of Schedule 18 to the Legal Services Act 2007 (loss of approved regulator status), the Secretary of State must, by order, remove it from the list.

(6) If the Secretary of State considers that a body which—

(a) is a qualifying regulator,

(b) is not a designated qualifying regulator, and

(c) is capable of providing effective regulation of relevant authorised persons in their provision of immigration advice or immigration services, ought to be designated, the Secretary of State may, by order, amend the list in subsection (2) to include the name of that body.

(7) If the Secretary of State is proposing to act under subsection (3) or (6), the Secretary of State must, before doing so, consult the Commissioner.

(8) If the Secretary of State is proposing to act under subsection (3), the Secretary of State must, before doing so, also —

(a) notify the body concerned of the proposal and give it a reasonable period within which to make representations, and

(b) consider any representations duly made.

(9) An order under subsection (3) or (6) requires the approval of the Lord Chancellor.

(10) If the Legal Services Board considers that a designated qualifying regulator is failing to provide effective regulation of relevant authorised persons in their provision of immigration advice or immigration services, the Legal Services Board must make a report to this effect to—

(a) the Secretary of State, and

(b) the Lord Chancellor.

(11) In this section—

'qualifying regulator' means a body which is a qualifying regulator for the purposes of this Part of this Act by virtue of Part 1 of Schedule 18 to the Legal Services Act 2007 (approved regulators approved by the Legal Services Board in relation to immigration matters);

'relevant authorised persons', in relation to a designated qualifying regulator, means persons who are authorised by the designated qualifying regulator to provide immigration advice or immigration services.]

Note: Section 86A inserted by Sch 18 Legal Services Act 2007 from 1 April 2011 (SI 2011/720).

[Appeals to the First-tier Tribunal]

87. [Appeals to the First-tier Tribunal]

(1) . . .

(2) Any person aggrieved by a relevant decision of the Commissioner may appeal to the [First-tier Tribunal] against the decision.

(3) 'Relevant decision' means a decision—

(a) to refuse an application for registration made under paragraph 1 of Schedule 6;

(b) . . .

(c) under paragraph 2(2) of that Schedule to register with limited effect;

(d) to refuse an application for continued registration made under paragraph 3 of that Schedule;

(e) to vary a registration on an application under paragraph 3 of that Schedule;

[(ea) to vary a registration under paragraph 3A of that Schedule;] or

[(eb) to cancel a registration under paragraph 4A(e) of that Schedule.]

(f) . . .

[(3A) A relevant decision of the Commissioner is not to have effect while the period within which an appeal may be brought against the decision is running.

(3B) In the case of an appeal under this section, Tribunal Procedure Rules may include provision permitting the First-tier Tribunal to direct that while the appeal is being dealt with—

(a) no effect is to be given to the decision appealed against; or

(b) only such limited effect is to be given to it as may be specified in the direction.

(3C) If provision is made in Tribunal Procedure Rules by virtue of subsection (3B), the rules must also include provision requiring the First-tier Tribunal to consider applications by the Commissioner for the cancellation or variation of directions given by virtue of that subsection;]

[(4) For [further functions] of the First-tier Tribunal under this Part, see paragraph 9(1)(e) of Schedule 5 (disciplinary charges laid by the Commissioner) [and paragraph 4B of Schedule 6 (suspension of registration by First-tier Tribunal)].]

(5) . . .

Note: Subsection (5) commenced 1 August 2000, remainder 30 October 2000 (SI 2000/1985). Words in square brackets inserted by Nationality, Immigration and Asylum Act 2002, s 140 from 8 January 2003 (SI 2003/1). Heading, words in square brackets in subsection (2) and subsection (4) substituted; subsections (3A)–(3C) inserted and subsections (1) and (5) revoked from 18 January 2010 (SI 2010/22). Subsection (3)(b) omitted and (3)(eb) inserted; by Sch 7 Immigration Act 2014 from 17 November 2014 (SI 2014/2771). First words in square brackets in subs-s (4) substituted and last words inserted by Sch 7 Immigration Act 2014 from 17 November 2014 (SI 2014/2771).

88. Appeal upheld by the [First-tier Tribunal]

(1) This section applies if the [First-tier Tribunal] allows an appeal under section 87.

(2) If the [First-tier Tribunal] considers it appropriate, it may direct the Commissioner—

(a) to register the applicant or to continue the applicant's registration;

(b) to make or vary the applicant's registration so as to have limited effect in any of the ways mentioned in paragraph 2(2) of Schedule 6;

(c) . . . or

(d) to quash a decision recorded under paragraph 9(1)(a) of Schedule 5 and the record of that decision.

Note: Commenced 30 October 2000 (SI 2000/1985). Words in square brackets substituted from 18 January 2010 (SI 2010/22). Subsection (2)(c) omitted by Sch 7 Immigration Act 2014 from a date to be appointed.

89. Disciplinary charge upheld by the [First-tier Tribunal]

(1) This section applies if the [First-tier Tribunal] upholds a disciplinary charge laid by the Commissioner under paragraph 9(1)(e) of Schedule 5 against a person ('the person charged').

[(2) Subsections (2A) and (2B) apply if the person charged was, at the time to which the charge relates, a registered person or a person acting on behalf of a registered person.

(2A) If the registered person mentioned in subsection (2) is still registered, the First-tier Tribunal may direct the Commissioner—

(a) to record the charge and the First-tier Tribunal's decision on it for consideration in connection with that person's next application for continued registration;

(b) to cancel that person's registration.

(2B) If the registered person mentioned in subsection (2) is no longer registered, the First-tier Tribunal may direct the Commissioner to record the charge and the First-tier Tribunal's decision on it for consideration in connection with any application by that person for registration.]

(4) . . . .

(5) If the person charged is found to have charged unreasonable fees for immigration advice or immigration services, the [First-tier Tribunal] may direct him to repay to the clients concerned such portion of those fees as it may determine.

(6) The [First-tier Tribunal] may direct the person charged to pay a penalty to the Commissioner of such sum as it considers appropriate.

(7) A direction given by the [First-tier Tribunal] under subsection (5) (or under subsection (6) may be enforced by the clients concerned (or by the Commissioner)—

(a) as if it were an order of a county court [in Northern Ireland or the county court in England and Wales]; or

(b) in Scotland, as if it were an extract registered decree arbitral bearing a warrant for execution issued by the sheriff court of any sheriffdom in Scotland.

(8) The [First-tier Tribunal] may direct that the person charged or any person [acting on his behalf or] under his supervision is to be—

(a) subject to such restrictions on the provision of immigration advice or immigration services as the [First-tier Tribunal] considers appropriate;

(b) suspended from providing immigration advice or immigration services for such period as the [First-tier Tribunal] may determine; or

(c) prohibited from providing immigration advice or immigration services indefinitely.

(9) The Commissioner must keep a record of the persons against whom there is in force a direction given by the [First-tier Tribunal] under subsection (8).

Note: Commenced 30 October 2000 (SI 2000/1985). 'First-tier Tribunal' substituted from 18 January 2010 (SI 2010/22). Subsection (2) substituted and subs-s (4) omitted by Sch 7 Immigration Act 2014 from 17 November 2014 (SI 2014/2771). Words in square brackets in subsection (7)(a) inserted by Sch 9 Crime and Courts Act 2013 from a date to be appointed.

90. Orders by disciplinary bodies

(1) A disciplinary body may make an order directing that a person subject to its jurisdiction is to be—

(a) subject to such restrictions on the provision of immigration advice or immigration services as the body considers appropriate;

(b) suspended from providing immigration advice or immigration services for such period as the body may determine; or

(c) prohibited from providing immigration advice or immigration services indefinitely.

(2) 'Disciplinary body' means any body—

[(a) appearing to the Secretary of State to be established for the purpose of hearing disciplinary charges against—

(i) members of a designated professional body, or

(ii) persons regulated by designated qualifying regulators; and]

(b) specified in an order made by the Secretary of State.

(3) The Secretary of State must consult the designated professional body [or designated qualifying regulator] concerned before making an order under subsection (2)(b).

(4) For the purposes of this section, a person is subject to the jurisdiction of a disciplinary body if he is an authorised person or [acting on his behalf or] an authorised person.

(5) 'Authorised person' means [—

(a)] , a person who is authorised by the designated professional body concerned to practise as a member of the profession whose members are regulated by that body [, or

(b) a person who is authorised by the designated qualifying regulator concerned to provide immigration advice or immigration services.]

Note: Commenced 1 August 2000 (SI 2000/1985). Words in square brackets in subsection (4) substituted by Asylum and Immigration (Treatment of Claimants etc.) Act 2004, s 37 from 1 October 2004 (SI 2004/2523). Others words in square brackets inserted and substituted by Sch 18 Legal Services Act 2007 from a date to be appointed.

Enforcement

91. Offences

(1) A person who provides immigration advice or immigration services in contravention of section 84 or of a restraining order is guilty of an offence and liable—

(a) on summary conviction, to imprisonment for a term not exceeding six months or to a fine not exceeding the statutory maximum, or to both; or

(b) on conviction on indictment, to imprisonment for a term not exceeding two years or to a fine, or to both.

(2) 'Restraining order' means—

(a) a direction given by the [First-tier Tribunal] under section 89(8) or paragraph 9(3) of Schedule 5; or

(b) an order made by a disciplinary body under section 90(1).

(3) If an offence under this section committed by a body corporate is proved—

(a) to have been committed with the consent or connivance of an officer, or

(b) to be attributable to neglect on his part, the officer as well as the body corporate is guilty of the offence and liable to be proceeded against and punished accordingly.

(4) 'Officer', in relation to a body corporate, means a director, manager, secretary or other similar officer of the body, or a person purporting to act in such a capacity.

(5) If the affairs of a body corporate are managed by its members, subsection (3) applies in relation to the acts and defaults of a member in connection with his functions of management as if he were a director of the body corporate.

(6) If an offence under this section committed by a partnership in Scotland is proved—

(a) to have been committed with the consent or connivance of a partner, or

(b) to be attributable to neglect on his part, the partner as well as the partnership is guilty of the offence and liable to be proceeded against and punished accordingly.

(7) 'Partner' includes a person purporting to act as a partner.

Note: Commenced 30 April 2001 (SI 2001/1394). Words in square brackets in subsection (2) substituted from 18 January 2010 (SI 2010/22).

92. Enforcement

(1) If it appears to the Commissioner that a person—

(a) is providing immigration advice or immigration services in contravention of section 84 or of a restraining order, and

(b) is likely to continue to do so unless restrained, the Commissioner may apply to a county court [in Northern Ireland or the county court in England and Wales] for an injunction, or to the sheriff for an interdict, restraining him from doing so.

(2) If the court is satisfied that the application is well-founded, it may grant the injunction or interdict in the terms applied for or in more limited terms.

(3) 'Restraining order' has the meaning given by section 91.

Note: Commenced 30 April 2001 (SI 2001/1394). Words in square brackets in subsection (1)(b) inserted by Sch 9 Crime and Courts Act 2013 from a date to be appointed.

[92A. Investigation of offence: power of entry

(1) On an application made by the Commissioner a justice of the peace may issue a warrant authorising the Commissioner to enter and search premises.

(2) A justice of the peace may issue a warrant in respect of premises only if satisfied that there are reasonable grounds for believing that—

(a) an offence under section 91 has been committed,

(b) there is material on the premises which is likely to be of substantial value (whether by itself or together with other material) to the investigation of the offence, and

(c) any of the conditions specified in subsection (3) is satisfied.

(3) Those conditions are—

(a) that it is not practicable to communicate with a person entitled to grant entry to the premises,

(b) that it is not practicable to communicate with a person entitled to grant access to the evidence,

(c) that entry to the premises will be prevented unless a warrant is produced, and

(d) that the purpose of a search may be frustrated or seriously prejudiced unless the Commissioner can secure immediate entry on arrival at the premises.

(4) The Commissioner may seize and retain anything for which a search is authorised under this section.

(5) A person commits an offence if without reasonable excuse he obstructs the Commissioner in the exercise of a power by virtue of this section.

(6) A person guilty of an offence under subsection (5) shall be liable on summary conviction to—

(a) imprisonment for a term not exceeding six months,

(b) a fine not exceeding level 5 on the standard scale, or

(c) both.

(7) In this section—

(a) a reference to the Commissioner includes a reference to a member of his staff authorised in writing by him,

(b) a reference to premises includes a reference to premises used wholly or partly as a dwelling, and

(c) a reference to material—

(i) includes material subject to legal privilege within the meaning of the Police and Criminal Evidence Act 1984 (c. 60),

(ii) does not include excluded material or special procedure material,

(iii) includes material whether or not it would be admissible in evidence at a trial.

(8) In the application of this section to Scotland—

(a) a reference to a justice of the peace shall be taken as a reference to the sheriff,

(b) for sub-paragraph (i) of subsection (7)(c) there is substituted—

'(i) includes material comprising items subject to legal privilege (as defined by section 412 of the Proceeds of Crime Act 2002 (c. 29)),' and

(c) sub-paragraph (ii) of subsection (7)(c) shall be ignored.

(9) In the application of this section to Northern Ireland the reference to the Police and Criminal Evidence Act 1984 shall be taken as a reference to the Police and Criminal Evidence (Northern Ireland) Order 1989 (S.I. 1989/1341 (N.I. 12)).]

Note: Section 92A inserted by Asylum and Immigration (Treatment of Claimants etc.) Act 2004, s 38 from 1 October 2004 (SI 2004/2523).

[92B. Advertising

(1) A person commits an offence if—

(a) he offers to provide immigration advice or immigration services, and

(b) provision by him of the advice or services would constitute an offence under section 91.

(2) For the purpose of subsection (1) a person offers to provide advice or services if he—

(a) makes an offer to a particular person or class of person,

(b) makes arrangements for an advertisement in which he offers to provide advice or services, or

(c) makes arrangements for an advertisement in which he is described or presented as competent to provide advice or services.

(3) A person guilty of an offence under this section shall be liable on summary conviction to a fine not exceeding level 4 on the standard scale.

(4) Subsections (3) to (7) of section 91 shall have effect for the purposes of this section as they have effect for the purposes of that section.

(5) An information relating to an offence under this section may in England and Wales be tried by a magistrates' court if—

(a) it is laid within the period of six months beginning with the date (or first date) on which the offence is alleged to have been committed, or

(b) it is laid—

(i) within the period of two years beginning with that date, and

(ii) within the period of six months beginning with a date certified by the Immigration Services Commissioner as the date on which the commission of the offence came to his notice.

(6) In Scotland, proceedings for an offence under this section may be commenced—

(a) at any time within the period of six months beginning with the date (or first date) on which the offence is alleged to have been committed, or

(b) at any time within both—

(i) the period of two years beginning with that date, and

(ii) the period of six months beginning with a date specified, in a certificate signed by or on behalf of the procurator fiscal, as the date on which evidence sufficient in his opinion to warrant such proceedings came to his knowledge, any such certificate purporting to be so signed shall be deemed so signed unless the contrary is proved and be conclusive as to the facts stated in it.

(7) Subsection (3) of section 136 of the Criminal Procedure (Scotland) Act 1995 (c. 46) (date on which proceedings are deemed commenced) has effect to the purposes of subsection (6) as it has effect for the purposes of that section.

(8) A complaint charging the commission of an offence under this section may in Northern Ireland be heard and determined by a magistrates' court if—

(a) it is made within the period of six months beginning with the date (or first date) on which the offence is alleged to have been committed, or

(b) it is made—

(i) within the period of two years beginning with that date, and

(ii) within the period of six months beginning with a date certified by the Immigration Services Commissioner as the date on which the commission of the offence came to his notice.]

Note: Section 92B inserted by Asylum and Immigration (Treatment of Claimants etc.) Act 2004, s 39 from 1 October 2004 (SI 2004/2523).

Miscellaneous

93. Information

(1) No enactment or rule of law prohibiting or restricting the disclosure of information prevents a person from—

(a) giving the Commissioner information which is necessary for the discharge of his functions; or

(b) giving the [First-tier Tribunal] information which is necessary for the discharge of its functions.

(2) No relevant person may at any time disclose information which—

(a) has been obtained by, or given to, the Commissioner under or for purposes of this Act,

(b) relates to an identified or identifiable individual or business, and

(c) is not at that time, and has not previously been, available to the public from other sources,

unless the disclosure is made with lawful authority.

(3) For the purposes of subsection (2), a disclosure is made with lawful authority only if, and to the extent that—

(a) it is made with the consent of the individual or of the person for the time being carrying on the business;

(b) it is made for the purposes of, and is necessary for, the discharge of any of the Commissioner's functions under this Act or any [EU] obligation of the Commissioner;

(c) it is made for the purposes of any civil or criminal proceedings arising under or by virtue of this Part, or otherwise; or

(d) having regard to the rights and freedoms or legitimate interests of any person, the disclosure is necessary in the public interest.

(4) A person who knowingly or recklessly discloses information in contravention of subsection (2) is guilty of an offence and liable—

(a) on summary conviction, to a fine not exceeding the statutory maximum; or

(b) on conviction on indictment, to a fine.

(5) 'Relevant person' means a person who is or has been—

(a) the Commissioner;

(b) a member of the Commissioner's staff; or

(c) an agent of the Commissioner.

Note: Commenced 22 May 2000 (SI 2000/1282). Words in square brackets in subsection (1)(b) substituted from 18 January 2010 (SI 2010/22). The term 'EU' substituted from 22 April 2011 (SI 2011/1043).

Part VI

Support for Asylum-Seekers

Interpretation

94. Interpretation of Part VI

(1) In this Part—

[. . .];

['asylum-seeker' means a person—

(a) who is at least 18 years old,

(b) who is in the United Kingdom,

(c) who has made a claim for asylum at a place designated by the Secretary of State,

(d) whose claim has been recorded by the Secretary of State, and

(e) whose claim has not been determined;]

'claim for asylum' means a claim that it would be contrary to the United Kingdom's obligations under the Refugee Convention, or under Article 3 of the Human Rights Convention, for the claimant to be removed from, or required to leave, the United Kingdom;

'the Department' means the Department of Health and Social Services for Northern Ireland;

['dependant' in relation to an asylum-seeker or a supported person means a person who—

(a) is in the United Kingdom, and
(b) is within a prescribed class;]

'the Executive' means the Northern Ireland Housing Executive;

'housing accommodation' includes flats, lodging houses and hostels;

'local authority' means—

(a) in England and Wales, a county council, a county borough council, a district council, a London borough council, the Common Council of the City of London or the Council of the Isles of Scilly;

(b) in Scotland, a council constituted under section 2 of the Local Government etc. (Scotland) Act 1994;

['Northern Ireland authority' has the meaning given by section 110(9).]

'supported person' means—

(a) an asylum-seeker, or
(b) a dependant of an asylum-seeker,

who has applied for support and for whom support is provided under section 95.

(2) References in this Part to support provided under section 95 include references to support which is provided under arrangements made by the Secretary of State under that section.

[(3) A claim for asylum shall be treated as determined for the purposes of subsection (1) at the end of such period as may be prescribed beginning with—

(a) the date on which the Secretary of State notifies the claimant of his decision on the claim, or

(b) if the claimant appeals against the Secretary of State's decision, the date on which the appeal is disposed of.

(3A) A person shall continue to be treated as an asylum-seeker despite paragraph (e) of the definition of 'asylum-seeker' in subsection (1) while—

(a) his household includes a dependant child who is under 18, and
(b) he does not have leave to enter or remain in the United Kingdom.]

(4) An appeal is disposed of when it is no longer pending for the purposes of the Immigration Acts or the Special Immigration Appeals Commission Act 1997.

(5) . . .

(6) . . .

(7) For the purposes of this Part, the Secretary of State may inquire into, and decide, the age of any person.

(8) A notice under subsection (3) must be given in writing.

(9) If such a notice is sent by the Secretary of State by first class post, addressed—

(a) to the asylum-seeker's representative, or
(b) to the asylum-seeker's last known address,

it is to be taken to have been received by the asylum-seeker on the second day after the day on which it was posted.

Note: Commenced 11 November 1999, s 170. Words in first and second square brackets in subsection (1) substituted by Nationality, Immigration and Asylum Act 2002, s 44 from a date to be appointed and words in third square brackets in subsection (1) inserted by the same Act, s 60 from 10 February 2003 (SI 2003/1). Subsection (3) substituted by and subsection (3A) inserted by and subsections (5) and (6) omitted by Nationality, Immigration and Asylum Act 2002, s 44 from a date to be appointed. Definition of 'asylum-seeker' modified in relation to ss 110 and 111 from 11 November 2002 so as not to exclude persons under 18 (Nationality, Immigration and Asylum Act 2002, s 48). Words omitted in subsection (1) from 3 November 2008 (SI 2008/2833).

Provision of support

95. Persons for whom support may be provided

(1) The Secretary of State may provide, or arrange for the provision of, support for—

(a) asylum-seekers, or

(b) dependants of asylum-seekers, who appear to the Secretary of State to be destitute or to be likely to become destitute within such period as may be prescribed.

[(2) Where a person has dependants, he and his dependants are destitute for the purpose of this section if they do not have and cannot obtain both—

(a) adequate accommodation, and

(b) food and other essential items.

(3) Where a person does not have dependants, he is destitute for the purpose of this section if he does not have and cannot obtain both—

(a) adequate accommodation, and

(b) food and other essential items.

(4) In determining whether accommodation is adequate for the purposes of subsection (2) or (3) the Secretary of State must have regard to any matter prescribed for the purposes of this subsection.

(5) In determining whether accommodation is adequate for the purposes of subsection (2) or (3) the Secretary of State may not have regard to—

(a) whether a person has an enforceable right to occupy accommodation,

(b) whether a person shares all or part of accommodation,

(c) whether accommodation is temporary or permanent,

(d) the location of accommodation, or

(e) any other matter prescribed for the purposes of this subsection.

(6) The Secretary of State may by regulations specify items which are or are not to be treated as essential items for the purposes of subsections (2) and (3).

(7) The Secretary of State may by regulations—

(a) provide that a person is not to be treated as destitute for the purposes of this Part in specified circumstances;

(b) enable or require the Secretary of State in deciding whether a person is destitute to have regard to income which he or a dependant of his might reasonably be expected to have;

(c) enable or require the Secretary of State in deciding whether a person is destitute to have regard to support which is or might reasonably be expected to be available to the person or a dependant of his;

(d) enable or require the Secretary of State in deciding whether a person is destitute to have regard to assets of a prescribed kind which he or a dependant of his has or might reasonably be expected to have;

(e) make provision as to the valuation of assets.]

(9) Support may be provided subject to conditions.

[(9A) A condition imposed under subsection (9) may, in particular, relate to—

(a) any matter relating to the use of the support provided, or

(b) compliance with a restriction imposed under paragraph 21 of Schedule 2 to the 1971 Act (temporary admission or release from detention) or paragraph 2 or 5 of Schedule 3 to that Act (restriction pending deportation).]

(10) The conditions must be set out in writing.

(11) A copy of the conditions must be given to the supported person.

(12) Schedule 8 gives the Secretary of State power to make regulations supplementing this section.

(13) Schedule 9 makes temporary provision for support in the period before the coming into force of this section.

Note: Commenced in part 11 November 1999 and 6 December 1999, remainder 1 January 2000 (SI 1999/3190). Subsections (2)–(8) substituted by Nationality, Immigration and Asylum Act 2002, s 44 from a date to be appointed and subsection 9A inserted by Nationality, Immigration and Asylum Act 2002, s 50 from 7 November 2002.

96. Ways in which support may be provided

(1) Support may be provided under section 95—

(a) by providing accommodation appearing to the Secretary of State to be adequate for the needs of the supported person and his dependants (if any);

[(b) by providing the supported person and his dependants (if any) with food or other essential items;]

(c) to enable the supported person (if he is the asylum-seeker) to meet what appear to the Secretary of State to be expenses (other than legal expenses or other expenses of a prescribed description) incurred in connection with his claim for asylum;

(d) to enable the asylum-seeker and his dependants to attend bail proceedings in connection with his detention under any provision of the Immigration Acts; or

(e) to enable the asylum-seeker and his dependants to attend bail proceedings in connection with the detention of a dependant of his under any such provision.

(2) If the Secretary of State considers that the circumstances of a particular case are exceptional, he may provide support under section 95 in such other ways as he considers necessary to enable the supported person and his dependants (if any) to be supported.

(3) . . .

(4) . . .

(5) . . .

(6) . . .

Note: Commenced 3 April 2000 (SI 2000/464). Subsection 1(b) substituted by Nationality, Immigration and Asylum Act 2002, s 45 from a date to be appointed. Subsection (3) repealed from 8 April 2002 (SI 2002/782). Subsections (4)–(6) repealed by the same Act, s 61 from 7 November 2002.

97. Supplemental

(1) When exercising his power under section 95 to provide accommodation, the Secretary of State must have regard to—

(a) the fact that the accommodation is to be temporary pending determination of the asylum-seeker's claim;

(b) the desirability, in general, of providing accommodation in areas in which there is a ready supply of accommodation; and

(c) such other matters (if any) as may be prescribed.

(2) But he may not have regard to—

(a) any preference that the supported person or his dependants (if any) may have as to the locality in which the accommodation is to be provided; or

(b) such other matters (if any) as may be prescribed.

(3) The Secretary of State may by order repeal all or any of the following—

(a) subsection (1)(a);

(b) subsection (1)(b);

(c) subsection (2)(a).

(4) When exercising his power under section 95 to provide [food and other essential items], the Secretary of State—

(a) must have regard to such matters as may be prescribed for the purposes of this paragraph; but

(b) may not have regard to such other matters as may be prescribed for the purposes of this paragraph.

(5) In addition, when exercising his power under section 95 to provide [food and other essential items], the Secretary of State may limit the overall amount of the expenditure which he incurs in connection with a particular supported person—

(za) to such portion of the maximum amount of an award of universal credit under section 8(1) of the Welfare Reform Act 2012, or]

(a) . . .

(b) to such portion of any components [or elements] of that amount, as he considers appropriate having regard to the temporary nature of the support that he is providing.

(6) For the purposes of subsection (5), any support of a kind falling within section 96(1)(c) is to be treated as if it were the provision of essential [items].

(7) In determining how to provide, or arrange for the provision of, support under section 95, the Secretary of State may disregard any preference which the supported person or his dependants (if any) may have as to the way in which the support is to be given.

Note: Commenced for the purposes of enabling subordinate legislation 1 January 2000 (SI 1999/3190), remainder 3 April 2000 (SI 2000/464). Words in square brackets in subsection (4) and (5) substituted by s 45 Nationality, Immigration and Asylum Act 2002 from a date to be appointed. Subsection (5)(za) and words in square brackets in s (5)(b) inserted by Sch 2 Welfare Reform Act from 29 April 2013 (SI 2013/983). Subsection (5)(a) omitted by Sch 14 Welfare Reform Act 2012 from a date to be appointed.

98. Temporary support

(1) The Secretary of State may provide, or arrange for the provision of, support for—

(a) asylum-seekers, or

(b) dependants of asylum-seekers, who it appears to the Secretary of State may be destitute.

(2) Support may be provided under this section only until the Secretary of State is able to determine whether support may be provided under section 95.

(3) Subsections (2) to (11) of section 95 apply for the purposes of this section as they apply for the purposes of that section.

Note: Subsection (3) commenced for the purposes of enabling subordinate legislation 1 March 2000, remainder 3 April 2000 (SI 2000/464).

Support and assistance by local authorities etc.

99. Provision of support by local authorities

(1) A local authority [or Northern Ireland authority] may provide support for [persons] in accordance with arrangements made by the Secretary of State under section [4,] 95 [or 98].

(2) Support may be provided by an authority in accordance with arrangements made with the authority or with another person.

(3) Support may be provided by an authority in accordance with arrangements made under section 95 only in one or more of the ways mentioned in section 96(1) and (2).

(4) [An authority] may incur reasonable expenditure in connection with the preparation of proposals for entering into arrangements under section [4,] 95 [or 98].

(5) The powers conferred on [an authority] by this section include power to—
- (a) provide services outside their area;
- (b) provide services jointly with one or more [other bodies];
- (c) form a company for the purpose of providing services;
- (d) tender for contracts (whether alone or with any other person).

Note: Subsections (1)–(3) commenced 3 April 2000 (SI 2000/464). Subsections (4) and (5) commenced 11 November 1999, s 170. Words in second and third square brackets in subsection (1) and second square brackets in subsection (4) substituted by Immigration, Nationality and Asylum Act 2006, s 43 from 16 June 2006 (SI 2006/1497). Subsections (2) and (3) substituted by and other words in square brackets substituted by Nationality, Immigration and Asylum Act 2002, s 56 from 7 November 2002.

100. Local authority and other assistance for Secretary of State

(1) This section applies if the Secretary of State asks—
- (a) a local authority,
- [(aa) a private registered provider of social housing,]
- (b) a registered social landlord,
- (c) a registered housing association in Scotland or Northern Ireland, or
- (d) the Executive, to assist him to exercise his power under section 95 to provide accommodation.

(2) The person to whom the request is made must cooperate in giving the Secretary of State such assistance in the exercise of that power as is reasonable in the circumstances.

(3) Subsection (2) does not require [a private registered provider of social housing, or] a registered social landlord to act beyond its powers.

(4) A local authority must supply to the Secretary of State such information about their housing accommodation (whether or not occupied) as he may from time to time request.

(5) The information must be provided in such form and manner as the Secretary of State may direct.

(6) 'Registered social landlord' has the same meaning as in Part I of the Housing Act 1996.

(7) 'Registered housing association' has the same meaning—

(a) in relation to Scotland, as in the Housing Associations Act 1985; and

(b) in relation to Northern Ireland, as in Part II of the Housing (Northern Ireland) Order 1992.

Note: Commenced 3 April 2000 (SI 2000/464). Words in square brackets inserted by SI 2010/866 from 1 April 2010.

101. Reception zones

(1) The Secretary of State may by order designate as reception zones—

(a) areas in England and Wales consisting of the areas of one or more local authorities;

(b) areas in Scotland consisting of the areas of one or more local authorities;

(c) Northern Ireland.

(2) Subsection (3) applies if the Secretary of State considers that—

(a) a local authority whose area is within a reception zone has suitable housing accommodation within that zone; or

(b) the Executive has suitable housing accommodation.

(3) The Secretary of State may direct the local authority or the Executive to make available such of the accommodation as may be specified in the direction for a period so specified—

(a) to him for the purpose of providing support under section 95; or

(b) to a person with whom the Secretary of State has made arrangements under section 95.

(4) A period specified in a direction under subsection (3)—

(a) begins on a date so specified; and

(b) must not exceed five years.

(5) A direction under subsection (3) is enforceable, on an application made on behalf of the Secretary of State, by injunction or in Scotland an order under section 45(b) of the Court of Session Act 1988.

(6) The Secretary of State's power to give a direction under subsection (3) in respect of a particular reception zone must be exercised by reference to criteria specified for the purposes of this subsection in the order designating that zone.

(7) The Secretary of State may not give a direction under subsection (3) in respect of a local authority in Scotland unless the Scottish Ministers have confirmed to him that the criteria specified in the designation order concerned are in their opinion met in relation to that authority.

(8) Housing accommodation is suitable for the purposes of subsection (2) if it—

(a) is unoccupied;

(b) would be likely to remain unoccupied for the foreseeable future if not made available; and

(c) is appropriate for the accommodation of persons supported under this Part or capable of being made so with minor work.

(9) If housing accommodation for which a direction under this section is, for the time being, in force—

(a) is not appropriate for the accommodation of persons supported under this Part, but

(b) is capable of being made so with minor work, the direction may require the body to whom it is given to secure that that work is done without delay.

(10) The Secretary of State must make regulations with respect to the general management of any housing accommodation for which a direction under subsection (3) is, for the time being, in force.

(11) Regulations under subsection (10) must include provision—

(a) as to the method to be used in determining the amount of rent or other charges to be payable in relation to the accommodation;

(b) as to the times at which payments of rent or other charges are to be made;

(c) as to the responsibility for maintenance of, and repairs to, the accommodation;

(d) enabling the accommodation to be inspected, in such circumstances as may be prescribed, by the body to which the direction was given;

(e) with respect to the condition in which the accommodation is to be returned when the direction ceases to have effect.

(12) Regulations under subsection (10) may, in particular, include provision—

(a) for the cost, or part of the cost, of minor work required by a direction under this section to be met by the Secretary of State in prescribed circumstances;

(b) as to the maximum amount of expenditure which a body may be required to incur as a result of a direction under this section.

(13) The Secretary of State must by regulations make provision ('the dispute resolution procedure') for resolving disputes arising in connection with the operation of any regulations made under subsection (10).

(14) Regulations under subsection (13) must include provision—

(a) requiring a dispute to be resolved in accordance with the dispute resolution procedure;

(b) requiring the parties to a dispute to comply with obligations imposed on them by the procedure; and

(c) for the decision of the person resolving a dispute in accordance with the procedure to be final and binding on the parties.

(15) Before—

(a) designating a reception zone in Great Britain,

(b) determining the criteria to be included in the order designating the zone, or

(c) making regulations under subsection (13),

the Secretary of State must consult such local authorities, local authority associations and other persons as he thinks appropriate.

(16) Before—

(a) designating Northern Ireland as a reception zone, or

(b) determining the criteria to be included in the order designating Northern Ireland,

the Secretary of State must consult the Executive and such other persons as he thinks appropriate.

(17) Before making regulations under subsection (10) which extend only to Northern Ireland, the Secretary of State must consult the Executive and such other persons as he thinks appropriate.

(18) Before making any other regulations under subsection (10), the Secretary of State must consult—

(a) such local authorities, local authority associations and other persons as he thinks appropriate; and

(b) if the regulations extend to Northern Ireland, the Executive.

Note: Commenced 3 April 2000 (SI 2000/464).

Appeals

102. . . .

Note: Commenced 3 April 2000 (SI 2000/464). Revoked from 3 November 2008 (SI 2008/2833).

[103. Appeals: general

[(1) This section applies where a person has applied for support under all or any of the following provisions—

(a) section 4,

(b) section 95, and

(c) section 17 of the Nationality, Immigration and Asylum Act 2002]

(2) The person may appeal to [the First-tier Tribunal] against a decision that the person is not qualified to receive the support for which he has applied.

(3) The person may also appeal to [the First-tier Tribunal] against a decision to stop providing support under a provision mentioned in subsection (1).

(4) But subsection (3) does not apply—

(a) to a decision to stop providing support under one of the provisions mentioned in subsection (1) if it is to be replaced immediately by support under [another of those provisions], or

(b) to a decision taken on the ground that the person is no longer an asylum-seeker or the dependant of an asylum-seeker.

(5) On an appeal under this section [the First-tier Tribunal] may—

(a) require the Secretary of State to reconsider a matter;

(b) substitute [its] decision for the decision against which the appeal is brought;

(c) dismiss the appeal.

(6) . . .

(7) If an appeal under this section is dismissed the Secretary of State shall not consider any further application by the appellant for support under a provision mentioned in [subsection (1)] unless the Secretary of State thinks there has been a material change in circumstances.

(8) An appeal under this section may not be brought or continued by a person who is outside the United Kingdom.]

Note: Section 103 substituted by Nationality, Immigration and Asylum Act 2002, s 53 from a date to be appointed. Subsection (1) and words in square brackets in subsection (7) substituted by Asylum and Immigration (Treatment of Claimants etc.) Act 2004, s 10 from 31 March 2005 (SI 2005/372). Other words in square brackets substituted from 3 November 2008 (SI 2008/2833).

[103A. Appeals: location of support under [section 4 or 95]

(1) The Secretary of State may by regulations provide for a decision as to where support provided under [section 4 or 95] is to be provided to be appealable to [the First-tier Tribunal] under this Part.

(2) Regulations under this section may provide for a provision of section 103 to have effect in relation to an appeal under the regulations with specified modifications.

Note: Section 103A inserted by Nationality, Immigration and Asylum Act 2002, s 53 from a date to be appointed. Words in first square brackets inserted by Asylum and Immigration (Treatment of Claimants etc.) Act 2004, s 10 from 31 March 2005 (SI 2005/372). Other words in square brackets substituted from 3 November 2008 (SI 2008/2833).

103B. Appeals: travelling expenses

The Secretary of State may pay reasonable travelling expenses incurred by an appellant in connection with attendance for the purposes of an appeal under or by virtue of section 103 or 103A.]

Note: Section 103B inserted by Nationality, Immigration and Asylum Act 2002, s 53 from a date to be appointed.

104. . . .

Note: Commenced 1 January 2000 (SI 1999/3190). Revoked from 3 November 2008 (SI 2008/2833).

Offences

105. False representations

(1) A person is guilty of an offence if, with a view to obtaining support for himself or any other person under any provision made by or under this Part, he—

(a) makes a statement or representation which he knows is false in a material particular;

(b) produces or gives to a person exercising functions under this Part, or knowingly causes or allows to be produced or given to such a person, any document or information which he knows is false in a material particular;

(c) fails, without reasonable excuse, to notify a change of circumstances when required to do so in accordance with any provision made by or under this Part; or

(d) without reasonable excuse, knowingly causes another person to fail to notify a change of circumstances which that other person was required to notify in accordance with any provision made by or under this Part.

(2) A person guilty of an offence under this section is liable on summary conviction to imprisonment for a term not exceeding [51 weeks] or to a fine not exceeding level 5 on the standard scale, or to both.

Note: Commenced 11 November 1999, s 170. Words in square brackets in subsection (2) substituted by Sch 26 Criminal Justice Act 2003, from a date to be appointed.

106. Dishonest representations

(1) A person is guilty of an offence if, with a view to obtaining any benefit or other payment or advantage under this Part for himself or any other person, he dishonestly—

(a) makes a statement or representation which is false in a material particular;

(b) produces or gives to a person exercising functions under this Part, or causes or allows to be produced or given to such a person, any document or information which is false in a material particular;

(c) fails to notify a change of circumstances when required to do so in accordance with any provision made by or under this Part; or

(d) causes another person to fail to notify a change of circumstances which that other person was required to notify in accordance with any provision made by or under this Part.

(2) A person guilty of an offence under this section is liable—

(a) on summary conviction, to imprisonment for a term not exceeding six months or to a fine not exceeding the statutory maximum, or to both; or

(b) on conviction on indictment, to imprisonment for a term not exceeding seven years or to a fine, or to both.

(3) In the application of this section to Scotland, in subsection (1) for 'dishonestly' substitute 'knowingly'.

Note: Commenced 11 November 1999, s 170.

107. Delay or obstruction

(1) A person is guilty of an offence if, without reasonable excuse, he—

(a) intentionally delays or obstructs a person exercising functions conferred by or under this Part; or

(b) refuses or neglects to answer a question, give any information or produce a document when required to do so in accordance with any provision made by or under this Part.

(2) A person guilty of an offence under subsection (1) is liable on summary conviction to a fine not exceeding level 3 on the standard scale.

Note: Commenced 11 November 1999, s 170.

108. Failure of sponsor to maintain

(1) A person is guilty of an offence if, during any period in respect of which he has given a written undertaking in pursuance of the immigration rules to be responsible for the maintenance and accommodation of another person—

(a) he persistently refuses or neglects, without reasonable excuse, to maintain that person in accordance with the undertaking; and

(b) in consequence of his refusal or neglect, support under any provision made by or under this Part is provided for or in respect of that person.

(2) A person guilty of an offence under this section is liable on summary conviction to imprisonment for a term not exceeding [51 weeks] or to a fine not exceeding level 4 on the standard scale, or to both.

(3) For the purposes of this section, a person is not to be taken to have refused or neglected to maintain another person by reason only of anything done or omitted in furtherance of a trade dispute.

Note: Commenced 11 November 1999, s 170. Words in square brackets in subsection (2) substituted by Sch 26 Criminal Justice Act 2003, from a date to be appointed.

109. Supplemental

(1) If an offence under section 105, 106, 107 or 108 committed by a body corporate is proved—

(a) to have been committed with the consent or connivance of an officer, or

(b) to be attributable to neglect on his part,

the officer as well as the body corporate is guilty of the offence and liable to be proceeded against and punished accordingly.

(2) 'Officer', in relation to a body corporate, means a director, manager, secretary or other similar officer of the body, or a person purporting to act in such a capacity.

(3) If the affairs of a body corporate are managed by its members, subsection (1) applies in relation to the acts and defaults of a member in connection with his functions of management as if he were a director of the body corporate.

(4) If an offence under section 105, 106, 107 or 108 committed by a partnership in Scotland is proved—

(a) to have been committed with the consent or connivance of a partner, or

(b) to be attributable to neglect on his part,

the partner as well as the partnership is guilty of the offence and liable to be proceeded against and punished accordingly.

(5) 'Partner' includes a person purporting to act as a partner.

Note: Commenced 11 November 1999, s 170.

[109A. Arrest

An immigration officer may arrest without warrant a person whom the immigration officer reasonably suspects has committed an offence under section 105 or 106.]

Note: Section 109A inserted from 31 January 2008 (SI 2008/99).

[109B. Entry, search and seizure

(1) An offence under section 105 or 106 shall be treated as—

(a) a relevant offence for the purposes of sections 28B and 28D of the Immigration Act 1971, and

(b) an offence under Part 3 of that Act (criminal proceedings) for the purposes of sections 28(4), 28E, 28G and 28H (search after arrest, &c.) of that Act.

(2) The following provisions of the Immigration Act 1971 (c. 77) shall have effect in connection with an offence under section 105 or 106 of this Act as they have effect in connection with an offence under that Act—

(a) section 28I (seized material: access and copying),

(b) section 28J (search warrants: safeguards),

(c) section 28K (execution of warrants), and

(d) section 28L(1) (interpretation).]

Note: Section 109B inserted from 31 January 2008 (SI 2008/99).

Expenditure

110. Payments to local authorities

(1) The Secretary of State may from time to time pay to any local authority or Northern Ireland authority such sums as he considers appropriate in respect of expenditure incurred, or to be incurred, by the authority in connection with—

(a) persons who are, or have been, asylum-seekers; and

(b) their dependants.

(2) The Secretary of State may from time to time pay to any—

(a) local authority,

(b) local authority association, or

(c) Northern Ireland authority,

such sums as he considers appropriate in respect of services provided by the authority or association in connection with the discharge of functions under this Part.

(3) The Secretary of State may make payments to any local authority towards the discharge of any liability of supported persons or their dependants in respect of council tax payable to that authority.

(4) The Secretary of State must pay to a body to which a direction under section 101(3) is given such sums as he considers represent the reasonable costs to that body of complying with the direction.

(5) The Secretary of State must pay to a directed body sums determined to be payable in relation to accommodation made available by that body under section 101(3)(a).

(6) The Secretary of State may pay to a directed body sums determined to be payable in relation to accommodation made available by that body under section 101(3)(b).

(7) In subsections (5) and (6)—

'determined' means determined in accordance with regulations made by virtue of subsection (11)(a) of section 101, and

'directed body' means a body to which a direction under subsection (3) of section 101 is given.

(8) Payments under subsection (1), (2) or (3) may be made on such terms, and subject to such conditions, as the Secretary of State may determine.

(9) 'Northern Ireland authority' means—

(a) the Executive; or

(b) a Health and Social Services Board established under Article 16 of the Health and Personal Social Services (Northern Ireland) Order 1972 [; or

(c) a Health and Social Services trust established under the Health and Personal Social Services (Northern Ireland) Order 1991 (S.I. 1991/194 (N.I. 1).]

Note: Subsections (1), (2) and (8) commenced 11 November 1999, s 170, subsection (9) 6 December 1999 (SI 1999/3190), remainder 3 April 2000 (SI 2000/464). Subsection (9)(c) inserted by Nationality, Immigration and Asylum Act 2002, s 60 from 7 November 2002.

111. Grants to voluntary organisations

(1) The Secretary of State may make grants of such amounts as he thinks appropriate to voluntary organisations in connection with—

(a) the provision by them of support (of whatever nature) to persons who are, or have been, asylum-seekers and to their dependants; and

(b) connected matters.

(2) Grants may be made on such terms, and subject to such conditions, as the Secretary of State may determine.

Note: Commenced 11 November 1999, s 170.

112. Recovery of expenditure on support: misrepresentation etc.

(1) This section applies if, on an application made by the Secretary of State, the court determines that—

(a) a person ('A') has misrepresented or failed to disclose a material fact (whether fraudulently or otherwise); and

(b) as a consequence of the misrepresentation or failure, support has been provided under section 95 or 98 (whether or not to A).

(2) If the support was provided by the Secretary of State, the court may order A to pay to the Secretary of State an amount representing the monetary value of the support which would not have been provided but for A's misrepresentation or failure.

(3) If the support was provided by another person ('B') in accordance with arrangements made with the Secretary of State under section 95 or 98, the court may order A to pay to the Secretary of State an amount representing the payment to B which would not have been made but for A's misrepresentation or failure.

(4) 'Court' means a county court [in Northern Ireland or the county court in England and Wales], or, in Scotland, the sheriff.

Note: Commenced 3 April 2000 (SI 2000/464). Words inserted in subsection (4) by Sch 9 Crime and Courts Act 2013 from a date to be appointed.

113. Recovery of expenditure on support from sponsor

(1) This section applies if—

(a) a person ('the sponsor') has given a written undertaking in pursuance of the immigration rules to be responsible for the maintenance and accommodation of another person; and

(b) during any period in relation to which the undertaking applies, support under section 95 is provided to or in respect of that other person.

(2) The Secretary of State may make a complaint against the sponsor to a magistrates' court for an order under this section.

(3) The court—

(a) must have regard to all the circumstances (and in particular to the sponsor's income); and

(b) may order him to pay to the Secretary of State such sum (weekly or otherwise) as it considers appropriate.

(4) But such a sum is not to include any amount attributable otherwise than to support provided under section 95.

(5) In determining—

(a) whether to order any payments to be made in respect of support provided under section 95 for any period before the complaint was made, or

(b) the amount of any such payments, the court must disregard any amount by which the sponsor's current income exceeds his income during that period.

(6) An order under this section is enforceable as a magistrates' court maintenance order within the meaning of section 150(1) of the Magistrates' Courts Act 1980.

(7) In the application of this section to Scotland—

(a) omit subsection (6);

(b) for references to a complaint substitute references to an application; and

(c) for references to a magistrates' court substitute references to the sheriff.

(8) In the application of this section to Northern Ireland, for references to a magistrates' court substitute references to a court of summary jurisdiction and for subsection (6) substitute—

'(6) An order under this section is an order to which Article 98(11) of the Magistrates' Courts (Northern Ireland) Order 1981 applies.'

Note: Commenced 3 April 2000 (SI 2000/464).

114. Overpayments

(1) Subsection (2) applies if, as a result of an error on the part of the Secretary of State, support has been provided to a person under section 95 or 98.

(2) The Secretary of State may recover from a person who is, or has been, a supported person an amount representing the monetary value of support provided to him as a result of the error.

(3) An amount recoverable under subsection (2) may be recovered as if it were a debt due to the Secretary of State.

(4) The Secretary of State may by regulations make provision for other methods of recovery, including deductions from support provided under section 95.

Note: Commenced 1 January 2000 for the purposes of enabling subordinate legislation (SI 1999/3190), otherwise commenced on 3 April 2000 (SI 2000/464).

Exclusions

115. Exclusion from benefits

(1) No person is entitled [to universal credit under Part 1 of the Welfare Reform Act 2012 or] [. . . to state pension credit under the State Pension Credit Act 2002] . . . [or to personal independence payment] or to

(a) attendance allowance,
(b) severe disablement allowance,
(c) [carer's allowance],
(d) . . .
(e) . . .
(f) . . .
(g) . . .
(h) a social fund payment,
[(ha) health in pregnancy grant,][or]
(i) child benefit,
(j) . . .
(j) . . .
(k) . . .

under the Social Security Contributions and Benefits Act 1992 while he is a person to whom this section applies.

(2) No person in Northern Ireland is entitled to [state pension credit under the State Pension Credit Act (Northern Ireland) 2002, or to]—

(a) income-based jobseeker's allowance under the Jobseekers (Northern Ireland) Order 1995, or

(b) [disability living allowance or] any of the benefits mentioned in paragraphs [(a) to (i)] of subsection (1), under the Social Security Contributions and Benefits (Northern Ireland) Act 1992 while he is a person to whom this section applies.

(3) This section applies to a person subject to immigration control unless he falls within such category or description, or satisfies such conditions, as may be prescribed.

(4) Regulations under subsection (3) may provide for a person to be treated for prescribed purposes only as not being a person to whom this section applies.

(5) In relation to [health in pregnancy grant or] [child benefit], 'prescribed' means prescribed by regulations made by the Treasury.

(6) In relation to the matters mentioned in subsection (2) (except so far as it relates to [health in pregnancy grant or] [child benefit]), 'prescribed' means prescribed by regulations made by the Department.

(7) Section 175(3) to (5) of the Social Security Contributions and Benefits Act 1992 (supplemental powers in relation to regulations) applies to regulations made by the Secretary of State or the Treasury under subsection (3) as it applies to regulations made under that Act.

(8) Sections 133(2), 171(2) and 172(4) of the Social Security Contributions and Benefits (Northern Ireland) Act 1992 apply to regulations made by the Department under subsection (3) as they apply to regulations made by the Department under that Act.

(9) 'A person subject to immigration control' means a person who is not a national of an EEA State and who—

(a) requires leave to enter or remain in the United Kingdom but does not have it;

(b) has leave to enter or remain in the United Kingdom which is subject to a condition that he does not have recourse to public funds;

(c) has leave to enter or remain in the United Kingdom given as a result of a maintenance undertaking; or

(d) has leave to enter or remain in the United Kingdom only as a result of paragraph 17 of Schedule 4.

(10) 'Maintenance undertaking', in relation to any person, means a written undertaking given by another person in pursuance of the immigration rules to be responsible for that person's maintenance and accommodation.

Note: Commenced for the purposes of enabling subordinate legislation 1 January 2000 (SI 1999/3190), remainder 3 April 2000 (SI 2000/464). First words in square brackets in subsection (1) inserted by s 4 State Pension Credit Act 2002, from 6 October 2003 (SI 2003/1766). Second words in square brackets in subsection (1) inserted by Sch 3 Welfare Reform Act 2007 from 27 October 2008 (SI 2008/787). Subsection (1)(c) substituted from 1 April 2003 (SI 2002/1457). Words in square brackets in subsection (2) substituted by s 4 State Pension Credit Act (Northern Ireland) 2002 from 2 December 2002 (SI 2002/366). Subsection (1)(ha) inserted and words in first square brackets in subsections (5) and (6) substituted by s 138 Health and Social Care Act 2008 from 1 January 2009 (SI 2009/2994). Words in second square brackets in subsections (5) and (6) substituted by Sch 4 Tax Credits Act 2002 from 7 April 2003 (SI 2003/392). Subsection (1)(e) revoked by Sch 7 Welfare Reform Act 2009 from a date to be appointed. Words in first square brackets in subsection (1) inserted by Sch 2 Welfare Reform Act 2012 from 29 April 2013 (SI 2013/983). Word inserted in subsection (1)(ha) and substituted in second square brackets in subsection (2)(b) by Sch 3 Welfare Reform Act 2012 from a date to be appointed. Words in third square brackets in subsection (1) and first square brackets in subsection (2)(b) inserted by Sch 9 Welfare Reform Act 2012 from 10 June 2013 (SI 2013/1250). Words deleted from subsection (1) and subsections (1)(d), (e), (j) and (k) repealed by Sch 14 Welfare Reform Act 2012 from a date to be appointed.

116. . . .

Note: Amends National Assistance Act 1948, s 21.

117. . . .

Note: Amends Health Services and Public Health Act 1968, s 4; Sch 8 National Health Service Act 1977; and Housing Act 1996, ss 161, 185–187.

118. Housing authority accommodation

(1) Each housing authority must secure that, so far as practicable, a tenancy of, or licence to occupy, housing accommodation provided under the accommodation provisions is not granted to a person subject to immigration control unless—

(a) he is of a class specified in an order made by the Secretary of State; or

(b) the tenancy of, or licence to occupy, such accommodation is granted in accordance with arrangements made under section [4, 95 or 98].

(2) 'Housing authority' means—

(a) in relation to England and Wales, a local housing authority within the meaning of the Housing Act 1985;

(b) in relation to Scotland, a local authority within the meaning of the Housing (Scotland) Act 1987; and

(c) in relation to Northern Ireland, the Executive.

(3) 'Accommodation provisions' means—

(a) in relation to England and Wales, Part II of the Housing Act 1985;

(b) in relation to Scotland, Part I of the Housing (Scotland) Act 1987;

(c) in relation to Northern Ireland, Part II of the Housing (Northern Ireland) Order 1981.

(4) 'Licence to occupy', in relation to Scotland, means a permission or right to occupy.

(5) 'Tenancy', in relation to England and Wales, has the same meaning as in the Housing Act 1985.

(6) 'Person subject to immigration control' means a person who under the 1971 Act requires leave to enter or remain in the United Kingdom (whether or not such leave has been given).

(7) This section does not apply in relation to any allocation of housing to which Part VI of the Housing Act 1996 (allocation of housing accommodation) applies.

Note: Commenced 1 January 2000 for purposes of enabling subordinate legislation (SI 1999/3190), remainder 1 March 2000 (SI 2000/464). Words in square brackets in subsection (1)(b) substituted by Immigration, Nationality and Asylum Act 2006, s 43 from 16 June 2006 (SI 2006/1497).

119. Homelessness: Scotland and Northern Ireland

(1) A person subject to immigration control—

(a) is not eligible for accommodation or assistance under the homelessness provisions, and

(b) is to be disregarded in determining for the purposes of those provisions, whether [a person falling within subsection (1A)] —

(i) is homeless or is threatened with homelessness, or

(ii) has a priority need for accommodation, unless he is of a class specified in an order made by the Secretary of State.

[(**1A**) A person falls within this subsection if the person—

(a) falls within a class specified in an order under subsection (1); but

(b) is not a national of an EEA State or Switzerland.]

(2) An order under subsection (1) may not be made so as to include in a specified class any person to whom section 115 applies.

(3) 'The homelessness provisions' means—

(a) in relation to Scotland, Part II of the Housing (Scotland) Act 1987; and

(b) in relation to Northern Ireland, Part II of the Housing (Northern Ireland) Order 1988.

(4) 'Person subject to immigration control' has the same meaning as in section 118.

Note: Commenced 1 January 2000 for purposes of enabling subordinate legislation, remainder 1 March 2000 (SI 2000/464). Words in square brackets substituted and s 1A inserted by Sch 15 Housing and Regeneration Act 2008 from 2 March 2009 in relation to applications (a) for accommodation or assistance in obtaining accommodation under Part I (provision of housing) or Part II (homeless persons) of the Housing (Scotland) Act 1987, or (b) for housing assistance under Part II (housing the homeless) of the Housing (Northern Ireland) Order 1988, made on or after 2 March 2009 (SI 2009/415).

120. . . .

Note: Amends Social Work (Scotland) Act 1968, ss 2 and 13, Mental Health (Scotland) Act 1984, ss 7–8 and Asylum and Immigration Appeals Act 1993, ss 4–5 and Sch 1.

121. . . .

Note: Amends Health and Personal Social Services (Northern Ireland) Order 1972.

[122. Family with children

(1) This section applies where a person ('the asylum-seeker') applies for support under section 95 of this Act or section 17 of the Nationality, Immigration and Asylum Act 2002 (accommodation centres) if—

(a) the Secretary of State thinks that the asylum-seeker is eligible for support under either or both of those sections, and

(b) the asylum-seeker's household includes a dependant child who is under 18.

(2) The Secretary of State must offer the provision of support for the child, as part of the asylum-seeker's household, under one of the sections mentioned in subsection (1).

(3) A local authority (or, in Northern Ireland, an authority) may not provide assistance for a child if—

(a) the Secretary of State is providing support for the child in accordance with an offer under subsection (2),

(b) an offer by the Secretary of State under subsection (2) remains open in respect of the child, or

(c) the Secretary of State has agreed that he would make an offer in respect of the child under subsection (2) if an application were made as described in subsection (1).

(4) In subsection (3) 'assistance' means assistance under—

(a) section 17 of the Children Act 1989 (c. 41) (local authority support),

(b) section 22 of the Children (Scotland) Act 1995 (c. 36) (similar provision for Scotland), or

(c) Article 18 of the Children (Northern Ireland) Order 1995 (similar provision for Northern Ireland).

(5) The Secretary of State may by order disapply subsection (3) in specified circumstances.

(6) Where subsection (3) ceases to apply to a child because the Secretary of State stops providing support, no local authority may provide assistance for the child except the authority for the area within which the support was provided.]

Note: Section 122 substituted by Nationality, Immigration and Asylum Act 2002, s 47 from a date to be appointed.

123. Back-dating of benefits where person recorded as refugee

. . .

Note: Section 123 ceased to have effect from 30 April 2003 Asylum and Immigration Act 2004, s 12.

Miscellaneous

124. Secretary of State to be corporation sole for purposes of Part VI

(1) For the purpose of exercising his functions under this Part, the Secretary of State is a corporation sole.

(2) Any instrument in connection with the acquisition, management or disposal of property, real or personal, heritable or moveable, by the Secretary of State under this Part may be executed on his behalf by a person authorised by him for that purpose.

(3) Any instrument purporting to have been so executed on behalf of the Secretary of State is to be treated, until the contrary is proved, to have been so executed on his behalf.

Note: Commenced 11 November 1999, s 170.

125. Entry of premises

(1) This section applies in relation to premises in which accommodation has been provided under section 95 or 98 for a supported person.

(2) If, on an application made by a person authorised in writing by the Secretary of State, a justice of the peace is satisfied that there is reason to believe that—

(a) the supported person or any dependants of his for whom the accommodation is provided is not resident in it,

(b) the accommodation is being used for any purpose other than the accommodation of the asylum-seeker or any dependant of his, or

(c) any person other than the supported person and his dependants (if any) is residing in the accommodation, he may grant a warrant to enter the premises to the person making the application.

(3) A warrant granted under subsection (2) may be executed—

(a) at any reasonable time;

(b) using reasonable force.

(4) In the application of subsection (2) to Scotland, read the reference to a justice of the peace as a reference to the sheriff or a justice of the peace.

Note: Commenced 3 April 2000 (SI 2000/464).

126. Information from property owners

(1) The power conferred by this section is to be exercised with a view to obtaining information about premises in which accommodation is or has been provided for supported persons.

(2) The Secretary of State may require any person appearing to him—

(a) to have any interest in, or

(b) to be involved in any way in the management or control of,

such premises, or any building which includes such premises, to provide him with such information with respect to the premises and the persons occupying them as he may specify.

(3) A person who is required to provide information under this section must do so in accordance with such requirements as may be prescribed.

(4) Information provided to the Secretary of State under this section may be used by him only in the exercise of his functions under this Part.

Note: Commenced 3 April 2000 (SI 2000/464).

127. Requirement to supply information about redirection of post

(1) The Secretary of State may require any person conveying postal packets to supply redirection information to the Secretary of State—

(a) for use in the prevention, detection, investigation or prosecution of criminal offences under this Part;

(b) for use in checking the accuracy of information relating to support provided under this Part; or

(c) for any other purpose relating to the provision of support to asylum-seekers.

(2) The information must be supplied in such manner and form, and in accordance with such requirements, as may be prescribed.

(3) The Secretary of State must make payments of such amount as he considers reasonable in respect of the supply of information under this section.

(4) 'Postal packet' has the same meaning as in the [Postal Services Act 2000].

(5) 'Redirection information' means information relating to arrangements made with any person conveying postal packets for the delivery of postal packets to addresses other than those indicated by senders on the packets.

Note: Commenced 3 April 2000 (SI 2000/464). Words in square brackets in subsection (4) substituted from 26 March 2001 (SI 2001/1149).

Part VII

Power to Arrest, Search and Fingerprint

Power to arrest

128. . . .

Note: Amends Immigration Act 1971, s 28.

Power to search and arrest

129. . . .

Note: Amends Immigration Act 1971, s 28.

130. . . .

Note: Amends Immigration Act 1971, s 28.

Power to enter and search premises

131. . . .

Note: Amends Immigration Act 1971, s 28.

132. . . .

Note: Amends Immigration Act 1971, s 28 and Sch 2, paragraph 25.

133. . . .

Note: Amends Immigration Act 1971, s 28.

Power to search persons

134. . . .

Note: Amends Immigration Act 1971, s 28 and Sch 2, paragraph 25.

135. . . .

Note: Amends Immigration Act 1971, s 28 and Sch 2, paragraph 25.

Seized material: access and copying

136. . . .

Note: Amends Immigration Act 1971, s 28 and Sch 2, paragraph 25.

Search warrants

137. . . .

Note: Amends Immigration Act 1971, s 28.

138. . . .

Note: Amends Immigration Act 1971, s 28.

139. . . .

Note: Amends Immigration Act 1971, s 28 and Sch 2, paragraph 25.

Detention

140. . . .

Note: Amends Immigration Act 1971, Sch 2, paragraphs 16–17.

Fingerprinting

141. Fingerprinting

(1) Fingerprints may be taken by an authorised person from a person to whom this section applies.

(2) Fingerprints may be taken under this section only during the relevant period.

(3) Fingerprints may not be taken under this section from a person under the age of sixteen ('the child') except in the presence of a person of full age who is—

(a) the child's parent or guardian; or

(b) a person who for the time being takes responsibility for the child.

(4) The person mentioned in subsection (3)(b) may not be—

(a) an officer of the Secretary of State who is not an authorised person;

(b) an authorised person.

(5) 'Authorised person' means—

(a) a constable;

(b) an immigration officer;

(c) a prison officer;

(d) an officer of the Secretary of State authorised for the purpose; or

(e) a person who is employed by a contractor in connection with the discharge of the contractor's duties under a [removal centre] contract.

(6) In subsection (5)(e) 'contractor' and '[removal centre] contract' have the same meaning as in Part VIII.

(7) This section applies to—

(a) any person ('A') who, on being required to do so by an immigration officer on his arrival in the United Kingdom, fails to produce a valid passport with photograph or some other document satisfactorily establishing his identity and nationality or citizenship;

(b) any person ('B') who has been refused leave to enter the United Kingdom but has been temporarily admitted under paragraph 21 of Schedule 2 to the 1971 Act if an immigration officer reasonably suspects that B might break any condition imposed on him relating to residence or as to reporting to the police or an immigration officer;

[(c) any person ("C") in respect of whom the Secretary of State has decided—

(i) to make a deportation order, or

(ii) that section 32(5) of the UK Borders Act 2007 (automatic deportation of foreign criminals) applies;

(ca) any person ("CA") who requires leave to enter or remain in the United Kingdom but does not have it;]

(d) any person ('D') who has been [detained under paragraph 16 of Schedule 2 to the 1971 Act or arrested under paragraph 17 of that Schedule;]

(e) any person ('E') who has made a claim for asylum;

(f) any person ('F') who is a dependant of any of those persons [, other than a dependant of a person who falls within [paragraph (c)(ii)]]

(8) 'The relevant period' begins—

(a) for A, on his failure to produce the passport or other document;

(b) for B, on the decision to admit him temporarily;

[(c) for C, when he is notified of the decision mentioned in subsection (7)(c);

(ca) for CA, when he becomes a person to whom this section applies,]

(d) for D, on his [detention or arrest;]

(e) for E, on the making of his claim for asylum; and

(f) for F, at the same time as for the person whose dependant he is.

(9) 'The relevant period' ends on the earliest of the following—

(a) the grant of leave to enter or remain in the United Kingdom;

(b) for A, B, C [, CA] or D, his removal or deportation from the United Kingdom;

[(c) for C—

(i) the time when the [decision mentioned in subsection (7)(c)] ceases to have effect, whether as a result of an appeal or otherwise, or

(ii) if a deportation order has been made against him, its revocation or its otherwise ceasing to have effect;]

[(ca) for CA, when he no longer requires leave to enter or remain in the United Kingdom;]

(d) for D, his release if he is no longer liable to be detained under paragraph 16 of Schedule 2 to the 1971 Act;

(e) for E, the final determination or abandonment of his claim for asylum; and

(f) for F, at the same time as for the person whose dependant he is.

(10) No fingerprints may be taken from A if the immigration officer considers that A has a reasonable excuse for the failure concerned.

(11) No fingerprints may be taken from B unless the decision to take them has been confirmed by a chief immigration officer.

(12) An authorised person may not take fingerprints from a person under the age of sixteen unless his decision to take them has been confirmed—

(a) if he is a constable, by a person designated for the purpose by the chief constable of his police force;

(b) if he is a person mentioned in subsection (5)(b) or (e), by a chief immigration officer;

(c) if he is a prison officer, by a person designated for the purpose by the governor of the prison;

(d) if he is an officer of the Secretary of State, by a person designated for the purpose by the Secretary of State.

(13) Neither subsection (3) nor subsection (12) prevents an authorised person from taking fingerprints if he reasonably believes that the person from whom they are to be taken is aged sixteen or over.

(14) For the purposes of subsection (7)(f), a person is a dependant of another person if—

(a) he is that person's spouse or child under the age of eighteen; and

(b) he does not have a right of abode in the United Kingdom or indefinite leave to enter or remain in the United Kingdom.

(15) 'Claim for asylum' has the same meaning as in Part VI.

[(16) . . .]

[(17) Section 157(1) applies to this section (in so far as it relates to removal centres by virtue of subsection (5)(e)) as it applies to Part VIII.]

Note: Commenced 11 December 2000 (SI 2000/3099). Words in first and second square brackets substituted by Nationality, Immigration and Asylum Act 2002, s 66 from 10 February 2003 (SI 2003/1). Words in square brackets in subsections (7)(c), (8)(c) and (9)(c) substituted and subsection (16) added by Asylum and Immigration (Treatment of Claimants etc.) Act 2004, s 15 from 1 October 2004 (SI 2004/2523), subsection (16) deleted by Sch 9 Immigration Act 2014 from 20 October 2014 with savings in articles 9-11 SI 2014/2771. Words in square brackets in subsections (7)(d) and (8)(d) substituted and subsection (17) added by Immigration, Asylum and Nationality Act 2006, s 28 from 31 August 2006 (SI 2006/2226). Words in square brackets in subsections (7)(f) inserted by s 51 Borders, Citizenship and Immigration Act 2009 from 15 November 2009 (SI 2009/2731). Subsections (7)(c), (8)(c) and words in second square brackets in (7)(f) and (9)(c)(i) substituted; letters in subsection (9)(b) and subsection (9)(ca) inserted by Sch 9 Immigration Act 2014 from 20 October 2014 with savings set out in articles 9-11 SI 2014/2771.

142. Attendance for fingerprinting

(1) The Secretary of State may, by notice in writing, require a person to whom section 141 applies to attend at a specified place for fingerprinting.

[(2) In the case of a notice given to a person of a kind specified in section 141(7)(a) to (d) or (f) (in so far as it applies to a dependant of a person of a kind specified in section 141(7)(a) to (d)), the notice—

(a) must require him to attend during a specified period of at least seven days beginning with a day not less than seven days after the date given in the notice as its date of issue, and

(b) may require him to attend at a specified time of day or during specified hours.

(2A) In the case of a notice given to a person of a kind specified in section 141(7)(e) or (f) (in so far as it applies to a dependant of a person of a kind specified in section 141(7)(e)), the notice—

(a) may require him to attend during a specified period beginning with a day not less than three days after the date given in the notice as its date of issue,

(b) may require him to attend on a specified day not less than three days after the date given in the notice as its date of issue, and

(c) may require him to attend at a specified time of day or during specified hours.]

(3) A constable or immigration officer may arrest without warrant a person who has failed to comply with a requirement imposed on him under this section (unless the requirement has ceased to have effect).

(4) Before a person arrested under subsection (3) is released—

(a) he may be removed to a place where his fingerprints may conveniently be taken; and
(b) his fingerprints may be taken (whether or not he is so removed).

(5) A requirement imposed under subsection (1) ceases to have effect at the end of the relevant period (as defined by section 141).

Note: Commenced 11 December 2000 (SI 2000/3099). Subsection (2) substituted and subsection 2A inserted by Immigration, Asylum and Nationality Act 2006, s 29 from 31 August 2006 (SI 2006/2226).

143. ...

Note: Repealed by Sch 9 Immigration Act 2014 from a date to be appointed.

144. Other methods of collecting data about physical characteristics

[(1)] The Secretary of State may make regulations containing provisions equivalent to sections 141, [and 142] in relation to such other methods of collecting [biometric information] as may be prescribed.

[(2) "Biometric information" has the meaning given by section 15 of the UK Borders Act 2007.]

Note: Commenced 11 December 2000 (SI 2000/3099). Subsection (2) inserted by Nationality, Immigration and Asylum Act 2002, s 128 from 10 February 2003 (SI 2003/1). Words in first square brackets in subsection (1) substituted by Sch 9 Immigraiton Act 2014 from a date to be appointed. Words in second square brackets in subsection (1) and subsection (2) substituted by Sch 2 Immigration Act 2014 from 28 July 2014 (SI 2014/1820).

[144A Use and retention of fingerprints etc.

(1) Section 8 of the UK Borders Act 2007 (power to make regulations about use and retention of biometric information) applies to—
(a) fingerprints taken by virtue of section 141, and
(b) biometric information taken by virtue of regulations under section 144,

as it applies to biometric information provided in accordance with regulations under section 5(1) of that Act.

(2) Regulations made by virtue of subsection (1)(a) must require fingerprints taken from a person ("F") by virtue of section 141(7)(f) to be destroyed when fingerprints taken from the person whose dependant F is are destroyed.

(3) Regulations made by virtue of subsection (1)(b) must make equivalent provision in relation to biometric information taken by virtue of any provision of regulations under section 144 which is equivalent to section 141(7)(f).]

Note: Section 144A inserted by s 14 Immigration Act 2014 from 28 July 2014 (SI 2014/1820).

Codes of practice

145. Codes of practice

(1) An immigration officer exercising any specified power to—
(a) arrest, question, search or take fingerprints from a person,

(b) enter and search premises, or

(c) seize property found on persons or premises,

must have regard to such provisions of a code as may be specified.

(2) Subsection (1) also applies to an authorised person exercising the power to take fingerprints conferred by section 141.

[(2A) A person exercising a power under regulations made by virtue of section 144 must have regard to such provisions of a code as may be specified.]

(3) Any specified provision of a code may have effect for the purposes of this section subject to such modifications as may be specified.

(4) 'Specified' means specified in a direction given by the Secretary of State.

(5) 'Authorised person' has the same meaning as in section 141.

(6) 'Code' means—

(a) in relation to England and Wales, any code of practice for the time being in force under the Police and Criminal Evidence Act 1984;

(b) in relation to Northern Ireland, any code of practice for the time being in force under the Police and Criminal Evidence (Northern Ireland) Order 1989.

(7) This section does not apply to any person exercising powers in Scotland.

Note: Commenced 11 November 1999, s 170. Subsection (2A) inserted by Nationality, Immigration and Asylum Act 2002, s 128 from 10 February 2003 (SI 2003/1).

Use of force

146. Use of force

(1) An immigration officer exercising any power conferred on him by [the Immigration Acts] may, if necessary, use reasonable force.

[(2) A person exercising a power under any of the following may if necessary use reasonable force—

(a) section 28CA, 28FA or 28FB of the 1971 Act (business premises: entry to arrest or search),

(b) section 141 or 142 of this Act, and

(c) regulations under section 144 of this Act.]

Note: Commenced 1 November 1999, s 170 (Royal Assent). Words in square brackets in sub-s(1) substituted by Sch 1 Immigration Act 2014 from 28 July 2014 (SI 2014/1820). Subsection (2) substituted by Nationality, Immigration and Asylum Act 2002, s 153 from 8 January 2003 (SI 2003/1).

PART VIII

[REMOVAL CENTRES] AND DETAINED PERSONS

Interpretation

147. Interpretation of Part VIII

In this Part—

'certificate of authorisation' means a certificate issued by the Secretary of State under section 154;

'certified prisoner custody officer' means a prisoner custody officer certified under section 89 of the Criminal Justice Act 1991, or section 114 of the Criminal Justice and Public Order Act 1994, to perform custodial duties;

'contract monitor' means a person appointed by the Secretary of State under section 149(4);

'contracted out [removal centre]' means a [removal centre] in relation to which a [removal centre] contract is in force;

'contractor', in relation to a [removal centre] which is being run in accordance with a [removal centre] contract, means the person who has contracted to run it;

'custodial functions' means custodial functions at a [removal centre];

['detained children' means detained persons who are under the age of 18;]

'detained persons' means persons detained or required to be detained under the 1971 Act [or under section 62 of the Nationality, Immigration and Asylum Act 2002 (detention by Secretary of State);]

'detainee custody officer' means a person in respect of whom a certificate of authorisation is in force;

. . .

'[removal centre] contract' means a contract entered into by the Secretary of State under section 149;

'[removal] centre rules' means rules made by the Secretary of State under section 153;

'directly managed [removal centre]' means a [removal centre] which is not a contracted out [removal centre];

'escort arrangements' means arrangements made by the Secretary of State under section 156;

'escort functions' means functions under escort arrangements;

'escort monitor' means a person appointed under paragraph 1 of Schedule 13;

["pre-departure accommodation" means a place used solely for the detention of detained children and their families for a period of—

(a) not more than 72 hours, or

(b) not more than seven days in cases where the longer period of detention is authorised personally by a Minister of the Crown (within the meaning of the Ministers of the Crown Act 1975);]

'prisoner custody officer'—

(a) in relation to England and Wales, has the same meaning as in the Criminal Justice Act 1991;

(b) in relation to Scotland, has the meaning given in section 114(1) of the Criminal Justice and Public Order Act 1994;

(c) in relation to Northern Ireland, has the meaning given in section 122(1) of that Act of 1994;

['removal centre' means a place which is used solely for the detention of detained persons but which is not a short-term holding [pre-departure accommodation,] facility, a prison or part of a prison;]

'short-term holding facility' means a place used

[–(a) solely for the detention of detained persons for a period of not more than seven days or for such other period as may be prescribed [, or

(b) for the detention of—

(i) detained persons for a period of not more than seven days or for such other period as may be prescribed, and

(ii) persons other than detained persons for any period] [but which is not pre-departure accommodation].

Note: Commenced 1 August 2000 (SI 2000/1985). Definition of removal centre inserted by Nationality, Immigration and Asylum Act 2002, s 66 from 10 February 2003 (SI 2003/1). Definition of detained persons amended by Nationality, Immigration and Asylum Act 2002, s 62 from 10 February 2003 (SI 2003/1). Definition of 'short term holding facility' amended by s 25 Borders, Citizenship and Immigration Act 2009 from 21 July 2009 (s 57). Definitions of 'detained children', 'pre-departure accommodation' and words in square brackets in definition of removal centre and words in last square brackets inserted by s 6 Immigration Act 2014 from 28 July 2014 (SI 2014/1820). Other words in square brackets inserted by Nationality, Immigration and Asylum Act 2002, s 66 from 10 February 2003 (SI 2003/1).

[Removal centres]

148. Management of [removal centres]

(1) A manager must be appointed for every [removal centre].

(2) In the case of a contracted out [removal centre], the person appointed as manager must be a detainee custody officer whose appointment is approved by the Secretary of State.

(3) The manager of a [removal centre] is to have such functions as are conferred on him by [removal centre] rules.

(4) The manager of a contracted out [removal centre] may not—

(a) enquire into a disciplinary charge laid against a detained person;

(b) conduct the hearing of such a charge; or

(c) make, remit or mitigate an award in respect of such a charge.

(5) The manager of a contracted out [removal centre] may not, except in cases of urgency, order—

(a) the removal of a detained person from association with other detained persons;

(b) the temporary confinement of a detained person in special accommodation; or

(c) the application to a detained person of any other special control or restraint (other than handcuffs).

Note: Subsection (3) commenced 1 August 2000 (SI 2000/1985). Remainder commenced 2 April 2001 (SI 2001/239). Words in square brackets substituted by Nationality, Immigration and Asylum Act 2002, s 66 from 10 February 2003 (SI 2003/1).

149. Contracting out of certain [removal centres]

(1) The Secretary of State may enter into a contract with another person for the provision or running (or the provision and running) by him, or (if the contract so provides) for the running by sub-contractors of his, of any [removal centre] or part of a [removal centre].

(2) While a [removal centre] contract for the running of a [removal centre] or part of a [removal centre] is in force—

(a) the [removal centre] or part is to be run subject to and in accordance with the provisions of or made under this Part; and

(b) in the case of a part, that part and the remaining part are to be treated for the purposes of those provisions as if they were separate [removal centres].

(3) If the Secretary of State grants a lease or tenancy of land for the purposes of a detention centre contract, none of the following enactments applies to the lease or tenancy—

(a) Part II of the Landlord and Tenant Act 1954 (security of tenure);

(b) section 146 of the Law of Property Act 1925 (restrictions on and relief against forfeiture);

(c) section 19(1), (2) and (3) of the Landlord and Tenant Act 1927 and the Landlord and Tenant Act 1988 (covenants not to assign etc.);

(d) the Agricultural Holdings Act 1986;

(e) sections 4 to 7 of the Law Reform (Miscellaneous Provisions) (Scotland) Act 1985 (irritancy clauses);

(f) the Agricultural Holdings (Scotland) Act 1991 [and the Agricultural Holdings (Scotland) Act 2003 (asp 11)];

(g) section 14 of the Conveyancing Act 1881;

(h) the Conveyancing and Law of Property Act 1892;

(i) the Business Tenancies (Northern Ireland) Order 1996.

(4) The Secretary of State must appoint a contract monitor for every contracted out [removal centre].

(5) A person may be appointed as the contract monitor for more than one [removal centre].

(6) The contract monitor is to have—

(a) such functions as may be conferred on him by [removal centre] rules;

(b) the status of a Crown servant.

(7) The contract monitor must—

(a) keep under review, and report to the Secretary of State on, the running of a [removal centre] for which he is appointed; and

(b) investigate, and report to the Secretary of State on, any allegations made against any person performing custodial functions at that centre.

(8) The contractor, and any sub-contractor of his, must do all that he reasonably can (whether by giving directions to the officers of the [removal centre] or otherwise) to facilitate the exercise by the contract monitor of his functions.

(9) 'Lease or tenancy' includes an underlease, sublease or sub-tenancy.

(10) In relation to a [removal centre] contract entered into by the Secretary of State before the commencement of this section, this section is to be treated as having been in force at that time.

Note: Subsections (1), (3), (6)(a) and (9) commenced 1 August 2000 (SI 2000/1985). Remainder commenced 2 April 2001, s 66 (SI 2001/239). Words in square brackets substituted by Nationality, Immigration and Asylum Act 2002, s 66 from 10 February 2003 (SI 2003/1). Words in square brackets in subsection (3)(f) inserted by Agricultural Holdings (Scotland) Act 2003 Schedule paragraph 52 from 27 November 2003 (SSI 2003/511).

150. Contracted out functions at directly managed [removal centres]

(1) The Secretary of State may enter into a contract with another person—

(a) for functions at, or connected with, a directly managed [removal centre] to be performed by detainee custody officers provided by that person; or

(b) for such functions to be performed by certified prisoner custody officers who are provided by that person.

(2) For the purposes of this section '[removal centre]' includes a short-term holding facility.

Note: Commenced 2 April 2001 (SI 2001/239). Words in square brackets substituted by Nationality, Immigration and Asylum Act 2002, s 66 from 10 February 2003 (SI 2003/1).

151. Intervention by Secretary of State

(1) The Secretary of State may exercise the powers conferred by this section if it appears to him that—

(a) the manager of a contracted out [removal centre] has lost, or is likely to lose, effective control of the centre or of any part of it; or

(b) it is necessary to do so in the interests of preserving the safety of any person, or of preventing serious damage to any property.

(2) The Secretary of State may appoint a person (to be known as the Controller) to act as manager of the [removal centre] for the period—

(a) beginning with the time specified in the appointment; and

(b) ending with the time specified in the notice of termination under subsection (5).

(3) During that period—

(a) all the functions which would otherwise be exercisable by the manager or the contract monitor are to be exercisable by the Controller;

(b) the contractor and any sub-contractor of his must do all that he reasonably can to facilitate the exercise by the Controller of his functions; and

(c) the staff of the detention centre must comply with any directions given by the Controller in the exercise of his functions.

(4) The Controller is to have the status of a Crown servant.

(5) If the Secretary of State is satisfied that a Controller is no longer needed for a particular detention centre, he must (by giving notice to the Controller) terminate his appointment at a time specified in the notice.

(6) As soon as practicable after making an appointment under this section, the Secretary of State must give notice of the appointment to those entitled to notice.

(7) As soon as practicable after terminating an appointment under this section, the Secretary of State must give a copy of the notice of termination to those entitled to notice.

(8) Those entitled to notice are the contractor, the manager, the contract monitor and the Controller.

Note: Commenced 2 April 2001 (SI 2001/239). Words in square brackets substituted by Nationality, Immigration and Asylum Act 2002, s 66 from 10 February 2003 (SI 2003/1).

152. Visiting Committees and inspections

(1) The Secretary of State must appoint a committee (to be known as the Visiting Committee) for each detention centre.

(2) The functions of the Visiting Committee for a [removal centre] are to be such as may be prescribed by the [removal centre] rules.

(3) Those rules must include provision—

(a) as to the making of visits to the centre by members of the Visiting Committee;

(b) for the hearing of complaints made by persons detained in the centre;

(c) requiring the making of reports by the Visiting Committee to the Secretary of State.

(4) Every member of the Visiting Committee for a [removal centre] may at any time enter the centre and have free access to every part of it and to every person detained there.

(5) . . .

Note: Sub-sections (2) and (3) commenced for the purposes of enabling subordinate legislation 1 August 2000 (SI 2000/1985). Otherwise commenced 2 April 2001 (SI 2001/239). Sub-section (5) amends the Prison Act 1952, s 5A. Words in square brackets substituted by Nationality, Immigration and Asylum Act 2002, s 66 from 10 February 2003 (SI 2003/1).

153. [Removal centre] rules

(1) The Secretary of State must make rules for the regulation and management of [removal centres].

(2) [Removal centre] rules may, among other things, make provision with respect to the safety, care, activities, discipline and control of detained persons.

Note: Commenced for the purposes of enabling subordinate legislation 1 August 2000 (SI 2000/1985). Otherwise commenced 2 April 2001 (SI 2001/239). Words in square brackets substituted by Nationality, Immigration and Asylum Act 2002, s 66 from 10 February 2003 (SI 2003/1).

[153A. Detained persons: national minimum wage

A detained person does not qualify for the national minimum wage in respect of work which he does in pursuance of removal centre rules.]

Note: Inserted by Immigration, Asylum and Nationality Act 2006, s 59 from 31 August 2006 (SI 2006/2226).

Custody and movement of detained persons

154. Detainee custody officers

(1) On an application made to him under this section, the Secretary of State may certify that the applicant—

(a) is authorised to perform escort functions; or

(b) is authorised to perform both escort functions and custodial functions.

(2) The Secretary of State may not issue a certificate of authorisation unless he is satisfied that the applicant—

(a) is a fit and proper person to perform the functions to be authorised; and

(b) has received training to such standard as the Secretary of State considers appropriate for the performance of those functions.

(3) A certificate of authorisation continues in force until such date, or the occurrence of such event, as may be specified in the certificate but may be suspended or revoked under paragraph 7 of Schedule 11.

(4) A certificate which authorises the performance of both escort functions and custodial functions may specify one date or event for one of those functions and a different date or event for the other.

[(5) The Secretary of State may confer functions of detainee custody officers on prison officers or prisoner custody officers.]

(6) A prison officer acting under arrangements made under subsection (5) has all the powers, authority, protection and privileges of a constable.

(7) Schedule 11 makes further provision about detainee custody officers.

Note: Commenced 2 April 2001 (SI 2001/239). Subsection (5) substituted by Nationality, Immigration and Asylum Act 2002, s 65 from 10 February 2003 (SI 2003/1).

155. Custodial functions and discipline etc. at [removal centres]

(1) Custodial functions may be discharged at a [removal centre] only by—

(a) a detainee custody officer authorised, in accordance with section 154(1), to perform such functions; or

(b) a prison officer, or a certified prisoner custody officer, exercising functions in relation to the [removal centre]—

(i) in accordance with arrangements made under section 154(5); or

(ii) as a result of a contract entered into under section 150(1)(b).

(2) Schedule 12 makes provision with respect to discipline and other matters at [removal centres] and short-term holding facilities [and in pre-departure accommodation.]

Note: Sub-section (2) commenced 1 August 2000 (SI 2000/1985). Remainder commenced 2 April 2001 (SI 2001/239). Words in last square brackets in subsection (2) inserted by s 6 Immigration Act 2014 from 28 July 2014 (SI 2014/1820). Other words in square brackets substituted by Nationality, Immigration and Asylum Act 2002, s 66 from 10 February 2003 (SI 2003/1).

156. Arrangements for the provision of escorts and custody

(1) The Secretary of State may make arrangements for—

(a) the delivery of detained persons to premises in which they may lawfully be detained;

(b) the delivery of persons from any such premises for the purposes of their removal from the United Kingdom in accordance with directions given under the 1971 Act or this Act;

(c) the custody of detained persons who are temporarily outside such premises;

(d) the custody of detained persons held on the premises of any court.

(2) Escort arrangements may provide for functions under the arrangements to be performed, in such cases as may be determined by or under the arrangements, by detainee custody officers.

(3) 'Court' includes—

[(a) the First-tier Tribunal;

(b) the Upper Tribunal; and]

(c) the Commission.

(4) Escort arrangements may include entering into contracts with other persons for the provision by them of—

(a) detainee custody officers; or

(b) prisoner custody officers who are certified under section 89 of the Criminal Justice Act 1991, or section 114 or 122 of the Criminal Justice and Public Order Act 1994, to perform escort functions.

(5) Schedule 13 makes further provision about escort arrangements.

(6) A person responsible for performing a function of a kind mentioned in subsection (1), in accordance with a transfer direction, complies with the direction if he does all that he reasonably can to secure that the function is performed by a person acting in accordance with escort arrangements.

(7) 'Transfer direction' means a transfer direction given under—

(a) section 48 of the Mental Health Act 1983 or section 71 of the Mental Health (Scotland) Act 1984 (removal to hospital of, among others, persons detained under the 1971 Act); or

(b) in Northern Ireland, article 54 of the Mental Health (Northern Ireland) Order 1986 (provision corresponding to section 48 of the 1983 Act).

Note: Subsection (5) commenced 1 August 2000 (SI 2000/1985). Remainder commenced 2 April 2001 (SI 2001/239). Words in square brackets substituted from 15 February 2010 (SI 2010/21).

157. Short-term holding facilities

(1) The Secretary of State may by regulations extend any provision made by or under this Part in relation to [removal centres] (other than one mentioned in subsection (2)) to short-term holding facilities.

(2) Subsection (1) does not apply to section 150.

(3) The Secretary of State may make rules for the regulation and management of short-term holding facilities.

Note: Commenced for the purposes of enabling subordinate legislation 1 August 2000 (SI 2000/1985). Otherwise commenced 2 April 2001 (SI 2001/239). Words in square brackets substituted by Nationality, Immigration and Asylum Act 2002, s 66 from 10 February 2003 (SI 2003/1).

[157A Pre-departure accommodation

(1) The following provisions of this Part apply to pre-departure accommodation as they apply to removal centres—

(a) section 149 (contracting out of certain removal centres);

(b) section 150 (contracting out functions at directly managed removal centres);

(c) section 151 (intervention by Secretary of State).

(2) In the application of those provisions to pre-departure accommodation—

(a) references to a removal centre contract are to be read as a contract made under section 149(1) for the provision or running of pre-departure accommodation;

(b) references to a contracted out removal centre are to be read as references to pre-departure accommodation in relation to which a contract under section 149(1) is in force;

(c) references to a directly managed removal centre are to be read as references to pre-departure accommodation in relation to which there is no contract under section 149(1) in force;

(d) references to removal centre rules are to be read as references to rules made under subsection (4).

(3) The Secretary of State may by regulations extend to pre-departure accommodation any other provision made by or under this Part in relation to removal centres.

(4) The Secretary of State may make rules for the regulation and management of pre-departure accommodation.]

Note: Section 157A inserted by s 6 Immigration Act from 28 July 2014 (SI 2014/1820).

Miscellaneous

158. Wrongful disclosure of information

(1) A person who is or has been employed (whether as a detainee custody officer, prisoner custody officer or otherwise)—

(a) in accordance with escort arrangements,

(b) at a contracted out [removal centre], or

(c) to perform contracted out functions at a directly managed detention centre, is guilty of an offence if he discloses, otherwise than in the course of his duty or as authorised by the Secretary of State, any information which he acquired in the course of his employment and which relates to a particular detained person.

(2) A person guilty of such an offence is liable—

(a) on conviction on indictment, to imprisonment for a term not exceeding two years or to a fine or to both;

(b) on summary conviction, to imprisonment for a term not exceeding six months or to a fine not exceeding the statutory maximum or to both.

(3) 'Contracted out functions' means functions which, as the result of a contract entered into under section 150, fall to be performed by detainee custody officers or certified prisoner custody officers.

Note: Commenced 2 April 2001 (SI 2001/239). Words in square brackets substituted by Nationality, Immigration and Asylum Act 2002, s 66 from 10 February 2003 (SI 2003/1).

159. Power of constable to act outside his jurisdiction

(1) For the purpose of taking a person to or from a [removal centre] under the order of any authority competent to give the order, a constable may act outside the area of his jurisdiction.

(2) When acting under this section, the constable concerned retains all the powers, authority, protection and privileges of his office.

Note: Commenced 2 April 2001 (SI 2001/239). Words in square brackets substituted by Nationality, Immigration and Asylum Act 2002, s 66 from 10 February 2003 (SI 2003/1).

Part IX

Registrar's Certificates: Procedure

160. . . .

Note: Amends Marriage Act 1949, ss 26–7, 31.

161. . . .

Note: Amends the Marriage Act 1949, ss 26–7 and the Marriage Law (Ireland) Amendment Act 1863, s 2.

162. . . .

Note: Amends the Marriage Act 1949, s 28 and the Marriage Law (Ireland) Amendment Act 1863 s 3.

163. . . .

Note: Amends the Marriage Act 1949, s 31 and the Marriages (Ireland) Act 1844, s 16.

Part X
Miscellaneous and Supplemental

164. . . .

Note: Amends the Prosecution of Offences Act 1985, s 3.

165. . . .

Note: Amends Immigration Act 1971, s 31.

166. Regulations and orders

(1) Any power to make rules, regulations or orders conferred by this Act is exercisable by statutory instrument.

(2) But subsection (1) does not apply in relation to [orders made under section 90(1),] rules made under paragraph 1 of Schedule 5 or immigration rules.

(3) Any statutory instrument made as a result of subsection (1) may—

(a) contain such incidental, supplemental, consequential and transitional provision as the person making it considers appropriate;

(b) make different provision for different cases or descriptions of case; and

(c) make different provision for different areas.

(4) No order is to be made under—

(a) section 20,

(b) section 21,

(c) section 31(10),

[(da) section 86A(3)]

(d) section 86(2),

(e) . . .

(f) section 97(3),

(g) . . .; or

(h) paragraph 4 of Schedule 5,

unless a draft of the order has been laid before Parliament and approved by a resolution of each House.

(5) No regulations are to be made under—

[(za) section 4(5),]

(a) section 9,

(b) section 46(8),

(c) section 53, or

(d) section 144,

unless a draft of the regulations has been laid before Parliament and approved by a resolution of each House.

(6) Any statutory instrument made under this Act, apart from one made—

(a) under any of the provisions mentioned in subsection (4) or (5), or

(b) under section 24(3) [, 24A(3)] or 170(4) or (7), shall be subject to annulment by a resolution of either House of Parliament.

Note: Commencement 11 November 1999, s 170. Subsection (4)(e) omitted by Nationality, Immigration and Asylum Act 2002, s 61 from 7 November 2002. Words in square brackets in subsection (2) inserted by Asylum and Immigration Act 2004, s 41 from 1 October 2004 (SI 2004/2523). Subsection (4)(da) inserted by Sch 18 Legal Services Act from 1 April 2011 (SI 2011/720). Subsection (5)(za) inserted by Asylum and Immigration Act 2004, s 10 from 1 December 2004 (SI 2004/2999). Words in square brackets in subsection 6(b) inserted by Civil Partnership Act 2004 Schedule 27 from 15 April 2005 SI 2005/1112). Subsection (4)(g) omitted by Sch 9 Immigration Act 2014 from a date to be appointed.

167. Interpretation

(1) In this Act—

'the 1971 Act' means the Immigration Act 1971;

'adjudicator' (except in Part VI) means an adjudicator appointed under section 57;

'Chief Adjudicator' means the person appointed as Chief Adjudicator under section 57(2);

'claim for asylum' (except in Parts V and VI and section 141) means a claim that it would be contrary to the United Kingdom's obligations under the Refugee Convention for the claimant to be removed from, or required to leave, the United Kingdom;

'the Commission' means the Special Immigration Appeals Commission;

'country' includes any territory;

'EEA State' means a State which is a Contracting Party to the Agreement on the European Economic Area signed at Oporto on 2nd May 1992 as it has effect for the time being;

'the Human Rights Convention' means the Convention for the Protection of Human Rights and Fundamental Freedoms, agreed by the Council of Europe at Rome on 4 November 1950 as it has effect for the time being in relation to the United Kingdom;

. . .

'prescribed' means prescribed by regulations made by the Secretary of State;

'the Refugee Convention' means the Convention relating to the Status of Refugees done at Geneva on 28 July 1951 and the Protocol to the Convention;

'voluntary organisations' means bodies (other than public or local authorities) whose activities are not carried on for profit.

(2) The following expressions have the same meaning as in the 1971 Act—

'certificate of entitlement';
'entry clearance';
'illegal entrant';
'immigration officer';
'immigration rules';
'port';
'United Kingdom passport';
'work permit'.

Note: Commencement 11 November 1999, s 170. Words omitted ceased to have effect from 30 March 2006, s 64 Immigration, Asylum and Nationality Act 2006 (Royal Assent).

168. Expenditure and receipts

(1) There is to be paid out of money provided by Parliament—

(a) any expenditure incurred by the Secretary of State or the Lord Chancellor in consequence of this Act; and

(b) any increase attributable to this Act in the sums so payable by virtue of any other Act.

(2) Sums received by the Secretary of State under section 5, 32, 40, 112 or 113 or by the Lord Chancellor under section 48(4) or 49(4) must be paid into the Consolidated Fund.

Note: Commencement 11 November 1999, s 170.

169. Minor and consequential amendments, transitional provisions and repeals

(1) Schedule 14 makes minor and consequential amendments.

(2) Schedule 15 contains transitional provisions and savings.

(3) The enactments set out in Schedule 16 are repealed.

170. Short title, commencement and extent

(1) This Act may be cited as the Immigration and Asylum Act 1999.

(2) Subsections (1) and (2) of section 115 come into force on the day on which the first regulations made under Schedule 8 come into force.

(3) The following provisions come into force on the passing of this Act—

(a) section 4;
(b) section 9;
(c) section 15;
(d) section 27;
(e) section 31;
(f) section 94;
(g) section 95(13);
(h) section 99(4) and (5);
(i) sections 105 to 109;
(j) section 110(1), (2) and (8) (so far as relating to subsections (1) and (2));
(k) section 111;
(l) section 124;

(m) section 140;
(n) section 145;
(o) section 146(1);
(p) sections 166 to 168;
(q) this section;
(r) Schedule 9;
(s) paragraphs 62(2), 73, 78, 79, 81, 82, 87, 88 and 102 of Schedule 14;
(t) paragraph 2 and 13 of Schedule 15.

(4) The other provisions of this Act, except section 10 and paragraph 12 of Schedule 15 (which come into force in accordance with section 9), come into force on such day as the Secretary of State may by order appoint.

(5) Different days may be appointed for different purposes.

(6) This Act extends to Northern Ireland.

(7) Her Majesty may by Order in Council direct that any of the provisions of this Act are to extend, with such modifications (if any) as appear to Her Majesty to be appropriate, to any of the Channel Islands or the Isle of Man.

Note: Commenced 11 November 1999.

SCHEDULES

Sections 37(6) and 42(8)

SCHEDULE 1

SALE OF TRANSPORTERS

. . .

Section 56(2)

SCHEDULE 2

THE IMMIGRATION APPEAL TRIBUNAL

. . .

Note: Schedule 2 repealed by Sch 9 Nationality, Immigration and Asylum Act 2002 from 1 April 2003 (SI 2003/754, which sets out transitional provisions).

SCHEDULE 3

ADJUDICATORS

. . .

Note: Schedule 3 repealed by Sch 9 Nationality, Immigration and Asylum Act 2002 from 1 April 2003 (SI 2003/754, which sets out transitional provisions).

SCHEDULE 4

APPEALS

. . .

Note: Schedule 4 repealed by Sch 9 Nationality, Immigration and Asylum Act 2002 from 1 April 2003 (SI 2003/754, which sets out transitional provisions).

Section 83

Schedule 5

The Immigration Services Commissioner

Part I

Regulatory Functions

The Commissioner's rules

1.—(1) The Commissioner may make rules regulating any aspect of the professional practice, conduct or discipline of—

(a) registered persons, and

[(b) those acting on behalf of registered persons.]

(2) Before making or altering any rules, the Commissioner must consult such persons appearing to him to represent the views of persons engaged in the provision of immigration advice or immigration services as he considers appropriate.

(3) In determining whether a registered person is competent or otherwise fit to provide immigration advice or immigration services, the Commissioner may take into account any breach of the rules by—

(a) that person; and

[(b) any person acting on behalf of that person.]

(4) The rules may, among other things, make provision requiring the keeping of accounts or the obtaining of indemnity insurance.

Note: Sub-paragraphs (1)(b) and (3)(b) substituted by s 37 Asylum and Immigration (Treatment of Claimants) Act 2004 from 1 October 2004 (SI 2004/2523).

2.—(1) The Commissioner's rules must be made or altered by an instrument in writing.

(2) Such an instrument must specify that it is made under this Schedule.

(3) Immediately after such an instrument is made, it must be printed and made available to the public.

(4) The Commissioner may charge a reasonable fee for providing a person with a copy of the instrument.

(5) A person is not to be taken to have contravened a rule made by the Commissioner if he shows that at the time of the alleged contravention the instrument containing the rule had not been made available in accordance with this paragraph.

(6) The production of a printed copy of an instrument purporting to be made by the Commissioner on which is endorsed a certificate signed by an officer of the Commissioner authorised by him for that purpose and stating—

(a) that the instrument was made by the Commissioner,

(b) that the copy is a true copy of the instrument, and

(c) that on a specified date the instrument was made available to the public in accordance with this paragraph, is evidence (or in Scotland sufficient evidence) of the facts stated in the certificate.

(7) A certificate purporting to be signed as mentioned in sub-paragraph (6) is to be treated as having been properly signed unless the contrary is shown.

(8) A person who wishes in any legal proceedings to rely on an instrument containing the Commissioner's rules may require him to endorse a copy of the instrument with a certificate of the kind mentioned in sub-paragraph (6).

Code of Standards

3.—(1) The Commissioner must prepare and issue a code setting standards of conduct which those to whom the code applies are expected to meet.

(2) The code is to be known as the Code of Standards but is referred to in this Schedule as 'the Code'.

(3) The Code is to apply to any person providing immigration advice or immigration services other than—

(a) a person who is authorised by a designated professional body to practise as a member of the profession whose members are regulated by that body;

[(aa) a person who is authorised by a designated qualifying regulator to provide immigration advice or immigration services;]

[(b) a person who is acting on behalf of a person who is within paragraph (a), [or (aa)]];

(4) It is the duty of any person to whom the Code applies to comply with its provisions in providing immigration advice or immigration services.

(5) If the Commissioner alters the Code, he must re-issue it.

(6) Before issuing the Code or altering it, the Commissioner must consult—

(a) each of the designated professional bodies;

[(aa) each of the designated qualifying regulators;]

(b) . . .

(c) the Lord President of the Court of Session;

(d) the Lord Chief Justice of Northern Ireland; and

(e) such other persons appearing to him to represent the views of persons engaged in the provision of immigration advice or immigration services as he considers appropriate.

(7) The Commissioner must publish the Code in such form and manner as the Secretary of State may direct.

Note: Subparagraphs (3)(aa), (6)(aa) and first words in square brackets in subparagraph (3)(b) inserted by Sch 18 Legal Services Act 2007 from 1 April 2011 (SI 2011/720). Subparagraph (3)(b) substituted by s 37 Asylum and Immigration (Treatment of Claimants) Act 2004 from 1 October 2004 (SI 2004/2523).

Extension of scope of the Code

4.—(1) The Secretary of State may by order provide for the provisions of the Code, or such provisions of the Code as may be specified by the order, to apply to—

(a) persons authorised by any designated professional body to practise as a member of the profession whose members are regulated by that body; and

[(b) persons acting on behalf of persons who are within paragraph (a)].

(2) If the Secretary of State is proposing to act under sub-paragraph (1) he must, before doing so, consult—

(a) the Commissioner;

(b) . . .

(c) the [Scottish Legal Complaints Commission], if the proposed order would affect a designated professional body in Scotland;

(d) the lay observers appointed under Article 42 of the Solicitors (Northern Ireland) Order 1976, if the proposed order would affect a designated professional body in Northern Ireland.

(3) An order under sub-paragraph (1) requires the approval of—

(a) the Lord Chancellor, if it affects a designated professional body in . . . Northern Ireland;

(b) the Scottish Ministers, if it affects a designated professional body in Scotland.

(4) Before deciding whether or not to give his approval under sub-paragraph (3)(a), the Lord Chancellor must consult—

(a) . . .

(b) the Lord Chief Justice of Northern Ireland, if it affects a designated professional body in Northern Ireland.

(5) Before deciding whether or not to give their approval under sub-paragraph (3)(b), the Scottish Ministers must consult the Lord President of the Court of Session.

Note: Subparagraph (1)(b) substituted by s 37 Asylum and Immigration (Treatment of Claimants) Act 2004 from 1 October 2004 (SI 2004/2523). Subparagraphs (2)(b), (4)(a), and words in (3)(a) omitted, words in square brackets in (2)(c) substituted by Sch 18 Legal Services Act 2007 from 1 April 2011 (SI 2011/720).

[**Inspections 4A.** The Commissioner may carry out inspections of the activities and businesses of registered persons.]

Note: Paragraph 4A inserted by Sch 7 Immigation Act 2014 from 28 July 2014 (SI 2014/1820).

Investigation of complaints

5.—(1) The Commissioner must establish a scheme ('the complaints scheme') for the investigation by him of relevant complaints made to him in accordance with the provisions of the scheme.

(2) Before establishing the scheme or altering it, the Commissioner must consult—

(a) each of the designated professional bodies; and

(b) such other persons appearing to him to represent the views of persons engaged in the provision of immigration advice or immigration services as he considers appropriate.

(3) A complaint is a relevant complaint if it relates to—

[(za) the competence or fitness to provide immigration advice or immigration services of a person who, at the time to which the complaint relates, was a registered person,]

(a) the competence or fitness of [any other person] to provide immigration advice or immigration services,

[(aa) the competence or fitness of a person who, at the time to which the complaint relates, was acting on behalf of a registered person,]

(b) the competence or fitness of [any other person] [acting on behalf of] a person providing immigration advice or immigration services,

(c) an alleged breach of the Code,

(d) an alleged breach of one or more of the Commissioner's rules by [a person who, at the time to which the complaint relates, was a registered person or a person acting on behalf of a registered person], or

[(e) an alleged breach of a rule of a relevant regulatory body.]

[but not if the complaint is excluded by sub-paragraph (3A).]

[(3A) A complaint is excluded if—

(a) it relates to a person who is excluded from the application of subsection (1) of section 84 by subsection (6) of that section, or

(b) it relates to a person within section 84(2)(ba).]

(4) The Commissioner may, on his own initiative, investigate any matter which he would have power to investigate on a complaint made under the complaints scheme.

(5) In investigating any such matter on his own initiative, the Commissioner must proceed as if his investigation were being conducted in response to a complaint made under the scheme.

Note: Subparagraphs (3)(za), (3)(aa) inserted, words in first square brackets in (3)(b) and square brackets in (3)(a) and (3)(d) substituted by Sch 7 Immigration Act 2014 from 17 November 2014

(SI 2014/2771). Words in second square brackets in subparagraph (3)(b) and subparagraph (3)(e) substituted by s 37 Asylum and Immigration (Treatment of Claimants) Act 2004 from 1 October 2004 (SI 2004/2523). Other words in square brackets in subparagraph (3) and (3A) inserted by Sch 18 Legal Services Act 2007 from 1 April 2011 (SI 2011/720).

6.—(1) The complaints scheme must provide for a person who is the subject of an investigation under the scheme to be given a reasonable opportunity to make representations to the Commissioner.

(2) Any person who is the subject of an investigation under the scheme must—
(a) take such steps as are reasonably required to assist the Commissioner in his investigation; and
(b) comply with any reasonable requirement imposed on him by the Commissioner.

(3) If a person fails to comply with sub-paragraph (2)(a) or with a requirement imposed under sub-paragraph (2)(b) the Commissioner may—
(a) in the ease of a registered person, cancel his registration;
(b) . . . or
[(c) in any other case, refer the matter to any relevant regulatory body.]

Note: Subparagraph (3)(c) substituted by s 37 Asylum and Immigration (Treatment of Claimants) Act 2004 from 1 October 2004 (SI 2004/2523). Subparagraph (3)(b) omitted by Sch 7 Immigration Act 2014 from 17 November 2014 (SI 2014/2771).

7. . . .

Note: Paragraph 7 and heading omitted by Sch 7 Immigration Act 2014 from 17 November 2014 (SI 2014/2771).

Determination of complaints

8.—(1) On determining a complaint under the complaints scheme, the Commissioner must give his decision in a written statement.

(2) The statement must include the Commissioner's reasons for his decision.

(3) A copy of the statement must be given by the Commissioner to—
(a) the person who made the complaint; and
(b) the person who is the subject of the complaint.

9.—(1) On determining a complaint under the complaints scheme, the Commissioner may—
[(a) if the person to whom the complaint relates was at the time to which the complaint relates—
(i) a registered person, or
(ii) a person acting on behalf of a registered person,
record the complaint and the decision on it to be considered in connection with the next relevant application;]
(b) . . .
[(c) refer the complaint and his decision on it to a relevant regulatory body;]
(d) . . .
(e) lay before the [First-tier Tribunal] a disciplinary charge against a relevant person.

[(1A) In sub-paragraph (1)(a) "relevant application" means—
(a) if the registered person referred to in that sub-paragraph is still registered, an application by that person for continued registration, and
(b) otherwise, an application by that person for registration.]

[(1B) Sub-paragraph (1)(a) is subject to paragraph 4A(e) of Schedule 6 (duty of Commissioner to cancel registration of a person who is no longer competent or is otherwise unfit).]

(2) Sub-paragraph (3) applies if—
(a) the [First-tier Tribunal] is considering a disciplinary charge against a relevant person; and
(b) the Commissioner asks it to exercise its powers under that subparagraph.

(3) The [First-tier Tribunal] may give directions (which are to have effect while it is dealing with the charge)—

[(a) imposing restrictions on the provision of immigration advice or immigration services by the relevant person or by a person acting on his behalf or under his supervision;

(b) prohibiting the provision of immigration advice or immigration services by the relevant person or a person acting on his behalf or under his supervision.]

[(4) 'Relevant person' means—

(a) a person who, at the time to which the charge relates, was providing immigration advice or immigration services and was—

(i) a registered person, or

(ii) a person acting on behalf of a registered person;

[(b) a person providing immigration advice or immigration services who is—

(i) a person to who section 84(4)(d) applies, or

(ii) a person employed by, or working under the supervision of, such a person.]

Note: Words in first and second square brackets substituted by s 37 Asylum and Immigration (Treatment of Claimants) Act 2004 from 1 October 2004 (SI 2004/2523). Other words in square brackets substituted from 6 April 2010 (SI 2010/22). Subparagraphs (1)(a) and (4) substituted, (1)(b) and (1)(d) omitted and (1A) and (1B) inserted by Sch 7 Immigration Act 2014 from 17 November 2014 (SI 2014/2771).

Complaints referred to designated professional bodies

10.—(1) This paragraph applies if the Commissioner refers a complaint to a designated professional body under paragraph 9(1)(c).

(2) The Commissioner may give directions setting a timetable to be followed by the designated professional body—

(a) in considering the complaint; and

(b) if appropriate, in taking disciplinary proceedings in connection with the complaint.

(3) In making his annual report to the Secretary of State under paragraph 21, the Commissioner must take into account any failure of a designated professional body to comply (whether wholly or in part) with directions given to it under this paragraph.

(4) Sub-paragraph (5) applies if the Commissioner or the Secretary of State considers that a designated professional body has persistently failed to comply with directions given to it under this paragraph.

(5) The Commissioner must take the failure into account in determining whether to make a report under section 86(9)(b) and the Secretary of State must take it into account in determining whether to make an order under section 86(2).

[Power of entry and inspection

10A.—(1) On an application made by the Commissioner a justice of the peace (or in Scotland, the sheriff) may issue a warrant authorising the Commissioner to enter premises.

(2) A justice of the peace or sheriff may issue a warrant in respect of premises if satisfied that there are reasonable grounds for believing that—

(a) the premises are being used, or have been used, in connection with the provision of immigration advice or immigration services by a registered person,

(b) entry to the premises is reasonably required for the exercise of any of the Commissioner's functions, and

(c) entry to the premises may be prevented or delayed unless a warrant is produced.

(3) The Commissioner may enter premises by virtue of this paragraph only at a reasonable hour.

(4) Where the Commissioner enters premises by virtue of this paragraph the Commissioner may—
(a) take onto the premises any equipment that appears to the Commissioner to be necessary;
(b) require any person on the premises to produce any relevant document and, if the document is produced, to provide any explanation of it;
(c) require any person on the premises to state, to the best of the person's knowledge and belief, where any relevant document is to be found;
(d) take copies of, or extracts from, any relevant document on the premises which is produced;
(e) require any relevant information which is held in a computer and is accessible from the premises to be produced in a form—
(i) in which it can be taken away; and
(ii) in which it is visible and legible.

(5) For the purposes of sub-paragraph (4), a document or information is "relevant" if the document or information relates to any matter connected with the provision of immigration advice or immigration services.

(6) The powers conferred on the Commissioner by sub-paragraphs (1) to (5) may also be exercised by—
(a) a member of the Commissioner's staff authorised by the Commissioner in writing, and
(b) if the Commissioner so determines, a person appointed by the Commissioner to make a report on the provision of immigration advice or immigration services from the premises in question.

(7) If a registered person fails without reasonable excuse to allow access under this paragraph to any premises under the person's occupation or control, the Commissioner may cancel the person's registration.

(8) The Commissioner may also cancel the registration of a registered person who—
(a) without reasonable excuse fails to comply with a requirement imposed under sub-paragraph (4);
(b) intentionally delays or obstructs any person exercising functions under this paragraph; or
(c) fails to take reasonable steps to prevent an employee of the registered person from obstructing any person exercising such functions.

(9) In this paragraph "premises" includes premises used wholly or partly as a dwelling.]

Note: Paragraph 10A inserted by Sch 7 Immigration Act 2014 from 17 November 2014 (SI 2014/2771).

Part II

Commissioner's Status, Remuneration and Staff etc

. . .

Section 85(3)

Schedule 6

Registration

Applications for registration

1.—(1) An application for registration under section 84(2)(a) . . . must—
(a) be made to the Commissioner in such form and manner, and
(b) be accompanied by such information and supporting evidence, as the Commissioner may from time to time determine.

(2) When considering an application for registration, the Commissioner may require the applicant to provide him with such further information or supporting evidence as the Commissioner may reasonably require.

Registration

2.—(1) If the Commissioner considers that an applicant for registration is competent and otherwise fit to provide immigration advice and immigration services, he must register the applicant.

(2) Registration may be made so as to have effect—
(a) only in relation to a specified field of advice or services;
(b) only in relation to the provision of advice or services to a specified category of person;
(c) only in relation to the provision of advice or services to a member of a specified category of person; or
(d) only in specified circumstances.

Review of qualifications

3.—(1) At such intervals as the Commissioner may determine, each registered person must submit an application for his registration to be continued.

(2) Different intervals may be fixed by the Commissioner in relation to different registered persons or descriptions of registered person.

(3) An application for continued registration must—
(a) be made to the Commissioner in such form and manner, and
(b) be accompanied by such information and supporting evidence, as the Commissioner may from time to time determine.

(4) When considering an application for continued registration, the Commissioner may require the applicant to provide him with such further information or supporting evidence as the Commissioner may reasonably require.

(5) . . .

(6) [Unless the Commissioner is required by paragraph 4A to cancel the applicant's registration], the Commissioner must continue the applicant's registration but may, in doing so, vary the registration—
(a) so as to make it have limited effect in any of the ways mentioned in paragraph 2(2); or
(b) so as to make it have full effect.

(7) If a registered person fails, without reasonable excuse—
(a) to make an application for continued registration as required by subparagraph (1) . . . , or
(b) to provide further information or evidence under sub-paragraph (4),

the Commissioner may cancel the person's registration as from such date as he may determine.

Note: Amended by Sch 7 Immigration Act 2014 from 17 November 2014 (SI 2014/2771).

[Variation of registration

3A. The Commissioner may vary a person's registration—
(a) so as to make it have limited effect in any of the ways mentioned in paragraph 2(2); or
(b) so as to make it have full effect.]

Disqualification of certain persons

4. A person convicted of an offence under section 25 or 26(1)(d) or (g) of the 1971 Act is disqualified for registration under paragraph 2 or for continued registration under paragraph 3.

[4A. The Commissioner must cancel a person's registration if—
(a) the person asks for it to be cancelled;
(b) the person dies (in a case where the person is an individual) or is dissolved or wound up (in any other case);

(c) the person is convicted of an offence under section 25 or 26(1)(d) or (g) of the 1971 Act;
(d) under section 89(2A)(b) the First-tier Tribunal directs the Commissioner to cancel the person's registration; or
(e) the Commissioner considers that the person is no longer competent or is otherwise unfit to provide immigration advice or immigration services.]

Note: Paragraph 4A inserted by Sch 7 Immigration Act 2014 from 17 October 2014 (SI 2014/2771).

[Suspension of registration

[**4B.**—(1) The First-tier Tribunal may, on an application made to it by the Commissioner, suspend a person's registration if the person is for the time being charged with—
(a) an offence involving dishonesty or deception;
(b) an indictable offence; or
(c) an offence under section 25 or 26(1)(d) or (g) of the 1971 Act.

(2) The suspension of the person's registration ceases to have effect if one of these occurs—
(a) the person is acquitted of the offence;
(b) the charge is withdrawn;
(c) proceedings in respect of the charge are discontinued;
(d) an order is made for the charge to lie on the file, or in relation to Scotland, the diet is deserted *pro loco et tempore.*

(3) If the person is convicted of an offence under section 25 or 26(1)(d) or (g) of the 1971 Act, the suspension of the person's registration continues to have effect until the Commissioner cancels the person's registration (as required by paragraph 4A(c)).

(4) If the person is convicted of any other offence within sub-paragraph (1)—
(a) the Commissioner must as soon as reasonably practicable consider whether the person is no longer competent or is otherwise unfit to provide immigration advice or immigration services (so that the person's registration must be cancelled under paragraph 4A(e));
(b) the suspension of the person's registration continues to have effect until the Commissioner either cancels the person's registration, or decides that the person is competent and otherwise fit to provide immigration advice and immigration services.

(5) A person whose registration is suspended is not to be treated as a registered person for the purposes of section 84 (but is to be treated as a registered person for the purposes of the other provisions of this Part).

(6) Where a person's registration is suspended the Commissioner must as soon as reasonably practicable record the suspension in the register.

(7) Where a suspension ceases to have effect (and the person's registration is not cancelled) the Commissioner must as soon as reasonably practicable remove the record of the suspension from the register.]

Note: Paragraph 4B inserted by Sch 7 Immigration Act 2014 from 17 November 2014 (SI 2014/2771).

Fees

5.—(1) The Secretary of State may by order
[a] specify fees for the registration or continued registration of persons on the register.
[(b) make provision for, and in connection with, requiring or authorising the Commissioner to waive all or part of the specified fee in particular cases.]

(2) No application under paragraph 1 or 3 is to be entertained by the Commissioner unless it is accompanied by the specified fee [(but this is subject to any waiver in accordance with provision under sub-paragraph (1)(b))].

Note: Amended by Sch 7 Immigration Act 2014 from 17 November 2014 (SI 2014/2771).

Open registers

6.—(1) The register must be made available for inspection by members of the public in a legible form at reasonable hours.

(2) A copy of the register or of any entry in the register must be provided—

(a) on payment of a reasonable fee;

(b) in written or electronic form; and

(c) in a legible form.

(3) Sub-paragraphs (1) and (2) also apply to—

(a) . . .

(b) the record kept by the Commissioner of the persons against whom there is in force a direction given by the [First-tier Tribunal] under section 89(8).

Note: Words omitted from subparagraph (1), by s 37 Asylum and Immigration (Treatment of Claimants) Act 2004 from 1 October 2004 (SI 2004/2523). Words in second square brackets in subparagraph (3)(7) substituted by s 37 Asylum and Immigration (Treatment of Claimants) Act 2004 from 1 October 2004 (SI 2004/2523). Paragraph 3A inserted by Nationality, Immigration and Asylum Act 2002, s 140 from 8 January 2003 (SI 2003/1). Other words in square brackets substituted from 6 April 2010 (SI 2010/22). Subparagraph (3)(a) omitted by Sch 7 Immigration Act 2014 from 17 November 2014 (SI 2014/2771).

Section 87(5)

SCHEDULE 7

. . .

Note: Revoked from 6 April 2010 (SI 2010/22).

Section 95(12)

SCHEDULE 8

PROVISION OF SUPPORT: REGULATIONS

. . .

Section 95(13)

SCHEDULE 9

ASYLUM SUPPORT: INTERIM PROVISIONS

. . .

Section 102(3)

SCHEDULE 10

ASYLUM SUPPORT ADJUDICATORS

. . .

Note: Revoked from 3 November 2008 (SI 2008/2833).

Section 154(7)

Schedule 11

Detainee Custody Officers

. . .

Section 155(2)

Schedule 12

Discipline etc. at [Removal Centres]

. . .

Section 156(5)

Schedule 13

Escort Arrangements

. . .

Section 169(1)

Schedule 14

Consequential Amendments

. . .

Section 169(2)

Schedule 15

Transitional Provisions and Savings

Leave to enter or remain

1.—(1) An order made under section 3A of the 1971 Act may make provision with respect to leave given before the commencement of section 1.

(2) An order made under section 3B of the 1971 Act may make provision with respect to leave given before the commencement of section 2.

Section 2 of the Asylum and Immigration Act 1996

2.—(1) This paragraph applies in relation to any time before the commencement of the repeal by this Act of section 2 of the Asylum and Immigration Act 1996.

(2) That section has effect, and is to be deemed always to have had effect, as if the reference to section 6 of the Asylum and Immigration Appeals Act 1993 were a reference to section 15, and any certificate issued under that section is to be read accordingly.

Adjudicators and the Tribunal

3. . . .

References to justices' chief executive

4. . . .

Duties under National Assistance Act 1948

5. . . .

Duties under Health Services and Public Health Act 1968

6. . . .

Duties under Social Work (Scotland) Act 1968

7. . . .

Duties under Health and Personal Social Services (Northern Ireland) Order 1972

8. . . .

Duties under National Health Service Act 1977

9. . . .

Duties under Mental Health (Scotland) Act 1984

10. . . .

Appeals relating to deportation orders

11. Section 15 of the 1971 Act, section 5 of the Immigration Act 1988 and the Immigration (Restricted Right of Appeal against Deportation) (Exemption) Order 1993 are to continue to have effect in relation to any person on whom the Secretary of State has, before the commencement of the repeal of those sections, served a notice of his decision to make a deportation order.

12.—(1) Sub-paragraph (2) applies if, on the coming into force of section 10, sections 15 of the 1971 Act and 5 of the Immigration Act 1988 have been repealed by this Act.

(2) Those sections are to continue to have effect in relation to any person—

(a) who applied during the regularisation period fixed by section 9, in accordance with the regulations made under that section, for leave to remain in the United Kingdom, and

(b) on whom the Secretary of State has since served a notice of his decision to make a deportation order.

Assistance under Part VII of the Housing Act 1996

13. . . .

Provision of support

14. . . .

Section 169(3)

SCHEDULE 16

REPEALS

. . .

British Overseas Territories Act 2002
(2002, c. 8)

An Act to make provision about the name 'British overseas territories' and British citizenship so far as relating to the British overseas territories. [26 February 2002]

Change of names

1. British overseas territories

(1) As the territories mentioned in Schedule 6 to the British Nationality Act 1981 (c. 61) are now known as 'British overseas territories'—

(a) . . .
(b) . . .
(c) . . .

(2) In any other enactment passed or made before the commencement of this section (including an enactment comprised in subordinate legislation), any reference to a dependent territory within the meaning of the British Nationality Act 1981 shall be read as a reference to a British overseas territory.

(3) . . .

Note: Subsection (1)(a)–(c) amends British Nationality Act 1981, subsection (3) amends Sch 1 Interpretation Act 1978. Commenced 26 February 2002.

2. British overseas territories citizenship

(1) Pursuant to section 1, British Dependent Territories citizenship is renamed 'British overseas territories citizenship'; and a person having that citizenship is a 'British overseas territories citizen'.

(2) . . .

(3) In any other enactment passed or made before the commencement of this section (including an enactment comprised in subordinate legislation), any reference to British Dependent Territories citizenship, or a British Dependent Territories citizen, shall be read as a reference to British overseas territories citizenship, or a British overseas territories citizen.

Note: Subsection (2) amends British Nationality Act 1981. Commenced 26 February 2002.

British citizenship

3. Conferral on British overseas territories citizens

(1) Any person who, immediately before the commencement of this section, is a British overseas territories citizen shall, on the commencement of this section, become a British citizen.

(2) Subsection (1) does not apply to a person who is a British overseas territories citizen by virtue only of a connection with the Sovereign Base Areas of Akrotiri and Dhekelia.

(3) A person who is a British citizen by virtue of this section is a British citizen by descent for the purposes of the British Nationality Act 1981 if, and only if—

(a) he was a British overseas territories citizen by descent immediately before the commencement of this section, and

(b) if at that time he was a British citizen as well as a British overseas territories citizen, he was a British citizen by descent.

Note: Commenced 21 May 2002 (SI 2002/1252).

4. Acquisition by British overseas territories citizens by registration

. . .

Note: Amends British Nationality Act 1981, s 4.

5. Acquisition by reference to the British overseas territories

Schedule 1 (which makes provision about the acquisition of British citizenship by reference to the British overseas territories) has effect.

Note: Commenced 21 May 2002 (SI 2002/1252).

Supplementary

6. The Ilois: citizenship

(1) A person shall become a British citizen on the commencement of this section if—

(a) he was born on or after 26 April 1969 and before 1 January 1983,

(b) he was born to a woman who at the time was a citizen of the United Kingdom and Colonies by virtue of her birth in the British Indian Ocean Territory, and

(c) immediately before the commencement of this section he was neither a British citizen nor a British overseas territories citizen.

(2) A person who is a British citizen by virtue of subsection (1) is a British citizen by descent for the purposes of the British Nationality Act 1981 (c. 61).

(3) A person shall become a British overseas territories citizen on the commencement of this section if—

(a) subsection (1)(a) and (b) apply in relation to him, and

(b) immediately before the commencement of this section he was not a British overseas territories citizen.

(4) A person who is a British overseas territories citizen by virtue of subsection (3) is such a citizen by descent for the purposes of the British Nationality Act 1981.

Note: Commenced 21 May 2002 (SI 2002/1252).

7. Repeals

The enactments mentioned in Schedule 2 (which include some which are spent or effectively superseded) are repealed to the extent specified there.

Note: Commenced 26 February 2002, save in relation to the British Nationality (Falkland Islands) Act 1983, where commencement was 21 May 2002 (SI 2002/1252).

8. Short title, commencement and extent

(1) This Act may be cited as the British Overseas Territories Act 2002.

(2) The following provisions of this Act are to come into force on such day as the Secretary of State may by order made by statutory instrument appoint—

(a) sections 3 to 5 and Schedule 1,

(b) section 6, and

(c) section 7 and Schedule 2, so far as relating to the British Nationality (Falkland Islands) Act 1983 (c. 6).

(3) An order under subsection (2) may—

(a) appoint different days for different purposes, and

(b) include such transitional provision as the Secretary of State considers expedient.

(4) This Act extends to—

(a) the United Kingdom,

(b) the Channel Islands and the Isle of Man, and

(c) the British overseas territories.

Schedules

Schedule 1

British Citizenship and The British Overseas Territories

Birth or adoption

1. . . .

Descent

2. . . .

Registration of minors

3. . . .

Commonwealth citizens

4. . . .

Interpretation

5. . . .

6. . . .

Note: Amends British Nationality Act 1981, ss 1, 2, 3, 37(1)(a), 50 and 51(3)(a) from 21 May 2002 (SI 2002/1252).

SCHEDULE 2
REPEALS

. . .

Note: Commencement 26 February 2002.

Nationality, Immigration and Asylum Act 2002

(2002, c. 41)

Arrangement of Sections

Part I. Nationality

Part II. Accommodation Centres

Establishment

Use of centres

Operation of centres

31. Financial contribution by resident
32. Tenure
33. Advisory Groups

General

34. . . .
35. Ancillary provisions
36. Education: general
37. Education: special cases
38. Local authority
39. 'Prescribed': orders and regulations
40. Scotland
41. Northern Ireland
42. Wales

PART III. OTHER SUPPORT AND ASSISTANCE

43. Asylum-seeker: form of support
44. . . .
45. . . .
46. . . .
47. . . .
48. Young asylum-seeker
49. . . .
50. . . .
51. Choice of form of support
52. . . .
53. . . .
54. Withholding and withdrawal of support
55. Late claim for asylum: refusal of support
56. . . .
57. . . .
58. Voluntary departure from United Kingdom
59. International projects
60. . . .
61. . . .

PART IV. DETENTION AND REMOVAL

Detention

62. Detention by Secretary of State
63. . . .
64. . . .
65. . . .
66. Detention centres: change of name
67. Construction of reference to person liable to detention

Work permit

Authority-to-carry scheme

Evasion of procedure

Provision of information by traveller

Disclosure of information by public authority

Disclosure of information by private person

Immigration services

Immigration control

Country information

Part VII. Offences

Substance

An Act to make provision about nationality, immigration and asylum; to create offences in connection with international traffic in prostitution; to make provision about international projects connected with migration; and for connected purposes. [7 November 2002]

PART I

NATIONALITY

1. Naturalisation: knowledge of language and society

. . .

Note: Amends British Nationality Act 1981, s 41 and Sch 1.

2. Naturalisation: spouse of citizen

. . .

Note: Amends Sch 1 British Nationality Act 1981.

3. Citizenship ceremony, oath and pledge

Schedule 1 (which makes provision about citizenship ceremonies, oaths and pledges) shall have effect.

Note: Commencement 1 January 2004 (SI 2003/3516).

4. Deprivation of citizenship

(1) . . .

Note: Amends British Nationality Act 1981, s 40.

(2) . . .

Note: Amends Special Immigration Appeals Commission Act 1997, s 2.

(3) . . .

Note: Amends Special Immigration Appeals Commission Act 1997, s 5.

(4) In exercising a power under section 40 of the British Nationality Act 1981 after the commencement of subsection (1) above the Secretary of State may have regard to anything which—

(a) occurred before commencement, and

(b) he could have relied on (whether on its own or with other matters) in making an order under section 40 before commencement.

Note: Commencement from 1 April 2003 (SI 2003/754).

5. Resumption of citizenship

. . .

Note: Amends British Nationality Act 1981, ss 10, 22.

6. Nationality decision: discrimination

. . .

Note: Amends Race Relations Act 1976, ss 19 and 71. Subsections (1)–(4) omitted from 4 April 2011 (SI 2011/1060).

7. Nationality decision: reasons and review

(1) . . .

Note: Amends British Nationality Act 1981, s 44.

(2) . . .

Note: Amends British Nationality (Hong Kong) Act 1990, s 1.

8. Citizenship: registration

. . .

Note: Amends paragraph 3, Sch 2 British Nationality Act 1981.

9. Legitimacy of child

(1) . . .

Note: Amends British Nationality Act 1981, s 50(9).

(2) . . .

Note: Amends British Nationality Act 1981, s 3(6).

(3) . . .

Note: Amends British Nationality Act 1981, s 17(6).

(4) . . .

Note: Amends British Nationality Act 1981, s 47.

(5) . . .

Note: Amends paragraphs 1, 2, Sch 2 British Nationality Act 1981.

10. Right of abode: certificate of entitlement

(1) The Secretary of State may by regulations make provision for the issue to a person of a certificate that he has the right of abode in the United Kingdom.

(2) The regulations may, in particular—

(a) specify to whom an application must be made;

(b) specify the place (which may be outside the United Kingdom) to which an application must be sent;

(c) provide that an application must be [accompanied by specified information;]

(d) provide that an application must be accompanied by specified documents;

(e) . . .

(f) specify the consequences of failure to comply with a requirement under any of paragraphs [(a) to (d)] above;

(g) provide for a certificate to cease to have effect after a period of time specified in or determined in accordance with the regulations;

(h) make provision about the revocation of a certificate.

(3) The regulations may—

(a) make provision which applies generally or only in specified cases or circumstances;

(b) make different provision for different purposes;

(c) include consequential, incidental or transitional provision.

(4) The regulations—

(a) must be made by statutory instrument, and

(b) shall be subject to annulment in pursuance of a resolution of either House of Parliament.

(5) . . .

(6) Regulations under this section may, in particular, include provision saving, with or without modification, the effect of a certificate which—

(a) is issued before the regulations come into force, and

(b) is a certificate of entitlement for the purposes of sections 3(9) and 33(1) of the Immigration Act 1971 as those sections have effect before the commencement of subsection (5) above.

Note: Subsection (5) amends Immigration Act 1971, ss 3, 33. Subsections (1)–(4) and (6) commenced on 7 November 2002, s 162. Subsection (2)(e) deleted by Immigration, Asylum and Nationality Act 2006, s 52 and Sch 2 from 2 April 2007 (SI 2007/182). Words in square brackets in subsection (2) substituted by Immigration, Asylum and Nationality Act 2006, s 50 from 5 November 2007 (SI 2007/3138).

11. Unlawful presence in United Kingdom

. . .

Note: Commenced 7 November 2002, s 162. Revoked by s 48 Borders, Citizenship and Immigration Act 2009 from 13 January 2010 (SI 2009/2731), with transitional provisions.

12. British citizenship: registration of certain persons without other citizenship

Note: Amends British Nationality Act 1981, ss 4, 14.

13. British citizenship: registration of certain persons born between 1961 and 1983

Note: Amends British Nationality Act 1981, ss 4, 14.

14. Hong Kong

A person may not be registered as a British overseas territories citizen under a provision of the British Nationality Act 1981 (c. 61) by virtue of a connection with Hong Kong.

Note: Commencement from 1 January 2004 (SI 2003/3156).

15. Repeal of spent provisions

Schedule 2 (which repeals spent provisions) shall have effect.

Note: Commencement 7 November 2002, s 162.

Part II

Accommodation Centres

Establishment

16. Establishment of centres

(1) The Secretary of State may arrange for the provision of premises for the accommodation of persons in accordance with this Part.

(2) A set of premises provided under this section is referred to in this Act as an 'accommodation centre'.

(3) The Secretary of State may arrange for—

(a) the provision of facilities at or near an accommodation centre for sittings of adjudicators appointed for the purpose of Part 5 in accordance with a determination . . . under paragraph 2 of Schedule 4;

(b) the provision of facilities at an accommodation centre for the taking of steps in connection with the determination of claims for asylum (within the meaning of section 18(3)).

Note: Commencement 7 November 2002, s 162. Words deleted by Sch 18 Constitutional Reform Act 2005 from 3 April 2006 (SI 2006/1014).

Use of centres

17. Support for destitute asylum-seeker

(1) The Secretary of State may arrange for the provision of accommodation for a person in an accommodation centre if—

(a) the person is an asylum-seeker or the dependant of an asylum-seeker, and

(b) the Secretary of State thinks that the person is destitute or is likely to become destitute within a prescribed period.

(2) The Secretary of State may make regulations about procedure to be followed in respect of the provision of accommodation under this section.

(3) The regulations may, in particular, make provision—

(a) specifying procedure to be followed in applying for accommodation in an accommodation centre;

(b) providing for an application to be combined with an application under or in respect of another enactment;

(c) requiring an applicant to provide information;

(d) specifying circumstances in which an application may not be considered (which provision may, in particular, provide for an application not to be considered where the Secretary of State is not satisfied that the information provided is complete or accurate or that the applicant is co-operating with enquiries under paragraph (e));

(e) about the making of enquiries by the Secretary of State;

(f) requiring a person to notify the Secretary of State of a change in circumstances.

(4) Sections 18 to 20 define the following expressions for the purpose of this Part—

(a) asylum-seeker,

(b) dependant, and

(c) destitute.

Note: Commencement from a date to be appointed.

18. Asylum-seeker: definition

(1) For the purposes of this Part a person is an 'asylum-seeker' if—

(a) he is at least 18 years old,

(b) he is in the United Kingdom,

(c) a claim for asylum has been made by him at a place designated by the Secretary of State,

(d) the Secretary of State has recorded the claim, and

(e) the claim has not been determined.

(2) A person shall continue to be treated as an asylum-seeker despite subsection (1)(e) while—

(a) his household includes a dependent child who is under 18, and

(b) he does not have leave to enter or remain in the United Kingdom.

(3) A claim for asylum is a claim by a person that to remove him from or require him to leave the United Kingdom would be contrary to the United Kingdom's obligations under—

(a) the Convention relating to the Status of Refugees done at Geneva on 28 July 1951 and its Protocol, or

(b) Article 3 of the Convention for the Protection of Human Rights and Fundamental Freedoms agreed by the Council of Europe at Rome on 4 November 1950.

Note: Commenced for the purposes of ss 55(9), 70(3) and paragraph 17(1)(b) of Sch 3 on 8 January 2003 (SI 2003/1). For the purposes of Immigration Act 1971, s 26A(2) and this Act, s 71(5), 10 February 2003 (SI 2003/01).

19. Destitution: definition

(1) Where a person has dependants, he and his dependants are destitute for the purpose of this Part if they do not have and cannot obtain both—

(a) adequate accommodation, and

(b) food and other essential items.

(2) Where a person does not have dependants, he is destitute for the purpose of this Part if he does not have and cannot obtain both—

(a) adequate accommodation, and

(b) food and other essential items.

(3) In determining whether accommodation is adequate for the purposes of subsection (1) or (2) the Secretary of State must have regard to any matter prescribed for the purposes of this subsection.

(4) In determining whether accommodation is adequate for the purposes of subsection (1) or (2) the Secretary of State may not have regard to—

(a) whether a person has an enforceable right to occupy accommodation,

(b) whether a person shares all or part of accommodation,

(c) whether accommodation is temporary or permanent,

(d) the location of accommodation, or

(e) any other matter prescribed for the purposes of this subsection.

(5) The Secretary of State may by regulations specify items which are or are not to be treated as essential items for the purposes of subsections (1) and (2).

(6) The Secretary of State may by regulations—

(a) provide that a person is not to be treated as destitute for the purposes of this Part in specified circumstances;

(b) enable or require the Secretary of State in deciding whether a person is destitute to have regard to income which he or a dependant of his might reasonably be expected to have;

(c) enable or require the Secretary of State in deciding whether a person is destitute to have regard to support which is or might reasonably be expected to be available to the person or a dependant of his;

(d) enable or require the Secretary of State in deciding whether a person is destitute to have regard to assets of a prescribed kind which he or a dependant of his has or might reasonably be expected to have;

(e) make provision as to the valuation of assets.

Note: Commencement at a date to be appointed.

20. Dependant: definition

For the purposes of this Part a person is a 'dependant' of an asylum-seeker if (and only if) that person—

(a) is in the United Kingdom, and

(b) is within a prescribed class.

Note: Commencement at a date to be appointed.

21. Sections 17 to 20: supplementary

(1) This section applies for the purposes of sections 17 to 20.

(2) The Secretary of State may inquire into and decide a person's age.

(3) A claim for asylum shall be treated as determined at the end of such period as may be prescribed beginning with—

(a) the date on which the Secretary of State notifies the claimant of his decision on the claim, or

(b) if the claimant appeals against the Secretary of State's decision, the date on which the appeal is disposed of.

(4) A notice under subsection (3)(a)—

(a) must be in writing, and

(b) if sent by first class post to the claimant's last known address or to the claimant's representative, shall be treated as being received by the claimant on the second day after the day of posting.

(5) An appeal is disposed of when it is no longer pending for the purpose of—

(a) Part 5 of this Act, or

(b) the Special Immigration Appeals Commission Act 1997 (c. 68).

Note: Commencement at a date to be appointed.

22. Immigration and Asylum Act 1999, s 95

The Secretary of State may provide support under section 95 of the Immigration and Asylum Act 1999 (c. 33) (destitute asylum-seeker) by arranging for the provision of accommodation in an accommodation centre.

Note: Commencement at a date to be appointed.

23. Person subject to United Kingdom entrance control

(1) A residence restriction may include a requirement to reside at an accommodation centre.

(2) In subsection (1) 'residence restriction' means a restriction imposed under—

(a) paragraph 21 of Schedule 2 to the Immigration Act 1971 (c. 77) (temporary admission or release from detention), or

(b) paragraph 2(5) of Schedule 3 to that Act (control pending deportation).

(3) Where a person is required to reside in an accommodation centre by virtue of subsection (1) the Secretary of State must arrange for the provision of accommodation for the person in an accommodation centre.

(4) But if the person is required to leave an accommodation centre by virtue of section 26 or 30 he shall be treated as having broken the residence restriction referred to in subsection (1).

(5) The Secretary of State may provide support under section 4 of the Immigration and Asylum Act 1999 (persons subject to entrance control) (including that section as amended by section 49 of this Act) by arranging for the provision of accommodation in an accommodation centre.

Note: Commencement at a date to be appointed.

24. Provisional assistance

(1) If the Secretary of State thinks that a person may be eligible for the provision of accommodation in an accommodation centre under section 17, he may arrange for the provision for the person, pending a decision about eligibility, of—

(a) accommodation in an accommodation centre, or

(b) other support or assistance (of any kind).

(2) Section 99 of the Immigration and Asylum Act 1999 (c. 33) (provision of support by local authority) shall have effect in relation to the provision of support for persons under subsection (1) above as it has effect in relation to the provision of support for asylum-seekers under sections 95 and 98 of that Act.

Note: Commencement at a date to be appointed.

25. Length of stay

(1) The Secretary of State may not arrange for the provision of accommodation for a person in an accommodation centre if he has been a resident of an accommodation centre for a continuous period of six months.

(2) But—

(a) subsection (1) may be disapplied in respect of a person, generally or to a specified extent, by agreement between the Secretary of State and the person, and

(b) if the Secretary of State thinks it appropriate in relation to a person because of the circumstances of his case, the Secretary of State may direct that subsection (1) shall have effect in relation to the person as if the period specified in that subsection were the period of nine months.

(3) Section 51 is subject to this section.

(4) The Secretary of State may by order amend subsection (1) or (2)(b) so as to substitute a shorter period for a period specified.

Note: Commencement at a date to be appointed.

26. Withdrawal of support

(1) The Secretary of State may stop providing support for a person under section 17 or 24 if—

(a) the Secretary of State suspects that the person or a dependant of his has committed an offence by virtue of section 35, or

(b) the person or a dependant of his has failed to comply with directions of the Secretary of State as to the time or manner of travel to accommodation provided under section 17 or 24.

(2) The Secretary of State may by regulations specify other circumstances in which he may stop providing support for a person under section 17 or 24.

(3) In determining whether or not to provide a person with support or assistance under section 17 or 24 of this Act or section 4, 95 or 98 of the Immigration and Asylum Act 1999 (asylum-seeker) the Secretary of State may take into account the fact that—

(a) he has withdrawn support from the person by virtue of this section or section 30(4) or (5), or

(b) circumstances exist which would have enabled the Secretary of State to withdraw support from the person by virtue of this section had he been receiving support.

(4) This section is without prejudice to section 103 of the Immigration and Asylum Act 1999 (c. 33) (appeal against refusal to support).

Note: Commencement at a date to be appointed.

Operation of centres

27. Resident of centre

A reference in this Part to a resident of an accommodation centre is a reference to a person for whom accommodation in the centre is provided—

(a) under section 17,
(b) by virtue of section 22,
(c) by virtue of section 23, or
(d) under section 24.

Note: Commencement at a date to be appointed.

28. Manager of centre

A reference in this Part to the manager of an accommodation centre is a reference to a person who agrees with the Secretary of State to be wholly or partly responsible for the management of the centre.

Note: Commencement at a date to be appointed.

29. Facilities

(1) The Secretary of State may arrange for the following to be provided to a resident of an accommodation centre—

(a) food and other essential items;

(b) money;

(c) assistance with transport for the purpose of proceedings under the Immigration Acts or in connection with a claim for asylum;

(d) transport to and from the centre;

(e) assistance with expenses incurred in connection with carrying out voluntary work or other activities;

(f) education and training;

(g) facilities relating to health;

(h) facilities for religious observance;

(i) anything which the Secretary of State thinks ought to be provided for the purpose of providing a resident with proper occupation and for the purpose of maintaining good order;

(j) anything which the Secretary of State thinks ought to be provided for a person because of his exceptional circumstances.

(2) The Secretary of State may make regulations specifying the amount or maximum amount of money to be provided under subsection (1)(b).

(3) The Secretary of State may arrange for the provision of facilities in an accommodation centre for the use of a person in providing legal advice to a resident of the centre.

(4) The Secretary of State shall take reasonable steps to ensure that a resident of an accommodation centre has an opportunity to obtain legal advice before any appointment made by an immigration officer or an official of the Secretary of State for the purpose of obtaining information from the resident to be used in determining his claim for asylum.

(5) The Secretary of State may by order amend subsection (1) so as to add a reference to facilities which may be provided.

Note: Commencement at a date to be appointed.

30. Conditions of residence

(1) The Secretary of State may make regulations about conditions to be observed by residents of an accommodation centre.

(2) Regulations under subsection (1) may, in particular, enable a condition to be imposed in accordance with the regulations by—

(a) the Secretary of State, or

(b) the manager of an accommodation centre.

(3) A condition imposed by virtue of this section may, in particular—

(a) require a person not to be absent from the centre during specified hours without the permission of the Secretary of State or the manager;

(b) require a person to report to an immigration officer or the Secretary of State.

(4) If a resident of an accommodation centre breaches a condition imposed by virtue of this section, the Secretary of State may—

(a) require the resident and any dependant of his to leave the centre;

(b) authorise the manager of the centre to require the resident and any dependant of his to leave the centre.

(5) If a dependant of a resident of an accommodation centre breaches a condition imposed by virtue of this section, the Secretary of State may—

(a) require the resident and any dependant of his to leave the centre;

(b) authorise the manager of the centre to require the resident and any dependant of his to leave the centre.

(6) Regulations under this section must include provision for ensuring that a person subject to a condition is notified of the condition in writing.

(7) A condition imposed by virtue of this section is in addition to any restriction imposed under paragraph 21 of Schedule 2 to the Immigration Act 1971 (c. 77) (control of entry to United Kingdom) or under paragraph 2(5) of Schedule 3 to that Act (control pending deportation).

(8) A reference in this Part to a condition of residence is a reference to a condition imposed by virtue of this section.

Note: Commencement at a date to be appointed.

31. Financial contribution by resident

(1) A condition of residence may, in particular, require a resident of an accommodation centre to make payments to—

(a) the Secretary of State, or

(b) the manager of the centre.

(2) The Secretary of State may make regulations enabling him to recover sums representing the whole or part of the value of accommodation and other facilities provided to a resident of an accommodation centre if—

(a) accommodation is provided for the resident in response to an application by him for support,

(b) when the application was made the applicant had assets which were not capable of being realised, and

(c) the assets have become realisable.

(3) In subsection (2) 'assets' includes assets outside the United Kingdom.

(4) An amount recoverable by virtue of regulations made under subsection (2) may be recovered—

(a) as a debt due to the Secretary of State;

(b) by another prescribed method (which may include the imposition or variation of a residence condition).

Note: Commencement at a date to be appointed.

32. Tenure

(1) A resident of an accommodation centre shall not be treated as acquiring a tenancy of or other interest in any part of the centre (whether by virtue of an agreement between the resident and another person or otherwise).

(2) Subsection (3) applies where—

(a) the Secretary of State decides to stop arranging for the provision of accommodation in an accommodation centre for a resident of the centre, or

(b) a resident of an accommodation centre is required to leave the centre in accordance with section 30.

(3) Where this subsection applies—

(a) the Secretary of State or the manager of the centre may recover possession of the premises occupied by the resident, and

(b) the right under paragraph (a) shall be enforceable in accordance with procedure prescribed by regulations made by the Secretary of State.

(4) Any licence which a resident of an accommodation centre has to occupy premises in the centre shall be an excluded licence for the purposes of the Protection from Eviction Act 1977 (c. 43).

(5) . . .

(6) . . .

(7) In this section a reference to an accommodation centre includes a reference to premises in which accommodation is provided under section 24(1)(b).

Note: Subsection (5) amends Protection from Eviction Act 1977, s 3A(7A), subsection (6) amends Rent (Scotland) Act 1984, s 23A(5A). Commencement at a date to be appointed.

33. Advisory Groups

(1) The Secretary of State shall appoint a group (to be known as an Accommodation Centre Advisory Group) for each accommodation centre.

(2) The Secretary of State may by regulations—
- (a) confer functions on Advisory Groups;
- (b) make provision about the constitution and proceedings of Advisory Groups.

(3) Regulations under subsection (2)(a) must, in particular, provide for members of an accommodation centre's Advisory Group—
- (a) to visit the centre;
- (b) to hear complaints made by residents of the centre;
- (c) to report to the Secretary of State.

(4) The manager of an accommodation centre must permit a member of the centre's Advisory Group on request—
- (a) to visit the centre at any time;
- (b) to visit any resident of the centre at any time, provided that the resident consents.

(5) A member of an Advisory Group shall hold and vacate office in accordance with the terms of his appointment (which may include provision about retirement, resignation or dismissal).

(6) The Secretary of State may—
- (a) defray expenses of members of an Advisory Group;
- (b) make facilities available to members of an Advisory Group.

Note: Commencement at a date to be appointed.

General

34. . . .

Note: Section 34 deleted by UK Borders Act 2007 s 54 from 1 April 2008 (SI 2008/309).

35. Ancillary provisions

(1) The following provisions of the Immigration and Asylum Act 1999 (c. 33) shall apply for the purposes of this Part as they apply for the purposes of Part VI of that Act (support for asylum-seeker)—
- (a) section 105 (false representation),
- (b) section 106 (dishonest representation),
- (c) section 107 (delay or obstruction),
- (d) section 108 (failure of sponsor to maintain),
- (e) section 109 (offence committed by body),
- (f) section 112 (recovery of expenditure),
- (g) section 113 (recovery of expenditure from sponsor),

(h) section 124 (corporation sole), and

(i) section 127 (redirection of post).

(2) In the application of section 112 a reference to something done under section 95 or 98 of that Act shall be treated as a reference to something done under section 17 or 24 of this Act.

(3) In the application of section 113 a reference to section 95 of that Act shall be treated as a reference to section 17 of this Act.

Note: Subsection (1)(h) commenced on 7 November 2002, s 162. Remainder to commence on a date to be appointed.

36. Education: general

(1) For the purposes of section 13 of the Education Act 1996 (c. 56) (general responsibility of [local authority]) a resident of an accommodation centre shall not be treated as part of the population of a [local authority's] area.

(2) A child who is a resident of an accommodation centre may not be admitted to a maintained school or a maintained nursery (subject to section 37).

(3) But subsection (2) does not prevent a child's admission to a school which is—

(a) a community special school or a foundation special school, and

(b) named in [an EHC plan maintained for the child under section 37 of the Children and Families Act 2014 or] a statement in respect of the child under section 324 of the Education Act 1996 (c. 56) (special educational needs).

(4) In subsections (2) and (3)—

(a) 'maintained school' means a maintained school within the meaning of section 20(7) of the School Standards and Framework Act 1998 (c. 31) (definition), and

(b) 'maintained nursery' means a facility for nursery education, within the meaning of section 117 of that Act, provided by a [local authority].

(5) The following shall not apply in relation to a child who is a resident of an accommodation centre (subject to section 37)—

(a) section 86(1) and (2) of the School Standards and Framework Act 1998 (parental preference),

(b) section 94 of that Act (appeal),

(c) section 19 of the Education Act 1996 (education out of school),

(d) section 316(2) and (3) of that Act (child with special educational needs to be educated in mainstream school),

(e) paragraphs 3 and 8 of Schedule 27 to that Act (special education needs: making of statement: parental preference).

[(f) sections 33 and 34 of the Children and Families Act 2014 (mainstream education for children with special educational needs), and

(g) sections 38 and 39 of that Act (EHC plan: request of parent for named school etc)].

[(5A) The powers of the First-tier Tribunal on determining an appeal under section 51(2)(c) of the Children and Families Act 2014 (appeals against certain aspects of content of EHC plan) are subject to subsection (2) above.]

(6) The power of [the Special Educational Needs Tribunal for Wales] under section 326(3) of the Education Act 1996 (appeal against content of statement) is subject to subsection (2) above.

(7) A person exercising a function under this Act [, Part 3 of the Children and Families Act 2014] or the Education Act 1996 shall (subject to section 37) secure that a child who

is a resident of an accommodation centre and who has special educational needs shall be educated by way of facilities provided under section 29(1)(f) of this Act unless that is incompatible with—

(a) his receiving the special educational provision [called for by his special educational needs or] which his learning difficulty calls for,

(b) the provision of efficient education for other children who are residents of the centre, or

(c) the efficient use of resources.

(8) A person may rely on subsection (7)(b) only where there is no action—

(a) which could reasonably be taken by that person or by another person who exercises functions, or could exercise functions, in respect of the accommodation centre concerned, and

(b) as a result of which subsection (7)(b) would not apply.

(9) An accommodation centre is not a school within the meaning of section 4 of the Education Act 1996 (definition); but—

(a) [Part 1 of the Education Act 2005 (school inspections)] shall apply to educational facilities provided at an accommodation centre as if the centre were a school (for which purpose a reference to the appropriate authority shall be taken as a reference to the person (or persons) responsible for the provision of education at the accommodation centre),

[(aa) section 36 of the Children and Families Act 2014 (assessment of education, health and care needs: England) shall have effect as if an accommodation centre were a school,]

(b) section 329A of the Education Act 1996 (review or assessment of educational needs at request of responsible body) shall have effect as if—

(i) an accommodation centre were a relevant school for the purposes of that section,

(ii) a child for whom education is provided at an accommodation centre under section 29(1)(f) were a registered pupil at the centre, and

(iii) a reference in section 329A to the responsible body in relation to an accommodation centre were a reference to any person providing education at the centre under section 29(1)(f), and

(c) section 140 of the Learning and Skills Act 2000 (c. 21) (learning difficulties: assessment of post-16 needs) shall have effect as if an accommodation centre were a school.

(10) Subsections (1), (2) and (5) shall not apply in relation to an accommodation centre if education is not provided for children who are residents of the centre under section 29(1)(f).

(11) An expression used in this section and in the Education Act 1996 (c. 56) shall have the same meaning in this section as in that Act.

Note: Commencement at a date to be appointed. Words in square brackets in subsection (9) substituted by Education Act 2005, s 61 and Sch 9 from 1 September 2005 (SI 2005/2034) and from 1 September 2006 (W) (SI 2006/1338). Words in square brackets in subsection (6) substituted from 3 November 2008 (SI 2008/2833). Term 'local authority' substituted from 5 April 2010 (SI 2010/1158). Other amendments made by Schedule 3 Children and Families Act 2014 from 1 September 2014 (SI 2014/899).

37. Education: special cases

(1) This section applies to a child if a person who provides education to residents of an accommodation centre recommends in writing to the [local authority] for the area in which the centre is that this section should apply to the child on the grounds that his special circumstances call for provision that can only or best be arranged by the authority.

(2) A [local authority] may—

(a) arrange for the provision of education for a child to whom this section applies;

(b) disapply a provision of section 36 in respect of a child to whom this section applies.

(3) In determining whether to exercise a power under subsection (2) in respect of a child a [local authority] shall have regard to any relevant guidance issued by the Secretary of State.

(4) The governing body of a maintained school shall comply with a requirement of the [local authority] to admit to the school a child to whom this section applies.

(5) Subsection (4) shall not apply where compliance with a requirement would prejudice measures taken for the purpose of complying with a duty arising under section 1(6) of the School Standards and Framework Act 1998 (c. 31) (limit on infant class size).

(6) A [local authority] may not impose a requirement under subsection (4) in respect of a school unless the authority has consulted the school in accordance with regulations made by the Secretary of State.

(7) In the case of a maintained school for which the [local authority] are the admission authority, the authority may not arrange for the admission of a child to whom this section applies unless the authority has notified the school in accordance with regulations made by the Secretary of State.

(8) In this section—

(a) 'maintained school' means a maintained school within the meaning of section 20(7) of the School Standards and Framework Act 1998 (definition), and

(b) an expression which is also used in the Education Act 1996 (c. 56) shall have the same meaning as it has in that Act.

Note: Commencement at a date to be appointed. Term 'local authority' substituted from 5 April 2010 (SI 2010/1158).

38. Local authority

(1) A local authority may in accordance with arrangements made by the Secretary of State—

(a) assist in arranging for the provision of an accommodation centre;

(b) make premises available for an accommodation centre;

(c) provide services in connection with an accommodation centre.

(2) In particular, a local authority may—

(a) incur reasonable expenditure;

(b) provide services outside its area;

(c) provide services jointly with another body;

(d) form a company;

(e) tender for or enter into a contract;

(f) do anything (including anything listed in paragraphs (a) to (e)) for a preparatory purpose.

(3) In this section 'local authority' means—

(a) a local authority within the meaning of section 94 of the Immigration and Asylum Act 1999 (c. 33), and

(b) a Northern Ireland authority within the meaning of section 110 of that Act and an Education and Library Board established under Article 3 of the Education and Libraries (Northern Ireland) Order 1986 (SI 1986/594 (N.I. 3)).

Note: Commenced 7 November 2002, s 162.

39. 'Prescribed': orders and regulations

(1) In this Part 'prescribed' means prescribed by the Secretary of State by order or regulations.

(2) An order or regulations under this Part may—

(a) make provision which applies generally or only in specified cases or circumstances (which may be determined wholly or partly by reference to location);

(b) make different provision for different cases or circumstances;

(c) include consequential, transitional or incidental provision.

(3) An order or regulations under this Part must be made by statutory instrument.

(4) An order or regulations under any of the following provisions of this Part shall be subject to annulment in pursuance of a resolution of either House of Parliament—

(a) section 17,
(b) section 19,
(c) section 20,
(d) section 21,
(e) section 26,
(f) section 29,
(g) section 31,
(h) section 32,
(i) section 33,
(j) section 37,
(k) section 40, and
(l) section 41.

(5) An order under section 25 or regulations under section 30 may not be made unless a draft has been laid before and approved by resolution of each House of Parliament.

Note: Commencement at a date to be appointed.

40. Scotland

(1) The Secretary of State may not make arrangements under section 16 for the provision of premises in Scotland unless he has consulted the Scottish Ministers.

(2) The Secretary of State may by order make provision in relation to the education of residents of accommodation centres in Scotland.

(3) An order under subsection (2) may, in particular—

(a) apply, disapply or modify the effect of an enactment (which may include a provision made by or under an Act of the Scottish Parliament);

(b) make provision having an effect similar to the effect of a provision of section 36 or 37.

Note: Subsection (1) commenced on 7 November 2002, s 162. Remainder at a date to be appointed.

41. Northern Ireland

(1) The Secretary of State may not make arrangements under section 16 for the provision of premises in Northern Ireland unless he has consulted the First Minister and the deputy First Minister.

(2) The Secretary of State may by order make provision in relation to the education of residents of accommodation centres in Northern Ireland.

(3) An order under subsection (2) may, in particular—

(a) apply, disapply or modify the effect of an enactment (which may include a provision made by or under Northern Ireland legislation);

(b) make provision having an effect similar to the effect of a provision of section 36 or 37.

Note: Subsection (1) commenced on 7 November 2002, s 162. Remainder at a date to be appointed.

42. Wales

The Secretary of State may not make arrangements under section 16 for the provision of premises in Wales unless he has consulted the National Assembly for Wales.

Note: Commenced 7 November 2002, s 162.

Part III

Other Support and Assistance

43. Asylum-seeker: form of support

(1) The Secretary of State may make an order restricting the application of section 96(1)(b) of the Immigration and Asylum Act 1999 (c. 33) (support for asylum-seeker: essential living needs)—

(a) in all circumstances, to cases in which support is being provided under section 96(1)(a) (accommodation), or

(b) in specified circumstances only, to cases in which support is being provided under section 96(1)(a).

(2) An order under subsection (1)(b) may, in particular, make provision by reference to—

(a) location;

(b) the date of an application.

(3) An order under subsection (1) may include transitional provision.

(4) An order under subsection (1)—

(a) must be made by statutory instrument, and

(b) may not be made unless a draft has been laid before and approved by resolution of each House of Parliament.

Note: Commenced 7 November 2002, s 162.

44. Destitute asylum-seeker

Note: Amends Immigration and Asylum Act 1999, ss 94, 95 (c. 33).

45. Section 44: supplemental

(1) . . .

Note: Amends Immigration and Asylum Act 1999, s 96.

(2) . . .

Note: Amends Immigration and Asylum Act 1999, s 97.

(3) . . .

Note: Amends Immigration and Asylum Act 1999, Sch 8, paragraphs 2, 6.

(4) . . .

Note: Amends paragraph 3, Sch 9 Immigration and Asylum Act 1999.

(5) . . .

Note: Amends National Assistance Act 1948, s 21(1B) (c. 29).

(6) . . .

Note: Amends Health Services and Public Health Act 1968, s 45(4B).

(7) . . .

Note: Amends paragraph 2(2B), Sch 8 National Health Service Act 1977.

46. Section 44: supplemental: Scotland and Northern Ireland

(1–3) . . .

Note: Amends the Social Work (Scotland) Act 1968.

(4–5) . . .

Note: Amends the Mental Health (Scotland) Act 1984.

(6–7) . . .

Note: Amends the Health and Personal Social Services (Northern Ireland) Order 1972 (SI 1972/1265 (NI 14)).

47. Asylum-seeker: family with children

Note: Amends Immigration and Asylum Act 1999, s 122.

48. Young asylum-seeker

The following provisions of the Immigration and Asylum Act 1999 (c. 33) shall have effect as if the definition of asylum-seeker in section 94(1) of that Act did not exclude persons who are under 18—

(a) section 110 (local authority expenditure on asylum-seekers), and
(b) section 111 (grants to voluntary organisations).

Note: Commenced on 7 November 2002, s 162.

49. Failed asylum-seeker

Note: Amends Immigration and Asylum Act 1999, s 4.

50. Conditions of support

Note: Amends Immigration and Asylum Act 1999, s 95 and Sch 9.

51. Choice of form of support

(1) The Secretary of State may refuse to provide support for a person under a provision specified in subsection (2) on the grounds that an offer has been made to the person of support under another provision specified in that subsection.

(2) The provisions are—

(a) sections 17 and 24 of this Act,

(b) section 4 of the Immigration and Asylum Act 1999 (accommodation for person temporarily admitted or released from detention), and

(c) sections 95 and 98 of that Act (support for destitute asylum-seeker).

(3) In deciding under which of the provisions listed in subsection (2) to offer support to a person the Secretary of State may—

(a) have regard to administrative or other matters which do not concern the person's personal circumstances;

(b) regard one of those matters as conclusive;

(c) apply different criteria to different persons for administrative reasons (which may include the importance of testing the operation of a particular provision).

Note: Commencement at a date to be appointed.

52. Back-dating of benefit for refugee

Note: Amends Immigration and Asylum Act 1999, s 123.

53. Asylum-seeker: appeal against refusal to support

Note: Amends Immigration and Asylum Act 1999, s 103.

54. Withholding and withdrawal of support

Schedule 3 (which makes provision for support to be withheld or withdrawn in certain circumstances) shall have effect.

Note: Commenced for the purpose of making subordinate legislation 8 December 2002. Remainder commenced 8 January 2003 (SI 2002/2811).

55. Late claim for asylum: refusal of support

(1) The Secretary of State may not provide or arrange for the provision of support to a person under a provision mentioned in subsection (2) if—

(a) the person makes a claim for asylum which is recorded by the Secretary of State, and

(b) the Secretary of State is not satisfied that the claim was made as soon as reasonably practicable after the person's arrival in the United Kingdom.

(2) The provisions are—

(a) sections 4, 95 and 98 of the Immigration and Asylum Act 1999 (c. 33) (support for asylum-seeker, &c.), and

(b) sections 17 and 24 of this Act (accommodation centre).

(3) An authority may not provide or arrange for the provision of support to a person under a provision mentioned in subsection (4) if—

(a) the person has made a claim for asylum, and

(b) the Secretary of State is not satisfied that the claim was made as soon as reasonably practicable after the person's arrival in the United Kingdom.

(4) The provisions are—

(a) section 29(1)(b) of the Housing (Scotland) Act 1987 (c. 26) (accommodation pending review),

(b) section 188(3) or 204(4) of the Housing Act 1996 (c. 52) (accommodation pending review or appeal), and

(c) section 2 of the Local Government Act 2000 (c. 22) (promotion of well-being) [and.

[(d) section 1 of the Localism Act 2011 (local authority's general power of competence)].

(5) This section shall not prevent—

(a) the exercise of a power by the Secretary of State to the extent necessary for the purpose of avoiding a breach of a person's Convention rights (within the meaning of the Human Rights Act 1998 (c. 42)),

(b) the provision of support under section 95 of the Immigration and Asylum Act 1999 (c. 33) or section 17 of this Act in accordance with section 122 of that Act (children), or

(c) the provision of support under section 98 of the Immigration and Asylum Act 1999 or section 24 of this Act (provisional support) to a person under the age of 18 and the household of which he forms part.

(6) An authority which proposes to provide or arrange for the provision of support to a person under a provision mentioned in subsection (4)—

(a) must inform the Secretary of State if the authority believes that the person has made a claim for asylum,

(b) must act in accordance with any guidance issued by the Secretary of State to determine whether subsection (3) applies, and

(c) shall not be prohibited from providing or arranging for the provision of support if the authority has complied with paragraph (a) and (b) and concluded that subsection (3) does not apply.

(7) The Secretary of State may by order—

(a) add, remove or amend an entry in the list in subsection (4);

(b) provide for subsection (3) not to have effect in specified cases or circumstances.

(8) An order under subsection (7)—

(a) may include transitional, consequential or incidental provision,

(b) must be made by statutory instrument, and

(c) may not be made unless a draft has been laid before and approved by resolution of each House of Parliament.

(9) For the purposes of this section 'claim for asylum' has the same meaning as in section 18.

(10) A decision of the Secretary of State that this section prevents him from providing or arranging for the provision of support to a person is not a decision that the person does not qualify for support for the purpose of section 103 of the Immigration and Asylum Act 1999 (appeals).

(11) This section does not prevent a person's compliance with a residence restriction imposed in reliance on section 70 (induction).

Note: Commenced 8 January 2003 (SI 2002/2811). Subsection (4)(d) inserted from 28 March 2012 (SI 2012/961).

56. Provision of support by local authority

. . .

Note: Amends Immigration and Asylum Act 1999, s 99.

57. Application for support: false or incomplete information

. . .

Note: Amends paragraph 12, Sch 8 Immigration and Asylum Act 1999.

58. Voluntary departure from United Kingdom

(1) A person is a 'voluntary leaver' for the purposes of this section if—

(a) he is not a British citizen or an EEA national,

(b) he leaves the United Kingdom for a place where he hopes to take up permanent residence (his 'new place of residence'), and

(c) the Secretary of State thinks that it is in the person's interest to leave the United Kingdom and that the person wishes to leave.

(2) The Secretary of State may make arrangements to—

(a) assist voluntary leavers;

(b) assist individuals to decide whether to become voluntary leavers.

(3) The Secretary of State may, in particular, make payments (whether to voluntary leavers or to organisations providing services for them) which relate to—

(a) travelling and other expenses incurred by or on behalf of a voluntary leaver, or a member of his family or household, in leaving the United Kingdom;

(b) expenses incurred by or on behalf of a voluntary leaver, or a member of his family or household, on or shortly after arrival in his new place of residence;

(c) the provision of services designed to assist a voluntary leaver, or a member of his family or household, to settle in his new place of residence;

(d) expenses in connection with a journey undertaken by a person (with or without his family or household) to prepare for, or to assess the possibility of, his becoming a voluntary leaver.

(4) In subsection (1)(a) 'EEA national' means a national of a State which is a contracting party to the Agreement on the European Economic Area signed at Oporto on 2nd May 1992 (as it has effect from time to time).

(5) . . .

Note: Subsection (5) repeals Immigration Act 1971, ss 29 and 31(d). Commenced 7 November 2002, s 162.

59. International projects

(1) The Secretary of State may participate in a project which is designed to—

(a) reduce migration,

(b) assist or ensure the return of migrants,

(c) facilitate co-operation between States in matters relating to migration,

(d) conduct or consider research about migration, or

(e) arrange or assist the settlement of migrants (whether in the United Kingdom or elsewhere).

(2) In particular, the Secretary of State may—

(a) provide financial support to an international organisation which arranges or participates in a project of a kind described in subsection (1);

(b) provide financial support to an organisation in the United Kingdom or another country which arranges or participates in a project of that kind;

(c) provide or arrange for the provision of financial or other assistance to a migrant who participates in a project of that kind;

(d) participate in financial or other arrangements which are agreed between Her Majesty's Government and the government of one or more other countries and which are or form part of a project of that kind.

(3) In this section—

(a) 'migrant' means a person who leaves the country where he lives hoping to settle in another country (whether or not he is a refugee within the meaning of any international Convention), and

(b) 'migration' shall be construed accordingly.

(4) Subsection (1) does not—

(a) confer a power to remove a person from the United Kingdom, or

(b) affect a person's right to enter or remain in the United Kingdom.

Note: Commenced 7 November 2002, s 162.

60. Northern Ireland authorities

. . .

Note: Amends Immigration and Asylum Act 1999, ss 94 and 110.

61. Repeal of spent provisions

. . .

Note: Repeals Immigration and Asylum Act 1999, ss 96(4)–(6), 166(4)(e).

Part IV

Detention and Removal

Detention

62. Detention by Secretary of State

(1) A person may be detained under the authority of the Secretary of State pending—

(a) a decision by the Secretary of State whether to give directions in respect of the person under [section 10 of the Immigration and Asylum Act 1999 (removal of persons unlawfully in the United Kingdom) or] paragraph 10, 10A or 14 of Schedule 2 to the Immigration Act 1971 (c. 77) (control of entry: removal), or

(b) removal of the person from the United Kingdom in pursuance of directions given by the Secretary of State under any of those [provisions].

(2) Where the Secretary of State is empowered under section 3A of [the Immigration Act 1971] (powers of Secretary of State) to examine a person or to give or refuse a person leave to enter the United Kingdom, the person may be detained under the authority of the Secretary of State pending—

(a) the person's examination by the Secretary of State,

(b) the Secretary of State's decision to give or refuse the person leave to enter,

(c) a decision by the Secretary of State whether to give directions in respect of the person under paragraph 8 or 9 of Schedule 2 to that Act (removal), or

(d) removal of the person in pursuance of directions given by the Secretary of State under either of those paragraphs.

(3) A provision of Schedule 2 to that Act about a person who is detained or liable to detention under that Schedule shall apply to a person who is detained or liable to detention under this section: and for that purpose—

(a) a reference to paragraph 16 of that Schedule shall be taken to include a reference to this section,

[(aa) a reference in paragraph 18B of that Schedule to an immigration officer shall be read as a reference to the Secretary of State,]

(b) a reference in paragraph 21 of that Schedule to an immigration officer shall be taken to include a reference to the Secretary of State, and

(c) a reference to detention under that Schedule or under a provision or Part of that Schedule shall be taken to include a reference to detention under this section.

(4) In the case of a restriction imposed under paragraph 21 of that Schedule by virtue of this section—

(a) a restriction imposed by an immigration officer may be varied by the Secretary of State, and

(b) a restriction imposed by the Secretary of State may be varied by an immigration officer.

(5) . . .

(6) . . .

(7) A power under this section which is exercisable pending a decision of a particular kind by the Secretary of State is exercisable where the Secretary of State has reasonable grounds to suspect that he may make a decision of that kind.

(8–16) . . .

Note: Subsections 8–16 amend Immigration Act 1971, ss 11, 24; Mental Health Act 1983, ss 48, 53; Mental Health (Scotland) Act 1984, ss 71, 74; Mental Health (Northern Ireland) Order 1986, Arts 54, 59; Immigration and Asylum Act 1999, ss 53, 147; Anti-terrorism, Crime and Security Act 2001, ss 23, 24. Commencement 10 February 2003 (SI 2003/1). Subsections (15)-(16) repealed by Prevention of Terrorism Act 2005, section 16(2) from 14 March 2005. Prevention of Terrorism Act, section 26(3). Words in square brackets in subsection (1)(a) and subsection (3)(aa) inserted, words in square brackets in subsections (1)(b) and (2) substituted, and subsections (5) and (6) omitted by Sch 9 Immigration Act 2014 from 20 October 2014 with savings set out in SI 2014/2771 articles 9-11.

63. Control of entry to United Kingdom, &c.: use of force

. . .

Note: Amends paragraph 17(2), Sch 2 Immigration Act 1971.

64. Escorts

. . .

Note: Amends paragraph 17, Sch 2 Immigration Act 1971.

65. Detention centres: custodial functions

. . .

Note: Amends Immigration and Asylum Act 1999, s 154 and Sch 11.

66. Detention centres: change of name

(1) –(3) . . .

(4) A reference in an enactment or instrument to a detention centre within the meaning of Part VIII of the Immigration and Asylum Act 1999 (c. 33) shall be construed as a reference to a removal centre within the meaning of that Part.

Note: Subsections (1)–(3) amend Immigration and Asylum Act 1999, ss 141, 147–53, 155, 157–9 and Schs 11–13 and Prison Act 1952, s 5A and Sch 4A Water Industry Act 1991. Commenced 10 February 2003 (SI 2003/01).

67. Construction of reference to person liable to detention

(1) This section applies to the construction of a provision which—

(a) does not confer power to detain a person, but

(b) refers (in any terms) to a person who is liable to detention under a provision of the Immigration Acts.

(2) The reference shall be taken to include a person if the only reason why he cannot not be detained under the provision is that—

(a) he cannot presently be removed from the United Kingdom, because of a legal impediment connected with the United Kingdom's obligations under an international agreement,

(b) practical difficulties are impeding or delaying the making of arrangements for his removal from the United Kingdom, or

(c) practical difficulties, or demands on administrative resources, are impeding or delaying the taking of a decision in respect of him.

(3) This section shall be treated as always having had effect.

Note: Commenced 7 November 2002, s 162.

Temporary release

68. Bail

(1) This section applies in a case where an immigration officer not below the rank of chief immigration officer has sole or shared power to release a person on bail in accordance with—

(a) a provision of Schedule 2 to the Immigration Act 1971 (c. 77) (control of entry) (including a provision of that Schedule applied by a provision of that Act or by another enactment), or

(b) section 9A of the Asylum and Immigration Appeals Act 1993 (c. 23) (pending appeal from Immigration Appeal Tribunal).

(2) In respect of an application for release on bail which is instituted after the expiry of the period of eight days beginning with the day on which detention commences, the power to release on bail—

(a) shall be exercisable by the Secretary of State (as well as by any person with whom the immigration officer's power is shared under the provision referred to in subsection (1)), and

(b) shall not be exercisable by an immigration officer (except where he acts on behalf of the Secretary of State).

(3) In relation to the exercise by the Secretary of State of a power to release a person on bail by virtue of subsection (2), a reference to an immigration officer shall be construed as a reference to the Secretary of State.

(4) The Secretary of State may by order amend or replace subsection (2) so as to make different provision for the circumstances in which the power to release on bail may be exercised by the Secretary of State and not by an immigration officer.

(5) An order under subsection (4)—

(a) may include consequential or transitional provision,

(b) must be made by statutory instrument, and

(c) may not be made unless a draft has been laid before and approved by resolution of each House of Parliament.

(6) . . .

Note: Subsection (6) repeals Immigration and Asylum Act 1999, ss 44–52, 53(5) and 55, from 10 February 2003 (SI 2003/1). Remainder of s 68 commenced 1 April 2003 (SI 2003/754).

69. Reporting restriction: travel expenses

(1) The Secretary of State may make a payment to a person in respect of travelling expenses which the person has incurred or will incur for the purpose of complying with a reporting restriction.

(2) In subsection (1) 'reporting restriction' means a restriction which—

(a) requires a person to report to the police, an immigration officer or the Secretary of State, and

(b) is imposed under a provision listed in subsection (3).

(3) Those provisions are—

(a) paragraph 21 of Schedule 2 to the Immigration Act 1971 (c. 77) (temporary admission or release from detention),

(b) paragraph 29 of that Schedule (bail), and

(c) paragraph 2 or 5 of Schedule 3 to that Act (pending deportation).

Note: Commenced 7 November 2002, s 162.

70. Induction

(1) A residence restriction may be imposed on an asylum-seeker or a dependant of an asylum-seeker without regard to his personal circumstances if—

(a) it requires him to reside at a specified location for a period not exceeding 14 days, and

(b) the person imposing the residence restriction believes that a programme of induction will be made available to the asylum-seeker at or near the specified location.

(2) In subsection (1) 'residence restriction' means a restriction imposed under—

(a) paragraph 21 of Schedule 2 to the Immigration Act 1971 (temporary admission or release from detention), or

(b) paragraph 2(5) of Schedule 3 to that Act (control pending deportation).

(3) In this section—

'asylum-seeker' has the meaning given by section 18 of this Act but disregarding section 18(1)(a),

'dependant of an asylum-seeker' means a person who appears to the Secretary of State to be making a claim or application in respect of residence in the United Kingdom by virtue of being a dependant of an asylum-seeker, and

'programme of induction' means education about the nature of the asylum process.

(4) Regulations under subsection (3)—

(a) may make different provision for different circumstances,

(b) must be made by statutory instrument, and

(c) shall be subject to annulment in pursuance of a resolution of either House of Parliament.

(5) Subsection (6) applies where the Secretary of State arranges for the provision of a programme of induction (whether or not he also provides other facilities to persons attending the programme and whether or not all the persons attending the programme are subject to residence restrictions).

(6) A local authority may arrange for or participate in the provision of the programme or other facilities.

(7) In particular, a local authority may—

(a) incur reasonable expenditure;

(b) provide services outside its area;

(c) provide services jointly with another body;

(d) form a company;

(e) tender for or enter into a contract;

(f) do anything (including anything listed in paragraphs (a) to (e)) for a preparatory purpose.

(8) In this section 'local authority' means—

(a) a local authority within the meaning of section 94 of the Immigration and Asylum Act 1999 (c. 33), and

(b) a Northern Ireland authority within the meaning of section 110 of that Act.

Note: Commenced 7 November 2002, s 162.

71. Asylum-seeker: residence, &c. restriction

(1) This section applies to—

(a) a person who makes a claim for asylum at a time when he has leave to enter or remain in the United Kingdom, and

(b) a dependant of a person within paragraph (a).

(2) The Secretary of State or an immigration officer may impose on a person to whom this section applies any restriction which may be imposed under paragraph 21 of Schedule 2

to the Immigration Act 1971 (c. 77) (control of entry: residence, reporting and occupation restrictions) on a person liable to detention under paragraph 16 of that Schedule.

(3) Where a restriction is imposed on a person under subsection (2)—

(a) the restriction shall be treated for all purposes as a restriction imposed under paragraph 21 of that Schedule, and

(b) if the person fails to comply with the restriction he shall be liable to detention under paragraph 16 of that Schedule.

(4) A restriction imposed on a person under this section shall cease to have effect if he ceases to be an asylum-seeker or the dependant of an asylum-seeker.

(5) In this section—

'asylum-seeker' has the same meaning as in section 70,

'claim for asylum' has the same meaning as in section 18, and

'dependant' means a person who appears to the Secretary of State to be making a claim or application in respect of residence in the United Kingdom by virtue of being a dependant of another person.

(6) Regulations under subsection (5)—

(a) may make different provision for different circumstances,

(b) must be made by statutory instrument, and

(c) shall be subject to annulment in pursuance of a resolution of either House of Parliament.

Note: Commenced 10 February 2003 (SI 2003/1).

Removal

72. Serious criminal

(1) This section applies for the purpose of the construction and application of Article 33(2) of the Refugee Convention (exclusion from protection).

(2) A person shall be presumed to have been convicted by a final judgment of a particularly serious crime and to constitute a danger to the community of the United Kingdom if he is—

(a) convicted in the United Kingdom of an offence, and

(b) sentenced to a period of imprisonment of at least two years.

(3) A person shall be presumed to have been convicted by a final judgment of a particularly serious crime and to constitute a danger to the community of the United Kingdom if—

(a) he is convicted outside the United Kingdom of an offence,

(b) he is sentenced to a period of imprisonment of at least two years, and

(c) he could have been sentenced to a period of imprisonment of at least two years had his conviction been a conviction in the United Kingdom of a similar offence.

(4) A person shall be presumed to have been convicted by a final judgment of a particularly serious crime and to constitute a danger to the community of the United Kingdom if—

(a) he is convicted of an offence specified by order of the Secretary of State, or

(b) he is convicted outside the United Kingdom of an offence and the Secretary of State certifies that in his opinion the offence is similar to an offence specified by order under paragraph (a).

(5) An order under subsection (4)—

(a) must be made by statutory instrument, and

(b) shall be subject to annulment in pursuance of a resolution of either House of Parliament.

(6) A presumption under subsection (2), (3) or (4) that a person constitutes a danger to the community is rebuttable by that person.

(7) A presumption under subsection (2), (3) or (4) does not apply while an appeal against conviction or sentence—

(a) is pending, or

(b) could be brought (disregarding the possibility of appeal out of time with leave).

(8) Section 34(1) of the Anti-terrorism, Crime and Security Act 2001 (c. 24) (no need to consider gravity of fear or threat of persecution) applies for the purpose of considering whether a presumption mentioned in subsection (6) has been rebutted as it applies for the purpose of considering whether Article 33(2) of the Refugee Convention applies.

(9) Subsection (10) applies where—

(a) a person appeals under section 82, . . . of this Act or under section 2 of the Special Immigration Appeals Commission Act 1997 (c. 68) wholly or partly on the ground [mentioned in section 84(1)(a) or (3)(a) of this Act (breach of the United Kingdom's obligations under the Refugee Convention), and]

(b) the Secretary of State issues a certificate that presumptions under subsection (2), (3) or (4) apply to the person (subject to rebuttal).

(10) The [. . .] Tribunal or Commission hearing the appeal—

(a) must begin substantive deliberation on the appeal by considering the certificate, and

(b) if in agreement that presumptions under subsection (2), (3) or (4) apply (having given the appellant an opportunity for rebuttal) must dismiss the appeal in so far as it relies on the ground specified in subsection (9)(a).

[(**10A**) Subsection (10) also applies in relation to the Upper Tribunal when it acts under section 12(2)(b)(ii) of the Tribunals, Courts and Enforcement Act 2007.]

(11) For the purposes of this section—

(a) 'the Refugee Convention' means the Convention relating to the Status of Refugees done at Geneva on 28 July 1951 and its Protocol, and

(b) a reference to a person who is sentenced to a period of imprisonment of at least two years—

(i) does not include a reference to a person who receives a suspended sentence [(unless a court subsequently orders that the sentence or any part of it is to take effect)],

[(ia) does not include a reference to a person who is sentenced to a period of imprisonment of at least two years only by virtue of being sentenced to consecutive sentences which amount in aggregate to more than two years,]

(ii) includes a reference to a person who is sentenced to detention, or ordered or directed to be detained, in an institution other than a prison (including, in particular, a hospital or an institution for young offenders), and

(iii) includes a reference to a person who is sentenced to imprisonment or detention, or ordered or directed to be detained, for an indeterminate period (provided that it may last for two years).

Note: Subsections (1)–(8) and (11) commenced 10 February 2003 (SI 2003/1), remainder on 1 April 2003 (SI 2003/754). Word in subsection (10) omitted by Sch 2 Asylum and Immigration (Treatment of Claimants etc.) Act 2004 from 4 April 2005 (SI 2005/565). Serious offences for the purposes of subsection (4)(a) set out in SI 2004/1910. Words in square brackets in subsection (9) omitted and substituted by Sch 9 Immigration Act 2014 from 20 October 2014 with savings set out in articles 9-11 SI 2014/2771. Words in subsection (11)(b)(i) substituted and subsection (11)(b)(ia) inserted by UK Borders Act 2007, s 39 from 1 August 2008 (SI 2008/1818). Subsection (10A) inserted from 15 February 2010 (SI 2010/21).

73. Family

. . .

Note: Amends Sch 2 Immigration Act 1971 (c. 77); Immigration and Asylum Act 1999, s 10.

74. Deception

. . .

Note: Amends Immigration and Asylum Act 1999, s 10(1).

75. Exemption from deportation

. . .

Note: Amends Immigration Act 1971, s 7; Immigration and Asylum Act 1999, s 10.

76. Revocation of leave to enter or remain

(1) The Secretary of State may revoke a person's indefinite leave to enter or remain in the United Kingdom if the person—

(a) is liable to deportation, but

(b) cannot be deported for legal reasons.

(2) The Secretary of State may revoke a person's indefinite leave to enter or remain in the United Kingdom if—

(a) the leave was obtained by deception,

(b) . . .

(c) . . .

(3) The Secretary of State may revoke a person's indefinite leave to enter or remain in the United Kingdom if the person, or someone of whom he is a dependant, ceases to be a refugee as a result of—

(a) voluntarily availing himself of the protection of his country of nationality,

(b) voluntarily re-acquiring a lost nationality,

(c) acquiring the nationality of a country other than the United Kingdom and availing himself of its protection, or

(d) voluntarily establishing himself in a country in respect of which he was a refugee.

(4) In this section—

'indefinite leave' has the meaning given by section 33(1) of the Immigration Act 1971 (c. 77) (interpretation),

'liable to deportation' has the meaning given by section 3(5) and (6) of that Act (deportation), 'refugee' has the meaning given by the Convention relating to the Status of Refugees done at Geneva on 28 July 1951 and its Protocol, and

. . .

(5) A power under subsection (1) or (2) to revoke leave may be exercised—
(a) in respect of leave granted before this section comes into force;
(b) in reliance on anything done before this section comes into force.

(6) A power under subsection (3) to revoke leave may be exercised—
(a) in respect of leave granted before this section comes into force, but
(b) only in reliance on action taken after this section comes into force.

(7) . . .

Note: Subsection (7) amends Immigration and Asylum Act 1999, s 10(1). Commencement 10 February 2003 (SI 2003/1). Subsections (2)(b)–(c) and definition of 'removed' omitted by Sch 9 Immigration Act from 20 October 2014 with savings set out in articles 9-11 SI 2014/2771.

77. No removal while claim for asylum pending

(1) While a person's claim for asylum is pending he may not be—

(a) removed from the United Kingdom in accordance with a provision of the Immigration Acts, or

(b) required to leave the United Kingdom in accordance with a provision of the Immigration Acts.

(2) In this section—

(a) 'claim for asylum' means a claim by a person that it would be contrary to the United Kingdom's obligations under the Refugee Convention to remove him from or require him to leave the United Kingdom, and

(b) a person's claim is pending until he is given notice of the Secretary of State's decision on it.

(3) In subsection (2) 'the Refugee Convention' means the Convention relating to the Status of Refugees done at Geneva on 28 July 1951 and its Protocol.

(4) Nothing in this section shall prevent any of the following while a claim for asylum is pending—
(a) the giving of a direction for the claimant's removal from the United Kingdom,
(b) the making of a deportation order in respect of the claimant, or
(c) the taking of any other interim or preparatory action.

(5) . . .

Note: Subsection (5) repeals Immigration and Asylum Act 1999, s 15. Commencement 1 April 2003 (SI 2003/754). Has effect in relation to a claim for asylum pending on 31 March 2003 as it has effect in relation to claims pending under the 2002 Act (SI 2003/754).

78. No removal while appeal pending

(1) While a person's appeal under section 82(1) is pending he may not be—

(a) removed from the United Kingdom in accordance with a provision of the Immigration Acts, or

(b) required to leave the United Kingdom in accordance with a provision of the Immigration Acts.

(2) In this section 'pending' has the meaning given by section 104.

(3) Nothing in this section shall prevent any of the following while an appeal is pending—

(a) the giving of a direction for the appellant's removal from the United Kingdom,

(b) the making of a deportation order in respect of the appellant (subject to section 79), or

(c) the taking of any other interim or preparatory action.

(4) This section applies only to an appeal brought while the appellant is in the United Kingdom in accordance with section 92.

Note: Commencement 1 April 2003 (SI 2003/754). Has effect in relation to appeals pending under the old appeal provisions as it has effect in relation to an appeal pending under s 82(1) of the 2002 Act.

[78A. Restriction on removal of children and their parents etc.

(1) This section applies in a case where—

(a) a child is to be removed from or required to leave the United Kingdom, and

(b) an individual who—

(i) is a parent of the child or has care of the child, and

(ii) is living in a household in the United Kingdom with the child, is also to be removed from or required to leave the United Kingdom (a "relevant parent or carer").

(2) During the period of 28 days beginning with the day on which the relevant appeal rights are exhausted—

(a) the child may not be removed from or required to leave the United Kingdom; and

(b) a relevant parent or carer may not be removed from or required to leave the United Kingdom if, as a result, no relevant parent or carer would remain in the United Kingdom.

(3) The relevant appeal rights are exhausted at the time when—

(a) neither the child, nor any relevant parent or carer, could bring an appeal under section 82 (ignoring any possibility of an appeal out of time with permission), and

(b) no appeal brought by the child, or by any relevant parent or carer, is pending within the meaning of section 104.

(4) Nothing in this section prevents any of the following during the period of 28 days mentioned in subsection (2)—

(a) the giving of a direction for the removal of a person from the United Kingdom,

(b) the making of a deportation order in respect of a person, or

(c) the taking of any other interim or preparatory action.

(5) In this section—

"child" means a person who is aged under 18;

references to a person being removed from or required to leave the United Kingdom are to the person being removed or required to leave in accordance with a provision of the Immigration Acts.]

Note: Section 78A inserted by s 2 Immigration Act 2014 from 28 July 2014 (SI 2014/1820).

79. Deportation order: appeal

(1) A deportation order may not be made in respect of a person while an appeal under section 82(1) [that may be brought or continued from within the United Kingdom relating to] the decision to make the order—

(a) could be brought (ignoring any possibility of an appeal out of time with permission), or

(b) is pending.

(2) In this section 'pending' has the meaning given by section 104.

[(3) This section does not apply to a deportation order which states that it is made in accordance with section 32(5) of the UK Borders Act 2007.]

[(4) But a deportation order made in reliance on subsection (3) does not invalidate leave to enter or remain, in accordance with section 5(1) of the Immigration Act 1971, if and for so long as section 78 above applies.]

Note: Commencement 1 April 2003 (SI 2003/754). Has effect in relation to an appeal pending under the old appeals provisions as it has effect in relation to an appeal pending under s 82(1) of the 2002 Act. Subsections (3) and (4) inserted by UK Borders Act 2007, s 35 from 1 August 2008 (SI 2008/1818). Words in square brackets in subsection (1) substituted by Sch 9 Immigration Act 2014 from 28 July 2014 (SI 2014/1820).

80. Removal of asylum-seeker to third country

. . .

Note: Amends Immigration and Asylum Act 1999, s 11.

PART V

[APPEALS IN RESPECT OF PROTECTION AND HUMAN RIGHTS CLAIMS]

Note: Heading substituted by Sch 9 Immigration Act 2014 from 20 October 2014 SI 2014/2771, with savings set out in articles 9-11.

[Appeal to Tribunal

[Meaning of 'the Tribunal'

81.

. . .

In this Part 'the Tribunal' means the First-tier Tribunal.]

Note: Section 81 substituted from 15 February 2010 (SI 2010/21).

[82. Right of appeal to the Tribunal

(1) A person ("P") may appeal to the Tribunal where—

(a) the Secretary of State has decided to refuse a protection claim made by P,

(b) the Secretary of State has decided to refuse a human rights claim made by P, or

(c) the Secretary of State has decided to revoke P's protection status.

(2) For the purposes of this Part—

(a) a "protection claim" is a claim made by a person ("P") that removal of P from the United Kingdom—

(i) would breach the United Kingdom's obligations under the Refugee Convention, or

(ii) would breach the United Kingdom's obligations in relation to persons eligible for a grant of humanitarian protection;

(b) P's protection claim is refused if the Secretary of State makes one or more of the following decisions—

(i) that removal of P from the United Kingdom would not breach the United Kingdom's obligations under the Refugee Convention;

(ii) that removal of P from the United Kingdom would not breach the United Kingdom's obligations in relation to persons eligible for a grant of humanitarian protection;

(c) a person has "protection status" if the person has been granted leave to enter or remain in the United Kingdom as a refugee or as a person eligible for a grant of humanitarian protection;

(d) "humanitarian protection" is to be construed in accordance with the immigration rules;

(e) "refugee" has the same meaning as in the Refugee Convention.

(3) The right of appeal under subsection (1) is subject to the exceptions and limitations specified in this Part.]

Note: Section 82 subsitutued by s 15 Immigration Act 2014 from 20 October 2014 with savings set out in SI 2014/2771, articles 9-11.

83. . . .

Note: Repealed by s 15 Immigration Act 2014 from 20 October 2014 with savings set out in SI 2014/2771, articles 9-11).

[83A.

Note: Repealed by s 15 Immigration Act 2014 from 20 October 2014 with savings set out in SI 2014/2771, articles 9-11.

[84 Grounds of appeal

(1) An appeal under section 82(1)(a) (refusal of protection claim) must be brought on one or more of the following grounds—

(a) that removal of the appellant from the United Kingdom would breach the United Kingdom's obligations under the Refugee Convention;

(b) that removal of the appellant from the United Kingdom would breach the United Kingdom's obligations in relation to persons eligible for a grant of humanitarian protection;

(c) that removal of the appellant from the United Kingdom would be unlawful under section 6 of the Human Rights Act 1998 (public authority not to act contrary to Human Rights Convention).

(2) An appeal under section 82(1)(b) (refusal of human rights claim) must be brought on the ground that the decision is unlawful under section 6 of the Human Rights Act 1998.

(3) An appeal under section 82(1)(c) (revocation of protection status) must be brought on one or more of the following grounds—

(a) that the decision to revoke the appellant's protection status breaches the United Kingdom's obligations under the Refugee Convention;

(b) that the decision to revoke the appellant's protection status breaches the United Kingdom's obligations in relation to persons eligible for a grant of humanitarian protection.]

Note: Section 84 substituted by s 15 Immigration Act 2014 from 20 October 2014 with savings set out in SI 2014/2771 articles 9-11.

85. Matters to be considered

(1) An appeal under section 82(1) against a decision shall be treated by [the Tribunal] as including an appeal against any decision in respect of which the appellant has a right of appeal under section 82(1).

(2) If an appellant under section 82(1) makes a statement under section 120, [the Tribunal] shall consider any matter raised in the statement which constitutes a ground of appeal of a kind listed in section [84] against the decision appealed against.

(3) Subsection (2) applies to a statement made under section 120 whether the statement was made before or after the appeal was commenced.

(4) On an appeal under section 82(1) . . . against a decision [the Tribunal] may consider . . . any matter which [it] thinks relevant to the substance of the decision, including . . . a matter arising after the date of the decision.

[(5) But the Tribunal must not consider a new matter unless the Secretary of State has given the Tribunal consent to do so.

(6) A matter is a "new matter" if—

(a) it constitutes a ground of appeal of a kind listed in section 84, and

(b) the Secretary of State has not previously considered the matter in the context of—

(i) the decision mentioned in section 82(1), or

(ii) a statement made by the appellant under section 120.]

Note: Commencement from 1 April 2003 (SI 2003/754, which sets out transitional provisions). Number in square brackets in subsection (2) substituted and words omitted from subsection (4) by Sch 9 Immigration Act 2014 from 20 October 2014, savings in articles 9-11 SI 2014/2771. Other words in square brackets substituted by Sch 2 Asylum and Immigration (Treatment of Claimants, etc.) Act 2004 from 4 April 2005 (SI 2005/565). Subsection (5) substituted by s 15 Immigration Act 2014 from 20 October 2014 with savings set out in SI 2014/2771.

[85A . . .

Note: Section 85A repealed by Sch 9 Immigration Act 2014 from 20 October 2014 with savings set out in articles 9-11 SI 2014/2771.

86. Determination of appeal

(1) This section applies on an appeal under section 82(1) . . .

(2) [the Tribunal] must determine—

(a) any matter raised as a ground of appeal . . ., and

(b) any matter which section 85 requires [it] to consider.

(3) . . .

(4) . . .

(5) . . .

(6) . . .

Note: Commencement from 1 April 2003 (SI 2003/754, which sets out transitional provisions). Words in square brackets in subsection (2) substituted by Sch 2 Asylum and Immigration (Treatment of Claimants, etc.) Act 2004 from 4 April 2005 (SI 2005/565). Words omitted from subsection (1) and (2) and subsections (3)–(6) omitted by Sch 9 Immigration Act 2014 from 20 October 2014, with savings in articles 9-11 of SI 2014/2771.

87. . . .

Note: Section 87 repealed by Sch 9 Immigration Act 2014 from 20 October 2014 with savings SI 2014/2771 articles 9-11.

Exceptions and limitations

88.

Note: Section 88 repealed by Sch 9 Immigration Act 2014 from 20 October 2014 with savings set out in articles 9-11 SI 2014/2771.

[88A.

Note: Section 88A repealed by Sch 9 Immigration Act 2014 from 20 October 2014 with savings set out in articles 9-11 SI 2014/2771.

[89.

Note: Section 89 repealed by Sch 9 Immigration Act 2014 from 20 October 2014 with savings in articles 9-11 SI 2014/2771.

90. . . .

Note: Section 90 repealed by Sch 9 Immigration Act 2014 from 20 October 2014 with savings set out in articles 9-11 SI 2014/2771.

91. . . .

Note: Section 91 repealed by Sch 9 Immigration Act 2014 from 20 October 2014 with savings set out in articles 9-11 SI 2014/2771.

[92. Place from which an appeal may be brought or continued

(1) This section applies to determine the place from which an appeal under section 82(1) may be brought or continued.

(2) In the case of an appeal under section 82(1)(a) (protection claim appeal), the appeal must be brought from outside the United Kingdom if—

(a) the claim to which the appeal relates has been certified under section 94(1) or (7) (claim clearly unfounded or removal to safe third country), or

(b) paragraph 5(3)(a), 10(3), 15(3) or 19(b) of Schedule 3 to the Asylum and Immigration (Treatment of Claimants, etc) Act 2004 (removal of asylum seeker to safe third country) applies.

Otherwise, the appeal must be brought from within the United Kingdom.

(3) In the case of an appeal under section 82(1)(b) (human rights claim appeal) where the claim to which the appeal relates was made while the appellant was in the United Kingdom, the appeal must be brought from outside the United Kingdom if—

(a) the claim to which the appeal relates has been certified under section 94(1) or (7) (claim clearly unfounded or removal to safe third country) or section 94B (certification of human rights claims made by persons liable to deportation), or

(b) paragraph 5(3)(b) or (4), 10(4), 15(4) or 19(c) of Schedule 3 to the Asylum and Immigration (Treatment of Claimants, etc.) Act 2004 (removal of asylum seeker to safe third country) applies.

Otherwise, the appeal must be brought from within the United Kingdom.

(4) In the case of an appeal under section 82(1)(b) (human rights claim appeal) where the claim to which the appeal relates was made while the appellant was outside the United Kingdom, the appeal must be brought from outside the United Kingdom.

(5) In the case of an appeal under section 82(1)(c) (revocation of protection status)—

(a) the appeal must be brought from within the United Kingdom if the decision to which the appeal relates was made while the appellant was in the United Kingdom;

(b) the appeal must be brought from outside the United Kingdom if the decision to which the appeal relates was made while the appellant was outside the United Kingdom.

(6) If, after an appeal under section 82(1)(a) or (b) has been brought from within the United Kingdom, the Secretary of State certifies the claim to which the appeal relates under section 94(1) or (7) or section 94B, the appeal must be continued from outside the United Kingdom.

(7) Where a person brings or continues an appeal under section 82(1)(a) (refusal of protection claim) from outside the United Kingdom, for the purposes of considering whether the grounds of appeal are satisfied, the appeal is to be treated as if the person were not outside the United Kingdom.

(8) Where an appellant brings an appeal from within the United Kingdom but leaves the United Kingdom before the appeal is finally determined, the appeal is to be treated as abandoned unless the claim to which the appeal relates has been certified under section 94(1) or (7) or section 94B.]

Note: Section 92 substituted by s 17 Immigration Act 2014 from 20 October 2014 with savings set out in SI 2014/2771 articles 9-11, and transitional provisions in art 4 SI 2014/1820.

93. Appeal from within United Kingdom: 'third country' removal

. . .

Note: Section 93 ceased to have effect from 1 October 2004, Asylum and Immigration Act 2004, s 33 (SI 2004/2523).

94. Appeal from within United Kingdom: unfounded human rights or [protection] claim

[(1) The Secretary of State may certify a protection claim or human rights claim as clearly unfounded.]

(3) If the Secretary of State is satisfied that [a] claimant is entitled to reside in a State listed in subsection (4) he shall certify the claim under subsection [(1)] unless satisfied that it is not clearly unfounded.

(4) Those States are—

(a)–(j) . . .

[(k) the Republic of Albania,

(l) . . .

(m) . . .

(n) Jamaica,

(o) Macedonia,

(p) the Republic of Moldova, and

(q) . . .]
[(r) . . .
(s) Bolivia,
(t) Brazil,
(u) Ecuador,
(v) . . .
(w) South Africa, and
(x) Ukraine.]
(y) India,
[(z) Mongolia,
(aa) Ghana (in respect of men),
(bb) Nigeria (in respect of men).]
[(cc) Bosnia-Herzegovina,
(dd) Gambia (in respect of men),
(ee) Kenya (in respect of men),
(ff) Liberia (in respect of men),
(gg) Malawi (in respect of men),
(hh) Mali (in respect of men),
(ii) Mauritius,
(jj) Montenegro,
(kk) Peru,
(ll) Serbia,
(mm) Sierra Leone (in respect of men)]
[(nn) Kosovo,
(oo) South Korea]

(5) The Secretary of State may by order add a State, or part of a State, to the list in subsection (4) if satisfied that—

(a) there is in general in that State or part no serious risk of persecution of persons entitled to reside in that State or part, and

(b) removal to that State or part of persons entitled to reside there will not in general contravene the United Kingdom's obligations under the Human Rights Convention.

[(**5A**) If the Secretary of State is satisfied that the statements in subsection (5)(a) and (b) are true of a State or part of a State in relation to a description of person, an order under subsection (5) may add the State or part to the list in subsection (4) in respect of that description of person.

(**5B**) Where a State or part of a State is added to the list in subsection (4) in respect of a description of person, subsection (3) shall have effect in relation to a claimant only if the Secretary of State is satisfied that he is within that description (as well as being satisfied that he is entitled to reside in the State or part).

(**5C**) A description for the purposes of subsection (5A) may refer to—

(a) gender,
(b) language,
(c) race,
(d) religion,
(e) nationality,
(f) membership of a social or other group,
(g) political opinion, or
(h) any other attribute or circumstance that the Secretary of State thinks appropriate.]

[(**5D**) In deciding whether the statements in subsection (5)(a) and (b) are true of a State or part of a State, the Secretary of State—

(a) shall have regard to all the circumstances of the State or part (including its laws and how they are applied), and

(b) shall have regard to information from any appropriate source (including other member States and international organisations).]

[(**6**) The Secretary of State may by order amend the list in subsection (4) so as to omit a State or part added under subsection (5); and the omission may be—

(a) general, or

(b) effected so that the State or part remains listed in respect of a description of person.]

[(**6A**) Subsection (3) shall not apply in relation to [a] claimant who—

(a) is the subject of a certificate under section 2 or 70 of the Extradition Act 2003 (c. 41),

(b) is in custody pursuant to arrest under section 5 of that Act,

(c) is the subject of a provisional warrant under section 73 of that Act,

(d) is the subject of an authority to proceed under section 7 of the Extradition Act 1989 (c. 33) or an order under paragraph 4(2) of Schedule 1 to that Act, or

(e) is the subject of a provisional warrant under section 8 of that Act or of a warrant under paragraph 5(1)(b) of Schedule 1 to that Act.]

[(**6B**) A certificate under subsection (1A) or (2) may not be issued (and subsection (3) shall not apply) in relation to an appeal under section 82(2)(d) or (e) against a decision relating to leave to enter or remain in the United Kingdom, where the leave was given in circumstances specified for the purposes of this subsection by order of the Secretary of State.]

(**7**) [The Secretary of State may certify a protection claim or human rights claim made by a person if]—

(a) it is proposed to remove the person to a country of which he is not a national or citizen, and

(b) there is no reason to believe that the person's rights under the Human Rights Convention will be breached in that country.

(**8**) In determining whether a person in relation to whom a certificate has been issued under subsection (7) may be removed from the United Kingdom, the country specified in the certificate is to be regarded as—

(a) a place where a person's life and liberty is not threatened by reason of his race, religion, nationality, membership of a particular social group, or political opinion, and

(b) a place from which a person will not be sent to another country otherwise than in accordance with the Refugee Convention [or with the United Kingdom's obligations in relation to persons eligible for a grant of humanitarian protection].

(**9**) . . .

Note: Subsection (5) commenced 10 February 2003 for the purposes of enabling subordinate legislation (SI 2003/249), remainder from 1 April 2003 (SI 2003/754, which sets out transitional provisions). Subsection (6B) inserted by Immigration, Asylum and Nationality Act 2006, s 13 from a date to be appointed. Subsection 4: words in first square brackets added by SI 2003/970 from 1 April 2003, words in second square brackets added by SI 2003/1919 from 23 July 2003, Bangladesh omitted and last words in square brackets inserted from December 2005 (SI 2005/3306). First words omitted and other words in square brackets substituted or added by Asylum and Immigration (Treatment of Claimants etc.) Act 2004, s 27 from 1 October 2004 (SI 2004/2523). Other words in subsection (4) omitted from 22 April 2005 (SI 2005/1016). Subsection (5D) inserted by SI 2007/3187 from 1 December 2007. India inserted from 15 February 2005 (SI 2005/330). Serbia and Montenegro omitted from subsection (4) and (cc)-(mm) inserted from 27 July 2007 (SI 2007/2221). Sri Lanka omitted from subsection (4) from 13 December 2006 (SI 2006/3275). Bulgaria and Romania omitted from sub-section (4) from 1 January 2007 (SI 2006/3215). Kosovo and South Korea inserted from 3 March 2010, but without effect to asylum claims made before that date, (SI 2010/561). Subsections (1)–(2) and words in square brackets in the heading, subsections (3), (6A), (7) substituted, words in square brackets in subsection (8)(b) inserted and subsection (9) omitted by Sch 9 Immigration Act 2014 from 20 October 2014 with savings set out in articles 9-11 SI 2014/2771.

[94A European Common List of Safe Countries of Origin

(1) The Secretary of State shall by order prescribe a list of States to be known as the 'European Common List of Safe Countries of Origin'.

(2) Subsections (3) and (4) apply where a person makes [a protection claim] or a human rights claim (or both) and that person is—

(a) a national of a State which is listed in the European Common List of Safe Countries of Origin, or

(b) a Stateless person who was formerly habitually resident in such a State.

(3) The Secretary of State shall consider the claim or claims mentioned in subsection (2) to be unfounded unless satisfied that there are serious grounds for considering that the State in question is not safe in the particular circumstances of the person mentioned in that subsection.

(4) The Secretary of State shall also certify the claim or claims mentioned in subsection (2) under section [94(1)] unless satisfied that the claim or claims is or are not clearly unfounded.

(5) An order under subsection (1) –

(a) may be made only if the Secretary of State thinks it necessary for the purpose of complying with the United Kingdom's obligations under [EU] law,

(b) may include transitional, consequential or incidental provision,

(c) shall be made by statutory instrument, and

(d) shall be subject to annulment in pursuance of a resolution of either House of Parliament.]

Note: Section 94A inserted by SI 2007/3187 from 1 December 2007. Words in square brackets in subsection (5)(a) substituted by SI 2011/1043 from 22 April 2011. Words in square brackets in subsections (2) and (4) substituted by Sch 9 Immigration Act 2014 from 20 October 2014 with savings set out in articles 9-11 SI 2014/2771.

[94B Appeal from within the United Kingdom: certification of human rights claims made by persons liable to deportation

(1) This section applies where a human rights claim has been made by a person ("P") who is liable to deportation under—

(a) section 3(5)(a) of the Immigration Act 1971 (Secretary of State deeming deportation conducive to public good), or

(b) section 3(6) of that Act (court recommending deportation following conviction).

(2) The Secretary of State may certify the claim if the Secretary of State considers that, despite the appeals process not having been begun or not having been exhausted, removal of P to the country or territory to which P is proposed to be removed, pending the outcome

of an appeal in relation to P's claim, would not be unlawful under section 6 of the Human Rights Act 1998 (public authority not to act contrary to Human Rights Convention).

(3) The grounds upon which the Secretary of State may certify a claim under subsection (2) include (in particular) that P would not, before the appeals process is exhausted, face a real risk of serious irreversible harm if removed to the country or territory to which P is proposed to be removed.]

Note: Section 94B inserted by s 17 Immigration Act 2014 from 28 July 2014 (SI 2014/1820).

95. . . .

Note: Section 95 repealed by Sch 9 Immigration Act 2014 from 20 October 2014 with savings set out in articles 9-11 SI 2014/2771.

96. Earlier right of appeal

[(1) [A person may not bring an appeal under section 82 against a decision ("the new decision")] if the Secretary of State or an immigration officer certifies—

(a) that the person was notified of a right of appeal under that section against another . . . decision ('the old decision') (whether or not an appeal was brought and whether or not any appeal brought has been determined),

(b) that the claim or application to which the new decision relates relies on a [ground] that could have been raised in an appeal against the old decision, and

(c) that, in the opinion of the Secretary of State or the immigration officer, there is no satisfactory reason for that [ground] not having been raised in an appeal against the old decision.

[(2) A person may not bring an appeal under section 82 if the Secretary of State or an immigration officer certifies—

(a) that the person has received a notice under section 120(2),

(b) that the appeal relies on a ground that should have been, but has not been, raised in a statement made under section 120(2) or (5), and

(c) that, in the opinion of the Secretary of State or the immigration officer, there is no satisfactory reason for that ground not having been raised in a statement under section 120(2) or (5).]

(4) In subsection (1) 'notified' means notified in accordance with regulations under section 105.

(5) [Subsections (1) and (2) apply to prevent] a person's right of appeal whether or not he has been outside the United Kingdom since an earlier right of appeal arose or since a requirement under section 120 was imposed.

(6) In this section a reference to an appeal under section 82(1) includes a reference to an appeal under section 2 of the Special Immigration Appeals Commission Act 1997 (c. 68) which is or could be brought by reference to an appeal under section 82(1).

[(7) A certificate under subsection (1) or (2) shall have no effect in relation to an appeal instituted before the certificate is issued.]

Note: Commencement from 1 April 2003 (SI 2003/754, which sets out transitional provisions). Word omitted from subsection (1)(a), words in square brackets in subsection (1) and subsection (2) substituted by Sch 9 Immigration Act 2014 from 20 October 2014, savings set out in articles 9-11 SI 2014/2771. Words in other square brackets substituted and subsection (7) added by Asylum and Immigration (Treatment of Claimants, etc.) Act 2004, s 30 from 1 October 2004 (SI 2004/2523).

97. National security, &c.

(1) An appeal under section 82(1) . . . against a decision in respect of a person may not be brought or continued if the Secretary of State certifies that the decision is or was taken—

(a) by the Secretary of State wholly or partly on a ground listed in subsection (2), or

(b) in accordance with a direction of the Secretary of State which identifies the person to whom the decision relates and which is given wholly or partly on a ground listed in subsection (2).

(2) The grounds mentioned in subsection (1) are that the person's exclusion or removal from the United Kingdom is—

(a) in the interests of national security, or

(b) in the interests of the relationship between the United Kingdom and another country.

(3) An appeal under section 82(1) . . . against a decision may not be brought or continued if the Secretary of State certifies that the decision is or was taken wholly or partly in reliance on information which in his opinion should not be made public—

(a) in the interests of national security,

(b) in the interests of the relationship between the United Kingdom and another country, or

(c) otherwise in the public interest.

(4) In subsections (1)(a) and (b) and (3) a reference to the Secretary of State is to the Secretary of State acting in person.

Note: Commencement from 1 April 2003 (SI 2003/754, which sets out transitional provisions). Words in square brackets in subsections (1) and (3) omitted by Sch 9 Immigration Act 2014 from 20 October 2014 with savings set out in articles 9-11 SI 2014/2771.

[97A. National security: deportation

(1) This section applies where the Secretary of State certifies that the decision to make a deportation order in respect of a person was taken on the grounds that his removal from the United Kingdom would be in the interests of national security.

[(1A) This section also applies where the Secretary of State certifies, in the case of a person in respect of whom a deportation order has been made which states that it is made in accordance with section 32(5) of the UK Borders Act 2007, that the person's removal from the United Kingdom would be in the interests of national security.]

(2) Where this section applies—

(a) section 79 shall not apply,

(b) the Secretary of State shall be taken to have certified the decision to make the deportation order under section 97, and

[(c) section 2(5) of the Special Immigration Appeals Commission Act 1997 (whether appeals brought against decisions certified under section 97 may be brought from within the United Kingdom) does not apply, but see instead the following provisions of this section.]

[(2A) The person while in the United Kingdom may not bring or continue an appeal under section 2 of the Special Immigration Appeals Commission Act 1997—

(a) against the decision to make the deportation order, or

(b) against any refusal to revoke the deportation order,

unless the person has made a human rights claim while in the United Kingdom.

(**2B**) Subsection (2A) does not allow the person while in the United Kingdom to bring or continue an appeal if the Secretary of State certifies that removal of the person—

(a) to the country or territory to which the person is proposed to be removed, and

(b) despite the appeals process not having been begun or not having been exhausted,

would not [be unlawful under section 6 of the Human Rights Act 1998 (public authority not to act contrary to Human Rights Convention)].

(**2C**) The grounds upon which a certificate may be given under subsection (2B) include (in particular)—

(a) that the person would not, before the appeals process is exhausted, face a real risk of serious irreversible harm if removed to the country or territory to which the person is proposed to be removed;

(b) that the whole or part of any human rights claim made by the person is clearly unfounded.

(**2D**) . . .

(**2E**) . . .

(**2F**) If a certificate in respect of a person is given under subsection (2B), the person may apply to the Special Immigration Appeals Commission to set aside the certificate.

(**2G**) If a person makes an application under subsection (2F) then the Commission, in determining whether the certificate should be set aside, must apply the principles that would be applied in judicial review proceedings.

(**2H**) The Commission's determination of a review under subsection (2F) is final.

(**2J**) The Commission may direct that a person who has made and not withdrawn an application under subsection (2F) is not to be removed from the United Kingdom at a time when the review has not been finally determined by the Commission.

(**2K**) Sections 5 and 6 of the Special Immigration Appeals Commission Act 1997 apply in relation to reviews under subsection (2F) (and to applicants for such reviews) as they apply in relation to appeals under section 2 or 2B of that Act (and to persons bringing such appeals).

(**2L**) Any exercise of power to make rules under section 5 of that Act in relation to reviews under subsection (2F) is to be with a view to securing that proceedings on such reviews are handled expeditiously.]

(3) . . .

(4) The Secretary of State may repeal this section by order.]

Note: Section 97A inserted by Immigration, Asylum and Nationality Act 2006, s 7 from 31 August 2006 (SI 2006/2226). Subsection (1A), (2A)–(2L) inserted, subsection (2)(c) substituted by s 54 Crime and Courts Act 2013 from 25 June 2013 (SI 2013/1042). Words in square brackets in subsection (2B) substituted and subsections (2D), (2E) and (3) omitted by Sch 9 Immigration Act 2014 from 20 October 2014 with savings set out in articles 9-11 SI 2014/2771.

[97B . . .

Note: Section 97B inserted by s 53 Crime and Courts Act 2013 from 25 June 2013 (SI 2013/1042), repealed by Sch 9 Immigration Act 2014 from 20 October 2014 with savings set out in articles 9-11 SI 2014/2771.

98. . . .

Note: Section 98 repealed by Schedule 9 Immigration Act 2014 from 20 October 2014 with savings set out in articles 9-11 SI 2014/2771.

99. [Section 97]: appeal in progress

(1) This section applies where a certificate is issued under section . . . [97] . . . in respect of a pending appeal.

(2) The appeal shall lapse.

Note: Commencement from 1 April 2003 (SI 2003/754, which sets out transitional provisions). Words in square brackets in title substituted and words omitted from subsection (1) by Sch 9 Immigration Act 2014 from 20 October 2014 with savings set out in articles 9-11 SI 2014/2771.

Appeal from adjudicator

100. Immigration Appeal Tribunal

. . .

Note: Section 100 ceased to have effect, Asylum and Immigration (Treatment of Claimants, etc.) Act 2004, s 26 from 4 April 2005 (SI 2005/565).

101. Appeal to Tribunal

. . .

Note: Section 101 ceased to have effect, Asylum and Immigration (Treatment of Claimants, etc.) Act 2004, s 26 from 4 April 2005 (SI 2005/565).

102. Decision

. . .

Note: Section 102 ceased to have effect from 4 April 2005 (SI 2005/565), Asylum and Immigration (Treatment of Claimants, etc.) Act 2004, s 26.

103. Appeal from Tribunal

. . .

Note: Section 103 ceased to have effect from 4 April 2005 (SI 2005/565), Asylum and Immigration (Treatment of Claimants, etc.) Act 2004, s 26.

[103A.–103E.]

Note: Sections 103A–E inserted by Asylum and Immigration (Treatment of Claimants, etc.) Act 2004, s 26 from 4 April 2005 (SI 2005/565). Revoked from 15 February 2010 (SI 2010/21).

Procedure

104. Pending appeal

(1) An appeal under section 82(1) is pending during the period—

(a) beginning when it is instituted, and

(b) ending when it is finally determined, withdrawn or abandoned (or when it lapses under section 99).

[(2) An appeal under section 82(1) is not finally determined for the purpose of subsection (1)(b) while—

(a) an application for permission to appeal under section 11 or 13 of the Tribunals, Courts and Enforcement Act 2007 could be made or is awaiting determination,

(b) permission to appeal under either of those sections has been granted and the appeal is awaiting determination, or

(c) an appeal has been remitted under section 12 or 14 of that Act and is awaiting determination.]

(3) . . .

[(4) . . .

(4A) An appeal under section 82(1) brought by a person while he is in the United Kingdom shall be treated as abandoned if the appellant is granted leave to enter or remain in the United Kingdom (subject to [subsection (4B)]).

(4B) Subsection (4A) shall not apply to an appeal in so far as it is brought on [a ground specified in section 84(1)(a) or (b) or 84(3) (asylum or humanitarian protection)] where the appellant—

(a) . . .

(b) gives notice, in accordance with [Tribunal Procedure Rules], that he wishes to pursue the appeal in so far as it is brought on that ground.

(4C) . . .

(5) . . .

Note: Commencement from 1 April 2003 (SI 2003/754). Subsection (3) omitted by Sch 2 Asylum and Immigration (Treatment of Claimants, etc.) Act 2004 from 4 April 2005 (SI 2005/565). Sub-section (4) substituted and subsections (4A)–(4C) inserted by Immigration, Asylum and Nationality Act 2006, s 9 from 13 November 2006 (SI 2006/2838). Subsection (2) and words in square brackets in subsections (4B)(b) substituted from 15 February 2010 (SI 2010/21). Words in square brackets in subsection (4B) substituted and subsections (4), (4B)(a), (4C) and (5) omitted by Sch 9 Immigration Act 2014 from 20 October 2014 with savings set out in articles 9-11 SI 2014/2771.

105. Notice of immigration decision

(1) The Secretary of State may make regulations requiring a person to be given written notice where an [appealable] decision is taken in respect of him.

(2) The regulations may, in particular, provide that a notice under subsection (1) of [an appealable decision] must state—

(a) that there is a right of appeal under [section 82], and

(b) how and when that right may be exercised.

(3) The regulations may make provision (which may include presumptions) about service.

[(4) In this section "appealable decision" means a decision mentioned in section 82(1).]

Note: Commencement from 1 April 2003 (SI 2003/754). Words in square brackets substituted and subsection (4) inserted by Sch 9 Immigration Act 2014 from 20 October 2014 with savings set out in articles 9-11 SI 2014/2771.

106. Rules

(1) . . .

[(1A) . . .

(2) . . .

[(3) In the case of an appeal under section 82 . . . or by virtue of section 109, Tribunal Procedure Rules may enable the Tribunal to certify that the appeal had no merit (and shall make provision for the consequences of the issue of a certificate).]

(4) A person commits an offence if without reasonable excuse he fails to comply with a requirement imposed in accordance with [Tribunal Procedure Rules in connection with proceedings under section 82 . . . or by virtue of section 109] to attend before . . . the Tribunal—

(a) to give evidence, or

(b) to produce a document.

(5) A person who is guilty of an offence under subsection (4) shall be liable on summary conviction to a fine not exceeding level 3 on the standard scale.

Note: Commencement from 1 April 2003 (SI 2003/754). Subsections (1), (1A) and (2) revoked, subsection (3) and words in square brackets in subsection (4) substituted from 15 February 2010 (SI 2010/21). Words omitted from subsection (3)–(4) by Schedule 9 Immigration Act 2014 from 20 October 2014 with savings set out in articles 9-11 SI 2014/2771.

107. Practice directions

(1) . . .

[(1A) . . .]

(2) . . .

[(3) In the case of proceedings under section 82 . . . or by virtue of section 109, or proceedings in the Upper Tribunal arising out of such proceedings, practice directions under section 23 of the Tribunals, Courts and Enforcement Act 2007—

(a) may require the Tribunal to treat a specified decision of the Tribunal or Upper Tribunal as authoritative in respect of a particular matter; and

(b) may require the Upper Tribunal to treat a specified decision of the Tribunal or Upper Tribunal as authoritative in respect of a particular matter.]

[(3A) In subsection (3) the reference to a decision of the Tribunal includes—

(a) a decision of the Asylum and Immigration Tribunal, and

(b) a decision of the Immigration Appeal Tribunal.]

(4) . . .

(5) . . .

(6) . . .

(7) . . .

Note: Commencement from 1 April 2003 (SI 2003/754). Subsections (1), (1A) and (4)—(7) revoked and subsection (3) substituted and (3A) inserted from 15 February 2010 (SI 2010/21). Words omitted from subsection (3) by Sch 9 Immigration Act 2014 from 20 October 2014 with savings set out in articles 9-11 SI 2014/2771.

108. Forged document: proceedings in private

(1) This section applies where it is alleged—

(a) that a document relied on by a party to an appeal under section 82 . . . is a forgery, and

(b) that disclosure to that party of a matter relating to the detection of the forgery would be contrary to the public interest.

(2) [The Tribunal]

(a) must investigate the allegation in private, and

(b) may proceed in private so far as necessary to prevent disclosure of the matter referred to in subsection (1)(b).

Note: Commencement from 1 April 2003 (SI 2003/754). Amended by Sch 2 Asylum and Immigration (Treatment of Claimants, etc.) Act 2004, from 4 April 2005 (SI 2005/565). Words in square brackets in subsection (1)(a) substituted by Sch 1 Immigration, Asylum and Nationality Act 2006 from 31 August 2006 (SI 2006/2226) and omitted by Sch 9 Immigration Act 2014 from 20 October 2014 with savings set out in articles 9-11 SI 2014/2771.

General

109. European Union and European Economic Area

(1) Regulations may provide for, or make provision about, an appeal against an immigration decision taken in respect of a person who has or claims to have a right under any of the [EU] Treaties.

(2) The regulations may—

(a) apply a provision of this Act or the Special Immigration Appeals Commission Act 1997 (c. 68) with or without modification;

(b) make provision similar to a provision made by or under this Act or that Act;

(c) disapply or modify the effect of a provision of this Act or that Act.

(3) In subsection (1) 'immigration decision' means a decision about—

(a) a person's entitlement to enter or remain in the United Kingdom, or

(b) removal of a person from the United Kingdom.

Note: Commencement from 1 April 2003 (SI 2003/754). Words in square brackets in subsection (1) substituted by SI 2011/1043 from 22 April 2011.

110. Grants

Note: Commencement from 1 April 2003 (SI 2003/754). Ceased to have effect from 16 June 2006, Immigration, Asylum and Nationality Act 2006, s 10 (SI 2006/1497).

111. . . .

Note: Section 111 deleted by UK Borders Act 2007 s 54(c) from 1 April 2008 (SI 2008/309).

112. Regulations, &c.

(1) Regulations under this Part shall be made by the Secretary of State.

(2) Regulations . . . under this Part . . . —

(a) must be made by statutory instrument, and

(b) shall be subject to annulment in pursuance of a resolution of either House of Parliament.

(3) Regulations . . . under this Part—

(a) may make provision which applies generally or only in a specified case or in specified circumstances,

(b) may make different provision for different cases or circumstances,

(c) may include consequential, transitional or incidental provision, and

(d) may include savings.

[(3A). . .

(4) An order under section 94(5) . . . —

(a) must be made by statutory instrument,

(b) may not be made unless a draft has been laid before and approved by resolution of each House of Parliament, and

(c) may include transitional provision.

(5) An order under section [94(6) or (6B)] . . . —

(a) must be made by statutory instrument,

(b) shall be subject to annulment in pursuance of a resolution of either House of Parliament, and

(c) may include transitional provision.

[(5A) If an instrument makes provision under section 94(5) and 94(6)—

(a) subsection (4)(b) above shall apply, and

(b) subsection (5)(b) above shall not apply.]

[(5B) An order under section 97A(4)—

(a) must be made by statutory instrument,

(b) shall be subject to annulment in pursuance of a resolution of either House of Parliament, and

(c) may include transitional provision.]

[(6) . . .

(7) . . .]

Note: Commenced 10 February 2003 (SI 2003/249). Subsection (3A) and (5A) inserted by Asylum and Immigration (Treatment of Claimants, etc.) Act 2004, ss 29 and 27 respectively from 1 October 2004 (SI 2004/2523). Words in square brackets in subsection (5) substituted and subsection (5B) inserted by Immigration, Asylum and Nationality Act 2006, ss 7, 14, 62 and Sch 1 from 31 August 2006 (SI 2006/2226). Words omitted from subsections (2) and (3) and subsections (6)–(7) revoked from 15 February 2010 (SI 2010/21, which contains savings). Subsection (3A) and words omitted from subsections (4) and (5) by Sch 9 Immigration Act 2014 from 20 October 2014 with savings set out in articles 9-11 SI 2014/2771.

113. Interpretation

(1) In this Part, unless a contrary intention appears—

['asylum claim'—

(a) means a claim made by a person that to remove him from or require him to leave the United Kingdom would breach the United Kingdom's obligations under the Refugee Convention, but

(b) does not include a claim which, having regard to a former claim, falls to be disregarded for the purposes of this Part in accordance with immigration rules,]

. . .

['human rights claim'—

(a) means a claim made by a person that to remove him from or require him to leave the United Kingdom [or to refuse him entry into the United Kingdom] would be unlawful under section 6 of the Human Rights Act 1998 (c. 42) (public authority not to act contrary to Convention) . . ., but

(b) does not include a claim which, having regard to a former claim, falls to be disregarded for the purposes of this Part in accordance with immigration rules,]

["humanitarian protection" has the meaning given in section 82(2);]

'the Human Rights Convention' has the same meaning as 'the Convention' in the Human Rights Act 1998 and 'Convention rights' shall be construed in accordance with section 1 of that Act,

. . .

'immigration rules' means rules under section 1(4) of that Act (general immigration rules),

. . .

['protection claim' has the meaning given in section 82(2)]

['protection status' has the meaning given in section 82(2)]

'the Refugee Convention' means the Convention relating to the Status of Refugees done at Geneva on 28 July 1951 and its Protocol,

. . .

. . .

(2) . . .

Note: Commenced 10 February 2003 (SI 2003/249). Definitions of asylum claim and human rights claim substituted by Immigration, Asylum and Nationality Act 2006, s 12 from a date to be appointed. Further amendments made in subsection (1) and omissions from subsection (2) by Sch 9 Immigration Act 2014 from 20 October 2014 with savings set out in articles 9-11 SI 2014/2771.

114. Repeal

(1) . . .

(2) Schedule 6 (which makes transitional provision in connection with the repeal of Part IV of that Act and its replacement by this Part) shall have effect.

(3) Schedule 7 (consequential amendments) shall have effect.

Note: Subsection (1) repeals Part IV of the Immigration and Asylum Act 1999. Subsection (3) Commenced 10 February 2003 (SI 2003/1). Remainder from 1 April 2003 (SI 2003/754).

115. . . .

Note: Section 115 repealed by Sch 9 Immigration Act 2014 from 20 October 2014 with savings set out in articles 9-11 SI 2014/2771.

116. Special Immigration Appeals Commission: Community Legal Service

. . .

Note: Amends paragraph 2(1), Sch 2 Access to Justice Act 1999. Repealed by Legal Aid, Sentencing and Punishment of Offenders Act 2012, Sch 5, Part 2 from a date to be appointed.

117. Northern Ireland appeals: legal aid

. . .

Note: Amends Part 1, Sch 1 Legal Aid, Advice and Assistance (Northern Ireland) Order 1981.

[PART VA

ARTICLE 8 OF THE ECHR; PUBLIC INTEREST CONSIDERATIONS

Note: Part 5A inserted by s 19 Immigration Act 2014 from 28 July 2014 (SI 2014/1820).

117A. Application of this Part

(1) This Part applies where a court or tribunal is required to determine whether a decision made under the Immigration Acts—

(a) breaches a person's right to respect for private and family life under Article 8, and

(b) as a result would be unlawful under section 6 of the Human Rights Act 1998.

(2) In considering the public interest question, the court or tribunal must (in particular) have regard—

(a) in all cases, to the considerations listed in section 117B, and

(b) in cases concerning the deportation of foreign criminals, to the considerations listed in section 117C.

(3) In subsection (2), "the public interest question" means the question of whether an interference with a person's right to respect for private and family life is justified under Article 8(2).

Note: Section 117A inserted by s 19 Immigration Act 2014 from 28 July 2014 (SI 2014/1820).

117B. Article 8: public interest considerations applicable in all cases

(1) The maintenance of effective immigration controls is in the public interest.

(2) It is in the public interest, and in particular in the interests of the economic well-being of the United Kingdom, that persons who seek to enter or remain in the United Kingdom are able to speak English, because persons who can speak English—

(a) are less of a burden on taxpayers, and

(b) are better able to integrate into society.

(3) It is in the public interest, and in particular in the interests of the economic well-being of the United Kingdom, that persons who seek to enter or remain in the United Kingdom are financially independent, because such persons—

(a) are not a burden on taxpayers, and

(b) are better able to integrate into society.

(4) Little weight should be given to—

(a) a private life, or

(b) a relationship formed with a qualifying partner,

that is established by a person at a time when the person is in the United Kingdom unlawfully.

(5) Little weight should be given to a private life established by a person at a time when the person's immigration status is precarious.

(6) In the case of a person who is not liable to deportation, the public interest does not require the person's removal where—

(a) the person has a genuine and subsisting parental relationship with a qualifying child, and

(b) it would not be reasonable to expect the child to leave the United Kingdom.

Note: Section 117B inserted by s 19 Immigration Act 2014 from 28 July 2014 (SI 2014/1820).

117C. Article 8: additional considerations in cases involving foreign criminals

(1) The deportation of foreign criminals is in the public interest.

(2) The more serious the offence committed by a foreign criminal, the greater is the public interest in deportation of the criminal.

(3) In the case of a foreign criminal ("C") who has not been sentenced to a period of imprisonment of four years or more, the public interest requires C's deportation unless Exception 1 or Exception 2 applies.

(4) Exception 1 applies where—

(a) C has been lawfully resident in the United Kingdom for most of C's life,

(b) C is socially and culturally integrated in the United Kingdom, and

(c) there would be very significant obstacles to C's integration into the country to which C is proposed to be deported.

(5) Exception 2 applies where C has a genuine and subsisting relationship with a qualifying partner, or a genuine and subsisting parental relationship with a qualifying child, and the effect of C's deportation on the partner or child would be unduly harsh.

(6) In the case of a foreign criminal who has been sentenced to a period of imprisonment of at least four years, the public interest requires deportation unless there are very compelling circumstances, over and above those described in Exceptions 1 and 2.

(7) The considerations in subsections (1) to (6) are to be taken into account where a court or tribunal is considering a decision to deport a foreign criminal only to the extent that the reason for the decision was the offence or offences for which the criminal has been convicted.

Note: Section 117C inserted by s 19 Immigration Act 2014 from 28 July 2014 (SI 2014/1820).

117D. Interpretation of this Part

(1) In this Part—

"Article 8" means Article 8 of the European Convention on Human Rights;

"qualifying child" means a person who is under the age of 18 and who—

(a) is a British citizen, or

(b) has lived in the United Kingdom for a continuous period of seven years or more;

"qualifying partner" means a partner who—

(a) is a British citizen, or

(b) who is settled in the United Kingdom (within the meaning of the Immigration Act 1971—see section 33(2A) of that Act).

(2) In this Part, "foreign criminal" means a person—

(a) who is not a British citizen,

(b) who has been convicted in the United Kingdom of an offence, and

(c) who—

(i) has been sentenced to a period of imprisonment of at least 12 months,

(ii) has been convicted of an offence that has caused serious harm, or

(iii) is a persistent offender.

(3) For the purposes of subsection (2)(b), a person subject to an order under—

(a) section 5 of the Criminal Procedure (Insanity) Act 1964 (insanity etc),

(b) section 57 of the Criminal Procedure (Scotland) Act 1995 (insanity etc.), or

(c) Article 50A of the Mental Health (Northern Ireland) Order 1986 (insanity etc.),

has not been convicted of an offence.

(4) In this Part, references to a person who has been sentenced to a period of imprisonment of a certain length of time—

(a) do not include a person who has received a suspended sentence (unless a court subsequently orders that the sentence or any part of it (of whatever length) is to take effect);

(b) do not include a person who has been sentenced to a period of imprisonment of that length of time only by virtue of being sentenced to consecutive sentences amounting in aggregate to that length of time;

(c) include a person who is sentenced to detention, or ordered or directed to be detained, in an institution other than a prison (including, in particular, a hospital or an institution for young offenders) for that length of time; and

(d) include a person who is sentenced to imprisonment or detention, or ordered or directed to be detained, for an indeterminate period, provided that it may last for at least that length of time.

(5) If any question arises for the purposes of this Part as to whether a person is a British citizen, it is for the person asserting that fact to prove it.]

Note: Section 117D inserted by s 19 Immigration Act 2014 from 28 July 2014 (SI 2014/1820).

PART VI

IMMIGRATION PROCEDURE

Applications

118. Leave pending decision on variation application

. . .

Note: Amends Immigration Act 1971, s 3C.

119. Deemed leave on cancellation of notice

. . .

Note: Amends paragraph 6(3), Sch 2 Immigration Act 1971.

[120. Requirement to state additional grounds for application etc.

(1) Subsection (2) applies to a person ("P") if—

(a) P has made a protection claim or a human rights claim,

(b) P has made an application to enter or remain in the United Kingdom, or

(c) a decision to deport or remove P has been or may be taken.

(2) The Secretary of State or an immigration officer may serve a notice on P requiring P to provide a statement setting out—

(a) P's reasons for wishing to enter or remain in the United Kingdom,

(b) any grounds on which P should be permitted to enter or remain in the United Kingdom, and

(c) any grounds on which P should not be removed from or required to leave the United Kingdom.

(3) A statement under subsection (2) need not repeat reasons or grounds set out in—

(a) P's protection or human rights claim,

(b) the application mentioned in subsection (1)(b), or

(c) an application to which the decision mentioned in subsection (1)(c) relates.

(4) Subsection (5) applies to a person ("P") if P has previously been served with a notice under subsection (2) and—

(a) P requires leave to enter or remain in the United Kingdom but does not have it, or

(b) P has leave to enter or remain in the United Kingdom only by virtue of section 3C or 3D of the Immigration Act 1971 (continuation of leave pending decision or appeal).

(5) Where P's circumstances have changed since the Secretary of State or an immigration officer was last made aware of them (whether in the application or claim mentioned in subsection (1) or in a statement under subsection (2) or this subsection) so that P has—

(a) additional reasons for wishing to enter or remain in the United Kingdom,

(b) additional grounds on which P should be permitted to enter or remain in the United Kingdom, or

(c) additional grounds on which P should not be removed from or required to leave the United Kingdom,

P must, as soon as reasonably practicable, provide a supplementary statement to the Secretary of State or an immigration officer setting out the new circumstances and the additional reasons or grounds.

(6) In this section—

"human rights claim" and "protection claim" have the same meanings as in Part 5;

references to "grounds" are to grounds on which an appeal under Part 5 may be brought (see section 84).]

Note: Commencement from 1 April 2003 (SI 2003/754). Substituted by Sch 9 Immigration Act 2014 from 20 October 2014 with savings set out in articles 9-11 SI 2014/2771.

121. Compliance with procedure

. . .

Note: Amends Immigration Act 1971, s 31A.

Work permit

122.

. . .

Note: Commenced 10 February 2003 (SI 2003/1). Ceased to have effect by Sch 2 Immigration, Asylum and Nationality Act 2006 from 2 April 2007 (SI 2007/1109).

123. Advice about work permit, &c.

. . .

Note: Amends Immigration and Asylum Act 1999, s 82.

Authority-to-carry scheme

124. Authority to carry

(1) Regulations made by the Secretary of State may authorise him to require a person (a 'carrier') to pay a penalty if the carrier brings a passenger to the United Kingdom and—

(a) the carrier was required by an authority-to-carry scheme to seek authority under the scheme to carry the passenger, and

(b) the carrier did not seek authority before the journey to the United Kingdom commenced or was refused authority under the scheme.

(2) An 'authority-to-carry scheme' is a scheme operated by the Secretary of State which requires carriers to seek authority to bring passengers to the United Kingdom.

(3) An authority-to-carry scheme must specify—

(a) the class of carrier to which it applies (which may be defined by reference to a method of transport or otherwise), and

(b) the class of passenger to which it applies (which may be defined by reference to nationality, the possession of specified documents or otherwise).

(4) The Secretary of State may operate different authority-to-carry schemes for different purposes.

(5) Where the Secretary of State makes regulations under subsection (1) he must—

(a) identify in the regulations the authority-to-carry scheme to which they refer, and

(b) lay the authority-to-carry scheme before Parliament.

(6) Regulations under subsection (1) may, in particular—

(a) apply or make provision similar to a provision of sections 40 to 43 of and Schedule 1 to the Immigration and Asylum Act 1999 (c. 33) (charge for passenger without document);

(b) do anything which may be done under a provision of any of those sections;

(c) amend any of those sections.

(7) Regulations by virtue of subsection (6)(a) may, in particular—

(a) apply a provision with modification;

(b) apply a provision which confers power to make legislation.

(8) The grant or refusal of authority under an authority-to-carry scheme shall not be taken to determine whether a person is entitled or permitted to enter the United Kingdom.

(9) Regulations under this section—

(a) must be made by statutory instrument, and

(b) may not be made unless a draft has been laid before and approved by resolution of each House of Parliament.

Note: Commencement at a date to be appointed.

Evasion of procedure

125. Carriers' liability

Schedule 8 (which amends Part II of the Immigration and Asylum Act 1999 (carriers' liability) shall have effect.

Note: Commencement 14 November 2002 for the purpose of enabling subordinate legislation; 8 December 2002 for certain purposes (SI 2002/2811) and 11 May 2012 for certain other purposes (2012/1263).

Provision of information by traveller

126. Physical data: compulsory provision

(1) The Secretary of State may by regulations—

(a) require an immigration application to be accompanied by specified [biometric information] of the applicant;

(b) enable an authorised person to require an individual who makes an immigration application to provide [biometric information];

(c) enable an authorised person to require an entrant to provide [biometric information].

(2) In subsection (1) 'immigration application' means an application for—

(a) entry clearance,

(b) leave to enter or remain in the United Kingdom, . . .

(c) variation of leave to enter or remain in the United Kingdom.

[(d) a transit visa (within the meaning of section 41 of the Immigration and Asylum Act 1999), or

(e) a document issued as evidence that a person who is not a national of an EEA state or Switzerland is entitled to enter or remain in the United Kingdom by virtue of an enforceable EU right or of any provision made under section 2(2) of the European Communities Act 1972.]

(3) Regulations under subsection (1) may not—

(a) impose a requirement in respect of a person to whom section 141 of the Immigration and Asylum Act 1999 (c. 33) (fingerprinting) applies, during the relevant period within the meaning of that section, or

(b) enable a requirement to be imposed in respect of a person to whom that section applies, during the relevant period within the meaning of that section.

(4) Regulations under subsection (1) may, in particular—

(a) require, or enable an authorised person to require, the provision of [biometric] information in a specified form;

(b) require an individual to submit, or enable an authorised person to require an individual to submit, to a specified process by means of which [biometric] information is obtained or recorded;

(c) make provision about the effect of failure to provide [biometric] information or to submit to a process (which may, in particular, include provision for an application to be disregarded or dismissed if a requirement is not satisfied);

(d) confer a function (which may include the exercise of a discretion) on an authorised person;

(e) require an authorised person to have regard to a code (with or without modification);

(f) require an authorised person to have regard to such provisions of a code (with or without modification) as may be specified by direction of the Secretary of State;

[(fa) provide for biometric information to be recorded on any document issued as a result of the application in relation to which the information was provided;]

(g) . . .

(h) make provision which applies generally or only in specified cases or circumstances;

(i) make different provision for different cases or circumstances.

(5) . . .

(6) In so far as regulations under subsection (1) require an individual under the age of 16 to submit to a process, the regulations must make provision similar to section 141(3) to (5) and (13) of the Immigration and Asylum Act 1999 (fingerprints: children).

(7) In so far as regulations under subsection (1) enable an authorised person to require an individual under the age of 16 to submit to a process, the regulations must make provision similar to section 141(3) to (5), (12) and (13) of that Act (fingerprints: children).

(8) Regulations under subsection (1)—

(a) must be made by statutory instrument, and

(b) shall not be made unless a draft of the regulations has been laid before and approved by resolution of each House of Parliament.

[(8A) Section 8 of the UK Borders Act 2007 (power to make regulations about use and retention of biometric information) applies to biometric information provided in accordance with regulations under subsection (1) as it applies to biometric information provided in accordance with regulations under section 5(1) of that Act.]

(9) In this section—

'authorised person' has the meaning given by section 141(5) of the Immigration and Asylum Act 1999 (authority to take fingerprints),

['biometric information' has the meaning given by section 15 of the UK Borders Act 2007,]

'code' has the meaning given by section 145(6) of that Act (code of practice),

['document' includes a card or sticker and any other method of recording information (whether in writing or by the use of electronic or other technology or by a combination of methods),]

'entrant' has the meaning given by section 33(1) of the Immigration Act 1971 (c. 77) (interpretation),

'entry clearance' has the meaning given by section 33(1) of that Act.

Note: Commencement from 1 April 2003 (SI 2003/754). Subsections (2)(d)–(e), (4)(fa) and definition of 'document' inserted by s 8 Immigration Act 2014, subsection (8A) inserted by s 14 of that Act and words in other square brackets substituted or inserted by Sch 2 of that Act from 28 July 2014 (SI 2014/1820). Subsections (4)(g) and (5) omitted by Sch 9 Immigration Act 2014 from a date to be appointed.

127. Physical data: voluntary provision

(1) The Secretary of State may operate a scheme under which an individual may supply, or submit to the obtaining or recording of, [biometric information] to be used (wholly or partly) in connection with entry to the United Kingdom.

(2) In particular, the Secretary of State may—

(a) require an authorised person to use [biometric] information supplied under a scheme;

(b) make provision about the collection, use and retention of [biometric] information supplied under a scheme (which may include provision requiring an authorised person to have regard to a code);

(c) charge for participation in a scheme.

(3) In this section the following expressions have the same meaning as in section 126—

(a) 'authorised person',

[(aa) 'biometric information' and]

(b) 'code',

(c) . . .

Note: Commencement from 10 December 2004 (SI 2004/2998). Amended by Sch 2 Immigration Act 2014 from 28 July 2014 (SI 2014/1820).

128. Data collection under Immigration and Asylum Act 1999

Note: Amends Immigration and Asylum Act 1999, ss 144, 145.

Disclosure of information by public authority

129. Local authority

(1) The Secretary of State may require a local authority to supply information for the purpose of establishing where a person is if the Secretary of State reasonably suspects that—

(a) the person has committed an offence under section 24(1)(a), (b), (c), (e) or (f), 24A(1) or 26(1)(c) or (d) of the Immigration Act 1971 (c. 77) (illegal entry, deception, &c.), and

(b) the person is or has been resident in the local authority's area.

(2) A local authority shall comply with a requirement under this section.

(3) In the application of this section to England and Wales 'local authority' means—

(a) a county council,

(b) a county borough council,

(c) a district council,

(d) a London borough council,

(e) the Common Council of the City of London, and

(f) the Council of the Isles of Scilly.

(4) In the application of this section to Scotland 'local authority' means a council constituted under section 2 of the Local Government etc. (Scotland) Act 1994 (c. 39).

(5) In the application of this section to Northern Ireland—

(a) a reference to a local authority shall be taken as a reference to the Northern Ireland Housing Executive, and

(b) the reference to a local authority's area shall be taken as a reference to Northern Ireland.

Note: Commencement from 30 July 2003 (SI 2003/1747).

130. . . .

Note: Section 130 deleted by UK Borders Act 2007, ss 40(6)(b), 58 and Schedule from 31 January 2008 (SI 2008/99).

131. Police, &c.

Information may be supplied under section 20 of the Immigration and Asylum Act 1999 (c. 33) (supply of information to Secretary of State) for use for the purpose of—

[(a) determining whether an applicant for naturalisation under the British Nationality Act 1981 is of good character;

[(b) determining whether, for the purposes of an application referred to in section 41A of the British Nationality Act 1981, the person for whose registration the application is made is of good character;

(ba) determining whether, for the purposes of an application under section 1 of the Hong Kong (War Wives and Widows) Act 1996, the woman for whose registration the application is made is of good character;

(bb) determining whether, for the purposes of an application under section 1 of the British Nationality (Hong Kong) Act 1997 for the registration of an adult or young person within the meaning of subsection (5A) of that section, the person is of good character;]

(c) determining whether to make an order in respect of a person under section 40 of the British Nationality Act 1981.]

Note: Commencement 10 February 2003 (SI 2001/1). Words in square brackets substituted by UK Borders Act 2007, s 43 from 31 January 2008 (SI 2008/99). Subsections (b)–(bb) substituted by s 47 Borders, Citizenship and Immigration Act 2009 from 13 January 2010 (SI 2009/2731).

132. Supply of document, &c. to Secretary of State

. . .

Note: Amends Immigration and Asylum Act 1999, s 20.

133. Medical inspectors

(1) This section applies to a person if an immigration officer acting under Schedule 2 to the Immigration Act 1971 (c. 77) (control on entry, &c.) has brought the person to the attention of—

(a) a medical inspector appointed under paragraph 1(2) of that Schedule, or

(b) a person working under the direction of a medical inspector appointed under that paragraph.

(2) A medical inspector may disclose to a health service body—

(a) the name of a person to whom this section applies,

(b) his place of residence in the United Kingdom,

(c) his age,

(d) the language which he speaks,

(e) the nature of any disease with which the inspector thinks the person may be infected,

(f) relevant details of the person's medical history,

(g) the grounds for an opinion mentioned in paragraph (e) (including the result of any test or examination which has been carried out), and

(h) the inspector's opinion about action which the health service body should take.

(3) A disclosure may be made under subsection (2) only if the medical inspector thinks it necessary for the purpose of—

(a) preventative medicine,

(b) medical diagnosis,

(c) the provision of care or treatment, or
(d) the management of health care services.

(4) For the purposes of this section 'health service body' in relation to a person means a body which carries out functions in an area which includes his place of residence and which is—

(a) in relation to England—
[(ai) the Secretary of State,]
(i) . . .
[(ia) the National Health Service Commissioning Board,
(ib) a clinical commissioning group established under section 14D of the National Health Service Act 2006,
(ic) a local authority in relation to the exercise of functions under section 2B or 111 of, or any of paragraphs 1 to 7B or 13 of Schedule 1 to, the National Health Service Act 2006,]
(ii) a National Health Service Trust established under [. . . section 18 of the National Health Service (Wales) Act 2006],
{(iia) an NHS foundation trust,}
(iii) . . . [or]
(iv) a Special Health Authority established under [section 28 of that Act or section 22 of the National Health Service (Wales) Act 2006], or
(v) . . .
(vi) . . .

(b) in relation to Wales—
[(i) a Local Health Board established under section 11 of the National Health Service (Wales) Act 2006], [or]
(ii) a National Health Service Trust established under [. . . section 18 of the National Health Service (Wales) Act 2006], or
(iii) . . .
(iv) . . .

(c) in relation to Scotland—
[(ai) the Secretary of State,]
(i) a Health Board, Special Health Board or National Health Service Trust established under section 2 or 12A of the National Health Service (Scotland) Act 1978 (c. 29), . . .
(ii) the Common Services Agency for the Scottish Health Service established under section 10 of that Act, or
[(iia) Healthcare Improvement Scotland established under section 10A of the 1978 Act, or]
[(iii) . . .

(d) in relation to Northern Ireland—
(i) a Health and Social Services Board established under the Health and Personal Social Services (Northern Ireland) Order 1972 (S.I. 1972/1265 (N.I. 14)),
(ii) a Health and Social Services Trust established under the Health and Personal Social Services (Northern Ireland) Order 1991 (S.I. 1991/194 (N.I. 1)),
[(iia) the Regional Agency for Public Health and Social Well-being established under section 12 of the Health and Social Care (Reform) Act (Northern Ireland) 2009, or].
(iii) the Department of Health, Social Services and Public Safety,
(iv) . . .

Note: Commencement 10 February 2003 (SI 2003/1). Words in square brackets inserted and words omitted by Sch 3 Health Protection Agency Act 2004 from 1 April 2005 (SI 2005/121). Words in square brackets in subsections (4)(a)(i)–(iv) and (4)(b)(i) and (ii) substituted by National Health Service (Consequential Provisions) Act Sch 1, paragraph 228 from 1 March 2007. Subsection (4)(a)(iia) inserted by Sch 4 Health and Social Care (Community Health and Standards) Act 2003 from 1 April 2004 (SI 2004/759). Subsection (4)(c)(iia) inserted from 28 October 2011 (SI 2011/2581). Words omitted from subsections (4)(a)(ii) and 4(b)(ii) by Sch 14 Health and Social Care Act 2012 from a date to be appointed. Further amendments to subsection (4) by Schs 5, 7 Health and Social Care Act 2012 from 1 April 2013 (SI 2013/160).

Disclosure of information by private person

134. Employer

(1) The Secretary of State may require an employer to supply information about an employee whom the Secretary of State reasonably suspects of having committed an offence under—

(a) section 24(1)(a), (b), (c), (e) or (f), 24A(1) or 26(1)(c) or (d) of the Immigration Act 1971 (c. 77) (illegal entry, deception, &c.),

(b) section 105(1)(a), (b) or (c) of the Immigration and Asylum Act 1999 (c. 33) (support for asylum-seeker: fraud), or

(c) section 106(1)(a), (b) or (c) of that Act (support for asylum-seeker: fraud).

(2) The power under subsection (1) may be exercised to require information about an employee only if the information—

(a) is required for the purpose of establishing where the employee is, or

(b) relates to the employee's earnings or to the history of his employment.

(3) In this section a reference to an employer or employee—

(a) includes a reference to a former employer or employee, and

(b) shall be construed in accordance with section 8(8) of the Asylum and Immigration Act 1996 (c. 49) (restrictions on employment).

(4) Where—

(a) a business (the 'employment agency') arranges for one person (the 'worker') to provide services to another (the 'client'), and

(b) the worker is not employed by the employment agency or the client, this section shall apply as if the employment agency were the worker's employer while he provides services to the client.

Note: Commencement from 30 July 2003 (SI 2003/1747).

135. Financial institution

(1) The Secretary of State may require a financial institution to supply information about a person if the Secretary of State reasonably suspects that—

(a) the person has committed an offence under section 105(1)(a), (b) or (c) or 106(1)(a), (b) or (c) of the Immigration and Asylum Act 1999 (c. 33) (support for asylum-seeker: fraud),

(b) the information is relevant to the offence, and

(c) the institution has the information.

(2) In this section 'financial institution' means—

(a) a person who has permission under [Part 4A] of the Financial Services and Markets Act 2000 (c. 8) to accept deposits, and

(b) a building society (within the meaning given by the Building Societies Act 1986 (c. 53).

Note: Commencement from 30 July 2003 (SI 2003/1747). Words in square brackets in subsection (2)(a) substituted by Sch 18 Financial Services Act 2012 from 1 April 2013 (SI 2013/423).

136. Notice

(1) A requirement to provide information under section 134 or 135 must be imposed by notice in writing specifying—

(a) the information,

(b) the manner in which it is to be provided, and

(c) the period of time within which it is to be provided.

(2) A period of time specified in a notice under subsection (1)(c)—

(a) must begin with the date of receipt of the notice, and

(b) must not be less than ten working days.

(3) A person on whom a notice is served under subsection (1) must provide the Secretary of State with the information specified in the notice.

(4) Information provided under subsection (3) must be provided—

(a) in the manner specified under subsection (1)(b), and

(b) within the time specified under subsection (1)(c).

(5) In this section 'working day' means a day which is not—

(a) Saturday,

(b) Sunday,

(c) Christmas Day,

(d) Good Friday, or

(e) a day which is a bank holiday under the Banking and Financial Dealings Act 1971 (c. 80) in any part of the United Kingdom.

Note: Commencement from 30 July 2003 (SI 2003/1747).

137. Disclosure of information: offences

(1) A person commits an offence if without reasonable excuse he fails to comply with section 136(3).

(2) A person who is guilty of an offence under subsection (1) shall be liable on summary conviction to—

(a) imprisonment for a term not exceeding 51 weeks,

(b) a fine not exceeding level 5 on the standard scale, or

(c) both.

Note: Commencement from 30 July 2003 (SI 2003/1747). Words is square brackets in subsection (2)(a) substituted by Sch 26 Criminal Justice Act from a date to be appointed.

138. Offence by body

(1) Subsection (2) applies where an offence under section 137 is committed by a body corporate and it is proved that the offence—

(a) was committed with the consent or connivance of an officer of the body, or

(b) was attributable to neglect on the part of an officer of the body.

(2) The officer, as well as the body, shall be guilty of the offence.

(3) In this section a reference to an officer of a body corporate includes a reference to—

(a) a director, manager or secretary,

(b) a person purporting to act as a director, manager or secretary, and

(c) if the affairs of the body are managed by its members, a member.

(4) Where an offence under section 137 is committed by a partnership (other than a limited partnership), each partner shall be guilty of the offence.

(5) Subsection (1) shall have effect in relation to a limited partnership as if—

(a) a reference to a body corporate were a reference to a limited partnership, and

(b) a reference to an officer of the body were a reference to a partner.

Note: Commencement from 30 July 2003 (SI 2003/1747).

139. Privilege against self-incrimination

(1) Information provided by a person pursuant to a requirement under section 134 or 135 shall not be admissible in evidence in criminal proceedings against that person.

(2) This section shall not apply to proceedings for an offence under section 137.

Note: Commencement from 30 July 2003 (SI 2003/1747).

Immigration services

140. Immigration Services Commissioner

. . .

Note: Amends, Immigration and Asylum Act 1999 s 87(3), Sch 5, paragraph 7 and Sch 6, paragraph 3.

Immigration control

141. EEA ports: juxtaposed controls

(1) The Secretary of State may by order make provision for the purpose of giving effect to an international agreement which concerns immigration control at an EEA port (whether or not it also concerns other aspects of frontier control at the port).

(2) An order under this section may make any provision which appears to the Secretary of State—

(a) likely to facilitate implementation of the international agreement (including those aspects of the agreement which relate to frontier control other than immigration control), or

(b) appropriate as a consequence of provision made for the purpose of facilitating implementation of the agreement.

(3) In particular, an order under this section may—

(a) provide for a law of England and Wales to have effect, with or without modification, in relation to a person in a specified area or anything done in a specified area;

(b) provide for a law of England and Wales not to have effect in relation to a person in a specified area or anything done in a specified area;

(c) provide for a law of England and Wales to be modified in its effect in relation to a person in a specified area or anything done in a specified area;

(d) disapply or modify an enactment in relation to a person who has undergone a process in a specified area;

(e) disapply or modify an enactment otherwise than under paragraph (b), (c) or (d);

(f) make provision conferring a function (which may include—

(i) provision conferring a discretionary function;

(ii) provision conferring a function on a servant or agent of the government of a State other than the United Kingdom);

(g) create or extend the application of an offence;

(h) impose or permit the imposition of a penalty;

(i) require the payment of, or enable a person to require the payment of, a charge or fee;

(j) make provision about enforcement (which may include—

(i) provision conferring a power of arrest, detention or removal from or to any place;

(ii) provision for the purpose of enforcing the law of a State other than the United Kingdom);

(k) confer jurisdiction on a court or tribunal;

(l) confer immunity or provide for indemnity;

(m) make provision about compensation;

(n) impose a requirement, or enable a requirement to be imposed, for a person to cooperate with or to provide facilities for the use of another person who is performing a function under the order or under the international agreement (which may include a requirement to provide facilities without charge);

(o) make provision about the disclosure of information.

(4) An order under this section may—

(a) make provision which applies generally or only in specified circumstances;

(b) make different provision for different circumstances;

(c) amend an enactment.

(5) An order under this section—

(a) must be made by statutory instrument,

(b) may not be made unless the Secretary of State has consulted with such persons as appear to him to be appropriate, and

(c) may not be made unless a draft has been laid before and approved by resolution of each House of Parliament.

(6) In this section—

'EEA port' means a port in an EEA State from which passengers are commonly carried by sea to or from the United Kingdom,

'EEA State' means a State which is a contracting party to the Agreement on the European Economic Area signed at Oporto on 2 May 1992 (as it has effect from time to time),

'frontier control' means the enforcement of law which relates to, or in so far as it relates to, the movement of persons or goods into or out of the United Kingdom or another State,

'immigration control' means arrangements made in connection with the movement of persons into or out of the United Kingdom or another State,

'international agreement' means an agreement made between Her Majesty's Government and the government of another State, and

'specified area' means an area (whether of the United Kingdom or of another State) specified in an international agreement.

Note: Commenced 8 January 2003 (SI 2002/2811).

Country information

142. . .

Note: Section 142 deleted by UK Borders Act 2007, s 54 from 1 April 2008 (SI 2008/309).

PART VII
OFFENCES

Substance

143. Assisting unlawful immigration, &c.

. . .

Note: Amends Immigration Act 1971, s 25.

144. Section 143: consequential amendments

. . .

Note: Amends Immigration Act 1971, ss 25A, 28A, 28B, 28C, 28D, 28F and 33.

145. . . .

Note: Commenced 10 February 2003 (SI 2003/1). Repealed by Sch 6 Sexual Offences Act 2003 from 1 May 2004 (SI 2004/874).

146. . . .

Note: Subsection (4) amends paragraph 2, Sch 4 Criminal Justice and Court Services Act 2000. Commenced 10 February 2003 (SI 2003/1). Repealed by Sexual Offences Act 2003, Sch 6 from 1 May 2004 (SI 2004/874).

147. Employment

. . .

Note: Amends Asylum and Immigration Act 1996, s 8.

148. Registration card

. . .

Note: Amends Immigration Act 1971, s 26.

149. Immigration stamp

. . .

Note: Inserts s 26B into the Immigration Act 1971.

150. Sections 148 and 149: consequential amendments

. . .

Note: Amends Immigration Act 1971, ss 28A, 28B and 28D.

151. False information

. . .

Note: Amends Immigration Act 1971, s 26(3).

Procedure

152. Arrest by immigration officer

. . .

Note: Inserts s 28AA into the Immigration Act 1971.

153. Power of entry

. . .

Note: Inserts s 28CA into the Immigration Act 1971; amends Immigration and Asylum Act 1999, s 146.

154. Power to search for evidence

. . .

Note: Inserts ss 28FA, 28FB into the Immigration Act 1971.

155. Sections 153 and 154: supplemental

. . .

Note: Amends Immigration Act 1971, s 28L.

156. Time limit on prosecution

. . .

Note: Amends Immigration Act 1971, ss 24A, 28(1).

Part VIII

General

157. Consequential and incidental provision

(1) The Secretary of State may by order make consequential or incidental provision in connection with a provision of this Act.

(2) An order under this section may, in particular—

(a) amend an enactment;

(b) modify the effect of an enactment.

(3) An order under this section must be made by statutory instrument.

(4) An order under this section which amends an enactment shall not be made unless a draft has been laid before and approved by resolution of each House of Parliament.

(5) Any other order under this section shall be subject to annulment pursuant to a resolution of either House of Parliament.

Note: Commenced 7 November 2002, s 162.

158. Interpretation: 'the Immigration Acts'

Note: Ceased to have effect by Immigration, Asylum and Nationality Act 2006, s 64 from 30 March 2006 (Royal Assent).

159. Applied provision

(1) Subsection (2) applies where this Act amends or refers to a provision which is applied by, under or for purposes of—

(a) another provision of the Act which contains the provision, or

(b) another Act.

(2) The amendment or reference shall have effect in relation to the provision as applied.

(3) Where this Act applies a provision of another Act, a reference to that provision in any enactment includes a reference to the provision as applied by this Act.

Note: Commenced 10 February 2003 (SI 2003/1).

160. Money

(1) Expenditure of the Secretary of State or the Lord Chancellor in connection with a provision of this Act shall be paid out of money provided by Parliament.

(2) An increase attributable to this Act in the amount payable out of money provided by Parliament under another enactment shall be paid out of money provided by Parliament.

(3) A sum received by the Secretary of State or the Lord Chancellor in connection with a provision of this Act shall be paid into the Consolidated Fund.

Note: Commenced 7 November 2002, s 162.

161. Repeals

The provisions listed in Schedule 9 are hereby repealed to the extent specified.

Note: Commenced 8 December 2002 (SI 2002/2811) and 10 February 2003 (SI 2003/1).

162. Commencement

(1) Subject to subsections (2) to (5), the preceding provisions of this Act shall come into force in accordance with provision made by the Secretary of State by order.

(2) The following provisions shall come into force on the passing of this Act—

(a) section 6,

(b) section 7,

(c) section 10(1) to (4) and (6),

(d) section 11,

(e) section 15 (and Schedule 2),

(f) section 16,

(g) section 35(1)(h),

(h) section 38,

(i) section 40(1),

(j) section 41(1),

(k) section 42,

(l) section 43,

(m) section 48,

(n) section 49,

(o) section 50,

(p) section 56,

(q) section 58,

(r) section 59,

(s) section 61,

(t) section 67,

(u) section 69,

(v) section 70,

(w) section 115 and paragraph 29 of Schedule 7 (and the relevant entry in Schedule 9),

(x) section 157, and

(y) section 160.

(3) Section 5 shall have effect in relation to—

(a) an application made after the passing of this Act, and

(b) an application made, but not determined, before the passing of this Act.

(4) Section 8 shall have effect in relation to—

(a) an application made on or after a date appointed by the Secretary of State by order, and

(b) an application made, but not determined, before that date.

(5) Section 9 shall have effect in relation to a child born on or after a date appointed by the Secretary of State by order.

(6) An order under subsection (1) may—

(a) make provision generally or for a specified purpose only (which may include the purpose of the application of a provision to or in relation to a particular place or area);

(b) make different provision for different purposes;

(c) include transitional provision;

(d) include savings;

(e) include consequential provision;

(f) include incidental provision.

(7) An order under this section must be made by statutory instrument.

Note: Commenced 7 November 2002 (Royal Assent). The date appointed for the purpose of subsection (5) is 1 July 2006 (SI 2006/1498).

163. Extent

(1) A provision of this Act which amends or repeals a provision of another Act or inserts a provision into another Act has the same extent as the provision amended or repealed or as the Act into which the insertion is made (ignoring, in any case, extent by virtue of an Order in Council).

(2) Sections 145 and 146 extend only to—

(a) England and Wales, and

(b) Northern Ireland.

(3) A provision of this Act to which neither subsection (1) nor subsection (2) applies extends to—

(a) England and Wales,

(b) Scotland, and

(c) Northern Ireland.

(4) Her Majesty may by Order in Council direct that a provision of this Act is to extend, with or without modification or adaptation, to—

(a) any of the Channel Islands;

(b) the Isle of Man.

(5) Subsection (4) does not apply in relation to the extension to a place of a provision which extends there by virtue of subsection (1).

164. Short title

This Act may be cited as the Nationality, Immigration and Asylum Act 2002.

SCHEDULES

Section 3

SCHEDULE 1

CITIZENSHIP CEREMONY, OATH AND PLEDGE

1.—7. . . .

8. The Secretary of State may make a payment to a local authority in respect of anything done by the authority in accordance with regulations made by virtue of section 41(3A) of the British Nationality Act 1981 (c. 61).

9.—(1) A local authority must—

(a) comply with a requirement imposed on it by regulations made by virtue of that section, and

(b) carry out a function imposed on it by regulations made by virtue of that section.

(2) A local authority on which a requirement or function is imposed by regulations made by virtue of that section—

(a) may provide facilities or make arrangements in addition to those which it is required to provide or make, and

(b) may make a charge for the provision of facilities or the making of arrangements under paragraph (a) which does not exceed the cost of providing the facilities or making the arrangements.

Note: Paragraphs 1–7 amend the British Nationality Act 1981. Commencement 1 January 2004 (SI 2003/3156).

Section 15

SCHEDULE 2
NATIONALITY: REPEAL OF SPENT PROVISIONS

1. . . .

2 Nothing in this Schedule has any effect in relation to a registration made under a provision before its repeal.

Note: Paragraph 1 repeals parts of British Nationality Act 1981. Commencement from 1 January 2004 (SI 2003/3156).

Section 54

SCHEDULE 3
WITHHOLDING AND WITHDRAWAL OF SUPPORT

Ineligibility for support

1.—(1) A person to whom this paragraph applies shall not be eligible for support or assistance under—

(a) section 21 or 29 of the National Assistance Act 1948 (c. 29) (local authority: accommodation and welfare),

(b) section 45 of the Health Services and Public Health Act 1968 (c. 46) (local authority: welfare of elderly),

(c) section 12 or 13A of the Social Work (Scotland) Act 1968 (c. 49) (social welfare services),

(d) Article 7 or 15 of the Health and Personal Social Services (Northern Ireland) Order 1972 (S.I. 1972/1265 (N.I. 14)) (prevention of illness, social welfare, &c.),

[(e) section 254 of, and Schedule 20 to, the National Health Service Act 2006, or section 192 of, and Schedule 15 to, the National Health Service (Wales) Act 2006 (social services),]

(f) section 29(1)(b) of the Housing (Scotland) Act 1987 (c. 26) (interim duty to accommodate in case of apparent priority need where review of a local authority decision has been requested),

(g) section 17, 23C, [23CA,] 24A or 24B of the Children Act 1989 (c. 41) (welfare and other powers which can be exercised in relation to adults),

(h) Article 18, 35 or 36 of the Children (Northern Ireland) Order 1995 (SI 1995/ 755 (N.I. 2)) (welfare and other powers which can be exercised in relation to adults),

(i) sections 22, 29 and 30 of the Children (Scotland) Act 1995 (c. 36) (provisions analogous to those mentioned in paragraph (g)),

(j) section 188(3) or 204(4) of the Housing Act 1996 (c. 52) (accommodation pending review or appeal),

(k) section 2 of the Local Government Act 2000 (c. 22) (promotion of well-being),

[(ka) section 1 of the Localism Act 2011 (local authority's general power of competence),]

(l) a provision of the Immigration and Asylum Act 1999 (c. 33), or

(m) a provision of this Act.

(2) A power or duty under a provision referred to in sub-paragraph (1) may not be exercised or performed in respect of a person to whom this paragraph applies (whether or not the person has previously been in receipt of support or assistance under the provision).

(3) An approval or directions given under or in relation to a provision referred to in sub-paragraph (1) shall be taken to be subject to sub-paragraph (2).

Exceptions

2.—(1) Paragraph 1 does not prevent the provision of support or assistance—

(a) to a British citizen, or

(b) to a child, or

(c) under or by virtue of regulations made under paragraph 8, 9 or 10 below, or

(d) in a case in respect of which, and to the extent to which, regulations made by the Secretary of State disapply paragraph 1, or
(e) in circumstances in respect of which, and to the extent to which, regulations made by the Secretary of State disapply paragraph 1.

(2) Regulations under sub-paragraph (1)(d) may confer a discretion on the Secretary of State.

(3) Regulations under sub-paragraph (1)(e) may, in particular, disapply paragraph 1 to the provision of support or assistance by a local authority to a person where the authority—
(a) has taken steps in accordance with guidance issued by the Secretary of State to determine whether paragraph 1 would (but for the regulations) apply to the person, and
(b) has concluded on the basis of those steps that there is no reason to believe that paragraph 1 would apply.

(4) Regulations under sub-paragraph (1)(d) or (e) may confer a discretion on an authority.

(5) A local authority which is considering whether to give support or assistance to a person under a provision listed in paragraph 1(1) shall act in accordance with any relevant guidance issued by the Secretary of State under sub-paragraph (3)(a).

(6) A reference in this Schedule to a person to whom paragraph 1 applies includes a reference to a person in respect of whom that paragraph is disapplied to a limited extent by regulations under sub-paragraph (1)(d) or (e), except in a case for which the regulations provide otherwise.

3. Paragraph 1 does not prevent the exercise of a power or the performance of a duty if, and to the extent that, its exercise or performance is necessary for the purpose of avoiding a breach of—
(a) a person's Convention rights, or
(b) a person's rights under the EU Treaties.

First class of ineligible person: refugee status abroad

4.—(1) Paragraph 1 applies to a person if he—
(a) has refugee status abroad, or
(b) is the dependant of a person who is in the United Kingdom and who has refugee status abroad.

(2) For the purposes of this paragraph a person has refugee status abroad if—
(a) he does not have the nationality of an EEA State, and
(b) the government of an EEA State other than the United Kingdom has determined that he is entitled to protection as a refugee under the Refugee Convention.

Second class of ineligible person: citizen of other EEA State

5. Paragraph 1 applies to a person if he—
(a) has the nationality of an EEA State other than the United Kingdom, or
(b) is the dependant of a person who has the nationality of an EEA State other than the United Kingdom.

Third class of ineligible person: failed asylum-seeker

6.—(1) Paragraph 1 applies to a person if—
(a) he was (but is no longer) an asylum-seeker, and
(b) he fails to cooperate with removal directions issued in respect of him.

(2) Paragraph 1 also applies to a dependant of a person to whom that paragraph applies by virtue of sub-paragraph (1).

Fourth class of ineligible person: person unlawfully in United Kingdom

7. Paragraph 1 applies to a person if—

(a) he is in the United Kingdom in breach of the immigration laws within the meaning of [section 50A of the British Nationality Act 1981], and
(b) he is not an asylum-seeker.

Fifth class of ineligible person: failed asylum-seeker with family

[**7A.**—(1) Paragraph 1 applies to a person if—
(a) he—
(i) is treated as an asylum-seeker for the purposes of Part VI of the Immigration and Asylum Act 1999 (c. 33) (support) by virtue only of section 94(3A) (failed asylum-seeker with dependent child), or
(ii) is treated as an asylum-seeker for the purposes of Part 2 of this Act by virtue only of section 18(2),
(b) the Secretary of State has certified that in his opinion the person has failed without reasonable excuse to take reasonable steps—
(i) to leave the United Kingdom voluntarily, or
(ii) to place himself in a position in which he is able to leave the United Kingdom voluntarily,
(c) the person has received a copy of the Secretary of State's certificate, and
(d) the period of 14 days, beginning with the date on which the person receives the copy of the certificate, has elapsed.

(2) Paragraph 1 also applies to a dependant of a person to whom that paragraph applies by virtue of sub-paragraph (1).

(3) For the purpose of sub-paragraph (1)(d) if the Secretary of State sends a copy of a certificate by first class post to a person's last known address, the person shall be treated as receiving the copy on the second day after the day on which it was posted.

(4) The Secretary of State may by regulations vary the period specified in sub-paragraph (1)(d).]

Travel assistance

8. The Secretary of State may make regulations providing for arrangements to be made enabling a person to whom paragraph 1 applies by virtue of paragraph 4 or 5 to leave the United Kingdom.

Temporary accommodation

9.—(1) The Secretary of State may make regulations providing for arrangements to be made for the accommodation of a person to whom paragraph 1 applies pending the implementation of arrangements made by virtue of paragraph 8.

(2) Arrangements for a person by virtue of this paragraph—
(a) may be made only if the person has with him a dependent child, and
(b) may include arrangements for a dependent child.

10.—(1) The Secretary of State may make regulations providing for arrangements to be made for the accommodation of a person if—
(a) paragraph 1 applies to him by virtue of paragraph 7, and
(b) he has not failed to cooperate with removal directions issued in respect of him.

(2) Arrangements for a person by virtue of this paragraph—
(a) may be made only if the person has with him a dependent child, and
(b) may include arrangements for a dependent child.

Assistance and accommodation: general

11. Regulations under paragraph 8, 9 or 10 may—

(a) provide for the making of arrangements under a provision referred to in paragraph 1(1) or otherwise;
(b) confer a function (which may include the exercise of a discretion) on the Secretary of State, a local authority or another person;
(c) provide that arrangements must be made in a specified manner or in accordance with specified principles;
(d) provide that arrangements may not be made in a specified manner;
(e) require a local authority or another person to have regard to guidance issued by the Secretary of State in making arrangements;
(f) require a local authority or another person to comply with a direction of the Secretary of State in making arrangements.

12.—(1) Regulations may, in particular, provide that if a person refuses an offer of arrangements under paragraph 8 or fails to implement or cooperate with arrangements made for him under that paragraph—
(a) new arrangements may not be made for him under paragraph 8, but
(b) new arrangements may not be made for him under paragraph 9.

(2) Regulations by virtue of this paragraph may include exceptions in the case of a person who—
(a) has a reason of a kind specified in the regulations for failing to implement or cooperate with arrangements made under paragraph 8, and
(b) satisfies any requirements of the regulations for proof of the reason.

Offences

13.—(1) A person who leaves the United Kingdom in accordance with arrangements made under paragraph 8 commits an offence if he—
(a) returns to the United Kingdom, and
(b) requests that arrangements be made for him by virtue of paragraph 8, 9 or 10.

(2) A person commits an offence if he—
(a) requests that arrangements be made for him by virtue of paragraph 8, 9 or 10, and
(b) fails to mention a previous request by him for the making of arrangements under any of those paragraphs.

(3) A person who is guilty of an offence under this paragraph shall be liable on summary conviction to imprisonment for a term not exceeding six months.

Information

14.—(1) If it appears to a local authority that paragraph 1 applies or may apply to a person in the authority's area by virtue of [paragraph 6, 7 or 7A], the authority must inform the Secretary of State.

(2) A local authority shall act in accordance with any relevant guidance issued by the Secretary of State for the purpose of determining whether paragraph 1 applies or may apply to a person in the authority's area by virtue of [paragraph 6, 7 or 7A].

Power to amend Schedule

15. The Secretary of State may by order amend this Schedule so as—
(a) to provide for paragraph 1 to apply or not to apply to a class of person;
(b) to add or remove a provision to or from the list in paragraph 1(1);
(c) to add, amend or remove a limitation of or exception to paragraph 1.

Orders and regulations

16.—(1) An order or regulations under this Schedule must be made by statutory instrument.

(2) An order or regulations under this Schedule may—
(a) make provision which applies generally or only in specified cases or circumstances or only for specified purposes;
(b) make different provision for different cases, circumstances or purposes;
(c) make transitional provision;
(d) make consequential provision (which may include provision amending a provision made by or under this or another Act).

(3) An order under this Schedule, regulations under paragraph 2(1)(d) or (e) or other regulations which include consequential provision amending an enactment shall not be made unless a draft has been laid before and approved by resolution of each House of Parliament.

(4) Regulations under this Schedule to which sub-paragraph (3) does not apply shall be subject to annulment in pursuance of a resolution of either House of Parliament.

Interpretation

17.—(1) In this Schedule—
'asylum-seeker' means a person—
(a) who is at least 18 years old,
(b) who has made a claim for asylum (within the meaning of section 18(3)), and
(c) whose claim has been recorded by the Secretary of State but not determined,
'Convention rights' has the same meaning as in the Human Rights Act 1998 (c. 42),
'child' means a person under the age of eighteen,
'dependant' and 'dependent' shall have such meanings as may be prescribed by regulations made by the Secretary of State,
'EEA State' means a State which is a contracting party to the Agreement on the European Economic Area signed at Oporto on 2 May 1992 (as it has effect from time to time),
'local authority'—
(a) in relation to England and Wales, has the same meaning as in section 129(3),
(b) in relation to Scotland, has the same meaning as in section 129(4), and
(c) in relation to Northern Ireland, means a health service body within the meaning of section 133(4)(d) and the Northern Ireland Housing Executive (for which purpose a reference to the authority's area shall be taken as a reference to Northern Ireland),
'the Refugee Convention' means the Convention relating to the status of Refugees done at Geneva on 28 July 1951 and its Protocol, and
'removal directions' means directions under Schedule 2 to the Immigration Act 1971 (c. 77) (control of entry, &c.), under Schedule 3 to that Act (deportation) or under section 10 of the Immigration and Asylum Act 1999 (c. 33) (removal of person unlawfully in United Kingdom).

(2) For the purpose of the definition of 'asylum-seeker' in sub-paragraph (1) a claim is determined if—
(a) the Secretary of State has notified the claimant of his decision,
(b) no appeal against the decision can be brought (disregarding the possibility of an appeal out of time with permission), and
(c) any appeal which has already been brought has been disposed of.

(3) For the purpose of sub-paragraph (2)(c) an appeal is disposed of when it is no longer pending for the purpose of—
(a) Part 5 of this Act, or
(b) the Special Immigration Appeals Commission Act 1997 (c. 68).

(4) The giving of directions in respect of a person under a provision of the Immigration Acts is not the provision of assistance to him for the purposes of this Schedule.

Note: Paragraphs 2, 8, 9, 10, 11, 12, 15 and 16 commenced on 8 December 2002, for the purpose of enabling subordinate legislation. Remainder of Schedule commenced 8 January 2003 (SI 2002/2811). Paragraph (7A) inserted and words in square brackets in paragraph 14 substituted by Asylum and Immigration Act 2004, s 9 from 1 December 2004 (SI 2004/2999). Words in square brackets in paragraph 7(a) substituted by Borders Citizenship and Immigration Act 2009, s 48 from 13 January 2010 (SI 2009/2731). Words in square brackets in paragraph 1(1)(g) inserted by Children and Young Persons Act 2008 s 22 from 1 April 2011 (SI 2010/2981). Paragraph (1)(1)(e) substituted by National Health Service Consequential Provisions Act 2006 Sch 1 from 1 March 2007. Paragraph 1 (ka) inserted from 28 March 2012 (SI 2012/961). Letters in square brackets in paragraph 3(b) substituted by SI 2011/1043, from 22 April 2011.

Section 81

[Schedule 4

. . .]

Note: Schedule 4 revoked from 15 February 2010 (SI 2010/21).

Section 100

Schedule 5

The Immigration Appeal Tribunal

. . .

Note: Schedule 5 ceased to have effect from 4 April 2005, subject to savings (SI 2005/565), Asylum and Immigration Act 2004, s 26.

Section 114

Schedule 6

Immigration and Asylum Appeals: Transitional Provision

'Commencement'

1. In this Schedule 'commencement' means the coming into force of Part 5 this Act.

Adjudicator

2. Where a person is an adjudicator under section 57 of the Immigration and Asylum Act 1999 (c. 33) immediately before commencement his appointment shall have effect after commencement as if made under section 81 of this Act.

Tribunal

3.—(1) Where a person is a member of the Immigration Appeal Tribunal immediately before commencement his appointment shall have effect after commencement as if made under Schedule 5.

(2) Where a person is a member of staff of the Immigration Appeal Tribunal immediately before commencement his appointment shall have effect after commencement as if made under Schedule 5.

Earlier appeal

4. In the application of section 96—

(a) a reference to an appeal or right of appeal under a provision of this Act includes a reference to an appeal or right of appeal under the Immigration and Asylum Act 1999,

(b) a reference to a requirement imposed under this Act includes a reference to a requirement of a similar nature imposed under that Act,

(c) a reference to a statement made in pursuance of a requirement imposed under a provision of this Act includes a reference to anything done in compliance with a requirement of a similar nature under that Act, and

(d) a reference to notification by virtue of this Act includes a reference to notification by virtue of any other enactment.

Saving

5.—(1) This Schedule is without prejudice to the power to include transitional provision in an order under section 162.

(2) An order under that section may, in particular, provide for a reference to a provision of Part 5 of this Act to be treated as being or including a reference (with or without modification) to a provision of the Immigration and Asylum Act 1999 (c. 33).

Note: Commencement from 1 April 2003 (SI 2003/754).

Section 114

SCHEDULE 7

IMMIGRATION AND ASYLUM APPEALS: CONSEQUENTIAL AMENDMENTS

. . .

Section 125

SCHEDULE 8

CARRIERS' LIABILITY

. . .

Note: Amends the Immigration and Asylum Act 1999.

Section 161

SCHEDULE 9

REPEALS

. . .

Asylum and Immigration (Treatment of Claimants, etc.) Act 2004
(2004, c. 19)

Arrangement of Sections

An Act to make provision about asylum and immigration.

[22 July 2004]

Offences

1. Assisting unlawful immigration

. . .

Note: Amends Immigration Act 1971, ss 25 and 25C.

2. Entering United Kingdom without passport, &c.

(1) A person commits an offence if at a leave or asylum interview he does not have with him an immigration document which—

(a) is in force, and

(b) satisfactorily establishes his identity and nationality or citizenship.

(2) A person commits an offence if at a leave or asylum interview he does not have with him, in respect of any dependent child with whom he claims to be travelling or living, an immigration document which—

(a) is in force, and

(b) satisfactorily establishes the child's identity and nationality or citizenship.

(3) But a person does not commit an offence under subsection (1) or (2) if—

(a) the interview referred to in that subsection takes place after the person has entered the United Kingdom, and

(b) within the period of three days beginning with the date of the interview the person provides to an immigration officer or to the Secretary of State a document of the kind referred to in that subsection.

(4) It is a defence for a person charged with an offence under subsection (1)—

(a) to prove that he is an EEA national,

(b) to prove that he is a member of the family of an EEA national and that he is exercising a right under the [EU] Treaties in respect of entry to or residence in the United Kingdom,

(c) to prove that he has a reasonable excuse for not being in possession of a document of the kind specified in subsection (1),

(d) to produce a false immigration document and to prove that he used that document as an immigration document for all purposes in connection with his journey to the United Kingdom, or

(e) to prove that he travelled to the United Kingdom without, at any stage since he set out on the journey, having possession of an immigration document.

(5) It is a defence for a person charged with an offence under subsection (2) in respect of a child—

(a) to prove that the child is an EEA national,

(b) to prove that the child is a member of the family of an EEA national and that the child is exercising a right under the [EU] Treaties in respect of entry to or residence in the United Kingdom,

(c) to prove that the person has a reasonable excuse for not being in possession of a document of the kind specified in subsection (2),

(d) to produce a false immigration document and to prove that it was used as an immigration document for all purposes in connection with the child's journey to the United Kingdom, or

(e) to prove that he travelled to the United Kingdom with the child without, at any stage since he set out on the journey, having possession of an immigration document in respect of the child.

(6) Where the charge for an offence under subsection (1) or (2) relates to an interview which takes place after the defendant has entered the United Kingdom—

(a) subsections (4)(c) and (5)(c) shall not apply, but

(b) it is a defence for the defendant to prove that he has a reasonable excuse for not providing a document in accordance with subsection (3).

(7) For the purposes of subsections (4) to (6)—

(a) the fact that a document was deliberately destroyed or disposed of is not a reasonable excuse for not being in possession of it or for not providing it in accordance with subsection (3), unless it is shown that the destruction or disposal was—

(i) for a reasonable cause, or

(ii) beyond the control of the person charged with the offence, and

(b) in paragraph (a)(i) 'reasonable cause' does not include the purpose of—

(i) delaying the handling or resolution of a claim or application or the taking of a decision,

(ii) increasing the chances of success of a claim or application, or

(iii) complying with instructions or advice given by a person who offers advice about, or facilitates, immigration into the United Kingdom, unless in the circumstances of the case it is unreasonable to expect non-compliance with the instructions or advice.

(8) A person shall be presumed for the purposes of this section not to have a document with him if he fails to produce it to an immigration officer or official of the Secretary of State on request.

(9) A person guilty of an offence under this section shall be liable—

(a) on conviction on indictment, to imprisonment for a term not exceeding two years, to a fine or to both, or

(b) on summary conviction, to imprisonment for a term not exceeding twelve months, to a fine not exceeding the statutory maximum or to both.

(10) If [an] immigration officer reasonably suspects that a person has committed an offence under this section he may arrest the person without warrant.

(11) An offence under this section shall be treated as—

(a) a relevant offence for the purposes of sections 28B and 28D of the Immigration Act 1971 (c. 77) (search, entry and arrest), and

(b) an offence under Part III of that Act (criminal proceedings) for the purposes of sections 28(4), 28E, 28G and 28H (search after arrest, &c.) of that Act.

(12) In this section—

'EEA national' means a national of a State which is a contracting party to the Agreement on the European Economic Area signed at Oporto on 2 May 1992 (as it has effect from time to time),

'immigration document' means—

(a) a passport, and

(b) a document which relates to a national of a State other than the United Kingdom and which is designed to serve the same purpose as a passport, and

'leave or asylum interview' means an interview with an immigration officer or an official of the Secretary of State at which a person—

(a) seeks leave to enter or remain in the United Kingdom, or

(b) claims that to remove him from or require him to leave the United Kingdom would breach the United Kingdom's obligations under the Refugee Convention or would be unlawful under section 6 of the Human Rights Act 1998 (c. 42) as being incompatible with his Convention rights.

(13) For the purposes of this section—

(a) a document which purports to be, or is designed to look like, an immigration document, is a false immigration document, and

(b) an immigration document is a false immigration document if and in so far as it is used—

(i) outside the period for which it is expressed to be valid,

(ii) contrary to provision for its use made by the person issuing it, or

(iii) by or in respect of a person other than the person to or for whom it was issued.

(14) Section 11 of the Immigration Act 1971 (c. 77) shall have effect for the purpose of the construction of a reference in this section to entering the United Kingdom.

(15) In so far as this section extends to England and Wales, subsection (9)(b) shall, until the commencement of section 154 of the Criminal Justice Act 2003 (c. 44) (increased limit on magistrates' power of imprisonment), have effect as if the reference to twelve months were a reference to six months.

(16) In so far as this section extends to Scotland, subsection (9)(b) shall have effect as if the reference to twelve months were a reference to six months.

(17) In so far as this section extends to Northern Ireland, subsection (9)(b) shall have effect as if the reference to twelve months were a reference to six months.

Note: Commenced 22 September 2004, s 48. Word in square brackets in subsection (10) substituted by Sch 7 Serious Organised Crime and Police Act 2005 from 1 January 2006 (SI 2005/3495). Words in square brackets in subsection (4)(b) and (5)(b) substituted by 2011/1043 from 22 April 2011.

3. Immigration documents: forgery

. . .

Note: Section 3 repealed from 7 June 2006, Identity Cards Act 2006, s 44 and Sch 2.

4. Trafficking people for exploitation

[**(1A)** A person ("A") commits an offence if A intentionally arranges or facilitates—

(a) the arrival in, or entry into, the United Kingdom or another country of another person ("B"),

(b) the travel of B within the United Kingdom or another country, or

(c) the departure of B from the United Kingdom or another country,

with a view to the exploitation of B.

(1B) For the purposes of subsection (1A)(a) and (c) A's arranging or facilitating is with a view to the exploitation of B if (and only if)—

(a) A intends to exploit B, after B's arrival, entry or (as the case may be) departure but in any part of the world, or

(b) A believes that another person is likely to exploit B, after B's arrival, entry or (as the case may be) departure but in any part of the world.

(1C) For the purposes of subsection (1A)(b) A's arranging or facilitating is with a view to the exploitation of B if (and only if)—

(a) A intends to exploit B, during or after the journey and in any part of the world, or

(b) A believes that another person is likely to exploit B, during or after the journey and in any part of the world.]

(4) For the purposes of this section a person is exploited if (and only if)—

(a) he is the victim of behaviour that contravenes Article 4 of the Human Rights Convention (slavery and forced labour),

(b) he is encouraged, required or expected to do anything

(i) as a result of which he or another person would commit an offence . . . [under section 32 or 33 of the Human Tissue Act 2004] [as it has effect in the law of England and Wales], [or

(ii) which, were it done in England and Wales, would constitute an offence within sub-paragraph (i),]

(c) he is subjected to force, threats or deception designed to induce him—

(i) to provide services of any kind,

(ii) to provide another person with benefits of any kind, or

(iii) to enable another person to acquire benefits of any kind, or

[(d) a person uses or attempts to use him for any purpose within sub-paragraph (i), (ii) or (iii) of paragraph (c), having chosen him for that purpose on the grounds that—

(i) he is mentally or physically ill or disabled, he is young or he has a family relationship with a person, and

(ii) a person without the illness, disability, youth or family relationship would be likely to refuse to be used for that purpose.]

[(**4A**) A person who is a UK national commits an offence under this section regardless of—

(a) where the arranging or facilitating takes place, or

(b) which country is the country of arrival, entry, travel or (as the case may be) departure.

(**4B**) A person who is not a UK national commits an offence under this section if—

(a) any part of the arranging or facilitating takes place in the United Kingdom, or

(b) the United Kingdom is the country of arrival, entry, travel or (as the case may be) departure.]

(5) A person guilty of an offence under this section shall be liable—

(a) on conviction on indictment, to imprisonment for a term not exceeding 14 years, to a fine or to both, or

(b) on summary conviction, to imprisonment for a term not exceeding twelve months, to a fine not exceeding the statutory maximum or to both.

Note: Commencement 1 December 2004 (SI 2004/2999). Words in first square brackets in subsection (4)(b)(i) substituted by Sch 6 Human Tissue Act 2004 from 1 September 2006 (SI 2006/1997). Subsection (4)(d) substituted by s 54 Borders, Citizenship and Immigration Act 2009 from 10 November 2009 (SI 2009/2731). Amended in relation to Scotland by the Criminal Justice and Licensing (Scotland) Act 2010 (asp). Subsections (1)–(3) substituted by (1A)–(1C), words omitted and words in second square brackets in subsection (4)(b)(i), subsection (4)(b)(ii), (4A) and (4B) inserted by s 110 Protection of Freedom Act 2012. Amendments to subsection (4)(b) by s 110 Protection of Freedoms Act 2012, from 6 April 2013 (SI 2013/470).

5. Section 4: supplemental

[(1) . . .

(2) . . .

(3) [In section 4—

country includes any territory or other part of the world,]

the Human Rights Convention means the Convention for the Protection of Human Rights and Fundamental Freedoms agreed by the Council of Europe at Rome on 4 November 1950

[UK national means—

(a) a British citizen,

(b) a person who is a British subject by virtue of Part 4 of the British Nationality Act 1981 and who has the right of abode in the United Kingdom, or

(c) a person who is a British overseas territories citizen by virtue of a connection with Gibraltar.]

(4) Section 25C and 25D of the Immigration Act 1971 (c. 77) (forfeiture or detention of vehicle, &c.) shall apply in relation to an offence under section 4 of this Act as they apply in relation to an offence under section 25 of that Act.

(5) . . .

Note: Amends Immigration Act 1971, s 25C(9)(b), (10)(b) and (11).

(6) . . .

Note: Amends paragraph 2, Sch 4 Criminal Justice and Court Services Act 2000.

(7) . . .

Note: Amends paragraph 4, Sch 2 Proceeds of Crime Act 2002.

(8) . . .

Note: Amends paragraph 4, Sch 4 Proceeds of Crime Act 2002.

(9) . . .

Note: Amends paragraph 4, Sch 5 Proceeds of Crime Act 2002.

(10) . . .

Note: Amends paragraph 2(1), Sch Protection of Children and Vulnerable Adults (Northern Ireland) Order 2003.

(11) . . . subsection (5)(b) shall, until the commencement of section 154 of the Criminal Justice Act 2003 (c. 44) (increased limit on magistrates' power of imprisonment), have effect as if the reference to twelve months were a reference to six months.

(12) . . .

(13) . . .

Note: Commenced 1 December 2004 (SI 2004/2999). Subsection (1) omitted, words in subsection (3) substituted, words in subsection (11) omitted and subsections (12)–(13) repealed by Protection of Freedoms Act 2012, ss 110, 115, Sch 9 from 6 April 2013 (SI 2013/470). Amended in relation to Scotland by the Criminal Justice and Licensing (Scotland) Act 2010 (asp).

6. Employment

. . .

Note: Amends Asylum and Immigration Act 1996, s 8.

7. Advice of Director of Public Prosecutions

. . .

Note: Amends Prosecution of Offences Act 1985, s 3(2).

Treatment of claimants

8. Claimant's credibility

(1) In determining whether to believe a statement made by or on behalf of a person who makes an asylum claim or a human rights claim, a deciding authority shall take account, as damaging the claimant's credibility, of any behaviour to which this section applies.

(2) This section applies to any behaviour by the claimant that the deciding authority thinks—

(a) is designed or likely to conceal information,

(b) is designed or likely to mislead, or

(c) is designed or likely to obstruct or delay the handling or resolution of the claim or the taking of a decision in relation to the claimant.

(3) Without prejudice to the generality of subsection (2) the following kinds of behaviour shall be treated as designed or likely to conceal information or to mislead—

(a) failure without reasonable explanation to produce a passport on request to an immigration officer or to the Secretary of State,

(b) the production of a document which is not a valid passport as if it were,

(c) the destruction, alteration or disposal, in each case without reasonable explanation, of a passport,

(d) the destruction, alteration or disposal, in each case without reasonable explanation, of a ticket or other document connected with travel, and

(e) failure without reasonable explanation to answer a question asked by a deciding authority.

(4) This section also applies to failure by the claimant to take advantage of a reasonable opportunity to make an asylum claim or human rights claim while in a safe country.

(5) This section also applies to failure by the claimant to make an asylum claim or human rights claim before being notified of an immigration decision, unless the claim relies wholly on matters arising after the notification.

(6) This section also applies to failure by the claimant to make an asylum claim or human rights claim before being arrested under an immigration provision, unless—

(a) he had no reasonable opportunity to make the claim before the arrest, or

(b) the claim relies wholly on matters arising after the arrest.

(7) In this section—

'asylum claim' has the meaning given by section 113(1) of the Nationality, Immigration and Asylum Act 2002 (c. 41) (subject to subsection (9) below),

'deciding authority' means—

(a) an immigration officer,

(b) the Secretary of State,

(c) [the First-tier Tribunal] or

(d) the Special Immigration Appeals Commission,

'human rights claim' has the meaning given by section 113(1) of the Nationality, Immigration and Asylum Act 2002 (subject to subsection (9) below),

'immigration decision' means—

(a) refusal of leave to enter the United Kingdom,

(b) refusal to vary a person's leave to enter or remain in the United Kingdom,

(c) grant of leave to enter or remain in the United Kingdom,

(d) a decision that a person is to be removed from the United Kingdom by way of directions under section 10 . . . of the Immigration and Asylum Act 1999 (c. 33) (removal of persons unlawfully in United Kingdom),

(e) a decision that a person is to be removed from the United Kingdom by way of directions under paragraphs 8 to 12 of Schedule 2 to the Immigration Act 1971 (c. 77) (control of entry: removal),

(f) a decision to make a deportation order under section 5(1) of that Act, and

(g) a decision to take action in relation to a person in connection with extradition from the United Kingdom,

'immigration provision' means—

(a) sections 28A, 28AA, 28B, 28C and 28CA of the Immigration Act 1971 (immigration offences: enforcement),

(b) paragraph 17 of Schedule 2 to that Act (control of entry),

(c) section 14 of this Act, and

(d) a provision of the Extradition Act 1989 (c. 33) or 2003 (c. 41),

'notified' means notified in such manner as may be specified by regulations made by the Secretary of State,

'passport' includes a document which relates to a national of a country other than the United Kingdom and which is designed to serve the same purpose as a passport, and

'safe country' means a country to which Part 2 of Schedule 3 applies.

(8) A passport produced by or on behalf of a person is valid for the purposes of subsection (3)(b) if it—

(a) relates to the person by whom or on whose behalf it is produced,

(b) has not been altered otherwise than by or with the permission of the authority who issued it, and

(c) was not obtained by deception.

(9) In subsection (4) a reference to an asylum claim or human rights claim shall be treated as including a reference to a claim of entitlement to remain in a country other than the United Kingdom made by reference to the rights that a person invokes in making an asylum claim or a human rights claim in the United Kingdom.

[(9A) In paragraph (c) of the definition of a "deciding authority" in subsection (7) the reference to the First-tier Tribunal includes a reference to the Upper Tribunal when acting under section 12(2)(b)(ii) of the Tribunals, Courts and Enforcement Act 2007.]

(10) Regulations under subsection (7) specifying a manner of notification may, in particular—

(a) apply or refer to regulations under section 105 of the Nationality, Immigration and Asylum Act 2002 (c. 41) (notice of immigration decisions);

(b) make provision similar to provision that is or could be made by regulations under that section;

(c) modify a provision of regulations under that section in its effect for the purpose of regulations under this section;

(d) provide for notice to be treated as received at a specified time if sent to a specified class of place in a specified manner.

(11) Regulations under subsection (7) specifying a manner of notification—

(a) may make incidental, consequential or transitional provision,

(b) shall be made by statutory instrument, and

(c) shall be subject to annulment in pursuance of a resolution of either House of Parliament.

(12) This section shall not prevent a deciding authority from determining not to believe a statement on the grounds of behaviour to which this section does not apply.

(13) . . .

Note: Commencement 1 January 2005 (SI 2004/3398). Words in square brackets in subsection (7)(c) substituted, subsection (9A) inserted and subsection (13) revoked from 15 February 2010 (SI 2010/21). Numbers omitted from subsection (7) by Sch 9 Immigration Act 2014 from 20 October 2014 with savings set out in SI 2014/2771 articles 9-11.

9. Failed asylum seekers: withdrawal of support

(1) . . .

Note: Amends Sch 3 Nationality, Immigration and Asylum Act 2002.

(2) . . .

Note: Amends Sch 3 Nationality, Immigration and Asylum Act 2002.

(3) No appeal may be brought under section 103 of the Immigration and Asylum Act 1999 (asylum support appeal) against a decision—

(a) that by virtue of a provision of Schedule 3 to the Nationality, Immigration and Asylum Act 2002 (c. 41) other than paragraph 7A a person is not qualified to receive support, or

(b) on the grounds of the application of a provision of that Schedule other than paragraph 7A, to stop providing support to a person.

(4) On an appeal under section 103 of the Immigration and Asylum Act 1999 (c. 33) against a decision made by virtue of paragraph 7A of Schedule 3 to the Nationality, Immigration and Asylum Act 2002 the [First-tier Tribunal] may, in particular—

(a) annul a certificate of the Secretary of State issued for the purposes of that paragraph;

(b) require the Secretary of State to reconsider the matters certified.

(5) An order under section 48 providing for this section to come into force may, in particular, provide for this section to have effect with specified modifications before the coming into force of a provision of the Nationality, Immigration and Asylum Act 2002.

Note: Commencement 1 December 2004 (SI 2004/2999). Words in square brackets in subsection (4) substituted from 3 November 2008 (SI 2008/2833).

10. Failed asylum seekers: accommodation

(1) . . .

Note: Amends Immigration and Asylum Act 1999, s 4.

(2) . . .

Note: Amends Immigration and Asylum Act 1999, s 166(5).

(3) . . .

Note: Amends Immigration and Asylum Act 1999, s 103.

(4) . . .

Note: Amends Immigration and Asylum Act 1999, s 103.

(5) . . .

Note: Amends Immigration and Asylum Act 1999, s 103A.

(6) In an amendment made by this section a reference to providing accommodation includes a reference to arranging for the provision of accommodation.

(7) Regulations under section 4(5)(b) of the Immigration and Asylum Act 1999 (c. 33) (as inserted by subsection (1) above) may apply to persons receiving support under section 4 when the regulations come into force.

Note: Subsections (1), (2), (6) and (7) commenced 1 December 2004 (SI 2004/2999), remainder 31 March 2005 (SI 2005/372).

11. Accommodation for asylum seekers: local connection

(1) . . .

Note: Amends Housing Act 1996, s 199.

(2) Subsection (3) applies where—

(a) a local housing authority would (but for subsection (3)) be obliged to secure that accommodation is available for occupation by a person under section 193 of the Housing Act 1996 (homeless persons),

(b) the person was (at any time) provided with accommodation in a place in Scotland under section 95 of the Immigration and Asylum Act 1999 (support for asylum seekers),

(c) the accommodation was not provided in an accommodation centre by virtue of section 22 of the Nationality, Immigration and Asylum Act 2002 (use of accommodation centres for section 95 support), and

(d) the person has neither—

(i) a local connection with the district of a local housing authority (in England or Wales) within the meaning of section 199 of the Housing Act 1996 as amended by subsection (1) above, nor

(ii) a local connection with a district (in Scotland) within the meaning of section 27 of the Housing (Scotland) Act 1987 (c. 26).

(3) Where this subsection applies—

(a) the duty of the local housing authority under section 193 of the Housing Act 1996 in relation to the person shall not apply, but

(b) the local housing authority—

(i) may secure that accommodation is available for occupation by the person for a period giving him a reasonable opportunity of securing accommodation for his occupation, and

(ii) may provide the person (or secure that he is provided with) advice and assistance in any attempts he may make to secure that accommodation becomes available for his occupation.

Note: Commenced 4 January 2005 (SI 2004/2999).

12. Refugee: back-dating of benefits

(1) . . .

Note: Repeals Immigration and Asylum Act 1999, s 123.

(2) . . .

Note: Amends SI 1987/1967, SR 1987/459, SI 1987/1968, SR 1987/465, SI 1987/1971, SR 1987/461, SI 1992/1814.

(3) . . .

Note: Amends SI 2000/636.

(4) . . .

Note: Amends SR 2000/71.

(5) An order under section 48 bringing this section into force may, in particular, provide for this section to have effect in relation to persons recorded as refugees after a specified date (irrespective of when the process resulting in the record was begun).

Note: Commencement 14 June 2007, but not with effect to a person recorded as a refugee on or before that date (SI 2007/1602), which sets out transitional provision.

13. [Integration loans for refugees]

(1) The Secretary of State may make regulations enabling him to make loans [—

(a) to refugees, and

(b) to such other classes of person, or to persons other than refugees in such circumstances, as the regulations may prescribe.]

(2) A person is a refugee for the purpose of subsection (1) if the Secretary of State has—

(a) recorded him as a refugee within the meaning of the Convention relating to the Status of Refugees done at Geneva on 28 July 1951, and

(b) [granted him leave to enter or remain] in the United Kingdom (within the meaning of section 33(1) of the Immigration Act 1971 (c. 77)).

(3) Regulations under subsection (1)—

(a) shall specify matters which the Secretary of State shall, in addition to other matters appearing to him to be relevant, take into account in determining whether or not to make a loan (and those matters may, in particular, relate to—

(i) a person's income or assets,

(ii) a person's likely ability to repay a loan, or

(iii) the length of time since a person was recorded as a refugee [or since some other event)],

(b) shall enable the Secretary of State to specify (and vary from time to time) a minimum and a maximum amount of a loan,

(c) shall prevent a person from receiving a loan if—

(i) he is under the age of 18,

(ii) he is insolvent, within a meaning given by the regulations, or

(iii) he has received a loan under the regulations,

(d) shall make provision about repayment of a loan (and may, in particular, make provision—

(i) about interest;

(ii) for repayment by deduction from a social security benefit or similar payment due to the person to whom the loan is made),

(e) shall enable the Secretary of State to attach conditions to a loan (which may include conditions about the use of the loan),

(f) shall make provision about—

(i) the making of an application for a loan, and

(ii) the information, which may include information about the intended use of a loan, to be provided in or with an application,

(g) may make provision about steps to be taken by the Secretary of State in establishing an applicant's likely ability to repay a loan,

(h) may make provision for a loan to be made jointly to more than one refugee, and

(i) may confer a discretion on the Secretary of State.

(4) Regulations under this section—

(a) shall be made by statutory instrument, and

(b) may not be made unless a draft has been laid before and approved by resolution of each House of Parliament.

Note: Commencement 29 June 2006 (SI 2006/1517). Words in square brackets substituted from 30 June 2006, Immigration, Nationality and Asylum Act 2006, s 45 (SI 2006/1497).

Enforcement powers

14. Immigration officer: power of arrest

(1) Where an immigration officer in the course of exercising a function under the Immigration Acts forms a reasonable suspicion that a person has committed or attempted to commit an offence listed in subsection (2), he may arrest the person without warrant.

(2) Those offences are—

(a) the offence of conspiracy at common law (in relation to conspiracy to defraud),

(b) at common law in Scotland, any of the following offences—

(i) fraud,

(ii) conspiracy to defraud,

(iii) uttering and fraud,

(iv) bigamy,

(v) theft, and

(vi) reset,

(c) an offence under section 57 of the Offences against the Person Act 1861 (c. 100) (bigamy),

(d) an offence under section 3 or 4 of the Perjury Act 1911 (c. 6) (false statements),

(e) an offence under section 7 of that Act (aiding, abetting &c.) if it relates to an offence under section 3 or 4 of that Act,

(f) an offence under section 53 of the Registration of Births, Deaths and Marriages (Scotland) Act 1965 (c. 49) (knowingly giving false information to district registrar, &c.),

(g) an offence under any of the following provisions of the Theft Act 1968 (c. 60)—

(i) . . . section 1 (theft),

(ii) . . .

(iii) . . .

(iv) section 17 (false accounting), and

(v) section 22 (handling stolen goods),

(h) an offence under section 1, . . . 17 or 21 of the Theft Act (Northern Ireland) 1969 (c. 16) (N.I.),

[(ha) an offence under either of the following provisions of the Fraud Act 2006—
(i) section 1 (fraud);
(ii) section 11 (obtaining services dishonestly),]
(i) . . .
(j) . . .
(k) an offence under Article 8 or 9 of the Perjury (Northern Ireland) Order 1979 (S.I. 1979/1714 (N.I. 19)),
(l) an offence under Article 12 of that Order if it relates to an offence under Article 8 or 9 of that Order,
(m) an offence under any of the following provisions of the Forgery and Counterfeiting Act 1981 (c. 45)—
(i) section 1 (forgery),
(ii) section 2 (copying false instrument),
(iii) section 3 (using false instrument),
(iv) section 4 (using copy of false instrument), and
(v) section 5(1) and (3) (false documents),
(n) an offence under any of sections 57 to [59A] of the Sexual Offences Act 2003 (c. 42) (trafficking for sexual exploitation),
(o) an offence under section 22 of the Criminal Justice (Scotland) Act 2003 (asp 7) (trafficking in prostitution), . . .
(p) an offence under section 4 of this Act.
[(q) an offence under any of sections 4 to 6 of the Identity Documents Act 2010].

(3) The following provisions of the Immigration Act 1971 (c. 77) shall have effect for the purpose of making, or in connection with, an arrest under this section as they have effect for the purpose of making, or in connection with, arrests for offences under that Act—
(a) section 28C (entry and search before arrest),
(b) sections 28E and 28F (entry and search after arrest),
(c) sections 28G and 28H (search of arrested person), and
(d) section 28I (seized material).

(4) . . .

Note: Commencement 1 December 2004 (SI 2004/2999). Subsection (4) amends Race Relations Act 1976, s 19D. Words in subsection 14(2)(o) omitted from 7 June 2006, Identity Cards Act 2006, s 30 and Sch 2, (SI 2006/1439). Subsections (2)(g), (ii)-(iii), (2)(i)-(j) omitted and words omitted in subsection (2)(h), subsection (2)(ha) inserted by Sch 1 Fraud Act 2006 from 15 January 2007 (SI 2006/3200). Subsection (2)(q) substituted by Identity Documents Act 2010, Schedule, paragraph 18 from 21 January 2011. Number in square brackets in subsection (2)(n) substituted by Protection of Freedoms Act 2012 Sch 9 from 6 April 2013 (SI 2013/470).

15. Fingerprinting

. . .

Note: Amends Immigration and Asylum Act 1999, s 141.

16. Information about passengers

. . .

Note: Amends paragraph 27B, Sch 2 Immigration Act 1971.

17. Retention of documents

Where a document comes into the possession of the Secretary of State or an immigration officer in the course of the exercise of an immigration function, the Secretary of State or an immigration officer may retain the document while he suspects that—

(a) a person to whom the document relates may be liable to removal from the United Kingdom in accordance with a provision of the Immigration Acts, and

(b) retention of the document may facilitate the removal.

Note: Commencement 1 December 2004 (SI 2004/2999).

18. Control of entry

. . .

Note: Amends paragraph 2A, Sch 2 Immigration Act 1971.

Procedure for marriage

19. England and Wales

[(1) This section applies to a marriage that is to be solemnised on the authority of certificates issued by a superintendent registrar under Part 3 of the Marriage Act 1949 (the "1949 Act") unless each party to the marriage falls within exception A or exception B.

(1A) A party to the marriage falls within exception A if the person is a relevant national.

(1B) A party to the marriage falls within exception B if—

(a) the person is exempt from immigration control, and

(b) the notice of marriage is accompanied by the specified evidence required by section 28C(2) of the 1949 Act that the person is exempt from immigration control.]

(2) In relation to a marriage to which this section applies, the notices under section 27 of the Marriage Act 1949—

(a) shall be given to the superintendent registrar of a registration district specified for the purpose of this paragraph by regulations made by the Secretary of State,

(b) shall be delivered to the superintendent registrar in person by the two parties to the marriage,

(c) may be given only if each party to the marriage has been resident in a registration district for the period of seven days immediately before the giving of his or her notice (but the district need not be that in which the notice is given and the parties need not have resided in the same district), and

(d) shall state, in relation to each party, the registration district by reference to which paragraph (c) is satisfied.

(3) . . .

[(4) In this section—

(a) a reference to a person being a relevant national, or being exempt from immigration control, has the same meaning as in section 49 of the Immigration Act 2014;

(b) "notice of marriage" means a notice of marriage given under section 27 of the 1949 Act.]

Note: Commencement 1 February 2005 (SI 2004/3398). Subsections (3) and (4)(c) and (d) repealed from 9 May 2011 (SI 2011/1158). Subsections (1) and (4) substituted by s 58 Immigration Act 2014 from a date to be appointed.

20. England and Wales: supplemental

(1) The Marriage Act 1949 (c. 76) shall have effect in relation to a marriage to which section 19 applies—

(a) subject to that section, and

(b) with any necessary consequential modification.

(2) In particular—

(a) section 28(1)(b) of that Act (declaration: residence) shall have effect as if it required a declaration that—

(i) the notice of marriage is given in compliance with section 19(2) above, . . .

(b) section 48 of that Act (proof of certain matters not essential to validity of marriage) shall have effect as if the list of matters in section 48(1)(a) to (e) included compliance with section 19 above.

(3) [Regulations under section 19(2(a)—

(a) may make transitional provision,

(b) shall be made by statutory instrument, and

(c) shall be subject to annulment in pursuance of a resolution of either House of Parliament.

(4) Before making regulations under section 19(2)(a) the Secretary of State shall consult the Registrar General.

(5) An expression used in section 19 or this section and in Part III of the Marriage Act 1949 (c. 76) has the same meaning in section 19 or this section as in that Part.

(6) . . .

Note: Commenced 1 February 2005 (SI 2004/3398). Subsection (6) repealed from 8 January 2007, ss 30, 33 Legislative and Regulatory Reform Act 2006. Words omitted from subsection (2) and words substituted in subsection (3) from 9 May 2011 (SI 2011/1158).

21. Scotland

(1) This section applies to a marriage—

(a) which is intended to be solemnised in Scotland, and

(b) a party to which is subject to immigration control.

(2) In relation to a marriage to which this section applies, notice under section 3 of the Marriage (Scotland) Act 1977 (c. 15)—

(a) may be submitted to the district registrar of a registration district prescribed for the purposes of this section, and

(b) may not be submitted to the district registrar of any other registration district.

(3) . . .

(4) Where the district registrar to whom notice is submitted by virtue of subsection (2) (here the 'notified registrar') is not the district registrar for the registration district in which the marriage is to be solemnised (here the 'second registrar')—

(a) the notified registrar shall . . . send the notices and any fee, certificate or declaration [submitted in pursuance of section 3 of the Marriage (Scotland) Act 1977 (c. 15) in relation to the marriage], to the second registrar, and

(b) the second registrar shall be treated as having received the notices from the parties to the marriage on the dates on which the notified registrar received them.

(5) Subsection (4) of section 19 applies for the purposes of this section as it applies for the purposes of that section.

Note: Commenced 1 February 2005 (SI 2004/3398). Words in square brackets in subsection (4)(a) substituted by s 59 Local Electoral Administration and Registration Services (Scotland) Act 2006 (asp) from 1 January 2007 (SSI 2006/469). Subsection (3) repealed and words omitted from subsections (4) and (5) from 9 May 2011 (SI 2011/1158).

22. Scotland: supplemental

(1) The Marriage (Scotland) Act 1977 shall have effect in relation to a marriage to which section 21 applies—

(a) subject to that section, and

(b) with any necessary consequential modification.

(2) In subsection (2)(a) of that section 'prescribed' means prescribed by regulations made by the Secretary of State after consultation with the Registrar General for Scotland; and other expressions used in subsections (1) to (4) of that section and in the Marriage (Scotland) Act 1977 have the same meaning in those subsections as in that Act.

(3) Regulations made by the Secretary of State under subsection (2)(a) . . . of that section—

(a) may make transitional provision,

(b) shall be made by statutory instrument, and

(c) shall be subject to annulment in pursuance of a resolution of either House of Parliament.

Note: Commenced 1 February 2005 (SI 2004/3398). Words omitted from subsection (3) from 9 May 2011 (SI 2011/1158).

23. Northern Ireland

(1) This section applies to a marriage—

(a) which is intended to be solemnised in Northern Ireland, and

(b) a party to which is subject to immigration control.

(2) In relation to a marriage to which this section applies, the marriage notices—

(a) shall be given only to a prescribed registrar, and

(b) shall, in prescribed cases, be given by both parties together in person at a prescribed register office.

(3) . . .

(4) . . . if the prescribed registrar is not the registrar for the purposes of Article 4 of that Order, the prescribed registrar shall send him the marriage notices and he shall be treated as having received them from the parties to the marriage on the dates on which the prescribed registrar received them.

(5) . . .

(6) For the purposes of this section—

(a) a person is subject to immigration control if—

(i) he is not an EEA national, and

(ii) under the Immigration Act 1971 (c. 77) he requires leave to enter or remain in the United Kingdom (whether or not leave has been given),

(b) 'EEA national' means a national of a State which is a contracting party to the Agreement on the European Economic Area signed at Oporto on 2 May 1992 (as it has effect from time to time),

(c) . . .

(d) . . .

Note: Commenced 1 February 2005 (SI 2004/3398). Subsections (3), (5) and (6)(c) and (d) repealed and words omitted from subsection (4) from 9 May 2011 (SI 2011/1158).

24. Northern Ireland: supplemental

(1) The Marriage (Northern Ireland) Order 2003 (SI 2003/413 (N.I. 3)) shall have effect in relation to a marriage to which section 23 applies—

(a) subject to section 23, and

(b) with any necessary consequential modification.

(2) In section 23 'prescribed' means prescribed for the purposes of that section by regulations made by the Secretary of State after consulting the Registrar General for Northern Ireland and other expressions used in that section or this section and the Marriage (Northern Ireland) Order 2003 have the same meaning in section 23 or this section as in that Order.

(3) Section 18(3) of the Interpretation Act (Northern Ireland) 1954 (c.33 (N.I.)) (provisions as to holders of offices) shall apply to section 23 as if that section were an enactment within the meaning of that Act.

(4) Regulations of the Secretary of State under section 23—

(a) may make transitional provision,

(b) shall be made by statutory instrument, and

(c) shall be subject to annulment in pursuance of a resolution of either House of Parliament.

Note: Commenced 1 February 2005 (SI 2004/3398).

25. Application for permission under section 19(3)(b), 21(3)(b) or 23(3)(b)

Note: Repealed by s 50 Immigration, Asylum and Nationality Act 2006 from 30 April 2007 subject to savings (SI 2007/1109), and repealed for all remaining purposes from 9 May 2011 (SI 2011/1158).

Appeals

26. Unification of appeal system

(1) . . .

Note: Amends Nationality, Immigration and Asylum Act 2002, s 81.

(2) . . .

Note: Amends Nationality, Immigration and Asylum Act 2002, s 82(1).

(3) . . .

Note: Amends Nationality, Immigration and Asylum Act 2002, s 83(2).

(4) . . .

(5) . . .

Note: Amends Nationality, Immigration and Asylum Act 2002, ss 100–103 and Sch 5.

(6) . . .

(7) Schedule 2 (which makes amendments consequential on this section, and transitional provision) shall have effect.

(8) . . .

(9) . . .

(10) . . .

Note: Commenced 4 April 2005 (SI 2005/565). Subsections (4), (6), (8)–(10) revoked from 15 February 2010 (SI 2010/21). Subsections (2)–(3) repealed by Sch 9 Immigration Act 2014 from a date to be appointed.

27. Unfounded human rights or asylum claim

. . .

Note: Amends Nationality, Immigration and Asylum Act 2002, ss 94 and 112 from 1 October 2004 (SI 2004/2523). Subsections (2)–(3) repealed by Sch 9 Immigration Act 2014 from a date to be appointed.

28. Appeal from within United Kingdom

. . .

Note: Amends Nationality, Immigration and Asylum Act 2002, s 92(3) from 1 October 2004 (SI 2004/2523). Repealed by Sch 9 Immigration Act 2014 from a date to be appointed.

29. Entry clearance

. . .

Note: Amends Nationality, Immigration and Asylum Act 2002, ss 88 and 112 from 1 October 2004 (SI 2004/2523). Repealed by Sch 9 Immigration Act 2014 from a date to be appointed.

30. Earlier right of appeal

. . .

Note: Amends Nationality, Immigration and Asylum Act 2002, s 96 from 1 October 2004 (SI 2004/2523).

31. Seamen and aircrews: right of appeal

. . .

Note: Amends Nationality, Immigration and Asylum Act 2002, s 82 from 1 October 2004 (SI 2004/2523) Repealed by Sch 9 Immigration Act 2014 from a date to be appointed.

32. Suspected international terrorist: bail

. . .

Note: Section 32 repealed from 14 March 2005, Prevention of Terrorism Act 2005, s 16(2).

Removal and detention

33. Removing asylum seeker to safe country

(1) Schedule 3 (which concerns the removal of persons claiming asylum to countries known to protect refugees and to respect human rights) shall have effect.

(2) . . .

Note: Repeals Immigration and Asylum Act 1999, ss 11 and 12.

(3) . . .

Note: Repeals Nationality, Immigration and Asylum Act 2002, ss 80 and 93. Commencement 1 October 2004 (SI 2004/2523).

34. Detention pending deportation

. . .

Note: Amends paragraph 2, Sch 3 Immigration Act 1971 from 1 October 2004 (SI 2004/2523).

35. Deportation or removal: cooperation

(1) The Secretary of State may require a person to take specified action if the Secretary of State thinks that—

(a) the action will or may enable a travel document to be obtained by or for the person, and

(b) possession of the travel document will facilitate the person's deportation or removal from the United Kingdom.

(2) In particular, the Secretary of State may require a person to—

(a) provide information or documents to the Secretary of State or to any other person;

(b) obtain information or documents;

[(c) provide biometric information (within the meaning of section 15 of the UK Borders Act 2007), or submit to a process by means of which such information is obtained or recorded];

(d) make, or consent to or cooperate with the making of, an application to a person acting for the government of a State other than the United Kingdom;

(e) cooperate with a process designed to enable determination of an application;

(f) complete a form accurately and completely;

(g) attend an interview and answer questions accurately and completely;

(h) make an appointment.

(3) A person commits an offence if he fails without reasonable excuse to comply with a requirement of the Secretary of State under subsection (1).

(4) A person guilty of an offence under subsection (3) shall be liable—

(a) on conviction on indictment, to imprisonment for a term not exceeding two years, to a fine or to both, or

(b) on summary conviction, to imprisonment for a term not exceeding twelve months, to a fine not exceeding the statutory maximum or to both.

(5) If [an] immigration officer reasonably suspects that a person has committed an offence under subsection (3) he may arrest the person without warrant.

(6) An offence under subsection (3) shall be treated as—

(a) a relevant offence for the purposes of sections 28B and 28D of the Immigration Act 1971 (c. 77) (search, entry and arrest), and

(b) an offence under Part III of that Act (criminal proceedings) for the purposes of sections 28(4), 28E, 28G and 28H (search after arrest, &c.) of that Act.

(7) In subsection (1)—

'travel document' means a passport or other document which is issued by or for Her Majesty's Government or the government of another State and which enables or facilitates travel from the United Kingdom to another State, and

'removal from the United Kingdom' means removal under—

(a) Schedule 2 to the Immigration Act 1971 (control on entry) (including a provision of that Schedule as applied by another provision of the Immigration Acts),

(b) section 10 of the Immigration and Asylum Act 1999 (c. 33) (removal of person unlawfully in United Kingdom), or

(c) Schedule 3 to this Act.

(8) While sections 11 and 12 of the Immigration and Asylum Act 1999 continue to have effect, the reference in subsection (7)(c) above to Schedule 3 to this Act shall be treated as including a reference to those sections.

(9) In so far as subsection (3) extends to England and Wales, subsection (4)(b) shall, until the commencement of section 154 of the Criminal Justice Act 2003 (c. 44) (increased limit on magistrates' power of imprisonment), have effect as if the reference to twelve months were a reference to six months.

(10) In so far as subsection (3) extends to Scotland, subsection (4)(b) shall have effect as if the reference to twelve months were a reference to six months.

(11) In so far as subsection (3) extends to Northern Ireland, subsection (4)(b) shall have effect as if the reference to twelve months were a reference to six months.

Note: Commencement 1 October 2004 (s 48). Word in square bracket in subsection (5) substituted by Sch 7 Serious Organised Crime and Police Act 2005 from 1 January 2006 (SI 2005/3495) and from 1 March 2007 (NI) (SI 2007/288 NI 2). Subsection (2)(c) substituted by Schedule 2 Immigration Act 2014 from 28 July 2014 (SI 2014/1820).

36. Electronic monitoring

(1) In this section—

(a) 'residence restriction' means a restriction as to residence imposed under—

(i) paragraph 21 of Schedule 2 to the Immigration Act 1971 (c. 77) (control on entry) (including that paragraph as applied by another provision of the Immigration Acts), or

(ii) Schedule 3 to that Act (deportation),

(b) 'reporting restriction' means a requirement to report to a specified person imposed under any of those provisions,

(c) 'employment restriction' means a restriction as to employment or occupation imposed under any of those provisions, and

(d) 'immigration bail' means—

(i) release under a provision of the Immigration Acts on entry into a recognizance or bail bond,

(ii) bail granted in accordance with a provision of the Immigration Acts by a court, a justice of the peace, the sheriff, [the First-tier Tribunal], the Secretary of State or an immigration officer (but not by a police officer), and

(iii) bail granted by the Special Immigration Appeals Commission.

(2) Where a residence restriction is imposed on an adult—

(a) he may be required to cooperate with electronic monitoring, and

(b) failure to comply with a requirement under paragraph (a) shall be treated for all purposes of the Immigration Acts as failure to observe the residence restriction.

(3) Where a reporting restriction could be imposed on an adult—

(a) he may instead be required to cooperate with electronic monitoring, and

(b) the requirement shall be treated for all purposes of the Immigration Acts as a reporting restriction.

(4) Immigration bail may be granted to an adult subject to a requirement that he cooperate with electronic monitoring; and the requirement may (but need not) be imposed as a condition of a recognizance or bail bond.

(5) In this section a reference to requiring an adult to cooperate with electronic monitoring is a reference to requiring him to cooperate with such arrangements as the person imposing the requirement may specify for detecting and recording by electronic means the location of the adult, or his presence in or absence from a location—

(a) at specified times,

(b) during specified periods of time, or

(c) throughout the currency of the arrangements.

(6) In particular, arrangements for the electronic monitoring of an adult—

(a) may require him to wear a device;

(b) may require him to make specified use of a device;

(c) may prohibit him from causing or permitting damage of or interference with a device;

(d) may prohibit him from taking or permitting action that would or might prevent the effective operation of a device;

(e) may require him to communicate in a specified manner and at specified times or during specified periods of time;

(f) may involve the performance of functions by persons other than the person imposing the requirement to cooperate with electronic monitoring (and those functions may relate to any aspect or condition of a residence restriction, of a reporting restriction, of an employment restriction, of a requirement under this section or of immigration bail).

(7) In this section 'adult' means an individual who is at least 18 years old.

(8) The Secretary of State—

(a) may make rules about arrangements for electronic monitoring for the purposes of this section, and

(b) when he thinks that satisfactory arrangements for electronic monitoring are available in respect of an area, shall notify persons likely to be in a position to exercise power under this section in respect of the area.

(9) Rules under subsection (8)(a) may, in particular, require that arrangements for electronic monitoring impose on a person of a specified description responsibility for specified aspects of the operation of the arrangements.

(10) A requirement to cooperate with electronic monitoring—

(a) shall comply with rules under subsection (8)(a), and

(b) may not be imposed in respect of an adult who is or is expected to be in an area unless the person imposing the requirement has received a notification from the Secretary of State under subsection (8)(b) in respect of that area.

(11) Rules under subsection (8)(a)—

(a) may include incidental, consequential or transitional provision,

(b) may make provision generally or only in relation to specified cases, circumstances or areas,

(c) shall be made by statutory instrument, and

(d) shall be subject to annulment in pursuance of a resolution of either House of Parliament.

(12) . . .

Note: Commencement 1 October 2004 (SI 2004/2523). Words in square brackets in subsection (1)(d) substituted and subsection (12) revoked from 15 February 2010 (SI 2010/21).

Immigration services

37. Provision of immigration services

Note: Amends Immigration and Asylum Act 1999, ss 84, 85, 89, 90 and Sch 5 and 6.

38. Immigration Services Commissioner: power of entry

. . .

Note: Amends Immigration and Asylum Act 1999, s 92 and Sch 5, paragraph 7.

39. Offence of advertising services

. . .

Note: Amends Immigration and Asylum Act 1999, s 92.

40. Appeal to Immigration Services Tribunal

. . .

Note: Repeals Immigration and Asylum Act 1999, s 87(3)(f).

41. Professional bodies

. . .

Note: Amends Immigration and Asylum Act 1999, ss 86, 166 and Sch 5, paragraph 21.

Fees

42. Amount of fees

(1) . . .

[(2) . . .

[(2A) . . .

(3) An Order in Council under section 1 of the Consular Fees Act 1980 (c. 23) (fees) which prescribes a fee in relation to an application for the issue of a certificate under section 10 of the Nationality, Immigration and Asylum Act 2002 (right of abode: certificate of entitlement) may prescribe an amount which is intended to—

(a) exceed the administrative costs of determining the application, and

(b) reflect benefits that in the opinion of Her Majesty in Council are likely to accrue to the applicant if the application is successful.

[(3A) The amount of a fee under section 1 of the Consular Fees Act 1980 in respect of a matter specified in subsection (3B) may be set so as to reflect costs referable to the exercise of any function in respect of which the Secretary of State has made an order under section 68 of the Immigration Act 2014.

(3B) The matters are—

(a) the determination of applications for entry clearances (within the meaning given by section 33(1) of the Immigration Act 1971),

(b) the determination of applications for transit visas under section 41 of the Immigration and Asylum Act 1999, or

(c) the determination of applications for certificates of entitlement to the right of abode in the United Kingdom under section 10 of the Nationality, Immigration and Asylum Act 2002.]

(4) Where an instrument prescribes a fee in reliance on this section it may include provision for the refund, where an application is unsuccessful or a process is not completed, of that part of the fee which is intended to reflect the matters specified in subsection . . . (3)(b).

(5) Provision included by virtue of subsection (4)—

(a) may determine, or provide for the determination of, the amount to be refunded;

(b) may confer a discretion on the Secretary of State or another person (whether in relation to determining the amount of a refund or in relation to determining whether a refund should be made).

(6) An instrument may not be made in reliance on this section unless the Secretary of State has consulted with such persons as appear to him to be appropriate.

(7) An instrument may not be made in reliance on this section unless a draft has been laid before and approved by resolution of each House of Parliament . . .

(8) This section is without prejudice to the power to make an order under section 102 of the Finance (No. 2) Act 1987 (c. 51) (government fees and charges) in relation to a power under a provision specified in this section.

Note: Commencement 1 October 2004 (SI 2004/2523). Subsections (2)(da), (2A) and (3A) inserted by s 20 UK Borders Act 2007 from 31 January 2008 (SI 2008/99). Subsections (1)–(2A) and words in subsections (4) and (7) omitted, subsection (3A) substituted by Sch 9 Immigration Act 2014 from 15 December 2014 (SI 2014/2771).

43. Transfer of leave stamps

. . .

Note: Amends Immigration and Asylum Act 1999, s 5.

General

44.

. . .

Note: Section 44 repealed by Immigration, Asylum and Nationality Act 2006, s 64(3) from 30 March 2006 (Royal Assent).

45. Interpretation: immigration officer

In this Act 'immigration officer' means a person appointed by the Secretary of State as an immigration officer under paragraph 1 of Schedule 2 to the Immigration Act 1971.

Note: Commencement 1 October 2004 (SI 2004/2523).

46. Money

There shall be paid out of money provided by Parliament—

(a) any expenditure incurred by a Minister of the Crown in connection with this Act, and

(b) any increase attributable to this Act in the sums payable under any other enactment out of money provided by Parliament.

Note: Commencement 1 October 2004 (SI 2004/2523).

47. Repeals

. . .

48. Commencement

(1) Sections 2, 32(2) and 35 shall come into force at the end of the period of two months beginning with the date on which this Act is passed.

(2) Section 32(1) shall have effect in relation to determinations of the Special Immigration Appeals Commission made after the end of the period of two months beginning with the date on which this Act is passed.

(3) The other preceding provisions of this Act shall come into force in accordance with provision made—

(a) in the case of section 26 or Schedule 1 or 2, by order of the Lord Chancellor,

(b) in the case of sections 4 and 5 in so far as they extend to Scotland, by order of the Scottish Ministers, and

(c) in any other case, by order of the Secretary of State.

(4) An order under subsection (3)—

(a) may make transitional or incidental provision,

(b) may make different provision for different purposes, and

(c) shall be made by statutory instrument.

(5) Transitional provision under subsection (4)(a) in relation to the commencement of section 26 may, in particular, make provision in relation to proceedings which, immediately before commencement—

(a) are awaiting determination by an adjudicator appointed, or treated as if appointed, under section 81 of the Nationality, Immigration and Asylum Act 2002 (c. 41),

(b) are awaiting determination by the Immigration Appeal Tribunal,

(c) having been determined by an adjudicator could be brought before the Immigration Appeal Tribunal,

(d) are awaiting the determination of a further appeal brought in accordance with section 103 of that Act,

(e) having been determined by the Immigration Appeal Tribunal could be brought before another court by way of further appeal under that section,

(f) are or could be made the subject of an application under section 101 of that Act (review of decision on permission to appeal to Tribunal), or

(g) are or could be made the subject of another kind of application to the High Court or the Court of Session.

(6) Provision made under subsection (5) may, in particular—

(a) provide for the institution or continuance of an appeal of a kind not generally available after the commencement of section 26,

(b) provide for the termination of proceedings, or
(c) make any other provision that the Lord Chancellor thinks appropriate.

49. Extent

(1) This Act extends (subject to subsection (2)) to—
(a) England and Wales,
(b) Scotland, and
(c) Northern Ireland.

(2) An amendment effected by this Act has the same extent as the enactment, or as the relevant part of the enactment, amended (ignoring extent by virtue of an Order in Council).

(3) Her Majesty may by Order in Council direct that a provision of this Act is to extend, with or without modification or adaptation, to—
(a) any of the Channel Islands;
(b) the Isle of Man.

50. Short title

This Act may be cited as the Asylum and Immigration (Treatment of Claimants, etc.) Act 2004.

Schedules

Schedule 1

. . .

Note: Schedule 1 amends Nationality, Immigration and Asylum Act 2002.

Section 26

Schedule 2

Asylum and Immigration Tribunal: Consequential Amendments and Transitional Provision

Part 1

Consequential Amendments

. . .

Part 2

Transitional Provision

26. In this Part 'commencement' means the coming into force of section 26.

27. A person who immediately before commencement is, or is to be treated as, an adjudicator appointed under section 81 of the Nationality, Immigration and Asylum Act 2002 (c. 41) (appeals) (as it has effect before commencement) shall be treated as having been appointed as

a member of the Asylum and Immigration Tribunal under paragraph 1 of Schedule 4 to that Act (as it has effect after commencement) immediately after commencement.

28. Where immediately before commencement a person is a member of the Immigration Appeal Tribunal—

(a) he shall be treated as having been appointed as a member of the Asylum and Immigration Tribunal under paragraph 1 of Schedule 4 to that Act immediately after commencement, and

(b) if he was a legally qualified member of the Immigration Appeal Tribunal (within the meaning of Schedule 5 to that Act) he shall be treated as having been appointed as a legally qualified member of the Asylum and Immigration Tribunal.

29. A person who immediately before commencement is a member of staff of adjudicators appointed or treated as appointed under section 81 of the Nationality, Immigration and Asylum Act 2002 (c. 41) or of the Immigration Appeal Tribunal shall be treated as having been appointed as a member of the staff of the Asylum and Immigration Tribunal under paragraph 9 of Schedule 4 to the Nationality, Immigration and Asylum Act 2002 immediately after commencement.

30. . . .

Note: Commencement 4 April 2005 (SI 2005/565). Paragraph 30 revoked from 15 February 2010 (SI 2010/21).

Section 33

Schedule 3

Removal of Asylum Seeker to Safe Country

Part 1

Introductory

1.—(1) In this Schedule—

'asylum claim' means a claim by a person that to remove him from or require him to leave the United Kingdom would breach the United Kingdom's obligations under the Refugee Convention,

'Convention rights' means the rights identified as Convention rights by section 1 of the Human Rights Act 1998 (c. 42) (whether or not in relation to a State that is a party to the Convention),

'human rights claim' means a claim by a person that to remove him from or require him to leave the United Kingdom would be unlawful under section 6 of the Human Rights Act 1998 (public authority not to act contrary to Convention) as being incompatible with his Convention rights,

'immigration appeal' means an appeal under section 82(1) of the Nationality, Immigration and Asylum Act 2002 (c. 41) (appeal against immigration decision), and

'the Refugee Convention' means the Convention relating to the Status of Refugees done at Geneva on 28 July 1951 and its Protocol.

(2) In this Schedule a reference to anything being done in accordance with the Refugee Convention is a reference to the thing being done in accordance with the principles of the Convention, whether or not by a signatory to it.

[(3) Section 92 of the Nationality, Immigration and Asylum Act 2002 makes further provision about the place from which an appeal relating to an asylum or human rights claim may be brought or continued.]

Note: Subparagraph (3) inserted by Sch 9 Immigration Act 2014 from 20 October 2014 with savings set out in articles 9-11 SI 2014/2771.

PART 2

FIRST LIST OF SAFE COUNTRIES (REFUGEE CONVENTION AND HUMAN RIGHTS (1))

2. This Part applies to—
(a) Austria,
(b) Belgium,
[(ba) Bulgaria,]
(c) Republic of Cyprus,
(d) Czech Republic,
(e) Denmark,
(f) Estonia,
(g) Finland,
(h) France,
(i) Germany,
(j) Greece,
(k) Hungary,
(l) Iceland,
(m) Ireland,
(n) Italy,
(o) Latvia,
(p) Lithuania,
(q) Luxembourg,
(r) Malta,
(s) Netherlands,
(t) Norway,
(u) Poland,
(v) Portugal,
[(va) Romania,]
(w) Slovak Republic,
(x) Slovenia,
(y) Spain, . . .
(z) Sweden.
{(z1) Switzerland}

Note: Words in square brackets inserted from 1 January 2007 (SI 2006/3393). Switzerland added from 20 November 2010 (SI 2010/2802); the amendment adding Switzerland (a) applies in relation to asylum and human rights claims made before 20 November 2010 (as well as those made after), but (b) does not apply in relation to an asylum or human rights claim if, before 20 November 2010, a decision is made to refuse the claimant leave to enter the United Kingdom or to remove the claimant from the United Kingdom: see Art 1(3) SI 2010/2802.

3.—(1) This paragraph applies for the purposes of the determination by any person, tribunal or court whether a person who has made an asylum claim or a human rights claim may be removed—
(a) from the United Kingdom, and
(b) to a State of which he is not a national or citizen.

(2) A State to which this Part applies shall be treated, in so far as relevant to the question mentioned in sub-paragraph (1), as a place—
(a) where a person's life and liberty are not threatened by reason of his race, religion, nationality, membership of a particular social group or political opinion,
(b) from which a person will not be sent to another State in contravention of his Convention rights, and

(c) from which a person will not be sent to another State otherwise than in accordance with the Refugee Convention.

4. Section 77 of the Nationality, Immigration and Asylum Act 2002 (c. 41) (no removal while claim for asylum pending) shall not prevent a person who has made a claim for asylum from being removed—

(a) from the United Kingdom, and

(b) to a State to which this Part applies;

provided that the Secretary of State certifies that in his opinion the person is not a national or citizen of the State.

5.—(1) This paragraph applies where the Secretary of State certifies that—

(a) it is proposed to remove a person to a State to which this Part applies, and

(b) in the Secretary of State's opinion the person is not a national or citizen of the State.

(2) . . .

(3) The person may not bring an immigration appeal [from within the United Kingdom] in reliance on—

(a) an asylum claim which asserts that to remove the person to a specified State to which this Part applies would breach the United Kingdom's obligations under the Refugee Convention, or

(b) a human rights claim in so far as it asserts that to remove the person to a specified State to which this Part applies would be unlawful under section 6 of the Human Rights Act 1998 because of the possibility of removal from that State to another State.

(4) The person may not bring an immigration appeal [from within the United Kingdom] in reliance on a human rights claim to which this sub-paragraph applies if the Secretary of State certifies that the claim is clearly unfounded; and the Secretary of State shall certify a human rights claim to which this sub-paragraph applies unless satisfied that the claim is not clearly unfounded.

(5) Sub-paragraph (4) applies to a human rights claim if, or in so far as, it asserts a matter other than that specified in sub-paragraph (3)(b).

Note: Subparagraph (2) omitted and words in square brackets in subparagraphs (3) and (4) substituted by Sch 9 Immigration Act 2014 from 20 October 2014 with savings set out in articles 9-11 SI 2014/2771.

6. A person who is outside the United Kingdom may not bring an immigration appeal on any ground that is inconsistent with treating a State to which this Part applies as a place—

(a) where a person's life and liberty are not threatened by reason of his race, religion, nationality, membership of a particular social group or political opinion,

(b) from which a person will not be sent to another State in contravention of his Convention rights, and

(c) from which a person will not be sent to another State otherwise than in accordance with the Refugee Convention.

PART 3

SECOND LIST OF SAFE COUNTRIES (REFUGEE CONVENTION AND HUMAN RIGHTS (2))

7.—(1) This Part applies to such States as the Secretary of State may by order specify.

(2) An order under this paragraph—

(a) shall be made by statutory instrument, and

(b) shall not be made unless a draft has been laid before and approved by resolution of each House of Parliament.

8.—(1) This paragraph applies for the purposes of the determination by any person, tribunal or court whether a person who has made an asylum claim may be removed—

(a) from the United Kingdom, and

(b) to a State of which he is not a national or citizen.

(2) A State to which this Part applies shall be treated, in so far as relevant to the question mentioned in sub-paragraph (1), as a place—

(a) where a person's life and liberty are not threatened by reason of his race, religion, nationality, membership of a particular social group or political opinion, and

(b) from which a person will not be sent to another State otherwise than in accordance with the Refugee Convention.

9. Section 77 of the Nationality, Immigration and Asylum Act 2002 (c. 41) (no removal while claim for asylum pending) shall not prevent a person who has made a claim for asylum from being removed—

(a) from the United Kingdom, and

(b) to a State to which this Part applies;

provided that the Secretary of State certifies that in his opinion the person is not a national or citizen of the State.

10.—(1) This paragraph applies where the Secretary of State certifies that—

(a) it is proposed to remove a person to a State to which this Part applies, and

(b) in the Secretary of State's opinion the person is not a national or citizen of the State.

(2) . . .

(3) The person may not bring an immigration appeal [from within the United Kingdom] in reliance on an asylum claim which asserts that to remove the person to a specified State to which this Part applies would breach the United Kingdom's obligations under the Refugee Convention.

(4) The person may not bring an immigration appeal [from within the United Kingdom] in reliance on a human rights claim if the Secretary of State certifies that the claim is clearly unfounded; and the Secretary of State shall certify a human rights claim where this paragraph applies unless satisfied that the claim is not clearly unfounded.

Note: Subparagraph (2) omitted and words in square brackets in subparagraphs (3) and (4) substituted by Sch 9 Immigration Act 2014 form a date to be appointed.

11. A person who is outside the United Kingdom may not bring an immigration appeal on any ground that is inconsistent with treating a State to which this Part applies as a place—

(a) where a person's life and liberty are not threatened by reason of his race, religion, nationality, membership of a particular social group or political opinion, and

(b) from which a person will not be sent to another State otherwise than in accordance with the Refugee Convention.

Part 4

Third List of Safe Countries (Refugee Convention Only)

12.—(1) This Part applies to such States as the Secretary of State may by order specify.

(2) An order under this paragraph—

(a) shall be made by statutory instrument, and

(b) shall not be made unless a draft has been laid before and approved by resolution of each House of Parliament.

13.—(1) This paragraph applies for the purposes of the determination by any person, tribunal or court whether a person who has made an asylum claim may be removed—

(a) from the United Kingdom, and

(b) to a State of which he is not a national or citizen.

(2) A State to which this Part applies shall be treated, in so far as relevant to the question mentioned in sub-paragraph (1), as a place—

(a) where a person's life and liberty are not threatened by reason of his race, religion, nationality, membership of a particular social group or political opinion, and

(b) from which a person will not be sent to another State otherwise than in accordance with the Refugee Convention.

14. Section 77 of the Nationality, Immigration and Asylum Act 2002 (c. 41) (no removal while claim for asylum pending) shall not prevent a person who has made a claim for asylum from being removed—

(a) from the United Kingdom, and

(b) to a State to which this Part applies;

provided that the Secretary of State certifies that in his opinion the person is not a national or citizen of the State.

15.—(1) This paragraph applies where the Secretary of State certifies that—

(a) it is proposed to remove a person to a State to which this Part applies, and

(b) in the Secretary of State's opinion the person is not a national or citizen of the State.

(2) . . .

(3) The person may not bring an immigration appeal [from within the United Kingdom] in reliance on an asylum claim which asserts that to remove the person to a specified State to which this Part applies would breach the United Kingdom's obligations under the Refugee Convention.

(4) The person may not bring an immigration appeal [from within the United Kingdom] in reliance on a human rights claim if the Secretary of State certifies that the claim is clearly unfounded.

Note: Subparagraph (2) omitted and words in square brackets in subparagraphs (3) and (4) substituted by Sch 9 Immigration Act 2014 from 20 October 2014 with savings set out in articles 9-11 SI 2014/2771.

16. A person who is outside the United Kingdom may not bring an immigration appeal on any ground that is inconsistent with treating a State to which this Part applies as a place—

(a) where a person's life and liberty are not threatened by reason of his race, religion, nationality, membership of a particular social group or political opinion, and

(b) from which a person will not be sent to another State otherwise than in accordance with the Refugee Convention.

Part 5

Countries Certified as Safe for Individuals

17. This Part applies to a person who has made an asylum claim if the Secretary of State certifies that—

(a) it is proposed to remove the person to a specified State,

(b) in the Secretary of State's opinion the person is not a national or citizen of the specified State, and

(c) in the Secretary of State's opinion the specified State is a place—

(i) where the person's life and liberty will not be threatened by reason of his race, religion, nationality, membership of a particular social group or political opinion, and

(ii) from which the person will not be sent to another State otherwise than in accordance with the Refugee Convention.

18. Where this Part applies to a person section 77 of the Nationality, Immigration and Asylum Act 2002 (c. 41) (no removal while claim for asylum pending) shall not prevent his removal to the State specified under paragraph 17.

19. Where this Part applies to a person—

(a) . . .

(b) he may not bring an immigration appeal [from within the United Kingdom] in reliance on an asylum claim which asserts that to remove the person to the State specified under paragraph 17 would breach the United Kingdom's obligations under the Refugee Convention,

(c) he may not bring an immigration appeal [from within the United Kingdom] in reliance on a human rights claim if the Secretary of State certifies that the claim is clearly unfounded, and

(d) he may not while outside the United Kingdom bring an immigration appeal on any ground that is inconsistent with the opinion certified under paragraph 17(c).

Note: Subparagraph (a) omitted and words in square brackets in subparagraphs (b) and (c) substituted by Sch 9 Immigration Act 2014 from 20 October 2014 with savings set out in articles 9-11 SI 2014/2771.

Part 6

Amendment of Lists

20.—(1) The Secretary of State may by order add a State to the list specified in paragraph 2.

(2) The Secretary of State may by order—

(a) add a State to a list specified under paragraph 7 or 12, or

(b) remove a State from a list specified under paragraph 7 or 12.

21.—(1) An order under paragraph 20(1) or (2)(a)—

(a) shall be made by statutory instrument,

(b) shall not be made unless a draft has been laid before and approved by resolution of each House of Parliament, and

(c) may include transitional provision.

(2) An order under paragraph 20(2)(b)—

(a) shall be made by statutory instrument,

(b) shall be subject to annulment in pursuance of a resolution of either House of Parliament, and

(c) may include transitional provision.

Note: Commencement 1 October 2004 (SI 2004/2523).

Section 47

Schedule 4

Repeals

. . .

Immigration, Asylum and Nationality Act 2006
(2006, c. 13)

Contents

Appeals

Employment

Information

An Act to make provision about immigration, asylum and nationality; and for connected purposes.

[30 March 2006]

Appeals

1. Variation of leave to enter or remain

. . .

Note: Amends Nationality, Immigration and Asylum Act 2002, s 83. Repealed by Sch 9 Immigration Act 2014 from 20 October 2014 with savings set out in articles 9-11 SI 2014/2771.

2. Removal

. . .

Note: Amends Nationality, Immigration and Asylum Act 2002, s 82(2). Repealed by Sch 9 Immigration Act 2014 from 20 October 2014 with savings set out in articles 9-11 SI 2014/2771.

3. Grounds of appeal

. . .

Note: Amends Nationality, Immigration and Asylum Act 2002, s 84(3). Repealed by Sch 9 Immigration Act 2014 from 20 October 2014 with savings set out in articles 9-11 SI 2014/2771.

4. Entry clearance

. . .

Note: Repealed by Sch 9 Immigration Act 2014 from 20 October 2014 with savings set out in articles 9-11 SI 2014/2771.

5. Failure to provide documents

. . .

Note: Amends Nationality, Immigration and Asylum Act 2002, s 88(2). Repealed by Sch 9 Immigration Act 2014 from 20 October 2014 with savings set out in articles 9-11 SI 2014/2771.

6. Refusal of leave to enter

. . .

Note: Amends Nationality, Immigration and Asylum Act 2002, s 89. Repealed by Sch 9 Immigration Act 2014 from 20 October 2014 with savings set out in articles 9-11 SI 2014/2771.

7. Deportation

. . .

Note: Amends Nationality, Immigration and Asylum Act 2002, ss 97, 112.

8. Legal aid

. . .

Note: Amends Nationality, Immigration and Asylum Act 2002, s 103D.

9. Abandonment of appeal

. . .

Note: Amends Nationality, Immigration and Asylum Act 2002, s 104(4).

10. Grants

. . .

Note: Amends Nationality, Immigration and Asylum Act 2002, s 110.

11. Continuation of leave

. . .

Note: Amends Immigration Act 1971, s 3C and Nationality, Immigration and Asylum Act 2002, s 82(3).

12. Asylum and human rights claims: definition

. . .

Note: Amends Nationality, Immigration and Asylum Act 2002, s 113.

13. Appeal from within United Kingdom: certification of unfounded claim

. . .

Note: Amends Nationality, Immigration and Asylum Act 2002, s 94.

14. Consequential amendments

Schedule 1 (which makes amendments consequential on the preceding provisions of this Act) shall have effect.

Note: Commencement 31 August 2006 (SI 2006/2226).

Employment

15. Penalty

(1) It is contrary to this section to employ an adult subject to immigration control if—

(a) he has not been granted leave to enter or remain in the United Kingdom, or

(b) his leave to enter or remain in the United Kingdom—

(i) is invalid,

(ii) has ceased to have effect (whether by reason of curtailment, revocation, cancellation, passage of time or otherwise), or

(iii) is subject to a condition preventing him from accepting the employment.

(2) The Secretary of State may give an employer who acts contrary to this section a notice requiring him to pay a penalty of a specified amount not exceeding the prescribed maximum.

(3) An employer is excused from paying a penalty if he shows that he complied with any prescribed requirements in relation to the employment.

(4) But the excuse in subsection (3) shall not apply to an employer who knew, at any time during the period of the employment, that it was contrary to this section.

(5) The Secretary of State may give a penalty notice without having established whether subsection (3) applies.

(6) A penalty notice must—

(a) state why the Secretary of State thinks the employer is liable to the penalty,

(b) state the amount of the penalty,

(c) specify a date, at least 28 days after the date specified in the notice as the date on which it is given, before which the penalty must be paid,

(d) specify how the penalty must be paid,

(e) explain how the employer may object to the penalty [or make an appeal against it], and

(f) explain how the Secretary of State may enforce the penalty.

(7) An order prescribing requirements for the purposes of subsection (3) may, in particular—

(a) require the production to an employer of a document of a specified description;

(b) require the production to an employer of one document of each of a number of specified descriptions;

(c) require an employer to take specified steps to verify, retain, copy or record the content of a document produced to him in accordance with the order;

(d) require action to be taken before employment begins;

(e) require action to be taken at specified intervals or on specified occasions during the course of employment.

Note: Commencement for the purposes of making an order under subsections (2), (3) and (7), 5 November 2007 (SI 2007/3138), remainder 29 February 2008, but without effect on employment which commenced before that date (SI 2008/310, which sets out transitional provisions). Words in square brackets in subsection (6)(e) inserted by sch 9 Immigration Act 2014 from 28 July 2014 (SI 2014/1820).

16. Objection

(1) This section applies where an employer to whom a penalty notice is given objects on the ground that—

(a) he is not liable to the imposition of a penalty,

(b) he is excused payment by virtue of section 15(3), or

(c) the amount of the penalty is too high.

(2) The employer may give a notice of objection to the Secretary of State.

(3) A notice of objection must—

(a) be in writing,

(b) give the objector's reasons,

(c) be given in the prescribed manner, and

(d) be given before the end of the prescribed period.

(4) Where the Secretary of State receives a notice of objection to a penalty he shall consider it and—

(a) cancel the penalty,

(b) reduce the penalty,

(c) increase the penalty, or

(d) determine to take no action.

(5) Where the Secretary of State considers a notice of objection he shall—

(a) have regard to the code of practice under section 19 (in so far as the objection relates to the amount of the penalty),

(b) inform the objector of his decision before the end of the prescribed period or such longer period as he may agree with the objector,

(c) if he increases the penalty, issue a new penalty notice under section 15, and

(d) if he reduces the penalty, notify the objector of the reduced amount.

Note: Commencement for the purposes of making an order under subsections (3) and (5), 5 November 2007 (SI 2007/3138), remainder 29 February 2008, but without effect on employment which commenced before that date (SI 2008/310, which sets out transitional provisions).

17. Appeal

(1) An employer to whom a penalty notice is given may appeal to the court on the ground that—

(a) he is not liable to the imposition of a penalty,

(b) he is excused payment by virtue of section 15(3), or

(c) the amount of the penalty is too high.

(2) The court may—

(a) allow the appeal and cancel the penalty,

(b) allow the appeal and reduce the penalty, or

(c) dismiss the appeal.

(3) An appeal shall be a re-hearing of the Secretary of State's decision to impose a penalty and shall be determined having regard to—

(a) the code of practice under section 19 that has effect at the time of the appeal (in so far as the appeal relates to the amount of the penalty),

and

(b) any other matters which the court thinks relevant (which may include matters of which the Secretary of State was unaware);

and this subsection has effect despite any provision of rules of court.

[(**4A**) An appeal may be brought only if the employer has given a notice of objection under section 16 and the Secretary of State—

(a) has determined the objection by issuing to the employer the penalty notice (as a result of increasing the penalty under section 16(4)(c)),

(b) has determined the objection by—

(i) reducing the penalty under section 16(4)(b), or

(ii) taking no action under section 16(4)(d), or

(c) has not informed the employer of a decision before the end of the period that applies for the purposes of section 16(5)(b).

(**4B**) An appeal must be brought within the period of 28 days beginning with the relevant date.

(**4C**) Where the appeal is brought under subsection (4A)(a), the relevant date is the date specified in the penalty notice issued in accordance with section 16(5)(c) as the date on which it is given.

(**4D**) Where the appeal is brought under subsection (4A)(b), the relevant date is the date specified in the notice informing the employer of the decision for the purposes of section 16(5)(b) as the date on which it is given.

(**4E**) Where the appeal is brought under subsection (4A)(c), the relevant date is the date on which the period that applies for the purposes of section 16(5)(b) ends.]

(6) In this section 'the court' means—

(a) where the employer has his principal place in England and Wales, [the county court],

(b) where the employer has his principal place of business in Scotland, the sheriff, and

(c) where the employer has his principal place of business in Northern Ireland, a county court.

Note: Commencement 29 February 2008, but without effect on employment which commenced before that date (SI 2008/310, which sets out transitional provisions). Subsections (4)–(5) substituted by s 44 Immigration Act 2014 from 28 July 2014 (SI 2014/1820).

18. Enforcement

[(1) This section applies where a sum is payable to the Secretary of State as a penalty under section 15.

(1A) In England and Wales the penalty is recoverable as if it were payable under an order of the county court.

(1B) In Scotland, the penalty may be enforced in the same manner as an extract registered decree arbitral bearing a warrant for execution issued by the sheriff court of any sheriffdom in Scotland.

(1C) In Northern Ireland the penalty is recoverable as if it were payable under an order of a county court in Northern Ireland.

(1D) Where action is taken under this section for the recovery of a sum payable as a penalty under section 15, the penalty is—

(a) in relation to England and Wales, to be treated for the purposes of section 98 of the Courts Act 2003 (register of judgments and orders etc) as if it were a judgment entered in the county court;

(b) in relation to Northern Ireland, to be treated for the purposes of Article 116 of the Judgments Enforcement (Northern Ireland) Order 1981 (S.I. 1981/226 (N.I. 6)) (register of judgments) as if it were a judgment in respect of which an application has been accepted under Article 22 or 23(1) of that Order.]

(3) Money paid to the Secretary of State by way of penalty shall be paid into the Consolidated Fund.

Note: Commencement 29 February 2008, but without effect on employment which commenced before that date (SI 2008/310, which sets out transitional provisions). Subsections (1)–(2) substituted by s 45 Immigration Act 2014 from 28 July 2014 (SI 2014/1820).

19. Code of practice

(1) The Secretary of State shall issue a code of practice specifying factors to be considered by him in determining the amount of a penalty imposed under section 15.

(2) The code—

(a) shall not be issued unless a draft has been laid before Parliament, and

(b) shall come into force in accordance with provision made by order of the Secretary of State.

(3) The Secretary of State shall from time to time review the code and may revise and re-issue it following a review; and a reference in this section to the code includes a reference to the code as revised.

Note: Commencement 31 August 2006 (SI 2006/2226).

20. Orders

(1) An order of the Secretary of State under section 15, 16 or 19—
(a) may make provision which applies generally or only in specified circumstances,
(b) may make different provision for different circumstances,
(c) may include transitional or incidental provision, and
(d) shall be made by statutory instrument.

(2) An order under section 15(2) may not be made unless a draft has been laid before and approved by resolution of each House of Parliament.

(3) Any other order shall be subject to annulment in pursuance of a resolution of either House of Parliament.

Note: Commencement 5 November 2007 (SI 2007/3138).

21. Offence

(1) A person commits an offence if he employs another ('the employee') knowing that the employee is an adult subject to immigration control and that—
(a) he has not been granted leave to enter or remain in the United Kingdom, or
(b) his leave to enter or remain in the United Kingdom—
(i) is invalid,
(ii) has ceased to have effect (whether by reason of curtailment, revocation, cancellation, passage of time or otherwise), or
(iii) is subject to a condition preventing him from accepting the employment.

(2) A person guilty of an offence under this section shall be liable—
(a) on conviction on indictment—
(i) to imprisonment for a term not exceeding two years,
(ii) to a fine, or
(iii) to both, or
(b) on summary conviction—
(i) to imprisonment for a term not exceeding 12 months in England and Wales or 6 months in Scotland or Northern Ireland,
(ii) to a fine not exceeding the statutory maximum, or
(iii) to both.

(3) An offence under this section shall be treated as—
(a) a relevant offence for the purpose of sections 28B and 28D of the Immigration Act 1971 (c. 77) (search, entry and arrest), and
(b) an offence under Part III of that Act (criminal proceedings) for the purposes of sections 28E, 28G and 28H (search after arrest).

(4) In relation to a conviction occurring before the commencement of section 154(1) of the Criminal Justice Act 2003 (c. 44) (general limit on magistrates' powers to imprison) the reference to 12 months in subsection (2)(b)(i) shall be taken as a reference to 6 months.

Note: Commencement 29 February 2008, but without effect on employment which commenced before that date (SI 2008/310, which sets out transitional provisions).

22. Offence: bodies corporate, &c.

(1) For the purposes of section 21(1) a body (whether corporate or not) shall be treated as knowing a fact about an employee if a person who has responsibility within the body for an aspect of the employment knows the fact.

(2) If an offence under section 21(1) is committed by a body corporate with the consent or connivance of an officer of the body, the officer, as well as the body, shall be treated as having committed the offence.

(3) In subsection (2) a reference to an officer of a body includes a reference to—

(a) a director, manager or secretary,

(b) a person purporting to act as a director, manager or secretary, and

(c) if the affairs of the body are managed by its members, a member.

(4) Where an offence under section 21(1) is committed by a partnership (whether or not a limited partnership) subsection (2) above shall have effect, but as if a reference to an officer of the body were a reference to—

(a) a partner, and

(b) a person purporting to act as a partner.

Note: Commencement 29 February 2008, but without effect on employment which commenced before that date (SI 2008/310, which sets out transitional provisions).

23. Discrimination: code of practice

(1) The Secretary of State shall issue a code of practice specifying what an employer should or should not do in order to ensure that, while avoiding liability to a penalty under section 15 and while avoiding the commission of an offence under section 21, he also avoids contravening—

(a) [the Equality Act 2010, so far as relating to race], or

(b) the Race Relations (Northern Ireland) Order 1997 (S.I. 869 (N.I. 6)).

(2) Before issuing the code the Secretary of State shall—

(a) consult—

(i) the Commission for Equality and Human Rights,

(ii) the Equality Commission for Northern Ireland,

(iii) such bodies representing employers as he thinks appropriate, and

(iv) such bodies representing workers as he thinks appropriate,

(b) publish a draft code (after that consultation),

(c) consider any representations made about the published draft, and

(d) lay a draft code before Parliament (after considering representations under paragraph (c) and with or without modifications to reflect the representations).

(3) The code shall come into force in accordance with provision made by order of the Secretary of State; and an order—

(a) may include transitional provision,

(b) shall be made by statutory instrument, and

(c) shall be subject to annulment in pursuance of a resolution of either House of Parliament.

(4) A breach of the code—

(a) shall not make a person liable to civil or criminal proceedings, but

(b) may be taken into account by a court or tribunal.

(5) The Secretary of State shall from time to time review the code and may revise and re-issue it following a review; and a reference in this section to the code includes a reference to the code as revised.

(6) Until the dissolution of the Commission for Racial Equality, the reference in subsection (2)(a)(i) to the Commission for Equality and Human Rights shall be treated as a reference to the Commission for Racial Equality.

Note: Commencement 31 August 2006 (SI 2006/2226). Words substituted in subsection (1)(a) from 1 October 2010 by the Equality Act 2010, Sch 26, paragraph 86 as inserted by SI 2010/2279.

24. Temporary admission, &c.

Where a person is at large in the United Kingdom by virtue of paragraph 21(1) of Schedule 2 to the Immigration Act 1971 (c. 77) (temporary admission or release from detention)—

(a) he shall be treated for the purposes of sections 15(1) and 21(1) as if he had been granted leave to enter the United Kingdom, and

(b) any restriction as to employment imposed under paragraph 21(2) shall be treated for those purposes as a condition of leave.

Note: Commencement 29 February 2008, but without effect on employment which commenced before that date (SI 2008/310, which sets out transitional provisions).

25. Interpretation

In sections 15 to 24—

(a) 'adult' means a person who has attained the age of 16,

(b) a reference to employment is to employment under a contract of service or apprenticeship, whether express or implied and whether oral or written,

(c) a person is subject to immigration control if under the Immigration Act 1971 he requires leave to enter or remain in the United Kingdom, and

(d) 'prescribed' means prescribed by order of the Secretary of State.

Note: Commencement 5 November 2007 (SI 2007/3138), but without effect on employment which commenced before 29 February 2008 (SI 2008/310, which sets out transitional provisions).

26. Repeal

. . .

Note: Repeals Asylum and Immigration Act 1996, ss 8 and 8A, but without effect on employment which commenced before 29 February 2008 (SI 2008/310), which sets out transitional provisions).

Information

27. Documents produced or found

. . .

Note: Amends paragraph 4, Sch 2 Immigration Act 1971.

28. Fingerprinting

. . .

Note: Amends Immigration and Asylum Act 1999, s 141.

29. Attendance for fingerprinting

. . .

Note: Amends Immigration and Asylum Act 1999, s 142(2).

30. Proof of right of abode

. . .

Note: Amends Immigration Act 1971, s 3(9).

31. Provision of information to immigration officers

. . .

Note: Subsections (1)–(3) amend paragraph 27, Sch 2 Immigration Act 1971, subsection (4) amends s 27 of that Act.

32. Passenger and crew information: police powers

(1) This section applies to ships and aircraft which are—

[(a) arriving, or expected to arrive, at any place in the United Kingdom (whether from a place in the United Kingdom or from outside the United Kingdom), or

(b) leaving, or expected to leave, from any place in the United Kingdom (whether for a place in the United Kingdom or for outside the United Kingdom).]

(2) The owner or agent of a ship or aircraft shall comply with any requirement imposed by a constable of the rank of superintendent or above to provide passenger or service information.

(3) A passenger or member of crew shall provide to the owner or agent of a ship or aircraft any information that he requires for the purpose of complying with a requirement imposed by virtue of subsection (2).

(4) A constable may impose a requirement under subsection (2) only if he thinks it necessary—

(a) in the case of a constable in England, Wales or Northern Ireland, for police purposes, or

(b) in the case of a constable in Scotland, for police purposes which are or relate to reserved matters.

(5) In this section—

(a) 'passenger or service information' means information which is of a kind specified by order of the Secretary of State and which relates to—

(i) passengers,

(ii) members of crew, or

(iii) a voyage or flight,

(b) 'police purposes' has the meaning given by section 21(3) of the Immigration and Asylum Act 1999 (c. 33) (disclosure by Secretary of State),. . .

(c) 'reserved matters' has the same meaning as in the Scotland Act 1998 (c. 46)[, and

(d) 'ship' includes—

(i) every description of vessel used in navigation, and

(ii) hovercraft.]

(6) A requirement imposed under subsection (2)—

(a) must be in writing,

(b) may apply generally or only to one or more specified ships or aircraft,

(c) must specify a period, not exceeding six months and beginning with the date on which it is imposed, during which it has effect,

(d) must state—

(i) the information required, and

(ii) the date or time by which it is to be provided.

(7) The Secretary of State may make an order specifying a kind of information under subsection (5)(a) only if satisfied that the nature of the information is such that there are likely to be circumstances in which it can be required under subsection (2) without breaching Convention rights (within the meaning of the Human Rights Act 1998 (c. 42)).

(8) An order under subsection (5)(a)—

(a) may apply generally or only to specified cases or circumstances,

(b) may make different provision for different cases or circumstances,

(c) may specify the form and manner in which information is to be provided,

(d) shall be made by statutory instrument, and

(e) shall be subject to annulment in pursuance of a resolution of either House of Parliament.

Note: Commencement for the purposes of making an order under subsection (5)(a), 5 November 2007 (SI 2007/3138), remainder 1 March 2008 (SI 2007/3580). Subsection (1)(a) and (b) substituted and subsection (5)(d) inserted and word omitted from subsection (5)(c) by Police and Justice Act 2006, s 14, Schedule 15 from a date to be appointed. Section 32 has effect in a form modified by and in circumstances specified by the Channel Tunnel (International Arrangements) Order (SI 1993/1813) as amended by SIs 1994/1405, 2000/913, 2001/178, 2001/3707, 2006/1003 and 2007/3759.

33. Freight information: police powers

(1) This section applies to ships, aircraft and vehicles which are—

(a) arriving, or expected to arrive, in the United Kingdom, or

(b) leaving, or expected to leave, the United Kingdom.

(2) If a constable of the rank of superintendent or above requires a person specified in subsection (3) to provide freight information he shall comply with the requirement.

(3) The persons referred to in subsection (2) are—

(a) in the case of a ship or aircraft, the owner or agent,

(b) in the case of a vehicle, the owner or hirer, and

(c) in any case, persons responsible for the import or export of the freight into or from the United Kingdom.

(4) A constable may impose a requirement under subsection (2) only if he thinks it necessary—

(a) in the case of a constable in England, Wales or Northern Ireland, for police purposes, or

(b) in the case of a constable in Scotland, for police purposes which are or relate to reserved matters.

(5) In this section—

(a) 'freight information' means information which is of a kind specified by order of the Secretary of State and which relates to freight carried,

(b) 'police purposes' has the meaning given by section 21(3) of the Immigration and Asylum Act 1999 (c. 33) (disclosure by Secretary of State), and

(c) 'reserved matters' has the same meaning as in the Scotland Act 1998 [, and

(d) 'ship' includes—

(i) every description of vessel used in navigation, and

(ii) hovercraft.]

(6) A requirement imposed under subsection (2)—

(a) must be in writing,

(b) may apply generally or only to one or more specified ships, aircraft or vehicles,

(c) must specify a period, not exceeding six months and beginning with the date on which it is imposed, during which it has effect, and

(d) must state—

(i) the information required, and

(ii) the date or time by which it is to be provided.

(7) The Secretary of State may make an order specifying a kind of information under subsection (5)(a) only if satisfied that the nature of the information is such that there are likely to be circumstances in which it can be required under subsection (2) without breaching Convention rights (within the meaning of the Human Rights Act 1998 (c. 42)).

(8) An order under subsection (5)(a)—

(a) may apply generally or only to specified cases or circumstances,

(b) may make different provision for different cases or circumstances,

(c) may specify the form and manner in which the information is to be provided,

(d) shall be made by statutory instrument, and

(e) shall be subject to annulment in pursuance of a resolution of either House of Parliament.

Note: Commencement for the purposes of making an order under subsection (5)(a) 1 April 2008 (SI 2008/310). Subsection (5)(d) inserted and word omitted from subsection (5)(c) by Police and Justice Act 2006 s 14, Schedule 15 from a date to be appointed.

34. Offence

(1) A person commits an offence if without reasonable excuse he fails to comply with a requirement imposed under section 32(2) or (3) or 33(2).

(2) But—

(a) a person who fails without reasonable excuse to comply with a requirement imposed under section 32(2) or 33(2) by a constable in England and Wales or Northern Ireland otherwise than in relation to a reserved matter (within the meaning of the Scotland Act 1998 (c. 46)) shall not be treated as having committed the offence in Scotland (but has committed the offence in England and Wales or Northern Ireland), and

(b) a person who fails without reasonable excuse to comply with a requirement which is imposed under section 32(3) for the purpose of complying with a requirement to which paragraph (a) applies—

(i) shall not be treated as having committed the offence in Scotland, but

(ii) shall be treated as having committed the offence in England and Wales or Northern Ireland.

(3) A person who is guilty of an offence under subsection (1) shall be liable on summary conviction to—

(a) imprisonment for a term not exceeding 51 weeks in England and Wales or 6 months in Scotland or Northern Ireland,

(b) a fine not exceeding level 4 on the standard scale, or

(c) both.

(4) In relation to a conviction occurring before the commencement of section 281(5) of the Criminal Justice Act 2003 (c. 44) (51 week maximum term of sentences) the reference to 51 weeks in subsection (2)(a) shall be taken as a reference to three months.

Note: Commencement 1 March 2008 (SI 2007/3580). Section 34 has effect in a form modified by and in circumstances specified by the Channel Tunnel (International Arrangements) Order (SI 1993/1813) as amended by SIs 1994/1405, 2000/913, 2001/178, 2001/3707, 2006/1003 and 2007/3759.

35. Power of Revenue and Customs to obtain information

. . .

Note: Amends Customs and Excise Management Act 1979, s 35.

36. Duty to share information

(1) This section applies to—

[(a) designated customs officials,

(aa) immigration officers,

(ab) the Secretary of State in so far as the Secretary of State has general customs functions,

(ac) the Secretary of State in so far as the Secretary of State has functions relating to immigration, asylum or nationality,

(ad) the Director of Border Revenue and any person exercising functions of the Director,]

(b) a chief officer of police, and

(c) Her Majesty's Revenue and Customs.

(2) The persons specified in subsection (1) shall share information to which subsection (4) applies and which is obtained or held by them in the course of their functions to the extent that the information is likely to be of use for—

(a) immigration purposes,

(b) police purposes, or

(c) Revenue and Customs purposes.

(3) But a chief officer of police in Scotland shall share information under subsection (2) only to the extent that it is likely to be of use for—

(a) immigration purposes,

(b) police purposes, in so far as they are or relate to reserved matters within the meaning of the Scotland Act 1998, or

(c) Revenue and Customs purposes other than the prosecution of crime.

(4) This subsection applies to information which—

(a) is obtained or held in the exercise of a power specified by the Secretary of State and the Treasury jointly by order and relates to—

(i) passengers on a ship or aircraft,

(ii) crew of a ship or aircraft,

(iii) freight on a ship or aircraft, or

(iv) flights or voyages, or

(b) relates to such other matters in respect of travel or freight as the Secretary of State and the Treasury may jointly specify by order.

(5) The Secretary of State and the Treasury may make an order under subsection (4) which has the effect of requiring information to be shared only if satisfied that—

(a) the sharing is likely to be of use for—

(i) immigration purposes,

(ii) police purposes, or

(iii) Revenue and Customs purposes, and

(b) the nature of the information is such that there are likely to be circumstances in which it can be shared under subsection (2) without breaching Convention rights (within the meaning of the Human Rights Act 1998 (c. 42)).

(6) Information shared in accordance with subsection (2)—

(a) shall be made available to each of the persons [or descriptions of persons] specified in subsection (1), and

(b) may be used for immigration purposes, police purposes or Revenue and Customs purposes (regardless of its source).

(7) An order under subsection (4) may not specify—

(a) a power of Her Majesty's Revenue and Customs if or in so far as it relates to a matter to which section 7 of the Commissioners for Revenue and Customs Act 2005 (c. 11) (former Inland Revenue matters) applies, or

(b) a matter to which that section applies.

(8) An order under subsection (4)—

(a) shall be made by statutory instrument, and

(b) may not be made unless a draft has been laid before and approved by resolution of each House of Parliament.

(9) In this section—

'chief officer of police' means—

(a) in England and Wales, the chief officer of police for a police area specified in section 1 of the Police Act 1996 (c. 16),

(b) in Scotland, the chief constable of a police force maintained under the Police (Scotland) Act 1967 (c. 77), and

(c) in Northern Ireland, the chief constable of the Police Service of Northern Ireland,

['designated customs official' and 'general customs function' have the meanings given by Part 1 of the Borders, Citizenship and Immigration Act 2009,]

'immigration purposes' has the meaning given by section 20(3) of the Immigration and Asylum Act 1999 (c. 33) (disclosure to Secretary of State),

'police purposes' has the meaning given by section 21(3) of that Act (disclosure by Secretary of State), and

'Revenue and Customs purposes' means those functions of Her Majesty's Revenue and Customs specified in section 21(6) of that Act.

(10) This section has effect despite any restriction on the purposes for which information may be disclosed or used.

Note: Commencement for the purposes of making an order under subsection (4), 5 November 2007 (SI 2007/3138), remainder 1 March 2008 (SI 2007/3580). Subsection (1)(a) substituted and words in square brackets in subsections (6) and (9) inserted by s 21 Borders, Citizenship and Immigration Act 21 July 2009, s 58(1). There is a prospective insertion of a definition, the definition of 'ship': see Police and Justice Act 2006 s 14(4). Section 36 has effect in a form modified by and in circumstances specified by the Channel Tunnel (International Arrangements) Order (SI 1993/1813) as amended by SIs 1994/1405, 2000/913, 2001/178, 2001/3707, 2006/1003 and 2007/3759.

37. Information sharing: code of practice

(1) The Secretary of State and the Treasury shall jointly issue one or more codes of practice about—

(a) the use of information shared in accordance with section 36(2), and

(b) the extent to which, or form or manner in which, shared information is to be made available in accordance with section 36(6).

(2) A code—

(a) shall not be issued unless a draft has been laid before Parliament, and

(b) shall come into force in accordance with provision made by order of the Secretary of State and the Treasury jointly.

(3) The Secretary of State and the Treasury shall jointly from time to time review a code and may revise and re-issue it following a review; and subsection (2) shall apply to a revised code.

(4) An order under subsection (2)—

(a) shall be made by statutory instrument, and

(b) shall be subject to annulment in pursuance of a resolution of either House of Parliament.

Note: Commencement for the purposes of laying a draft code before Parliament and making an order under subsection (2), 5 November 2007 (SI 2007/3138), remainder 1 March 2008 (SI 2007/3580). Section 37 has effect in a form modified by and in circumstances specified by the Channel Tunnel (International Arrangements) Order (SI 1993/1813) as amended by SIs 1994/1405, 2000/913, 2001/178, 2001/3707, 2006/1003 and 2007/3759.

38. . . .

Note: Commencement for the purposes of making an order under subsection (4) 5 November 2007 (SI 2007/3138), remainder 1 March 2008 (SI 2007/3580). Revoked by Sch 1 Counter-Terrorism Act 2008 from 24 December 2008, SI 2008/3296.

39. Disclosure to law enforcement agencies

(1) A chief officer of police may disclose information obtained in accordance with section 32 or 33 to—

(a) the States of Jersey police force;

(b) the salaried police force of the Island of Guernsey;

(c) the Isle of Man constabulary;

(d) any other foreign law enforcement agency.

(2) In subsection (1) 'foreign law enforcement agency' means a person outside the United Kingdom with functions similar to functions of—

(a) a police force in the United Kingdom, or

(b) the [National Crime Agency]

(3) In subsection (1) 'chief officer of police' means—

(a) in England and Wales, the chief officer of police for a police area specified in section 1 of the Police Act 1996,

(b) in Scotland, the chief constable of [the Police Service of Scotland], a police force maintained under the Police (Scotland) Act 1967, and

(c) in Northern Ireland, the chief constable of the Police Service of Northern Ireland.

Note: Commencement 1 March 2008 (SI 2007/3580). Section 39 has effect in a form modified by and in circumstances specified by the Channel Tunnel (International Arrangements) Order (SI 1993/1813) as amended by SIs 1994/1405, 2000/913, 2001/178, 2001/3707, 2006/1003 and 2007/3759. Words in square brackets in subsection (2)(b) substituted by Crime and Courts Act 2013 Sch 8 from 7 October 2013 SI 2013/1682. Words in square brackets in subsection (3)(b) substituted from 1 April 2013 SI 2013/602.

40. Searches: contracting out

(1) An authorised person may, in accordance with arrangements made under this section, search a searchable ship, aircraft, vehicle or other thing for the purpose of satisfying himself whether there are individuals whom an immigration officer might wish to examine under paragraph 2 of Schedule 2 to the Immigration Act 1971 (c. 77) (control of entry: administrative provisions).

(2) For the purposes of subsection (1)—

(a) 'authorised' means authorised for the purpose of this section by the Secretary of State, and

(b) a ship, aircraft, vehicle or other thing is 'searchable' if an immigration officer could search it under paragraph 1(5) of that Schedule.

(3) The Secretary of State may authorise a specified class of constable for the purpose of this section.

(4) The Secretary of State may, with the consent of the Commissioners for Her Majesty's Revenue and Customs, authorise a specified class of officers of Revenue and Customs for the purpose of this section.

(5) The Secretary of State may authorise a person other than a constable or officer of Revenue and Customs for the purpose of this section only if—

(a) the person applies to be authorised, and

(b) the Secretary of State thinks that the person is—

(i) fit and proper for the purpose, and

(ii) suitably trained.

(6) The Secretary of State—

(a) may make arrangements for the exercise by authorised constables of the powers under subsection (1),

(b) may make arrangements with the Commissioners for Her Majesty's Revenue and Customs for the exercise by authorised officers of Revenue and Customs of the powers under subsection (1), and

(c) may make arrangements with one or more persons for the exercise by authorised persons other than constables and officers of Revenue and Customs of the power under subsection (1).

(7) Where in the course of a search under this section an authorised person discovers an individual whom he thinks an immigration officer might wish to examine under paragraph 2 of that Schedule, the authorised person may—

(a) search the individual for the purpose of discovering whether he has with him anything of a kind that might be used—

(i) by him to cause physical harm to himself or another,

(ii) by him to assist his escape from detention, or

(iii) to establish information about his identity, nationality or citizenship or about his journey;

(b) retain, and as soon as is reasonably practicable deliver to an immigration officer, anything of a kind described in paragraph (a) found on a search under that paragraph;

(c) detain the individual, for a period which is as short as is reasonably necessary and which does not exceed three hours, pending the arrival of an immigration officer to whom the individual is to be delivered;

(d) take the individual, as speedily as is reasonably practicable, to a place for the purpose of delivering him to an immigration officer there;

(e) use reasonable force for the purpose of doing anything under paragraphs (a) to (d).

(8) Despite the generality of subsection (7)—

(a) an individual searched under that subsection may not be required to remove clothing other than an outer coat, a jacket or a glove (but he may be required to open his mouth), and

(b) an item may not be retained under subsection (7)(b) if it is subject to legal privilege—

(i) in relation to a search carried out in England and Wales, within the meaning of the Police and Criminal Evidence Act 1984 (c. 60),

(ii) in relation to a search carried out in Scotland, within the meaning of section 412 of the Proceeds of Crime Act 2002 (c. 29), and

(iii) in relation to a search carried out in Northern Ireland, within the meaning of the Police and Criminal Evidence (Northern Ireland) Order 1989 (SI 1989/1341 (N.I. 12)).

Note: Commencement 31 August 2006 (SI 2006/2226).

41. Section 40: supplemental

(1) Arrangements under section 40(6)(c) must include provision for the appointment of a Crown servant to—

(a) monitor the exercise of powers under that section by authorised persons (other than constables or officers of Revenue and Customs),

(b) inspect from time to time the way in which the powers are being exercised by authorised persons (other than constables or officers of Revenue and Customs), and

(c) investigate and report to the Secretary of State about any allegation made against an authorised person (other than a constable or officer of Revenue and Customs) in respect of anything done or not done in the purported exercise of a power under that section.

(2) The authorisation for the purpose of section 40 of a constable or officer of Revenue and Customs or of a class of constable or officer of Revenue and Customs—

(a) may be revoked, and

(b) shall have effect, unless revoked, for such period as shall be specified (whether by reference to dates or otherwise) in the authorisation.

(3) The authorisation of a person other than a constable or officer of Revenue and Customs for the purpose of section 40—

(a) may be subject to conditions,

(b) may be suspended or revoked by the Secretary of State by notice in writing to the authorised person, and

(c) shall have effect, unless suspended or revoked, for such period as shall be specified (whether by reference to dates or otherwise) in the authorisation.

(4) A class may be specified for the purposes of section 40(3) or (4) by reference to—

(a) named individuals,

(b) the functions being exercised by a person,

(c) the location or circumstances in which a person is exercising functions, or

(d) any other matter.

(5) An individual or article delivered to an immigration officer under section 40 shall be treated as if discovered by the immigration officer on a search under Schedule 2 to the Immigration Act 1971 (c. 77).

(6) A person commits an offence if he—

(a) absconds from detention under section 40(7)(c),

(b) absconds while being taken to a place under section 40(7)(d) or having been taken to a place in accordance with that paragraph but before being delivered to an immigration officer,

(c) obstructs an authorised person in the exercise of a power under section 40, or

(d) assaults an authorised person who is exercising a power under section 40.

(7) But a person does not commit an offence under subsection (6) by doing or failing to do anything in respect of an authorised person who is not readily identifiable—

(a) as a constable or officer of Revenue and Customs, or

(b) as an authorised person (whether by means of a uniform or badge or otherwise).

(8) A person guilty of an offence under subsection (6) shall be liable on summary conviction to—

(a) imprisonment for a term not exceeding 51 weeks, in the case of a conviction in England and Wales, or six months, in the case of a conviction in Scotland or Northern Ireland,

(b) a fine not exceeding level 5 on the standard scale, or

(c) both.

(9) In relation to a conviction occurring before the commencement of section 281(5) of the Criminal Justice Act 2003 (c. 44) (51 week maximum term of sentences) the reference in subsection (8)(a) to 51 weeks shall be treated as a reference to six months.

Note: Commencement 31 August 2006 (SI 2006/2226).

42. Information: embarking passengers

. . .

Note: Amends Sch 2 Immigration Act 1971 (c. 77).

Claimants and applicants

43. Accommodation

(1) . . .

(2) . . .

(3) . . .

(4) . . .

(5) A tenancy is not a Scottish secure tenancy (within the meaning of the Housing (Scotland) Act 2001 (asp 10)) if it is granted in order to provide accommodation under section 4 of the Immigration and Asylum Act 1999 (accommodation).

(6) A tenancy which would be a Scottish secure tenancy but for subsection (4) becomes a Scottish secure tenancy if the landlord notifies the tenant that it is to be regarded as such.

(7) . . .

Note: Subsections (1) and (2) amend Immigration and Asylum Act 1999, s 99. Subsection (3) amends s 118 and subsection 7 amends s 4 of that Act. Subsection (4) amends Protection from Eviction Act 1977, s 3A; paragraph 3A, Sch 2 Housing (Northern Ireland Order 1983 (SI 1983/1118, N.I. 15); Rent (Scotland) Act 1984, s 23A; paragraph 4A, Sch 1 Housing Act 1985; paragraph 1B, Sch 4 Housing (Scotland) Act 1988; paragraph 12A, Sch 1 Housing Act 1988. Commenced 16 June 2006 (SI 2006/1497).

44. Failed asylum-seekers: withdrawal of support

(1) The Secretary of State may by order provide for paragraph 7A of Schedule 3 to the Nationality, Immigration and Asylum Act 2002 (c. 41) (failed asylum seeker with family: withdrawal of support) to cease to have effect.

(2) An order under subsection (1) shall also provide for the following to cease to have effect—

(a) section 9(1), (2) and (4) of the Asylum and Immigration (Treatment of Claimants, etc.) Act 2004 (c. 19) (which insert paragraph 7A of Schedule 3 and make consequential provision), and

(b) in section 9(3)(a) and (b) of that Act, the words 'other than paragraph 7A.'

(3) An order under subsection (1)—

(a) may include transitional provision,

(b) shall be made by statutory instrument, and

(c) shall be subject to annulment in pursuance of a resolution of either House of Parliament.

Note: Commencement at a date to be appointed.

45. Integration loans

. . .

Note: Amends Asylum and Immigration (Treatment of Claimants, etc.) Act 2004, s 13.

46. Inspection of detention facilities

. . .

Note: Amends Prison Act 1952, ss 5 and 5A.

47. Removal: persons with statutorily extended leave

Note: Subsection (6) amends Nationality, Immigration and Asylum Act 2002, s 82, subsection (7) amends s 92 and subsection (8) amends s 94(1A) of that Act. Commenced 1 April 2008 (SI 2008/310). Repealed by Sch 9 Immigration Act 2014 from 20 October 2014 with savings set out in articles 9-11 SI 2014/2771.

48. Removal: cancellation of leave

. . .

Note: Amends Immigration and Asylum Act 1999, s 10(8). Repealed by Sch 9 Immigration Act 2014 from 20 October 2014 with savings set out in SI 2014/2771 articles 9-11.

49. Capacity to make nationality application

. . .

Note: Amends British Nationality Act 1981, s 44.

50. Procedure

(1) Rules under section 3 of the Immigration Act 1971 (c. 77)—

(a) may require a specified procedure to be followed in making or pursuing an application or claim (whether or not under those rules or any other enactment),

(b) may, in particular, require the use of a specified form and the submission of specified information or documents,

(c) may make provision about the manner in which a fee is to be paid, and

(d) may make provision for the consequences of failure to comply with a requirement under paragraph (a), (b) or (c).

(2) In respect of any application or claim in connection with immigration (whether or not under the rules referred to in subsection (1) or any other enactment) the Secretary of State—

(a) may require the use of a specified form,

(b) may require the submission of specified information or documents, and

(c) may direct the manner in which a fee is to be paid; and the rules referred to in subsection (1) may provide for the consequences of failure to comply with a requirement under paragraph (a), (b) or (c).

(3) . . .

(4) . . .

(5) . . .

(6) . . .

Note: Subsection (3) repeals Immigration Act 1971, s 31A and Asylum and Immigration (Treatment of Claimants etc) Act 2004, s 25. Subsection (4) amends British Nationality Act 1981, s 41. Subsection (5) amends Nationality, Immigration and Asylum Act 2002, s 10. Subsection (6) repeals paragraph 2(3), Sch 23 Civil Partnership Act 2004. Commencement 31 January 2007 (SI 2007/182).

51. Fees

Note: Commencement 31 January 2007 (SI 2007/182). Repealed by Sch 9 Immigration Act 2014 from 15 December 2014 (SI 2014/2771).

52. Fees: supplemental

Note: Subsections (1)–(6) commenced 31 January 2007, (SI 2007/182), remainder 2 April 2007 (SI 2007/1109). Repealed by Sch 9 Immigration Act 2014 from 15 December 2014 (SI 2014/2771).

Miscellaneous

53. Arrest pending deportation

. . .

Note: Amends paragraph 2(4), Sch 3 Immigration Act 1971.

54. Refugee Convention: construction

(1) In the construction and application of Article 1(F)(c) of the Refugee Convention the reference to acts contrary to the purposes and principles of the United Nations shall be taken as including, in particular—

(a) acts of committing, preparing or instigating terrorism (whether or not the acts amount to an actual or inchoate offence), and

(b) acts of encouraging or inducing others to commit, prepare or instigate terrorism (whether or not the acts amount to an actual or inchoate offence).

(2) In this section—

'the Refugee Convention' means the Convention relating to the Status of Refugees done at Geneva on 28 July 1951, and

'terrorism' has the meaning given by section 1 of the Terrorism Act 2000 (c. 11).

Note: Commencement 31 August 2006 (SI 2006/2226).

55. Refugee Convention: certification

(1) This section applies to an asylum appeal where the Secretary of State issues a certificate that the appellant is not entitled to the protection of Article 33(1) of the Refugee Convention because—

(a) Article 1(F) applies to him (whether or not he would otherwise be entitled to protection), or

(b) Article 33(2) applies to him on grounds of national security (whether or not he would otherwise be entitled to protection).

(2) In this section—

(a) 'asylum appeal' means an appeal—

(i) which is brought under section 82, . . . of the Nationality, Immigration and Asylum Act 2002 (c. 41) or section 2 of the Special Immigration Appeals Commission Act 1997 (c. 68), and

[(ii) which is brought on the ground mentioned in section 84(1)(a) or (3)(a) of that Act (breach of United Kingdom's obligations under the Refugee Convention);]

(b) 'the Refugee Convention' means the Convention relating to the Status of Refugees done at Geneva on 28 July 1951.

(3) The [First-tier Tribunal] or the Special Immigration Appeals Commission must begin substantive deliberations on the asylum appeal by considering the statements in the Secretary of State's certificate.

(4) If the Tribunal or Commission agrees with those statements it must dismiss such part of the asylum appeal as amounts to an asylum claim (before considering any other aspect of the case).

(5) Section 72(10)(a) of the Nationality, Immigration and Asylum Act 2002 (serious criminal: Tribunal or Commission to begin by considering certificate) shall have effect subject to subsection (3) above.

[(5A) Subsections (3) and (4) also apply in relation to the Upper Tribunal when it acts under section 12(2)(b)(ii) of the Tribunals, Courts and Enforcement Act 2007.]

(6) . . .

Note: Subsection (6) repeals Anti-terrorism, Crime and Security Act 2001, s 33. Commencement 31 August 2006 (SI 2006/2226). Words in square brackets in subsection (3) substituted and subsection (5A) inserted from 15 February 2010 (SI 2010/21). In subsection (2) words omitted and (2)(a)(ii) substituted by Sch 9 Immigration Act 2014 from 20 October 2014 with savings set out in articles 9-11 SI 2014/2771.

56. Deprivation of citizenship

(1) . . .

(2) . . .

Note: Subsection (1) amends the British Nationality Act 1981, s 42(2) subsection (2) amends s 40A of that Act.

57. Deprivation of right of abode

(1) . . .

(2) . . .

Note: Subsection (1) amends Immigration Act 1971, s 2 subsection (2) amends Nationality, Immigration and Asylum Act 2002, s 82, repealed by Sch 9 Immigration Act 2014 from 20 October 2014 with savings set out in articles 9-11 SI 2014/2771.

58. . . .

Note: Commencement from 4 December 2006, but without effect in relation to any application under the provisions listed in subsection (2) which was made before that date (SI 2006/2838). Section 50(8) of the British Nationality Act 1981 applies for the purpose of this section. Revoked by Schedule Borders, Citizenship and Immigration Act 2009 from 13 January 2010 (SI 2009/2731).

59. Detained persons: national minimum wage

(1) . . .

(2) . . .

Note: Subsection (1) amends Immigration and Asylum Act 1999, s 153. Subsection (2) amends National Minimum Wage Act 1998, s 45A.

General

60. Money

There shall be paid out of money provided by Parliament—

(a) any expenditure of the Secretary of State in connection with this Act, and

(b) any increase attributable to this Act in sums payable under another enactment out of money provided by Parliament.

Note: Commenced 16 June 2006 (SI 2006/1497).

61. Repeals

Schedule 3 (repeals) shall have effect.

Note: Commenced with regard to British Nationality Act 1981, s 40A(3) 16 June 2006 (SI 2006/1497). Remainder from 31 August 2006 (SI 2006/2226).

62. Commencement

(1) The preceding provisions of this Act shall come into force in accordance with provision made by order of the Secretary of State.

(2) An order under subsection (1)—

(a) may make provision generally or only for specified purposes,

(b) may make different provision for different purposes,

(c) may include transitional or incidental provision or savings, and

(d) shall be made by statutory instrument.

63. Extent

(1) This Act extends to—

(a) England and Wales,

(b) Scotland, and

(c) Northern Ireland.

(2) But—

(a) an amendment by this Act of another Act has the same extent as that Act or as the relevant part of that Act (ignoring extent by virtue of an Order in Council), and

(b) a provision of this Act shall, so far as it relates to nationality, have the same extent as the British Nationality Act 1981 (c. 61) (disregarding excepted provisions under section 53(7) of that Act).

(3) Her Majesty may by Order in Council direct that a provision of this Act is to extend, with or without modification or adaptation, to—

(a) any of the Channel Islands;

(b) the Isle of Man.

[(3A) In subsection (3), the reference to this Act includes—

(a) a reference to this Act as it has effect with the amendments and repeals made in it by the Police and Justice Act 2006, and

(b) a reference to this Act as it has effect without those amendments and repeals.]

(4) Subsection (3) does not apply in relation to the extension to a place of a provision which extends there by virtue of subsection (2)(b).

Note: Commencement 30 March 2006, s 62 (Royal Assent). Subsection (3A) inserted by Police and Justice Act 2006 s54 from 8 November 2006 (Royal Assent).

64. Citation

(1) This Act may be cited as the Immigration, Asylum and Nationality Act 2006.

(2) . . .

(3) . . .

(4) . . .

Note: Subsection (2) repealed from 30 October 2007 (s 61 UK Borders Act 2007). Subsection (3) repeals the definition of the Immigration Acts in Immigration Act 1971, s 32(5) Immigration and Asylum Act 1999, s 167(1) Nationality, Immigration and Asylum Act 2002, s 158 and Asylum and Immigration (Treatment of Claimants, etc) Act 2004, s 44. Subsection (4) amends Sch 1 Interpretation Act 1978. Commencement 30 March 2006, s 62 (Royal Assent).

SCHEDULES

Section 14

SCHEDULE 1

IMMIGRATION AND ASYLUM APPEALS: CONSEQUENTIAL AMENDMENTS

. . .

Section 52

SCHEDULE 2

FEES: CONSEQUENTIAL AMENDMENTS

. . .

Section 61

SCHEDULE 3

REPEALS

. . .

UK Borders Act 2007

(2007, c. 30)

Contents

An Act to make provision about immigration and asylum; and for connected purposes.

[30 October 2007]

Detention at ports

1. Designated immigration officers

(1) The Secretary of State may designate immigration officers for the purposes of section 2.

(2) The Secretary of State may designate only officers who the Secretary of State thinks are—

(a) fit and proper for the purpose, and

(b) suitably trained.

(3) A designation—

(a) may be permanent or for a specified period, and

(b) may (in either case) be revoked.

Note: Commencement 31 January 2008 (SI 2008/99).

2. Detention

(1) A designated immigration officer at a port in England, Wales or Northern Ireland may detain an individual if the immigration officer thinks that the individual—

(a) may be liable to arrest by a constable under section 24(1), (2) or (3) of the Police and Criminal Evidence Act 1984 or Article 26(1), (2) or (3) of the Police and Criminal Evidence (Northern Ireland) Order 1989 (S.I. 1989/1341 (N.I. 12)), or

(b) is subject to a warrant for arrest.

[(**1A**) A designated immigration officer at a port in Scotland may detain an individual if the immigration officer thinks that the individual is subject to a warrant for arrest.]

(2) A designated immigration officer who detains an individual—

(a) must arrange for a constable to attend as soon as is reasonably practicable,

(b) may search the individual for, and retain, anything that might be used to assist escape or to cause physical injury to the individual or another person,

(c) must retain anything found on a search which the immigration officer thinks may be evidence of the commission of an offence, and

(d) must, when the constable arrives, deliver to the constable the individual and anything retained on a search.

(3) An individual may not be detained under this section for longer than three hours.

(4) A designated immigration officer may use reasonable force for the purpose of exercising a power under this section.

(5) Where an individual whom a designated immigration officer has detained or attempted to detain under this section leaves the port, a designated immigration officer may—

(a) pursue the individual, and

(b) return the individual to the port.

(6) Detention under this section shall be treated as detention under the Immigration Act 1971 for the purposes of Part 8 of the Immigration and Asylum Act 1999 (detained persons).

Note: Commencement 31 January 2008 (SI 2008/99). Subsection (1A) inserted by s 52 Borders, Citizenship and Immigration Act 2009 from a date to be appointed.

3. Enforcement

(1) An offence is committed by a person who—

(a) absconds from detention under section 2,

(b) assaults an immigration officer exercising a power under section 2, or

(c) obstructs an immigration officer in the exercise of a power under section 2.

(2) A person guilty of an offence under subsection (1)(a) or (b) shall be liable on summary conviction to—

(a) imprisonment for a term not exceeding 51 weeks,

(b) a fine not exceeding level 5 on the standard scale, or

(c) both.

(3) A person guilty of an offence under subsection (1)(c) shall be liable on summary conviction to—

(a) imprisonment for a term not exceeding 51 weeks,

(b) a fine not exceeding level 3 on the standard scale, or

(c) both.

(4) In the application of this section to Northern Ireland—

(a) the reference in subsection (2)(a) to 51 weeks shall be treated as a reference to six months, and

(b) the reference in subsection (3)(a) to 51 weeks shall be treated as a reference to one month.

[(**4A**) In the application of this section to Scotland, the references in subsections (2)(a) and (3)(a) to 51 weeks shall be treated as references to 12 months.]

(5) In relation to an offence committed before the commencement of section 281(5) of the Criminal Justice Act 2003 (51 week maximum term of sentences)—

(a) the reference in subsection (2)(a) to 51 weeks shall be treated as a reference to six months, and

(b) the reference in subsection (3)(a) to 51 weeks shall be treated as a reference to one month.

Note: Commencement 31 January 2008 (SI 2008/99). Subsection (4A) inserted by s 52 Borders, Citizenship and Immigration Act 2009 from a date to be appointed.

4. Interpretation: 'port'

(1) In section 2 'port' includes an airport and a hoverport.

(2) A place shall be treated for the purposes of that section as a port in relation to an individual if a designated immigration officer believes that the individual—

(a) has gone there for the purpose of embarking on a ship or aircraft, or

(b) has arrived there on disembarking from a ship or aircraft.

Note: Commencement 31 January 2008 (SI 2008/99).

Biometric registration

5. Registration regulations

(1) The Secretary of State may make regulations—

(a) requiring a person subject to immigration control to apply for the issue of a document recording biometric information (a 'biometric immigration document');

(b) requiring a biometric immigration document to be used—

(i) for specified immigration purposes,

(ii) in connection with specified immigration procedures, or

(iii) in specified circumstances, where a question arises about a person's status in relation to nationality or immigration;

(c) requiring a person who produces a biometric immigration document by virtue of paragraph (b) to provide information for comparison with information provided in connection with the application for the document.

(2) Regulations under subsection (1)(a) may, in particular—

(a) apply generally or only to a specified class of persons subject to immigration control (for example, persons making or seeking to make a specified kind of application for immigration purposes);

(b) specify the period within which an application for a biometric immigration document must be made;

(c) make provision about the issue of biometric immigration documents;

(d) make provision about the content of biometric immigration documents (which may include non-biometric information);

(e) make provision permitting a biometric immigration document to be combined with another document;

(f) make provision for biometric immigration documents to begin to have effect, and cease to have effect, in accordance with the regulations;

(g) require a person who acquires a biometric immigration document, without the consent of the person to whom it relates or of the Secretary of State, to surrender it to the Secretary of State as soon as is reasonably practicable;

(h) permit the Secretary of State to require the surrender of a biometric immigration document in other specified circumstances;

(i) permit the Secretary of State on issuing a biometric immigration document to require the surrender of other documents connected with immigration or nationality.

(3) Regulations under subsection (1)(a) may permit the Secretary of State to cancel a biometric immigration document—

(a) if the Secretary of State thinks that information provided in connection with the document was or has become false, misleading or incomplete,

(b) if the Secretary of State thinks that the document has been lost or stolen,

(c) if the Secretary of State thinks that the document (including any information recorded in it) has been altered, damaged or destroyed (whether deliberately or not),

(d) if the Secretary of State thinks that an attempt has been made (whether successfully or not) to copy the document or to do anything to enable it to be copied,

(e) if the Secretary of State thinks that a person has failed to surrender the document in accordance with subsection (2)(g) or (h),

(f) if the Secretary of State thinks that the document should be re-issued (whether because the information recorded in it requires alteration or for any other reason),

(g) if the Secretary of State thinks that the holder is to be given leave to enter or remain in the United Kingdom,

(h) if the Secretary of State thinks that the holder's leave to enter or remain in the United Kingdom is to be varied, cancelled or invalidated or to lapse,

(i) if the Secretary of State thinks that the holder has died,

(j) if the Secretary of State thinks that the holder has been removed from the United Kingdom (whether by deportation or otherwise),

(k) if the Secretary of State thinks that the holder has left the United Kingdom without retaining leave to enter or remain, and

(l) in such other circumstances as the regulations may specify.

(4) Regulations under subsection (1)(a) may require notification to be given to the Secretary of State by the holder of a biometric immigration document—

(a) who knows or suspects that the document has been lost or stolen,

(b) who knows or suspects that the document has been altered or damaged (whether deliberately or not),

(c) who knows or suspects that information provided in connection with the document was or has become false, misleading or incomplete,

(d) who was given leave to enter or remain in the United Kingdom in accordance with a provision of rules under section 3 of the Immigration Act 1971 (immigration rules) and knows or suspects that owing to a change of the holder's circumstances the holder would no longer qualify for leave under that provision, or

(e) in such other circumstances as the regulations may specify.

(5) Regulations under subsection (1)(a) may require a person applying for the issue of a biometric immigration document to provide information (which may include biographical or other non-biometric information) to be recorded in it or retained by the Secretary of State; and, in particular, the regulations may—

(a) require, or permit an authorised person to require, the provision of information in a specified form;

(b) require an individual to submit, or permit an authorised person to require an individual to submit, to a specified process by means of which biometric information is obtained or recorded;

(c) confer a function (which may include the exercise of a discretion) on an authorised person;

(d) permit the Secretary of State, instead of requiring the provision of information, to use or retain information which is (for whatever reason) already in the Secretary of State's possession.

(6) Regulations under subsection (1)(b) may, in particular, require the production or other use of a biometric immigration document that is combined with another document . . .

(7) Regulations under subsection (1)(b) may not make provision the effect of which would be to require a person to carry a biometric immigration document at all times.

(8) Regulations under subsection (1)(c) may, in particular, make provision of a kind specified in subsection (5)(a) or (b).

(9) Rules under section 3 of the Immigration Act 1971 may require a person applying for the issue of a biometric immigration document to provide non-biometric information to be recorded in it or retained by the Secretary of State.

(10) Subsections (5) to (9) are without prejudice to the generality of section 50 of the Immigration, Asylum and Nationality Act 2006 (procedure).

Note: Commencement 31 January 2008 (SI 2008/99). Words omitted from subsection (6) by the Identity Documents Act 2010, Schedule, paragraph 19 from 21 January 2011 (s 14(2)).

6. Regulations: supplemental

(1) This section applies to regulations under section 5(1).

(2) Regulations amending or replacing earlier regulations may require a person who holds a biometric immigration document issued under the earlier regulations to apply under the new regulations.

(3) In so far as regulations require an individual under the age of 16 to submit to a process for the recording of biometric information, or permit an authorised person to require an individual under the age of 16 to submit to a process of that kind, the regulations must make provision similar to section 141(3) to (5) and (13) of the Immigration and Asylum Act 1999 (fingerprints: children).

(4) Rules under section 3 of the Immigration Act 1971 (immigration rules) may make provision by reference to compliance or non-compliance with regulations.

(5) Information in the Secretary of State's possession which is used or retained in accordance with regulations under section 5(5)(d) shall be treated, for the purpose of requirements about treatment and destruction, as having been provided in accordance with the regulations at the time at which it is used or retained in accordance with them.

(6) Regulations—

(a) may make provision having effect generally or only in specified cases or circumstances,

(b) may make different provision for different cases or circumstances,

(c) may include incidental, consequential or transitional provision,

(d) shall be made by statutory instrument, and

(e) may not be made unless a draft has been laid before and approved by resolution of each House of Parliament.

Note: Commencement 31 January 2008 (SI 2008/99).

7. Effect of non-compliance

(1) Regulations under section 5(1) must include provision about the effect of failure to comply with a requirement of the regulations.

(2) In particular, the regulations may—

(a) require or permit an application for a biometric immigration document to be refused;

(b) require or permit an application or claim in connection with immigration to be disregarded or refused;

(c) require or permit the cancellation or variation of leave to enter or remain in the United Kingdom;

(d) require the Secretary of State to consider giving a notice under section 9;

(e) provide for the consequence of a failure to be at the discretion of the Secretary of State.

[(2A) If the regulations require a biometric immigration document to be used in connection with an application or claim, they may require or permit the application or claim to be disregarded or refused if that requirement is not complied with.]

(3) The regulations may also permit the Secretary of State to designate an adult as the person responsible for ensuring that a child complies with requirements of the regulations; and for that purpose—

(a) 'adult' means an individual who has attained the age of 18,

(b) 'child' means an individual who has not attained the age of 18, and

(c) sections 9 to 13 shall apply (with any necessary modifications) to a designated adult's failure to ensure compliance by a child with a requirement of regulations as they apply to a person's own failure to comply with a requirement.

Note: Commencement 31 January 2008 (SI 2008/99). Subsection (2A) inserted by s 11 Immigration Act 2014 from 28 July 2014 (SI 2014/1820).

[8 Use and retention of biometric information

(1) The Secretary of State must by regulations make provision about the use and retention by the Secretary of State of biometric information provided in accordance with regulations under section 5(1).

(2) The regulations must provide that biometric information may be retained only if the Secretary of State thinks that it is necessary to retain it for use in connection with—

(a) the exercise of a function by virtue of the Immigration Acts, or

(b) the exercise of a function in relation to nationality.

(3) The regulations may include provision permitting biometric information retained by virtue of subsection (2) also to be used—

(a) in connection with the prevention, investigation or prosecution of an offence,

(b) for a purpose which appears to the Secretary of State to be required in order to protect national security,

(c) in connection with identifying persons who have died, or are suffering from illness or injury,

(d) for the purpose of ascertaining whether a person has acted unlawfully, or has obtained or sought anything to which the person is not legally entitled, and

(e) for such other purposes (whether in accordance with functions under an enactment or otherwise) as the regulations may specify.

(4) The regulations must include provision about the destruction of biometric information.

(5) In particular the regulations must require the Secretary of State to take all reasonable steps to ensure that biometric information is destroyed if the Secretary of State—

(a) no longer thinks that it is necessary to retain the information for use as mentioned in subsection (2), or

(b) is satisfied that the person to whom the information relates is a British citizen, or a Commonwealth citizen who has a right of abode in the United Kingdom as a result of section 2(1)(b) of the Immigration Act 1971.

(6) The regulations must also—

(a) require that any requirement to destroy biometric information by virtue of the regulations also applies to copies of the information, and

(b) require the Secretary of State to take all reasonable steps to ensure—

(i) that data held in electronic form which relates to biometric information which has to be destroyed by virtue of the regulations is destroyed or erased, or

(ii) that access to such data is blocked.

(7) But a requirement to destroy biometric information or data is not to apply if and in so far as the information or data is retained in accordance with and for the purposes of another power.

(8) The regulations must include provision—

(a) entitling a person whose biometric information has to be destroyed by virtue of the regulations, on request, to a certificate issued by the Secretary of State to the effect that the Secretary of State has taken the steps required by virtue of subsection (6)(b), and

(b) requiring such a certificate to be issued within the period of 3 months beginning with the date on which the request for it is received by the Secretary of State.

(9) Section 6(6) applies to regulations under this section as it applies to regulations under section 5(1).]

Note: Commencement 31 January 2008 (SI 2008/99). Section 8 substituted by s 14 Immigration Act 2014 from 28 July 2014 (SI 2014/1820).

9. Penalty

(1) The Secretary of State may by notice require a person to pay a penalty for failing to comply with a requirement of regulations under section 5(1).

(2) The notice must—

(a) specify the amount of the penalty,

(b) specify a date before which the penalty must be paid to the Secretary of State,

(c) specify methods by which the penalty may be paid,

(d) explain the grounds on which the Secretary of State thinks the person has failed to comply with a requirement of the regulations, and

(e) explain the effect of sections 10 to 12.

(3) The amount specified under subsection (2)(a) may not exceed £1,000.

(4) The date specified under subsection (2)(b) must be not less than 14 days after the date on which the notice is given.

(5) A person who has been given a notice under subsection (1) for failing to comply with regulations may be given further notices in the case of continued failure; but a person may not be given a new notice—

(a) during the time available for objection or appeal against an earlier notice, or

(b) while an objection or appeal against an earlier notice has been instituted and is neither withdrawn nor determined.

(6) The Secretary of State may by order amend subsection (3) to reflect a change in the value of money.

Note: Commencement 25 November 2009 (SI 2008/2822).

10. Penalty: objection

(1) A person ("P") who is given a penalty notice under section 9(1) may by notice to the Secretary of State object on the grounds—

(a) that P has not failed to comply with a requirement of regulations under section 5(1),

(b) that it is unreasonable to require P to pay a penalty, or

(c) that the amount of the penalty is excessive.

(2) A notice of objection must—

(a) specify the grounds of objection and P's reasons,

(b) comply with any prescribed requirements as to form and content, and

(c) be given within the prescribed period.

(3) The Secretary of State shall consider a notice of objection and—

(a) cancel the penalty notice,

(b) reduce the penalty by varying the penalty notice,

(c) increase the penalty by issuing a new penalty notice, or

(d) confirm the penalty notice.

(4) The Secretary of State shall act under subsection (3) and notify P—

(a) in accordance with any prescribed requirements, and

(b) within the prescribed period or such longer period as the Secretary of State and P may agree.

Note: Commencement for the purposes of making an order under subsections (2) and (4) 31 January 2008 (SI 2008/99), remainder 25 November 2008 (SI 2008/2822).

11. Penalty: appeal

(1) A person ("P") who is given a penalty notice under section 9(1) may appeal to—

(a) [the county court in England and Wales or a county court in] Northern Ireland, or

(b) the sheriff, in Scotland.

(2) An appeal may be brought on the grounds—

(a) that P has not failed to comply with a requirement of regulations under section 5(1),

(b) that it is unreasonable to require P to pay a penalty, or

(c) that the amount of the penalty is excessive.

(3) The court or sheriff may—

(a) cancel the penalty notice,

(b) reduce the penalty by varying the penalty notice,

(c) increase the penalty by varying the penalty notice (whether because the court or sheriff thinks the original amount insufficient or because the court or sheriff thinks that the appeal should not have been brought), or

(d) confirm the penalty notice.

(4) An appeal may be brought—

(a) whether or not P has given a notice of objection, and

(b) irrespective of the Secretary of State's decision on any notice of objection.

(5) The court or sheriff may consider matters of which the Secretary of State was not and could not have been aware before giving the penalty notice.

(6) Rules of court may make provision about the timing of an appeal under this section.

Note: Commencement for the purposes of making rules under subsection (6) 31 January 2008 (SI 2008/99), remainder 25 November 2008 (SI 2008/2822). Words in square brackets in subsection (1)(a) substituted by Sch 9 Crime and Courts Act 2013 from a date to be appointed.

12. Penalty: enforcement

(1) Where a penalty has not been paid before the date specified in the penalty notice in accordance with section 9(2)(b), it may be recovered as a debt due to the Secretary of State.

(2) Where a notice of objection is given in respect of a penalty notice, the Secretary of State may not take steps to enforce the penalty notice before—

(a) deciding what to do in response to the notice of objection, and

(b) informing the objector.

(3) The Secretary of State may not take steps to enforce a penalty notice while an appeal under section 11—

(a) could be brought (disregarding any possibility of an appeal out of time with permission), or

(b) has been brought and has not been determined or abandoned.

(4) In proceedings for the recovery of a penalty no question may be raised as to the matters specified in sections 10 and 11 as grounds for objection or appeal.

(5) Money received by the Secretary of State in respect of a penalty shall be paid into the Consolidated Fund.

Note: Commencement 25 November 2008 (SI 2008/2822).

13. Penalty: code of practice

(1) The Secretary of State shall issue a code of practice setting out the matters to be considered in determining—

(a) whether to give a penalty notice under section 9(1), and

(b) the amount of a penalty.

(2) The code may, in particular, require the Secretary of State to consider any decision taken by virtue of section 7.

(3) A court or the sheriff shall, when considering an appeal under section 11, have regard to the code.

(4) The Secretary of State may revise and re-issue the code.

(5) Before issuing or re-issuing the code the Secretary of State must—

(a) publish proposals,

(b) consult members of the public, and

(c) lay a draft before Parliament.

(6) The code (or re-issued code) shall come into force at the prescribed time.

Note: Commencement for the purposes of issuing a code of practice under subsection (1) and making an order under subsection (6) 31 January 2008 (SI 2008/99), remainder 25 November 2008 (SI 2008/2822).

14. Penalty: prescribed matters

(1) In sections 10 to 13 'prescribed' means prescribed by the Secretary of State by order.

(2) An order under subsection (1) or under section 9(6)—

(a) may make provision generally or only for specified purposes,

(b) may make different provision for different purposes,

(c) shall be made by statutory instrument, and

(d) shall be subject to annulment in pursuance of a resolution of either House of Parliament.

(3) But the first order under section 13(6) shall not be made unless a draft has been laid before and approved by resolution of each House of Parliament (and shall not be subject to annulment).

Note: Commencement 31 January 2008 (SI 2008/99).

15. Interpretation

(1) For the purposes of section 5—

(a) 'person subject to immigration control' means a person who under the Immigration Act 1971 requires leave to enter or remain in the United Kingdom (whether or not such leave has been given),

(b) . . .

(c) . . .

(d) 'document' includes a card or sticker and any other method of recording information (whether in writing or by the use of electronic or other technology or by a combination of methods),

(e) 'authorised person' has the meaning given by section 141(5) of the Immigration and Asylum Act 1999 (authority to take fingerprints),

(f) 'immigration' includes asylum, and

(g) regulations permitting something to be done by the Secretary of State may (but need not) permit it to be done only where the Secretary of State is of a specified opinion.

[(**1A**) For the purposes of section 5 "biometric information" means—

(a) information about a person's external physical characteristics (including in particular fingerprints and features of the iris), and

(b) any other information about a person's physical characteristics specified in an order made by the Secretary of State.

(**1B**) An order under subsection (1A)(b)—

(a) may specify only information that can be obtained or recorded by an external examination of a person;

(b) must not specify information about a person's DNA.

(**1C**) Section 6(6) applies to an order under subsection (1A)(b) as it applies to regulations under section 5(1).]

(2) An application for a biometric immigration document is an application in connection with immigration for the purposes of—

(a) section 50(1) and (2) of the Immigration, Asylum and Nationality Act 2006 (procedure), and

[(b) section 68 of the Immigration Act 2014 (fees);]

and in the application of either of those sections to an application for a biometric immigration document, the prescribed consequences of non-compliance may include any of the consequences specified in section 7(2) above.

Note: Commencement 31 January 2008 (SI 2008/99). Subsections (1)(b)–(c) omitted, (1A), (1B) and (1C) inserted by s 12 Immigration Act 2014 from 28 July 2014 (SI 2014/1820). Subsection (2)(b) substituted by Sch 9 of that Act from 15 December 2014 (SI 2014/2771).

Treatment of claimants

16. Conditional leave to enter or remain

Note: Amends s 3(1)(c) Immigration Act 1971.

17. Support for failed asylum-seekers

(1) This section applies for the purposes of—

(a) Part 6 (and section 4) of the Immigration and Asylum Act 1999 (support and accommodation for asylum-seekers),

(b) Part 2 of the Nationality, Immigration and Asylum Act 2002 (accommodation centres), and

(c) Schedule 3 to that Act (withholding and withdrawal of support).

(2) A person (A-S) remains (or again becomes) an asylum-seeker, despite the fact that the claim for asylum made by A-S has been determined, during any period when—

(a) A-S can bring an in-country appeal . . . under section 82 of the 2002 Act or section 2 of the Special Immigration Appeals Commission Act 1997, or

(b) an in-country appeal, brought by A-S under either of those sections . . ., is pending (within the meaning of section 104 of the 2002 Act).

(3) For the purposes of subsection (2)—

(a) 'in-country' appeal means an appeal brought while the appellant is in the United Kingdom, and

(b) the possibility of an appeal out of time with permission shall be ignored.

(4) For the purposes of the provisions mentioned in subsection (1)(a) and (b), a person's status as an asylum-seeker by virtue of subsection (2)(b) continues for a prescribed period after the appeal ceases to be pending.

(5) In subsection (4) 'prescribed' means prescribed by regulations made by the Secretary of State; and the regulations—

(a) may contain incidental or transitional provision,

(b) may make different provision for different classes of case,

(c) shall be made by statutory instrument, and

(d) shall be subject to annulment in pursuance of a resolution of either House of Parliament.

(6) This section shall be treated as always having had effect.

Note: The prescribed period for the purposes of subsection (4) is 28 days where an appeal has been disposed of by being allowed, and 21 days in all other cases (SI 2007/3102). Commencement 30 October 2007, s 59 (Royal Assent). Words omitted from subsection (2) by Sch 9 Immigration Act 2014 from 20 October 2014 with savings set out in articles 9-11 SI 2014/2771.

18. Support for asylum-seekers: enforcement

Note: Amends s 109 Immigration and Asylum Act 1999.

19. Points-based applications: no new evidence on appeal

Note: Amends ss 85 and 106 of the Nationality, Immigration and Asylum Act 2002. Repealed by Sch 9 Immigration Act 2014 from 20 October 2014 with savings set out in articles 9-11 SI 2014/2771.

20. Fees

Note: Amends s 42 of the Asylum and Immigration (Treatment of Claimants, etc.) Act 2004. Repealed by Sch 9 Immigration Act 2014 from 15 December 2014 (SI 2014/2771).

21. Children

. . .

Note: Revoked by s 55 Borders, Citizenship and Immigration Act 2009 from 2 November 2009 (SI 2009/2731).

Enforcement

22. Assaulting an immigration officer: offence

(1) A person who assaults an immigration officer commits an offence.

(2) A person guilty of an offence under this section shall be liable on summary conviction to—

(a) imprisonment for a period not exceeding 51 weeks,

(b) a fine not exceeding level 5 on the standard scale, or

(c) both.

(3) In the application of this section to Northern Ireland the reference in subsection (2)(a) to 51 weeks shall be treated as a reference to 6 months.

(4) In the application of this section to Scotland the reference in subsection (2)(a) to 51 weeks shall be treated as a reference to 12 months.

(5) In relation to an offence committed before the commencement of section 281(5) of the Criminal Justice Act 2003 (51 week maximum term of sentences) the reference in subsection (2)(a) to 51 weeks shall be treated as a reference to 6 months.

Note: Commencement 31 January 2008 (SI 2008/99).

23. Assaulting an immigration officer: powers of arrest, &c.

(1) An immigration officer may arrest a person without warrant if the officer reasonably suspects that the person has committed or is about to commit an offence under section 22.

(2) An offence under section 22 shall be treated as—

(a) a relevant offence for the purposes of sections 28B and 28D of the Immigration Act 1971 (search, entry and arrest), and

(b) an offence under Part 3 of that Act (criminal proceedings) for the purposes of sections 28(4), 28E, 28G and 28H (search after arrest, &c.) of that Act.

(3) The following provisions of the Immigration Act 1971 shall have effect in connection with an offence under section 22 of this Act as they have effect in connection with an offence under that Act—

(a) section 28I (seized material: access and copying),

(b) section 28J (search warrants: safeguards),

(c) section 28K (execution of warrants), and

(d) section 28L(1) (interpretation).

Note: Commencement 31 January 2008 (SI 2008/99).

24. Seizure of cash

(1) Chapter 3 of Part 5 of the Proceeds of Crime Act 2002 (recovery of cash) shall apply in relation to an immigration officer as it applies in relation to a constable.

(2) For that purpose—

[(a) "unlawful conduct", in or in relation to section 289, means conduct which—

(i) relates to the entitlement of one or more persons who are not nationals of the United Kingdom to enter, transit across, or be in, the United Kingdom (including conduct which relates to conditions or other controls on any such entitlement), or

(ii) is undertaken for the purposes of, or otherwise in relation to, a relevant nationality enactment, and (in either case) constitutes an offence,]

(c) 'senior officer' in [sections 290 and 297A] means an official of the Secretary of State who is a civil servant [at or above the grade which is designated by the Secretary of State as being equivalent to the rank of police inspector],

(d) in section 292 the words '(in relation to England and Wales . . .' shall be disregarded,

(e) [sections 293 and 293A] shall not apply,

(f) an application for an order under section 295(2) must be made—

(i) in relation to England and Wales or Northern Ireland, by an immigration officer, and

(ii) in relation to Scotland, by the Scottish Ministers in connection with their functions under section 298 or by a procurator fiscal,

(g) an application for forfeiture under section 298 must be made—

(i) in relation to England and Wales or Northern Ireland, by an immigration officer, and

(ii) in relation to Scotland, by the Scottish Ministers, and

(h) any compensation under section 302 shall be paid by the Secretary of State.

[(2A) In subsection (2)(a)(ii) "relevant nationality enactment" means any enactment in—

(a) the British Nationality Act 1981,

(b) the Hong Kong Act 1985,

(c) the Hong Kong (War Wives and Widows) Act 1996,

(d) the British Nationality (Hong Kong) Act 1997,

(e) the British Overseas Territories Act 2002, or

(f) an instrument made under any of those Acts.]

(3) The Secretary of State may by order amend subsection (2)(c) to reflect a change in nomenclature; and an order—

(a) shall be made by statutory instrument, and

(b) shall be subject to annulment in pursuance of a resolution of either House of Parliament.

Note: Commencement 1 April 2010 (SI 2010/606). Words in square brackets in subsection (2)(c) substituted by paragraph 113 Sch 7 Policing and Crime Act 2009 from a date to be appointed. Subsections (2)(a)–(b), words in square brackets in subsection (2)(c) substituted and (2A) inserted by Crime and Courts Act 2013, s 55, Sch 21 from 25 June 2013 (SI 2013/1042). Words omitted from subsection (2)(d) and substituted in (2)(e) by SI 2012/2595 from 18 October 2012.

25. Forfeiture of detained property

(1) A court making a forfeiture order about property may order that the property be taken into the possession of the Secretary of State (and not of the police).

(2) An order may be made under subsection (1) only if the court thinks that the offence in connection with which the order is made—

(a) related to immigration or asylum, or

(b) was committed for a purpose connected with immigration or asylum.

(3) In subsection (1) 'forfeiture order' means an order under—

(a) section 143 of the Powers of Criminal Courts (Sentencing) Act 2006 or

(b) Article 11 of the Criminal Justice (Northern Ireland) Order 1994 (S.I. 1994/2795 (N.I. 15)).

Note: Commencement 31 March 2008 (SI 2008/309).

26. Disposal of property

(1) In this section 'property' means property which—

(a) has come into the possession of an immigration officer, or

(b) has come into the possession of the Secretary of State in the course of, or in connection with, a function under the Immigration Acts.

(2) A magistrates' court may, on the application of the Secretary of State or a claimant of property—

(a) order the delivery of property to the person appearing to the court to be its owner, or

(b) if its owner cannot be ascertained, make any other order about property.

(3) An order shall not affect the right of any person to take legal proceedings for the recovery of the property, provided that the proceedings are instituted within the period of six months beginning with the date of the order.

(4) An order may be made in respect of property forfeited under section 25, or under section 25C of the Immigration Act 1971 (vehicles, &c.), only if—

(a) the application under subsection (2) above is made within the period of six months beginning with the date of the forfeiture order, and

(b) the applicant (if not the Secretary of State) satisfies the court—

(i) that the applicant did not consent to the offender's possession of the property, or

(ii) that the applicant did not know and had no reason to suspect that the property was likely to be used, or was intended to be used, in connection with an offence.

(5) The Secretary of State may make regulations for the disposal of property—

(a) where the owner has not been ascertained,

(b) where an order under subsection (2) cannot be made because of subsection (4)(a), or

(c) where a court has declined to make an order under subsection (2) on the grounds that the court is not satisfied of the matters specified in subsection (4)(b).

(6) The regulations may make provision that is the same as or similar to provision that may be made by regulations under section 2 of the Police (Property) Act 1897 (or any similar enactment applying in relation to Scotland or Northern Ireland); and the regulations—

(a) may apply, with or without modifications, regulations under that Act,

(b) may, in particular, provide for property to vest in the Secretary of State,

(c) may make provision about the timing of disposal (which, in particular, may differ from provision made by or under the Police (Property) Act 1897),

(d) shall have effect only in so far as not inconsistent with an order of a court (whether or not under subsection (2) above),

(e) shall be made by statutory instrument, and

(f) shall be subject to annulment in pursuance of a resolution of either House of Parliament.

(7) For the purposes of subsection (1) it is immaterial whether property is acquired as a result of forfeiture or seizure or in any other way.

(8) In the application of this section to Scotland a reference to a magistrates' court is a reference to the sheriff.

Note: Commencement for the purposes of making regulations under subsection (5) 31 January 2008 (SI 2008/99). Remainder from 1 April 2008 (SI 2008/309) which sets out transitional provisions.

27. Employment: arrest

Note: Amends s 28AA of the Immigration Act 1971.

28. Employment: search for personnel records

Note: Amends s 28FA(7) of the Immigration Act 1971.

29. Facilitation: arrival and entry

Note: Amends s 25A(1)(a) of the Immigration Act 1971.

30. Facilitation: territorial application

Note: Amends ss 25, 25A and 25B of the Immigration Act 1971.

31. People trafficking

Note: Amends ss 4 and 5 of the Asylum and Immigration (Treatment of Claimants, etc.) Act 2004, ss 57 and 60 of the Sexual Offences Act 2003.

Deportation of criminals

32. Automatic deportation

(1) In this section 'foreign criminal' means a person—
(a) who is not a British citizen,
(b) who is convicted in the United Kingdom of an offence, and
(c) to whom Condition 1 or 2 applies.

(2) Condition 1 is that the person is sentenced to a period of imprisonment of at least 12 months.

(3) Condition 2 is that—
(a) the offence is specified by order of the Secretary of State under section 72(4)(a) of the Nationality, Immigration and Asylum Act 2002 (serious criminal), and
(b) the person is sentenced to a period of imprisonment.

(4) For the purpose of section 3(5)(a) of the Immigration Act 1971 (c. 77), the deportation of a foreign criminal is conducive to the public good.

(5) The Secretary of State must make a deportation order in respect of a foreign criminal (subject to section 33).

(6) The Secretary of State may not revoke a deportation order made in accordance with subsection (5) unless—
(a) he thinks that an exception under section 33 applies,
(b) the application for revocation is made while the foreign criminal is outside the United Kingdom, or
(c) section 34(4) applies.

(7) Subsection (5) does not create a private right of action in respect of consequences of non-compliance by the Secretary of State.

Note: Commencement in respect of a person for whom condition 1 applies, if the person has not been served with a notice of intention to make a deportation order before 1 August 2008, is in custody on, or has a suspended sentence at 1 August 2008 (SI 2008/1818), which sets out transitional provisions.

33. Exceptions

(1) Section 32(4) and (5)—

(a) do not apply where an exception in this section applies (subject to subsection (7) below), and

(b) are subject to sections 7 and 8 of the Immigration Act 1971 (Commonwealth citizens, Irish citizens, crew and other exemptions).

(2) Exception 1 is where removal of the foreign criminal in pursuance of the deportation order would breach—

(a) a person's Convention rights, or

(b) the United Kingdom's obligations under the Refugee Convention.

(3) Exception 2 is where the Secretary of State thinks that the foreign criminal was under the age of 18 on the date of conviction.

(4) Exception 3 is where the removal of the foreign criminal from the United Kingdom in pursuance of a deportation order would breach rights of the foreign criminal under the [EU] treaties.

(5) Exception 4 is where the foreign criminal—

(a) is the subject of a certificate under section 2 or 70 of the Extradition Act 2003,

(b) is in custody pursuant to arrest under section 5 of that Act,

(c) is the subject of a provisional warrant under section 73 of that Act,

(d) is the subject of an authority to proceed under section 7 of the Extradition Act 1989 or an order under paragraph 4(2) of Schedule 1 to that Act, or

(e) is the subject of a provisional warrant under section 8 of that Act or of a warrant under paragraph 5(1)(b) of Schedule 1 to that Act.

(6) Exception 5 is where any of the following has effect in respect of the foreign criminal—

(a) a hospital order or guardianship order under section 37 of the Mental Health Act 1983,

(b) a hospital direction under section 45A of that Act,

(c) a transfer direction under section 47 of that Act,

(d) a compulsion order under section 57A of the Criminal Procedure (Scotland) Act 1995,

(e) a guardianship order under section 58 of that Act,

(f) a hospital direction under section 59A of that Act,

(g) a transfer for treatment direction under section 136 of the Mental Health (Care and Treatment) (Scotland) Act 2003, or

(h) an order or direction under a provision which corresponds to a provision specified in paragraphs (a) to (g) and which has effect in relation to Northern Ireland.

[(6A) Exception 6 is where the Secretary of State thinks that the application of section 32(4) and (5) would contravene the United Kingdom's obligations under the Council of Europe Convention on Action against Trafficking in Human Beings (done at Warsaw on 16 May 2005).]

(7) The application of an exception—

(a) does not prevent the making of a deportation order;

(b) results in it being assumed neither that deportation of the person concerned is conducive to the public good nor that it is not conducive to the public good; but section 32(4) applies despite the application of Exception 1 or 4.

Note: Commencement in respect of a person for whom condition 1 of s 32 applies, 1 August 2008 (SI 2008/1818), which sets out transitional provisions. Subsection (6A) inserted by s 146 Criminal Justice and Immigration Act 2008 from 1 April 2009 (SI 2009/860). Term 'EU' substituted from 22 April 2011 (SI 2011/1043).

34. Timing

(1) Section 32(5) requires a deportation order to be made at a time chosen by the Secretary of State.

(2) A deportation order may not be made under section 32(5) while an appeal or further appeal against the conviction or sentence by reference to which the order is to be made—

(a) has been instituted and neither withdrawn nor determined, or

(b) could be brought.

(3) For the purpose of subsection (2)(b)—

(a) the possibility of an appeal out of time with permission shall be disregarded, and

(b) a person who has informed the Secretary of State in writing that the person does not intend to appeal shall be treated as being no longer able to appeal.

(4) The Secretary of State may withdraw a decision that section 32(5) applies, or revoke a deportation order made in accordance with section 32(5), for the purpose of—

(a) taking action under the Immigration Acts or rules made under section 3 of the Immigration Act 1971 (immigration rules), and

(b) subsequently taking a new decision that section 32(5) applies and making a deportation order in accordance with section 32(5).

Note: Commencement in respect of a person for whom condition 1 of s 32 applies, 1 August 2008 (SI 2008/1818) which sets out transitional provisions.

35. Appeal

Note: Amends ss 79 and 82 of the Nationality, Immigration and Asylum Act 2002.

36. Detention

(1) A person who has served a period of imprisonment may be detained under the authority of the Secretary of State—

(a) while the Secretary of State considers whether section 32(5) applies, and

(b) where the Secretary of State thinks that section 32(5) applies, pending the making of the deportation order.

(2) Where a deportation order is made in accordance with section 32(5) the Secretary of State shall exercise the power of detention under paragraph 2(3) of Schedule 3 to the Immigration Act 1971 (detention pending removal) unless in the circumstances the Secretary of State thinks it inappropriate.

(3) A court determining an appeal against conviction or sentence may direct release from detention under subsection (1) or (2).

(4) Provisions of the Immigration Act 1971 which apply to detention under paragraph 2(3) of Schedule 3 to that Act shall apply to detention under subsection (1) (including provisions about bail).

(5) Paragraph 2(5) of Schedule 3 to that Act (residence, occupation and reporting restrictions) applies to a person who is liable to be detained under subsection (1).

Note: Commencement in respect of a person for whom condition 1 of s 32 applies, 1 August 2008 (SI 2008/1818) which sets out transitional provisions.

37. Family

(1) Where a deportation order against a foreign criminal states that it is made in accordance with section 32(5) ('the automatic deportation order') this section shall have effect in place of the words from 'A deportation order' to 'after the making of the deportation order against him' in section 5(3) of the Immigration Act 1971 (period during which family members may also be deported).

(2) A deportation order may not be made against a person as belonging to the family of the foreign criminal after the end of the relevant period of 8 weeks.

(3) In the case of a foreign criminal who has not appealed in respect of the automatic deportation order, the relevant period begins when an appeal can no longer be brought (ignoring any possibility of an appeal out of time with permission).

(4) In the case of a foreign criminal who has appealed in respect of the automatic deportation order, the relevant period begins when the appeal is no longer pending (within the meaning of section 104 of the Nationality, Immigration and Asylum Act 2002.

Note: Commencement in respect of a person for whom condition 1 of s 32 applies, 1 August 2008 (SI 2008/1818) which sets out transitional provisions.

38. Interpretation

(1) In section 32(2) the reference to a person who is sentenced to a period of imprisonment of at least 12 months—

(a) does not include a reference to a person who receives a suspended sentence (unless a court subsequently orders that the sentence or any part of it (of whatever length) is to take effect),

(b) does not include a reference to a person who is sentenced to a period of imprisonment of at least 12 months only by virtue of being sentenced to consecutive sentences amounting in aggregate to more than 12 months,

(c) includes a reference to a person who is sentenced to detention, or ordered or directed to be detained, in an institution other than a prison (including, in particular, a hospital or an institution for young offenders) for at least 12 months, and

(d) includes a reference to a person who is sentenced to imprisonment or detention, or ordered or directed to be detained, for an indeterminate period (provided that it may last for 12 months).

(2) In section 32(3)(b) the reference to a person who is sentenced to a period of imprisonment—

(a) does not include a reference to a person who receives a suspended sentence (unless a court subsequently orders that the sentence or any part of it is to take effect), and

(b) includes a reference to a person who is sentenced to detention, or ordered or directed to be detained, in an institution other than a prison (including, in particular, a hospital or an institution for young offenders).

(3) For the purposes of section 32 a person subject to an order under section 5 of the Criminal Procedure (Insanity) Act 1964 (insanity, &c.) has not been convicted of an offence.

(4) In sections 32 and 33—

(a) 'British citizen' has the same meaning as in section 3(5) of the Immigration Act 1971 (and section 3(8) (burden of proof) shall apply),

(b) 'Convention rights' has the same meaning as in the Human Rights Act 1998,

(c) 'deportation order' means an order under section 5, and by virtue of section 3(5), of the Immigration Act 1971, and

(d) 'the Refugee Convention' means the Convention relating to the Status of Refugees done at Geneva on 28 July 1951 and its Protocol.

Note: Commencement in respect of a person for whom condition 1 of s 32 applies, 1 August 2008 (SI 2008/1818) which sets out transitional provisions.

39. Consequential amendments

Note: Amends s 72(11) of the Nationality, Immigration and Asylum Act 2002.

Information

40. Supply of Revenue and Customs information

(1) Her Majesty's Revenue and Customs (HMRC) and the Revenue and Customs Prosecutions Office (the RCPO) may each supply the Secretary of State with information for use for the purpose of—

(a) administering immigration control under the Immigration Acts;

(b) preventing, detecting, investigating or prosecuting offences under those Acts;

(c) determining whether to impose, or imposing, penalties or charges under Part 2 of the Immigration and Asylum Act 1999 (carriers' liability);

(d) determining whether to impose, or imposing, penalties under section 15 of the Immigration, Asylum and Nationality Act 2006 (restrictions on employment);

(e) providing facilities, or arranging for the provision of facilities, for the accommodation of persons under section 4 of the Immigration and Asylum Act 1999;

(f) providing support for asylum-seekers and their dependants under Part 6 of that Act;

(g) determining whether an applicant for naturalisation under the British Nationality Act 1981 is of good character;

[(h) determining whether, for the purposes of an application referred to in section 41A of the British Nationality Act 1981, the person for whose registration the application is made is of good character;

(ha) determining whether, for the purposes of an application under section 1 of the Hong Kong (War Wives and Widows) Act 1996, the woman for whose registration the application is made is of good character;

(hb) determining whether, for the purposes of an application under section 1 of the British Nationality (Hong Kong) Act 1997 for the registration of an adult or young person within the meaning of subsection (5A) of that section, the person is of good character;]

(i) determining whether to make an order in respect of a person under section 40 of the British Nationality Act 1981 (deprivation of citizenship);

(j) doing anything else in connection with the exercise of immigration and nationality functions.

(2) This section applies to a document or article which comes into the possession of, or is discovered by, HMRC or the RCPO, or a person acting on behalf of HMRC or the RCPO, as it applies to information.

(3) The Secretary of State—

(a) may retain for a purpose within subsection (1) a document or article supplied by virtue of subsection (2);

(b) may dispose of a document or article supplied by virtue of subsection (2).

(4) In subsection (1) 'immigration and nationality functions' means functions exercisable by virtue of—

(a) the Immigration Acts,

(b) the British Nationality Act 1981,

(c) the Hong Kong Act 1985,

(d) the Hong Kong (War Wives and Widows) Act 1996, or

(e) the British Nationality (Hong Kong) Act 1997.

(5) A power conferred by this section on HMRC or the RCPO may be exercised on behalf of HMRC or the RCPO by a person who is authorised (generally or specifically) for the purpose.

(6) . . .

Note: Subsection (6) amends s 20(1)(d) of the Immigration and Asylum Act 1999, s 130 of the Nationality, Immigration and Asylum Act 2002 and paragraphs 17 and 20 of Sch 2 to the Commissioners for Revenue and Customs Act 2005. Commencement 31 January 2008 (SI 2008/99). Subsections (1)(h)–(hb) substituted by s 47 Borders, Citizenship and Immigration Act 2009 from 13 January 2010 (SI 2009/2731).

41. Confidentiality

(1) A person to whom relevant information is supplied (whether before or after the commencement of this section) may not disclose that information.

(2) Information is relevant information if it is supplied by or on behalf of HMRC or the RCPO under—

(a) section 20 of the Immigration and Asylum Act 1999,

(b) section 130 of the Nationality, Immigration and Asylum Act 2002,

(c) section 36 of the Immigration, Asylum and Nationality Act 2006 (except in so far as that section relates to information supplied to a chief officer of police), or

(d) section 40 of this Act.

(3) But subsection (1) does not apply to a disclosure—

(a) which is made for a purpose within section 40(1),

(b) which is made for the purposes of civil proceedings (whether or not within the United Kingdom) relating to an immigration or nationality matter,

(c) which is made for the purposes of a criminal investigation or criminal proceedings (whether or not within the United Kingdom) relating to an immigration or nationality matter,

(d) which is made in pursuance of an order of a court,

(e) which is made with the consent (which may be general or specific) of HMRC or the RCPO, depending on by whom or on whose behalf the information was supplied, or

(f) which is made with the consent of each person to whom the information relates.

(4) Subsection (1) is subject to any other enactment permitting disclosure.

(5) The reference in subsection (1) to a person to whom relevant information is supplied includes a reference to a person who is or was acting on behalf of that person.

(6) The reference in subsection (2) to information supplied under section 40 of this Act includes a reference to documents or articles supplied by virtue of subsection (2) of that section.

(7) In subsection (3) 'immigration or nationality matter' means a matter in respect of which the Secretary of State has immigration and nationality functions (within the meaning given in section 40(4)).

(8) In subsection (4) 'enactment' does not include—

(a) an Act of the Scottish Parliament,

(b) an Act of the Northern Ireland Assembly, or

(c) an instrument made under an Act within paragraph (a) or (b).

Note: Commencement 31 January 2008 (SI 2008/1999).

[41A. Supply of information to UK Border Agency

(1) HMRC and the RCPO may each supply a person to whom this section applies with information for use for the purpose of the customs functions exercisable by that person.

(2) This section applies to—

(a) a designated customs official,

(b) the Secretary of State by whom general customs functions are exercisable,

(c) the Director of Border Revenue, and

(d) a person acting on behalf of a person mentioned in paragraphs (a) to (c).

(3) This section applies to a document or article which comes into the possession of, or is discovered by, HMRC or the RCPO, or a person acting on behalf of HMRC or the RCPO, as it applies to information.

(4) A person to whom this section applies—

(a) may retain for a purpose within subsection (1) a document or article supplied by virtue of subsection (3);

(b) may dispose of a document or article supplied by virtue of subsection (3).

(5) A power conferred by this section on HMRC or the RCPO may be exercised on behalf of HMRC or the RCPO by a person who is authorised (generally or specifically) for the purpose.

(6) In this section and section 41B "customs function" and "general customs function" have the meanings given by Part 1 of the Borders, Citizenship and Immigration Act 2009.

41B. UK Border Agency: onward disclosure

(1) A person to whom information is supplied under section 41A may not disclose that information.

(2) But subsection (1) does not apply to a disclosure—

(a) which is made for the purpose of a customs function, where the disclosure does not contravene any restriction imposed by the Commissioners for Her Majesty's Revenue and Customs;

(b) which is made for the purposes of civil proceedings (whether or not within the United Kingdom) relating to a customs function;

(c) which is made for the purpose of a criminal investigation or criminal proceedings (whether or not within the United Kingdom);

(d) which is made in pursuance of an order of a court;

(e) which is made with the consent (which may be general or specific) of HMRC or the RCPO, depending on by whom or on whose behalf the information was supplied;

(f) which is made with the consent of each person to whom the information relates.

(3) Subsection (1) is subject to any other enactment permitting disclosure.

(4) The reference in subsection (1) to information supplied under section 41A includes a reference to documents or articles supplied by virtue of subsection (3) of that section.

(5) The reference in that subsection to a person to whom information is supplied includes a reference to a person who is or was acting on behalf of that person.

(6) In subsection (3) "enactment" does not include—

(a) an Act of the Scottish Parliament,

(b) an Act of the Northern Ireland Assembly, or

(c) an instrument made under an Act within paragraph (a) or (b).]

Note : Sections 41A and 41B inserted by s 20 Borders, Citizenship and Immigration Act 2009 from 21 July 2009 (s 58).

42. Wrongful disclosure

(1) An offence is committed by a person who contravenes section 41 [or 41B] by disclosing information relating to a person whose identity—

(a) is specified in the disclosure, or

(b) can be deduced from it.

(2) Subsection (1) does not apply to the disclosure of information about internal administrative arrangements of HMRC or the RCPO (whether relating to Commissioners, officers, members of the RCPO or others).

(3) It is a defence for a person ("P") charged with an offence under this section of disclosing information to prove that P reasonably believed—

(a) that the disclosure was lawful, or

(b) that the information had already and lawfully been made available to the public.

(4) A person guilty of an offence under this section shall be liable—

(a) on conviction on indictment, to imprisonment for a term not exceeding two years, to a fine or to both, or

(b) on summary conviction, to imprisonment for a term not exceeding 12 months, to a fine not exceeding the statutory maximum or to both.

(5) The reference in subsection (4)(b) to 12 months shall be treated as a reference to six months—

(a) in the application of this section to Northern Ireland;

(b) in the application of this section to England and Wales, in relation to an offence under this section committed before the commencement of section 282 of the

Criminal Justice Act 2003 (imprisonment on summary conviction for certain offences in England and Wales);

(c) in the application of this section to Scotland, until the commencement of section 45(1) of the Criminal Proceedings etc. (Reform) (Scotland) Act 2007 (corresponding provision in Scotland).

(6) A prosecution for an offence under this section may be instituted—

(a) in England and Wales, only with the consent of the Director of Public Prosecutions;

(b) in Northern Ireland, only with the consent of the Director of Public Prosecutions for Northern Ireland.

Note: Commencement 31 January 2008 (SI 2008/1999). Words in square brackets in subsection (1) inserted by s 20 Borders, Citizenship and Immigration Act 2009 from 21 July 2009 (s 58).

43. Supply of police information, etc.

. . .

Note: Amends s 131 of the Nationality, Immigration and Asylum Act 2002.

44. Search for evidence of nationality

(1) This section applies where an individual has been arrested on suspicion of the commission of an offence and an immigration officer or a constable suspects—

(a) that the individual may not be a British citizen, and

(b) that nationality documents relating to the individual may be found on—

(i) premises occupied or controlled by the individual,

(ii) premises on which the individual was arrested, or

(iii) premises on which the individual was, immediately before being arrested.

(2) The immigration officer or constable may enter and search the premises for the purpose of finding those documents.

(3) The power of search may be exercised only with the written authority of a senior officer; and for that purpose—

(a) 'senior officer' means—

(i) in relation to an immigration officer, an immigration officer of at least the rank of chief immigration officer, and

(ii) in relation to a constable, a constable of at least the rank of inspector, and

(b) a senior officer who gives authority must arrange for a written record to be made of—

(i) the grounds for the suspicions in reliance on which the power of search is to be exercised, and

(ii) the nature of the documents sought.

(4) The power of search may not be exercised where the individual has been released without being charged with an offence.

(5) In relation to an individual 'nationality document' means a document showing—

(a) the individual's identity, nationality or citizenship,

(b) the place from which the individual travelled to the United Kingdom, or

(c) a place to which the individual is proposing to go from the United Kingdom.

Note: Commencement 29 February 2008 (SI 2008/309), which sets out transitional provisions.

45. Search for evidence of nationality: other premises

(1) This section applies where an individual—

(a) has been arrested on suspicion of the commission of an offence, and

(b) has not been released without being charged with an offence.

(2) If, on an application made by an immigration officer or a constable, a justice of the peace is satisfied that there are reasonable grounds for believing that—

(a) the individual may not be a British citizen,

(b) nationality documents relating to the individual may be found on premises specified in the application,

(c) the documents would not be exempt from seizure under section 46(2), and

(d) any of the conditions in subsection (3) below applies,

the justice of the peace may issue a warrant authorising an immigration officer or constable to enter and search the premises.

(3) The conditions are that—

(a) it is not practicable to communicate with any person entitled to grant entry to the premises;

(b) it is practicable to communicate with a person entitled to grant entry to the premises but it is not practicable to communicate with any person entitled to grant access to the nationality documents;

(c) entry to the premises will not be granted unless a warrant is produced;

(d) the purpose of a search may be frustrated or seriously prejudiced unless an immigration officer or constable arriving at the premises can secure immediate entry.

(4) Sections 28J and 28K of the Immigration Act 1971 (warrants: application and execution) apply, with any necessary modifications, to warrants under this section.

(5) In the application of this section to Scotland a reference to a justice of the peace shall be treated as a reference to the sheriff or a justice of the peace.

Note: Commencement 29 February 2008 (SI 2008/309), which sets out transitional provisions.

46. Seizure of nationality documents

(1) An immigration officer or constable searching premises under section 44 or 45 may seize a document which the officer or constable thinks is a nationality document in relation to the arrested individual.

(2) Subsection (1) does not apply to a document which—

(a) in relation to England and Wales or Northern Ireland, is subject to legal professional privilege, or

(b) in relation to Scotland, is an item subject to legal privilege within the meaning of section 412 of the Proceeds of Crime Act 2002.

(3) An immigration officer or constable may retain a document seized under subsection (1) while the officer or constable suspects that—

(a) the individual to whom the document relates may be liable to removal from the United Kingdom in accordance with a provision of the Immigration Acts, and

(b) retention of the document may facilitate the individual's removal.

(4) Section 28I of the Immigration Act 1971 (seized material: access and copying) shall have effect in relation to a document seized and retained by an immigration officer.

(5) Section 21 of the Police and Criminal Evidence Act 1984 or Article 23 of the Police and Criminal Evidence (Northern Ireland) Order 1989 (S.I. 1989/1341 (N.I. 12)) (seized material: access and copying) shall have effect in relation to a document seized and retained by a constable in England and Wales or Northern Ireland.

Note: Commencement 29 February 2008 (SI 2008/309), which sets out transitional provisions.

47. Police civilians

. . .

Note: Amends Schedule 4 to the Police Reform Act 2002.

Border and Immigration Inspectorate

48. Establishment

(1) The Secretary of State shall appoint a person as Chief Inspector of [the UK Border Agency].

[(**1A**) The Chief Inspector shall monitor and report on the efficiency and effectiveness of the performance of functions by the following—

(a) designated customs officials, and officials of the Secretary of State exercising customs functions;

(b) immigration officers, and officials of the Secretary of State exercising functions relating to immigration, asylum or nationality;

(c) the Secretary of State in so far as the Secretary of State has general customs functions;

(d) the Secretary of State in so far as the Secretary of State has functions relating to immigration, asylum or nationality;

(e) the Director of Border Revenue and any person exercising functions of the Director.

(**1B**) The Chief Inspector shall monitor and report on the efficiency and effectiveness of the services provided by a person acting pursuant to arrangements relating to the discharge of a function within subsection (1A).]

(2) . . .; in particular, the Chief Inspector shall consider and make recommendations about—

(a) consistency of approach [among the persons listed in subsections (1A) and (1B) (the 'listed persons')],

(b) the practice and performance of [the listed persons] compared to other persons doing similar things,

(c) practice and procedure in making decisions,

(d) the treatment of claimants and applicants,

(e) certification under section 94 of the Nationality, Immigration and Asylum Act 2002 (unfounded claim),

(f) compliance with law about discrimination in the exercise of functions, including reliance on [paragraph 17 of Schedule 3 of the Equality Act 2010] (exception for immigration functions),

(g) practice and procedure in relation to the exercise of enforcement powers (including powers of arrest, entry, search and seizure),

[(ga) practice and procedure in relation to the prevention, detection and investigation of offences, (gb) practice and procedure in relation to the conduct of criminal proceedings,

(gc) whether customs functions have been appropriately exercised by the Secretary of State and the Director of Border Revenue,]

(h) the provision of information,

(i) the handling of complaints, and

(j) the content of information about conditions in countries outside the United Kingdom which the Secretary of State compiles and makes available, for purposes connected with immigration and asylum, to immigration officers and other officials.

[(2A) Unless directed to do so by the Secretary of State, the Chief Inspector shall not monitor and report on the exercise by the listed persons of—

(a) functions at removal centres and short term holding facilities [and in pre-departure accommodation], and under escort arrangements, in so far as Her Majesty's Chief Inspector of Prisons has functions under section 5A of the Prison Act 1952 in relation to such functions, and

(b) functions at detention facilities, in so far as Her Majesty's Inspectors of Constabulary, the Scottish inspectors or the Northern Ireland inspectors have functions by virtue of section 29 of the Borders, Citizenship and Immigration Act 2009 in relation to such functions.]

(3) . . .

[(3A) In this section "customs function", "designated customs official" and "general customs function" have the meanings given by Part 1 of the Borders, Citizenship and Immigration Act 2009.]

(4) The Chief Inspector shall not aim to investigate individual cases (although this subsection does not prevent the Chief Inspector from considering or drawing conclusions about an individual case for the purpose of, or in the context of, considering a general issue).

Note: Commencement 1 April 2008 (SI 2008/309). Words in square brackets in subsection (1)–(2); subsections (1A), (1B), (2)(ga)–(gc), (2A) and (3A) inserted and words in subsection (2) and (3) omitted by s 28 Borders, Citizenship and Immigration Act 2009 from 21 July 2009 (s 58). Words substituted in subsection (2)(f) from 1 October 2010 by the Equality Act 2010, Sch 26, paragraph 86 as inserted by SI 2010/2279. Words in square brackets in subsection (2A)(a) inserted by Sch 9 Immigration Act 2014 from 28 July 2014 (SI 2014/1820).

49. Chief Inspector: supplemental

(1) The Secretary of State shall pay remuneration and allowances to the Chief Inspector.

(2) The Secretary of State—

(a) shall before the beginning of each financial year specify a maximum sum which the Chief Inspector may spend on functions for that year,

(b) may permit that to be exceeded for a specified purpose, and

(c) shall defray the Chief Inspector's expenditure for each financial year subject to paragraphs (a) and (b).

(3) The Chief Inspector shall hold and vacate office in accordance with terms of appointment (which may include provision about retirement, resignation or dismissal).

(4) The Chief Inspector may appoint staff.

(5) A person who is employed by or in any of the following may not be appointed as Chief Inspector—

(a) a government department,
(b) the Scottish Administration,
(c) the National Assembly for Wales, and
(d) a department in Northern Ireland.

Note: Commencement 1 April 2008 (SI 2008/309).

50. Reports

(1) The Chief Inspector shall report in writing to the Secretary of State—

(a) once each calendar year, in relation to the performance of the functions under section 48 generally, and

(b) at other times as requested by the Secretary of State in relation to specified matters.

(2) The Secretary of State shall lay before Parliament a copy of any report received under subsection (1).

(3) But a copy may omit material if the Secretary of State thinks that its publication—
(a) is undesirable for reasons of national security, or
(b) might jeopardise an individual's safety.

Note: Commencement 1 April 2008 (SI 2008/309).

51. Plans

(1) The Chief Inspector shall prepare plans describing the objectives and terms of reference of proposed inspections.

(2) Plans shall be prepared—
(a) at prescribed times and in respect of prescribed periods, and
(b) at such other times, and in respect of such other periods, as the Chief Inspector thinks appropriate.

(3) A plan must—
(a) be in the prescribed form, and
(b) contain the prescribed information.

(4) In preparing a plan the Chief Inspector shall consult—
(a) the Secretary of State, and
(b) prescribed persons.

(5) As soon as is reasonably practicable after preparing a plan the Chief Inspector shall send a copy to—
(a) the Secretary of State, and
(b) each prescribed person.

(6) The Chief Inspector and a prescribed person may by agreement disapply a requirement—
(a) to consult the person, or
(b) to send a copy of a plan to the person.

(7) Nothing in this section prevents the Chief Inspector from doing anything not mentioned in a plan.

Note: Commencement for the purposes of making an order under subsections (2)-(6) 1 April 2008 (SI 2008/309).

52. Relationship with other bodies: general

(1) The Chief Inspector shall cooperate with prescribed persons in so far as the Chief Inspector thinks it consistent with the efficient and effective performance of the functions under section 48.

(2) The Chief Inspector may act jointly with prescribed persons where the Chief Inspector thinks it in the interests of the efficient and effective performance of the functions under section 48.

(3) The Chief Inspector may assist a prescribed person.

(4) The Chief Inspector may delegate a specified aspect of the functions under section 48 to a prescribed person.

Note: Commencement for the purposes of making an order under these provisions 1 April 2008 (SI 2008/309).

53. Relationship with other bodies: non-interference notices

(1) Subsection (2) applies if the Chief Inspector believes that—

(a) a prescribed person proposes to inspect any aspect of the work of [a person listed in section 48(1A) or (1B)], and

(b) the inspection may impose an unreasonable burden on [such a person].

(2) The Chief Inspector may give the prescribed person a notice prohibiting a specified inspection.

(3) The prescribed person shall comply with the notice, unless the Secretary of State cancels it on the grounds that the inspection would not impose an unreasonable burden on [a person listed in section 48(1A) or (1B)].

(4) A notice must—

(a) be in the prescribed form, and

(b) contain the prescribed information.

(5) The Secretary of State may by order make provision about—

(a) the timing of notices;

(b) the publication of notices;

(c) the revision or withdrawal of notices.

Note: Commencement for the purposes of making an order under these provisions 1 April 2008 (SI 2008/309). Words in square brackets in subsections (1) and (3) substituted by s 28 Borders, Citizenship and Immigration Act 2009 from 21 July 2009 (s 58).

54. Abolition of other bodies

Note: Amends s 19E of the Race Relations Act 1976, ss 34, 111, 142 of the Nationality, Immigration and Asylum Act 2002.

55. Prescribed matters

(1) In sections 48 to 53 'prescribed' means prescribed by order of the Secretary of State.

(2) An order under any of those sections—

(a) may make provision generally or only for specified purposes,

(b) may make different provision for different purposes, and

(c) may include incidental or transitional provision.

(3) An order under any of those sections prescribing a person may specify—

(a) one or more persons, or

(b) a class of person.

(4) An order under any of those sections—

(a) shall be made by statutory instrument, and

(b) shall be subject to annulment in pursuance of a resolution of either House of Parliament.

Note: Commencement 1 April 2008 (SI 2008/309).

56. Senior President of Tribunals

(1) . . .

(2) In exercising the function under section 43 of the Tribunals, Courts and Enforcement Act 2007 the Senior President of Tribunals shall have regard to—

(a) the functions of the Chief Inspector of [the UK Border Agency], and

(b) in particular, the Secretary of State's power to request the Chief Inspector to report about specified matters.

Note: Subsection (1) amends s 43(3) of the Tribunals, Courts and Enforcement Act 2007. Commencement 1 April 2008 (SI 2008/309). Words in square brackets substituted by s 28 Borders, Citizenship and Immigration Act 2009 from 21 July 2009 (s 58).

General

56A. No rehabilitation for certain immigration or nationality purposes

(1) Section 4(1), (2) and (3) of the Rehabilitation of Offenders Act 1974 (effect of rehabilitation) do not apply—

(a) in relation to any proceedings in respect of a relevant immigration decision or a relevant nationality decision, or

(b) otherwise for the purposes of, or in connection with, any such decision.

(2) In this section—

'immigration officer' means a person appointed by the Secretary of State as an immigration officer under paragraph 1 of Schedule 2 to the Immigration Act 1971,

'relevant immigration decision' means any decision, or proposed decision, of the Secretary of State or an immigration officer under or by virtue of the Immigration Acts, or rules made under section 3 of the Immigration Act 1971 (immigration rules), in relation to the entitlement of a person to enter or remain in the United Kingdom (including, in particular, the removal of a person from the United Kingdom, whether by deportation or otherwise),

'relevant nationality decision' means any decision, or proposed decision, of the Secretary of State under or by virtue of—

(a) the British Nationality Act 1981,

(b) the British Nationality (Hong Kong) Act 1990, or

(c) the Hong Kong (War Wives and Widows) Act 1996,

in relation to the good character of a person.

(3) The references in subsection (2) to the Immigration Acts and to the Acts listed in the definition of 'relevant nationality decision' include references to any provision made under section 2(2) of the European Communities Act 1972, or of EU law, which relates to the subject matter of the Act concerned.]

Note: Section 56A inserted from 1 October 2012 by the Legal Aid, Sentencing and Punishment of Offenders Act 2012, s 140, subject to transitional and consequential provisions set out in s 141(7)–(9) of that Act.

57. Money

The following shall be paid out of money provided by Parliament—

(a) any expenditure of a Minister of the Crown in consequence of this Act, and

(b) any increase attributable to this Act in sums payable out of money provided by Parliament under another enactment.

Note: Commencement at a date to be appointed.

58. Repeals

. . .

59. Commencement

(1) Section 17 comes into force on the day on which this Act is passed.

(2) The other preceding provisions of this Act shall come into force in accordance with provision made by the Secretary of State by order.

(3) An order—

(a) may make provision generally or only for specified purposes,

(b) may make different provision for different purposes, and

(c) may include incidental, consequential or transitional provision.

(4) In particular, transitional provision—

(a) in the case of an order commencing section 16, may permit the adding of a condition to leave given before the passing of this Act;

(b) in the case of an order commencing section 25, may permit an order to be made in proceedings instituted before the passing of this Act;

(c) in the case of an order commencing section 26, may permit an order or regulations to have effect in relation to property which came into the possession of an immigration officer or the Secretary of State before the passing of this Act;

(d) in the case of an order commencing section 32—

(i) may provide for the section to apply to persons convicted before the passing of this Act who are in custody at the time of commencement or whose sentences are suspended at the time of commencement;

(ii) may modify the application of the section in relation to those persons so as to disapply, or apply only to a specified extent, Condition 2.

(5) An order shall be made by statutory instrument.

Note: Commencement 30 October 2007 (s 59, Royal Assent).

60. Extent

(1) Sections . . . 25 and 31(1) and (2) extend to—
(a) England and Wales, and
(b) Northern Ireland.

(2) Other provisions of this Act extend (subject to subsection (3)) to—
(a) England and Wales,
(b) Scotland, and
(c) Northern Ireland.

(3) A provision of this Act which amends another Act shall (subject to subsection (1)) have the same extent as the relevant part of the amended Act (ignoring extent by virtue of an Order in Council).

(4) Her Majesty may by Order in Council direct that a provision of this Act is to extend, with or without modification or adaptation, to—
(a) any of the Channel Islands;
(b) the Isle of Man.

Note: Commencement 30 October 2007 (s 59, Royal Assent). Numbers in subsection (1) omitted by s 52 Borders, Citizenship and Immigration Act 2009 from a date to be appointed.

61. Citation

(1) This Act may be cited as the UK Borders Act 2007.

(2) A reference (in any enactment, including one passed or made before this Act) to 'the Immigration Acts' is to—
(a) the Immigration Act 1971,
(b) the Immigration Act 1988,
(c) the Asylum and Immigration Appeals Act 1993,
(d) the Asylum and Immigration Act 1996,
(e) the Immigration and Asylum Act 1999,
(f) the Nationality, Immigration and Asylum Act 2002,
(g) the Asylum and Immigration (Treatment of Claimants, etc.) Act 2004,
(h) the Immigration, Asylum and Nationality Act 2006, . . .
(i) this Act[, and
(j) the Immigration Act 2014.]

(3) . . . Section 64(2) (meaning of 'Immigration Acts') shall cease to have effect.

(4) . . .

Note: Subsection (3) repeals s 64(2) of the Immigration, Asylum and Nationality Act 2006. Subsection (4) amends Sch 1 of the Interpretation Act 1978. Commencement 30 October 2007, (s 59 Royal Assent). Subsection (2)(j) inserted by s 73 Immigration Act 2014 from 14 May 2014, s 75.

SCHEDULE

REPEALS

Tribunals, Courts and Enforcement Act 2007
(2007, c. 15)

Chapter 2 First-tier Tribunal and Upper Tribunal

Establishment

3. The First-tier Tribunal and the Upper Tribunal

(1) There is to be a tribunal, known as the First-tier Tribunal, for the purpose of exercising the functions conferred on it under or by virtue of this Act or any other Act.

(2) There is to be a tribunal, known as the Upper Tribunal, for the purpose of exercising the functions conferred on it under or by virtue of this Act or any other Act.

(3) Each of the First-tier Tribunal, and the Upper Tribunal, is to consist of its judges and other members.

(4) The Senior President of Tribunals is to preside over both of the First-tier Tribunal and the Upper Tribunal.

(5) The Upper Tribunal is to be a superior court of record.

Note: Commenced 3 November 2008 (SI 2008/2696).

Members and composition of tribunals

4. Judges and other members of the First-tier Tribunal

(1) A person is a judge of the First-tier Tribunal if the person—

(a) is a judge of the First-tier Tribunal by virtue of appointment under paragraph 1(1) of Schedule 2,

(b) is a transferred-in judge of the First-tier Tribunal (see section 31(2)),

(c) is a judge of the Upper Tribunal,

[(ca) is within section 6A,]

(d) . . . or

(e) is a member of a panel of [Employment Judges].

(2) A person is also a judge of the First-tier Tribunal, but only as regards functions of the tribunal in relation to appeals such as are mentioned in subsection (1) of section 5 of the Criminal Injuries Compensation Act 1995 (c. 53), if the person is an adjudicator appointed under that section by the Scottish Ministers.

(3) A person is one of the other members of the First-tier Tribunal if the person—

(a) is a member of the First-tier Tribunal by virtue of appointment under paragraph 2(1) of Schedule 2,

(b) is a transferred-in other member of the First-tier Tribunal (see section 31(2)),

(c) is one of the other members of the Upper Tribunal, or

(d) is a member of a panel of members of employment tribunals that is not a panel of [Employment Judges].

(4) Schedule 2—

contains provision for the appointment of persons to be judges or other members of the First-tier Tribunal, and

makes further provision in connection with judges and other members of the First-tier Tribunal.

Note: Commenced 3 November 2008 (SI 2008/2696). Subsection (1)(d) omitted from 15 February 2010 (SI 2010/21). Subsection (1)(ca) inserted and words in square brackets in subsections (1)(e) and (3)(d) substituted by Crime and Courts Act 2013, Sch 14 from 1 October 2013 (SI 2013/2200).

5. Judges and other members of the Upper Tribunal

(1) A person is a judge of the Upper Tribunal if the person—

(a) is the Senior President of Tribunals,

(b) is a judge of the Upper Tribunal by virtue of appointment under paragraph 1(1) of Schedule 3, [or]

(c) is a transferred-in judge of the Upper Tribunal (see section 31(2)),

(d) . . .

(f) is a Social Security Commissioner appointed under section 50(2) of that Act (deputy Commissioners),

(g) is within section 6(1),

(h) is a deputy judge of the Upper Tribunal (whether under paragraph 7 of Schedule 3 or under section 31(2)), or

(i) is a Chamber President or a Deputy Chamber President, whether of a chamber of the Upper Tribunal or of a chamber of the First-tier Tribunal, and does not fall within any of paragraphs (a) to (h).

(2) A person is one of the other members of the Upper Tribunal if the person—

(a) is a member of the Upper Tribunal by virtue of appointment under paragraph 2(1) of Schedule 3,

(b) is a transferred-in other member of the Upper Tribunal (see section 31(2)), [or]

(c) is a member of the Employment Appeal Tribunal appointed under section 22(1)(c) of the Employment Tribunals Act 1996 (c. 17),. . .

(d) . . .

(3) Schedule 3—

contains provision for the appointment of persons to be judges (including deputy judges), or other members, of the Upper Tribunal, and

makes further provision in connection with judges and other members of the Upper Tribunal.

Note: Commenced 3 November 2008 (SI 2008/2696). Subsections (1)(d) and 2(d) omitted from 15 February 2010 (SI 2010/21).

6. Certain judges who are also judges of First-tier Tribunal and Upper Tribunal

(1) A person is within this subsection (and so, by virtue of sections 4(1)(c) and 5(1)(g), is a judge of the First-tier Tribunal and of the Upper Tribunal) if the person—

[(za) is the Lord Chief Justice of England and Wales,

(zb) is the Master of the Rolls,

(zc) is the President of the Queen's Bench Division of the High Court in England and Wales,

(zd) is the President of the Family Division of the High Court in England and Wales,

(ze) is the Chancellor of the High Court in England and Wales,]

(a) is an ordinary judge of the Court of Appeal in England and Wales (including the vice-president, if any, of either division of that Court),

(b) is a Lord Justice of Appeal in Northern Ireland,

(c) is a judge of the Court of Session,

(d) is a puisne judge of the High Court in England and Wales or Northern Ireland,

[(da) is a deputy judge of the High Court in England and Wales,

(db) is the Judge Advocate General,]

(e) is a circuit judge,

(f) is a sheriff in Scotland,

(g) is a county court judge in Northern Ireland,

(h) is a district judge in England and Wales or Northern Ireland, or

(i) is a District Judge (Magistrates' Courts).

(2) References in subsection (1)(c) to (i) to office-holders do not include deputies or temporary office-holders.

Note: Commenced 3 November 2008 (SI 2008/2696). Subsections (za)–(ze) and (da)–(db) inserted by Crime and Courts Act 2013, Sch 14 from 1 October 2013 (SI 2013/2200).

[6A Certain judges who are also judges of the First-tier Tribunal

A person is within this section (and so, by virtue of section 4(1)(ca), is a judge of the First-tier Tribunal) if the person—

(a) is a deputy Circuit judge,

(b) is a Recorder,

(c) is a person who holds an office listed—

(i) in the first column of the table in section 89(3C) of the Senior Courts Act 1981 (senior High Court Masters etc), or

(ii) in column 1 of Part 2 of Schedule 2 to that Act (High Court Masters etc),

(d) is a deputy district judge appointed under section 102 of that Act or section 8 of the County Courts Act 1984,

(e) is a Deputy District Judge (Magistrates' Courts), or

(f) is a person appointed under section 30(1)(a) or (b) of the Courts-Martial (Appeals) Act 1951 (assistants to the Judge Advocate General).]

Note: Section 6A inserted by Crime and Courts Act 2013, Sch 14 from 1 October 2013 (SI 2013/2200).

7. Chambers: jurisdiction and Presidents

(1) The Lord Chancellor may, with the concurrence of the Senior President of Tribunals, by order make provision for the organisation of each of the First-tier Tribunal and the Upper Tribunal into a number of chambers.

(2) There is—

(a) for each chamber of the First-tier Tribunal, and

(b) for each chamber of the Upper Tribunal,

to be a person, or two persons, to preside over that chamber.

(3) A person may not at any particular time preside over more than one chamber of the First-tier Tribunal and may not at any particular time preside over more than one chamber of the Upper Tribunal (but may at the same time preside over one chamber of the First-tier Tribunal and over one chamber of the Upper Tribunal).

(4) A person appointed under this section to preside over a chamber is to be known as a Chamber President.

(5) Where two persons are appointed under this section to preside over the same chamber, any reference in an enactment to the Chamber President of the chamber is a reference to a person appointed under this section to preside over the chamber.

(6) The Senior President of Tribunals may (consistently with subsections (2) and (3)) appoint a person who is the Chamber President of a chamber to preside instead, or to preside also, over another chamber.

(7) The [Senior President of Tribunals] may (consistently with subsections (2) and (3)) appoint a person who is not a Chamber President to preside over a chamber.

(8) Schedule 4 (eligibility for appointment under subsection (7), appointment of Deputy Chamber Presidents and Acting Chamber Presidents, assignment of judges and other members of the First-tier Tribunal and Upper Tribunal, and further provision about Chamber Presidents and chambers) has effect.

(9) Each of the Lord Chancellor and the Senior President of Tribunals may, with the concurrence of the other, by order—

(a) make provision for the allocation of the First-tier Tribunal's functions between its chambers;

(b) make provision for the allocation of the Upper Tribunal's functions between its chambers;

(c) amend or revoke any order made under this subsection.

Note: Subsections (1) and (9) in force from 19 September 2007 (SI 2007/2709). Remainder in force from 3 November 2008 (SI 2008/2696). Words in square brackets in subsection (7) substituted by Sch 13 Crime and Courts Act 2013 from 1 October 2013 (SI 2013/2200).

8. Senior President of Tribunals: power to delegate

(1) The Senior President of Tribunals may delegate any function he has in his capacity as Senior President of Tribunals—

(a) to any judge, or other member, of the Upper Tribunal or First-tier Tribunal;

(b) to staff appointed under section 40(1).

[(**1A**) A function under paragraph 1(1) or 2(1) of Schedule 2 may be delegated under subsection (1) only to a Chamber President of a chamber of the Upper Tribunal.]

(2) Subsection (1) does not apply to functions of the Senior President of Tribunals [under any of the following—

section 7(7);
section 7(9);
paragraph 2(1) of Schedule 3;
paragraph 7(1) of Schedule 3;
paragraph 2 of Schedule 4;
paragraph 5(1) and (3) of Schedule 4;
paragraph 5(5) to (8) of Schedule 4;

paragraph 5A(2)(a) of Schedule 4;
paragraph 5A(3)(a) of Schedule 4.]

(3) A delegation under subsection (1) is not revoked by the delegator's becoming incapacitated.

(4) Any delegation under subsection (1) that is in force immediately before a person ceases to be Senior President of Tribunals continues in force until varied or revoked by a subsequent holder of the office of Senior President of Tribunals.

(5) The delegation under this section of a function shall not prevent the exercise of the function by the Senior President of Tribunals.

Note: Commenced 3 November 2008 (SI 2008/2696). Subsection (1A) inserted and words in square brackest in subsection (2) substituted by Crime and Courts Act 2013 from 1 October 2013 (SI 2013/2200).

Review of decisions and appeals

9. Review of decision of First-tier Tribunal

(1) The First-tier Tribunal may review a decision made by it on a matter in a case, other than a decision that is an excluded decision for the purposes of section 11(1) (but see subsection (9)).

(2) The First-tier Tribunal's power under subsection (1) in relation to a decision is exercisable—

(a) of its own initiative, or

(b) on application by a person who for the purposes of section 11(2) has a right of appeal in respect of the decision.

(3) Tribunal Procedure Rules may—

(a) provide that the First-tier Tribunal may not under subsection (1) review (whether of its own initiative or on application under subsection (2)(b)) a decision of a description specified for the purposes of this paragraph in Tribunal Procedure Rules;

(b) provide that the First-tier Tribunal's power under subsection (1) to review a decision of a description specified for the purposes of this paragraph in Tribunal Procedure Rules is exercisable only of the tribunal's own initiative;

(c) provide that an application under subsection (2)(b) that is of a description specified for the purposes of this paragraph in Tribunal Procedure Rules may be made only on grounds specified for the purposes of this paragraph in Tribunal Procedure Rules;

(d) provide, in relation to a decision of a description specified for the purposes of this paragraph in Tribunal Procedure Rules, that the First-tier Tribunal's power under subsection (1) to review the decision of its own initiative is exercisable only on grounds specified for the purposes of this paragraph in Tribunal Procedure Rules.

(4) Where the First-tier Tribunal has under subsection (1) reviewed a decision, the First-tier Tribunal may in the light of the review do any of the following—

(a) correct accidental errors in the decision or in a record of the decision;

(b) amend reasons given for the decision;

(c) set the decision aside.

(5) Where under subsection (4)(c) the First-tier Tribunal sets a decision aside, the First-tier Tribunal must either—

(a) re-decide the matter concerned, or

(b) refer that matter to the Upper Tribunal.

(6) Where a matter is referred to the Upper Tribunal under subsection (5)(b), the Upper Tribunal must re-decide the matter.

(7) Where the Upper Tribunal is under subsection (6) re-deciding a matter, it may make any decision which the First-tier Tribunal could make if the First-tier Tribunal were re-deciding the matter.

(8) Where a tribunal is acting under subsection (5)(a) or (6), it may make such findings of fact as it considers appropriate.

(9) This section has effect as if a decision under subsection (4)(c) to set aside an earlier decision were not an excluded decision for the purposes of section 11(1), but the First-tier Tribunal's only power in the light of a review under subsection (1) of a decision under subsection (4)(c) is the power under subsection (4)(a).

(10) A decision of the First-tier Tribunal may not be reviewed under subsection (1) more than once, and once the First-tier Tribunal has decided that an earlier decision should not be reviewed under subsection (1) it may not then decide to review that earlier decision under that subsection.

(11) Where under this section a decision is set aside and the matter concerned is then re-decided, the decision set aside and the decision made in re-deciding the matter are for the purposes of subsection (10) to be taken to be different decisions.

Note: Subsection (3) in force from 19 September 2007 (SI 2007/2709). Remainder in force from 3 November 2008 (SI 2008/2696).

10. Review of decision of Upper Tribunal

(1) The Upper Tribunal may review a decision made by it on a matter in a case, other than a decision that is an excluded decision for the purposes of section 13(1) (but see subsection (7)).

(2) The Upper Tribunal's power under subsection (1) in relation to a decision is exercisable—

(a) of its own initiative, or

(b) on application by a person who for the purposes of section 13(2) has a right of appeal in respect of the decision.

(3) Tribunal Procedure Rules may—

(a) provide that the Upper Tribunal may not under subsection (1) review (whether of its own initiative or on application under subsection (2)(b)) a decision of a description specified for the purposes of this paragraph in Tribunal Procedure Rules;

(b) provide that the Upper Tribunal's power under subsection (1) to review a decision of a description specified for the purposes of this paragraph in Tribunal Procedure Rules is exercisable only of the tribunal's own initiative;

(c) provide that an application under subsection (2)(b) that is of a description specified for the purposes of this paragraph in Tribunal Procedure Rules may be made only on grounds specified for the purposes of this paragraph in Tribunal Procedure Rules;

(d) provide, in relation to a decision of a description specified for the purposes of this paragraph in Tribunal Procedure Rules, that the Upper Tribunal's power under subsection (1) to review the decision of its own initiative is exercisable only on grounds specified for the purposes of this paragraph in Tribunal Procedure Rules.

(4) Where the Upper Tribunal has under subsection (1) reviewed a decision, the Upper Tribunal may in the light of the review do any of the following—

(a) correct accidental errors in the decision or in a record of the decision;

(b) amend reasons given for the decision;

(c) set the decision aside.

(5) Where under subsection (4)(c) the Upper Tribunal sets a decision aside, the Upper Tribunal must re-decide the matter concerned.

(6) Where the Upper Tribunal is acting under subsection (5), it may make such findings of fact as it considers appropriate.

(7) This section has effect as if a decision under subsection (4)(c) to set aside an earlier decision were not an excluded decision for the purposes of section 13(1), but the Upper Tribunal's only power in the light of a review under subsection (1) of a decision under subsection (4)(c) is the power under subsection (4)(a).

(8) A decision of the Upper Tribunal may not be reviewed under subsection (1) more than once, and once the Upper Tribunal has decided that an earlier decision should not be reviewed under subsection (1) it may not then decide to review that earlier decision under that subsection.

(9) Where under this section a decision is set aside and the matter concerned is then re-decided, the decision set aside and the decision made in re-deciding the matter are for the purposes of subsection (8) to be taken to be different decisions.

Note: Subsection (3) in force from 19 September 2007 (SI 2007/2709). Remainder in force from 3 November 2008 (SI 2008/2696).

11. Right to appeal to Upper Tribunal

(1) For the purposes of subsection (2), the reference to a right of appeal is to a right to appeal to the Upper Tribunal on any point of law arising from a decision made by the First-tier Tribunal other than an excluded decision.

(2) Any party to a case has a right of appeal, subject to subsection (8).

(3) That right may be exercised only with permission (or, in Northern Ireland, leave).

(4) Permission (or leave) may be given by—

(a) the First-tier Tribunal, or

(b) the Upper Tribunal, on an application by the party.

(5) For the purposes of subsection (1), an "excluded decision" is—

(a) any decision of the First-tier Tribunal on an appeal made in exercise of a right conferred by the Criminal Injuries Compensation Scheme in compliance with section 5(1)(a) of the Criminal Injuries Compensation Act 1995 (c. 53) (appeals against decisions on reviews),

[(aa) any decision of the First-tier Tribunal on an appeal made in exercise of a right conferred by the Victims of Overseas Terrorism Compensation Scheme in compliance with section 52(3) of the Crime and Security Act 2010,]

(b) any decision of the First-tier Tribunal on an appeal under section 28(4) or (6) of the Data Protection Act 1998 (c. 29) (appeals against national security certificate),

(c) any decision of the First-tier Tribunal on an appeal under section 60(1) or (4) of the Freedom of Information Act 2000 (c. 36) (appeals against national security certificate),

(d) a decision of the First-tier Tribunal under section 9—

(i) to review, or not to review, an earlier decision of the tribunal,

(ii) to take no action, or not to take any particular action, in the light of a review of an earlier decision of the tribunal,

(iii) to set aside an earlier decision of the tribunal, or

(iv) to refer, or not to refer, a matter to the Upper Tribunal,

(e) a decision of the First-tier Tribunal that is set aside under section 9 (including a decision set aside after proceedings on an appeal under this section have been begun), or

(f) any decision of the First-tier Tribunal that is of a description specified in an order made by the Lord Chancellor.

(6) A description may be specified under subsection (5)(f) only if—

(a) in the case of a decision of that description, there is a right to appeal to a court, the Upper Tribunal or any other tribunal from the decision and that right is, or includes, something other than a right (however expressed) to appeal on any point of law arising from the decision, or

(b) decisions of that description are made in carrying out a function transferred under section 30 and prior to the transfer of the function under section 30(1) there was no right to appeal from decisions of that description.

(7) Where—

(a) an order under subsection (5)(f) specifies a description of decisions, and

(b) decisions of that description are made in carrying out a function transferred under section 30, the order must be framed so as to come into force no later than the time when the transfer under section 30 of the function takes effect (but power to revoke the order continues to be exercisable after that time, and power to amend the order continues to be exercisable after that time for the purpose of narrowing the description for the time being specified).

(8) The Lord Chancellor may by order make provision for a person to be treated as being, or to be treated as not being, a party to a case for the purposes of subsection (2).

Note: Subsection (5)(f) and (6)–(8) in force from 19 September 2007 (SI 2007/2709). Remainder in force from 3 November 2008 (SI 2008/2696). Application of s 11 modified by SI 2010/22 Sch 5, paragraph 5(a) from 18 January 2010. Subsection (5)(aa) inserted from 8 April 2010 by Crime and Security Act 2010. There are other modifications/exclusions not relevant to immigration law.

12. Proceedings on appeal to Upper Tribunal

(1) Subsection (2) applies if the Upper Tribunal, in deciding an appeal under section 11, finds that the making of the decision concerned involved the making of an error on a point of law.

(2) The Upper Tribunal—

(a) may (but need not) set aside the decision of the First-tier Tribunal, and

(b) if it does, must either—

(i) remit the case to the First-tier Tribunal with directions for its reconsideration, or

(ii) re-make the decision.

(3) In acting under subsection (2)(b)(i), the Upper Tribunal may also—

(a) direct that the members of the First-tier Tribunal who are chosen to reconsider the case are not to be the same as those who made the decision that has been set aside;

(b) give procedural directions in connection with the reconsideration of the case by the First-tier Tribunal.

(4) In acting under subsection (2)(b)(ii), the Upper Tribunal—

(a) may make any decision which the First-tier Tribunal could make if the First-tier Tribunal were re-making the decision, and

(b) may make such findings of fact as it considers appropriate.

Note: Commenced 3 November 2008 (SI 2008/2696).

13. Right to appeal to Court of Appeal etc.

(1) For the purposes of subsection (2), the reference to a right of appeal is to a right to appeal to the relevant appellate court on any point of law arising from a decision made by the Upper Tribunal other than an excluded decision.

(2) Any party to a case has a right of appeal, subject to subsection (14).

(3) That right may be exercised only with permission (or, in Northern Ireland, leave).

(4) Permission (or leave) may be given by—

(a) the Upper Tribunal, or

(b) the relevant appellate court, on an application by the party.

(5) An application may be made under subsection (4) to the relevant appellate court only if permission (or leave) has been refused by the Upper Tribunal.

(6) The Lord Chancellor may, as respects an application under subsection (4) that falls within subsection (7) and for which the relevant appellate court is the Court of Appeal in England and Wales or the Court of Appeal in Northern Ireland, by order make provision for permission (or leave) not to be granted on the application unless the Upper Tribunal or (as the case may be) the relevant appellate court considers—

(a) that the proposed appeal would raise some important point of principle or practice, or

(b) that there is some other compelling reason for the relevant appellate court to hear the appeal.

[(**6A**) Rules of court may make provision for permission not to be granted on an application under subsection (4) to the Court of Session that falls within subsection (7) unless the court considers—

(a) that the proposed appeal would raise some important point of principle, or

(b) that there is some other compelling reason for the court to hear the appeal.]

(7) An application falls within this subsection if the application is for permission (or leave) to appeal from any decision of the Upper Tribunal on an appeal under section 11.

(8) For the purposes of subsection (1), an "excluded decision" is—

(a) any decision of the Upper Tribunal on an appeal under section 28(4) or (6) of the Data Protection Act 1998 (c. 29) (appeals against national security certificate),

(b) any decision of the Upper Tribunal on an appeal under section 60(1) or (4) of the Freedom of Information Act 2000 (c. 36) (appeals against national security certificate),

(c) any decision of the Upper Tribunal on an application under section 11(4)(b) (application for permission or leave to appeal),

(d) a decision of the Upper Tribunal under section 10—

(i) to review, or not to review, an earlier decision of the tribunal,

(ii) to take no action, or not to take any particular action, in the light of a review of an earlier decision of the tribunal, or

(iii) to set aside an earlier decision of the tribunal,

(e) a decision of the Upper Tribunal that is set aside under section 10 (including a decision set aside after proceedings on an appeal under this section have been begun), or

(f) any decision of the Upper Tribunal that is of a description specified in an order made by the Lord Chancellor.

(9) A description may be specified under subsection (8)(f) only if—

(a) in the case of a decision of that description, there is a right to appeal to a court from the decision and that right is, or includes, something other than a right (however expressed) to appeal on any point of law arising from the decision, or

(b) decisions of that description are made in carrying out a function transferred under section 30 and prior to the transfer of the function under section 30(1) there was no right to appeal from decisions of that description.

(10) Where—

(a) an order under subsection (8)(f) specifies a description of decisions, and

(b) decisions of that description are made in carrying out a function

transferred under section 30, the order must be framed so as to come into force no later than the time when the transfer under section 30 of the function takes effect (but power to revoke the order continues to be exercisable after that time, and power to amend the order continues to be exercisable after that time for the purpose of narrowing the description for the time being specified).

(11) Before the Upper Tribunal decides an application made to it under subsection (4), the Upper Tribunal must specify the court that is to be the relevant appellate court as respects the proposed appeal.

(12) The court to be specified under subsection (11) in relation to a proposed appeal is whichever of the following courts appears to the Upper Tribunal to be the most appropriate—

(a) the Court of Appeal in England and Wales;

(b) the Court of Session;

(c) the Court of Appeal in Northern Ireland.

(13) In this section except subsection (11), "the relevant appellate court", as respects an appeal, means the court specified as respects that appeal by the Upper Tribunal under subsection (11).

(14) The Lord Chancellor may by order make provision for a person to be treated as being, or to be treated as not being, a party to a case for the purposes of subsection (2).

(15) Rules of court may make provision as to the time within which an application under subsection (4) to the relevant appellate court must be made.

Note: Subsections (6), (8)(f), (9), (10), (14) and (15) in force from 19 September 2007 (SI 2007/2709). Remainder in force from 3 November 2008 (SI 2008/2696). Application of s 11 modified by SI 2010/22 Sch 5, paragraph 5(a) from 18 January 2010. Subsection (6A) inserted by s 23 Crime and Courts Act 2013 from 15 July 2013.

14. Proceedings on appeal to Court of Appeal etc.

(1) Subsection (2) applies if the relevant appellate court, in deciding an appeal under section 13, finds that the making of the decision concerned involved the making of an error on a point of law.

(2) The relevant appellate court—

(a) may (but need not) set aside the decision of the Upper Tribunal, and

(b) if it does, must either—

(i) remit the case to the Upper Tribunal or, where the decision of the Upper Tribunal was on an appeal or reference from another tribunal or some other person, to the Upper Tribunal or that other tribunal or person, with directions for its reconsideration, or

(ii) re-make the decision.

(3) In acting under subsection (2)(b)(i), the relevant appellate court may also—

(a) direct that the persons who are chosen to reconsider the case are not to be the same as those who—

(i) where the case is remitted to the Upper Tribunal, made the decision of the Upper Tribunal that has been set aside, or

(ii) where the case is remitted to another tribunal or person, made the decision in respect of which the appeal or reference to the Upper Tribunal was made;

(b) give procedural directions in connection with the reconsideration of the case by the Upper Tribunal or other tribunal or person.

(4) In acting under subsection (2)(b)(ii), the relevant appellate court—

(a) may make any decision which the Upper Tribunal could make if the Upper Tribunal were re-making the decision or (as the case may be) which the other tribunal or person could make if that other tribunal or person were re-making the decision, and

(b) may make such findings of fact as it considers appropriate.

(5) Where—

(a) under subsection (2)(b)(i) the relevant appellate court remits a case to the Upper Tribunal, and

(b) the decision set aside under subsection (2)(a) was made by the Upper Tribunal on an appeal or reference from another tribunal or some other person,

the Upper Tribunal may (instead of reconsidering the case itself) remit the case to that other tribunal or person, with the directions given by the relevant appellate court for its reconsideration.

(6) In acting under subsection (5), the Upper Tribunal may also—

(a) direct that the persons who are chosen to reconsider the case are not to be the same as those who made the decision in respect of which the appeal or reference to the Upper Tribunal was made;

(b) give procedural directions in connection with the reconsideration of the case by the other tribunal or person.

(7) In this section "the relevant appellate court", as respects an appeal under section 13, means the court specified as respects that appeal by the Upper Tribunal under section 13(11).

Note: Commenced 3 November 2008 (SI 2008/2696).

Judicial review

15. Upper Tribunal's "judicial review" jurisdiction

(1) The Upper Tribunal has power, in cases arising under the law of England and Wales or under the law of Northern Ireland, to grant the following kinds of relief—

(a) a mandatory order;
(b) a prohibiting order;
(c) a quashing order;
(d) a declaration;
(e) an injunction.

(2) The power under subsection (1) may be exercised by the Upper Tribunal if—

(a) certain conditions are met (see section 18), or

(b) the tribunal is authorised to proceed even though not all of those conditions are met (see section 19(3) and (4)).

(3) Relief under subsection (1) granted by the Upper Tribunal—

(a) has the same effect as the corresponding relief granted by the High Court on an application for judicial review, and

(b) is enforceable as if it were relief granted by the High Court on an application for judicial review.

(4) In deciding whether to grant relief under subsection (1)(a), (b) or (c), the Upper Tribunal must apply the principles that the High Court would apply in deciding whether to grant that relief on an application for judicial review.

(5) In deciding whether to grant relief under subsection (1)(d) or (e), the Upper Tribunal must—

(a) in cases arising under the law of England and Wales apply the principles that the High Court would apply in deciding whether to grant that relief under section 31(2) of the [Senior Courts Act 1981] (c. 54) on an application for judicial review, and

(b) in cases arising under the law of Northern Ireland apply the principles that the High Court would apply in deciding whether to grant that relief on an application for judicial review.

(6) For the purposes of the application of subsection (3)(a) in relation to cases arising under the law of Northern Ireland—

(a) a mandatory order under subsection (1)(a) shall be taken to correspond to an order of mandamus,

(b) a prohibiting order under subsection (1)(b) shall be taken to correspond to an order of prohibition, and

(c) a quashing order under subsection (1)(c) shall be taken to correspond to an order of certiorari.

Note: Commenced 3 November 2008 (SI 2008/2696). Words in square brackets is subsection (5)(a) substituted by Sch 11 Constitutional Reform Act 2005 from 1 October 2009 (SI 2009/1604).

16. Application for relief under section 15(1)

(1) This section applies in relation to an application to the Upper Tribunal for relief under section 15(1).

(2) The application may be made only if permission (or, in a case arising under the law of Northern Ireland, leave) to make it has been obtained from the tribunal.

(3) The tribunal may not grant permission (or leave) to make the application unless it considers that the applicant has a sufficient interest in the matter to which the application relates.

(4) Subsection (5) applies where the tribunal considers—

(a) that there has been undue delay in making the application, and

(b) that granting the relief sought on the application would be likely to cause substantial hardship to, or substantially prejudice the rights of, any person or would be detrimental to good administration.

(5) The tribunal may—

(a) refuse to grant permission (or leave) for the making of the application;

(b) refuse to grant any relief sought on the application.

(6) The tribunal may award to the applicant damages, restitution or the recovery of a sum due if—

(a) the application includes a claim for such an award arising from any matter to which the application relates, and

(b) the tribunal is satisfied that such an award would have been made by the High Court if the claim had been made in an action begun in the High Court by the applicant at the time of making the application.

(7) An award under subsection (6) may be enforced as if it were an award of the High Court.

(8) Where—

(a) the tribunal refuses to grant permission (or leave) to apply for relief under section 15(1),

(b) the applicant appeals against that refusal, and

(c) the Court of Appeal grants the permission (or leave),

the Court of Appeal may go on to decide the application for relief under section 15(1).

(9) Subsections (4) and (5) do not prevent Tribunal Procedure Rules from limiting the time within which applications may be made.

Note: Commenced 3 November 2008 (SI 2008/2696).

17. Quashing orders under section 15(1): supplementary provision

(1) If the Upper Tribunal makes a quashing order under section 15(1)(c) in respect of a decision, it may in addition—

(a) remit the matter concerned to the court, tribunal or authority that made the decision, with a direction to reconsider the matter and reach a decision in accordance with the findings of the Upper Tribunal, or

(b) substitute its own decision for the decision in question.

(2) The power conferred by subsection (1)(b) is exercisable only if—

(a) the decision in question was made by a court or tribunal,

(b) the decision is quashed on the ground that there has been an error of law, and

(c) without the error, there would have been only one decision that the court or tribunal could have reached.

(3) Unless the Upper Tribunal otherwise directs, a decision substituted by it under subsection (1)(b) has effect as if it were a decision of the relevant court or tribunal.

Note: Commenced 3 November 2008 (SI 2008/2696).

18. Limits of jurisdiction under section 15(1)

(1) This section applies where an application made to the Upper Tribunal seeks (whether or not alone)—

(a) relief under section 15(1), or

(b) permission (or, in a case arising under the law of Northern Ireland, leave) to apply for relief under section 15(1).

(2) If Conditions 1 to 4 are met, the tribunal has the function of deciding the application.

(3) If the tribunal does not have the function of deciding the application, it must by order transfer the application to the High Court.

(4) Condition 1 is that the application does not seek anything other than—

(a) relief under section 15(1);

(b) permission (or, in a case arising under the law of Northern Ireland, leave) to apply for relief under section 15(1);

(c) an award under section 16(6);

(d) interest;

(e) costs.

(5) Condition 2 is that the application does not call into question anything done by the Crown Court.

(6) Condition 3 is that the application falls within a class specified for the purposes of this subsection in a direction given in accordance with Part 1 of Schedule 2 to the Constitutional Reform Act 2005 (c. 4).

(7) The power to give directions under subsection (6) includes—

(a) power to vary or revoke directions made in exercise of the power, and

(b) power to make different provision for different purposes.

(8) Condition 4 is that the judge presiding at the hearing of the application is either—

(a) a judge of the High Court or the Court of Appeal in England and Wales or Northern Ireland, or a judge of the Court of Session, or

(b) such other persons as may be agreed from time to time between the Lord Chief Justice, the Lord President, or the Lord Chief Justice of Northern Ireland, as the case may be, and the Senior President of Tribunals.

(9) Where the application is transferred to the High Court under subsection (3)—

(a) the application is to be treated for all purposes as if it—

(i) had been made to the High Court, and

(ii) sought things corresponding to those sought from the tribunal, and

(b) any steps taken, permission (or leave) given or orders made by the tribunal in relation to the application are to be treated as taken, given or made by the High Court.

(10) Rules of court may make provision for the purpose of supplementing subsection (9).

(11) The provision that may be made by Tribunal Procedure Rules about amendment of an application for relief under section 15(1) includes, in particular, provision about amendments that would cause the application to become transferrable under subsection (3).

(12) For the purposes of subsection (9)(a)(ii), in relation to an application transferred to the High Court in Northern Ireland—

(a) an order of mandamus shall be taken to correspond to a mandatory order under section 15(1)(a),

(b) an order of prohibition shall be taken to correspond to a prohibiting order under section 15(1)(b), and

(c) an order of certiorari shall be taken to correspond to a quashing order under section 15(1)(c).

Note: Subsections (10) and (11) in force from 19 September 2007 (SI 2007/2709). Remainder in force from 3 November 2008 (SI 2008/2696).

19. Transfer of judicial review applications from High Court

(1) . . .

(2) . . .

(3) Where an application is transferred to the Upper Tribunal under 31A of the [Senior Courts Act 1981] or section 25A of the Judicature (Northern Ireland) Act 1978 (transfer from the High Court of judicial review applications)—

(a) the application is to be treated for all purposes as if it—

(i) had been made to the tribunal, and

(ii) sought things corresponding to those sought from the High Court,

(b) the tribunal has the function of deciding the application, even if it does not fall within a class specified under section 18(6), and

(c) any steps taken, permission given, leave given or orders made by the High Court in relation to the application are to be treated as taken, given or made by the tribunal.

(4) Where—

(a) an application for permission is transferred to the Upper Tribunal under section 31A of the [Senior Courts Act 1981] and the tribunal grants permission, or

(b) an application for leave is transferred to the Upper Tribunal under section 25A of the Judicature (Northern Ireland) Act 1978 (c. 23) and the tribunal grants leave, the tribunal has the function of deciding any subsequent application brought under the permission or leave, even if the subsequent application does not fall within a class specified under section 18(6).

(5) Tribunal Procedure Rules may make further provision for the purposes of supplementing subsections (3) and (4).

(6) For the purposes of subsection (3)(a)(ii), in relation to an application transferred to the Upper Tribunal under section 25A of the Judicature (Northern Ireland) Act 1978—

(a) a mandatory order under section 15(1)(a) shall be taken to correspond to an order of mandamus,

(b) a prohibiting order under section 15(1)(b) shall be taken to correspond to an order of prohibition, and

(c) a quashing order under section 15(1)(c) shall be taken to correspond to an order of certiorari.

Note: Commenced 3 November 2008 (SI 2008/2696). Subsection (1) amends the Supreme Court Act 1981. Subsection (2) amends the Judicature (Northern Ireland) Act 1978. Words in square brackets in subsections (3) and (4) substituted by Sch 11 Constitutional Reform Act 2005 from 1 October 2009 (SI 2009/1064).

20. Transfer of judicial review applications from the Court of Session

(1) Where an application is made to the supervisory jurisdiction of the Court of Session, the Court—

(a) must, if Conditions 1 [and 2 are met, and]

[aa . . .]

(b) may, if Conditions 1 [and 3] are met, but Condition 2 is not, by order transfer the application to the Upper Tribunal.

(2) Condition 1 is that the application does not seek anything other than an exercise of the supervisory jurisdiction of the Court of Session.

(3) Condition 2 is that the application falls within a class specified for the purposes of this subsection by act of sederunt made with the consent of the Lord Chancellor.

(4) Condition 3 is that the subject matter of the application is not a devolved Scottish matter.

(5) . . .

[(5A) . . .]

(6) There may not be specified under subsection (3) any class of application which includes an application the subject matter of which is a devolved Scottish matter.

(7) For the purposes of this section, the subject matter of an application is a devolved Scottish matter if it—

(a) concerns the exercise of functions in or as regards Scotland, and

(b) does not relate to a reserved matter within the meaning of the Scotland Act 1998 (c. 46).

(8) In subsection (2), the reference to the exercise of the supervisory jurisdiction of the Court of Session includes a reference to the making of any order in connection with or in consequence of the exercise of that jurisdiction.

Note: Subsections (3), (6) and (7) in force from 19 September 2007 (SI 2007/2709). Remainder in force from 3 November 2008 (SI 2008/2696). Subsections (1)(aa) and (5A) inserted by the UK Borders Act 8 November 2009 (SI 2011/1741) and omitted by s 22 Crime and Courts Act 2013 from 1 November 2013 (SI 2013/2200). Words in square brackets in subsection (1) substituted and subsection (5) omitted from 1 November 2013 (SI 2013/2200).

21. Upper Tribunal's "judicial review" jurisdiction: Scotland

(1) The Upper Tribunal has the function of deciding applications transferred to it from the Court of Session under section 20(1).

(2) The powers of review of the Upper Tribunal in relation to such applications are the same as the powers of review of the Court of Session in an application to the supervisory jurisdiction of that Court.

(3) In deciding an application by virtue of subsection (1), the Upper Tribunal must apply principles that the Court of Session would apply in deciding an application to the supervisory jurisdiction of that Court.

(4) An order of the Upper Tribunal by virtue of subsection (1)—

(a) has the same effect as the corresponding order granted by the Court of Session on an application to the supervisory jurisdiction of that Court, and

(b) is enforceable as if it were an order so granted by that Court.

(5) Where an application is transferred to the Upper Tribunal by virtue of section 20(1), any steps taken or orders made by the Court of Session in relation to the application (other than the order to transfer the application under section 20(1)) are to be treated as taken or made by the tribunal.

(6) Tribunal Procedure Rules may make further provision for the purposes of supplementing subsection (5).

Note: Subsection (6) in force from 19 September 2007 (SI 2007/2709). Remainder in force from 3 November 2008 (SI 2008/2696).

Miscellaneous

22. Tribunal Procedure Rules

(1) There are to be rules, to be called "Tribunal Procedure Rules", governing—

(a) the practice and procedure to be followed in the First-tier Tribunal, and

(b) the practice and procedure to be followed in the Upper Tribunal.

(2) Tribunal Procedure Rules are to be made by the Tribunal Procedure Committee.

(3) In Schedule 5—

Part 1 makes further provision about the content of Tribunal Procedure Rules,

Part 2 makes provision about the membership of the Tribunal Procedure Committee,

Part 3 makes provision about the making of Tribunal Procedure Rules by the Committee, and

Part 4 confers power to amend legislation in connection with Tribunal Procedure Rules.

(4) Power to make Tribunal Procedure Rules is to be exercised with a view to securing—

(a) that, in proceedings before the First-tier Tribunal and Upper Tribunal, justice is done,

(b) that the tribunal system is accessible and fair,

(c) that proceedings before the First-tier Tribunal or Upper Tribunal are handled quickly and efficiently,

(d) that the rules are both simple and simply expressed, and

(e) that the rules where appropriate confer on members of the First-tier Tribunal, or Upper Tribunal, responsibility for ensuring that proceedings before the tribunal are handled quickly and efficiently.

(5) In subsection (4)(b) "the tribunal system" means the system for deciding matters within the jurisdiction of the First-tier Tribunal or the Upper Tribunal.

Note: Commenced 19 September 2007 (SI 2007/2709).

23. Practice directions

(1) The Senior President of Tribunals may give directions—

(a) as to the practice and procedure of the First-tier Tribunal;

(b) as to the practice and procedure of the Upper Tribunal.

(2) A Chamber President may give directions as to the practice and procedure of the chamber over which he presides.

(3) A power under this section to give directions includes—

(a) power to vary or revoke directions made in exercise of the power, and

(b) power to make different provision for different purposes (including different provision for different areas).

(4) Directions under subsection (1) may not be given without the approval of the Lord Chancellor.

(5) Directions under subsection (2) may not be given without the approval of—

(a) the Senior President of Tribunals, and

(b) the Lord Chancellor.

(6) Subsections (4) and (5)(b) do not apply to directions to the extent that they consist of guidance about any of the following—

(a) the application or interpretation of the law;

(b) the making of decisions by members of the First-tier Tribunal or Upper Tribunal.

(7) Subsections (4) and (5)(b) do not apply to directions to the extent that they consist of criteria for determining which members of the First-tier Tribunal or Upper Tribunal may be chosen to decide particular categories of matter; but the directions may, to that extent, be given only after consulting the Lord Chancellor.

Note: Commenced 3 November 2008 (SI 2008/2696).

24. Mediation

(1) A person exercising power to make Tribunal Procedure Rules or give practice directions must, when making provision in relation to mediation, have regard to the following principles—

(a) mediation of matters in dispute between parties to proceedings is to take place only by agreement between those parties;

(b) where parties to proceedings fail to mediate, or where mediation between parties to proceedings fails to resolve disputed matters, the failure is not to affect the outcome of the proceedings.

(2) Practice directions may provide for members to act as mediators in relation to disputed matters in a case that is the subject of proceedings.

(3) The provision that may be made by virtue of subsection (2) includes provision for a member to act as a mediator in relation to disputed matters in a case even though the member has been chosen to decide matters in the case.

(4) Once a member has begun to act as a mediator in relation to a disputed matter in a case that is the subject of proceedings, the member may decide matters in the case only with the consent of the parties.

(5) Staff appointed under section 40(1) may, subject to their terms of appointment, act as mediators in relation to disputed matters in a case that is the subject of proceedings.

(6) In this section—

'member' means a judge or other member of the First-tier Tribunal or a judge or other member of the Upper Tribunal;

'practice direction' means a direction under section 23(1) or (2);

'proceedings' means proceedings before the First-tier Tribunal or proceedings before the Upper Tribunal.

Note: Commenced 3 November 2008 (SI 2008/2696).

25. Supplementary powers of Upper Tribunal

(1) In relation to the matters mentioned in subsection (2), the Upper Tribunal—

(a) has, in England and Wales or in Northern Ireland, the same powers, rights, privileges and authority as the High Court, and

(b) has, in Scotland, the same powers, rights, privileges and authority as the Court of Session.

(2) The matters are—

(a) the attendance and examination of witnesses,

(b) the production and inspection of documents, and

(c) all other matters incidental to the Upper Tribunal's functions.

(3) Subsection (1) shall not be taken—

(a) to limit any power to make Tribunal Procedure Rules;

(b) to be limited by anything in Tribunal Procedure Rules other than an express limitation.

(4) A power, right, privilege or authority conferred in a territory by subsection (1) is available for purposes of proceedings in the Upper Tribunal that take place outside that territory (as well as for purposes of proceedings in the tribunal that take place within that territory).

Note: Commenced 3 November 2008 (SI 2008/2696).

26. First-tier Tribunal and Upper Tribunal: sitting places

Each of the First-tier Tribunal and the Upper Tribunal may decide a case—

(a) in England and Wales,

(b) in Scotland, or

(c) in Northern Ireland, even though the case arises under the law of a territory other than the one in which the case is decided.

Note: Commenced 3 November 2008 (SI 2008/2696).

27. Enforcement

(1) A sum payable in pursuance of a decision of the First-tier Tribunal or Upper Tribunal made in England and Wales—

(a) shall be recoverable as if it were payable under an order of [the county court] in England and Wales;

(b) shall be recoverable as if it were payable under an order of the High Court in England and Wales.

(2) An order for the payment of a sum payable in pursuance of a decision of the First-tier Tribunal or Upper Tribunal made in Scotland (or a copy of such an order certified in accordance with Tribunal Procedure Rules) may be enforced as if it were an extract registered decree arbitral bearing a warrant for execution issued by the sheriff court of any sheriffdom in Scotland.

(3) A sum payable in pursuance of a decision of the First-tier Tribunal or Upper Tribunal made in Northern Ireland—

(a) shall be recoverable as if it were payable under an order of a county court in Northern Ireland;

(b) shall be recoverable as if it were payable under an order of the High Court in Northern Ireland.

(4) This section does not apply to a sum payable in pursuance of—

(a) an award under section 16(6), or

(b) an order by virtue of section 21(1).

(5) The Lord Chancellor may by order make provision for subsection (1) or (3) to apply in relation to a sum of a description specified in the order with the omission of one (but not both) of paragraphs (a) and (b).

(6) Tribunal Procedure Rules—

(a) may make provision as to where, for purposes of this section, a decision is to be taken to be made;

(b) may provide for all or any of subsections (1) to (3) to apply only, or not to apply except, in relation to sums of a description specified in Tribunal Procedure Rules. Tribunals, Courts and Enforcement Act 2007 (c. 15).

Note: Subsections (5) and (6) in force from 19 September 2007 (SI 2007/2709). Remainder in force from 3 November 2008 (SI 2008/2696). Words in square brackets substituted by Schedule 9 Crime and Courts Act 2013 from 22 April 2014 (SI 2014/954).

28. Assessors

(1) If it appears to the First-tier Tribunal or the Upper Tribunal that a matter before it requires special expertise not otherwise available to it, it may direct that in dealing with that matter it shall have the assistance of a person or persons appearing to it to have relevant knowledge or experience.

(2) The remuneration of a person who gives assistance to either tribunal as mentioned in subsection (1) shall be determined and paid by the Lord Chancellor.

(3) The Lord Chancellor may—

(a) establish panels of persons from which either tribunal may (but need not) select persons to give it assistance as mentioned in subsection (1);

(b) under paragraph (a) establish different panels for different purposes;

(c) after carrying out such consultation as he considers appropriate, appoint persons to a panel established under paragraph (a);

(d) remove a person from such a panel.

Note: Commenced 3 November 2008 (SI 2008/2696).

29. Costs or expenses

(1) The costs of and incidental to—

(a) all proceedings in the First-tier Tribunal, and

(b) all proceedings in the Upper Tribunal, shall be in the discretion of the Tribunal in which the proceedings take place.

(2) The relevant Tribunal shall have full power to determine by whom and to what extent the costs are to be paid.

(3) Subsections (1) and (2) have effect subject to Tribunal Procedure Rules.

(4) In any proceedings mentioned in subsection (1), the relevant Tribunal may—

(a) disallow, or

(b) (as the case may be) order the legal or other representative concerned to meet, the whole of any wasted costs or such part of them as may be determined in accordance with Tribunal Procedure Rules.

(5) In subsection (4) "wasted costs" means any costs incurred by a party—

(a) as a result of any improper, unreasonable or negligent act or omission on the part of any legal or other representative or any employee of such a representative, or

(b) which, in the light of any such act or omission occurring after they were incurred, the relevant Tribunal considers it is unreasonable to expect that party to pay.

(6) In this section "legal or other representative", in relation to a party to proceedings, means any person exercising a right of audience or right to conduct the proceedings on his behalf.

(7) In the application of this section in relation to Scotland, any reference in this section to costs is to be read as a reference to expenses.

Note: Commenced 3 November 2008 (SI 2008/2696).

Criminal Justice and Immigration Act 2008
(2008, c. 4)

Part 10

Special Immigration Status

130. Designation

(1) The Secretary of State may designate a person who satisfies Condition 1 or 2 (subject to subsections (4) and (5)).

(2) Condition 1 is that the person

(a) is a foreign criminal within the meaning of section 131, and

(b) is liable to deportation, but cannot be removed from the United Kingdom because of section 6 of the Human Rights Act 1998 (c. 42) (public authority not to act contrary to Convention).

(3) Condition 2 is that the person is a member of the family of a person who satisfies Condition 1.

(4) A person who has the right of abode in the United Kingdom may not be designated.

(5) The Secretary of State may not designate a person if the Secretary of State thinks that an effect of designation would breach—

(a) the United Kingdom's obligations under the Refugee Convention, or

(b) the person's rights under the [EU] treaties.

Note: Commencement at a date to be appointed. Letters in square brackets substituted by SI 2011/1043 from 22 April 2013.

131. 'Foreign criminal'

(1) For the purposes of section 130 'foreign criminal' means a person who—

(a) is not a British citizen, and

(b) satisfies any of the following Conditions.

(2) Condition 1 is that section 72(2)(a) and (b) or (3)(a) to (c) of the Nationality, Immigration and Asylum Act 2002 (c. 41) applies to the person (Article 33(2) of the Refugee Convention: imprisonment for at least two years).

(3) Condition 2 is that—

(a) section 72(4)(a) or (b) of that Act applies to the person (person convicted of specified offence), and

(b) the person has been sentenced to a period of imprisonment.

(4) Condition 3 is that Article 1F of the Refugee Convention applies to the person (exclusions for criminals etc.).

(5) Section 72(6) of that Act (rebuttal of presumption under section 72(2) to (4)) has no effect in relation to Condition 1 or 2.

(6) Section 72(7) of that Act (non-application pending appeal) has no effect in relation to Condition 1 or 2.

Note: Commencement at a date to be appointed.

132. Effect of designation

(1) A designated person does not have leave to enter or remain in the United Kingdom.

(2) For the purposes of a provision of the Immigration Acts and any other enactment which concerns or refers to immigration or nationality (including any provision which applies or refers to a provision of the Immigration Acts or any other enactment about immigration or nationality) a designated person—

(a) is a person subject to immigration control,

(b) is not to be treated as an asylum-seeker or a former asylum-seeker, and

(c) is not in the United Kingdom in breach of the immigration laws.

(3) Despite subsection (2)(c), time spent in the United Kingdom as a designated person may not be relied on by a person for the purpose of an enactment about nationality.

(4) A designated person—

(a) shall not be deemed to have been given leave in accordance with paragraph 6 of Schedule 2 to the Immigration Act 1971 (c. 77) (notice of leave or refusal), and

(b) may not be granted temporary admission to the United Kingdom under paragraph 21 of that Schedule.

(5) Sections 134 and 135 make provision about support for designated persons and their dependants.

Note: Commencement at a date to be appointed.

133. Conditions

(1) The Secretary of State or an immigration officer may by notice in writing impose a condition on a designated person.

(2) A condition may relate to—

(a) residence,

(b) employment or occupation, or

(c) reporting to the police, the Secretary of State or an immigration officer.

(3) Section 36 of the Asylum and Immigration (Treatment of Claimants, etc.) Act 2004 (c. 19) (electronic monitoring) shall apply in relation to conditions imposed under this section as it applies to restrictions imposed under paragraph 21 of Schedule 2 to the

Immigration Act 1971 (with a reference to the Immigration Acts being treated as including a reference to this section).

(4) Section 69 of the Nationality, Immigration and Asylum Act 2002 (c. 41) (reporting restrictions: travel expenses) shall apply in relation to conditions imposed under subsection (2)(c) above as it applies to restrictions imposed under paragraph 21 of Schedule 2 to the Immigration Act 1971.

(5) A person who without reasonable excuse fails to comply with a condition imposed under this section commits an offence.

(6) A person who is guilty of an offence under subsection (5) shall be liable on summary conviction to—

(a) a fine not exceeding level 5 on the standard scale,

(b) imprisonment for a period not exceeding 51 weeks, or

(c) both.

(7) A provision of the Immigration Act 1971 (c. 77) which applies in relation to an offence under any provision of section 24(1) of that Act (illegal entry etc.) shall also apply in relation to the offence under subsection (5) above.

(8) In the application of this section to Scotland or Northern Ireland the reference in subsection (6)(b) to 51 weeks shall be treated as a reference to six months.

Note: Commencement at a date to be appointed. In the application of this section in England and Wales to offences committed before the commencement of s 281(5) of the Criminal Justice Act 2003, the maximum term of sentence in subsection (6)(b) shall be read as 6 months, Sch 27 paragraph 36.

134. Support

(1) Part VI of the Immigration and Asylum Act 1999 (c. 33) (support for asylum seekers) shall apply in relation to designated persons and their dependants as it applies in relation to asylum-seekers and their dependants.

(2) But the following provisions of that Part shall not apply—

(a) section 96 (kinds of support),

(b) section 97(1)(b) (desirability of providing accommodation in well-supplied area),

(c) section 100 (duty to cooperate in providing accommodation),

(d) section 101 (reception zones),

(e) section 108 (failure of sponsor to maintain),

(f) section 111 (grants to voluntary organisations), and

(g) section 113 (recovery of expenditure from sponsor).

(3) Support may be provided under section 95 of the 1999 Act as applied by this section—

(a) by providing accommodation appearing to the Secretary of State to be adequate for a person's needs;

(b) by providing what appear to the Secretary of State to be essential living needs;

(c) in other ways which the Secretary of State thinks necessary to reflect exceptional circumstances of a particular case.

(4) Support by virtue of subsection (3) may not be provided wholly or mainly by way of cash unless the Secretary of State thinks it appropriate because of exceptional circumstances.

(5) Section 4 of the 1999 Act (accommodation) shall not apply in relation to designated persons.

(6) . . .

Note: Commencement at a date to be appointed. Subsection (6) repealed by Housing and Regeneration Act 2008 Sch 15 paragraph 24 from 2 March 2009 (SI 2009/415).

135. Support: supplemental

(1) A reference in an enactment to Part VI of the 1999 Act or to a provision of that Part includes a reference to that Part or provision as applied by section 134 above; and for that purpose—

(a) a reference to section 96 shall be treated as including a reference to section 134(3) above,

(b) a reference to a provision of section 96 shall be treated as including a reference to the corresponding provision of section 134(3), and

(c) a reference to asylum-seekers shall be treated as including a reference to designated persons.

(2) A provision of Part VI of the 1999 Act which requires or permits the Secretary of State to have regard to the temporary nature of support shall be treated, in the application of Part VI by virtue of section 134 above, as requiring the Secretary of State to have regard to the nature and circumstances of support by virtue of that section.

(3) . . .

(4) Any . . . instrument under Part VI of the 1999 Act—

(a) may make provision in respect of that Part as it applies by virtue of section 134 above, as it applies otherwise than by virtue of that section, or both, and

(b) may make different provision for that Part as it applies by virtue of section 134 above and as it applies otherwise than by virtue of that section.

(5) In the application of paragraph 9 of Schedule 8 to the 1999 Act (regulations: notice to quit accommodation) the reference in paragraph (2)(b) to the determination of a claim for asylum shall be treated as a reference to ceasing to be a designated person.

(6) The Secretary of State may by order repeal, modify or disapply (to any extent) section 134(4).

(7) . . .

Note: Commencement at a date to be appointed. Subsection (3) omitted and words omitted from subsection (4) by The Transfer of Tribunal Functions (Lands Tribunal and Miscellaneous Amendments) Order 2009 Sch 1 paragraph 288(a) from 1 June 2009 (SI 2009/1307). Subsection (7) repealed by Housing and Regeneration Act 2008 Sch 15 paragraph 25 from 2 March 2009 (SI 2009/415).

136. End of designation

(1) Designation lapses if the designated person—

(a) is granted leave to enter or remain in the United Kingdom,

(b) is notified by the Secretary of State or an immigration officer of a right of residence in the United Kingdom by virtue of the [EU] treaties,

(c) leaves the United Kingdom, or

(d) is made the subject of a deportation order under section 5 of the Immigration Act 1971 (c. 77).

(2) After designation lapses support may not be provided by virtue of section 134, subject to the following exceptions.

(3) Exception 1 is that, if designation lapses under subsection (1)(a) or (b), support may be provided in respect of a period which—

(a) begins when the designation lapses, and

(b) ends on a date determined in accordance with an order of the Secretary of State.

(4) Exception 2 is that, if designation lapses under subsection (1)(d), support may be provided in respect of—

(a) any period during which an appeal against the deportation order may be brought (ignoring any possibility of an appeal out of time with permission),

(b) any period during which an appeal against the deportation order is pending, and

(c) after an appeal ceases to be pending, such period as the Secretary of State may specify by order.

Note: Commencement at a date to be appointed. Words in square brackets in subsection (1)(b) substituted from 22 April 2011 (SI 2011/1043).

137 Interpretation: general

(1) This section applies to sections 130 to 136.

(2) A reference to a designated person is a reference to a person designated under section 130.

(3) 'Family' shall be construed in accordance with section 5(4) of the Immigration Act 1971 (c. 77) (deportation: definition of 'family').

(4) 'Right of abode in the United Kingdom' has the meaning given by section 2 of that Act.

(5) 'The Refugee Convention' means the Convention relating to the Status of Refugees done at Geneva on 28 July 1951 and its Protocol.

(6) 'Period of imprisonment' shall be construed in accordance with section 72(11)(b)(i) and (ii) of the Nationality, Immigration and Asylum Act 2002 (c. 41).

(7) A voucher is not cash.

(8) A reference to a pending appeal has the meaning given by section 104(1) of that Act.

(9) A reference in an enactment to the Immigration Acts includes a reference to sections 130 to 136.

Note: Commencement at a date to be appointed.

Borders, Citizenship and Immigration Act 2009
(2009, c. 11)

Contents

Part 1. Border Functions

Part 2. Citizenship

Acquisition of British citizenship by naturalisation

Acquisition of British citizenship by birth

Acquisition of British citizenship etc. by registration

Interpretation etc.

Part 3. Immigration

Studies

Fingerprinting

An Act to provide for customs functions to be exercisable by the Secretary of State, the Director of Border Revenue and officials designated by them; to make provision about the use and disclosure of customs information; to make provision for and in connection with the exercise of customs functions and functions relating to immigration, asylum or nationality; to make provision about citizenship and other nationality matters; to make further provision about immigration and asylum; and for connected purposes. [21 July 2009] BE IT ENACTED by the Queen's Most Excellent Majesty, by and with the advice and consent of the Lords Spiritual and Temporal, and Commons, in this present Parliament assembled, and by the authority of the same, as follows:—

PART 1

BORDER FUNCTIONS

Note: Part 1 makes provision relating to the exercise of customs functions and related matters and only the sections below are reproduced. Sections are also identified that amend or repeal statutory provisions that appear elsewhere in this book.

20. Supply of Revenue and Customs information

Note: Inserts sections 41A and 41B and amends section 42(1) of the UK Borders Act 2007. Repealed by Sch 9 Immigration Act 2014 from a date to be appointed.

21. Duty to share information

Note: Amends section 36 of the Immigration Asylum and Nationality Act 2006.

25. Short-term holding facilities

Note: Amends section 147 of the Immigration and Asylum Act 1999.

Inspection and oversight

28. Inspections by the Chief Inspector of the UK Border Agency

(1)–(6) . . .

(7)–(8) . . .

(9) . . .

(10) The person holding the office of the Chief Inspector of the Border and Immigration Agency immediately before the day on which this section comes into force is to be treated, on and after that day, as if appointed as the Chief Inspector of the UK Border Agency under section 48(1) of the UK Borders Act 2007 (c. 30).

Note: Commenced 21 July 2009 (s 58). Subsections (1)–(6) amend section 48 of the UK Borders Act 2007. Subsections (7)–(8) amend section 53 of the UK Borders Act 2007. Subsection (9) amends section 56(2)(a) of the UK Borders Act 2007.

34. Children

. . .

. . .

Note: Commenced 21 July 2009 (s 58). Subsections (1)–(5) amend section 21 of the UK Borders Act 2007. Ceased to have effect 2 November 2009 (s 34(6)).

PART 2

CITIZENSHIP

Acquisition of British citizenship by naturalisation

39. Application requirements: general

. . .

Note: Amends paragraphs 1 and 2 and inserts paragraph 2A of Schedule 1 of the British Nationality Act 1981.

40. Application requirements: family members etc.

(1)–(2) . . .

(3)–(5) . . .

Note: Subsections (1)–(2) amends section 6 of the British Nationality Act 1981. Subsections (3)–(5) amend paragraph 3 and 4 and inserts paragraph 4A of Schedule 1 of the British Nationality Act 1981.

41. The qualifying period

(1) . . .

(2)–(5) . . .

Note: Subsection (1) inserts paragraph 4B of Schedule 1 to the British Nationality Act 1981. Subsections (2)–(5) amend section 41 of the British nationality Act 1981.

Acquisition of British citizenship by birth

42. Children born in UK etc. to members of the armed forces

Note: Amends section 1 of the British Nationality Act 1981.

Acquisition of British citizenship etc. by registration

43. Minors

Note: Amends section 3 of the British Nationality Act 1981.

44. British Nationals (Overseas) without other citizenship

Note: Amends section 4B of the British Nationality Act 1981.

45. Descent through the female line

Note: Amends section 4C of the British Nationality Act 1981.

46. Children born outside UK etc. to members of the armed forces

Note: Inserts section 4D of the British Nationality Act 1981.

47. Good character requirement

(1) . . .

(2) . . .

(3) . . .

(4) . . .

(5) . . .

Note: Subsection (1) inserts section 41A of the British Nationality Act 1981. Subsection (2) amends section 1 of the Hong Kong (War Wives and Widows) Act 1996. Subsection (3) amends section 1 of the British Nationality (Hong Kong) Act 1997. Subsection (4) amends section 131 of the Nationality, Immigration and Asylum Act 2002. Subsection (5) amends section 40 of the UK Borders Act 2007.

Interpretation etc.

48. Meaning of references to being in breach of immigration laws

(1) . . .

(2) . . .

(3) Notwithstanding its repeal, section 11 of the 2002 Act is to continue to have effect for the purpose of determining on or after the relevant day—

(a) whether a person born before the relevant day is a British citizen under section 1(1) of the British Nationality Act 1981 (c. 61),

(b) whether, on an application under section 1(3) or 4(2) of that Act made but not determined before the relevant day, a person is entitled to be registered as a British citizen,

(c) whether, on an application under section 6(1) or (2) of that Act made but not determined before the relevant day, the applicant fulfils the requirements of Schedule 1 for naturalisation as a British citizen under section 6(1) or (2) of that Act, or

(d) whether, in relation to an application under section 1(3) or 6(1) or (2) of that Act made on or after the relevant day, a person was in the United Kingdom "in breach of the immigration laws" at a time before 7 November 2002 (the date of commencement of section 11 of the 2002 Act).

(4) Where section 11 of the 2002 Act continues to have effect by virtue of paragraph (d) of subsection (3) for the purpose of determining on or after the relevant day the matter mentioned in that paragraph, section 50A of the British Nationality Act 1981 is not to apply for the purpose of determining that matter.

(5) The relevant day for the purposes of subsection (3) is the day appointed for the commencement of this section.

(6) . . .

Note: Commenced 13 January 2010 (SI 2009/2731). Subsection (1) inserts section 50A of the British Nationality Act 1981. Subsection (2) repeals section 11 of the Nationality, Immigration and Asylum Act 2002, subject to subsection (3). Subsection (6) amends paragraph 7(a) of Schedule 3 to the Nationality, Immigration and Asylum Act 2002.

49. Other interpretation etc.

(1) . . .

(2) . . .

(3) . . .

Note: Subsection (1) commenced 13 January 2010 (SI 2009/2731), remainder on a date to be appointed. Subsection (1) amends section 50 of the British Nationality Act 1981. Subsection (2) amends Schedule 1 to the British Nationality Act 1981. Subsection (3) inserts paragraph 11 of Schedule 1 to the British Nationality Act 1981.

Part 3

Immigration

Studies

50. Restriction on studies

(1) . . .

(2) A condition under section 3(1)(c)(ia) of that Act may be added as a condition to leave given before the passing of this Act (as well as to leave given on or after its passing).

Note: Commenced 21 July 2009 (s 58). Subsection (1) amends section 3(1)(c) of the Immigration Act 1971.

Fingerprinting

51. Fingerprinting of foreign criminals liable to automatic deportation

. . .

Note: Amends section 141 of the Immigration and Asylum Act 1999.

Detention at ports in Scotland

52. Extension of sections 1 to 4 of the UK Borders Act 2007 to Scotland

(1)–(2) . . .

(3) . . .

Note: Subsections (1) and (2) amend sections 2 and 3 of the UK Borders Act 2007. Subsection (3) amends section 60(1) of the UK Borders Act 2007.

Part 4

Miscellaneous and General

Judicial review

53. Transfer of certain immigration judicial review applications

(1) . . .

(2) . . .

(3) . . .

Note: Subsection (1) amends section 31A of the Supreme Court Act 1981. Subsection (2) amends section 25A of the Judicature (Northern Ireland) Act 1978. Subsection (3) amends section 20 of the Tribunals, Courts and Enforcement Act 2007.

Trafficking people for exploitation

54. Trafficking people for exploitation

Note: Amends section 4(4) of the Asylum and Immigration (Treatment of Claimants, etc.) Act 2004.

Children

[54A. Independent Family Returns Panel

(1) The Independent Family Returns Panel is established.

(2) The Secretary of State must consult the Independent Family Returns Panel—

(a) in each family returns case, on how best to safeguard and promote the welfare of the children of the family, and

(b) in each case where the Secretary of State proposes to detain a family in pre-departure accommodation, on the suitability of so doing, having particular regard to the need to safeguard and promote the welfare of the children of the family.

(3) A family returns case is a case where—

(a) a child who is living in the United Kingdom is to be removed from or required to leave the United Kingdom, and

(b) an individual who—

(i) is a parent of the child or has care of the child, and

(ii) is living in a household in the United Kingdom with the child, is also to be removed from or required to leave the United Kingdom.

(4) The Secretary of State may by regulations make provision about—

(a) additional functions of the Independent Family Returns Panel,

(b) its status and constitution,

(c) the appointment of its members,

(d) the payment of remuneration and allowances to its members, and

(e) any other matters in connection with its establishment and operation.

(5) Regulations under this section must be made by statutory instrument.

(6) An instrument containing regulations under this section is subject to annulment in pursuance of a resolution of either House of Parliament.

(7) In this section—

"child" means a person who is under the age of 18;

"pre-departure accommodation" has the same meaning as in Part 8 of the Immigration and Asylum Act 1999;

references to a person being removed from or required to leave the United Kingdom are to the person being removed or required to leave in accordance with a provision of the Immigration Acts.]

Note: Section 54A inserted by s 3 Immigration Act 2014 from 28 July 2014 (SI 2014/1820).

55. Duty regarding the welfare of children

(1) The Secretary of State must make arrangements for ensuring that—

(a) the functions mentioned in subsection (2) are discharged having regard to the need to safeguard and promote the welfare of children who are in the United Kingdom; and

(b) any services provided by another person pursuant to arrangements which are made by the Secretary of State and relate to the discharge of a function mentioned in subsection (2) are provided having regard to that need.

(2) The functions referred to in subsection (1) are—

(a) any function of the Secretary of State in relation to immigration, asylum or nationality;

(b) any function conferred by or by virtue of the Immigration Acts on an immigration officer;

(c) any general customs function of the Secretary of State; and

(d) any customs function conferred on a designated customs official.

(3) A person exercising any of those functions must, in exercising the function, have regard to any guidance given to the person by the Secretary of State for the purpose of subsection (1).

(4) The Director of Border Revenue must make arrangements for ensuring that—

(a) the Director's functions are discharged having regard to the need to safeguard and promote the welfare of children who are in the United Kingdom; and

(b) any services provided by another person pursuant to arrangements made by the Director in the discharge of such a function are provided having regard to that need.

(5) A person exercising a function of the Director of Border Revenue must, in exercising the function, have regard to any guidance given to the person by the Secretary of State for the purpose of subsection (4).

(6) In this section—

'children' means persons who are under the age of 18;

'customs function', 'designated customs official' and 'general customs function' have the meanings given by Part 1.

(7) A reference in an enactment (other than this Act) to the Immigration Acts includes a reference to this section.

(8) . . .

Note: Commenced 2 November 2009 (SI 2009/2731). Subsection (8) repeals section 21 of the UK Borders Act 2007.

General

56. Repeals

The Schedule contains repeals.

Note: Commenced 2 November 2009 (SI 2009/2731).

57. Extent

(1) Subject to the following provisions of this section, this Act extends to—

(a) England and Wales,

(b) Scotland, and

(c) Northern Ireland.

(2) Sections 22 (application of the PACE orders) and 23 (investigations and detention: England and Wales and Northern Ireland) extend to England and Wales and Northern Ireland only.

(3) An amendment, modification or repeal by this Act has the same extent as the enactment or relevant part of the enactment to which it relates (ignoring extent by virtue of an Order in Council under any of the Immigration Acts).

(4) Subsection (3) does not apply to—

(a) the amendments made by section 52 (detention at ports in Scotland);

(b) the amendment made by section 54 (trafficking people for exploitation), which extends to England and Wales and Northern Ireland only.

(5) Her Majesty may by Order in Council provide for any of the provisions of this Act, other than any provision of Part 1 (border functions) or section 53 (transfer of certain immigration judicial review applications), to extend, with or without modifications, to any of the Channel Islands or the Isle of Man.

(6) Subsection (5) does not apply in relation to the extension to a place of a provision which extends there by virtue of subsection (3).

Note: Commenced 21 July 2009 (s 58).

58. Commencement

(1) Part 1 (border functions) comes into force on the day this Act is passed.

(2) The provisions of Part 2 (citizenship) come into force on such day as the Secretary of State may by order appoint.

(3) In Part 3 (immigration)—

(a) section 50 (restriction on studies) comes into force on the day this Act is passed;

(b) sections 51 (fingerprinting of foreign criminals) and 52 (detention at ports in Scotland) come into force on such day as the Secretary of State may by order appoint.

(4) In this Part—

(a) section 53 (transfer of certain immigration judicial review applications) comes into force on such day as the Lord Chancellor may by order appoint;

(b) sections 54 (trafficking people for exploitation) and 55 (duty regarding the welfare of children) come into force on such day as the Secretary of State may by order appoint.

(5) Any repeal in the Schedule (and section 56 so far as relating to the repeal) comes into force in the same way as the provisions of this Act to which the repeal relates.

(6) The other provisions of this Part come into force on the day this Act is passed.

(7) An order under this section must be made by statutory instrument.

(8) An order under this section—

(a) may appoint different days for different purposes;

(b) may include transitional or incidental provision or savings.

(9) An order commencing sections 39 to 41 (acquisition of British citizenship by naturalisation) must include provision that the amendments made by those sections do not have effect in relation to an application for naturalisation as a British citizen if—

(a) the date of the application is before the date on which those sections come into force in accordance with the order ("the date of commencement"), or

(b) the date of the application is before the end of the period of 24 months beginning with the date of commencement and the application is made by a person who falls within subsection (10) or (11).

(10) A person falls within this subsection if on the date of commencement the person has indefinite leave to remain in the United Kingdom.

(11) A person falls within this subsection if the person is given indefinite leave to remain in the United Kingdom on an application—

(a) the date of which is before the date of commencement, and

(b) which is decided after the date of commencement.

(12) The reference in subsection (9) to an order commencing sections 39 to 41 does not include an order commencing those sections for the purpose only of enabling regulations to be made under the British Nationality Act 1981 (c. 61).

(13) In the case of an order commencing sections 39 to 41, transitional provision may, in particular—

(a) provide that the qualifying period for the purposes of paragraph 1 or 3 of Schedule 1 to the British Nationality Act 1981 includes time before that commencement;

(b) provide for leave to enter or remain in the United Kingdom granted before that commencement to be treated as qualifying temporary residence leave or probationary citizenship leave for the purposes of that Schedule.

(14) In the case of an order commencing section 45 (acquisition of British citizenship through the female line), transitional provision may, in particular, provide that section 45 is to apply to an application made, but not determined, under section 4C of the British Nationality Act 1981 before that commencement.

(15) No order may be made commencing section 52 (detention at ports in Scotland) unless the Secretary of State has consulted the Scottish Ministers.

(16) No order may be made commencing section 53 (transfer of certain immigration judicial review applications) unless the functions of the Asylum and Immigration Tribunal in relation to appeals under Part 5 of the Nationality, Immigration and Asylum Act 2002 (c. 41) have been transferred under section 30(1) of the Tribunals, Courts and Enforcement Act 2007 (c. 15).

Note: Commenced 21 July 2009 (s 58).

59. Short title

This Act may be cited as the Borders, Citizenship and Immigration Act 2009.

Note: Commenced 21 July 2009 (s 58).

Section 56 SCHEDULE

Note: The Schedule sets out repeals of provisions of the UK Borders Act 2007, British Nationality Act 1981, Hong Kong (War Wives and Widows) Act 1996, Nationality, Asylum and Immigration Act 2002, and the Immigration, Asylum and Nationality Act 2006.

Immigration Act 2014
(2014, c. 22)

Contents

PART 1

REMOVAL AND OTHER POWERS

Removal

Powers of immigration officers

Detention and bail

Biometrics

PART 2

APPEALS ETC.

CHAPTER 3

Other Provisions

Persons not relevant nationals etc.: marriage on superintendent registrar's certificates

Information

Miscellaneous

PART 5

OVERSIGHT

Office of the Immigration Services Commissioner

Police Ombudsman for Northern Ireland

PART 6

MISCELLANEOUS

CITIZENSHIP

Embarkation checks

Fees

SCHEDULE 9

TRANSITIONAL AND CONSEQUENTIAL PROVISION

Part 1—Provision relating to removal
Part 2—Provision relating to detention and bail
Part 3—Provision relating to biometrics
Part 4—Provision relating to appeals
Part 5—Provision relating to employment
Part 6—Provision relating to driving licences
Part 7—Provision relating to marriage and civil partnership
Part 8—Provision relating to immigration advisers and immigration service providers
Part 9—Provision relating to persons unable to acquire nationality because natural father not married to mother
Part 10—Provision relating to embarkation checks
Part 11—Provision relating to fees

An Act to make provision about immigration law; to limit, or otherwise make provision about, access to services, facilities and employment by reference to immigration status; to make provision about marriage and civil partnership involving certain foreign nationals; to make provision about the acquisition of citizenship by persons unable to acquire it because their fathers and mothers were not married to each other and provision about the removal of citizenship from persons whose conduct is seriously prejudicial to the United Kingdom's vital interests; and for connected purposes.

[14th May 2014]

PART 1

REMOVAL AND OTHER POWERS

Removal

1. Removal of persons unlawfully in the United Kingdom

. . .

Note: Amends s 10 of the Immigration and Asylum Act 1999 from a date to be appointed.

2. Restriction on removal of children and their parents etc.

. . .

Note: Inserts s 78A of the Nationality, Immigration and Asylum Act 2002 from a date to be appointed.

3. Independent Family Returns Panel

Note: Inserts s 54A of the Borders, Citizenship and Immigration Act 2009 from a date to be appointed.

Powers of immigration officers

4. Enforcement powers

Schedule 1 (enforcement powers) has effect.

Note: Commencement at a date to be appointed.

Detention and bail

5. Restrictions on detention of unaccompanied children

. . .

Note: Amends Sch 2 to the Immigration Act 1971 from a date to be appointed.

6. Pre-departure accommodation for families

. . .

Note: Amends Part 8 of the Immigration and Asylum Act 1999 (removal centres and detained persons) from a date to be appointed.

7. Immigration bail: repeat applications and effect of removal directions

. . .

Note: Amends Sch 2 to the Immigration Act 1971 from a date to be appointed.

Biometrics

8. Provision of biometric information with immigration applications

. . .

Note: Amends s 126 of the Nationality, Immigration and Asylum Act 2002 from a date to be appointed.

9. Identifying persons liable to detention

. . .

Note: Amends paragraph 18(2) of Sch 2 to the Immigration Act 1971 from a date to be appointed.

10. Provision of biometric information with citizenship applications

. . .

Note: Amends s 41 of the British Nationality Act 1981 from a date to be appointed.

11. Biometric immigration documents

. . .

Note: Amends s 7 of the UK Borders Act 2007 from a date to be appointed.

12. Meaning of "biometric information"

. . .

Note: Amends s 15 of the UK Borders Act 2007 from a date to be appointed.

13. Safeguards for children

. . .

Note: Amends Sch 2 to the Immigration Act 1971 from a date to be appointed.

14. Use and retention of biometric information

(1) . . .

(2) . . .

(3) . . .

Note: Subsection (1) substitutes s 8 of the UK Borders Act 2007; subsection (2) inserts 144A of the Immigration and Asylum Act 1999; subsection (3) amends s 126 of the Nationality, Immigration and Asylum Act 2002 from a date to be appointed.

PART 2

APPEALS ETC.

15. Right of appeal to First-tier Tribunal

. . .

Note: Amends Part 5 of the Nationality, Immigration and Asylum Act 2002 (immigration and asylum appeals) from a date to be appointed.

16. Report by Chief Inspector on administrative review

(1) Before the end of the period of 12 months beginning on the day on which section 15 comes into force, the Secretary of State must commission from the Chief Inspector a report that addresses the following matters—

(a) the effectiveness of administrative review in identifying case working errors;

(b) the effectiveness of administrative review in correcting case working errors;

(c) the independence of persons conducting administrative review (in terms of their separation from the original decision-maker).

(2) On completion of the report, the Chief Inspector must send it to the Secretary of State.

(3) The Secretary of State must lay before Parliament a copy of the report received under subsection (2).

(4) In this section—

"administrative review" means review conducted under the immigration rules;

"case working error" has the meaning given in the immigration rules;

the "Chief Inspector" means the Chief Inspector established under section 48 of the UK Borders Act 2007;

"immigration rules" has the same meaning as in the Immigration Act 1971.

Note: Commencement from 20 October 2014 (SI 2014/2771).

17. Place from which appeal may be brought or continued

. . .

Note: Amends Part 5 of the Nationality, Immigration and Asylum Act 2002 (immigration and asylum appeals) from a date to be appointed.

18. Review of certain deportation decisions by Special Immigration Appeals Commission

. . .

Note: Inserts s 2E into the Special Immigration Appeals Commission Act 1997 from a date to be appointed.

19. Article 8 of the ECHR: public interest considerations

. . .

Note: Inserts Part 5A of the Nationality, Immigration and Asylum Act 2002 from a date to be appointed.

PART 3

ACCESS TO SERVICES ETC.

CHAPTER 1

RESIDENTIAL TENANCIES

Key interpretation

20. Residential tenancy agreement

(1) This section applies for the purposes of this Chapter.

(2) "Residential tenancy agreement" means a tenancy which—

(a) grants a right of occupation of premises for residential use,

(b) provides for payment of rent (whether or not a market rent), and

(c) is not an excluded agreement.

(3) In subsection (2), "tenancy" includes—

(a) any lease, licence, sub-lease or sub-tenancy, and

(b) an agreement for any of those things, and in this Chapter references to "landlord" and "tenant", and references to premises being "leased", are to be read accordingly.

(4) For the purposes of subsection (2)(a), an agreement grants a right of occupation of premises "for residential use" if, under the agreement, one or more adults have the right to occupy the premises as their only or main residence (whether or not the premises may also be used for other purposes).

(5) In subsection (2)(b) "rent" includes any sum paid in the nature of rent.

(6) In subsection (2)(c) "excluded agreement" means any agreement of a description for the time being specified in Schedule 3.

(7) The Secretary of State may by order amend Schedule 3 so as to—

(a) add a new description of excluded agreement,

(b) remove any description, or

(c) amend any description.

Note: Commencement from 1 December 2014 for premises in local authorities set out in article 6 SI 2014/2771.

21. Persons disqualified by immigration status or with limited right to rent

(1) For the purposes of this Chapter, a person ("P") is disqualified as a result of their immigration status from occupying premises under a residential tenancy agreement if—

(a) P is not a relevant national, and

(b) P does not have a right to rent in relation to the premises.

(2) P does not have a "right to rent" in relation to premises if—

(a) P requires leave to enter or remain in the United Kingdom but does not have it, or

(b) P's leave to enter or remain in the United Kingdom is subject to a condition preventing P from occupying the premises.

(3) But P is to be treated as having a right to rent in relation to premises (in spite of subsection (2)) if the Secretary of State has granted P permission for the purposes of this Chapter to occupy premises under a residential tenancy agreement.

(4) References in this Chapter to a person with a "limited right to rent" are references to—

(a) a person who has been granted leave to enter or remain in the United Kingdom for a limited period, or

(b) a person who—

(i) is not a relevant national, and

(ii) is entitled to enter or remain in the United Kingdom by virtue of an enforceable EU right or of any provision made under section 2(2) of the European Communities Act 1972.

(5) In this section "relevant national" means—

(a) a British citizen,

(b) a national of an EEA State other than the United Kingdom, or

(c) a national of Switzerland.

Note: Commencement from 1 December 2014 for premises in local authorities set out in article 6 SI 2014/2771.

Penalty notices

22. Persons disqualified by immigration status not to be leased premises

(1) A landlord must not authorise an adult to occupy premises under a residential tenancy agreement if the adult is disqualified as a result of their immigration status.

(2) A landlord is to be taken to "authorise" an adult to occupy premises in the circumstances mentioned in subsection (1) if (and only if) there is a contravention of this section.

(3) There is a contravention of this section in either of the following cases.

(4) The first case is where a residential tenancy agreement is entered into that, at the time of entry, grants a right to occupy premises to—

(a) a tenant who is disqualified as a result of their immigration status,

(b) another adult named in the agreement who is disqualified as a result of their immigration status, or

(c) another adult not named in the agreement who is disqualified as a result of their immigration status (subject to subsection (6)).

(5) The second case is where—

(a) a residential tenancy agreement is entered into that grants a right to occupy premises on an adult with a limited right to rent,

(b) the adult later becomes a person disqualified as a result of their immigration status, and

(c) the adult continues to occupy the premises after becoming disqualified.

(6) There is a contravention as a result of subsection (4)(c) only if—

(a) reasonable enquiries were not made of the tenant before entering into the agreement as to the relevant occupiers, or

(b) reasonable enquiries were so made and it was, or should have been, apparent from the enquiries that the adult in question was likely to be a relevant occupier.

(7) Any term of a residential tenancy agreement that prohibits occupation of premises by a person disqualified by their immigration status is to be ignored for the purposes of determining whether there has been a contravention of this section if—

(a) the landlord knew when entering into the agreement that the term would be breached, or

(b) the prescribed requirements were not complied with before entering into the agreement.

(8) It does not matter for the purposes of this section whether or not—

(a) a right of occupation is exercisable on entering into an agreement or from a later date;

(b) a right of occupation is granted unconditionally or on satisfaction of a condition.

(9) A contravention of this section does not affect the validity or enforceability of any provision of a residential tenancy agreement by virtue of any rule of law relating to the validity or enforceability of contracts in circumstances involving illegality.

(10) In this Chapter—

"post-grant contravention" means a contravention in the second case mentioned in subsection (5);

"pre-grant contravention" means a contravention in the first case mentioned in subsection (4);

"relevant occupier", in relation to a residential tenancy agreement, means any adult who occupies premises under the agreement (whether or not named in the agreement).

Note: Commencement from 1 December 2014 for premises in local authorities set out in article 6 SI 2014/2771.

23. Penalty notices: landlords

(1) If there is a contravention of section 22, the Secretary of State may give the responsible landlord a notice requiring the payment of a penalty.

(2) The amount of the penalty is such an amount as the Secretary of State considers appropriate, but the amount must not exceed £3,000.

(3) "Responsible landlord" means—

(a) in relation to a pre-grant contravention, the landlord who entered into the residential tenancy agreement;

(b) in relation to a post-grant contravention, the person who is the landlord under the agreement at the time of the contravention.

(4) But if there is a superior landlord in relation to the residential tenancy agreement who is responsible for the purposes of this section, the "responsible landlord" means that superior landlord (and references to the landlord in the following provisions of this Chapter are to be read accordingly).

(5) A superior landlord is "responsible for the purposes of this section" if arrangements in writing have been made in relation to the residential tenancy agreement between the landlord and the superior landlord under which the superior landlord accepts responsibility for—

(a) contraventions of section 22 generally, or

(b) contraventions of a particular description and the contravention in question is of that description.

(6) The Secretary of State may by order amend the amount for the time being specified in subsection (2).

Note: Commencement from 1 December 2014 for premises in local authorities set out in article 6 SI 2014/2771.

24. Excuses available to landlords

(1) This section applies where a landlord is given a notice under section 23 requiring payment of a penalty.

(2) Where the notice is given for a pre-grant contravention, the landlord is excused from paying the penalty if the landlord shows that—

(a) the prescribed requirements were complied with before the residential tenancy agreement was entered into, or

(b) a person acting as the landlord's agent is responsible for the contravention (see section 25(2)).

(3) The prescribed requirements may be complied with for the purposes of subsection (2)(a) at any time before the residential tenancy agreement is entered into.

(4) But where compliance with the prescribed requirements discloses that a relevant occupier is a person with a limited right to rent, the landlord is excused under subsection (2)(a) only if the requirements are complied with in relation to that occupier within such period as may be prescribed.

(5) The excuse under subsection (2)(a) or (b) is not available if the landlord knew that entering into the agreement would contravene section 22.

(6) Where the notice is given for a post-grant contravention, the landlord is excused from paying the penalty if any of the following applies—

(a) the landlord has notified the Secretary of State of the contravention as soon as reasonably practicable;

(b) a person acting as the landlord's agent is responsible for the contravention;

(c) the eligibility period in relation to the limited right occupier whose occupation caused the contravention has not expired.

(7) For the purposes of subsection (6)(a), the landlord is to be taken to have notified the Secretary of State of the contravention "as soon as reasonably practicable" if the landlord—

(a) complied with the prescribed requirements in relation to each limited right occupier at the end of the eligibility period, and

(b) notified the Secretary of State of the contravention without delay on it first becoming apparent that the contravention had occurred.

(8) Notification under subsection (6)(a) must be in the prescribed form and manner.

(9) In this Chapter "limited right occupier", in relation to a residential tenancy agreement, means a relevant occupier who had a limited right to rent at the time when the occupier was first granted a right to occupy the premises under the agreement.

Note: Commencement from 1 December 2014 for premises in local authorities set out in article 6 SI 2014/2771.

25. Penalty notices: agents

(1) Subsection (3) applies where—

(a) a landlord contravenes section 22, and

(b) a person acting as the landlord's agent ("the agent") is responsible for the contravention.

(2) For the purposes of this Chapter, an agent is responsible for a landlord's contravention of section 22 if (and only if)—

(a) the agent acts in the course of a business, and

(b) under arrangements made with the landlord in writing, the agent was under an obligation for the purposes of this Chapter to comply with the prescribed requirements on behalf of the landlord.

(3) The Secretary of State may give the agent a notice requiring the agent to pay a penalty.

(4) The amount of the penalty is such an amount as the Secretary of State considers appropriate, but the amount must not exceed £3,000.

(5) The Secretary of State may by order amend the amount for the time being specified in subsection (4).

Note: Commencement from 1 December 2014 for premises in local authorities set out in article 6 SI 2014/2771.

26. Excuses available to agents

(1) This section applies where an agent is given a notice under section 25 requiring payment of a penalty.

(2) Where the notice is given for a pre-grant contravention, the agent is excused from paying the penalty if the agent shows that the prescribed requirements were complied with before the residential tenancy agreement was entered into.

(3) The prescribed requirements may be complied with for the purposes of subsection (2) at any time before the residential tenancy agreement is entered into.

(4) But where compliance with the prescribed requirements discloses that a relevant occupier is a person with a limited right to rent, the agent is excused under subsection (2) only if the requirements are complied with in relation to that occupier within such period as may be prescribed.

(5) The excuse under subsection (2) is not available if the agent—

(a) knew that the landlord would contravene section 22 by entering into the agreement,

(b) had sufficient opportunity to notify the landlord of that fact before the landlord entered into the agreement, but

(c) did not do so.

(6) Where the notice is given for a post-grant contravention, the agent is excused from paying the penalty if either of the following applies—

(a) the agent has notified the Secretary of State and the landlord of the contravention as soon as reasonably practicable;

(b) the eligibility period in relation to the limited right occupier whose occupation caused the contravention has not expired.

(7) For the purposes of subsection (6)(a), the agent is to be taken to have notified the Secretary of State and the landlord of the contravention "as soon as reasonably practicable" if the agent—

(a) complied with the prescribed requirements in relation to each limited right occupier at the end of the eligibility period, and

(b) notified the Secretary of State and the landlord of the contravention without delay on it first becoming apparent that the contravention had occurred.

(8) Notification under subsection (6)(a) must be in the prescribed form and manner.

Note: Commencement from 1 December 2014 for premises in local authorities set out in article 6 SI 2014/2771.

27. Eligibility period

(1) An eligibility period in relation to a limited right occupier is established if the prescribed requirements are complied with in relation to the occupier.

(2) An eligibility period established under subsection (1) may be renewed (on one or more occasions) by complying with the prescribed requirements again.

(3) But an eligibility period in relation to a limited right occupier is only established or renewed under this section at any time if it reasonably appears from the information obtained in complying with the prescribed requirements at that time that the occupier is a person with a limited right to rent.

(4) The length of an eligibility period established or renewed under this section in relation to a limited right occupier is the longest of the following periods—

(a) the period of one year beginning with the time when the prescribed requirements were last complied with in relation to the occupier;

(b) so much of any leave period as remains at that time;

(c) so much of any validity period as remains at that time.

(5) In subsection (4)—

"leave period" means a period for which the limited right occupier was granted leave to enter or remain in the United Kingdom;

"validity period" means the period for which an immigration document issued to the limited right occupier by or on behalf of the Secretary of State is valid.

(6) In subsection (5) "immigration document" means a document of a prescribed description which—

(a) is issued as evidence that a person who is not a national of an EEA state or Switzerland is entitled to enter or remain in the United Kingdom by virtue of an enforceable EU right or of any provision made under section 2(2) of the European Communities Act 1972, or

(b) grants to the holder a right to enter or remain in the United Kingdom for such period as the document may authorise.

Note: Commencement from 1 December 2014 for premises in local authorities set out in article 6 SI 2014/2771.

28. Penalty notices: general

(1) The Secretary of State may give a penalty notice—

(a) to a landlord under section 23 without having established whether the landlord is excused from paying the penalty under section 24;

(b) to an agent under section 25 without having established whether the agent is excused from paying the penalty under section 26.

(2) A penalty notice must—

(a) be in writing,

(b) state why the Secretary of State thinks the recipient is liable to the penalty,

(c) state the amount of the penalty,

(d) specify a date, at least 28 days after the date specified in the notice as the date on which it is given, before which the penalty must be paid,

(e) specify how a penalty must be paid,

(f) explain how the recipient may object to the penalty or make an appeal against it, and

(g) explain how the Secretary of State may enforce the penalty.

(3) A separate penalty notice may be given in respect of each adult disqualified by their immigration status in relation to whom there is a contravention of section 22.

(4) Where a penalty notice is given to two or more persons who jointly constitute the landlord or agent in relation to a residential tenancy agreement, those persons are jointly and severally liable for any sum payable to the Secretary of State as a penalty imposed by the notice.

(5) A penalty notice may not be given in respect of any adult if—

(a) the adult has ceased to occupy the premises concerned, and

(b) a period of 12 months or more has passed since the time when the adult last occupied the premises,

but this subsection is not to be taken as affecting the validity of a penalty notice given before the end of that period.

(6) Subsection (5) does not apply to a penalty notice given after the end of the 12 month period mentioned in that subsection if—

(a) it is a new penalty notice given by virtue of section 29(6)(b) on the determination of an objection to another penalty notice, and

(b) that other penalty notice was given before the end of the period.

Note: Commencement from 1 December 2014 for premises in local authorities set out in article 6 SI 2014/2771.

Objections, appeals and enforcement

29. Objection

(1) The recipient of a penalty notice ("the recipient") may object on the ground that—

(a) the recipient is not liable to the imposition of the penalty,

(b) the recipient is excused by virtue of section 24 or 26, or

(c) the amount of the penalty is too high.

(2) An objection must be made by giving a notice of objection to the Secretary of State.

(3) A notice of objection must—

(a) be in writing,

(b) give the reasons for the objection,

(c) be given in the prescribed manner, and

(d) be given before the end of the prescribed period.

(4) In considering a notice of objection to a penalty the Secretary of State must have regard to the code of practice under section 32.

(5) On considering a notice of objection the Secretary of State may—

(a) cancel the penalty,

(b) reduce the penalty,

(c) increase the penalty, or

(d) determine to take no action.

(6) After reaching a decision as to how to proceed under subsection (5) the Secretary of State must—

(a) notify the recipient of the decision (including the amount of any increased or reduced penalty) before the end of the prescribed period or such longer period as the Secretary of State may agree with the recipient, and

(b) if the penalty is increased, issue a new penalty notice under section 23 or (as the case may be) section 25.

Note: Commencement from 1 December 2014 for premises in local authorities set out in article 6 SI 2014/2771.

30. Appeals

(1) The recipient may appeal to the court on the ground that—

(a) the recipient is not liable to the imposition of a penalty,

(b) the recipient is excused payment as a result of section 24 or 26, or

(c) the amount of the penalty is too high.

(2) The court may

(a) allow the appeal and cancel the penalty,

(b) allow the appeal and reduce the penalty, or

(c) dismiss the appeal.

(3) An appeal is to be a re-hearing of the Secretary of State's decision to impose a penalty and is to be determined having regard to—

(a) the code of practice under section 32 that has effect at the time of the appeal, and

(b) any other matters which the court thinks relevant (which may include matters of which the Secretary of State was unaware).

(4) Subsection (3) has effect despite any provisions of rules of court.

(5) An appeal may be brought only if the recipient has given a notice of objection under section 29 and the Secretary of State—

(a) has determined the objection by issuing to the recipient the penalty notice (as a result of increasing the penalty under section 29(5)(c)),

(b) has determined the objection by—

(i) reducing the penalty under section 29(5)(b), or

(ii) taking no action under section 29(5)(d), or

(c) has not informed the recipient of a decision before the end of the period that applies for the purposes of section 29(6)(a).

(6) An appeal must be brought within the period of 28 days beginning with the relevant date.

(7) Where the appeal is brought under subsection (5)(a), the relevant date is the date specified in the penalty notice issued in accordance with section 29(6)(b) as the date on which it is given.

(8) Where the appeal is brought under subsection (5)(b), the relevant date is the date specified in the notice informing the recipient of the decision for the purposes of section 29(6)(a) as the date on which it is given.

(9) Where the appeal is brought under subsection (5)(c), the relevant date is the date on which the period that applies for the purposes of section 29(6)(a) ends.

(10) In this section "the court" means—

(a) the county court, if the appeal relates to a residential tenancy agreement in relation to premises in England and Wales;

(b) the sheriff, if the appeal relates to a residential tenancy agreement in relation to premises in Scotland;

(c) a county court in Northern Ireland, if the appeal relates to a residential tenancy agreement in relation to premises in Northern Ireland.

Note: Commencement from 1 December 2014 for premises in local authorities set out in article 6 SI 2014/2771.

31. Enforcement

(1) This section applies where a sum is payable to the Secretary of State as a penalty under this Chapter.

(2) In England and Wales the penalty is recoverable as if it were payable under an order of the county court in England and Wales.

(3) In Scotland the penalty may be enforced in the same manner as an extract registered decree arbitral bearing a warrant for execution issued by the sheriff court of any sheriffdom in Scotland.

(4) In Northern Ireland the penalty is recoverable as if it were payable under an order of a county court in Northern Ireland.

(5) Where action is taken under this section for the recovery of a sum payable as a penalty under this Chapter, the penalty is—

(a) in relation to England and Wales, to be treated for the purposes of section 98 of the Courts Act 2003 (register of judgments and orders etc) as if it were a judgment entered in the county court;

(b) in relation to Northern Ireland, to be treated for the purposes of Article 116 of the Judgments Enforcement (Northern Ireland) Order 1981 (S.I. 1981/226 (N.I. 6)) (register of judgments) as if it were a judgment in respect of which an application has been accepted under Article 22 or 23(1) of that Order.

(6) Money paid to the Secretary of State by way of a penalty must be paid into the Consolidated Fund.

Note: Commencement from 1 December 2014 for premises in local authorities set out in article 6 SI 2014/2771.

Codes of practice

32. General matters

(1) The Secretary of State must issue a code of practice for the purposes of this Chapter.

(2) The code must specify factors that the Secretary of State will consider when determining the amount of a penalty imposed under this Chapter.

(3) The code may contain guidance about—

(a) factors that the Secretary of State will consider when determining whether—

(i) a residential tenancy agreement grants a right of occupation of premises for residential use, or

(ii) a person is occupying premises as an only or main residence;

(b) the reasonable enquiries that a landlord should make to determine the identity of relevant occupiers in relation to a residential tenancy agreement (so far as they are not named in the agreement);

(c) any other matters in connection with this Chapter that the Secretary of State considers appropriate.

(4) Guidance under subsection (3)(a) may in particular relate to the treatment for the purposes of this Chapter of arrangements that are made in connection with holiday lettings or lettings for purposes connected with business travel.

(5) The Secretary of State must from time to time review the code and may revise and re-issue it following a review.

(6) The code (or revised code)—

(a) may not be issued unless a draft has been laid before Parliament, and

(b) comes into force in accordance with provision made by order of the Secretary of State.

Note: Commencement from 1 December 2014 (SI 2014/2771).

33. Discrimination

(1) The Secretary of State must issue a code of practice specifying what a landlord or agent should or should not do to ensure that, while avoiding liability to pay a penalty under this Chapter, the landlord or agent also avoids contravening—

(a) the Equality Act 2010, so far as relating to race, or

(b) the Race Relations (Northern Ireland) Order 1997 (S.I. 1997/869 (N.I. 6)).

(2) The Secretary of State must from time to time review the code and may revise and re-issue it following a review.

(3) Before issuing the code (or a revised code) the Secretary of State must consult—

(a) the Commission for Equality and Human Rights,

(b) the Equality Commission for Northern Ireland, and

(c) such persons representing the interests of landlords and tenants as the Secretary of State considers appropriate.

(4) After consulting under subsection (3) the Secretary of State must—

(a) publish a draft code, and

(b) consider any representations made about the published draft.

(5) The code (or revised code)—

(a) may not be issued unless a draft has been laid before Parliament (prepared after considering representations under subsection (4)(b) and with or without modifications to reflect the representations), and

(b) comes into force in accordance with provision made by order of the Secretary of State.

(6) A breach of the code—

(a) does not make a person liable to civil or criminal proceedings, but

(b) may be taken into account by a court or tribunal.

Note: Commencement from 1 December 2014 (SI 2014/2771).

General

34. Orders

(1) An order prescribing requirements for the purposes of this Chapter may, in particular, require a landlord or agent to—

(a) obtain a document of a prescribed description from relevant occupiers before or during the course of a residential tenancy agreement;

(b) obtain one document of each of a number of prescribed descriptions from relevant occupiers before or during the course of a residential tenancy agreement;

(c) take steps to verify, retain, copy or record the content of a document obtained in accordance with the order;

(d) take such other steps before or during the course of a residential tenancy agreement as the order may specify.

(2) If the draft of an instrument containing an order under or in connection with this Chapter would, apart from this subsection, be a hybrid instrument for the purposes of the standing orders of either House of Parliament, it is to proceed in that House as if it were not a hybrid instrument.

Note: Commencement from 1 December 2014 (SI 2014/2771).

35. Transitional provision

(1) This Chapter does not apply in relation to a residential tenancy agreement entered into before the commencement day.

(2) This Chapter does not apply in relation to a residential tenancy agreement entered into on or after the commencement day ("the renewed agreement") if—

(a) another residential tenancy agreement was entered into before the commencement day between the same parties ("the original agreement"), and

(b) the tenant has always had a right of occupation of the premises leased under the renewed agreement since entering into the original agreement.

(3) In this section "the commencement day" means such day as the Secretary of State may by order appoint; and different days may be appointed for different purposes or areas.

Note: Commencement from 1 December 2014 (SI 2014/2771).

36. Crown application

This Chapter binds the Crown, except where the Crown is the responsible landlord for the purposes of section 23.

Note: Commencement from 1 December 2014 (SI 2014/2771).

37. Interpretation

(1) In this Chapter—

"adult" means a person who has attained the age of 18;

"agreement" includes an agreement in any form (whether or not in writing);

"eligibility period", in relation to a limited right occupier, is to be read in accordance with section 27;

"limited right occupier" has the meaning given in section 24(9);

"occupy" means occupy as an only or main residence;

"penalty notice" means a penalty notice given under this Chapter;

"person with a limited right to rent" has the meaning given in section 21(4);

"post-grant contravention" has the meaning given in section 22(10);

"pre-grant contravention" has the meaning given in section 22(10);

"premises" includes land, buildings, moveable structures, vehicles and vessels;

"prescribed" means prescribed in an order made by the Secretary of State;

"recipient" means the recipient of a penalty notice;

"relevant occupier" has the meaning given in section 22(10);

(2) For the purposes of this Chapter a residential tenancy agreement grants a person a right to occupy premises if—

(a) the agreement expressly grants that person the right (whether or not by naming the person), or

(b) the person is permitted to occupy the premises by virtue of an express grant given to another person, and references to a person occupying premises under an agreement are to be read accordingly.

(3) A reference in this Chapter to the "prescribed requirements", in connection with compliance with the requirements at a particular time, is a reference only to such of the requirements as are capable of being complied with at that time.

(4) Where two or more persons jointly constitute the landlord in relation to a residential tenancy agreement—

(a) the references to the landlord in—

(i) section 22(7)(a),

(ii) section 24(5), (6)(a) and (7), and

(iii) section 26(6)(a) and (7)(b), are to be taken as references to any of those persons;

(b) any other references to the landlord in this Chapter are to be taken as references to all of those persons.

(5) Where two or more persons jointly constitute the agent in relation to a residential tenancy agreement—

(a) the references to the agent in section 26(5), (6)(a) and (7) are to be taken as references to any of those persons;

(b) any other references to the agent in this Chapter are to be taken as references to all of those persons.

(6) The Secretary of State may by order prescribe cases in which—

(a) a residential tenancy agreement is, or is not, to be treated as being entered into for the purposes of this Chapter;

(b) a person is, or is not, to be treated as occupying premises as an only or main residence for the purposes of this Chapter.

(7) An order under subsection (6) prescribing a case may modify the application of this Chapter in relation to that case.

(8) The cases mentioned in subsection (6)(a) include, in particular, cases where—

(a) an option to renew an agreement is exercised;

(b) rights of occupation under an agreement are varied;

(c) an agreement is assigned (whether by the landlord or the tenant);

(d) a periodic tenancy arises at the end of a fixed term;

(e) an agreement grants a right of occupation on satisfaction of a condition;

(f) there is a change in the persons in occupation of the premises leased under an agreement or in the circumstances of any such person.

Note: Commencement from 1 December 2014 (SI 2014/2771).

Chapter 2

Other Services etc

National Health Service

38. Immigration health charge

(1) The Secretary of State may by order provide for a charge to be imposed on—

(a) persons who apply for immigration permission, or

(b) any description of such persons.

(2) "Immigration permission" means—

(a) leave to enter or remain in the United Kingdom for a limited period,

(b) entry clearance which, by virtue of provision made under section 3A(3) of the Immigration Act 1971, has effect as leave to enter the United Kingdom for a limited period, or

(c) any other entry clearance which may be taken as evidence of a person's eligibility for entry into the United Kingdom for a limited period.

(3) An order under this section may in particular—

(a) impose a separate charge on a person in respect of each application made by that person;

(b) specify the amount of any charge (and different amounts may be specified for different purposes);

(c) make provision about when or how a charge may or must be paid to the Secretary of State;

(d) make provision about the consequences of a person failing to pay a charge (including provision for the person's application to be refused);

(e) provide for exemptions from a charge;

(f) provide for the reduction, waiver or refund of part or all of a charge (whether by conferring a discretion or otherwise).

(4) In specifying the amount of a charge under subsection (3)(b) the Secretary of State must (among other matters) have regard to the range of health services that are likely to be available free of charge to persons who have been given immigration permission.

(5) Sums paid by virtue of an order under this section must—

(a) be paid into the Consolidated Fund, or

(b) be applied in such other way as the order may specify.

(6) In this section—

"entry clearance" has the meaning given by section 33(1) of the Immigration Act 1971;

"health services" means services provided as part of the health service in England, Wales, Scotland and Northern Ireland;

and the references to applying for leave to enter or remain for a limited period include references to applying for a variation of leave to enter or remain which would result in leave to enter or remain for a limited period.

Note: Commencement from 20 October 2014 (SI 2014/2771).

39. Related provision: charges for health services

(1) A reference in the NHS charging provisions to persons not ordinarily resident in Great Britain or persons not ordinarily resident in Northern Ireland includes (without prejudice to the generality of that reference) a reference to—

(a) persons who require leave to enter or remain in the United Kingdom but do not have it, and

(b) persons who have leave to enter or remain in the United Kingdom for a limited period.

(2) The "NHS charging provisions" are—

(a) section 175 of the National Health Service Act 2006 (charges in respect of persons not ordinarily resident in Great Britain);

(b) section 124 of the National Health Service (Wales) Act 2006 (charges in respect of persons not ordinarily resident in Great Britain);

(c) section 98 of the National Health Service (Scotland) Act 1978 (charges in respect of persons not ordinarily resident in Great Britain);

(d) Article 42 of the Health and Personal Social Services (Northern Ireland) Order 1972 (S.I. 1972/1265 (N.I. 14)) (provision of services to persons not ordinarily resident in Northern Ireland).

Note: Commencement from a date to be appointed.

Bank accounts

40. Prohibition on opening current accounts for disqualified persons

(1) A bank or building society ("B") must not open a current account for a person ("P") who is within subsection (2) unless—

(a) B has carried out a status check which indicates that P is not a disqualified person, or

(b) at the time when the account is opened B is unable, because of circumstances that cannot reasonably be regarded as within its control, to carry out a status check in relation to P.

(2) A person is within this subsection if he or she—

(a) is in the United Kingdom, and

(b) requires leave to enter or remain in the United Kingdom but does not have it.

(3) For the purposes of this section—

(a) carrying out a "status check" in relation to P means checking with a specified anti-fraud organisation or a specified data-matching authority whether, according to information supplied to that organisation or authority by the Secretary of State, P is a disqualified person;

(b) a "disqualified person" is a person within subsection (2) for whom the Secretary of State considers that a current account should not be opened by a bank or building society;

(c) opening an account for P includes—

(i) opening a joint account for P and others;

(ii) opening an account in relation to which P is a signatory or is identified as a beneficiary;

(iii) adding P as an account holder or as a signatory or identified beneficiary in relation to an account.

(4) In subsection (3)(a)—

"anti-fraud organisation" has the same meaning as in section 68 of the Serious Crime Act 2007;

"data-matching authority" means a person or body conducting data matching exercises, within the meaning of Schedule 9 to the Local Audit and Accountability Act 2014, under or by virtue of that or any other Act;

"specified" means specified by an order made by the Secretary of State for the purposes of this section.

(5) Subsection (1)(b) does not apply where—

(a) a bank or building society is required to pay a reasonable fee for carrying out status checks, and

(b) its inability to carry out a status check is due to its failure to pay the fee.

(6) A bank or building society that refuses to open a current account for someone on the ground that he or she is a disqualified person must tell the person, if it may lawfully do so, that that is the reason for its refusal.

Note: Commencement from a date to be appointed.

41. Regulation by Financial Conduct Authority

(1) The Treasury may make regulations to enable the Financial Conduct Authority to make arrangements for monitoring and enforcing compliance with the prohibition imposed on banks and building societies by section 40.

(2) The regulations may (in particular)—

(a) provide for the Financial Conduct Authority to be given free access to the information to which banks and building societies are given access when carrying out status checks under section 40;

(b) apply, or make provision corresponding to, any of the provisions of the Financial Services and Markets Act 2000, including in particular those mentioned in subsection (3), with or without modification.

(3) The provisions are—

(a) provisions about investigations, including powers of entry and search and criminal offences;

(b) provisions for the grant of an injunction (or, in Scotland, an interdict) in relation to a contravention or anticipated contravention;

(c) provisions giving the Financial Conduct Authority powers to impose disciplinary measures (including financial penalties) or to give directions;

(d) provisions giving a Minister of the Crown (within the meaning of the Ministers of the Crown Act 1975) or the Financial Conduct Authority powers to make subordinate legislation;

(e) provisions for the Financial Conduct Authority to charge fees.

Note: Commencement from a date to be appointed.

42. "Bank" and "building society"

(1) In sections 40 and 41 "bank" means an authorised deposit-taker that has its head office or a branch in the United Kingdom. This is subject to subsection (4).

(2) In subsection (1) "authorised deposit-taker" means—

(a) a person who under Part 4A of the Financial Services and Markets Act 2000 has permission to accept deposits;

(b) an EEA firm of the kind mentioned in paragraph 5(b) of Schedule 3 to that Act that has permission under paragraph 15 of that Schedule (as a result of qualifying for authorisation under paragraph 12(1) of that Schedule) to accept deposits.

(3) A reference in subsection (2) to a person or firm with permission to accept deposits does not include a person or firm with permission to do so only for the purposes of, or in the course of, an activity other than accepting deposits.

(4) "Bank" does not include—

(a) a building society;

(b) a person who is specified, or is within a class of persons specified, by an order under section 38 of the Financial Services and Markets Act 2000 (exemption orders);

(c) a credit union within the meaning given by section 31(1) of the Credit Unions Act 1979 or by Article 2(2) of the Credit Unions (Northern Ireland) Order 1985;

(d) a friendly society within the meaning given by section 116 of the Friendly Societies Act 1992.

(5) In sections 40 and 41, and in subsection (4), "building society" means a building society incorporated (or deemed to be incorporated) under the Building Societies Act 1986.

Note: Commencement at a date to be appointed.

43. Power to amend

(1) The Treasury may by order amend any of sections 40 to 42 so as—

(a) to alter the categories of financial institution to which those sections apply;

(b) to alter the categories of account to which the prohibition in section 40(1) applies;

(c) to include provision defining a category of account specified in that section;

(d) to provide for the prohibition in section 40(1) not to apply in the case of an account to be operated (or an account that is operated) by or for a person or body of a specified description.

(2) An order under subsection (1) may amend a section so that it provides for a matter to be specified in a further order to be made by the Treasury.

(3) In subsection (1) "account" includes a financial product by means of which a payment may be made.

Note: Commencement from a date to be appointed.

Work

44. Appeals against penalty notices

. . .

Note: Amends s 17 of the Immigration, Asylum and Nationality Act 2006 from a date to be appointed.

45. Recovery of sums payable under penalty notices

. . .

Note: Amends s 18 of the Immigration, Asylum and Nationality Act 2006 from a date to be appointed.

Driving licences

46. Grant of driving licences: residence requirement

. . .

Note: Amends s 97 of the Road Traffic Act 1988, Road Traffic (Northern Ireland) Order 1981 (SI 1981/154 (NI 1)) from a date to be appointed.

47. Revocation of driving licences on grounds of immigration status

. . .

Note: Amends ss 99–100 of the Road Traffic Act 1988, Road Traffic (Northern Ireland) Order 1981 (SI 1981/154 (NI 1)), from a date to be appointed.

PART 4

MARRIAGE AND CIVIL PARTNERSHIP

CHAPTER 1

REFERRAL AND INVESTIGATION OF PROPOSED MARRIAGES AND CIVIL PARTNERSHIPS

Investigation

48. Decision whether to investigate

(1) This section applies if—

(a) a superintendent registrar refers a proposed marriage to the Secretary of State under section 28H of the Marriage Act 1949, or

(b) a registration authority refers a proposed civil partnership to the Secretary of State under section 12A of the Civil Partnership Act 2004.

(2) The Secretary of State must decide whether to investigate whether the proposed marriage or civil partnership is a sham.

(3) The Secretary of State may not decide to conduct such an investigation unless conditions A and B are met.

(4) Condition A is met if the Secretary of State is satisfied that—

(a) only one of the parties to the proposed marriage or civil partnership is an exempt person, or

(b) neither of the parties are exempt persons.

(5) Condition B is met if the Secretary of State has reasonable grounds for suspecting that the proposed marriage or civil partnership is a sham.

(6) In making the decision whether to investigate, regard must be had to any guidance published by the Secretary of State for this purpose.

(7) In the case of a proposed marriage, the Secretary of State must give notice of the decision made under this section to—

(a) both of the parties to the proposed marriage, and

(b) the superintendent registrar who referred the proposed marriage to the Secretary of State.

(8) In the case of a proposed civil partnership, the Secretary of State must give notice of the decision made under this section to—

(a) both of the parties to the proposed civil partnership,

(b) the registration authority who referred the proposed civil partnership to the Secretary of State, and

(c) if different, the registration authority responsible for issuing the civil partnership schedule under section 14(1) of the Civil Partnership Act 2004 in relation to the proposed civil partnership.

(9) The Secretary of State must make the decision, and give the notice, required by this section within the relevant statutory period.

Note: Commencement from a date to be appointed.

49. Exempt persons

(1) A person who is a party to a proposed marriage or civil partnership is an exempt person if the person—

(a) is a relevant national;

(b) has the appropriate immigration status; or

(c) holds a relevant visa in respect of the proposed marriage or civil partnership.

(2) A person has the appropriate immigration status if the person—

(a) has a right of permanent residence in the United Kingdom by virtue of an enforceable EU right or of any provision made under section 2(2) of the European Communities Act 1972;

(b) is exempt from immigration control; or

(c) is settled in the United Kingdom (within the meaning of the Immigration Act 1971 — see section 33(2A) of that Act).

(3) The question of whether a person is exempt from immigration control is to be determined in accordance with regulations made for this purpose by the Secretary of State.

(4) A person holds a relevant visa if the person holds a visa or other authorisation that is of a kind specified for this purpose in regulations made by the Secretary of State.

(5) The Secretary of State may not specify a visa or other authorisation under subsection (4) unless the Secretary of State considers that the purpose of issuing that kind of visa or authorisation is, or includes, enabling a person to enter or remain in the United Kingdom to marry or form a civil partnership.

Note: Commencement from 20 October 2014 for the purpose of making regulations (SI 2014/2771).

50. Conduct of investigation

(1) An investigation must be conducted in accordance with any regulations made by the Secretary of State for this purpose.

(2) In conducting an investigation, regard must also be had to any guidance published by the Secretary of State for this purpose.

(3) A relevant party must comply with a requirement specified in regulations made under section 51(4) if—

(a) the section 48 notice given to the relevant party states that he or she must do so, or

(b) the Secretary of State subsequently notifies the relevant party (orally or in writing) that he or she must do so; and the relevant party must comply with that requirement in the manner stated in the section 48 notice or in the Secretary of State's notification (if such a manner is stated there).

(4) As part of an investigation, the Secretary of State must decide whether or not each of the relevant parties has complied with the investigation (the "compliance question").

(5) The compliance question must be decided in accordance with any regulations made by the Secretary of State for this purpose.

(6) In deciding the compliance question, regard must also be had to any guidance published by the Secretary of State for this purpose.

(7) Within the 70 day period, the Secretary of State must—

(a) decide the compliance question; and

(b) give notice of that decision to the persons to whom the Secretary of State gave the section 48 notice relating to the proposed marriage or civil partnership.

(8) If the Secretary of State's decision is that one or both of the relevant parties have not complied with the investigation, the notice under subsection (7) must include a statement of the Secretary of State's reasons for reaching that decision.

(9) Regulations made under this section may, in particular, make provision about—

(a) the circumstances in which a relevant party is to be taken to have failed to comply with a relevant requirement;

(b) the consequences of a relevant party's failure to comply with a relevant requirement.

(10) The provision that may be made under subsection (9)(b) includes provision for the compliance question to be decided (in whole or in part) by reference to a relevant party's compliance or non-compliance with one or more relevant requirements.

(11) In this section—

"70 day period" means the period of 70 days beginning with the day on which the relevant statutory period begins;

"investigation" means an investigation, conducted following a decision by the Secretary of State under section 48, whether a proposed marriage or civil partnership is a sham;

"relevant party" means a person who is a party to a proposed marriage or civil partnership that is the subject of an investigation;

"relevant requirement" means any requirement imposed by law, including a requirement imposed by or in accordance with—

(a) subsection (3);

(b) section 27E, 28B or 28C of the Marriage Act 1949;

(c) regulations under section 28D of that Act;

(d) section 8A, or any of sections 9 to 9B, of the Civil Partnership Act 2004.

Note: Commencement from 20 October 2014 for the purpose of making regulations (SI 2014/2771).

51. Investigations: supplementary

(1) A section 48 notice which states that the Secretary of State has decided to investigate whether a proposed marriage or civil partnership is a sham must include—

(a) notice that the compliance question must be decided within the period of 70 days mentioned in section 50(7);

(b) notice of the date on which that period will end;

(c) notice that a relevant party may be required to comply with one or more requirements imposed by the Secretary of State subsequently in accordance with section 50(3); and

(d) prescribed information about the investigation.

(2) The section 48 notice may also include such other information as the Secretary of State considers appropriate.

(3) For the purposes of subsection (1)(d) "prescribed information" means information prescribed by the Secretary of State by regulations; and the information that may be prescribed includes information about—

(a) the conduct of the investigation;

(b) requirements with which the relevant parties must comply in relation to the investigation;

(c) the consequence of a failure to comply with those or any other requirements;

(d) the possible outcomes of the investigation;
(e) the consequences of those outcomes.

(4) The Secretary of State may, by regulations, specify requirements relating to the conduct of investigations which may be imposed on a relevant party by the section 48 notice or by the Secretary of State subsequently in accordance with section 50(3).

(5) Regulations made under subsection (4) may, in particular, specify any of the following requirements—

(a) a requirement to make contact with a particular person or description of persons in a particular way (including by telephoning a particular number) within a particular time period;
(b) a requirement to be present at a particular place at a particular time;
(c) a requirement to be visited at home;
(d) a requirement to be interviewed;
(e) a requirement to provide information (whether orally or in writing);
(f) a requirement to provide photographs;
(g) a requirement to provide evidence.

(6) The provisions of this Part, and any investigation or other steps taken under those provisions (including the decision of the compliance question), do not limit the powers of the Secretary of State in relation to marriages or civil partnerships that are, or are suspected to be, a sham (including any powers to investigate such marriages or civil partnerships).

(7) In this section "investigation", "relevant party" and "compliance question" have the same meanings as in section 50.

Note: Commencement from 20 October 2014 for the purpose of making regulations (SI 2014/2771).

Referral

52. Referral of proposed marriages and civil partnerships in England and Wales

Schedule 4 (referral of proposed marriages and civil partnerships in England and Wales) has effect.

Note: Commencement from 20 October 2014 for the purpose of making regulations for part of Schedule 4 (article 3 SI 2014/2771).

Scotland and Northern Ireland

53. Extension of scheme to Scotland and Northern Ireland

(1) The Secretary of State may, by order, make such provision as the Secretary of State considers appropriate for extending the referral and investigation scheme to any of the following—
(a) proposed marriages under the law of Scotland;
(b) proposed civil partnerships under the law of Scotland;
(c) proposed marriages under the law of Northern Ireland;
(d) proposed civil partnerships under the law of Northern Ireland.

(2) An order under this section may—
(a) make provision having a similar effect to the provision made by section 58, Schedule 4, or Parts 1, 2 and 4 of Schedule 6;
(b) confer functions on any person;
(c) amend, repeal or revoke any enactment (including an enactment contained in this Act).

(3) The power under subsection (2)(b) to confer functions includes power to impose a duty of referral on persons exercising functions in Scotland or Northern Ireland in relation to marriage or civil partnership.

(4) But an order under this section may not impose that or any other duty, or otherwise confer functions, on—

(a) the Scottish Ministers,

(b) the First Minister and deputy First Minister in Northern Ireland,

(c) a Northern Ireland Minister, or

(d) a Northern Ireland department.

(5) In this section—

"duty of referral" means a duty to refer a proposed marriage or proposed civil partnership to the Secretary of State in a case where—

(a) one of the parties is not an exempt person, or

(b) both of the parties are not exempt persons;

"enactment" includes—

(a) an enactment contained in subordinate legislation within the meaning of the Interpretation Act 1978;

(b) an enactment contained in, or in an instrument made under, an Act of the Scottish Parliament;

(c) an enactment contained in, or in an instrument made under, Northern Ireland legislation;

"referral and investigation scheme" means the provision made by sections 48 to 51.

Note: Commencement from 20 October 2014 for the purpose of making orders (SI 2014/2771).

54. Supplementary provision

(1) This section applies if the referral and investigation scheme is extended by an order under section 53 (an "extension order").

(2) The Secretary of State may make administrative regulations in connection with the application of the scheme—

(a) to proposed marriages or civil partnerships under the law of Scotland (insofar as the scheme is extended to them), and

(b) to proposed marriages or civil partnerships under the law of Northern Ireland (insofar as the scheme is extended to them).

(3) For that purpose "administrative regulations" means regulations of any kind set out in Schedule 5 (sham marriage and civil partnership: administrative regulations).

(4) The Secretary of State may by order make provision about—

(a) the information that must or may be given, or

(b) the matters in respect of which evidence must or may be given, in relation to proposed marriages or civil partnerships under the law of Scotland or Northern Ireland in cases where one or both of the parties is not a relevant national.

(5) An order under subsection (4) may amend, repeal or revoke any enactment (including an enactment contained in this Act or in provision made by an extension order or an order under subsection (4)).

(6) If an extension order makes provision ("information disclosure provision") having similar effect to the provision made by paragraph 2 of Schedule 6 about the disclosure of

information for immigration purposes, the Secretary of State may by order specify other immigration purposes (in addition to those specified in provision made by an extension order or in any provision made under this subsection) for which information may be disclosed under the information disclosure provision.

(7) The Secretary of State must consult—

(a) the Registrar General for Scotland before making administrative regulations, or an order under subsection (4), in relation to proposed marriages or civil partnerships under the law of Scotland;

(b) the Registrar General for Northern Ireland before making administrative regulations, or an order under subsection (4), in relation to proposed marriages or civil partnerships under the law of Northern Ireland.

(8) Expressions used in this section or Schedule 5 that are also used in section 53 have the same meanings in this section or Schedule 5 as in section 53.

Note: Gives power to make regulations in connection with the scheme where s 53 Order made, from 20 October 2014 for the purpose of making regulations (SI 2014/2771).

CHAPTER 2

SHAM MARRIAGE AND CIVIL PARTNERSHIP

55. Meaning of "sham marriage" and "sham civil partnership"

. . .

Note: Amends the Immigration and Asylum Act 1999 from a date to be appointed.

56. Duty to report suspicious marriages and civil partnerships

. . .

Note: Amends the Immigration and Asylum Act 1999 from 14 July 2014 (s 75).

CHAPTER 3

OTHER PROVISIONS

Persons not relevant nationals etc.: marriage on superintendent registrar's certificates

57. Solemnization of marriage according to rites of Church of England

. . .

Note: Amends the Marriage Act 1949 from a date to be appointed.

58. Requirement as to giving of notice of marriage or civil partnership

Note: Subsections (2)–(3) amend s 19 of the Asylum and Immigration (Treatment of Claimants, etc.) Act 2004 and subsections (5)–(9) amend Sch 23 to the Civil Partnership Act 2004 from a date to be appointed.

Information

59. Information

Schedule 6 (information) has effect.
Note: Commencement from 14 July 2014 (s 75).

Miscellaneous

60. Regulations about evidence

(1) The Secretary of State may make regulations about evidence relevant to the determination of any of the following questions for a purpose of this Part—

(a) whether a person is a relevant national;

(b) whether a person has the appropriate immigration status;

(c) whether a person has a relevant visa.

(2) The regulations may, in particular, make provision about—

(a) the kind of evidence which is to be supplied;

(b) the form in which evidence is to be supplied;

(c) the manner in which evidence is to be supplied;

(d) the period within which evidence is to be supplied;

(e) the supply of further evidence;

(f) the sufficiency of evidence supplied;

(g) the consequences of failing to supply sufficient evidence in accordance with the regulations (including provision to secure that, in such a case, a particular decision is made or is to be treated as having been made);

(h) the retention or copying of evidence supplied.

(3) The Secretary of State must consult the Registrar General before making regulations under this section.

(4) In this section "evidence" includes a photograph or other image.

Note: Commencement from 20 October 2014 (SI 2014/2771).

61. Notices

(1) The Secretary of State may, by regulations, make provision about the giving of—

(a) notices under any provision of this Part;

(b) notices relating to the referral of proposed marriages under section 28H of the Marriage Act 1949 which are given under any provision of that Act;

(c) notices relating to the referral of proposed civil partnerships under section 12A of the Civil Partnership Act 2004 which are given under any provision of that Act.

(2) The regulations may, in particular, make provision that a notice given inaccordance with the regulations is to be presumed to have been received by the person to whom it is given.

(3) The Secretary of State must consult the Registrar General before making regulations under this section.

Note: Appointment from 20 October 2014 (SI 2014/2771).

62. Interpretation of this Part

(1) These expressions have the meanings given—

"exempt person" has the meaning given in section 49;

"registrar" means a registrar of births, deaths and marriages;

"Registrar General" means the Registrar General for England and Wales;

"registration authority" has the same meaning as in the Civil Partnership Act 2004 (see section 28 of that Act);

"relevant national" means—

(a) a British citizen,

(b) a national of an EEA State other than the United Kingdom, or

(c) a national of Switzerland;

"relevant statutory period" means—

(a) in relation to a proposed marriage, the period—

(i) beginning the day after notice of the proposed marriage is entered in the marriage book in accordance with Part 3 of the Marriage Act 1949, or is entered in an approved electronic form by virtue of section 27(4A) of that Act, and

(ii) ending at the end of the period of 28 days beginning with that day;

(b) in relation to a proposed civil partnership, the period—

(i) beginning the day after notice of the proposed civil partnership is recorded in the register in accordance with Chapter 1 of Part 2 of the Civil Partnership Act 2004, and

(ii) ending at the end of the period of 28 days beginning with that day;

"section 48 notice" means a notice given under section 48(7) or (8);

"superintendent registrar" means a superintendent registrar of births, deaths and marriages.

(2) A reference to a person being a party to a proposed marriage or civil partnership is a reference to a person who would be a party to the marriage or civil partnership if it took place as proposed.

(3) A reference to a proposed marriage or civil partnership being a sham is a reference to a marriage or civil partnership which would (if it took place as proposed) be a sham marriage or sham civil partnership (within the meaning of the Immigration and Asylum Act 1999 — see section 24 or 24A of that Act).

(4) For provision about the interpretation of the following expressions, see section 49—

(a) the appropriate immigration status;

(b) a relevant visa.

(5) This section, and the provision mentioned in subsection (4), apply for the purposes of this Part.

Note: Commencement 15 July 2014 (s 75).

Part 5

Oversight

Office of the Immigration Services Commissioner

63. Immigration advisers and immigration service providers

Schedule 7 (immigration advisers and immigration service providers) has effect.

Note: Commencement from 20 October 2014 for paragraphs 1 and 3, 17 November 2014 for the remainder of Schedule 7 (SI 2014/2771).

Police Ombudsman for Northern Ireland

64. Police Ombudsman for Northern Ireland

. . .

Note: Amends the Police (Northern Ireland) Act 1998 from a date to be notified.

PART 6

MISCELLANEOUS

Citizenship

65. Persons unable to acquire citizenship: natural father not married to mother

. . .

Note: Inserts ss 4E–4J of the British Nationality Act 1981 from a date to be appointed.

66. Deprivation if conduct seriously prejudicial to vital interests of the UK

(1) . . .

(2) In deciding whether to make an order under subsection (2) of section 40 of the British Nationality Act 1981 in a case which falls within subsection (4A) of that Act, the Secretary of State may take account of the manner in which a person conducted him or herself before this section came into force.

(3) . . .

Note: Subsection (1) amends s 40 of the British Nationality Act 1981, subsection (3) inserts s 40B of the same Act from a date to be appointed.

Embarkation checks

67. Embarkation checks

Schedule 8 (embarkation checks) has effect.

Note: Commencement at a date to be appointed.

Fees

68. Fees

(1) The Secretary of State may provide, in accordance with this section, for fees to be charged in respect of the exercise of functions in connection with immigration or nationality.

(2) The functions in respect of which fees are to be charged are to be specified by the Secretary of State by order ("a fees order").

(3) A fees order—

(a) must specify how the fee in respect of the exercise of each specified function is to be calculated, and

(b) may not provide for a fee to be charged in respect of the exercise of a function otherwise than in connection with an application or claim, or on request.

(4) For any specified fee, a fees order must provide for it to comprise one or more amounts each of which is—

(a) a fixed amount, or

(b) an amount calculated by reference to an hourly rate or other factor.

(5) Where a fees order provides for a fee (or part of a fee) to be a fixed amount, it—

(a) must specify a maximum amount for the fee (or part), and

(b) may specify a minimum amount.

(6) Where a fees order provides for a fee (or part of a fee) to be calculated as mentioned in subsection (4)(b), it—

(a) must specify—

(i) how the fee (or part) is to be calculated, and

(ii) a maximum rate or other factor, and

(b) may specify a minimum rate or other factor.

(7) For any specified fee, the following are to be set by the Secretary of State by regulations ("fees regulations")—

(a) if the fee (or any part of it) is to be a fixed amount, that amount;

(b) if the fee (or any part of it) is to be calculated as mentioned in subsection (4)(b), the hourly rate or other factor by reference to which it (or that part) is to be calculated.

(8) An amount, or rate or other factor, set by fees regulations for a fee in respect of the exercise of a specified function—

(a) must not—

(i) exceed the maximum specified for that amount, or rate or other factor;

(ii) be less than the minimum, if any, so specified;

(b) subject to that, may be intended to exceed, or result in a fee which exceeds, the costs of exercising the function.

(9) In setting the amount of any fee, or rate or other factor, in fees regulations, the Secretary of State may have regard only to—

(a) the costs of exercising the function;

(b) benefits that the Secretary of State thinks are likely to accrue to any person in connection with the exercise of the function;

(c) the costs of exercising any other function in connection with immigration or nationality;

(d) the promotion of economic growth;

(e) fees charged by or on behalf of governments of other countries in respect of comparable functions;

(f) any international agreement. This is subject to section 69(5).

(10) In respect of any fee provided for under this section, fees regulations may—

(a) provide for exceptions;

(b) provide for the reduction, waiver or refund of part or all of a fee (whether by conferring a discretion or otherwise);

(c) make provision about—

(i) the consequences of failure to pay a fee;

(ii) enforcement;

(iii) when a fee may or must be paid.

(11) Any provision that may be made by fees regulations by virtue of subsection (10) may be included instead in a fees order (and any provision so included may be amended or revoked by fees regulations).

(12) In this section and sections 69 and 70—

"costs" includes—

(a) the costs of the Secretary of State, and

(b) the costs of any other person (whether or not funded from public money);

"fees order" has the meaning given by subsection (2);

"fees regulations" has the meaning given by subsection (7);

"function" includes a power or a duty;

"function in connection with immigration or nationality" includes a function in connection with an enactment (including an enactment of a jurisdiction outside the United Kingdom) that relates wholly or partly to immigration or nationality;

"specified" means specified in a fees order.

(13) Any reference in this section or section 70 to the exercise of a function includes a reference to its exercise in particular circumstances, including its exercise—

(a) at particular times or in a particular place;

(b) under particular arrangements;

(c) otherwise in particular ways,

and, for this purpose, "arrangements" includes arrangements for the convenience of applicants, claimants or persons making requests for the exercise of a function.

Note: Commencement from 15 December 2014 (SI 2014/2771).

69. Fees orders and fees regulations: supplemental

(1) A fees order or fees regulations may be made only with the consent of the Treasury.

(2) A fee under section 68 may relate to something done outside the United Kingdom.

(3) Fees payable by virtue of section 68 may be recovered as a debt due to the Secretary of State.

(4) Fees paid to the Secretary of State by virtue of section 68 must—

(a) be paid into the Consolidated Fund, or

(b) be applied in such other way as the relevant order may specify.

(5) Section 68 is without prejudice to—

(a) section 1 of the Consular Fees Act 1980 (fees for consular acts etc);

(b) section 102 of the Finance (No. 2) Act 1987 (government fees and charges), or

(c) any other power to charge a fee.

Note: Commencement from 15 December 2014 (SI 2014/2771).

70. Power to charge fees for attendance services in particular cases

(1) This section applies where a person exercises a function in connection with immigration or nationality in respect of which a fee is chargeable by virtue of a fees order (a "chargeable function") in a particular case and—

(a) in doing so attends at a place outside the United Kingdom, and time, agreed with a person ("the client"), and

(b) does so at the request of the client. It is immaterial whether or not the client is a person in respect of whom the chargeable function is exercised.

(2) In this section "attendance service" means the service described in subsection (1) except so far as it consists of the exercise of a chargeable function.

(3) The following are to be disregarded in determining whether a fee is chargeable in respect of a function by virtue of a fees order—

(a) any exception provided for by a fees order or fees regulations;

(b) any power so provided to waive or refund a fee.

(4) The person exercising the chargeable function may charge the client such fee for the purposes of recovering the costs of providing the attendance service as the person may determine.

(5) Fees paid to the Secretary of State by virtue of this section must be paid into the Consolidated Fund.

(6) A fee payable by virtue of this section may be recovered as a debt due to the Secretary of State.

(7) This section is without prejudice to—

(a) section 68;

(b) section 1 of the Consular Fees Act 1980 (fees for consular acts etc);

(c) section 102 of the Finance (No. 2) Act 1987 (government fees and charges), or

(d) any other power to charge a fee.

Note: Commencement from a date to be notified.

Welfare of children

71. Duty regarding the welfare of children

For the avoidance of doubt, this Act does not limit any duty imposed on the Secretary of State or any other person by section 55 of the Borders, Citizenship and Immigration Act 2009 (duty regarding the welfare of children).

Note: Commencement from a date to be notified.

Part 7

Final Provisions

72. Financial provision

The following are to be paid out of money provided by Parliament—

(a) expenditure incurred under or by virtue of this Act by the Secretary of State, and

(b) any increase attributable to this Act in the sums payable under any other Act out of money so provided.

Note: Commencement 14 May 2013 (s 75).

73. Transitional and consequential provision

(1) The Secretary of State may, by order, make such transitional, transitory or saving provision as the Secretary of State considers appropriate in connection with the coming into force of any provision of this Act.

(2) The Secretary of State may, by order, make such provision as the Secretary of State considers appropriate in consequence of this Act.

(3) The provision that may be made by an order under subsection (2) includes provision amending, repealing or revoking any enactment.

(4) "Enactment" includes—

(a) an enactment contained in subordinate legislation within the meaning of the Interpretation Act 1978;

(b) an enactment contained in, or in an instrument made under, an Act of the Scottish Parliament;

(c) an enactment contained in, or in an instrument made under, a Measure or Act of the National Assembly for Wales;

(d) an enactment contained in, or in an instrument made under, Northern Ireland legislation.

(5) . . .

(6) Schedule 9 (transitional and consequential provision) has effect.

Note: Subsection (5) amends s 61 of the UK Borders Act 2007. Subsection (6) commences from 20 October 2014 and 17 November 2014 with saving provisions, (SI 2014/2771), remainder 14 May 2014 (s 75).

74. Orders and regulations

(1) Any power of the Secretary of State or Treasury to make an order or regulations under this Act is exercisable by statutory instrument.

(2) A statutory instrument containing any of the following orders or regulations may not be made unless a draft of the instrument has been laid before each House of Parliament and approved by a resolution of each House of Parliament—

(a) an order under section 20(7), 23(6) or 25(5);
(b) an order under section 38;
(c) regulations under section 41;
(d) an order under section 43, or under a section amended by such an order;
(e) the first regulations under section 50(1);
(f) the first regulations under section 50(5);
(g) the first regulations under section 51(3);
(h) the first regulations under section 51(4);
(i) an order under section 53 or 54(4) or (6);
(j) a fees order (within the meaning of section 68);
(k) an order under section 73(2) which amends or repeals primary legislation;
(l) an order under paragraph 2(3)(e) of Schedule 6.

(3) "Primary legislation" means any of the following—

(a) a public general Act;
(b) an Act of the Scottish Parliament;
(c) a Measure or Act of the National Assembly for Wales;
(d) Northern Ireland legislation.

(4) A statutory instrument containing any other order or regulations made by the Secretary of State or Treasury under this Act is subject to annulment in pursuance of a resolution of either House of Parliament.

(5) But subsection (4) does not apply to a statutory instrument containing an order under any of sections 35(3), 73(1) and 75(3) (subject to subsection (7)).

(6) Subsection (7) applies if an order under section 75(3) is made which—

(a) brings into force a provision of Chapter 1 of Part 3,

(b) brings that provision into force only in relation to a particular area or areas within England and Wales, Scotland or Northern Ireland, and

(c) is the first order to be made bringing into force a provision of that Chapter only in relation to an area or areas within England and Wales, Scotland or Northern Ireland.

(7) A statutory instrument containing any subsequent order under section 75(3) (after the order mentioned in subsection (6)) that brings into force a provision of Chapter 1 of Part 3 for anywhere other than the area or areas mentioned in paragraph (b) of that subsection is subject to annulment in pursuance of a resolution of either House of Parliament.

(8) An order or regulations made by the Secretary of State or Treasury under this Act may—

(a) make different provision for different purposes or areas,

(b) make provision which applies generally or only for particular purposes or areas,

(c) make transitional, transitory or saving provision, or

(d) make incidental, supplementary or consequential provision.

Note: Commencement from 14 May 2014, s 75.

75. Commencement

(1) This Part, other than section 73(6) and Schedule 9, comes into force on the day on which this Act is passed.

(2) Section 56, section 59 and Schedule 6, and section 62 come into force at the end of the period of two months beginning with the day on which this Act is passed.

(3) Subject to subsections (1) and (2), this Act comes into force on such day as the Secretary of State may by order appoint; and different days may be appointed for different purposes or areas.

Note: Commencement 14 May 2014.

76. Extent

(1) This Act extends to England and Wales, Scotland and Northern Ireland.

(2) Subsection (1) is subject to subsection (3).

(3) Section 59 and Schedule 6 extend to England and Wales only.

(4) Subsections (1) to (3) do not apply to an amendment, repeal or revocation made by this Act.

(5) An amendment, repeal or revocation made by this Act has the same extent as the provision amended, repealed or revoked (ignoring extent by virtue of an Order in Council).

(6) Her Majesty may by Order in Council provide for any of the provisions of this Act to extend, with or without modifications, to any of the Channel Islands or the Isle of Man.

(7) Subsection (6) does not apply in relation to the extension to a place of a provision which extends there by virtue of subsection (5).

Note: Commencement 14 May 2014, s 75.

77. Short title

This Act may be cited as the Immigration Act 2014.

Note: Commencement 14 May 2014, s 75.

SCHEDULES

SCHEDULE 1

Section 4 ENFORCEMENT POWERS

Note: Commencement from a date to be appointed.

SCHEDULE 2

Section 12 MEANING OF BIOMETRIC INFORMATION

. . .

Note: Commencement from a date to be appointed.

SCHEDULE 3

Section 20 EXCLUDED RESIDENTIAL TENANCY AGREEMENTS

Social housing

1.—(1) An agreement that grants a right of occupation in social housing.

(2) "Social housing" means accommodation provided to a person by virtue of a relevant provision.

(3) "Relevant provision" means a provision of—
- (a) in relation to England and Wales—
  - (i) Part 2 of the Housing Act 1985, or
  - (ii) Part 6 or 7 of the Housing Act 1996;
- (b) in relation to Scotland, Part 1 or 2 of the Housing (Scotland) Act 1987;
- (c) in relation to Northern Ireland—
  - (i) Chapter 4 of Part 2 of the Housing (Northern Ireland) Order 1981 (S.I. 1981/156 (N.I. 3)), or
  - (ii) Part 2 of the Housing (Northern Ireland) Order 1988 (S.I. 1988/1990 (N.I. 23)).

(4) Accommodation provided to a person by virtue of a relevant provision includes accommodation provided in pursuance of arrangements made under any such provision.

2.—(1) This paragraph applies for the purposes of paragraph 1.

(2) An allocation of housing accommodation by a local housing authority in England to a person who is already—
- (a) a secure or introductory tenant, or
- (b) an assured tenant of housing accommodation held by a private registered provider of social housing or a registered social landlord, is to be treated as an allocation of housing accommodation by virtue of Part 6 of the Housing Act 1996 (and accordingly section 159(4A) of that Act is to be ignored).

(3) An allocation of housing accommodation that falls within a case specified in, or prescribed under, section 160 of the Housing Act 1996 (cases where provisions about allocation under Part 6 of that Act do not apply) is to be treated as an allocation of housing accommodation by virtue of Part 6 of that Act (and accordingly that section is to be ignored).

(4) An allocation of housing accommodation by virtue of Part 1 of the Housing (Scotland) Act 1987 is to be treated as provided by virtue of a relevant provision only if it is provided by a local authority within the meaning of that Act (or in pursuance of arrangements made under or for the purposes of that Part with a local authority).

(5) Accommodation provided to a person in Northern Ireland by a registered housing association is to be treated as provided to the person by virtue of a relevant provision.

(6) Terms used in sub-paragraphs (2) and (3) have the same meanings as in Part 6 of the Housing Act 1996.

(7) In sub-paragraph (5) "registered housing association" means a housing association, within the meaning of Part 2 of the Housing (Northern Ireland) Order 1992 (S.I. 1992/1725 (N.I. 15)), that is registered in the register of housing associations maintained under Article 14 of that Order.

Care homes

3.—(1) An agreement that grants a right of occupation in a care home.

(2) "Care home" means—

(a) in relation to England and Wales, an establishment that is a care home for the purposes of the Care Standards Act 2000;

(b) in relation to Scotland, accommodation that is provided as a care home service within the meaning of Part 5 of the Public Services Reform (Scotland) Act 2010;

(c) in relation to Northern Ireland, an establishment that is a residential care home, or a nursing home, for the purposes of the Health and Personal Social Services (Quality, Improvement and Regulation) (Northern Ireland) Order 2003 (S.I. 2003/431 (N.I. 9)).

Hospitals and hospices

4.—(1) An agreement that grants a right of occupation of accommodation in a hospital or hospice.

(2) "Hospital"—

(a) in relation to England, has the meaning given in section 275 of the National Health Service Act 2006;

(b) in relation to Wales, has the meaning given in section 206 of the National Health Service (Wales) Act 2006;

(c) in relation to Scotland, has the meaning given in section 108 of the National Health Service (Scotland) Act 1978;

(d) in relation to Northern Ireland, has the meaning given in Article 2(2) of the Health and Personal Social Services (Northern Ireland) Order 1972 (S.I. 1972/1265 (N.I. 14)).

(3) "Hospice" means an establishment other than a hospital whose primary function is the provision of palliative care to persons resident there who are suffering from a progressive disease in its final stages.

Other accommodation relating to healthcare provision

5.—(1) An agreement—

(a) under which accommodation is provided to a person as a result of a duty imposed on a relevant NHS body by an enactment, and (b) which is not excluded by another provision of this Schedule.

(2) "Relevant NHS body" means—

(a) in relation to England—

(i) a clinical commissioning group, or
(ii) the National Health Service Commissioning Board;
(b) in relation to Wales, a local health board;
(c) in relation to Scotland, a health board constituted by order made under section 2 of the National Health Service (Scotland) Act 1978;
(d) in relation to Northern Ireland, a Health and Social Services trust.

Hostels and refuges

6.—(1) An agreement that grants a right of occupation of accommodation in a hostel or refuge.

(2) "Hostel" means a building which satisfies the following two conditions.

(3) The first condition is that the building is used for providing to persons generally, or to a class of persons—
(a) residential accommodation otherwise than in separate and selfcontained premises, and
(b) board or facilities for the preparation of food adequate to the needs of those persons (or both).

(4) The second condition is that any of the following applies in relation to the building—
(a) it is managed by a registered housing association;
(b) it is not operated on a commercial basis and its costs of operation are provided wholly or in part by a government department or agency, or by a local authority;
(c) it is managed by a voluntary organisation or charity.

(5) "Refuge" means a building which satisfies the second condition in subparagraph (4) and is used wholly or mainly for providing accommodation to persons who have been subject to any incident, or pattern of incidents, of—
(a) controlling, coercive or threatening behaviour,
(b) physical violence,
(c) abuse of any other description (whether physical or mental in nature), or
(d) threats of any such violence or abuse.

(6) In this paragraph—
"government department" includes—
(a) any part of the Scottish Administration;
(b) a Northern Ireland department;
(c) the Welsh Assembly Government;
(d) any body or authority exercising statutory functions on behalf of the Crown;
"registered housing association" means—
(a) a private registered provider of social housing;
(b) a registered social landlord within the meaning of Part 1 of the Housing Act 1996 or section 165 of the Housing (Scotland) Act 2010;
(c) a housing association which is registered in a register maintained under Article 14 of the Housing (Northern Ireland) Order 1992 (S.I. 1992/1725 (N.I. 15));
"voluntary organisation" means a body, other than a public or local authority, whose activities are not carried on for profit.

Accommodation from or involving local authorities

7.—(1) An agreement—
(a) under which accommodation is provided to a person as a result of a duty or relevant power that is imposed or conferred on a local authority by an enactment (whether or not provided by the local authority), and
(b) which is not excluded by another provision of this Schedule.

Accommodation provided by virtue of immigration provisions

8. An agreement granting a right of occupation of accommodation that is provided to an individual by virtue of any of the following provisions of the Immigration and Asylum Act 1999—
   (a) section 4 (provision of accommodation to persons granted temporary admission etc.);
   (b) section 95 (provision of support to asylum seekers etc.);
   (c) section 98 (provision of temporary support to asylum seekers etc.).

Mobile homes

9. An agreement to which the Mobile Homes Act 1983 applies.

Tied accommodation

10.—(1) An agreement that grants a right of occupation of tied accommodation.

(2) "Tied accommodation" means accommodation that is provided—
   (a) by an employer to an employee in connection with a contract of employment, or
   (b) by a body providing training in a trade, profession or vocation to an individual in connection with that training.

(3) In this paragraph "employer" and "employee" have the same meanings as in the Employment Rights Act 1996 (see section 230 of that Act).

Student accommodation

11.—(1) An agreement that grants a right of occupation in a building which—
   (a) is used wholly or mainly for the accommodation of students, and
   (b) satisfies either of the following conditions.

(2) The first condition is that the building is owned or managed by any of the following—
   (a) an institution within the meaning of paragraph 5 of Schedule 1 to the Local Government Finance Act 1992;
   (b) a body that is specified in regulations made under Article 42(2A) of the Rates (Northern Ireland) Order 1977 (SI 1977/2157 (NI 28));
   (c) a body established for charitable purposes only.

(3) The second condition is that the building is a hall of residence.

(4) In this paragraph and paragraph 12 "student"—
   (a) in relation to England and Wales or Scotland, has the same meaning as in paragraph 4 of Schedule 1 to the Local Government Finance Act 1992;
   (b) in relation to Northern Ireland, means a person who satisfies such conditions as to education or training as may be specified in regulations made under Article 42(2A) of the Rates (Northern Ireland) Order 1977 (SI 1977/2157 (NI 28)).

12. An agreement under which accommodation is provided to a student who has been nominated to occupy it by an institution or body of the kind mentioned in paragraph 11(2).

Long leases

13.—(1) An agreement that—
   (a) is, or is for, a long lease, or
   (b) grants a right of occupation for a term of 7 years or more.

(2) "Long lease" means—
   (a) in relation to England and Wales, a lease which is a long lease for the purposes of Chapter 1 of Part 1 of the Leasehold Reform, Housing and Urban Development Act 1993 or which, in the case of a shared ownership lease (within the meaning given by section 7(7) of that Act),

would be such a lease if the tenant's total share (within the meaning given by that section) were 100 per cent;

(b) in relation to Scotland, has the meaning given by section 9(2) of the Land Registration (Scotland) Act 2012.

(3) An agreement does not grant a right of occupation for a term of 7 years or more if the agreement can be terminated at the option of a party before the end of 7 years from the commencement of the term.

Interpretation

14.—(1) This paragraph applies for the purposes of this Schedule.

(2) "Building" includes a part of a building.

(3) "Enactment" includes—

(a) an enactment contained in subordinate legislation within the meaning of the Interpretation Act 1978;

(b) an enactment contained in, or in an instrument made under, an Act of the Scottish Parliament;

(c) an enactment contained in, or in an instrument made under, a Measure or Act of the National Assembly for Wales;

(d) an enactment contained in, or in an instrument made under, Northern Ireland legislation.

(4) "Local authority" means—

(a) in relation to England—

(i) a county, district or parish council in England,

(ii) a London borough council,

(iii) the Common Council of the City of London in its capacity as a local authority, or

(iv) the Council of the Isles of Scilly;

(b) in relation to Wales, any county, county borough or community council in Wales;

(c) in relation to Scotland, a council constituted under section 2 of the Local Government etc. (Scotland) Act 1994;

(d) in relation to Northern Ireland, a district council constituted under section 1 of the Local Government Act (Northern Ireland) 1972 (c. 9 (N.I.)).

Note: Commencement from 1 December 2014 for premises in local authorities set out in article 6 SI 2014/2771.

SCHEDULE 4

Section 52

REFERRAL OF PROPOSED MARRIAGES AND CIVIL PARTNERSHIPS IN ENGLAND AND WALES

. . .

Note: Commencement from a date to be appointed.

SCHEDULE 5

Section 54

SHAM MARRIAGE AND CIVIL PARTNERSHIP: ADMINISTRATIVE REGULATIONS

Note: This Schedule sets out the kinds of regulations which may be made by the Secretary of State under s 54(2). Commencement from 20 October 2014 (SI 2014/2771).

Schedule 6

Section 59

Information

Part 1

Disclosure of Information etc. Where Proposed Marriage or Civil Partnership Referred to Secretary of State

1.—(1) This paragraph applies if—

(a) a superintendent registrar refers a proposed marriage to the Secretary of State under section 28H of the Marriage Act 1949, or

(b) a registration authority refers a proposed civil partnership to the Secretary of State under section 12A of the Civil Partnership Act 2004.

(2) The Secretary of State may—

(a) disclose relevant information to a registration official, or

(b) supply a document containing relevant information to a registration official.

(3) In this paragraph "relevant information" means any of the following information—

(a) the fact that the proposed marriage or civil partnership has been referred to the Secretary of State;

(b) the names of the parties to the proposed marriage or civil partnership;

(c) in the case of a proposed marriage—

(i) any information included with the referral in accordance with regulations under section 28H of the Marriage Act 1949;

(ii) any address of a party to the proposed marriage notified to the Secretary of State in accordance with such regulations or regulations under section 28D of the Marriage Act 1949;

(d) in the case of a proposed civil partnership—

(i) any information included with the referral in accordance with regulations under section 12A of the Civil Partnership Act 2004;

(ii) any address of a party to the proposed civil partnership notified to the Secretary of State in accordance with such regulations or regulations under section 9B of the Civil Partnership Act 2004;

(e) details of any immigration enforcement action taken by the Secretary of State in respect of a party to the proposed marriage or civil partnership (including any action taken after solemnization of the marriage or formation of the civil partnership);

(f) details of any immigration decision taken wholly or partly by reference to the marriage or civil partnership (whether while it was proposed or after it was solemnized or formed).

Part 2

Disclosure of Information etc. for Immigration Purposes etc.

Disclosures by registration officials

2.—(1) A registration official may—

(a) disclose any information held by the registration official, or

(b) supply any document held by the registration official,

to the Secretary of State, or to another registration official, for use for either of the following purposes.

(2) Those purposes are—

(a) immigration purposes;

(b) purposes connected with the exercise of functions relating to—
(i) the referral of proposed marriages to the Secretary of State under section 28H of the Marriage Act 1949, or
(ii) the referral of proposed civil partnerships to the Secretary of State under section 12A of the Civil Partnership Act 2004.

(3) In this paragraph "immigration purposes" means—
(a) the administration of immigration control under the Immigration Acts;
(b) the prevention, detection, investigation or prosecution of criminal offences relating to immigration;
(c) the imposition of penalties or charges under Part 3 of the Immigration and Asylum Act 1999;
(d) the provision of support for asylum-seekers and their dependants under Part 6 of that Act;
(e) such other purposes as may be specified by the Secretary of State by order.

3. A registration official may disclose to another registration official—
(a) the fact that a suspicion about a marriage or civil partnership has been reported to the Secretary of State under section 24 or 24A of the Immigration and Asylum Act 1999, and
(b) the content of any such report,

(whether or not the suspicion was reported by the registration official making the disclosure).

Disclosures by the Secretary of State

4.—(1) The Secretary of State may—
(a) disclose any information held by the Secretary of State, or
(b) supply any document held by the Secretary of State, to a registration official for use for verification purposes.

(2) In this paragraph "verification purposes" means—
(a) assisting in the verification of information provided to a relevant official by a person giving—
(i) notice of marriage under section 27 of the Marriage Act 1949, or
(ii) notice under section 8 of the Civil Partnership Act 2004;
(b) assisting in the verification of the immigration status of a person who contacts a relevant official in connection with the exercise of a function by a registration official;
(c) assisting in the verification of whether a person who contacts a relevant official in connection with the exercise of a function by a registration official—
(i) is suspected of involvement in crime relating to immigration, or
(ii) has been convicted of an offence relating to immigration.

(3) In this paragraph "relevant official" means—
(a) a registration official, or
(b) any other person employed to assist the exercise of functions by registration officials.

Part 3

Disclosure of Information etc. for Prevention of Crime etc.

5.—(1) A registration official may—
(a) disclose any information held by the registration official, or
(b) supply any document held by the registration official,

to an eligible person, or to another registration official in England and Wales, for use for crime-fighting purposes.

(2) Information is disclosed, or a document is supplied, for use for crimefighting purposes if condition A and condition B are met.

(3) Condition A is met if the registration official disclosing the information or supplying the document has reasonable grounds for suspecting that a criminal offence has been, is being, or is going to be committed.

(4) Condition B is met if the registration official discloses the information or supplies the document for use for one or both of these purposes—

(a) assisting in the verification of information supplied to that or any other registration official;

(b) assisting in the prevention, detection, investigation or prosecution of a criminal offence.

(5) In this section "eligible person" means—

(a) the Secretary of State;

(b) the Commissioners for Her Majesty's Revenue and Customs;

(c) a member of a police force operating in England and Wales or any part of it;

(d) a county council, a district council or a county borough council;

(e) the Greater London Authority, a London borough council or the Common Council of the City of London.

Part 4
General Provisions

Limitations on powers

6. This Schedule does not authorise—

(a) a disclosure, in contravention of any provisions of the Data Protection Act 1998, of personal data which are not exempt from those provisions, or

(b) a disclosure which is prohibited by Part 1 of the Regulation of Investigatory Powers Act 2000.

No breach of confidentiality etc.

7. A disclosure of information which is authorised by this Schedule does not breach—

(a) an obligation of confidence owed by the person making the disclosure, or

(b) any other restriction on the disclosure of information (however imposed).

Retention, copying and disposal of documents

8. A person to whom a document is supplied under any provision of this Schedule may—

(a) retain the document;

(b) copy the document;

(c) dispose of the document in such manner as the person thinks appropriate.

Saving for existing powers

9. This Schedule does not limit any other power under which—

(a) information may be disclosed, or

(b) documents may be supplied.

Meaning of "registration official"

10. A "registration official" is any of the following—

(a) the Registrar General;

(b) a superintendent registrar;

(c) a registrar;

(d) a registration authority or a person exercising the functions of a registration authority;

(e) a civil partnership registrar (within the meaning of Chapter 1 of Part 2 of the Civil Partnership Act 2004—see section 29 of that Act).

Note: Commencement from 14 July 2014 (s 75).

Schedule 7

Section 63

Immigration Advisers and Immigration Service Providers

. . .

Note: Amends Part 5 of the Immigration and Asylum Act 1999 from a date to be appointed.

Schedule 8

Section 67

Embarkation Checks

. . .

Note: Amends Sch 2 and s 27 to the Immigration Act 1971 from a date to be appointed.

Schedule 9

Section 73

Transitional and Consequential Provision

. . .

Note: Commencement from a date to be appointed.

PROCEDURE RULES AND PRACTICE DIRECTIONS

The Tribunal Procedure (First-tier Tribunal) (Immigration and Asylum Chamber) Rules 2014
2014 No. 2604 (L. 31)

Contents

Having consulted in accordance with paragraph 28(1) of Schedule 5 to the Tribunals, Courts and Enforcement Act 2007, the Tribunal Procedure Committee has made the following Rules in exercise of the powers conferred by—

(a) sections 9, 22, 29(3) and (4) of and Schedule 5 to the Tribunals, Courts and Enforcement Act 2007,

(b) paragraph 25 of Schedule 2 to the Immigration Act 1971,

(c) section 106(3) of the Nationality, Immigration and Asylum Act 2002,

(d) section 40A(3) of the British Nationality Act 1981, and

(e) Schedule 1 to the Immigration (European Economic Area) Regulations 2006.

The Lord Chancellor has allowed the Rules in accordance with paragraph 28(3) of Schedule 5 to the Tribunals, Courts and Enforcement Act 2007.

PART I

INTRODUCTION

Citation, commencement, application and interpretation

1.—(1) These Rules may be cited as the Tribunal Procedure (First-tier Tribunal) (Immigration and Asylum Chamber) Rules 2014 and come into force on 20th October 2014.

(2) They apply to proceedings before the Immigration and Asylum Chamber of the First-tier Tribunal.

(3) The Schedule of Fast Track Rules has effect in the circumstances and in the manner specified in that Schedule.

(4) In these Rules—

"the 1999 Act" means the Immigration and Asylum Act 1999;

"the 2002 Act" means the Nationality, Immigration and Asylum Act 2002;

"the 2004 Act" means the Asylum and Immigration (Treatment of Claimants, etc.) Act 2004;

"the 2006 Regulations" means the Immigration (European Economic Area) Regulations 2006;

"the 2007 Act" means the Tribunals, Courts and Enforcement Act 2007;

"appealable decision" means a decision from which there is a right of appeal to the Immigration and Asylum Chamber of the First-tier Tribunal;

"appellant" means a person who has provided a notice of appeal to the Tribunal against an appealable decision in accordance with these Rules;

"asylum claim" has the meaning given in section 113(1) of the 2002 Act;

"certificate of fee satisfaction" means a certificate of fee satisfaction issued by the Lord Chancellor under article 8 of the Fees Order;

"decision maker" means the maker of a decision against which an appeal is brought;

"dispose of proceedings" includes, unless indicated otherwise, disposing of a part of the proceedings;

"document" means anything in which information is recorded in any form, and an obligation under these Rules to provide or allow access to a document or a copy of a document for any purpose means, unless the Tribunal directs otherwise, an obligation to provide or allow access to such document or copy in a legible form or in a form which can be readily made into a legible form;

"Fast Track Rules" means the rules contained in the Schedule to this statutory instrument;

"the Fees Order" means the First-tier Tribunal (Immigration and Asylum Chamber) Fees Order 2011;

"hearing" means an oral hearing and includes a hearing conducted in whole or in part by video link, telephone or other means of instantaneous two-way electronic communication;

"the Immigration Acts" means the Acts referred to in section 61 of the UK Borders Act 2007;

"party" means—

(a) an appellant or respondent to proceedings;

(b) a party to a bail application as provided for in rule 37(3) and 37(4); and

(c) the UNHCR where notice has been given to the Tribunal in accordance with rule 8(3); "practice direction" means a direction given under section 23 of the 2007 Act;

"qualified representative" means a person who is a qualified person in accordance with section 84(2) of the 1999 Act;

"respondent" means—

(a) the decision maker specified in the notice of decision against which a notice of appeal has been provided; and

(b) a person substituted or added as a respondent in accordance with rule 8.

"Tribunal" means the First-tier Tribunal;

"the UNHCR" means the United Kingdom Representative of the United Nations High Commissioner for Refugees; and

"working day" means any day except—

(a) a Saturday or Sunday, Christmas Day, Good Friday or a bank holiday under section 1 of the Banking and Financial Dealings Act 1971; and

(b) 27th to 31st December inclusive.

(5) A rule or Part referred to by number alone, means a rule in, or Part of, these Rules.

Overriding objective and parties' obligation to cooperate with the Tribunal

2.—(1) The overriding objective of these Rules is to enable the Tribunal to deal with cases fairly and justly.

(2) Dealing with a case fairly and justly includes—

(a) dealing with the case in ways which are proportionate to the importance of the case, the complexity of the issues, the anticipated costs and the resources of the parties and of the Tribunal;

(b) avoiding unnecessary formality and seeking flexibility in the proceedings;

(c) ensuring, so far as practicable, that the parties are able to participate fully in the proceedings;

(d) using any special expertise of the Tribunal effectively; and

(e) avoiding delay, so far as compatible with proper consideration of the issues.

(3) The Tribunal must seek to give effect to the overriding objective when it—

(a) exercises any power under these Rules; or

(b) interprets any rule or practice direction.

(4) Parties must—

(a) help the Tribunal to further the overriding objective; and

(b) cooperate with the Tribunal generally.

PART 2

GENERAL POWERS AND PROVISIONS

Delegation to staff

3.—(1) Anything of a formal or administrative nature which is required or permitted to be done by the Tribunal under these Rules may be done by a member of the Tribunal's staff.

(2) Staff appointed by the Lord Chancellor may, with the approval of the Senior President of Tribunals, carry out functions of a judicial nature permitted or required to be done by the Tribunal.

(3) The approval referred to at paragraph (2) may apply generally to the carrying out of specified functions by members of staff of a specified description in specified circumstances.

(4) Within 14 days after the date on which the Tribunal sends notice of a decision made by a member of staff under paragraph (2) to a party, that party may apply in writing to the Tribunal for that decision to be considered afresh by a judge.

Case management powers

4.—(1) Subject to the provisions of the 2007 Act and any other enactment, the Tribunal may regulate its own procedure.

(2) The Tribunal may give a direction in relation to the conduct or disposal of proceedings at any time, including a direction amending, suspending or setting aside an earlier direction.

(3) In particular, and without restricting the general powers in paragraphs (1) and (2), the Tribunal may—

(a) extend or shorten the time for complying with any rule, practice direction or direction;

(b) consolidate or hear together two or more sets of proceedings or parts of proceedings raising common issues;

(c) permit or require a party to amend a document;

(d) permit or require a party or another person to provide documents, information, evidence or submissions to the Tribunal or a party;

(e) provide for a particular matter to be dealt with as a preliminary issue;

(f) hold a hearing to consider any matter, including a case management issue;

(g) decide the form of any hearing;

(h) adjourn or postpone a hearing;

(i) require a party to produce a bundle for a hearing;

(j) stay (or, in Scotland, sist) proceedings;

(k) transfer proceedings to another court or tribunal if that other court or tribunal has jurisdiction in relation to the proceedings and—

(i) because of a change of circumstances since the proceedings were started, the Tribunal no longer has jurisdiction in relation to the proceedings; or

(ii) the Tribunal considers that the other court or tribunal is a more appropriate forum for the determination of the case; or

(l) suspend the effect of its own decision pending the determination by the Tribunal or the Upper Tribunal of an application for permission to appeal against, and any appeal or review of, that decision.

Procedure for applying for and giving directions

5.—(1) The Tribunal may give a direction on the application of one or more of the parties or on its own initiative.

(2) An application for a direction may be made—

(a) by sending or delivering a written application to the Tribunal; or

(b) orally during the course of a hearing.

(3) An application for a direction must include the reason for making that application.

(4) Unless the Tribunal considers that there is good reason not to do so, the Tribunal must send written notice of any direction to every party and to any other person affected by the direction.

(5) If a party or any other person sent notice of the direction under paragraph (4) wishes to challenge the direction which the Tribunal has given, they may do so by applying for another direction which amends, suspends or sets aside the first direction.

Failure to comply with rules etc.

6.—(1) An irregularity resulting from a failure to comply with any requirement in these Rules, a practice direction or a direction does not of itself render void the proceedings or any step taken in the proceedings.

(2) If a party has failed to comply with a requirement in these Rules, a practice direction or a direction, the Tribunal may take such action as it considers just, which may include—

(a) waiving the requirement;

(b) requiring the failure to be remedied; or

(c) exercising its power under paragraph (3).

(3) The Tribunal may refer to the Upper Tribunal, and ask the Upper Tribunal to exercise its power under section 25 (supplementary powers of Upper Tribunal) of the 2007 Act in relation to, any failure by a person to comply with a requirement imposed by the Tribunal—

(a) to attend at any place for the purpose of giving evidence;

(b) otherwise to make themselves available to give evidence;

(c) to swear an oath in connection with the giving of evidence;

(d) to give evidence as a witness;

(e) to produce a document; or

(f) to facilitate the inspection of a document or any other thing (including any premises).

Striking out of an appeal for non-payment of fee and reinstatement

7.—(1) Where the Tribunal is notified by the Lord Chancellor that a certificate of fee satisfaction has been revoked, the appeal shall automatically be struck out without order of the Tribunal and the Tribunal must notify each party that the appeal has been struck out.

(2) Where an appeal has been struck out in accordance with paragraph (1), the appeal may be reinstated if—

(a) the appellant applies to have the appeal reinstated; and

(b) the Lord Chancellor has issued a new certificate of fee satisfaction.

(3) An application made under paragraph (2)(a) must be made in writing and received by the Tribunal within 14 days, or if the appellant is outside the United Kingdom within

28 days, of the date on which the Tribunal sent notification of the striking out to the appellant.

Substitution and addition of parties

8.—(1) The Tribunal may give a direction substituting a respondent if—

(a) the wrong person has been named as a respondent; or

(b) the substitution has become necessary because of a change in circumstances since the start of proceedings.

(2) The Tribunal may give a direction adding a person to the proceedings as a respondent.

(3) The UNHCR may give notice to the Tribunal that they wish to participate in any proceedings where the appellant has made an asylum claim and on giving such notice becomes a party to the proceedings.

(4) If—

(a) the Tribunal gives a direction under paragraph (1) or (2); or

(b) the UNHCR gives notice to the Tribunal under paragraph (3),

the Tribunal may give such consequential directions as it considers appropriate.

Orders for payment of costs and interest on costs (or, in Scotland, expenses)

9.—(1) If the Tribunal allows an appeal, it may order a respondent to pay by way of costs to the appellant an amount no greater than—

(a) any fee paid under the Fees Order that has not been refunded; and

(b) any fee which the appellant is or may be liable to pay under that Order.

(2) The Tribunal may otherwise make an order in respect of costs only—

(a) under section 29(4) of the 2007 Act (wasted costs) and costs incurred in applying for such costs; or

(b) if a person has acted unreasonably in bringing, defending or conducting proceedings.

(3) The Tribunal may make an order under this rule on an application or on its own initiative.

(4) A person making an application for an order for costs—

(a) must, unless the application is made orally at a hearing, send or deliver an application to the Tribunal and to the person against whom the order is sought to be made; and

(b) may send or deliver together with the application a schedule of the costs claimed in sufficient detail to allow summary assessment of such costs by the Tribunal.

(5) An application for an order for costs may be made at any time during the proceedings but must be made within 28 days after the date on which the Tribunal sends—

(a) a notice of decision recording the decision which disposes of the proceedings; or

(b) notice that a withdrawal has taken effect under rule 17 (withdrawal).

(6) The Tribunal may not make an order for costs against a person (in this rule called the "paying person") without first giving that person an opportunity to make representations.

(7) The amount of costs to be paid under an order under this rule may be determined by—

(a) summary assessment by the Tribunal;

(b) agreement of a specified sum by the paying person and the person entitled to receive the costs (in this rule called the "receiving person");

(c) detailed assessment of the whole or a specified part of the costs (including the costs of the assessment) incurred by the receiving person, if not agreed.

(8) Except in relation to paragraph (9), in the application of this rule in relation to Scotland, any reference to costs is to be read as a reference to expenses.

(9) Following an order for detailed assessment made by the Tribunal under paragraph (7)(c) the paying person or the receiving person may apply—

(a) in England and Wales, to the county court for a detailed assessment of the costs on the standard basis or, if specified in the order, on the indemnity basis; and the Civil Procedure Rules 1998, section 74 (interest on judgment debts, etc.) of the County Courts Act 1984 and the County Court (Interest on Judgment Debts) Order 1991 shall apply, with necessary modifications, to that application and assessment as if the proceedings in the Tribunal had been proceedings in a court to which the Civil Procedure Rules 1998 apply;

(b) in Scotland, to the Auditor of the Sheriff Court or the Court of Session (as specified in the order) for the taxation of the expenses according to the fees payable in that court; or

(c) in Northern Ireland, to the Taxing Office of the High Court of Northern Ireland for taxation on the standard basis or, if specified in the order, on the indemnity basis.

Representatives

10.—(1) A party may be represented by any person not prohibited from representing by section 84 of the 1999 Act.

(2) Where a party is or has been represented by a person prohibited from representing by section 84 of the 1999 Act, that does not of itself render void the proceedings or any step taken in the proceedings.

(3) If a party appoints a representative, that party (or the representative if the representative is a qualified representative) must send or deliver to the Tribunal written notice of the representative's name and address, which may be done at a hearing.

(4) Anything permitted or required to be done by a party under these Rules, a practice direction or a direction may be done by the representative of that party, except signing a witness statement.

(5) A person who receives notice of the appointment of a representative—

(a) must provide to the representative any document which is required to be provided to the represented party, and need not provide that document to the represented party; and

(b) may assume that the representative is and remains authorised as such until they receive written notification that this is not so from the representative or the represented party.

(6) As from the date on which a person has notified the Tribunal that they are acting as the representative of an appellant and has given an address for service, if any document is provided to the appellant a copy must also at the same time be provided to the appellant's representative.

Calculating time

11.—(1) An act required or permitted to be done on or by a particular day by these Rules, a practice direction or a direction must, unless otherwise directed, be done by midnight on that day.

(2) Subject to the Tribunal directing that this paragraph does not apply, if the time specified by these Rules, a practice direction or a direction for doing any act ends on a day other than a working day, the act is done in time if it is done on the next working day.

Sending, delivery and language of documents

12.—(1) Any document to be provided to the Tribunal or any person under these Rules, a practice direction or a direction must be—

(a) delivered, or sent by post, to an address;

(b) sent via a document exchange to a document exchange number or address;

(c) sent by fax to a fax number;

(d) sent by e-mail to an e-mail address; or

(e) sent or delivered by any other method,

identified for that purpose by the Tribunal or person to whom the document is directed.

(2) A document to be provided to an individual may be provided by leaving it with that individual.

(3) If the respondent believes that the address specified under paragraph (1) for the provision of documents to the appellant is not appropriate for that purpose, the respondent must notify the Tribunal in writing of that fact and, if aware of it, an address which would be appropriate.

(4) If any document is provided to a person who has notified the Tribunal that they are acting as the representative of a party, it shall be deemed to have been provided to that party.

(5) Subject to paragraph (6)—

(a) any notice of appeal or application notice provided to the Tribunal must be completed in English; and

(b) if a document provided to the Tribunal is not written in English, it must be accompanied by an English translation.

(6) In proceedings that are in Wales or have a connection with Wales, a document or translation may be provided to the Tribunal in Welsh.

Use of documents and information

13.—(1) The Tribunal may make an order prohibiting the disclosure or publication of—

(a) specified documents or information relating to the proceedings; or

(b) any matter likely to lead members of the public to identify any person whom the Tribunal considers should not be identified.

(2) The Tribunal may give a direction prohibiting the disclosure of a document or information to a person if—

(a) the Tribunal is satisfied that such disclosure would be likely to cause that person or some other person serious harm; and

(b) the Tribunal is satisfied, having regard to the interests of justice, that it is proportionate to give such a direction.

(3) If a party ("the first party") considers that the Tribunal should give a direction under paragraph (2) prohibiting the disclosure of a document or information to another party ("the second party"), the first party must—

(a) exclude the relevant document or information from any documents to be provided to the second party; and

(b) provide to the Tribunal the excluded document or information, and the reason for its exclusion, so that the Tribunal may decide whether the document or information should be disclosed to the second party or should be the subject of a direction under paragraph (2).

(4) The Tribunal must conduct proceedings as appropriate in order to give effect to a direction given under paragraph (2).

(5) If the Tribunal gives a direction under paragraph (2) which prevents disclosure to a party who has appointed a representative, the Tribunal may give a direction that the documents or information be disclosed to that representative if the Tribunal is satisfied that—

(a) disclosure to the representative would be in the interests of the party; and

(b) the representative will act in accordance with paragraph (6).

(6) Documents or information disclosed to a representative in accordance with a direction under paragraph (5) must not be disclosed either directly or indirectly to any other person without the Tribunal's consent.

(7) The Tribunal may, on the application of a party or on its own initiative, give a direction that certain documents or information must or may be disclosed to the Tribunal on the basis that the Tribunal will not disclose such documents or information to other persons, or specified other persons.

(8) A party making an application for a direction under paragraph (7) may withhold the relevant documents or information from other parties until the Tribunal has granted or refused the application.

(9) In a case involving matters relating to national security, the Tribunal must ensure that information is not disclosed contrary to the interests of national security.

(10) The Tribunal must conduct proceedings and record its decision and reasons appropriately so as not to undermine the effect of an order made under paragraph (1), a direction given under paragraph (2), (5) or (7) or the duty imposed by paragraph (9).

Evidence and submissions

14.—(1) Without restriction on the general powers in rule 4 (case management powers), the Tribunal may give directions as to—

(a) issues on which it requires evidence or submissions;

(b) the nature of the evidence or submissions it requires;

(c) whether the parties are permitted or required to provide expert evidence;

(d) any limit on the number of witnesses whose evidence a party may put forward, whether in relation to a particular issue or generally;

(e) the manner in which any evidence or submissions are to be provided, which may include a direction for them to be given—

(i) orally at a hearing; or

(ii) by witness statement or written submissions; and

(f) the time at which any evidence or submissions are to be provided.

(2) The Tribunal may admit evidence whether or not—

(a) the evidence would be admissible in a civil trial in the United Kingdom; or

(b) subject to section 85A(4) of the 2002 Act, the evidence was available to the decision maker.

(3) The Tribunal may consent to a witness giving, or require any witness to give, evidence on oath or affirmation, and may administer an oath or affirmation for that purpose.

Summoning or citation of witnesses and orders to answer questions or produce documents

15.—(1) On the application of a party or on its own initiative, the Tribunal may—

(a) by summons (or, in Scotland, citation) require any person to attend as a witness at a hearing at the time and place specified in the summons or citation; or

(b) order any person to answer any questions or produce any documents in that person's possession or control which relate to any issue in the proceedings.

(2) A summons or citation under paragraph (1)(a) must—

(a) give the person required to attend 14 days' notice of the hearing or such shorter period as the Tribunal may direct; and

(b) where the person is not a party, make provision for the person's necessary expenses of attendance to be paid, and state who is to pay them.

(3) No person may be compelled to give any evidence or produce any document that the person could not be compelled to give or produce on a trial of an action in a court of law in the part of the United Kingdom where the proceedings are to be determined.

(4) A summons, citation or order under this rule must—

(a) state that the person on whom the requirement is imposed may apply to the Tribunal to vary or set aside the summons, citation or order, if they have not had an opportunity to object to it; and

(b) state the consequences of failure to comply with the summons, citation or order.

Appeal treated as abandoned or finally determined

16.—(1) A party must notify the Tribunal if they are aware that—

(a) the appellant has left the United Kingdom;

(b) the appellant has been granted leave to enter or remain in the United Kingdom;

(c) a deportation order has been made against the appellant; or

(d) a document listed in paragraph 4(2) of Schedule 2 to the 2006 Regulations has been issued to the appellant.

(2) Where an appeal is treated as abandoned pursuant to section 104(4A) of the 2002 Act or paragraph 4(2) of Schedule 2 to 2006 Regulations, the Tribunal must send the parties a notice informing them that the appeal is being treated as abandoned or finally determined, as the case may be.

(3) Where an appeal would otherwise fall to be treated as abandoned pursuant to section 104(4A) of the 2002 Act, but the appellant wishes to pursue their appeal, the appellant must provide a notice, which must comply with any relevant practice direction, to the Tribunal and each other party so that it is received within 28 days of the date on which the appellant was sent notice of the grant of leave to enter or remain in the United Kingdom or was sent the document listed in paragraph 4(2) of Schedule 2 to the 2006 Regulations, as the case may be.

Withdrawal

17.—(1) A party may give notice of the withdrawal of their appeal—

(a) by providing to the Tribunal a written notice of withdrawal of the appeal; or

(b) orally at a hearing,

and in either case must specify the reasons for that withdrawal.

(2) The Tribunal must (save for good reason) treat an appeal as withdrawn if the respondent notifies the Tribunal and each other party that the decision (or, where the appeal relates to more than one decision, all of the decisions) to which the appeal relates has been withdrawn and specifies the reasons for the withdrawal of the decision.

(3) The Tribunal must notify each party in writing that a withdrawal has taken effect under this rule and that the proceedings are no longer regarded by the Tribunal as pending.

Certification of pending appeal

18.—(1) The Secretary of State must, upon issuing a certificate under section 97 or 98 of the 2002 Act which relates to a pending appeal, provide notice of the certification to the Tribunal.

(2) Where a notice of certification is provided under paragraph (1), the Tribunal must—

(a) notify the parties; and

(b) take no further action in relation to the appeal.

PART 3

PROCEEDINGS BEFORE THE TRIBUNAL

CHAPTER 1

Before the Hearing

Notice of appeal

19.—(1) An appellant must start proceedings by providing a notice of appeal to the Tribunal.

(2) If the person is in the United Kingdom, the notice of appeal must be received not later than 14 days after they are sent the notice of the decision against which the appeal is brought.

(3) If the person is outside the United Kingdom, the notice of appeal must be received—

(a) not later than 28 days after their departure from the United Kingdom if the person—

(i) was in the United Kingdom when the decision against which they are appealing was made, and

(ii) may not appeal while they are in the United Kingdom by reason of a provision of the 2002 Act; or

(b) in any other case, not later than 28 days after they receive the notice of the decision.

(4) The notice of appeal must—

(a) set out the grounds of appeal;

(b) be signed and dated by the appellant or their representative;

(c) if the notice of appeal is signed by the appellant's representative, the representative must certify in the notice of appeal that it has been completed in accordance with the appellant's instructions;

(d) state whether the appellant requires an interpreter at any hearing and if so for which language and dialect;

(e) state whether the appellant intends to attend at any hearing; and

(f) state whether the appellant will be represented at any hearing.

(5) The appellant must provide with the notice of appeal—

(a) the notice of decision against which the appellant is appealing or if it is not practicable to include the notice of decision, the reasons why it is not practicable;

(b) any statement of reasons for that decision;

(c) any documents in support of the appellant's case which have not been supplied to the respondent;

(d) an application for the Lord Chancellor to issue a certificate of fee satisfaction;

(e) any further information or documents required by an applicable practice direction.

(6) The Tribunal must send a copy of the notice of appeal and the accompanying documents or information provided by the appellant to the respondent.

(7) An appellant may, with the permission of the Tribunal, vary the grounds on which they rely in the notice of appeal.

Late notice of appeal

20.—(1) Where a notice of appeal is provided outside the time limit in rule 19, including any extension of time directed under rule 4(3)(a) (power to extend time), the notice of appeal must include an application for such an extension of time and the reason why the notice of appeal was not provided in time.

(2) If, upon receipt of a notice of appeal, the notice appears to the Tribunal to have been provided outside the time limit but does not include an application for an extension of time, the Tribunal must (unless it extends time of its own initiative) notify the person in writing that it proposes to treat the notice of appeal as being out of time.

(3) Where the Tribunal gives notification under paragraph (2), the person may by written notice to the Tribunal contend that—

(a) the notice of appeal was given in time; or

(b) time for providing the notice of appeal should be extended,

and, if so, that person may provide the Tribunal with written evidence in support of that contention.

(4) The Tribunal must decide any issue under this rule as to whether a notice of appeal was given in time, or whether to extend the time for appealing, as a preliminary issue, and may do so without a hearing.

(5) Where the Tribunal makes a decision under this rule it must provide to the parties written notice of its decision, including its reasons.

Special provision for imminent removal cases (late notice of appeal)

21.—(1) This rule applies in any case to which rule 20 applies, where the respondent notifies the Tribunal that directions have been given for the removal of that person from the United Kingdom on a date within 5 days of the date on which the notice of appeal was received.

(2) The Tribunal must, if reasonably practicable, make any decision under rule 20 before the date and time proposed for the removal.

(3) Rule 20 shall apply, subject to the modifications that the Tribunal may—

(a) give notification under rule 20(2) orally, which may include giving it by telephone,

(b) direct a time for providing evidence under rule 20(3), and

(c) direct that evidence in support of a contention under rule 20(3) is to be given orally, which may include requiring the evidence to be given by telephone, and hold a hearing for the purpose of receiving such evidence.

Circumstances in which the Tribunal may not accept a notice of appeal

22.—(1) Where a person has provided a notice of appeal to the Tribunal and any of the circumstances in paragraph (2) apply, the Tribunal may not accept the notice of appeal.

(2) The circumstances referred to in paragraph (1) are that—

(a) there is no appealable decision; or

(b) the Lord Chancellor has refused to issue a certificate of fee satisfaction.

(3) Where the Tribunal does not accept a notice of appeal, it must—

(a) notify the person providing the notice of appeal and the respondent; and

(b) take no further action on that notice of appeal.

Response: entry clearance cases

23.—(1) This rule applies to an appeal against a refusal of entry clearance or a refusal of an EEA family permit (which has the meaning given in regulation 2(1) of the 2006 Regulations).

(2) When a respondent is provided with a copy of a notice of appeal from a refusal of entry clearance or a refusal of an EEA family permit, the respondent must provide the Tribunal with—

(a) the notice of the decision to which the notice of appeal relates and any other document the respondent provided to the appellant giving reasons for that decision;

(b) a statement of whether the respondent opposes the appellant's case and, if so, the grounds for such opposition;

(c) any statement of evidence or application form completed by the appellant;

(d) any record of an interview with the appellant in relation to the decision being appealed;

(e) any other unpublished document which is referred to in a document mentioned in sub-paragraph (a) or relied upon by the respondent; and

(f) the notice of any other appealable decision made in relation to the appellant.

(3) The respondent must send to the Tribunal and the other parties the documents listed in paragraph (2) within 28 days of the date on which the respondent received from the Tribunal a copy of the notice of appeal and any accompanying documents or information provided under rule 19(6).

Response: other cases

24.—(1) Except in appeals to which rule 23 applies, when a respondent is provided with a copy of a notice of appeal, the respondent must provide the Tribunal with—

(a) the notice of the decision to which the notice of appeal relates and any other document the respondent provided to the appellant giving reasons for that decision;

(b) any statement of evidence or application form completed by the appellant;

(c) any record of an interview with the appellant in relation to the decision being appealed;

(d) any other unpublished document which is referred to in a document mentioned in sub-paragraph (a) or relied upon by the respondent; and

(e) the notice of any other appealable decision made in relation to the appellant.

(2) The respondent must, if the respondent intends to change or add to the grounds or reasons relied upon in the notice or the other documents referred to in paragraph (1)(a), provide the Tribunal and the other parties with a statement of whether the respondent opposes the appellant's case and the grounds for such opposition.

(3) The documents listed in paragraph (1) and any statement required under paragraph (2) must be provided in writing within 28 days of the date on which the Tribunal sent to the respondent a copy of the notice of appeal and any accompanying documents or information provided under rule 19(6).

CHAPTER 2

Hearings

Consideration of decision with or without a hearing

25.—(1) The Tribunal must hold a hearing before making a decision which disposes of proceedings except where—

(a) each party has consented to, or has not objected to, the matter being decided without a hearing;

(b) the appellant has not consented to the appeal being determined without a hearing but the Lord Chancellor has refused to issue a certificate of fee satisfaction for the fee payable for a hearing;

(c) the appellant is outside the United Kingdom and does not have a representative who has an address for service in the United Kingdom;

(d) it is impracticable to give the appellant notice of the hearing;

(e) a party has failed to comply with a provision of these Rules, a practice direction or a direction and the Tribunal is satisfied that in all the circumstances, including the extent of the failure and any reasons for it, it is appropriate to determine the appeal without a hearing;

(f) the appeal is one to which rule 16(2) or 18(2) applies; or

(g) subject to paragraph (2), the Tribunal considers that it can justly determine the matter without a hearing.

(2) Where paragraph (1)(g) applies, the Tribunal must not make the decision without a hearing without first giving the parties notice of its intention to do so, and an opportunity to make written representations as to whether there should be a hearing.

(3) This rule does not apply to decisions under Part 4 or Part 5.

Notice of hearings

26. The Tribunal must give each party entitled to attend a hearing reasonable notice of the time and place of the hearing (including any adjourned or postponed hearing) and any changes to the time and place of the hearing.

Public and private hearings

27.—(1) Subject to the following paragraphs and to section 108 of the 2002 Act, all hearings must be held in public.

(2) The Tribunal may give a direction that a hearing, or part of it, is to be held in private.

(3) Where a hearing, or part of it, is to be held in private, the Tribunal may determine who is permitted to attend the hearing or part of it.

(4) The Tribunal may give a direction excluding from any hearing, or part of it—

(a) any person whose conduct the Tribunal considers is disrupting or is likely to disrupt the hearing;

(b) any person whose presence the Tribunal considers is likely to prevent another person from giving evidence or making submissions freely;

(c) any person who the Tribunal considers should be excluded in order to give effect to a direction under rule 13(2) (withholding a document or information likely to cause serious harm); or

(d) any person where the purpose of the hearing would be defeated by the attendance of that person.

(5) The Tribunal may give a direction excluding a witness from a hearing until that witness gives evidence.

Hearing in a party's absence

28. If a party fails to attend a hearing the Tribunal may proceed with the hearing if the Tribunal—

(a) is satisfied that the party has been notified of the hearing or that reasonable steps have been taken to notify the party of the hearing; and

(b) considers that it is in the interests of justice to proceed with the hearing.

Chapter 3
Decisions

Decisions and notice of decisions

29.—(1) The Tribunal may give a decision orally at a hearing.

(2) Subject to rule 13(2) (withholding information likely to cause serious harm), the Tribunal must provide to each party as soon as reasonably practicable after making a decision (other than a decision under Part 4) which disposes of the proceedings—

(a) a notice of decision stating the Tribunal's decision; and

(b) notification of any right of appeal against the decision and the time within which, and the manner in which, such right of appeal may be exercised.

(3) Where the decision of the Tribunal relates to—

(a) an asylum claim or a humanitarian protection claim, the Tribunal must provide, with the notice of decision in paragraph (2)(a), written reasons for its decision;

(b) any other matter, the Tribunal may provide written reasons for its decision but, if it does not do so, must notify the parties of the right to apply for a written statement of reasons.

(4) Unless the Tribunal has already provided a written statement of reasons, a party may make a written application to the Tribunal for such statement following a decision which disposes of the proceedings.

(5) An application under paragraph (4) must be received within 28 days of the date on which the Tribunal sent or otherwise provided to the party a notice of decision relating to the decision which disposes of the proceedings.

(6) If a party makes an application in accordance with paragraphs (4) and (5) the Tribunal must, subject to rule 13(2) (withholding a document or information likely to cause serious harm), send a written statement of reasons to each party as soon as reasonably practicable.

PART 4

CORRECTING, SETTING ASIDE, REVIEWING AND APPEALING TRIBUNAL DECISIONS

Interpretation

30. In this Part—

"appeal" means the exercise of a right of appeal on a point of law under section 11 of the 2007 Act;

"review" means the review of a decision by the Tribunal under section 9 of the 2007 Act.

Clerical mistakes and accidental slips or omissions

31. The Tribunal may at any time correct any clerical mistake or other accidental slip or omission in a decision, direction or any document produced by it, by—

(a) providing notification of the amended decision or direction, or a copy of the amended document, to all parties; and

(b) making any necessary amendment to any information published in relation to the decision, direction or document.

Setting aside a decision which disposes of proceedings

32.—(1) The Tribunal may set aside a decision which disposes of proceedings, or part of such a decision, and re-make the decision, or the relevant part of it, if—

(a) the Tribunal considers that it is in the interests of justice to do so; and

(b) one or more of the conditions in paragraph (2) are satisfied.

(2) The conditions are—

(a) a document relating to the proceedings was not provided to, or was not received at an appropriate time by, a party or a party's representative;

(b) a document relating to the proceedings was not provided to the Tribunal at an appropriate time;

(c) a party, or a party's representative, was not present at a hearing related to the proceedings; or

(d) there has been some other procedural irregularity in the proceedings.

(3) An application for a decision, or part of a decision, to be set aside under paragraph (1) must be made—

(a) if the appellant is outside the United Kingdom, within 28 days; or

(b) in any other case, within 14 days,

of the date on which the party was sent the notice of decision.

Application for permission to appeal to the Upper Tribunal

33.—(1) A party seeking permission to appeal to the Upper Tribunal must make a written application to the Tribunal for permission to appeal.

(2) Subject to paragraph (3), an application under paragraph (1) must be provided to the Tribunal so that it is received no later than 14 days after the date on which the party making the application was provided with written reasons for the decision.

(3) Where an appellant is outside the United Kingdom, an application to the Tribunal under paragraph (1) must be provided to the Tribunal so that it is received no later than 28 days after the date on which the party making the application was provided with written reasons for the decision.

(4) The time within which a party may apply for permission to appeal against an amended notice of decision runs from the date on which the party is sent the amended notice of decision.

(5) An application under paragraph (1) must—

(a) identify the decision of the Tribunal to which it relates;

(b) identify the alleged error or errors of law in the decision; and

(c) state the result the party making the application is seeking and include any application for an extension of time and the reasons why such an extension should be given.

(6) If a person makes an application under paragraph (1) when the Tribunal has not given a written statement of reasons for its decision—

(a) the Tribunal must, if no application for a written statement of reasons has been made, treat the application for permission as such an application; and

(b) may—

(i) direct under rule 36 that the application is not to be treated as an application for permission to appeal; or

(ii) determine the application for permission to appeal.

(7) If an application for a written statement of reasons has been, or is, refused because the application was received out of time, the Tribunal must only admit the application for permission if the Tribunal considers that it is in the interests of justice to do so.

Tribunal's consideration of an application for permission to appeal to the Upper Tribunal

34.—(1) On receiving an application for permission to appeal the Tribunal must first consider whether to review the decision in accordance with rule 35.

(2) If the Tribunal decides not to review the decision, or reviews the decision and decides to take no action in relation to the decision, or part of it, the Tribunal must consider whether to give permission to appeal in relation to the decision or that part of it.

(3) The Tribunal must send a record of its decision to the parties as soon as practicable.

(4) If the Tribunal refuses permission to appeal it must send with the record of its decision—

(a) a statement of its reasons for such refusal; and

(b) notification of the right to make an application to the Upper Tribunal for permission to appeal and the time within which, and the manner in which, such application must be made.

(5) The Tribunal may give permission to appeal on limited grounds, but must comply with paragraph (4) in relation to any grounds on which it has refused permission.

Review of a decision

35.—(1) The Tribunal may only undertake a review of a decision—

(a) pursuant to rule 34 (review on an application for permission to appeal); and

(b) if it is satisfied that there was an error of law in the decision.

(2) The Tribunal must notify the parties in writing of the outcome of any review, and of any right of appeal in relation to the outcome.

(3) If the Tribunal takes any action in relation to a decision following a review without first giving every party an opportunity to make representations—

(a) the notice under paragraph (2) must state that any party that did not have an opportunity to make representations may apply for such action to be set aside; and

(b) the Tribunal may regard the review as incomplete and act accordingly.

Power to treat an application as a different type of application

36. The Tribunal may treat an application for a decision to be corrected, set aside or reviewed, or for permission to appeal against a decision, as an application for any other one of those things.

Part 5

Bail

Scope of this Part and interpretation

37.—(1) This Part applies to bail proceedings, meaning bail applications and any matter relating to bail which the Tribunal is considering on its own initiative.

(2) In this Part, "bail party" means a person released on bail or applying to the Tribunal to be released on bail.

(3) Except where paragraph (4) applies, the parties to bail proceedings are the bail party and the Secretary of State.

(4) Where the proceedings concern forfeiture of a recognizance, the parties are the Secretary of State and any person who entered into the recognizance in question, whether as principal or surety.

Bail applications

38.—(1) A bail application must be made by sending or delivering to the Tribunal an application notice containing the information specified below.

(2) A bail application must specify whether it is for—

(a) the bail party to be released on bail;

(b) variation of bail conditions;

(c) continuation of bail; or

(d) forfeiture of a recognizance.

(3) Subject to paragraph (4), a bail application must contain the following details—

(a) the bail party's—

(i) full name;

(ii) date of birth; and

(iii) date of their most recent arrival in the United Kingdom;

(b) the address of any place where the bail party is detained;

(c) the address where the bail party will reside if the bail application is granted, or, if unable to give such an address, the reason why an address is not given;

(d) the amount of any recognizance in which the bail party is, or is proposed to be, bound;

(e) whether the bail party has a pending appeal to the Tribunal or any pending application for further appeal relating to such an appeal;

(f) the full name, address, date of birth and any occupation of any person who is acting or is proposed to act as a surety for the recognizance and the amount in which the surety is, or is proposed to be, bound;

(g) where the bail party is aged 18 or over, whether the bail party will, if required, agree as a condition of bail to cooperate with electronic monitoring under section 36 of the 2004 Act;

(h) the grounds on which the application is made and, where a previous application has been refused, when it was refused and details of any material change in circumstances since the refusal; and

(i) whether an interpreter will be required at the hearing, and in respect of what language and dialect.

(4) Where the application is for forfeiture of a recognizance, paragraph (3) applies except for sub-paragraphs (a)(iii), (b), (c), (e) and (g) of that paragraph.

(5) An application made by the bail party must be signed by the bail party or their representative.

(6) On receipt of a bail application, the Tribunal must record the date on which it was received and provide a copy of the application to the Secretary of State as soon as reasonably practicable.

Bail hearings

39.—(1) Subject to paragraph (3), where a bail application is for the bail party to be released on bail, the Tribunal must, as soon as reasonably practicable, hold a hearing of the application.

(2) In all other bail proceedings, the Tribunal may determine the matter without a hearing if it considers it can justly do so.

(3) Where an application for release on bail is received by the Tribunal within 28 days after a Tribunal decision made at a hearing under paragraph (1) not to release the bail party on bail, the Tribunal—

(a) must determine whether the bail party has demonstrated that there has been a material change in circumstances since the decision;

(b) if the Tribunal so determines, must apply paragraph (1);

(c) otherwise, must dismiss the application without a hearing.

(4) Paragraph (3) has no effect until the date on which section 7(3)(c) of the Immigration Act 2014 (inserting paragraph 25(2) of Schedule 2 to the Immigration Act 1971) comes into force.

Response to a bail application

40.—(1) If the Secretary of State opposes a bail application, the Secretary of State must provide the Tribunal and the bail party with a written statement of the reasons for doing so—

(a) not later than 2.00 pm on the working day before the hearing; or

(b) if the Secretary of State was provided with notice of the hearing less than 24 hours before that time, as soon as reasonably practicable.

(2) Where the Secretary of State's reasons for opposition include that directions are in force for the removal of the bail party from the United Kingdom, the Secretary of State must provide a copy of the notice of those directions.

Decision in bail proceedings

41.—(1) The Tribunal must provide written notice of its decision to—

(a) the parties; and

(b) if the bail application is for the bail party to be released on bail, the person having custody of the bail party.

(2) Where bail is granted, varied or continued, the notice must state any bail conditions, including any amounts in which the bail party and any sureties are to be bound.

(3) Where bail is refused or where the Tribunal orders forfeiture of the recognizance, the notice must include reasons for the decision.

(4) Where, instead of granting or refusing bail, the Tribunal fixes the amount and conditions of the bail with a view to the recognizance being taken subsequently by a person specified by the Tribunal, the notice must include the matters stated in paragraph (2) and the name or office of the person so specified.

(5) Paragraph (6) applies where the Tribunal determines that directions for the removal of the bail party from the United Kingdom are for the time being in force and the directions require the bail party to be removed from the United Kingdom within 14 days of the date of the decision to release the bail party on bail or under paragraph (4).

(6) The notice provided under paragraph (1) must state—

(a) the determination of the Tribunal under paragraph (5);

(b) whether the Secretary of State has consented to the release of the bail party;

(c) where the Secretary of State has not consented to that release, that the bail party must therefore not be released on bail.

Recognizances

42.—(1) Any recognizance must be in writing and must state—

(a) the bail conditions, including the amount of the recognizance and any amount in which any surety agrees to be bound; and

(b) that the bail party and any surety understand the bail conditions and that, if the bail party fails to comply with those conditions, they may be ordered to pay all or part of the amount in which they are bound.

(2) The recognizance must be signed by the bail party and any surety and provided to the Tribunal, and a copy provided to—

(a) the parties,

(b) any person having custody of the bail party, and

(c) any surety.

Release of bail party

43. The person having custody of the bail party must release the bail party upon—

(a) being provided with a notice of decision to grant bail; or

(b) being—

(i) provided with a notice of decision fixing the amount and conditions of the bail, and

(ii) satisfied that the recognizance required by that decision has been entered into.

Application of this Part to Scotland

44. This Part applies to Scotland with the following modifications—

(a) in rule 37, for paragraph (4) substitute—

"(4) Where the proceedings concern forfeiture of bail, the parties are the Secretary of State and any person who entered into the bail bond in question, whether that is the bail party or cautioner."

(b) in rule 38—

(i) for paragraph (2)(d) substitute— "(d) forfeiture of bail.";

(ii) for paragraph (3)(d) substitute—

"(d) the amount, if any, deposited or to be deposited if bail is granted;";

(iii) for paragraph (3)(f) substitute—

"(f) the full name, address, date of birth and any occupation of any person acting or offering to act as a cautioner if the application for bail is granted, and the amount, if any, deposited or to be deposited;"; and

(iv) for paragraph (4) substitute—

"(4) Where the application is for forfeiture of bail, paragraph (3) applies with the exception of sub-paragraphs (a)(iii) and (b), (c), (e) and (g) of that paragraph";

(c) in rule 41, for paragraphs (2), (3) and (4) substitute—

"(2) Where bail is granted, varied or continued, the notice must state any bail conditions, including the amounts (if any) to be deposited by the bail party and any cautioners.

(3) Where bail is refused or where the Tribunal orders forfeiture of bail, the notice must include reasons for the decision.

(4) Where, instead of granting or refusing bail, the Tribunal fixes the amount and conditions of bail with a view to a bail bond being entered into subsequently before a person specified by the Tribunal, the notice must include the matters stated in paragraph (2) and the name or office of the person so specified.";

(d) for rule 42 substitute—

"Bail bond

42.—(1) Any bail bond of a bail party or cautioner must be in writing and, where the deposit of money is required as a condition of bail, must state—

(a) the amount to be deposited; and

(b) that the bail party and any cautioner understand that, if the bail party fails to answer to bail, all or part of the amount deposited may be forfeited.

(2) The bail bond must be signed by the bail party and any cautioner and provided to the Tribunal, and a copy provided to—

(a) the parties,

(b) any person having custody of the bail party, and

(c) any cautioner."

(e) in rule 43, for sub-paragraph (b) substitute— "(b) being—

(i) provided with the notice of decision fixing the amount and conditions of the bail, and

(ii) satisfied that the amount, if any, to be deposited in accordance with those conditions has been deposited.".

PART 6

FINAL

Revocations

45. The statutory instruments listed in the left hand column of Table 1 below are revoked to the extent specified in the right hand column.

Table 1 Revocations

Statutory Instrument	*Extent of revocation*
The Asylum and Immigration Tribunal (Procedure) Rules 2005 (S.I. 2005/230)	The entire Rules
The Asylum and Immigration Tribunal (Procedure) (Amendment) Rules 2006 (S.I. 2006/2788)	The entire Rules
The Asylum and Immigration Tribunal (Procedure) Rules 2007 (S.I. 2007/835)	The entire Rules
The Asylum and Immigration Tribunal (Procedure) (Amendment No. 2) Rules 2007 (S.I. 2007/3170)	The entire Rules
The Asylum and Immigration Tribunal (Procedure) (Amendment) Rules 2008 (S.I. 2008/1088)	The entire Rules
The Tribunal Procedure (Amendment No. 2) Rules 2010 (S.I. 2010/44)	Rules 23 to 28 inclusive
The Tribunal Procedure (Amendment No. 3) Rules 2010 (S.I. 2010/2653)	Rule 4

Statutory Instrument	*Extent of revocation*
The Tribunal Procedure (Amendment) (No. 2) Rules 2011 (S.I. 2011/2840)	The entire Rules
The Asylum and Immigration Tribunal (Fast Track Procedure) Rules 2005 (S.I. 2005/560)	The entire Rules
The Asylum and Immigration Tribunal (Fast Track Procedure) (Amendment) Rules 2006 (S.I. 2006/2789)	The entire Rules
The Asylum and Immigration Tribunal (Fast Track Procedure) (Amendment) Rules 2008 (S.I. 2008/1089)	The entire Rules

Transitional provisions

46.—(1) The Tribunal may give any direction to ensure that proceedings are dealt with fairly and, in particular, may—

(a) apply any provision of the Asylum and Immigration Tribunal (Procedure) Rules 2005 or the Asylum and Immigration Tribunal (Fast Track Procedure) Rules 2005 which applied to the proceedings immediately before the date these Rules came into force; or

(b) disapply provisions of these Rules (including the Fast Track Rules).

(2) A time period which has started to run before the date on which these Rules come into force and which has not expired shall continue to apply.

SCHEDULE RULE 1(3)

THE FAST TRACK RULES

PART 1

INTRODUCTION AND SCOPE

Interpretation and relationship with the Principal Rules

1.—(1) The rules in this Schedule are the Fast Track Rules.

(2) A rule or Part referred to in this Schedule by number alone means a rule in, or Part of, the Fast Track Rules.

(3) In these Rules, the "Principal Rules" means rules 1 to 46 of the Tribunal Procedure (First-tier Tribunal) (Immigration and Asylum Chamber) Rules 2014.

(4) The Principal Rules, except for those provisions referred to in Table 2 below apply for the purposes of and the interpretation of the Fast Track Rules.

(5) Where the Fast Track Rules cease to apply to an appeal or application because—

(a) the condition referred to in rule 2(1)(b) ceases to apply; or

(b) the Tribunal makes an order under rule 14,

the Principal Rules shall apply to the appeal or application.

(6) Where—

(a) a period of time for taking a step has started to run under a provision of the Fast Track Rules, and

(b) that provision ceases to apply in the circumstances to which paragraph (5) refers, if the Principal Rules contain a time limit for taking such step, the time limit in the Principal Rules shall apply, and the relevant period of time shall be treated as running from the date on which the period of time under the Fast Track Rules started to run.

Table 2 Principal Rules which do not apply in the fast track

Rule numbers refer to the Principal Rules	*Notes*
Rule 3(2) – (4) (delegation to staff)	
Rule 4(3)(a) (case management powers: reducing or extending time)	Rule 5(2) – (6) of the Fast Track Rules (time limits) applies
Rule 4(3)(h) (case management powers: adjourning or postponing hearing)	Rule 12 of the Fast Track Rules (adjournment) applies
Rule 4(3)(j) (case management powers: stay or sist proceedings)	
Rule 4(3)(k) (case management powers: transfer of proceedings)	
Rule 4(3)(l) (suspending effect of decision pending onward appeal etc.)	
Rule 7 (striking out of appeal for non-payment of fee and reinstatement)	
Rule 9(1) (costs orders for payment of Tribunal fees)	
Rule 19 (notice of appeal)	Rules 3 to 6 of the Fast Track Rules apply
Rules 20 and 21 (late notice of appeal; special provision for imminent removal cases)	Rule 5 of the Fast Track Rules (time limits) applies
Rule 22, except for the purposes of paragraph (2)(a) (no appealable decision)	
Rules 23 – 24 (response: entry clearance and other cases)	Rule 7 of the Fast Track Rules (filing of documents by respondent) applies
Rule 29(2) to (6) (provision of written statement of reasons for Tribunal's decision)	Rule 10 of the Fast Track Rules (decisions and notice of decisions) applies
Rule 33(2) and (3) (time limit for applying to the Tribunal for permission to appeal to the Upper Tribunal)	Rule 11 of the Fast Track Rules (time limit for making an application for permission to appeal) applies
Rule 34(1) (Tribunal to consider first whether to review decision)	

Scope of Fast Track Rules

2.—(1) The Fast Track Rules apply to an appeal to the Tribunal or an application for permission to appeal to the Upper Tribunal where the appellant—

(a) was detained under the Immigration Acts at a place specified in paragraph (3) when provided with notice of the appealable decision against which the appellant is appealing; and

(b) has been continuously detained under the Immigration Acts at a place or places specified in paragraph (3) since that notice was served on the appellant.

(2) An appellant does not, for the purposes of this rule, cease to satisfy the condition in paragraph (1)(b) by reason only of—

(a) being transported from one place of detention specified in paragraph (3) to another place which is so specified; or

(b) leaving and returning to such a place of detention for any purpose between the hours of 6 am and 10 pm.

(3) The places specified for the purposes of this rule are—

(a) Colnbrook House Immigration Removal Centre, Harmondsworth, Middlesex;

(b) Harmondsworth Immigration Removal Centre, Harmondsworth, Middlesex;

(c) Yarl's Wood Immigration Removal Centre, Clapham, Bedfordshire.

Part 2

Appeals to the Tribunal

Notice of appeal

3.—(1) An appellant must start proceedings by providing a notice of appeal to the Tribunal.

(2) The notice of appeal must—

(a) set out the grounds of appeal;

(b) be signed and dated by the appellant or their representative;

(c) if a notice of appeal is signed by the appellant's representative, the representative must certify in the notice of appeal that it has been completed in accordance with the appellant's instructions;

(d) state whether the appellant requires an interpreter at any hearing and if so for which language and dialect;

(e) state whether the appellant intends to attend at any hearing; and

(f) state whether the appellant will be represented at any hearing.

(3) The appellant must provide with the notice of appeal—

(a) the notice of decision against which the appellant is appealing or if it is not practicable to include the notice of decision, the reasons why it is not practicable;

(b) any statement of reasons for that decision;

(c) any documents in support of the appellant's case which have not been supplied to the respondent;

(d) an application for the Lord Chancellor to issue a certificate of fee satisfaction;

(e) any further information or documents required by an applicable practice direction.

(4) An appellant may, with the permission of the Tribunal, vary the grounds on which they rely in the notice of appeal.

Providing notice of appeal

4.—(1) An appellant may provide a notice of appeal to the Tribunal either—

(a) by providing it to the Tribunal; or

(b) by providing it to the person having custody of the appellant.

(2) Where a notice of appeal is provided under paragraph (1)(b), the person having custody of the appellant must—

(a) endorse on the notice the date that it is provided to the person having custody of the appellant; and

(b) provide it to the Tribunal immediately.

Time limits

5.—(1) The notice of appeal must be provided not later than 2 working days after the day on which the appellant was provided with notice of the decision against which the appeal is brought.

(2) Where a notice of appeal is provided outside the time limit in paragraph (1), the Tribunal must not extend the time for appealing unless it considers that it is in the interests of justice to do so.

(3) Subject to paragraph (5), the Tribunal must consider any issue as to—

(a) whether a notice of appeal was given outside the time limit in paragraph (1); and

(b) whether to extend the time for appealing,

at the hearing fixed for the hearing of the appeal under the Fast Track Rules under rule 8, and rules 9, 12 and 14 apply to the consideration and decision of such an issue as they apply to the consideration and decision of an appeal.

(4) Where a notice of appeal is provided outside the time limit in paragraph (1) and the respondent notifies the Tribunal that directions have been given for the removal of that person from the United Kingdom on a date within 5 working days of the date on which the notice of appeal was received, the Tribunal must, if reasonably practicable, make any decision on an issue referred to in paragraph (3) before the date and time proposed for the removal, and may do so as a preliminary issue.

(5) Where the Tribunal decides that the notice of appeal was provided outside the time limit and does not extend the time for appealing, the Tribunal must provide to the parties notice of its decision, including its reasons, not later than 1 working day after the date on which that decision was made, after which it shall take no further action in relation to the notice of appeal.

(6) In a case to which paragraph (5) applies, the notice of decision may be given orally at a hearing.

Service of notice of appeal etc. on respondent

6. When the Tribunal receives a notice of appeal and any further documents or information from the appellant under rule 4, it must immediately provide a copy to the respondent.

Filing of documents by respondent

7. The respondent must, not later than 2 working days after the day on which the Tribunal provides the respondent with the notice of appeal, provide the following documents to the Tribunal—

(a) the notice of the decision to which the notice of appeal relates, and any other document the respondent provided to the appellant giving reasons for that decision;

(b) any statement of evidence or application form completed by the appellant;

(c) any record of an interview with the appellant, in relation to the decision being appealed;

(d) any other unpublished document which is referred to in a document mentioned in sub-paragraph (a) or relied upon by the respondent; and

(e) the notice of any other appealable decision made in relation to the appellant.

Fixing date of appeal hearing

8.—(1) The Tribunal must fix a date for the hearing of the appeal which is—

(a) not later than 3 working days after the day on which the respondent provides the documents under rule 7; or

(b) if the Tribunal is unable to arrange a hearing within that time, as soon as practicable.

(2) The Tribunal must provide notice of the date, time and place of the hearing to every party as soon as practicable and in any event not later than noon on the working day before the hearing.

(3) A practice direction may provide that, as regards—

(a) all appellants detained at one of the places specified in rule 2(3); or

(b) a class or category of appellants detained in any of those specified places,

a period of 6 working days shall apply instead of the period of 3 working days provided for in paragraph (1).

Consideration with or without a hearing

9.—(1) The Tribunal must conclude the hearing of the appeal on the date fixed under the Fast Track Rules.

(2) Where—

(a) the appeal—

(i) lapses pursuant to section 99 of the 2002 Act;

(ii) is treated as abandoned pursuant to section 104(4A) of the 2002 Act; or

(iii) is withdrawn by the appellant or treated as withdrawn in accordance with rule 17 of the Principal Rules;

(b) the Tribunal postpones or adjourns the hearing under rule 12 or 14(2)(a); or

(c) all of the parties to the appeal consent to the Tribunal deciding the appeal without a hearing;

the requirement referred to in paragraph (1) ceases.

Decisions and notice of decisions

10.—(1) Where the Tribunal decides an appeal, it must provide to each party—

(a) a notice of decision and the reasons for it;

(b) notification of any right of appeal against the decision and the time within which, and the manner in which, such right of appeal may be exercised.

(2) The Tribunal must provide the notice and the notification—

(a) where rule 9(1) applies, not later than 2 working days after the day on which the hearing of the appeal was concluded; or

(b) in any other case, not later than 2 working days after the day on which the appeal was decided.

Part 3

Appeals to the Upper Tribunal

Time limit for making an application for permission to appeal

11. An application for permission to appeal to the Upper Tribunal must be provided to the Tribunal so that it is received no later than 3 working days after the date on which the party making the application was provided with the notice of decision.

Part 4

General Provisions

Adjournment

12. Unless the Tribunal makes an order under rule 14, the Tribunal may postpone or adjourn the hearing of the appeal only where the Tribunal is satisfied that—

(a) the appeal could not justly be decided if the hearing were to be concluded on the date fixed under the Fast Track Rules; and

(b) there is an identifiable future date, not more than 10 working days after the date so fixed, upon which the Tribunal can conclude the hearing and justly decide the appeal within the timescales provided for in the Fast Track Rules.

Correction of errors and determinations

13. Where a notice of decision is amended under the Principal Rules, the Tribunal must, not later than one working day after making the amendment, provide an amended version to every party to whom it provided the original.

Part 5

TRANSFER OUT OF FAST TRACK

Transfer out of fast track

14.—(1) Where the Fast Track Rules apply to an appeal or application, the Tribunal must order that the Fast Track Rules shall cease to apply—

(a) if all the parties consent; or

(b) if the Tribunal is satisfied that the case cannot justly be decided within the time-scales provided for in the Fast Track Rules.

(2) When making an order under paragraph (1), the Tribunal may, notwithstanding rule 1(5) or (6) of the Fast Track Rules or the application of the Principal Rules—

(a) postpone or adjourn any hearing of the appeal or application; and

(b) give directions in relation to the conduct of the proceedings.

The Tribunal Procedure (Upper Tribunal) Rules 2008
(SI 2008 No. 2698 [L. 15])

Contents

Part 1

Introduction

Part 2

General Powers and Provisions

Part 3

[Procedure for Cases in] the Upper Tribunal

SCHEDULES

PART I

INTRODUCTION

Citation, commencement, application and interpretation

1.—(1) These Rules may be cited as the Tribunal Procedure (Upper Tribunal) Rules 2008 and came into force on 3rd November 2008.

(2) These Rules apply to proceedings before the Upper Tribunal [except proceedings in the Lands Chamber].

(3) In these Rules—

"the 2007 Act" means the Tribunals, Courts and Enforcement Act 2007;

["appellant" means—

(a) a person who makes an appeal, or applies for permission to appeal, to the Upper Tribunal;

(b) in proceedings transferred or referred to the Upper Tribunal from the First-tier Tribunal, a person who started the proceedings in the First-tier Tribunal; or

(c) a person substituted as an appellant under rule 9(1) (substitution and addition of parties);]

["applicant" means—

(a) a person who applies for permission to bring, or does bring, judicial review proceedings before the Upper Tribunal and, in judicial review proceedings transferred to the Upper Tribunal from a court, includes a person who was a claimant or petitioner in the proceedings immediately before they were transferred; or

(b) a person who refers a financial services [or a wholesale energy case] case to the Upper Tribunal;]

["appropriate national authority" means, in relation to an appeal, the Secretary of State, the Scottish Ministers[, the Department of the Environment in Northern Ireland] or the Welsh Ministers, as the case may be;

["asylum case" means proceedings before the Upper Tribunal on appeal against a decision in proceedings under section 82, 83 or 83A of the Nationality, Immigration and Asylum Act 2002 in which a person claims that removal from, or a requirement to leave, the United Kingdom would breach the United Kingdom's obligations under the Convention relating to the Status of Refugees done at Geneva on 28 July 1951 and the Protocol to the Convention;]

["authorised person" means—

(a) an examiner appointed by the Secretary of State under section 66A of the Road Traffic Act 1988;

(b) an examiner appointed by the Department of the Environment in Northern Ireland under Article 74 of the Road Traffic (Northern Ireland) Order 1995; or

(c) any person authorised in writing by the Department of the Environment in Northern Ireland for the purposes of the Goods Vehicles (Licensing of Operators) Act (Northern Ireland) 2010;

and includes a person acting under the direction of such an examiner or other authorised person, who has detained the vehicle to which an appeal relates;] . . .

["disability discrimination in schools case" means proceedings concerning discrimination in the education of a child or young person or related matters;] . . .

"dispose of proceedings" includes, unless indicated otherwise, disposing of a part of the proceedings;

"document" means anything in which information is recorded in any form, and an obligation under these Rules or any practice direction or direction to provide or allow access to a document or a copy of a document for any purpose means, unless the Upper Tribunal directs otherwise, an obligation to provide or allow access to such document or copy in a legible form or in a form which can be readily made into a legible form;

"fast-track case" means an asylum case or an immigration case where the person who appealed to the First-tier Tribunal—

(a) was detained under the Immigration Acts at a place specified in [rule 2(3) of the Schedule to the Tribunal Procedure (First-tier Tribunal) (Immigration and Asylum Chamber) Rules 2014] when the notice of decision that was the subject of the appeal to the First-tier Tribunal was served on the appellant;

(b) remains so detained; and

(c) the First-tier Tribunal or the Upper Tribunal has not directed that the case cease to be treated as a fast-track case;]

["financial services case" means a reference to the Upper Tribunal in respect of—

[(a) a decision of the Financial Conduct Authority;

(aa) a decision of the Prudential Regulation Authority;]

(b) a decision of the Bank of England;

(c) a decision of the Pensions Regulator; or

(d) a decision of a person relating to the assessment of any compensation or consideration under the Banking (Special Provisions) Act 2008 or the Banking Act 2009;] or

[(e) any determination, calculation or dispute which may be referred to the Upper Tribunal under the Financial Services and Markets Act 2000 (Contribution to Costs of Special Resolution Regime) Regulations 2010(b) (and in these Rules a decision in respect of which a reference has been made to the Upper Tribunal in a financial services case includes any such determination, calculation or, except for the purposes of rule 5(5), dispute relating to the making of payments under the Regulations);]

"hearing" means an oral hearing and includes a hearing conducted in whole or in part by video link, telephone or other means of instantaneous two-way electronic communication;

["immigration case" means proceedings before the Upper Tribunal on appeal against a decision in proceedings under section 40A of the British Nationality Act 1981, section 82 of the Nationality, Immigration and Asylum Act 2002, or regulation 26 of the Immigration (European Economic Area) Regulations 2006 that are not an asylum case;]

["immigration judicial review proceedings" means judicial review proceedings which are designated as an immigration matter—

(a) In a direction made in accordance with Part 1 of Schedule 2 to the Constitutional Reform Act 2005 specifying a class of case for the purposes of section 18(6) of the 2007 Act; or

(b) in an order of the High Court in England and Wales made under section 31A(3) of the Senior Courts Act 1981, transferring to the Upper Tribunal an application of a kind described in section 31A(1) of that Act;]

"interested party" means—

(a) a person who is directly affected by the outcome sought in judicial review proceedings, and has been named as an interested party under rule 28 or 29 (judicial review), or has been substituted or added as an interested party under rule 9 [(addition, substitution and removal of parties)];

(b) in judicial review proceedings transferred to the Upper Tribunal under section 25A(2) or (3) of the Judicature (Northern Ireland) Act 1978 or section 31A(2) or (3) of the Supreme Court Act 1981, a person who was an interested party in the proceedings immediately before they were transferred to the Upper Tribunal;

[and

(c) in a financial services case, [or a wholesale energy case] any person other than the applicant who could have referred the case to the Upper Tribunal and who has been added or substituted as an interested party under rule 9 (addition, substitution and removal of parties);]

"judicial review proceedings" means proceedings within the jurisdiction of the Upper Tribunal pursuant to section 15 or 21 of the 2007 Act, whether such proceedings are started in the Upper Tribunal or transferred to the Upper Tribunal;

. . .

"mental health case" means proceedings before the Upper Tribunal on appeal against a decision in proceedings under the Mental Health Act 1983 or paragraph 5(2) of the Schedule to the Repatriation of Prisoners Act 1984;

["national security certificate appeal" means an appeal under section 28 of the Data Protection Act 1998 or section 60 of the Freedom of Information Act 2000 (including that section as applied and modified by regulation 18 of the Environmental Information Regulations 2004);]

"party" means a person who is an appellant, an applicant, a respondent or an interested party in proceedings before the Upper Tribunal, a person who has referred a question [or matter] to the Upper Tribunal or, if the proceedings have been concluded, a person who was an appellant, an applicant, a respondent or an interested party when the [Upper] Tribunal finally disposed of all issues in the proceedings;

"permission" includes leave in cases arising under the law of Northern Ireland;

"practice direction" means a direction given under section 23 of the 2007 Act;

["reference", in a financial services case, includes an appeal;]

["relevant minister" means the Minister or designated person responsible for the signing of the certificate to which a national security certificate appeal relates;]

"respondent" means—

(a) in an appeal, or application for permission to appeal, against a decision of another tribunal, any person other than the appellant who—

(i) was a party before that other tribunal;

(ii) . . .

(iii) otherwise has a right of appeal against the decision of the other tribunal and has given notice to the Upper Tribunal that they wish to be a party to the appeal;

(b) in an appeal [other than a road transport case], the person who made the decision;

(c) in judicial review proceedings—

(i) in proceedings started in the Upper Tribunal, the person named by the applicant as the respondent;

(ii) in proceedings transferred to the Upper Tribunal under section 25A(2) or (3) of the Judicature (Northern Ireland) Act 1978 or section 31A(2) or (3) of the Supreme Court Act 1981, a person who was a defendant in the proceedings immediately before they were transferred;

(iii) in proceedings transferred to the Upper Tribunal under section 20(1) of the 2007 Act, a person to whom intimation of the petition was made before the proceedings were transferred, or to whom the Upper Tribunal has required intimation to be made.

[(ca) in proceedings transferred or referred to the Upper Tribunal from the First-tier Tribunal, a person who was a respondent in the proceedings in the First-tier Tribunal;]

(d) in a reference under the Forfeiture Act 1982, the person whose eligibility for a benefit or advantage is in issue;

[(da) in a financial services case—

(i) where the case is a multiple regulator case, both the primary and secondary regulator as defined in Schedule 3 to these rules (but subject to the operation of paragraph 4A(3) of that Schedule);

(ii) where the case is a single regulator case, the maker of the decision in respect of which a reference has been made; or]

[(db) in a wholesale energy case, in relation to Great Britain, the Gas and Electricity Markets Authority or, in relation to Northern Ireland, the Northern Ireland Authority for Utility Regulation; or]

(e) a person substituted or added as a respondent under rule 9 (substitution and addition of parties);

["road transport case" means an appeal against a decision of a traffic commissioner or the Department of the Environment in Northern Ireland;]

["special educational needs case" means proceedings concerning the education of a child or young person who has or may have special educational needs, including proceedings relating to—

(a) an EHC needs assessment within the meaning of section 36(2) of the Children and Families Act 2014; or

(b) an EHC plan within the meaning of section 37(2) of that Act,

of such a child or young person;]

["tribunal" does not include a traffic commissioner;]

["wholesale energy case" means a reference to the Upper Tribunal in respect of a decision of—

(a) in relation to Great Britain, the Gas and Electricity Markets Authority under the Electricity and Gas (Market Integrity and Transparency) (Enforcement etc.) Regulations 2013; or

(b) in relation to Northern Ireland, the Northern Ireland Authority for Utility Regulation under the Electricity and Gas (Market Integrity and Transparency) (Enforcement etc.) Regulations (Northern Ireland) 2013;]

. . .

"working day" means any day except a Saturday or Sunday, Christmas Day, Good Friday or a bank holiday under section 1 of the Banking and Financial Dealings Act 1971;

["young person" means, in relation to a special educational needs case or a disability discrimination in schools case, a person over compulsory school age but under 25.]

Note: Words in square brackets in paragraph (2), definitions of 'appropriate national authority', 'authorised person' and 'tribunal' and words in square brackets in subparagraph (b) of definition of respondent inserted from 1 September 2009 (SI 2009/1975). Definition of appellant substituted, definitions of 'disability discrimination in schools cases', 'legal representative', 'special education needs case' omitted and in definition of respondent subparagraph (a)(ii) omitted and (ca) inserted from 1 April 2009 (SI 2009/274). Definitions of 'national security certificate appeal' and 'relevant minister' inserted from 18 January 2010 (SI 2010/43). Definitions of 'asylum case', 'immigration case' and 'fast-track case' inserted from 15 February 2010 (SI 2010/44). Definition of 'applicant' and words in square brackets in subparagraph (a) of definition of interested party substituted; definitions of 'financial services case' and 'reference', subparagraph (c) of definition of interested party. Words in square brackets in definition of party and subparagraph (da) in definition of respondent inserted from 6 April 2010 (SI 2010/747). Subparagraph (e) in definition of 'financial services case' inserted from 1 April 2011 (SI 2011/651). Definition of 'fresh claim proceedings' inserted from 17 October 2011 (SI 2011/2343) and omitted by SI 2013/2067 from 1 November 2013. Words inserted in the definition of 'appropriate national authority', definition of 'authorised person' substituted, definition of 'respondent' further amended and definition of 'road transport case' inserted from 1 July 2012 (SI 2012/1363). Definition of 'immigration review proceedings' and word in square brackets in definition of party inserted by SI 2013/2067 from 1 November 2013. Subparagraphs (a)–(aa) of 'financial services case' substituted by SI 2013/606 from 1 April 2013. Subparagraph (db) of 'respondent', definition of 'wholesale energy case' and words in first square brackets in subparagraphs (b) of 'applicant' and (c) of 'interested party' inserted and word omitted from subparagraph (c) of 'financial services case' by SI 2014/514 from 6 April 2014. Definitions of 'disability discrimination in a school case', 'special educational needs case' and 'young person' inserted by SI 2014/2128 from 1 September 2014. Words in square brackets in 'fast track case' substituted by SI 2014 from 20 October 2014.

Overriding objective and parties' obligation to cooperate with the Upper Tribunal

2.—(1) The overriding objective of these Rules is to enable the Upper Tribunal to deal with cases fairly and justly.

(2) Dealing with a case fairly and justly includes—

(a) dealing with the case in ways which are proportionate to the importance of the case, the complexity of the issues, the anticipated costs and the resources of the parties;

(b) avoiding unnecessary formality and seeking flexibility in the proceedings;

(c) ensuring, so far as practicable, that the parties are able to participate fully in the proceedings;

(d) using any special expertise of the Upper Tribunal effectively; and

(e) avoiding delay, so far as compatible with proper consideration of the issues.

(3) The Upper Tribunal must seek to give effect to the overriding objective when it—

(a) exercises any power under these Rules; or

(b) interprets any rule or practice direction.

(4) Parties must—

(a) help the Upper Tribunal to further the overriding objective; and

(b) cooperate with the Upper Tribunal generally.

Alternative dispute resolution and arbitration

3.—(1) The Upper Tribunal should seek, where appropriate—

(a) to bring to the attention of the parties the availability of any appropriate alternative procedure for the resolution of the dispute; and

(b) if the parties wish and provided that it is compatible with the overriding objective, to facilitate the use of the procedure.

(2) Part 1 of the Arbitration Act 1996 does not apply to proceedings before the Upper Tribunal.

Part 2

General Powers and Provisions

Delegation to staff

4.—(1) Staff appointed under section 40(1) of the 2007 Act (tribunal staff and services) may, with the approval of the Senior President of Tribunals, carry out functions of a judicial nature permitted or required to be done by the Upper Tribunal.

(2) The approval referred to at paragraph (1) may apply generally to the carrying out of specified functions by members of staff of a specified description in specified circumstances.

(3) Within 14 days after the date on which the Upper Tribunal sends notice of a decision made by a member of staff under paragraph (1) to a party, that party may apply in writing to the Upper Tribunal for that decision to be considered afresh by a judge.

Case management powers

5.—(1) Subject to the provisions of the 2007 Act and any other enactment, the Upper Tribunal may regulate its own procedure.

(2) The Upper Tribunal may give a direction in relation to the conduct or disposal of proceedings at any time, including a direction amending, suspending or setting aside an earlier direction.

(3) In particular, and without restricting the general powers in paragraphs (1) and (2), the Upper Tribunal may—

(a) extend or shorten the time for complying with any rule, practice direction or direction;

(b) consolidate or hear together two or more sets of proceedings or parts of proceedings raising common issues, or treat a case as a lead case;

(c) permit or require a party to amend a document;

(d) permit or require a party or another person to provide documents, information, evidence or submissions to the Upper Tribunal or a party;

(e) deal with an issue in the proceedings as a preliminary issue;

(f) hold a hearing to consider any matter, including a case management issue;

(g) decide the form of any hearing;

(h) adjourn or postpone a hearing;

(i) require a party to produce a bundle for a hearing;

(j) stay (or, in Scotland, sist) proceedings;

(k) transfer proceedings to another court or tribunal if that other court or tribunal has jurisdiction in relation to the proceedings; and—

(i) because of a change of circumstances since the proceedings were started, the Upper Tribunal no longer has jurisdiction in relation to the proceedings; or

(ii) the Upper Tribunal considers that the other court or tribunal is a more appropriate forum for the determination of the case;

(l) suspend the effect of its own decision pending an appeal or review of that decision;

(m) in an appeal, or an application for permission to appeal, against the decision of another tribunal, suspend the effect of that decision pending the determination of the application for permission to appeal, and any appeal;

[(n) require any person, body or other tribunal whose decision is the subject of proceedings before the Upper Tribunal to provide reasons for the decision, or other information or documents in relation to the decision or any proceedings before that person, body or tribunal.]

[(4) The Upper Tribunal may direct that a fast-track case cease to be treated as a fast-track case if—

(a) all the parties consent; [or]

(b) the Upper Tribunal is satisfied that . . . the appeal or application could not be justly determined if it were treated as a fast-track case . . .

(c) . . .]

[(5) In a financial services case, the Upper Tribunal may direct that the effect of the decision in respect of which the reference has been made is to be suspended pending the determination of the reference, if it is satisfied that to do so would not prejudice—

(a) the interests of any persons (whether consumers, investors or otherwise) intended to be protected by that notice; or

(b) the smooth operation or integrity of any market intended to be protected by that notice[; or

(c) the stability of the financial system of the United Kingdom.]

(6) Paragraph (5) does not apply in the case of a reference in respect of a decision of the Pensions Regulator.].

[(7) In a wholesale energy case, the Upper Tribunal may direct that the effect of the decision in respect of which the reference has been made is to be suspended pending the determination of the reference.]

Note: Paragraph (3)(n) substituted from 1 September 2009 (SI 2009/1975). Paragraph (4) inserted from 15 February 2010 (SI 2010/44). Paragraph (5) inserted from 6 April 2010 (SI 2010/747). Subparagraph (5)(c) inserted by SI 2013/606 from 1 April 2013 subparagraph (7) inserted by SI 2014/514 from 6 April 2014. Subparagraph (4)(c) and words in square brackets in subparagraph (4)(b) omitted by SI 2014/2128 from 20 October 2014.

Procedure for applying for and giving directions

6.—(1) The Upper Tribunal may give a direction on the application of one or more of the parties or on its own initiative.

(2) An application for a direction may be made—

(a) by sending or delivering a written application to the Upper Tribunal; or

(b) orally during the course of a hearing.

(3) An application for a direction must include the reason for making that application.

(4) Unless the Upper Tribunal considers that there is good reason not to do so, the Upper Tribunal must send written notice of any direction to every party and to any other person affected by the direction.

(5) If a party or any other person sent notice of the direction under paragraph (4) wishes to challenge a direction which the Upper Tribunal has given, they may do so by applying for another direction which amends, suspends or sets aside the first direction.

Failure to comply with rules etc.

7.—(1) An irregularity resulting from a failure to comply with any requirement in these Rules, a practice direction or a direction, does not of itself render void the proceedings or any step taken in the proceedings.

(2) If a party has failed to comply with a requirement in these Rules, a practice direction or a direction, the Upper Tribunal may take such action as it considers just, which may include—

(a) waiving the requirement;

(b) requiring the failure to be remedied;

(c) exercising its power under rule 8 (striking out a party's case); or

(d) except in [a mental health case, an asylum case or an immigration case], restricting a party's participation in the proceedings.

(3) Paragraph (4) applies where the First-tier Tribunal has referred to the Upper Tribunal a failure by a person to comply with a requirement imposed by the First-tier Tribunal—

(a) to attend at any place for the purpose of giving evidence;

(b) otherwise to make themselves available to give evidence;

(c) to swear an oath in connection with the giving of evidence;

(d) to give evidence as a witness;

(e) to produce a document; or

(f) to facilitate the inspection of a document or any other thing (including any premises).

(4) The Upper Tribunal may exercise its power under section 25 of the 2007 Act (supplementary powers of the Upper Tribunal) in relation to such non-compliance as if the requirement had been imposed by the Upper Tribunal.

Note: Words in square brackets in paragraph (2)(d) inserted from 15 February 2010 (SI 2010/44).

Striking out a party's case

8.—[(1A) Except for paragraph (2), this rule does not apply to an asylum case or an immigration case.]

[(1) The proceedings, or the appropriate part of them, will automatically be struck out—

(a) if the appellant or applicant has failed to comply with a direction that stated that failure by the appellant or applicant to comply with the direction would lead to the striking out of the proceedings or part of them; or

[(b) in immigration judicial review proceedings, when a fee has not been paid, as required, in respect of an application under rule 30(4) or upon the grant of permission.]]

(2) The Upper Tribunal must strike out the whole or a part of the proceedings if the Upper Tribunal—

(a) does not have jurisdiction in relation to the proceedings or that part of them; and

(b) does not exercise its power under rule 5(3)(k)(i) (transfer to another court or tribunal) in relation to the proceedings or that part of them.

(3) The Upper Tribunal may strike out the whole or a part of the proceedings if—

(a) the appellant or applicant has failed to comply with a direction which stated that failure by the appellant or applicant to comply with the direction could lead to the striking out of the proceedings or part of them;

(b) the appellant or applicant has failed to cooperate with the Upper Tribunal to such an extent that the Upper Tribunal cannot deal with the proceedings fairly and justly; or

(c) in proceedings which are not an appeal from the decision of another tribunal or judicial review proceedings, the Upper Tribunal considers there is no reasonable prospect of the appellant's or the applicant's case, or part of it, succeeding.

(4) The Upper Tribunal may not strike out the whole or a part of the proceedings under paragraph (2) or (3)(b) or (c) without first giving the appellant or applicant an opportunity to make representations in relation to the proposed striking out.

(5) If the proceedings have been struck out under paragraph (1) or (3)(a), the appellant or applicant may apply for the proceedings, or part of them, to be reinstated.

(6) An application under paragraph (5) must be made in writing and received by the Upper Tribunal within 1 month after the date on which the Upper Tribunal sent notification of the striking out to the appellant or applicant.

(7) This rule applies to a respondent [or an interested party] as it applies to an appellant or applicant except that—

(a) a reference to the striking out of the proceedings is to be read as a reference to the barring of the respondent [or interested party] from taking further part in the proceedings; and

(b) a reference to an application for the reinstatement of proceedings which have been struck out is to be read as a reference to an application for the lifting of the bar on the respondent [or interested party] . . . taking further part in the proceedings.

(8) If a respondent [or an interested party] has been barred from taking further part in proceedings under this rule and that bar has not been lifted, the Upper Tribunal need not consider any response or other submission made by that respondent [or interested party, and may summarily determine any or all issues against that respondent or interested party].

Note: Paragraph (1A) inserted from 15 February 2010 (SI 2010/44). Words in square brackets in paragraphs (7)–(8) inserted from 1 April 2009 (SI 2009/274). Paragraph 1 substituted from 17 October 2011 (SI 2011/2343). Subparagraph (1)(b) substituted by SI 2013/2067 from 1 November 2013.

[Addition, substitution and removal of parties

9.—(1) The Upper Tribunal may give a direction adding, substituting or removing a party as an appellant, a respondent or an interested party.

(2) If the Upper Tribunal gives a direction under paragraph (1) it may give such consequential directions as it considers appropriate.

(3) A person who is not a party may apply to the Upper Tribunal to be added or substituted as a party.

(4) If a person who is entitled to be a party to proceedings by virtue of another enactment applies to be added as a party, and any conditions applicable to that entitlement have been satisfied, the Upper Tribunal must give a direction adding that person as a respondent or, if appropriate, as an appellant.]

[(5) In an asylum case, the United Kingdom Representative of the United Nations High Commissioner for Refugees ("the United Kingdom Representative") may give notice to the Upper Tribunal that the United Kingdom Representative wishes to participate in the proceedings.

(6) If the United Kingdom Representative gives notice under paragraph (5)—

(i) the United Kingdom Representative is entitled to participate in any hearing; and

(ii) all documents which are required to be sent or delivered to parties must be sent or delivered to the United Kingdom Representative.]

Note: Rule 9 substituted from 1 September 2009 (SI 2009/1975). Paragraph (5) inserted from 15 February 2010 (SI 2010/44).

[Orders for costs

10.—(1) The Upper Tribunal may not make an order in respect of costs (or, in Scotland, expenses) in proceedings [transferred or referred by, or on appeal from,] another tribunal except—

[(aa) in a national security certificate appeal, to the extent permitted by paragraph (1A);]

(a) in proceedings [transferred by, or on appeal from,] the Tax Chamber of the First-tier Tribunal; or

(b) to the extent and in the circumstances that the other tribunal had the power to make an order in respect of costs (or, in Scotland, expenses).

[(1A) In a national security certificate appeal—

(a) the Upper Tribunal may make an order in respect of costs or expenses in the circumstances described at paragraph (3)(c) and (d);

(b) if the appeal is against a certificate, the Upper Tribunal may make an order in respect of costs or expenses against the relevant Minister and in favour of the appellant if the Upper Tribunal allows the appeal and quashes the certificate to any extent or the Minister withdraws the certificate;

(c) if the appeal is against the application of a certificate, the Upper Tribunal may make an order in respect of costs or expenses—

(i) against the appellant and in favour of any other party if the Upper Tribunal dismisses the appeal to any extent; or

(ii) in favour of the appellant and against any other party if the Upper Tribunal allows the appeal to any extent.]

(2) The Upper Tribunal may not make an order in respect of costs or expenses under section 4 of the Forfeiture Act 1982.

(3) In other proceedings, the Upper Tribunal may not make an order in respect of costs or expenses except—

(a) in judicial review proceedings;

(b) . . . ;

(c) under section 29(4) of the 2007 Act (wasted costs) [and costs incurred in applying for such costs];

(d) if the Upper Tribunal considers that a party or its representative has acted unreasonably in bringing, defending or conducting the proceedings [; or

(e) if, in a financial services case [or a wholesale energy case], the Upper Tribunal considers that the decision in respect of which the reference was made was unreasonable.]

(4) The Upper Tribunal may make an order for costs (or, in Scotland, expenses) on an application or on its own initiative.

(5) A person making an application for an order for costs or expenses must—

(a) send or deliver a written application to the Upper Tribunal and to the person against whom it is proposed that the order be made; and

(b) send or deliver with the application a schedule of the costs or expenses claimed sufficient to allow summary assessment of such costs or expenses by the Upper Tribunal.

(6) An application for an order for costs or expenses may be made at any time during the proceedings but may not be made later than 1 month after the date on which the Upper Tribunal sends—

(a) a decision notice recording the decision which finally disposes of all issues in the proceedings; or

[(b) notice under rule 17(5) that a withdrawal which ends the proceedings has taken effect.]

(7) The Upper Tribunal may not make an order for costs or expenses against a person (the "paying person") without first—

(a) giving that person an opportunity to make representations; and

(b) if the paying person is an individual and the order is to be made under paragraph (3)(a), (b) or (d), considering that person's financial means.

(8) The amount of costs or expenses to be paid under an order under this rule may be ascertained by—

(a) summary assessment by the Upper Tribunal;

(b) agreement of a specified sum by the paying person and the person entitled to receive the costs or expenses ("the receiving person"); or

(c) assessment of the whole or a specified part of the costs or expenses[, including the costs or expenses of the assessment,] incurred by the receiving person, if not agreed.

(9) Following an order for assessment under paragraph (8)(c), the paying person or the receiving person may apply—

(a) in England and Wales, to the High Court or the Costs Office of the Supreme Court (as specified in the order) for a detailed assessment of the costs on the standard basis or, if specified in the order, on the indemnity basis; and the Civil Procedure Rules 1998 shall apply, with necessary modifications, to that application and assessment as if the proceedings in the tribunal had been proceedings in a court to which the Civil Procedure Rules 1998 apply;

(b) in Scotland, to the Auditor of the Court of Session for the taxation of the expenses according to the fees payable in that court; or

(c) in Northern Ireland, to the Taxing Office of the High Court of Northern Ireland for taxation on the standard basis or, if specified in the order, on the indemnity basis.]

[(10) Upon making an order for the assessment of costs, the [Upper] Tribunal may order an amount to be paid on account before the costs or expenses are assessed.]

Note: Rule 10 substituted from 1 April 2009 (SI 2009/274). Words in square brackets in paragraph (1) and (1)(a) substituted and paragraph (3)(a) omitted from 1 September 2009 (SI 2009/1975). Paragraph(1)(aa) and (1A) inserted from 18 January 2010 (SI 2010/43). Paragraph (3)(e) inserted from 6 April 2010 (SI 2010/747). Paragraph (6)(b) substituted, paragraph (10) and words in square brackets in (3)(c) inserted by SI 2013/477 from 1 April 2013. Word in square brackets in (10) inserted by 2013/2067 from 1 November 2013. Words in square brackets in (3)(e) inserted by SI 2014/514 from 6 April 2014.

Representatives

11.—(1) [Subject to paragraph 5A] a party may appoint a representative (whether a legal representative or not) to represent that party in the proceedings [save that a party in an asylum or immigration case may not be represented by any person prohibited from representing by section 84 of the Immigration and Asylum Act 1999].

(2) If a party appoints a representative, that party (or the representative if the representative is a legal representative) must send or deliver to the Upper Tribunal . . . written notice of the representative's name and address.

[(**2A**) If the Upper Tribunal receives notice that a party has appointed a representative under paragraph (2), it must send a copy of that notice to each other party.]

(3) Anything permitted or required to be done by a party under these Rules, a practice direction or a direction may be done by the representative of that party, except signing a witness statement.

(4) A person who receives due notice of the appointment of a representative—

(a) must provide to the representative any document which is required to be provided to the represented party, and need not provide that document to the represented party; and

(b) may assume that the representative is and remains authorised as such until they receive written notification that this is not so from the representative or the represented party.

(5) [Subject to paragraph (5B)] At a hearing a party may be accompanied by another person whose name and address has not been notified under paragraph (2) but who, subject to paragraph (8) and with the permission of the Upper Tribunal, may act as a representative or otherwise assist in presenting the party's case at the hearing.

[(**5A**) In [immigration judicial review] proceedings, a party may appoint as a representative only a person authorised under the Legal Services Act 2007 to undertake the conduct of litigation in the High Court.]

[(**5B**) At a hearing of [immigration judicial review] proceedings, rights of audience before the Upper Tribunal are restricted to persons authorised to exercise those rights in the High Court under the Legal Services Act 2007.]

(6) Paragraphs (2) to (4) do not apply to a person who accompanies a party under paragraph (5).

(7) In a mental health case if the patient has not appointed a representative the Upper Tribunal may appoint a legal representative for the patient where—

(a) the patient has stated that they do not wish to conduct their own case or that they wish to be represented; or

(b) the patient lacks the capacity to appoint a representative but the Upper Tribunal believes that it is in the patient's best interests for the patient to be represented.

(8) In a mental health case a party may not appoint as a representative, or be represented or assisted at a hearing by—

(a) a person liable to be detained or subject to guardianship or after-care under supervision, or who is a community patient, under the Mental Health Act 1983; or

(b) a person receiving treatment for mental disorder at the same hospital [or] home as the patient.

[(9) In this rule "legal representative" means [a person who, for the purposes of the Legal Services Act 2007, is an authorised person in relation to an activity which constitutes the exercise of a right of audience or the conduct of litigation within the meaning of that Act] [a qualified person as defined in section 84(2) of the Immigration and Asylum Act 1999,] an advocate or solicitor in Scotland or a barrister or solicitor in Northern Ireland.]

[(10) In an asylum case or an immigration case, an appellant's representative before the First-tier Tribunal will be treated as that party's representative before the Upper Tribunal, unless the Upper Tribunal receives notice—

(a) of a new representative under paragraph (2) of this rule; or

(b) from the appellant stating that they are no longer represented.]

Note: Words omitted from paragraph (2), paragraphs (2A) and (9) inserted from 1 April 2009 (SI 2009/274). Word in square brackets in paragraph (8)(b) inserted from 1 September 2009 (SI 2009/275). Words in first square brackets in paragraph (9) substituted from 18 January 2010 (SI 2010/43). Paragraph (10), words in square brackets in paragraph (1) and second square brackets in paragraph (9) inserted from 15 February 2010 (SI 2010/44). Words inserted in paragraphs (1) and (5) and paragraphs (5A) and (5B) inserted from 17 October 2011 (SI 2011/2343). Words in square brackets in paragraphs 5A and 5B substituted by 2013/2067 from 1 November 2013.

Calculating time

12.—(1) An act required by these Rules, a practice direction or a direction to be done on or by a particular day must be done by 5pm on that day.

(2) If the time specified by these Rules, a practice direction or a direction for doing any act ends on a day other than a working day, the act is done in time if it is done on the next working day.

(3) In a special educational needs case or a disability discrimination in schools case, the following days must not be counted when calculating the time by which an act must be done—

(a) 25th December to 1st January inclusive; and

(b) any day in August.

[(3A) In an asylum case or an immigration case, when calculating the time by which an act must be done, in addition to the days specified in the definition of "working days" in rule 1 (interpretation), the following days must also not be counted as working days—

(a) 27th to 31st December inclusive; . . .

(b) . . .]

(4) Paragraph (3) [or (3A)] does not apply where the Upper Tribunal directs that an act must be done by or on a specified date.

[(5) . . .]

Note: Paragraph (5) inserted from 1 April 2009 (SI 2009/274) and omitted from 1 September 2014 by SI 2014/2128. Paragraph (3A) and words in square brackets in paragraph (4) inserted from 15 February 2010 (SI 2010/44). Subparagraph (3A) (b) omitted from 20 October 2014 by SI 2014/2128.

Sending and delivery of documents

13.—(1) Any document to be provided to the Upper Tribunal under these Rules, a practice direction or a direction must be—

(a) sent by pre-paid post or [by document exchange, or delivered by hand,] to the address specified for the proceedings;

(b) sent by fax to the number specified for the proceedings; or

(c) sent or delivered by such other method as the Upper Tribunal may permit or direct.

(2) Subject to paragraph (3), if a party provides a fax number, email address or other details for the electronic transmission of documents to them, that party must accept delivery of documents by that method.

(3) If a party informs the Upper Tribunal and all other parties that a particular form of communication, other than pre-paid post or delivery by hand, should not be used to provide documents to that party, that form of communication must not be so used.

(4) If the Upper Tribunal or a party sends a document to a party or the Upper Tribunal by email or any other electronic means of communication, the recipient may request that the sender provide a hard copy of the document to the recipient. The recipient must make such a request as soon as reasonably practicable after receiving the document electronically.

(5) The Upper Tribunal and each party may assume that the address provided by a party or its representative is and remains the address to which documents should be sent or delivered until receiving written notification to the contrary.

[(6) Subject to paragraph (7), if a document submitted to the Upper Tribunal is not written in English, it must be accompanied by an English translation.

(7) In proceedings that are in Wales or have a connection with Wales, a document or translation may be submitted to the [Upper] Tribunal in Welsh.]

Note: Words in square brackets in paragraph (1)(a) substituted from 1 April 2009 (SI 2009/274). Paragraphs (6) and (7) inserted from 15 February 2010 (SI 2010/44). Word in square brackets inserted by SI 2013/2067 from 1 November 2013.

Use of documents and information

14.—(1) The Upper Tribunal may make an order prohibiting the disclosure or publication of—

(a) specified documents or information relating to the proceedings; or

(b) any matter likely to lead members of the public to identify any person whom the Upper Tribunal considers should not be identified.

(2) The Upper Tribunal may give a direction prohibiting the disclosure of a document or information to a person if—

(a) the Upper Tribunal is satisfied that such disclosure would be likely to cause that person or some other person serious harm; and

(b) the Upper Tribunal is satisfied, having regard to the interests of justice, that it is proportionate to give such a direction.

(3) If a party ("the first party") considers that the Upper Tribunal should give a direction under paragraph (2) prohibiting the disclosure of a document or information to another party ("the second party"), the first party must—

(a) exclude the relevant document or information from any documents that will be provided to the second party; and

(b) provide to the Upper Tribunal the excluded document or information, and the reason for its exclusion, so that the Upper Tribunal may decide whether the document or information should be disclosed to the second party or should be the subject of a direction under paragraph (2).

(4) . . .

(5) If the Upper Tribunal gives a direction under paragraph (2) which prevents disclosure to a party who has appointed a representative, the Upper Tribunal may give a direction that the documents or information be disclosed to that representative if the Upper Tribunal is satisfied that—

(a) disclosure to the representative would be in the interests of the party; and

(b) the representative will act in accordance with paragraph (6).

(6) Documents or information disclosed to a representative in accordance with a direction under paragraph (5) must not be disclosed either directly or indirectly to any other person without the Upper Tribunal's consent.

(7) Unless the Upper Tribunal gives a direction to the contrary, information about mental health cases and the names of any persons concerned in such cases must not be made public.

[(8) The Upper Tribunal may, on its own initiative or on the application of a party, give a direction that certain documents or information must or may be disclosed to the Upper Tribunal on the basis that the Upper Tribunal will not disclose such documents or information to other persons, or specified other persons.

(9) A party making an application for a direction under paragraph (8) may withhold the relevant documents or information from other parties until the Upper Tribunal has granted or refused the application.

(10) In a case involving matters relating to national security, the Upper Tribunal must ensure that information is not disclosed contrary to the interests of national security.

(11) The Upper Tribunal must conduct proceedings and record its decision and reasons appropriately so as not to undermine the effect of an order made under paragraph (1), a direction given under paragraph (2) or (8) or the duty imposed by paragraph (10).]

Note: Paragraph (4) omitted and paragraphs (8)–(11) inserted from 1 September 2009 (2009/1975).

Evidence and submissions

15.—(1) Without restriction on the general powers in rule 5(1) and (2) (case management powers), the Upper Tribunal may give directions as to—

(a) issues on which it requires evidence or submissions;

(b) the nature of the evidence or submissions it requires;

(c) whether the parties are permitted or required to provide expert evidence, and if so whether the parties must jointly appoint a single expert to provide such evidence;

(d) any limit on the number of witnesses whose evidence a party may put forward, whether in relation to a particular issue or generally;

(e) the manner in which any evidence or submissions are to be provided, which may include a direction for them to be given—

(i) orally at a hearing; or

(ii) by written submissions or witness statement; and

(f) the time at which any evidence or submissions are to be provided.

(2) The Upper Tribunal may—

(a) admit evidence whether or not—

(i) the evidence would be admissible in a civil trial in the United Kingdom; or

(ii) the evidence was available to a previous decision maker; or

(b) exclude evidence that would otherwise be admissible where—

(i) the evidence was not provided within the time allowed by a direction or a practice direction;

(ii) the evidence was otherwise provided in a manner that did not comply with a direction or a practice direction; or

(iii) it would otherwise be unfair to admit the evidence.

[(2A) In an asylum case or an immigration case—

(a) if a party wishes the Upper Tribunal to consider evidence that was not before the First-tier Tribunal, that party must send or deliver a notice to the Upper Tribunal and any other party—

(i) indicating the nature of the evidence; and

(ii) explaining why it was not submitted to the First-tier Tribunal; and

(b) when considering whether to admit evidence that was not before the First-tier Tribunal, the Upper Tribunal must have regard to whether there has been unreasonable delay in producing that evidence.]

(3) The Upper Tribunal may consent to a witness giving, or require any witness to give, evidence on oath, and may administer an oath for that purpose.

Note: Paragraph 2A inserted from 15 February 2010 (SI 2010/44).

Summoning or citation of witnesses and orders to answer questions or produce documents

16.—(1) On the application of a party or on its own initiative, the Upper Tribunal may—

(a) by summons (or, in Scotland, citation) require any person to attend as a witness at a hearing at the time and place specified in the summons or citation; or

(b) order any person to answer any questions or produce any documents in that person's possession or control which relate to any issue in the proceedings.

(2) A summons or citation under paragraph (1)(a) must—

(a) give the person required to attend 14 days' notice of the hearing or such shorter period as the Upper Tribunal may direct; and

(b) where the person is not a party, make provision for the person's necessary expenses of attendance to be paid, and state who is to pay them.

(3) No person may be compelled to give any evidence or produce any document that the person could not be compelled to give or produce on a trial of an action in a court of law in the part of the United Kingdom where the proceedings are due to be determined.

[(4) A person who receives a summons, citation or order may apply to the Upper Tribunal for it to be varied or set aside if they did not have an opportunity to object to it before it was made or issued.

(5) A person making an application under paragraph (4) must do so as soon as reasonably practicable after receiving notice of the summons, citation or order.

(6) A summons, citation or order under this rule must—

(a) state that the person on whom the requirement is imposed may apply to the Upper Tribunal to vary or set aside the summons, citation or order, if they did not have an opportunity to object to it before it was made or issued; and

(b) state the consequences of failure to comply with the summons, citation or order.]

Note: Paragraph (4) substituted from 1 April 2009 (SI 2009/274).

Withdrawal

17.—(1) Subject to paragraph (2), a party may give notice of the withdrawal of its case, or any part of it—

(a) . . . by sending or delivering to the Upper Tribunal a written notice of withdrawal; or

(b) orally at a hearing.

(2) Notice of withdrawal will not take effect unless the Upper Tribunal consents to the withdrawal except in relation to an application for permission to appeal.

(3) A party which has withdrawn its case may apply to the Upper Tribunal for the case to be reinstated.

(4) An application under paragraph (3) must be made in writing and be received by the Upper Tribunal within 1 month after—

(a) the date on which the Upper Tribunal received the notice under paragraph (1)(a); or

(b) the date of the hearing at which the case was withdrawn orally under paragraph (1)(b).

(5) The Upper Tribunal must notify each party in writing [that a withdrawal has taken effect] under this rule.

[(6) Paragraph (3) does not apply to a financial services case other than a reference against a penalty.]

Note: Paragraph (6) inserted from 6 April 2010 (SI 2010/747). Words omitted from (1)(a) and substituted in (5) from 1 April 2013 (SI 2013/477).

[Appeal treated as abandoned or finally determined in an asylum case or an immigration case

17A.—(1) A party to an asylum case or an immigration case before the Upper Tribunal must notify the [Upper] Tribunal if they are aware that—

(a) the appellant has left the United Kingdom;

(b) the appellant has been granted leave to enter or remain in the United Kingdom;

(c) a deportation order has been made against the appellant; or

(d) a document listed in paragraph 4(2) of Schedule 2 to the Immigration (European Economic Area) Regulations 2006 has been issued to the appellant.

(2) Where an appeal is treated as abandoned pursuant to section 104(4) or (4A) of the Nationality, Immigration and Asylum Act 2002 or paragraph 4(2) of Schedule 2 to the Immigration (European Economic Area) Regulations 2006, or as finally determined pursuant to section 104(5) of the Nationality, Immigration and Asylum Act 2002, the Upper

Tribunal must send the parties a notice informing them that the appeal is being treated as abandoned or finally determined.

(3) Where an appeal would otherwise fall to be treated as abandoned pursuant to section 104(4A) of the Nationality, Immigration and Asylum Act 2002, but the appellant wishes to pursue their appeal, the appellant must send or deliver a notice, which must comply with any relevant practice directions, to the Upper Tribunal and the respondent so that it is received within thirty days of the date on which the notice of the grant of leave to enter or remain in the United Kingdom was sent to the appellant.

(4) Where a notice of grant of leave to enter or remain is sent electronically or delivered personally, the time limit in paragraph (3) is twenty eight days.

(5) Notwithstanding rule 5(3)(a) (case management powers) and rule 7(2) (failure to comply with rules etc.), the Upper Tribunal must not extend the time limits in paragraph (3) and (4).]

Note: Rule 17A inserted from 15 February 2010 (SI 2010/44). Word inserted in (1) by SI 2013/2067 from 1 November 2013.

Notice of funding of legal services

18. If a party is granted funding of legal services at any time, that party must as soon as practicable—

(a)(i) if [civil legal services (within the meaning of section 8 of the Legal Aid, Sentencing and Punishment of Offenders Act 2012) are provided under arrangements made for the purposes of Part 1 of that Act or by] the Northern Ireland Legal Services Commission, send a copy of the [certificate or] funding notice to the Upper Tribunal; or

(ii) if funding is granted by the Scottish Legal Aid Board, send a copy of the legal aid certificate to the Upper Tribunal; and

(b) notify every other party in writing that funding has been granted.

Note: Words in first square brackets substituted and words in second square brackets inserted by SI 2013/477 from 1 April 2013.

[Confidentiality in social security and child support cases

19.—(1) Paragraph (4) applies to an appeal against a decision of the First-tier Tribunal—

(a) in proceedings under the Child Support Act 1991 in the circumstances described in paragraph (2), other than an appeal against a reduced benefit decision (as defined in section 46(10)(b) of the Child Support Act 1991, as that section had effect prior to the commencement of section 15(b) of the Child Maintenance and Other Payments Act 2008); or

(b) in proceedings where the parties to the appeal include former joint claimants who are no longer living together in the circumstances described in paragraph (3).

(2) The circumstances referred to in paragraph (1)(a) are that—

(a) in the proceedings in the First-tier Tribunal in respect of which the appeal has been brought, there was an obligation to keep a person's address confidential; or

(b) an absent parent, non-resident parent or person with care would like their address or the address of the child to be kept confidential and has given notice to that effect to the Upper Tribunal—

(i) in an application for permission to appeal or notice of appeal;

(ii) within 1 month after an enquiry by the Upper Tribunal; or

(iii) when notifying any subsequent change of address after proceedings have been started.

(3) The circumstances referred to in paragraph (1)(b) are that—

(a) in the proceedings in the First-tier Tribunal in respect of which the appeal has been brought, there was an obligation to keep a person's address confidential; or

(b) one of the former joint claimants would like their address to be kept confidential and has given notice to that effect to the Upper Tribunal—

(i) in an application for permission to appeal or notice of appeal;

(ii) within 1 month after an enquiry by the Upper Tribunal; or

(iii) when notifying any subsequent change of address after proceedings have been started.

(4) Where this paragraph applies, the Secretary of State or other decision maker and the Upper Tribunal must take appropriate steps to secure the confidentiality of the address and of any information which could reasonably be expected to enable a person to identify the address, to the extent that the address or that information is not already known to each other party.

(5) In this rule—

"absent parent", "non-resident parent" and "person with care" have the meanings set out in section 3 of the Child Support Act 1991;

"joint claimants" means the persons who made a joint claim for a jobseeker's allowance under the Jobseekers Act 1995, a tax credit under the Tax Credits Act 2002 or in relation to whom an award of universal credit is made under Part 1 of the Welfare Reform Act 2012.]

Note: Rule 19 substituted by SI 2014/2128 from 20 October 2014.

Power to pay expenses and allowances

20.—(1) In proceedings brought under section 4 of the Safeguarding Vulnerable Groups Act 2006 . . ., the Secretary of State may pay such allowances for the purpose of or in connection with the attendance of persons at hearings as the Secretary of State may, with the consent of the Treasury, determine.

(2) Paragraph (3) applies to proceedings on appeal from a decision of—

(a) the First-tier Tribunal in proceedings under the Child Support Act 1991, section 12 of the Social Security Act 1998 or paragraph 6 of Schedule 7 to the Child Support, Pensions and Social Security Act 2000;

(b) the First-tier Tribunal in a war pensions and armed forces case (as defined in the Tribunal Procedure (First-tier Tribunal) (War Pensions and Armed Forces Compensation Chamber) Rules 2008; or

(c) a Pensions Appeal Tribunal for Scotland or Northern Ireland.

(3) The Lord Chancellor (or, in Scotland, the Secretary of State) may pay to any person who attends any hearing such travelling and other allowances, including compensation for loss of remunerative time, as the Lord Chancellor (or, in Scotland, the Secretary of State) may determine.

Note: Words omitted from paragraph (1) from 1 April 2009 (SI 2009/274).

[Procedure for applying for a stay of a decision pending an appeal

20A.—(1) This rule applies where another enactment provides in any terms for the Upper Tribunal to stay or suspend, or to lift a stay or suspension of, a decision which is or may be the subject of an appeal to the Upper Tribunal ("the substantive decision") pending such appeal.

(2) A person who wishes the Upper Tribunal to decide whether the substantive decision should be stayed or suspended must make a written application to the Upper Tribunal which must include—

(a) the name and address of the person making the application;

(b) the name and address of any representative of that person;

(c) the address to which documents for that person should be sent or delivered;

(d) the name and address of any person who will be a respondent to the appeal;

(e) details of the substantive decision and any decision as to when that decision is to take effect, and copies of any written record of, or reasons for, those decisions; and

(f) the grounds on which the person making the application relies.

(3) In the case of an application under paragraph (2) [in a road transport case]—

(a) the person making the application must notify the [decision maker] when making the application;

(b) within 7 days of receiving notification of the application the [decision maker] must send or deliver written reasons for refusing or withdrawing the stay—

(i) to the Upper Tribunal; and

(ii) to the person making the application, if the [decision maker] has not already done so.

(4) If the Upper Tribunal grants a stay or suspension following an application under this rule—

(a) the Upper Tribunal may give directions as to the conduct of the appeal of the substantive decision; and

(b) the Upper Tribunal may, where appropriate, grant the stay or suspension subject to conditions.

(5) Unless the Upper Tribunal considers that there is good reason not to do so, the Upper Tribunal must send written notice of any decision made under this rule to each party.]

Note: Rule 20A inserted from 1 September 2009 (SI 2009/1975). Paragraph (3) amended from 1 July 2012 (SI 2012/1363).

PART 3

[PROCEDURE FOR CASES IN] THE UPPER TRIBUNAL

Application to the Upper Tribunal for permission to appeal

21.—(1) . . .

(2) A person may apply to the Upper Tribunal for permission to appeal to the Upper Tribunal against a decision of another tribunal only if—

(a) they have made an application for permission to appeal to the tribunal which made the decision challenged; and

(b) that application has been refused or has not been admitted [or has been granted only on limited grounds].

(3) An application for permission to appeal must be made in writing and received by the Upper Tribunal no later than—

(a) in the case of an application under section 4 of the Safeguarding Vulnerable Groups Act 2006, 3 months after the date on which written notice of the decision being challenged was sent to the appellant;

[(aa) . . ., in an asylum case or an immigration case where the appellant is in the United Kingdom at the time that the application is made—

(i) [14] days after the date on which notice of the First-tier Tribunal's refusal of permission was sent to the appellant; or

(ii) if the case is a fast-track case, four working days after the date on which notice of the First-tier Tribunal's refusal of permission was sent to the appellant;

(ab) . . .]

(b) otherwise, a month after the date on which the tribunal that made the decision under challenge sent notice of its refusal of permission to appeal, or refusal to admit the application for permission to appeal, to the appellant.

[(3A) . . .

(4) The application must state—

(a) the name and address of the appellant;

(b) the name and address of the representative (if any) of the appellant;

(c) an address where documents for the appellant may be sent or delivered;

(d) details (including the full reference) of the decision challenged;

(e) the grounds on which the appellant relies; and

(f) whether the appellant wants the application to be dealt with at a hearing.

(5) The appellant must provide with the application a copy of—

(a) any written record of the decision being challenged;

(b) any separate written statement of reasons for that decision; and

(c) if the application is for permission to appeal against a decision of another tribunal, the notice of refusal of permission to appeal, or notice of refusal to admit the application for permission to appeal, from that other tribunal.

(6) If the appellant provides the application to the Upper Tribunal later than the time required by paragraph (3) or by an extension of time allowed under rule 5(3)(a) (power to extend time)—

(a) the application must include a request for an extension of time and the reason why the application was not provided in time; and

(b) unless the Upper Tribunal extends time for the application under rule 5(3)(a) (power to extend time) the Upper Tribunal must not admit the application.

(7) If the appellant makes an application to the Upper Tribunal for permission to appeal against the decision of another tribunal, and that other tribunal refused to admit the appellant's application for permission to appeal because the application for permission or for a written statement of reasons was not made in time—

(a) the application to the Upper Tribunal for permission to appeal must include the reason why the application to the other tribunal for permission to appeal or for a written statement of reasons, as the case may be, was not made in time; and

(b) the Upper Tribunal must only admit the application if the Upper Tribunal considers that it is in the interests of justice for it to do so.

[(8) In this rule, a reference to notice of a refusal of permission to appeal is to be taken to include a reference to notice of a grant of permission to appeal on limited grounds.]

Note: Paragraph (1) omitted from 1 September 2009 (SI 2009/1975). Paragraphs (3)(aa)–(ab) and (3A) inserted from 15 February 2010 (SI 2010/44). Paragraph (8) and words in para (2)(b) inserted from 6 April 2014 (SI 2014/514). Words omitted from (3)(aa), number substituted in (3)(aa)(i), paragraphs 3(ab) and (3A) omitted by SI 2014/2128 from 20 October 2014.

Decision in relation to permission to appeal

22.—(1) [Except where rule 22A (special procedure for providing notice of a refusal of permission to appeal in an asylum case) applies], if the Upper Tribunal refuses permission to appeal [or refuses to admit a late application for permission], it must send written notice of the refusal and of the reasons for the refusal to the appellant.

(2) If the Upper Tribunal gives permission to appeal—

(a) the Upper Tribunal must send written notice of the permission, and of the reasons for any limitations or conditions on such permission, to each party;

(b) subject to any direction by the Upper Tribunal, the application for permission to appeal stands as the notice of appeal and the Upper Tribunal must send to each respondent a copy of the application for permission to appeal and any documents provided with it by the appellant; and

(c) the Upper Tribunal may, with the consent of the appellant and each respondent, determine the appeal without obtaining any further response.

[(3) Paragraph (4) applies where the Upper Tribunal, without a hearing, determines an application for permission to appeal—

(a) against a decision of—

(i) the Tax Chamber of the First-tier Tribunal;

(ii) the Health, Education and Social Care Chamber of the First-tier Tribunal;

[(iia) the General Regulatory Chamber of the First-tier Tribunal;]

[(iib) the Property Chamber of the First-tier Tribunal;]

(iii) the Mental Health Review Tribunal for Wales; or

(iv) the Special Educational Needs Tribunal for Wales; or

(b) under section 4 of the Safeguarding Vulnerable Groups Act 2006.]

(4) In the circumstances set out at paragraph (3) the appellant may apply for the decision to be reconsidered at a hearing if the Upper Tribunal—

(a) refuses permission to appeal [or refuses to admit a late application for permission];

(b) gives permission to appeal on limited grounds or subject to conditions.

(5) An application under paragraph (4) must be made in writing and received by the Upper Tribunal within 14 days after the date on which the Upper Tribunal sent written notice of its decision regarding the application to the appellant.

Note: Paragraph (3) substituted from 1 April 2009 (SI 2009/274). Paragraph (3)(a)(ii) inserted from 1 September 2009 (SI 2009/1975). Words in first square brackets in paragraph (1) substituted by SI 2128 from 20 October 2014. Paragraph (3)(iib) and words in other square brackets in (1) and (4)(a) inserted from 6 April 2014 (2014/514).

[Special procedure for providing notice of a refusal of permission to appeal in an asylum case

22A.—(1) This rule applies to a decision in an asylum case to refuse permission to appeal

or to refuse to admit a late application for permission to appeal, where—

(a) the appellant is not the Secretary of State;

(b) at the time the application is made the appellant is in the United Kingdom; and

(c) the decision is not made in a fast-track case.

(2) The Upper Tribunal must provide written notice of the refusal and of the reasons for the refusal ("the notice") to the Secretary of State as soon as reasonably practicable.

(3) The Secretary of State must—

(a) send the notice to the appellant not later than 30 days after the Upper Tribunal provided it to the Secretary of State; and

(b) as soon as practicable after doing so, inform the Upper Tribunal of the date on which, and the means by which, it was sent.

(4) If the Secretary of State does not give the Upper Tribunal the information required by paragraph (3)(b) within 31 days after the notice was provided to the Secretary of State, the Upper Tribunal must send the notice to the appellant as soon as reasonably practicable.]

Note: Rule 22A inserted by SI 2014/2128 from 20 October 2014.

Notice of appeal

23.—[(1) This rule applies—

(a) to proceedings on appeal to the Upper Tribunal for which permission to appeal is not required, except proceedings to which rule 26A [or (26B)] applies;

(b) if another tribunal has given permission for a party to appeal to the Upper Tribunal; or

(c) subject to any other direction by the Upper Tribunal, if the Upper Tribunal has given permission to appeal and has given a direction that the application for permission to appeal does not stand as the notice of appeal.

[(1A) In an asylum case or an immigration case in which the First-tier Tribunal has given permission to appeal, subject to any direction of the First-tier Tribunal or the Upper Tribunal, the application for permission to appeal sent or delivered to the First-tier Tribunal stands as the notice of appeal and accordingly paragraphs (2) to (6) of this rule do not apply.]

(2) The appellant must provide a notice of appeal to the Upper Tribunal so that it is received within 1 month after—

(a) the date that the tribunal that gave permission to appeal sent notice of such permission to the appellant; or

(b) if permission to appeal is not required, the date on which notice of decision to which the appeal relates was sent to the appellant.]

(3) The notice of appeal must include the information listed in rule 21(4)(a) to (e) (content of the application for permission to appeal) and, where the Upper Tribunal has given permission to appeal, the Upper Tribunal's case reference.

(4) If another tribunal has granted permission to appeal, the appellant must provide with the notice of appeal a copy of—

(a) any written record of the decision being challenged;

(b) any separate written statement of reasons for that decision; and

(c) the notice of permission to appeal.

(5) If the appellant provides the notice of appeal to the Upper Tribunal later than the time required by paragraph (2) or by an extension of time allowed under rule 5(3)(a) (power to extend time)—

(a) the notice of appeal must include a request for an extension of time and the reason why the notice was not provided in time; and

(b) unless the Upper Tribunal extends time for the notice of appeal under rule 5(3)(a) (power to extend time) the Upper Tribunal must not admit the notice of appeal.

[(6) When the Upper Tribunal receives the notice of appeal it must send a copy of the notice and any accompanying documents—

(a) to each respondent; or

[(b) in a road transport case, to—

(i) the decision maker;

(ii) the appropriate national authority; and

(iii) in a case relating to the detention of a vehicle, the authorised person.]

Note: Paragraphs (1), (2) and (6) substituted from 1 September 2009 (SI 2009/1975). Paragraph (1A) inserted from 15 February 2010 (SI 2010/44). Number in square brackets in paragraph (1)(a) inserted from 6 April 2010 (SI 2010/747). Paragraph 6(b) substituted from 1 July 2012 (SI 2012/1363).

Response to the notice of appeal

24.—[(1) This rule and rule 25 do not apply to {a road transport case}, in respect of which Schedule 1 makes alternative provision.

(1A) Subject to any direction given by the Upper Tribunal, a respondent may provide a response to a notice of appeal.]

(2) Any response provided under paragraph [(1A)] must be in writing and must be sent or delivered to the Upper Tribunal so that it is received—

[(a) if an application for permission to appeal stands as the notice of appeal, no later than one month after the date on which the respondent was sent notice that permission to appeal had been granted;]

[(aa) in a fast-track case, [two days] before the hearing of the appeal; or].

(b) in any other case, no later than 1 month after the date on which the Upper Tribunal sent a copy of the notice of appeal to the respondent.

(3) The response must state—

(a) the name and address of the respondent;

(b) the name and address of the representative (if any) of the respondent;

(c) an address where documents for the respondent may be sent or delivered;

(d) whether the respondent opposes the appeal;

(e) the grounds on which the respondent relies, including [(in the case of an appeal against the decision of another tribunal)], any grounds on which the respondent was unsuccessful in the proceedings which are the subject of the appeal, but intends to rely in the appeal; and

(f) whether the respondent wants the case to be dealt with at a hearing.

(4) If the respondent provides the response to the Upper Tribunal later than the time required by paragraph (2) or by an extension of time allowed under rule 5(3)(a) (power to extend time), the response must include a request for an extension of time and the reason why the [response] was not provided in time.

(5) When the Upper Tribunal receives the response it must send a copy of the response and any accompanying documents to the appellant and each other party.

Note: Paragraph (1) substituted and words in square brackets in paragraph (3)(e) substituted from 1 September 2009 (SI 2009/1975). Words in curly brackets in paragraph 1 substituted from 1 July 2012 (SI 2012/1363). Paragraph (2)(a) substituted and (2)(aa) inserted from 15 February 2010 (SI 2010/44). Word in square bracket in paragraph (4) substituted from 1 April 2009 (SI 2009/274). Words in square brackets in paragraph (2)(aa) substituted from 20 October 2014 (SI 2014/2128).

Appellant's reply

25.—(1) Subject to any direction given by the Upper Tribunal, the appellant may provide a reply to any response provided under rule 24 (response to the notice of appeal).

(2) [Subject to paragraph (2A), any] reply provided under paragraph (1) must be in writing and must be sent or delivered to the Upper Tribunal so that it is received within one month after the date on which the Upper Tribunal sent a copy of the response to the appellant.

[(2A) In an asylum case or an immigration case, the time limit in paragraph (2) is—

(a) one month after the date on which the Upper Tribunal sent a copy of the response to the appellant, or five days before the hearing of the appeal, whichever is the earlier; and

(b) in a fast-track case, the day of the hearing.]

(3) When the Upper Tribunal receives the reply it must send a copy of the reply and any accompanying documents to each respondent.

Note: Words in square brackets in paragraph (2) substituted and (2A) inserted from 15 February 2010 (SI 2010/44).

References under the Forfeiture Act 1982

26.—(1) If a question arises which is required to be determined by the Upper Tribunal under section 4 of the Forfeiture Act 1982, the person to whom the application for the relevant benefit or advantage has been made must refer the question to the Upper Tribunal.

(2) The reference must be in writing and must include—

(a) a statement of the question for determination;

(b) a statement of the relevant facts;

(c) the grounds upon which the reference is made; and

(d) an address for sending documents to the person making the reference and each respondent.

(3) When the Upper Tribunal receives the reference it must send a copy of the reference and any accompanying documents to each respondent.

(4) Rules 24 (response to the notice of appeal) and 25 (appellant's reply) apply to a reference made under this rule as if it were a notice of appeal.

[Cases transferred or referred to the Upper Tribunal, applications made directly to the Upper Tribunal and proceedings without notice to a respondent

26A.—[(1) Paragraphs (2) and (3) apply to—

(a) a case transferred or referred to the Upper Tribunal from the First-tier Tribunal; or

(b) a case, other than an appeal or a case to which rule 26 (references under the Forfeiture Act 1982) applies, which is started by an application made directly to the Upper Tribunal.]

(2) In a case to which this paragraph applies—

(a) the Upper Tribunal must give directions as to the procedure to be followed in the consideration and disposal of the proceedings;

[(aa) in a reference under Schedule 1D of the Charities Act 1993, the Upper Tribunal may give directions providing for an application to join the proceedings as a party and the time within which it may be made; and]

(b) the preceding rules in this Part will only apply to the proceedings to the extent provided for by such directions.

(3) If a case or matter to which this paragraph applies is to be determined without notice to or the involvement of a respondent—

(a) any provision in these Rules requiring a document to be provided by or to a respondent; and

(b) any other provision in these Rules permitting a respondent to participate in the proceedings

does not apply to that case or matter.]

[(4) Schedule 2 makes further provision for national security certificate appeals transferred to the Upper Tribunal.]

Note: Rule 26A inserted from 1 April 2009 (SI 2009/274). Paragraph (1) substituted from 1 September 2009 (SI 2009/1975). Paragraph (4) inserted from 18 January 2010 (SI 2010/43). Subparagraph (2) (aa) inserted from 6 April 2012 (SI 2012/500).

[Financial services cases [and wholesale energy cases]

26B. Schedule 3 makes provision for financial services cases [and wholesale energy cases].]

Note: Rule 26B inserted from 6 April 2010 (SI 2010/747). Words inserted from 6 April 2014 (SI 2014/514).

PART 4

JUDICIAL REVIEW PROCEEDINGS IN THE UPPER TRIBUNAL

Application of this Part to judicial review proceedings transferred to the Upper Tribunal

27.—(1) When a court transfers judicial review proceedings to the Upper Tribunal, the Upper Tribunal—

(a) must notify each party in writing that the proceedings have been transferred to the Upper Tribunal; and

(b) must give directions as to the future conduct of the proceedings.

(2) The directions given under paragraph (1)(b) may modify or disapply for the purposes of the proceedings any of the provisions of the following rules in this Part.

(3) In proceedings transferred from the Court of Session under section 20(1) of the 2007 Act, the directions given under paragraph (1)(b) must—

(a) if the Court of Session did not make a first order specifying the required intimation, service and advertisement of the petition, state the Upper Tribunal's requirements in relation to those matters;

(b) state whether the Upper Tribunal will consider summary dismissal of the proceedings; and

(c) where necessary, modify or disapply provisions relating to permission in the following rules in this Part.

Applications for permission to bring judicial review proceedings

28.—(1) A person seeking permission to bring judicial review proceedings before the Upper Tribunal under section 16 of the 2007 Act must make a written application to the Upper Tribunal for such permission.

(2) Subject to paragraph (3), an application under paragraph (1) must be made promptly and, unless any other enactment specifies a shorter time limit, must be sent or delivered to the Upper Tribunal so that it is received no later than 3 months after the date of the decision[, action or omission] to which the application relates.

(3) An application for permission to bring judicial review proceedings challenging a decision of the First-tier Tribunal may be made later than the time required by paragraph (2) if it is made within 1 month after the date on which the First-tier Tribunal sent—

(a) written reasons for the decision; or

(b) notification that an application for the decision to be set aside has been unsuccessful, provided that that application was made in time.

(4) The application must state—

(a) the name and address of the applicant, the respondent and any other person whom the applicant considers to be an interested party;

(b) the name and address of the applicant's representative (if any);

(c) an address where documents for the applicant may be sent or delivered;

(d) details of the decision challenged (including the date, the full reference and the identity of the decision maker);

(e) that the application is for permission to bring judicial review proceedings;

(f) the outcome that the applicant is seeking; and

(g) the facts and grounds on which the applicant relies.

(5) If the application relates to proceedings in a court or tribunal, the application must name as an interested party each party to those proceedings who is not the applicant or a respondent.

(6) The applicant must send with the application—

(a) a copy of any written record of the decision in the applicant's possession or control; and

(b) copies of any other documents in the applicant's possession or control on which the applicant intends to rely.

(7) If the applicant provides the application to the Upper Tribunal later than the time required by paragraph (2) or (3) or by an extension of time allowed under rule 5(3)(a) (power to extend time)—

(a) the application must include a request for an extension of time and the reason why the application was not provided in time; and

(b) unless the Upper Tribunal extends time for the application under rule 5(3)(a) (power to extend time) the Upper Tribunal must not admit the application.

(8) [Except where rule 28A(2)(a) (special provisions for [immigration judicial review] proceedings) applies,] when the Upper Tribunal receives the application it must send a copy of the application and any accompanying documents to each person named in the application as a respondent or interested party.

Note: Words in square brackets in paragraph (2) inserted from 1 April 2009 (SI 2009/274). Words inserted in paragraph (8) from 17 October 2011 (SI 2011/2343). Words in second square brackets in paragraph (8) substituted from 1 November 2013 (2013/2067).

[Special provisions for [immigration judicial review] proceedings

28A.—(1) The Upper Tribunal must not accept an application for permission to bring [immigration judicial review] proceedings unless it is either accompanied by any required fee or the Upper Tribunal accepts an undertaking that the fee will be paid.

(2) Within 9 days of making an application referred to in paragraph (1), an applicant must provide—

(a) a copy of the application and any accompanying documents to each person named in the application as a respondent or an interested party; and

(b) the Upper Tribunal with a written statement of when and how this was done.]

Note: Rule 28A inserted from 17 October 2011 (SI 2011/2343). Words in square brackets substituted from 1 November 2013 (2013/2067).

Acknowledgment of service

29.—(1) A person who is sent [or provided with] a copy of an application for permission under rule 28(8) (application for permission to bring judicial review proceedings) [or rule 28A(2)(a) (special provisions for {immigration judicial review} proceedings)] and wishes to take part in the proceedings must [provide] to the Upper Tribunal an acknowledgment of service so that it is received no later than 21 days after the date on which the Upper Tribunal sent, [or in {immigration judicial review} proceedings the applicant provided,] a copy of the application to that person.

(2) An acknowledgment of service under paragraph (1) must be in writing and state—

(a) whether the person intends to [support or] oppose the application for permission;

(b) their grounds for any [support or] opposition under sub-paragraph (a), or any other submission or information which they consider may assist the Upper Tribunal; and

(c) the name and address of any other person not named in the application as a respondent or interested party whom the person providing the acknowledgment considers to be an interested party.

[(2A) In {immigration judicial review} proceedings, a person who provides an acknowledgement of service under paragraph (1) must also provide a copy to—

(a) the applicant; and

(b) any other person named in the application under rule 28(4)(a) or acknowledgement of service under paragraph (2)(c) no later than the time specified in paragraph (1).]

(3) A person who is {provided with} a copy of an application for permission under rule 28(8) [or 28A(2)(a)] but does not provide an acknowledgment of service [to the Upper Tribunal] may not take part in the application for permission {unless allowed to do so by the Upper Tribunal}, but may take part in the subsequent proceedings if the application is successful.

Note: Word in square brackets in paragraph (2) inserted from 1 April 2009 (SI 2009/274). Words in curly brackets in paragraph (3) inserted from 1 April 2011 (SI 2011/651). Words inserted/substituted in paragraph (1), paragraph (2A) inserted and words in square brackets in paragraph (3) inserted/substituted from 17 October 2011 (SI 2011 2343). Words in curly brackets in (1) and (2A) substituted from 1 November 2013 (SI 2013/2067).

Decision on permission or summary dismissal, and reconsideration of permission or summary dismissal at a hearing

30.—(1) The Upper Tribunal must send to the applicant, each respondent and any other person who provided an acknowledgment of service to the Upper Tribunal, and may send to any other person who may have an interest in the proceedings, written notice of—

(a) its decision in relation to the application for permission; and

[(b) the reasons for any—

(i) refusal of the application or refusal to admit the late application, or

(ii) limitations or conditions on permission.]

(2) In proceedings transferred from the Court of Session under section 20(1) of the 2007 Act, where the Upper Tribunal has considered whether summarily to dismiss of the proceedings, the Upper Tribunal must send to the applicant and each respondent, and may send to any other person who may have an interest in the proceedings, written notice of—

(a) its decision in relation to the summary dismissal of proceedings; and

(b) the reasons for any decision summarily to dismiss part or all of the proceedings, or any limitations or conditions on the continuation of such proceedings.

(3) Paragraph (4) applies where the Upper Tribunal, without a hearing—

[(a) determines an application for permission to bring judicial review proceedings by—

(i) refusing permission or refusing to admit the late application, or

(ii) giving permission on limited grounds or subject to conditions;] or

(b) in proceedings transferred from the Court of Session, summarily dismisses part or all of the proceedings, or imposes any limitations or conditions on the continuation of such proceedings.

(4) [Subject to paragraph (4A), in] the circumstances specified in paragraph (3) the applicant may apply for the decision to be reconsidered at a hearing.

[(4A) Where the Upper Tribunal refuses permission to bring immigration judicial review proceedings [or refuses to admit a late application for permission to bring such proceedings] and considers the application to be totally without merit, it shall record that fact in its decision notice and, in those circumstances, the applicant may not request the decision to be reconsidered at a hearing.]

(5) An application under paragraph (4) must be made in writing and must be sent or delivered to the Upper Tribunal so that it is received within 14 days, [or in [immigration judicial review] proceedings 9 days,] after the date on which the Upper Tribunal sent written notice of its decision regarding the application to the applicant.

Note: Words inserted in paragraph (5) from 17 October 2011 (SI 2011/2343). Paragraph (4A) inserted and words in square brackets in (4) and second square brackets in (5) substituted from 1 November 2013 (SI 2013/2067). Paragraphs (1)(b) and 3(a) substituted and words in square brackets in (4A) inserted from 6 April 2014 (SI 2014/514).

Responses

31.—(1) Any person to whom the Upper Tribunal has sent notice of the grant of permission under rule 30(1) (notification of decision on permission), and who wishes to contest the application or support it on additional grounds, must provide detailed grounds for contesting or supporting the application to the Upper Tribunal.

(2) Any detailed grounds must be provided in writing and must be sent or delivered to the Upper Tribunal so that they are received not more than 35 days after the Upper Tribunal sent notice of the grant of permission under rule 30(1).

Applicant seeking to rely on additional grounds

32. The applicant may not rely on any grounds, other than those grounds on which the applicant obtained permission for the judicial review proceedings, without the consent of the Upper Tribunal.

Right to make representations

33. Each party and, with the permission of the Upper Tribunal, any other person, may—

(a) submit evidence, except at the hearing of an application for permission;

(b) make representations at any hearing which they are entitled to attend; and

(c) make written representations in relation to a decision to be made without a hearing.

[Amendments and additional grounds resulting in transfer of proceedings to the High Court in England and Wales

33A.—(1) This rule applies only to judicial review proceedings arising under the law of England and Wales.

(2) In relation to such proceedings—

(a) the powers of the Upper Tribunal to permit or require amendments under rule 5(3)(c) extend to amendments which would, once in place, give rise to an obligation or power to transfer the proceedings to the High Court in England and Wales under section 18(3) of the 2007 Act or paragraph (3);

(b) except with the permission of the Upper Tribunal, additional grounds may not be advanced, whether by an applicant or otherwise, if they would give rise to an obligation or power to transfer the proceedings to the High Court in England and Wales under section 18(3) of the 2007 Act or paragraph (3).

(3) Where the High Court in England and Wales has transferred judicial review proceedings to the Upper Tribunal under any power or duty and subsequently the proceedings are amended or any party advances additional grounds—

(a) if the proceedings in their present form could not have been transferred to the Upper Tribunal under the relevant power or duty had they been in that form at the time of the transfer, the Upper Tribunal must transfer the proceedings back to the High Court in England and Wales;

(b) subject to sub-paragraph, where the proceedings were transferred to the Upper Tribunal under section 31A(3) of the Senior Courts Act 1981 (power to transfer judicial review proceedings to the Upper Tribunal), the Upper Tribunal may transfer proceedings back to the High Court in England and Wales if it appears just and convenient to do so.]

Note: Rule 33A inserted from 17 October 2011 (SI 2011/2343).

Part 5

Hearings

Decision with or without a hearing

34.—(1) Subject to [paragraphs (2) and (3)], the Upper Tribunal may make any decision without a hearing.

(2) The Upper Tribunal must have regard to any view expressed by a party when deciding whether to hold a hearing to consider any matter, and the form of any such hearing.

[(3) In immigration judicial review proceedings, the Upper Tribunal must hold a hearing before making a decision which disposes of proceedings.

(4) Paragraph (3) does not affect the power of the Upper Tribunal to—

(a) strike out a party's case, pursuant to rule 8(1)(b) or 8(2);

(b) consent to withdrawal, pursuant to rule 17;

(c) determine an application for permission to bring judicial review proceedings, pursuant to rule 30; or

(d) make a consent order disposing of proceedings, pursuant to rule 39, without a hearing.]

Note: Words substituted in (1) and paragraphs (3)-(4) inserted from 1 November 2013 (SI 2013/2067).

Entitlement to attend a hearing

35.—[(1)] Subject to rule 37(4) (exclusion of a person from a hearing), each party is entitled to attend a hearing.

[(2) In a national security certificate appeal the relevant Minister is entitled to attend any hearing.]

Note: Paragraph (2) inserted from 18 January 2010 (SI 2010/43).

Notice of hearings

36.—(1) The Upper Tribunal must give each party entitled to attend a hearing reasonable notice of the time and place of the hearing (including any adjourned or postponed hearing) and any change to the time and place of the hearing.

(2) The period of notice under paragraph (1) must be at least 14 days except that—

(a) in applications for permission to bring judicial review proceedings, the period of notice must be at least 2 working days;

[(aa) in a fast-track case the period of notice must be at least one working day; and]

(b) [in any case other than a fast-track case] the Upper Tribunal may give shorter notice—

(i) with the parties' consent; or

(ii) in urgent or exceptional cases.

Note: Words in square brackets inserted from 15 February 2010 (SI 2010/44).

[Special time limits for hearing an appeal in a fast-track case

36A.—(1) Subject to rule 36(2)(aa) (notice of hearings) and paragraph (2) of this rule, where permission to appeal to the Upper Tribunal has been given in a fast-track case, the Upper Tribunal must start the hearing of the appeal not later than—

(a) [five] working days after the date on which the First-tier Tribunal or the Upper Tribunal sent notice of its grant of permission to appeal to the appellant; or

(b) where the notice of its grant of permission to appeal is sent electronically or delivered personally, two working days after the date on which the First-tier Tribunal or the Upper Tribunal sent notice of its grant of permission to appeal to the appellant.

(2) If the Upper Tribunal is unable to arrange for the hearing to start within the time specified in paragraph (1), it must set a date for the hearing as soon as is reasonably practicable.]

Note: Rule 36A inserted from 15 February 2010 (SI 2010/44). Word in square brackets in paragraph (1)(a) substituted from 20 October 2014 (SI 2014/2128).

Public and private hearings

37.—(1) Subject to the following paragraphs, all hearings must be held in public.

(2) The Upper Tribunal may give a direction that a hearing, or part of it, is to be held in private.

[(2A) In a national security certificate appeal, the Upper Tribunal must have regard to its duty under rule 14(10) (no disclosure of information contrary to the interests of national security) when considering whether to give a direction that a hearing, or part of it, is to be held in private.]

(3) Where a hearing, or part of it, is to be held in private, the Upper Tribunal may determine who is entitled to attend the hearing or part of it.

(4) The Upper Tribunal may give a direction excluding from any hearing, or part of it—

(a) any person whose conduct the Upper Tribunal considers is disrupting or is likely to disrupt the hearing;

(b) any person whose presence the Upper Tribunal considers is likely to prevent another person from giving evidence or making submissions freely;

(c) any person who the Upper Tribunal considers should be excluded in order to give effect to [the requirement at rule 14(11) (prevention of disclosure or publication of documents and information)];

(d) any person where the purpose of the hearing would be defeated by the attendance of that person [; or

(e) a person under [18, other than a young person who is a party in a special educational needs case or a disability discrimination in schools case]].

(5) The Upper Tribunal may give a direction excluding a witness from a hearing until that witness gives evidence.

Note: Paragraph (2A) inserted from 18 January 2010 (SI 2010/43). Words in square brackets in paragraph (4)(c) substituted from 1 September 2009 (SI 2009/1975). Paragraph (4)(e) inserted from 1 April 2009 (SI 2009/274). Words in square brackets in para(4)(e) substituted from 1 September 2014 (SI 2014/2128).

Hearings in a party's absence

38. If a party fails to attend a hearing, the Upper Tribunal may proceed with the hearing if the Upper Tribunal—

(a) is satisfied that the party has been notified of the hearing or that reasonable steps have been taken to notify the party of the hearing; and

(b) considers that it is in the interests of justice to proceed with the hearing.

PART 6
DECISIONS

Consent orders

39.—(1) The Upper Tribunal may, at the request of the parties but only if it considers it appropriate, make a consent order disposing of the proceedings and making such other appropriate provision as the parties have agreed.

(2) Notwithstanding any other provision of these Rules, the [Upper] Tribunal need not hold a hearing before making an order under paragraph (1). . .

Note: Words omitted from paragraph (2) from 1 April 2009 (SI 2009/274). Word inserted in (2) from 1 November 2013 (2013/2067).

Decisions

40.—(1) The Upper Tribunal may give a decision orally at a hearing.

[(**1A**) Subject to paragraph (1B), in immigration judicial review proceedings, a decision which disposes of proceedings shall be given at a hearing.

(**1B**) Paragraph (1A) does not affect the power of the Upper Tribunal to—

(a) strike out a party's case, pursuant to rule 8(1)(b) or 8(2);

(b) consent to withdrawal, pursuant to rule 17;

(c) determine an application for permission to bring judicial review proceedings, pursuant to rule 30; or

(d) make a consent order disposing of proceedings, pursuant to rule 39, without a hearing.]

(2) [Except where [rule 22 (decision in relation to permission to appeal) or rule 22A (special procedure for providing notice of a refusal of permission to appeal in an asylum case)] applies,] the Upper Tribunal must provide to each party as soon as reasonably practicable after making [a decision (other than a decision under Part 7) which finally disposes of all issues in the proceedings or of a preliminary issue dealt with following a direction under rule 5(3)(e)]

(a) a decision notice stating the [Upper] Tribunal's decision; and

(b) notification of any rights of review or appeal against the decision and the time and manner in which such rights of review or appeal may be exercised.

(3) [Subject to rule [14(11) (prevention of disclosure or publication of documents and information)] the Upper Tribunal must provide written reasons for its decision with a decision notice provided under paragraph (2)(a) unless—

(a) the decision was made with the consent of the parties; or

(b) the parties have consented to the Upper Tribunal not giving written reasons.

(4) The [Upper] Tribunal may provide written reasons for any decision to which paragraph (2) does not apply.

[(5) In a national security certificate appeal, when the Upper Tribunal provides a notice or reasons to the parties under this rule, it must also provide the notice or reasons to the relevant Minister and the Information Commissioner, if they are not parties.]

Note: Words in square brackets in paragraphs (3) substituted and in (4) inserted from 1 September 2009 (SI 2009/1975). Paragraph (5) inserted from 18 January 2010 (SI 2010/43). Paragraphs (1A)–(1B) inserted from 1 November 2013 (2013/2067). Words in first and third square brackets in (2) substituted and word in second square brackets in (2)(a) inserted from 1 April 2013 (2013/477). Words in second square brackets in paragraph (2) substituted from 20 October 2014 (SI 2014/2128).

[Special procedure for providing notice of a decision relating to an asylum case

40A

Note: Rule 40A inserted from 15 February 2010 (SI 2010/44), and omitted from 20 October 2014 (SI 2014/2128).

PART 7

CORRECTING, SETTING ASIDE, REVIEWING AND APPEALING DECISIONS OF THE UPPER TRIBUNAL

Interpretation

41. In this Part—

"appeal" [, except in rule 44(2) (application for permission to appeal),] means the exercise of a right of appeal under section 13 of the 2007 Act; and

"review" means the review of a decision by the Upper Tribunal under section 10 of the 2007 Act.

Note: Words in square brackets inserted from 1 April 2009 (SI 2009/274).

Clerical mistakes and accidental slips or omissions

42. The Upper Tribunal may at any time correct any clerical mistake or other accidental slip or omission in a decision or record of a decision by—

(a) sending notification of the amended decision, or a copy of the amended record, to all parties; and

(b) making any necessary amendment to any information published in relation to the decision or record.

Setting aside a decision which disposes of proceedings

43.—(1) The Upper Tribunal may set aside a decision which disposes of proceedings, or part of such a decision, and re-make the decision or the relevant part of it, if—

(a) the Upper Tribunal considers that it is in the interests of justice to do so; and

(b) one or more of the conditions in paragraph (2) are satisfied.

(2) The conditions are—

(a) a document relating to the proceedings was not sent to, or was not received at an appropriate time by, a party or a party's representative;

(b) a document relating to the proceedings was not sent to the Upper Tribunal at an appropriate time;

(c) a party, or a party's representative, was not present at a hearing related to the proceedings; or

(d) there has been some other procedural irregularity in the proceedings.

(3) [Except where paragraph (4) applies,] a party applying for a decision, or part of a decision, to be set aside under paragraph (1) must make a written application to the Upper Tribunal so that it is received no later than 1 month after the date on which the [Upper] Tribunal sent notice of the decision to the party.

[(4) In an asylum case or an immigration case, the written application referred to in paragraph (3) must be sent or delivered so that it is received by the Upper Tribunal—

(a) where the person who appealed to the First-tier Tribunal is in the United Kingdom at the time that the application is made, no later than twelve days after the date on which the Upper Tribunal or, as the case may be in an asylum case, the Secretary of State for the Home Department, sent notice of the decision to the party making the application; or

(b) where the person who appealed to the First-tier Tribunal is outside the United Kingdom at the time that the application is made, no later than thirty eight days after the date on which the Upper Tribunal sent notice of the decision to the party making the application.

(5) Where a notice of decision is sent electronically or delivered personally, the time limits in paragraph (4) are ten working days.].

Note: Paragraph (4) and words in square brackets in paragraph (3) inserted from 15 February 2010 (SI 2010/44). Word in second square brackets in (3) inserted from 1 November 2013 (2013/2067).

Application for permission to appeal

44.—(1) [Subject to [paragraphs (4A) and (4B)] a person seeking permission to appeal must make a written application to the Upper Tribunal for permission to appeal.

(2) Paragraph (3) applies to an application under paragraph (1) in respect of a decision—

(a) on an appeal against a decision in a social security and child support case (as defined in the Tribunal Procedure (First-tier Tribunal) (Social Entitlement Chamber) Rules 2008);

(b) on an appeal against a decision in proceedings in the War Pensions and Armed Forces Compensation Chamber of the First-tier Tribunal;

[(ba) on an appeal against a decision of a Pensions Appeal Tribunal for Scotland or Northern Ireland; or]

(c) in proceedings under the Forfeiture Act 1982.

(3) Where this paragraph applies, the application must be sent or delivered to the Upper Tribunal so that it is received within 3 months after the date on which the Upper Tribunal sent to the person making the application—

(a) written notice of the decision;

(b) notification of amended reasons for, or correction of, the decision following a review; or

(c) notification that an application for the decision to be set aside has been unsuccessful.

[(**3A**) An application under paragraph (1) in respect of a decision in an asylum case or an immigration case must be sent or delivered to the Upper Tribunal so that it is received within the appropriate period after the Upper Tribunal or, as the case may be in an asylum case, the Secretary of State for the Home Department, sent any of the documents in paragraph (3) to the party making the application.

(**3B**) The appropriate period referred to in paragraph (3A) is as follows—

(a) where the person who appealed to the First-tier Tribunal is in the United Kingdom at the time that the application is made—

(i) [twelve working days]; or

(ii) if the party making the application is in detention under the Immigration Acts, seven working days; and

(b) where the person who appealed to the First-tier Tribunal is outside the United Kingdom at the time that the application is made, thirty-eight days.

(**3C**) Where a notice of decision is sent electronically or delivered personally, the time limits in paragraph (3B) are—

(a) in sub-paragraph (a)(i), ten working days;

(b) in sub-paragraph (a)(ii), five working days; and

(c) in sub-paragraph (b), ten working days.]

[(**3D**) An application under paragraph (1) in respect of a decision in a financial services case must be sent or delivered to the Upper Tribunal so that it is received within 14 days after the date on which the Upper Tribunal sent to the person making the application—

(a) written notice of the decision;

(b) notification of amended reasons for, or correction of, the decision following a review; or

(c) notification that an application for the decision to be set aside has been unsuccessful.]

(**4**) Where paragraph (3)[, (3A)[, (3D) or (4C)] does not apply, an application under paragraph (1) must be sent or delivered to the Upper Tribunal so that it is received within 1 month after the latest of the dates on which the Upper Tribunal sent to the person making the application—

(a) written reasons for the decision;

(b) notification of amended reasons for, or correction of, the decision following a review; or

(c) notification that an application for the decision to be set aside has been unsuccessful.

[(**4A**) Where a decision that disposes of immigration judicial review proceedings is given at a hearing, a party may apply at that hearing for permission to appeal, and the Upper Tribunal must consider at the hearing whether to give or refuse permission to appeal.

(**4B**) Where a decision that disposes of immigration judicial review proceedings is given at a hearing and no application for permission to appeal is made at that hearing—

(a) the Upper Tribunal must nonetheless consider at the hearing whether to give or refuse permission to appeal; and

(b) if permission to appeal is given to a party, it shall be deemed for the purposes of section 13(4) of the 2007 Act to be given on application by that party.

(4C) Where a decision that disposes of immigration judicial review proceedings is given pursuant to rule 30 and the Upper Tribunal records under rule 30(4A) that the application is totally without merit, an application under paragraph (1) must be sent or delivered to the Upper Tribunal so that it is received within 7 days after the later of the dates on which the Upper Tribunal sent to the applicant—

(a) written reasons for the decision; or

(b) notification of amended reasons for, or correction of, the decision following a review.]

(5) The date in paragraph (3)(c) or (4)(c) applies only if the application for the decision to be set aside was made within the time stipulated in rule 43 (setting aside a decision which disposes of proceedings) or any extension of that time granted by the Upper Tribunal.

(6) If the person seeking permission to appeal provides the application to the Upper Tribunal later than the time required by paragraph (3)[, [3A]{, 3D}] or (4), or by any extension of time under rule 5(3)(a) (power to extend time)—

(a) the application must include a request for an extension of time and the reason why the application notice was not provided in time; and

(b) unless the Upper Tribunal extends time for the application under rule 5(3)(a) (power to extend time) the Upper Tribunal must refuse the application.

(7) An application under paragraph (1) [or (4A)] must—

(a) identify the decision of the [Upper] Tribunal to which it relates;

(b) identify the alleged error or errors of law in the decision; and

(c) state the result the party making the application is seeking.

Note: Paragraph (2)(ba) inserted from 1 April 2009 (SI 2009/274). Paragraphs (3A)–(3C) and numbers in square brackets in paragraph (6) inserted from 15 February 2010 (SI 2010/44). Paragraph (3D) and numbers in curly brackets in paragraph (6) inserted and numbers in square brackets in paragraph (4) substituted from 6 April 2010 (SI 2010/747). Subparagraph (3B)(a)(i) amended from 1 April 2011 (SI 2011/651). Paragraph (4A) and words in first square brackets in paragraphs (1) and (7) inserted from 11 December 2012 (SI 2012/2890). Paragraph (4A), words in second square brackets in (1) and (4) substituted from 1 November 2013 (SI 2013/2067). Word in first square brackets in (7) inserted from 11 December 2012 (SI 2012/2890), word in second square brackets in (7) inserted from 1 November 2013 (2013/2067).

Upper Tribunal's consideration of application for permission to appeal

45.—(1) On receiving an application for permission to appeal the Upper Tribunal may review the decision in accordance with rule 46 (review of a decision), but may only do so if—

(a) when making the decision the Upper Tribunal overlooked a legislative provision or binding authority which could have had a material effect on the decision; or

(b) since the Upper Tribunal's decision, a court has made a decision which is binding on the Upper Tribunal and which, had it been made before the Upper Tribunal's decision, could have had a material effect on the decision.

(2) If the Upper Tribunal decides not to review the decision, or reviews the decision and decides to take no action in relation to the decision or part of it, the Upper Tribunal must consider whether to give permission to appeal in relation to the decision or that part of it.

(3) The Upper Tribunal must [provide] a record of its decision to the parties as soon as practicable.

(4) If the Upper Tribunal refuses permission to appeal it must [provide] with the record of its decision—

(a) a statement of its reasons for such refusal; and

(b) notification of the right to make an application to the relevant appellate court for permission to appeal and the time within which, and the method by which, such application must be made.

(5) The Upper Tribunal may give permission to appeal on limited grounds, but must comply with paragraph (4) in relation to any grounds on which it has refused permission.

Note: Word in square brackets in paragraphs (3) and (4) substituted from 1 November 2013 (SI 2013/2067).

[Setting aside] of a decision

46.—[(1) The Upper Tribunal may only undertake a review of a decision pursuant to rule 45(1) (review on an application for permission to appeal).]

(2) The Upper Tribunal must notify the parties in writing of the outcome of any review and of any rights of review or appeal in relation to the outcome.

(3) If the Upper Tribunal decides to take any action in relation to a decision following a review without first giving every party an opportunity to make representations, the notice under paragraph (2) must state that any party that did not have an opportunity to make representations may apply for such action to be set aside and for the decision to be reviewed again.

Note: Paragraph (1) substituted from 17 October 2011 (SI 2011/2343).

[Setting aside] a decision in proceedings under the Forfeiture Act 1982

47.—(1) A person who referred a question to the Upper Tribunal under rule 26 (references under the Forfeiture Act 1982) must refer the Upper Tribunal's previous decision in relation to the question to the Upper Tribunal if they—

(a) consider that the decision should be[set aside and re-made under this rule]; or

(b) have received a written application for the decision to be [set aside and re-made under this rule] from the person to whom the decision related.

(2) The Upper Tribunal may [set aside the decision, either in whole or in part, and re-make it] if—

(a) . . .

(b) the decision was made in ignorance of, or was based on a mistake as to, some material fact; or

(c) there has been a relevant change in circumstances since the decision was made.

[(3) Rule 26(2) to (4), Parts 5 and 6 and this Part apply to a reference under this rule as they apply to a reference under rule 26(1).]

(4) . . .

(5) . . .

Note: Words inserted/substituted in heading, paragraphs (1) and (2), subparagraph 2(a) omitted, paragraph (3) substituted and paragraphs (4) and (5) omitted from 17 October 2011 (SI 2011/2343).

[Power to treat an application as a different type of application

48. The [Upper] Tribunal may treat an application for a decision to be corrected, set aside or reviewed, or for permission to appeal against a decision, as an application for any other one of those things.]

Note: Rule 48 inserted from 29 November 2010 (SI 2010/2653). Word in square brackets inserted from 1 November 2013 (SI 2013/2067).

[Schedule 1

Procedure after the notice of appeal in appeals against decisions of traffic commissioners]

. . .

Rule 26a(4)

[Schedule 2

Additional procedure in national security certificate cases

. . .

Schedule 3

Procedure in financial services cases]

. . .

Practice Direction

Immigration and Asylum Chambers of the First-Tier Tribunal and The Upper Tribunal

---

Contents

Part 1

Preliminary

Part 2

Practice Directions for the Immigration and Asylum Chamber of the First-Tier Tribunal

Part 3

Practice Directions for the Immigration and Asylum Chamber of the Upper Tribunal

Part 4

Practice Directions for the Immigration and Asylum Chamber of the First-Tier Tribunal and The Upper Tribunal

---

Part 1

Preliminary

1. *Interpretation, etc.*

1.1 In these Practice Directions:-

"the 2002 Act" means the Nationality, Immigration and Asylum Act 2002;

"the 2007 Act" means the Tribunals, Courts and Enforcement Act 2007;

"adjudicator" means an adjudicator appointed, or treated as appointed, under section 81 of the 2002 Act (as originally enacted);

"AIT" means the Asylum and Immigration Tribunal;

"CMR hearing" means a case management review hearing;

"fast track appeal" means an appeal to which Part 2 of the Fast Track Rules applies;

"Fast Track Rules" means the Asylum and Immigration Tribunal (Fast Track Procedure) Rules 2005;

"First-tier rule", followed by a number, means the rule bearing that number in the Asylum and Immigration Tribunal (Procedure) Rules 2005;

"IAT" means the Immigration Appeal Tribunal;

"Practice Statements" means the Practice Statements – *Immigration and Asylum Chambers of the First-tier Tribunal and the Upper Tribunal* (dated 10 February 2010); and "Practice Statement", followed by a number, means the Statement bearing that number in the Practice Statements;

"Transfer of Functions Order" means the Transfer of Functions of the Asylum and Immigration Tribunal Order 2010 (SI/2010/21);

"The Tribunal" means the Immigration and Asylum Chamber of the First-tier Tribunal or of the Upper Tribunal, as the case may be;

"UT rule", followed by a number, means the rule bearing that number in the Tribunal Procedure (Upper Tribunal) Rules 2008.

1.2 Except where expressly stated to the contrary, any reference in these Practice Directions to an enactment is a reference to that enactment as amended by or under any other enactment.

1.3 Other expressions in these Practice Statements have the same meanings as in the 2007 Act.

1.4 These Practice Directions come into force on 15 February 2010.

1.5 These Practice Directions apply, as appropriate, in relation to transitional cases to which Schedule 4 to the Transfer of Functions Order applies; and references to the First-tier Tribunal and the Upper Tribunal shall be construed accordingly.

Part 2

Practice Directions for the Immigration and Asylum Chamber of The First-Tier Tribunal

2. *Standard directions in fast track appeals*

2.1 In the case of a fast track appeal, the parties must respectively serve the material specified in Practice Direction 7.5(a) and (b) either at the hearing or, if practicable, on the business day immediately preceding the date of the hearing.

2.2 Subject to the exception mentioned in Practice Direction 7.7, witness statements served in pursuance of paragraph 2.1 shall stand as evidence-in-chief at the hearing.

Part 3

Practice Directions for the Immigration and Asylum Chamber of The Upper Tribunal

3. *Procedure on appeal*

3.1 Where permission to appeal to the Upper Tribunal has been granted, then, unless and to the extent that they are directed otherwise, for the purposes of preparing for a hearing in the Upper Tribunal the parties should assume that:-

(a) the Upper Tribunal will decide whether the making of the decision of the First-tier Tribunal involved the making of an error on a point of law, such that the decision should be set aside under section 12(2)(a) of the 2007 Act;
(b) except as specified in Practice Statement 7.2 (disposal of appeals by Upper Tribunal), the Upper Tribunal will proceed to re-make the decision under section 12(2)(b)(ii), if satisfied that the original decision should be set aside; and
(c) in that event, the Upper Tribunal will consider whether to re-make the decision by reference to the First-tier Tribunal's findings of fact and any new documentary evidence submitted under UT rule 15(2A) which it is reasonably practicable to adduce for consideration at that hearing.

3.2 The parties should be aware that, in the circumstances described in paragraph 3.1(c), the Upper Tribunal will generally expect to proceed, without any further hearing, to re-make the decision, where this can be undertaken without having to hear oral evidence. In certain circumstances, the Upper Tribunal may give directions for the giving of oral evidence at the relevant hearing, where it appears appropriate to do so. Such directions may be given before or at that hearing.

3.3 In a case where no oral evidence is likely to be required in order for the Upper Tribunal to re-make the decision, the Upper Tribunal will therefore expect any documentary evidence relevant to the re-making of the decision to be adduced in accordance with Practice Direction 4 so that it may be considered at the relevant hearing; and, accordingly, the party seeking to rely on such documentary evidence will be expected to show good reason why it is not reasonably practicable to adduce the same in order for it to be considered at that hearing.

3.4 If the Upper Tribunal nevertheless decides that it cannot proceed as described in paragraph 3.1(c) because findings of fact are needed which it is not in a position to make, the Upper Tribunal will make arrangements for the adjournment of the hearing, so that the proceedings may be completed before the same constitution of the Tribunal; or, if that is not reasonably practicable, for their transfer to a different constitution, in either case so as to enable evidence to be adduced for that purpose.

3.5 Where proceedings are transferred in the circumstances described in paragraph 3.4, any documents sent to or given by the Tribunal from which the proceedings are transferred shall be deemed to have been sent to or given by the Tribunal to which those proceedings are transferred.

3.6 Where such proceedings are transferred, the Upper Tribunal shall prepare written reasons for finding that the First-tier Tribunal made an error of law, such that its decision fell to be set aside, and those written reasons shall be sent to the parties before the next hearing.

3.7 The written reasons shall be incorporated **in full** in, and form part of, the determination of the Upper Tribunal that re-makes the decision. Only in very exceptional cases can the decision contained in those written reasons be departed from or varied by the Upper Tribunal which re-makes the decision under section 12(2)(b)(ii) of the 2007 Act.

3.8 Unless directed otherwise, the parties to any fast track appeal which is before the Upper Tribunal will be expected to attend with all necessary witnesses and evidence that may be required if the Upper Tribunal should decide that it is necessary to set aside the decision of the First-tier Tribunal and re-make the decision. It will be unusual for the Upper Tribunal to adjourn or transfer, but, if it does so, paragraph 3.6 and 3.7 will, so far as appropriate, apply.

3.9 In this Practice Direction and Practice Direction 4, "the relevant hearing" means a hearing fixed by the Upper Tribunal at which it will consider if the First-tier Tribunal made an error of law.

3.10 Without prejudice to the generality of paragraph 1.5, where, by virtue of any transitional provisions in Schedule 4 to the Transfer of Functions Order, the Upper Tribunal is undertaking the reconsideration of a decision of the AIT, references in this Practice Direction and Practice Direction 4 to the First-tier Tribunal shall be construed as references to the AIT.

4. *Evidence*

4.1 UT rule 15(2A) imposes important procedural requirements where the Upper Tribunal is asked to consider evidence that was not before the First-tier Tribunal. UT rule 15(2A) must be complied with in **every case** where permission to appeal is granted and a party wishes the Upper Tribunal to consider such evidence. Notice under rule 15(2A)(a), indicating the nature of the evidence and explaining why it was not submitted to the First-tier Tribunal, must be filed with the Upper Tribunal and served on the other party within the time stated in any specific directions given by the Upper Tribunal; or, if no such direction has been given, as soon as practicable after permission to appeal has been granted.

4.2 A party who wishes the Upper Tribunal to consider any evidence that was not before the First-tier Tribunal must indicate in the notice whether the evidence is sought to be adduced:-

(a) in connection with the issue of whether the First-tier Tribunal made an error of law, requiring its decision to be set aside; or

(b) in connection with the re-making of the decision by the Upper Tribunal, in the event of the First-tier Tribunal being found to have made such an error.

4.3 The notice must clearly indicate whether the party concerned wishes the evidence to be considered at the relevant hearing and state whether the evidence is in oral or documentary form.

4.4 Where a party wishes, in the circumstances described in paragraph 4.2(b), to adduce only documentary evidence, Practice Direction 3.3 will apply.

4.5 Where a party wishes, in the circumstances described in paragraph 4.2(b), to adduce oral evidence at the relevant hearing, the notice must explain why it is considered desirable to proceed in such a manner and give details of the oral evidence and a time estimate.

4.6 Where the Upper Tribunal acts under Practice Direction 3 to adjourn or transfer the hearing, it shall consider any notice given under UT rule 15(2A) and give any directions arising therefrom, if and to the extent that this has not already been done.

4.7 This Practice Direction does not apply in the case of a fast track appeal (as to which, see Practice Direction 3.8).

5. *Pursuing appeal after grant of leave*

5.1 This Practice Direction applies where:-

(a) an appeal would otherwise fall to be treated as abandoned pursuant to section 104(4A) of the 2002 Act because the appellant is granted leave to remain in the United Kingdom; but

(b) the appellant wishes, in pursuance of section 104(4B) or (4C), to pursue the appeal, insofar as it is brought on asylum grounds or on grounds of unlawful discrimination.

5.2 Where this Practice Direction applies, the appellant must comply with the following requirements (which are the relevant practice directions for the purposes of UT rule 17A(3)).

5.3 Where section 104(4B) of the 2002 Act (asylum grounds) applies, the notice required by UT rule 17A(3) to be sent or delivered to the Upper Tribunal must state:-

(a) the appellant's full name and date of birth;

(b) the Tribunal's reference number;

(c) the Home Office reference number, if applicable;

(d) the Foreign and Commonwealth Office reference number, if applicable;

(e) the date on which the appellant was granted leave to enter or remain in the United Kingdom for a period exceeding 12 months; and

(f) that the appellant wishes to pursue the appeal in so far as it is brought on the ground specified in section 84(1)(g) of the 2002 Act which relates to the Refugee Convention.

5.4 Where section 104(4C) of the 2002 Act (grounds of unlawful discrimination) applies, the notice required by UT rule 17A(3) to be sent or delivered to the Upper Tribunal must state:-

(a) the appellant's full name and date of birth;

(b) the Tribunal's reference number;
(c) the Home Office reference number, if applicable;
(d) the Foreign and Commonwealth Office reference number, if applicable;
(e) the date on which the appellant was granted leave to enter or remain in the United Kingdom; and
(f) that the appellant wishes to pursue the appeal in so far as it is brought on the ground specified in section 84(1)(b) of the 2002 Act which relates to section 19B of the Race Relations Act 1976 (discrimination by public authorities).

5.5 Where an appellant has sent or delivered a notice under UT rule 17A(3), the Upper Tribunal will notify the appellant of the date on which it received the notice.

5.6 The Upper Tribunal will send a copy of the notice issued under paragraph 5.5 to the respondent.

5.7 In this Practice Direction:-

"appellant" means the party who was the appellant before the First- tier Tribunal; and

"respondent" means the party who was the respondent before the First-tier Tribunal.

PART 4

PRACTICE DIRECTIONS FOR THE IMMIGRATION AND ASYLUM CHAMBER OF THE FIRST-TIER TRIBUNAL AND THE UPPER TRIBUNAL

6. *Form of notice of appeal etc.*

6.1 The form of notice approved for the purpose of:-
(a) First-tier rule 8 (notice of appeal);
(b) First-tier rule 24 (application for permission to appeal to the Upper Tribunal);
(c) First-tier rule 38 (application for bail); and
(d) UT rule 21 (application to the Upper Tribunal for permission to appeal).

as the case may be, is the appropriate form as displayed on the Tribunal's website at the time when the notice is given, or that form with any variations that circumstances may require.

7. *Case management review hearings and directions*

7.1 Where the Tribunal so directs, a CMR hearing will be held in the case of an appeal where the party who is or was the appellant before the First-tier Tribunal:-
(a) is present in the United Kingdom; and
(b) has a right of appeal whilst in the United Kingdom.

7.2 It is important that the parties and their representatives understand that a CMR hearing is a hearing in the appeal and that the appeal may be determined under the relevant Procedure Rules if a party does not appear and is not represented at that hearing.

7.3 In addition to any information required by First-tier rule 8 (form of contents and notice of appeal), the appellant before the First-tier Tribunal must provide that Tribunal and the respondent at the CMR hearing with:-
(a) particulars of any application for permission to vary the grounds of appeal;
(b) particulars of any amendments to the reasons in support of the grounds of appeal;
(c) particulars of any witnesses to be called or whose written statement or report is proposed to be relied upon at the full hearing; and
(d) the draft of any directions that the appellant is requesting the Tribunal to make at the CMR hearing.

7.4 In addition to any documents required by relevant Procedure Rules, the party who is or was the respondent before the First-tier Tribunal must provide the Tribunal and the other party at the CMR hearing with:-

(a) any amendment that has been made or is proposed to be made to the notice of decision to which the appeal relates or to any other document served on the person concerned giving reasons for that decision; and

(b) a draft of any directions that the Tribunal is requested to make at the CMR hearing.

7.5 In most cases, including those appeals where a CMR hearing is to be held, the Tribunal will normally have given to the parties the following directions with the notice of hearing:-

(a) not later than 5 working days before the full hearing (or 10 days in the case of an out-of-country appeal) the appellant shall serve on the Tribunal and the respondent:

(i) witness statements of the evidence to be called at the hearing, such statements to stand as evidence in chief at the hearing;

(ii) a paginated and indexed bundle of all the documents to be relied on at the hearing with a schedule identifying the essential passages;

(iii) a skeleton argument, identifying all relevant issues including human rights claims and citing all the authorities relied upon; and

(iv) a chronology of events;

(b) not later than 5 working days before the full hearing, the respondent shall serve on the Tribunal and the appellant a paginated and indexed bundle of all the documents to be relied upon at the hearing, with a schedule identifying the relevant passages, and a list of any authorities relied upon.

7.6 At the end of the CMR hearing, the Tribunal will give the parties any further written directions relating to the conduct of the appeal.

7.7 Although in normal circumstances a witness statement should stand as evidence-in-chief, there may be cases where it will be appropriate for appellants or witnesses to have the opportunity of adding to or supplementing their witness statements.

7.8 In addition to the directions referred to above, at the end of the CMR hearing the Tribunal will also give to the parties written confirmation of:-

(a) any issues that have been agreed at the CMR hearing as being relevant to the determination of the appeal; and

(b) any concessions made at the CMR hearing by a party.

8. *Trial bundles*

8.1 The parties must take all reasonably practicable steps to act in accordance with paragraph 8.2 to 8.6 in the preparation of trial bundles for hearings before the Tribunal.

8.2 The best practice for the preparation of bundles is as follows:-

(a) all documents must be relevant, be presented in logical order and be legible;

(b) where the document is not in the English language, a typed translation of the document signed by the translator, and certifying that the translation is accurate, must be inserted in the bundle next to the copy of the original document, together with details of the identity and qualifications of the translator;

(c) if it is necessary to include a lengthy document, that part of the document on which reliance is placed should, unless the passages are outlined in any skeleton argument, be highlighted or clearly identified by reference to page and/or paragraph number;

(d) bundles submitted must have an index showing the page numbers of each document in the bundle;

(e) the skeleton argument or written submission should define and confine the areas at issue in a numbered list of brief points and each point should refer to any documentation in the bundle on which the appellant proposes to rely (together with its page number);

(f) where reliance is placed on a particular case or text, photocopies of the case or text must be provided in full for the Tribunal and the other party; and

(g) large bundles should be contained in a ring binder or lever arch file, capable of lying flat when opened.

8.3 The Tribunal recognises the constraints on those representing the parties in appeals in relation to the preparation of trial bundles and this Practice Direction does not therefore make it mandatory in every case that bundles in exactly the form prescribed must be prepared. Where the issues are particularly complex it is of the highest importance that comprehensive bundles are prepared. If parties to appeals fail in individual cases to present documentation in a way which complies with the direction, it will be for the Tribunal to deal with any such issue.

8.4 Much evidence in immigration and asylum appeals is in documentary form. Representatives preparing bundles need to be aware of the position of the Tribunal, which may be coming to the case for the first time. The better a bundle has been prepared, the greater it will assist the Tribunal. Bundles should contain all the documents that the Tribunal will require to enable it to reach a decision without the need to refer to any other file or document. The Tribunal will not be assisted by repetitious, outdated or irrelevant material.

8.5 It may not be practical in many appeals to require there to be an agreed trial bundle but it nevertheless remains vital that the parties inform each other at an early stage of all and any documentation upon which they intend to rely.

8.6 The parties cannot rely on the Tribunal having any prior familiarity with any country information or background reports in relation to the case in question. If either party wishes to rely on such country or background information, copies of the relevant documentation must be provided.

9. *Adjournments*

9.1 Applications for the adjournment of appeals (other than fast track appeals) listed for hearing before the Tribunal must be made not later than 5.00p.m. one clear working day before the date of the hearing.

9.2 For the avoidance of doubt, where a case is listed for hearing on, for example, a Friday, the application must be received by 5.00p.m. on the Wednesday.

9.3 The application for an adjournment must be supported by full reasons and must be made in accordance with relevant Procedure Rules.

9.4 Any application made later than the end of the period mentioned in paragraph 9.1 must be made to the Tribunal at the hearing and will require the attendance of the party or the representative of the party seeking the adjournment.

9.5 It will be only in the most exceptional circumstances that a late application for an adjournment will be considered without the attendance of a party or representative.

9.6 Parties must not assume that an application, even if made in accordance with paragraph 9.1, will be successful and they must always check with the Tribunal as to the outcome of the application.

9.7 Any application for the adjournment of a fast track appeal must be made to the Tribunal at the hearing and will be considered by the Tribunal in accordance with relevant Procedure Rules.

9.8 If an adjournment is not granted and the party fails to attend the hearing, the Tribunal may in certain circumstances proceed with the hearing in that party's absence.

10. *Expert evidence*

10.1 A party who instructs an expert must provide clear and precise instructions to the expert, together with all relevant information concerning the nature of the appellant's case, including the appellant's immigration history, the reasons why the appellant's claim or application has been refused by the respondent and copies of any relevant previous reports prepared in respect of the appellant.

10.2 It is the duty of an expert to help the Tribunal on matters within the expert's own expertise. This duty is paramount and overrides any obligation to the person from whom the expert has received instructions or by whom the expert is paid.

10.3 Expert evidence should be the independent product of the expert uninfluenced by the pressures of litigation.

10.4 An expert should assist the Tribunal by providing objective, unbiased opinion on matters within his or her expertise, and should not assume the role of an advocate.

10.5 An expert should consider all material facts, including those which might detract from his or her opinion.

10.6 An expert should make it clear:-

(a) when a question or issue falls outside his or her expertise; and

(b) when the expert is not able to reach a definite opinion, for example because of insufficient information.

10.7 If, after producing a report, an expert changes his or her view on any material matter, that change of view should be communicated to the parties without delay, and when appropriate to the Tribunal.

10.8 An expert's report should be addressed to the Tribunal and not to the party from whom the expert has received instructions.

10.9 An expert's report must:-

(a) give details of the expert's qualifications;

(b) give details of any literature or other material which the expert has relied on in making the report;

(c) contain a statement setting out the substance of all facts and instructions given to the expert which are material to the opinions expressed in the report or upon which those opinions are based;

(d) make clear which of the facts stated in the report are within the expert's own knowledge;

(e) say who carried out any examination, measurement or other procedure which the expert has used for the report, give the qualifications of that person, and say whether or not the procedure has been carried out under the expert's supervision;

(f) where there is a range of opinion on the matters dealt with in the report:

(i) summarise the range of opinion, so far as reasonably practicable, and

(ii) give reasons for the expert's own opinion;

(g) contain a summary of the conclusions reached;

(h) if the expert is not able to give an opinion without qualification, state the qualification; and

(j) contain a statement that the expert understands his or her duty to the Tribunal, and has complied and will continue to comply with that duty.

10.10 An expert's report must be verified by a Statement of Truth as well as containing the statements required in paragraph 10.9(h) and (j).

10.11 The form of the Statement of Truth is as follows:-

'I confirm that insofar as the facts stated in my report are within my own knowledge I have made clear which they are and I believe them to be true, and that the opinions I have expressed represent my true and complete professional opinion.'

10.12 The instructions referred to in paragraph 10.9(c) are not protected by privilege but cross-examination of the expert on the contents of the instructions will not be allowed unless the Tribunal permits it (or unless the party who gave the instructions consents to it). Before it gives permission the Tribunal must be satisfied that there are reasonable grounds to consider that the statement in the report or the substance of the instructions is inaccurate or incomplete. If the Tribunal is so satisfied, it will allow the cross-examination where it appears to be in the interests of justice to do so.

10.13 In this Practice Direction:-

"appellant" means the party who is or was the appellant before the First-tier Tribunal; and

"respondent" means the party who is or was the respondent before the First-tier Tribunal.

11. *Citation of unreported determinations*

11.1 A determination of the Tribunal which has not been reported may not be cited in proceedings before the Tribunal unless:-

(a) the person who is or was the appellant before the First-tier Tribunal, or a member of that person's family, was a party to the proceedings in which the previous determination was issued; or

(b) the Tribunal gives permission.

11.2 An application for permission to cite a determination which has not been reported must:-

(a) include a full transcript of the determination;

(b) identify the proposition for which the determination is to be cited; and

(c) certify that the proposition is not to be found in any reported determination of the Tribunal, the IAT or the AIT and had not been superseded by the decision of a higher authority.

11.3 Permission under paragraph 11.1 will be given only where the Tribunal considers that it would be materially assisted by citation of the determination, as distinct from the adoption in argument of the reasoning to be found in the determination. Such instances are likely to be rare; in particular, in the case of determinations which were unreportable (see Practice Statement 11 (reporting of determinations)). It should be emphasised that the Tribunal will not exclude good arguments from consideration but it will be rare for such an argument to be capable of being made only by reference to an unreported determination.

11.4 The provisions of paragraph 11.1 to 11.3 apply to unreported and unreportable determinations of the AIT, the IAT and adjudicators, as those provisions apply respectively to unreported and unreportable determinations of the Tribunal.

11.5 A party citing a determination of the IAT bearing a neutral citation number prior to [2003] (including all series of "bracket numbers") must be in a position to certify that the matter or proposition for which the determination is cited has not been the subject of more recent, reported, determinations of the IAT, the AIT or the Tribunal.

11.6 In this Practice Direction and Practice Direction 12, "determination" includes any decision of the AIT or the Tribunal.

12. *Starred and Country Guidance determinations*

12.1 Reported determinations of the Tribunal, the AIT and the IAT which are "starred" shall be treated by the Tribunal as authoritative in respect of the matter to which the "starring" relates, unless inconsistent with other authority that is binding on the Tribunal.

12.2 A reported determination of the Tribunal, the AIT or the IAT bearing the letters "CG" shall be treated as an authoritative finding on the country guidance issue identified in the determination, based upon the evidence before the members of the Tribunal, the AIT or the IAT that determine the appeal. As a result, unless it has been expressly superseded or replaced by any later "CG" determination, or is inconsistent with other authority that is binding on the Tribunal, such a country guidance case is authoritative in any subsequent appeal, so far as that appeal:-

(a) relates to the country guidance issue in question; and
(b) depends upon the same or similar evidence.

12.3 A list of current CG cases will be maintained on the Tribunal's website. Any representative of a party to an appeal concerning a particular country will be expected to be conversant with the current "CG" determinations relating to that country.

12.4 Because of the principle that like cases should be treated in like manner, any failure to follow a clear, apparently applicable country guidance case or to show why it does not apply to the case in question is likely to be regarded as grounds for appeal on a point of law.

13. *Bail applications*

13.1 An application for bail must if practicable be listed for hearing within three working days of receipt by the Tribunal of the notice of application.

13.2 Any such notice which is received by the Tribunal after 3.30p.m. on a particular day will be treated for the purposes of this paragraph as if it were received on the next business day.

13.3 An Upper Tribunal judge may exercise bail jurisdiction under the Immigration Act 1971 by reason of being also a First-tier judge.

13.4 Notwithstanding paragraph 13.3, it will usually be appropriate for a bail application to be made to an Upper Tribunal judge only where the appeal in question is being heard by the Upper Tribunal, or where a hearing before the Upper Tribunal is imminent. In case of doubt, a potential applicant should consult the bails section of the First-tier Tribunal.

14 This Practice Direction is made by the Senior President of Tribunals with the agreement of the Lord Chancellor. It is made in the exercise of powers conferred by the Tribunals, Courts and Enforcement Act 2007.

Practice Directions

Immigration Judicial Review in the Immigration and Asylum Chamber of the Upper Tribunal

Contents

PART 1

PRELIMINARY

1. *Interpretation*

1.1 In these Practice Directions:

"applicant" has the same meaning as in the UT Rules;

"the application" means the written application under rule 28 for permission to bring judicial review proceedings; "immigration judicial review proceedings" has the same meaning as

in the UT Rules; "party" has the same meaning as in the UT Rules; "respondent" has the same meaning as in the UT Rules;

"the Tribunal" means the Immigration and Asylum Chamber of the Upper Tribunal;

"UKBA" means the UK Border Agency of the Home Office;

"UT Rules" means the Tribunal Procedure (Upper Tribunal) Rules 2008 and "rule", followed by a number, means the rule bearing that number in the UT Rules.

PART 2

SCOPE

2. *Scope*

2.1 Parts 3 and 4 of these Practice Directions apply to immigration judicial review proceedings.

2.2 Part 5 of these Practice Directions applies to proceedings to which Part 3 applies, where:

(a) a person has been served with a copy of directions for that person's removal from the United Kingdom by UKBA and notified that Part 5 applies; and

(b) that person makes an application to the Tribunal or a court for permission to bring judicial review proceedings or to apply for judicial review, before the removal takes effect.

2.3 In the case of proceedings transferred to the Tribunal by a court, the Tribunal will expect the applicant to have complied with all relevant Practice Directions of that court that applied up to the point of transfer. In the event of non-compliance, the Tribunal will make such directions pursuant to rule 27(1)(b) as are necessary and which may, in particular, include applying provisions of these Practice Directions.

PART 3

GENERAL PROVISIONS

The application to bring judicial review proceedings

3. *Form of application*

3.1 The application must be made using the form displayed on the Upper Tribunal's website at the time the application is made.

4. *Additional materials to be filed with the application*

4.1 Without prejudice to rule 28, the application must be accompanied by:

(a) any written evidence on which it is intended to rely (but see paragraph 4.2 below);
(b) copies of any relevant statutory material; and
(c) a list of essential documents for advance reading by the Tribunal (with page references to the passages relied on).

4.2 The applicant may rely on the matters set out in the application as evidence under this Practice Direction if the application is verified by a statement of truth.

5. *Bundle of documents to be sent etc. with the application*

5.1 The applicant must file two copies of a paginated and indexed bundle containing all the documents required by rule 28 and these Practice Directions to be sent or delivered with the application.

6. *Permission without a hearing*

6.1 The Tribunal will generally, in the first instance, consider the question of permission without a hearing.

The substantive hearing

7. *Additional grounds at the substantive hearing*

7.1 Where an applicant who has been given permission to bring judicial review proceedings intends to apply under rule 32 to rely on additional grounds at the substantive hearing, the applicant must give written notice to the Tribunal and to any other person served with the application, not later than 7 working days before that hearing.

8. *Skeleton arguments for the substantive hearing*

8.1 The applicant must serve a skeleton argument on the Tribunal and on any other person served with the application, not later than 21 days before the substantive hearing.

8.2 The respondent and any other party wishing to make representations at the hearing must serve a skeleton argument on the Tribunal and on the applicant, not later than 14 days before the hearing.

8.3 Skeleton arguments must contain:

(a) a time estimate for the complete hearing, including the giving of the decision by the Tribunal;
(b) a list of issues;
(c) a list of the legal points to be taken (together with any relevant authorities with page references to the passages relied on);
(d) a chronology of events (with page references to the bundle of documents (see Practice Direction 9 below);
(e) a list of essential documents for the advance reading of the Tribunal (with page references to the passages relied on) (if different from that served with the application) and a time estimate for that reading; and
(f) a list of persons referred to.

9. *Bundle of documents for the substantive hearing*

9.1 The applicant must serve on the Tribunal and any other person served with the application a paginated and indexed bundle of all relevant documents required for the substantive hearing, when the applicant's skeleton argument is served.

9.2 The bundle must also include those documents required by the respondent and any other person who is expected to make representations at the hearing.

10. *Agreed final order*

10.1 If the parties agree about the final order to be made, the applicant must file at the Tribunal a document (with 2 copies) signed by all the parties setting out the terms of the proposed agreed order, together with a short statement of the matters relied on as justifying the proposed agreed order and copies of any authorities or statutory provisions relied on.

10.2 The Tribunal will consider the documents referred to in paragraph 10.1 above and will make the order if satisfied that the order should be made.

10.3 If the Tribunal is not satisfied that the order should be made, a hearing date will be set.

Part 4

Urgent Applications For Permission To Bring Judicial Review Proceedings

11. *Request for Urgent Consideration*

11.1 Where it is intended to request the Tribunal to deal urgently with the application or where an interim injunction is sought, the applicant must serve with the application a written "Request for Urgent Consideration", in the form displayed on the Upper Tribunal's website at the time the application is made, which states:

(a) the need for urgency;

(b) the timescale sought for the consideration of the application (e.g. within 72 hours or sooner if necessary); and

(c) the date by which the substantive hearing should take place.

11.2 Where an interim injunction is sought, the applicant must, in addition, provide:

(a) the draft order; and

(b) the grounds for the injunction.

12. *Notifying the other parties*

12.1 The applicant must serve (by fax and post) the application form and the Request for Urgent Consideration on the respondent and interested parties, advising them of the application and that they may make representations.

12.2 Where an interim injunction is sought, the applicant must serve (by fax and post) the draft order and grounds for the injunction on the respondent and interested parties, advising them of the application and that they may make representations.

13. *Consideration by Tribunal*

13.1 The Tribunal will consider the application within the time requested and may make such order as it considers appropriate.

13.2 If the Tribunal specifies that a hearing shall take place within a specified time, the representatives of the parties must liaise with the Tribunal and each other to fix a hearing of the application within that time.

PART 5
APPLICATIONS WHICH CHALLENGE REMOVAL

14. *General*

14.1 The requirements contained in this Part are additional to those contained in Part 3 and (where applicable) Part 4 of these Practice Directions.

14.2 Nothing in these Practice Directions prevents a person from making the application after that person has been removed from the United Kingdom.

15. *Special requirements regarding the application*

15.1 Without prejudice to rule 28, the application must:
- (a) indicate on its face that this Part of these Practice Directions applies; and
- (b) be accompanied by:
  - (i) a copy of the removal directions and the decisions to which the application relates; and
  - (ii) any document served with the removal directions including any document which contains UKBA's factual summary of the case; and
- (c) contain or be accompanied by the detailed statement of the applicant's grounds for making the application.

15.2 If the applicant is unable to comply with paragraph 15.1(b) or (c) above, the application must contain or be accompanied by a statement of the reasons why.

15.3 Notwithstanding rule 28A, immediately upon issue of the application, the applicant must send copies of the issued application form and accompanying documents to the address specified by the United Kingdom Border Agency.

16. Referral in case of non-compliance

16.1 Where the applicant has not complied with Practice Direction 15.1(b) or (c) above and has provided reasons for not complying, and the Tribunal has issued the application form, the Tribunal's staff will:
- (a) refer the matter to a Judge for consideration as soon as practicable; and
- (b) notify the parties that they have done so.

17. Application clearly without merit

17.1 If, upon a refusal to grant permission to bring judicial review proceedings, the Tribunal considers that the application is totally without merit, that fact will be included in the decision notice.

These Practice Directions are made by the Senior President of Tribunals with the agreement of the Lord Chancellor. They are made in the exercise of powers conferred by the Tribunals, Courts and Enforcement Act 2007.

Lord Justice Carnwath Senior President of Tribunals
17 October 2011

Amended By Sir Jeremy Sullivan Senior President of Tribunals
01 November 2013

Practice Statement

Fresh Claim Judicial Reviews in the Immigration and Asylum Chamber of the Upper Tribunal on or After 29 April 2013

1. *Introduction*

1.1 This Practice Statement supplements the Senior President's Practice Direction (PD) in respect of applications for judicial review of fresh claim decisions within the meaning of the Direction made by the Lord Chief Justice 17 October 2011 (hereafter the proceedings).[1]

1.2 The Direction and the PD are available on the Senior President's web site at: <http://www.judiciary.gov.uk/publications-and-reports/practicedirections/tribunals/tribunals-pd>.

1.3 References in this statement to the Upper Tribunal Rules are to the Tribunal Procedure (Upper Tribunal) Rules 2008 as amended, available at the same location.

2. *Permission applications*

Lodging

2.1 Applications for permission to bring the proceedings, whether commenced in the High Court or the Upper Tribunal, are submitted to the Administrative Court Office in London and the Regional Centres and transferred to Upper Tribunal Field House for decision. The relevant forms for an application to the Upper Tribunal may be found at <http:// www.justice.gov.uk/forms/hmcts/upper> where there is also some guidance on their completion and submission.

Considering permission

2.2 The application for permission will not be considered before the time for lodging an Acknowledgment of Service (AOS) has expired[2] unless:-

i. the Respondent has indicated that no AOS will be lodged or has asked for urgent consideration of the application;

ii. an application for urgent relief to prevent removal has been refused and the judge considers it is appropriate to refuse the application for permission at the same time.

2.3 An application for an extension of time to lodge the application will be determined at the same time as the application for permission and permission will not be granted unless extension of time is allowed.[3]

[1] For the content of the application see UT rule 28(4).

[2] 21 days after sending see UT rule 29(1).

[3] UT rule 28(7).

Extension of time

2.4 An application for an extension of time will be refused unless:-

i. Satisfactory written reasons are given why the application was not made promptly and in any event within three months of the decision under challenge. In deciding what is "prompt" regard may be had to any relevant time limits for statutory appeals.

ii. Any factual assertion made in the explanation is supported by evidence or an explanation of why such evidence has not been lodged.

No jurisdiction

2.5 A judge considering an application for permission must transfer the application to the Administrative Court if relief is claimed other than relief that can be granted by the Upper Tribunal under the Direction of the Lord Chief Justice.[4]

Permission decisions

2.6 Where the Upper Tribunal is entitled to grant the relief sought, the Upper Tribunal judge may, on considering the permission application:

i. Grant the application.

ii. Grant the application on some grounds and refuse it on others.

iii. Adjourn the application for permission to an oral hearing.

iv. Refuse the application.

2.7 Where the application is refused the judge may also:

i. Make any order for costs of the Acknowledgement of Service as is appropriate in all the circumstances.

ii. Curtail the period for renewal of the application from the 9 days permitted under the Upper Tribunal Rules.[5] In order to reflect the practice of the Administrative Court CPR 54.12 the Upper Tribunal judge will normally curtail time for renewal to five working days and may curtail time to two working days where there is a compelling case for expedition.

iii. Direct that the application is wholly without merit and if so that any renewal of the application shall not operate as a bar on removal.

2.8 The judge must give brief written reasons for refusing the application or any part of it[6] and may give reasons for the other decisions made if considered appropriate to identify the issues or otherwise assist the preparation for the next hearing.

Renewed applications

2.9 Where a judge refuses the application on some or all grounds without a hearing, the applicant may apply by notice in writing for that decision to be renewed at an oral hearing.

[4] TCEA s 18(3).

[5] UT rule 30(5).

[6] UT rule 30(1) (b).

2.10 Such notice must explain:-
  i. The grounds on which permission is being renewed;
  ii. The basis on which the application is renewed; and
  iii. The response the applicant makes to any reasons given by the judge in refusing permission.

2.11 A renewed application for permission will be listed promptly in a permission list at Field House, London. Save with the parties' consent or in urgent or exceptional cases, at least two days notice of such a hearing will be given to the applicant and any party that has served an AOS.[7]

2.12 Legal representatives based outside London who wish to be heard by video link shall notify the Upper Tribunal in good time, giving details of the proposed arrangements. The Upper Tribunal will have regard to the guidance to be found in CPR 32PD32 (see in particular paragraphs 8-14 of Annex 3).

2.13 A renewed permission application shall be assigned a time estimate of 45 minutes, unless either party has previously applied to the Upper Tribunal explaining:-
  i. why a longer hearing is necessary;
  ii. what steps have or will be taken to keep the extension of time to the minimum necessary; and
  iii. giving a realistic revised time estimate.

Decisions on renewed application

2.14 If permission is refused, at the conclusion of the hearing of the application, or at such other time promptly thereafter as the judge directs, the judge shall:
  i. deliver a judgment giving the decision and explaining in summary terms why the application or any part of it has been refused;[8]
  ii. arrange for service of a written notice of the decision refusing permission;[9]
  iii. consider any costs orders to be made arising from the application;
  iv. consider any application for a stay on removal pending an application made to the Court of Appeal for permission to appeal.

In addition, the judge may curtail the time for applying in writing to the Upper Tribunal for permission to appeal against the refusal of permission to the Court of Appeal.[10]

2.15 The Tribunal's permission is required if an applicant seeks to rely on grounds other than those for which the applicant has been given permission to proceed.

2.16 When a written notice is served refusing permission on all grounds at the oral hearing the decision is a decision of the Upper Tribunal which disposes of proceedings.

[7] UT rule 36 (a) and (b).
[8] UT rule 40 (1).
[9] UT rule 40 (2).
[10] For the UT's general case management powers see UT rule 5(3). See also UT rule 44(4A).

2.17 An application for permission to appeal to the Court of Appeal against a refusal of permission to bring judicial review proceedings shall be made orally at the hearing or in writing.[11]

2.18 Having regard to the subject matter of the application and the practice of the Administrative Court, at the conclusion of the renewed permission hearing the Upper Tribunal judge will normally have exercised case management powers to curtail the period of one month[12] for making an application for permission to appeal to the Court of Appeal against the Upper Tribunal's refusal of permission to six working days from the date of sending of the written decision refusing permission. The Upper Tribunal judge will take into account that reasons will already have been given orally at the hearing.

3. Urgent applications

3.1 An application for urgent consideration (an "urgent application") under 11.1 of the Senior President's PD, can only be considered by a judge of the Upper Tribunal on the papers where the judicial review proceedings have been issued. Applications for urgent relief made before an application for judicial review has been made should accordingly be made to the Administrative Court.

3.2 An application for a stay on removal or an injunction must be accompanied by statement from the applicant's legal representative (i) explaining why the application is made urgently; (ii) stating when the decision under challenge came to the claimant's notice and justifying any delay since that date; and (iii) certifying that there is nothing in the application that the legal representative does not consider to be properly arguable. Such applications must be served on the respondent together with the application for permission.

3.3 An urgent application lodged after 9.30am and before 4.15pm on a working day will be considered by a judge of the Upper Tribunal that day. An urgent application lodged outside these times will be referred to a duty judge of the Queen Bench Division to consider, acting as a judge of the Upper Tribunal.

3.4 Special arrangements have been made for applications lodged at centres outside London for urgent applications made before permission is granted to be considered by judges at those centres before the case is transferred to Field House.

3.5 An urgent application for a stay on removal will be considered on the papers by a judge of the Upper Tribunal, unless the judge adjourns the application for an oral hearing at which both sides can makes submissions.

3.6 An application for an injunction requiring the respondent to return a person who has been previously removed from the United Kingdom may only be made after an oral hearing of which the respondent has notice.

11 UT rule 44 (1), (4A).
12 UT rule 44 (4).

3.7 Where a judge considers an urgent application on the papers, and concludes that further information is needed from the respondent, the judge may telephone the Home Office and seek the further information. A note shall be kept of any information supplied.

3.8 Where an urgent application is granted, the judge shall forthwith draw up an order and give short reasons for it that shall be sent to both parties.

3.9 Where an urgent application is refused, the judge shall give short written reasons for the decision and shall append to those reasons any material information obtained from the Home Office.

3.10 An urgent application that is refused on the papers may be renewed orally to a judge of the Upper Tribunal upon application being made promptly to the Tribunal and notice given to the respondent. The Tribunal will list such application as soon as practicable in all the circumstances of the case.

3.11 A refusal of an oral urgent application is final.

3.12 The provisions of paragraphs 2.14 to 2.18 of this Guidance Note shall, so far as relevant, apply to urgent applications.

4. Costs

4.1 Where a judge of the Upper Tribunal makes an order that the applicant is to pay a sum to the respondent in respect of the acknowledgment of service or the costs of resisting an urgent application, pursuant to rule 10(3)(a) of the Upper Tribunal Rules and there has been no prior opportunity on the paying party to make representations or to have an inquiry into that party's means, the order takes effect as a provisional order subject to representations to be made in writing within 10 working days of the order.

4.2 Where no representations have been received within the time specified in the order, the order for costs shall become absolute. In other cases, the representations shall be referred promptly to the judge making the order or such other judge as is available for determination.

Sir Jeremy Sullivan
Senior President of Tribunals
26 April 2013

IMMIGRATION RULES

Immigration Rules
(HC 395)

Note: The version of the Immigration Rules set out below includes all amendments to the Rules published up to 27 October 2014, including amendments that take effect after that date. The annotations identify the amendments made since the last edition of this work, that is to say the changes resulting from the 18 *Statement of Changes to the Immigration Rules* published between 22 November 2012 (HC 760) and 16 October 2014 (HC 693). Amendments made prior to that are incorporated in the text but not identified in the annotations. Where amendments are subject to savings or transitional provisions (normally for applications for entry clearance or leave to remain made before a specified date) this is indicated in the annotations. In such cases users may need to consult previous versions of the Rules: these are archived on the gov.uk website and can be accessed at <www.gov.uk/government/collections/archive-immigration-rules>. The Rules are subject to frequent amendment. Users of this work should be aware of the importance of checking what further amendments have been made after HC 693; all *Statement of Changes to the Immigration Rules* are published on the gov.uk website and can be accessed at <www.gov.uk/government/collections/immigration-rules-statement-of-changes>.

Laid before Parliament on 23 May 1994 under section 3(2) of the Immigration Act 1971.

Arrangement of Rules

Part 1. General Provisions Regarding Leave to enter or Remain in the United Kingdom

Part 2. Persons Seeking to Enter or Remain in the United Kingdom for Visits

Part 3. Persons Seeking to Enter or Remain in the United Kingdom for Studies

Part 4. Persons Seeking to Enter or Remain in the United Kingdom in an "Au Pair" Placement, as a Working Holidaymaker, or for Training or Work Experience

Part 5. Persons Seeking to Enter or Remain in the United Kingdom for Employment

Part 6. Persons Seeking to Enter or Remain in The United Kingdom as a Businessman, Self-Employed Person, Investor, Writer, Composer or Artist

Part 6A. Points-Based System

Part 7. Other Categories

Introduction

1. The Home Secretary has made changes in the Rules laid down by him as to the practice to be followed in the administration of the Immigration Acts for regulating entry into and the stay of persons in the United Kingdom and contained in the statement laid before Parliament on 23 March 1990 (HC 251) (as amended). This statement contains the Rules as changed and replaces the provisions of HC 251 (as amended).

2. Immigration Officers, Entry Clearance Officers and all staff of the Home Office Immigration and Nationality Directorate will carry out their duties without regard to the race, colour or religion of persons seeking to enter or remain in the United Kingdom and in compliance with the provisions of the Human Rights Act 1998.

3. In these Rules words importing the masculine gender include the feminine unless the contrary intention appears.

Implementation and transitional provisions

4. These Rules come into effect on 1 October 1994 and will apply to all decisions taken on or after that date save that any application made before 1 October 1994 for entry clearance, leave to enter or remain or variation of leave to enter or remain other than an application for leave by a person seeking asylum shall be decided under the provisions of HC 251, as amended, as if these Rules had not been made.

Application

5. Save where expressly indicated, these Rules do not apply to those persons who are entitled to enter or remain in the United Kingdom by virtue of the provisions of the 2006 EEA Regulations. But any person who is not entitled to rely on the provisions of those Regulations is covered by these Rules.

Interpretation

6. In these Rules the following interpretations apply:

"**the Immigration Acts**" has the same meaning as it has in the Interpretation Act 1978;

"**the 1993 Act**" is the Asylum and Immigration Appeals Act 1993;

"**the 1996 Act**" is the Asylum and Immigration Act 1996;

"**the 2006 EEA Regulations**" means the Immigration (European Economic Area) Regulations 2006;

"**adoption**" unless the contrary intention appears, includes a de facto adoption in accordance with the requirements of paragraph 309A of these Rules, and "adopted" and "adoptive parent" should be construed accordingly.

In Appendix FM references to "**application for leave to remain**" include an application for variation of leave to enter or remain of a person in the UK.

"**Approved Destination Status Agreement with China**" means the Memorandum of Understanding on visa and related issues concerning tourist groups from the People's Republic of China to the United Kingdom as a approved destination, signed on 21 January 2005.

"**a bona fide private education institution**" is a private education institution which:

a) maintains satisfactory records of enrolment and attendance of students, and supplies these to the Border and Immigration Agency when requested;

b) provides courses which involve a minimum of 15 hours organised daytime study per week;

c) ensures a suitably qualified tutor is present during the hours of study to offer teaching and instruction to the students;

d) offers courses leading to qualifications recognised by the appropriate accreditation bodies;

e) employs suitably qualified staff to provide teaching, guidance and support to the students;

f) provides adequate accommodation, facilities, staffing levels and equipment to support the numbers of students enrolled at the institution; and

g) if it offers tuition support to external students at degree level, ensures that such students are registered with the UK degree awarding body.

"**Business day**" means any day other than Saturday or Sunday, a day which is a bank holiday under the Banking and Financial Dealings Act 1971 in the part of the United Kingdom to which the notice is sent, Christmas Day or Good Friday.

"**civil partner**" means a civil partnership which exists under or by virtue of the Civil Partnership Act 2004 (and any reference to a civil partner is to be read accordingly);

"**conviction**" means conviction for a criminal offence in the UK or any other country.

"**curtailment**" in relation to the curtailment of a person's leave to enter or remain in the UK, means curtailing their leave such that they will have a shorter period of, or no, leave remaining.

"**degree level study**" means a course which leads to a recognised United Kingdom degree at bachelor's level or above, or an equivalent qualification at level 6 or above of the revised National Qualifications Framework, or levels 9 or above of the Scottish Credit and Qualifications Framework.

Under Part 8 of these Rules, "**post-graduate level study**" means a course at level 7 or above of the revised National Qualifications Framework or Qualifications and Credit Framework, or level 11 or above of the Scottish Credit and Qualifications Framework, which leads to a recognised United Kingdom postgraduate degree at Master's level or above, or an equivalent qualification at the same level.

"**foundation degree**" means a programme of study which leads to a qualification awarded by an English higher education institution with degree awarding powers which is at a minimum of level 5 on the revised National Qualifications Framework, or awarded on a directly equivalent basis in the devolved administrations.

"**primary degree**" means a qualification obtained from a course of degree level study, which did not feature as an entry requirement a previous qualification obtained from degree level study. An undergraduate degree is a primary degree. A Masters degree that has a Bachelor degree as an entry requirement is not a primary degree.

A "**UK recognised body**" is an institution that has been granted degree awarding powers by either a Royal Charter, an Act of Parliament or the Privy Council. For the purposes of these Rules we will consider the Foundation Programme Office, South London Local Education and Training Board and the Yorkshire and Humber Strategic Health Authority as equivalent to UK Recognised Bodies.

A "**UK listed body**" is an institution that is not a UK recognised body but which provides full courses that lead to the award of a degree by a UK recognised body.

"**EEA national**" has the meaning given in regulation 2(1) of the 2006 EEA Regulations.

"**an external student**" is a student studying for a degree from a UK degree awarding body without any requirement to attend the UK degree awarding body's premises or a UK Listed Body's premises for lectures and tutorials.

"**United Kingdom passport**" bears the meaning it has in the Immigration Act 1971.

"**a UK Bachelors degree**" means

(a) A programme of study or research which leads to the award, by or on behalf of a university, college or other body which is authorised by Royal Charter or by or under an Act of Parliament to grant degrees, of a qualification designated by the awarding institution to be of Bachelors degree level; or

(b) A programme of study or research, which leads to a recognised award for the purposes of section 214(2)(c) of the Education Reform Act 1988, of a qualification designated by the awarding institution to be of Bachelors degree level.

"**Immigration Officer**" includes a Customs Officer acting as an Immigration Officer.

"**Multiple Entry work permit employment**" is work permit employment where the person concerned does not intend to spend a continuous period in the United Kingdom in work permit employment.

"**public funds**" means

(a) housing under Part VI or VII of the Housing Act 1996 and under Part II of the Housing Act 1985, Part I or II of the Housing (Scotland) Act 1987, Part II of the Housing (Northern Ireland) Order 1981 or Part II of the Housing (Northern Ireland) Order 1988;

(b) attendance allowance, severe disablement allowance, carer's allowance and disability living allowance under Part III of the Social Security Contribution and Benefits Act 1992; income support, council tax benefit and housing benefit under Part VII of that Act; a social fund payment under Part VIII of that Act; child benefit under Part IX of that Act; income based jobseeker's allowance under the Jobseekers Act 1995, income related allowance under Part 1 of the Welfare Reform Act 2007 (employment and support allowance) state pension credit under the State Pension Credit Act 2002; or child tax credit and working tax credit under Part 1 of the Tax Credits Act 2002;

(c) attendance allowance, severe disablement allowance, carer's allowance and disability living allowance under Part III of the Social Security Contribution and Benefits (Northern Ireland) Act 1992; income support, council tax benefit and, housing benefit under Part VII of that Act; a social fund payment under Part VIII of that Act; child benefit under Part IX of that Act; income based jobseeker's allowance under the Jobseekers (Northern Ireland) Order 1995 or income related allowance under Part 1 of the Welfare Reform Act (Northern Ireland) 2007;

(d) Universal Credit under Part 1 of the Welfare Reform Act 2012 or Personal Independence Payment under Part 4 of that Act;

(e) Universal Credit, Personal Independence Payment or any domestic rate relief under the Northern Ireland Welfare Reform Act 2013;

(f) a council tax reduction under a council tax reduction scheme made under section 13A of the Local Government Finance Act 1992 in relation to England or Wales or a council tax reduction pursuant to the Council Tax Reduction (Scotland) Regulations 2012 or the Council Tax Reduction (State Pension Credit) (Scotland) Regulations 2012.

"**settled in the United Kingdom**" means that the person concerned:

(a) is free from any restriction on the period for which he may remain save that a person entitled to an exemption under Section 8 of the Immigration Act 1971 (otherwise than as a member of the home forces) is not to be regarded as settled in the United Kingdom except in so far as Section 8(5A) so provides; and

(b) is either:

(i) ordinarily resident in the United Kingdom without having entered or remained in breach of the immigration laws; or

(ii) despite having entered or remained in breach of the immigration laws, has subsequently entered lawfully or has been granted leave to remain and is ordinarily resident.

"a parent" includes

(a) the stepfather of a child whose father is dead and the reference to stepfather includes a relationship arising through civil partnership;

(b) the stepmother of a child whose mother is dead and the reference to stepmother includes a relationship arising through civil partnership and;

(c) the father as well as the mother of an illegitimate child where he is proved to be the father;

(d) an adoptive parent, where a child was adopted in accordance with a decision taken by the competent administrative authority or court in a country whose adoption orders are recognised by the United Kingdom or where a child is the subject of a de facto adoption in accordance with the requirements of paragraph 309A of these Rules (except that an adopted child or a child who is the subject of a de facto adoption may not make an application for leave to enter or remain in order to accompany, join or remain with an adoptive parent under paragraphs 297–303);

(e) in the case of a child born in the United Kingdom who is not a British citizen, a person to whom there has been a genuine transfer of parental responsibility on the ground of the original parent(s)' inability to care for the child.

"date of application" means the date of application determined in accordance with paragraph 30 or 34G of these rules as appropriate.

"a valid application" means an application made in accordance with the requirements of Part 1 of these Rules.

"refugee leave" means limited leave granted pursuant to paragraph 334 or 335 of these rules and has not been revoked pursuant to paragraph 339A or 339B of these rules.

"humanitarian protection" means limited leave granted pursuant to paragraph 339C of these rules and has not been revoked pursuant to paragraph 339G or 339H of these rules.

"a period of imprisonment" referred to in these rules has the same meaning as set out in section 38(2) of the UK Borders Act 2007.

"Overstayed" or **"Overstaying"** means the applicant has stayed in the UK beyond the latest of:

(i) the time limit attached to the last period of leave granted, or

(ii) beyond the period that his leave was extended under sections 3C or 3D of the Immigration Act 1971,

"intention to live permanently with the other" or **"intend to live together permanently"** means an intention to live together, evidenced by a clear commitment from both parties that they will live together permanently in the UK immediately following the outcome of the application in question or as soon as circumstances permit thereafter. However, where an application is made under Appendix Armed Forces the words "in the UK" in this definition do not apply. [Where an application is made under Appendix FM and the sponsor is a permanent member of HM Diplomatic Service, or a comparable UK-based staff member of the British Council, the Department for International Development or the Home Office on a tour of duty outside the UK, the words "in the UK" in this definition do not apply.]

"present and settled" or **"present and settled in the UK"** means that the person concerned is settled in the United Kingdom and, at the time that an application under these Rules is made, is physically present here or is coming here with or to join the applicant and intends to make the UK their home with the applicant if the application is successful.

Where the person concerned is a British Citizen or settled in the UK and is:

(i) a member of HM Forces serving overseas, or

(ii) a permanent member of HM Diplomatic Service, or a comparable UK-based staff member of the British Council, the Department for International Development or the

Home Office on a tour of duty outside the UK, and the applicant has provided the evidence specified in paragraph 26A of Appendix FM-SE,

then for the purposes of Appendix FM the person is to be regarded as present and settled in the UK, and in paragraphs R-LTRP.1.1.(a) and R-ILRP.1.1.(a) of Appendix FM the words "and their partner must be in the UK" are to be disregarded.

For the purposes of an application as a fiancé(e) or proposed civil partner under paragraphs 289AA to 295 or Appendix FM, an EEA national who holds a document certifying permanent residence issued under the 2006 EEA Regulations is to be regarded as present and settled in the UK.

"**sponsor**" means the person in relation to whom an applicant is seeking leave to enter or remain as their spouse, fiance, civil partner, proposed civil partner, unmarried partner, same-sex partner or dependent relative, as the case may be, under paragraphs 277 to 295O or 317 to 319 or the person in relation to whom an applicant is seeking entry clearance or leave as their partner or dependent relative under Appendix FM.

"**overcrowded**" means overcrowded within the meaning of the Housing Act 1985, the Housing (Scotland) Act 1987 or the Housing (Northern Ireland) Order 1988 (as appropriate).

"**working illegally**" means working in breach of conditions of leave or working when in the UK without valid leave where such leave is required.

"**in breach of immigration laws**" means without valid leave where such leave is required, or in breach of the conditions of leave.

"**adequate**" and "**adequately**" in relation to a maintenance and accommodation requirement shall mean that, after income tax, national insurance contributions and housing costs have been deducted, there must be available to the family the level of income that would be available to them if the family was in receipt of income support.

"**occupy exclusively**" in relation to accommodation shall mean that part of the accommodation must be for the exclusive use of the family.

"**must not be leading an independent life**" or "is not leading an independent life" means that the applicant does not have a partner as defined in Appendix FM; is living with their parents (except where they are at boarding school, college or university as part of their full-time education); is not employed full-time (unless aged 18 years or over); is wholly or mainly dependent upon their parents for financial support (unless aged 18 years or over); and is wholly or mainly dependent upon their parents for emotional support. [Where a relative other than a parent may act as the sponsor of the applicant, references in this definition to "parents" shall be read as applying to that other relative.]

"**prohibited degree of relationship**" has the same meaning as in the Marriage Act 1949, the Marriage (Prohibited Degrees of Relationship) Act 1986 and the Civil Partnership Act 2004.

"**visa nationals**" are the persons specified in Appendix 1 to these Rules who need a visa for the United Kingdom.

"**non-visa nationals**" are persons who are not specified in Appendix 1 to these Rules.

"**specified national**" is a person specified in Appendix 3 to these Rules who seeks leave to enter the United Kingdom for a period of more than 6 months.

"**employment**" unless the contrary intention appears, includes paid and unpaid employment, paid and unpaid work placements undertaken as part of a course or period of study, self employment and engaging in business or any professional activity.

"**the Human Rights Convention**" means the Convention for the Protection of Human Rights and Fundamental Freedoms, agreed by the Council of Europe at Rome on 4th November 1950 as it has effect for the time being in relation to the United Kingdom.

"**immigration employment document**" means a work permit or any other document which relates to employment and is issued for the purpose of these Rules or in connection with leave to enter or remain in the United Kingdom.

"Employment as a Doctor in Training" means employment in a medical post or training programme which has been approved by the Postgraduate Medical Education and Training Board, or employment in a postgraduate training programme in dentistry.

"these Rules" means these immigration rules (HC 395) made under section 3(2) of the Immigration Act 1971.

A **"refugee"** is a refugee as defined in regulation 2 of The Refugee or Person in Need of International Protection (Qualification) Regulation 2006.

In part 6A of these Rules, **"relevant grant allocation period"** means a specified period of time, which will be published by the Secretary of State on the visas and immigration pages of the gov.uk website, during which applications for entry clearance or leave to enter in respect of a particular route may be granted subject to the grant allocation for that period;

In part 6A of these Rules, **"grant allocation"** means a limit, details of which will be published by the Secretary of State on the visas and immigration pages of the gov.uk website, on the number of grants of entry clearance or leave to enter which may be granted in respect of a particular route during the relevant grant allocation period;

Under Part 6A of these Rules, **"Highly Skilled Migrant"** means a migrant granted leave under paragraphs 135A to 135G of the Rules in force before 30th June 2008.

Under Part 6A of these Rules, **"Highly Skilled Migrant Programme Approval Letter"** means a letter issued by the Home Office confirming that the applicant meets the criteria specified by the Secretary of State for entry to or stay in the UK under the Highly Skilled Migrant Programme.

Under Part 6A of these Rules, **"Innovator"** means a migrant granted leave under paragraphs 210A to 210F of the Rules in force before 30th June 2008.

Under Part 6A of these Rules, **"Participant in the Fresh Talent Working in Scotland Scheme"** means a migrant granted leave under paragraphs 143A to 143F of the Rules in force before 30th June 2008.

Under Part 6A of these Rules, **"Participant in the International Graduates Scheme"** means a migrant granted leave under paragraphs 135O to 135T of the Rules in force before 30th June 2008.

Under Part 6A of these Rules, **"Postgraduate Doctor or Dentist"** means a migrant who is granted leave under paragraphs 70 to 75 of these Rules.

Under Part 6A of these Rules, **"Self-Employed"** means an applicant is registered as self-employed with HM Revenue & Customs, or is employed by a company of which the applicant is a controlling shareholder.

Under Part 6A of these Rules, **"Student"** means a migrant who is granted leave under paragraphs 57 to 62 of these Rules.

Under Part 6A of these Rules, **"Student Nurse"** means a migrant who is granted leave under paragraphs 63 to 69 of these Rules.

Under Part 6A of these Rules, **"Student Re-Sitting an Examination"** means a migrant who is granted leave under paragraphs 69A to 69F of these Rules.

Under Part 6A of these Rules, **"Student Writing-Up a Thesis"** means a migrant who is granted leave under paragraphs 69G to 69L of these Rules.

Under Part 6A of these Rules, **"Work Permit Holder"** means a migrant who is granted leave under paragraphs 128 to 133 of these Rules.

Under Part 6A of these Rules, **"Prospective Student"** means a migrant who is granted leave under paragraphs 82 to 87 of these rules.

Under Part 6A of these Rules, an **"A-rated Sponsor"** is a Sponsor which is recorded as being "A-rated" on the register of licensed Sponsors maintained by the United Kingdom Border Agency.

Under Part 6A and Appendix A of these Rules, a "**B-rated Sponsor**" is a sponsor which is recorded as being "B-rated" on the register of licensed sponsors maintained by the United Kingdom Border Agency.

Under Part 6A of these Rules, "**Highly Trusted Sponsor**" means a sponsor which is recorded as being "Highly Trusted" on the register of licensed sponsors maintained by the United Kingdom Border Agency.

Under paragraph 34K of these Rules, a "**Premium Sponsor**" is a Sponsor which is recorded as holding Premium status on the register of licensed Sponsors maintained by the United Kingdom Border Agency.

Under Part 6A of these Rules, "**Certificate of Sponsorship**" means an authorisation issued by the Secretary of State to a Sponsor in respect of one or more applications, or potential applications, for entry clearance, leave to enter or remain as a Tier 2 migrant or a Tier 5 migrant in accordance with these Rules.

Under Part 6A and Appendix A of these Rules, "**Confirmation of Acceptance for Studies**" means a unique reference number electronically issued by a sponsor via the Sponsor Management System to an applicant for entry clearance, leave to enter or remain as a Tier 4 Migrant in accordance with these Rules.

Under Parts 6A and 9 of these Rules, "**Certificate of Sponsorship Checking Service**" means a computerised interface with the Points Based System computer database which allows a United Kingdom Border Agency caseworker or entry clearance officer assessing a migrant's application for entry clearance, leave to enter or leave to remain to access and review details of the migrant's Certificate of Sponsorship, including details of the migrant's Sponsor, together with details of the job and other details associated with the circumstances in which the Certificate of Sponsorship was issued.

Under Part 6A and Appendix A of these Rules, "**length of the period of engagement**" is the period beginning with the employment start date as recorded on the Certificate of Sponsorship Checking service entry which relates to the Certificate of Sponsorship reference number for which the migrant was awarded points under Appendix A and ending on the employment end date as recorded in the same entry.

Under Part 6A and Appendix A of these Rules, a "**genuine vacancy**" is a vacancy which exists in practice (or would exist in practice were it not filled by the applicant) for a position which:

(a) requires the jobholder to undertake the specific duties and responsibilities, for the weekly hours and length of the period of engagement, described by the Sponsor in the Certificate of Sponsorship relating to the applicant; and

(b) does not include dissimilar and/or unequally skilled duties such that the Standard Occupational Classification (SOC) code used by the Sponsor as stated in the Certificate of Sponsorship relating to the applicant is inappropriate.

Under Part 6A and Appendix A of these Rules, working for "**the same employer**" or "**the same Sponsor**" includes working for a different employer or Sponsor in circumstances which constitute a "relevant transfer" under Regulation 3(1) of the Transfer of Undertakings (Protection of Employment) Regulations 2006, or similar protection, provided the worker's duties remain unchanged.

Under Part 6A and Appendix A of these Rules, "**Designated Competent Body**" means an organisation which has been approved by the UK Border Agency to endorse applicants as a Tier 1 (Exceptional Talent) Migrant.

Under Part 6A and Appendix A of these Rules, "**Tier 1 (Exceptional Talent) Unique Reference Number**" means a unique reference number issued for the purposes of managing the Tier 1 (Exceptional Talent) Limit and provided by the UK Border Agency to an applicant prior to making his application as a Tier 1 (Exceptional Talent) Migrant.

For the purpose of paragraph 320(7B) of these Rules "**Removal Decision**" means (a) a decision to remove in accordance with section 10 of the Immigration and Asylum Act 1999; (b) a decision to remove an illegal entrant by way of directions under paragraphs 8 to 10 of Schedule 2 to the Immigration Act 1971 or (c) a decision to remove in accordance with section 47 of the Immigration, Asylum and Nationality Act 2006. Pending appeal has the same meaning as in section 104 of the nationality, immigration and asylum act 2002.

Under Part 6A of these Rules, "**Confirmation of Acceptance for Studies Checking Service**" means a computerised interface with the Points Based System computer database which allows a United Kingdom Border Agency caseworker or entry clearance officer assessing a migrant's application for entry clearance, leave to enter or leave to remain as a Tier 4 migrant under these Rules to access and review details of the migrant's Confirmation of Acceptance for Studies, including details of the migrant's Sponsor, together with details of the course of study and other details associated with the circumstances in which the Confirmation of Acceptance for Studies was issued.

Under Part 6A of these Rules, "**Established Entertainer**" means an applicant who is applying for leave to remain as a Tier 2 (General) Migrant or a Tier 2 (Intra-Company Transfer) Migrant in respect of whom the following conditions are satisfied:

(a) the Certificate of Sponsorship Checking Service entry to which the applicant's Certificate of Sponsorship reference number relates, records that the applicant is being sponsored in an occupation which is defined in the United Kingdom Border Agency's Transitional Guidance as being a job in the entertainment sector,

(b) the applicant has, or has previously had, entry clearance, leave to enter or leave to remain in the UK as a Work Permit Holder, and the work permit that led to that grant was issued in the sports and entertainment category to enable him to work in the occupation in which he is, at the date of the application for leave to remain, currently being sponsored,

(c) the applicant's last grant of leave was:

(i) as a Work Permit Holder in the sports and entertainment category, provided the work permit on the basis of which that leave was granted was issued in the sports and entertainment category to enable him to work either in the occupation in which he is, at the date of the current application for leave to remain, currently being sponsored, or in another occupation which is defined in the UK Border Agency's Transitional Guidance as being a job in the entertainment sector, or

(ii) leave to remain as a Tier 2 (General) Migrant or a Tier 2 (Intra-Company Transfer) Migrant, provided (in either case):

(1) he previously had leave as a Work Permit Holder in the sports and entertainment category to work as described in (i) above,

(2) he has not been granted entry clearance in this or any other route since his last grant of leave as a Work Permit Holder, and

(3) his last grant of leave was made to enable him to work either in the occupation in which he is, at the date of the current application for leave to remain, currently being sponsored or in another occupation which is defined in the UK Border Agency's Transitional Guidance as being a job in the entertainment sector,

(d) the Certificate of Sponsorship Checking Service entry to which the applicant's Certificate of Sponsorship reference number relates records:

(i) that the applicant will be paid a salary for the job that is at or above the appropriate entertainments industry rate, as listed in the United Kingdom Border Agency's Transitional Guidance; and

(ii) that before agreeing to employ the applicant, the Sponsor consulted with such bodies as the United Kingdom Border Agency's Transitional Guidance indicates that it should consult with before employing someone in this capacity, and

(e) the applicant has not spent a period of 5 years or more in the UK, beginning with the last grant of entry clearance, as a Qualifying Work Permit Holder, Tier 2 (General) Migrant or Tier 2 (Intra-Company Transfer) Migrant, or in any combination of these.

Under Part 6A of these Rules, "**Qualifying Work Permit Holder**" means a Work Permit Holder who was issued a work permit in the business and commercial or sports and entertainment work permit categories.

Under Part 6A of these Rules, "**Senior Care Worker**" means an applicant who is applying for leave to remain as a Tier 2 (General) Migrant or a Tier 2 (Intra-Company Transfer) Migrant in respect of whom the following conditions are satisfied:

(a) the Certificate of Sponsorship Checking Service entry to which the applicant's Certificate of Sponsorship reference number relates, records that the applicant is being sponsored in an occupation which is defined in the codes of practice for Tier 2 sponsors published by the UK Border Agency as being a Senior Care Worker role,

(b) the applicant's last grant of leave was:

(i) as a Qualifying Work Permit Holder, or

(ii) leave to remain as a Tier 2 (General) Migrant or a Tier 2 (Intra-Company Transfer) Migrant, provided (in either case):

(1) he previously had leave as a Qualifying Work Permit Holder, and

(2) he has not been granted entry clearance in this or any other route since his last grant of leave as a Qualifying Work Permit Holder.

(c) the work permit or Certificate of Sponsorship that led to the last grant of leave was issued to enable the applicant to work as a senior care worker, and

(d) the applicant has not spent a period of 5 years or more in the UK, beginning with the last grant of entry clearance, as a Qualifying Work Permit Holder, Tier 2 (General) Migrant or Tier 2 (Intra-Company Transfer) Migrant, or in any combination of these.

Under Part 6A of these Rules, "**Sponsor**" means the person or Government that the Certificate of Sponsorship Checking Service or Confirmation of Acceptance for Studies Checking Service records as being the Sponsor for a migrant.

Under Part 6A of these Rules, a reference to a "**sponsor licence**" means a licence granted by the Secretary of State to a person who, by virtue of such a grant, is licensed as a Sponsor under Tiers 2, 4 or 5 of the Points Based System.

In Part 6A and Appendices A and J of these Rules, "**settled worker**" means a person who:

(i) is a national of the UK,

(ii) is a person with a right of residence in accordance with the Immigration (European Economic Area) Regulations 2006 or, except where that person is subject to worker authorisation, the regulations made under section 2 of the European Union (Accessions) Act 2006 in combination with section 2(2) of the European Communities Act 1972 or the regulations made under section 4 of the European Union (Croatian Accession and Irish Protocol) Act 2013,

(iii) is a British overseas territories citizen, except those from Sovereign Base Areas in Cyprus,

(iv) is a Commonwealth citizen with leave to enter or remain granted on the basis of UK Ancestry (paragraphs 186 to 193 of these Rules), or

(v) has settled status in the UK within the meaning of the Immigration Act 1971, as amended by the Immigration and Asylum Act 1999, and the Nationality, Immigration and Asylum Act 2002.

Under Part 6A of these Rules, “**supplementary employment**” means other employment in a job which appears on the Shortage Occupation List in Appendix K, or in the same profession and at the same professional level as that which the migrant is being sponsored to do provided that:

(a) the migrant remains working for the Sponsor in the employment that the Certificate of Sponsorship Checking Service records that the migrant is being sponsored to do,

(b) the other employment does not exceed 20 hours per week and takes place outside of the hours when the migrant is contracted to work for the Sponsor in the employment the migrant is being sponsored to do.

Under part 6A and Appendix A of these Rules, “**overseas higher education institution**” means an institution which holds overseas accreditation confirmed by UK NARIC as offering degree programmes which are equivalent to UK degree level qualifications, and which teach no more than half of a degree programme in the UK as a study abroad programme.

“**Business person**” means a migrant granted leave under paragraphs 200 to 208 of the Rules in force before 30th June 2008.

“**Investor**” means a migrant granted leave under paragraphs 224 to 229 of the Rules in force before 30th June 2008.

“**Self-employed Lawyer**” means a migrant granted entry clearance, or leave to enter or remain, outside the Rules under the concession for Self-employed lawyers that formerly appeared in Chapter 6, Section 1 Annex D of the Immigration Directorate instructions.

“**Points Based System Migrant**” means a migrant applying for or granted leave as a Tier 1 Migrant, a Tier 2 Migrant, a Tier 4 Migrant or a Tier 5 Migrant.

“**Tier 1 Migrant**” means a migrant who is granted leave as a Tier 1 (Exceptional Talent) Migrant, a Tier 1 (General) Migrant, a Tier 1 (Entrepreneur) Migrant, a Tier 1 (Investor) Migrant, a Tier 1 (Graduate Entrepreneur) Migrant or a Tier 1 (Post-Study Work) Migrant.

“**Tier 1 (Exceptional Talent) Migrant**” means a migrant who is granted leave under paragraphs 245B to 245BF of these Rules.

“**Tier 1 (General) Migrant**” means a migrant who is granted leave under paragraphs 245C to 245CE of these Rules.

“**Tier 1 (Entrepreneur) Migrant**” means a migrant who is granted leave under paragraphs 245D to 245DF of these Rules.

“**Tier 1 (Investor) Migrant**” means a migrant who is granted leave under paragraphs 245E to 245EF of these Rules.

“**Tier 1 (Graduate Entrepreneur) Migrant**” means a migrant who is granted leave under paragraphs 245F to 245FB of these Rules in place on or after 6 April 2012.

“**Tier 1 (Post-Study Work) Migrant**” means a migrant who is granted leave under paragraphs 245F to 245FE of the Rules in place before 6 April 2012.

“**Tier 2 Migrant**” means a migrant who is granted leave as a Tier 2 (Intra-Company Transfer) Migrant, a Tier 2 (General) Migrant, a Tier 2 (Minister of Religion) Migrant or a Tier 2 (Sportsperson) Migrant.

“**Tier 2 (Intra-Company Transfer) Migrant**” means a migrant granted leave under paragraphs 245G to 245GF of these Rules.

“**Tier 2 (General) Migrant**” means a migrant granted leave under paragraphs 245H to 245HF of these Rules and who obtains points under paragraphs 76 to 84A of Appendix A.

"**Tier 2 (Minister of Religion) Migrant**" means a migrant granted leave under paragraphs 245H to 245HF of these Rules and who obtains points under paragraphs 85 to 92 of Appendix A.

"**Tier 2 (Sportsperson) Migrant**" means a migrant granted leave under paragraphs 245H to 245HF of these Rules and who obtains points under paragraphs 93 to 100 of Appendix A.

"**Tier 4 (General) Student**" means a migrant granted leave under paragraphs 245ZT to 245ZY of these Rules.

"**Tier 4 (Child) Student**" means a migrant granted leave under paragraphs 245ZZ to 245ZZD of these Rules.

"**Tier 4 Migrant**" means a Tier 4 (General) Student or a Tier 4 (Child) Student.

"**expected end date of a course leading to the award of a PhD**" means the date the PhD is expected to be formally confirmed, by the sponsor, as completed to the standard required for the award of a PhD and recorded on the confirmation of acceptance for studies accompanying the application for leave to remain as a Tier 4 (General) Student on the doctorate extension scheme.

"**Tier 5 (Youth Mobility) Temporary Migrant**" means a migrant granted leave under paragraphs 245ZI to 245ZL of these Rules.

"Tier 5 (Temporary Worker) Migrant" means a migrant granted leave under paragraphs 245ZM to 245ZS of these Rules.

"**Deemed sponsorship status**" means that the country or territory is not required to issue its nationals or passport holders with a Certificate of Sponsorship in order to enable a successful application under the Tier 5 Youth Mobility Scheme and is held by a country or territory listed as such at Appendix G of these Rules.

"**Tier 5 Migrant**" means a migrant who is either a Tier 5 (Temporary Worker) Migrant or a Tier 5 (Youth Mobility) Temporary Migrant.

Under Part 6A of these Rules "**Government Authorised Exchange Scheme**" means a scheme under the Tier 5 (Temporary Worker) Government Authorised Exchange sub-category which is endorsed by a Government Department in support of Government objectives and provides temporary work in an occupation which appears on the list of occupations skilled to National Qualifications Framework level 3, as stated in the codes of practice for Tier 2 Sponsors published by the UK Border Agency, and where the migrant will be supernumerary.

Under Part 6A of these Rules "**Work Experience Programme**" means work experience including volunteering and job-shadowing, internships and work exchange programmes under a Government Authorised Exchange Scheme.

Under Part 6A of these Rules "**Research Programme**" means research programmes and fellowships under a Government Authorised Exchange Scheme where the migrant is working on a scientific, academic, medical, or government research project/s at either a UK Higher Education Institution or another research institution operating under the authority and/or financial sponsorship of a relevant Government Department.

Under Part 6A of these Rules "**Training Programme**" means a training programme under a Government Authorised Exchange Scheme where the migrant either receives formal, practical training in the fields of science and/or medicine or will be trained by HM Armed Forces or by UK emergency services, or meets the requirements of paragraph 245ZQ(b)(vi)(2) to (4).

Under Part 6A of these Rules "**Overseas Government Language Programme**" means an overseas Government sponsored professional language development programme under the Government Authorised Exchange Scheme where the migrant delivers language training and participates in a cultural exchange programme that is fully or partially paid for by the overseas government or an organisation affiliated to an overseas government.

Under Part 6A of these Rules, "**Temporary Engagement as a Sports Broadcaster**" means providing guest expert commentary on a particular sporting event.

"**Contractual Service Supplier**" means a migrant who is granted entry clearance, leave to enter or leave to remain under paragraphs 245ZP(e) and 245ZR(b)(ii)(3) of these Rules on the basis that the circumstances in which such leave is sought engage the United Kingdom's commitments in respect of contractual service suppliers under the relevant provisions of one of the agreements specified in paragraph 111(f)(i) of Appendix A of these Rules.

"**Independent Professional**" means a migrant who is granted entry clearance, leave to enter or leave to remain under paragraphs 245ZP(e) and 245ZR(b)(ii)(3) of these Rules on the basis that the circumstances in which such leave is sought engage the United Kingdom's commitments in respect of independent professionals under the relevant provisions of one of the agreements specified in paragraph 111(f)(i) of Appendix A of these Rules.

"**Jewish Agency Employee**" means a migrant granted leave outside of these Rules under the concession that formerly appeared in Chapter 17 Section 5 Part 2 of the Immigration Directorate Instructions.

"**Member of the Operational Ground Staff of an Overseas-owned Airline**" means a migrant granted leave under paragraphs 178 to 185 of the Rules in force before 27 November 2008.

"**Minister of Religion, Missionary or Member of a Religious Order**" means a migrant granted leave under paragraphs 170 to 177A of the Rules in force before 27 November 2008.

"**Overseas Qualified Nurse or Midwife**" means a migrant granted leave under paragraphs 69M to 69R of the Rules in force before 27 November 2008.

"**Participant in the Science and Engineering Graduates Scheme**" means a migrant granted leave under paragraphs 135O to 135T of the Rules in force before 1 May 2007.

"**Representative of an Overseas Newspaper, News Agency or Broadcasting Organisation**" means a migrant granted leave under paragraphs 136 to 143 of the Rules in force before 27 November 2008.

"**Student Union Sabbatical Officer**" means a migrant granted leave under paragraphs 87A to 87F of the Rules in force before 27 November 2008.

"**Working Holidaymaker**" means a migrant granted leave under paragraphs 95 to 97 of the Rules in force before 27 November 2008.

A "**visitor**" is a person granted leave to enter or remain in the UK under paragraphs 40–56Z, 75A–M or 82–87 of these Rules.

A "**Business Visitor**" is a person granted leave to enter or remain in the UK under paragraphs 46G–46L, 75A–F or 75G–M of these Rules.

An "**Academic Visitor**" is a person who is from an overseas academic institution or who is highly qualified within his own field of expertise seeking leave to enter the UK to carry out research and associated activities for his own purposes.

A "**Visiting Professor**" is a person who is seeking leave to enter the UK as an academic professor to accompany students who are studying here on Study Abroad Programmes.

A "**Sports Visitor**" is a person granted leave to enter or remain in the UK under paragraphs 46M–46R of these Rules.

An "**Amateur**" is a person who engages in a sport or creative activity solely for personal enjoyment and who is not seeking to derive a living from the activity.

A "**Series of events**" is two or more linked events, such as a tour, or rounds of a competition, which do not add up to a league or a season.

An "**Entertainer Visitor**" is a person granted leave to enter or remain in the UK under paragraphs 46S–46X of these Rules.

A "**Special Visitor**" is a person granted leave for a short-term visit in the following circumstances:

"**A visitor undertaking permitted paid engagements**" is someone who is granted leave to enter under paragraphs 56X–56Z of these Rules.

(a) A person granted leave to enter or remain in the UK as a visitor for private medical treatment under paragraphs 51–56 of these Rules,

(b) A person granted leave to enter or remain in the UK for the purpose of marriage or to enter into civil partnership under paragraphs 56D–56F of these Rules,

(c) A person granted leave to enter or remain in the UK as a Parent of a child at school under paragraphs 56A–56C of these Rules,

(d) A person granted leave to enter or remain in the UK as a Child Visitor under paragraphs 46A–46F of these Rules,

(e) A person granted leave to enter or remain in the UK as a Student Visitor under paragraphs 56K–56M of these Rules,

(f) A person granted leave to enter or remain in the UK as a Prospective Student under paragraphs 82–87 of these Rules,

(g) A person granted leave to enter the UK as a Visitor in transit under paragraphs 47–50 of these Rules, or

(h) A person granted entry clearance, leave to enter or leave to remain in the UK as a Prospective Entrepreneur under paragraphs 56N–56Q of these Rules.

"**Writer, Composer or Artist**" means a migrant granted leave under paragraphs 232 to 237 of the Rules in force before 30th June 2008.

In paragraph 320(7B) and paragraph 320(11) of these Rules:

"**Deception**" means making false representations or submitting false documents (whether or not material to the application), or failing to disclose material facts.

"**Illegal Entrant**" has the same definition as in section 33(1) of the Immigration Act 1971.

In paragraph 320(22) and 322(12) of these Rules, and in paragraphs S-EC.2.3., S-LTR.2.3. and S-ILR.2.3. of Appendix FM to these Rules:

"**relevant NHS body**" means

a) in relation to England—

(i) a National Health Service Trust established under section 25 of the National Health Service Act 2006,

(ii) a NHS foundation trust.

b) in relation to Wales—

(i) a Local Health Board established under section 11 of the National Health Service (Wales) Act 2006,

(ii) a National Health Service Trust established under section 18 of the National Health Service (Wales) Act 2006,

(iii) a Special Health Authority established under 22 of the National Health Service (Wales) Act 2006.

c) in relation to Scotland—

(i) a Health Board or Special Health Board established under section 2 of the National Health Service (Scotland) Act 1978 (c. 29),

(ii) the Common Services Agency for the Scottish Health Service established under section 10 of that Act,

(iii) Healthcare Improvement Scotland established under section 10A of that Act.

d) in relation to Northern Ireland—

(i) the Regional Health and Social Care Board established under the Health and Social Care (Reform) Act (Northern Ireland) 2009,

(ii) a Health and Social Care trust established under the Health and Personal Social Services (Northern Ireland) Order 1991 (S.I. 1991/194 (N.I. 1)) and renamed under the Health and Social Care (Reform) Act (Northern Ireland) 2009.

"relevant NHS regulations" means

(i) The National Health Service (Charges to Overseas Visitors) (Amendment) (Wales) Regulations 2004 (2004 No. 1433);

(ii) The National Health Service (Charges to Overseas Visitors) (Scotland) Regulations 1989 as amended (1989 No. 364);

(iii) The Health and Personal Social Services (Provision of Health Services to Persons not Ordinarily Resident) Regulations (Northern Ireland) 2005 (2005 No. 551); or

(iv) The National Health Service (Charges to Overseas Visitors) Regulations (2011 No. 1556).

"administrative review" means a review conducted in accordance with Appendix AR of these Rules;

"eligible decision" means a decision eligible for administrative review as referred to in paragraph AR3.2 of Appendix AR of these Rules;

"working day" means a business day in the part of the UK in which the applicant resides or (as the case may be) is detained.

Note: Definitions of 'primary degree', 'contractual services supplier', inserted and definitions of 'supplementary employment' and 'training programme' amended from 13 December 2012 subject to savings for applications made before that date (HC 760). Definition of public funds amended from 13 April 2013 (HC 1038). Definition of 'settled worker' amended and definitions of 'expected end date of a course leading to a PhD' and 'independent professional' inserted from 6 April 2013 subject to savings for applications made before that date (HC 1039). Definition of 'relevant NHS body'amended from 1 July 2013 (HC 244). Definition of 'visitor' inserted and definition of 'UK recognised body' amended from 1 October 2013 subject to savings for applications made before that date (HC 628). Definitions of 'must not be leading an independent life' and 'intention to live permanently with the other' substituted from 1 December 2013 subject to savings for applications made before that date (HC 803). Definition of 'working for the same employer' substituted, definition of 'overseas government language programme' and 'curtailment' inserted, definitions of 'certificate of sponsorship checking service', 'relevant grant allocation period'. 'grant allocation' amended, the sentence after the definition of 'present and settled' inserted and words at the end of paragraph 6 deleted from 6 April 2014 (HC 1138; see implementation section of HC 1138 as amended by HC 1201 for provisions as to savings). Definition of 'overstayed' amended and definitions of 'administrative review', 'eligible decision' and 'working day' inserted from 20 October 2014, definition of 'intention to live permanently with the other' amended, definition of 'present and settled' substituted, and definition of 'must not be leading an independent life' amended from 6 November 2014 (HC 693). Definition of 'genuine vacancy' inserted from 6 November 2014 subject to savings for applications made before that date (HC 693).

6A. For the purpose of these Rules, a person ("P") is not to be regarded as having (or potentially having) recourse to public funds merely because P is (or will be) reliant in whole or in part on public funds provided to P's sponsor unless, as a result of P's presence in the United Kingdom, the sponsor is (or would be) entitled to increased or additional public funds (save where such entitlement to increased or additional public funds is by virtue of P and the sponsor's joint entitlement to benefits under the regulations referred to in paragraph 6B).

6B. Subject to paragraph 6C, a person (P) shall not be regarded as having recourse to public funds if P is entitled to benefits specified under section 115 of the Immigration and

Asylum Act 1999 by virtue of regulations made under sub-sections (3) and (4) of that section or section 42 of the Tax Credits Act 2002.

6C. A person (P) making an application from outside the United Kingdom will be regarded as having recourse to public funds where P relies upon the future entitlement to any public funds that would be payable to P or to P's sponsor as a result of P's presence in the United Kingdom, (including those benefits to which P or the sponsor would be entitled as a result of P's presence in the United Kingdom under the regulations referred to in paragraph 6B).

Part 1

General Provisions Regarding Leave to Enter or Remain in the United Kingdom

Leave to enter the United Kingdom

7. A person who is neither a British citizen nor a Commonwealth citizen with the right of abode nor a person who is entitled to enter or remain in the United Kingdom by virtue of the provisions of the 2006 EEA Regulations requires leave to enter the United Kingdom.

8. Under Sections 3 and 4 of the Immigration Act 1971 an Immigration Officer when admitting to the United Kingdom a person subject to immigration control under that Act may give leave to enter for a limited period and, if he does, may impose all or any of the following conditions:

(i) a condition restricting employment or occupation in the United Kingdom;

(ii) a condition requiring the person to maintain and accommodate himself, and any dependants of his, without recourse to public funds; and

(iii) a condition requiring the person to register with the police.

He may also require him to report to the appropriate Medical Officer of Environmental Health. Under Section 24 of the 1971 Act it is an offence knowingly to remain beyond the time limit or fail to comply with such a condition or requirement.

9. The time limit and any conditions attached will be made known to the person concerned either:

(i) by written notice given to him or endorsed by the Immigration Officer in his passport or travel document; or

(ii) in any other manner permitted by the Immigration (Leave to Enter and Remain) Order 2000.

Exercise of the power to refuse leave to enter the United Kingdom or to cancel leave to enter or remain which is in force

10. The power to refuse leave to enter the United Kingdom or to cancel leave to enter or remain which is already in force is not to be exercised by an Immigration Officer acting on his own. The authority of a Chief Immigration Officer or of an Immigration Inspector must always be obtained.

Suspension of leave to enter or remain in the United Kingdom

10A. Where a person has arrived in the United Kingdom with leave to enter or remain which is in force but which was given to him before his arrival he may be examined by an Immigration Officer under paragraph 2A of Schedule 2 to the Immigration Act 1971. An Immigration Officer examining a person under paragraph 2A may suspend that person's leave to enter or remain in the United Kingdom until the examination is completed.

Cancellation of leave to enter or remain in the United Kingdom

10B. Where a person arrives in the United Kingdom with leave to enter or remain in the United Kingdom which is already in force, an Immigration Officer may cancel that leave.

Requirement for persons arriving in the United Kingdom or seeking entry through the Channel Tunnel to produce evidence of identity and nationality

11. A person must, on arrival in the United Kingdom or when seeking entry through the Channel Tunnel, produce on request by the Immigration Officer:

(i) a valid national passport or other document satisfactorily establishing his identity and nationality; and

(ii) such information as may be required to establish whether he requires leave to enter the United Kingdom and, if so, whether and on what terms leave to enter should be given.

Requirement for a person not requiring leave to enter the United Kingdom to prove that he has the right of abode

12. A person claiming to be a British citizen must prove that he has the right of abode in the United Kingdom by producing either:

(i) a United Kingdom passport describing him as a British citizen or as a citizen of the United Kingdom and Colonies having the right of abode in the United Kingdom; or

(ii) a certificate of entitlement duly issued by or on behalf of the Government of the United Kingdom certifying that he has the right of abode.

13. A person claiming to be a Commonwealth citizen with the right of abode in the United Kingdom must prove that he has the right of abode by producing a certificate of entitlement duly issued to him by or on behalf of the Government of the United Kingdom certifying that he has the right of abode.

14. A Commonwealth citizen who has been given limited leave to enter the United Kingdom may later claim to have the right of abode. The time limit on his stay may be removed if he is able to establish a claim to the right of abode, for example by showing that:

(i) immediately before the commencement of the British Nationality Act 1981 he was a Commonwealth citizen born to or legally adopted by a parent who at the time of the birth had citizenship of the United Kingdom and Colonies by his birth in the United Kingdom or any of the Islands; and

(ii) he has not ceased to be a Commonwealth citizen in the meanwhile.

Common travel area

15. The United Kingdom, the Channel Islands, the Isle of Man and the Republic of Ireland collectively form a common travel area. A person who has been examined for the purpose of immigration control at the point at which he entered the area does not normally require leave to enter any other part of it. However certain persons subject to the Immigration (Control of Entry through the Republic of Ireland) Order 1972 (as amended) who enter the United Kingdom through the Republic of Ireland do require leave to enter. This includes:

(i) those who merely passed through the Republic of Ireland;

(ii) persons requiring visas;

(iii) persons who entered the Republic of Ireland unlawfully;

(iv) persons who are subject to directions given by the Secretary of State for their exclusion from the United Kingdom on the ground that their exclusion is conducive to the public good;

(v) persons who entered the Republic from the United Kingdom and Islands after entering there unlawfully or overstaying their leave.

Admission of certain British passport holders

16. A person in any of the following categories may be admitted freely to the United Kingdom on production of a United Kingdom passport issued in the United Kingdom and Islands or the Republic of Ireland prior to 1 January 1973, unless his passport has been endorsed to show that he was subject to immigration control:

(i) a British Dependent Territories citizen;

(ii) a British National (Overseas);

(iii) a British Overseas citizen;

(iv) a British protected person;

(v) a British subject by virtue of Section 30(a) of the British Nationality Act 1981, (who, immediately before the commencement of the 1981 Act would have been a British subject not possessing citizenship of the United Kingdom and Colonies or the citizenship of any other Commonwealth country or territory).

17. British Overseas citizens who hold United Kingdom passports wherever issued and who satisfy the Immigration Officer that they have, since 1 March 1968, been given indefinite leave to enter or remain in the United Kingdom may be given indefinite leave to enter.

Persons outside the United Kingdom

17A. Where a person is outside the United Kingdom but wishes to travel to the United Kingdom an Immigration Officer may give or refuse him leave to enter. An Immigration Officer may exercise these powers whether or not he is, himself, in the United Kingdom. However, an Immigration Officer is not obliged to consider an application for leave to enter from a person outside the United Kingdom.

17B. Where a person having left the common travel area, has leave to enter the United Kingdom which remains in force under article 13 of the Immigration (Leave to Enter and Remain) Order 2000, an Immigration Officer may cancel that leave. An Immigration Officer may exercise these powers whether or not he is, himself, in the United Kingdom. If a person outside the United Kingdom has leave to remain in the United Kingdom which is in force in this way, the Secretary of State may cancel that leave.

Returning residents

18. A person seeking leave to enter the United Kingdom as a returning resident may be admitted for settlement provided the Immigration Officer is satisfied that the person concerned:

(i) had indefinite leave to enter or remain in the United Kingdom when he last left; and

(ii) has not been away from the United Kingdom for more than 2 years; and

(iii) did not receive assistance from public funds towards the cost of leaving the United Kingdom; and

(iv) now seeks admission for the purpose of settlement.

19. A person who does not benefit from the preceding paragraph by reason only of having been away from the United Kingdom too long may nevertheless be admitted as a returning resident if, for example, he has lived here for most of his life.

19A. Where a person who has indefinite leave to enter or remain in the United Kingdom accompanies, on a tour of duty abroad, a spouse, civil partner, unmarried partner or same-sex partner who is a member of HM Forces serving overseas, or a permanent member of HM Diplomatic Service, or a comparable United Kingdom-based staff member of the British Council, or a staff member of the Department for International Development who is a British Citizen or is settled in the United Kingdom, sub-paragraphs (ii) and (iii) of paragraph 18 shall not apply.

20. The leave of a person whose stay in the United Kingdom is subject to a time limit lapses on his going to a country or territory outside the common travel area if the leave was given for a period of six months or less or conferred by a visit visa. In other cases, leave lapses on the holder remaining outside the United Kingdom for a continuous period of more than two years. A person whose leave has lapsed and who returns after a temporary absence abroad within the period of this earlier leave has no claim to admission as a returning resident. His application to re-enter the United Kingdom should be considered in the light of all the relevant circumstances. The same time limit and any conditions attached will normally be reimposed if he meets the requirements of these Rules, unless he is seeking admission in a different capacity from the one in which he was last given leave to enter or remain.

Non-lapsing leave

20A. Leave to enter or remain in the United Kingdom will usually lapse on the holder going to a country or territory outside the common travel area. However, under article 13 of the Immigration (Leave to Enter and Remain) Order 2000 such leave will not lapse where it was given for a period exceeding six months or where it was conferred by means of an entry clearance (other than a visit visa).

Holders of restricted travel documents and passports

21. The leave to enter or remain in the United Kingdom of the holder of a passport or travel document whose permission to enter another country has to be exercised before a given date may be restricted so as to terminate at least 2 months before that date.

22. If his passport or travel document is endorsed with a restriction on the period for which he may remain outside his country of normal residence, his leave to enter or remain in the United Kingdom may be limited so as not to extend beyond the period of authorised absence.

23. The holder of a travel document issued by the Home Office should not be given leave to enter or remain for a period extending beyond the validity of that document. This paragraph and paragraphs 21–22 do not apply to a person who is eligible for admission for settlement or to a spouse or civil partner who is eligible for admission under paragraph 282 or to a person who qualifies for the removal of the time limit on his stay.

Leave to enter granted on arrival in the United Kingdom

23A. A person who is not a visa national and who is seeking leave to enter on arrival in the United Kingdom for a period not exceeding 6 months for a purpose for which prior entry clearance is not required under these Rules may be granted such leave, for a period not exceeding 6 months. This paragraph does not apply where the person is a British National (Overseas), a British overseas territories citizen, a British Overseas citizen, a British protected person, or a person who under the British Nationality Act 1981 is a British subject.

23B. A person who is a British National (Overseas), a British overseas territories citizen, a British Overseas citizen, a British protected person, or a person who under the British Nationality Act 1981 is a British subject, and who is seeking leave to enter on arrival in the United Kingdom for a purpose for which prior entry clearance is not required under these Rules may be granted such leave, irrespective of the period of time for which he seeks entry, for a period not exceeding 6 months.

Entry clearance

24. The following must produce to the Immigration Officer a valid passport or other identity document endorsed with a United Kingdom entry clearance issued to him for the purpose for which he seeks entry:

(i) a visa national;

(ii) any other person (other than British Nationals (Overseas), a British overseas territories citizen, a British Overseas citizen, a British protected person or a person who under the British Nationality Act 1981 is a British subject) who is seeking entry for a period exceeding six months or is seeking entry for a purpose for which prior entry clearance is required under these Rules.

Such a person will be refused leave to enter if he has no such current entry clearance. Any other person who wishes to ascertain in advance whether he is eligible for admission to the United Kingdom may apply for the issue of an entry clearance.

25. Entry clearance takes the form of a visa (for visa nationals) or an entry certificate (for non visa nationals). These documents are to be taken as evidence of the holder's eligibility for entry into the United Kingdom, and accordingly accepted as "entry clearances" within the meaning of the Immigration Act 1971.

25A. An entry clearance which satisfies the requirements set out in article 3 of the Immigration (Leave to Enter and Remain) Order 2000 will have effect as leave to enter the United Kingdom. The requirements are that the entry clearance must specify the purpose for which the holder wishes to enter the United Kingdom and should be endorsed with the conditions to which it is subject or with a statement that it has effect as indefinite leave to enter the United Kingdom. The holder of such an entry clearance will not require leave to enter on arrival in the United Kingdom and, for the purposes of these Rules, will be treated as a person who has arrived in the United Kingdom with leave to enter the United Kingdom which is in force but which was given to him before his arrival.

26. An application for entry clearance will be considered in accordance with the provisions in these Rules governing the grant or refusal of leave to enter. Where appropriate, the term "Entry Clearance Officer" should be substituted for "Immigration Officer".

27. An application for entry clearance is to be decided in the light of the circumstances existing at the time of the decision, except that an applicant will not be refused an entry clearance where entry is sought in one of the categories contained in paragraphs 296–316 or paragraph EC-C of Appendix FM solely on account of his attaining the age of 18 years between receipt of his application and the date of the decision on it.

28. An applicant for an entry clearance must be outside the United Kingdom and Islands at the time of the application. An applicant for an entry clearance who is seeking entry as a visitor must apply to a post designated by the Secretary of State to accept applications for entry clearance for that purpose and from that category of applicant. Subject to paragraph 28A, any other application must be made to the post in the country or territory where the applicant is living which has been designated by the Secretary of State to accept applications for entry clearance for that purpose and from that category of applicant. Where there is no such post the applicant must apply to the appropriate designated post outside the country or territory where he is living.

28A.

(a) An application for entry clearance as a Tier 5 (Temporary Worker) Migrant in the creative and sporting sub-category of Tier 5 may also be made at the post in the country or territory where the applicant is situated at the time of the application, provided that:

(i) the post has been designated by the Secretary of State to accept applications for entry clearance for that purpose and from that category of applicant,

(ii) the applicant is in that country or territory for a similar purpose to the activity he proposes to undertake in the UK, and

(iii) the applicant is able to demonstrate to the Entry Clearance Officer that he has authority to be living in that country or territory in accordance with its immigration laws. Those applicants who are known to the authorities of that country or territory but who have not been given permission to live in that country or territory will not be eligible to make an application.

(b) An application for entry clearance [as a Tier 1 (Exceptional Talent) Migrant or] as a Tier 5 (Youth Mobility Scheme) Temporary Migrant may also be made at the post in the country or territory where the applicant is situated at the time of the application, provided that:

(i) the post has been designated by the Secretary of State to accept applications for entry clearance for that purpose and from that category of applicant, and

(ii) the applicant is able to demonstrate to the Entry Clearance Officer that he has authority to be living in that country or territory in accordance with its immigration laws and that when he was given authority to live in that country or territory he was given authority to live in that country or territory for a period of more than 6 months. Those applicants who are known to the authorities of that country or territory but who have not been given permission to live in that country or territory will not be eligible to make an application.

Note: Words in square brackets in (b) inserted from 6 April 2014 (HC 1138; see implementation section of HC 1138 as amended by HC 1201 for provisions as to savings).

29. For the purposes of paragraph 28 "post" means a British Diplomatic Mission, British Consular post or the office of any person outside the United Kingdom and Islands who has been authorised by the Secretary of State to accept applications for entry clearance. A list of designated posts is published by the Foreign and Commonwealth Office.

30. An application for an entry clearance is not made until any fee required to be paid under the Consular Fees Act 1980 (including any Regulations or Orders made under that Act) has been paid.

30A. An entry clearance may be revoked if the Entry Clearance Officer is satisfied that:

(i) whether or not to the holder's knowledge, false representations were employed or material facts were not disclosed, either in writing or orally, for the purpose of obtaining the entry clearance; or

(ii) a change of circumstances since the entry clearance was issued has removed the basis of the holder's claim to be admitted to the United Kingdom, except where the change of circumstances amounts solely to his exceeding the age for entry in one of the categories contained in paragraphs 296–316 of these Rules since the issue of the entry clearance; or

(iii) the holder's exclusion from the United Kingdom would be conducive to the public good.

30B. An entry clearance shall cease to have effect where the entry clearance has effect as leave to enter and an Immigration Officer cancels that leave in accordance with paragraph 2A(8) of Schedule 2 to the Immigration Act 1971.

30C. An Immigration Officer may cancel an entry clearance which is capable of having effect as leave to enter if the holder arrives in the United Kingdom before the day on which the entry clearance becomes effective or if the holder seeks to enter the United Kingdom for a purpose other than the purpose specified in the entry clearance.

Variation of leave to enter or remain in the United Kingdom

31. Under Section 3(3) of the 1971 Act a limited leave to enter or remain in the United Kingdom may be varied by extending or restricting its duration, by adding, varying or revoking conditions or by removing the time limit (where upon any condition attached to the leave ceases to apply). When leave to enter or remain is varied an entry is to be made in the applicant's passport or travel document (and his registration certificate where appropriate) or the decision may be made known in writing in some other appropriate way.

31A. Where a person has arrived in the United Kingdom with leave to enter or remain in the United Kingdom which is in force but was given to him before his arrival, he may apply, on arrival at the port of entry in the United Kingdom, for variation of that leave. An Immigration Officer acting on behalf of the Secretary of State may vary the leave at the port of entry but is not obliged to consider an application for variation made at the port of entry. If an Immigration Officer acting on behalf of the Secretary of State has declined to consider an application for variation of leave at a port of entry but the leave has not been cancelled under paragraph 2A(8) of Schedule 2 to the Immigration Act 1971, the person seeking variation should apply to the Home office under paragraph 32.

32. DELETED

33. DELETED

33A. Where a person having left the common travel area, has leave to enter or remain in the United Kingdom which remains in force under article 13 of the Immigration (Leave to Enter and Remain) Order 2000, his leave may be varied (including any condition to which it is subject in such form and manner as permitted for the giving of leave to enter. However, the Secretary of State is not obliged to consider an application for variation of leave to enter or remain from a person outside the United Kingdom.

33B–33G. DELETED

Note: Paragraphs 33B–33G deleted from 28 October 2013 subject to savings for applications made before that date (HC 628).

Specified forms and procedures for applications or claims in connection with immigration

A34. An application for leave to remain in the United Kingdom . . . under . . . these Rules must be made either by completing the relevant online application process in accordance with paragraph A34(iii) or by using the specified application form in accordance with paragraphs 34A to 34D.

(i) "The relevant online application process" means the application process accessible via the [visas and immigration pages of the gov.uk website] and identified there as relevant for applications for leave to remain [for the immigration category under which the applicant wishes to apply.]

(ii) "Specified" in relation to the relevant online application process means specified in the online guidance accompanying that process.

(iii) When the application is made via the relevant online application process:

(a) any specified fee in connection with the application must be paid in accordance with the method specified;

(b) if the online application process requires the applicant to provide biometric information that information must be provided as specified;

(c) if the online application process requires supporting documents to be submitted by post then any such documents specified as mandatory must be submitted in the specified manner within 15 working days of submission of the online application;

(d) if the online application process requires the applicant to make an appointment to attend a public enquiry office of the United Kingdom Border Agency the applicant must, within 45 working days of submission of the online application, make and attend that appointment; and comply with any specified requirements in relation to the provision of biometric information and documents specified as mandatory.

(iv) . . .

Notice of invalidity will be given in writing and deemed to be received on the date it is given, except where it is sent by post, in which case it will be deemed to be received on the second day after it was posted excluding any day which is not a business day.

Note: Words omitted, words in square brackets in sub-paragraph (i) substituted and subparagraph (iv) inserted from 13 December 2012 subject to savings for applications made before that date (HC 760). Words in square brackets in subparagraph (i) substituted from 6 April 2014 (HC 1138; see implementation section of HC 1138 as amended by HC 1201 for savings). Sub-paragraph (iv) deleted from 6 November 2014 subject to savings for applications made before that date (HC 693).

34. An application form is specified when:

(i) it is posted on the [visas and immigration pages of the gov.uk website],

(ii) it is marked on the form that it is a specified form for the purpose of the immigration rules,

(iii) it comes into force on the date specified on the form and/or in any accompanying announcement.

Note: Subparagraph (iv) inserted from 13 December 2012 subject to savings for applications made before that date (HC 760).

34A. Where an application form is specified, the application or claim must also comply with the following requirements:

(i) Subject to paragraph A34 the application or claim must be made using the specified form,

(ii) any specified fee in connection with the application or claim must be paid in accordance with the method specified in the application form, separate payment form and/or related guidance notes, as applicable,

(iii) any section of the form which is designated as mandatory in the application form and/or related guidance notes must be completed as specified,

(iv) if the application form and/or related guidance notes require the applicant to provide biometric information, such information must be provided as specified,

(v) an appointment for the purposes stated in subparagraph (iv) must be made and must take place by the dates specified in any subsequent notification by the Secretary of State following receipt of the application, or as agreed by the Secretary of State,

(vi) where the application or claim is made by post or courier, or submitted in person:

(a) the application or claim must be accompanied by the photographs and documents specified as mandatory in the application form and/or related guidance notes,

(ab) those photographs must be in the same format specified as mandatory in the application form and/or related guidance notes, and

(b) the form must be signed by the applicant, and where applicable, the applicant's spouse, civil partner, same-sex partner or unmarried partner, save that where the applicant is under the age of eighteen, the form may be signed by the parent or legal guardian of the applicant on his behalf,

Note: Word replaced in subparagraph (iv) from 6 November 2014 subject to savings for applications made before that date (HC 693).

34B. Where an application form is specified, it must be sent by prepaid post to the United Kingdom Border Agency of the Home Office, or submitted in person at a public enquiry office of the United Kingdom Border Agency of the Home Office, save for the following exceptions:

(i) an application may be sent by courier to . . . the Home Office [at the address specified on the application form for such purposes] if it is an application for:

(a) limited or indefinite leave to remain as a sole representative, retired person of independent means or as a Tier 1 Migrant or Tier 2 Migrant;

(b) limited leave to remain for work permit employment, as a seasonal agricultural worker, for the purpose of employment under the Sectors-Based Scheme.

(c) Indefinite leave to remain as a businessperson, investor or innovator, or

(d) limited leave to remain as a Tier 5 (Temporary Worker) Migrant.

(ii) an applicant may submit an application online where this option is available on the [visas and immigration pages of the gov.uk website];

(iii) an application may not be sent by pre-paid post, and must be made online, if it is an application for a Tier 2, Tier 4 or Tier 5 (Temporary Worker) sponsorship licence.

Note: Subparagraph (i) deleted and previous subparagraphs (ii), (iii) and (iv) renumbered as (i), (ii) and (iii) and words deleted from and inserted in subparagraph (i) from 6 November 2014 subject to savings for applications made before that date (HC 693).

34C. Where an application or claim in connection with immigration for which an application form is specified does not comply with the requirements in paragraph 34A, or where an application for leave to remain in the United Kingdom is made by completing the relevant online application process, and does not comply with the requirements of paragraph A34(iii), the following provisions apply:

(a) Subject to sub-paragraph (b), the application will be invalid if it does not comply with the relevant requirements of A34(iii) or 34A, as applicable, and will not be considered. Notice of invalidity will be given in writing and deemed to be received on the date it is given, except where it is sent by post, in which case it will be deemed to be received on the second day after it was posted excluding any day which is not a business day, unless the contrary is proved.

(b) The decision maker may contact the applicant or their representative in writing and give the applicant a single opportunity to correct any omission or error which renders the application invalid. The amended application and/or any requested documents must be received at the address specified in the request within 10 business days of the date on which the request was sent.

Note: Paragraph 34C substituted from 6 November 2014 subject to savings for applications made before that date (HC 693).

34CA.

Note: Paragraph 34CA deleted from 13 December 2012 (HC 760).

34D. Where the main applicant wishes to include applications or claims by any members of his family as his dependants on his own application form, the applications or claims of the dependants must meet the following requirements or they will be invalid and will not be considered:

(i) the application form must expressly permit the applications or claims of dependants to be included, and

(ii) such dependants must be:

(a) the spouse, civil partner, unmarried or same-sex partner of the main applicant; and/or

(b) children of the main applicant aged under 18; and/or

(c) where permitted by the Rules for the immigration category under which the applicant wishes to apply, any dependants of the main applicant aged 18 or over.

Note: Subparagraph (ii) substituted from 6 November 2014 subject to savings for applications made before that date (HC 693).

Variation of applications or claims for leave to remain

34E. If a person wishes to vary the purpose of an application or claim for leave to remain in the United Kingdom and an application form is specified for such new purpose or paragraph A34 applies, the variation must comply with the requirements of paragraph 34A or paragraph A34 (as they apply at the date the variation is made) as if the variation were a new application or claim, or the variation will be invalid and will not be considered.

34F. Any valid variation of a leave to remain application will be decided in accordance with the immigration rules in force at the date such variation is made.

Determination of the date of an application or claim (or variation of an application or claim) in connection with immigration

34G. For the purposes of these rules, the date on which an application or claim (or a variation in accordance with paragraph 34E) is made is as follows:

(i) where the application form is sent by post, the date of posting,

(ii) where the application form is submitted in person, the date on which it is accepted by a . . . Home Office [premium service centre],

(iii) where the application form is sent by courier, the date on which it is delivered to the . . . Home Office, or

(iv) where the application is made via the online application process, on the date on which the online application is submitted.

Note: Words omitted from and inserted in subparagraph (ii) and words omitted from subparagraph (iii) from 6 November 2014 (HC 693).

34H. Applications or claims for leave to remain made before 29 February 2008 for which a form was prescribed prior to 29 February 2008 shall be subject to the forms and procedures as in force on the date on which the application or claim was made.

34I. Where an application or claim is made no more than 21 days after the date on which a form is specified under the immigration rules and on a form that was permitted for such application or claim immediately prior to the date of such specification, the application or claim shall be deemed to have been made on the specified form.

Withdrawn applications or claims for leave to remain in the United Kingdom

34J. Where a person whose application or claim for leave to remain is being considered requests the return of his passport for the purpose of travel outside the common travel area, the application for leave shall, provided it has not already been determined, be treated as withdrawn as soon as the passport is returned in response to that request.

34K. Paragraph 34J does not apply to an applicant who is applying as a Tier 2 Migrant or a Tier 5 Migrant and whose application is supported by a Certificate of Sponsorship from a Premium Sponsor.

Specified forms and procedures in connection with applications for administrative review

Notice of an eligible decision

34L. (1) Unless sub-paragraph (2) applies, written notice must be given to a person of any eligible decision. The notice given must:

(a) include or be accompanied by a statement of reasons for the decision to which it relates, and

(b) include information on how to apply for an administrative review and the time limit for making an application.

(2) Sub-paragraph (1) does not apply where the eligible decision is a grant of leave to remain.

Note: Paragraphs 34L to 34Y inserted from 20 October 2014 (HC 693).

Making an application

34M. (1) Unless sub-paragraph (2) applies only one valid application for administrative review may be made in respect of an eligible decision.

(2) A further application for administrative review in respect of an eligible decision may be made where the outcome of the administrative review is as set out in paragraph AR2.2(d) of Appendix AR of these Rules.

Note: Paragraphs 34L to 34Y inserted from 20 October 2014 (HC 693).

34N. An application for administrative review must be made in accordance with the requirements set out in paragraphs 34O to 34S. If it is not it will be invalid and will not be considered.

Note: Paragraphs 34L to 34Y inserted from 20 October 2014 (HC 693).

34O. The application must be made in accordance with paragraph 34U or paragraph 34V.

Note: Paragraphs 34L to 34Y inserted from 20 October 2014 (HC 693).

34P. The application must be made in relation to an eligible decision.

Note: Paragraphs 34L to 34Y inserted from 20 October 2014 (HC 693).

34Q. The application must be made while the applicant is in the UK.

Note: Paragraphs 34L to 34Y inserted from 20 October 2014 (HC 693).

34R. (1) The application must be made:

(a) where the applicant is not detained, no more than 14 calendar days after receipt by the applicant of the notice of the eligible decision; or

(b) where the applicant is in detention under the Immigration Acts, no more than 7 calendar days after receipt by the applicant of the notice of the eligible decision.

(2) But the application may be accepted out of time if the Secretary of State is satisfied that it would be unjust not to waive the time limit and the application was made as soon as reasonably practicable.

(3) For the purposes of this paragraph, where notice of the eligible decision is sent by post to an address in the UK, it is deemed to have been received, unless the contrary is shown, on the second working day after the day on which it was posted.

(4) For provision about when an application is made see paragraph 34W.

Note: Paragraphs 34L to 34Y inserted from 20 October 2014 (HC 693).

34S. An application may only include an application on behalf of a dependant of the applicant if that dependant was also a dependant on the application which resulted in the eligible decision.

Note: Paragraphs 34L to 34Y inserted from 20 October 2014 (HC 693).

Notice of invalidity

34T. (1) A notice informing an applicant that their application is invalid will be given in writing (which includes, where an email address has been provided for correspondence, by electronic mail).

(2) A notice of invalidity is deemed to have been received, unless the contrary is shown:

(a) where it is sent by post, on the second working day after the day on which it was posted;

(b) where it is sent by electronic mail, on the day on which it is sent; and

(c) where it is given in person, on the day on which it is given.

Note: Paragraphs 34L to 34Y inserted from 20 October 2014 (HC 693).

Online applications for administrative review

34U. (1) In this paragraph:

"the relevant online application process" means the application process accessible via the gov.uk website and identified there as relevant for applications for administrative review; and

"specified" in relation to the relevant online application process means specified in the online guidance accompanying that process.

(2) An application may be made online by completing the relevant online application process.

(3) Where an application is made online:

(a) any specified fee in connection with the application must be paid in accordance with the method specified;

(b) any section of the online application which is designated as mandatory must be completed as specified; and

(c) documents specified as mandatory on the online application or in the related guidance must be submitted either electronically with the online application and in the specified manner, where this is permitted, or received by post and in the specified manner no more than 7 working days after the day on which the online application is submitted.

Note: Paragraphs 34L to 34Y inserted from 20 October 2014 (HC 693).

Postal applications for administrative review

34V. (1) An application may be made by post or courier in accordance with this paragraph.

(2) Where an application is made by post or courier:

(a) it must be made on the application form as specified within the meaning of paragraph 34 (but see paragraph 34Y);

(b) any specified fee in connection with the application must be paid in accordance with the method specified in the application form, separate payment form or related guidance notes (as applicable);

(c) any section of the application form which is designated as mandatory in the form itself or related guidance notes must be completed;

(d) the form must be signed by the applicant or their representative;

(e) the application must be accompanied by the documents specified as mandatory in the application form or related guidance notes; and

(f) the application must be sent to the address specified on the form.

Note: Paragraphs 34L to 34Y inserted from 20 October 2014 (HC 693).

Determining the date of an application

34W. (1) An application for administrative review is made:

(a) where it is made by post in accordance with paragraph 34V, on the marked date of posting;

(b) where it is made by courier in accordance with paragraph 34V, on the date on which it is delivered; and

(c) where it is made online in accordance with paragraph 34U, on the date on which it is submitted.

(2) Accepting an application has been made does not mean that it is accepted as being valid.

Note: Paragraphs 34L to 34Y inserted from 20 October 2014 (HC 693).

Withdrawal of applications

34X. (1) An application which has not been determined will be treated as withdrawn if the applicant requests the return of their passport for the purpose of travel outside the UK.

(2) An application which may only be brought from within the UK and which has not been determined will be treated as withdrawn if the applicant leaves the UK.

(3) The application for administrative review may be withdrawn by the applicant. A request to withdraw an application must be made in writing to the Home Office at the address provided for that purpose on the visas and immigration pages of the gov.uk website. The application will be treated as withdrawn on the date on which the request is received.

Note: Paragraphs 34L to 34Y inserted from 20 October 2014 (HC 693).

Transitional arrangements for specified forms used in postal and courier applications

34Y. Where an application is made no more than 21 days after the date on which a form is specified (within the meaning of paragraph 34) and on a form that was specified immediately prior to the date of the new specification, the application is deemed to have been made on the specified form (and is therefore not to be treated as invalid by reason only of being made on the "wrong" form).

Note: Paragraphs 34L to 34Y inserted from 20 October 2014 (HC 693).

Undertakings

35. A sponsor of a person seeking leave to enter or remain in the United Kingdom may be asked to give an undertaking in writing to be responsible for that person's maintenance, accommodation and (as appropriate) personal care for the period of any leave granted, including any further variation or for a period of 5 years from date of grant where indefinite leave to enter or remain is granted. Under the Social Security Administration Act 1992 and the Social Security Administration (Northern Ireland) Act 1992, the Department of Social Security or, as the case may be, the Department of Health and Social Services in Northern Ireland, may seek to recover from the person giving such an undertaking any income support paid to meet the needs of the person in respect of whom the undertaking has been given. Under the Immigration and Asylum Act 1999 the Home Office may seek to recover from the person giving such an undertaking amounts attributable to any support provided under section 95 of the Immigration and Asylum Act 1999 (support for asylum seekers) to, or in respect of, the person in respect

of whom the undertaking has been given. Failure by the sponsor to maintain that person in accordance with the undertaking, may also be an offence under section 105 of the Social Security Administration Act 1992 and/or under section 108 of the Immigration and Asylum Act 1999 if, as a consequence, asylum support and/or income support is provided to, or in respect of, that person.

Medical

36. A person who intends to remain in the United Kingdom for more than 6 months should normally be referred to the Medical Inspector for examination. If he produces a medical certificate he should be advised to hand it to the Medical Inspector. Any person seeking entry who mentions health or medical treatment as a reason for his visit, or who appears not to be in good mental or physical health, should also be referred to the Medical Inspector; and the Immigration Officer has discretion, which should be exercised sparingly, to refer for examination in any other case.

37. Where the Medical Inspector advises that a person seeking entry is suffering from a specified disease or condition which may interfere with his ability to support himself or his dependants, the Immigration Officer should take account of this, in conjunction with other factors, in deciding whether to admit that person. The Immigration Officer should also take account of the Medical Inspector's assessment of the likely course of treatment in deciding whether a person seeking entry for private medical treatment has sufficient means at his disposal.

38. A returning resident should not be refused leave to enter or have existing leave to enter or remain cancelled on medical grounds. But where a person would be refused leave to enter or have existing leave to enter or remain cancelled on medical grounds if he were not a returning resident or in any case where it is decided on compassionate grounds not to exercise the power to refuse leave to enter or to cancel existing leave to enter or remain, or in any other case where the Medical Inspector so recommends, the Immigration Officer should give the person concerned a notice requiring him to report to the Medical Officer of Environmental Health designated by the Medical Inspector with a view to further examination and any necessary treatment.

[A39. Any person from a country listed in Appendix T Part 1 making an application for entry clearance to come to the UK for more than six months or as a fiance(e) or proposed civil partner applying for leave to enter under Section EC-P: Entry clearance as a partner under Appendix FM or leave to enter under paragraphs 290–291 in Part 8 of these Rules, must present, at the time of application, a valid medical certificate issued by a medical practitioner listed in Appendix T Part 2 confirming that they have undergone screening for active pulmonary tuberculosis and that this tuberculosis is not present in the applicant.]

Note: Paragraph A39 substituted from 30 April 2013 (Cm 8599).

B39. Applicants seeking leave to enter as a returning resident under paragraph 19 of these rules, having been absent from the United Kingdom for more than two years are also subject to the requirements in paragraph A39.

39. The Entry Clearance Officer has the same discretion as an Immigration Officer to refer applicants for entry clearance for medical examination and the same principles will apply to the decision whether or not to issue an entry clearance.

Students

39A. An application for a variation of leave to enter or remain made by a student who is sponsored by a government or international sponsorship agency may be refused if the sponsor has not given written consent to the proposed variation.

Specified documents

39B.

(a) Where these Rules state that specified documents must be provided, that means documents specified in these Rules as being specified documents for the route under which the applicant is applying. If the specified documents are not provided, the applicant will not meet the requirement for which the specified documents are required as evidence.

(b) Where these Rules specify documents that are to be provided, those documents are considered to be specified documents, whether or not they are named as such, and as such are subject to the requirements in (c) to (f) below.

(c) If the Entry Clearance Officer or Secretary of State has reasonable cause to doubt the genuineness of any document submitted by an applicant which is, or which purports to be, a specified document under these Rules, and having taken reasonable steps to verify the document is unable to verify that it is genuine, the document will be discounted for the purposes of this application.

(d) Specified documents must be originals, not copies, except where stated otherwise.

(e) Specified documents must contain, or the applicant must provide, full contact details to allow each document to be verified.

(f) Where any specified documents provided are not in English or Welsh, the applicant must provide the original and a full translation that can be independently verified by the Entry Clearance Officer, Immigration Officer or the Secretary of State.

The translation must be dated and include:

(i) confirmation that it is an accurate translation of the original document;

(ii) the full name and original signature of the translator or an authorised official of the translation company;

(iii) the translator or translation company's contact details; and

(iv) if the applicant is applying for leave to remain or indefinite leave to remain, certification by a qualified translator and details of the translator or translation company's credentials.

Note: Note Subparagraph (f) substituted from 1 October 2013 (HC 628).

Indefinite leave to enter or remain

39C. (a) An applicant for indefinite leave to enter or remain must, unless the applicant provides a reasonable explanation, comply with any request made by the Secretary of State to attend an interview.

(b) If the decision-maker has reasonable cause to doubt (on examination or interview or on any other basis) that any document submitted by an applicant for the purposes of satisfying the requirements of Appendix KoLL of these Rules was genuinely obtained, that document may be discounted for the purposes of the application.

(c) Where sub-paragraph (b) applies, the decision-maker may request the applicant to provide additional evidence of knowledge of the English language and/or knowledge about life in the UK (as set out in paragraphs 3.2(b)(ii) and 3.3 of Appendix KoLL) for the purposes of demonstrating sufficient knowledge of the English language requirement and sufficient knowledge about life in the United Kingdom in accordance with Appendix KoLL.

(d) A decision-maker will not request evidence under sub-paragraph (c) where the decision-maker does not anticipate that the supply of that evidence will lead to a grant of leave to enter or remain in the United Kingdom because the application may be refused for other reasons.

Note: Paragraph 39C inserted from 6 November 2014 (HC 693).

PART 2

PERSONS SEEKING TO ENTER OR REMAIN IN THE UNITED KINGDOM FOR VISITS

Visitors

Requirement for leave to enter as a general visitor

40. For the purposes of paragraphs 41–46 a general visitor includes a person living and working outside the United Kingdom who comes to the United Kingdom as a tourist. A person seeking leave to enter the United Kingdom as a Business Visitor, which includes Academic Visitors, must meet the requirements of paragraph 46G. A person seeking entry as a Sports Visitor must meet the requirements of paragraph 46M. A person seeking entry as an Entertainer Visitor must meet the requirements of paragraph 46S. A visitor seeking leave to enter for the purposes of marriage or to enter into a civil partnership must meet the requirements of paragraph 56D. [A person seeking entry to study as a student visitor must meet the requirements of paragraph 56K.]

Note: Words in square brackets inserted from 1 October 2013 (HC 628).

41. The requirements to be met by a person seeking leave to enter the United Kingdom as a general visitor are that he:

(i) is genuinely seeking entry as a general visitor for a limited period as stated by him, not exceeding 6 months or not exceeding 12 months in the case of a person seeking entry to accompany an academic visitor [(as their child, spouse or partner)], provided in the latter case the visitor accompanying the academic visitor has entry clearance; and

(ii) intends to leave the United Kingdom at the end of the period of the visit as stated by him; and [does not intend to live for extended periods in the United Kingdom through frequent or successive visits; and]

(iii) does not intend to take employment in the United Kingdom; and

(iv) does not intend to produce goods or provide services within the United Kingdom, including the selling of goods or services direct to members of the public; and

(v) [Save to the extent provided by paragraph 43A,] does not intend to undertake a course of study; and

(vi) will maintain and accommodate himself and any dependants adequately out of resources available to him without recourse to public funds or taking employment; or will, with any dependants, be maintained and[/or] accommodated adequately by relatives or friends[who can demonstrate they are able and intend to do so, and are legally present in the United Kingdom, or will be at the time of their visit; and]

(vii) can meet the cost of the return or onward journey; and

(viii) is not a child under the age of 18.

(ix) does not intend to do any of the activities provided for in paragraphs 46G(iii), 46M(iii) or 46S(iii); and

(x) does not, during his visit, intend to marry or form a civil partnership, or to give notice of marriage or civil partnership; and

(xi) does not intend to receive private medical treatment during his visit; and

(xii) is not in transit to a country outside the common travel area.

(xiii) where he is seeking leave to enter as a general visitor to take part in archaeological excavations, provides a letter from the director or organiser of the excavation stating the length of their visit and, where appropriate, what arrangements have been made for their accommodation and maintenance.

Note: Words inserted in subparagraph (v) from 1 October 2013 (HC 628). Words substituted in subparagraphs (ii) and (vi) from 6 April 2013 subject to savings for applications made before that date (HC 1039). Words inserted in sub-paragraph (ii) from 6 November 2014 subject to savings for applications made before that date (HC 693).

41A. The requirements to be met by a person seeking leave to enter the United Kingdom as a general visitor who is acting as an organ donor, or is to be assessed as a suitable organ donor, are that the person:

(a) meets the requirements in paragraph 41(i) to (xii); and

(b) genuinely intends to donate an organ, or be assessed as a suitable organ donor to an identified recipient in the UK, with whom the visitor has a genetic or pre-existing emotional relationship; and

(c) is confirmed as a donor match to the identified recipient through medical tests, or is undergoing further tests to be assessed as a potential donor to the intended recipient; and

(d) provides a letter, dated no more than three months prior to the person's intended date of arrival in the UK, from either:

(i) the lead nurse or coordinator of the UK's NHS Trust's Living Donor Kidney Transplant team; or

(ii) a UK registered medical practitioner who holds an NHS consultant post or who appears in the Specialist Register of the General Medical Council; which:

(aa) confirms that the visitor meets the requirements in subparagraphs (b) and (c); and

(bb) confirms when and where the planned organ transplant or medical tests will take place; and

(e) can demonstrate, if required to do so, that the identified recipient is legally present in the United Kingdom or will be at the time of the visitor's planned organ transplant.

Note: Paragraph 41A inserted from 6 November 2014 subject to savings for applications made before that date (HC 693).

Leave to enter as a general visitor

42. A person seeking leave to enter to the United Kingdom as a general visitor may be admitted for a period not exceeding 6 months, or not exceeding 12 months in the case of a person accompanying an academic visitor [(as their child, spouse or partner)], subject to a condition prohibiting employment . . . and recourse to public funds, provided the Immigration Officer is satisfied that each of the requirements of paragraph 41 is met.

Note: Word deleted from 1 October 2013 (HC 628). Words inserted from 6 November 2014 subject to savings for applications made before that date (HC 693).

Refusal of leave to enter as a general visitor

43. Leave to enter as a general visitor is to be refused if the Immigration Officer is not satisfied that each of the requirements of paragraph 41 is met.

Permitted study as a general visitor

43A. (1) A person who has been granted leave to enter the United Kingdom under paragraph 42 may undertake a course of study to the extent permitted by this paragraph.

(2) A course of study is permitted under this paragraph if it—

(a) does not exceed 30 days in duration (either alone or taken together with any other course and whether continuous or otherwise); and

(b) is a recreational course; but

(c) is not an English language course.

(3) A course of study is also permitted under this paragraph if it—

(a) does not exceed 30 days in duration (either alone or taken together with any other course and whether continuous or otherwise); and

(b) is provided by an institution which is—

(i) the holder of a Sponsor licence for Tier 4 of the Points-Based System,

(ii) the holder of valid accreditation from Accreditation UK, the Accreditation Body for Language Services (ABLS), the British Accreditation Council (BAC), or the Accreditation Service for International Colleges (ASIC),

(iii) the holder of a valid and satisfactory full institutional inspection, review or audit by the Bridge Schools Inspectorate, the Education and Training Inspectorate, Estyn, Education Scotland, the Independent Schools Inspectorate, Office for Standards in Education, the Quality Assurance Agency for Higher Education, the Schools Inspection Service or the Education and Training Inspectorate Northern Ireland, or

(iv) an overseas higher education institution offering only part of its programmes in the United Kingdom, holding its own national accreditation and offering programmes that are an equivalent level to a United Kingdom degree.

(4) For the purposes of this paragraph a "recreational course" is one which a person undertakes purely for leisure purposes.

Note: Paragraph 43A inserted from 1 October 2013 (HC 628).

Requirements for an extension of stay as a general visitor

44. Six months is the maximum permitted leave which may be granted to a general visitor. The requirements for an extension of stay as a general visitor are that the applicant:

(i) meets the requirements of paragraph 41(ii)–(vii) and (ix)–(xii); and

(ii) has not already spent, or would not as a result of an extension of stay spend, more than 6 months in total in the United Kingdom or not more than 12 months in the case of a person accompanying an academic visitor as a general visitor. Any periods spent as a child visitor are to be counted as a period spent as a general visitor; and

(iii) has, or was last granted, entry clearance, leave to enter or leave to remain as a general visitor or as a child visitor; and

(iv) must not be in the UK in breach of immigration laws except that any period of overstaying for a period of 28 days or less will be disregarded.

Extension of stay as a general visitor

45. An extension of stay as a general visitor may be granted, subject to a condition prohibiting employment . . . and recourse to public funds, provided the Secretary of State is satisfied that each of the requirements of paragraph 44 is met.

Note: Words deleted from 1 October 2013 (HC 628).

Refusal of extension of stay as a general visitor

46. An extension of stay as a general visitor is to be refused if the Secretary of State is not satisfied that each of the requirements of paragraph 44 is met.

Child visitors

Requirements for leave to enter as a child visitor

46A. (1) The requirements to be met by a person seeking leave to enter the United Kingdom as a child visitor are that the applicant:

(i) is genuinely seeking entry as a child visitor for a limited period as stated, not exceeding 6 months or not exceeding 12 months to accompany an academic visitor, provided in the latter case the applicant has entry clearance; and

(ii) meets the requirements of paragraph 41(ii)–(iv), (vi)–(vii) and (x)–(xii); and

(iii) is under the age of 18; and

(iv) can demonstrate that suitable arrangements have been made for their travel to, and reception and care in the United Kingdom; and;

(v) has a parent or guardian in their home country or country of habitual residence who is responsible for their care and who confirms that they consent to the arrangements for the applicant's travel, reception and care in the United Kingdom; and

(vi) if a visa national:

(a) the applicant holds a valid United Kingdom entry clearance for entry as an accompanied child visitor and is travelling in the company of the adult identified on the entry clearance, who is on the same occasion being admitted to the United Kingdom; or

(b) the applicant holds a valid United Kingdom entry clearance for entry as an unaccompanied child visitor; and

(via) except to the extent permitted by sub-paragraph (viii), does not intend to study at a maintained school; and

(vii) if the applicant has been accepted for or [intends to follow] a course of study, this is to be provided by an institution which is outside the maintained sector and is:

(a) the holder of a Sponsor Licence for Tier 4 of the Points Based System, or

(b) the holder of valid accreditation from Accreditation UK; the Accreditation Body for Language Services (ABLS); the British Accreditation Council (BAC) or the Accreditation Service for International Colleges (ASIC), or

(c) the holder of a valid and satisfactory full institutional inspection, review or audit by one of the following bodies: the Bridge Schools Inspectorate; the Education and Training Inspectorate; Estyn; Education Scotland; the Independent Schools Inspectorate; Office for Standards in Education; the Schools Inspection Service or the Education and Training Inspectorate Northern Ireland.

(viii) if the applicant is undertaking an exchange or educational visit only, this is to be provided by one of the following schools:

(a) For England and Wales, maintained schools as defined under section 20(7) of the School Standards and Framework Act 1998; non-maintained special schools approved under section 342 of the Education Act 1996; independent schools as defined under section 463 of the Education Act 1996 and registered independent schools entered on the register of independent schools maintained under section 158 of the Education Act 2002; academies as defined in section 1(10) of the Academies Act 2010; city technology colleges and city colleges for technology of the arts as established under the Education Act 1996 and treated as academies under section 15(4) of the Academies Act.

(b) For Scotland, [public] schools, grant-aided schools and independent fee paying schools as defined under Section 135 of the Education (Scotland) Act 1980.

(c) For Northern Ireland, grant-aided schools as defined under Articles 10 and 11 of and Schedules 4 to 7 to the Education and Libraries (NI) Order in Council 1986; grant maintained integrated schools as defined under Article 69 of and Schedule 5 to the Education Reform (NI) Order 1989; independent fee paying schools as defined under Article 38 of the Education and Libraries (NI) Order 1986.

[(2) In sub-paragraph (1)(via) a "maintained school" is one which provides free education and is primarily funded from public funds.]

Note: Subparagraph (via) inserted, words inserted in subparagraph (vii), words substituted in subparagraph (viii)(b) and subparagraph (2) inserted from 1 December 2013 (HC 803).

Leave to enter as a child visitor

46B. An applicant seeking leave to enter the United Kingdom as a child visitor may be admitted for a period not exceeding 6 months, or not exceeding 12 months in the case of a child visitor accompanying an academic visitor subject to a condition prohibiting employment and recourse to public funds, providing that the Immigration Officer is satisfied that each of the requirements of paragraph 46A is met.

Refusal of leave to enter as a child visitor

46C. Leave to enter as a child visitor is to be refused if the Immigration Officer is not satisfied that each of the requirements of paragraph 46A is met.

Requirements for an extension of stay as a child visitor

46D. Six months is the maximum permitted leave which may be granted to a child visitor. The requirements for an extension of stay as a child visitor are that the applicant:

(i) meets the requirements of paragraph 41(ii)–(vii) and (x)–(xii); and

(ii) is under the age of 18; and

(iii) can demonstrate that there are suitable arrangements for his care in the United Kingdom; and

(iv) has a parent or guardian in his home country or country of habitual residence who is responsible for his care, and who confirms that they consent to the arrangements for the applicant's travel, reception and care in the United Kingdom; and

(v) has not already spent, or would not as a result of an extension of stay spend, more than 6 months in total in the United Kingdom, or not more than 12 months in the case of a child visitor accompanying an academic visitor, as a child visitor; and

(vi) has, or was last granted, entry clearance, leave to enter or leave to remain as a child visitor; and

(vii) must not be in the UK in breach of immigration laws except that any period of overstaying for a period of 28 days or less will be disregarded.

Extension of stay as a child visitor

46E. An extension of stay as a child visitor may be granted, subject to a condition prohibiting employment and recourse to public funds, provided the Secretary of State is satisfied that each of the requirements of paragraph 46D is met.

Refusal of extension of stay as a child visitor

46F. An extension of stay as a child visitor is to be refused if the Secretary of State is not satisfied that each of the requirements of paragraph 46D is met.

Business Visitors

Requirements for leave to enter as a Business Visitor

46G. The requirements to be met by a person seeking leave to enter the United Kingdom as a business visitor are that he:

(i) is genuinely seeking entry as a Business Visitor for a limited period as stated by him:

(a) not exceeding 6 months; or

(b) not exceeding 12 months if seeking entry as an Academic Visitor

(ii) meets the requirements of [paragraphs 41(ii)–(iv), subject to paragraph 46HA, (v), (vi)–and (x)–(xii)];

(iii) intends to do one or more of the following during his visit:

(a) to carry out one of the following activities;

(i) to attend meetings, conferences and interviews, provided they were arranged before arrival in the UK and, if the applicant is a board-level director attending board meetings in the UK, provided they are not employed by a UK company (although they may be paid a fee for attending the meeting);

(ii) to attend trade fairs for promotional work only, provided they are not directly selling;

(iii) to arrange deals, or negotiating or signing trade agreements or contracts;

(iv) to carry out fact-finding missions;

(v) to conduct site visits;

(vi) to work as a driver on a genuine international route delivering goods or passengers from abroad;

(vii) to work as a tour group courier, providing the applicant is contracted to a firm with headquarters outside the UK, is seeking entry to accompany a tour group, and will depart with that tour, or another tour organised by the same company;

(viii) to speak at a one-off conference which is not organised as a commercial concern, and is not making a profit for the organiser;

(ix) to represent a foreign manufacturer by:

(i) carrying out installing, debugging or enhancing work for computer software companies,

(ii) servicing or repairing the manufacturer's products within the initial guarantee period, or

(iii) being briefed on the requirements of a UK customer, provided this is limited to briefing and does not include work involving use of the applicant's expertise to make a detailed assessment of a potential customer's requirements;

(x) to represent a foreign machine manufacturer, as part of the contract of purchase and supply, in erecting and installing machinery too heavy to be delivered in one piece;

(xi) to act as an interpreter or translator for visiting business people, provided they are all employed by, and doing the business of, the same overseas company;

(xii) to erect, dismantle, install, service, repair or advise on the development of foreign-made machinery, provided they will only do so in the UK for up to six months;

(b) to take part in a location shoot as a member of a film crew meaning he is a film actor, producer, director or technician paid or employed by an overseas firm other than one established in the UK and is coming to the UK for location sequences only for an overseas film;

(c) to represent overseas news media including as a journalist, correspondent, producer or cameraman provided he is employed or paid by an overseas company and is gathering information for an overseas publication;

(d) to act as an Academic Visitor but only if

(1) he is an academic who is:

(a) on sabbatical leave from an overseas academic institution to carry out research;

(b) taking part in formal exchange arrangements with UK counterparts (including doctors);

(c) coming to share knowledge or experience, or to hold informal discussions with their UK counterparts, or

(d) taking part in a single conference or seminar that is not a commercial or non-profit venture;

(e) an eminent senior doctor or dentist taking part in research, teaching or clinical practice; and

(2) he has been working as an academic in an institution of higher education overseas or in the field of their academic expertise immediately prior to seeking entry;"

(e) to act as a Visiting Professor; subject to undertaking only a small amount of teaching for the institution hosting the students he is supervising, being employed and paid by the overseas academic institution and not intending to base himself or seek employment in the UK.

(f) to be a secondee to a UK company which is directly contracted with the visitor's overseas company,with which it has no corporate relationship, to provide goods or services, provided the secondee remains employed and paid by the overseas company throughout the secondee's visit;

(g) to undertake some preaching or pastoral work as a religious worker, provided his base is abroad and he is not taking up an office, post or appointment;

(h) To act as an adviser, consultant, trainer, [internal auditor] or trouble shooter, to the UK branch of the same group of companies as the visitor's overseas company, provided the visitor remains employed and paid by the overseas company and does not undertake work, paid or unpaid with the UK company's clients;

(i) [To receive] specific, one-off training on techniques and work practices used in the UK where:

(a) the training is to be delivered by the UK branch of the same group of companies to which the individual's employer belongs; or

(b) the training is to be provided by a UK company contracted to provide goods or services to the overseas company; or

(c) a UK company is contracted to provide training facilities only, to an overseas company; or

(d) the training is corporate training which is being delivered by an outside provider to overseas and UK employees of the same group of companies; [or

(e) the training is corporate training provided for the purposes of the person's employment overseas and delivered by a UK company that is neither part of the person's employer's corporate group nor whose main activity is the provision of training.]

(j) To share knowledge or experience relevant to, or advise on, an international project that is being led from the UK as an overseas scientist or researcher, provided the visitor remains paid and employed overseas and is not carrying out research in the United Kingdom;

(k) To advise a UK client on litigation and/or international transactions as an employee of an international law firm which has offices in the UK, provided the visitor remains paid and employed overseas.

Note: Words substituted in subparagraph (ii), words inserted in subparagraph (iii)(h) and subparagraph (iii)(i) and subparagraph (iii)(i)(e) inserted from 1 October 2013 (HC 628). Subparagraphs (iii)(j) and (iii)(k) inserted from 6 November 2014 subject to savings for applications made before that date (HC 693).

Leave to enter as a Business Visitor

46H. A person seeking leave to enter to the United Kingdom as a Business Visitor may be admitted for a period not exceeding 6 months, subject to a condition prohibiting employment . . . and recourse to public funds, provided the Immigration Officer is satisfied that each of the requirements of paragraph 46G is met. A person seeking leave to enter the United Kingdom as an Academic Visitor who does not have entry clearance may, if otherwise eligible, be admitted for a period not exceeding 6 months, subject to a condition prohibiting employment . . . and recourse to public funds, provided the Immigration Officer is satisfied that each of the requirements of paragraph 46G are met. An Academic Visitor who has entry clearance may be admitted for up to 12 months subject to a condition prohibiting employment . . . and recourse to public funds.

Note: Words omitted from 1 October 2013 (HC 628).

Permitted study as a business visitor

46HA. A person granted leave to enter under paragraph 46H may undertake a course of study to the same extent permitted by paragraph 43A.

Note: Paragraph 46HA inserted from 1 October 2013 (HC 628).

Refusal of leave to enter as a Business Visitor

46HI. Leave to enter as a Business Visitor is to be refused if the Immigration Officer is not satisfied that each of the requirements of paragraph 46G are met.

Requirements for an extension of stay as a Business Visitor

46J. Twelve months is the maximum permitted leave which may be granted to an Academic Visitor and six months is the maximum that may be granted to any other form of Business Visitor. The requirements for an extension of stay as a Business Visitor are that the applicant:

(i) meets the requirements of paragraph 46G(ii)–(iii); and

(ii) if he is a Business Visitor other than an Academic Visitor, has not already spent, or would not as a result of an extension of stay spend, more than 6 months in total in the United Kingdom as a Business Visitor; and

(iii) if he is an Academic Visitor, has not already spent, or would not as a result of an extension of stay spend, more than 12 months in total in the United Kingdom as a Business Visitor; and

(iv) has, or was last granted, entry clearance, leave to enter or leave to remain as a Business Visitor; and

(v) must not be in the UK in breach of immigration laws except that any period of overstaying for a period of 28 days or less will be disregarded.

Extension of stay as a Business Visitor

46K. An extension of stay as a Business Visitor may be granted, subject to a condition prohibiting employment. . . and recourse to public funds, provided the Secretary of State is satisfied that each of the requirements of paragraph 46J is met.

Note: Words omitted from 1 October 2013 (HC 628).

Refusal of extension of stay as a Business Visitor

46L. An extension of stay as a Business Visitor is to be refused if the Secretary of State is not satisfied that each of the requirements of paragraph 46J is met.

Sports Visitors

Requirements for leave to enter as a Sports Visitor

46M. The requirements to be met by a person seeking leave to enter the United Kingdom as a Sports Visitor are that he:

(i) is genuinely seeking entry as a Sports Visitor for a limited period as stated by him, not exceeding six months; and

(ii) meets the requirements of paragraphs 41(ii)–(viii) and (x)–(xii) [(except that the requirement in paragraph 41(v) is to be read as if it were not qualified by paragraph 43A)]; and

(iii) intends to do one or more of the following during his visit:

a. to take part in a sports tournament, a particular sporting event or series of sporting events in which the applicant is either:

(i) taking part, either as an individual or as part of a team;

(ii) making personal appearances and promotions, such as book signings, television interviews, guest commentaries, negotiating contracts, or to discuss sponsorship deals;

(iii) taking part in 'trials', providing it is not in front of an audience, either paying or non-paying;

(iv) undertaking short periods of training, either as an individual or as part of a team, providing the applicant is not intending to settle in the UK, being paid by a UK sporting body, or joining a UK team where they are involved in friendly or exhibition matches.

b. To take part in a specific one off charity sporting event, provided no payment is received other than for travelling and other expenses;

c. To join, as an Amateur, a wholly or predominantly amateur team provided no payment is received other than for board and lodging and reasonable expenses;

d. To serve as a member of the technical or personal staff, or as an official, attending the same event as a visiting sportsperson coming for one or more of the purposes listed in (a), (b) or (c) or attending the same event as a sports-person carrying out permitted paid engagements as a visitor.

Note: Words inserted in subparagraph (ii) from 1 October 2013 (HC 628).

Leave to enter as a Sports Visitor

46N. A person seeking leave to enter to the United Kingdom as a Sports Visitor may be admitted for a period not exceeding 6 months, subject to a condition prohibiting employment, study and recourse to public funds, provided the Immigration Officer is satisfied that each of the requirements of paragraph 46M is met.

Refusal of leave to enter as a Sports Visitor

46O. Leave to enter as a Sports Visitor is to be refused if the Immigration Officer is not satisfied that each of the requirements of paragraph 46M is met.

Requirements for an extension of stay as a Sports Visitor

46P. Six months is the maximum permitted leave which may be granted to a Sports Visitor. The requirements for an extension of stay as a sports visitor are that the applicant:

(i) meets the requirements of paragraph 46M(ii)–(iii); and

(ii) has not already spent, or would not as a result of an extension of stay spend, more than 6 months in total in the United Kingdom as a Sports Visitor; and

(iii) has, or was last granted, entry clearance, leave to enter or leave to remain as a Sports Visitor; and

(iv) must not be in the UK in breach of immigration laws except that any period of overstaying for a period of 28 days or less will be disregarded.

Extension of stay as a Sports Visitor

46Q. An extension of stay as a Sports Visitor may be granted, subject to a condition prohibiting employment, study and recourse to public funds, provided the Secretary of State is satisfied that each of the requirements of paragraph 46P is met.

Refusal of extension of stay as a Sports Visitor

46R. An extension of stay as a Sports Visitor is to be refused if the Secretary of State is not satisfied that each of the requirements of paragraph 46P is met.

Entertainer Visitors

Requirements for leave to enter as an Entertainer Visitor

46S. The requirements to be met by a person seeking leave to enter the United Kingdom as an Entertainer Visitor are that he:

(i) is genuinely seeking entry as an Entertainer Visitor for a limited period as stated by him, not exceeding six months and

(ii) meets the requirements of paragraphs 41(ii)–(viii) and (x)–(xii) [(except that the requirement in paragraph 41(v) is to be read as if it were not qualified by paragraph 43A)] and

(iii) intends to do one or more of the following during his visit:

a. to take part as a professional entertainer in one or more music competitions; and/or

b. to fulfil one or more specific engagements as either an individual Amateur entertainer or as an Amateur group; and/or

c. to take part, as an amateur or professional entertainer, in one or more cultural events or festivals on the list of permit free festivals at Appendix R to these Rules.

d. serve as a member of the technical or personal staff, or of the production team, of an entertainer coming for one or more of the purposes listed in (a), (b), or (c), or attending the same event as an entertainer carrying out permitted paid engagements as a visitor.

Note: Words inserted in subparagraph (ii) from 1 October 2013 (HC 628).

Leave to enter as an Entertainer Visitor

46T. A person seeking leave to enter to the United Kingdom as an Entertainer Visitor may be admitted for a period not exceeding 6 months, subject to a condition prohibiting employment, study and recourse to public funds, provided the Immigration Officer is satisfied that each of the requirements of paragraph 46S is met.

Refusal of leave to enter as an Entertainer Visitor

46U. Leave to enter as an Entertainer Visitor is to be refused if the Immigration Officer is not satisfied that each of the requirements of paragraph 46S is met.

Requirements for an extension of stay as an Entertainer Visitor

46V. Six months is the maximum permitted leave which may be granted to an Entertainer Visitor. The requirements for an extension of stay as an Entertainer Visitor are that the applicant:

(i) meets the requirements of paragraph 46S(ii)–(iii); and

(ii) has not already spent, or would not as a result of an extension of stay spend, more than 6 months in total in the United Kingdom as an Entertainer Visitor; and

(iii) has, or was last granted, entry clearance, leave to enter or leave to remain as an Entertainer Visitor; and

(iv) must not be in the UK in breach of immigration laws except that any period of overstaying for a period of 28 days or less will be disregarded.

Extension of stay as an Entertainer Visitor

46W. An extension of stay as an Entertainer Visitor may be granted, subject to a condition prohibiting employment, study and recourse to public funds, provided the Secretary of State is satisfied that each of the requirements of paragraph 46V is met.

Refusal of extension of stay as an Entertainer Visitor

46X. An extension of stay as an Entertainer Visitor is to be refused if the Secretary of State is not satisfied that each of the requirements of paragraph 46V is met.

Visitors in transit

Transit by visa nationals

47ZA. A visa national who seeks to enter the UK for the purpose of transit (that is, to travel via the UK en route to another destination country) must be in possession of a visa enabling their admission to the United Kingdom as a visitor in transit under paragraph 47, or must meet the requirements for admission under the transit without visa scheme provided for by paragraphs 50A to 50D when seeking leave to enter the UK.

Note: Paragraph 47A inserted from 1 December 2014 (HC 693).

Requirements for admission as a visitor in transit to another country

47. The requirements to be met by a person (not being a member of the crew of a ship, aircraft, hovercraft, hydrofoil or train) seeking leave to enter the United Kingdom as a visitor in transit to another country are that he:

(i) is [genuinely] in transit to a country outside the common travel area; and

(ii) has both the means and the intention of proceeding at once to another country; and

(iii) is assured of entry there; and

(iv) intends and is able to leave the United Kingdom within 48 hours.

Note: Word inserted in subparagraph (i) from 1 December 2014 (HC 693).

Leave to enter as a visitor in transit

48. A person seeking leave to enter the United Kingdom as a visitor in transit may be admitted for a period not exceeding 48 hours with a prohibition on employment, study and recourse to public funds, provided the Immigration Officer is satisfied that each of the requirements of paragraph 47 is met.

Refusal of leave to enter as a visitor in transit

49. Leave to enter as a visitor in transit is to be refused if the Immigration Officer is not satisfied that each of the requirements of paragraph 47 is met.

Extension of stay as a visitor in transit

50. The maximum permitted leave which may be granted to a visitor in transit is 48 hours. An application for an extension of stay beyond 48 hours from a person admitted in this category is to be refused.

Transit Without Visa Scheme

50A. A visa national must meet the requirements in paragraphs 50B and 50C when seeking leave to enter the UK in order to be granted leave to enter under the transit without visa scheme.

Note: Paragraphs 50A to 50F inserted from 1 December 2014 (HC 693).

50B. The requirements to be met by a visa national seeking leave to enter the United Kingdom under the transit without visa scheme are that he:

(i) has arrived and will depart by air; and

(ii) is genuinely in transit to another country, meaning the purpose of his visit is to travel via the UK en route to another destination country, and he is taking a reasonable transit route; and

(iii) does not intend to access public funds, undertake employment or study in the UK; and

(iv) intends and is able to leave the UK before 23:59 hours on the day after the day when he arrived; and

(v) has a confirmed booking on a flight departing the UK before 23:59 hours on the day after the day when he arrived; and

(vi) is assured entry to his country of destination and any other countries he is transiting through on his way there.

Note: Paragraphs 50A to 50F inserted from 1 December 2014 (HC 693).

50C. The visa national must also:

(i) be travelling to (or on part of a reasonable journey to) Australia, Canada, New Zealand or the USA and have a valid visa for that country; or

(ii) be travelling from (or on part of a reasonable journey from) Australia, Canada, New Zealand or the USA and it is less than 6 months since he last entered that country with a valid entry visa; or

(iii) hold a valid residence permit issued by either:

(a) Australia;

(b) Canada, issued after 28 June 2002;

(c) New Zealand;

(d) USA, issued after 21 April 1998 including: a valid USA I-551 Temporary Immigrant visa (a wet-ink stamp version will NOT be accepted by UK border control); a permanent residence card; an expired I-551 Permanent Residence card provided it is accompanied by a valid I-797 letter authorising extension; a standalone US Immigration Form 155A/155B; or

(e) an EEA state or Switzerland; or

(iv) hold a valid uniform format category D visa for entry to a state in the European Economic Area (EEA) or Switzerland; or

(v) be travelling on to the Republic of Ireland and have a valid Irish biometric visa; or

(vi) be travelling from the Republic of Ireland and it is less than 3 months since the applicant was last given permission to land or be in the Republic by the Irish authorities with a valid Irish biometric visa.

Note: Paragraphs 50A to 50F inserted from 1 December 2014 (HC 693).

Leave to enter under the transit without visa scheme

50D. A person seeking leave to enter the United Kingdom on arrival under the transit without visa scheme may be admitted for a period ending no later than 23:59 hours on the day after the day on which he arrived, with a prohibition on employment, study and recourse to public funds, provided the Immigration Officer is satisfied that the requirements of paragraphs 50B and 50C are met.

Note: Paragraphs 50A to 50F inserted from 1 December 2014 (HC 693).

Refusal of leave to enter under the transit without visa scheme

50E. Leave to enter under the transit without visa scheme is to be refused if the Immigration Officer is not satisfied that the requirements of paragraphs 50B and 50C are met.

Note: Paragraphs 50A to 50F inserted from 1 December 2014 (HC 693).

Extension of stay under the transit without visa scheme

50F. The maximum permitted leave which may be granted to a person under the transit without visa scheme is for a period ending no later than 23:59 hours on the day after the day on which they arrived. An application for an extension of stay beyond this period by a person admitted in this category is to be refused.

Note: Paragraphs 50A to 50F inserted from 1 December 2014 (HC 693).

Visitors seeking to enter or remain for private medical treatment

Requirements for leave to enter as a visitor for private medical treatment

51. The requirements to be met by a person seeking leave to enter the UK as a visitor for private medical treatment are that the person:

(i) is genuinely seeking entry as a visitor who will be receiving private medical treatment in the UK for an initial period as stated by him that is:

(a) not exceeding six months; or

(b) not exceeding 11 months, where the visitor's medical practitioner has confirmed that the period of treatment is likely to exceed six months and provided the person has entry clearance as a visitor; and

(ii) meets the requirements set out in paragraph 41(iii)–(vii), (ix)–(x) and (xii) (except that the requirement in paragraph 41(v) is to be read as if it were not qualified by paragraph 43A for entry as a general visitor); and

(iii) in the case of a person suffering from a communicable disease, has satisfied the Medical Inspector that there is no danger to public health; and

(iv) can show, if required to do so, that any proposed course of treatment is of finite duration; and

(v) intends to leave the UK at the end of the treatment; and

(vi) can produce satisfactory evidence, if required to do so, of:

(a) the medical condition requiring consultation or treatment; and

(b) satisfactory arrangements for the necessary consultation or treatment at his own expense; and

(c) the estimated costs of such consultation or treatment; and

(d) the likely duration of the treatment; and

(e) sufficient funds available to the person in the UK to meet the estimated costs and the person's undertaking to do so.

Note: Paragraph 51 substituted from 6 November 2014 subject to savings for applications made before that date (HC 693).

Leave to enter as a visitor for private medical treatment

52. A person seeking leave to enter the UK as a visitor for private medical treatment may be admitted for a period not exceeding six months, or for a period not exceeding 11 months where paragraph 51(i)(b) applies, subject to a condition prohibiting employment, study and recourse to public funds, provided the Immigration Officer is satisfied that each of the requirements of paragraph 51 is met.

Note: Paragraph 52 substituted from 6 November 2014 subject to savings for applications made before that date (HC 693).

Refusal of leave to enter as a visitor for private medical treatment

53. Leave to enter as a visitor for private medical treatment is to be refused if the Immigration Officer is not satisfied that each of the requirements of paragraph 51 is met.

Requirements for an extension of stay as a visitor for private medical treatment

54. The requirements for an extension of stay as a visitor to undergo or continue private medical treatment are that the applicant:

(i) meets the requirements set out in paragraph 41(iii)–(vii), (ix)–(x) and (xii) and paragraph 51(ii)–(v); and

(ii) has produced evidence in the form of a letter on headed notepaper giving a private practice or hospital address from a registered medical practitioner who holds an NHS consultant post or who appears in the Specialist Register of the General Medical Council that provides full details of the:

(a) nature of the illness;

(b) proposed or continuing treatment;

(c) frequency of consultations;

(d) probable duration of the treatment;

(e) details of the cost of treatment and confirmation that all expenses are being met; and

(f) where treatment amounts to private visits to a consultant for a relatively minor ailment, details of the progress being made and;

(iii) has provided evidence that he has met, out of the resources available to him, any costs and expenses incurred in relation to his treatment in the United Kingdom; and

(iv) has provided evidence that he has sufficient funds available to him in the United Kingdom or if relying on funds from abroad has provided evidence that those funds are fully transferable to the United Kingdom, to meet the likely costs of his treatment and intends to meet those costs; and

(v) was not last admitted to the United Kingdom under the Approved Destination Status Agreement with China; and

(vi) must not be in the UK in breach of immigration laws except that any period of overstaying for a period of 28 days or less will be disregarded.

Extension of stay as a visitor for private medical treatment

55. An extension of stay to undergo or continue private medical treatment may be granted for a period not exceeding six months, with a prohibition on employment, study and recourse to public funds, provided the Secretary of State is satisfied that each of the requirements of paragraph 54 is met.

Note: Paragraph 55 substituted from 6 November 2014 subject to savings for applications made before that date (HC 693).

Refusal of extension of stay as a visitor for private medical treatment

56. An extension of stay as a visitor to undergo or continue private medical treatment is to be refused if the Secretary of State is not satisfied that each of the requirements of paragraph 54 is met.

Parent of a child at school

Requirements for leave to enter or remain as the parent of a child at school

56A. The requirements to be met by a person seeking leave to enter or remain in the United Kingdom as the parent of a child at school are that:

(i) the parent meets the requirements set out in paragraph 41(ii)–(xii) [(except that the requirement in paragraph 41(v) is to be read as if it were not qualified by paragraph 43A)]; and

(ii) (1) if the child has leave under paragraphs 57 to 62 of these Rules, the child is attending an independent fee paying day school and meets the requirements set out in paragraph 57(i) to (ix), or

(2) if the child is a Tier 4 (Child) Student, the child is attending an independent fee paying day school and meets the requirements set out in paragraph 245ZZA (if seeking leave to enter) or 245ZZC (if seeking leave to remain); and

(iii) the child is under 12 years of age; and

(iv) the parent can provide satisfactory evidence of adequate and reliable funds for maintaining a second home in the United Kingdom; and

(v) the parent is not seeking to make the United Kingdom his main home; and

(vi) the parent was not last admitted to the United Kingdom under the Approved Destination Status Agreement with China; and

(vii) if seeking leave to remain must not be in the UK in breach of immigration laws except that any period of overstaying for a period of 28 days or less will be disregarded.

Note: Words inserted in subparagraph (i) from 1 October 2013 (HC 628).

Leave to enter or remain as the parent of a child at school

56B. A person seeking leave to enter or remain in the United Kingdom as the parent of a child at school may be admitted or allowed to remain for a period not exceeding 12 months, subject to a condition prohibiting employment, study and recourse to public funds, provided the Immigration Officer or, in the case of an application for limited leave to remain, the Secretary of State is satisfied that each of the requirements of paragraph 56A is met.

Refusal of leave to enter or remain as the parent of a child at school

56C. Leave to enter or remain in the United Kingdom as the parent of a child at school is to be refused if the Immigration Officer or, in the case of an application for limited leave to remain, the Secretary of State is not satisfied that each of the requirements of paragraph 56A is met.

Visitors seeking to enter for the purposes of marriage or to enter into a civil partnership

Requirements for leave to enter as a visitor for marriage or to enter a civil partnership

56D. The requirements to be met by a person seeking leave to enter the United Kingdom as a visitor for marriage or civil partnership are that he:

(i) meets the requirements set out in paragraph 41(i)–(ix) and (xi)–(xii) [(except that the requirement in paragraph 41(v) is to be read as if it were not qualified by paragraph 43A)]; and

(ii) can show that he intends to give notice of marriage or civil partnership, or marry or form a civil partnership, in the United Kingdom within the period for which entry is sought; and

(iii) can produce satisfactory evidence, if required to do so, of the arrangements for giving notice of marriage or civil partnership, or for his wedding or civil partnership to take place, in the United Kingdom during the period for which entry is sought; and

(iv) does not intend to enter into a sham marriage or sham civil partnership within the meaning of sections 24(5) and 24A(5) of the Immigration and Asylum Act 1999; and

(v) holds a valid United Kingdom entry clearance for entry in this capacity.

Note: Words inserted in subparagraph (i) from 1 October 2013 (HC 628). Sub-paragraph (iv) substituted and subparagraph (v) inserted from 6 November 2014 subject to savings for applications made before that date (HC 693).

Leave to enter as a visitor for marriage or civil partnership

56E. A person seeking leave to enter the United Kingdom as a visitor for marriage or civil partnership may be admitted for a period not exceeding 6 months, subject to a condition prohibiting employment, study and recourse to public funds, provided the Immigration Officer is satisfied that each of the requirements of paragraph 56D is met.

Refusal of leave to enter as a visitor for marriage or civil partnership

56F. Leave to enter as a visitor for marriage or civil partnership is to be refused if the Immigration Officer is not satisfied that each of the requirements of paragraph 56D is met.

Visitors seeking leave to enter under the Approved Destination Status (ADS) Agreement with China

Requirements for leave to enter as a visitor under the Approved Destination Status Agreement with China ("ADS Agreement")

56G. The requirements to be met by a person seeking leave to enter the United Kingdom as a visitor under the ADS agreement with China are that he:

(i) meets the requirements set out in paragraph 41(ii)–(xii) [(except that the requirement in paragraph 41(v) is to be read as if it were not qualified by paragraph 43A)]; and

(ii) is a national of the People's Republic of China; and

(iii) is genuinely seeking entry as a visitor for a limited period as stated by him, not exceeding 30 days; and

(iv) intends to enter, leave and travel within the territory of the United Kingdom as a member of a tourist group under the ADS agreement; and

(v) holds a valid ADS agreement visit visa.

Note: Words inserted in subparagraph (i) from 1 October 2013 (HC 628). Sub-paragraph (iv) substituted and subparagraph (v) inserted from 6 November 2014 subject to savings for applications made before that date (HC 693).

Leave to enter as a visitor under the ADS agreement with China

56H. A person seeking leave to enter the United Kingdom as a visitor under the ADS Agreement may be admitted for a period not exceeding 30 days, subject to a condition prohibiting employment, study and recourse to public funds, provided they hold an ADS Agreement visit visa.

Refusal of leave to enter as a visitor under the ADS agreement with China

56I. Leave to enter as a visitor under the ADS agreement with China is to be refused if the person does not hold an ADS Agreement visit visa.

Extension of stay as a visitor under the ADS agreement with China

56J. Any application for an extension of stay as a visitor under the ADS Agreement with China is to be refused.

Student visitors

Requirements for leave to enter as a student visitor

56K(1) The requirements to be met by a person seeking leave to enter the United Kingdom as a student visitor are that he:

(i) is genuinely seeking entry as a student visitor for a limited period as stated by him, not exceeding six months; and

(ii) has been accepted on a course of study which is to be provided by an institution which is:

(a) the holder of a Sponsor licence for Tier 4 of the Points Based System, or

(b) the holder of valid accreditation from Accreditation UK, the Accreditation Body for Language Services (ABLS), the British Accreditation Council (BAC) or the Accreditation Service for International Colleges (ASIC), or

(c) the holder of a valid and satisfactory full institutional inspection, review or audit by one of the following bodies: Bridge Schools Inspectorate; the Education and Training Inspectorate; Estyn; Education Scotland; the Independent Schools Inspectorate; Office for Standards in Education; the Quality Assurance Agency for Higher Education; the Schools Inspection Service or the Education and Training Inspectorate Northern Ireland, or

(d) an overseas Higher Education Institution offering only part of their programmes in the United Kingdom, holding its own national accreditation and offering programmes that are an equivalent level to a United Kingdom degree, or

[(iia)–

(a) is enrolled on a course of study abroad equivalent to at least UK degree level study, and

(b) has been accepted by a UK recognised body or a body in receipt of public funding as a higher education institution from the Department for Employment and Learning in Northern Ireland, the Higher Education Funding Council for England, the Higher Education Funding Council for Wales or the Scottish Funding Council to undertake research or research tuition at the UK institution, providing that—

(c) the overseas course provider confirms that the research or research tuition is part of or relevant to the course of study mentioned in sub-paragraph (a) above, and

(d) the student is not to be employed as a sponsored researcher under the relevant Tier 5 Government Authorised Exchange scheme, or under Tier 2 of the Points-Based System, at the UK institution; and]

(iii) intends to leave the United Kingdom at the end of his visit as stated by him; and

(iv) does not intend to take employment in the United Kingdom; and

(v) does not intend to engage in business, to produce goods or provide services within the United Kingdom, including the selling of goods or services direct to members of the public; and

(vi) does not intend to study at a maintained school; and

(vii) will maintain and accommodate himself and any dependants adequately out of resources available to him without recourse to public funds or taking employment; or will, with any dependants, be maintained and accommodated adequately by relatives or friends; and

(viii) can meet the cost of the return or onward journey; and

(ix) is not a child under the age of 18; and

(x) meets the requirements set out in paragraph 41(ix)–(xii).

(2) In sub-paragraph (1)(iia) "research tuition" means tuition given to the applicant about how to conduct research.

Note: Subparagraphs (1)(iia) and (2) inserted from 1 October 2013 (HC 628).

Leave to enter as a student visitor

56L. A person seeking leave to enter to the United Kingdom as a student visitor may be admitted for a period not exceeding 6 months, subject to a condition prohibiting employment, and recourse to public funds, provided the Immigration Officer is satisfied that each of the requirements of paragraph 56K is met.

Refusal of leave to enter as a student visitor

56M. Leave to enter as a student visitor is to be refused if the Immigration Officer is not satisfied that each of the requirements of paragraph 56K is met.

Prospective Entrepreneurs

Purpose

56N. This Special Visitor route is to enable individuals who are at the time of applying for leave under this route in discussions with:

(i) one or more registered venture capitalist firms regulated by the [Financial Conduct Authority], and/or

(ii) one or more UK entrepreneurial seed funding competitions which is listed as endorsed on the UK Trade & Investment website, and/or

(iii) one or more UK Government Departments,

to secure funding in order to join, set up or take over, and be actively involved in the running of, a business in the UK.

Note: Words substituted in subparagraph (i) from 1 October 2013 (HC 628).

Requirements for leave to enter as a Prospective Entrepreneur

56O. The requirements to be met by a person seeking leave to enter the United Kingdom as a Prospective Entrepreneur are that:

(a) The applicant must provide an original, letter on headed paper signed by an authorised official of that institution supporting the application from:

(i) one or more registered venture capitalist firms regulated by the [financial conduct authority],

(ii) one or more UK entrepreneurial seed funding competitions which is listed as endorsed on the UK Trade & Investment website, or

(iii) one or more UK Government Departments;

(b) The letter referred to in (a) must be dated no earlier than three months before the date of the application, be signed by an authorised official, and contain:

(i) a description of the nature of the individual(s) and/or organisation(s) supporting the application;

(ii) a description of the background and nature of the proposed business;

(iii) a description of the applicant's suitability to be involved with the proposed business;

(iv) a commitment by the individual(s) and/or organisation(s) supporting the applicant to make a decision whether to make a decision whether to provide a minimum of £50,000 funding for the proposed business within 6 months of the applicant entering the UK. (if more than one individual and/or organisation is supporting the applicant, each amount proposed may be less than £50k, provided that the total amount is a minimum of £50k);

(v) a commitment by the individual(s) or organisation(s) supporting the applicant that the proposed business will be set up and run from the UK;

(vi) details of a contact name, telephone number and e-mail address for the individual(s) and/or organisation(s) supporting the applicant; and

(vii) confirmation that the individual(s) and/or organisation(s) supporting the applicant is content to be contacted about the applicant;

(c) The applicant's primary intention in applying as a Prospective Entrepreneur is to secure funding in order to join, set up or take over, and be actively involved in the running of a business in the UK;

(d) The applicant intends to carry out one of the activities as listed in paragraph 56O(d)(i), specifying the activities that a Prospective Entrepreneur may undertake during a visit to the UK;

56O(d)(i). The permitted activities are:

(1) attending meetings, including meetings arranged while in the UK, interviews arranged before arriving in the UK and conferences;

(2) attending trade fairs provided this is restricted to promotional work and does not involve selling directly to members of the public;

(3) arranging deals and negotiating or signing trade agreements and contracts;

(4) conducting site visits;

(5) speaking at a one-off conference which is not organised as a commercial concern;

(6) undertaking fact finding missions;

(7) purchasing, checking the details of or examining goods; and

(8) recruiting staff for the proposed business activity which is the object of the visa.

(e) The applicant intends to leave the United Kingdom at the end of the period of the visit as stated by him, unless he makes a successful application for leave to remain as a Tier 1 (Entrepreneur) Migrant before the end of the period of the visit;

(f) The applicant will maintain and accommodate himself and any dependants adequately out of resources available to him without recourse to public funds or taking employment; or will, with any dependants, be maintained and accommodated adequately by relatives or friends;

(g) The applicant does not intend during his visit to:

(i) take employment in the United Kingdom;

(ii) produce goods or provide services within the United Kingdom, including the selling of goods or services direct to members of the public;

(iii) undertake a course of study;

(iv) marry or form a civil partnership, or to give notice of marriage or civil partnership; or

(v) receive private medical treatment.

(h) The applicant is not under the age of 18;

(i) The applicant is not in transit to a country outside the common travel area; and

(j) The applicant holds a valid United Kingdom entry clearance for entry in this capacity.

Note: Words substituted in subparagraph (i) from 1 October 2013 (HC 628).

Leave to enter as a Prospective Entrepreneur

56P. A person seeking leave to enter to the United Kingdom as a Prospective Entrepreneur may be admitted for a period not exceeding 6 months, subject to a condition prohibiting employment, study and recourse to public funds, provided the secretary of state is satisfied that each of the requirements of paragraph 56O is met.

Refusal of leave to enter as a Prospective Entrepreneur

56Q. Leave to enter as a Prospective Entrepreneur is to be refused if the secretary of state is not satisfied that each of the requirements of paragraph 56O is met.

Paragraphs 56R to 56W DELETED.

Note: Paragraphs 56R to 56W deleted from 6 April 2013 subject to savings for applications made before that date (HC 1039).

Visitors undertaking permitted paid engagements

Requirements for leave to enter as a visitor undertaking permitted paid engagements

56X. The requirements to be met by a person seeking leave to enter the United Kingdom as a visitor undertaking permitted paid engagements are that the applicant:

i. is genuinely seeking entry as a visitor undertaking a permitted paid engagement for a limited period, not exceeding one month; and

ii. meets the requirements of paragraphs 41(ii), (v), (vii), (viii), (x)–(xii) [(except that the requirement in paragraph 41(v) is to be read as if it were not qualified by paragraph 43A)]; and

iii. intends to do one of the following pre-arranged permitted paid engagements which can be evidenced by a formal invitation, and can show that the engagement relates to his or her area of expertise and/or qualifications, and full time occupation overseas:

(a) examine students and/or participate in or chair selection panels as a visiting academic, who is highly qualified within his or her own field of expertise, invited by a United Kingdom Higher Education Institution or a United Kingdom based research or arts organisation as part of that institution or organisation's quality assurance processes;

(b) give one or more lectures in his or her field of expertise as a visiting lecturer, invited by a United Kingdom Higher Education Institution or a United Kingdom based research or arts organisation provided this is not in a formal teaching role;

(c) as an overseas designated pilot examiner, assess United Kingdom based pilots to ensure they meet the national aviation regulatory requirements of other countries, by invitation of an approved training organisation based in the United Kingdom that is regulated by the United Kingdom Civil Aviation Authority for that purpose;

(d) provide advocacy in a particular area of law as a qualified lawyer for the purposes of a court or tribunal hearing, arbitration or other form of alternative dispute resolution for legal proceedings within the United Kingdom, at the invitation of a client in the United Kingdom or foreign based client;

(e) undertake an activity relating to the arts, entertainment or sporting professions, by invitation of an arts or sports organisation or broadcaster based in the United Kingdom; and

iv. does not intend to take employment, produce goods or provide services within the United Kingdom, including the selling of goods or services direct to members of the public other than as permitted for by the pre-arranged paid engagement; and

v. will maintain and accommodate him or herself adequately out of resources available to the applicant without recourse to public funds or taking employment; or will be maintained and accommodated adequately by relatives or friends.

Note: Words inserted in subparagraph (ii) from 1 October 2013 (HC 628).

Leave to enter as a visitor undertaking permitted paid engagements

56Y. A person seeking leave to enter the United Kingdom as a visitor undertaking permitted paid engagements may be admitted for a single entry and for a period not exceeding 1 month, with a condition prohibiting study and recourse to public funds provided the Immigration Officer is satisfied that each of the requirements of paragraph 56X are met.

Refusal of leave to enter as a visitor undertaking permitted paid engagements

56Z. Leave to enter as a visitor undertaking permitted paid engagements is to be refused if the Immigration Officer is not satisfied that each of the requirements at paragraph 56X are met.

Commonwealth Games Family Member Visitor

Note: Paragraphs 56ZA to 56ZH deleted from 6 November 2014 subject to savings for applications made before that date (HC 693).

PART 3

PERSONS SEEKING TO ENTER OR REMAIN IN THE UNITED KINGDOM FOR STUDIES

Students

Paragraphs 57–62. DELETED

Student nurses

Paragraphs 63–69. DELETED

Re-sits of examinations

Paragraphs 69A–69F. DELETED

Writing up a thesis

Paragraphs 69G–69L. DELETED

Overseas qualified nurse or midwife

Paragraphs 69M–69R. DELETED

Postgraduate doctors and dentists

Paragraphs 70–75M. DELETED

Requirements for leave to enter the United Kingdom to take the Professional and Linguistic Assessments Board (PLAB Test) or an Objective Structured Clinical Examination (OSCE).

75A. The requirements to be met by a person seeking leave to enter in order to take the PLAB Test [or an OSCE] are that the applicant:

(i) is a graduate of a medical school and intends to take the PLAB Test, or is a graduate of an overseas nursing school and intends to take an OSCE, in the UK; and

(ii) can provide documentary evidence of a confirmed test date or of his eligibility to take the PLAB Test by way of a letter or email from the General Medical Council or a test admission card; or can provide evidence of a confirmed test date or of his eligibility to take an OSCE by way of a letter from the Nursing and Midwifery Council; and

(iii) meets the requirements of paragraph 41(ii)-(viii) and (x)-(xi) for entry as a visitor; and

(iv) intends to leave the United Kingdom at the end of the leave granted under this paragraph unless he is successful in the PLAB Test and granted leave to remain to undertake a clinical attachment in accordance with paragraphs 75G to 75M of these Rules.

Note: Heading substituted, words inserted and subparagraphs (i)-(iii) substituted from 6 November 2014 subject to savings for applications made before that date (HC 693).

Leave to enter to take the PLAB Test [or an OSCE]

75B. A person seeking leave to enter the United Kingdom to take the PLAB Test [or an OSCE] may be admitted for a period not exceeding 6 months subject to a condition prohibiting employment, study and recourse to public funds, provided the Immigration Officer is satisfied that each of the requirements of paragraph 75A is met.

Note: Paragraph 75B amended from 6 November 2014 subject to savings for applications made before that date (HC 693).

Refusal of leave to enter to take the PLAB Test [or an OSCE]

75C. Leave to enter the United Kingdom to take the PLAB Test [or an OSCE] is to be refused if the Immigration Officer is not satisfied that each of the requirements of paragraph 75A is met.

Note: Paragraph 75C amended from 6 November 2014 (HC 693).

Requirements for an extension of stay in order to take the PLAB Test

75D. The requirements for an extension of stay in the United Kingdom in order to take the PLAB Test are that the applicant:

(i) was given leave to enter the United Kingdom for the purposes of taking the PLAB Test in accordance with paragraph 75B of these Rules; and

(ii) intends to take the PLAB Test and can provide documentary evidence of a confirmed test date, by way of a letter or email from the General Medical Council or a test admission card; and

(iii) meets the requirements set out in paragraph 41(iii)–(vii); and

(iv) intends to leave the United Kingdom at the end of the leave granted under this paragraph unless he is successful in the PLAB Test and granted leave to remain to undertake a clinical attachment in accordance with paragraphs 75G to 75M of these Rules; and

(v) would not as a result of an extension of stay spend more than 18 months in the United Kingdom for the purpose of taking the PLAB Test; and

(vi) must not be in the UK in breach of immigration laws except that any period of overstaying for a period of 28 days or less will be disregarded.

Extension of stay to take the PLAB Test

75E. A person seeking leave to remain in the United Kingdom to take the PLAB Test may be granted an extension of stay for a period not exceeding 6 months, subject to a condition prohibiting employment, study and recourse to public funds, provided the Secretary of State is satisfied that each of the requirements of paragraph 75D is met.

Refusal of extension of stay to take the PLAB Test

75F. Leave to remain in the United Kingdom to take the PLAB Test is to be refused if the Secretary of State is not satisfied that each of the requirements of paragraph 75D is met.

Requirements for leave to enter to undertake a clinical attachment or dental observer post

75G. The requirements to be met by a person seeking leave to enter to undertake a clinical attachment or dental observer post are that the applicant:

(i) is a graduate from a medical or dental school and intends to undertake a clinical attachment or dental observer post in the United Kingdom; and

(ii) can provide documentary evidence of the clinical attachment or dental observer post which will:

(a) be unpaid; and

(b) only involve observation, not treatment, of patients; and

(iii) meets the requirements of paragraph 41(iii)–(vii) of these Rules; and

(iv) intends to leave the United Kingdom at the end of the leave granted under this paragraph;

(v) if he has previously been granted leave in this category, is not seeking leave to enter which, when amalgamated with those previous periods of leave, would total more than 6 months.

Leave to enter to undertake a clinical attachment or dental observer post

75H. A person seeking leave to enter the United Kingdom to undertake a clinical attachment or dental observer post may be admitted for the period of the clinical attachment or dental observer post, [up to a maximum of 3 months at a time], or 6 months in total in this category, subject to a condition prohibiting employment, study and recourse to public funds, provided the Immigration Officer is satisfied that each of the requirements of paragraph 75G is met.

Note: Words substituted from 6 April 2013 subject to savings for applications made before that date (HC 1039).

Refusal of leave to enter to undertake a clinical attachment or dental observer post

75J. Leave to enter the United Kingdom to undertake a clinical attachment or dental observer post is to be refused if the Immigration Officer is not satisfied that each of the requirements of paragraph 75G is met.

Requirements for an extension of stay in order to undertake a clinical attachment or dental observer post

75K. The requirements to be met by a person seeking an extension of stay to undertake a clinical attachment or dental observer post are that the applicant:

(i) was given leave to enter or remain in the United Kingdom to undertake a clinical attachment or dental observer post or:

(a) for the purposes of taking the PLAB Test in accordance with paragraphs 75A to 75F and has passed both parts of the PLAB Test;

(b) as a postgraduate doctor, dentist or trainee general practitioner in accordance with paragraphs 70 to 75; or

(c) as a work permit holder for employment in the UK as a doctor or dentist in accordance with paragraphs 128 to 135; and

(ii) is a graduate from a medical or dental school and intends to undertake a clinical attachment or dental observer post in the United Kingdom; and

(iii) can provide documentary evidence of the clinical attachment or dental observer post which will:

(a) be unpaid; and

(b) only involve observation, not treatment, of patients; and

(iv) intends to leave the United Kingdom at the end of the leave granted under this paragraph; and

(v) meets the requirements of paragraph 41(iii)–(vii) of these Rules; and

(vi) if he has previously been granted leave in this category, is not seeking an extension of stay which, when amalgamated with those previous periods of leave, would total more than 6 months; and

(vii) must not be in the UK in breach of immigration laws except that any period of overstaying for a period of 28 days or less will be disregarded.

Extension of stay to undertake a clinical attachment or dental observer post

75L. A person seeking leave to remain in the United Kingdom to undertake a clinical attachment or dental observer post [up to a maximum of 3 months at a time] or 6 months in total in this category, subject to a condition prohibiting employment, study and recourse to public funds, may be granted an extension of stay for the period of their clinical attachment or dental observer post, provided that the Secretary of State is satisfied that each of the requirements of paragraph 75K is met.

Note: Words substituted from 6 April 2013 subject to savings for applications made before that date (HC 1039).

Refusal of extension of stay to undertake a clinical attachment or dental observer post

75M. Leave to remain in the United Kingdom to undertake a clinical attachment or dental observer post is to be refused if the Secretary of State is not satisfied that each of the requirements of paragraph 75K is met.

Spouses or civil partners of students or prospective students granted leave under this part of the Rules

[Requirements for leave to enter or remain as the spouse or civil partner of a student and for leave to remain as the spouse or civil partner of a prospective student]

76. The requirements to be met by a person seeking leave to enter or remain in the United Kingdom as the spouse or civil partner of a student or [leave to remain as the spouse or civil partner of] a prospective student are that:

(i) the applicant is married to or the civil partner of a person admitted to or allowed to remain in the United Kingdom under paragraphs 57–75 or 82–87F; and

(ii) each of the parties intends to live with the other as his or her spouse or civil partner during the applicant's stay and the marriage or the civil partner of is subsisting; and

(iii) there will be adequate accommodation for the parties and any dependants without recourse to public funds; and

(iv) the parties will be able to maintain themselves and any dependants adequately without recourse to public funds; and

(v) the applicant does not intend to take employment except as permitted under paragraph 77 below; and

(vi) the applicant intends to leave the United Kingdom at the end of any period of leave granted to him; and

(vii) if seeking leave to remain must not be in the UK in breach of immigration laws except that any period of overstaying for a period of 28 days or less will be disregarded.

Note: Heading amended and words inserted from 1 October 2013 subject to savings for applications made before that date (HC 628).

Leave to enter or remain as the spouse or civil partner of a student or [leave to remain as the spouse or civil partner of a] prospective student

77. A person seeking leave to enter or remain in the United Kingdom as the spouse or civil partner of a student or [leave to remain as the spouse or civil partner of] a prospective student may be admitted or allowed to remain for a period not in excess of that granted to the student or prospective student provided the Immigration Officer or, in the case of an application for limited leave to remain, the Secretary of State is satisfied that each of the requirements of paragraph 76 is met. Employment may be permitted where the period of leave granted to the student or prospective student is, or was, 12 months or more.

Note: Words inserted from 1 October 2013 subject to savings for applications made before that date (HC 628).

Refusal of leave to enter or remain as the spouse or civil partner of a student or [leave to remain as the spouse or civil partner of a] prospective student

78. Leave to enter or remain as the spouse or civil partner of a student or [leave to remain as the spouse or civil partner of a] prospective student is to be refused if the Immigration Officer or, in the case of an application for limited leave to remain, the Secretary of State is not satisfied that each of the requirements of paragraph 76 is met.

Note: Heading amended and words inserted from 1 October 2013 subject to savings for applications made before that date (HC 628).

Children of students or prospective students granted leave under this part of the Rules

[Requirements for leave to enter or remain as the child of a student and for leave to remain as the child of a prospective student]

79. The requirements to be met by a person seeking leave to enter or remain in the United Kingdom as the child of a student or [leave to remain as the child of a prospective student] are that he:

(i) is the child of a parent admitted to or allowed to remain in the United Kingdom as a student or prospective student under paragraphs 57–75 or 82–87F; and

(ii) is under the age of 18 or has current leave to enter or remain in this capacity; and

(iii) is not married or in a civil partnership, has not formed an independent family unit and is not leading an independent life; and

(iv) can, and will, be maintained and accommodated adequately without recourse to public funds; and

(v) will not stay in the United Kingdom beyond any period of leave granted to his parent; and

(vi) meets the requirements of paragraph 79A; and

(vii) if seeking leave to remain must not be in the UK in breach of immigration laws except that any period of overstaying for a period of 28 days or less will be disregarded.

Note: Words inserted from 1 October 2013 subject to savings for applications made before that date (HC 628).

79A. Both of the applicant's parents must either be lawfully present in the UK, or being granted entry clearance or leave to remain at the same time as the applicant or one parent must be lawfully present in the UK and the other being granted entry clearance or leave to remain at the same time as the applicant, unless:

(i) The student or prospective student is the applicant's sole surviving parent, or

(ii) The student or prospective student parent has and has had sole responsibility for the applicant's upbringing, or

(iii) there are serious or compelling family or other considerations which would make it desirable not to refuse the application and suitable arrangements have been made in the UK for the applicant's care.

Leave to enter or remain as the child of a student or [leave to remain as the child of a] prospective student

80. A person seeking leave to enter or remain in the United Kingdom as the child of a student or [leave to remain as the child of a] prospective student may be admitted or allowed to remain for a period not in excess of that granted to the student or prospective student provided the Immigration Officer or, in the case of an application for limited leave to remain, the Secretary of State is satisfied that each of the requirements of paragraph 79 is met. Employment may be permitted where the period of leave granted to the student or prospective student is, or was, 12 months or more.

Note: Words inserted from 1 October 2013 subject to savings for applications made before that date (HC 628).

Refusal of leave to enter or remain as the child of a student or prospective student

81. Leave to enter or remain in the United Kingdom as the child of a student or [leave to remain as the child of a] prospective student is to be refused if the Immigration Officer or, in the case of an application for limited leave to remain, the Secretary of State, is not satisfied that each of the requirements of paragraph 79 is met.

Note: Words inserted from 1 October 2013 subject to savings for applications made before that date (HC 628).

Prospective students

A82. In this Part "prospective student" means a person who was granted leave to enter as a prospective student under paragraph 83 as it was at 30 September 2013 (and see further Part 5 of Appendix F to these Rules).

82–84. DELETED.

Note: Paragraphs 82–84 deleted from 1 October 2013 subject to savings for applications made before that date (HC 628).

Requirements for extension of stay as a prospective student

85. Six months is the maximum permitted leave which may be granted to a prospective student. The requirements for an extension of stay as a prospective student are that the applicant:

(i) was admitted to the United Kingdom with a valid prospective student entry clearance; and

(ii) meets the requirements of paragraph 82; and

(iii) would not, as a result of an extension of stay, spend more than 6 months in the United Kingdom; and

(iv) must not be in the UK in breach of immigration laws except that any period of overstaying for a period of 28 days or less will be disregarded.

Extension of stay as a prospective student

86. An extension of stay as a prospective student may be granted, with a prohibition on employment, provided the Secretary of State is satisfied that each of the requirements of paragraph 85 is met.

Refusal of extension of stay as a prospective student

87. An extension of stay as a prospective student is to be refused if the Secretary of State is not satisfied that each of the requirements of paragraph 85 is met.

Students' Unions sabbatical officers

Paragraphs 87A–87F. DELETED

Part 4

Persons Seeking to Enter or Remain in the United Kingdom in an "Au Pair" Placement, as a Working Holidaymaker or for Training or Work experience

"Au pair" placements

Paragraphs 88–94. DELETED

Working holidaymakers

Paragraphs 95–100. DELETED

Children of working holidaymakers

Paragraphs 101–103. DELETED

Seasonal agricultural workers

Paragraphs 104–109. DELETED

Teachers and language assistants coming to the United Kingdom under approved exchange schemes

Paragraphs 110–115. DELETED

Home Office approved training or work experience

Paragraphs 116–121. DELETED

Spouses of persons with limited leave to enter or remain under paragraphs 110–121

Requirements for leave to enter or remain as the spouse or civil partners of a person with limited leave to enter or remain in the United Kingdom under paragraphs 110–121

122. The requirements to be met by a person seeking leave to enter or remain in the United Kingdom as the spouse or civil partners of a person with limited leave to enter or remain in the United Kingdom under paragraphs 110–121 are that:

(i) the applicant is married or the civil partner of to a person with limited leave to enter or remain in the United Kingdom under paragraphs 110–121; and

(ii) each of the parties intends to live with the other as his or her spouse or civil partners during the applicant's stay and the marriage or civil partnership is subsisting; and

(iii) there will be adequate accommodation for the parties and any dependants without recourse to public funds in accommodation which they own or occupy exclusively; and

(iv) the parties will be able to maintain themselves and any dependants adequately without recourse to public funds; and

(v) the applicant does not intend to stay in the United Kingdom beyond any period of leave granted to his spouse; and

(vi) if seeking leave to enter, the applicant holds a valid United Kingdom entry clearance for entry in this capacity or, if seeking leave to remain, was admitted with a valid United Kingdom entry clearance for entry in this capacity; or

(vii) if seeking leave to remain, must not be in the UK in breach of immigration laws except that any period of overstaying for a period of 28 days or less will be disregarded.

Leave to enter or remain as the spouse of a person with limited leave to enter or remain in the United Kingdom under paragraphs 110–121

123. A person seeking leave to enter or remain in the United Kingdom as the spouse of a person with limited leave to enter or remain in the United Kingdom under paragraphs 110–121 may be given leave to enter or remain in the United Kingdom for a period of leave not in excess of that granted to the person with limited leave to enter or remain under paragraphs 110–121 provided that, in relation to an application for leave to enter, he is able, on arrival, to produce to the Immigration Officer a valid United Kingdom entry clearance for entry in this capacity or, in the case of an application for limited leave to remain, was admitted with a valid United Kingdom entry clearance for entry in this capacity and he is able to satisfy the Secretary of State that each of the requirements of paragraph 122(i)–(v) and (vii) is met.

Refusal of leave to enter or remain as the spouse of a person with limited leave to enter or remain in the United Kingdom under paragraphs 110–121

124. Leave to enter or remain in the United Kingdom as the spouse of a person with limited leave to enter or remain in the United Kingdom under paragraphs 110–121 is to

be refused if, in relation to an application for leave to enter, a valid United Kingdom entry clearance for entry in this capacity is not produced to the Immigration Officer on arrival or, in the case of an application for limited leave to remain, if the applicant was not admitted with a valid United Kingdom entry clearance for entry in this capacity or is unable to satisfy the Secretary of State that each of the requirements of paragraph 122(i)–(v) and (vii) is met.

Children of persons with limited leave to enter or remain under paragraphs 110–121

Requirements for leave to enter or remain as the child of a person with limited leave to enter or remain in the United Kingdom under paragraphs 110–121

125. The requirements to be met by a person seeking leave to enter or remain in the United Kingdom as the child of a person with limited leave to enter or remain in the United Kingdom under paragraphs 110–121 are that:

(i) he is the child of a parent who has limited leave to enter or remain in the United Kingdom under paragraphs 110–121; and

(ii) he is under the age of 18 or has current leave to enter or remain in this capacity; and

(iii) he is unmarried and is not a civil partner, has not formed an independent family unit and is not leading an independent life; and

(iv) he can, and will, be maintained and accommodated adequately without recourse to public funds in accommodation which his parent(s) own or occupy exclusively; and

(v) he will not stay in the United Kingdom beyond any period of leave granted to his parent(s); and

(vi) both parents are being or have been admitted to or allowed to remain in the United Kingdom save where:

(a) the parent he is accompanying or joining is his sole surviving parent; or

(b) the parent he is accompanying or joining has had sole responsibility for his upbringing; or

(c) there are serious and compelling family or other considerations which make exclusion from the United Kingdom undesirable and suitable arrangements have been made for his care; and

(vii) if seeking leave to enter, he holds a valid United Kingdom entry clearance for entry in this capacity or, if seeking leave to remain, was admitted with a valid United Kingdom entry clearance for entry in this capacity; or

(viii) if seeking leave to remain, must not be in the UK in breach of immigration laws except that any period of overstaying for a period of 28 days or less will be disregarded.

Leave to enter or remain as the child of a person with limited leave to enter or remain in the United Kingdom under paragraphs 110–121

126. A person seeking leave to enter or remain in the United Kingdom as the child of a person with limited leave to enter or remain in the United Kingdom under paragraphs 110–121 may be given leave to enter or remain in the United Kingdom for a period of leave not in excess of that granted to the person with limited leave to enter or remain under paragraphs 110–121 provided that, in relation to an application for leave to enter, he is

able, on arrival, to produce to the Immigration Officer a valid United Kingdom entry clearance for entry in this capacity or, in the case of an application for limited leave to remain, he was admitted with a valid United Kingdom entry clearance for entry in this capacity and is able to satisfy the Secretary of State that each of the requirements of paragraph 125 (i)–(vi) and (viii) is met.

Refusal of leave to enter or remain as the child of a person with limited leave to enter or remain in the United Kingdom under paragraphs 110–121

127. Leave to enter or remain in the United Kingdom as the child of a person with limited leave to enter or remain in the United Kingdom under paragraphs 110–121 is to be refused if, in relation to an application for leave to enter, a valid United Kingdom entry clearance for entry in this capacity is not produced to the Immigration Officer on arrival, or, in the case of an application for limited leave to remain, if the applicant was not admitted with a valid United Kingdom entry clearance for entry in this capacity or is unable to satisfy the Secretary of State that each of the requirements of paragraph 125(i)–(vi) and (viii) is met.

Part 5

Persons seeking to enter or remain in the United Kingdom for employment

Work permit employment

General requirements for indefinite leave to remain

[128A. For the purposes of references in this Part to requirements for indefinite leave to remain:

(a) "continuous period of 5 years or 4 years lawfully in the UK" means, subject to paragraph (aa), residence in the United Kingdom for an unbroken period with valid leave, and for these purposes a period shall not be considered to have been broken where:

(i) the applicant has been absent from the UK for a period of 180 days or less in any of the five consecutive 12 calendar month periods (or four consecutive 12 calendar month periods [where the applicant received a Highly Skilled Migrant Programme approval letter issued on the basis of an application made before 3 April 2006, and was subsequently granted entry clearance or leave to remain on the basis of that letter]) preceding the date of the application for indefinite leave to remain; and

(ii) the applicant has existing limited leave to enter or remain upon their departure and return, except that where that leave expired no more than 28 days prior to a further application for entry clearance, that period and any period pending the determination of that application shall be disregarded; and

(iii) the applicant has any period of overstaying between periods of entry clearance, leave to enter or leave to remain of up to 28 days and any period of overstaying pending the determination of an application made within that 28 day period disregarded.

(aa) For the purposes of paragraph (a), time spent with valid leave in the Bailiwick of Guernsey, Bailiwick of Jersey or the Isle of Man may be included in the continuous period of 5 or 4 years residence in the UK, provided that:

(i) the leave granted in the Bailiwick of Guernsey, Bailiwick of Jersey or the Isle of Man was granted in a category equivalent to those specified in the indefinite leave to remain provisions in this Part; and

(ii) any period of leave granted in the Bailiwick of Guernsey, Bailiwick of Jersey or the Isle of Man as a work permit holder was for employment:

(a) in a job which appears on the list of occupations skilled to National Qualifications Framework level 3 or above, as stated in the Codes of Practice in Appendix J, or

(b) in a job which appears in the Creative Sector Codes of Practice in Appendix J, or

(c) as a professional sportsperson (including as a sports coach); and

(iii) in the case of leave granted in the Bailiwick of Guernsey, Bailiwick of Jersey and the Isle of Man as an overseas domestic worker in a private household, it was granted before 6 April 2012; and

(iv) the most recent period of leave in the relevant continuous period of 5 years or 4 years has been granted in the United Kingdom.

(b) Except for periods when the applicant had leave as a highly skilled migrant, a self-employed lawyer, a writer, composer or artist, an innovator or on the grounds of his UK Ancestry, [and subject to paragraph (ba)]:

[(ba) For the purposes of paragraph (b), continuous employment in the UK may include employment in the Bailiwick of Guernsey, Bailiwick of Jersey and the Isle of Man under the terms of his work permit or in the employment for which he was given leave to enter or remain, provided that the most recent work permit or period of leave was granted in the UK; and, in any such case, paragraph (b) shall apply to employment in the Bailiwick of Guernsey, Bailiwick of Jersey and the Isle of Man in the same way as it applies to employment in the UK.]

(i) the applicant must have been employed in the UK continuously throughout the five years, under the terms of his work permit or in the employment for which he was given leave to enter or remain, except that any breaks in employment in which he applied for leave as a work permit holder or as an employee under any provision of this section to work for a new employer shall be disregarded provided this is within 60 days of the end of his employment with his previous employer.

(ii) any absences from the UK must have been for a purpose that is consistent with the continuous permitted employment in (i), including paid annual leave or for serious or compelling reasons.]

Note: Paragraph 128A inserted from 13 December 2012 subject to savings for applications made before that date (HC 760). Words inserted in subparagraph (b) and subparagraphs (aa) and (ba) inserted from 6 April 2013 (HC 1039). Words inserted in subparagraph (a) from 6 April 2014 (HC 1138; for savings see implementation section of HC 1138 as amended by HC 1201).

Requirements for leave to enter the United Kingdom for work permit employment

128. A person coming to the UK to seek or take employment must be otherwise eligible for admission under these Rules or eligible for admission as a seaman under contract to join a ship due to leave British waters. The requirements for applications for work permit employment set out in paragraphs 128 to 133 of these Rules were deleted on 6 April 2012 by Statement of Changes HC 1888 except insofar as relevant to paragraphs 134 to 135.

Indefinite leave to remain for a work permit holder

134. Indefinite leave to remain may be granted on application . . . [provided] the applicant:

(i) . . . has spent a continuous period of 5 years lawfully in the UK, of which the most recent period must have been spent with leave as a work permit holder (under paragraphs 128 to 133 of these rules), and the remainder must be any combination of leave as a work permit holder or leave as a highly skilled migrant (under paragraphs 135A to 135F of these rules) or leave as a self-employed lawyer (under the concession that appeared in Chapter 6, Section 1 Annex D of the Immigration Directorate Instructions), or leave as a writer, composer or artist (under paragraphs 232 to 237 of these rules);

(ii) . . . has met the requirements of paragraph 128(i) to (v) throughout [their] leave as a work permit holder, and has met the requirements of paragraph 135G(ii) throughout any leave as a highly skilled migrant;

(iii) . . . is still required for the employment in question, as certified by [the] employer; and

(iv) [provides certification from the employer] that the applicant is paid at or above the appropriate rate for the job as stated in the Codes of Practice in Appendix J[, or where [the applicant] is on maternity, paternity or adoption leave at the time of the application and not being paid the appropriate rate, the date that leave started and that they were paid at the appropriate rate immediately before the start of that leave].

(v) . . . provides the specified documents in paragraph 134-SD to evidence the employer's certification in sub-section (iv), [and the reason for the absences set out in paragraph 128A], and

(vi) has demonstrated sufficient knowledge of the English language and sufficient knowledge about life in the United Kingdom, in accordance with Appendix KoLL; and

(vii) [does not fall for refusal under the general grounds for refusal]; and

(viii) must not be in the UK in breach of immigration laws except that any period of overstaying for a period of 28 days or less will be disregarded.

Note: Words omitted and word inserted in first sentence, words deleted from subparagraphs (i), (ii) and (iii), words inserted/substituted in subparagraphs (ii)–(vi) from 13 December 2012 subject to savings for applications made before that date (HC 760). Subparagraph (vi) substituted from 28 October 2013 subject to savings for applications made before that date (HC 628). Words inserted in subparagraph (iv) from 6 April 2013 (HC 628).

134-SD Specified documents

The specified documents referred to in paragraph 134(v) are [A, B and C below]:

A. Either a payslip and a personal bank or building society statement, or a payslip and a building society pass book.

(a) Payslips must be:

(i) the applicant's most recent payslip,

(ii) dated no earlier than one calendar month before the date of the application, and

(iii) either:

(1) an original payslip,

(2) on company-headed paper, or

(3) accompanied by a letter from the applicant's Sponsor, on company headed paper and signed by a senior official, confirming the payslip is authentic.

(b) Personal bank or building society statements must:
   (i) be the applicant's most recent statement,
   (ii) be dated no earlier than one calendar month before the date of the application,
   (iii) clearly show:
      (1) the applicant's name,
      (2) the applicant's account number,
      (3) the date of the statement,
      (4) the financial institution's name,
      (5) the financial institution's logo, and
      (6) transactions by the Sponsor covering the period no earlier than one calendar month before the date of the application, including the amount shown on the specified payslip as at 134-SD A(a),
   (iv) be either:
      (1) printed on the bank's or building society's letterhead,
      (2) electronic bank or building society statements, accompanied by a supporting letter from the bank or building society, on company headed paper, confirming the statement provided is authentic, or
      (3) electronic bank or building society statements, bearing the official stamp of the bank or building society on every page, and
   (v) not be mini-statements from automatic teller machines (ATMs).

(c) Building society pass books must
   (i) clearly show:
      (1) the applicant's name,
      (2) the applicant's account number,
      (3) the financial institution's name,
      (4) the financial institution's logo, and
      (5) transactions by the sponsor covering the period no earlier than one calendar month before the date of the application, including the amount shown on the specified payslip as at 134-SD A(a),
      and
   (ii) be either:
      (1) the original pass book, or
      (2) a photocopy of the pass book which has been certified by the issuing building society on company headed paper, confirming the statement provided is authentic.

B. A letter from the employer detailing the purpose and period of absences in connection with the employment, including periods of annual leave. Where the absence was due to a serious or compelling reason, a personal letter from the applicant which includes full details of the reason for the absences and all original supporting documents in relation to those reasons – e.g. medical certificates, birth/death certificates, information about the reasons which led to the absence from the UK.

C. Where the applicant is not being paid the appropriate rate in Appendix J due to maternity, paternity or adoption leave:

(a) Payslips must be:
   (i) the applicant's payslip from the month immediately preceding the leave,
   (ii) the applicant's payslips for each month of the period of the leave,
   (iii) as set out in A(a)(iii) above.

(b) Bank or building society statements must be:
   (i) the applicant's statement from the month immediately preceding the leave,

(ii) the applicant's statement for each month of the period of the leave,
(iii) as set out in A(b)(iii) above.

Note: Paragraph 134-SD substituted from 13 December 2012 subject to savings for applications made before that date. Words substituted in the first sentence and subparagraph C inserted from 6 April 2013 (HC1039). Words omitted from subparagraphs A(b)(iv)(2) and (3) from 28 October 2013 (subject to savings for applications made before that date (HC 628).

Refusal of indefinite leave to remain for a work permit holder

135. Indefinite leave to remain in the United Kingdom for a work permit holder is to be refused if the Secretary of State is not satisfied that each of the requirements of paragraph 134 is met.

Highly skilled migrants

135A–135F. DELETED

Requirements for indefinite leave to remain as a highly skilled migrant

135G. The requirements for indefinite leave to remain for a person who has been granted leave as a highly skilled migrant are that the applicant:

(a) has spent a continuous period of 5 years (or 4 years where the applicant received a Highly Skilled Migrant Programme approval letter issued on the basis of an application made before 3 April 2006, and was subsequently granted entry clearance or leave to remain on the basis of that letter) lawfully in the United Kingdom; and

(b) on the date that the continuous period of 5 years (or 4 years as appropriate, as set out in (a)) ends, has leave as a highly skilled migrant, and has spent the remainder of the period with leave as a highly skilled migrant, a work permit holder or an Innovator; and

(c) throughout the 5 years (or 4 years where applicable, as set out in (a)) spent in the United Kingdom, has maintained and accommodated himself and any dependants adequately without recourse to public funds; and

(d) is lawfully economically active in the United Kingdom in employment, self-employment or a combination of both; and

(e) has demonstrated sufficient knowledge of the English language and sufficient knowledge about life in the United Kingdom, in accordance with Appendix KoLL, unless the applicant received a Highly Skilled Migrant Programme approval letter issued on the basis of an application made before 7 November 2006, and was subsequently granted entry clearance or leave to remain on the basis of that letter; and

(f) does not fall for refusal under the general grounds for refusal, except that paragraph 322(1C) shall not apply if the applicant received a Highly Skilled Migrant Programme approval letter issued on the basis of an application made before 7 November 2006, and was subsequently granted entry clearance or leave to remain on the basis of that letter; and

(g) must not be in the UK in breach of immigration laws except that any period of overstaying for a period of 28 days or less will be disregarded, unless the applicant received a Highly Skilled Migrant Programme approval letter issued on the basis of an application made before 7 November 2006, and was subsequently granted entry clearance or leave to remain on the basis of that letter; and

(h) has made the application for indefinite leave to remain before 6 April 2018.

Note: Paragraph 135G substituted from 6 April 2014 (HC 1138; for savings see implementation section of HC 1138 as amended by HC 1201).

Indefinite leave to remain as a highly skilled migrant

135GA. Indefinite leave to remain may be granted provided that the Secretary of State is satisfied that each of the requirements of paragraph 135G is met and that the application does not fall for refusal under paragraph 135HA.

Refusal of indefinite leave to remain as a highly skilled migrant

135H. Indefinite leave to remain in the United Kingdom is to be refused if the Secretary of State is not satisfied that each of the requirements of paragraph 135G is met or if the application falls for refusal under paragraph 135HA.

Additional grounds for refusal for highly skilled migrants

135HA. An application under paragraphs 135A–135C or 135G–135H of these Rules is to be refused, even if the applicant meets all the requirements of those paragraphs, if the Immigration Officer or Secretary of State has cause to doubt the genuineness of any document submitted by the applicant and, having taken reasonable steps to verify the document, has been unable to verify that it is genuine.

Sectors-Based Scheme

135I–135N. DELETED

135J. DELETED

135K. DELETED

135L. DELETED

International Graduates Scheme

135O–135T. DELETED

Representatives of overseas newspapers, news agencies and broadcasting organisations

Requirements for leave to enter as a representative of an overseas newspaper, news agency or broadcasting organisation

136–141. Deleted from 27 November 2008 by HC1113 except insofar as relevant to paragraphs 142 and 143.

Indefinite leave to remain for a representative of an overseas newspaper, news agency or broadcasting organisation

142. Indefinite leave to remain may be granted, on application, to a representative of an overseas newspaper, news agency or broadcasting organisation provided [the applicant]:

(i) . . . has spent a continuous period of 5 years [lawfully] in the United Kingdom in this capacity; and

(ii) . . . has met the requirements of paragraph 139 throughout the 5 year period; and

(iii) . . . is still required for the employment in question, as certified by [the] employer; and

(iv) has demonstrated sufficient knowledge of the English language and sufficient knowledge about life in the United Kingdom, in accordance with Appendix KoLL; and

(v) [does not fall for refusal under the general grounds for refusal]; and

(vi) . . . is not in the UK in breach of immigration laws except that any period of overstaying for a period of 28 days or less will be disregarded; and

(vii) provides the specified documents in paragraph 142-SD to evidence the reason for the absences set out in paragraph 128A.

Note: Words deleted from subparagraphs (i)–(iii) and (vi), words substituted/inserted in subparagraphs (i), (iii) and (v) and subparagraph (vii) inserted from 13 December 2012 (change to subparagraph (v) subject to savings for applications made before that date) (HC 760). Subparagraph (iv) substituted from 28 October 2013 subject to savings for applications made before that date (HC 628).

142-SD Specified documents

The specified documents referred to in paragraph 142(vii) are:

a) A letter from the employer detailing the purpose and period of absences in connection with the employment, including periods of annual leave.

b) Where the absence was due to a serious or compelling reason, a personal letter from the applicant which includes full details of the reason for the absences and all original supporting documents in relation to those reasons – e.g. medical certificates, birth/death certificates, information about the reasons which led to the absence from the UK.

Note: Paragraph 142-SD inserted from 13 December 2012 (HC 760).

Refusal of indefinite leave to remain for a representative of an overseas newspaper, news agency or broadcasting organisation.

143. Indefinite leave to remain in the United Kingdom for a representative of an overseas newspaper, news agency or broadcasting organisation is to be refused if the Secretary of State is not satisfied that each of the requirements of paragraph 142 is met.

143A. DELETED

Leave to enter as a Fresh Talent: Working in Scotland scheme participant

143B. DELETED

Refusal of leave to enter as a Fresh Talent: Working in Scotland scheme participant

143C. DELETED

Requirements for an extension of stay as a Fresh Talent: Working in Scotland scheme participant

143D. DELETED

Extension of stay as a Fresh Talent: Working in Scotland scheme participant

143E. DELETED

Refusal of an extension of stay as a Fresh Talent: Working in Scotland scheme participant

143F. DELETED

Representatives of overseas businesses

Requirements for leave to enter as a representative of an overseas business

144. The requirements to be met by a person seeking leave to enter the United Kingdom as a representative of an overseas business are that he:

(i) has been recruited and taken on as an employee outside the United Kingdom of a business which has its headquarters and principal place of business outside the United Kingdom; and

(ii) is seeking entry to the United Kingdom:

(a) as a senior employee of an overseas business which has no branch, subsidiary or other representative in the United Kingdom with full authority to take operational decisions on behalf of the overseas business for the purpose of representing it in the United Kingdom by establishing and operating a registered branch or wholly owned subsidiary of that overseas business, the branch or subsidiary of which will be concerned with same type of business activity as the overseas business; or

(b) as an employee of an overseas newspaper, news agency or broadcasting organisation being posted on a long-term assignment as a representative of their overseas employer.

(iii) where entry is sought under (ii)(a), the person:

(a) will be the sole representative of the employer present in the United Kingdom under the terms of this paragraph;

(b) intends to be employed full time as a representative of that overseas business; and

(c) is not a majority shareholder in that overseas business.

(iv) where entry is sought under (ii)(b), the person intends to work full-time as a representative of their overseas employer.

(v) does not intend to take employment except within the terms of this paragraph; and

(vi) has competence in the English language to the required standard on the basis that

(a) the applicant is a national of one of the following countries: Antigua and Barbuda; Australia; The Bahamas; Barbados; Belize; Canada; Dominica; Grenada; Guyana; Jamaica; New Zealand; St Kitts and Nevis; St Lucia; St Vincent and the Grenadines; Trinidad and Tobago; United States of America; and provides the specified documents in paragraph 144-SD(a), or

(b) the applicant has a knowledge of English equivalent to level A1 or above of the Council of Europe's Common European Framework for Language Learning, and

(1) [provides the specified documents from an English language test provider approved by the Secretary of State for these purposes, as listed in Appendix O, which clearly show] the applicant's name, the qualification obtained (which must meet or exceed the standard described above) and the date of the award, or

(2) has obtained an academic qualification (not a professional or vocational qualification) which is deemed by UK NARIC to meet the recognised standard of a Bachelor's degree in the UK, and

(i) provides the specified documents in paragraph 144-SD(b) to show he has the qualification, and

(ii) UK NARIC has confirmed that the qualification was taught or researched in English to level C1 of the Council of Europe's Common European Framework for Language learning or above, or

(3) has obtained an academic qualification (not a professional or vocational qualification) which is deemed by UK NARIC to meet or exceed the recognised standard of a Bachelor's or Master's degree in the UK, and provides the specified documents in paragraph 144-SD(c) to show that:

(i) he has the qualification, and

(ii) the qualification was taught or researched in English, or

(4) has obtained an academic qualification (not a professional or vocational qualification), which is deemed by UK NARIC to meet the recognised standard of a Bachelor's or Master's degree or PhD in the UK, from an educational establishment in one of the following countries: Antigua and Barbuda; Australia; The Bahamas; Barbados; Belize; Dominica; Grenada; Guyana; Ireland; Jamaica; New Zealand; St Kitts and Nevis; St Lucia; St Vincent and The Grenadines; Trinidad and Tobago; the UK; the USA; and provides the specified documents in paragraph 144-SD(b).

(vii) can maintain and accommodate himself and any dependants adequately without recourse to public funds; and

(viii) holds a valid United Kingdom entry clearance for entry in this capacity.

Note: Words substituted in subparagraph (vi)(b)(1) from 1 October 2013 subject to savings for applications made before that date (HC 628).

144-SD Specified documents

a) The specified documents in paragraph 144(vi)(a) as evidence of nationality are the applicant's current valid original passport or travel document. If the applicant is unable to provide these, the UK Border Agency may exceptionally consider this requirement to have been met where the applicant provides full reasons in the passport section of the application form, and either:

i) a current national identity document, or

ii) an original letter from his home government or embassy, on the letter-headed paper of the government or embassy, which has been issued by an authorised official of that institution and confirms the applicant's full name, date of birth and nationality.

b) The specified documents in paragraph 144(vi)(b)(2)(i) and paragraph 144(vi)(4) as evidence of qualifications taught in English are:

1) the original certificate of the award, or

2) if the applicant is awaiting graduation having successfully completed

the qualification, or no longer has the certificate and the awarding institution is unable to provide a replacement, an academic transcript (or original letter in the case of a PhD qualification) from the awarding institution on its official headed paper, which clearly shows:

(a) the applicant's name,
(b) the name of the awarding institution,
(c) the title of the award,
(d) confirmation that the qualification has been or will be awarded, and
(e) the date that the certificate will be issued (if the applicant has not yet graduated) or confirmation that the institution is unable to re-issue the original certificate or award.

c) The specified documents in paragraph 144(vi)(b)(3)(i) as evidence of qualifications taught in English are:

1) the specified documents in (b) above, and
2) an original letter from the awarding institution on its official headed paper, which clearly shows:

(a) the applicant's name,
(b) the name of the awarding institution,
(c) the title of the award,
(d) the date of the award, and
(e) confirmation that the qualification was taught in English.

Leave to enter as a representative of an overseas business

145. A person seeking leave to enter the United Kingdom as a representative of an overseas business may be admitted for a period not exceeding 3 years provided he is able to produce to the Immigration Officer, on arrival, a valid United Kingdom entry clearance for entry in this capacity, and his leave may be subject to the following conditions:

(i) no recourse to public funds,
(ii) registration with the police, if this is required by paragraph 326 of these Rules, and
(iii) no employment other than working for the business which the applicant has been admitted to represent.

Refusal of leave to enter as a representative of an overseas business

146. Leave to enter as a representative of an overseas business is to be refused if a valid United Kingdom entry clearance for entry in this capacity is not produced to the Immigration Officer on arrival.

Requirements for an extension of stay as a representative of an overseas business

147. The requirements for an extension of stay as a representative of an overseas business are that the applicant:

(i) entered the United Kingdom with a valid United Kingdom entry clearance as:

(a) a sole representative of an overseas business, including entry under the rules providing for the admission of sole representatives in force prior to 1 October 2009; or
(b) a representative of an overseas newspaper, news agency or broadcasting organisation;

(ii) the person was admitted in accordance with paragraph 144(ii)(a) and can show that:

(a) the overseas business still has its headquarters and principal place of business outside the United Kingdom; and

(b) he is employed full time as a representative of that overseas business and has established and is in charge of its registered branch or wholly owned subsidiary; and

(c) he is still required for the employment in question, as certified by his employer;

(iii) the person was admitted in accordance with paragraph 144(ii)(b) and can show that:

(a) he is still engaged in the employment for which the entry clearance was granted; and

(b) he is still required for the employment in question, as certified by his employer.

(iv) does not intend to take employment except within the terms of this paragraph; and

(v) can maintain and accommodate himself and any dependants adequately without recourse to public funds; and

(vi) must not be in the UK in breach of immigration laws except that any period of overstaying for a period of 28 days or less will be disregarded.

Extension of stay as a representative of an overseas business

148. An extension of stay as a representative of an overseas business may be granted provided the Secretary of State is satisfied that each of the requirements of paragraph 147 is met. The extension of stay will be granted for:

(i) a period not exceeding 2 years, unless paragraph (ii) applies.

(ii) a period not exceeding 3 years, if the applicant was last granted leave prior to 1 October 2009, and will be subject to the following conditions:

(i) no recourse to public funds,

(ii) registration with the police, if this is required by paragraph 326 of these Rules, and

(iii) no employment other than working for the business which the applicant has been admitted to represent.

Refusal of extension of stay as a representative of an overseas business

149. An extension of stay as a representative of an overseas business is to be refused if the Secretary of State is not satisfied that each of the requirements of paragraph 147 is met.

Indefinite leave to remain for a representative of an overseas business

150. Indefinite leave to remain may be granted, on application, to a representative of an overseas business provided the applicant:

(i) . . . has spent a continuous period of 5 years [lawfully] in the United Kingdom in this capacity; and

(ii) . . . has met the requirements of paragraph 147 throughout the 5 year period; and

(iii) . . . is still required for the employment in question, as certified by [the] employer; and

(iv) has demonstrated sufficient knowledge of the English language and sufficient knowledge about life in the United Kingdom, in accordance with Appendix KoLL; and

(v) does not fall for refusal under the general grounds for refusal; and

(vi) . . . is not in the UK in breach of immigration laws except that any period of overstaying for a period of 28 days or less will be disregarded; and

(vii) provides the specified documents in paragraph 150-SD to evidence the reason for the absences set out in paragraph 128A.

Note: Words deleted from subparagraphs (i)–(iii) and (vi), words substituted/inserted in subparagraphs (i), (iii) and (v) and subparagraph (vii) inserted from 13 December 2012 (change to subparagraph (v) subject to savings for applications made before that date) (HC 760). Subparagraph (iv) substituted from 28 October 2013 subject to savings for applications made before that date (HC 628).

150-SD Specified documents

The specified documents referred to in paragraph 150(vii) are:

(a) A letter from the employer detailing the purpose and period of absences in connection with the employment, including periods of annual leave.

(b) Where the absence was due to a serious or compelling reason, a personal letter from the applicant which includes full details of the reason for the absences and all original supporting documents in relation to those reasons – e.g. medical certificates, birth/death certificates, information about the reasons which led to the absence from the UK.

Note: Paragraph 150-SD inserted from 13 December 2012 (HC 760).

Refusal of indefinite leave to remain for a sole representative of an overseas business

151. Indefinite leave to remain in the United Kingdom for a representative of an overseas business is to be refused if the Secretary of State is not satisfied that each of the requirements of paragraph 150 is met.

Private servants in diplomatic households

Requirements for leave to enter as a private servant in a diplomatic household

152. Deleted on 27 November 2008 by paragraph 39 of Statement of Changes HC 1113 except insofar as relevant to paragraph 158 and 159.

Indefinite leave to remain for a servant in a diplomatic household

158. Indefinite leave to remain may be granted, on application, to a private servant in a diplomatic household provided [the applicant]:

(i) . . . has spent a continuous period of 5 years [lawfully] in the United Kingdom in this capacity; and

(ii) . . . has met the requirements of paragraph 155 throughout the 5 year period; and

(iii) . . . is still required for the employment in question, as certified by [the employer]; and

(iv) has demonstrated sufficient knowledge of the English language and sufficient knowledge about life in the United Kingdom, in accordance with Appendix KoLL; and

(v) . . . does not fall for refusal under the general grounds for refusal; and

(vi) . . . is not in the UK in breach of immigration laws except that any period of overstaying for a period of 28 days or less will be disregarded; and

(vii) provides the specified documents in paragraph 158-SD to evidence the reason for the absences set out in paragraph 128A.

Note: Words deleted from subparagraphs (i)–(iii) and (vi), words substituted/inserted in subparagraphs (i), (iii) and (v) and subparagraph (vii) inserted from 13 December 2012 (change to subparagraph (v) subject to savings for applications made before that date) (HC 760). Subparagraph (iv) substituted from 28 October 2013 subject to savings for applications made before that date (HC 628).

158-SD Specified documents

The specified documents referred to in paragraph 158(vii) are:

(a) A letter from the employer detailing the purpose and period of absences in connection with the employment, including periods of annual leave.

(b) Where the absence was due to a serious or compelling reason, a personal letter from the applicant which includes full details of the reason for the absences and all original supporting documents in relation to those reasons – e.g. medical certificates, birth/death certificates, information about the reasons which led to the absence from the UK.

Note: Paragraph 158-SD inserted from 13 December 2012 (HC 760).

Refusal of indefinite leave to remain for a servant in a diplomatic household

159. Indefinite leave to remain in the United Kingdom for a private servant in a diplomatic household is to be refused if the Secretary of State is not satisfied that each of the requirements of paragraph 158 is met.

Domestic workers in private households

Requirements for leave to enter as a domestic worker in a private household

159A. The requirements to be met by a person seeking leave to enter the United Kingdom as a domestic worker in a private household are that the applicant:

(i) is aged 18–65 inclusive; and

(ii) has been employed as a domestic worker for one year or more immediately prior to the application for entry clearance under the same roof as the employer or in a household that the employer uses for himself on a regular basis and where evidence is produced to demonstrate the connection between employer and employee in the form of:

(a) a letter from the employer confirming that the domestic worker has been employed by them in that capacity for the twelve months immediately prior to the date of application; and

(b) one of the following documents covering the same period of employment as that in (a):

(i) pay slips or bank statements showing payment of salary;

(ii) confirmation of tax paid;

(iii) confirmation of health insurance paid;

(iv) contract of employment;

(v) work visa, residence permit or equivalent passport endorsement for the country in which the domestic worker has been employed by that employer; or

(vi) visas or equivalent passport endorsement to confirm that the domestic worker has travelled with the employer; and

(iii) intends to work for the employer whilst the employer is in the United Kingdom and intends to travel in the company of either;

(a) a British or EEA national employer, or that employer's British or EEA national spouse, civil partner or child, where the employer's usual place of residence is outside the UK and where the employer does not intend to remain in the UK beyond six months; or

(b) a British or EEA national employer's foreign national spouse, civil partner or child where the employer does not intend to remain in the UK beyond six months; or

(c) a foreign national employer or the employer's spouse, civil partner or child where the employer is seeking or has been granted entry clearance or leave to enter under Part 2 of these Rules; and

(iv) intends to leave the UK at the end of six months in the United Kingdom or at the same time as the employer, whichever is the earlier [and does not intend to live for extended periods in the United Kingdom through frequent and successive visits; and]

(v) has agreed in writing terms and conditions of employment in the UK with the employer, including specifically that the applicant will be paid in accordance with the National Minimum Wage Act 1998 and any Regulations made under it, and provides evidence of this in the form set out in Appendix 7 with the entry clearance application; and

(vi) will not take employment other than within the terms of this paragraph to work full time as a domestic worker for the employer in a household that the employer intends to live in; and

(vii) can maintain and accommodate him or herself adequately without recourse to public funds; and

(viii) holds a valid entry clearance for entry in this capacity.

Note: Sub-paragraph (iv) amended from 6 November 2014 subject to savings for applications made before that date (HC 693).

Leave to enter as a domestic worker in a private household

159B. A person seeking leave to enter the United Kingdom as a domestic worker in a private household may be given leave to enter for that purpose for a period not exceeding 6 months provided he is able to produce to the Immigration Officer, on arrival, a valid United Kingdom entry clearance for entry in this capacity.

Refusal of leave to enter as a domestic worker in a private household

159C. Leave to enter as a domestic worker in a private household is to be refused if a valid United Kingdom entry clearance for entry in this capacity is not produced to the Immigration Officer on arrival.

Requirements for extension of stay as a domestic worker in a private household

159D. The requirements for an extension of stay as a domestic worker in a private household are that the applicant:

(i) entered the United Kingdom with a valid entry clearance as a domestic worker in a private household; and

(ii) was granted less than 6 months leave to enter in this capacity; and

(iii) has continued to be employed for the duration of leave granted as a domestic worker in the private household of the employer with whom the applicant entered or joined in the UK; and

(iv) continues to be required for employment for the period of the extension sought as a domestic worker in a private household that the employer lives in, where there is evidence of this in the form of written terms and conditions of employment in the UK as set out in Appendix 7 and evidence that the employer is living in the UK; and

(v) does not intend to take employment except as a domestic worker in the private household of the employer; and

(vi) meets the requirements of paragraph 159A(iv) and (vii); and

(vii) must not be in the UK in breach of immigration laws except that any period of overstaying for a period of 28 days or less will be disregarded.

Extension of stay as a domestic worker in a private household

159E. An extension of stay as a domestic worker in a private household may be granted for a period of six months less the period already spent in the UK in this capacity.

Requirements for extension of stay as a domestic worker in a private household for applicants who entered the United Kingdom under the Rules in place before 6 April 2012

159EA. The requirements for an extension of stay as a domestic worker in a private household for applicants who entered the United Kingdom under Rules in place before 6 April 2012 are that the applicant:

(i) [last] entered the UK with a valid entry clearance as a domestic worker in a private household under Rules in place before 6 April 2012; and

(ii) has continued to be employed for the duration of leave granted as a domestic worker in a private household; and

(iii) continues to be required for employment for the period of the extension sought as a [full time] domestic worker in a private household under the same roof as the employer or in the same household that the employer has lived in and where evidence of this in the form of written terms and conditions of employment in the UK as set out in Appendix 7 and evidence that the employer resides in the UK; and

(iv) does not intend to take employment except as a full time domestic worker in the private household referred to in sub-paragraph 159EA(iii); and

(v) meets the requirements of paragraph 159A(i) and (vii); and

(vi) must not be in the UK in breach of immigration laws except that any period of overstaying for a period of 28 days or less will be disregarded.

Note: Words inserted in subparagraphs (i) and (iii) and subparagraph (iv) substituted from 1 October 2013 subject to savings for applications made before that date (HC 628).

Extension of stay as a domestic worker in a private household for applicants who entered the United Kingdom under the Rules in place before 6 April 2012

159EB(i) An extension of stay as a domestic worker in a private household may be granted for a period not exceeding 12 months at a time provided the Secretary of State is satisfied that each of the requirements of paragraph 159EA are met.

(ii) Except, where the application is decided before the current leave expires, the extension of stay granted may be for a period not exceeding 12 months plus the time remaining before the expiry of the current leave (so if the application is decided on March 31st and the current leave does not expire until April 30th, an additional period of one month's leave may be granted).

Note: Subparagraph (ii) inserted from 1 October 2013 subject to savings for applications made before that date.

Refusal of extension of stay as a domestic worker in a private household

159F. An extension of stay as a domestic worker may be refused if the Secretary of State is not satisfied that each of the requirements of paragraph either paragraph 159D or, where applicable, paragraph 159EA, is met.

Indefinite leave to remain for a domestic worker in a private household

159G. The requirements for indefinite leave to remain as a domestic worker in a private household are that the applicant:

(i) entered the United Kingdom with a valid entry clearance as a domestic worker in a private household under the Rules in place before 6 April 2012; and

(ii) has spent a continuous period of 5 years [lawfully] in the United Kingdom employed in this capacity; and

(iii) . . . has met the requirements of paragraph 159A(vi) and (vii) throughout the 5 year period; and

(iv) continues to be required for employment as a domestic worker in a private household as certified by the current employer; and

(v) has demonstrated sufficient knowledge of the English language and sufficient knowledge about life in the United Kingdom, in accordance with Appendix KoLL; and

(vi) [does not fall for refusal under the general grounds for refusal]; and

(vii) must not be in the UK in breach of immigration laws except that any period of overstaying for a period of 28 days or less will be disregarded; and

(viii) provides the specified documents in paragraph 159G-SD to evidence the reason for the absences set out in paragraph 128A.

Note: Words inserted/substituted in subparagraphs (ii) and (vi) and subparagraph (viii) inserted from 13 December 2012 (change to subparagraph (vi) subject to savings for applications made before that date) (HC 760). Subparagraph (v) substituted from 1 October 2013 subject to savings for applications made before that date (HC 628).

159G-SD Specified documents

The specified documents referred to in paragraph 159G(viii) are:

(a) A letter from the employer detailing the purpose and period of absences in connection with the employment, including periods of annual leave.

(b) Where the absence was due to a serious or compelling reason, a personal letter from the applicant which includes full details of the reason for the absences and all original supporting documents in relation to those reasons – e.g. medical certificates, birth/death certificates, information about the reasons which led to the absence from the UK.

Note: Paragraph 159G-SD inserted from 13 December 2012 (HC 760).

Refusal of indefinite leave to remain for a domestic worker in a private household

159H. Indefinite leave to remain in the United Kingdom for a domestic worker in a private household is to be refused if the Secretary of State is not satisfied that each of the requirements of paragraph 159G is met.

Overseas government employees

Requirements for leave to enter as an overseas government employee

160–166. Deleted from 27 November 2008 by HC 1113 except insofar as relevant to paragraphs 167 and 168.

Indefinite leave to remain for an overseas government employee

167. Indefinite leave to remain may be granted, on application, to an overseas government employee provided [the applicant]:

(i) . . . has spent a continuous period of 5 years [lawfully] in the United Kingdom in this capacity; and

(ii) . . . has met the requirements of paragraph 164 throughout the 5 year period; and

(iii) . . . is still required for the employment in question, as certified by the employer; and

(iv) has demonstrated sufficient knowledge of the English language and sufficient knowledge about life in the United Kingdom, in accordance with Appendix KoLL; and

(v) [does not fall for refusal under the general grounds for refusal]; and

(vi) is not in the UK in breach of immigration laws except that any period of overstaying for a period of 28 days or less will be disregarded; and

(vii) provides the specified documents in paragraph 167-SD to evidence the reason for the absences set out in paragraph 128A.

Note: Words deleted from subparagraphs (i)–(iii) and (vi), words substituted/inserted in subparagraphs (i), (iii) and (v) and subparagraph (vii) inserted from 13 December 2012 (change to subparagraph (v) subject to savings for applications made before that date) (HC 760). Subparagraph (iv) substituted from 28 October 2013 subject to savings for applications made before that date (HC 628).

167-SD Specified documents

The specified documents referred to in paragraph 167(vii) are:

(a) A letter from the employer detailing the purpose and period of absences in connection with the employment, including periods of annual leave.

(b) Where the absence was due to a serious or compelling reason, a personal letter from the applicant which includes full details of the reason for the absences and all original supporting documents in relation to those reasons – e.g. medical certificates, birth/death certificates, information about the reasons which led to the absence from the UK.

Note: Paragraph 167-SD inserted from 13 December 2013 (HC 760).

Refusal of indefinite leave to remain for an overseas government employee

168. Indefinite leave to remain in the United Kingdom for an overseas government employee is to be refused if the Secretary of State is not satisfied that each of the requirements of paragraph 167 is met.

Ministers of religion, missionaries and members of religious orders

169. For the purposes of these Rules:

(i) a minister of religion means a religious functionary whose main regular duties comprise the leading of a congregation in performing the rites and rituals of the faith and in preaching the essentials of the creed;

(ii) a missionary means a person who is directly engaged in spreading a religious doctrine and whose work is not in essence administrative or clerical;

(iii) a member of a religious order means a person who is coming to live in a community run by that order.

Requirements for leave to enter as a minister of religion, missionary, or member of a religious order

170. Deleted on 27 November 2008 by paragraph 39 of Statement of Changes HC 1113 except insofar as relevant to paragraphs 176 and 177.

Refusal of extension of stay as a minister of religion, missionary or member of a religious order

175. An extension of stay as a minister of religion, missionary or member of a religious order is to be refused if the Secretary of State is not satisfied that each of the requirements of paragraph 173 or 174A is met.

Indefinite leave to remain for a minister of religion, missionary or member of a religious order

176. Indefinite leave to remain may be granted, on application, to a person admitted as a minister of religion, missionary or member of a religious order provided [the applicant]:

(i) . . . has spent a continuous period of 5 years [lawfully] in the United Kingdom in this capacity; and

(ii) . . . has met the requirements of paragraph 173 or 174A throughout the 5 year period; and

(iii) . . . is still required for the employment in question as certified by the leadership of the congregation, [the] employer or the head of the religious order to which [the applicant] belongs; and

(iv) has demonstrated sufficient knowledge of the English language and sufficient knowledge about life in the United Kingdom, in accordance with Appendix KoLL; and

(v) [does not fall for refusal under the general grounds for refusal]; and

(vi) is not in the UK in breach of immigration laws except that any period of overstaying for a period of 28 days or less will be disregarded; and

(vii) provides the specified documents in paragraph 176-SD to evidence the reason for the absences set out in paragraph 128A.

Note: Words deleted from subparagraphs (i)–(iii) and (vi), words substituted/inserted in subparagraphs (i), (iii) and (v) and subparagraph (vii) inserted from 13 December 2012 (change to subparagraph (v) subject to savings for applications made before that date) (HC 760). Subparagraph (iv) substituted from 1 October 2013 subject to savings for applications made before that date (HC 628).

176-SD Specified documents

The specified documents referred to in paragraph 176(vii) are:

(a) A letter from the leadership of the congregation, the employer or the head of the religious order to which the applicant belongs, detailing the purpose and period of absences in connection with the employment, including periods of annual leave.

(b) Where the absence was due to a serious or compelling reason, a personal letter from the applicant which includes full details of the reason for the absences and all original supporting documents in relation to those reasons – e.g. medical certificates, birth/death certificates, information about the reasons which led to the absence from the UK.

Note: Paragraph 176-SD inserted from 13 December 2012 (HC 760).

Refusal of indefinite leave to remain for a minister of religion, missionary or member of a religious order

177. Indefinite leave to remain in the United Kingdom for a minister of religion, missionary or member of a religious order is to be refused if the Secretary of State is not satisfied that each of the requirements of paragraph 176 is met.

Requirements for leave to enter the United Kingdom as a visiting religious worker or a religious worker in a non-pastoral role

177A–177G. DELETED

Airport-based operational ground staff of overseas-owned airlines

Requirements for leave to enter the United Kingdom as a member of the operational ground staff of an overseas-owned airline

178–183. Deleted from 27 November 2008 by HC 1113 except insofar as relevant to paragraphs 184 and 185.

Indefinite leave to remain for a member of the operational ground staff of an overseas owned airline

184. Indefinite leave to remain may be granted, on application, to a member of the operational ground staff of an overseas-owned airline provided [the applicant]:

(i) . . . has spent a continuous period of 5 years [lawfully] in the United Kingdom in this capacity; and

(ii) . . . has met the requirements of paragraph 181 throughout the 5 year period; and

(iii) . . . is still required for the employment in question as certified by the employer; and

(iv) has demonstrated sufficient knowledge of the English language and sufficient knowledge about life in the United Kingdom, in accordance with Appendix KoLL; and

(v) [does not fall for refusal under the general grounds for refusal]; and

(vi) . . . is not in the UK in breach of immigration laws except that any period of overstaying for a period of 28 days or less will be disregarded; and

(vii) provides the specified documents in paragraph 184-SD to evidence the reason for the absences set out in paragraph 128A.

Note: Words deleted from subparagraphs (i)–(iii) and (vi), words substituted/inserted in subparagraphs (i) and (v) and subparagraph (vii) inserted from 13 December 2012 (change to subparagraph (v) subject to savings for applications made before that date) (HC 760). Subparagraph (iv) substituted from 28 October 2013 subject to savings for applications made before that date (HC 628).

184-SD Specified documents

The specified documents referred to in paragraph 184(vii) are:

(a) A letter from the employer detailing the purpose and period of absences in connection with the employment, including periods of annual leave.

(b) Where the absence was due to a serious or compelling reason, a personal letter from the applicant which includes full details of the reason for the absences and all original supporting documents in relation to those reasons – e.g. medical certificates, birth/death certificates, information about the reasons which led to the absence from the UK.

Note: Paragraph 184-SD inserted from 13 December 2012 (HC 760).

Refusal of indefinite leave to remain for a member of the operational ground staff of an overseas owned airline

185. Indefinite leave to remain in the United Kingdom for a member of the operational ground staff of an overseas owned airline is to be refused if the Secretary of State is not satisfied that each of the requirements of paragraph 184 is met.

Persons with United Kingdom ancestry

Requirements for leave to enter on the grounds of United Kingdom ancestry

186. The requirements to be met by a person seeking leave to enter the United Kingdom on the grounds of his United Kingdom ancestry are that he:

(i) is a Commonwealth citizen; and

(ii) is aged 17 or over; and

(iii) is able to provide proof that one of his grandparents was born in the United Kingdom and Islands and that any such grandparent is the applicant's blood grandparent or grandparent by reason of an adoption recognised by the laws of the United Kingdom relating to adoption; and

(iv) is able to work and intends to take or seek employment in the United Kingdom; and

(v) will be able to maintain and accommodate himself and any dependants adequately without recourse to public funds; and

(vi) holds a valid United Kingdom entry clearance for entry in this capacity.

Leave to enter the United Kingdom on the grounds of United Kingdom ancestry

187. A person seeking leave to enter the United Kingdom on the grounds of his United Kingdom ancestry may be given leave to enter for a period not exceeding 5 years provided he is able to produce to the Immigration Officer, on arrival, a valid United Kingdom entry clearance for entry in this capacity.

Refusal of leave to enter on the grounds of United Kingdom ancestry

188. Leave to enter the United Kingdom on the grounds of United Kingdom ancestry is to be refused if a valid United Kingdom entry clearance for entry in this capacity is not produced to the Immigration Officer on arrival.

Requirements for an extension of stay on the grounds of United Kingdom ancestry

189. The requirements to be met by a person seeking an extension of stay on the grounds of United Kingdom ancestry are that:

(i) he is able to meet each of the requirements of paragraph 186 (i)–(v); and

(ii) he was admitted to the United Kingdom on the grounds of United Kingdom ancestry in accordance with paragraphs 186 to 188 or has been granted an extension of stay in this capacity; and

(iii) he is not in the UK in breach of immigration laws except that any period of overstaying for a period of 28 days or less will be disregarded.

Extension of stay on the grounds of United Kingdom ancestry

190. An extension of stay on the grounds of United Kingdom ancestry may be granted for a period not exceeding 5 years provided the Secretary of State is satisfied that each of the requirements of paragraph 189 is met.

Refusal of extension of stay on the grounds of United Kingdom ancestry

191. An extension of stay on the grounds of United Kingdom ancestry is to be refused if the Secretary of State is not satisfied that each of the requirements of paragraph 189 is met.

Indefinite leave to remain on the grounds of United Kingdom ancestry

192. Indefinite leave to remain may be granted, on application, to a Commonwealth citizen with a United Kingdom born grandparent provided [the applicant]:

(i) . . . meets the requirements of paragraph 186 (i)–(v); and

(ii) . . . has spent a continuous period of 5 years [lawfully] in the United Kingdom in this capacity; and

(iii) has demonstrated sufficient knowledge of the English language and sufficient knowledge about life in the United Kingdom, in accordance with Appendix KoLL; and

(iv) [does not fall for refusal under the general grounds for refusal]; and

(v) . . . is not in the UK in breach of immigration laws except that any period of overstaying for a period of 28 days or less will be disregarded; and

(vi) provides the specified documents in paragraph 192-SD to evidence the reason for the absences set out in paragraph 128A, where the absence was due to a serious or compelling reason.

Note: Words deleted from subparagraphs (i)–(iii) and (v), words substituted/inserted in subparagraphs (ii) and (iv) and subparagraph (vi) inserted from 13 December 2012 (change to subparagraph (iv) subject to savings for applications made before that date) (HC 760). Subparagraph (iii) substituted from 28 October 2013 subject to savings for applications made before that date (HC 628).

192-SD Specified documents

The specified documents referred to in paragraph 192(vi) are:

A personal letter from the applicant which includes full details of the reason for the absences and all original supporting documents in relation to those reasons – e.g. medical certificates, birth/death certificates, information about the reasons which led to the absence from the UK.

Note: Paragraph 192-SD inserted from 13 December 2013 (HC 760).

Refusal of indefinite leave to remain on the grounds of United Kingdom ancestry

193. Indefinite leave to remain in the United Kingdom on the grounds of a United Kingdom born grandparent is to be refused if the Secretary of State is not satisfied that each of the requirements of paragraph 192 is met.

[Partners] of persons who have or have had leave to enter or remain under paragraphs 128–193 (but not paragraphs 135I–135K)

193A. Nothing in paragraphs 194–196F is to be construed as allowing a person to be granted entry clearance, leave to enter, leave to remain or variation of leave as a [partner] of a person granted entry clearance or leave to enter under Paragraph 159A where that entry clearance or leave to enter was granted under 159A on or after 6 April 2012.

Note: 'Partner' substituted from 1 October 2013 subject to savings for applications made before that date (HC 628).

Requirements for leave to enter as the [partner] of a person with limited leave to enter or remain in the United Kingdom under paragraphs 128–193 (but not paragraphs 135I–135K)

194. The requirements to be met by a person seeking leave to enter the United Kingdom as the partner of a person with limited leave to enter or remain in the United Kingdom under paragraphs 128–193 (but not paragraphs 135I–135K) are that:

(i) the applicant is the spouse, civil partner, unmarried or same-sex partner of a person with limited leave to enter or remain in the United Kingdom under paragraphs 128–193 (but not paragraphs 135I–135K); and

(ii) if an unmarried or same-sex partner:

(1) any previous marriage or civil partnership (or similar relationship) by either partner has permanently broken down; and

(2) the parties are not involved in a consanguineous relationship with one another; and

(3) the parties have been living together in a relationship akin to marriage or civil partnership which has subsisted for 2 years or more; and

(iii) each of the parties intends to live with the other as his or her partner during the applicant's stay and the relationship is subsisting; and

(iv) there will be adequate accommodation for the parties and any dependants without recourse to public funds in accommodation which they own or occupy exclusively; and

(v) the parties will be able to maintain themselves and any dependants adequately without recourse to public funds; and

(vi) the applicant does not intend to stay in the United Kingdom beyond any period of leave granted to his partner; and

(vii) the applicant does not fall for refusal under the general grounds for refusal; and

(viii) the applicant holds a valid United Kingdom entry clearance for entry in this capacity.

Note: 'Partner' and the words 'is the spouse, civil partner, unmarried or same-sex partner of' substituted and subparagraphs (ii)–(vi) substituted from 1 October 2013 subject to savings for applications made before that date (HC 628).

Leave to enter as the [partner] of a person with limited leave to enter or remain in the United Kingdom under paragraphs 128–193 (but not paragraphs 135I–135K)

195. A person seeking leave to enter the United Kingdom as the [partner] of a person with limited leave to enter or remain in the United Kingdom under paragraphs 128–193 (but not paragraphs 135I–135K) may be given leave to enter for a period not in excess of that granted to the person with limited leave to enter or remain under paragraphs 128–193 (but not paragraphs 135I–135K) provided the Immigration Officer is satisfied that each of the requirements of paragraph 194 is met. If the person is seeking leave to enter as the [partner] of a Highly Skilled Migrant, leave which is granted will be subject to a condition prohibiting Employment as a Doctor or Dentist in Training, unless the applicant has obtained a degree in medicine or dentistry at bachelor's level or above from a UK institution that is a UK recognised or listed body, or which holds a sponsor licence under Tier 4 of the Points Based System and provides evidence of this degree.

Note: 'Partner' substituted from 1 October 2013 subject to savings for applications made before that date (HC 628).

Refusal of leave to enter as the [partner] of a person with limited leave to enter or remain in the United Kingdom under paragraphs 128–193 (but not paragraphs 135I–135K)

196. Leave to enter the United Kingdom as the [partner] of a person with limited leave to enter or remain in the United Kingdom under paragraphs 128–193 (but not paragraphs 135I–135K) is to be refused if the Immigration Officer is not satisfied that each of the requirements of paragraph 194 is met.

Note: 'Partner' and substituted from 1 October 2013 subject to savings for applications made before that date (HC 628).

Requirements for extension of stay as the [partner] of a person who has or has had leave to enter or remain in the United Kingdom under paragraphs 128–193 (but not paragraphs 135I–135K)

196A. The requirements to be met by a person seeking an extension of stay in the United Kingdom as the [partner] of a person who has or has had leave to enter or remain in the United Kingdom under paragraphs 128–193 (but not paragraphs 135I–135K) are that the applicant:

(i) is the spouse, civil partner, unmarried or same sex partner of a person who:

(1) has limited leave to enter or remain in the United Kingdom under paragraphs 128–193 (but not paragraphs 135I–135K); or

(2) has indefinite leave to remain in the United Kingdom or has become a British citizen, and who had limited leave to enter or remain in the United Kingdom under paragraphs 128–193 (but not paragraphs 135I–135K) immediately before being granted indefinite leave to remain; and

(ii) meets the requirements of paragraph 194(ii)–(vii); and

(iii) was not last granted:

(1) entry clearance or leave as a visitor,

(2) temporary admission, or

(3) temporary release; and

(iv) must not be in the UK in breach of immigration laws except that any period of overstaying for a period of 28 days or less will be disregarded.

Note: 'Partner' substituted and subparagraphs (i)–(iv) substituted and subparagraphs (v)–(vi) deleted from 1 October 2013 subject to savings for applications made before that date (HC 628).

Extension of stay as the [partner] of a person who has or has had leave to enter or remain in the United Kingdom under paragraphs 128–193 (but not paragraphs 135I–135K)

196B. An extension of stay in the United Kingdom as:

(i) the [partner] of a person who has limited leave to enter or remain under paragraphs 128–193 (but not paragraphs 135I–135K) may be granted for a period not in excess of that granted to the person with limited leave to enter or remain; or

(ii) the [partner] of a person who is being admitted at the same time for settlement, or the [partner] of a person who has indefinite leave to remain [or has become a

British citizen], may be granted for a period not exceeding 2 years, in both instances, provided the Secretary of State is satisfied that each of the requirements of paragraph 196A is met.

If the person is seeking an extension of stay as the [partner], of a Highly Skilled Migrant, leave which is granted will be subject to a condition prohibiting Employment as a Doctor or Dentist in Training, unless the applicant:

(1) has obtained a primary degree in medicine or dentistry at bachelor's level or above from a UK institution that is a UK recognised or listed body, or which holds a sponsor licence under Tier 4 of the Points Based System; or

(2) has, or has last been granted, entry clearance, leave to enter or leave to remain that was not subject to any condition restricting him from taking employment as a Doctor in Training, and has been employed during that leave as a Doctor in Training; or

(3) has, or has last been granted, entry clearance, leave to enter or leave to remain that was not subject to any condition restricting him from taking employment as a Dentist in Training, and has been employed during that leave as a Dentist in Training.

Note: 'Partner' and the words 'is the spouse, civil partner, unmarried or same-sex partner of' substituted and words inserted in subparagraph (ii) from 1 October 2013 subject to savings for applications made before that date (HC 628).

Refusal of extension of stay as the partner of a person who has or has had leave to enter or remain in the United Kingdom under paragraphs 128–193 (but not paragraphs 135I–135K)

196C. An extension of stay in the United Kingdom as the partner of a person who has or has had leave to enter or remain in the United Kingdom under paragraphs 128–193 (but not paragraphs 135I–135K) is to be refused if the Secretary of State is not satisfied that each of the requirements of paragraph 196A is met.

Note: 'Partner' and the words 'is the spouse, civil partner, unmarried or same-sex partner of' substituted from 1 October 2013 subject to savings for applications made before that date (HC 628).

Requirements for indefinite leave to remain for the partner of a person who has or has had leave to enter or remain in the United Kingdom under paragraphs 128–193 (but not paragraphs 135I–135K)

196D. The requirements to be met by a person seeking indefinite leave to remain in the United Kingdom as the partner of a person who has or has had leave to enter or remain in the United Kingdom under paragraphs 128–193 (but not paragraphs 135I–135K) are that the applicant:

(i) is the spouse, civil partner, unmarried or same-sex partner of a person who:

(1) has limited leave to enter or remain in the United Kingdom under paragraphs 128–193 (but not paragraphs 135I–135K) and who is being granted indefinite leave to remain at the same time; or

(2) is the spouse, civil partner, unmarried or same-sex partner of a person who has indefinite leave to remain in the United Kingdom or has become a British citizen, and who had limited leave to enter or remain in the United Kingdom under paragraphs

128–193 (but not paragraphs 135I–135K) immediately before being granted indefinite leave to remain; and

(ii) meets the requirements of paragraph 194(ii)–(vii); and

(iii) has demonstrated sufficient knowledge of the English language and sufficient knowledge about life in the United Kingdom, in accordance with Appendix KoLL; and

(iv) was not last granted:

(1) entry clearance or leave as a visitor,

(2) temporary admission, or

(3) temporary release; and

(v) must not be in the UK in breach of immigration laws except that any period of overstaying for a period of 28 days or less will be disregarded.

Note: 'Partner' and the words 'is the spouse, civil partner, unmarried or same-sex partner of' substituted and subparagraphs (i)–(v) substituted and subparagraphs (vi)–(vii) deleted from 1 October 2013 subject to savings for applications made before that date. (HC 628). Subparagraph (iii) further amended from 28 October 2013 with savings for applications made before that date (HC 628).

Indefinite leave to remain as the [partner] of a person who has or has had leave to enter or remain in the United Kingdom under paragraphs 128–193 (but not paragraphs 135I–135K)

196E. Indefinite leave to remain in the United Kingdom [as] the [partner] of a person who has or has had leave to enter or remain in the United Kingdom under paragraphs 128–193 (but not paragraphs 135I–135K) may be granted provided the Secretary of State is satisfied that each of the requirements of paragraph 196D is met.

Note: Words 'partner' and 'as' substituted from 1 October 2013 subject to savings for applications made before that date. (HC 628).

Refusal of indefinite leave to remain as the [partner] of a person who has or has had leave to enter or remain in the United Kingdom under paragraphs 128–193 (but not paragraphs 135I–135K)

196F. Indefinite leave to remain in the United Kingdom [as] the [partner] of a person who has or has had limited leave to enter or remain in the United Kingdom under paragraphs 128–193 (but not paragraphs 135I–135K) is to be refused if the Secretary of State is not satisfied that each of the requirements of paragraph 196D is met.

Note: Words 'partner' and 'as' substituted from 1 October 2013 subject to savings for applications made before that date (HC 628).

Children of persons with limited leave to enter or remain in the United Kingdom under paragraphs 128–193 (but not paragraphs 135I–135K)

196G. Nothing in paragraphs 197–199 is to be construed as allowing a person to be granted entry clearance, leave to enter, leave to remain or variation of leave as the child of a person granted entry clearance or leave to enter under Paragraph 159A where that entry clearance or leave to enter was granted under 159A on or after 6 April 2012.

Requirements for leave to enter or remain as the child of a person with limited leave to enter or remain in the United Kingdom under paragraphs 128–193 (but not paragraphs 135I–135K)

197. The requirements to be met by a person seeking leave to enter or remain in the United Kingdom as a child of a person with limited leave to enter or remain in the United Kingdom under paragraphs 128–193 (but not paragraphs 135I–135K) are that:

(i) he is the child of a parent with limited leave to enter or remain in the United Kingdom under paragraphs 128–193 (but not paragraphs 135I–135K) [or, in respect of applications for leave to remain only, of a parent who has indefinite leave to remain in the UK but who immediately before that grant had limited leave to rener or remain under those paragraphs]; and

(ii) he is under the age of 18 or has current leave to enter or remain in this capacity; and

(iii) he is unmarried and is not a civil partner, has not formed an independent family unit and is not leading an independent life; and

(iv) he can and will be maintained and accommodated adequately without recourse to public funds in accommodation which his parent(s) own or occupy exclusively; and

(v) he will not stay in the United Kingdom beyond any period of leave granted to his parent(s); and

(vi) both parents are being or have been admitted to or allowed to remain in the United Kingdom save where:

(a) the parent he is accompanying or joining is his sole surviving parent; or

(b) the parent he is accompanying or joining has had sole responsibility for his upbringing;

or

(c) there are serious and compelling family or other considerations which make exclusion from the United Kingdom undesirable and suitable arrangements have been made for his care; and

(vii) if seeking leave to enter, he holds a valid United Kingdom entry clearance for entry in this capacity or, if seeking leave to remain, he was not last granted:

(1) entry clearance or leave as a visitor,

(2) temporary admission, or

(3) temporary release; and

(viii) if seeking leave to remain, must not be in the UK in breach of immigration laws except that any period of overstaying for a period of 28 days or less will be disregarded.

Note: Words inserted in subparagraph (i) (from 28 October 2013) and subparagraph (vii) substituted (from 1 October 2013) subject to savings for applications made before those dates (HC 628).

Leave to enter or remain as the child of a person with limited leave to enter or remain in the United Kingdom under paragraphs 128–193 (but not paragraphs 135I–135K)

198. (a) A person seeking leave to enter or remain in the United Kingdom as the child of a person with limited leave to enter or remain in the United Kingdom under paragraphs 128–193 (but not paragraphs 135I–135K) may be given leave to enter or remain in the United Kingdom for a period of leave not in excess of that granted to the person

with limited leave to enter or remain under paragraphs 128–193 (but not paragraphs 135I–135K) provided that:

i) in relation to an application for leave to enter, he is able to produce to the Immigration Officer, on arrival, a valid United Kingdom entry clearance for entry in this capacity; or

ii) in the case of an application for limited leave to remain, he was not last granted:

(1) entry clearance or leave as a visitor,

(2) temporary admission, or

(3) temporary release,

and is able to satisfy the Secretary of State that each of the requirements of paragraph 197(i)–(vi) and(viii) is met.

(b) A person seeking leave to remain as the child of a parent who has indefinite leave to remain in the UK and who had limited leave under paragraphs 128–193 (but not paragraphs 135l–135K) immediately before being granted indefinite leave may be given leave to remain in the UK for a period of 30 months provided he is in the UK with valid leave under paragraph 198 and is able to satisfy the Secretary of State that each of the requirements of paragraph 197(i) and 197(ii)–(vi) and (viii) is met.

Note: Paragraphs 198–199B inserted/substituted from 1 October 2013 subject to savings for applications made before that date (HC 628). Subparagraph (b) inserted from 28 October 2013 subject to savings for applications made before that date.

Refusal of leave to enter or remain as the child of a person with limited leave to enter or remain in the United Kingdom under paragraphs 128–193 (but not paragraphs 135I–135K)

198A. Leave to enter or remain in the United Kingdom as the child of a person with limited leave to enter or remain in the United Kingdom under paragraphs 128–193 (but not paragraphs 135I–135K) is to be refused if:

(i) in relation to an application for leave to enter, a valid United Kingdom entry clearance for entry in this capacity is not produced to the Immigration Officer on arrival; or

(ii) in the case of an application for limited leave to remain, if the applicant was last granted:

(1) entry clearance or leave as a visitor,

(2) temporary admission, or

(3) temporary release,

or is unable to satisfy the Secretary of State that each of the requirements of paragraph 197(i)–(vi) and (viii) is met.

Note: Paragraphs 198–199B inserted/substituted from 1 October 2013 subject to savings for applications made before that date (HC 628).

Requirements for indefinite leave to remain as the child of a person who has or has had leave to enter or remain in the United Kingdom under paragraphs 128–193 (but not paragraphs 135I–135K)

199. The requirements to be met by a person seeking indefinite leave to remain in the United Kingdom as the child of a person who has or has had leave to enter or remain in

the United Kingdom under paragraphs 128–193 (but not paragraphs 135I–135K) are that the applicant:

(i) is the child of a person who:

(1) has limited leave to enter or remain in the United Kingdom under paragraphs 128–193 (but not paragraphs 135I–135K) and who is being granted indefinite leave to remain at the same time; or

(2) has indefinite leave to remain in the United Kingdom and who had limited leave to enter or remain in the United Kingdom under paragraphs 128–193 (but not paragraphs 135I–135K) immediately before being granted indefinite leave to remain; and

(ii) meets the requirements of paragraph 197(i)–(vi) and (viii); and

(iii) was not last granted:

(1) entry clearance or leave as a visitor,

(2) temporary admission, or

(3) temporary release; and

(iv) does not fall for refusal under the general grounds for refusal; and

(v) must not be in the UK in breach of immigration laws except that any period of overstaying for a period of 28 days or less will be disregarded; and

(vi) has demonstrated sufficient knowledge of the English language and sufficient knowledge about life in the United Kingdom, in accordance with Appendix KoLL, unless he is under the age of 18 at the date on which the application is made.

Note: Paragraphs 198–199B inserted/substituted from 1 October 2013 subject to savings for applications made before that date (HC 628). Subparagraph (vi) inserted from 28 October 2013 subject to savings for applications made before that date (HC 628).

Indefinite leave to remain as the child of a person who has or has had leave to enter or remain in the United Kingdom under paragraphs 128–193 (but not paragraphs 135I–135K)

199A. Indefinite leave to remain in the United Kingdom as the child of a person who has or has had leave to enter or remain in the United Kingdom under paragraphs 128–193 (but not paragraphs 135I–135K) may be granted provided the Secretary of State is satisfied that each of the requirements of paragraph 199 is met.

Note: Paragraphs 198–199B inserted/substituted from 1 October 2013 subject to savings for applications made before that date (HC 628).

Refusal of indefinite leave to remain as the child of a person who has or has had leave to enter or remain in the United Kingdom under paragraphs 128–193 (but not paragraphs 135I–135K)

199B. Indefinite leave to remain in the United Kingdom as the child of a person who has or has had limited leave to enter or remain in the United Kingdom under paragraphs 128–193 (but not paragraphs 135I–135K) is to be refused if the Secretary of State is not satisfied that each of the requirements of paragraph 199 is met.

Note: Paragraphs 198–199B inserted/substituted from 1 October 2013 subject to savings for applications made before that date (HC 628).

Part 6

Persons seeking to enter or remain in the United Kingdom as a businessman, self-employed person, investor, writer or composer or artist

200A. DELETED

Person intending to establish themselves in business

Requirements for leave to enter the United Kingdom as a person intending to establish himself in business

200–208. Deleted from 30 June 2008 by HC 607 except insofar as relevant to paragraph 209. See Appendix F for the wording of these Rules in a case in which they are relevant.

Note: Paragraphs 200–208 fully deleted from 1 October 2013 subject to savings for applications made before that date (HC 628).

209–210. DELETED

Note: Paragraphs 209–210 deleted from 1 October 2013 subject to savings for applications made before that date (HC 628).

Innovators

Requirements for leave to enter the United Kingdom as an innovator

210A–210F: Deleted from 30 June 2008 by HC 607 except insofar as relevant to paragraph 210G. See Appendix F for the wording of these Rules in a case in which they are relevant.

Note: Paragraphs 210A–210F fully deleted from 1 October 2013 subject to savings for applications made before that date (HC 628).

210G–210H. DELETED

Note: Paragraphs 210G–210H deleted from 1 October 2013 subject to savings for applications made before that date (HC 628).

Persons intending to establish themselves in business under provisions of EC Association Agreements

Requirements for leave to enter the United Kingdom as a person intending to establish himself in business under the provisions of an EC Association Agreement

211–221. DELETED

222–223A. DELETED

Note: Paragraphs 222–223A deleted from 1 October 2013 subject to savings for applications made before that date (HC 628).

Investors

224–229: Deleted from 30 June 2008 by HC 607 except insofar as relevant to paragraph 230. See Appendix F for the wording of these Rules in a case in which they are relevant.

Note: Paragraphs 224–229 fully deleted from 1 October 2013 subject to savings for applications made before that date (HC 628).

230–231. DELETED

Note: Paragraphs 230–231 deleted from 1 October 2013 subject to savings for applications made before that date (HC 628).

Writers, composers and artists

Requirements for leave to enter the United Kingdom as a writer, composer or artist

232–237: Deleted from 30 June 2008 by HC 607 except insofar as relevant to paragraph 238. See Appendix F for the wording of these Rules in a case in which they are relevant.

Note: Paragraphs 232–237 fully deleted from 1 October 2013 subject to savings for applications made before that date (HC 628).

238–245. DELETED

Note: Paragraphs 238–245 deleted from 1 October 2013 subject to savings for applications made before that date (HC 628).

Part 6A
Points-Based System

245AAA. General requirements for indefinite leave to remain

For the purposes of references in this Part to requirements for indefinite leave to remain, except for those in paragraphs 245BF, 245DF and 245EF:

(a) "continuous period of 5 years lawfully in the UK" means, [subject to paragraphs 245CD, 245GF and 245HF,] residence in the United Kingdom for an unbroken period with valid leave, and for these purposes a period shall not be considered to have been broken where:

(i) the applicant has been absent from the UK for a period of 180 days or less in any of the five consecutive 12 month periods preceding the date of the application for leave to remain;

(ii) the applicant has existing limited leave to enter or remain upon their departure and return except that where that leave expired no more than 28 days prior to a further application for entry clearance, that period and any period pending the determination of an application made within that 28 day period shall be disregarded; and

(iii) the applicant has any period of overstaying between periods of entry clearance, leave to enter or leave to remain of up to 28 days and any period of overstaying pending the determination of an application made within that 28 day period disregarded

(b) Except for periods when the applicant had leave as a Tier 1 (General) Migrant, a Tier 1 (Investor) Migrant, a Tier 1 (Entrepreneur) Migrant, a Tier 1 (Exceptional Talent) Migrant, a highly skilled migrant, a Businessperson, an Innovator, an Investor, a self-employed lawyer or a writer, composer or artist, the applicant must have been employed in the UK continuously throughout the five years, under the terms of their Certificate of Sponsorship, work permit or in the employment for which they were given leave to enter or remain, except that any breaks in employment in which they applied for leave as a Tier 2 Migrant, or, under Tier 5 Temporary Worker (International Agreement) Migrant as a private servant in a diplomatic household, where in the latter case they applied to enter the UK before 6 April 2012, to work for a new employer shall be disregarded, provided this is within 60 days of the end of their employment with their previous employer or Sponsor.

(c) Except for periods where the applicant had leave as a Tier 1 (Investor) Migrant, a Tier 1 (Entrepreneur) Migrant, a Tier 1 (Exceptional Talent) Migrant or a highly skilled migrant, any absences from the UK during the five years must have been for a purpose that is consistent with the applicant's basis of stay here, including paid annual leave, or for serious or compelling reasons.

Note: Paragraph 245AAA inserted from 13 December 2012 (HC 760). Words inserted in subparagraph (a) and subparagraphs (b) and (c) inserted/substituted from 6 April 2013 (the amendment to (b) and (c) subject to savings for applications made before that date) (HC 1039).

245AA. Documents not submitted with applications

(a) Where Part 6A or any appendices referred to in Part 6A state that specified documents must be provided, [the Entry Clearance Officer, Immigration Officer or the Secretary of State] will only consider documents that have been submitted with the application, and will only consider documents submitted after the application {where they are submitted in accordance with subparagraph (b)}.

(b) If the applicant has submitted specified documents in which:

(i) Some of the documents in a sequence have been omitted (for example, if one bank statement from a series is missing);

(ii) A document is in the wrong format (for example, if a letter is not on letterhead paper as specified); or

(iii) A document is a copy and not an original document; or

(iv) A document does not contain all of the specified information;

the Entry Clearance Officer, Immigration Officer or the Secretary of State may contact the applicant or his representative in writing, and request the correct documents. The requested documents must be received at the address specified in the request within 7 working days of the date of the request.

(c) Documents will not be requested where a specified document has not been submitted (for example an English language certificate is missing), or where the Entry Clearance Officer, Immigration Officer or the Secretary of State does not anticipate that addressing the omission or error referred to in subparagraph (b) will lead to a grant because the application will be refused for other reasons.

(d) If the applicant has submitted a specified document:

(i) in the wrong format; or

(ii) which is a copy and not an original document; or

(iii) which does not contain all of the specified information, but the missing information is verifiable from:

(1) other documents submitted with the application,

(2) the website of the organisation which issued the document, or

(3) the website of the appropriate regulatory body;

the application may be granted exceptionally, providing the Entry Clearance Officer, Immigration Officer or the Secretary of State is satisfied that the specified documents are genuine and the applicant meets all the other requirements. The Entry Clearance Officer, Immigration Officer or the Secretary of State reserves the right to request the specified original documents in the correct format in all cases where (b) applies, and to refuse applications if these documents are not provided as set out in (b).

Note: Words in curly brackets in subparagraph (a) substituted from 13 December 2012 subject to savings for applications made before that date (HC 760). Words in square brackets substituted in subparagraph (a) and subparagraphs (b)–(d) substituted from 1 October 2013 (HC 628).

245A. Specified documents for students previously sponsored by an overseas government or international scholarship agency

Where Part 6A of these Rules state that specified documents must be provided to show that a sponsoring government or international scholarship agency has provided its unconditional written consent to the application, the specified documents are original letters, on the official letter-headed paper or stationery of the organisation(s), bearing the official stamp of that organisation and issued by an authorised official of that organisation. The documents must confirm that the organisation gives the applicant unconditional consent to remain in or re-enter the UK for an unlimited time.

Tier 1 (Exceptional Talent) Migrants

245B. Purpose

This route is for exceptionally talented individuals in . . . the particular fields, who wish to work in the UK. These individuals are those who are already internationally recognised at the highest level as world leaders in their particular field, or who have already demonstrated exceptional promise . . . and are likely to become world leaders in their particular area.

Note: Words deleted from 1 October 2013 (HC 628) and from 6 April 2014 subject to savings for applications made before that date (HC 1138 as amended by HC 1201).

245BA. Entry to the UK

All migrants arriving in the UK and wishing to enter as a Tier 1 (Exceptional Talent) Migrant must have a valid entry clearance for entry under this route. If they do not have a valid entry clearance, entry will be refused.

245BB. Requirements for entry clearance

To qualify for entry clearance as a Tier 1 (Exceptional Talent) Migrant, an applicant must meet the requirements listed below. If the applicant meets these requirements, entry clearance will be granted. If the applicant does not meet these requirements, the application will be refused.

Requirements:

(a) The applicant must not fall for refusal under the general grounds for refusal.

(c) The applicant must have a minimum of 75 points under paragraphs 1 to 6 of Appendix A.

(d) an applicant who has, or was last granted, leave as a student or a Postgraduate Doctor or Dentist, a Student Nurse, a Student Writing-Up a Thesis, a Student Re-Sitting an Examination or as a Tier 4 Migrant and:

(i) is currently being sponsored by a government or international scholarship agency, or

(ii) was being sponsored by a government or international scholarship agency, and that sponsorship came to an end 12 months ago or less,

must provide the unconditional written consent of the sponsoring Government or agency to the application and must provide the specified documents as set out in paragraph 245A above to show that this requirement has been met.

245BC. Period and conditions of grant

[Entry clearance will be granted for a period of 5 years and 4 months] and will be subject to the following conditions:

(i) no recourse to public funds,
(ii) registration with the police, if this is required by paragraph 326,
(iii) no employment as a Doctor or Dentist in Training, and
(iv) no employment as a professional sportsperson (including as a sports coach).

Note: Words substituted from 6 November 2014 subject to savings for applications made before that date (HC 693).

245BD. Requirements for leave to remain

To qualify for leave to remain as a Tier 1 (Exceptional Talent) Migrant, an applicant must meet the requirements listed below. If the applicant meets these requirements, leave to remain will be granted. If the applicant does not meet these requirements, the application will be refused.

Requirements:

(a) The applicant must not fall for refusal under the general grounds for refusal, and must not be an illegal entrant.

(b) The applicant must have a minimum of 75 points under paragraphs 1 to 6 of Appendix A.

(c) The applicant must have, or have last been granted, entry clearance, leave to enter or remain as:

(i) a Tier 1 Migrant,

(ii) a Tier 2 Migrant, or

(iii) as a Tier 5 (Temporary Worker) Migrant, sponsored in the Government Authorised Exchange sub-category in an exchange scheme for sponsored researchers.

(d) The applicant must not be in the UK in breach of immigration laws except that any period of overstaying for a period of 28 days or less will be disregarded.

Note: Subparagraph (c)(ii) substituted from 6 April 2013 subject to savings for applications made before that date (HC 1039). Subparagraph (c)(i) substituted from 6 April 2014 subject to savings for applications made before that date (HC 1138 as amended by HC 1201). Original subparagraph (c) deleted and subsequent subparagraphs renumbered accordingly from 6 November 2014 (HC 693).

245BE. Period and conditions of grant

(a) Leave to remain will be granted for a period of 5 years.
(b) Leave to remain under this route will be subject to the following conditions:
(i) no recourse to public funds,
(ii) registration with the police, if this is required by paragraph 326,
(iii) no employment as a Doctor or Dentist in Training, and
(iv) no employment as a professional sportsperson (including as a sports coach).

Note: Paragraph 245BE substituted from 13 December 2012 (HC 760). Subparagraph (a) substituted from 6 November 2014 subject to savings for applications made before that date (HC 693).

245BF. Requirements for indefinite leave to remain

To qualify for indefinite leave to remain, a Tier 1 (Exceptional Talent) Migrant must meet the requirements listed below. If the applicant meets these requirements, indefinite leave to remain will be granted. If the applicant does not meet these requirements, the application will be refused.

Requirements:

(a) DELETED

(b) The applicant must not fall for refusal under the general grounds for refusal, and must not be an illegal entrant.

(c) The applicant must have spent a continuous period of 5 years lawfully in the UK as follows:

(i) The applicant must have, or have last been granted, leave as a Tier 1 (Exceptional Talent) Migrant;

(ii) The 5 years must have been spent with leave as a Tier 1 Migrant (excluding as a Tier 1 (Graduate Entrepreneur) Migrant or Tier 1 (Post-Study Work) Migrant) or as a Tier 2 Migrant (excluding as a Tier 2 (Intra-Company Transfer) Migrant); and

(iii) The applicant must have had absences from the UK of no more than 180 days in any 12 calendar months during the 5 years.

(d) The applicant must have a minimum of 75 points under paragraphs 1 to 6 of Appendix A.

(e) The applicant must have demonstrated sufficient knowledge of the English language and sufficient knowledge about life in the United Kingdom, in accordance with Appendix KoLL.

(f) The applicant must not be in the UK in breach of immigration laws except that any period of overstaying for a period of 28 days or less will be disregarded.

Note: Subparagraph (a) deleted from 13 December 2012 subject to savings for applications made before that date (HC 760). Subparagraph (e) substituted from 28 October 2013 subject to savings for applications made before that date (HC 628). Subparagraph (c) substituted from 6 April 2014 subject to savings for applications made before that date (HC 1138 as amended by HC 1201).

Tier 1 (General) Migrants

245C. Purpose

This route is for highly skilled migrants who wish to work, or become self-employed, to extend their stay in the UK.

245CA. Requirements for leave to remain

To qualify for leave to remain as a Tier 1 (General) Migrant, an applicant must meet the requirements listed below. If the applicant meets these requirements, leave to remain will be granted. If the applicant does not meet these requirements, the application will be refused.

Requirements:

(a) The applicant must not fall for refusal under the general grounds for refusal, and must not be an illegal entrant.

(b) if the applicant has, or has had, leave as a Highly Skilled Migrant, as a Writer, Composer or Artist, Self-Employed Lawyer, or as a Tier 1 (General) Migrant under the Rules in place before 19 July 2010, and has not been granted leave in any categories other than these under the Rules in place since 19 July 2010, the applicant must have 75 points under paragraphs 7 to 34 of Appendix A.

(c) in all cases other than those referred to in (b) above, the applicant must have 80 points under paragraphs 7 to 34 of Appendix A.

(d) The applicant must have 10 points under paragraphs 1 to 15 of Appendix B.

(e) The applicant must have 10 points under paragraphs 1 to 3 of appendix C.

(f) The applicant must have, or have last been granted, entry clearance, leave to enter or remain:

(i) as a Tier 1 (General) Migrant,

(ii) as a Highly Skilled Migrant,

(iii) as a Writer, Composer or Artist, or

(iv) as a self-employed lawyer.

(g) The applicant must not be in the UK in breach of immigration laws except that any period of overstaying for a period of 28 days or less will be disregarded.

(h) The application for leave to remain must have been made before 6 April 2015.

Note: Subparagraph (h) substituted from 6 April 2014 subject to savings for applications made before that date (HC 1138 as amended by HC 1201).

245CB. Period and conditions of grant

(a) Leave to remain will be granted for:

(i) a period of 3 years, or

(ii) the period the applicant needs to take his total leave granted in this category to 5 years.

(b) DELETED.

(c) leave to remain under this route will be subject to the following conditions:

(i) no recourse to public funds,

(ii) registration with the police, if this is required by paragraph 326, and

(iii) no Employment as a Doctor or Dentist in Training, unless the applicant:

(1) has obtained a primary degree in medicine or dentistry at bachelor's level or above from a UK institution that is a UK recognised or listed body, or which holds a sponsor licence under Tier 4 of the Points Based System, and provides evidence of this degree; or

(2) has, or has last been granted, entry clearance, leave to enter or leave to remain that was not subject to any condition restricting him from taking employment as a Doctor in Training, has been employed during that leave as a Doctor in Training, and provides a

letter from the Postgraduate Deanery or NHS Trust employing them which confirms that they have been working in a post or programme that has been approved by the [General Medical Council] as a training programme or post; or

(3) has, or has last been granted, entry clearance, leave to enter or leave to remain that was not subject to any condition restricting him from taking employment as a Dentist in Training, has been employed during that leave as a Dentist in Training, and provides a letter from the Postgraduate Deanery or NHS Trust employing them which confirms that they have been working in a post or programme that has been approved by the [Joint Committee for Postgraduate Training in Dentistry] as a training programme or post.

(iv) no employment as a professional sportsperson (including as a sports coach).

Note: Words substituted in subparagraph (c)(iii)(2) and (3) from 13 December 2012 (HC 760). Subparagraph (a) substituted and subparagraph (b) deleted from 6 November 2014 subject to savings for applications made before that date (HC 693).

245CD. Requirements for indefinite leave to remain

To qualify for indefinite leave to remain, a Tier 1 (General) Migrant must meet the requirements listed below. If the applicant meets these requirements, indefinite leave to remain will be granted. If the applicant does not meet these requirements, the application will be refused.

Requirements:

(a) DELETED

(b) The applicant must not fall for refusal under the general grounds for refusal [(except that paragraph 322(1C) shall not apply if the applicant meets the conditions in (f)(i)–(iii) below], and must not be an illegal entrant.

(c) . . . The applicant must have spent a continuous period as specified in (d) lawfully in the UK, of which the most recent period must have been spent with leave as a Tier 1 (General) Migrant, in any combination of the following categories:

(i) as a Tier 1 (General) Migrant,

(ii) as a Highly Skilled Migrant,

(iii) as a Work Permit Holder,

(iv) as an innovator,

(v) as a Self-Employed Lawyer,

(vi) as a Writer, Composer or Artist,

(vii) as a Tier 2 (General) Migrant, a Tier 2 (Minister of Religion) Migrant or a Tier 2 (Sportsperson) Migrant, or

(viii) as a Tier 2 (Intra-Company Transfer) Migrant, provided the continuous period of 5 years spent lawfully in the UK includes a period of leave as a Tier 2 (Intra-Company Transfer) Migrant granted under the Rules in place before 6 April 2010, or as a Work Permit Holder where the work permit was granted because the applicant was the subject of an Intra-Company Transfer.

(d) The continuous period in (c) is:

(i) 4 years, if the applicant:

(1) received a Highly Skilled Migrant Programme approval letter issued on the basis of an application made before 3 April 2006,

(2) was subsequently granted entry clearance or leave to remain on the basis of that letter, and

(3) has not since been granted entry clearance or leave to remain in any category other than as a Highly Skilled Migrant or Tier 1 (General) Migrant; or

(ii) 5 years, in all other cases.

(e) If the applicant has or has had leave as a Highly Skilled Migrant, a Writer, Composer or artist, a self-employed lawyer or as a Tier 1 (General) Migrant under the Rules in place before 19 July 2010, and has not been granted leave in any categories other than these under the Rules in place since 19 July 2010, the applicant must have 75 points under paragraphs 7 to 34 of Appendix A.

(f) Where the applicant:

(i) received a Highly Skilled Migrant Programme approval letter issued on the basis of an application made before 7 November 2006,

(ii) was subsequently granted entry clearance or leave to remain on the basis of that letter, and

(iii) has not since been granted entry clearance or leave to remain in any category other than as a Highly Skilled Migrant or Tier 1 (General) Migrant, the applicant must be economically active in the UK, in employment or self-employment or both.

(g) in all cases other than those referred to in (e) or (f) above, the applicant must have 80 points under paragraphs 7 to 34 of Appendix A.

(h) The applicant must have sufficient knowledge of the English language and sufficient knowledge about life in the United Kingdom, in accordance with Appendix KoLL of these Rules, unless the applicant meets the conditions in (f)(i)–(iii) above.

(i) The applicant must not be in the UK in breach of immigration laws except that any period of overstaying for a period of 28 days or less will be disregarded, unless the applicant meets the conditions in (f)(i)–(iii) above.

(j) The applicant must provide the specified documents in paragraph 245CD-SD to evidence the reason for the absences set out in paragraph 245AAA, unless the applicant meets the conditions in (f)(i)–(iii) above.

(k) For the purposes of sub-paragraph (c), time spent with valid leave in the Bailiwick of Guernsey, the Bailiwick of Jersey or the Isle of Man in a category equivalent to those set out in (c)(i) to (viii) may be included in the continuous period of 5 years lawful residence in the UK, provided that:

(i) the most recent period of leave was granted in the UK as a Tier 1 (General) Migrant; and

(ii) any period of leave granted in the Bailiwick of Guernsey, the Bailiwick of Jersey or the Isle of Man as a work permit holder or a Tier 2 Migrant was for employment:

(a) in a job which appears on the list of occupations skilled to National Qualifications Framework level 3 or above (or from 6 April 2011, National Qualifications Framework level 4 or above or from 14 June 2012, National Qualifications Framework level 6 or above), as stated in the Codes of Practice in Appendix J, or

(b) in a job which appears in the Creative Sector Codes of Practice in Appendix J, or

(c) as a professional sportsperson (including as a sports coach).

(iii) In any such case, references to the "UK" in paragraph 245AAA shall include a reference to the Bailiwick of Guernsey, Bailiwick of Jersey or the Isle of Man, as the case may be.

(l) For the purposes of paragraph (e), time spent with valid leave in the Bailiwick of Guernsey, the Bailiwick of Jersey and the Isle of Man in a category equivalent to those set out in (e)(i) to (iv) may be included in the continuous period of [5 years (or 4 years as the case may be)] lawful residence in the UK, provided that:

(i) the most recent period of leave was granted in the UK as a Tier 1 (General) Migrant; and

(ii) any period of leave granted in the Bailiwick of Guernsey, the Bailiwick of Jersey or the Isle of Man as a work permit holder or a Tier 2 Migrant was for employment:

(a) in a job which appears on the list of occupations skilled to National Qualifications Framework level 3 or above (or from 6 April 2011, National Qualifications Framework level 4 or above or from 14 June 2012, National Qualifications Framework level 6 or above), as stated in the Codes of Practice in Appendix J, or

(b) in a job which appears in the Creative Sector Codes of Practice in Appendix J, or

(c) as a professional sportsperson (including as a sports coach).

(iii) In any such case, references to the "UK" in paragraph 245AAA shall include a reference to the Bailiwick of Guernsey, Bailiwick of Jersey or the Isle of Man, as the case may be.

(m) The application for indefinite leave to remain must have been made before 6 April 2018.

Note: Subparagraph (a) deleted from 13 December 2012 (HC 760). Subparagraphs (k) and (l) inserted from 6 April 2013 (HC 1039). Words inserted in subparagraph (b), words deleted from subparagraph (c), subparagraphs (d)–(j) substituted, words substituted in subparagraph (l) and subparagraph (m) inserted from 6 April 2014 (HC 1138).

245CD-SD Specified documents

The specified documents referred to in paragraph 245CD(j) are:

(a) For periods where the applicant was in employment in the UK, a letter from the employer detailing the purpose and period of absences in connection with the employment, including periods of annual leave.

(b) For periods where the applicant was self-employed or in business in the UK, or looking for work or setting up in business in the UK, a personal letter from the applicant detailing the purpose and period of absences in relation to those activities.

(c) A personal letter from the applicant which includes full details of the reason for the absences and all original supporting documents in relation to those reasons – e.g. medical certificates, birth/death certificates, information about the reasons which led to the absence from the UK.

Note: Paragraph 245CD-SD inserted from 13 December 2012 (HC 760) and substituted from 6 April 2013 subject to savings for applications made before that date (HC 1039).

245CE. Transitional arrangements

Note: Paragraph 245CE deleted from 6 April subject to savings for applications made before that date (HC 1138).

Tier 1 (Entrepreneur) Migrants

245D. Purpose of this route and meaning of business

(a) This route is for migrants who wish to establish, join or take over one or more businesses in the UK.

(b) For the purpose of paragraphs 245D to 245DF and paragraphs 35 to 53 of Appendix A 'business' means an enterprise as:

(i) a sole trader,

(ii) a partnership, or

(iii) a company registered in the UK.

(c) Where paragraphs 245D to 245DF and paragraphs 35 to 53 of Appendix A, refer to money remaining available to the applicant until such time as it is spent for the purposes of his business or businesses:

(i) 'Available' means that the funds are:

(1) in the applicant's own possession,

(2) in the financial accounts of a UK incorporated business of which he is the director, or

(3) available from the third party or parties named in the application under the terms of the declaration(s) referred to in paragraph 41-SD(b) of Appendix A.

(ii) 'Spent' excludes spending on:

(1) the applicant's own remuneration,

(2) buying the business from a previous owner, where the money goes to that previous owner rather than into the business,

(3) investing in other businesses, and

(4) any spending which is not directly for the purpose of establishing or running the applicant's own business or businesses.

Note: Subparagraph (c) inserted from 6 April 2014 (HC 1138 as amended by HC 1201).

245DA. Entry to the UK

All migrants arriving in the UK and wishing to enter as a Tier 1 (Entrepreneur) Migrant must have a valid entry clearance for entry under this route. If they do not have a valid entry clearance, entry will be refused.

245DB. Requirements for entry clearance

To qualify for entry clearance as a Tier 1 (Entrepreneur) Migrant, an applicant must meet the requirements listed below. If the applicant meets those requirements, entry clearance will be granted. If the applicant does not meet these requirements, the application will be refused.

Requirements:

(a) The applicant must not fall for refusal under the general grounds for refusal.

(b) The applicant must have a minimum of 75 points under paragraphs 35 to 53 of Appendix A.

(c) The applicant must have a minimum of 10 points under paragraphs 1 to 15 of Appendix B.

(d) The applicant must have a minimum of 10 points under paragraphs 1 to 2 of Appendix C.

(e) An applicant who has, or was last granted, leave as a Student or a Postgraduate Doctor or Dentist, a Student Nurse, a Student Writing-Up a Thesis, a Student Re-Sitting an Examination or as a Tier 4 Migrant and:

(i) is currently being sponsored by a government or international scholarship agency, or

(ii) was being sponsored by a government or international scholarship agency, and that sponsorship came to an end 12 months ago or less,

must provide the unconditional written consent of the sponsoring Government or agency to the application and must provide the specified documents as set out in paragraph 245A above, to show that this requirement has been met.

(f) Except where the applicant has had entry clearance, leave to enter or leave to remain as a Tier 1 (Entrepreneur) Migrant, a Businessperson or an Innovator in the 12 months immediately before the date of application and is being assessed under Table 5 of Appendix A, the Entry Clearance Officer must be satisfied that:

(i) the applicant genuinely intends and is able to establish, take over or become a director of one or more businesses in the UK within the next six months;

(ii) the applicant genuinely intends to invest the money referred to in Table 4 of Appendix A in the business or businesses referred to in (i);

(iii) that the money referred to in Table 4 of Appendix A is genuinely available to the applicant, and will remain available to him until such time as it is spent for the purposes of his business or businesses.

(iv) that the applicant does not intend to take employment in the United Kingdom other than under the terms of paragraph 245DC;

(g) In making the assessment in (f), the Entry Clearance Officer will assess the balance of probabilities. The Entry Clearance Officer may take into account the following factors:

(i) the evidence the applicant has submitted;

(ii) the viability and credibility of the source of the money referred to in Table 4 of Appendix A;

(iii) the viability and credibility of the applicant's business plans and market research into their chosen business sector;

(iv) the applicant's previous educational and business experience (or lack thereof);

(v) the applicant's immigration history and previous activity in the UK; and

(vi) any other relevant information.

(h) The Entry Clearance Officer reserves the right to request additional information and evidence to support the assessment in (f), and to refuse the application if the information or evidence is not provided. Any requested documents must be received by the UK Border Agency at the address specified in the request within 28 [calendar] days of the date of the request.

(i) If the Entry Clearance Officer is not satisfied with the genuineness of the application in relation to a points-scoring requirement in Appendix A, those points will not be awarded.

(j) The Entry Clearance Officer [may decide not to carry out] the assessment in (f) if the application already falls for refusal on other grounds, but reserves the right to carry out this assessment in any reconsideration of the decision.

(k) The applicant must be at least 16 years old.

(l) Where the applicant is under 18 years of age, the application must be supported by the applicant's parents or legal guardian or by one parent if that parent has sole legal responsibility for the child.

(m) Where the applicant is under 18 years of age, the applicant's parents or legal guardian, or one parent if that parent has sole legal responsibility for the child, must confirm that they consent to the arrangements for the applicant's care in the UK.

Note: Subparagraphs (f)–(j) inserted from 31 January 2013 (HC 943). Words substituted in subparagraph (j) from 1 October 2013 (HC 628). Subparagraph (f)(iii) substituted and subparagraphs (k)–(m) inserted from 6 April 2014 (insertion of (k)–(m) subject to savings for applications made before that date) (HC 1138 as amended by HC 1201). Word substituted in subparagraph (h) from 6 November 2014 subject to savings for applications made before that date (HC 693).

245DC. Period and conditions of grant

(a) Entry clearance will be granted for a period of 3 years and four months and will be subject to the following conditions:

(i) no recourse to public funds,

(ii) registration with the police, if this is required by paragraph 326 of these Rules, and

(iii) no employment other than working for the business(es) the applicant has established, joined or taken over, [but working for such business(es) does not include anything undertaken by the applicant pursuant to a contract of service or apprenticeship, whether express or implied and whether or written, with another business,] and

(iv) no employment as a professional sportsperson (including as a sports coach).

Note: Words inserted in subparagraph (a)(iii) from 11 July 2014 subject to savings for applications made before that date (HC 532).

245DD. Requirements for leave to remain

To qualify for leave to remain as a Tier 1 (Entrepreneur) Migrant under this rule, an applicant must meet the requirements listed below. If the applicant meets these requirements, leave to remain will be granted. If the applicant does not meet these requirements, the application will be refused.

Requirements:

(a) The applicant must not fall for refusal under the general grounds for refusal, except that paragraph 322(10) shall not apply, and must not be an illegal entrant.

(b) The applicant must have a minimum of 75 points under paragraphs 35 to 53 of Appendix A.

(c) The applicant must have a minimum of 10 points under paragraphs 1 to 15 of Appendix B.

(d) The applicant must have a minimum of 10 points under paragraphs 1 to 2 of Appendix C.

(e) The applicant who is applying for leave to remain must have, or have last been granted, entry clearance, leave to enter or remain:

(i) as a Highly Skilled Migrant,

(ii) as a Tier 1 (General) Migrant,

(iii) as a Tier 1 (Entrepreneur) Migrant,

(iv) as a Tier 1 (Investor) Migrant,

(v) as a Tier 1 (Graduate Entrepreneur) Migrant

(vi) as a Tier 1 (Post-Study Work) Migrant,

(vii) as a Businessperson,

(viii) as an Innovator,

(ix) as an Investor,

(x) as a Participant in the Fresh Talent: Working in Scotland Scheme,

(xi) as a Participant in the International Graduates Scheme (or its predecessor, the Science and Engineering Graduates Scheme),

(xii) as a Postgraduate Doctor or Dentist,

(xiii) as a Self-employed Lawyer,

(xiv) as a Student,

(xv) as a Student Nurse,

(xvi) as a Student Re-sitting an Examination,

(xvii) as a Student Writing Up a Thesis,

(xviii) as a Work Permit Holder,

(xix) as a Writer, Composer or Artist,

(xx) as a Tier 2 Migrant

(xxi) as a Tier 4 Migrant, or

(xxii) as a Prospective Entrepreneur.

(f) An applicant who has, or was last granted, leave as a Student or a Postgraduate Doctor or Dentist, Student Nurse, Student Re-Sitting an Examination, a Student Writing-Up a Thesis or as a Tier 4 Migrant and:

(i) is currently being sponsored by a government or international scholarship agency, or

(ii) was being sponsored by a government or international scholarship agency, and that sponsorship came to an end 12 months ago or less,

must provide the unconditional written consent of the sponsoring Government or agency to the application and must provide the specified documents as set out in paragraph 245A above, to show that this requirement has been met.

(g) The applicant must not be in the UK in breach of immigration laws except that any period of overstaying for a period of 28 days or less will be disregarded.

(h) Except where the applicant has, or was last granted, leave as a Tier 1 (Entrepreneur) Migrant, a Businessperson or an Innovator and is being assessed under Table 5 of Appendix A, the Secretary of State must be satisfied that:

(i) the applicant genuinely:

(1) intends and is able to establish, take over or become a director of one or more businesses in the UK within the next six months, or

(2) has established, taken over or become a director of one or more businesses in the UK and continues to operate that business or businesses; and

(ii) the applicant genuinely intends to invest the money referred to in Table 4 of Appendix A in the business or businesses referred to in (i);

(iii) the money referred to in Table 4 of Appendix A is genuinely available to the applicant, and will remain available to him until such time as it is spent for the purposes of his business or businesses.

(iv) that the applicant does not intend to take employment in the United Kingdom other than under the terms of paragraph 245DE.

(i) In making the assessment in (h), the Secretary of State will assess the balance of probabilities. The Secretary of State may take into account the following factors:

(i) the evidence the applicant has submitted;

(ii) the viability and credibility of the source of the money referred to in Table 4 of Appendix A;

(iii) the viability and credibility of the applicant's business plans and market research into their chosen business sector;

(iv) the applicant's previous educational and business experience (or lack thereof);

(v) the applicant's immigration history and previous activity in the UK;

(vi) where the applicant has already registered in the UK as self-employed or as the director of a business, and the nature of the business requires mandatory accreditation, registration and/or insurance, whether that accreditation, registration and/or insurance has been obtained; and

(vii) any other relevant information.

(j) The Secretary of State reserves the right to request additional information and evidence to support the assessment in (h), and to refuse the application if the information or evidence is not provided. Any requested documents must be received by the Secretary of State at the address specified in the request within 28 [calendar] days of the date of the request.

(k) If the Secretary of State is not satisfied with the genuineness of the application in relation to a points-scoring requirement in Appendix A, those points will not be awarded.

(l) The Secretary of State may decide not to carry out the assessment in (h) if the application already falls for refusal on other grounds, but reserves the right to carry out this assessment in any reconsideration of the decision.

(m) The applicant must, unless he provides a reasonable explanation, comply with any request made by the Secretary of State to attend for interview.

(n) The applicant must be at least 16 years old.

(o) Where the applicant is under 18 years of age, the application must be supported by the applicant's parents or legal guardian or by one parent if that parent has sole legal responsibility for the child.

(p) Where the applicant is under 18 years of age, the applicant's parents or legal guardian, or one parent if that parent has sole legal responsibility for the child, must confirm that they consent to the arrangements for the applicant's care in the UK.

Note: Subparagraphs (h)–(l) inserted from 31 January 2013 (HC 943). Subparagraph (a) substituted and subparagraph (m) inserted from 6 April 2013 subject to savings for applications made before that date (HC 1039). Subparagraph (h)(iii) substituted and subparagraphs (n)–(p) inserted from 6 April 2014 (insertion of (n) to (p) subject to savings for applications made before that date) (HC 1138 as amended by HC 1201). Word substituted in subparagraph (j) from 6 November 2014 subject to savings for applications made before that date (HC 693).

245DE. Period, conditions and curtailment of grant

(a) Leave to remain will be granted:

(i) for a period of 2 years, to an applicant who has, or was last granted, leave as a Tier 1 (Entrepreneur) Migrant,

(ii) for a period of 3 years, to any other applicant.

(b) Leave to remain under this route will be subject to the following conditions:

(i) no recourse to public funds,

(ii) registration with the police, if this is required by paragraph 326 of these Rules, and

(iii) no employment, other than working for the business or businesses which he has established, joined or taken over, [but working for such business(es) does not include anything undertaken by the applicant pursuant to a contract of service or apprenticeship, whether express or implied and whether oral or written, with another business,] and

(iv) no employment as a professional sportsperson (including as a sports coach).

(c) Without prejudice to the grounds for curtailment in paragraph 323 of these Rules, leave to enter or remain granted to a Tier 1 (Entrepreneur) Migrant may be curtailed if:

(i) within 6 months of the date specified in paragraph (d), the applicant has not done one or more of the following things:

(1) registered with HM Revenue and Customs as self-employed,

(2) registered a new business in which he is a director, or

(3) registered as a director of an existing business, or

(ii) the funds referred to in the relevant sections of Appendix A cease to be available to him, except where they have been spent for the purposes of his business or businesses.

(d) The date referred to in paragraph (c) is:

(i) the date of the applicant's entry to the UK, in the case of an applicant granted entry clearance as a Tier 1 (Entrepreneur) Migrant where there is evidence to establish the applicant's date of entry to the UK,

(ii) the date of the grant of entry clearance to the applicant, in the case of an applicant granted entry clearance as a Tier 1 (Entrepreneur) Migrant where there is no evidence to establish the applicant's date of entry to the UK, or

(iii) the date of the grant of leave to remain to the applicant, in any other case.

(e) Paragraph 245DE(c) does not apply where the applicant's last grant of leave prior to the grant of the leave that he currently has was as a Tier 1 (Entrepreneur) Migrant, a Businessperson or an Innovator.

Note: Subparagraphs (c) substituted from 31 January 2013 (HC 943). Subparagraph (c)(ii) substituted from 6 April 2014 (HC 1138 as amended by HC 1201). Words inserted in subparagraph (b)(iii) from 11 July 2014 subject to savings for applications made before that date (HC 532).

245DF. Requirements for indefinite leave to remain

To qualify for indefinite leave to remain as a Tier 1 (Entrepreneur) Migrant, an applicant must meet the requirements listed below. If the applicant meets these requirements, indefinite leave to remain will be granted. If the applicant does not meet these requirements, the application will be refused.

Requirements:

(a) DELETED

(b) The applicant must not fall for refusal under the general grounds for refusal, and must not be an illegal entrant.

(c) The applicant must have a minimum of 75 points under paragraphs 35 to 53 of Appendix A.

(d) The applicant must have demonstrated sufficient knowledge of the English language and sufficient knowledge about life in the United Kingdom, in accordance with Appendix KoLL.

(e) The applicant must not be in the UK in breach of immigration laws except that any period of overstaying for a period of 28 days or less will be disregarded.

Note: Subparagraph (a) deleted from 13 December 2012 subject to savings for applications made before that date (HC 760). Subparagraph (d) substituted from 28 October 2013 subject to savings for applications made before that date (HC 628).

Tier 1 (Investor) Migrants

245E. Purpose

This route is for high net worth individuals making a substantial financial investment to the UK.

245EA. Entry to the UK

All migrants arriving in the UK and wishing to enter as a Tier 1 (Investor) Migrant must have a valid entry clearance for entry under this route. If they do not have a valid entry clearance, entry will be refused.

245EB. Requirements for entry clearance

To qualify for entry clearance or leave to remain as a Tier 1 (Investor) Migrant, an applicant must meet the requirements listed below. If the applicant meets these requirements, entry clearance will be granted. If the applicant does not meet these requirements, the application will be refused.

Requirements:

(a) The applicant must not fall for refusal under the general grounds for refusal.

(b) The applicant must have a minimum of 75 points under paragraphs 54 to [65-SD] of Appendix A.

(c) An applicant who has, or was last granted, leave as a Student or a Postgraduate Doctor or Dentist, a Student Nurse, a Student Re-Sitting an Examination, a Student Writing-Up a Thesis or as a Tier 4 Migrant and:

(i) is currently being sponsored by a government or international scholarship agency, or

(ii) was being sponsored by a government or international scholarship agency, and that sponsorship came to an end 12 months ago or less

must provide the unconditional written consent of the sponsoring Government or agency to the application and must provide the specified documents to as set out in paragraph 245A above, show that this requirement has been met.

(d) The applicant must be at least 16 years old and the assets and investment he is claiming points for must be wholly under his control.

(e) Where the applicant is under 18 years of age, the application must be supported by the applicant's parents or legal guardian or by one parent if that parent has sole legal responsibility for the child.

(f) Where the applicant is under 18 years of age, the applicant's parents or legal guardian, or one parent if that parent has sole legal responsibility for the child, must confirm that they consent to the arrangements for the applicant's care in the UK.

(g) The Entry Clearance Officer must not have reasonable grounds to believe that:

(i) notwithstanding that the applicant has provided the relevant specified documents required under Appendix A, the applicant is not in control of and at liberty to freely invest the money specified in their application for the purposes of meeting the requirements of Table 7 of Appendix A to these Rules (where relevant); or

(ii) any of the money specified in the application for the purposes of meeting the requirements of Table 7 of Appendix A to these Rules held by:

(1) the applicant; or

(2) where any of the specified money has been made available to the applicant by another party, that party,

has been acquired by means of conduct which is unlawful in the UK, or would constitute unlawful conduct if it occurred in the UK; or

(iii) where any of the money specified in the application for the purposes of meeting the requirements of Table 7 of Appendix A to these Rules has been made available by another party, the character, conduct or associations of that party are such that approval of the application would not be conducive to the public good,

and where the Entry Clearance Officer does have reasonable grounds to believe one or more of the above applies, no points from Table 7 (where relevant) will be awarded.

Note: Subparagraphs (d)–(f) substituted from 6 April 2014 subject to savings for applications made before that date (HC 1138). Word substituted in subparagraph (b) and subparagraph (g) inserted from 6 November 2014 subject to savings for applications made before that date (HC 693).

245EC. Period and conditions of grant

(a) Entry clearance will be granted for a period of 3 years and four months and will be subject to the following conditions:

(i) no recourse to public funds,

(ii) registration with the police, if this is required by paragraph 326 of these Rules,

(iii) no Employment as a Doctor or Dentist in Training, unless the applicant has obtained a primary degree in medicine or dentistry at bachelor's level or above from a UK institution that is a UK recognised or listed body, or which holds a sponsor licence under Tier 4 of the Points Based System, and

(iv) no employment as a professional sportsperson (including as a sports coach).

Note: Subparagraph (iv) inserted from 13 December 2012 (HC 760).

245ED. Requirements for leave to remain

To qualify for leave to remain as a Tier 1 (Investor) Migrant, an applicant must meet the requirements listed below. If the applicant meets these requirements, leave to remain will be granted. If the applicant does not meet these requirements, the application will be refused.

Requirements:

(a) The applicant must not fall for refusal under the general grounds for refusal, and must not be an illegal entrant.

(b) The applicant must have a minimum of 75 points under paragraphs 54 to [65-SD] of Appendix A.

(c) The applicant must have, or have last been granted, entry clearance, leave to enter or remain:

(i) as a Highly Skilled Migrant,

(ii) as a Tier 1 (General) Migrant,

(iii) as a Tier 1 (Entrepreneur) Migrant,
(iv) as a Tier 1 (Investor) Migrant,
(v) as a Tier 1 (Post-Study Work) Migrant,
(vi) as a Businessperson,
(vii) as an Innovator,
(viii) as an Investor,
(ix) as a Student,
(x) as a Student Nurse,
(xi) as a Student Re-Sitting an Examination,
(xii) as a Student Writing Up a Thesis,
(xiii) as a Work Permit Holder,
(xiv) as a Writer, Composer or Artist,
(xv) as a Tier 2 Migrant, or
(xvi) as a Tier 4 Migrant.

(d) An applicant who has, or was last granted, leave as a Student Nurse, Student Re-Sitting an Examination, Student Writing-Up a Thesis or as a Tier 4 Migrant and:

(i) is currently being sponsored by a government or international scholarship agency, or

(ii) was being sponsored by a government or international scholarship agency, and that sponsorship came to an end 12 months ago or less,

must provide the unconditional written consent of the sponsoring Government or agency to the application and must provide the specified documents as set out in paragraph 245A above, to show that this requirement has been met.

(e) The applicant must be at least 16 years old and the assets and investment he is claiming points for must be wholly under his control.

(f) Where the applicant is under 18 years of age, the application must be supported by the applicant's parents or legal guardian or by one parent if that parent has sole legal responsibility for the child.

(g) Where the applicant is under 18 years of age, the applicant's parents or legal guardian, or one parent if that parent has sole legal responsibility for the child, must confirm that they consent to the arrangements for the applicant's care in the UK.

(h) The applicant must not be in the UK in breach of immigration laws except that any period of overstaying for a period of 28 days or less will be disregarded.

(i) The Secretary of State must not have reasonable grounds to believe that:

(i) notwithstanding that the applicant has provided the relevant specified documents required under Appendix A, the applicant is not in control of and at liberty to freely invest the money specified in their application for the purposes of meeting the requirements of Table 7 of Appendix A to these Rules (where relevant); or

(ii) any of the money specified in the application for the purposes of meeting the requirements of Table 7 of Appendix A to these Rules held by:

(1) the applicant; or

(2) where any of the specified money has been made available to the applicant by another party, that party,

has been acquired by means of conduct which is unlawful in the UK, or would constitute unlawful conduct if it occurred in the UK; or

(iii) where any of the money specified in the application for the purposes of meeting the requirements of Table 7 of Appendix A to these Rules has been made available by another party, the character, conduct or associations of that party are such that approval of the application would not be conducive to the public good,

and where the Secretary of State does have reasonable grounds to believe one or more of the above applies, no points from Table 7 (where relevant) will be awarded.

Note: Subparagraphs (e)–(g) inserted and subparagraph (h) renumbered from 6 April 2014 (HC 1138 as amended by HC 1201). Word substituted in subparagraph (b) and subparagraph (i) inserted from 6 November 2014 subject to savings for applications made before that date (HC 693).

245EE. Period, conditions and curtailment of grant

(a) Leave to remain will be granted:

(i) for a period of 2 years, to an applicant who has, or was last granted, leave as a Tier 1 (Investor) Migrant,

(ii) for a period of 3 years, to any other applicant.

(b) Leave to remain under this route will be subject to the following conditions:

(i) no recourse to public funds,

(ii) registration with the police, if this is required by paragraph 326 of these Rules,

(iii) no Employment as a Doctor or Dentist in Training, unless the applicant:

(1) has obtained a primary degree in medicine or dentistry at bachelor's level or above from a UK institution that is a UK recognised or listed body, or which holds a sponsor licence under Tier 4 of the Points Based System, and provides evidence of this degree; or

(2) has, or has last been granted, entry clearance, leave to enter or leave to remain that was not subject to any condition restricting him from taking employment as a Doctor in Training, has been employed during that leave as a Doctor in Training, and provides a letter from the Postgraduate Deanery or NHS Trust employing them which confirms that they have been working in a post or programme that has been approved by the [General Medical Council] as a training programme or post; or

(3) has, or has last been granted, entry clearance, leave to enter or leave to remain that was not subject to any condition restricting him from taking employment as a Dentist in Training, has been employed during that leave as a Dentist in Training, and provides a letter from the Postgraduate Deanery or NHS Trust employing them which confirms that they have been working in a post or programme that has been approved by the [Joint Committee for Postgraduate Training in Dentistry] as a training programme or post, and

(iv) no employment as a professional sportsperson (including as a sports coach).

(c) Without prejudice to the grounds for curtailment in paragraph 323 of these Rules, leave to enter or remain as a Tier 1 (Investor) Migrant may be curtailed if:

(i) within 3 months of the date specified in paragraph (d), the applicant has not invested, or had invested on his behalf, at least [the amount of capital specified in paragraph (e)] in the UK by way of UK Government bonds, share capital or loan capital in active and trading UK registered companies other than those principally engaged in property investment, or

(ii) the applicant does not maintain [at least the level of] investment in (i) throughout the remaining period of his leave.

(d) The date referred to in paragraph (c) is:

(i) the date of the applicant's entry to the UK, in the case of an applicant granted entry clearance as a Tier 1 (Investor) Migrant where there is evidence to establish the applicant's date of entry to the UK,

(ii) the date of the grant of entry clearance to the applicant, in the case of an applicant granted entry clearance as a Tier 1 (Investor) Migrant where there is no evidence to establish the applicant's date of entry to the UK, or

(iii) the date of the grant of leave to remain to the applicant, in any other case.

(e) The amount of capital referred to in paragraph (c) is:

(i) at least £2 million if the applicant was last granted leave under the Rules in place from 6 November 2014 and was awarded points as set out in Table 7 or Table 8A of Appendix A to these Rules in that last grant, or

(ii) at least £750,000 if the applicant was last granted leave under the Rules in place before 6 November 2014 or was awarded points as set out in Table 8B of Appendix A to these Rules in his last grant.

(f) Paragraph 245EE(c) does not apply where the applicant's two most recent grants of leave were either as a Tier 1 (Investor) Migrant and/or as an Investor.

Note: Words substituted in subparagraphs (b)(iii)(2) and (iii), subparagraph (b)(iv) inserted and subparagraph (c) substituted from 13 December 2012 (HC 760). Words substituted in subparagraph (c)(ii), subparagraph (e) substituted and subparagraph (f) inserted from 6 November 2014 subject to savings for applications made before that date (HC 693).

245EF. Requirements for indefinite leave to remain

To qualify for indefinite leave to remain, a Tier 1 (Investor) Migrant must meet the requirements listed below. if the applicant meets these requirements, indefinite leave to remain will be granted. if the applicant does not meet these requirements, the application will be refused.

Requirements:

(a) DELETED

(b) The applicant must not fall for refusal under the general grounds for refusal, and must not be an illegal entrant.

(c) The applicant must have a minimum of 75 points under paragraphs 54 to [65-SD] of Appendix A.

(d) The applicant must have demonstrated sufficient knowledge of the English language and sufficient knowledge about life in the United Kingdom, in accordance with Appendix KoLL.

(e) The applicant must not be in the UK in breach of immigration laws except that any period of overstaying for a period of 28 days or less will be disregarded.

Note: Subparagraph (a) deleted 13 December 2012 subject to savings for applications made before that date (HC 760). Subparagraph (d) substituted from 28 October 2013 subject to savings for applications made before that date (HC 628). Subparagraph (c) amended from 6 November 2014 subject to savings for applications made before that date (HC 693).

Tier 1 (Graduate Entrepreneur) Migrants

245F. Purpose of the route and meaning of business

(a) This route is for:

(i) UK graduates who have been identified by Higher Education Institutions as having developed genuine and credible business ideas and entrepreneurial skills to extend their stay in the UK after graduation to establish one or more businesses in the UK; and

(ii) Graduates who have been identified by UK Trade and Investment as elite global graduate entrepreneurs to establish one or more businesses in the UK.

(b) For the purpose of paragraphs 245F to [245FC] and paragraphs 66 to 72 of Appendix A 'business' means an enterprise as:

(i) a sole trader,

(ii) a partnership, or

(iii) a company registered in the UK.

Note: Words substituted in subparagraph (b) from 6 April 2013 subject to savings for applications made before that date (HC 1039). Subparagraph (a) substituted from 6 April 2014 subject to savings for applications made before that date (HC 1138 as amended by HC 1201).

245FA. Entry to the UK

All migrants arriving in the UK and wishing to enter as a Tier 1 (Graduate Entrepreneur) Migrant must have a valid entry clearance for entry under this route. If they do not have a valid entry clearance, entry will be refused.

Note: New paragraph 245FA inserted from 6 April 2013 subject to savings for applications made before that date (HC 1039).

245FB. [Requirements for entry clearance or leave to remain

To qualify for entry clearance or leave to remain as a Tier 1 (Graduate Entrepreneur) Migrant, an applicant must meet the requirements listed below. If the applicant meets these requirements, entry clearance or leave to remain will be granted. If the applicant does not meet these requirements, the application will be refused.]

Requirements:

(a) The applicant must not fall for refusal under the general grounds for refusal, and must not be an illegal entrant.

(b) The applicant must have a minimum of 75 points under paragraphs 66 to 72 of Appendix A.

(c) The applicant must have a minimum of 10 points under paragraphs 1 to 15 of Appendix B.

(d) The applicant must have a minimum of 10 points under [paragraphs 1 to 2 of Appendix C.]

(e) [If applying for leave to remain, the applicant] must have, or have last been granted, entry clearance, leave to enter or remain:

- (i) as a Tier 4 Migrant,
- (ii) as a Student,
- (iii) as a Student Nurse,
- (iv) as a Student Re-sitting an Examination,
- (v) as a Student Writing Up a Thesis,
- (vi) as a Postgraduate Doctor or Dentist,
- (vii) as a Tier 1 (Graduate Entrepreneur) Migrant, or
- (viii) as a Tier 2 (General) Migrant.

(f) [An applicant who is applying for leave to remain and has], or was last granted, entry clearance or leave to remain as a Tier 2 (General) Migrant must have been granted leave to work as a post-doctoral researcher for the same institution which is endorsing his application as a Tier 1 (Graduate Entrepreneur) Migrant.

(g) The applicant must not have previously been granted entry clearance, leave to enter or remain as a Tier 1 (Post-Study Work) Migrant, a Participant in the Fresh Talent: Working in Scotland Scheme, or a Participant in the International Graduates Scheme (or its predecessor, the Science and Engineering Graduates Scheme).

(h) The applicant must not previously have been granted leave as a Tier 1 (Graduate Entrepreneur) Migrant on more than 1 occasion.

(i) An applicant who does not have, or was not last granted, leave to remain as a Tier 1 (Graduate Entrepreneur) Migrant and:

(i) is currently being sponsored in his studies by a government or international scholarship agency, or

(ii) was being sponsored in his studies by a government or international scholarship agency, and that sponsorship came to an end 12 months ago or less,

must provide the unconditional written consent of the sponsoring government or agency to the application and must provide the specified documents as set out in paragraph 245A above, to show that this requirement has been met.

(j) The applicant must not be in the UK in breach of immigration laws except that any period of overstaying for a period of 28 days or less will be disregarded.

Note: Paragraph 245FB renumbered, words in opening paragraph and in subparagraphs (c) and (e) substituted, subparagraph (e)(viii) inserted and subparagraphs (g)–(j) renumbered from 6 April 2013 subject to savings for applications made before that date (HC 1039). Subparagraph (f) substituted from 6 April 2014 subject to savings for applications made before that date (HC 1138 as amended by HC 1201). Words substituted in subparagraph (f) from 11 July 2014 (HC 532).

245FC. Period and conditions of grant

Entry clearance or leave to remain will be granted for a period of 1 year and will be subject to the following conditions:

(i) no recourse to public funds,
(ii) registration with the police, if this is required by paragraph 326 of these Rules,
(iii) no employment as a Doctor or Dentist in Training, and
(iv) no employment as a professional sportsperson (including as a sports coach).

Note: Paragraph 245FC renumbered and text substituted from 6 April 2013 subject to savings for applications made before that date (HC 1039).

Tier 2 Migrants

Tier 2 (Intra-Company Transfer) Migrants

245G. Purpose of this route and definitions

This route enables multinational employers to transfer their existing employees from outside the EEA to their UK branch for training purposes or to fill a specific vacancy that cannot be filled by a British or EEA worker. There are four sub-categories in this route:

(i) Short Term staff: for established employees of multi-national companies who are being transferred to a skilled job in the UK for 12 months or less that could not be carried out by a new recruit from the resident workforce;

(ii) Long Term staff: for established employees of multi-national companies who are being transferred to a skilled job in the UK which will, or may, last for more than 12 months and could not be carried out by a new recruit from the resident workforce;

(iii) Graduate Trainee: for recent graduate recruits of multi-national companies who are being transferred to the UK branch of the same organisation as part of a structured graduate training programme, which clearly defines progression towards a managerial or specialist role;

(iv) Skills Transfer: for overseas employees of multi-national companies who are being transferred to the UK branch of the same organisation in a graduate occupation to learn the skills and knowledge they will need to perform their jobs overseas, or to impart their specialist skills to the UK workforce.

245GA. Entry clearance

All migrants arriving in the UK and wishing to enter as a Tier 2 (Intra-Company Transfer) Migrant must have a valid entry clearance for entry under this route. If they do not have a valid entry clearance, entry will be refused.

245GB. Requirements for entry clearance

To qualify for entry clearance as a Tier 2 (Intra-Company Transfer) Migrant, an applicant must meet the requirements listed below. If the applicant meets these requirements, entry clearance will be granted. if the applicant does not meet these requirements, the application will be refused.

Requirements:

(a) The applicant must not fall for refusal under the general grounds for refusal.

(b) The applicant must have a minimum of 50 points under paragraphs 73 to 75E of Appendix A.

(c) The applicant must have a minimum of 10 points under paragraphs 4 to 5 of Appendix C.

(d) The applicant must not have had entry clearance or leave to remain as a Tier 2 Migrant at any time during the 12 months immediately before the date of the application . . ., unless paragraph (e) below applies.

(e) Paragraph (d) above does not apply to an applicant who:

(i) was not in the UK with leave as a Tier 2 migrant at any time during the above 12-month period, and provides evidence to show this,

(ii) is applying under the Long Term Staff sub-category and who has, or last had entry clearance or leave to remain as a Tier 2 (Intra-Company Transfer) Migrant in the Short Term staff, Graduate Trainee or Skills Transfer sub-categories, or under the Rules in place before 6 April 2011, or

(iii) will be paid a gross annual salary (as recorded by the Certificate of Sponsorship Checking Service entry, and including such allowances as are specified as acceptable for this purpose in paragraph 75 of Appendix A) of [£153,500] or higher.

(f) an applicant who has, or was last granted, leave as a Student, a Student Nurse, a Student Re-Sitting an Examination, a Student Writing-Up a Thesis, a Postgraduate Doctor or Dentist or a Tier 4 Migrant and:

(i) is currently being sponsored by a government or international scholarship agency, or

(ii) was being sponsored by a government or international scholarship agency, and that sponsorship came to an end 12 months ago or less,

must provide the unconditional written consent of the sponsoring Government or agency to the application and must provide the specified documents as set out in paragraph 245A above, to show that this requirement has been met.

(g) The applicant must be at least 16 years old.

(h) Where the applicant is under 18 years of age, the application must be supported by the applicant's parents or legal guardian, or by one parent if that parent has sole legal responsibility for the child.

(i) Where the applicant is under 18 years of age, the applicant's parents or legal guardian, or just one parent if that parent has sole responsibility for the child, must confirm that they consent to the arrangements for the applicant's travel to, and reception and care in, the UK.

Note: Words deleted from subparagraph (d) and subparagraph (e) substituted from 13 December 2012 subject to savings for applications made before that date (HC 760). Words substituted in subparagraph (e)(iii) from 6 April 2014 subject to savings for applications made on ar after that date using a certificate of sponsorship assigned to the applicant before that date (HC 1138 as amended by HC 1201).

245GC. Period and conditions of grant

(a) Entry clearance will be granted for whichever is the shorter of:

(i) a period equal to the length of the period of engagement plus 1 month, or

(ii) the maximum time, as set out in (b).

(b) The maximum time referred to in (a)(ii) is:

(i) 6 months, if the applicant is applying in the Skills Transfer subcategory,

(ii) 12 months, if the applicant is applying in either of the Graduate Trainee or Short Term Staff sub-categories, or

(iii) 5 years and 1 month, if the applicant is applying in the Long Term Staff sub-category.

(c) entry clearance will be granted with effect from 14 days before the date that the Certificate of Sponsorship Checking Service records as the start date for the applicant's employment in the UK, unless entry clearance is being granted less than 14 days before that date, in which case it will be granted with immediate effect.

(d) Entry clearance will be subject to the following conditions:

(i) no recourse to public funds,

(ii) registration with the police, if this is required by paragraph 326, and

(iii) no employment except:

(1) working for the sponsor in the employment that the Certificate of Sponsorship Checking Service records that the migrant is being sponsored to do, subject to any notification of a change to the details of that employment, other than prohibited changes as defined in paragraph 323AA, (2) supplementary employment, and

(2) voluntary work.

Note Subparagraphs (a)–(c) substituted from 6 April 2014 subject to savings for applications made before that date (HC 1138 as amended by HC 1201).

245GD. Requirements for leave to remain

To qualify for leave to remain as a Tier 2 (Intra-Company Transfer) Migrant under this rule, an applicant must meet the requirements listed below. If the applicant meets these requirements, leave to remain will be granted. If the applicant does not meet these requirements, the application will be refused.

Requirements:

(a) The applicant must not fall for refusal under the general grounds for refusal, and must not be an illegal entrant.

(b) if the applicant is applying for leave to remain as a Tier 2 (Intra-Company Transfer) Migrant in the Long Term Staff sub-category:

(i) the applicant must have, or have last been granted, entry clearance, leave to enter or leave to remain as either:

(1) a Tier 2 (Intra-Company Transfer) Migrant in the Long Term Staff sub-category, or

(2) a Tier 2 (Intra-Company Transfer) Migrant in the established Staff sub-category under the Rules in place before 6 April 2011, or

(3) a Tier 2 (Intra-Company Transfer) Migrant granted under the Rules in place before 6 April 2010, or

(4) a Qualifying Work Permit Holder, provided that the work permit was granted because the applicant was the subject of an Intra-Company Transfer, or

(5) as a representative of an overseas Business, and

(ii) the applicant must still be working for the same employer as he was at the time of that earlier grant of leave.

(c) if the applicant is applying for leave to remain as a Tier 2 (Intra-Company Transfer) Migrant in the Short Term Staff sub-category:

(i) the applicant must have, or have last been granted, entry clearance, leave to enter or leave to remain as a Tier 2 (Intra-Company Transfer) Migrant in the Short Term Staff sub-category, and

(ii) the applicant must still be working for the same employer as he was at the time of that earlier grant of leave.

(d) if the applicant is applying for leave to remain as a Tier 2 (Intra-Company Transfer) Migrant in the Graduate Trainee sub-category:

(i) the applicant must have, or have last been granted, entry clearance, leave to enter or leave to remain as a Tier 2 (Intra-Company Transfer) Migrant in the Graduate Trainee sub-category, and

(ii) the applicant must still be working for the same employer as he was at the time of that earlier grant of leave.

(e) if the applicant is applying for leave to remain as a Tier 2 (Intra-Company Transfer) Migrant in the Skills Transfer sub-category:

(i) the applicant must have, or have last been granted, entry clearance, leave to enter or leave to remain as a Tier 2 (Intra-Company Transfer) Migrant in the skills Transfer sub-category, and

(ii) the applicant must still be working for the same employer as he was at the time of that earlier grant of leave.

(f) in all cases the applicant must have a minimum of 50 points under paragraphs 73 to 75E of Appendix A.

(g) DELETED

(h) The applicant must have a minimum of 10 points under paragraphs 4 to 5 of Appendix C.

(i) The applicant must be at least 16 years old.

(j) Where the applicant is under 18 years of age, the application must be supported by the applicant's parents or legal guardian or by one parent if that parent has sole legal responsibility for the child.

(k) Where the applicant is under 18 years of age, the applicant's parents or legal guardian, or one parent if that parent has sole legal responsibility for the child, must confirm that they consent to the arrangements for the applicant's care in the UK.

(l) The applicant must not be in the UK in breach of immigration laws except that any period of overstaying for a period of 28 days or less will be disregarded.

Note Subparagraph (g) deleted from 1 October 2013 subject to savings for applications made before that date (HC 628).

245GE. Period and conditions of grant

(a) Leave to remain will be granted for whichever of the following is the shortest:

(i) the length of the period of engagement plus 14 days,

(ii) 5 years, or

(iii) the difference between the continuous period of leave that the applicant has already been granted (notwithstanding any breaks between periods of leave of up to 28 days) as a Tier 2 (Intra-Company Transfer) Migrant, and the maximum time, as set out in (b).

If the calculation of period of leave comes to zero or a negative number, leave to remain will be refused.

(b) The maximum time referred to in (a)(iii) is:

(i) 6 months, if the applicant is applying in the Skills Transfer subcategory,

(ii) 12 months, if the applicant is applying in either of the Graduate Trainee or Short Term Staff sub-categories,

(iii) 5 years, if:

(1) the applicant is applying in the Long Term Staff subcategory,

(2) the Certificate of Sponsorship Checking Service entry records that the applicant's gross annual salary (including such allowances as are specified as acceptable for this purpose in paragraph 75 of Appendix A) to be paid by the Sponsor is less than £153,500, (or £152,100 if the Certificate of Sponsorship used in support of the application was assigned to him before 6 April 2014) and

(3) Paragraph (v) below does not apply,

(iv) 9 years, if:

(1) the applicant is applying in the Long Term Staff subcategory,

(2) the Certificate of Sponsorship Checking Service entry records that the applicant's gross annual salary (including such allowances as are specified as acceptable for this purpose in paragraph 75 of Appendix A) to be paid by the Sponsor is £153,500, (or £152,100 if the Certificate of Sponsorship used in support of the application was assigned to him before 6 April 2014) or higher, and

(3) Paragraph (v) below does not apply,

or

(v) No limit, if the applicant:

(1) is applying in the Long Term Staff sub-category,

(2) previously had leave as a Tier 2 (Intra-Company Transfer) Migrant under the Rules in place before 6 April 2011 or as a Qualifying Work Permit Holder, and

(3) has not been granted entry clearance in this or any other route since the grant of leave referred to in (2) above.

(c) In addition to the period in (a), leave to remain will be granted for the period between the date that the application is decided and the date that the Certificate of Sponsorship

Checking Service records as the start date of employment in the UK, provided this is not a negative value.

(d) Leave to remain will be granted subject to the following conditions:

(i) no recourse to public funds,

(ii) registration with the police, if this is required by paragraph 326, and

(iii) no employment except:

(1) working for the sponsor in the employment that the Certificate of Sponsorship Checking Service records that the migrant is being sponsored to do, subject to any notification of a change to the details of that employment, other than prohibited changes as defined in paragraph 323AA,

(2) supplementary employment, and

(3) voluntary work.

Note: Paragraph 245GE substituted from 6 April 2014 subject to savings for applications made before that date (HC 1138 as amended by HC 1201).

245GF. Requirements for indefinite leave to remain

To qualify for indefinite leave to remain as a Tier 2 (Intra-Company Transfer) Migrant, an applicant must meet the requirements listed below. If the applicant meets these requirements, indefinite leave to remain will be granted. if the applicant does not meet these requirements, the application will be refused.

Requirements:

(a) DELETED

(b) The applicant must not fall for refusal under the general grounds for refusal, and must not be an illegal entrant.

(c) The applicant must have spent a continuous period of 5 years lawfully in the UK, of which the most recent period must have been spent with leave as a Tier 2 (Intra-Company Transfer) Migrant, in any combination of the following categories:

(i) as a Tier 2 (Intra-Company Transfer) Migrant,

(ii) as a Qualifying Work Permit Holder, or

(iii) as a representative of an overseas Business.

(d) The continuous period of 5 years referred to in paragraph (c) must include a period of leave as:

(i) a Tier 2 (Intra-Company Transfer) Migrant granted under the Rules in place before 6 April 2010, or

(ii) a Qualifying Work Permit Holder, provided that the work permit was granted because the applicant was the subject of an Intra-Company Transfer.

(e) The Sponsor that issued the Certificate of Sponsorship that led to the applicant's last grant of leave must:

(i) still hold, or have applied for a renewal of, a Tier 2 (Intra-Company Transfer) Sponsor licence; and

(ii) certify in writing that:

(1) he still requires the applicant for the employment in question, and

(2) the applicant is paid at or above the appropriate rate for the job as stated in the Codes of Practice in Appendix J, or where the applicant is not paid at that rate only due to maternity, paternity or adoption leave, the date that leave started and that the applicant was paid at the appropriate rate immediately before the leave.

(f) The applicant provides the specified documents in paragraph 245GF-SD to evidence the sponsor's certification in subsection (e)(ii) and to evidence the reason for the absences set out in paragraph 245AAA.

(g) The applicant must have sufficient knowledge of the English language and sufficient knowledge about life in the United Kingdom, in accordance with Appendix KoLL.

(h) The applicant must not be in the UK in breach of immigration laws except that any period of overstaying for a period of 28 days or less will be disregarded.

(i) For the purposes of sub-paragraph (c), time spent with valid leave in the Bailiwick of Guernsey, the Bailiwick of Jersey or the Isle of Man in a category equivalent to the categories set out in (c)(i) to (iii) above, may be included in the continuous period of 5 years lawful residence, provided that:

(i) the continuous period of 5 years includes a period of leave as a Tier 2 (Intra-Company Transfer) Migrant granted before 6 April 2010, or a Qualifying Work Permit Holder (provided the work permit was granted because the applicant was the subject of an Intra-Company Transfer); and

(ii) any period of leave granted in the Bailiwick of Guernsey, the Bailiwick of Jersey or the Isle of Man as a work permit holder or as a Tier 2 Migrant was for employment:

(a) in a job which appears on the list of occupations skilled to National Qualifications Framework level 3 or above (or from 6 April 2011, National Qualifications Framework level 4 or above or from 14 June 2012, National Qualifications Framework level 6 or above), as stated in the Codes of Practice in Appendix J, or

(b) in a job which appears in the Creative Sector Codes of Practice in Appendix J, or

(c) as a professional sportsperson (including as a sports coach); and

(iii) the most recent period of leave was granted in the UK as a Tier 2 (Intra-Company Transfer) Migrant.

In such cases, references to the "UK" in paragraph 245AAA shall include a reference to the Bailiwick of Guernsey, Bailiwick of Jersey or the Isle of Man, as the case may be.

Note: Subparagraph (a) deleted and subparagraphs (d) and (f) amended from 13 December 2012 (deletion of (a) subject to savings for applications made before that date) (HC 760). Subparagraph (e) substituted from 1 October 2013 and subparagraph (g) substituted from 28 October 2013 subject to savings for applications made before those dates (HC 628). Words inserted in subparagraph (e) and subparagraph (i) inserted from 6 April 2013 (HC 1039).

245GF-SD Specified documents

The specified documents referred to in paragraph 245GF(f) are set out in [A, B and C below]:

A. Either a payslip and a personal bank or building society statement, or a payslip and a building society pass book.

(a) Payslips must be:

(i) the applicant's most recent payslip,

(ii) dated no earlier than one calendar month before the date of the application, and

(iii) either:

(1) an original payslip,

(2) on company-headed paper, or

(3) accompanied by a letter from the applicant's Sponsor, on company headed paper and signed by a senior official, confirming the payslip is authentic.

(b) Personal bank or building society statements must:

(i) be the applicant's most recent statement,

(ii) be dated no earlier than one calendar month before the date of the application,

(iii) clearly show:

(1) the applicant's name,

(2) the applicant's account number,

(3) the date of the statement,

(4) the financial institution's name,

(5) the financial institution's logo, and

(6) transactions by the Sponsor covering the period no earlier than one calendar month before the date of the application, including the amount shown on the specified payslip as at 245GF-SD A.(a)

(iv) be either:

(1) printed on the bank's or building society's letterhead,

(2) electronic bank or building society statements, accompanied by a supporting letter from the bank or building society, on company headed paper, confirming the statement provided is authentic, or

(3) electronic bank or building society statements, bearing the official stamp of the bank or building society on every page,

and

(v) not be mini-statements from automatic teller machines (ATMs).

(c) Building society pass books must:

(i) clearly show:

(1) the applicant's name,

(2) the applicant's account number,

(3) the financial institution's name,

(4) the financial institution's logo, and

(5) transactions by the sponsor covering the period no earlier than one calendar month before the date of the application, including the amount shown on the specified payslip as at 245GF-SD A.(a)

and

(ii) be either:

(1) the original pass book, or

(2) a photocopy of the pass book which has been certified by the issuing building society on company headed paper, confirming the statement provided is authentic.

B. A letter from the employer detailing the purpose and period of absences in connection with the employment, including periods of annual leave. Where the absence was due to a serious or compelling reason, a personal letter from the applicant which includes full details of the reason for the absences and all original supporting documents in relation to those reasons – e.g. medical certificates, birth/death certificates, information about the reasons which led to the absence from the UK.

C. Where the applicant is not being paid the appropriate rate in Appendix J due to maternity, paternity or adoption leave:

(a) Payslips must be:

(i) the applicant's payslip from the month immediately preceding the leave,

(ii) the applicant's payslips for each month of the period of the leave,

(iii) as set out in A(a)(iii) above.

(b) Bank or building society statements must be:

(i) the applicant's statement from the month immediately preceding the leave,

(ii) the applicant's statement for each month of the period of the leave,
(iii) as set out in A(b)(iii) above.

Note: Paragraph 245GF-SD substituted from 13 December 2012 (HC 760). Words deleted from subparagraphs (b)(iv)(2) and (3) from1 October 2013 subject to savings for applications made before that date (HC 628). Words substituted in opening sentence and subparagraph C inserted from 6 April 2013 (HC 1039).

Tier 2 (General) Migrants, Tier 2 (Minister of Religion) Migrants and Tier 2 (Sportsperson) Migrants

245H. Purpose of these routes and definitions

These routes enable UK employers to recruit workers from outside the EEA to fill a particular vacancy that cannot be filled by a British or EEA worker.

245HA. Entry clearance

All Migrants arriving in the UK and wishing to enter as a Tier 2 (General) Migrant, Tier 2 (Minister of Religion) Migrant or Tier 2 (Sportsperson) Migrant must have a valid entry clearance for entry under the relevant one of these routes. If they do not have a valid entry clearance, entry will be refused.

245HB. Requirements for entry clearance

To qualify for entry clearance as a Tier 2 (General) Migrant, Tier 2 (Minister of Religion) Migrant or Tier 2 (Sportsperson) Migrant, an applicant must meet the requirements listed below. If the applicant meets these requirements, entry clearance will be granted. if the applicant does not meet these requirements, the application will be refused.

Requirements:

(a) The applicant must not fall for refusal under the general grounds for refusal.

(b) If applying as a Tier 2 (General) Migrant, the applicant must have a minimum of 50 points under paragraphs 76 to 84A of Appendix A.

(c) If applying as a Tier 2 (Minister of religion) Migrant, the applicant must have a minimum of 50 points under paragraphs 85 to [92A] of Appendix A.

(d) If applying as a Tier 2 (sportsperson) Migrant, the applicant must have a minimum of 50 points under paragraphs 93 to 100 of Appendix A.

(e) The applicant must have a minimum of 10 points under paragraphs 1 to 18 of Appendix B.

(f) The applicant must have a minimum of 10 points under paragraphs 4 to 5 of Appendix C.

(g) The applicant must not have had entry clearance or leave to remain as a Tier 2 Migrant at any time during the 12 months immediately before the date of the application, unless the applicant:

(i) was not in the UK with leave as a Tier 2 Migrant during this period, and provides evidence to show this, or

(ii) will be paid a gross annual salary (as recorded by the Certificate of Sponsorship Checking Service entry, and including such allowances as are specified as acceptable for this purpose in paragraph 79 of Appendix A) of [£153,500] or higher.

(h) An applicant who has, or was last granted, leave as a Student, a Student Nurse, a Student Re-Sitting an Examination, a Student Writing-Up a Thesis, a Postgraduate Doctor or Dentist or a Tier 4 Migrant and:

(i) is currently being sponsored by a government or international scholarship agency, or

(ii) was being sponsored by a government or international scholarship agency, and that sponsorship came to an end 12 months ago or less

must provide the unconditional written consent of the sponsoring Government or agency to the application and must provide the specified documents as set out in paragraph 245A above, to show that this requirement has been met.

(i) The applicant must be at least 16 years old.

(j) Where the applicant is under 18 years of age, the application must be supported by the applicant's parents or legal guardian, or by one parent if that parent has sole legal responsibility for the child.

(k) Where the applicant is under 18 years of age, the applicant's parents or legal guardian, or one parent if that parent has sole responsibility for the child, must confirm that they consent to the arrangements for the applicant's travel to, and reception and care in, the UK.

(l) If the Sponsor is a limited company, the applicant must not own more than 10% of its shares{, unless the gross annual salary (as recorded by the Certificate of Sponsorship Checking Service entry, and including such allowances as are specified as acceptable for this purpose in paragraph 79 of Appendix A) is [£153,500] or higher.}

(m) If the applicant is applying as a Tier 2 (Minister of Religion) Migrant, the Entry Clearance Officer must be satisfied that the applicant:

(i) genuinely intends to undertake, and is capable of undertaking, the role recorded by the Certificate of Sponsorship Checking Service; and

(ii) will not undertake employment in the United Kingdom other than under the terms of paragraph [245HC(d)(iii)].

(n) To support the assessment in paragraph 245HB(m), the Entry Clearance Officer may:

(i) request additional information and evidence, and refuse the application if the information or evidence is not provided. Any requested documents must be received by the Home Office at the address specified in the request within 28 [calendar] days of the date the request is sent, and

(ii) request the applicant attends an interview, and refuse the application if the applicant fails to comply with any such request without providing a reasonable explanation.

(o) If the Entry Clearance Officer is not satisfied following the assessment in paragraph 245HB(m), no points will be awarded under paragraphs 85 to 92A of Appendix A.

(p) The Entry Clearance Officer may decide not to carry out the assessment in paragraph 245HB(m) if the application already falls for refusal on other grounds, but reserves the right to carry out this assessment in any reconsideration of the decision.

Note: Words substituted in subparagraph (c), words in curly brackets in subparagraph (l) inserted (both changes subject to savings for applications made before 1 October 2013) and subparagraph (m) inserted from 1 October 2013 (HC 628). Subparagraph (g) substituted from 6 April 2013 subject to savings for applications made before that date (HC 1039). Words substituted in subparagraphs (g)(ii) subparagraph (l) from 6 April 2014 subject to savings for applications made on ar after that date using a Certificate of Sponsorship assigned to the applicant before that date (HC 1138 as amended by HC 1201). Subparagraphs (m)(ii) and (n)(i) amended from 6 November 2014 subject to savings for applications made before that date (HC 693).

245HC. Period and conditions of grant

(a) Entry clearance will be granted for whichever of the following is the shorter:
(i) a period equal to the length of the period of engagement plus 1 month, or
(ii) the maximum time, as set out in (b).
(b) The maximum time referred to in (a)(ii) is:
(i) 5 years and 1 month, if the applicant is applying as a Tier 2 (General) Migrant; or
(ii) 3 years and 1 month, if the applicant is applying as a Tier 2 (Minister of Religion) Migrant or a Tier 2 (Sportsperson) Migrant.

(c) Entry clearance will be granted with effect from 14 days before the date that the Certificate of Sponsorship Checking Service records as the start date for the applicant's employment in the UK, unless entry clearance is being granted less than 14 days before that date, in which case it will be granted with immediate effect.

(d) Entry clearance will be subject to the following conditions:
(i) no recourse to public funds,
(ii) registration with the police, if this is required by paragraph 326 of these Rules, and
(iii) no employment except:
(1) working for the sponsor in the employment that the Certificate of Sponsorship Checking Service records that the migrant is being sponsored to do, subject to any notification of a change to the details of that employment, other than prohibited changes as defined in paragraph 323AA,
(2) supplementary employment,
(3) voluntary work, and
(4) if the applicant is applying as a Tier 2 (Sportsperson) Migrant, employment as a sportsperson for his national team while his national team is in the UK [and Temporary Engagement as a Sports Broadcaster].

(e) (i) Applicants who meet the requirements for entry clearance and who obtain points under paragraphs 76 to 79D of Appendix A shall be granted entry clearance as a Tier 2 (General) Migrant.

(ii) Applicants who meet the requirements for entry clearance and who obtain points under paragraphs 85 to 92 of Appendix A shall be granted entry clearance as a Tier 2 (Minister of Religion) Migrant.

(iii) Applicants who meet the requirements for entry clearance and who obtain points under paragraphs 93 to 100 of Appendix A shall be granted entry clearance as a Tier 2 (Sportsperson) Migrant.

Note: Subparagraphs (a)–(b) substituted and subsequent subparagraphs renumbered from 6 April 2014 subject to savings for applications made before that date (HC 1138 as amended by HC 1201). Words inserted in subparagraph (d)(iii)(iv) from 6 November 2014 subject to savings for applications made before that date (HC 693).

245HD. Requirements for leave to remain

To qualify for leave to remain as a Tier 2 (General) Migrant, Tier 2 (Minister of Religion Migrant or Tier 2 (Sportsperson) Migrant under this rule, an applicant must meet the requirements listed below. if the applicant meets these requirements, leave to remain will be granted. if the applicant does not meet these requirements, the application will be refused.

Requirements:

(a) The applicant must not fall for refusal under the general grounds for refusal, and must not be an illegal entrant.

(b) the applicant must:

(i) have, or have last been granted, entry clearance, leave to enter or leave to remain as:

(1) a Tier 1 Migrant,

(2) a Tier 2 Migrant,

(3) a Highly Skilled Migrant,

(4) an Innovator,

(5) a Jewish Agency Employee,

(6) a Member of the Operational Ground Staff of an Overseas-owned Airline,

(7) a Minister of Religion, Missionary or Member of a Religious Order,

(8) a Participant in the Fresh Talent: Working in Scotland Scheme,

(9) a Participant in the International Graduates Scheme (or its predecessor, the Science and Engineering Graduates Scheme),

(10) a Qualifying Work Permit Holder,

(11) a Representative of an Overseas Business

(12) a Representative of an Overseas Newspaper, News Agency or Broadcasting Organisation,

(13) a Tier 5 (Temporary Worker) Migrant, or

(14) the partner of a Relevant Points Based System Migrant if the relevant Points Based System Migrant is a Tier 4 Migrant,

or

(ii) [have, or have last been granted, entry clearance, leave to enter or leave to remain as]:

(1) a Tier 4 Migrant,

(2) a Student,

(3) a Student Nurse,

(4) a Student Re-Sitting an Examination,

(5) a Person Writing Up a Thesis,

(6) an Overseas Qualified Nurse or Midwife,

(7) a Postgraduate Doctor or Dentist, or

(8) a Student Union Sabbatical Officer.

(c) An applicant who has, or was last granted leave as a Tier 2 (Intra-Company Transfer) Migrant must:

(i) have previously had leave as a Tier 2 (Intra-Company Transfer) Migrant under the Rules in place before 6 April 2010, or in the Established Staff sub-category under the Rules in place before 6 April 2011,

(ii) not have been granted entry clearance in this or any other route since the grant of leave referred to in (i) above; and

(iii) not be applying to work for the same Sponsor as sponsored him when he was last granted leave.

(d) An applicant under the provisions in (b)(ii) above must meet the following requirements:

(i) The applicant must have completed and passed:

(1) a UK recognised [bachelor's or master's degree] (not a qualification of equivalent level which is not a degree),

(2) a UK Postgraduate Certificate in Education or Professional Graduate Diploma of Education (not a qualification of equivalent level),

or the applicant must have completed a minimum of 12 months study in the UK towards a UK PhD.

(ii) The applicant must have studied for the course in (d)(i) at a UK institution that is a UK recognised or listed body, or which holds a sponsor licence under Tier 4 of the Points Based System.

(iii) The applicant must have studied the course referred to in (d)(i) during:

(1) his last grant of leave, or

(2) a period of continuous leave which includes his last grant of leave, [(for these purposes continuous leave will not be considered to have been broken if any of the circumstances set out in paragraphs 245AAA(a)(i) to (iii) of these Rules apply.)].

(iv) The applicant's periods of UK study and/or research towards the course in (i) must have been undertaken whilst he had entry clearance, leave to enter or leave to remain in the UK that was not subject to a restriction preventing him from undertaking that course of study and/or research.

(v) If the institution studied at is removed from the Tier 4 Sponsor Register, the applicant's qualification must not have been obtained on or after the date of removal from the Sponsor Register.

(vi) If the applicant:

(1) is currently being sponsored by a government or international scholarship agency, or

(2) was being sponsored by a government or international scholarship agency, and that sponsorship came to an end 12 months ago or less,

the applicant must provide the unconditional written consent of the sponsoring Government or agency to the application and must provide the specified documents as set out in paragraph 245A above, to show that this requirement has been met.

(vii) The applicant must provide an original degree certificate, academic transcript or an academic reference on official headed paper of the institution, which clearly shows:

(1) The applicant's name,

(2) the course title/award,

(3) the course duration (except in the case of a degree certificate), and

(4) unless the course is a PhD course, the date of course completion and pass (or the date of award in the case of a degree certificate).

(e) an applicant who was last granted leave as a Tier 5 (Temporary Worker) Migrant must have been granted such leave in the Creative and Sporting sub-category of Tier 5 in order to allow the applicant to work as a professional footballer, and the applicant must be applying for leave to remain as a Tier 2 (Sportsperson) Migrant.

(f) If applying as a Tier 2 (General) Migrant, the applicant must have a minimum of 50 points under paragraphs 76 to 79D of Appendix A.

(g) If applying as a Tier 2 (Minister of Religion) Migrant, the applicant must have a minimum of 50 points under paragraphs 85 to [92A] of Appendix A.

(h) If applying as a Tier 2 (Sportsperson) Migrant, the applicant must have a minimum of 50 points under paragraphs 93 to 100 of Appendix A.

(i) The applicant must have a minimum of 10 points under paragraphs 1 to 16 of Appendix B.

(j) The applicant must have a minimum of 10 points under paragraphs 4 to 5 of Appendix C.

(k) The applicant must not have had entry clearance or leave to remain as a Tier 2 Migrant at any time during the 12 months immediately before the date of the application, unless:

(i) the applicant's last grant of leave was as a Tier 2 Migrant,

(ii) the applicant was not in the UK with leave as a Tier 2 Migrant during this period, and provides evidence to show this, or

(iii) the applicant will be paid a gross annual salary (as recorded by the Certificate of Sponsorship Checking Service entry, and including such allowances as are specified as acceptable for this purpose in paragraph 79 of Appendix A) of [£153,500] or higher.

(l) The applicant must be at least 16 years old.

(m) Where the applicant is under 18 years of age, the application must be supported by the applicant's parents or legal guardian, or by just one parent if that parent has sole legal responsibility for the child.

(n) Where the applicant is under 18 years of age, the applicant's parents or legal guardian, or just one parent if that parent has sole legal responsibility for the child, must confirm that they consent to the arrangements for the applicant's care in the UK.

(o) if the sponsor is a limited company, the applicant must not own more than 10% of its shares, [unless the gross annual salary (as recorded by the Certificate of Sponsorship Checking Service entry, and including such allowances as are specified as acceptable for this purpose in paragraph 79 of Appendix A) is [£153,500] or higher].

(p) The applicant must not be in the UK in breach of immigration laws except that any period of overstaying for a period of 28 days or less will be disregarded.

(q) If the applicant is applying as a Tier 2 (Minister of Religion) Migrant, the Secretary of State must be satisfied that the applicant:

(i) genuinely intends to undertake, and is capable of undertaking, the role recorded by the Certificate of Sponsorship Checking Service; and

(ii) will not undertake employment in the United Kingdom other than under the terms of paragraph [245HE(d)(iii)].

(r) To support the assessment in paragraph 245HD(q), the Secretary of State may:

(i) request additional information and evidence, and refuse the application if the information or evidence is not provided. Any requested documents must be received by the Home Office at the address specified in the request within 28 [calendar] days of the date the request is sent, and

(ii) request the applicant attends an interview, and refuse the application if the applicant fails to comply with any such request without providing a reasonable explanation.

(s) If the Secretary of State is not satisfied following the assessment in paragraph 245HD(q), no points will be awarded under paragraphs 85 to 92A of Appendix A.

(t) The Secretary of State may decide not to carry out the assessment in paragraph 245HD(q) if the application already falls for refusal on other grounds, but reserves the right to carry out this assessment in any reconsideration of the decision.

Note: Subparagraphs (d)(vii)(3) and (4) substituted from 13 December 2012 (subject to savings for applications made before that date) and subparagraph (k) substituted from 13 December 2012 (HC 760). Subparagraphs (b)(ii), (d)(i)(1), (d)(iii)(2) amended and (k)(iii) inserted from 6 April 2013 subject to savings for applications made before that date (HC 1039). Words substituted/inserted in subparagraphs (g) and (o) (both changes subject to savings for applications made before 1 October 2013) and subparagraph (q)–(t) inserted from 1 October 2013 (HC 628). Words substituted in subparagraphs (k)(iii) and (o) subject to savings for applications made on or after that date using a Certificate of Sponsorship assigned to the applicant before that date (HC 1138 as amended by

HC 1201). Words substituted in subparagraphs (q)(ii) and (r)(i) from 6 November 2014 subject to savings for applications made before that date (HC 693).

245HE. Period and conditions of grant

(a) Leave to remain will be granted for whichever of the following is the shortest:

(i) the length of the period of engagement plus 14 days,

(ii) 5 years if the applicant is applying as a Tier 2 (General) Migrant, or

(iii) 3 years if the applicant is applying as a Tier 2 (Minister of Religion) Migrant or a Tier 2 (Sportsperson) Migrant, or

(iv) except where (b) applies, the difference between the continuous period of leave that the applicant has already been granted (notwithstanding any breaks between periods of leave of up to 28 days) as a Tier 2 Migrant [(other than as a Tier 2 (Intra-Company Transfer) Migrant)], and 6 years.

If the calculation of period of leave comes to zero or a negative number, leave to remain will be refused.

(b) The 6 year restriction set out in (a)(iv) will not apply if the applicant:

(i) previously had leave under the Rules in place before 6 April 2011 as:

(1) a Tier 2 (General) Migrant,

(2) a Tier 2 (Minister of Religion) Migrant,

(3) a Tier 2 (Sportsperson) Migrant,

(4) a Jewish Agency Employee,

(5) a Member of the Operational Ground Staff of an Overseas-owned Airline,

(6) a Minister of Religion, Missionary or Member of a Religious Order,

(7) a Qualifying Work Permit Holder, or

(8) a Representative of an Overseas Newspaper, News Agency or Broadcasting Organisation,

and

(ii) has not been granted entry clearance as a Tier 2 (General) Migrant, Tier 2 (Minister of Religion) Migrant or Tier 2 (Sportsperson) Migrant under the Rules in place from 6 April 2011, and

(iii) has not been granted entry clearance, leave to enter or leave to remain in any other category since the grant of leave referred to in (i) above.

(c) In addition to the period in (a), leave to remain will be granted for the period between the date that the application is decided and the date that the Certificate of Sponsorship Checking Service records as the start date of employment in the UK, provided this is not a negative value.

(d) leave to remain will be granted subject to the following conditions:

(i) no recourse to public funds,

(ii) registration with the police, if this is required by paragraph 326 of these Rules, and

(iii) no employment except:

(1) working for the sponsor in the employment that the Certificate of Sponsorship Checking Service records that the migrant is being sponsored to do, subject to any notification of a change to the details of that employment, other than prohibited changes as defined in paragraph 323AA,

(2) supplementary employment,

(3) voluntary work,

(4) until the start date of the period of engagement, any employment which the applicant was lawfully engaged in on the date of his application, and

(5) if the applicant is applying as a Tier 2 (Sportsperson) Migrant, employment as a sportsperson for his national team while his national team is in the UK [and Temporary Engagement as a Sports Broadcaster].

(e) (i) Applicants who meet the requirements for leave to remain and who obtain points under paragraphs 76 to 79D of Appendix A shall be granted leave to remain as a Tier 2 (General) Migrant.

(ii) Applicants who meet the requirements for leave to remain and who obtain points under paragraphs 85 to 92 of Appendix A shall be granted leave to remain as a Tier 2 (Minister of Religion) Migrant.

(iii) Applicants who meet the requirements for leave to remain and who obtain points under paragraphs 93 to 100 of Appendix A shall be granted leave to remain as a Tier 2 (Sportsperson) Migrant.

Note: Subparagraphs (a)–(f) substituted and subparagraphs (d) and (e) renumbered from 6 April 2014 subject to savings for applications made before that date (HC 1138 as amended by HC 1201). Words inserted in subparagraphs (a)(iv) and (d)(iii)(5) from 6 November 2014 subject to savings for applications made before that date (HC 693).

245HF. Requirements for indefinite leave to remain

To qualify for indefinite leave to remain as a Tier 2 (General) Migrant, Tier 2 (Minister of Religion) Migrant or Tier 2 (Sportsperson) Migrant, an applicant must meet the requirements listed below. If the applicant meets these requirements, indefinite leave to remain will be granted. If the applicant does not meet these requirements, the application will be refused.

Requirements:

(a) DELETED

(b) The applicant must not fall for refusal under the general grounds for refusal, and must not be an illegal entrant.

(c) The applicant must have spent a continuous period of 5 years lawfully in the UK, of which the most recent period must have been spent with leave as a Tier 2 Migrant, in any combination of the following categories:

(i) as a Member of the Operational Ground Staff of an Overseas-owned Airline,

(ii) as a Minister of Religion, Missionary or Member of a Religious Order,

(iii) as a Qualifying Work Permit Holder,

(iv) as a Representative of an Overseas Business,

(v) as a Representative of an Overseas Newspaper, News Agency or Broadcasting Organisation,

(vi) as a Tier 1 Migrant, other than a Tier 1 (Post Study Work) Migrant,

(vii) as a Highly Skilled Migrant,

(viii) as an innovator,

(ix) as a Tier 2 (General) Migrant, a Tier 2 (Minister of Religion) Migrant or a Tier 2 (Sportsperson) Migrant, or

(x) as a Tier 2 (Intra-Company Transfer) Migrant, provided the continuous period of 5 years spent lawfully in the UK includes a period of leave as:

(1) a Tier 2 (Intra-Company Transfer) Migrant granted under the Rules in place before 6 April 2010, or

(2) a Qualifying Work Permit Holder, provided that the work permit was granted because the applicant was the subject of an Intra-Company Transfer.

(d) The Sponsor that issued the Certificate of Sponsorship that led to the applicant's last grant of leave must:

(i) still hold, or have applied for a renewal of, a Tier 2 Sponsor licence in the relevant category; and

(ii) certify in writing that:

(1) he still requires the applicant for the employment in question, and

(2) in the case of a Tier 2 (General) Migrant applying for settlement, the applicant is paid at or above the appropriate rate for the job as stated in the Codes of Practice in Appendix J, or where the applicant is not paid at that rate only due to maternity, paternity or adoption leave, the date that leave started and that the applicant was paid at the appropriate rate immediately before the leave.

(e) The applicant provides the specified documents in paragraph 245HF-SD to evidence the sponsor's certification in subsection (d)(ii) and to evidence the reason for the absences set out in paragraph 245AAA.

(f) The applicant must have sufficient knowledge of the English language and sufficient knowledge about life in the United Kingdom, in accordance with Appendix KoLL.

(g) The applicant must not be in the UK in breach of immigration laws except that any period of overstaying for a period of 28 days or less will be disregarded.

(h) For the purposes of sub-paragraph (c), time spent with valid leave in the Bailiwick of Guernsey, the Bailiwick of Jersey or the Isle of Man in a category equivalent to any of the categories set out in (c)(i) to (x), may be included in the continuous period of 5 years lawful residence, provided that:

(i) where the leave is in category (x), the continuous period of 5 years includes a period of leave as a Tier 2 (Intra-Company Transfer) Migrant granted before 6 April 2010, or a Qualifying Work Permit Holder (provided the work permit was granted because the applicant was the subject of an Intra-Company Transfer); and

(ii) any period of leave granted in the Bailiwick of Guernsey, the Bailiwick of Jersey or the Isle of Man as a work permit holder or as a Tier 2 Migrant was for employment:

(a) in a job which appears on the list of occupations skilled to National Qualifications Framework level 3 or above (or from 6 April 2011, National Qualifications Framework level 4 or above or from 14 June 2012, National Qualifications Framework level 6 or above), as stated in the Codes of Practice in Appendix J, or

(b) in a job which appears in the Creative Sector Codes of Practice in Appendix J, or

(c) as a professional sportsperson (including as a sports coach); and

(iii) the most recent period of leave was granted in the UK as a Tier 2 Migrant.

In any such case, references to the "UK" in paragraph 245AAA shall include a reference to the Bailiwick of Guernsey, Bailiwick of Jersey or the Isle of Man, as the case may be.

Note: Subparagraph (d) substituted from 1 October 2013 (subject to savings for applications made before that date) and subparagraph (f) substituted from 28 October 2013 (subject to savings for applications made before that date) (HC 628). Words inserted in subparagraph (d)(ii) and subparagraph (h) inserted from 6 April 2013 (HC 1039).

245HF-SD Specified documents

The specified documents referred to in paragraph 245HF(e) are set out in A, B and C below:

A. Either a payslip and a personal bank or building society statement, or a payslip and a building society pass book.

(a) Payslips must be:
(i) the applicant's most recent payslip,
(ii) dated no earlier than one calendar month before the date of the application, and
(iii) either:
(1) an original payslip,
(2) on company-headed paper, or
(3) accompanied by a letter from the applicant's Sponsor, on company headed paper and signed by a senior official, confirming the payslip is authentic.
(b) Personal bank or building society statements must:
(i) be the applicant's most recent statement,
(ii) be dated no earlier than one calendar month before the date of the application,
(iii) clearly show:
(1) the applicant's name,
(2) the applicant's account number,
(3) the date of the statement,
(4) the financial institution's name,
(5) the financial institution's logo, and
(6) transactions by the Sponsor covering the period no earlier than one calendar month before the date of the application, including the amount shown on the specified payslip as at 245HF-SD A.(a)
(iv) be either:
(1) printed on the bank's or building society's letterhead,
(2) electronic bank or building society statements . . ., accompanied by a supporting letter from the bank or building society, on company headed paper, confirming the statement provided is authentic, or
(3) electronic bank or building society statements . . ., bearing the official stamp of the bank or building society on every page,
and
(v) not be mini-statements from automatic teller machines (ATMs).
(c) Building society pass books must
(i) clearly show:
(1) the applicant's name,
(2) the applicant's account number,
(3) the financial institution's name,
(4) the financial institution's logo, and
(5) transactions by the sponsor covering the period no earlier than one calendar month before the date of the application, including the amount shown on the specified payslip as at 245HF-SD A.(a)
and
(ii) be either:
(1) the original pass book, or
(2) a photocopy of the pass book which has been certified by the issuing building society on company headed paper, confirming the statement provided is authentic.

B. A letter from the employer detailing the purpose and period of absences in connection with the employment, including periods of annual leave. Where the absence was due to a serious or compelling reason, a personal letter from the applicant which includes full details of the reason for the absences and all original supporting documents in relation to those reasons – e.g. medical certificates, birth/death certificates, information about the reasons which led to the absence from the UK.

C. Where the applicant is not being paid the appropriate rate in Appendix J due to maternity, paternity or adoption leave:

(a) Payslips must be:

(i) the applicant's payslip from the month immediately preceding the leave,

(ii) the applicant's payslips for each month of the period of the leave,

(iii) as set out in A(a)(iii) above.

(b) Bank or building society statements must be:

(i) the applicant's statement from the month immediately preceding the leave,

(ii) the applicant's statements for each month of the period of the leave,

(iii) as set out in A(b)(iii) above.

Note: Paragraph 245HF-SD substituted from 13 December 2012 (HC 760). Subparagraphs A(b)(iv)(2) and (3) subject to savings for applications made before 1 October 2013 (HC 628). Subparagraph C inserted from 6 April 2013 (HC 1039).

Tier 5 (Youth Mobility Scheme) Temporary Migrants

245ZI. Purpose of this route

This route is for sponsored young people from participating countries and territories who wish to live and work temporarily in the UK.

245ZJ. Entry clearance

All migrants arriving in the UK and wishing to enter as a Tier 5 (Youth Mobility Scheme) Temporary Migrant must have a valid entry clearance for entry under this route. If a migrant does not have a valid entry clearance, entry will be refused.

245ZK. Requirements for entry clearance

To qualify for entry clearance as a Tier 5 (Youth Mobility Scheme) Temporary Migrant, an applicant must meet the requirements listed below. However, whether or not the requirements listed below are met, if a citizen of a country or the rightful holder of a passport issued by a territory listed in Appendix G makes an application for entry clearance which, if granted, would mean that the annual allocation of places under this route as specified in Appendix G for citizens of that country or rightful holders of passports issued by that territory would be exceeded, the application will be refused. The applicant will also be refused if the requirements listed below are not met.

Requirements:

(a) The applicant must not fall for refusal under the general grounds for refusal; and

(b) The applicant must be:

(i) a citizen of a country or rightful holder of a passport issued by a territory listed in Appendix G to these Rules, or

(ii) a British Overseas Citizen, British Overseas Territories Citizen or British National (Overseas), as defined by the British Nationality Act 1981 and must provide a valid passport to show that this requirement has been met; and

(c) The applicant must be sponsored by his country of citizenship or the territory of which he is a rightful passport holder as follows:

(i) If the applicant is a citizen of a country or the rightful holder of a passport issued by a territory that does not have Deemed Sponsorship Status, the applicant must hold a valid Certificate of Sponsorship issued by that country or territory and must use that Certificate of Sponsorship in support of an application lodged in the country or territory of issue; or

(ii) If the applicant is a citizen of a country or the rightful holder of a passport issued by a territory that has Deemed Sponsorship Status, his valid passport issued by the country or territory holding such status will stand as evidence of sponsorship and the application for leave may be made at any post worldwide; and

(ca) A Certificate of Sponsorship will only be considered to be valid if:

(i) the country or territory issued it to the applicant no more than 3 months before the application for entry clearance is made, and

(ii) it has not have been cancelled by the country or territory since it was issued.

(d) The applicant must have a minimum of 40 points under paragraphs 101 to 104 of Appendix A; and

(e) The applicant must have a minimum of 10 points under paragraphs 6 to 7 of Appendix C; and

(f) The applicant must have no children under the age of 18 who are either living with him or for whom he is financially responsible; and

(g) The applicant must not previously have spent time in the UK as a Working Holidaymaker or a Tier 5 (Youth Mobility Scheme) Temporary Migrant.

245ZL. Period and conditions of grant

Entry clearance will be granted for a period of 2 years subject to the following conditions:

(a) no recourse to public funds,

(b) registration with the police, if this is required by paragraph 326 of these Rules,

(c) no employment as a professional sportsperson (including as a sports coach), and

(d) no employment as a Doctor or Dentist in Training, unless the applicant has obtained a degree in medicine or dentistry at bachelor's level or above from a UK institution that is a UK recognised or listed body, or which holds a sponsor licence under Tier 4 of the Points Based System, and provides evidence of this degree.

(e) no self employment, except where the following conditions are met:

(i) the migrant has no premises which he owns, other than his home, from which he carries out his business,

(ii) the total value of any equipment used in the business does not exceed £5,000, and

(iii) the migrant has no employees.

Tier 5 (Temporary Worker) Migrants

245ZM. Purpose of this route and definitions

(a) This route is for certain types of temporary worker whose entry helps to satisfy cultural, charitable, religious or international objectives including volunteering and job shadowing.

(b) For the purposes of paragraphs 245ZM to 245ZS and paragraphs 105 to 112 of Appendix A:

a migrant has "consecutive engagements" if:

(i) more than one Certificate of Sponsorship reference number has been allocated in respect of the migrant,

(ii) there is no gap of more than 14 days between any of the periods of engagement, and

(iii) all the Certificate of Sponsorship Checking Service references record that the migrant is being sponsored in the creative and sporting subcategory of the Tier 5 (Temporary Worker) Migrant route.

"Period of engagement" means a period beginning with the employment start date as recorded on the Certificate of Sponsorship Checking Service entry which relates to the Certificate of Sponsorship reference number for which the migrant was awarded points under paragraphs 105 to 111 of Appendix A, and ending on the employment end date as recorded in the same entry.

245ZN. Entry clearance

(a) Subject to paragraph (b), all migrants arriving in the UK and wishing to enter as a Tier 5 (Temporary Worker) Migrant must have a valid entry clearance for entry under this route. If they do not have a valid entry clearance, entry will be refused.

(b) A migrant arriving in the UK and wishing to enter as a Tier 5 (Temporary Worker) Migrant who does not have a valid entry clearance will not be refused entry if the following conditions are met:

(i) the migrant is not a visa national,

(ii) the Certificate of Sponsorship reference number provided by the migrant leading to points being obtained under Appendix A links to an entry in the Certificate of Sponsorship Checking Service recording that their Sponsor has sponsored them in the creative and sporting subcategory of the Tier 5 (Temporary Worker) Migrant route,

(iii) if the migrant has consecutive engagements, the total length of all the periods of engagement, together with any gap between those engagements, is 3 months or less,

(iv) if the migrant does not have consecutive engagements, the total length of the period of engagement is 3 months or less, and

(v) the migrant meets the requirements in paragraph 245ZO below.

245ZO. Requirements for entry clearance or leave to enter

To qualify for entry clearance or, as the case may be, leave to enter, as a Tier 5 (Temporary Worker) Migrant, an applicant must meet the requirements listed below. If the applicant meets these requirements, entry clearance will be granted. If the applicant does not meet these requirements, the application will be refused.

Requirements:

(a) The applicant must not fall for refusal under the general grounds for refusal.

(b) The applicant must have a minimum of 30 points under paragraphs 105 to 112 of Appendix A.

(c) The applicant must have a minimum of 10 points under paragraphs 8 to 9 of Appendix C.

(d) Where the applicant is under 18 years of age, the application must be supported by the applicant's parents or legal guardian, or by just one parent if that parent has sole legal responsibility for the child.

(e) Where the applicant is under 18 years of age, the applicant's parents or legal guardian, or just one parent if that parent has sole responsibility for the child, must confirm that they consent to the arrangements for the applicant's travel to, and reception and care in, the UK.

(f) An applicant being sponsored in the international agreement sub-category of Tier 5 (Temporary Workers) as a private servant in a diplomatic household must:

(i) be no less than 18 years of age at the time of application, and

(ii) provide evidence of agreed written terms and conditions of employment in the UK with his employer including specifically that the applicant will be paid in accordance with the National Minimum Wage Act 1998 and regulations made under that Act, in the form set out in Appendix Q.

(g) The employer referred to in (f)(ii) must be:

(i) a diplomat, or

(ii) an employee of an international organisation recognised by Her Majesty's Government, who enjoys certain privileges or immunity under UK or international law.

(h) Where the Certificate of Sponsorship Checking Service reference number for which the applicant was awarded points under Appendix A records that the applicant is being sponsored as a Contractual Service Supplier, or Independent Professional in the International Agreement sub-category of the Tier 5 (Temporary Worker) Migrant route, the grant of leave to enter will not result in the applicant being granted leave to enter or remain as a Contractual Service Supplier, or Independent Professional under the International Agreement sub-category of the Tier 5 (Temporary Worker) Migrant route for a cumulative period exceeding 6 months in any 12 month period ending during the period of leave to enter requested.

(i) The Entry Clearance Officer or Immigration Officer must be satisfied that the applicant:

(i) genuinely intends to undertake, and is capable of undertaking, the role recorded by the Certificate of Sponsorship Checking Service; and

(ii) will not undertake employment in the United Kingdom other than under the terms of paragraph 245ZP(f)(iii).

(j) To support the assessment in paragraph 245ZO(i), the Entry Clearance Officer or Immigration Officer may:

(i) request additional information and evidence, and refuse the application if the information or evidence is not provided. Any requested documents must be received by the Home Office at the address specified in the request within 28 [calendar] days of the date the request is sent, and

(ii) request the applicant attends an interview, and refuse the application if the applicant fails to comply with any such request without providing a reasonable explanation.

(k) If the Entry Clearance Officer or Immigration Officer is not satisfied following the assessment in paragraph 245ZO(i), no points will be awarded under paragraphs 105 to 112 of Appendix A.

(l) The Entry Clearance Officer or Immigration Officer may decide not to carry out the assessment in paragraph 245ZO(i) if the application already falls for refusal on other grounds, but reserves the right to carry out this assessment in any reconsideration of the decision.

Note: Subparagraphs (g) and (h) inserted from 13 December 2012 subject to savings for applications made before that date (HC 760). Subparagraphs (i)–(i) inserted from 1 October 2013 (HC 628). Words 'or independent professional' inserted from 6 April 2013 subject to savings for applications made before that date (HC 1039). Word substituted in subparagraph (j)(i) from 6 November 2014 subject to savings for applications made before that date (HC 693).

245ZP. Period and conditions of grant

(a) Where paragraph 245ZN(b) applies and the applicant has consecutive engagements, leave to enter will be granted for:

(i) a period commencing not more than 14 days before the beginning of the first period of engagement and ending 14 days after the end of the last period of engagement, or

(ii) 3 months

whichever is the shorter.

(b) Where paragraph 245ZN(b) applies and the applicant does not have consecutive engagements, leave to enter will be granted for:

(i) a period commencing not more than 14 days before the beginning of the period of engagement and ending 14 days after the end of that period of engagement, or

(ii) 3 months

whichever is the shorter.

(c) Where paragraph 245ZN(b) does not apply and the Certificate of Sponsorship Checking Service reference number for which the applicant was awarded points under Appendix A records that the applicant is being sponsored in the Creative and Sporting subcategory, the Government Authorised Exchange subcategory for a Work Experience Programme, or the Charity Workers sub-category of the Tier 5 (Temporary Worker) Migrant route, entry clearance or leave to enter will be granted for:

(i) a period commencing 14 days before the beginning of the period of engagement (or of the first period of engagement, where the applicant has consecutive engagements) and ending 14 days after the end of that period of engagement (or of the last period of engagement, where the applicant has consecutive engagements), or

(ii) 12 months

whichever of (i) or (ii) is the shorter.

(d) Where paragraph 245ZN(b) does not apply and the Certificate of Sponsorship Checking Service reference number for which the applicant was awarded points under Appendix A records that the applicant is being sponsored in the religious workers, {the Government Authorised Exchange subcategory} [for a Research Programme, Training Programme or Overseas Government Language Programme], or other than as a Contractual Service Supplier, or Independent Professional, in the international agreement subcategory of the Tier 5 (Temporary Worker) Migrant route, entry clearance will be granted for:

(i) a period commencing 14 days before the beginning of the period of engagement and ending 14 days after the end of that period of engagement, or

(ii) 2 years,

whichever is the shorter.

(e) Where paragraph 245ZN(b) does not apply and the Certificate of Sponsorship Checking Service reference number for which the applicant was awarded points under Appendix A records that the applicant is being sponsored as a Contractual Service Supplier, or Independent Professional in the International Agreement sub-category of the Tier 5 (Temporary Worker) Migrant route, entry clearance will be granted for:

(i) a period commencing 14 days before the beginning of the period of engagement and ending 14 days after the end of that period of engagement, or

(ii) 6 months,

whichever is the shorter.

(f) Leave to enter and entry clearance will be granted subject to the following conditions:

(i) no recourse to public funds,

(ii) registration with the police if this is required by paragraph 326 of these Rules, and

(iii) no employment except:

(1) unless paragraph (2) applies, working for the person who for the time being is the Sponsor in the employment that the Certificate of Sponsorship Checking Service records that the migrant is being sponsored to do for that Sponsor,

(2) in the case of a migrant whom the Certificate of Sponsorship Checking Service records as being sponsored in the Government Authorised Exchange subcategory of Tier 5 (Temporary Workers), the work, volunteering or job shadowing authorised by the Sponsor and that the Certificate of Sponsorship Checking Service records that the migrant is being sponsored to do,

(3) supplementary employment except in the case of a migrant whom the Certificate of Sponsorship Checking Service records as being sponsored in the international agreement sub-category, to work as a private servant in a diplomatic household or as a Contractual Service Supplier, or Independent Professional, and

(4) in the case of a migrant whom the Certificate of Sponsorship Checking Service records as being sponsored in the creative and sporting subcategory of Tier 5 (Temporary Workers), employment as a sportsperson for his national team while his national team is in the UK and Temporary Engagement as a Sports Broadcaster.

(iv) in the case of an applicant whom the Certificate of Sponsorship Checking Service records as being sponsored in the international agreement sub-category of Tier 5 (Temporary Workers), to work as a private servant in a diplomatic household, the employment in (iii)(1) above means working only in the household of the employer recorded by the Certificate of Sponsorship Checking Service.

Note: Subparagraph (d) substituted from 13 December 2013 subject to savings for applications made before that date (HC 760). Words 'or independent professional' inserted and words in curly brackets in subparagraph (d) substituted from 6 April 2013 subject to savings for applications made before that date (HC 1039). Words substituted in subparagraph (d) from 6 April 2014 subject to savings for applications made before that date (HC 1138 as amended by HC 1201).

245ZQ. Requirements for leave to remain

To qualify for leave to remain as a Tier 5 (Temporary Worker) Migrant under this rule, an applicant must meet the requirements listed below. Subject to paragraph 245ZR(a), if the applicant meets these requirements, leave to remain will be granted. If the applicant does not meet these requirements, the application will be refused.

Requirements:

(a) The applicant must not fall for refusal under the general grounds for refusal, and must not be an illegal entrant.

(b) The applicant must have, or have last been granted.

(i) entry clearance or leave to remain as a Tier 5 (Temporary Worker) Migrant, or

(ii) entry clearance, leave to enter or leave to remain as a Sports Visitor or Entertainer Visitor, provided:

(1) the Certificate of Sponsorship Checking Service reference for which he is being awarded points in this application shows that he is being sponsored in the creative and sporting subcategory; and

(2) the Certificate of Sponsorship reference number was allocated to the applicant before he entered the UK as a Sports Visitor or Entertainer Visitor, or

(iii) entry clearance, leave to enter or leave to remain as an Overseas Government Employee, provided

(a) the Certificate of Sponsorship Checking Service reference for which he is being awarded points in this application shows he is being sponsored in the international agreement sub-category, and

(b) the applicant is continuing employment with the same overseas government or international organisation for which earlier leave was granted, or

(iv) entry clearance, leave to enter or leave to remain as a Qualifying Work Permit Holder, provided, or

(a) the applicant was previously issued with a work permit for the purpose of employment by an overseas government, and

(b) the Certificate of Sponsorship Checking Service reference for which he is being awarded points in this application shows he is being sponsored in the international agreement sub-category, and

(c) the applicant is continuing employment with the same overseas government or international organisation for which earlier leave was granted

(v) entry clearance, leave to enter or leave to remain as a Qualifying Work Permit Holder, provided

(1) the applicant was previously issued with a work permit for the purpose of employment as a sponsored researcher, and

(2) the Certificate of Sponsorship Checking Service reference for which he is being awarded points in this application shows he is being sponsored in the government authorised exchange sub-category, and

(3) the applicant is continuing employment with the same organisation for which his most recent period of leave was granted, or

(vi) entry clearance, leave to enter or leave to remain as a Student, a Student Re-Sitting an Examination, a Person Writing Up a Thesis, a Postgraduate Doctor or Dentist, a Student Nurse, a Student Union Sabbatical Officer, or a Tier 4 (General) Migrant, provided the Certificate of Sponsorship Checking Service reference for which he is being awarded points in this application confirms:

(1) he is being sponsored in the government authorised exchange sub-category, and

(2) he lawfully obtained a UK recognised bachelor or postgraduate degree (not a qualification of equivalent level which is not a degree) during his last grant of leave, and

(3) he is being sponsored to:

(a) undertake a period of postgraduate professional training or work experience which is required to obtain a professional qualification or professional registration in the same professional field as the qualification in (2) above, and will not be filling a permanent vacancy, such that the employer he is directed to work for by the Sponsor does not intend to employ him in the UK once the training or work experience for which he is being sponsored has concluded, or

(b) undertake an internship for up to 12 months which directly relates to the qualification in (2) above, and will not be filling a permanent vacancy, such that the employer he is directed to work for by the Sponsor does not intend to employ him in the UK once the training or work experience for which he is being sponsored has concluded,

(c) The applicant must have a minimum of 30 points under paragraphs 105 to 112 of Appendix A.

(d) The applicant must have a minimum of 10 points under paragraphs 8 to 9 of Appendix C.

(e) The Certificate of Sponsorship Checking Service entry to which the Certificate of Sponsorship reference number for which points under Appendix A were awarded relates must:

(i) record that the applicant is being sponsored in the same subcategory of the Tier 5 (Temporary Worker) Migrant route as the one in which he was being sponsored to work for when he was last granted entry clearance or leave to remain as a Tier 5 (Temporary Worker) Migrant, and

(ii) in the case of an applicant who the Certificate of Sponsorship Checking Service records as being sponsored in the international agreement sub-category of Tier 5 (Temporary Workers), to work as a private servant in a diplomatic household, who entered the UK with a valid entry clearance in that capacity under the Rules in place from 6 April 2012, record that the applicant is being sponsored to work for the same employer [as set out in paragraph 245ZO (g) who] he was being sponsored to work for when he was last granted entry clearance or leave to remain as a Tier 5 (Temporary Worker) Migrant, and the applicant must have continued to work for that employer throughout his period of leave and must provide evidence of agreed written terms and conditions of employment in the UK with his employer in the form set out in Appendix Q.

(f) Where the applicant is under 18 years of age, the application must be supported by the applicant' parents or legal guardian, or by just one parent if that parent has sole legal responsibility for the child.

(g) Where the applicant is under 18 years of age, the applicant's parents or legal guardian, or just one parent if that parent has sole legal responsibility for the child, must confirm that they consent to the arrangements for the applicant's care in the UK.

(h) An applicant who has, or was last granted, leave as a Student, a Student Re-Sitting an Examination, a Person Writing Up a Thesis, a Postgraduate Doctor or Dentist, a Student Nurse, a Student Union Sabbatical Officer, or a Tier 4 (General) Migrant and:

(i) is currently being sponsored by a government or international scholarship agency, or

(ii) was being sponsored by a government or international scholarship agency, and that sponsorship came to an end 12 months ago or less

must provide the unconditional written consent of the sponsoring Government or agency to the application and must provide the specified documents as set out in paragraph 245A above, to show that this requirement has been met.

(i) The applicant must not be in the UK in breach of immigration laws except that any period of overstaying for a period of 28 days or less will be disregarded.

(j) Where the Certificate of Sponsorship Checking Service reference number for which the applicant was awarded points under Appendix A records that the applicant is being sponsored as a Contractual Service Supplier, or Independent Professional in the International Agreement subcategory of the Tier 5 (Temporary Worker) Migrant route, the grant of leave to remain will not result in the applicant being granted leave to enter or remain as a Contractual Service Supplier, or Independent Professional under the international agreement sub-category of the Tier 5 (Temporary Worker) Migrant route for a cumulative period exceeding 6 months in any 12 month period ending during the period of leave to remain requested.

(k) The Secretary of State must be satisfied that the applicant:

(i) genuinely intends to undertake, and is capable of undertaking, the role recorded by the Certificate of Sponsorship Checking Service; and

(ii) will not undertake employment in the United Kingdom other than under the terms of paragraph 245ZR(h)(iii).

(l) To support the assessment in paragraph 245ZQ(k), the Secretary of State may:

(i) request additional information and evidence, and refuse the application if the information or evidence is not provided. Any requested documents must be received by the Home Office at the address specified in the request within 28 [calendar] days of the date the request is sent, and

(ii) request the applicant attends an interview, and refuse the application if the applicant fails to comply with any such request without providing a reasonable explanation.

(m) If the Secretary of State is not satisfied following the assessment in paragraph 245ZQ(k), no points will be awarded under paragraphs 105 to 112 of Appendix A.

(n) The Secretary of State may decide not to carry out the assessment in paragraph 245ZQ(k) if the application already falls for refusal on other grounds, but reserves the right to carry out this assessment in any reconsideration of the decision.

Note: Words inserted in subparagraph (e)(ii) and subparagraph (j) inserted from 13 December 2013 subject to savings for applications made before that date (HC 760). Subparagraphs (b)(vi)(3) and (4) substituted and subparagraph (k) inserted from 1 October 2013 subject to savings for applications made before that date (HC 628). Words 'or independent professional' in subparagraph (j) inserted from 6 April 2013 subject to savings for applications made before that date (HC 1039). Word substituted in subparagraph (l)(i) from 6 November 2014 subject to savings for applications made before that date (HC 693).

245ZR. Period and conditions of grant

(a) If any calculation of period of leave comes to zero or a negative number, leave to remain will be refused.

(b) Subject to paragraphs (c) to (f) below, leave to remain will be granted for:

(i) the length of the period of engagement, as recorded in the Certificate of Sponsorship Checking Service entry, plus 14 days (or, where the applicant has consecutive engagements, a period beginning on the first day of the first period of engagement and ending 14 days after the last day of the last period of engagement) or

(ii) the difference between the period that the applicant has already spent in the UK since his last grant of entry clearance or leave to enter as a Tier 5 (Temporary Worker) Migrant and:

(1) 12 months, if he is being sponsored in the Government Authorised exchange sub-category for a Work Experience Programme where the initial grant of leave was granted under the Rules in place from 6 April 2012, the Creative and Sporting subcategory, or the Charity Workers subcategory, or

(2) 2 years, if he is being sponsored in the Government Authorised Exchange sub-category where the initial grant of leave was made under the Rules in place before 6 April 2012 or for a Research Programme, [Training Programme or Overseas Government Language Programme], the Religious Workers subcategory, or the International Agreement subcategory other than as a Contractual Service Supplier, {or Independent Professional}, or

(3) 6 months, if the applicant is being sponsored in the International Agreement subcategory and is a Contractual Service Supplier [or Independent Professional],

whichever of (i) or (ii) is the shorter.

(c) Where the provisions in paragraph 245ZQ(b)(ii) apply, the migrant will be granted leave to remain for:

(i) the period of engagement plus 14 days (or, where the applicant has consecutive engagements, a period beginning on the first day of the first period of engagement and ending 14 days after the last day of the last period of engagement), or

(ii) 12 months

whichever of (i) or (ii) is the shorter.

(d) Where the Certificate of Sponsorship Checking Service reference records that the migrant is being sponsored in the international agreement subcategory of the Tier 5 (Temporary Worker) Migrant route as an overseas government employee, [employee of an international organisation] or a private servant in a diplomatic household where in the case of the latter he entered the UK with a valid entry clearance in that capacity under the Rules in place before 6 April 2012, leave to remain will be granted for:

(i) the period of engagement plus 14 days, or

(ii) [24 months],

whichever of (i) or (ii) is the shorter, unless at the date of the application for leave to remain the applicant has spent more than [4 years] continuously in the UK with leave as a Tier 5 (Temporary Worker) Migrant, in which case leave to remain will be granted for:

(iii) the period of engagement plus 14 days, or

(iv) a period equal to 6 years less X, where X is the period of time, beginning with the date on which the applicant was last granted entry clearance or leave to enter as a Tier 5 (Temporary Worker) Migrant, that the applicant has already spent in the UK as a Tier 5 (Temporary Worker) Migrant

whichever of (iii) or (iv) is the shorter.

(e) Where the Certificate of Sponsorship Checking Service reference records that the applicant is being sponsored in the international agreement sub-category of the Tier 5 (Temporary Worker) Migrant route as a private servant in a diplomatic household to work in a domestic capacity in the household of a named individual and where he entered the UK with a valid entry clearance in that capacity under the Rules in place from 6 April 2012, leave to remain will be granted for:

(i) the period of engagement plus 14 days, or

(ii) [24 months],

whichever of (i) or (ii) is the shorter, unless at the date of the application the applicant has spent more than [3 years] continuously in the UK with leave as a Tier 5 (Temporary Worker) migrant, in which case leave will be granted for:

(iii) the period of engagement plus 14 days, or

(iv) a period equal to 5 years less X, where X is the period of time, beginning with the date on which the applicant was first granted entry clearance as a Tier 5 (Temporary Worker) Migrant, that the applicant has already spent in the UK as a Tier 5 (Temporary Worker) Migrant

whichever of (iii) or (iv) is the shorter. Where the calculation at (iv) above results in zero or a negative number, the application for leave to remain will be refused.

(f) Where:

(i) the Certificate of Sponsorship Checking Service reference number records that the applicant is being sponsored in the creative and sporting subcategory of the Tier 5 (Temporary Worker) Migrant route as a creative worker, and

(ii) the Sponsor is the Sponsor who sponsored the applicant when he received his last grant of leave

leave to remain will be granted for the period set out [in paragraph (g)] below.

(g) Where the conditions [in paragraph (f)] above are met, leave to remain will be granted for:

(i) the period of engagement plus 14 days (or, where the applicant has consecutive engagements, a period beginning on the first day of the first period of engagement and ending 14 days after the last day of the last period of engagement), or

(ii) 12 months

whichever of (i) or (ii) is the shorter, unless the applicant has spent more than 1 year continuously in the UK with leave as a Tier 5 (Temporary Worker) Migrant, in which case leave to remain will be granted for:

(iii) the period of engagement plus 14 days (or, where the applicant has consecutive engagements, a period beginning on the first day of the first period of engagement and ending 14 days after the last day of the last period of engagement), or

(iv) a period equal to 2 years less X, where X is the period of time, beginning with the date on which the applicant was last granted entry clearance or leave to enter as a Tier 5 (Temporary Worker) Migrant, that the applicant has already spent in the UK as a Tier 5 (Temporary Worker) Migrant

whichever of (iii) or (iv) is the shorter.

(h) Leave to remain will be granted subject to the following conditions:

(i) no recourse to public funds,

(ii) registration with the police if this is required by paragraph 326 of these Rules, and

(iii) no employment except:

(1) unless paragraph (2) applies, working for the person who for the time being is the Sponsor in the employment that the Certificate of Sponsorship Checking Service records that the migrant is being sponsored to do for that Sponsor,

(2) in the case of a migrant whom the Certificate of Sponsorship Checking Service records as being sponsored in the government authorised exchange subcategory of Tier 5 (Temporary Workers), the work, volunteering or job shadowing authorised by the Sponsor and that the Certificate of Sponsorship Checking Service records that the migrant is being sponsored to do,

(3) supplementary employment, and

(4) in the case of a migrant whom the Certificate of Sponsorship Checking Service records as being sponsored in the creative and sporting subcategory of Tier 5 (Temporary Workers), employment as a sportsperson for his national team while his national team is in the UK and Temporary Engagement as a Sports Broadcaster.

(iv) in the case of a migrant whom the Certificate of Sponsorship Checking Service records as being sponsored in the international agreement sub-category of Tier 5 (Temporary Workers), to work as a private servant in a diplomatic household, the employment in (iii)(1) above means working only in the household of the employer recorded by the Certificate of Sponsorship Checking Service.

Note: Words 'other than as a Contractual Service Supplier' inserted in subparagraph (b)(ii)(2) and subparagraph (b)(ii)(3) inserted from 13 December 2013 subject to savings for applications made before that date (HC 760). Words inserted in subparagraph (b)(ii)(3) from 1 July 2013 (HC 244). Words in curly brackets inserted in subparagraph (b)(ii)(2), and words in square brackets inserted/substituted in subparagraph (d), in subparagraph (f) and subparagraph (g) from 6 April 2013 subject to savings for applications made before that date (HC 1039). Words substituted in subparagraph (b) (ii)(2) from 6 April 2014 subject to savings for applications made before that date (HC 1138 as amended by HC 1201).

245ZS. Requirements for indefinite leave to remain

To qualify for indefinite leave to remain as a Tier 5 (Temporary Worker) Migrant, an applicant must meet the requirements listed below. If the applicant meets these requirements, indefinite leave to remain will be granted. If the applicant does not meet these requirements, the application will be refused.

Requirements:

(aa) DELETED

(a) The applicant must not fall for refusal under the general grounds for refusal and must not be an illegal entrant.

(b) The applicant must have spent a continuous period of 5 years lawfully in the UK with leave in the international agreement sub-category of Tier 5 and working as a private servant in a diplomatic household and have last been granted entry clearance in this capacity under the Rules in place before 6 April 2012.

(c) The applicant must have demonstrated sufficient knowledge of the English language and sufficient knowledge about life in the United Kingdom, in accordance with Appendix KoLL.

(d) The applicant must not be in the UK in breach of immigration laws except that any period of overstaying for a period of 28 days or less will be disregarded.

(e) the applicant must provide a letter from the employer detailing the purpose and period of absences in connection with the employment, including periods of annual leave. Where the absence was due to a serious or compelling reason, the applicant must provide a personal letter which includes full details of the reason for the absences and all original supporting documents in relation to those reasons – e.g. medical certificates, birth/death certificates, information about the reasons which led to the absence from the UK.

Note: Subparagraph (aa) deleted and subparagraph (e) inserted from 13 December 2012 (deletion of (aa) subject to savings for applications made before that date) (HC 760). Subparagraph (c) substituted from 28 October 2013 subject to savings for applications made before that date (HC 628).

Tier 4 (General) Student

245ZT. Purpose of this route

This route is for migrants aged 16 or over who wish to study in the UK.

245ZU. Entry clearance

All migrants arriving in the UK and wishing to enter as a Tier 4 (General) Student must have a valid entry clearance for entry under this route. If they do not have a valid entry clearance, entry will be refused.

245ZV. Requirements for entry clearance

To qualify for entry clearance as a Tier 4 (General) Student, an applicant must meet the requirements listed below. If the applicant meets these requirements, entry clearance will be granted. If the applicant does not meet these requirements, the application will be refused.

Requirements:

(a) The applicant must not fall for refusal under the general grounds for refusal.

(b) The applicant must have a minimum of 30 points under paragraphs 113 to 120 of Appendix A.

(c) The applicant must have a minimum of 10 points under paragraphs 10 to 14 of Appendix C.

(ca) The applicant must, if required to do so on examination or interview, be able to demonstrate without the assistance of an interpreter English language proficiency of a standard to be expected from an individual who has reached the standard specified in a Confirmation of Acceptance for Studies assigned in accordance with Appendix A paragraph [118(b)] (for the avoidance of doubt, the applicant will not be subject to a test at the standard set out in Appendix A, paragraph [118(b)].

(da) If the applicant wishes to undertake a course:

(i) undergraduate or postgraduate studies leading to a Doctorate or Masters degree by research in one of the disciplines listed in paragraph 1 of Appendix 6 of these Rules, or

(ii) undergraduate or postgraduate studies leading to a taught Masters degree or other postgraduate qualification in one of the disciplines listed in paragraph 2 of Appendix 6 of these Rules, or

(iii) a period of study or research in excess of 6 months in one of the disciplines listed in paragraphs 1 or 2 of Appendix 6 of these Rules at an institution of higher education where this forms part of an overseas postgraduate qualification

the applicant must hold a valid Academic Technology Approval Scheme clearance certificate from the Counter-Proliferation Department of the Foreign and Commonwealth Office which relates to the course, or area of research, that the applicant will be taking and at the institution at which the applicant wishes to undertake it and must provide a print-out of his Academic Technology Approval Scheme clearance certificate to show that these requirements have been met.

(e) If the applicant wishes to be a postgraduate doctor or dentist on a recognised Foundation Programme:

(i) the applicant must have successfully completed a recognised UK degree in medicine or dentistry from:

(1) an institution with a Tier 4 General Sponsor Licence,

(2) a UK publicly funded institution of further or higher education or

(3) a UK bona fide private education institution which maintains satisfactory records of enrolment and attendance,

(ii) the applicant must have previously been granted leave:

(1) as a Tier 4 (General) Student, or as a Student, for the final academic year of the studies referred to in paragraph (i) above, and

(2) as a Tier 4 (General) Student, or as a Student, for at least one other academic year (aside from the final year) of the studies referred to in paragraph (i) above,

(iii) if the applicant has previously been granted leave as a Postgraduate Doctor or Dentist, the applicant must not be seeking entry clearance or leave to enter or remain to a date beyond 3 years from the date on which he was first granted leave to enter or remain in that category, and

(iv) if the applicant has previously been granted leave as a Tier 4 (General) Student to undertake a course as a postgraduate doctor or dentist, the applicant must not be seeking entry clearance or leave to enter or remain to a date beyond 3 years from the date on which the applicant was first granted leave to undertake such a course.

(f) If the applicant is currently being sponsored by a Government or international scholarship agency, or within the last 12 months has come to the end of such a period of sponsorship, the applicant must provide the written consent of the sponsoring Government or agency to the application and must provide the specified documents as set out in paragraph 245A above, to show that this requirement has been met.

(g) If the course is below degree level the grant of entry clearance the applicant is seeking must not lead to the applicant having spent more than 3 years in the UK as a Tier 4 Migrant since the age of 18 studying courses that did not consist of degree level study.

(ga) If the course is at degree level or above, the grant of entry clearance the applicant is seeking must not lead to the applicant having spent more than 5 years in the UK as a Tier 4 (General) Migrant, or as a Student, studying courses at degree level or above unless:

(i) the applicant has successfully completed a course at degree level in the UK of a minimum duration of 4 academic years, and will follow a course of study at Masters degree level sponsored by a Sponsor that is a Recognised Body or a body in receipt of public funding as a higher education institution from the Department of Employment and Learning in Northern Ireland, the Higher Education Funding Council for England, the Higher Education Funding Council for Wales or the Scottish Funding Council, and the grant of entry clearance must not lead to the applicant having spent more than 6 years in the UK as a Tier 4 (General) Migrant, or as a Student, studying courses at degree level or above; or

(ii) the grant of entry clearance is to follow a course leading to the award of a PhD, and the applicant is sponsored by a Sponsor that is a Recognised Body or a body in receipt of public funding as a higher education institution from the Department of Employment and Learning in Northern Ireland, the Higher Education Funding Council for England, the Higher Education Funding Council for Wales or the Scottish Funding Council; or

(iii) the applicant is following a course of study in;

(1) Architecture;

(2) Medicine;

(3) Dentistry;

(4) Law, where the applicant has completed a course at degree level in the UK and is progressing to:

a. a law conversion course validated by the Joint Academic Stage Board in England and Wales, a Masters in Legal Science (MLegSc) in Northern Ireland, or an accelerated graduate LLB in Scotland; or

b. the Legal Practice Course in England and Wales, the Solicitors Course in Northern Ireland, or a Diploma in Professional Legal Practice in Scotland; or

c. the Bar Professional Training Course in England and Wales, or the Bar Course in Northern Ireland.

(5) Veterinary Medicine & Science; or

(6) Music at a music college that is a member of Conservatoires UK (CUK).

(gb) If the applicant has completed a course leading to the award of a PhD in the UK, the grant of entry clearance the applicant is seeking must not lead to the applicant having spent more than 8 years in the UK as a Tier 4 (General) Migrant, or as a Student.

(h) The applicant must be at least 16 years old.

(i) Where the applicant is under 18 years of age, the application must be supported by the applicant's parents or legal guardian, or by just one parent if that parent has sole legal responsibility for the child.

(j) Where the applicant is under 18 years of age, the applicant's parents or legal guardian, or just one parent if that parent has sole responsibility for the child, must confirm that they consent to the arrangements for the applicant's travel to, and reception and care in, the UK.

(k) The Entry Clearance Officer must be satisfied that the applicant is a genuine student.

. . .

Note: Subparagraph (ca) amended from 13 December (HC 760). Subparagraph (ga)(iii)(4) substituted from 1 July 2013 (HC 244). Words at end of subparagraph (k) deleted from 6 April 2014 subject to savings for applications made before that date (HC 1138 as amended by HC 1201).

245ZW. Period and conditions of grant

(a) Subject to paragraph (b), entry clearance will be granted for the duration of the course.

(b) In addition to the period of entry clearance granted in accordance with paragraph (a), entry clearance will also be granted for the periods set out in the following table. Notes to accompany the table appear below the table.

Type of course	Period of entry clearance to be granted before the course starts	Period of entry clearance to be granted after the course ends
12 months or more	1 month	4 months
6 months or more but less than 12 months	1 month	2 months
Pre-sessional course of less than 6 months	1 month	1 month
Course of less than 6 months that is not a pre-sessional course	7 days	7 days
Postgraduate doctor or dentist	1 month	1 month

Notes

(i) If the grant of entry clearance is made less than 1 month or, in the case of a course of less than 6 months that is not a pre-sessional course, less than 7 days before the start of the course, entry clearance will be granted with immediate effect.

(ii) A pre-sessional course is a course which prepares a student for the student's main course of study in the UK.

(iii) The additional periods of entry clearance granted further to the table above will be disregarded for the purposes of calculating whether a migrant has exceeded the limits specified at 245ZV(g) to 245ZV(gb).

(c) Entry clearance will be granted subject to the following conditions:

(i) no recourse to public funds,

(ii) registration with the police, if this is required by paragraph 326 of these Rules,

(iii) no employment except:

(1) employment during term time of no more than 20 hours per week and employment (of any duration) during vacations, where the student is following a course of degree level study and is either:

(a) sponsored by a Sponsor that is a Recognised Body or a body in receipt of public funding as a higher education institution from the Department of Employment and Learning in Northern Ireland, the Higher Education Funding Council for England, the Higher Education Funding Council for Wales or the Scottish Funding Council; or

(b) sponsored by an overseas higher education institution to undertake a short-term Study Abroad Programme in the United Kingdom.

(2) employment during term time of no more than 10 hours per week and employment (of any duration) during vacations, where the student is following a course of below degree level study and is sponsored by a Sponsor that is a Recognised Body or a body in receipt of public funding as a higher education institution from the Department of Employment and Learning in Northern Ireland, the Higher Education Funding Council for England, the Higher Education Funding Council for Wales or the Scottish Funding Council,

(3) employment during term time of no more than 10 hours per week and employment (of any duration) during vacations, where the student is following a course of study at any academic level and is sponsored by a Sponsor that is a publicly funded further education college,

(4) employment as part of a course-related work placement which forms an assessed part of the applicant's course and provided that any period that the applicant spends on that placement does not exceed one third of the total length of the course undertaken in the UK except:

(i) where it is a United Kingdom statutory requirement that the placement should exceed one third of the total length of the course; or

(ii) where the placement does not exceed one half of the total length of the course undertaken in the UK and the student is following a course of degree level study and is either: (a) sponsored by a Sponsor that is a Recognised Body or a body in receipt of public funding as a higher education institution from the Department of Employment and Learning in Northern Ireland, the Higher Education Funding Council for England, the Higher Education Funding Council for Wales or the Scottish Funding Council; or (b) sponsored by an overseas higher education institution to undertake a short-term Study Abroad Programme in the United Kingdom.

(5) employment as a Student Union Sabbatical Officer, for up to 2 years, provided the post is elective and is at the institution which is the applicant's Sponsor [or they must be elected to a national National Union of Students (NUS) position].

(6) employment as a postgraduate doctor or dentist on a recognised Foundation Programme

(7) until such time as a decision is received from the UK Border Agency on an application which is supported by a Certificate of Sponsorship assigned by a licensed Tier 2 Sponsor and which is made following successful completion of course at degree level or above at a Sponsor that is a Recognised Body or a body in receipt of public funding as a higher education institution from the Department of Employment and Learning in Northern Ireland, the Higher Education Funding Council for England, the Higher Education Funding Council for Wales or the Scottish Funding Council and while the applicant has extant leave, and any appeal [or administrative review] against that decision has been determined, employment with the Tier 2 Sponsor, in the role for which they assigned the Certificate of Sponsorship to the Tier 4 migrant,

(8) self-employment, providing the migrant has made an application for leave to remain as a Tier 1 (Graduate Entrepreneur) Migrant which:

(a) is supported by an endorsement from a qualifying Higher Education Institution,

(b) is made following successful completion of a UK recognised Bachelor degree, Masters degree or PhD (not a qualification of equivalent level which is not a degree) course at a Sponsor that is a Recognised Body or a body in receipt of public funding as a higher education institution from the Department of Employment and Learning in Northern Ireland, the Higher Education Funding Council for England, the Higher Education Funding Council for Wales or the Scottish Funding Council, and

(c) is made while the applicant has extant leave,

until such time as a decision is received from the UK Border Agency on that application and any appeal [or administrative review] against that decision has been determined,

provided that the migrant is [not self-employed other than under the conditions of (8) above, or employed as a Doctor or Dentist in Training other than under the conditions of (v) below], professional sportsperson (including a sports coach) or an entertainer, and provided that the migrant's employment would not fill a permanent full time vacancy other than under the conditions of (7) above, or a vacancy on a recognised Foundation Programme or as a sabbatical officer; and

(iv) no study except:

(1) study at the institution that the Confirmation of Acceptance for Studies Checking Service records as the migrant's Sponsor, or where the migrant was awarded points for a visa letter, study at the institution which issued that visa letter unless the migrant is studying at an institution which is a partner institution of the migrant's Sponsor;

(2) until such time as a decision is received from the Home Office on an application which is supported by a Confirmation of Acceptance for Studies assigned by a Highly Trusted Sponsor and which is made while the applicant has extant leave, and any appeal or administrative review against that decision has been determined, study at the Highly Trusted Sponsor institution which the Confirmation of Acceptance for Studies Checking Service records as having assigned a Confirmation of Acceptance for Studies to the Tier 4 migrant;

(3) supplementary study;

(4) study of the course, or courses where a pre-sessional is included, for which the Confirmation of Acceptance for Studies was assigned or the visa letter was issued, unless the student:

(a) has yet to complete the course for which the Confirmation of Acceptance for Studies was assigned or the visa letter was issued;

(b) continues studying at the institution referred to in (1) above; and

(c) begins studying a new course, instead of the course for which the Confirmation of Acceptance for Studies was assigned or the visa letter was issued, that represents academic progress (as set out paragraph 120A(b) of Appendix A to these Rules) on the course(s) preceding the migrant's last grant of Tier 4 (General) Student or Student leave, and:

i. the new course is either:

(1) at a higher or the same level as the course for which the Confirmation of Acceptance for Studies was assigned or the visa letter issued; or

(2) at a lower level than the course for which the Confirmation of Acceptance for Studies was assigned or the visa letter was issued, provided that the requirements and conditions of the migrant's grant of leave as at the date of commencement of the new course are the same requirements and conditions to which the migrant's leave would have been subject had he made an application to study at that lower level under the Rules in force at the time of commencement of the new course; and

ii. where the new course (or period of research) is of a type specified in paragraph 245ZV(da), the student obtains an Academic Technology Approval Scheme clearance certificate from the Counter-Proliferation Department of the Foreign and Commonwealth Office relating to that new course (or area of research) prior to commencing the new course.

(5) in the case of a course (or period of research) of a type specified in paragraph 245ZV(da), study or research to which the Academic Technology Approval Scheme certificate issued to the migrant relates. If the migrant's course (or research) completion date reported on the Confirmation of Acceptance for Studies is postponed for a period of more

than three calendar months, or if there are any changes to the course contents (or the research proposal), the migrant must apply for a new Academic Technology Approval Scheme certificate within 28 calendar days.

(v) no employment as a Doctor or Dentist in Training unless:

(1) the course that the migrant is being sponsored to do (as recorded by the Confirmation of Acceptance for Studies Checking Service) is a recognised Foundation Programme, or

(2) the migrant has made an application as a Tier 4 (General) Student which is supported by a Confirmation of Acceptance for Studies assigned by a Highly Trusted Sponsor to sponsor the applicant to do a recognised Foundation Programme, and this study satisfies the requirements of (iv)(2) above, or

(3) the migrant has made an application as a Tier 2 (General) Migrant which is supported by a Certificate of Sponsorship assigned by a licensed Tier 2 Sponsor to sponsor the applicant to work as a Doctor or Dentist in Training, and this employment satisfies the conditions of (iii)(7) above.

Note: Subparagraph (c)(iii)(5) amended, subparagraph (c)(iii)(8) inserted, subparagraph (c)(iii) substituted (subject to savings), paragraph at the end of subparagraph (c)(iii) amended (subject to savings), subparagraph (c)(v) inserted (subject to savings), subparagraph (c)(iv)(2) amended and subparagraph (c)(iv)(3) inserted from 13 December 2012 (HC 760). Subparagraph (c)(iv)(4) inserted from 6 April 2013 subject to savings for applications made before that date (HC 1039). Words 'or administrative review' inserted from 20 October 2014 (HC 693); subparagraph (c)(iv) substituted from 6 November 2014 subject to savings for applications made before that date (HC 693).

245ZX. Requirements for leave to remain

To qualify for leave to remain as a Tier 4 (General) Student under this rule, an applicant must meet the requirements listed below. If the applicant meets these requirements, leave to remain will be granted. If the applicant does not meet these requirements, the applicant will be refused.

Requirements:

(a) The applicant must not fall for refusal under the general grounds for refusal and must not be an illegal entrant.

(b) The applicant must have, or have last been granted, entry clearance, leave to enter or leave to remain:

(i) as a Tier 4 (General) Student,
(ii) as a Tier 4 (Child) Student,
(iii) as a Tier 1 (Post-study Work) Migrant,
(iv) as a Tier 2 Migrant,
(v) as a Participant in the International Graduates Scheme (or its predecessor, the Science and Engineering Graduates Scheme),
(vi) as a Participant in the Fresh Talent: Working in Scotland Scheme,
(vii) as a Postgraduate Doctor or Dentist,
(viii) as a Prospective Student,
(ix) as a Student,
(x) as a Student Nurse,
(xi) as a Student Re-sitting an Examination,
(xii) as a Student Writing-Up a Thesis,
(xiii) as a Student Union Sabbatical Officer, or
(xiv) as a Work Permit Holder.

(c) The applicant must have a minimum of 30 points under paragraphs 113 to 120 of Appendix A.

(d) The applicant must have a minimum of 10 points under paragraphs 10 to 14 of Appendix C.

(da) The applicant must, if required to do so on examination or interview, be able to demonstrate without the assistance of an interpreter English language proficiency of a standard to be expected from an individual who has reached the standard specified in a Confirmation of Acceptance for Studies assigned in accordance with Appendix A paragraph 118(b) (for the avoidance of doubt, the applicant will not be subject to a test at the standard set out in Appendix A, paragraph 118(b)).

(ea) if the applicant wishes to undertake a course:

(i) undergraduate or postgraduate studies leading to a Doctorate or Masters degree by research in one of the disciplines listed in paragraph 1 of Appendix 6 of these Rules, or

(ii) undergraduate or postgraduate studies leading to a taught Masters degree or other postgraduate qualification in one of the disciplines listed in paragraph 2 of Appendix 6 of these Rules, or

(iii) a period of study or research in excess of 6 months in one of the disciplines listed in paragraphs 1 or 2 of Appendix 6 of these Rules at an institution of higher education where this forms part of an overseas postgraduate qualification

the applicant must hold a valid Academic Technology Approval Scheme clearance certificate from the Counter-Proliferation Department of the Foreign and Commonwealth Office which relates to the course, or area of research, that the applicant will be taking and at the institution at which the applicant wishes to undertake it and must provide a print-out of his Academic Technology Approval Scheme clearance certificate to show that these requirements have been met.

Applicants applying for leave to remain under the doctorate extension scheme must, where required, meet the conditions of paragraph 245ZX(ea), unless they are applying for a course of study of 28 days or less.

(f) If the applicant wishes to be a postgraduate doctor or dentist on a recognised Foundation Programme:

(i) the applicant must have successfully completed a recognised UK degree in medicine or dentistry from:

(1) an institution with a Tier 4 General Sponsor Licence,

(2) a UK publicly funded institution of further or higher education, or

(3) a UK bona fide private education institution which maintains satisfactory records of enrolment and attendance,

(ii) the applicant must have previously been granted leave:

(1) as a Tier 4 (General) Student, or as a Student, for the final academic year of the studies referred to in paragraph (i) above, and

(2) as a Tier 4 (General) Student, or as a Student, for at least one other academic year (aside from the final year) of the studies referred to in paragraph (i) above,

(iii) if the applicant has previously been granted leave as a Postgraduate Doctor or Dentist the applicant must not be seeking entry clearance or leave to enter or remain to a date beyond 3 years from the date on which he was first granted leave to enter or remain in that category, and

(iv) if the applicant has previously been granted leave as a Tier 4 (General) Student to undertake a course as a postgraduate doctor or dentist, the applicant must not be seeking entry clearance or leave to enter or remain to a date beyond 3 years from the date on which he was first granted leave to undertake such a course.

(g) If the applicant is currently being sponsored by a Government or international scholarship agency, or within the last 12 months has come to the end of such a period of sponsorship, the applicant must provide the unconditional written consent of the sponsoring Government or agency to the application and must provide the specified documents as set out in paragraph 245A above, to show that this requirement has been met.

(h) If the course is below degree level the grant of leave to remain the applicant is seeking must not lead to the applicant having spent more than 3 years in the UK as a Tier 4 Migrant since the age of 18 studying courses that did not consist of degree level study.

(ha) If the course is at degree level or above, the grant of leave to remain the applicant is seeking must not lead to the applicant having spent more than 5 years in the UK as a Tier 4 (General) Migrant, or as a Student, studying courses at degree level or above unless:

(i) the applicant has successfully completed a course at degree level in the UK of a minimum duration of 4 academic years, and will follow a course of study at Masters degree level sponsored by a Sponsor that is a Recognised Body or a body in receipt of public funding as a higher education institution from the Department of Employment and Learning in Northern Ireland, the Higher Education Funding Council for England, the Higher Education Funding Council for Wales or the Scottish Funding Council, and the grant of leave to remain must not lead to the applicant having spent more than 6 years in the UK as a Tier 4 (General) Migrant, or as a Student, studying courses at degree level or above; or

(ii) the grant of leave to remain is to follow a course leading to the award of a PhD and the applicant is sponsored by a Sponsor that is a Recognised Body or a body in receipt of public funding as a higher education institution from the Department of Employment and Learning in Northern Ireland, the Higher Education Funding Council for England, the Higher Education Funding Council for Wales or the Scottish Funding Council; or

(iii) the applicant is following a course of study in;

(1) Architecture;

(2) Medicine;

(3) Dentistry;

(4) Law, where the applicant has completed a course at degree level in the UK and is progressing to:

a. a law conversion course validated by the Joint Academic Stage Board in England and Wales, a Masters in Legal Science (MLegSc) in Northern Ireland, or an accelerated graduate LLB in Scotland; or

b. the Legal Practice Course in England and Wales, the Solicitors Course in Northern Ireland, or a Diploma in Professional Legal Practice in Scotland; or

c. the Bar Professional Training Course in England and Wales, or the Bar Course in Northern Ireland.

(5) Veterinary Medicine & Science; or

(6) Music at a music college that is a member of Conservatoires UK (CUK).

(hb) If the applicant has completed a course leading to the award of a PhD in the UK, the grant of leave to remain the applicant is seeking must not lead to the applicant having spent more than 8 years in the UK as a Tier 4 (General) Migrant, or as a Student.

(i) The applicant must be at least 16 years old.

(j) Where the applicant is under 18 years of age, the application must be supported by the applicant's parents or legal guardian, or by just one parent if that parent has sole legal responsibility for the child.

(k) Where the applicant is under 18 years of age, the applicant's parents or legal guardian, or just one parent if that parent has sole legal responsibility for the child, must confirm that they consent to the arrangements for the applicant's care in the UK.

(l) [Unless applying for leave to remain as a Tier 4 (General) Student on the doctorate extension scheme, the applicant] must be applying for leave to remain for the purpose of studies which commence within 28 days of the expiry of the applicant's current leave to enter or remain or, where the applicant has overstayed, within 28 days of when that period of overstaying began.

(m) The applicant must not be in the UK in breach of immigration laws except that any period of overstaying for a period of 28 days or less will be disregarded.

(n) Where the applicant is applying for leave to remain as a Tier 4 (General) Student on the doctorate extension scheme:

(i) leave to remain as a Tier 4 (General) Student on the doctorate extension scheme must not have previously been granted;

(ii) the applicant must be following a course leading to the award of a PhD;

(iii) the applicant must be sponsored by a Sponsor that is a Recognised Body or a body in receipt of public funding as a higher education institution from the Department of Employment and Learning in Northern Ireland, the Higher Education Funding Council for England, the Higher Education Funding Council for Wales or the Scottish Funding Council and that sponsor will be the sponsor awarding the PhD; and

(iv) the date of the application must be within 60 days of the expected end date of a course leading to the award of a PhD.

(o) the Secretary of State must be satisfied that the applicant is a genuine student.

Note: Subparagraph (ha)(iii)(4) substituted from 13 December 2012 (HC 760). Words inserted in subparagraph (l) and subparagraph (n) inserted from 6 April 2013 subject to savings for applications made before that date (HC 1039). Subparagraphs (da) and (o) inserted from 1 October 2013 (HC 628). Words deleted at the end of subparagraph (o) from 6 April 2014 subject to savings for applications made before that date (HC 1138).

245ZY. Period and conditions of grant

(a) Subject to paragraphs (b), [(ba)] and (c) below, leave to remain will be granted for the duration of the course.

(b) In addition to the period of leave to remain granted in accordance with paragraph (a), leave to remain will also be granted for the periods set out in the following table. Notes to accompany the table appear below the table.

Type of course	Period of leave to remain to be granted before the course starts	Period of leave to remain to be granted after the course ends
12 months or more	1 month	4 months
6 months or more but less than 12 months	1 month	2 months
Pre-sessional course of less than 6 months	1 month	1 month
Course of less than 6 months that is not a pre-sessional course	7 days	7 days
Postgraduate doctor or dentist	1 month	1 month

Notes

(i) If the grant of leave to remain is being made less than 1 month or, in the case of a course of less than 6 months that is not a pre-sessional course, less than 7 days before the start of the course, leave to remain will be granted with immediate effect.

(ii) A pre-sessional course is a course which prepares a student for the student's main course of study in the UK.

(iii) The additional periods of [leave to remain] granted further to the table above will be disregarded for the purposes of calculating whether a migrant has exceeded the limits specified at 245ZX(h) to 245ZX(hb).

(ba) Leave to remain as a Tier 4 (General) Student on the doctorate extension scheme will be granted for 12 months, commencing on the expected end date of a course leading to the award of a PhD.

(bb) Leave to remain as a Tier 4 (General) Student on the doctorate extension scheme will not be subject to the conditions on the limited time that can be spent as a Tier 4 (General) Student or as a student, specified at 245ZX (hb).

(c) Leave to remain will be granted subject to the following conditions:

(i) no recourse to public funds,

(ii) registration with the police, if this is required by paragraph 326 of these Rules,

(iii) no employment except:

(1) employment during term time of no more than 20 hours per week and employment (of any duration) during vacations, where the student is following a course of degree level study and is either:

(a) sponsored by a Sponsor that is a Recognised Body or a body in receipt of public funding as a higher education institution from the Department of Employment and Learning in Northern Ireland, the Higher Education Funding Council for England, the Higher Education Funding Council for Wales or the Scottish Funding Council; or

(b) sponsored by an overseas higher education institution to undertake a short-term Study Abroad Programme in the United Kingdom.

(2) employment during term time of no more than 10 hours per week and employment (of any duration) during vacations, where the student is following a course of below degree level study and is sponsored by a Sponsor that is a Recognised Body or a body in receipt of public funding as a higher education institution from the Department of Employment and Learning in Northern Ireland, the Higher Education Funding Council for England, the Higher Education Funding Council for Wales or the Scottish Funding Council,

(3) employment during term time of no more than 10 hours per week and employment (of any duration) during vacations, where the student is following a course of study at any academic level and is sponsored by a Sponsor that is a publicly funded further education college,

(4) employment as part of a course-related work placement which forms an assessed part of the applicant's course and provided that any period that the applicant spends on that placement does not exceed one third of the total length of the course undertaken in the UK except:

(i) where it is a United Kingdom statutory requirement that the placement should exceed one third of the total length of the course; or

(ii) where the placement does not exceed one half of the total length of the course undertaken in the UK and the student is following a course of degree level study and is either:

(a) sponsored by a Sponsor that is a Recognised Body or a body in receipt of public funding as a higher education institution from the Department of Employment and Learning in Northern Ireland, the Higher Education Funding Council for England, the Higher Education Funding Council for Wales or the Scottish Funding Council; or

(b) sponsored by an overseas higher education institution to undertake a short-term Study Abroad Programme in the United Kingdom.

(5) employment as a Student Union Sabbatical Officer for up to 2 years provided the post is elective and is at the institution which is the applicant's Sponsor [or they must be elected to a national National Union of Students (NUS) position],

(6) employment as a postgraduate doctor or dentist on a recognised Foundation Programme,

(7) until such time as a decision is received from the UK Border Agency on an application which is supported by a Certificate of Sponsorship assigned by a licensed Tier 2 Sponsor and which is made following successful completion of course at degree level or above at a Sponsor that is a Recognised Body or a body in receipt of public funding as a higher education institution from the Department of Employment and Learning in Northern Ireland, the Higher Education Funding Council for England, the Higher Education Funding Council for Wales or the Scottish Funding Council and while the applicant has extant leave, and any appeal [or administrative review] against that decision has been determined, employment with the Tier 2 Sponsor institution, in the role for which they assigned the Certificate of Sponsorship to the Tier 4 migrant,

(8) self-employment, providing the migrant has made an application for leave to remain as a Tier 1 (Graduate Entrepreneur) Migrant which is supported by an endorsement from a qualifying Higher Education Institution and which is made following successful completion of a course at degree level or above at a Sponsor that is a Recognised Body or a body in receipt of public funding as a higher education institution from the Department of Employment and Learning in Northern Ireland, the Higher Education Funding Council for England, the Higher Education Funding Council for Wales or the Scottish Funding Council and while the applicant has extant leave, until such time as a decision is received from the UK Border Agency on an application and any appeal [or administrative review] against that decision has been determined,

provided that the migrant is not [self-employed other than under the conditions of (8) above, or employed as a Doctor or Dentist in Training other than under the conditions of (v) below], a professional sportsperson (including a sports coach) or an entertainer, and provided that the migrant's employment would not fill a permanent full time vacancy other than under the conditions of (7) above, or a vacancy on a recognised Foundation Programme or as a sabbatical officer.

(9) where, during the current period of leave, the migrant has successfully completed a PhD at a Sponsor that is a Recognised Body or a body in receipt of public funding as a higher education institution from the Department of Employment and Learning in Northern Ireland, the Higher Education Funding Council for England, the Higher Education Funding Council for Wales or the Scottish Funding Council, and has been granted leave to remain as a Tier 4 (General) Student on the doctorate extension scheme or has made a valid application for leave to remain as a Tier 4 (General) Student on the doctorate extension scheme but has not yet received a decision from the UK Border Agency on that application, there will be no limitation on the type of employment that may be taken, except for:

(a) no employment as a Doctor or Dentist in Training other than under the conditions of (v) below;

(b) no employment as a professional sportsperson (including a sports coach).

(iv) no study except:

(1) study at the institution that the Confirmation of Acceptance for Studies Checking Service records as the migrant's Sponsor, or where the migrant was awarded points for a visa letter, study at the institution which issued that visa letter unless the migrant is studying at an institution which is a partner institution of the migrant's Sponsor;

(2) until such time as a decision is received from the Home Office on an application which is supported by a Confirmation of Acceptance for Studies assigned by a Highly Trusted Sponsor and which is made while the applicant has extant leave, and any appeal or administrative review against that decision has been determined, study at the Highly Trusted Sponsor institution which the Confirmation of Acceptance for Studies Checking Service records as having assigned a Confirmation of Acceptance for Studies to the Tier 4 migrant;

(3) supplementary study;

(4) study of the course, or courses where a pre-sessional is included, for which the Confirmation of Acceptance for Studies was assigned or the visa letter was issued, unless the student:

(a) has yet to complete the course for which the Confirmation of Acceptance for Studies was assigned or the visa letter was issued;

(b) continues studying at the institution referred to in (1) above; and

(c) begins studying a new course, instead of the course for which the Confirmation of Acceptance for Studies was assigned or the visa letter was issued, that represents academic progress (as set out paragraph 120A(b) of Appendix A to these Rules) on the course(s) preceding the migrant's last grant of Tier 4 (General) Student or Student leave, and:

i. the new course is either:

(1) at a higher or the same level as the course for which the Confirmation of Acceptance for Studies was assigned or the visa letter issued; or

(2) at a lower level than the course for which the Confirmation of Acceptance for Studies was assigned or the visa letter was issued, provided that the requirements and conditions of the migrant's grant of leave as at the date of commencement of the new course are the same requirements and conditions to which the migrant's leave would have been subject had he made an application to study at that lower level under the Rules in force at the time of commencement of the new course; and

ii. where the new course (or period of research) is of a type specified in paragraph 245ZX(ea), the student obtains an Academic Technology Approval Scheme clearance certificate from the Counter-Proliferation Department of the Foreign and Commonwealth Office relating to that new course (or area of research) prior to commencing the new course.

(5) in the case of a course (or period of research) of a type specified in paragraph 245ZX(ea), study or research to which the Academic Technology Approval Scheme certificate issued to the migrant relates. If the migrant's course (or research) completion date reported on the Confirmation of Acceptance for Studies is postponed for a period of more than three calendar months, or if there are any changes to the course contents (or the research proposal), the migrant must apply for a new Academic Technology Approval Scheme certificate within 28 calendar days.

(v) no employment as a Doctor or Dentist in Training unless:

(1) the course that the migrant is being sponsored to do (as recorded by the Confirmation of Acceptance for Studies Checking Service) is a recognised Foundation Programme, or

(2) the migrant has made an application as a Tier 4 (General) Student which is supported by a Confirmation of Acceptance for Studies assigned by a Highly Trusted

Sponsor to sponsor the applicant to do a recognised Foundation Programme, and this study satisfies the requirements of (iv)(2) above, or

(3) the migrant has made an application as a Tier 2 (General) Migrant which is supported by a Certificate of Sponsorship assigned by a licensed Tier 2 Sponsor to sponsor the applicant to work as a Doctor or Dentist in Training, and this employment satisfies the conditions of (iii)(7) above.

Note: Words inserted in subparagraph (c)(iii)(5), subparagraph (c)(iii)(8) inserted (subject to savings), words substituted in the paragraph following subparagraph (c)(iii)(8) (subject to savings), words deleted from subparagraph (c)(iv)(2), subparagraph (c)(iv)(3) inserted and subparagraph (c)(v) inserted (subject to savings) from 13 December 2012 (HC 760). Subparagraph (bb) inserted and subparagraph (c)(v)(4) deleted from 1 July 2013 (HC 244). Subparagraphs (a) and (b)(iii) amended and subparagraphs (ba) and (c)(iii)(9) inserted from 6 April 2013 subject to savings for applications made before that date (HC 1039). Words 'administrative review' inserted from 20 October 2014 (HC 693); subparagraph (c)(iv) substituted from 6 November 2014 subject to savings for applications made before that date (HC 693).

Tier 4 (Child) Student

245ZZ. Purpose of route

This route is for children at least 4 years old and under the age of 18 who wish to be educated in the UK.

245ZZA. Entry clearance

All migrants arriving in the UK and wishing to enter as a Tier 4 (Child) Student must have a valid entry clearance for entry under this route. If they do not have a valid entry clearance, entry will be refused.

Requirements:

(a) The applicant must not fall for refusal under the general grounds for refusal.

(b) The applicant must have a minimum of 30 points under paragraphs 121 to 126 of Appendix A.

(c) The applicant must have a minimum of 10 points under paragraphs 15 to 22 of Appendix C.

(d) The applicant must be at least 4 years old and under the age of 18.

(e) The applicant must have no children under the age of 18 who are either living with the applicant or for whom the applicant is financially responsible.

(f) If a foster carer or a relative (not a parent or guardian) of the applicant will be responsible for the care of the applicant:

(i) the arrangements for the care of the applicant by the foster carer or relative must meet the requirements in paragraph 245ZZE and the applicant must provide the specified documents in paragraph 245ZZE to show that this requirement has been met, and

(ii) the applicant must provide details of the care arrangements as specified in paragraph 245ZZE.

(g) The application must be supported by the applicant's parents or legal guardian, or by just one parent if that parent has sole legal responsibility for the child.

(h) The applicant's parents or legal guardian, or just one parent if that parent has sole responsibility for the child, must confirm that they consent to the arrangements for the applicant's travel to, and reception and care in, the UK.

(i) If the applicant is currently being sponsored by a Government or international scholarship agency, or within the last 12 months has come to the end of such a period of sponsorship, the applicant must provide the written consent of the sponsoring Government or agency to the application and must provide the specified documents as set out in paragraph 245A above, to show that this requirement has been met

245ZZB. Period and conditions of grant

(a) Where the applicant is under the age of 16, entry clearance will be granted for:
  (i) a period of no more than 1 month before the course starts, plus
  (ii) a period:
    (1) requested by the applicant,
    (2) equal to the length of the programme the applicant is following, or
    (3) of 6 years
  whichever is the shorter, plus
  (iii) 4 months.
(b) Where the applicant is aged 16 or over, entry clearance will be granted for:
  (i) a period of no more than 1 month before the course starts, plus
  (ii) a period:
    (1) requested by the applicant,
    (2) equal to the length of the programme the applicant is following, or
    (3) of 3 years
  whichever is the shorter, plus
  (iii) 4 months.
(c) Entry clearance will be granted subject to the following conditions:
  (i) no recourse to public funds,
  (ii) registration with the police, if this is required by paragraph 326 of these Rules,
  (iii) no employment whilst the migrant is aged under 16,
  (iv) no employment whilst the migrant is aged 16 or over except:
    (1) employment during term time of no more than 10 hours per week,
    (2) employment (of any duration) during vacations,
    (3) employment as part of a course-related work placement which forms an assessed part of the applicant's course and provided that any period that the applicant spend on that placement does not exceed half of the total length of the course undertaken in the UK except where it is a United Kingdom statutory requirement that the placement should exceed half the total length of the course
    (4) employment as a Student Union Sabbatical Officer for up to 2 years provided the post is elective and is at the institution which is the applicant's Sponsor [or they must be elected to a national National Union of Students (NUS) position],

    provided that the migrant is not self employed, or employed as a Doctor in Training, a professional sportsperson (including a sports coach) or an entertainer, and provided that the migrant's employment would not fill a permanent full time vacancy other than a vacancy as a sabbatical officer.
  (v) no study except:
    (1) study at the institution that the Confirmation of Acceptance for Studies Checking Service records as the migrant's Sponsor, or where the migrant was awarded points for a visa letter, study at the institution which issued that visa letter unless the migrant is studying at an institution which is a partner institution of the migrant's Sponsor;

(2) until such time as a decision is received from the Home Office on an application which is supported by a Confirmation of Acceptance for Studies assigned by a Highly Trusted Sponsor and which is made while the applicant has extant leave, and any appeal or administrative review against that decision has been determined, study at the Highly Trusted Sponsor institution which the Confirmation of Acceptance for Studies Checking Service records as having assigned a Confirmation of Acceptance for Studies to the Tier 4 migrant;

(3) supplementary study;

(4) study of the course, or courses where a pre-sessional is included, for which the Confirmation of Acceptance for Studies was assigned or the visa letter was issued, unless the student:

(a) has yet to complete the course for which the Confirmation of Acceptance for Studies was assigned or the visa letter was issued;

(b) continues studying at the institution referred to in (1) above; and

(c) begins studying a new course, instead of the course for which the Confirmation of Acceptance for Studies was assigned or the visa letter was issued, and the new course is either:

(1) at a higher or the same level as the course for which the Confirmation of Acceptance for Studies was assigned or the visa letter issued; or

(2) at a lower level than the course for which the Confirmation of Acceptance for Studies was assigned or the visa letter was issued, provided that the requirements and conditions of the migrant's grant of leave as at the date of commencement of the new course are the same requirements and conditions to which the migrant's leave would have been subject had he made an application to study at that lower level under the Rules in force at the time of commencement of the new course.

Note: Words inserted in subparagraph (c)(iv)(4) from 13 December 2012 (HC 760). Subparagraph (c)(v) substituted from 6 November 2014 subject to savings for applications made before that date (HC 693).

245ZZC. Requirements for leave to remain

To qualify for leave to remain as a Tier 4 (Child) Student under this rule, an applicant must meet the requirements listed below. If the applicant meets these requirements, leave to remain will be granted. If the applicant does not meet these requirements, leave to remain will be refused.

Requirements:

(a) The applicant must not fall for refusal under the general grounds for refusal and must not be an illegal entrant.

(b) The applicant must have, or have last been granted, entry clearance, leave to enter or leave to remain:

(i) as a Tier 4 Migrant,

(ii) as a Student, or

(iii) as a Prospective Student.

(c) The applicant must have a minimum of 30 points under paragraphs 121 to 126 of Appendix A.

(d) The applicant must have a minimum of 10 points under paragraphs 15 to 22 of Appendix C.

(e) The applicant must be under the age of 18.

(f) The applicant must have no children under the age of 18 who are either living with the applicant or for whom the applicant is financially responsible.

(g) If a foster carer or a relative (not a parent or guardian) of the applicant will be responsible for the care of the applicant:

(i) the arrangements for the care of the applicant by the foster carer or relative must meet the requirements in paragraph 245ZZE and the applicant must provide the specified documents in paragraph 245ZZE to show that this requirement has been met, and

(ii) the applicant must provide details of the care arrangements as specified in paragraph 245ZZE.

(h) The application must be supported by the applicant's parents or legal guardian, or by just one parent if that parent has sole legal responsibility for the child.

(i) The applicant's parents or legal guardian, or just one parent if that parent has sole legal responsibility for the child, must confirm that they consent to the arrangements for the applicant's care in the UK.

(j) The applicant must be applying for leave to remain for the purpose of studies which commence within 28 days of the expiry of the applicant's current leave to enter or remain or, where the applicant has overstayed, within 28 days of when that period of overstaying began.

(k) If the applicant is currently being sponsored by a Government or international scholarship agency, or within the last 12 months has come to the end of such a period of sponsorship, the applicant must provide the written consent of the sponsoring Government or agency to the application and must provide the specified documents as specified in paragraph 245A above, to show that this requirement has been met.

(l) The applicant must not be in the UK in breach of immigration laws except that any period of overstaying for a period of 28 days or less will be disregarded.

245ZZD. Period and conditions of grant

(a) Where the applicant is under the age of 16, leave to remain will be granted for:

(i) a period of no more than 1 month before the course starts, plus

(ii) a period:

(1) requested by the applicant,

(2) equal to the length of the programme the applicant is following, or

(3) of 6 years

whichever is the shorter, plus

(iii) 4 months.

(b) Where the applicant is aged 16 or over, leave to remain will be granted for:

(i) a period of no more than 1 month before the course starts, plus

(ii) a period:

(1) requested by the applicant,

(2) equal to the length of the programme the applicant is following, or

(3) of 3 years

whichever is the shorter, plus

(iii) 4 months.

(c) Leave to remain will be granted subject to the following conditions:

(i) no recourse to public funds,

(ii) registration with the police, if this is required by paragraph 326 of these Rules,

(iii) no employment whilst the migrant is aged under 16,

(iv) no employment whilst the migrant is aged 16 or over except:

(1) employment during term time of no more than 10 hours per week,

(2) employment (of any duration) during vacations,

(3) employment as part of a course-related work placement which forms an assessed part of the applicant's course, and provided that any period that the applicant spend on that placement does not exceed half of the total length of the course undertaken in the UK except where it is a United Kingdom statutory requirement that the placement should exceed half the total length of the course,

(4) employment as a Student Union Sabbatical Officer for up to 2 years provided the post is elective and is at the institution which is the applicant's Sponsor, [or they must be elected to a National Union of Students (NUS) position]

provided that the migrant is not self-employed, or employed as a Doctor in Training, a professional sportsperson (including a sports coach) or an entertainer, and provided that the migrant's employment would not fill a permanent full time vacancy other than a vacancy as a sabbatical officer.

(v) no study except:

(1) study at the institution that the Confirmation of Acceptance for Studies Checking Service records as the migrant's Sponsor, or where the migrant was awarded points for a visa letter, study at the institution which issued that visa letter unless the migrant is studying at an institution which is a partner institution of the migrant's Sponsor;

(2) until such time as a decision is received from the Home Office on an application which is supported by a Confirmation of Acceptance for Studies assigned by a Highly Trusted Sponsor and which is made while the applicant has extant leave, and any appeal or administrative review against that decision has been determined, study at the Highly Trusted Sponsor institution which the Confirmation of Acceptance for Studies Checking Service records as having assigned a Confirmation of Acceptance for Studies to the Tier 4 migrant;

(3) supplementary study;

(4) study of the course, or courses where a pre-sessional is included, for which the Confirmation of Acceptance for Studies was assigned or the visa letter was issued, unless the student:

(a) has yet to complete the course for which the Confirmation of Acceptance for Studies was assigned or the visa letter was issued;

(b) continues studying at the institution referred to in (1) above; and

(c) begins studying a new course, instead of the course for which the Confirmation of Acceptance for Studies was assigned or the visa letter was issued, and the new course is either:

(1) at a higher or the same level as the course for which the Confirmation of Acceptance for Studies was assigned or the visa letter issued; or

(2) at a lower level than the course for which the Confirmation of Acceptance for Studies was assigned or the visa letter was issued, provided that the requirements and conditions of the migrant's grant of leave as at the date of commencement of the new course are the same requirements and conditions to which the migrant's leave would have been subject had he made an application to study at that lower level under the Rules in force at the time of commencement of the new course.

Note: Words inserted in subparagraph (c)(iv) from 13 December 2012 (HC 760). Subparagraph (c)(v) substituted from 6 November 2014 subject to savings for applications made before that date (HC 693).

245ZZE. Specified documents, details and requirements of care arrangements

The specified documents, details and requirements of care arrangements referred to in paragraph 245ZZA(f) and paragraph 245ZZC(g) are:

(i) The applicant must provide a written letter of undertaking from the intended carer confirming the care arrangement, which shows:

(1) the name, current address and contact details of the intended carer,

(2) the address where the carer and the Tier 4 (Child) student will be living in the UK if different from the intended carer's current address,

(3) confirmation that the accommodation offered to the Tier 4 (Child) student is a private address, and not operated as a commercial enterprise, such as a hotel or a youth hostel,

(4) the nature of the relationship between the Tier 4 (Child) student's parent(s) or legal guardian and the intended carer,

(5) that the intended carer agrees to the care arrangements for the Tier 4 (Child) student,

(6) that the intended carer has at least £500 per month (up to a maximum of nine months) available to look after and accommodate the Tier 4 (Child) student for the length of the course,

(7) a list of any other people that the intended carer has offered support to, and

(8) the signature and date of the undertaking.

(ii) The applicant must provide a letter from his parent(s) or legal guardian confirming the care arrangement, which shows:

(1) the nature of their relationship with the intended carer,

(2) the address in the UK where the Tier 4 (Child) student and the Tier 4 (Child) student's intended carer will be living,

(3) that the parent(s) or legal guardian support the application, and authorise the intended carer to take responsibility for the care of the Tier 4 (Child) student during his stay in the UK,

(4) the intended carer's current passport, travel document or certificate of naturalisation, confirming that they are settled in the UK. The UK Border Agency will accept a notarised copy of the original passport or travel document, but reserves the right to request the original.

(iii) If the applicant will be staying in a private foster care arrangement, he must receive permission from the private foster carer's UK local authority, as set out in the Children (Private Arrangements for Fostering) Regulations 2005.

(iv) If the applicant will be staying in a private foster care arrangement and is under 16 years old, he must provide:

(1) a copy of the letter of notification from his parent(s), legal guardian or intended carer to the UK local authority, which confirms that the applicant will be in the care of a private foster carer while in the UK, and

(2) the UK local authority's confirmation of receipt, which confirms that the local authority has received notification of the foster care arrangement.

Note: Word 'settled' substituted in subparagraph (ii)(4) from 6 April 2014 subject to savings for applications made before that date.

Part 7
Other Categories

Persons exercising rights of access to a child resident in the United Kingdom

Requirements for leave to enter the United Kingdom as a person exercising rights of access to a child resident in the United Kingdom

A246. Paragraphs 246 to 248F apply only to a person who has made an application before 9 July 2012 for leave to enter or remain or indefinite leave to remain as a person exercising rights of access to a child resident in the UK, or who before 9 July 2012 has been granted leave to enter or remain as a person exercising rights of access to a child resident in the UK.

AB246. Where an application for leave to enter or remain is made on or after 9 July 2012 as a person exercising rights of access to a child resident in the UK Appendix FM will apply.

246. The requirements to be met by a person seeking leave to enter the United Kingdom to exercise access rights to a child resident in the United Kingdom are that:

(i) the applicant is the parent of a child who is resident in the United Kingdom; and

(ii) the parent or carer with whom the child permanently resides is resident in the United Kingdom; and

(iii) the applicant produces evidence that he has access rights to the child in the form of:

(a) a Residence Order or a Contact Order granted by a Court in the United Kingdom; or

(b) a certificate issued by a district judge confirming the applicant's intention to maintain contact with the child; and

(iv) the applicant intends to take an active role in the child's upbringing; and

(v) the child is under the age of 18; and

(vi) there will be adequate accommodation for the applicant and any dependants without recourse to public funds in accommodation which the applicant owns or occupies exclusively; and

(vii) the applicant will be able to maintain himself and any dependants adequately without recourse to public funds; and

(viii) the applicant holds a valid United Kingdom entry clearance for entry in this capacity.

Leave to enter the United Kingdom as a person exercising rights of access to a child resident in the United Kingdom

247. Leave to enter as a person exercising access rights to a child resident in the United Kingdom may be granted for 12 months in the first instance, provided that a valid United Kingdom entry clearance for entry in this capacity is produced to the Immigration Officer on arrival.

Refusal of leave to enter the United Kingdom as a person exercising rights of access to a child resident in the United Kingdom

248. Leave to enter as a person exercising rights of access to a child resident in the United Kingdom is to be refused if a valid United Kingdom entry clearance for entry in this capacity is not produced to the Immigration Officer on arrival.

Requirements for leave to remain in the United Kingdom as a person exercising rights of access to a child resident in the United Kingdom

248A. The requirements to be met by a person seeking leave to remain in the United Kingdom to exercise access rights to a child resident in the United Kingdom are that:

(i) the applicant is the parent of a child who is resident in the United Kingdom; and

(ii) the parent or carer with whom the child permanently resides is resident in the United Kingdom; and

(iii) the applicant produces evidence that he has access rights to the child in the form of:

(a) a Residence Order or a Contact Order granted by a Court in the United Kingdom; or

(b) a certificate issued by a district judge confirming the applicant's intention to maintain contact with the child; or

(c) a statement from the child's other parent (or, if contact is supervised, from the supervisor) that the applicant is maintaining contact with the child; and

(iv) the applicant takes and intends to continue to take an active role in the child's upbringing; and

(v) the child visits or stays with the applicant on a frequent and regular basis and the applicant intends this to continue; and

(vi) the child is under the age of 18; and

(vii) the applicant has limited leave to remain in the United Kingdom as the spouse, civil partner, unmarried partner or same-sex partner of a person present and settled in the United Kingdom who is the other parent of the child; and

(viii) the applicant has not remained in breach of the immigration laws; and

(ix) there will be adequate accommodation for the applicant and any dependants without recourse to public funds in accommodation which the applicant owns or occupies exclusively; and

(x) the applicant will be able to maintain himself and any dependants adequately without recourse to public funds.

Leave to remain in the United Kingdom as a person exercising rights of access to a child resident in the United Kingdom

248B. Leave to remain as a person exercising access rights to a child resident in the United Kingdom may be granted for 12 months in the first instance, provided the Secretary of State is satisfied that each of the requirements of paragraph 248A is met.

Refusal of leave to remain in the United Kingdom as a person exercising rights of access to a child resident in the United Kingdom

248C. Leave to remain as a person exercising rights of access to a child resident in the United Kingdom is to be refused if the Secretary of State is not satisfied that each of the requirements of paragraph 248A is met.

Indefinite leave to remain in the United Kingdom as a person exercising rights of access to a child resident in the United Kingdom

248D. The requirements for indefinite leave to remain in the United Kingdom as a person exercising rights of access to a child resident in the United Kingdom are that:

(i) the applicant was admitted to the United Kingdom or granted leave to remain in the United Kingdom for a period of 12 months as a person exercising rights of access to a child and has completed a period of 12 months as a person exercising rights of access to a child; and

(ii) the applicant takes and intends to continue to take an active role in the child's upbringing; and

(iii) the child visits or stays with the applicant on a frequent and regular basis and the applicant intends this to continue; and

(iv) there will be adequate accommodation for the applicant and any dependants without recourse to public funds in accommodation which the applicant owns or occupies exclusively; and

(v) the applicant will be able to maintain himself and any dependants adequately without recourse to public funds; and

(vi) the child is under 18 years of age; and

(vii) the applicant must have demonstrated sufficient knowledge of the English language and sufficient knowledge about life in the United Kingdom, in accordance with Appendix KoLL; and

(viii) the applicant does not fall for refusal under the general grounds for refusal.

Note: Subparagraph (viii) inserted from 13 December 2012 subject to savings for applications made before that date (HC 760). Subparagraph (vii) substituted from 13 December 2012 and then substituted from 28 October 2013 subject to savings for applications made before those dates (HC 760 and HC 628).

Indefinite leave to remain as a person exercising rights of access to a child resident in the United Kingdom

248E. Indefinite leave to remain as a person exercising rights of access to a child may be granted provided the Secretary of State is satisfied that each of the requirements of paragraph 248D is met.

Refusal of indefinite leave to remain in the United Kingdom as a person exercising rights of access to a child resident in the United Kingdom

248F. Indefinite leave to remain as a person exercising rights of access to a child is to be refused if the Secretary of State is not satisfied that each of the requirements of paragraph 248D is met.

Holders of special vouchers

Requirements for indefinite leave to enter as the holder of a special voucher

249. DELETED

Indefinite leave to enter as the holder of a special voucher

250. DELETED

Refusal of indefinite leave to enter as the holder of a special voucher

251. DELETED

Requirements for indefinite leave to enter as the spouse or child of a special voucher holder

252. DELETED

Indefinite leave to enter as the spouse or child of a special voucher holder

253. DELETED

Refusal of indefinite leave to enter as the spouse or child of a special voucher holder

254. DELETED

EEA Nationals and their families

Settlement

255–255B. DELETED

256. DELETED

257–257B. DELETED

257C–257E. DELETED

Note: Paragraphs 257C–257E deleted from 6 April 2013 subject to savings for applications made before that date (HC 1039).

The EEA family permit

258–262. DELETED

Retired persons of independent means

263–265. DELETED

Requirements for an extension of stay as a retired person of independent means

266. The requirements for an extension of stay as a retired person of independent means are that the applicant:

(i) entered the United Kingdom with a valid United Kingdom entry clearance as a retired person of independent means; and

(ii) meets the following requirements:

(a) has under his control and disposable in the United Kingdom an income of his own of not less than £25,000 per annum; and

(b) is able and willing to maintain and accommodate himself and any dependants indefinitely in the United Kingdom from his own resources with no assistance from any other person and without taking employment or having recourse to public funds; and

(c) can demonstrate a close connection with the United Kingdom; and

(iii) has made the United Kingdom his main home; and

(iv) must not be in the UK in breach of immigration laws, except that any period of overstaying for a period of 28 days or less will be disregarded.

Extension of stay as a retired person of independent means

266A–266E. DELETED

267. An extension of stay as a retired person of independent means, with a prohibition on the taking of employment, may be granted so as to bring the person's stay in this category up to a maximum of 5 years in aggregate, provided the Secretary of State is satisfied that each of the requirements of paragraph 266 is met.

Refusal of extension of stay as a retired person of independent means

268. An extension of stay as a retired person of independent means is to be refused if the Secretary of State is not satisfied that each of the requirements of paragraph 266 is met.

Indefinite leave to remain for a retired person of independent means

269. Indefinite leave to remain may be granted, on application, to a person admitted as a retired person of independent means provided [the applicant]:

(i) has spent a continuous period of 5 years [lawfully] in the United Kingdom in this capacity; and

(ii) . . . has met the requirements of paragraph 266 throughout the 5 year period and continues to do so; and

(iii) [does not fall for refusal under the general grounds for refusal]; and

(iv) must not be in the UK in breach of immigration laws, except that any period of overstaying for a period of 28 days or less will be disregarded; and

(v) in the case of absences for serious or compelling reasons, submits a personal letter which includes full details of the reason for the absences and all original supporting documents in relation to those reasons – e.g. medical certificates, birth/death certificates, information about the reasons which led to the absence from the UK

"continuous period of 5 years lawfully in the UK" means residence in the United Kingdom for an unbroken period with valid leave, and for these purposes a period shall not be considered to have been broken where:

(i) the applicant has been absent from the UK for a period of 180 days or less in any of the five consecutive 12 calendar month periods preceding the date of the application for indefinite leave to remain; and

(ii) the applicant has existing limited leave to enter or remain upon their departure and return, except that where that leave expired no more than 28 days prior to a further application for entry clearance, that period and any period pending the determination of an application made within that 28 day period shall be disregarded; and

(iii) the applicant has any period of overstaying between periods of entry clearance, leave to enter or leave to remain of up to 28 days and any period of overstaying pending the determination of an application made within that 28 day period disregarded.

Note: Words substituted in the opening sentence, words inserted in subparagraph (i), words substituted in subparagraph (iii) (subject to savings for applications made before 13 December 2012), subparagraph (v) and definition following it inserted from 13 December 2012 (HC 760).

Refusal of indefinite leave to remain for a retired person of independent means

270. Indefinite leave to remain in the United Kingdom for a retired person of independent means is to be refused if the Secretary of State is not satisfied that each of the requirements of paragraph 269 is met.

Partners of persons with limited leave to enter or remain in the United Kingdom as retired persons of independent means

Requirements for leave to enter or remain as the partners of a person with limited leave to enter or remain in the United Kingdom as a retired person of independent means

271. The requirements to be met by a person seeking leave to enter the United Kingdom as the partner of a person with limited leave to enter or remain in the United Kingdom as a retired person of independent means are that:

(i) the applicant is the spouse, civil partner, unmarried or same-sex partner of a person with limited leave to enter or remain in the United Kingdom as a retired person of independent means; and

(ii) if an unmarried or same-sex partner:

(1) any previous marriage or civil partnership (or similar relationship) by either partner has permanently broken down; and

(2) the parties are not involved in a consanguineous relationship with one another; and

(3) the parties have been living together in a relationship akin to marriage or civil partnership which has subsisted for 2 years or more; and

(iii) each of the parties intends to live with the other as his or her partner during the applicant's stay and the relationship is subsisting; and

(iv) there will be adequate accommodation for the parties and any dependants without recourse to public funds in accommodation which they own or occupy exclusively; and

(v) the parties will be able to maintain themselves and any dependants adequately without recourse to public funds; and

(vi) the applicant does not intend to stay in the United Kingdom beyond any period of leave granted to his partner; and

(vii) the applicant does not fall for refusal under the general grounds for refusal; and

(viii) the applicant holds a valid United Kingdom entry clearance for entry in this capacity.

Note: Paragraphs 271 to 273F: all references to 'spouse or civil partner' substituted with 'partner' from 1 October 2013 (HC 628); paragraphs 271 to 273D: all references to 'is married to or a civil partner of' substituted with 'is the spouse, civil partner, unmarried or same-sex partner of' from 1 October 2013; both changes subject to savings for applications made before that date. Paragraph 271: subparagraphs (ii)–(vi) substituted and (vii)–(viii) inserted from 1 October 2013 subject to savings for applications made before that date (HC 628).

Leave to enter as the partner of a person with limited leave to enter or remain in the United Kingdom as a retired person of independent means

272. A person seeking leave to enter the United Kingdom as the partner of a person with limited leave to enter or remain in the United Kingdom as a retired person of independent means may be given leave to enter for a period not in excess of that granted to the person with limited leave to enter or remain as a retired person of independent means, provided the Immigration Officer is satisfied that each of the requirements of paragraph 271 is met.

Refusal of leave to enter as the partner of a person with limited leave to enter or remain in the United Kingdom as a retired person of independent means

273. Leave to enter as the partner of a person with limited leave to enter or remain in the United Kingdom as a retired person of independent means is to be refused if the Immigration Officer is not satisfied that each of the requirements of paragraph 271 is met.

Requirements for extension of stay as the partner of a person who has or has had leave to enter or remain in the United Kingdom as a retired person of independent means

273A. The requirements to be met by a person seeking an extension of stay in the United Kingdom as the partner of a person who has or has had leave to enter or remain in the United Kingdom as a retired person of independent means are that the applicant:

(i) is the spouse, civil partner, unmarried or same sex partner of a person who:

(1) has limited leave to enter or remain in the United Kingdom as a retired person of independent means; or

(2) has indefinite leave to remain in the United Kingdom or has become a British citizen, and who had limited leave to enter or remain in the United Kingdom as a retired person of independent means immediately before being granted indefinite leave to remain; and

(ii) meets the requirements of paragraph 271(ii)–(vii); and

(iii) was not last granted:

(1) entry clearance or leave as a visitor,

(2) temporary admission, or

(3) temporary release; and

(iv) must not be in the UK in breach of immigration laws except that any period of overstaying for a period of 28 days or less will be disregarded.

Note: Subparagraphs (i)–(vi) substituted and (vii)–(viii) inserted from 1 October 2013 subject to savings for applications made before that date (HC 628).

Extension of stay as the partner of a person who has or has had leave to enter or remain in the United Kingdom as a retired person of independent means

273B. An extension of stay in the United Kingdom as:

(i) the partner of a person who has limited leave to enter or remain as a retired person of independent means may be granted for a period not in excess of that granted to the person with limited leave to enter or remain; or

(ii) the partner of a person who is being admitted at the same time for settlement or the partner of a person who has indefinite leave to remain [or has become a British citizen] may be granted for a period not exceeding 2 years, in both instances, provided the Secretary of State is satisfied that each of the requirements of paragraph 273A is met.

Note: Words inserted in subparagraph (ii) from 1 October 2013 subject to savings for applications made before that date (HC 628).

Refusal of extension of stay as the partner of a person who has or has had leave to enter or remain in the United Kingdom as a retired person of independent means

273C. An extension of stay in the United Kingdom as the partner of a person who has or has had leave to enter or remain in the United Kingdom as a retired person of independent means is to be refused if the Secretary of State is not satisfied that each of the requirements of paragraph 273A is met.

Requirements for indefinite leave to remain for the partner of a person who has or has had leave to enter or remain in the United Kingdom as a retired person of independent means

273D. The requirements to be met by a person seeking indefinite leave to remain in the United Kingdom as the partner of a person who has or has had leave to enter or remain in the United Kingdom as a retired person of independent means are that the applicant:

(i) is the spouse, civil partner, unmarried or same-sex partner of a person who:

(1) has limited leave to enter or remain in the United Kingdom as a retired person of independent means and who is being granted indefinite leave to remain at the same time; or

(2) is the spouse, civil partner, unmarried or same-sex partner of a person who has indefinite leave to remain in the United Kingdom or has become a British citizen, and who had limited leave to enter or remain in the United Kingdom as a retired person of independent means immediately before being granted indefinite leave to remain; and

(ii) meets the requirements of paragraph 271(ii)–(vii); and

(iii) has demonstrated sufficient knowledge of the English language and sufficient knowledge about life in the United Kingdom, in accordance with Appendix KoLL; and

(iv) was not last granted:

(1) entry clearance or leave as a visitor,

(2) temporary admission, or

(3) temporary release; and

(v) must not be in the UK in breach of immigration laws except that any period of overstaying for a period of 28 days or less will be disregarded.

Note: Subparagraphs (i)–(vii) substituted from 1 October 2013 subject to savings for applications made before that date (HC 628). Subparagraph (iii) then substituted from 28 October 2013 subject to savings for applications made before that date (HC 628).

Indefinite leave to remain as the partner of a person who has or has had leave to enter or remain in the United Kingdom as a retired person of independent means

273E. Indefinite leave to remain in the United Kingdom [as] the partner of a person who has or has had leave to enter or remain in the United Kingdom as a retired person of independent means may be granted provided the Secretary of State is satisfied that each of the requirements of paragraph 273D is met.

Note: Word substituted from 1 October 2013 subject to savings for applications made before that date (HC 628).

Refusal of indefinite leave to remain as the partner of a person who has or has had leave to enter or remain in the United Kingdom as a retired person of independent means

273F. Indefinite leave to remain in the United Kingdom [as] the partner of a person who has or has had leave to enter or remain in the United Kingdom as a retired person of independent means is to be refused if the Secretary of State is not satisfied that each of the requirements of paragraph 273D is met.

Note: Word substituted from 1 October 2013 subject to savings for applications made before that date (HC 628).

Children of persons with limited leave to enter or remain in the United Kingdom as retired persons of independent means

Requirements for leave to enter or remain as the child of a person with limited leave to enter or remain in the United Kingdom as a retired person of independent means

274. The requirements to be met by a person seeking leave to enter or remain in the United Kingdom as the child of a person with limited leave to enter or remain in the United Kingdom as a retired person of independent means are that:

(i) he is the child of a parent who has been admitted to or allowed to remain in the United Kingdom as a retired person of independent means [or, for applications for leave to remain, of a parent with indefinite leave to remain in the UK and who had limited leave as a retired person of independent means immediately before being granted indefinite leave; and]

(ii) he is under the age of 18 or has current leave to enter or remain in this capacity; and

(iii) he is unmarried and is not a civil partner, has not formed an independent family unit and is not leading an independent life; and

(iv) he can, and will, be maintained and accommodated adequately without recourse to public funds in accommodation which his parent(s) own or occupy exclusively; and

(v) he will not stay in the United Kingdom beyond any period of leave granted to his parent(s); and

(vi) both parents are being or have been admitted to or allowed to remain in the United Kingdom save where:

(a) the parent he is accompanying or joining is his sole surviving parent; or

(b) the parent he is accompanying or joining has had sole responsibility for his upbringing; or

(c) there are serious and compelling family or other considerations which make exclusion from the United Kingdom undesirable and suitable arrangements have been made for his care; and

(vii) if seeking leave to enter, he holds a valid United Kingdom entry clearance for entry in this capacity or, if seeking leave to remain, he was not last granted:

(1) entry clearance or leave as a visitor,

(2) temporary admission, or

(3) temporary release;

and

(viii) if seeking leave to remain, must not be in the UK in breach of immigration laws except that any period of overstaying for a period of 28 days or less will be disregarded.

Note: Words inserted in subparagraph (i) and subparagraph (vii) from 28 October 2013 subject to savings for applications made before that date (HC 628).

Leave to enter or remain as the child of a person with limited leave to enter or remain in the United Kingdom as a retired person of independent means

275. (a) A person seeking leave to enter or remain in the United Kingdom as the child of a person with limited leave to enter or remain in the United Kingdom as a retired person of independent means may be given leave to enter or remain in the United Kingdom for a period of leave not in excess of that granted to the person with limited leave to enter or remain as a retired person of independent means if:

(i) in relation to an application for leave to enter, he is able to produce to the Immigration Officer, on arrival, a valid United Kingdom entry clearance for entry in this capacity; or

(ii) in the case of an application for limited leave to remain, he was not last granted:

(1) entry clearance or leave as a visitor,

(2) temporary admission, or

(3) temporary release,

and is able to satisfy the Secretary of State that each of the requirements of paragraph 274(i)–(vi) and (viii) is met.

(b) A person seeking limited leave to remain as the child of a parent who has indefinite leave to remain in the UK and who had limited leave as a retired person of independent means immediately before being granted indefinite leave may be given leave to remain in the UK for a period of 30 months provided he is in the UK with valid leave under paragraph 275 and is able to satisfy the Secretary of State that each of the requirements of paragraph 274(i) to (vi) and (viii) are satisfied.

Note: Paragraph 275 substituted from 28 October 2013 subject to savings for applications made before that date (HC 628).

275A. An application for indefinite leave to remain in this category may be granted provided the applicant meets the requirements listed below. If the applicant meets these requirements, indefinite leave to remain will be granted. If the applicant does not meet these requirements, the application will be refused.

Requirements

(i) he is the child of a parent with limited leave to enter or remain in the United Kingdom as a retired person of independent means who is, at the same time, being granted indefinite leave to remain, or he is the child of a parent who has indefinite leave to remain in the United Kingdom and who had limited leave under paragraphs 263–269 immediately before being granted indefinite leave; and

(ii) he is under the age of 18 or has current leave to enter or remain in this capacity; and

(iii) he is unmarried and is not a civil partner, has not formed an independent family unit and is not leading an independent life; and

(iv) he can and will be maintained and accommodated adequately without recourse to public funds in accommodation which his parent(s) own or occupy exclusively; and

(v) he will not stay in the United Kingdom beyond any period of leave granted to his parent(s); and

(vi) both parents are being or have been admitted to or allowed to remain in the United Kingdom save where:

(a) the parent he is accompanying or joining is his sole surviving parent; or

(b) the parent he is accompanying or joining has had sole responsibility for his upbringing; or

(c) there are serious and compelling family or other considerations which make exclusion from the United Kingdom undesirable and suitable arrangements have been made for his care;

(vii) he must not be in the UK in breach of immigration laws except that any period of overstaying for a period of 28 days or less will be disregarded;

(viii) if aged 18 or over, he has sufficient knowledge of the English language and sufficient knowledge about life in the United Kingdom in accordance with Appendix KoLL of these Rules;

(ix) indefinite leave to remain is, at the same time, being granted to the person with limited leave as a retired person of independent means unless, at the time when indefinite leave to remain was granted to that person, the applicant was aged 18 or over and unable to satisfy paragraph 275A(viii) and the applicant has continued to be in the United Kingdom with leave to remain as a child of that person.

Note: Paragraph 275A substituted from 28 October 2013 subject to savings for applications made before that date (HC 628).

Refusal of leave to enter or remain as the child of a person with limited leave to enter or remain in the United Kingdom as a retired person of independent means

276. Leave to enter or remain in the United Kingdom as the child of a person with limited leave to enter or remain in the United Kingdom as a retired person of independent means is to be refused if, in relation to an application for leave to enter, a valid United Kingdom entry clearance for entry in this capacity is not produced to the Immigration Officer on arrival, or in the case of an application for limited leave to remain, if the applicant was not admitted with a valid United Kingdom entry clearance for entry in this capacity or is unable to satisfy the Secretary of State that each of the requirements of paragraph 274(i)–(vi) and (viii) is met. [An application for indefinite leave to remain in this category is to be refused if the applicant was not admitted with a valid United Kingdom entry clearance for entry in this capacity or is unable to satisfy the Secretary of State that each of the requirements of paragraph 275 is met.]

Note: Words substituted from 28 October 2013 subject to savings for applications made before that date (HC 628).

Long residence

Long residence in the United Kingdom

276A. For the purposes of paragraphs 276B to 276D and [276ADE (1)] . . .

(a) "continuous residence" means residence in the United Kingdom for an unbroken period, and for these purposes a period shall not be considered to have been broken where an applicant is absent from the United Kingdom for a period of 6 months or less at any one time, provided that the applicant in question has existing limited leave to enter or remain upon their departure and return, but shall be considered to have been broken if the applicant:

(i) has been removed under Schedule 2 of the 1971 Act, section 10 of the 1999 Act, has been deported or has left the United Kingdom having been refused leave to enter or remain here; or

(ii) has left the United Kingdom and, on doing so, evidenced a clear intention not to return; or

(iii) left the United Kingdom in circumstances in which he could have had no reasonable expectation at the time of leaving that he would lawfully be able to return; or

(iv) has been convicted of an offence and was sentenced to a period of imprisonment or was directed to be detained in an institution other than a prison (including, in particular, a hospital or an institution for young offenders), provided that the sentence in question was not a suspended sentence; or

(v) has spent a total of more than 18 months absent from the United Kingdom during the period in question.

(b) "lawful residence" means residence which is continuous residence pursuant to:

(i) existing leave to enter or remain; or

(ii) temporary admission within section 11 of the 1971 Act where leave to enter or remain is subsequently granted; or

(iii) an exemption from immigration control, including where an exemption ceases to apply if it is immediately followed by a grant of leave to enter or remain.

(c) 'lived continuously' and 'living continuously' mean 'continuous residence', except that paragraph 276A(a)(iv) shall not apply.

Note: Words deleted from the end of 1st sentence from 11 July 2014 (HC 532). Words substituted in the 1st sentence from 6 November 2014 (HC 693).

276A0. For the purposes of paragraph 276ADE(1) the requirement to make a valid application will not apply when the Article 8 claim is raised:

(i) as part of an asylum claim, or as part of a further submission in person after an asylum claim has been refused;

(ii) where a migrant is in immigration detention. A migrant in immigration detention or their representative must submit any application or claim raising Article 8 to a prison officer, a prisoner custody officer, a detainee custody officer or a member of Home Office staff at the migrant's place of detention; or

(iii) in an appeal (subject to the consent of the Secretary of State where applicable).

Note: Paragraph 276A0 inserted from 6 April 2013 (HC 1039) and then substituted from 6 November 2014 (HC 693).

[**276A00.** Where leave to remain is granted under paragraphs 276ADE–276DH, or where an applicant does not meet the requirements in paragraph 276ADE(1) but the Secretary of State grants leave to remain outside the rules on Article 8 grounds, (and without prejudice to the specific provision that is made in paragraphs 276ADE–276DH in respect of a no recourse to public funds condition), that leave may be subject to such conditions as the Secretary of State considers appropriate in a particular case.]

Note: Paragraph 276A00 inserted from 28 July 2014 and applies to all applications to which paragraphs 276ADE–276DH and Appendix FM apply (or can be applied by virtue of the Immigration Rules), and to any other ECHR Article 8 claims (save for those from foreign criminals), and which are decided on or after that date (HC 532).

Requirements for an extension of stay on the ground of long residence in the United Kingdom

276A1. The requirement to be met by a person seeking an extension of stay on the ground of long residence in the United Kingdom is that the applicant meets each of the requirements in paragraph 276B(i)–(ii) and (v).

Extension of stay on the ground of long residence in the United Kingdom

276A2. An extension of stay on the ground of long residence in the United Kingdom may be granted for a period not exceeding 2 years provided that the Secretary of State is satisfied that the requirement in paragraph 276A1 is met, and a person granted such an extension of stay following an application made before 9 July 2012 will remain subject to the rules in force on 8 July 2012.

Conditions to be attached to extension of stay on the ground of long residence in the United Kingdom

276A3. Where an extension of stay is granted under paragraph 276A2:

(i) if the applicant has spent less than 20 years in the UK, the grant of leave should be subject to the same conditions attached to his last period of lawful leave, or

(ii) if the applicant has spent 20 years or more in the UK, the grant of leave should not contain any restriction on employment.

Refusal of extension of stay on the ground of long residence in the United Kingdom

276A4. An extension of stay on the ground of long residence in the United Kingdom is to be refused if the Secretary of State is not satisfied that the requirement in paragraph 276A1 is met.

Requirements for indefinite leave to remain on the ground of long residence in the United Kingdom

276B. The requirements to be met by an applicant for indefinite leave to remain on the ground of long residence in the United Kingdom are that:

(i) (a) he has had at least 10 years continuous lawful residence in the United Kingdom.

(ii) having regard to the public interest there are no reasons why it would be undesirable for him to be given indefinite leave to remain on the ground of long residence, taking into account his:

(a) age; and

(b) strength of connections in the United Kingdom; and

(c) personal history, including character, conduct, associations and employment record; and

(d) domestic circumstances; and

(e) compassionate circumstances; and

(f) any representations received on the person's behalf; and

(iii) the applicant does not fall for refusal under the general grounds for refusal.

(iv) the applicant has demonstrated sufficient knowledge of the English language and sufficient knowledge about life in the United Kingdom, in accordance with Appendix KoLL.

(v) the applicant must not be in the UK in breach of immigration laws except that any period of overstaying for a period of 28 days or less will be disregarded [, as will any period of overstaying between periods of entry clearance, leave to enter or leave to remain of up to 28 days and any period of overstaying pending the determination of an application made within that 28 day period.]

Note: Words substituted in subparagraph (iii) from 13 December 2012 (subject to savings for applications made before that date (HC 760). Words inserted in subparagraph (v) from 6 April 2013 (HC 1039). Subparagraph (iv) substituted from 28 October 2013 subject to savings for applications made before that date (HC 628).

Indefinite leave to remain on the ground of long residence in the United Kingdom

276C. Indefinite leave to remain on the ground of long residence in the United Kingdom may be granted provided that the Secretary of State is satisfied that each of the requirements of paragraph 276B is met.

Refusal of indefinite leave to remain on the ground of long residence in the United Kingdom

276D. Indefinite leave to remain on the ground of long residence in the United Kingdom is to be refused if the Secretary of State is not satisfied that each of the requirements of paragraph 276B is met.

Private life

Requirements to be met by an applicant for leave to remain on the grounds of private life

276ADE (1). The requirements to be met by an applicant for leave to remain on the grounds of private life in the UK are that at the date of application, the applicant:

(i) does not fall for refusal under any of the grounds in Section S-LTR.1.2 to S-LTR.2.3. and S-LTR.3.1. in Appendix FM; and

(ii) has made a valid application for leave to remain on the grounds of private life in the UK; and

(iii) has lived continuously in the UK for at least 20 years (discounting any period of imprisonment); or

(iv) is under the age of 18 years and has lived continuously in the UK for at least 7 years (discounting any period of imprisonment) [and it would not be reasonable to expect the applicant to leave the UK]; or

(v) is aged 18 years or above and under 25 years and has spent at least half of his life living continuously in the UK (discounting any period of imprisonment); or

(vi) [subject to sub-paragraph (2),] is aged 18 years or above, has lived continuously in the UK for less than 20 years (discounting any period of imprisonment) but [there would be very significant obstacles to the applicant's integration into] the country to which he would have to go if required to leave the UK.

276ADE(2). Sub-paragraph (1)(vi) does not apply, and may not be relied upon, in circumstances in which it is proposed to return a person to a third country pursuant to Schedule 3 to the Asylum and Immigration (Treatment of Claimants, etc.) Act 2004.

Note: Words inserted in subparagraph (1)(iv) from 13 December 2012 subject to savings for applications made before that (HC 760). Subparagraph (1)(ii) substituted from 6 April 2013 subject to savings for applications made before that date (HC 1039). Subparagraph (2) inserted and words inserted in subparagraph (1)(vi) from 13 December 2013 (HC 803). Words substituted in subparagraph (1)(vi) from28 July 2014, amendment applying to all applications to which paragraphs 276ADE–276DH and Appendix FM apply (or can be applied by virtue of the Immigration Rules), and to any other ECHR Article 8 claims (save for those from foreign criminals), and which are decided on or after that date (HC 532).

Leave to remain on the grounds of private life in the UK

276BE(1). Limited leave to remain on the grounds of private life in the UK may be granted for a period not exceeding 30 months provided that the Secretary of State is satisfied that the requirements in paragraph {276ADE(1)} are met or, in respect of the requirements in paragraph {276ADE(1)(iv) and (v)}, were met in a previous application which led to a grant of limited leave to remain under [this sub-paragraph]. Such leave shall be given subject to [a condition of no recourse to public funds unless the Secretary of State considers that the person should not be subject to such a condition].

Note: Paragraph 276BE(1) renumbered and words substituted from 28 July 2014, which amendments apply to all applications to which paragraphs 276ADE–276DH and Appendix FM apply (or can be applied by virtue of the Immigration Rules), and to any other ECHR Article 8 claims (save for those from foreign criminals), and which are decided on or after that date (HC 532). Words in curly brackets substituted from 6 November 2014 (HC 693).

276BE(2). Where an applicant does not meet the requirements in paragraph 276ADE(1) but the Secretary of State grants leave to remain outside the rules on Article 8 grounds, the applicant will normally be granted leave for a period not exceeding 30 months and subject to a condition of no recourse to public funds unless the Secretary of State considers that the person should not be subject to such a condition.

Note: Paragraph 276BE(2) inserted from 28 July 2014, and applies to all applications to which paragraphs 276ADE–276DH and Appendix FM apply (or can be applied by virtue of the Immigration Rules), and to any other ECHR Article 8 claims (save for those from foreign criminals), and which are decided on or after that date.

276BE(3). Where an applicant has extant leave at the date of decision, the remaining period of that extant leave up to a maximum of 28 days will be added to the period of limited leave to remain granted under paragraph 276BE(1) or 276BE(2) (which may therefore exceed 30 months).

Note: Paragraph 276BE(3) inserted from 6 November 2014 (HC 693).

Refusal of limited leave to remain on the grounds of private life in the UK

276CE. Limited leave to remain on the grounds of private life in the UK is to be refused if the Secretary of State is not satisfied that the requirements in paragraph [276ADE(1)] are met.

Note: Amended from 6 November 2014 (HC 693).

Requirements for indefinite leave to remain on the grounds of private life in the UK

276DE. The requirements to be met for the grant of indefinite leave to remain on the grounds of private life in the UK are that:

(a) the applicant has been in the UK with continuous leave on the grounds of private life for a period of at least 120 months [. This continuous leave will disregard any period of overstaying between periods of leave on the grounds of private life where the application was made no later than 28 days after the expiry of the previous leave. Any period pending the determination of the application will also be disregarded];

(b) the applicant meets the requirements of paragraph {276ADE(1)} [or, in respect of the requirements in paragraph {276ADE(1)(iv) and (v)}, the applicant met the requirements in a previous application which led to a grant of limited leave to remain under paragraph {276BE(1)}];

(c) the applicant does not fall for refusal under any of the grounds in Section S-ILR: Suitability-indefinite leave to remain in Appendix FM;

(d) the applicant has demonstrated sufficient knowledge of the English language and sufficient knowledge about life in the United Kingdom, in accordance with Appendix KoLL; and

(e) there are no reasons why it would be undesirable to grant the applicant indefinite leave to remain based on the applicant's conduct, character or associations or because the applicant represents a threat to national security.

Note: Words inserted in subparagraphs (a) and (c) from 13 December 2012 subject to savings for applications made before that date (HC 760). Words inserted in subparagraph (b) from 6 April 2013 (HC 1039). Subparagraph (d) substituted from 1 October 2013 subject to savings for applications made before that date (HC 628). Words in curly brackets substituted from 6 November 2014 (HC 693).

Indefinite leave to remain on the grounds of private life in the UK

276DF. Indefinite leave to remain on the grounds of private life in the UK may be granted provided that the Secretary of State is satisfied that each of the requirements of paragraph 276DE is met.

276DG. If the applicant does not meet the requirements for indefinite leave to remain on the grounds of private life in the UK only for one or both of the following reasons—

(a) paragraph S-ILR 1.5. or S-ILR 1.6. in Appendix FM applies;

(b) the applicant has not met the requirements of paragraphs 33B to 33G of these Rules,

the applicant may be granted further limited leave to remain on the grounds of private life in the UK for a period not exceeding 30 months, and subject to [a condition of no recourde to public funds unless the Secretary of State considers that the person should not be subject to such a condition].

Note: Subparagraph (a) substituted from 13 December 2012 subject to savings for applications made before that date (HC 760). Words substituted from 28 July 2014; this change applies to all applications to which paragraphs 276ADE–276DH and Appendix FM apply (or can be applied by virtue of the Immigration Rules), and to any other ECHR Article 8 claims (save for those from foreign criminals), and which are decided on or after that date: see HC 532.

Refusal of indefinite leave to remain on the grounds of private life in the UK

276DH. Indefinite leave to remain on the grounds of private life in the UK is to be refused if the Secretary of State is not satisfied that each of the requirements of paragraph 276DE is met, subject to paragraph 276DG.

HM Forces

Transitional provisions and interaction between paragraphs 276E to 276AI of Part 7 and Appendix Armed Forces

276DI. From 1 December 2013, Appendix Armed Forces will apply to all applications to which paragraphs 276E to 276AI of this Part applied on or before 30 November 2013, except where the provisions of 276E to 276AI are preserved and continue to apply in accordance with paragraph 276DL.

Note: Paragraphs 276DI–276DL inserted from 1 December 2013 subject to savings for applications made before that date (HC 803).

276DJ. The requirements to be met under paragraphs 276E to 276AI from 1 December 2013 may be modified or supplemented by the requirements in Appendix Armed Forces or Appendix FM-SE.

Note: Paragraphs 276DI–276DL inserted from 1 December 2013 subject to savings for applications made before that date (HC 803).

276DK. The requirements in paragraphs 8 and 9 of Appendix Armed Forces apply to applications made under paragraphs 276E to 276AI where the decision is made on or after 1 December 2013 (and irrespective of the date of the application).

Note: Paragraphs 276DI–276DL inserted from 1 December 2013 subject to savings for applications made before that date (HC 803).

276DL. Paragraphs 276E–276AI also continue to apply to applications:

(i) made before 1 December 2013 under paragraphs 276E to 276AI but which have not been decided before that date; and

(ii) by persons who have been granted entry clearance or limited leave to enter or remain under paragraphs 276E to 276AI before 1 December 2013 or in accordance with sub-paragraph (i) above and, where it is a requirement of Part 7, that leave to enter or remain is extant.

Note: Paragraphs 276DI–276DL inserted from 1 December 2013 subject to savings for applications made before that date (HC 803).

Definition of Gurkha

276E. For the purposes of these Rules the term "Gurkha" means a citizen or national of Nepal who has served in the Brigade of Gurkhas of the British Army under the Brigade of Gurkhas' terms and conditions of service.

Leave to enter or remain in the United Kingdom as a Gurkha discharged from the British Army

Requirements for indefinite leave to enter the United Kingdom as a Gurkha discharged from the British Army

276F. The requirements for indefinite leave to enter the United Kingdom as a Gurkha discharged from the British Army are that:

(i) the applicant has completed at least four years' service as a Gurkha with the British Army; and

(ii) was discharged from the British Army in Nepal on completion of engagement on or after 1 July 1997; and

(iii) was not discharged from the British Army more than 2 years prior to the date on which the application is made; and

(iv) holds a valid United Kingdom entry clearance for entry in this capacity; and

(v) does not fall for refusal under the general grounds for refusal.

Note: Words substituted in subparagraph (v) from 13 December 2012 subject to savings for applications made before that date (HC 760).

Indefinite leave to enter the United Kingdom as a Gurkha discharged from the British Army

276G. A person seeking indefinite leave to enter the United Kingdom as a Gurkha discharged from the British Army may be granted indefinite leave to enter provided a valid United Kingdom entry clearance for entry in this capacity is produced to the Immigration Officer on arrival.

Refusal of indefinite leave to enter the United Kingdom as a Gurkha discharged from the British Army

276H. Indefinite leave to enter the United Kingdom as a Gurkha discharged from the British Army is to be refused if a valid United Kingdom entry clearance for entry in this capacity is not produced to the Immigration Officer on arrival.

Requirements for indefinite leave to remain in the United Kingdom as a Gurkha discharged from the British Army

276I. The requirements for indefinite leave to remain in the United Kingdom as a Gurkha discharged from the British Army are that [the applicant]:

(i) . . . has completed at least four years' service as a Gurkha with the British Army; and

(ii) was discharged from the British Army in Nepal on completion of engagement on or after 1 July 1997; and

(iii) was not discharged from the British Army more than 2 years prior to the date on which the application is made [unless they are applying following a grant of limited leave to remain under paragraph 276KA]; and

(iv) is not in the UK in breach of immigration laws except that any period of overstaying for a period of 28 days or less will be disregarded; and

(v) does not fall for refusal under the general grounds for refusal.

Note: Words inserted in opening sentence, word deleted from subparagraph (i), words inserted in subparagraph (iii) and subparagraphs (iv) and (v) from 13 December 2012 subject to savings for applications made before that date (HC 760).

Indefinite leave to remain in the United Kingdom as a Gurkha discharged from the British Army

276J. A person seeking indefinite leave to remain in the United Kingdom as a Gurkha discharged from the British Army may be granted indefinite leave to remain provided the Secretary of State is satisfied that each of the requirements of paragraph 276I is met.

Refusal of indefinite leave to remain in the United Kingdom as a Gurkha discharged from the British Army

276K. Indefinite leave to remain in the United Kingdom as a Gurkha discharged from the British Army is to be refused if the Secretary of State is not satisfied that each of the requirements of paragraph 276I is met.

Leave to remain in the United Kingdom as a Gurkha discharged from the British Army

276KA. If a Gurkha discharged from the British Army does not meet the requirements for indefinite leave to remain only because paragraph 322(1C)(iii) or 322(1C)(iv) applies, the applicant may be granted limited leave to remain for a period not exceeding 30 months.

Note: Subparagraph 276KA inserted from 13 December 2012 subject to savings for applications made before that date (HC 760).

Leave to enter or remain in the United Kingdom as a foreign or Commonwealth citizen discharged from HM Forces

Requirements for indefinite leave to enter the United Kingdom as a foreign or Commonwealth citizen discharged from HM Forces

276L. The requirements for indefinite leave to enter the United Kingdom as a foreign or Commonwealth citizen discharged from HM Forces are that [the applicant]:

(i) . . . has completed at least four years' service with HM Forces; and

(ii) was discharged from HM Forces on completion of engagement; and

(iii) was not discharged from HM Forces more than 2 years prior to the date on which the application is made; and

(iv) holds a valid United Kingdom entry clearance for entry in this capacity; and

(v) does not fall for refusal under the general grounds for refusal.

Note: Words substituted in opening sentence, words deleted from subparagraph (i) and words substituted in subparagraph (v) from 13 December 2012 subject to savings for applications made before that date (HC 760).

Indefinite leave to enter the United Kingdom as a foreign or Commonwealth citizen discharged from HM Forces

276M. A person seeking indefinite leave to enter the United Kingdom as a foreign or Commonwealth citizen discharged from HM Forces may be granted indefinite leave to enter provided a valid United Kingdom entry clearance for entry in this capacity is produced to the Immigration Officer on arrival.

Refusal of indefinite leave to enter the United Kingdom as a foreign or Commonwealth citizen discharged from HM Forces

276N. Indefinite leave to enter the United Kingdom as a foreign or Commonwealth citizen discharged from HM Forces is to be refused if a valid United Kingdom entry clearance for entry in this capacity is not produced to the Immigration Officer on arrival.

Requirements for indefinite leave to remain in the United Kingdom as a foreign or Commonwealth citizen discharged from HM Forces

276O. The requirements for indefinite leave to remain in the United Kingdom as a foreign or Commonwealth citizen discharged from HM Forces are that the applicant:

(i) has completed at least four years' service with HM Forces; and

(ii) was discharged from HM Forces on completion of engagement; and

(iii) was not discharged from HM Forces more than 2 years prior to the date on which the application is made [unless they are applying following a grant of limited leave to remain under paragraph 276QA]; and

(iv) is not in the UK in breach of immigration laws except that any period of overstaying for a period of 28 days or less will be disregarded; and

(v) does not fall for refusal under the general grounds for refusal.

Note: Words substituted in opening sentence, words deleted from subparagraph (i), words inserted in subparagraph (iii) and words substituted in subparagraph (v) from 13 December 2012 subject to savings for applications made before that date (HC 760).

Indefinite leave to remain in the United Kingdom as a foreign or Commonwealth citizen discharged from HM Forces

276P. A person seeking indefinite leave to remain in the United Kingdom as a foreign or Commonwealth citizen discharged from HM Forces may be granted indefinite leave to remain provided the Secretary of State is satisfied that each of the requirements of paragraph 276O is met.

Refusal of indefinite leave to remain in the United Kingdom as a foreign or Commonwealth citizen discharged from HM Forces

276Q. Indefinite leave to remain in the United Kingdom as a foreign or Commonwealth citizen discharged from HM Forces is to be refused if the Secretary of State is not satisfied that each of the requirements of paragraph 276O is met.

Leave to remain in the United Kingdom as a foreign or Commonwealth citizen discharged from HM Forces

276QA. If a foreign or Commonwealth citizen discharged from HM Forces does not meet the requirements for indefinite leave to remain only because paragraph 322(1C)(iii) or 322(1C)(iv) applies, the applicant may be granted limited leave to remain for a period not exceeding 30 months.

Note: Paragraph 276QA inserted from 13 December 2012 subject to savings for applications made before that date (HC 760).

Spouses, civil partners, unmarried or same-sex partners of persons settled or seeking settlement in the United Kingdom in accordance with paragraphs 276E to 276Q (HM Forces rules) or of members of HM Forces who are exempt from immigration control under section 8(4)(a) of the Immigration Act 1971 and have at least 5 years' continuous service

Leave to enter or remain in the UK as the spouse, civil partner, unmarried or same-sex partner of a person present and settled in the United Kingdom or being granted settlement on the same occasion in accordance with paragraphs 276E to 276Q or of a member of HM Forces who is exempt from immigration control under section 8(4)(a) of the Immigration Act 1971 and has at least 5 years' continuous service.

Requirements for indefinite leave to enter the United Kingdom as the spouse, civil partner, unmarried or same-sex partner of a person present and settled in the United Kingdom or being admitted on the same occasion for settlement under paragraphs 276E to 276Q or of a member of HM Forces who is exempt from immigration control under section 8(4)(a) of the Immigration Act 1971 and has at least 5 years' continuous service

276R. The requirements to be met by a person seeking indefinite leave to enter the United Kingdom as the spouse, civil partner, unmarried or same-sex partner of a person present and settled in the United Kingdom or being admitted on the same occasion for settlement in accordance with paragraphs 276E to 276Q or of a member of HM Forces who is exempt from immigration control under section 8(4)(a) of the Immigration Act 1971 and has at least 5 years' continuous service are that:

(i) the applicant is married to, or the civil partner, unmarried or same-sex partner of, a person present and settled in the United Kingdom or who is being admitted on the same occasion for settlement in accordance with paragraphs 276E to 276Q or of a member of HM Forces who is exempt from immigration control under section 8(4)(a) of the Immigration Act 1971 and has at least 5 years' continuous service; and

(ii) the parties to the marriage, or civil partnership or relationship akin to marriage or civil partnership have met; and

(iii) the parties were married or formed a civil partnership or a relationship akin to marriage or civil partnership at least 2 years ago; and

(iv) each of the parties intends to live permanently with the other as his or her spouse, civil partner, unmarried or same-sex partner; and

(v) the marriage, civil partnership or relationship akin to marriage or civil partnership is subsisting; and

(vi) the applicant holds a valid United Kingdom entry clearance for entry in this capacity;

and

(vii) the applicant does not [fall for refusal under the general grounds for refusal].

Note: Words substituted in subparagraph (vii) from 13 December 2012 subject to savings for applications made before that date (HC 760).

Indefinite leave to enter the United Kingdom as the spouse, civil partner, unmarried or same-sex partner of a person present and settled in the United Kingdom or being admitted on the same occasion for settlement in accordance with paragraphs 276E to 276Q or of a member of HM Forces who is exempt from immigration control under section 8(4)(a) of the Immigration Act 1971 and has at least 5 years' continuous service

276S. A person seeking leave to enter the United Kingdom as the spouse, civil partner, unmarried or same-sex partner of a person present and settled in the United Kingdom or being admitted on the same occasion for settlement in accordance with paragraphs 276E to 276Q or of a member of HM Forces who is exempt from immigration control under section 8(4)(a) of the Immigration Act 1971 and has at least 5 years' continuous service may be granted indefinite leave to enter provided a valid United Kingdom entry clearance for entry in this capacity is produced to the Immigration Officer on arrival.

Refusal of indefinite leave to enter the United Kingdom as the spouse, civil partner, unmarried or same-sex partner of a person present and settled in the UK or being admitted on the same occasion for settlement in accordance with paragraphs 276E to 276Q or of a member of HM Forces who is exempt from immigration control under section 8(4)(a) of the Immigration Act 1971 and has at least 5 years' continuous service

276T. Leave to enter the United Kingdom as the spouse, civil partner, unmarried or same-sex partner of a person present and settled in the United Kingdom or being admitted on the same occasion for settlement in accordance with paragraphs 276E to 276Q or of a member of HM Forces who is exempt from immigration control under section 8(4)(a) of the Immigration Act 1971 and has at least 5 years' continuous service is to be refused if a valid United Kingdom entry clearance for entry in this capacity is not produced to the Immigration Officer on arrival.

Requirement for indefinite leave to remain in the United Kingdom as the spouse, civil partner, unmarried or same-sex partner of a person present and settled in the United Kingdom under paragraphs 276E to 276Q or being granted settlement on the same occasion in accordance with paragraphs 276E to 276Q or of a member of HM Forces who is exempt from immigration control under section 8(4)(a) of the Immigration Act 1971 and has at least 5 years' continuous service

276U. The requirements to be met by a person seeking indefinite leave to remain in the United Kingdom as the spouse, civil partner, unmarried or same-sex partner of a person present and settled in the United Kingdom or being granted settlement on the same occasion in accordance with paragraphs 276E to 276Q or of a member of HM Forces who is exempt from immigration control under section 8(4)(a) of the Immigration Act 1971 and has at least 5 years' continuous service are that:

(i) the applicant is married to or the civil partner or unmarried or same-sex partner of a person present and settled in the United Kingdom or being granted settlement on the same occasion in accordance with paragraphs 276E to 276Q or of a member of HM Forces who is exempt from immigration control under section 8(4)(a) of the Immigration Act 1971 and has at least 5 years' continuous service; and

(ii) the parties to the marriage, civil partnership or relationship akin to marriage or civil partnership have met; and

(iii) the parties were married or formed a civil partnership or relationship akin to marriage or civil partnership at least 2 years ago; and

(iv) each of the parties intends to live permanently with the other as his or her spouse, civil partner, unmarried or same-sex partner; and

(v) the marriage, civil partnership or relationship akin to marriage or civil partnership is subsisting; and

(vi) has, or has last been granted, leave to enter or remain in the United Kingdom as the spouse, civil partner, unmarried or same-sex partner; and

(vii) the applicant [does not fall for refusal under the general grounds for refusal].

Note: Words substituted in subparagraph (vii) from 13 December 2012 subject to savings for applications made before that date (HC 760).

Indefinite leave to remain in the United Kingdom as the spouse, civil partner, unmarried or same-sex partner of a person present and settled in the United Kingdom or being granted settlement on the same occasion in accordance with paragraphs 276E to 276Q or of a member of HM Forces who is exempt from immigration control under section 8(4)(a) of the Immigration Act 1971 and has at least 5 years' continuous service

276V. Indefinite leave to remain in the United Kingdom as the spouse, civil partner, unmarried or same-sex partner of a person present and settled in the United Kingdom or being granted settlement on the same occasion in accordance with paragraphs 276E to 276Q or of a member of HM Forces who is exempt from immigration control under section 8(4)(a) of the Immigration Act 1971 and has at least 5 years' continuous service

may be granted provided the Secretary of State is satisfied that each of the requirements of paragraph 276U is met.

Refusal of indefinite leave to remain in the United Kingdom as the spouse, civil partner, unmarried or same-sex partner of a person present and settled in the United Kingdom or being granted settlement on the same occasion in accordance with paragraphs 276E to 276Q or of a member of HM Forces who is exempt from immigration control under section 8(4)(a) of the Immigration Act 1971 and has at least 5 years' continuous service

276W. Indefinite leave to remain in the United Kingdom as the spouse, civil partner, unmarried or same-sex partner of a person present and settled in the United Kingdom or being granted settlement on the same occasion in accordance with paragraphs 276E to 276Q or of a member of HM Forces who is exempt from immigration control under section 8(4)(a) of the Immigration Act 1971 and has at least 5 years' continuous service is to be refused if the Secretary of State is not satisfied that each of the requirements of paragraph 276U is met.

Children of a parent, parents or a relative settled or seeking settlement in the United Kingdom under paragraphs 276E to 276Q (HM Forces rules) or of members of HM Forces who are exempt from immigration control under section 8(4)(a) of the Immigration Act 1971 and have at least 5 years' continuous service

Leave to enter or remain in the United Kingdom as the child of a parent, parents or a relative present and settled in the United Kingdom or being granted settlement on the same occasion in accordance with paragraphs 276E to 276Q or of a member of HM Forces who is exempt from immigration control under section 8(4)(a) of the Immigration Act 1971 and has at least 5 years' continuous service

Requirements for indefinite leave to enter the United Kingdom as the child of a parent, parents or a relative present and settled in the United Kingdom or being admitted for settlement on the same occasion in accordance with paragraphs 276E to 276Q or of a member of HM Forces who is exempt from immigration control under section 8(4)(a) of the Immigration Act 1971 and has at least 5 years' continuous service

276X. The requirements to be met by a person seeking indefinite leave to enter the United Kingdom as the child of a parent, parents or a relative present and settled in the United Kingdom or being admitted for settlement on the same occasion in accordance with paragraphs 276E to 276Q or of a member of HM Forces who is exempt from immigration control under section 8(4)(a) of the Immigration Act 1971 and has at least 5 years' continuous service are that:

(i) the applicant is seeking indefinite leave to enter to accompany or join a parent, parents or a relative in one of the following circumstances:

(a) both parents are present and settled in the United Kingdom; or

(b) both parents are being admitted on the same occasion for settlement; or

(c) one parent is present and settled in the United Kingdom or is a member of HM Forces who is exempt from immigration control under section 8(4)(a) of the Immigration

Act 1971 and has at least 5 years' continuous service and the other is being admitted on the same occasion for settlement or is a member of HM Forces who is exempt from immigration control under section 8(4)(a) of the Immigration Act 1971 and has at least 5 years' continuous service; or

(d) one parent is present and settled in the United Kingdom or being admitted on the same occasion for settlement or is a member of HM Forces who is exempt from immigration control under section 8(4)(a) of the Immigration Act 1971 and has at least 5 years' continuous service and the other parent is dead; or

(e) one parent is present and settled in the United Kingdom or being admitted on the same occasion for settlement or is a member of HM Forces who is exempt from immigration control under section 8(4)(a) of the Immigration Act 1971 and has at least 5 years' continuous service and has had sole responsibility for the child's upbringing; or

(f) one parent or a relative is present and settled in the United Kingdom or being admitted on the same occasion for settlement or is a member of HM Forces who is exempt from immigration control under section 8(4)(a) of the Immigration Act 1971 and has at least 5 years' continuous service and there are serious and compelling family or other considerations which make exclusion of the child undesirable and suitable arrangements have been made for the child's care; and

(ii) is under the age of 18; and

(iii) is not leading an independent life, is unmarried and is not a civil partner, and has not formed an independent family unit; and

(iv) holds a valid United Kingdom entry clearance for entry in this capacity; and

(v) the applicant [does not fall for refusal under the general grounds for refusal].

Note: Words substituted in subparagraph (v) from 13 December 2012 subject to savings for applications made before that date (HC 760).

Indefinite leave to enter the United Kingdom as the child of a parent, parents or a relative present and settled in the United Kingdom or being admitted for settlement on the same occasion in accordance with paragraphs 276E to 276Q or of a member of HM Forces who is exempt from immigration control under section 8(4)(a) of the Immigration Act 1971 and has at least 5 years' continuous service

276Y. Indefinite leave to enter the United Kingdom as the child of a parent, parents or a relative present and settled in the United Kingdom or being admitted for settlement on the same occasion in accordance with paragraphs 276E to 276Q or of a member of HM Forces who is exempt from immigration control under section 8(4)(a) of the Immigration Act 1971 and has at least 5 years' continuous service may be granted provided a valid United Kingdom entry clearance for entry in this capacity is produced to the Immigration Officer on arrival.

Refusal of indefinite leave to enter the United Kingdom as the child of a parent, parents or a relative present and settled in the United Kingdom or being admitted for settlement on the same occasion in accordance with paragraphs 276E to 276Q or of a member of HM Forces who is exempt from immigration control under section 8(4)(a) of the Immigration Act 1971 and has at least 5 years' continuous service

276Z. Indefinite leave to enter the United Kingdom as the child of a parent, parents, or a relative present and settled in the United Kingdom or being admitted for settlement on the same occasion in accordance with paragraphs 276E to 276Q or of a member of HM

Forces who is exempt from immigration control under section 8(4)(a) of the Immigration Act 1971 and has at least 5 years' continuous service is to be refused if a valid United Kingdom entry clearance for entry in this capacity is not produced to the Immigration Officer on arrival.

Requirements for indefinite leave to remain in the United Kingdom as the child of a parent, parents or a relative present and settled in the United Kingdom or being granted settlement on the same occasion in accordance with paragraphs 276E to 276Q or of a member of HM Forces who is exempt from immigration control under section 8(4)(a) of the Immigration Act 1971 and has at least 5 years' continuous service

276AA. The requirements to be met by a person seeking indefinite leave to remain in the United Kingdom as the child of a parent, parents or a relative present and settled in the United Kingdom or being granted settlement on the same occasion in accordance with paragraphs 276E to 276Q or of a member of HM Forces who is exempt from immigration control under section 8(4)(a) of the Immigration Act 1971 and has at least 5 years' continuous service are that:

(i) the applicant is seeking indefinite leave to remain with a parent, parents or a relative in one of the following circumstances:

(a) both parents are present and settled in the United Kingdom or being granted settlement on the same occasion; or

(ab) one parent is present and settled in the United Kingdom or is a member of HM Forces who is exempt from immigration control under section 8(4)(a) of the Immigration Act 1971 and has at least 5 years' continuous service and the other is being granted settlement on the same occasion or is a member of HM Forces who is exempt from immigration control under section 8(4)(a) of the Immigration Act 1971 and has at least 5 years' continuous service; or

(b) one parent is present and settled in the United Kingdom or being granted settlement on the same occasion or is a member of HM Forces who is exempt from immigration control under section 8(4)(a) of the Immigration Act 1971 and has at least 5 years' continuous service and the other parent is dead; or

(c) one parent is present and settled in the United Kingdom or being granted settlement on the same occasion or is a member of HM Forces who is exempt from immigration control under section 8(4)(a) of the Immigration Act 1971 and has at least 5 years' continuous service and has had sole responsibility for the child's upbringing; or

(d) one parent or a relative is present and settled in the United Kingdom or being granted settlement on the same occasion or is a member of HM Forces who is exempt from immigration control under section 8(4)(a) of the Immigration Act 1971 and has at least 5 years' continuous service and there are serious and compelling family or other considerations which make exclusion of the child undesirable and suitable arrangements have been made for the child's care; and

(ii) is under the age of 18; and

(iii) is not leading an independent life, is unmarried and is not a civil partner, and has not formed an independent family unit; and

(iv) is not in the UK in breach of immigration laws except that any period of overstaying for a period of 28 days or less will be disregarded; and

(v) the applicant [does not fall for refusal under the general grounds for refusal].

Note: Words substituted in subparagraph (v) from 13 December 2012 subject to savings for applications made before that date (HC 760).

Indefinite leave to remain in the United Kingdom as the child of a parent, parents or a relative present and settled in the United Kingdom or being granted settlement on the same occasion in accordance with paragraphs 276E to 276Q or of a member of HM Forces who is exempt from immigration control under section 8(4)(a) of the Immigration Act 1971 and has at least 5 years' continuous service

276AB. Indefinite leave to remain in the United Kingdom as the child of a parent, parents or a relative present and settled in the United Kingdom or being granted settlement on the same occasion in accordance with paragraphs 276E to 276Q or of a member of HM Forces who is exempt from immigration control under section 8(4)(a) of the Immigration Act 1971 and has at least 5 years' continuous service may be granted if the Secretary of State is satisfied that each of the requirements of paragraph 276AA is met.

Refusal of indefinite leave to remain in the United Kingdom as the child of a parent, parents or a relative present and settled in the United Kingdom or being granted settlement on the same occasion in accordance with paragraphs 276E to 276Q or of a member of HM Forces who is exempt from immigration control under section 8(4)(a) of the Immigration Act 1971 and has at least 5 years' continuous service

276AC. Indefinite leave to remain in the United Kingdom as the child of a parent, parents or a relative present and settled in the United Kingdom or being granted settlement on the same occasion in accordance with paragraphs 276E to 276Q or of a member of HM Forces who is exempt from immigration control under section 8(4)(a) of the Immigration Act 1971 and has at least 5 years' continuous service is to be refused if the Secretary of State is not satisfied that each of the requirements of paragraph 276AA is met.

Spouses, civil partners, unmarried or same-sex partners of armed forces members who are exempt from immigration control under section 8(4) of the Immigration Act 1971

Requirements for leave to enter or remain as the spouse, civil partner, unmarried or same-sex partner of an armed forces member who is exempt from immigration control under section 8(4) of the Immigration Act 1971

276AD. The requirements to be met by a person seeking leave to enter or remain in the United Kingdom as the spouse, civil partner, unmarried or same-sex partner of an armed forces member who is exempt from immigration control under section 8(4) of the Immigration Act 1971 are that:

(i) the applicant is married to or the civil partner, unmarried or same-sex partner of an armed forces member who is exempt from immigration control under section 8(4) of the Immigration Act 1971; and

(ii) each of the parties intends to live with the other as his or her spouse or civil partner, unmarried or same-sex partner during the applicant's stay and the marriage, civil partnership, or relationship akin to a marriage or civil partnership is subsisting; and

(iii) there will be adequate accommodation for the parties and any dependants without recourse to public funds in accommodation which they own or occupy exclusively; and

(iv) the parties will be able to maintain themselves and any dependants adequately without recourse to public funds;

(v) the applicant does not intend to stay in the United Kingdom beyond his or her spouse's, civil partner's, unmarried or same-sex partner's enlistment in the home forces, or period of posting or training in the United Kingdom; and

(vi) where the applicant is the unmarried or same-sex partner of an armed forces member who is exempt from immigration control under section 8(4) of the Immigration Act 1971, the following requirements are also met:

(a) any previous marriage or civil partnership or relationship akin to a marriage by the applicant or the exempt armed forces member must have permanently broken down,

(b) the applicant and the exempt armed forces member must not be so closely related that they would be prohibited from marrying each other in the UK, and

(c) the applicant and the exempt armed forces member must have been living together in a relationship akin to marriage or civil partnership for a period of at least 2 years.

Leave to enter or remain as the spouse, civil partner, unmarried or same-sex partner of an armed forces member who is exempt from immigration control under section 8(4) of the Immigration Act 1971

276AE. A person seeking leave to enter or remain in the United Kingdom as the spouse, civil partner, unmarried or same-sex partner of an armed forces member who is exempt from immigration control under section 8(4) of the Immigration Act 1971 may be given leave to enter or remain in the United Kingdom for a period not exceeding 4 years or the expected duration of the enlistment, posting or training of his or her spouse, civil partner, unmarried or same-sex partner, whichever is shorter, provided that the Immigration Officer, or in the case of an application for leave to remain, the Secretary of State, is satisfied that each of the requirements of paragraph 276AD (i)–(vi) is met.

Refusal of leave to enter or remain as the spouse, civil partner, unmarried or same-sex partner of an armed forces member who is exempt from immigration control under section 8(4) of the Immigration Act 1971

276AF. Leave to enter or remain in the United Kingdom as the spouse, civil partner, unmarried or same-sex partner of an armed forces member who is exempt from immigration control under section 8(4) of the Immigration Act 1971 is to be refused if the Immigration Officer, or in the case of an application for leave to remain, the Secretary of State, is not satisfied that each of the requirements of paragraph 276AD(i)–(vi) is met.

Children of armed forces members who are exempt from immigration control under section 8(4) of the Immigration Act 1971

Requirements for leave to enter or remain as the child of an armed forces member exempt from immigration control under section 8(4) of the Immigration Act 1971

276AG. The requirements to be met by a person seeking leave to enter or remain in the United Kingdom as the child of an armed forces member exempt from immigration control under section 8(4) of the Immigration Act 1971 are that:

(i) he is the child of a parent who is an armed forces member exempt from immigration control under section 8(4) of the Immigration Act 1971; and

(ii) he is under the age of 18 or has current leave to enter or remain in this capacity; and

(iii) he is unmarried and is not a civil partner, has not formed an independent family unit and is not leading an independent life; and

(iv) he can and will be maintained and accommodated adequately without recourse to public funds in accommodation which his parent(s) own or occupy exclusively; and

(v) he will not stay in the United Kingdom beyond the period of his parent's enlistment in the home forces, or posting or training in the United Kingdom; and

(vi) his other parent is being or has been admitted to or allowed to remain in the United Kingdom save where:

(a) the parent he is accompanying or joining is his sole surviving parent; or

(b) the parent he is accompanying or joining has had sole responsibility for his upbringing; or

(c) there are serious and compelling family or other considerations which make exclusion from the United Kingdom undesirable and suitable arrangements have been made for his care.

Leave to enter or remain as the child of an armed forces member exempt from immigration control under section 8(4) of the Immigration Act 1971

276AH. A person seeking leave to enter or remain in the United Kingdom as the child of an armed forces member exempt from immigration control under section 8(4) of the Immigration Act 1971 may be given leave to enter or remain in the United Kingdom for a period not exceeding 4 years or the duration of the enlistment, posting or training of his parent, whichever is the shorter, provided that the Immigration Officer, or in the case of an application for leave to remain, the Secretary of State, is satisfied that each of the requirements of 276AG (i)–(vi) is met.

Refusal of leave to enter or remain as the child of an armed forces member exempt from immigration control under section 8(4) of the Immigration Act 1971

276AI. Leave to enter or remain in the United Kingdom as the child of an armed forces member exempt from immigration control under section 8(4) of the Immigration Act 1971 is to be refused if the Immigration Officer, or in the case of an application for leave to remain, the Secretary of State, is not satisfied that each of the requirements of paragraph 276AG (i)–(vi) is met.

Limited leave to enter for relevant Afghan citizens

Limited leave to enter the United Kingdom as a relevant Afghan citizen

276BA1. Limited leave to enter the United Kingdom for a period not exceeding 5 years will be granted to relevant Afghan citizens, unless the application falls for refusal under paragraph 276BC1.

Note: Paragraphs 276BA1–276BS1 inserted from 1 October 2013 subject to savings for applications made before that date (HC 628).

Definition of a "relevant Afghan citizen"

276BB1. A relevant Afghan citizen is a person who:

(i) is in Afghanistan;

(ii) is an Afghan citizen;

(iii) is aged 18 years or over;

(iv) was employed in Afghanistan directly by the Ministry of Defence, the Foreign and Commonwealth Office or the Department for International Development;

(v) was made redundant on or after 19 December 2012; and

(vi) the Ministry of Defence, the Foreign and Commonwealth Office, or the Department for International Development has determined should qualify for the resettlement redundancy package as described in the written Ministerial statement of the Secretary of State for Defence dated 4th June 2013.

Note: Paragraphs 276BA1–276BS1 inserted from 1 October 2013 subject to savings for applications made before that date (HC 628).

Refusal of limited leave to enter the United Kingdom as a relevant Afghan citizen

276BC1. An applicant will be refused leave to enter as a relevant Afghan citizen if:

(i) their application falls for refusal under the general grounds of refusal contained in Part 9 of these Rules;

(ii) there are serious reasons for considering that the applicant has committed a crime against peace, a war crime, a crime against humanity, or any other serious crime or instigated or otherwise participated in such crimes;

(iii) there are serious reasons for considering that the applicant is guilty of acts contrary to the purposes and principles of the United Nations or has committed, prepared or instigated such acts or encouraged or induced others to commit, prepare or instigate such acts; or

(iv) there are serious reasons for considering that the applicant constitutes a danger to the community or to the security of the United Kingdom.

Note: Paragraphs 276BA1–276BS1 inserted from 1 October 2013 subject to savings for applications made before that date (HC 628).

Curtailment of leave to enter the United Kingdom as a relevant Afghan citizen

276BD1. Limited leave to enter the United Kingdom as a relevant Afghan citizen under paragraph 276BA1 may be curtailed where the person is a danger to the security or public order of the United Kingdom or leave may be curtailed where:

(i) the relevant Afghan citizen has made false representations or failed to disclose any material fact for the purpose of obtaining leave to enter; and/or

(ii) it is undesirable to permit the relevant Afghan citizen to remain in the United Kingdom in the light of his conduct, character or associations or the fact that he represents a threat to national security.

Note: Paragraphs 276BA1–276BS1 inserted from 1 October 2013 subject to savings for applications made before that date (HC 628).

Dependants of a relevant Afghan citizen

276BE1. A relevant Afghan citizen may include a partner or minor dependant child in his or her application for limited leave to enter as his or her dependants.

Note: Paragraphs 276BA1–276BS1 inserted from 1 October 2013 subject to savings for applications made before that date (HC 628).

276BF1. All dependants included in the application for limited leave to enter the United Kingdom must be:

(i) Afghan citizens; and
(ii) in Afghanistan.

276BG1. The application must include the details of all dependents seeking relocation at the time the application is made. Additional dependants cannot normally be added after the application has been made.

Note: Paragraphs 276BA1–276BS1 inserted from 1 October 2013 subject to savings for applications made before that date (HC 628).

276BH1. If the application is successful, the relevant Afghan citizen and his eligible dependents must all travel at the same time.

Note: Paragraphs 276BA1–276BS1 inserted from 1 October 2013 subject to savings for applications made before that date (HC 628).

276BI1. If the relevant Afghan citizen is in a polygamous marriage, his or her application for limited leave may only include one partner.

Note: Paragraphs 276BA1–276BS1 inserted from 1 October 2013 subject to savings for applications made before that date (HC 628).

Limited leave to enter the United Kingdom as the partner of a relevant Afghan citizen

276BJ1. Limited leave to enter the United Kingdom for a period not exceeding 5 years will be granted to the partner of a relevant Afghan citizen where;

(i) the relationship requirements under paragraph 276BL1 are met; and
(ii) the application does not fall for refusal under paragraph 276BM1.

Note: Paragraphs 276BA1–276BS1 inserted from 1 October 2013 subject to savings for applications made before that date (HC 628).

Definition of "partner" of a relevant Afghan citizen

276BK1. For the purposes of this section a partner of a relevant Afghan citizen (the principal applicant) is a person who:

(i) is the principal applicant's spouse; or

(ii) is the principal applicant's civil partner; or

(iii) has been living together with the principal applicant in a relationship akin to a marriage or civil partnership for at least two years prior to the date of application.

Note: Paragraphs 276BA1–276BS1 inserted from 1 October 2013 subject to savings for applications made before that date (HC 628).

Relationship requirements for a partner of a relevant Afghan citizen

276BL1. The relationship requirements for a partner of a relevant Afghan citizen (the principal applicant) are that:

(i) they are aged 18 or over at the date of application;

(ii) they are in a relationship with the principal applicant that is not within the prohibited degree of relationship;

(iii) they have met the principal applicant in person;

(iv) they are in a genuine and subsisting relationship with the principal applicant;

(v) if the principal applicant and partner are married or in a civil partnership, they must be in a valid marriage or civil partnership and must provide reasonable evidence to the equivalent of a marriage certificate or civil partnership certificate issued in the United Kingdom and valid under the law in force in the relevant country;

(vi) any previous relationship of the principal applicant or their partner must have broken down permanently, unless it is a relationship which falls with paragraph 278(i) of these Rules; and

(vii) they must intend to live together permanently in the UK with the principal applicant.

Note: Paragraphs 276BA1–276BS1 inserted from 1 October 2013 subject to savings for applications made before that date (HC 628).

Refusal of limited leave to enter the United Kingdom as the partner of a relevant Afghan citizen

276BM1. A partner of a relevant Afghan citizen (the principal applicant) will be refused limited leave to enter the United Kingdom if:

(i) their application falls for refusal under the general grounds of refusal contained in Part 9 of these Rules;

(ii) there are serious reasons for considering that the partner of the principal applicant has committed a crime against peace, a war crime, a crime against humanity, or any other serious crime or instigated or otherwise participated in such crimes;

(iii) there are serious reasons for considering that the partner of the principal applicant is guilty of acts contrary to the purposes and principles of the United Nations or has committed, prepared or instigated such acts or encouraged or induced others to commit, prepare or instigate such acts; or

(iv) there are serious reasons for considering that the partner of the principal applicant constitutes a danger to the community or to the security of the United Kingdom.

Note: Paragraphs 276BA1–276BS1 inserted from 1 October 2013 subject to savings for applications made before that date (HC 628).

Curtailment of limited leave to enter the United Kingdom as the partner of a relevant Afghan citizen

276BN1. Limited leave to enter the United Kingdom as the partner of a relevant Afghan citizen and who has been granted leave in accordance with paragraph 276BJ1 may be curtailed where the person is a danger to the security or public order of the United Kingdom or leave may be curtailed where:

(i) the partner of a relevant Afghan citizen has made false representations or failed to disclose any material fact for the purpose of obtaining leave to enter; and/or

(ii) it is undesirable to permit the partner of a relevant Afghan citizen to remain in the United Kingdom in the light of his conduct, character or associations or the fact that he represents a threat to national security.

Note: Paragraphs 276BA1–276BS1 inserted from 1 October 2013 subject to savings for applications made before that date (HC 628).

Limited leave to enter the United Kingdom as the minor dependant child of a relevant Afghan citizen or their partner

276BO1. Limited leave to enter the United Kingdom for a period not exceeding 5 years will be granted to the minor dependant child of a relevant Afghan citizen or their partner where;

(i) the relationship requirements under paragraph 276BQ1 are met; and

(ii) the application does not fall for refusal under paragraph 276BR1.

Note: Paragraphs 276BA1–276BS1 inserted from 1 October 2013 subject to savings for applications made before that date (HC 628).

Definition of "minor dependant child" of a relevant Afghan citizen or their partner

276BP1. For the purposes of paragraphs 276BO1, 276BQ1, 276BR1 and 276BS1 a minor dependant child of a relevant Afghan citizen (the principal applicant) or their partner is a person who:

(i) is the child of the principal applicant or the partner of the principal applicant who is also seeking leave to enter the United Kingdom on the same application; and who

(ii) was under the age of 18 at 19 December 2012;

(iii) is not married or in a civil partnership;

(iv) has not formed an independent family unit; and

(v) must not be leading an independent life.

Note: Paragraphs 276BA1–276BS1 inserted from 1 October 2013 subject to savings for applications made before that date (HC 628).

Relationship requirements for a minor dependant child of a relevant Afghan citizen or their partner

276BQ1. The relationship requirements for a minor dependant child of a relevant Afghan citizen (the principal applicant) or their partner are that the person:

(i) is the child of the principal applicant and the child's other parent is the principal applicant's partner; or

(ii) is the child of the principal applicant; and

(a) the child's other parent is dead; or

(b) the principal applicant has sole responsibility for the child's upbringing; or

(iii) is the child of the principal applicant's partner; and

(a) the child's other parent is dead; or

(b) the principle applicant's partner has sole responsibility for the child's upbringing; or

(iv) is the adopted child of the principal applicant as defined at paragraphs 309A or 309B of these Rules and where the requirements at paragraph 310(vi)–(xi) of these Rules are fulfilled; or

(v) is the adopted child of the principal applicant's partner who is also seeking leave to enter the UK on the same application and as defined at paragraphs 309A or 309B of these Rules and where the requirements at paragraph 310(vi)–(xi) of these Rules are fulfilled.

Note: Paragraphs 276BA1–276BS1 inserted from 1 October 2013 subject to savings for applications made before that date (HC 628).

Refusal of limited leave to enter the United Kingdom as the minor dependant child of a relevant Afghan citizen or their partner

276BR1. A minor dependant child of a relevant Afghan citizen (the principal applicant) or their partner will be refused limited leave to enter the United Kingdom if:

(i) their application falls for refusal under the general grounds of refusal contained in Part 9 of these Rules;

(ii) there are serious reasons for considering that the minor dependant child of the principal applicant or their partner has committed a crime against peace, a war crime, a crime against humanity, or any other serious crime or instigated or otherwise participated in such crimes;

(iii) there are serious reasons for considering that the minor dependant child of the principal applicant or their partner is guilty of acts contrary to the purposes and principles of the United Nations or has committed, prepared or instigated such acts or encouraged or induced others to commit, prepare or instigate such acts; or

(iv) there are serious reasons for considering that the minor dependant child of the principal applicant or their partner constitutes a danger to the community or to the security of the United Kingdom.

Note: Paragraphs 276BA1–276BS1 inserted from 1 October 2013 subject to savings for applications made before that date (HC 628).

Curtailment of limited leave to enter the United Kingdom as the minor dependant child of a relevant Afghan citizen or their partner

276BS1. Limited leave to enter the United Kingdom as the minor dependant child of a relevant Afghan citizen or their partner and who has been granted leave in accordance with paragraph 276BO1 may be curtailed where the person is a danger to the security or public order of the United Kingdom or leave may be curtailed where:

(i) the minor dependant child of a relevant Afghan citizen has made false representations or failed to disclose any material fact for the purpose of obtaining leave to enter; and/or

(ii) it is undesirable to permit the minor dependant child of a relevant Afghan citizen to remain in the United Kingdom in the light of his conduct, character or associations or the fact that he represents a threat to national security.

Note: Paragraphs 276BA1–276BS1 inserted from 1 October 2013 subject to savings for applications made before that date (HC 628).

Part 8

Family members

Transitional provisions and interaction between Part 8, Appendix FM and Appendix FM-SE

A277. From 9 July 2012 Appendix FM will apply to all applications to which Part 8 of these rules applied on or before 8 July 2012 except where the provisions of Part 8 are preserved and continue to apply, as set out in [paragraphs A280 to A280B].

Note: Amended from 6 November 2014 (HC 693).

A277A. Where the Secretary of State is considering [an application for limited leave to remain or indefinite leave to remain] to which Part 8 of these rules continues to apply (excluding an application from a family member of a Relevant Points Based System Migrant), and where the applicant:

(a) does not meet the requirements of Part 8 for indefinite leave to remain [(where the application is for indefinite leave to remain)], and

(b) [meets or continues to meet the requirements for limited leave to remain under Part 8 in force at the date of decision,]

further limited leave to remain under Part 8 may be granted of such a period and subject to such conditions as the Secretary of State deems appropriate. [For the purposes of this sub-paragraph an applicant last granted limited leave to enter under Part 8 will be considered as if they had last been granted limited leave to remain under Part 8;] or

(c) if the applicant does not meet the requirements of Part 8 for indefinite leave to remain as a bereaved partner [(where the application is for indefinite leave to remain as a bereaved partner)] only because paragraph 322(1C)(iii) or 322(1C)(iv) of these rules applies, the applicant will be granted limited leave to remain under Part 8 for a period not exceeding 30 months and subject to such conditions as the Secretary of State deems appropriate.

Note: Words inserted in subparagraph (b) and subparagraph (c) inserted from 13 December 2012 subject to savings for applications made before that date (HC 760). Words inserted in subparagraphs (a) and (c) and words substituted in subparagraph (b) from 6 November 2014 (HC 693).

A277B. Where the Secretary of State is considering [an application for limited leave to remain or indefinite leave to remain] to which Part 8 of these rules continues to apply (excluding an application from a family member of a Relevant Points Based System Migrant) and where the application does not meet [the requirements for indefinite leave to remain (where the application is for indefinite leave to remain) or limited leave to remain under Part 8 in force at the date of decision]:

(a) the application will also be considered under paragraphs R-LTRP.1.1.(a), (b) and (d), R-LTRPT.1.1.(a), (b) and (d) and EX.1. of Appendix FM (family life) and paragraphs 276ADE to 276DH (private life) of these rules;

(b) if the applicant meets the requirements for leave under those paragraphs of Appendix FM or paragraphs 276ADE to 276DH (except the requirement for a valid application under that route), the applicant will be granted leave under those provisions; and

(c) if the applicant is granted leave under those provisions, the period of the applicant's continuous leave under Part 8 at the date of application will be counted towards the period of continuous leave which must be completed before the applicant can apply for indefinite leave to remain under [paragraph 276B].

(d) Except sub-paragraph (c) does not apply to a person last granted leave as the family member of a Relevant Points Based System Migrant.

Note: Subparagraph (d) inserted from 6 April 2014 (HC 1138 as amended by HC 1201). Words substituted in 1st sentence and in subparagraph (c) from 6 November 2014 (HC 693).

A277C. Subject to paragraphs A277 to A280B, {paragraph 276A0} and paragraph GEN.1.9. of Appendix FM of these rules, where the Secretary of State [deems it appropriate, the Secretary of State will consider] any application to which the provisions of Appendix FM (family life) and paragraphs 276ADE(1) to 276DH (private life) of these rules do not already apply, [under paragraphs R-LTRP.1.1.(a), (b) and (d), R-LTRPT.1.1.(a), (b) and (d) and EX.1. of Appendix FM (family life) and paragraph 276ADE (private life) of these rules.] If the applicant meets the requirements for leave under those provisions (except the requirement for a valid application), the applicant will be granted leave under paragraph D-LTRP.1.2. or D-LTRPT.1.2. of Appendix FM or under paragraph [276BE(1)] of these rules.

Note: Words in first two sets of square brackets inserted/substituted 13 December 2012 subject to savings for applications made before that date (HC 760). Words in curly brackets inserted from 6 April 2013 (HC 1039). Words in final set of square brackets substituted from28 July 2014; this amendment applies to all applications to which paragraphs 276ADE to 276DH and Appendix FM apply (or can be applied by virtue of the Immigration Rules), and to any other ECHR Article 8 claims (save for those from foreign criminals), and which are decided on or after that date (HC 532). Words 'A280B' and '276ADE(1)' substituted from 6 November 2014 (HC 693).

A278. The requirements to be met under Part 8 after 9 July 2012 may be modified or supplemented by the requirements in Appendix FM and Appendix FM-SE.

[**A279.** Paragraphs 398–399D apply to all immigration decisions made further to applications under Part 8 and paragraphs 276A–276D where a decision is made on or after 28 July 2014, irrespective of the date the application was made.]

Note: Paragraph A279 substituted from 28 July 2014 (HC 532).

A280 The following provisions of Part 8 apply in the manner and circumstances specified:

(a) The following paragraphs apply in respect of all applications made under Part 8 and Appendix FM, irrespective of the date of application or decision:

277–280
289AA
295AA
296

(b) The following paragraphs of Part 8 continue to apply to all applications made on or after 9 July 2012. The paragraphs apply in their current form unless an additional requirement by reference to Appendix FM is specified:

Paragraph number	Additional requirement
295J	None
297–300	None
304–309	None
309A–316F	Where: (1) the applicant: • falls under paragraph 314(i)(a); or • falls under paragraph 316A(i)(d) or (e); and • is applying on or after 9 July 2012; and (2) the "other parent" mentioned in paragraph 314(i)(a), or one of the prospective parents mentioned in paragraph 316A(i)(d) or (e), has or is applying for entry clearance or limited leave to remain as a partner under Appendix FM, the application must also meet the requirements of paragraphs E-ECC 2.1–2.3 (entry clearance applications) or E-LTRC 2.1–2.3 (leave to remain applications) of Appendix FM. Where the applicant: • falls under paragraph 314(i)(d); • is applying on or after 9 July 2012; and • has two parents or prospective parents and one of the applicant's parents or prospective parents does not have right of abode, indefinite leave to enter or remain, is not present and settled in the UK or being admitted for settlement on the same occasion as the applicant is seeking admission, but otherwise has or is applying for entry clearance or limited leave to remain as a partner under Appendix FM, the application must also meet the requirements of paragraphs E-ECC 2.1–2.3 (entry clearance applications) or E-LTRC 2.1–2.3 (leave to remain applications) of Appendix FM.
319X	None

(c) The following provisions of Part 8 continue to apply on or after 9 July 2012, and are not subject to any additional requirement listed in (b) above:

(i) to persons who have made an application before 9 July 2012 under Part 8 which was not decided as at 9 July 2012; and

(ii) to applications made by persons [in the UK] who have been granted entry clearance or limited leave to enter or remain under Part 8 before 9 July 2012 and [, where this is a requirement of Part 8,] this leave to enter or limited leave to remain is extant:

281–289
289A–289C
290–295
295A–295O
297–316F

317–319
319L–319U
319V–319Y

(d)(i) The following provisions of Part 8 continue to apply to applications made [in the period beginning with 9 July 2012 and ending on 30 November 2013, including those that have not been decided before 1 December 2013], and are not subject to any additional requirement listed in (b) above, by persons who have made an application for entry clearance, leave to enter or remain as the fiancé(e), proposed civil partner, spouse, civil partner, unmarried partner, same sex partner, or child or other dependant relative of a British citizen or settled person who is a full-time member of HM Forces:

281–289
289A–289C
290–295
295A–295O
297–316F
317–319

(ii) Subject to the following provisions, from 1 December 2013, Appendix Armed Forces applies to all applications for entry clearance, leave to enter or remain as the fiancé(e), proposed civil partner, spouse, civil partner, unmarried partner, same sex partner or child of a British citizen or settled person who is a full-time member of HM Forces.

(iii) Except, from 1 December 2013, the provisions in paragraph A280(d)(i) continue to apply to persons who were granted entry clearance, limited leave to enter or remain under Part 8 before 1 December 2013, and where it is a requirement of Part 8, that leave to enter or remain is extant.

(iv) Applications may continue to be made under paragraphs 297 to 316F of Part 8 by the child of a British citizen or settled person who is a full-time member of HM Forces regardless of the date of application and paragraph A280(b) continues to apply to these applications as appropriate.

(v) A new application by a dependent relative of a British citizen or settled person who is a full time member of HM Forces may no longer be made under paragraphs 317–319 on or after 1 December 2013. Those applications must meet the requirements of Appendix FM unless an application was submitted on or before 30 November 2013. An application made by a dependent relative of a British citizen or settled person who is a full time member of HM Forces on or before 30 November 2013 will be considered under the relevant paragraphs 317–319 which apply.

(vi) For the avoidance of doubt, paragraph A280(e) will continue to apply to the spouse, civil partner, unmarried partner or same sex partner of a British citizen or settled person who is a full-time member of HM Forces who was admitted to the UK under paragraph 282(c) or 295B(c) who has not yet applied for indefinite leave to remain, including where an application relying on paragraph A280(e) is made on or after 1 December 2013.

(vii) The requirements in paragraphs 8 and 9 of Appendix Armed Forces apply to applications for entry clearance, leave to enter or remain as the fiancé(e), proposed civil partner, spouse, civil partner, unmarried partner, same sex partner, or child or other dependent relative of a British citizen or settled person who is a full-time member of HM Forces making an application under Part 8 (where paragraph A280 (d) has permitted such an application) where the decision is made on or after 1 December 2013 (and irrespective of the date of the application).

(e) The following provisions of Part 8 shall continue to apply to applications made on or after 9 July 2012, and are not subject to any additional requirement listed in (b) above, by a spouse, civil partner, unmarried partner or same sex partner who was admitted to the UK before 9 July 2012 further to paragraph 282(c) or 295B(c) of these Rules who has not yet applied for indefinite leave to remain:

284–286
287(a)(i)(c)
287(a)(ii)–(vii)
287(b)
288–289
289A–289C
295D–295F
295G(i)(c)
295G(ii)–(vii)
295H–295I

(f) Paragraphs 301–303F continue to apply to applications made under this route on or after 9 July 2012, and are not subject to any additional requirement listed in (b) above, by a child of a person to whom those paragraphs relate who has been granted limited leave to enter or remain or an extension of stay following an application made before 9 July 2012.

(g) For the avoidance of doubt, notwithstanding the introduction of Appendix FM, paragraphs 319AA–319J of Part 8 continue to apply, and are not subject to any additional requirement listed in paragraph (b) above, to applications for entry clearance or leave to enter or remain as the spouse, civil partner, unmarried partner, same sex partner, or child of a Relevant Points Based System Migrant.

Note: Words inserted in subparagraph (c)(ii) from 6 April 2013 (HC 1039). Words substituted in subparagraph (d) and subparagraphs (d)(ii)–(vii) inserted from 1 December 2013 (HC 803). Subparagraph (d)(iii) substituted from 1 January 2014 (HC 887). Table entry relating to 309A–316F amended from 6 April 2014 (HC 1138 as amended by HC 1201).

A280A. The sponsor of an applicant under Part 8 for limited or indefinite leave to remain as a spouse, civil partner, unmarried partner or same sex partner must be the same person as the sponsor of the applicant's last grant of leave in that category.

Note: Paragraphs A280A-A280B inserted from 6 November 2014 (HC 693).

A280B. An applicant aged 18 or over may not rely on paragraph A280 where, since their last grant of limited leave to enter or remain under Part 8, they have been granted or refused leave under Appendix FM, Appendix Armed Forces or paragraph 276BE to CE of these rules, or been granted limited leave to enter or remain in a category outside their original route to settlement.

Note: Paragraphs A280A-A280B inserted from 6 November 2014 (HC 693).

A281. In Part 8 "specified" means specified in Appendix FM-SE, unless otherwise stated, and "English language test provider approved by the Secretary of State" means a provider specified in Appendix O.

Spouses and civil partners

277. Nothing in these Rules shall be construed as permitting a person to be granted entry clearance, leave to enter, leave to remain or variation of leave as a spouse or civil partner of another if either the applicant or the sponsor will be aged under 18 on the date of arrival in the United Kingdom or (as the case may be) on the date on which the leave to remain or variation of leave would be granted. In these rules the term "sponsor" includes "partner" as defined in GEN 1.2 of Appendix FM.

278. Nothing in these Rules shall be construed as allowing a person to be granted entry clearance, leave to enter, leave to remain or variation of leave as the spouse and civil partner of a man or woman (the sponsor) if:

(i) his or her marriage or civil partnership to the sponsor is polygamous; and

(ii) there is another person living who is the husband or wife of the sponsor and who:

(a) is, or at any time since his or her marriage or civil partnership to the sponsor has been, in the United Kingdom; or

(b) has been granted a certificate of entitlement in respect of the right of abode mentioned in Section 2(1)(a) of the Immigration Act 1988 or an entry clearance to enter the United Kingdom as the husband or wife of the sponsor.

For the purpose of this paragraph a marriage or civil partnership may be polygamous although at its inception neither party had any other spouse or civil partner.

279. Paragraph 278 does not apply to any person who seeks entry clearance, leave to enter, leave to remain or variation of leave where:

(i) he or she has been in the United Kingdom before 1 August 1988 having been admitted for the purpose of settlement as the husband or wife of the sponsor; or

(ii) he or she has, since their marriage or civil partnership to the sponsor, been in the United Kingdom at any time when there was no such other spouse or civil partner living as is mentioned in paragraph 278(ii).

But where a person claims that paragraph 278 does not apply to them because they have been in the United Kingdom in circumstances which cause them to fall within sub paragraphs (i) or (ii) of that paragraph it shall be for them to prove that fact.

280. For the purposes of paragraphs 278 and 279 the presence of any wife or husband in the United Kingdom in any of the following circumstances shall be disregarded:

(i) as a visitor; or

(ii) an illegal entrant; or

(iii) in circumstances whereby a person is deemed by Section 11(1) of the Immigration Act 1971 not to have entered the United Kingdom.

Spouses or civil partners of persons present and settled in the United Kingdom or being admitted on the same occasion for settlement

Requirements for leave to enter the United Kingdom with a view to settlement as the spouse or civil partner of a person present and settled in the United Kingdom or being admitted on the same occasion for settlement

281. The requirements to be met by a person seeking leave to enter the United Kingdom with a view to settlement as the spouse or civil partner of a person present and settled in the United Kingdom or who is on the same occasion being admitted for settlement are that:

(i) (a)(i) the applicant is married to or the civil partner of a person present and settled in the United Kingdom or who is on the same occasion being admitted for settlement; and

(ii) the applicant provides an original English language test certificate in speaking and listening from an English language test provider approved by the Secretary of State for these purposes, which clearly shows the applicant's name and the qualification obtained (which must meet or exceed level A1 of the Common European Framework of Reference) unless:

(a) the applicant is aged 65 or over at the time he makes his application; or

(b) the applicant has a physical or mental condition that would prevent him from meeting the requirement; or;

(c) there are exceptional compassionate circumstances that would prevent the applicant from meeting the requirement; or

(iii) the applicant is a national of one of the following countries: Antigua and Barbuda; Australia; The Bahamas; Barbados; Belize; Canada; Dominica; Grenada; Guyana; Jamaica; New Zealand; St Kitts and Nevis; St Lucia; St Vincent and the Grenadines; Trinidad and Tobago; United States of America; or

(iv) the applicant has obtained an academic qualification (not a professional or vocational qualification), which is deemed by UK NARIC to meet the recognised standard of a Bachelor's or Master's degree or PhD in the UK, from an educational establishment in one of the following countries: Antigua and Barbuda; Australia; The Bahamas; Barbados; Belize; Dominica; Grenada; Guyana; Ireland; Jamaica; New Zealand; St Kitts and Nevis; St Lucia; St Vincent and The Grenadines; Trinidad and Tobago; the UK; the USA; and provides the specified documents; or

(v) the applicant has obtained an academic qualification (not a professional or vocational qualification) which is deemed by UK NARIC to meet the recognised standard of a Bachelor's or Master's degree or PhD in the UK, and

(1) provides the specified evidence to show he has the qualification, and

(2) UK NARIC has confirmed that the qualification was taught or researched in English, or

(vi) has obtained an academic qualification (not a professional or vocational qualification) which is deemed by UK NARIC to meet the recognised standard of a Bachelor's or Master's degree or PhD in the UK, and provides the specified evidence to show:

(1) he has the qualification, and

(2) that the qualification was taught or researched in English.

or

(b)(i) the applicant is married to or the civil partner of a person who has a right of abode in the United Kingdom or indefinite leave to enter or remain in the United Kingdom and is on the same occasion seeking admission to the United Kingdom for the purposes of settlement and the parties were married or formed a civil partnership at least 4 years ago, since which time they have been living together outside the United Kingdom; and

(b)(ii) the applicant has demonstrated sufficient knowledge of the English language and sufficient knowledge about life in the United Kingdom, in accordance with Appendix KoLL; and

(b)(iii) DELETED

(ii) the parties to the marriage or civil partnership have met; and

(iii) each of the parties intends to live permanently with the other as his or her spouse or civil partner and the marriage or civil partnership is subsisting; and

(iv) there will be adequate accommodation for the parties and any dependants without recourse to public funds in accommodation which they own or occupy exclusively; and

(v) the parties will be able to maintain themselves and any dependants adequately without recourse to public funds; and

(vi) the applicant holds a valid United Kingdom entry clearance for entry in this capacity; and

(vii) the applicant does not fall for refusal under the general grounds for refusal.

For the purposes of this paragraph and paragraphs 282–289 a member of HM Forces serving overseas, or a permanent member of HM Diplomatic Service or a comparable UK-based staff member of the British Council on a tour of duty abroad, or a staff member of the Department for International Development who is a British Citizen or is settled in the United Kingdom, is to be regarded as present and settled in the United Kingdom.

Note: Subparagraph (i)(b)(iii) deleted and subparagraph (vii) inserted from 13 December 2012 subject to savings for applications made before that date (HC 760). Subparagraph (b)(ii) substituted from 28 October 2013 subject to savings for applications made before that date (HC 628).

Leave to enter as the spouse or civil partner of a person present and settled in the United Kingdom or being admitted for settlement on the same occasion

282. A person seeking leave to enter the United Kingdom as the spouse or civil partner of a person present and settled in the United Kingdom or who is on the same occasion being admitted for settlement may:

(a) in the case of a person who meets the requirements of paragraph 281(i)(a)(i) and one of the requirements of paragraph 281(i)(a)(ii)–(vi) be admitted for an initial period not exceeding 27 months, or

(b) in the case of a person who meets all of the requirements in paragraph 281(i)(b), be granted indefinite leave to enter, or

(c) in the case of a person who meets the requirement in paragraph 281(i)(b)(i), but not the requirement in paragraph 281(i)(b)(ii) to have sufficient knowledge of the English language and about life in the United Kingdom, be admitted for an initial period not exceeding 27 months, in all cases provided the Immigration Officer is satisfied that each of the relevant requirements of paragraph 281 is met.

Refusal of leave to enter as the spouse or civil partner of a person present and settled in the United Kingdom or being admitted on the same occasion for settlement

283. Leave to enter the United Kingdom as the spouse or civil partner of a person present and settled in the United Kingdom or who is on the same occasion being admitted for settlement is to be refused if the Immigration Officer is not satisfied that each of the requirements of paragraph 281 is met.

Requirements for an extension of stay as the spouse or civil partner of a person present and settled in the United Kingdom

284. The requirements for an extension of stay as the spouse or civil partner of a person present and settled in the United Kingdom are that:

(i) the applicant has or was last granted limited leave to enter or remain in the United Kingdom which meets the following requirements:

(a) The leave was given in accordance with any of the provisions of these Rules; and

(b) The leave was granted for a period of 6 months or more, unless it was granted as a fiancé(e) or proposed civil partner; and

(c) The leave was not as the spouse, civil partner, unmarried or same-sex partner of a Relevant Points-Based System Migrant; and

(ii) [the applicant] is married to or the civil partner of a person present and settled in the United Kingdom; and

(iii) the parties to the marriage or civil partnership have met; and

(iv) the applicant has not remained in breach of the immigration laws, disregarding any period of overstaying for a period of 28 days or less; and

(v) the marriage or civil partnership has not taken place after a decision has been made to deport the applicant or he has been recommended for deportation or been given notice under Section 6(2) of the Immigration Act 1971 or been given directions for his removal under section 10 of the Immigration and Asylum Act 1999; and

(vi) each of the parties intends to live permanently with the other as his or her spouse or civil partner and the marriage or civil partnership is subsisting; and

(vii) there will be adequate accommodation for the parties and any dependants without recourse to public funds in accommodation which they own or occupy exclusively; and

(viii) the parties will be able to maintain themselves and any dependants adequately without recourse to public funds; and

(ix)(a) the applicant provides an original English language test certificate in speaking and listening from an English language test provider approved by the Secretary of State for these purposes, which clearly shows the applicant's name and the qualification obtained (which must meet or exceed level A1 of the Common European Framework of Reference) unless:

(i) the applicant is aged 65 or over at the time he makes his application; or

(ii) the applicant has a physical or mental condition that would prevent him from meeting the requirement; or

(iii) there are exceptional compassionate circumstances that would prevent the applicant from meeting the requirement; or

(ix)(b) the applicant is a national of one of the following countries: Antigua and Barbuda; Australia; The Bahamas; Barbados; Belize; Canada; Dominica; Grenada; Guyana; Jamaica; New Zealand; St Kitts and Nevis; St Lucia; St Vincent and the Grenadines; Trinidad and Tobago; United States of America; or

(ix)(c) the applicant has obtained an academic qualification (not a professional or vocational qualification), which is deemed by UK NARIC to meet the recognised standard of a Bachelor's or Master's degree or PhD in the UK, from an educational establishment in one of the following countries: Antigua and Barbuda; Australia; The Bahamas; Barbados; Belize; Dominica; Grenada; Guyana; Ireland; Jamaica; New Zealand; St Kitts and Nevis; St Lucia; St Vincent and The Grenadines; Trinidad and Tobago; the UK; the USA; and provides the specified documents; or

(ix)(d) the applicant has obtained an academic qualification (not a professional or vocational qualification) which is deemed by UK NARIC to meet the recognised standard of a Bachelor's or Master's degree or PhD in the UK, and

(1) provides the specified evidence to show he has the qualification, and

(2) UK NARIC has confirmed that the qualification was taught or researched in English, or

(ix)(e) has obtained an academic qualification (not a professional or vocational qualification) which is deemed by UK NARIC to meet the recognised standard of a Bachelor's or Master's degree or PhD in the UK, and provides the specified evidence to show:

(1) he has the qualification, and
(2) that the qualification was taught or researched in English.

Note: Words inserted in subparagraph (iv) from 6 April 2013 (HC 1039). Words inserted in subparagraph (ii) from 1 July 2013 (HC 244). Subparagraph (i) substituted from 6 April 2014 subject to savings for applications made before that date (HC 1138 as amended by HC 1201).

Extension of stay as the spouse or civil partner of a person present and settled in the United Kingdom

285. An extension of stay as the spouse or civil partner of a person present and settled in the United Kingdom may be granted for a period of 2 years in the first instance, provided the Secretary of State is satisfied that each of the requirements of paragraph 284 is met.

Refusal of extension of stay as the spouse or civil partner of a person present and settled in the United Kingdom

286. An extension of stay as the spouse or civil partner of a person present and settled in the United Kingdom is to be refused if the Secretary of State is not satisfied that each of the requirements of paragraph 284 is met.

Requirements for indefinite leave to remain for the spouse or civil partner of a person present and settled in the United Kingdom

287. (a) The requirements for indefinite leave to remain for the spouse or civil partner of a person present and settled in the United Kingdom are that:

(i) (a) the applicant was admitted to the United Kingdom for a period not exceeding 27 months or given an extension of stay for a period of 2 years in accordance with paragraphs 281 to 286 of these Rules and has completed a period of 2 years as the spouse or civil partner of a person present and settled in the United Kingdom; or

(b) the applicant was admitted to the United Kingdom for a period not exceeding 27 months or given an extension of stay for a period of 2 years in accordance with paragraphs 295AA to 295F of these Rules and during that period married or formed a civil partnership with the person whom he or she was admitted or granted an extension of stay to join and has completed a period of 2 years as the unmarried or same-sex partner and then the spouse or civil partner of a person present and settled in the United Kingdom; or

(c) was admitted to the United Kingdom in accordance with leave granted under paragraph 282(c) of these rules; [or]

(d) the applicant was admitted to the UK or given an extension of stay as the spouse or civil partner of a Relevant Points Based System Migrant; and then obtained an extension of stay under paragraphs 281 to 286 of these Rules and has completed a period of 2 years as the spouse or civil partner of the person who is now present and settled here; or

(e) the applicant was admitted to the UK or given an extension of stay as the unmarried or same-sex partner of a Relevant Points Based System Migrant; and during that period married or formed a civil partnership with the person whom he or she was admitted or granted an extension of stay to join and has completed a period of 2 years as the unmarried or same-sex partner and then the spouse or civil partner of the person who is now present and settled in the UK; or

(f) the applicant was admitted into the UK in accordance with paragraph 319L and has completed a period of 2 years limited leave as the spouse or civil partner of a refugee or beneficiary of humanitarian protection who is now present and settled in the UK or as the spouse or civil partner of a former refugee or beneficiary of humanitarian protection who is now a British Citizen.

(ii) the applicant is still the spouse or civil partner of the person he or she was admitted or granted an extension of stay to join and the marriage or civil partnership is subsisting; and

(iii) each of the parties intends to live permanently with the other as his or her spouse or civil partner; and

(iv) there will be adequate accommodation for the parties and any dependants without recourse to public funds in accommodation which they own or occupy exclusively; and

(v) the parties will be able to maintain themselves and any dependants adequately without recourse to public funds; and

(vi) the applicant has demonstrated sufficient knowledge of the English language and sufficient knowledge about life in the United Kingdom, in accordance with Appendix KoLL; and

(vii) the applicant [does not fall for refusal under the general grounds for refusal].

(b) The requirements for indefinite leave to remain for the bereaved spouse or civil partner of a person who was present and settled in the United Kingdom are that:

(i) (a) the applicant was admitted to the United Kingdom for a period not exceeding 27 months or given an extension of stay for a period of 2 years as the spouse or civil partner of a person present and settled in the United Kingdom in accordance with paragraphs 281 to 286 of these Rules; or

(b) the applicant was admitted to the United Kingdom for a period not exceeding 27 months or given an extension of stay for a period of 2 years as the unmarried or same-sex partner of a person present and settled in the United Kingdom in accordance with paragraphs 295AA to 295F of these Rules and during that period married or formed a civil partnership with the person whom he or she was admitted or granted an extension of stay to join; and

(ii) the person whom the applicant was admitted or granted an extension of stay to join died during that period; and

(iii) the applicant was still the spouse or civil partner of the person he or she was admitted or granted an extension of stay to join at the time of the death; and

(iv) each of the parties intended to live permanently with the other as his or her spouse or civil partner and the marriage or civil partnership was subsisting at the time of the death; and

(v) the applicant [does not fall for refusal under the general grounds for refusal].

Note: Words substituted in subparagraphs (a) (vii) and (b)(v) from 13 December 2012 subject to savings for applications made before that date (HC 760). Subparagraph (vi) substituted from 28 October 2013 subject to savings for applications made before that date (HC 628). Subparagraphs (a)(i)(d) and (a)(i)(e) substituted from 6 April 2013 subject to savings for applications made before that date (HC 1039). Word 'or' at the end of subparagraph (a)(i)(c) substituted from 6 November 2014 (HC 693).

Indefinite leave to remain for the spouse or civil partner of a person present and settled in the United Kingdom

288. Indefinite leave to remain for the spouse or civil partner of a person present and settled in the United Kingdom may be granted provided the Secretary of State is satisfied that each of the requirements of paragraph 287 is met.

Refusal of indefinite leave to remain for the spouse or civil partner of a person present and settled in the United Kingdom

289. Indefinite leave to remain for the spouse or civil partner of a person present and settled in the United Kingdom is to be refused if the Secretary of State is not satisfied that each of the requirements of paragraph 287 is met.

Victims of domestic violence

Requirements for indefinite leave to remain in the United Kingdom as the victim of domestic violence

289A. The requirements to be met by a person who is the victim of domestic violence and who is seeking indefinite leave to remain in the United Kingdom are that the applicant:

(i) (a) the applicant was last admitted to the UK for a period not exceeding 27 months in accordance with sub-paragraph 282(a), 282(c), 295B(a) or 295B(c) of these Rules; or

(b) the applicant was last granted leave to remain as the spouse or civil partner or unmarried partner or same-sex partner of a person present and settled in the UK in accordance with paragraph 285 or 295E of these Rules, except where that leave extends leave originally granted to the applicant as the partner of a Relevant Points Based System Migrant; or

(c) the applicant was last granted leave to enable access to public funds pending an application under paragraph 289A and the preceding grant of leave was given in accordance with paragraph 282(a), 282(c), 285, 295B(a), 295B(c) or 295E of these Rules, except where that leave extends leave originally granted to the applicant as the partner of a Relevant Points Based System Migrant; and

(ii) the relationship with their spouse or civil partner or unmarried partner or same-sex partner, as appropriate, was subsisting at the beginning of the last period of leave granted in accordance with paragraph 282(a), 282(c), 285, 295B(a), 295B(c) or 295E of these Rules; and

(iii) is able to produce evidence to establish that the relationship was caused to permanently break down before the end of that period as a result of domestic violence; and

(iv) DELETED

Note: Subparagraph (v) deleted from 13 December 2012 subject to savings for applications made before that date (HC 760). Subparagraphs (i) and (ii) substituted, original subparagraph (iii) deleted and original subparagraph (iv) renumbered as (iii) from 6 November 2014 (HC 693).

Indefinite leave to remain as the victim of domestic violence

289B. Indefinite leave to remain as the victim of domestic violence may be granted provided the Secretary of State is satisfied that each of the requirements of paragraph 289A is met.

Refusal of indefinite leave to remain as the victim of domestic violence

289C. Indefinite leave to remain as the victim of domestic violence is to be refused if the Secretary of State is not satisfied that each of the requirements of paragraph 289A is met.

289D. If the applicant does not meet the requirements for indefinite leave to remain as a victim of domestic violence only because paragraph 322(1C)(iii) or 322(1C)(iv) applies, they may be granted further limited leave to remain for a period not exceeding 30 months and subject to such conditions as the Secretary of State deems appropriate.

Note: Paragraph 289D inserted from 13 December 2012 subject to savings for applications made before that date (HC 760).

Fiance(e)s and proposed civil partners

289AA. Nothing in these Rules shall be construed as permitting a person to be granted entry clearance, leave to enter or variation of leave as a fiance(e) or proposed civil partner if either the applicant or the sponsor will be aged under 18 on the date of arrival of the applicant in the United Kingdom or (as the case may be) on the date on which the leave to enter or variation of leave would be granted.

Requirements for leave to enter the United Kingdom as a fiance(e) or proposed civil partner (i.e. with a view to marriage or civil partnership and permanent settlement in the United Kingdom)

290. The requirements to be met by a person seeking leave to enter the United Kingdom as a fiance(e) or proposed civil partner are that:

(i) the applicant is seeking leave to enter the United Kingdom for marriage or civil partnership to a person present and settled in the United Kingdom or who is on the same occasion being admitted for settlement; and

(ii) the parties to the proposed marriage or civil partnership have met; and

(iii) each of the parties intends to live permanently with the other as his or her spouse or civil partner after the marriage or civil partnership; and

(iv) adequate maintenance and accommodation without recourse to public funds will be available for the applicant until the date of the marriage or civil partnership; and

(v) there will, after the marriage or civil partnership, be adequate accommodation for the parties and any dependants without recourse to public funds in accommodation which they own or occupy exclusively; and

(vi) the parties will be able after the marriage or civil partnership to maintain themselves and any dependants adequately without recourse to public funds; and

(vii)(a) the applicant provides an original English language test certificate in speaking and listening from an English language test provider approved by the Secretary of State for these purposes, which clearly shows the applicant's name and the qualification obtained (which must meet or exceed level A1 of the Common European Framework of Reference) unless:

(i) the applicant is aged 65 or over at the time he makes his application; or

(ii) the applicant has a physical or mental condition that would prevent him from meeting the requirement; or;

(iii) there are exceptional compassionate circumstances that would prevent the applicant from meeting the requirement; or (vii)(b) the applicant is a national of one of the following countries: Antigua and Barbuda; Australia; The Bahamas; Barbados; Belize; Canada; Dominica; Grenada; Guyana; Jamaica; New Zealand; St Kitts and Nevis; St Lucia; St Vincent and the Grenadines; Trinidad and Tobago; United States of America; or

(vii)(c) the applicant has obtained an academic qualification (not a professional or vocational qualification), which is deemed by UK NARIC to meet the recognised standard of a Bachelor's or Master's degree or PhD in the UK, from an educational establishment in one of the following countries: Antigua and Barbuda; Australia; The Bahamas; Barbados; Belize; Dominica; Grenada; Guyana; Ireland; Jamaica; New Zealand; St Kitts and Nevis; St Lucia; St Vincent and The Grenadines; Trinidad and Tobago; the UK; the USA; and provides the specified documents; or

(vii)(d) the applicant has obtained an academic qualification (not a professional or vocational qualification) which is deemed by UK NARIC to meet the recognised standard of a Bachelor's or Master's degree or PhD in the UK, and

(1) provides the specified evidence to show he has the qualification, and

(2) UK NARIC has confirmed that the qualification was taught or researched in English, or

(vii)(e) has obtained an academic qualification (not a professional or vocational qualification) which is deemed by UK NARIC to meet the recognised standard of a Bachelor's or Master's degree or PhD in the UK, and provides the specified evidence to show:

(1) he has the qualification, and

(2) that the qualification was taught or researched in English.

and

(viii) the applicant holds a valid United Kingdom entry clearance for entry in this capacity.

290A. DELETED

Note: Paragraph 290A deleted from 6 April 2014 subject to savings for applications made before that date (HC 1138 as amended by HC 1201).

Leave to enter as a fiance(e) or proposed civil partner

291. A person seeking leave to enter the United Kingdom as a fiance(e) or proposed civil partner may be admitted, with a prohibition on employment, for a period not exceeding 6 months to enable the marriage or civil partnership to take place provided a valid United Kingdom entry clearance for entry in this capacity is produced to the Immigration Officer on arrival.

Refusal of leave to enter as a fiance(e) or proposed civil partner

292. Leave to enter the United Kingdom as a fiance(e) or proposed civil partner is to be refused if a valid United Kingdom entry clearance for entry in this capacity is not produced to the Immigration Officer on arrival.

Requirements for an extension of stay as a fiance(e) or proposed civil partner

293. The requirements for an extension of stay as a fiance(e) or proposed civil partner are that:

(i) the applicant was admitted to the United Kingdom with a valid United Kingdom entry clearance as a fiance(e) or proposed civil partner; and

(ii) good cause is shown why the marriage or civil partnership did not take place within the initial period of leave granted under paragraph 291; and

(iii) there is satisfactory evidence that the marriage or civil partnership will take place at an early date; and

(iv) the requirements of paragraph 290 (ii)–(vii) are met.

Extension of stay as a fiance(e) or proposed civil partner

294. An extension of stay as a fiance(e) or proposed civil partner may be granted for an appropriate period with a prohibition on employment to enable the marriage or civil partnership to take place provided the Secretary of State is satisfied that each of the requirements of paragraph 293 is met.

Refusal of extension of stay as a fiance(e) or proposed civil partner

295. An extension of stay is to be refused if the Secretary of State is not satisfied that each of the requirements of paragraph 293 is met.

Unmarried and same-sex partners

Leave to enter as the unmarried or same-sex partner of a person present and settled in the United Kingdom or being admitted on the same occasion for settlement

295AA. Nothing in these Rules shall be construed as permitting a person to be granted entry clearance, leave to enter or variation of leave as an unmarried or same-sex partner if either the applicant or the sponsor will be aged under 18 on the date of arrival of the applicant in the United Kingdom or (as the case may be) on the date on which the leave to enter or variation of leave would be granted.

Requirements for leave to enter the United Kingdom with a view to settlement as the unmarried or same-sex partner of a person present and settled in the United Kingdom or being admitted on the same occasion for settlement

295A. The requirements to be met by a person seeking leave to enter the United Kingdom with a view to settlement as the unmarried or same-sex partner of a person present and settled in the United Kingdom or being admitted on the same occasion for settlement, are that:

(i)(a)(i) the applicant is the unmarried or same-sex partner of a person present and settled in the United Kingdom or who is on the same occasion being admitted for settlement and the parties have been living together in a relationship akin to marriage or civil partnership which has subsisted for two years or more; and

(ii) the applicant provides an original English language test certificate in speaking and listening from an English language test provider approved by the Secretary of State for these purposes, which clearly shows the applicant's name and the qualification obtained (which must meet or exceed level A1 of the Common European Framework of Reference) unless:

(a) the applicant is aged 65 or over at the time he makes his application; or

(b) the applicant has a physical or mental condition that would prevent him from meeting the requirement; or

(c) there are exceptional compassionate circumstances that would prevent the applicant from meeting the requirement; or

(iii) the applicant is a national of one of the following countries: Antigua and Barbuda; Australia; The Bahamas; Barbados; Belize; Canada; Dominica; Grenada; Guyana; Jamaica; New Zealand; St Kitts and Nevis; St Lucia; St Vincent and the Grenadines; Trinidad and Tobago; United States of America; or

(iv) the applicant has obtained an academic qualification (not a professional or vocational qualification), which is deemed by UK NARIC to meet the recognised standard of a Bachelor's or Master's degree or PhD in the UK, from an educational establishment in one of the following countries: Antigua and Barbuda; Australia; The Bahamas; Barbados; Belize; Dominica; Grenada; Guyana; Ireland; Jamaica; New Zealand; St Kitts and Nevis; St Lucia; St Vincent and The Grenadines; Trinidad and Tobago; the UK; the USA; and provides the specified documents; or

(v) the applicant has obtained an academic qualification (not a professional or vocational qualification) which is deemed by UK NARIC to meet the recognised standard of a Bachelor's or Master's degree or PhD in the UK, and

(1) provides the specified evidence to show he has the qualification, and

(2) UK NARIC has confirmed that the qualification was taught or researched in English, or

(vi) has obtained an academic qualification (not a professional or vocational qualification) which is deemed by UK NARIC to meet the recognised standard of a Bachelor's or Master's degree or PhD in the UK, and provides the specified evidence to show:

(1) he has the qualification, and

(2) that the qualification was taught or researched in English.

or

(b)(i) the applicant is the unmarried or same-sex partner of a person who has a right of abode in the United Kingdom or indefinite leave to enter or remain in the United Kingdom and is on the same occasion seeking admission to the United Kingdom for the purposes of settlement and the parties have been living together outside the United Kingdom in a relationship akin to marriage or civil partnership which has subsisted for 4 years or more; and

(b)(ii) the applicant has demonstrated sufficient knowledge of the English language and sufficient knowledge about life in the United Kingdom, in accordance with Appendix KoLL; and

(b)(iii) DELETED

(ii) any previous marriage or civil partnership (or similar relationship) by either partner has permanently broken down; and

(iii) the parties are not involved in a consanguineous relationship with one another; and

(iv) DELETED

(v) there will be adequate accommodation for the parties and any dependants without recourse to public funds in accommodation which they own or occupy exclusively; and

(vi) the parties will be able to maintain themselves and any dependants adequately without recourse to public funds; and

(vii) the parties intend to live together permanently; and

(viii) the applicant holds a valid United Kingdom entry clearance for entry in this capacity; and

(ix) the applicant does not fall for refusal under the general grounds for refusal.

For the purposes of this paragraph and paragraphs 295B–295I, a member of HM Forces serving overseas, or a permanent member of HM Diplomatic Service or a comparable UK-based staff member of the British Council on a tour of duty abroad, or a staff member of the Department for International Development who is a British Citizen or is settled in the United Kingdom, is to be regarded as present and settled in the United Kingdom.

Note: Subparagraph (i)(b)(iii) deleted and subparagraph (ix) inserted from 13 December 2012 subject to savings for applications made before that date (HC 760). Subparagraph (i)(b)(ii) substituted from 28 October 2013 subject to savings for applications made before that date (HC 628).

Leave to enter the United Kingdom with a view to settlement as the unmarried or same-sex partner of a person present and settled in the United Kingdom or being admitted on the same occasion for settlement

295B. A person seeking leave to enter the United Kingdom as the unmarried or same-sex partner of a person present and settled in the United Kingdom or who is on the same occasion being admitted for settlement may:

(a) in the case of a person who meets the requirements of paragraph 295A(i)(a)(i), and one of the requirements of paragraph 295A(i)(a)(ii)–(vi) be admitted for an initial period not exceeding 27 months, or

(b) in the case of a person who meets all of the requirements in paragraph 295A(i)(b), be granted indefinite leave to enter, or

(c) in the case of a person who meets the requirement in paragraph 295A(i)(b)(i), but not the requirement in paragraph 295A(i)(b)(ii) to have sufficient knowledge of the English language and about life in the United Kingdom, be admitted for an initial period not exceeding 27 months, in all cases provided the Immigration Officer is satisfied that each of the relevant requirements of paragraph 295A is met.

Refusal of leave to enter the United Kingdom with a view to settlement as the unmarried or same-sex partner of a person present and settled in the United Kingdom or being admitted on the same occasion for settlement

295C. Leave to enter the United Kingdom with a view to settlement as the unmarried or same-sex partner of a person present and settled in the United Kingdom or being admitted on the same occasion for settlement, is to be refused if the Immigration Officer is not satisfied that each of the requirements of paragraph 295A is met.

Leave to remain as the unmarried or same-sex partner of a person present and settled in the United Kingdom

Requirements for leave to remain as the unmarried or same-sex partner of a person present and settled in the United Kingdom

295D. The requirements to be met by a person seeking leave to remain as the unmarried or same-sex partner of a person present and settled in the United Kingdom are that:

(i) the applicant has or was last granted limited leave to enter or remain in the United Kingdom which was given in accordance with any of the provisions of these Rules, unless:

(a) as a result of that leave he would not have been in the United Kingdom beyond 6 months from the date on which he was admitted to the United Kingdom; or

(b) the leave was granted as the unmarried or same-sex partner of a Relevant Points Based System Migrant; and

(ii) any previous marriage or civil partnership (or similar relationship) by either partner has permanently broken down; and

(iii) the applicant is the unmarried or same-sex partner of a person who is present and settled in the United Kingdom; and

(iv) the applicant has not remained in breach of the immigration laws [, disregarding any period of overstaying for a period of 28 days or less]; and

(v) the parties are not involved in a consanguineous relationship with one another; and

(vi) the parties have been living together in a relationship akin to marriage or civil partnership which has subsisted for two years or more; and

(vii) the parties' relationship pre-dates any decision to deport the applicant, recommend him for deportation, give him notice under Section 6(2) of the Immigration Act 1971, or give directions for his removal under section 10 of the Immigration and Asylum Act 1999; and

(viii) there will be adequate accommodation for the parties and any dependants without recourse to public funds in accommodation which they own or occupy exclusively; and

(ix) the parties will be able to maintain themselves and any dependants adequately without recourse to public funds; and

(x) the parties intend to live together permanently; and

(xi)(a) the applicant provides an original English language test certificate in speaking and listening from an English language test provider approved by the Secretary of State for these purposes, which clearly shows the applicant's name and the qualification obtained (which must meet or exceed level A1 of the Common European Framework of Reference) unless:

(i) the applicant is aged 65 or over at the time he makes his application; or

(ii) the applicant has a physical or mental condition that would prevent him from meeting the requirement; or

(iii) there are exceptional compassionate circumstances that would prevent the applicant from meeting the requirement; or

(xi)(b) the applicant is a national of one of the following countries: Antigua and Barbuda; Australia; The Bahamas; Barbados; Belize; Canada; Dominica; Grenada; Guyana; Jamaica; New Zealand; St Kitts and Nevis; St Lucia; St Vincent and the Grenadines; Trinidad and Tobago; United States of America; or

(xi)(c) the applicant has obtained an academic qualification (not a professional or vocational qualification), which is deemed by UK NARIC to meet the recognised standard of a Bachelor's or Master's degree or PhD in the UK, from an educational establishment in one of the following countries: Antigua and Barbuda; Australia; The Bahamas; Barbados; Belize; Dominica; Grenada; Guyana; Ireland; Jamaica; New Zealand; St Kitts and Nevis; St Lucia; St Vincent and The Grenadines; Trinidad and Tobago; the UK; the USA; and provides the specified documents; or

(xi)(d) the applicant has obtained an academic qualification (not a professional or vocational qualification) which is deemed by UK NARIC to meet the recognised standard of a Bachelor's or Master's degree or PhD in the UK, and

(1) provides the specified evidence to show he has the qualification, and

(2) UK NARIC has confirmed that the qualification was taught or researched in English, or

(xi)(e) has obtained an academic qualification (not a professional or vocational qualification) which is deemed by UK NARIC to meet the recognised standard of a Bachelor's or Master's degree or PhD in the UK, and provides the specified evidence to show:

(1) he has the qualification, and

(2) that the qualification was taught or researched in English.

Note: Words inserted in subparagraph (iv) from 6 April 2013 (HC 1039). Subparagraph (i) substituted from 6 April 2014 subject to savings for applications made before that date (HC 1138 as amended by HC 1201).

Leave to remain as the unmarried or same-sex partner of a person present and settled in the United Kingdom

295E. Leave to remain as the unmarried or same-sex partner of a person present and settled in the United Kingdom may be granted for a period of 2 years in the first instance provided that the Secretary of State is satisfied that each of the requirements of paragraph 295D are met.

Refusal of leave to remain as the unmarried or same-sex partner of a person present and settled in the United Kingdom

295F. Leave to remain as the unmarried or same-sex partner of a person present and settled in the United Kingdom is to be refused if the Secretary of State is not satisfied that each of the requirements of paragraph 295D is met.

Indefinite leave to remain as the unmarried or same-sex partner of a person present and settled in the United Kingdom

Requirements for indefinite leave to remain as the unmarried or same-sex partner of a person present and settled in the United Kingdom

295G. The requirements to be met by a person seeking indefinite leave to remain as the unmarried partner of a person present and settled in the United Kingdom are that:

(i) (a) the applicant was admitted to the United Kingdom for a period not exceeding 27 months or given an extension of stay for a period of 2 years in accordance with paragraphs 295AA to 295F of these Rules and has completed a period of 2 years as the unmarried or same-sex partner of a person present and settled here; or

(b) the applicant was admitted to the UK or given an extension of stay as the unmarried or same-sex partner of a Relevant Points Based System Migrant; and then obtained an extension of stay under paragraphs 295AA to 295F of these Rules; and the person has completed a period of 2 years as the unmarried or same-sex partner of the person who is now present and settled here; or

(c) the applicant was admitted to the United Kingdom in accordance with leave granted under paragraph 295B(c) of these rules; or

(d) the applicant was admitted into the UK in accordance with paragraph 319O and has completed a period of 2 years limited leave as the unmarried or same-sex partner of a refugee or beneficiary of humanitarian protection who is now present and settled in the UK or as the unmarried or same-sex partner of a former refugee or beneficiary of humanitarian protection who is now a British Citizen.

(ii) the applicant is still the unmarried or same-sex partner of the person he was admitted or granted an extension of stay to join and the relationship is still subsisting; and

(iii) each of the parties intends to live permanently with the other as his partner; and

(iv) there will be adequate accommodation for the parties and any dependants without recourse to public funds in accommodation which they own or occupy exclusively; and

(v) the parties will be able to maintain themselves and any dependants adequately without recourse to public funds; and

(vi) the applicant has demonstrated sufficient knowledge of the English language and sufficient knowledge about life in the United Kingdom, in accordance with Appendix KoLL; and

(vii) the applicant does not fall for refusal under the general grounds for refusal.

Note: Subparagraph (i)(b) substituted from 6 April 2013 subject to savings for applications made before that date. Subparagraph (vi) substituted from 28 October 2013 subject to savings for applications made before that date (HC 628).

Indefinite leave to remain as the unmarried or same-sex partner of a person present and settled in the United Kingdom

295H. Indefinite leave to remain as the unmarried or same-sex partner of a person present and settled in the United Kingdom may be granted provided that the Secretary of State is satisfied that each of the requirements of paragraph 295G is met.

Refusal of indefinite leave to remain as the unmarried or same-sex partner of a person present and settled in the United Kingdom

295I. Indefinite leave to remain as the unmarried or same-sex partner of a person present and settled in the United Kingdom is to be refused if the Secretary of State is not satisfied that each of the requirements of paragraph 295G is met.

Leave to enter or remain as the unmarried or same-sex partner of a person with limited leave to enter or remain in the United Kingdom under paragraphs 128–193; 200–239; or 263–270

Requirements for leave to enter or remain as the unmarried or same-sex partner of a person with limited leave to enter or remain in the United Kingdom under paragraphs 128–193; 200–239; or 263–270

295J–295L. DELETED

Note: Paragraphs 295J–295L deleted from 1 October 2013 subject to savings for applications made before that date (HC 628).

Indefinite leave to remain for the bereaved unmarried or same-sex partner of a person present and settled in the United Kingdom

Requirements for indefinite leave to remain for the bereaved unmarried or same-sex partner of a person present and settled in the United Kingdom

295M. The requirements to be met by a person seeking indefinite leave to remain as the bereaved unmarried or same-sex partner of a person present and settled in the United Kingdom, are that:

(i) the applicant was admitted to the United Kingdom for a period not exceeding 27 months; or given an extension of stay for a period of 2 years in accordance with paragraphs 295AA to 295F of these Rules as the unmarried partner of a person present and settled in the United Kingdom; and

(ii) the person whom the applicant was admitted or granted an extension of stay to join died during that period of leave; and

(iii) the applicant was still the unmarried or same-sex partner of the person he was admitted or granted an extension of stay to join at the time of the death; and

(iv) each of the parties intended to live permanently with the other as his partner and the relationship was subsisting at the time of the death; and

(v) the applicant does not fall for refusal under the general grounds for refusal.

Note: Subparagraph (v) substituted from 13 December 2012 subject to savings for applications made before that date (HC 760).

Indefinite leave to remain for the bereaved unmarried or same-sex partner of a person present and settled in the United Kingdom

295N. Indefinite leave to remain for the bereaved unmarried partner of a person present and settled in the United Kingdom, may be granted provided that the Secretary of State is satisfied that each of the requirements of paragraph 295M is met.

Refusal of indefinite leave to remain for the bereaved unmarried or same-sex partner of a person present and settled in the United Kingdom

295O. Indefinite leave to remain for the bereaved unmarried or same-sex partner of a person present and settled in the United Kingdom, is to be refused if the Secretary of State is not satisfied that each of the requirements of paragraph 295M is met.

Children

296. Nothing in these Rules shall be construed as permitting a child to be granted entry clearance, leave to enter or remain, or variation of leave where his parent is party to a polygamous marriage or civil partnership and any application by that parent for admission or leave to remain for settlement or with a view to settlement would be refused pursuant to paragraphs 278 or 278A.

Leave to enter or remain in the United Kingdom as the child of a parent, parents or a relative present and settled or being admitted for settlement in the United Kingdom

Requirements for indefinite leave to enter the United Kingdom as the child of a parent, parents or a relative present and settled or being admitted for settlement in the United Kingdom

297. The requirements to be met by a person seeking indefinite leave to enter the United Kingdom as the child of a parent, parents or a relative present and settled or being admitted for settlement in the United Kingdom are that he:

(i) is seeking leave to enter to accompany or join a parent, parents or a relative in one of the following circumstances:

(a) both parents are present and settled in the United Kingdom; or

(b) both parents are being admitted on the same occasion for settlement; or

(c) one parent is present and settled in the United Kingdom and the other is being admitted on the same occasion for settlement; or

(d) one parent is present and settled in the United Kingdom or being admitted on the same occasion for settlement and the other parent is dead; or

(e) one parent is present and settled in the United Kingdom or being admitted on the same occasion for settlement and has had sole responsibility for the child's upbringing; or

(f) one parent or a relative is present and settled in the United Kingdom or being admitted on the same occasion for settlement and there are serious and compelling family or other considerations which make exclusion of the child undesirable and suitable arrangements have been made for the child's care; and

(ii) is under the age of 18; and

(iii) is not leading an independent life, is unmarried and is not a civil partner, and has not formed an independent family unit; and

(iv) can, and will, be accommodated adequately by the parent, parents or relative the child is seeking to join without recourse to public funds in accommodation which the parent, parents or relative the child is seeking to join, own or occupy exclusively; and

(v) can, and will, be maintained adequately by the parent, parents, or relative the child is seeking to join, without recourse to public funds; and

(vi) holds a valid United Kingdom entry clearance for entry in this capacity; and

(vii) does not [fall for refusal under the general grounds for refusal].

Note: Subparagraph (vii) amended from 13 December 2012 subject to savings for applications made before that date (HC 760).

Requirements for indefinite leave to remain in the United Kingdom as the child of a parent, parents or a relative present and settled or being admitted for settlement in the United Kingdom

298. The requirements to be met by a person seeking indefinite leave to remain in the United Kingdom as the child of a parent, parents or a relative present and settled in the United Kingdom are that he:

(i) is seeking to remain with a parent, parents or a relative in one of the following circumstances:

(a) both parents are present and settled in the United Kingdom; or

(b) one parent is present and settled in the United Kingdom and the other parent is dead; or

(c) one parent is present and settled in the United Kingdom and has had sole responsibility for the child's upbringing [or the child normally lives with this parent and not their other parent]; or

(d) one parent or a relative is present and settled in the United Kingdom and there are serious and compelling family or other considerations which make exclusion of the child undesirable and suitable arrangements have been made for the child's care; and

(ii) has [or has had] limited leave to enter or remain in the United Kingdom, and

(a) is under the age of 18; or

(b) was given leave to enter or remain with a view to settlement under paragraph 302 or Appendix FM; or

(c) was admitted into the UK in accordance with paragraph 319R and has completed a period of 2 years limited leave as the child of a refugee or beneficiary of humanitarian protection who is now present and settled in the UK or as the child of a former refugee or beneficiary of humanitarian protection who is now a British Citizen, or

(d) the applicant has limited leave to enter or remain in the United Kingdom in accordance with paragraph 319X, as the child of a relative with limited leave to remain as a refugee or beneficiary of humanitarian protection in the United Kingdom and who is now present and settled here; or

(e) was last given limited leave to remain under paragraph 298A; and

(iii) is not leading an independent life, is unmarried, and has not formed an independent family unit; and

(iv) can, and will, be accommodated adequately by the parent, parents or relative the child was admitted to join, without recourse to public funds in accommodation which the parent, parents or relative the child was admitted to join, own or occupy exclusively; and

(v) can, and will, be maintained adequately by the parent, parents or relative the child was admitted to join, without recourse to public funds; and

(vi) does not [fall for refusal under the general grounds for refusal], [and]

(vii) if aged 18 or over, was admitted to the United Kingdom under paragraph 302, or Appendix FM, or 319R or 319X and has demonstrated sufficient knowledge of the English language and sufficient knowledge about life in the United Kingdom in accordance with Appendix KoLL.

Note: Words inserted in subparagraph (i)(c), and in subparagraph (ii) and words substituted in subparagraph (vi) from 13 December 2012 subject to savings for applications made before that date (HC 760). Subparagraph (vii) inserted from 28 October 2013 subject to savings for applications made before that date (HC 628). Subparagraph (ii)(e) inserted, and word 'and' inserted at end of subparagraph (vi) from 6 April 2014 (HC 1138 as amended by HC 1201).

298A. If an applicant does not meet the requirements of paragraph 298 only because:

(a) the applicant does not meet the requirement in paragraph 298(vi) by reason of a sentence or disposal of a type mentioned in paragraph 322(1C)(iii) or (iv); or

(b) an applicant aged 18 or over does not meet the requirement in paragraph 298(vii); or

(c) the applicant would otherwise be refused indefinite leave to remain under paragraph 322(1C)(iii) or (iv),

the applicant may be granted limited leave to remain for a period not exceeding 30 months and subject to a condition of no recourse to public funds.

Note: Paragraph 298A inserted from 6 April 2014 (HC 1138 as amended by HC 1201).

Indefinite leave to enter or remain in the United Kingdom as the child of a parent, parents or a relative present and settled or being admitted for settlement in the United Kingdom

299. Indefinite leave to enter the United Kingdom as the child of a parent, parents or a relative present and settled or being admitted for settlement in the United Kingdom may be granted provided a valid United Kingdom entry clearance for entry in this capacity is produced to the Immigration Officer on arrival. Indefinite leave to remain in the

United Kingdom as the child of a parent, parents or a relative present and settled in the United Kingdom may be granted provided the Secretary of State is satisfied that each of the requirements of paragraph 298 is met.

Refusal of indefinite leave to enter or remain in the United Kingdom as the child of a parent, parents or a relative present and settled or being admitted for settlement in the United Kingdom

300. Indefinite leave to enter the United Kingdom as the child of a parent, parents or a relative present and settled or being admitted for settlement in the United Kingdom is to be refused if a valid United Kingdom entry clearance for entry in this capacity is not produced to the Immigration Officer on arrival. Indefinite leave to remain in the United Kingdom as the child of a parent, parents or a relative present and settled in the United Kingdom is to be refused if the Secretary of State is not satisfied that each of the requirements of paragraph 298 is met.

Requirements for limited leave to enter or remain in the United Kingdom with a view to settlement as the child of a parent or parents given limited leave to enter or remain in the United Kingdom with a view to settlement

301. The requirements to be met by a person seeking limited leave to enter or remain in the United Kingdom with a view to settlement as the child of a parent or parents given limited leave to enter or remain in the United Kingdom with a view to settlement are that he:

(i) is seeking leave to enter to accompany or join or remain with a parent or parents in one of the following circumstances:

(a) one parent is present and settled in the United Kingdom or being admitted on the same occasion for settlement and the other parent is being or has been given limited leave to enter or remain in the United Kingdom with a view to settlement; or

(b) one parent is being or has been given limited leave to enter or remain in the United Kingdom with a view to settlement and has had sole responsibility for the child's upbringing; or

(c) one parent is being or has been given limited leave to enter or remain in the United Kingdom with a view to settlement and there are serious and compelling family or other considerations which make exclusion of the child undesirable and suitable arrangements have been made for the child's care; and

(ii) is under the age of 18; and

(iii) is not leading an independent life, is unmarried and is not a civil partner, and has not formed an independent family unit; and

(iv) can, and will, be accommodated adequately without recourse to public funds, in accommodation which the parent or parents own or occupy exclusively; and

(iva) can, and will, be maintained adequately by the parent or parents without recourse to public funds; and

(ivb) does not qualify for limited leave to enter as a child of a parent or parents given limited leave to enter or remain as a refugee or beneficiary of humanitarian protection under paragraph 319R; and

(v) (where an application is made for limited leave to remain with a view to settlement) has limited leave to enter or remain in the United Kingdom; and

(vi) if seeking leave to enter, holds a valid United Kingdom entry clearance for entry in this capacity.

Limited leave to enter or remain in the United Kingdom with a view to settlement as the child of a parent or parents given limited leave to enter or remain in the United Kingdom with a view to settlement

302. A person seeking limited leave to enter the United Kingdom with a view to settlement as the child of a parent or parents given limited leave to enter or remain in the United Kingdom with a view to settlement may be admitted for a period not exceeding 27 months provided he is able, on arrival, to produce to the Immigration Officer a valid United Kingdom entry clearance for entry in this capacity. A person seeking limited leave to remain in the United Kingdom with a view to settlement as the child of a parent or parents given limited leave to enter or remain in the United Kingdom with a view to settlement may be given limited leave to remain for a period not exceeding 27 months provided the Secretary of State is satisfied that each of the requirements of paragraph 301 (i)–(v) is met.

Refusal of limited leave to enter or remain in the United Kingdom with a view to settlement as the child of a parent or parents given limited leave to enter or remain in the United Kingdom with a view to settlement

303. Limited leave to enter the United Kingdom with a view to settlement as the child of a parent or parents given limited leave to enter or remain in the United Kingdom with a view to settlement is to be refused if a valid United Kingdom entry clearance for entry in this capacity is not produced to the Immigration Officer on arrival. Limited leave to remain in the United Kingdom with a view to settlement as the child of a parent or parents given limited leave to enter or remain in the United Kingdom with a view to settlement is to be refused if the Secretary of State is not satisfied that each of the requirements of paragraph 301 (i)–(v) is met.

Leave to enter and extension of stay in the United Kingdom as the child of a parent who is being, or has been admitted to the United Kingdom as a fiance(e) or proposed civil partner

Requirements for limited leave to enter the United Kingdom as the child of a fiance(e) or proposed civil partner

303A. The requirements to be met by a person seeking limited leave to enter the United Kingdom as the child of a fiance(e) or proposed civil partner, are that:

(i) he is seeking to accompany or join a parent who is, on the same occasion that the child seeks admission, being admitted as a fiance(e) or proposed civil partner, or who has been admitted as a fiance(e) or proposed civil partner; and

(ii) he is under the age of 18; and

(iii) he is not leading an independent life, is unmarried and is not a civil partner, and has not formed an independent family unit; and

(iv) he can and will be maintained and accommodated adequately without recourse to public funds with the parent admitted or being admitted as a fiance(e) or proposed civil partner; and

(v) there are serious and compelling family or other considerations which make the child's exclusion undesirable, that suitable arrangements have been made for his care in the United Kingdom, and there is no other person outside the United Kingdom who could reasonably be expected to care for him; and

(vi) he holds a valid United Kingdom entry clearance for entry in this capacity.

Limited leave to enter the United Kingdom as the child of a parent who is being, or has been admitted to the United Kingdom as a fiance(e) or proposed civil partner

303B. A person seeking limited leave to enter the United Kingdom as the child of a fiance(e) or proposed civil partner, may be granted limited leave to enter the United Kingdom for a period not in excess of that granted to the fiance(e) or proposed civil partner, provided that a valid United Kingdom entry clearance for entry in this capacity is produced to the Immigration Officer on arrival. Where the period of limited leave granted to a fiance(e) will expire in more than 6 months, a person seeking limited leave to enter as the child of the fiance(e) or proposed civil partner should be granted leave for a period not exceeding six months.

Refusal of limited leave to enter the United Kingdom as the child of a parent who is being, or has been admitted to the United Kingdom as a fiance(e) or proposed civil partner

303C. Limited leave to enter the United Kingdom as the child of a fiance(e) or proposed civil partner, is to be refused if a valid United Kingdom entry clearance for entry in this capacity is not produced to the Immigration Officer on arrival.

Requirements for an extension of stay in the United Kingdom as the child of a fiance(e) or proposed civil partner

303D. The requirements to be met by a person seeking an extension of stay in the United Kingdom as the child of a fiance(e) or proposed civil partner are that:

(i) the applicant was admitted with a valid United Kingdom entry clearance as the child of a fiance(e) or proposed civil partner; and

(ii) the applicant is the child of a parent who has been granted limited leave to enter, or an extension of stay, as a fiance(e) or proposed civil partner; and

(iii) the requirements of paragraph 303A (ii)–(v) are met.

Extension of stay in the United Kingdom as the child of a fiance(e) or proposed civil partner

303E. An extension of stay as the child of a fiance(e) or proposed civil partner may be granted provided that the Secretary of State is satisfied that each of the requirements of paragraph 303D is met.

Refusal of an extension of stay in the United Kingdom as the child of a fiance(e) or proposed civil partner

303F. An extension of stay as the child of a fiance(e) or proposed civil partner is to be refused if the Secretary of State is not satisfied that each of the requirements of paragraph 303D is met.

Children born in the United Kingdom who are not British citizens

304. This paragraph and paragraphs 305–309 apply only to dependent children under 18 years of age who are unmarried and are not civil partners and who were born in the

United Kingdom on or after 1 January 1983 (when the British Nationality Act 1981 came into force) but who, because neither of their parents was a British Citizen or settled in the United Kingdom at the time of their birth, are not British Citizens and are therefore subject to immigration control. Such a child requires leave to enter where admission to the United Kingdom is sought, and leave to remain where permission is sought for the child to be allowed to stay in the United Kingdom. If he qualifies for entry clearance, leave to enter or leave to remain under any other part of these Rules, a child who was born in the United Kingdom but is not a British Citizen may be granted entry clearance, leave to enter or leave to remain in accordance with the provisions of that other part.

Requirements for leave to enter or remain in the United Kingdom as the child of a parent or parents given leave to enter or remain in the United Kingdom

305. The requirements to be met by a child born in the United Kingdom who is not a British Citizen who seeks leave to enter or remain in the United Kingdom as the child of a parent or parents given leave to enter or remain in the United Kingdom are that he:

(i)(a) is accompanying or seeking to join or remain with a parent or parents who have, or are given, leave to enter or remain in the United Kingdom; or

(b) is accompanying or seeking to join or remain with a parent or parents one of whom is a British Citizen or has the right of abode in the United Kingdom; or

(c) is a child in respect of whom the parental rights and duties are vested solely in a local authority; and

(ii) is under the age of 18; and

(iii) was born in the United Kingdom; and

(iv) is not leading an independent life, is unmarried and is not a civil partner, and has not formed an independent family unit; and

(v) (where an application is made for leave to enter) has not been away from the United Kingdom for more than 2 years.

Leave to enter or remain in the United Kingdom

306. A child born in the United Kingdom who is not a British Citizen and who requires leave to enter or remain in the circumstances set out in paragraph 304 may be given leave to enter for the same period as his parent or parents where paragraph 305(i)(a) applies, provided the Immigration Officer is satisfied that each of the requirements of paragraph 305(ii)–(v) is met. Where leave to remain is sought, the child may be granted leave to remain for the same period as his parent or parents where paragraph 305(i)(a) applies, provided the Secretary of State is satisfied that each of the requirements of paragraph 305(ii)–(iv) is met. Where the parent or parents have or are given periods of leave of different duration, the child may be given leave to whichever period is longer except that if the parents are living apart the child should be given leave for the same period as the parent who has day to day responsibility for him.

307. If a child does not qualify for leave to enter or remain because neither of his parents has a current leave, (and neither of them is a British Citizen or has the right of abode), he will normally be refused leave to enter or remain, even if each of the requirements of paragraph 305(ii)–(v) has been satisfied. However, he may be granted leave to enter or remain for a period not exceeding 3 months if both of his parents are in the United Kingdom and it appears unlikely that they will be removed in the immediate future, and there is no other person outside the United Kingdom who could reasonably be expected to care for him.

308. A child born in the United Kingdom who is not a British Citizen and who requires leave to enter or remain in the United Kingdom in the circumstances set out in paragraph 304 may be given indefinite leave to enter where paragraph 305(i)(b) or (i)(c) applies provided the Immigration Officer is satisfied that each of the requirements of paragraph 305(ii)–(v) is met. Where an application is for leave to remain, such a child may be granted indefinite leave to remain where paragraph 305(i)(b) or (i)(c) applies, provided the Secretary of State is satisfied that each of the requirements of paragraph 305(ii)–(iv) is met.

Refusal of leave to enter or remain in the United Kingdom

309. Leave to enter the United Kingdom where the circumstances set out in paragraph 304 apply is to be refused if the Immigration Officer is not satisfied that each of the requirements of paragraph 305 is met. Leave to remain for such a child is to be refused if the Secretary of State is not satisfied that each of the requirements of paragraph 305(i)–(iv) is met.

Adopted children

309A. For the purposes of adoption under paragraphs 310–316C a de facto adoption shall be regarded as having taken place if:

(a) at the time immediately preceding the making of the application for entry clearance under these Rules the adoptive parent or parents have been living abroad (in applications involving two parents both must have lived abroad together) for at least a period of time equal to the first period mentioned in sub-paragraph (b)(i) and must have cared for the child for at least a period of time equal to the second period material in that sub-paragraph; and

(b) during their time abroad, the adoptive parent or parents have:

(i) lived together for a minimum period of 18 months, of which the 12 months immediately preceding the application for entry clearance must have been spent living together with the child; and

(ii) have assumed the role of the child's parents, since the beginning of the 18 month period, so that there has been a genuine transfer of parental responsibility.

309B. Inter-country adoptions which are not a de facto adoption under paragraph 309A are subject to the Adoption and Children Act 2002 and the Adoptions with a Foreign Element Regulations 2005. As such all prospective adopters must be assessed as suitable to adopt by a competent authority in the UK, and obtain a Certificate of Eligibility from the Department for Education, before travelling abroad to identify a child for adoption. This Certificate of Eligibility must be provided with all entry clearance adoption applications under paragraphs 310–316F.

Requirements for indefinite leave to enter the United Kingdom as the adopted child of a parent or parents present and settled or being admitted for settlement in the United Kingdom

310. The requirements to be met in the case of a child seeking indefinite leave to enter the United Kingdom as the adopted child of a parent or parents present and settled or being admitted for settlement in the United Kingdom are that he:

(i) is seeking leave to enter to accompany or join an adoptive parent or parents in one of the following circumstances;

(a) both parents are present and settled in the United Kingdom; or

(b) both parents are being admitted on the same occasion for settlement; or

(c) one parent is present and settled in the United Kingdom and the other is being admitted on the same occasion for settlement; or

(d) one parent is present and settled in the United Kingdom or being admitted on the same occasion for settlement and the other parent is dead; or

(e) one parent is present and settled in the United Kingdom or being admitted on the same occasion for settlement and has had sole responsibility for the child's upbringing; or

(f) one parent is present and settled in the United Kingdom or being admitted on the same occasion for settlement and there are serious and compelling family or other considerations which make exclusion of the child undesirable and suitable arrangements have been made for the child's care; or

(g) in the case of a de facto adoption one parent has a right of abode in the United Kingdom or indefinite leave to enter or remain in the United Kingdom and is seeking admission to the United Kingdom on the same occasion for the purposes of settlement; and

(ii) is under the age of 18; and

(iii) is not leading an independent life, is unmarried and is not a civil partner, and has not formed an independent family unit; and

(iv) can, and will, be accommodated and maintained adequately without recourse to public funds in accommodation which the adoptive parent or parents own or occupy exclusively; and

(v) DELETED

(vi) (a) was adopted in accordance with a decision taken by the competent administrative authority or court in his country of origin or the country in which he is resident, being a country whose adoption orders are recognised by the United Kingdom; or

(b) is the subject of a de facto adoption; and

(vii) was adopted at a time when:

(a) both adoptive parents were resident together abroad; or

(b) either or both adoptive parents were settled in the United Kingdom; and

(viii) has the same rights and obligations as any other child of the adoptive parent's or parents' family; and

(ix) was adopted due to the inability of the original parent(s) or current carer(s) to care for him and there has been a genuine transfer of parental responsibility to the adoptive parents; and

(x) has lost or broken his ties with his family of origin; and

(xi) was adopted, but the adoption is not one of convenience arranged to facilitate his admission to or remaining in the United Kingdom; and

(xii) holds a valid United Kingdom entry clearance for entry in this capacity; and

(xiii) does not [fall for refusal under the general grounds for refusal].

Note: Words substituted in subparagraph (xiii) from 13 December 2012 subject to savings for applications made before that date (HC 760).

Requirements for indefinite leave to remain in the United Kingdom as the adopted child of a parent or parents present and settled in the United Kingdom

311. The requirements to be met in the case of a child seeking indefinite leave to remain in the United Kingdom as the adopted child of a parent or parents present and settled in the United Kingdom are that he:

(i) is seeking to remain with adoptive parent or parents in one of the following circumstances:

(a) both parents are present and settled in the United Kingdom; or

(b) one parent is present and settled in the United Kingdom and the other parent is dead; or

(c) one parent is present and settled in the United Kingdom and has had sole responsibility for the child's upbringing; or

(d) one parent is present and settled in the United Kingdom and there are serious and compelling family or other considerations which make exclusion of the child undesirable and suitable arrangements have been made for the child's care; or

(e) in the case of a de facto adoption one parent has a right of abode in the United Kingdom or indefinite leave to enter or remain in the United Kingdom and is seeking admission to the United Kingdom on the same occasion for the purpose of settlement; and

(ii) has limited leave to enter or remain in the United Kingdom, and

(a) is under the age of 18; or

(b) was given leave to enter or remain with a view to settlement under paragraph 315 or paragraph 316B; and

(iii) is not leading an independent life, is unmarried and is not a civil partner, and has not formed an independent family unit; and

(iv) can, and will, be accommodated and maintained adequately without recourse to public funds in accommodation which the adoptive parent or parents own or occupy exclusively; and

(v) DELETED

(vi) (a) was adopted in accordance with a decision taken by the competent administrative authority or court in his country of origin or the country in which he is resident, being a country whose adoption orders are recognised by the United Kingdom; or

(b) is the subject of a de facto adoption; and

(vii) was adopted at a time when:

(a) both adoptive parents were resident together abroad; or

(b) either or both adoptive parents were settled in the United Kingdom; and

(viii) has the same rights and obligations as any other child of the adoptive parent's or parents' family; and

(ix) was adopted due to the inability of the original parent(s) or current carer(s) to care for him and there has been a genuine transfer of parental responsibility to the adoptive parents; and

(x) has lost or broken his ties with his family of origin; and

(xi) was adopted, but the adoption is not one of convenience arranged to facilitate his admission to or remaining in the United Kingdom; and

(xii) [does not fall for refusal under the general grounds for refusal].

Note: Words substituted in subparagraph (xii) from 13 December 2012 subject to savings for applications made before that date (HC 760).

Indefinite leave to enter or remain in the United Kingdom as the adopted child of a parent or parents present and settled or being admitted for settlement in the United Kingdom

312. Indefinite leave to enter the United Kingdom as the adopted child of a parent or parents present and settled or being admitted for settlement in the United Kingdom may be granted provided a valid United Kingdom entry clearance for entry in this capacity is produced to the Immigration Officer on arrival. Indefinite leave to remain in the United Kingdom as the adopted child of a parent or parents present and settled in the

United Kingdom may be granted provided the Secretary of State is satisfied that each of the requirements of paragraph 311 is met.

Refusal of indefinite leave to enter or remain in the United Kingdom as the adopted child of a parent or parents present and settled or being admitted for settlement in the United Kingdom

313. Indefinite leave to enter the United Kingdom as the adopted child of a parent or parents present and settled or being admitted for settlement in the United Kingdom is to be refused if a valid United Kingdom entry clearance for entry in this capacity is not produced to the Immigration Officer on arrival. Indefinite leave to remain in the United Kingdom as the adopted child of a parent or parents present and settled in the United Kingdom is to be refused if the Secretary of State is not satisfied that each of the requirements of paragraph 311 is met.

Requirements for limited leave to enter or remain in the United Kingdom with a view to settlement as the adopted child of a parent or parents given limited leave to enter or remain in the United Kingdom with a view to settlement

314. The requirements to be met in the case of a child seeking limited leave to enter or remain in the United Kingdom with a view to settlement as the adopted child of a parent or parents given limited leave to enter or remain in the United Kingdom with a view to settlement are that he:

(i) is seeking leave to enter to accompany or join or remain with a parent or parents in one of the following circumstances:

(a) one parent is present and settled in the United Kingdom or being admitted on the same occasion for settlement and the other parent is being or has been given limited leave to enter or remain in the United Kingdom with a view to settlement; or

(b) one parent is being or has been given limited leave to enter or remain in the United Kingdom with a view to settlement and has had sole responsibility for the child's upbringing; or

(c) one parent is being or has been given limited leave to enter or remain in the United Kingdom with a view to settlement and there are serious and compelling family or other considerations which make exclusion of the child undesirable and suitable arrangements have been made for the child's care; or

(d) in the case of a de facto adoption one parent has a right of abode in the United Kingdom or indefinite leave to enter or remain in the United Kingdom and is seeking admission to the United Kingdom on the same occasion for the purpose of settlement; and

(ii) is under the age of 18; and

(iii) is not leading an independent life, is unmarried and is not a civil partner, and has not formed an independent family unit; and

(iv) can, and will, be accommodated and maintained adequately without recourse to public funds in accommodation which the adoptive parent or parents own or occupy exclusively; and

(v) (a) was adopted in accordance with a decision taken by the competent administrative authority or court in his country of origin or the country in which he is resident, being a country whose adoption orders are recognised by the United Kingdom; or

(b) is the subject of a de facto adoption; and

(vi) was adopted at a time when:

(a) both adoptive parents were resident together abroad; or

(b) either or both adoptive parents were settled in the United Kingdom; and

(vii) has the same rights and obligations as any other child of the adoptive parent's or parents' family; and

(viii) was adopted due to the inability of the original parent(s) or current carer(s) to care for him and there has been a genuine transfer of parental responsibility to the adoptive parents; and

(ix) has lost or broken his ties with his family of origin; and

(x) was adopted, but the adoption is not one of convenience arranged to facilitate his admission to the United Kingdom; and

(xi) (where an application is made for limited leave to remain with a view to settlement) has limited leave to enter or remain in the United Kingdom; and

(xii) if seeking leave to enter, holds a valid United Kingdom entry clearance for entry in this capacity.

Limited leave to enter or remain in the United Kingdom with a view to settlement as the adopted child of a parent or parents given limited leave to enter or remain in the United Kingdom with a view to settlement

315. A person seeking limited leave to enter the United Kingdom with a view to settlement as the adopted child of a parent or parents given limited leave to enter or remain in the United Kingdom with a view to settlement may be admitted for a period not exceeding 12 months provided he is able, on arrival, to produce to the Immigration Officer a valid United Kingdom entry clearance for entry in this capacity. A person seeking limited leave to remain in the United Kingdom with a view to settlement as the adopted child of a parent or parents given limited leave to enter or remain in the United Kingdom with a view to settlement may be granted limited leave for a period not exceeding 12 months provided the Secretary of State is satisfied that each of the requirements of paragraph 314(i)–(xi) is met.

Refusal of limited leave to enter or remain in the United Kingdom with a view to settlement as the adopted child of a parent or parents given limited leave to enter or remain in the United Kingdom with a view to settlement

316. Limited leave to enter the United Kingdom with a view to settlement as the adopted child of a parent or parents given limited leave to enter or remain in the United Kingdom with a view to settlement is to be refused if a valid United Kingdom entry clearance for entry in this capacity is not produced to the Immigration Officer on arrival. Limited leave to remain in the United Kingdom with a view to settlement as the adopted child of a parent or parents given limited leave to enter or remain in the United Kingdom with a view to settlement is to be refused if the Secretary of State is not satisfied that each of the requirements of paragraph 314(i)–(xi) is met.

Requirements for limited leave to enter the United Kingdom with a view to settlement as a child for adoption

316A. The requirements to be satisfied in the case of a child seeking limited leave to enter the United Kingdom for the purpose of being adopted (which, for the avoidance of doubt, does not include a de facto adoption) in the United Kingdom are that he:

(i) is seeking limited leave to enter to accompany or join a person or persons who wish to adopt him in the United Kingdom (the "prospective parent(s)"), in one of the following circumstances:

(a) both prospective parents are present and settled in the United Kingdom; or

(b) both prospective parents are being admitted for settlement on the same occasion that the child is seeking admission; or

(c) one prospective parent is present and settled in the United Kingdom and the other is being admitted for settlement on the same occasion that the child is seeking admission; or

(d) one prospective parent is present and settled in the United Kingdom and the other is being given limited leave to enter or remain in the United Kingdom with a view to settlement on the same occasion that the child is seeking admission, or has previously been given such leave; or

(e) one prospective parent is being admitted for settlement on the same occasion that the other is being granted limited leave to enter with a view to settlement, which is also on the same occasion that the child is seeking admission; or

(f) one prospective parent is present and settled in the United Kingdom or is being admitted for settlement on the same occasion that the child is seeking admission, and has had sole responsibility for the child's upbringing; or

(g) one prospective parent is present and settled in the United Kingdom or is being admitted for settlement on the same occasion that the child is seeking admission, and there are serious and compelling family or other considerations which would make the child's exclusion undesirable, and suitable arrangements have been made for the child's care; and

(ii) is under the age of 18; and

(iii) is not leading an independent life, is unmarried and is not a civil partner, and has not formed an independent family unit; and

(iv) can, and will, be maintained and accommodated adequately without recourse to public funds in accommodation which the prospective parent or parents own or occupy exclusively; and

(v) will have the same rights and obligations as any other child of the marriage or civil partnership; and

(vi) is being adopted due to the inability of the original parent(s) or current carer(s) (or those looking after him immediately prior to him being physically transferred to his prospective parent or parents) to care for him, and there has been a genuine transfer of parental responsibility to the prospective parent or parents; and

(vii) has lost or broken or intends to lose or break his ties with his family of origin; and

(viii) will be adopted in the United Kingdom by his prospective parent or parents in accordance with the law relating to adoption in the United Kingdom, but the proposed adoption is not one of convenience arranged to facilitate his admission to the United Kingdom.

Limited leave to enter the United Kingdom with a view to settlement as a child for adoption

316B. A person seeking limited leave to enter the United Kingdom with a view to settlement as a child for adoption may be admitted for a period not exceeding 24 months provided he is able, on arrival, to produce to the Immigration Officer a valid United Kingdom entry clearance for entry in this capacity.

Refusal of limited leave to enter the United Kingdom with a view to settlement as a child for adoption

316C. Limited leave to enter the United Kingdom with a view to settlement as a child for adoption is to be refused if a valid United Kingdom entry clearance for entry in this capacity is not produced to the Immigration Officer on arrival.

Requirements for limited leave to enter the United Kingdom with a view to settlement as a child for adoption under the Hague Convention

316D The requirements to be satisfied in the case of a child seeking limited leave to enter the United Kingdom for the purpose of being adopted in the United Kingdom under the Hague Convention are that he:

(i) is seeking limited leave to enter to accompany one or two people each of whom are habitually resident in the United Kingdom and who wish to adopt him under the Hague Convention ("the prospective parents");

(ii) is the subject of an agreement made under Article 17(c) of the Hague Convention; and

(iii) has been entrusted to the prospective parents by the competent administrative authority of the country from which he is coming to the United Kingdom for adoption under the Hague Convention; and

(iv) is under the age of 18; and

(v) can, and will, be maintained and accommodated adequately without recourse to public funds in accommodation which the prospective parent or parents own or occupy exclusively; and

(vi) holds a valid United Kingdom entry clearance for entry in this capacity.

Limited leave to enter the United Kingdom with a view to settlement as a child for adoption under the Hague Convention

316E A person seeking limited leave to enter the United Kingdom with a view to settlement as a child for adoption under the Hague Convention may be admitted for a period not exceeding 24 months provided he is able, on arrival, to produce to the Immigration Officer a valid United Kingdom entry clearance for entry in this capacity.

Refusal of limited leave to enter the United Kingdom with a view to settlement as a child for adoption under the Hague Convention

316F Limited leave to enter the United Kingdom with a view to settlement as a child for adoption under the Hague Convention is to be refused if a valid United Kingdom entry clearance for entry in this capacity is not produced to the Immigration Officer on arrival.

Parents, grandparents and other dependent relatives of persons present and settled in the United Kingdom

Requirements for indefinite leave to enter or remain in the United Kingdom as the parent, grandparent or other dependent relative of a person present and settled in the United Kingdom

317. The requirements to be met by a person seeking indefinite leave to enter or remain in the United Kingdom as the parent, grandparent or other dependent relative of a person present and settled in the United Kingdom are that the person:

(i) is related to a person present and settled in the United Kingdom in one of the following ways:

(a) parent or grandparent who is divorced, widowed, single or separated aged 65 years or over; or

(b) parents or grandparents travelling together of whom at least one is aged 65 or over;

or

(c) a parent or grandparent aged 65 or over who has entered into a second relationship of marriage or civil partnership but cannot look to the spouse, civil partner or children of that second relationship for financial support; and where the person settled in the United Kingdom is able and willing to maintain the parent or grandparent and any spouse or civil partner or child of the second relationship who would be admissible as a dependant; or

(d) parent or grandparent under the age of 65 if living alone outside the United Kingdom in the most exceptional compassionate circumstances; or

(e) parents or grandparents travelling together who are both under the age of 65 if living in the most exceptional compassionate circumstances; or

(f) the son, daughter, sister, brother, uncle or aunt over the age of 18 if living alone outside the United Kingdom in the most exceptional compassionate circumstances; and

(ii) is joining or accompanying a person who is present and settled in the United Kingdom or who is on the same occasion being admitted for settlement; and

(iii) is financially wholly or mainly dependent on the relative present and settled in the United Kingdom; and

(iv) can, and will, be accommodated adequately, together with any dependants, without recourse to public funds, in accommodation which the sponsor owns or occupies exclusively; and

(iva) can, and will, be maintained adequately, together with any dependants, without recourse to public funds; and

(v) has no other close relatives in his own country to whom he could turn for financial support; and

(vi) if seeking leave to enter, holds a valid United Kingdom entry clearance for entry in this capacity; and

(vii) does not [fall for refusal under the general grounds for refusal].

Note: Words substituted in subparagraph (vii) from 13 December 2012 subject to savings for applications made before that date (HC 760).

Indefinite leave to enter or remain as the parent, grandparent or other dependent relative of a person present and settled in the United Kingdom

318. Indefinite leave to enter the United Kingdom as the parent, grandparent or other dependent relative of a person present and settled in the United Kingdom may be granted provided a valid United Kingdom entry clearance for entry in this capacity is produced to the Immigration Officer on arrival. Indefinite leave to remain in the United Kingdom as the parent, grandparent or other dependent relative of a person present and settled in the United Kingdom may be granted provided the Secretary of State is satisfied that each of the requirements of paragraph 317(i)–(v) is met.

Refusal of indefinite leave to enter or remain in the United Kingdom as the parent, grandparent or other dependent relative of a person present and settled in the United Kingdom

319. Indefinite leave to enter the United Kingdom as the parent, grandparent or other dependent relative of a person settled in the United Kingdom is to be refused if a valid United Kingdom entry clearance for entry in this capacity is not produced to the Immigration Officer on arrival. Indefinite leave to remain in the United Kingdom as the parent, grandparent or other dependent relative of a person present and settled in the United Kingdom is to be refused if the Secretary of State is not satisfied that each of the requirements of paragraph 317(i)–(v) is met.

Family members of relevant points-based system migrants

Partners of relevant points-based system migrants

319AA. In paragraphs 319A to 319K and Appendix E, 'Relevant Points Based System Migrant' means a migrant granted leave as a Tier 1 Migrant, a Tier 2 Migrant, a Tier 4 (General) Student or a Tier 5 (Temporary Worker) Migrant.

319A. Purpose

This route is for the spouse, civil partner, unmarried or same-sex partner of a Relevant Points Based System Migrant (Partner of a Relevant Points Based System Migrant). Paragraphs 277 to 280 of these Rules apply to spouses or civil partners of Relevant Points Based System Migrant; paragraph 277 of these Rules applies to civil partners of Relevant Points Based System Migrant; and paragraph 295AA of these Rules applies to unmarried and same-sex partners of Relevant Points Based System Migrants.

319B. Entry to the UK

(a) Subject to paragraph (b), all migrants wishing to enter as the Partner of a relevant Points Based System Migrant must have a valid entry clearance for entry under this route. If they do not have a valid entry clearance, entry will be refused.

(b) A Migrant arriving in the UK and wishing to enter as a partner of a Tier 5 (Temporary Worker) Migrant, who does not have a valid entry clearance will not be refused entry if the following conditions are met:

(i) the migrant wishing to enter as partner is not a visa national,

(ii) the migrant wishing to enter as a Partner is accompanying an applicant who at the same time is being granted leave to enter under paragraph 245ZN(b), and

(iii) the migrant wishing to enter as a Partner meets the requirements of entry clearance in paragraph 319C.

319C. Requirements for entry clearance or leave to remain

To qualify for entry clearance or leave to remain as the Partner of a Relevant Points Based System Migrant, an applicant must meet the requirements listed below. If the applicant meets these requirements, entry clearance or leave to remain will be granted. If the applicant does not meet these requirements, the application will be refused.

Requirements:

(a) The applicant must not fall for refusal under the general grounds for refusal, and if applying for leave to remain, must not be an illegal entrant.

(b) The applicant must be the spouse or civil partner, unmarried or same-sex partner of a person who:

(i) has valid leave to enter or remain as a Relevant Points Based System Migrant, or

(ii) is, at the same time, being granted entry clearance or leave to remain as a Relevant Points Based System Migrant, or

(iii) has indefinite leave to remain as a Relevant Points Based System Migrant, or is at the same time being granted indefinite leave to remain as a Relevant Points Based System Migrant, where the applicant is applying for further leave to remain [, or has been refused indefinite leave to remain solely because the applicant has not met the requirements of paragraph 319E(g),] and was last granted leave:

(1) as the partner of that same Relevant Points Based System Migrant: or

(2) as the spouse or civil partner, unmarried or same-sex partner of that person at a time when that person had leave under another category of these Rules; or

(iv) has become a British Citizen where prior to that they held indefinite leave to Remain as a Relevant Points Based System Migrant and where the applicant is applying for further leave to remain and was last granted leave:

(1) as the partner of that same Relevant Points Based System Migrant, or

(2) as the spouse or civil partner, unmarried or same-sex partner of that person at a time when that person had leave under another category of these Rules.

(c) An applicant who is the unmarried or same-sex partner of a Relevant Points Based System Migrant must also meet the following requirements:

(i) any previous marriage or civil partnership or similar relationship by the applicant or the Relevant Points Based System Migrant with another person must have permanently broken down,

(ii) the applicant and the Relevant Points Based System Migrant must not be so closely related that they would be prohibited from marrying each other in the UK, and

(iii) the applicant and the Relevant Points Based System Migrant must have been living together in a relationship similar to marriage or civil partnership for a period of at least 2 years.

(d) The marriage or civil partnership, or relationship similar to marriage or civil partnership, must be subsisting at the time the application is made.

(e) The applicant and the Relevant Points Based System Migrant must intend to live with the other as their spouse or civil partner, unmarried or same-sex partner throughout the applicants stay in the UK.

(f) The applicant must not intend to stay in the UK beyond any period of leave granted to the Relevant Points Based System Migrant.

(g) Unless the Relevant Points Based System Migrant is a Tier 1 (Investor) Migrant or a Tier 1 (Exceptional Talent) Migrant, there must be a sufficient level of funds available to the applicant, as set out in Appendix E.

(h) An applicant who is applying for leave to remain must not have last been granted:

(i) entry clearance or leave as a visitor, unless the Relevant Points Based System Migrant has, or is being granted, leave to remain as a Tier 5 (Temporary Worker) Migrant in the creative and sporting subcategory on the basis of having met the requirement at paragraph 245ZQ(b)(ii);

(ii) temporary admission; or

(iii) temporary release.

(i) Where the relevant Points Based System Migrant is applying for, or has been granted, entry clearance, leave to enter, or leave to remain in the United Kingdom as a Tier 4 (General) Student either:

(i) the relevant Points Based System Migrant must be a government sponsored student who is applying for, or who has been granted, entry clearance or leave to remain to undertake a course of study longer than six months;

(ii) the relevant Points Based System Migrant must:

(1) be applying for, or have been granted entry clearance or leave to remain in order to undertake a course of study at post-graduate level [that is 12 months or longer in duration]; and

(2) be sponsored by a sponsor who is a Recognised Body or a body in receipt of funding as a higher education institution from either:

(a) the Department for Employment and Learning in Northern Ireland;

(b) the Higher Education Funding Council for England;

(c) the Higher Education Funding Council for Wales; or

(d) the Scottish Funding Council;

(iii) the relevant Points Based System Migrant must be applying for, or have been granted leave to remain as a Tier 4 (General) Student on the doctorate extension scheme; or

(iv) the following conditions must be met:

(1) the relevant Points Based System Migrant must be applying for entry clearance, leave to enter, or leave to remain, to undertake a course of study that is longer than six months and either:

(a) have entry clearance, leave to enter, or leave to remain as a Tier 4 (General) Student or as a student to undertake a course of study longer than six months; or

(b) have last had entry clearance, leave to enter, or leave to remain within the three months preceding the application as a Tier 4 (General) Student or as a student to undertake a course of study longer than six months; and

(2) the Partner must either:

(a) have entry clearance, leave to enter, or leave to remain as the Partner of a Tier 4 (General) Student or a student with entry clearance, leave to enter, or leave to remain, to undertake a course of study longer than six months; or

(b) have last had entry clearance, leave to enter, or leave to remain within the three months preceding the application as the Partner of a Tier 4 (General) Student or as a student to undertake a course of study longer than six months; and

(3) the relevant Points Based System Migrant and the Partner must be applying at the same time.

(j) The applicant must not be in the UK in breach of immigration laws except that any period of overstaying for a period of 28 days will be disregarded.

Note: Subparagraph (i) substituted from 1 July 2013 (HC 244). Words substituted in subparagraph (i)(ii)(1) from 1 August 2013 Cm 8690; see implementation section of Cm 8690 for savings for applications made on or after 1 July 2013 and before 1 August 2013. Subparagraph (h) inserted from 1 October 2013 subject to savings for applications made before that date (HC 628). Words inserted in subparagraph (b)(iii) from 6 November 2014 (HC 693); paragraph 95 of HC 693 purports to insert words in subparagraph (b)(iv) but it is unclear from the text where the insertion is intended to be.

319D. Period and conditions of grant

(a) (i) Entry clearance or limited leave to remain will be granted for a period which expires on the same day as the leave granted to the Relevant Points Based System Migrant, or

(ii) If the Relevant Points-Based System Migrant has indefinite leave to remain as a Relevant Points Based System Migrant, or is, at the same time being granted indefinite leave to remain as a Relevant Points Based System Migrant, or where the Relevant Points-Based System Migrant has since become a British Citizen, leave to remain will be granted to the applicant for a period of 3 years.

(b) Entry clearance and leave to remain under this route will be subject to the following conditions:

(i) no recourse to public funds,

(ii) registration with the police, if this is required under paragraph 326 of these Rules,

(iii) no Employment as a Doctor or Dentist in Training, unless the applicant:

(1) has obtained a primary degree in medicine or dentistry at bachelor's level or above from a UK institution that is a UK recognised or listed body, or which holds a sponsor licence under Tier 4 of the Points Based System, and provides evidence of this degree; or

(2) is applying for leave to remain and has, or has last been granted, entry clearance, leave to enter or leave to remain that was not subject to any condition restricting him from taking employment as a Doctor in Training, has been employed during that leave as a Doctor in Training, and provides a letter from the Postgraduate Deanery or NHS Trust employing them which confirms that they have been working in a post or programme that has been approved by the [General Medical Council] as a training programme or post; or

(3) is applying for leave to remain and has, or has last been granted, entry clearance, leave to enter or leave to remain that was not subject to any condition restricting him from taking employment as a Dentist in Training, has been employed during that leave as a Dentist in Training, and provides a letter from the Postgraduate Deanery or NHS Trust employing them which confirms that they have been working in a post or programme that has been approved by the [Joint Committee for Postgraduate Training in Dentistry] as a training programme or post.

(iv) if the Relevant Points Based System Migrant is a Tier 4 (General) Student and the Partner meets the requirements of paragraphs [319C(i)(iv)(1), (2) and (3)] and:

(1) the Relevant Points Based System Migrant is a Tier 4 (General) Student applying for leave for less than 12 months, no employment, or

(2) the Relevant Points Based System Migrant is a Tier 4 (General) Student who is following a course of below degree level study, no employment.

(v) no employment as a professional sportsperson (including as a sports coach).

Note: Words substituted in subparagraphs (b)(iii)(2) and (b)(iii)(3) from 13 December 2012 (HC 760). Words substituted in subparagraph (b)(iv) from 1 October 2013 subject to savings for applications made before that date (HC 628). Subparagraph (v) inserted, from 6 April 2014 subject to savings for applications made before that date (HC 1138 as amended by HC 1201).

319E. Requirements for indefinite leave to remain

To qualify for indefinite leave to remain as the Partner of a Relevant Points Based System Migrant, an applicant must meet the requirements listed below. If the applicant meets these requirements, indefinite leave to remain will be granted. If the applicant does not meet these requirements, the application will be refused.

Requirements:

(a) The applicant must not fall for refusal under the general grounds for refusal, and must not be an illegal entrant.

(b) The applicant must be the spouse or civil partner, unmarried or same-sex partner of a person who:

(i) has indefinite leave to remain as a Relevant Points Based System Migrant; or

(ii) is, at the same time being granted indefinite leave to remain as a Relevant Points Based System Migrant, or

(iii) has become a British Citizen where prior to that they held indefinite leave to remain as a Relevant Points Based System Migrant.

(c) The applicant must have, or have last been granted, leave as the partner of the Relevant Points Based System Migrant who:

(i) has indefinite leave to remain as a Relevant Points Based System Migrant; or

(ii) is, at the same time being granted indefinite leave to remain as a Relevant Points Based System Migrant, or

(iii) has become a British Citizen where prior to that they held indefinite leave to remain as a Relevant Points Based System Migrant.

(d) The applicant and the Relevant Points Based System Migrant must have been living together in the UK in a marriage or civil partnership, or in a relationship similar to marriage or civil partnership, for at least the period specified in (i) or (ii):

(i) If the applicant was granted leave as:

(a) the Partner of that Relevant Points Based System Migrant, or

(b) the spouse or civil partner, unmarried or same-sex partner of that person at a time when that person had leave under another category of these Rules under the Rules in place before 9 July 2012, and since then has had continuous leave as the Partner of that Relevant Points based System Migrant, the specified period is 2 years.

(ii) If (i) does not apply, the specified period is a [continuous period of 5 years], during which the applicant must:

(a) have been in a relationship with the same Relevant Points Based System Migrant for this entire period,

(b) have spent the most recent part of the 5 year period with leave as the Partner of that Relevant Points Based System Migrant, and during that part of the period have met all of the requirements of paragraph 319C(a) to (e), and

(c) have spent the remainder of the 5 year period, where applicable, [with leave] as the spouse or civil partner, unmarried or same-sex partner of that person at a time when that person had leave under another category of these Rules.

(e) The marriage or civil partnership, or relationship similar to marriage or civil partnership, must be subsisting at the time the application is made.

(f) The applicant and the Relevant Points Based System Migrant must intend to live permanently with the other as their spouse or civil partner, unmarried or same-sex partner.

(g) The applicant has demonstrated sufficient knowledge of the English language and sufficient knowledge about life in the United Kingdom, in accordance with Appendix KoLL.

(h) DELETED

(i) The applicant must not be in the UK in breach of immigration laws except that any period of overstaying for a period of 28 days will be disregarded.

Note: Words inserted in subparagraph (i)(c), and in subparagraph (ii) and words substituted in subparagraph (vi) from 13 December 2012 subject to savings for applications made before that date (HC 760). Words substituted in subparagraph (d)(ii) and words inserted in subparagraph (d)(ii)(c) from 1 October 2013 subject to savings for applications made before that date (HC 628). Subparagraph (g) substituted from 28 October 2013 subject to savings for applications made before that date (HC 628).

Children of relevant points-based system migrants

319F. Purpose

This route is for the children of a Relevant Points Based System Migrant who are under the age of 18 when they apply to enter under this route. Paragraph 296 of these Rules applies to children of a Relevant Points Based System Migrants.

319G. Entry to the UK

(a) Subject to paragraph (b), all migrants wishing to enter as the child of a relevant Points Based System Migrant must have a valid entry clearance for entry under this route. If they do not have a valid entry clearance, entry will be refused.

(b) A Migrant arriving in the UK and wishing to enter as a child of a Tier 5 (Temporary Worker) Migrant, who does not have a valid entry clearance will not be refused entry if the following conditions are met:

(i) the migrant wishing to enter as a child is not a visa national,

(ii) the migrant wishing to enter as a child is accompanying an applicant who at the same time is being granted leave to enter under paragraph 245ZN(b), and

(iii) the migrant wishing to enter as a child meets the requirements of entry clearance in paragraph 319H.

319H. Requirements for entry clearance or leave to remain

To qualify for entry clearance or leave to remain under this route, an applicant must meet the requirements listed below. If the applicant meets these requirements, entry clearance or leave to remain will be granted. If the applicant does not meet these requirements, the application will be refused.

Requirements:

(a) The applicant must not fall for refusal under the general grounds for refusal, and if applying for leave to remain, must not be an illegal entrant.

(b) The applicant must be the child of a parent who has, or is at the same time being granted, valid entry clearance, leave to enter or remain, or indefinite leave to remain, as:

(i) a Relevant Points Based System Migrant, or

(ii) the partner of a Relevant Points Based System Migrant.

or who has obtained British citizenship having previously held indefinite leave to remain as above.

(c) The applicant must be under the age of 18 on the date the application is made, or if over 18 and applying for leave to remain, must have, or have last been granted, leave as the child of a Relevant Points Based System Migrant or as the child of the parent who had leave under another category of these Rules and who has since been granted, or, is at the same time being granted, leave to remain as a Relevant Points Based System Migrant.

(d) The applicant must not be married or in a civil partnership, must not have formed an independent family unit, and must not be leading an independent life [, and, if he is over the age of 16 on the date the application is made, he must provide the specified documents and information in paragraph 319H-SD to show that this requirement is met.]

(e) The applicant must not intend to stay in the UK beyond any period of leave granted to the Relevant Points Based System Migrant parent.

(f) Both of the applicant's parents must either be lawfully present in the UK, or being granted entry clearance or leave to remain at the same time as the applicant or one parent must be lawfully present in the UK and the other is being granted entry clearance or leave to remain at the same time as the applicant, unless:

(i) The Relevant Points Based System Migrant is the applicant's sole surviving parent, or

(ii) The Relevant Points Based System Migrant parent has and has had sole responsibility for the applicant's upbringing, or

(iii) there are serious or compelling family or other considerations which would make it desirable not to refuse the application and suitable arrangements have been made in the UK for the applicant's care.

(g) Unless the Relevant Points Based System Migrant is a Tier 1 (Investor) Migrant or a Tier 1 (Exceptional Talent) Migrant, there must be a sufficient level of funds available to the applicant, as set out in Appendix E.

(h) An applicant who is applying for leave to remain must not have last been granted:

(i) entry clearance or leave as a visitor, unless the Relevant Points Based System Migrant has, or is being granted, leave to remain as a Tier 5 (Temporary Worker) Migrant in the creative and sporting subcategory on the basis of having met the requirement at paragraph 245ZQ(b)(ii);

(ii) temporary admission; or

(iii) temporary release.

(i) Where the relevant Points Based System Migrant is applying for, or has been granted, entry clearance, leave to enter, or leave to remain in the United Kingdom as a Tier 4 (General) Student either:

(i) the relevant Points Based System Migrant must be a government sponsored student who is applying for, or who has been granted, entry clearance or leave to remain to undertake a course of study longer than six months;

(ii) the relevant Points Based System Migrant must:

(1) be applying for, or have been granted entry clearance or leave to remain in order to undertake a course of study at post-graduate level that is [12 months or longer in duration]; and

(2) be sponsored by a sponsor who is a Recognised Body or a body in receipt of funding as a higher education institution from either:

(a) the Department for Employment and Learning in Northern Ireland;

(b) the Higher Education Funding Council for England;

(c) the Higher Education Funding Council for Wales; or

(d) the Scottish Funding Council;

(iii) the relevant Points Based System Migrant must be applying for, or have been granted leave to remain as a Tier 4 (General) Student on the doctorate extension scheme; or

(iv) the following conditions must be met:

(1) the relevant Points Based System Migrant must be applying for entry clearance, leave to enter, or leave to remain, to undertake a course of study that is longer than six months and either:

(a) have entry clearance, leave to enter, or leave to remain as a Tier 4 (General) Student or as a student to undertake a course of study longer than six months; or

(b) have last had entry clearance, leave to enter, or leave to remain within the three months preceding the application as a Tier 4 (General) Student or as a student to undertake a course of study longer than six months; and

(2) the Child must either:

(a) have entry clearance, leave to enter, or leave to remain as the Child of a Tier 4 (General) Student or a student with entry clearance, leave to enter, or leave to remain, to undertake a course of study longer than six months; or

(b) have last had entry clearance, leave to enter, or leave to remain within the three months preceding the application as the Child of a Tier 4 (General) Student or as a student to undertake a course of study longer than six months; and

(3) the relevant Points Based System Migrant and the Child must be applying at the same time.

(j) A Child whose parent is a Relevant Points Based System Migrant, who is a Tier 4 General) Student or Student, and who does not otherwise meet the requirements of paragraph 319H(i):

(1) must have been born during the Relevant Points Based System Migrant's most recent grant of entry clearance, leave to enter or leave to remain as a Tier 4 (General) Student or Student with leave for a course of more than six months duration; or

(2) where the Relevant Points Based System Migrant's most recent grant of entry clearance, leave to enter or leave to remain was to re-sit examinations or repeat a module of a course, must either have been born during a period of leave granted for the purposes of re-sitting examinations or repeating a module of a course or during the Relevant Points Based System Migrant's grant of leave for a course of more than six months, where that course is the same as the one for which the most recent grant of leave was to re-sit examinations or repeat a module; or

(3) must have been born no more than three months after the expiry of that most recent grant of leave; and

(4) must be applying for entry clearance.

(k) If the applicant is a child born in the UK to a Relevant Points Based System migrant and their partner, the applicant must provide a full UK birth certificate showing the names of both parents.

(l) All arrangements for the child's care and accommodation in the UK must comply with relevant UK legislation and regulations.

(m) The applicant must not be in the UK in breach of immigration laws except that any period of overstaying for a period of 28 days will be disregarded.

Note: Subparagraphs (b) and (k)–(m) substituted and subparagraph (f) inserted from 13 December 2012 (HC 760; substitution of (k)–(m) subject to savings for applications made before that date). Words inserted at the end of subparagraph (d) from 6 April 2013 subject to savings for applications made before that date (HC 1039). Subparagraph (i) substituted from 1 July 2013 (HC 244). Words substituted in subparagraph (i)(ii)(1) from 1 August 2013 Cm 8690; see implementation section of Cm 8690 for savings for applications made on or after 1 July 2013 and before 1 August 2013. Subparagraph (h) inserted from 1 October 2013 subject to savings for applications made before that date (HC 628). Subparagraph (b) inserted from 6 April 2014 subject to savings for applications made before that date (HC 1138 as amended by HC 1201).

319H-SD Specified documents and information

Applicants who are over the age of 16 on the date the application is made must provide the following specified documents and information:

(a) The applicant must provide two items from the list below confirming his residential address:

(i) bank statements,

(ii) credit card bills,

(iii) driving licence,

(iv) NHS Registration document,

(v) letter from his current school, college or university, on official headed paper and bearing the official stamp of that organisation, and issued by an authorised official of that organisation.

(b) The documents submitted must be from two separate sources and dated no more than one calendar month before the date of the application.

(c) If the applicant pays rent or board, he must provide details of how much this amounts to each calendar month.

(d) If the applicant is residing separately from the Relevant Points Based System Migrant, he must provide:

(i) reasons for residing away from the family home. Where this is due to academic endeavours he must provide confirmation from his university or college confirming his enrolment and attendance on the specific course, on official headed paper and bearing the official stamp of that organisation, and issued by an authorised official of that organisation,

(ii) the following evidence that he has been supported financially by his parents whilst residing away from the family home:

(1) bank statements for the applicant covering the three months before the date of the application clearly showing the origin of the deposits; and

(2) bank statements for the applicant's parent covering the three months before the date of the application also showing corroborating payments out of their account.

Note: Paragraph 319H-SD inserted from 6 April 2013 subject to savings for applications made before that date (HC 1039).

319I. Period and conditions of grant

(a) Entry clearance and leave to remain will be granted for:

(i) a period which expires on the same day as the leave granted to the parent whose leave expires first, or

(ii) Where both parents have, or are at the same time being granted, indefinite leave to remain, or have since become British citizens, leave to remain will be granted to the applicant for a period of 3 years.

(b) Entry clearance and leave to remain under this route will be subject to the following conditions:

(i) no recourse to public funds,

(ii) registration with the police, if this is required under paragraph 326 of these Rules, and

(iii) if the Relevant Points Based System Migrant is a Tier 4 (General) Student and the Child meets the requirements of paragraphs [319H(i)(iv)(1), (2) and (3) or 319H(j)] and:

(1) the Relevant Points Based System Migrant is a Tier 4 (General) Student applying for leave for less than 12 months, no employment, or

(2) the Relevant Points Based System Migrant is a Tier 4 (General) Student who is following a course of below degree level study, no employment.

Note: Words substituted in subparagraph (b)(iii) from 1 October 2013 subject to savings for applications made before that date (HC 628). Subparagraph (a) substituted from 6 April 2014 subject to savings for applications made before that date (HC 1138 as amended by HC 1201).

319J. Requirements for indefinite leave to remain

To qualify for indefinite leave to remain under this route, an applicant must meet the requirements listed below. If the applicant meets these requirements, indefinite leave to remain will be granted. If the applicant does not meet these requirements, the application will be refused.

Requirements:

(a) The applicant must not fall for refusal under the general grounds for refusal, and must not be an illegal entrant.

(b) The applicant must be the child of a parent who has, or is at the same time being granted, indefinite leave to remain as:

(i) a Relevant Points Based System Migrant, or

(ii) the partner of a Relevant Points Based System Migrant.

(c) The applicant must have, or have last been granted, leave as the child of or have been born in the United Kingdom to, the Points Based System Migrant, [or the partner of a Points Based System migrant] who is being granted indefinite leave to remain.

(d) The applicant must not be married or in a civil partnership, must not have formed an independent family unit, and must not be leading an independent life [, and if he is over the age of 16 on the date the application is made, he must provide the specified documents and information in paragraph 319H-SD to show that this requirement is met.]

(e) Both of an applicant's parents must either be lawfully [settled] in the UK, or being granted . . . indefinite leave to remain at the same time as the applicant, unless:

(i) The Points Based System Migrant is the applicant's sole surviving parent, or

(ii) The Points Based System Migrant parent has and has had sole responsibility for the applicant's upbringing, or

(iii) there are serious and compelling family or other considerations which would make it desirable not to refuse the application and suitable arrangements have been made for the applicant's care, or

(iv) One parent is, at the same time, being granted indefinite leave to remain as a Relevant Points Based System Migrant, the other parent is lawfully present in the UK or being granted leave at the same time as the applicant, and the applicant was granted leave as the child of a Relevant Points Based System Migrant under the Rules in place before 9 July 2012.

(f) The applicant has demonstrated sufficient knowledge of the English language and sufficient knowledge about life in the United Kingdom, in accordance with Appendix KoLL, unless he is under the age of 18 at the date on which the application is made.

(g) If the applicant is a child born in the UK to a Relevant Points Based System migrant and their partner, the applicant must provide a full UK birth certificate showing the names of both parents.

(h) All arrangements for the child's care and accommodation in the UK must comply with relevant UK legislation and regulations.

(i) The applicant must not be in the UK in breach of immigration laws except that any period of overstaying for a period of 28 days will be disregarded.

Please note in the printed version of Cm 5829 these points appear in error numbered as an alternative version of 316D(iii) and (iv).

Note: Subparagraph (b) substituted, words inserted in subparagraph (c), words substituted and deleted in subparagraph (e), subparagraph (e)(iv) inserted and subparagraphs (g)–(i) substituted from 13 December 2012 (HC 760; amendment of (g)–(i) subject to savings for applications made before 13 December 2012). Words inserted at the end of subparagraph (d) from 6 April 2013 (HC 1039).

Subparagraph (f) substituted from 28 October 2013 subject to savings for applications made before that date (HC 628).

Other family members of persons with limited leave to enter or remain in the United Kingdom as a refugee or beneficiary of humanitarian protection

Requirements for leave to enter the United Kingdom as the spouse or civil partner of a person with limited leave to enter or remain in the United Kingdom as a refugee or beneficiary of humanitarian protection

319L. The requirements to be met by a person seeking leave to enter the United Kingdom as the spouse or civil partner of a person with limited leave to enter or remain in the United Kingdom as a refugee or beneficiary of humanitarian protection, are that:

(i) (a) the applicant is married to or the civil partner of a person who has limited leave to enter or remain in the United Kingdom as a refugee or beneficiary of humanitarian protection granted such status under the immigration rules and the parties are married or have formed a civil partnership after the person granted asylum or humanitarian protection left the country of his former habitual residence in order to seek asylum or humanitarian protection; and

(b) the applicant provides an original English language test certificate in speaking and listening from an English language test provider approved by the Secretary of State for these purposes, which clearly shows the applicant's name and the qualification obtained (which must meet or exceed level A1 of the Common European Framework of Reference) unless:

(i) the applicant is aged 65 or over at the date he makes his application; or

(ii) the Secretary of State or Entry Clearance Officer considers that the applicant has a physical or mental condition that would prevent him from meeting the requirement; or

(iii) the Secretary of State or entry Clearance officer considers there are exceptional compassionate circumstances that would prevent the applicant from meeting the requirement; or

(iv) the applicant is a national of one of the following countries: Antigua and Barbuda; Australia; The Bahamas; Barbados; Belize; Canada; Dominica; Grenada; Guyana; Jamaica; New Zealand; St Kitts and Nevis; St Lucia; St Vincent and the Grenadines; Trinidad and Tobago; USA; or

(v) the applicant has obtained an academic qualification (not a professional or vocational qualification), which is deemed by UK NARIC to meet the recognised standard of a Bachelor's or Masters degree or PhD in the UK, from an educational establishment in one of the following countries: Antigua and Barbuda; Australia; The Bahamas; Barbados; Belize; Dominica; Grenada; Guyana; Ireland; Jamaica; New Zealand; St Kitts and Nevis; St Lucia; St Vincent and The Grenadines; Trinidad and Tobago; the UK; the USA; and provides the specified documents; or

(vi) the applicant has obtained an academic qualification (not a professional or vocational qualification) which is deemed by UK NARIC to meet the recognised standard of a Bachelor's or Masters degree or PhD in the UK, and

(1) provides the specified evidence to show he has the qualification, and

(2) UK NARIC has confirmed that the degree was taught or researched in English,

or

(vii) has obtained an academic qualification (not a professional or vocational qualification) which is deemed by UK NARIC to meet the recognised standard of a Bachelor's or Masters degree or PhD in the UK, and provides the specified evidence to show:

(1) he has the qualification, and

(2) that the qualification was taught or researched in English; and

(ii) the parties to the marriage or civil partnership have met; and

(iii) each of the parties intends to live permanently with the other as his or her spouse or civil partner and the marriage or civil partnership is subsisting; and

(iv) there will be adequate accommodation for the parties and any dependants without recourse to public funds in accommodation which they own or occupy exclusively; and

(v) the parties will be able to maintain themselves and any dependants adequately without recourse to public funds; and

(vi) the applicant holds a valid United Kingdom entry clearance for entry in this capacity.

L319M. Leave to enter the United Kingdom as the spouse or civil partner of a refugee or beneficiary of humanitarian protection may be granted for 63 months provided the Immigration Officer is satisfied that each of the requirements of paragraph 319L(i)–(vi) are met.

319N. Leave to enter the United Kingdom as the spouse or civil partner of a refugee or beneficiary of humanitarian protection is to be refused if the Immigration Officer is not satisfied that each of the requirements of paragraph 319L(i)–(vi) are met.

Requirements for leave to enter the United Kingdom as the unmarried or same-sex partner of a person with limited leave to enter or remain in the United Kingdom as a refugee or beneficiary of humanitarian protection.

319O. The requirements to be met by a person seeking leave to enter the United Kingdom as the unmarried or same-sex partner of a person with limited leave to enter or remain in the United Kingdom as a refugee or beneficiary of humanitarian protection, are that:

(i) (a) the applicant is the unmarried or same-sex partner of a person who has limited leave to enter or remain in the United Kingdom as a refugee or beneficiary of humanitarian protection granted such status under the immigration rules, and the parties have been living together in a relationship akin to either a marriage or civil partnership subsisting for two years or more after the person granted asylum or humanitarian protection left the country of his former habitual residence in order to seek asylum or humanitarian protection; and

(b) the applicant provides an original English language test certificate in speaking and listening from an English language test provider approved by the Secretary of State for these purposes, which clearly shows the applicant's name and the qualification obtained (which must meet or exceed level A1 of the Common European Framework of Reference) unless:

(i) the applicant is aged 65 or over at the time he makes his application;

(ii) the Secretary of State or entry Clearance officer considers that the applicant has a physical or mental condition that would prevent him from meeting the requirement;

(iii) the Secretary of State or Entry Clearance Officer considers there are exceptional compassionate circumstances that would prevent the applicant from meeting the requirement;

(iv) the applicant is a national of one of the following countries: Antigua and Barbuda; Australia; The Bahamas; Barbados; Belize; Canada; Dominica; Grenada; Guyana; Jamaica; New Zealand; St Kitts and Nevis; St Lucia; St Vincent and the Grenadines; Trinidad and Tobago; the USA;

(v) the applicant has obtained an academic qualification (not a professional or vocational qualification), which is deemed by UK NARIC to meet the recognised standard of a Bachelor's or Masters degree or PhD in the UK, from an educational establishment in one of the following countries: Antigua and Barbuda; Australia; The Bahamas; Barbados; Belize; Dominica; Grenada; Guyana; Ireland; Jamaica; New Zealand; St Kitts and Nevis; St Lucia; St Vincent and The Grenadines; Trinidad and Tobago; the UK; the USA; and provides the specified documents; or

(vi) the applicant has obtained an academic qualification (not a professional or vocational qualification) which is deemed by UK NARIC to meet the recognised standard of a Bachelor's or Masters degree or PhD in the UK, and

(1) provides the specified evidence to show he has the qualification, and

(2) UK NARIC has confirmed that the degree was taught or researched in English,

or

(vii) has obtained an academic qualification (not a professional or vocational qualification) which is deemed by UK NARIC to meet the recognised standard of a Bachelor's or Masters degree or PhD in the UK, and provides the specified evidence to show:

(1) he has the qualification, and

(2) that the qualification was taught or researched in English; and

(ii) any previous marriage or civil partnership (or similar relationship) by either partner has permanently broken down; and

(iii) the parties are not involved in a consanguineous relationship with one another; and

(iv) there will be adequate accommodation for the parties and any dependants without recourse to public funds in accommodation which they own or occupy exclusively; and

(v) the parties will be able to maintain themselves and any dependants adequately without recourse to public funds; and

(vi) the parties intend to live together permanently; and

(vii) the applicant holds a valid United Kingdom entry clearance for entry in this capacity.

319P. Leave to enter the United Kingdom as the unmarried or same-sex partner of a refugee or beneficiary of humanitarian protection may be granted for 63 months provided the Immigration Officer is satisfied that each of the requirements of paragraph 319O (i)–(vii) are met.

319Q. Leave to enter the United Kingdom as the unmarried or same-sex partner of a refugee or beneficiary of humanitatrian protection is to be refused if the Immigration Officer is not satisfied that each of the requirements of paragraph 319O (i)–(vii) are met.

Requirements for leave to enter the United Kingdom as the child of a parent or parents given limited leave to enter or remain in the United Kingdom as a refugee or beneficiary of humanitarian protection

319R. The requirements to be met by a person seeking leave to enter the United Kingdom as the child of a parent or parents given limited leave to enter or remain in the United Kingdom as a refugee or beneficiary of humanitarian protection, are that the applicant:

(i) is the child of a parent or parents granted limited leave to enter or remain as a refugee or beneficiary of humanitarian protection granted as such under the immigration rules; and

(ii) is under the age of 18, and

(iii) is not leading an independent life, is unmarried, is not in a civil partnership, and has not formed an independent family unit; and

(iv) was conceived after the person granted asylum or humanitarian protection left the country of his habitual residence in order to seek asylum in the UK; and

(v) can, and will, be accommodated adequately by the parent or parents the child is seeking to join without recourse to public funds in accommodation which the parent or parents the child is seeking to join, own or occupy exclusively; and

(vi) can, and will, be maintained adequately by the parent or parents the child is seeking to join, without recourse to public funds; and

(vii) if seeking leave to enter, holds a valid United Kingdom entry clearance for entry in this capacity.

319S. Limited leave to enter the United Kingdom as the child of a refugee or beneficiary of humanitarian protection may be granted for 63 months provided the Immigration Officer is satisfied that each of the requirements in paragraph 319R(i)–(vii) are met.

319T. Limited leave to enter the United Kingdom as the child of a refugee or beneficiary humanitarian protection is to be refused if the Immigration Officer is not satisfied that each of the requirements in paragraph 319R(i)–(vii) are met.

Requirements for indefinite leave to remain in the United Kingdom as the spouse or civil partner, unmarried or same-sex partner or child of a refugee or beneficiary of humanitatrian protection present and settled in the United Kingdom

319U. To qualify for indefinite leave to remain in the UK, an applicant must meet the requirements set out in paragraph 287 if the applicant is a spouse or civil partner, paragraph 295G if they are an unmarried or same-sex partner, or 298 if the applicant is a child and the sponsor must be present and settled in the United Kingdom at the time the application is made. If an applicant meets the requirements as set out in the relevant paragraphs, indefinite leave to remain will be granted. If the applicant does not meet these requirements, the application will be refused.

Parents, grandparents and other dependent relatives of persons with limited leave to enter or remain in the United Kingdom as a refugee or beneficiary of humanitarian protection

Requirements for leave to enter or remain in the United Kingdom as the parent, grandparent or other dependent relative of a person with limited leave to enter or remain in the United Kingdom as a refugee or beneficiary of humanitarian protection

319V. The requirements to be met by a person seeking leave to enter or remain in the United Kingdom as the parent, grandparent or other dependent relative of a person with limited leave to enter or remain in the United Kingdom as a refugee or beneficiary of humanitarian protection are that the person:

(i) is related to a refugee or beneficiary of humanitarian protection with limited leave to enter or remain in the United Kingdom in one of the following ways:

(a) parent or grandparent who is divorced, widowed, single or separated aged 65 years or over; or

(b) parents or grandparents travelling together of whom at least one is aged 65 or over; or

(c) a parent or grandparent aged 65 or over who has entered into a second relationship of marriage or civil partnership but cannot look to the spouse, civil partner or children of that second relationship for financial support; and where the person with limited leave to enter or remain in the United Kingdom is able and willing to maintain the parent or grandparent and any spouse or civil partner or child of the second relationship who would be admissible as a dependant; or

(d) a parent or grandparent under the age of 65 if living alone outside the United Kingdom in the most exceptional compassionate circumstances; or

(e) parents or grandparents travelling together who are both under the age of 65 if living in the most exceptional compassionate circumstances; or

(f) the son, daughter, sister, brother, uncle or aunt over the age of 18 if living alone outside the United Kingdom in the most exceptional compassionate circumstances; and

(ii) is joining a refugee or beneficiary of humanitarian protection with limited leave to enter or remain in the United Kingdom; and

(iii) is financially wholly or mainly dependent on the relative who has limited leave to enter or remain as a refugee or beneficiary of humanitarian protection in the United Kingdom; and

(iv) can, and will, be accommodated adequately, together with any dependants, without recourse to public funds, in accommodation which the sponsor owns or occupies exclusively; and

(v) can, and will, be maintained adequately, together with any dependants, without recourse to public funds; and

(vi) has no other close relatives in his own country to whom he could turn for financial support; and

(vii) if seeking leave to enter, holds a valid United Kingdom entry clearance for entry in this capacity, or, if seeking leave to remain, holds valid leave to remain in another capacity.

319VA. Limited leave to enter the United Kingdom as the parent, grandparent or other dependent relative of a refugee or beneficiary of humanitarian protection with limited leave to enter or remain in the United Kingdom may be granted for 5 years provided a valid United Kingdom entry clearance for entry in this capacity is produced to the Immigration Officer on arrival. Limited leave to remain in the United Kingdom as the parent, grandparent or other dependent relative of a refugee or beneficiary of humanitarian protection with limited leave to enter or remain in the United Kingdom may be granted provided the Secretary of State is satisfied that each of the requirements of paragraph 319V(i)–(vii) is met.

319VB. Limited leave to enter the United Kingdom as the parent, grandparent or other dependent relative of a refugee or beneficiary of humanitarian protection with limited leave to enter or remain in the United Kingdom is to be refused if a valid United Kingdom entry clearance for entry in this capacity is not produced to the Immigration Officer on arrival. Limited leave to remain in the United Kingdom as the parent, grandparent or other dependent relative of a refugee or beneficiary of humanitarian protection with limited leave to enter or remain in the United Kingdom is to be refused if the Secretary of State is not satisfied that each of the requirements of paragraph 319V(i)–(vii) is met.

Requirements for indefinite leave to remain in the United Kingdom as the parent, grandparent or other dependent relative of a refugee or beneficiary of humanitarian protection who is present and settled in the United Kingdom or of a former refugee or beneficiary humanitarian protection, who is now a British Citizen.

319W. The requirements for indefinite leave to remain in the United Kingdom as the parent, grandparent or other dependent relative of a refugee or beneficiary of humanitarian protection who is now present and settled in the United Kingdom or who is now a British Citizen are that:

(i) the applicant has limited leave to enter or remain in the United Kingdom in accordance with paragraph 319V as a dependent relative of a refugee or beneficiary of humanitarian protection with limited leave to enter or remain in the United Kingdom; and

(ii) the sponsor the applicant was admitted to join is now present and settled in the United Kingdom, or is now a British Citizen; and

(iii) the applicant is financially wholly or mainly dependent on the relative who is present and settled in the United Kingdom; and

(iv) the applicant can, and will, be accommodated adequately, together with any dependants, without recourse to public funds, in accommodation which the sponsor owns or occupies exclusively; and

(v) the applicant can, and will, be maintained adequately, together with any dependants, without recourse to public funds; and

(vi) the applicant has no other close relatives in their country of former habitual residence to whom he could turn for financial support; and

(vii) does not [fall for refusal under the general grounds for refusal].

Note: Words substituted in subparagraph (vii) from 13 December 2012 subject to savings for applications made before that date (HC 760).

319WA. Indefinite leave to remain in the United Kingdom as the parent, grandparent or other dependent relative of a refugee or beneficiary of humanitarian protection who is present and settled in the United Kingdom, or who is now a British Citizen may be granted provided the Secretary of State is satisfied that each of the requirements of paragraph 319W(i)–(vii) is met.

319WB. Indefinite leave to remain in the United Kingdom as the parent, grandparent or other dependent relative of a person present and settled in the United Kingdom is to be refused if the Secretary of State is not satisfied that each of the requirements of paragraph 319W(i)–(vii) is met.

Requirements for leave to enter or remain in the United Kingdom as the child of a relative with limited leave to enter or remain in the United Kingdom as a refugee or beneficiary of humanitarian protection.

319X. The requirements to be met by a person seeking leave to enter or remain in the United Kingdom as the child of a relative with limited leave to remain as a refugee or beneficiary of humanitarian protection in the United Kingdom are that:

(i) the applicant is seeking leave to enter or remain to join a relative with limited leave to enter or remain as a refugee or person with humanitarian protection; and

(ii) the relative has limited leave in the United Kingdom as a refugee or beneficiary of humanitarian protection and there are serious and compelling family or other considerations which make exclusion of the child undesirable and suitable arrangements have been made for the child's care; and

(iii) the relative is not the parent of the child who is seeking leave to enter or remain in the United Kingdom; and

(iv) the applicant is under the age of 18; and

(v) the applicant is not leading an independent life, is unmarried and is not a civil partner, and has not formed an independent family unit; and

(vi) the applicant can, and will, be accommodated adequately by the relative the child is seeking to join without recourse to public funds in accommodation which the relative in the United Kingdom owns or occupies exclusively; and

(vii) the applicant can, and will, be maintained adequately by the relative in the United Kingdom without recourse to public funds; and

(viii) if seeking leave to enter, the applicant holds a valid United Kingdom entry clearance for entry in this capacity or, if seeking leave to remain, holds valid leave to remain in [this or] another capacity.

319XA. Limited leave to enter the United Kingdom as the child of a relative with limited leave to enter or remain as a refugee or beneficiary of humanitarian protection in the United Kingdom may be granted for 5 years provided a valid United Kingdom entry clearance for entry in this capacity is produced to the Immigration Officer on arrival. Limited leave to remain in the United Kingdom as the child of a relative with limited leave to enter or remain as a refugee or beneficiary of humanitarian protection in the United Kingdom may be granted provided the Secretary of State is satisfied that each of the requirements of paragraph 319X(i)–(viii) is met.

Note: Words inserted in subparagraph (viii) from 6 November 2014 (HC 693).

319XB. Limited leave to enter the United Kingdom as the child of a relative with limited leave to enter or remain as a refugee or beneficiary of humanitarian protection in the United Kingdom is to be refused if a valid United Kingdom entry clearance for entry in this capacity is not produced to the Immigration Officer on arrival. Limited leave to remain in the United Kingdom as the child of a relative with limited leave to enter or remain as a refugee or beneficiary of humanitarian protection in the United Kingdom is to be refused if the Secretary of State is not satisfied that each of the requirements of paragraph 319X(i)–(viii) is met.

Requirements for indefinite leave to remain in the United Kingdom as the child of a relative who is present and settled in the United Kingdom or as a former refugee or beneficiary of humanitarian protection who is now a British Citizen

319Y. To qualify for indefinite leave to remain as the child of a relative who is present and settled in the United Kingdom, an applicant must meet the requirements set out in paragraph 298.

PART 9

GENERAL GROUNDS FOR THE REFUSAL OF ENTRY CLEARANCE, LEAVE TO ENTER OR VARIATION OF LEAVE TO ENTER OR REMAIN IN THE UNITED KINGDOM

Refusal of entry clearance or leave to enter the United Kingdom

A320. Paragraphs 320 (except subparagraph (3), (10) and (11)) and 322 do not apply to an application for entry clearance, leave to enter or leave to remain as a Family Member under Appendix FM, and Part 9 (except for paragraph 322(1)) does not apply to an application for leave to remain on the grounds of private life under paragraphs 276ADE-276DH.

B320(1). Subject to sub-paragraph (2), paragraphs 320 (except sub-paragraphs (3), (7B), (10) and (11)) and 322 (except sub-paragraphs (2) and (3)) do not apply to an application for entry clearance, leave to enter or leave to remain under Appendix Armed Forces.

(2) As well as the sub-paragraphs mentioned above, sub-paragraph (13) of paragraph 320 also applies to applications for entry clearance, leave to enter or leave to remain under Part 9 or 10 of Appendix Armed Forces.

Note: Paragraph B320 inserted from 30 December 2013 (HC 887).

320. In addition to the grounds of refusal of entry clearance or leave to enter set out in Parts 2–8 of these Rules, and subject to paragraph 321 below, the following grounds for the refusal of entry clearance or leave to enter apply:

Grounds on which entry clearance or leave to enter the United Kingdom is to be refused

(1) the fact that entry is being sought for a purpose not covered by these Rules;

(2) the fact that the person seeking entry to the United Kingdom:

(a) is currently the subject of a deportation order; or

(b) has been convicted of an offence for which they have been sentenced to a period of imprisonment of at least 4 years; or

(c) has been convicted of an offence for which they have been sentenced to a period of imprisonment of at least 12 months but less than 4 years, unless a period of 10 years has passed since the end of the sentence; or

(d) has been convicted of an offence for which they have been sentenced to a period of imprisonment of less than 12 months, unless a period of 5 years has passed since the end of the sentence.

Where this paragraph applies, unless refusal would be contrary to the Human Rights Convention or the Convention and Protocol Relating to the Status of Refugees, it will only be in exceptional circumstances that the public interest in maintaining refusal will be outweighed by compelling factors.

(3) failure by the person seeking entry to the United Kingdom to produce to the Immigration Officer a valid national passport or other document satisfactorily establishing his identity and nationality;

(4) failure to satisfy the Immigration Officer, in the case of a person arriving in the United Kingdom or seeking entry through the Channel Tunnel with the intention of entering any other part of the common travel area, that he is acceptable to the immigration authorities there;

(5) failure, in the case of a visa national, to produce to the Immigration Officer a passport or other identity document endorsed with a valid and current United Kingdom entry clearance issued for the purpose for which entry is sought;

(6) where the Secretary of State has personally directed that the exclusion of a person from the United Kingdom is conducive to the public good;

(7) save in relation to a person settled in the United Kingdom or where the Immigration Officer is satisfied that there are strong compassionate reasons justifying admission, confirmation from the Medical Inspector that, for medical reasons, it is undesirable to admit a person seeking leave to enter the United Kingdom.

(7A) where false representations have been made or false documents or information have been submitted (whether or not material to the application, and whether or not to the applicant's knowledge), or material facts have not been disclosed, in relation to the application or in order to obtain documents from the Secretary of State or a third party required in support of the application.

(7B) where the applicant has previously breached the UK's immigration laws (and was [18 or over] at the time of his most recent breach) by:

(a) overstaying;

(b) breaching a condition attached to his leave;

(c) being an illegal entrant;

(d) using deception in an application for entry clearance, leave to enter or remain, or in order to obtain documents from the Secretary of State or a third party required in support of the application (whether successful or not);

unless the applicant:

(i) overstayed for 90 days or less and left the UK voluntarily, not at the expense (directly or indirectly) of the Secretary of State;

(ii) used deception in an application for entry clearance more than 10 years ago;

(iii) left the UK voluntarily, not at the expense (directly or indirectly) of the Secretary of State, more than 12 months ago;

(iv) left the UK voluntarily, at the expense (directly or indirectly) of the Secretary of State, more than 2 years ago; and the date the person left the UK was no more than 6 months after the date on which the person was given notice of the removal decision, or no more than 6 months after the date on which the person no longer had a pending appeal [or administrative review]; whichever is the later;

(v) left the UK voluntarily, at the expense (directly or indirectly) of the Secretary of State, more than 5 years ago;

(vi) was removed or deported from the UK more than 10 years ago or;

(vii) left or was removed from the UK as a condition of a caution issued in accordance with [section 22 of the Criminal Justice Act 2003] more than 5 years ago.

Where more than one breach of the UK's immigration laws has occurred, only the breach which leads to the longest period of absence from the UK will be relevant under this paragraph.

(7C) DELETED

(7D) failure, without providing a reasonable explanation, to comply with a request made on behalf of the Entry Clearance Officer to attend for interview.

Grounds on which entry clearance or leave to enter the United Kingdom should normally be refused

(8) failure by a person arriving in the United Kingdom to furnish the Immigration Officer with such information as may be required for the purpose of deciding whether he requires leave to enter and, if so, whether and on what terms leave should be given;

(8A) where the person seeking leave is outside the United Kingdom, failure by him to supply any information, documents, copy documents or medical report requested by an Immigration Officer;

(9) failure by a person seeking leave to enter as a returning resident to satisfy the Immigration Officer that he meets the requirements of paragraph 18 of these Rules, or that he seeks leave to enter for the same purpose as that for which his earlier leave was granted;

(10) production by the person seeking leave to enter the United Kingdom of a national passport or travel document issued by a territorial entity or authority which is not recognised by Her Majesty's Government as a state or is not dealt with as a government by them, or which does not accept valid United Kingdom passports for the purpose of its own immigration control; or a passport or travel document which does not comply with international passport practice;

(11) where the applicant has previously contrived in a significant way to frustrate the intentions of the Rules by:

(i) overstaying; or

(ii) breaching a condition attached to his leave; or

(iii) being an illegal entrant; or

(iv) using deception in an application for entry clearance, leave to enter or remain or in order to obtain documents from the Secretary of State or a third party required in support of the application (whether successful or not); and

there are other aggravating circumstances, such as absconding, not meeting temporary admission/reporting restrictions or bail conditions, using an assumed identity or multiple identities, switching nationality, making frivolous applications or not complying with the re-documentation process.

(12) DELETED

(13) failure, except by a person eligible for admission to the United Kingdom for settlement, to satisfy the Immigration Officer that he will be admitted to another country after a stay in the United Kingdom;

(14) refusal by a sponsor of a person seeking leave to enter the United Kingdom to give, if requested to do so, an undertaking in writing to be responsible for that person's maintenance and accommodation for the period of any leave granted;

(16) failure, in the case of a child under the age of 18 years seeking leave to enter the United Kingdom otherwise than in conjunction with an application made by his parent(s) or legal guardian to provide the Immigration Officer, if required to do so, with written consent to the application from his parent(s) or legal guardian; save that the requirement as to written consent does not apply in the case of a child seeking admission to the United Kingdom as an asylum seeker;

(17) save in relation to a person settled in the United Kingdom, refusal to undergo a medical examination when required to do so by the Immigration Officer;

(18) DELETED

(18A) [within the 12 months prior to the date on which the application is decided,] the person has been convicted of or admitted an offence for which they received a non-custodial sentence or other out of court disposal that is recorded on their criminal record;

(18B) in the view of the Secretary of State:

(a) the person's offending has caused serious harm; or

(b) the person is a persistent offender who shows a particular disregard for the law.

(19) The immigration officer deems the exclusion of the person from the United Kingdom to be conducive to the public good. For example, because the person's conduct (including convictions which do not fall within paragraph 320(2)), character, associations, or other reasons, make it undesirable to grant them leave to enter.

(20) failure by a person seeking entry into the United Kingdom to comply with a requirement relating to the provision of physical data to which he is subject by regulations made under section 126 of the Nationality, Immigration and Asylum Act 2002.

(21) DELETED

(22) where one or more relevant NHS body has notified the Secretary of State that the person seeking entry or leave to enter has failed to pay a charge or charges with a total value of at least £1000 in accordance with the relevant NHS regulations on charges to overseas visitors.

Note: Subparagraph 320(2) substituted, subparagraph (7B)(vii) inserted, subparagraph (18) deleted, subparagraphs (18A) and (18B) inserted and subparagraph (19) substituted from 13 December 2012 subject to savings for applications made before that date (HC 760). Words substituted in opening sentence of subparagraph (7B) from 6 April 2013 subject to savings for applications made before that date (HC 1039). Words substituted in subparagraphs (7B)(vii) and (18A) from 1 December 2013 (HC 803; amendment of subparagraph (7B)(vii) subject to savings for applications made before 1 December 2013). Words inserted in subparagraph (7B)(iv) from 20 October 2014 (HC 693).

Refusal of leave to enter in relation to a person in possession of an entry clearance

321. A person seeking leave to enter the United Kingdom who holds an entry clearance which was duly issued to him and is still current may be refused leave to enter only where the Immigration Officer is satisfied that:

(i) False representations were made or false documents or information were submitted (whether or not material to the application, and whether or not to the holder's knowledge), or material facts were not disclosed, in relation to the application for entry clearance; or in order to obtain documents from the Secretary of State or a third party required in support of the application.

(ii) a change of circumstances since it was issued has removed the basis of the holder's claim to admission, except where the change of circumstances amounts solely to the person becoming over age for entry in one of the categories contained in paragraphs 296–316 of these Rules since the issue of the entry clearance; or

(iii) {on grounds which would have led to a refusal under paragraphs 320(2), 320(6), 320(18A), 320(18B) or 320(19)} [(except where this sub-paragraph applies in respect of an entry clearance issued under Appendix Armed Forces it is to be read as if for "paragraphs 320(2), 320(6), 320(18A), 320(18B) or 320(19)" it said "paragraph 8(a), (b), (c) or (g) and paragraph 9(d)")]

Note: Words in curly brackets inserted in subparagraph (iii) from 13 December 2012 subject to savings for applications made before that date (HC 760). Words in square brackets inserted at the end of subparagraph (iii) from 30 December 2013 (HC 887).

Grounds on which leave to enter or remain which is in force is to be cancelled at port or while the holder is outside the United Kingdom

321A. The following grounds for the cancellation of a person's leave to enter or remain which is in force on his arrival in, or whilst he is outside, the United Kingdom apply;

(1) there has been such a change in the circumstances of that person's case since the leave was given, that it should be cancelled; or

(2) false representations were made or false documents were submitted (whether or not material to the application, and whether or not to the holder's knowledge), or material facts were not disclosed, in relation to the application for leave; or in order to obtain documents from the Secretary of State or a third party required in support of the application or,

(3) save in relation to a person settled in the United Kingdom or where the Immigration Officer or the Secretary of State is satisfied that there are strong compassionate reasons justifying admission, where it is apparent that, for medical reasons, it is undesirable to admit that person to the United Kingdom; or

(4) where the Secretary of State has personally directed that the exclusion of that person from the United Kingdom is conducive to the public good; or

(4A) Grounds which would have led to a refusal under paragraphs 320(2), 320(6), 320(18A), 320(18B) or 320(19) if the person concerned were making a new application for leave to enter or remain [(except where this sub-paragraph applies in respect of leave to enter or remain granted under Appendix Armed Forces it is to be read as if for "paragraphs 320(2), 320(6), 320(18A), 320(18B) or 320(19)" it said "paragraph 8(a), (b), (c) or (g) and paragraph 9(d)")]; or

(5) The Immigration Officer or the Secretary of State deems the exclusion of the person from the United Kingdom to be conducive to the public good. For example, because the person's conduct (including convictions which do not fall within paragraph 320(2)), character, associations, or other reasons, make it undesirable to grant them leave to enter the United Kingdom; or

(6) where that person is outside the United Kingdom, failure by that person to supply any information, documents, copy documents or medical report requested by an Immigration Officer or the Secretary of State.

Note: Subparagraph (4A) inserted and subparagraph (5) substituted from 13 December 2012 subject to savings for applications made before that date (HC 760). Words in square brackets inserted at the end of subparagraph (4A) from 30 December 2013 (HC 887).

Refusal of leave to remain, variation of leave to enter or remain or curtailment of leave

322. In addition to the grounds for refusal of extension of stay set out in Parts 2–8 of these Rules, the following provisions apply in relation to the refusal of an application for leave to remain, variation of leave to enter or remain or, where appropriate, the curtailment of leave: Grounds on which leave to remain and variation of leave to enter or remain in the United Kingdom are to be refused;

(1) the fact that variation of leave to enter or remain is being sought for a purpose not covered by these Rules;

(1A) where false representations have been made or false documents or information have been submitted (whether or not material to the application, and whether or not to the applicant's knowledge), or material facts have not been disclosed, in relation to the application or in order to obtain documents from the Secretary of State or a third party required in support of the application;

(1B) the applicant is, at the date of application, the subject of a deportation order or a decision to make a deportation order;

(1C) where the person is seeking indefinite leave to enter or remain:

(i) they have been convicted of an offence for which they have been sentenced to imprisonment for at least 4 years; or

(ii) they have been convicted of an offence for which they have been sentenced to imprisonment for at least 12 months but less than 4 years, unless a period of 15 years has passed since the end of the sentence; or

(iii) they have been convicted of an offence for which they have been sentenced to imprisonment for less than 12 months, unless a period of 7 years has passed since the end of the sentence; or

(iv) they have, within the 24 months [prior to the date on which the application is decided], been convicted of or admitted an offence for which they have received a non-custodial sentence or other out of court disposal that is recorded on their criminal record.

(1D) DELETED

Grounds on which leave to remain and variation of leave to enter or remain in the United Kingdom should normally be refused

(2) the making of false representations or the failure to disclose any material fact for the purpose of obtaining leave to enter or a previous variation of leave or in order to obtain documents from the Secretary of State or a third party required in support of the application for leave to enter or a previous variation of leave;

(2A) the making of false representations or the failure to disclose any material fact for the purpose of obtaining a document from the Secretary of State that indicates the person has a right to reside in the United Kingdom;

(3) failure to comply with any conditions attached to the grant of leave to enter or remain;

(4) failure by the person concerned to maintain or accommodate himself and any dependants without recourse to public funds;

(5) the undesirability of permitting the person concerned to remain in the United Kingdom in the light of his conduct (including convictions which do not fall within paragraph 322(1C), character or associations or the fact that he represents a threat to national security;

(5A) it is undesirable to permit the person concerned to enter or remain in the United Kingdom because, in the view of the Secretary of State:

(a) their offending has caused serious harm; or

(b) they are a persistent offender who shows a particular disregard for the law;

(6) refusal by a sponsor of the person concerned to give, if requested to do so, an undertaking in writing to be responsible for his maintenance and accommodation in the United Kingdom or failure to honour such an undertaking once given;

(7) failure by the person concerned to honour any declaration or undertaking given orally or in writing as to the intended duration and/or purpose of his stay;

(8) failure, except by a person who qualifies for settlement in the United Kingdom or by the spouse or civil partner of a person settled in the United Kingdom, to satisfy the Secretary of State that he will be returnable to another country if allowed to remain in the United Kingdom for a further period;

(9) failure by an applicant to produce within a reasonable time information, documents or other evidence required by the Secretary of State to establish his claim to remain under these Rules;

(10) failure, without providing a reasonable explanation, to comply with a request made on behalf of the Secretary of State to attend for interview;

(11) failure, in the case of a child under the age of 18 years seeking a variation of his leave to enter or remain in the United Kingdom otherwise than in conjunction with an application by his parent(s) or legal guardian, to provide the Secretary of State, if required to do so, with written consent to the application from his parent(s) or legal guardian; save that the requirement as to written consent does not apply in the case of a child who has been admitted to the United Kingdom as an asylum seeker;

(12) where one or more relevant NHS body has notified the Secretary of State that the person seeking leave to remain or a variation of leave to enter or remain has failed to pay a charge or charges with a total value of at least £1000 in accordance with the relevant NHS regulations on charges to overseas visitors.

Note: Subparagraphs (1B), (1C) and (5A) inserted and words substituted in subparagraph (5) from 13 December 2012 subject to savings for applications made before that date (HC 760). Subparagraph (1D) inserted from 31 January 2013 (HC 943). Words substituted in subparagraph (1C)(iv) from 1 December 2013 HC 803. Subparagraph (2A) inserted from 6 April 2014 subject to savings for applications made before that date (HC 1138 as amended by HC 1201).

Grounds on which leave to enter or remain may be curtailed

323. A person's leave to enter or remain may be curtailed:

(i) on any of the grounds set out in paragraph 322(2)–[(5A)] above [(except where this paragraph applies in respect of a person granted leave under Appendix Armed Forces "paragraph 322(2)–(5A) above" is to read as if it said "paragraph 322(2) and (3) above and paragraph 8(e) and (g) of Appendix Armed Forces")]; or

(ii) if he ceases to meet the requirements of the Rules under which his leave to enter or remain was granted; or

(iii) if he is the dependant, or is seeking leave to remain as the dependant, of an asylum applicant whose claim has been refused and whose leave has been curtailed under section 7 of the1993 Act, and he does not qualify for leave to remain in his own right, or

(iv) on any of the grounds set out in paragraph 339A (i)–(vi) and paragraph 339G (i)–(vi),

or

(v) where a person has, within the first 6 months of being granted leave to enter, committed an offence for which they are subsequently sentenced to a period of imprisonment, or

(vi) if he was granted his current period of leave as the dependent of a person ("P") and P's leave to enter or remain is being, or has been, curtailed.

Note: Subparagraph (v) inserted from 13 December 2012 subject to savings for applications made before that date (HC 760). '(5A)' substituted in subparagraph (i) from 1 October 2013 subject to savings for applications made before that date (HC 628). Words inserted at the end of subparagraph (i) from 30 December 2013 (HC 887). Subparagraph (ia) inserted from 6 April 2014 subject to savings for applications made before that date and subparagraph (vi) inserted from the date on which s 1 of the Immigration Act 2014 comes into force (HC 1138 as amended by HC 1201).

Curtailment of leave . . . in relation to a Tier 2 Migrant, a Tier 5 Migrant or a Tier 4 Migrant

323A. In addition to the grounds specified in paragraph 323, the leave to enter or remain of a Tier 2 Migrant, a Tier 4 Migrant or a Tier 5 Migrant:

(a) is to be curtailed . . . if:

(i) in the case of a Tier 2 Migrant or a Tier 5 Migrant:

(1) the migrant fails to commence, or

(2) the migrant ceases, or will cease, before the end date recorded on the Certificate of Sponsorship Checking Service,

the employment, volunteering, training or job shadowing (as the case may be) that the migrant has been sponsored to do.

(ii) in the case of a Tier 4 Migrant:

(1) the migrant fails to commence studying with the Sponsor, or

(2) the Sponsor has excluded or withdrawn the migrant, or the migrant has withdrawn, from the course of studies, or

(2A) the migrant's course of study has ceased, or will cease, before the end date recorded on the Certificate of Sponsorship Checking Service, or

(3) the Sponsor withdraws their sponsorship of a migrant on the doctorate extension scheme, or

(4) the Sponsor withdraws their sponsorship of a migrant who, having completed a pre-sessional course as provided in paragraph 120(b)(i) of Appendix A, does not have a knowledge of English equivalent to level B2 of the Council of Europe's Common European Framework for Language Learning in all four components (reading, writing, speaking and listening) or above.

(b) may be curtailed . . . if:

(i) the migrant's Sponsor ceases to have a sponsor licence (for whatever reason); or

(ii) the migrant's Sponsor transfers the business for which the migrant works, or at which the migrant is studying, to another person; and

(1) that person does not have a sponsor licence; and

(2) fails to apply for a sponsor licence within 28 days of the date of the transfer of the business; or

(3) applies for a sponsor licence but is refused; or

(4) makes a successful application for a sponsor licence, but the Sponsor licence granted is not in a category that would allow the Sponsor to issue a Certificate of Sponsorship [or Confirmation of Acceptance for Studies] to the migrant;

(iii) in the case of a Tier 2 Migrant or a Tier 5 Migrant, if the employment that the Certificate of Sponsorship Checking Service records that the migrant is being sponsored to do undergoes a prohibited change as specified in paragraph 323AA;

(iv) paragraph (a) above applies but:

(1) the migrant is under the age of 18;

(2) the migrant has a dependant child under the age of 18;

(3) leave is to be varied such that when the variation takes effect the migrant will have leave to enter or remain and the migrant has less than 60 days extant leave remaining;

(4) the migrant has been granted leave to enter or remain with another Sponsor or under another immigration category; or

(5) the migrant has a pending application for leave to remain, or variation of leave, with the UK Border Agency, or has a pending appeal under Section 82 of

the Nationality, Immigration and Asylum Act 2002 [, or has a pending administrative review].

Note: Subparagraph (a)(ii)(3) inserted from 6 April 2013 subject to savings for applications made before that date (HC 1039). Subparagraph (a)(ii)(4) inserted from 1 October 2013 (HC 628). Words in heading and in subparagraphs (a) and (b) deleted, subparagraphs (a)(i)(1), (a)(i)(2) and (a)(ii)(2) substituted, subparagraph (a)(ii)(2A) inserted and words inserted in subparagraph (b)(ii)(4) from 6 April 2014 subject to savings for applications made before that date (HC 1138 as amended by HC 1201). Words inserted in subparagraph (b)(iv)(5) from 20 October 2014 (HC 693).

323AA Prohibited changes to employment for Tier 2 Migrants and Tier 5 Migrants

The following are prohibited changes, unless a further application for leave to remain is granted which expressly permits the changes:

(a) The migrant is absent from work without pay for one calendar month or more in total (whether over a single period or more than one period), during any calendar year (1 January to 31 December), unless the absence from work is due solely to:

(i) maternity leave,

(ii) paternity leave,

(iii) adoption leave, or

(iv) long term sick leave of one calendar month or more during any one period.

(b) The employment changes such that the migrant is working for a different employer or Sponsor, unless:

(i) the migrant is a Tier 5 (Temporary Worker) Migrant in the Government Authorised Exchange sub-category and the change of employer is authorised by the Sponsor and under the terms of the work, volunteering or job shadowing that the Certificate of Sponsorship Checking Service records that the migrant is being sponsored to do,

(ii) the migrant is working for a different Sponsor under arrangements covered by the Transfer of Undertakings (Protection of Employment) Regulations 2006 or similar protection to continue in the same job, or

(iii) the migrant is a Tier 2 (Sportsperson) Migrant or a Tier 5 (Temporary Worker) Migrant in the creative and sporting sub-category and the following conditions are met:

(1) The migrant's sponsor is a sports club;

(2) The migrant is sponsored as a player only and is being temporarily loaned as a player to another sports club;

(3) Player loans are specifically permitted in rules set down by the relevant sports governing body listed in Appendix M;

(4) The migrant's sponsor has made arrangements with the loan club to enable the sponsor to continue to meet its sponsor duties; and

(5) The migrant will return to working for the sponsor at the end of the loan.

(c) The employment changes to a job in a different Standard Occupational Classification (SOC) code to that recorded by the Certificate of Sponsorship Checking Service.

(d) If the migrant is a Tier 2 (Intra-Company Transfer) Migrant or a Tier 2 (General) Migrant, the employment changes to a different job in the same Standard Occupational Classification code to that recorded by the Certificate of Sponsorship Checking Service, and the gross annual salary (including such allowances as are specified as acceptable for this purpose in Appendix A) is below the appropriate salary rate for that new job as specified in the Codes of Practice in Appendix J.

(e) If the migrant was required to be Sponsored for a job at a minimum National Qualification Framework level in the application which led to his last grant of entry clearance or leave to remain, the employment changes to a job which the Codes of Practice in Appendix J record as being at a lower level.

(f) If the migrant is a Tier 2 (General) Migrant and scored points from the shortage occupation provisions of Appendix A, the employment changes to a job which does not appear in the Shortage Occupation List in Appendix K.

(g) Except where (h) applies, the gross annual salary (including such allowances as are specified as acceptable for this purpose in Appendix A) reduces below:

(i) any minimum salary threshold specified in Appendix A of these Rules, where the applicant was subject to or relied on that threshold in the application which led to his current grant of entry clearance or leave to remain, or

(ii) the appropriate salary rate for the job as specified in the Codes of Practice in Appendix J, or

(iii) in cases where there is no applicable threshold in Appendix A and no applicable salary rate in Appendix J, the salary recorded by the Certificate of Sponsorship Checking Service.

(h) Other reductions in salary are permitted if the reduction coincides with a period of:

(i) maternity leave,

(ii) paternity leave,

(iii) adoption leave,

(iv) long term sick leave of one calendar month or more,

(v) working for the sponsor's organisation while the migrant is not physically present,

(vi) undertaking professional examinations before commencing work for the sponsor, where such examinations are a regulatory requirement of the job the migrant is being sponsored to do, and providing the migrant continues to be sponsored during that period.

Note: Paragraph 323AA substituted from 6 April 2013 subject to savings for applications made before that date (HC 1039). Subparagraphs (b)(iii) and (h)(v) inserted and subparagraph (vi) renumbered from 6 April 2014 subject to savings for applications made before that date (HC 1138 as amended by HC 1201). Subparagraph (h)(vi) substituted from 6 November 2014 subject to savings for applications made before that date (HC 693).

Curtailment of leave in relation to a Tier 1 (Exceptional Talent) Migrant

323B. In addition to the grounds specified in paragraph 323, the leave to enter or remain of a Tier 1 (Exceptional Talent) Migrant may be curtailed if the Designated Competent Body that endorsed the application which led to the migrant's current grant of leave withdraws its endorsement of the migrant.

Curtailment of leave in relation to a Tier 1 (Graduate Entrepreneur) Migrant

323C. In addition to the grounds specified in paragraph 323, the leave to enter or remain of a Tier 1 (Graduate Entrepreneur) Migrant may be curtailed if the [endorsing body] that endorsed the application which led to the migrant's current grant of leave:

(a) loses its status as an endorsing institution for Tier 1 (Graduate Entrepreneur) Migrants,

(b) loses its status as a Highly Trusted Sponsor under Tier 4 of the Points-Based System (for whatever reason),

(c) ceases to be an A-rated Sponsor under Tier 2 or Tier 5 of the Points-Based System because its Tier 2 or Tier 5 Sponsor licence is downgraded or revoked by the UK Border Agency, or

(d) withdraws its endorsement of the migrant.

Note: Words substituted from 6 April 2013 subject to savings for applications made before that date (HC 1039).

Crew members

324. A person who has been given leave to enter to join a ship, aircraft, hovercraft, hydrofoil or international train service as a member of its crew, or a crew member who has been given leave to enter for hospital treatment, repatriation or transfer to another ship, aircraft, hovercraft, hydrofoil or international train service in the United Kingdom, is to be refused leave to remain unless an extension of stay is necessary to fulfil the purpose for which he was given leave to enter or unless he meets the requirements for an extension of stay as a spouse or civil partner in paragraph 284.

Part 10

Registration with the police

325. For the purposes of paragraph 326, a "relevant foreign national" is a person aged 16 or over who is:

(i) a national or citizen of a country or territory listed in Appendix 2 to these Rules;

(ii) a stateless person; or

(iii) a person holding a non-national travel document.

326. (1) Subject to sub-paragraph (2) below, a condition requiring registration with the police should normally be imposed on any relevant foreign national who is:

(i) given limited leave to enter the United Kingdom for longer than six months; or

(ii) given limited leave to remain which has the effect of allowing him to remain in the United Kingdom for longer than six months, reckoned from the date of his arrival (whether or not such a condition was imposed when he arrived).

(2) Such a condition should not normally be imposed where the leave is given:

(i) as a seasonal agricultural worker;

(ii) as a Tier 5 (Temporary Worker) Migrant, provided the Certificate of Sponsorship Checking System reference for which points were awarded records that the applicant is being sponsored as an overseas goverment employee or a private servant is a diplomatic household;

(iii) as a Tier 2 (Minister of Religion) Migrant;

(iv) on the basis of marriage to or civil partnership with a person settled in the United Kingdom or as the unmarried or same-sex partner of a person settled in the United Kingdom;

(v) as a person exercising access rights to a child resident in the United Kingdom;

(vi) as the parent of a child at school; or

(vii) following the grant of asylum.

(3) Such a condition should also be imposed on any foreign national given limited leave to enter the United Kingdom where, exceptionally, the Immigration Officer considers it necessary to ensure that he complies with the terms of the leave.

Part 11
Asylum

Procedure

326A. The procedures set out in these Rules shall apply to the consideration of asylum and humanitarian protection.

326B. Where the Secretary of State is considering a claim for asylum or humanitarian protection under this Part, she will consider any Article 8 elements of that claim in line with the provisions of Appendix FM (family life) [which are relevant to those elements and in line with] paragraphs 276ADE to 276DH (private life) of these Rules {unless the person is someone to whom Part 13 of these Rules applies}].

Note: Words substituted from 13 December 2012 subject to savings for applications made before that date (HC 760). Words in curly brackets inserted from 28 July 2014; this change applies to all ECHR article 8 claims from foreign criminals that are decided on or after that date (HC 532).

Definition of asylum applicant

327. Under the Rules an asylum applicant is a person who either;

(a) makes a request to be recognised as a refugee under the Geneva Convention on the basis that it would be contrary to the United Kingdom's obligations under the Geneva Convention for him to be removed from or required to leave the United Kingdom, or

(b) otherwise makes a request for international protection. "Application for asylum" shall be construed accordingly.

327A. Every person has the right to make an application for asylum on his own behalf.

Applications for asylum

328. All asylum applications will be determined by the Secretary of State in accordance with the Geneva Convention. Every asylum application made by a person at a port or airport in the United Kingdom will be referred by the Immigration Officer for determination by the Secretary of State in accordance with these Rules.

328A. The Secretary of State shall ensure that authorities which are likely to be addressed by someone who wishes to make an application for asylum are able to advise that person how and where such an application may be made.

329. Until an asylum application has been determined by the Secretary of State or the Secretary of State has issued a certificate under Part 2, 3, 4 or 5 of Schedule 3 to the Asylum and Immigration (Treatment of Claimants, etc.) Act 2004 no action will be taken to require the departure of the asylum applicant or his dependants from the United Kingdom.

330. If the Secretary of State decides to grant asylum and the person has not yet been given leave to enter, the Immigration Officer will grant limited leave to enter.

331. If a person seeking leave to enter is refused asylum or their application for asylum is withdrawn or treated as withdrawn under paragraph 333C of these Rules, the Immigration Officer will consider whether or not he is in a position to decide to give or refuse leave to enter without interviewing the person further. If the Immigration Officer decides that a further interview is not required he may serve the notice giving or refusing leave to enter by post. If the Immigration Officer decides that a further interview is required, he will then resume his examination to determine whether or not to grant the person leave to enter under any other provision of these Rules. If the person fails at any time to comply with a requirement to report to an Immigration Officer for examination, the Immigration Officer may direct that the person's examination shall be treated as concluded at that time. The Immigration Officer will then consider any outstanding applications for entry on the basis of any evidence before him.

332. If a person who has been refused leave to enter applies for asylum and that application is refused or withdrawn or treated as withdrawn under paragraph 333C of these Rules, leave to enter will again be refused unless the applicant qualifies for admission under any other provision of these Rules.

333. Written notice of decisions on applications for asylum shall be given in reasonable time. Where the applicant is legally represented, notice may instead be given to the representative. Where the applicant has no legal representative and free legal assistance is not available, he shall be informed of the decision on the application for asylum and, if the application is rejected, how to challenge the decision, in a language that he may reasonably be supposed to understand.

333A. The Secretary of State shall ensure that a decision is taken by him on each application for asylum as soon as possible, without prejudice to an adequate and complete examination.

Where a decision on an application for asylum cannot be taken within six months of the date it was recorded, the Secretary of State shall either:

(a) inform the applicant of the delay; or

(b) if the applicant has made a specific written request for it, provide information on the timeframe within which the decision on his application is to be expected. The provision of such information shall not oblige the Secretary of State to take a decision within the stipulated time-frame.

333B. Applicants for asylum shall be allowed an effective opportunity to consult, at their own expense or at public expense in accordance with provision made for this by the Legal Services Commission or otherwise, a person who is authorised under Part V of the Immigration and Asylum Act 1999 to give immigration advice. This paragraph shall also apply where the Secretary of State is considering revoking a person's refugee status in accordance with these Rules.

Withdrawal of applications

333C. If an application for asylum is withdrawn either explicitly or implicitly, consideration of it may be discontinued. An application will be treated as explicitly withdrawn if the applicant signs the relevant form provided by the Secretary of State. An application may be treated as impliedly withdrawn if an applicant fails to attend the personal interview as provided in paragraph 339NA of these Rules unless the applicant demonstrates within a reasonable time that that failure was due to circumstances beyond his or her control. The Secretary of State will indicate on the applicant's asylum file that the application for asylum has been withdrawn and consideration of it has been discontinued.

Grant of asylum

334. An asylum applicant will be granted asylum in the United Kingdom if the Secretary of State is satisfied that:

(i) he is in the United Kingdom or has arrived at a port of entry in the United Kingdom;

(ii) he is a refugee, as defined in regulation 2 of The Refugee or Person in Need of International Protection (Qualification) Regulations 2006;

(iii) there are no reasonable grounds for regarding him as a danger to the security of the United Kingdom;

(iv) he does not, having been convicted by a final judgment of a particularly serious crime, constitute danger to the community of the United Kingdom; and

(v) refusing his application would result in him being required to go (whether immediately or after the time limited by any existing leave to enter or remain) in breach of the Geneva Convention, to a country in which his life or freedom would threatened on account of his race, religion, nationality, political opinion or membership of a particular social group.

335. If the Secretary of State decides to grant asylum to a person who has been given leave to enter (whether or not the leave has expired) or to a person who has entered without leave, the Secretary of State will vary the existing leave or grant limited leave to remain.

Refusal of asylum

336. An application which does not meet the criteria set out in paragraph 334 will be refused. Where an application for asylum is refused, the reasons in fact and law shall be stated in the decision and information provided in writing on how to challenge the decision.

337. DELETED

338. When a person in the United Kingdom is notified that asylum has been refused he may, if he is liable to removal as an illegal entrant, removal under section 10 of the Immigration and Asylum Act 1999 or to deportation, at the same time be notified of removal directions, served with a notice of intention to make a deportation order, or served with a deportation order, as appropriate.

339. DELETED

Revocation or refusal to renew a grant of asylum

339A. A person's grant of asylum under paragraph 334 will be revoked or not renewed if the Secretary of State is satisfied that:

(i) he has voluntarily re-availed himself of the protection of the country of nationality;

(ii) having lost his nationality, he has voluntarily re-acquired it; or

(iii) he has acquired a new nationality, and enjoys the protection of the country of his new nationality;

(iv) he has voluntarily re-established himself in the country which he left or outside which he remained owing to a fear of persecution;

(v) he can no longer, because the circumstances in connection with which he has been recognised as a refugee have ceased to exist, continue to refuse to avail himself of the protection of the country of nationality;

(vi) being a stateless person with no nationality, he is able, because the circumstances in connection with which he has been recognised a refugee have ceased to exist, to return to the country of former habitual residence;

(vii) he should have been or is excluded from being a refugee in accordance with regulation 7 of The Refugee or Person in Need of International Protection (Qualification) Regulations 2006;

(viii) his misrepresentation or omission or facts, including the use of false documents, were decisive for the grant of asylum;

(ix) there are reasonable grounds for regarding him as a danger to the security of the United Kingdom; or

(x) having been convicted by a final judgment of a particularly serious crime he constitutes danger to the community of the United Kingdom.

In considering (v) and (vi), the Secretary of State shall have regard to whether the change of circumstances is of such a significant and non-temporary nature that the refugee's fear of persecution can no longer be regarded as well-founded.

Where an application for asylum was made on or after the 21st October 2004, the Secretary of State will revoke or refuse to renew a person's grant of asylum where he is satisfied that at least one of the provisions in sub-paragraph (i)–(vi) apply.

339B. When a person's grant of asylum is revoked or not renewed any limited leave which they have may be curtailed.

339BA. Where the Secretary of State is considering revoking refugee status in accordance with these Rules, the person concerned shall be informed in writing that the Secretary of State is reconsidering his qualification for refugee status and the reasons for the reconsideration. That person shall be given the opportunity to submit, in a personal interview or in a written statement, reasons as to why his refugee status should not be revoked. If there is a personal interview, it shall be subject to the safeguards set out in these Rules. However, where a person acquires British citizenship status, his refugee status is automatically revoked in accordance with paragraph 339A(iii) upon acquisition of that status without the need to follow the procedure set out above.

Grant of humanitarian protection

339C. A person will be granted humanitarian protection in the United Kingdom if the Secretary of State is satisfied that:

(i) he is in the United Kingdom or has arrived at a port of entry in the United Kingdom;

(ii) he does not qualify as a refugee as defined in regulation 2 of The Refugee or Person in Need of International Protection (Qualification) Regulations 2006;

(iii) substantial grounds have been shown for believing that the person concerned, if he returned to the country of return, would face a real risk of suffering serious harm and is unable, or, owing to such risk, unwilling to avail himself of the protection of that country; and

(iv) he is not excluded from a grant of humanitarian protection.

Serious harm consists of:

(i) the death penalty or execution;

(ii) unlawful killing;

(iii) torture or inhuman or degrading treatment or punishment of a person in the country of return; or

(iv) serious and individual threat to a civilian's life or person by reason of indiscriminate violence in situations of international or internal armed conflict.

Exclusion from humanitarian protection

339D. A person is excluded from a grant of humanitarian protection under paragraph 339C (iv) where the Secretary of State is satisfied that:

(i) there are serious reasons for considering that he has committed a crime against peace, a war crime, a crime against humanity, or any other serious crime or instigated or otherwise participated in such crimes;

(ii) there are serious reasons for considering that he is guilty of acts contrary to the purposes and principles of the United Nations or has committed, prepared or instigated such acts or encouraged or induced others to commit, prepare or instigate instigated such acts;

(iii) there are serious reasons for considering that he constitutes a danger to the community or to the security of the United Kingdom; or

(iv) prior to his admission to the United Kingdom the person committed a crime outside the scope of (i) and (ii) that would be punishable by imprisonment were it committed in the United Kingdom and the person left his country of origin solely in order to avoid sanctions resulting from the crime.

339E. If the Secretary of State decides to grant humanitarian protection and the person has not yet been given leave to enter, the Secretary of State or an Immigration Officer will grant limited leave to enter. If the Secretary of State decides to grant humanitarian protection to a person who has been given limited leave to enter (whether or not that leave has expired) or a person who has entered without leave, the Secretary of State will vary the existing leave or grant limited leave to remain.

Refusal of humanitarian protection

339F. Where the criteria set out in paragraph 339C is not met humanitarian protection will be refused.

Revocation of humanitarian protection

339G. A person's humanitarian protection granted under paragraph 339C will be revoked or not renewed if the Secretary of State is satisfied that at least one of the following applies:

(i) the circumstances which led to the grant of humanitarian protection have ceased to exist or have changed to such a degree that such protection is no longer required;

(ii) the person granted humanitarian protection should have been or is excluded from humanitarian protection because there are serious reasons for considering that he has committed a crime against peace, a war crime, a crime against humanity, or any other serious crime or instigated or otherwise participated in such crimes;

(iii) the person granted humanitarian protection should have been or is excluded from humanitarian protection because there are serious reasons for considering that he is guilty of acts contrary to the purposes and principles of the United Nations or has committed, prepared or instigated such acts or encouraged or induced others to commit, prepare or instigate such acts;

(iv) the person granted humanitarian protection should have been or is excluded from humanitarian protection because there are serious reasons for considering that he constitutes a danger to the community or to the security of the United Kingdom;

(v) the person granted humanitarian protection misrepresented or omitted facts, including the use of false documents, which were decisive to the grant of humanitarian protection; or

(vi) the person granted humanitarian protection should have been or is excluded from humanitarian protection because prior to his admission to the United Kingdom the person committed a crime outside the scope of (ii) and (iii) that would be punishable by imprisonment had it been committed in the United Kingdom and the person left his country of origin solely in order to avoid sanctions resulting from the crime.

In applying (i) the Secretary of State shall have regard to whether the change of circumstances is of such a significant and non-temporary nature that the person no longer faces a real risk of serious harm.

339H. When a person's humanitarian protection is revoked or not renewed any limited leave which they have may be curtailed.

Consideration of applications

339HA. The Secretary of State shall ensure that the personnel examining applications for asylum and taking decisions on his behalf have the knowledge with respect to relevant standards applicable in the field of asylum and refugee law.

339I. When the Secretary of State considers a person's asylum claim, eligibility for a grant of humanitarian protection or human rights claim it is the duty of the person to submit to the Secretary of State as soon as possible all material factors needed to substantiate the asylum claim or establish that he is a person eligible for humanitarian protection or substantiate the human rights claim, which the Secretary of State shall assess in cooperation with the person.

The material factors include:

(i) the person's statement on the reasons for making an asylum claim or on eligibility for a grant of humanitarian protection or for making a human rights claim;

(ii) all documentation at the person's disposal regarding the person's age, background (including background details of relevant relatives), identity, nationality(ies), country(ies) and place(s) of previous residence, previous asylum applications, travel routes; and

(iii) identity and travel documents.

339IA. For the purposes of examining individual applications for asylum

(i) information provided in support of an application and the fact that an application has been made shall not be disclosed to the alleged actor(s) of persecution of the applicant, and

(ii) information shall not be obtained from the alleged actor(s) of persecution that would result in their being directly informed that an application for asylum has been made by the applicant in question and would jeopardise the physical integrity of the applicant and his dependants, or the liberty and security of his family members still living in the country of origin.

This paragraph shall also apply where the Secretary of State is considering revoking a person's refugee status in accordance with these Rules.

339J. The assessment by the Secretary of State of an asylum claim, eligibility for a grant of humanitarian protection or a human rights claim will be carried out on an individual, objective and impartial basis. This will include taking into account in particular:

(i) all relevant facts as they relate to the country of origin or country of return at the time of taking a decision on the grant; including laws and regulations of the country of origin or country of return and the manner in which they are applied;

(ii) relevant statements and documentation presented by the person including information on whether the person has been or may be subject to persecution or serious harm;

(iii) the individual position and personal circumstances of the person, including factors such as background, gender and age, so as to assess whether, on the basis of the person's personal circumstances, the acts to which the person has been or could be exposed would amount to persecution or serious harm;

(iv) whether the person's activities since leaving the country of origin or country of return were engaged in for the sole or main purpose of creating the necessary conditions for making an asylum claim or establishing that he is a person eligible for humanitarian protection or a human rights claim, so as to assess whether these activities will expose the person to persecution or serious harm if he returned to that country; and

(v) whether the person could reasonably be expected to avail himself of the protection of another country where he could assert citizenship.

339JA. Reliable and up-to-date information shall be obtained from various sources as to the general situation prevailing in the countries of origin of applicants for asylum and, where necessary, in countries through which they have transited. Such information shall be made available to the personnel responsible for examining applications and taking decisions and may be provided to them in the form of a consolidated country information report.

This paragraph shall also apply where the Secretary of State is considering revoking a person's refugee status in accordance with these Rules.

339K. The fact that a person has already been subject to persecution or serious harm, or to direct threats of such persecution or such harm, will be regarded as a serious indication of the person's well-founded fear of persecution or real risk of suffering serious harm, unless there are good reasons to consider that such persecution or serious harm will not be repeated.

339L. It is the duty of the person to substantiate the asylum claim or establish that he is a person eligible for humanitarian protection or substantiate his human rights claim. Where aspects of the person's statements are not supported by documentary or other evidence, those aspects will not need confirmation when all of the following conditions are met:

(i) the person has made a genuine effort to substantiate his asylum claim or establish that he is a person eligible for humanitarian protection or substantiate his human rights claim;

(ii) all material factors at the person's disposal have been submitted, and a satisfactory explanation regarding any lack of other relevant material has been given;

(iii) the person's statements are found to be coherent and plausible and do not run counter to available specific and general information relevant to the person's case;

(iv) the person has made an asylum claim or sought to establish that he is a person eligible for humanitarian protection or made a human rights claim at the earliest possible time, unless the person can demonstrate good reason for not having done so; and

(v) the general credibility of the person has been established.

339M. The Secretary of State may consider that a person has not substantiated his asylum claim or established that he is a person eligible for humanitarian protection or substantiated his human rights claim, and thereby reject his application for asylum, determine that he is not eligible for humanitarian protection or reject his human rights claim, if he fails, without reasonable explanation, to make a prompt and full disclosure of material facts, either orally or in writing, or otherwise to assist the Secretary of State in establishing the facts of the case; this includes, for example, failure to report to a designated place to be fingerprinted, failure to complete an asylum questionnaire or failure to comply with a requirement to report to an immigration officer for examination.

339MA. Applications for asylum shall be neither rejected nor excluded from examination on the sole ground that they have not been made as soon as possible.

339N. In determining whether the general credibility of the person has been established the Secretary of State will apply the provisions in s 8 of the Asylum and Immigration (Treatment of Claimants, etc.) Act 2004.

Personal interview

339NA. Before a decision is taken on the application for asylum, the applicant shall be given the opportunity of a personal interview on his application for asylum with a representative of the Secretary of State who is legally competent to conduct such an interview.

The personal interview may be omitted where:

(i) the Secretary of State is able to take a positive decision on the basis of evidence available;

(ii) the Secretary of State has already had a meeting with the applicant for the purpose of assisting him with completing his application and submitting the essential information regarding the application;

(iii) the applicant, in submitting his application and presenting the facts, has only raised issues that are not relevant or of minimal relevance to the examination of whether he is a refugee, as defined in regulation 2 of the Refugee or Person in Need of International Protection (Qualification) Regulations 2006;

(iv) the applicant has made inconsistent, contradictory, improbable or insufficient representations which make his claim clearly unconvincing in relation to his having been the object of persecution;

(v) the applicant has submitted a subsequent application which does not raise any relevant new elements with respect to his particular circumstances or to the situation in his country of origin;

(vi) the applicant is making an application merely in order to delay or frustrate the enforcement of an earlier or imminent decision which would result in his removal; and

(vii) it is not reasonably practicable, in particular where the Secretary of State is of the opinion that the applicant is unfit or unable to be interviewed owing to enduring circumstances beyond his control.

The omission of a personal interview shall not prevent the Secretary of State from taking a decision on the application.

Where the personal interview is omitted, the applicant and dependants shall be given a reasonable opportunity to submit further information.

339NB. (i) The personal interview mentioned in paragraph 339NA above shall normally take place without the presence of the applicant's family members unless the Secretary of State considers it necessary for an appropriate examination to have other family members present.

(ii) The personal interview shall take place under conditions which ensure appropriate confidentiality.

339NC. (i) A written report shall be made of every personal interview containing at least the essential information regarding the asylum application as presented by the applicant in accordance with paragraph 339I of these Rules.

(ii) The Secretary of State shall ensure that the applicant has timely access to the report of the personal interview and that access is possible as soon as necessary for allowing an appeal to be prepared and lodged in due time.

339ND. The Secretary of State shall provide at public expense an interpreter for the purpose of allowing the applicant to submit his case, wherever necessary. The Secretary of State shall select an interpreter who can ensure appropriate communication between the applicant and the representative of the Secretary of State who conducts the interview.

Internal relocation

339O. (i) The Secretary of State will not make:

(a) a grant of asylum if in part of the country of origin a person would not have a well founded fear of being persecuted, and the person can reasonably be expected to stay in that part of the country;

or

(b) a grant of humanitarian protection if in part of the country of return a person would not face a real risk of suffering serious harm, and the person can reasonably be expected to stay in that part of the country.

(ii) In examining whether a part of the country of origin or country of return meets the requirements in (i) the Secretary of State, when making his decision on whether to grant asylum or humanitarian protection, will have regard to the general circumstances prevailing in that part of the country and to the personal circumstances of the person.

(iii) (i) applies notwithstanding technical obstacles to return to the country of origin or country of return.

Sur place claims

339P. A person may have a well-founded fear of being persecuted or a real risk of suffering serious harm based on events which have taken place since the person left the country of origin or country of return and/or activities which have been engaged in by a person since he left the country of origin or country of return, in particular where it is established that the activities relied upon constitute the expression and continuation of convictions or orientations held in the country of origin or country of return.

Residence Permits

339Q. (i) The Secretary of State will issue to a person granted asylum in the United Kingdom a United Kingdom Residence Permit (UKRP) as soon as possible after the grant of asylum. The UKRP will be valid for five years and renewable, unless compelling reasons of national security or public order otherwise require or where there are reasonable grounds for considering that the applicant is a danger to the security of the UK or having been convicted by a final judgment of a particularly serious crime, the applicant constitutes a danger to the community of the UK.

(ii) The Secretary of State will issue to a person granted humanitarian protection in the United Kingdom a UKRP as soon as possible after the grant of humanitarian protection. The UKRP will be valid for five years and renewable, unless compelling reasons of national security or public order otherwise require or where there are reasonable grounds for considering that the person granted humanitarian protection is a danger to the security of the UK or having been convicted by a final judgment of a serious crime, this person constitutes a danger to the community of the UK.

(iii) The Secretary of State will issue a UKRP to a family member of a person granted asylum or humanitarian protection where the family member does not qualify for such status. A UKRP will be granted for a period of five years. The UKRP is renewable on the terms set out in (i) and (ii) respectively. "Family member" for the purposes of this sub-paragraph refers only to those who are treated as dependants for the purposes of paragraph 349.

(iv) The Secretary of State may revoke or refuse to renew a person's UKRP where their grant of asylum or humanitarian protection is revoked under the provisions in the immigration rules.

Requirements for indefinite leave to remain for persons granted asylum or humanitarian protection

339R. The requirements for indefinite leave to remain for a person granted asylum or humanitarian protection, or their dependants granted asylum or humanitarian protection in line with the main applicant, are that:

(i) the applicant has held a UK Residence Permit (UKRP) issued under paragraph 339Q for a continuous period of five years in the UK; and

(ii) the applicant's UKRP has not been revoked or not renewed under paragraphs 339A or 339G of the immigration rules; and

(iii) the applicant has not:

a. been convicted of an offence for which they have been sentenced to imprisonment for at least 4 years; or

b. been convicted of an offence for which they have been sentenced to imprisonment for at least 12 months but less than 4 years, unless a period of 15 years has passed since the end of the sentence; or

c. been convicted of an offence for which they have been sentenced to imprisonment for less than 12 months, unless a period of 7 years has passed since the end of the sentence; or

d. been convicted of an offence for which they have received a non-custodial sentence or other out of court disposal that is recorded on their criminal record, unless a period of 24 months has passed since they received their sentence; or

e. in the view of the Secretary of State persistently offended and shown a particular disregard for the law, unless a period of seven years has passed since the most recent sentence was received.

Note: Paragraphs 339R to 339T inserted from 1 October 2013 subject to savings for applications made before that date (HC 628).

Indefinite leave to remain for a person granted asylum or humanitarian protection

339S. Indefinite leave to remain for a person granted asylum or humanitarian protection will be granted where each of the requirements in paragraph 339R is met.

Note: Paragraphs 339R to 339T inserted from 1 October 2013 subject to savings for applications made before that date (HC 628).

Refusal of indefinite leave to remain for a person granted asylum or humanitarian protection

339T. (i) Indefinite leave to remain for a person granted asylum or humanitarian protection is to be refused if any of the requirements of paragraph 339R is not met.

(ii) An applicant refused indefinite leave to remain under paragraph 339T(i) may apply to have their UK Residence Permit extended in accordance with paragraph 339Q.

Note: Paragraphs 339R to 339T inserted from 1 October 2013 subject to savings for applications made before that date (HC 628).

Consideration of asylum applications and human rights claims

340. DELETED

341. DELETED

342. The actions of anyone acting as an agent of the asylum applicant or human rights claimant may also be taken into account in regard to the matters set out in paragraphs 340 and 341.

343. DELETED

344. DELETED

Travel documents

344A (i). After having received a complete application for a travel document, the Secretary of State will issue to a person granted asylum in the United Kingdom and their family members travel documents, in the form set out in the Schedule to the Geneva Convention, for the purpose of travel outside the United Kingdom, unless compelling reasons of national security or public order otherwise require.

(ii) After having received a complete application for a travel document, the Secretary of State will issue travel documents to a person granted humanitarian protection in the United Kingdom where that person is unable to obtain a national passport or other identity documents which enable him to travel, unless compelling reasons of national security or public order otherwise require.

(iii) Where the person referred to in (ii) can obtain a national passport or identity documents but has not done so, the Secretary of State will issue that person with a travel document where he can show that he has made reasonable attempts to obtain a national passport or identity document and there are serious humanitarian reasons for travel.

Access to Employment

344B. The Secretary of State will not impose conditions restricting the employment or occupation in the United Kingdom of a person granted asylum or humanitarian protection.

Information

344C. A person who is granted asylum or humanitarian protection will be provided with access to information in a language that they may reasonably be supposed to understand which sets out the rights and obligations relating to that status. The Secretary of State will provide the information as soon as possible after the grant of asylum or humanitarian protection.

Third country cases

345. (1) In a case where the Secretary of State is satisfied that the conditions set out in Paragraphs 4 and 5(1), 9 and 10(1), 14 and 15(1) or 17 of Schedule 3 to the Asylum and Immigration (Treatment of Claimants, etc.) Act 2004 are fulfilled, he will normally decline to examine the asylum application substantively and issue a certificate under Part 2, 3, 4 or 5 of Schedule 3 to the Asylum and Immigration (Treatment of Claimants, etc.) Act 2004 as appropriate.

(2) The Secretary of State shall not issue a certificate under Part 2, 3, 4 or 5 of Schedule 3 to the Asylum and Immigration (Treatment of Claimants, etc.) Act 2004 unless:

(i) the asylum applicant has not arrived in the United Kingdom directly from the country in which he claims to fear persecution and has had an opportunity at the border or within the third country or territory to make contact with the authorities of that third country or territory in order to seek their protection; or

(ii) there is other clear evidence of his admissibility to a third country or territory.

Provided that he is satisfied that a case meets these criteria, the Secretary of State is under no obligation to consult the authorities of the third country or territory before the removal of an asylum applicant to that country or territory.

345(2A) Where a certificate is issued under Part 2, 3, 4 or 5 of Schedule 3 to the Asylum and Immigration (Treatment of Claimants, etc.) Act 2004 the asylum applicant shall:

(i) be informed in a language that he may reasonably be expected to understand regarding his removal to a safe third country;

(ii) be provided with a document informing the authorities of the safe third country, in the language of that country, that the asylum application has not been examined in substance by the authorities in the United Kingdom;

(iii) sub-paragraph 345(2A)(ii) shall not apply if removal takes place with reference to the arrangements set out in Regulation (EC) No. 343/2003 (the Dublin Regulation) [or Regulation (EC) No. 604/2013]; and

(iv) if an asylum applicant removed under this paragraph is not admitted to the safe third country (not being a country to which the Dublin Regulation applies as specified in paragraph 345(2A)(iii)), subject to determining and resolving the reasons for his nonadmission, the asylum applicant shall be admitted to the asylum procedure in the United Kingdom.

(3) Where a certificate is issued under Part 2, 3, 4 or 5 of Schedule 3 to the Asylum and Immigration (Treatment of Claimants, etc.) Act 2004 in relation to the asylum claim and the person is seeking leave to enter the Immigration Officer will consider whether or not he is in a position to decide to give or refuse leave to enter without interviewing the person further. If the Immigration Officer decides that a further interview is not required he may serve the notice giving or refusing leave to enter by post. If the Immigration Officer decides that a further interview is required, he will then resume his examination to determine whether or not to grant the person leave to enter under any other provision

of these Rules. If the person fails at any time to comply with a requirement to report to an Immigration Officer for examination, the Immigration Officer may direct that the person's examination shall be treated as concluded at that time. The Immigration Officer will then consider any outstanding applications for entry on the basis of any evidence before him.

(4) Where a certificate is issued under Part 2, 3, 4 or 5 of Schedule 3 to the Asylum and Immigration (Treatment of Claimants, etc.) Act 2004 the person may, if liable to removal as an illegal entrant, or removal under section 10 of the Immigration and Asylum Act 1999 or to deportation, at the same time be notified of removal directions, served with a notice of intention to make a deportation order, or served with a deportation order, as appropriate.

Note: Words inserted in subparagraph (2A)(iii) from 1 December 2013 (HC 803).

Previously rejected applications

346. DELETED

347. DELETED

Rights of appeal

348. DELETED

Dependants

349. A spouse, civil partner, unmarried or same-sex partner, or minor child accompanying a principal applicant may be included in his application for asylum as his dependant, provided, in the case of an adult dependant with legal capacity, the dependant consents to being treated as such at the time the application is lodged. A spouse, civil partner, unmarried or same-sex partner or minor child may also claim asylum in his own right. If the principal applicant is granted asylum or humanitarian protection and leave to enter or remain any spouse, civil partner, unmarried or same-sex partner or minor child will be granted leave to enter or remain for the same duration. The case of any dependant who claims asylum in his own right will be also considered individually in accordance with paragraph 334 above. An applicant under this paragraph, including an accompanied child, may be interviewed where he makes a claim as a dependant or in his own right.

If the spouse, civil partner, unmarried or same-sex partner, or minor child in question has a claim in his own right, that claim should be made at the earliest opportunity. Any failure to do so will be taken into account and may damage credibility if no reasonable explanation for it is given. Where an asylum or humanitarian protection application is unsuccessful, at the same time that asylum or humanitarian protection is refused the applicant may be notified of removal directions or served with a notice of the Secretary of State's intention to deport him, as appropriate. In this paragraph and paragraphs 350–352 a child means a person who is under 18 years of age or who, in the absence of documentary evidence establishing age, appears to be under that age. An unmarried or same sex partner for the purposes of this paragraph, is a person who has been living together with the principal applicant in a subsisting relationship akin to marriage or a civil partnership for two years or more.

Unaccompanied children

350. Unaccompanied children may also apply for asylum and, in view of their potential vulnerability, particular priority and care is to be given to the handling of their cases.

351. A person of any age may qualify for refugee status under the Convention and the criteria in paragraph 334 apply to all cases. However, account should be taken of the applicant's maturity and in assessing the claim of a child more weight should be given to objective indications of risk than to the child's state of mind and understanding of his situation. An asylum application made on behalf of a child should not be refused solely because the child is too young to understand his situation or to have formed a well founded fear of persecution. Close attention should be given to the welfare of the child at all times.

352. Any child over the age of 12 who has claimed asylum in his own right shall be interviewed about the substance of his claim unless the child is unfit or unable to be interviewed. When an interview takes place it shall be conducted in the presence of a parent, guardian, representative or another adult independent of the Secretary of State who has responsibility for the child. The interviewer shall have specialist training in the interviewing of children and have particular regard to the possibility that a child will feel inhibited or alarmed. The child shall be allowed to express himself in his own way and at his own speed. If he appears tired or distressed, the interview will be suspended. The interviewer should then consider whether it would be appropriate for the interview to be resumed the same day or on another day.

352ZA. The Secretary of State shall as soon as possible after an unaccompanied child makes an application for asylum take measures to ensure that a representative represents and/or assists the unaccompanied child with respect to the examination of the application and ensure that the representative is given the opportunity to inform the unaccompanied child about the meaning and possible consequences of the interview and, where appropriate, how to prepare himself for the interview. The representative shall have the right to be present at the interview and ask questions and make comments in the interview, within the framework set by the interviewer.

352ZB. The decision on the application for asylum shall be taken by a person who is trained to deal with asylum claims from children.

Requirements for limited leave to remain as an unaccompanied asylum seeking child.

352ZC The requirements to be met in order for a grant of limited leave to remain to be made in relation to an unaccompanied asylum seeking child under paragraph 352ZE are:

a) the applicant is an unaccompanied asylum seeking child under the age of 17½ years throughout the duration of leave to be granted in this capacity;

b) the applicant must have applied for asylum and been refused Refugee Leave and Humanitarian Protection;

c) there are no adequate reception arrangements in the country to which they would be returned if leave to remain was not granted;

d) the applicant must not be excluded from a grant of asylum under Regulation 7 of the Refugee or Person in Need of International Protection (Qualification) Regulations 2006 or excluded from a grant of Humanitarian Protection under paragraph 339D or both;

e) there are no reasonable grounds for regarding the applicant as a danger to the security of the United Kingdom;

f) the applicant has not been convicted by a final judgment of a particularly serious crime, and the applicant does not constitute a danger to the community of the United Kingdom; and

g) the applicant is not, at the date of their application, the subject of a deportation order or a decision to make a deportation order.

Note: Paragraphs 352ZC to 352ZF inserted from 6 April 2013 subject to savings for applications made before that date (HC 1039).

352ZD An unaccompanied asylum seeking child is a person who:

a) is under 18 years of age when the asylum application is submitted;

b) is applying for asylum in their own right; and

c) is separated from both parents and is not being cared for by an adult who in law or by custom has responsibility to do so.

Note: Paragraphs 352ZC to 352ZF inserted from 6 April 2013 subject to savings for applications made before that date (HC 1039).

352ZE. Limited leave to remain should be granted for a period of 30 months or until the child is 17½ years of age whichever is shorter, provided that the Secretary of State is satisfied that the requirements in paragraph 352ZC are met.

Note: Paragraphs 352ZC to 352ZF inserted from 6 April 2013 subject to savings for applications made before that date (HC 1039).

352ZF. Limited leave granted under this provision will cease if

a) any one or more of the requirements listed in paragraph 352ZC cease to be met, or

b) a misrepresentation or omission of facts, including the use of false documents, were decisive for the grant of leave under 352ZE.

Note: Paragraphs 352ZC to 352ZF inserted from 6 April 2013 subject to savings for applications made before that date (HC 1039).

352A. The requirements to be met by a person seeking leave to enter or remain in the United Kingdom as the spouse civil partner of a refugee are that:

(i) the applicant is married to or the civil partner of a person who is currently a refugee granted status as such under the immigration rules in the United Kingdom; and

(ii) the marriage or civil partnership did not take place after the person granted asylum left the country of his former habitual residence in order to seek asylum; an

(iii) the applicant would not be excluded from protection by virtue of article 1F of the United Nations Convention and Protocol relating to the Status of Refugees if he were to seek asylum in his own right; and

(iv) each of the parties intends to live permanently with the other as his or her spouse civil partner and the marriage is subsisting; and

(v) if seeking leave to enter, the applicant holds a valid United Kingdom entry clearance for entry in this capacity.

352AA. The requirements to be met by a person seeking leave to enter or remain in the United Kingdom as the unmarried or the same-sex partner of a refugee are that:

(i) the applicant is the unmarried or same-sex partner of a person who is currently a refugee granted status as such under the immigration rules in the United Kingdom and was granted that status in the UK on or after 9th October 2006; and

(ii) the parties have been living together in a relationship akin to either a marriage or a civil partnership which has subsisted for two years or more; and

(iii) the relationship existed before the person granted asylum left the country of his former habitual residence in order to seek asylum; and

(iv) the applicant would not be excluded from protection by virtue of paragraph 334(iii) or of these Rules or article 1F of the Geneva Convention if he were to seek asylum in his own right; and

(v) each of the parties intends to live permanently with the other as his or her unmarried or same-sex partner and the relationship is subsisting; and

(vi) the parties are not involved in a consanguineous relationship with one another; and

(vii) if seeking leave to enter, the applicant holds a valid United Kingdom entry clearance for entry in this capacity.

352B. Limited leave to enter the United Kingdom as the spouse civil partner of a refugee may be granted provided a valid United Kingdom entry clearance for entry in this capacity is produced to the Immigration Officer on arrival. Limited leave to remain in the United Kingdom as the spouse of a refugee may be granted provided the Secretary of State is satisfied that each of the requirements of paragraph 352A(i)–(v) are met.

352BA. Limited leave to enter the United Kingdom as the unmarried or same-sex partner of a refugee may be granted provided a valid United Kingdom entry clearance for entry in this capacity is produced to the Immigration Officer on arrival. Limited leave to remain in the United Kingdom as the unmarried or same sex partner of a refugee may be granted provided the Secretary of State is satisfied that each of the requirements of paragraph 352AA(i)–(vii) are met.

352C. Limited leave to enter the United Kingdom as the spouse civil partner of a refugee is to be refused if a valid United Kingdom entry clearance for entry in this capacity is not produced to the Immigration Officer on arrival. Limited leave to remain as the spouse civil partner of a refugee is to be refused if the Secretary of State is not satisfied that each of the requirements of paragraph 352A(i)–(v) are met.

352CA Limited leave to enter the United Kingdom as the unmarried or same-sex partner of a refugee is to be refused if a valid United Kingdom entry clearance for entry in this capacity is not produced to the Immigration Officer on arrival. Limited leave to remain as the unmarried or same sex partner of a refugee is to be refused if the Secretary of State is not satisfied that each of the requirements of paragraph 352AA(i)–(vi) are met.

352D. The requirements to be met by a person seeking leave to enter or remain in the United Kingdom in order to join or remain with the parent who is currently a refugee granted status as such under the immigration rules in the United Kingdom are that the applicant:

(i) is the child of a parent who is currently a refugee granted status as such under the immigration rules in the United Kingdom; and

(ii) is under the age of 18, and

(iii) is not leading an independent life, is unmarried and is not a civil partner, and has not formed an independent family unit; and

(iv) was part of the family unit of the person granted asylum at the time that the person granted asylum left the country of his habitual residence in order to seek asylum; and

(v) would not be excluded from protection by virtue of article 1F of the United Nations Convention and Protocol relating to the Status of Refugees if he were to seek asylum in his own right; and

(vi) if seeking leave to enter, holds a valid United Kingdom entry clearance for entry in this capacity.

352E. Limited leave to enter the United Kingdom as the child of a refugee may be granted provided a valid United Kingdom entry clearance for entry in this capacity is produced to the Immigration Officer on arrival. Limited leave to remain in the United Kingdom as the child of a refugee may be granted provided the Secretary of State is satisfied that each of the requirements of paragraph 352D(i)–(v) are met.

352F. Limited leave to enter the United Kingdom as the child of a refugee is to be refused if a valid United Kingdom entry clearance for entry in this capacity is not produced to the Immigration Officer on arrival. Limited leave to remain as the child of a refugee is to be refused if the Secretary of State is not satisfied that each of the requirements of paragraph 352D(i)–(v) are met.

352FA. The requirements to be met by a person seeking leave to enter or remain in the United Kingdom as the spouse or civil partner of a person who is currently a beneficiary of humanitarian protection granted under the immigration rules in the United Kingdom and was granted that status on or after 30 August 2005 are that:

(i) the applicant is married to or the civil partner of a person who is currently a beneficiary of humanitarian protection granted under the immigration rules and was granted that status on or after 30 August 2005; and

(ii) the marriage or civil partnership did not take place after the person granted humanitarian protection left the country of his former habitual residence in order to seek asylum in the UK; and

(iii) the applicant would not be excluded from a grant of humanitarian protection for any of the reasons in paragraph 339D; and

(iv) each of the parties intend to live permanently with the other as his or her spouse or civil partner and the marriage or civil partnership is subsisting; and

(v) if seeking leave to enter, the applicant holds a valid United Kingdom entry clearance for entry in this capacity.

352FB. Limited leave to enter the United Kingdom as the spouse or civil partner of a person granted humanitarian protection may be granted provided a valid United Kingdom entry clearance for entry in this capacity is produced to the Immigration Officer on arrival. Limited leave to remain in the United Kingdom as the spouse or civil partner of a person granted humanitarian protection may be granted provided the Secretary of State is satisfied that each of the requirements in sub paragraphs 352FA(i)–(iv) are met.

352FC. Limited leave to enter the United Kingdom as the spouse or civil partner of a person granted humanitarian protection is to be refused if a valid United Kingdom entry clearance for entry in this capacity is not produced to the Immigration Officer on arrival. Limited leave to remain as the spouse or civil partner of a person granted humanitarian protection is to be refused if the Secretary of State is not satisfied that each of the requirements in sub paragraphs 352FA(i)–(iv) are met.

352FD. The requirements to be met by a person seeking leave to enter or remain in the United Kingdom as the unmarried or same-sex partner of a person who is currently a beneficiary of humanitarian protection granted under the immigration rules in the United Kingdom are that:

(i) the applicant is the unmarried or same-sex partner of a person who is currently a beneficiary of humanitarian protection granted under the immigration rules and was granted that status on or after 9th October 2006; and

(ii) the parties have been living together in a relationship akin to either a marriage or a civil partnership which has subsisted for two years or more; and

(iii) the relationship existed before the person granted humanitarian protection left the country of his former habitual residence in order to seek asylum; and

(iv) the applicant would not be excluded from a grant of humanitarian protection for any of the reasons in paragraph 339D; and

(v) each of the parties intends to live permanently with the other as his or her unmarried or same-sex partner and the relationship is subsisting; and

(vi) the parties are not involved in a consanguineous relationship with one another; and

(vii) if seeking leave to enter, the applicant holds a valid United Kingdom entry clearance for entry in this capacity.

352FE. Limited leave to enter the United Kingdom as the unmarried or same-sex partner of a person granted humanitarian protection may be granted provided a valid United Kingdom entry clearance for entry in this capacity is produced to the Immigration Officer on arrival. Limited leave to remain in the United Kingdom as the unmarried or same sex partner of a person granted humanitarian protection may be granted provided the Secretary of State is satisfied that each of the requirements in subparagraphs 352FD(i)–(vi) are met.

352FF. Limited leave to enter the United Kingdom as the unmarried or same-sex partner of a person granted humanitarian protection is to be refused if a valid United Kingdom entry clearance for entry in this capacity is not produced to the Immigration Officer on arrival. Limited leave to remain as the unmarried or same sex partner of a person granted humanitarian protection is to be refused if the Secretary of State is not satisfied that each of the requirements in sub paragraphs 352FD(i)–(vi) are met.

352FG. The requirements to be met by a person seeking leave to enter or remain in the United Kingdom in order to join or remain with their parent who is currently a beneficiary of humanitarian protection granted under the immigration rules in the United Kingdom and was granted that status on or after 30 August 2005 are that the applicant:

(i) is the child of a parent who is currently a beneficiary of humanitarian protection granted under the immigration rules in the United Kingdom and was granted that status on or after 30 August 2005; and

(ii) is under the age of 18, and

(iii) is not leading an independent life, is unmarried or is not in a civil partnership, and has not formed an independent family unit; and

(iv) was part of the family unit of the person granted humanitarian protection at the time that the person granted humanitarian protection left the country of his habitual residence in order to seek asylum in the UK; and

(v) would not be excluded from a grant of humanitarian protection for any of the reasons in paragraph 339D; and

(vi) if seeking leave to enter, holds a valid United Kingdom entry clearance for entry in this capacity.

352FH. Limited leave to enter the United Kingdom as the child of a person granted humanitarian protection may be granted provided a valid United Kingdom entry clearance for entry in this capacity is produced to the Immigration Officer on arrival. Limited leave to remain in the United Kingdom as the child of a person granted humanitarian protection may be granted provided the Secretary of State is satisfied that each of the requirements in sub paragraphs 352FG(i)–(v) are met.

352FI. Limited leave to enter the United Kingdom as the child of a person granted humanitarian protection is to be refused if a valid United Kingdom entry clearance for entry in this capacity is not produced to the Immigration Officer on arrival. Limited leave to remain as the child of a person granted humanitarian protection is to be refused if the Secretary of State is not satisfied that each of the requirements in sub paragraphs 352FG (i)–(v) are met.

352FJ. Nothing in paragraphs 352A–352FI shall allow a person to be granted leave to enter or remain in the United Kingdom as the spouse or civil partner, unmarried or same sex partner or child of a refugee, or of a person granted humanitarian protection under the immigration rules in the United Kingdom on or after 30 August 2005, if the refugee or, as the case may be, person granted humanitarian protection, is a British Citizen.

Interpretation

352G. For the purposes of this Part:

(a) "Geneva Convention" means the United Nations Convention and Protocol relating to the Status of Refugees;

(b) "Country of return" means a country or territory listed in paragraph 8(c) of Schedule 2 of the Immigration Act 1971;

(c) "Country of origin" means the country or countries of nationality or, for a stateless person, or former habitual residence.

Part 11A

Temporary Protection

Definition of Temporary Protection Directive

354. For the purposes of paragraphs 355 to 356B, "Temporary Protection Directive" means Council Directive 2001/55/EC of 20 July 2001 regarding the giving of temporary protection by Member States in the event of a mass influx of displaced persons.

Grant of temporary protection

355. An applicant for temporary protection will be granted temporary protection if the Secretary of State is satisfied that:

(i) the applicant is in the United Kingdom or has arrived at a port of entry in the United Kingdom; and

(ii) the applicant is a person entitled to temporary protection as defined by, and in accordance with, the Temporary Protection Directive; and

(iii) the applicant does not hold an extant grant of temporary protection entitling him to reside in another Member State of the European Union. This requirement is subject to the provisions relating to dependants set out in paragraphs 356 to 356B and to any agreement to the contrary with the Member State in question; and

(iv) the applicant is not excluded from temporary protection under the provisions in paragraph 355A.

355A. An applicant or a dependant may be excluded from temporary protection if:

(i) there are serious reasons for considering that:

(a) he has committed a crime against peace, a war crime, or a crime against humanity, as defined in the international instruments drawn up to make provision in respect of such crimes; or

(b) he has committed a serious non-political crime outside the United Kingdom prior to his application for temporary protection; or

(c) he has committed acts contrary to the purposes and principles of the United Nations, or

(ii) there are reasonable grounds for regarding the applicant as a danger to the security of the United Kingdom or, having been convicted by a final judgment of a particularly serious crime, to be a danger to the community of the United Kingdom.

Consideration under this paragraph shall be based solely on the personal conduct of the applicant concerned. Exclusion decisions or measures shall be based on the principle of proportionality.

355B. If temporary protection is granted to a person who has been given leave to enter or remain (whether or not the leave has expired) or to a person who has entered without leave, the Secretary of State will vary the existing leave or grant limited leave to remain.

355C. A person to whom temporary protection is granted will be granted limited leave to enter or remain, which is not to be subject to a condition prohibiting employment, for a period not exceeding 12 months. On the expiry of this period, he will be entitled to apply for an extension of this limited leave for successive periods of 6 months thereafter.

355D. A person to whom temporary protection is granted will be permitted to return to the United Kingdom from another Member State of the European Union during the period of a mass influx of displaced persons as established by the Council of the European Union pursuant to Article 5 of the Temporary Protection Directive.

355E. A person to whom temporary protection is granted will be provided with a document in a language likely to be understood by him in which the provisions relating to temporary protection and which are relevant to him are set out. A person with temporary protection will also be provided with a document setting out his temporary protection status.

355F. The Secretary of State will establish and maintain a register of those granted temporary protection. The register will record the name, nationality, date and place of birth and marital status of those granted temporary protection and their family relationship to any other person who has been granted temporary protection.

355G. If a person who makes an asylum application is also eligible for temporary protection, the Secretary of State may decide not to consider the asylum application until the applicant ceases to be entitled to temporary protection.

Dependants

356. In this part:

"dependant" means a family member or a close relative.

"family member" means:

(i) the spouse or civil partner of an applicant for, or a person who has been granted, temporary protection; or

(ii) the unmarried or same-sex partner of an applicant for, or a person who has been granted, temporary protection where the parties have been living together in a relationship akin to marriage which has subsisted for 2 years or more; or

(iii) the minor child (who is unmarried and not a civil partner); of an applicant for, or a person who has been granted, temporary protection or his spouse,

who lived with the principal applicant as part of the family unit in the country of origin immediately prior to the mass influx.

"close relative" means:

(i) the adult child (who is unmarried and not a civil partner), parent or grandparent of an applicant for, or person who has been granted, temporary protection; or

(ii) sibling (who is unmarried and not a civil partner or the uncle or aunt of an applicant for, or person who has been granted, temporary protection, who lived with the principal applicant as part of the family unit in the country of origin immediately prior to the mass influx and was wholly or mainly dependent upon the principal applicant at that time, and would face extreme hardship if reunification with the principal applicant did not take place.

356A. A dependant may apply for temporary protection. Where the dependant falls within paragraph 356 and does not fall to be excluded under paragraph 355A, he will be granted temporary protection for the same duration and under the same conditions as the principal applicant.

356B. When considering any application by a dependant child, the Secretary of State shall take into consideration the best interests of that child.

Part 11B

Asylum

Reception Conditions for non-EU asylum applicants

357. Part 11B only applies to asylum applicants (within the meaning of these Rules) who are not nationals of a member State.

Information to be provided to asylum applicants

357A. The Secretary of State shall inform asylum applicants in a language they may reasonably be supposed to understand and within a reasonable time after their claim for asylum has been recorded of the procedure to be followed, their rights and obligations during the procedure, and the possible consequences of non-compliance and non-co-operation. They shall be informed of the likely timeframe for consideration of the application and the means at their disposal for submitting all relevant information.

358. The Secretary of State shall inform asylum applicants within a reasonable time not exceeding fifteen days after their claim for asylum has been recorded of the benefits and services that they may be eligible to receive and of the rules and procedures with which they must comply relating to them. The Secretary of State shall also provide information on non-governmental organisations and persons that provide legal assistance to asylum applicants and which may be able to help asylum applicants or provide information on available benefits and services.

358A. The Secretary of State shall ensure that the information referred to in paragraph 358 is available in writing and, to the extent possible, will provide the information in a language that asylum applicants may reasonably be supposed to understand. Where appropriate, the Secretary of State may also arrange for this information to be supplied orally.

Information to be provided by asylum applicants

358B. An asylum applicant must notify the Secretary of State of his current address and of any change to his address or residential status. If not notified beforehand, any change must be notified to the Secretary of State without delay after it occurs.

The United Nations High Commissioner for Refugees

358C. A representative of the United Nations High Commissioner for Refugees (UNHCR) or an organisation working in the United Kingdom on behalf of the UNHCR pursuant to an agreement with the government shall:

(a) have access to applicants for asylum, including those in detention;

(b) have access to information on individual applications for asylum, on the course of the procedure and on the decisions taken on applications for asylum, provided that the applicant for asylum agrees thereto;

(c) be entitled to present his views, in the exercise of his supervisory responsibilities under Article 35 of the Geneva Convention, to the Secretary of State regarding individual applications for asylum at any stage of the procedure.

This paragraph shall also apply where the Secretary of State is considering revoking a person's refugee status in accordance with these Rules.

Documentation

359. The Secretary of State shall ensure that, within three working days of recording an asylum application, a document is made available to that asylum applicant, issued in his own name, certifying his status as an asylum applicant or testifying that he is allowed to remain in the United Kingdom while his asylum application is pending. For the avoidance of doubt, in cases where the Secretary of State declines to examine an application it will no longer be pending for the purposes of this rule.

359A. The obligation in paragraph 359 above shall not apply where the asylum applicant is detained under the Immigration Acts, the Immigration and Asylum Act 1999 or the Nationality, Immigration and Asylum Act 2002.

359B. A document issued to an asylum applicant under paragraph 359 does not constitute evidence of the asylum applicant's identity.

359C. In specific cases the Secretary of State or an Immigration Officer may provide an asylum applicant with evidence equivalent to that provided under rule 359. This might be, for example, in circumstances in which it is only possible or desirable to issue a time-limited document.

Right to request permission to take up employment

360. An asylum applicant may apply to the Secretary of State for permission to take up employment if a decision at first instance has not been taken on the applicant's asylum application within one year of the date on which it was recorded. The Secretary of State shall only consider such an application if, in the Secretary of State's opinion, any delay in reaching a decision at first instance cannot be attributed to the applicant.

360A. If permission to take up employment is granted under paragraph 360, that permission will be subject to the following restrictions:

(i) employment may only be taken up in a post which is, at the time an offer of employment is accepted, included on the list of shortage occupations published by the United Kingdom Border Agency (as that list is amended from time to time);

(ii) no work in a self-employed capacity; and

(iii) no engagement in setting up a business.

360B. If an asylum applicant is granted permission to take up employment under paragraph 360 this shall only be until such time as his asylum application has been finally determined.

360C. Where an individual makes further submissions which raise asylum grounds and which fall to be considered under paragraph 353 of these Rules, that individual may apply to the Secretary of State for permission to take up employment if a decision pursuant to paragraph 353 of these Rules has not been taken on the further submissions within one year of the date on which they were recorded. The Secretary of State shall only consider such an application if, in the Secretary of State's opinion, any delay in reaching a decision pursuant to paragraph 353 of these Rules cannot be attributed to the individual.

360D. If permission to take up employment is granted under paragraph 360C, that permission will be subject to the following restrictions:

(i) employment may only be taken up in a post which is, at the time an offer of employment is accepted, included on the list of shortage occupations published by the United Kingdom Border Agency (as that list is amended from time to time);

(ii) no work in a self-employed capacity; and

(iii) no engagement in setting up a business.

360E. Where permission to take up employment is granted pursuant to paragraph 360C, this shall only be until such time as:

(i) a decision has been taken pursuant to paragraph 353 that the further submissions do not amount to a fresh claim; or

(ii) where the further submissions are considered to amount to a fresh claim for asylum pursuant to paragraph 353, all rights of appeal from the immigration decision made in consequence of the rejection of the further submissions have been exhausted.

Interpretation

361. For the purposes of this Part—

(a) 'working day' means any day other than a Saturday or Sunday, a bank holiday, Christmas day or Good Friday;

(b) 'member State' has the same meaning as in Schedule 1 to the European Communities Act 1972.

PART 12

PROCEDURE AND RIGHTS OF APPEAL

Fresh Claims

353. When a human rights or asylum claim has been refused or withdrawn or treated as withdrawn under paragraph 333C of these Rules and any appeal relating to that claim is no longer pending, the decision maker will consider any further submissions and, if rejected, will then determine whether they amount to a fresh claim. The submissions will amount to a fresh claim if they are significantly different from the material that has previously been considered. The submissions will only be significantly different if the content:

(i) had not already been considered; and

(ii) taken together with the previously considered material, created a realistic prospect of success, notwithstanding its rejection.

This paragraph does not apply to claims made overseas.

353A. Consideration of further submissions shall be subject to the procedures set out in these Rules. An applicant who has made further submissions shall not be removed before the Secretary of State has considered the submissions under paragraph 353 or otherwise.

Exceptional Circumstances

353B. Where further submissions have been made and the decision maker has established whether or not they amount to a fresh claim under paragraph 353 of these Rules, or in cases with no outstanding further submissions whose appeal rights have been exhausted and which are subject to a review, the decision maker will also have regard to the migrant's:

(i) character, conduct and associations including any criminal record and the nature of any offence of which the migrant concerned has been convicted;

(ii) compliance with any conditions attached to any previous grant of leave to enter or remain and compliance with any conditions of temporary admission or immigration bail where applicable;

(iii) length of time spent in the United Kingdom spent for reasons beyond the migrant's control after the human rights or asylum claim has been submitted or refused;

in deciding whether there are exceptional circumstances which mean that removal from the United Kingdom is no longer appropriate.

This paragraph does not apply to submissions made overseas.

This paragraph does not apply where the person is liable to deportation.

PART 13

DEPORTATION

A deportation order

A362. Where Article 8 is raised in the context of deportation under Part 13 of these Rules, the claim under Article 8 will only succeed where the requirements of these rules as at [28 July 2014] are met, regardless of when the notice of intention to deport or the deportation order, as appropriate, was served.

Note: Words substituted from 28 July 2014; this change applies to all ECHR Article 8 claims from foreign criminals which are decided on or after that date (HC 532).

362. A deportation order requires the subject to leave the United Kingdom and authorises his detention until he is removed. It also prohibits him from re-entering the country for as long as it is in force and invalidates any leave to enter or remain in the United Kingdom given him before the Order is made or while it is in force.

363. The circumstances in which a person is liable to deportation include:

(i) where the Secretary of State deems the person's deportation to be conducive to the public good;

(ii) where the person is the spouse or civil partner or child under 18 of a person ordered to be deported; and

(iii) where a court recommends deportation in the case of a person over the age of 17 who has been convicted of an offence punishable with imprisonment.

363A. Prior to 2 October 2000, a person would have been liable to deportation in certain circumstances in which he is now liable to administrative removal . . . However, such a person remains liable to deportation, rather than administrative removal where:

(i) a decision to make a deportation order against him was taken before 2 October 2000;

or

(ii) the person has made a valid application under the Immigration (Regularisation Period for Overstayers) Regulations 2000.

Note: Words deleted from 6 April 2013 subject to savings for applications made before that date (HC 1039).

Deportation of family members

364. DELETED

364A. DELETED

365. . . . The Secretary of State will not normally decide to deport the spouse or civil partner of a deportee [under section 5 of the Immigration Act 1971] where:

(i) he has qualified for settlement in his own right; or

(ii) he has been living apart from the deportee.

Note: Words deleted and words inserted from 20 October 2014 (HC 693).

366. The Secretary of State will not normally decide to deport the child of a deportee [under section 5 of the Immigration Act 1971] where:

(i) he and his mother or father are living apart from the deportee; or

(ii) he has left home and established himself on an independent basis; or

(iii) he married or formed a civil partnership before deportation came into prospect.

Note: Words inserted from 20 October 2014 (HC 693).

367. DELETED

368. DELETED (from 20 October 2014 (HC 693)).

Right of appeal against destination

369. DELETED

Restricted right of appeal against deportation in cases of breach of limited leave

370. DELETED

Exemption to the restricted right of appeal

371. DELETED

372. DELETED

A deportation order made on the recommendation of a Court

373. DELETED

Where deportation is deemed to be conducive to the public good

374. DELETED

375. DELETED

Hearing of appeals

376. DELETED

377. DELETED

378. DELETED (from 20 October 2014 (HC 693)).

Persons who have claimed asylum

379. DELETED

379A. DELETED

380. DELETED

Procedure

381. When a decision to make a deportation order has been taken (otherwise than on the recommendation of a court) a notice will be given to the person concerned informing him of the decision . . .

Note: Words deleted from 20 October 2014 (HC 693).

382. Following the issue of such a notice the Secretary of State may authorise detention or make an order restricting a person as to residence, employment or occupation and requiring him to report to the police, pending the making of a deportation order.

383. DELETED

384. DELETED (from 20 October 2014 (HC 693)).

Arrangements for removal

385. A person against whom a deportation order has been made will normally be removed from the United Kingdom. The power is to be exercised so as to secure the person's return to the country of which he is a national, or which has most recently provided him with a travel document, unless he can show that another country will receive him. In considering any departure from the normal arrangements, regard will be had to the public interest generally, and to any additional expense that may fall on public funds.

386. DELETED (from 20 October 2014 (HC 693)).

Supervised departure

387. DELETED

Returned deportees

388. Where a person returns to this country when a deportation order is in force against him, he may be deported under the original order. The Secretary of State will consider every such case in the light of all the relevant circumstances before deciding whether to enforce the order.

Returned family members

389. Persons deported in the circumstances set out in paragraphs 365-368 above (deportation of family members) may be able to seek re-admission to the United Kingdom under the Immigration Rules where:

(i) a child reaches 18 (when he ceases to be subject to the deportation order); or

(ii) in the case of a spouse or civil partner, the marriage or civil partnership comes to an end.

Revocation of deportation order

390. An application for revocation of a deportation order will be considered in the light of all the circumstances including the following:

(i) the grounds on which the order was made;

(ii) any representations made in support of revocation;

(iii) the interests of the community, including the maintenance of an effective immigration control;

(iv) the interests of the applicant, including any compassionate circumstances.

390A. Where paragraph 398 applies the Secretary of State . . . will consider whether paragraph 399 or 399A applies and, if it does not, it will only be in exceptional circumstances that the public interest in maintaining the deportation order will be outweighed by other factors.

Note: Words deleted from 13 December 2012 subject to savings for applications made before that date (HC 760).

391. In the case of a person who has been deported following conviction for a criminal offence, the continuation of a deportation order against that person will be the proper course:

(a) in the case of a conviction for an offence for which the person was sentenced to a period of imprisonment of less than 4 years, unless 10 years have elapsed since the making of the deportation order [when, if an application for revocation is received, consideration will be given on a case by case basis to whether the deportation order should be maintained], or

(b) in the case of a conviction for an offence for which the person was sentenced to a period of imprisonment of at least 4 years, at any time,

Unless, in either case, the continuation would be contrary to the Human Rights Convention or the Convention and Protocol Relating to the Status of Refugees, or there are other exceptional circumstances that mean the continuation is outweighed by compelling factors.

Note: Paragraph 391 substituted from 13 December 2012 subject to savings for applications made before that date (HC 760). Words inserted in subparagraph (a) from 20 October 2014 (HC 693).

391A. In other cases, revocation of the order will not normally be authorised unless the situation has been materially altered, either by a change of circumstances since the order was made, or by fresh information coming to light which was not before the appellate authorities or the Secretary of State. The passage of time since the person was deported may also in itself amount to such a change of circumstances as to warrant revocation of the order.

Note: Paragraph 391A inserted from 13 December 2012 subject to savings for applications made before that date (HC 760).

392. Revocation of a deportation order does not entitle the person concerned to re-enter the United Kingdom; it renders him eligible to apply for admission under the Immigration Rules. Application for revocation of the order may be made to the Entry Clearance Officer or direct to the Home Office.

Rights of appeal in relation to a decision not to revoke a deportation order

393. DELETED

394. DELETED

395. DELETED (from 20 October 2014 (HC 693)).

396. Where a person is liable to deportation the presumption shall be that the public interest requires deportation. It is in the public interest to deport where the Secretary of

State must make a deportation order in accordance with section 32 of the UK Borders Act 2007.

397. A deportation order will not be made if the person's removal pursuant to the order would be contrary to the UK's obligations under the Refugee Convention or the Human Rights Convention. Where deportation would not be contrary to these obligations, it will only be in exceptional circumstances that the public interest in deportation is outweighed.

[Deportation and Article 8]

Note: New heading from 13 December 2012 subject to savings for applications made before that date (HC 760).

A398. These rules apply where:

(a) a foreign criminal liable to deportation claims that his deportation would be contrary to the United Kingdom's obligations under Article 8 of the Human Rights Convention;

(b) a foreign criminal applies for a deportation order made against him to be revoked.

Note: Paragraph A398 inserted from 28 July 2014; this change applies to all ECHR Article 8 claims from foreign criminals which are decided on or after that date (HC 532).

398. Where a person claims that their deportation would be contrary to the UK's obligations under Article 8 of the Human Rights Convention, and

(a) the deportation of the person from the UK is conducive to the public good [and in the public interest] because they have been convicted of an offence for which they have been sentenced to a period of imprisonment of at least 4 years;

(b) the deportation of the person from the UK is conducive to the public good [and in the public interest] because they have been convicted of an offence for which they have been sentenced to a period of imprisonment of less than 4 years but at least 12 months;

or

(c) the deportation of the person from the UK is conducive to the public good [and in the public interest] because, in the view of the Secretary of State, their offending has caused serious harm or they are a persistent offender who shows a particular disregard for the law,

the Secretary of State in assessing that claim will consider whether paragraph 399 or 399A applies and, if it does not, [the public interest in deportation will only be outweighed by other factors where there are very compelling circumstances over and above those described in paragraphs 399 and 399A].

Note: Words inserted in subparagraphs (a), (b) and (c) and words substituted in the last sentence from 28 July 2014; change applies to all ECHR Article 8 claims from foreign criminals which are decided on or after that date (HC 532).

399. This paragraph applies where paragraph 398(b) or (c) applies if –

(a) the person has a genuine and subsisting parental relationship with a child under the age of 18 years who is in the UK, and

(i) the child is a British Citizen; or

(ii) the child has lived in the UK continuously for at least the 7 years immediately preceding the date of the immigration decision; and in either case

(a) [it would be unduly harsh for the child to live in the country to which the person is to be deported]; and

(b) [it would be unduly harsh for the child to remain in the UK without the person who is to be deported]; or

(b) the person has a genuine and subsisting relationship with a partner who is in the UK and is a [British citizen or settled in the UK], and

(i) [the relationship was formed at a time when the person (deportee) was in the UK lawfully and their immigration status was not precarious; and]

(ii) [it would be unduly harsh for that partner to live in the country to which the person is to be deported, because of compelling circumstances over and above those described in paragraph EX.2. of Appendix FM; and]

(iii) [it would be unduly harsh for that partner to remain in the UK without the person who is to be deported.]

Note: Words substituted in subparagraphs (a)(ii)(a) and (a)(ii)(b) and subparagraph (b), subparagraphs (b)(i) and (b)(ii) substituted and subparagraph (b)(iii) inserted from 28 July 2014; changes apply to all ECHR Article 8 claims from foreign criminals which are decided on or after that date (HC 532).

399A. This paragraph applies where paragraph 398(b) or (c) applies if—

[(a) the person has been lawfully resident in the UK for most of his life; and]

[(b) he is socially and culturally integrated in the UK; and]

[(c) there would be very significant obstacles to his integration into the country to which it is proposed he is deported.]

Note: Subparagraphs (a) and (b) substituted and subparagraph (c) inserted from 28 July 2014; changes apply to all ECHR Article 8 claims from foreign criminals which are decided on or after that date (HC 532).

399B. [Where an Article 8 claim from a foreign criminal is successful:

(a) in the case of a person who is in the UK unlawfully or whose leave to enter or remain has been cancelled by a deportation order, limited leave may be granted for periods not exceeding 30 months and subject to such conditions as the Secretary of State considers appropriate;

(b) in the case of a person who has not been served with a deportation order, any limited leave to enter or remain may be curtailed to a period not exceeding 30 months and conditions may be varied to such conditions as the Secretary of State considers appropriate;

(c) indefinite leave to enter or remain may be revoked under section 76 of the 2002 Act and limited leave to enter or remain granted for a period not exceeding 30 months subject to such conditions as the Secretary of State considers appropriate;

(d) revocation of a deportation order does not confer entry clearance or leave to enter or remain or re-instate any previous leave.]

Note: Paragraph 399B substituted from 28 July 2014; change applies to all ECHR Article 8 claims from foreign criminals which are decided on or after that date (HC 532).

399C. DELETED

Note: Paragraph 399C deleted from 13 December 2012 subject to savings for applications made before that date (HC 760), then re-inserted with a substituted wording from 28 July 2014; change applies to all ECHR Article 8 claims from foreign criminals which are decided on or after that date (HC 532).

399D. Where a foreign criminal has been deported and enters the United Kingdom in breach of a deportation order enforcement of the deportation order is in the public interest and will be implemented unless there are very exceptional circumstances.

Note: Paragraph 399D inserted from 28 July 2014; change applies to all ECHR Article 8 claims from foreign criminals which are decided on or after that date (HC 532).

400. Where a person claims that their removal under paragraphs 8 to 10 of Schedule 2 to the Immigration Act 1971, section 10 of the Immigration and Asylum Act 1999 or section 47 of the Immigration, Asylum and Nationality Act 2006 would be contrary to the UK's obligations under Article 8 of the Human Rights Convention, the Secretary of State may require an application under paragraph 276ADE(1) (private life) or under paragraphs RLTRP.1.1.(a), (b) and (d), R-LTRPT.1.1.(a), (b) and (d) and EX.1. of Appendix FM (family life as a partner or parent) of these rules. Where an application is not required, in assessing that claim the Secretary of State or an immigration officer will, subject to paragraph 353, consider that claim against the requirements to be met (except the requirement to make a valid application) under paragraph 276ADE(1) (private life) or paragraphs RLTRP.1.1.(a), (b) and (d), R-LTRPT.1.1.(a), (b) and (d) and EX.1. of Appendix FM (family life as a partner or parent) of these rules as appropriate and if appropriate the removal decision will be cancelled.

Note: Paragraph 400 substituted from 6 November 2014 (HC 693).

Part 14

Note: Part 14 comprising paragraphs 401–416 inserted from 6 April 2013 subject to savings for applications made before that date (HC 1039).

Stateless persons

Definition of a stateless person

401. For the purposes of this Part a stateless person is a person who:

(a) satisfies the requirements of Article 1(1) of the 1954 United Nations Convention relating to the Status of Stateless Persons, as a person who is not considered as a national by any State under the operation of its law;

(b) is in the United Kingdom; and

(c) is not excluded from recognition as a Stateless person under paragraph 402.

Exclusion from recognition as a stateless person

402. A person is excluded from recognition as a stateless person if there are serious reasons for considering that they:

(a) are at present receiving from organs or agencies of the United Nations, other than the United Nations High Commissioner for Refugees, protection or assistance, so long as they are receiving such protection or assistance;

(b) are recognised by the competent authorities of the country of their former habitual residence as having the rights and obligations which are attached to the possession of the nationality of that country;

(c) have committed a crime against peace, a war crime, or a crime against humanity, as defined in the international instruments drawn up to make provisions in respect of such crimes;

(d) have committed a serious non-political crime outside the UK prior to their arrival in the UK;

(e) have been guilty of acts contrary to the purposes and principles of the United Nations.

Requirements for limited leave to remain as a stateless person

403. The requirements for leave to remain in the United Kingdom as a stateless person are that the applicant:

(a) has made a valid application to the Secretary of State for limited leave to remain as a stateless person;

(b) is recognised as a stateless person by the Secretary of State in accordance with paragraph 401;

(c) is not admissible to their country of former habitual residence or any other country; and

(d) has obtained and submitted all reasonably available evidence to enable the Secretary of State to determine whether they are stateless.

Refusal of limited leave to remain as a stateless person

404. An applicant will be refused leave to remain in the United Kingdom as a stateless person if:

(a) they do not meet the requirements of paragraph 403;

(b) there are reasonable grounds for considering that they are:

(i) a danger to the security of the United Kingdom;

(ii) a danger to the public order of the United Kingdom; or

(c) their application would fall to be refused under any of the grounds set out in paragraph 322 of these Rules.

Grant of limited leave to remain to a stateless person

405. Where an applicant meets the requirements of paragraph 403 they may be granted limited leave to remain in the United Kingdom for a period not exceeding 30 months.

Curtailment of limited leave to remain as a stateless person

406. Limited leave to remain as a stateless person under paragraph 405 may be curtailed where the stateless person is a danger to the security or public order of the United Kingdom or where leave would be curtailed pursuant to paragraph 323 of these Rules.

Requirements for indefinite leave to remain as a stateless person

407. The requirements for indefinite leave to remain as a stateless person are that the applicant:

(a) has made a valid application to the Secretary of State for indefinite leave to remain as a stateless person;

(b) was last granted limited leave to remain as a stateless person inaccordance with paragraph 405;

(c) has spent a continuous period of five years in the United Kingdom with lawful leave, except that any period of overstaying for a period of 28 days or less will be disregarded;

(d) continues to meet the requirements of paragraph 403.

Grant of indefinite leave remain as a stateless person

408. Where an applicant meets the requirements of paragraph 407 they may be granted indefinite leave to remain.

Refusal of indefinite leave to remain as a stateless person

409. An applicant will be refused indefinite leave to remain if:

(a) the applicant does not meet the requirements of paragraph 407;

(b) there are reasonable grounds for considering that the applicant is:

(i) a danger to the security of the United Kingdom;

(ii) a danger to the public order of the United Kingdom; or

(c) the application would fall to be refused under any of the grounds set out in paragraph 322 of these Rules.

Requirements for limited leave to enter or remain as the family member of a stateless person

410. For the purposes of this Part a family member of a stateless person means their:

(a) spouse;

(b) civil partner;

(c) unmarried or same sex partner with whom they have lived together in a subsisting relationship akin to marriage or a civil partnership for two years or more;

(d) child under 18 years of age who:

(i) is not leading an independent life;

(ii) is not married or a civil partner; and

(iii) has not formed an independent family unit.

411. The requirements for leave to enter or remain in the United Kingdom as the family member of a stateless person are that the applicant:

(a) has made a valid application to the Secretary of State for leave to enter or remain as the family member of a stateless person;

(b) is the family member of a person granted leave to remain under paragraphs 405 or 408;

(c) if seeking leave to enter, holds a valid United Kingdom entry clearance for entry in this capacity.

Refusal of leave to enter or remain as the family member of a stateless person

412. A family member will be refused leave to enter or remain if:

(a) they do not meet the requirements of paragraph 411;

(b) there are reasonable grounds for considering that:

(i) they are a danger to the security of the United Kingdom;

(ii) they are a danger to the public order of the United Kingdom; or

(c) their application would fall to be refused under any of the grounds set out in paragraph 320, 321 or 322 of these Rules.

Grant of leave to enter or remain as the family member of a stateless person

413. A person who meets the requirements of paragraph 411 may be granted leave to enter or remain for a period not exceeding 30 months.

Curtailment of limited leave to enter or remain as the family member of a stateless person

414. Limited leave to remain as the family member of a stateless person under paragraph 413 may be curtailed where the family member is a danger to the security or public order of the United Kingdom or where leave would be curtailed pursuant to paragraph 323 of these Rules.

Requirements for indefinite leave to remain as the family member of a stateless person

415. The requirements for indefinite leave to remain as the family member of a stateless person are that the applicant:

(a) has made a valid application to the Secretary of State for indefinite leave to remain as the family member of a stateless person;

(b) was last granted limited leave to remain as a family member of a stateless person in accordance with paragraph 413; and

(i) is still a family member of a stateless person; or

(ii) is over 18 and was last granted leave as the family member of a stateless person; and

(a) is not leading an independent life;

(b) is not married or a civil partner;

(c) has not formed an independent family unit; and

(c) has spent a continuous period of five years with lawful leave in the United Kingdom, except that any period of overstaying for a period of 28 days or less will be disregarded.

Refusal of indefinite leave to remain as the family member of a stateless person

416. An applicant will be refused indefinite leave to remain as a family member of a stateless person if:

(a) they do not meet the requirements of paragraph 415;

(b) there are reasonable grounds for considering that:

(i) they are a danger to the security of the United Kingdom;

(ii) they are a danger to the public order of the United Kingdom; or

(c) the application would fall to be refused under any of the grounds set out in paragraph 322 of these Rules.

Appendix 1

Visa requirements for the United Kingdom

1. Subject to paragraph 2 below, the following persons need a visa for the United Kingdom:

(a) Nationals or citizens of the following countries or territorial entities:

Afghanistan
Albania
Algeria
Angola
Armenia
Azerbaijan
Bahrain [(except those referred to in sub-paragraph 2(w) of this Appendix)]
Bangladesh
Belarus
Benin
Bhutan
Bolivia
Bosnia Herzegovina
Burkina Faso
Burma
Burundi
Cambodia
Cameroon
Cape Verde
Central African Republic
Chad
People's Republic of China (except those referred to in sub-paragraphs 2(d) and (e) of this Appendix)
Colombia
Comoros
Congo
Cuba
Democratic Republic of the Congo
Djibouti
Dominican Republic
Ecuador
Egypt
Equatorial Guinea
Eritrea
Ethiopia
Fiji
Gabon
Gambia
Georgia
Ghana
Guinea
Guinea Bissau
Guyana
Haiti
India
Indonesia
Iran
Iraq
Ivory Coast
Jamaica
Jordan
Kazakhstan
Kenya
Korea (North)
Kuwait (except those referred to in sub-paragraph 2(r) of this Appendix)
Kyrgyzstan
Laos
Lebanon
Lesotho
Liberia
Libya
Macedonia
Madagascar
Malawi
Mali
Mauritania
Moldova
Mongolia
Morocco
Mozambique
Nepal
Niger
Nigeria
Oman (except those referred to in sub-paragraphs 2(j) and (u) of this Appendix)
Pakistan
Peru
Philippines
Qatar (except those referred to in sub-paragraph 2(k) and (u) of this Appendix)
Russia
Rwanda
Sao Tome e Principe
Saudi Arabia
Senegal
Serbia
Sierra Leone
Somalia
South Africa
South Sudan
Sri Lanka
Sudan
Surinam
Swaziland
Syria
Taiwan (except those referred to in sub-paragraph 2(h) of this Appendix)
Tajikistan
Tanzania
Thailand
Togo
Tunisia
Turkey (except those referred to in sub-paragraph 2(q) of this Appendix)
Turkmenistan
Uganda

Ukraine	Uzbekistan	Zimbabwe
United Arab Emirates (except those referred to in sub-paragraph 2(l) and (u) of this Appendix)	Venezuela . . .	The territories formerly comprising the socialist Federal Republic of Yugoslavia
	Vietnam	
	Yemen	
	Zambia	

(b) Persons who hold passports or travel documents issued by the former Soviet Union or by the former Socialist Federal Republic of Yugoslavia.

(c) Stateless persons.

(d) Persons travelling on any document other than a national passport, regardless of whether the document is issued by, or evidences nationality of, a state not listed in paragraph (a), except where that document has been issued by the UK.

Note: Words inserted next to the entry for Kuwait from 1 October 2013 subject to savings for applications made before that date (HC 628). Words inserted immediately after Bahrein from 6 April 2014 subject to savings for applications made before that date (HC 1138 as amended by HC 1201). Words omitted immediately after Venezuela from 5 May 2014 (HC 1138 as amended by HC 1201). Subparagraph (d) substituted from 6 November 2014 subject to savings for applications made before that date (HC 693).

2. The following persons do not need a visa for the United Kingdom:

(a) those who qualify for admission to the United Kingdom as returning residents in accordance with paragraph 18;

(b) those who seek leave to enter the United Kingdom within the period of their earlier leave and for the same purpose as that for which that leave was granted, unless it

(i) was for a period of six months or less; or

(ii) was extended by statutory instrument or by section 3C of the Immigration Act 1971 (inserted by section 3 of the Immigration and Asylum Act 1999);

(c) DELETED

(d) those nationals or citizens of the People's Republic of China holding passports issued by Hong Kong Special Administrative Region;

(e) those nationals or citizens of the People's Republic of China holding passports issued by Macao Special Administrative Region;

(f) those who arrive in the United Kingdom with leave to enter which is in force but which was given before arrival, so long as those in question arrive within the period of their earlier leave and for the same purpose as that for which leave was granted, unless that leave—

(i) was for a period of six months or less, or

(ii) was extended by statutory instrument or by section 3C of the Immigration Act 1971 (inserted by section 3 of the Immigration and Asylum Act 1999);

(g) DELETED

(h) those nationals or citizens of Taiwan who hold a passport by Taiwan that includes the number of the identification card issued by the competent authority in Taiwan in it;

(i) DELETED

(j) those nationals or citizens of Oman, who hold diplomatic and special passports issued by Oman when travelling to the UK for the purpose of a general visit in accordance with paragraph 41;

(k) those nationals or citizens of Qatar who hold diplomatic and special passports issued by Qatar when travelling to the UK for the purpose of a general visit in accordance with paragraph 41;

(l) those nationals or citizens of the United Arab Emirates who hold diplomatic and special passports issued by the United Arab Emirates when travelling to the UK for the purpose of a general visit in accordance with paragraph 41;

(m) DELETED
(n) DELETED
(o) DELETED
(p) DELETED

(q) those nationals or citizens of Turkey, who hold diplomatic passports issued by Turkey when travelling to the UK for the purpose of a general visit in accordance with paragraph 41;

(r) those nationals of Kuwait who hold diplomatic and special passports issued by Kuwait when travelling to the UK for the purpose of a general visit in accordance with paragraph 41;

(s) for the period beginning with 4 March 2014 and ending with 3 August 2014, nationals or citizens of the countries or territorial entities listed in paragraph 1 who hold a XX (20th) Commonwealth Games Identity and Accreditation Card issued by the Organising Committee of the Commonwealth Games (Glasgow 2014 Ltd) save for those who are accredited under (and whose card indicates accreditation under) category code WKF or S;

(t) for the period beginning with 4 August 2014 and ending with 3 September 2014 nationals or citizens of the countries or territorial entities listed in paragraph 1 who hold a Commonwealth Games Identity and Accreditation Card issued by Glasgow 2014 Ltd unless

(i) the holder is accredited under (and the card indicates accreditation under) category code WKF or S; or

(ii) the holder had not had leave to enter, leave to remain or entry clearance under paragraph 56ZC or 56ZF at any time during the period beginning with 4 March 2014 and ending with 3 August 2014;

(u) those passport holders of Oman, Qatar or the United Arab Emirates who hold and use an Electronic Visa Waiver (EVW) Document in accordance with paragraphs 3 to 9. Where the passport holder does not hold and use an EVW Document in accordance with paragraphs 3 to 9, the passport holder is a visa national and requires entry clearance;

(v) persons who hold Service, Temporary Service and Diplomatic passports issued by the Holy See;

(w) those nationals or citizens of Bahrain who hold diplomatic and special passports issued by Bahrain when travelling to the UK for the purpose of a general visit in accordance with paragraph 41.

Note: Subparagraphs 2(m) to 2(p) deleted from 6 April 2013 subject to savings for applications made before that date (HC 1039). Subparagraphs 2(r) and 2(s) inserted from 1 October 2013 subject to savings for applications made before that date (HC 628). Subparagraphs 2(s) and 2(t) renumbered from 1 December 2013 (HC 803). Subparagraph 2(u) inserted from 1 January 2013 and subparagraph 2(v) inserted from 30 December 2013 (HC 887). Subparagraphs 2(i) and 2(w) inserted from 6 April 2014 subject to savings for applications made before that date (HC 1138 as amended by HC 1201).

Exception where the applicant holds an Electronic Visa Waiver Document (Oman, Qatar and United Arab Emirates passport holders only)

3. To obtain an Electronic Visa Waiver ("EVW") Document, a person (the "holder") or their agent must provide the required biographic and travel information at the Visa4UK website established by the United Kingdom Government at <http://www.visa4uk.fco.gov.uk/home/evw>. The EVW Document must also specify:

(a) the flight, train or ship on which the holder intends to arrive in the United Kingdom, including the port of departure and arrival, and the scheduled date and time of departure and arrival, unless (b) or (c) applies;

(b) where the holder is seeking to arrive in the UK by entering a control zone in France or Belgium or supplementary control zone in France, the train or ship on which the holder intends to arrive in the United Kingdom, including:

(i) the railway station or port where the holder enters the control zone or supplementary control zone and from which the holder intends to depart for the United Kingdom, and

(ii) the railway station or port at which the holder intends to leave the train or ship after arrival in the United Kingdom, and

(iii) the scheduled date and time of departure from, and of arrival at, the specified railway stations or ports; or

(c) where the holder intends to cross the land border from the Republic of Ireland to the United Kingdom by train, car or any other means, the place at which it is intended to cross and the intended date and time of arrival in the United Kingdom.

When the EVW Document is issued it must be printed in a legible form and in English.

Note: Paragraphs 3–9 inserted from 1 January 2014 (HC 887).

4. An EVW Document is only valid if issued at least 48 hours before the holder departs on a flight, train or ship to the United Kingdom or crosses the United Kingdom land border from the Republic of Ireland by train, car or any other means. An EVW Document may not be issued more than 3 months before the date of the holder's scheduled departure to the United Kingdom as specified on the EVW Document or, where the holder intends to cross the land border with the Republic of Ireland, before the intended date of the holder's arrival in the United Kingdom as specified on the EVW Document.

Note: Paragraphs 3–9 inserted from 1 January 2014 (HC 887).

5. An EVW Document relates to one person and may only be used for one application for leave to enter the United Kingdom or, where applicable, one crossing of the land border from the Republic of Ireland. A child must have a separate EVW Document.

Note: Paragraphs 3–9 inserted from 1 January 2014 (HC 887).

6. The holder must present the EVW Document to an Immigration Officer on request upon the holder's arrival in the United Kingdom or, where the holder is seeking to arrive in the United Kingdom by entering a control zone in France or Belgium or a supplementary control zone in France, upon arrival in that zone. The EVW Document must be surrendered to an Immigration Officer upon request.

Note: Paragraphs 3–9 inserted from 1 January 2014 (HC 887).

7. The holder will be a visa national, and so will require entry clearance, if the biographic details on the EVW Document do not match those on the valid national passport also presented by the holder to the Immigration Officer.

Note: Paragraphs 3–9 inserted from 1 January 2014 (HC 887).

8. The holder will be a visa national, and so will require entry clearance, unless:

(a) the holder travels on the flight, train or ship specified on the EVW Document; or

(b) save where paragraphs (c) or (d) apply, the holder travels on a different flight, train or ship which departs from the same port and arrives at the same United Kingdom port as specified on the EVW Document, and which departs after the departure time specified on the EVW Document but arrives in the United Kingdom no more than 8 hours after the arrival time specified on the EVW Document; or

(c) where the holder is seeking to arrive in the United Kingdom by entering a control zone in France or Belgium or a supplementary control zone in France, the holder travels on a different ship or train which departs from the same railway station or port and arrives in the same United Kingdom railway station or port as specified on the EVW Document, and which departs after, but no more than 8 hours after, the departure time specified on the EVW Document; or

(d) where the holder is seeking to arrive in the United Kingdom by crossing the land border from the Republic of Ireland, the holder crosses the border at the time

specified on the EVW Document or no more than 8 hours after the time specified on the EVW Document.

Note: Paragraphs 3–9 inserted from 1 January 2014 (HC 887).

9. For the purposes of paragraphs 3, 6 and 8, "control zone" means a control zone defined by Article 2(1) and Schedule 1 to the Channel Tunnel (International Arrangements) Order 1993 (SI 1993/1813) and Article 2 of the Nationality Immigration and Asylum Act 2002 (Juxtaposed Controls) Order 2003 (SI 2003/2818), and "supplementary control zone" means a supplementary control zone defined by Article 2(1) and Schedule 1 to the Channel Tunnel (International Agreements) Order 1993 (SI 1993/1813).

Note: Paragraphs 3–9 inserted from 1 January 2014 (HC 887).

Appendix 2

Countries or Territories Whose Nationals or Citizens are Relevant Foreign Nationals for the Purposes of Part 10 of These Rules (Registration with the Police)

Afghanistan	Colombia	Kyrgyzstan
Algeria	Cuba	Lebanon
Argentina	Egypt	Libya
Armenia	Georgia	Moldova
Azerbaijan	Iran	Morocco
Bahrain	Iraq	North Korea
Belarus	Israel	Oman
Bolivia	Jordan	Palestine
Brazil	Kazakhstan	Peru
China	Kuwait	Qatar

Russia
Saudi Arabia
Sudan
Syria
Tajikistan
Tunisia
Turkey
Turkmenistan
United Arab Emirates
Ukraine
Uzbekistan
Yemen

Appendix 6

Disciplines for which an Academic Technology Approval Scheme certificate from the Counter-Proliferation Department of the Foreign and Commonwealth Office is required for the purposes of paragraphs 245ZV and 245ZX of these Rules:

1. Doctorate or Masters by research:

Subjects allied to Medicine:

JACs codes beginning
- B1 – Anatomy, Physiology and Pathology
- B2 – Pharmacology, Toxicology and Pharmacy
- B9 – Others in subjects allied to Medicine

Biological Sciences:

JACs codes beginning
- C1 – Biology
- C2 – Botany
- C4 – Genetics
- C5 – Microbiology
- C7 – Molecular Biology, Biophysics and Biochemistry
- C9 – Others in Biological Sciences

Veterinary Sciences, Agriculture and related subjects:

JACs codes beginning
- D3 – Animal Science
- D9 – Others in Veterinary Sciences, Agriculture and related subjects

Physical Sciences:

JACs codes beginning
- F1 – Chemistry
- F2 – Materials Science
- F3 – Physics

F5 – Astronomy

F8 – Physical and Terrestrial Geographical and Environmental Sciences

F9 – Others in Physical Sciences

Mathematical and Computer Sciences:

JACs codes beginning

G1 – Mathematics

G2 – Operational Research

G4 – Computer Science

G7 – Artificial Intelligence

G9 – Others in Mathematical and Computing Sciences

Engineering:

JACs codes beginning

H1 – General Engineering

H2 – Civil Engineering

H3 – Mechanical Engineering

H4 – Aerospace Engineering

H5 – Naval Architecture

H6 – Electronic and Electrical Engineering

H7 – Production and Manufacturing Engineering

H8 – Chemical, Process and Energy Engineering

H9 – Others in Engineering

Technologies:

JACs codes beginning

J2 – Metallurgy

J4 – Polymers and Textiles

J5 – Materials Technology not otherwise specified

J7 – Industrial Biotechnology

J9 – Others in Technology

2. Taught Masters:

F2 – Materials Science

F3 – Physics (including Nuclear Physics)

H3 – Mechanical Engineering

H4 – Aerospace Engineering

J5 – Materials Technology/Materials Science not otherwise specified

For courses commencing on or after 1 January 2012

1. Doctorate or Masters by Research:

JACs codes beginning:

G0 – Mathematical and Computer Sciences

I1 – Computer Science

I4 – Artificial Intelligence

I9 – Others in Computer Science

2. Taught Masters:

H8 – Chemical, Process and Energy Engineering

Appendix 7

Statement of Written Terms and Conditions of employment required in [paragraphs 159A(v), 159D(iv) and 159EA(iii)]

Statement of the terms and conditions of employment of an overseas domestic worker in a private household in the United Kingdom

This form must be completed and signed by the employer, signed by the overseas domestic worker and submitted with the entry clearance application or with the leave to remain application as required by [paragraphs 159A(v), 159D(iv) and 159EA(iii)] of the Immigration Rules.

Please complete this form in capitals

Name of employee:

Name of employer:

1. Job Title:
2. Duties/Responsibilities:
3. Date of start of employment in the UK:
4. Employer's address in the UK:
5. Employee's address in the UK (if different from 4 please explain):
6. Employee's place of work in the UK (if different from 4 please explain):
7. Rate of Pay per week/month:

Note: By signing this document, the employer is declaring that the employee will be paid in accordance with the National Minimum Wage Act 1998 and any Regulations made under it for the duration of the employment.

8. Hours of work per day/week:

   Free periods per day:
   Free periods per week:
9. Details of sleeping accommodation:

10. Details of Holiday entitlement:

11. Ending the employment:

Employee must give ________ weeks notice if he/she decides to leave his/her job.

Employee is entitled to ________ weeks notice if the employer decides to dismiss him/her.

Employee is employed on a fixed-term contract until (date) [if applicable].

Signed ________ Date ________ (Employer)

I confirm that the above reflects my conditions of employment:

Signed ________ Date ________ (Employee)

Note: Words in square brackets substituted from 13 December 2012 subject to savings for applications made before that date (HC 760).

Appendix A

Attributes

Attributes for Tier 1 (Exceptional Talent) Migrants

1. An applicant applying for entry clearance, leave to remain or indefinite leave to remain as a Tier 1 (Exceptional Talent) Migrant must score 75 points for attributes.

2. Available points are shown in Table 1.

3. Notes to accompany the table are shown below the table.

Table 1

[Applications for entry clearance and leave to remain where the applicant does not have, or has not last had, leave as a Tier 1 (Exceptional Talent) Migrant]

Criterion	Points
Endorsed by Designated Competent Body according to that Body's criteria as set out in Appendix L.	75

[All other applications for entry clearance and leave to remain and applications for indefinite leave to remain]

Criterion	Points
(i) During his most recent period of leave as a Tier 1 (Exceptional Talent) Migrant, the applicant has earned money in the UK as a result of employment or self-employment in his expert field as previously endorsed by a Designated Competent Body; and (ii) That Designated Competent Body has not withdrawn its endorsement of the applicant.	75

Note: Headings substituted from 6 April 2014 subject to savings for applications made before that date (HC 1138 as amended by HC 1201).

Notes

Tier 1 (Exceptional Talent) Limit

4. (a) The Secretary of State shall be entitled to limit the total number of Tier 1 (Exceptional Talent) endorsements Designated Competent Bodies may make in support of successful applications, [for entry clearance and leave to remain] in a particular period, to be referred to as the Tier 1 (Exceptional Talent) Limit.

(b) The Tier 1 (Exceptional Talent) Limit is 1,000 endorsements in total per year (beginning on 6 April and ending on 5 April) which will be allocated to the Designated Competent Bodies as follows:

(i) 250 endorsements to The Arts Council for the purpose of endorsing applicants with exceptional talent in the fields of arts and culture;

(ii) 250 endorsements to The Royal Society for the purpose of endorsing applicants with exceptional talent in the fields of natural sciences and medical science research;

(iii) 150 endorsements to The Royal Academy of Engineering for the purpose of endorsing applicants with exceptional talent in the field of engineering

(iv) 150 endorsements to The British Academy for the purpose of endorsing applicants with exceptional talent in the fields of humanities and social sciences; and

(v) 200 endorsements to Tech City UK for the purpose of endorsing applicants with exceptional talent in the field of digital technology.

(c) The Tier 1 (Exceptional Talent) Limit will be operated according to the practice set out in paragraph 5 below.

(d) If a Designated Competent Body chooses to transfer part of its unused allocation of endorsements to another Designated Competent Body by mutual agreement of both bodies and the Secretary of State, the allocations of both bodies will be adjusted accordingly and the adjusted allocations will be published on the [visas and immigration pages of the gov.uk website].

Note: Words inserted in subparagraph (a) from 6 April 2013 subject to savings for applications made before that date (HC 1039). Subparagraph (b) substituted and words in square brackets in subparagraph (d) substituted from 6 April 2014 subject to savings for applications made before that date (HC 1138 as amended by HC 1201).

5. (a) Before an applicant applies for entry clearance or leave to remain (unless he has, or last had, leave as a Tier 1 (Exceptional Talent) Migrant), he must make an application for a Designated Competent Body endorsement, and this application must:

(i) be made to the UK Border Agency using the specified form,

(ii) state which Designated Competent Body he wishes to endorse his application, and

(iii) provide the specified evidence set out in Appendix L.

(b) A number of endorsements will be made available for each Designated Competent Body, as follows:

(i) From 6 April to 30 September each year, half that body's allocated endorsements under paragraph 4 above.

(ii) From 1 October to 5 April each year, that body's remaining unused allocated endorsements under paragraph 4 above.

(c) Unused endorsements will not be carried over from one year to the next.

(d) If a Designated Competent Body endorses an application for an endorsement, the applicant subsequently uses that endorsement to make an application for entry clearance or leave to remain which is refused, and that refusal is not subsequently overturned, the used endorsement will be returned to the number of endorsements available for the relevant Designated Competent Body, providing the end of the period (6 April to 5 April) to which it relates has not yet passed.

(e) An application for a Designated Competent Body endorsement will be refused if the Designated Competent Body has reached or exceeded the number of endorsements available to it.

(f) The number of endorsements available for each Designated Competent Body to endorse Tier 1 (Exceptional Talent) applicants in a particular period, will be reduced by one for each Croatian national that body endorses in that period for the purposes of applying to be deemed a highly skilled person under the Accession of Croatia (Immigration and Worker Authorisation) Regulations 2013.

Note: Subparagraphs (a), (d) and (e) substituted from 6 April 2013 subject to savings for applications made before that date (HC 1039). Subparagraph (f) inserted from 1 October 2013 subject to savings for applications made before that date (HC 628).

Endorsement by the relevant Designated Competent Body

6. Points will only be awarded in an application for entry clearance or leave to remain (except where the applicant has, or last had, leave as a Tier 1 (Exceptional Talent) Migrant) for an endorsement from the relevant Designated Competent Body if:

(a) the applicant provides a valid approval letter from the UK Border Agency for a Designated Competent Body endorsement, which was granted to him no more than three months before the date of the application for entry clearance or leave to remain, and

(b) the endorsement has not been withdrawn by the relevant Designated Competent Body at the time the application is considered by the UK Border Agency.

Note: Paragraph 6 substituted from 6 April 2013 subject to savings for applications made before that date (HC 1039).

Money earned in the UK

6A. Points will only be awarded for money earned in the UK if the applicant provides the following specified documents:

(a) If the applicant is a salaried employee, the specified documents are at least one of the following:

(i) payslips confirming his earnings, which must be either:

(1) original formal payslips issued by the employer and showing the employer's name, or

(2) accompanied by a letter from the applicant's employer, on company headed paper and signed by a senior official, confirming the payslips are authentic;

or

(ii) personal bank statements on official bank stationery, showing the payments made to the applicant; or

(iii) electronic bank statements . . ., which either:

(1) are accompanied by a supporting letter from the bank on company headed paper confirming that the documents are authentic, or

(2) bear the official stamp of the issuing bank on every page of the document;

or

(iv) an official tax document produced by HM Revenue & Customs or the applicant's employer, which shows earnings on which tax has been paid or will be paid in a tax year, and is either:

(1) a document produced by HM Revenue & Customs that shows details of declarable taxable income on which tax has been paid or will be paid in a tax year, such as a tax refund letter or tax demand,

(2) a P60 document produced by an employer as an official return to HM Revenue & Customs, showing details of earnings on which tax has been paid in a tax year, or

(3) a document produced by a person, business, or company as an official return to HM Revenue & Customs, showing details of earnings on which tax has been paid or will be paid in a tax year, and which has been approved, registered, or stamped by HM Revenue & Customs;

or

(v) Dividend vouchers, confirming the gross and net dividend paid by a company to the applicant, normally from its profits. The applicant must provide a separate dividend voucher or payment advice slip for each dividend payment.

(b) If the applicant has worked in a self-employed capacity, the specified documents are at least one of the following:

(i) A letter from the applicant's accountant (who must be either a fully qualified chartered accountant or a certified accountant who is a member of a registered body in the UK), on headed paper, which shows a breakdown of the gross and net earnings. The letter should give a breakdown of salary, dividends, profits, tax credits and dates of net payments earned. If the applicant's earnings are a share of the net profit of the company, the letter should also explain this; or

(ii) Company or business accounts that meet statutory requirements and clearly show:

(1) the net profit of the company or business made over the earnings period to be assessed,

(2) both a profit and loss account (or income and expenditure account if the organisation is not trading for profit), and

(3) a balance sheet signed by a director;

or

(iii) If the applicant has worked as a sponsored researcher, a letter on official headed paper to the applicant from the institution providing the funding, which confirms:

(1) the applicant's name,

(2) the name of the sponsoring institution providing the funding,

(3) the name of the host institution where the applicant's sponsored research is based,

(4) the title of the post, and

(5) details of the funding provided.

(c) All applicants must also provide at least one of the following specified documents:

(i) A contract of service or work between the applicant and a UK employer or UK institution which indicates the field of work he has undertaken; or

(ii) A letter from a UK employer or UK institution on its official headed paper, confirming that the applicant has earned money in his expert field.

Note: Subparagraph (a)(i)(1) substituted, original subparagraph (a)(i)(2) deleted and subparagraph (a)(i)(3) renumbered as subparagraph (a)(i)(2) and words deleted from subparagraph (a)(iii) from 1 October 2013 subject to savings for applications made before that date (HC 628).

Attributes for Tier 1 (General) Migrants

7. An applicant applying for leave to remain or indefinite leave to remain as a Tier 1 (General) Migrant must score 75 points for attributes, if the applicant has, or has had, leave as a Highly Skilled Migrant, as a Writer, Composer or Artist, Self-employed Lawyer, or as a Tier 1 (General) Migrant under the rules in place before 19 July 2010, and has not been granted leave in any categories other than these under the rules in place since 19 July 2010.

8. An applicant applying for leave to remain or indefinite leave to remain as a Tier 1 (General) Migrant who does not fall within the scope of paragraph 7 above or paragraph 9 below must score 80 points for attributes.

9. An applicant applying for indefinite leave to remain as a Tier 1 (General) Migrant is not required to score points for attributes if he:

(a) received a Highly Skilled Migrant Programme approval letter issued on the basis of an application made before 7 November 2006,

(b) was subsequently granted entry clearance or leave to remain on the basis of that letter, and

(c) has not since been granted entry clearance or leave to remain in any category other than as a Highly Skilled Migrant or Tier 1 (General) Migrant.

Note: Paragraph 9 substituted from 6 April 2014 subject to savings for applications made before that date (HC 1138 as amended by HC 1201).

10. Available points are shown in Table 2 and Table 3 below. only one set of points will be awarded per column in each table. For example, points will only be awarded for one qualification.

11. Notes to accompany Table 2 and Table 3 appear below Table 3.

Table 2: Applications for leave to remain and indefinite leave to remain where the applicant has, or has had, leave as a Highly Skilled Migrant, as a Writer, Composer or Artist, Self-employed Lawyer, or as a Tier 1 (General) Migrant under the rules in place before 6 April 2010, and has not been granted leave in any categories other than these since 6 April 2010

Qualification	Points	Previous earnings	Points	UK experience	Points	Age (at date of application for first grant)	Points
Bachelor's degree (see paragraph 13 below)	30	£16,000–£17,999.99 (see paragraph 18 below)	5	If £16,000 or more of the previous earnings for which points are claimed were earned in the UK	5	Under 28 years of age	20

Master's Degree	35	£18,000–£19,999.99 (see paragraph 18 below)	10	If £16,000 or more of the previous earnings for which points are claimed were earned in the UK	28 or 29 years of age	10
PhD	50	£20,000–£22,999.99	15		30 or 31 years of age	5
		£23,000–£25,999.99	20			
		£26,000–£28,999.99	25			
		£29,000–£31,999.99	30			
		£32,000–£34,999.99	35			
		£35,000–£39,999.99	40			
		£40,000 or more	45			

Table 3: All other applications for leave to remain and indefinite leave to remain

Qualification	Points	Previous earnings	Points	UK experience	Points	Age (at date of application for first grant)	Points
Bachelor's Degree	30		5	If £25,000 or more of the previous earnings for which points are claimed were earned in the UK	5	Under 30 years of age	20
Master's Degree	35	£30,000–£34,999.99	15			30 to 34 years of age	10
PhD	45	£35,000–£39,999.99	20			35 to 39 years of age	5
		£40,000–£49,999.99	25				
		£50,000–£54,999.99	30				
		£55,000–£64,999.99	35				
		£65,000–£74,999.99	40				
		£75,000–£149,999.99	45				
		£150,000 or more	80				

Notes

12. Qualifications and/or earnings will not be taken into account if the applicant was in breach of the UK's immigration laws at the time those qualifications were studied for or those earnings were made.

Qualifications: notes

13. An applicant will be awarded no points for a Bachelor's degree if:

(a) his last grant of entry clearance was as a Tier 1 (General) Migrant under the rules in place between 31 March 2009 and 5 April 2010, or

(b)

(i) he has had leave to remain as a Tier 1 (General) Migrant under the rules in place between 31 March 2009 and 5 April 2010, and

(ii) his previous entry clearance, leave to enter or leave to remain before that leave was not as a Highly skilled Migrant, as a Writer, Composer or artist, as a self-employed lawyer, or as a Tier 1 (General) Migrant.

14. The specified documents in paragraph 14-SD must be provided as evidence of the qualification, unless the applicant has, or was last granted, leave as a Highly skilled Migrant or a Tier 1 (General) Migrant and previously scored points for the same qualification in respect of which points are being claimed in this application.

14-SD. (a) The specified documents in paragraph 14 are:

(i) The original certificate of award of the qualification, which clearly shows the:

(1) applicant's name,

(2) title of the award,

(3) date of the award, and

(4) name of the awarding institution,

or

(ii) if:

(1) the applicant is awaiting graduation having successfully completed his degree, or

(2) the applicant no longer has the certificate and the institution who issued the certificate is unable to produce a replacement,

an original academic reference from the institution that is awarding the degree together with an original academic transcript, unless (d) applies.

(b) The academic reference referred to in (a)(ii) must be on the official headed paper of the institution and clearly show the:

(1) applicant's name,

(2) title of award,

(3) date of award, confirming that it has been or will be awarded, and

(4) either the date that the certificate will be issued (if the applicant has not yet graduated) or confirmation that the institution is unable to re-issue the original certificate or award.

(c) The academic transcript referred to in (a)(ii) must be on the institution's official paper and must show the:

(1) applicant's name,

(2) name of the academic institution,

(3) course title, and

(4) confirmation of the award.

(d) If the applicant cannot provide his original certificate for one of the reasons given in (a)(ii) and is claiming points for a qualification with a significant research bias, such as a doctorates, an academic transcript is not required, providing the applicant provides an academic reference which includes all the information detailed in (b) above.

(e) Where an applicant cannot find details of his academic qualification on the points based calculator on the [visas and immigration pages of the gov.uk website], he must, in addition to the document or documents in (a), provide an original letter or certificate from UK NARIC confirming the equivalency of the level of his qualification.

(f) Where an applicant cannot find details of his professional or vocational qualification on the points based calculator, he must, in addition to the document or documents in (a), provide an original letter from the appropriate UK professional body confirming the equivalence to UK academic levels of his qualification, which clearly shows:

(1) the name of the qualification, including the country and awarding body, and

(2) confirmation of which UK academic level this qualification is equivalent to.

Note: Words substituted in subparagraph (e) from 6 April 2014 subject to savings for applications made before that date (HC 1138 as amended by HC 1201).

15. Points will only be awarded for an academic qualification if an applicant's qualification is deemed by the national academic recognition information Centre for the United Kingdom (UK NARIC) to meet or exceed the recognised standard of a Bachelor's or Master's degree or a PhD, as appropriate, in the UK.

16. Points will also be awarded for vocational and professional qualifications that are deemed by UK NARIC or the appropriate UK professional body to be equivalent to a Bachelor's or Master's degree or a PhD in the UK.

17. If the applicant has, or was last granted, leave as a Tier 1 (General) Migrant or a Highly skilled Migrant and the qualification for which points are now claimed was, in the applicant's last successful application for leave or for a Highly Skilled Migrant Programme approval letter, assessed to be of a higher level than now indicated by UK NARIC, the higher score of points will be awarded in this application too.

Previous earnings: notes

18. An applicant will be awarded no points for previous earnings of less than £20,000 if:

(a) his last grant of entry clearance was as a Tier 1 (General) Migrant under the rules in place between 31 March 2009 and 5 April 2010, or

(b) (i) he has had leave to remain as a Tier 1 (General) Migrant under the rules in place between 31 March 2009 and 5 April 2010, and

(ii) his previous entry clearance, leave to enter or leave to remain before that leave was not as a Highly Skilled Migrant, as a Writer, Composer or artist, as a self-employed lawyer, or as a Tier 1 (General) Migrant.

19. (a) In all cases, the applicant must provide at least two different types of the specified documents in paragraph 19-SD(a) from two or more separate sources as evidence for each source of previous earnings.

(b) If the applicant is claiming points for self-employed earnings made in the UK, he must also provide the specified documents in paragraph 19-SD(b) to show that:

(i) he is registered as self-employed,

(ii) he was registered as self-employed during the period(s) of self-employment used to claim points, and

(iii) he was paying Class 2 National Insurance contributions during the period(s) of self-employment used to claim points.

(c) Each piece of supporting evidence must support all the other evidence and, where appropriate, be accompanied by any information or explanation of the documents submitted, including further documents such as a letter of explanation from the applicant's accountant, so that together the documents clearly prove the earnings claimed.

(d) Full contact details must be provided for each supporting document for verification purposes.

(e) Where an applicant is providing bank statements as evidence, the bank statements provided must:

(i) be on official bank stationery, and must show each of the payments that the applicant is claiming, or

(ii) electronic bank statements . . ., which either:

(1) are accompanied by a supporting letter from the bank on company headed paper confirming that the documents are authentic, or

(2) bear the official stamp of the issuing bank on every page of the statement.

(f) Where an applicant is providing official tax documents as evidence, the documents must be:

(i) a document produced by a tax authority that shows details of declarable taxable income on which tax has been paid or will be paid in a tax year (for example a tax refund letter or tax demand),

(ii) a document produced by an employer as an official return to a tax authority, showing details of earnings on which tax has been paid in a tax year (for example a P60 in the United Kingdom), or

(iii) a document produced by a person, business, or company as an official return to a tax authority, showing details of earnings on which tax has been paid or will be paid in a tax year, and which has been approved, registered, or stamped by the tax authority.

(g) (i) Where an applicant is providing evidence from an accountant or accountancy firm, the accountant must be either a fully qualified chartered accountant or a certified accountant who is a member of a registered body.

(ii) If the earnings were for work done while the applicant was in the UK, such evidence must come from an accountant or accountancy firm in the UK who is a member of one of the following recognised supervisory bodies:

(1) The Institute of Chartered Accountants in England and Wales (ICAEW),

(2) The Institute of Chartered Accountants in Scotland (ICAS),

(3) The Institute of Chartered Accountants in Ireland (ICAI),

(4) The Association of Chartered Certified Accountants (ACCA),

(5) The Chartered Institute of Public Finance and Accountancy (CIPFA),

(6) The Institute of Financial Accountants (IFA),

(7) The Chartered Institute of Management Accountants (CIMA), or

(8) The Association of International Accountants (AIA).

(iii) If the earnings were made while the applicant was not in the UK, the evidence must come from an accountant or accountancy firm which meets the requirements in (ii) or appears on the list of full members given on the website of the International Federation of Accountants.

(h) If the applicant has exchanged some of his UK employment rights for shares as an employee-owner, the value of those shares will not be included when calculating the applicant's previous earnings.

(i) The Secretary of State must be satisfied that the earnings are from genuine employment. If the Secretary of State is not satisfied, points for those earnings will not be awarded.

(j) In making the assessment in paragraph 19(i), the Secretary of State will assess on the balance of probabilities and may take into account the following factors:

(i) the evidence the applicant has submitted;

(ii) whether the money appears to have been earned through genuine employment, rather than being borrowed, gifted, or otherwise shown in the applicant's financial transactions or records without being earned;

(iii) whether the business from which the earnings are claimed can be shown to exist and be lawfully and genuinely trading;

(iv) verification of previous earnings claims with declarations made in respect of the applicant to other Government Departments, including declarations made in respect of earnings claimed by the applicant in previous applications;

(v) the applicant's previous educational and business experience (or lack thereof) in relation to the claimed business activity;

(vi) the applicant's immigration history and previous activity in the UK;

(vii) where the nature of the applicant's employment or business requires him to have mandatory accreditation, registration or insurance, whether that accreditation, registration or insurance has been obtained;

(viii) any payments made by the applicant to other parties; and

(ix) any other relevant information.

(k) To support the assessment in paragraph 19(i), the Secretary of State may:

(i) request additional information and evidence, and refuse the application if the information or evidence is not provided. Any requested documents must be received by the Secretary of State at the address specified in the request within 28 [calendar] days of the date the request is sent, and

(ii) request the applicant attends an interview, and refuse the application if the applicant fails to comply with any such request without providing a reasonable explanation.

(l) The Secretary of State may decide not to carry out the assessment in paragraph 19(i) if the application already falls for refusal on other grounds, but reserves the right to carry out this assessment in any reconsideration of the decision.

Note: Subparagraph (h) inserted from 6 April 2013 subject to savings for applications made before that date (HC 1039). Words deleted from subparagraph (e)(ii) and subparagraphs (i) to (l) inserted from 1 October 2013 (change to subparagraph (e)(ii) subject to savings for applications made before that date) (HC 628). Subparagraph (g)(ii)(8) inserted from 6 April 2014 subject to savings for applications made before that date (HC 1138 as amended by HC 1201). Word substituted in subparagraph (k)(i) from 6 November 2014 subject to savings for applications made before that date (HC 693).

19-SD. (a) The specified documents in paragraph 19(a) are:

(i) Payslips covering the whole period claimed, which must be either:

(1) original formal payslips issued by the employer and showing the employer's name, or

(2) accompanied by a letter from the applicant's employer, on the employer's headed paper and signed by a senior official, confirming the payslips are authentic;

(ii) Personal bank statements showing the payments made to the applicant;

(iii) A letter from the applicant's employer(s) during the period claimed (or in the case of winnings, the relevant awarding body), on company headed paper, which:

(1) is dated after the period for which earnings are being claimed, and

(2) clearly confirms the applicant's gross and net earnings during the period claimed, and the date and amount of each payment;

(iv) Official tax document produced by the relevant tax authority or employer, showing earnings on which tax has been paid or will be paid in a tax year;

(v) Dividend vouchers which show the amount of money paid by the company to the applicant, normally from its profits, and which confirm both the gross and net dividend paid. The applicant must provide a separate dividend voucher or payment advice slip for each dividend payment, to cover the whole period claimed;

(vi) If the applicant is claiming points for self-employed earnings, a letter from his accountant on headed paper, confirming that the applicant received the exact amount he is claiming, or the net profit to which he is entitled. This is a letter from the applicant's accountant on headed paper confirming the gross and net pay for the period claimed. The letter should give a breakdown of salary, dividends, profits, tax credits and dates of net payments earned. If the applicant's earnings are a share of the net profit of the company, the letter should also explain this;

(vii) Invoice explanations or payment summaries from the applicant's accountant, which include a breakdown of the gross salary, tax deductions and dividend payments made to the applicant, and which enable the UK Border Agency to check that the total gross salary and dividend payments correspond with the net payments into the applicant's personal bank account.

(viii) Company or business accounts that meet statutory requirements and clearly show:

(1) the net profit of the company or business made over the earnings period to be assessed,

(2) both a profit and loss account (or income and expenditure account if the organisation is not trading for profit), and

(3) a balance sheet signed by a director;

(ix) Business bank statements showing the payments made to the applicant;

(x) If the applicant provides a combination of bank statements and a letter or invoice summary from his accountant, he must also provide any invoices generated during the period for which earnings are being claimed.

(b) The specified documents in paragraph 19(b) are:

(i) If the applicant's National Insurance is paid by bill, the original bill from the billing period immediately before the application.

(ii) If the applicant's National Insurance is paid by direct debit, the most recent bank statement issued before the application, showing the direct debit payment of National Insurance to HM Revenue & Customs.

(iii) If the applicant has low earnings, an original small earnings exception certificate issued by HM Revenue & Customs for the most recent return date.

(iv) If the applicant has not yet received the documents in (i) to (iii), the original, dated welcome letter from HM Revenue & Customs containing the applicant's unique taxpayer reference number.

Note: Subparagraph (a)(i) substituted from 1 October 2013 subject to savings for applications made before that date (HC 628).

Period for assessment

20. Applicants should indicate in the application form for which 12-month period their earnings should be assessed.

21. (a) for all applicants the period for assessment of earnings must:

(i) consist of no more than 12 months which must run consecutively, and

(ii) fall within the 15 months immediately preceding the application.

(b) if the applicant:

(i) has been on maternity or adoption leave at some point within the 12 months preceding the application, and

(ii) has provided the specified documents, or where due to exceptional circumstances the specified documents in paragraph 21-SD are not available, has provided alternative documents which show that the circumstances provided for in (i) apply,

the applicant may choose for a period of no more than 12 months spent on maternity or adoption leave to be disregarded when calculating both the 12-month and 15-month period.

21-SD (a) Where paragraph 21(b)(ii) states that specified documents must be provided, the applicant must provide:

(i) The document in (b) below, if it has been issued, and

(ii) If the document in (b) has been issued and is provided, the documents in either (c)(i) or (c)(ii) below, or

(iii) If the document in (b) has not been issued, the documents in both (c)(i) and (ii) below, or

(iv) If the applicant is unable to satisfy (ii) or (iii) above:

(1) the documents in either (b) or (c)(i) or (c)(ii),

(2) a satisfactory explanation as to why the other types of document cannot be provided, and

(3) one of the types of documents in (d) below.

The specified documents are:

(b) The original full birth certificate or original full certificate of adoption (as appropriate), containing the names of parents or adoptive parents of the child for whom the period of maternity or adoption-related absence was taken;

(c) (i) An original letter from the applicant's employer, on the company headed paper, which confirms the start and end dates of the period of maternity or adoption-related absence;

(ii) Original payslips or other payment or remittance documents, on the official letter-headed paper of the issuing authority, and covering the entire period for which the maternity or adoption-related absence is being claimed and showing the statutory maternity or adoption payments to the applicant;

(d) One of the following documents, from an official source and which is independently verifiable:

(i) official adoption papers issued by the relevant authority;

(ii) any relevant medical documents

(iii) a relevant extract from a register of birth accompanied by an original letter from the issuing authority.

22. If the applicant has not indicated a period for assessment of earnings, or has indicated a period which does not meet the conditions in paragraph 21 above, their earnings

will be assessed against the 12-month period immediately preceding their application, assuming the specified documents in paragraph 19-SD above have been provided. Where the specified documents in paragraph 19-SD above have not been provided, points will not be awarded for previous earnings.

Earnings

23. Earnings include, but are not limited to:

(a) salaries (includes full-time, part-time and bonuses),

(b) earnings derived through self-employment,

(c) earnings derived through business activities,

(d) statutory and contractual maternity pay, statutory and contractual adoption pay,

(e) allowances (such as accommodation, schooling or car allowances) which form part of an applicant's remuneration package and are specified in the applicant's payslips,

(f) dividends paid by a company in which the applicant is active in the day-to-day management, or where the applicant receives the dividend as part or all of their remuneration package,

(g) property rental income, where this constitutes part of the applicant's business, and

(h) payments in lieu of notice.

24. Where the earnings take the form of a salary or wages, they will be assessed before tax (i.e. gross salary).

25. Where the earnings are the profits of a business derived through self-employment or other business activities:

(a) the earnings that will be assessed are the profits of the business before tax. Where the applicant only has a share of the business, the earnings that will be assessed are the profits of the business before tax to which the applicant is entitled, and

(b) the applicant must be registered as self-employed in the UK, and must provide the specified evidence.

26. Earnings do not include unearned sources of income, such as:

(a) allowances (such as accommodation, schooling or car allowances) which are paid as reimbursement for monies the applicant has previously paid,

(b) any other allowances, unless part of the applicant's remuneration package and specified in the applicant's payslips,

(c) dividends, unless paid by a company in which the applicant is active in the day-to-day management, or unless the applicant receives the dividend as part or all of their remuneration package,

(d) property rental income, unless this constitutes part of the applicant's business,

(e) interest on savings and investments,

(f) funds received through inheritance,

(g) employer pension contributions or monies paid to the applicant as a pension,

(h) expenses where the payment constitutes a reimbursement for monies the applicant has previously outlaid,

(i) redundancy payment,

(j) sponsorship for periods of study,

(k) state benefits, or

(l) prize money or competition winnings, other than where they are directly related to the applicant's main profession or occupation.

Note: Subparagraph (g) substituted from 13 December 2012 (HC 760).

Converting foreign currencies

27. Earnings in a foreign currency will be converted to pound sterling (£) using the closing spot exchange rate for the last day of the period for which the applicant has claimed earnings in that currency.

28. If the applicant's earnings fall either side of a period of maternity or adoption leave, earnings in a foreign currency will be converted to pounds sterling (£) using the closing spot exchange rate which exists:

(a) for the earnings earned before maternity or adoption leave, on the last day of the period before maternity leave, and

(b) for the earnings earned after maternity or adoption leave, on the last day of the period after maternity leave.

29. The spot exchange rate which will be used is that which appears on <www.oanda.com>*

30. Where the previous earnings claimed are in different currencies, any foreign currencies will be converted before being added together, and then added to any UK earnings, to give a total amount.

UK experience: notes

31. Previous earnings will not be taken into account for the purpose of awarding points for UK experience if the applicant was not physically present in the UK at the time those earnings were made.

32. Previous earnings will not be taken into account for the purpose of awarding points for UK experience if the applicant was physically present in the Isle of Man or the Channel Islands at the time those earnings were made.

Age: notes

33. If the applicant was first granted leave in the categories of Highly Skilled Migrant, Writer, Composer or Artist, Self-employed Lawyer or Tier 1 (General) Migrant and has not been granted leave in any category other than those listed here since the first grant of leave, points will be awarded based on the applicant's age at the date of the application for that first grant of leave. If the applicant has been granted leave since his first grant of leave in a category not listed in this paragraph, points will be awarded based on his age at the date of application for a grant of leave in a category listed in this paragraph where leave has not been granted in any category not listed in this paragraph between that grant of leave and the current application.

34. The specified documents in paragraph 34-SD must be provided as evidence of age.

34-SD. The specified documents in paragraph 34 are:

(i) The applicant's Biometric Residence Permit, which contains the date of approval of the last grant of leave and the age of the applicant; or

(ii) The applicant's current valid original passport or travel document containing the last [entry clearance] granted to the applicant.

Note: Words substituted in subparagraph (ii) from 13 December 2012 (HC 760).

Attributes for Tier 1 (Entrepreneur) Migrants

35. An applicant applying for entry clearance, leave to remain or indefinite leave to remain as a Tier 1 (Entrepreneur) Migrant must score 75 points for attributes.

36. Subject to paragraph 37, available points for applications for entry clearance or leave to remain are shown in Table 4.

36A. An applicant who is applying for leave to remain and has, or was last granted, entry clearance, leave to enter or leave to remain as:

(i) a Tier 4 Migrant,

(ii) a Student,

(iii) a Student Nurse,

(iv) a Student Re-sitting an Examination, or

(v) a Student Writing Up a Thesis,

will only be awarded points under [the provisions in (b)(ii) or (b)(iii)] in Table 4.

Note: Paragraph 36A inserted from 13 December 2012 subject to savings for applications made before that date (HC 760). Words substituted from 11 July 2014 subject to savings for applications made before that date (HC 532).

36B. An applicant who is applying for leave to remain and has, or was last granted, entry clearance, leave to enter or leave to remain as a Tier 1 (Post-Study Work) Migrant will only be awarded points under the provisions in (b)(ii), (b)(iii) or (d) in Table 4.

Note: Paragraph 36B inserted from 11 July 2014 subject to savings for applications made before that date (HC 532).

37. Available points are shown in Table 5 for an applicant who:

(a) has had entry clearance, leave to enter or leave to remain as a Tier 1 (Entrepreneur) Migrant, a Businessperson or an Innovator in the 12 months immediately before the date of application, or

(b) is applying for leave to remain and has, or was last granted, entry clearance, leave to enter or leave to remain as a Tier 1 (Entrepreneur) Migrant, a Businessperson or an Innovator.

38. Available points for applications for indefinite leave to remain are shown in Table 6.

39. (a) Notes to accompany Table 4 appear below Table 4.

(b) Notes to accompany Tables 4, 5 and 6 appear below Table 6.

40. In all cases, an applicant cannot use the same funds to score points for attributes under this Appendix and to score points for maintenance funds for himself or his dependants under Appendices C or E.

Note: Paragraph 40 inserted from 1 October 2013 subject to savings for applications made before that date (HC 628).

Table 4: Applications for entry clearance or leave to remain referred to in paragraph 36

Investment and business activity	Points
(a) The applicant has access to not less than £200,000, or (b) The applicant has access to not less than £50,000 from: (i) one or more registered venture capitalist firms [regulated by the Financial Conduct Authority (FCA)], (ii) one or more UK Entrepreneurial seed funding competitions which is listed as endorsed on the UK Trade & Investment website, or (iii) one or more UK Government Departments, [or Devolved Government Departments in Scotland, Wales or Northern Ireland,] and made available by the Department(s) for the specific purpose of establishing or expanding a UK business, or (c) The applicant: (i) is applying for leave to remain, (ii) has, or was last granted, leave as a Tier 1 (Graduate Entrepreneur) Migrant, and (iii) has access to not less than £50,000, or (d) The applicant: (i) is applying for leave to remain, (ii) has, or was lasted granted, leave as a Tier 1 (Post-Study Work) Migrant, (iii) since before 11 July 2014 and up to the date of his application, has been continuously engaged in business activity which was not, or did not amount to, activity pursuant to a contract of service with a business other than his own and, during such period, has been continuously: (1) registered with HM Revenue & Customs as self-employed, or (2) registered with Companies House as the Director of a new or existing business. Directors who are on the list of disqualified directors provided by Companies House will not be awarded points, (iv) [since before 11 July 2014 and up to the date of his application, has continuously been working] in an occupation which appears on the list of occupations skilled to National Qualifications Framework level 4 or above, as stated in the Codes of Practice in Appendix J, and provides the specified evidence in paragraph 41-SD. "Working" in this context means that the core service his business provides to its customers or clients involves the business delivering a service in an occupation at this level. It excludes any work involved in administration, marketing or website functions for the business, and (v) has access to not less than £50,000.	25
The money is held in one or more regulated financial institutions	25
The money is disposable in the UK	25
[If the applicant is applying for leave to remain, the money must be held in the UK]	

Note: In the first row of Table 4 words inserted in paragraph (b)(iii) and paragraph (d) substituted from 13 December 2012 (HC 760). Words substituted in the first row of Table 4 in paragraph (b)(i) from 1 July 2013 (HC 244). Paragraph (d)(iii) and words in paragraph (d)(iv) substituted from 11 July 2014 subject to savings for applications made before that date (HC 532). Words inserted at the end of Table 4 from 6 November 2014 subject to savings for applications made before that date (HC 693).

Investment: notes

41. An applicant will only be considered to have access to funds if:

(a) The specified documents in paragraph 41-SD are provided to show cash money to the amount required (this must not be in the form of assets [and, where multiple documents are provided, they must show the total amount required is available on the same date]);

(b) The specified documents in paragraph 41-SD are provided to show that the applicant has permission to use the money to invest in a business in the UK;

(c) The money is either held in a UK regulated financial institution or is transferable to the UK; and

(d) The money will remain available to the applicant until such time as it is spent for the purposes of the applicant's business or businesses. The Secretary of State reserves the right to request further evidence or otherwise verify that the money will remain available, and to refuse the application if this evidence is not provided or it is unable to satisfactorily verify.

Note: Subparagraph (d) substituted from 6 April 2014 (HC 1138 as amended by HC 1201), having previously been inserted from 31 January 2013 (HC 943). Words inserted in subparagraph (a) from 6 November 2014 subject to savings for applications made before that date (HC 693).

41-SD. The specified documents in Table 4 and paragraph 41, and associated definitions, are as follows:

(a) Where this paragraph refers to funding being available, unless stated otherwise, this means funding available to:

(i) the applicant;

(ii) the entrepreneurial team, if the applicant is applying under the provisions in paragraph 52 of this Appendix; or

(iii) the applicant's business.

(b) Where sub-paragraph (a)(iii) above applies and this paragraph refers to the applicant's business, the business must be a company and the applicant must be registered as a director of that business in the UK, and provide a Companies House document showing the address of the registered office in the UK, or head office in the UK if it has no registered office, and the applicant's name, as it appears on the application form, as a director.

(c) The specified documents to show evidence of the funding available to invest [, whether from the applicant's own funds or from one or more third parties,] are one or more of the following specified documents:

(i) A letter from each financial institution holding the funds, to confirm the amount of money available. Each letter must:

(1) be an original document and not a copy,

(2) be on the institution's headed paper,

(3) have been issued by an authorised official of that institution,

(4) have been produced within the three months immediately before the date of application,

(5) confirm that the institution is regulated by the appropriate body,

(6) state the applicant's name, and his team partner's name where relevant,

(7) show the account number and,

(8) state the date of the document,

(9) confirm the amount of money available from the applicant's own funds (if applicable) that are held in that institution,

(10) for money available from any third party (if applicable) that is held in that institution, confirm that the third party has informed the institution of the amount of money it intends to make available, and that the institution is not aware of the third party having promised to make that money available to any other person,

(11) confirm the name of each third party and their contact details, including their full address including postal code, and where available landline phone number and any email address, and

(12) confirm that if the money is not in an institution regulated by the Financial Conduct Authority (FCA) and the Prudential Regulation Authority (PRA), the money can be transferred into the UK; or

(ii) For money held in the UK only, a recent personal bank or building society statement from each UK financial institution holding the funds, which confirms the amount of money available. Each statement must satisfy the following requirements:

(1) the statements must be original documents and not copies;

(2) the bank or building society holding the money must be based in the UK and regulated by the Financial Conduct Authority (FCA) and the Prudential Regulation Authority (PRA);

(3) the money must be in cash in the account, not Individual Savings Accounts or assets such as stocks and shares;

(4) the account must be in the applicant's own name only (or both names for an entrepreneurial team [or where it is a joint account with the applicant's spouse, civil partner or partner as set out in paragraph 53 below]), not in the name of a business or third party;

(5) each statement must be on the institution's official stationery showing the institution's name and logo, and confirm the applicant's name (and, where relevant, the applicant's entrepreneurial team partner's name), the account number and the date of the statement;

(6) each statement must have been issued by an authorised official of that institution and produced within the three months immediately before the date of the application; and

(7) if the statements are printouts of electronic statements, they must either be accompanied by a supporting letter from the bank, on the bank's headed paper, confirming the authenticity of the statements, or bear the official stamp of the bank in question on each page of the statement; or

(iii) For £50,000 from a Venture Capital firm, Seed Funding Competition or UK Government Department only, a recent letter from an accountant, who is a member of a recognised UK supervisory body, or other authorised official in the case of a UK Government Department, confirming the amount of money made available. Each letter must:

(1) be an original document and not a copy,

(2) be on the institution's official headed paper,

(3) have been issued by an accountant engaged by the Venture Capital firm, Seed Funding Competition or UK Government Department or other official of the UK Government Department authorised to provide the information,

(4) have been produced within the three months immediately before the date of the application,

(5) state the applicant's name, and his team partner's name where relevant, or the name of the applicant's business,

(6) state the date of the document,

(7) confirm the amount of money available to the applicant, the entrepreneurial team or the applicant's business from the Venture Capital firm, Seed funding competition or UK Government Department, and

(8) confirm the name of the Venture Capital firm, Seed funding competition or UK Government Department and the contact details of an official of that organisation, including their full address, postal code and, where available, landline phone number and any email address,

(d) If the applicant is applying using money from a third party, he must provide all of the following specified documents [in addition to the specified documents in (c) above]:

(i) An original written declaration from every third party that they have made the money available to invest in a business in the United Kingdom, containing:

(1) the names of the third party and the applicant (and his team partner's name where relevant), or the name of the applicant's business,

(2) the date of the declaration,

(3) the applicant's signature and the signature of the third party (and the signature of the applicant's team partner where relevant),

(4) the amount of money available in pounds sterling,

(5) the relationship(s) of the third party to the applicant,

(6) if the third party is a venture capitalist firm, confirmation of whether [this body is registered with the Financial Conduct Authority (FCA) and its entry in the register includes a permission to arrange, deal in or manage investments, or to manage alternative investment funds],

(7) if the third party is a UK Seed Funding Competition, confirmation that the applicant, the entrepreneurial team or the applicant's business has been awarded money and that the competition is listed as endorsed on the UK Trade & Investment website, together with the amount of the award and naming the applicant, the entrepreneurial team or the applicant's business as a winner,

(8) if the third party is a UK Government Department, confirmation that it has made money available for the specific purpose of establishing or expanding a UK business, and the amount,

(9) if the third party is another business in which the applicant is self-employed or a director, evidence of the applicant's status within that business and that the applicant is the sole controller of that business's finances, or, where the applicant is not the sole controller, the letter must be signed by another authorised official of that business who is not the applicant, and

(10) confirmation that the money will remain available until such time as it is transferred to the applicant, the entrepreneurial team or the applicant's business.

and

(ii) A letter from a legal representative [who is independent from the third party or third parties,] confirming the validity of signatures on each third-party declaration provided, which confirms that the declaration(s) from the third party or parties contains the signatures of the people stated. It can be a single letter covering all third-party permissions, or several letters from several legal representatives. It must be an original letter and not a copy, and it must be from a legal representative permitted to practise in the country where the third party or the money is. The letter must clearly show the following:

(1) the name of the legal representative confirming the details,

(2) the registration or authority of the legal representative to practise legally in the country in which the permission or permissions was or were given,

(3) the date of the confirmation letter,

(4) the applicant's name (and the name of the applicant's team partner's name where relevant) and, where (b) applies, that the applicant is a director of the business named in each third-party declaration,

(5) the third party's name (which cannot be the legal representative themselves or their client),

(6) that the declaration from the third party is signed and valid, and

(7) if the third party is not a Venture Capitalist Firm, Seed Funding Competition or UK Government Department, the number of the third party or their authorised representative's identity document (such as a passport or national identity card), the place of issue and dates of issue and expiry.

(e) If the applicant is applying under the provisions in (d) in Table 4, he must also provide:

(i) his job title,

(ii) the Standard Occupational Classification (SOC) code of the occupation that the applicant [has been working in since before 11 July 2014 up to the date of his application], which must appear on the list of occupations skilled to National Qualifications Framework level 4 or above, as stated in the Codes of Practice in Appendix J,

(iii) one or more of the following specified documents [covering (either together or individually) a continuous period commencing before 11 July 2014 up to no earlier than three months before the date of his application]:

(1) advertising or marketing material, including printouts of online advertising, that has been published locally or nationally, showing the applicant's name (and the name of the business if applicable) together with the business activity or, where his business is trading online, confirmation of his ownership of the domain name of the business's website,

(2) article(s) or online links to article(s) in a newspaper or other publication showing the applicant's name (and the name of the business if applicable) together with the business activity,

(3) information from a trade fair, at which the applicant has had a stand or given a presentation to market his business, showing the applicant's name (and the name of the business if applicable) together with the business activity, or

(4) personal registration with a UK trade body linked to the applicant's occupation; and

(iv) one or more of the following documents showing trading which must cover (either together or individually) a continuous period before 11 July 2014 up to no earlier than three months before the date of his application:

(1) one or more contracts for service. If a contract is not an original the applicant must sign each page. Each contract must show:

(a) the applicant's name and the name of the business;

(b) the service provided by the applicant's business;

(c) the name of the other party or parties involved in the contract and their contact details, including their full address, postal code and, where available, landline phone number and any email address; and

(d) the duration of the contract; or

(2) one or more original letters from UK-regulated financial institutions with which the applicant has a business bank account, on the institution's headed paper, confirming the dates the business was trading during the period referred to at (iv) above;

(v)

(1) if claiming points for being self-employed, the following specified documents to show the applicant's compliance with National Insurance requirements:

(a) the original bills covering the continuous billing period during which the applicant claims to have been self-employed, if his Class 2 National Insurance is paid by bill;

(b) bank statements covering the continuous period during which the applicant claims to have been self-employed, showing the direct debit payment of Class 2 National Insurance to HM Revenue & Customs;

(c) all original small earnings exception certificates issued to the applicant by HM Revenue & Customs covering the continuous tax period during which the applicant claims to have been self-employed, if he has low earnings; or

(d) if applying before 31 January 2015, the original, dated welcome letter from HM Revenue & Customs containing the applicant's unique taxpayer reference number, if he has not yet become liable for paying National Insurance, or has not yet received the documents in (c);

or

(2) (a) if claiming points for being a director of a UK company at the time of his application, a printout of a Current Appointment Report from Companies House, dated no earlier than three months before the date of the application, listing the applicant as a director of a company that is actively trading and not dormant, or struck-off, or dissolved or in liquidation, and showing the date of his appointment as a director of that company; and

(b) if claiming points for being a director of a UK company other than the company referred to in (a) above, at any time before the date of his application, a printout from Companies House of the applicant's appointments history, showing that the applicant has held directorships continuously during the period in which he claims to have been a director;

and the evidence at (1) and (2) above must cover (either together or individually) a continuous period commencing before 11 July 2014 up to no earlier than three months before the date of his application, unless the applicant is claiming points for being self-employed at the time of his application and the evidence consists of documents issued by HM Revenue & Customs referred to at (v)(1)(_a), (_c) or (_d) above, in which case the applicant must submit the most recent document issued before the date of his application;

and

(vi) if the applicant is currently a director, the following evidence that his business has business premises in the UK and is subject to UK taxation:

(1) a printout of a Companies House document showing the address of the registered office in the UK, or head office in the UK if it has no registered office, and the applicant's name, as it appears on the application form, as a director; and

(2) documentation from HM Revenue & Customs which confirms that the business is registered for corporation tax;

and

(vii) the following evidence that the business has a UK bank account of which the applicant is a signatory:

(1) if the applicant is currently self employed, a personal bank statement showing transactions for his business (which must be currently active), or a business bank statement, or a letter from [the UK bank in question, on its headed paper] confirming that he has a business and acts through that bank for the purposes of that business, or

(2) if the applicant is currently a director, a company bank statement showing that the company has a UK account, or a letter from [the UK bank in question, on its headed paper,] confirming that the company has a bank account and the applicant is a signatory of that account,

and the evidence at (vi) and (vii)(2) above must relate to a company that is actively trading and not dormant, or struck-off, or dissolved or in liquidation.

Note: Paragraph 41-SD substituted from 1 October 2013 subject to savings for applications made before that date (HC 628). Words inserted in subparagraph (c), subparagraph (c)(i)(10) substituted and words inserted in subparagraph (d) from 6 April 2014 (HC 1138 as amended by HC 1201). Words inserted in subparagraph (d)(ii) and subparagraph (d)(ii)(5) substituted from 6 April 2014 subject to savings for applications made before that date (HC 1138 as amended by HC 1201). Subparagraph (b) substituted, words substituted in subparagraph (e)(ii), words inserted in subparagraph (e)(iii), subparagraphs (e)(iv) and (v) substituted and subparagraphs (e)(vi) and (vii) inserted from 11 July 2014 subject to savings for applications made before that date (HC 532). Words substituted in subparagraphs (c)(ii)(4) and (d)(i)(6), new subparagraph (d)(i)(9) inserted and previous (d)(i)(9) renumbered and words substituted in subparagraphs (e)(vii)(1) and (e)(vii)(2) from 6 November 2014 subject to savings for applications made before that date (HC 693).

42. [Subject to paragraphs 36A and 36B above, points will only be awarded] to an applicant to whom Table 4, paragraph (b) applies if the total sum of those funds derives from one or more of the sources listed in (b)(i) to (iii) in Table 4.

Note: Words substituted from 11 July 2014 subject to savings for applications made before that date (HC 532).

43. A regulated financial institution is one, which is regulated by the appropriate regulatory body for the country in which the financial institution operates.

44. Money is disposable in the UK if all of the money is held in a UK based financial institution or if the money is freely transferable to the UK and convertible to sterling. Funds in a foreign currency will be converted to pounds sterling (£) using the spot exchange rate which appeared on <www.oanda.com>* on the date on which the application was made.

45. If the applicant has invested the money referred to in Table 4 in the UK before the date of the application, points will be awarded for funds available as if the applicant had not yet invested the funds, providing:

(a) the investment was made no more than 12 months (or 24 months if the applicant was last granted leave as a Tier 1 (Graduate Entrepreneur) Migrant) before the date of the application; and

(b) all of the specified documents required in paragraphs 46-SD(a) to (g) are provided to show:

(i) the amount of money invested; and

(ii) that the applicant has established a business in the UK, in which the money was invested.

Note: Paragraph 45 substituted from 6 November 2014 subject to savings for applications made before that date (HC 693).

45A. No points will be awarded where the specified documents show that the funds are held in a financial institution listed in Appendix P as being an institution with which the UK Border Agency is unable to make satisfactory verification checks.

Note: Paragraph 45A inserted from 13 December 2012 (HC 760).

[Table 5: Applications for entry clearance or leave to remain referred to in paragraph 37]

Investment and business activity	Points
The applicant has invested, or had invested on his behalf, not less than £200,000 (or £50,000) if, in his last grant of leave, he was awarded points for funds of £50,000 . . . above in cash directly into one or more businesses in the UK.	25
The applicant has: (a) registered with HM Revenue and Customs as self-employed, or (b) registered with Companies House as a director of a new or an existing business. Directors who are on the list of disqualified directors provided by Companies House will not be awarded points. Where the applicant's last grant of entry clearance, leave to enter or leave to remain was as a Tier 1 (Entrepreneur) Migrant, the above condition must have been met within 6 months of his entry to the UK (if he was granted entry clearance as a Tier 1 (Entrepreneur) Migrant and there is evidence to establish his date of arrival to the UK), or, in any other case, the date of the grant of leave to remain.	20
On a date no earlier than three months prior to the date of application, the applicant was: (a) registered with HM Revenue and Customs as self-employed, or (b) registered with Companies House as a director of a new or an existing business. Directors who are on the list of disqualified directors provided by Companies House will not be awarded points.	15
The applicant has: (a) established a new business or businesses that has or have created the equivalent of at least two new full-time jobs for persons settled in the UK, or (b) taken over or invested in an existing business or businesses and his services or investment have resulted in a net increase in the employment provided by the business or businesses for persons settled in the UK by creating the equivalent of at least two new full-time jobs. Where the applicant's last grant of entry clearance or leave to enter or remain was as a Tier 1 (Entrepreneur) Migrant, the jobs must have existed for at least 12 months of the period for which the previous leave was granted.	20

Note: Title of Table 5 substituted from 13 December 2012 (HC 760). Words deleted from the first row, paragraph (b) in the second and third row substituted and paragraph (c) in the second and third row deleted from 11 July 2014 subject to savings for applications made before that date (HC 532).

Table 6: Applications for indefinite leave to remain as referred to in paragraph 38

Row	Investment and business activity	Points
1	The applicant has invested, or had invested on his behalf, not less than £200,000 (or £50,000 if, in his last grant of leave, he was awarded points for funds of £50,000) in cash directly into one or more businesses in the UK. The applicant will not need to provide evidence of this investment if he was awarded points for it, as set out in Table 5, in his previous grant of entry clearance or leave to remain as a Tier 1 (Entrepreneur) Migrant.	20
2	On a date no earlier than three months prior to the date of application, the applicant was: (a) registered with HM Revenue and Customs as self-employed, or (b) registered with Companies House as a director of a new or an existing business. Directors who are on the list of disqualified directors provided by Companies House will not be awarded points.	20
3	The applicant has: (a) established a new UK business or businesses that has or have created the equivalent of X new full-time jobs for persons settled in the UK, or (b) taken over or invested in an existing UK business or businesses and his services or investment have resulted in a net increase in the employment provided by the business or businesses for persons settled in the UK by creating the equivalent of X new full-time jobs where X is at least 2. Where the applicant's last grant of entry clearance or leave to enter or remain was as a Tier 1 (Entrepreneur) Migrant, the jobs must have existed for [for at least 12 months during that last grant of leave].	20
4	The applicant has spent the specified continuous period lawfully in the UK, with absences from the UK of no more than 180 days in any 12 calendar months during that period. The specified period must have been spent with leave as a Tier 1 (Entrepreneur) Migrant, as a Businessperson and/or as an Innovator, of which the most recent period must have been spent with leave as a Tier (1) (Entrepreneur) Migrant. The specified continuous period is: (a) 3 years if the number of new full-time jobs, X, referred to in [row 3 above] is at least 10, [or] (b) 3 years if the applicant has: (i) established a new UK business that has had an income from business activity of at least £5 million during a 3 year period in which the applicant has had leave as a Tier 1 (Entrepreneur) Migrant, or (ii) taken over or invested in an existing UK business and his services or investment have resulted in a net increase in income from business activity to that business of £5 million during a 3 year period in which the applicant has had leave as a Tier 1 (Entrepreneur) Migrant, when compared to the immediately preceding 3 year period, or (c) 5 years in all other cases.	35

[Time spent with valid leave in the Bailiwick of Guernsey, the Bailiwick of Jersey or the Isle of Man in a category equivalent to the categories set out above may be included in the continuous period of lawful residence, provided the most recent period of leave was as a Tier 1 (Entrepreneur) Migrant in the UK. In any such case, the applicant must have absences from the Bailiwick of Guernsey, the Bailiwick of Jersey or the Isle of Man (as the case may be) of no more than 180 days in any 12 calendar months during the specified continuous period.]

Note: New paragraph inserted at the end of Row 3 (now row 4) from 6 April 2013 (HC 1039). Word 'or' inserted at the end of subparagraph (a) in row 3 (now row 4) of Table 6 from 1 October 2013 subject to savings for applications made before that date (HC 628). Paragraph (b) in the first (now the second) row substituted and paragraph (c) in the first (now the second) row deleted from 11 July 2014 subject to savings for applications made before that date (HC 532). New Row 1 inserted and subsequent Rows renumbered and words substituted in Rows 3 and 4 from 6 November 2014 subject to savings for applications made before that date (HC 693).

Investment and business activity: notes

46. Documentary evidence must be provided in all cases. The specified documents in paragraph 46-SD must be provided as evidence of any investment and business activity that took place when the applicant had leave as a Tier 1 (Entrepreneur) Migrant or a Tier 1 (Post-Study Work) Migrant, and any investment made no more than 12 months [(or 24 months if the applicant was last granted leave as a Tier 1 (Graduate Entrepreneur) Migrant)] before the date of the application for which the applicant is claiming points.

Note: Words inserted from 6 April 2014 subject to savings for applications made before that date (HC 1138 as amended by HC 1201).

46-SD. The specified documents in paragraphs 45 and 46 are as follows:

(a) The applicant must provide all the appropriate specified documents needed to establish the amount of money he has invested from the following list:

(i) If the applicant's business is a registered company that is required to produce audited accounts, the audited accounts must be provided;

(ii) If the applicant's business is not required to produce audited accounts, unaudited accounts and an accounts compilation report must be provided from an accountant who is a member of a UK Recognised Supervisory Body (as defined in the Companies Act 2006);

(iii) If the applicant has made the investment in the form of a director's loan, it must be shown in the relevant set of accounts provided, and the applicant must also provide a legal agreement, between the applicant (in the name that appears on his application) and the company, showing:

(1) the terms of the loan,

(2) any interest that is payable,

(3) the period of the loan, and

(4) that the loan is unsecured and subordinated in favour of third-party creditors.

(iv) If the applicant is claiming points for investing £50,000 from a Venture Capital firm, Seed Funding Competition or UK Government Department, and has not been awarded points in a previous application for having those funds available, he must provide a letter as specified in paragraph 41-SD(c)(iii) (except that the letter does not need to have been produced within the three months immediately before the date of the application) as evidence of the source of those funds.

(b) Audited or unaudited accounts must show the investment in money made directly by the applicant, in his own name [or on his behalf (and showing his name)]. If he has invested by way of share capital the business accounts must show the shareholders, the amount and value of the shares (on the date of purchase) in the applicant's name as it appears on his application. If the value of the applicant's share capital is not shown in the accounts, then share certificates must be submitted as documentary evidence. The accounts must clearly show the name of the accountant, the date the accounts were produced, and how much the applicant has invested in the business. [The accounts must be prepared and signed off in accordance with statutory requirements,]

(c) The applicant must provide the following specified documents to show that he has established a UK business:

(i) Evidence that the business has business premises in the United Kingdom:

(1) If the applicant is self employed, his registration with HM Revenue and Customs to show that the business is based in the UK, or

(2) If the applicant is a director, printout of a Companies House document showing the address of the registered office in the UK, or head office in the UK if it has no registered office, and the applicant's name, as it appears on the application form, as a director,

and

(ii) Evidence that the business has a UK bank account of which the applicant is a signatory:

(1) If the applicant is self employed, a personal bank statement showing transactions for his business, or a business bank statement, or a letter from a UK-regulated financial institution, on the institution's headed paper, confirming that he has a business and acts through that bank for the purposes of that business, or

(2) If the applicant is a director, a company bank statement showing that the company has a UK account, or a letter from a UK-regulated financial institution, on the institution's headed paper, confirming that the company has a bank account and the applicant is a signatory of that account,

and

(iii) Evidence that the business is subject to UK taxation:

(1) If the applicant is self-employed, he must be registered as self-employed for National Insurance assessment and provide either the welcome letter from HM Revenue & Customs, the Small Earnings Exception certificate, a copy of the National Insurance bill from HM Revenue & Customs, or the applicant's bank statement showing that National Insurance is taken by HM Revenue & Customs by direct debit, or

(2) If the applicant is a director of a business, the business must be registered for corporation tax and the applicant must provide documentation from HM Revenue & Customs which confirms this.

(d) If the applicant has bought property that includes residential accommodation the value of this part of the property will not be counted towards the amount of the business investment. The applicant must provide an estimate of the value of the living accommodation if it is part of the premises also used for the business, from a surveyor who is a member of the Royal Institution of Chartered Surveyors. This valuation must be produced in the three months prior to the date of application.

(e) If some of the money has been invested into a business in the UK, the balance of funds must be held in a regulated financial institution and disposable in the UK, and the applicant must provide the specified documents required in paragraph 41-SD for the previous investment of money together with the specified documents required in paragraph 41-SD required for his access to the balance of sufficient funds.

(f) Where Table 5 applies and the applicant's last grant of entry clearance, leave to enter or leave to remain was as a Tier 1 (Entrepreneur) Migrant . . . , he must provide the following specified documents as evidence of his registration as self-employed or as a director within the 6 months after the specified date [in the relevant table]:

(i) If the applicant was self-employed, he must provide one of the following:

(1) an original, dated welcome letter from HM Revenue & Customs containing the applicant's unique taxpayer reference number, {dated no more than 8 months from the specified date in the relevant table},

(2) an original Exception Certificate from HM Revenue & Customs, dated no more than 8 months from the specified date [in the relevant table],

(3) an original National Insurance bill from the HM Revenue & Customs dated during the 6 months after the specified date [in the relevant table], or

(4) a bank statement dated in the 6 months after the specified date [in the relevant table], showing the direct debit payment of National Insurance to HM Revenue & Customs.

(ii) If the applicant was a director of a new or existing company, he must provide a Current Appointment Report from Companies House, listing the applicant as the Director of the company and the date of his appointment, which must be no more than 8 months after the specified date [in the relevant table].

(g) The applicant must provide the following specified documents as evidence of his current registration as self-employed or as a director:

(i) If the applicant is claiming points for being currently self-employed, he must provide the following specified documents to show that he is paying Class 2 National Insurance contributions:

(1) the original bill from the billing period immediately before the application, if his Class 2 National Insurance is paid by . . . bill,

(2) the most recent bank statement issued before the application, showing the direct debit payment of National Insurance to HM Revenue & Customs, if his National Insurance is paid by direct debit,

(3) an original small earnings exception certificate issued by HM Revenue & Customs for the most recent return date, if he has low earnings, or

(4) the original, dated welcome letter from HM Revenue & Customs containing the applicant's unique taxpayer reference number, if he has not yet received the documents in (1) to (3).

(ii) If the applicant is claiming points for currently being a director of a UK company, he must provide a printout of a Current Appointment Report from Companies House, dated no earlier than three months before the date of the application, listing the applicant as a director of the company, and confirming the date of his appointment. The company must be actively trading and not struck-off, or dissolved or in liquidation on the date that the printout was produced . . .

(h) If the applicant is required to score points for creating the net increase in employment in Table 5 or Table 6, he must provide the following information and specified documents:

(i) A HM Revenue & Customs [Employee Payment Record], showing details of the earnings for the settled worker for each week that he worked for the applicant, and signed and dated by the applicant;

(ii) If the date of the start of the employment is not shown in the [Employee Payment Record], an original HM Revenue & Customs form P45 or form P46 (also called a Full Payment Submission) for the settled worker, showing the starting date of the employment;

(iii) If the employer is taking part in the Real Time Initiative pilot, printouts of the Full Payment Submission, sent to HM Revenue & Customs, which include the start date of the settled worker and are initialled by the applicant;

(iv) Duplicate payslips or wage slips for each settled worker for whom points are being claimed, covering the full period of the employment for which points are being claimed;

(v) Confirmation of the hourly rate for each settled worker used to claim points, including any changes in the hourly rate and the dates of the changes, enabling calculation of the hours of work created for each settled worker;

(vi) Documents which show that the employment was created for settled workers, such as the passport pages from a UK passport that contain the employee's personal details, and the page containing the UK Government stamp or endorsement, if appropriate, or the worker's full birth certificate, showing the name of at least one parent;

(vii) If the applicant was a director of a company, the information from the Companies House Current Appointment Report to confirm that he was a Director of the company that employed the settled worker at the time that he was employed;

(viii) If the applicant was self-employed, the specified documents in (c) above showing the dates that the applicant became self-employed, the names on the [Employee Payment Record] and bank account, and the address of the business;

(ix) If the applicant took over or joined a business that employed workers before he joined it, he must also provide one of the following types of payroll documentation:

(1) a duplicate HM Revenue & Customs [Full Payment Submission] for the year before the jobs were created and the year that the jobs were created, showing the net increase in employment, and signed and dated by the applicant (If the posts were created too recently for [a Full Payment Submission] to have been produced, the applicant must provide a draft copy), or

(2) a printout of the information sent to HM Revenue & Customs, initialled by the applicant, if the employer is taking part in the Real Time Initiative pilot;

(x) If the applicant took over or joined a business that employed workers before he joined it, he must also provide an original accountant's letter verifying the net increase in employment and confirming the number of posts. The accountant must be a member of the Institute of Chartered Accountants in England and Wales, the Institute of Chartered Accountants in Scotland, the Institute of Chartered Accountants in Ireland, the Association of Chartered Certified Accountants, or the Association of Authorised Public Accountants. The letter must contain:

(1) the name and contact details of the business,

(2) the applicant's status in the business,

(3) the number of posts created in the business and the hours worked,

(4) the dates of the employment created,

(5) the registration or permission of the accountant to operate in the United Kingdom,

(6) the date that the accountant created the letter on the applicant's behalf, and

(7) that the accountant will confirm the content of the letter to the UK Border Agency on request.

Note: Words inserted in subparagraph (b), words in curly brackets in subparagraph (f)(i)(1) inserted and words 'in the relevant table' substituted in subparagraph (f) from 13 December 2012 (HC 760). Subparagraph (c)(iii)(2) substituted, words deleted in subparagraphs (f) (deleted words had previously been inserted from 13 December 2012 by HC 760) and (h)(i) and words substituted in subparagraphs (h)(ii), (h)(viii) and (h)(ix) from 1 October 2013 subject to savings for applications made before that date (HC 628). Subparagraph (a)(ii) substituted, subparagraph (a)(iv) inserted and words at the end of subparagraph (b) from 6 April 2014 subject to savings for applications made before that date (HC 1138 as amended by HC 1201). Subparagraph (c)(ii) substituted, words omitted from subparagraphs (g)(i)(1) and (g)(ii) from 11 July 2014 subject to savings for applications made before that date (HC 532).

47. For the purposes of Tables 4, 5 and 6, "investment and business activity" does not include investment in any residential accommodation, property development or property management, and must not be in the form of a director's loan unless it is unsecured and subordinated in favour of the business. "Property development or property management" in this context means any development of property owned by the applicant or his business to increase the value of the property with a view to earning a return either through rent or a future sale or both, or management of property (whether or not it is owned by the applicant or his business) for the purposes of renting it out or resale.

Note: Paragraph 47 substituted from 6 November 2014 subject to savings for applications made before that date (HC 693).

48. Points will only be awarded in respect of a UK business or businesses.

(a) A business will be considered to be a UK business if:

(i) it is trading within the UK economy, and

(ii) it has a registered office in the UK, except where the applicant is registered with HM revenue & Customs as self-employed and does not have a business office, and

(iii) it has a UK bank account, and

(iv) it is subject to UK taxation.

(b) Multinational companies that are registered as UK companies with either a registered office or head office in the UK are considered to be UK businesses for the purposes of Tables 4, 5 and 6.

(c) Subject to (d) below, a business will only be considered to be a "new" business for the purposes of Tables 5 and 6 if it was established no earlier than 12 months before the start of a period throughout which the applicant has had continuous leave as a Tier 1 (Entrepreneur) Migrant, and which includes the applicant's last grant of leave. (For these purposes continuous leave will not be considered to have been broken if any of the circumstances set out in paragraphs 245AAA(a)(i) to (iii) of these Rules apply.)

(d) If the applicant held entry clearance or leave to remain as a Tier 1 (Graduate Entrepreneur) Migrant no more than 28 days before the application which led to the start of the period of continuous leave as a Tier 1 (Entrepreneur) Migrant referred to in (c) above, a business will only be considered to be a "new" business for the purposes of Tables 5 and 6 if it was established no earlier than 24 months before the start of the period in (c).

Note: Paragraph 47 substituted from 6 November 2014 subject to savings for applications made before that date (HC 693).

49. A full-time job is one involving at least 30 hours of work a week. Two or more part-time jobs that add up to 30 hours a week will count as one full-time job but one full-time job of more than 30 hours work a week will not count as more than one full-time job.

50. Where the applicant's last grant of entry clearance or leave was as a Tier (Entrepreneur) Migrant, the jobs must have existed for a total of at least 12 months during the period in which the migrant had leave in that category. This need not consist of 12

consecutive months and the jobs need not exist at the date of application, provided they existed for at least 12 months during the period in which the migrant had leave as a Tier 1 (Entrepreneur) Migrant.

51. The jobs must comply with all relevant UK legislation including, but not limited to, the national Minimum Wage and the Working Time Directive.

Entrepreneurial teams: Notes

52. Two applicants [, and no more than two applicants,] may claim points for the same investment and business activity in Tables 4, 5 or 6 providing the following requirements are met.

Requirements:

(a) The applicants have equal level of control over the funds and/or the business or businesses in question;

(b) The applicants are both shown by name in each other's applications and in the specified evidence required in the relevant table; and

(c) Neither applicant has previously been granted leave as a Tier 1 (Entrepreneur) Migrant on the basis of investment and/or business activity linked in this way with any applicant other than each other if the same funds are being relied on as in a previous application.

Note: Words inserted from 1 October 2013 subject to savings for applications made before that date (HC 628).

53. (a) No points will be awarded for funds that are made available to any individual other than the applicant, except:

(i) under the terms of paragraph 52 above; or

where the money is held in a joint account with the applicant's [spouse, civil partner or partner (defined as a person who has been living together with the applicant in a relationship akin to a marriage or civil partnership for at least two years prior to the date of application)]

(ii) , and that spouse or partner is not (or is not applying to be) another Tier 1 (Entrepreneur) Migrant.

(b) No points will be awarded for investment and business activity shared with another Tier 1 (Entrepreneur) applicant, except under the terms of paragraph 52 above.

(c) If the applicant is not the sole partner or director in the business, he must state:

(i) the names of the other partners or directors,

(ii) whether any of the other partners or directors are also Tier 1 (Entrepreneur) Migrants, and

(iii) if so:

(1) the dates they became partners or directors,

(2) whether they are applying under the provisions in paragraph 52 above, and

(3) if they have made (or are making at the same time) an application in which they claimed points for creating jobs, the names of the jobholders in question.

Note: Paragraph 53 substituted from 13 December 2012 (HC 760) and then substituted again from 6 April 2014 subject to savings for applications made before that date (HC 1138 as amended by HC 1201). Words substituted in subparagraph (ii)(a) from 11 July 2014 subject to savings for applications made before that date (HC 532).

Attributes for Tier 1 (Investor) Migrants

54. An applicant applying for entry clearance, leave to remain or indefinite leave to remain as a Tier 1 (Investor) Migrant must score 75 points for attributes.

55. Except where paragraph 56 applies, available points for applications for entry clearance or leave to remain are shown in Table 7.

Note: Paragraphs 55-58 substituted from 6 November 2014 subject to savings for applications made before that date (HC 693).

56. (a) Available points for entry clearance or leave to remain are shown in Table 8A for an applicant who:

(i) has had entry clearance, leave to enter or leave to remain as a Tier 1 (Investor) Migrant, which was granted under the Rules in place from 6 November 2014, in the 12 months immediately before the date of application, or

(ii) is applying for leave to remain and has, or was last granted, entry clearance, leave to enter or leave to remain as a Tier 1 (Investor) Migrant, which was granted under the Rules in place from 6 November 2014.

(b) Available points for entry clearance or leave to remain are shown in Table 8B for an applicant who:

(i) has had entry clearance, leave to enter or leave to remain as a Tier 1 (Investor) Migrant, under the Rules in place before 6 November 2014, or as an Investor, in the 12 months immediately before the date of application;, or

(ii) is applying for leave to remain and has, or was last granted, entry clearance, leave to enter or leave to remain as a Tier 1 (Investor) Migrant, under the Rules in place before 6 November 2014, or as an Investor.

Note: Paragraphs 55-58 substituted from 6 November 2014 subject to savings for applications made before that date (HC 693).

57. (a) Available points for applications for indefinite leave to remain are shown in Table 9A for an applicant who was last granted as a Tier 1 (Investor) Migrant under the Rules in place from 6 November 2014, and was awarded points as set out in Table 7 or Table 8A of Appendix A to these Rules in that last grant.

(b) Available points for applications for indefinite leave to remain are shown in Table 9B for an applicant who was last granted as a Tier 1 (Investor) Migrant under the Rules in place before 6 November 2014, or was awarded points as set out in Table 8B of Appendix A in his last grant.

Note: Paragraphs 55-58 substituted from 6 November 2014 subject to savings for applications made before that date (HC 693).

58. Notes to accompany Tables 7 to Table 9B appear below Table 9B.

Note: Paragraphs 55-58 substituted from 6 November 2014 subject to savings for applications made before that date (HC 693).

Table 7: Applications for entry clearance or leave to remain referred to in paragraph 55

Assets	Points
The applicant has money of his own under his control held in a regulated financial institution and disposable in the UK amounting to not less than £2 million.	75

Note: Table 7 substituted from 6 November 2014 subject to savings for applications made before that date (HC 693).

Table 8A: Applied to enter the category from 6 November 2014 as referred to in paragraph 56(a)

Money and investment	Points
The applicant has invested not less than £2 million in the UK by way of UK Government bonds, share capital or loan capital in active and trading UK registered companies, subject to the restrictions set out in paragraph 65 below. The investment referred to above was made: (1) within 3 months of the applicant's entry to the UK, if he was granted entry clearance as a Tier 1 (Investor) Migrant and there is evidence to establish his date of entry to the UK, unless there are exceptionally compelling reasons for the delay in investing, or (2) where there is no evidence to establish his date of entry in the UK or where the applicant was granted entry clearance in a category other than Tier 1 (Investor) Migrant, within 3 months of the date of the grant of entry clearance or leave to remain as a Tier 1 (Investor) Migrant, unless there are exceptionally compelling reasons for the delay in investing, or (3) where the investment was made prior to the application which led to the first grant of leave as a Tier 1 (Investor) Migrant, no earlier than 12 months before the date of such application, and in each case the level of investment has been at least maintained for the whole of the remaining period of that leave. "Compelling reasons for the delay in investing" must be unforeseeable and outside of the applicant's control. Delays caused by the applicant failing to take timely action will not be accepted. Where possible, the applicant must have taken reasonable steps to mitigate such delay.	75

Table 8B: Applications for entry clearance or leave to remain from applicants who initially applied to enter the category before 6 November 2014 as referred to in paragraph 56(b)

Money and investment	Points
The applicant: (a) has money of his own under his control in the UK amounting to not less than £1 million, or (b) (i) owns personal assets which, taking into account any liabilities to which they are subject, have a value of not less than £2 million; and (ii) has money under his control and disposable in the UK amounting to not less than £1 million which has been loaned to him by a UK regulated financial institution.	30
The applicant has invested not less than £750,000 of his capital in the UK by way of UK Government bonds, share capital or loan capital in active and trading UK registered companies, subject to the restrictions set out in paragraph 65 below and has invested the remaining balance of £1,000,000 in the UK by the purchase of assets or by maintaining the money on deposit in a UK regulated financial institution.	30
(i) The investment referred to above was made: (1) within 3 months of the applicant's entry to the UK, if he was granted entry clearance as a Tier 1 (Investor) Migrant and there is evidence to establish his date of entry to the UK, unless there are exceptionally compelling reasons for the delay in investing; or (2) where there is no evidence to establish his date of entry in the UK or where the applicant was granted entry clearance in a category other than Tier 1 (Investor) Migrant, within 3 months of the date of the grant of entry clearance or leave to remain as a Tier 1 (Investor) Migrant, unless there are exceptionally compelling reasons for the delay in investing; or (3) where the investment was made prior to the application which led to the first grant of leave as a Tier 1 (Investor) Migrant, no earlier than 12 months before the date of such application, and in each case the level of investment has been at least maintained for the whole of the remaining period of that leave; or (ii) The migrant has, or was last granted, entry clearance, leave to enter or leave to remain as an Investor. "Compelling reasons for the delay in investing" must be unforeseeable and outside of the applicant's control. Delays caused by the applicant failing to take timely action will not be accepted. Where possible, the applicant must have taken reasonable steps to mitigate such delay.	15

Note: Tables 8A and 8B substituted from 6 November 2014 subject to savings for applications made before that date (HC 693).

Table 9A: Applications for indefinite leave to remain from applicants who initially applied to enter the category from 6 November 2014 as referred to in paragraph 57(a)

Row	Money and investment	Points
1	The applicant has invested money of his own under his control amounting to at least: (a) £10 million; or (b) £5 million; or (c) £2 million in the UK by way of UK Government bonds, share capital or loan capital in active and trading UK registered companies, subject to the restrictions set out in paragraph 65 below.	40
2	The applicant has spent the specified continuous period lawfully in the UK, with absences from the UK of no more than 180 days in any 12 calendar months during that period. The specified continuous period must have been spent with leave as a Tier 1 (Investor) Migrant. The specified continuous period is: (a) 2 years if the applicant scores points from row 1(a) above; (b) 3 years if the applicantscores points from row 1(b) above; or (c) 5 years if the applicant scores points from row 1(c) above. Time spent with valid leave in the Bailiwick of Guernsey, the Bailiwick of Jersey or the Isle of Man in a category equivalent to the categories set out above may be included in the continuous period of lawful residence, provided the most recent period of leave was as a Tier 1 (Investor) Migrant in the UK. In any such case, the applicant must have absences from the Bailiwick of Guernsey, the Bailiwick of Jersey or the Isle of Man (as the case may be) of no more than 180 days in any 12 calendar months during the specified continuous period.	20
3	The investment referred to above was made no earlier than 12 months before the date of the application which led to the first grant of leave as a Tier 1 (Investor) Migrant. The level of investment has been at least maintained throughout the relevant specified continuous period referred to in row 2, other than in the first 3 months of that period, and the applicant has provided the specified documents to show that this requirement has been met. When calculating the specified continuous period, the first day of that period will be taken to be the later of: (a) the date the applicant first entered the UK as a Tier 1 (Investor) Migrant, (or the date entry clearance was granted as a Tier 1 (Investor) Migrant) or the date the applicant first entered the Bailiwick of Guernsey, the Bailiwick of Jersey or the Isle of Man with leave in a category equivalent to Tier 1 (Investor) if this is earlier; or (b) the date 3 months before the full specified amount was invested in the UK, or before the full required amount in an equivalent category was invested in the Bailiwick of Guernsey, the Bailiwick of Jersey or the Isle of Man.	15

Table 9B: Applications for indefinite leave to remain from applicants who initially applied to enter the category before 6 November 2014 as referred to in paragraph 57(b)

Row	Money and investment	Points
1	The applicant: (a) (i) has money of his own under his control in the UK amounting to not less than £10 million; or (ii) (1) owns personal assets which, taking into account any liabilities to which they are subject, have a value of not less than £20 million; and (2) has money under his control and disposable in the UK amounting to not less than £10 million which has been loaned to him by a UK regulated financial institution, or (b) (i) has money of his own under his control in the UK amounting to not less than £5 million; or (ii) (1) owns personal assets which, taking into account any liabilities to which they are subject, have a value of not less than £10 million; and (2) has money under his control and disposable in the UK amounting to not less than £5 million which has been loaned to him by a UK regulated financial institution; or (c) (i) has money of his own under his control in the UK amounting to not less than £1 million; or (ii) (1) owns personal assets which, taking into account any liabilities to which they are subject, have a value of not less than £2 million; and (2) has money under his control and disposable in the UK amounting to not less than £1 million which has been loaned to him by a UK regulated financial institution.	20
2	The applicant has invested not less than 75% of the specified invested amount of his capital in the UK by way of UK Government bonds, share capital or loan capital in active and trading UK registered companies, subject to the restrictions set out in paragraph 65 below, and has invested the remaining balance of the specified invested amount in the UK by the purchase of assets or by maintaining the money on deposit in a UK regulated financial institution. The specified invested amount is: (a) £10,000,000 if the applicant scores points from row 1(a) above, (b) £5,000,000 if the applicant scores points from row 1(b) above, or (c) £1,000,000 if the applicant scores points from row 1(c) above.	20

3	The applicant has spent the specified continuous period lawfully in the UK, with absences from the UK of no more than 180 days in any 12 calendar months during that period. The specified continuous period must have been spent with leave as a Tier 1 (Investor) Migrant and/or as an Investor, of which the most recent period must have been spent with leave as a Tier 1 (Investor) Migrant. The specified continuous period is: (a) 2 years if the applicant scores points from row 1(a) above, (b) 3 years if the applicant scores points from row 1(b) above, or (c) 5 years if the applicant scores points from row 1(c) above. Time spent with valid leave in the Bailiwick of Guernsey, the Bailiwick of Jersey or the Isle of Man in a category equivalent to the categories set out above may be included in the continuous period of lawful residence, provided the most recent period of leave was as a Tier 1 (Investor) Migrant in the UK. In any such case, the applicant must have absences from the Bailiwick of Guernsey, the Bailiwick of Jersey or the Isle of Man (as the case may be) of no more than 180 days in any 12 calendar months during the specified continuous period.	20
4	The investment referred to above was made no earlier than 12 months before the date of the application which led to the first grant of leave as a Tier 1 (Investor) Migrant. The level of investment has been at least maintained throughout the time spent with leave as a Tier 1 (Investor) Migrant in the UK in the relevant specified continuous period referred to in row 3, other than in the first 3 months of that period. In relation to time spent with leave as a Tier 1 (Investor) Migrant in the UK, the applicant has provided the specified documents to show that this requirement has been met. When calculating the specified continuous period, the first day of that period will be taken to be the later of: (a) the date the applicant first entered the UK as a Tier 1 (Investor) Migrant (or the date entry clearance was granted as a Tier 1 (Investor) Migrant), or the date the applicant first entered the Bailiwick of Guernsey, the Bailiwick of Jersey or the Isle of Man with leave in a category equivalent to Tier 1 (Investor) if this is earlier, or (b) the date 3 months before the full specified amount was invested in the UK, or before the full required amount in an equivalent category was invested in the Bailiwick of Guernsey, the Bailiwick of Jersey or the Isle of Man.	15

Note: Tables 9A and 9B substituted for Table 9 from 6 November 2014 subject to savings for applications made before that date (HC 693).

[Money and Assets:] notes

59. DELETED

60. Money is disposable in the UK if all of the money is held in a UK based financial institution or if the money is freely transferable to the UK and convertible to sterling. Funds in a foreign currency will be converted to pounds sterling (£) using the spot exchange rate which appeared on <www.oanda.com>* on the date on which the application was made.

61. "Money of his own", "personal assets" and 'his capital' include money or assets belonging to the applicant's spouse, civil partner or unmarried or same-sex partner, provided that:

(a) the applicant's spouse, civil partner or unmarried or same-sex partner meets the requirements of paragraphs 319C(c) and (d) of these rules, and the specified documents in paragraph 61-SD are provided, and

(b) specified documents in paragraph 61-SD are provided to show that the money or assets are under the applicant's control and that he is free to invest them.

61A. In Tables {7 to 9B}, "money of his own under his control" and "money under his control" exclude money that a loan has been secured against, where another party would have a claim on the money if loan repayments were not met[, except where:

(i) the applicant made an application before 13 December 2012 which is undecided or which led to a grant of entry clearance or leave to remain as an Investor or a Tier 1 (Investor) migrant,

(ii) the applicant has not been granted entry clearance, leave to enter or leave to remain in any other category since the grant referred to in (i), and

(iii) the money is under the applicant's control, except for the fact that the loan referred to {in paragraph (b) in Table 8B or row 1 in Table 9B} has been secured against it.]

Note: Paragraph 61A inserted from 13 December 2012 (HC 760). Words in square brackets inserted from 13 December 2012 (HC 820). Words in curly brackets substituted from 6 November 2014 subject to savings for applications made before that date (HC 693).

61-SD. The specified documents in paragraph 61, as evidence of the relationship and to show that the money or assets are under the applicant's control and that he is free to invest them, are as follows:

(a) The applicant must provide:

(i) The original certificate of marriage or civil partnership, to confirm the relationship, which includes the name of the applicant and the husband, wife or civil partner, or

(ii) At least three of the following types of specified documents to demonstrate a relationship similar in nature to marriage or civil partnership, including unmarried and same-sex relationships, covering a full two-year period immediately before the date of the application:

(1) a bank statement or letter from a bank confirming a joint bank account held in both names,

(2) an official document such as a mortgage agreement showing a joint mortgage,

(3) official documents such as deeds of ownership or a mortgage agreement showing a joint investment, such as in property or business,

(4) a joint rent (tenancy) agreement,

(5) any other official correspondence linking both partners to the same address, such as example bills for council tax or utilities,

(6) a life insurance policy naming the other partner as beneficiary,

(7) birth certificates of any children of the relationship, showing both partners as parents, or

(8) any other evidence that adequately demonstrates the couple's long-term commitment to one another.

(b) The applicant must provide an original declaration from the applicant's husband, wife, civil partner, or unmarried or same-sex partner that he will permit all joint or personal money used to claim points for the application to be under the control of the applicant in the UK, known as a gift of beneficial ownership of the money while retaining the legal title, which clearly shows:

(1) the names of husband, wife, civil partner, or unmarried or same-sex partner and the applicant,

(2) the date of the declaration,

(3) the signatures of the husband, wife, civil partner, or unmarried or same-sex partner and applicant,

(4) the amount of money available, and

(5) a statement that the husband, wife, civil partner, or unmarried or same-sex partner agrees that the applicant has sole control over the money.

(c) The applicant must provide a letter, from a legal adviser who is permitted to practise in the country where the declaration was made, confirming that the declaration is valid and which clearly shows:

(1) the name of the legal adviser confirming that the declaration is valid,

(2) the registration or authority of the legal adviser to practise legally in the country in which the document was drawn up,

(3) the date of the confirmation of the declaration,

(4) the names of the applicant and husband, wife, civil partner, or unmarried or same-sex partner, and

(5) that the declaration is signed and valid according to the laws of the country in which it was made.

62. "Regulated financial institution" is defined in paragraph 43, Appendix A.

62A. DELETED (from 6 November 2014 subject to savings for aplications made before that date (HC 693)).

63. In the case of an application where Table 7 applies, where the money referred to in Table 7 has already been invested in the UK before the date of application, points will only be awarded if it was invested in the UK no more than 12 months before the date of application.

Note: Paragraph 63 substituted from 6 November 2014 subject to savings for applications made before that date (HC 693).

[Source of money: notes]

64. In the case of an application where Table 7 applies, points will only be awarded if the applicant:

(a) has had the money ... referred to in Table 7 for a consecutive 90-day period of time, ending no earlier than one calendar month before the date of application, and provides the specified documents in paragraph 64-SD; or

(b) provides the additional specified documents in paragraph 64A-SD of the source of the money ...

Note: Heading inserted and words omitted from subparagraphs (a) and (b) from 6 November 2014 subject to savings for applications made before that date (HC 693).

64-SD. The specified document requirements in paragraph 64(a), as evidence of having held the money . . . for the specified 90-day period, are as follows:

(a) [The applicant must provide:]

(i) A portfolio report produced by a UK regulated financial institution, or a breakdown of investments in an original letter produced by a UK regulated financial institution, on the official letter-headed paper of the institution, issued by an authorised official of that institution. The portfolio report or letter must cover the three consecutive months before the date of application. The report must be no more than one calendar month old at the time of application. The portfolio report or letter must confirm all the following:

(1) the amount of the money held in the investments,

(2) the beneficial owner of the funds,

(3) the date of the investment period covered,

(4) that the institution is a UK regulated financial institution, with the details of the registration shown on the documentation, and

(5) that the money can be transferred into the UK should the application be successful, if it is held abroad, or that the money has already been invested in the UK in the form of UK Government bonds, share capital or loan capital in active and trading UK registered companies, and the dates of these investments;

(ii) If the applicant manages his own investments, or has a portfolio manager who does not operate in the UK and is not therefore [regulated by the Financial Conduct Authority (FCA) (and the Prudential Regulation Authority (PRA) where applicable)], he must provide one or more of the documents from the list below, as relevant to their type of investments, covering the three consecutive months in the period immediately before the date of application:

(1) certified copies of bond documents showing the value of the bonds, the date of purchase and the owner;

(2) share documents showing the value of the shares, the date of purchase and the owner,

(3) the latest audited annual accounts of the organisation in which the investment has been made, clearly showing the amount of money held in the investments, the name of the applicant (or applicant and/or husband, wife, civil partner, or unmarried or same-sex partner), and the date of investment, or, if no accounts have been produced, a certificate from an accountant showing the amount of money held in the investments, and

(4) original trust fund documents from a legal adviser showing the amount of money in the fund, the date that the money is available and the beneficial owner, and including the name and contact details of the legal adviser and at least one of the trustees;

(iii) Original personal bank statements on the official bank stationery from a bank that is regulated by the official regulatory body for the country in which the institution operates and the funds are located, showing the amount of money available in the name of the applicant (or applicant and/or husband, wife, civil partner, or unmarried or same-sex partner), covering the three full consecutive months before the date of application. The most recent statement must be no more than one calendar month old at the date of application. Electronic bank statements . . . must be accompanied by a supporting letter from the bank on the institution's official headed paper, issued by an authorising official of that institution, confirming the content and that the document is genuine;

(iv) If the applicant cannot provide bank statements, an original letter from a bank that is regulated by the official regulatory body for the country in which the institution operates and the funds are located, on the institution's official headed paper, issued by an authorised official of that institution, stating that the account has held the required amount of money on the day the letter was produced and for the three full consecutive months immediately before the date of the letter. The letter must be dated no more than one calendar month before the date of application. The letter must confirm:

(1) the name of the applicant (or applicant and/or husband, wife, civil partner, or unmarried or same-sex partner), and that the money is available in their name(s),

(2) that the bank is regulated by the official regulatory body for the country in which the institution operates and the funds are located,

(3) the dates of the period covered, including both the day the letter was produced and three full consecutive months immediately before the date of the letter, and

(4) the balance of the account to cover the amount claimed as a credit balance on the date of the letter and the three full consecutive months before the date of the letter;

(v) If the funds are not held in the UK, the applicant must provide an original letter from a bank or financial institution that is regulated by the official regulatory body for the country in which the institution operates and the funds are located, on the institution's official headed paper, issued by an authorised official of that institution, which confirms:

(1) the name of the beneficial owner, which should be the applicant (or applicant and/or husband, wife, civil partner, or unmarried or same-sex partner),

(2) the date of the letter,

(3) the amount of money to be transferred,

(4) that the money can be transferred to the UK if the application is successful, and

(5) that the institution will confirm the content of the letter to the UK Border Agency on request.

(b) If specified documents are provided from accountants, the accountant must:

(i) if based in the UK, be a member of the Institute of Chartered Accountants in England and Wales, the Institute of Chartered Accountants in Scotland, the Institute of Chartered Accountants in Ireland, the Association of Chartered Certified Accountants, or the Association of Authorised Public Accountants, or

(ii) if not based in the UK, be a member of an equivalent, appropriate supervisory or regulatory body in the country in which they operate.

Note: Words substituted in subparagraph (a)(ii) from 1 July 2013 (HC 244). Words deleted from subparagraph (a)(iii) from 1 October 2013 (HC 628). Words substituted at the start of subparagraph (a), original subparagraph (b) deleted and subparagraph (c) renumbered as (b) from 6 November 2014 subject to savings fro applications made before that date (HC 693).

64A-SD. Where paragraph 64(b) states that specified documents are required as evidence [that the money is under the applicant's control and that he is free to invest it] the applicant must provide all the specified documents from the following list, with contact details that enable verification:

(a) Original documents in the form of:

(i) Money given to the applicant (or applicant and/or husband, wife, civil partner, or unmarried or same-sex partner) within the three months immediately before the application must be shown in an irrevocable memorandum of gift, which clearly shows:

(1) the name and signature of the person receiving the gift,

(2) the name and signature of the person giving the gift,

(3) the date of the memorandum,

(4) the amount of money being given,

(5) a statement that the legal ownership of the gift is transferred and that the document is the memorandum of transfer,

(6) a clear description of the gift, and

(7) a statement that the gift is irrevocable;

(ii) If a memorandum of gift in (i) is provided, it must be accompanied by an original confirmation letter from a legal adviser permitted to practise in the country where the gift was made, which clearly shows:

(1) the name of the legal adviser who is confirming the details,

(2) the registration or authority of the legal adviser to practise legally in the country in which the gift was made,

(3) the date of the confirmation of the memorandum,

(4) the names of the person giving the gift and the person receiving it,

(5) the amount of money given,

(6) the date that the money was transferred to the applicant, or to the husband, wife, civil partner, or unmarried partner or same-sex partner of the applicant,

(7) that the memorandum is signed and valid,

(8) that the gift is irrevocable, and

(9) that the memorandum is binding according to the laws of the country in which it was made;

(iii) Deeds of sale of assets such as business or property, if the applicant has generated these funds within the three months immediately before the date of application, which meet the relevant legal requirements of the country of sale and clearly show:

(1) the name of the applicant (or applicant and/or husband, wife, civil partner, or unmarried or same-sex partner),

(2) the amount of money raised, and

(3) the date of the sale;

(iv) If a deed of sale in (iii) is provided, it must be accompanied by an original confirmation letter from a legal adviser permitted to practise in the country where the sale was made, which clearly shows:

(1) the name of the legal adviser confirming the details,

(2) the registration or authority of the legal adviser to practise legally in the country in which the sale was made,

(3) the date of the sale,

(4) the date of production of the letter confirming the sale,

(5) the details of what was sold and the amount of money received from the sale,

(6) the name of the person receiving the money from the sale,

(7) the date that the money was transferred, and

(8) that the sale was valid according to the laws of the country in which it was made;

(v) If the funds are currently held in the applicant's business (or the business of the applicant and/or the applicant's husband, wife, civil partner, or unmarried or same-sex partner), the applicant must provide business accounts, which:

(1) are profit and loss accounts (or income and expenditure accounts if the organisation is not trading for profit),

(2) are prepared and signed off in accordance with statutory requirements, and

(3) clearly show the amount of money available for investment;

(vi) If business accounts in (v) are provided, they must be accompanied by an original letter from a legal adviser who is permitted to practise in the country where business was operating, confirming that the applicant (or applicant and/or husband, wife, civil partner, or unmarried or same-sex partner) can lawfully extract the money from the business, which clearly shows:

(1) the name of the legal adviser who is confirming the details,

(2) the registration or authority of the legal adviser to practise legally in the country in which the business is operating,

(3) the date on which the details are confirmed, and

(4) that the applicant (or applicant and/or husband, wife, civil partner, or unmarried or same-sex partner) can lawfully extract the money from the business in question;

(vii) If the applicant (or applicant and/or husband, wife, civil partner, or unmarried or same sex partner) has been the beneficiary of a will within the three months before making the application, and has received money as a result, the applicant must provide a notarised copy of the will. If the applicant (or applicant and/or husband, wife, civil partner, or unmarried or same-sex partner) has received possessions or assets, rather than money, then the applicant (or applicant and/or husband, wife, civil partner, or unmarried or same-sex partner) may not use estimates of the value of the items as evidence of funds for investment. The notarised copy of the will must clearly show:

(1) the date of the will,

(2) the beneficiary of the will (this should be the applicant or applicant and/or husband, wife, civil partner, or unmarried or same-sex partner),

(3) the amount of money that the applicant (or applicant and/or husband, wife, civil partner, or unmarried or same-sex partner) has inherited, and

(4) the names of any executors, plus any codicils (additions) to the will that affect the amount of money that was received;

(viii) If a notarised copy of a will in (vii) is provided, it must be accompanied by an original confirmation letter from a legal adviser who is permitted to practise in the country where the will was made, confirming the validity of the will, which clearly shows:

(1) the name of the legal adviser confirming the details,

(2) the registration or authority of the legal adviser to practise legally in the country in which the will was made,

(3) the date of the document produced by the legal adviser confirming the will,

(4) the date that the applicant received the money as a result of the settlement of the will,

(5) the names of the person making the will and the beneficiary,

(6) confirmation of the amount of money received by the applicant (or applicant and/or husband, wife, civil partner, or unmarried or same-sex partner).

(7) that the will is signed and valid, and

(8) that the will is valid according to the laws of the country in which it was made;

(ix) If the applicant (or applicant and/or husband, wife, civil partner, or unmarried or same-sex partner) has obtained money as a result of a divorce settlement within the three months immediately before the date of application, the applicant must provide a notarised copy of a financial agreement following a divorce. If the applicant (or applicant and/or husband, wife, civil partner, or unmarried or same-sex partner) has received possessions or assets, rather than money, estimates of the value of the items will not be accepted as evidence of money for investment.

(x) If a divorce settlement in (ix) is provided, it must be accompanied by an original confirmation letter from a legal adviser who is permitted to practise in the country where the divorce took place, which clearly shows:

(1) the name of the legal adviser confirming the details,

(2) the registration or authority of the legal adviser to practise legally in the country in which the divorce took place,

(3) the date of the document produced by the legal adviser confirming the divorce settlement,

(4) the date that the applicant received the money as a result of the settlement,

(5) the names of the persons who are divorced,

(6) confirmation of the amount of money received by the applicant (or applicant and/or husband, wife, civil partner, or unmarried or same-sex partner),

(7) that the divorce settlement is complete and valid, and

(8) that the divorce settlement is valid according to the laws of the country in which it was made;

(xi) If the applicant is relying on a financial award or winnings as a source of funds, he must provide an original letter from the organisation issuing the financial award or winnings, which clearly shows:

(1) the name of the applicant (or applicant and/or husband, wife, civil partner, or unmarried or same-sex partner),

(2) the date of the award,

(3) the amount of money won,

(4) the winnings are genuine, and

(5) the contact details for the organisation issuing the award or winnings;

(xii) If a letter showing a financial award or winnings in (xi) is provided, it must be accompanied by an original confirmation letter from a legal adviser who is permitted to practise in the country where the award was made, which clearly shows:

(1) the name of the legal adviser confirming the details,

(2) the registration or authority of the legal adviser to practise legally in the country in which the award was made,

(3) the date of the letter of confirmation,

(4) the date of the award,

(5) the name of the recipient of the award,

(6) the amount of the winnings,

(7) the source of the winnings, and

(8) the date that the money was transferred to the applicant, or husband, wife, civil partner, or unmarried or same-sex partner;

(xiii) If the applicant (or applicant and/or husband, wife, civil partner, or unmarried or same-sex partner) has received money from a source not listed above, the applicant must provide relevant original documentation as evidence of the source of the money, together with independent supporting evidence, which both clearly confirm:

(1) the amount of money received,

(2) the date that the money was received,

(3) the source of the money, and

(4) that the applicant (or applicant and/or husband, wife, civil partner, or unmarried or same-sex partner) was the legal recipient of the money.

Note: Words substituted in opening sentence from 6 November 2014 subject to savings for applications made before that date (HC 693).

64B-SD. In the case of an application where Table 9A, row 1 (a) or (b), or Table 9B, row 1 (a)(i) or (b)(i) applies, points will only be awarded if the applicant:

(a) (i) has had the additional money (or the additional assets in respect of an application to which either row 1 (a)(i) or (b)(i) of Table 9B applies) that he was not awarded points for in his previous grant of leave for a consecutive 90-day period of time, ending on the date(s) this additional capital was invested (as set out in row 1 of Table 9A or row 2 of Table 9B), and

(ii) provides the specified documents in paragraph 64-SD (or the additional assets in respect of an application to which either row 1 (a)(i) or (b)(i) of Table 9B applies), with the difference that references to "date of application" in that paragraph are taken to read "date of investment"; or

(b) provides the additional specified documents in paragraph 64A-SD of the source of the additional money (with the difference that references to "date of application" in that paragraph are taken to read "date of investment").

Note: Paragraph 64B-SD inserted from 13 December 2012 subject to savings for applications made before that date (HC 760) and then substituted from 6 November 2014 subject to savings for applications made before that date (HC 693).

64C-SD. In the case of an application where Table 9B, row 1 (a)(ii) or (b)(ii) applies, points will only be awarded if the applicant provides an original letter of confirmation from each UK regulated financial institution the applicant has taken out a loan with to obtain the additional funds that he was not awarded points for in his previous grant of leave. The letter must have been issued by an authorised official, on the official letter-headed paper of the institution(s), and confirm:

(i) the amount of money that the institution(s) has loaned to the applicant,

(ii) the date(s) the loan(s) was taken out by the applicant, which must be no later than the date(s) this additional capital was invested (as set out in Table 9B, row 2),

(iii) that the institution is a UK regulated financial institution for the purpose of granting loans,

(iv) that the applicant has personal assets with a net value of at least £2 million, £10 million or £20 million (as appropriate), and

that the institution(s) will confirm the content of the letter to the Home Office on request.

Note: Paragraph 64C-SD inserted from 6 November 2014 subject to savings for applications made before that date (HC 693).

Qualifying investments (Table 8A to Table 9B): notes

65. Investment excludes investment by the applicant by way of:

(a) an offshore company or trust, {or investments that are held in offshore custody} [except that investments held in offshore custody shall not be excluded where the applicant made an application before 13 December 2012 which is undecided or which led to a grant of entry clearance or leave to remain as an Investor or a Tier 1 (Investor) migrant and has not since been granted entry clearance, leave to enter or leave to remain in any other category.]

(b) Open-ended investment companies, investment trust companies or pooled investment vehicles,

(c) Companies mainly engaged in property investment, property management or property development,

(d) Deposits with a bank, building society or other enterprise whose normal course of business includes the acceptance of deposits,

(e) ISAs, premium bonds and saving certificates issued by the National Savings and Investment Agency (NS&I), for an applicant who has, or last had leave as a Tier 1 (Investor) Migrant, or

(f) Leveraged investment funds, except where the leverage in question is the security against the loan referred to in paragraph (b) in Table 8B or row 1 of Table 9B (as appropriate), and paragraph 61A(i)-(iii) apply.

Note: Words in curly brackets in subparagraph (a) inserted from 13 December 2012 (HC 760) and words in square brackets in subparagraphs (a) and (f) inserted from 13 December 2012 (HC 820). Subparagraph (f) substituted from 6 November 2014 subject to savings for applications made before that date (HC 693).

65A. No points will be awarded where the specified documents show that the funds are held in a financial institution listed in Appendix P as being an institution with which the UK Border Agency is unable to make satisfactory verification checks.

Note: Paragraph 65A inserted from 13 December 2012 (HC 760).

65-SD. The following specified documents must be provided as evidence of investment:

(a) The applicant must provide a portfolio of investments certified as correct by a UK regulated financial institution, which must:

(i) Cover the required period, beginning no later than the end of the 3 month timescale specified in [the relevant table];

(ii) Continue to the last reporting date of the most recent billing period of the year directly before the date of the application;

(iii) Include the value of the investments;

(iv) Show that any shortfall in investments below the specified investment amount was made up by the next reporting period [as required by paragraph 65C (a) or (b) as applicable];

(v) Show the dates that the investments were made;

(vi) Show the destination of the investments;

(vii) Include, for investments made as loan funds to companies, audited accounts or unaudited accounts with an [accounts compilation report] for the investments made, giving the full details of the applicant's investment. The accountant must be a member of the Institute of Chartered Accountants in England and Wales, the Institute of Chartered Accountants in Scotland, the Institute of Chartered Accountants in Ireland, the Association of Chartered Certified Accountants, or the Association of Authorised Public Accountants;

(viii) Show the name and contact details of the financial institution that has certified the portfolio as correct, and confirmation that this institution is [regulated by the Financial Conduct Authority (FCA) (and the Prudential Regulation Authority (PRA) where applicable)];

(ix) Show that the investments were made in the applicant's name and/or that of his spouse, civil partner, unmarried or same-sex partner and not in the name of an offshore company or trust even if this is wholly owned by the applicant;

(x) include the date that the portfolio was certified by the financial institution; and

(xi) state that the institution will confirm the content of the letter to the [Home Office] on request.

(b) [Where the applicant is applying under Table 8B or Table 9B, previously had leave as an Investor and is unable to provide the evidence listed above because he manages his own investments, or because he has a portfolio manager who does not operate in the UK] and is therefore not [regulated by the Financial Conduct Authority (FCA) (and the Prudential Regulation Authority (PRA) where applicable)], the applicant must provide the following specified documents showing his holdings used to claim points, as relevant to the type of investment:

(i) Certified copies of bond documents showing the value of the bonds, the date of purchase and the owner;

(ii) Share documents showing the value of the shares, the date of purchase and the owner;

(iii) The latest audited annual accounts of the organisation in which the investment has been made, [which have been prepared and signed off in accordance with statutory requirements, and clearly show]:

(1) the amount of money held in the investments,

(2) the name of the applicant (or applicant and/or husband, wife, civil partner, or unmarried or same-sex partner), and

(3) the date of investment.

(iv) If the organisation in (iii) is not required to produce accounts, the applicant must provide a certificate showing the amount of money held in the investments, from an accountant who is a member of the Institute of Chartered Accountants in England and Wales, the Institute of Chartered Accountants in Scotland, the Institute of Chartered Accountants in Ireland, the Association of Chartered Certified Accountants, or the Association of Authorised Public Accountants.

(c) [Where the applicant is applying under Table 8B or Table 9B and has invested] at least 75% of the specified investment amount but less than 100%, he must provide one or more of the following specified documents as evidence of the balance of the funds required to bring his total investment in the UK up to the specified investment amount:

(i) Documents confirming the purchase of assets in the UK, showing the assets purchased, the value of these assets and the dates of purchase. When using property only the unmortgaged portion of the applicant's own home can be considered and the valuation must be provided on a report issued by a surveyor (who is a member of the Royal Institution of Chartered Surveyors) in the six months prior to the date of application;

(ii) If the applicant maintained money on deposit in the UK, a statement or statements of account on the official stationery of the institution that holds the funds. These statements must be in the name of the applicant (or applicant and/or the husband, wife, civil partner, or unmarried or same-sex partner of the applicant) and confirm the dates and amount of money held. The applicant must ensure that the institution will confirm the content of the statement to the [Home Office] on request;

(iii) An original letter from the financial institution that holds the cash on deposit, on the institution's official headed paper, issued by an authorised official of that institution, which confirms the dates and amount of money held and that the institution will confirm the content of the letter to the UK Border Agency on request.

(d) If the applicant wishes the start of the 3 month timescale specified in [Table 8A, Table 8B, Table 9A or Table 9B] to be taken as the date he entered the UK, he must provide evidence which proves this date, such as a stamp in the applicant's passport, or an aircraft boarding card.

(e) Evidence of the investment having been maintained, from the date that the funds were invested for the full period of remaining leave, will be determined using the portfolio provided in (a).

Note: Words substituted in subparagraphs (a)(viii) and (b) from 1 July 2013 (HC 244). Words substituted in subparagraphs (a)(vii) and (b)(iii) from 6 April 2014 subject to savings for applications made before that date (HC 1138 as amended by HC 1201). Words substituted in subparagraphs (a)(i), (a)(iv), (a)(xi), (b), (c), (c)(ii) and (d) from 6 November 2014 subject to savings for applications made before that date (HC 693).

Attributes for Tier 1 (Graduate Entrepreneur) Migrants

66. An applicant applying [for entry clearance or leave to remain] as a Tier 1 (Graduate Entrepreneur) Migrant must score 75 points for attributes.

Note: Words in square brackets substituted from 6 November 2014 subject to savings for applications made before that date (HC 693).

67. Available points are shown in Table 10.

68. Notes to accompany the table appear below the table.

Table 10

Criterion	Points
(a) The applicant has been endorsed by a UK Higher Education Institution which: (i) has Highly Trusted Sponsor status under Tier 4 of the Points-Based System, (ii) is an A-rated Sponsor under Tier 2 of the Points-Based System if a Tier 2 licence is held, (iii) is an A-rated Sponsor under Tier 5 of the Points-Based System if a Tier 5 licence is held, (iv) has degree-awarding powers, and (v) has established processes and competence for identifying, nurturing and developing entrepreneurs among its undergraduate and postgraduate population; Or (b) The applicant has been endorsed by UK Trade and Investment.	25
The applicant has been awarded a degree qualification (not a qualification of equivalent level which is not a degree) which meets or exceeds the recognised standard of a Bachelor's degree in the UK. For overseas qualifications, the standard must be confirmed by UK NARIC.	25
The endorsement must confirm that the endorsing body has assessed the applicant and considers that: (a) the applicant has a genuine and credible business idea, and (b) the applicant will spend the majority of his working time on developing business ventures, and (c) if the applicant is applying for leave to remain and his last grant of leave was as a Tier 1 (Graduate Entrepreneur), he has made satisfactory progress in developing his business since that leave was granted.	25

Note: Table 10 substituted from 6 April 2014 subject to savings for applications made before that date (HC 1138 as amended by HC 1201).

Notes Tier 1 (Graduate Entrepreneur) Limit

69. (a) The Secretary of State shall be entitled to limit the total number of Tier 1 (Graduate Entrepreneur) endorsements qualifying [endorsing bodies] may make in support of successful applications in a particular period, to be referred to as the Tier 1 (Graduate Entrepreneur) Limit.

(b) The Tier 1 (Graduate Entrepreneur) Limit is 2,000 places per year (beginning on 6 April and ending on 5 April), which will be allocated as follows:

(i) 1, 900 places will be allocated to qualifying Higher Education Institutions as set out in (c) below; and

(ii) 100 places will be allocated to UK Trade and Investment.

(c) Places for qualifying Higher Education Institutions will be allocated as follows:

(i) The UK Border Agency will, on an annual basis, invite all UK Higher Education Institutions which meet the requirements in (a)(i) to (iv) in the first row of Table 10 to take part as endorsing institutions, with responses required by 5 April for the year beginning the next day.

(ii) The endorsements will be allocated between all invited Higher Education Institutions who confirm that:

(1) They wish to take part, and

(2) They meet the requirement in (a)(v) in the first row of Table 10 above.

(iii) Each qualifying body in (ii) will be allocated the smallest of:

(1) The number of . . . endorsements it has requested,

(2) Its equal share of the number of endorsements available (if the result is not an integer it will be rounded down to the next lowest integer), or

(3) 20 endorsements.

(iv) If the result of (i) to (iii) is that there are fewer than 1,850 endorsements allocated to qualifying Higher Education Institutions for the year, the Home Office will invite all UK Higher Education Institutions which meet the requirements in (a)(i) to (iv) in the first row of Table 10 to request the remaining endorsements for the year ending 5 April, with responses required by 30 September.

(v) The remaining endorsements will be allocated between all invited Higher Education Institutions who meet the criteria in (ii), regardless of whether they were previously allocated endorsements for the year.

(vi) If all requests can be met without exceeding the number of remaining places available, each Higher Education Institution in (v) will be allocated the number of endorsements it has requested.

(vii) If all requests cannot be met without exceeding the number of remaining places available, each Higher Education Institution in (v) will be allocated the smaller of:

(1) The number of endorsements it has requested, or

(2) Its equal share of the remaining number of endorsements available (if the result is not an integer it will be rounded down to the next lowest integer).

(viii) If the result of (iv) to (vii) is that there are still remaining places in the Tier 1 (Graduate Entrepreneur) Limit for the year, those places will not be allocated.

(d) If:

(i) an applicant does not make a valid application within 3 months of the date of his endorsement, or

(ii) an application is refused, and that refusal is not subsequently overturned,

the endorsement used in that application will be cancelled and the relevant endorsing body's unused allocation of endorsements will be increased by one, providing the end of the period (6 April to 5 April) to which it relates has not yet passed.

(e) The Tier 1 (Graduate Entrepreneur) limit will not apply to applications for leave to remain where the applicant has, or last had, leave to remain as a Tier 1 (Graduate Entrepreneur).

(f) Endorsements which have not been used by endorsing bodies cannot be carried over from one year (beginning on 6 April and ending on 5 April) to the next.

Note: Words substituted in subparagraph (a) and subparagraph (d) substituted from 6 April 2013 subject to savings for applications made before that date (HC 1039). Subparagraphs (b) to (c) substituted from 6 April 2014 subject to savings for applications made before that date (HC 1138 as amended by HC 1201). Words deleted from subparagraph (c)(iii)(1) from 6 November 2014 subject to savings for applications made before that date (HC 693).

Endorsement

70. Points will only be awarded for an endorsement if:

(a) the endorsement was issued to the applicant no more than 3 months before the date of application,

(b) the endorsement has not been withdrawn by the relevant [endorsing body] at the time the application is considered by [the entry clearance officer or the Secretary of State], and

(c) the applicant provides an original endorsement from the [relevant endorsing body], which shows:

(i) the endorsement reference number,

(ii) the date of issue (including a statement on how long the letter is valid for),

(iii) the applicant's name,

(iv) the applicant's date of birth,

(v) the applicant's nationality,

(vi) the applicant's current passport number,

(vii) details of any dependants of the applicant who are already in the UK or who the applicant intends to bring to the UK,

(viii) the name of the endorsing body,

(ix) the name and contact details of the authorising official of the endorsing body,

(x) the name, level and date of award of the applicant's qualification, this was shown in a previous successful Tier 1 (Graduate Entrepreneur) application,

(xi) the applicant's intended business sector or business intention,

(xii) what has led the endorsing body to endorse the application, and

(xiii) [if the applicant is applying for leave to remain and was last granted leave] as a Tier 1 (Graduate Entrepreneur) Migrant, confirmation that the endorsing body is satisfied that he has made satisfactory progress.

Note: Words in first square brackets in subparagraph (b) substituted and words substituted in opening pargraph of subparagraph (c) and subparagraphs (c)(viii) to (c)(xiii) substituted from 6 April 2013 subject to savings for applications made before that date (HC 1039). Words in second square brackets substituted in subparagraph (b) and subparagraph (c)(x) substituted from 6 April 2014 subject to savings for applications made before that date (HC 1138 as amended by

HC 1201). Words substituted in subparagraph (c)(xiii) from 6 November 2014 subject to savings for applications made before that date (HC 693).

Qualifications

71. Points will be awarded for a degree qualification if the endorsement:

(a) is by the UK Higher Education Institution which awarded the qualification; and

(b) contains the specified details of the qualification, as set out in paragraph 70(c).

Note: Paragraph 71 substituted from 6 April 2014 subject to savings for applications made before that date (HC 1138 as amended by HC 1201).

72. (a) [In cases other than those in paragraph 71, points will only be awarded for a degree qualification if the applicant provides the following specified documents:]

(i) The original certificate of award of the qualification, which clearly shows the:

(1) applicant's name,

(2) title of the award,

(3) date of the award, and

(4) name of the awarding institution,

or

(ii) if:

(1) the applicant is awaiting graduation having successfully completed his degree,

or

(2) the applicant no longer has the certificate and the institution who issued the certificate is unable to produce a replacement, an original academic reference from the institution that is awarding, or has awarded, the degree together with an original academic transcript, unless (d) applies.

(b) The academic reference referred to in (a)(ii) must be on the official headed paper of the institution and clearly show the:

(1) applicant's name,

(2) title of award,

(3) date of award, confirming that it has been or will be awarded, and

(4) either the date that the certificate will be issued (if the applicant has not yet graduated) or confirmation that the institution is unable to re-issue the original certificate or award.

(c) The academic transcript referred to in (a)(ii) must be on the institution's official paper and must show the:

(1) applicant's name,

(2) name of the academic institution,

(3) course title, and

(4) confirmation of the award.

(d) If the applicant cannot provide his original certificate for one of the reasons given in (a)(ii) and is claiming points for a qualification with a significant research bias, such as a doctorate, an academic transcript is not required, providing the applicant provides an academic reference which includes all the information detailed in (b) above.

(e) Where the degree is an overseas qualification and an applicant cannot find details of it on the points based calculator on the visas and immigration pages of the gov.uk website, he must, in addition to the document or documents in (a), provide an original letter or certificate from UK NARIC confirming the equivalency of the level of his qualification.

Note: Paragraph 72 inserted from 6 April 2013 subject to savings for applications made before that date (HC 1039). Words substituted in subparagraph (a) and subparagraph (e) substituted from 6 April 2014 subject to savings for applications made before that date (HC 1138 as amended by HC 1201).

Attributes for Tier 2 (Intra-Company Transfer) Migrants

73. An applicant applying for entry or leave to remain as a Tier 2 (Intra-Company Transfer) Migrant must score 50 points for attributes.

73A. Available points for entry clearance or leave to remain are shown in Table 11.

73B. Notes to accompany Table 11 appear below the table.

Table 11

Criterion	Points
Certificate of Sponsorship	30
Appropriate salary	20

Notes

Certificate of Sponsorship

74. In order to obtain points for a Certificate of Sponsorship, the applicant must provide a valid Certificate of Sponsorship reference number.

74A. A Certificate of Sponsorship reference number will only be considered to be valid if:

(a) the number supplied links to a Certificate of Sponsorship Checking Service entry that names the applicant as the migrant and confirms that the Sponsor is Sponsoring him as a Tier 2 (Intra-Company Transfer) Migrant and specifies the sub-category of Tier 2 (Intra-Company Transfer) under which he is applying,

(b) the Sponsor assigned the Certificate of Sponsorship reference number to the migrant no more than 3 months before the application for entry clearance or leave to remain is made,

(c) the application for entry clearance or leave to remain is made no more than 3 months before the start of the employment as stated on the Certificate of Sponsorship,

(d) The migrant must not previously have applied for entry clearance, leave to enter or leave to remain using the same Certificate of Sponsorship reference number, if that application was either approved or refused (not rejected as an invalid application declared void or withdrawn),

(e) that reference number must not have been withdrawn or cancelled by the Sponsor or by the UK Border Agency since it was assigned, including where it has been cancelled by the UK Border Agency due to having been used in a previous application, and

(f) the Sponsor is an A-rated Sponsor, unless the application is for leave to remain and the applicant has, or was last granted, leave as a Tier 2 (Intra-Company) Migrant or a Qualifying Work Permit Holder.

74B. No points will be awarded for a Certificate of Sponsorship unless:

(a) the job that the Certificate of Sponsorship Checking Service entry records that the person is being sponsored to do appears on:

(i) the list of occupations skilled to National Qualifications Framework level 6 or above, as stated in the codes of practice in Appendix J, or

(ii) one of the following creative sector occupations skilled to National Qualifications Framework level 4 or above:

(1) 3411 Artists,

(2) 3412 Authors, writers and translators,

(3) 3413 Actors, entertainers and presenters,

(4) 3414 Dancers and choreographers, or

(5) 3422 Product, clothing and related designers,

or

(b) (i) the applicant is applying for leave to remain,

(ii) the applicant previously had leave as a Tier 2 (Intra-Company Transfer) Migrant under the Rules in place between 6 April 2011 and [13 June 2012], and has not since been granted leave to remain in any other route, or entry clearance or leave to enter in any route, and

(iii) the job that the Certificate of Sponsorship Checking Service entry records that the person is being sponsored to do appears on the list of occupations skilled to National Qualifications Framework level 4 or above, as stated in the codes of practice in Appendix J.

(c) (i) the applicant is applying for leave to remain as a Tier 2 (Intra-Company Transfer) Migrant in the Long Term Staff sub-category,

(ii) the applicant previously had leave as:

(1) a Tier 2 (Intra-Company Transfer) Migrant under the rules in place before 6 April 2011, or

(2) a Qualifying Work Permit Holder,

and has not since been granted leave to remain in any other route, or entry clearance or leave to enter in any route, and

(iii) the job that the Certificate of Sponsorship Checking Service entry records that the person is being sponsored to do appears on the list of occupations skilled to National Qualifications Framework level 3 or above, as stated in the codes of practice in Appendix J, or the applicant is a Senior Care Worker or an Established Entertainer as defined in paragraph 6 of these Rules [, or]

(d) (i) the applicant was last granted entry clearance or leave as a Tier 2 (Intra-Company Transfer) Migrant,

(ii) the applicant is applying for leave to remain to work in the same occupation for the same Sponsor as in the application which led to his previous grant of leave,

(iii) the Certificate of Sponsorship used in support of the applicant's previous application was assigned by the Sponsor before 6 April 2013, and

(iv) the occupation fails to meet the required skill level in (a) to (c) above solely due to reclassification from the SOC 2000 system to the SOC 2010 system.

Note: Words substituted in sub-paragraph (b)(ii) from 13 December 2012 subject to savings for applications made before that date (HC 760). Sub-paragraph (a)(ii) substituted and sub-paragraph (d) inserted from 6 April 2013 subject to savings for applications made on or after 6 April 2013 using a Certificate of Sponsorship issued to the applicant before that date (HC 1039). Word 'or' deleted from the end of sub-paragraph (b) and word 'or' inserted at the end of sub-paragraph (c) from 6 April 2014 subject to savings for applications made before that date (HC 1138 as amended by HC 1201).

74C. (a) if the applicant is applying as a Tier 2 (Intra-Company Transfer) Migrant in either the Short Term Staff or Long Term Staff sub-categories, no points will be awarded for a Certificate of Sponsorship unless:

(i) the Certificate of Sponsorship Checking Service entry confirms that the applicant has been working for the Sponsor for at least 12 months as specified in paragraphs (b) and (c) below, and

(ii) the applicant provides, if requested to do so, the specified documents as set out in paragraph 74C-SD(a) below, unless he was last granted leave to work for the same Sponsor in the same sub-category as he is currently applying under. The application may be granted without these specified documents, but the Home Office reserves the right to request the specified documents, and to refuse applications if these documents are not received at the address specified in the request within 7 working days of the date of the request.

(b) Throughout the 12 months referred to in paragraph (a)(i) above, the applicant must have been working for the Sponsor:

(i) outside the UK, or

(ii) in the UK, provided he had leave to work for the Sponsor as:

(1) a Tier 2 (Intra-Company Transfer) Migrant in either of the Short Term Staff or Long Term Staff sub-categories,

(2) a Tier 2 (Intra-Company Transfer) Migrant in the established staff sub-category under the rules in place before 6 April 2011,

(3) a Tier 2 (Intra-Company Transfer) Migrant under the rules in place before 6 April 2010,

(4) a Qualifying Work Permit Holder (provided that the work permit was granted because the holder was the subject of an Intra-Company Transfer), and/or

(5) a representative of an Overseas Business, and

(c) The specified period referred to in paragraph (a)(i) above is:

(i) a continuous period of 12 months immediately prior to the date of application, or

(ii) an aggregated period of at least 12 months within the 24 month period immediately before the date of application, if at some point within the 12 months preceding the date of application, the applicant has been:

(1) on maternity, paternity or adoption leave,

(2) on long-term sick leave lasting one month or longer, or

(3) working for the Sponsor in the UK as a Tier 2 (Intra-Company Transfer) Migrant in either of the Graduate Trainee or Skills Transfer sub-categories,

and if requested to provide the specified documents set out in paragraph 74C-SD(a) below, also provides, at the same time, the specified documents as set out in paragraph 74C-SD(c) below, or

(iii) an aggregated period of at least 12 months during the time the applicant has been continuously working for the Sponsor, if at some point within the 12 months preceding the date of application, the applicant has been working in the UK for the Sponsor lawfully under any other category of these Rules not listed in paragraph (b)(ii) above.

Note: Paragraph 74C substituted from 6 April 2014 subject to savings for applications made before that date (HC 1138 as amended by HC 1201).

74C-SD (a) The specified documents in paragraph 74C(a) are:

(i) [Original formal payslips issued by the employer and showing the employer's name] covering the full specified period (The most recent payslip must be dated no earlier than 31 days before the date of the application);

(ii) [Other payslips] covering the full specified period (The most recent payslip must be dated no earlier than 31 days before the date of the application), accompanied by a letter from the Sponsor, on company headed paper and signed by a senior official, confirming the authenticity of the payslips;

(iii) Personal bank or building society statements covering the full specified period, which clearly show:

(1) the applicant's name,

(2) the account number,

(3) the date of the statement (The most recent statement must be dated no earlier than 31 days before the date of the application),

(4) the financial institution's name and logo, and

(5) transactions by the Sponsor covering the full specified period; [or]

(iv) A building society pass book, which clearly shows:

(1) the applicant's name,

(2) the account number,

(3) the financial institution's name and logo, and

(4) transactions by the Sponsor covering the full specified period.

(b) If the applicant provides the bank or building society statements in (a)(iii):

(i) The statements must:

(1) be printed on paper bearing the bank or building society's letterhead,

(2) bear the official stamp of the bank on every page, or

(3) be accompanied by a supporting letter from the issuing bank or building society, on company headed paper, confirming the authenticity of the statements provided;

(ii) The statements must not be mini-statements obtained from an Automated Teller Machine.

(c) The specified documents as evidence of periods of maternity, paternity or adoption leave, as required in paragraph 74C(b), are:

(i) The original full birth certificate or original full certificate of adoption (as appropriate) containing the names of the parents or adoptive parents of the child for whom the leave was taken, if this is available; and

(ii) At least one (or both, if the document in (i) is unavailable) of the following, if they are available:

(1) An original letter from the applicant and his sponsor, on company headed paper, confirming the start and end dates of the applicant's leave,

(2) One of the types of documents set out in (a) above, covering the entire period of leave, and showing the maternity, paternity or adoption payments,

and

(iii) If the applicant cannot provide two of the types of specified document in (i) and (ii), at least one of the types of specified documents in either (i) or (ii), a full explanation of why the other documents cannot be provided, and at least one of the following specified documents, from an official source and which is independently verifiable:

(1) official adoption papers issued by the relevant authority,

(2) any relevant medical documents, or

(3) a relevant extract from a register of birth which is accompanied by an original letter from the issuing authority.

(d) The specified documents as evidence of periods of long term sick leave, as required in paragraph 74C(b), are:

(i) An original letter from the applicant's Sponsor, on company headed paper, confirming the start and end dates of the applicant's leave, if this is available;

(ii) One of the types of documents set out in (a) above, covering the entire period of leave, and showing the statutory sick pay and/or sick pay from health insurance, if these documents are available; and

(iii) If the applicant cannot provide the specified documents in both (i) and (ii), the specified documents in either (i) or (ii), a full explanation of why the other documents cannot be provided, and any relevant medical documents, from an official source and which are independently verifiable.

Note: Words substituted in subparagraphs (a)(i) and (a)(ii) and word 'or' inserted at the end of sub-paragraph (a)(iii)(5) from 1 October 2013 subject to savings for applications made before that date (HC 628).

74D. If the applicant is applying as a Tier 2 (Intra-Company Transfer) Migrant in the Graduate Trainee sub-category, no points will be awarded for a Certificate of Sponsorship unless:

(a) the job that the Certificate of Sponsorship Checking Service entry records that the person is being Sponsored to do is part of a structured graduate training programme, with clearly defined progression towards a managerial or specialist role within the organisation,

(b) the Sponsor has assigned Certificates of Sponsorship to 5 applicants or fewer, including the applicant in question, under the Graduate Trainee sub-category in the current year, beginning 6 April and ending 5 April each year, and

(c) the Certificate of Sponsorship Checking Service entry confirms that the applicant has been working for the Sponsor outside the UK for a continuous period of 3 months immediately prior to the date of application and, if requested to do so, the applicant provides the specified documents in paragraph 74C-SD(a) above to prove this. The application may be granted without these specified documents, but the UK Border Agency reserves the right to request the specified documents, and to refuse applications if these documents are not received at the address specified in the request within 7 working days of the date of the request.

74E. If the applicant is applying as a Tier 2 (Intra-Company Transfer) Migrant in the Skills Transfer subcategory, no points will be awarded for a Certificate of Sponsorship unless the job that the Certificate of Sponsorship Checking Service entry records that the person is being Sponsored to do is for the sole purpose of transferring skills to or from the Sponsor's UK work environment. The appointment must be additional to staffing requirements that is the role in the UK would not exist but for the need for skills transfer.

74F. An applicant cannot score points for a Certificate of Sponsorship from Table 11 if the job that the Certificate of Sponsorship Checking Service entry records that he is being Sponsored to do is as a sports person or a Minister of Religion.

74G. No points will be awarded for a Certificate of Sponsorship if the job that the Certificate of Sponsorship Checking Service entry records that the applicant is being sponsored to do amounts to:

(a) the hire of the applicant to a third party who is not the sponsor to fill a position with that party, whether temporary or permanent, or

(b) contract work to undertake an ongoing routine role or to provide an ongoing routine service for a third party who is not the sponsor,

regardless of the nature or length of any arrangement between the sponsor and the third party.

Note: Paragraphs 74G to 74I inserted from 6 November 2014 subject to savings for applications made before that date (HC 693).

74H. No points will be awarded for a Certificate of Sponsorship if the Entry Clearance Officer or the Secretary of State has reasonable grounds to believe, notwithstanding that the applicant has provided the evidence required under the relevant provisions of Appendix A, that:

(a) the job as recorded by the Certificate of Sponsorship Checking Service is not a genuine vacancy, if the applicant is applying as a Tier 2 (Intra-Company Transfer) Migrant in either of the Short Term Staff or Long Term Staff subcategories, or

(b) the applicant is not appropriately qualified to do the job in question.

Note: Paragraphs 74G to 74I inserted from 6 November 2014 subject to savings for applications made before that date (HC 693).

74I. To support the assessment in paragraph 74H, the Entry Clearance Officer or the Secretary of State may request additional information and evidence from the applicant or the Sponsor, and refuse the application if the information or evidence is not provided. Any requested documents must be received by the Entry Clearance Officer or the Secretary of State at the address specified in the request within 28 calendar days of the date the request is sent.

Note: Paragraphs 74G to 74I inserted from 6 November 2014 subject to savings for applications made before that date (HC 693).

Appropriate salary

75. The points awarded for appropriate salary will be based on the applicant's gross annual salary to be paid by the Sponsor, subject to the following conditions:

(i) Points will be awarded based on basic pay (excluding overtime);

(ii) Allowances will be included in the salary for the awarding of points where they are part of the guaranteed salary package and:

(1) would be paid to a local settled worker in similar circumstances, or

(2) are paid to cover the additional cost of living in the UK;

(iii) Where allowances are made available solely for the purpose of accommodation, they will only be included up to a value of:

(1) 40% of the total salary package for which points are being awarded, if the applicant is applying in either the Short Term Staff, Graduate Trainee or Skills Transfer sub-categories, or

(2) 30% of the total salary package for which points are being awarded, if the applicant is applying in the Long Term Staff sub-category;

(iv) [Other allowances and benefits, such as bonus or incentive pay, employer pension contributions, and allowances] to cover business expenses, including (but not limited to) travel to and from the sending country, will not be included;

(v) If the applicant has exchanged some of his UK employment rights for shares as an employee-owner, the value of those shares will not be included.

Note: Words substituted in sub-paragraph (iv) from 13 December 2012 subject to savings for applications made before that date (HC 760). Sub-paragraph (v) inserted from 6 April 2013 subject to savings for applications made after that date (HC 1039).

75A. No points will be awarded if the salary referred to in paragraph 75 above is less than [£41,000] per year where the applicant is applying in the Long Term Staff sub-category, unless the applicant is applying for leave to remain and previously had leave as:

(i) a Qualifying Work Permit Holder, or

(ii) a Tier 2 (Intra-Company Transfer) Migrant under the rules in place before 6 April 2011, and has not been granted entry clearance in this or any other route since that grant of leave.

Note: Paragraph 75A substituted from 13 December 2012 subject to savings for applications made before that date (HC 760). Words '£41,000' substituted from 6 April 2014 (previous words having been substituted from 6 April 2013 by HC 1039 subject to savings: see implementation section of HC 1039) subject to savings for applications made before that date (HC 1138 as amended by HC 1201).

75B. No points will be awarded if the salary referred to in paragraph 75 above is less than £24,500 per year where the applicant is applying in the Short Term Staff, Graduate Trainee or Skills Transfer sub-categories, unless the applicant is applying for leave to remain and has, or last had entry clearance, leave to enter or leave to remain as a Tier 2 (Intra-Company Transfer) Migrant under the rules in place before 6 April 2011.

Note: Paragraph 75A substituted from 13 December 2012 subject to savings for applications made before that date (HC 760). Words '£24,500' substituted from 6 April 2014 (previous words having been substituted from 6 April 2013 by HC 1039 subject to savings: see implementation section of HC 1039) subject to savings for applications made before that date (HC 1138 as amended by HC 1201).

75C. No points will be awarded if the salary referred to in paragraph 75 above is less than the appropriate rate for the job as stated in the codes of practice in Appendix J, unless the applicant is an established entertainer as defined in paragraph 6 of these Rules.

75D. Where the applicant is paid hourly, the appropriate salary consideration will be based on earnings up to a maximum of 48 hours a week, even if the applicant works for longer than this. For example, an applicant who works 60 hours a week for £8 per hour will be considered to have a salary of £19,968 (8x48x52) and not £25,960 (8x60x52), and will therefore not be awarded points for appropriate salary.

75E. No points will be awarded for appropriate salary if the applicant does not provide a valid Certificate of Sponsorship reference number with his application.

Attributes for Tier 2 (General) Migrants

76. An applicant applying for entry or leave to remain as a Tier 2 (General) Migrant must score 50 points for attributes.

76A. Available points for entry clearance or leave to remain are shown in Table 11A.

76B. Notes to accompany Table 11A appear below the table.

Table 11A

Certificate of Sponsorship	Points	Appropriate Salary	Points
Job offer passes Resident Labour Market Test	30	Appropriate Salary	20
Resident Labour Market Test exemption applies	30		
Continuing to work in the same occupation for the same Sponsor	30		

Note: Table 11A substituted from 6 April 2013 subject to savings for applications made on or after 6 April 13 using a Certificate of Sponsorship assigned to the applicant before that date (HC 1039).

Notes

Certificate of Sponsorship

77. Points may only be scored for one entry in the Certificate of Sponsorship column.

77A. In order to obtain points for a Certificate of Sponsorship, the applicant must provide a valid Certificate of Sponsorship reference number.

77B. The only Certificates of Sponsorship to be allocated to Sponsors for applicants to be Sponsored as Tier 2 (General) Migrants . . . are:

(a) Certificates of Sponsorship to be assigned to applicants as a Tier 2 (General) Migrant, as allocated to Sponsors under the Tier 2 (General) limit, which is set out in paragraphs 80 to 84A below.

(b) Certificates of Sponsorship to be assigned to specified applicants for leave to remain as a Tier 2 (General) Migrant, as set out in paragraph 77D of Appendix A,

(c) Certificates of Sponsorship to be assigned to an applicant to do a job for which the gross annual salary (including such allowances as are specified as acceptable for this purpose {in paragraph 79 of this Appendix}) is [£153,500 (or £152,100, if the recruitment took place before 6 April 2014)] or higher,

and [*sic*]

Note: Words in opening sentence deleted from 6 April 2013 subject to savings for applications made before that date (HC 1039). Words in curly brackets in sub-paragraph (c) substituted from 1 October 2013 subject to savings for applications before that date (HC 628). Words in square brackets in sub-paragraph (c) substituted from 6 April 2014 (previous words having been substituted from 6 April 2013 by HC 1039) subject to savings for applications made before that date (HC 1138 as amended by HC 1201).

77C. A Certificate of Sponsorship reference number will only be considered to be valid if:

(a) the number supplied links to a Certificate of Sponsorship Checking Service entry that names the applicant as the migrant and confirms that the Sponsor is Sponsoring him as a Tier 2 (General) Migrant,

(b) the Sponsor assigned that reference number to the migrant no more than 3 months after the Sponsor was allocated the Certificate of Sponsorship, if the Certificate of Sponsorship was allocated to the Sponsor under the Tier 2 (General) limit,

(c) the Sponsor assigned that reference number to the migrant no more than 3 months before the application for entry clearance or leave to remain is made,

(d) the application for entry clearance or leave to remain is made no more than 3 months before the start of the employment as stated on the Certificate of Sponsorship,

(e) the migrant must not previously have applied for entry clearance, leave to enter or leave to remain using the same Certificate of Sponsorship reference number, if that application was either approved or refused (not rejected as an invalid application, declared void or withdrawn),

(f) that reference number must not have been withdrawn or cancelled by the Sponsor or by the UK Border Agency since it was assigned, including where it has been cancelled by the UK Border Agency due to having been used in a previous application, and

(g) the Sponsor is an A-rated Sponsor, unless:

(1) the application is for leave to remain, and

(2) the applicant has, or was last granted, leave as a Tier 2 (General) Migrant, a Jewish Agency Employee, a Member of the Operational Ground Staff of an Overseas-owned Airline, a Representative of an Overseas Newspaper, News Agency or Broadcasting Organisation, or a Qualifying Work Permit Holder, and

(3) the applicant is applying to work for the same employer named on the Certificate of Sponsorship or Work Permit document which led to his last grant of leave or, in the case of an applicant whose last grant of leave was as a Jewish Agency Employee, a Member of the Operational Ground Staff of an Overseas-owned Airline, a Representative of an Overseas Newspaper, News Agency or Broadcasting Organisation, the same employer for whom the applicant was working or stated he was intending to work when last granted leave.

77D. No points will be awarded for a Certificate of Sponsorship unless:

(a) in the case of a Certificate of Sponsorship which was allocated to the Sponsor under the Tier 2 (General) limit, the number supplied links to a Certificate of Sponsorship Checking Service entry which contains the same job and at least the same salary details as stated in the Sponsor's application for that Certificate of Sponsorship,

(b) in the case of a Certificate of Sponsorship which was not allocated to the Sponsor under the Tier 2 (General) limit:

(i) the applicant:

(1) is applying for leave to remain, and

(2) does not have, or was not last granted, entry clearance, leave to enter or leave to remain as the Partner of a Relevant Points Based System Migrant,

or

(ii) the number supplied links to a Certificate of Sponsorship Checking Service entry which shows that the applicant's gross annual salary (including such allowances as are specified as acceptable for this purpose in paragraph 79 of this appendix) to be paid by the Sponsor is [£153,500 (or £152,100 if the recruitment took place before 6 April 2014)] or higher.

Note: Words substituted in sub-paragraph (b)(ii) from 6 April 2014 subject to savings for applications made before that date (HC 1138 as amended by HC 1201). The words substituted had previously been substituted from 6 April 2013 (HC 1039, subject to savings: see implementation section of HC 1039). Subparagraph (b)(i) substituted from 6 November 2014 subject to savings for applications made before that date (HC 693).

77E. No points will be awarded for a Certificate of Sponsorship unless:

(a) the job that the Certificate of Sponsorship Checking Service entry records that the person is being sponsored to do appears on:

(i) the list of occupations skilled to National Qualifications Framework level 6 or above, as stated in the codes of practice in Appendix J, or

(ii) one of the following creative sector occupations skilled to National Qualifications Framework level 4 or above:

(1) 3411 Artists,

(2) 3412 Authors, writers and translators,

(3) 3413 Actors, entertainers and presenters,

(4) 3414 Dancers and choreographers, or

(5) 3422 Product, clothing and related designers,

or

(b) the job that the Certificate of Sponsorship Checking Service entry records that the person is being sponsored to do is skilled to National Qualifications Framework level 4 or above, and appears on the shortage occupation list in Appendix K,

or

(c) (i) the applicant is applying for leave to remain,

(ii) the applicant previously had leave as a Tier 2 (General) Migrant or a Qualifying Work Permit Holder, and has not since been granted leave to remain in any other route, or entry clearance or leave to enter in any route,

(iii) at the time a Certificate of Sponsorship or Work Permit which led to a grant of leave in (ii) was issued, the job referred to in that Certificate of Sponsorship or Work Permit appeared on the shortage occupation list in Appendix K, and

(iv) the job that the Certificate of Sponsorship Checking service entry records that the person is being sponsored to do in his current application is the same as the job referred to in (iii), for either the same or a different employer,

or

(d) (i) the applicant is applying for leave to remain,

(ii) the applicant previously had leave as a Tier 2 (General) Migrant under the Rules in place between 6 April 2011 and [13 June 2012], and has not since been granted leave to remain in any other route, or entry clearance or leave to enter in any route, and

(iii) the job that the Certificate of Sponsorship Checking Service entry records that the person is being sponsored to do appears on the list of occupations skilled to National Qualifications Framework level 4 or above, as stated in the codes of practice in Appendix J,

or

(e) (i) the applicant is applying for leave to remain,

(ii) the applicant previously had leave as:

(1) a Tier 2 (General) Migrant under the rules in place before 6 April 2011,

(2) a Qualifying Work Permit Holder,

(3) a Representative of an Overseas Newspaper, News Agency or Broadcasting Organisation,

(4) a Member of the Operational Ground Staff of an Overseas-owned Airline,

(5) a Jewish Agency Employee,

and has not since been granted leave to remain in any other route, or entry clearance or leave to enter in any route, and

(iii) the job that the Certificate of Sponsorship Checking Service entry records that the person is being sponsored to do appears on the list of occupations skilled to National Qualifications Framework level 3 or above, as stated in the codes of practice in Appendix J, or the applicant is a Senior Care Worker or an Established Entertainer as defined in paragraph 6 of these Rules.

(f) (i) the applicant was last granted as a Tier 2 (General) Migrant,

(ii) the applicant is applying for leave to remain to work in the same occupation for the same Sponsor as in the application which led to his previous grant of leave,

(iii) the Certificate of Sponsorship used in support of the applicant's previous application was assigned by the Sponsor before 6 April 2013, and

(iv) the occupation fails to meet the required skill level in (a) to (e) above solely due to reclassification from the SOC 2000 system to the SOC 2010 system.

Note: Words substituted in sub-paragraph (d)(ii) from 13 December 2012 subject to savings for applications made before that date (HC 760). Sub-paragraph (a)(ii) substituted and sub-paragraph (f) inserted from 6 April 2013 subject to savings for applications made on or after that date using a Certificate of Sponsorship assigned to the applicant before that date (HC 1039).

77F. An applicant cannot score points for a Certificate of Sponsorship from Table 11A if the job that the Certificate of Sponsorship Checking Service entry records that he is being sponsored to do is as a sports person or a Minister of Religion.

77G. No points will be awarded for a Certificate of Sponsorship if the job that the Certificate of Sponsorship Checking Service entry records that the applicant is being sponsored to do amounts to:

(a) the hire of the applicant to a third party who is not the sponsor to fill a position with that party, whether temporary or permanent, or

(b) contract work to undertake an ongoing routine role or to provide an ongoing routine service for a third party who is not the sponsor,

regardless of the nature or length of any arrangement between the sponsor and the third party.

Note: Paragraphs 77G to 77J inserted from 6 November 2014 subject to savings for applications made before that date (HC 693).

77H. No points will be awarded for a Certificate of Sponsorship if the Entry Clearance Officer or the Secretary of State has reasonable grounds to believe, notwithstanding that the applicant has provided the evidence required under the relevant provisions of Appendix A, that:

(a) the job as recorded by the Certificate of Sponsorship Checking Service is not a genuine vacancy,

(b) the applicant is not appropriately qualified or registered to do the job in question (or will not be, by the time they begin the job), or

(c) the stated requirements of the job as recorded by the Certificate of Sponsorship Checking Service and in any advertisements for the job are inappropriate for the job on offer and / or have been tailored to exclude resident workers from being recruited.

Note: Paragraphs 77G to 77J inserted from 6 November 2014 subject to savings for applications made before that date (HC 693).

77I. To support the assessment in paragraph 77H(b), if the applicant is not yet appropriately qualified or registered to do the job in question, he must provide evidence with his application showing that he can reasonably be expected to obtain the appropriate qualifications or registrations by the time he begins the job, for example, a letter from the relevant body providing written confirmation that the applicant has registered to sit the relevant examinations.

Note: Paragraphs 77G to 77J inserted from 6 November 2014 subject to savings for applications made before that date (HC 693).

77J. To support the assessment in paragraph 77H(a)-(c), the Entry Clearance Officer or the Secretary of State may request additional information and evidence from the applicant or the Sponsor, and refuse the application if the information or evidence is not provided. Any requested documents must be received by the Entry Clearance Officer or the Secretary of State at the address specified in the request within 28 calendar days of the date the request is sent.

Note: Paragraphs 77G to 77J inserted from 6 November 2014 subject to savings for applications made before that date (HC 693).

Job offer passes Resident Labour Market Test

78. Points will only be awarded for a job offer that passes the Resident Labour Market Test if:

(a) the Sponsor has advertised (or had advertised on its behalf) the job as set out in Tables 11B and 11C below; and

(b) The advertisements have stated:

(i) the job title,

(ii) the main duties and responsibilities of the job (job description),

(iii) the location of the job,

(iv) an indication of the salary package or salary range or terms on offer,

(v) the skills, qualifications and experience required for the job, and

(vi) the closing date for applications, unless it is part of the Sponsor's rolling recruitment programme, in which case the advertisement should show the period of the recruitment programme;

and

(c) The advertisements were published in English (or Welsh if the job is based in Wales); and

(d) The Sponsor can show that no suitable settled worker is available to fill the job unless the job is in a PhD-level occupation listed in Appendix J. Settled workers will not be considered unsuitable on the basis that they lack qualifications, experience or skills (including language skills) that were not specifically requested in the job advertisement; and

(e) The Certificate of Sponsorship Checking Service entry contains full details of when and where the job was advertised, and any advertisement reference numbers, including the Universal Jobmatch (or other Jobcentre Plus online service) or JobCentre Online vacancy reference number where relevant.

Table 11B: Advertising methods and duration which satisfy the Resident Labour Market Test

Type of job	Methods of advertising / Recruitment	Duration / timing of Advertising
New graduate jobs or internships	• University milkround visits to at least 3 UK universities (or all UK universities which provide the relevant course, whichever is the lower number), • At least one of the following websites: – <www.jobs.ac.uk>, – <www.milkround.com>, – <www.prospects.ac.uk>, or – <www.targetjobs.co.uk> And • At least one other medium listed in Table 11C	At least 28 days within the 4 years immediately before the Sponsor assigned the Certificate of Sponsorship to the Applicant

Pupillages for trainee barristers	• At least two media (or one medium if the job was advertised before 6 April 2013) listed in Table 11C	At least 28 days within the **2 years** immediately before the Sponsor assigned the Certificate of Sponsorship to the Applicant
Jobs in PhD-level occupations as listed in Appendix J	• At least two media (or one medium if the job was advertised before 6 April 2013) listed in Table 11C	At least 28 days within the 1 year immediately before the Sponsor assigned the Certificate of Sponsorship to the Applicant
Jobs where the appropriate salary, as determined by paragraphs 79 to 79D of Appendix A, is [at least £71,600 per year (or £71,000 per year if the job was advertised before 6 April 2014)] or there is a stock exchange disclosure requirement	• At least two media (or one medium if the job was advertised before 6 April 2013) listed in Table 11C	At least 28 days within the **6 months** immediately before the Sponsor assigned the Certificate of Sponsorship to the Applicant
Creative sector jobs covered by Table 9 of Appendix J	• As set out in Table 9 of Appendix J	As set out in Table 9 of Appendix J
Orchestral musicians	• Universal Jobmatch (or other Jobcentre Plus online service) for jobs based in England, Scotland or Wales, or JobCentre Online for jobs based in Northern Ireland, and • At least one other medium listed in Table 11C	At least 28 days within the **2 years** immediately before the Sponsor assigned the Certificate of Sponsorship to the applicant
Positions in the NHS where the Resident Labour Market Test includes advertising on NHS Jobs between 19 November 2012 and [6 April 2015]	• NHS Jobs	At least 28 days within the **6 months** immediately before the Sponsor assigned the Certificate of Sponsorship to the applicant
All other jobs	• Universal Jobmatch (or other Jobcentre Plus online service) for jobs based in England, Scotland or Wales, or JobCentre Online for jobs based in Northern Ireland, and • At least one other medium listed in Table 11C	At least 28 days within the **6 months** immediately before the Sponsor assigned the Certificate of Sponsorship to the applicant

Table 11C: Advertising media which satisfy the Resident Labour Market Test

Type of Medium	Criteria for suitable media
Newspaper	Must be: • marketed throughout the UK or throughout the whole of the devolved nation in which the job is located, and • published at least once a week
Professional Journal	Must be: • available nationally through retail outlets or through subscription, • published at least once a month, and • related to the nature of the job i.e. a relevant trade journal, official journal of a professional occupational body, or subject-specific Publication
Website	Must be one of the following: • Universal Jobmatch (or other Jobcentre Plus online service), for jobs based in England, Scotland or Wales, • JobCentre Online, for jobs based in Northern Ireland, • an online version of a newspaper or professional journal which would satisfy the criteria above, • the website of a prominent professional or recruitment organisation, which does not charge a fee to jobseekers to view job advertisements or to apply for jobs via those advertisements, or • if the Sponsor is a multinational organisation or has over 250 permanent employees in the UK, the Sponsor's own website

Note: Paragraphs 78 to 78C (including headings and Tables 11B and 11C substituted from 6 April 2013 subject to savings for applications made on or after that date using a Certificate of Sponsorship assigned to the applicant before that date (HC 1039). Words substituted in the fourth row of Table B from 6 April 2014 subject to savings for applications made before that date (HC 1138 as amended by HC 1201). Words substituted in the 7th row of Table 11B from 6 November 2014 (HC 693).

Resident Labour Market Test exemption applies

Shortage occupation

78A. In order for a Resident Labour Market Test exemption to apply for a job offer in a shortage occupation:

(a) the job must, at the time the Certificate of Sponsorship was assigned to the applicant, have appeared on the shortage occupation list in Appendix K,

(b) in all cases, contracted working hours must be for at least 30 hours a week, and

(c) in all cases, if the UK Border Agency list of shortage occupations indicates that the job appears on the 'Scotland only' shortage occupation list, the job offer must be for employment in which the applicant will be working at a location in Scotland.

Note: Paragraphs 78 to 78C (including headings and Tables 11B and 11C substituted from 6 April 2013 subject to savings for applications made on or after that date using a Certificate of Sponsorship assigned to the applicant before that date (HC 1039).

Post-Study Work

78B. In order for a Resident Labour Market Test exemption to apply for post-study work:

(a) the applicant must be applying for leave to remain,

(b) the applicant must have, or have last been granted, entry clearance, leave to enter or leave to remain as:

(1) a Tier 1 (Graduate Entrepreneur) Migrant,

(2) a Tier 1 (Post-Study Work) Migrant,

(3) a Participant in the International Graduates Scheme (or its predecessor, the Science and Engineering Graduates Scheme),

(4) a Participant in the Fresh Talent: Working in Scotland Scheme,

(5) a Tier 4 Migrant,

(6) a Student,

(7) a Student Nurse,

(8) a Student Re-Sitting an Examination,

(9) a Person Writing Up a Thesis,

(10) an Overseas Qualified Nurse or Midwife,

(11) a Postgraduate Doctor or Dentist, or

(12) a Student Union Sabbatical Officer,

and

(c) Where (b)[(5) to (12)] apply, the applicant must meet the requirements of paragraph 245HD(d) of these Rules.

Note: Paragraphs 78 to 78C (including headings and Tables 11B and 11C substituted from 6 April 2013 subject to savings for applications made on or after that date using a Certificate of Sponsorship assigned to the applicant before that date (HC 1039). Sub-paragraph (b)(1) inserted and subsequent subas (b)(2) to (b)(12) renumbered and words substituted in sub-paragraph (c) from 1 October 2013 subject to savings for applications made before that date (HC 628).

Other exemptions

78C. In order for another Resident Labour Market Test exemption to apply, either:

(a) the Certificate of Sponsorship Checking Service entry must show that the applicant's gross annual salary (including such allowances as are specified as acceptable for this purpose in paragraph 79 of this appendix) to be paid by the Sponsor is [£153,500 (or £152,100, if the recruitment took place before 6 April 2014)] or higher; or

(b) the job offer must be in a supernumerary research position where the applicant has been issued a non-transferable scientific research Award or Fellowship by an external organisation which is not the Sponsor, meaning that the role is over and above the Sponsor's normal requirements and if the applicant was not there, the role would not be filled by anyone else; or

(c) the job offer must be to continue working as a Doctor or Dentist in training, under the same NHS Training Number which was assigned to the applicant for previous lawful employment as a Doctor or Dentist in Training in the UK; or

(d) the job offer must be as a Doctor in Speciality Training where the applicant's salary and the costs of his training are being met by the government of another country under an agreement with that country and the United Kingdom Government; [or]

(e) the job offer must be to resume a post in a Higher Education Institution, working for the same Sponsor as in a previous grant of entry clearance or leave to remain as a Tier 2 (General) Migrant, where the break in employment is due solely to a period of academic leave;

and the Certificate of Sponsorship Checking Service entry must provide full details of why an exemption applies.

Note: Paragraphs 78 to 78C (including headings and Tables 11B and 11C substituted from 6 April 2013 subject to savings for applications made on or after that date using a Certificate of Sponsorship assigned to the applicant before that date (HC 1039). Sub-paragraph (b) substituted from 1 July 2013 subject to savings for applications for entry clearance made using a Certificate of sponsorship assigned to the applicant before that date (HC 244). Words substituted in sub-paragraph (a) and sub-paragraph (e) inserted from 6 April 2014 subject to savings for applications made before that date (HC 1138 as amended by HC 1201).

Continuing to work in the [same occupation] for the same Sponsor

78D. In order for the applicant to be awarded points for continuing to work in the [same occupation] for the same Sponsor:

(a) the applicant must be applying for leave to remain,

(b) the applicant must have [, or have last been granted,] entry clearance or leave to remain as:

(i) a Tier 2 (General) Migrant,

(ii) a Qualifying Work Permit Holder,

(iii) a Representative of an Overseas Newspaper, News Agency or Broadcasting Organisation,

(iv) a Member of the Operational Ground Staff of an Overseas-owned Airline or

(v) a Jewish Agency Employee,

(c) the Sponsor must be the same employer:

(i) as the Sponsor on the previous application that was granted, in the case of an applicant whose last grant of leave was as a Tier 2 (General) Migrant,

(ii) that the work permit was issued to, in the case of an applicant whose last grant of leave was as a Qualifying Work Permit Holder,

(iii) for whom the applicant was working or stated he was intending to work when last granted leave, in the case of an applicant whose last grant of leave was a Representative of an Overseas Newspaper, News Agency or Broadcasting Organisation, a Member of the Operational Ground Staff of an Overseas-owned Airline, or a Jewish Agency Employee.

(d) the job that the Certificate of Sponsorship Checking Service entry records the applicant as having been engaged to do must be [in the same occupation]:

(i) in respect of which the Certificate of Sponsorship that led to the previous grant was issued, in the case of an applicant whose last grant of leave was as a Tier 2 (General) Migrant,

(ii) in respect of which the previous work permit was issued, in the case of an applicant whose last grant of leave was as a Qualifying Permit Holder, or

(iii) that the applicant was doing, or intended to do, when he received his last grant of leave, in the case of an applicant whose last grant of leave was a Representative of an Overseas Newspaper, News Agency or Broadcasting Organisation, a Member of the Operational Ground Staff of an Overseas-owned Airline, or a Jewish Agency Employee.

Note: Words in heading and in opening sentence and in sub-paragraph (d) substituted from 6 April 2013 subject to savings for applications made before that date (HC 1039). Words inserted in subparagraph (b) from 6 November 2014 subject to savings for applications made before that date (HC 693).

Appropriate salary

79. The points awarded for appropriate salary will be based on the applicant's gross annual salary to be paid by the Sponsor, subject to the following conditions:

(i) Points will be awarded based on basic pay (excluding overtime);

(ii) Allowances, such as London weighting, will be included in the salary for the awarding of points where they are part of the guaranteed salary package and would be paid to a local settled worker in similar circumstances;

(iii) Other allowances and benefits, such as bonus or incentive pay, [employer pension contributions,] travel and subsistence (including travel to and from the applicant's home country), will not be included.

(iv) If the applicant has exchanged some of his UK employment rights for shares as an employee-owner, the value of those shares will not be included.

Note: Words inserted in sub-paragraph (iii) from 13 December 2012 subject to savings for applications made before that date (HC 760). Sub-paragraph (iv) inserted from 6 April 2013 subject to savings for applications made before that date (HC 1039).

79A. No points will be awarded if the salary referred to in paragraph 79 above is less than £20,500 per year, unless:

(a) the applicant:

(i) is applying for leave to remain, and

(ii) previously had leave as:

(1) a Qualifying Work Permit Holder,

(2) a Representative of an Overseas Newspaper, News Agency or Broadcasting Organisation,

(3) a Member of the operational Ground Staff of an Overseas-owned Airline,

(4) a Jewish Agency Employee, or

(5) a Tier 2 (General) Migrant under the Rules in place before 6 April 2011; and

(iii) has not been granted entry clearance in this or any other route since that grant of leave; or

(b) the Certificate of Sponsorship checking service entry records that the applicant:

(i) obtained a Nursing and Midwifery Council permission before 30 March 2015 to undertake the Overseas Nursing Programme or the Adaptation to Midwifery Programme;

(ii) is being sponsored as a nurse or midwife in a supervised practice placement approved by the Nursing and Midwifery Council;

(iii) will continue to be sponsored as a registered nurse or midwife by the Sponsor after achieving Nursing and Midwifery Council registration; and

(iv) will be paid at least £20,500 per year once that registration is achieved,

and the applicant provides evidence of the above, if requested to do so.

Note: Paragraph 79A substituted from 6 November 2014 subject to savings for applications made before that date (HC 693).

79B. No points will be awarded for appropriate salary if the salary referred to in paragraph 79 above is less than the appropriate rate for the job as stated in the codes of practice in Appendix J, unless the applicant is an established entertainer as defined in paragraph 6 of these Rules.

79C. Where the applicant is paid hourly, the appropriate salary consideration will be based on earnings up to a maximum of 48 hours a week, even if the applicant works for longer than this. for example, an applicant who works 60 hours a week for £8 per hour will be considered to have a salary of £19,968 (8x48x52) and not £25,960 (8x60x52), and will therefore not be awarded points for appropriate salary.

79D. No points will be awarded for appropriate salary if the applicant does not provide a valid Certificate of Sponsorship reference number with his application.

Tier 2 (General) limit

Overview

80. The Secretary of State shall be entitled to limit the number of Certificates of Sponsorship available to be allocated to Sponsors in any specific period under the Tier 2 (General) limit referred to in paragraph 77B(a) above;

80A. The Tier 2 (General) limit is 20,700 Certificates of Sponsorship in each year (beginning on 6 April and ending on 5 April).

Note: Paragraph 80A substituted from 6 April 2013 subject to savings for applications made before that date (HC 1039).

80B. The process by which Certificates of Sponsorship shall be allocated to Sponsors under the Tier 2 (General) limit is set out in paragraphs 80C to 84a and Table 11D below.

Note: Words substituted from 6 April 2013 subject to savings for applications before that date (HC 1039).

80C. A Sponsor must apply to the Secretary of State for a Certificate of Sponsorship.

80D. Available points for an application for a Certificate of Sponsorship are shown in Table [11D]. No application will be granted unless it scores a minimum of 30 points under the heading "Type of Job" and a minimum of 2 points under the heading "Salary on Offer".

Note: '11D' substituted from 6 April 2013 subject to savings for applications made before that date (HC 1039).

80E. Notes to accompany Table [11D] appear below the table.

Note: '11D' substituted from 6 April 2013 subject to savings for applications made before that date (HC 1039).

Table 11D Applications for Certificates of Sponsorship under the Tier 2 (General) limit

Type of job	Points	Salary on offer	Points
Shortage Occupation	75	{[£20,500]–£20,999.99]}	2
PhD-level occupation code and job passes Resident Labour Market Test	50	£21,000–£21,999.99	3
Job passes Resident Labour Market Test or an exemption applies as set out in paragraphs [78B or 78C]	30	£22,000–£22,999.99	4
		£23,000–£23,999.99	5
		£24,000–£24,999.99	6

£25,000–£25,999.99	7
£26,000–£26,999.99	8
£27,000–£27,999.99	9
£28,000–£31,999.99	10
£32,000–£45,999.99	15
£46,000–£74,999.99	20
£75,000–£99,999.99	25
{£100,000–[£153,499.99]}	30

Note: Renumbered as Table 11D from and words in curly brackets substituted in the third column of the first row and the last row from 6 April 2013 subject to savings for applications made before that date (HC 1039). Words substituted in the first column of the third row from 1 October 2013 subject to savings for applications made before that date (HC 628). Words in square brackets in the third column of the first and last rows substituted from 6 April 2014.

Notes

81. Points may only be scored for one entry in each column.

81A. No points will be awarded under the heading "Type of Job" unless the job described in the Sponsor's application for a Certificate of Sponsorship:

(a) appears on:

(i) the list of occupations skilled to National Qualifications Framework level 6 or above, as stated in the codes of practice in Appendix J, or

(ii) one of the following creative sector occupations skilled to National Qualifications Framework level 4 or above:

(1) 3411 Artists,

(2) 3412 Authors, writers and translators,

(3) 3413 Actors, entertainers and presenters,

(4) 3414 Dancers and choreographers, or

(5) 3422 Product, clothing and related designers,

or

(b) is skilled to National Qualifications Framework level 4 or above, and appears on the shortage occupation list in Appendix K.

Note: Sub-paragraph (a)(ii) substituted from 6 April 2013 subject to savings for applications made before that date (HC 1039).

81B. In order for the Sponsor's application to be awarded points for a job in a shortage occupation, the job must, at the time the application for a Certificate of Sponsorship is decided, appear on the the shortage occupation list in Appendix K, and contracted working hours must be for at least 30 hours a week. Furthermore, if the shortage occupation list in Appendix K, indicates that the job appears on the 'Scotland only' shortage occupation list, the job must be for employment in Scotland.

81C. In order for the Sponsor's application to be awarded points for a job in a PhD-level occupation code, the job must be in an occupation code which appears on the list of PhD-level occupation codes as stated in the codes of practice in Appendix J. The Sponsor's application must also meet the requirements of paragraph 81D.

81D. In order for the Sponsor's application to be awarded points for a job that passes the resident labour market test or an exemption applies, the Sponsor must certify that it has met the requirements of that test, as defined in guidance published by the UK Border Agency, in respect of the job, or that one of the exemptions set out in [paragraphs 78B or 78C] of this Appendix applies.

Note: Words substituted from 1 October 2013 subject to savings for applications made before that date (HC 628).

81E. The points awarded under the heading "Salary on Offer" will be based on the gross annual salary on offer to be paid by the Sponsor, as stated in the Sponsor's application, subject to the following conditions:

(i) Points will be awarded based on basic pay (excluding overtime);

(ii) Allowances, such as London weighting, will be included in the salary for the awarding of points where they are part of the guaranteed salary package and would be paid to a local settled worker in similar circumstances;

(iii) Other allowances and benefits, such as bonus or incentive pay, travel and subsistence (including travel to and from the applicant's home country), will not be included.

81F. No points will be awarded for the salary on offer if the salary referred to in paragraph 81e above is less than the appropriate rate for the job as stated in the codes of practice for Tier 2 Sponsors published by the UK Border Agency.

81G. Where the salary on offer will be paid hourly, the salary on offer will be calculated on the basis of earnings up to a maximum of 48 hours a week, even if the jobholder works for longer than this.

81H. No points will be awarded for a Certificate of Sponsorship if the Secretary of State has reasonable grounds to believe that:

(a) the job described in the application is not a genuine vacancy, or

(b) the stated requirements of the job described in the application and in any advertisements for the job are inappropriate for the job on offer and / or have been tailored to exclude resident workers from being recruited.

Note: Paragraphs 81H and 81I inserted from 6 November 2014 subject to savings for applications made before that date (HC 693).

81I. To support the assessment in paragraph 81H, the Secretary of State may request additional information and evidence from the Sponsor. This request will follow the procedure for verification checks as set out in paragraph 82C.

Note: Paragraphs 81H and 81I inserted from 6 November 2014 subject to savings for applications made before that date (HC 693).

Monthly allocations

82. The Tier 2 (General) limit will be divided into monthly allocations.

82A. (i) There will be a monthly allocation specifying the number of Certificates of Sponsorship available to be allocated in respect of applications for Certificates of Sponsorship received during each previous month.

(ii) The monthly application and allocation periods begin on the 6th date of each calendar month and end on the 5th date of the next calendar month.

(iii) The provisional monthly allocation, subject to the processes set out in paragraphs 83 to 84a below, is 1,725 Certificates of Sponsorship each month.

Note: Paragraphs 82A to 83 substituted from 6 April 2013 subject to savings for applications made before that date (HC 1039).

82B. Applications by Sponsors for Certificates of Sponsorship each month will be accepted for consideration against each monthly allocation in the following month.

Note: Paragraphs 82A to 83 substituted from 6 April 2013 subject to savings for applications made before that date (HC 1039).

82C. (i) An application that would fall to be considered as having been received in a particular month may be deferred for consideration as if it had been received in the following month if the Secretary of State considers that the information stated in the application requires verification checks, and may be refused if the information cannot be verified or is confirmed as false.

(ii) If the verification checks are prolonged due to the failure of the Sponsor to cooperate with the verification process such that the application cannot be considered as if it had been received in the next month, the application will be refused.

Note: Paragraphs 82A to 83 substituted from 6 April 2013 subject to savings for applications made before that date (HC 1039).

82D. These provisional monthly allocations may be adjusted according to the processes set out in paragraphs 83 to 84A below.

Note: Paragraphs 82A to 83 substituted from 6 April 2013 subject to savings for applications made before that date (HC 1039).

83. In paragraphs 83A to 84A below:

(a) "number of applications" means the number of applications by Sponsors for a Certificate of Sponsorship under the Tier 2 (General) limit in a single monthly application period.

(b) "monthly allocation" means 1,725 Certificates of Sponsorship, adjusted according to the processes set out in these paragraphs following the assigning of Certificates of Sponsorship under the Tier 2 (General) limit, or to Croatian nationals as set out in (c) below, in the previous monthly period.

(c) (i) Subject to (ii) and (iii) below, each monthly allocation will be reduced by the number of Certificates of Sponsorship assigned by Tier 2 (General) Sponsors to Croatian nationals in the previous monthly allocation period.

(ii) Paragraph (i) does not apply to the first monthly allocation under the Tier 2 (General) limit for 6 April to 5 April each year, to which the application period of 6 March to 5 April relates, or to Certificates of Sponsorship assigned by Tier 2 (General) Sponsors to Croatian nationals before 1 July 2013.

Note: Paragraphs 82A to 83 substituted from 6 April 2013 subject to savings for applications made before that date (HC 1039).

83A. Subject to paragraph 83e below, if the number of applications is equal to or less than the monthly allocation:

(a) All applications by Sponsors which score 32 points or more from the points available in Table [11D] above will be granted, and

(b) If the number of applications granted under (a) above is less than the monthly allocation, the next monthly allocation will be increased by a number equivalent to the Certificates of Sponsorship remaining for allocation in the undersubscribed current month.

Note: '11D' substituted from 6 April 2013 subject to savings for applications made before that date (HC 1039).

83B. Subject to paragraph 83E below, if the number of applications is greater than the monthly allocation:

(a) The minimum points level at which applications for Certificates of Sponsorship will be granted will be calculated as follows:

(i) if the number of applications scoring 32 points or more is no more than 100 greater than the monthly allocation, all applications which score 32 points or more will be granted,

(ii) if the number of applications scoring 32 points or more is more than 100 greater than the monthly allocation, X (being both the number of points scored in Table [11D] above and the minimum number of points required for an application to be granted) will be increased by 1 point incrementally until the number of applications scoring X points is:

(1) less than or equal to the monthly allocation; or

(2) no more than 100 greater than the monthly allocation;

whichever results in the higher value of X, at which stage all applications which score X points or more will be granted,

(b) if the number of applications granted under (a) above is less than the monthly allocation, the number remaining under the monthly allocation will be added to the next monthly allocation,

(c) if the number of applications granted under (a) above is more than the monthly allocation, the number by which the monthly allocation is exceeded will be subtracted from the next monthly allocation.

Note: '11D' substituted from 6 April 2013 subject to savings for applications made before that date (HC 1039).

83C. If a Sponsor is allocated one or more Certificates of Sponsorship under the Tier 2 (General) limit which it then elects not to assign to a migrant it may return them to the Secretary of State and the Secretary of State will subsequently add such Certificates of Sponsorship to the following monthly allocation.

83D. If:

(i) a Sponsor is allocated one or more Certificates of Sponsorship under the Tier 2 (General) limit; and

(ii) the application(s) by the Sponsor scored points from [Table 11D] for a job in a shortage occupation; and

(iii) the Sponsor has not assigned the Certificate(s) of Sponsorship to a migrant(s); and

(iv) the job(s) in question no longer appear on the list of shortage occupations published by the UK Border Agency,

the Certificate(s) of Sponsorship in question will be cancelled and the Secretary of State will subsequently add such Certificates of Sponsorship to the following monthly allocation.

Note: Words substituted in sub-paragraph (ii) from 6 April 2013 subject to savings for applications made before that date (HC 1039).

83E. With regard to the final monthly allocation under the Tier 2 (General) limit for 6 April to 5 April each year, to which the application period of 6 February to 5 March relates:

(i) Paragraphs 83a(b), 83B(b) and 83B(c) do not apply to this monthly allocation, such that no adjustments will be made to the next monthly allocation, and

(ii) References to 'more than 100 greater than the monthly allocation' in paragraphs 83B(a)(ii) to (iii) are amended to 'greater than the monthly allocation', such that the total Tier 2 (General) limit in the period 6 April to 5 April each year will not be exceeded.

84. The Secretary of State is entitled (but not required) to grant an application for a Certificate of Sponsorship under the Tier 2 (General) limit exceptionally outside of the processes set out in paragraphs 82a to 83B above if:

(a) the application is considered by the Secretary of State to require urgent treatment when considered in line with the Tier 2 (Sponsor) guidance published on the [visas and immigration pages of the gov.uk website], and

(b) the application scores enough points from Table [11D] above that it would have met the requirements to be granted under the previous monthly allocation.

Note: '11D' substituted from 6 April 2013 subject to savings for applications made before that date (HC 1039). Words substituted in sub-paragraph (a) from 6 April 2014 subject to savings for applications made before that date (HC 1138 as amended by HC 1201).

84A. For each Certificate of Sponsorship application granted under the urgent treatment process set out in paragraph 84 above:

(i) the current monthly allocation for granting Certificates of Sponsorship further to requests for urgent treatment will be reduced by one, if the current monthly allocation has not yet been reached; or

(ii) In all other cases, the subsequent monthly allocation for granting Certificates of Sponsorship further to requests for urgent treatment will be reduced by one.

Attributes for Tier 2 (Ministers of Religion) Migrants

85. An applicant applying for entry clearance or leave to remain as a Tier 2 (Ministers of Religion) Migrant must score 50 points for attributes.

86. Available points are shown in Table 12 below.

87. Notes to accompany Table 12 appear below that table.

Table 12

Criterion	Points
Certificate of Sponsorship	50

Notes

88. In order to obtain points for sponsorship. the applicant will need to provide a valid Certificate of Sponsorship reference number in this category.

89. A Certificate of Sponsorship reference number will only be considered to be valid for the purposes of this sub-category if:

(a) the number supplied links to a Certificate of Sponsorship Checking Service entry that names the applicant as the Migrant and confirms that the sponsor is sponsoring him as a Tier 2 (Minister of Religion) Migrant, and

(b) the Sponsor is an A-rated Sponsor, unless:

(1) the application is for leave to remain, and

(2) the applicant has, or was last granted, leave as a Tier 2 (Minister of Religion) Migrant, a Minister of Religion, Missionary or Member of a Religious Order, and

(3) the applicant is applying to work for the same employer named on the Certificate of Sponsorship which led to his last grant of leave or, in the case of an applicant whose last grant of leave was as a Minister of Religion, Missionary or Member of a Religious Order, the same employer for whom the applicant was working or stated he was intending to work when last granted leave.

90. The sponsor must have assigned the Certificate of Sponsorship reference number to the migrant no more than 3 months before the application is made and the reference number must not have been cancelled by the Sponsor or by the United Kingdom Border Agency since then.

91. The migrant must not previously have applied for entry clearance, leave to enter or leave to remain using the same Certificate of Sponsorship reference number, if that application was either approved or refused (not rejected as an invalid application, declared void or withdrawn).

92. in addition, the Certificate of Sponsorship Checking Service entry must:

(a) confirm that the applicant is being sponsored to perform religious duties, which:

(i) must be work which is within the Sponsor's organisation, or directed by the Sponsor's organisation,

(ii) may include preaching, pastoral work and non-pastoral work,

(iii) must not involve mainly non-pastoral duties, such as school teaching, media production, domestic work, or administrative or clerical work, unless the role is a senior position in the Sponsor's organisation, and

(b) provide an outline of the duties in (a),

(c) if the Sponsor's organisation is a religious order, confirm that the applicant is a member of that order,

(d) confirm that the applicant will receive pay and conditions at least equal to those given to settled workers in the same role, that the remuneration complies with or is exempt from National Minimum Wage regulations, and provide details of the remuneration,

(e) confirm that the requirements of the resident labour market test, as set out in paragraph 92A below, in respect of the job, have been complied with, unless the applicant is applying for leave to remain and the Sponsor is the same Sponsor as in his last grant of leave,

(f) confirm that the migrant:

(i) is qualified to do the job in respect of which he is seeking leave as a Tier 2 (Minister of Religion) Migrant,

(ii) intends to base himself in the UK, and

(iii) will comply with the conditions of his leave, if his application is successful, and

(g) confirm that the Sponsor will maintain or accommodate the migrant.

Note: Subparagraphs (f) and (g) substituted from 13 December 2012 subject to savings for applications made before that date (HC 1039).

92A. To confirm that the Resident Labour Market Test has been passed or the role is exempt from the test, and for points to be awarded, the Certificate of Sponsorship Checking Service entry must confirm:

(a) That the role is supernumerary, such that it is over and above the Sponsor's normal staffing requirements and if the person filling the role was not there, it would not need to be filled by anyone else, with a full explanation of why it is supernumerary; or

(b) That the role involves living mainly within and being a member of a religious order, which must be a lineage of communities or of people who live in some way set apart from society in accordance with their specific religious devotion, for example an order of nuns or monks; or

(c) That the Sponsor holds national records of all available individuals, details of those records and confirmation that the records show that no suitable settled worker is available to fill the role; or

(d) That a national recruitment search was undertaken, including the following details:

(i) Where the role was advertised, which must be at least one of the following:

(1) a national form of media appropriate to the Sponsor's religion or denomination,

(2) the Sponsor's own website, if that is how the Sponsor usually reaches out to its community on a national scale, that is where it normally advertises vacant positions, and the pages containing the advertisement are free to view without paying a subscription fee or making a donation, or

(3) Jobcentre Plus (or in Northern Ireland, JobCentre Online) or in the employment section of a national newspaper, if there is no suitable national form of media appropriate to the Sponsor's religion or denomination;

(ii) any reference numbers of the advertisements;

(iii) the period the role was advertised for, which must include at least 28 days during the 6 month period immediately before the date the Sponsor assigned the Certificate of Sponsorship to the applicant; and

(iv) confirmation that no suitable settled workers are available to be recruited for the role;

or the applicant must be applying for leave to remain and the Sponsor must be the same Sponsor as in his last grant of leave.

Note: Paragraph 92A substituted from 1 July 2013 (HC 244).

Attributes for Tier 2 (Sportsperson) Migrants

93. An applicant applying for entry clearance or leave to remain as a Tier 2 (Sportsperson) Migrant must score 50 points for attributes.

94. Available points are shown in Table 13 below.

95. Notes to accompany Table 13 appear below that table.

Table 13

Criterion	Points
Certificate of Sponsorship	50

Notes

96. In order to obtain points for sponsorship, the applicant will need to provide a valid Certificate of Sponsorship reference number for sponsorship in this subcategory.

97. A Certificate of Sponsorship reference number will only be considered to be valid for the purposes of this subcategory if:

(a) the number supplied links to a Certificate of Sponsorship Checking Service entry that names the applicant as the Migrant and confirms that the sponsor is sponsoring him as a Tier 2 (Sportsperson) Migrant, and

(b) the Sponsor is an A-rated Sponsor, unless:

(1) the application is for leave to remain, and

(2) the applicant has, or was last granted, leave as a Tier 2 (Sportsperson) Migrant or a Qualifying Work Permit Holder, and

(3) the applicant is applying to work for the same employer named on the Certificate of Sponsorship or Work Permit document which led to his last grant of leave.

98. The Sponsor must have assigned the Certificate of Sponsorship reference number to the migrant no more than 3 months before the application is made and the reference number must not have been cancelled by the Sponsor or by the United Kingdom Border Agency since then.

99. The migrant must not previously have applied for entry clearance, leave to enter or leave to remain using the same Certificate of Sponsorship reference number, if that application was either approved or refused (not rejected as an invalid application, declared void or withdrawn).

100. In addition the Certificate of Sponsorship Checking Service entry must confirm that the migrant:

(a) is qualified to do the job in question,

(b) has been endorsed by the Governing Body for his Sport (that is, the organisation which is specified in Appendix M as being the Governing Body for the sport in question),

(c) The endorsement referred to in (b) above must confirm that the player or coach is internationally established at the highest level whose employment will make a significant contribution to the development of his sport at the highest level in the UK, and that the post could not be filled by a suitable settled worker,

(d) intends to base himself in the UK, and

(e) will comply with the conditions of his leave, if his application is successful.

Attributes for Tier 5 (Youth Mobility Scheme) Temporary Migrants

101. An applicant applying for entry clearance as a Tier 5 (Youth Mobility Scheme) Temporary Migrant must score 40 points for attributes.

102. Available points are shown in Table 14 below.

103. Notes to accompany Table 14 below.

Table 14

Criterion	Points
Citizen of a country or rightful holder of a passport issued by a territory listed in Appendix G or Is a British Overseas Citizen, British Territories Overseas Citizen or British National (Overseas)	30
Will be 18 or over when his entry clearance becomes valid for use and was under the age of 31 on the date his application was made	10

Notes

104. The applicant must provide a valid passport as evidence of all of the above.

Attributes for Tier 5 (Temporary Worker) Migrants

105. An applicant applying for entry clearance or leave enter or remain as a Tier 5 (Temporary Worker) Migrant must score 30 points for attributes.

106. Available points are shown in Table 15 below.

107. Notes to accompany Table 15 appear below in that table.

Table 15

Criterion	Points awarded
Holds a Tier 5 (Temporary Worker) Certificate of Sponsorship	30

Notes

108. In order to meet the 'holds a Certificate of Sponsorship' requirement, the applicant will provide a valid Certificate of Sponsorship reference number for sponsorship in this category.

109. A Certificate of Sponsorship reference number will only be considered to be valid if the number supplied links to a Certificate of Sponsorship Checking Service reference that names the applicant as the migrant and confirms that the Sponsor is sponsoring him as a Tier 5 (Temporary Worker) Migrant in the subcategory indicated by the migrant in his application for entry clearance or leave.

109A. A Certificate of Sponsorship reference number will only be considered to be valid if:

(a) the Sponsor assigned the reference number to the migrant no more than 3 months before the application for entry clearance or leave to remain is made, unless the migrant is applying for leave to enter and has previously been granted leave to enter using the same Certificate of Sponsorship reference number,

(b) the application for entry clearance or leave to remain is made no more than 3 months before the start date of the employment as stated on the Certificate of Sponsorship,

(c) that reference number must not have been cancelled by the Sponsor or by the United Kingdom Border Agency since it was assigned, and

(d) the Sponsor is an A-rated sponsor, unless the application is for leave to remain and the applicant has, or was last granted, leave as a Tier 5 Migrant, an Overseas Government Employee or a Qualifying Work Permit Holder.

110. The migrant must not previously have applied for entry clearance or leave to remain using the same Certificate of Sponsorship reference number, if that application was either approved or refused (not rejected as an invalid application, declared void or withdrawn).

111. In addition, a Certificate of Sponsorship reference number will only be considered to be valid:

(a) where the Certificate of Sponsorship Checking Service entry shows that the Certificate of Sponsorship has been issued in the Creative and Sporting subcategory to enable the applicant to work as a sportsperson, if:

(i) The Certificate of Sponsorship Checking Service entry shows that the applicant has been endorsed by the Governing Body for his sport (that is, the organisation which is specified in Appendix M as being the Governing Body for the sport in question), and

(ii) The endorsement referred to in (i) above confirms that the player or coach is internationally established at the highest level and/or will make a significant contribution to the development of his sport at the highest level in the UK, and that the post could not be filled by a suitable settled worker.

(b) where the Certificate of Sponsorship Checking Service entry shows that the Certificate of Sponsorship has been issued in the Creative and Sporting subcategory to enable the applicant to work as a creative worker, if the entry confirms that:

(i) where a relevant creative sector Codes of Practice exists in Appendix J, the Sponsor has complied with that Code of Practice; or

(ii) where no relevant creative sector Codes of Practice exists in Appendix J, the Sponsor has otherwise taken into account the needs of the resident labour market in that field, and the work could not be carried out by a suitable settled worker.

(c) where the Certificate of Sponsorship Checking Service entry shows that the Certificate of Sponsorship has been issued in the Charity Workers subcategory, if the work the applicant is being sponsored to do is:

(i) voluntary fieldwork directly related to the purpose of the charity which is sponsoring him,

(ii) not paid (except reasonable expenses outlined in section 44 of the National Minimum Wage Act), and

(iii) not a permanent position.

(d) where the Certificate of Sponsorship Checking Service entry shows that the Certificate of Sponsorship has been issued in the Religious Workers subcategory, if the entry confirms:

(i) that the applicant is being sponsored to perform religious duties, which:

(1) must be work which is within the Sponsor's organisation, or directed by the Sponsor's organisation,

(2) may include preaching, pastoral work and non-pastoral work, and

(ii) an outline of the duties in (i),

(iii) if the Sponsor's organisation is a religious order, that the applicant is a member of that order;

(iv) that the applicant will receive pay and conditions at least equal to those given to settled workers in the same role,

(v) that the remuneration complies with or is exempt from National Minimum Wage regulations, and provides details of the remuneration,

(vi) details of how the resident labour market test has been complied with or why the role is exempt from the test, as set out in paragraph 92A of this Appendix.

(e) where the Certificate of Sponsorship Checking Service entry shows that the Certificate of Sponsorship has been issued in the Government Authorised Exchange subcategory, if the entry confirms that the work, volunteering or job shadowing the applicant is being sponsored to do:

(i) meets the requirements of the individual exchange scheme, as set out in Appendix N,

(ii) does not fill a vacancy in the workforce,

(iii) is skilled to National Qualifications Framework level 3, as stated in the codes of practice in Appendix J, unless the applicant is being sponsored under an individual exchange scheme set up as part of the European Commission's Lifelong Learning Programme,

(iv) conforms with all relevant UK and EU legislation, such as the National Minimum Wage Act and the Working Time Directive.

(f) where the Certificate of Sponsorship Checking Service entry shows that the Certificate of Sponsorship has been issued in the International Agreement subcategory and the applicant is applying for entry clearance or leave to enter or remain for the purpose of work as a Contractual Service Supplier, [or Independent Professional] if either:

(i) the work is pursuant to a contract to supply services to the sponsor in the United Kingdom by an overseas undertaking established on the territory of a party to the General Agreement on Trade in Services or a similar trade agreement which has been concluded between the EU and another party or parties and which is in force, and which has no commercial presence in the European Union; and

(ii) the service which that undertaking is contracted to supply to the sponsor in the United Kingdom is a service falling within the scope of the sectors specified in the relevant commitments in respect of Contractual Service Suppliers [or Independent Professionals] as set out in the agreements mentioned at (i) above; and

(iii) the sponsor has, through an open tendering procedure or other procedure which guarantees the bona fide character of the contract, awarded a services contract for a period not exceeding 12 months to the applicant's employer; and

(iv) the sponsor will be the final consumer of the services provided under that contract; and

(v) the applicant is a national of the country in which the overseas undertaking is established; and

(vi) where the applicant is a Contractual Service Supplier, he possesses:

(1) a university degree or a technical qualification demonstrating knowledge of an equivalent level, and provides the original certificate of that qualification, except where (4) applies;

(2) where they are required by any relevant law, regulations or requirements in force in the United Kingdom in order to exercise the activity in question, professional qualifications;

(3) 3 years' professional experience in the sector concerned, except where (4) applies; and

(4) (a) in the case of advertising and translation services, relevant qualifications and 3 years' professional experience, and provides the original certificate of those qualifications;

(b) in the case of management consulting services and services related to management consulting (managers and senior consultants), a university degree and 3 years' professional experience, and provides the original certificate of that qualification;

(c) in the case of technical testing and analysis services, a university degree or technical qualifications demonstrating technical knowledge and 3 years' professional experience, and provides the original certificate of that qualification;

(d) in the case of fashion model services and entertainment services other than audiovisual services, 3 years' relevant experience;

(e) in the case of chef de cuisine services, an advanced technical qualification and 6 years' relevant experience at the level of chef de cuisine, and provides the original certificate of that qualification; and

(vii) where the applicant is a Contractual Service Supplier, he has been employed, and provides the specified documents in paragraph 111-SD to show that he has been employed, by the service supplier for a period of at least one year immediately prior to the date of application; or

(viii) where the applicant is an Independent Professional, he possesses:

(1) a university degree or a technical qualification demonstrating knowledge of an equivalent level, and provide the original certificate of that qualification,

(2) where they are required by any relevant law, regulations or requirements in force in the United Kingdom in order to exercise the activity in question, professional qualifications; and

(3) at least six years professional experience in the sector concerned; or

(ix) the applicant is applying for leave to remain and holds a Certificate of Sponsorship issued in the International Agreement sub-category by the same sponsor, and for the purpose of the same contract to supply services, as was the case when the applicant was last granted entry clearance, leave to enter or remain.

(g) where the Certificate of Sponsorship Checking Service entry shows that the Certificate of Sponsorship has been issued in the International Agreement subcategory and the applicant is coming for a purpose other than work as a Contractual Service Supplier, or Independent Profession if the entry confirms that applicant is being sponsored:

(i) as an employee of an overseas government, or

(ii) as an employee of an international organisation established by international treaty signed by the UK or European Union, or

(iii) as a private servant in a diplomatic household under the provisions of the Vienna Convention on Diplomatic Relations, 1961, or in the household of an employee of an international organisation recognised by Her Majesty's Government, who enjoys certain privileges or immunity under UK or international law, and confirms the name of the individual who is employing them.

Note: Sub-paragraph (f) substituted from 13 December 2012 (subject to savings for applications made before that date (HC 760). Words inserted in subparagraphs (f) and (f)(ii) and (g) and subparagraphs (f)(vi) to (ix) substituted from 6 April 2013 subject to savings for applications made before that date (HC 1039). Sub-paragraph (b) substituted from 1 October 2013 subject to savings for applications made before that date (HC 628). Sub-paragraph (d)(vi) substituted from 1 July 2013 (HC 244).

111-SD (a) Where paragraph 111(f)(vii) refers to specified documents, those specified documents are:

(i) original formal payslips issued by the employer and showing the employer's name; or

(ii) payslips accompanied by a letter from the applicant's employer, on the employer's headed paper and signed by a senior official, confirming the payslips are authentic; or

(iii) Personal bank or building society statements covering the full specified period, which clearly show:

(1) the applicant's name,

(2) the account number,

(3) the date of the statement (The most recent statement must be dated no earlier than 31 days before the date of the application),

(4) the financial institution's name and logo, and

(5) transactions by the service supplier covering the full specified period;

or

(iv) A building society pass book, which clearly shows:

(1) the applicant's name,

(2) the account number,

(3) the financial institution's name and logo, and

(4) transactions by the service supplier covering the full specified period.

(b) If the applicant provides the bank or building society statements in (a)(iii):

(i) The statements must:

(1) be printed on paper bearing the bank or building society's letterhead,

(2) bear the official stamp of the bank on every page, or

(3) be accompanied by a supporting letter from the issuing bank or building society, on company headed paper, confirming the authenticity of the statements provided;

(ii) The statements must not be mini-statements obtained from an Automated Teller Machine.

Note: Paragraph 111SD inserted from 13 December 2012 subject to savings for applications made before that date (HC 760). Subparagraphs (a)(i) and (a)(ii) substituted from 1 October 2013 subject to savings for applications made before that date (HC 628).

112. Points will not be awarded for a Tier 5 (Temporary Worker) Certificate of Sponsorship where the claimed basis for its issuance are the provisions under Mode 4 of the General Agreement on Trade in Services relating to intra-corporate transfers.

Attributes for Tier 4 (General) Students

113. An applicant applying for entry clearance or leave to remain as a Tier 4 (General) Student must score 30 points for attributes. Available points are shown in Table 16 below.

114. Notes to accompany Table 16 appear below that table.

Table 16

Criterion	Points awarded
Confirmation of Acceptance for Studies	30

Notes

115A. In order to obtain points for a Confirmation of Acceptance for Studies, the applicant must provide a valid Confirmation of Acceptance for Studies reference number.

Tier 4 Interim Limit

115B. The Secretary of State shall be entitled to limit the number of Confirmations of Acceptance for Studies allocated to any specific Sponsor in any one period.

Note: Paragraphs 115B to 115I substituted from 1 January 2013 subject to savings for applications made before that date (HC 760).

115C. The limit on the number of Confirmations of Acceptance for Studies allocated to specific Sponsors shall be known as the Tier 4 Interim Limit.

Note: Paragraphs 115B to 115I substituted from 1 January 2013 subject to savings for applications made before that date (HC 760).

115CA. The interim limit implemented by HC 1888 and effective in relation to Tier 4 between 6 April 2012 and 31 December 2012 shall be known as the Former Interim Limit.

Note: Paragraphs 115B to 115I substituted from 1 January 2013 subject to savings for applications made before that date (HC 760).

115D. The Tier 4 Interim Limit will apply from 1 January 2013 to 30 June 2013 (inclusive) (the "Tier 4 Interim Limit Period").

Note: Paragraphs 115B to 115I substituted from 1 January 2013 subject to savings for applications made before that date (HC 760).

115E. The Tier 4 Interim Limit will be applied to any Tier 4 Sponsor who

(i) is still subject to the former interim limit on 31 December 2012 and has applied for but not yet achieved HTS status and a valid and satisfactory full institutional inspection, review or audit from one of the following bodies:

(a) the Bridge Schools Inspectorate; or
(b) the Education and Training Inspectorate; or
(c) Estyn; or
(d) Education Scotland; or
(e) the Independent Schools Inspectorate; or
(f) Ofsted; or
(g) the Quality Assurance Agency for Higher Education; or
(h) The Schools Inspection Service;

or is not:

(ii) the Foundation Programme Office;
(iii) the Yorkshire and Humber Strategic Health Authority;
(iv) an overseas higher education institution which has Highly Trusted Sponsor Status.

Note: Paragraphs 115B to 115I substituted from 1 January 2013 subject to savings for applications made before that date (HC 760).

115F. A Tier 4 Sponsor who does not satisfy the requirements of paragraph 115E and is therefore subject to the Tier 4 Interim Limit is known as a Limited Sponsor.

Note: Paragraphs 115B to 115I substituted from 1 January 2013 subject to savings for applications made before that date (HC 760).

115FA. No Confirmations of Acceptance for Studies will be allocated to a Limited Sponsor where:

(i) The Limited Sponsor did not apply for inspection, review or audit by the appropriate specified body by the relevant deadline, as listed below:

Specified body	Deadline
Quality Assurance Agency	9 September 2011
Independent Schools Inspectorate	9 September 2011
Bridge Schools Inspectorate	7 October 2011
School Inspection Service	7 October 2011
Education Scotland	11 November 2011
Education and Training Inspectorate N.I.	30 April 2012

or

(ii) The Limited Sponsor applied by the deadline specified in (i) above, and failed to meet the required standard to obtain a full institutional audit, inspection or review, except for where The Limited Sponsor requires a second institutional audit, inspection or review within 6 months of the initial audit, inspection or review as determined by the relevant body listed above; or

(iii) The Limited Sponsor applied for Highly Trusted Sponsor status on two occasions and has not been granted Highly Trusted Sponsor status.

Note: Paragraphs 115B to 115I substituted from 1 January 2013 subject to savings for applications made before that date (HC 760).

115FB. A Limited Sponsor that is allocated no Confirmations of Acceptance for Studies further to paragraph 115FA is known as a Legacy Sponsor.

Note: Paragraphs 115B to 115I substituted from 1 January 2013 subject to savings for applications made before that date (HC 760).

115G. All Confirmations of Acceptance for Studies allocated by the Secretary of State to Limited Sponsors prior to 1 January 2013 and which have not been assigned to an applicant for entry clearance, leave to enter or leave to remain under Tier 4 prior to 1 January 2013 are withdrawn and the only Confirmations of Acceptance for Studies allocated to a Limited Sponsor are the Confirmations of Acceptance for Studies allocated in accordance with paragraph 115H below.

Note: Paragraphs 115B to 115I substituted from 1 January 2013 subject to savings for applications made before that date (HC 760).

115H. The Tier 4 Interim Limit will be calculated as follows:

(i) A Limited Sponsor who has that status as at 1 January 2013 will be allocated:

(a) where the Limited Sponsor was subject to the Former Tier 4 Interim Limit for the entirety of the period 6 April 2012 to 31 December 2012, a number of Confirmations of Acceptance for Studies equal to two thirds of the number of Confirmations of Acceptance for Studies allocated to that Limited Sponsor for the period 6 April 2012 to 31 December 2012;

(b) where the Limited Sponsor had a Tier 4 Sponsor Licence for only part of the period 6 April 2012 to 31 December 2012, and was subject to the Former Tier 4 Interim Limit from the date on which it was granted a sponsor licence, a number of Confirmations of Acceptance for Studies equal to:

(i) the number of Confirmations of Acceptance for Studies allocated to that Limited Sponsor for the period it was licenced between 6 April 2012 to 31 December 2012;

(ii) multiplied by the appropriate factor such that the figure in (i) is equal to the number of Confirmations of Acceptance for Studies that would have been granted to that Limited Sponsor for a period of 6 months;

(c) where the Limited Sponsor had a Tier 4 Sponsor Licence for the entirety of the period 6 April 2012 to 31 December 2012 and was subject to the Former Tier 4 Interim Limit for only part of that period, a number of Confirmations of Acceptance for Studies equal to:

(i) the number of Confirmations of Acceptance for Studies allocated to that Limited Sponsor under the Tier 4 Interim Limit;

(ii) multiplied by the appropriate factor such that the figure in (i) is equal to the number of Confirmations of Acceptance for Studies that would have been granted to that Limited Sponsor for a period of 6 months;

(d) where the calculation in paragraphs (a) to (c) results in 0 or a negative number, the Limited Sponsor will be allocated 0 Confirmations of Acceptance for Studies under the Tier 4 Interim Limit;

(e) where the calculation in paragraphs (a) to (c) does not result in a whole number, the Limited Sponsor will be allocated a number of Confirmations of Acceptance for Studies equal to the nearest whole number (fractions will be rounded up to the nearest whole number).

Note: Paragraphs 115B to 115I substituted from 1 January 2013 subject to savings for applications made before that date (HC 760).

115I. A Limited Sponsor will, on provision to the UK Border Agency of evidence that it meets the criteria set out in paragraph 115E above, be exempt from the Tier 4 Interim Limit from the date the UK Border Agency provides written confirmation that it is so exempt.

Note: Paragraphs 115B to 115I substituted from 1 January 2013 subject to savings for applications made before that date (HC 760).

116. A Confirmation of Acceptance for Studies will only be considered to be valid if:

(a) it was issued no more than 6 months before the application is made,

(b) the application for entry clearance or leave to remain is made no more than 3 months before the start date of the course of study as stated on the Confirmation of Acceptance for Studies,

(c) the Sponsor has not withdrawn the offer since the Confirmation of Acceptance for Studies was issued,

(d) it was issued by an institution with a Tier 4 (General) Student Sponsor Licence,

(da) where the application for entry clearance or leave to remain is for the applicant to commence a new course of study, not for completion of a course already commenced by way of re-sitting examinations or repeating a module of a course, the Sponsor must hold an A-rated or Highly Trusted Sponsor Licence and must not be a Legacy Sponsor,

(db) where the Confirmation of Acceptance for Studies is issued by a Legacy Sponsor or a B-rated sponsor, the Confirmation of Acceptance for Studies will only be valid if it is issued for completion of a course already commenced by way of re-sitting examinations or repeating a module of a course and the Confirmation of Acceptance for Studies must be for the same course as the course for which the last period of leave was granted to study with that same sponsor,

(e) the institution must still hold such a licence at the time the application for entry clearance or leave to remain is determined,

(ea) the migrant must not previously have applied for entry clearance, leave to enter or leave to remain using the same Confirmation of Acceptance for Studies reference number where that application was either approved or refused (not rejected as an invalid application declared void or withdrawn),

(f) it contains the following mandatory information:

(i) the applicant's:

(1) name,

(2) date of birth,

(3) gender,

(4) nationality, and

(5) passport number;

(ii) the course:

(1) title,

(2) level,

(3) start and end dates, and

(4) hours per week, including confirmation that the course is full-time;

(iii) confirmation if the course is one in which the applicant must hold a valid Academic Technology Approval Scheme clearance certificate from the Counter-Proliferation Department of the Foreign and Commonwealth Office;

(iv) confirmation if the course is a recognised Foundation Programme for post-graduate doctors or dentists, and requires a certificate from the Postgraduate Dean;

(v) the main study address;

(vi) details of how the Tier 4 Sponsor has assessed the applicant's English language ability including, where relevant, the applicant's English language test scores in all four components (reading, writing, speaking and listening);

(vii) details of any work placements relating to the course;

(viii) accommodation, fees and boarding costs;

(ix) details of any partner institution, if the course will be provided by an education provider that is not the Tier 4 Sponsor; and

(x) the name and address of the overseas higher education institution, if the course is part of a study abroad programme.

(g) . . . it was not issued for a course of studies, it was issued for a full-time, salaried, elected executive position as a student union sabbatical officer to an applicant who is part-way through their studies or who is being sponsored to fill the position in the academic year immediately after their graduation [, or]

(h) it was not issued for a course of studies, it was issued within 60 days of the expected end date of a course leading to the award of a PhD and the migrant is sponsored by a Sponsor that is a Recognised Body or a body in receipt of public funding as a higher education institution from the Department of Employment and Learning in Northern Ireland, the Higher Education Funding Council for England, the Higher Education Funding Council for Wales or the Scottish Funding Council, to enable the migrant to remain in the UK as a Tier 4 (General) Student on the doctorate extension scheme.

Note: Words omitted from and inserted in sub-paragraph (g) and sub-paragraph (h) inserted from 6 April 2013 subject to savings for applications made before that date (HC 1039).

117. A Confirmation of Acceptance for Studies reference number will only be considered to be valid if:

(a) the number supplied links to a Confirmation of Acceptance for Studies Checking Service entry that names the applicant as the migrant and confirms that the Sponsor is sponsoring him in the Tier 4 category indicated by the migrant in his application for leave to remain (that is, as a Tier 4 (General) Student or a Tier 4 (Child) Student), and

(b) that reference number must not have been withdrawn or cancelled by the Sponsor or the UK Border Agency since it was assigned.

118. No points will be awarded for a Confirmation of Acceptance for Studies unless:

(a) the applicant supplies, as evidence of previous qualifications, the specified documents, as set out in paragraph 120-SD(a), that the applicant used to obtain the offer of a place on a course from the Sponsor unless the applicant is sponsored by a Highly Trusted Sponsor, is a national of one of the countries or the rightful holder of a qualifying passport issued by one of the relevant competent authorities, as appropriate, listed in Appendix H, and is applying for entry clearance in his country of nationality or in the territory related to the passport he holds, as appropriate, or leave to remain in the UK. The UK Border Agency reserves the right to request the specified documents from these applicants. The application will be refused if the specified documents are not provided in accordance with the request made; and

(b) One of the requirements in (i) to (iii) below is met:

(i) the course is degree level study and the Confirmation of Acceptance for Studies has been assigned by a Sponsor which is a Recognised Body or a body in receipt of funding as a higher education institution from the Department for Employment and Learning in Northern Ireland, the Higher Education Funding Council for England, the Higher Education Funding Council for Wales, or the Scottish Funding Council, and:

(1) the applicant is a national of one of the following countries: Antigua and Barbuda; Australia; The Bahamas; Barbados; Belize; Canada; Dominica; Grenada; Guyana; Jamaica; New Zealand; St Kitts and Nevis; St Lucia; St Vincent and the Grenadines; Trinidad and Tobago; the United States of America, and provides the specified documents set out in paragraph 120-SD(b); or

(2) has obtained an academic qualification (not a professional or vocational qualification), which is deemed by UK NARIC to meet or exceed the recognised standard of a Bachelor's or Master's degree or a PhD in the UK, from an educational establishment in one of the following countries: Antigua and Barbuda; Australia; The Bahamas; Barbados; Belize; Dominica; Grenada; Guyana; Ireland; Jamaica; New Zealand; St Kitts and Nevis; St Lucia; St Vincent and The Grenadines; Trinidad and Tobago; the UK; the USA, and provides the specified documents set out in paragraph 120-SD(a); or

(3) the applicant has successfully completed a course as a Tier 4 (Child) Student (or under the student rules that were in force before 31 March 2009, where the student was granted permission to stay whilst he was under 18 years old) which:

i. was at least six months in length, and

ii. ended within two years of the date the sponsor assigned the Confirmation of Acceptance for Studies; or

(4) the Confirmation of Acceptance for Studies Checking Service entry confirms that the applicant has a knowledge of English equivalent to level B2 of the Council of Europe's Common European Framework for Language Learning in all four components (reading, writing, speaking and listening), or above, [or that the Sponsor is satisfied that on completion of a pre-sessional course as provided for in paragraph 120(b)(i) of this Appendix, the applicant will have a knowledge of English as set out in this paragraph]; or

(ii) the course is degree level study and the Confirmation of Acceptance for Studies has been assigned by a Sponsor which is not a Recognised Body or is not a body in receipt of funding as a higher education institution from the Department for Employment and Learning in Northern Ireland, the Higher Education Funding Council for England, the Higher Education Funding Council for Wales, or the Scottish Funding Council, and:

(1) the applicant is a national of one of the following countries: Antigua and Barbuda; Australia; The Bahamas; Barbados; Belize; Canada; Dominica; Grenada; Guyana; Jamaica; New Zealand; St Kitts and Nevis; St Lucia; St Vincent and the Grenadines; Trinidad and Tobago; the United States of America, and provides the specified documents set out in paragraph 120-SD(b); or

(2) has obtained an academic qualification (not a professional or vocational qualification), which is deemed by UK NARIC to meet or exceed the recognised standard of a Bachelor's or Master's degree or a PhD in the UK, from an educational establishment in one of the following countries: Antigua and Barbuda; Australia; The Bahamas; Barbados; Belize; Dominica; Grenada; Guyana; Ireland; Jamaica; New Zealand; St Kitts and Nevis; St Lucia; St Vincent and The Grenadines; Trinidad and Tobago; the UK; the USA, and provides the specified documents set out in paragraph 120-SD(a); or

(3) the applicant has successfully completed a course as a Tier 4 (Child) Student (or under the student rules that were in force before 31 March 2009, where the student was granted permission to stay whilst he was under 18 years old) which:

i. was at least six months in length, and

ii. ended within two years of the date the sponsor assigned the Confirmation of Acceptance for Studies; or

(4) the applicant provides the specified documents from an English language test provider approved by the Secretary of State for these purposes as listed in Appendix O, which clearly show:

i. the applicant's name,

ii. that the applicant has achieved or exceeded level B2 of the Council of Europe's Common European Framework for Language learning in all four components (reading, writing, speaking and listening), unless exempted from sitting a component on the basis of the applicant's disability,

iii. the date of the award, and

iv. that the test is within its validity date (where applicable).

Or

(iii) the course is for below degree level study and:

(1) the applicant is a national of one of the following countries: Antigua and Barbuda; Australia; The Bahamas; Barbados; Belize; Canada; Dominica; Grenada; Guyana; Jamaica; New Zealand; St Kitts and Nevis; St Lucia; St Vincent and the Grenadines; Trinidad and Tobago; the United States of America, and provides the specified documents set out in paragraph 120-SD(b); or

(2) has obtained an academic qualification (not a professional or vocational qualification), which is deemed by UK NARIC to meet or exceed the recognised standard of a Bachelor's or Master's degree or a PhD in the UK, from an educational establishment in one of the following countries: Antigua and Barbuda; Australia; The Bahamas; Barbados; Belize; Dominica; Grenada; Guyana; Ireland; Jamaica; New Zealand; St Kitts and Nevis; St Lucia; St Vincent and The Grenadines; Trinidad and Tobago; the UK; the USA, and provides the specified documents set out in paragraph 120-SD(a); or

(3) the applicant has successfully completed a course as a Tier 4 (Child) student (or under the student rules that were in force before 31 March 2009, where the student was granted permission to stay whilst he was under 18 years old) which:

i. was at least six months in length, and

ii. ended within two years of the date the sponsor assigned the Confirmation of Acceptance for Studies; or

(4) the applicant provides the specified documents from an English language test provider approved by the Secretary of State for these purposes as listed in Appendix O, which clearly show:

i. the applicant's name,

ii. that the applicant has achieved or exceeded level B1 of the Council of Europe's Common European Framework for Language learning in all four components (reading, writing, speaking and listening), unless exempted from sitting a component on the basis of the applicant's disability,

iii. the date of the award, and

iv. that the test is within its validity date (where applicable).

Note: Subparagraphs (b)(ii)(4) and (b)(iii)(4) substituted from 1 July 2013 (HC 244). Words inserted in subparagraph (b)(i)(4) from 1 October 2013 (HC 628).

119. If the applicant is re-sitting examinations or repeating a module of a course, the applicant must not previously have re-sat the same examination or repeated the same module more than once, unless the Sponsor is a Highly Trusted Sponsor. If this requirement is not met then no points will be awarded for the Confirmation of Acceptance for Studies, unless the Sponsor is a Highly Trusted Sponsor.

120. Points will only be awarded for a Confirmation of Acceptance for Studies (even if all the requirements in paragraphs 116 to 119 above are met) if the course in respect of which it is issued meets each of the following requirements:

(a) The course must meet the following minimum academic requirements:

i. for applicants applying to study in England, Wales or Northern Ireland, the course must be at National Qualifications Framework (NQF) / Qualifications and Credit Framework (QCF) Level 3 or above if the Sponsor is a Highly Trusted Sponsor; or

ii. for applicants applying to study in England, Wales or Northern Ireland, the course must be at National Qualifications Framework (NQF) / Qualifications and Credit Framework (QCF) Level 4 or above if the Sponsor is an A-Rated Sponsor or a B-Rated Sponsor; or

iii. for applicants applying to study in Scotland, the course must be accredited at Level 6 or above in the Scottish Credit and Qualifications Framework (SCQF) by the Scottish Qualifications Authority and the Sponsor must be a Highly Trusted Sponsor; or

iv. for applicants applying to study in Scotland, the course must be accredited at Level 7 or above in the Scottish Credit and Qualifications Framework (SCQF) by the Scottish Qualifications Authority if the Sponsor is an A-Rated Sponsor or B-Rated Sponsor; or

v. the course must be a short-term Study Abroad Programme in the United Kingdom as part of the applicant's qualification at an overseas higher education institution, and that qualification must be confirmed as the same as a United Kingdom degree level by the National Recognition Information Centre for the United Kingdom (UK NARIC); or

vi. the course must be an English language course at level B2 or above of the Common European Framework of Reference for Languages; or

vii. the course must be a recognised Foundation Programme for postgraduate doctors or dentists.

(b) The Confirmation of Acceptance for Studies must be for a single course of study except where the Confirmation of Acceptance for Studies is:

(i) issued by a Sponsor which is a Recognised Body or a body in receipt of funding as a higher education institution from the Department for Employment and Learning in Northern Ireland, the Higher Education Funding Council for England, the Higher Education Funding Council for Wales, or the Scottish Funding Council to cover both a pre-sessional course of no longer than three months' duration and a course of degree level study at that Sponsor; and

(ii) the applicant has an unconditional offer of a place on a course of degree level study at that Sponsor [or that where the offer is made in respect of an applicant whose knowledge of English is not at B2 level of the Council of Europe's Common European Framework for Language Learning in all four components (reading, writing, speaking and listening) or above, the Sponsor is satisfied that on completion of a pre-sessional course as provided for in (i) above, the applicant will have a knowledge of English at as set out in this paragraph]; and

(iii) the course of degree level study commences no later than one month after the end date of the pre-sessional course.

(c) The course must, except in the case of a pre-sessional course, lead to an approved qualification as defined in (cb) below.

(ca) If a student is specifically studying towards an Association of Certified Chartered Accountants (ACCA) qualification or an ACCA Foundations in Accountancy . . . qualification, the sponsor must be an ACCA approved learning partner - student tuition (ALP-st) at either Gold or Platinum level.

(cb) An approved qualification as one that is:

(1) validated by Royal Charter,

(2) awarded by a body that is on the list of recognised bodies produced by the Department for Business, Innovation and Skills,

(3) recognised by one or more recognised bodies through a formal articulation agreement with the awarding body,

(4) in England, Wales and Northern Ireland, on the Register of Regulated Qualifications (<http://register.ofqual.gov.uk/>) at National Qualifications Framework (NQF) / Qualifications and Credit Framework (QCF) level 3 or above,

(5) in Scotland, accredited at Level 6 or above in the Scottish Credit and Qualifications Framework (SCQF) by the Scottish Qualifications Authority,

(6) an overseas qualification that UK NARIC assesses as valid and equivalent to National Qualifications Framework (NQF) / Qualifications and Credit Framework (QCF) level 3 or above, or

(7) covered by a formal legal agreement between a UK-recognised body and another education provider or awarding body. An authorised signatory for institutional agreements within the recognised body must sign this. The agreement must confirm the recognised body's own independent assessment of the level of the Tier 4 Sponsor's or the awarding body's programme compared to the National Qualifications Framework (NQF) / Qualifications and Credit Framework (QCF) or its equivalents. It must also state that the recognised body would admit any student who successfully completes the Tier 4 Sponsor's or the awarding body's named course onto a specific or a range of degree-level courses it offers.

(d) Other than when the applicant is on a course-related work placement or a pre-sessional course, all study that forms part of the course must take place on the premises of the sponsoring educational institution or an institution which is a partner institution of the migrant's Sponsor.

(e) The course must meet one of the following requirements:

i. be a full-time course of degree level study that leads to an approved qualification as defined in (cb) above;

ii. be an overseas course of degree level study that is recognised as being equivalent to a UK Higher Education course and is being provided by an overseas Higher Education Institution; or

iii. be a full-time course of study involving a minimum of 15 hours per week organised daytime study and, except in the case of a pre-sessional course, lead to an approved qualification, below bachelor degree level as defined in (cb) above.

(f) Where the student is following a course of below degree level study including course-related work placement, the course can only be offered by a Highly Trusted Sponsor. If the course contains a course-related work placement, any period that the applicant will be spending on that placement must not exceed one third of the total length of the course spent in the United Kingdom except:

(i) where it is a United Kingdom statutory requirement that the placement should exceed one third of the total length of the course; or

(ii) where the placement does not exceed one half of the total length of the course undertaken in the UK and the student is following a course of degree level study and is either:

(a) sponsored by a Sponsor that is a Recognised Body or a body in receipt of public funding as a higher education institution from the Department of Employment and Learning in Northern Ireland, the Higher Education Funding Council for England, the Higher Education Funding Council for Wales or the Scottish Funding Council; or

(b) sponsored by an overseas higher education institution to undertake a short-term Study Abroad Programme in the United Kingdom.

Note: Word omitted from sub-paragraph (ca) from 13 December 2012 (HC 760). Words inserted in sub-paragraph (b)(ii) and from 1 October 2013 (HC 628).

Specified documents

120-SD. Where paragraphs 118 to 120 of this Appendix refer to specified documents, those specified documents are as follows:

(a) In the case of evidence relating to previous qualifications, the applicant must provide, for each qualification, either:

(i) The original certificate(s) of qualification, which clearly shows:

(1) the applicant's name,

(2) the title of the award,

(3) the date of the award, and

(4) the name of the awarding institution;

(ii) The transcript of results, which clearly shows:

(1) the applicant's name,

(2) the name of the academic institution,

(3) their course title, and

(4) confirmation of the award.

This transcript must be original unless the applicant has applied for their course through UCAS (Universities and Colleges Admissions Service), and:

(a) the applicant is applying in the UK to study at a Higher Education Institution which has Highly Trusted Sponsor status, and

(b) the qualification is issued by a UK awarding body for a course that the applicant has studied in the UK;

or

(iii) If the applicant's Tier 4 sponsor has assessed the applicant by using one or more references, and the Confirmation of Acceptance for Studies Checking Service entry includes details of the references assessed, the original reference(s) (or a copy, together with an original letter from the Tier 4 sponsor confirming it is a true copy of the reference they assessed), which must contain:

(1) the applicant's name,

(2) confirmation of the type and level of course or previous experience; and dates of study or previous experience,

(3) date of the letter, and

(4) contact details of the referee.

(b) In the case of evidence of the applicant's nationality, the specified documents are the applicant's current valid original passport or travel document. If the applicant is unable to provide this, the UK Border Agency may exceptionally consider this requirement to have been met where the applicant provides full reasons in the passport section of the application form, and either:

(1) a current national identity document, or

(2) an original letter from his home government or embassy, on the letter-headed paper of the government or embassy, which has been issued by an authorised official of that institution and confirms the applicant's full name, date of birth and nationality.

Note: Sub-paragraph (a) substituted from 1 July 2013 (HC 244).

120A. (a) Points will only be awarded for a valid Confirmation of Acceptance for Studies (even if all the requirements in paragraphs 116 to 120A above are met) if the Sponsor has confirmed that the course for which the Confirmation of Acceptance for Studies has been assigned represents academic progress from previous study, as defined in (b) below undertaken during the last period of leave as a Tier 4 (General) Student or as a Student where the applicant has had such leave, except where:

(i) the applicant is re-sitting examinations or repeating modules in accordance with paragraph 119 above, or

(ii) the applicant is making a first application to move to a new institution to complete a course commenced elsewhere.

(b) For a course to represent academic progress from previous study, the course must:

(i) be above the level of the previous course for which the applicant was granted leave as a Tier 4 (General) Student or as a Student, or

(ii) involve further study at the same level, which the Tier 4 Sponsor confirms as complementing the previous course for which the applicant was granted leave as a Tier 4 (General) Student or as a Student.

Attributes for Tier 4 (Child) Students

121. An applicant applying for entry clearance or leave to remain as a Tier 4 (Child) Student must score 30 points for attributes.

122. Available points are show in Table 17 below.

123. Notes to accompany Table 17 appear below that table.

123A. In order to obtain points for a Confirmation of Acceptance for Studies, the applicant must provide a valid Confirmation of Acceptance for Studies reference number.

Table 17

Criterion	Points awarded
Confirmation of Acceptance for Studies	30

Notes

124. A Confirmation of Acceptance for Studies will be considered to be valid only if:

(a) where the applicant is under 16, it was issued by an independent, fee paying school,

(b) it was issued no more than 6 months before the application is made,

(c) the application for entry clearance or leave to remain is made no more than 3 months before the start date of the course of study as stated on the Confirmation of Acceptance for Studies,

(d) the Sponsor has not withdrawn the offer since the Confirmation of Acceptance for Studies was issued,

(e) it was issued by an institution with a Tier 4 (Child) Student Sponsor Licence,

(f) the institution must still hold such a licence at the time the application for entry clearance or leave to remain is determined, and

(fa) the migrant must not previously have applied for entry clearance, leave to enter or leave to remain using the same Confirmation of Acceptance for Studies reference number, if that application was either approved or refused (not rejected as an invalid application declared void or withdrawn), and

(g) it contains such information as is specified as mandatory in these immigration rules.

Note: Sub-paragraph (g) substituted from 13 December 2012 (HC 760).

125. A Confirmation of Acceptance for Studies reference number will only be considered to be valid if:

(a) the number supplied links to a Confirmation of Acceptance for Studies Checking Service entry that names the applicant as the migrant and confirms that the Sponsor is sponsoring him in the Tier 4 category indicated by the migrant in his application for leave to remain (that is, as a Tier 4 (General) Student or a Tier 4 (Child) Student), and

(b) that reference number must not have been withdrawn or cancelled by the Sponsor or the UK Border Agency since it was assigned.

125A. Points will only be awarded for a Confirmation of Acceptance for Studies if the applicant:

(a) supplies, as evidence of previous qualifications, the specified documents set out in paragraph 125-SD that the applicant used to obtain the offer of a place on a course from the Sponsor,

(b) is sponsored by a Highly Trusted Sponsor, is a national of one of the countries or the rightful holder of a qualifying passport issued by one of the relevant competent authorities, as appropriate, listed in Appendix H and is applying for entry clearance in his country of nationality or in the territory related to the passport he holds, as appropriate, or leave to remain in the UK. The UK Border Agency reserves the right to request the specified documents set out in paragraph 125-SD from these applicants. The application will be refused if the specified documents are not provided in accordance with the request made; or

(c) where the application for entry clearance or leave to remain is for the applicant to commence a new course of study, not for completion of a course already commenced by way of re-sitting examinations or repeating a module of a course, the Sponsor must hold an A-rated or Highly Trusted Sponsor Licence and must not be a Legacy Sponsor, or

(d) where the Confirmation of Acceptance for Studies is issued by a Legacy Sponsor or a B-rated sponsor, the Confirmation of Acceptance for Studies will only be valid if it is issued for completion of a course already commenced by way of re-sitting examinations or repeating a module of a course and the Confirmation of Acceptance for Studies must be for the same course as the course for which the last period of leave was granted to study with that same sponsor.

Specified documents

125-SD. Where paragraph 125 of this Appendix refers to specified documents evidence relating to previous qualifications, those specified documents are:

(i) The original certificate(s) of qualification, which clearly shows:

(1) the applicant's name,

(2) the title of the award,

(3) the date of the award, and

(4) the name of the awarding institution;

(ii) The original transcript of results, which clearly shows:

(1) the applicant's name,

(2) the name of the academic institution,

(3) their course title, and

(4) confirmation of the award;

126. Points will not be awarded under Table 17 unless the course that the student will be pursuing meets one of the following requirements:

(a) be taught in accordance with the National Curriculum,

(b) be taught in accordance with the National Qualification Framework (NQF),

(c) be accepted as being of equivalent academic status to (a) or (b) above by Ofsted (England), the Education and Training Inspectorate (Northern Ireland), Education Scotland (Scotland) or Estyn (Wales),

(d) be provided as required by prevailing independent school education inspection standards.

(e) is a single course of study, except where the Confirmation of Acceptance for Studies is:

(i) issued by an independent school to cover both a pre-sessional course and a course at an independent school; and

(ii) the applicant has an unconditional offer of a place at the independent school; and

(iii) the duration of the pre-sessional course and period of study at the independent school does not exceed the maximum period of entry clearance or leave to remain that can be granted under paragraphs 245ZZB and 245ZZD of the Immigration Rules.

* This is an external website for which the Home Office is not responsible.

Appendix AR

Administrative Review

Note: Appendix AR inserted from 20 October 2014 (HC 693).

Introduction

Administrative review is available where an eligible decision has been made. Decisions eligible for administrative review are listed in paragraph AR3.2 of this Appendix.

Administrative review will consider whether an eligible decision is wrong because of a case working error and, if it is considered to be wrong, the decision will be withdrawn or amended as set out in paragraph AR2.2 of this Appendix.

Rules about how to make a valid application for administrative review are set out at paragraphs 34M to 34Y of these Rules.

Definitions

AR1.1 For the purpose of this Appendix the following definitions apply:

Applicant	the individual applying for administrative review.
Case working error	an error in decision-making listed in paragraph AR3.4 (for administrative review in the UK).
Valid application	an application for administrative review made in accordance with paragraphs 34M to 34Y of these Rules.
Pending	as defined in paragraph AR2.9.
Reviewer	the Home Office case worker or Immigration Officer conducting the administrative review.
Original decision maker	the Home Office case worker or Immigration Officer who made the *eligible decision.*

General Principles

What is Administrative Review?

AR2.1 Administrative review is the review of an *eligible decision* to decide whether the decision is wrong due to a *case working error.*

Outcome of Administrative Review

AR2.2 The outcome of an administrative review will be:

(a) Administrative review succeeds and the *eligible decision* is withdrawn; or

(b) Administrative review does not succeed and the *eligible decision* remains in force and all of the reasons given for the decision are maintained; or

(c) Administrative review does not succeed and the *eligible decision* remains in force but one or more of the reasons given for the decision are withdrawn; or

(d) Administrative review does not succeed and the *eligible decision* remains in force but with different or additional reasons to those specified in the decision under review.

What will be Considered on Administrative Review?

AR2.3 The *eligible decision* will be reviewed to establish whether there is a *case working error*, either as identified in the application for administrative review, or identified by the *Reviewer* in the course of conducting the administrative review.

AR2.4 The *Reviewer* will not consider any evidence that was not before the *original decision maker* except where evidence that was not before the *original decision maker* is submitted to demonstrate that a *case working error* as defined in paragraph AR3.4(e), (g), (h) and (j) has been made.

AR2.5 If the *applicant* has identified a *case working error* as defined in paragraph AR3.4 (e), (g), (h) and (j), the *Reviewer* may contact the applicant or his representative in writing, and request relevant evidence. The requested evidence must be received at the address specified in the request within 7 working days of the date of the request.

AR2.6 The *Reviewer* will not consider whether the applicant is entitled to leave to remain on some other basis and nothing in these rules shall be taken to mean that the *applicant* may make an application for leave or vary an existing application for leave, or make a protection or human rights claim, by seeking administrative review.

Applying for Administrative Review

AR2.7 The rules setting out the process to be followed for making an application for administrative review are at 34M to 34Y of these Rules.

Effect of Pending Administrative Review on Liability for Removal

AR2.8 Where administrative review is pending (as defined in AR2.9) the Home Office will not seek to remove the *applicant* from the United Kingdom.

When is Administrative Review Pending?

AR2.9 Administrative review is pending for the purposes of sections 3C(2)(d) and 3D(2)(c) of the Immigration Act 1971:

(a) While an application for administrative review can be made in accordance with 34M to 34Y of these Rules, ignoring any possibility of an administrative review out-of-time under paragraph 34R(2);

(b) While a further application for administrative review can be made in accordance with paragraph 34M(2) of these Rules following a notice of outcome at AR2.2(d) served in accordance with Articles 8ZA to 8ZC of the Immigration (Leave to Enter and Remain) Order 2000 (SI 2000/1161) (as amended);

(c) When an application for administrative review has been made until:

(i) the application for administrative review is rejected as invalid because it does not meet the requirements of paragraph 34N to 34S of these Rules;

(ii) the application for administrative review is withdrawn in accordance with paragraph 34X; or

(iii) the notice of outcome at AR2.2(a), (b) or (c) is served in accordance with Articles 8ZA to 8ZC of the Immigration (Leave to Enter and Remain) Order 2000 (SI 2000/1161) (as amended).

AR2.10 Administrative review is not pending when an administrative review waiver form has been signed by an individual in respect of whom an *eligible decision* has been made. An administrative review waiver form is a form where the person can declare that although they can make an application in accordance with paragraphs 34M to 34Y of these Rules, they will not do so.

Administrative Review in the UK

Decisions Eligible for Administrative Review in the United Kingdom

AR3.1 Administrative review is only available where an *eligible decision* has been made.

AR3.2 (a) *An eligible decision* is a refusal of an application made on or after 20th October 2014 for:

(i) leave to remain as a Tier 4 Migrant under the Points Based System; or

(ii) leave to remain as the partner of a Tier 4 Migrant under paragraph 319C of the Immigration Rules; or

(iii) leave to remain as the child of a Tier 4 Migrant under paragraph 319H of the Immigration Rules.

(b) An eligible decision is also a decision to grant leave to remain in relation to an application referred to in sub-paragraph (a) where a review is requested of the period of leave granted.

AR3.3 Any decision not listed in AR3.2. is not an *eligible decision* and administrative review is not available in respect of that decision.

What is a Case Working Error?

AR3.4 The following is a complete list of case working errors for the purposes of these Rules:

(a) Where the *original decision maker* applied the wrong Immigration Rules;

(b) Where the *original decision maker* applied the Immigration Rules incorrectly;

(c) Where the *original decision maker* incorrectly added up the points to be awarded under the Immigration Rules;

(d) Where there has been an error in calculating the correct period of immigration leave either held or to be granted;

(e) Where the *original decision maker* has not considered all the evidence that was submitted as evidenced in the *eligible decision*;

(f) Where the *original decision maker* has considered some or all of the evidence submitted incorrectly as evidenced in the *eligible decision*;

(g) Where the Immigration Rules provide for the *original decision maker* to consider the credibility of the applicant in deciding the application and the *original decision maker* has reached an unreasonable decision on the credibility of the applicant;

(h) Where the *original decision maker*'s decision to refuse an application on the basis that the supporting documents were not genuine was incorrect;

(i) Where the *original decision maker*'s decision to refuse an application on the basis that the supporting documents did not meet the requirements of the Immigration Rules was incorrect;

(j) Where the *original decision maker* has incorrectly refused an application on the basis that it was made more than 28 days after leave expired; and

(k) Where the *original decision maker* failed to apply the Secretary of State's relevant published policy and guidance in relation to the application.

Appendix Armed Forces

Note: Appendix Armed Forces inserted from 1 December 2013 subject to savings for applications made before that date (HC 803). Subsequent amendments of Appendix Armed Forces are identified after each affected paragraph.

Part 1 General

Who these rules apply to

1. The rules contained in this Appendix apply to those seeking to enter or remain in the United Kingdom as:

(a) a foreign or Commonwealth member of HM Forces (on discharge);

(b) a partner or child of a member of HM Forces;

(c) a partner or child of a member of non-HM Forces who is exempt from immigration control by virtue of section 8(4)(b) or (c) of the Immigration Act 1971;

(d) a member of non-HM Forces who is not exempt from immigration control; . . .

(e) a partner or child of a member of non-HM Forces who is not exempt from immigration control;

(f) a Relevant Civilian Employee as defined in paragraph 2(j)(a); and

(g) a partner or child of a Relevant Civilian Employee.

Note: Word 'and' deleted from subparagraph (d) and subparagraphs (f) and (g) inserted from 6 April 2014 subject to savings for applications made before that date (HC 1138 as amended by HC 1201).

Interpretation and general provisions

2. In this Appendix (including as it applies to applications under Part 7 or 8 of these Rules):

(a) an application for leave to enter or remain includes an application for variation of leave to enter or remain;

(b) a reference to a British Citizen in the United Kingdom includes:

(i) a British Citizen who is coming to the United Kingdom with the applicant as the applicant's partner or parent; and

(ii) a British Citizen who has naturalised having accrued 5 years' reckonable service in HM Forces;

(ba) a reference to a civilian employee of NATO includes an employee of the American National Red Cross working with US Forces in the United Kingdom;

(c) "Gurkha" means a member of HM Forces who is serving or has served in the Brigade of Gurkhas of the British Army under the Brigade of Gurkhas' terms and conditions of service;

(d) "a member of HM Forces" is a person who, subject to sub-paragraphs (e) and (f), is a member of the regular forces within the meaning of the Armed Forces Act 2006;

(e) a person is not to be regarded as a member of HM Forces if the person is treated as a member of a regular force by virtue of:

(i) section 369 of the Armed Forces Act 2006, or

(ii) section 4(3) of the Visiting Forces (British Commonwealth) Act 1933;

(f) a reference to a member of HM Forces includes a person who was a member of HM Forces but was discharged within the period of 2 years prior to the date of the application under these Rules made in relation to that member;

(g) "a member of non-HM Forces" means a member of other armed forces who is:

(i) exempt from immigration control under section 8(4)(b) or (c) of the Immigration Act 1971, or

(ii) not exempt from immigration control;

(h) "partner" means (unless a different meaning of partner applies elsewhere in this Appendix):

(i) the applicant's spouse;

(ii) the applicant's civil partner;

(iii) the applicant's fiancé(e) or proposed civil partner; or

(iv) a person who has been living together with the applicant in a relationship akin to a marriage or civil partnership for at least 2 years prior to the date of the application;

(i) a reference to a person who is present and settled in the UK includes a person who is being admitted for settlement on the same occasion as the applicant;

(j) "reckonable service" is the service which counts towards pension, which starts from the first day of paid service in HM Forces;

(ja) a reference to a Relevant Civilian Employee means a civilian who is being employed to work in the United Kingdom by:

(i) [a NATO force]

(ii) a company under contract to [a NATO force]; or

(iii) the Australian Department of Defence;

(k) "specified" means specified in Appendix FM-SE and Appendix O to these Rules;

(l) where a financial or maintenance requirement applies in this Appendix, paragraphs A. to 21 of Appendix FM-SE to these Rules shall apply as appropriate.

Note: Subparagraphs (ba) and (ja) inserted and words substituted in subparagraph (h) from 6 April 2014 subject to savings (in the case of the insertion of subparagraphs (ba) and (ja)) for applications made before that date (HC 1138 as amended by HC 1201). Words inserted in subparagraphs (ja)(i) and (ii) from 6 November 2014 subject to savings for applications made before that date (HC 693).

3. If an Entry Clearance Officer, or the Secretary of State, has reasonable cause to doubt the genuineness of any document submitted in support of an application, and having taken reasonable steps to verify the document, is unable to verify that it is genuine, the document will be discounted for the purposes of the application.

4. A reference to an application being considered under this Appendix includes, where relevant, an application considered under Part 7 or 8 of these Rules which requires compliance with this Appendix.

5. Paragraphs 277–280, 289AA, 295AA and 296 of Part 8 of these Rules apply to applications made under this Appendix.

Leave to enter

6. The requirements to be met by a person seeking leave to enter the United Kingdom under this Appendix are that the person:

(a) must have a valid entry clearance for entry in a route under this Appendix; [, unless they are: (i) a non-visa national; (ii) not seeking entry for a period exceeding 6 months; and (iii) applying for leave to enter under paragraphs 56, 61B or 64 of this Appendix; and]

(b) must produce to the Immigration Officer on arrival a valid national passport or other document satisfactorily establishing their identity and nationality.

Note: Words inserted in subparagraph (b) from 6 November 2014 subject to savings for applications made before that date (HC 693).

7. If a person does not meet the requirements of paragraph 6, entry will be refused.

Part 2 Suitability requirements

8. An application under this Appendix will be refused on the grounds of suitability if any of the provisions in this paragraph apply:

(a) in respect of applications for entry clearance, the Secretary of State has personally directed that the exclusion of the applicant from the United Kingdom is conducive to the public good;

(b) the applicant is currently the subject of a deportation order;

(c) subject to sub-paragraph (d), permitting the applicant to enter, or remain in, the United Kingdom is not conducive to the public good because he or she has been convicted of an offence for which he or she has been sentenced to a period of imprisonment of:

(i) at least 4 years; or

(ii) at least 12 months, but less than 4 years, unless:

(aa) in respect of applications for entry clearance: a period of 10 years has passed since the end of the sentence; or

(bb) in respect of applications for indefinite leave to remain: a period of 15 years has passed since the end of the sentence; or

(iii) in respect of applications for entry clearance or indefinite leave to remain, less than 12 months, unless: (aa) in respect of applications for entry clearance: a period of 5 years has passed since the end of the sentence; or (bb) in respect of applications for indefinite leave to remain: a period of 7 years has passed since the end of the sentence;

(d) in respect of applications for entry clearance, where sub-paragraph (c) applies, unless refusal would be contrary to the Human Rights Convention or the Convention and Protocol Relating to the Status of Refugees, it will only be in exceptional circumstances that the public interest in maintaining refusal will be outweighed by compelling factors;

(e) in respect of applications for limited leave to remain or indefinite leave to remain, in the view of the Secretary of State,

(i) the applicant's offending has caused serious harm; or

(ii) the applicant is a persistent offender who shows a particular disregard for the law;

(f) in respect of applications for indefinite leave to remain, the applicant has, within the 24 months prior to the date on which the application is decided, been convicted of or admitted an offence for which they received a non-custodial sentence or other out of court disposal that is recorded on their criminal record;

(g) permitting the applicant to enter, or remain in, the UK is not conducive to the public good because, for example, their conduct (including convictions which do not fall within sub-paragraph (c) or (f) as appropriate, character, associations, or other reasons, make it undesirable to grant them entry clearance or allow them to remain in the UK;

(h) in respect of applications for entry clearance, the applicant left or was removed from the United Kingdom pursuant to a condition attached to a conditional caution given under section 22 of the Criminal Justice Act 2003 less than 5 years before the date on which the application is decided;

(i) the applicant has failed without reasonable excuse to comply with a requirement to:

(i) attend an interview;

(ii) provide information;

(iii) provide physical data; or

(iv) undergo a medical examination or provide a medical report; or

(j) it is undesirable to grant entry clearance to the applicant for medical reasons.

9. An application under this Appendix will normally be refused on the grounds of suitability if any of the provisions in this paragraph apply:

(a) whether or not to the applicant's knowledge:

(i) false information, representations or documents have been submitted in relation to the application (including false information submitted to any person to obtain a document used in support of the application); or

(ii) there has been a failure to disclose material facts in relation to the application;

(b) one or more relevant NHS bodies (within the meaning of paragraph 6 of these Rules) has notified the Secretary of State that:

(i) the applicant has failed to pay charges in accordance with the relevant NHS regulations on charges to overseas visitors; and

(ii) the outstanding charges have a total value of at least £1000;

(c) a maintenance and accommodation undertaking has been requested or required under this Appendix or paragraph 35 of these Rules or otherwise and has not been provided;

(d) in respect of applications for entry clearance, the exclusion of the applicant from the United Kingdom is conducive to the public good because:

(i) within the 12 months prior to the date on which the application is decided, the person has been convicted of or admitted an offence for which they received a non-custodial sentence or other out of court disposal that is recorded on their criminal record; or

(ii) in the view of the Secretary of State: (aa) the person's offending has caused serious harm; or (bb) the person is a persistent offender who shows a particular disregard for the law.

10. In respect of applications for limited leave to remain or indefinite leave to remain, when considering whether the presence of the applicant in the UK is not conducive to the public good any legal or practical reasons why the applicant cannot presently be removed from the United Kingdom must be ignored.

Part 3 Discharged members of HM Forces

General eligibility requirements

11. The general eligibility requirements to be met for entry clearance (and limited or indefinite leave to enter) or for limited or indefinite leave to remain as a discharged member of HM Forces are that:

(a) the applicant:

(i) has completed at least 4 years' reckonable service in HM Forces; or

(ii) meets the medical discharge criteria in paragraph 12; and

(b) on the date on which the application is made:

(i) the applicant has been discharged from HM Forces for a period of less than 2 years; or

(ii) in the case of an applicant who was medically discharged more than 2 years before, new information regarding his or her prognosis is being considered by the Secretary of State; or

(iii) the applicant has been granted his or her most recent period of limited leave:

(aa) under paragraph 15 or 19 of this Appendix as a foreign or Commonwealth citizen who has been discharged from HM Forces; or

(bb) under paragraph 276KA or 276QA of these Rules; or

(cc) under the concession which existed outside these Rules, whereby the Secretary of State exercised her discretion to grant leave to enter or remain to members of HM Forces who have been medically discharged; and

(c) in relation to an application made by a Gurkha, the Gurkha is a citizen or national of Nepal.

Medical discharge

12. The medical discharge criteria are satisfied where the applicant was medically discharged from HM Forces:

(a) where the cause was attributable to service in HM Forces and it came about owing to deployment in an operational theatre; or

(b) where the cause was attributable to service in HM Forces, it did not come about owing to deployment in an operational theatre but it is appropriate to grant leave to enter or remain in the United Kingdom following an assessment of the following factors:

(i) the seriousness of the illness or injury;

(ii) the need for further medical treatment in relation to the illness or injury and the availability of such medical treatment in the applicant's country of origin;

(iii) the prognosis for recovery, including whether the injury or illness will affect the applicant's ability to support themselves in their country of origin; and

(iv) the length of reckonable service in HM Forces at the time of the applicant's discharge.

Indefinite leave to enter

13. Entry clearance and indefinite leave to enter as a foreign or Commonwealth citizen discharged from HM Forces will be granted to an applicant who:

(a) is outside the United Kingdom;

(b) has made a valid application for entry clearance and indefinite leave to enter as a foreign or Commonwealth citizen discharged from HM Forces;

(c) does not fall to be refused on the grounds of suitability under paragraph 8 or 9; and

(d) meets the general eligibility requirements in paragraph 11.

Leave to remain

14. Limited leave to remain as a foreign or Commonwealth citizen discharged from HM Forces will be granted to an applicant who:

(a) is in the United Kingdom;

(b) is not in breach of immigration laws, except that any period of overstaying for a period of 28 days or less will be disregarded;

(c) has made a valid application for limited leave to remain as a foreign or Commonwealth citizen discharged from HM Forces;

(d) does not fall to be refused on the grounds of suitability under paragraph 8 or 9; and

(e) meets the general eligibility requirements in paragraph 11.

15. Limited leave to remain granted under paragraph 14 will normally be granted for a period not exceeding 30 months and will be subject to such conditions as the Secretary of State considers appropriate.

Indefinite leave to remain

16. Indefinite leave to remain as a foreign or Commonwealth citizen discharged from HM Forces will be granted to an applicant who:

(a) is in the United Kingdom;

(b) is not in breach of immigration laws, except that any period of overstaying for a period of 28 days or less will be disregarded;

(c) has made a valid application for indefinite leave to remain as a foreign or Commonwealth citizen discharged from HM Forces;

(d) does not fall to be refused on the grounds of suitability under paragraph 8 or 9; and

(e) meets the general eligibility requirements in paragraph 11.

Circumstances in which limited leave to remain may be granted to applicants for indefinite leave to remain under Paragraph 16

17. Limited leave to remain as a foreign or Commonwealth citizen discharged from HM Forces may be granted to a person who fails to meet the requirements for indefinite leave to remain in paragraph 16 of this Appendix by reason only of failing to meet the suitability requirements in paragraph 8 or 9 in respect of a grant of indefinite leave to remain (but not a grant of limited leave to remain).

18. Limited leave to remain as a foreign or Commonwealth citizen discharged from HM Forces may be granted to a person ("P") who fails to meet the requirements for indefinite leave to remain in paragraph 16 of this Appendix by reason only of being unable to meet the medical discharge criteria in paragraph 12, provided that the following conditions are met:

(a) P has been medically discharged from HM Forces;

(b) the cause of P's discharge was attributable to service in HM Forces; and

(c) before P can return to P's country of origin it is appropriate to grant limited leave to remain to facilitate:

(i) further medical treatment for P; or

(ii) a period of recovery for P.

19. Limited leave to remain granted under paragraph 17 or 18 will normally be granted for a period not exceeding 30 months and will be subject to such conditions as the Secretary of State considers appropriate.

Part 4 Partners of members of HM Forces

General eligibility requirements

20. The general eligibility requirements to be met by the partner ("P") of a member of HM Forces are that on the date the application is made:

(a) P's sponsor is a member of HM Forces (as defined in paragraph 2(d) of this Appendix) who:

(i) is exempt from immigration control; or

(ii) has leave to enter or remain under paragraphs 13–19 of this Appendix or paragraphs 276E–QA of these Rules [or under the concession which existed outside these Rules whereby the Secretary of State exercised her discretion to grant leave to enter or remain to a member of HM Forces who has been medically discharged]; or

(iii) is being granted leave to enter or remain under paragraphs 13-19 of this Appendix or paragraphs 276E–QA of these Rules at the same time as P; or

(iv) is a British Citizen;

(b) P and P's sponsor:

(i) are both aged 18 or over;

(ii) must not be within a prohibited degree of relationship;

(iii) must intend to live together permanently; and

(iv) must have met in person;

(c) the relationship between P and P's sponsor is genuine and subsisting; and

(d) any previous relationship of P or P's sponsor must have broken down permanently, unless it is a relationship which falls within paragraph 278(i) of these Rules.

Note: Words inserted in subparagraph (a)(ii) from 30 December 2013 (HC 887).

21. If P and P's sponsor are married or in a civil partnership, it must be a valid marriage or civil partnership as specified in Appendix FM-SE.

22. If P is the fiancé(e) or proposed civil partner of P's sponsor, P must be seeking entry to the UK to enable their marriage or civil partnership to take place.

Leave to enter

23. Entry clearance and leave to enter as the partner of a member of HM Forces will be granted to an applicant who:

(a) is outside the United Kingdom;

(b) has made a valid application for entry clearance and leave to enter as the partner of a member of HM Forces;

(c) does not fall to be refused on the grounds of suitability under paragraph 8 or 9;

(d) meets the general eligibility requirements in paragraph 20;

(e) meets the English language requirement in Part 11 of this Appendix; and

(f) meets the financial requirements in Part 12 of this Appendix.

24. Entry clearance and leave to enter granted under paragraph 23 will normally be:

(a) for whichever is the shortest period of:

(i) 5 years;

(ii) the remaining duration of the applicant's partner's enlistment;

(iii) the remaining duration of the applicant's partner's extant leave under paragraph 276KA or 276QA of these Rules or paragraph 15 or 19 of this Appendix or under the concession which existed outside these Rules whereby the Secretary of State exercised her discretion to grant leave to enter or remain to a member of HM Forces who has been medically discharged; or

(iv) in the case of a fiancé(e) or proposed civil partner, a period not exceeding 6 months; and

(b) subject to the following conditions:

(i) no recourse to public funds; and

(ii) in the case of a fiancé(e) or proposed civil partner, a prohibition on employment.

Indefinite leave to enter

25. Entry clearance and indefinite leave to enter as the partner of a member of HM Forces will be granted to an applicant who:

(a) is outside the United Kingdom;

(b) has made a valid application for entry clearance and indefinite leave to enter as the partner of a member of HM Forces;

(c) has a partner who:

(i) is a foreign or Commonwealth citizen who is a member of HM Forces with at least 5 years' reckonable service in HM Forces; or

(ii) has been granted indefinite leave to enter or remain under paragraph 13 or 16 of this Appendix or paragraphs 276E–Q of these Rules and is in the United Kingdom; or

(iii) is a British Citizen;

(d) does not fall to be refused on the grounds of suitability under paragraph 8 or 9;

(e) meets the general eligibility requirements in paragraph 20;

(f) can demonstrate sufficient knowledge of the English language and sufficient knowledge about life in the UK in accordance with the requirements of Appendix KoLL to these Rules;

(g) meets the financial requirements in Part 12 of this Appendix; and

(h) has completed a continuous period of 60 months with leave under this Appendix as the partner of the same member of HM Forces, excluding any period of entry clearance or limited leave as a fiancé(e) or proposed civil partner.

26. Entry clearance and limited leave to enter as a partner (excluding as a fiancé(e) or proposed civil partner) of a member of HM Forces for a period of 30 months may be granted:

(a) where an applicant fails to meet the requirements of paragraph 25 by reason only of failing to meet the requirements of paragraph 25(c)(i) or (ii), provided that the applicant's sponsor has been granted leave to enter or remain under paragraph 15 or 19 of this Appendix; or

(b) where an applicant fails to meet the requirements of paragraph 25 by reason only of failing to meet the requirements of paragraph 25(f).

27. Entry clearance and limited leave to enter granted under paragraph 26 will be subject to a condition of no recourse to public funds.

Leave to remain

28. Limited leave to remain as the partner of a member of HM Forces will be granted to an applicant who:

(a) is in the United Kingdom, but not:

(i) as a visitor;

(ii) with valid leave that was granted for a period of 6 months or less, unless that leave:

(aa) is as a fiancé(e) or proposed civil partner; or

(bb) was granted pending the outcome of family court or divorce proceedings; or

(iii) on temporary admission or temporary release;

(b) is not in breach of immigration laws, except that any period of overstaying for a period of 28 days or less is to be disregarded;

(c) has made a valid application for limited leave to remain as the partner of a member of HM Forces;

(d) does not fall to be refused on the grounds of suitability under paragraph 8 or 9;

(e) meets the general eligibility requirements in paragraph 20;

(f) is not a fiancé(e) or proposed civil partner of the member of HM Forces, unless:

(i) the applicant is in the United Kingdom with leave as a fiancé(e) or proposed civil partner under paragraph 23 (and that earlier leave was granted in respect of the current sponsor);

(ii) there is good reason why the marriage or civil partnership has not taken place during that period of leave; and

(iii) there is evidence that the marriage or civil partnership will take place within the next 6 months;

(g) meets the English language requirement in Part 11 of this Appendix; and

(h) meets the financial requirements in Part 12 of this Appendix.

29. Limited leave to remain granted under paragraph 28 will normally be granted:

(a) for whichever is the shortest period of:

(i) 5 years;

(ii) the remaining duration of the applicant's partner's enlistment; or

(iii) the remaining duration of the applicant's partner's extant leave under paragraph 276KA or 276QA of these Rules or paragraph 15 or 19 of this Appendix or under the concession which existed outside these Rules whereby the Secretary of State exercised her discretion to grant leave to enter or remain to a member of HM Forces who has been medically discharged; or

(iv) in the case of a fiancé(e) or proposed civil partner, a period not exceeding 6 months; and

(b) subject to the following conditions:

(i) no recourse to public funds; and

(ii) in the case of a fiancé(e) or proposed civil partner, a prohibition on employment.

30. An applicant granted limited leave to remain under paragraph 29 will be eligible to apply for settlement after a continuous period of 60 months with such leave under this Appendix as the partner of the same member of HM Forces, excluding any period of entry clearance or limited leave as a fiancé(e) or proposed civil partner.

Indefinite leave to remain

31. Indefinite leave to remain as the partner of a member of HM Forces will be granted to an applicant who:

(a) is in the United Kingdom;

(b) is not in breach of immigration laws, except that any period of overstaying for a period of 28 days or less is to be disregarded;

(c) has a partner who:

(i) is a foreign or Commonwealth citizen who is a member of HM Forces with at least 5 years' reckonable service in HM Forces; or

(ii) has been granted, or is being granted at the same time as the applicant, indefinite leave to enter or remain under paragraph 13 or 16 of this Appendix or paragraphs 276E–Q of these Rules; or

(iii) is a British Citizen;

(d) does not fall to be refused on the grounds of suitability under paragraph 8 or 9;

(e) meets the general eligibility requirements in paragraph 20;

(f) can demonstrate sufficient knowledge of the English language and sufficient knowledge about life in the UK in accordance with the requirements of Appendix KoLL to these Rules;

(g) meets the financial requirements in Part 12 of this Appendix; and

(h) has completed a continuous period of 60 months with leave under this Appendix as the partner of the same member of HM Forces, excluding any period of entry clearance or limited leave as a fiancé(e) or proposed civil partner.

32. Limited leave to remain as the partner (excluding as a fiancé(e) or proposed civil partner) of a member of HM Forces for a period of 30 months may be granted where the applicant fails to meet the requirements for indefinite leave to remain in paragraph 31:

(a) by reason only of failing to satisfy the suitability requirements in paragraph 8 or 9 in respect of a grant of indefinite leave to remain (but not a grant of limited leave to remain); or

(b) by reason only of failing to meet the requirements of paragraph 31(c)(i) or (ii), provided that the applicant's sponsor has been granted leave to enter or remain under paragraph 15 or 19 of this Appendix; or

(c) by reason only of failing to meet the requirements of paragraph 31(f).

33. Limited leave to remain granted under paragraph 32 will be subject to a condition of no recourse to public funds.

Part 5 Bereaved partners of members of HM Forces

General eligibility requirements

34. The general eligibility requirements to be met by a bereaved partner of a member of HM Forces are that:

(a) the applicant's partner at the time of the applicant's last grant of leave as a partner (other than as a fiancé(e) or proposed civil partner) was:

(i) a foreign or Commonwealth citizen who was a serving member of HM Forces;

or

(ii) a discharged member of HM Forces who had been granted, or was seeking at the same time as the applicant, leave to enter or remain under paragraphs 13–19 of this Appendix or paragraphs 276E–QA of these Rules; or

(iii) a British Citizen in HM Forces;

(b) the applicant's partner has died;

(c) at the time of the applicant's partner's death the applicant and the partner:

(i) were both aged 18 or over;

(ii) were not within a prohibited degree of relationship; and

(iii) had met in person; and

(d) at the time of the applicant's partner's death the relationship between the applicant and the partner was genuine and subsisting and each of the parties intended to live together permanently.

Indefinite leave to enter

35. Entry clearance and indefinite leave to enter as a bereaved partner of a member of HM Forces will be granted to an applicant who:

(a) is outside the United Kingdom as a result of accompanying their sponsor on an overseas posting;

(b) has made a valid application for entry clearance and indefinite leave to enter as the bereaved partner of a member of HM Forces;

(c) does not fall to be refused on the grounds of suitability under paragraph 8 or 9; and

(d) meets the general eligibility requirements in paragraph 34.

Indefinite leave to remain

36. Indefinite leave to remain as a bereaved partner of a member of HM Forces will be granted to an applicant who:

(a) is in the United Kingdom;

(b) has made a valid application for indefinite leave to remain as the bereaved partner of a member of HM Forces;

(c) does not fall to be refused on the grounds of suitability under paragraph 8 or 9; and

(d) meets the general eligibility requirements in paragraph 34.

37. Limited leave to remain as a bereaved partner of a member of HM Forces for a period of 30 months may be granted to a person who fails to meet the requirements for indefinite leave to remain in paragraph 36 by reason only of failing to meet the suitability requirements in paragraph 8 or 9 in respect of a grant of indefinite leave to remain (but not a grant of limited leave to remain).

38. Limited leave to remain granted under paragraph 37 will be subject to a condition of no recourse to public funds.

Part 6 Partners of members of HM Forces who are the victim of domestic violence

General eligibility requirements

39. The general eligibility requirements to be met by the partner of a member of HM Forces who is a victim of domestic violence are that:

(a) the applicant is in the UK and was:

(i) last admitted to the UK under paragraph 276AD of these Rules or paragraph 23, 26, 28 or 32 of this Appendix; or

(ii) last granted leave to enable access to public funds pending an application under this paragraph and the preceding grant of leave was given in accordance with paragraph 276AD of these Rules or paragraph 23, 26, 28 or 32 of this Appendix;

(b) the leave referred to in sub-paragraph (a) [(i) or, where applicable, the preceding grant of leave referred to in sub paragraph (a)(ii)] was as the partner (other than a fiancé(e) or proposed civil partner) of a member of HM Forces who is:

(i) a British Citizen; or

(ii) a foreign or Commonwealth citizen with at least 4 years' reckonable service in HM Forces at the date of application under this paragraph;

(c) the applicant does not fall to be refused on grounds of suitability under paragraph 8 or 9;

(d) the applicant has made a valid application for indefinite leave to remain as a victim of domestic violence; and

(e) the applicant must provide evidence that during the last period of limited leave as a partner the applicant's relationship with their partner broke down permanently as a result of domestic violence.

Note: Subparagraph (a)(ii) substituted and words inserted in subparagraph (b) from 6 November 2014 (HC 693).

Indefinite leave to remain

40. Indefinite leave to remain as the partner of a member of HM Forces who is a victim of domestic violence will be granted to an applicant who meets the general eligibility requirements in paragraph 39.

41. Limited leave to remain for a period of 30 months may be granted to a partner of a member of HM Forces who is a victim of domestic violence who fails to meet the requirements for indefinite leave to remain in paragraph 40 by reason only of failing to meet the suitability requirements in paragraph 8 or 9 in respect of a grant of indefinite leave to remain (but not a grant of limited leave to remain). This will be subject to such conditions as the Secretary of State considers appropriate.

Part 7 Children of members of HM Forces

General eligibility requirements

42. The general eligibility requirements to be met by the child of a member of HM Forces are that:

(a) the applicant is the child of a parent who is:

(i) a foreign or Commonwealth citizen who is a serving member of HM Forces; or

(ii) a discharged member of HM Forces who has been granted, or who is being granted at the same time as the applicant, leave to enter or remain under paragraphs 13–19 of this Appendix or paragraphs 276E–QA of these Rules [or under the concession which existed outside these Rules whereby the Secretary of State exercised her discretion to grant leave to enter or remain to a member of HM Forces who has been medically discharged]; or

(iii) a member of HM Forces who is a British Citizen; and

(b) the applicant meets one of the following criteria:

(i) the applicant's other parent must:

(aa) also come within paragraph 42(a); or

(bb) have been granted leave to enter or remain under paragraphs 23–33 of this Appendix or paragraph 276S, 276V or 276AE of these Rules; or (cc) be being granted leave to enter or remain under paragraphs 23–33 of this Appendix or paragraph 276S, 276V or 276AE of these Rules at the same time as the applicant; or

(dd) have died; or

(ii) the parent under paragraph 42(a) has sole responsibility for the applicant's upbringing; or

(iii) there are serious and compelling family or other considerations which make the applicant's exclusion from the United Kingdom undesirable and suitable arrangements have been made for their care.

Note: Words inserted in subparagraph (a)(ii) from 30 December 2013 (HC 887).

Leave to enter

43. Entry clearance and leave to enter as the child of a member of HM Forces will be granted to an applicant who:

(a) was either:

(i) under 18 years of age at the date of application; or

(ii) aged 18 or over at the date of application; and was last granted leave to remain under paragraph 43 or 47 of this Appendix or paragraph 276AH of these Rules;

(b) is outside the United Kingdom;

(c) is not married or in a civil partnership;

(d) has not formed an independent family unit;

(e) is not leading an independent life;

(f) has made a valid application for entry clearance and leave to enter as the child of a member of HM Forces;

(g) does not fall to be refused on the grounds of suitability under paragraph 8 or 9;

(h) meets the general eligibility requirements in paragraph 42;

(i) either:

(a) meets the financial requirement in Part 12 of this Appendix; or

(b) in a case in which sub-paragraph (b)(i)(aa), (b)(i)(dd) or (b)(ii) of paragraph 42 applies will be:

(i) accommodated adequately by the parent or parents the applicant will be joining without recourse to public funds in accommodation which the parent or parents own or occupy exclusively; and

(ii) maintained adequately by that parent or those parents without recourse to public funds; and

(j) has not applied and does not qualify for indefinite leave to enter under paragraph 45

Note: Subparagraph (i) substituted from 30 December 2013 (HC 887).

44. Entry clearance and leave to enter granted under paragraph 43 will be granted:

(a) for whichever is the shortest period of:

(i) 5 years; or

(ii) the remaining duration of the applicant's parent's enlistment; or

(iii) the remaining duration of the applicant's parent's leave; and

(b) subject to a condition of no recourse to public funds.

Indefinite leave to enter

45. Entry clearance and indefinite leave to enter as the child of a member of HM Forces will be granted to an applicant who:

(a) was either:

(i) under 18 years of age at the date of application; or

(ii) aged 18 or over at the date of application and was last granted leave to remain under paragraph 43 or 47 of this Appendix or paragraph 276AH of these Rules;

(b) is outside the United Kingdom;

(c) is not married or in a civil partnership;

(d) has not formed an independent family unit;

(e) is not leading an independent life;

(f) has made a valid application for entry clearance and indefinite leave to enter as the child of a member of HM Forces;

(g) is the child of:

(i) a foreign or Commonwealth citizen who is a serving member of HM Forces who has completed at least 5 years' reckonable service; or

(ii) a person who has been granted indefinite leave to enter or remain under paragraph 13 or 16 of this Appendix or paragraphs 276E–Q of these Rules and is in the UK; or

(iii) a member of HM Forces who is a British Citizen;

(h) meets one of the following criteria:

(i) the applicant's other parent must:

(aa) come within paragraph 45(g); or

(bb) have been granted indefinite leave to enter or remain under paragraph 25 or 31 of this Appendix or paragraph 276S or 276V of these Rules; or

(cc) be being granted indefinite leave to enter or remain under paragraph 25 or 31 of this Appendix or paragraph 276S or 276V of these Rules at the same time as the applicant; or

(dd) have died; or

(ii) the parent under paragraph 45(g) has sole responsibility for the applicant's upbringing; or

(iii) there are serious and compelling family or other considerations which make the applicant's exclusion from the United Kingdom undesirable and suitable arrangements have been made for their care;

(i) does not fall to be refused on the grounds of suitability under paragraph 8 or 9;

(j) meets the general eligibility requirements in paragraph 42;

(k) where the applicant is aged 18 or over, can demonstrate sufficient knowledge of the English language and about life in the United Kingdom, in accordance with the requirements of Appendix KoLL to these Rules;

(l) will be accommodated adequately by the parent or parents the applicant is seeking to join without recourse to public funds in accommodation which the parent or parents the applicant is seeking to join, own or occupy exclusively; and

(m) will be maintained adequately by the parent or parents the applicant is seeking to join, without recourse to public funds.

46. Entry clearance and limited leave to enter as a child of a member of HM Forces for a period of 30 months may be granted subject to a condition of no recourse to public funds where:

a) an applicant fails to meet the requirements for indefinite leave to enter in paragraph 45 by reason solely of failing to meet the requirements of paragraph 45(k); or

b) an applicant fails to meet the requirements of paragraph 45 by reason only of failing to meet the requirements of paragraph 45(g)(i) or (ii), provided that the applicant's sponsor has been granted leave to enter or remain under paragraph 15 or 19 of this Appendix.

Leave to remain

47. Limited leave to remain as the child of a member of HM Forces will be granted to an applicant who:

(a) was either:

(i) under 18 years of age at the date of application; or

(ii) aged 18 or over at the date of application and who was last granted leave under paragraph 43 or 47 of this Appendix or paragraph 276AH of these Rules;

(b) is not married or in a civil partnership;

(c) has not formed an independent family unit;

(d) is not leading an independent life;

(e) is not in breach of immigration laws, except that any period of overstaying for 28 days or less will be disregarded;

(f) is in the United Kingdom;

(g) has made a valid application for leave to remain as the child of a member of HM Forces;

(h) does not fall to be refused on the grounds of suitability under paragraph 8 or 9;

(i) meets: (aa) the general eligibility requirements in paragraph 42; or (bb) meets those general eligibility requirements, except that subparagraph (b)(ii) does not apply but the parent of the applicant falls under paragraph 49(h) and the applicant normally lives with this parent and not their other parent; and

(j) either:

(a) meets the financial requirement in Part 12 of this Appendix; or

(b) in a case in which sub-paragraph (b)(i)(aa), (b)(i)(dd) or (b)(ii) of paragraph 42 applies (and including the application of sub-paragraph b(ii) as modified by sub-paragraph (i) above) will be:

(i) accommodated adequately by the parent or parents the applicant is seeking to remain with without recourse to public funds in accommodation which the parent or parents own or occupy exclusively; and

(ii) maintained adequately by that parent or those parents without recourse to public funds.

Note: Subparagraph (j) substituted from 30 December 2013 (HC 887).

48. Leave to remain granted under paragraph 47 will be:

(a) for whichever is the shortest period of:

(i) 5 years; or

(ii) the remaining duration of the applicant's parent's enlistment; or

(iii) the remaining duration of the applicant's parent's leave; and

(b) subject to a condition of no recourse to public funds.

Indefinite leave to remain

49. Indefinite leave to remain as the child of a member of HM Forces will be granted to an applicant who has or has had leave to enter or remain under paragraph 43 or 47 of this Appendix or paragraph 276AH of these Rules and who:

(a) was either:

(i) under 18 years of age at the date of application; or

(ii) aged 18 or over at the date of application and who was last granted leave under paragraph 43 or 47 of this Appendix or paragraph 276AH of these Rules;

(b) is not married or in a civil partnership;

(c) has not formed an independent family unit;

(d) is not leading an independent life;

(e) is in the United Kingdom;

(f) has made a valid application for indefinite leave to remain as the child of a member of HM Forces;

(g) is not in breach of immigration laws, except that any period of overstaying for 28 days or less will be disregarded;

(h) is the child of:

(i) a foreign or Commonwealth citizen who is a serving member of HM Forces who has completed at least 5 years' reckonable service; or

(ii) a person who has been granted, or is being granted at the same time as the applicant, indefinite leave to enter or remain under paragraph 13 or 16 of this Appendix or paragraphs 276E–Q of these Rules; or

(iii) a member of HM Forces who is a British Citizen;

(i) meets one of the following criteria:

(i) the applicant's other parent must:

(aa) also come within paragraph 49(h); or

(bb) have been granted indefinite leave to enter or remain under paragraph 25 or 31 of this Appendix or paragraph 276S or 276V of these Rules; or

(cc) be being granted indefinite leave to enter or remain under paragraph 25 or 31 of this Appendix or paragraph 276S or 276V of these Rules at the same time as the applicant; or (dd) have died; or

(ii) the parent under paragraph 49(h) has sole responsibility for the applicant's upbringing or the applicant normally lives with this parent and not their other parent; or

(iii) there are serious and compelling family or other considerations which make the applicant's exclusion from the United Kingdom undesirable and suitable arrangements have been made for their care;

(j) does not fall to be refused on the grounds of suitability under paragraph 8 or 9;

(k) meets the general eligibility requirements in paragraph 42;

(l) where the applicant is aged 18 or over, can demonstrate sufficient knowledge of the English language and about life in the United Kingdom, in accordance with the requirements of Appendix KoLL to these Rules;

(m) will be accommodated adequately by the parent or parents the applicant is seeking to remain with without recourse to public funds in accommodation which the parent or parents the applicant is seeking to join own or occupy exclusively; and

(n) will be maintained adequately by the parent or parents the applicant is seeking to join, without recourse to public funds.

50. Limited leave to remain as a child of a member of HM Forces for a period of 30 months and subject to a condition of no recourse to public funds will be granted:

(a) where an applicant fails to meet the requirements for indefinite leave to remain in paragraph 49 by reason only of failing to satisfy the suitability requirements in paragraph 8 or 9 in respect of a grant of indefinite leave to remain (but not a grant of limited leave to remain); or

(b) where an applicant fails to meet the requirements for indefinite leave to remain by reason only of failing to meet the requirements in paragraph 49(l); or

(c) by reason only of failing to meet the requirements of paragraph 49(h)(i) or (ii), provided that the applicant's sponsor has been granted leave to enter or remain under paragraph 15 or 19 of this Appendix.

Part 8 Bereaved children of members of HM Forces

General eligibility requirements

51. The general eligibility requirements to be met by a bereaved child of a member of HM Forces are that:

(a) one of their parents has died and at the time of their death was:

(i) a foreign or Commonwealth citizen who was a serving member of HM Forces; or

(ii) a discharged member of HM Forces who had been granted, or was seeking at the same time as the applicant, leave to enter or remain under paragraphs 13–19 of this Appendix or paragraphs 276E–QA of these Rules; or

(iii) a British Citizen who was a member of HM Forces; and

(b) they meet one of the following criteria:

(i) their other parent must:

(aa) also come within sub-paragraph 51(a); or

(bb) have been granted, or be being granted at the same time as the applicant, leave to enter or remain under paragraphs 23–33 or 35–37 of this Appendix, under paragraph 276S, 276V or 276AE of these Rules or under any concession that existed outside these Rules whereby the Secretary of State exercised her discretion to grant leave to enter or remain to bereaved partners of foreign or Commonwealth members of HM Forces; or

(cc) have died; or

(ii) the parent referred to in sub-paragraph (a) had sole responsibility for their upbringing; or

(iii) there are serious and compelling family or other considerations which make exclusion of the applicant from the United Kingdom undesirable and suitable arrangements have been made for their care.

Indefinite leave to enter

52. Entry clearance and indefinite leave to enter as a bereaved child of a member of HM Forces will be granted to an applicant who:

(a) was either:

(i) under 18 years of age at the date of application; or

(ii) aged 18 or over at the date of application and was last granted leave to enter or remain under paragraph 43 or 47 of this Appendix or paragraph 276AH of these Rules;

(b) is outside the United Kingdom;

(c) is not married or in a civil partnership;

(d) has not formed an independent family unit;

(e) is not leading an independent life;

(f) has made a valid application for entry clearance and indefinite leave to enter as the bereaved child of a member of HM Forces;

(g) does not fall to be refused on the grounds of suitability under paragraph 8 or 9; and

(h) meets the general eligibility requirements in paragraph 51.

Indefinite leave to remain

53. Indefinite leave to remain as a bereaved child of a member of HM Forces will be granted to an applicant who:

(a) is in the United Kingdom;

(b) was either:

(i) under 18 years of age at the date of application; or

(ii) aged 18 or over at the date of application and was last granted leave to remain under paragraph 43 or 47 of this Appendix or paragraph 276AH of these Rules; and

(c) is not married or in a civil partnership;

(d) has not formed an independent family unit;

(e) is not leading an independent life;

(f) has made a valid application for indefinite leave to remain as the bereaved child of a member of HM Forces;

(g) does not fall to be refused on the grounds of suitability under paragraph 8 or 9; and

(h) meets the general eligibility requirements in paragraph 51.

54. Limited leave to remain as a bereaved child of a member of HM Forces for a period of 30 months will be granted subject to a condition of no recourse to public funds to an applicant who fails to meet the requirements for indefinite leave to remain in paragraph 53 by reason solely of failing to meet the suitability requirements in paragraph 8 or 9 in respect of a grant of indefinite leave (but not a grant of limited leave to remain).

Part 9 Members of Armed Forces who are not exempt from immigration control

General eligibility requirements

55. The general eligibility requirements for members of armed forces who are not exempt from immigration control are that they:

(a) are a member of a foreign armed force;

(b) have been invited by:

(i) HM Forces to undergo training in the United Kingdom which HM Forces will provide; or

(ii) the Ministry of Defence to study, or become familiarised with military equipment being supplied by a firm in the United Kingdom;

(c) will leave the United Kingdom after the period of training, study or familiarisation;

(d) can provide evidence that they are able to maintain themselves and any dependants adequately in the United Kingdom without recourse to public funds;

(e) can provide evidence that there will be adequate accommodation, without recourse to public funds, for themselves and any dependants in the United Kingdom, including any other dependants who are not included in the application but who will live in the same household in the United Kingdom, which the applicant and their dependants own or occupy exclusively: accommodation will not be regarded as adequate if:

(i) it is, or will be, overcrowded; or

(ii) it contravenes public health regulations.

Leave to enter

56. Entry clearance and/or leave to enter as a member of an armed force not exempt from immigration control will be granted to an applicant who:

(a) is outside the United Kingdom;

(b) has made a valid application for entry clearance and leave to enter as a member of an armed force not exempt from immigration control;

(c) does not fall to be refused on the grounds of suitability under paragraph 8 or 9; and

(d) meets the general eligibility requirements in paragraph 55.

57. Entry clearance and/or leave to enter granted under paragraph 56 will be granted:

(a) for whichever is the shorter period of:

(i) 4 years; and

(ii) the duration of the training, study or familiarisation; and

(b) subject to the following conditions:

(i) no recourse to public funds; and

(ii) a prohibition on employment other than that for the purposes for which the applicant was granted leave to enter.

58. Entry clearance and/or leave to enter granted under paragraph 56 may be granted subject to the conditions in paragraph 57(b) for an additional period of 3 months beyond the end of the training, study or familiarisation where:

(a) such leave is required in order to enable the applicant to meet third country transit regulations which require passengers to have 3 months' extant leave in the United Kingdom;

(b) travel to the third country forms part of the training, study or familiarisation; and

(c) the total period of leave granted does not exceed 4 years.

Leave to remain

59. Limited leave to remain as a member of an armed force not exempt from immigration control will be granted to an applicant who:

(a) is in the United Kingdom;

(b) was last granted leave to enter or remain under paragraph 56 or 59 of this Appendix or under the concession which existed outside these Rules whereby the Secretary of State exercised her discretion to grant leave to enter or remain to members of armed forces who are not exempt from immigration control;

(c) is not in breach of immigration laws, except that any period of overstaying for 28 days or less will be disregarded;

(d) has made a valid application for leave to remain as a member of an armed force not exempt from immigration control;

(e) does not fall to be refused on the grounds of suitability under paragraph 8 or 9; and

(f) meets the general eligibility requirements in paragraph 55.

60. Limited leave to remain granted under paragraph 59 will be granted:

(a) for whichever is the shorter period of:

(i) 4 years; or

(ii) the duration of the training, study or familiarisation; and provided the total period of leave granted (including any leave granted under paragraph 57 or 59) does not exceed 4 years; and

(b) subject to the following conditions:

(i) no recourse to public funds; and

(ii) a prohibition on employment other than that for the purposes for which the applicant was granted leave to remain.

61. Limited leave to remain granted under paragraph 59 may be granted subject to the conditions in paragraph 60(b) for an additional 3 months beyond the end of the training, study or familiarisation where:

(a) such leave is required in order to enable the applicant to meet third country transit regulations which require passengers to have 3 months' extant leave in the United Kingdom;

(b) travel to the third country forms part of the training, study or familiarisation; and

(c) the total period of leave granted (including any leave granted under paragraph 57 [or 59 or the concession which existed outside these Rules) whereby the Secretary of State exercised her discretion to grant leave to enter or remain to members of armed forces who are not exempt from immigration control] does not exceed 4 years.

Part 9A Relevant Civilian Employees

Note: Part 9A inserted from 6 April 2014 (subject to savings for applications made before that date (HC 1138 as amended by HC 1201).

General Eligibility Requirements

61A. The general eligibility requirements for Relevant Civilian Employees are that the applicant:

(a) is a Relevant Civilian Employee;

(b) will leave the United Kingdom at the end of their period of employment;

(c) can provide evidence that they are able to maintain themselves and any dependants adequately in the United Kingdom without recourse to public funds; and

(d) can provide evidence that there will be adequate accommodation, without recourse to public funds, for themselves and any dependants in the United Kingdom, including any other dependants who are not included in the application but who will live in the same household in the United Kingdom, which the applicant and their dependants own or occupy exclusively: accommodation will not be regarded as adequate if:

(i) it is, or will be, overcrowded; or

(ii) it contravenes public health regulations.

Leave to enter

61B. Entry clearance and/or leave to enter as a Relevant Civilian Employee will be granted to an applicant who:

(a) is outside the United Kingdom;

(b) has made a valid application for entry clearance and/or leave to enter as a Relevant Civilian Employee;

(c) does not fall to be refused on the grounds of suitability under paragraph 8 or 9; and

(d) meets the general eligibility requirements in paragraph 61A.

61C. Entry clearance and/or leave to enter granted under paragraph 61B will be granted:

(a) for

(i) in respect of an application from a civilian employee of a NATO force or the Australian Department of Defence: (aa) 6 months, where the duration of their period of employment in the United Kingdom does not exceed 6 months; or (bb) five years, where the duration of their period of employment in the United Kingdom exceeds 6 months; or

(ii) in respect of a civilian employee of a company under contract to a NATO force, the duration of their period of employment in the United Kingdom or, if the shorter period, 4 years; and

(b) subject to the following conditions:

(i) no recourse to public funds; and

(ii) a prohibition on employment other than for the purposes for which the applicant was last granted leave to enter.

Note: Subparagraph (a) substituted from 6 November 2014 subject to savings for applications made before that date (HC 693).

Leave to remain

61D. Leave to remain as a Relevant Civilian Employee will be granted to an applicant who:

(a) is in the United Kingdom;

(b) was last:

(i) granted leave to enter or remain under paragraph 61C or 61E of this Appendix or under the concessions which existed outside these Rules whereby the Secretary of State exercised her discretion to grant leave to enter or remain to Relevant Civilian Employees; or

(ii) exempt from control under section 8(4)(b) of the Immigration Act 1971 and has been offered employment as a Relevant Civilian Employee;

(c) is not in breach of any immigration laws, except that any period of overstaying for 28 days or less will be disregarded;

(d) has made a valid application for leave to remain as a Relevant Civilian Employee;

(e) does not fall to be refused on the grounds of suitability under paragraph 8 or 9; and

(f) meets the general eligibility requirements set out in paragraph 61A.

61E. Leave to remain granted under paragraph 61D will be granted:

(a) for . . . :

(i) in respect of an application from a civilian employee of NATO or the Australian Department of Defence, five years; or

(ii) in respect of an application from a civilian employee of a company under contract to NATO, [the duration of their period of employment in the United Kingdom, or, if the shorter period, four years; and]

. . .

(b) subject to the following conditions:

(i) no recourse to public funds; and

(ii) a prohibition on employment other than for the purposes for which the applicant was last granted leave to enter or remain.

Note: Words omitted from subparagraph (a), words substituted in subparagraph (a)(ii) and a second erroneously numbered subparagraph (a)(ii) deleted from 6 November 2014 subject to savings for applications made before that date (HC 693).

Part 10 Dependants of non-HM Forces [and of Relevant Civilian Employees]

Note: Words inserted in heading to Part 10 from 6 April 2014 subject to savings for applications made before that date (HC 1138 as amended by HC 1201).

General eligibility requirements

62. The general eligibility requirements to be met by dependants of a member of non-HM Forces [or of a Relevant Civilian Employee] are that:

(a) the applicant is sponsored by:

(i) a serving armed forces member who is exempt from immigration control under section 8(4)(b) or (c) of the Immigration Act 1971; or

(ii) a serving armed forces member who: (aa) has leave to enter or remain under paragraph 56 or 59 of this Appendix or under any concession that existed outside these Rules whereby the Secretary of State exercised her discretion to grant leave to enter or remain to members of armed forces who are not exempt from immigration control; or (bb) is being granted leave to enter or remain under paragraph 56 or 59 of this Appendix at the same time as the applicant; [or]

(iii) a Relevant Civilian Employee who: (aa) has been granted leave to enter or remain under paragraph 61B or 61D or under the concession which existed outside these Rules whereby the Secretary of State exercised her discretion to grant leave to enter or remain to a Relevant Civilian Employee; or (bb) is being granted leave to enter or remain under paragraph 61B or 61D at the same time as the applicant;

(b) the applicant's sponsor is:

(i) the applicant's partner (except a fiancé(e) or proposed civil partner) where: (aa) both parties are aged 18 or over; (bb) both parties intend to live with the other during their stay in the United Kingdom; and (cc) the relationship is genuine and subsisting; or

(ii) the applicant's parent and the applicant:

(aa) is under 18 years of age at the date of application;

(bb) is not married or in a civil partnership;

(cc) has not formed an independent family unit; and

(dd) is not living an independent life; or

(iii) a serving armed forces member who is exempt from immigration control under section 8(4)(b) or (c) of the Immigration Act 1971 or a civilian employed to work in the UK by a NATO force or the Australian Department of Defence and the applicant: (aa) is a dependant other than a partner within the meaning of section 12(4)(b) of the Visiting Forces Act 1952 or Article I(c) of the NATO Status of Forces Agreement; and (bb) is listed as a dependant of the sponsor on the sponsor's military movement orders or equivalent civilian posting letter;

(c) the applicant must provide evidence that their [sponsor] is able to maintain and accommodate themselves, the applicant and any dependants adequately in the United Kingdom without recourse to public funds;

(d) the applicant must provide evidence that there will be adequate accommodation, without recourse to public funds, for the applicant, the applicant's sponsor and any other family members of the applicant, including other family members who are not included in the application but who will live in the same household, which the applicant, the applicant's sponsor and the other family members own or occupy exclusively: accommodation will not be regarded as adequate if—

(i) it is, or will be, overcrowded; or

(ii) it contravenes public health regulations; and

(e) the applicant intends to leave the United Kingdom at the end of their sponsor's period of posting, [employment,] training, study or familiarisation in the United Kingdom.

Note: Words inserted in opening sentence, subparagraph (a)(iii) inserted and word 'employment' inserted in subparagraph (e) from 6 April 2014 subject to savings for applications made before that date (HC 1138 as amended by HC 1201). Subparagraph (b)(ii) substituted, subparagraph (b)(iii) inserted and words substituted in subparagraph (c) from 6 November 2014 subject to savings for applications made before that date (HC 693).

63. Where the sponsor is the applicant's parent, the applicant must meet one of the following criteria:

(a) their other parent must:

(i) also meet the criteria set out in paragraph 62(a)(i) [, (ii) or (iii)]; or

(ii) either: (aa) have been granted leave to enter or remain as a partner in relation to that member of non-HM Forces [or Relevant Civilian Employee] under [paragraph 64 or 66] of this Appendix or paragraph 276AE of these Rules or under any concession that existed outside these Rules whereby the Secretary of State exercised her discretion to grant leave to enter or remain to partners of non-exempt members of armed forces [or Relevant Civilian Employees]; or (bb) be being granted leave to enter or remain under [paragraph 64 or 66] at the same time as the applicant; or

(iii) have died; or

(b) the parent they are joining in paragraph 62(a) has sole responsibility for their upbringing; or

(c) there are serious and compelling family or other considerations which make the applicant's exclusion from the United Kingdom undesirable and suitable arrangements have been made for their care.

Note: Words substituted/inserted in subparagraphs (a)(i), (a)(ii)(aa) and (a)(ii)(bb) from 6 April 2014 subject to savings for applications made before that date (HC 1138 as amended by HC 1201).

Leave to enter

64. Entry clearance and[/or] leave to enter as the dependant of a member of non-HM Forces [or of a Relevant Civilian Employee] will be granted to an applicant who:

(a) is outside the United Kingdom;

(b) has made a valid application for entry clearance and[/or] leave to enter as the dependant of a member of non-HM Forces [or of a Relevant Civilian Employee];

(c) does not fall to be refused on the grounds of suitability under paragraph 8 or 9; and

(d) meets the general eligibility requirements in paragraph 62 and where relevant one of the criteria in paragraph 63.

Note: Words inserted in opening sentence and in original subparagraph (c) from 6 April 2014 subject to savings for applications made before that date (HC 1138 as amended by HC 1201). Original subparagraph (b) deleted and subsequent subparagraphs renumbered from 6 November 2014 subject to savings for applications made before that date (HC 693).

65. Entry clearance and[/or] leave to enter granted under paragraph 64 will be granted:

(a) for

(i) in respect of an application from the dependant of an armed forces member who is not exempt from immigration control or of a civilian employee of a company under contract to a NATO force, the duration of the sponsor's period of posting, employment, training, study or familiarisation in the United Kingdom or, if the shorter period, 4 years; or

(ii) in respect of an application from the dependant of an armed forces member who is exempt from immigration control under section 8(4)(b) or (c) of the Immigration Act 1971 or of a civilian employee of a NATO force or the Australian Department of Defence: (aa) 6 months, where the duration of the sponsor's period of posting, employment, training, study or familiarisation in the United Kingdom does not exceed 6 months; or (bb) a maximum of 5 years, where the duration of the sponsor's period of posting, employment, training, study or familiarisation in the United Kingdom exceeds 6 months; and

(iii) the duration of the sponsor's period of posting, [employment,] training, study or familiarisation in the United Kingdom; and

(b) subject to the following conditions:

(i) no recourse to public funds; and

(ii) in respect of applications from dependants [of Relevant Civilian Employees or] of armed forces members who are not exempt from immigration control and are being granted leave to enter for less than 6 months, a prohibition on employment.

Note: Words inserted in opening sentence and in subparagraphs (a)(i), (a)(ii), (a)(iii) and (b)(ii) from 6 April 2014 subject to savings for applications made before that date (HC 1138 as amended by HC 1201). Subparagraph (b) substituted from 6 November 2014 subject to savings for applications made before that date (HC 693).

Leave to remain

66. Leave to remain as the dependant of a member of non-HM Forces [or of Relevant Civilian Employees] will be granted to an applicant who:

(a) is in the United Kingdom;

(b) in relation to an application to which sub-paragraph 62(a)(ii) applies, was last granted leave to enter or remain under paragraph 64 or 66 of this Appendix or under the concession which existed outside these Rules whereby the Secretary of State exercised her discretion to grant leave to enter or remain to the dependant of a member of the armed forces who is not exempt from immigration control;

(c) is not in breach of immigration laws, except that any period of overstaying for 28 days or less will be disregarded;

(d) has made a valid application for leave to remain as the dependant of a member of non-HM Forces [or of a Relevant Civilian Employee];

(e) does not fall to be refused on the grounds of suitability under paragraph 8 or 9; and

(f) meets the general eligibility criteria in paragraph 62 and, where the sponsor is the applicant's parent, one of the criteria in paragraph 63, except that the applicant does not need to be under 18 years of age at the date of application where:

(i) paragraph 66(b) applies; or

(ii) sub-paragraph 62(a)(iii) applies and the applicant was last granted leave to enter or remain under paragraph 64 or 66 of this Appendix or under the concession which existed outside these Rules whereby the Secretary of State exercised her discretion to grant leave to enter or remain to the dependant of an employee of a company under contract to a NATO force.

Note: Words inserted in opening sentence and in subparagraphs (b)(ii) and (d) from 6 April 2014 subject to savings for applications made before that date (HC 1138 as amended by HC 1201). Subparagraphs (b) and (f) substituted from 6 November 2014 subject to savings for applications made before that date (HC 693).

67. Leave to remain granted under paragraph 66 will be granted:

(a) . . .

(i) in respect of an application from the dependant of an armed forces member who is not exempt from immigration control [or of a civilian employee of a company under contract to NATO], [the duration of the sponsor's period of posting, employment, training, study or familiarisation in the United Kingdom, or, if the shorter period, 4 years; or] or

(ii) in respect of an application from the dependant of an armed forces member who is exempt from immigration control under section 8(4)(b) or (c) of the Immigration Act 1971 [or of a civilian employee of NATO or the Australian Department of Defence], [a maximum of 5 years; and]

(b) subject to the following conditions:

(i) no recourse to public funds; and

(ii) in respect of applications from dependants [of Relevant Civilian Employees or] of armed forces members who are not exempt from immigration control and are being granted leave to remain for less than 6 months, a prohibition on employment.

Note: Words inserted in subparagraphs (a)(i), (a)(ii), (a)(iii) and (b)(ii) from 6 April 2014 subject to savings for applications made before that date (HC 1138 as amended by HC 1201). Words deleted/ substituted in subparagraphs (a), (a)(i) and (ii) and subparagraph (a)(iii) deleted from 6 November 2014 subject to savings for applications made before that date (HC 693).

Part 11 English language requirements

Meeting the English language requirement in applications for leave to enter or remain

68. Where an English language requirement applies to an application for leave to enter or remain made by a partner under this Appendix, and if the applicant has not met the requirement in a previous application for leave as a partner, the applicant must provide specified evidence set out in Appendix FM-SE and Appendix O that they:

(a) are a national of a majority English speaking country listed in paragraph 70 of this Part;

(b) have passed an English language test in speaking and listening at a minimum of level A1 of the Common European Framework of Reference for Languages with a provider approved by the Secretary of State;

(c) have an academic qualification recognised by UK NARIC to be equivalent to the standard of a Bachelor's or Master's degree or PhD in the UK, which was taught in English; or

(d) are exempt from the English language requirement under paragraph 69 of this Part.

Exemptions from the English language requirement

69. The applicant is exempt from the English language requirement if at the date of application:

(a) the applicant is aged 65 or over;

(b) the applicant has a disability (physical or mental condition) which prevents the applicant from meeting the requirement; or

(c) there are exceptional circumstances which prevent the applicant from being able to meet the requirement, which for an application for entry clearance is prior to entry to the UK.

Majority English speaking countries

70. For the purposes of paragraph 68(a) of this Part the applicant must be a national of:

Antigua and Barbuda, Australia, the Bahamas, Barbados, Belize, Canada, Dominica, Grenada, Guyana, Jamaica, New Zealand, St Kitts and Nevis, St Lucia, St Vincent and the Grenadines, Trinidad and Tobago, or the United States of America.

Part 12 Financial requirements

This Part applies where the financial requirements in Part 12 must be met in an application for leave to enter or remain [or for indefinite leave to enter or remain] made under this Appendix by a partner or child of a member of HM Forces. Paragraphs A to 21 of Appendix FM-SE to these Rules apply to applications to which this Part applies. References in this Part to the applicant's parent or the applicant's parent's partner relate only to applications made by a child under this Appendix. References in this Part to a partner or to the applicant's partner do not refer to the partner of a child making an application under this Appendix.

Note: Words inserted in introduction to Part 12 from 6 April (HC 1138 as amended by HC 1201).

Financial requirements for applications for leave to enter

71. The applicant must provide specified evidence, from the sources listed in paragraph 73, of:

(a) a specified gross annual income of at least:

(i) £18,600;

(ii) an additional £3,800 for the first child; and

(iii) an additional £2,400 for each additional child; alone or in combination with

(b) specified savings of:

(i) £16,000; and

(ii) additional savings of an amount equivalent to the difference – multiplied by the length in years of the period of limited leave for which the applicant has applied [(or by the part-year equivalent if the applicant has applied for less than 12 months' limited leave)] – between the gross annual income from the sources listed in paragraph 73(a)–(f) and the total amount required under paragraph 71(a); or

(c) the requirements in paragraph 74 are met.

Note: Words inserted in subparagraph (b)(ii) from 6 April 2014 (HC 1138 as amended by HC 1201).

72. In paragraph 71 "child" means a dependent child of the applicant or of the applicant's parent who is:

(a) under the age of 18 years, or who was under the age of 18 years when they were first granted entry under this route;

(b) applying for entry clearance or has limited leave to enter or remain in the United Kingdom under this Appendix;

(c) not a British Citizen or settled in the United Kingdom; and

(d) not an EEA national with a right to be admitted under the Immigration (EEA) Regulations 2006.

73. When determining whether the financial requirements in paragraph 71 are met only the following sources will be taken into account:

(a) income of the applicant's partner or the applicant's parent's partner from specified employment or self-employment, which, in respect of a partner (or applicant's parent's partner) returning to the United Kingdom with the applicant, can include specified employment or self-employment overseas and in the United Kingdom;

(b) income of the applicant's parent from specified employment or self-employment if they are in the United Kingdom unless they are working illegally;

(c) specified pension income of the applicant and their partner or of the applicant's parent and that parent's partner;

(d) any specified maternity allowance or bereavement benefit in the UK, or any specified benefit relating to service in HM Forces, received by the applicant and their partner or by the applicant's parent and that parent's partner;

(e) other specified income of the applicant and their partner or of the applicant's parent and that parent's partner; and

(f) income from the sources at sub-paragraphs (b), (d) and (e) of a dependent child of the applicant or the applicant's parent under paragraph 72 who is aged 18 or over; and

(g) specified savings of the applicant and their partner; or of the applicant's parent and that parent's partner; or of a dependent child of the applicant or the applicant's parent under paragraph 72 who is aged 18 or over.

74. The requirements to be met under this paragraph are:

(a) the applicant's partner or the applicant's parent's partner must be receiving one or more of the following:

(i) Disability Living Allowance;

(ii) Severe Disablement Allowance;

(iii) Industrial Injury Disablement Benefit;

(iv) Attendance Allowance;

(v) Carer's Allowance;

(vi) Personal Independence Payment;

(vii) Armed Forces Independence Payment or Guaranteed Income Payment under the Armed Forces Compensation Scheme; or

(viii) Constant Attendance Allowance, Mobility Supplement or War Disablement Pension under the War Pensions Scheme; and

(b) the applicant must provide evidence that their partner (or their parent's partner) is able to maintain and accommodate themselves, the applicant (and their parent) and any dependants adequately in the UK without recourse to public funds.

75. The applicant must provide evidence that there will be adequate accommodation, without recourse to public funds, for the family, including other family members who are not included in the application but who live in the same household, which the family own or occupy exclusively: accommodation will not be regarded as adequate if:

(a) it is, or will be, overcrowded; or

(b) it contravenes public health regulations.

Financial requirements for applications for leave to remain

76. The applicant must provide specified evidence, from the sources listed in paragraph 78, of:

(a) a specified gross annual income of at least:

(i) £18,600;

(ii) an additional £3,800 for the first child; and

(iii) an additional £2,400 for each additional child; alone or in combination with

(b) specified savings of:

(i) £16,000; and

(ii) additional savings of an amount equivalent to the difference – multiplied by the length in years of any period of limited leave for which the applicant has applied [(or by the part-year equivalent if the applicant has applied for less than 12 months' limited leave)] – between the gross annual income from the sources listed in paragraph 78(a)–(f) and the total amount required under paragraph 76(a); or

(c) the requirements in paragraph 79 are met.

Note: Words inserted in subparagraph (b)(ii) from 6 April 2014 (HC 1138 as amended by HC 1201).

77. In paragraph 76, "child" means a dependent child of the applicant or of the applicant's parent who is:

(a) under the age of 18 years, or who was under the age of 18 years when they were first granted entry under this route;

(b) applying for entry clearance or is in the United Kingdom;

(c) not a British Citizen or settled in the United Kingdom; and

(d) not an EEA national with a right to remain in the United Kingdom under the Immigration (EEA) Regulations 2006.

78. When determining whether the financial requirements in paragraph 76 are met only the following sources may be taken into account:

(a) income of the applicant's partner or of the applicant's parent's partner from specified employment or self-employment;

(b) income of the applicant (where aged 18 or over) or of the applicant's parent from specified employment or self-employment unless they are working illegally;

(c) specified pension income of the applicant and their partner or of the applicant's parent and that parent's partner;

(d) any specified maternity allowance or bereavement benefit in the UK, or any specified benefit relating to service in HM Forces, received by the applicant or their partner or by the applicant's parent and that parent's partner;

(e) other specified income of the applicant and their partner or of the applicant's parent and that parent's partner;

(f) income from the sources at sub-paragraphs (b), (d) or (e) of a dependent child of the applicant or their parent under paragraph 77 who is aged 18 years or over; and

(g) specified savings of the applicant and their partner; of the applicant's parent and that parent's partner; or of a dependent child of the applicant or the applicant's parent under paragraph 77 who is aged 18 or over.

79. The requirements to be met under this paragraph are:

(a) the applicant's partner or the applicant's parent's partner must be receiving one or more of the following:

(i) Disability Living Allowance;

(ii) Severe Disablement Allowance;

(iii) Industrial Injury Disablement Benefit;

(iv) Attendance Allowance;

(v) Carer's Allowance;

(vi) Personal Independence Payment;

(vii) Armed Forces Independence Payment or Guaranteed Income Payment under the Armed Forces Compensation Scheme; or

(viii) Constant Attendance Allowance, Mobility Supplement or War Disablement Pension under the War Pensions Scheme; and

(b) the applicant must provide evidence that their partner (or their parent's partner) is able to maintain and accommodate themselves, the applicant (and their parent) and any dependants adequately in the UK without recourse to public funds.

80. The applicant must provide evidence that there will be adequate accommodation, without recourse to public funds, for the family, including other family members who are not included in the application but who live in the same household, which the family own or occupy exclusively: accommodation will not be regarded as adequate if:

(a) it is, or will be, overcrowded; or

(b) it contravenes public health regulations.

Financial requirements for applications for indefinite leave to enter or remain

81. The applicant must meet all of the requirements of paragraphs 71 to 75 (for indefinite leave to enter) or paragraphs 76 to 80 (for indefinite leave to remain), except that instead of the requirement in paragraph 71(b) or 76(b) the applicant must provide specified evidence from the sources listed in paragraph 73 or 78, (as the case may be) of specified savings of:

(i) £16,000; and

(ii) additional savings of an amount equivalent to the difference between the gross annual income from the sources listed in paragraph 73(a)–(f) or 78(a)–(f) and the total amount required under paragraph 71(a) or 76(a).

Note: Paragraph 81 inserted from 6 April 2014 (HC 1138 as amended by HC 1201).

Appendix B

English Language

Appendix B – English language

1. An applicant applying as a Tier 1 Migrant or Tier 2 Migrant must have 10 points for English language, unless applying for entry clearance or leave to remain:

(i) as a Tier 1 (Exceptional Talent) Migrant,

(ii) as a Tier 1 (Investor) Migrant, or

(iii) as a Tier 2 (Intra-Company Transfer) Migrant.

Note: Subparagraph (i) substituted from 6 April 2013 subject to savings for applications made before that date (HC 1039) and then substituted again from 6 November 2014 subject to savings for applications made before that date (HC 693).

2. The levels of English language required are shown in Table 1.
3. Available points for English language are shown in Table 2.
4. Notes to accompany the tables are shown below each table.

Table 1 Level of English language required to score points

Tier 1

Row	Category	Applications	Level of English language Required
A	Tier 1 (General)	Entry clearance and leave to remain	A knowledge of English equivalent to level C1 or above of the Council of Europe's Common European Framework for Language Learning
B	Tier 1 (Entrepreneur)	Entry clearance and leave to remain	A knowledge of English equivalent to [level B1] or above of the Council of Europe's Common European Framework for Language Learning
C	Tier 1 (Graduate Entrepreneur)	[Entry clearance and leave to remain]	A knowledge of English equivalent to [level B1] or above of the Council of Europe's Common European Framework for Language Learning

Tier 2

Row	Category	Applications	Level of English language Required
E	Tier 2 (Minister of Religion)	Entry clearance and leave to remain	A knowledge of English equivalent to level B2 or above of the Council of Europe's Common European Framework for Language Learning
F	Tier 2 (General)	Entry clearance and leave to remain, other than the cases in paragraph 5 below	A knowledge of English equivalent to level B1 or above of the Council of Europe's Common European Framework for Language Learning
G	Tier 2 (General)	Leave to remain cases in paragraph 5 below	A knowledge of English equivalent to level A1 or above of the Council of Europe's Common European Framework for Language Learning
H	Tier 2 (Sportsperson)	Entry clearance and leave to remain	A knowledge of English equivalent to level A1 or above of the Council of Europe's Common European Framework for Language Learning

Note: Words substituted in the third column of Rows B and C from 13 December 2012 subject to savings for applications made before that date (HC 760). Words substituted/inserted in the second column of Rows C and D from 6 April 2013 subject to savings for applications made before that date (HC 1039). Original Row G deleted and subsequent Rows H and I renumbered as Rows G and H from 1 October 2013 subject to savings for applications made before that date (HC 628). Row D deleted from 6 November 2014 subject to savings for applications made before that date (HC 693).

Notes

5. An applicant applying for leave to remain as a Tier 2 (General) Migrant must have competence of English to a level A1 or above as set out in Table 1 above if:

(i) he previously had leave as:

(1) a Tier 2 (General) Migrant under the rules in place before 6 April 2011,

(2) a Qualifying Work Permit Holder,

(3) a representative of an overseas newspaper, news agency or Broadcasting organisation,

(4) a Member of the Operational Ground Staff of an Overseas-owned Airline, or

(5) a Jewish Agency Employee,

and

(ii) he has not been granted leave to remain in any other routes, or entry clearance or leave to enter in any route, since the grant of leave referred to in (i) above.

Table 2 Points available for English language

Factor	Points
National of a majority English speaking country	10
Degree taught in English	10
Passed an English language test	10
Met requirement in a previous grant of leave	10
Transitional arrangements	10

Notes

National of a majority English speaking country

6. 10 points will only be awarded for being a national of a majority English speaking country if the applicant has the relevant level of English language shown in Table 1 and:

(i) is a national of one of the following countries:

Antigua and Barbuda
Australia
The Bahamas
Barbados
Belize
Canada

Dominica
Grenada
Guyana
Jamaica
New Zealand
St Kitts and Nevis
St Lucia
St Vincent and the Grenadines
Trinidad and Tobago
USA

and

(ii) provides his current valid original passport or travel document to show that this requirement is met. If the applicant is unable to do so, the UK Border Agency may exceptionally consider this requirement to have been met where the applicant provides full reasons in the passport section of the application form, and either:

(1) a current national identity document, or

(2) an original letter from his home government or embassy, on the letter-headed paper of the government or embassy, which has been issued by an authorised official of that institution and confirms the applicant's full name, date of birth and nationality.

Degree taught in English

7. 10 points will be awarded for a degree taught in English if the applicant has the relevant level of English language shown in Table 1 and:

(i) has obtained an academic qualification (not a professional or vocational qualification) which either:

(1) is deemed by UK NARIC to meet the recognised standard of a Bachelor's degree (not a Master's degree or a PhD) in the UK, and UK NARIC has confirmed that the degree was taught or researched in English to level C1 of the Council of Europe's Common European Framework for Language learning or above

or:

(2) is deemed by UK NARIC to meet or exceed the recognised standard of a Bachelor's or Master's degree or a PhD in the UK, and is from an educational establishment in one of the following countries:

Antigua and Barbuda
Australia
The Bahamas
Barbados
Belize
Dominica
Grenada
Guyana
Ireland
Jamaica
New Zealand
St Kitts and Nevis

St Lucia
St Vincent and The Grenadines
Trinidad and Tobago
the UK
the USA,

and

(ii) provides the following specified documents to show he has the qualification:

(1) the original certificate of the award, or

(2) if the applicant is awaiting graduation having successfully completed the qualification, or no longer has the certificate and the awarding institution is unable to provide a replacement, an academic transcript (or original letter in the case of a PhD qualification) from the awarding institution on its official headed paper, which clearly shows:

(a) the applicant's name,

(b) the name of the awarding institution,

(c) the title of the award,

(d) confirmation that the qualification has been or will be awarded, and

(e) the date that the certificate will be issued (if the applicant has not yet graduated) or confirmation that the institution is unable to reissue the original certificate or award.

8. If the applicant is required to have competence of English to level A1 as set out in Table 1 above [(rows G and H)], 10 points will be awarded for a degree taught in English if the applicant has the relevant level of English language shown in Table 1 and:

(i) has obtained an academic qualification (not a professional or vocational qualification) which is deemed by UK NARIC to meet or exceed the recognised standard of a Bachelor's or Master's degree or a PhD in the UK,

(ii) provides the specified documents in paragraph 7(ii) evidence to show that he has the qualification, and

(iii) provides provide an original letter from the awarding institution on its official headed paper, which clearly shows:

(1) the applicant's name,

(2) the name of the awarding institution,

(3) the title of the award,

(4) the date of the award, and

(5) confirmation that the qualification was taught in English.

Note: Words substituted in the opening sentence from 1 October 2013 subject to savings for applications made before that date (HC 628).

9. An applicant for entry clearance or leave to remain as a Tier 1 (Graduate Entrepreneur) Migrant does not need to provide evidence of a qualification taught in English if:

(a) the applicant scores points from Appendix A for an endorsement by the UK Higher Education Institution which awarded the qualification; and

(b) the endorsement letter contains the specified details of the qualification, as set out in paragraph 70(c) of Appendix A.

Note: Paragraph 9 substituted from 6 April 2014 subject to savings for applications made before that date (HC 1138 as amended by HC 1201).

Passed an English language test

10. 10 points will only be awarded for passing an English language test if the applicant has the relevant level of English language shown in Table 1 and provides the specified documents from an English language test provider approved by the Secretary of State for these purposes, as listed in Appendix O, which clearly show:

(1) the applicant's name,

(2) the qualification obtained, which must meet or exceed the relevant level shown in Table 1 in all four components (reading, writing, speaking and listening), unless the applicant was exempted from sitting a component on the basis of his disability,

(3) the date of the award, and

(4) that the test is within its validity date (where applicable).

Note: Subparagraph 10 substituted from 1 July 2013 (HC 244).

Met requirement in a previous grant of leave

11. Subject to [paragraph 15 below], 10 points will be awarded for meeting the requirement in a previous grant of leave if the applicant:

(i) has ever been granted leave as a Tier 1 (General) Migrant, a Tier 1 (Entrepreneur) Migrant or Business person, or a Tier 1 (Post-Study Work) Migrant, or

(ii) has ever been granted leave as a Highly Skilled Migrant under the Rules in place on or after 5 December 2006.

Note: Words substituted in the opening sentence from 1 October 2013 subject to savings for applications made before that date (HC 628). Subparagraph (i) substituted from 6 April 2014 subject to savings for applications made before that date (HC 1138 as amended by HC 1201).

12. Subject to paragraph 15 below, where the application falls under rows B to H of Table 1 above, 10 points will be awarded for meeting the requirement in a previous grant of leave if the applicant has ever been granted leave:

(a) as a Minister of Religion (not as a Tier 2 (Minister of Religion) Migrant) under the Rules in place on or after 19 April 2007,

(b) as a Tier 2 (Minister of Religion) Migrant, provided that when he was granted that leave he obtained points for English language for being a national of a majority English speaking country, a degree taught in English, or passing an English language test, or

(c) as a Tier 4 (General) student, and the Confirmation of Acceptance for Studies used to support that application was assigned on or after 21 April 2011 for a course of at least degree level study.

Note: Paragraph 12 substituted from 1 October 2013 subject to savings for applications made before that date (HC 628).

13. Subject to paragraph 15 below, where the application falls under rows B to C or rows F to H of Table 1 above, 10 points will be awarded for meeting the requirement in a previous grant of leave if the applicant has ever been granted leave:

(a) as a Tier 1 (Graduate Entrepreneur) Migrant,

(b) as a Tier 2 (General) Migrant under the Rules in place on or after 6 April 2011, or

(c) as a Tier 4 (General) student, and the Confirmation of Acceptance for Studies used to support that application was assigned on or after 21 April 2011, provided that when he was granted that leave he obtained points for having knowledge of English equivalent to level B1 of the Council of Europe's Common European Framework for Language Learning or above.

Note: Paragraph 13 substituted from 1 October 2013 subject to savings for applications made before that date (HC 628) and then substituted again from 6 November 2014 subject to savings for applications made before that date (HC 693).

14. [Subject to paragraph 15 below, where the application] falls under rows [G and H] of table 1 above, 10 points will be awarded for meeting the requirement in a previous grant of leave if the applicant has ever been granted:

(i) leave as a Minister of Religion (not as a Tier 2 (Minister of Religion) Migrant) under the Rules in place on or after 23 August 2004,

(ii) leave as a Tier 2 Migrant, provided that when he was granted that leave he obtained points for English language for being a national of a majority English speaking country, a degree taught in English, or passing an English language test.

Note: Words substituted from 1 October 2013 subject to savings for applications made before that date (HC 628).

15. No points will be awarded for meeting the requirement in a previous grant of leave if false representations were made or false documents or information were submitted (whether or not to the applicant's knowledge) in relation to the requirement in the application for that previous grant of leave.

Transitional arrangements

16. 10 points will be awarded for English language if the applicant:

(a) is applying for leave to remain as a [Tier 2 (General) Migrant], and

(b) has previously been granted entry clearance, leave to enter or leave to remain as:

(i) a Jewish Agency Employee,

(ii) a Member of the Operational Ground Staff of an Overseas-owned Airline,

(iii) a Minister of Religion, Missionary or Member of a Religious Order,

(iv) a Qualifying Work Permit Holder,

(v) a Representative of an Overseas Newspaper, News Agency or Broadcasting Organisation

and

(c) has not been granted leave in any categories other than Tier 2 (General), Tier 2 (Intra-Company Transfer) and those listed in (b) above under the Rules in place since 28 November 2008.

Note: Words substituted in subparagraph (a) from 1 October 2013 subject to savings for applications made before that date (HC 628).

17. 10 points will be awarded for English language if the applicant:

(a) is applying for leave to remain as a Tier 2 (Minister of Religion) Migrant,

(b) has previously been granted entry clearance, leave to enter and/or leave to remain as a Minister of Religion, Missionary or Member of a Religious Order, and

(c) has not been granted leave in any categories other than Tier 2 (Minister of Religion) and those listed in (b) above under the Rules in place since 28 November 2008.

18. 10 points will be awarded for English language if the applicant:

(a) is applying for leave to remain as a Tier 2 (Sportsperson) Migrant,

(b) has previously been granted entry clearance, leave to enter and/or leave to remain as a Qualifying Work Permit Holder, and

(c) has not been granted leave in any categories other than Tier 2 (Sportsperson) and as a Qualifying Work Permit Holder under the Rules in place since 28 November 2008.

* This is an external website for which the Home Office is not responsible.

Appendix C

Maintenance (funds)

1A. In all cases where an applicant is required to obtain points under Appendix C, the applicant must meet the requirements listed below:

(a) The applicant must have the funds specified in the relevant part of Appendix C at the date of the application;

(b) If the applicant is applying as a Tier 1 Migrant, a Tier 2 Migrant or a Tier 5 (Temporary Worker) Migrant, the applicant must have had the funds referred to in (a) above for a consecutive 90-day period of time, unless applying as a Tier 1 (Exceptional Talent) Migrant or a Tier 1 (Investor) Migrant;

(c) If the applicant is applying as a Tier 4 Migrant, the applicant must have had the funds referred to in (a) above for a consecutive 28-day period of time;

(ca) If the applicant is applying for entry clearance or leave to remain as a Tier 4 Migrant, he must confirm that the funds referred to in (a) above are:

(i) available in the manner specified in paragraph 13 below for his use in studying and living in the UK; and

(ii) that the funds will remain available in the manner specified in paragraph 13 below unless used to pay for course fees and living costs;

(d) If the funds were obtained when the applicant was in the UK, the funds must have been obtained while the applicant had valid leave and was not acting in breach of any conditions attached to that leave;

(e) Where the funds are in one or more foreign currencies, the applicant must have the specified level of funds when converted to pound sterling (£) using the spot exchange rate which appears on <www.oanda.com>* for the date of the application;

(f) Where the applicant is applying as a Tier 1 Migrant, a Tier 2 Migrant or a Tier 5 Migrant, the funds must have been under his own control on the date of the application and for the period specified in (b) above; and

(g) Where the application is made at the same time as applications by the partner or child of the applicant (such that the applicant is a Relevant Points Based System Migrant for the purposes of paragraph 319AA), each applicant must have the total requisite funds specified in the relevant parts of appendices C and E. If each applicant does not individually meet the requirements of appendices C and/or E, as appropriate, all the applications (the application by the Relevant Points Based System Migrant and applications as the partner or child of that relevant Points Based system Migrant) will be refused.

(h) the end date of the 90-day and 28-day periods referred to in (b) and (c) above will be taken as the date of the closing balance on the most recent of the specified documents (where specified documents from two or more accounts are submitted, this will be the end date for the account that most favours the applicant), and must be no earlier than 31 days before the date of application.

(i) No points will be awarded where the specified documents show that the funds are held in a financial institution listed in Appendix P as being an institution with which the UK Border Agency is unable to make satisfactory verification checks.

(j) Maintenance must be in the form of cash funds. Other accounts or financial instruments such as shares, bonds, [credit cards,] pension funds etc., regardless of notice period are not acceptable.

(k) If the applicant wishes to rely on a joint account as evidence of available funds, the applicant (or for children under 18 years of age, the applicant's parent or legal guardian who is legally present in the United Kingdom) must be named on the account as one of the account holders.

(l) Overdraft facilities will not be considered towards funds that are available or under an applicant's own control.

Note: Subparagraph (l) inserted from 6 April 2013 subject to savings for applications made before that date (HC 1039). Words inserted in subparagraph (j) from 6 April 2014 (HC 1138 as amended by HC 1201).

1B. In all cases where Appendix C or Appendix E states that an applicant is required to provide specified documents, the specified documents are:

(a) Personal bank or building society statements which satisfy the following requirements:

(i) The statements must cover:

(1) a consecutive 90-day period of time, if the applicant is applying as a Tier 1 Migrant, a Tier 2 Migrant a Tier 5 (Temporary Worker) Migrant, or the Partner or Child of a Relevant Points Based System Migrant in any of these categories,

(2) a single date within 31 days of the date of the application, if the applicant is applying as a Tier 5 (Youth Mobility Scheme) Migrant, or

(3) a consecutive 28-day period of time, if the applicant is applying as a Tier 4 Migrant or the Partner or Child of a Relevant Points Based System Migrant who is a Tier 4 Migrant

(ii) The most recent statement must be dated no earlier than 31 days before the date of the application;

(iii) The statements must clearly show:

(1) the name of:

i. the applicant,

ii. the applicant's parent(s) or legal guardian's name, if the applicant is applying as Tier 4 Migrant,

iii. the name of the Relevant Points-Based System Migrant, if the applicant is applying as a Partner or Child of a Relevant Points-Based System Migrant, or

iv. the name of the applicant's other parent who is legally present in the UK, if the applicant is applying as a Child of a Relevant Points-Based System Migrant,

(2) the account number,

(3) the date of each statement,

(4) the financial institution's name,

(5) the financial institution's logo,

(6) any transactions during the specified period, and

(7) that the funds in the account have been at the required level throughout the specified period;

(iv) The statements must be be either:

(1) printed on the bank's or building society's letterhead,

(2) electronic bank or building society statements . . ., accompanied by a supporting letter from the bank or building society, on company headed paper, confirming the statement provided is authentic, or

(3) electronic bank or building society statements . . ., bearing the official stamp of the bank or building society on every page,

(v) The statements must not be mini-statements from automatic teller machines (ATMs);

or

(b) A building society pass book which satisfies the following requirements:

(i) The building society pass book must cover:

(1) a consecutive 90-day period of time, if the applicant is applying as a Tier 1 Migrant, a Tier 2 Migrant a Tier 5 (Temporary Worker) Migrant, or the Partner or Child of a Relevant Points Based System Migrant in any of these categories,

(2) a single date within 31 days of the date of the application, if the applicant is applying as a Tier 5 (Youth Mobility Scheme) Migrant, or

(3) a consecutive 28-day period of time, if the applicant is applying as a Tier 4 Migrant or the Partner or Child of a Relevant Points Based System Migrant who is a Tier 4 Migrant.

(ii) The period covered by the building society pass book must end no earlier than 31 days before the date of the application;

(iii) The building society pass book must clearly show:

(1) the name of:

i. the applicant,

ii. the applicant's parent(s) or legal guardian's name, if the applicant is applying as Tier 4 Migrant,

iii. the name of the Relevant Points-Based System Migrant, if the applicant is applying as a Partner or Child of a Relevant Points-Based System Migrant, or

iv. the name of the applicant's other parent who is legally present in the UK, if the applicant is applying as a Child of a Relevant Points-Based System Migrant,

(2) the account number,

(3) the building society's name and logo,

(4) any transactions during the specified period, and

(5) that there have been enough funds in the applicant's account throughout the specified period;

or

(c) A letter from the applicant's bank or building society, or a letter from a financial institution [regulated for the purpose of personal savings accounts by the Financial Conduct Authority (FCA) and the Prudential Regulation Authority (PRA)] or, for overseas accounts, the official regulatory body for the country in which the institution operates and the funds are located, which satisfies the following requirements:

(i) The letter must confirm the level of funds and that they have been held for:

(1) a consecutive 90-day period of time, if the applicant is applying as a Tier 1 Migrant, a Tier 2 Migrant a Tier 5 (Temporary Worker) Migrant, or the Partner or Child of a Relevant Points Based System Migrant in any of these categories,

(2) a single date within 31 days of the date of the application, if the applicant is applying as a Tier 5 (Youth Mobility Scheme) Migrant, or

(3) a consecutive 28-day period of time, if the applicant is applying as a Tier 4 Migrant or the Partner or Child of a Relevant Points Based System Migrant who is a Tier 4 Migrant;

(ii) The period covered by the letter must end no earlier than 31 days before the date of the application;

(iii) The letter must be dated no earlier than 31 days before the date of the application;

(iv) The letter must be on the financial institution's letterhead or official stationery;

(v) The letter must clearly show:

(1) the name of:

i. the applicant,

ii. the applicant's parent(s) or legal guardian's name, if the applicant is applying as Tier 4 Migrant,

iii. the name of the Relevant Points-Based System Migrant, if the applicant is applying as a Partner or Child of a Relevant Points-Based System Migrant, or

iv. the name of the applicant's other parent who is legally present in the UK, if the applicant is applying as a Child of a Relevant Points-Based System Migrant,

(2) the account number,

(3) the date of the letter,

(4) the financial institution's name and logo,

(5) the funds held in the applicant's account, and

(6) confirmation that there have been enough funds in the applicant's account throughout the specified period;

or

(d) If the applicant is applying as a Tier 4 Migrant, an original loan letter from a financial institution [regulated for the purpose of student loans by either the Financial Conduct Authority (FCA) and the Prudential Regulation Authority (PRA)] or, in the case of overseas accounts, the official regulatory body for the country the institution is in and where the money is held, which is dated no more than 6 months before the date of the application and clearly shows:

(1) the applicant's name,

(2) the date of the letter,

(3) the financial institution's name and logo,

(4) the money available as a loan,

(5) for applications for entry clearance, that the loan funds are or will be available to the applicant before he travels to the UK, unless the loan is an academic or student loan from the applicant's country's national government and will be released to the applicant on arrival in the UK,

(6) there are no conditions placed upon the release of the loan funds to the applicant, other than him making a successful application as a Tier 4 Migrant, and

(7) the loan is provided by the national government, the state or regional government or a government sponsored student loan company or is part of an academic or educational loans scheme.

Note: Subparagraph (d) substituted from 13 December 2012 (HC 760). Words substituted in subparagraphs (c) and (d) from 1 July 2013 (HC 244). Words deleted from subparagraphs (a)(iv)(2) and (a)(iv)(3) from 1 October 2013 subject to savings for applications made before that date (HC 628).

Tier 1 Migrants

1. An applicant applying for entry clearance or leave to remain as a Tier 1 Migrant must score 10 points for funds, unless applying as a Tier 1 (Exceptional Talent) Migrant or a Tier 1 (Investor) Migrant.

2. 10 points will only be awarded if an applicant:

(a) applying for entry clearance, has the level of funds shown in the table below and provides the specified documents in paragraph 1B above, or

Category	Level of funds	Points
Tier 1 (Entrepreneur)	[£3,310]	10
Tier 1 (Graduate Entrepreneur)	[£1,890]	10

(b) applying for leave to remain, has the level of funds shown in the table below and provides the specified documents in paragraph 1B above, or

Level of funds	Points
[£945]	10

(c) applying as a Tier 1 (Graduate Entrepreneur) Migrant scores points from Appendix A {for an endorsement from UK Trade and Investment}, and UK Trade and Investment has confirmed in the endorsement letter that it has awarded funding of [at least £1,890 (for entry clearance applications) or £900 (for leave to remain applications)] to the applicant.

Note: Table following subparagraph (a) substituted and subparagraph (c) inserted from 6 April 2013 subject to savings for applications made before that date (HC 1039). Words in curly brackets in subparagraph (c) substituted from 6 April 2014 subject to savings for applications made before that date and words in square brackets substituted in the Tables and in subparagraph (c) from 1 July 2014 subject to savings for applications made before that date (HC 1138 as amended by HC 1201).

3. Where the applicant is applying as a Tier 1 (Entrepreneur) Migrant, he cannot use the same funds to score points for attributes under Appendix A and to score points for maintenance funds for himself or his dependants under this Appendix or Appendix E.

Note: Paragraph 3 inserted from 1 October 2013 subject to savings for applications made before that date (HC 628).

Tier 2 Migrants

4. An applicant applying for entry clearance or leave to remain as a Tier 2 Migrant must score 10 points for Funds.

5. 10 points will only be awarded if:

(a) the applicant has the level of funds shown in the table below and provides the specified documents in paragraph 1B above, or

Level of funds	Points awarded
[£945]	10

(b) the applicant has entry clearance, leave to enter or leave to remain as:

(i) a Tier 2 Migrant,

(ii) a Jewish Agency Employee,

(iii) A member of the Operational Ground Staff of an Overseas-owned Airline,

(iv) a Minister of Religion, Missionary or Member of a Religious Order,

(v) a Representative of an Overseas Newspaper, News Agency or Broadcasting Organisation, or

(vi) a Work Permit Holder, or

(c) the Sponsor is an A-rated Sponsor and has certified on the Certificate of Sponsorship that, should it become necessary, it will maintain and accommodate the migrant up to the end of the first month of his employment. The Sponsor may limit the amount of the undertaking but any limit must be at least [£945]. Points will only be awarded if the applicant provides a valid Certificate of Sponsorship reference number with his application.

Note: Words substituted in the Table and in subparagraph (c) from 1 July 2014 subject to savings for applications made before that date (HC 1138 as amended by HC 1201).

Tier 5 (Youth Mobility) Temporary Migrants

6. An applicant applying for entry clearance as a Tier 5 (Youth Mobility) Temporary Migrant must score 10 points for funds.

7. 10 points will only be awarded if an applicant has the level of funds shown in the table below and provides the specified documents in paragraph 1B above:

Level of funds	Points awarded
[£1890]	10

Note: Words substituted in the Table from 1 July 2014 subject to savings for applications made before that date (HC 1138 as amended by HC 1201).

Tier 5 (Temporary Worker) Migrants

8. A migrant applying for entry clearance or leave to remian as a Tier 5 (Temporary Worker) Migrant must score 10 points for funds.

9. 10 points will only be awarded if an applicant has the level of funds shown in the table below and provides the specified documents in paragraph 1B above:

Criterion	Points Awarded
Meets one of the following criteria: • Has [£945]; or • The Sponsor is an A rated Sponsor and the Certificate of Sponsorship Checking Service confirms that the Sponsor has certified that the applicant will not claim public funds during his period of leave as a Tier 5 (Temporary Worker) Migrant. Points will only be awarded if the applicant provides a valid Certificate of Sponsorship reference number with his application.	10

Note: Words substituted in the Table from 1 July 2014 subject to savings for applications made before that date (HC 1138 as amended by HC 1201).

Tier 4 (General) Students

10. A Tier 4 (General) Student must score 10 points for funds.

11. 10 points will only be awarded if the funds shown in the table below are available in the manner specified in paragraph 13 and 13A below to the applicant. The applicant must either:

(a) provide the specified documents in paragraph 1B above to show that the funds are available to him, or

(b) where the applicant is sponsored by a Highly Trusted Sponsor, is a national of one of the countries or the rightful holder of a qualifying passport issued by one of the relevant competent authorities, as appropriate, listed in Appendix H, and is applying for entry clearance in his country of nationality or in the territory related to the passport he holds, as appropriate, or leave to remain in the UK, confirm that the funds are available to him in the specified manner. The UK Border Agency reserves the right to request the specified documents in paragraph 1B above from these applicants to support this confirmation. The application will be refused if the specified documents are not provided in accordance with the request made.

Criterion	Points
If studying in inner London:	10
i) Where the applicant does not have an established presence studying in the United Kingdom, the applicant must have funds amounting to the full course fees for the first academic year of the course, or for the entire course if it is less than a year long, plus [£1020] for each month of the course up to a maximum of nine months.	
ii) Where the applicant has an established presence studying in the United Kingdom, the applicant must have funds amounting to the course fees required either for the remaining academic year if the applicant is applying part-way through, or for the next academic year if the applicant will continue or commence a new course at the start of the next academic year, or for the entire course if it is less than a year long, plus [£1020] for each month of the course up to a maximum of two months.	
If studying in outer London and elsewhere in the United Kingdom:	10
i) Where the applicant does not have an established presence studying in the United Kingdom, the applicant must have funds amounting to the full course fees for the first academic year of the course, or for the entire course if it is less than a year long, plus [£820] for each month of the course up to a maximum of nine months.	
ii) Where the applicant has an established presence studying in the United Kingdom, the applicant must have funds amounting to the course fees required either for the remaining academic year if the applicant is applying part-way through, or for the next academic year if the applicant will continue or commence a new course at the start of the next academic year, or for the entire course if it is less than a year long, plus [£820] for each month of the course up to a maximum of two months.	

Note: Words substituted in the Table from 1 July 2014 subject to savings for applications made before that date (HC 1138 as amended by HC 1201).

Notes

12. An applicant will be considered to be studying in inner London if the institution, or branch of the institution, at which the applicant will be studying is situated in any of the London boroughs of Camden, City of London, Hackney, Hammersmith and Fulham, Haringey, Islington, Kensington and Chelsea, Lambeth, Lewisham, Newham Southwark, Tower Hamlets, Wandsworth, or Westminster. If the applicant will be studying at more than one site, one or more of which is in inner London and one or more outside, then the applicant will be considered to be studying in inner London if the applicant's Confirmation of Acceptance for Studies states that the applicant will be spending the majority of time studying at a site or sites situated in inner London.

12A. If the length of the applicant's course includes a part of a month, the time will be rounded up to the next full month.

13. Funds will be available to the applicant only where the specified documents show or, where permitted by these Rules, the applicant confirms that the funds are held or provided by:

(i) the applicant (whether as a sole or joint account holder); and/or

(ii) the applicant's parent(s) or legal guardian(s), and the parent(s) or legal guardian(s) have provided written consent that their funds may be used by the applicant in order to study in the UK; and/or

(iii) an official financial sponsor which must be Her Majesty's Government, the applicant's home government, the British Council or any international organisation, international company, University or Independent school.

13A. In assessing whether the requirements of Appendix C, paragraph 11 are met, where an applicant pays a deposit on account to the sponsor for accommodation costs this amount, up to a maximum of [£1020], can be offset against the total maintenance requirement if he will be staying in accommodation arranged by the Tier 4 sponsor and he has paid this money to that Tier 4 sponsor.

Note: Paragraph 13A substituted from 13 December 2012 (HC 760). Words substituted from 1 July 2014 subject to savings for applications made before that date (HC 1138 as amended by HC 1201).

13B. If the applicant is relying on the provisions in paragraph 13(ii) above, he must provide:

(a) one of the following original (or notarised copy) documents:

(i) his birth certificate showing names of his parent(s),

(ii) his certificate of adoption showing the names of both parent(s) or legal guardian, or

(iii) a Court document naming his legal guardian;

and

(b) a letter from his parent(s) or legal guardian, confirming:

(1) the relationship between the applicant and his parent(s) or legal guardian, and

(2) that the parent(s) or legal guardian give their consent to the applicant using their funds to study in the UK.

13C. If the applicant has already paid all or part of the course fees to his Tier 4 Sponsor:

(a) the Confirmation of Acceptance for Studies Checking Service entry must confirm details of the fees already paid; or

(b) the applicant must provide an original paper receipt issued by the Tier 4 Sponsor, confirming details of the fees already paid.

13D. If the applicant has an official financial sponsor as set out in paragraph 13(iii) above:

(a) the Confirmation of Acceptance for Studies Checking Service entry must confirm details of the official financial sponsorship, if it is the Tier 4 Sponsor who is the official financial sponsor; or

(b) the applicant must provide a letter of confirmation from his official financial sponsor, on official letter-headed paper or stationery of that organisation and bearing the official stamp of that organisation, which clearly shows:

(1) the applicant's name,

(2) the name and contact details of the official financial sponsor,

(3) the date of the letter,

(4) the length of the official financial sponsorship, and

(5) the amount of money the official financial sponsor is giving to the applicant, or a statement that the official financial sponsor will cover all of the applicant's fees and living costs.

14. An applicant will have an established presence studying in the UK if the applicant has current entry clearance, leave to enter or leave to remain as a Tier 4 migrant, Student or as a Postgraduate Doctor or Dentist and at the date of application:

(i) has finished a single course that was at least six months long within the applicant's last period of entry clearance, leave to enter or leave to remain, or

(ii) is applying for continued study on a single course where the applicant has completed at least six months of that course [, or]

(iii) is applying for leave to remain as a Tier 4 (General) Student on the doctorate extension scheme.

Note: Subparagraph (iii) inserted from 6 April 2013 subject to savings for applications made before that date (HC 1039).

Tier 4 (Child) Students

15. A Tier 4 (Child) Student must score 10 points for funds.

16. 10 points will only be awarded if the funds shown in the table below are available in the manner specified in paragraph 21 and 21A below to the applicant. The applicant must either:

(a) provide the specified documents in paragraph 1B above to show that the funds are available to him, or

(b) where the applicant is sponsored by a Highly Trusted Sponsor, is a national of one of the countries or the rightful holder of a qualifying passport issued by one of the relevant competent authorities, as appropriate, listed in Appendix H, and is applying for entry clearance in his country of nationality or in the territory related to the passport he holds, as appropriate, or leave to remain in the UK, confirm that the funds are available to him in the specified manner. The UK Border Agency reserves the right to request the specified documents in paragraph 1B above from these applicants to support this confirmation. The application will be refused if the specified documents are not provided in accordance with the request made.

Criterion	Points
Where the child is (or will be) studying at a residential independent school: sufficient funds are available to the applicant to pay boarding fees (being course fees plus board/ lodging fees) for an academic year.	10
Where the child is (or will be) studying at a non-residential independent school and is in a private foster care arrangement (see notes below) or staying with and cared for by a close relative (see notes below): sufficient funds are available to the applicant to pay school fees for an academic year, the foster carer or relative (who must meet the requirements specified in paragraph 19 of this Appendix) has undertaken to maintain and accommodate the child for the duration of the course, and that foster carer or relative has funds equivalent to at least [£560] per month, for up to a maximum of nine months, to support the child while he is in the United Kingdom.	10
Where the child is (or will be) studying at a non-residential independent school, is under the age of 12 and is (or will be) accompanied by a parent, sufficient funds are available to the applicant to pay school fees for an academic year, plus: • if no other children are accompanying the applicant and the parent, [£1535] per Month of stay up to a maximum of nine months; or • if other children are accompanying the applicant and the parent, [£1535] per month, plus [£615] per month for each additional child, up to a maximum of nine months.	10
Where the child is aged 16 or 17 years old and is living independently and studying in inner London: i) Where the applicant does not have an established presence studying in the United Kingdom, the applicant must have funds amounting to the full course fees for the first academic year of the course, or for the entire course if it is less than a year long, plus [£920] for each month of the course up to a maximum of nine months. ii) Where the applicant has an established presence studying in the United Kingdom, the applicant must have funds amounting to the course fees required either for the remaining academic year if the applicant is applying part-way through, or for the next academic year if the applicant will continue or commence a new course at the start of the next academic year, or for the entire course if it is less than a year long, plus [£920] for each month of the course up to a maximum of two months.	10

Where the child is aged 16 or 17 years old, is living independently and studying in outer London or elsewhere in the United Kingdom: iii) Where the applicant does not have an established presence studying in the United Kingdom, the applicant must have funds amounting to the full course fees for the first academic year of the course, or for the entire course if it is less than a year long, plus [£715] for each month of the course up to a maximum of nine months. iv) Where the applicant has an established presence studying in the United Kingdom, the applicant must have funds amounting to the course fees required either for the remaining academic year if the applicant is applying part-way through, or for the next academic year if the applicant will continue or commence a new course at the start of the next academic year, or for the entire course if it is less than a year long, plus [£715] for each month of the course up to a maximum of two months.	10

Note: Words substituted in the Table from 1 July 2014 subject to savings for applications made before that date (HC 1138 as amended by HC 1201).

Notes

17. Children (under 16, or under 18 if disabled) are privately fostered when they are cared for on a full-time basis by a person or persons aged 18 or over, who are not their parents or a close relative, for a period of 28 days or more.

18. A close relative is a grandparent, brother, sister, step-parent, uncle (brother or half-brother of the child's parent) or aunt (sister or half-sister of the child's parent) who is aged 18 or over.

19. The care arrangement made for the child's care in the UK must comply with the following requirements:

(a) In all cases, the applicant must provide a letter from their parent(s) or legal guardian, confirming:

(1) the relationship between the parent(s) or legal guardian and the applicant,

(2) that the parent(s) or legal guardian have given their consent to the application,

(3) that the parent(s) or legal guardian agrees to the applicant's living arrangements in the UK, and

(4) if the application is for entry clearance, that the parent(s) or legal guardian agrees to the arrangements made for the applicant's travel to and reception in the UK,

(5) if a parent(s) or legal guardian has legal custody or sole responsibility for the applicant,

(6) that each parent or legal guardian with legal custody or responsibility for the applicant agrees to the contents of the letter, and signs the letter, and

(7) the applicant's parent(s) or legal guardian's consent to the applicant travelling to and living in the UK independently, if the applicant is 16 or 17 years old and living independently.

(b) If the applicant is under 16 years old or is not living in the UK independently, the applicant must provide:

(i) a written letter of undertaking from his intended carer confirming the care arrangement, which clearly shows:

(1) the name, current address and contact details of the intended carer,

(2) the address where the carer and the applicant will be living in the UK if different from the intended carer's current address,

(3) confirmation that the accommodation offered to the applicant is a private address, and not operated as a commercial enterprise, such as a hotel or a youth hostel,

(4) the nature of the relationship between the applicant's parent(s) or legal guardian and the intended carer,

(5) that the intended carer agrees to the care arrangements for the applicant,

(6) that the intended carer has at least [£560] per month (up to a maximum of nine months) available to look after and accommodate the applicant for the length of the course,

(7) a list of any other people that the intended carer has offered support to, and

(8) the carer's signature and date of the undertaking;

(ii) A letter from his parent(s) or legal guardian, which confirms the care arrangement and clearly shows:

(1) the nature of parent(s) or legal guardian's relationship with the intended carer,

(2) the address in the UK where the applicant and the intended carer will be living,

(3) that the parent(s) or legal guardian support the application, and authorise the intended carer to take responsibility for the care of the applicant during his stay in the UK; and

(iii) The intended carer's original (or notarised copy, although the UK Border Agency reserves the right to request the original):

(1) current UK or European Union passport,

(2) current passport or travel document to confirm that they are [settled in the United Kingdom], or

(3) certificate of naturalisation.

(c) If the applicant is staying in a private foster care arrangement, he must receive permission from the private foster carer's UK local authority, as set out in the Children (Private Arrangements for Fostering) Regulations 2005.

(d) If the applicant is staying in a private foster care arrangement and is under 16 years old, he must provide:

(i) A copy of the letter of notification from his parent(s), legal guardian or intended carer to the UK local authority, confirming that the applicant will be in the care of a private foster carer while in the UK, and

(ii) The UK local authority's confirmation of receipt, confirming that the local authority has received notification of the foster care arrangement.

Note: Words substituted in subparagraph (b)(iii)(2) from 6 April 2013 subject to savings for applications made before that date (HC 1039). Words substituted in subparagraph (b)(i)(6) from 1 July 2014 subject to savings for applications made before that date (HC 1138 as amended by HC 1201).

19A. (a) An applicant will be considered to be studying in inner London if the institution, or branch of the institution, at which the applicant will be studying is situated in any of the London boroughs of Camden, City of London, Hackney, Hammersmith and Fulham, Haringey, Islington, Kensington and Chelsea, Lambeth, Lewisham, Newham Southwark, Tower Hamlets, Wandsworth, or Westminster.

(b) If the applicant will be studying at more than one site, one or more of which is in inner London and one or more outside, then the applicant will be considered to be studying in inner London if the applicant's Confirmation of Acceptance for Studies states that the applicant will be spending the majority of time studying at a site or sites situated in inner London.

20. If the length of the applicant's course includes a part of a month, the time will be rounded up to the next full month.

21. Funds will be available to the applicant only where the specified documents show or, where permitted by these Rules, the applicant confirms that the funds are held or provided by:

(i) the applicant (whether as a sole or joint account holder); and/or

(ii) the applicant's parent(s) or legal guardian(s), and the parent(s) or legal guardian(s) have provided written consent that their funds may be used by the applicant in order to study in the UK; and/or

(iii) an official financial sponsor which must be Her Majesty's Government, the applicant's home government, the British Council or any international organisation, international company, University or Independent school.

21A. In assessing whether the requirements of Appendix C, paragraph 16 are met, where an applicant pays a deposit on account to the sponsor for accommodation costs this amount, up to a maximum of [£1020], can be offset against the total maintenance requirement if he will be staying in accommodation arranged by the Tier 4 sponsor and he has paid this money to that Tier 4 sponsor.

Note: Paragraph 21A substituted from 13 December 2012 (HC 760). Words substituted from 1 July 2014 subject to savings for applications made before that date (HC 1138 as amended by HC 1201).

21B. If the applicant has already paid all or part of the course fees to his Tier 4 Sponsor:

(a) the Confirmation of Acceptance for Studies Checking Service entry must confirm details of the fees already paid; or

(b) the applicant must provide an original paper receipt issued by the Tier 4 Sponsor, confirming details of the fees already paid.

21C. If the applicant has an official financial sponsor as set out in paragraph 21(iii) above:

(a) the Confirmation of Acceptance for Studies Checking Service entry must confirm details of the official financial sponsorship, if it is the Tier 4 Sponsor who is the official financial sponsor; or

(b) the applicant must provide a letter of confirmation from his official financial sponsor, on official letter-headed paper or stationery of that organisation and bearing the official stamp of that organisation, which clearly shows:

(1) the applicant's name,

(2) the name and contact details of the official financial sponsor,

(3) the date of the letter,

(4) the length of the official financial sponsorship, and

(5) the amount of money the official financial sponsor is giving to the applicant, or a statement that the official financial sponsor will cover all of the applicant's fees and living costs.

22. An applicant will have an established presence studying in the UK if the applicant has current entry clearance, leave to enter or leave to remain as a Tier 4 migrant or Student and at the date of application:

(i) has finished a single course that was at least six months long within the applicant's last period of entry clearance, leave to enter or leave to remain, or

(ii) is applying for continued study on a single course where the applicant has completed at least six months of that course.

Appendix D

Immigration Rules for leave to enter as a Highly Skilled Migrant as at 31 March 2008, and Immigration Rules for leave to remain as a Highly Skilled Migrant as at 28 February

Requirements for an extension of stay as a highly skilled migrant

135A. The requirements to be met by a person seeking leave to enter as a highly skilled migrant are that the applicant:

(i) must produce a valid document issued by the Home Office confirming that he meets, at the time of the issue of that document, the criteria specified by the Secretary of State for entry to the United Kingdom under the Highly Skilled Migrant Programme; and

(ii) intends to make the United Kingdom his main home; and

(iii) is able to maintain and accommodate himself and any dependants adequately without recourse to public funds; and

(iv) holds a valid United Kingdom entry clearance for entry in this capacity.

Leave to enter as a highly skilled migrant

135B. A person seeking leave to enter the United Kingdom as a highly skilled migrant may be admitted for a period not exceeding 2 years, subject to a condition prohibiting Employment as a Doctor in Training, (unless the applicant has submitted with this application a valid Highly Skilled Migrant Programme Approval Letter, where the application for that approval letter was made on or before 6 February 2008), provided the Immigration Officer is satisfied that each of the requirements of paragraph 135A is met and that the application does not fall for refusal under paragraph 135HA.

Refusal of leave to enter as a highly skilled migrant

135C. Leave to enter as a highly skilled migrant is to be refused if the Immigration Officer is not satisfied that each of the requirements of paragraph 135A is met or if the application falls for refusal under paragraph 135HA.

135D. The requirements for an extension of stay as a highly skilled migrant for a person who has previously been granted entry clearance or leave in this capacity, are that the applicant:

(i) entered the United Kingdom with a valid United Kingdom entry clearance as a highly skilled migrant, or has previously been granted leave in accordance with paragraphs 135DA–135DH of these Rules; and

(ii) has achieved at least 75 points in accordance with the criteria specified in Appendix 4 of these Rules, having provided all the documents which are set out in Appendix 5 (Part I) of these Rules which correspond to the points which he is claiming; and

(iii) (a) has produced an International English Language Testing System certificate issued to him to certify that he has achieved at least band 6 competence in English; or

(b) has demonstrated that he holds a qualification which was taught in English and which is of an equivalent level to a UK Bachelors degree by providing both documents which are set out in Appendix 5 (Part II) of these Rules; and

(iv) meets the requirements of paragraph 135A(ii)–(iii).

135DA. The requirements for an extension of stay as a highly skilled migrant for a work permit holder are that the applicant:

(i) entered the United Kingdom or was given leave to remain as a work permit holder in accordance with paragraphs 128 to 132 of these Rules; and

(ii) meets the requirements of paragraph 135A (i)–(iii).

135DB. The requirements for an extension of stay as a highly skilled migrant for a student are that the applicant:

(i) entered the United Kingdom or was given leave to remain as a student in accordance with paragraphs 57 to 62 of these Rules; and

(ii) has obtained a degree qualification on a recognised degree course at either a United Kingdom publicly funded further or higher education institution or a bona fide United Kingdom private education institution which maintains satisfactory records of enrolment and attendance; and

(iii) has the written consent of his official sponsor to remain as a highly skilled migrant if he is a member of a government or international scholarship agency sponsorship and that sponsorship is either ongoing or has recently come to an end at the time of the requested extension; and

(iv) meets the requirements of paragraph 135A(i)–(iii).

135DC. The requirements for an extension of stay as a highly skilled migrant for a postgraduate doctor or postgraduate dentist are that the applicant:

(i) entered the United Kingdom or was given leave to remain as a postgraduate doctor or a postgraduate dentist in accordance with paragraphs 70 to 75 of these Rules; and

(ii) has the written consent of his official sponsor to such employment if he is a member of a government or international scholarship agency sponsorship and that sponsorship is either ongoing or has recently come to an end at the time of the requested extension; and

(iii) meets the requirements of paragraph 135A(i)–(iii).

135DD. The requirements for an extension of stay as a highly skilled migrant for a working holidaymaker are that the applicant:

(i) entered the United Kingdom as a working holidaymaker in accordance with paragraphs 95 to 96 of these Rules; and

(ii) meets the requirements of paragraph 135A(i)–(iii).

135DE. The requirements for an extension of stay as a highly skilled migrant for a participant in the Science and Engineering Graduates Scheme or International Graduates Scheme are that the applicant:

(i) entered the United Kingdom or was given leave to remain as a participant in the Science and Engineering Graduates Scheme or International Graduates Scheme in accordance with paragraphs 135O to 135T of these Rules; and

(ii) meets the requirements of paragraph 135A(i)–(iii).

135DF. The requirements for an extension of stay as a highly skilled migrant for an innovator are that the applicant:

(i) entered the United Kingdom or was given leave to remain as an innovator in accordance with paragraphs 210A to 210E of these Rules; and

(ii) meets the requirements of paragraph 135A(i)–(iii).

135DG. Deleted

135DH. The requirements for an extension of stay as a highly skilled migrant for a participant in the Fresh Talent: Working in Scotland scheme are that the applicant:

(i) entered the United Kingdom or was given leave to remain as a Fresh Talent: Working in Scotland scheme participant in accordance with paragraphs 143A to 143F of these Rules; and

(ii) has the written consent of his official sponsor to such employment if the studies which led to him being granted leave under the Fresh Talent: Working in Scotland scheme in accordance with paragraphs 143A to 143F of these Rules, or any studies he has subsequently undertaken, were sponsored by a government or international scholarship agency; and

(iii) meets the requirements of paragraph 135A(i)–(iii).

Extension of stay as a highly skilled migrant

135E. An extension of stay as a highly skilled migrant may be granted for a period not exceeding 3 years, provided that the Secretary of State is satisfied that each of the requirements of paragraph 135D, 135DA, 135DB, 135DC, 135DD, 135DE, 135DF or 135DH is met and that the application does not fall for refusal under paragraph 135HA.

Refusal of extension of stay as a highly skilled migrant

135F. An extension of stay as a highly skilled migrant is to be refused if the Secretary of State is not satisfied that each of the requirements of paragraph 135D, 135DA, 135DB, 135DC, 135DD, 135DE, 135DF or 135DH is met or if the application falls for refusal under paragraph 135HA.

Additional grounds for refusal for highly skilled migrants

135HA. An application under paragraphs 135A–135H of these Rules is to be refused, even if the applicant meets all the requirements of those paragraphs, if:

(i) the applicant submits any document which, whether or not it is material to his application, is forged or not genuine, unless the Immigration Officer or Secretary of State is satisfied that the applicant is unaware that the document is forged or not genuine; or

(ii) the Immigration Officer or Secretary of State has cause to doubt the genuineness of any document submitted by the applicant and, having taken reasonable steps to verify the document, has been unable to verify that it is genuine.

Appendix E

Maintenance (funds) for the family of Relevant Points Based Systems Migrants

A sufficient level of funds must be available to an applicant applying as the Partner or Child of a Relevant Points Based System Migrant. A sufficient level of funds will only be available if the requirements below are met.

(aa) Paragraphs 1A and 1B of Appendix C also apply to this Appendix.

(ab) Where the application is connected to a Tier 1 (Entrepreneur) Migrant, the applicant cannot use the same funds to score points for maintenance funds from this Appendix as the Tier 1 (Entrepreneur) Migrant used to score points for attributes under Appendix A.

(a) Where the application is connected to a Tier 1 Migrant (other than a Tier 1 (Investor) Migrant or a Tier 1 (Exceptional Talent) Migrant) who is outside the UK or who has been in the UK for a period of less than 12 months, {there must be:

(i) [£1,260] in funds, where the application is connected to a Tier 1 (Graduate Entrepreneur) Migrant;

(ii) [£1,890 in funds in other cases.}

(b) Where:

(i) paragraph (a) does not apply, and

(ii) the application is connected to a Relevant Points Based System Migrant who is not a Tier 1 (Investor) Migrant a Tier 1 (Exceptional Talent) Migrant or a Tier 4 (General) Student there must be [£630] in funds.

(ba) (i) Where the application is connected to a Tier 4 (General) Student:

(1) if the Tier 4 (General) Student is studying in inner London (as defined in paragraph 12 of Appendix C), there must be [£615] in funds for each month for which the applicant would, if successful, be granted leave under paragraph 319D(a), up to a maximum of [£5,535], or

(2) if the Tier 4 (General) Student is not studying in inner London, there must be [£460] in funds for each month for which the applicant would, if successful, be granted leave under paragraph 319D(a), up to a maximum of [£4,140],

and in each case

(3) the applicant must confirm that the funds referred to in (1) or (2) above are:

(i) available in the manner specified in paragraph (f) below for use in living costs in the UK; and

(ii) that the funds will remain available in the manner specified in paragraph (f) below unless used to pay for living costs.

(c) Where the applicant is applying as the Partner of a Relevant Points Based System Migrant the relevant amount of funds must be available to either the applicant or the Relevant Points Based System Migrant.

(d) Where the applicant is applying as the Child of a Relevant Points Based System Migrant, the relevant amount of funds must be available to the applicant, the Relevant

Points Based System Migrant, or the applicant's other parent who is Lawfully present in the UK or being granted entry clearance, or leave to enter or remain, at the same time.

(e) Where the Relevant Points Based System Migrant is applying for entry clearance or leave to remain at the same time as the applicant, the amount of funds available to the applicant must be in addition to the level of funds required separately of the Relevant Points Based System Migrant.

(f) In all cases, the funds in question must be available to:

(i) the applicant, or

(ii) where he is applying as the partner of a Relevant Points Based System Migrant, either to him or to that Relevant Points Based System Migrant, or

(iii) where he is applying as the child of a Relevant Points Based System Migrant, either to him, to the Relevant Points Based System Migrant or to the child's other parent who is lawfully present in the UK or being granted entry clearance, or leave to enter or remain, at the same time;

(g) The funds in question must have been available to the person referred to in (f) above on the date of the application and for:

(i) a consecutive 90-day period of time, if the applicant is applying as the Partner or Child of a Tier 1 Migrant (other than a Tier 1 (Investor) Migrant) or a Tier 1 (Exceptional Talent) Migrant, a Tier 2 Migrant or a Tier 5 (Temporary Worker) Migrant;

(ii) a consecutive 28-day period of time, if the applicant is applying as the Partner or Child of a Tier 4 (General) Student;

(h) If the funds in question were obtained when the person referred to in (f) above was in the UK, the funds must have been obtained while that person had valid leave and was not acting in breach of any conditions attached to that leave; and

(i) In the following cases, sufficient funds will be deemed to be available where all of the following conditions are met:

(1) the Relevant Points Based System Migrant to whom the application is connected has, or is being granted, leave as a Tier 2 Migrant,

(2) the Sponsor of that Relevant Points Based System Migrant is A-rated, and

(3) that Sponsor has certified on the Certificate of Sponsorship that, should it become necessary, it will maintain and accommodate the dependants of the relevant Points Based System Migrant up to the end of the first month of the dependant's leave, if granted. The undertaking may be limited provided the limit is at least [£630] per dependant. If the relevant Points Based System Migrant is applying at the same time as the applicant, points will only be awarded if the Relevant Points Based System Migrant provides a valid Certificate of Sponsorship reference number with his application.

(ia) Sufficient funds will not be deemed to be available to the Partner or Child if the specified documents, as set out in paragraph 1B of Appendix C, show that the funds are held in a financial institution listed in Appendix P as being an institution with which the UK Border Agency is unable to make satisfactory verification checks.

(ib) Sufficient funds will be deemed to be available where the application is connected to a Tier 1 (Graduate Entrepreneur) Migrant who scores, or scored, points from Appendix A [for an endorsement from UK Trade and Investment], and UK Trade and Investment has confirmed in the endorsement letter that it has awarded funding that is at least sufficient to cover the required maintenance funds for the Tier 1 (Graduate Entrepreneur) Migrant, the applicant and any other dependants.

(j) In all cases the applicant must provide the specified documents as set out in paragraph 1B of Appendix C, unless the applicant is applying at the same time as the Relevant Points Based System Migrant who is a Tier 4 (General) Student sponsored by a Highly

Trusted Sponsor, is a national of one of the countries or the rightful holder of a qualifying passport issued by one of the relevant competent authorities, as appropriate, listed in Appendix H, and is applying for entry clearance in his country of nationality or in the territory related to the passport he holds, as appropriate, or leave to remain in the UK and the applicant is also a national of the same country, and confirms these requirements are met, in which case the specified documents shall not be required. The UK Border Agency reserves the right to request the specified documents from these applicants. The application will be refused if the specified documents are not provided in accordance with the request made.

(k) Where the funds are in one or more foreign currencies, the applicant must have the specified level of funds when converted to pound sterling (£) using the spot exchange rate which appears on <www.oanda.com>* for the date of the application.

(l) Where the application is one of a number of applications made at the same time as a partner or child of a Relevant Points Based System Migrant (as set out in paragraphs 319A and 319F) each applicant, including the Relevant Points Based System Migrant if applying at the same time, must have the total requisite funds specified in the relevant parts of appendices C and E. If each applicant does not individually meet the requirements of appendices C and/or E, as appropriate, all the applications (the application by the Relevant Points Based System Migrant and applications as the partner or child of that Relevant Points Based System Migrant) will be refused.

(m) The end date of the 90-day and 28-day periods referred to in (g) above will be taken as the date of the closing balance on the most recent of the specified documents (where specified documents from two or more accounts are submitted, this will be the end date for the account that most favours the applicant), as set out in paragraph 1B of Appendix C, and must be no earlier than 31 days before the date of application.

(n) If:

(i) the Relevant Points-Based System Migrant is a Tier 4 (General) Student who has official financial sponsorship as set out in paragraph 13(iii) of Appendix C, and

(ii) this sponsorship is intended to cover costs of the Relevant Points-Based System Migrant's family member(s),

the applicant must provide a letter of confirmation from the Tier 4 (General) Student's official financial sponsor which satisfies the requirements in paragraph 13D of Appendix C, and confirms that the sponsorship will cover costs of the applicant in addition to costs of the Relevant Points-Based System Migrant.

(o) Where the Relevant Points Based System Migrant is applying for entry clearance or leave to remain at the same time as the applicant, and is not required to provide evidence of maintenance funds because of the provisions in paragraph 5(b) of Appendix C, the applicant is also not required to provide evidence of maintenance funds.

(p) Overdraft facilities will not be considered towards funds that are available or under an applicant's own control.

* This is an external website for which the Home Office is not responsible.

Note: Subparagraph (o) inserted from 13 December 2013 subject to savings for applications made before that date (HC 760). Words in curly brackets in subparagraph (a) substituted and subparagraphs (ib) and (p) inserted from 6 April 2013 subject to savings for applications made before that date (HC 139). Subparagraph (ab) inserted from 1 October 2013 subject to savings for applications made before that date (HC 628). Words substituted in subparagraphs (a)(i), (a)(ii), (b)(ii), (ba)(i)(1), (ba)(i)(2), (i)(3) and (ib) from 1 July 2014, these amendments (apart from the change to subparagraph (i)(b)) being subject to savings for applications made before that date (HC 1138 as amended by HC 1201).

APPENDIX F

[ARCHIVED IMMIGRATION RULES]

[PART 1 – IMMIGRATION RULES RELATING TO HIGHLY SKILLED MIGRANTS, THE INTERNATIONAL GRADUATES SCHEME, THE FRESH TALENT: WORKING IN SCOTLAND SCHEME, BUSINESSPERSONS, INNOVATORS, INVESTORS AND WRITERS, COMPOSERS AND ARTISTS AS AT 29 JUNE 2008]

Note: Headings substituted from 1 October 2013 subject to savings for applications made before that date (HC 628).

Highly skilled migrants

Requirements for leave to enter the United Kingdom as a highly skilled migrant

135A. The requirements to be met by a person seeking leave to enter as a highly skilled migrant are that the applicant:

(i) must produce a valid document issued by the Home Office confirming that he meets, at the time of the issue of that document, the criteria specified by the Secretary of State for entry to the United Kingdom under the Highly Skilled Migrant Programme; and

(ii) intends to make the United Kingdom his main home; and

(iii) is able to maintain and accommodate himself and any dependants adequately without recourse to public funds; and

(iv) holds a valid United Kingdom entry clearance for entry in this capacity; and

(v) if he makes an application for leave to enter on or after 29 February 2008, is not applying in India.

Immigration Officers at port should not refuse entry to passengers on the basis that they applied in India, if those passengers have a valid entry clearance for entry in this capacity.

Leave to enter as a highly skilled migrant

135B. A person seeking leave to enter the United Kingdom as a highly skilled migrant may be admitted for a period not exceeding 2 years, subject to a condition prohibiting Employment as a Doctor in Training (unless the applicant has submitted with this application a valid Highly Skilled Migrant Programme Approval Letter, where the application for that approval letter was made on or before 6 February 2008), provided the Immigration Officer is satisfied that each of the requirements of paragraph 135A is met and that the application does not fall for refusal under paragraph 135HA.

Refusal of leave to enter as a highly skilled migrant

135C. Leave to enter as a highly skilled migrant is to be refused if the Immigration Officer is not satisfied that each of the requirements of paragraph 135A is met or if the application falls for refusal under paragraph 135HA.

International Graduates Scheme

Requirements for leave to enter as a participant in the International Graduates Scheme

135O. The requirements to be met by a person seeking leave to enter as a participant in the International Graduates Scheme are that he:

(i) has successfully completed and obtained either:

(a) a recognised UK degree (with second class honours or above) in a subject approved by the Department for Education and Skills for the purposes of the Science and Engineering Graduates scheme, completed before 1 May 2007; or

(b) a recognised UK degree, Master's degree, or PhD in any subject completed on or after 1 May 2007; or

(c) a postgraduate certificate or postgraduate diploma in any subject completed on or after 1 May 2007;

at a UK education institution which is a recognised or listed body.

(ii) intends to seek and take work during the period for which leave is granted in this capacity;

(iii) can maintain and accommodate himself and any dependants without recourse to public funds;

(iv) completed his degree, Master's degree, PhD or postgraduate certificate or diploma, in the last 12 months;

(v) if he has previously spent time in the UK as a participant in the Science and Engineering Graduates Scheme or International Graduates Scheme, is not seeking leave to enter to a date beyond 12 months from the date he was first given leave to enter or remain under the Science and Engineering Graduates Scheme or the International Graduates Scheme;

(vi) intends to leave the United Kingdom if, on expiry of his leave under this scheme, he has not been granted leave to remain in the United Kingdom in accordance with paragraphs 128–135, 200–210H or 245A–245G of these Rules;

(vii) has the written consent of his official sponsor to enter or remain in the United Kingdom under the Science and Engineering Graduates Scheme or International Graduates Scheme if his approved studies, or any studies he has subsequently undertaken, were sponsored by a government or international scholarship agency; and

(viii) holds a valid entry clearance for entry in this capacity except where he is a British National (Overseas), a British overseas territories citizen, a British Overseas citizen, a British protected person or a person who under the British Nationality Act 1981 is a British subject.

Leave to enter as a participant in the International Graduates Scheme

135P. A person seeking leave to enter the United Kingdom as a participant in the International Graduates Scheme may be admitted for a period not exceeding 12 months provided he is able to produce to the Immigration Officer, on arrival, a valid United Kingdom entry clearance for entry in this capacity.

Refusal of leave to enter as a participant in the International Graduates Scheme

135Q. Leave to enter as a participant in the International Graduates Scheme is to be refused if the Immigration Officer is not satisfied that each of the requirements of paragraph 135O is met.

Requirements for leave to remain as a participant in the International Graduates Scheme

135R. The requirements to be met by a person seeking leave to remain as a participant in the International Graduates Scheme are that he:

(i) meets the requirements of paragraph 135O(i) to (vii); and

(ii) has leave to enter or remain as a student or as a participant in the Science and Engineering Graduates Scheme or International Graduates Scheme in accordance with paragraphs 57–69L or 135O–135T of these Rules;

(iii) would not, as a result of an extension of stay, remain in the United Kingdom as a participant in the International Graduates Scheme to a date beyond 12 months from the date on which he was first given leave to enter or remain in this capacity or under the Science and Engineering Graduates Scheme.

Leave to remain as a participant in the International Graduates Scheme

135S. Leave to remain as a participant in the International Graduates Scheme may be granted if the Secretary of State is satisfied that the applicant meets each of the requirements of paragraph 135R.

Refusal of leave to remain as a participant in the International Graduates Scheme

135T. Leave to remain as a participant in the International Graduates Scheme is to be refused if the Secretary of State is not satisfied that each of the requirements of paragraph 135R is met.

Requirements for leave to enter the United Kingdom as a Fresh Talent: Working in Scotland scheme participant

143A. The requirements to be met by a person seeking leave to enter as a Fresh Talent: Working in Scotland scheme participant are that the applicant:

(i) has been awarded:

(a) a HND, by a Scottish publicly funded institution of further or higher education, or a Scottish bona fide private education institution; or

(b) a recognised UK undergraduate degree, Master's degree or PhD or postgraduate certificate or diploma, by a Scottish education institution which is a recognised or listed body; and

(ii) has lived in Scotland for an appropriate period of time whilst studying for the HND, undergraduate degree, Master's degree PhD or postgraduate certificate or diploma referred to in (i) above; and

(iii) intends to seek and take employment in Scotland during the period of leave granted under this paragraph; and

(iv) is able to maintain and accommodate himself and any dependants adequately without recourse to public funds; and

(v) has completed the HND, undergraduate degree, Master's degree PhD or postgraduate certificate or diploma referred to in (i) above in the last 12 months; and

(vi) intends to leave the United Kingdom if, on expiry of his leave under this paragraph, he has not been granted leave to remain in the United Kingdom as:

(a) a work permit holder in accordance with paragraphs 128–135 of these Rules; or

(b) a Tier 1 (General) Migrant; or

(c) a person intending to establish themselves in business in accordance with paragraphs 200–210 of these Rules; or

(d) an innovator in accordance with paragraphs 210A–210H of these Rules; and

(vii) has the written consent of his official sponsor to enter or remain in the United Kingdom as a Fresh Talent: Working in Scotland scheme participant, if the studies which led to his qualification under (i) above (or any studies he has subsequently undertaken) were sponsored by a government or international scholarship agency; and

(viii) if he has previously been granted leave as either:

(a) a Fresh Talent: Working in Scotland scheme participant in accordance with this paragraph; and/or

(b) a participant in the Science and Engineering Graduates Scheme or International Graduates Scheme in accordance with paragraphs 135O–135T of these Rules is not seeking leave to enter under this paragraph which, when amalgamated with any previous periods of leave granted in either of these two categories, would total more than 24 months; and

(ix) holds a valid entry clearance for entry in this capacity except where he is a British National (Overseas), a British overseas territories citizen, a British Overseas citizen, a British protected person or a person who under the British Nationality Act 1981 is a British subject.

Leave to enter as a Fresh Talent: Working in Scotland scheme participant

143B. A person seeking leave to enter the United Kingdom as a Fresh Talent: Working in Scotland scheme participant may be admitted for a period not exceeding 24 months provided the Immigration Officer is satisfied that each of the requirements of paragraph 143A is met.

Refusal of leave to enter as a Fresh Talent: Working in Scotland scheme participant

143C. Leave to enter as a Fresh Talent: Working in Scotland scheme participant is to be refused if the Immigration Officer is not satisfied that each of the requirements of paragraph 143A is met.

Requirements for an extension of stay as a Fresh Talent: Working in Scotland scheme participant

143D. The requirements to be met by a person seeking an extension of stay as a Fresh Talent: Working in Scotland scheme participant are that the applicant:

(i) meets the requirements of paragraph 143A(i) to (vii); and

(ii) has leave to enter or remain in the United Kingdom as either:

(a) a student in accordance with paragraphs 57–69L of these Rules; or

(b) a participant in the Science and Engineering Graduates Scheme or International Graduates Scheme in accordance with paragraphs 135O–135T of these Rules; or

(c) a Fresh Talent: Working in Scotland scheme participant in accordance with paragraphs 143A–143F of these Rules; and

(iii) if he has previously been granted leave as either:

(a) a Fresh Talent: Working in Scotland scheme participant in accordance with paragraphs 143A–143F of these Rules; and/or

(b) a Science and Engineering Graduates Scheme or International Graduates Scheme participant in accordance with paragraphs 135O–135T of these Rules is not seeking leave to remain under this paragraph which, when amalgamated with any previous periods of leave granted in either of these two categories, would total more than 24 months.

Extension of stay as a Fresh Talent: Working in Scotland scheme participant

143E. An extension of stay as a Fresh Talent: Working in Scotland scheme participant may be granted for a period not exceeding 24 months if the Secretary of State is satisfied that each of the requirements of paragraph 143D is met.

Refusal of an extension of stay as a Fresh Talent: Working in Scotland scheme participant

143F. An extension of stay as a Fresh Talent: Working in Scotland scheme participant is to be refused if the Secretary of State is not satisfied that each of the requirements of paragraph 143D is met.

Persons intending to establish themselves in business

Requirements for leave to enter the United Kingdom as a person intending to establish himself in business

200. For the purpose of paragraphs 201–210 a business means an enterprise as:

- a sole trader; or
- a partnership; or
- a company registered in the United Kingdom.

201. The requirements to be met by a person seeking leave to enter the United Kingdom to establish himself in business are:

(i) that he satisfies the requirements of either paragraph 202 or paragraph 203; and

(ii) that he has not less than £200,000 of his own money under his control and disposable in the United Kingdom which is held in his own name and not by a trust or other investment vehicle and which he will be investing in the business in the United Kingdom; and

(iii) that until his business provides him with an income he will have sufficient additional funds to maintain and accommodate himself and any dependants without recourse to employment (other than his work for the business) or to public funds; and

(iv) that he will be actively involved full-time in trading or providing services on his own account or in partnership, or in the promotion and management of the company as a director; and

(v) that his level of financial investment will be proportional to his interest in the business; and

(vi) that he will have either a controlling or equal interest in the business and that any partnership or directorship does not amount to disguised employment; and

(vii) that he will be able to bear his share of liabilities; and

(viii) that there is a genuine need for his investment and services in the United Kingdom; and

(ix) that his share of the profits of the business will be sufficient to maintain and accommodate himself and any dependants without recourse to employment (other than his work for the business) or to public funds; and

(x) that he does not intend to supplement his business activities by taking or seeking employment in the United Kingdom other than his work for the business; and

(xi) that he holds a valid United Kingdom entry clearance for entry in this capacity.

202. Where a person intends to take over or join as a partner or director an existing business in the United Kingdom he will need, in addition to meeting the requirements at paragraph 201, to produce:

(i) a written statement of the terms on which he is to take over or join the business; and

(ii) audited accounts for the business for previous years; and

(iii) evidence that his services and investment will result in a net increase in the employment provided by the business to persons settled here to the extent of creating at least 2 new full-time jobs.

203. Where a person intends to establish a new business in the United Kingdom he will need, in addition to meeting the requirements at paragraph 201 above, to produce evidence:

(i) that he will be bringing into the country sufficient funds of his own to establish a business; and

(ii) that the business will create full-time paid employment for at least 2 persons already settled in the United Kingdom.

Leave to enter the United Kingdom as a person seeking to establish himself in business

204. A person seeking leave to enter the United Kingdom to establish himself in business may be admitted for a period not exceeding 2 years with a condition restricting his freedom to take employment provided he is able to produce to the Immigration Officer, on arrival, a valid United Kingdom entry clearance for entry in this capacity.

Refusal of leave to enter the United Kingdom as a person seeking to establish himself in business

205. Leave to enter the United Kingdom as a person seeking to establish himself in business is to be refused if a valid United Kingdom entry clearance for entry in this capacity is not produced to the Immigration Officer on arrival.

Requirements for an extension of stay in order to remain in business

206. The requirements for an extension of stay in order to remain in business in the United Kingdom are that the applicant can show:

(i) that he entered the United Kingdom with a valid United Kingdom entry clearance as a businessman; and

(ii) audited accounts which show the precise financial position of the business and which confirm that he has invested not less than £200,000 of his own money directly into the business in the United Kingdom; and

(iii) that he is actively involved on a full-time basis in trading or providing services on his own account or in partnership or in the promotion and management of the company as a director; and

(iv) that his level of financial investment is proportional to his interest in the business; and

(v) that he has either a controlling or equal interest in the business and that any partnership or directorship does not amount to disguised employment; and

(vi) that he is able to bear his share of any liability the business may incur; and

(vii) that there is a genuine need for his investment and services in the United Kingdom; and

(viii) (a) that where he has established a new business, new full-time paid employment has been created in the business for at least 2 persons settled in the United Kingdom; or

(b) that where he has taken over or joined an existing business, his services and investment have resulted in a net increase in the employment provided by the business to persons settled here to the extent of creating at least 2 new full-time jobs; and

(ix) that his share of the profits of the business is sufficient to maintain and accommodate him and any dependants without recourse to employment (other than his work for the business) or to public funds; and

(x) that he does not and will not have to supplement his business activities by taking or seeking employment in the United Kingdom other than his work for the business.

206A. The requirements for an extension of stay as a person intending to establish himself in business in the United Kingdom for a person who has leave to enter or remain for work permit employment are that the applicant:

(i) entered the United Kingdom or was given leave to remain as a work permit holder in accordance with paragraphs 128 to 133 of these Rules; and

(ii) meets each of the requirements of paragraph 201(i)–(x).

206B. The requirements for an extension of stay as a person intending to establish himself in business in the United Kingdom for a highly skilled migrant are that the applicant:

(i) entered the United Kingdom or was given leave to remain as a highly skilled migrant in accordance with paragraphs 135A to 135F of these Rules; and

(ii) meets each of the requirements of paragraph 201(i)–(x).

206C. The requirements for an extension of stay as a person intending to establish himself in business in the United Kingdom for a participant in the Science and Engineering Graduates Scheme or International Graduates Scheme are that the applicant:

(i) entered the United Kingdom or was given leave to remain as a participant in the Science and Engineering Graduates Scheme or International Graduates Scheme in accordance with paragraphs 135O to 135T of these Rules; and

(ii) meets each of the requirements of paragraph 201(i)–(x).

206D. The requirements for an extension of stay as a person intending to establish himself in business in the United Kingdom for an innovator are that the applicant:

(i) entered the United Kingdom or was given leave to remain as an innovator in accordance with paragraphs 210A to 210F of these Rules; and

(ii) meets each of the requirements of paragraph 201(i)–(x).

206E. The requirements for an extension of stay as a person intending to establish himself in business in the United Kingdom for a student are that the applicant:

(i) entered the United Kingdom or was given leave to remain as a student in accordance with paragraphs 57 to 62 of these Rules; and

(ii) has obtained a degree qualification on a recognised degree course at either a United Kingdom publicly funded further or higher education institution or a bona fide United Kingdom private education institution which maintains satisfactory records of enrolment and attendance; and

(iii) has the written consent of his official sponsor to such self employment if he is a member of a government or international scholarship agency sponsorship and that sponsorship is either ongoing or has recently come to an end at the time of the requested extension; and

(iv) meets each of the requirements of paragraph 201(i)–(x).

206F. The requirements for an extension of stay as a person intending to establish himself in business in the United Kingdom for a working holidaymaker are that the applicant:

(i) entered the United Kingdom or was given leave to remain as a working holidaymaker in accordance with paragraphs 95 to 100 of these Rules; and

(ii) has spent more than 12 months in total in the UK in this capacity; and

(iii) meets each of the requirements of paragraph 201(i)–(x).

206G. The requirements for an extension of stay as a person intending to establish himself in business in the United Kingdom in the case of a person who has leave to enter or remain as a Fresh Talent: Working in Scotland scheme participant are that the applicant:

(i) entered the United Kingdom or was given leave to remain as a Fresh Talent: Working in Scotland scheme participant in accordance with paragraphs 143A to 143F of these Rules; and

(ii) has the written consent of his official sponsor to such employment if the studies which led to him being granted leave under the Fresh Talent: Working in Scotland scheme in accordance with paragraphs 143A to 143F of these Rules, or any studies he has subsequently undertaken, were sponsored by a government or international scholarship agency; and

(iii) meets each of the requirements of paragraph 201(i)–(x).

206H. The requirements for an extension of stay as a person intending to establish himself in business in the United Kingdom for a Postgraduate Doctor or Dentist are that the applicant:

(i) entered the United Kingdom or was given leave to remain as a Postgraduate Doctor or Dentist in accordance with paragraphs 70 to 75 of these Rules; and

(ii) has the written consent of his official sponsor to such self employment if he is a member of a government or international scholarship agency sponsorship and that sponsorship is either ongoing or has recently come to an end at the time of the requested extension; and

(iii) meets each of the requirements of paragraph 201(i)–(x).

206I. The requirements for an extension of stay as a person intending to establish himself in business in the United Kingdom for a Tier 1 (General) Migrant are that the applicant:

(i) entered the United Kingdom or was given leave to remain as a Tier 1 (General) Migrant; and

(ii) meets each of the requirements of paragraph 201(i)–(x).

Extension of stay in order to remain in business

207. An extension of stay in order to remain in business with a condition restricting his freedom to take employment may be granted for a period not exceeding 3 years at a time provided the Secretary of State is satisfied that each of the requirements of paragraph 206, 206A, 206B, 206C, 206D, 206E, 206F, 206G, 206H or 206I is met.

Refusal of extension of stay in order to remain in business

208. An extension of stay in order to remain in business is to be refused if the Secretary of State is not satisfied that each of the requirements of paragraph 206, 206A, 206B, 206C, 206D, 206E, 206F, 206G, 206H or 206I is met.

Innovators

Requirements for leave to enter the United Kingdom as an innovator

210A. The requirements to be met by a person seeking leave to enter as an innovator are that the applicant:

(i) is approved by the Home Office as a person who meets the criteria specified by the Secretary of State for entry under the innovator scheme at the time that approval is sought under that scheme;

(ii) intends to set up a business that will create full-time paid employment for at least 2 persons already settled in the UK; and

(iii) intends to maintain a minimum five per cent shareholding of the equity capital in that business, once it has been set up, throughout the period of his stay as an innovator; and

(iv) will be able to maintain and accommodate himself and any dependants adequately without recourse to public funds or to other employment; and

(v) holds a valid United Kingdom entry clearance for entry in this capacity.

Leave to enter as an innovator

210B. A person seeking leave to enter the United Kingdom as an innovator may be admitted for a period not exceeding 2 years, provided the Immigration Officer is satisfied that each of the requirements of paragraph 210A is met.

Refusal of leave to enter as an innovator

210C. Leave to enter as an innovator is to be refused if the Immigration Officer is not satisfied that each of the requirements of paragraph 210A are met.

Requirements for an extension of stay as an innovator

210D. The requirements for an extension of stay in the United Kingdom as an innovator, in the case of a person who was granted leave to enter under paragraph 210A, are that the applicant:

(i) has established a viable trading business, by reference to the audited accounts and trading records of that business; and

(ii) continues to meet the requirements of paragraph 210A(i) and (iv); and has set up a business that will create full-time paid employment for at least 2 persons already settled in the UK; and

(iii) has maintained a minimum five per cent shareholding of the equity capital in that business, once it has been set up, throughout the period of his stay.

210DA. The requirements for an extension of stay in the United Kingdom as an innovator, in the case of a person who has leave for the purpose of work permit employment are that the applicant:

(i) entered the United Kingdom or was given leave to remain as a work permit holder in accordance with paragraphs 128 to 132 of these Rules; and

(ii) meets the requirements of paragraph 210A(i)–(iv).

210DB. The requirements for an extension of stay in the United Kingdom as an innovator in the case of a person who has leave as a student are that the applicant:

(i) entered the United Kingdom or was given leave to remain as a student in accordance with paragraphs 57 to 62 of these Rules; and

(ii) has obtained a degree qualification on a recognised degree course at either a United Kingdom publicly funded further or higher education institution or a bona fide United Kingdom private education institution which maintains satisfactory records of enrolment and attendance; and

(iii) has the written consent of his official sponsor to remain under the Innovator category if he is a member of a government or international scholarship agency sponsorship and that sponsorship is either ongoing or has recently come to an end at the time of the requested extension; and

(iv) meets the requirements of paragraph 210A(i)–(iv).

210DC. The requirements to be met for an extension of stay as an innovator, for a person who has leave as a working holidaymaker are that the applicant:

(i) entered the United Kingdom as a working holidaymaker in accordance with paragraphs 95 to 96 of these Rules; and

(ii) meets the requirements of paragraph 210A(i)–(iv).

210DD. The requirements to be met for an extension of stay as an innovator, for a postgraduate doctor, postgraduate dentist or trainee general practitioner are that the applicant:

(i) entered the United Kingdom or was given leave to remain as a postgraduate doctor, postgraduate dentist or trainee general practitioner in accordance with paragraphs 70 to 75 of these Rules; and

(ii) has the written consent of his official sponsor to remain under the innovator category if he is a member of a government or international scholarship agency sponsorship and that sponsorship is either ongoing or has recently come to an end at the time of the requested extension; and

(iii) meets the requirements of paragraph 210A(i)–(iv).

210DE. The requirements to be met for an extension of stay as an innovator, for a participant in the Science and Engineering Graduate Scheme or International Graduates Scheme are that the applicant:

(i) entered the United Kingdom or was given leave to remain as a participant in the Science and Engineering Graduate Scheme or International Graduates Scheme in accordance with paragraphs 135O to 135T of these Rules; and

(ii) meets the requirements of paragraph 210A(i)–(iv).

210DF. The requirements to be met for an extension of stay as an innovator, for a highly skilled migrant are that the applicant:

(i) entered the United Kingdom or was given leave to remain as a highly skilled migrant in accordance with paragraphs 135A to 135E of these Rules; and

(ii) meets the requirements of paragraph 210A(i)–(iv)

Requirements for leave to enter the United Kingdom as an investor

224. The requirements to be met by a person seeking leave to enter the United Kingdom as an investor are that he:

(i) (a) has money of his own under his control in the United Kingdom amounting to no less than £1 million; or

(b) (i) owns personal assets which, taking into account any liabilities to which he is subject, have a value exceeding £2 million; and

(ii) has money under his control in the United Kingdom amounting to no less than £1 million, which may include money loaned to him provided that it was loaned by a financial institution regulated by the Financial Services Authority; and

(ii) intends to invest not less than £750,000 of his capital in the United Kingdom by way of United Kingdom Government bonds, share capital or loan capital in active and trading United Kingdom registered companies (other than those principally engaged in property investment and excluding investment by the applicant by way of deposits with a bank, building society or other enterprise whose normal course of business includes the acceptance of deposits); and

(iii) intends to make the United Kingdom his main home; and

(iv) is able to maintain and accommodate himself and any dependants without taking employment (other than self employment or business) or recourse to public funds; and

(v) holds a valid United Kingdom entry clearance for entry in this capacity.

Leave to enter as an investor

225. A person seeking leave to enter the United Kingdom as an investor may be admitted for a period not exceeding 2 years with a restriction on his right to take employment, provided he is able to produce to the Immigration Officer, on arrival, a valid United Kingdom entry clearance for entry in this capacity.

Refusal of leave to enter as an investor

226. Leave to enter as an investor is to be refused if a valid United Kingdom entry clearance for entry in this capacity is not produced to the Immigration Officer on arrival.

Requirements for an extension of stay as an investor

Extension of stay as an investor

227. The requirements for an extension of stay as an investor are that the applicant:

(i) entered the United Kingdom with a valid United Kingdom entry clearance as an investor; and

(ii) (a) has money of his own under his control in the United Kingdom amounting to no less than £1 million; or

(b) (i) owns personal assets which, taking into account any liabilities to which he is subject, have a value exceeding £2 million; and

(ii) has money under his control in the United Kingdom amounting to no less than £1 million, which may include money loaned to him provided that it was loaned by a financial institution regulated by the Financial Services Authority; and

(iii) has invested not less than £750,000 of his capital in the United Kingdom on the terms set out in paragraph 224 (ii) above and intends to maintain that investment on the terms set out in paragraph 224 (ii); and

(iv) has made the United Kingdom his main home; and

(v) is able to maintain and accommodate himself and any dependants without taking employment (other than his self employment or business) or recourse to public funds.

227A. The requirements to be met for an extension of stay as an investor, for a person who has leave to enter or remain in the United Kingdom as a work permit holder are that the applicant:

(i) entered the United Kingdom or was granted leave to remain as a work permit holder in accordance with paragraphs 128 to 133 of these Rules; and

(ii) meets the requirements of paragraph 224(i)–(iv).

227B. The requirements to be met for an extension of stay as an investor, for a person in the United Kingdom as a highly skilled migrant are that the applicant:

(i) entered the United Kingdom or was granted leave to remain as a highly skilled migrant in accordance with paragraphs 135A to 135F of these Rules; and

(ii) meets the requirements of paragraph 224(i)–(iv).

227C. The requirements to be met for an extension of stay as an investor, for a person in the United Kingdom to establish themselves or remain in business are that the applicant:

(i) entered the United Kingdom or was granted leave to remain as a person intending to establish themselves or remain in business in accordance with paragraphs 201 to 208 of these Rules; and

(ii) meets the requirements of paragraph 224(i)–(iv).

227D. The requirements to be met for an extension of stay as an investor, for a person in the United Kingdom as an innovator are that the applicant:

(i) entered the United Kingdom or was granted leave to remain as an innovator in accordance with paragraphs 210A to 210F of these Rules; and

(ii) meets the requirements of paragraph 224(i)–(iv).

227E. The requirements to be met for an extension of stay as an investor, for a person in the United Kingdom as a Tier 1 (General) Migrant are that the applicant:

(i) entered the United Kingdom or was granted leave to remain as a Tier 1 (General) Migrant; and

(ii) meets the requirements of paragraph 224(i)–(iv).

228. An extension of stay as an investor, with a restriction on the taking of employment, may be granted for a period not exceeding 3 years at a time of 3 years, provided the Secretary of State is satisfied that each of the requirements of paragraph 227, 227A, 227B, 227C, 227D or 227E is met.

Refusal of extension of stay as an investor

229. An extension of stay as an investor is to be refused if the Secretary of State is not satisfied that each of the requirements of paragraph 227, 227A, 227B, 227C, 227D or 227E is met.

Writers, composers and artists

Requirements for leave to enter the United Kingdom as a writer, composer or artist

232. The requirements to be met by a person seeking leave to enter the United Kingdom as a writer, composer or artist are that he:

(i) has established himself outside the United Kingdom as a writer, composer or artist primarily engaged in producing original work which has been published (other than exclusively in newspapers or magazines), performed or exhibited for its literary, musical or artistic merit; and

(ii) does not intend to work except as related to his self employment as a writer, composer or artist; and

(iii) has for the preceding year been able to maintain and accommodate himself and any dependants from his own resources without working except as a writer, composer or artist; and

(iv) will be able to maintain and accommodate himself and any dependants from his own resources without working except as a writer, composer or artist and without recourse to public funds; and

(v) holds a valid United Kingdom entry clearance for entry in this capacity.

Leave to enter as a writer, composer or artist

233. A person seeking leave to enter the United Kingdom as a writer, composer or artist may be admitted for a period not exceeding 2 years, subject to a condition restricting his freedom to take employment, provided he is able to produce to the Immigration Officer, on arrival, a valid United Kingdom entry clearance for entry in this capacity.

Refusal of leave to enter as a writer, composer or artist

234. Leave to enter as a writer, composer or artist is to be refused if a valid United Kingdom entry clearance for entry in this capacity is not produced to the Immigration Officer on arrival.

Requirements for an extension of stay as a writer, composer or artist

235. The requirements for an extension of stay as a writer, composer or artist are that the applicant:

(i) entered the United Kingdom with a valid United Kingdom entry clearance as a writer, composer or artist; and

(ii) meets the requirements of paragraph 232 (ii)–(iv).

Extension of stay as a writer, composer or artist

236. An extension of stay as a writer, composer or artist may be granted for a period not exceeding 3 years with a restriction on his freedom to take employment, provided the Secretary of State is satisfied that each of the requirements of paragraph 235 is met.

Refusal of extension of stay as a writer, composer or artist

237. An extension of stay as a writer, composer or artist is to be refused if the Secretary of State is not satisfied that each of the requirements of paragraph 235 is met.

Part 2

Note: Words 'Part 2' inserted from 1 October 2013 subject to savings for applications made before that date (HC 628).

Immigration rules as at 26 November 2008 relating to routes deleted on 27 November 2008

A) Requirements for leave to enter as an overseas qualified nurse or midwife

69M. The requirements to be met by a person seeking leave to enter as an qualified nurse or midwife are that the applicant:

(i) has obtained confirmation from the Nursing and Midwifery Council that he is eligible:

(a) for admission to the Overseas Nurses Programme; or

(b) to undertake a period of supervided practice; or

(c) to undertake an adaptation programme leading to registration as a midwife; and

(ii) as been offered:

(a) a supervised practice placement through an education provider that is recognised by the Nursing and Midwifery Council; or

(b) a supervised practice placement in a setting approved by the Nursing and Midwifery Council; or

(c) a midwifery adaptation programme placement is a setting approved by the Nursing and Midwifery Council; and

(iii) did not obtain acceptance of the offer referred to in paragraph 69 (ii) by misrepresentation; and

(iv) is able and intends to undertake the supervised practice placement or midwife adaptation programme; and

(v) does not intend to engage in business or take employment, except

(a) in connection with the supervised practice placement or midwife adaptation programme; or

(b) part-time work of a similar nature to the work undertaken on the supervised practice placement or midwife adaptation programme; and

(vi) is able to maintain and accommodate himself and any dependants without recourse to public funds.

Leave to enter the United Kingdom as an overseas qualified nurse or midwife

69N. Leave to enter the United Kingdom as an overseas qualified nurse or midwife may be granted for a period not exceeding 18 months, provided the Immigration Officer is satisfied that each of the requirements of paragraph 69M is met.

Refusal of leave to enter as an overseas qualified nurse or midwife

69O. Leave to enter the United Kingdom as an overseas qualified nurse or midwife is to be refused if the Immigration Officer is not is satisfied that each of the requirements of paragraph 69M is met.

B) Requirements for an extension of stay as an overseas qualified nurse or midwife

69P. The requirements to be met by a person seeking an extension of stay as an overseas qualified nurse or midwife are that the applicant:

(i) has leave to enter or remain in the United Kingdom as a prospective student in accordance with paragraphs 82–87 of these Rules; or

(ii) has leave to enter or remain in the United Kingdom as a student in accordance with paragraphs 57 to 69L of these Rules; or

(iii) (a) has leave to enter or remain in the United Kingdom as a work permit holder in accordance with paragraphs 128 to 135 of these Rules; or

C) Requirements for leave to enter the United Kingdom to take the PLAB Test

75A. The requirements to be met by a person seeking leave to enter in order to take the PLAB Test are that the applicant:

(iv) intends to leave the United Kingdom at the end of his leave granted under this paragraph unless he is successful in the PLAB Test and granted leave to remain:

(c) as a work permit holder for employment in the United Kingdom as a doctor in accordance with paragraphs 128 to 135.

Requirements for an extension of stay in order to take the PLAB Test

75D. The requirements for an extension of stay in the United Kingdom in order to take the PLAB Test are that the applicant:

(iv) intends to leave the United Kingdom at the end of his leave granted under this paragraph unless he is successful in the PLAB Test and granted leave to remain:

(c) as a work permit holder for employment in the United Kingdom as a doctor in accordance with paragraphs 128 to 135; and

Requirements for leave to enter to undertake a clinical or dental observer post

75G. The requirements to be met by a person seeking leave to enter to undertake a clinical attachment or dental observer post are that the applicant:

(iv) intends to leave the United Kingdom at the end of his leave granted under this paragraph unless he is granted leave to remain:

(b) as a work permit holder for employment in the United Kingdom as a doctor or dentist in accordance with paragraphs 128 to 135; and

Requirements for an extension of stay in order to undertake a clinical attachment or dental observer post

75K. The requirements to be met by a person seeking an extension of stay to undertake a clinical attachment or dental observer post are that the applicant:

(iv) intends to leave the United Kingdom at the end of his period of leave granted under this paragraph unless he is granted leave to remain:

(b) as a work permit holder for employment in the United Kingdom as a doctor or dentist in accordance with paragraphs 128 to 135; and

D) *Definition of an 'au pair' placement*

88. For the purposes of these Rules an 'au pair' placement as an arrangement whereby a young person:

(a) comes to the United Kingdom for the purpose of learning the English language; and

(b) lives for a time as a member of an English speaking family with appropriate opportunities for study; and

(c) helps in the home for a maximum of 5 hours per day in return for a reasonable allowance and with two free days a week.

Requirements for leave to enter as an 'au pair'

89. The requirements to be met by a person seeking leave to enter the United Kingdom as an 'au pair' are that he:

(i) is seeking entry for the purpose of taking up an arranged placement which can be shown to fall within the definition set out in paragraph 88; and

(ii) is aged between 17–27 inclusive or was so aged when first given leave to enter this category; and

(iii) is unmarried and is not a civil partner; and

(iv) is without dependants; and

(v) is a national of one of the following countries: Andorra, Bosnia-Herzegovina, Croatia, The Faroes, Greenland, Macedonia, Monaco, San Marino or Turkey; and

(vi) does not intend to stay in the United Kingdom for more than 2 years as an 'au pair';

and

(vii) intends to leave the United Kingdom on completion of his stay as an 'au pair'; and

(viii) if he has previously spent time in the United Kingdom as an 'au pair', is not seeking leave to enter to a date beyond 2 years from the date on which he was first given leave to enter the United Kingdom in this capacity; and

ix) is able to maintain and accommodate himself without recourse to public funds.

Leave to enter as an 'au pair'

90. A person seeking leave to enter the United Kingdom as an 'au pair' may be admitted for a period not exceeding 2 years with a prohibition on employment except as an 'au pair' provided the Immigration Officer is satisfied that each of the requirements of paragraph 89 is met. (A non-visa national who wishes to ascertain in advance whether a proposed 'au pair' placement is likely to meet the requirements of paragraph 89 is advised to obtain an entry clearance before travelling to the United Kingdom.)

Refusal of leave to enter as an 'au pair'

91. An application for leave to enter as an 'au pair' is to be refused if the Immigration Officer is not satisfied that each of the requirements of paragraph 89 is met.

E) Working Holidaymakers

Requirements for leave to enter as a working holidaymaker

95. The requirements to be met by a person seeking leave to enter the United Kingdom as a working holidaymaker are that he:

(i) is a national or citizen of a country listed in Appendix 3 of these Rules, or a British Overseas Citizen; a British Overseas Territories Citizen; or a British National; and

(ii) is aged between 17 and 30 inclusive or was so aged at the date of his application for leave to enter; and

(iii) (a) is unmarried and is not a civil partner, or

(b) is married to, or the civil partner of, a person who meets the requirements of this paragraph and the parties to the marriage or civil partnership intend to take a working holiday together; and

(iv) has the means to pay for his return or onward journey, and

(v) is able and intends to maintain and accommodate himself without recourse to public funds; and

(vi) is intending only to take employment incidental to a holiday, and not to engage in business, or to provide services as a professional sportsperson, and in any event not to work for more than 12 months during his stay; and

(vii) does not have dependent children any of whom are 5 years of age or over or who will reach 5 years of age before the applicant completes his working holiday; and

(viii) intends to leave the UK at the end of his working holiday; and

(ix) has not spent time in the United Kingdom on a previous working holidaymaker entry clearance; and

(x) holds a valid United Kingdom entry clearance, granted for a limited period not exceeding 2 years, for entry in this capacity.

Leave to enter as a working holidaymaker

96. A person seeking to enter the United Kingdom as a working holidaymaker may be admitted provided he is able to produce on arrival a valid United Kingdom entry clearance granted for a period not exceeding 2 years for entry in this capacity.

Refusal of leave to enter as a working holidaymaker

97. Leave to enter as a working holidaymaker is to be refused if a valid United Kingdom entry clearance for entry in this capacity is not produced to the Immigration Officer on arrival.

F) Children of working holidaymakers

Requirements for leave to enter or remain as the child of a working holidaymaker

101. The requirements to be met by a person seeking leave to enter or remain in the United Kingdom as the child of a working holidaymaker are that:

(i) he is the child of a parent admitted to, and currently present in, the United Kingdom as a working holidaymaker; and

(ii) he is under the age of 5 and will leave the United Kingdom before reaching that age; and

(iii) he can and will be maintained and accommodated adequately without recourse to public funds or without his parent(s) engaging in employment except as provided by paragraph 95 above; and

(iv) both parents are being or have been admitted to the United Kingdom, save where:

(a) the parent he is accompanying or joining is his sole surviving parent; or

(b) the parent he is accompanying or joining has had sole responsibility for his upbringing; or

(c) there are serious and compelling family or other considerations which make exclusion from the United Kingdom undesirable and suitable arrangements have been made for his care; and

(v) he holds a valid United Kingdom entry clearance for entry in this capacity or, if seeking leave to remain, was admitted with a valid United Kingdom entry clearance for entry in this capacity, and is seeking leave to a date not beyond the date to which his parent(s) have leave to enter in the working holidaymaker category.

Leave to enter or remain as the child of a working holidaymaker

102. A person seeking to enter the United Kingdom as the child of working holidaymaker/s must be able to produce on arrival a valid United Kingdom entry clearance for entry in this capacity.

Refusal of leave to enter or remain as the child of a working holidaymaker

103. Leave to enter or remain in the United Kingdom as the child of a working holidaymaker is to be refused if, in relation to an application for leave to enter, a valid United Kingdom entry clearance for entry in this capacity is not produced to the Immigration Officer on arrival or, in the case of an application for leave to remain, the applicant was not admitted with a valid United Kingdom entry clearance for entry in this capacity or is unable to satisfy the Secretary of State that each of the requirements of paragraph 101(i)–(iv) is met.

G) Requirements for leave to enter as a teacher or language assistant under an approved exchange scheme

110. The requirements to be met by a person seeking leave to enter the United Kingdom as a teacher or language assistant on an approved exchange scheme are that he:

(i) is coming to an educational establishment in the United Kingdom under an exchange scheme approved by the Department for Education and Skills, the Scottish or Welsh Office of Education or the Department of Education, Northern Ireland, or administered by the British Council's Education and Training Group or the League for the Exchange of Commonwealth Teachers; and

(ii) intends to leave the United Kingdom at the end of his exchange period; and

(iii) does not intend to take employment except in the terms of this paragraph; and

(iv) is able to maintain and accommodate himself and any dependants without recourse to public funds; and

(v) holds a valid United Kingdom entry clearance for entry in this capacity.

Leave to enter as a teacher or language assistant under an exchange scheme

111. A person seeking leave to enter the United Kingdom as a teacher or language assistant under an approved exchange scheme may be given leave to enter for a period not exceeding 12 months provided he is able to produce to the Immigration Officer, on arrival, a valid United Kingdom entry clearance for entry in this capacity.

Refusal of leave to enter as a teacher or language assistant under an approved exchange scheme

112. Leave to enter the United Kingdom as a teacher or language assistant under an approved exchange scheme is to be refused if a valid United Kingdom entry clearance for entry in this capacity is not produced to the Immigration Officer on arrival.

Requirements for extension of stay as a teacher or language assistant under an approved exchange scheme

113. The requirements for an extension of stay as a teacher or language assistant under an approved exchange scheme are that the applicant:

(i) entered the United Kingdom with a valid United Kingdom entry clearance as a teacher or language assistant; and

(ii) is still engaged in the employment for which his entry clearance was granted; and

(iii) is still required for the employment in question, as certified by the employer; and

(iv) meets the requirements of paragraph 110 (ii)–(iv); and

(v) would not, as a result of an extension of stay, remain in the United Kingdom as an exchange teacher or language assistant for more than 2 years from the date on which he was first given leave to enter the United Kingdom in this capacity.

Extension of stay as a teacher or language assistant under an approved exchange scheme

114. An extension of stay as a teacher or language assistant under an approved exchange scheme may be granted for a further period not exceeding 12 months provided the Secretary of State is satisfied that each of the requirements of paragraph 113 is met.

Refusal of extension of stay as a teacher or language assistant under an approved exchange scheme

115. An extension of stay as a teacher or language assistant under an approved exchange scheme is to be refused

if the Secretary of State is not satisfied that each of the requirements of paragraph 113 is met.

H) Requirements for leave to enter for Home Office approved training or work experience

116. The requirements to be met by a person seeking leave to enter the United Kingdom for Home Office approved training or work experience are that he:

(i) holds a valid work permit from the Home Office issued under the Training and Work Experience Scheme; and

(ii) DELETED

(iii) is capable of undertaking the training or work experience as specified in his work permit; and

(iv) intends to leave the United Kingdom on the completion of his training or work experience;

and

(v) does not intend to take employment except as specified in his work permit; and

(vi) is able to maintain and accommodate himself and any dependants adequately without recourse to public funds; and

(vii) holds a valid United Kingdom entry clearance for entry in this capacity except where he holds a work permit valid for 6 months or less or he is a British National (Overseas), a British overseas territories citizen, a British Overseas citizen, a British protected person or a person who under the British Nationality Act 1981 is a British subject.

Leave to enter for Home Office approved training or work experience

117. A person seeking leave to enter the United Kingdom for the purpose of approved training or approved work experience under the Training or Work Experience Scheme may be admitted to the United Kingdom for a period not exceeding the period of training or work experience approved by the Home Office for this purpose (as specified in his work permit), subject to a condition restricting him to that approved employment, provided he is able to produce to the Immigration Officer, on arrival, a valid United Kingdom entry clearance for entry in this capacity or, where entry clearance is not required, provided the Immigration Officer is satisfied that each of the requirements of paragraph 116(i)–(vi) is met.

Refusal of leave to enter for Home Office approved training or work experience

118. Leave to enter the United Kingdom for Home Office approved training or work experience under the Training and Work Experience scheme is to be refused if a valid United Kingdom entry clearance for entry in this capacity is not produced to the Immigration Officer on arrival or, where entry clearance is not required, if the Immigration Officer is not satisfied that each of the requirements of paragraph 116(i)–(vi) is met.

Requirements for extension of stay for Home Office approved training or work experience

119. The requirements for an extension of stay for Home Office approved training or work experience are that the applicant:

(i) entered the United Kingdom with a valid work permit under paragraph 117 or was admitted or allowed to remain in the United Kingdom as a student; and

(ii) has written approval from the Home Office for an extension of stay in this category; and

(iii) meets the requirements of paragraph 116(ii)–(vi).

Extension of stay for Home Office approved training or work experience

120. An extension of stay for approved training or approved work experience under the Training and Work Experience scheme may be granted for a further period not exceeding the extended period of training or work experience approved by the Home Office for this purpose (as specified in his work permit), provided that in each case the Secretary of State is satisfied that the requirements of paragraph 119 are met. An extension of stay is to be subject to a condition permitting the applicant to take or change employment only with the permission of the Home Office.

Refusal of extension of stay for Home Office approved training or work experience

121. An extension of stay for approved training or approved work experience under the Training and Work Experience scheme is to be refused if the Secretary of State is not satisfied that each of the requirements of paragraph 119 is met.

I) Representatives of overseas newspapers, news agencies and broadcasting organisations

Requirements for leave to enter as a representative of an overseas newspaper, news agency or broadcasting organisation

136. The requirements to be met by a person seeking leave to enter the United Kingdom as a representative of an overseas newspaper, news agency or broadcasting organisation are that he:

(i) has been engaged by that organisation outside the United Kingdom and is being posted to the United Kingdom on a long term assignment as a representative; and

(ii) intends to work full-time as a representative of that overseas newspaper, news agency or broadcasting organisation; and

(iii) does not intend to take employment except within the terms of this paragraph; and

(iv) can maintain and accommodate himself and any dependants adequately without recourse to public funds; and

(v) holds a valid United Kingdom entry clearance for entry in this capacity.

Leave to enter as a representative of an overseas newspaper, news agency or broadcasting organisation

137. A person seeking leave to enter the United Kingdom as a representative of an overseas newspaper, news agency or broadcasting organisation may be admitted for a period not exceeding 2 years, provided he is able to produce to the Immigration Officer, on arrival, a valid United Kingdom entry clearance for entry in this capacity.

Refusal of leave to enter as a representative of an overseas newspaper, news agency or broadcasting organisation

138. Leave to enter as a representative of an overseas newspaper, news agency or broadcasting organisation is to be refused if a valid United Kingdom entry clearance for entry in this capacity is not produced to the Immigration Officer on arrival.

Requirements for an extension of stay as a representative of an overseas newspaper, news agency or broadcasting organisation

139. The requirements for an extension of stay as a representative of an overseas newspaper, news agency or broadcasting organisation are that the applicant:

(i) entered the United Kingdom with a valid United Kingdom entry clearance as a representative of an overseas newspaper, news agency or broadcasting organisation; and

(ii) is still engaged in the employment for which his entry clearance was granted; and

(iii) is still required for the employment in question, as certified by his employer; and
(iv) meets the requirements of paragraph 136 (ii)–(iv).

Extension of stay as a representative of an overseas newspaper, news agency or broadcasting organisation

140. An extension of stay as a representative of an overseas newspaper, news agency or broadcasting organisation may be granted for a period not exceeding 3 years provided the Secretary of State is satisfied that each of the requirements of paragraph 139 is met.

Refusal of extension of stay as a representative of an overseas newspaper, news agency or broadcasting organisation

141. An extension of stay as a representative of an overseas newspaper, news agency or broadcasting organisation is to be refused if the Secretary of State is not satisfied that each of the requirements of paragraph 139 is met.

J) Private servants in diplomatic households

Requirements for leave to enter as a private servant in a diplomatic household

152. The requirements to be met by a person seeking leave to enter the United Kingdom as a private servant in a diplomatic household are that he:

(i) is aged 18 or over; and

(ii) is employed as a private servant in the household of a member of staff of a diplomatic or consular mission

who enjoys diplomatic privileges and immunity within the meaning of the Vienna Convention on Diplomatic and Consular Relations or a member of the family forming part of the household of such a person; and

(iii) intends to work full-time as a private servant within the terms of this paragraph; and

(iv) does not intend to take employment except within the terms of this paragraph; and

(v) can maintain and accommodate himself and any dependants adequately without recourse to public funds; and

(vi) holds a valid United Kingdom entry clearance for entry in this capacity.

Leave to enter as a private servant in a diplomatic household

153. A person seeking leave to enter the United Kingdom as a private servant in a diplomatic household may be given leave to enter for a period not exceeding 12 months provided he is able to produce to the Immigration Officer, on arrival, a valid United Kingdom entry clearance for entry in this capacity.

Refusal of leave to enter as a private servant in a diplomatic household

154. Leave to enter as a private servant in a diplomatic household is to be refused if a valid United Kingdom entry clearance for entry in this capacity is not produced to the Immigration Officer on arrival.

Requirements for an extension of stay as a private servant in a diplomatic household

155. The requirements for an extension of stay as a private servant in a diplomatic household are that the applicant:

(i) entered the United Kingdom with a valid United Kingdom entry clearance as a private servant in a diplomatic household; and

(ii) is still engaged in the employment for which his entry clearance was granted; and

(iii) is still required for the employment in question, as certified by the employer; and

(iv) meets the requirements of paragraph 152(iii)–(v).

Extension of stay as a private servant in a diplomatic household

156. An extension of stay as a private servant in a diplomatic household may be granted for a period not exceeding 12 months at a time provided the Secretary of State is satisfied that each of the requirements of paragraph 155 is met.

Refusal of extension of stay as a private servant in a diplomatic household

157. An extension of stay as a private servant in a diplomatic household is to be refused if the Secretary of State is not satisfied that each of the requirements of paragraph 155 is met.

K) Overseas government employees

Requirements for leave to enter as an overseas government employee

160. For the purposes of these Rules an overseas government employee means a person coming for employment by an overseas government or employed by the United Nations Organisation or other international organisation of which the United Kingdom is a member.

161. The requirements to be met by a person seeking leave to enter the United Kingdom as an overseas government employee are that he:

(i) is able to produce either a valid United Kingdom entry clearance for entry in this capacity or satisfactory documentary evidence of his status as an overseas government employee; and

(ii) intends to work full-time for the government or organisation concerned; and

(iii) does not intend to take employment except within the terms of this paragraph; and

(iv) can maintain and accommodate himself and any dependants adequately without recourse to public funds.

Leave to enter as an overseas government employee

162. A person seeking leave to enter the United Kingdom as an overseas government employee may be given leave to enter for a period not exceeding 2 years, provided he is able, on arrival, to produce to the Immigration Officer a valid United Kingdom entry clearance for entry in this capacity or satisfy the Immigration Officer that each of the requirements of paragraph 161 is met.

Refusal of leave to enter as an overseas government employee

163. Leave to enter as an overseas government employee is to be refused if a valid United Kingdom entry clearance for entry in this capacity is not produced to the Immigration Officer on arrival or if the Immigration Officer is not satisfied that each of the requirements of paragraph 161 is met.

Requirements for an extension of stay as an overseas government employee

164. The requirements to be met by a person seeking an extension of stay as an overseas government employee are that the applicant:

(i) was given leave to enter the United Kingdom under paragraph 162 as an overseas government employee; and

(ii) is still engaged in the employment in question; and

(iii) is still required for the employment in question, as certified by the employer; and

(iv) meets the requirements of paragraph 161(ii)–(iv).

Extension of stay as an overseas government employee

165. An extension of stay as an overseas government employee may be granted for a period not exceeding 3 years provided the Secretary of State is satisfied that each of the requirements of paragraph 164 is met.

Refusal of extension of stay as an overseas government employee

166. An extension of stay as an overseas government employee is to be refused if the Secretary of State is not satisfied that each of the requirements of paragraph 164 is met.

L) Requirements for leave to enter as a minister of religion, missionary, or member of a religious order

170. The requirements to be met by a person seeking leave to enter the United Kingdom as a minister of religion, missionary or member of a religious order are that he:

(i) (a) if seeking leave to enter as a Minister of Religion has either been working for at least one year as a minister of religion in any of the 5 years immediately prior to the date on which the application is made or, where ordination is prescribed by a religious faith as the sole means of entering the ministry, has been ordained as a minister of religion following at least one years full-time or two years' part-time training for the ministry; or

(b) if seeking leave to enter as a missionary has been trained as a missionary or has worked as a missionary and is being sent to the United Kingdom by an overseas organisation; or

(c) if seeking leave to enter as a member of a religious order is coming to live in a community maintained by the religious order of which he is a member and, if intending to teach, does not intend to do so save at an establishment maintained by his order; and

(ii) intends to work full-time as a minister of religion, missionary or for the religious order of which he is a member; and

(iii) does not intend to take employment except within the terms of this paragraph; and

(iv) can maintain and accommodate himself and any dependants adequately without recourse to public funds; and

(iva) if seeking leave as a Minister of Religion can produce an International English Language Testing System certificate issued to him to certify that he has achieved level 6 competence in spoken and written English and that it is dated not more than two years prior to the date on which the application is made.

(v) holds a valid United Kingdom entry clearance for entry in this capacity.

Leave to enter as a minister of religion, missionary, or member of a religious order

171. A person seeking leave to enter the United Kingdom as a minister of religion, missionary or member of a religious order may be admitted for a period not exceeding 2 years provided he is able to produce to the Immigration Officer, on arrival, a valid United Kingdom entry clearance for entry in this capacity.

Refusal of leave to enter as a minister of religion, missionary or member of a religious order

172. Leave to enter as a minister of religion, missionary or member of a religious order is to be refused if a valid United Kingdom entry clearance for entry in this capacity is not produced to the Immigration Officer on arrival.

Requirements for an extension of stay as a minister of religion where entry to the United Kingdom was granted in that capacity

173. The requirements for an extension of stay as a minister of religion, where entry to the United Kingdom was granted in that capacity, missionary or member of a religious order are that the applicant:

(i) entered the United Kingdom with a valid United Kingdom entry clearance as a minister of religion, missionary or member of a religious order; and

(ii) is still engaged in the employment for which his entry clearance was granted; and

(iii) is still required for the employment in question as certified by the leadership of his congregation, his employer or the head of his religious order; and

(iv) (a) if he entered the United Kingdom as a minister of religion, missionary or member of a religious order in accordance with sub-paragraph (i) prior to 23 August 2004 meets the requirements of paragraph 170(ii)–(iv); or

(b) if he entered the United Kingdom as a minister of religion, missionary or member of a religious order in accordance with sub-paragraph (i), on or after 23 August 2004 but prior to 19 April 2007, or was granted leave to remain in accordance with paragraph 174B between those dates, meets the requirements of paragraph 170(ii)–(iv), and if a minister of religion met the requirement to produce an International English Language Testing System certificate certifying that he achieved level 4 competence in spoken English at the time he was first granted leave in this capacity; or

(c) if he entered the United Kingdom as a minister of religion, missionary or member of a religious order in accordance with sub-paragraph (i) on or after 19 April 2007, or was granted leave to remain in accordance with paragraph 174B on or after that date, meets the requirements of paragraph 170(ii)–(iv), and if a minister of religion met the requirement to produce an International English Language Testing System certificate certifying that he achieved level 6 competence in spoken and written English at the time he was first granted leave in this capacity.

Extension of stay as a minister of religion, missionary or member of a religious order

174. An extension of stay as a minister of religion, missionary or member of a religious order may be granted for a period not exceeding 3 years provided the Secretary of State is satisfied that each of the requirements of paragraph 173 is met.

Requirements for an extension of stay as a minister of religion where entry to the United Kingdom was not granted in that capacity

174A. The requirements for an extension of stay as a minister of religion for an applicant who did not enter the United Kingdom in that capacity are that he:

(i) entered the United Kingdom, or was given an extension of stay, in accordance with these Rules, except as a minister of religion or as a visitor under paragraphs 40–56 of these Rules, and has spent a continuous period of at least 12 months here pursuant to that leave immediately prior to the application being made; and

(ii) has either been working for at least one year as a minister of religion in any of the 5 years immediately prior to the date on which the application is made (provided that, when doing so, he was not in breach of a condition of any subsisting leave to enter or remain) or, where ordination is prescribed by a religious faith as the sole means of entering the ministry, has been ordained as a minister of religion following at least one year's full-time or two years part-time training for the ministry; and

(iii) is imminently to be appointed, or has been appointed, to a position as a minister of religion in the United Kingdom and is suitable for such a position, as certified by the leadership of his prospective congregation; and

(iv) meets the requirements of paragraph 170(ii)–(iva)

Extension of stay as a minister of religion where leave to enter was not granted in that capacity

174B. An extension of stay as a minister of religion may be granted for a period not exceeding 3 years at a time provided the Secretary of State is satisfied that each of the requirements of paragraph 174A is met.

Refusal of extension of stay as a minister of religion, missionary or member of a religious order

175. An extension of stay as a minister of religion, missionary or member of a religious order is to be refused if the Secretary of State is not satisfied that each of the requirements of paragraph 173 or 174A is met.

M) Refusal of indefinite leave to remain for a minister of religion, missionary or member of a religious order

177. Indefinite leave to remain in the United Kingdom for a minister of religion, missionary or member of a religious order is to be refused if the Secretary of State is not satisfied that each of the requirements of paragraph 176 is met.

177A. For the purposes of these Rules: Visiting religious workers and religious workers in non-pastoral roles:

(i) a visiting religious worker means a person coming to the UK for a short period to perform religious duties at one or more locations in the UK;

(ii) a religious worker in a non-pastoral role means a person employed in the UK by the faith he is coming here to work for, whose duties include performing religious rites within the religious community, but not preaching to a congregation.

Requirements for leave to enter the United Kingdom as a visiting religious worker or a religious worker in a non-pastoral role

177B. The requirements to be met by a person seeking leave to enter as a visiting religious worker or a religious worker in a non-pastoral role are that the applicant:

(i) (a) if seeking leave to enter as a visiting religious worker:

(i) is an established religious worker based overseas; and

(ii) submits a letter(s) from a senior member or senior representative of one or more local religious communities in the UK confirming that he is invited to perform religious duties as a visiting religious worker at one or more locations in the UK and confirming the expected duration of that employment; and

(iii) if he has been granted leave as a visiting religious worker in the last 12 months, is not seeking leave to enter which, when amalgamated with his previous periods of leave in this category in the last 12 months, would total more than 6 months; or

(b) if seeking leave to enter as a religious worker in a non-pastoral role:

(i) has at least one year of full-time training or work experience, or a period of part-time training or work experience equivalent to one year full-time training or work experience, accrued in the five years preceding the application in the faith with which he has employment in the UK; and

(ii) can show that, at the time of his application, at least one full-time member of staff of the local religious community which the applicant is applying to join in the UK has a sufficient knowledge of English; and

(iii) submits a letter from a senior member or senior representative of the local religious community which has invited him to the UK, confirming that he has been offered employment as religious worker in a non-pastoral role in that religious community, and confirming the duration of that employment; and

(ii) does not intend to take employment except as a visiting religious worker or religious worker in a non-pastoral role, whichever is the basis of his application; and

(iii) does not intend to undertake employment as a Minister of Religion, Missionary or Member of a Religious Order, as described in paragraphs 169–177 of these Rules; and

(iv) is able to maintain and accommodate himself and any dependants without recourse to public funds, or will, with any dependants, be maintained and accommodated adequately by the religious community employing him; and

(v) intends to leave the UK at the end of his leave in this category; and

(vi) holds a valid entry clearance for entry in this capacity except where he is a British National (Overseas), a British overseas territories citizen, a British Overseas citizen, a British protected person or a person who under the British Nationality Act 1981 is a British subject.

Leave to enter as a visiting religious worker or a religious worker in a non-pastoral role

177C. Leave to enter the United Kingdom as a visiting religious worker or a religious worker in a non-pastoral role may be granted:

(a) as a visiting religious worker, for a period not exceeding 6 months; or

(b) as a religious worker in a non-pastoral role, for a period not exceeding 12 months;

provided the Immigration Officer is satisfied that each of the requirements of paragraph 177B is met.

Refusal of leave to enter as a visiting religious worker or a religious worker in a non-pastoral role

177D. Leave to enter as a visiting religious worker or a religious worker in a non-pastoral role is to be refused if the Immigration Officer is not satisfied that each of the requirements of paragraph 177B is met.

Requirements for an extension of stay as a visiting religious worker or a religious worker in a non-pastoral role

177E. The requirements to be met by a person seeking an extension of stay as a visiting religious worker or a religious worker in a non-pastoral role are that the applicant:

(i) entered the United Kingdom with a valid entry clearance in this capacity or was given leave to enter as a visiting religious worker or a religious worker in a non-pastoral role; and

(ii) intends to continue employment as a visiting religious worker or a religious worker in a non-pastoral role; and

(iii) if seeking an extension of stay as a visiting religious worker:

(a) meets the requirement of paragraph 177B(i)(a)(i) above; and

(b) submits a letter from a senior member or senior representative of one or more local religious communities in the UK confirming that he is still wanted to perform religious duties as a visiting religious worker at one or more locations in the UK and confirming the expected duration of that employment; and

(c) would not, as the result of an extension of stay, be granted leave as a visiting religious worker which, when amalgamated with his previous periods of leave in this category in the last 12 months, would total more than 6 months; or

(iv) if seeking an extension of stay as a religious worker in a non-pastoral role:

(a) meets the requirements of paragraph 177B(i)(b)(i) and (ii); and

(b) submits a letter from a senior member or senior representative of the local religious community for which he works in the UK confirming that his employment as a religious worker in a non-pastoral role in that religious community will continue, and confirming the duration of that employment; and

(c) would not, as the result of an extension of stay, remain in the UK for a period of more than 24 months as a religious worker in a non-pastoral role; and

(v) meets the requirements of paragraph 177B(ii) to (v); and

Extension of stay as a visiting religious worker or a religious worker in a non-pastoral role

177F. An extension of stay as a visiting religious worker or a religious worker in a non-pastoral role may be granted:

(a) as a visiting religious worker, for a period not exceeding 6 months; or

(b) as a religious worker in a non-pastoral role, for a period not exceeding 24 months;

if the Secretary of State is satisfied that each of the requirements of paragraph 177E is met.

Refusal of an extension of stay as a visiting religious worker or a religious worker in a non-pastoral role

177G. An extension of stay as a visiting religious worker or a religious worker in a non-pastoral role is to be refused if the Secretary of State is not satisfied that each of the requirements of paragraph 177E is met.

N) Airport based operational ground staff of overseas-owned airlines

Requirements for leave to enter the United Kingdom as a member of the operational ground staff of an overseas-owned airline

178. The requirements to be met by a person seeking leave to enter the United Kingdom as a member of the operational ground staff of an overseas-owned airline are that he:

(i) has been transferred to the United Kingdom by an overseas-owned airline operating services to and from the United Kingdom to take up duty at an international airport as station manager, security manager or technical manager; and

(ii) intends to work full-time for the airline concerned; and

(iii) does not intend to take employment except within the terms of this paragraph; and

(iv) can maintain and accommodate himself and any dependants without recourse to public funds; and

(v) holds a valid United Kingdom entry clearance for entry in this capacity.

Leave to enter as a member of the operational ground staff of an overseas-owned airline

179. A person seeking leave to enter the United Kingdom as a member of the operational ground staff of an overseas-owned airline may be given leave to enter for a period not exceeding 2 years, provided he is able to produce to the Immigration Officer, on arrival, a valid United Kingdom entry clearance for entry in this capacity.

Refusal of leave to enter as a member of the operational ground staff of an overseas-owned airline

180. Leave to enter as a member of the operational ground staff of an overseas-owned airline is to be refused if a valid United Kingdom entry clearance for entry in this capacity is not produced to the Immigration Officer on arrival.

Requirements for an extension of stay as a member of the operational ground staff of an overseas-owned airline

181. The requirements to be met by a person seeking an extension of stay as a member of the operational ground staff of an overseas-owned airline are that the applicant:

(i) entered the United Kingdom with a valid United Kingdom entry clearance as a member of the operational ground staff of an overseas-owned airline; and

(ii) is still engaged in the employment for which entry was granted; and
(iii) is still required for the employment in question, as certified by the employer; and
(iv) meets the requirements of paragraph 178(ii)–(iv).

Extension of stay as a member of the operational ground staff of an overseas-owned airline

182. An extension of stay as a member of the operational ground staff of an overseas-owned airline may be granted for a period not exceeding 3 years, provided the Secretary of State is satisfied that each of the requirements of paragraph 181 is met.

Refusal of extension of stay as a member of the operational ground staff of an overseas-owned airline

183. An extension of stay as a member of the operational ground staff of an overseas-owned airline is to be refused if the Secretary of State is not satisfied that each of the requirements of paragraph 181 is met.

O) Retired persons of independent means

Requirements for leave to enter the United Kingdom as a retired person of independent means

263. The requirements to be met by a person seeking leave to enter the United Kingdom as a retired person of independent means are that he:
(i) is at least 60 years old; and
(ii) has under his control and disposable in the United Kingdom an income of his own of not less than £25,000 per annum; and
(iii) is able and willing to maintain and accommodate himself and any dependants indefinitely in the United Kingdom from his own resources with no assistance from any other person and without taking employment or having recourse to public funds; and
(iv) can demonstrate a close connection with the United Kingdom; and
(v) intends to make the United Kingdom his main home; and
(vi) holds a valid United Kingdom entry clearance for entry in this capacity.

Leave to enter as a retired person of independent means

264. A person seeking leave to enter the United Kingdom as a retired person of independent means may be admitted subject to a condition prohibiting employment for a period not exceeding 5 years, provided he is able to produce to the Immigration Officer, on arrival, a valid United Kingdom entry clearance for entry in this capacity.

Refusal of leave to enter as a retired person of independent means

265. Leave to enter as a retired person of independent means is to be refused if a valid United Kingdom entry clearance for entry in this capacity is not produced to the Immigration Officer on arrival.

Requirements for an extension of stay as a retired person of independent means

266. The requirements for an extension of stay as a retired person of independent means are that the applicant:

(i) entered the United Kingdom with a valid United Kingdom entry clearance as a retired person of independent means; and

(ii) meets the requirements of paragraph 263(ii)–(iv); and

(iii) has made the United Kingdom his main home.

Extension of stay as a retired person of independent means

266A. The requirements for an extension of stay as a retired person of independent means for a person in the United Kingdom as a work permit holder are that the applicant:

(i) entered the United Kingdom or was granted leave to remain as a work permit holder in accordance with paragraphs 128 to 133 of these Rules; and

(ii) meets the requirements of paragraph 263(i)–(v).

266B. The requirements for an extension of stay as a retired person of independent means for a person in the United Kingdom as a highly skilled migrant are that the applicant:

(i) entered the United Kingdom or was granted leave to remain as a highly skilled migrant in accordance with paragraphs 135A to 135F of these Rules; and

(ii) meets the requirements of paragraph 263(i)–(v).

266C. The requirements for an extension of stay as a retired person of independent means for a person in the United Kingdom to establish themselves or remain in business are that the applicant:

(i) entered the United Kingdom or was granted leave to remain as a person intending to establish themselves or remain in business in accordance with paragraphs 201 to 208 of these Rules; and

(ii) meets the requirements of paragraph 263(i)–(v).

266D. The requirements for an extension of stay as a retired person of independent means for a person in the United Kingdom as an innovator are that the applicant:

(i) entered the United Kingdom or was granted leave to remain as an innovator in accordance with paragraphs 210A to 210F of these Rules; and

(ii) meets the requirements of paragraph 263(i)–(v).

266E. The requirements for an extension of stay as a retired person of independent means for a person in the UK as a Tier 1 (General) Migrant, Tier 1 (Entrepreneur) Migrant or Tier 1 (Investor) Migrant are that the applicant:

(i) entered the UK or was granted leave to remain as a Tier 1 (General) Migrant, Tier 1 (Entrepreneur) Migrant or Tier 1 (Investor) Migrant; and

(ii) meets the requirements of paragraphs 263(i)–(v).

267. An extension of stay as a retired person of independent means, with a prohibition on the taking of employment, may be granted so as to bring the person's stay in this category up to a maximum of 5 years in aggregate, provided the Secretary of State is satisfied that each of the requirements of paragraph 266 is met. An extension of stay as a retired person of independent means, with a prohibition on the taking of employment, may be granted for a maximum period of 5 years, provided the Secretary of State is satisfied that each of the requirements of paragraph 266A, 266B, 266C, 266D or 266E is met.

Refusal of extension of stay as a retired person of independent means

268. An extension of stay as a retired person of independent means is to be refused if the Secretary of State is not satisfied that each of the requirements of paragraph 266, 266A, 266B, 266C, 266D or 266E is met.

Indefinite leave to remain for a retired person of independent means

269. Indefinite leave to remain may be granted, on application, to a person admitted as a retired person of independent means provided he:

(i) has spent a continuous period of 5 years in the United Kingdom in this capacity; and

(ii) has met the requirements of paragraph 266 throughout the 5 year period and continues to do so.

Refusal of indefinite leave to remain for a retired person of independent means

270. Indefinite leave to remain in the United Kingdom for a retired person of independent means is to be refused if the Secretary of State is not satisfied that each of the requirements of paragraph 269 is met.

PART 3

Note: Words 'Part 3' inserted from 1 October 2013 subject to savings for applications made before that date (HC 628).

IMMIGRATION RULES AS AT 30 MARCH 2009 RELATING TO STUDENTS, STUDENT NURSES, STUDENTS RE-SITTING AN EXAMINATION, STUDENTS WRITING-UP A THESIS, POSTGRADUATE DOCTORS OR DENTISTS, SABBATICAL OFFICERS AND APPLICANTS UNDER THE SECTORS-BASED SCHEME

Specified forms and procedures for applications or claims in connection with immigration

34B. Where an application form is specified, it must be sent by prepaid post to the United Kingdom Border Agency of the Home Office, or submitted in person at a public enquiry office of the United Kingdom Border Agency of the Home Office, save for the following exceptions:

(i) an application may not be submitted at a public enquiry office of the United Kingdom Border Agency of the Home Office if it is an application for:

(f) limited leave to remain as a Tier 5 (Temporary Worker) Migrant.

Requirements for leave to enter as a student

57. The requirements to be met by a person seeking leave to enter the United Kingdom as a student are that he:

(i) has been accepted for a course of study, or a period of research, which is to be provided by or undertaken at an organisation which is included on the Register of Education and Training Providers, and is at either;

(a) a publicly funded institution of further or higher education which maintains satisfactory records of enrolment and attendance of students and supplies these to the United Kingdom Border Agency when requested; or

(b) a bona fide private education institution; or

(c) an independent fee paying school outside the maintained sector which maintains satisfactory records of enrolment and attendance of students and supplies these to the United Kingdom Border Agency when requested; and

(ii) is able and intends to follow either:

(a) a recognised full-time degree course or postgraduate studies at a publicly funded institution of further or higher education; or

(b) a period of study and/or research in excess of 6 months at a publicly funded institution of higher education where this forms part of an overseas degree course; or

(c) a weekday full-time course involving attendance at a single institution for a minimum of 15 hours organised daytime study per week of a single subject, or directly related subjects; or

(d) a full-time course of study at an independent fee paying school; and

(iii) if under the age of 16 years is enrolled at an independent fee paying school on a full-time course of studies which meets the requirements of the Education Act 1944; and

(iv) if he has been accepted to study externally for a degree at a private education institution, he is also registered as an external student with the UK degree awarding body; and

(v) he holds a valid Academic Technology Approval Scheme (ATAS) clearance certificate from the Counter-Proliferation Department of the Foreign and Commonwealth Office which relates to the course, or area of research, he intends to undertake and the institution at which he wishes to undertake it; if he intends to undertake either,

(i) postgraduate studies leading to a Doctorate or Masters degree by research in one of the disciplines listed in paragraph 1 of Appendix 6 to these Rules; or

(ii) postgraduate studies leading to a taught Masters degree in one of the disciplines listed in paragraph 2 of Appendix 6 to these Rules; or

(iii) a period of study or research, as described in paragraph 57(ii)(b), in one of the disciplines listed in paragraph 1 or 2 of Appendix 6 to these Rules, that forms part of an overseas postgraduate qualification; and

(vi) intends to leave the United Kingdom at the end of his studies; and

(vii) does not intend to engage in business or to take employment, except part-time or vacation work undertaken with the consent of the Secretary of State; and

(viii) is able to meet the costs of his course and accommodation and the maintenance of himself and any dependants without taking employment or engaging in business or having recourse to public funds; and

(ix) holds a valid United Kingdom entry clearance for entry in this capacity.

Leave to enter as a student

58. A person seeking leave to enter the United Kingdom as a student may be admitted for an appropriate period depending on the length of his course of study and his means, and with a condition restricting his freedom to take employment, provided he is able to produce to the Immigration Officer on arrival a valid United Kingdom entry clearance for entry in this capacity.

Refusal of leave to enter as a student

59. Leave to enter as a student is to be refused if the Immigration Officer is not satisfied that each of the requirements of paragraph 57 is met.

Requirements for an extension of stay as a student

60. The requirements for an extension of stay as a student are that the applicant:

(i) (a) was last admitted to the United Kingdom in possession of a valid student entry clearance in accordance with paragraphs 57–62 or valid prospective student entry clearance in accordance with paragraphs 82–87 of these Rules; or

(b) has previously been granted leave to enter or remain in the United Kingdom to re-sit an examination in accordance with paragraphs 69A–69F of these Rules; or

(c) if he has been accepted on a course of study at degree level or above, has previously been granted leave to enter or remain in the United Kingdom in accordance with paragraphs 87A–87F, 128–135, 135O–135T and 143A to 143F or 245V to 245ZA of these Rules; or

(d) has valid leave as a student in accordance with paragraphs 57–62 of these Rules; and

(ii) meets the requirements for admission as a student set out in paragraph 57(i)–(viii); and

(iii) has produced evidence of his enrolment on a course which meets the requirements of paragraph 57; and

(iv) can produce satisfactory evidence of regular attendance during any course which he has already begun; or any other course for which he has been enrolled in the past; and

(v) can show evidence of satisfactory progress in his course of study including the taking and passing of any relevant examinations; and

(vi) would not, as a result of an extension of stay, spend more than 2 years on short courses below degree level (i.e. courses of less than 1 years duration, or longer courses broken off before completion); and

(vii) has not come to the end of a period of government or international scholarship agency sponsorship, or has the written consent of his official sponsor for a further period of study in the United Kingdom and satisfactory evidence that sufficient sponsorship funding is available.

Extension of stay as a student

61. An extension of stay as a student may be granted, subject to a restriction on his freedom to take employment, provided the Secretary of State is satisfied that the applicant meets each of the requirements of paragraph 60.

Refusal of extension of stay as a student

62. An extension of stay as a student is to be refused if the Secretary of State is not satisfied that each of the requirements of paragraph 60 is met.

Student nurses

Definition of student nurse

63. For the purposes of these Rules the term student nurse means a person accepted for training as a student nurse or midwife leading to a registered nursing qualification.

Requirements for leave to enter as a student nurse

64. The requirements to be met by a person seeking leave to enter the United Kingdom as a student nurse are that the person:

(i) comes within the definition set out in paragraph 63 above; and

(ii) has been accepted for a course of study in a recognised nursing educational establishment offering nursing training which meets the requirements of the Nursing and Midwifery Council.

(iii) did not obtain acceptance on the course of study referred to in (ii) above by misrepresentation;

(iv) is able and intends to follow the course; and

(v) does not intend to engage in business or take employment except in connection with the training course; and

(vi) intends to leave the United Kingdom at the end of the course; and

(vii) has sufficient funds available for accommodation and maintenance for himself and any dependants without engaging in business or taking employment (except in connection with the training course) or having recourse to public funds. The possession of a Department of Health bursary may be taken into account in assessing whether the student meets the maintenance requirement.

Leave to enter the United Kingdom as a student nurse

65. A person seeking leave to enter the United Kingdom as a student nurse may be admitted for the duration of the course, with a restriction on his freedom to take employment, provided the Immigration Officer is satisfied that each of the requirements of paragraph 64 is met.

Refusal of leave to enter as a student nurse

66. Leave to enter as a student nurse is to be refused if the Immigration Officer is not satisfied that each of the requirements of paragraph 64 is met.

Requirements for an extension of stay as a student nurse

67. The requirements for an extension of stay as a student nurse are that the applicant:

(i) was last admitted to the United Kingdom in possession of a valid student entry clearance, or valid prospective student entry clearance in accordance with paragraphs 82 to 87 of these Rules, if he is a person specified in Appendix 1 to these Rules; and

(ii) meets the requirements set out in paragraph 64(i)–(vii); and

(iii) has produced evidence of enrolment at a recognised nursing educational establishment; and

(iv) can provide satisfactory evidence of regular attendance during any course which he has already begun; or any other course for which he has been enrolled in the past; and

(v) would not, as a result of an extension of stay, spend more than 4 years in obtaining the relevant qualification; and

(vi) has not come to the end of a period of government or international scholarship agency sponsorship, or has the written consent of his official sponsor for a further period of study in the United Kingdom and evidence that sufficient sponsorship funding is available.

Extension of stay as a student nurse

68. An extension of stay as a student nurse may be granted, subject to a restriction on his freedom to take employment, provided the Secretary of State is satisfied that the applicant meets each of the requirements of paragraph 67.

Refusal of extension of stay as a student nurse

69. An extension of stay as a student nurse is to be refused if the Secretary of State is not satisfied that each of the requirements of paragraph 67 is met.

Re-sits of examinations

Requirements for leave to enter to re-sit an examination

69A. The requirements to be met by a person seeking leave to enter the United Kingdom in order to re-sit an examination are that the applicant:

(i) (a) meets the requirements for admission as a student set out in paragraph 57(i)–(viii); or

(b) met the requirements for admission as a student set out in paragraph 57(i)–(iii) in the previous academic year and continues to meet the requirements of paragraph 57(iv)–(viii) save, for the purpose of paragraphs (i) (a) or (b) above, where leave was last granted in accordance with paragraphs 57–62 of these Rules before 30 November 2007, the requirements of paragraph 57(v) do not apply; and

(ii) has produced written confirmation from the education institution or independent fee paying school which he attends or attended in the previous academic year that he is required to re-sit an examination; and

(iii) can provide satisfactory evidence of regular attendance during any course which he has already begun; or any other course for which he has been enrolled in the past; and

(iv) has not come to the end of a period of government or international scholarship agency sponsorship, or has the written consent of his official sponsor for a further period of study in the United Kingdom and satisfactory evidence that sufficient sponsorship funding is available; and

(v) has not previously been granted leave to re-sit the examination.

Leave to enter to re-sit an examination

69B. A person seeking leave to enter the United Kingdom in order to re-sit an examination may be admitted for a period sufficient to enable him to re-sit the examination at the first available opportunity with a condition restricting his freedom to take employment, provided the Immigration Officer is satisfied that each of the requirements of paragraph 69A is met.

Refusal of leave to enter to re-sit an examination

69C. Leave to enter to re-sit an examination is to be refused if the Immigration Officer is not satisfied that each of the requirements of paragraph 69A is met.

Requirements for an extension of stay to re-sit an examination

69D. The requirements for an extension of stay to re-sit an examination are that the applicant:

(i) was admitted to the United Kingdom with a valid student entry clearance if he was then a visa national; and

(ii) meets the requirements set out in paragraph 69A(i)–(v).

Extension of stay to re-sit an examination

69E. An extension of stay to re-sit an examination may be granted for a period sufficient to enable the applicant to re-sit the examination at the first available opportunity, subject to a restriction on his freedom to take employment, provided the Secretary of State is satisfied that the applicant meets each of the requirements of paragraph 69D.

Refusal of extension of stay to re-sit an examination

69F. An extension of stay to re-sit an examination is to be refused if the Secretary of State is not satisfied that each of the requirements of paragraph 69D is met.

Writing up a thesis

Requirements for leave to enter to write up a thesis

69G. The requirements to be met by a person seeking leave to enter the United Kingdom in order to write up a thesis are that the applicant:

(i) (a) meets the requirements for admission as a student set out in paragraph 57(i)–(viii); or

(b) met the requirements for admission as a student set out in paragraph 57(i)–(iii) in the previous academic year and continues to meet the requirements of paragraph 57(iv)–(viii)

save, for the purpose of paragraphs (i)(a) or (b) above, where leave was last granted in accordance with paragraphs 57–62 of these Rules before 30 November 2007, the requirements of paragraph 57(v) do not apply; and

(ii) can provide satisfactory evidence that he is a postgraduate student enrolled at an education institution as either a full-time, part-time or writing up student; and

(iii) can demonstrate that his application is supported by the education institution; and

(iv) has not come to the end of a period of government or international scholarship agency sponsorship, or has the written consent of his official sponsor for a further period of study in the United Kingdom and satisfactory evidence that sufficient sponsorship funding is available; and

(v) has not previously been granted 12 months leave to write up the same thesis.

Leave to enter to write up a thesis

69H. A person seeking leave to enter the United Kingdom in order to write up a thesis may be admitted for 12 months with a condition restricting his freedom to take employment, provided the Immigration Officer is satisfied that each of the requirements of paragraph 69G is met.

Refusal of leave to enter to write up a thesis

69I. Leave to enter to write up a thesis is to be refused if the Immigration Officer is not satisfied that each of the requirements of paragraph 69G is met.

Requirements for an extension of stay to write up a thesis

69J. The requirements for an extension of stay to write up a thesis are that the applicant:

(i) was admitted to the United Kingdom with a valid student entry clearance if he was then a visa national; and

(ii) meets the requirements set out in paragraph 69G(i)–(v).

Extension of stay to write up a thesis

69K. An extension of stay to write up a thesis may be granted for 12 months subject to a restriction on his freedom to take employment, provided the Secretary of State is satisfied that the applicant meets each of the requirements of paragraph 69J.

Refusal of extension of stay to write up a thesis

69L. An extension of stay to write up a thesis is to be refused if the Secretary of State is not satisfied that each of the requirements of paragraph 69J is met.

Postgraduate doctors, dentists and trainee general practitioners

Requirements for leave to enter the United Kingdom as a postgraduate doctor or dentist

70. The requirements to be met by a person seeking leave to enter the UK as a postgraduate doctor or dentist are that the applicant:

(i) has successfully completed and obtained a recognised UK degree in medicine or dentistry from either:

(a) a UK publicly funded institution of further or higher education; or

(b) a UK bona fide private education institution which maintains satisfactory records of enrolment and attendance; and

(ii) has previously been granted leave:

(a) in accordance with paragraphs 57 to 69L of these Rules for the final academic year of the studies referred to in (i) above; and

(b) as a student under paragraphs 57 to 62 of these Rules for at least one other academic year (aside from the final year) of the studies referred to in (i) above; and

(iii) holds a letter from the Postgraduate Dean confirming he has a full-time place on a recognised Foundation Programme; and

(iv) intends to train full-time in his post on the Foundation Programme; and

(v) is able to maintain and accommodate himself and any dependants without recourse to public funds; and

(vi) intends to leave the United Kingdom if, on expiry of his leave under this paragraph, he has not been granted leave to remain in the United Kingdom as:

(a) a doctor or dentist undertaking a period of clinical attachment or a dental observer post in accordance with paragraphs 75G to 75M of these Rules; or

(b) a Tier 2 Migrant

(c) a Tier 1 (General) Migrant or Tier (1) (Entrepreneur) Migrant; and

(vii) if his study at medical school or dental school, or any subsequent studies he has undertaken, were sponsored by a government or international scholarship agency, he has the written consent of his sponsor to enter or remain in the United Kingdom as a postgraduate doctor or dentist; and

(viii) if he has not previously been granted leave in this category has completed his medical or dental degree in the 12 months preceding this application; and

(ix) if he has previously been granted leave as a postgraduate doctor or dentist, is not seeking leave to enter to a date beyond 3 years from that date on which he was first granted leave to enter or remain in this category; and

(x) holds a valid entry clearance for entry in this capacity except where he is a British National (Overseas), a British Overseas Territories Citizen, a British Overseas Citizen, a British Protected Person or a person who under the British Nationality Act 1981 is a British Subject.

Leave to enter as a postgraduate doctor or dentist

71. Leave to enter the United Kingdom as a postgraduate doctor or dentist may be granted for the duration of the Foundation Programme, for a period not exceeding 26 months, provided the Immigration Officer is satisfied that each of the requirements of paragraph 70 is met.

Refusal of leave to enter as a postgraduate doctor or dentist

72. Leave to enter as a postgraduate doctor or dentist is to be refused if the Immigration Officer is not satisfied that each of the requirements of paragraph 70 is met.

Requirements for an extension of stay as a postgraduate doctor or dentist

73. The requirements to be met by a person seeking an extension of stay as a postgraduate doctor or dentist are that the applicant:

(i) meets the requirements of paragraph 70(i) to (vii); and

(ii) has leave to enter or remain in the United Kingdom as either:

(a) a student in accordance with paragraphs 57 to 69L of these Rules; or

(b) as a postgraduate doctor or dentist in accordance with paragraphs 70 to 75 of these Rules;

or

(c) as a doctor or dentist undertaking a period of clinical attachment or a dental observer post in accordance with paragraphs 75G to 75M of these Rules.

(iii) if he has not previously been granted leave in this category, has completed his medical or dental degree in the last 12 months;

(iv) would not, as a result of an extension of stay, remain in the United Kingdom as a postgraduate doctor or dentist to a date beyond 3 years from the date on which he was first given leave to enter or remain in this capacity.

Extension of stay as a postgraduate doctor or dentist

74. An extension of stay as a postgraduate doctor or dentist may be granted for the duration of the Foundation Programme, for a period not exceeding 3 years, provided the Secretary of State is satisfied that each of the requirements of paragraph 73 is met.

Refusal of an extension of stay as a postgraduate doctor or dentist

75. An extension of stay as a postgraduate doctor or dentist is to be refused if the Secretary of State is not satisfied that each of the requirements of paragraph 73 is met.

Requirements for leave to enter the United Kingdom to take the PLAB Test

75A. The requirements to be met by a person seeking leave to enter in order to take the PLAB Test are that the applicant:

(i) is a graduate from a medical school and intends to take the PLAB Test in the United Kingdom; and

(ii) can provide documentary evidence of a confirmed test date or of his eligibility to take the PLAB Test; and

(iii) meets the requirements of paragraph 41(iii)–(vii) for entry as a visitor; and

(iv) intends to leave the United Kingdom at the end of his leave granted under this paragraph unless he is successful in the PLAB Test and granted leave to remain:

(a) as a postgraduate doctor or trainee general practitioner in accordance with paragraphs 70 to 75; or

(b) to undertake a clinical attachment in accordance with paragraphs 75G to 75M of these Rules; or

Leave to enter to take the PLAB Test

75B. A person seeking leave to enter the United Kingdom to take the PLAB Test may be admitted for a period not exceeding 6 months, provided the Immigration Officer is satisfied that each of the requirements of paragraph 75A is met.

Refusal of leave to enter to take the PLAB Test

75C. Leave to enter the United Kingdom to take the PLAB Test is to be refused if the Immigration Officer is not satisfied that each of the requirements of paragraph 75A is met.

Requirements for an extension of stay in order to take the PLAB Test

75D. The requirements for an extension of stay in the United Kingdom in order to take the PLAB Test are that the applicant:

(i) was given leave to enter the United Kingdom for the purposes of taking the PLAB Test in accordance with paragraph 75B of these Rules; and

(ii) intends to take the PLAB Test and can provide documentary evidence of a confirmed test date; and

(iii) meets the requirements set out in paragraph 41(iii)–(vii); and

(iv) intends to leave the United Kingdom at the end of his leave granted under this paragraph unless he is successful in the PLAB Test and granted leave to remain:

(a) as a postgraduate doctor or trainee general practitioner in accordance with paragraphs 70 to 75; or

(b) to undertake a clinical attachment in accordance with paragraphs 75G to 75M of these Rules; or

(v) would not as a result of an extension of stay spend more than 18 months in the United Kingdom for the purpose of taking the PLAB Test.

Extension of stay to take the PLAB Test

75E. A person seeking leave to remain in the United Kingdom to take the PLAB Test may be granted an extension of stay for a period not exceeding 6 months, provided the Secretary of State is satisfied that each of the requirements of paragraph 75D is met.

Refusal of extension of stay to take the PLAB Test

75F. Leave to remain in the United Kingdom to take the PLAB Test is to be refused if the Secretary of State is not satisfied that each of the requirements of paragraph 75D is met.

Requirements for leave to enter to undertake a clinical attachment or dental observer post

75G. The requirements to be met by a person seeking leave to enter to undertake a clinical attachment or dental observer post are that the applicant:

(i) is a graduate from a medical or dental school and intends to undertake a clinical attachment or dental observer post in the United Kingdom; and

(ii) can provide documentary evidence of the clinical attachment or dental observer post which will:

(a) be unpaid; and

(b) only involve observation, not treatment, of patients; and

(iii) meets the requirements of paragraph 41(iii)–(vii) of these Rules; and

(iv) intends to leave the United Kingdom at the end of his leave granted under this paragraph unless he is granted leave to remain:

(a) as a postgraduate doctor, dentist or trainee general practitioner in accordance with paragraphs 70 to 75;

(v) if he has previously been granted leave in this category, is not seeking leave to enter which, when amalgamated with those previous periods of leave, would total more than 6 months.

Leave to enter to undertake a clinical attachment or dental observer post

75H. A person seeking leave to enter the United Kingdom to undertake a clinical attachment or dental observer post may be admitted for the period of the clinical attachment or dental observer post, up to a maximum of 6 weeks at a time or 6 months in total in this category, provided the Immigration Officer is satisfied that each of the requirements of paragraph 75G is met.

Refusal of leave to enter to undertake a clinical attachment or dental observer post

75J. Leave to enter the United Kingdom to undertake a clinical attachment or dental observer post is to be refused if the Immigration Officer is not satisfied that each of the requirements of paragraph 75G is met.

Requirements for an extension of stay in order to undertake a clinical attachment or dental observer post

75K. The requirements to be met by a person seeking an extension of stay to undertake a clinical attachment or dental observer post are that the applicant:

(i) was given leave to enter or remain in the United Kingdom to undertake a clinical attachment or dental observer post or:

(a) for the purposes of taking the PLAB Test in accordance with paragraphs 75A to 75F and has passed both parts of the PLAB Test;

(b) as a postgraduate doctor, dentist or trainee general practitioner in accordance with paragraphs 70 to 75; or

(c) as a work permit holder for employment in the UK as a doctor or dentist in accordance with paragraphs 128 to 135; and

(ii) is a graduate from a medical or dental school and intends to undertake a clinical attachment or dental observer post in the United Kingdom; and

(iii) can provide documentary evidence of the clinical attachment or dental observer post which will:

(a) be unpaid; and

(b) only involve observation, not treatment, of patients; and

(iv) intends to leave the United Kingdom at the end of his period of leave granted under this paragraph unless he is granted leave to remain:

(a) as a postgraduate doctor, dentist or trainee general practitioner in accordance with paragraphs 70 to 75; or

(v) meets the requirements of paragraph 41(iii)–(vii) of these Rules; and

(vi) if he has previously been granted leave in this category, is not seeking an extension of stay which, when amalgamated with those previous periods of leave, would total more than 6 months.

Extension of stay to undertake a clinical attachment or dental observer post

75L. A person seeking leave to remain in the United Kingdom to undertake a clinical attachment or dental observer post up to a maximum of 6 weeks at a time or 6 months in total in this category, may be granted an extension of stay for the period of their clinical attachment or dental observer post, provided that the Secretary of State is satisfied that each of the requirements of paragraph 75K is met.

Refusal of extension of stay to undertake a clinical attachment or dental observer post

75M. Leave to remain in the United Kingdom to undertake a clinical attachment or dental observer post is to be refused if the Secretary of State is not satisfied that each of the requirements of paragraph 75K is met.

Requirements for leave to enter as a prospective student

82. The requirements to be met by a person seeking leave to enter the United Kingdom as a prospective student are that he:

(i) can demonstrate a genuine and realistic intention of undertaking, within 6 months of his date of entry:

(b) a supervised practice placement or midwife adaptation course which would meet the requirements for an extension of stay as an overseas qualified nurse or midwife under paragraphs 69P to 69R of these Rules; and

(ii) intends to leave the United Kingdom on completion of his studies or on the expiry of his leave to enter if he is not able to meet the requirements for an extension of stay:

(b) as an overseas qualified nurse or midwife in accordance with paragraph 69P of these Rules; and

Students' unions sabbatical officers

Requirements for leave to enter as a sabbatical officer

87A. The requirements to be met by a person seeking leave to enter the United Kingdom as a sabbatical officer are that the person:

(i) has been elected to a full-time salaried post as a sabbatical officer at an educational establishment at which he is registered as a student;

(ii) meets the requirements set out in paragraph 57(i)–(ii) or met the requirements set out in paragraph 57(i)–(ii) in the academic year prior to the one in which he took up or intends to take up sabbatical office; and

(iii) does not intend to engage in business or take employment except in connection with his sabbatical post; and

(iv) is able to maintain and accommodate himself and any dependants adequately without recourse to public funds; and

(v) at the end of the sabbatical post he intends to:

(a) complete a course of study which he has already begun; or

(b) take up a further course of study which has been deferred to enable the applicant to take up the sabbatical post; or

(c) leave the United Kingdom; and

(vi) has not come to the end of a period of government or international scholarship agency sponsorship, or has the written consent of his official sponsor to take up a sabbatical post in the United Kingdom; and

(vii) has not already completed 2 years as a sabbatical officer.

Leave to enter the United Kingdom as a sabbatical officer

87B. A person seeking leave to enter the United Kingdom as a sabbatical officer may be admitted for a period not exceeding 12 months on conditions specifying his employment provided the Immigration Officer is satisfied that each of the requirements of paragraph 87A is met.

Refusal of leave to enter the United Kingdom as a sabbatical officer

87C. Leave to enter as a sabbatical officer is to be refused if the Immigration Officer is not satisfied that each of the requirements of paragraph 87A is met.

Requirements for an extension of stay as a sabbatical officer

87D. The requirements for an extension of stay as a sabbatical officer are that the applicant:

(i) was admitted to the United Kingdom with a valid student entry clearance if he was then a visa national; and

(ii) meets the requirements set out in paragraph 87A(i)–(vi); and

(iii) would not, as a result of an extension of stay, remain in the United Kingdom as a sabbatical officer to a date beyond 2 years from the date on which he was first given leave to enter the United Kingdom in this capacity.

Extension of stay as a sabbatical officer

87E. An extension of stay as a sabbatical officer may be granted for a period not exceeding 12 months on conditions specifying his employment provided the Secretary of State is satisfied that the applicant meets each of the requirements of paragraph 87D.

Refusal of extension of stay as a sabbatical officer

87F. An extension of stay as a sabbatical officer is to be refused if the Secretary of State is not satisfied that each of the requirements of paragraph 87D is met

Requirements for leave to enter the United Kingdom for the purpose of employment under the Sectors-Based Scheme

135I. The requirements to be met by a person seeking leave to enter the United Kingdom for the purpose of employment under the Sectors-Based Scheme are that he:

(i) holds a valid Home Office immigration employment document issued under the Sectors-Based Scheme; and

(ii) is aged between 18 and 30 inclusive or was so aged at the date of his application for leave to enter; and

(iii) is capable of undertaking the employment specified in the immigration employment document; and

(iv) does not intend to take employment except as specified in his immigration employment document; and

(v) is able to maintain and accommodate himself adequately without recourse to public funds; and

(vi) intends to leave the United Kingdom at the end of his approved employment; and

(vii) holds a valid United Kingdom entry clearance for entry in this capacity.

Leave to enter for the purpose of employment under the Sectors-Based Scheme

135J. A person seeking leave to enter the United Kingdom for the purpose of employment under the Sectors-Based Scheme may be admitted for a period not exceeding 12 months (normally as specified in his work permit), subject to a condition restricting him to employment approved by the Home Office, provided the Immigration Officer is satisfied that each of the requirements of paragraph 135I is met.

Refusal of leave to enter for the purpose of employment under the Sectors-Based Scheme

135K. Leave to enter the United Kingdom for the purpose of employment under the Sectors-Based Scheme is to be refused if the Immigration Officer is not satisfied that each of the requirements of paragraph 135I is met.

Requirements for an extension of stay for Sector-Based employment

135L. The requirements for an extension of stay for Sector-Based employment are that the applicant:

(i) entered the United Kingdom with a valid Home Office immigration employment document issued under the sectors-Based Scheme and;

(ii) has written approval from the Home Office for the continuation of his employment under the Sectors-Based Scheme; and

(iii) meets the requirements of paragraph 135I(ii) to (vi); and

(iv) would not, as a result of the extension of stay sought, remain in the United Kingdom for Sector-Based Scheme employment to a date beyond 12 months from the date on which he was given leave to enter the United Kingdom on this occasion in this capacity.

Extension of stay for Sectors-Based Scheme employment

135M. An extension of stay for Sectors-Based Scheme employment may be granted for a period not exceeding the period of approved employment recommended by the Home Office provided the Secretary of State is satisfied that each of the requirements of paragraph 135L are met. An extension of stay is to be subject to a condition restricting the applicant to employment approved by the Home Office.

Refusal of extension of stay for Sectors-Based Scheme employment

135N. An extension of stay for Sector-Based Scheme employment is to be refused if the Secretary of State is not satisfied that each of the requirements of paragraph 135L is met.

Period and conditions of grant

245ZG.

(b) The cases referred to in paragraph (a) are those where the applicant has, or was last granted, entry clearance, leave to enter or leave to remain as:

(iii) a Minister of Religion, Missionary or Member of a Religious Order, provided he is still working for the same employer,

Attributes for Tier 1 (Investor) Migrants

47. A regulated financial institution is one which is regulated by the appropriate regulatory body for the country in which the financial institution operates. For example, where a financial institution does business in the UK, the appropriate regulator is the Financial Services Authority.

Part 4

Note: Words 'Part 4' inserted from 1 October 2013 subject to savings for applications made before that date (HC 628).

Immigration Rules as at 5 April 2012 relating to Overseas qualified nurses or midwives, Seasonal agricultural workers, Work permit employment, Multiple Entry work permit Employment, and Tier 1 (Post Study Work) Migrants

Overseas qualified nurse or midwife

Requirements for leave to enter as an overseas qualified nurse or midwife

69M. Deleted on 27 November 2008 by paragraph 39 of Statement of Changes HC 1113 except insofar as relevant to paragraph 69P.

Leave to enter the United Kingdom as an overseas qualified nurse or midwife

69N. DELETED

Refusal of leave to enter as an overseas qualified nurse or midwife

69O. DELETED.

Requirements for an extension of stay as an overseas qualified nurse or midwife

69P. The requirements to be met by a person seeking an extension of stay as an overseas qualified nurse or midwife are that the applicant:

(i)–(iii) Deleted by HC 1113

(iv) has leave to enter or remain as an overseas qualified nurse or midwife in accordance with paragraphs 69M–69R of these Rules; and

(v) meets the requirements set out in paragraph 69M(i)–(vi); and

(vi) can provide satisfactory evidence of regular attendance during any previous period of supervised practice or midwife adaptation course; and

(vii) if he has previously been granted leave:

(a) as an overseas qualified nurse or midwife under paragraphs 69M–69R of these Rules, or

(b) to undertake an adaptation course as a student nurse under paragraphs 63–69 of these Rules; and is not seeking an extension of stay in this category which, when amalgamated with those previous periods of leave, would total more than 18 months; and

(viii) if his previous studies, supervised practice placement or midwife adaptation programme placement were sponsored by a government or international scholarship agency, he has the written consent of his official sponsor to remain in the United Kingdom as an overseas qualified nurse or midwife.

Extension of stay as an overseas qualified nurse or midwife

69Q. An extension of stay as an overseas qualified nurse or midwife may be granted for a period not exceeding 18 months, provided that the Secretary of State is satisfied that each of the requirements of paragraph 69P is met.

Refusal of extension of stay as an overseas qualified nurse or midwife

69R. An extension of stay as an overseas qualified nurse or midwife is to be refused if the Secretary of State is not satisfied that each of the requirements of paragraph 69P is met.

Seasonal agricultural workers

Requirements for leave to enter as a seasonal agricultural worker

104. The requirements to be met by a person seeking leave to enter the United Kingdom as a seasonal agricultural worker are that he:

(i) is a student in full-time education aged 18 or over; and

(ii) holds an immigration employment document in the form of a valid Home Office work card issued by the operator of a scheme approved by the Secretary of State; and

(iii) intends to leave the United Kingdom at the end of his period of leave as a seasonal worker; and

(iv) does not intend to take employment except as permitted by his work card and within the terms of this paragraph; and

(v) is not seeking leave to enter on a date less than 3 months from the date on which an earlier period of leave to enter or remain granted to him in this capacity expired; and

(vi) is able to maintain and accommodate himself without recourse to public funds.

Leave to enter as a seasonal agricultural worker

105. A person seeking leave to enter the United Kingdom as a seasonal agricultural worker may be admitted with a condition restricting his freedom to take employment for a period not exceeding 6 months providing the Immigration Officer is satisfied that each of the requirements of paragraph 104 is met.

Refusal of leave to enter as a seasonal agricultural worker

106. Leave to enter the United Kingdom as a seasonal agricultural worker is to be refused if the Immigration Officer is not satisfied that each of the requirements of paragraph 104 is met.

Requirements for extension of stay as a seasonal agricultural worker

107. The requirements for an extension of stay as a seasonal agricultural worker are that the applicant:

(i) entered the United Kingdom as a seasonal agricultural worker under paragraph 105; and

(ii) meets the requirements of paragraph 104(iii)–(vi); and

(iii) would not, as a result of an extension of stay sought, remain in the United Kingdom as a seasonal agricultural worker beyond 6 months from the date on which he was given leave to enter the United Kingdom on this occasion in this capacity.

Extension of stay as a seasonal agricultural worker

108. An extension of stay as a seasonal agricultural worker may be granted with a condition restricting his freedom to take employment for a period which does not extend

beyond 6 months from the date on which he was given leave to enter the United Kingdom on this occasion in this capacity, provided the Secretary of State is satisfied that the applicant meets each of the requirements of paragraph 107.

Refusal of extension of stay as a seasonal worker

109. An extension of stay as a seasonal worker is to be refused if the Secretary of State is not satisfied that each of the requirements of paragraph 107 is met.

Work permit employment

Requirements for leave to enter the United Kingdom for work permit employment

128. The requirements to be met by a person coming to the United Kingdom to seek or take employment (unless he is otherwise eligible for admission for employment under these Rules or is eligible for admission as a seaman under contract to join a ship due to leave British waters) are that he:

(i) holds a valid Home Office work permit; and

(ii) is not of an age which puts him outside the limits for employment; and

(iii) is capable of undertaking the employment specified in the work permit; and

(iv) does not intend to take employment except as specified in his work permit; and

(v) is able to maintain and accommodate himself and any dependants adequately without recourse to public funds; and

(vi) in the case of a person in possession of a work permit which is valid for a period of 12 months or less, intends to leave the United Kingdom at the end of his approved employment; and

(vii) holds a valid United Kingdom entry clearance for entry in this capacity except where he holds a work permit valid for 6 months or less or he is a British National (Overseas), a British overseas territories citizen, a British Overseas citizen, a British protected person or a person who under the British Nationality Act 1981 is a British subject.

Leave to enter for work permit employment

129. A person seeking leave to enter the United Kingdom for the purpose of work permit employment may be admitted for a period not exceeding the period of employment approved by the Home Office (as specified in his work permit), subject to a condition restricting him to that approved employment, provided he is able to produce to the Immigration Officer, on arrival, a valid United Kingdom entry clearance for entry in this capacity or, where entry clearance is not required, provided the Immigration Officer is satisfied that each of the requirements of paragraph 128(i)–(vi) is met.

Refusal of leave to enter for employment

130. Leave to enter for the purpose of work permit employment is to be refused if a valid United Kingdom entry clearance for entry in this capacity is not produced to the Immigration Officer on arrival or, where entry clearance is not required, if the Immigration Officer is not satisfied that each of the requirements of paragraph 128(i)–(vi) is met.

Requirements for an extension of stay for work permit employment

131. The requirements for an extension of stay to seek or take employment (unless the applicant is otherwise eligible for an extension of stay for employment under these Rules) are that the applicant:

(i) entered the United Kingdom with a valid work permit under paragraph 129; and

(ii) has written approval from the Home Office for the continuation of his employment; and

(iii) meets the requirements of paragraph 128(ii)–(v).

131A. The requirements for an extension of stay to take employment (unless the applicant is otherwise eligible for an extension of stay for employment under these Rules) for a student are that the applicant:

(i) entered the United Kingdom or was given leave to remain as a student in accordance with paragraphs 57 to 62 of these Rules; and

(ii) has obtained a degree qualification on a recognised degree course at either a United Kingdom publicly funded further or higher education institution or a bona fide United Kingdom private education institution which maintains satisfactory records of enrolment and attendance; and

(iii) holds a valid Home Office immigration employment document for employment; and

(iv) has the written consent of his official sponsor to such employment if he is a member of a government or international scholarship agency sponsorship and that sponsorship is either ongoing or has recently come to an end at the time of the requested extension; and

(v) meets each of the requirements of paragraph 128(ii) to (vi).

131B. The requirements for an extension of stay to take employment (unless the applicant is otherwise eligible for an extension of stay for employment under these Rules) for a student nurse overseas qualified nurse or midwife, postgraduate doctor or postgraduate dentist are that the applicant:

(i) entered the United Kingdom or was given leave to remain as a student nurse in accordance with paragraphs 63 to 69 of these Rules; or

(ia) entered the United Kingdom or was given leave to remain as an overseas qualified nurse or midwife in accordance with paragraphs 69M to 69R of these Rules; and

(ii) entered the United Kingdom or was given leave to remain as a postgraduate doctor or a postgraduate dentist in accordance with paragraphs 70 to 75 of these Rules; and

(iii) holds a valid Home Office immigration employment document for employment as a nurse, doctor or dentist; and

(iv) has the written consent of his official sponsor to such employment if he is a member of a government or international scholarship agency sponsorship and that sponsorship is either ongoing or has recently come to an end at the time of the requested extension; and

(v) meets each of the requirements of paragraph 128(ii) to (vi).

131C The requirements for an extension of stay to take employment for a Science and Engineering Graduate Scheme or International Graduates Scheme participant are that the applicant:

(i) entered the United Kingdom or was given leave to remain as a Science and Engineering Graduate Scheme or International Graduates Scheme participant in accordance with paragraphs 135O to 135T of these Rules; and

(ii) holds a valid Home Office immigration employment document for employment; and

(iii) meets each of the requirements of paragraph 128(ii) to (vi).

131D. The requirements for an extension of stay to take employment (unless the applicant is otherwise eligible for an extension of stay for employment under these Rules) for a working holidaymaker are that the applicant:

(i) entered the United Kingdom as a working holidaymaker in accordance with paragraphs 95 to 96 of these Rules; and

(ii) he has spent more than 12 months in total in the UK in this capacity; and

(iii) holds a valid Home Office immigration employment document for employment in an occupation listed on the Work Permits (UK) shortage occupations list; and

(iv) meets each of the requirements of paragraph 128(ii) to (vi).

131E. The requirements for an extension of stay to take employment for a highly skilled migrant are that the applicant:

(i) entered the United Kingdom or was given leave to remain as a highly skilled migrant in accordance with paragraphs 135A to 135E of these Rules; and

(ii) holds a valid work permit; and

(iii) meets each of the requirements of paragraph 128(ii) to (vi).

131F. The requirements for an extension of stay to take employment (unless the applicant is otherwise eligible for an extension of stay for employment under these Rules) for an Innovator are that the applicant:

(i) entered the United Kingdom or was given leave to remain as an Innovator in accordance with paragraphs 210A to 210E of these Rules; and

(ii) holds a valid Home Office immigration employment document for employment; and

(iii) meets each of the requirements of paragraph 128(ii) to (vi).

131G. The requirements for an extension of stay to take employment (unless the applicant is otherwise eligible for an extension of stay for employment under these Rules) for an individual who has leave to enter or leave to remain in the United Kingdom to take the PLAB Test or to undertake a clinical attachment or dental observer post are that the applicant:

(i) entered the United Kingdom or was given leave to remain for the purposes of taking the PLAB Test in accordance with paragraphs 75A to 75F of these Rules; or

(ii) entered the United Kingdom or was given leave to remain to undertake a clinical attachment or dental observer post in accordance with paragraphs 75G to 75M of these Rules; and

(iii) holds a valid Home Office immigration employment document for employment as a doctor or dentist; and

(iv) meets each of the requirements of paragraph 128(ii) to (vi).

131H. The requirements for an extension of stay to take employment (unless the applicant is otherwise eligible for an extension of stay for employment under these Rules) in the case of a person who has leave to enter or remain as a Fresh Talent: Working in Scotland scheme participant are that the applicant:

(i) entered the United Kingdom or was given leave to remain as a Fresh Talent: Working in Scotland scheme participant in accordance with paragraphs 143A to 143F of these Rules; and

(ii) holds a valid Home Office immigration employment document for employment in Scotland; and

(iii) has the written consent of his official sponsor to such employment if the studies which led to him being granted leave under the Fresh Talent: Working in Scotland scheme in accordance with paragraphs 143A to 143F of these Rules, or any studies he has subsequently undertaken, were sponsored by a government or international scholarship agency; and

(iv) meets each of the requirements of paragraph 128(ii) to (vi).

131I. The requirements for an extension of stay to take employment for a Tier 1 Migrant are that the applicant:

(i) entered the UK or was given leave to remain as a Tier 1 Migrant; and

(ii) holds a valid work permit; and

(iii) meets each of the requirements of paragraph 128(ii) to (vi).

Extension of stay for work permit employment

132. An extension of stay for work permit employment may be granted for a period not exceeding the period of approved employment recommended by the Home Office provided the Secretary of State is satisfied that each of the requirements of paragraphs 131, 131A, 131B, 131C, 131D, 131E, 131F, 131G, 131H or 131I is met. An extension of stay is to be subject to a condition restricting the applicant to employment approved by the Home Office.

133. An extension of stay for employment is to be refused if the Secretary of State is not satisfied that each of the requirements of paragraphs 131, 131A, 131B, 131C, 131D, 131E, 131F, 131G, 131H or 131I is met (unless the applicant is otherwise eligible for an extension of stay for employment under these Rules).

Multiple Entry work permit employment

Requirements for leave to enter for Multiple Entry work permit employment

199A. The requirements to be met by a person coming to the United Kingdom to seek or take Multiple Entry work permit employment are that he:

(i) holds a valid work permit;

(ii) is not of an age which puts him outside the limits for employment;

(iii) is capable of undertaking the employment specified in the work permit;

(iv) does not intend to take employment except as specified in his work permit;

(v) is able to maintain and accommodate himself adequately without recourse to public funds; and

(vi) intends to leave the United Kingdom at the end of the employment covered by the Multiple Entry work permit and holds a valid United Kingdom Entry clearance for entry into this capacity excepts where he holds a work permit valid for 6 months or less or he is a British National (Overseas), a British overseas territories citizen, a British Overseas citizen, a British protected person or a person who under the British Nationality Act 1981 is a British subject.

Leave to enter for Multiple Entry work permit employment

199B. A person seeking leave to enter the United Kingdom for the purpose of Multiple Entry work permit employment may be admitted for a period not exceeding 2 years provided that the Immigration Officer is satisfied that each of the requirements of paragraph 199A are met.

Refusal of leave to enter for Multiple Entry work permit employment

199C. Leave to enter for the purpose of Multiple Entry work permit employment is to be refused if the Immigration Officer is not satisfied that each of the requirements of paragraph 199A is met.

Tier 1 (Post-Study Work) Migrants

245F. Purpose

The purpose of this route is to encourage international graduates who have studied in the UK to stay on and do skilled or highly skilled work.

245FA. Entry to the UK

All migrants arriving in the UK and wishing to enter as a Tier 1 (Post-Study Work) Migrant must have a valid entry clearance for entry under this route. If they do not have a valid entry clearance, entry will be refused.

245FB. Requirements for entry clearance

To qualify for entry clearance as a Tier 1 (Post-Study Work) Migrant, an applicant must meet the requirements listed below. If the applicant meets these requirements, entry clearance will be granted. If the applicant does not meet these requirements, the application will be refused.

Requirements:

(a) The applicant must not fall for refusal under the general grounds for refusal.

(b) The applicant must not previously have been granted entry clearance or leave to remain as a Tier 1 (Post-Study Work) Migrant as a Participant in the International Graduates Scheme (or its predecessor, the Science and Engineering Graduates Scheme), or as a Participant in the Fresh Talent: Working in Scotland Scheme.

(c) The applicant must have a minimum of 75 points under paragraphs 66 to 72 of Appendix A.

(d) The applicant must have a minimum of 10 points under paragraphs 1 to 3 of Appendix B.

(e) The applicant must have a minimum of 10 points under paragraphs 1 to 2 of Appendix C.

(f) If:

(i) the studies that led to the qualification for which the applicant obtains points under paragraphs 66 to 72 of Appendix A were sponsored by a Government or international scholarship agency, and

(ii) those studies came to an end 12 months ago or less the applicant must provide the unconditional written consent of the sponsoring Government or agency to the application and must provide the specified documents to show that this requirement has been met.

245FC. Period and conditions of grant

Entry clearance will be granted for a period of 2 years and will be subject to the following conditions:

(a) no recourse to public funds,

(b) registration with the police, if this is required by paragraph 326 of these Rules, and

(c) no Employment as a Doctor or Dentist in Training, unless the applicant has obtained a degree in medicine or dentistry at bachelor's level or above from a UK institution that is a UK recognised or listed body, or which holds a sponsor licence under Tier 4 of the Points Based System.

245FD. Requirements for leave to remain

To qualify for leave to remain as a Tier 1 (Post-Study Work) Migrant, an applicant must meet the requirements listed below. Subject to paragraph 245FE(a)(i), if the applicant meets these requirements, leave to remain will be granted. If the applicant does not meet these requirements, the application will be refused.

Requirements:

(a) The applicant must not fall for refusal under the general grounds for refusal, and must not be an illegal entrant.

(b) The applicant must not previously have been granted entry clearance or leave to remain as a Tier 1 (Post-Study Work) migrant.

(c) The applicant must have a minimum of 75 points under paragraphs 66 to 72 of Appendix A.

(d) The applicant must have a minimum of 10 points under paragraphs 1 to 3 of Appendix B.

(e) The applicant must have a minimum of 10 points under paragraphs 1 to 2 of Appendix C.

(f) The applicant must have, or have last been granted, entry clearance, leave to enter or leave to remain:

(i) as a Participant in the Fresh Talent: Working in Scotland Scheme,

(ii) as a Participant in the International Graduates Scheme (or its predecessor, the Science and Engineering Graduates Scheme),

(iii) as a Student, provided the applicant has not previously been granted leave in any of the categories referred to in paragraphs (i) and (ii) above,

(iv) as a Student Nurse, provided the applicant has not previously been granted leave in any of the categories referred to in paragraphs (i) and (ii) above,

(v) as a Student Re-Sitting an Examination, provided the applicant has not previously been granted leave in any of the categories referred to in paragraphs (i) and (ii) above,

(vi) as a Student Writing Up a Thesis, provided the applicant has not previously been granted leave as a Tier 1 Migrant or in any of the categories referred to in paragraphs (i) and (ii) above,

(vii) as a Tier 4 Migrant, provided the applicant has not previously been granted leave as a Tier 1 (Post-Study Work) Migrant or in any of the categories referred to in paragraphs (i) and (ii) above, or

(viii) as a Postgraduate Doctor or Dentist, provided the applicant has not previously been granted leave as a Tier 1 (Post-Study Work) Migrant or in any of the categories referred to in paragraphs (i) and (ii) above.

(g) An applicant who has, or was last granted leave as a Participant in the Fresh Talent: Working in Scotland Scheme must be a British National (Overseas), British overseas territories citizen, British Overseas citizen, British protected person or a British subject as defined in the British Nationality Act 1981.

(h) If:

(i) the studies that led to the qualification for which the applicant obtains points under paragraphs 66 to 72 of Appendix A were sponsored by a Government or international scholarship agency, and

(ii) those studies came to an end 12 months ago or less the applicant must provide the unconditional written consent of the sponsoring Government or agency to the application and must provide the specified documents to show that this requirement has been met.

245FE. Period and conditions of grant

(a) Leave to remain will be granted:

(i) for a period of the difference between 2 years and the period of the last grant of entry clearance, leave to enter or remain, to an applicant who has or was last granted leave as a Participant in the Fresh Talent: Working in Scotland Scheme, as a Participant in the International Graduates Scheme (or its predecessor the Science and Engineering Graduates Scheme). If this calculation results in no grant of leave then leave to remain is to be refused;

(ii) for a period of 2 years, to any other applicant.

(b) Leave to remain under this route will be subject to the following conditions:

(i) no access to public funds,

(ii) registration with the police, if this is required by paragraph 326 of these Rules, and

(iii) no Employment as a Doctor or Dentist in Training, unless the applicant:

(1) has obtained a primary degree in medicine or dentistry at bachelor's level or above from a UK institution that is a UK recognised or listed body, or which holds a sponsor licence under Tier 4 of the Points Based System; or

(2) has, or has last been granted, entry clearance, leave to enter or leave to remain that was not subject to any condition restricting him from taking employment as a Doctor in Training, and has been employed during that leave as a Doctor in Training; or

(3) has, or has last been granted, entry clearance, leave to enter or leave to remain that was not subject to any condition restricting him from taking employment as a Dentist in Training, and has been employed during that leave as a Dentist in Training.

Appendix A

Attributes for Tier 1 (Post-Study Work) Migrants

66. An applicant applying for entry clearance or leave to remain as a Tier 1 (Post-Study Work) Migrant must score 75 points for attributes.

67. Available points are shown in Table 10.

68. Notes to accompany the table appear below the table.

Table 10

Qualifications	Points
The applicant has been awarded: (a) a UK recognised bachelor or postgraduate degree, or (b) a UK postgraduate certificate in education or Professional Graduate Diploma of Education, or (c) a Higher National Diploma ('HND') from a Scottish institution.	20
(a) The applicant studied for his award at a UK institution that is a UK recognised or listed body, or which holds a sponsor licence under Tier 4 of the Points Based System, or (b) If the applicant is claiming points for having been awarded a Higher National Diploma from a Scottish Institution, he studied for that diploma at a Scottish publicly funded institution of further or higher education, or a Scottish bona fide private education institution which maintains satisfactory records of enrolment and attendance. The Scottish institution must: (i) be on the list of Education and Training Providers list on the Department of Business, Innovation and Skills website, or (ii) hold a Sponsor licence under Tier 4 of the Points Based System.	20
The applicant's periods of UK study and/or research towards his eligible award were undertaken whilst he had entry clearance, leave to enter or leave to remain in the UK that was not subject to a restriction preventing him from undertaking a course of study and/or research.	20
The applicant made the application for entry clearance or leave to remain as a Tier 1 (Post-Study Work) Migrant within 12 months of obtaining the relevant qualification or within 12 months of completing a United Kingdom Foundation Programme Office affiliated Foundation Programme as a postgraduate doctor or dentist.	15
The applicant is applying for leave to remain and has, or was last granted, leave as a Participant in the International Graduates Scheme (or its predecessor, the Science and Engineering Graduates Scheme) or as a Participant in the Fresh Talent: Working in Scotland Scheme.	75

Qualification: notes

69. Specified documents must be provided as evidence of the qualification and, where relevant, completion of the United Kingdom Foundation Programme Office affiliated Foundation Programme as a postgraduate doctor or dentist.

70. A qualification will have been deemed to have been 'obtained' on the date on which the applicant was first notified in writing, by the awarding institution, that the qualification had been awarded.

71. If the institution studied at is removed from one of the relevant lists referred to in Table 10, or from the Tier 4 Sponsor Register, no points will be awarded for a qualification obtained on or after the date the institution was removed from the relevant list or from the Tier 4 Sponsor Register.

72. To qualify as an HND from a Scottish institution, a qualification must be at level 8 on the Scottish Credit and Qualifications Framework.

Part 5
Immigration Rules relating to prospective students as at 30 September 2013

Note: Part 5 inserted from 1 October 2013 subject to savings for applications made before that date (HC 628).

Requirements for leave to enter as a prospective student

82. The requirements to be met by a person seeking leave to enter the United Kingdom as a prospective student are that he:

(i) can demonstrate a genuine and realistic intention of undertaking, within 6 months of his date of entry:

(a) a course of study which would meet the requirements for an extension of stay as a student under paragraph 245ZX or paragraph 245ZZC; and

(b) DELETED

(ii) intends to leave the United Kingdom on completion of his studies or on the expiry of his leave to enter if he is not able to meet the requirements for an extension of stay:

(a) as a student in accordance with paragraph 245ZX or paragraph 245ZZC; and

(b) DELETED

(iii) is able without working or recourse to public funds to meet the costs of his intended course and accommodation and the maintenance of himself and any dependants while making arrangements to study and during the course of his studies; and

(iv) holds a valid United Kingdom entry clearance for entry in this capacity.

Leave to enter as a prospective student

83. A person seeking leave to enter the United Kingdom as a prospective student may be admitted for a period not exceeding 6 months with a condition prohibiting employment, provided he is able to produce to the Immigration Officer on arrival a valid United Kingdom entry clearance for entry in this capacity.

Refusal of leave to enter as a prospective student

84. Leave to enter as a prospective student is to be refused if the Immigration Officer is not satisfied that each of the requirements of paragraph 82 is met.

APPENDIX FM
FAMILY MEMBERS

General

Section GEN: General

Purpose

GEN.1.1. This route is for those seeking to enter or remain in the UK on the basis of their family life with a person who is a British Citizen, is settled in the UK, or is in the UK with limited leave as a refugee or person granted humanitarian protection [(and the applicant cannot seek leave to enter or remain in the UK as their family member under Part 11 of these rules)]. It sets out the requirements to be met and, in considering applications under this route, it reflects how, under Article 8 of the Human Rights Convention, the balance will be struck between the right to respect for private and family life and the legitimate aims of protecting national security, public safety and the economic well-being of the UK; the prevention of disorder and crime; the protection of health or morals; and the protection of the rights and freedoms of others {(and in doing also reflects the relevant public interest considerations as set out in Part 5A of the Nationality, Immigration and Asylum Act 2002)}. It also takes into account the need to safeguard and promote the welfare of children in the UK {, in line with the Secretary of State's duty under section 55 of the Borders, Citizenship and Immigration Act 2009}.

Note: Words in square brackets inserted from 13 December 2013 (HC 760). Words in curly brackets inserted from 28 July 2014; this change applies to all applications to which paragraphs 276ADE to 276DH and Appendix FM apply (or can be applied by virtue of the Immigration Rules), and to any other ECHR Article 8 claims (save for those from foreign criminals), and which are decided on or after that date (HC 532).

Definitions

GEN.1.2. For the purposes of this Appendix "partner" means—

(i) the applicant's spouse;

(ii) the applicant's civil partner;

(iii) the applicant's fiancé(e) or proposed civil partner; or

(iv) a person who has been living together with the applicant in a relationship akin to a marriage or civil partnership for at least two years prior to the date of application, [unless a different meaning of partner applies elsewhere in this Appendix.]

Note: Words substituted from 6 April 2014 (HC 1138 as amended by HC 1201).

GEN.1.3. For the purposes of this Appendix

(a) "application for leave to remain" also includes an application for variation of leave to enter or remain by a person in the UK;

(b) references to a person being present and settled in the UK also include a person who is being admitted for settlement on the same occasion as the applicant; and

(c) references to a British Citizen in the UK also include a British Citizen who is coming to the UK with the applicant as their partner or parent.

GEN.1.4. In this Appendix "specified" means specified in Appendix FM-SE, unless otherwise stated.

GEN.1.5. If the Entry Clearance Officer, or Secretary of State, has reasonable cause to doubt the genuineness of any document submitted in support of an application, and having taken reasonable steps to verify the document, is unable to verify that it is genuine, the document will be discounted for the purposes of the application.

GEN.1.6. For the purposes of paragraph E-ECP.4.1.(a); E-LTRP.4.1.(a); EECPT. 4.1(a) and E-LTRPT.5.1.(a) the applicant must be a national of Antigua and Barbuda; Australia; the Bahamas; Barbados; Belize; Canada; Dominica; Grenada; Guyana; Jamaica; New Zealand; St Kitts and Nevis; St Lucia; St Vincent and the Grenadines; Trinidad and Tobago; or the United States of America.

GEN.1.7. In this Appendix references to paragraphs are to paragraphs of this Appendix unless the context otherwise requires.

GEN.1.8. Paragraphs 277–280, 289AA, 295AA and 296 of Part 8 of these Rules shall apply to this Appendix.

GEN.1.9. In this Appendix:

(a) the requirement to make a valid application will not apply when the Article 8 claim is raised:

(i) as part of an asylum claim, or as part of a further submission in person after an asylum claim has been refused;

(ii) where a migrant is in immigration detention. A migrant in immigration detention or their representative must submit any application or claim raising Article 8 to a prison officer, a prisoner custody officer, a detainee custody officer or a member of Home Office staff at the migrant's place of detention; or

(iii) in an appeal (subject to the consent of the Secretary of State where applicable); and

(b) where an application or claim raising Article 8 is made in any of the circumstances specified in paragraph GEN.1.9.(a), or is considered by the Secretary of State under paragraph A277C of these rules, the requirements of paragraphs R-LTRP.1.1.(c) and R-LTRPT.1.1.(c) are not met.

Note: Paragraph GEN.1.9. substituted from 6 November 2014 (HC 693).

GEN.1.10. Where an applicant does not meet the requirements of this Appendix as a partner or parent but the decision-maker grants entry clearance or leave to enter or remain outside the rules on Article 8 grounds, the applicant will normally be granted entry clearance for a period not exceeding 33 months, or leave to enter or remain for a period not exceeding 30 months, and subject to a condition of no recourse to public funds unless the decision-maker considers that the person should not be subject to such a condition.

Note: Paragraphs GEN 1.10 to GEN 1.12 inserted from 28 July 2014; this change applies to all applications to which paragraphs 276ADE–276DH and Appendix FM apply (or can be applied by virtue of the Immigration Rules), and to any other ECHR Article 8 claims (save for those from foreign criminals), and which are decided on or after that date (HC 532).

GEN.1.11. Where entry clearance or leave to enter or remain is granted under this Appendix, or where an applicant does not meet the requirements of this Appendix as a partner or parent but the decision-maker grants entry clearance or leave to enter or remain outside the rules on Article 8 grounds, (and without prejudice to the specific provision that is made in this Appendix in respect of a no recourse to public funds condition), that leave may be subject to such conditions as the decision-maker considers appropriate in a particular case.

Note: Paragraphs GEN 1.10 to GEN 1.12 inserted from 28 July 2014; this change applies to all applications to which paragraphs 276ADE–276DH and Appendix FM apply (or can be applied by virtue of the Immigration Rules), and to any other ECHR Article 8 claims (save for those from foreign criminals), and which are decided on or after that date (HC 532).

GEN.1.12. In paragraphs GEN.1.10. and GEN.1.11. "decision-maker" refers to the Secretary of State or an Entry Clearance Officer.

Note: Paragraphs GEN 1.10 to GEN 1.12 inserted from 28 July 2014; this change applies to all applications to which paragraphs 276ADE–276DH and Appendix FM apply (or can be applied by virtue of the Immigration Rules), and to any other ECHR Article 8 claims (save for those from foreign criminals), and which are decided on or after that date (HC 532).

GEN.1.13. For the purposes of paragraphs D-LTRP.1.1., D-LTRP.1.2., D ILRP.1.2., D-LTRPT.1.1., D-LTRPT.1.2., and D-ILRPT.1.2. (excluding a grant of limited leave to remain as a fiancé(e) or proposed civil partner), where the applicant has extant leave at the date of decision, the remaining period of that extant leave up to a maximum of 28 days will be added to the period of limited leave to remain granted under that paragraph (which may therefore exceed 30 months).

Note: Paragraph GEN.1.13. inserted from 6 November 2014 (HC 693).

Leave to enter

GEN.2.1. The requirements to be met by a person seeking leave to enter the UK under this route are that the person—

(a) must have a valid entry clearance for entry under this route; and

(b) must produce to the Immigration Officer on arrival a valid national passport or other document satisfactorily establishing their identity and nationality.

GEN.2.2. If a person does not meet the requirements of paragraph GEN.2.1. entry will be refused.

Family life with a partner

Section EC-P: Entry clearance as a partner

EC-P.1.1. The requirements to be met for entry clearance as a partner are that—

(a) the applicant must be outside the UK;

(b) the applicant must have made a valid application for entry clearance as a partner;

(c) the applicant must not fall for refusal under any of the grounds in Section S-EC: Suitability–entry clearance; and

(d) the applicant must meet all of the requirements of Section E-ECP: Eligibility for entry clearance as a partner.

Section S-EC: Suitability-entry clearance

S-EC.1.1. The applicant will be refused entry clearance on grounds of suitability if any of paragraphs S-EC.1.2. to 1.8. apply.

Note: Paragraph S-EC.1.1 substituted from 6 April 2013 subject to savings for applications made before that date (HC 1039).

S-EC.1.2. The Secretary of State has personally directed that the exclusion of the applicant from the UK is conducive to the public good.

S-EC.1.3. The applicant is [currently] the subject of a deportation order.

Note: Words substituted from 1 December 2013 subject to savings for applications made before that date (HC 803).

S-EC.1.4. The exclusion of the applicant from the UK is conducive to the public good because they have:

(a) been convicted of an offence for which they have been sentenced to a period of imprisonment of at least 4 years; or

(b) been convicted of an offence for which they have been sentenced to a period of imprisonment of at least 12 months but less than 4 years, unless a period of 10 years has passed since the end of the sentence; or

(c) been convicted of an offence for which they have been sentenced to a period of imprisonment of less than 12 months, unless a period of 5 years has passed since the end of the sentence.

Where this paragraph applies, unless refusal would be contrary to the Human Rights Convention or the Convention and Protocol Relating to the Status of Refugees, it will only be in exceptional circumstances that the public interest in maintaining refusal will be outweighed by compelling factors.

Note: Words from and including subparagraph (a) onwards substituted from 13 December 2012 subject to savings for applications made before that date (HC 760).

S-EC.1.5. The exclusion of the applicant from the UK is conducive to the public good because, for example, the applicant's conduct (including convictions which do not fall within paragraph S-EC.1.4.), character, associations, or other reasons, make it undesirable to grant them entry clearance.

S-EC.1.6. The applicant has failed without reasonable excuse to comply with a requirement to—

(a) attend an interview;

(b) provide information;

(c) provide physical data; or

(d) undergo a medical examination or provide a medical report.

S-EC.1.7. It is undesirable to grant entry clearance to the applicant for medical reasons.

S-EC.1.8. The applicant left or was removed from the UK as a condition of a caution issued in accordance with [section 22 of the Criminal Justice Act 2003] less than 5 years prior to the date on which the application is decided.

Note: Paragraph S-EC.1.8 inserted from 6 April 2013 subject to savings for applications made before that date (HC 1039). Words substituted from 1 December 2013 subject to savings for applications made before that date (HC 803).

S-EC.2.1. The applicant will normally be refused on grounds of suitability if any of paragraphs S-EC.2.2. to [2.5. apply].

Note: Words substituted from 13 December 2012 subject to savings for applications made before that date (HC 760).

S-EC.2.2. Whether or not to the applicant's knowledge—

(a) false information, representations or documents have been submitted in relation to the application (including false information submitted to any person to obtain a document used in support of the application); or

(b) there has been a failure to disclose material facts in relation to the application.

S-EC.2.3. One or more relevant NHS body has notified the Secretary of State that the applicant has failed to pay charges in accordance with the relevant NHS regulations on charges to overseas visitors and the outstanding charges have a total value of at least £1000.

S-EC.2.4. A maintenance and accommodation undertaking has been requested or required under paragraph 35 of these Rules or otherwise and has not been provided.

S-EC.2.5. The exclusion of the applicant from the UK is conducive to the public good because:

(a) [within the 12 months prior to the date on which the application is decided], the person has been convicted of or admitted an offence for which they received a non-custodial sentence or other out of court disposal that is recorded on their criminal record; or

(b) in the view of the Secretary of State:

(i) the person's offending has caused serious harm; or

(ii) the person is a persistent offender who shows a particular disregard for the law.

Note: Paragraph S-EC.2.5 inserted from 13 December 2012 subject to savings for applications made before that date (HC 760). Words substituted in subparagraph (a) from 1 December 2013 (HC 803).

Section E-ECP: Eligibility for entry clearance as a partner

E-ECP.1.1. To meet the eligibility requirements for entry clearance as a partner all of the requirements in paragraphs E-ECP.2.1. to 4.2. must be met.

Relationship requirements

E-ECP.2.1. The applicant's partner must be—

(a) a British Citizen in the UK, subject to paragraph GEN.1.3.(c); or

(b) present and settled in the UK, subject to paragraph GEN.1.3.(b); or

(c) in the UK with refugee leave or with humanitarian protection.

E-ECP.2.2. The applicant must be aged 18 or over at the date of application.

E-ECP.2.3. The partner must be aged 18 or over at the date of application.

E-ECP.2.4. The applicant and their partner must not be within the prohibited degree of relationship.

E-ECP.2.5. The applicant and their partner must have met in person.

E-ECP.2.6. The relationship between the applicant and their partner must be genuine and subsisting.

E-ECP.2.7. If the applicant and partner are married or in a civil partnership it must be a valid marriage or civil partnership, as specified.

E-ECP.2.8. If the applicant is a fiancé(e) or proposed civil partner they must be seeking entry to the UK to enable their marriage or civil partnership to take place.

E-ECP.2.9. Any previous relationship of the applicant or their partner must have broken down permanently, unless it is a relationship which falls within paragraph 278(i) of these Rules.

E-ECP.2.10. The applicant and partner must intend to live together permanently in the UK.

Financial requirements

E-ECP.3.1. The applicant must provide specified evidence, from the sources listed in paragraph E-ECP.3.2., of—

(a) a specified gross annual income of at least—
(i) £18,600;
(ii) an additional £3,800 for the first child; and
(iii) an additional £2,400 for each additional child; alone or in combination with
(b) specified savings of—
(i) £16,000; and
(ii) additional savings of an amount equivalent to 2.5 times the amount which is the difference between the gross annual income from the sources listed in paragraph E-ECP.3.2.(a)–(d) and the total amount required under paragraph E-ECP.3.1.(a); or
(c) the requirements in paragraph E-ECP.3.3. being met.

In this paragraph "child" means a dependent child of the applicant who is—
(a) under the age of 18 years, or who was under the age of 18 years when they were first granted entry under this route;
(b) applying for entry clearance as a dependant of the applicant, or has limited leave to enter or remain in the UK;
(c) not a British Citizen or settled in the UK; and
(d) not an EEA national with a right to be admitted under the Immigration (EEA) Regulations 2006.

E-ECP.3.2. When determining whether the financial requirement in paragraph EECP 3.1. is met only the following sources will be taken into account—
(a) income of the partner from specified employment or self-employment, which, in respect of a partner returning to the UK with the applicant, can include specified employment or self-employment overseas and in the UK;
(b) specified pension income of the applicant and partner;
(c) any specified maternity allowance or bereavement benefit received by the partner in the UK [or any specified payment relating to service in HM Forces received by the applicant or partner];
(d) other specified income of the applicant and partner; and
(e) specified savings of the applicant and partner.

Note: Words inserted in subparagraph (c) from 1 December 2013 (HC 803).

E-ECP.3.3. The requirements to be met under this paragraph are—
(a) the applicant's partner must be receiving one or more of the following—
(i) disability living allowance;
(ii) severe disablement allowance;
(iii) industrial injury disablement benefit;
(iv) attendance allowance; . . .
(v) carer's allowance . . . ;
(vi) personal independence payment . . . ;
(vii) Armed Forces Independence Payment or Guaranteed Income Payment under the Armed Forces Compensation Scheme; or
(viii) Constant Attendance Allowance, Mobility Supplement or War Disablement Pension under the War Pensions Scheme; and
(b) the applicant must provide evidence that their partner is able to maintain and accommodate themselves, the applicant and any dependants adequately in the UK without recourse to public funds.

Note: Words 'or' deleted from subparagraph (a)(iv) and subparagraph (vi) inserted from 6 April 2013 (HC 1039). Word 'or' deleted from subparagraph subparagraph (a)(v), word 'and' deleted from subparagraph (a)(vi) and subparagraphs (a)(vii) and (a)(viii) inserted from 1 December 2013 (HC 803).

E-ECP.3.4. The applicant must provide evidence that there will be adequate accommodation, without recourse to public funds, for the family, including other family members who are not included in the application but who live in the same household, which the family own or occupy exclusively: accommodation will not be regarded as adequate if—

(a) it is, or will be, overcrowded; or

(b) it contravenes public health regulations.

English language requirement

E-ECP.4.1. The applicant must provide specified evidence that they—

(a) are a national of a majority English speaking country listed in paragraph GEN.1.6.;

(b) have passed an English language test in speaking and listening at a minimum of level A1 of the Common European Framework of Reference for Languages with a provider approved by the [Secretary of State];

(c) have an academic qualification recognised by [UK NARIC] to be equivalent to the standard of a Bachelor's or Master's degree or PhD in the UK, which was taught in English; or

(d) are exempt from the English language requirement under paragraph E-ECP. 4.2.

Note: Words substituted in subparagraph (c) from 6 April 2013 (HC 1039). Words substituted in subparagraph (b) from 1 October 2013 (HC 803).

E-ECP.4.2. The applicant is exempt from the English language requirement if at the date of application—

(a) the applicant is aged 65 or over;

(b) the applicant has a disability (physical or mental condition) which prevents the applicant from meeting the requirement; or

(c) there are exceptional circumstances which prevent the applicant from being able to meet the requirement prior to entry to the UK.

Section D-ECP: Decision on application for entry clearance as a partner

D-ECP.1.1. If the applicant meets the requirements for entry clearance as a partner the applicant will be granted entry clearance for an initial period not exceeding 33 months, and subject to a condition of no recourse to public funds; or, where the applicant is a fiancé(e) or proposed civil partner, the applicant will be granted entry clearance for a period not exceeding 6 months, and subject to a condition of no recourse to public funds and a prohibition on employment.

D-ECP.1.2. Where the applicant does not meet the requirements for entry clearance as a partner the application will be refused.

Section R-LTRP: Requirements for limited leave to remain as a partner

R-LTRP.1.1. The requirements to be met for limited leave to remain as a partner are—

(a) the applicant and their partner must be in the UK;

(b) the applicant must have made a valid application for limited [or indefinite] leave to remain as a partner; and either

(c) (i) the applicant must not fall for refusal under Section S-LTR: Suitability leave to remain; and

(ii) the applicant meets all of the requirements of Section E-LTRP: Eligibility for leave to remain as a partner; or

(d) (i) the applicant must not fall for refusal under Section S-LTR: Suitability leave to remain; and

(ii) the applicant meets the requirements of paragraphs E-LTRP.1.2–1.12. and E-LTRP.2.1.; and

(iii) paragraph EX.1. applies.

Note: Words inserted in subparagraph (b), words substituted in subparagraph (c)(ii) and subparagraph (c)(iii) deleted from 13 December 2012 (HC 760).

Section S-LTR: Suitability-leave to remain

S-LTR.1.1. The applicant will be refused limited leave to remain on grounds of suitability if any of paragraphs S-LTR.1.2. to 1.7. apply.

S-LTR.1.2. The applicant is [currently] the subject of a deportation order.

Note: Words substituted from 1 December 2013 subject to savings for applications made before that date (HC 803).

S-LTR.1.3. The presence of the applicant in the UK is not conducive to the public good because they have been convicted of an offence for which they have been sentenced to imprisonment for at least 4 years.

S-LTR.1.4. The presence of the applicant in the UK is not conducive to the public good because they have been convicted of an offence for which they have been sentenced to imprisonment for less than 4 years but at least 12 months.

S-LTR.1.5. The presence of the applicant in the UK is not conducive to the public good because, in the view of the Secretary of State, their offending has caused serious harm or they are a persistent offender who shows a particular disregard for the law.

S-LTR.1.6. The presence of the applicant in the UK is not conducive to the public good because their conduct (including convictions which do not fall within paragraphs S-LTR.1.3. to 1.5.), character, associations, or other reasons, make it undesirable to allow them to remain in the UK.

S-LTR.1.7. The applicant has failed without reasonable excuse to comply with a requirement to—

(a) attend an interview;

(b) provide information;

(c) provide physical data; or

(d) undergo a medical examination or provide a medical report.

S-LTR.2.1. The applicant will normally be refused on grounds of suitability if any of paragraphs S-LTR.2.2. to 2.4. apply.

S-LTR.2.2. Whether or not to the applicant's knowledge—

(a) false information, representations or documents have been submitted in relation to the application (including false information submitted to any person to obtain a document used in support of the application); or

(b) there has been a failure to disclose material facts in relation to the application.

S-LTR.2.3. One or more relevant NHS body has notified the Secretary of State that the applicant has failed to pay charges in accordance with the relevant NHS regulations on charges to overseas visitors and the outstanding charges have a total value of at least £1000.

S-LTR.2.4. A maintenance and accommodation undertaking has been requested under paragraph 35 of these Rules and has not been provided.

S-LTR.3.1. When considering whether the presence of the applicant in the UK is not conducive to the public good any legal or practical reasons why the applicant cannot presently be removed from the UK must be ignored.

Section E-LTRP: Eligibility for limited leave to remain as a partner

E-LTRP.1.1. To qualify for limited leave to remain as a partner all of the requirements of paragraphs E-LTRP.1.2. to 4.2. must be met.

Relationship requirements

E-LTRP.1.2. The applicant's partner must be—

(a) a British Citizen in the UK;
(b) present and settled in the UK; or
(c) in the UK with refugee leave or as a person with humanitarian protection.

E-LTRP.1.3. The applicant must be aged 18 or over at the date of application.

E-LTRP.1.4. The partner must be aged 18 or over at the date of application.

E-LTRP.1.5. The applicant and their partner must not be within the prohibited degree of relationship.

E-LTRP.1.6. The applicant and their partner must have met in person.

E-LTRP.1.7. The relationship between the applicant and their partner must be genuine and subsisting.

E-LTRP.1.8. If the applicant and partner are married or in a civil partnership it must be a valid marriage or civil partnership, as specified.

E-LTRP.1.9. Any previous relationship of the applicant or their partner must have broken down permanently, unless it is a relationship which falls within paragraph 278(i) of these Rules.

E-LTRP.1.10. The applicant and their partner must intend to live together permanently in the UK and, in any application for further leave to remain as a partner (except where the applicant is in the UK as a fiancé(e) or proposed civil partner) and in any application for indefinite leave to remain as a partner, the applicant must provide evidence that, since entry clearance as a partner was granted under paragraph D-ECP1.1. or since the last grant of limited leave to remain as a partner, the applicant and their partner have lived together in the UK or there is good reason, consistent with a continuing intention to live together permanently in the UK, for any period in which they have not done so.

E-LTRP.1.11. If the applicant is in the UK with leave as a fiancé(e) or proposed civil partner and the marriage or civil partnership did not take place during that period of leave, there must be good reason why and evidence that it will take place within the next 6 months.

E-LTRP.1.12. The applicant's partner cannot be the applicant's fiancé(e) or proposed civil partner, unless the applicant was granted entry clearance as that person's fiancé(e) or proposed civil partner.

Immigration status requirements

E-LTRP.2.1. The applicant must not be in the UK—

(a) as a visitor; or

(b) with valid leave granted for a period of 6 months or less, unless that leave is as a fiancé(e) or proposed civil partner [, or was granted pending the outcome of family court or divorce proceedings]; . . .

(c) . . .

Note: Words inserted in subparagraphs (b) and (c) from 13 December 2012 (HC 760). Word 'or' inserted at the end of subparagraph (a), word 'or' deleted at the end of subparagraph (b) and subparagraph (c) deleted from 28 July 2014; this amendment applies to all applications to which paragraphs 276ADE to 276DH and Appendix FM apply (or can be applied by virtue of the Immigration Rules), and to any other ECHR Article 8 claims (save for those from foreign criminals), and which are decided on or after that date (HC 532).

E-LTRP.2.2. The applicant must not be in the UK—

(a) on temporary admission or temporary release, unless paragraph EX.1. applies; or

(b) in breach of immigration laws (disregarding any period of overstaying for a period of 28 days or less), unless paragraph EX.1. applies.

Note: Paragraph E-LTRP.2.2 substituted from 28 July 2014; this amendment applies to all applications to which paragraphs 276ADE to 276DH and Appendix FM apply (or can be applied by virtue of the Immigration Rules), and to any other ECHR Article 8 claims (save for those from foreign criminals), and which are decided on or after that date HC 532).

Financial requirements

E-LTRP.3.1. The applicant must provide specified evidence, from the sources listed in paragraph E-LTRP.3.2., of—

(a) a specified gross annual income of at least—

(i) £18,600;

(ii) an additional £3,800 for the first child; and

(iii) an additional £2,400 for each additional child; alone or in combination with

(b) specified savings of—

(i) £16,000; and

(ii) additional savings of an amount equivalent to 2.5 times the amount which is the difference between the gross annual income from the sources listed in paragraph E-LTRP.3.2.(a)–(f) and the total amount required under paragraph E-LTRP.3.1.(a); or

(c) the requirements in paragraph E-LTRP.3.3. being met, unless paragraph EX.1. applies.

In this paragraph "child" means a dependent child of the applicant who is—

(a) under the age of 18 years, or who was under the age of 18 years when they were first granted entry under this route;

(b) applying for entry clearance or is in the UK as a dependant of the applicant;

(c) not a British Citizen or settled in the UK; and

(d) not an EEA national with a right to remain in the UK under the Immigration (EEA) Regulations 2006.

E-LTRP.3.2. When determining whether the financial requirement in paragraph ELTRP.3.1 is met only the following sources may be taken into account—

(a) income of the partner from specified employment or self-employment;

(b) income of the applicant from specified employment or self-employment unless they are working illegally;

(c) specified pension income of the applicant and partner;

(d) any specified maternity allowance or bereavement benefit received by the applicant and partner in the UK [or any specified payment relating to service in HM Forces received by the applicant or partner];

(e) other specified income of the applicant and partner;

(f) income from the sources at (b), (d) or (e) of a dependent child of the applicant under paragraph E-LTRP.3.1. who is aged 18 years or over; and

(g) specified savings of the applicant, partner and a dependent child of the applicant under paragraph E-LTRP.3.1. who is aged 18 years or over.

Note: Words substituted in subparagraph (d) from 1 December 2013 (HC 803).

E-LTRP.3.3. The requirements to meet this paragraph are—

(a) the applicant's partner must be receiving one or more of the following—

(i) disability living allowance;

(ii) severe disablement allowance;

(iii) industrial injury disablement benefit;

(iv) attendance allowance;

(v) carer's allowance; . . .

(vi) personal independence payment; . . .

(vii) Armed Forces Independence Payment or Guaranteed Income Payment under the Armed Forces Compensation Scheme; or

(viii) Constant Attendance Allowance, Mobility Supplement or War Disablement Pension under the War Pensions Scheme; and

(b) the applicant must provide evidence that their partner is able to maintain and accommodate themselves, the applicant and any dependants adequately in the UK without recourse to public funds.

Note: Word 'or' deleted from subparagraph (a)(iv), word 'or' substituted in subparagraph (a)(v) and subparagraph (a)(vi) inserted from 6 April 2013 (HC 1039; amendment to subparagraph (a)(v) later superseded). Word 'or' omitted from subparagraph (a)(v), word 'and' deleted from subparagraph (a)(vi) and subparagraphs (a)(vii) and (a)(viii) inserted from 1 December 2013 (HC 803).

E-LTRP.3.4. The applicant must provide evidence that there will be adequate accommodation, without recourse to public funds, for the family, including other family members who are not included in the application but who live in the same household, which the family own or occupy exclusively, unless paragraph EX.1. applies: accommodation will not be regarded as adequate if—

(a) it is, or will be, overcrowded; or

(b) it contravenes public health regulations.

English language requirement

E-LTRP.4.1. If the applicant has not met the requirement in a previous application for leave as a partner [or parent], the applicant must provide specified evidence that they—

(a) are a national of a majority English speaking country listed in paragraph GEN.1.6.;

(b) have passed an English language test in speaking and listening at a minimum of level A1 of the Common European Framework of Reference for Languages with a provider approved by the [Secretary of State];

(c) have an academic qualification recognised by [UK NARIC] to be equivalent to the standard of a Bachelor's or Master's degree or PhD in the UK, which was taught in English; or

(d) are exempt from the English language requirement under paragraph E-LTRP. 4.2.; unless paragraph EX.1. applies.

Note: Words substituted in subparagraph (c) from 6 April 2013 (HC 1039). Words substituted on subparagraph (b) from 1 October 2013 (HC 628). Words inserted in opening sentence from 6 April 2014 (HC 1138 as amended by HC 1201).

E-LTRP.4.2. The applicant is exempt from the English language requirement if at the date of application—

(a) the applicant is aged 65 or over;

(b) the applicant has a disability (physical or mental condition) which prevents the applicant from meeting the requirement; or

(c) there are exceptional circumstances which prevent the applicant from being able to meet the requirement.

Section D-LTRP: Decision on application for limited leave to remain as a partner

D-LTRP.1.1. If the applicant meets the requirements in paragraph R-LTRP.1.1.(a) to (c) for limited leave to remain as a partner the applicant will be granted limited leave to remain for a period not exceeding 30 months, and subject to a condition of no recourse to public funds, and they will be eligible to apply for settlement after a continuous period of at least 60 months with such leave or in the UK with entry clearance as a partner under paragraph D-ECP1.1. (excluding in all cases any period of entry clearance or limited leave as a fiance(e) or proposed civil partner); or, if paragraph E-LTRP.1.11. applies, the applicant will be granted limited leave for a period not exceeding 6 months and subject to a condition of no recourse to public funds and a prohibition on employment.

D-LTRP.1.2. If the applicant meets the requirements in paragraph R-LTRP.1.1.(a), (b) and (d) for limited leave to remain as a partner they will be granted leave to remain for a period not exceeding 30 months [and subject to a condition of no recourse to public funds {unless the Secretary of State considers that the person should not be subject to such a condition},] and [they] will be eligible to apply for settlement after a continuous period of at least 120 months with such leave, with limited leave as a partner under paragraph D-LTRP.1.1., or in the UK with entry clearance as a partner under paragraph D-ECP1.1. (excluding in all cases any period of entry clearance or limited leave as a fiancé(e) or proposed civil partner), or, if paragraph E-LTRP.1.11. applies, the applicant will be granted limited leave for a period not exceeding 6 months and subject to a condition of no recourse to public funds and a prohibition on employment.

Note: Words in square brackets inserted from 13 December 2012 (HC 760). Words in curly brackets inserted from 28 July 2014; this amendment applies to all applications to which paragraphs 276ADE–276DH and Appendix FM apply (or can be applied by virtue of the Immigration Rules), and to any other ECHR Article 8 claims (save for those from foreign criminals), and which are decided on or after that date (HC 532).

D-LTRP.1.3. If the applicant does not meet the requirements for limited leave to remain as a partner the application will be refused.

Section R-ILRP: Requirements for indefinite leave to remain (settlement) as a partner

R-ILRP.1.1. The requirements to be met for indefinite leave to remain as a partner are that—

(a) the applicant and their partner must be in the UK;

(b) the applicant must have made a valid application for indefinite leave to remain as a partner;

(c) the applicant must not fall for refusal under any of the grounds in Section S-ILR: Suitability for indefinite leave to remain;

(d) the applicant:

(i) must meet all of the requirements of Section E-LTRP: Eligibility for leave to remain as a partner (but in applying paragraph E LTRP.3.1.(b)(ii) delete the words "2.5 times"); or

(ii) must meet the requirements of paragraphs E-LTRP.1.2.-1.12. and E-LTRP.2.1. and paragraph EX.1. applies; and

(e) the applicant must meet all of the requirements of Section E-ILRP: Eligibility for indefinite leave to remain as a partner.

Note: Paragraph R-ILRP.1.1. substituted from 6 November 2014 (HC 693).

Section S-ILR: Suitability for indefinite leave to remain

Note: Paragraph R-ILRP.1.1. substituted from 6 November 2014 (HC 693).

S-ILR.1.1. The applicant will be refused indefinite leave to remain on grounds of suitability if any of paragraphs S-ILR.1.2. to 1.9. apply.

S-ILR.1.2. The applicant is currently the subject of a deportation order.

S-ILR.1.3. The presence of the applicant in the UK is not conducive to the public good because they have been convicted of an offence for which they have been sentenced to imprisonment for at least 4 years.

S-ILR.1.4. The presence of the applicant in the UK is not conducive to the public good because they have been convicted of an offence for which they have been sentenced to imprisonment for less than 4 years but at least 12 months, unless a period of 15 years has passed since the end of the sentence.

S-ILR.1.5. The presence of the applicant in the UK is not conducive to the public good because they have been convicted of an offence for which they have been sentenced to imprisonment for less than 12 months, unless a period of 7 years has passed since the end of the sentence.

S-ILR.1.6. The applicant has, within the 24 months prior to the date on which the application is decided, been convicted of or admitted an offence for which they received a non-custodial sentence or other out of court disposal that is recorded on their criminal record.

S-ILR.1.7. The presence of the applicant in the UK is not conducive to the public good because, in the view of the Secretary of State, their offending has caused serious harm or they are a persistent offender who shows a particular disregard for the law.

S-ILR.1.8. The presence of the applicant in the UK is not conducive to the public good because their conduct (including convictions which do not fall within paragraphs S-ILR.1.3. to 1.6.), character, associations, or other reasons, make it undesirable to allow them to remain in the UK.

S-ILR.1.9. The applicant has failed without reasonable excuse to comply with a requirement to—

(a) attend an interview;
(b) provide information;
(c) provide physical data; or
(d) undergo a medical examination or provide a medical report.

S-ILR.2.1. The applicant will normally be refused on grounds of suitability if any of paragraphs S-ILR.2.2. to 2.4. apply.

S-ILR.2.2. Whether or not to the applicant's knowledge –

(a) false information, representations or documents have been submitted in relation to the application (including false information submitted to any person to obtain a document used in support of the application); or

(b) there has been a failure to disclose material facts in relation to the application.

S-ILR.2.3. One or more relevant NHS body has notified the Secretary of State that the applicant has failed to pay charges in accordance with the relevant NHS regulations on charges to overseas visitors and the outstanding charges have a total value of at least £1000.

S-ILR.2.4. A maintenance and accommodation undertaking has been requested under paragraph 35 of these Rules and has not been provided.

S-ILR.3.1. When considering whether the presence of the applicant in the UK is not conducive to the public good, any legal or practical reasons why the applicant cannot presently be removed from the UK must be ignored.

Section E-ILRP: Eligibility for indefinite leave to remain as a partner

E-ILRP.1.1. To meet the eligibility requirements for indefinite leave to remain as a partner all of the requirements of paragraphs E-ILRP.1.2. to 1.6. must be met.

E-ILRP.1.2. The applicant must be in the UK with valid leave to remain as a partner (disregarding any period of overstaying for a period of 28 days or less).

E-ILRP.1.3. The applicant must have completed a continuous period of at least 60 months with limited leave as a partner under paragraph R-LTRP.1.1.(a) to (c) or in the UK with entry clearance as a partner under paragraph D-ECP.1.1.; or a continuous period of at least 120 months with limited leave as a partner under paragraph R-LTR.P.1.1(a), (b) and (d) or in the UK with entry clearance as a partner under paragraph D-ECP.1.1.; or a continuous period of at least 120 months with limited leave as a partner under a combination of these paragraphs, excluding in all cases any period of entry clearance or limited leave as a fiancé(e) or proposed civil partner.

E-ILRP.1.4. In calculating the periods under paragraph E-ILRP.1.3. only the periods when the applicant's partner is the same person as the applicant's partner for the previous period of limited leave shall be taken into account.

E-ILRP.1.5. In calculating the periods under paragraph E-ILRP.1.3. the words "in the UK" in that paragraph shall not apply to any period(s) to which the evidence in paragraph 26A of Appendix FM-SE applies.

Note: Paragraph 1.5 deleted from 13 December 2012 (HC 760) and then reinserted from 6 November 2014 (HC 693).

E-ILRP.1.6. The applicant must have [demonstrated] sufficient knowledge of the English language and sufficient knowledge about life in the [United Kingdom] in accordance with the requirements of [Appendix KoLL] of these Rules.

Note Words inserted/substituted from 28 October 2013 subject to savings for applications made before that date (HC 628).

Section D-ILRP: Decision on application for indefinite leave to remain as a partner

D-ILRP.1.1. If the applicant meets all of the requirements for indefinite leave to remain as a partner the applicant will be granted indefinite leave to remain.

D-ILRP.1.2. If the applicant does not meet the requirements for indefinite leave to remain as a partner only for one or both of the following reasons—

(a) [paragraph S-ILR.1.5. or S-ILR.1.6. applies];

(b) the applicant has not demonstrated sufficient knowledge of the English language or about life in the United Kingdom in accordance with Appendix KoLL,

the applicant will be granted further limited leave to remain as a partner for a period not exceeding 30 months, and subject to a condition of no recourse to public funds.

Note: Words substituted in subparagraph (a) from 13 December 2012 subject to savings for applications made before that date (HC 760). Subparagraph (b) substituted from 28 October 2013 subject to savings for applications made before that date (HC 628).

D-ILRP.1.3. If the applicant does not meet [all the eligibility requirements for indefinite leave to remain as a partner, and does not qualify for] further limited leave to remain as a partner under paragraph DILRP. 1.2., the application will be refused, [unless the applicant meets the requirements in paragraph R-LTRP.1.1.(a), (b) and (d) for limited leave to remain as a partner. Where they do,] the applicant will be granted further limited leave to remain as a partner for a period not exceeding 30 months under paragraph D-LTRP.1.2. [and subject to a condition of no recourse to public funds {unless the Secretary of State considers that the person should not be subject to such a condition}.]

Note: Words in square brackets inserted/substituted from 13 December 2012 (HC 760). Words in curly brackets substituted from 28 July 2014; this amendment applies to all applications to which paragraphs 276ADE–276DH and Appendix FM apply (or can be applied by virtue of the Immigration Rules), and to any other ECHR Article 8 claims (save for those from foreign criminals), and which are decided on or after that date HC 532).

Section EX: [Exceptions to certain eligibility requirements for leave to remain as a partner or parent]

Note: Heading substituted from 28 July 2014 (HC 532).

EX.1. This paragraph applies if

(a) (i) the applicant has a genuine and subsisting parental relationship with a child who—

(aa) is under the age of 18 years [, or was under the age of 18 years when the applicant was first granted leave on the basis that this paragraph applied];

(bb) is in the UK;

(cc) is a British Citizen or has lived in the UK continuously for at least the 7 years immediately preceding the date of application; and

(ii) it would not be reasonable to expect the child to leave the UK; or

(b) the applicant has a genuine and subsisting relationship with a partner who is in the UK and is a British Citizen, settled in the UK or in the UK with refugee leave or humanitarian protection, and there are insurmountable obstacles to family life with that partner continuing outside the UK.

Note: Words substituted in subparagraph (a)(i)(aa) from 13 December 2012 (HC 760).

EX.2. For the purposes of paragraph EX.1.(b) "insurmountable obstacles" means the very significant difficulties which would be faced by the applicant or their partner in continuing their family life together outside the UK and which could not be overcome or would entail very serious hardship for the applicant or their partner.

Note: Paragraph EX.2 inserted from 28 July 2014; this amendment applies to all applications to which paragraphs 276ADE–276DH and Appendix FM apply (or can be applied by virtue of the Immigration Rules), and to any other ECHR Article 8 claims (save for those from foreign criminals), and which are decided on or after that date (HC 532).

Bereaved partner

Section BPILR: Indefinite leave to remain (settlement) as a bereaved partner

BPILR.1.1. The requirements to be met for indefinite leave to remain in the UK as a bereaved partner are that—

(a) the applicant must be in the UK;

(b) the applicant must have made a valid application for indefinite leave to remain as a bereaved partner;

(c) the applicant must not fall for refusal under any of the grounds in [Section S-ILR: Suitability – indefinite leave to remain]; and

(d) the applicant must meet all of the requirements of Section E-BPILR: Eligibility for indefinite leave to remain as a bereaved partner.

Note: Words substituted in subparagraph (c) from 13 December 2012 subject to savings for applications made before that date (HC 760).

Section E-BPILR: Eligibility for indefinite leave to remain as a bereaved partner

E-BPILR.1.1. To meet the eligibility requirements for indefinite leave to remain as a bereaved partner all of the requirements of paragraphs E-BPILR1.2. to [1.4.] must be met.

Note: Figures substituted from 13 December 2012 subject to savings for applications made before that date (HC 760).

E-BPILR.1.2. The applicant's last grant of limited leave must have been as—

(a) a partner (other than a fiancé(e) or proposed civil partner) of a British Citizen or a person settled in the UK; or

(b) a bereaved partner.

E-BPILR.1.3. The person who was the applicant's partner at the time of the last grant of limited leave as a partner must have died.

E-BPILR.1.4. At the time of the partner's death the relationship between the applicant and the partner must have been genuine and subsisting and each of the parties must have intended to live permanently with the other in the UK.

E-BPILR.1.5. . . .

Note: Paragraph E-BPILR.1.5 deleted from 13 December 2012 subject to savings for applications made before that date (HC 760).

Section D-BPILR: Decision on application for indefinite leave to remain as a bereaved partner

D-BPILR.1.1. If the applicant meets all of the requirements for indefinite leave to remain as a bereaved partner the applicant will be granted indefinite leave to remain.

D-BPILR.1.2. If the applicant does not meet the requirements for indefinite leave to remain as a bereaved partner only because [paragraph S-ILR.1.5. or S-ILR.1.6. applies], the applicant will be granted further limited leave to remain for a period not exceeding 30 months, and subject to a condition of no recourse to public funds.

Note: Words substituted from 13 December 2012 subject to savings for applications made before that date (HC 760).

D-BPILR.1.3. If the applicant does not meet the requirements for indefinite leave to remain as a bereaved partner, or limited leave to remain as a bereaved partner under paragraph D-BPILR.1.2., the application will be refused.

Victim of domestic violence

Section DVILR: Indefinite leave to remain (settlement) as a victim of domestic violence

DVILR.1.1. The requirements to be met for indefinite leave to remain in the UK as a victim of domestic violence are that—

(a) the applicant must be in the UK;

(b) the applicant must have made a valid application for indefinite leave to remain as a victim of domestic violence;

(c) the applicant must not fall for refusal under any of the grounds in [Section S-ILR: Suitability – indefinite leave to remain]; and

(d) the applicant must meet all of the requirements of Section E-DVILR: Eligibility for indefinite leave to remain as a victim of domestic violence.

Note: Words substituted in subparagraph (c) from 13 December 2012 subject to savings for applications made before that date (HC 760).

Section E-DVILR: Eligibility for indefinite leave to remain as a victim of domestic violence

E-DVILR.1.1. To meet the eligibility requirements for indefinite leave to remain as a victim of domestic violence all of the requirements of paragraphs E-DVILR.1.2. [and 1.3.] must be met.

Note: Words substituted from 13 December 2012 subject to savings for applications made before that date (HC 760).

E-DVILR.1.2. [The applicant's first grant of limited leave under this Appendix must have been as a partner (other than a fiancé(e) or proposed civil partner) of a British Citizen or a person settled in the UK under paragraph D-ECP.1.1., D LTRP.1.1. or D-LTRP.1.2. of this Appendix and any subsequent grant of limited leave must have been:]

(a) granted as a partner (other than a fiancé(e) or proposed civil partner) of a British Citizen or a person settled in the UK under paragraph D-ECP.1.1., D LTRP.1.1. or D-LTRP.1.2. of this Appendix; or

(b) granted to enable access to public funds pending an application under DVILR and the preceding grant of leave was granted as a partner (other than a fiancé(e) or proposed civil partner) of a British Citizen or a person settled in the UK under paragraph D-ECP.1.1., D-LTRP.1.1. or D-LTRP.1.2. of this Appendix; or

(c) granted under paragraph D-DVILR.1.2.

Note: Opening words substituted and subparagraphs (a) and (b) substituted fom 6 November 2014 (HC 693).

E-DVILR.1.3. The applicant must provide evidence that during the last period of limited leave as a partner [of a British Citizen or a person settled in the UK under paragraph D-ECP.1.1., D-LTRP.1.1. or D-LTRP.1.2. of this Appendix] the applicant's relationship with their partner broke down permanently as a result of domestic violence.

Note: Words inserted from 6 November 2014 (HC 693).

E-DVILR.1.4.

Note: Paragraph E-DVILR.1.4 deleted from 13 December 2012 subject to savings for applications made before that date (HC 760).

Section D-DVILR: Decision on application for indefinite leave to remain as a victim of domestic violence

D-DVILR.1.1. If the applicant meets all of the requirements for indefinite leave to remain as a victim of domestic violence the applicant will be granted indefinite leave to remain.

D-DVILR.1.2. If the applicant does not meet the requirements for indefinite leave to remain as a victim of domestic violence only because [paragraph S-ILR.1.5. or S-ILR.1.6. applies], the applicant will be granted further limited leave to remain for a period not exceeding 30 months.

Note: Words substituted from 13 December 2012 subject to savings for applications made before that date (HC 760).

D-DVILR.1.3. If the applicant does not meet the requirements for indefinite leave to remain as a victim of domestic violence, or further limited leave to remain under paragraph D-DVILR.1.2. the application will be refused.

Family life as a child of a person with limited leave as a partner or parent

This route is for a child whose parent is applying for entry clearance or leave, or who has limited leave, as a partner or parent. For further provision on a child seeking to enter or remain in the UK for the purpose of their family life see Part 8 of these Rules.

Section EC-C: Entry clearance as a child

EC-C.1.1. The requirements to be met for entry clearance as a child are that—

(a) the applicant must be outside the UK;

(b) the applicant must have made a valid application for entry clearance as a child;

(c) the applicant must not fall for refusal under any of the grounds in Section S-EC: Suitability for entry clearance; and

(d) the applicant must meet all of the requirements of Section E-ECC: Eligibility for entry clearance as a child.

Section E-ECC: Eligibility for entry clearance as a child

E-ECC.1.1. To meet the eligibility requirements for entry clearance as a child all of the requirements of paragraphs E-ECC.1.2. to 2.4. must be met.

Relationship requirements

E-ECC.1.2. The applicant must be under the age of 18 at the date of application.

E-ECC.1.3. The applicant must not be married or in a civil partnership.

E-ECC.1.4. The applicant must not have formed an independent family unit.

E-ECC.1.5. The applicant must not be leading an independent life.

E-ECC.1.6. One of the applicant's parents must be in the UK with limited leave to enter or remain, or be applying, or have applied, for entry clearance, as a partner or a parent under this Appendix (referred to in this section as the "applicant's parent"), [and]

(a) the applicant's parent's partner under Appendix FM is also a parent of the applicant; or

(b) the applicant's parent has had and continues to have sole responsibility for the child's upbringing; or

(c) there are serious and compelling family or other considerations which make exclusion of the child undesirable and suitable arrangements have been made for the child's care.

Note: Subparagraphs (a)–(c) inserted from 13 December 2012 (HC 760).

Financial requirement

E-ECC.2.1. The applicant must provide specified evidence, from the sources listed in paragraph E-ECC.2.2., of—

(a) a specified gross annual income of at least—

(i) £18,600;

(ii) an additional £3,800 for the first child; and

(iii) an additional £2,400 for each additional child; alone or in combination with

(b) specified savings of

(i) £16,000; and

(ii) additional savings of an amount equivalent to 2.5 times the amount which is the difference between the gross annual income from the sources listed in paragraph E-ECC.2.2.(a)–(f) and the total amount required under paragraph E-ECC.2.1.(a); or

(c) the requirements in paragraph E-ECC.2.3. being met.

In this paragraph "child" means the applicant and any other dependent child of the applicant's parent who is—

(a) under the age of 18 years, or who was under the age of 18 years when they were first granted entry under this route;

(b) in the UK;

(c) not a British Citizen or settled in the UK; and

(d) not an EEA national with a right to remain in the UK under the Immigration (EEA) Regulations 2006.

E-ECC.2.2. When determining whether the financial requirement in paragraph EECC. 2.1. is met only the following sources may be taken into account—

(a) income of the applicant's parent's partner from specified employment or self-employment, which, in respect of an applicant's parent's partner returning to the UK with the applicant, can include specified employment or self-employment overseas and in the UK;

(b) income of the applicant's parent from specified employment or self employment if they are in the UK unless they are working illegally;

(c) specified pension income of the applicant's parent and that parent's partner;

(d) any specified maternity allowance or bereavement benefit received by the applicant's parent and that parent's partner in the UK [or any specified payment relating to service in HM Forces received by the applicant's parent and that parent's partner];

(e) other specified income of the applicant's parent and that parent's partner;

(f) income from the sources at (b), (d) or (e) of a dependent child of the applicant's parent under paragraph E-ECC.2.1. who is aged 18 years or over; and

(g) specified savings of the applicant's parent, that parent's partner and a dependent child of the applicant's parent under paragraph E-ECC.2.1. who is aged 18 years or over.

Note: Words inserted in subparagraph (d) from 1 December 2013 (HC 803).

E-ECC.2.3. The requirements to be met under this paragraph are—

(a) the applicant's parent's partner must be receiving one or more of the following—

(i) disability living allowance;

(ii) severe disablement allowance;

(iii) industrial injury disablement benefit;

(iv) attendance allowance; . . .

(v) carer's allowance; . . .

(vi) personal independence payment; . . .

(vii) Armed Forces Independence Payment or Guaranteed Income Payment under the Armed Forces Compensation Scheme; or

(viii) Constant Attendance Allowance, Mobility Supplement or War Disablement Pension under the War Pensions Scheme; and

(b) the applicant must provide evidence that their parent's partner is able to maintain and accommodate themselves, the applicant's parent, the applicant and any dependants adequately in the UK without recourse to public funds.

Note: Word 'or' deleted from subparagraph (a)(iv) and word 'or' inserted in subparagraph (a)(v) (subsequently deleted) and subparagraph (a)(vi) inserted from 6 April 2013 (HC 1039). Word 'or' deleted from subparagraph (a)(v) and word 'and' deleted from subparagraph (a)(vi) and subparagraphs (a)(vii) and (a)(viii) inserted from 1 December 2013 (HC 803).

E-EEC.2.4. The applicant must provide evidence that there will be adequate accommodation, without recourse to public funds, for the family, including other family members who are not included in the application but who live in the same household, which the family own or occupy exclusively: accommodation will not be regarded as adequate if—

(a) it is, or will be, overcrowded; or

(b) it contravenes public health regulations.

Section D-ECC: Decision on application for entry clearance as a child

D-ECC.1.1. If the applicant meets the requirements for entry clearance as a child they will be granted entry clearance of a duration which will expire at the same time as the leave granted to the applicant's parent, and subject to a condition of no recourse to public funds.

D-ECC.1.2. If the applicant does not meet the requirements for entry clearance as a child the application will be refused.

[Section R-LTRC]: Requirements for leave to remain as a child

Note: Words in heading substituted from 13 December 2012 subject to savings for applications made before that date (HC 760).

[R-LTRC.1.1.] The requirements to be met for leave to remain as a child are that—

(a) the applicant must be in the UK;

(b) the applicant must have made a valid application for leave to remain as a child; [and either]

(c) (i) the applicant must not fall for refusal under any of the grounds in Section S-LTR: Suitability – leave to remain; and

(ii) the applicant meets all of the requirements of Section E-LTRC: Eligibility for leave to remain as a child; or

(d) (i) the applicant must not fall for refusal under any of the grounds in Section S-LTR: Suitability – leave to remain; and

(ii) the applicant meets the requirements of paragraphs E-LTRC.1.2.–1.6.; and

(iii) a parent of the applicant has been or is at the same time being granted leave to remain under paragraph D-LTRP.1.2. or D-LTRPT.1.2. or indefinite leave to remain under this Appendix (except as an adult dependent relative).

Note: Paragraph number amended and subparagraphs (c) and (d) and words preceding them substituted from 13 December (HC 760).

Section E-LTRC: Eligibility for leave to remain as a child

E-LTRC.1.1. To qualify for limited leave to remain as a child all of the requirements of paragraphs E-LTRC.1.2. to 2.4. must be met [(except where paragraph R-LTRC.1.1.(d) (ii) applies)].

Note: Words inserted from 13 December 2012 (HC 760).

Relationship requirements

E-LTRC.1.2. The applicant must be under the age of 18 at the date of application or when first granted leave as a child under this route.

E-LTRC.1.3. The applicant must not be married or in a civil partnership.

E-LTRC.1.4. The applicant must not have formed an independent family unit.

E-LTRC.1.5. The applicant must not be leading an independent life.

E-LTRC.1.6. One of the applicant's parents (referred to in this section as the "applicant's parent") must be in the UK and have leave to enter or remain or indefinite leave to remain, or is at the same time being granted leave to remain or indefinite leave to remain, under this Appendix (except as an adult dependent relative), and

(a) the applicant's parent's partner under Appendix FM is also a parent of the applicant; or

(b) the applicant's parent has had and continues to have sole responsibility for the child's upbringing or the applicant normally lives with this parent and not their other parent; or

(c) there are serious and compelling family or other considerations which make exclusion of the child undesirable and suitable arrangements have been made for the child's care.

Note: Paragraph E-LTRC.1.6. substituted from 13 December 2012 (HC 760).

Financial requirements

E-LTRC.2.1. The applicant must provide specified evidence, from the sources listed in paragraph E-LTRC.2.2., of—

(a) a specified gross annual income of at least—

(i) £18,600;

(ii) an additional £3,800 for the first child; and

(iii) an additional £2,400 for each additional child; alone or in combination with

(b) specified savings of—

(i) £16,000; and

(ii) additional savings of an amount equivalent to 2.5 times (or if the parent is applying for indefinite leave to remain 1 times) the amount which is the difference between the gross annual income from the sources listed in paragraph E-LTRC.2.2.(a)–(f) and the total amount required under paragraph E-LTRC.2.1.(a); or

(c) the requirements in paragraph E-LTRC.2.3. being met.

In this paragraph "child" means the applicant and any other dependent child of the applicant's parent who is—

(i) under the age of 18 years, or who was under the age of 18 years when they were first granted entry under this route;

(ii) in the UK;

(iii) not a British Citizen or settled in the UK; and

(iv) not an EEA national with a right to remain in the UK under the Immigration (EEA) Regulations 2006.

E-LTRC.2.2. When determining whether the financial requirement in paragraph ELTRC. 2.1. is met only the following sources may be taken into account—

(a) income of the applicant's parent's partner from specified employment or self-employment;

(b) income of the applicant's parent from specified employment or self employment;

(c) specified pension income of the applicant's parent and that parent's partner;

(d) any specified maternity allowance or bereavement benefit received by the applicant's parent and that parent's partner in the UK [or any specified payment relating to service in HM Forces received by the applicant's parent and that parent's partner];

(e) other specified income of the applicant's parent and that parent's partner;

(f) income from the sources at (b), (d) or (e) of a dependent child of the applicant's parent under paragraph E-LTRC.2.1. who is aged 18 years or over; and

(g) specified savings of the applicant's parent, that parent's partner and a dependent child of the applicant's parent under paragraph E-ECC.2.1. who is aged 18 years or over.

Note: Words inserted in subparagraph (d) from 1 December 2013 (HC 803).

E-LTRC.2.3. The requirements to be met under this paragraph are—

(a) the applicant's parent's partner must be receiving one or more of the following—

(i) disability living allowance;

(ii) severe disablement allowance;

(iii) industrial injury disablement benefit;

(iv) attendance allowance; . . .

(v) carer's allowance; . . .

(vi) personal independence payment; . . .

(vii) Armed Forces Independence Payment or Guaranteed Income Payment under the Armed Forces Compensation Scheme; or

(viii) Constant Attendance Allowance, Mobility Supplement or War Disablement Pension under the War Pensions Scheme; and

(b) the applicant must provide evidence that their parent's partner is able to maintain and accommodate themselves, the applicant's parent, the applicant and any dependants adequately in the UK without recourse to public funds.

Note: Word 'or' deleted from subparagraph (a) (iv) and word 'or' inserted in subparagraph (a) (v) (subsequently deleted) and subparagraph (a) (vi) inserted from 6 April 2013 (HC 1039). Word 'or' deleted from subparagraph (a)(v) and word 'and' deleted from subparagraph (a)(vi) and subparagraphs (a)(vii) and (a)(viii) inserted from 1 December 2013 (HC 803).

E-LTRC.2.4. The applicant must provide evidence that there will be adequate accommodation in the UK, without recourse to public funds, for the family, including other family members who are not included in the application but who live in the same household, which the family own or occupy exclusively: accommodation will not be regarded as adequate if—

(a) it is, or will be, overcrowded; or

(b) it contravenes public health regulations.

Section D-LTRC: Decision on application for leave to remain as a child

D-LTRC.1.1. If the applicant meets the requirements for leave to remain as a child the applicant will be granted leave to remain of a duration which will expire at the same time as the leave granted to the applicant's parent, and subject to a condition of no recourse to public funds. [To qualify for indefinite leave to remain as a child of a person with indefinite leave to remain as a partner or parent, the applicant must meet the requirements of paragraph 298 of these rules.]

Note: Words substituted from 13 December 2012 (HC 760).

D-LTRC.1.2. If the applicant does not meet the requirements for leave to remain as a child the application will be refused.

Family life as a parent of a child in the UK

Section EC-PT: Entry clearance as a parent of a child in the UK

EC-PT.1.1. The requirements to be met for entry clearance as a parent are that—

(a) the applicant must be outside the UK;

(b) the applicant must have made a valid application for entry clearance as a parent;

(c) the applicant must not fall for refusal under any of the grounds in Section S-EC: Suitability–entry clearance; and

(d) the applicant must meet all of the requirements of Section E-ECPT: Eligibility for entry clearance as a parent.

Section E-ECPT: Eligibility for entry clearance as a parent

E-ECPT.1.1. To meet the eligibility requirements for entry clearance as a parent all of the requirements in paragraphs E-ECPT.2.1. to 4.2. must be met.

Relationship requirements

E-ECPT.2.1. The applicant must be aged 18 years or over.

E-ECPT.2.2. The child of the applicant must be—

(a) under the age of 18 years at the date of application;

(b) living in the UK; and

(c) a British Citizen or settled in the UK.

E-ECPT.2.3. Either—

(a) the applicant must have sole parental responsibility for the child; or

(b) the parent or carer with whom the child normally lives must be—

(i) a British Citizen in the UK or settled in the UK;

(ii) not the partner of the applicant; and

(iii) the applicant must not be eligible to apply for entry clearance as a partner under this Appendix.

E-ECPT.2.4.

(a) The applicant must provide evidence that they have either—

(i) sole parental responsibility for the child; or

(ii) access rights to the child; and

(b) The applicant must provide evidence that they are taking, and intend to continue to take, an active role in the child's upbringing.

Financial requirements

E-ECPT.3.1. The applicant must provide evidence that they will be able to adequately maintain and accommodate themselves and any dependants in the UK without recourse to public funds.

E-ECPT.3.2. The applicant must provide evidence that there will be adequate accommodation in the UK, without recourse to public funds, for the family, including other family members who are not included in the application but who live in the same household, which the family own or occupy exclusively: accommodation will not be regarded as adequate if—

(a) it is, or will be, overcrowded; or

(b) it contravenes public health regulations.

English language requirement

E-ECPT.4.1. The applicant must provide specified evidence that they—

(a) are a national of a majority English speaking country listed in paragraph GEN.1.6.;

(b) have passed an English language test in speaking and listening at a minimum of level A1 of the Common European Framework of Reference for Languages with a provider approved by the [Secretary of State];

(c) have an academic qualification recognised by [UK NARIC] to be equivalent to the standard of a Bachelor's or Master's degree or PhD in the UK, which was taught in English; or

(d) are exempt from the English language requirement under paragraph E-ECPT. 4.2.

Note: Words substituted in subparagraph (c) from 6 April 2013 (HC 1039). Words substituted in subparagraph (b) from 1 October 2013 (HC 628).

E-ECPT.4.2. The applicant is exempt from the English language requirement if at the date of application—

(a) the applicant is aged 65 or over;

(b) the applicant has a disability (physical or mental condition) which prevents the applicant from meeting the requirement; or

(c) there are exceptional circumstances which prevent the applicant from being able to meet the requirement prior to entry to the UK.

Section D-ECPT: Decision on application for entry clearance as a parent

D-ECPT.1.1. If the applicant meets the requirements for entry clearance as a parent they will be granted entry clearance for an initial period not exceeding 33 months, and subject to a condition of no recourse to public funds.

D-ECPT.1.2. If the applicant does not meet the requirements for entry clearance as a parent the application will be refused.

Section R-LTRPT: Requirements for limited leave to remain as a parent

R-LTRPT.1.1. The requirements to be met for limited or indefinite leave to remain as a parent or partner are—

(a) the applicant and the child must be in the UK;

(b) the applicant must have made a valid application for limited [or indefinite] leave to remain as a parent [or partner]; and either

(c) (i) the applicant must not fall for refusal under Section S-LTR: Suitability leave to remain; and

(ii) the applicant [meets] all of the requirements of Section ELTRPT: Eligibility for leave to remain as a parent, [or]

(iii) . . .

(d) (i) the applicant must not fall for refusal under S-LTR: Suitability leave to remain; and

(ii) the applicant meets the requirements of paragraphs E-LTRPT.2.2–2.4. and E-LTRPT.3.1.; and

(iii) paragraph EX.1. applies.

Note: Words inserted in subparagraph (b), words substituted in subparagraph (c)(ii) and subparagraph (c)(iii) deleted from 13 December 2012 (HC 760).

Section E-LTRPT: Eligibility for limited leave to remain as a parent

E-LTRPT.1.1. To qualify for limited leave to remain as a parent all of the requirements of paragraphs E-LTRPT.2.2. to 5.2. must be met.

Relationship requirements

E-LTRPT.2.2. The child of the applicant must be—

(a) under the age of 18 years at the date of application [, or where the child has turned 18 years of age since the applicant was first granted entry clearance or leave to remain as a parent under this Appendix, must not have formed an independent family unit or be leading an independent life];

(b) living in the UK; and

(c) a British Citizen or settled in the UK; or

(d) has lived in the UK continuously for at least the 7 years immediately preceding the date of application and paragraph EX.1. applies.

Note: Words inserted in subparagraph (a) from 13 December 2012 (HC 760).

E-LTRPT.2.3. Either—

(a) the applicant must have sole parental responsibility for the child [or the child normally lives with the applicant and not their other parent (who is a British Citizen or settled in the UK)]; or

(b) the parent or carer with whom the child normally lives must be—

(i) a British Citizen in the UK or settled in the UK;

(ii) not the partner of the applicant [(which here includes a person who has been in a relationship with the applicant for less than two years prior to the date of application)]; and

(iii) the applicant must not be eligible to apply for leave to remain as a partner under this Appendix.

Note: Words inserted in subparagraph (a) and subparagraph (b)(ii) from 13 December 2012 (HC 760).

E-LTRPT.2.4.

(a) The applicant must provide evidence that they have either—

(i) sole parental responsibility for the child [, or that the child normally lives with them]; or

(ii) access rights to the child; and

(b) The applicant must provide evidence that they are taking, and intend to continue to take, an active role in the child's upbringing.

Note: Words inserted in subparagraph (a)(i) from 13 December 2012 (HC 760).

Immigration status requirement

E-LTRPT.3.1. The applicant must not be in the UK—

(a) as a visitor; [or]

(b) with valid leave granted for a period of 6 months or less [, unless that leave was granted pending the outcome of family court or divorce proceedings];

(c) . . .

Note: Words inserted in subparagraph (b) from 13 December 2012 (HC 760). Word 'or' inserted at the end of subparagraph (a) and subparagraph (c) deleted from 28 July 2014; this amendment applies to all applications to which paragraphs 276ADE to 276DH and Appendix FM apply (or can be applied by virtue of the Immigration Rules), and to any other ECHR Article 8 claims (save for those from foreign criminals), and which are decided on or after that date (HC 532).

E-LTRPT.3.2. The applicant must not be in the UK—

(a) on temporary admission or temporary release, unless paragraph EX.1. applies; or

(b) in breach of immigration laws (disregarding any period of overstaying for a period of 28 days or less), unless paragraph EX.1. applies.

Note: Paragraph E-LTRPT.3.2. inserted from 28 July 2014; this amendment applies to all applications to which paragraphs 276ADE–276DH and Appendix FM apply (or can be applied by virtue of the Immigration Rules), and to any other ECHR Article 8 claims (save for those from foreign criminals), and which are decided on or after that date (HC 532).

Financial requirements

E-LTRPT.4.1. The applicant must provide evidence that they will be able to adequately maintain and accommodate themselves and any dependants in the UK without recourse to public funds, unless paragraph EX.1. applies.

E-LTRPT.4.2. The applicant must provide evidence that there will be adequate accommodation in the UK, without recourse to public funds, for the family, including other family members who are not included in the application but who live in the same household, which the family own or occupy exclusively, unless paragraph EX.1. applies: accommodation will not be regarded as adequate if—

(a) it is, or will be, overcrowded; or

(b) it contravenes public health regulations.

English language requirement

E-LTRPT.5.1. [If the applicant has not met the requirement in a previous application for leave as a parent or partner, the applicant] must provide specified evidence that they—

(a) are a national of a majority English speaking country listed in paragraph GEN.1.6.;

(b) have passed an English language test in speaking and listening at a minimum of level A1 of the Common European Framework of Reference for Languages with a provider approved by the [Secretary of State];

(c) have an academic qualification recognised by [UK NARIC] to be equivalent to the standard of a Bachelor's or Master's degree or PhD in the UK, which was taught in English; or

(d) are exempt from the English language requirement under paragraph E-LTRPT. 5.2., unless paragraph EX.1. applies.

Note: Words substituted in subparagraph (c) from 6 April 2013 (HC 1039). Words substituted in subparagraph (b) from 1 October 2013 (HC 628). Words substituted in the opening sentence from 6 April 2014 (HC 1138 as amended by HC 1201).

E-LTRPT.5.2. The applicant is exempt from the English language requirement if at the date of application—

(a) the applicant is aged 65 or over;

(b) the applicant has a disability (physical or mental condition) which prevents the applicant from meeting the requirement; or

(c) there are exceptional circumstances which prevent the applicant from being able to meet the requirement.

Section D-LTRPT: Decision on application for limited leave to remain as a parent

D-LTRPT.1.1. If the applicant meets the requirements in paragraph [R-]LTRPT.1.1.(a) to (c) for limited leave to remain as a parent the applicant will be granted limited leave to remain for a period not exceeding 30 months, and subject to a condition of no recourse to public funds, and they will be eligible to apply for settlement after a continuous period of at least 60 months with such leave or in the UK with entry clearance as a parent under paragraph D-ECPT.1.1.

Note: 'R-' inserted from 6 April 2014 (HC 1138 as amended by HC 1201).

D-LTRPT.1.2. If the applicant meets the requirements in paragraph [R-]LTRPT.1.1.(a), (b) and (d) for limited leave to remain as a parent they will be granted leave to remain for a period not exceeding 30 months [and subject to a condition of no recourse to public funds {unless the Secretary of State considers that the person should not be subject to such a condition},] and [they] will be eligible to apply for settlement after a continuous period of at least 120 months with such leave, with limited leave as a parent under paragraph D-LTRPT.1.1., or in the UK with entry clearance as a parent under paragraph D-ECPT.1.1.

Note: Words in square brackets inserted from 13 December 2013 (HC 760). 'R-' inserted from 6 April 2014 subject (HC 1138 as amended by HC 1201). Words in curly brackets substituted from 28 July 2014; this amendment applies to all applications to which paragraphs 276ADE–276DH and Appendix FM apply (or can be applied by virtue of the Immigration Rules), and to any other ECHR Article 8 claims (save for those from foreign criminals), and which are decided on or after that date (HC 532).

D-LTRPT.1.3. If the applicant does not meet the requirements for limited leave to remain as a parent the application will be refused.

Section R-ILRPT: Requirements for indefinite leave to remain (settlement) as a parent

R-ILRPT.1.1. The requirements to be met for indefinite leave to remain as a parent are that—

(a) the applicant must be in the UK;

(b) the applicant must have made a valid application for indefinite leave to remain as a parent;

(c) the applicant must not fall for refusal under any of the grounds in [Section S-ILR: Suitability – indefinite leave to remain];

(d) the applicant must meet all of the requirements of Section E-LTRPT: Eligibility for leave to remain as a parent; and

(e) the applicant must meet all of the requirements of Section E-ILRPT: Eligibility for indefinite leave to remain as a parent.

Note: Words substituted in subparagraph (c) from 13 December 2012 subject to savings for applications made before that date (HC 760).

Section E-ILRPT: Eligibility for indefinite leave to remain as a parent

E-ILRPT.1.1. To meet the eligibility requirements for indefinite leave to remain as a parent all of the requirements of paragraphs E-ILRPT.1.2. to 1.5. must be met.

E-ILRPT.1.2. The applicant must be in the UK with valid leave to remain as a parent (disregarding any period of overstaying for 28 days or less).

E-ILRPT.1.3. The applicant must have completed a continuous period of at least 60 months with limited leave as a parent under paragraph R-LTRPT.1.1.(a) to (c) or in the UK with entry clearance as a parent under paragraph D-ECPT.1.1.; or a continuous period of at least 120 months with limited leave as a parent, under paragraphs R-LTRPT.1.1(a), (b) and (d) or in the UK with entry clearance as a parent under paragraph D-ECPT.1.1.; or a continuous period of at least 120 months with limited leave as a parent under a combination of these paragraphs.

E-ILRPT.1.4. DELETED

Note: Paragraph E-ILRPT.1.4 deleted from 13 December 2012 subject to savings for applications made before that date (HC 760).

E-ILRPT.1.5. The applicant must have [demonstrated] sufficient knowledge of the English language and sufficient knowledge about life in the [United Kingdom] in accordance with the requirements of [Appendix KoLL] of these Rules.

Note: Words substituted from 28 October 2013 (HC 628).

Section D-ILRPT: Decision on application for indefinite leave to remain as a parent

D-ILRPT.1.1. If the applicant meets all of the requirements for indefinite leave to remain as a parent the applicant will be granted indefinite leave to remain.

D-ILRPT.1.2. If the applicant does not meet the requirements for indefinite leave to remain as a parent only for one or both of the following reasons—

(a) [paragraph S-ILR.1.5. or S-ILR.1.6. applies]; or

(b) the applicant has not demonstrated sufficient knowledge of the English language or about life in the United Kingdom in accordance with Appendix KoLL, the applicant will be granted further limited leave to remain as a parent for a period not exceeding 30 months, and subject to a condition of no recourse to public funds.

Note: Words substituted from 13 December 2012 subject to savings for applications made before that date (HC 760).

D-ILRPT.1.3. If the applicant does not meet [all the eligibility requirements for indefinite leave to remain as a parent, and does not qualify] for further limited leave to remain under paragraph D-ILRPT.1.2., the application will be refused, [unless the applicant meets the requirements in paragraph R-LTRPT.1.1.(a), (b) and (d) for limited leave to remain as a parent. Where they do,] the applicant will be granted further limited leave to remain as a parent for a period not exceeding 30 months under paragraph D-LTRPT.1.2. [and subject to a condition of no recourse to public funds {unless the Secreatry of State considers that the person should not be subject to such a condition}].

Note: Words in square brackets substituted from 13 December 2012 (HC 760). Words in curly brackets substituted from 28 July 2014; this amendment applies to all applications to which paragraphs 276ADE–276DH and Appendix FM apply (or can be applied by virtue of the Immigration Rules), and to any other ECHR Article 8 claims (save for those from foreign criminals), and which are decided on or after that date (HC 532).

Adult dependent relative

Section EC-DR: Entry clearance as an adult dependent relative

EC-DR.1.1. The requirements to be met for entry clearance as an adult dependent relative are that—

(a) the applicant must be outside the UK;

(b) the applicant must have made a valid application for entry clearance as an adult dependent relative;

(c) the applicant must not fall for refusal under any of the grounds in Section S-EC: Suitability for entry clearance; and

(d) the applicant must meet all of the requirements of Section E-ECDR: Eligibility for entry clearance as an adult dependent relative.

Section E-ECDR: Eligibility for entry clearance as an adult dependent relative

E-ECDR.1.1. To meet the eligibility requirements for entry clearance as an adult dependent relative all of the requirements in paragraphs E-ECDR.2.1. to 3.2. must be met.

Relationship requirements

E-ECDR.2.1. The applicant must be the—

(a) parent aged 18 years or over;

(b) grandparent;

(c) brother or sister aged 18 years or over; or

(d) son or daughter aged 18 years or over

of a person ("the sponsor") who is in the UK.

E-ECDR.2.2. If the applicant is the sponsor's parent or grandparent they must not be in a subsisting relationship with a partner unless that partner is also the sponsor's parent or grandparent and is applying for entry clearance at the same time as the applicant.

E-ECDR.2.3. The sponsor must at the date of application be—

(a) aged 18 years or over; and

(b) (i) a British Citizen in the UK; or

(ii) present and settled in the UK; or

(iii) in the UK with refugee leave or humanitarian protection.

E-ECDR.2.4. The applicant or, if the applicant and their partner are the sponsor's parents or grandparents, the applicant's partner, must as a result of age, illness or disability require long-term personal care to perform everyday tasks.

E-ECDR.2.5. The applicant or, if the applicant and their partner are the sponsor's parents or grandparents, the applicant's partner, must be unable, even with the practical and financial help of the sponsor, to obtain the required level of care in the country where they are living, because—

(a) it is not available and there is no person in that country who can reasonably provide it; or

(b) it is not affordable.

Financial requirements

E-ECDR.3.1. The applicant must provide evidence that they can be adequately maintained, accommodated and cared for in the UK by the sponsor without recourse to public funds.

E-ECDR.3.2. If the applicant's sponsor is a British Citizen or settled in the UK, the applicant must provide an undertaking signed by the sponsor confirming that the applicant will have no recourse to public funds, and that the sponsor will be responsible for their maintenance, accommodation and care, for a period of 5 years from the date the applicant enters the UK if they are granted indefinite leave to enter.

Section D-ECDR: Decision on application for entry clearance as an adult dependent relative

D-ECDR.1.1. If the applicant meets the requirements for entry clearance as an adult dependent relative of a British Citizen or person settled in the UK they will be granted indefinite leave to enter.

D-ECDR.1.2. If the applicant meets the requirements for entry clearance as an adult dependent relative and the sponsor has limited leave the applicant will be granted limited leave of a duration which will expire at the same time as the sponsor's limited leave, and subject to a condition of no recourse to public funds. If the sponsor applies for further limited leave, the applicant may apply for further limited leave of the same duration, if the requirements in EC-DR.1.1. (c) and (d) continue to be met, and subject to no recourse to public funds.

D-ECDR.1.3. If the applicant does not meet the requirements for entry clearance as an adult dependent relative the application will be refused.

Section R-ILRDR: Requirements for indefinite leave to remain as an adult dependent relative

R-ILRDR.1.1. The requirements to be met for indefinite leave to remain as an adult dependent relative are that—

(a) the applicant is in the UK;

(b) the applicant must have made a valid application for indefinite leave to remain as an adult dependent relative;

(c) the applicant must not fall for refusal under any of the grounds in [Section S-ILR: Suitability – indefinite leave to remain]; and

(d) the applicant must meet all of the requirements of Section E-ILRDR: Eligibility for indefinite leave to remain as an adult dependent relative.

Note: Words substituted in subparagraph (c) from 13 December 2012 subject to savings for applications made before that date (HC 760).

Section E-ILRDR: Eligibility for indefinite leave to remain as an adult dependent relative

E-ILRDR.1.1. To qualify for indefinite leave to remain as an adult dependent relative all of the requirements of paragraphs E-ILRDR.1.2. to [1.5.] must be met.

Note: Figures substituted from 13 December 2012 subject to savings for applications made before that date (HC 760).

E-ILRDR.1.2. The applicant must be in the UK with valid leave to remain as an adult dependent relative (disregarding any period of overstaying for a period of 28 days or less).

E-ILRDR.1.3. The applicant's sponsor must at the date of application be

(a) present and settled in the UK; or

(b) in the UK with refugee leave or as a person with humanitarian protection and have made an application for indefinite leave to remain.

E-ILRDR.1.4. The applicant must provide evidence that they can be adequately maintained, accommodated and cared for in the UK by the sponsor without recourse to public funds.

E-ILRDR.1.5. The applicant must provide an undertaking signed by the sponsor confirming that the applicant will have no recourse to public funds, and that the sponsor will be responsible for their maintenance, accommodation and care, for a period ending 5 years from the date the applicant entered the UK with limited leave as an adult dependent relative.

E-ILR DR.1.6. . . .

Note: Paragraph E-ILRDR.1.6. deleted from 13 December 2012 subject to savings for applications made before that date (HC 760).

Section D-ILRDR: Decision on application for indefinite leave to remain as an adult dependent relative

D-ILRDR.1.1. If the applicant meets the requirements for indefinite leave to remain as an adult dependent relative and the applicant's sponsor is settled in the UK, the applicant will be granted indefinite leave to remain as an adult dependent relative.

D-ILRDR.1.2. If the applicant does not meet the requirements for indefinite leave to remain as an adult dependent relative because [paragraph S-ILR.1.5. or S-ILR.1.6. applies], the applicant will be granted further limited leave to remain as an adult dependent relative for a period not exceeding 30 months, and subject to a condition of no recourse to public funds.

Note: Words substituted from 13 December 2012 subject to savings for applications made before that date (HC 760).

D-ILRDR.1.3. If the applicant's sponsor has made an application for indefinite leave to remain and that application is refused, the applicant's application for indefinite leave to remain will be refused. If the sponsor is granted limited leave, the applicant will be granted further limited leave as an adult dependent relative of a duration which will expire at the same time as the sponsor's further limited leave, and subject to a condition of no recourse to public funds.

D-ILRDR.1.4. Where an applicant does not meet the requirements for indefinite leave to remain, or further limited leave to remain under paragraphs D-ILRDR.1.2. or 1.3., the application will be refused.

Deportation and removal

Where the Secretary of State or an immigration officer is considering deportation or removal of a person who claims that their deportation or removal from the UK would be a breach of the right to respect for private and family life under Article 8 of the Human Rights Convention that person may be required to make an application under this Appendix or paragraph [276ADE(1)], but if they are not required to make an application Part 13 of these Rules will apply.

Note: '276ADE(1)' substituted from 6 November 2014 (HC 693).

Appendix FM-SE

Family members – specified evidence

Family Members – Specified Evidence

A. This Appendix sets out the specified evidence applicants need to provide to meet the requirements of rules contained in Appendix FM and, where those requirements are also contained in other rules [, including Appendix Armed Forces,] and unless otherwise stated, the specified evidence applicants need to provide to meet the requirements of those rules.

Note: Words inserted in paragraph A from1 December 2013 (HC 803).

B. Where evidence is not specified by Appendix FM, but is of a type covered by this Appendix, the requirements of this Appendix shall apply.

C. In this Appendix references to paragraphs are to paragraphs of this Appendix unless the context otherwise requires.

D. (a) In deciding an application in relation to which this Appendix states that specified documents must be provided, the Entry Clearance Officer or Secretary of State ("the decision-maker") will consider documents that have been submitted with the application, and will only consider documents submitted after the application where sub-paragraph (b) or (e) applies.

(b) If the applicant:

(i) Has submitted:

(aa) A sequence of documents and some of the documents in the sequence have been omitted (e.g. if one bank statement from a series is missing);

(bb) A document in the wrong format [(for example, if a letter is not on letter-head paper as specified)]; or

(cc) A document that is a copy and not an original document; or

(dd) A document which does not contain all of the specified information; or

(ii) Has not submitted a specified document,

the decision-maker may contact the applicant or his representative in writing or otherwise, and request the document(s) or the correct version(s). The material requested must be received . . . at the address specified in the request within a reasonable timescale specified in the request.

(c) The decision-maker will not request documents where he or she does not anticipate that addressing the error or omission referred to in sub-paragraph (b) will lead to a grant because the application will be refused for other reasons.

(d) If the applicant has submitted:

(i) A document in the wrong format; or

(ii) A document that is a copy and not an original document, or

(iii) A document that does not contain all of the specified information, but the missing information is verifiable from:

(1) other documents submitted with the application,

(2) the website of the organisation which issued the document, or

(3) the website of the appropriate regulatory body,

the application may be granted exceptionally, providing the decision-maker is satisfied that the document(s) is genuine and that the applicant meets the requirement to which the document relates. The decision-maker reserves the right to request the specified original document(s) in the correct format in all cases where sub-paragraph (b) applies, and to refuse applications if this material is not provided as set out in sub-paragraph (b).

(e) Where the decision-maker is satisfied that there is a valid reason why a specified document(s) cannot be supplied, e.g. because it is not issued in a particular country or has been permanently lost, he or she may exercise discretion not to apply the requirement for the document(s) or to request alternative or additional information or document(s) be submitted by the applicant.

(f) Before making a decision under Appendix FM or this Appendix, the decision-maker may contact the applicant or their representative in writing or otherwise to request further information or documents. The material requested must be received . . . at the address specified in the request within a reasonable timescale specified in the request.

Note: Paragraph D inserted from 13 December 2012 (HC 760). Subparagraph (f) inserted from 6 April 2013 (HC 1039). Words inserted in subparagraph (b)(i)(bb), subparagraph (b)(i)(dd) inserted, words deleted from subparagraph (b)(ii) and subparagraph (f) and subparagraph (d)(iii) inserted from 1 October 2013 (HC 628).

Evidence of Financial Requirements under Appendix FM

A1. To meet the financial requirement under paragraphs E-ECP.3.1., E-LTRP.3.1., E-ECC.2.1. and E-LTRC.2.1. of Appendix FM, the applicant must meet:

(a) The level of financial requirement applicable to the application under Appendix FM; and

(b) The requirements specified in Appendix FM and this Appendix as to:

(i) The permitted sources of income and savings;

(ii) The time periods and permitted combinations of sources applicable to each permitted source relied upon; and

(iii) The evidence required for each permitted source relied upon.

1. In relation to evidencing the financial requirements in Appendix FM the following general provisions shall apply:

(a) Bank statements must:

(i) be from a financial institution regulated by the appropriate regulatory body for the country in which that institution is operating.

(ii) not be from a financial institution on the list of excluded institutions in Appendix P of these rules.

(iii) in relation to personal bank statements be only in the name of:

(1) the applicant's partner, the applicant or both as appropriate; or

(2) if the applicant is a child the applicant parent's partner, the applicant's parent or both as appropriate; or

(3) if the applicant is an adult dependent relative, the applicant's sponsor or the applicant,

unless otherwise stated.

(iv) cover the period(s) specified.

(v) be:

(1) on official bank stationery; or

(2) electronic bank statements which are either accompanied by a letter from the bank on its headed stationery confirming that the documents are authentic or which bear the official stamp of the issuing bank on every page.

(aa) Where a bank statement is specified in this Appendix, a building society statement, a building society pass book, a letter from the applicant's bank or building society, or a letter from a financial institution regulated by the Financial Conduct Authority and the Prudential Regulation Authority or, for overseas accounts, the appropriate regulatory body for the country in which the institution operates and the funds are located, may be submitted as an alternative to a bank statement(s) provided that:

(1) the requirements in paragraph 1(a)(i)–(iv) are met as if the document were a bank statement; and

(2) a building society pass book must clearly show:

(i) the account number;

(ii) the building society's name and logo; and

(iii) the information required on transactions, funds held and time period(s) or as otherwise specified in this Appendix in relation to bank statements; and/or

(3) a letter must be on the headed stationery of the bank, building society or other financial institution and must clearly show:

(i) the account number;

(ii) the date of the letter;

(iii) the financial institution's name and logo; and

(iv) the information required on transactions, funds held and time period(s) or as otherwise specified in this Appendix in relation to bank statements.

(b) Promises of third party support will not be accepted. Third party support will only be accepted in the form of:

(i) payments from a former partner of the applicant for the maintenance of the applicant or any children of the applicant and the former partner, and payments from a former partner of the applicant's partner for the maintenance of that partner;

(ii) income from a dependent child who has turned 18, remains in the same UK household as the applicant and continues to be counted towards the financial requirement under Appendix FM;

(iii) gift of cash savings (whose source must be declared) evidenced at paragraph 1(a)(iii), provided that the cash savings have been held by the person or persons at paragraph 1(a)(iii) for at least 6 months prior to the date of application and are under their control; and

(iv) a maintenance grant or stipend associated with undergraduate study or postgraduate study or research.

(bb) Payslips must be:

(i) original formal payslips issued by the employer and showing the employer's name; or

(ii) accompanied by a letter from the employer, on the employer's headed paper and signed by a senior official, confirming the payslips are authentic;

(c) [Employment or self-employment income of an applicant] will only be taken into account if they are in the UK, aged 18 years or over and working legally, and prospective employment income will not be taken into account (except that of an applicant's partner or parent's partner who is returning to employment or self-employment in the UK at paragraphs E-ECP.3.2.(a) and E-ECC.2.2.(a) of Appendix FM).

(cc) The income of an applicant or sponsor working in the UK in salaried or non-salaried employment or in self-employment can include income from work undertaken overseas, provided paragraph E-LTRP.1.10 of Appendix FM and the other requirements of this Appendix are met.

(d) All income and savings must be lawfully derived.

(e) Savings must be held in cash.

(f) Income or cash savings in a foreign currency will be converted to pounds sterling using the closing spot exchange rate which appears on <www.oanda.com>* on the date of application.

(g) Where there is income or cash savings in different foreign currencies, each will be converted into pounds sterling before being added together, and then added to any UK income or savings to give a total amount.

(h) All documentary evidence must be original, unless otherwise stated.

(i) Evidence of profit from the sale of a business, property, investment, bond, stocks, shares or other asset will:

(i) not be accepted as evidence of income, but

(ii) the associated funds will be accepted as cash savings subject to the requirements of this Appendix and Appendix FM.

(j) Where any specified documents provided are not in English or Welsh, the applicant must provide the original and a full translation that can be independently verified by the Entry Clearance Officer, Immigration Officer or the Secretary of State. The translation must be dated and include:

(i) confirmation that it is an accurate translation of the original document;

(ii) the full name and original signature of the translator or an authorised official of the translation company;

(iii) the translator or translation company's contact details; and

(iv) if the applicant is applying for leave to remain or indefinite leave to remain, certification by a qualified translator and details of the translator or translation company's credentials.

(k) Where the gross (pre-tax) amount of any income cannot be properly evidenced, the net (post-tax) amount will be counted, including towards a gross income requirement.

(l) Where this Appendix requires the applicant to provide specified evidence relating to a period which ends with the date of application, that evidence, or the most recently dated part of it, must be dated no earlier than 28 days before the date of application.

(m) Cash income on which the correct tax has been paid may be counted as income under this Appendix, subject to the relevant evidential requirements of this Appendix.

(n) The gross amount of any cash income may be counted where the person's specified bank statements show the net amount which relates to the gross amount shown on their payslips (or in the relevant specified evidence provided in addition to the specified bank statements in relation to non-employment income). Otherwise, only the net amount shown on the specified bank statements may be counted.

(o) In this Appendix, a reference to the "average" is a reference to the mean average.

Note: Subparagraphs (a)(iv) and (a)(v) substituted, subparagraphs (aa) and (bb) inserted and what was subparagraph (k) deleted and what was subparagraph (l) renumbered as (k) from 13 December 2012 (HC 760). Words substituted in subparagraph (aa) from 1 July 2013 (HC 244). Words deleted from subparagraph (a)(v)(2), subparagraphs (bb) and (j) substituted and subparagraph (n) inserted from 1 October 2013 subject to savings for applications made before that date (HC 628). Subparagraph (b) substituted, subparagraph (m) inserted and subparagraph (n) renumbered as (o) from 6 April 2014 (HC 1138 as amended by HC 1201). Words substituted in subparagraph (c) and subparagraph (cc) inserted from 6 November 2014 (HC 693).

2. In respect of salaried employment in the UK [(except where paragraph 9 applies)], all of the following evidence must be provided:

(a) [Payslips] covering:

(i) a period of 6 months prior to the date of application if the [person] has been employed by their current employer for at least 6 months (and where paragraph 13(b) of this Appendix does not apply); or

(ii) any period of salaried employment in the period of 12 months prior to the date of application if the [person] has been employed by their current employer for less than 6 months (or at least 6 months but the person does not rely on paragraph 13(a) of this Appendix), or in the financial year(s) relied upon by a self-employed person.

(b) A letter from the employer(s) who issued the [payslips] at paragraph 2(a) confirming:

(i) the person's employment and gross annual salary;

(ii) the length of their employment;

(iii) the period over which they have been or were paid the level of salary relied upon in the application; and

(iv) the type of employment (permanent, fixed-term contract or agency).

(c) Personal bank statements corresponding to the same period(s) as the [payslips] at paragraph 2(a), showing that the salary has been paid into an account in the name of the person or in the name of the person and their partner jointly.

(d) Where the person is a director of a limited company based in the UK, evidence that the company is not of a type specified in paragraph 9(a). This can include the latest Annual Return filed at Companies House.

Note: Paragraph 2 substituted from 13 December 2012 (HC 760). Words inserted in the opening sentence, words substituted in subparagraphs (a)(i) and (a)(ii) and subparagraph (d) inserted from 6 April 2013 (HC 1039). Words substituted in subparagraphs (a), (b) and (c) from 1 October 2013 (HC 628).

2A. (i) In respect of salaried employment in the UK (paragraph 2 of this Appendix), statutory or contractual maternity, paternity, adoption or sick pay in the UK (paragraph 5 or 6 of this Appendix), or a director's salary paid to a self-employed person (paragraph 9 of this Appendix), the applicant may, in addition to the payslips and personal bank statements required under that paragraph, submit the P60 for the relevant period(s) of employment relied upon (if issued). If they do not, the Entry Clearance Officer or Secretary of State may grant the application if otherwise satisfied that the requirements of this Appendix relating to that employment are met. The Entry Clearance Officer or Secretary of State may request that the applicant submit the document(s) in accordance with paragraph D of this Appendix.

(ii) In respect of salaried employment in the UK (paragraph 2 of this Appendix), or statutory or contractual maternity, paternity, adoption or sick pay in the UK (paragraph 5 or 6 of this Appendix), the applicant may, in addition to the letter from the employer(s) required under that paragraph, submit a signed contract of employment. If they do not, the Entry Clearance Officer or Secretary of State may grant the application if otherwise satisfied that the requirements of this Appendix relating to that employment are met. The Entry Clearance Officer or Secretary of State may request that the applicant submit the document(s) in accordance with paragraph D of this Appendix.

Note: Paragraph 2A inserted from 13 December 2012 (HC 760). Words substituted from 1 October 2013 (HC 628).

3. In respect of salaried employment outside of the UK, evidence should be a reasonable equivalent to that set out in paragraph 2 [and (where relevant) paragraph 2A]. {In respect of an equity partner whose income from the partnership is treated as salaried employment under paragraph 17, the payslips and employer's letter referred to in paragraph 2 may be replaced by other evidence providing the relevant information in paragraph 2 (which may include, but is not confined to, a letter on official stationery from an accountant, solicitor or business manager acting for the partnership).}

Note: Words in square brackets inserted from 1 October 2013 (HC 628). Words in curly brackets inserted from 6 November 2014 (HC 693).

4. In respect of a job offer in the UK (for an applicant's partner or parent's partner returning to salaried employment in the UK at paragraphs E-ECP.3.2.(a) and E-ECC.2.2.(a) of Appendix FM) a letter from the employer must be provided:

(a) confirming the job offer, the gross annual salary and the starting date of the employment which must be within 3 months of the applicant's partner's return to the UK; or

(b) enclosing a signed contract of employment, which must have a starting date within 3 months of the applicant's partner's return to the UK.

5. In respect of statutory or contractual maternity, paternity or adoption pay . . . all of the following [, and in respect of parental leave in the UK only the evidence at paragraph 5(c),] must be provided:

(a) Personal bank statements corresponding to the same period(s) as the [payslips] at paragraph 5(b), showing that the salary has been paid into an account in the name of the person or in the name of the person and their partner jointly.

(b) [Payslips] covering:

(i) a period of 6 months prior to [the date of application or to] the commencement of the maternity, paternity or adoption leave, if the applicant has been employed by their current employer for at least 6 months [(and where paragraph 13(b) does not apply)]; or

(ii) any period of salaried employment in the period of 12 months prior to [the date of application or to] the commencement of the maternity, paternity or adoption leave, if the applicant has been employed by their current employer for less than 6 months (or at least 6 months but the person does not rely on paragraph 13(a)).

(c) A letter from the employer confirming:

(i) the length of the person's employment;

(ii) the gross annual salary and the period over which it has been paid at this level;

(iii) the entitlement to maternity, paternity [, parental] or adoption leave; and

(iv) the date of commencement and the end-date of the maternity [, paternity,] parental or adoption leave.

Note: Subparagraph (a) substituted from 13 December 2012 (HC 760). Words inserted in the opening sentence, in subparagraphs (b)(i), (b)(ii), (c)(iii) and (c)(iv) from 6 April 2013 (HC 1039). Words substituted in subparagraphs (a) and (b) from 1 October 2013 (HC 628). Words deleted from opening sentence from 6 April 2014 (HC 1138 as amended by HC 1201).

6. In respect of statutory or contractual sick pay in the UK all of the following must be provided:

(a) Personal bank statements corresponding to the same period(s) as the [payslips] at paragraph 6(b), showing that the salary has been paid into an account in the name of the person or in the name of the person and their partner jointly.

(b) [Payslips] covering:

(i) a period of 6 months prior to [the date of application or to] the commencement of the sick leave, if the applicant has been employed by their current employer for at least 6 months [(and where paragraph 13(b) does not apply)]; or,

(ii) any period of salaried employment in the period of 12 months prior to [the date of application or to] the commencement of the sick leave, if the applicant has been employed by their current employer for less than 6 months [(or at least 6 months but the person does not rely on paragraph 13(a))].

(c) A letter from employer confirming:

(i) the length of the person's employment;

(ii) the gross annual salary and the period over which it has been paid at this level;

(iii) that the person is in receipt of statutory or contractual sick pay; and

(iv) the date of commencement of the sick leave.

Note: Subparagraph (a) substituted from 13 December 2012 (HC 760).Words inserted in subparagraphs (b)(i) and (b)(ii) from 6 April 2013 (HC 1039). Words substituted in subparagraphs (a) and (b) from 1 October 2013 (HC 628).

7. In respect of self-employment in the UK as a partner, as a sole trader or in a franchise all of the following must be provided:

(a) Evidence of the amount of tax payable, paid and unpaid for the last [full] financial year.

(b) The following documents for the last full financial year, or for the last two such years (where those documents show the necessary level of gross income as an average of those two years):

(i) annual self-assessment tax return to HMRC (a copy or print-out); and

(ii) Statement of Account (SA300 or SA302).

(c) Proof of registration with HMRC as self-employed [if available] . . .

(d) Each partner's Unique Tax Reference Number (UTR) and/or the UTR of the partnership or business.

(e) Where the person holds or held a separate business bank account(s), . . . bank statements for the same 12-month period as the tax return(s).

(f) . . . personal bank statements for the same 12-month period as the tax return(s) showing that the income from self-employment has been paid into an account in the name of the person or in the name of the person and their partner jointly.

(g) Evidence of ongoing self-employment through evidence of payment of Class 2 National Insurance contributions [, or (where the person has reached state pension age) through alternative evidence (which may include, but is not confined to, evidence of ongoing payment of business rates, business-related insurance premiums, employer National Insurance contributions or franchise payments to the parent company)].

(h) One of the following documents must also be submitted:

(i) (aa) If the {business} is required to produce annual audited accounts, [such accounts for the last full financial year]; or

(bb) If the . . . business is not required to produce annual audited accounts, [unaudited accounts for the last full financial year] and an accountant's certificate of confirmation, from an accountant who is a member of a UK Recognised Supervisory Body (as defined in the Companies Act 2006);

(ii) A certificate of VAT registration and the . . . VAT return [for the last full financial year] {(a copy or print-out)} confirming the VAT registration number, if turnover is in excess of [£79,000 or was in excess of the threshold which applied during the last full financial year];

(iii) Evidence to show appropriate planning permission or local planning authority consent is held to operate the type/class of business at the trading address (where this is a local authority requirement); or

(iv) A franchise agreement signed by both parties.

(i) The document referred to in paragraph 7(h)(iv) must be provided if the organisation is a franchise.

Note: Words inserted in and deleted from subparagraph (c), words deleted from subparagraphs (e) and (f), subparagraph (h)(i) substituted and words in curly brackets in subparagraph (h)(ii) inserted from 13 December 2012 (HC 760). Subparagraph (g) substituted, word in curly brackets substituted in subparagraph (h)(i)(aa) and words deleted from subparagraph (h)(i)(bb) from 6 April 2013 (HC 1039). Words inserted in subparagraph (a), subparagraph (b) substituted, words substituted in subparagraphs (h)(i)(aa) and (h)(i)(bb), and words deleted from and inserted/substituted in subparagraph (h)(ii) from 6 April 2014 (HC 1138 as amended by HC 1201). Words inserted in subparagraph (g) from 6 November 2014 (HC 693).

8. In respect of self-employment outside of the UK, evidence should be a reasonable equivalent to that set out in paragraph 7.

9. In respect of income from employment and/or shares in a limited company based in the UK of a type specified in paragraph 9(a), the requirements of paragraph 9(b)–(d) shall apply in place of the requirements of paragraphs 2 and 10(b).

(a) The specified type of limited company is one in which:

(i) the person is a director of the company (or another company within the same group); and

(ii) shares are held (directly or indirectly) by the person, their partner or the following family members of the person or their partner: parent, grandparent, child, stepchild, grandchild, brother, sister, uncle, aunt, nephew, niece or first cousin; and

(iii) any remaining shares are held (directly or indirectly) by fewer than five other persons.

(b) All of the following must be provided:

(i) Company Tax Return CT600 (a copy or print-out) for the last full financial year and evidence this has been filed with HMRC, such as electronic or written acknowledgment from HMRC.

(ii) Evidence of registration with the Registrar of Companies at Companies House.

(iii) If the company is required to produce annual audited accounts, [such accounts for the last full financial year].

(iv) If the company is not required to produce annual audited accounts, [unaudited accounts for the last full financial year] and an accountant's certificate of confirmation, from an accountant who is a member of a UK Recognized Supervisory Body (as defined in the Companies Act 2006).

(v) Corporate/business bank statements covering the same 12-month period as the Company Tax Return CT600.

(vi) A current Appointment Report from Companies House.

(vii) One of the following documents must also be provided:

(1) A certificate of VAT registration and the . . . VAT return [for the last full financial year] (a copy or print-out) confirming the VAT registration number, if turnover is in excess of [£79,000 or was in excess of the threshold which applied during the last full financial year].

(2) Proof of ownership or lease of business premises.

(3) Original proof of registration with HMRC as an employer for the purposes of PAYE and National Insurance, proof of PAYE reference number and Accounts Office reference number. This evidence may be in the form of a certified copy of the documentation issued by HMRC.

(c) Where the person is listed as a director of the company and receives a salary from the company, all of the following documents must also be provided:

(i) Payslips and P60 (if issued) covering the same period as the Company Tax Return CT600.

(ii) Personal bank statements covering the same 12-month period as the Company Tax Return CT600 showing that the salary as a director was paid into an account in the name of the person or in the name of the person and their partner jointly.

(d) Where the person receives dividends from the company, all of the following documents must also be provided:

(i) Dividend vouchers for all dividends declared in favour of the person during or in respect of the period covered by the Company Tax Return CT600 showing the company's and the person's details with the person's net dividend amount and tax credit.

(ii) Personal bank statement(s) showing that those dividends were paid into an account in the name of the person or in the name of the person and their partner jointly.

Note: Paragraph 9 substituted from 6 April 2013 (HC 1039). Words substituted in subparagraph (c)(i) from 1 October 2013 (HC 628). Words substituted in subparagraph (b)(iii) and (b)(iv) and words deleted from and substituted in subparagraph (b)(vii)(1) from 6 April 2014 (HC 1138 as amended by HC 1201).

10. In respect of non-employment income all the following evidence, in relation to the form of income relied upon, must be provided:

(a) To evidence property rental income:

(i) Confirmation that the person or the person and their partner jointly own the property for which the rental income is received, through:

(1) A copy of the title deeds of the property or of the title register from the Land Registry (or overseas equivalent); or

(2) A mortgage statement.

(ii) . . . personal bank statements for the 12-month period prior to the date of application showing the rental income was paid into an account in the name of the person or of the person and their partner jointly.

(iii) A rental agreement or contract.

(b) To evidence dividends [(except where paragraph 9 applies)] or other income from investments, stocks, shares, bonds or trust funds:

(i) A certificate showing proof of ownership and the amount(s) of any investment(s).

(ii) A portfolio report (for a financial institution regulated by [the Financial Conduct Authority (and the Prudential Regulation Authority where applicable)] in the UK) {or a dividend voucher showing the company and person's details with the person's net dividend amount and tax credit}.

(iii) . . . personal bank statements for the 12-month period prior to the date of application showing that the income relied upon was paid into an account in the name of the person or of the person and their partner jointly.

(iv) Where the person is a director of a limited company based in the UK, evidence that the company is not of a type specified in paragraph 9(a). This can include the latest Annual Return filed at Companies House.

(c) To evidence interest from savings:

(i) . . . personal bank statements for the 12-month period prior to the date of application showing the amount of the savings held and that the interest was paid into an account in the name of the person or of the person and their partner jointly.

(d) To evidence maintenance payments (from a former partner of the applicant to maintain their and the applicant's child or children or the applicant, or from a former partner of the applicant's partner to maintain the applicant's partner):

(i) Evidence of a maintenance agreement through any of the following:

(1) A court order;

(2) Written voluntary agreement; or

(3) Child Support Agency documentation.

(ii) . . . personal bank statements for the 12-month period prior to the date of application showing the income relied upon was paid into an account in the name of the applicant.

(e) To evidence a pension:

(i) Official documentation from:

(1) [The Department for Work and Pensions] (in respect of the Basic State Pension and the Additional or Second State Pension) {or other government department or agency}[, including the Veterans Agency];

(2) An overseas pension authority; or

(3) A pension company,

confirming pension entitlement and amount.

(ii) At least one . . . personal bank statement in the 12-month period prior to the date of application showing payment of the pension into the person's account.

(iii) For the purposes of sub-paragraph (i), War Disablement Pension, War Widow's/Widower's Pension and any other pension or equivalent payment for life made under the War Pensions Scheme, the Armed Forces Compensation Scheme or the Armed Forces Attributable Benefits Scheme may be treated as a pension, unless excluded under paragraph 21 of this Appendix.

(f) To evidence UK Maternity Allowance, Bereavement Allowance, Bereavement Payment and Widowed Parent's Allowance:

(i) Department for Work and Pensions documentation confirming the person or their partner is or was in receipt of the benefit in the 12-month period prior to the date of application.

(ii) . . . personal bank statements for the 12-month period prior to the date of application showing the income was paid into the person's account.

(ff) Subject to paragraph 12, to evidence payments under the War Pensions Scheme, the Armed Forces Compensation Scheme or the Armed Forces Attributable Benefits Scheme which are not treated as a pension for the purposes of paragraph 10(e)(i):

(i) Veterans Agency or Department for Work and Pensions documentation in the form of an award notification letter confirming the person or their partner is or was in receipt of the payment at the date of application.

(ii) personal bank statements for the 12-month period prior to the date of application showing the income was paid into the person's account.

(g) To evidence a maintenance grant or stipend (not a loan) associated with undergraduate study or postgraduate study or research:

(i) Documentation from the body or company awarding the grant or stipend confirming that the person is currently in receipt of the grant or stipend or will be within 3 months of the date of application, confirming that the grant or stipend will be paid for a period of at least 12 months [or for at least one full academic year] from the date of application or from the date on which payment of the grant or stipend will commence, and confirming the annual amount of the grant or stipend. [Where the grant or stipend is or will be paid on a tax-free basis, the amount of the gross equivalent may be counted as income under this Appendix.]

(ii) . . . personal bank statements for any part of the 12-month period prior to the date of the application during which the person has been in receipt of the grant or stipend showing the income was paid into the person's account.

(h) To evidence ongoing insurance payments (such as, but not exclusively, payments received under an income protection policy):

(i) documentation from the insurance company confirming:

(a) that in the 12 months prior to the date of application the person has been in receipt of insurance payments and the amount and frequency of the payments.

(b) the reason for the payments and their expected duration.

(c) that, provided any relevant terms and conditions continue to be met, the payment(s) will continue for at least the 12 months following the date of application.

(ii) personal bank statements for the 12-month period prior to the date of application showing the insurance payments were paid into the person's account.

(i) To evidence ongoing payments (other than maintenance payments under paragraph 10(d)) arising from a structured legal settlement (such as, but not exclusively, one arising from settlement of a personal injury claim):

(i) documentation from a court or the person's legal representative confirming:

(a) that in the 12 months prior to the date of application the person has been in receipt of structured legal settlement payments and the amount and frequency of those payments.

(b) the reason for the payments and their expected duration.

(c) that the payment(s) will continue for at least the 12 months following the date of application.

(ii) personal bank statements for the 12-month period prior to the date of application showing the payments were paid into the person's account, either directly or via the person's legal representative.

Note: Subparagraph (a)(i)(1) substituted, words deleted from subparagraphs (a)(ii), (b)(iii), (c)(i), (d)(ii), (e)(ii), (f)(ii) and (g)(ii) and words substituted in subparagraph (e)(i)(1) from 13 December 2012 (HC 760). Words inserted in subparagraph (b), words in curly brackets inserted in subparagraph (b)(ii), subparagraph (b)(iv) inserted and words inserted at the end of subparagraph (g)(i) from 6 April 2013 (HC 1039). Words substituted in subparagraph (b)(ii) and words in curly brackets inserted in subparagraph (e)(i)(1) from 1 July 2013 (HC 244). Words in square brackets in subparagraph (e)(i)(1) inserted and subparagraphs (e)(iii) and (ff) inserted from 1 December 2013 (HC 803). Words inserted in subparagraph (d) and subparagraphs (h) and (i) inserted from 6 April 2014 (HC 1138 as amended by HC 1201). Words inserted in subparagraph (g) from 6 November 2014 (HC 693).

11. In respect of cash savings the following must be provided:

(a) personal bank statements showing that at least the level of cash savings relied upon in the application has been held in an account(s) in the name of the person or of the person and their partner jointly throughout the period of 6 months prior to the date of application.

(b) A declaration by the account holder(s) of the source(s) of the cash savings.

Note: Subparagraph (a) from 1 October 2013 (HC 628).

11A. In respect of cash savings:

(a) The savings may be held in any form of bank/savings account [(whether a deposit or investment account)], provided that the account allows the savings to be accessed immediately (with or without a penalty for withdrawing funds without notice). This can include . . . savings held in a pension savings account which can be immediately withdrawn.

(b) Paid out competition winnings or a legacy which has been paid can contribute to cash savings.

(c) Funds held as cash savings by the applicant, their partner or both jointly at the date of application can have been transferred from investments, stocks, shares, bonds or trust funds within the period of 6 months prior to the date of application, provided that:

(i) The funds have been in the ownership and under the control of the applicant, their partner or both jointly for at least the period of 6 months prior to the date of application.

(ii) The ownership of the funds in the form of investments, stocks, shares, bonds or trust funds; the cash value of the funds in that form at or before the beginning of the period of 6 months prior to the date of application; and the transfer of the funds into cash, are evidenced by a portfolio report or other relevant documentation from a financial institution regulated by the appropriate regulatory body for the country in which that institution is operating.

(iii) The requirements of this Appendix in respect of the cash savings held at the date of application are met, except that the period of . . . 6 months prior to the date of application in paragraph 11(a) will be reduced by the amount of that period in which the relevant funds were held in the form of investments, stocks, shares, bonds or trust funds.

(iv) For the purposes of sub-paragraph 11A(c), "investments" includes funds held in an investment account which does not meet the requirements of paragraphs and 11A(a).

(d) Funds held as cash savings by the applicant, their partner or both jointly at the date of application can be from the proceeds of the sale of property, in the form only of a dwelling, other building or land, which took place within the period of 6 months prior to the date of application, provided that:

(i) The property (or relevant share of the property) was owned at the beginning of the period of 6 months prior to the date of application and at the date of sale by the applicant, their partner or both jointly.

(ii) Where ownership of the property was shared with a third party, only the proceeds of the sale of the share of the property owned by the applicant, their partner or both jointly may be counted.

(iii) The funds deposited as cash savings are the net proceeds of the sale, once any mortgage or loan secured on the property (or relevant share of the property) has been repaid and once any taxes and professional fees associated with the sale have been paid.

(iv) The decision-maker is satisfied that the requirements in sub-paragraphs (i)–(iii) are met on the basis of information and documents submitted in support of the application. These may include for example:

(1) Registration information or documentation (or a copy of this) from the Land Registry (or overseas equivalent).

(2) A letter from a solicitor (or other relevant professional, if the sale takes place overseas) instructed in the sale of the property confirming the sale price and other relevant information.

(3) A letter from a lender (a bank or building society) on its headed stationery regarding the repayment of a mortgage or loan secured on the property.

(4) Confirmation of payment of taxes or professional fees associated with the sale.

(5) Any other relevant evidence that the requirements in subparagraphs (i)–(iii) are met.

(v) The requirements of this Appendix in respect of the cash savings held at the date of application are met, except that the period of 6 months mentioned in paragraph

11(a) will be reduced by the amount of time which passed between the start of that 6-month period and the deposit of the proceeds of the sale in an account mentioned in paragraph 11(a).

Note: Subparagraph (c) inserted from 6 April 2013 (HC 1039). Words deleted from subparagraph (a) from 1 July 2013 (HC 244). Words inserted in subparagraph (a), words deleted from subparagraph (c)(iii) and subparagraph (d) inserted from 1 October 2013 (HC 628). Subparagraph (c)(iv) inserted from 6 November 2014 (HC 693).

12. Where [a person] is in receipt of Carer's Allowance, Disability Living Allowance, Severe Disablement Allowance, Industrial Injuries Disablement Benefit . . ., Attendance Allowance {or Personal Independence Payment} [or Armed Forces Independence Payment or Guaranteed Income Payment under the Armed Forces Compensation Scheme or Constant Attendance Allowance, Mobility Supplement or War Disablement Pension under the War Pensions Scheme,] all the following must be provided:

(a) Official documentation from the Department for Work and Pensions [or Veterans Agency] confirming [the current entitlement and the amount currently received]

(b) At least one . . . personal bank statement in the 12-month period prior to the date of application showing [payment of the amount of the benefit or allowance to which the person is currently entitled into their account].

Note: Words deleted from sub-paragraph (b) from 13 December 2012 (HC 760). Words deleted from and words in curly brackets in opening sentence inserted from 6 April 2013 (HC 1039). Words substituted and inserted in opening sentence and words inserted in subparagraph (a) from 1 December 2013 (HC 803). Words substituted in subparagraphs (a) and (b) from 6 November 2014 (HC 693).

12A. Where the financial requirement the applicant must meet under Appendix FM relates to adequate maintenance, paragraphs 2 to 12 apply only to the extent and in the manner specified by this paragraph. Where such a financial requirement applies, the applicant must provide the following evidence:

(a) Where the current salaried employment in the UK of the applicant or their partner, parent, parent's partner or sponsor is relied upon:

(i) A letter from the employer confirming the employment, the gross annual salary and the annual salary after income tax and National Insurance contributions have been paid, how long the employment has been held, and the type of employment (permanent, fixed-term contract or agency).

(ii) [Payslips] covering the period of 6 months prior to the date of application or such shorter period as the current employment has been held.

(iii) . . . personal bank statement covering the same period as the [payslips], showing that the salary has been paid into an account in the name of the person or in the name of the person and their partner jointly.

(b) Where statutory or contractual maternity, paternity, adoption or sick pay in the UK of the applicant or their partner, parent, parent's partner or sponsor are relied upon, paragraph 5(b)(i) and (c) or paragraph 6(b)(i) and (c) apply as appropriate.

(c) Where self-employment in the UK of the applicant or their partner, parent, parent's partner or sponsor [, or income from employment and/or shares in a limited company based in the UK of a type to which paragraph 9 applies,] is relied upon, paragraph 7 or 9 applies as appropriate.

(d) Where the non-employment income of the applicant or their partner, parent, parent's partner or sponsor is relied upon, paragraph 10 applies and paragraph 10 shall apply as if it referred to any UK welfare benefit or tax credit relied upon and to HMRC as well as Department for Work and Pensions [or other official] documentation.

(e) Where the cash savings of the applicant or their partner, parent, parent's partner or sponsor are relied upon, paragraphs 11 and 11A apply.

(f) The monthly housing and Council Tax costs for the accommodation in the UK in which the applicant (and any other family members who are or will be part of the same household) lives or will live if the application is granted.

(g) Where the applicant is an adult dependent relative applying for entry clearance, the applicant must in addition provide details of the care arrangements in the UK planned for them by their sponsor (which can involve other family members in the UK), of the cost of these arrangements and of how that cost will be met by the sponsor.

Note: Words deleted from sub-paragraph (a)(iii) from 13 December 2012 (HC 760). Words inserted in subparagraph (c) from 6 April 2013 (HC 1039). Words substituted in subparagraphs (a)(ii) and (a)(iii) from 1 October 2013 (HC 628). Words inserted in subparagraph (d) from 1 December 2013 (HC 803).

12B. Where the financial requirement an applicant must meet under Part 8 (excluding an applicant who is a family member of a Relevant Points Based System Migrant) or under Appendix FM relates to adequate maintenance and where cash savings are relied upon to meet the requirement in full or in part, the decision-maker will:

(a) Establish the total cash savings which meet the requirements of paragraphs 11 and 11A;

(b) Divide this figure by the number of weeks of limited leave which would be issued if the application were granted, or by 52 if the application is for indefinite leave to enter or remain;

(c) Add the figure in sub-paragraph 12B(b) to the weekly net income (before the deduction of housing costs) available to meet the requirement.

Note: Paragraph 12B inserted from 6 November 2014 (HC 693).

Calculating Gross Annual Income under Appendix FM

13. Based on evidence that meets the requirements of this Appendix, and can be taken into account with reference to the applicable provisions of Appendix FM, gross annual income under paragraphs E-ECP.3.1., E-LTRP.3.1., E-ECC.2.1. and E-LTRC.2.1. will be calculated in the following ways:

(a) Where the person is in salaried employment in the UK at the date of application . . . , has been employed by their current employer for at least 6 months [and has been paid throughout the period of 6 months prior to the date of application at a level of gross annual salary which equals or exceeds the level relied upon in paragraph 13(a)(i),] their gross annual income will be {(where paragraph 13(b) does not apply)} the total of:

(i) [The level of gross annual salary relied upon in the application];

(ii) The gross amount of any specified non-employment income (other than pension income) received by them or their partner in the 12 months prior to the date of application; and

(iii) The gross annual income from a UK or foreign State pension or a private pension received by them or their partner.

(b) Where the person is in salaried employment in the UK at the date of application and has been employed by their current employer for less than 6 months [(or at least 6 months but the person does not rely on paragraph 13(a)),] their gross annual income will be the total of:

(i) The gross annual salary from employment as it was at the date of application;

(ii) The gross amount of any specified non-employment income (other than pension income) received by them or their partner in the 12 months prior to the date of application; and

(iii) The gross annual income from a UK or foreign State pension or a private pension received by them or their partner.

In addition, the requirements of paragraph 15 must be met.

(c) Where the person is the applicant's partner, is in salaried employment outside of the UK at the date of application, has been employed by their current employer for at least 6 months, and is returning to the UK to take up salaried employment in the UK starting within 3 months of their return, the person's gross annual income will be calculated:

(i) On the basis set out in paragraph 13(a); and also

(ii) On that basis but substituting for the gross annual salary at paragraph 13(a)(i) the gross annual salary in the salaried employment in the UK to which they are returning.

(d) Where the person is the applicant's partner, has been in salaried employment outside of the UK within 12 months of the date of application, and is returning to the UK to take up salaried employment in the UK starting within 3 months of their return, the person's gross annual income will be calculated:

(i) On the basis set out in paragraph 13(a) but substituting for the gross annual salary at paragraph 13(a)(i) the gross annual salary in the salaried employment in the UK to which they are returning; and also

(ii) On the basis set out in paragraph 15(b).

(e) Where the person is self-employed, their gross annual income will be the total of their gross income from their self-employment, [from any salaried or non-salaried employment they have had or their partner has had (if their partner is in the UK with permission to work),] from specified non-employment income received by them or their partner, and from income from a UK or foreign State pension or a private pension received by them or their partner, in the last full financial year or as an average of the last two full financial years. {The requirements of this Appendix for specified evidence relating to these forms of income shall apply as if references to the date of application were references to the end of the relevant financial year(s).} [The relevant financial year(s) cannot be combined with any financial year(s) to which paragraph 9 applies and vice versa.]

(f) Where the person is self-employed, they cannot combine their gross annual income at paragraph 13(e) with specified savings in order to meet the level of income required under Appendix FM.

(g) Where the person is not relying on income from salaried employment or self-employment, their gross annual income will be the total of:

(i) The gross amount of any specified non-employment income (other than pension income) received by them or their partner in the 12 months prior to the date of application; and

(ii) The gross annual income from a UK or foreign State pension or a private pension received by them or their partner.

(h) Where the person is the applicant's partner and is in self-employment outside the UK at the date of application and is returning to the UK to take up salaried employment in the UK starting within 3 months of their return, the person's gross annual income will be calculated:

(i) On the basis set out in paragraph 13(a) but substituting for the gross annual salary at paragraph 13(a)(i) the gross annual salary in the salaried employment in the UK to which they are returning; and also

(ii) On the basis set out in paragraph 13(e).

(i) Any period of unpaid maternity, paternity, adoption, parental or sick leave in the 12 months prior to the date of application will not be counted towards any period relating to employment, or any period relating to income from employment, for which this Appendix provides.

(j) The provisions of paragraph 13 which apply to self-employment and to a person who is self-employed also apply to income from employment and/or shares in a limited company based in the UK of a type to which paragraph 9 applies and to a person in receipt of such income.

(k) Where the application relies on the employment income of the applicant and the sponsor, all of that income must be calculated either under sub-paragraph 13(a) or under sub-paragraph 13(b) and paragraph 15, and not under a combination of these methods.

Note: Words in curly brackets in subparagraphs (a) and (e) inserted and words in square brackets in subparagraph (b) inserted from13 December 2012 (HC 760). Word deleted from and words inserted in subparagraph (a), words substituted in subparagraph (a)(i), words inserted at the end of subparagraph (e) and subparagraphs (h)–(j) inserted from 6 April 2013 (HC 1039). Words substituted in subparagraph (e) from 6 April 2014 (HC 1138 as amended by HC 1201). Subparagraph (k) inserted from 6 November 2014 (HC 693).

14. Where the requirements of this Appendix and Appendix FM are met by the combined income or cash savings of more than one person, the income or the cash savings must only be counted once unless stated otherwise.

15. In respect of paragraph 13(b) and paragraph 13(d), the provisions in this paragraph also apply:

(a) In order to evidence the level of gross annual income required by Appendix FM, the person must meet the requirements in paragraph 13(b) or paragraph 13(d)(i); and

(b) The person must also meet the level of gross annual income required by Appendix FM on the basis that their income is the total of:

(i) The gross income from salaried employment [in the UK or overseas] earned by the person in the 12 months prior to the date of application;

(ii) The gross amount of any specified non-employment income (other than pension income) received by the person or their partner in the 12 months prior to the date of application;

(iii) The gross amount received from a UK or foreign State pension or a private pension by the person or their partner in the 12 months prior to the date of application; and

(iv) The person cannot combine the gross annual income at paragraph 15(b)(i)–(iii) with specified savings in order to meet the level of income required.

Note: Words inserted in subparagraph (b)(i) from 6 April 2013 (HC 1039).

16. Where a person is in receipt of maternity, paternity, adoption or sick pay [or has been so in the 6 months prior to the date of application,] this paragraph applies:

(a) the relevant date for considering the length of employment with their current employer will be the date that the maternity, paternity, adoption or sick leave commenced [or] the date of application; and

(b) the relevant period for calculating income from their salaried employment will be the period prior to the commencement of the maternity, paternity, adoption or sick pay [or to] the date of application.

Note: Words inserted in the opening sentence and words substituted in subparagraphs (a) and (b) from 6 April 2013 (HC 1039).

17. If a person is an equity partner, for example in a law firm, the income they draw from the partnership will be treated as salaried employment for the purposes of this Appendix and Appendix FM.

17A. Where a person is a subcontractor under the Construction Industry Scheme administered by HMRC and does not rely on paragraph 13(e), the income they receive as a subcontractor under the Construction Industry Scheme may be treated as income from salaried employment for the purposes of this Appendix and Appendix FM. In that case, the requirements for specified evidence in paragraph 2 must be met, subject to applying those requirements so as to reflect the person's status as a subcontractor under the Construction Industry Scheme.

Note: Paragraph 17A inserted from 1 October 2013 (HC 628).

18. When calculating income from salaried employment under paragraphs 12A and 13 to 16, this paragraph applies:

(a) Basic pay, skills-based allowances, and UK location-based allowances will be counted as income provided that:

(i) They are contractual; and

(ii) Where these allowances make up more than 30% of the total salary, only the amount up to 30% is counted.

(b) Overtime, commission-based pay and bonuses [(which can include tips and gratuities paid via a tronc scheme registered with HMRC)] will be counted as income {, where they have been received in the relevant period(s) of employment or self-employment relied upon in the application.}

(bb) In respect of a person in salaried employment at the date of application, the amount of income in sub-paragraph (b) which may be added to their gross annual salary, and counted as part of that figure for the purposes of paragraph 13(a)(i) or 13(b)(i), is the annual equivalent of the person's average gross monthly income from that income in their current employment in the 6 months prior to the date of application.

(c) UK and overseas travel, subsistence and accommodation allowances, and allowances relating to the cost of living overseas will not be counted as income.

(d) Gross income from non-salaried employment will be calculated on the same basis as income from salaried employment, except as provided in paragraph 18(e) and 18(f), and the requirements of this Appendix for specified evidence relating to salaried employment shall apply as if references to salary were references to income from non-salaried employment. Non-salaried employment includes that paid at an hourly or other rate [(and the number and/or pattern of hours required to be worked may vary)], or paid an amount which varies according to the work undertaken [, whereas salaried employment includes that paid at a minimum fixed rate (usually annual) and is subject usually to a contractual minimum number of hours to be worked].

(e) For the purpose of paragraph 13(a)(i), in respect of a person in non-salaried employment at the date of application "the level of gross annual salary relied upon in the application" shall be no greater than the annual equivalent of the person's average gross monthly income from non-salaried employment in the 6 months prior to the date of application, where that employment was held throughout that period.

(f) For the purpose of paragraph 13(b)(i), "the gross annual salary from employment as it was at the date of application" of a person in non-salaried employment at the date of application shall be considered to be the annual equivalent of the person's average gross monthly income from non-salaried employment in the 6 months prior to the date of application, regardless of whether that employment was held throughout that period.

(g) For the purpose of paragraphs 13(c)(ii) and 13(d)(i), "the gross annual salary in the salaried employment in the UK to which they are returning" of a person who is returning to the UK to take up non-salaried employment in the UK starting within 3 months of their return is the gross annual income from that employment, based on the rate or amount of pay, and the standard or core hours of work, set out in the document(s) from the employer provided under paragraph 4. Notwithstanding paragraph 18(b), this may include the gross "on-target" earnings which may be expected from satisfactory performance in the standard or core hours of work.

Note: Subparagraphs (d)–(f) substituted from 6 April 2013 (HC 1039). Words in curly brackets in sub-paragraph (b) inserted, sub-paragraphs (bb) and (g) inserted and words in sub-paragraph (d) inserted from 1 October 2013 (HC 628). Words inserted in sub-paragraph (b) from 6 April 2014 (HC 1138 as amended by HC 1201). Subparagraph (k) inserted from 6 November 2014 (HC 693).

19. When calculating income from self-employment under paragraphs 12A and 13(e) [, and in relation to income from employment and/or shares in a limited company based in the UK of a type to which paragraph 9 applies, this paragraph applies]:

(a) There must be evidence of ongoing self-employment [, and (where income from salaried employment is also relied upon or where paragraph 9(c) applies) ongoing employment,] at the date of application.

(b) Where the self-employed person is a sole trader or is in a partnership or franchise agreement, the income will be:

(i) the gross taxable profits from their share of the business; and

(ii) allowances or deductable expenses which are not taxed will not be counted towards income.

(c) Where [income to which paragraph 19 applies] is being used to meet the financial requirement for an initial application for leave to remain as a partner under Appendix FM by an applicant who used such income to meet that requirement in an application for entry clearance as a fiancé(e) or proposed civil partner under that Appendix in the last 12 months, the Secretary of State may continue to accept the same level and evidence of [income to which paragraph 19 applies] that was accepted in granting the application for entry clearance, provided that there is evidence of ongoing self-employment [, and (where income from salaried employment is also relied upon or where paragraph 9(c) applies) ongoing employment,] at the date of the application for leave to remain.

(d) The financial year(s) to which paragraph 7 refers is the period of the last full financial year(s) to which the required Statement(s) of Account (SA300 or SA302) relates.

(e) The financial year(s) to which paragraph 9 refers is the period of the last full financial year(s) to which the required Company Tax Return(s) CT600 relates.

Note: Words inserted in opening sentence, words inserted in sub-paragraph (a), original subparagraph (c) deleted and original subparagraph (d) (which had been inserted by HC 760 from 13 December 2012) renumbered as (c), words substituted in what is now subparagraph (c) and new subparagraphs (d) and (e) inserted from 6 April 2013 (HC 1039).

20. When calculating income from specified non-employment sources under paragraphs 12A and 13 to 15, this paragraph applies:

(a) Assets or savings must be in the name of the person, or jointly with their partner.

(b) Any asset or savings on which income is based must be held or owned by the person at the date of application.

(c) Any rental income from property, in the UK or overseas, must be from a property that is:

(i) owned by the person;

(ii) not their main residence [and will not be so if the application is granted, except in the circumstances specified in paragraph 20(e)]; and

(iii) if ownership of the property is shared with a third party, only income received from their share of the property can be counted.

(cc) The amount of rental income from property received before any management fee was deducted may be counted.

(d) Equity in a property cannot be used to meet the financial requirement.

(e) Where the applicant and their partner are resident outside the UK at the date of application, rental income from a property in the UK that will become their main residence if the application is granted may only be counted under paragraph 13(c)(i) and paragraph 13(d)(ii).

(f) Any future entitlement to a maintenance grant or stipend of the type specified in paragraph 10(g) may be counted as though the person had received the annual amount of that grant or stipend in the 12 months prior to the date of application.

Note: Subparagraph (cc) inserted from 13 December 2012 (HC 760). Words inserted in subparagraph (c)(ii) and subparagraphs (e) and (f) inserted from 6 April 2013 (HC 1039).

20A. When calculating the gross annual income from pension under paragraph 13, the gross annual amount of any pension received may be counted where the pension has become a source of income at least 28 days prior to the date of application.

21. When calculating income under paragraphs 13 to 16, the following sources will not be counted:

(a) Loans and credit facilities.

(b) Income-related benefits: Income Support, income-related Employment and Support Allowance, Pension Credit, Housing Benefit, Council Tax Benefit and income-based Jobseeker's Allowance.

(c) The following contributory benefits: contribution-based Jobseeker's Allowance, contribution-based Employment and Support Allowance and Incapacity Benefit.

(cc) Unemployability Allowance, Allowance for a Lowered Standard of Occupation and Invalidity Allowance under the War Pension Scheme.

(d) Child Benefit.

(e) Working Tax Credit.

(f) Child Tax Credit.

(g) Any other source of income not specified in this appendix.

Note: Subparagraph (cc) inserted from 1 December 2013 (HC 803).

Evidence of Marriage or Civil Partnerships

22. A claim to have been married in the United Kingdom must be evidenced by a marriage certificate.

23. A claim to be divorced in the United Kingdom must be evidenced by a decree absolute from a civil court.

24. A civil partnership in the United Kingdom must be evidenced by a civil partnership certificate.

25. The dissolution of a civil partnership in the UK must be evidenced by a final order of civil partnership dissolution from a civil court.

26. Marriages, civil partnerships or evidence of divorce or dissolution from outside the UK must be evidenced by a reasonable equivalent to the evidence detailed in paragraphs 22 to 25, valid under the law in force in the relevant country.

Evidence of the Applicant Living Overseas with a Crown Servant

26A. Where.

(a) An applicant for entry clearance, limited leave to enter or remain or indefinite leave to remain as a partner under Appendix FM (except as a fiancé(e) or proposed civil partner) intends to enter or remain in the UK to begin their probationary period (or has done so) and then to live outside the UK for the time being with their sponsor (or is doing so or has done so) before the couple live together permanently in the UK; and

(b) The sponsor, who is a British Citizen or settled in the UK, is a permanent member of HM Diplomatic Service or a comparable UK-based staff member of the British Council, the Department for International Development or the Home Office on a tour of duty outside the UK, the applicant must provide a letter on official stationery from the sponsor's head of mission confirming the information at (a) and (b) and confirming the start date and expected end date of the sponsor's tour of duty outside the UK.

Note: Paragraph 26A inserted from 6 November 2014 (HC 693).

Evidence of English Language Requirements

27. Evidence of passing an English language test in speaking and listening must take the form of either:

(a) a certificate [and/or other document(s) for the relevant test as specified in Appendix O] that:

(i) is from an English language test provider approved by the Secretary of State for these purposes as specified in Appendix O of these rules;

(ii) is a test approved by the Secretary of State for these purposes as specified in Appendix O of these rules:

(iii) shows the applicant's name;

(iv) shows the qualification obtained (which must meet or exceed level A1 of the Common European Framework of Reference); and

(v) shows the date of award.

or,

(b) a print out of the online score from a PTE (Pearson) test which:

(i) is a test approved by the Secretary of State for these purposes as specified in Appendix O of these rules;

(ii) can be used to show that the qualification obtained (which must meet or exceed level A1 of the Common European Framework of Reference); and,

(iii) is from an English language test provider approved by the Secretary of State for these purposes as specified in Appendix O of these rules.

Note: Words substituted in sub-paragraph (a) from 1 July 2013 (HC 244).

28. The evidence required to show that a person is a citizen or national of a majority English speaking country is a valid passport or travel document, unless paragraphs 29 and 30 apply. A dual national may invoke either of their nationalities.

29. If the applicant has not provided their passport or travel document other evidence of nationality can be supplied in the following circumstances only (as indicated by the applicant on their application form):

(a) where the passport {or travel document} has been lost or stolen;

(b) where the passport {or travel document} has expired and been returned to the relevant authorities; or

(c) where the passport {or travel document} is with another part of the [Home Office].

Note: Words in square brackets substituted in subparagraph (c) from 1 October 2013 (HC 628). Words in curly brackets inserted from 6 November 2014 (HC 693).

30. Alternative evidence as proof of nationality, if acceptable, must be either:

(a) A current national identity document; or

(b) An original letter from the applicant's [national government, Embassy or High Commission] confirming the applicant's full name, date of birth and nationality.

Note: Words in square brackets in subparagraph (b) substituted from 6 November 2014 (HC 693).

31. Evidence of an academic qualification (recognised by [UK NARIC] to be equivalent to the standard of a Bachelor's or Master's degree or PhD in the UK) and was taught in English must be either:

(a) A certificate issued by the relevant institution confirming the award of the academic qualification showing:

(i) the applicant's name;
(ii) the title of award;
(iii) the date of award;
(iv) the name of the awarding institution; and
(v) that the qualification was taught in English

or,

(b) If the applicant is awaiting graduation or no longer has the certificate and cannot get a new one, the evidence must be:

(i) an original academic reference from the institution awarding the academic qualification that;

(1) is on official letter headed paper;
(2) shows the applicant's name;
(3) shows the title of award;
(4) confirms that the qualification was taught in English;
(5) explains when the academic qualification has been, or will be awarded; and
(6) states either the date that the certificate will be issued (if the applicant has not yet graduated) or confirms that the institution is unable to re-issue the original certificate of award.

or

(ii) an original academic transcript that;

(1) is on official letter headed paper;
(2) shows the applicant's name;
(3) the name of the academic institution;
(4) the course title;
(5) confirms that the qualification was taught in English; and
(6) provides confirmation of the award.

Note: Words substituted from 6 April 2013 subject (HC 1039).

32. If the qualification was taken in one of the following countries, it will be assumed for the purpose of paragraph 31 that it was taught in English: Antigua and Barbuda, Australia, the Bahamas, Barbados, Belize, Dominica, Grenada, Guyana, Ireland, Jamaica, New Zealand, St Kitts and Nevis, St Lucia, St Vincent and the Grenadines, Trinidad and Tobago, the UK, the USA.

32A. For the avoidance of doubt paragraphs 27 to 32D of this Appendix apply to fiancé(e), proposed civil partner, spouse, civil partner, unmarried partner and same sex partner applications for limited leave to enter or remain made under Part 8 of these Rules where English language requirements apply, regardless of the date of application. Paragraphs 27 to 32D of this Appendix also apply to spouse, civil partner, unmarried partner and same sex partner applications which do not meet the requirements of Part 8 of these Rules for indefinite leave to remain (where the application is for indefinite leave to remain) and are being considered for a grant of limited leave to remain where paragraph A277A(b) of these Rules applies. Any references in paragraphs 27 to 32D of this Appendix to "limited leave to enter or remain" shall therefore be read as referring to all applicants referred to in this paragraph.

Note: Paragraphs 32A to 32D inserted from 6 November 2014 (HC 693).

32B. Where the decision-maker has:

(a) reasonable cause to doubt that an English language test in speaking and listening at a minimum of level A1 of the Common Framework of Reference for Languages relied on at any time to meet a requirement for limited leave to enter or remain in Part 8 or Appendix FM was genuinely obtained; or

(b) information that the test certificate or result awarded to the applicant has been withdrawn by the test provider for any reason,

the decision-maker may discount the document and the applicant must provide a new test certificate or result from an approved provider which shows that they meet the requirement, if they are not exempt from it.

Note: Paragraphs 32A to 32D inserted from 6 November 2014 (HC 693).

32C. If an applicant applying for limited leave to enter or remain under Part 8 or Appendix FM submits an English language test certificate or result which has ceased by the date of application to be:

(a) from an approved test provider, or

(b) in respect of an approved test,

the decision-maker will not accept that certificate or result as valid, unless the decision-maker does so in accordance with paragraph 32D of this Appendix and subject to any transitional arrangements made in respect of the test provider or test in question.

Note: Paragraphs 32A to 32D inserted from 6 November 2014 (HC 693).

32D. If an applicant applying for limited leave to enter or remain under Part 8 or Appendix FM submits an English language test certificate or result and the Home Office has already accepted it as part of a successful previous partner or parent application (but not where the application was refused, even if on grounds other than the English language requirement), the decision-maker may accept that certificate or result as valid if it is:

(a) from a provider which is no longer approved, or

(b) from a provider who remains approved but the test the applicant has taken with that provider is no longer approved, or

(c) past its validity date (if a validity date is required under Appendix O), provided that when the subsequent application is made:

(i) the applicant has had continuous leave (disregarding any period of overstaying of no more than 28 days) as a partner or parent since the Home Office accepted the test certificate as valid; and

(ii) the award to the applicant does not fall within the circumstances set out in paragraph 32B of this Appendix.

Note: Paragraphs 32A to 32D inserted from 6 November 2014 (HC 693).

Adult dependent relatives

33. Evidence of the family relationship between the applicant(s) and the sponsor should take the form of birth or adoption certificates, or other documentary evidence.

34. Evidence that, as a result of age, illness or disability, the applicant requires long-term personal care should take the form of:

(a) [Independent] medical evidence that the applicant's physical or mental condition means that they cannot perform everyday tasks; and

(b) This must be from a doctor or other health professional.

Note: Word inserted in sub-paragraph (a) from 6 April 2014 (HC 1138 as amended by HC 1201).

35. [Independent] evidence that the applicant is unable, even with the practical and financial help of the sponsor in the UK, to obtain the required level of care in the country where they are living should be from:

(a) a central or local health authority;

(b) a local authority; or

(c) a doctor or other health professional.

Note: Word inserted in from 6 April 2014 (HC 1138 as amended by HC 1201).

36. If the applicant's required care has previously been provided through a private arrangement, the applicant must provide details of that arrangement and why it is no longer available.

37. If the applicant's required level of care is not, or is no longer, affordable because payment previously made for arranging this care is no longer being made, the applicant must provide records of that payment and an explanation of why that payment cannot continue. If financial support has been provided by the sponsor or other close family in the UK, the applicant must provide an explanation of why this cannot continue or is no longer sufficient to enable the required level of care to be provided.

* This is an external website for which the Home Office is not responsible.

Appendix G

Countries and Territories participating in the Tier 5 Youth Mobility Scheme and annual allocations of places for 2015

Note: Appendix G substituted from 1 January 2015 (HC 693).

Places available for use by Countries and Territories with Deemed Sponsorship Status:

- Australia – 38,000 places
- Canada – 5,000 places
- Japan – 1,000 places
- New Zealand – 11,000 places
- Monaco – 1,000 places

Places available for use by Countries and Territories without Deemed Sponsorship Status:

- Taiwan – 1,000 places
- South Korea – 1,000 places
- Hong Kong – 1,000 places

Appendix H

Applicants who are subject to different documentary requirements under Tier 4 of the Points Based System

An applicant will be subject to different documentary requirements under Tier 4 of the Points Based System where he is a national of one of the following countries and he is applying for entry clearance in his country of nationality or leave to remain in the UK:

- Argentina
- Australia
- [Barbados]
- Botswana
- Brunei
- Canada
- Chile
- Japan
- Malaysia
- New Zealand
- [Oman]
- [Qatar]
- Singapore
- South Korea
- Trinidad and Tobago
- [United Arab Emirates]
- United States of America

Note: Barbados inserted in list and Croatia deleted from 1 October 2013 subject to savings for applications made before that date (HC 628). Oman, Qatar and United Arab Emirates inserted from 6 April 2014 subject to savings for applications made before that date (HC 1138 as amended by HC 1201).

Where an applicant is a dual national, and only one of their nationalities is listed above, he will be able to apply using the different documentary requirements that apply to these nationals, provided he is applying either for entry clearance in his country of nationality listed above or for leave to remain in the UK.

An applicant will be subject to different documentary requirements under Tier 4 of the Points Based System where he is the rightful holder of one of the following passports, which has been issued by the relevant competent authority, and where he is applying for leave to remain in the UK or for entry clearance in the territory related to the passport he holds:

- British National (Overseas)
- Hong Kong
- Taiwan (those who hold a passport issued by Taiwan that includes the number of the identification card issued by the competent authority in Taiwan).

Where an applicant is the rightful holder of a passport issued by a relevant competent authority listed above and also holds another passport or is the national of a country not listed above, he will be able to apply using the different documentary requirements that apply to rightful holders of those passports listed in this Appendix provided he is applying either for entry clearance in the territory related to the passport he holds or for leave to remain in the UK.

Appendix I

Pay requirements which the Secretary of State intends to apply to applications for indefinite leave to remain from Tier 2 (General) and Tier 2 (Sportspersons) migrants made on or after 6 April 2016

The Immigration Rules are subject to change and applicants will need to meet the Rules in force at the date of application. However, it is the Secretary of State's intention that these rules, as they relate to pay, will replace paragraph 245HF from that date.

245HF. Requirements for indefinite leave to remain as a Tier 2 (General) or Tier 2 (Sportsperson) Migrant

To qualify for indefinite leave to remain as a Tier 2 (General) Migrant or Tier 2 (Sportsperson) Migrant an applicant must meet the requirements listed below. If the applicant meets these requirements, indefinite leave to remain will be granted. If the applicant does not meet these requirements, the application will be refused.

Requirements:

(a) The applicant must not have one or more unspent convictions within the meaning of the Rehabilitation of Offenders Act 1974.

(b) The applicant must not fall for refusal under the general grounds for refusal, and must not be an illegal entrant.

(c) The applicant must have spent a continuous period of 5 years lawfully in the UK, in any combination of the following categories of which the most recent period must have been spent with leave as a Tier 2 Migrant either:

(i) as a Tier 1 Migrant, other than a Tier 1 (Post Study Work) Migrant,

(ii) as a Tier 2 (General) Migrant, a Tier 2 (Minister of Religion) Migrant or a Tier 2 (Sportsperson) Migrant.

(d) The Sponsor that issued the Certificate of Sponsorship that led to the applicant's last grant of leave must certify in writing:

(i) that he still requires the applicant for the employment in question, and

(ii) subject to sub-paragraph (iii), in the case of a Tier 2 (General) or Tier 2 (Sportsperson) Migrant applying for settlement, that they are being paid for the employment in question either:

(1) at or above the appropriate rate for the job, as stated in the the Codes of Practice in Appendix J, or

(2) a gross annual salary of at least:

(a) £35,000 if applying on or after 6 April 2016,

(b) £35,500 if applying on or after 6 April 2018,

(c) £35,800 if applying on or after 6 April 2019,

whichever is higher, where the appropriate rate or salary includes basic pay and allowances as set out in paragraph 79E or paragraph 100A of Appendix A.

(iii) where a Tier 2 (General) Migrant applying for settlement is recorded (at the time of application for settlement) by the Certificate of Sponsorship Checking Service as being sponsored to do a job that either:

(1) appears on the Shortage Occupation List in Appendix K, or has appeared on that list during any time the applicant was being sponsored to do that job and during the continuous period of 5 years referred to in paragraph (c) above, or

(2) appears on the occupations skilled to PhD-level as stated in the Codes of Practice in Appendix J, or has appeared on that list during any time the applicant was

being sponsored to do that job and during the continuous period of 5 years referred to in paragraph (c) above,

sub paragraph (d)(ii) does not apply and the Sponsor that issued the Certificate of Sponsorship for the employment in question must certify that the Tier 2 (General) migrant applying for Indefinite Leave to Remain is being paid at or above the appropriate rate for the job as stated in the Codes of Practice in Appendix J, where the appropriate rate or salary includes basic pay and allowances as set out in paragraph 79E of Appendix A.

(e) The applicant provides the specified documents in paragraph 245HF-SD to evidence the sponsor's certification in subsection (d)(ii).

(f) The applicant must have sufficient knowledge of the English language and sufficient knowledge about life in the United Kingdom, in accordance with paragraph 33BA of these Rules, unless the applicant is under the age of 18 or aged 65 or over at the time the application is made.

Note: Subparagraph (d)(ii)(d) substituted from 6 April 2014 subject to savings for applications made before that date (HC 1138 as amended by HC 1201).

245HG. Requirements for indefinite leave to remain as a Tier 2 (Minister of Religion) Migrant

To qualify for indefinite leave to remain as a Tier 2 (Minister of Religion) Migrant, an applicant must meet the requirements listed below. If the applicant meets these requirements, indefinite leave to remain will be granted. If the applicant does not meet these requirements, the application will be refused.

Requirements:

(a) The applicant must not have one or more unspent convictions within the meaning of the Rehabilitation of Offenders Act 1974.

(b) The applicant must not fall for refusal under the general grounds for refusal, and must not be an illegal entrant.

(c) The applicant must have spent a continuous period of 5 years lawfully in the UK, in any combination of the following categories of which the most recent period must have been spent with leave as a Tier 2 Migrant (Minister of Religion):

(i) as a Tier 1 Migrant, other than a Tier 1 (Post Study Work) Migrant, or

(ii) as a Tier 2 (General) Migrant, a Tier 2 (Minister of Religion) Migrant or a Tier 2 (Sportsperson) Migrant,

(d) The Sponsor that issued the Certificate of Sponsorship that led to the applicant's last grant of leave must certify in writing that he still requires the applicant for the employment in question, and

(e) The applicant must have sufficient knowledge of the English language and sufficient knowledge about life in the United Kingdom, in accordance with paragraph 33BA of these Rules, unless the applicant is under the age of 18 or aged 65 or over at the time the application is made.

2. *In Appendix A – Attributes, after 79D insert:*

79E. Appropriate salary for indefinite leave to remain

An applicant applying for Indefinite Leave to Remain under paragraph 245HF is expected to demonstrate that he is being paid either at or above the appropriate rate for the job, as stated in the Codes of Practice in Appendix J, or [a gross annual salary as set out in paragraph 245HF(d)(ii)(2)], whichever is higher. The appropriate rate [or gross annual salary as set out in paragraph 245HF(d)(ii)(2)] will be based on the applicant's gross annual salary to be paid by the Sponsor, as recorded in the Certificate of Sponsorship Checking Service entry to which the applicant's Certificate of Sponsorship reference number relates, subject to the following conditions:

(i) Salary will be based on basic pay (excluding overtime);

(ii) Allowances, such as London weighting, will be included in the salary where they are part of the guaranteed salary package and would be paid to a local settled worker in similar circumstances;

(iii) Other allowances and benefits, such as a bonus or incentive pay, travel expenses and subsistence (including travel to and from the applicant's home country), will not be included.

Note: Words in square brackets substituted from 6 April 2014 subject to savings for applications made before that date (HC 1138 as amended by HC 1201).

3. In Appendix A – Attributes, after paragraph 100 insert:

Appropriate salary for indefinite leave to remain

100A. An applicant applying for Indefinite Leave to Remain under 245HF is expected to demonstrate that he is being paid either at or above the appropriate rate for the job, as stated in the Codes of Practice in Appendix J, or [a gross annual salary as set out in paragraph 245HF(d)(ii)(2)], whichever is higher. The appropriate rate [or gross annual salary as set out in paragraph 245HF(d)(ii)(2)] will be based on the applicant's gross annual salary to be paid by the Sponsor, as recorded in the Certificate of Sponsorship Checking Service entry to which the applicant's Certificate of Sponsorship reference number relates, subject to the following conditions:

(i) Salary will be based on basic pay (excluding overtime);

(ii) Allowances, such as London weighting, will be included in the salary where they are part of the guaranteed salary package and would be paid to a local settled worker in similar circumstances;

(iii) Other allowances and benefits, such as a bonus or incentive pay, travel expenses and subsistence (including travel to and from the applicant's home country), will not be included.

Note: Words in square brackets substituted from 6 April 2014 subject to savings for applications made before that date (HC 1138 as amended by HC 1201).

Appendix J

Codes of practice for Tier 2 Sponsors, Tier 5 Sponsors and employers of work permit holders

Introduction

1. This Appendix sets out the skill level and appropriate salary rate for jobs, as referred to elsewhere in these Rules.

Note: Paragraphs 1–14 substituted from 6 April 2013 subject to savings for applications made on or after 6 April 2013 using a Certificate of Sponsorship assigned to the applicant before that date (HC 1039).

2. The Standard Occupational Classification (SOC) codes are based on the SOC 2010 system designed by the Office for National Statistics, except where otherwise stated. This system is designed to cover all possible jobs. The related job titles listed in Tables 1 to 7 of this Appendix are taken from guidance published by the Office for National Statistics.

Note: Paragraphs 1–14 substituted from 6 April 2013 subject to savings for applications made on or after 6 April 2013 using a Certificate of Sponsorship assigned to the applicant before that date (HC 1039).

3. References to "job" refer to the most appropriate match for the job in question, as it appears in the tables in this Appendix. The job description must correlate with the most appropriate match, according to further guidance on the SOC 2010 system published by the Office for National Statistics, and reproduced in codes of practice for Sponsors published by the UK Border Agency. The most appropriate match may be applied based on the job description in an application, even if this is not the match stated by the applicant or his Sponsor.

Note: Paragraphs 1 to 14 substituted from 6 April 2013 subject to savings for applications made on or after 6 April 2013 using a Certificate of Sponsorship assigned to the applicant before that date (HC 1039).

4. Table 8 of this Appendix also sets out advertising and evidential requirements for creative sector jobs, as referred to elsewhere in these Rules.

Note: Paragraphs 1–14 substituted from 6 April 2013 subject to savings for applications made on or after 6 April 2013 using a Certificate of Sponsorship assigned to the applicant before that date (HC 1039).

Tables

5. Table 1 sets out PhD-level occupation codes.

Note: Paragraphs 1–14 substituted from 6 April 2013 subject to savings for applications made on or after 6 April 2013 using a Certificate of Sponsorship assigned to the applicant before that date (HC 1039).

6. Table 2 sets out occupations skilled to National Qualifications Framework level 6 or above.

Note: Paragraphs 1–14 substituted from 6 April 2013 subject to savings for applications made on or after 6 April 2013 using a Certificate of Sponsorship assigned to the applicant before that date (HC 1039).

7. Table 3 sets out occupations skilled to National Qualifications Framework level 4 or above.

Note: Paragraphs 1–14 substituted from 6 April 2013 subject to savings for applications made on or after 6 April 2013 using a Certificate of Sponsorship assigned to the applicant before that date (HC 1039).

8. Table 4 sets out occupations skilled to National Qualifications Framework level 3 or above.

Note: Paragraphs 1–14 substituted from 6 April 2013 subject to savings for applications made on or after 6 April 2013 using a Certificate of Sponsorship assigned to the applicant before that date (HC 1039).

9. Table 5 sets out occupations in which some jobs are skilled to National Qualifications Framework level 3 and some jobs are lower-skilled.

Note: Paragraphs 1–14 substituted from 6 April 2013 subject to savings for applications made on or after 6 April 2013 using a Certificate of Sponsorship assigned to the applicant before that date (HC 1039).

10. Table 6 sets out occupations skilled below National Qualifications Framework level 3.

Note: Paragraphs 1–14 substituted from 6 April 2013 subject to savings for applications made on or after 6 April 2013 using a Certificate of Sponsorship assigned to the applicant before that date (HC 1039).

11. Table 7 sets out occupations which are ineligible for Sponsorship in Tier 2 (General) and Tier 2 (Intra-Company Transfer) applications, for reasons other than skill level.

Note: Paragraphs 1–14 substituted from 6 April 2013 subject to savings for applications made on or after 6 April 2013 using a Certificate of Sponsorship assigned to the applicant before that date (HC 1039).

12. (a) Table 8 sets out the equivalent SOC 2010 codes in comparison to the SOC 2000 system, for all occupations that appear in Tables 1 to 5. This table is provided for applicants and Sponsors who relied on a SOC 2000 code in a previous application, and need to know the equivalent SOC 2010 code if the applicant is applying to continue working in the same occupation.

(b) Where Appendix A of these Rules refers to an applicant continuing to work in the same occupation, this means:

(i) the same SOC 2010 code as stated in the Certificate of Sponsorship Checking Service entry that led to the applicant's previous grant, . . .

(ii) a SOC 2010 code which Table 8 shows as being equivalent to the SOC 2000 code stated in the Certificate of Sponsorship Checking Service entry that led to the applicant's previous grant, [or]

(iii) any SOC 2010 code, providing the change is due solely to the move from SOC 2000 to SOC 2010 and not due to a change in the applicant's job.

Note: Paragraphs 1–14 substituted from 6 April 2013 subject to savings for applications made on or after 6 April 2013 using a Certificate of Sponsorship assigned to the applicant before that date (HC 1039). Words deleted and subparagraph (iii) inserted from 6 April 2014 (HC 1138 as amended by HC 1201).

13. Table 9 sets out creative sector codes of practice.

Note: Paragraphs 1–14 substituted from 6 April 2013 subject to savings for applications made on or after 6 April 2013 using a Certificate of Sponsorship assigned to the applicant before that date (HC 1039).

Appropriate salary rates

14. Where these Rules state that an applicant must be paid the appropriate rate for a job as set out in this Appendix, the rate will be determined as follows:

(a) Where the most appropriate match for the job in question appears in Tables 1 to 5 or Table 9, the appropriate rate is as stated in the relevant Table.

(b) Where the most appropriate match for the job in question appears in one of Tables 1 to 5 and also appears in Table 9, the appropriate rate is as stated in Table 9, and the rates stated in Tables 1 to 5 do not apply.

(c) Table 8 is to be used for identifying the equivalent SOC 2010 code only. The appropriate rate must then be identified for that SOC 2010 code using the other tables, where relevant.

(d) Where both "new entrant" and "experienced worker" rates are stated in Tables 1 to 5, the "new entrant" rate will only apply if the applicant:

(i) is applying as a Tier 2 (General) Migrant and scores points from the Post-Study Work provisions of Appendix A,

(ii) is applying as a Tier 2 (General) Migrant and scores points from the Resident Labour Market Test provisions of Appendix A, on the basis that his Sponsor has carried out a university milkround,

(iii) is applying as a Tier 2 (Intra-Company Transfer) Migrant in the Graduate Trainee sub-category, or

(iv) was under the age of 26 on the date the application was made,

and is not applying for a grant of leave that would extend his total stay in Tier 2 and/or as a Work Permit Holder beyond 3 years and 1 month.

The "experienced worker" rate will apply in all other cases.

(e) The rates stated are per year and are based on the following weekly hours:

(i) Where the source is the Annual Survey of Hours and Earnings...a 39-hour week;

(ii) Where the source is NHS Agenda for Change or the Royal Institute of British Architects, a 37.5-hour week;

(iii) Where the source is teachers' national pay scales, on the definition of a full-time teacher as used when determining those pay scales;

(iv) where the source is the National Grid submission to the Migration Advisory Committee, a 37-hour week;

(v) In all other cases, a 40-hour week.

Where the applicant has contracted weekly hours or is paid an hourly rate, the rates must be pro-rated accordingly. [The exception is 'Skilled chef as defined in the Shortage Occupation List in Appendix K', where the appropriate rate cannot be pro-rated down for shorter working hours as it forms a key part of the shortage occupation criteria recommended by the Migration Advisory Committee.]

(f) In all cases, the pay must be compliant with National Minimum Wage regulations.

Note: Paragraphs 1–14 substituted from 6 April 2013 subject to savings for applications made on or after 6 April 2013 using a Certificate of Sponsorship assigned to the applicant before that date (HC 1039). Subparagraph (e) substituted from 1 October 2013 (HC 628). Words inserted at the end of subparagraph (e) from 6 April 2014 subject to savings for applications made before that date (HC 1138 as amended by HC 1201). Words deleted from subparagraph (e)(i) from 6 November 2014 subject to savings for applications made before that date (HC 693).

Table 1 Occupational skilled to PhD-level

Note: Tables 1–5 substituted from 6 April 2014 subject to savings for applications made on or after 6 April 2014 using a Certificate of Sponsorship assigned to the applicant before that date (HC 1138 as amended by HC 1201). The current version of this Table can be accessed online at <www.gov.uk/government/publications/immigration-rules-appendix-j>.

Table 2 Occupations skilled to National Qualifications Framework (NQF) level 6 and above

Note: Tables 1–5 substituted from 6 April 2014 subject to savings for applications made on or after 6 April 2014 using a Certificate of Sponsorship assigned to the applicant before that date (HC 1138 as amended by HC 1201). The current version of this Table can be accessed online at <www.gov.uk/government/publications/immigration-rules-appendix-j>.

Table 3 Occupations skilled to National Qualifications Framework (NQF) level 4 and above

Note: Tables 1–5 substituted from 6 April 2014 subject to savings for applications made on or after 6 April 2014 using a Certificate of Sponsorship assigned to the applicant before that date (HC 1138 as amended by HC 1201). The current version of this Table can be accessed online at <www.gov.uk/government/publications/immigration-rules-appendix-j>.

Table 4 Occupations skilled to National Qualifications Framework (NQF) level 3 and above

Note: Tables 1–5 substituted from 6 April 2014 subject to savings for applications made on or after 6 April 2014 using a Certificate of Sponsorship assigned to the applicant before that date (HC 1138 as amended by HC 1201). The current version of this Table can be accessed online at <www.gov.uk/government/publications/immigration-rules-appendix-j>.

Table 5 Occupations in which some jobs are skilled to National Qualifications Framework (NQF) level 3 and some jobs are lower-skilled

Note: Tables 1–5 substituted from 6 April 2014 subject to savings for applications made on or after 6 April 2014 using a Certificate of Sponsorship assigned to the applicant before that date (HC 1138 as amended by HC 1201). The current version of this Table can be accessed online at <www.gov.uk/government/publications/immigration-rules-appendix-j>.

Table 6 Lower-skilled occupations

Note: The current version of this table can be accessed online at <www.gov.uk/government/publications/immigration-rules-appendix-j>.

Table 7 Occupations which are ineligible for Tier 2 (General) and Tier 2 (Intra-Company Transfer) applications for reasons other than skill level

Note: The current version of this table can be accessed online at <www.gov.uk/government/publications/immigration-rules-appendix-j>.

Table 8 Transition from SOC 2000 to SOC 2010 for applicants continuing to work in the same occupation

Note: Table 8 amended from 1 July 2013 (HC 244). The current version of this table can be accessed online at <www.gov.uk/government/publications/immigration-rules-appendix-j>.

Table 9 Creative sector codes of practice

Note: The current version of this table can be accessed online at <www.gov.uk/government/publications/immigration-rules-appendix-j>.

Appendix K

Shortage Occupation List

1. Where these Rules refer to jobs which appear on the Shortage Occupation List, this means only those specific jobs within each Standard Occupational Classification code stated in Tables 1 and 2 below and, where stated, where the further specified criteria are met.

2. Jobs which appear on the United Kingdom Shortage Occupation List are set out in Table 1.

3. Jobs which appear on the Scotland Only Shortage Occupation List are set out in Table 2.

Table 1 United Kingdom Shortage Occupation List

Standard Occupational Classification (SOC) code and description	**Job titles included on the United Kingdom Shortage Occupation List and further criteria**
Production managers and directors in mining and energy (1123)	**Only** the following jobs in this occupation code: The following jobs in the decommissioning and waste management areas of the nuclear industry: • managing director • programme director • site director The following jobs in the electricity transmission and distribution industry: • project manager • site manager
2112 Biological scientists and biochemists	**Only** the following job in this occupation code: • clinical neurophysiologist
2113 Physical Scientists	**Only** the following jobs in this occupation code: The following jobs in the construction-related ground engineering industry: • engineering geologist • hydrogeologist • geophysicist The following jobs in the oil and gas industry: • geophysicist • geoscientist • geologist • geochemist • technical services manager in the decommissioning and waste areas of the nuclear industry • nuclear medicine scientist • radiotherapy physicist • senior resource geologist and staff geologist in the mining sector
2119 Natural and social science professionals not elsewhere classified	**Only** the following jobs in this occupation code: • informatician • bio-informatician
2121 Civil engineers	**Only** the following jobs in this occupation code: The following jobs in the construction-related ground engineering industry: • geotechnical engineer • tunnelling engineer

	The following jobs in the oil and gas industry: • petroleum engineer • drilling engineer • completions engineer • fluids engineer • reservoir engineer • offshore and subsea engineer • control and instrument engineer • process safety engineer • wells engineer • senior mining engineer in the mining sector
2122 Mechanical engineers	**Only** the following job in this occupation code: • mechanical engineer in the oil and gas industry
2123 Electrical engineers	**Only** the following jobs in this occupation code: • electrical engineer in the oil and gas industry The following jobs in the electricity transmission and distribution industry: • power system engineer • control engineer • protection engineer The following jobs in the aerospace industry: • electrical machine design engineer • power electronics engineer
2124 Electronics Engineers	**Only** the following jobs in this occupation code: The following jobs in the railway industry: • signalling design manager • signalling design engineer • signalling principles designer • senior signalling design checker • signalling design checker • signalling systems engineer • specialist electronics engineer in the automotive manufacturing and design industry
2126 Design and development engineers	**Only** the following jobs in this occupation code: • design engineer in the electricity transmission and distribution industry The following jobs in the automotive design and manufacturing industry: • product development engineer • product design engineer The following jobs in the electronics system industry: • integrated circuit design engineer • integrated circuit test engineer

2127 Production and process engineers	**Only** the following jobs in this occupation code: • chemical engineer • manufacturing engineer (process planning) in the aerospace industry • technical services representative in the decommissioning and waste areas of the nuclear industry
2129 Engineering professionals not elsewhere classified	**Only** the following jobs in this occupation code: The following jobs in the electricity transmission and distribution industry: • project engineer • proposals engineer The following jobs in the aerospace industry: • aerothermal engineer • stress engineer • chief of engineering • advance tool and fixturing engineer The following jobs in the decommissioning and waste management areas of the civil nuclear industry: • operations manager • decommissioning specialist manager • project/planning engineer • radioactive waste manager • radiological protection advisor The following jobs in the civil nuclear industry: • nuclear safety case engineer • mechanical design engineer (pressure vehicles) • piping design engineer • mechanical design engineer (stress) • thermofluids/process engineer
2135 IT Business analysts, architects and systems designers	**Only** the following jobs in this occupation code: • systems engineer in visual effects and 2D/3D computer animation for the film, television or video games sectors
2136 Programmers and software development professionals	**Only** the following jobs in this occupation code: The following jobs in visual effects and 2D/3D computer animation for the film, television or video games sectors: • software developer • shader writer • games designer The following jobs in the electronics system industry: • driver developer • embedded communications engineer

2142 Environmental Professionals	**Only** the following jobs in this occupation code: the following jobs in the construction-related ground engineering industry: • contaminated land specialist • geoenvironmental specialist • landfill engineer
2211 Medical practitioners	**Only** the following jobs in this occupation code: consultant in the following specialities: • emergency medicine • haematology • old age psychiatry Non-consultant, non-training, medical staff post in the following specialities: • anaesthetics • general medicine specialities delivering acute care services (intensive care medicine, general internal medicine (acute), emergency medicine (including specialist doctors working in accident and emergency)) • rehabilitation medicine • psychiatry
2217 Medical Radiographers	**Only** the following jobs in this occupation code: • HPC registered diagnostic radiographer • HPC registered therapeutic radiographer • sonographer Sponsors must retain evidence of the individual's HPC registration and provide this to the UK Border Agency on request. (Registration may need to be done after the individual has entered the United Kingdom but must be done before starting work).
2231 Nurses	**Only** the following job in this occupation code: • specialist nurse working in neonatal intensive care Units Sponsors must retain evidence of the individual's provisional/full NMC registration and provide this to the UK Border Agency on request.
2314 Secondary education teaching professionals	**Only** the following jobs in this occupation code: • secondary education teachers in the subjects of maths and science (chemistry and physics only)
2442 Social workers	**Only** the following jobs in this occupation code: • social worker working in children's and family services

2461 Quality control and planning engineers	**Only** the following jobs in this occupation code: The following jobs in the electricity transmission and distribution industry: • planning / development engineer • quality, health, safety and environment (QHSE) engineer
3113 Engineering technicians	**Only** the following jobs in this occupation code: The following jobs in the electricity transmission and distribution industry: • commissioning engineer • substation electrical engineer
3218 Medical and dental technicians	**Only** the following jobs in this occupation code: • nuclear medicine technologist • radiotherapy technologist
3411 Artist	**Only** the following jobs in this occupation code: • animator in visual effects and 2D/3D computer animation for the film, television or video games sectors
3414 Dancers and choreographers	**Only** the following jobs in this occupation code: Skilled classical ballet dancers who meet the standard required by internationally recognised United Kingdom ballet companies (e.g. Birmingham Royal Ballet, English National Ballet, Northern Ballet Theatre, The Royal Ballet and Scottish Ballet). The company must either: • have performed at or been invited to perform at venues of the calibre of the Royal Opera House, Sadler's Wells or Barbican, either in the United Kingdom or overseas; or • attract dancers and/or choreographers and other artists from other countries; or • be endorsed as being internationally recognised by a United Kingdom industry body such as the Arts Councils (of England, Scotland and/or Wales) Skilled contemporary dancers who meet the standard required by internationally recognised United Kingdom contemporary dance companies (e.g. Shobana Jeyasingh Dance Company, Scottish Dance Theatre and Rambert Dance Company). The company must either: • have performed at or been invited to perform at venues of the calibre of Sadler's Wells, the Southbank Centre or The Place, either in the United Kingdom or overseas; or • attract dancers and/or choreographers and other artists from all over the world; or • be endorsed as being internationally recognised by a United Kingdom industry body such as the Arts Councils (of England, Scotland and/or Wales)

3415 Musicians	**Only** the following jobs in this occupation code: • skilled orchestral musicians who are leaders, principals, sub-principals or numbered stringpositions, and who meet the standard required by internationally recognised UK orchestras (including London Symphony Orchestra, London Philharmonic Orchestra, Philharmonia Orchestra and Royal Philharmonic Orchestra)
3416 Arts officers, producers and directors	**Only** the following jobs in this occupation code: The following jobs in visual effects and 2D/3D computer animation for the film, television or video games sectors: • 2D supervisor • 3D supervisor • computer graphics supervisor • producer • production manager • technical director • visual effects supervisor
3421 Graphic designers	**Only** the following jobs in this occupation code: The following jobs in visual effects and 2D/3D computer animation for the film, television or video games sectors: • compositing artist • matte painter • modeller • rigger • stereo artist • texture artist
3541 Buyers and purchasing officers	**Only** the following job in this occupation code: • manufacturing engineer (purchasing) in the aerospace industry
5215 Welding trades	**Only** the following job in this occupation code: • high integrity pipe welder where the job requires three or more years' related on-the-job experience Sponsors must retain references from the individual's past employer(s) detailing three or more years' related on-the-job experience and provide these to the UK Border Agency on request. Sponsors must also retain relevant evidence to enable them to justify the following: 1) why does the job require someone with three or more years' related on-the-job experience? What elements of the job require this experience and why? 2) why could the job not be carried out to the required standard by someone with less experience? 3) how would you expect a settled worker to gain this experience before being appointed to the post?

5235 Aircraft maintenance and related trades	**Only** the following jobs in this occupation code: • licensed and military certifying engineer/inspector technician
5249 Line repairers and cable jointers	**Only** the following job in this occupation code: • overhead lines worker, working on high voltage lines that carry at least 275,000 volts
5434 Chefs	**Only** the following job in this occupation code: Skilled chef where: • the pay is at least £29,570 per year after deductions for accommodation, meals etc; and • the job requires five or more years relevant experience in a role of at least equivalent status to the one they are entering; and • the job is not in either a fast food outlet, a standard fare outlet, or an establishment which provides a take-away service; and The job is in one of the following roles: • executive chef - limited to one per establishment • head chef - limited to one per establishment • sous chef - limited to one for every four kitchen staff per establishment • specialist chef - limited to one per speciality per establishment A fast food outlet is one where food is prepared in bulk for speed of service, rather than to individual order. A standard fare outlet is one where the menu is designed centrally for outlets in a chain/franchise, rather than by a chef or chefs in the individual restaurant. Standard fare outlets also include those where dishes and/or cooking sauces are bought in ready-made, rather than prepared from fresh/raw ingredients. Sponsors must retain references from the individual's past employer(s) detailing five or more years' relevant experience in a role of at least equivalent status and provide these to the UK Border Agency on request. Sponsors must also retain relevant evidence to enable them to justify the following: 1) why does the job require someone with at least five years' previous experience in a role of at least equivalent status? What elements of the job require this experience and why? 2) why could the job not be carried out to the required standard by someone with less experience? 3) how would you expect a settled worker to gain this experience before being appointed to the post?

Note: Entry relating to musicians substituted from 1 July 2013 (HC 244). Entry relating to metal working production and maintenance fitters deleted and entry relating to aircraft maintenance and related trades inserted from 1 July 2013 subject to savings for applications made on or after 1 July 2013 using a Certificate of Sponsorhip assigned to the applicant before that date (HC 244).

Table 2 Scotland only Shortage Occupation List

Standard Occupational Classification (SOC) code and description	Job titles included on the Scotland only Shortage Occupation List and further criteria
All	All job titles and occupations on the United Kingdom Shortage Occupation List
2113 Physical scientists	**Only** the following jobs in this occupation code: • jobs on the United Kingdom Shortage Occupation List • staff working in diagnostics radiology (including magnetic resonance imaging)
2211 Medical practitioners	**Only** the following jobs in this occupation code: • jobs on the United Kingdom Shortage Occupation List • ST3, ST4, ST5 and ST6 trainees in paediatrics or anaesthetics • SAS staff doctors in paediatrics or anaesthetics • consultants in paediatrics or anaesthetics • non-consultant, non-training doctors in the specialty obstetrics and gynaecology

Appendix KoLL

Knowledge of language and life

Note: Appendix KoLL inserted from 28 October 2013 subject to savings for applications made before that date (HC 628).

Part 1 – general

1.1

Purpose

This Appendix sets out [how] an applicant for [indefinite] leave to enter or remain must demonstrate sufficient knowledge of the English language and about life in the United Kingdom where it is a requirement of the Rules to demonstrate this for the purposes of an application for indefinite leave to enter or remain. It also sets out general exemptions to the requirement on grounds of age and enables the decision maker to waive the requirement in light of special circumstances in any particular case.

"Specified" in this Appendix means "specified in Part 4 of this appendix".

Note: Words in square brackets substituted/inserted from 6 November 2014 (HC 693).

Part 2 – knowledge of language and life

2.1 An applicant for leave to enter or remain has sufficient knowledge of the English language and about life in the United Kingdom for the purpose of an application for indefinite leave to enter or remain made under these Rules if the requirements set out in paragraphs 2.2 and 2.3 are met unless the exceptions set out in Part 3 apply.

2.2 For the purposes of paragraph 2.1, an applicant [demonstrates] sufficient knowledge of the English language if:

(a) the applicant has provided specified documentary evidence that:

i) the applicant is a national or citizen of one of the following countries:

- Antigua and Barbuda
- Australia
- The Bahamas
- Barbados
- Belize
- Canada
- Dominica
- Grenada
- Guyana
- Jamaica
- New Zealand
- St Kitts and Nevis
- St Lucia
- St Vincent and the Grenadines
- Trinidad and Tobago
- USA.

or

ii) the applicant has passed an English language test in speaking and listening at a minimum level B1 of the Common European Framework of Reference for Languages with a provider approved by the Secretary of State as specified in Appendix O to these Rules; or

iii) the applicant has obtained an academic qualification (not a professional or vocational qualification), which is deemed by UK NARIC to meet the recognised standard of a Bachelor's or Master's degree or PhD in the UK, from an educational establishment in one of the following countries: Antigua and Barbuda; Australia; The Bahamas; Barbados; Belize; Dominica; Grenada; Guyana; Ireland; Jamaica; New Zealand; St Kitts and Nevis; St Lucia; St Vincent and The Grenadines; Trinidad and Tobago; the UK; the USA; and provides the specified documents; or

iv) the applicant has obtained an academic qualification (not a professional or vocational qualification) which is deemed by UK NARIC to meet the recognised standard of a Bachelor's or Master's degree or PhD in the UK, and

(1) provides the specified documentary evidence to show he has the qualification, and

(2) UK NARIC has confirmed that the qualification was taught or researched in English; or

v) the applicant has obtained an academic qualification (not a professional or vocational qualification) which is deemed by UK NARIC to meet the recognised standard of a Bachelor's or Master's degree or PhD in the UK, and provides the specified evidence to show:

(1) he has the qualification, and

(2) that the qualification was taught or researched in English; or.

vi) the applicant has taken and passed in England, Wales or Northern Ireland a qualification in English for Speakers of Other Languages (ESOL) which:

(aa) includes speaking and listening;

(bb) is at ESOL Entry level 3, level 1, level 2 or level 3,

(cc) is regulated by the Office of Qualifications and Examinations Regulation (OFQUAL), the Welsh Government or the Council for Curriculum, Examinations and Assessment (CCEA), and

(dd) is listed as an ESOL qualification on the Register of Regulated Qualifications,

or

vii) the applicant has passed in Scotland a National Qualification in English for Speakers of Other Languages at Scottish Credit and Qualifications Framework (SCQF) level 4, 5 or 6 awarded by the Scottish Qualifications Authority;

or

(b) the applicant—

(i) has limited leave to enter or remain in the UK, and

(ii) that leave (or a grant of leave which preceded it provided any periods of leave since have been unbroken) was given on the basis that the applicant had an English language qualification at a minimum level of B1 on the Common European Framework of Reference for Languages [, and]

(iii) at the date of application, the provider of that qualification continues to be approved by the Secretary of State as specified in Appendix O to these Rules.

Note: Words in square brackets in introductory wording and in subparagraph (b)(ii) inserted and subparagraph (b)(iii) inserted from 6 November 2014 (HC 693).

2.3 For the purposes of sub-paragraph (1), an applicant [demonstrates] sufficient knowledge about life in the United Kingdom if:

(a) the applicant has passed the test known as the "Life in the UK test" administered by learndirect limited; or

(b) in respect of an applicant who was resident in the Isle of Man, the applicant took and passed the test in the Isle of Man known as the "Life in the UK test" and which was administered by an educational institution or other person approved for that purpose by the Lieutenant Governor; or

(c) in respect of an applicant who was resident in the Bailiwick of Guernsey or in the Bailiwick of Jersey, the applicant took and passed the test known as the "Citizenship Test" and which was administered by an educational institution or other person approved for that purpose by the Lieutenant Governor of Guernsey or Jersey (as the case may be).

Note: Word in square brackets in introductory wording substituted from 6 November 2014 (HC 693).

Part 3 – exceptions

3.1 Notwithstanding any requirement to the contrary in these Rules, for the purposes of this appendix, an applicant will not be required to demonstrate sufficient knowledge of the English language and about life in the UK where:

(a) the applicant is under 18 years of age at the date of his or her application, or

(b) the applicant is at least 65 years of age at the date of his or her application, or

(c) in all the circumstances of the case, the decision maker considers that, because of the applicant's mental or physical condition, it would be unreasonable to expect the applicant to fulfil that requirement.

3.2 In the following circumstances an applicant will be deemed to have demonstrated sufficient knowledge of the English language and about life in the UK:

(a) Where the application for indefinite leave to [enter or] remain in the United Kingdom is made under:

(i) paragraph 196D and the applicant has had, as at the day on which the application is made, continuous leave to enter or remain in the United Kingdom for at least 15 years as the spouse or civil partner of a person who has or has had leave to enter or remain under paragraphs 128–193 (but not paragraphs 135I–135K), or

(ii) paragraph 198 and the applicant has had, as at the day on which the application was made, continuous leave to enter or remain in the United Kingdom for at least 15 years as the child of a person who has or has had leave to enter or remain in the United Kingdom under paragraphs 128–193 (but not paragraphs 135l–135K), or

(iii) paragraph 248D and the applicant has had, as at the day on which the application was made, continuous leave to enter or remain in the United Kingdom for at least 15 years as a person exercising rights of access to a child resident in the United Kingdom and that child is under the age of 18 at the day on which the applicant's application for indefinite leave is made under paragraph 248D, or

(iv) paragraph 273D and the applicant has had, as at the day on which the application is made, continuous leave to enter or remain in the United Kingdom for at least 15 years as a spouse or civil partner of a person who has or has had leave to enter or remain in the United Kingdom as a retired person of independent means, or

(v) paragraph 275A and the applicant has had, as at the day on which the application was made, continuous leave to enter or remain in the United Kingdom for at least 15 years as the child of a person who has or has had leave to enter or remain in the United Kingdom as a retired person of independent means, or

(vi) paragraph 287 and the applicant has had, as at the day on which the application is made, continuous leave to enter or remain in the United Kingdom for at least 15 years under paragraph 281 or paragraph 284, or

(vii) paragraph 295G and the applicant has had, as at the day on which the application is made, continuous leave to enter or remain in the United Kingdom for at least 15 years under paragraph 295B or paragraph 295D, or

(viii) paragraph 298 and the applicant has had, as at the day on which the application is made, continuous leave to enter or remain in the United Kingdom for at least 15 years under paragraph 302 or Appendix FM or paragraph 319R or paragraph 319X, or

(ix) paragraph 319E and the applicant has had, as at the day on which the application is made, continuous leave to enter or remain in the United Kingdom for at least 15 years as the partner of a relevant points based system migrant, or

(x) paragraph 319J and the applicant has had, as at the day on which the application is made, continuous leave to enter or remain in the United Kingdom for at least 15 years as the child of a relevant points based system migrant, or

(xi) section E-ILRP of Appendix FM and the applicant has had, as at the day on which the application is made, continuous leave to enter or remain in the United Kingdom for at least 15 years on the day on which the application is made as a partner (except where leave is as a fiancé or proposed civil partner) under section D-LTRP of Appendix FM; or

(xii) section E-ILRPT of Appendix FM and the applicant has had, as at the day on which the application is made, continuous leave to enter or remain in the United Kingdom for at least 15 years on the day on which the application is made as a parent under section D-ILRPT of Appendix FM, or

(xiii) paragraph 25 or 31 of Appendix Armed Forces and the applicant has completed, on the date on which the application is made, a continuous period of leave to enter or remain in the United Kingdom of at least 15 years as the partner of a member of HM Forces under that Appendix, or

(xiv) paragraph 45 or 49 of Appendix Armed Forces and the applicant has completed, on the date on which the application is made, a continuous period of leave to enter or remain in the United Kingdom of at least 15 years as the child of a member of HM Forces under that Appendix, and

(b) (i) the applicant has provided specified documentary evidence of an English language speaking and listening qualification at A2 CEFR or ESOL entry level 2 or Scottish Credit and Qualification Framework level 3; or

(ii) where paragraph 39C(c) of these Rules applies, the applicant has provided specified documentary evidence of an English language speaking and listening qualification at A2 CEFR with a provider approved by the Secretary of State as specified in Appendix O to these Rules,

and

(c) the applicant has provided specified documentary evidence from a qualified English language teacher that the applicant has made efforts to learn English but does not yet have sufficient knowledge of the English language to pass a qualification at B1 CEFR, or ESOL entry level 3 or Scottish Credit and Qualification Framework level 4.

and

(d) the applicant is not a national or a citizen of one of the following countries:

- Antigua and Barbuda
- Australia
- The Bahamas
- Barbados
- Belize
- Canada
- Dominica
- Grenada
- Guyana
- Jamaica
- New Zealand
- St Kitts and Nevis
- St Lucia
- St Vincent and the Grenadines
- Trinidad and Tobago
- USA.

Note: Words inserted in subparagraph 3.2(a) and subparagraphs 3.2(a)(xiii) and (xiv) from 6 April 2014 subject to savings for applications made before that date (HC 1138 as amended by HC 1201). Subparagraph 3.2(b) substituted from 6 November 2014 (HC 693).

3.3 Where paragraph 39C(c) of these Rules applies, an applicant demonstrates sufficient knowledge of the English language and about life in the UK where:

(i) upon a request by the decision-maker to provide additional evidence of knowledge of the English language, he or she has provided specified documentary evidence that he or she has passed an English language test in speaking and listening at a minimum B1 of the Common European Framework of Reference for Languages with a provider approved by the Secretary of State as specified in Appendix O to these Rules, unless paragraph 3.2 of this Appendix applies; or

(ii) upon a request by the decision-maker to provide additional evidence of knowledge about life in the UK, he or she has provided specified evidence that he or she has passed the test known as the "Life in the UK test" administered by learndirect limited under arrangements approved by the decision-maker; or

(iii) upon a request by the decision-maker to provide additional evidence of knowledge of the English language and about life in the UK, he or she has provided the evidence set out in sub-paragraphs (i) and (ii).

Part 4 – specified documents

4.1 Where these Rules require an applicant to demonstrate sufficient knowledge of the English language and of life in the United Kingdom, the applicant must supply the documents specified in paragraphs 4.6 to 4.14 below.

4.2 The decision maker will only consider evidence submitted after the date on which an application is made where the circumstances in [paragraph 39(C)(c) of these Rules or paragraphs 4.3 or 4.6 of this Appendix apply].

Note: Words substituted from 6 November 2014 (HC 693).

4.3 Where an applicant has submitted:

(i) a document in the wrong format (for example, if a letter is not on letterhead paper as specified); or

(ii) a document that is a copy and not an original document, or

(iii) a document which does not contain all of the specified information,

or

(iv) fails to submit a specified document,

the decision-maker may contact the applicant or his or her representative (in writing or otherwise), and request the document or the correct version of the document. The document must be received by the Home Office at the address specified in the request within such timescale (which will not be unreasonable) as is specified.

4.4 A decision-maker may decide not to request a document under paragraph 4.3 where he or she does not anticipate that the supply of that document will lead to a grant of leave to enter or remain in the United Kingdom because the application may be refused for other reasons.

4.5 Without prejudice to the decision maker's discretion under paragraph 4.2 and also his or her right in all cases to request the original or specified document and refuse an application in circumstances in which they are not provided, where an applicant submits a specified document:

(i) in the wrong format, or

(ii) which is a copy and not an original document, or

(iii) which does not contain all of the specified information but the missing information is verifiable from,

(aa) other documents submitted with the application,

(bb) the website of the organisation which issued the document,

or

(cc) the website of the appropriate regulatory body;

the application for leave to enter or remain in the United Kingdom may be granted exceptionally providing the decision-maker is satisfied that the specified documents are genuine and that the applicant meets all the other requirements.

4.6 Where the decision-maker is satisfied that there is a valid reason why a document has not been and cannot be supplied, (for example, because the document has been permanently lost or destroyed), he or she may waive the requirement for the document to be provided or may instead request alternative or additional evidence (which may include confirmation of evidence from the organisation which issued the original document).

4.7 The evidence specified for the purposes of paragraph 2.2 of this Appendix is:

(a) a certificate that:

(i) is from an English language test provider approved by the Secretary of State for the purposes of limited leave to enter or remain as specified in Appendix O of these Rules, and is in respect of a test approved by the Secretary of State as specified in that Appendix, and

(ii) shows the applicant's name; and

(iii) shows the qualification obtained, and

(iv) shows that the level of speaking and listening skills attained by the applicant met or exceeded level B1 of the Common European Framework of Reference, and

(v) shows the date of award of the qualification;

or,

(b) a print out of the online score from a PTE Academic (Pearson) test which:

(i) is from an English language test provider approved by the Secretary of State for the purposes of limited leave to enter or remain as specified in Appendix O of these rules, and

(ii) is in respect of a test approved by the Secretary of State as specified in that Appendix, and

(iii) can be used to show the qualification obtained; and,

(iv) shows that the level of speaking and listening skills attained by the applicant met or exceeded level B1 of the Common European Framework of Reference;

or

(c) a certificate or other document issued by an awarding organisation that is recognised either by Ofqual, the Welsh Government, or CCEA that

(i) is issued in England, Wales or Northern Ireland in respect of a qualification listed as an ESOL qualification in the OFQUAL Register of Regulated Qualifications, and

(ii) shows that the level of speaking and listening skills attained by the applicant met or exceeded ESOL entry level 3; or

(d) a certificate that

(i) is issued in Scotland in respect of a National Qualification in English for Speakers of Other Languages awarded by the Scottish Qualifications Authority, and

(ii) shows that the level of speaking and listening skills attained by the applicant met or exceeded Scottish Credit and Qualifications Framework level 4.

4.8 Subject to paragraphs 4.9 and 4.10 the documentary evidence specified for the purposes of paragraph 2.2 of this Appendix as showing that a person is a national or a citizen of one of the countries listed in paragraph 2.2 is a valid passport or travel document which satisfactorily establishes the applicant's nationality.

4.9 If the applicant cannot provide their passport or travel document other evidence of nationality of the type described in paragraph 4.10 may exceptionally be supplied in the following circumstances (the reason for which must be indicated by the applicant on their application form), where:

(a) the applicant's passport has been lost or stolen, or

(b) the applicant's passport has expired and has been returned to the relevant authorities, or

(c) the applicant's passport is with another part of the Home Office.

4.10 Where paragraph 4.9 applies, the alternative evidence specified for the purposes of establishing the applicant's nationality is:

(a) a valid national identity document; or

(b) an original letter from the applicant's Home Government or Embassy confirming the applicant's full name, date of birth and nationality.

4.11. The evidence specified for the purposes of paragraph [2.2(a)(iii) to 2.2(a)(v)] (academic qualification recognised by UK NARIC) is:

(a) a certificate issued by the relevant institution confirming the award of the academic qualification and showing:

(i) the applicant's name,

(ii) the title of the award,

(iii) the date of the award,

(iv) the name of the awarding institution, and,

(v) for paragraph [2.2(a)(iii)] that the qualification was taught in English

or,

(b) where an applicant has not, at the date of application, formally graduated or no longer has his or her certificate and is unable to obtain a duplicate certificate:

(i) an original academic reference from the institution awarding the academic qualification that:

(aa) is on official letter headed paper,

(bb) shows the applicant's name,

(cc) shows the title of the award,

(dd) confirms that the qualification was taught in English,

(ee) states when the academic qualification was (or as the case may be, will be) awarded,

and

(ff) confirms that the institution is unable to issue a duplicate certificate of award or (as the case may be in respect of an applicant who has not yet graduated) the date on which the certificate will be issued.

or

(ii) an original academic transcript that;

(aa) is on official letter headed paper,

(bb) shows the applicant's name,

(cc) shows the name of the academic institution,

(dd) shows the course title,

(ee) confirms that the qualification was taught in English, and,

(ff) confirms the award given.

Note: Words substituted in the introductory wording and in subparagraph (a)(v) from 6 November 2014 (HC 693).

4.12 In the absence of any evidence to the contrary, a qualification obtained in one of the following countries will be assumed for the purposes of this Appendix to have been taught in English: Antigua and Barbuda, Australia, the Bahamas, Barbados, Belize, Dominica, Grenada, Guyana, Ireland, Jamaica, New Zealand, St Kitts and Nevis, St Lucia, St Vincent and the Grenadines, Trinidad and Tobago, the UK or the USA.

4.13 The evidence specified for the purposes of paragraph [3.2(b)(i)] (evidence of English language speaking and listening) is the same as that specified for the purposes of [paragraphs 2.2(a)(vi) and 2.2(a)(vii)] except that:

(a) references to B1 are to be read as references to A2,

(b) references to ESOL levels Entry 3, level 1, level 2 and level 3 are to be read as references to ESOL Entry level 2, and

(c) references to Scottish Credit and Qualification Framework Level 4, 5 and 6 are to be read as references to Scottish Qualification Framework Level 3.

Note: Words substituted in introductory wording from 6 November 2014 (HC 693).

4.13A The evidence specified for the purposes of paragraph 3.2(b)(ii) (evidence of English language speaking and listening) is the same as that specified for the purposes of paragraph 2.2(a)(ii) except that references to B1 are to be read as references to A2.

Note: Paragraph 4.13A inserted from 6 November 2014 (HC 693).

4.14 (a) The evidence specified for the purposes of paragraph [3.2(c)] (evidence from qualified English teacher) is a letter from the teacher which is signed by him or her and dated no more than 3 months before the date on which the application for indefinite leave to remain is made and which includes the following information:

(i) the applicant's name,

(ii) confirmation that the applicant has attended an English language class taught by that teacher for at least 75 guided learning hours and which was taught during the period of 12 months immediately preceding the date on which the application for indefinite leave to remain was made,

(iii) confirmation that the teacher has assessed that the speaking and listening level attained by the applicant is not at B1 level or above,

(iv) confirmation that the applicant is considered unlikely to attain B1 level through further study, and

(v) confirmation of the teacher's qualifications as an English language teacher within the meaning of this Appendix.

(b) For the purposes of paragraph (a)(ii) "guided learning hours" means the time during which a person is taught or given instruction and does not include any time spent on unsupervised preparation or study.

Note: Words substituted in introductory wording from 6 November 2014 (HC 693).

4.15 The documentary evidence specified for the purposes of paragraph 2.3 of this Appendix is:

(a) a pass notification letter issued by learndirect limited in respect of the test known as the "Life in the UK test", or

(b) where the "Life in the UK test" was taken and passed in the Isle of Man, a pass certificate in respect of the test issued by the relevant educational institution or other person approved for that purpose by the Lieutenant Governor, or

(c) where the "Citizenship test" was taken in the Bailiwick of Guernsey or, as the case may be, in the Bailiwick of Jersey, a pass certificate issued by the relevant educational institution or other person approved for that purpose by the Lieutenant Governor of Guernsey or Jersey (as the case may be).

4.16 The evidence specified for the purposes of paragraph 3.3(i) of this Appendix (evidence of English language speaking and listening) is the same as that specified for the purpose of paragraph 2.2(a)(ii) of this Appendix.

Note: Paragraphs 4.16 and 4.17 inserted from 6 November 2014 (HC 693).

4.17 The evidence specified for the purposes of paragraph 3.3(ii) of this Appendix (evidence of knowledge about life in the UK) is the same as that specified at paragraph 4.15(a) of this Appendix.

Note: Paragraphs 4.16 and 4.17 inserted from 6 November 2014 (HC 693).

Part 5 – Interpretation

5.1 For the purposes of this Appendix "decision maker" means an Entry Clearance Officer or the Secretary of State.

5.2 For the purposes of this Appendix, "qualified English language teacher" means a person who holds a qualification in teaching English as a foreign language or in teaching English to speakers of other languages which was awarded by an awarding organisation regulated by OFQUAL or the Welsh Government or the CCEA or the Scottish Qualification Authority.

Appendix L

Designated Competent Body criteria for Tier 1 (Exceptional Talent) applications

Criteria for endorsement by The Royal Society, The Royal Academy of Engineering or The British Academy

1. [To be considered for endorsement, the application must first:]

(a) satisfy all of the mandatory "Exceptional Talent (world leader)" criteria, and at least one of the qualifying criteria, in the table below, or

(b) satisfy all of the "Exceptional Promise (potential world leader)" criteria in the table below.

Note: Words substituted/inserted from 6 November 2014 subject to savings for applications made before that date (HC 693).

Exceptional Talent (world leader) Mandatory	Exceptional Promise (potential world leader) Mandatory
The applicant must: • Be an active researcher in a relevant field, typically within a university, research institute or within industry; • Have a PhD or equivalent research experience; • Provide a dated letter of personal recommendation from an eminent person resident in the UK [supporting the Tier 1 (Exceptional Talent) application] who is familiar with his work and his contribution to his field, and is qualified to assess his claim to be a world leader in his field;	The applicant must: • Be an active researcher in a relevant field, typically within a university, research institute or within industry; • Have a PhD or equivalent research experience (including industrial research); • Provide a dated letter of personal recommendation from an eminent person resident in the UK [supporting the Tier 1 (Exceptional Talent) application] who is familiar with his work and his contribution to his field, and is qualified to assess his claim that he has the potential to be a world leader in his field;
• Meet one or more of the following Qualifying Criteria.	• Be at an early stage in his career; • Have been awarded, hold, or have held in the past five years, a prestigious UK-based Research Fellowship, or an international Fellowship or advanced research post judged by the competent bodies to be of equivalent standing.

Qualifying • Be a member of his national academy or a foreign member of academies of other countries (in particular any of the UK national academies); • Have been awarded a prestigious internationally recognised prize; • Provide a written recommendation from a reputable UK organisation concerned with research in his field. The dated letter must be written by an authorised senior member of the organisation, such as a Chief Executive, Vice-Chancellor or similar, on official paper.

2. [To be considered for endorsement, the applicant] must provide the following documents:

(a) A completed Designated Competent Bodies' Tier 1 (Exceptional Talent) application form;

(b) A short curriculum vitae outlining his career and publication history (of no more than 3 A4 sides in length);

(c) [A mandatory dated letter of recommendation written in support of the application] from an eminent person resident in the UK who is familiar with his work and his contribution to his field, and is qualified to assess his claim to be a world leader or a potential world leader in his field. The letter should include be dated and details of how the eminent person knows the applicant; the applicant's achievements in the specialist field, and how in the opinion of the eminent person the applicant exhibits exceptional talent; how the applicant would benefit from living in the UK; and the contribution they would make to UK research excellence and to wider society.

(d) Evidence in relation to at least one of the qualifying criteria listed above.

Note: Words substituted in subparagraph (c) from 1 October 2013 subject to savings for applications made before that date (HC 628). Words substituted in opening sentence from 6 November 2014 subject to savings for applications made before that date (HC 693).

3. The documents in paragraph 2 above must be:

(a) Hard copy,

(b) Printed (not hand-written), and

(c) Written in English or accompanied by authorised English translations.

4. [If the eligibility criteria in paragraph 1 are met, and the documents outlined in paragraph 2 are provided in accordance with the requirements at paragraph 3, then the Designated Competent Body will assess the applicant for endorsement, taking into consideration the following assessment criteria:]

(a) The applicant's track record/career history (including his international standing, the significance of his publications, prizes and research funding awarded, patents, and the impact of past innovation activity, in a company, academia or as an individual);

(b) The strength of the supporting statements in the letter of personal recommendation, and evidence in relation to qualifying criteria, including a written recommendation from a reputable UK organisation concerned with research in the applicant's field (if relevant);

(c) The expected benefits of the applicant's presence in the UK in terms of the contribution to UK research excellence and to wider society, including potential economic benefits from exploitation of intellectual capital; and

(d) The additional factors in the table below.

Exceptional Talent (world leader)	Exceptional Promise (potential world leader)
• Whether the applicant is the winner of a prestigious prize or award; • Whether the applicant has secured significant funding for his work in the past ten years; • Whether the applicant is regarded as a world leader in your field.	• Whether the applicant has provided evidence sufficient to demonstrate that he has the potential to be a future world leader in the field; • The level of additional funding secured during or following tenure of a relevant fellowship; • Whether he can provide evidence of a relevant prize or award for early career researchers; • The significance of his contribution to his field relative to his career stage.

Note: Words substituted in opening sentence from 6 November 2014 subject to savings for applications made before that date (HC 693).

4A. The Designated Competent Body will advise the Home Office whether or not it endorses the applicant. If the applicant is judged by the Designated Competent Body to have met the published eligibility criteria for consideration as well as assessed to have met the assessment criteria to a level considered demonstrable of a world leader in their field or a potential world leader in their field then the Designated Competent Body will endorse the applicant. If the applicant is judged by the Designated Competent Body not to have met the eligibility criteria or assessed not to have met the assessment criteria to a level considered demonstrable of a world leader in their field or a potential world leader in their field, then the Designated Competent Body will not endorse the applicant.

Note: Paragraph 4A inserted from 6 November 2014 subject to savings for applications made before that date (HC 693).

Criteria for endorsement by The Arts Council

5. The applicant must either:

(a) be established as, or demonstrate potential to become, a world-leading artist or an internationally-recognised expert within the fields of the arts (encompassing dance, music, theatre, visual arts and literature), museums or galleries; or

(b) be established as a world-leading artist or an internationally-recognised expert within the film, television, animation, post-production and visual effects industry.

Note: Paragraphs 5–9 substituted from 1 October 2013 subject to savings for applications made before that date (HC 628).

6. The applicant must:

(a) be professionally engaged in producing work of outstanding quality which has been published (other than exclusively in newspapers or magazines), performed, presented, distributed or exhibited internationally;

(b) show recent and regular activity of being engaged professionally as a practitioner in his field;

(c) show a substantial (if applying under the exceptional talent criteria) or developing (if applying under the exceptional promise criteria) track record in at least one country other than his country of residence.

Note: Paragraphs 5–9 substituted from 1 October 2013 subject to savings for applications made before that date (HC 628).

7. If the applicant's field is within the arts, museums or galleries, he must provide the evidence specified in the table below to demonstrate that his work is of exceptional quality and has national or international recognition. This evidence must consist of no more than 10 documents in total, and must be submitted as paper-based documents in hard copy with the application.

Evidence cannot include other objects, Digital Versatile Discs (DVDs) or Compact Discs (CDs), digital files or web links. (If an applicant wishes to use the content of a webpage as one of his 10 permitted supporting documents, he must provide a printed copy of the page which clearly shows the Uniform Resource Locator (URL) for the page.) [A document in this context is defined as a single article, review, letter, etc. If more than the permitted ten documents are submitted, only the first ten documents listed will be considered; additional evidence in excess of the permitted ten documents will be disregarded.]

Exceptional talent within the fields of the arts, museums or galleries	Exceptional Promise (potential world leader)
The applicant must provide evidence to support **two or more** of the following: 1) Examples of significant media recognition such as features, articles and/or reviews from national publications or broadcasting companies in at least one country other than the applicant's country of residence. Event listings or advertisements are not acceptable. 2) Proof of having won international awards for excellence, for example the Booker Prize, a Grammy Award; or domestic awards in another country, for example a Tony Award. The Arts Council will judge whether a particular award provides appropriate evidence of international recognition in the applicant's field. 3) Proof of appearances, performances, publications or exhibitions in the past five years in contexts which are recognised as internationally significant in the applicant's field or evidence of extensive international distribution and	The applicant must provide evidence to support **two or more** of the following: 1) Two or more examples of media recognition such as articles and/or reviews from national publications or broadcasting companies in at least one country other than the applicant's country of residence. Event listings or advertisements are not acceptable. 2) Proof of having won or been nominated or shortlisted for international awards for excellence, for example the Booker Prize, a Grammy Award; or domestic awards in another country, for example a Tony Award. The Arts Council will judge whether a particular award provides appropriate evidence of recognition in the applicant's field. 3) Proof of appearances, performances, publications or exhibitions in the past three years in contexts which are internationally recognised in the applicant's field or evidence of international distribution and audiences for the applicant's work.

audiences for the applicant's work. The Arts Council will judge whether such appearances, performances, exhibitions or distribution provide appropriate evidence of international significance in the applicant's field.	The Arts Council will judge whether such appearances, performances, exhibitions or distribution provide appropriate evidence of international recognition in the applicant's field.

Note: Paragraphs 5–9 substituted from 1 October 2013 subject to savings for applications made before that date (HC 628). Words in square brackets in paragraph 7 inserted from 6 November 2014 subject to savings for applications made before that date (HC 693).

8. If the applicant's field is within the film, television, animation, post-production and visual effects industry, he must:

(a) have won, or within the last five years from the year of application, have received a nomination for:

(i) an Academy Award,

(ii) a British Academy of Film and Television Arts (BAFTA) award,

(iii) a Golden Globe, or

(iv) an Emmy award

and provide:

(1) full details of the production nomination or award, including category and year of nomination or award,

(2) evidence of the applicant's involvement if the nomination or award was as part of a group, and

(3) evidence of the credit the applicant received for the nomination or award;

or

(b) have, within the last five years from the year of application, made a significant and direct contribution to winning or being nominated for:

(i) an Academy Award,

(ii) a British Academy of Film and Television Arts (BAFTA) award,

(iii) a Golden Globe, or

(iv) an Emmy award

and provide evidence from the named person on the award(s) or nomination(s) which demonstrates that the applicant has significantly influenced or directly resulted in the award or nomination to the named person; or

(c) demonstrate notable industry recognition by providing evidence of:

(i) international distribution sales and recognition, and

(ii) having achieved one of the following combinations:

(1) won a minimum of two,

(2) won one, and, within the last five years before the date of application, have been nominated for one other, or

(3) within the last three years before the date of application, have been nominated for a minimum of three, of the following Notable Industry Recognition Awards:

- Akil Koci Prize
- American Academy of Arts and Letters Gold Medal in Music
- Angers Premiers Plans
- ARIA Music Awards (Australian Recording Industry Association)
- ASCAP awards (American Society of Composers, Authors and Publishers)
- Australian Academy of Cinema and Television Arts (AACTS)

- Awit Awards (Philippine Association of the Record Industry)
- BAFTA Cymru
- BAFTA Games Awards
- BAFTA Interactive Awards
- BAFTA Scotland
- BAFTA Television Craft Awards
- Berlin International Film Festival
- BET Awards (Black Entertainment Television, United States)
- BFI London Film Festival
- Brit Awards
- British Composer Awards – For excellence in classical and jazz music
- Brooklyn International Film Festival
- Cannes International Film Festival / Festival de Cannes
- Chicago International Film Festival
- Cinema Jove International Film Festival
- Classic Rock Roll of Honour Awards – An annual awards program bestowed by Classic Rock
- Comet (Viva, Germany)
- Cork International Film Festival
- Country Music Awards of Australia (Country Music Association of Australia)
- DICE Awards organised by the Academy of Interactive Arts and Sciences
- Directors Guild of America Award
- Distinguished Service to Music Medal (Kappa Kappa Psi) – For exceptional service to American bands and band music
- Echo (German Phonographic Academy)
- Edinburgh International Film Festival
- Ernst von Siemens Music Prize
- Fédération Internationale de la Presse Cinématographique or International Film Critics Award given by the International Federation of Film Critics
- GDC Awards
- George Peabody Medal (Peabody Institute)
- Gold Badge Awards – For outstanding contributions to the music and the entertainment industry of the United Kingdom
- Golden Melody Awards (Taiwan)
- Grammy Awards
- Grand Prix du Disque (France)
- Grawemeyer Award for Music Composition
- IGF Awards
- Independent Music Awards
- Independent Spirit Awards
- International Film Music Critics Association Awards
- Ivor Novello Awards
- Juno Awards (Canadian Academy of Recording Arts and Sciences)
- Latin Grammy Award (Latin Academy of Recording Arts & Sciences)
- Léonie Sonning Music Prize (Léonie Sonning Music Foundation)
- Locarno Film Festival
- Los Premios MTV Latinoamérica – Previously known as MTV Video Music Awards Latinoamérica (MTV)

- Melbourne International Film Festival
- Mercury Prize
- MTV Music Awards (MTV)
- Otaka Prize – An annual composition prize for Japanese composers
- Polar Music Prize
- Praemium Imperiale
- Preis der deutschen Schallplattenkritik – For achievement in recorded music
- Prix de Rome
- Pulitzer Prize for Music
- Raindance Film Festival
- Rolf Schock Prize in Musical Arts
- Rotterdam International Film Festival
- Sanremo Music Festival (Italy)
- Sao Paulo International Film Festival
- Satellite Awards
- Saturn Awards
- Sibelius Prize
- South by Southwest Film Festival
- Stockholm International Film Festival
- Sundance Film Festival
- Suntory Music Award (Japan)
- Sydney Film Festival
- The Annime Awards
- Toronto International Film Festival
- Tribeca Film Festival
- Venice International Film Festival
- Visual Effects Society Awards
- Women in Film and Television Awards
- Writers Guild Awards of Great Britain
- Writers Guild of America Awards

Note: Paragraphs 5–9 substituted from 1 October 2013 subject to savings for applications made before that date (HC 628). Subparagraph (c)(ii) substituted from 6 November 2014 subject to savings for applications made before that date (HC 693).

9. The applicant must provide letters of endorsement as specified in the table below, which must:

(a) be written on headed paper, dated, and signed by the author who must be an authorised member of the organisation such as the Chief Executive, Artistic Director, Principal or Chair;

(b) include details of the author's credentials (for example, a Curriculum Vitae or résumé) and how they know the applicant (whether through personal relationship or reputation);

(c) detail the applicant's achievements in his specialist field and how in the opinion of the author he has demonstrated that he is, or has the potential to become, a world leader in his field;

(d) describe how the applicant would benefit from living in the UK and the contribution he could make to cultural life in the UK, including details of any future professional engagements in the UK that the author is aware of;

Letters of endorsement for exceptional talent and exceptional promise
The applicant must provide 3 letters of endorsement (as described in paragraph 9 above). • The **first letter** must be from a **UK based** arts or cultural organisation, institution or company which is well-established nationally and/or internationally and widely acknowledged as possessing expertise in its field. • The **second letter** must be from another arts or cultural organisation, institution or company which is well-established nationally and/or internationally and widely acknowledged as possessing expertise in its field. This second organisation may be UK or overseas based. • The **third letter** may be **either** from a third arts or cultural organisation, institution or company (UK or overseas based) which is well-established nationally and/or internationally and widely acknowledged as possessing expertise in its field **or** from an eminent individual with internationally recognised expertise in the applicant's specialist field.

(e) include full contact details of the author including personal email address and direct telephone number so that personal contact can be made; and

(f) be written specifically for the purpose of supporting the application, not as a general all-purpose reference letter.

Note: Paragraphs 5–9 substituted from 1 October 2013 subject to savings for applications made before that date (HC 628). Table in paragraph 9 substituted from 6 November 2014 (HC 693).

Criteria for endorsement by Tech City UK

10. The applicant must satisfy all of the mandatory criteria, and at least two of the qualifying criteria, in the table below:

Exceptional Talent (world leader)
Mandatory The applicant must have a proven track record of innovation working for a digital technology company. The applicant must provide a dated letter of personal recommendation from a recognised expert resident in the UK who is familiar with his work and his contribution to his field, and is qualified to assess his claim to be a world leader in his field. The applicant must meet two or more of the following Qualifying Criteria. **Qualifying** The applicant: • Has led in the development of new or leading-edge technology; • Has had significant commercial success in the digital technology sector; • Has received or been nominated for a prestigious internationally recognised prize in the digital technology sector; • Has been recognised as a world-leading talent in the digital technology sector.

Note: Paragraphs 10–13 substituted from 6 April 2014 subject to savings for applications made before that date (HC 1138 as amended by HC 1201).

11. The applicant must provide the following documents:

(a) A completed Designated Competent Bodies' Tier 1 (Exceptional Talent) application form;

(b) A short curriculum vitae outlining his career and publication history (of no more than 3 A4 sides in length).

(c) Evidence of any active businesses established or businesses that have been dissolved in the last five years or evidence of share ownership through employment in a digital technology sector company.

(d) A dated letter of recommendation written in support of the application from a recognised expert in the UK who is familiar with his work and his contribution to his field, and is qualified to assess his claim to be a world leader in his field. The letter should include be dated and include details of how the recognised expert knows the applicant; the applicant's achievements in the specialist field, and how in the opinion of the recognised expert the applicant exhibits exceptional talent; how the applicant would benefit from living in the UK; and the contribution they would make to the UK digital technology sector.

(e) Evidence in relation to at least two of the qualifying criteria listed above.

Note: Paragraphs 10–13 substituted from 6 April 2014 subject to savings for applications made before that date (HC 1138 as amended by HC 1201).

12. The documents in paragraph 11 above must be written in English or accompanied by authorised English translations.

Note: Paragraphs 10–13 substituted from 6 April 2014 subject to savings for applications made before that date (HC 1138 as amended by HC 1201).

13. When assessing applicants Tech City UK will take into consideration the following:

(a) The applicant's track record/career history (including his international standing, the significance of his work and the impact of his activity in a company or as an individual);

(b) The strength of the supporting statements in the letter of personal recommendation, and evidence in relation to qualifying criteria; and

(c) The expected benefits of the applicant's presence in the UK in terms of the contribution to the UK digital technology sector.

Note: Paragraphs 10–13 substituted from 6 April 2014 subject to savings for applications made before that date (HC 1138 as amended by HC 1201).

Appendix M

Sports Governing Bodies for Tier 2 (Sportsperson) and Tier 5 (Temporary Worker - Creative and Sporting) applications

1. Applicants in these categories must be endorsed by the relevant Governing Body from the table below, and the Certificate of Sponsorship Checking Service entry relating to the application must confirm this endorsement.

2. Each Governing Body may only endorse applicants in the Tier(s) specified in the table.

Sport	Governing body	Tiers
Archery	Grand National Archery Society	Tier 2 (Sportsperson) and Tier 5 (Temporary Worker – Creative and Sporting)
Athletics	UK Athletics	Tier 2 (Sportsperson) and Tier 5 (Temporary Worker – Creative and Sporting)
Badminton	Badminton England	Tier 2 (Sportsperson) and Tier 5 (Temporary Worker – Creative and Sporting)
Badminton	Badminton Scotland	Tier 2 (Sportsperson) and Tier 5 (Temporary Worker – Creative and Sporting)
Baseball	BaseballSoftball UK	Tier 2 (Sportsperson) and Tier 5 (Temporary Worker – Creative and Sporting)
Basketball	Basketball England	Tier 2 (Sportsperson) and Tier 5 (Temporary Worker – Creative and Sporting)
Basketball	Basketball Ireland	Tier 2 (Sportsperson) and Tier 5 (Temporary Worker – Creative and Sporting)
Boxing	British Boxing Board of Control	Tier 2 (Sportsperson) and Tier 5 (Temporary Worker – Creative and Sporting)
Canoeing	British Canoeing	Tier 2 (Sportsperson) and Tier 5 (Temporary Worker– Creative and Sporting)
Chinese Martial Arts	British Council for Chinese Martial Arts	Tier 2 (Sportsperson) and Tier 5 (Temporary Worker – Creative and Sporting)
Cricket	England and Wales Cricket Board (ECB)	Tier 2 (Sportsperson) and Tier 5 (Temporary Worker – Creative and Sporting)
Cricket	Cricket Scotland	Tier 2 (Sportsperson) and Tier 5 (Temporary Worker – Creative and Sporting)
Cricket	Cricket Ireland	Tier 2 (Sportsperson) and Tier 5 (Temporary Worker – Creative and Sporting)
Curling	Royal Caledonian Curling Club	Tier 2 (Sportsperson)
Cycling	British Cycling	Tier 2 (Sportsperson) and Tier 5 (Temporary Worker – Creative and Sporting)
Equestrianism	British Horse Society	Tier 2 (Sportsperson) and Tier 5 (Temporary Worker – Creative and Sporting)

Fencing	British Fencing	Tier 2 (Sportsperson) and Tier 5 (Temporary Worker – Creative and Sporting)
Field Hockey England	England Hockey	Tier 2 (Sportsperson) and Tier 5 (Temporary Worker – Creative and Sporting)
Field Hockey Scotland	Scottish Hockey Union	Tier 2 (Sportsperson) and Tier 5 (Temporary Worker – Creative and Sporting)
Field Hockey Wales	Welsh Hockey Union	Tier 2 (Sportsperson) and Tier 5 (Temporary Worker – Creative and Sporting)
Field Hockey Ireland	Irish Hockey Association	Tier 2 (Sportsperson) and Tier 5 (Temporary Worker – Creative and Sporting)
Football England	The Football Association	Tier 2 (Sportsperson) and Tier 5 (Temporary Worker – Creative and Sporting)
Football Scotland	Scottish Football Association	Tier 2 (Sportsperson) and Tier 5 (Temporary Worker – Creative and Sporting)
Football Wales	The Football Association of Wales	Tier 2 (Sportsperson) and Tier 5 (Temporary Worker – Creative and Sporting)
Football Northern Ireland	Irish Football Association	Tier 2 (Sportsperson) and Tier 5 (Temporary Worker – Creative and Sporting)
Gymnastics	British Gymnastics	Tier 2 (Sportsperson) and Tier 5 (Temporary Worker – Creative and Sporting)
Handball	British Handball Association	Tier 2 (Sportsperson) and Tier 5 (Temporary Worker – Creative and Sporting)
Ice Hockey	Ice Hockey (UK)	Tier 2 (Sportsperson) and Tier 5 (Temporary Worker – Creative and Sporting)
Ice Skating	National Ice Skating Association of Great Britain and Northern Ireland	Tier 5 (Temporary Worker – Creative and Sporting)
Jockeys and Trainers	British Horseracing Authority	Tier 2 (Sportsperson) and Tier 5 (Temporary Worker – Creative and Sporting)
Judo	British Judo Association	Tier 2 (Sportsperson) and Tier 5 (Temporary Worker – Creative and Sporting)
Kabbadi	England Kabaddi Federation (UK) Registered	Tier 2 (Sportsperson) and Tier 5 (Temporary Worker – Creative and Sporting)
Karate	Scottish Karate	Tier 5 (Temporary Worker – Creative and Sporting)
Lacrosse	English Lacrosse	Tier 2 (Sportsperson) and Tier 5 (Temporary Worker – Creative and Sporting)
Motorcycling (except speedway)	Auto-cycle Union	Tier 2 (Sportsperson)

Motorsports	The Royal Automobile Club Motor Sports Association Ltd	Tier 2 (Sportsperson) and Tier 5 (Temporary Worker – Creative and Sporting)
Netball	Welsh Netball Association	Tier 2 (Sportsperson) and Tier 5 (Temporary Worker – Creative and Sporting)
Netball	England Netball	Tier 2 (Sportsperson) and Tier 5 (Temporary Worker – Creative and Sporting)
Netball	Netball Northern Ireland	Tier 2 (Sportsperson) and Tier 5 (Temporary Worker – Creative and Sporting)
Netball	Netball Scotland	Tier 2 (Sportsperson) and Tier 5 (Temporary Worker – Creative and Sporting)
Polo	Hurlingham Polo Association	Tier 2 (Sportsperson) and Tier 5 (Temporary Worker – Creative and Sporting)
Rowing	British Rowing	Tier 2 (Sportsperson) and Tier 5 (Temporary Worker – Creative and Sporting)
Rugby League	Rugby Football League	Tier 2 (Sportsperson) and Tier 5 (Temporary Worker – Creative and Sporting)
Rugby Union England	Rugby Football Union	Tier 2 (Sportsperson) and Tier 5 (Temporary Worker – Creative and Sporting)
Rugby Union Scotland	Scottish Rugby Union	Tier 2 (Sportsperson) and Tier 5 (Temporary Worker – Creative and Sporting)
Rugby Union Wales	Welsh Rugby Union	Tier 2 (Sportsperson) and Tier 5 (Temporary Worker – Creative and Sporting)
Rugby Union Ireland	Ulster Rugby	Tier 2 (Sportsperson) and Tier 5 (Temporary Worker – Creative and Sporting)
Sailing, windsurfing and powerboating	Royal Yachting Association	Tier 2 (Sportsperson) and Tier 5 (Temporary Worker – Creative and Sporting)
Shooting	British Shooting	Tier 2 (Sportsperson) and Tier 5 (Temporary Worker – Creative and Sporting)
Snooker	World Snooker	Tier 2 (Sportsperson)
Speedway	British Speedway Promoters Association	Tier 2 (Sportsperson)
Squash and racketball	England Squash and Racketball	Tier 2 (Sportsperson) and Tier 5 (Temporary Worker – Creative and Sporting)
Swimming, water polo, diving and synchronised swimming	British Swimming	Tier 2 (Sportsperson) and Tier 5 (Temporary Worker – Creative and Sporting)

Table Tennis	English Table Tennis Federation	Tier 2 (Sportsperson) and Tier 5 (Temporary Worker – Creative and Sporting)
Taekwondo	GB Taekwondo	Tier 2 (Sportsperson)
Tennis	Lawn Tennis Association	Tier 2 (Sportsperson) and Tier 5 (Temporary Worker – Creative and Sporting)
Triathlon	British Triathlon	Tier 2 (Sportsperson) and Tier 5 (Temporary Worker – Creative and Sporting)
Water Skiing	British Water Ski	Tier 5 (Temporary Worker – Creative and Sporting)
Wheelchair Basketball	British Wheelchair Basketball	Tier 2 (Sportsperson) and Tier 5 (Temporary Worker – Creative and Sporting)
Wrestling	British Wrestling Association	Tier 2 (Sportsperson) and Tier 5 (Temporary Worker – Creative and Sporting)
Yoga	The British Wheel of Yoga	Tier 2 (Sportsperson) and Tier 5 (Temporary Worker – Creative and Sporting)

Note: Paragraph 2 inserted and Table substituted from 6 November 2014 subject to savings for applications made before that date (HC 693).

Appendix N

Approved Tier 5 government authorised exchange schemes

Name of scheme	Scheme summary	Name of overarching body (sponsor)	Type of scheme	Area of UK covered
AIESEC internships	The scheme is part of AIESEC's global exchange programme in which 4,000 graduates participate every year. It develops the leadership skills of recent graduates from overseas, with typically at least a years' experience in management	AIESEC	Work experience programme Maximum 12 months	All UK

	(marketing, finance, sales), technical (IT, engineering) and development (charity) through work with UK companies and organisations.			
American Institute for Foreign Study (AIFS	A programme for US undergraduate education majors and postgraduate students run jointly with the Institute of Education, with whom they spend an initial 4 weeks and followed by around 10 weeks undertaking placements working with teachers in English secondary schools.	AIFS (UK) Ltd	Work experience programme Maximum 12 months	England
Bar Council	The scheme is an umbrella for three types of programmes involving overseas law, overseas students and lawyers undertaking pupillages (both funded and unfunded) and mini pupillages within barristers chambers and other legal training programmes.	Bar Council	Work experience programme Maximum 12 months	All UK
[BAE Systems Training, Intern and Graduate Programme]	[Programme designed to allow individuals to train alongside BAE Systems in the UK.]	[BAE systems]	[Research and training programme. Maximum 24 Months]	[UK]

BNSC Satellite KHTT Programme	A secondment programme for employees of foreign space agencies to undertake practical training and work experience working alongside specialist UK staff	British National Space Centre (DBIS)	Research and training programmes Maximum 24 months	All UK
BOND business internships	Overseas Industrial Placement scheme (BOND) is a UK Trade & Investment initiative whereby high quality professionals, selected through the British Council offices overseas, are assigned to UK companies for up to a year. Participants gain an understanding of UK business practices and the programme aims to foster links between them and the British business community.	British Council	Work experience programme Maximum 12 months	All UK
British Council – Speak European	This programme will provide practical, on-the-job training to a group of mid-career government employees from Serbia working in key departments of the central government, as well as in local self- government institutions.	British Council	Work experience programme Maximum 12 months	All UK

Broadening Horizons	The Broadening Horizons scheme brings to the UK Taiwanese teachers who are professionally qualified to teach Mandarin as a second language, to provide children at participating schools with a unique opportunity to study Mandarin Chinese and to explore the culture of Taiwan, which also brings benefits to teachers and language assistants.	The Sir Bernard Lovell Language School	Work experience programme Maximum 12 months	England
BUNAC Blue Card Internships – 'Intern in Britain'	BUNAC has over 40 years' experience of running international work programmes. The Blue Card Internships scheme provides a well-controlled pathway for a wide range of organisations in the UK to offer and to benefit from work experience opportunities (internships) for eligible students and recent graduates.	BUNAC	Work experience programme Maximum 12 months	All UK
[Cabinet Office Interchange Programme]	[To bring in relevant expertise and cutting edge thinking from the private sector and] academia to help deliver the Government's Efficiency and Reform agenda.	[Cabinet Office]	[Work experience programme Maximum 12 Months]	[All UK]

Chatham House Fellowship	The scheme provides opportunities for overseas government and non-government experts, drawn from policy communities, the private sector, academia and civil society, to participate in and undertake research at Chatham House relevant to their government or non-government area(s) of expertise.	The Royal Institute of International Affairs (Chatham House)	Research & Training Programmes Maximum 24 months	All UK
Chevening Programme	The programme includes scholars and researchers attending the UK Environment Programme's World Conservation Monitoring Centre in Cambridge, the Oxford Centre for Islamic Studies and the Clore Leadership programme.	Association of Commonwealth Universities (ACU)	Research and training programmes Maximum 24 months	All UK
City Fellowships Scheme	The scheme aims to strengthen Anglo-American financial relations by bringing young minority financiers from the US to the City of London to work at Goldman Sachs and Morgan Stanley.	Sponsors for Educational Opportunity (SEO) London	Work experience programme Maximum 12 months	All UK

Commonwealth Exchange Programme	The programme offers teachers the opportunity to work in different education systems, exchange ideas and knowledge and observe teaching practices in another country. Teachers exchange positions and homes with those from Australia, Canada or New Zealand for between one term and one year. Exchanges to Canada take place from September toAugust. Those to Australia and New Zealand run from January to December.	Commonwealth Youth Exchange Council (CYEC)	Work experience programme Maximum 12 months	All UK
Commonwealth Scholarships and Fellowships Plan	This is an annual scheme made available to developing Common wealth countries by the Common wealth Scholarships Commission. Participants Undertake academic, medical or professional research fellowships.	[Association of Commonwealth Universities]	Research and training programmes Maximum 24 Months	All UK
Competition Commission and US Federal Trade Commission scheme	A work exchange scheme with the USA, primarily with the Federal Trade Commission and the Journal	Competition Commission	Work experience programme Maximum 12 months	All UK

	of Economists, to promote cooperation and mutual understanding with the objective of learning from one another's expertise in competition regulation.			
Defence Academy		Defence Academy	Research and training programmes Maximum 24 months	All UK
De La Rue Internship	Internship Programme for Post Graduate students at the University of West Indies, to build on and consolidate the support De La Rue already provides to high achieving students in the Caribbean through a scholarship programme	De La Rue International	Work experience programme Maximum 12 months	All UK
Encouraging Dynamic Global Entrepreneurs (EDGE)	EDGE is a unique business development and entrepreneurial programme involving undergraduates from Scottish and overseas universities and 5th- and 6th-year school pupils. They work in consultancy teams implementing key business development for companies,	Scottish Enterprise	Work experience programme Maximum 12 months	Scotland

	providing experiential learning for students and businesses.			
Engineering work placement scheme	This scheme offers overseas engineering students (both undergraduates and graduates) short work experience opportunities with engineering companies in the UK.	Twin Training International	Work experience programme Maximum 12 months	UK
Erasmus	Erasmus is a European Commission educational exchange programme for higher education students and teachers. It aims to increase student mobility within Europe through opportunities for work and study and promotes trans-national cooperation projects among universities across Europe. Erasmus Mundus is for joint cooperation and mobility programmes for postgraduate students, researchers and staff.	British Council Wales British Council Scotland British Council British Council Northern Ireland	Work experience programme Maximum 12 months	All UK
EU-China Managers Exchange and Training Programme (METP)	The programme is co-funded by the EU and the People's Republic of China with the aim of training Chinese	Manchester Metropolitan University	Work experience programme Maximum 12 months	All UK

	and EU business managers, especially in small and medium-sized companies, in their languages, culture and business practices and to build networks.			
European Voluntary Service (Youth in Action Programme)	Part of the European Union's Youth in Action Programme, funded by the European Commission, the EVS scheme offers people aged 18-30 the opportunity to undertake voluntary work placements in the social, cultural, environmental and sports sectors for a period of 2 to 12 months. Placements of 2 weeks to 2 months are also available.	British Council	Work experience programme Maximum 12 months	All UK
Finance Ministries and Central Banks schemes	The schemes includes secondments by employees of other central banks and financial institutions, research fellowships and PhD research internships for economists who will undertake placements with the Bank of England for between 1 and 18 months' duration.	HM Treasury	Research and training programmes Maximum 24 months	All UK

Food Standards Australia and New Zealand	A secondment programme for government bodies, to promote cooperation and mutual understanding with the objective of learning from one another's expertise in food safety.	Food Standards Agency	Work experience programme Maximum 12 months	All UK
Foreign & Commonwealth Office		Foreign & Commonwealth Office	Work experience programme Maximum 12 months	All UK
Foreign Language Assistants Programme	Working with partner organisations overseas to provide opportunities for young people to work as language assistants in the UK, the programme aims to improve both the language ability of the assistants and students in addition to expanding their cultural awareness.	British Council Wales British Council Scotland British Council British Council Northern Ireland	Work experience programme Maximum 12 months	All UK
Fullbright UK-US Teacher Exchange Programme	Run by the British Council in collaboration with the US Department of State, the programme offers outstanding UK teachers the opportunity to trade places. Teachers can spend the autumn term or one full academic	British Council Wales British Council Scotland British Council British Council Northern Ireland	Work experience programme Maximum 12 months	All UK

	year teaching in the United States. Exchanges involve elementary and secondary schools, including community and further education colleges throughout the US.			
Glasgow Caledonian University International exchange programme	To offer students, through the exchange programme, work experience, cultural diversity and personal development to strengthen their employability.	Glasgow Caledonian University	Work experience programme Maximum 12 months	Scotland
Grundtvig	Grundtvig, part of the European Commission's Lifelong Learning Programme, aims to strengthen the European dimension in adult education and lifelong learning. Funding is open to any organisation based in one of the countries participating in the programme involved in adult education. The programme funds a range of activities: assistantships, in-service training, learner workshops, visits and exchanges.	Ecorys UK Ltd	Work experience programme Maximum 12 months	All UK

[Hanban: Mandarin teachers Scheme]	[The scheme is part of Hanban's global Exchange Programme through which it sponsors volunteer and professional Mandarin teachers to undertake placements at Confucius institutes and classrooms in the UK, and at institutions in the UK which are covered by Hanban UK's teaching Exchange programme. These roles are not filling Teaching vacancies. The scheme aims to build and/or enhance foreign language] skills and foster good cultural relations in between the UK and China.	[Hanban UK Ltd]	[Overseas Government language programme. Maximum 24 Months]	[All UK]
Highways Agency Scheme	The scheme is intended to honour the historic and future commitments to facilitating the sharing of experience, scientific information, technology, working practice and organisational cultures between Highways Agency and similar administrations outside of the EEA.	Highways Agency	Work experience programme Maximum 12 months	All UK

HMC Projects in Central and Eastern Europe – Teachers' Work Exchange Scheme	This scheme offers teachers from Central and Eastern Europe a year of work experience in UK independent schools to enable them to experience the UK educational system.	HMC Projects in Central and Eastern Europe	Work experience programme Maximum 12 months	All UK
HMRC Exchange Scheme	The scheme facilitates the sharing of experience, working practices and organisational cultures between HM Revenue & Customs and tax, customs and similar administrations outside the EEA	HM Revenue & Customs	Work experience programme	All UK
IAESTE	IAESTE UK provides science, engineering and applied arts graduates with training experience relevant to their studies through work placements.	British Council Wales British Council Scotland British Council British Council Northern Ireland	Work experience programme Maximum 12 months	England Northern Ireland Scotland Wales
[Intensive Korean Public School English Teacher Training Programme]	[A customised in-service continuing professional development programme for very experienced Korean English teachers who have been specially selected.]	[University of Chichester]	[Work Experience Programme Maximum 12 Months]	[England]
International Cross-Posting Programme for Kazakhstan	UK Trade & Investment	Work experience programme Maximum 12 Months	All UK	

International Defence and Security Scheme (IDSS)	The aim of the IDSS scheme is to share knowledge, experience and best practice between the UK and foreign defence, aerospace, security and space industries in cooperative programmes.	ADS Group	Work experience programme Maximum 12 months	All UK
International Exchange Programme (UK) Ltd	Providing international training and career development through guided practical work experience across the environmental and land-based sector. Programmes monitored and industry endorsed via individuals' IntSCA personal development programme, encouraging continued skills progression.	IEPUK Ltd	Work experience programme Maximum 12 months	All UK
International Fire and Rescue Training Scheme		[Capita]	Research and training programmes Maximum 24 months	England with scope to include devolved administrations if required.
International Horticulture Scheme	This is an international horticultural and education skills development and exchange scheme designed to develop practical skills and to further academic studies within	Lantra	Work experience programme Maximum 12 months	Gardens or establishments linked to the Royal Botanic Gardens, Kew the Royal Horticultural Society's gardens.

	the designated establishments of the Royal Botanic Gardens, Kew and the Royal Horticultural Society.			
International Internship Scheme	A scheme for young people and future business leaders from outside the EEA to experience	Fragomen LLP	Work experience programme Maximum 12 months	All UK
	working for UK companies in the UK working environment.			
International Science and Innovation Unit		International Science and Innovation Unit	Work experience programme Maximum 12 months	All UK
[International Student Internship Scheme (ISIS)]	[This internship scheme will offer supernumerary work placements to: Chinese students from the top 211 universities; Chinese graduates from UK universities (who will transfer from Tier 4 to Tier 5 GAE) and Chinese nationals (students and graduates) applying direct from China. Interns will spend time with large UK businesses looking to expand their Chinese presence and to grow their trade links with China.]	[Denning Legal & Overseas Student Service Centre]	[Work experience programme Maximum 12 Months]	[UK]

International Optometrists Scheme	Scheme for registration for optometry graduates with a 2.2 degree or above. The scheme ensures they have the knowledge and skills to enter the General Optical Council's (GOC) Register and practise optometry without supervision.	College of Optometrists	Research and training programmes Maximum 24 months	All UK
Jiangsu Centre for Chinese Studies in Essex	To promote the teaching and learning of Mandarin and an appreciation of Chinese culture in Essex schools and to the wider local community, including businesses; underpin the links of friendship, education, culture and business between the County of Essex and the Province of Jiangsu.	Essex County Council	Work experience programme Maximum 12 months	All UK
Korean Teacher Exchange Programme	The scheme contributes to the DfE objective of strengthening maths teaching in schools.	Institute of Education University of London	Work experience programme Maximum 12 months	All UK
Law Society Tier 5 scheme for migrant lawyers	This scheme for migrant lawyers is open to law firms based in England and Wales. It covers placements, internships and secondments	The Law Society of England and Wales	Work experience programme Maximum 12 months	England and Wales

	offered to lawyers and law students from other countries coming to the UK for primarily non-economic purposes for limited periods to share knowledge, experience and best practice.			
Leonardo da Vinci	Leonardo is part of the European Commission's Lifelong Learning Programme. UK organisations work with European partners to exchange best practice, increase staff expertise and develop learners' skills. The programme is open to any organisation involved in vocational training in the countries participating in the programme and includes activities such as mobility projects, preparatory visits and transfer of innovation.	Ecorys Ltd	Work experience programme Maximum 12 months	All UK
London Organising Committee of the Olympic and Paralympic Olympic Games (LOCOG)	Secondment programme for employees of future organising committees, allowing them to undertake practical training and work experience working		Work experience programme Maximum 12 months	All UK

	alongside London 2012 staff. They will then cascade this learning back to their home organising committee.			
Lord Chancellor's Training Scheme for Young Chinese Lawyers	The programme is organised to enable the Chinese lawyers to obtain practical experience in commercial law, litigation and court procedure as well as the management of a legal practice.	British Council	Work experience programme Maximum 12 months	All UK
Mathematics Teacher Exchange Programme (England–China)	Mathematics teachers from China will support the teaching and learning of mathematics, and promote their approaches to the teaching of mathematics, in a network of Maths Hubs across England which are funded by the Department for Education (DfE). There will also be reciprocal arrangements for teachers from England to spend time in schools in China.	National College for Teaching and Leadership, Department of Education	Work Experience 12 months	England
Medical Training Initiative	The scheme allows post-graduate medical graduates to undertake a fixed period of training or development in the UK, normally	Academy of Medical Royal Colleges	Research and training programmes Maximum 24 months	All UK

	within the NHS. It covers all schemes and arrangements sponsored or administered by the medical royal colleges and similar organisations for the training of overseas doctors. MTI placements are temporary and require the approval of the employer and the local postgraduate dean of the relevant medical royal college.			
Medical Training Initiative for Dentistry	International Training Fellows: the Faculty of Dental Surgery (FDS) of the Royal College of Surgeons of England is able to sponsor suitably qualified postgraduate dentists to come to the UK for clinical training in an approved hospital training post.	The Royal College of Surgeons of England	Research and training programmes Maximum 24 months	England
Mountbatten Programme		Mountbatten Institute	Work experience programme Maximum 12 months	All UK
National Assembly for Wales Intern Programme	The scheme enables students from Ohio University to undertake intern placements for up to three months with assembly members.	National Assembly for Wales	Work experience programme Maximum 12 months	Wales

National Policing Improvement Agency (NPIA)	To support the NPIA in establishing a UK Police Training and Development Exchange Scheme, aligned to one of its core strategic aims of improving international police training and development partnerships. The aim is to increase shared good practice, improve interoperability and enhance the impact of UK international policing assistance aligned to HMG security and development priorities.	National Policing Improvement Agency (NPIA)	Work experience programme Maximum 12 months	All UK
NHS Tayside International Staff Exchange Scheme	The scheme aims to share different ways of working and approaches to care needs. This would provide an insight into how different health systems operate and use this to develop local services.	NHS Tayside	Work experience programme Maximum 12 months	All UK
NIM China Secondee Programme		LGC Ltd	Work experience programme Maximum 12 months	All UK
NPL Guest Worker and Secondment Scheme	This reciprocal scheme aims to encourage closer collaboration between UK and overseas organisations interested in	National Physical Laboratory (NPL) Management Limited	Research and training programmes Maximum 24 months	England

	metrology by allowing scientists, industrial experts and students to undertake placements with the NPL.			
Overseas Fellows Post	The opportunity is accredited by [the General Medical Council] and approved by the Royal College of Surgeons of Edinburgh International Medical Graduate Sponsorship Scheme.	National Health Service (NHS) Highland	Research and training programmes Maximum 24 months	Scotland
REX Programme	The REX programme enables highly qualified teachers from Japan to work temporarily in countries where English is spoken to teach Japanese language and culture.	Ceredigion County Council	Work experience programme Maximum 12 months	All UK
Royal Pharmaceutical Society international pre-registration scheme	Pre-registration placements are supernumerary training positions, under the supervision of a pre-registration tutor, which enables the pre-registration trainee pharmacist to undergo training as mandated by the General Pharmaceutical Council (GPhC).	Royal Pharmaceutical Society	Research and training programmes Maximum 24 months	All UK

[Scottish Government Interchange Scheme]	[A scheme to share knowledge, experience and best practice with other governments and organisations on the full range of policy areas for which the Scottish Government has responsibility.]	[Scottish Government]	[Work Experience Programme Maximum 12 months]	
Scottish Schools Education Research Centre (SSERC) Work Exchange programme with China	Offers employees of the Educational Equipment Research and Development Centre (EERDC) in China to come to Scotland to share best practices and educational resources with their Scottish counterparts and to develop new educational resources	Scottish Schools Education Research Centre (SSERC)	Work experience programme Maximum 12 months	Scotland
[Serious Fraud Office]	[This is an exchange programme between the Serious fraud Office and law enforcement partners in overseas jurisdictions. The programme will help to promote greater cooperation with investigations, and to share and Develop investigative techniques and approaches in the fight against fraud and corruption in the UK and overseas.]	[Serious Fraud Office]	[Work experience Maximum 12 Months]	[UK]

Sponsored researcher	A scheme to enable higher Education institutions to recruit sponsored researchers, or visiting academics giving lectures, acting as examiners or working on supernumerary Research collaborations. Institutions do not need individual support from the Department for Business, Innovation and Skills to operate a scheme.	Higher education institutions	Research and training programmes Maximum 24 months	All UK
Sponsored Scientific Researcher Initiative	This scheme enables organisations to engage overseas postgraduate scientists in formal research projects and/or collaborations within an internationally recognised host institute/ laboratory for sharing knowledge, experience and best practice, and enabling the individual to experience the social and cultural life of the United Kingdom	UK Shared Business Services Limited (UKSBS)	Research & Training Programmes Maximum 24 months	UK

The Ofgem International Staff Exchange Scheme	A scheme to promote cooperation and mutual understanding between Ofgem and similar regulatory agencies overseas.	Office of Gas & Electricity Markets (Ofgem)	Work experience programme Maximum 12 months	England
Tier 5 interns scheme	Designed for employers, the Tier 5 intern programme is a government approved scheme which allows graduates and undergraduates from countries outside the EEA to gain intern experience working within UK industry and provides organisations with the scope to deploy the brightest and best talent on key initiatives and learn skills they can take back to their home country.	GTI Recruiting Solutions	Work experience programme Maximum 12 months	All UK
UK-India Education and Research Initiative	This 5-year initiative is designed to facilitate education and research cooperation between the 2 countries through collaboration	British Council British Council Wales British Council Scotland British Council N Ireland	Work experience programme Maximum 12 months	England Wales Scotland N Ireland

	between schools, professional and technical skills, HE research and graduate work experience.			
US-UK Education Commission (also known as the US-UK Fulbright Commission)	To foster mutual understanding between the US and the UK through academic exchange by the awarding of merit based scholarships.	US-UK Education Commission (also known as the US-UK Fulbright Commission)	Research and training programmes Maximum 24 months	All UK
Welsh Language Teaching Programme in Patagonia	The scheme aims to strengthen the use of Welsh in Patagonia by bringing Patagonians to Wales to improve their language fluency and bilingual environments. Participants are teachers, tutors or those suitable to work in activities which develop the use of Welsh in the wider social and business situations.	British Council Wales	Work experience programme Maximum 12 months	Wales

Note: Entry relating to Intensive Korean Public School English Teacher Training Programme inserted and entry relating to Overseas Fellows Post amended in the second column from 13 December 2012 subject to savings for applications made before that date (HC 760). Entries relating to Commonwealth Scholarships and Fellowships Plan and International Fire and Rescue Training Scheme amended and entry relating to Scottish Government Interchange Scheme inserted from 6 April 2013 subject to savings for applications made before that date (HC 1039). Entries relating to De La Rue Internship and Mandarin Teachers Programme (University of Ulster) inserted and entries relating to UK-China Graduate Work Experience Programme and UK-India Graduate Work Experience Programme deleted from 1 October 2013 subject to savings for applications made before that date (HC 628). Entry relating to Cabinet Office Interchange Programme substituted from 1 July 2013 (HC 244). Entries relating to BAE Systems Training, Intern and Graduate Programme, Hanban, International Student Internship Scheme, Mandarin Teachers Programme at South Bank University, and Serious Fraud Office inserted from 6 April 2014 (HC 1138 as amended by HC 1201). Entry relating to Mathematics Teacher Exchange Programme (England–China) inserted from 1 August 2014 subject to savings for applications made before that date (HC 532). Entries relating to Engineering work placement scheme and SSERC inserted, entry relating to Sponsored Scientific Researcher Initiative substituted and entries relating to Mandarin Teachers Programmes—London Southbank University, Mandarin Teaching Programme—University of Edinburgh, Mandarin Teachers Programme—Strathclyde University and Mandarin Teachers Programme—University of Ulster deleted from 6 November 2014 subject to savings for applications made before that date (HC 693).

Appendix O

List of English language tests that have been approved by the Home Office for English language requirements for limited leave to enter or remain under the Immigration Rules

Note: Appendix O substituted from 1 July 2013 (HC 244).

. . .

Note: Introductory words deleted from 1 October 2013 subject to savings for applications made before that date (HC 628).

1. Where two or more components (reading, writing, speaking and listening) of an English language test are examined and awarded together, for example a combined exam and certificate for reading and writing skills, the specified evidence submitted by the applicant must show that he achieved the required scores in all the relevant components during a single sitting of that examination, unless exempted from sitting a component on the basis of his disability. This requirement does not apply to applications made under part 8 or Appendix FM unless Appendix KoLL applies.

Note: Paragraph 1 inserted from 1 October 2013 subject to savings for applications made before that date (HC 628).

2. Only the level(s) of Test specified for each Test are approved.

Note: Paragraph 2 inserted from 1 October 2013 subject to savings for applications made before that date (HC 628).

English language Test	Awarded by	Levels covered by test	Test Validity	Documents required with application
Cambridge English: Key (also known as Key English Test)	Cambridge English (previously known as Cambridge ESOL)	A1 A2 B1	No expiry	For tests taken before 6 April 2013: Certificate, Statement of results, Candidate ID number and Candidate's secret number (applicants should provide

				Statement of Entry if possible) For tests taken on or after 6 April 2013: no documents required (Scores will be verified using the Cambridge English online system using name, date of birth and passport number).
Cambridge English: Preliminary (also known as Preliminary English Test)	Cambridge English (previously known as Cambridge ESOL)	A2 B1 B2	No expiry	For tests taken before 6 April 2013: Certificate, Statement of results, Candidate ID number and Candidate's secret number (applicants should provide Statement of Entry if possible) For tests taken on or after 6 April 2013: no documents required (Scores will be verified using the Cambridge English online system using name, date of birth and passport number)
Cambridge English: First (also known as First Certificate in English)	Cambridge English (previously known as Cambridge ESOL)	B1 B2 C1	No expiry	For tests taken before 6 April 2013: Certificate, Statement of results, Candidate ID number and Candidate's secret number (applicants should provide Statement of Entry if possible) For tests taken on or after 6 April 2013: no documents required (Scores will be verified using the Cambridge English online system using name, date of birth and passport number)
Cambridge English: Advanced (also known as Certificate in Advanced English)	Cambridge English (previously known as Cambridge ESOL)	B2 C1 C2	No expiry	For tests taken before 6 April 2013: Certificate, Statement of results, Candidate ID number and Candidate's secret number (applicants should provide Statement of Entry if possible)

				For tests taken on or after 6 April 2013: no documents required (Scores will be verified using the Cambridge English online) system using name, date of birth and passport number
Cambridge English: Proficiency (also known as Certificate of Proficiency in English)	Cambridge English (previously known as Cambridge ESOL)	C1 C2	No expiry	For tests taken before 6 April 2013: Certificate, Statement of results, Candidate ID number and Candidate's secret number (applicants should provide Statement of Entry if possible) For tests taken on or after 6 April 2013: no documents required (Scores will be verified using the Cambridge English online system using name, date of birth and passport number)
Cambridge English: Business Preliminary (also known as Business English Certificate Preliminary)	Cambridge English (previously known as Cambridge ESOL)	A2 B1 B2	No expiry	For tests taken before 6 April 2013: Certificate, Statement of results, Candidate ID number and Candidate's secret number (applicants should provide Statement of Entry if possible) For tests taken on or after 6 April 2013: no documents required (Scores will be verified using the Cambridge English online system using name, date of birth and passport number)
Cambridge English: Business Vantage (also known as Business English Certificate Vantage)	Cambridge English (previously known as Cambridge ESOL)	B1 B2 C1	No expiry	For tests taken before 6 April 2013: Certificate, Statement of results, Candidate ID number and Candidate's secret number (applicants should provide Statement of Entry if possible) For tests taken on or after 6 April 2013: no documents required (Scores will be verified using the Cambridge English online system using name, date of birth and passport number)

Cambridge English: Business Higher (also known as Business English Certificate Higher)	Cambridge English (previously known as Cambridge ESOL)	B2 C1 C2	No expiry	For tests taken before 6 April 2013: Certificate, Statement of results, Candidate ID number and Candidate's secret number (applicants should provide Statement of Entry if possible) For tests taken on or after 6 April 2013: no documents required (Scores will be verified using the Cambridge English online system using name, date of birth and passport number)
Cambridge English Legal (also known as International Legal English Certificate)	Cambridge English (previously known as Cambridge ESOL)	B2 C1	No expiry	For tests taken before 6 April 2013: Certificate, Statement of results, Candidate ID number and Candidate's secret number (applicants should provide Statement of Entry if possible) For tests taken on or after 6 April 2013: no documents required (Scores will be verified using the Cambridge English online system using name, date of birth and passport number)
Cambridge English: Financial (also known as International Certificate in Financial English)	Cambridge English (previously known as Cambridge ESOL)	B2 C1	No expiry	For tests taken before 6 April 2013: Certificate, Statement of results, Candidate ID number and Candidate's secret number (applicants should provide Statement of Entry if possible) For tests taken on or after 6 April 2013: no documents required (Scores will be verified using the Cambridge English online system using name, date of birth and passport number)
Cambridge IGCSE English as a First Language (Syllabus 0500 & 0522)	Cambridge International Examinations	B1 B2	No expiry	Certificate Supplementary Certifying Statement with breakdown of component grades

Cambridge IGCSE English as a Second Language (Syllabus 0510 & 0511)	Cambridge International Examinations	A2 B1 B2	No expiry	Certificate Supplementary Certifying Statement with breakdown of component grades
ESOL Skills for Life Entry 1	Cambridge English (previously known as Cambridge ESOL)	A1	No expiry	For tests taken before 6 April 2013: Certificate, Statement of Results for each component (reading, writing, speaking, listening), Name of test centre For tests taken on or after 6 April 2013: no documents required (Scores will be verified using the Cambridge English online system using name, date of birth and passport number)
ESOL Skills for Life Entry 2	Cambridge English (previously known as Cambridge ESOL)	A2	No expiry	For tests taken before 6 April 2013: Certificate, Statement of Results for each component (reading, writing, speaking, listening), Name of test centre For tests taken on or after 6 April 2013: no documents required (Scores will be verified using the Cambridge English online system using name, date of birth and passport number)
ESOL Skills for Life Entry 3	Cambridge English (previously known as Cambridge ESOL)	B1	No expiry	For tests taken before 6 April 2013: Certificate, Statement of Results for each component (reading, writing, speaking, listening), Name of test centre For tests taken on or after 6 April 2013: no documents required (Scores will be verified using the Cambridge English online system using name, date of birth and passport number)

ESOL Skills for Life Level 1	Cambridge English (previously known as Cambridge ESOL)	B2	No expiry	For tests taken before 6 April 2013: Certificate, Statement of Results for each component (reading, writing, speaking, listening), Name of test centre For tests taken on or documents required (Scores will be verified using the Cambridge English online system using name, date of birth and passport number)
ESOL Skills for Life Level 2	Cambridge English (previously known as Cambridge ESOL)	C1	No expiry	For tests taken before 6 April 2013: Certificate, Statement of Results for each component (reading, writing, speaking, listening), Name of test centre For tests taken on or after 6 April 2013: no documents required (Scores will be verified using the Cambridge English online system using name, date of birth and passport number)
BULATS Online (certificated version) Only tests taken with certifying BULATS agents detailed on the BULATS website	Cambridge English (previously known as Cambridge ESOL)	A1 A2 B1 B2 C1 C2	2 years	For tests taken before 6 April 2013: Certificate, Test report form for each component (reading, writing, speaking, listening), Name of test centre, Country where test was taken For tests taken on or after 6 April 2013: no documents required (Scores will be verified using the Cambridge English online system using name, date of birth and passport number)
IELTS (Academic and General Training)	Cambridge English (previously known as Cambridge ESOL)	B1 B2 C1 C2	2 years	For tests taken before 6 April 2013: Test report form For tests taken on or after 6 April 2013: no documents required (Scores will be verified using the Cambridge English online system using name, date of birth and passport number)

City & Guilds International Speaking and Listening IESOL Diploma at A1 level	City & Guilds	A1 (spouse/ partner)	No expiry	One of the following document combinations: (1) 'International Speaking and Listening IESOL Diploma' certificate Or (2) ISESOL certificate plus IESOL Listening (A1) certificate
City & Guilds International ESOL (IESOL) Diploma	City & Guilds	A1 (spouse / partner)	No expiry	For tests booked or taken before 6 April 2013 by Points-Based System applicants, and for all spouse and partner applicants: One of the following document combinations: (1) IESOL Diploma certificate plus IESOL notification of candidate results sheet Or (2) ISESOL certificate plus IESOL certificate plus IESOL candidate results sheet Or (3) ISESOL certificate plus IESOL notification of candidate results sheet For tests booked and taken online on or after 6 April 2013 by Points-Based System applicants: One of the following document combinations (1) IESOL Diploma certificate Or (2) ISESOL certificate plus IESOL certificate
City & Guilds International ESOL (IESOL) Diploma	City & Guilds	A1 (all other categories) A2 B1 B2 C1 C2	No expiry	For tests booked or taken before 6 April 2013: One of the following document combinations: (1) IESOL Diploma certificate plus IESOL notification of candidate results sheet Or (2) ISESOL certificate plus IESOL certificate plus IESOL notification of candidate results sheet

				A1 booked and taken online on or after 6 April 2013: One of the following Document combinations: (1) IESOL Diploma certificate Or (2) ISESOL certificate plus IESOL certificate For A1 (all other categories) tests booked and taken online on or after 6 April 2013: (1) IESOL Diploma certificate Or (2) ISESOL certificate plus IESOL certificate plus Notification of candidate results sheet
Pearson Test of English Academic (PTE Academic)	Pearson	A1 A2 B1 B2 C1 C2	2 years	Print-out of online score report Scores must also be sent to the Home Office online Pearson does not issue paper certificates
Entry Level Certificate in ESOL Skills for Life	Trinity College London	A1 A2 B1	For UK immigration purposes, the tests are valid for 2 years only	For tests taken before 1 July 2013: Summary slip and certificate For tests taken on or after 1 July 2013: Certificate which must show the candidate's name, qualification, date of award and the candidate Trinity ID
Level 1 Certificate in ESOL Skills for life	Trinity College London	B2	For UK immigration purposes, the tests are valid for 2 years only	For tests taken before 1 July 2013: Summary slip and certificate For tests taken on or after 1 July 2013: Certificate which must show the candidate's name, qualification, date of award and the candidate Trinity ID
Level 2 Certificate in ESOL Skills for life	Trinity College London	C1	For UK immigration purposes, the tests are valid for 2 years only	For tests taken before 1 July 2013: Summary slip and certificate For tests taken on or after 1 July 2013: Certificate which must show the candidate's name, qualification, date of award and the candidate Trinity ID

Integrated skills in English	Trinity College London	A2 B1 B2 C1 C2	For UK immigration purposes, the tests are valid for 2 years only	For tests taken before 1 July 2013: Summary slip and certificate For tests taken on or after 1 July 2013: Certificate which must show the candidate's name, qualification, date of award and the candidate Trinity ID [For tests taken on or after 6 November 2014: Certificate as above which must also state "SELT Centre" on the test certificate and the test must be able to be verified on the online verification tool.]
Graded examinations in Spoken English	Trinity College London	A1 or higher	For UK immigration purposes, the tests are valid for 2 years only	Certificate [For tests taken on or after 6 November 2014: Certificate as above which must also state "SELT Centre" on the test certificate and the test must be able to be verified on the online verification tool.]

Note: Entries relating to TOEIC and TOEFL iBT Test deleted from 1 July 2014 (HC 198). This amendment is subject to detailed transitional provisions for which see the Implementation Section of HC 198 which can be accessed at <http:www.gov.uk/government/collections/immigration-rules-statement-of-changes>. Words inserted in the last column for the final two entries from 6 November 2014 subject to savings for applications made before that date (HC 693).

Appendix P

Lists of financial institutions that do not satisfactorily verify financial statements, or whose financial statements are accepted

1. An institution may be included on the relevant list of those that do not satisfactorily verify financial statements if:

(a) on the basis of experience, that it does not verify financial statements to the UK Border Agency's satisfaction in more than 50 per cent of a sample of cases; or

(b) it does not participate in specified schemes or arrangements in the country of origin, where the UK Border Agency trusts the verification checks provided by banks that do participate in those schemes.

2. An institution may be (but is not required to be) included on the relevant list of those whose financial statements are accepted if it:

(a) is an international bank;

(b) is a national bank with a UK private banking presence;
(c) is a regulated national or state bank that provides a core banking service; or
(d) has a history of providing satisfactory verification checks to the UK Border Agency.

3. The addition or removal of each institution to or from the relevant lists will be considered on its own facts.

4. An applicant will not satisfy any requirement in these rules which requires him to provide documents if those documents relate to a financial institution on a list of those that do not satisfactorily verify financial statements.

5. Where stated in the lists below, the 'effective date' is the date from which the UK Border Agency will not accept financial statements relating to the stated institution.

6. The UK Border Agency will continue to verify financial information from other institutions on a case-by-case basis, and may refuse applications on the basis of these individual checks.

7. The following lists have been established and are set out below:
(i) Financial institutions in Cameroon whose financial statements are accepted, set out in Table 1;
(ii) Financial institutions in India that do not satisfactorily verify financial statements, set out in Table 2;
(iii) Financial institutions in India whose financial statements are accepted, set out in Table 3;
(iv) Financial institutions in Ghana whose financial statements are accepted, set out in Table 4;
(v) Financial institutions in Pakistan that do not satisfactorily verify financial statements, set out in Table 5;
(vi) Financial institutions in Pakistan whose financial statements are accepted, set out in Table 6;
(vii) Financial institutions in Iran that do not satisfactorily verify financial statements, set out in Table 7;
(viii) Financial institutions in Iran whose financial statements are accepted, set out in Table 8;
(ix) Financial institutions in the Philippines that do not satisfactorily verify financial statements, set out in Table 9;
(x) Financial institutions in the Philippines whose financial statements are accepted, set out in Table 10;
(xi) Financial institutions in Bangladesh that do not satisfactorily verify financial statements, set out in Table 11;
(xii) Financial institutions in Bangladesh whose financial statements are accepted, set out in Table 12;
(xiii) Financial institutions in Sri Lanka whose financial statements are accepted, set out in Table 13.

Tables 1 to 13

Note: Tables 1 to 13 of Appendix P are not reproduced here. The contents are subject to regular amendment and users of this Handbook should consult the current version of the Tables which can be accessed online at <http://www.gov.uk/government/publications/immigration-rules-appendix-p>.

Appendix Q

Statement of written terms and conditions of employment required in paragraph 245ZO(f)(ii) and paragraph 245ZQ(e)(ii)

Statement of the terms and conditions of employment of an overseas domestic worker in a diplomatic household in the United Kingdom

This form must be completed and signed by the employer, signed by the overseas domestic worker and submitted with the entry clearance application or with the leave to remain application as required by paragraphs 245ZO(f)(ii) and 245ZQ(e)(ii) of the Immigration Rules.

Please complete this form in capitals.

Name of employee:

Name of employer:

1. Job Title:

2. Duties/Responsibilities:

3. Date of start of employment in the UK:

4. Employer's address in the UK:

5. Employee's address in the UK (if different from 4 please explain):

6. Employee's place of work in the UK (if different from 4 please explain):

7. Rate of Pay per week/month:

   Note: By signing this document, the employer is declaring that the employee will be paid in accordance with the National Minimum Wage Act 1998 and any Regulations made under it for the duration of the employment.

8. Hours of work per day/week:

Free periods per day:
Free periods per week:

9. Sleeping accommodation:

10. Holidays:

11. Ending the employment:

Employee must give . . . . weeks' notice if he/she decides to leave his/her job.

Employee is entitled to . . . . weeks' notice if the employer decides to dismiss him/her.

Employee is employed on a fixed-term contract until (date) (if applicable) . . . .

Signed . . . . Date . . . . (Employer)

I confirm that my conditions of employment are as described above:

Signed . . . . Date . . . . (Employee).

Appendix R

List of recognised festivals for which entry by amateur and professional entertainer visitors is permitted

Note: Appendix R substituted from 6 April 2014 subject to savings for applications made before that date (HC 1138 as amended by HC 1201).

- Aberdeen International Youth Festival
- Aldeburgh Festival
- Alnwick International Music Festival
- Barbican Festivals (Only Connect; Explorations; The Sound of Nonesuch Records;
- Summer festival; Autumn 1: Transcender, Autumn 2; Music and Film).
- Belfast Festival at Queens
- Bestival
- Billingham International Folklore Festival
- Birmingham International Jazz Festival
- Breakin' Convention
- Brighton Festival
- Brighton Fringe
- Brouhaha International Festival
- Calling Festival
- Cambridge Folk Festival
- Camp Bestival
- Celtic Connections Festival
- Cheltenham Festivals (Jazz/Science/Music/Literature)
- City of London Festival
- Cornwall International Male Voice Choral Festival
- Dance Umbrella
- Download
- Edinburgh Festival Fringe
- Edinburgh International Festival
- Edinburgh International Jazz and Blues Festival
- Edinburgh Military Tattoo,
- Glasgow International Jazz Festival
- Glastonbury
- Glyndebourne
- Greenbelt Festival
- Harrogate International Festival
- Hay Festival
- Huddersfield Contemporary Music Festival
- Latitude
- Leeds Festival

- LIFT
- London Jazz
- Manchester International Festival
- Meltdown
- National Eisteddfod of Wales
- Norfolk and Norwich Festival
- Reading Festival
- Salisbury International Arts Festival
- Snape Festival
- T in the Park
- V Festivals
- Wireless
- WOMAD Festival

Appendix T

Tuberculosis screening

Part I – applicable countries

[Migrants applying to enter the UK for more than 6 months from the countries listed below, or who are applying in a category which may lead to them being settled in the United Kingdom in accordance with the definition of "settled in the United Kingdom" contained in paragraph 6 of the Immigration Rules, must present at the time of application a valid medical certificate issued by a medical practitioner listed in Part 2 of this Appendix confirming that they have undergone screening for active pulmonary tuberculosis and that such tuberculosis is not present in the applicant.]

- Afghanistan
- Algeria
- Angola
- Armenia
- Azerbaijan
- Bangladesh
- Belarus
- Benin
- Bhutan
- Bolivia
- Botswana
- Brunei Darussalam
- Burkina Faso
- Burma
- Burundi
- Cambodia
- Cape Verde
- Central African Republic
- Chad
- Cameroon
- China
- Congo
- Congo Democratic Republic
- Côte d'Ivoire
- Democratic People's Republic of Korea
- Djibouti
- Dominican Republic
- Ecuador
- Equatorial Guinea
- Eritrea
- Ethiopia
- Gabon
- Gambia
- Georgia
- Ghana
- Guatemala
- Guinea
- Guinea Bissau
- Guyana
- Haiti
- Hong Kong or Macau
- India
- Indonesia
- Iraq
- Kazakhstan
- Kenya
- Kiribati
- Korea
- Kyrgyzstan

- Laos
- Lesotho
- Liberia
- Madagascar
- Malawi
- Malaysia
- Mali
- Marshall Islands
- Mauritania
- Micronesia
- Moldova
- Mongolia
- Morocco
- Mozambique
- Namibia
- Nepal
- Niger
- Nigeria
- Pakistan
- Palau
- Papua New Guinea
- Panama
- Paraguay
- Peru
- Russian Federation
- Rwanda
- Sao Tome and Principe
- Senegal
- Sierra Leone
- Solomon Islands
- Somalia
- South Africa
- South Sudan
- Sri Lanka
- Sudan
- Tajikistan
- Swaziland
- Tanzania
- Timor Leste
- Togo
- Thailand
- The Philippines
- Turkmenistan
- Tuvalu
- Uganda
- Ukraine
- Uzbekistan
- Vanuatu
- Vietnam
- Zambia
- Zimbabwe

Applicants from Burkina Faso, Côte d'Ivoire, Niger, Togo are screened in Ghana, those from Eritrea and Somalia are screened in Kenya, those in Lesotho and Swaziland are screened in South Africa and those from Laos are screened in Thailand.

Note: Introductory wording substituted from 31 December 2013 (HC 901). List of countries amended by the following rule changes: HC 847 (from 31 December 2012), HC 967 (from 28 February 2013), HC 244 (from 1 July 2013), Cm 8690 (from 1 August 2013), HC 686 (from 31 October 2013), HC 803 (from 1 December 2013, subject to savings for applications made before that date), HC 901 (from 31 December 2013), HC 938 (from 31 December 2013) and HC 1130 (from 31 March 2014).

Part 2 – List of Screening Clinics

Migrants applying to enter the UK for more than 6 months from the countries listed in Part 1 of this Appendix [, and, in the case of China, Hong Kong and Macau, a migrant who is applying in a category which may lead to him being settled in the United Kingdom in accordance with the definition of "settled in the United Kingdom" contained in paragraph 6 of the Immigration Rules,] must present at the time of application a valid medical certificate issued by a medical practitioner from a medical clinic listed below confirming that they have undergone screening for active pulmonary tuberculosis and that such tuberculosis is not present in the applicant.

Note: Words inserted in the introductory wording from 1 August 2013 (Cm 8690). The list of clinics is not reproduced here; it is subject to frequent change and users of the Handbook are advised to consult the current list which can be accessed online at <www.gov.uk/government/publications/immigration-rules-appendix-t>.

STATUTORY INSTRUMENTS

Immigration (Control of Entry through Republic of Ireland) Order 1972
(SI 1972, No. 1610)

Note: See SI 2014/2475 for amendments to this Order not included in the text.

1. This Order may be cited as the Immigration (Control of Entry through Republic of Ireland) Order 1972 and shall come into operation on 1 January 1973.

2.—(1) In this Order—

'the Act' means the Immigration Act 1971; and

['EEA national' means a national of an EEA State who is not also a British citizen;]

['EEA State' means a member State (other than the United Kingdom), Norway, Iceland, Liechtenstein or Switzerland.]

'visa national' means a person who, in accordance with the immigration rules, is required on entry into the United Kingdom to produce a passport or other document of identity endorsed with a United Kingdom visa and includes a stateless person.

(2) In this Order any reference to an Article shall be construed as a reference to an Article of this Order and any reference in an Article to a paragraph as a reference to a paragraph of that Article.

(3) ...

Note: Definitions inserted and paragraph (3) omitted from 12 October 2014 (SI 2014/2475).

3.—(1) This Article applies to—

(a) any person (other than a citizen of the Republic of Ireland) who arrives in the United Kingdom on an aircraft which began its flight in that Republic if he entered that Republic in the course of a journey to the United Kingdom which began outside the common travel area and was not given leave to land in that Republic in accordance with the law in force there;

(b) any person (other than a person to whom sub-paragraph (a) of this paragraph applies) who arrives in the United Kingdom on a local journey from the Republic of Ireland if he satisfies any of the following conditions, that is to say—

(i) he is a visa national who has no valid visa for his entry into the United Kingdom [, save for a visa national to whom article 3A applies];

(ii) he entered that Republic unlawfully from a place outside the common travel area;

(iii) he entered that Republic from a place in the United Kingdom and Islands after entering there unlawfully, [or if he had a limited leave to enter or remain there, after the expiry of the leave, provided that in either case] he has not subsequently been given leave to enter or remain in the United Kingdom or any of the Islands; . . .

(iv) he is a person in respect of whom directions have been given by the Secretary of State for him not to be given entry to the United Kingdom on the ground that his exclusion is conducive to the public good. [or

(v) he is a person who has been prohibited from entering the United Kingdom by an order made by the Secretary of State under any provision made under section 2(2) of the European Communities Act 1972.]

(2) In relation only to persons to whom this Article applies, the Republic of Ireland shall be excluded from section 1(3) of the Act (provisions relating to persons travelling on local journeys in the common travel area).

Note: Words in square brackets in subparagraph (1)(b)(iii) inserted by SI 1979/730. Words inserted in subparagraph (1)(b)(i) and paragraph (1)(b)(v) inserted from 12 October 2014 (SI 2014/2475).

[**3A.** This article applies to a visa national who is a citizen of a country specified in the Schedule who—

(a) has applied to the Republic of Ireland authorities for a visa to travel to the Republic;

(b) has made the application mentioned in sub-paragraph (a) to the Republic of Ireland authorities based in the country listed in the Schedule where the visa national is a citizen;

(c) has been granted a visa to travel to the Republic of Ireland by the Republic of Ireland authorities for the purpose of a stay of a period of 90 days or fewer, as a result of the application mentioned in sub-paragraph (a), which is ndorsed with the letters "BIVS";

(d) has since been given permission by the Republic of Ireland authorities, endorsed on his passport, to land or be in the Republic of Ireland pursuant to the visa mentioned in sub-paragraph (c); and

(e) is in possession of both the valid Irish visa mentioned in sub-paragraph (c) and the valid endorsement from the Republic of Ireland authorities conferring permission to land or to be in the Republic mentioned in sub-paragraph (d), at the time when he enters the United Kingdom on a local journey from the Republic of Ireland.]

Note: Article 3A inserted from 12 October 2014 (SI 2014/2475).

4.—(1) Subject to paragraph (2), this Article applies to [any person who does not have the right of abode in the United Kingdom under section 2 of the Act] and is not [an EEA national, or a person who is entitled to enter or remain in the United Kingdom by virtue of an enforceable EU right or any provision made under section 2(2) of the European Communities Act 1972,] and who enters the United Kingdom on a local journey from the Republic of Ireland after having entered that Republic—

(a) on coming from a place outside the common travel area; or

(b) after leaving the United Kingdom whilst having a limited leave to enter or remain there which has since expired.

(2) This Article shall not apply to any person [who arrives in the United Kingdom with leave to enter or remain in the United Kingdom which is in force but which was given to him before arrival or] who requires leave to enter the United Kingdom by virtue of Article 3 or section 9(4) of the Act.

(3) A person to whom this Article applies by virtue only of paragraph (1)(a) shall, unless he is a visa national [without a valid visa for entry to the United Kingdom, who is also a visa national to whom article 3A applies,] be subject to the restriction and to the condition set out in paragraph (4).

(4) The restriction and the condition referred to in paragraph (3) are—

(a) the period for which he may remain in the United Kingdom shall not be more than three months from the date on which he entered the United Kingdom; and

[(b) . . . he shall not engage in any occupation for reward; and

(c) . . . he shall not engage in any employment.]

(5) . . .

(6) . . .

[(**6A**) In relation to a person who is a visa national without a valid visa for entry to the United Kingdom and who is also a visa national to whom article 3A applies, the restriction and condition in paragraph (6B) apply instead of the provisions contained in paragraph (4).

(**6B**) The restriction and condition referred to in paragraph (6A) are—

(a) the period for which the visa national may remain in the United Kingdom ends on the date of the expiry of the permission to land or to be in the Republic of Ireland mentioned in article 3A(d);

(b) the person shall not engage in any occupation for reward or any employment.]

(7) The preceding provisions of this Article shall have effect in relation to a person to whom this Article applies by virtue of sub-paragraph (b) of paragraph (1) (whether or not he is also a person to whom this Article applies by virtue of subparagraph (a) thereof) as they have effect in relation to a person to whom this Article applies by virtue only of the said subparagraph (a), but as if for the [reference] in [paragraph (4)] to three months . . . there were substituted a reference to seven days.

[(8) The restriction and condition mentioned in paragraphs (4) and (6B) shall cease to apply to a person if that person becomes entitled to enter or remain in the United Kingdom by virtue of an enforceable EU right or of any provision made under section 2(2) of the European Communities Act 1972.]

Note: Words in square brackets in paragraph (1) substituted by SI 1982/1028. Words in square brackets in paragraph (2) inserted by SI 2000/1776 from 30 July 2000. Subparagraphs (4)(b) and (c) substituted by SI 1980/1859. Words in curly brackets in paragraph (1) substituted, words substituted in paragraph (3), words omitted from paragraphs (4)(b) and (c), paragraphs (5) and (6) omitted, paragraphs (6A), (6B) and (8)inserted and words substituted/omitted in paragraph (7) from 12 October 2014 (SI 2014/2475).

[SCHEDULE

The countries specified for the purposes of article 3A are:

India

People's Republic of China]

Note: Schedule inserted from 12 October 2014 (SI 2014/2475).

Immigration (Exemption from Control) Order 1972

(SI 1972, No. 1613)

1. This Order may be cited as the Immigration (Exemption from Control) Order 1972 and shall come into operation on 1 January 1973.

2.—(1) In this Order—

'the Act' means the Immigration Act 1971; and

'consular employee' and 'consular officer' have the meanings respectively assigned to them by Article 1 of the Vienna Convention on Consular Relations as set out in Schedule 1 to the Consular Relations Act 1968.

(2) In this Order any reference to an Article or to the Schedule shall be construed as a reference to an Article of this Order or, as the case may be, to the Schedule thereto and any reference in an Article to a paragraph as a reference to a paragraph of that Article.

(3) In this Order any reference to an enactment is a reference to it as amended, and includes a reference to it as applied, by or under any other enactment and any reference to

an instrument made under or by virtue of any enactment is a reference to any such instrument for the time being in force.

(4) The Interpretation Act 1889 shall apply to the interpretation of this Order as it applies to the interpretation of an Act of Parliament.

3.—(1) The following persons shall be exempt from any provision of the Act relating to those who are not [British citizens], that is to say:—

(a) any consular officer in the service of any of the states specified in the Schedule (being states with which consular conventions have been concluded by Her Majesty);

(b) any consular employee in such service as is mentioned in sub-paragraph (a) of this paragraph; and

(c) any member of the family of a person exempted under sub-paragraph (a) or (b) of this paragraph forming part of his household.

(2) In paragraph (1) and in Article 4 any reference to a consular employee shall be construed as a reference to such an employee who is in the full-time service of the state concerned and is not engaged in the United Kingdom in any private occupation for gain.

Note: Words in square brackets in paragraph (1) substituted by SI 1982/1649.

4. The following persons shall be exempt from any provision of the Act relating to those who are not [British citizens] except any provision relating to deportation, that is to say:—

(a) unless the Secretary of State otherwise directs, any member of the government of a country or territory outside the United Kingdom and Islands who is visiting the United Kingdom on the business of that government;

(b) any person entitled to immunity from legal process with respect to acts performed by him in his official capacity under any Order in Council made under section 3(1) of the Bretton Woods Agreements Act 1945 (which empowers Her Majesty by Order in Council to make provision relating to the immunities and privileges of the governors, executive directors, alternates, officers and employees of the International Monetary Fund and the International Bank for Reconstruction and Development);

(c) any person entitled to immunity from legal process with respect to acts performed by him in his official capacity under any Order in Council made under section 3(1) of the International Finance Corporation Act 1955 (which empowers Her Majesty by Order in Council to make provision relating to the immunities and privileges of the governors, directors, alternates, officers and employees of the International Finance Corporation);

(d) any person entitled to immunity from legal process with respect to acts performed by him in his official capacity under any Order in Council made under section 3(1) of the International Development Association Act 1960 (which empowers Her Majesty by Order in Council to make provision relating to the immunities and privileges of the governors, directors, alternates, officers and employees of the International Development Association);

(e) any person (not being a person to whom section 8(3) of the Act applies) who is the representative or a member of the official staff of the representative of the government of a country to which section 1 of the Diplomatic Immunities (Conferences with Commonwealth Countries and Republic of Ireland) Act 1961 applies (which provides for representatives of certain Commonwealth countries and their staff attending conferences in the United Kingdom to be entitled to diplomatic immunity) so long as he is included in a list complied and published in accordance with that section;

(f) any person on whom any immunity from jurisdiction is conferred by any Order in Council made under section 12(1) of the Consular Relations Act 1968 (which empowers Her Majesty by Order in Council to confer on certain persons connected with the service of the government of Commonwealth countries or the Republic of Ireland all or any of the immunities and privileges which are conferred by or may be conferred under that Act on persons connected with consular posts);

(g) any person (not being a person to whom section 8(3) of the Act applies) on whom any immunity from suit and legal process is conferred by any Order in Council made under section 1(2), 5(1) or 6(2) of the International Organisations Act 1968 (which empower Her Majesty by Order in Council to confer certain immunities and privileges on persons connected with certain international organisations and international tribunals and on representatives of foreign countries and their staffs attending certain conferences in the United Kingdom) except any such person as is mentioned in section 5(2)(c) to (e) of the said Act of 1968 [or by any Order in Council continuing to have effect by virtue of section 12(5) of the said Act of 1968];

(h) any consular officer (not being an honorary consular officer) in the service of a state other than such a state as is mentioned in the Schedule;

(i) any consular employee in such service as is mentioned in paragraph (h);

[(j) any officer or servant of the Commonwealth Secretariat falling within paragraph 6 of the Schedule to the Commonwealth Secretariat Act 1966 (which confers certain immunities on those members of the staff of the Secretariat who are not entitled to full diplomatic immunity);]

[(k) any person on whom any immunity from suit and legal process is conferred by the European Communities (Immunities and Privileges of the North Atlantic Salmon Conservation Organisation) Order 1985 (which confers certain immunities and privileges on the representatives and officers of the North Atlantic Salmon Conservation Organisation);]

[(l) any member of the Hong Kong Economic and Trade Office as defined by paragraph 8 of the Schedule to the Hong Kong Economic and Trade Office Act 1996,]

[(m)

(i) Any member or servant of the Independent International Commission on Decommissioning ('the Commission') established under an Agreement between the Government of the United Kingdom of Great Britain and Northern Ireland and the Government of the Republic of Ireland concluded on 26 August 1997,

(ii) in sub-paragraph (i) above, 'servant' includes any agent of or person carrying out work for or giving advice to the Commission,

(n) any member of the family of a person exempted under any of the preceding paragraphs forming part of his household.']

[(o) any person falling within Article 4A below.]

Note: First words in square brackets substituted by SI 1982/1649. Words in square brackets in Art 4(g) added by SI 1977/693. Article 4(j) substituted by SI 1977/693. Article 4(k) substituted by SI 1985/1809. Art 4(l) substituted by SI 1402/1997. Art 4(m) substituted by SI 2207/1997. Article 4(o) inserted from 25 January 2008 (SI 2004/3171).

[**4A.** —(1) In relation to the court ('the ICC') established by the Rome Statute of the International Criminal Court done at Rome on 17 July 1998 ('the Rome Statute');

(a) except in so far as in any particular case the exemption given by this Article is waived by the State or intergovernmental organisation they represent,

(i) any representative of a State party to the Rome Statute attending meetings of the Assembly or one of its subsidiary organs,

(ii) any representative of another State attending meetings of the Assembly or one of its subsidiary organs as an observer, and

(iii) any representative of a State or of an intergovernmental organisation invited to a meeting of the Assembly or one of its subsidiary organs,

while exercising their official functions and during their journey to and from the place of the meeting;

(b) except in so far as in any particular case the exemption given by this Article is waived by the State they represent, any representative of a State participating in the proceedings of the ICC while exercising their official functions and during their journeys to and from the place of the proceedings of the ICC;

(c) except in so far as in any particular case the exemption given by this Article is waived by an absolute majority of the judges, any judge and the Prosecutor, when engaged on or with respect to the business of the ICC;

(d) except in so far as in any particular case the exemption given by this Article is waived by the Prosecutor, any Deputy Prosecutor, when engaged on or with respect to the business of the ICC;

(e) except in so far as in any particular case the exemption given by this Article is waived by the Presidency, the Registrar, when engaged on or with respect to the business of the ICC;

(f) except in so far as in any particular case the exemption given by this Article is waived by the Registrar, the Deputy Registrar, so far as necessary for the performance of his functions;

(g) except in so far as in any particular case the exemption given by this Article is waived by the Prosecutor, any member of the staff of the office of the Prosecutor, so far as necessary for the performance of their functions;

(h) except in so far as in any particular case the exemption given by this Article is waived by the Registrar, any member of the staff of the Registry, so far as necessary for the performance of their functions;

(i) except in so far as in any particular case the exemption given by this Article is waived by the Presidency and subject to the production of the certificate under seal of the Registrar provided to counsel and persons assisting defence counsel upon appointment, counsel and any person assisting defence counsel, so far as necessary for the performance of their functions;

(j) except in so far as in any particular case the exemption given by this Article is waived by the Presidency and subject to the production of a document provided by the ICC certifying that the person's appearance before the ICC is required by the ICC and specifying a time period during which such appearance is necessary, any witness, to the extent necessary for their appearance before the ICC for the purposes of giving evidence;

(k) except in so far as in any particular case the exemption given by this Article is waived by the Presidency and subject to the production of a document provided by the ICC certifying the participation of the person in the proceedings of the ICC and specifying a time period for that participation, any victim, to the extent necessary for their appearance before the ICC;

(l) except in so far as in any particular case the exemption given by this Article is waived by the head of the organ of the ICC appointing the person and subject to the production of a document provided by the ICC certifying that the person is performing functions for the ICC and specifying a time period during which those functions will last, any expert performing functions for the ICC, to the extent necessary for the exercise of those functions;

(m) any member of the family of a person exempted under any of paragraphs (c) to (h) above forming part of their household.

(2) In paragraph (1) above:

'the Assembly' means the assembly of State parties to the Rome Statute;

'the Presidency' means the organ of the ICC composed of the president and the first and second vice-presidents of the ICC elected in accordance with Article 38, paragraph 1, of the Rome Statute;

'the Prosecutor' and 'Deputy Prosecutors' mean the prosecutor and deputy prosecutors respectively elected by the assembly of State parties to the Rome Statute in accordance with Article 42, paragraph 4, of the Rome Statute;

'the Registrar' and 'the Deputy Registrar' mean the registrar and deputy registrar respectively elected by the ICC in accordance with Article 43, paragraph 4, of the Rome Statute.]

Note: Inserted from 25 January 2008 (SI 2004/3171).

5.—(1) Subject to the provisions of this Article the following persons who are not [British citizens] shall, on arrival in the United Kingdom, be exempt from the provisions of section 3(1)(a) of the Act (which requires persons who are not [British citizens] to obtain leave to enter the United Kingdom), that is to say—

(a) any citizen of the United Kingdom and Colonies who holds a passport issued to him in the United Kingdom and Islands and expressed to be a British Visitor's Passport;

(b) any Commonwealth citizen who is included in a passport issued in the United Kingdom by the Government of the United Kingdom or in one of the Islands by the Lieutenant-Governor thereof which is expressed to be a Collective Passport;

(c) any Commonwealth citizen or citizen of the Republic of Ireland returning to the United Kingdom from an excursion to France or Belgium [or the Netherlands] who holds a valid document of identity issued in accordance with arrangements approved by the United Kingdom Government and in a form authorised by the Secretary of State and enabling him to travel on such an excursion without a passport;

(d) any Commonwealth citizen who holds a British seaman's card or any citizen of the Republic of Ireland if (in either case) he was engaged as a member of the crew of a ship in a place within the common travel area and, on arrival in the United Kingdom, is, or is to be, discharged from his engagement;

(e) any person who, having left the United Kingdom after having been given a limited leave to enter, returns to the United Kingdom within the period for which he had leave as a member of the crew of an aircraft under an engagement requiring him to leave on that or another aircraft as a member of its crew within a period exceeding seven days.

(2) Paragraph (1) shall not apply so as to confer any exemption on any person against whom there is a deportation order in force or who has previously entered the United Kingdom unlawfully and has not subsequently been given leave to enter or remain in the United Kingdom and sub-paragraphs (d) and (e) of that paragraphs shall not apply to a person who is required by an immigration officer to submit to examination in accordance with Schedule 2 to the Act.

(3) In this Article any reference to a Commonwealth citizen shall be construed as including a reference to a British protected person and in paragraph (1)(d) 'British seaman's card' means a valid card issued under any regulations in force under section 70 of the Merchant Shipping Act 1970 or any card having effect by virtue of the said regulations

as a card so issued and 'holder of a British seaman's card' has the same meaning as in the said regulations.

Note: Words in square brackets in Art 5(1) substituted by SI 1982/1649. Words in square brackets in Art 5(1)(c) added by SI 1975/617.

6.—**(1)** For the purposes of section 1(1) of the British Nationality Act 1981 (which relates to acquisition of British citizenship by birth in the United Kingdom), a person to whom a child is born in the United Kingdom on or after 1 January 1983 is to be regarded (notwithstanding the preceding provisions of this Order) as settled in the United Kingdom at the time of the birth if—

(a) he would fall to be so regarded but for his being at that time entitled to an exemption by virtue of this Order; and

(b) immediately before he became entitled to that exemption he was settled in the United Kingdom; and

(c) he was ordinarily resident in the United Kingdom from the time when he became entitled to that exemption to the time of the birth;

but this Article shall not apply if at the time of the birth the child's father or mother is a person on whom any immunity from jurisdiction is conferred by or under the Diplomatic Privileges Act 1964.

(2) Expressions used in this Article shall be construed in accordance with section 50 of the British Nationality Act 1981.

Note: Article 6 added by SI 1982/1649.

Articles 3 and 4

SCHEDULE

STATES WITH WHICH CONSULAR CONVENTIONS HAVE BEEN CONCLUDED BY HER MAJESTY

Austria
Belgium
Bulgaria
[Czechoslovakia]
Denmark
France
[German Democratic Republic]
Greece
Federal Republic of Germany
Hungary
Italy
Japan
Mexico
[Mongolia]
Norway
Poland
Romania
Sweden
Spain
Union of Soviet Socialist Republics
United States of America
Yugoslavia

Note: Words in square brackets in the Sch added by SI 1977/693.

The Channel Tunnel (International Arrangements) Order 1993
(SI 1993 No. 1813)

Note: The Channel Tunnel (International Arrangements) Order 1993 includes provisions modifying the application of specified statutory provisions in specified circumstances. Only the text relevant to the modification of statutes and statutory instruments included in this book are reproduced.

Citation and commencement

1. . . .

Note: Order in force from 2 August 1993 being the date notified in the London, Edinburgh and Belfast Gazettes.

Interpretation

2. . . .

Application of international articles

3. . . .

Application of supplementary articles

3A. . . .

4.— Application of enactments

(1) All frontier control enactments [except those relating to transport and road traffic controls] shall for the purpose of enabling officers belonging to the United Kingdom to carry out frontier controls extend to France within a control zone.

[(1A) All frontier control enactments relating to transport and road traffic controls shall for the purpose of enabling officers belonging to the United Kingdom to carry out such controls extend to France within the control zone in France within the tunnel system.]

[(1B) All immigration control enactments shall, for the purpose of enabling immigration officers to carry out immigration controls, extend to France within a supplementary control zone.]

[(1C) The Race Relations Act 1976 shall apply to the carrying out by immigration officers of their functions in a control zone or a supplementary control zone outside the United Kingdom as it applies to the carrying out of their functions within the United Kingdom.]

[(2–4]. . .

Note: Paragraphs (2)–(4) concern processing of data. Words inserted in paragraph (1) and paragraph (1A) inserted from 2 October 1996 (SI 1996/2283). Paragraph (1B) inserted from 25 May 2001 (SI 2001/1544). Paragraph (1C) inserted from 10 December 2001 (SI 2001/3707).

Role of the Office of Rail Regulation

4A. . . .

Application of criminal law

5. . . .

Persons boarding a through train

5A. . . .

Powers of officers and supplementary controls

6. . . .

7.— Enactments modified

(1) Without prejudice to the generality of [articles 4(1), 4(1B) and 5(1)], the frontier control enactments mentioned in Schedule 4 shall–

(a) in their application to France by virtue of article 4(1) [or article 4(1B)], and

(b) in their application to the United Kingdom–

(i) within the tunnel system, and

(ii) elsewhere for the authorised purposes,

have effect with the modifications set out in Schedule 4.

[(1A) Nothing in paragraph (1)(b)(ii) implies the existence of a supplementary control zone in the station of London-Waterloo on British Territory.]

(2) . . .

(3) . . .

[(3A) . . .

(4) . . .

Note: Paragraphs (2)–(3A) concern the application of the Firearms Act 1968. Paragraph 4 concerns transport and road traffic controls. Words inserted in paragraph (1) from 25 May 2001 (SI 2001/1544). Paragraph (1A) inserted from 14 November 2007 (SI 2007/2907).

Schedule 1

Expressions Defined

Schedule 2

International Articles

Schedule 2A

Supplementary Articles

Schedule 3

Powers of Officers

Article 4

Schedule 4

Enactments Modified

(1) In this paragraph "the 1971 Act" means the Immigration Act 1971.

(2) In section 3 of the 1971 Act (general provision for regulation and control)–

(a) after subsection (4) insert–

"(4A) For the purposes of subsection (4) above a person seeking to leave the United Kingdom through the tunnel system who is refused admission to France shall be treated as having gone to a country outside the common travel area."

; and

(b) after subsection (7) insert–

"(7A) Any reference in an Order in Council under subsection (7) above to embarking or being about to embark shall be construed as including a reference to leaving or seeking to leave the United Kingdom through the tunnel system."

(3) In section 4 of the 1971 Act (administration of control) in subsection (2)(b)–

(a) for the words "the United Kingdom by ship or aircraft" substitute ", or seeking to arrive in or leave, the United Kingdom through the tunnel system"; and

(b) for the words after "arrive as" substitute "members of the crews of through trains or shuttle trains".

(4) In section 8 of the 1971 Act (exceptions for seamen etc.) in subsection (1)–

(a) for the words from "of a ship" to "its crew" substitute "of a through train or shuttle train under an engagement requiring him to leave within seven days as a member of the crew of that or another such train"; and

(b) for the words "departure of the ship or aircraft" substitute "departure of the through train or shuttle train".

(5) In section 11 of the 1971 Act (construction of references to entry etc.)–

(a) in subsection (1)–

(i) for the words "by ship or aircraft" substitute "through the tunnel system", and

(ii) for the words from "he disembarks" to "immigration officer" substitute–

"(a) he leaves any control area designated under paragraph 26 of Schedule 2 to this Act, or

(b) he remains on a through train after it has ceased to be such a control area";

(b) omit subsections (2) and (3); and

(c) in subsection (4) omit the words after "section 1(3)".

(6) In section 13 of the 1971 Act (appeals against exclusion from United Kingdom) in subsection (3) omit the words "at a port of entry and".

(7) In section 24 of the 1971 Act (illegal entry and similar offences)–

(a) in subsection (1)(f) for the words from "disembarks" to "aircraft" substitute "leaves a train in the United Kingdom"; and

(b) in subsection (1)(g) for the word "embarks" substitute "leaves or seeks to leave the United Kingdom through the tunnel system".

(8) In section 25 of the 1971 Act (assisting illegal entry and harbouring)–

[. . .]

(b) for subsection (6) substitute–

"(6) Where a person convicted on indictment of an offence under subsection (1) above is at the time of the offence–

(a) the owner or one of the owners of a through train, shuttle train or vehicle used or intended to be used in carrying out the arrangements in respect of which the offence is committed; or

(b) a director or manager of a company which is the owner or one of the owners of any such train or vehicle; or

(c) the train manager of any such train;

then subject to subsections (7) and (8) below the court before which he is convicted may order the forfeiture of the train or vehicle.

In this subsection (but not in subsection (7) below)–

"owner" in relation to a train or vehicle which is the subject of a hire-purchase agreement includes the person in possession of it under that agreement, and in relation to a train, includes a charterer; and

"vehicle" includes a railway vehicle capable of being uncoupled from a train and a road vehicle carried on a train.";

(c) in subsection (7)–

(i) for the words "ship or aircraft", wherever occurring, substitute "train",

(ii) omit paragraph (a), and

(iii) omit the words from "In this subsection" to "in respect of the aircraft"; and

(d) in subsection (8) for the words "ship, aircraft", wherever occurring, substitute "train".

(9) In section 27 of the 1971 Act (offences by persons connected with ships etc.)–

(a) in paragraph (a)–

(i) for the words "captain of a ship or aircraft" substitute "train manager of a through train or shuttle train", and

(ii) in sub-paragraph (i) for the word "disembark" substitute "leave the train";

(b) in paragraph (b)–

(i) for the words "as owner or agent of a ship or aircraft" substitute "as, or as agent of, a person operating an international service";

(ii) in sub-paragraph (i) for the words from "the ship" to "port of entry" substitute "a through train to stop at a place other than a terminal control point [or an international station]"; and

(c) in paragraph (c)–

[(i) for the words "as a person" to "port" substitute "as an occupier or person concerned with the management of a terminal control point or of an international station"], and

(ii) for the words "the embarkation or disembarkation of passengers" substitute "persons arriving or seeking to arrive in, or leaving or seeking to leave, the United Kingdom through the tunnel system" [; and

(d) in paragraph (ca) for the words "as a person" to "port" substitute "as an occupier or person concerned with the management of a terminal control point or of an international station".]

[(9A) In section 28A of the 1971 Act (arrest without warrant), in subsection (3) after the words "immigration officer" insert "or a constable".]

(10) In section 33 of the 1971 Act (interpretation)–

(a) in subsection (1)–

(i) omit the definitions of "airport" and "port",

(ii) in the definition of "crew" after the word "captain," insert "and in relation to a through train or a shuttle train, means all persons on the train who are actually employed in its service or working, including the train manager,", and

(iii) in the definition of "illegal entrant" after the words "unlawfully entering or seeking" insert "(whether or not he has arrived in the United Kingdom)"; and

(b) [in subsection (3) for the words "ports of entry for purposes of this Act" substitute "international stations for purposes of this Act shall be such railway stations as may from time to time be designated by order of the Secretary of State".]

(11) In Schedule 2 to the 1971 Act (administrative provisions as to control on entry etc.)—

(a) in paragraph 1(4) and where first occurring in paragraph 1(5) for the words "ship or aircraft" substitute "through train or shuttle train";

(b) in paragraph 1(5) for the words after "vehicle" substitute

"which–

(a) is in a control zone in France within the tunnel system, or

(b) has arrived in, or is seeking to leave, the United Kingdom through the tunnel system.";

(c) in paragraph 2(1) for the words from "in the United Kingdom" to "seeking to enter the United Kingdom)" substitute ", or who are seeking to arrive, in the United Kingdom through the tunnel system";

[(d) after paragraph 2(1) insert—

"(1A) The power conferred by sub-paragraph (1) is exercisable—

(a) as respects persons who have arrived in the United Kingdom, in a control area, and

(b) as respects persons seeking to arrive in the United Kingdom (who may first be questioned to ascertain whether they are seeking to do so), in a control zone in France or Belgium, or in a supplementary control zone in France.";]

(e) in paragraph 2(3)[after the words "further examination" insert "(or, if examined by an immigration officer in a supplementary control zone, may be required to submit to a [further examination before or after arrival] in the United Kingdom)" and]–

(i) for the words "crew of a ship or aircraft" substitute "crew of a through train or shuttle train",

(ii) after the words "joining a ship or aircraft" insert "or a shuttle train or through train", and

(iii) after the words "intended ship or aircraft" insert "or train";

[(ea) after paragraph 2A(1) insert—

"(1A) This paragraph also applies to a person who seeks to arrive in the United Kingdom and who is in a control zone in France or Belgium, or in a supplementary control zone in France.";

and after paragraph 2A(5) insert—

"(5A) A person examined by an immigration officer under this paragraph in a supplementary control zone may be required to submit to a [further examination before or after arrival] in the United Kingdom.";]

(eb) in paragraph 2A(6)–

(i) [after the words "sub-paragraph (5)" insert "or sub-paragraph (5A)"] for the words "crew of a ship or aircraft" substitute "crew of a through train or shuttle train";

(ii) after the words "joining a ship or aircraft" insert "or a shuttle train or through train"; and

(iii) after the words "intended ship or aircraft", insert "or train";]

(f) in paragraph 3(1) and (2) for the words "embarking or seeking to embark in the United Kingdom" substitute "leaving or seeking to leave the United Kingdom through the tunnel system";

[(g) in paragraph 5—

(i) in sub-paragraph (a) for the words "passengers disembarking" to "such passengers" substitute "persons arriving in or leaving or seeking to arrive in or leave the United Kingdom through the tunnel system, or any class of such persons",

(ii) in sub-paragraph (b) for the words "passengers embarking" to "such passengers" substitute "persons leaving or seeking to leave the United Kingdom through the tunnel system, or any class of such persons", and

(iii) for the words "the owners or agents of ships and aircraft to supply such cards to those passengers" substitute "persons operating international services to supply such cards to those persons";]

[(ga) in paragraph 5B–

(i) in sub-paragraph (1)(a) for the words "an owner or agent of a ship or aircraft" substitute "a person operating, or a person acting as agent of a person operating, an international service", and

(ii) in sub-paragraph (1)(b) for the words "a person concerned in the management of a port" substitute "an occupier of, or a person concerned with the management of a terminal control point or of an international station", and

(iii) in sub-paragraph (2)(a) for the words "the port" substitute "the terminal control point or the international station".]

(h) in paragraph 8(1)–

(i) after the words "in the United Kingdom" insert "through the tunnel system", and

(ii) for the words after "sub-paragraph (2) below" substitute

"give the person operating the international service by which he arrived ("the carrier") directions requiring the carrier–

(a) to remove him from the United Kingdom through the tunnel system; or

(b) to make arrangements for his removal from the United Kingdom in any ship or aircraft specified or indicated in the directions to a country or territory so specified, being either–

(i) a country of which he is a national or citizen; or

(ii) a country or territory in which he has obtained a passport or other document of identity; or

(iii) the country from which he departed for the United Kingdom; or

(iv) a country or territory to which there is reason to believe he will be admitted.";

(i) after paragraph 8(1) insert–

"(1A) Where a person seeking to arrive in the United Kingdom through the tunnel system is refused leave to enter and is then in a control zone in France within the tunnel system, an immigration officer may give the Concessionaires directions requiring them to secure that the person is taken out of the control zone to a place where he may be accepted back by the competent French authorities as provided in Article 18 of the international articles.";

(j) in paragraph 8(2)–

(i) for the words "sub-paragraph (1)(b) or (a)" substitute "sub-paragraph (1)", and

(ii) for the words "the owners or agents in question" substitute "the carrier";

(k) in paragraph 9 for the words after "an immigration officer" substitute

"may–

(a) if the illegal entrant has arrived in the United Kingdom, give such directions in respect of him as in a case within sub-paragraph (1) of paragraph 8 above are authorised by that sub-paragraph, or

(b) if the illegal entrant is in a control zone in France within the tunnel system, give such directions in respect of him as in a case within sub-paragraph (1A) of paragraph 8 above are authorised by that sub-paragraph.";

(l) in paragraph 10(1)–

(i) omit the words from "either" to "or (b)",

(ii) for the words "owners or agents of any ship or aircraft" substitute "person operating the international service by which he arrived", and

(iii) for the words "paragraph 8(1)(c)" substitute "paragraph 8(1)";

(m) in paragraph 11 after the words "ship or aircraft" insert "or through train or shuttle train";

(n) in paragraph 13 omit sub-paragraph (1) and in sub-paragraph (2)–

(i) for the words "crew of a ship or aircraft, and either" substitute "crew of a through train or shuttle train, and",

(ii) omit the words from "or (B)" to "do so", and

(iii) for the words after "an immigration officer may" substitute–

"(a) give the train manager of the train in which that person ("the crew member") arrived directions requiring the train manager to remove him from the United Kingdom in that train; or

(b) give the person operating the international service on which that train is engaged directions requiring that person to remove the crew member from the United Kingdom in any train specified or indicated in the directions, being a train engaged on that international service; or

(c) give that person directions requiring him to make arrangements for the removal of the crew member from the United Kingdom in any ship or aircraft or through train or shuttle train specified in the directions to a country or territory so specified, being either–

(i) a country of which he is a national or citizen; or

(ii) a country or territory in which he has obtained a passport or other document of identity; or

(iii) the country from which he departed for the United Kingdom; or

(iv) a country or territory in which he was engaged as a member of the crew of the through train or shuttle train in which he arrived in the United Kingdom; or

(v) a country or territory to which there is reason to believe he will be admitted.";

(o) in paragraph 15 after the words "ship or aircraft" insert "or through train or shuttle train";

(p) in paragraph 16–

(i) in sub-paragraph (2) for the words "his removal in pursuance of" substitute "the taking of any action in respect of him required by",

(ii) for sub-paragraph (3) substitute–

"(3) A person may under the authority of an immigration officer be removed for detention under this paragraph–

(a) from a vehicle in a control zone in the tunnel system in France; or

(b) from a train or vehicle in which he arrives in the United Kingdom through the tunnel system."

, and

(iii) after sub-paragraph (4) insert–

"(5) Where a person has under paragraph 11 or 15 above been placed on a through train or shuttle train sub-paragraph (4) of this paragraph has effect with the substitution–

(a) for the word "captain", wherever occurring, of the words "train manager"; and

(b) for the words "ship or aircraft", wherever occurring, of the word "train"; and

(c) for the word "disembarking", of the words "leaving the train".";

(q) in paragraphs 19(1) and 20(1) for the words "owners or agents of the ship or aircraft in" substitute "person operating the international service by"; [. . .]

(r) for paragraphs 26 and 27 substitute–

"26.—(1) Persons operating international services shall not, without the approval of the Secretary of State, arrange for any through train to stop for the purpose of enabling passengers to leave it except at a terminal control point.

(2) The Secretary of State may from time to time give written notice to persons operating international services designating all or any through trains as control areas while they are within any area in the United Kingdom specified in the notice or while they constitute a control zone.

(3) The Secretary of State may from time to time give written notice designating a control area–

(a) to the Concessionaires as respects any part of the tunnel system in the United Kingdom or of a control zone within the tunnel system in France, or

(b) to any occupier or person concerned with the management of a terminal control point in the United Kingdom.

(4) A notice under sub-paragraph (2) or (3) above may specify conditions and restrictions to be observed in a control area, and any person to whom such a notice is given shall take all reasonable steps to secure that any such conditions or restrictions are observed.

[27.—(1) The train manager of a through train or shuttle train arriving in the United Kingdom—

(a) shall take such steps as may be necessary to secure that persons, other than members of the crew who may lawfully enter the United kingdom by virtue of section 8(1) of this Act, do not leave the train except in accordance with any arrangements approved by an immigration officer; and

(b) where persons are to be examined by an immigration officer on the train, shall take such steps as may be necessary to secure that they are ready for examination.

(2) The Secretary of State may by order require, or enable an immigration officer to require, the train manager of a through train or shuttle train or a person operating an international service or his agent to supply—

(a) a passenger list showing the names and nationality or citizenship of passengers arriving or leaving on board the train; and

(b) particulars of members of the crew of the train.

(3) An order under sub-paragraph (2) may relate—

(a) to all through trains or shuttle trains arriving or expected to arrive in the United Kingdom;

(b) to all through trains or shuttle trains leaving or expected to leave the United Kingdom.

(4) An order under sub-paragraph (2)—

(a) may specify the time at which or period during which information is to be provided,

(b) may specify the form and manner in which information is to be provided,

(c) shall be made by statutory instrument, and

(d) shall be subject to annulment in pursuance of a resolution of either House of Parliament.".]

[(s) In paragraph 27B (passenger information)–

(i) in sub-paragraph (1) for the words "ships or aircraft" substitute "through trains or shuttle trains";

(ii) in sub-paragraph (2) for the words "owner or agent ("the carrier") of a ship or aircraft" substitute "person operating an international service or his agent ("the carrier")";

(iii) in sub-paragraph (3)(a) for the words "ship or particular aircraft" substitute "train";

(iv) in sub-paragraph (3)(b) and (c) for the words "ships or aircraft" substitute "trains"; and

(v) in sub-paragraphs (4) and (9) for the words "ship or aircraft", wherever occurring, substitute "train"; [. . .]

[(vi) in sub-paragraph (9A) for "voyage or flight" substitute "international service" and for the words "ship or aircraft" substitute "through train or shuttle train"; and]

(t) In paragraph 27C (notification of non-EEA arrivals)–

(i) in sub-paragraph (1)–

(a) for the words "owner or agent ("the carrier") of a ship or aircraft" substitute "person operating an international service other than a shuttle service or his agent ("the carrier")", and

(b) for the second occurrence of the words "ship or aircraft" substitute "through train";

(ii) in sub-paragraph (2)(a) for the words "ship or particular aircraft" substitute "through train";

(iii) in sub-paragraph (2)(b) and (c) for the words "ships or aircraft" substitute "through trains"; and

(iv) in sub-paragraphs (6), (7) and (9) for the words "ship or aircraft" substitute "through trains".]

(12) In Schedule 3 to the 1971 Act (supplementary provisions as to deportation)–

(a) in paragraph 1(1) after the words "any person" insert "who arrived in the United Kingdom through the tunnel system";

(b) in paragraph 1(2) after sub-paragraph (b) insert–

"(bb) directions to the person operating the international service by which the person in question arrived ("the carrier") requiring the carrier to make arrangements for the removal of the person in question through the tunnel system; or"

; and

(c) in paragraph 1(4) after the word "voyage" insert "or journey".

Note: Words omitted from paragraph 1(8) from 25 May 2001 (SI 2001/1544). Words inserted in paragraph 1(9)(b)(ii) from 1 July 1994 (SI 1994/1405). Paragraph 1(9)(c)(i) substituted and paragraph 1(9)(d) inserted from 5 August 2014 (SI 2014/1814). Paragraph 1(9A) inserted from 25 May 2001 (SI 2001/1544). Paragraph 1(10)(iii)(b) inserted from 1 July 1994 (SI 1994/1405). Paragraph 1(11)(d) substituted and words inserted in paragraph 1(11)(e) from 25 May 2001 (SI 2001/1544). Paragraph 1(11)(ea) and (eb) inserted from 30 July 2000 (SI 2000/1775). Words substituted in paragraph 1(11)(ea) from 10 December 2001 (SI 2001/3707). Words substituted in paragraph 1(11)(eb) from 25 May 2001 (SI 2001/1544). Paragraph 1(11)(g) substituted and paragraph 1(11)(ga) inserted from 5 August 2014 (SI 2014/1814). Words omitted from paragraph 1(11)(q) from 28 April 2000 (SI 2000/913). Words substituted in paragraph 1(11)(r) and words inserted in paragraph 1(11)(s) from 2 January 2008 (SI 2007/3579). Paragraph 1(11)(s) inserted from 28 April 2000 (SI 2000/913).

[2A. In the Immigration and Asylum Act 1999 in section 141 (fingerprinting)—

(a) in subsection (7)(a) for "on his arrival in the United Kingdom" substitute "in a control zone or a supplementary control zone";

(b) in subsection (9)(b) for his "removal or deportation from the United Kingdom" substitute "his leaving a control zone or a supplementary control zone".]

Note: Paragraph 2A inserted from 26 October 2006 (SI 2006/2626).

[3A. In the Immigration, Asylum and Nationality Act 2006—

(a) in section 32 (passenger and crew information: police powers)—

(i) in subsection (1) for "ships and aircraft" substitute "through trains and shuttle trains";

(ii) in subsections (2) and (3) for "owner or agent of a ship or aircraft" substitute "person operating an international service or his agent";

(iii) in subsection (5)(a)(iii) for "a voyage or flight" substitute "an international service"; and

(iv) in subsection (6)(b) for "ships or aircraft" substitute "through trains or shuttle trains";

(b) in section 34 (offence) the reference to section 32 includes a reference to that provision as modified by paragraph (a);

(c) in section 36 (duty to share information)—

(i) in subsection (4) for "ship or aircraft", wherever occurring, substitute "through train or shuttle train"; and

(ii) in subsection (4) for "flights or voyages" substitute "international services";

(d) in section 37 (information sharing: code of practice) the references to section 36 include references to that provision as modified by paragraph (c);

(e) in section 38 (disclosure of information for security purposes) in subsection (4)—

(i) for "ship or aircraft", wherever occurring, substitute "through train or shuttle train"; and

(ii) for "flights or voyages" substitute "international services"; and

(f) in section 39 (disclosure to law enforcement agencies) the reference to section 32 includes a reference to that provision as modified by paragraph (a).]

Note: Paragraph 3A inserted from 2 January 2008 (SI 2007/3579).

[4. In the Immigration (Leave to Enter and Remain) Order 2000—

(a) in article 4(2)—

(i) after the words "arrives in the United Kingdom", insert "or enters a control zone in France or Belgium, or a supplementary control zone in France, seeking to arrive in the United Kingdom through the tunnel system";

(ii) after the words "before arrival", insert "or entry into the control zone or supplementary control zone"; and

(iii) after the words "date of arrival", insert "or entry into the control zone or supplementary control zone";

(b) in article 4(3)—

(i) after the words "on arrival in the United Kingdom", insert "or entry into a control zone in France or Belgium, or a supplementary control zone in France, seeking to arrive in the United Kingdom through the tunnel system"; and

(ii) after the words "before arrival", insert "or entry into the control zone or supplementary control zone"; and

(c) in article 6(2)(a) after the words "arrives in the United Kingdom", insert "or enters a control zone in France or Belgium, or a supplementary control zone in France, seeking to arrive in the United Kingdom through the tunnel system".]

Note: Paragraph 4 substituted from 25 May 2001 (SI 200/1544).

[5. In the [Immigration (European Economic Area) Regulations 2006] [. . .]—

(a) after [regulation 11(2)] insert—

{(2A)} Any passport, identity card, family permit, [residence card{, permanent residence card or qualifying EEA State residence card}] which is required to be produced under this regulation as a condition for admission to the United Kingdom ("the required documents") may, for the same purpose, be required to be produced in a control zone or a supplementary control zone.;

[(b) in regulations 11(4) and 19(2) after the word "arrival" and in regulations 20(4) and (5) after the words "United Kingdom" insert "or the time of his production of the required documents in a control zone or a supplementary control zone".]]

Note: Paragraph 5 inserted from 10 December 2001 (SI 2001/3707). Words in square brackets substituted from 30 April 2006 (SI 2006/1003 Schedule 5). Words '(2A)' in curly brackets substituted from 1 January 2014 and other words in curly brackets substituted from 7 April 2014 (SI 2013/3032).

SCHEDULE 5

AMENDMENTS OF ENACTMENTS AND INSTRUMENTS

. . .

The Asylum Support Regulations 2000
(SI 2000, No. 704)

Arrangement of Regulations

General

Initial application for support

Determining whether persons are destitute

Provision of support

Change of circumstances

General

Citation and commencement

1. These Regulations may be cited as the Asylum Support Regulations 2000 and shall come into force on 3 April 2000.

Interpretation

2.—(1) In these Regulations—

'the Act' means the Immigration and Asylum Act 1999;

'asylum support' means support provided under section 95 of the Act;

["civil partnership couple" means two people of the same sex who are civil partners of each other and who are members of the same household;]

'dependant' has the meaning given by paragraphs (4) and (5);

'the interim Regulations' means the Asylum Support (Interim Provisions) Regulations 1999;

'married couple' means a man and woman who are married to each other and are members of the same household; and

["same-sex couple" means two people of the same sex who, though not civil partners of each other, are living together as if they were;]

'unmarried couple' means a man and woman who, though not married to each other, are living together as if married.

[(2) The period prescribed under section 94(3) of the Act (day on which a claim for asylum is determined) for the purposes of Part VI of the Act is 28 days where paragraph (2A) applies, and 21 days in any other case.

(2A) This paragraph applies where:

(a) the Secretary of State notifies the claimant that his decision is to accept the asylum claim;

(b) the Secretary of State notifies the claimant that his decision is to reject the asylum claim but at the same time notifies him that he is giving him limited leave to enter or remain in the United Kingdom; or

(c) an appeal by the claimant against the Secretary of State's decision has been disposed of by being allowed.]

(3) Paragraph (2) does not apply in relation to a case to which the interim Regulations apply (for which case, provision corresponding to paragraph (2) is made by regulation 2(6) of those Regulations).

(4) In these Regulations 'dependant', in relation to an asylum-seeker, a supported person or an applicant for asylum support, means, subject to paragraph (5), a person in the United Kingdom ('the relevant person') who—

(a) is his spouse [or civil partner];

(b) is a child of his or of his spouse [or civil partner], is dependant on him and is, or was at the relevant time, under 18;

(c) is a member of his or his spouse's [or civil partner] close family and is, or was at the relevant time, under 18;

(d) had been living as part of his household—

(i) for at least six of the twelve months before the relevant time, or

(ii) since birth,

and is, or was at the relevant time, under 18;

(e) is in need of care and attention from him or a member of his household by reason of a disability and would fall within sub-paragraph (c) or (d) but for the fact that he is not, and was not at the relevant time, under 18;

(f) had been living with him as a member of an unmarried couple for at least two of the three years before the relevant time;

[(fa) had been living with him as a member of a same-sex couple for at least two of the three years before the relevant time;]

(g) is living as part of his household and was, immediately before 6 December 1999 (the date when the interim Regulations came into force), receiving assistance from a local authority under section 17 of the Children Act 1989;

(h) is living as part of his household and was, immediately before the coming into force of these Regulations, receiving assistance from a local authority under—

(i) section 22 of the Children (Scotland) Act 1995; or

(ii) Article 18 of the Children (Northern Ireland) Order 1995; or

(i) has made a claim for leave to enter or remain in the United Kingdom, or for variation of any such leave, which is being considered on the basis that he is dependant on the asylum-seeker;

and in relation to a supported person, or an applicant for asylum support, who is himself a dependant of an asylum-seeker, also includes the asylum-seeker if in the United Kingdom.

(5) Where a supported person or applicant for asylum support is himself a dependant of an asylum-seeker, a person who would otherwise be a dependant of the supported person, or of the applicant, for the purposes of these Regulations is not such a dependant unless he is also a dependant of the asylum-seeker or is the asylum-seeker.

(6) In paragraph (4), 'the relevant time', in relation to the relevant person, means—

(a) the time when an application for asylum support for him was made in accordance with regulation 3(3); or

(b) if he has joined a person who is already a supported person in the United Kingdom and sub-paragraph (a) does not apply, the time when he joined that person in the United Kingdom.

(7) Where a person, by falling within a particular category in relation to an asylum-seeker or supported person, is by virtue of this regulation a dependant of the asylum-seeker or supported person for the purposes of these Regulations, that category is also a prescribed category for the purposes of paragraph (c) of the definition of 'dependant' in section 94(1) of the Act and, accordingly, the person is a dependant of the asylum-seeker or supported person for the purposes of Part VI of the Act.

(8) Paragraph (7) does not apply to a person who is already a dependant of the asylum-seeker or supported person for the purposes of Part VI of the Act because he falls within either of the categories mentioned in paragraphs (a) and (b) of the definition of 'dependant' in section 94(1) of the Act.

(9) Paragraph (7) does not apply for the purposes of any reference to a 'dependant' in Schedule 9 to the Act.

Note: Regulation 2(2) substituted from 8 April 2002 (SI 2002/472). Definitions of 'civil partnership couple' and 'same-sex couple' inserted and words inserted in subparagraphs (4)(a), (b) and (c) and subparagraph (4)(fa) inserted from 5 December 2005 (SI 2005/2114).

Initial application for support

Initial application for support: individual and group applications

3.—(1) Either of the following—

(a) an asylum-seeker, or

(b) a dependant of an asylum-seeker,

may apply to the Secretary of State for asylum support.

(2) An application under this regulation may be—

(a) for asylum support for the applicant alone; or

(b) for asylum support for the applicant and one or more dependants of his.

(3) The application must be made by completing in full and in English the form for the time being issued by the Secretary of State for the purpose.

[(4) The application may not be entertained by the Secretary of State—

(a) where it is made otherwise than in accordance with paragraph (3); or

(b) where the Secretary of State is not satisfied that the information provided is complete or accurate or that the applicant is co-operating with enquiries made under paragraph (5).]

(5) The Secretary of State may make further enquiries of the applicant about any matter connected with the application.

[(5A) Where the Secretary of State makes further enquiries under paragraph (5) the applicant shall reply to those enquiries within five working days of his receipt of them.

(5B) The Secretary of State shall be entitled to conclude that the applicant is not cooperating with his enquiries under paragraph (5) if he fails, without reasonable excuse, to reply within the period prescribed by paragraph (5A).

(5C) In cases where the Secretary of State may not entertain an application for asylum support he shall also discontinue providing support under section 98 of the Act.]

(6) Paragraphs (3) and (4) do not apply where a person is already a supported person and asylum support is sought for a dependant of his for whom such support is not already provided (for which case, provision is made by regulation 15).

[(7) For the purposes of this regulation, working day means any day other than a Saturday, a Sunday, Christmas Day, Good Friday or a day which is a bank holiday under section 1 of the Banking and Financial Dealings Act 1971 in the locality in which the applicant is living.]

Note: Subparagraph (4) substituted from 8 January 2003 (SI 2002/3110). Subparagraphs (5A), (5B), (5C) and (7) inserted from 5 February 2005 (SI 2005/11). Words omitted from subparagraph (3) from 9 April 2007 (SI 2007/863).

Persons excluded from support

4.—(1) The following circumstances are prescribed for the purposes of subsection (2) of section 95 of the Act as circumstances where a person who would otherwise fall within subsection (1) of that section is excluded from that subsection (and, accordingly, may not be provided with asylum support).

(2) A person is so excluded if he is applying for asylum support for himself alone and he falls within paragraph (4) by virtue of any sub-paragraph of that paragraph.

(3) A person is so excluded if—

(a) he is applying for asylum support for himself and other persons, or he is included in an application for asylum support made by a person other than himself;

(b) he falls within paragraph (4) (by virtue of any sub-paragraph of that paragraph); and

(c) each of the other persons to whom the application relates also falls within paragraph (4) (by virtue of any sub-paragraph of that paragraph).

(4) A person falls within this paragraph if at the time when the application is determined—

(a) he is a person to whom interim support applies; or

(b) he is a person to whom social security benefits apply; or

(c) he has not made a claim for leave to enter or remain in the United Kingdom, or for variation of any such leave, which is being considered on the basis that he is an asylum-seeker or dependent on an asylum-seeker.

(5) For the purposes of paragraph (4), interim support applies to a person if—

(a) at the time when the application is determined, he is a person to whom, under the interim Regulations, support under regulation 3 of those Regulations must be provided by a local authority;

(b) sub-paragraph (a) does not apply, but would do so if the person had been determined by the local authority concerned to be an eligible person; or

(c) sub-paragraph (a) does not apply, but would do so but for the fact that the person's support under those Regulations was (otherwise than by virtue of regulation 7(1)(d) of those Regulations) refused under regulation 7, or suspended or discontinued under regulation 8, of those Regulations;

and in this paragraph 'local authority', 'local authority concerned' and 'eligible person' have the same meanings as in the interim Regulations.

(6) For the purposes of paragraph (4), a person is a person to whom social security benefits apply if he is—

(a) a person who by virtue of regulation 2 of the Social Security (Immigration and Asylum) Consequential Amendments Regulations 2000 is not excluded by section 115(1) of the Act from entitlement to—

(i) income-based jobseeker's allowance under the Jobseekers Act 1995; or

(ii) income support, housing benefit or council tax benefit under the Social Security Contributions and Benefits Act 1992;

(iii) income-related employment and support allowance payable under Part 1 of the Welfare Reform Act 2007] [or

(iv) universal credit under Part 1 of the Welfare Reform Act 2012;]

(b) a person who, by virtue of regulation 2 of the Social Security (Immigration and Asylum) Consequential Amendments Regulations (Northern Ireland) 2000 is not excluded by section 115(2) of the Act from entitlement to—

(i) income-based jobseeker's allowance under the Jobseekers (Northern Ireland) Order 1995; or

(ii) income support or housing benefit under the Social Security Contributions and Benefits (Northern Ireland) Act 1992;

(7) A person is not to be regarded as falling within paragraph (2) or (3) if, when asylum support is sought for him, he is a dependant of a person who is already a supported person.

(8) The circumstances prescribed by paragraphs (2) and (3) are also prescribed for the purposes of section 95(2), as applied by section 98(3), of the Act as circumstances where a person who would otherwise fall within subsection (1) of section 98 is excluded from that subsection (and, accordingly, may not be provided with temporary support under section 98).

(9) For the purposes of paragraph (8), paragraphs (2) and (3) shall apply as if any reference to an application for asylum support were a reference to an application for support under section 98 of the Act.

Note: Subparagraph (6)(a)(iii) inserted from 27 October 2008 (SI 2008/1879). Subparagraph (6)(a)(iv) inserted from 29 April 2013 (SI 2013/630).

Determining whether persons are destitute

Determination where application relates to more than one person, etc.

5.—(1) Subject to paragraph (2), where an application in accordance with regulation 3(3) is for asylum support for the applicant and one or more dependants of his, in applying section 95(1) of the Act the Secretary of State must decide whether the applicant and all those dependants, taken together, are destitute or likely to become destitute within the period prescribed by regulation 7.

(2) Where a person is a supported person, and the question falls to be determined whether asylum support should in future be provided for him and one or more other persons who are his dependants and are—

(a) persons for whom asylum support is also being provided when that question falls to be determined; or

(b) persons for whom the Secretary of State is then considering whether asylum support should be provided,

in applying section 95(1) of the Act the Secretary of State must decide whether the supported person and all those dependants, taken together, are destitute or likely to become destitute within the period prescribed by regulation 7.

Income and assets to be taken into account

6.—(1) This regulation applies where it falls to the Secretary of State to determine for the purposes of section 95(1) of the Act whether—

(a) a person applying for asylum support, or such an applicant and any dependants of his, or

(b) a supported person, or such a person and any dependants of his, is or are destitute or likely to become so within the period prescribed by regulation 7.

(2) In this regulation 'the principal' means the applicant for asylum support (where paragraph (1)(a) applies) or the supported person (where paragraph (1)(b) applies).

(3) The Secretary of State must ignore—

(a) any asylum support, and

(b) any support under section 98 of the Act, which the principal or any dependant of his is provided with or, where the question is whether destitution is likely within a particular period, might be provided with in that period.

(4) But he must take into account—

(a) any other income which the principal, or any dependant of his, has or might reasonably be expected to have in that period;

(b) any other support which is available to the principal or any dependant of his, or might reasonably be expected to be so available in that period; and

(c) any assets mentioned in paragraph (5) (whether held in the United Kingdom or elsewhere) which are available to the principal or any dependant of his otherwise than by way of asylum support or support under section 98, or might reasonably be expected to be so available in that period.

(5) Those assets are—

(a) cash;

(b) savings;

(c) investments;

(d) land;

(e) cars or other vehicles; and

(f) goods held for the purpose of a trade or other business.

(6) The Secretary of State must ignore any assets not mentioned in paragraph (5).

Period within which applicant must be likely to become destitute

7. The period prescribed for the purposes of section 95(1) of the Act is—

(a) where the question whether a person or persons is or are destitute or likely to become so falls to be determined in relation to an application for asylum support and sub-paragraph (b) does not apply, 14 days beginning with the day on which that question falls to be determined;

(b) where that question falls to be determined in relation to a supported person, or in relation to persons including a supported person, 56 days beginning with the day on which that question falls to be determined.

Adequacy of existing accommodation

8.—(1) Subject to paragraph (2), the matters mentioned in paragraph (3) are prescribed for the purposes of subsection (5)(a) of section 95 of the Act as matters to which the Secretary of State must have regard in determining for the purposes of that section whether the accommodation of—

(a) a person applying for asylum support, or

(b) a supported person for whom accommodation is not for the time being provided by way of asylum support, is adequate.

(2) The matters mentioned in paragraph (3)(a) and (d) to (g) are not so prescribed for the purposes of a case where the person indicates to the Secretary of State that he wishes to remain in the accommodation.

(3) The matters referred to in paragraph (1) are—

(a) whether it would be reasonable for the person to continue to occupy the accommodation;

(b) whether the accommodation is affordable for him;

(c) whether the accommodation is provided under section 98 of the Act, or otherwise on an emergency basis, only while the claim for asylum support is being determined;

(d) whether the person can secure entry to the accommodation;

(e) where the accommodation consists of a moveable structure, vehicle or vessel designed or adapted for human habitation, whether there is a place where the person is entitled or permitted both to place it and reside in it;

(f) whether the accommodation is available for occupation by the person's dependants together with him;

(g) whether it is probable that the person's continued occupation of the accommodation will lead to domestic violence against him or any of his dependants.

(4) In determining whether it would be reasonable for a person to continue to occupy accommodation, regard may be had to the general circumstances prevailing in relation to housing in the district of the local housing authority where the accommodation is.

(5) In determining whether a person's accommodation is affordable for him, the Secretary of State must have regard to—

(a) any income, or any assets mentioned in regulation 6(5) (whether held in the United Kingdom or elsewhere), which is or are available to him or any dependant of his otherwise than by way of asylum support or support under section 98 of the Act, or might reasonably be expected to be so available;

(b) the costs in respect of the accommodation; and

(c) the person's other reasonable living expenses.

(6) In this regulation—

(a) 'domestic violence' means violence from a person who is or has been a close family member, or threats of violence from such a person which are likely to be carried out; and

(b) 'district of the local housing authority' has the meaning given by section 217(3) of the Housing Act 1996.

(7) The reference in paragraph (1) to subsection (5)(a) of section 95 of the Act does not include a reference to that provision as applied by section 98(3) of the Act.

Essential living needs

9. (1) The matter mentioned in paragraph (2) is prescribed for the purposes of subsection (7)(b) of section 95 of the Act as a matter to which the Secretary of State may not have regard in determining for the purposes of that section whether a person's essential living needs (other than accommodation) are met.

(2) That matter is his personal preference as to clothing (but this shall not be taken to prevent the Secretary of State from taking into account his individual circumstances as regards clothing).

(3) None of the items and expenses mentioned in paragraph (4) is to be treated as being an essential living need of a person for the purposes of Part VI of the Act.

(4) Those items and expenses are—

(a) the cost of faxes;
(b) computers and the cost of computer facilities;
(c) the cost of photocopying;
(d) travel expenses, except the expense mentioned in paragraph (5);
(e) toys and other recreational items;
(f) entertainment expenses.

(5) The expense excepted from paragraph (4)(d) is the expense of an initial journey from a place in the United Kingdom to accommodation provided by way of asylum support or (where accommodation is not so provided) to an address in the United Kingdom which has been notified to the Secretary of State as the address where the person intends to live.

(6) Paragraph (3) shall not be taken to affect the question whether any item or expense not mentioned in paragraph (4) or (5) is, or is not, an essential living need.

(7) The reference in paragraph (1) to subsection (7)(b) of section 95 of the Act includes a reference to that provision as applied by section 98(3) of the Act and, accordingly, the reference in paragraph (1) to 'that section' includes a reference to section 98.

Provision of support

Kind and levels of support for essential living needs

10.—(1) This regulation applies where the Secretary of State has decided that asylum support should be provided in respect of the essential living needs of a person.

[(2) As a general rule, asylum support in respect of the essential living needs of that person may be expected to be provided weekly in the form of [cash, equal to] the amount shown in the second column of the following table opposite the entry in the first column which for the time being describes that person, [. . .].

Table

Qualifying couple	£72.52
Lone parent aged 18 or over	£43.94
Single person aged 25 or over (where the decision to grant support was made prior to 5th October 2009 and the person reached age 25 prior to that date)	£42.62
Any other single person aged 18 or over	£36.62
Person aged at least 16 but under 18 (except a member of a qualifying couple)	£39.80
Person aged under 16	£52.96

(3) In paragraph (1) and the provisions of paragraph (2) preceding the table, 'person' includes 'couple'.

(4) In this regulation—

(a) ["qualifying couple" means a married couple, an unmarried couple, a civil partnership couple or a same-sex couple, at least one of whom is aged 18 or over and neither of whom is aged under 16; and]

[(b) "lone parent" means a parent who is not a member of a married couple, an unmarried couple, a civil partnership couple or a same-sex couple;]

(c) 'single person' means a person who is not a parent or a member of a qualifying couple; and

(d) 'parent' means a parent of a relevant child, that is to say a child who is aged under 18 and for whom asylum support is provided.

(5) Where the Secretary of State has decided that accommodation should be provided for a person (or couple) by way of asylum support, and the accommodation is provided in a form which also meets other essential living needs (such as bed and breakfast, or half or full board), the amounts shown in the table in paragraph (2) shall be treated as reduced accordingly.

(6) . . .

Note: Regulation 10(6) omitted from 8 April 2002 (SI 2002/472). Regulation 10(2) substituted from 7 April 2005 (SI 2003/755). Words in square brackets in reg 10(2) substituted from 4 June 2004 (SI 2004/1313). Subparagraphs (4)(a) and (4)(b) substituted from 5 December 2005 (SI 2005/2114). Table substituted from 18 April 2011 (SI 2011/907).

[Additional support for pregnant women and children under 3

10A.—(1) In addition to the [cash support which the Secretary of State may be expected to provide weekly as] described in regulation 10(2), in the case of any pregnant woman or child aged under 3 for whom the Secretary of State has decided asylum support should be provided, there shall, as a general rule, be added to the [cash support] for any week the amount shown in the second column of the following table opposite the entry in the first column which for the time being describes that person.

(2) In this regulation, 'pregnant woman' means a woman who has provided evidence to satisfy the Secretary of State that she is pregnant.]

Note: Regulation 10A inserted from 3 March 2003 (SI 2003/241). Words in square brackets substituted from 4 June 2004 (SI 2004/1313).

Pregnant woman	£3.00
Child aged under 1	£5.00
Child aged at least 1 and under 3	£3.00

Additional single payments in respect of essential living needs

11. . . .

Note: Regulation 11 revoked from 4 June 2004 (SI 2004/1313), save to enable the Secretary of State to make a payment to a person whose qualifying period ends on or before that date.

Income and assets to be taken into account in providing support

12.—(1) This regulation applies where it falls to the Secretary of State to decide the level or kind of asylum support to be provided for—

(a) a person applying for asylum support, or such an applicant and any dependants of his,

(b) a supported person, or such a person and any dependants of his.

(2) In this regulation 'the principal' means the applicant for asylum support (where paragraph (1)(a) applies) or the supported person (where paragraph (1)(b) applies).

(3) The Secretary of State must take into account—

(a) any income which the principal or any dependant of his has or might reasonably be expected to have,

(b) support which is or might reasonably be expected to be available to the principal or any dependant of his, and

(c) any assets mentioned in regulation 6(5) (whether held in the United Kingdom or elsewhere) which are or might reasonably be expected to be available to the principal or any dependant of his, otherwise than by way of asylum support.

Accommodation

13.—(1) The matters mentioned in paragraph (2) are prescribed for the purposes of subsection (2)(b) of section 97 of the Act as matters to which regard may not be had when exercising the power under section 95 of the Act to provide accommodation for a person.

(2) Those matters are—

(a) his personal preference as to the nature of the accommodation to be provided; and

(b) his personal preference as to the nature and standard of fixtures and fittings; but this shall not be taken to prevent the person's individual circumstances, as they relate to his accommodation needs, being taken into account.

Services

14.—(1) The services mentioned in paragraph (2) may be provided or made available by way of asylum support to persons who are otherwise receiving such support, but may be so provided only for the purpose of maintaining good order among such persons.

(2) Those services are—

(a) education, including English language lessons,

(b) sporting or other developmental activities.

Change of circumstances

Change of circumstances

15.—(1) If a relevant change of circumstances occurs, the supported person concerned or a dependant of his must, without delay, notify the Secretary of State of that change of circumstances.

(2) A relevant change of circumstances occurs where a supported person or a dependant of his—

(a) is joined in the United Kingdom by a dependant or, as the case may be, another dependant, of the supported person;

(b) receives or gains access to any money, or other asset mentioned in regulation 6(5), that has not previously been declared to the Secretary of State;

(c) becomes employed;

(d) becomes unemployed;

(e) changes his name;

(f) gets married;

[(fa) forms a civil partnership;]

(g) starts living with a person as if married to that person;

[(ga) starts living with a person as if a civil partner of that person;]

(h) gets divorced;

[(ha) becomes a former civil partner on the dissolution of his civil partnership;]

(i) separates from a spouse, or from a person with whom he has been living as if married to that person;

[(ia) separates from his civil partner or from the person with whom he has been living as if a civil partner of that person;]

(j) becomes pregnant;

(k) has a child;

(l) leaves school;

(m) starts to share his accommodation with another person;

(n) moves to a different address, or otherwise leaves his accommodation;

(o) goes into hospital;

(p) goes to prison or is otherwise held in custody;

(q) leaves the United Kingdom; or

(r) dies.

(3) If, on being notified of a change of circumstances, the Secretary of State considers that the change may be one—

(a) as a result of which asylum support should be provided for a person for whom it was not provided before, or

(b) as a result of which asylum support should no longer be provided for a person, or

(c) which may otherwise affect the asylum support which should be provided for a person, he may make further enquiries of the supported person or dependant who gave the notification.

(4) The Secretary of State may, in particular, require that person to provide him with such information as he considers necessary to determine whether, and if so, what, asylum support should be provided for any person.

Note: Subparagraphs (2)(fa), (ga), (ha) and (ia) inserted from 5 December 2005 (SI 2005/2114).

Contributions

Contributions

16.—(1) This regulation applies where, in deciding the level of asylum support to be provided for a person who is or will be a supported person, the Secretary of State is required to take into account income, support or assets as mentioned in regulation 12(3).

(2) The Secretary of State may—

(a) set the asylum support for that person at a level which does not reflect the income, support or assets; and

(b) require from that person payments by way of contributions towards the cost of the provision for him of asylum support.

(3) A supported person must make to the Secretary of State such payments by way of contributions as the Secretary of State may require under paragraph (2).

(4) Prompt payment of such contributions may be made a condition (under section 95(9) of the Act) subject to which asylum support for that person is provided.

Recovery of sums by Secretary of State

Recovery where assets become realisable

17.—(1) This regulation applies where it appears to the Secretary of State at any time (the relevant time)—

(a) that a supported person had, at the time when he applied for asylum support, assets of any kind in the United Kingdom or elsewhere which were not capable of being realised; but

(b) that those assets have subsequently become, and remain, capable of being realised.

(2) The Secretary of State may recover from that person a sum not exceeding the recoverable sum.

(3) Subject to paragraph (5), the recoverable sum is a sum equal to whichever is the less of—

(a) the monetary value of all the asylum support provided to the person up to the relevant time; and

(b) the monetary value of the assets concerned.

(4) As well as being recoverable as mentioned in paragraph 11(2)(a) of Schedule 8 to the Act, an amount recoverable under this regulation may be recovered by deduction from asylum support.

(5) The recoverable sum shall be treated as reduced by any amount which the Secretary of State has by virtue of this regulation already recovered from the person concerned (whether by deduction or otherwise) with regard to the assets concerned.

[Recovery of asylum support

17A.—(1) The Secretary of State may require a supported person to refund asylum support if it transpires that at any time during which asylum support was being provided for him he was not destitute.

(2) If a supported person has dependants, the Secretary of State may require him to refund asylum support if it transpires that at any time during which asylum support was being provided for the supported person and his dependants they were not destitute.

(3) The refund required shall not exceed the monetary value of all the asylum support provided to the supported person or to the supported person and his dependants for the relevant period.

(4) In this regulation the relevant period is the time during which asylum support was provided for the supported person or the supported person and his dependants and during which he or they were not destitute.

(5) If not paid within a reasonable period, the refund required may be recovered from the supported person as if it were a debt due to the Secretary of State.]

Note: Regulation 17A inserted from 5 April 2005 (SI 2005/11).

Overpayments: method of recovery

18. As well as being recoverable as mentioned in subsection (3) of section 114 of the Act, an amount recoverable under subsection (2) of that section may be recovered by deduction from asylum support.

Breach of conditions and suspension and discontinuation of support

Breach of conditions: decision whether to provide support

19.—(1) When deciding—

(a) whether to provide, or to continue to provide, asylum support for any person or persons, or

(b) the level or kind of support to be provided for any person or persons, the Secretary of State may take into account [the extent to which a] relevant condition has been complied with.

[(2) A relevant condition is one which makes the provision of asylum support subject to actual residence by the supported person or a dependant of his for whom support is being provided in a specific place or location.]

Note: Words in square brackets in paragraphs (1) and (2) substituted from 5 February 2005 (SI 2005/11).

[Suspension or discontinuation of support

20.—(1) Asylum support for a supported person and any dependant of his or for one or more dependants of a supported person may be suspended or discontinued if—

(a) support is being provided for the supported person or a dependant of his in collective accommodation and the Secretary of State has reasonable grounds to believe that the supported person or his dependant has committed a serious breach of the rules of that accommodation;

(b) the Secretary of State has reasonable grounds to believe that the supported person or a dependant of his for whom support is being provided has committed an act of seriously violent behaviour whether or not that act occurs in accommodation provided by way of asylum support or at the authorised address or elsewhere;

(c) the supported person or a dependant of his has committed an offence under Part VI of the Act;

(d) the Secretary of State has reasonable grounds to believe that the supported person or any dependant of his for whom support is being provided has abandoned the authorised address without first informing the Secretary of State or, if requested, without permission;

(e) the supported person has not complied within a reasonable period, which shall be no less than five working days beginning with the day on which the request was received by him, with requests for information made by the Secretary of State and which relate to the supported person's or his dependant's eligibility for or receipt of asylum support including requests made under regulation 15;

(f) the supported person fails, without reasonable excuse, to attend an interview requested by the Secretary of State relating to the supported person's or his dependant's eligibility for or receipt of asylum support;

(g) the supported person or, if he is an asylum seeker, his dependant, has not complied within a reasonable period, which shall be no less than ten working days beginning with the day on which the request was received by him, with a request for information made by the Secretary of State relating to his claim for asylum;

(h) the Secretary of State has reasonable grounds to believe that the supported person or a dependant of his for whom support is being provided has concealed financial resources and that the supported person or a dependant of his or both have therefore unduly benefited from the receipt of asylum support;

(i) the supported person or a dependant of his for whom support is being provided has not complied with a reporting requirement;

(j) the Secretary of State has reasonable grounds to believe that the supported person or a dependant of his for whom support is being provided has made a claim for asylum ('the first claim') and before the first claim has been determined makes or seeks to make a further claim for asylum not being part of the first claim in the same or a different name; or

(k) the supported person or a dependant of his for whom support is being provided has failed without reasonable excuse to comply with a relevant condition.

(2) If a supported person is asked to attend an interview of the type referred to in paragraph (1)(f) he shall be given no less than five working days notice of it.

(3) Any decision to discontinue support in the circumstances referred to in paragraph (1) above shall be taken individually, objectively and impartially and reasons shall be given. Decisions will be based on the particular situation of the person concerned and particular regard shall be had to whether he is a vulnerable person as described by Article 17 of Council Directive 2003/9/EC of 27 January 2003 laying down minimum standards for the reception of asylum seekers.

(4) No person's asylum support shall be discontinued before a decision is made under paragraph (1).

(5) Where asylum support for a supported person or his dependant is suspended or discontinued under paragraph (1)(d) or (i) and the supported person or his dependant are traced or voluntarily report to the police, the Secretary of State or an immigration officer, a duly motivated decision based on the reasons for the disappearance shall be taken as to the reinstatement of some or all of the supported person's or his dependant's or both of their asylum support.

(6) For the purposes of this regulation—

(a) the authorised address is—

(i) the accommodation provided for the supported person and his dependants (if any) by way of asylum support; or

(ii) if no accommodation is so provided, the address notified by the supported person to the Secretary of State in his application for asylum support or, where a change of address has been notified to the Secretary of State under regulation 15 or under the Immigration Rules or both, the address for the time being so notified;

(b) 'collective accommodation' means accommodation which a supported person or any dependant of his for whom support is being provided shares with any other supported person and includes accommodation in which only facilities are shared;

(c) 'relevant condition' has the same meaning as in regulation 19(2);

(d) 'reporting requirement' is a condition or restriction which requires a person to report to the police, an immigration officer or the Secretary of State and is imposed under—

(i) paragraph 21 of Schedule 2 to the Immigration Act 1971 (temporary admission or release from detention);

(ii) paragraph 22 of that Schedule; or

(iii) paragraph 2 or 5 of Schedule 3 to that Act (pending deportation).

(e) 'working day' has the same meaning as in regulation 3(7) save that the reference to the applicant shall be a reference to the supported person or his dependant.]

Note: Regulation 20 substituted from 5 February 2005 (SI 2005/11).

[Temporary Support

20A. Regulations 19 and 20 shall apply to a person or his dependant who is provided with temporary support under section 98 of the Act in the same way as they apply to a person and his dependant who is in receipt of asylum support and any reference to asylum support in regulations 19 and 20 shall include a reference to temporary support under section 98.]

Note: Regulation 20A inserted from 5 April 2005 (SI 2005/11).

Effect of previous suspension or discontinuation

21.—(1) [Subject to regulation 20(5) where—]

(a) an application for asylum support is made,

(b) the applicant or any other person to whom the application relates has previously had his asylum support suspended or discontinued under regulation 20, and

(c) there has been no material change of circumstances since the suspension or discontinuation,

the application need not be entertained unless the Secretary of State considers that there are exceptional circumstances which justify its being entertained.

(2) A material change of circumstances is one which, if the applicant were a supported person, would have to be notified to the Secretary of State under regulation 15.

(3) This regulation is without prejudice to the power of the Secretary of State to refuse the application even if he has entertained it.

Note: Words in square brackets in paragraph (1) substituted from 5 February 2005 (SI 2005/11).

Notice to quit

Notice to quit

22.—(1) If—

(a) as a result of asylum support, a person has a tenancy or licence to occupy accommodation,

(b) one or more of the conditions mentioned in paragraph (2) is satisfied, and

(c) he is given notice to quit in accordance with paragraph (3) or (4),

his tenancy or licence is to be treated as ending with the period specified in that notice, regardless of when it could otherwise be brought to an end.

(2) The conditions are that—

(a) the asylum support is suspended or discontinued as a result of any provision of regulation 20;

(b) the relevant claim for asylum has been determined;

(c) the supported person has ceased to be destitute; or

(d) he is to be moved to other accommodation.

(3) A notice to quit is in accordance with this paragraph if it is in writing and—

(a) in a case where sub-paragraph (a), (c) or (d) of paragraph (2) applies, specifies as the notice period a period of not less than seven days; or

(b) in a case where the Secretary of State has notified his decision on the relevant claim for asylum to the claimant, specifies as the notice period a period at least as long as whichever is the greater of—

(i) seven days; or

(ii) the period beginning with the date of service of the notice to quit and ending with the date of determination of the relevant claim for asylum (found in accordance with section 94(3) of the Act).

(4) A notice to quit is in accordance with this paragraph if—

(a) it is in writing;

(b) it specifies as the notice period a period of less than seven days; and

(c) the circumstances of the case are such that that notice period is justified.

Meaning of 'destitute' for certain other purposes

Meaning of 'destitute' for certain other purposes

23.—(1) In this regulation 'the relevant enactments' means—

(a) section 21(1A) of the National Assistance Act 1948;

(b) section 45(4A) of the Health Services and Public Health Act 1968;

(c) paragraph 2(2A) of Schedule 8 to the National Health Service Act 1977;

(d) sections 12(2A), 13A(4) and 13B(3) of the Social Work (Scotland) Act 1968;

(e) sections 7(3) and 8(4) of the Mental Health (Scotland) Act 1984; and

(f) Articles 7(3) and 15(6) of the Health and Personal Social Services (Northern Ireland) Order 1972.

(2) The following provisions of this regulation apply where it falls to an authority, or the Department, to determine for the purposes of any of the relevant enactments whether a person is destitute.

(3) Paragraphs (3) to (6) of regulation 6 apply as they apply in the case mentioned in paragraph (1) of that regulation, but as if references to the principal were references to the person whose destitution or otherwise is being determined and references to the Secretary of State were references to the authority or (as the case may be) Department.

(4) The matters mentioned in paragraph (3) of regulation 8 (read with paragraphs (4) to (6) of that regulation) are prescribed for the purposes of subsection (5)(a) of section 95 of the Act, as applied for the purposes of any of the relevant enactments, as matters to which regard must be had in determining for the purposes of any of the relevant enactments whether a person's accommodation is adequate.

(5) The matter mentioned in paragraph (2) of regulation 9 is prescribed for the purposes of subsection (7)(b) of section 95 of the Act, as applied for the purposes of any of the relevant enactments, as a matter to which regard may not be had in determining for the purposes of any of the relevant enactments whether a person's essential living needs (other than accommodation) are met.

(6) Paragraphs (3) to (6) of regulation 9 shall apply as if the reference in paragraph (3) to Part VI of the Act included a reference to the relevant enactments.

(7) The references in regulations 8(5) and 9(2) to the Secretary of State shall be construed, for the purposes of this regulation, as references to the authority or (as the case may be) Department.

SCHEDULE

Regulation 3(3)

Note: Schedule revoked from 9 April 2007 (SI 2007/863).

. . .

The Immigration (Leave to Enter and Remain) Order 2000
(SI 2000, No. 1161)

PART I

GENERAL

1. Citation, commencement and interpretation

(1) This Order may be cited as the Immigration (Leave to Enter and Remain) Order 2000.

(2) Articles 1 to 12, 14 and 15(1) of this Order shall come into force on 28 April 2000 or, if later, on the day after the day on which it is made and articles 13 and 15(2) shall come into force on 30 July 2000.

(3) In this Order—

'the Act' means the Immigration Act 1971;

['ADS Agreement with China' means the Memorandum of Understanding on visa and related issues concerning tourist groups from the People's Republic of China to the United Kingdom as an approved destination, signed on 21 January 2005;]

'control port' means a port in which a control area is designated under paragraph 26(3) of Schedule 2 to the Act;

['convention travel document' means a travel document issued pursuant to Article 28 of the Refugee Convention, except where that travel document was issued by the United Kingdom Government;]

{'decision-maker' means— (a) the Secretary of State; (b) an immigration officer;}

'the Immigration Acts' means:

(a) the Act;

(b) the Immigration Act 1988;

(c) the Asylum and Immigration Appeals Act 1993;

(d) the Asylum and Immigration Act 1996; and

(e) the Immigration and Asylum Act 1999.

['Refugee Convention' means the Convention relating to the Status of Refugees done at Geneva on 28 July 1951 and its Protocol;]

{"representative" means a person who appears to the decision-maker— (a) to be the representative of the person referred to in article 8ZA(1); and (b) not to be prohibited from acting as a representative by section 84 of the Immigration and Asylum Act 1999;}

'responsible third party' means a person appearing to an immigration officer to be:

(a) in charge of a group of people arriving in the United Kingdom together or intending to arrive in the United Kingdom together;

(b) a tour operator;

(c) the owner or agent of a ship, aircraft, train, hydrofoil or hovercraft;

(d) the person responsible for the management of a control port or his agent; or

(e) an official at a British Diplomatic Mission or at a British Consular Post or at the office of any person outside the United Kingdom and Islands who has been authorised by the Secretary of State to accept applications for entry clearance;

'tour operator' means a person who, otherwise than occasionally, organises and provides holidays to the public or a section of it; and

'visit visa' means an entry clearance granted for the purpose of entry to the United Kingdom as a visitor under the immigration rules.

Note: Words in first square brackets inserted from 1 April 2005 (SI 2005/1159). Other words in square brackets inserted from 27 February 2004 (SI 2004/475). Definitions of 'decision-maker' and 'representative' inserted from 12 July 2013 (SI 2013/1749).

PART II

ENTRY CLEARANCE AS LEAVE TO ENTER

2. Entry clearance as Leave to Enter

Subject to article 6(3), an entry clearance which complies with the requirements of article 3 shall have effect as leave to enter the United Kingdom to the extent specified in article 4, but subject to the conditions referred to in article 5.

3. Requirements

[(1) Subject to paragraph (4), an entry clearance shall only have effect as leave to enter if it complies with the requirements of this article.]

(2) The entry clearance must specify the purpose for which the holder wishes to enter the United Kingdom.

(3) The entry clearance must be endorsed with:

(a) the conditions to which it is subject; or

(b) a statement that it is to have effect as indefinite leave to enter the United Kingdom.

[(4) Subject to paragraph (5), an entry clearance shall not have effect as leave to enter if it is endorsed on a convention travel document.

(5) An entry clearance endorsed on a convention travel document before 27 February 2004 shall have effect as leave to enter.]

Note: Article 3(1) substituted and Art 3(4) and (5) inserted from 27 February 2004 (SI 2004/475).

4. Extent to which entry clearance is to be leave to enter

(1) A visit visa, [(other than a visit visa granted pursuant to the ADS Agreement with China) unless endorsed with a statement that it is to have effect as a single-entry visa] during its period of validity, shall have effect as leave to enter the United Kingdom on an unlimited number of occasions, in accordance with paragraph (2).

(2) On each occasion the holder arrives in the United Kingdom, he shall be treated for the purposes of the Immigration Acts as having been granted, before arrival, leave to enter the United Kingdom for a limited period beginning on the date of arrival, being:

(a) six months if six months or more remain of the visa's period of validity; or

(b) the visa's remaining period of validity, if less than six months.

[(**2A**) A visit visa granted pursuant to the ADS Agreement with China endorsed with a statement that it is to have effect as a dual-entry visa, shall have effect as leave to enter the United Kingdom on two occasions during its period of validity, in accordance with paragraph (2B).

(2B) On arrival in the United Kingdom on each occasion, the holder shall be treated for the purposes of the Immigration Acts as having been granted, before arrival, leave to enter the United Kingdom for a limited period, being the period beginning on the date on which the holder arrives in the United Kingdom and ending on the date of expiry of the entry clearance.]

(3) In the case of [any form of entry clearance to which this paragraph applies], it shall have effect as leave to enter the United Kingdom on one occasion during its period of validity; and, on arrival in the United Kingdom, the holder shall be treated for the purposes of the Immigration Acts as having been granted, before arrival, leave to enter the United Kingdom:

(a) in the case of an entry clearance which is endorsed with a statement that it is to have effect as indefinite leave to enter the United Kingdom, for an indefinite period; or

(b) in the case of an entry clearance which is endorsed with conditions, for a limited period, being the period beginning on the date on which the holder arrives in the United Kingdom and ending on the date of expiry of the entry clearance.

[(**3A**) Paragraph (3) applies to—

(a) a visit visa (other than a visit visa granted pursuant to the ADS Agreement with China) endorsed with a statement that it is to have effect as a single entry visa;

(b) a visit visa granted pursuant to the ADS Agreement with China unless endorsed with a statement to the effect that it is to have effect as a dual entry visa; and

(c) any other form of entry clearance.]

(4) In this article 'period of validity' means the period beginning on the day on which the entry clearance becomes effective and ending on the day on which it expires.

Note: Words in square brackets inserted from 1 April 2005 (SI 2005/1159). Paragraphs (2) and (3) have effect in a form modified by and in circumstances specified by the Channel Tunnel (International Arrangements) Order (SI 1993/1813) as amended.

5. Conditions

An entry clearance shall have effect as leave to enter subject to any conditions, being conditions of a kind that may be imposed on leave to enter given under section 3 of the Act, to which the entry clearance is subject and which are endorsed on it.

6. Incidental, supplementary and consequential provisions

(1) Where an immigration officer exercises his power to cancel leave to enter under paragraph 2A(8) of Schedule 2 to the Act or article 13(7) below in respect of an entry clearance which has effect as leave to enter, the entry clearance shall cease to have effect.

(2) If the holder of an entry clearance—

(a) arrives in the United Kingdom before the day on which it becomes effective; or

(b) seeks to enter the United Kingdom for a purpose other than the purpose specified in the entry clearance, an immigration officer may cancel the entry clearance.

(3) If the holder of an entry clearance which does not, at the time, have effect as leave to enter the United Kingdom seeks leave to enter the United Kingdom at any time before his departure for, or in the course of his journey to, the United Kingdom and is refused leave to enter under article 7, the entry clearance shall not have effect as leave to enter.

Note: Paragraph (2)(a) has effect in a form modified by and in circumstances specified by the Channel Tunnel (International Arrangements) Order (SI 1993/1813) as amended.

Part III

Form and Manner of Giving and Refusing Leave to Enter

7. Grant and refusal of leave to enter before arrival in the United Kingdom

(1) An immigration officer, whether or not in the United Kingdom, may give or refuse a person leave to enter the United Kingdom at any time before his departure for, or in the course of his journey to, the United Kingdom.

(2) In order to determine whether or not to give leave to enter under this article (and, if so, for what period and subject to what conditions), an immigration officer may seek such information, and the production of such documents or copy documents, as an immigration officer would be entitled to obtain in an examination under paragraph 2 or 2A of Schedule 2 to the Act.

(3) An immigration officer may also require the person seeking leave to supply an up to date medical report.

(4) Failure by a person seeking leave to supply any information, documents, copy documents or medical report requested by an immigration officer under this article shall be a ground, in itself, for refusal of leave.

Oral grant or refusal of leave

[8.(1) A notice giving or refusing leave to enter the United Kingdom as a visitor may, instead of being given in writing as required by section 4(1) of the Act, be given orally, including by means of a telephone.

(2) In paragraph (1), "leave to enter the United Kingdom as a visitor" means leave to enter as a visitor under the immigration rules for a period not exceeding six months, subject to conditions prohibiting employment and recourse to public funds (within the meaning of the immigration rules).]

Note: Article 8 substituted from 12 July 2013 (SI 2013/1749).

Grant, refusal or variation of leave by notice in writing

[8ZA.(1) A notice in writing—

(a) giving leave to enter or remain in the United Kingdom;

(b) refusing leave to enter or remain in the United Kingdom;

(c) refusing to vary a person's leave to enter or remain in the United Kingdom; or

(d) varying a person's leave to enter or remain in the United Kingdom, may be given to the person affected as required by section 4(1) of the Act as follows.

(2) The notice may be—

(a) given by hand;

(b) sent by fax;

(c) sent by postal service to a postal address provided for correspondence by the person or the person's representative;

(d) sent electronically to an e-mail address provided for correspondence by the person or the person's representative;

(e) sent by document exchange to a document exchange number or address; or

(f) sent by courier.

(3) Where no postal or e-mail address for correspondence has been provided, the notice may be sent—

(a) by postal service to—

(i) the last-known or usual place of abode, place of study or place of business of the person; or

(ii) the last-known or usual place of business of the person's representative; or

(b) electronically to—

(i) the last-known e-mail address for the person (including at the person's last-known place of study or place of business); or

(ii) the last-known e-mail address of the person's representative.

(4) Where attempts to give notice in accordance with paragraphs (2) and (3) are not possible or have failed, when the decision-maker records the reasons for this and places the notice on file the notice shall be deemed to have been given.

(5) Where a notice is deemed to have been given in accordance with paragraph (4) and then subsequently the person is located, the person shall as soon as is practicable be given a copy of the notice and details of when and how it was given.

(6) A notice given under this article may, in the case of a person who is under 18 years of age and does not have a representative, be given to the parent, guardian or another adult who for the time being takes responsibility for the child.]

Note: Article 8ZA inserted from 12 July 2013 (SI 2013/1749).

Presumptions about receipt of notice

[**8ZB.**(1) Where a notice is sent in accordance with article 8ZA, it shall be deemed to have been given to the person affected, unless the contrary is proved—

(a) where the notice is sent by postal service—

(i) on the second day after it was sent by postal service in which delivery or receipt is recorded if sent to a place within the United Kingdom;

(ii) on the 28th day after it was posted if sent to a place outside the United Kingdom;

(b) where the notice is sent by fax, e-mail, document exchange or courier, on the day it was sent.

(2) For the purposes of paragraph (1)(a) the period is to be calculated excluding the day on which the notice is posted.

(3) For the purposes of paragraph (1)(a)(i) the period is to be calculated excluding any day which is not a business day.

(4) In paragraph (3) "business day" means any day other than a Saturday, a Sunday, Christmas Day, Good Friday or a day which is a bank holiday under the Banking and Financial Dealings Act 1971(2) in the part of the United Kingdom to which the notice is sent.]

Note: Article 8ZB inserted from 12 July 2013 (SI 2013/1749).

Notice not given

[**8ZC.** No notice under article 8(1) or 8ZA(1)(a) shall be given where a person is given leave to enter the United Kingdom by passing through an automated gate in accordance with article 8A.]

Note: Article 8ZC inserted from 12 July 2013 (SI 2013/1749).

[Automatic grant of leave

8A.—(1) An immigration officer may authorise a person to be a person who may obtain leave to enter the United Kingdom by passing through an automated gate.

(2) Such an authorisation may—

(a) only authorise a person to obtain leave to enter the United Kingdom as one of the categories of person under the immigration rules mentioned in paragraph (5);

(b) set out the conditions of use for an automated gate;

(c) list the automated gates for which the authorisation is valid;

(d) remain in force for up to 24 months; and

(e) be varied or withdrawn at any time, with or without notice being given to the person.

(3) Where a person passes through an automated gate—

(a) having been authorised under paragraph (1) as a person who may obtain leave to enter the United Kingdom by passing through an automated gate;

(b) in accordance with the conditions of use for an automated gate;

(c) which is an automated gate for which the authorisation is valid; and

(d) while the authorisation remains in force; the person shall be given leave to enter the United Kingdom for six months as the category of person under the immigration rules for which the person has been authorised under paragraph (1).

(4) Such leave shall be subject to conditions prohibiting employment and recourse to public funds (within the meaning of the immigration rules).

(5) The categories of person under the immigration rules mentioned in this paragraph are—

(a) a general visitor;

(b) a business visitor;

(c) an academic visitor;

(d) a sports visitor;

(e) an entertainer visitor;

(f) a person seeking leave to enter as a visitor for private medical treatment;

(g) a person seeking leave to enter as the parent of a child at school in the United Kingdom.]

Note: Article 8A inserted from 25 March 2010 (SI 2010/957).

9. Grant or refusal of leave by notice to a responsible third party

(1) Leave to enter may be given or refused to a person by means of a notice given (in such form and manner as permitted by the Act or this Order for a notice giving or refusing leave to enter) to a responsible third party acting on his behalf.

(2) A notice under paragraph (1) may refer to a person to whom leave is being granted or refused either by name or by reference to a description or category of persons which includes him.

10. Notice of refusal of leave

(1) Where a notice refusing leave to enter to a person is given under [article 8(1)] or 9, an immigration officer shall as soon as practicable give to him a notice in writing stating that he has been refused leave to enter the United Kingdom and stating the reasons for the refusal.

(2) Where an immigration officer serves a notice under the Immigration (Appeals) Notices Regulations 1984 or under regulations made under paragraph 1 of Schedule 4 to the Immigration and Asylum Act 1999 in respect of the refusal, he shall not be required to serve a notice under paragraph (1).

(3) Any notice required by paragraph (1) to be given to any person may be [given in accordance with article 8ZA.]

Note: Words in square brackets in paragraphs (1) and (3) substituted from 12 July 2013 (SI 2013/1749).

11. Burden of proof

Where any question arises under the Immigration Acts as to whether a person has leave to enter the United Kingdom and he alleges that he has such leave by virtue of a notice given under article {8(1)} or 9, [or by virtue of article 8A,] the onus shall lie upon him to show the manner and date of his entry into the United Kingdom.

Note: Words in square brackets inserted from 25 March 2010 (SI 2010/957). Words in curly brackets substituted from 12 July 2013 (SI 2013/1749).

12.—(1) This article applies where—

(a) an immigration officer has commenced examination of a person ('the applicant') under paragraph 2(1)(c) of Schedule 2 to the Act (examination to determine whether or not leave to enter should be given);

(b) that examination has been adjourned, or the applicant has been required (under paragraph 2(3) of Schedule 2 to the Act) to submit to a further examination, whilst further inquiries are made (including, where the applicant has made an asylum claim, as to the Secretary of State's decision on that claim); and

(c) upon the completion of those inquiries, an immigration officer considers he is in a position to decide whether or not to give or refuse leave to enter without interviewing the applicant further.

(2) Where this article applies, any notice giving or refusing leave to enter which is on any date thereafter sent by post to the applicant (or is communicated to him in such form or manner as is permitted by this Order) shall be regarded, for the purposes of the Act, as having been given within the period of 24 hours specified in paragraph 6(1) of Schedule 2 to the Act (period within which notice giving or refusing leave to enter must be given after completion of examination).

Part IV

Leave Which does not Lapse on Travel Outside Common Travel Area

13.—(1) In this article 'leave' means—

(a) leave to enter the United Kingdom (including leave to enter conferred by means of an entry clearance under article 2); and

(b) leave to remain in the United Kingdom.

(2) Subject to paragraph (3), where a person has leave which is in force and which was:

(a) conferred by means of an entry clearance (other than a visit visa) under article 2; or

(b) given by an immigration officer or the Secretary of State for a period exceeding six months,

such leave shall not lapse on his going to a country or territory outside the common travel area.

(3) Paragraph (2) shall not apply:

(a) where a limited leave has been varied by the Secretary of State; and

(b) following the variation the period of leave remaining is six months or less.

(4) Leave which does not lapse under paragraph (2) shall remain in force either indefinitely (if it is unlimited) or until the date on which it would otherwise have expired (if limited), but—

(a) where the holder has stayed outside the United Kingdom for a continuous period of more than two years, the leave (where the leave is unlimited) or any leave then remaining (where the leave is limited) shall thereupon lapse; and

(b) any conditions to which the leave is subject shall be suspended for such time as the holder is outside the United Kingdom.

(5) For the purposes of paragraphs 2 and 2A of Schedule 2 to the Act (examination by immigration officers, and medical examination), leave to remain which remains in force under this article shall be treated, upon the holder's arrival in the United Kingdom, as leave to enter which has been granted to the holder before his arrival.

(6) Without prejudice to the provisions of section 4(1) of the Act, where the holder of leave which remains in force under this article is outside the United Kingdom, the Secretary of State may vary that leave (including any conditions to which it is subject) in such form and manner as permitted by the Act or this Order for the giving of leave to enter.

(7) Where a person is outside the United Kingdom and has leave which is in force by virtue of this article, that leave may be cancelled:

(a) in the case of leave to enter, by an immigration officer; or

(b) in the case of leave to remain, by the Secretary of State.

(8) In order to determine whether or not to vary (and, if so, in what manner) or cancel leave which remains in force under this article and which is held by a person who is outside the United Kingdom, an immigration officer or, as the case may be, the Secretary of State may seek such information, and the production of such documents or copy documents, as an immigration officer would be entitled to obtain in an examination under paragraph 2 or 2A of Schedule 2 to the Act and may also require the holder of the leave to supply an up to date medical report.

(9) Failure to supply any information, documents, copy documents or medical report requested by an immigration officer or, as the case may be, the Secretary of State under this article shall be a ground, in itself, for cancellation of leave.

(10) Section 3(4) of the Act (lapsing of leave upon travelling outside the common travel area) shall have effect subject to this article.

Part V

Consequential and Transitional Provisions

14. Section 9(2) of the Act (further provisions as to common travel area: conditions applicable to certain arrivals on a local journey) shall have effect as if, after the words 'British Citizens', there were inserted 'and do not hold leave to enter or remain granted to them before their arrival'.

15.—(1) Article 12 shall apply where an applicant's examination has begun before the date that article comes into force, as well as where it begins on or after that date.

(2) Article 13 shall apply with respect to leave to enter or remain in the United Kingdom which is in force on the date that article comes into force, as well as to such leave given after that date.

The Immigration (Removal Directions) Regulations 2000
(SI 2000, No. 2243)

1. Citation and commencement

These Regulations may be cited as the Immigration (Removal Directions) Regulations 2000 and shall come into force on 2 October 2000.

2. Interpretation

(1) In these Regulations—

'the Act' means the Immigration and Asylum Act 1999;

'aircraft' includes hovercraft;

'captain' means master (of a ship) or commander (of an aircraft);

'international service' has the meaning given by section 13(6) of the Channel Tunnel Act 1987;

'ship' includes every description of vessel used in navigation; and

'the tunnel system' has the meaning given by section 1(7) of the Channel Tunnel Act 1987.

(2) In these Regulations, a reference to a section number is a reference to a section of the Act.

3. Persons to whom directions may be given

For the purposes of section 10(6)(a) (classes of person to whom directions may be given), the following classes of person are prescribed—

(a) owners of ships;
(b) owners of aircraft;
(c) agents of ships;
(d) agents of aircraft;
(e) captains of ships about to leave the United Kingdom;
(f) captains of aircraft about to leave the United Kingdom; and
(g) persons operating an international service.

4. Requirements that may be imposed by directions

(1) For the purposes of section 10(6)(b) (requirements that may be imposed by directions), the following kinds of requirements are prescribed—

(a) in the case where directions are given to a captain of a ship or aircraft about to leave the United Kingdom, a requirement to remove the relevant person from the United Kingdom in that ship or aircraft;

(b) in the case where directions are given to a person operating an international service, a requirement to make arrangements for the removal of the relevant person through the tunnel system;

(c) in the case where directions are given to any other person who falls within a class prescribed in regulation 3, a requirement to make arrangements for the removal of the relevant person in a ship or aircraft specified or indicated in the directions; and

(d) in all cases, a requirement to remove the relevant person in accordance with arrangements to be made by an immigration officer.

(2) Paragraph (1) only applies if the directions specify that the relevant person is to be removed to a country or territory being—

(i) a country of which he is a national or citizen; or

(ii) a country or territory to which there is reason to believe that he will be admitted.

(3) Paragraph (1)(b) only applies if the relevant person arrived in the United Kingdom through the tunnel system.

(4) 'Relevant person' means a person who may be removed from the United Kingdom in accordance with section 10(1).

The Asylum (Designated Safe Third Countries) Order 2000
(SI 2000, No. 2245)

---

1. This Order may be cited as the Asylum (Designated Safe Third Countries) Order 2000 and shall come into force on 2 October 2000.

2. The Asylum (Designated Countries of Destination and Designated Safe Third Countries) Order 1996 is hereby revoked.

3. The following countries are designated for the purposes of section 12(1)(b) of the Immigration and Asylum Act 1999 (designation of countries other than EU Member States for the purposes of appeal rights):

Canada
Norway
Switzerland
United States of America.

The Immigration (Leave to Enter) Order 2001
(SI 2001, No. 2590)

1.—(1) This Order may be cited as the Immigration (Leave to Enter) Order 2001 and shall come into force on the day after the day on which it is made.

(2) In this Order—

(a) 'the 1971 Act' means the Immigration Act 1971; and

(b) 'claim for asylum' and 'the Human Rights Convention' have the meanings assigned by section 167 of the Immigration and Asylum Act 1999.

Note: Commencement 18 July 2001.

2.—(1) Where this article applies to a person, the Secretary of State may give or refuse him leave to enter the United Kingdom.

(2) This article applies to a person who seeks leave to enter the United Kingdom and who—

(a) has made a claim for asylum; or

(b) has made a claim that it would be contrary to the United Kingdom's obligations under the Human Rights Convention for him to be removed from, or required to leave, the United Kingdom.

(3) This article also applies to a person who seeks leave to enter the United Kingdom for a purpose not covered by the immigration rules or otherwise on the grounds that those rules should be departed from in his case.

(4) In deciding whether to give or refuse leave under this article the Secretary of State may take into account any additional grounds which a person has for seeking leave to enter the United Kingdom.

(5) The power to give or refuse leave to enter the United Kingdom under this article shall be exercised by notice in writing to the person affected or in such manner as is permitted by the Immigration (Leave to Enter and Remain) Order 2000.

3. In relation to the giving or refusing of leave to enter by the Secretary of State under article 2, paragraphs 2 (examination by immigration officers, and medical examination), 4 (information and documents), 7(1), (3) and (4) (power to require medical examination after entry), 8 (removal of persons refused leave to enter), 9 (removal of illegal entrants) and 21 (temporary admission of persons liable to detention) of Schedule 2 to the 1971 Act shall be read as if references to an immigration officer included references to the Secretary of State.

4.—(1) This article applies where—

(a) an immigration officer has commenced examination of a person ('the applicant') under paragraph 2(1)(c) of Schedule 2 to the 1971 Act (examination to determine whether or not leave to enter should be given);

(b) that examination has been adjourned, or the applicant has been required (under paragraph 2(3) of Schedule 2 to the Immigration Act 1971) to submit to a further examination;

(c) the Secretary of State subsequently examines the applicant or conducts a further examination in relation to him; and

(d) the Secretary of State thereafter gives or refuses the applicant leave to enter.

(2) Where this article applies, the notice giving or refusing leave to enter shall be regarded for the purposes of the 1971 Act as having been given within the period of 24 hours specified in paragraph 6(1) of Schedule 2 to that Act (period within which notice giving or refusing leave to enter must be given after completion of examination by an immigration officer).

The Immigration (Entry Otherwise than by Sea or Air) Order 2002

(SI 2002, No. 1832)

---

1. This Order may be cited as the Immigration (Entry Otherwise than by Sea or Air) Order 2002 and shall come into force on the day after the day on which it is made.

Note: Commencement 17 July 2002.

2.—(1) This article applies where—

(a) a person who requires leave to enter the United Kingdom by virtue of section 9(4) of the Immigration Act 1971 or by virtue of article 3 of the Immigration (Control of Entry through Republic of Ireland) Order 1972; or

(b) a person in respect of whom a deportation order is in force, has entered or is seeking to enter the United Kingdom from the Republic of Ireland.

(2) Where this article applies, paragraphs 8, 9 and 11 of Schedule 2 to the Immigration Act 1971 shall have effect in relation to persons entering or seeking to enter the United Kingdom on arrival otherwise than by ship or aircraft as they have effect in the case of a person arriving by ship or aircraft, with the modifications set out in the Schedule to this Order.

3. Article 2 shall apply where an illegal entrant entered the United Kingdom before the date when this Order comes into force, as well as where he entered the United Kingdom on or after that date.

(3) Article 2 shall not apply where a person has arrived in, but not entered, the United Kingdom before the date on which this Order comes into force.

Article 2(2) SCHEDULE

MODIFICATIONS TO SCHEDULE 2 OF THE IMMIGRATION ACT 1971

1. In this Schedule 'Schedule 2' means Schedule 2 to the Immigration Act 1971.

2. For paragraph 8 of Schedule 2, substitute:

'8.—(1) Where a person arriving in the United Kingdom is refused leave to enter, an immigration officer or the Secretary of State may give the owners or agents of any train, vehicle, ship or aircraft directions requiring them to make arrangements for that person's removal from the United Kingdom in any train, vehicle, ship or aircraft specified or indicated in the direction to a country or territory so specified being—

(a) a country of which he is a national or citizen; or

(b) a country or territory in which he has obtained a passport or other document of identify; or

(c) a country or territory in which he embarked for the United Kingdom; or

(d) a country or territory to which there is reason to believe that he will be admitted.

(2) The costs of complying with any directions given under this paragraph shall be defrayed by the Secretary of State.'.

3. In paragraph 9(1) of Schedule 2:

(a) after 'immigration officer', insert 'or the Secretary of State'; and

(b) after 'authorised by paragraph 8(1)', insert 'and the costs of complying with any directions given under this paragraph shall be defrayed by the Secretary of State'.

4. In paragraph 11 of Schedule 2, after 'on board any', insert 'train, vehicle,'.

The British Nationality (General) Regulations 2003
(SI 2003, No. 548)

Arrangement of Regulations

Part I

General

Citation and commencement

1. These Regulations may be cited as the British Nationality (General) Regulations 2003 and shall come into force on 1 April 2003.

Interpretation

2.—(1) In these Regulations, the following expressions have the meanings hereby assigned to them, that is to say—

'the Act' means the British Nationality Act 1981;

'applicant' in relation to an application made on behalf of a person not of full age or capacity means that person;

'High Commissioner' means, in relation to a country mentioned in Schedule 3 to the Act, the High Commissioner for Her Majesty's Government in the United Kingdom appointed to that country, and includes the acting High Commissioner.

(2) In the application of the provisions of regulation 6(2) [6(3), 6A(1), (3) and (5), paragraph 3 of Schedule 3] [. . .] where a function of the Secretary of State under the Act is exercised by the Lieutenant-Governor of any of the Islands by virtue of arrangements made under section 43(1) of the Act, any reference in those provisions to the Secretary of State shall be construed as a reference to the Lieutenant-Governor.

Note: Words in square brackets inserted from 1 January 2004 (SI 2003/3158), words omitted from 3 December 2007 (SI 2007/3137).

Part II

Registration and Naturalisation

Applications

3. Any application for registration as a British citizen, British Overseas citizen or British subject or for a certificate of naturalisation as a British citizen shall—

(a) be made to the appropriate authority specified in regulation 4; and

(b) satisfy the requirements of Part I and, if made on behalf of a person not of full age or capacity, Part II of Schedule 1 and such further requirements, if any, as are specified in relation thereto in Schedule 2.

Authority to whom application is to be made

4.—(1) Except as provided by paragraphs (2) and (3), the authority to whom an application is to be made is as follows:

(a) if the application is in Great Britain or Northern Ireland, to the Secretary of State at the Home Office;

(b) if the applicant is in any of the Islands, to the Lieutenant-Governor;

(c) if the applicant is in a British overseas territory, to the Governor;

[(d) if the applicant is in Hong Kong to any consular officer, any established officer in the Diplomatic Service of Her Majesty's Government in the United Kingdom or any person authorised by the Secretary of State in that behalf;]

[(e) if the applicant is elsewhere, to the Secretary of State at the Home Office.]

(2) The authority to whom an application under section 4(5) of the Act (acquisition by registration: British overseas territories citizens, etc.), on grounds of Crown Service under the government of a British overseas territory or service as a member of a body established by law in a British overseas territory, is to be made is in all cases the Governor of that territory.

(3) The authority to whom an application under section 5 of the Act (acquisition by registration: nationals for purposes of the [EU] Treaties) is to be made is in all cases the Governor of Gibraltar.

Note: Subparagraphs (1)(d) and (e) substituted from 16 July 2012 (SI 2012/1588).

Persons not of full age or capacity

5. An application may be made on behalf of someone not of full age or capacity by his father or mother or any person who has assumed responsibility for his welfare.

[Knowledge of language and life in the United Kingdom

5A.—(1) A person has sufficient knowledge of the English language for the purpose of an application for naturalisation as a British citizen under section 6 of the Act if that person—

(a) possesses a qualification or has passed a test specified in Schedule 2A; or

(b) possesses an academic qualification deemed by UK NARIC(d) to meet the recognised standard of a Bachelor's or Master's degree or PhD in the United Kingdom and—

(i) UK NARIC has confirmed that the qualification was taught or, as the case may be, researched in English; or

(ii) the qualification was taught or, as the case may be, researched in an English speaking country specified in Schedule 2A other than Canada; or

(c) is ordinarily resident outside the United Kingdom and a person designated by the Secretary of State certifies in writing that the person has sufficient knowledge of the English language for the purpose of an application for naturalisation; or

(d) satisfied the Secretary of State when making a successful application for indefinite leave to remain within the meaning of section 33(1) of the Immigration Act 1971 that he or she possessed a qualification or had passed a test in English at a level equivalent to Level B1 or above on the Council of Europe's Common European Framework of Reference for Languages: Learning, Teaching, Assessment; or

(e) is a national of an English speaking country specified in Schedule 2A.

(2) A person has sufficient knowledge about life in the United Kingdom for the purpose of an application for naturalisation as a British citizen under section 6 of the Act if that person—

(a) has passed the test known as the "Life in the UK Test" administered by an educational institution or other person approved for this purpose by the Secretary of State or the Lieutenant Governor of the Isle of Man; or

(b) has passed the test known as the "Citizenship Test" administered by an educational institution or other person approved for this purpose by the Lieutenant Governor of Guernsey or Jersey; or

(c) is ordinarily resident outside the United Kingdom and a person designated by the Secretary of State certifies in writing that the person has sufficient knowledge about life in the United Kingdom for the purpose of an application for naturalisation.]

Note: Regulation 5A substituted from 28 October 2013 (SI 2013/2541).

[Citizenship oaths and pledges

6.—(1) Where a citizenship oath or pledge is required by section 42 of the Act to be made by an applicant for registration or for a certificate of naturalisation, it shall be administered in accordance with the requirements of Schedule 3.

(2) If, on an application for a registration or for a certificate of naturalisation by an applicant who is required to make a citizenship oath or pledge, the Secretary of State decides that the registration should be effected or the certificate should be granted, he shall cause notice in writing of the decision to be given to the applicant.

(3) The requirement to make a citizenship oath or pledge shall be satisfied within three months of the giving of the notice referred to in paragraph (2) or such longer time as the Secretary of State may allow.

(4) Any notice required by paragraph (2) to be given to an applicant may be given—

(a) in any case where the applicant's whereabouts are known, by causing the notice to be delivered to him personally or by sending it to him by post;

(b) in a case where the applicant's whereabouts are not known, by sending it by post in a letter addressed to him at his last known address.

(5) In this regulation, references to the requirement to make a citizenship oath or pledge include the requirement to make a citizenship oath and pledge at a citizenship ceremony.]

Note: Regulation 6 substituted from 1 January 2004 (SI 2003/3158).

Arrangements for, and conduct of, citizenship ceremonies

6A.—(1) The Secretary of State may designate or authorise a person to exercise a function (which may include a discretion) in connection with a citizenship ceremony or a citizenship oath or pledge, and the reference in paragraph (3)(b) to 'designated person' shall be construed accordingly.

(2) Each local authority (within the meaning of section 41(3B) of the Act) shall—

(a) make available, or make arrangements for, premises at which citizenship ceremonies may be conducted; and

(b) arrange for citizenship ceremonies to be conducted with sufficient frequency so as to enable applicants in their area who are required to make a citizenship oath and pledge at a citizenship ceremony to meet the time limit laid down by regulation 6(3).

(3) Where an applicant is required by section 42 of the Act to make a citizenship oath and pledge at a citizenship ceremony, the Secretary of State shall—

(a) issue to the applicant an invitation in writing to attend a citizenship ceremony (a 'ceremony invitation');

(b) notify the applicant of the local authority or designated person which the applicant should contact to arrange attendance at a citizenship ceremony (the 'relevant authority'); and

(c) notify the relevant authority of his decision in relation to the applicant.

(4) An applicant who has arranged attendance at a citizenship ceremony shall bring with him to the ceremony his ceremony invitation; and if the applicant fails to do so, the person conducting the ceremony may refuse admittance to, or participation in, the ceremony if he is not reasonably satisfied as to the identity of the applicant.

(5) Where an applicant makes the relevant citizenship oath and pledge at a citizenship ceremony as required by section 42 of the Act—

(a) the person conducting the ceremony shall grant to the applicant a certificate of registration or naturalisation, duly dated with the date of the ceremony; and

(b) the relevant authority shall notify the Secretary of State in writing within 14 days of the date of the ceremony that the applicant has made the relevant citizenship oath and pledge at a citizenship ceremony and the date on which the ceremony took place.

(6) In this regulation, 'the person conducting the ceremony' is the person who administers the citizenship oath and pledge at the citizenship ceremony in accordance with paragraph 3 of Schedule 3.]

Note: Regulation 6A inserted from 1 January 2004 (SI 2003/3158).

[Certificates of naturalisation

7. A certificate of naturalisation shall include the following information relating to the person to whom the certificate is being granted—

(a) full name;
(b) date of birth; and
(c) place and country of birth.]

Note: Regulation 7 substituted from 3 December 2007 (SI 2007/3137).

Part III

Renunciation and Deprivation

Declarations of renunciation

8. Any declaration of renunciation of British citizenship, British Overseas citizenship or the status of a British subject shall—

(a) be made to the appropriate authority specified in regulation 9; and
(b) satisfy the requirements of Schedule 5.

Authority to whom declaration of renunciation is to be made

9. The authority to whom a declaration of renunciation is to be made is as follows:

(a) if the declarant is in Great Britain or Northern Ireland, to the Secretary of State at the Home Office;

(b) if the declarant is in any of the Islands, to the Lieutenant-Governor;

(c) if the declarant is in a British overseas territory, to the Governor;

[(d) if the declarant is in Hong Kong to any consular officer, any established officer in the Diplomatic Service of Her Majesty's Government in the United Kingdom or any person authorised by the Secretary of State in that behalf;]

[(e) if the declarant is elsewhere, to the Secretary of State at the Home Office.]

Note: Subparagraphs (d) and (e) substituted from 16 July 2012 (SI 2012/1588).

Notice of proposed deprivation of citizenship

10.—(1) Where it is proposed to make an order under section 40 of the Act depriving a person of a citizenship status, the notice required by section 40(5) of the Act to be given to that person may be given—

(a) in a case where that person's whereabouts are known, by causing the notice to be delivered to him personally or by sending it to him by post;

(b) in a case where that person's whereabouts are not known, by sending it by post in a letter addressed to him at his last known address.

(2) If a notice required by section 40(5) of the Act is given to a person appearing to the Secretary of State or, as appropriate, the Governor or Lieutenant-Governor to represent the person to whom notice under section 40(5) is intended to be given, it shall be deemed to have been given to that person.

(3) A notice required to be given by section 40(5) of the Act shall, unless the contrary is proved, be deemed to have been given—

(a) where the notice is sent by post from and to a place within the United Kingdom, on the second day after it was sent;

(b) where the notice is sent by post from or to a place outside the United Kingdom, on the twenty-eighth day after it was sent, and

(c) in any other case on the day on which the notice was delivered.

Cancellation of registration of person deprived of citizenship

11. Where an order has been made depriving a person who has a citizenship status by virtue of registration (whether under the Act or under the former nationality Acts) of that citizenship status, the name of that person shall be removed from the relevant register.

Cancellation of certificate of naturalisation in case of deprivation of citizenship

12. Where an order has been made depriving a person who has a citizenship status by virtue of the grant of a certificate of naturalisation (whether under the Act or under the former nationality Acts) of that citizenship status, the person so deprived or any other person in possession of the relevant certificate of naturalisation shall, if required by notice in writing given by the authority by whom the order was made, deliver up the said certificate to such person, and within such time, as may be specified in the notice; and the said certificate shall thereupon be cancelled or amended.

Part IV

Supplemental

Evidence

13. A document may be certified to be a true copy of a document for the purpose of section 45(2) of the Act by means of a statement in writing to that effect signed by a person authorised by the Secretary of State, the Lieutenant-Governor, the High Commissioner or the Governor in that behalf.

[Manner of signifying parental consent to registration

14. Where a parent, in pursuance of section 3(5)(c) or 4D(3) {or 4G(3)} of the Act, consents to the registration of a person as a British citizen under subsection 3(5) or section 4D {or 4G}, the consent shall be expressed in writing and signed by the parent.]

Note: Regulation 14 substituted from 13 January 2010 (SI 2009/3363). Words in curly brackets inserted by Immigration Act 2014, Sch 9 paragraph 71 from a date to be appointed.

Revocation

15. The British Nationality (General) Regulations 1982 are hereby revoked.

Regulation 3

Schedule 1

General Requirements As Respects Applications

Part I

All applications

1. An application shall be made in writing and shall state the name, address and date and place of birth of the applicant.

2. An application shall contain a declaration that the particulars stated therein are true.

Part II

Applications by persons not of full age or capacity

3. An application in respect of someone not of full age or capacity made by another person on his behalf shall state that that is the case and the name and address of that person.

4. An application made by a person on behalf of someone not of full age or capacity shall indicate the nature of that person's connection with him and, if that person has any responsibility for him otherwise than as a parent, the nature of that responsibility and the manner in which it was assumed.

Regulation 3

SCHEDULE 2

PARTICULAR REQUIREMENTS AS RESPECTS APPLICATIONS

Application under section 1(3) of the Act

1. An application under section 1(3) of the Act shall contain information showing:

[(a)] that the applicant's father or mother became a British citizen, or became settled in the United Kingdom, after the applicant's birth[; and

(b) where the applicant is aged 10 or over, that he is of good character.]

Note: Words in square brackets inserted from 3 December 2007 (SI 2007/3137).

Application under section 1(3A) of the Act

1A. An application under section 1(3A) shall contain information showing—

(a) that the applicant's father or mother became a member of the armed forces after the applicant's birth; and

(b) where the applicant is aged 10 or over, that he is of good character.]

Note: Paragraph 1A inserted from 13 January 2010 (SI 2009/3363).

Application under section 1(4) of the Act

2. An application under section 1(4) of the Act shall contain information showing:

[(a)] that the applicant possesses the requisite qualifications in respect of residence [; and

(b) where the applicant is aged 10 or over, that he is of good character.]

Note: Words in square brackets inserted from 3 December 2007 (SI 2007/3137).

3. If the applicant was absent from the United Kingdom on more than 90 days in all in any one of the first 10 years of his life and it is desired that the application should nevertheless be considered under section 1(7) of the Act, it shall specify the special circumstances to be taken into consideration.

Application under section 3(2) of the Act

4. An application under section 3(2) of the Act shall contain information showing—

(a) that the applicant's father or mother ('the parent in question') was a British citizen by descent at the time of the applicant's birth;

(b) that the father or mother of the parent in question—

(i) was a British citizen otherwise than by descent at the time of the birth of the parent in question; or

(ii) became a British citizen otherwise than by descent at commencement; or

(iii) would have become a British citizen otherwise than by descent at commencement but for his or her death;

(c) either—

(i) that the parent in question possesses the requisite qualifications in respect of residence; or

(ii) that the applicant was born stateless.

5. . . .

Note: Paragraph 5 omitted from 13 January 2010 (SI 2009/3363).

Application under section 3(5) of the Act

6. An application under section 3(5) of the Act shall contain information showing—

(a) that the applicant's father or mother was a British citizen by descent at the time of the applicant's birth;

(b) that the applicant and his father and mother possess the requisite qualifications in respect of residence;

(c) that the consent of the applicant's father and/or mother (as required by section 3(5)(c) and (6) of the Act) has been signified in accordance with regulation 14 and, if the consent of one parent only has been signified, the reason for that fact [; and

(d) where the applicant is aged 10 or over, that he is of good character.]

Note: Words in square brackets inserted from 3 December 2007 (SI 2007/3137).

Application under section 4(2) of the Act

7.—(1) An application under section 4(2) of the Act shall contain information showing—

(a) that the applicant is a British overseas territories citizen, a British Overseas citizen, a British subject under the Act or a British protected person;

(b) that the applicant possesses the requisite qualifications in respect of residence, freedom from immigration restrictions and compliance with the immigration laws [; and

(c) where the applicant is aged 10 or over, that he is of good character.]

(2) If the applicant does not possess the requisite qualifications in respect of residence, freedom from immigration restrictions and compliance with the immigration laws and it is desired that the application should nevertheless be considered under section 4(4) of the Act, it shall specify the special circumstances to be taken into consideration.

Note: Words in square brackets inserted from 3 December 2007 (SI 2007/3137).

Application under section 4(5) of the Act

8.—(1) An application under section 4(5) of the Act shall contain information showing—

(a) that the applicant is a British overseas territories citizen, a British Overseas citizen, a British subject under the Act or a British protected person;

(b) that the applicant possesses the requisite qualifications in respect of service [; and

(c) where the applicant is aged 10 or over, that he is of good character.]

(2) The application shall specify the special circumstances to be taken into consideration.

Note: Words in square brackets inserted from 3 December 2007 (SI 2007/3137).

Application under section 4A of the Act

9. An application under section 4A of the Act shall contain information showing—

(a) that the applicant is a British overseas territories citizen who is not such a citizen by virtue only of a connection with the Sovereign Base Areas of Akrotiri and Dhekelia;

(b) that the applicant has not ceased to be a British citizen as a result of a declaration of renunciation [; and

(c) where the applicant is aged 10 or over, that he is of good character].

Note: Words in square brackets inserted from 3 December 2007 (SI 2007/3137).

[Application under section 4B of the Act

10. An application under section 4B of the Act shall contain information showing—

(a) that the applicant is a British Overseas citizen, a British subject under the Act, a British protected person or a British National (Overseas) and does not have any other citizenship or nationality; and

(b) (i) in the case of an application made by virtue of subsection (1)(a), (b) or (c), that the applicant has not, after 4th July 2002, renounced, voluntarily relinquished or lost through action or inaction, any citizenship or nationality; or

(ii) in the case of an application made by virtue of subsection (1)(d), that the applicant has not, after 19th March 2009, renounced, voluntarily relinquished or lost through action or inaction, any citizenship or nationality].

Note: Paragraph 10 substituted from 13 January 2010 (SI 2009/3363).

[Application under section 4C of the Act

11. An application under section 4C of the Act shall contain information showing—

(a) that the applicant was born before 1 January 1983;

(b) that the applicant would at some time before 1 January 1983 have become a citizen of the United Kingdom and Colonies—

(i) under section 5 or 12(2) of, or paragraph 3 of Schedule 3 to, the British Nationality Act 1948 if (as the case may be) that section or paragraph provided for citizenship by descent from a mother in the same terms as it provided for citizenship by descent from a father and if references in that provision to a father were references to the applicant's mother; or

(ii) under section 12(2), (3), (4) or (5) of the British Nationality Act 1948 if a provision of the law at some time before 1 January 1949, which provided for a nationality status to be acquired by descent from a father, provided in the same terms for its acquisition by descent from a mother and if references in that provision to a father were references to the applicant's mother;

(c) that immediately before 1st January 1983 the applicant would have had the right of abode in the United Kingdom by virtue of section 2 of the Immigration Act 1971 had he become a citizen of the United Kingdom and Colonies as described in either sub-paragraph (b)(i) or (ii) above; and

(d) that he is of good character.]

Note: Paragraph 11 substituted from 13 January 2010 (SI 2009/3363).

[Application under section 4D of the Act

11A.—(1) An application under section 4D of the Act shall contain information showing—

(a) that the applicant's father or mother was a member of the armed forces and serving outside of the United Kingdom and qualifying territories at the time of the applicant's birth;

(b) that the consent of the applicant's father and/or mother (as required by section 4D(3) and (4) of the Act) has been signified in accordance with regulation 14 and, if the consent of one parent only has been signified, the reason for that fact; and

(c) where the applicant is aged 10 or over, that he is of good character.

(2) If the application is made without the consent of the applicant's father and/or mother and it is desired that the application should nevertheless be considered under section 4D(5) of the Act, it shall specify the special circumstances to be taken into consideration.]

Note: Paragraph 11A inserted from 13 January 2010 (SI 2009/3363).

Application under section 5 of the Act

12. An application under section 5 of the Act shall contain information showing

[(a)] that the applicant is a British overseas territories citizen who falls to be treated as a national of the United Kingdom for the purposes of the {EU}Treaties [; and

(b) where the applicant is aged 10 or over, that he is of good character.]

Note: Words in square brackets inserted from 3 December 2007 (SI 2007/3137).

Application under section 6(1)

13.—(1) An application under section 6(1) of the Act shall contain information showing—

(a) that the applicant possesses the requisite qualifications in respect of residence or Crown service, freedom from immigration restrictions, compliance with the immigration laws, good character, knowledge of language [, knowledge about life in the United Kingdom] and intention with respect to residence or occupation in the event of a certificate of naturalisation being granted to him;

(b) that the applicant is of full capacity.

(2) If the applicant does not possess the requisite qualifications in respect of residence, freedom from immigration restrictions, compliance with the immigration laws and knowledge of language and it is desired that the application should nevertheless be

considered under paragraph 2 of Schedule 1 to the Act, it shall specify the special circumstances to be taken into consideration.

[(3) If the applicant is not of full capacity and it is desired that the requirement of full capacity be waived in accordance with section 44A of the Act (waiver of requirement for full capacity), the application shall specify why it would be in the applicant's best interests for the requirement to be waived in his case.]

Note: Words in square brackets substituted from 1 May 2006 (SI 2005/2785). Subparagraph (3) inserted from 3 December 2007 (SI 2007/3137).

Application under section 6(2) of the Act

14.—(1) An application under section 6(2) of the Act shall contain information showing—

(a) that the applicant is married to a British citizen;

(b) that the applicant possesses the requisite qualifications in respect of residence, freedom from immigration restrictions, compliance with the [immigration laws, good character, knowledge of language and knowledge about life in the United Kingdom].

(c) that the applicant is of full capacity.

(2) If the applicant does not possess the requisite qualifications in respect of residence and compliance with the immigration laws and it is desired that the application should nevertheless be considered under paragraph 4 of Schedule 1 to the Act, it shall specify the special circumstances to be taken into consideration.

(3) If the applicant does not possess the requisite qualifications in respect of residence and it is desired that the application should nevertheless be considered under paragraph 4(d) of Schedule 1 to the Act on the grounds of marriage to a person who is serving in Crown Service under the government of the United Kingdom or other designated service, it shall specify the nature of the service and contain information showing that recruitment for that service took place in the United Kingdom.

[(4) If the applicant is not of full capacity and it is desired that the requirement of full capacity be waived in accordance with section 44A of the Act (waiver of requirement for full capacity), the application shall specify why it would be in the applicant's best interests for the requirement to be waived in his case.]

Note: Words in square brackets substituted from 1 May 2006 (SI 2005/2785). Subparagraph (4) inserted from 3 December 2007 (SI 2007/3137).

Application under section 10(1) of the Act

15. An application under section 10(1) of the Act shall contain information showing—

(a) that the applicant renounced citizenship of the United Kingdom and Colonies;

(b) that at the time when he renounced it the applicant was, or was about to become, a citizen of a country mentioned in section 1(3) of the British Nationality Act 1948;

(c) that the applicant could not have remained or become such a citizen but for renouncing it or had reasonable cause to believe that he would be deprived of his citizenship of that country unless he renounced it;

(d) that the applicant possessed the requisite qualifying connection with the United Kingdom immediately before commencement or was married before commencement to a person who possessed the requisite qualifying connection with the United Kingdom immediately before commencement or would if living have possessed such a connection;

(e) that the applicant has not previously been registered under section 10(1) of the Act [; and

(f) where the applicant is aged 10 or over, that he is of good character].

Note: Subparagraph (f) inserted from 3 December 2007 (SI 2007/3137).

Application under section 10(2) of the Act

16. [(1)] An application under section 10(2) of the Act shall contain information showing—

(a) that the applicant has renounced citizenship of the United Kingdom and Colonies and his reason for so doing;

(b) that the applicant possesses the requisite qualifying connection with the United Kingdom or has been married to a person who has, or would if living have, such a connection;

(c) that the applicant is of full capacity [; and

(d) where the applicant is aged 10 or over, that he is of good character];

[(2) If the applicant is not of full capacity and it is desired that the requirement of full capacity be waived in accordance with section 44A of the Act (waiver of requirement for full capacity), the application shall specify why it would be in the applicant's best interests for the requirement to be waived in his case.]

Note: Words in square brackets inserted from 3 December 2007 (SI 2007/3137).

Application under section 13(1) of the Act

17. [(1)] An application under section 13(1) of the Act shall contain information showing—

(a) that the applicant has renounced British citizenship;

(b) that, at the time when he renounced it, the applicant had or was about to acquire some other citizenship or nationality;

(c) that the renunciation of British citizenship was necessary to enable him to retain or acquire that other citizenship or nationality;

(d) that the applicant has not previously been registered under section 13(1) of the Act;

(e) that the applicant is of full capacity [; and

(f) where the applicant is aged 10 or over, that he is of good character];

[(2) If the applicant is not of full capacity and it is desired that the requirement of full capacity be waived in accordance with section 44A of the Act (waiver of requirement for full capacity), the application shall specify why it would be in the applicant's best interests for the requirement to be waived in his case.]

Note: Words in square brackets inserted from 3 December 2007 (SI 2007/3137).

Application under section 13(3) of the Act

18. [(1)] An application under section 13(3) of the Act shall contain information showing—

(a) that the applicant has renounced British citizenship and his reason for so doing;

(b) that the applicant is of full capacity [; and

(c) where the applicant is aged 10 or over, that he is of good character.]

[(2) If the applicant is not of full capacity and it is desired that the requirement of full capacity be waived in accordance with section 44A of the Act (waiver of requirement for full capacity), the application shall specify why it would be in the applicant's best interests for the requirement to be waived in his case.]

Note: Words in square brackets inserted from 3 December 2007 (SI 2007/3137).

Application under paragraph 3 of Schedule 2 to the Act

19.—(1) An application under paragraph 3 of Schedule 2 to the Act shall contain information showing—

(a) that the applicant is and always has been stateless;

(b) that the applicant seeks British citizenship and possesses the requisite qualifications in respect of residence.

(2) If the applicant does not possess the requisite qualifications in respect of residence and it is desired that the application should nevertheless be considered under paragraph 6 of Schedule 2 to the Act, it shall specify the special circumstances to be taken into consideration.

Application under paragraph 4 of Schedule 2

20.—(1) An application under paragraph 4 of Schedule 2 to the Act shall contain information showing—

(a) that the applicant is and always has been stateless;

(b) in respect of both the father and mother of the applicant, which of the following statuses, namely, British citizenship, British overseas territories citizenship, British Overseas citizenship or the status of a British subject under the Act, was held at the time of the applicant's birth;

(c) that the applicant possesses the requisite qualifications in respect of residence;

(d) if more than one of the statuses mentioned in sub-paragraph (b) above are available to the applicant, which status or statuses is or are wanted.

(2) If the applicant does not possess the requisite qualifications in respect of residence and it is desired that the application should nevertheless be considered under paragraph 6 of Schedule 2 to the Act, it shall specify the special circumstances to be taken into consideration.

Application under paragraph 5 of Schedule 2

21. An application under paragraph 5 of Schedule 2 to the Act shall contain information showing—

(a) that the applicant is and always has been stateless;

(b) if he was not born at a place which is at the date of the application within the United Kingdom and British overseas territories—

(i) that the applicant's mother was a citizen of the United Kingdom and Colonies at the time of his birth; or

(ii) that he possesses the requisite qualifications in respect of parentage or residence and parentage;

(c) that the applicant seeks British citizenship or British Overseas citizenship and that that citizenship is available to the applicant in accordance with paragraph 5(2) of Schedule 2 to the Act.

Regulation 5A [SCHEDULE 2A

SPECIFIED ENGLISH LANGUAGE TESTS AND QUALIFICATIONS AND ENGLISH SPEAKING COUNTRIES

Specified English Language Tests and Qualifications

1. The following tests and qualifications are specified for the purposes of regulation 5A(1)(a)—

(a) a qualification included on the register maintained by the Office of Qualifications and Examinations Regulation under section 148 of the Apprenticeships, Skills, Children and Learning Act 2009 ("the Register of Regulated Qualifications") which—

(i) is classified on the Register of Regulated Qualifications as a qualification in English for speakers of other languages;

(ii) was obtained in England, Wales or Northern Ireland; and

(iii) is at a level equivalent to level B1 or above on the Council of Europe's Common European Framework of Reference for Languages: Learning, Teaching, Assessment;

(b) a National Qualification in English awarded by the Scottish Qualifications Authority(a) which—

(i) was obtained in Scotland; and

(ii) is at level 4, 5 or 6 on the Scottish Credit and Qualifications Framework;

(c) a qualification or test specified in the following table which is at a level equivalent to level B1 or above on the Council of Europe's Common European Framework of Reference for Languages: Learning, Teaching, Assessment.

Recognised English Language Tests and Qualifications

Awarding body	Specified English language test or qualification
Cambridge English (previously known as Cambridge ESOL)	Business Language Testing Service (BULATS) Online Test (Certificated version)
	Cambridge English: Key (also known as Key English Test)
	Cambridge English: Preliminary (also known as Preliminary English Test)
	Cambridge English: First (also known as First Certificate in English)
	Cambridge English: Advanced (also known as Certificate in Advanced English)
	Cambridge English: Proficiency (also known as Certificate of Proficiency in English)
	Cambridge English: Business Preliminary (also known as Business English Certificate Preliminary)
	Cambridge English: Business Vantage (also known as Business English Certificate Vantage)
	Cambridge English: Business Higher (also known as Business English Certificate Higher)
	Cambridge English: Legal (also known as International Legal English Certificate)
	Cambridge English: Financial (also known as International Certificate in Financial English)
	ESOL Skills for Life at Entry level 3, level 1 or level 2
	IELTS (International English Language Testing System)
Cambridge International Examinations	Cambridge IGCSE: English as a First Language
	Cambridge IGCSE: English as a Second Language
City and Guilds	City and Guilds International ESOL (IESOL) Diploma
Pearson	Pearson Test of English Academic (PTE Academic)
Trinity College London	ESOL Skills for Life at Entry level 3, level 1 or level 2
	Integrated Skills in English

Specified English Speaking Countries

2. The following countries are specified English speaking countries for the purposes of regulation 5A(1)(b)(ii) and (e)—

(a) Antigua and Barbuda;

(b) Australia;

(c) the Bahamas;

(d) Barbados;

(e) Belize;
(f) Canada;
(g) Dominica;
(h) Grenada;
(i) Guyana;
(j) Jamaica;
(k) New Zealand;
(l) the Republic of Ireland;
(m) Saint Christopher and Nevis;
(n) Saint Lucia;
(o) Saint Vincent and the Grenadines;
(p) Trinidad and Tobago; or
(q) the United States of America]

Note: Schedule 2A inserted from 18 October 2013 (SI 2013/2541). Entry relating to 'Educational Testing Service' omitted from Table in paragraph 1 from 1 July 2014 (SI 2014/1465).

Regulation 6

SCHEDULE 3

ADMINISTRATION OF [CITIZENSHIP OATH OR PLEDGE]

1. Subject to [paragraphs 2 and 3] [a citizenship oath or pledge] shall be administered by one of the following persons:

(a) in England and Wales or Northern Ireland—any justice of the peace, commissioner for oaths or notary public;

(b) in Scotland—any sheriff principal, sheriff, justice of the peace or notary public;

(c) in the Channel Islands, the Isle of Man or any British overseas territory—any judge of any court of civil or criminal jurisdiction, any justice of the peace or magistrate, or any person for the time being authorised by the law of the place where the applicant, declarant or deponent is, to administer an oath for any judicial or other legal purpose;

(d) in any country mentioned in Schedule 3 to the Act of which Her Majesty is Queen, or in any territory administered by the government of any such country—any person for the time being authorised by the law of the place where the deponent is to administer an oath for any judicial or other legal purpose, any consular officer or any established officer of the Diplomatic Service of Her Majesty's Government in the United Kingdom;

(e) elsewhere—any consular officer, any established officer of the Diplomatic Service of Her Majesty's Government in the United Kingdom or any person authorised by the Secretary of State in that behalf.

2. If the deponent is serving in Her Majesty's naval, military or air forces, the oath [or pledge] may be administered by any officer holding a commission in any of those forces, whether the oath [or pledge] is made [. . .] in the United Kingdom or elsewhere.

[3. Where a citizenship oath and pledge is required by section 42 of the Act to be made at a citizenship ceremony, it shall be administered at the ceremony:

(a) in the case of a ceremony held in England, Wales or Scotland, by a registrar (within the meaning of section 41(3B) of the Act); and

(b) in the case of a ceremony held elsewhere, by a person authorised to do so by the Secretary of State.]

Note: Words in square brackets substituted and inserted, and words omitted from 1 January 2004 (SI 2003/3158).

Regulation 7 SCHEDULE 4

. . .

Note: Schedule 4 revoked from 3 December 2007 (SI 2007/3137).

Regulation 8 SCHEDULE 5

REQUIREMENTS AS RESPECTS DECLARATIONS OF RENUNCIATION

1. A declaration shall be made in writing and shall state the name, address, date and place of birth of the declarant.

2. A declaration shall contain information showing that the declarant—

(a) is a British citizen, British Overseas citizen or British subject, as the case may be;

(b) is of full age or, if not, has been married;

(c) is of full capacity;

(d) will, after the registration of the declaration, have or acquire some citizenship or nationality other than British citizenship, British Overseas citizenship or British subject status, as the case may be.

[**2A.** If the declarant is not of full capacity and it is desired that the requirement of full capacity be waived in accordance with section 44A of the Act (waiver of requirement for full capacity), the declaration shall specify why it would be in the applicant's best interests for the requirement to be waived in his case.]

Note: Paragraph 2A inserted from 3 December 2007 (SI 2007/3137).

3. A declaration shall contain a declaration that the particulars stated therein are true.

The Immigration (Notices) Regulations 2003

(SI 2003, No. 658)

Citation and commencement

1. These Regulations may be cited as the Immigration (Notices) Regulations 2003 and shall come into force on the 1 April 2003.

Interpretation

2. In these Regulations—

'the 1971 Act' means the Immigration Act 1971;

'the 1997 Act' means the Special Immigration Appeals Commission Act 1997;
'the 1999 Act' means the Immigration and Asylum Act 1999;
'the 2002 Act' means the Nationality, Immigration and Asylum Act 2002;
'decision-maker' means—
(a) the Secretary of State;
(b) an immigration officer;
(c) an entry clearance officer;

['EEA decision' has the same meaning as in regulation 2(1) of the Immigration (European Economic Area) Regulations 2006];

'entry clearance officer' means a person responsible for the grant or refusal of entry clearance;

...

'minor' means a person who is under 18 years of age;

'notice of appeal' means a notice in the appropriate prescribed form in accordance with the [Procedure Rules];

'Procedure Rules' means rules made under section [22 of, and Schedule 5 to, the Tribunals, Courts and Enforcement Act 2007];

'representative' means a person who appears to the decision-maker—
(a) to be the representative of a person referred to in regulation 4(1) below; and
(b) not to be prohibited from acting as a representative by section 84 of the 1999 Act.

Note: Definition of 'EEA Decision' substituted from 16 July 2012 (SI 2012/1547). Other words in square brackets inserted from 1 August 2008 (SI 2008/1819). Definition of 'immigration decision' deleted and definitions of 'notice of appeal' and 'Procedure Rules' amended from 6 November 2014 (SI 2014/2768).

3. ...

Note: Regulation 3 omitted from 6 November 2014 (SI 2014/2768).

Notice of decisions

4.—(1) Subject to regulation 6, the decision-maker must give written notice to a person of any [decision taken in respect of him which is appealable under section 82(1) of the 2002 Act or any] EEA decision taken in respect of him which is appealable.

(2) ...

(2A) ...

(3) If the notice is given to the representative of the person, it is to be taken to have been given to the person.

Note: Words substituted in paragraph (1) and paragraphs (2) and (2A) omitted from 6 November 2014 subject to transitional provisions (SI 2014/2768).

Contents of notice

5.—[(1) A notice given under regulation 4(1)—

(a) is to include or be accompanied by a statement of the reasons for the decision to which it relates;...

(b) ...

(2) ...

(2A) ...

(3) ...the notice given under regulation 4 shall also include, or be accompanied by, a statement which advises the person of—

(a) his right of appeal and the statutory provision on which his right of appeal is based;

(b) whether or not such an appeal may be brought while in the United Kingdom;

(c) the grounds on which such an appeal may be brought; and

(d) the facilities available for advice and assistance in connection with such an appeal.

[(4) The notice given under regulation 4 shall be accompanied by information about the process for providing a notice of appeal to the Tribunal and the time limit for providing that notice.]

(5) ...

(6) ...

(7) ...

(8) ...

Note: Paragraph (1) substituted from 31 August 2006 (SI 2006/2168). Words omitted from paragraphs (1)(a) and (3), paragraph (4) substituted and paragraphs (1)(b), (2), (2A), (5), (6), (7) and (8) omitted from 6 November 2014 subject to transitional provisions (SI 2014/2768).

Certain notices under the 1971 Act deemed to comply with the regulations

6.—(1) This regulation applies where the power to—

(a) refuse leave to enter; or

(b) vary leave to enter or remain in the United Kingdom;

is exercised by notice in writing under section 4 of (administration of control), or paragraph 6(2) (notice of decisions of leave to enter or remain) of Schedule 2 to, the 1971 Act.

(2) If—

(a) the statement required by regulation 5(3) is included in or accompanies that notice; and

(b) the notice is given in accordance with the provision of regulation 7; the notice is to be taken to have been given under regulation 4(1) for the purposes of these Regulations.

Service of notice

7.—(1) A notice required to be given under regulation 4 may be—

(a) given by hand;

(b) sent by fax;

(c) sent by postal service in which delivery or receipt is recorded to—

(i) an address provided for correspondence by the person or his representative; or

(ii) where no address for correspondence has been provided by the person, the last-known or usual place of abode or place of business of the person or his representative [;

[(c) sent electronically;

(d) sent by document exchange to a document exchange number or address;

(e) sent by courier; or

(f) collected by the person who is the subject of the decision or their representative.]

(2) Where—

(a) a person's whereabouts are not known; and

(b)

(i) no address has been provided for correspondence and the decision-maker does not know the last-known or usual place of abode or place of business of the person; or

(ii) the address provided to the decision-maker is defective, false or no longer in use by the person; and

(c) no representative appears to be acting for the person,

the notice shall be deemed to have been given when the decision-maker enters a record of the above circumstances and places the . . . notice on the relevant file.

[(3) Where a notice has been given in accordance with paragraph (2) and then subsequently the person is located—

(a) he shall be given a copy of the notice and details of when and how it was given as soon as practicable; and

(b) the time limit for appeal under the Procedure Rules shall be calculated from the date the notice is deemed to have been given in accordance with paragraph (2).]

[(4) Where a notice is sent by post to a place outside the United Kingdom in accordance with paragraph (1)(c) it shall be deemed to have been received on the twenty-eighth day after it was posted, unless the contrary is proved.]

(5) For the purposes of paragraph (4) the period is to be calculated—

(a) excluding the day on which the notice is posted;. . .

(b) . . .

(6) . . .

(7) A notice given under regulation 4 may, in the case of a minor who does not have a representative, be given to the parent, guardian or another adult who for the time being takes responsibility for the child.

Note: Words in square brackets in paragraph (1) inserted from 1 April 2008 (SI 2008/684). Words omitted from paragraph (2)(c) from 28 April 2013 (SI 2013/793). Paragraphs (3) and (4) substituted and paragraphs (5)(b) and (6) omitted from 6 November 2014 (SI 2014/2768).

. . .

The Immigration and Asylum Act 1999 (Part V Exemption: Relevant Employers) Order 2003
(SI 2003, No. 3214)

Citation and commencement

1. This Order may be cited as the Immigration and Asylum Act 1999 (Part V Exemption: Relevant Employers) Order 2003 and shall come into force on 1 January 2004.

Interpretation

2. In this Order—

'the Act' means the Immigration and Asylum Act 1999;

'immigration advice' and 'immigration services' have the same meanings as in section 82 of the Act;

'work permit' has the same meaning as in section 33(1) of the Immigration Act 1971;

'immediate family' means a person's spouse, and children below eighteen years of age;

'EEA national' means a person to whom the [Immigration (European Economic Area) Regulations 2006] apply;

'family member of an EEA national' has the same meaning as in the Immigration (European Economic Area) Regulations 2006.

Note: Words in square brackets inserted from 30 April 2006 (SI 2006/1003).

Exemption of relevant employers

3.—(1) Subject to paragraph (2), the following category of person is hereby specified for the purposes of section 84(4)(d) of the Act (provision of immigration services), namely, a person who provides immigration advice or immigration services free of charge to an employee or prospective employee who—

(a) is the subject of an application for a work permit submitted by the prospective employer;

(b) has been granted a work permit entitling him to work with the employer; or

(c) is an EEA national or the family member of an EEA national,

where the immigration advice or immigration services are restricted to matters which concern that employee or prospective employee or his immediate family.

(2) For the purposes of paragraph (1), the person providing the immigration advice or immigration services must be the employer or prospective employer of the person receiving the advice or services, or an employee of that employer acting as such.

The Immigration (Claimant's Credibility) Regulations 2004
(SI 2004, No. 3263)

Citation and commencement

1. These Regulations may be cited as the Immigration (Claimant's Credibility) Regulations 2004 and shall come into force on the 1 January 2005.

Interpretation

2. In these Regulations—

'the 2004 Act' means the Asylum and Immigration (Treatment of Claimants, etc.) Act 2004;

'representative' means a person who appears to the decision-maker—

(a) to be the representative of a person; and

(b) not to be prohibited from acting as a representative by section 84 of the Immigration and Asylum 1999 Act.

Manner of notifying immigration decision

3.—(1) For the purpose of section 8(5) of the 2004 Act a person may be notified of an immigration decision in any of the following ways—

(a) orally, including by means of a telecommunications system;

(b) in writing given by hand; or

(c) in writing

(i) sent by fax to a fax number;

(ii) sent by electronic mail to an electronic mail address; or

(iii) delivered or sent by postal service to an address,

provided for correspondence by the person or his representative.

(2) Where no fax number, electronic mail or postal address for correspondence has been provided by the person, notice of an immigration decision under paragraph (1)(c) may be delivered or sent by postal service to the last known or usual place of abode or place of business of the person or his representative.

(3) Notice given in accordance with paragraph (1) or (2) to the representative of the person, is to be taken to have been given to the person.

(4) In the case of a minor who does not have a representative, notice given in accordance with paragraph (1) or (2) to the parent, guardian or another adult who for the time being takes responsibility for the minor is taken to have been given to the minor.

Presumptions about receipt of notice

4.—(1) For the purpose of section 8(5) of the 2004 Act notice of an immigration decision shall, unless the contrary is proved, be treated as received;

(a) where the notice is sent by postal service in which delivery or receipt is recorded to an address, on the recorded date of delivery or receipt, or on the second day after the day it was posted, whichever is the earlier;

(b) in any other case in which the notice is sent by postal service on the second day after the day it was posted; or

(c) in any other case, on the day and time that it was communicated orally, given by hand or sent by electronic mail or fax.

(2) For the purposes of determining the second day after a notice is posted under paragraph (1)(a) and (b) any day which is not a business day shall be excluded.

(3) In this regulation 'business day' means any day other than Saturday or Sunday, a day which is a bank holiday under the Banking and Financial Dealings Act 1971 in the part of the United Kingdom from or to which the notice is sent, Christmas Day or Good Friday.

The Asylum Seekers (Reception Conditions) Regulations 2005

(SI 2005, No. 7)

Citation and commencement

1.—(1) These Regulations may be cited as the Asylum Seekers (Reception Conditions) Regulations 2005 and shall come into force on 5 February 2005.

(2) These Regulations shall only apply to a person whose claim for asylum is recorded on or after 5 February 2005.

Interpretation

2.—(1) In these Regulations—

(a) 'the 1999 Act' means the Immigration and Asylum Act 1999;

(b) 'asylum seeker' means a person who is at least 18 years old who has made a claim for asylum which has been recorded by the Secretary of State but not yet determined;

(c) 'claim for asylum' means a claim made by a third country national or a stateless person that to remove him or require him to leave the United Kingdom would be contrary to the United Kingdom's obligations under the Convention relating to the Status of Refugees done at Geneva on 28 July 1951 and its Protocol;

(d) 'family members' means, in so far as the family already existed in the country of origin, the following members of the asylum seeker's family who are present in the United Kingdom and who are asylum seekers or dependants on the asylum seeker's claim for asylum:

(i) the spouse of the asylum seeker or his unmarried partner in a stable relationship;

(ii) the minor child of the couple referred to in paragraph (2)(d)(i) or of the asylum seeker as long as the child is unmarried and dependent on the asylum seeker;

(e) 'Immigration Acts' has the same meaning as in section 44 of the Asylum and Immigration (Treatment of Claimants, etc.) Act 2004; and

(f) 'third country national' means a person who is not a national of a member State.

(2) For the purposes of these Regulations—

(a) a claim is determined on the date on which the Secretary of State notifies the asylum seeker of his decision on his claim or, if the asylum seeker appeals against the Secretary of State's decision, the date on which that appeal is disposed of; and

(b) an appeal is disposed of when it is no longer pending for the purposes of the Immigration Acts.

Families

3.—(1) When the Secretary of State is providing or arranging for the provision of accommodation for an asylum seeker and his family members under section 95 or 98 of the 1999 Act, he shall have regard to family unity and ensure, in so far as it is reasonably practicable to do so, that family members are accommodated together.

(2) Paragraph (1) shall only apply to those family members who confirm to the Secretary of State that they agree to being accommodated together.

(3) This regulation shall not apply in respect of a child when the Secretary of State is providing or arranging for the provision of accommodation for that child under section 122 of the 1999 Act.

Provisions for persons with special needs

4.—(1) This regulation applies to an asylum seeker or the family member of an asylum seeker who is a vulnerable person.

(2) When the Secretary of State is providing support or considering whether to provide support under section 95 or 98 of the 1999 Act to an asylum seeker or his family member who is a vulnerable person, he shall take into account the special needs of that asylum seeker or his family member.

(3) A vulnerable person is—

(a) a minor;

(b) a disabled person;

(c) an elderly person;

(d) a pregnant woman;

(e) a lone parent with a minor child; or

(f) a person who has been subjected to torture, rape or other serious forms of psychological, physical or sexual violence;

who has had an individual evaluation of his situation that confirms he has special needs.

(4) Nothing in this regulation obliges the Secretary of State to carry out or arrange for the carrying out of an individual evaluation of a vulnerable person's situation to determine whether he has special needs.

Asylum support under section 95 or 98 of the 1999 Act

5.—(1) If an asylum seeker or his family member applies for support under section 95 of the 1999 Act and the Secretary of State thinks that the asylum seeker or his family member is eligible for support under that section he must offer the provision of support to the asylum seeker or his family member.

(2) If the Secretary of State thinks that the asylum seeker or his family member is eligible for support under section 98 of the 1999 Act he must offer the provision of support to the asylum seeker or his family member.

Tracing family members of unaccompanied minors

6.—(1) So as to protect an unaccompanied minor's best interests, the Secretary of State shall endeavour to trace the members of the minor's family as soon as possible after the minor makes his claim for asylum.

(2) In cases where there may be a threat to the life or integrity of the minor or the minor's close family, the Secretary of State shall take care to ensure that the collection, processing and circulation of information concerning the minor or his close family is undertaken on a confidential basis so as not to jeopardise his or their safety.

(3) For the purposes of this regulation—

(a) an unaccompanied minor means a person below the age of eighteen who arrives in the United Kingdom unaccompanied by an adult responsible for him whether by law or custom and makes a claim for asylum;

(b) a person shall be an unaccompanied minor until he is taken into the care of such an adult or until he reaches the age of 18 whichever is the earlier;

(c) an unaccompanied minor also includes a minor who is left unaccompanied after he arrives in or enters the United Kingdom but before he makes his claim for asylum.

The Immigration and Asylum (Provision of Accommodation to Failed Asylum-Seekers) Regulations 2005

(SI 2005, No. 930)

Citation and commencement

1.—(1) These Regulations may be cited as the Immigration and Asylum (Provision of Accommodation to Failed Asylum-Seekers) Regulations 2005 and shall come into force on 31 March 2005.

(2) These Regulations apply to a person who is receiving accommodation when these Regulations come into force to the same extent as they apply to a person provided with accommodation after these Regulations come into force.

Interpretation

2. In these Regulations—

'the 1999 Act' means the Immigration and Asylum Act 1999;

'destitute' is to be construed in accordance with section 95(3) of the 1999 Act; and

'reporting requirement' means a condition or restriction which requires a person to report to the police, an immigration officer or the Secretary of State, and is imposed under—

(a) paragraph 21 of Schedule 2 to the Immigration Act 1971 (temporary admission or release from detention),

(b) paragraph 22 of that Schedule, or

(c) paragraph 2 or 5 of Schedule 3 to that Act (pending deportation).

Eligibility for and provision of accommodation to a failed asylum-seeker

3.—(1) Subject to regulations 4 and 6, the criteria to be used in determining the matters referred to in paragraphs (a) and (b) of section 4(5) of the 1999 Act in respect of a person falling within section 4(2) or (3) of that Act are—

(a) that he appears to the Secretary of State to be destitute, and

(b) that one or more of the conditions set out in paragraph (2) are satisfied in relation to him.

(2) Those conditions are that—

(a) he is taking all reasonable steps to leave the United Kingdom or place himself in a position in which he is able to leave the United Kingdom, which may include complying with attempts to obtain a travel document to facilitate his departure;

(b) he is unable to leave the United Kingdom by reason of a physical impediment to travel or for some other medical reason;

(c) he is unable to leave the United Kingdom because in the opinion of the Secretary of State there is currently no viable route of return available;

(d) he has made an application for judicial review of a decision in relation to his asylum claim—

(i) in England and Wales, and has been granted permission to proceed pursuant to Part 54 of the Civil Procedure Rules 1998,

(ii) in Scotland, pursuant to Chapter 58 of the Rules of the Court of Session 1994 or

(iii) in Northern Ireland, and has been granted leave pursuant to Order 53 of the Rules of Supreme Court (Northern Ireland) 1980; or

(e) the provision of accommodation is necessary for the purpose of avoiding a breach of a person's Convention rights, within the meaning of the Human Rights Act 1998.

Community activities: general

4.—(1) Where the Secretary of State so determines, the continued provision of accommodation to a person falling within section 4(2) or (3) of the 1999 Act is to be conditional upon that person's performance of or participation in such community activity as is described in this regulation and is from time to time notified to the person in accordance with regulation 5.

(2) In making the determination referred to in paragraph (1), regard will be had to the following matters—

(a) the length of time that he believes the person will continue to be eligible for accommodation,

(b) the arrangements that have been made for the performance of or participation in community activities in the area in which the person is being provided with accommodation,

(c) any relevant health and safety standards which are agreed between the Secretary of State and a person with whom he has made arrangements for the provision of community activities in the person's area,

(d) whether the person is in the Secretary of State's belief unable to perform or participate in community activities because of a physical or mental impairment or for some other medical reason,

(e) whether the person is in the Secretary of State's belief unable to perform or participate in community activities because of a responsibility for the care of a dependant child or of a dependant who because of a physical or mental impairment is unable to look after himself, and

(f) any relevant information provided to the Secretary of State, regarding the person's suitability to perform or participate in particular tasks, activities or a range of tasks or activities.

(3) Paragraph (1) does not apply in relation to a person who is under the age of 18.

(4) No condition on the continued provision of accommodation will require a person to perform or participate in community activities for more than 35 hours in any week, including the weekend.

Community activities: Relevant information

5. A notice under regulation 4(1) falls within this regulation if it contains the following information—

(a) the task, activity or range of tasks or activities in the area in which the person lives which are to be performed or participated in as community activities,

(b) the geographical location at which the community activities will be performed or participated in,

(c) the maximum number of hours per week that the person will be expected to perform or participate in community activities, where it is possible for the Secretary of State to so specify, and

(d) the date upon which the task, activity or range of tasks or activities to be performed or participated in as community activities will commence and, where it is possible for the Secretary of State to so specify, the length of time such community activities will last.

Other conditions on continued provision of accommodation

6.—(1) The continued provision of accommodation to a person falling within section 4(2) or (3) of the 1999 Act is to be subject to such other conditions falling within paragraph (2) as—

(a) the Secretary of State may from time to time determine, and

(b) are set out in a notice to that person in writing.

(2) A condition falls within this paragraph to the extent that it relates to—

(a) complying with specified standards of behaviour,

(b) complying with a reporting requirement,

(c) complying with a requirement—

(i) to reside at an authorised address, or

(ii) if he is absent from an authorised address without the permission of the Secretary of State, to ensure that that absence is for no more than seven consecutive days and nights or for no more than a total of fourteen days and nights in any six month period, or

(d) complying with specified steps to facilitate his departure from the United Kingdom.

The Immigration (European Economic Area) Regulations 2006
(SI 2006, No. 1003)

Contents

PART 1

INTERPRETATION ETC.

Citation and commencement

1. These Regulations may be cited as the Immigration (European Economic Area) Regulations 2006 and shall come into force on 30 April 2006.

General interpretation

2.—(1) In these Regulations—

'the 1971 Act' means the Immigration Act 1971;

'the 1999 Act' means the Immigration and Asylum Act 1999;

'the 2002 Act' means the Nationality, Immigration and Asylum Act 2002;

['the Accession Regulations' means the Accession (Immigration and Worker Registration) Regulations 2004;]

['civil partner' does not include—

(a) a party to a civil partnership of convenience; or

(b) the civil partner ("C") of a person ("P") where a spouse, civil partner or durable partner of C or P is already present in the United Kingdom;]

'decision maker' means the Secretary of State, an immigration officer or an entry clearance officer (as the case may be);

['deportation order' means an order made pursuant to regulation 24(3);]

['derivative residence card' means a card issued to a person, in accordance with regulation 18A, as proof of the holder's derivative right to reside in the United Kingdom as at the date of issue;]

'document certifying permanent residence' means a document issued to an EEA national, in accordance with regulation 18, as proof of the holder's permanent right of residence under regulation 15 as at the date of issue;

['durable partner' does not include the durable partner ("D") of a person ("P") where a spouse, civil partner or durable partner of D or P is already present in the United Kingdom and where that marriage, civil partnership or durable partnership is subsisting;]

['EEA decision' means a decision under these Regulations that concerns—

(a) a person's entitlement to be admitted to the United Kingdom;

(b) a person's entitlement to be issued with or have renewed, or not to have revoked, a registration certificate, residence card, derivative residence card, document certifying permanent residence or permanent residence card;

(c) a person's removal from the United Kingdom; or

(d) the cancellation, pursuant to regulation 20A, of a person's right to reside in the United Kingdom;]

{but does not include decisions under regulations 24AA (human rights considerations and interim orders to suspend removal) or 29AA (temporary admission in order to submit case in person);}

'EEA family permit' means a document issued to a person, in accordance with regulation 12, in connection with his admission to the United Kingdom;

'EEA national' means a national of an EEA State [who is not also a British citizen ;]

'EEA State' means—

(a) a member State, other than the United Kingdom;

(b) Norway, Iceland or Liechtenstein; or

(c) Switzerland;

'entry clearance' has the meaning given in section 33(1) of the 1971 Act;

'entry clearance officer' means a person responsible for the grant or refusal of entry clearance;

['exclusion order' means an order made under regulation 19(1B)];

'immigration rules' has the meaning given in section 33(1) of the 1971 Act;

'military service' means service in the armed forces of an EEA State;

'permanent residence card' means a card issued to a person who is not an EEA national, in accordance with regulation 18, as proof of the holder's permanent right of residence under regulation 15 as at the date of issue;

['. . . qualifying EEA State residence card' means—

(a) a document called a 'Residence card of a family member of a Union Citizen' issued under Article 10 of Council Directive 2004/38/EC (as applied, where relevant, by the EEA Agreement) by an EEA State listed in sub-paragraph (b) to a non-EEA family member of an EEA national as proof of the holder's right of residence in that State;

(b) Germany and Estonia;]

'registration certificate' means a certificate issued to an EEA national, in accordance with regulation 16, as proof of the holder's right of residence in the United Kingdom as at the date of issue;

'relevant EEA national' in relation to an extended family member has the meaning given in regulation 8(6);

'residence card' means a card issued to a person who is not an EEA national, in accordance with regulation 17, as proof of the holder's right of residence in the United Kingdom as at the date of issue;

'spouse' does not include—

[(a) a party to a marriage of convenience; or

(b) the spouse ("S") of a person ("P") where a spouse, civil partner or durable partner of S or P is already present in the United Kingdom;]

(2) Paragraph (1) is subject to paragraph 1(a) of Schedule 4 (transitional provisions).

[(3) Section 11 of the 1971 Act (construction of references to entry) shall apply for the purpose of determining whether a person has entered the United Kingdom for the purpose of these Regulations as it applies for the purpose of determining whether a person has entered the United Kingdom for the purpose of that Act.]

Note: Paragraph (3) and definitions of 'deportation order' and 'exclusion order' inserted from 1 June 2009 (SI 1009/1117). Definition of 'Accession Regulations' inserted from 1 May 2011 (SI 2011/544). Definitions of 'derivative residence card' and 'durable partner' inserted and definitions of 'civil partner', 'spouse' and 'EEA decision' amended from 16 July 2012 (SI 2012/1547). Definition of EEA decision (end of subparagraph (d)) further amended from 28 July 2014 (SI 2014/1976) subject to transitional provisions: 'The amendments made by these Regulations have no effect in relation to any decision under the 2006 Regulations to remove a person from the United Kingdom taken before these Regulations came into force' (regulation 4 of SI 2014/1976). Definition of 'EEA national' amended from 16 October 2012 (SI 2012/1547). Definition of United Kingdom national deleted from 8 November 2012 (SI 2012/2560). Definition of 'a qualifying EEA State residence card' inserted from 7 April 2014 (SI 2013/3032).

Continuity of residence

3.—(1) This regulation applies for the purpose of calculating periods of continuous residence in the United Kingdom under regulation 5(1) and regulation 15.

(2) Continuity of residence is not affected by—

(a) periods of absence from the United Kingdom which do not exceed six months in total in any year;

(b) periods of absence from the United Kingdom on military service; or

(c) any one absence from the United Kingdom not exceeding twelve months for an important reason such as pregnancy and childbirth, serious illness, study or vocational training or an overseas posting.

(3) But continuity of residence is broken if a person is removed from the United Kingdom under [these Regulations].

Note: Words in square brackets substituted from 1 June 2009 (SI 1009/1117).

'Worker', 'self-employed person', 'self-sufficient person' and 'student'

4.—(1) In these Regulations—

(a) 'worker' means a worker within the meaning of [Article 45 of the Treaty on the Functioning of the European Union];

(b) 'self-employed person' means a person who establishes himself in order to pursue activity as a self-employed person in accordance with [Aticle 49 of Treaty on the Functioning of the European Union];

(c) 'self-sufficient person' means a person who has—

(i) sufficient resources not to become a burden on the social assistance system of the United Kingdom during his period of residence; and

(ii) comprehensive sickness insurance cover in the United Kingdom;

(d) 'student' means a person who—

[(i) is enrolled, for the principal purpose of following a course of study (including vocational training), at a public or private establishment which is—(aa) financed from public funds; or (bb) otherwise recognised by the Secretary of State as an establishment which has been accredited for the purpose of providing such courses or training within the law or administrative practice of the part of the United Kingdom in which the establishment is located;]

(ii) has comprehensive sickness insurance cover in the United Kingdom; and

(iii) assures the Secretary of State, by means of a declaration, or by such equivalent means as the person may choose, that he has sufficient resources not to become a burden on the social assistance system of the United Kingdom during his period of residence.

(2) For the purposes of paragraph (1)(c), where family members of the person concerned reside in the United Kingdom and their right to reside is dependent upon their being family members of that person—

(a) the requirement for that person to have sufficient resources not to become a burden on the social assistance system of the United Kingdom during his period of residence shall only be satisfied if his resources and those of the family members are sufficient to avoid him and the family members becoming such a burden;

(b) the requirement for that person to have comprehensive sickness insurance cover in the United Kingdom shall only be satisfied if he and his family members have such cover.

(3) For the purposes of paragraph (1)(d), where family members of the person concerned reside in the United Kingdom and their right to reside is dependent upon their being family members of that person, the requirement for that person to assure the Secretary of State that he has sufficient resources not to become a burden on the social assistance system of the United Kingdom during his period of residence shall only be satisfied if he assures the Secretary of State that his resources and those of the family members are sufficient to avoid him and the family members becoming such a burden.

[(4) For the purposes of paragraphs (1)(c) and (d) and paragraphs (2) and (3), the resources of the person concerned and, where applicable, any family members, are to be regarded as sufficient if—

(a) they exceed the maximum level of resources which a {British citizen} and his family members may possess if he is to become eligible for social assistance under the United Kingdom benefit system; or

(b) paragraph (a) does not apply but, taking into account the personal situation of the person concerned and, where applicable, any family members, it appears to the decision maker that the resources of the person or persons concerned should be regarded as sufficient.]

[(5) For the purpose of regulation 15A(2) references in this regulation to "family members" includes a "primary carer" as defined in regulation 15A(7).]

Note: Paragraph (4) substituted from 2 June 2011 (SI 2011/1247). Words in square brackets in paragraph 4(1)(a) and (b) substituted from 1 August 2012 (SI 2012/1809). Paragraph (1)(d) substituted and paragraph 5 inserted from 16 July 2012 (SI 2012/1547). Words 'British citizen' substituted from 8 November 2012 (SI 2012/2560).

'Worker or self-employed person who has ceased activity'

5.—(1) In these Regulations, 'worker or self-employed person who has ceased activity' means an EEA national who satisfies the conditions in paragraph (2), (3), (4) or (5).

(2) A person satisfies the conditions in this paragraph if he—

(a) terminates his activity as a worker or self-employed person and—

(i) has reached the age at which he is entitled to a state pension on the date on which he terminates his activity; or

(ii) in the case of a worker, ceases working to take early retirement;

(b) pursued his activity as a worker or self-employed person in the United Kingdom for at least twelve months prior to the termination; and

(c) resided in the United Kingdom continuously for more than three years prior to the termination.

(3) A person satisfies the conditions in this paragraph if—

(a) he terminates his activity in the United Kingdom as a worker or self-employed person as a result of a permanent incapacity to work; and

(b) either—

(i) he resided in the United Kingdom continuously for more than two years prior to the termination; or

(ii) the incapacity is the result of an accident at work or an occupational disease that entitles him to a pension payable in full or in part by an institution in the United Kingdom.

(4) A person satisfies the conditions in this paragraph if—

(a) he is active as a worker or self-employed person in an EEA State but retains his place of residence in the United Kingdom, to which he returns as a rule at least once a week; and

(b) prior to becoming so active in that EEA State, he had been continuously resident and continuously active as a worker or self-employed person in the United Kingdom for at least three years.

(5) A person who satisfies the condition in paragraph (4)(a) but not the condition in paragraph (4)(b) shall, for the purposes of paragraphs (2) and (3), be treated as being active and resident in the United Kingdom during any period in which he is working or self-employed in the EEA State.

(6) The conditions in paragraphs (2) and (3) as to length of residence and activity as a worker or self-employed person shall not apply in relation to a person whose spouse or civil partner is a [British citizen].

(7) [Subject to {regulations 6(2), 7A(3) or 7B(3)}, for the purposes of this regulation—]

(a) periods of inactivity for reasons not of the person's own making;

(b) periods of inactivity due to illness or accident; and

(c) in the case of a worker, periods of involuntary unemployment duly recorded by the relevant employment office,

shall be treated as periods of activity as a worker or self-employed person, as the case may be.

Note: Words in square brackets in paragraph (7) substituted from 1 May 2011 (SI 2011/544). Words in paragraph (6) substituted from 8 November 2012 (SI 2012/2560). Words in curly brackets in paragraph (7) substituted from 1 January 2014 (SI 2013/3032).

'Qualified person'

6.—(1) In these Regulations, 'qualified person' means a person who is an EEA national and in the United Kingdom as—

(a) a jobseeker;

(b) a worker;

(c) a self-employed person;

(d) a self-sufficient person; or

(e) a student.

(2) [Subject to regulation 7A(4) {and 7B(4)}, a person who is no longer working shall not cease to be treated as a worker for the purpose of paragraph (1)(b) if—]

(a) he is temporarily unable to work as the result of an illness or accident;

(b) {he is in duly recorded involuntary unemployment after having been employed in the United Kingdom for at least one year, provided that he—

(i) has registered as a jobseeker with the relevant employment office; and

(ii) satisfies conditions A and B;}

{(ba) he is in duly recorded involuntary unemployment after having been employed in the United Kingdom for less than one year, provided that he—

(i) has registered as a jobseeker with the relevant employment office; and

(ii) satisfies conditions A and B;}

(c) he is involuntarily unemployed and has embarked on vocational training; or

(d) he has voluntarily ceased working and embarked on vocational training that is related to his previous employment.

[(2A) A person to whom paragraph (2)(ba) applies may only retain worker status for a maximum of 6 months.]

(3) A person who is no longer in self-employment shall not cease to be treated as a self-employed person for the purpose of paragraph (1)(c) if he is temporarily unable to pursue his activity as a self-employed person as the result of an illness or accident.

[(4) For the purpose of paragraph (1)(a), a "jobseeker" is a person who satisfies conditions A and B {and where relevant C}.]

(5) Condition A is that the person—

(a) entered the United Kingdom in order to seek employment; or

(b) is present in the United Kingdom seeking employment, immediately after enjoying a right to reside pursuant to paragraph (1)(b) to (e) (disregarding any period during which worker status was retained pursuant to paragraph (2)(b) or (ba).

(6) Condition B is that the person can provide evidence that he is seeking employment and has a genuine chance of being engaged.

(7) A person may not retain the status of a worker pursuant to paragraph (2)(b), or jobseeker pursuant to paragraph (1)(a), for longer than {the relevant period}unless he can provide compelling evidence that he is continuing to seek employment and has a genuine chance of being engaged.]

[(8) In paragraph (7), "the relevant period" means—

(a) in the case of a person retaining worker status pursuant to paragraph (2)(b), a continuous period of six months;

(b) in the case of a jobseeker, [91] days, minus the cumulative total of any days during which the person concerned previously enjoyed a right to reside as a jobseeker, not including any days prior to a continuous absence from the United Kingdom of at least 12 months.]

[(9) Condition C applies where the person concerned has, previously, enjoyed a right to reside under this regulation as a result of satisfying conditions A and B—

(a) in the case of a person to whom paragraph (2)(b) or (ba) applied, for at least six months; or

(b) in the case of a jobseeker, for at least [91] days in total,

unless the person concerned has, since enjoying the above right to reside, been continuously absent from the United Kingdom for at least 12 months.]

[(10) Condition C is that the person has had a period of absence from the United Kingdom.]

[(11) Where condition C applies—

(a) paragraph (7) does not apply; and

(b) condition B has effect as if "compelling" were inserted before "evidence".]

Note: Words in square brackets in paragraph (2) substituted from 1 May 2011 (SI 2011/544). Words in curly brackets in paragraph (2) substituted, paragraph (2A) inserted and paragraphs (4)–(7) substituted from 1 January 2014 (SI 2013/3032). Words in curly brackets in paragraph (4) and paragraph (7) substituted and paragraphs (8) to (11) inserted from 1 July 2014 (SI 2014/1451) subject to the following transitional provisions: 'Any period after 31st December 2013 during which a person was a jobseeker for the purposes of regulation 6(1)(a) of the 2006 Regulations is, where relevant, to be taken into consideration when determining—(a) the length of the relevant period; and (b) whether condition C applies, for the purposes of regulation 6 of the 2006 Regulations as amended by these Regulations.' (Regulation 4 of SI 2014/1451). Word '91' in paragraphs (8)(b) and (9)(b) substituted from 10 November 2014 subject to transitional provisions (SI 2014/2761).

Family member

7.—(1) Subject to paragraph (2), for the purposes of these Regulations the following persons shall be treated as the family members of another person—

(a) his spouse or his civil partner;

(b) direct descendants of his, his spouse or his civil partner who are—

(i) under 21; or

(ii) dependants of his, his spouse or his civil partner;

(c) dependent direct relatives in his ascending line or that of his spouse or his civil partner;

(d) a person who is to be treated as the family member of that other person under paragraph (3).

(2) A person shall not be treated under paragraph (1)(b) or (c) as the family member of a student residing in the United Kingdom after the period of three months beginning on the date on which the student is admitted to the United Kingdom unless—

(a) in the case of paragraph (b), the person is the dependent child of the student or of his spouse or civil partner; or

(b) the student also falls within one of the other categories of qualified persons mentioned in regulation 6(1).

(3) Subject to paragraph (4), a person who is an extended family member and has been issued with an EEA family permit, a registration certificate or a residence card shall be treated as the family member of the relevant EEA national for as long as he continues to satisfy the conditions in regulation 8(2), (3), (4) or (5) in relation to that EEA national and the permit, certificate or card has not ceased to be valid or been revoked.

(4) Where the relevant EEA national is a student, the extended family member shall only be treated as the family member of that national under paragraph (3) if either the EEA family permit was issued under regulation 12(2), the registration certificate was issued under regulation 16(5) or the residence card was issued under regulation 17(4).

[Application of the Accession Regulations

7A.—(1) This regulation applies to an EEA national who was an accession State worker requiring registration on 30th April 2011 ('an accession worker').

(2) In this regulation—

'accession State worker requiring registration' has the same meaning as in regulation 1(2)(d) of the Accession Regulations;

'legally working' has the same meaning as in regulation 2(7) of the Accession Regulations.

(3) In regulation 5(7)(c), where the worker is an accession worker, periods of involuntary unemployment duly recorded by the relevant employment office shall be treated only as periods of activity as a worker—

(a) during any period in which regulation 5(4) of the Accession Regulations applied to that person; or

(b) when the unemployment began on or after 1st May 2011.

(4) Regulation 6(2) applies to an accession worker where he—

(a) was a person to whom regulation 5(4) of the Accession Regulations applied on 30th April 2011; or

(b) became unable to work, became unemployed or ceased to work, as the case maybe, on or after 1st May 2011.

(5) For the purposes of regulation 15, an accession worker shall be treated as having resided in accordance with these Regulations during any period before 1st May 2011 in which the accession worker—

(a) was legally working in the United Kingdom; or

(b) was a person to whom regulation 5(4) of the Accession Regulations applied.

(6) Subject to paragraph (7), a registration certificate issued to an accession worker under regulation 8 of the Accession Regulations shall, from 1st May 2011, be treated as if it was a registration certificate issued under these Regulations where the accession worker was legally working in the United Kingdom for the employer specified in that certificate on—

(a) 30th April 2011; or

(b) the date on which the certificate is issued where it is issued after 30th April 2011.

(7) Paragraph (6) does not apply—

(a) if the Secretary of State issues a registration certificate in accordance with regulation 16 to an accession worker on or after 1st May 2011; and

(b) from the date of registration stated on that certificate.]

Note: Regulation 7A inserted from 1 May 2011 (SI 2011/544). To the extent necessary for the purpose of reg 7A the Accession (Immigration and Worker Registration) Regulations 2004 (SI 2004/1219 as amended) continue in force, subject to amendment, after repeal from 1 May 2011 (SI 2011/544).

[7B. Application of the EU2 Regulations

(1) This regulation applies to an EEA national who was an accession State national subject to worker authorisation before 1st January 2014.

(2) In this regulation—

"accession State national subject to worker authorisation" has the same meaning as in regulation 2 of the EU2 Regulations;

"the EU2 Regulations" means the Accession (Immigration and Worker Authorisation) Regulations 2006.

(3) Regulation 2(12) of the EU2 Regulations (accession State national subject to worker authorisation: legally working) has effect for the purposes of this regulation as it does for regulation 2(3) and (4) of the EU2 Regulations.

(4) In regulation 5(7)(c), where the worker is an accession State national subject to worker authorisation, periods of involuntary unemployment duly recorded by the relevant employment office must only be treated as periods of activity as a worker when the unemployment began on or after 1st January 2014.

(5) Regulation 6(2) applies to an accession State national subject to worker authorisation where the accession State national subject to worker authorisation became unable to work, became unemployed or ceased to work, as the case may be, on or after 1st January 2014.

(6) For the purposes of regulation 15, an accession State national subject to worker authorisation must be treated as having resided in accordance with these Regulations during any period before 1st January 2014 in which the accession State national subject to worker authorisation was legally working in the United Kingdom.

(7) An accession worker card issued to an accession State national subject to worker authorisation under regulation 11 of the EU2 Regulations before 1st January 2014 must be treated as if it were a registration certificate issued under these Regulations so long as it has not expired.]

Note: Regulation 7B inserted from 1 January 2014 (SI 2013/3032).

'Extended family member'

8.—(1) In these Regulations 'extended family member' means a person who is not a family member of an EEA national under regulation 7(1)(a), (b) or (c) and who satisfies the conditions in paragraph (2), (3), (4) or (5).

(2) A person satisfies the condition in this paragraph if the person is a relative of an EEA national, his spouse or his civil partner and—

(a) the person is residing in [a country other than the United Kingdom] . . . and is dependent upon the EEA national or is a member of his household;

(b) the person satisfied the condition in paragraph (a) and is accompanying the EEA national to the United Kingdom or wishes to join him there; or

(c) the person satisfied the condition in paragraph (a), has joined the EEA national in the United Kingdom and continues to be dependent upon him or to be a member of his household.

(3) A person satisfies the condition in this paragraph if the person is a relative of an EEA national or his spouse or his civil partner and, on serious health grounds, strictly requires the personal care of the EEA national, his spouse or his civil partner.

(4) A person satisfies the condition in this paragraph if the person is a relative of an EEA national and would meet the requirements in the immigration rules (other than those relating to entry clearance) for indefinite leave to enter or remain in the United Kingdom as a dependent relative of the EEA national were the EEA national a person present and settled in the United Kingdom.

(5) A person satisfies the condition in this paragraph if the person is the partner of an EEA national (other than a civil partner) and can prove to the decision maker that he is in a durable relationship with the EEA national.

(6) In these Regulations 'relevant EEA national' means, in relation to an extended family member, the EEA national who is or whose spouse or civil partner is the relative of the

extended family member for the purpose of paragraph (2), (3) or (4) or the EEA national who is the partner of the extended family member for the purpose of paragraph (5).

Note: Words substituted in paragraph (2)(a) from 2 June 2011 (SI 2011/1247). Words omitted from paragraph (2)(a) from 8 November 2012 (SI 2012/2560).

[Family members of British citizens

9.—(1) If the conditions in paragraph (2) are satisfied, these Regulations apply to a person who is the family member of a British citizen as if the British citizen ("P") were an EEA national.

(2) The conditions are that—

(a) P is residing in an EEA State as a worker or self-employed person or was so residing before returning to the United Kingdom;

(b) if the family member of P is P's spouse or civil partner, the parties are living together in the EEA State or had entered into the marriage or civil partnership and were living together in the EEA State before the British citizen returned to the United Kingdom; and

(c) the centre of P's life has transferred to the EEA State where P resided as a worker or self-employed person.

(3) Factors relevant to whether the centre of P's life has transferred to another EEA State include—

(a) the period of residence in the EEA State as a worker or self-employed person;

(b) the location of P's principal residence;

(c) the degree of integration of P in the EEA State.

(4) Where these Regulations apply to the family member of P, P is to be treated as holding a valid passport issued by an EEA State for the purpose of the application of regulation 13 to that family member.]

Note: Regulation 9 substituted from 1 January 2014, subject to transitional provisions (SI 2013/3032).

'Family member who has retained the right of residence'

10.—(1) In these Regulations, 'family member who has retained the right of residence' means, subject to paragraph (8), a person who satisfies the conditions in paragraph (2), (3), (4) or (5).

(2) A person satisfies the conditions in this paragraph if—

[(a) he was a family member of a qualified person or of an EEA national with a permanent right residence when that person died;]

(b) he resided in the United Kingdom in accordance with these Regulations for at least the year immediately before the death of the qualified person [or the EEA national with a permanent right of residence]; and

(c) he satisfies the condition in paragraph (6).

(3) A person satisfies the conditions in this paragraph if—

(a) he is the direct descendant of—

(i) a qualified person [or an EEA national with a permanent right of residence] who has died;

(ii) a person who ceased to be a qualified person on ceasing to reside in the United Kingdom; or

(iii) the person who was the spouse or civil partner of the qualified person [or the EEA national with a permanent right of residence] mentioned in sub-paragraph (i) when he died or is the spouse or civil partner of the person mentioned in sub-paragraph (ii); and

(b) he was attending an educational course in the United Kingdom immediately before the qualified person [or the EEA national with a permanent right of residence] died or ceased to be a qualified person and continues to attend such a course.

(4) A person satisfies the conditions in this paragraph if the person is the parent with actual custody of a child who satisfies the condition in paragraph (3).

(5) A person satisfies the conditions in this paragraph if—

[(a) he ceased to be a family member of a qualified person or of an EEA national with a permanent right of residence on the termination of the marriage or civil partnership of that person;]

(b) he was residing in the United Kingdom in accordance with these Regulations at the date of the termination;

(c) he satisfies the condition in paragraph (6); and

(d) either—

(i) prior to the initiation of the proceedings for the termination of the marriage or the civil partnership the marriage or civil partnership had lasted for at least three years and the parties to the marriage or civil partnership had resided in the United Kingdom for at least one year during its duration;

(ii) the former spouse or civil partner of the qualified person [or the EEA national with a permanent right of residence] has custody of a child of the qualified person;

[(iii) the former spouse or civil partner of the qualified person or the EEA national with a permanent right of residence has the right of access to a child of the qualified person or the EEA national with a permanent right of residence, where the child is under the age of 18 and where a court has ordered that such access must take place in the United Kingdom; or]

(iv) the continued right of residence in the United Kingdom of the person is warranted by particularly difficult circumstances, such as he or another family member having been a victim of domestic violence while the marriage or civil partnership was subsisting.

(6) The condition in this paragraph is that the person—

(a) is not an EEA national but would, if he were an EEA national, be a worker, a self-employed person or a self-sufficient person under regulation 6; or

(b) is the family member of a person who falls within paragraph (a).

(7) In this regulation, 'educational course' means a course within the scope of Article 12 of Council Regulation (EEC) No. 1612/68 on freedom of movement for workers.

(8) A person with a permanent right of residence under regulation 15 shall not become a family member who has retained the right of residence on the death or departure from the United Kingdom of the qualified person [or the EEA national with a permanent right of residence] or the termination of the marriage or civil partnership, as the case may be, and a family member who has retained the right of residence shall cease to have that status on acquiring a permanent right of residence under regulation 15.

Note: Paragraphs 2(a), 5(a) and 5(d)(iii) substituted and words inserted in paragraphs 2(b), 3(a)(iii), 3(b), 5(d(ii), 8 and 3(a)(i) from 16 July 2012 (SI 2012/1547).

Part 2
EEA Rights

Right of admission to the United Kingdom

11.—(1) An EEA national must be admitted to the United Kingdom if he produces on arrival a valid national identity card or passport issued by an EEA State.

[(2) A person who is not an EEA national must be admitted to the United Kingdom if he is—

(a) a family member of an EEA national and produces on arrival a valid passport and a qualifying EEA State residence card, provided the conditions in regulation 19(2)(a) (non-EEA family member to be accompanying or joining EEA national in the United Kingdom) and (b) (EEA national must have a right to reside in the United Kingdom under these Regulations) are met; or

(b) a family member of an EEA national, a family member who has retained the right of residence, a person who meets the criteria in paragraph (5) or a person with a permanent right of residence under regulation 15 and produces on arrival—

(i) a valid passport; and

(ii) an EEA family permit, a residence card, a derivative residence card or a permanent residence card.]

[(3) An immigration officer must not place a stamp in the passport of a person admitted to the United Kingdom under this regulation who is not an EEA national if the person produces a residence card, a derivative residence card, a permanent residence card or a qualifying EEA State residence card.]

(4) Before an immigration officer refuses admission to the United Kingdom to a person under this regulation because the person does not produce on arrival a document mentioned in paragraph (1) or (2), the immigration officer must give the person every reasonable opportunity to obtain the document or have it brought to him within a reasonable period of time or to prove by other means that he is—

(a) an EEA national;

(b) a family member of an EEA national with a right to accompany that national or join him in the United Kingdom;

[(ba) a person who meets the criteria in paragraph (5); or]

(c) a family member who has retained the right of residence or a person with a permanent right of residence under regulation 15.

[(5) A person ("P") meets the criteria in this paragraph where—

(a) P previously resided in the United Kingdom pursuant to regulation 15A(3) and would be entitled to reside in the United Kingdom pursuant to that regulation were P in the country;

(b) P is accompanying an EEA national to, or joining an EEA national in, the United Kingdom and P would be entitled to reside in the United Kingdom pursuant to regulation 15A(2) were P and the EEA national both in the United Kingdom;

(c) P is accompanying a person ("the relevant person") to, or joining the relevant person in, the United Kingdom and—

(i) the relevant person is residing, or has resided, in the United Kingdom pursuant to regulation 15A(3); and

(ii) P would be entitled to reside in the United Kingdom pursuant to regulation 15A(4) were P and the relevant person both in the United Kingdom.

(d) P is accompanying a person who meets the criteria in (b) or (c) ("the relevant person") to the United Kingdom and—

(i) P and the relevant person are both—

(aa) seeking admission to the United Kingdom in reliance on this paragraph for the first time; or

(bb) returning to the United Kingdom having previously resided there pursuant to the same provisions of regulation 15A in reliance on which they now base their claim to admission; and

(ii) P would be entitled to reside in the United Kingdom pursuant to regulation 15A(5) were P and the relevant person there or]

[(e) P is accompanying a British citizen to, or joining a British citizen in, the United Kingdom and P would be entitled to reside in the United Kingdom pursuant to regulation 15A(4A) were P and the British citizen both in the United Kingdom.]

[(6) Paragraph (7) applies where—

(a) a person ("P") seeks admission to the United Kingdom in reliance on paragraph (5)(b) or (c); and

(b) if P were in the United Kingdom, P would have a derived right of residence by virtue of regulation 15A(7)(b)(ii).]

[(7) Where this paragraph applies a person ("P") will only be regarded as meeting the criteria in paragraph (5)(b) or (c) where P—

(a) is accompanying the person with whom P would on admission to the United Kingdom jointly share care responsibility for the purpose of regulation 15A(7)(b)(ii); or

(b) has previously resided in the United Kingdom pursuant to regulation 15A(2) or (4) as a joint primary carer and seeks admission to the United Kingdom in order to reside there again on the same basis.]

(8) But this regulation is subject to regulations 19(1){, (1A)} [(1AB)] and (2).

Note: Words inserted at the end of paragraph (5)(d)(ii) and paragraph (5)(e) inserted from 8 November 2012 (SI 2012/2560). Paragraphs (2) and (3) substituted from 7 April 2014 (SI 2013/3032). Words in square brackets in paragraph (8) substituted from 1 January 2014 (SI 2013/3032). Words in curly brackets in paragraph (8) inserted from 28 July 2014 (SI 2014/1976) subject to transitional provisions: 'The amendments made by these Regulations have no effect in relation to any decision under the 2006 Regulations to remove a person from the United Kingdom taken before these Regulations came into force' (regulation 4 of SI 2014/1976).

Issue of EEA family permit

12.—(1) An entry clearance officer must issue an EEA family permit to a person who applies for one if the person is a family member of an EEA national and—

(a) the EEA national—

(i) is residing in the UK in accordance with these Regulations; or

(ii) will be travelling to the United Kingdom within six months of the date of the application and will be an EEA national residing in the United Kingdom in accordance with these Regulations on arrival in the United Kingdom; and

[(b) the family member will be accompanying the EEA national to the United Kingdom or joining the EEA national there.]

[(**1A**) An entry clearance officer must issue an EEA family permit to a person who applies and provides proof that, at the time at which he first intends to use the EEA family permit, he—

(a) would be entitled to be admitted to the United Kingdom by virtue of regulation 11(5); and

(b) will (save in the case of a person who would be entitled to be admitted to the United Kingdom by virtue of regulation 11(5)(a)) be accompanying to, or joining in, the United Kingdom any person from whom his right to be admitted to the United Kingdom under regulation 11(5) will be derived.]

[(**1B**) An entry clearance officer must issue an EEA family permit to a family member who has retained the right of residence.]

(2) An entry clearance officer may issue an EEA family permit to an extended family member of an EEA national who applies for one if—

(a) the relevant EEA national satisfies the condition in paragraph (1)(a);

(b) the extended family member wishes to accompany the relevant EEA national to the United Kingdom or to join him there; and

(c) in all the circumstances, it appears to the entry clearance officer appropriate to issue the EEA family permit.

(3) Where an entry clearance officer receives an application under paragraph (2) he shall undertake an extensive examination of the personal circumstances of the applicant and if he refuses the application shall give reasons justifying the refusal unless this is contrary to the interests of national security.

(4) An EEA family permit issued under this regulation shall be issued free of charge and as soon as possible.

(5) But an EEA family permit shall not be issued under this regulation if the applicant or the EEA national concerned {is not entitled to be admitted to the United Kingdom as a result of regulation 19(1A) or [(1AB) or] falls to be excluded in accordance with regulation 19(1B).}

[(**6**) An EEA family permit will not be issued under this regulation to a person ("A") who is the spouse, civil partner or durable partner of a person ("B") where a spouse, civil partner or durable partner of A or B holds a valid EEA family permit.]

Note: Paragraph (1)(b) substituted from 2 June 2011 (SI 2011/1247). Paragraphs (1A) and (1B) inserted, words in curly brackets in paragraph (5) substituted and paragraph (6) inserted from 16 July 2012 (SI 2012/1547). Words in square brackets inserted in paragraph (5) from 1 January 2014 (SI 2013/3032).

Initial right of residence

13.—(1) An EEA national is entitled to reside in the United Kingdom for a period not exceeding three months beginning on the date on which he is admitted to the United Kingdom provided that he holds a valid national identity card or passport issued by an EEA State.

(2) A family member of an EEA national [or a family member who has retained the right of residence who is] residing in the United Kingdom under paragraph (1) who is not himself an EEA national is entitled to reside in the United Kingdom provided that he holds a valid passport.

[(3) An EEA national or his family member who becomes an unreasonable burden on the social assistance system of the United Kingdom will cease to have a right to reside under this regulation.]

[(4) A person who otherwise satisfies the criteria in this regulation will not be entitled to reside in the United Kingdom under this regulation where the Secretary of State has made a decision under—

{(a) regulation 19(3)(b), 20(1) or 20A(1); or

(b) regulation 21B(2), where that decision was taken in the preceding twelve months.}]

Note: Words inserted in paragraph (2), paragraph (3) substituted and paragraph (4) inserted from 16 July 2012 (SI 2012/1547). Words in paragraph (4) substituted from 1 January 2014 (SI 2013/3032).

Extended right of residence

14.—(1) A qualified person is entitled to reside in the United Kingdom for so long as he remains a qualified person.

(2) A family member of a qualified person residing in the United Kingdom under paragraph (1) or of an EEA national with a permanent right of residence under regulation 15 is entitled to reside in the United Kingdom for so long as he remains the family member of the qualified person or EEA national.

(3) A family member who has retained the right of residence is entitled to reside in the United Kingdom for so long as he remains a family member who has retained the right of residence.

(4) A right to reside under this regulation is in addition to any right a person may have to reside in the United Kingdom under regulation 13 or 15.

[(5) A person who otherwise satisfies the criteria in this regulation will not be entitled to a right to reside in the United Kingdom under this regulation where the Secretary of State has made a decision under—

{(a) regulation 19(3)(b), 20(1) or 20A(1); or

(b) regulation 21B(2) (not including such a decision taken on the basis of regulation 21B(1)(a) or (b)), where that decision was taken in the preceding twelve months.}]

Note: Paragraph (5) substituted from 16 July 2012 (SI 2012/1547) and amended from 1 January 2014 (SI 2013/3032).

Permanent right of residence

15.—(1) The following persons shall acquire the right to reside in the United Kingdom permanently—

(a) an EEA national who has resided in the United Kingdom in accordance with these Regulations for a continuous period of five years;

(b) a family member of an EEA national who is not himself an EEA national but who has resided in the United Kingdom with the EEA national in accordance with these Regulations for a continuous period of five years;

(c) a worker or self-employed person who has ceased activity;

(d) the family member of a worker or self-employed person who has ceased activity;

(e) a person who was the family member of a worker or self-employed person where—

(i) the worker or self-employed person has died;

(ii) the family member resided with him immediately before his death; and

(iii) the worker or self-employed person had resided continuously in the United Kingdom for at least the two years immediately before his death or the death was the result of an accident at work or an occupational disease;

(f) a person who—

(i) has resided in the United Kingdom in accordance with these Regulations for a continuous period of five years; and

(ii) was, at the end of that period, a family member who has retained the right of residence.

[(**1A**) Residence in the United Kingdom as a result of a derivative right of residence does not constitute residence for the purpose of this regulation;]

(2) [The] right of permanent residence under this regulation shall be lost only through absence from the United Kingdom for a period exceeding two consecutive years.

[(3) A person who satisfies the criteria in this regulation will not be entitled to a permanent right to reside in the United Kingdom where the Secretary of State has made a decision under—

{(a) regulation 19(3)(b), 20(1) or 20A(1); or

(b) regulation 21B(2) (not including such a decision taken on the basis of regulation 21B(1)(a) or (b)), where that decision was taken in the preceding twelve months.}]

Note: Paragraph (1A) inserted, words substituted in paragraph (2) and paragraph (3) substituted from 16 July 2012 (SI 2012/1547). Words in paragraph (3) substituted from 1 January 2014 (SI 2013/3032).

[15A. Derivative right of residence

(1) A person ("P") who is not [an exempt person] and who satisfies the criteria in paragraph (2), (3), [(4A)] or (5) of this regulation is entitled to a derivative right to reside in the United Kingdom for as long as P satisfies the relevant criteria.

(2) P satisfies the criteria in this paragraph if—

(a) P is the primary carer of an EEA national ("the relevant EEA national"); and

(b) the relevant EEA national—

(i) is under the age of 18;

(ii) is residing in the United Kingdom as a self-sufficient person; and

(iii) would be unable to remain in the United Kingdom if P were required to leave.

(3) P satisfies the criteria in this paragraph if—

(a) P is the child of an EEA national ("the EEA national parent");

(b) P resided in the United Kingdom at a time when the EEA national parent was residing in the United Kingdom as a worker; and

(c) P is in education in the United Kingdom and was in education there at a time when the EEA national parent was in the United Kingdom.

(4) P satisfies the criteria in this paragraph if—

(a) P is the primary carer of a person meeting the criteria in paragraph (3) ("the relevant person"); and

(b) the relevant person would be unable to continue to be educated in the United Kingdom if P were required to leave.

[(**4A**) P satisfies the criteria in this paragraph if—

(a) P is the primary carer of a British citizen ("the relevant British citizen");

(b) the relevant British citizen is residing in the United Kingdom; and

(c) the relevant British citizen would be unable to reside in the UK or in another EEA State if P were required to leave.]

(**5**) P satisfies the criteria in this paragraph if—

(a) P is under the age of 18;

(b) P's primary carer is entitled to a derivative right to reside in the United Kingdom by virtue of paragraph (2) or (4);

(c) P does not have leave to enter, or remain in, the United Kingdom; and

(d) requiring P to leave the United Kingdom would prevent P's primary carer from residing in the United Kingdom.

(**6**) For the purpose of this regulation—

(a) "education" excludes nursery education; and

(b) "worker" does not include a jobseeker or a person who falls to be regarded as a worker by virtue of regulation 6(2); and

(c) an "exempt person" is a person—

(i) who has a right to reside in the United Kingdom as a result of any other provision of these Regulations;

(ii) who has a right of abode in the United Kingdom by virtue of section 2 of the 1971 Act;

(iii) to whom section 8 of the 1971 Act, or any order made under subsection (2) of that provision, applies; or

(iv) who has indefinite leave to enter or remain in the United Kingdom.]

(**7**) P is to be regarded as a "primary carer" of another person if

(a) P is a direct relative or a legal guardian of that person; and

(b) P—

(i) is the person who has primary responsibility for that person's care; or

[(ii) shares equally the responsibility for that person's care with one other person who is not an exempt person.]

[(**7A**) Where P is to be regarded as a primary carer of another person by virtue of paragraph (7)(b)(ii) the criteria in paragraphs (2)(b)(iii), (4)(b) and (4A)(c) shall be considered on the basis that both P and the person with whom care responsibility is shared would be required to leave the United Kingdom.

(**7B**) Paragraph (7A) does not apply if the person with whom care responsibility is shared acquired a derivative right to reside in the United Kingdom as a result of this regulation prior to P assuming equal care responsibility.]

(**8**) P will not be regarded as having responsibility for a person's care for the purpose of paragraph (7) on the sole basis of a financial contribution towards that person's care.

(**9**) A person who otherwise satisfies the criteria in paragraph (2), (3), (4) [(4A)] or (5) will not be entitled to a derivative right to reside in the United Kingdom where the Secretary of State has made a decision under—

{(a) regulation 19(3)(b), 20(1) or 20A(1); or

(b) regulation 21B(2), where that decision was taken in the preceding twelve months.}

Note: Regulation 15A inserted from 16 July 2012 (SI 2012/1547). Words in paragraphs (1), (6), (7) and (9) inserted/substituted and paragraphs (4A), (7A) and (7B) inserted from 8 November 2012 (SI 2012/2560). Words in curly brackets substituted in paragraph (9) from 1 January 2014 (SI 2013/3032).

[15B. Continuation of a right of residence

(1) This regulation applies during any period in which, but for the effect of regulation 13(4), 14(5), 15(3) or 15A(9), a person ("P") who is in the United Kingdom would be entitled to reside here pursuant to these Regulations.

(2) Where this regulation applies, any right of residence will (notwithstanding the effect of regulation 13(4), 14(5), 15(3) or 15A(9) be deemed to continue during any period in which—

(a) an appeal under regulation 26 could be brought, while P is in the United Kingdom, against a relevant decision (ignoring any possibility of an appeal out of time with permission); or

(b) an appeal under regulation 26 against a relevant decision, brought while P is in the United Kingdom, is pending . . .

(3) Periods during which residence pursuant to regulation 14 is deemed to continue as a result of paragraph (2) will not constitute residence for the purpose of regulation 15 unless and until—

(a) a relevant decision is withdrawn by the Secretary of State; or

(b) an appeal against a relevant decision is allowed and that appeal is finally determined . . .

(4) Periods during which residence is deemed to continue as a result of paragraph (2) will not constitute residence for the purpose of regulation 21(4)(a) unless and until—

(a) a relevant decision is withdrawn by the Secretary of State; or

(b) an appeal against a relevant decision is allowed and that appeal is finally determined . . .

(5) A "relevant decision" for the purpose of this regulation means a decision pursuant to regulation [19(3)(b) or (c)], 20(1) or 20A(1) which would, but for the effect of paragraph (2), prevent P from residing in the United Kingdom pursuant to these Regulations.]

[(6) This regulation does not affect the ability of the Secretary of State to give directions for P's removal while an appeal is pending or before it is finally determined.]

[(7) In this regulation, "pending" and "finally determined" have the meanings given in section 104 of the 2002 Act.]

Note: Regulation 15B inserted from 16 July 2012 (SI 2012/1547). Words in paragraph (5) substituted from 1 January 2014 (SI 2013/3032). Words omitted from subparagraphs (2)(b), (3)(b) and (4)(b) and paragraphs (6) and (7) inserted from 28 July 2014 (SI 2014/1976) subject to transitional provisions: 'The amendments made by these Regulations have no effect in relation to any decision under the 2006 Regulations to remove a person from the United Kingdom taken before these Regulations came into force' (regulation 4 of SI 2014/1976).

PART 3
RESIDENCE DOCUMENTATION

Issue of registration certificate

16.—(1) The Secretary of State must issue a registration certificate to a qualified person immediately on application and production of—

(a) a valid identity card or passport issued by an EEA State;

(b) proof that he is a qualified person.

(2) In the case of a worker, confirmation of the worker's engagement from his employer or a certificate of employment is sufficient proof for the purposes of paragraph (1)(b).

(3) The Secretary of State must issue a registration certificate to an EEA national who is the family member of a qualified person or of an EEA national with a permanent right of residence under regulation 15 immediately on application and production of—

(a) a valid identity card or passport issued by an EEA State; and

(b) proof that the applicant is such a family member.

(4) The Secretary of State must issue a registration certificate to an EEA national who is a family member who has retained the right of residence on application and production of—

(a) a valid identity card or passport; and

(b) proof that the applicant is a family member who has retained the right of residence.

(5) The Secretary of State may issue a registration certificate to an extended family member not falling within regulation 7(3) who is an EEA national on application if—

(a) the relevant EEA national in relation to the extended family member is a qualified person or an EEA national with a permanent right of residence under regulation 15; and

(b) in all the circumstances it appears to the Secretary of State appropriate to issue the registration certificate.

(6) Where the Secretary of State receives an application under paragraph (5) he shall undertake an extensive examination of the personal circumstances of the applicant and if he refuses the application shall give reasons justifying the refusal unless this is contrary to the interests of national security.

(7) A registration certificate issued under this regulation shall state the name and address of the person registering and the date of registration . . .

(8) [But this regulation is subject to regulations 7A(6) and 20(1).]

Note: Paragraph (8) substituted from 1 May 2011 (SI 2011/544). Words omitted from paragraph (7) from 1 July 2013 (SI 2013/1391).

Issue of residence card

17.—(1) The Secretary of State must issue a residence card to a person who is not an EEA national and is the family member of a qualified person or of an EEA national with a permanent right of residence under regulation 15 on application and production of—

(a) a valid passport; and

(b) proof that the applicant is such a family member.

(2) The Secretary of State must issue a residence card to a person who is not an EEA national but who is a family member who has retained the right of residence on application and production of—

(a) a valid passport; and

(b) proof that the applicant is a family member who has retained the right of residence.

(3) On receipt of an application under paragraph (1) or (2) and the documents that are required to accompany the application the Secretary of State shall immediately issue the applicant with a certificate of application for the residence card and the residence card shall be issued no later than six months after the date on which the application and documents are received.

(4) The Secretary of State may issue a residence card to an extended family member not falling within regulation 7(3) who is not an EEA national on application if—

(a) the relevant EEA national in relation to the extended family member is a qualified person or an EEA national with a permanent right of residence under regulation 15; and

(b) in all the circumstances it appears to the Secretary of State appropriate to issue the residence card.

(5) Where the Secretary of State receives an application under paragraph (4) he shall undertake an extensive examination of the personal circumstances of the applicant and if he refuses the application shall give reasons justifying the refusal unless this is contrary to the interests of national security.

(6) A residence card issued under this regulation may take the form of a stamp in the applicant's passport and shall be . . . valid for—

(a) five years from the date of issue; or

(b) in the case of a residence card issued to the family member or extended family member of a qualified person, the envisaged period of residence in the United Kingdom of the qualified person,

whichever is the shorter.

[(6A) A residence card issued under this regulation shall be entitled 'Residence card of a family member of an EEA national' or 'Residence card of a family member who has retained the right of residence', as the case may be.]

(7) . . .

(8) But this regulation is subject to regulation 20(1) and (1A)].

Note: Words omitted from paragraph (6), paragraph (6A) inserted and words in square brackets in paragraph (8) substituted from 1 June 2009 (SI 2009/1117). Paragraph (7) omitted from 1 July 2013 (SI 2013/1391).

Issue of a document certifying permanent residence and a permanent residence card

18.—(1) The Secretary of State must issue an EEA national with a permanent right of residence under regulation 15 with a document certifying permanent residence as soon as possible after an application for such a document and proof that the EEA national has such a right is submitted to the Secretary of State.

(2) The Secretary of State must issue a person who is not an EEA national who has a permanent right of residence under regulation 15 with a permanent residence card no later than six months after the date on which an application for a permanent residence card and proof that the person has such a right is submitted to the Secretary of State.

(3) Subject to paragraph (5) . . . , a permanent residence card shall be valid for ten years from the date of issue and must be renewed on application.

(4) . . .

(5) A document certifying permanent residence and a permanent residence card shall cease to be valid if the holder ceases to have a right of permanent residence under regulation 15.

[(**6**) But this regulation is subject to regulation 20.]

Note: Words omitted from paragraph (3) and paragraph (6) inserted from 1 June 2009 (SI 2009/1117). Paragraph (4) omitted from 1 July 2013 (SI 2013/1391).

[18A. Issue of a derivative residence card

(1) The Secretary of State must issue a person with a derivative residence card on application and on production of—

(a) a valid identity card issued by an EEA State or a valid passport; and

(b) proof that the applicant has a derivative right of residence under regulation 15A.

(2) On receipt of an application under paragraph (1) the Secretary of State must issue the applicant with a certificate of application as soon as possible.

(3) A derivative residence card issued under paragraph (1) may take the form of a stamp in the applicant's passport and will be valid until—

(a) a date five years from the date of issue; or

(b) any other date specified by the Secretary of State when issuing the derivative residence card.

(4) A derivative residence card issued under paragraph (1) must be issued . . . as soon as practicable.

(5) But this regulation is subject to regulations 20(1) and 20(1A).]

Note: Regulation 18A inserted from 16 July 2012 (SI 2012/1547). Words omitted from paragraph (4) from 1 July 2013 (SI 2013/1391).

Part 4

Refusal of Admission and Removal etc.

Exclusion and removal from the United Kingdom

19.—(1) A person is not entitled to be admitted to the United Kingdom by virtue of regulation 11 if his exclusion is justified on grounds of public policy, public security or public health in accordance with regulation 21.

[(**1A**) A person is not entitled to be admitted to the United Kingdom by virtue of regulation 11 if that person is subject to a deportation or exclusion order [, except where the person is temporarily admitted pursuant to regulation 29AA]].

[(**1AB**) A person is not entitled to be admitted to the United Kingdom by virtue of regulation 11 if the Secretary of State considers there to be reasonable grounds to suspect that his admission would lead to the abuse of a right to reside in accordance with regulation 21B(1).]

[(**1B**) If the Secretary of State considers that the exclusion of an EEA national or the family member of an EEA national is justified on the grounds of public policy, public security or public health in accordance with regulation 21 the Secretary of State may make an order for the purpose of these Regulations prohibiting that person from entering the United Kingdom.]

(2) A person is not entitled to be admitted to the United Kingdom as the family member of an EEA national under regulation 11(2) unless, at the time of his arrival—

(a) he is accompanying the EEA national or joining him in the United Kingdom; and

(b) the EEA national has a right to reside in the United Kingdom under these Regulations.

[(3) Subject to paragraphs (4) and (5), an EEA national who has entered the United Kingdom or the family member of such a national who has entered the United Kingdom may be removed if –

{(a) that person does not have or ceases to have a right to reside under these Regulations;

(b) the Secretary of State has decided that the person's removal is justified on grounds of public policy, public security or public health in accordance with regulation 21;

or

(c) the Secretary of State has decided that the person's removal is justified on grounds of abuse of rights in accordance with regulation 21B(2).}]

(4) A person must not be removed under paragraph (3) as the automatic consequence of having recourse to the social assistance system of the United Kingdom.

(5) A person must not be removed under paragraph (3) if he has a right to remain in the United Kingdom by virtue of leave granted under the 1971 Act unless his removal is justified on the grounds of public policy, public security or public health in accordance with regulation 21.

Note: Paragraph (1A) and (1B) inserted and paragraph (3) substituted from 1 June 2009 (SI 2009/1117). Paragraph (1AB) inserted and paragraph (3) amended from 1 January 2014 (SI 2013/3032). Words inserted in paragraph (1A) from 28 July 2014 (SI 2014/1976) subject to transitional provisions: 'The amendments made by these Regulations have no effect in relation to any decision under the 2006 Regulations to remove a person from the United Kingdom taken before these Regulations came into force' (regulation 4 of SI 2014/1976).

Refusal to issue or renew and revocation of residence documentation

20.—(1) The Secretary of State may refuse to issue, revoke or refuse to renew a registration certificate, a residence card, a document certifying permanent residence or a permanent residence card if the refusal or revocation is justified on grounds of public policy, public security or public health [or on grounds of abuse of rights in accordance with regulation 21B(2)].

[(**1A**) {A decision under regulation 19(3) to remove a person from the United Kingdom will (save during any period in which a right of residence is deemed to continue as a result of regulation 15B(2)) invalidate} a registration certificate, residence card, document certifying permanent residence or permanent residence card held by that person or an application made by that person for such a certificate, card or document.]

(2) The Secretary of State may revoke a registration certificate or a residence card or refuse to renew a residence card if the holder of the certificate or card has ceased to have [, or never had,] a right to reside under these Regulations.

(3) The Secretary of State may revoke a document certifying permanent residence or a permanent residence card or refuse to renew a permanent residence card if the holder of the certificate or card has ceased to have [, or never had], a right of permanent residence under regulation 15.

(4) An immigration officer may, at the time of a person's arrival in the United Kingdom—

(a) revoke that person's residence card if he is not at that time the family member of a qualified person or of an EEA national who has a right of permanent residence under regulation 15, a family member who has retained the right of residence or a person with a right of permanent residence under regulation 15;

(b) revoke that person's permanent residence card if he is not at that time a person with a right of permanent residence under regulation 15.

(5) [An entry clearance officer or immigration officer may at any time revoke a person's] EEA family permit if—

(a) the revocation is justified on grounds of public policy, public security or public health; or

(b) the person is not at that time the family member of an EEA national with the right to reside in the United Kingdom under these Regulations or is not accompanying that national or joining him in the United Kingdom.

(6) Any action taken under this regulation on grounds of public policy, public security or public health shall be in accordance with regulation 21.

Note: Paragraph (1A) inserted and words in square brackets in paragraph (5) substituted from 1 June 2009 (SI 2009/1117). Words in curly brackets in paragraph (1A) substituted from 16 July 2012 (SI 2012/1547). Words inserted in paragraphs (1), (2) and (3) from 1 January 2014 (SI 2013/3032).

[20A. Cancellation of a right of residence

(1) Where the conditions in paragraph (2) are met the Secretary of State may cancel a person's right to reside in the United Kingdom pursuant to these Regulations.

(2) The conditions in this paragraph are met where—

(a) a person has a right to reside in the United Kingdom as a result of these Regulations;

(b) the Secretary of State has decided that the cancellation of that person's right to reside in the United Kingdom is justified on grounds of public policy, public security or public health in accordance with regulation 21 [or on grounds of abuse of rights in accordance with regulation 21B(2)];

(c) the circumstances are such that the Secretary of State cannot make a decision under regulation 20(1); and

(d) it is not possible for the Secretary of State to remove the person from the United Kingdom pursuant to regulation 19(3)(b) [or (c)].]

Note: Regulation 20A inserted from 16 July 2012 (SI 2012/1547). Words inserted in paragraph (2)(b) and (d) from 1 January 2014 (SI 2013/3032).

[Verification of a right of residence

20B.—(1) This regulation applies when the Secretary of State—

(a) has reasonable doubt as to whether a person ("A") has a right to reside under regulation 14(1) or (2); or

(b) wants to verify the eligibility of a person ("A") to apply for documentation issued under Part 3.

(2) The Secretary of State may invite A to—

(a) provide evidence to support the existence of a right to reside, or to support an application for documentation under Part 3; or

(b) attend an interview with the Secretary of State.

(3) If A purports to be entitled to a right to reside on the basis of a relationship with another person ("B"), the Secretary of State may invite B to—

(a) provide information about their relationship with A; or

(b) attend an interview with the Secretary of State.

(4) If, without good reason, A or B fail to provide the additional information requested or, on at least two occasions, fail to attend an interview if so invited, the Secretary of State may draw any factual inferences about A's entitlement to a right to reside as appear appropriate in the circumstances.

(5) The Secretary of State may decide following an inference under paragraph (4) that A does not have or ceases to have a right to reside.

(6) But the Secretary of State must not decide that A does not have or ceases to have a right to reside on the sole basis that A failed to comply with this regulation.

(7) This regulation may not be invoked systematically.

(8) In this regulation, "a right to reside" means a right to reside under these Regulations.]

Note: Regulation 20B inserted from 1 January 2014 (SI 2013/3032).

Decisions taken on public policy, public security and public health grounds

21.—(1) In this regulation a 'relevant decision' means an EEA decision taken on the grounds of public policy, public security or public health.

(2) A relevant decision may not be taken to serve economic ends.

(3) A relevant decision may not be taken in respect of a person with a permanent right of residence under regulation 15 except on serious grounds of public policy or public security.

(4) A relevant decision may not be taken except on imperative grounds of public security in respect of an EEA national who—

(a) has resided in the United Kingdom for a continuous period of at least ten years prior to the relevant decision; or

(b) is under the age of 18, unless the relevant decision is necessary in his best interests, as provided for in the Convention on the Rights of the Child adopted by the General Assembly of the United Nations on 20th November 1989.

(5) Where a relevant decision is taken on grounds of public policy or public security it shall, in addition to complying with the preceding paragraphs of this regulation, be taken in accordance with the following principles—

(a) the decision must comply with the principle of proportionality;

(b) the decision must be based exclusively on the personal conduct of the person concerned;

(c) the personal conduct of the person concerned must represent a genuine, present and sufficiently serious threat affecting one of the fundamental interests of society;

(d) matters isolated from the particulars of the case or which relate to considerations of general prevention do not justify the decision;

(e) a person's previous criminal convictions do not in themselves justify the decision.

(6) Before taking a relevant decision on the grounds of public policy or public security in relation to a person who is resident in the United Kingdom the decision maker must take account of considerations such as the age, state of health, family and economic situation of the person, the person's length of residence in the United Kingdom, the person's social and cultural integration into the United Kingdom and the extent of the person's links with his country of origin.

(7) In the case of a relevant decision taken on grounds of public health—

(a) a disease that does not have epidemic potential as defined by the relevant instruments of the World Health Organisation or is not a disease [listed in Schedule 1 to the Health Protection (Notification) Regulations 2010] shall not constitute grounds for the decision; and

(b) if the person concerned is in the United Kingdom, diseases occurring after the three month period beginning on the date on which he arrived in the United Kingdom shall not constitute grounds for the decision.

Note: Words substituted (England, Scotland and Northern Ireland only) in paragraph (7)(a) from 6 April 2010 (SI 2010/708) and (Wales) from 26 July 2010 (SI 2010/1593).

[21A. Application of Part 4 to persons with a derivative right of residence

(1) Where this regulation applies Part 4 of these Regulations applies subject to the modifications listed in paragraph (3).

(2) This regulation applies where a person—

(a) would, notwithstanding Part 4 of these Regulations, have a right to be admitted to, or reside in, the United Kingdom by virtue of a derivative right of residence arising under regulation 15A(2), (4)[, (4A)] or (5);

(b) holds a derivative residence card; or

(c) has applied for a derivative residence card.

(3) Where this regulation applies Part 4 applies in relation to the matters listed in paragraph (2) as if—

(a) references to a matter being "justified on grounds of public policy, public security or public health in accordance with regulation 21" referred instead to a matter being "conducive to the public good";

(b) the reference in regulation 20(5)(a) to a matter being "justified on grounds of public policy, public security or public health" referred instead to a matter being "conducive to the public good";

(c) references to "the family member of an EEA national" referred instead to "a person with a derivative right of residence";

(d) references to "a registration certificate, a residence card, a document certifying permanent residence or a permanent residence card" referred instead to "a derivative residence card";

(e) the reference in regulation 19(1A) to a deportation or exclusion order referred also to a deportation or exclusion order made under any provision of the immigration Acts.

(f) regulation 20(4) instead conferred on an immigration officer the power to revoke a derivative residence card where the holder is not at that time a person with a derivative right of residence; and

(g) regulations 20(3), 20(6) and 21 were omitted.]

Note: Regulation 21A inserted from 16 July 2012 (SI 2012/1547). Words inserted in paragraph (2)(a) from 8 November 2012 (SI 2012/2560).

[Abuse of rights or fraud

21B.—(1) The abuse of a right to reside includes—

(a) engaging in conduct which appears to be intended to circumvent the requirement to be a qualified person;

(b) attempting to enter the United Kingdom within 12 months of being removed pursuant to regulation 19(3)(a), where the person attempting to do so is unable to provide evidence that, upon re-entry to the United Kingdom, the conditions for any right to reside, other than the initial right of residence under regulation 13, will be met;

(c) entering, attempting to enter or assisting another person to enter or attempt to enter, a marriage or civil partnership of convenience; or

(d) fraudulently obtaining or attempting to obtain, or assisting another to obtain or attempt to obtain, a right to reside.

(2) The Secretary of State may take an EEA decision on the grounds of abuse of rights where there are reasonable grounds to suspect the abuse of a right to reside and it is proportionate to do so.

(3) Where these Regulations provide that an EEA decision taken on the grounds of abuse in the preceding twelve months affects a person's right to reside, the person who is the subject of that decision may apply to the Secretary of State to have the effect of that decision set aside on grounds that there has been a material change in the circumstances which justified that decision.

(4) An application under paragraph (3) may only be made whilst the applicant is outside the United Kingdom.

(5) This regulation may not be invoked systematically.

(6) In this regulation, "a right to reside" means a right to reside under these Regulations.]

Note: Regulation 21B inserted from 1 January 2014 (SI 2013/3032).

PART 5
PROCEDURE IN RELATION TO EEA DECISIONS

Person claiming right of admission

22.—(1) This regulation applies to a person who claims a right of admission to the United Kingdom under regulation 11 as—

[(a) a person, not being an EEA national, who—

(i) is a family member of an EEA national;

(ii) is a family member who has retained the right of residence;

(iii) has a derivative right of residence;

(iv) has a permanent right of residence under regulation 15; or

(v) is in possession of a qualifying EEA State residence card; . . .]

[(b) an EEA national, where there is reason to believe that he may fall to be excluded under regulation 19(1) {(1A) or (1B)}][; or

(c) a person to whom regulation 29AA applies.]

(2) A person to whom this regulation applies is to be treated as if he were a person seeking leave to enter the United Kingdom under the 1971 Act for the purposes of paragraphs 2, 3, 4, 7, 16 to 18 and 21 to 24 of Schedule 2 to the 1971 Act (administrative provisions as to control on entry etc.), except that—

(a) the reference in paragraph 2(1) to the purpose for which the immigration officer may examine any persons who have arrived in the United Kingdom is to be read as a reference to the purpose of determining whether he is a person who is to be granted admission under these Regulations;

(b) the references in paragraphs 4(2A), 7 and 16(1) to a person who is, or may be, given leave to enter are to be read as references to a person who is, or may be, granted admission under these Regulations; and

(c) a medical examination is not to be carried out under paragraph 2 or paragraph 7 as a matter of routine and may only be carried out within three months of a person's arrival in the United Kingdom.

(3) For so long as a person to whom this regulation applies is detained, or temporarily admitted or released while liable to detention, under the powers conferred by Schedule 2 to the 1971 Act, he is deemed not to have been admitted to the United Kingdom.

Note: Paragraph (1)(b) substituted from 1 June 2009 (SI 2009/1117). Paragraph (1)(a) substituted from 7 April 2014 (SI 2013/3032). Words in paragraph (1)(b) substituted from 1 January 2014 (SI 2013/3032). Word omitted at the end of paragraph (1)(a) and paragraph (1)(c) inserted from 28 July 2014 (SI 2014/1976) subject to transitional provisions: 'The amendments made by these Regulations have no effect in relation to any decision under the 2006 Regulations to remove a person from the United Kingdom taken before these Regulations came into force' (regulation 4 of SI 2014/1976).

Person refused admission

23.—(1) This regulation applies to a person who is in the United Kingdom and has been refused admission to the United Kingdom—

(a) because he does not meet the requirement of regulation 11 (including where he does not meet those requirements because his EEA family permit, residence card

[, derivative residence card] or permanent residence card has been revoked by an immigration officer in accordance with regulation 20); or

(b) in accordance with regulation [19(1), (1A){, (1AB),} or (2)].

(2) A person to whom this regulation applies, is to be treated as if he were a person refused leave to enter under the 1971 Act for the purpose of paragraphs 8, 10, 10A, 11, 16 to 19 and 21 to 24 of Schedule 2 to the 1971 Act, except that the reference in paragraph 19 to a certificate of entitlement, entry clearance or work permit is to be read as a reference to an EEA family permit, residence card[, derivative residence card][, a qualifying EEA State residence card, or a permanent residence card].

Note: Words in square brackets in paragraph (1)(b) substituted from 1 June 2009 (SI 2009/1117). Words inserted in paragraph 1(a) and paragraph (2) from 16 July 2012 (SI 2012/1547). Words inserted in paragraph (1)(b) from 1 January 2014 and words substituted in paragraph (2) from 7 April 2014 (SI 2013/3032).

Person subject to removal

24.—[(1) If there are reasonable grounds for suspecting that a person is someone who may be removed from the United Kingdom under {regulation 19(3)(b)}, that person may be detained under the authority of {the Secretary of State} pending a decision whether or not to remove the person under that regulation, and paragraphs 17 and 18 of Schedule 2 to the 1971 Act shall apply in relation to the detention of such a person as those paragraphs apply in relation to a person who may be detained under paragraph 16 of that Schedule.]

(2) [Where a decision is taken to remove a person] under regulation 19(3)(a), {or (c)}, the person is to be treated as if he were a person to whom section 10(1)(a) of the 1999 Act applied, and section 10 of that Act (removal of certain persons unlawfully in the United Kingdom) is to apply accordingly.

(3) [Where a decision is taken to remove a person] under regulation 19(3)(b), the person is to be treated as if he were a person to whom section 3(5)(a) of the 1971 Act (liability to deportation) applied, and section 5 of that Act (procedure for deportation) and Schedule 3 to that Act (supplementary provision as to deportation) are to apply accordingly.

(4) A person who enters the United Kingdom in breach of a deportation or exclusion order shall be removable as an illegal entrant under Schedule 2 to the 1971 Act and the provisions of that Schedule shall apply accordingly].

(5) Where such a deportation order is made against a person but he is not removed under the order during the two year period beginning on the date on which the order is made, the Secretary of State shall only take action to remove the person under the order after the end of that period if, having assessed whether there has been any material change in circumstances since the deportation order was made, he considers that the removal continues to be justified on the grounds of public policy, public security or public health.

(6) A person to whom this regulation applies shall be allowed one month to leave the United Kingdom, beginning on the date on which he is notified of the decision to remove him, before being removed pursuant to that decision except—

(a) in duly substantiated cases of urgency;

(b) where the person is detained pursuant to the sentence or order of any court;

(c) where a person is a person to whom regulation 24(4) applies.

[(7—Paragraph (6) of this regulation does not apply where a decision has been taken under regulation 19(3) on the basis that the relevant person—

(a) has ceased to have a derivative right of residence; or

(b) is a person who would have had a derivative right of residence but for the effect of a decision to remove under regulation 19(3)(b).]

Note: Words in square brackets substituted from 1 June 2009 (SI 2009/1117). Paragraph (1) amended and paragraph (7) inserted from 16 July 2012 (SI 2012/1547). Words in curly brackets in paragraph (2) inserted from 1 January 2014 (SI 2013/3032).

Human rights considerations and interim orders to suspend removal

[24AA.—(1) This regulation applies where the Secretary of State intends to give directions for the removal of a person ("P") to whom regulation 24(3) applies, in circumstances where—

(a) P has not appealed against the EEA decision to which regulation 24(3) applies, but would be entitled, and remains within time, to do so from within the United Kingdom (ignoring any possibility of an appeal out of time with permission); or

(b) P has so appealed but the appeal has not been finally determined.

(2) The Secretary of State may only give directions for P's removal if the Secretary of State certifies that, despite the appeals process not having been begun or not having been finally determined, removal of P to the country or territory to which P is proposed to be removed, pending the outcome of P's appeal, would not be unlawful under section 6 of the Human Rights Act 1998(a) (public authority not to act contrary to Human Rights Convention).

(3) The grounds upon which the Secretary of State may certify a removal under paragraph (2) include (in particular) that P would not, before the appeal is finally determined, face a real risk of serious irreversible harm if removed to the country or territory to which P is proposed to be removed.

(4) If P applies to the appropriate court or tribunal (whether by means of judicial review or otherwise) for an interim order to suspend enforcement of the removal decision, P may not be removed from the United Kingdom until such time as the decision on the interim order has been taken, except—

(a) where the expulsion decision is based on a previous judicial decision;

(b) where P has had previous access to judicial review; or

(c) where the removal decision is based on imperative grounds of public security.

(5) In this regulation, "finally determined" has the same meaning as in Part 6.]

Note: Paragraph 24AA inserted from 28 July 2014 (SI 2014/1976) subject to transitional provisions: 'The amendments made by these Regulations have no effect in relation to any decision under the 2006 Regulations to remove a person from the United Kingdom taken before these Regulations came into force' (regulation 4 of SI 2014/1976).

[24A.—(1) A deportation or exclusion order shall remain in force unless it is revoked by the Secretary of State under this regulation.

(2) A person who is subject to a deportation or exclusion order may apply to the Secretary of State to have it revoked if the person considers that there has been a material change in the circumstances that justified the making of the order.

(3) An application under paragraph (2) shall set out the material change in circumstances relied upon by the applicant and may only be made whilst the applicant is outside the United Kingdom.

(4) On receipt of an application under paragraph (2), the Secretary of State shall revoke the order if the Secretary of State considers that the criteria for making such an order are no longer satisfied].

(5) The Secretary of State shall take a decision on an application under paragraph (2) no later than six months after the date on which the application is received.]

Note: Regulation (24A) inserted from 1 June 2009 (SI 2009/1117). Words substituted in paragraph (4) from 16 July 2012 (SI 2012/1547).

Part 6

Appeals Under These Regulations

Interpretation of Part 6

25.—(1) In this Part—

. . .

['Asylum claim' has the meaning given in section 113(1) of the 2002 Act;]

'Commission' has the same meaning as in the Special Immigration Appeals Commission Act 1997;

. . .

['Human rights claim' has the meaning given in section 113(1) of the 2002 Act.]

(2) For the purposes of this Part, and subject to paragraphs (3) and (4), an appeal is to be treated as pending during the period when notice of appeal is given and ending when the appeal is finally determined, withdrawn or abandoned.

(3) An appeal is not to be treated as finally determined while a further appeal may be brought; and, if such a further appeal is brought, the original appeal is not to be treated as finally determined until the further appeal is determined, withdrawn or abandoned.

(4) A pending appeal is not to be treated as abandoned solely because the appellant leaves the United Kingdom.

Note: Words omitted from 15 February 2010 (SI 2010/21) and from 16 July 2012 (SI 2012/1547). Definitions of 'asylum claim' and 'human rights claim' inserted from 16 July 2012 (SI 2012/1547).

Appeal rights

26.—(1) Subject to the following paragraphs of this regulation, a person may appeal under these Regulations against an EEA decision.

(2) If a person claims to be an EEA national, he may not appeal under these Regulations unless he produces a valid national identity card or passport issued by an EEA State.

[(2A) If a person claims to be in a durable relationship with an EEA national he may not appeal under these Regulations unless he produces—

(a) a passport; and

(b) either—

(i) an EEA family permit; or

(ii) sufficient evidence to satisfy the Secretary of State that he is in a relationship with that EEA national.]

[(3) If a person [to whom paragraph (2) does not apply] claims to be a family member who has retained the right of residence or the family member or relative of an EEA national he may not appeal under these Regulations unless he produces—

(a) . . . a passport; and

(b) either—

(i) an EEA family permit;

[(ia) a qualifying EEA State residence card;]

(ii) proof that he is the family member or relative of an EEA national; or

(iii) in the case of a person claiming to be a family member who has retained the right of residence, proof that he was a family member of the relevant person.]

[3A) If a person claims to be a person with a derivative right of [entry or] residence he may not appeal under these Regulations unless he produces a passport, and either—

(a) an EEA family permit; or

(b) proof that—

(i) where the person claims to have [a derivative right of entry or residence as a result of] regulation 15A(2), he is a direct relative or guardian of an EEA national who is under the age of 18;

(ii) where the person claims to have [a derivative right of entry or residence as a result of] regulation 15A(3), he is the child of an EEA national;

(iii) where the person claims to have [a derivative right of entry or residence as a result of] residence under regulation 15A(4), he is a direct relative or guardian of the child of an EEA national;

(iv) where the person claims to have [a derivative right of entry or residence as a result of] regulation 15A(5), he is under the age of 18 and is a dependant of a person satisfying the criteria in (i) or (iii).]

[(v) where the person claims to have a derivative right of entry or residence as a result of regulation 15A(4A), he is a direct relative or guardian of a British citizen.]

(4) A person may not bring an appeal under these Regulations on a ground certified under paragraph (5) or rely on such a ground in an appeal brought under these Regulations.

(5) The Secretary of State or an immigration officer may certify a ground for the purposes of paragraph (4) if it has been considered in a previous appeal brought under these Regulations or under section 82(1) of the 2002 Act.

(6) Except where an appeal lies to the Commission, an appeal under these Regulations lies to the [First-tier Tribunal].

(7) The provisions of or made under the 2002 Act referred to in Schedule 1 shall have effect for the purposes of an appeal under these Regulations to the [First-tier Tribunal] in accordance with that Schedule.

Note: Words in square brackets in paragraphs (6) and (7) substituted from 15 February 2010 (SI 2010/21). Paragraph (3) substituted and paragraph (3A) inserted from 16 July 2012 (SI 2012/1547). Paragraph (2A) inserted and words in paragraphs (3) and (3A) inserted/substituted from 8 November 2012 (SI 2012/2560). Paragraph (3)(b)(ia) inserted from 7 April 2014 (SI 2013/3032).

Out of country appeals

27.—(1) Subject to paragraphs (2) and (3), a person may not appeal under regulation 26 whilst he is in the United Kingdom against an EEA decision—

(a) to refuse to admit him to the United Kingdom;

[(aa) to make an exclusion order against him;]

(b) to refuse to revoke a deportation [or exclusion] order made against him;

(c) to refuse to issue him with an EEA family permit;

{(ca) to revoke, or to refuse to issue or renew any document under these Regulations where that decision is taken at a time when the relevant person is outside the United Kingdom; or}

[(d) to remove him from the United Kingdom after he has entered the United Kingdom in breach of a deportation or exclusion order].

(2) [Paragraphs (1)(a) and (aa) do not apply where the person is in the United Kingdom and]

(a) the person held [a valid EEA family permit, registration certificate, residence card, {derivative residence card,} document certifying permanent residence{, permanent residence card or qualifying EEA State residence card}, on his arrival in the United Kingdom or can otherwise prove that he is resident in the United Kingdom;

(b) the person is deemed not to have been admitted to the United Kingdom under regulation 22(3) but at the date on which notice of the decision to refuse to admit him is given he has been in the United Kingdom for at least 3 months; [or]

{(c) has made an asylum or human rights claim (or both), unless the Secretary of State has certified that the claim or claims is or are clearly unfounded.}

{(3) Paragraph (1)(d) does not apply where the person has made an asylum or human rights claim (or both), unless the Secretary of State has certified that the claim or claims is or are clearly unfounded.

Note: Paragraph (1)(aa) and words in square brackets in paragraphs (1)(b) and (2)(c) inserted and other words in square brackets substituted from 1 June 2009 (SI 2009/1117). Paragraph (1)(ca) inserted, words in paragraph (2) inserted and paragraphs (2)(c) and (3) substituted from 16 July 2012 (SI 2012/1547). The words 'permanent residence card or qualifying EEA State residence card' in paragraph (2)(a) inserted from 7 April 2014 (SI 2013/3032).}

Appeals to the Commission

28.—(1) An appeal against an EEA decision lies to the Commission where paragraph (2) or (4) applies.

(2) This paragraph applies if the Secretary of State certifies that the EEA decision was taken—

(a) by the Secretary of State wholly or partly on a ground listed in paragraph (3); or

(b) in accordance with a direction of the Secretary of State which identifies the person to whom the decision relates and which is given wholly or partly on a ground listed in paragraph (3).

(3) The grounds mentioned in paragraph (2) are that the person's exclusion or removal from the United Kingdom is—

(a) in the interests of national security; or

(b) in the interests of the relationship between the United Kingdom and another country.

(4) This paragraph applies if the Secretary of State certifies that the EEA decision was taken wholly or partly in reliance on information which in his opinion should not be made public—

(a) in the interests of national security;

(b) in the interests of the relationship between the United Kingdom and another country; or

(c) otherwise in the public interest.

(5) In paragraphs (2) and (4) a reference to the Secretary of State is to the Secretary of State acting in person.

(6) Where a certificate is issued under paragraph (2); or (4); in respect of a pending appeal to the [First-tier Tribunal or Upper Tribunal] the appeal shall lapse.

(7) An appeal against an EEA decision lies to the Commission where an appeal lapses by virtue of paragraph (6).

(8) The Special Immigration Appeals Commission Act 1997 shall apply to an appeal to the Commission under these Regulations as it applies to an appeal under section 2 of that Act to which subsection (2) of that section applies (appeals against an immigration decision) but paragraph (i) of that subsection shall not apply in relation to such an appeal.

Note: Words in square brackets substituted from 15 February 2010 (SI 2010/21).

[National security: EEA Decisions

28A.—(1) Section 97A(a) of the 2002 Act applies to an appeal against an EEA decision where the Secretary of State has certified under regulation 28(2) or (4) that the EEA decision was taken in the interests of national security.

(2) Where section 97A so applies, it has effect as if—

(a) the references in that section to a deportation order were to an EEA decision;

(b) subsections (1), (1A), (2)(b) and (4) were omitted;

(c) the reference in subsection (2)(a) to section 79 were a reference to regulations 27(2) and (3) and 29 of these Regulations; and

(d) in subsection (2A), for sub-paragraphs (a) and (b), "against an EEA decision" were substituted.]

Note: Regulation 28A inserted from 1 January 2013 (SI 2013/3032).

Effect of appeals to the [First-tier Tribunal or Upper Tribunal]

29.—(1) This Regulation applies to appeals under these Regulations made to the [First-tier Tribunal or Upper Tribunal].

(2) If a person in the United Kingdom appeals against an EEA decision to refuse to admit him to the United Kingdom [(other than a decision under regulation 19(1), (1A) or (1B))], any directions for his removal from the United Kingdom previously given by virtue of the refusal cease to have effect, except in so far as they have already been carried out, and no directions may be so given while the appeal is pending.

(3) If a person in the United Kingdom appeals against an EEA decision to remove him from the United Kingdom [(other than a decision under regulation 19(3)(b))], any

directions given under section 10 of the 1999 Act or Schedule 3 to the 1971 Act for his removal from the United Kingdom are to have no effect, except in so far as they have already been carried out, while the appeal is pending.

(4) But the provisions of Part I of Schedule 2, or as the case may be, Schedule 3 to the 1971 Act with respect to detention and persons liable to detention apply to a person appealing against a refusal to admit him or a decision to remove him as if there were in force directions for his removal from the United Kingdom, except that he may not be detained on board a ship or aircraft so as to compel him to leave the United Kingdom while the appeal is pending.

[(4A) In paragraph (4), the words "except that he" to the end do not apply to an EEA decision to which regulation 24AA applies.]

(5) In calculating the period of two months limited by paragraph 8(2) of Schedule 2 to the 1971 Act for—

(a) the giving of directions under that paragraph for the removal of a person from the United Kingdom; and

(b) the giving of a notice of intention to give such directions,

any period during which there is pending an appeal by him is to be disregarded [(except in cases where the EEA decision was taken pursuant to regulation 19(1), (1A), (1B) or (3)(b))].

(6) If a person in the United Kingdom appeals against an EEA decision to remove him from the United Kingdom, a deportation order is not to be made against him under section 5 of the 1971 Act while the appeal is pending.

(7) Paragraph 29 of Schedule 2 to the 1971 Act (grant of bail pending appeal) applies to a person who has an appeal pending under these Regulations as it applies to a person who has an appeal pending under section 82(1) of the 2002 Act.

Note: Words in square brackets in paragraph (1) substituted from 15 February 2010 (SI 2010/21). Words in square brackets in paragraphs (2), (3) and (5) inserted and paragraph (4A) inserted from 28 July 2014 (SI 2014/1976) subject to transitional provisions: 'The amendments made by these Regulations have no effect in relation to any decision under the 2006 Regulations to remove a person from the United Kingdom taken before these Regulations came into force' (regulation 4 of SI 2014/1976).

Temporary admission in order to submit case in person

[**29AA.**—(1) This regulation applies where—

(a) a person ("P") was removed from the United Kingdom pursuant to regulation 19(3)(b);

(b) P has appealed against the decision referred to in sub-paragraph (a);

(c) a date for P's appeal has been set by the First Tier Tribunal or Upper Tribunal; and

(d) P wants to make submissions before the First Tier Tribunal or Upper Tribunal in person.

(2) P may apply to the Secretary of State for permission to be temporarily admitted (within the meaning of paragraphs 21 to 24 of Schedule 2 to the 1971 Act(a), as applied by this regulation) to the United Kingdom in order to make submissions in person.

(3) The Secretary of State must grant P permission, except when P's appearance may cause serious troubles to public policy or public security.

(4) When determining when P is entitled to be given permission, and the duration of P's temporary admission should permission be granted, the Secretary of State must have regard to the dates upon which P will be required to make submissions in person.

(5) Where—

(a) P is temporarily admitted to the United Kingdom pursuant to this regulation;

(b) a hearing of P's appeal has taken place; and

(c) the appeal is not finally determined,

P may be removed from the United Kingdom pending the remaining stages of the redress procedure (but P may apply to return to the United Kingdom to make submissions in person during the remaining stages of the redress procedure in accordance with this regulation).

(6) Where the Secretary of State grants P permission to be temporarily admitted to the United Kingdom under this regulation, upon such admission P is to be treated as if P were a person refused leave to enter under the 1971 Act for the purposes of paragraphs 8, 10, 10A, 11, 16 to 18 and 21 to 24 of Schedule 2(b) to the 1971 Act.

(7) Where Schedule 2 to the 1971 Act so applies, it has effect as if—

(a) the reference in paragraph 8(1) to leave to enter were a reference to admission to the United Kingdom under these Regulations; and

(b) the reference in paragraph 16(1) to detention pending a decision regarding leave to enter or remain in the United Kingdom were to detention pending submission of P's case in person in accordance with this regulation.

(8) P will be deemed not to have been admitted to the United Kingdom during any time during which P is temporarily admitted pursuant to this regulation.]

Note: Paragraph 29AA inserted from 28 July 2014 (SI 2014/1976) subject to transitional provisions: 'The amendments made by these Regulations have no effect in relation to any decision under the 2006 Regulations to remove a person from the United Kingdom taken before these Regulations came into force' (regulation 4 of SI 2014/1976).

[Alternative evidence of identity and nationality

29A.—(1) Subject to paragraph (2), where a provision of these Regulations requires a person to hold or produce a valid identity card issued by an EEA State or a valid passport the Secretary of State may accept alternative evidence of identity and nationality where the person is unable to obtain or produce the required document due to circumstances beyond his or her control.

(2) This regulation does not apply to regulation 11.]

Note: Regulation 29A inserted from 8 November 2012 (SI 2012/2560).

Part 7
General

Effect on other legislation

30. Schedule 2 (effect on other legislation) shall have effect.

Revocations, transitional provisions and consequential amendments

31.—(1) The Regulations listed in column 1 of the table in Part 1 of Schedule 3 are revoked to the extent set out in column 3 of that table, subject to Part 2 of that Schedule and to Schedule 4.

(2) Schedule 4 (transitional provisions) and Schedule 5 (consequential amendments) shall have effect.

Regulation 26(7) SCHEDULE 1

APPEALS TO THE [FIRST-TIER TRIBUNAL OR UPPER TRIBUNAL]

[1.] The following provisions of, or made under, the 2002 Act have effect in relation to an appeal under these Regulations to the [First-tier Tribunal or Upper Tribunal] Asylum and Immigration Tribunal as if it were an appeal against an immigration decision under section 82(1) of that Act:

section 84(1), except paragraphs (a) and (f);
sections 85 to 87;
. . . ;
section 105 and any regulations made under that section; and
section 106 and any rules made under that section.

[2. Tribunal Procedure Rules have effect in relation to appeals under these Regulations.]

Note: Words in square brackets substituted, other words omitted and paragraph 2 inserted from 15 February 2010 (SI 2010/21).

Regulation 30 SCHEDULE 2

EFFECT ON OTHER LEGISLATION

Leave under the 1971 Act

1.—(1) In accordance with section 7 of the Immigration Act 1988, a person who is admitted to or acquires a right to reside in the United Kingdom under these Regulations shall not require leave to remain in the United Kingdom under the 1971 Act during any period in which he has a right to reside under these Regulations but such a person shall require leave to remain under the 1971 Act during any period in which he does not have such a right.

(2) [Subject to sub-paragraph (3),] Where a person has leave to enter or remain under the 1971 Act which is subject to conditions and that person also has a right to reside under these Regulations, those conditions shall not have effect for as long as the person has that right to reside.

[(3) Where the person mentioned in sub-paragraph (2) is an accession State national subject to worker authorisation working in the United Kingdom during the accession period and the document endorsed to show that the person has leave is an accession worker authorisation document, any conditions to which that leave is subject restricting his employment shall continue to apply.

(4) In sub-paragraph (3)—

(a) 'accession period' has the meaning {given in—

(i) regulation 1(2)(c) of the Accession (Immigration and Worker Authorisation) Regulations 2006, in relation to a person who is an accession State national subject to worker authorisation within the meaning of regulation 2 of those Regulations; and

(ii) regulation 1(2) of the Accession of Croatia (Immigration and Worker Authorisation) Regulations 2013, in relation to a person who is an accession State national subject to worker authorisation within the meaning of regulation 2 of those Regulations;}

(b) 'accession State national subject to worker authorisation' has the meaning {given in—

(i) regulation 2 of the Accession (Immigration and Worker Authorisation) Regulations 2006; and

(ii) regulation 2 of the Accession of Croatia (Immigration and Worker Authorisation) Regulations 2013; and}

(c) 'accession worker authorisation document' has the meaning {given in—

(i) regulation 9(2) of the Accession (Immigration and Worker Authorisation) Regulations 2006, in relation to a person who is an accession State national subject to worker authorisation within the meaning of regulation 2 of those Regulations; and

(ii) regulation 1(2) of the Accession of Croatia (Immigration and Worker Authorisation) Regulations 2013, in relation to a person who is an accession State national subject to worker authorisation within the meaning of regulation 2 of those Regulations.}

Persons not subject to restriction on the period for which they may remain.

2.—(1) For the purposes of the 1971 Act and the British Nationality Act 1981, a person who has a permanent right of residence under regulation 15 shall be regarded as a person who is in the United Kingdom without being subject under the immigration laws to any restriction on the period for which he may remain.

(2) But a qualified person, the family member of a qualified person [, a person with a derivative right of residence] and a family member who has retained the right of residence shall not, by virtue of that status, be so regarded for those purposes.

Carriers' liability under the 1999 Act

3. For the purposes of satisfying a requirement to produce a visa under section 40(1)(b) of the 1999 Act (charges in respect of passenger without proper documents), 'a visa of the required kind' includes an EEA family permit, a residence card [, a derivative residence card] {, permanent residence card or qualifying EEA State residence card} or a permanent residence card required for admission under regulation 11(2).

Appeals under the 2002 Act and previous immigration Acts

4.—(1) The following EEA decisions shall not be treated as immigration decisions for the purpose of section 82(2) of the 2002 Act (right of appeal against an immigration decision)—

(a) a decision that a person is to be removed under regulation 19(3)(a) {or 19(3)(c)} by way of a direction under section 10(1)(a) of the 1999 Act (as provided for by regulation 24(2));

(b) a decision to remove a person under regulation 19(3)(b) by making a deportation order under section 5(1) of the 1971 Act (as provided for by regulation 24(3));

(c) a decision to remove a person mentioned in regulation 24(4) by way of directions under paragraphs 8 to 10 of Schedule 2 to the 1971 Act.

(2) A person who has been issued with a registration certificate, residence card, [derivative residence card,] a document certifying permanent residence or a permanent residence card under these Regulations {(including a registration certificate under these Regulations as applied by regulation 7 of the Accession of Croatia (Immigration and Worker Authorisation) Regulations 2013)} or a registration certificate under the Accession (Immigration and Worker Registration) Regulations 2004, [or an accession worker card under the Accession (Immigration and Worker Authorisation) Regulations 2006,] {or a worker authorisation registration certificate under the Accession of Croatia (Immigration and Worker Authorisation) Regulations 2013,} or a person whose passport has been stamped with a family member residence stamp, shall have no right of appeal under section 2 of the Special Immigration Appeals Commission Act 1997 or section 82(1) of the 2002 Act. Any existing appeal under those sections of those Acts or under the Asylum and Immigration Appeals Act 1993, the Asylum and Immigration Act 1996 or the 1999 Act shall be treated as abandoned.

(3) Subject to paragraph (4), a person may appeal to the [First-tier Tribunal] under section 83(2) of the 2002 Act against the rejection of his asylum claim where—

(a) that claim has been rejected, but

(b) he has a right to reside in the United Kingdom under these Regulations.

(4) Paragraph (3) shall not apply if the person is an EEA national and the Secretary of State certifies that the asylum claim is clearly unfounded.

(5) The Secretary of State shall certify the claim under paragraph (4) unless satisfied that it is not clearly unfounded.

(6) In addition to the national of a State which is a contracting party to the Agreement referred to in section 84(2) of the 2002 Act, a Swiss national shall also be treated as an EEA national for the purposes of section 84(1)(d) of that Act.

(7) An appeal under these Regulations against an EEA decision (including an appeal made on or after 1 April 2003 which is treated as an appeal under these Regulations under Schedule 4 but not an appeal made before that date) shall be treated as an appeal under section 82(1) of the 2002 Act against an immigration decision for the purposes of section 96(1)(a) of the 2002 Act.

(8) Section 120 of the 2002 Act shall apply to a person if an EEA decision has been taken or may be taken in respect of him and, accordingly, the Secretary of State or an immigration officer may by notice require a statement from that person under subsection (2) of that section and that notice shall have effect for the purpose of section 96(2) of the 2002 Act.

(9) In sub-paragraph [(2)], 'family member residence stamp' means a stamp in the passport of a family member of an EEA national confirming that he is the family member of an accession State worker requiring registration [or an accession State national subject to worker authorisation working in the United Kingdom] with a right of residence under these Regulations as the family member of that worker; and in this sub-paragraph 'accession State worker requiring registration' has the same meaning as in regulation 2 of the Accession (Immigration and Worker Registration) Regulations 2004 [and 'accession State national subject to worker authorisation' has the meaning given in regulation 2 of the Accession (Immigration and Worker Authorisation) Regulations 2006].

Note: Words in paragraph 4(3) substituted from 15 February 2010 (SI 2010/21). Words inserted in paragraphs 2(2), 3 and 4(2) inserted and paragraph 2(9) amended from 16 July 2012 (SI 2012/1547). Other words in square brackets in Schedule 2 inserted from 1 January 2007 (SI 2006/3317). Words in curly brackets in paragraphs 3 and 4(1)(a) inserted from 7 April 2014 (SI 2013/3032). Words in paragraph 1(4)(a), (b) and (c) substituted from 1 July 2013 (SI 2013/1460). Words in curly brackets in paragraph 4(2) inserted from 1 July 2014 (SI 2013/1460).

Regulation 31(2)

Schedule 3

Revocations and Savings

Part 1

Table of Revocations

. . .

Part 2

Savings

1. The—

(a) Immigration (Swiss Free Movement of Persons) (No. 3) Regulations 2002 are not revoked insofar as they apply the 2000 Regulations to posted workers; and

(b) the 2000 Regulations and the Regulations amending the 2000 Regulations are not revoked insofar as they are so applied to posted workers;

and, accordingly, the 2000 Regulations, as amended, shall continue to apply to posted workers in accordance with the Immigration (Swiss Free Movement of Persons) (No. 3) Regulations 2002.

2. In paragraph 1, 'the 2000 Regulations' means the Immigration (European Economic Area) Regulations 2000 and 'posted worker' has the meaning given in regulation 2(4)(b) of the Immigration (Swiss Free Movement of Persons) (No. 3) Regulations 2002.

Regulation 31(2)

Schedule 4

Transitional Provisions

Interpretation

1. In this Schedule—

(a) the '2000 Regulations' means the Immigration (European Economic Area) Regulations 2000 and expressions used in relation to documents issued or applied for under those Regulations shall have the meaning given in regulation 2 of those Regulations;

(b) the 'Accession Regulations' means the Accession (Immigration and Worker Registration) Regulations 2004.

Existing documents

2.—(1) An EEA family permit issued under the 2000 Regulations shall, after 29 April 2006, be treated as if it were an EEA family permit issued under these Regulations.

(2) Subject to paragraph (4), a residence permit issued under the 2000 Regulations shall, after 29 April 2006, be treated as if it were a registration certificate issued under these Regulations.

(3) Subject to paragraph (5), a residence document issued under the 2000 Regulations shall, after 29 April 2006, be treated as if it were a residence card issued under these Regulations.

(4) Where a residence permit issued under the 2000 Regulations has been endorsed under the immigration rules to show permission to remain in the United Kingdom indefinitely it shall, after 29 April 2006, be treated as if it were a document certifying permanent residence issued under these Regulations and the holder of the permit shall be treated as a person with a permanent right of residence under regulation 15.

(5) Where a residence document issued under the 2000 Regulations has been endorsed under the immigration rules to show permission to remain in the United Kingdom indefinitely it shall, after 29 April 2006, be treated as if it were a permanent residence card issued under these Regulations and the holder of the permit shall be treated as a person with a permanent right of residence under regulation 15.

(6) Paragraphs (4) and (5) shall also apply to a residence permit or residence document which is endorsed under the immigration rules on or after 30 April 2006 to show permission to remain in the United Kingdom indefinitely pursuant to an application for such an endorsement made before that date.

Outstanding applications

3.—(1) An application for an EEA family permit, a residence permit or a residence document made but not determined under the 2000 Regulations before 30 April 2006 shall be treated as an application under these Regulations for an EEA family permit, a registration certificate or a residence card, respectively.

(2) But the following provisions of these Regulations shall not apply to the determination of an application mentioned in sub-paragraph (1)—

(a) the requirement to issue a registration certificate immediately under regulation 16(1); and

(b) the requirement to issue a certificate of application for a residence card under regulation 17(3).

Decisions to remove under the 2000 Regulations

4.—(1) A decision to remove a person under regulation 21(3)(a) of the 2000 Regulations shall, after 29 April 2006, be treated as a decision to remove that person under regulation 19(3)(a) of these Regulations.

(2) A decision to remove a person under regulation 21(3)(b) of the 2000 Regulations, including a decision which is treated as a decision to remove a person under that regulation by virtue of regulation 6(3)(a) of the Accession Regulations, shall, after 29 April 2006, be treated as a decision to remove that person under regulation 19(3)(b) of these Regulations.

(3) A deportation order made under section 5 of the 1971 Act by virtue of regulation 26(3) of the 2000 Regulations shall, after 29 April 2006, be treated as a deportation made under section 5 of the 1971 Act by virtue of regulation 24(3) of these Regulations.

Appeals

5.—(1) Where an appeal against an EEA decision under the 2000 Regulations is pending immediately before 30 April 2006 that appeal shall be treated as a pending appeal against the corresponding EEA Decision under these Regulations.

(2) Where an appeal against an EEA decision under the 2000 Regulations has been determined, withdrawn or abandoned it shall, on and after 30 April 2006, be treated as an appeal against the corresponding EEA decision under these Regulations which has been determined, withdrawn or abandoned, respectively.

(3) For the purpose of this paragraph—

(a) a decision to refuse to admit a person under these Regulations corresponds to a decision to refuse to admit that person under the 2000 Regulations;

(b) a decision to remove a person under regulation 19(3)(a) of these Regulations corresponds to a decision to remove that person under regulation 21(3)(a) of the 2000 Regulations;

(c) a decision to remove a person under regulation 19(3)(b) of these Regulations corresponds to a decision to remove that person under regulation 21(3)(b) of the 2000 Regulations, including a decision which is treated as a decision to remove a person under regulation 21(3)(b) of the 2000 Regulations by virtue of regulation 6(3)(a) of the Accession Regulations;

(d) a decision to refuse to revoke a deportation order made against a person under these Regulations corresponds to a decision to refuse to revoke a deportation order made against that person under the 2000 Regulations, including a decision which is treated as a decision to refuse to revoke a deportation order under the 2000 Regulations by virtue of regulation 6(3)(b) of the Accession Regulations;

(e) a decision not to issue or renew or to revoke an EEA family permit, a registration certificate or a residence card under these Regulations corresponds to a decision not to issue or renew or to revoke an EEA family permit, a residence permit or a residence document under the 2000 Regulations, respectively.

[6. Periods of residence prior to the entry into force of these Regulations

(1) Any period during which a person ("P"), who is an EEA national, carried out an activity or was resident in the United Kingdom in accordance with the conditions in subparagraph (2) or (3) is to be treated as a period during which the person carried out that activity or was resident in the United Kingdom in accordance with these Regulations for the purpose of calculating periods of activity and residence there under.

(2) P carried out an activity, or was resident, in the United Kingdom in accordance with this subparagraph where such activity or residence was at that time in accordance with—

(a) the 2000 Regulations;

(b) the Immigration (European Economic Area) Order 1994(5) ("the 1994 Order"); or

(c) where such activity or residence preceded the entry into force of the 1994 Order, any of the following Directives which was at the relevant time in force in respect of the United Kingdom—

(i) Council Directive 64/221/EEC;
(ii) Council Directive 68/360/EEC;
(iii) Council Directive 72/194/EEC;
(iv) Council Directive 73/148/EEC;
(v) Council Directive 75/34/EEC;
(vi) Council Directive 75/35/EEC;
(vii) Council Directive 90/364/EEC;
(viii) Council Directive 90/365/EEC; and
(ix) Council Directive 93/96/EEC.

(3) P carried out an activity or was resident in the United Kingdom in accordance with this subparagraph where P—

(a) had leave to enter or remain in the United Kingdom; and

(b) would have been carrying out that activity or residing in the United Kingdom in accordance with these Regulations had the relevant state been an EEA State at that time and had these Regulations at that time been in force.

(4) Any period during which P carried out an activity or was resident in the United Kingdom in accordance with subparagraph (2) or (3) will not be regarded as a period during which P carried out that activity or was resident in the United Kingdom in accordance with these Regulations where it was followed by a period—

(a) which exceeded two consecutive years and for the duration of which P was absent from the United Kingdom; or

(b) which exceeded two consecutive years and for the duration of which P's residence in the United Kingdom—

(i) was not in accordance with subparagraph (2) or (3); or
(ii) was not otherwise in accordance with these Regulations.

(5) The relevant state for the purpose of subparagraph (3) is the state of which P is, and was at the relevant time, a national.]

Note: Paragraph 6 substituted from 16 July 2012 (SI 2012/1547).

Regulation 31(2)

Schedule 5

Consequential Amendments

. . .

The British Nationality (Proof of Paternity) Regulations 2006

(SI 2006, No. 1496)

---

1. These Regulations may be cited as the British Nationality (Proof of Paternity) Regulations 2006 and shall come into force on 1 July 2006.

2. The following requirements are prescribed as to proof of paternity for the purposes of section 50(9A)(c) of the British Nationality Act 1981—

(a) the person must be named as the father of the child in a birth certificate issued within one year of the date of the child's birth; or

(b) the person must satisfy the Secretary of State that he is the father of the child.

3. The Secretary of State may determine whether a person is the father of a child for the purpose of regulation 2(b), and for this purpose the Secretary of State may have regard to any evidence which he considers to be relevant, including, but not limited to—

(a) DNA test reports; and

(b) court orders.

The Immigration (Provision of Physical Data) Regulations 2006

(SI 2006, No. 1743)

Citation, commencement and interpretation

1. These Regulations may be cited as the Immigration (Provision of Physical Data) Regulations 2006 and shall come into force on the day after they are made.

2. In these Regulations:

['accreditation card' means an Olympic Identity and Accreditation Card or a Paralympic Identity and Accreditation Card issued by the London Organising Committee of the Olympic Games and Paralympic Games Limited;]

'application' means:

(a) an application for entry clearance;

(b) an application for leave to enter the United Kingdom where the person seeking leave to enter presents a Convention travel document endorsed with an entry clearance for that journey to the United Kingdom;

[(c) an application for leave to enter the United Kingdom made during the period commencing on 30th March 2012 and ending on 8th November 2012 where the person seeking leave to enter holds an accreditation card and would be required to obtain a visa to enter the United Kingdom under Appendix 1 to the immigration rules were that person not exempted from that requirement in accordance with the provisions of paragraph 2 of that Appendix applicable to holders of accreditation cards; or

(d) an application for leave to remain in the United Kingdom made during the period commencing on 30th March 2012 and ending on 8th November 2012 where—

(i) the person has been granted leave to enter the United Kingdom following an application mentioned in paragraph (c);

(ii) an authorised person did not require a record of the person's fingerprints and photograph of the person's face to accompany that application for leave to enter; and

(iii) the person seeking leave to remain holds an accreditation card and would have been required to obtain a visa to enter the United Kingdom under Appendix 1 to the immigration rules were that person not exempted from that requirement in accordance with the provisions of paragraph 2 of that Appendix applicable to holders of accreditation cards;]

'Convention travel document' means a travel document issued pursuant to Article 28 of the Refugee Convention, except where that travel document was issued by the United Kingdom Government;

['immigration rules' means rules made under section 3(2) of the Immigration Act 1971;]

'Refugee Convention' means the Convention relating to the Status of Refugees done at Geneva on 28 July 1951 and its Protocol.

Note: Definitions of 'accreditation card' and 'immigration rules' inserted and definition of 'application' amended from 30 March 2012 (SI 2011/1779).

Power for an authorised person to require an individual to provide a record of his fingerprints and a photograph of his face

3. Subject to regulations 4 and 5, an authorised person may require an individual who makes an application to provide a record of his fingerprints and a photograph of his face.

Provision in relation to applicants under the age of sixteen

4.—(1) An applicant under the age of sixteen shall not be required to provide a record of his fingerprints or a photograph of his face except where the authorised person is satisfied that the fingerprints or the photograph will be taken in the presence of a person aged eighteen or over who is—

(a) the child's parent or guardian; or

(b) a person who for the time being takes responsibility for the child.

(2) The person mentioned in paragraph (1)(b) may not be—

(a) an officer of the Secretary of State who is not an authorised person;

(b) an authorised person; or

(c) any other person acting on behalf of an authorised person as part of a process specified under regulation 6(2).

(3) An authorised person shall not require a person under the age of sixteen to provide a record of his fingerprints or a photograph of his face unless his decision to do so has been confirmed by a person designated for the purpose by the Secretary of State.

(4) This regulation shall not apply if the authorised person reasonably believes that the applicant is aged sixteen or over.

Provision in relation to section 141 of the Immigration and Asylum Act 1999

5. An applicant shall not be required to provide a record of his fingerprints or a photograph of his face under regulation 3 if he is a person to whom section 141 of the Immigration and Asylum Act 1999 applies, during the relevant period within the meaning of that section.

Process by which the applicant's fingerprints and photograph may be obtained and recorded

6.—(1) An authorised person who requires an individual to provide a record of his fingerprints or a photograph of his face under regulation 3 may require that individual to submit to any process specified in paragraph (2).

(2) A process by which the individual who makes the application:

(a) attends a British Diplomatic mission or British Consular post where a record of his fingerprints or a photograph of his face is taken;

(b) attends a Diplomatic mission or Consular post of another State where a record of his fingerprints or a photograph of his face is taken by an official of that State on behalf of an authorised person; or

[(c) attends any other place nominated by an authorised person where a record of his fingerprints or a photograph of his face is taken by an authorised person or by a person on behalf of an authorised person.]

Note: Paragraph 2(c) substituted from 30 March 2012 (SI 2011/1779).

Consequences of failure to comply with these Regulations

7.—(1) Subject to paragraphs (2) and (3), where an individual does not provide a record of his fingerprints or a photograph of his face in accordance with a requirement imposed under these Regulations, his application may be treated as invalid.

(2) An application shall not be treated as invalid under paragraph (1) if it is for leave to enter the United Kingdom where the person seeking leave to enter presents a Convention travel document endorsed with an entry clearance for that journey to the United Kingdom.

(3) Where an application is of a type described in paragraph (2) and the applicant does not provide a record of his fingerprints or a photograph of his face in accordance with a requirement imposed under these Regulations, that application may be refused.

Destruction of information

8. Subject to regulation 9, any record of fingerprints, photograph, copy of fingerprints or copy of a photograph held by the Secretary of State pursuant to these Regulations must be destroyed by the Secretary of State at the end of ten years beginning with the date on which the original record or photograph was provided.

9. If an applicant proves that he is—

(a) a British citizen; or

(b) a Commonwealth citizen who has a right of abode in the United Kingdom as a result of section 2(1)(b) of the Immigration Act 1971, any record of fingerprints, photograph, copy of fingerprints or copy of a photograph held by the Secretary of State pursuant to these Regulations must be destroyed as soon as reasonably practicable.

10.—(1) The Secretary of State must take all reasonably practicable steps to secure:

(a) that data held in electronic form which relate to any record of fingerprints or photograph which have to be destroyed in accordance with regulation 8 or 9 are destroyed or erased; or

(b) that access to such data is blocked.

(2) The applicant to whom the data relates is entitled, on written request, to a certificate issued by the Secretary of State to the effect that he has taken the steps required by paragraph (1).

(3) A certificate issued under paragraph (2) must be issued within three months of the date on which the request was received by the Secretary of State.

Revocation and transitional provisions

11.—(1) . . .

(2) For the purposes of paragraph (3) only, 'application' means an application within the meaning of regulation 2 of the Immigration (Provision of Physical Data) Regulations 2003 (the '2003 Regulations').

(3) Where a person made an application before these Regulations came into force, the 2003 Regulations will continue to apply for the purposes of that application as if they had not been revoked by paragraph (1).

The Immigration (Continuation of Leave) (Notices) Regulations 2006
(SI 2006, No. 2170)

Citation and Commencement

1. These Regulations may be cited as the Immigration (Continuation of Leave) (Notices) Regulations 2006 and shall come into force on 31 August 2006.

Decision on an application for variation of leave

2. For the purpose of section 3C of the Immigration Act 1971 an application for variation of leave is decided—

(a) when notice of the decision has been given in accordance with regulations made under section 105 of the Nationality, Immigration and Asylum Act 2002; or where no such notice is required,

(b) when notice of the decision has been given in accordance with section 4(1) of the Immigration Act 1971.

The Refugee or Person in Need of International Protection (Qualification) Regulations 2006
(SI 2006, No. 2525)

Citation and commencement

1.—(1) These Regulations may be cited as The Refugee or Person in Need of International Protection (Qualification) Regulations 2006 and shall come into force on 9 October 2006.

(2) These Regulations apply to any application for asylum which has not been decided and any immigration appeal brought under the Immigration Acts (as defined in section 64(2) of the Immigration, Asylum and Nationality Act 2006) which has not been finally determined.

Interpretation

2. In these Regulations—

'application for asylum' means the request of a person to be recognised as a refugee under the Geneva Convention;

'Geneva Convention' means the Convention Relating to the Status of Refugees done at Geneva on 28 July 1951 and the New York Protocol of 31 January 1967;

'immigration rules' means rules made under section 3(2) of the Immigration Act 1971;

'persecution' means an act of persecution within the meaning of Article 1(A) of the Geneva Convention;

'person eligible for humanitarian protection' means a person who is eligible for a grant of humanitarian protection under the immigration rules;

'refugee' means a person who falls within Article 1(A) of the Geneva Convention and to whom regulation 7 does not apply;

'residence permit' means a document confirming that a person has leave to enter or remain in the United Kingdom whether limited or indefinite;

'serious harm' means serious harm as defined in the immigration rules;

'person' means any person who is not a British citizen.

Actors of persecution or serious harm

3. In deciding whether a person is a refugee or a person eligible for humanitarian protection, persecution or serious harm can be committed by:

(a) the State;

(b) any party or organisation controlling the State or a substantial part of the territory of the State;

(c) any non-State actor if it can be demonstrated that the actors mentioned in paragraphs (a) and (b), including any international organisation, are unable or unwilling to provide protection against persecution or serious harm.

Actors of protection

4.—(1) In deciding whether a person is a refugee or a person eligible for humanitarian protection, protection from persecution or serious harm can be provided by:

(a) the State; or

(b) any party or organisation, including any international organisation, controlling the State or a substantial part of the territory of the State.

(2) Protection shall be regarded as generally provided when the actors mentioned in paragraph (1)(a) and (b) take reasonable steps to prevent the persecution or suffering of serious harm by operating an effective legal system for the detection, prosecution and punishment of acts constituting persecution or serious harm, and the person mentioned in paragraph (1) has access to such protection.

(3) In deciding whether a person is a refugee or a person eligible for humanitarian protection the Secretary of State may assess whether an international organisation controls a State or a substantial part of its territory and provides protection as described in paragraph (2).

Act of persecution

5.—(1) In deciding whether a person is a refugee an act of persecution must be:

(a) sufficiently serious by its nature or repetition as to constitute a severe violation of a basic human right, in particular a right from which derogation cannot be made under Article 15 of the Convention for the Protection of Human Rights and Fundamental Freedoms; or

(b) an accumulation of various measures, including a violation of a human right which is sufficiently severe as to affect an individual in a similar manner as specified in (a).

(2) An act of persecution may, for example, take the form of:

(a) an act of physical or mental violence, including an act of sexual violence;

(b) a legal, administrative, police, or judicial measure which in itself is discriminatory or which is implemented in a discriminatory manner;

(c) prosecution or punishment, which is disproportionate or discriminatory;

(d) denial of judicial redress resulting in a disproportionate or discriminatory punishment;

(e) prosecution or punishment for refusal to perform military service in a conflict, where performing military service would include crimes or acts falling under regulation 7.

(3) An act of persecution must be committed for at least one of the reasons in Article 1(A) of the Geneva Convention.

Reasons for persecution

6.—(1) In deciding whether a person is a refugee:

(a) the concept of race shall include consideration of, for example, colour, descent, or membership of a particular ethnic group;

(b) the concept of religion shall include, for example, the holding of theistic, non-theistic and atheistic beliefs, the participation in, or abstention from, formal worship in private or in public, either alone or in community with others, other religious acts or expressions of view, or forms of personal or communal conduct based on or mandated by any religious belief;

(c) the concept of nationality shall not be confined to citizenship or lack thereof but shall include, for example, membership of a group determined by its cultural, ethnic, or linguistic identity, common geographical or political origins or its relationship with the population of another State;

(d) a group shall be considered to form a particular social group where, for example:

(i) members of that group share an innate characteristic, or a common background that cannot be changed, or share a characteristic or belief that is so fundamental to identity or conscience that a person should not be forced to renounce it, and

(ii) that group has a distinct identity in the relevant country, because it is perceived as being different by the surrounding society;

(e) a particular social group might include a group based on a common characteristic of sexual orientation but sexual orientation cannot be understood to include acts considered to be criminal in accordance with national law of the United Kingdom;

(f) the concept of political opinion shall include the holding of an opinion, thought or belief on a matter related to the potential actors of persecution mentioned in regulation 3 and to their policies or methods, whether or not that opinion, thought or belief has been acted upon by the person.

(2) In deciding whether a person has a well-founded fear of being persecuted, it is immaterial whether he actually possesses the racial, religious, national, social or political characteristic which attracts the persecution, provided that such a characteristic is attributed to him by the actor of persecution.

Exclusion

7.—(1) A person is not a refugee, if he falls within the scope of Article 1D, 1E or 1F of the Geneva Convention.

(2) In the construction and application of Article 1F(b) of the Geneva Convention:

(a) the reference to serious non-political crime includes a particularly cruel action, even if it is committed with an allegedly political objective;

(b) the reference to the crime being committed outside the country of refuge prior to his admission as a refugee shall be taken to mean the time up to and including the day on which a residence permit is issued.

(3) Article 1F(a) and (b) of the Geneva Convention shall apply to a person who instigates or otherwise participates in the commission of the crimes or acts specified in those provisions.

The Immigration (Certificate of Entitlement to Right of Abode in the United Kingdom) Regulations 2006

(SI 2006, No. 3145)

Citation, commencement and interpretation

1. These Regulations may be cited as the Immigration (Certificate of Entitlement to Right of Abode in the United Kingdom) Regulations 2006 and shall come into force on 21 December 2006.

2. In these Regulations—

'the 1971 Act' means the Immigration Act 1971;

'the 1981 Act' means the British Nationality Act 1981;

'the 2002 Act' means the Nationality, Immigration and Asylum Act 2002;

['the 2008 Act' means the Human Fertilisation and Embryology Act 2008;]

'appropriate authority' means the authority to whom an application for a certificate of entitlement must be made, as determined in accordance with regulation 3;

'certificate of entitlement' means a certificate, issued in accordance with these Regulations, that a person has the right of abode in the United Kingdom;

'Governor', in relation to a territory, includes the officer for the time being administering the government of that territory;

'High Commissioner' means, in relation to a country mentioned in Schedule 3 to the 1981 Act, the High Commissioner for Her Majesty's Government in the United Kingdom appointed to that country, and includes the acting High Commissioner; and

'passport' includes a document which relates to a national of a country other than the United Kingdom and which is designed to serve the same purpose as a passport.

Note: Definition of '2008 Act' inserted from 1 September 2009 (SI 2009/1892).

Authority to whom an application must be made

3. An application for a certificate of entitlement must be made—

(a) if the applicant is in the United Kingdom, to the Secretary of State for the Home Department;

[(b) if the applicant is in any of the Channel Islands or the Isle of Man, to the Lieutenant-Governor or the Secretary of State for the Home Department;]

(c) if the applicant is in a British overseas territory, to the Governor;

(d) if the applicant is in a country mentioned in Schedule 3 to the 1981 Act, to the High Commissioner, or, if there is no High Commissioner, to the Secretary of State for the Home Department; and

(e) if the applicant is elsewhere, to any consular officer, any established officer in the Diplomatic Service of Her Majesty's Government in the United Kingdom or any other person authorised by the Secretary of State in that behalf.

Note: Regulation 3(b) substituted from 12 December 2011 (SI 2011/2682).

Form of application

[4.—(1) Subject to paragraph (2), an application for a certificate of entitlement must be accompanied by—

(a) the applicant's passport or travel document;

(b) two photographs of the applicant taken no more than 6 months prior to making the application; and

(c) the additional documents which are specified in the right-hand column of the Schedule in respect of an application of a description specified in the corresponding entry in the left hand column.

(2) The requirement in paragraph (1)(c) may be waived in relation to a particular document if the appropriate authority—

(a) is satisfied that it is appropriate to do so in light of the facts of the particular case; and

(b) is otherwise satisfied that the applicant has a right of abode in the United Kingdom.]

Note: Regulation 4 substituted from 12 December 2011 (SI 2011/2682).

5. A passport produced by or on behalf of a person is valid for the purposes of regulation 4 if it—

(a) relates to the person by whom or on whose behalf it is produced;

(b) has not been altered otherwise than by or with the permission of the authority who issued it; and

(c) was not obtained by deception.

Issue of certificate of entitlement

6. A certificate of entitlement will only be issued where the appropriate authority is satisfied that the applicant—

(a) has a right of abode in the United Kingdom under section 2(1) of the 1971 Act;

[(b) is not a person who holds:

(i) a United Kingdom passport describing him as a British citizen,

(ii) a United Kingdom passport describing him as a British subject with the right of abode in the United Kingdom, or

(iii) a certificate of entitlement;]

(c) is not a person whose exercise of his right of abode is restricted under section 2 of the Immigration Act 1988 (restrictions on exercise of right of abode in cases of polygamy); and

(d) is not a person who is deprived of his right of abode by an order under section 2A of the 1971 Act.

7. A certificate of entitlement is to be issued by means of being affixed to the passport or travel document of the applicant.

Note: Regulation 6(b) substituted from 12 December 2011 (SI 2011/2682).

Expiry and revocation of certificate of entitlement

8. A certificate of entitlement shall cease to have effect on the expiry of the passport or travel document to which it is affixed.

9. A certificate of entitlement may be revoked by the Secretary of State for the Home Department, an immigration officer, a consular officer or a person responsible for the grant or refusal of entry clearance, where the person who revokes the certificate is satisfied that the person in possession of the certificate (whether or not this is the person to whom the certificate was issued)—

(a) does not have the right of abode in the United Kingdom under section 2(1) of the 1971 Act;

[(b) is the holder of:

(i) a United Kingdom passport describing him as a British citizen,

(ii) a United Kingdom passport describing him as a British subject with the right of abode in the United Kingdom,

(iii) another certificate of entitlement;]

(c) is a person whose exercise of his right of abode is restricted under section 2 of the Immigration Act 1988; or

(d) is a person who is deprived of his right of abode by an order under section 2A of the 1971 Act.

Note: Regulation 9(b) substituted from 12 December 2011 (SI 2011/2682).

Savings

10. The effect of a certificate described in section 10(6) of the 2002 Act is that it will cease to have effect on the expiry of the passport or travel document to which it is affixed.

Schedule

Additional documents which must accompany an application for a certificate of entitlement.

[Regulation 4(1)(c)]

Basis of application	Documents
Applicant was registered or naturalised as a British citizen on or after 1st January 1983	Applicant's registration or naturalisation certificate
Applicant was born in the United Kingdom before 1st January 1983	Applicant's full birth certificate, showing parents' details
Applicant was registered or naturalised as a citizen of the United Kingdom and Colonies in the United Kingdom before 1st January 1983	Applicant's registration or naturalisation certificate
Applicant is a Commonwealth (not British) citizen born before 1st January 1983 to a parent who was born in the United Kingdom	(i) Applicant's full birth certificate showing parents' details; and (ii) Parents' full UK birth certificate
Applicant is a female Commonwealth citizen who was married before 1st January 1983 to a man with right of abode in the United Kingdom	(i) Applicant's marriage certificate; and (ii) Evidence of applicant's husband's right of abode, eg passport or UK birth certificate
Applicant was born in the United Kingdom or the Falkland Islands on or after 1st January 1983, or in another qualifying British overseas territory on or after 21st May 2002	(i) Applicant's full birth certificate showing parents' details; (ii) Evidence of either parent's British citizenship or settled status at time of applicant's birth, eg a passport describing the relevant parent as a British citizen or indicating that he or she then had indefinite leave to remain; and [(iii) Parents' marriage or civil partnership certificate (if claiming through father or if claiming through woman who is a parent of the applicant by virtue of section 42 or 43 of the 2008 Act.]
Applicant was born outside the United Kingdom and the Falkland Islands on or after 1st January 1983, or outside the United Kingdom and any qualifying	(i) Applicant's full birth certificate showing parents' details;

British overseas territory on or after 21st May 2002, to a parent born in the United Kingdom or the Falkland Islands (or, on/after 21 May 2002, any qualifying British overseas territory) or to a parent registered or naturalised in the United Kingdom prior to the applicant's birth	[(ii) Parents' marriage or civil partnership certificate (if claiming through father or if claiming through woman who is a parent of the applicant by virtue of section 42 or 43 of the 2008 Act);] and (iii) Parents' full birth certificate, registration or naturalisation certificate
Applicant was born outside the United Kingdom and the Falkland Islands on or after 1st January 1983, or outside the United Kingdom and any qualifying British overseas territory on or after 21 May 2002, to a parent who, at the time of the birth, was a British citizen in service to which section 2(1)(b) of the British Nationality Act 1981 applies	(i) Applicant's full birth certificate; [(ii) Parents' marriage or civil partnership certificate (if claiming through father or if claiming through woman who is a parent of the applicant by virtue of section 42 or 43 of the 2008 Act);] and (iii) Evidence of parents' relevant employment at the time of the birth, eg a letter from the employer
Applicant was adopted in the United Kingdom, a qualifying British overseas territory, or otherwise under the terms of the Hague Convention on Intercountry Adoption(1)	(i) Applicant's adoption certificate; and (ii) Evidence of adoptive parents' citizenship and, if a Convention adoption, of their place of habitual residence at the time of the adoption, eg in respect of citizenship, a passport, and in respect of habitual residence at the time of the Convention adoption, the adoption certificate
Applicant was a citizen of the United Kingdom and Colonies and was ordinarily resident in the United Kingdom for a continuous period of 5 years before 1st January 1983 and was settled in the United Kingdom at the end of that period	(i) Evidence of citizenship of the United Kingdom and Colonies, eg a passport or certificate of naturalisation or registration; and (ii) Evidence of settlement and 5 years' ordinary residence in the UK before 1983, eg, passport, P60s, details of National Insurance contributions, DSS claims, employers' letters
Applicant was a citizen of the United Kingdom and Colonies and had a parent who was born, adopted, registered or naturalised in the United Kingdom prior to the applicant's birth/adoption	(i) Applicant's full birth certificate or adoption certificate; [(ii) Parents' marriage or civil partnership certificate (if claiming through father or if claiming through woman who is a parent of the applicant by virtue of section 42 or 43 of the 2008 Act);] and (iii) Parents' full birth certificate, adoption, registration or naturalisation certificate

Applicant was a citizen of the United Kingdom and Colonies and had a grandparent born, adopted, registered or naturalised in the United Kingdom before the applicant's parents' birth/adoption	(i) Parents' marriage certificate (if claiming through father); [(ii) Parents' marriage or civil partnership certificate (if claiming through father or if claiming through woman who is a parent of the applicant by virtue of section 42 or 43 of the 2008 Act);] (iii) Applicant's full birth certificate or adoption certificate; (iv) Grandparents' marriage certificate (if claiming through grandfather); and (v) Grandparents' full birth certificate, adoption, registration or naturalisation certificate.

Note: Schedule amended from 1 September 2009 by SI 2009/1892 and from 12 December 2011 by SI 2011/2682.

The Immigration (Leave to Remain) (Prescribed Forms and Procedures) Regulations 2007

(SI 2007, No. 882)

Citation, commencement and interpretation

1. These Regulations may be cited as the Immigration (Leave to Remain) (Prescribed Forms and Procedures) Regulations 2007 and shall come into force on 2 April 2007.

2. In these Regulations:

'asylum claimant' means a person making a claim for asylum which has not been determined or has been granted;

'claim for asylum' has the meaning given in section 94(1) of the Immigration and Asylum Act 1999, and a claim for asylum is taken to be determined—

(a) on the day on which the Secretary of State notifies the claimant of his decision on the claim,

(b) if the claimant has appealed against the Secretary of State's decision, on the day on which the appeal is disposed of, or

(c) if the claimant has brought an in-country appeal against an immigration decision under section 82 of the Nationality, Immigration and Asylum Act 2002 or section 2 of the Special Immigration Appeals Commission Act 1997, on the day on which the appeal is disposed of; 'dependant', in respect of a person, means—

(a) the spouse, civil partner, unmarried partner or same sex partner, or

(b) a child under the age of eighteen,

of that person; and

'public enquiry office' means a public enquiry office of the Border and Immigration Agency of the Home Office.

Prescribed forms

3.—(1) Subject to paragraph (2), the form set out in Schedule 1 is prescribed for an application for limited or indefinite leave to remain in the United Kingdom as:

(a) a business person,

(b) a sole representative,

(c) a retired person of independent means,

(d) an investor, or

(e) an innovator,for the purposes of the immigration rules.

(2) Paragraph (1) does not apply to an application for limited or indefinite leave to remain in the United Kingdom as a business person where the application is made under the terms of a European Community Association Agreement.

4. The form set out in Schedule 2 is prescribed for an application for limited leave to remain in the United Kingdom:

(a) for work permit employment,

(b) as a seasonal agricultural worker,

(c) for the purpose of employment under the Sectors Based Scheme, or

(d) for Home Office approved training or work experience, for the purposes of the immigration rules.

5. The form set out in Schedule 3 is prescribed for an application for limited leave to remain in the United Kingdom as a highly skilled migrant for the purposes of the immigration rules.

6. The form set out in Schedule 4 is prescribed for an application for limited leave to remain in the United Kingdom as:

(a) the spouse or civil partner of a person present and settled in the United Kingdom, or

(b) the unmarried partner or same sex partner of a person present and settled in the United Kingdom, for the purposes of the immigration rules.

7. The form set out in Schedule 5 is prescribed for an application for limited leave to remain in the United Kingdom:

(a) as a student,

(b) as a student nurse,

(c) to re-sit an examination,

(d) to write up a thesis,

(e) as a student union sabbatical officer, or

(f) as a prospective student, for the purposes of the immigration rules.

8. The form set out in Schedule 6 is prescribed for an application for limited leave to remain in the United Kingdom as a participant in the [International Graduates Scheme] for the purposes of the immigration rules.

Note: Words in square brackets inserted from 1 May 2007 (SI 2007/1122).

9. The form set out in Schedule 7 is prescribed for an application for limited leave to remain in the United Kingdom as a participant in the Fresh Talent: Working in Scotland Scheme for the purposes of the immigration rules.

10.—(1) The form set out in Schedule 8 is prescribed for an application for limited leave to remain in the United Kingdom as:

(a) a visitor,

(b) a visitor seeking to undergo or continue private medical treatment,

(c) a postgraduate doctor or dentist or a trainee general practitioner,

(d) an au pair,

(e) a teacher or language assistant under an approved exchange scheme,

(f) a representative of an overseas newspaper, news agency or broadcasting organisation,

(g) a private servant in a diplomatic household,

(h) a domestic worker in a private household,

(i) an overseas government employee,

(j) a minister of religion, missionary or member of a religious order,

(k) a visiting religious worker or a religious worker in a non-pastoral role,

(l) a member of the operational ground staff of an overseas-owned airline,

(m) a person with United Kingdom ancestry,

(n) a writer, composer or artist,

(o) an overseas qualified nurse or midwife, or

(p) the spouse, civil partner or child of an armed forces member who is exempt from immigration control under section 8(4) of the Immigration Act 1971, for the purposes of the immigration rules.

(2) Subject to paragraph (3), the form set out in Schedule 8 is prescribed for an application for limited leave to remain in the United Kingdom for any other reason or purpose for which provision is made in the immigration rules but which is not covered by the forms prescribed by regulations 3 to 9.

(3) Paragraph (2) does not apply to an application for limited leave to remain in the United Kingdom where:

(a) the application is made under the terms of a European Community Association Agreement, or

(b) the basis on which the application is made is that the applicant is an asylum claimant or a dependant of an asylum claimant.

11. The form set out in Schedule 9 is prescribed for an application for indefinite leave to remain in the United Kingdom as:

(a) the spouse or civil partner of a person present and settled in the United Kingdom, or

(b) the unmarried partner or same sex partner of a person present and settled in the United Kingdom, for the purposes of the immigration rules.

12. The form set out in Schedule 10 is prescribed for an application for indefinite leave to remain in the United Kingdom as:

(a) the child under the age of eighteen of a parent, parents or relative present and settled in the United Kingdom,

(b) the adopted child under the age of eighteen of a parent or parents present and settled in the United Kingdom, or

(c) the parent, grandparent or other dependent relative of a person present and settled in the United Kingdom, for the purposes of the immigration rules.

13. The form set out in Schedule 11 is prescribed for an application for indefinite leave to remain in the United Kingdom as a victim of domestic violence.

14.—(1) The form set out in Schedule 12 is prescribed for an application for indefinite leave to remain in the United Kingdom:

(a) as a work permit holder,

(b) as a highly skilled migrant,

(c) as a representative of an overseas newspaper, news agency or broadcasting organisation,

(d) as a private servant in a diplomatic household,

(e) as a domestic worker in a private household,

(f) as an overseas government employee,

(g) as a minister of religion, missionary or member of a religious order,

(h) as a member of the operational ground staff of an overseas-owned airline,

(i) as a person with United Kingdom ancestry,

(j) as a writer, composer or artist,

(k) on the basis of long residence in the United Kingdom, or

(l) as a foreign or Commonwealth citizen discharged from HM Forces, for the purposes of the immigration rules.

(2) Subject to paragraph (3), the form set out in Schedule 12 is prescribed for an application for indefinite leave to remain in the United Kingdom for any other reason or purpose for which provision is made in the immigration rules but which is not covered by the forms prescribed by regulations 11, 12 or 13.

(3) Paragraph (2) does not apply to an application for indefinite leave to remain in the United Kingdom where:

(a) the application is made under the terms of a European Community Association Agreement,

(b) the basis on which the application is made is that the applicant is an asylum claimant or a dependant of an asylum claimant.

15. An application for leave to remain in the United Kingdom which is made by a person ('the main applicant') on a form prescribed by any of the regulations 3 to 14 above may include an application in respect of any person applying for leave to remain in the United Kingdom as a dependant of the main applicant.

Prescribed procedures

16.—(1) The following procedures are prescribed in relation to an application for which a form is prescribed by regulations 3 to 14:

(a) the form shall be signed and dated by the applicant, save that where the applicant is under the age of eighteen, the form may be signed and dated by the parent or legal guardian of the applicant on behalf of the applicant;

(b) the application shall be accompanied by such documents and photographs as specified in the form; and

(c) each part of the form shall be completed as specified in the form.

(2) The following procedures are prescribed in relation to delivery of an application for which a form is prescribed:

(a) in relation to an application for which a form is prescribed by regulation 3, the application shall be sent by prepaid post or by courier to the Border and Immigration Agency of the Home Office; it may not be submitted in person at a public enquiry office,

(b) in relation to an application for which a form is prescribed by regulation 4, the application shall be:

(i) sent by prepaid post or by courier to Work Permits (UK) at the Border and Immigration Agency of the Home Office, or

(ii) submitted in person at the Croydon public enquiry office (but no other public enquiry office),

(c) in relation to an application for which a form is prescribed by regulation 5, the application shall be sent by prepaid post or by courier to Work Permits (UK) at the Border and Immigration Agency of the Home Office, and may not be submitted in person at a public enquiry office,

(d) in relation to an application for which a form is prescribed by regulations 6 to 12 and regulation 14, the application shall be:

(i) sent by prepaid post to the Border and Immigration Agency of the Home Office, or

(ii) submitted in person at a public enquiry office,

(e) in relation to an application for which a form is prescribed by regulation 13, the application shall be sent by prepaid post to the Border and Immigration Agency of the Home Office; it may not be submitted in person at a public enquiry office.

17.—(1) A failure to comply with any of the requirements of regulation 16(1) to any extent will only invalidate an application if:

(a) the applicant does not provide, when making the application, an explanation for the failure which the Secretary of State considers to be satisfactory,

(b) the Secretary of State notifies the applicant, or the person who appears to the Secretary of State to represent the applicant, of the failure within 28 days of the date on which the application is made, and

(c) the applicant does not comply with the requirements within a reasonable time, and in any event within 28 days, of being notified by the Secretary of State of the failure.

(2) For the purposes of this regulation, the date on which the application is made is:

(a) in the case of an application sent by post, the date of posting,

(b) in the case of an application submitted in person, the date on which the application is delivered to, and accepted by, a public enquiry office, and

(c) in the case of an application sent by courier, the date on which the application is delivered to Work Permits (UK) at the Border and Immigration Agency of the Home Office.

Revocation and transitional provision

18.—(1) . . .

(2) . . .

(3) An application made on a form prescribed by the Immigration (Leave to Remain) (Prescribed Forms and Procedures) Regulations 2006 shall be deemed to have been made on the corresponding form prescribed by these Regulations if made within 21 days of these Regulations coming into force for the purposes of section 31A of the Immigration Act 1971.

Note: Paragraphs (1) and (2) revoke SI 2006/1421, SI 2006/1548, SI 2006/2889.

Schedules

. . .

The Asylum (Procedures) Regulations 2007
(SI 2007, No. 3187)

Citation and commencement

1. These Regulations may be cited as the Asylum (Procedures) Regulations 2007 and shall come into force on 1 December 2007.

Interpretation

2. In these Regulations –

'the 1997 Act' means the Special Immigration Appeals Commission Act 1997;

'the 2002 Act' means the Nationality, Immigration and Asylum Act 2002;

'asylum claim' and 'human rights claim' have the meanings given to them in section 113 of the 2002 Act.

Designation of States or parts of States for the purposes of section 94 of the 2002 Act

3. . . .

Note: Amends s 94 Nationality, Immigration and Asylum Act 2002.

European Common List of Safe Countries of Origin

4. . . .

Note: Amends s 94 Nationality, Immigration and Asylum Act 2002.

Interpreters

5.—(1) Paragraph (2) applies where a person who has made an asylum or a human rights claim (or both)—

(a) appeals under section 82, 83 or 83A of the 2002 Act or section 2 of the 1997 Act, and

(b) by virtue of Rules made under section 106 of the 2002 Act or sections 5 and 8 of the 1997 Act is entitled to the services of an interpreter for the purposes of bringing his appeal.

(2) The Secretary of State shall defray the costs of providing the interpreter.

(3) Paragraph (5) applies where a person who has made an asylum claim or a human rights claim (or both) is party to –

(a) an appeal under section 103B, 103C or 103E of the 2002 Act, or

(b) an appeal under section 7 of the 1997 Act.

(4) Paragraph (5) also applies where a person who has made an asylum or a human rights claim (or both) makes –

(a) an application to the supervisory jurisdiction of the Court of Session made by petition for judicial review,

(b) an application under section 31 of the Supreme Court Act 1981, or

(c) an application under section 18 of the Judicature (Northern Ireland) Act 1978.

(5) The person mentioned in paragraphs (3) and (4) shall be entitled to the services of an interpreter for the purposes of the appeal or application —

(a) when giving evidence, and

(b) in such other circumstances as the court hearing the appeal or application considers it necessary.

(6) Where a person is entitled to the services of an interpreter under paragraph (5), the Secretary of State shall defray the costs of providing such interpreter.

Amendment to the Immigration (Notices) Regulations 2003

6. . . .

Note: Amends SI 2003/658.

The Immigration and Asylum (Provision of Services or Facilities) Regulations 2007

(SI 2007, No. 3627)

Citation and commencement

1. These Regulations may be cited as the Immigration and Asylum (Provision of Services or Facilities) Regulations 2007 and shall come into force on 31 January 2008.

Interpretation

2. In these Regulations—

'the 1999 Act' means the Immigration and Asylum Act 1999;

'ante-natal eligible period' means the period from eight weeks before the expected date of birth to the date of birth;

'child' means an individual who is less than 18 years old;

'destitute' is to be construed in accordance with section 95(3) of the 1999 Act;

'full birth certificate' means a birth certificate issued in the United Kingdom, which specifies the names of the child's parents;

'immigration officer' means a person appointed as an immigration officer under paragraph 1(1) of Schedule 2 to the Immigration Act 1971;

'maternity payment' means a payment of £250 made by the Secretary of State to a person supported under section 95 or section 98 of the 1999 Act to help with the costs arising from the birth of a child;

'mother' means a woman who is a supported person and who has provided evidence to satisfy the Secretary of State that she has given birth to a child;

'post-natal eligible period' means the period from the date of the birth to six weeks after the birth;

'pregnant woman' means a woman who is a supported person who has provided evidence to satisfy the Secretary of State that she is pregnant;

'provider' means a person providing facilities for the accommodation of persons by arrangement with the Secretary of State under section 4 of the 1999 Act;

'qualified person' has the same meaning as in section 84(2) of the 1999 Act;

'qualifying journey' means where—

(a) a single journey of a distance of not less than three miles; or

(b) where there is a specified need, a single journey of a distance of less than three miles; 'specified need' means where—

(a) the supported person is unable or virtually unable to walk a distance of up to three miles by reason of a physical impediment or for some other reason; or

(b) the supported person has one or more child dependants—

(i) aged under five; or

(ii) who are unable or virtually unable to walk a distance of up to three miles by reason of a physical impediment or for some other reason;

'supported person' means a person who is being provided with accommodation under section 4 of the 1999 Act and who is destitute; and

'voluntary sector partner' means an organisation funded by the Secretary of State to deliver aspects of asylum support services.

Travel

3.—(1) The Secretary of State may supply, or arrange for the supply of, facilities for travel for a qualifying journey to a supported person to—

(a) receive healthcare treatment, provided that the supported person has provided evidence that the qualifying journey is necessary; or

(b) register a birth.

(2) Subject to paragraph (3), if the Secretary of State supplies, or arranges for the supply of, facilities for travel for a qualifying journey to a supported person under paragraph (1) then, if necessary, the Secretary of State may also supply, or arrange for the supply of, facilities for travel for that qualifying journey to—

(a) one or more dependants of that supported person; and

(b) in the case of a supported person who is a child—

(i) a parent or guardian of that supported person or a person who for the time being takes parental responsibility for that supported person; and

(ii) if the parent, guardian or person who for the time being takes parental responsibility for that supported person himself has dependants then one or more of his dependants.

(3) The Secretary of State may only supply, or arrange for the supply of, facilities for travel under paragraph (2) to persons who are supported persons.

Birth certificates

4. The Secretary of State may arrange for the provision to a supported person of his child's full birth certificate.

Telephone calls and letters

5.—(1) The Secretary of State may supply, or arrange for the supply of, facilities to make telephone calls—

(a) regarding medical treatment or care,
(b) to a qualified person,
(c) to a court or tribunal,
(d) to a voluntary sector partner,
(e) to a citizens advice bureau,
(f) to a local authority,
(g) to an immigration officer, or
(h) to the Secretary of State,

to a supported person aged 18 or over.

(2) The Secretary of State may supply, or arrange for the supply of, stationery and postage for correspondence—

(a) regarding medical treatment or care,
(b) to a qualified person,
(c) to a court or tribunal,
(d) to a voluntary sector partner,
(e) to a citizens advice bureau,
(f) to a local authority,
(g) to an immigration officer, or
(h) to the Secretary of State,

to a supported person aged 18 or over.

One-off supply of vouchers for pregnant women and new mothers

6.—(1) During the ante-natal eligible period, on application, the Secretary of State may supply, or arrange for the supply of, vouchers redeemable for goods to the value of £250 in respect of each expected child to a pregnant woman.

(2) In a case where such support has not been provided under paragraph (1), during the post-natal eligible period, on application, the Secretary of State may supply, or arrange for the supply of, vouchers redeemable for goods to the value of £250 in respect of each new born child to a mother.

(3) Paragraphs (1) and (2) shall not apply if a maternity payment has been made in respect of the child in question.

Additional weekly vouchers for pregnant women and children under three

7.—(1) For the duration of the pregnancy, on application, the Secretary of State may supply, or arrange for the supply of, vouchers redeemable for goods or services to the value of £3 per week to a pregnant woman.

(2) Until the first birthday of a child who is a supported person, on application, the Secretary of State may supply, or arrange for the supply of, vouchers redeemable for goods or services to the value of £5 per week to him.

(3) From the day after the first birthday of a child who is a supported person, until the third birthday, on application, the Secretary of State may supply, or arrange for the supply of, vouchers redeemable for goods or services to the value of £3 per week to him.

Additional weekly vouchers for clothing for children

8. Until the sixteenth birthday of a child who is a supported person, on application, the Secretary of State may supply, or arrange for the supply of, vouchers redeemable for clothing to the value of £5 per week to him.

Exceptional specific needs

9.—(1) If the Secretary of State is satisfied that a supported person has an exceptional need for:

(a) facilities for travel,

(b) facilities to make telephone calls,

(c) stationery and postage, or

(d) essential living needs, she may provide for that need, notwithstanding that the conditions for the supply of those services or facilities referred to respectively in regulations 3, 5, and 6 are not satisfied.

(2) In determining what are or are not to be treated as essential living needs, the Secretary of State shall have regard to regulations made under section 95(7) of the 1999 Act.

The Immigration, Asylum and Nationality Act 2006 (Commencement No. 8 and Transitional and Saving Provisions) Order 2008

2008 No. 310 (C. 10)

Citation and interpretation

1.—(1) This Order may be cited at the Immigration, Asylum and Nationality Act 2006 (Commencement No. 8 and Transitional and Saving Provisions) Order 2008.

(2) In this Order—

'the 2006 Act' means the Immigration, Asylum and Nationality Act 2006;

'the 2002 Act' means the Nationality, Immigration and Asylum Act 2002;

'the 1999 Act' means the Immigration and Asylum Act 1999;

'the 1996 Act' means the Asylum and Immigration Act 1996; and 'immigration rules' means rules made under section 3(2) of the Immigration Act 1971.

Commencement

2.—(1) Subject to article 5 the following provisions of the 2006 Act shall come into force on 29 February 2008—

(a) sections 15 to 18 to the extent to which they are not already in force (penalty for employment of adult subject to immigration control);

(b) sections 21 and 22 (offence of employing adult subject to immigration control);

(c) section 24 (employment of adult subject to immigration control: temporary admission);

(d) section 26 (repeal); and

(e) in Schedule 3, the entries relating to the 1996 Act.

(2) The following provisions of the 2006 Act shall come into force on 29 February 2008—

(a) section 50(3)(a) (repeal); and

(b) in Schedule 3, the entries relating to section 31A of the Immigration Act 1971.

3. The following provisions of the 2006 Act shall come in to force on 1 April 2008—

(a) subject to article 4, section 4 (entry clearance);

(b) section 33 (freight information: police powers) for the purposes of making an order under subsection (5)(a); and

(c) section 47 (removal: person with statutorily extended leave).

Saving and Transitional Provision

4. Notwithstanding the commencement of section 4 of the 2006 Act and the substitution of section 88A of the 2002 Act and section 23 of the 1999 Act, section 4(1) (appeals: entry clearance) and section 4(2) of the 2006 Act (monitoring refusals of entry clearance) shall have effect only so far as they relate to applications of a kind identified in immigration rules as requiring to be considered under a 'Points Based System' [and applications made for the purpose of entering the United Kingdom as a visitor, including applications made for the purpose of visiting a person of a class or description prescribed by regulations for the purpose of section 88A(1)(a)(3) of the 2002 Act].

5.—(1) Notwithstanding the commencement of section 26 of the 2006 Act (repeal) the following provisions and instruments continue to have effect in relation to employment which commenced before 29th February 2008, including employment which continued on or after that date—

(a) sections 8 (restrictions on employment) and 8A (code of practice) of the 1996 Act;

(b) any Code of Practice in force immediately before 29 February 2008 under section 8A of the 1996 Act;

(c) the Immigration (Restrictions on Employment) Order 2004; and

(d) the Immigration (Restrictions on Employment) (Code of Practice) Order 2001.

(2) Sections 15 to 18, 21, 22, 24, 25 and 26 of the 2006 Act are of no effect in relation to employment of a kind mentioned in paragraph (1).

Note: Words inserted in Art 4 from 9 July 2012 (SI 2012/1531).

The Appeals from the Upper Tribunal to the Court of Appeal Order 2008
2008 No. 2834

1. This Order may be cited as the Appeals from the Upper Tribunal to the Court of Appeal Order 2008 and shall come into force on 3 November 2008.

2. Permission to appeal to the Court of Appeal in England and Wales or leave to appeal to the Court of Appeal in Northern Ireland shall not be granted unless the Upper Tribunal or, where the Upper Tribunal refuses permission, the relevant appellate court, considers that—

(a) the proposed appeal would raise some important point of principle or practice; or

(b) there is some other compelling reason for the relevant appellate court to hear the appeal.

The Immigration (Biometric Registration) Regulations 2008
SI 2008 No. 3048

Made	*24th November 2008*
Coming into force	*25th November 2008*

Citation, commencement and interpretation

1. These Regulations may be cited as the Immigration (Biometric Registration) Regulations 2008 and shall come into force on the day after the day on which they are made.

[2. In these Regulations—

'Certificate of Travel' means a travel document issued in the United Kingdom at the discretion of the Secretary of State to persons who have been formally and, in the view of the Secretary of State, unreasonably refused a passport by their own authorities and who have—

(a) been refused recognition as a refugee or as a stateless person but have been granted discretionary leave to remain or humanitarian protection; or

(b) been granted indefinite leave to enter or remain;

'Convention travel document' means a travel document issued pursuant to Article 28 of the Geneva Convention;

'dependant' means a spouse, a civil partner, an unmarried or same sex partner, or a child;

'Geneva Convention' means the Convention relating to the Status of Refugees done at Geneva on 28th July 1951 and the New York Protocol of 31st January 1967;

'humanitarian protection' means protection granted in accordance with paragraph 339C of the immigration rules;

'immigration rules' means the rules for the time being laid down as mentioned in section 3(2) of the Immigration Act 1971;

'leave to remain' means limited or indefinite leave to remain in the United Kingdom given in accordance with the provisions of the Immigration Act 1971 or the immigration rules;

'refugee' means a person who falls within Article 1(A) of the Geneva Convention and to whom regulation 7 of the Refugee or Person in Need of International Protection (Qualification) Regulations 2006 does not apply;

'Stateless Convention' means the Convention relating to the Status of Stateless Persons done at New York on 28th September 1954; and

'Stateless Person's Travel Document' means a travel document issued pursuant to Article 28 of the Stateless Convention.]

Note: Regulation 2 substituted from 28 February 2012 (SI 2012/594).

Requirement to apply for a biometric immigration document

[3.—(1) Subject to paragraph (6), a person subject to immigration control must apply for the issue of a biometric immigration document where he—

(a) satisfies the condition in paragraph (2); or

(b) is a person falling within paragraph (3).

(2) The condition is that whilst in the United Kingdom the person makes an application—

(a) for limited leave to remain for a period which, together with any preceding period of leave to enter or remain, exceeds a cumulative total of 6 months leave in the United Kingdom;

(b) for indefinite leave to remain;

(c) to replace a stamp, sticker or other attachment in a passport or other document which indicated that he had been granted limited or indefinite leave to enter or remain in the United Kingdom;

(d) to replace a letter which indicated that he had been granted limited or indefinite leave to enter or remain in the United Kingdom;

(e) to be recognised as a refugee or a person in need of humanitarian protection;

(f) to be recognised as a stateless person in accordance with Article 1 of the Stateless Convention;

(g) for a Convention Travel Document, Stateless Person's Travel Document or a Certificate of Travel and does not already hold a valid biometric immigration document; or

(h) as the dependant of a person who is making an application in accordance with subparagraph (a), (b), (e) or (f).

(3) Subject to paragraph (4), a person falls within this paragraph if he has been notified on or after 1st December 2012 that the Secretary of State has decided to grant him—

(a) limited leave to remain for a period which, together with any preceding period of leave to enter or remain, exceeds a cumulative total of 6 months leave in the United Kingdom; or

(b) indefinite leave to remain.

(4) A person does not fall within paragraph (3) if—

(a) he was required to apply for a biometric immigration document in respect of his application for that leave; or

(b) he was required to apply for a biometric immigration document in respect of any application mentioned in paragraph (2).

(5) Where a person is required to apply for a biometric immigration document, that application must be made on the form or in the manner specified for that purpose (if one is specified) in the immigration rules.

(6) These Regulations do not apply to a person who applies for or is granted leave to remain in accordance with paragraphs 56R and 56U of the immigration rules (Olympic or Paralympic Games Family Member Visitor or an Olympic or Paralympic Games Family Member Child Visitor).]

Note: Regulation 3 substituted from 28 February 2012 (SI 2012/594).

[Specified categories

4 . . .

Note: Regulation 4 omitted from 28 February 2012 (SI 2012/594).

Power for an authorised person to require a person to provide biometric information

5.—(1) Subject to regulation 7, where a person makes an application for the issue of a biometric immigration document in accordance with regulation 3, an authorised person may require him to provide a record of his fingerprints and a photograph of his face.

(2) Where an authorised person requires a person to provide biometric information in accordance with paragraph (1), the person must provide it.

Power for the Secretary of State to use and retain existing biometric information

6.—(1) This regulation applies where —

(a) a person makes an application for the issue of a biometric immigration document in accordance with regulation 3; and

(b) the Secretary of State already has a record of the person's fingerprints or a photograph of the person's face in his possession (for whatever reason).

(2) Where this regulation applies the Secretary of State may use or retain that information for the purposes of these Regulations.

Provision in relation to persons under the age of sixteen

7.—(1) A person under the age of sixteen ('the child') must not be required to provide a record of his fingerprints or a photograph of his face in accordance with regulation 5 except where the authorised person is satisfied that the fingerprints or the photograph will be taken in the presence of a person aged eighteen or over who is —

(a) the child's parent or guardian; or

(b) a person who for the time being takes responsibility for the child.

(2) The person mentioned in paragraph (1)(b) may not be —

(a) an officer of the Secretary of State who is not an authorised person;

(b) an authorised person; or

(c) any other person acting on behalf of an authorised person under regulation 8(2)(d).

(3) This regulation does not apply if the authorised person reasonably believes that the person who is to be fingerprinted or photographed is aged sixteen or over.

Process by which a person's fingerprints and photograph may be obtained and recorded

8.—(1) An authorised person who requires a person to provide a record of his fingerprints or a photograph of his face under regulation 5 may require the person to submit to any process, or any combination of processes, specified in paragraph (2).

(2) An authorised person may —

(a) require a person to make an appointment before a specified date, which the person must attend, to enable a record of his fingerprints or a photograph of his face to be taken;

(b) specify the date, time and place for the appointment;

(c) specify any documents which the person must bring to the appointment, or action which the person must take, to confirm his appointment and identity;

[(d) require a person to attend premises before a specified date where a record of his fingerprints or a photograph of his face is taken by a person on behalf of an authorised person; and

(e) specify any documents which the person must bring to the premises, or action which the person must take to confirm his identity.]

(3) An authorised person may require a record of fingerprints or photograph to be of a particular specification.

(4) Where an authorised person requires a person to submit to any process, or any combination of processes, in accordance with paragraph (1), the person must submit to it.

Note: Subparagraph (2)(d) substituted and 2(e) inserted from 28 February 2012 (SI 2012/594).

Use and retention of biometric information

9. Subject to regulations 10 and 11, the Secretary of State may use a record of a person's fingerprints or a photograph of a person's face provided in accordance with these Regulations —

(a) in connection with the exercise of a function by virtue of the Immigration Acts;

(b) in connection with the control of the United Kingdom's borders;

(c) in connection with the exercise of a function related to nationality;

(d) in connection with the prevention, investigation, or prosecution of an offence;

(e) for a purpose which appears to the Secretary of State to be required in order to protect national security;

(f) in connection with identifying victims of an event or situation which has caused loss of human life or human illness or injury;

(g) for the purpose of ascertaining whether any person has failed to comply with the law or has gained, or sought to gain, a benefit or service, or has asserted an entitlement, to which he is not by law entitled.

10. Subject to regulation 11, any record of a person's fingerprints or his photograph, or any copy of them, held by the Secretary of State pursuant to these Regulations must be destroyed if the Secretary of State thinks it is no longer likely to be of use in accordance with regulation 9.

11. If a person proves that he is —

(a) a British citizen; or

(b) a Commonwealth citizen who has a right of abode in the United Kingdom as a result of section 2(1)(b) of the Immigration Act 1971 (statement of right of abode in the United Kingdom).

Any record of the person's fingerprints or his photograph, or any copy of them, held by the Secretary of State pursuant to these Regulations must be destroyed as soon as reasonably practicable.

12.—(1) The Secretary of State must take all reasonably practicable steps to secure —

(a) that data held in an electronic form which relate to any record of fingerprints or photograph which has to be destroyed in accordance with regulation 10 or 11 are destroyed or erased; or

(b) that access to such data is blocked.

(2) The person to whom the data relate is entitled, on written request, to a certificate issued by the Secretary of State to the effect that he has taken the steps required by paragraph (1).

(3) A certificate issued under paragraph (2) must be issued within three months of the date on which the request was received by the Secretary of State.

Issue of a biometric immigration document

13.—(1) The Secretary of State may issue a biometric immigration document to a person who has applied in accordance with regulation 3, provided the Secretary of State has decided to—

[(a) grant limited leave to remain to the person for a period which, together with any preceding period of leave to enter or remain, exceeds a cumulative total of 6 months leave in the United Kingdom; or

(b) grant indefinite leave to remain to the person; or

(c) issue or replace a document to the person following an application mentioned in regulation 3(2)(c), (d) or (g).]

(2) A biometric immigration document begins to have effect on the date of issue.

(3) A biometric immigration document ceases to have effect on one of the dates specified in paragraph (4), whichever date occurs earliest.

(4) The specified dates are —

(a) the date that the person's leave to remain ceases to have effect, including where the leave to remain is varied, cancelled or invalidated, or is to lapse;

(b) in the case of a biometric immigration document which was issued to a person aged [sixteen] or over, the date after the expiry of ten years beginning with the date of issue; or

(c) in the case of a biometric immigration document which was issued to a person aged under [sixteen], the date after the expiry of five years beginning with the date of issue.

Note: Subparagraphs (1)(a)–(c) substituted/inserted from 28 February 2012 (SI 2012/594). Words in square brackets in paragraph (4) substituted from 31 March 2009, but without effect to biometric immigration documents issued before that date (SI 2009/819).

Requirement to surrender documents connected with immigration and nationality

14.—(1) On issuing the biometric immigration document, the Secretary of State may require the surrender of other documents connected with immigration or nationality.

(2) Where the Secretary of State requires the surrender of other documents, the person must comply with the requirement.

Content of a biometric immigration document

15.—(1) A biometric immigration document may contain some or all of the following information on the face of the document—

(a) the title of the document;

(b) the document number;

(c) the name of the holder;

(d) the holder's date of birth;

(e) the holder's place of birth;

(f) the holder's nationality;

(g) the sex of the holder;

(h) the period of leave to remain which the person is granted;

(i) the class of leave to remain which the person is granted;

(j) any conditions to which the limited leave to remain is subject or remarks relating to those conditions;

(k) the place and date of issue of the document;

(l) the period for which the document is valid;

(m) the holder's facial image;

(n) the signature of the holder;

(o) a machine readable code;

(p) a hologram;

(q) an emblem of the United Kingdom and the words 'United Kingdom';

(r) the symbol of the International Civil Aviation Organization denoting a machine readable travel document which contains a contactless microchip; and

(s) any additional security features.

(2) A biometric immigration document may contain some or all of the following within a radio frequency electronic microchip embedded in the document—

(a) any of the information specified in paragraph (1)(a) to (m);

(b) information relating to a record of any two of the holder's fingerprints; and

(c) any additional security features.

Surrender of a biometric immigration document

16.—(1) The Secretary of State may require the surrender of a biometric immigration document as soon as reasonably practicable if he thinks that —

(a) information provided in connection with the document was or has become false, misleading or incomplete;

(b) the document (including any information recorded in it) has been altered, damaged or destroyed (whether deliberately or not);

(c) an attempt has been made (whether successfully or not) to copy the document or to do anything to enable it to be copied;

(d) the document should be re-issued (whether because the information recorded in it requires alteration or for any other reason);

(e) the holder's leave to remain is to be varied, cancelled or invalidated, or is to lapse;

(f) a person has acquired the biometric immigration document without the consent of the holder or of the Secretary of State;

(g) the document has ceased to have effect under regulation 13(3) or has been cancelled under regulation 17; . . .

(h) the holder has died.

[(i) the holder has failed to produce a valid passport or travel document when required to do so by an immigration officer; or

(j) the holder has proved that he is a British citizen or a Commonwealth citizen who has a right of abode in the United Kingdom as a result of section 2(1)(b) of the Immigration Act 1971 (statement of right of abode in the United Kingdom).]

(2) Where a person is required to surrender the biometric immigration document under paragraph (1), the person must comply with the requirement.

Note: Subparagraphs (1)(i)–(j) inserted from 31 March 2009 (SI 2009/819).

Cancellation of a biometric immigration document

17. The Secretary of State may cancel a biometric immigration document if he thinks that—

(a) information provided in connection with the document was or has become false, misleading or incomplete;

(b) the document has been lost or stolen;

(c) the document (including any information recorded in it) has been altered, damaged or destroyed (whether deliberately or not);

(d) an attempt has been made (whether successfully or not) to copy the document or to do anything to enable it to be copied;

(e) a person has failed to surrender the document when required to do so under regulation [16(a) to (f), (h), (i) or (j);]

(f) the document should be re-issued (whether because the information recorded in it requires alteration or for any other reason);

(g) a person has acquired the biometric immigration document without the consent of the holder or of the Secretary of State; [. . .]

(h) the holder has died [or

(i) the holder has proved that he is a British citizen or a Commonwealth citizen who has a right of abode in the United Kingdom as a result of section 2(1)(b) of the Immigration Act 1971 (statement of right of abode in the United Kingdom).]

Note: Words in square brackets substituted and inserted from 31 March 2009 (SI 2009/819).

Requirement for the holder of a document to notify the Secretary of State

18. The holder of a biometric immigration document must notify the Secretary of State as soon as reasonably practicable if he —

(a) knows or suspects that information provided in connection with the document was or has become false, misleading or incomplete;

(b) knows or suspects that the document has been lost or stolen;

(c) knows or suspects that the document (including any information recorded in it) has been altered or damaged (whether deliberately or not);

(d) was given leave to enter or remain in the United Kingdom in accordance with a provision of the immigration rules and knows or suspects that owing to a change of his circumstances he would no longer qualify for leave under that provision; or

(e) knows or suspects that another person has acquired the biometric immigration document without his consent or the consent of the Secretary of State.

Requirement to apply for a replacement biometric immigration document

19.—(1) A person who has been issued with a biometric immigration document under regulation 13(1) is required to apply for a replacement biometric immigration document where his original document—

(a) has been cancelled under [paragraphs (a) to (g) of] regulation 17; or

(b) has ceased to have effect under regulation 13(4)(b) or (c).

(2) A person required to apply for a biometric immigration document under paragraph (1) must do so within 3 months beginning with the date that the original document was cancelled or ceased to have effect.

Note: Words in square brackets inserted from 31 March 2009 (SI 2009/819).

Application of these Regulations to a person who is required to apply for a replacement biometric immigration document

20.—(1) These Regulations apply to a person who makes an application for a biometric immigration document in accordance with regulation 19 just as they apply to a person who makes an application for a document in accordance with regulation 3, with the modification in paragraph (2).

(2) The Secretary of State may issue a biometric immigration document to a person who has applied in accordance with regulation 19, provided the person has limited leave to remain.

Requirement to use a biometric immigration document

21.—(1) The holder of a biometric immigration document must provide his document to an immigration officer or the Secretary of State, as applicable—

(a) where he is examined by an immigration officer under paragraph 2, 2A or 3 of Schedule 2 to the Immigration Act 1971;

(b) where he is examined by an immigration officer under Article 7(2) of the Immigration (Leave to Enter and Remain) Order 2000;

(c) where he is examined by the Secretary of State under Article 3 of the Immigration (Leave to Enter) Order 2001;

[(d) where he makes an application for entry clearance, leave to enter or leave to remain;

(da) where he makes an application to be recognised as a refugee, as a person in need of humanitarian protection, or as a stateless person in accordance with Article 1 of the Stateless Convention;

(db) where he applies as a dependant of a person who makes an application mentioned in sub-paragraph (d) or (da);

(dc) where he makes an application for a Convention Travel Document, Stateless Person's Travel Document or a Certificate of Travel;

(e) when his dependant makes an application—

(i) for entry clearance, leave to enter, leave to remain; or

(ii) to be recognised as a refugee, as a person in need of humanitarian protection, or as a stateless person in accordance with Article 1 of the Stateless Convention;]

(f) when he is the sponsor under the immigration rules of a person who seeks entry clearance, leave to enter or leave to remain in the United Kingdom.

(2) Where the holder of a biometric immigration document attends premises to take a test known under the immigration rules as the 'Life in the UK Test', he must provide his document to the representative of the educational institution, or other person, who is administering the test.

(3) The holder of a biometric immigration document must provide his document to a prospective employer or employer—

(a) prior to the commencement of his employment; and

(b) [where he has limited leave to remain,] on the anniversary of the date that the document was first produced, provided he is still working for that employer on that date.

[(4) Where the holder of a biometric immigration document makes—

(a) an application for a certificate of entitlement under section 10 of the Nationality, Immigration and Asylum Act 2002(a) that a person has the right of abode in the United Kingdom;

(b) an application for a letter or other document confirming a person's immigration or nationality status or that a person is not a British citizen;

(c) an application for naturalisation as a British citizen under section 6(1) or (2) of the British Nationality Act 1981(b), or as a British overseas territories citizen under section 18(1) or (2) of that Act; or

(d) an application for registration under any provision of the British Nationality Act 1981, he must provide his biometric immigration document to the Secretary of State or a person acting on behalf of the Secretary of State in connection with that application.]

Note: Subparagraphs (1)(d)–(e) substituted/inserted, words inserted in subparagraph (3)(b) and paragraph (4) inserted from 28 February 2012 (SI 2012/594).

Requirement to provide information for comparison

22.—(1) A person who provides a biometric immigration document in accordance with [regulation 21] is required to provide biometric information for comparison with biometric information provided in connection with the application for the document.

(2) Where the document is provided to an authorised person, the authorised person may require the provision of the information in a specified form.

(3) Regulation 8 applies to a person required to provide information under paragraph (1) as it applies to a person who is required to provide biometric information under regulation 5.

Note: Words substituted in paragraph (1) from 28 February 2012 (SI 2012/594).

Consequences of a failure to comply with a requirement of these Regulations

[**23.**—(1) Subject to paragraphs (3) and (4), where a person who is required to make an application for the issue of a biometric immigration document fails to comply with a requirement of these Regulations, the Secretary of State—

(a) may take any, or any combination, of the actions specified in paragraph (2); and
(b) must consider giving a notice under section 9 of the UK Borders Act 2007.

(2) The actions specified are to—

(a) refuse an application for a biometric immigration document;
(b) treat the person's application for leave to remain as invalid;
(c) refuse the person's application for leave to remain; and
(d) cancel or vary the person's leave to enter or remain.

(3) Where a person is required to apply for a biometric immigration document under regulation 3(2)(a) or (b) or as a dependant of a person who has made an application in accordance with regulation 3(2)(a) or (b) and fails to comply with a requirement of these Regulations, the Secretary of State—

(a) must refuse the person's application for a biometric immigration document;
(b) must treat the person's application for leave to remain as invalid; and
(c) may cancel or vary the person's leave to enter or remain.

(4) Where a person is required to apply for a biometric immigration document under regulation 3(2)(e), (f) or (g) or as the dependant of a person who has made an application in accordance with regulation 3(2)(e) or (f) and fails to comply with a requirement of these Regulations the Secretary of State—

(a) may refuse the application for a biometric immigration document; and
(b) must consider giving a notice under section 9 of the UK Borders Act 2007.

(5) Where any person apart from a person referred to in paragraph (1), (3) or (4) fails to comply with a requirement of these Regulations, the Secretary of State must consider giving a notice under section 9 of the UK Borders Act 2007.

(6) The Secretary of State may designate an adult as the person responsible for ensuring that a child complies with the requirements of these Regulations.]

Note: Regulation 23 substituted from 28 February 2012 (SI 2012/594).

Revocation and transitional provisions

24.—(1) Subject to paragraph (2), the Immigration (Biometric Registration) (Pilot) Regulations 2008 are revoked.

(2) The Immigration (Biometric Registration) (Pilot) Regulations 2008 continue to apply to a person who was required to apply for a biometric immigration document in accordance with regulation 3 of those Regulations before the coming into force of these Regulations, subject to paragraph (3).

(3) These Regulations apply to any application for leave to remain falling within regulation 3 of these Regulations, which is made by a person referred to in paragraph (2) on or after the coming into force of these Regulations.

The Appeals (Excluded Decisions) Order 2009
2009 No. 275

Citation and commencement

1. This Order may be cited as the Appeals (Excluded Decisions) Order 2009 and comes into force on 1 April 2009.

[Excluded decisions

2. For the purposes of section 11(1) of the Tribunals, Courts and Enforcement Act 2007, the following decisions of the First-tier Tribunal are excluded decisions—

(a) a decision under section 103 of the Immigration and Asylum Act 1999 (appeals); and

(b) a decision under paragraphs 22, 23, 24, 29, 30, 31, 32 and 33 of Schedule 2 to the Immigration Act 1971.]

Note: Article 2 substituted from 15 February 2010 (SI 2010/41).

3. For the purposes of sections 11(1) and 13(1) of the Tribunals, Courts and Enforcement Act 2007, the following decisions of the First-tier Tribunal or the Upper Tribunal are excluded decisions—

(a) . . .
(b) . . .
(c) . . .
(d) . . .
(e) . . .
(f) . . .
(g) . . .
(h) . . .
(i) . . .
(j) . . .
(k) . . .
(l) . . .
[(m) any procedural, ancillary or preliminary decision made in relation to an appeal against a decision under section 40A of the British Nationality Act 1981, section 82, 83 or 83A of the Nationality, Immigration and Asylum Act 2002, or regulation 26 of the Immigration (European Economic Area) Regulations 2006.]

Note: Paragraphs (a)–(l) not relevant to immigration law. Paragraph (m) inserted from 15 February 2010 (SI 2010/41).

Revocations

4. . . .

The Immigration and Asylum Act 1999 (Part V Exemption: Licensed Sponsors Tiers 2 and 4) Order 2009

SI 2009 No. 506

Citation and Commencement

1. This Order may be cited as the Immigration and Asylum Act 1999 (Part V Exemption: Licensed Sponsors Tiers 2 and 4) Order 2009 and shall come into force on 31 March 2009.

Interpretation

2. In this Order—

'the Act' means the Immigration and Asylum Act 1999;

'immediate family' means a Tier 2 or Tier 4 migrant's spouse, civil partner, unmarried partner, same-sex partner, dependant child under 18 or parent of a Tier 4 (Child) Student;

'immigration advice' and 'immigration services' have the same meanings as in section 82 of the Act;

'immigration rules' means rules made under section 3(2) of the Immigration Act 1971;

'licensed sponsor' means a person who has been granted a sponsor licence;

'Points based system' means the points-based system under Part 6A of the immigration rules;

'sponsor licence' means a licence granted by the Secretary of State to a person who, by virtue of such a grant, is licensed as a Sponsor under Tiers 2, 4 or 5 of the Points Based System;

'Tier 2 migrant' means a migrant who (i) makes an application of a kind identified in the immigration rules as requiring to be considered under 'Tier 2' of the immigration rules' points-based system or (ii) has been granted leave under the relevant paragraphs of the immigration rules;

'Tier 4 migrant' means a migrant who (i) makes an application of a kind identified in the immigration rules as requiring to be considered under 'Tier 4' of the immigration rules' points-based system or (ii) has been granted leave under the relevant paragraphs of the immigration rules;

Exemption of licensed sponsors

3.—(1) Subject to paragraphs (2) and (3) and for the purposes of section 84(4)(d) of the Act the following persons shall be specified, namely persons who are licensed sponsors of Tier 2 and Tier 4 migrants and who provide immigration advice or immigration services free of charge to those migrants or their immediate family.

(2) The immigration advice or services given must be restricted to matters relating to the migrant's application under Tier 2 or Tier 4 of the Points-based system or to an application for entry clearance, leave to enter or leave to remain made by that person's immediate family and which is dependent on the migrant's application under Tier 2 or Tier 4 of the Points-based system.

(3) For the purposes of paragraph (1), the person providing the immigration advice or immigration services must be the licensed sponsor.

The Transfer of Functions of the Asylum and Immigration Tribunal Order 2010
2010 No. 21

Citation and commencement

1. This Order may be cited as the Transfer of Functions of the Asylum and Immigration Tribunal Order 2010 and comes into force on 15th February 2010.

Transfer of functions and abolition of tribunal

2.—(1) The functions of the Asylum and Immigration Tribunal are transferred to the First-tier Tribunal.

(2) The Asylum and Immigration Tribunal is abolished.

Transfer of persons into the First-tier Tribunal and the Upper Tribunal

3. . . .

Transfer of Rules

4. The Asylum and Immigration Tribunal (Procedure) Rules 2005 and the Asylum and Immigration Tribunal (Procedure) (Fast-track) Rules 2005 have effect as if they were Tribunal Procedure Rules.

Consequential and transitional provisions

. . .

Schedule 4
Transitional and saving provisions

Appeals and applications for bail

1. An appeal under section 40A of the British Nationality Act 1981, section 82, 83 or 83A of the 2002 Act or regulation 26 of the Immigration (European Economic Area) Regulations 2006, or an application for bail under Schedule 2 to the Immigration Act 1971, made to the Asylum and Immigration Tribunal before 15 February 2010 but not determined before that date shall continue as an appeal or application before the First-tier Tribunal.

Section 103A applications

2. An application for review made to the Asylum and Immigration Tribunal under section 103A of the 2002 Act and Schedule 2 to the 2004 Act before 15 February 2010 but not determined before that date shall continue as an application to the First-tier Tribunal for permission to appeal to the Upper Tribunal under section 11 of the 2007 Act.

3. Where the Asylum and Immigration Tribunal or the appropriate court has made an order for reconsideration under section 103A of the 2002 Act before 15 February 2010, but reconsideration has not taken place before that date, the order for reconsideration shall be treated as an order granting permission to appeal to the Upper Tribunal under section 11 of the 2007 Act and sections 12 and 13 of the 2007 Act shall apply.

4. Where the reconsideration of an appeal by the Asylum and Immigration Tribunal under section 103A of the 2002 Act has commenced before 15 February 2010 but has not been determined, the reconsideration shall continue as an appeal to the Upper Tribunal under section 12 of the 2007 Act and section 13 of the 2007 Act shall apply.

5. An application for review made to the appropriate court under section 103A of the 2002 Act before 15 February 2010 but not determined before that date shall continue as an application for review under section 103A of the 2002 Act.

6. An order for reconsideration made by the appropriate court on or after 15 February 2010 which, if it had been made before that date would have been for reconsideration by the Asylum and Immigration Tribunal, shall be treated as an order granting permission to appeal to the Upper Tribunal under section 11 of the 2007 Act and sections 12 and 13 of the 2007 Act shall apply.

Section 103C references

7. A reference made by the appropriate court to the appropriate appellate court under section 103C of the 2002 Act before 15 February 2010 shall continue to be considered as a reference under section 103C of the 2002 Act.

8. A case remitted or restored by the appropriate appellate court on or after 15 February 2010 which, if it had been remitted or restored before that date would have been remitted to the Asylum and Immigration Tribunal or restored to the appropriate court, shall be remitted to the Upper Tribunal and sections 12 and 13 of the 2007 Act shall apply.

Section 103B and 103E applications

9. An application for permission to appeal to the appropriate appellate court made to the Asylum and Immigration Tribunal under section 103B or 103E of the 2002 Act before 15 February 2010 but not determined before that date shall continue as an application to the Upper Tribunal for permission to appeal to the relevant appellate court under section 13 of the 2007 Act.

10. An application for permission to appeal to the appropriate appellate court made to that court under section 103B or 103E of the 2002 Act before 15 February 2010 but not determined before that date shall continue as an application for permission to appeal to the appropriate appellate court under section 103B or 103E of the 2002 Act.

11. An appeal which is proceeding before the appropriate appellate court under section 103B or 103E of the 2002 Act before 15 February 2010 but which is not determined

before that date shall continue as an appeal to the appropriate appellate court under section 103B or 103E of the 2002 Act.

12. A case remitted by the appropriate appellate court on or after 15 February 2010 which, if it had been remitted before that date would have been remitted to the Asylum and Immigration Tribunal, shall be remitted to the Upper Tribunal and sections 12 and 13 of the 2007 Act shall apply.

Time limits

13.—(1) Where the time period for making an appeal or application has begun but not expired before 15 February 2010, in the case of—

(a) an appeal to the Asylum and Immigration Tribunal under section 40A of the British Nationality Act 1981, section 82, 83 or 83A of the 2002 Act or regulation 26 of the Immigration (European Economic Area) Regulations 2006, an appeal may be made within that period to the First-tier Tribunal;

(b) an application to the Asylum and Immigration Tribunal for review under section 103A of the 2002 Act and Schedule 2 to the 2004 Act, an application for permission to appeal to the Upper Tribunal under section 11 of the 2007 Act may be made within that period to the First-tier Tribunal;

(c) an application to the appropriate court for review under section 103A of the 2002 Act, an application may be made within that period under section 103A of the 2002 Act to the appropriate court;

(d) an application to the Asylum and Immigration Tribunal for permission to appeal to the appropriate appellate court under section 103B or 103E of the 2002 Act, an application for permission to appeal to the relevant appellate court under section 13 of the 2007 Act may be made within that period to the Upper Tribunal; and

(e) an application to the appropriate appellate court for permission to appeal to that court under section 103B or 103E of the 2002 Act, an application for permission to appeal to the relevant appellate court under section 13 of the 2007 Act may be made within that period to that court.

(2) Where an appeal or application mentioned in sub-paragraphs (1)(a) to (e) is made after the time period in question has expired, it must be made and decided in accordance with the relevant procedural rules or other enactments, as they apply on and after the transfer date.

(3) Where an appeal or application has been determined by the Asylum and Immigration Tribunal before the transfer date but the determination has not been served on the parties before that date, the determination shall be treated as if it were a determination of the First-tier Tribunal or (if it follows reconsideration) a determination of the Upper Tribunal, as the case may be, and the determination may be served accordingly.

(4) Sub-paragraph (3) applies, subject to any necessary modifications, to any other decision of the Asylum and Immigration Tribunal that has been made but not served before the transfer date.

General

14.—(1) This paragraph applies where proceedings are commenced or continued in the First-tier Tribunal or the Upper Tribunal by virtue of the provisions of this Schedule.

(2) The First-tier Tribunal or Upper Tribunal, as the case may be, may give any direction to ensure that the proceedings are dealt with fairly and, in particular, may apply any provision in procedural rules which applied to the proceedings before 15 February 2010.

(3) In sub-paragraph (2) "procedural rules" includes any provision (whether called rules or not) regulating practice or procedure before the Asylum and Immigration Tribunal.

(4) Any direction or order given or made in the proceedings which is in force immediately before 15 February 2010 remains in force on and after that date as if it were a direction or order of the First-tier Tribunal or Upper Tribunal, as the case may be, and may be varied accordingly.

(5) A time period which has started to run before 15 February 2010 and which has not expired shall continue to apply.

15. Any procedural, ancillary or preliminary matter before the Asylum and Immigration Tribunal before 15 February 2010 may, on or after that date, be considered by the First-tier Tribunal or the Upper Tribunal, as the case may be, as appropriate.

16.—(1) This paragraph applies when—

(a) the Asylum and Immigration Tribunal has started to reconsider or has reconsidered an appeal before 15 February 2010, but has not produced a determination before that date; and

(b) the reconsideration of the appeal continues as an appeal to the Upper Tribunal by virtue of paragraph 4.

(2) A member of the Asylum and Immigration Tribunal who was hearing or otherwise considering the appeal may take all such steps as the member considers necessary to determine the appeal and produce a determination on or after 15 February 2010.

17. In any judicial review proceedings before the High Court, the Court of Session or the High Court of Northern Ireland before 15 February 2010 where a matter could be remitted to the Asylum and Immigration Tribunal, on or after that date the matter may be remitted to the First-tier Tribunal or the Upper Tribunal as the court considers appropriate.

18. Staff appointed to the Asylum and Immigration Tribunal before 15 February 2010 are to be treated on and after that date, for the purpose of any enactment, as if they had been appointed by the Lord Chancellor under section 40(1) of the Tribunals, Courts and Enforcement Act 2007 (tribunal staff and services).

Saving provisions

19. In accordance with the provisions of this Schedule, sections 87(3) and (4), 103A, 103B, 103C and 103E of the 2002 Act, shall continue to apply to proceedings to which paragraphs 5, 7, 10 to 12 and 13(1)(c) and (2) (in relation to sub-paragraph (1)(c)) apply as if the repeals in Schedule 1 in respect of those sections of the 2002 Act had not been made.

20. Section 103D of the 2002 Act and the Community Legal Service (Asylum and Immigration Appeals) Regulations 2005 ("the 2005 Regulations") (legal aid funding arrangements) shall continue to apply to proceedings to which paragraphs 2 to 8 and 13(1)(b),

(c) and (2) (in relation to sub-paragraphs (1)(b) to (e)) apply until the proceedings are finally determined —

(a) as if the repeals in Schedule 1 in respect of sections 103A and 103D of the 2002 Act and rule 33 of the Asylum and Immigration Tribunal (Procedure) Rules 2005 ("the 2005 Rules"), and the repeals and revocations in Schedule 3 in respect of paragraph 30 of Schedule 2 to the 2004 Act and the 2005 Regulations had not been made;

(b) as if the references to the Tribunal in section 103D of the 2002 Act, paragraph 30 of Schedule 2 to the 2004 Act, the 2005 Regulations and rule 33 of the 2005 Rules were references to the First-tier Tribunal or the Upper Tribunal as appropriate, and the references to the appropriate court and the High Court were references to the Upper Tribunal where appropriate; and

(c) subject to any necessary modifications to the 2005 Regulations and the 2005 Rules.

Interpretation

21. In this Schedule—

'appropriate court' means—

(i) in relation to an appeal decided in England or Wales, the High Court;

(ii) in relation to an appeal decided in Scotland, the Outer House of the Court of Session; and

(iii) in relation to an appeal decided in Northern Ireland, the High Court of Northern Ireland;

'appropriate appellate court' means—

(iv) in relation to an appeal decided in England or Wales, the Court of Appeal;

(v) in relation to an appeal decided in Scotland, the Inner House of the Court of Session; and

(vi) in relation to an appeal decided in Northern Ireland, the Court of Appeal of Northern Ireland;

'the 2002 Act' means the Nationality, Immigration and Asylum Act 2002;

'the 2004 Act' means the Asylum and Immigration (Treatment of Claimants, etc.) Act 2004 (; and

'the 2007 Act' means the Tribunals, Courts and Enforcement Act 2007.

The First-tier Tribunal and Upper Tribunal (Chambers) Order 2010

SI 2010 No. 2655

Note: This is the text that has direct relevance to the Immigration and Asylum Chamber of the Tribunal.

Citation, commencement and revocations

1.—(1) This Order may be cited as the First-tier Tribunal and Upper Tribunal (Chambers) Order 2010 and comes into force on 29th November 2010.

(2) . . .

First-tier Tribunal Chambers

2. The First-tier Tribunal shall be organised into the following chambers—

. . .

(c) the Immigration and Asylum Chamber;

. . .

Functions of the Immigration and Asylum Chamber of the First-tier Tribunal

5. To the Immigration and Asylum Chamber of the First-tier Tribunal are allocated all functions related to immigration and asylum matters, with the exception of matters allocated to—

(a) the Social Entitlement Chamber by article 6(a);

(b) the General Regulatory Chamber by article 3(a).

Upper Tribunal Chambers

9. The Upper Tribunal shall be organised into the following chambers—

. . .

(b) the Immigration and Asylum Chamber of the Upper Tribunal;

. . .

Functions of the Immigration and Asylum Chamber of the Upper Tribunal

11. To the Immigration and Asylum Chamber of the Upper Tribunal are allocated all functions related to—

(a) an appeal against a decision of the First-tier Tribunal made in the Immigration and Asylum Chamber of the First-tier Tribunal;

(b) a matter referred to the Upper Tribunal under section 9(5)(b) of the Tribunals, Courts and Enforcement Act 2007 or under Tribunal Procedure Rules by the Immigration and Asylum Chamber of the First-tier Tribunal;

[(c) an application for the Upper Tribunal to grant relief mentioned in section 15(1) of the Tribunals, Courts and Enforcement Act 2007 (Upper Tribunal's "judicial review" jurisdiction), or to exercise the power of review under section 21(2) of that Act (Upper Tribunal's "judicial review" jurisdiction: Scotland), which is made by a person who claims to be a minor from outside the United Kingdom challenging a defendant's assessment of that person's age;]

[(d) an application for the Upper Tribunal to exercise the powers of review under section 21(2) of the Tribunals, Court and Enforcement Act (Upper Tribunal's "judicial review" jurisdiction: Scotland), which relates to a decision of the First-tier Tribunal mentioned in paragraph (a);]

[(e) an application for the Upper Tribunal to grant relief mentioned in section 15(1) of the Tribunals, Courts and Enforcement Act 2007 (Upper Tribunal's "judicial review" jurisdiction), which is designated as an immigration matter—

(i) in a direction made in accordance with Part 1 of Schedule 2 to the Constitutional Reform Act 2005 specifying a class of case for the purposes of section 18(6) of the Tribunals, Courts and Enforcement Act 2007; or

(ii) in an order of the High Court in England and Wales made under section 31A(3) of the Senior Courts Act 1981, transferring to the Upper Tribunal an application of a kind described in section 31A(1) of that Act.

Note: Subparagraphs (c), (d) and (e) substituted/inserted from 1 November 2013 (SI 2013/2068).

The First-tier Tribunal (Immigration and Asylum Chamber) Fees Order 2011
2011 No. 2841

Citation and commencement

1. This Order may be cited as the First-tier Tribunal (Immigration and Asylum Chamber) Fees Order 2011 and shall come into force on the day after the date on which it is made.

Interpretation

2. In this Order—

'an immigration or asylum matter' means a matter in respect of which functions are allocated to the Immigration and Asylum Chamber of the First-tier Tribunal under article 5 of the First-tier Tribunal and Upper Tribunal (Chambers) Order 2010(b);

'appellant' means any person identified in the notice of appeal as appealing in relation to an immigration and asylum matter to the First-tier Tribunal;

'BACS' means the method of payment known as 'Banks Automated Clearing System' by which money is transferred from one bank in the United Kingdom to another by means of an automated system;

'international money transfer' means a method of payment by which money is transferred from a bank account outside the United Kingdom to a bank account in the United Kingdom by means of an automated system;

'the 1971 Act' means the Immigration Act 1971;

'the 1999 Act' means the Immigration and Asylum Act 1999;

'the 2002 Act' means the Nationality, Immigration and Asylum Act 2002.

Fees for appeals

3.—(1) A fee is payable in respect of an appeal to the First-tier Tribunal where the appeal relates to an immigration or asylum matter and the decision against which the appeal is made was taken on or after the coming into force of this Order.

(2) The fee is payable by or in respect of each appellant on the date on which the Notice of Appeal is given.

(3) The fee payable is—

(a) where the appellant consents to the appeal being determined without a hearing, £80; or

(b) where the appellant does not consent to the appeal being determined without a hearing, £140.

(4) Subject to paragraph (5), where after making payment in accordance with paragraph (3)(a), the appellant withdraws their consent to the appeal being determined without a hearing, the difference between the amounts specified in subparagraphs (a) and (b) of paragraph (3) ('the balance') becomes payable on the withdrawal of that consent.

(5) The balance referred to in paragraph (4) ceases to be payable if the Tribunal decides that the appeal can be justly determined without a hearing.

(6) This article is subject to articles 5, 6 and 7.

Method of paying fee

4.—(1) The fee payable must be paid by one of the following methods—

(a) credit card;

(b) debit card;

(c) BACS; or

(d) international money transfer.

(2) For the purposes of enabling payment to be made by or in respect of the appellant—

(a) authorisation to take payment and details of the credit or debit card, or

(b) an undertaking by or on behalf of each appellant to pay by BACS or an international money transfer, must be provided at the same time as the giving of the notice of appeal or the subsequent withdrawal of their consent to the appeal being determined without a hearing (as the case may be).

Exemption from fees

5.—(1) No fee is payable for—

(a) an appeal against a decision made under—

(i) section 2A of the 1971 Act(d) (deprivation of right of abode);

(ii) section 5(1) of the 1971 Act (a decision to make a deportation order);

(iii) paragraphs 8, 9,10, 10A or 12(2) of Schedule 2 to the 1971 Act(a) (a decision that an illegal entrant, any family or seaman and aircrew is or are to be removed from the United Kingdom by way of directions);

(iv) section 40 of the British Nationality Act 1981(b) (deprivation of citizenship);

(v) section 10(1) of the 1999 Act (removal of certain persons unlawfully in the United Kingdom);

(vi) section 76 of the 2002 Act (revocation of indefinite leave to enter or remain in the United Kingdom);

(vii) section 47 of the Immigration, Asylum and Nationality Act 2006(d) (removal: persons with statutorily extended leave);

(viii) regulation 19(3) of the Immigration (European Economic Area) Regulations 2006 (a decision to remove an EEA national or the family member of such a national); or

(b) an appeal to which Part 2 of the Asylum and Immigration Tribunal (Fast Track Procedure) Rules 2005 applies.

(2) No fee is payable where, at the time the fee would otherwise become payable, the appellant is, under the 1999 Act—

(a) a 'supported person' as defined in section 94(1); or

(b) provided with temporary support under section 98.

(3) No fee is payable where, for the purpose of proceedings before the Tribunal, the appellant is in receipt of—

(a) [civil legal services (within the meaning of Part 1 of the Legal Aid, Sentencing and Punishment of Offenders Act 2012) made available under arrangements made for the purposes of that Part of that Act;]

(b) legal aid under Part 2 of the Legal Aid, Advice and Assistance (Northern Ireland) Order 1981; or

(c) civil legal aid or advice and assistance under the Legal Aid (Scotland) Act 1986.

(4) No fee is payable where the appellant is the person for whose benefit services are provided by a local authority under section 17 of the Children Act 1989.

(5) Where by any convention, treaty or other instrument entered into by Her Majesty with any foreign power it is provided that no fee is required to be paid in respect of any proceedings, the fees specified in this Order are not payable in respect of those proceedings.

Note: Subparagraph (3)(a) substituted from 1 April 2013 (SI 2013/534).

Power to defer payment in certain cases

6. The Lord Chancellor may defer payment of a fee where the appeal is brought on the grounds that the removal of the appellant from, or a requirement for the appellant to leave, the United Kingdom would breach the United Kingdom's obligations under either—

(a) the Convention relating to the Status of Refugees done at Geneva on 28 July 1951 and the Protocol to the Convention; or

(b) article 21 of Directive 2004/83/EC of the European Parliament and Council of 29 April 2004.

Reduction or remission of fees

7. A fee specified in this Order may be reduced or remitted where the Lord Chancellor is satisfied that there are exceptional circumstances which justify doing so.

Certificate of fee satisfaction

8.—(1) The Lord Chancellor must issue a certificate of fee satisfaction if satisfied that—

(a) the appropriate fee payable under article 3 has been paid;

(b) in view of an undertaking given by or on behalf of the appellant, payment will be promptly made by BACS or an international money transfer;

(c) no fee is payable;

(d) payment is to be deferred in accordance with article 6; or

(e) the appellant has, at the time a fee would otherwise be payable under article 3, applied for the fee to be reduced or remitted in accordance with article 7.

(2) The issuing of such a certificate is without prejudice to the power to recover the amount of any payable fee or part of such fee which remains unpaid and unremitted.

(3) The Lord Chancellor may revoke a certificate of fee satisfaction and if a certificate is revoked, the Tribunal shall be notified accordingly.

Refunds

9.—(1) Subject to paragraph (2) —

(a) where the fee payable under article 3(3)(b) has been paid but the appeal is determined without a hearing, the difference between the amounts specified in article 3(3)(a) and 3(3)(b) may be refunded; and

(b) where a fee has been paid which the Lord Chancellor, if all the circumstances had been known, would have reduced or remitted under article 7, the fee or the amount by which the fee would have been reduced, as the case may be, shall be refunded.

(2) No refund will be made under this article unless the appellant applies in writing to the Lord Chancellor within 6 months of the date the fee becomes payable.

(3) The Lord Chancellor may extend the period of 6 months mentioned in paragraph (2) if the Lord Chancellor considers there is a good reason for the application being made after the end of the period of 6 months.

The Immigration Appeals (Family Visitor) Regulations 2012

2012 No. 1532

The Secretary of State, in exercise of the powers conferred by sections 88A(1)(a), 2(a) and (c) and 112(1) and (3) of the Nationality, Immigration and Asylum Act 2002(1), makes the following Regulations:

Citation and commencement

1. These Regulations may be cited as the Immigration Appeals (Family Visitor) Regulations 2012 and shall come into force on 9th July 2012.

Class or description of person to be visited

2.—(1) A person ("P") is of a class or description prescribed for the purposes of section 88A(1)(a) of the Nationality, Immigration and Asylum Act 2002 (entry clearance), if—

(a) the applicant for entry clearance ("A") is a member of the family of P; and

(b) P's circumstances match those specified in regulation 3.

(2) For the purposes of paragraph (1), A is a member of the family of P if A is the—

(a) spouse, civil partner, father, mother, son, daughter, grandfather, grandmother, grandson, granddaughter, brother or sister;

(b) father-in-law, mother-in-law, brother-in-law or sister-in-law;

(c) son-in-law or daughter-in-law; or

(d) stepfather, stepmother, stepson, stepdaughter, stepbrother or stepsister; of P.

(3) For the purposes of paragraph (1), A is also a member of the family of P if A is the partner of P.

(4) In this regulation, A is the partner of P if—

(a) A and P have been in a relationship that is akin to a marriage or civil partnership for at least the two years before the day on which A's application for entry clearance was made; and

(b) such relationship is genuine and subsisting.

(5) In this regulation—

(a) "father-in-law of P" includes the father of P's civil partner;

(b) "mother-in-law of P" includes the mother of P's civil partner;

(c) "brother-in-law of P" includes the brother of P's civil partner;

(d) "sister-in-law of P" includes the sister of P's civil partner;

(e) "son-in-law of P" includes the son of P's civil partner;

(f) "daughter-in-law of P" includes the daughter of P's civil partner;

(g) "stepfather of P" includes the person who is the civil partner of A's father (but is not A's parent);

(h) "stepmother of P" includes the person who is the civil partner of A's mother (but is not A's parent);

(i) "stepson of P" includes the person who is the son of A's civil partner (but is not A's son);

(j) "stepdaughter of P" includes the person who is the daughter of A's civil partner (but is not A's daughter);

(k) "stepbrother of P" includes the person who is the son of the civil parent of A's parent (but is not the son of either of A's parents); and

(l) "stepsister of P" includes the person who is the daughter of the civil partner of A's parent (but is not the daughter of either of A's parents).

Circumstances of the person to be visited

3. The circumstances of P mentioned in regulation 2(1)(b) are that P–

(a) is settled in the United Kingdom as defined in paragraph 6(2) of the immigration rules;

(b) has been granted asylum in the United Kingdom under paragraph 334(3) of the immigration rules; or

(c) has been granted humanitarian protection in the United Kingdom under paragraph 339C(4) of the immigration rules.

Transitional provision

4. These Regulations apply only to an application for entry clearance made on or after the day on which they come into force.

The Immigration, Asylum and Nationality Act 2006 (Commencement No. 8 and Transitional and Saving Provisions) (Amendment) Order 2012

2012 No. 1531 (C. 57)

The Secretary of State, in exercise of the powers conferred by section 62 of the Immigration, Asylum and Nationality Act 2006, makes the following Order:

Citation and commencement

1. This Order may be cited as the Immigration, Asylum and Nationality Act 2006 (Commencement No. 8 and Transitional and Saving Provisions) (Amendment) Order 2012 and shall come into force on 9th July 2012.

Amendment of the Immigration, Asylum and Nationality Act 2006 (Commencement No. 8 and Transitional and Saving Provisions) Order 2008

2. . . .

Note: Article 2 amends Art 4 of SI 2008/310.

Saving provision

3. Notwithstanding the substitution of section 88A of the Nationality, Immigration and Asylum Act 2002 for section 90 of that Act, section 90 and the Immigration Appeals (Family Visitor) Regulations 2003 continue to have effect in relation to an appeal brought in respect of an application for entry clearance made before 9th July 2012.

The Immigration (European Economic Area) (Amendment) Regulations 2012
(SI 2012, No. 1547)

Citation

1. These Regulations may be cited as the Immigration (European Economic Area) (Amendment) Regulations 2012.

2–4. . . .

Note: Articles 2–4 and Schs 1 and 2 amend the Immigration (European Economic Area) Regulations 2006 (SI 2006/1003) and make consequential amendments.

Schedule 3
Transitional Provisions

Interpretation

1. In this Schedule—

(a) the "2006 Regulations" means the Immigration (European Economic Area) Regulations 2006; and

(b) the terms "EEA family permit", "EEA State", "family member", "registration certificate" and "residence card" have the meanings given in regulation 2(1) of the 2006 Regulations.

Amendments to the definition of EEA national

2.—(1) Where the right of a family member ("F") to be admitted to, or reside in, the United Kingdom pursuant to the 2006 Regulations depends on the fact that a person ("P") is an EEA national, P will, notwithstanding the effect of paragraph 1(d) of Schedule 1 to these Regulations, continue to be regarded as an EEA national for the purpose of the 2006 Regulations where the criteria in subparagraphs (2), (3) or (4) are met and for as long as they remain satisfied in accordance with subparagraph (5).

(2) The criterion in this subparagraph is met where F was on 16th July 2012 a person with a permanent right to reside in the United Kingdom under the 2006 Regulations.

(3) The criteria in this subparagraph are met where F—

(a) was on the 16th July 2012 a person with a right to reside in the United Kingdom under the 2006 Regulations; and

(b) on the 16th October 2012—

(i) held a valid registration certificate or residence card issued under the 2006 Regulations;

(ii) had made an application under the 2006 Regulations for a registration certificate or residence card which had not been determined; or

(iii) had made an application under the 2006 Regulations for a registration certificate or residence card which had been refused and in respect of which an appeal under regulation 26 could be brought while the appellant is in the United Kingdom (excluding the possibility of an appeal out of time with permission) or was pending (within the meaning of section 104 of the Nationality, Immigration and Asylum Act 2002(19)).

(4) The criteria in this sub-paragraph are met where F—

(a) had, prior to the 16th July 2012, applied for an EEA family permit pursuant to regulation 12 of the 2006 Regulations; or

(b) has applied for and been refused an EEA family permit and where, on the 16th July 2012, an appeal under regulation 26 against that decision could be brought (excluding the possibility of an appeal out of time with permission) or was pending (within the meaning of section 104 of the 2002 Act).

(5) Where met, the criteria in subparagraph (2), (3) and (4) remain satisfied until the occurrence of the earliest of the following events—

(a) the date six months after an EEA family permit has been issued if F has not within that period been admitted to the United Kingdom;

(b) the date on which an appeal against a decision referred to in subparagraph (3)(b)(iii) or (4)(b) can no longer be brought (ignoring the possibility of an appeal out of time with permission) where no such appeal has been brought;

(c) the date on which any appeal against a decision referred to in sub-paragraph (3)(b)(iii) or (4)(b) is finally determined, is withdrawn or is abandoned (within the meaning of section 104 of the 2002 Act) (save where the outcome of the appeal process is that the document in question falls to be granted);

(d) the date on which F ceases to be the family member of an EEA national; or

(e) the date on which a right of permanent residence under regulation 15 of the 2006 Regulations is lost in accordance with regulation 15(2) of those Regulations.

(6) P will only continue to be regarded as an EEA national for the purpose of considering the position of F under the 2006 Regulations.

Note: Schedule 3 in force from 16 July 2012 (Article 2).

The Accession of Croatia (Immigration and Worker Authorisation) Regulations 2013
(SI 2013/1460)

The Secretary of State makes the following Regulations in exercise of the powers conferred by section 4 of the European Union (Croatian Accession and Irish Protocol) Act 2013.

In accordance with section 5(1) of that Act, a draft of this instrument was laid before Parliament and approved by resolution of each House of Parliament.

PART 1
INTERPRETATION ETC.

Citation, commencement, interpretation and consequential amendments

1.—(1) These Regulations may be cited as the Accession of Croatia (Immigration and Worker Authorisation) Regulations 2013 and come into force on 1st July 2013.

(2) In these Regulations—

"the 1971 Act" means the Immigration Act 1971(b);

"the 2006 Act" means the Immigration, Asylum and Nationality Act 2006(c);

"accession period" means the period beginning with 1st July 2013 and ending with 30th June 2018;

"accession State national subject to worker authorisation" has the meaning given in regulation 2;

"accession worker authorisation document" has the meaning given in regulation 8(2);

"authorised category of employment" means—

(a) employment for which the applicant has been issued by a sponsor with a valid certificate of sponsorship under Tier 2 or Tier 5 of the Points-Based System; or

(b) employment as—

(i) a representative of an overseas business;

(ii) a postgraduate doctor or dentist; or

(iii) a domestic worker in a private household;

"certificate of sponsorship" has the meaning given in paragraph 6 of the immigration rules, except that the reference to an application or potential application for entry clearance or leave to enter or remain as a Tier 2 migrant or a Tier 5 migrant is to be read as including a reference to an application or potential application for a worker authorisation registration certificate;

"certificate of sponsorship checking service" has the meaning given in paragraph 6 of the immigration rules, except that the reference to an application or potential application for entry clearance or leave to enter or remain as a Tier 2 migrant or a Tier 5 migrant is to be read as including a reference to an application or potential application for a worker authorisation registration certificate;

"civil partner" does not include a party to a civil partnership of convenience;

"EEA registration certificate" means a certificate issued in accordance with regulation 16 of the EEA Regulations;

"the EEA Regulations" means the Immigration (European Economic Area) Regulations 2006;

"EEA State" excludes the United Kingdom and includes Switzerland;

"employer" means, in relation to a worker, the person who directly pays the wage or salary of that worker, and "employ", "employment" and "employs" shall be construed accordingly;

"the EU2 Regulations" means the Accession (Immigration and Worker Authorisation) Regulations 2006;

"extended family member" has the meaning given in regulation 8 of the EEA Regulations;

"family member" has the meaning given in regulation 7 of the EEA Regulations;

"highly skilled person" has the meaning given in regulation 3;

"immigration rules" means the rules laid down as mentioned in section 3(2) of the 1971 Act applying (except for in the definition of "relevant requirements") on 1st July 2013;

"Points-Based System" means the system established under Part 6A of the immigration rules;

"relevant requirements" means, in relation to an authorised category of employment, the requirements which, subject to any necessary modifications, a person in that category of employment was obliged to meet under the immigration rules in force on 9th December 2011 in order to obtain entry clearance or leave to enter or remain in the United Kingdom and which are set out in the relevant statement;

["relevant statement" means the statement entitled "the Statement of relevant requirements" dated April 2014 and published by the Secretary of State;]

"right to reside" shall be interpreted in accordance with the EEA Regulations and "entitled to reside" and "right of residence" shall be construed accordingly;

"sponsor" means the holder of a sponsor licence(e);

"sponsor licence" has the meaning given in paragraph 6 of the immigration rules;

"spouse" does not include a party to a marriage of convenience;

"student" has the meaning given in regulation 4(1)(d) of the EEA Regulations;

"Tier 2" and "Tier 5" shall be construed in accordance in paragraph 6 of the immigration rules, except that the reference to the grant of leave is to be read as including a reference to the issuing of a worker authorisation registration certificate;

"unmarried or same sex partner" means a person who is in a durable relationship with another person;

"work" and "working" shall be construed in accordance with the meaning of "worker"; and

"worker authorisation registration certificate" means a certificate issued in accordance with regulation 10 of these Regulations.

(3) The Schedule (consequential amendments) shall have effect.

Note: Definition of 'relevant statement' substituted from 6 April 2014 (SI 2014/530).

"Accession State national subject to worker authorisation"

2.—(1) Subject to the following paragraphs of this regulation, other than where these Regulations expressly refer to an accession State national subject to worker authorisation within the meaning of regulation 2 of the EU2 Regulations, in these Regulations "accession State national subject to worker authorisation" means a Croatian national.

(2) A Croatian national is not an accession State national subject to worker authorisation if, on 30th June 2013, he had leave to enter or remain in the United Kingdom under the 1971 Act that was not subject to any condition restricting his employment [(other than a condition restricting his employment as a doctor in training or as a dentist in training or as a professional sportsperson (including as a sports coach))], or he is given such leave after that date.

(3) A Croatian national is not an accession State national subject to worker authorisation if he was legally working in the United Kingdom on 30th June 2013 and had been legally working in the United Kingdom without interruption throughout the preceding period of 12 months ending on that date.

(4) A Croatian national who legally works in the United Kingdom without interruption for a period of 12 months falling partly or wholly after 30th June 2013 ceases to be an accession State national subject to worker authorisation at the end of that period of 12 months.

(5) For the purposes of paragraphs (3) and (4) of this regulation—

(a) a person working in the United Kingdom during a period falling before 1st July 2013 was legally working in the United Kingdom during that period if—

(i) he had leave to enter or remain in the United Kingdom under the 1971 Act for that period, that leave allowed him to work in the United Kingdom, and he was working in accordance with any condition of that leave restricting his employment;

(ii) he was exempt from the provisions of the 1971 Act by virtue of section 8(2) or (3) of that Act (persons exempted by order or membership of diplomatic mission); or

(iii) he was entitled to reside in the United Kingdom for that period under the EEA Regulations without the requirement for such leave;

(b) a person working in the United Kingdom on or after 1st July 2013 is legally working in the United Kingdom during any period in which he—

(i) falls within any of paragraphs (6) to (16) or (18); or

(ii) holds an accession worker authorisation document and is working in accordance with the conditions set out in that document; and

(c) a person shall be treated as having worked in the United Kingdom without interruption for a period of 12 months if—

(i) he was legally working in the United Kingdom at the beginning and end of that period; and

(ii) during that period of 12 months, if his work in the United Kingdom was interrupted, any intervening periods of interruption did not exceed 30 days in total.

(6) Other than during any period in which he is also an accession State national subject to worker authorisation within the meaning of regulation 2 of the EU2 Regulations, a Croatian national is not an accession State national subject to worker authorisation during any period in which he is also a national of—

(a) the United Kingdom; or

(b) an EEA State, other than Croatia.

(7) A Croatian national is not an accession State national subject to worker authorisation during any period in which he is also an accession State national subject to worker authorisation within the meaning of regulation 2 of the EU2 Regulations and is working in accordance with those Regulations.

(8) A Croatian national is not an accession State national subject to worker authorisation during any period in which he is the spouse, civil partner, unmarried or same sex

partner, or child under 18 of a person who has leave to enter or remain in the United Kingdom under the 1971 Act and that leave allows him to work in the United Kingdom.

(9) A Croatian national is not an accession State national subject to worker authorisation during any period in which he is the spouse, civil partner, unmarried or same sex partner of—

(a) a national of the United Kingdom; or

(b) a person that is settled in the United Kingdom in accordance with the meaning given in section 33(2A) (interpretation – meaning of "settled") of the 1971 Act.

(10) A Croatian national is not an accession State national subject to worker authorisation during any period in which he is a member of a mission or other person mentioned in section 8(3) (member of a diplomatic mission, the family member of such a person, or a person otherwise entitled to diplomatic immunity) of the 1971 Act, other than a person who, under section 8(3A) (conditions of membership of a mission) of that Act, does not count as a member of a mission for the purposes of section 8(3).

(11) A Croatian national is not an accession State national subject to worker authorisation during any period in which he is a person who is exempt from all or any of the provisions of the 1971 Act by virtue of an order made under section 8(2) (exemption for persons specified by order) of that Act.

(12) A Croatian national is not an accession State national subject to worker authorisation during any period in which he has a permanent right of residence under regulation 15 of the EEA Regulations.

(13) Subject to paragraph (14), a Croatian national is not an accession State national subject to worker authorisation during any period in which he is a family member (X) of an EEA national (Y) who has a right to reside in the United Kingdom.

(14) Where Y is an accession State national subject to worker authorisation under these Regulations or an accession State national subject to worker authorisation within the meaning of regulation 2 of the EU2 Regulations, paragraph (13) only applies where X is the—

(a) spouse or civil partner of Y;

(b) unmarried or same sex partner of Y; or

(c) a direct descendant of Y, Y's spouse or Y's civil partner who is—

(i) under 21; or

(ii) dependant of Y, Y's spouse or Y's civil partner.

(15) A Croatian national is not an accession State national subject to worker authorisation during any period in which he is a highly skilled person and holds an EEA registration certificate issued in accordance with regulation 7 that includes a statement that he has unconditional access to the United Kingdom labour market.

(16) A Croatian national is not an accession State national subject to worker authorisation during any period in which he is in the United Kingdom as a student and either—

(a) holds an EEA registration certificate that includes a statement that he is a student who may work in the United Kingdom whilst a student in accordance with the condition set out in paragraph (17) and complies with that condition; or

(b) has leave to enter or remain under the 1971 Act as a student and is working in accordance with any conditions attached to that leave.

(17) The condition referred to in paragraph (16)(a) is that the student shall not work for more than 20 hours a week unless—

(a) he is following a course of vocational training and is working as part of that training; or

(b) he is working during his vacation.

(18) A Croatian national who ceases to be a student at the end of his course of study is not an accession State national subject to worker authorisation during the period of four months beginning with the date on which his course ends provided he holds an EEA registration certificate that was issued to him before the end of the course that includes a statement that he may work during that period.

(19) A Croatian national is not an accession State national subject to worker authorisation during any period in which he is a posted worker.

(20) In paragraph (19), "posted worker" means a worker who is posted to the United Kingdom, within the meaning of Article 1(3) of the Council Directive 96/71/EC of the European Parliament and of the Council of 16 December 1996 concerning the posting of workers in the framework of the provision of services, by an undertaking established in an EEA State.

Note: Words in square brackets in paragraph (2) inserted from 6 April 2014 (SI 2014/530).

"Highly skilled person"

3.—(1) In these Regulations "highly skilled person" means a person who—

(a) meets the requirements specified by the Secretary of State for the purpose of paragraph 245BB(c) (requirements for entry clearance as a Tier 1 (Exceptional Talent) migrant) of the immigration rules; or

(b) has been awarded one of the following qualifications and applies for an EEA registration certificate within 12 months of being awarded the qualification—

(i) a recognised bachelor, masters or doctoral degree;

(ii) a postgraduate certificate in education or professional graduate diploma of education; or

(iii) a higher national diploma awarded by a Scottish higher education institution.

(2) For the purposes of paragraph (1)(b), the qualification must have been awarded by a higher education institution which, on the date of the award, is a UK recognised body or an institution that is not a UK recognised body but which provides full courses that lead to the award of a degree by a UK recognised body.

(3) For the purposes of paragraph (1)(b)(iii), to qualify as a higher national diploma from a Scottish institution, a qualification must be at level 8 on the Scottish credit and qualifications framework.

(4) In this regulation, a "UK recognised body" means an institution that has been granted degree awarding powers by a Royal Charter, an Act of Parliament or the Privy Council.

Part 2

Application of the EEA Regulations and Other Instruments

Derogation from provisions of European Union law relating to workers

4. Pursuant to Annex V of the treaty concerning the accession of the Republic of Croatia to the European Union, signed at Brussels on 9 December 2011, Regulations 5 and 7 to 10 derogate during the accession period from Article 45 of the Treaty on the Functioning of the European Union, Articles 1 to 6 of Regulation (EEC) No. 1612/68 of the Council of 15

October 1968 on freedom of movement for workers within the Community and Directive 2004/38/EC of the European Parliament and of the Council of 29 April 2004 on the right of citizens of the Union and their family members to move and reside freely within the territory of the member States, amending Regulation (EEC) No. 1612/68, and repealing Directives 64/221/EEC, 68/360/EEC, 72/194/EEC, 73/148/EEC, 75/34/EEC, 75/35/EEC, 90/364/EEC, 90/365/EEC and 93/96/EEC.

Right of residence of an accession State national subject to worker authorisation

[5. During the accession period, an accession State national subject to worker authorisation who is seeking employment in the United Kingdom shall not be treated as a jobseeker and shall be treated as a worker only in so far as it gives him a right to reside and only during a period in which he holds an accession worker authorisation document and is working in accordance with the conditions set out in that document.]

Note: Regulation 5 substituted from 6 April 2014 (SI 2014/530).

Transitional provisions to take account of the application of the EEA Regulations to Croatian nationals and their family members on 1st July 2013

6.—(1) Where, before 1st July 2013, any direction has been given for the removal of a Croatian national or the family member of such a national under paragraphs 8 to 10A of Schedule 2 (removal of persons refused leave to enter and illegal entrants) to the 1971 Act, section 10 (removal of certain persons unlawfully in the United Kingdom) of the 1999 Act or section 47 (removal: persons with statutorily extended leave) of the 2006 Act, that direction shall cease to have effect on that date.

(2) Where before 1st July 2013 the Secretary of State has made a deportation order against a Croatian national or the family member of such a national under section 5(1) (deportation orders) of the 1971 Act—

(a) that order shall, on and after 1st July 2013, be treated as if it were a decision under regulation 19(3)(b) of the EEA Regulations; and

(b) any appeal against that order, or against the refusal of the Secretary of State to revoke the deportation order, made before 1st July 2013 under section 63 (deportation orders) of the 1999 Act, or under section 82(2)(j) or (k) (right of appeal: general) of the 2002 Act shall, on or after that date, be treated as if it had been made under regulation 26 of the EEA Regulations.

(3) In this regulation—

(a) "the 1999 Act" means the Immigration and Asylum Act 1999;

(b) "the 2002 Act" means the Nationality, Immigration and Asylum Act 2002; and

(c) any reference to the family member of a Croatian national is, in addition to the definition set out in regulation 1(2), a reference to a person who on 1st July 2013 acquires a right to reside in the United Kingdom under the EEA Regulations as the family member of a Croatian national.

Issuing EEA registration certificates and residence cards

7.—(1) During the accession period, regulation 6 of the EEA Regulations has effect as if, in paragraph (1), after "EEA national", there were inserted ", except an accession

State national subject to worker authorisation within the meaning of regulation 2 of the Croatian Regulations," and after paragraph (1), there were inserted—

"(**1A**) In these Regulations, a "qualified person" also means a person who is an accession State national subject to worker authorisation within the meaning of regulation 2 of the Croatian Regulations and in the United Kingdom as—

(a) a self-employed person;

(b) a self-sufficient person;

(c) a student; or

(d) a highly skilled person who is seeking employment or is employed in the United Kingdom.

[(**1B**) In regulation 14(2), regulation 16(3) and (5) and regulation 17(1) and (4) a "qualified person" includes an accession State national subject to worker authorisation within the meaning of regulation 2 of the Croatian Regulations where that accession State national subject to worker authorisation has a right to reside.]

(**1C**) In these Regulations—

(a) "the Croatian Regulations" means the Accession of Croatia (Immigration and Worker Authorisation) Regulations 2013; and

(b) "highly skilled worker" has the meaning given in regulation 1 of the Croatian Regulations."

(**2**) Subject to paragraph (6), an EEA registration certificate issued to a Croatian national during the accession period shall include a statement that the holder of the certificate has unconditional access to the United Kingdom labour market, unless that person is not an accession State national subject to worker authorisation solely by virtue of falling within paragraph (16) or (18) of regulation 2.

(**3**) A Croatian national who holds an EEA registration certificate that does not include a statement that he has unconditional access to the United Kingdom labour market may, during the accession period, submit the certificate to the Secretary of State for the inclusion of such a statement.

(**4**) The Secretary of State must re-issue a EEA certificate submitted to her under paragraph (3) with the inclusion of a statement that the holder has unconditional access to the United Kingdom labour market if she is satisfied that the holder—

(a) is a qualified person within the meaning of paragraph (1A) of regulation 6 of the EEA Regulations as applied by paragraph (1); or

(b) has ceased to be an accession State national subject to worker authorisation other than solely by virtue of falling within paragraph (16) or (18) of regulation 2.

(**5**) An EEA registration certificate issued to a Croatian national who is a student during the accession period shall include a statement that the holder of the certificate is a student who may work in the United Kingdom whilst a student in accordance with the condition set out in paragraph (17) of regulation 2 and who, on ceasing to be a student, may work during the period referred to in paragraph (18) of regulation 2, unless it includes a statement under paragraph (2) or (4) that the holder has unconditional access to the United Kingdom labour market.

(**6**) Where under paragraph (5) of regulation 16 of the EEA Regulations an EEA registration certificate is issued to a Croatian national extended family member [with the exception of an extended family member who is an unmarried partner (including a same sex partner),] of an accession State national subject to worker authorisation, the certificate must include a statement that the certificate does not confer a permission to work.

[(7) Where under paragraph (1) or (4) of regulation 17 of the EEA Regulations a residence card is issued to a family member or an extended family member of an accession State national subject to worker authorisation—

(a) paragraph (6) of regulation 17 of the EEA Regulations shall not apply;

(b) the duration of that card shall be twelve months from the date of issue; and

(c) that card shall be entitled "Accession Residence Card".]

Note: Words in square brackets in paragraph (1) substituted, words in square brackets in paragraph (6) inserted and paragraph (7) inserted from 6 April 2014 (SI 2014/530).

Part 3

Accession State Worker Authorisation and Associated Documentation

Requirement for an accession State national subject to worker authorisation to be authorised to work

8.—(1) An accession State national subject to worker authorisation shall only be authorised to work in the United Kingdom during the accession period if he holds an accession worker authorisation document and is working in accordance with the conditions set out in that document.

(2) For the purpose of these Regulations, an accession worker authorisation document means—

(a) a passport or other travel document endorsed before 1st July 2013 to show that the holder has leave to enter or remain in the United Kingdom under the 1971 Act, subject to a condition restricting his employment in the United Kingdom to a particular employer or category of employment; or

(b) a worker authorisation registration certificate endorsed with a condition restricting the holder's employment to a particular employer and authorised category of employment.

(3) In the case of a document mentioned in paragraph (2)(a), the document ceases to be a valid accession worker authorisation document at the point at which—

(a) the period of leave to enter or remain expires; or

(b) the document holder ceases working for the employer, or in the employment, specified in the document for a period of time that exceeds 30 days in total.

(4) In the case of a document mentioned in paragraph (2)(b), the document ceases to be a valid accession worker authorisation document at the point at which—

(a) the document expires;

(b) the document holder ceases working for the employer, or in the authorised category of employment, specified in the document for a period of time that exceeds 30 days in total; or

(c) the document is revoked.

(5) For the purposes of this regulation, and regulations 9 and 11, the reference to a travel document other than a passport is a reference to a document which relates to a Croatian national and which can serve the same purpose as a passport.

Application for a worker authorisation registration certificate as an accession worker authorisation document

9.—(1) An application for a worker authorisation registration certificate may be made by an accession State national subject to worker authorisation who wishes to work for an employer in the United Kingdom if the employment concerned falls within an authorised category of employment.

(2) The application shall be in writing and shall be made to the Secretary of State.

(3) The application shall state—

(a) the name, address in the United Kingdom or in Croatia, and date of birth, of the applicant;

(b) the name and address of the employer for whom the applicant wishes to work; and

(c) the authorised category of employment covered by the application.

(4) The application shall be accompanied by—

(a) proof of the applicant's identity in the form of—

(i) a national identity card;

(ii) a passport; or

(iii) other travel document as defined by regulation 8(5);

(b) two passport size photographs of the applicant;

(c) where the relevant requirements require the applicant to hold a certificate of sponsorship, the certificate of sponsorship reference number;

(d) where sub-paragraph (c) does not apply, a letter from the employer specified in the application confirming that the applicant has an offer of employment with the employer; and

(e) a fee of £55.

(5) In this regulation "address" means, in relation to an employer which is a body corporate or partnership, the head or main office of that employer.

Issuing and revoking a worker authorisation registration certificate

10.—(1) Subject to paragraph (3), the Secretary of State shall issue a worker authorisation registration certificate pursuant to an application made in accordance with the provisions of regulation 9 if the Secretary of State is satisfied that the applicant is an accession State national subject to worker authorisation who meets the relevant requirements.

(2) A worker authorisation registration certificate shall include—

(a) a condition restricting the employment of the document holder to the employer and the authorised category of employment specified in the application;

(b) a statement that the document holder has a right of residence in the United Kingdom as a worker whilst working in accordance with any conditions specified in the certificate;

(c) where the authorised category of employment specified in the application is one for which a certificate of sponsorship is required, a statement that the holder of the document has a right to engage in supplementary employment; and

(d) where the period of authorised employment is less than 12 months, a statement specifying the date on which the worker authorisation registration certificate expires.

(3) The Secretary of State may—

(a) refuse to issue, revoke or refuse to renew a worker authorisation registration certificate if the refusal or revocation is justified on grounds of public policy, public security or public health,

(b) refuse the application where the Secretary of State is not satisfied that regulation 9 or this regulation has been complied with or satisfied, or

(c) revoke a worker authorisation registration certificate where—

(i) the document holder ceases working for the employer, or in the employment, specified in the document for a period of time that exceeds 30 days in total,

(ii) deception was used in order to obtain the document, or

(iii) the document was obtained on the basis of sponsorship by a sponsor whose licence has been withdrawn, and where the Secretary of State has refused to issue, revoked or refused to renew a worker authorisation registration certificate, she shall issue a notice setting out the reasons.

(4) A worker authorisation registration certificate or notice of refusal or revocation issued under this regulation shall be sent to the applicant by post together with the identity card or passport that accompanied the application.

(5) Subject to paragraph (6), in this regulation, "supplementary employment" means—

(a) employment in a job which appears on the shortage occupation list in Appendix K of the immigration rules; or

(b) employment in the same profession and at the same professional level as the employment for which the applicant has been issued with a certificate of sponsorship.

(6) "Supplementary employment" is subject to the condition that—

(i) the applicant remains working for the sponsor in the employment that the certificate of sponsorship checking service records that the applicant has been sponsored to do; and

(ii) the supplementary employment does not exceed 20 hours per week and takes place outside of the hours when the applicant is contracted to work for the sponsor in the employment the applicant is being sponsored to do.

(7) The Secretary of State shall ensure that the relevant statement is available to the public through her website and the library of the Home Office.

Part 4

Penalties and Offences

Unauthorised employment of accession State national - penalty for employer

11.—(1) It is contrary to this regulation to employ an accession State national subject to worker authorisation during the accession period if that person is not the holder of a valid accession worker authorisation document or, where that person holds such a document, the person would be in breach of a condition of that document in undertaking the employment.

(2) The Secretary of State may give an employer who acts contrary to this regulation a notice requiring him to pay a penalty of a specified amount not exceeding £5,000.

(3) The Secretary of State may give a penalty notice without having established whether the employer is excused under paragraph (5).

(4) A penalty notice must—

(a) state why the Secretary of State thinks the employer is liable to the penalty;

(b) state the amount of the penalty;

(c) specify a date, at least 28 days after the date specified in the notice as the date on which it is given, before which the penalty must be paid;

(d) specify how the penalty must be paid;

(e) provide a reference number;

(f) explain how the employer may object to the penalty; and

(g) explain how the Secretary of State may enforce the penalty.

(5) Subject to paragraph (7), an employer is excused from paying a penalty under this regulation if—

(a) before the commencement of the employment, the employee or prospective employee produces to the employer any of the following documents—

(i) an accession worker authorisation document that authorises the employee or prospective employee to take the employment in question;

(ii) an EEA registration certificate which includes a statement that the holder has unconditional access to the United Kingdom labour market; or

(iii) one of the following documents confirming that the document holder is not an accession State national subject to worker authorisation by virtue of regulation 2(6)—

(aa) a passport;

(bb) a national identity card; or

(cc) other travel document as defined by regulation 8(5); and

(b) the employer complies with the requirements set out in paragraph (6) of this regulation.

(6) The requirements are that—

(a) the employer takes all reasonable steps to check the validity of the document;

(b) the employer has satisfied himself that the photograph on the document is of the employee or prospective employee;

(c) the employer has satisfied himself that the date of birth on the document is consistent with the appearance of the employee or prospective employee;

(d) the employer takes all other reasonable steps to check that the employee or prospective employee is the rightful holder of the document; and

(e) the employer securely retains a dated copy of the whole of the document in a format which cannot be subsequently altered for a period of not less than two years after the employment has come to an end.

(7) An employer is not excused from paying a penalty if the employer knew, at any time during the period of the employment, that the employment was contrary to this regulation.

(8) Nothing in these regulations permits an employer to retain documents produced by an employee or prospective employee for the purposes of paragraph (5) for any period longer than is necessary for the purposes of ensuring compliance with paragraph (6).

(9) The Secretary of State may issue a code of practice specifying factors to be considered by her in determining the amount of a penalty imposed under paragraph (2) of this regulation.

(10) The Secretary of State shall lay a code issued under paragraph (9) before Parliament and publish it.

(11) The Secretary of State may from time to time review the code and may revoke, or revise and re-issue it, following a review; and a reference in this section to the code includes a reference to the code as revised.

Unauthorised employment of accession State national - penalty for employer - objection

12.—(1) This regulation applies where an employer to whom a penalty notice is given objects on the ground that—

(a) he is not liable to the imposition of a penalty;

(b) he is excused payment by virtue of regulation 11(5); or

(c) the amount of the penalty is too high.

(2) The employer may give a notice of objection to the Secretary of State.

(3) A notice of objection shall—

(a) be in writing;

(b) give the full grounds of objection;

(c) give the reference number of the notice given under regulation 11(4);

(d) give the name and address of the head or main office of the employer;

(e) give the name and address of the employee in respect of whom the penalty was issued;

(f) contain details of any appeal made by the employer under regulation 13; and

(g) be given within 28 days, beginning with the date specified in the penalty notice as the date on which it was given.

(4) Where the Secretary of State receives a notice of objection to a penalty she shall consider it and—

(a) cancel the penalty;

(b) reduce the penalty;

(c) increase the penalty; or

(d) determine to take no action.

(5) Where the Secretary of State considers a notice of objection she shall—

(a) have regard to any code of practice issued under regulation 11(9) (in so far as the objection relates to the amount of the penalty);

(b) inform the objector in writing of her decision within 28 days, beginning with the date on which the notice of objection was given to the Secretary of State, or such longer period as she may agree with the objector;

(c) if she increases the penalty, issue a new penalty notice under regulation 11; and

(d) if she reduces the penalty, notify the objector of the reduced amount.

Unauthorised employment of accession State national - penalty for employer - appeal

13.—(1) An employer to whom a penalty notice is given may appeal to the court on the ground that—

(a) he is not liable to the imposition of a penalty;

(b) he is excused payment by virtue of regulation 11(5); or

(c) the amount of the penalty is too high.

(2) The court may—

(a) allow the appeal and cancel the penalty;

(b) allow the appeal and reduce the penalty; or

(c) dismiss the appeal.

(3) An appeal shall be a re-hearing of the Secretary of State's decision to impose a penalty and shall be determined having regard to—

(a) any code of practice issued under regulation 11(9) that has effect at the time of the appeal

(in so far as the appeal relates to the amount of the penalty), and

(b) any other matters which the court thinks relevant (which may include matters of which the Secretary of State was unaware), and this paragraph has effect despite any provision of rules of Court.

(4) An appeal must be brought within the period of 28 days beginning with—

(a) the date specified in the penalty notice as the date upon which it is given; or

(b) if the employer gives a notice of objection and the Secretary of State reduces the penalty, the date specified in the notice of reduction as the date upon which it is given; or

(c) if the employer gives a notice of objection and the Secretary of State determines to take no action, the date specified in the notice of that determination as the date upon which it is given.

(5) An appeal may be brought by an employer whether or not—

(a) he has given a notice of objection under regulation 12; or

(b) the penalty has been increased or reduced under that regulation.

(6) In this section "the court" means—

(a) where the employer has his principal place of business in England and Wales, a county court;

(b) where the employer has his principal place of business in Scotland, the sheriff and sheriff court; and

(c) where the employer has his principal place of business in Northern Ireland, a county court.

Unauthorised employment of accession State national - penalty for employer - enforcement

14.—(1) A sum payable to the Secretary of State as a penalty under regulation 11 may be recoverable as if payable under a court order.

(2) In proceedings for the enforcement of a penalty, no question may be raised as to—

(a) liability to the imposition of the penalty;

(b) the application of the excuse in regulation 11(5); or

(c) the amount of the penalty.

(3) Money paid to the Secretary of State by way of penalty shall be paid into the Consolidated Fund.

Unauthorised employment of accession State national - employer offence

15.—(1) A person commits an offence if he employs another ("the employee") knowing that the employee is an accession State national subject to worker authorisation and that—

(a) the employee is not the holder of a valid accession worker authorisation document; or

(b) the employee is prohibited from undertaking the employment because of a condition in his accession worker authorisation document.

(2) A person guilty of an offence under this section shall be liable on summary conviction—

(a) to imprisonment for a term not exceeding 51 weeks in England and Wales or 6 months in Scotland or Northern Ireland;

(b) to a fine not exceeding level 5 on the standard scale; or

(c) to both.

(3) An offence under this regulation shall be treated as—

(a) a relevant offence for the purpose of sections 28B (search and arrest by warrant) and 28D (entry and search of premises) of the 1971 Act; and

(b) an offence under Part 3 of that Act (criminal proceedings) for the purposes of sections 28E (entry and search of premises following arrest), 28G (searching arrested persons) and 28H (searching persons in police custody).

(4) In relation to an offence committed before the commencement of section 281(5) (alteration of penalties for other summary offences) of the Criminal Justice Act 2003, the reference to 51 weeks in paragraph (2)(a) shall be read as a reference to 6 months.

(5) For the purposes of paragraph (1), a body (whether corporate or not) shall be treated as knowing a fact about an employee if a person who has responsibility within the body for an aspect of the employment knows the fact.

Unauthorised working by accession State national - employee offence and penalty

16.—(1) Subject to paragraph (2), an accession State national subject to worker authorisation who works in the United Kingdom during the accession period shall be guilty of an offence if he does not hold a valid accession worker authorisation document.

(2) A person guilty of an offence under this regulation shall be liable on summary conviction—

(a) to imprisonment for a term not exceeding more than three months;

(b) to a fine not exceeding level 5 on the standard scale; or

(c) to both.

(3) A constable or immigration officer who has reason to believe that a person has committed an offence under this regulation may give that person a notice offering him the opportunity of discharging any liability to conviction for that offence by payment of a penalty of £1000 in accordance with the notice.

(4) Where a person is given a notice under paragraph (3) in respect of an offence under this regulation—

(a) no proceedings may be instituted for that offence before the expiration of the period of 21 days beginning with the day after the date of the notice; and

(b) he may not be convicted of that offence if, before the expiration of that period, he pays the penalty in accordance with the notice.

(5) A notice under paragraph (3) must give such particulars of the circumstances alleged to constitute the offence as are necessary for giving reasonable information of the offence.

(6) A notice under paragraph (3) must also state—

(a) the period during which, by virtue of paragraph (4), proceedings will not be instituted for the offence;

(b) the amount of the penalty; and

(c) that the penalty is payable to the Secretary of State at the address specified in the notice.

(7) Without prejudice to payment by any other method, payment of a penalty in pursuance of a notice under paragraph (3) may be made by pre-paying and posting a letter by registered post or the recorded delivery service containing the amount of the penalty (in cash or otherwise) to the Secretary of State at the address specified in the notice.

(8) Where a letter is sent in accordance with paragraph (7) payment is to be regarded as having been made at the time at which that letter would be delivered in the ordinary course of registered post or the recorded delivery service.

(9) A constable or immigration officer may withdraw a penalty notice given under paragraph (3) if the constable or immigration officer decides that—

(a) the notice was issued in error;

(b) the notice contains material errors; or

(c) he has reasonable grounds to believe that the employee has committed an offence under regulation 17.

(10) A penalty notice may be withdrawn—

(a) whether or not the period specified in paragraph (4)(a) has expired;

(b) under paragraph (9)(a) and (b), whether or not the penalty has been paid; and

(c) under paragraph (9)(c), only where the penalty has not yet been paid.

(11) Where a penalty notice has been withdrawn under paragraph (9)—

(a) notice of the withdrawal must be given to the recipient; and

(b) any amount paid by way of penalty in pursuance of that notice must be repaid to the person who paid it.

(12) Subject to paragraph (13), proceedings shall not be continued or instituted against an employee for an offence under paragraph (1) in connection with which a withdrawal notice was issued.

(13) Proceedings may be continued or instituted for an offence in connection with which a withdrawal notice was issued if—

(a) where the withdrawal notice was withdrawn pursuant to paragraph (9)(b)—

(i) a further penalty notice in respect of the offence was issued at the same time as the penalty notice was withdrawn; and

(ii) the penalty has not been paid pursuant to that further penalty notice in accordance with paragraph (4)(a); or

(b) the withdrawal notice was withdrawn pursuant to paragraph (9)(c).

Deception - employee offence

17.—(1) A person is guilty of an offence if, by means which include deception by him, he obtains or seeks to obtain a worker authorisation registration certificate.

(2) A person guilty of an offence under this regulation shall be liable on summary conviction—

(a) to imprisonment for a term not exceeding three months;

(b) to a fine not exceeding level 5 on the standard scale; or

(c) to both.

Offences under regulations 16 and 17 - search, entry and arrest

18. An offence under regulation 16 or 17 shall be treated as—

(a) a relevant offence for the purposes of sections 28B (search and arrest by warrant) and 28D (entry and search of premises) of the 1971 Act;

(b) an offence under Part 3 of the 1971 Act (criminal proceedings) for the purposes of sections 28E (entry and search of premises following arrest), 28G (searching arrested persons) and 28H (searching persons in police custody) of that Act; and

(c) an offence under section 24(1)(b) of the 1971 Act for the purposes of sections 28A(1) (arrest without warrant), 28CA (business premises: entry to arrest) and 28FA (search for personnel records: warrant unnecessary) of that Act.

SCHEDULE

REGULATION 1(3)

CONSEQUENTIAL AMENDMENTS

Note: Amends Sch 2 of the EEA Regulations.

The Immigration (European Economic Area) (Amendment) (No. 2) Regulations 2013
(SI 2013/3032)

Citation

1. These Regulations may be cited as the Immigration (European Economic Area) (Amendment) (No. 2) Regulations 2013.

Commencement

2.—(1) Except as provided by paragraph (2), these Regulations come into force on 1st January 2014.

(2) Paragraphs 1, 6(a) and (b), 19(a), 20(b), 22, 23 and 25(a) of Schedule 1 and paragraphs 1(b) and 2(c) of Schedule 2, come into force on 7th April 2014.

Interpretation

3. In these Regulations, "the 2006 Regulations" means the Immigration (European Economic Area) Regulations 2006.

4.–6. ...

Note: Regulations 4–5 and Schs 1 and 2 amend the Immigration (European Economic Area) Regulations 2006 (SI 2006/1003) and make consequential amendments. These are subject to the transitional provisions and savings set out below in Sch 3.

SCHEDULE 3

REGULATION 6

TRANSITIONAL PROVISIONS

Qualified person

1. For the purposes of paragraph 3(b) to (e) of Schedule 1—

(a) any period of employment in the United Kingdom before the coming into force of these Regulations is to be treated as a period of employment under regulation 6 of the 2006 Regulations as amended by these Regulations; and

(b) any period—

(i) of duly recorded involuntary unemployment; or

(ii) during which a person was a jobseeker for the purposes of regulation 6(1)(a) of the 2006 Regulations, before the coming into force of these Regulations is to be disregarded.

Family members of British citizens

2.—(1) The substitution of regulation 9 of the 2006 Regulations by paragraph 5 of Schedule 1 has no effect in relation to the family member ("F") of a British citizen where the criteria in subparagraphs (2) or (3) are met.

(2) The criterion in this subparagraph is met where, upon the coming into force of these Regulations, F was a person with a permanent right to reside in the United Kingdom under the 2006 Regulations.

(3) The criteria in this subparagraph are met where, upon the coming into force of these Regulations, F was a person with a right to reside under the 2006 Regulations; and

(a) held a valid registration certificate, residence card or EEA family permit issued under the 2006 Regulations;

(b) had made an application under the 2006 Regulations for a registration certificate, residence card or EEA family permit which had not been determined; or (c) had made an application under the 2006 Regulations for a registration certificate or residence card which had been refused and in respect of which an appeal under regulation 26 of the 2006 Regulations could be brought while the appellant is in the United Kingdom (excluding the possibility of an appeal out of time with permission) or was pending (within the meaning of regulation 25(2) of the 2006 Regulations).

(4) Where met, the criteria in subparagraphs (2) and (3) remain satisfied until the occurrence of the earliest of the following events—

(a) the date six months after an EEA family permit has been issued if F has not within that period been admitted to the United Kingdom;

(b) the date on which an appeal against a decision referred to in subparagraph (3)(c) can no longer be brought (ignoring the possibility of an appeal out of time with permission) where no such appeal has been brought;

(c) the date on which any appeal against a decision referred to in subparagraph 3(c) is finally determined, is withdrawn or is abandoned (within the meaning of regulation 25(2) of the 2006 Regulations), save where the outcome of the appeal process is that the document in question falls to be granted;

(d) the date on which F ceases to be the family member of an EEA national or a family member who has retained the right of residence, within the meaning of regulation 10 of the 2006 Regulations; or

(e) the date on which F's right of residence under regulation 15 of the 2006 Regulations (permanent right of residence) is lost in accordance with paragraph (2) of that regulation (right of permanent residence lost through more than two years' consecutive absence).

Abuse of rights or fraud

3. For the purposes of paragraph 18 of Schedule 1, insofar as it inserts regulation 21B(1)(b) into the 2006 Regulations, any removal pursuant to regulation 19(3)(a) of the 2006 Regulations before the coming into force of these Regulations is to be disregarded.

The Immigration (Passenger Transit Visa) Order 2014

2014 No. 2702

The Secretary of State, in exercise of the powers conferred by section 41 of the Immigration and Asylum Act 1999 Act, makes the following Order:

Citation and commencement

1.—(1) This Order may be cited as the Immigration (Passenger Transit Visa) Order 2014.

(2) This Order comes into force on 1st December 2014.

Interpretation

2.—(1) Subject to paragraph (5), in this Order a "transit passenger" means a person to whom paragraph (2), (3) or (4) applies and who on arrival in the United Kingdom passes through to another country or territory without entering the United Kingdom.

(2) This paragraph applies to a person who is a citizen or national of a country or territory listed in Schedule 1 to this Order.

(3) This paragraph applies to a person holding a travel document issued by the purported "Turkish Republic of Northern Cyprus".

(4) This paragraph applies to a person who holds a passport issued by the Republic of Venezuela that does not contain biometric information contained in an electronic chip.

(5) A person to whom paragraph (2), (3) or (4) applies will not be a transit passenger if he—

(a) has the right of abode in the United Kingdom under the Immigration Act 1971;

(b) is a citizen or national of an EEA State; or

(c) in the case of a citizen or national of the People's Republic of China, holds a passport issued by either the Hong Kong Special Administrative Region or the Macao Special Administrative Region.

(6) In this Order—

"Approved Destination Status Scheme" means a scheme for issuing visas to Chinese tour groups under—

(a) the Memorandum of Understanding between the European Community and the National Tourism Administration of the People's Republic of China on visa and related issues concerning tourist groups from the People's Republic of China (ADS) signed at Beijing on 12th February 2004; or

(b) a similar agreement between the People's Republic of China and a Schengen Acquis State;

"EEA State" means a country which is a contracting party to the Agreement on the European Economic Area signed at Oporto on 2nd May 1992(**b**) as adjusted by the Protocol signed at Brussels on 17th March 1993;

"Schengen Acquis State" means an EEA State (excluding the United Kingdom and Republic of Ireland) or Switzerland.

Requirement for a transit passenger to hold a transit visa

3. Subject to article 4, a transit passenger is required to hold a transit visa.

Exemption from the requirement for a transit passenger to hold a transit visa

4. A transit passenger is not required to hold a transit visa if he holds or a person with whom he arrives in the United Kingdom holds on his behalf—

(a) a valid visa for entry to Australia, Canada, New Zealand or the United States of America;

(b) a valid Australian Permanent Resident Visa;

(c) a valid Canadian Permanent Resident Card issued on or after 28th June 2002;

(d) a valid New Zealand Permanent Resident Visa;

(e) a valid USA I-551 Permanent Resident Card issued on or after 21st April 1998;

(f) an expired USA I-551 Permanent Resident Card provided it is accompanied by a valid I-797 letter authorising an extension of the period of permanent residency;

(g) a valid USA I-551 Temporary Immigrant Visa;

(h) a valid standalone US Immigration Form 155A/155B attached to a brown sealed envelope;

(i) a valid common format Category D visa for entry to an EEA state or Switzerland;

(j) a valid common format residence permit issued by an EEA State pursuant to Council Regulation (EC) No 1030/2002 or Switzerland;

(k) a valid biometric visa issued by the Republic of Ireland;

(l) a valid visa issued by a Schengen Acquis State under the Approved Destination Status Scheme where the transit passenger is undertaking a journey via the United Kingdom to a Schengen Acquis State;

(m) a valid airline ticket for travel via the United Kingdom as part of a journey from a Schengen Acquis State to another country or territory, provided that the transit passenger does not seek to travel via the United Kingdom on a date more than 30 days from the date on which he last entered a Schengen Acquis State with a valid visa issued by a Schengen Acquis State under the Approved Destination Status Scheme;

(n) a diplomatic or service passport issued by the People's Republic of China;

(o) a diplomatic or official passport issued by India; or

(p) a diplomatic or official passport issued by Vietnam.

Method of application for a transit visa

5. An application for a transit visa may be made to any British High Commission, Embassy or Consulate which accepts such applications.

Revocations

6. The Orders specified in Schedule 2 to this Order are revoked.

SCHEDULE 1

ARTICLE 2(2)

Countries or territories whose nationals or citizens need transit visas

Afghanistan
Albania
Algeria
Angola
Bangladesh
Belarus
Burma
Burundi
Cameroon
China
Congo
Democratic Republic of the Congo
Egypt
Eritrea
Ethiopia
Former Yugoslav Republic of Macedonia
Gambia
Ghana
Guinea
Guinea-Bissau
India
Iran
Iraq
Ivory Coast
Jamaica
Kenya
Kosovo
Lebanon
Lesotho
Liberia
Libya
Malawi
Moldova
Mongolia

Nepal
Nigeria
Pakistan
Palestinian Territories
Rwanda
Senegal
Serbia
Sierra Leone
Somalia
South Africa
South Sudan
Sri Lanka
Sudan
Swaziland
Syria
Tanzania
Turkey
Uganda
Vietnam
Yemen
Zimbabwe

SCHEDULE 2

REVOCATIONS

. . .

2014 No. 2771 (C. 122)
The Immigration Act 2014 (Commencement No. 3, Transitional and Saving Provisions) Order 2014
2014 No. 2771

See SI 2014/2928 The Immigration Act 2014 (Transitional and Savings Provisions) Order 2014, published too late for inclusion, which amends defects in this Order.

PART 1

INTRODUCTION AND DAYS APPOINTED

Citation and interpretation

1.—(1) This Order may be cited as the Immigration Act 2014 (Commencement No. 3, Transitional and Saving Provisions) Order 2014.

(2) In this Order—

(a) "the 1971 Act" means the Immigration Act 1971;

(b) "the 2002 Act" means the Nationality, Immigration and Asylum Act 2002;

(c) "the Act" means the Immigration Act 2014;

(d) "the relevant provisions" means section 1 (removal of persons unlawfully in the UK), section 15 (right of appeal to First-tier Tribunal) and section 17(2) (place from which appeal may be brought or continued) of, and paragraphs 3, 4, 5, 6 and 7 and Part 4 of Schedule 9 (apart from paragraph 26(2), (3) and (5)) (transitional and consequential provision relating to appeals) to, the Act;

(e) "the saved provisions" means section 10 of the Immigration and Asylum Act 1999, sections 62, 72 and 76, and Part 5 of the 2002 Act, section 8(7) of the Asylum and Immigration (Treatment of Claimants, etc.) Act 2004, section 47 of the Immigration, Asylum and Nationality Act 2006 and paragraph 19(10) of Schedule 1 to the Legal Aid, Sentencing and Punishment of Offenders Act 2012 as in force immediately prior to 20th October 2014.

2.–5. . . .

6. (1) . . . .

(2) The relevant local authorities are–

(a) Birmingham City Council;

(b) Dudley Metropolitan Borough Council;

(c) Sandwell Metropolitan Borough Council;

(d) Walsall Metropolitan Borough Council; and

(e) Wolverhampton City Council

7.–8. . . . .

PART 2

TRANSITIONAL AND SAVING PROVISIONS AND REPEALS

Transitional and saving provision

9. Notwithstanding the commencement of the relevant provisions, the saved provisions continue to have effect, and the relevant provisions do not have effect, other than so far as they relate to the persons set out respectively in articles 10 and 11, unless article 11(2) or (3) applies.

10. The persons referred to in article 9 are—

(a) a person ("P1") who becomes a foreign criminal within the definition in section 117D(2) of the 2002 Act on or after 20th October 2014; and

(b) a person who is liable to deportation from the United Kingdom under section 3(5)(b) of the 1971 Act because they belong to the family of P1.

11.—(1) The persons referred to in article 9 are a person ("P2") who makes an application on or after 20th October 2014 for leave to remain—

(a) as a Tier 4 Migrant;

(b) as the partner of a Tier 4 Migrant under paragraph 319C of the immigration rules; or (c) as the child of a Tier 4 Migrant under paragraph 319H of the immigration rules.

(2) The saved provisions have effect, and the relevant provisions do not have effect, where P2, having made an application of a kind mentioned in paragraph (1), at any time thereafter makes—

(a) an application for leave to enter; or

(b) any further application for leave to remain which is not of a kind that is mentioned in paragraph (1);

provided the subsequent application is not a protection claim or human rights claim, made while P2 is in the United Kingdom, other than at a port.

(3) Where paragraph (2) applies, the saved provisions also have effect, and the relevant provisions do not have effect, where a decision is taken in relation to P2—

(a) which constitutes an immigration decision under section 82(2) of the 2002 Act as in force immediately prior to 20th October 2014; or

(b) to which section 83 or 83A of the 2002 Act as in force immediately prior to 20th October 2014 applies.

(4) Where the relevant provisions apply, and an appeal has already been brought against an immigration decision under section 82(1) of the 2002 Act but before the relevant provisions applied, the reference to a "decision" in section 96(1)(a) of the 2002 Act is to be read as a reference to an "immigration decision".

(5) In this article—

(a) "human rights claim" means—

(i) a claim made by a person to the Secretary of State that to remove the person from or require him to leave the United Kingdom would be unlawful under section 6 of the Human Rights Act 1998 (public authority not to act contrary to Convention); or

(ii) an application for leave to remain made under paragraph 276ADE of, or Appendix FM to, the immigration rules;

(b) "immigration decision" has the same meaning as in section 82(2) of the 2002 Act as in force immediately prior to 20th October 2014;

(c) "immigration rules" means the rules for the time being laid down by the Secretary of State as mentioned in section 3(2) of the 1971 Act;

(d) "Leave to enter the United Kingdom" means leave to enter the United Kingdom given in accordance with the provisions of, or made under, the 1971 Act;

(e) "Leave to remain in the United Kingdom" means leave to remain in the United Kingdom given in accordance with the provisions of, or made under, the 1971 Act and any variation of leave to enter or remain by the Secretary of State;

(f) "port" has the meaning in section 33(1) of the 1971 Act;

(g) "protection claim" has the meaning given in section 82(2) of the 2002 Act;

(h) "protection status" has the meaning given in section 82(2) of the 2002 Act;

(i) "Tier 4 Migrant" has the same meaning as provided in the immigration rules.

12. For the purposes of section 35(3) of the Act, the day appointed as "the commencement day" is 1st December 2014.

13. Notwithstanding the commencement of Part 11 of Schedule 9 to the Act, the following statutory instruments remain in force—

(a) the Immigration and Nationality (Fees) Regulations 2014;

(b) the Immigration and Nationality (Cost Recovery Fees) Regulations 2014;

(c) the Immigration and Nationality (Fees) Order 2011, so far as is necessary for the purposes of preserving the Regulations mentioned in sub-paragraphs (a) and (b).

Consequential revocation and saving

14. Article 4 of the Immigration Act 2014 (Commencement No. 1, Transitory and Saving Provisions) Order 2014 is revoked.

15. But in any case in which a foreign criminal as defined in section 117D(2) of the 2002 Act has made a human rights claim which the Secretary of State certified under section 94B of that Act prior to 20th October 2014, section 92 of the 2002 Act (appeal from within the United Kingdom: general) continues to have effect as if the following provisions of that Act were omitted—

(a) the reference in subsection (2) to an immigration decision of a kind specified in section 82(2)(j);

(b) the reference in subsection (4)(a) to a human rights claim; and

(c) subsection (4)(b).

The Immigration (Removal of Family Members) Regulations 2014

2014 No. 2816

The Secretary of State, in exercise of the powers conferred by section 10(10)(b) of the Immigration and Asylum Act 1999, makes the following Regulations:

Citation, commencement and interpretation

1. These Regulations may be cited as the Immigration (Removal of Family Members) Regulations 2014 and come into force on 14th November 2014.

2. In these Regulations—

"the Act" means the Immigration and Asylum Act 1999;

"family member" means a person who meets the conditions set out in section 10(3), (4) and (5) of the Act;

"P" means a person who is liable to be or has been removed from the United Kingdom under section 10(1) of the Act.

Giving of notice to a family member

3. A notice given to a family member in accordance with section 10(2) of the Act may be given—

(a) at any time prior to P's removal, or

(b) during the period of eight weeks beginning with the date on which P is removed.

Service of notice

4.—(1) A notice given to a family member in accordance with section 10(2) of the Act may be—

(a) given by hand,

(b) sent by fax,

(c) sent by postal service in which delivery or receipt is recorded to—

(i) an address provided for correspondence by the person or the person's representative, or

(ii) where no address for correspondence has been provided, the last-known or usual place of abode or place of business of the person or the person's representative,

(d) sent electronically,

(e) sent by document exchange to a document exchange number or address,

(f) sent by courier,

(g) collected by the person who is the subject of the decision or the person's representative.

(2) Where—

(a) a person's whereabouts are not known, and

(b) no address is available for correspondence with either the person or the person's representative under paragraph (1)(c),

the notice shall be deemed to have been given when the Secretary of State or immigration officer enters a record of the above circumstances and places the signed notice on the relevant file.

(3) Where notice is deemed to have been given in accordance with paragraph (2) and subsequently the person is located, the person is to be given a copy of the notice and details of when and how it was deemed to be served as soon as is practicable.

(4) Where a notice is sent by post in accordance with paragraph (1)(c) it shall be deemed to have been served, unless the contrary is proved, on the second day after it was posted.

(5) For the purposes of paragraph (4) the period is to be calculated—

(a) excluding the day on which the notice is posted, and

(b) excluding any day which is not a business day.

(6) In this regulation, "business day" means any day other than Saturday or Sunday, a day which is a bank holiday under the Banking and Financial Dealings Act 1971 in the part of the United Kingdom to which the notice is sent, Christmas Day or Good Friday.

(7) A notice to be given to a family member in accordance with section 10(2) of the Act may, in the case of a child below the age of 18 who does not have a representative, be given to P.

EUROPEAN MATERIALS

Consolidated Version of the Treaty on the Functioning of the European Union*

Part Two

Non-Discrimination and Citizenship of the Union

Article 18

(ex Article 12 TEC)

Within the scope of application of the Treaties, and without prejudice to any special provisions contained therein, any discrimination on grounds of nationality shall be prohibited.

The European Parliament and the Council, acting in accordance with the ordinary legislative procedure, may adopt rules designed to prohibit such discrimination.

Article 19

(ex Article 13 TEC)

1. Without prejudice to the other provisions of the Treaties and within the limits of the powers conferred by them upon the Union, the Council, acting unanimously in accordance with a special legislative procedure and after obtaining the consent of the European Parliament, may take appropriate action to combat discrimination based on sex, racial or ethnic origin, religion or belief, disability, age or sexual orientation.

2. By way of derogation from paragraph 1, the European Parliament and the Council, acting in accordance with the ordinary legislative procedure, may adopt the basic principles of Union incentive measures, excluding any harmonisation of the laws and regulations of the Member States, to support action taken by the Member States in order to contribute to the achievement of the objectives referred to in paragraph 1.

Article 20

(ex Article 17 TEC)

1. Citizenship of the Union is hereby established. Every person holding the nationality of a Member State shall be a citizen of the Union. Citizenship of the Union shall be additional to and not replace national citizenship.

2. Citizens of the Union shall enjoy the rights and be subject to the duties provided for in the Treaties. They shall have, *inter alia*:

(a) the right to move and reside freely within the territory of the Member States;

* © European Union, http://eur-lex.europa.eu/, 1998–2014').

'Only European Union legislation printed in the paper edition of the *Official Journal of the European Union* is deemed authentic.'

(b) the right to vote and to stand as candidates in elections to the European Parliament and in municipal elections in their Member State of residence, under the same conditions as nationals of that State;

(c) the right to enjoy, in the territory of a third country in which the Member State of which they are a nationals is not represented, the protection of the diplomatic and consular authorities of any Member State on the same conditions as the nationals of that State;

(d) the right to petition the European Parliament, to apply to the European Ombudsman, and to address the institutions and advisory bodies of the Union in any of the Treaty languages and to obtain a reply in the same language.

These rights shall be exercised in accordance with the conditions and limits defined by the Treaties and by the measures adopted thereunder.

Article 21

(ex Article 18 TEC)

1. Every citizen of the Union shall have the right to move and reside freely within the territory of the Member States, subject to the limitations and conditions laid down in the Treaties and by the measures adopted to give them effect.

2. If action by the Union should prove necessary to attain this objective and the Treaties have not provided the necessary powers, the European Parliament and the Council, acting in accordance with the ordinary legislative procedure, may adopt provisions with a view to facilitating the exercise of the rights referred to in paragraph 1.

3. For the same purposes as those referred to in paragraph 1 and if the Treaties have not provided the necessary powers, the Council, acting in accordance with a special legislative procedure, may adopt measures concerning social security or social protection. The Council shall act unanimously after consulting the European Parliament.

Part Three

Title IV

Free Movement of Persons, Services and Capital

Chapter 1

Workers

Article 45

(ex Article 39 TEC)

1. Freedom of movement for workers shall be secured within the Union.

2. Such freedom of movement shall entail the abolition of any discrimination based on nationality between workers of the Member States as regards employment, remuneration and other conditions of work and employment.

3. It shall entail the right, subject to limitations justified on grounds of public policy, public security or public health:

(a) to accept offers of employment actually made;

(b) to move freely within the territory of Member States for this purpose;

(c) to stay in a Member State for the purpose of employment in accordance with the provisions governing the employment of nationals of that State laid down by law, regulation or administrative action;

(d) to remain in the territory of a Member State after having been employed in that State, subject to conditions which shall be embodied in regulations to be drawn up by the Commission.

4. The provisions of this Article shall not apply to employment in the public service.

Article 46

(ex Article 40 TEC)

The European Parliament and the Council shall, acting in accordance with the ordinary legislative procedure and after consulting the Economic and Social Committee, issue directives or make regulations setting out the measures required to bring about freedom of movement for workers, as defined in Article 45, in particular:

(a) by ensuring close cooperation between national employment services;

(b) by abolishing those administrative procedures and practices and those qualifying periods in respect of eligibility for available employment, whether resulting from national legislation or from agreements previously concluded between Member States, the maintenance of which would form an obstacle to liberalisation of the movement of workers;

(c) by abolishing all such qualifying periods and other restrictions provided for either under national legislation or under agreements previously concluded between Member States as imposed on workers of other Member States conditions regarding the free choice of employment other than those imposed on workers of the State concerned;

(d) by setting up appropriate machinery to bring offers of employment into touch with applications for employment and to facilitate the achievement of a balance between supply and demand in the employment market in such a way as to avoid serious threats to the standard of living and level of employment in the various regions and industries.

Article 47

(ex Article 41 TEC)

Member States shall, within the framework of a joint programme, encourage the exchange of young workers.

Article 48

(ex Article 42 TEC)

The European Parliament and the Council shall, acting in accordance with the ordinary legislative procedure, adopt such measures in the field of social security as are necessary to provide freedom of movement for workers; to this end, they shall make arrangements to secure for employed and self-employed migrant workers and their dependants:

(a) aggregation, for the purpose of acquiring and retaining the right to benefit and of calculating the amount of benefit, of all periods taken into account under the laws of the several countries;

(b) payment of benefits to persons resident in the territories of Member States.

Where a member of the Council declares that a draft legislative act referred to in the first subparagraph would affect important aspects of its social security system, including its scope, cost or financial structure, or would affect the financial balance of that system, it may request that the matter be referred to the European Council. In that case, the ordinary legislative procedure shall be suspended. After discussion, the European Council shall, within four months of this suspension, either:

(a) refer the draft back to the Council, which shall terminate the suspension of the ordinary legislative procedure; or

(b) take no action or request the Commission to submit a new proposal; in that case, the act originally proposed shall be deemed not to have been adopted.

Chapter 3
Services

Article 56

(ex Article 49 TEC)

Within the framework of the provisions set out below, restrictions on freedom to provide services within the Union shall be prohibited in respect of nationals of Member States who are established in a Member State other than that of the person for whom the services are intended.

The European Parliament and the Council, acting in accordance with the ordinary legislative procedure, may extend the provisions of the Chapter to nationals of a third country who provide services and who are established within the Union.

Article 57

(ex Article 50 TEC)

Services shall be considered to be 'services' within the meaning of the Treaties where they are normally provided for remuneration, in so far as they are not governed by the provisions relating to freedom of movement for goods, capital and persons.

'Services' shall in particular include:

(a) activities of an industrial character;

(b) activities of a commercial character;

(c) activities of craftsmen;

(d) activities of the professions.

Without prejudice to the provisions of the Chapter relating to the right of establishment, the person providing a service may, in order to do so, temporarily pursue his activity in the Member State where the service is provided, under the same conditions as are imposed by that State on its own nationals.

Article 58

(ex Article 51 TEC)

1. Freedom to provide services in the field of transport shall be governed by the provisions of the Title relating to transport.

2. The liberalisation of banking and insurance services connected with movements of capital shall be effected in step with the liberalisation of movement of capital.

Article 59

(ex Article 52 TEC)

1. In order to achieve the liberalisation of a specific service, the European Parliament and the Council, acting in accordance with the ordinary legislative procedure and after consulting the Economic and Social Committee, shall issue directives.

2. As regards the directives referred to in paragraph 1, priority shall as a general rule be given to those services which directly affect production costs or the liberalisation of which helps to promote trade in goods.

Article 60

(ex Article 53 TEC)

The Member States shall endeavour to undertake the liberalisation of services beyond the extent required by the directives issued pursuant to Article 59(1), if their general economic situation and the situation of the economic sector concerned so permit.

To this end, the Commission shall make recommendations to the Member States concerned.

Article 61

(ex Article 54 TEC)

As long as restrictions on freedom to provide services have not been abolished, each Member State shall apply such restrictions without distinction on grounds of nationality or residence to all persons providing services within the meaning of the first paragraph of Article 56.

Article 62

(ex Article 55 TEC)

The provisions of Articles 51 to 54 shall apply to the matters covered by this Chapter.

Title V

Area of Freedom, Security and Justice

Chapter 1

General Provisions

Article 67

(ex Article 61 TEC and ex Article 29 TEU)

1. The Union shall constitute an area of freedom, security and justice with respect for fundamental rights and the different legal systems and traditions of the Member States.

2. It shall ensure the absence of internal border controls for persons and shall frame a common policy on asylum, immigration and external border control, based on solidarity between Member States, which is fair towards third-country nationals. For the purpose of this Title, stateless persons shall be treated as third-country nationals.

3. The Union shall endeavour to ensure a high level of security through measures to prevent and combat crime, racism and xenophobia, and through measures for coordination and cooperation between police and judicial authorities and other competent authorities, as well as through the mutual recognition of judgments in criminal matters and, if necessary, through the approximation of criminal laws.

4. The Union shall facilitate access to justice, in particular through the principle of mutual recognition of judicial and extrajudicial decisions in civil matters.

Article 68

The European Council shall define the strategic guidelines for legislative and operational planning within the area of freedom, security and justice.

Article 69

National Parliaments ensure that the proposals and legislative initiatives submitted under Chapters 4 and 5 comply with the principle of subsidiarity, in accordance with the arrangements laid down by the Protocol on the application of the principles of subsidiarity and proportionality.

Article 72

(ex Article 64(1) TEC and ex Article 33 TEU)

This Title shall not affect the exercise of the responsibilities incumbent upon Member States with regard to the maintenance of law and order and the safeguarding of internal security.

Chapter 2

Policies on Border Checks, Asylum and Immigration

Article 77

(ex Article 62 TEC)

1. The Union shall develop a policy with a view to:

(a) ensuring the absence of any controls on persons, whatever their nationality, when crossing internal borders;

(b) carrying out checks on persons and efficient monitoring of the crossing of external borders;

(c) the gradual introduction of an integrated management system for external borders.

2. For the purposes of paragraph 1, the European Parliament and the Council, acting in accordance with the ordinary legislative procedure, shall adopt measures concerning:

(a) the common policy on visas and other short-stay residence permits;

(b) the checks to which persons crossing external borders are subject;

(c) the conditions under which nationals of third countries shall have the freedom to travel within the Union for a short period;

(d) any measure necessary for the gradual establishment of an integrated management system for external borders;

(e) the absence of any controls on persons, whatever their nationality, when crossing internal borders.

3. If action by the Union should prove necessary to facilitate the exercise of the right referred to in Article 20(2)(a), and if the Treaties have not provided the necessary powers, the Council, acting in accordance with a special legislative procedure, may adopt provisions concerning passports, identity cards, residence permits or any other such document. The Council shall act unanimously after consulting the European Parliament.

4. This Article shall not affect the competence of the Member States concerning the geographical demarcation of their borders, in accordance with international law.

Article 78

(ex Articles 63, points 1 and 2, and 64(2) TEC)

1. The Union shall develop a common policy on asylum, subsidiary protection and temporary protection with a view to offering appropriate status to any third-country national requiring international protection and ensuring compliance with the principle of *non-refoulement*. This policy must be in accordance with the Geneva Convention of 28 July 1951 and the Protocol of 31 January 1967 relating to the status of refugees, and other relevant treaties.

2. For the purposes of paragraph 1, the European Parliament and the Council, acting in accordance with the ordinary legislative procedure, shall adopt measures for a common European asylum system comprising:

(a) a uniform status of asylum for nationals of third countries, valid throughout the Union;

(b) a uniform status of subsidiary protection for nationals of third countries who, without obtaining European asylum, are in need of international protection;

(c) a common system of temporary protection for displaced persons in the event of a massive inflow;

(d) common procedures for the granting and withdrawing of uniform asylum or subsidiary protection status;

(e) criteria and mechanisms for determining which Member State is responsible for considering an application for asylum or subsidiary protection;

(f) standards concerning the conditions for the reception of applicants for asylum or subsidiary protection;

(g) partnership and cooperation with third countries for the purpose of managing inflows of people applying for asylum or subsidiary or temporary protection.

3. In the event of one or more Member States being confronted by an emergency situation characterised by a sudden inflow of nationals of third countries, the Council, on a proposal from the Commission, may adopt provisional measures for the benefit of the Member State(s) concerned. It shall act after consulting the European Parliament.

Article 79

(ex Article 63, points 3 and 4, TEC)

1. The Union shall develop a common immigration policy aimed at ensuring, at all stages, the efficient management of migration flows, fair treatment of third-country nationals residing legally in Member States, and the prevention of, and enhanced measures to combat, illegal immigration and trafficking in human beings.

2. For the purposes of paragraph 1, the European Parliament and the Council, acting in accordance with the ordinary legislative procedure, shall adopt measures in the following areas:

(a) the conditions of entry and residence, and standards on the issue by Member States of long-term visas and residence permits, including those for the purpose of family reunification;

(b) the definition of the rights of third-country nationals residing legally in a Member State, including the conditions governing freedom of movement and of residence in other Member States;

(c) illegal immigration and unauthorised residence, including removal and repatriation of persons residing without authorisation;

(d) combating trafficking in persons, in particular women and children.

3. The Union may conclude agreements with third countries for the re-admission to their countries of origin or provenance of third-country nationals who do not or who no longer fulfil the conditions for entry, presence or residence in the territory of one of the Member States.

4. The European Parliament and the Council, acting in accordance with the ordinary legislative procedure, may establish measures to provide incentives and support for the action of Member States with a view to promoting the integration of third-country nationals residing legally in their territories, excluding any harmonisation of the laws and regulations of the Member States.

5. This Article shall not affect the right of Member States to determine volumes of admission of third-country nationals coming from third countries to their territory in order to seek work, whether employed or self-employed. . . .

Council Directive 2001/55/EC of 20 July 2001

on minimum standards for giving temporary protection in the event of a mass influx of displaced persons and on measures promoting a balance of efforts between Member States in receiving such persons and bearing the consequences thereof

---

Note: Entered into force on 7 August 2001 (Article 33).

THE COUNCIL OF THE EUROPEAN UNION,

Having regard to the Treaty establishing the European Community, and in particular point 2(a) and (b) of Article 63 thereof,

Having regard to the proposal from the Commission,[1]

Having regard to the opinion of the European Parliament,[2]

Having regard to the opinion of the Economic and Social Committee,[3]

Having regard to the opinion of the Committee of the Regions,[4]

Whereas:

(1) The preparation of a common policy on asylum, including common European arrangements for asylum, is a constituent part of the European Union's objective of

[1] OJ C 311 E, 31.10.2000, p. 251.

[2] Opinion delivered on 13 March 2001 (not yet published in the Official Journal).

[3] OJ C 155, 29.5.2001, p. 21.

[4] Opinion delivered on 13 June 2001 (not yet published in the Official Journal).

establishing progressively an area of freedom, security and justice open to those who, forced by circumstances, legitimately seek protection in the European Union.

(2) Cases of mass influx of displaced persons who cannot return to their country of origin have become more substantial in Europe in recent years. In these cases it may be necessary to set up exceptional schemes to offer them immediate temporary protection.

(3) In the conclusions relating to persons displaced by the conflict in the former Yugoslavia adopted by the Ministers responsible for immigration at their meetings in London on 30 November and 1 December 1992 and Copenhagen on 1 and 2 June 1993, the Member States and the Community institutions expressed their concern at the situation of displaced persons.

(4) On 25 September 1995 the Council adopted a Resolution on burden-sharing with regard to the admission and residence of displaced persons on a temporary basis,[5] and, on 4 March 1996, adopted Decision 96/198/JHA on an alert and emergency procedure for burden-sharing with regard to the admission and residence of displaced persons on a temporary basis.[6]

(5) The Action Plan of the Council and the Commission of 3 December 1998[7] provides for the rapid adoption, in accordance with the Treaty of Amsterdam, of minimum standards for giving temporary protection to displaced persons from third countries who cannot return to their country of origin and of measures promoting a balance of effort between Member States in receiving and bearing the consequences of receiving displaced persons.

(6) On 27 May 1999 the Council adopted conclusions on displaced persons from Kosovo. These conclusions call on the Commission and the Member States to learn the lessons of their response to the Kosovo crisis in order to establish the measures in accordance with the Treaty.

(7) The European Council, at its special meeting in Tampere on 15 and 16 October 1999, acknowledged the need to reach agreement on the issue of temporary protection for displaced persons on the basis of solidarity between Member States.

(8) It is therefore necessary to establish minimum standards for giving temporary protection in the event of a mass influx of displaced persons and to take measures to promote a balance of efforts between the Member States in receiving and bearing the consequences of receiving such persons.

(9) Those standards and measures are linked and interdependent for reasons of effectiveness, coherence and solidarity and in order, in particular, to avert the risk of secondary movements. They should therefore be enacted in a single legal instrument.

(10) This temporary protection should be compatible with the Member States' international obligations as regards refugees. In particular, it must not prejudge the recognition of refugee status pursuant to the Geneva Convention of 28 July 1951 on the status of refugees, as amended by the New York Protocol of 31 January 1967, ratified by all the Member States.

(11) The mandate of the United Nations High Commissioner for Refugees regarding refugees and other persons in need of international protection should be respected,

[5] OJ C 262, 7.10.1995, p. 1.
[6] OJ L 63, 13.3.1996, p. 10.
[7] OJ C 19, 20.1.1999, p. 1.

and effect should be given to Declaration No. 17, annexed to the Final Act to the Treaty of Amsterdam, on Article 63 of the Treaty establishing the European Community which provides that consultations are to be established with the United Nations High Commissioner for Refugees and other relevant international organisations on matters relating to asylum policy.

(12) It is in the very nature of minimum standards that Member States have the power to introduce or maintain more favourable provisions for persons enjoying temporary protection in the event of a mass influx of displaced persons.

(13) Given the exceptional character of the provisions established by this Directive in order to deal with a mass influx or imminent mass influx of displaced persons from third countries who are unable to return to their country of origin, the protection offered should be of limited duration.

(14) The existence of a mass influx of displaced persons should be established by a Council Decision, which should be binding in all Member States in relation to the displaced persons to whom the Decision applies. The conditions for the expiry of the Decision should also be established.

(15) The Member States' obligations as to the conditions of reception and residence of persons enjoying temporary protection in the event of a mass influx of displaced persons should be determined. These obligations should be fair and offer an adequate level of protection to those concerned.

(16) With respect to the treatment of persons enjoying temporary protection under this Directive, the Member States are bound by obligations under instruments of international law to which they are party and which prohibit discrimination.

(17) Member States should, in concert with the Commission, enforce adequate measures so that the processing of personal data respects the standard of protection of Directive 95/46/EC of the European Parliament and the Council of 24 October 1995 on the protection of individuals with regard to the processing of personal data and on the free movement of such data.[8]

(18) Rules should be laid down to govern access to the asylum procedure in the context of temporary protection in the event of a mass influx of displaced persons, in conformity with the Member States' international obligations and with the Treaty.

(19) Provision should be made for principles and measures governing the return to the country of origin and the measures to be taken by Member States in respect of persons whose temporary protection has ended.

(20) Provision should be made for a solidarity mechanism intended to contribute to the attainment of a balance of effort between Member States in receiving and bearing the consequences of receiving displaced persons in the event of a mass influx. The mechanism should consist of two components. The first is financial and the second concerns the actual reception of persons in the Member States.

(21) The implementation of temporary protection should be accompanied by administrative cooperation between the Member States in liaison with the Commission.

(22) It is necessary to determine criteria for the exclusion of certain persons from temporary protection in the event of a mass influx of displaced persons.

[8] OJ L 281, 23.11.1995, p. 31.

(23) Since the objectives of the proposed action, namely to establish minimum standards for giving temporary protection in the event of a mass influx of displaced persons and measures promoting a balance of efforts between the Member States in receiving and bearing the consequences of receiving such persons, cannot be sufficiently attained by the Member States and can therefore, by reason of the scale or effects of the proposed action, be better achieved at Community level, the Community may adopt measures in accordance with the principle of subsidiarity as set out in Article 5 of the Treaty. In accordance with the principle of proportionality as set out in that Article, this Directive does not go beyond what is necessary in order to achieve those objectives.

(24) In accordance with Article 3 of the Protocol on the position of the United Kingdom and Ireland, annexed to the Treaty on European Union and to the Treaty establishing the European Community, the United Kingdom gave notice, by letter of 27 September 2000, of its wish to take part in the adoption and application of this Directive.

(25) Pursuant to Article 1 of the said Protocol, Ireland is not participating in the adoption of this Directive. Consequently and without prejudice to Article 4 of the aforementioned Protocol, the provisions of this Directive do not apply to Ireland.

(26) In accordance with Articles 1 and 2 of the Protocol on the position of Denmark, annexed to the Treaty on European Union and to the Treaty establishing the European Community, Denmark is not participating in the adoption of this Directive, and is therefore not bound by it nor subject to its application,

HAS ADOPTED THIS DIRECTIVE:

Chapter I
General Provisions

Article 1

The purpose of this Directive is to establish minimum standards for giving temporary protection in the event of a mass influx of displaced persons from third countries who are unable to return to their country of origin and to promote a balance of effort between Member States in receiving and bearing the consequences of receiving such persons.

Article 2

For the purpose of this Directive:

(a) 'temporary protection' means a procedure of exceptional character to provide, in the event of a mass influx or imminent mass influx of displaced persons from third countries who are unable to return to their country of origin, immediate and temporary protection to such persons, in particular if there is also a risk that the asylum system will be unable to process this influx without adverse effects for its efficient operation, in the interests of the persons concerned and other persons requesting protection;

(b) 'Geneva Convention' means the Convention of 28 July 1951 relating to the status of refugees, as amended by the New York Protocol of 31 January 1967;

(c) 'displaced persons' means third-country nationals or state-less persons who have had to leave their country or region of origin, or have been evacuated, in particular in response to an appeal by international organisations, and are unable to return in safe and durable conditions because of the situation prevailing in that country, who may fall within the scope of Article 1A of the Geneva Convention or other international or national instruments giving international protection, in particular:

(i) persons who have fled areas of armed conflict or endemic violence;

(ii) persons at serious risk of, or who have been the victims of, systematic or generalised violations of their human rights;

(d) 'mass influx' means arrival in the Community of a large number of displaced persons, who come from a specific country or geographical area, whether their arrival in the Community was spontaneous or aided, for example through an evacuation programme;

(e) 'refugees' means third-country nationals or stateless persons within the meaning of Article 1A of the Geneva Convention;

(f) 'unaccompanied minors' means third-country nationals or stateless persons below the age of eighteen, who arrive on the territory of the Member States unaccompanied by an adult responsible for them whether by law or custom, and for as long as they are not effectively taken into the care of such a person, or minors who are left unaccompanied after they have entered the territory of the Member States;

(g) 'residence permit' means any permit or authorisation issued by the authorities of a Member State and taking the form provided for in that State's legislation, allowing a third country national or a stateless person to reside on its territory;

(h) 'sponsor' means a third-country national enjoying temporary protection in a Member State in accordance with a decision taken under Article 5 and who wants to be joined by members of his or her family.

Article 3

1. Temporary protection shall not prejudge recognition of refugee status under the Geneva Convention.

2. Member States shall apply temporary protection with due respect for human rights and fundamental freedoms and their obligations regarding non-refoulement.

3. The establishment, implementation and termination of temporary protection shall be the subject of regular consultations with the Office of the United Nations High Commissioner for Refugees (UNHCR) and other relevant international organisations.

4. This Directive shall not apply to persons who have been accepted under temporary protection schemes prior to its entry into force.

5. This Directive shall not affect the prerogative of the Member States to adopt or retain more favourable conditions for persons covered by temporary protection.

Chapter II

Duration and Implementation of Temporary Protection

Article 4

1. Without prejudice to Article 6, the duration of temporary protection shall be one year. Unless terminated under the terms of Article 6(1)(b), it may be extended automatically by six monthly periods for a maximum of one year.

2. Where reasons for temporary protection persist, the Council may decide by qualified majority, on a proposal from the Commission, which shall also examine any request by a Member State that it submit a proposal to the Council, to extend that temporary protection by up to one year.

Article 5

1. The existence of a mass influx of displaced persons shall be established by a Council Decision adopted by a qualified majority on a proposal from the Commission, which shall also examine any request by a Member State that it submit a proposal to the Council.

2. The Commission proposal shall include at least:

(a) a description of the specific groups of persons to whom the temporary protection will apply;

(b) the date on which the temporary protection will take effect;

(c) an estimation of the scale of the movements of displaced persons.

3. The Council Decision shall have the effect of introducing temporary protection for the displaced persons to which it refers, in all the Member States, in accordance with the provisions of this Directive. The Decision shall include at least:

(a) a description of the specific groups of persons to whom the temporary protection applies;

(b) the date on which the temporary protection will take effect;

(c) information received from Member States on their reception capacity;

(d) information from the Commission, UNHCR and other relevant international organisations.

4. The Council Decision shall be based on:

(a) an examination of the situation and the scale of the movements of displaced persons;

(b) an assessment of the advisability of establishing temporary protection, taking into account the potential for emergency aid and action on the ground or the inadequacy of such measures;

(c) information received from the Member States, the Commission, UNHCR and other relevant international organisations.

5. The European Parliament shall be informed of the Council Decision.

Article 6

1. Temporary protection shall come to an end:

(a) when the maximum duration has been reached; or

(b) at any time, by Council Decision adopted by a qualified majority on a proposal from the Commission, which shall also examine any request by a Member State that it submit a proposal to the Council.

2. The Council Decision shall be based on the establishment of the fact that the situation in the country of origin is such as to permit the safe and durable return of those granted temporary protection with due respect for human rights and fundamental freedoms and Member States' obligations regarding non-refoulement. The European Parliament shall be informed of the Council Decision.

Article 7

1. Member States may extend temporary protection as provided for in this Directive to additional categories of displaced persons over and above those to whom the Council Decision provided for in Article 5 applies, where they are displaced for the same reasons and from the same country or region of origin. They shall notify the Council and the Commission immediately.

2. The provisions of Articles 24, 25 and 26 shall not apply to the use of the possibility referred to in paragraph 1, with the exception of the structural support included in the European Refugee Fund set up by Decision 2000/596/EC,[9] under the conditions laid down in that Decision.

CHAPTER III

OBLIGATIONS OF THE MEMBER STATES TOWARDS PERSONS ENJOYING TEMPORARY PROTECTION

Article 8

1. The Member States shall adopt the necessary measures to provide persons enjoying temporary protection with residence permits for the entire duration of the protection. Documents or other equivalent evidence shall be issued for that purpose.

2. Whatever the period of validity of the residence permits referred to in paragraph 1, the treatment granted by the Member States to persons enjoying temporary protection may not be less favourable than that set out in Articles 9 to 16.

3. The Member States shall, if necessary, provide persons to be admitted to their territory for the purposes of temporary protection with every facility for obtaining the necessary visas, including transit visas. Formalities must be reduced to a minimum because of the urgency of the situation. Visas should be free of charge or their cost reduced to a minimum.

Article 9

The Member States shall provide persons enjoying temporary protection with a document, in a language likely to be understood by them, in which the provisions relating to temporary protection and which are relevant to them are clearly set out.

Article 10

To enable the effective application of the Council Decision referred to in Article 5, Member States shall register the personal data referred to in Annex II, point (a), with respect to the persons enjoying temporary protection on their territory.

[9] OJ L 252, 6.10.2000, p. 12.

Article 11

A Member State shall take back a person enjoying temporary protection on its territory, if the said person remains on, or, seeks to enter without authorisation onto, the territory of another Member State during the period covered by the Council Decision referred to in Article 5. Member States may, on the basis of a bilateral agreement, decide that this Article should not apply.

Article 12

The Member States shall authorise, for a period not exceeding that of temporary protection, persons enjoying temporary protection to engage in employed or self-employed activities, subject to rules applicable to the profession, as well as in activities such as educational opportunities for adults, vocational training and practical workplace experience. For reasons of labour market policies, Member States may give priority to EU citizens and citizens of States bound by the Agreement on the European Economic Area and also to legally resident third-country nationals who receive unemployment benefit. The general law in force in the Member States applicable to remuneration, access to social security systems relating to employed or self-employed activities and other conditions of employment shall apply.

Article 13

1. The Member States shall ensure that persons enjoying temporary protection have access to suitable accommodation or, if necessary, receive the means to obtain housing.

2. The Member States shall make provision for persons enjoying temporary protection to receive necessary assistance in terms of social welfare and means of subsistence, if they do not have sufficient resources, as well as for medical care. Without prejudice to paragraph 4, the assistance necessary for medical care shall include at least emergency care and essential treatment of illness.

3. Where persons enjoying temporary protection are engaged in employed or self-employed activities, account shall be taken, when fixing the proposed level of aid, of their ability to meet their own needs.

4. The Member States shall provide necessary medical or other assistance to persons enjoying temporary protection who have special needs, such as unaccompanied minors or persons who have undergone torture, rape or other serious forms of psychological, physical or sexual violence.

Article 14

1. The Member States shall grant to persons under 18 years of age enjoying temporary protection access to the education system under the same conditions as nationals of the host Member State. The Member States may stipulate that such access must be confined to the state education system.

2. The Member States may allow adults enjoying temporary protection access to the general education system.

Article 15

1. For the purpose of this Article, in cases where families already existed in the country of origin and were separated due to circumstances surrounding the mass influx, the following persons shall be considered to be part of a family:

(a) the spouse of the sponsor or his/her unmarried partner in a stable relationship, where the legislation or practice of the Member State concerned treats unmarried couples in a way comparable to married couples under its law relating to aliens; the minor unmarried children of the sponsor or of his/her spouse, without distinction as to whether they were born in or out of wedlock or adopted;

(b) other close relatives who lived together as part of the family unit at the time of the events leading to the mass influx, and who were wholly or mainly dependent on the sponsor at the time.

2. In cases where the separate family members enjoy temporary protection in different Member States, Member States shall reunite family members where they are satisfied that the family members fall under the description of paragraph 1(a), taking into account the wish of the said family members. Member States may reunite family members where they are satisfied that the family members fall under the description of paragraph 1(b), taking into account on a case by case basis the extreme hardship they would face if the reunification did not take place.

3. Where the sponsor enjoys temporary protection in one Member State and one or some family members are not yet in a Member State, the Member State where the sponsor enjoys temporary protection shall reunite family members, who are in need of protection, with the sponsor in the case of family members where it is satisfied that they fall under the description of paragraph 1(a). The Member State may reunite family members, who are in need of protection, with the sponsor in the case of family members where it is satisfied that they fall under the description of paragraph 1(b), taking into account on a case by case basis the extreme hardship which they would face if the reunification did not take place.

4. When applying this Article, the Member States shall take into consideration the best interests of the child.

5. The Member States concerned shall decide, taking account of Articles 25 and 26, in which Member State the reunification shall take place.

6. Reunited family members shall be granted residence permits under temporary protection. Documents or other equivalent evidence shall be issued for that purpose. Transfers of family members onto the territory of another Member State for the purposes of reunification under paragraph 2, shall result in the withdrawal of the residence permits issued, and the termination of the obligations towards the persons concerned relating to temporary protection, in the Member State of departure.

7. The practical implementation of this Article may involve cooperation with the international organisations concerned.

8. A Member State shall, at the request of another Member State, provide information, as set out in Annex II, on a person receiving temporary protection which is needed to process a matter under this Article.

Article 16

1. The Member States shall as soon as possible take measures to ensure the necessary representation of unaccompanied minors enjoying temporary protection by legal guardianship, or, where necessary, representation by an organisation which is responsible for the care and well-being of minors, or by any other appropriate representation.

2. During the period of temporary protection Member States shall provide for unaccompanied minors to be placed:

(a) with adult relatives;

(b) with a foster-family;

(c) in reception centres with special provisions for minors, or in other accommodation suitable for minors;

(d) with the person who looked after the child when fleeing.

The Member States shall take the necessary steps to enable the placement. Agreement by the adult person or persons concerned shall be established by the Member States. The views of the child shall be taken into account in accordance with the age and maturity of the child.

Chapter IV

Access to the Asylum Procedure in the Context of Temporary Protection

Article 17

1. Persons enjoying temporary protection must be able to lodge an application for asylum at any time.

2. The examination of any asylum application not processed before the end of the period of temporary protection shall be completed after the end of that period.

Article 18

The criteria and mechanisms for deciding which Member State is responsible for considering an asylum application shall apply. In particular, the Member State responsible for examining an asylum application submitted by a person enjoying temporary protection pursuant to this Directive, shall be the Member State which has accepted his transfer onto its territory.

Article 19

1. The Member States may provide that temporary protection may not be enjoyed concurrently with the status of asylum seeker while applications are under consideration.

2. Where, after an asylum application has been examined, refugee status or, where applicable, other kind of protection is not granted to a person eligible for or enjoying temporary protection, the Member States shall, without prejudice to Article 28, provide for that person to enjoy or to continue to enjoy temporary protection for the remainder of the period of protection.

Chapter V

Return and Measures after Temporary Protection has Ended

Article 20

When the temporary protection ends, the general laws on protection and on aliens in the Member States shall apply, without prejudice to Articles 21, 22 and 23.

Article 21

1. The Member States shall take the measures necessary to make possible the voluntary return of persons enjoying temporary protection or whose temporary protection has ended. The Member States shall ensure that the provisions governing voluntary return of persons enjoying temporary protection facilitate their return with respect for human dignity.

The Member State shall ensure that the decision of those persons to return is taken in full knowledge of the facts. The Member States may provide for exploratory visits.

2. For such time as the temporary protection has not ended, the Member States shall, on the basis of the circumstances prevailing in the country of origin, give favourable consideration to requests for return to the host Member State from persons who have enjoyed temporary protection and exercised their right to a voluntary return.

3. At the end of the temporary protection, the Member States may provide for the obligations laid down in Chapter III to be extended individually to persons who have been covered by temporary protection and are benefiting from a voluntary return programme. The extension shall have effect until the date of return.

Article 22

1. The Member States shall take the measures necessary to ensure that the enforced return of persons whose temporary protection has ended and who are not eligible for admission is conducted with due respect for human dignity.

2. In cases of enforced return, Member States shall consider any compelling humanitarian reasons which may make return impossible or unreasonable in specific cases.

Article 23

1. The Member States shall take the necessary measures concerning the conditions of residence of persons who have enjoyed temporary protection and who cannot, in view of their state of health, reasonably be expected to travel; where for example they would suffer serious negative effects if their treatment was interrupted. They shall not be expelled so long as that situation continues.

2. The Member States may allow families whose children are minors and attend school in a Member State to benefit from residence conditions allowing the children concerned to complete the current school period.

Chapter VI

Solidarity

Article 24

The measures provided for in this Directive shall benefit from the European Refugee Fund set up by Decision 2000/596/EC, under the terms laid down in that Decision.

Article 25

1. The Member States shall receive persons who are eligible for temporary protection in a spirit of Community solidarity. They shall indicate—in figures or in general terms—their capacity to receive such persons. This information shall be set out in the Council Decision referred to in Article 5. After that Decision has been adopted, the Member States may indicate additional reception capacity by notifying the Council and the Commission. This information shall be passed on swiftly to UNHCR.

2. The Member States concerned, acting in cooperation with the competent international organisations, shall ensure that the eligible persons defined in the Council Decision referred to in Article 5, who have not yet arrived in the Community have expressed their will to be received onto their territory.

3. When the number of those who are eligible for temporary protection following a sudden and massive influx exceeds the reception capacity referred to in paragraph 1, the Council shall, as a matter of urgency, examine the situation and take appropriate action, including recommending additional support for Member States affected.

Article 26

1. For the duration of the temporary protection, the Member States shall cooperate with each other with regard to transferral of the residence of persons enjoying temporary protection from one Member State to another, subject to the consent of the persons concerned to such transferral.

2. A Member State shall communicate requests for transfers to the other Member States and notify the Commission and UNHCR. The Member States shall inform the requesting Member State of their capacity for receiving transferees.

3. A Member State shall, at the request of another Member State, provide information, as set out in Annex II, on a person enjoying temporary protection which is needed to process a matter under this Article.

4. Where a transfer is made from one Member State to another, the residence permit in the Member State of departure shall expire and the obligations towards the persons concerned relating to temporary protection in the Member State of departure shall come to an end. The new host Member State shall grant temporary protection to the persons concerned.

5. The Member States shall use the model pass set out in Annex I for transfers between Member States of persons enjoying temporary protection.

Chapter VII
Administrative Cooperation

Article 27

1. For the purposes of the administrative cooperation required to implement temporary protection, the Member States shall each appoint a national contact point, whose address they shall communicate to each other and to the Commission. The Member States shall, in liaison with the Commission, take all the appropriate measures to establish direct cooperation and an exchange of information between the competent authorities.

2. The Member States shall, regularly and as quickly as possible, communicate data concerning the number of persons enjoying temporary protection and full information on the national laws, regulations and administrative provisions relating to the implementation of temporary protection.

Chapter VIII
Special Provisions

Article 28

1. The Member States may exclude a person from temporary protection if:

(a) there are serious reasons for considering that:

(i) he or she has committed a crime against peace, a war crime, or a crime against humanity, as defined in the international instruments drawn up to make provision in respect of such crimes;

(ii) he or she has committed a serious non-political crime outside the Member State of reception prior to his or her admission to that Member State as a person enjoying temporary protection. The severity of the expected persecution is to be weighed against the nature of the criminal offence of which the person concerned is suspected. Particularly cruel actions, even if committed with an allegedly political objective, may be classified as serious non-political crimes. This applies both to the participants in the crime and to its instigators;

(iii) he or she has been guilty of acts contrary to the purposes and principles of the United Nations;

(b) there are reasonable grounds for regarding him or her as a danger to the security of the host Member State or, having been convicted by a final judgment of a particularly serious crime, he or she is a danger to the community of the host Member State.

2. The grounds for exclusion referred to in paragraph 1 shall be based solely on the personal conduct of the person concerned. Exclusion decisions or measures shall be based on the principle of proportionality.

Chapter IX

Final Provisions

Article 29

Persons who have been excluded from the benefit of temporary protection or family reunification by a Member State shall be entitled to mount a legal challenge in the Member State concerned.

Article 30

The Member States shall lay down the rules on penalties applicable to infringements of the national provisions adopted pursuant to this Directive and shall take all measures necessary to ensure that they are implemented. The penalties provided for must be effective, proportionate and dissuasive.

Article 31

1. Not later than two years after the date specified in Article 32, the Commission shall report to the European Parliament and the Council on the application of this Directive in the Member States and shall propose any amendments that are necessary. The Member States shall send the Commission all the information that is appropriate for drawing up this report.

2. After presenting the report referred to at paragraph 1, the Commission shall report to the European Parliament and the Council on the application of this Directive in the Member States at least every five years.

Article 32

1. The Member States shall bring into force the laws, regulations and administrative provisions necessary to comply with this Directive by 31 December 2002 at the latest. They shall forthwith inform the Commission thereof.

2. When the Member States adopt these measures, they shall contain a reference to this Directive or shall be accompanied by such reference on the occasion of their official publication. The methods of making such a reference shall be laid down by the Member States.

Article 33

This Directive shall enter into force on the day of its publication in the *Official Journal of the European Communities.*

Article 34

This Directive is addressed to the Member States in accordance with the Treaty establishing the European Community.

Done at Brussels, 20 July 2001.

For the Council
The President
J. VANDE LANOTTE

Council Directive 2003/9/EC of 27 January 2003

laying down minimum standards for the reception of asylum seekers

Note: Entered into force on 6 February 2003 (Article 27). The United Kingdom continues to be bound by this Directive as it has opted out of the recast Reception Conditions Directive 2013/33/EU. It has been repealed for those EU States that are bound by the recast Directive with effect from 21 July 2015.

THE COUNCIL OF THE EUROPEAN UNION,

Having regard to the Treaty establishing the European Community, and in particular point (1)(b) of the first sub-paragraph of Article 63 thereof,

Having regard to the proposal from the Commission,[1]

Having regard to the opinion of the European Parliament,[2]

Having regard to the opinion of the Economic and Social Committee,[3]

Having regard to the opinion of the Committee of the Regions,[4]

Whereas:

(1) A common policy on asylum, including a Common European Asylum System, is a constituent part of the European Union's objective of progressively establishing an area of freedom, security and justice open to those who, forced by circumstances, legitimately seek protection in the Community.

(2) At its special meeting in Tampere on 15 and 16 October 1999, the European Council agreed to work towards establishing a Common European Asylum System, based on the full and inclusive application of the Geneva Convention relating to the Status of Refugees of 28 July 1951, as supplemented by the New York Protocol of 31 January 1967, thus maintaining the principle of non-refoulement.

(3) The Tampere Conclusions provide that a Common European Asylum System should include, in the short term, common minimum conditions of reception of asylum seekers.

(4) The establishment of minimum standards for the reception of asylum seekers is a further step towards a European asylum policy.

(5) This Directive respects the fundamental rights and observes the principles recognised in particular by the Charter of Fundamental Rights of the European Union. In particular, this Directive seeks to ensure full respect for human dignity and to promote the application of Articles 1 and 18 of the said Charter.

(6) With respect to the treatment of persons falling within the scope of this Directive, Member States are bound by obligations under instruments of international law to which they are party and which prohibit discrimination.

(7) Minimum standards for the reception of asylum seekers that will normally suffice to ensure them a dignified standard of living and comparable living conditions in all Member States should be laid down.

[1] OJ C 213 E, 31.7.2001, p. 286.

[2] Opinion delivered on 25 April 2002 (not yet published in the Official Journal).

[3] OJ C 48, 21.2.2002, p. 63.

[4] OJ C 107, 3.5.2002, p. 85.

(8) The harmonisation of conditions for the reception of asylum seekers should help to limit the secondary movements of asylum seekers influenced by the variety of conditions for their reception.

(9) Reception of groups with special needs should be specifically designed to meet those needs.

(10) Reception of applicants who are in detention should be specifically designed to meet their needs in that situation.

(11) In order to ensure compliance with the minimum procedural guarantees consisting in the opportunity to contact organisations or groups of persons that provide legal assistance, information should be provided on such organisations and groups of persons.

(12) The possibility of abuse of the reception system should be restricted by laying down cases for the reduction or withdrawal of reception conditions for asylum seekers.

(13) The efficiency of national reception systems and cooperation among Member States in the field of reception of asylum seekers should be secured.

(14) Appropriate coordination should be encouraged between the competent authorities as regards the reception of asylum seekers, and harmonious relationships between local communities and accommodation centres should therefore be promoted.

(15) It is in the very nature of minimum standards that Member States have the power to introduce or maintain more favourable provisions for third-country nationals and stateless persons who ask for international protection from a Member State.

(16) In this spirit, Member States are also invited to apply the provisions of this Directive in connection with procedures for deciding on applications for forms of protection other than that emanating from the Geneva Convention for third country nationals and stateless persons.

(17) The implementation of this Directive should be evaluated at regular intervals.

(18) Since the objectives of the proposed action, namely to establish minimum standards on the reception of asylum seekers in Member States, cannot be sufficiently achieved by the Member States and can therefore, by reason of the scale and effects of the proposed action, be better achieved by the Community, the Community may adopt measures in accordance with the principles of subsidiarity as set out in Article 5 of the Treaty. In accordance with the principle of proportionality, as set out in that Article, this Directive does not go beyond what is necessary in order to achieve those objectives.

(19) In accordance with Article 3 of the Protocol on the position of the United Kingdom and Ireland, annexed to the Treaty on European Union and to the Treaty establishing the European Community, the United Kingdom gave notice, by letter of 18 August 2001, of its wish to take part in the adoption and application of this Directive.

(20) In accordance with Article 1 of the said Protocol, Ireland is not participating in the adoption of this Directive. Consequently, and without prejudice to Article 4 of the aforementioned Protocol, the provisions of this Directive do not apply to Ireland.

(21) In accordance with Articles 1 and 2 of the Protocol on the position of Denmark, annexed to the Treaty on European Union and to the Treaty establishing the European Community, Denmark is not participating in the adoption of this Directive and is therefore neither bound by it nor subject to its application,

HAS ADOPTED THIS DIRECTIVE:

Chapter I

Purpose, Definitions and Scope

Article 1

Purpose

The purpose of this Directive is to lay down minimum standards for the reception of asylum seekers in Member States.

Article 2

Definitions

For the purposes of this Directive:

(a) 'Geneva Convention' shall mean the Convention of 28 July 1951 relating to the status of refugees, as amended by the New York Protocol of 31 January 1967;

(b) 'application for asylum' shall mean the application made by a third-country national or a stateless person which can be understood as a request for international protection from a Member State, under the Geneva Convention. Any application for international protection is presumed to be an application for asylum unless a third-country national or a stateless person explicitly requests another kind of protection that can be applied for separately;

(c) 'applicant' or 'asylum seeker' shall mean a third country national or a stateless person who has made an application for asylum in respect of which a final decision has not yet been taken;

(d) 'family members' shall mean, in so far as the family already existed in the country of origin, the following members of the applicant's family who are present in the same Member State in relation to the application for asylum:

(i) the spouse of the asylum seeker or his or her unmarried partner in a stable relationship, where the legislation or practice of the Member State concerned treats unmarried couples in a way comparable to married couples under its law relating to aliens;

(ii) the minor children of the couple referred to in point (i) or of the applicant, on condition that they are unmarried and dependent and regardless of whether they were born in or out of wedlock or adopted as defined under the national law;

(e) 'refugee' shall mean a person who fulfils the requirements of Article 1(A) of the Geneva Convention;

(f) 'refugee status' shall mean the status granted by a Member State to a person who is a refugee and is admitted as such to the territory of that Member State;

(g) 'procedures' and 'appeals', shall mean the procedures and appeals established by Member States in their national law;

(h) 'unaccompanied minors' shall mean persons below the age of eighteen who arrive in the territory of the Member States unaccompanied by an adult responsible for them whether by law or by custom, and for as long as they are not effectively taken into the care of such a person; it shall include minors who are left unaccompanied after they have entered the territory of Member States;

(i) 'reception conditions' shall mean the full set of measures that Member States grant to asylum seekers in accordance with this Directive;

(j) 'material reception conditions' shall mean the reception conditions that include housing, food and clothing, provided in kind, or as financial allowances or in vouchers, and a daily expenses allowance;

(k) 'detention' shall mean confinement of an asylum seeker by a Member State within a particular place, where the applicant is deprived of his or her freedom of movement;

(l) 'accommodation centre' shall mean any place used for collective housing of asylum seekers.

Article 3

Scope

1. This Directive shall apply to all third country nationals and stateless persons who make an application for asylum at the border or in the territory of a Member State as long as they are allowed to remain on the territory as asylum seekers, as well as to family members, if they are covered by such application for asylum according to the national law.

2. This Directive shall not apply in cases of requests for diplomatic or territorial asylum submitted to representations of Member States.

3. This Directive shall not apply when the provisions of Council Directive 2001/55/EC of 20 July 2001 on minimum standards for giving temporary protection in the event of a mass influx of displaced persons and on measures promoting a balance of efforts between Member States in receiving such persons and bearing the consequences thereof[5] are applied.

4. Member States may decide to apply this Directive in connection with procedures for deciding on applications for kinds of protection other than that emanating from the Geneva Convention for third-country nationals or stateless persons who are found not to be refugees.

Article 4

More favourable provisions

Member States may introduce or retain more favourable provisions in the field of reception conditions for asylum seekers and other close relatives of the applicant who are present in the same Member State when they are dependent on him or for humanitarian reasons insofar as these provisions are compatible with this Directive.

[5] OJ L 212, 7.8.2001, p. 12.

Chapter II

General Provisions on Reception Conditions

Article 5

Information

1. Member States shall inform asylum seekers, within a reasonable time not exceeding fifteen days after they have lodged their application for asylum with the competent authority, of at least any established benefits and of the obligations with which they must comply relating to reception conditions.

Member States shall ensure that applicants are provided with information on organisations or groups of persons that provide specific legal assistance and organisations that might be able to help or inform them concerning the available reception conditions, including health care.

2. Member States shall ensure that the information referred to in paragraph 1 is in writing and, as far as possible, in a language that the applicants may reasonably be supposed to understand. Where appropriate, this information may also be supplied orally.

Article 6

Documentation

1. Member States shall ensure that, within three days after an application is lodged with the competent authority, the applicant is provided with a document issued in his or her own name certifying his or her status as an asylum seeker or testifying that he or she is allowed to stay in the territory of the Member State while his or her application is pending or being examined. If the holder is not free to move within all or a part of the territory of the Member State, the document shall also certify this fact.

2. Member States may exclude application of this Article when the asylum seeker is in detention and during the examination of an application for asylum made at the border or within the context of a procedure to decide on the right of the applicant legally to enter the territory of a Member State. In specific cases, during the examination of an application for asylum, Member States may provide applicants with other evidence equivalent to the document referred to in paragraph 1.

3. The document referred to in paragraph 1 need not certify the identity of the asylum seeker.

4. Member States shall adopt the necessary measures to provide asylum seekers with the document referred to in paragraph 1, which must be valid for as long as they are authorised to remain in the territory of the Member State concerned or at the border thereof.

5. Member States may provide asylum seekers with a travel document when serious humanitarian reasons arise that require their presence in another State.

Article 7

Residence and freedom of movement

1. Asylum seekers may move freely within the territory of the host Member State or within an area assigned to them by that Member State. The assigned area shall not affect the unalienable sphere of private life and shall allow sufficient scope for guaranteeing access to all benefits under this Directive.

2. Member States may decide on the residence of the asylum seeker for reasons of public interest, public order or, when necessary, for the swift processing and effective monitoring of his or her application.

3. When it proves necessary, for example for legal reasons or reasons of public order, Member States may confine an applicant to a particular place in accordance with their national law.

4. Member States may make provision of the material reception conditions subject to actual residence by the applicants in a specific place, to be determined by the Member States. Such a decision, which may be of a general nature, shall be taken individually and established by national legislation.

5. Member States shall provide for the possibility of granting applicants temporary permission to leave the place of residence mentioned in paragraphs 2 and 4 and/or the assigned area mentioned in paragraph 1. Decisions shall be taken individually, objectively and impartially and reasons shall be given if they are negative.

The applicant shall not require permission to keep appointments with authorities and courts if his or her appearance is necessary.

6. Member States shall require applicants to inform the competent authorities of their current address and notify any change of address to such authorities as soon as possible.

Article 8

Families

Member States shall take appropriate measures to maintain as far as possible family unity as present within their territory, if applicants are provided with housing by the Member State concerned. Such measures shall be implemented with the asylum seeker's agreement.

Article 9

Medical screening

Member States may require medical screening for applicants on public health grounds.

Article 10

Schooling and education of minors

1. Member States shall grant to minor children of asylum seekers and to asylum seekers who are minors access to the education system under similar conditions as nationals of the host Member State for so long as an expulsion measure against them or their parents is not actually enforced. Such education may be provided in accommodation centres.

The Member State concerned may stipulate that such access must be confined to the State education system.

Minors shall be younger than the age of legal majority in the Member State in which the application for asylum was lodged or is being examined. Member States shall not withdraw secondary education for the sole reason that the minor has reached the age of majority.

2. Access to the education system shall not be postponed for more than three months from the date the application for asylum was lodged by the minor or the minor's parents. This period may be extended to one year where specific education is provided in order to facilitate access to the education system.

3. Where access to the education system as set out in paragraph 1 is not possible due to the specific situation of the minor, the Member State may offer other education arrangements.

Article 11

Employment

1. Member States shall determine a period of time, starting from the date on which an application for asylum was lodged, during which an applicant shall not have access to the labour market.

2. If a decision at first instance has not been taken within one year of the presentation of an application for asylum and this delay cannot be attributed to the applicant, Member States shall decide the conditions for granting access to the labour market for the applicant.

3. Access to the labour market shall not be withdrawn during appeals procedures, where an appeal against a negative decision in a regular procedure has suspensive effect, until such time as a negative decision on the appeal is notified.

4. For reasons of labour market policies, Member States may give priority to EU citizens and nationals of States parties to the Agreement on the European Economic Area and also to legally resident third-country nationals.

Article 12

Vocational training

Member States may allow asylum seekers access to vocational training irrespective of whether they have access to the labour market.

Access to vocational training relating to an employment contract shall depend on the extent to which the applicant has access to the labour market in accordance with Article 11.

Article 13

General rules on material reception conditions and health care

1. Member States shall ensure that material reception conditions are available to applicants when they make their application for asylum.

2. Member States shall make provisions on material reception conditions to ensure a standard of living adequate for the health of applicants and capable of ensuring their subsistence. Member States shall ensure that that standard of living is met in the specific situation of persons who have special needs, in accordance with Article 17, as well as in relation to the situation of persons who are in detention.

3. Member States may make the provision of all or some of the material reception conditions and health care subject to the condition that applicants do not have sufficient means to have a standard of living adequate for their health and to enable their subsistence.

4. Member States may require applicants to cover or contribute to the cost of the material reception conditions and of the health care provided for in this Directive, pursuant to the provision of paragraph 3, if the applicants have sufficient resources, for example if they have been working for a reasonable period of time.

If it transpires that an applicant had sufficient means to cover material reception conditions and health care at the time when these basic needs were being covered, Member States may ask the asylum seeker for a refund.

5. Material reception conditions may be provided in kind, or in the form of financial allowances or vouchers or in a combination of these provisions.

Where Member States provide material reception conditions in the form of financial allowances or vouchers, the amount thereof shall be determined in accordance with the principles set out in this Article.

Article 14

Modalities for material reception conditions

1. Where housing is provided in kind, it should take one or a combination of the following forms:

(a) premises used for the purpose of housing applicants during the examination of an application for asylum lodged at the border;

(b) accommodation centres which guarantee an adequate standard of living;

(c) private houses, flats, hotels or other premises adapted for housing applicants.

2. Member States shall ensure that applicants provided with the housing referred to in paragraph 1(a), (b) and (c) are assured:

(a) protection of their family life;

(b) the possibility of communicating with relatives, legal advisers and representatives of the United Nations High Commissioner for Refugees (UNHCR) and non-governmental organisations (NGOs) recognised by Member States. Member States shall pay particular attention to the prevention of assault within the premises and accommodation centres referred to in paragraph 1(a) and (b).

3. Member States shall ensure, if appropriate, that minor children of applicants or applicants who are minors are lodged with their parents or with the adult family member responsible for them whether by law or by custom.

4. Member States shall ensure that transfers of applicants from one housing facility to another take place only when necessary. Member States shall provide for the possibility for applicants to inform their legal advisers of the transfer and of their new address.

5. Persons working in accommodation centres shall be adequately trained and shall be bound by the confidentiality principle as defined in the national law in relation to any information they obtain in the course of their work.

6. Member States may involve applicants in managing the material resources and non-material aspects of life in the centre through an advisory board or council representing residents.

7. Legal advisors or counsellors of asylum seekers and representatives of the United Nations High Commissioner for Refugees or non-governmental organisations designated by the latter and recognised by the Member State concerned shall be granted access to accommodation centres and other housing facilities in order to assist the said asylum seekers. Limits on such access may be imposed only on grounds relating to the security of the centres and facilities and of the asylum seekers.

8. Member States may exceptionally set modalities for material reception conditions different from those provided for in this Article, for a reasonable period which shall be as short as possible, when:

— an initial assessment of the specific needs of the applicant is required,

— material reception conditions, as provided for in this Article, are not available in a certain geographical area,

— housing capacities normally available are temporarily exhausted,

— the asylum seeker is in detention or confined to border posts. These different conditions shall cover in any case basic needs.

Article 15

Health care

1. Member States shall ensure that applicants receive the necessary health care which shall include, at least, emergency care and essential treatment of illness.

2. Member States shall provide necessary medical or other assistance to applicants who have special needs.

Chapter III

Reduction or Withdrawal of Reception Conditions

Article 16

Reduction or withdrawal of reception conditions

1. Member States may reduce or withdraw reception conditions in the following cases:

(a) where an asylum seeker:

— abandons the place of residence determined by the competent authority without informing it or, if requested, without permission, or

— does not comply with reporting duties or with requests to provide information or to appear for personal interviews concerning the asylum procedure during a reasonable period laid down in national law, or

— has already lodged an application in the same Member State.

When the applicant is traced or voluntarily reports to the competent authority, a duly motivated decision, based on the reasons for the disappearance, shall be taken on the reinstallation of the grant of some or all of the reception conditions;

(b) where an applicant has concealed financial resources and has therefore unduly benefited from material reception conditions.

If it transpires that an applicant had sufficient means to cover material reception conditions and health care at the time when these basic needs were being covered, Member States may ask the asylum seeker for a refund.

2. Member States may refuse conditions in cases where an asylum seeker has failed to demonstrate that the asylum claim was made as soon as reasonably practicable after arrival in that Member State.

3. Member States may determine sanctions applicable to serious breaching of the rules of the accommodation centres as well as to seriously violent behaviour.

4. Decisions for reduction, withdrawal or refusal of reception conditions or sanctions referred to in paragraphs 1, 2 and 3 shall be taken individually, objectively and impartially and reasons shall be given. Decisions shall be based on the particular situation of the person concerned, especially with regard to persons covered by Article 17, taking into account the principle of proportionality. Member States shall under all circumstances ensure access to emergency health care.

5. Member States shall ensure that material reception conditions are not withdrawn or reduced before a negative decision is taken.

Chapter IV

Provisions for Persons with Special Needs

Article 17

General principle

1. Member States shall take into account the specific situation of vulnerable persons such as minors, unaccompanied minors, disabled people, elderly people, pregnant women, single parents with minor children and persons who have been subjected to torture, rape or other serious forms of psychological, physical or sexual violence, in the national legislation implementing the provisions of Chapter II relating to material reception conditions and health care.

2. Paragraph 1 shall apply only to persons found to have special needs after an individual evaluation of their situation.

Article 18

Minors

1. The best interests of the child shall be a primary consideration for Member States when implementing the provisions of this Directive that involve minors.

2. Member States shall ensure access to rehabilitation services for minors who have been victims of any form of abuse, neglect, exploitation, torture or cruel, inhuman and degrading treatment, or who have suffered from armed conflicts, and ensure that appropriate mental health care is developed and qualified counselling is provided when needed.

Article 19

Unaccompanied minors

1. Member States shall as soon as possible take measures to ensure the necessary representation of unaccompanied minors by legal guardianship or, where necessary, representation by an organisation which is responsible for the care and well-being of minors, or by any other appropriate representation. Regular assessments shall be made by the appropriate authorities.

2. Unaccompanied minors who make an application for asylum shall, from the moment they are admitted to the territory to the moment they are obliged to leave the host Member State in which the application for asylum was made or is being examined, be placed:

(a) with adult relatives;
(b) with a foster-family;
(c) in accommodation centres with special provisions for minors;
(d) in other accommodation suitable for minors.

Member States may place unaccompanied minors aged 16 or over in accommodation centres for adult asylum seekers.

As far as possible, siblings shall be kept together, taking into account the best interests of the minor concerned and, in particular, his or her age and degree of maturity. Changes of residence of unaccompanied minors shall be limited to a minimum.

3. Member States, protecting the unaccompanied minor's best interests, shall endeavour to trace the members of his or her family as soon as possible. In cases where there may be a threat to the life or integrity of the minor or his or her close relatives, particularly if they have remained in the country of origin, care must be taken to ensure that the collection, processing and circulation of information concerning those persons is undertaken on a confidential basis, so as to avoid jeopardising their safety.

4. Those working with unaccompanied minors shall have had or receive appropriate training concerning their needs, and shall be bound by the confidentiality principle as defined in the national law, in relation to any information they obtain in the course of their work.

Article 20

Victims of torture and violence

Member States shall ensure that, if necessary, persons who have been subjected to torture, rape or other serious acts of violence receive the necessary treatment of damages caused by the aforementioned acts.

Chapter V

Appeals

Article 21

Appeals

1. Member States shall ensure that negative decisions relating to the granting of benefits under this Directive or decisions taken under Article 7 which individually affect asylum seekers may be the subject of an appeal within the procedures laid down in the national law. At least in the last instance the possibility of an appeal or a review before a judicial body shall be granted.

2. Procedures for access to legal assistance in such cases shall be laid down in national law.

Chapter VI

Actions to Improve the Efficiency of the Reception System

Article 22

Cooperation

Member States shall regularly inform the Commission on the data concerning the number of persons, broken down by sex and age, covered by reception conditions and provide full information on the type, name and format of the documents provided for by Article 6.

Article 23

Guidance, monitoring and control system

Member States shall, with due respect to their constitutional structure, ensure that appropriate guidance, monitoring and control of the level of reception conditions are established.

Article 24

Staff and resources

1. Member States shall take appropriate measures to ensure that authorities and other organisations implementing this Directive have received the necessary basic training with respect to the needs of both male and female applicants.

2. Member States shall allocate the necessary resources in connection with the national provisions enacted to implement this Directive.

Chapter VII

Final Provisions

Article 25

Reports

By 6 August 2006, the Commission shall report to the European Parliament and the Council on the application of this Directive and shall propose any amendments that are necessary.

Member States shall send the Commission all the information that is appropriate for drawing up the report, including the statistical data provided for by Article 22 by 6 February 2006.

After presenting the report, the Commission shall report to the European Parliament and the Council on the application of this Directive at least every five years.

Article 26

Transposition

1. Member States shall bring into force the laws, regulations and administrative provisions necessary to comply with this Directive by 6 February 2005. They shall forthwith inform the Commission thereof.

When the Member States adopt these measures, they shall contain a reference to this Directive or shall be accompanied by such a reference on the occasion of their official publication. Member States shall determine how such a reference is to be made.

2. Member States shall communicate to the Commission the text of the provisions of national law which they adopt in the field relating to the enforcement of this Directive.

Article 27

Entry into force

This Directive shall enter into force on the day of its publication in the *Official Journal of the European Union.*

Article 28

Addresses

This Directive is addressed to the Member States in accordance with the Treaty establishing the European Union.

Done at Brussels, 27 January 2003.

For the Council
The President
G. PAPANDREOU

Commission Regulation (EC) No. 1560/2003 of 2 September 2003

laying down detailed rules for the application of Council Regulation (EC) No. 343/2003 establishing the criteria and mechanisms for determining the Member State responsible for examining an asylum application lodged in one of the Member States by a third-country national

Note: Entered into force on 6 September 2003 (Article 23).

THE COMMISSION OF THE EUROPEAN COMMUNITIES,

Having regard to the Treaty establishing the European Community,

Having regard to Council Regulation (EC) No. 343/2003 of 18 February 2003 establishing the criteria and mechanisms for determining the Member State responsible for examining an asylum application lodged in one of the Member States by a third-country national,[1] and in particular Article 15(5), Article 17(3), Article 18(3), Article 19(3) and (5), Article 20(1), (3) and (4) and Article 22(2) thereof,

Whereas:

(1) A number of specific arrangements must be established for the effective application of Regulation (EC) No. 343/2003. Those arrangements must be clearly defined so as to facilitate cooperation between the authorities in the Member States competent for implementing that Regulation as regards the transmission and processing of requests for the purposes of taking charge and taking back, requests for information and the carrying out of transfers.

(2) To ensure the greatest possible continuity between the Convention determining the State responsible for examining applications for asylum lodged in one of the Member States of the European Communities,[2] signed in Dublin on 15 June 1990, and Regulation (EC) No. 343/2003, which replaces that Convention, this Regulation should be based on the common principles, lists and forms adopted by the committee set up by Article 18 of that Convention, with the inclusion of amendments necessitated by the introduction of new criteria, the wording of certain provisions and of the lessons drawn from experience.

(3) The interaction between the procedures laid down in Regulation (EC) No. 343/2003 and the application of Council Regulation (EC) No. 2725/2000 of 11 December 2000 concerning the establishment of 'Eurodac' for the comparison of fingerprints for the effective application of the Dublin Convention[3] must be taken into account.

(4) It is desirable, both for the Member States and the asylum seekers concerned, that there should be a mechanism for finding a solution in cases where Member States

[1] OJ L 50, 25.2.2003, p. 1.
[2] OJ C 254, 19.8.1997, p. 1.
[3] OJ L 316, 15.12.2000, p. 1.

differ over the application of the humanitarian clause in Article 15 of Regulation (EC) No. 343/2003.

(5) The establishment of an electronic transmission network to facilitate the implementation of Regulation (EC) No. 343/2003 means that rules must be laid down relating to the technical standards applicable and the practical arrangements for using the network.

(6) Directive 95/46/EC of the European Parliament and of the Council of 24 October 1995 on the protection of individuals with regard to the processing of personal data and on the free movement of such data[4] applies to processing carried out pursuant to the present Regulation in accordance with Article 21 of Regulation (EC) No. 343/2003.

(7) In accordance with Articles 1 and 2 of the Protocol on the position of Denmark annexed to the Treaty on European Union and to the Treaty establishing the European Community, Denmark, which is not bound by Regulation (EC) No. 343/2003, is not bound by the present Regulation or subject to its application, until such time as an agreement allowing it to participate in Regulation (EC) No. 343/2003 is reached.

(8) In accordance with Article 4 of the Agreement of 19 January 2001 between the European Community and the Republic of Iceland and the Kingdom of Norway concerning the criteria and mechanisms for establishing the State responsible for examining an application for asylum lodged in a Member State or in Iceland or Norway,[5] this Regulation is to be applied by Iceland and Norway as it is applied by the Member States of the European Community. Consequently, for the purposes of this Regulation, Member States also include Iceland and Norway.

(9) It is necessary for the present Regulation to enter into force as quickly as possible to enable Regulation (EC) No. 343/2003 to be applied.

(10) The measures set out in this Regulation are in accordance with the opinion of the Committee set up by Article 27 of Regulation (EC) No. 343/2003,

has adopted this regulation:

Title I

Procedures

Chapter I

Preparation of Requests

Article 1

Preparation of requests for taking charge

1. Requests for taking charge shall be made on a standard form in accordance with the model in Annex I. The form shall include mandatory fields which must be duly filled in and other fields to be filled in if the information is available. Additional information may be entered in the field set aside for the purpose.

[4] OJ L 281, 23.11.1995, p. 31.
[5] OJ L 93, 3.4.2001, p. 40.

The request shall also include: (a) a copy of all the proof and circumstantial evidence showing that the requested Member State is responsible for examining the application for asylum, accompanied, where appropriate, by comments on the circumstances in which it was obtained and the probative value attached to it by the requesting Member State, with reference to the lists of proof and circumstantial evidence referred to in Article 18(3) of Regulation (EC) No. 343/2003, which are set out in Annex II to the present Regulation; (b) where necessary, a copy of any written declarations made by or statements taken from the applicant.

2. Where the request is based on a positive result (hit) transmitted by the Eurodac Central Unit in accordance with Article 4(5) of Regulation (EC) No. 2725/2000 after comparison of the asylum seeker's fingerprints with fingerprint data previously taken and sent to the Central Unit in accordance with Article 8 of that Regulation and checked in accordance with Article 4(6) of that Regulation, it shall also include the data supplied by the Central Unit.

2a. Where the request is based on a positive result (hit) transmitted by the Visa Information System (VIS) in accordance with Article 21 of Regulation (EC) No. 767/2008 of the European Parliament and of the Council after comparison of the fingerprints of the applicant for international protection with fingerprint data previously taken and sent to the VIS in accordance with Article 9 of that Regulation and checked in accordance with Article 21 of that Regulation, it shall also include the data supplied by the VIS.

3. Where the requesting Member State asks for an urgent reply in accordance with Article 17(2) of Regulation (EC) No. 343/2003, the request shall describe the circumstances of the application for asylum and shall state the reasons in law and in fact which warrant an urgent reply.

Note: Paragraph 2A inserted from 9 February 2014 by Commission Implementing Regulation No. 118/2014.

Article 2

Preparation of requests for taking back

Requests for taking back shall be made on a standard form in accordance with the model in Annex III, setting out the nature of the request, the reasons for it and the provisions of Regulation (EU) No. 604/2013 of the European Parliament and of the Council on which it is based.

The request shall also include, as applicable:

(a) a copy of all the proof and circumstantial evidence showing that the requested Member State is responsible for examining the application for international protection, accompanied, where appropriate, by comments on the circumstances in which it was obtained and the probative value attached to it by the requesting Member State, with reference to the lists of proof and circumstantial evidence referred to in Article 22(3) of Regulation (EU) No. 604/2013, which are set out in Annex II to this Regulation;

(b) the positive result (hit) transmitted by the Eurodac Central Unit, in accordance with Article 4(5) of Regulation (EC) No. 2725/2000, after comparison of the applicant's fingerprints with fingerprint data previously taken and sent to the Central Unit in accordance with Article 4(1) and (2) of that Regulation and checked in accordance with Article 4(6) of that Regulation.

Note: Paragraph 2 substituted from 9 February 2014 by Commission Implementing Regulation No. 118/2014.

Chapter II

Reaction to Requests

Article 3

Processing requests for taking charge

1. The arguments in law and in fact set out in the request shall be examined in the light of the provisions of Regulation (EC) No. 343/2003 and the lists of proof and circumstantial evidence which are set out in Annex II to the present Regulation.

2. Whatever the criteria and provisions of Regulation (EC) No. 343/2003 that are relied on, the requested Member State shall, within the time allowed by Article 18(1) and (6) of that Regulation, check exhaustively and objectively, on the basis of all information directly or indirectly available to it, whether its responsibility for examining the application for asylum is established. If the checks by the requested Member State reveal that it is responsible under at least one of the criteria of that Regulation, it shall acknowledge its responsibility.

Article 4

Processing of requests for taking back

Where a request for taking back is based on data supplied by the Eurodac Central Unit and checked by the requesting Member State, in accordance with Article 4(6) of Regulation (EC) No. 2725/2000, the requested Member State shall acknowledge its responsibility unless the checks carried out reveal that its obligations have ceased under the second subparagraph of Article 4(5) or under Article 16(2), (3) or (4) of Regulation (EC) No. 343/2003. The fact that obligations have ceased on the basis of those provisions may be relied on only on the basis of material evidence or substantiated and verifiable statements by the asylum seeker.

Article 5

Negative reply

1. Where, after checks are carried out, the requested Member State considers that the evidence submitted does not establish its responsibility, the negative reply it sends to the requesting Member State shall state full and detailed reasons for its refusal.

2. Where the requesting Member State feels that such a refusal is based on a misappraisal, or where it has additional evidence to put forward, it may ask for its request to be re-examined. This option must be exercised within three weeks following receipt of the negative reply. The requested Member State shall endeavour to reply within two weeks. In any event, this additional procedure shall not extend the time limits laid down in Article 18(1) and (6) and Article 20(1)(b) of Regulation (EC) No. 343/2003.

Article 6

Positive reply

Where the Member State accepts responsibility, the reply shall say so, specifying the provision of Regulation (EC) No. 343/2003 that is taken as a basis, and shall include practical details regarding the subsequent transfer, such as contact particulars of the department or person to be contacted.

Chapter III
Transfers

Article 7

Practical arrangements for transfers

1. Transfers to the Member State responsible may be carried out in one of the following ways:

(a) at the request of the asylum seeker, by a certain specified date;

(b) by supervised departure, with the asylum seeker being accompanied to the point of embarkation by an official of the requesting Member State, the responsible Member State being notified of the place, date and time of the asylum seeker's arrival within an agreed time limit;

(c) under escort, the asylum seeker being accompanied by an official of the requesting Member State or by a representative of an agency empowered by the requesting Member State to act in that capacity and handed over to the authorities in the responsible Member State.

2. In the cases referred to in paragraph 1(a) and (b), the applicant shall be supplied with the laissez-passer referred to in Article 19(3) and Article 20(1)(e) of Regulation (EC) No. 343/2003, a model of which is set out in Annex IV to the present Regulation, to allow him to enter the Member State responsible and to identify himself on his arrival at the place and time indicated to him at the time of notification of the decision on taking charge or taking back by the Member State responsible.

In the case referred to in paragraph 1(c), a laissez-passer shall be issued if the asylum seeker is not in possession of identity documents. The time and place of transfer shall be agreed in advance by the Member States concerned in accordance with the procedure set out in Article 8.

3. The Member State making the transfer shall ensure that all the asylum seeker's documents are returned to him before his departure, given into the safe keeping of members of the escort to be handed to the competent authorities of the Member State responsible, or sent by other appropriate means.

Article 8

Cooperation on transfers

1. It is the obligation of the Member State responsible to allow the asylum seeker's transfer to take place as quickly as possible and to ensure that no obstacles are put in his way. That Member State shall determine, where appropriate, the location on its territory to which the asylum seeker will be transferred or handed over to the competent authorities, taking account of geographical constraints and modes of transport available to the Member State making the transfer. In no case may a requirement be imposed that the escort accompany the asylum seeker beyond the point of arrival of the international

means of transport used or that the Member State making the transfer meet the costs of transport beyond that point.

2. The Member State organising the transfer shall arrange the transport for the asylum seeker and his escort and decide, in consultation with the Member State responsible, on the time of arrival and, where necessary, on the details of the handover to the competent authorities. The Member State responsible may require that three working days' notice be given.

3. The standard form set out in Annex VI shall be used for the purpose of transmitting to the responsible Member State the data essential to safeguard the rights and immediate needs of the person to be transferred. This standard form shall be considered a notice in the meaning of paragraph 2.

Note: Paragraph 3 inserted from 9 February 2014 by Commission Implementing Regulation No. 118/2014.

Article 9

Postponed and delayed transfers

1. The Member State responsible shall be informed without delay of any postponement due either to an appeal or review procedure with suspensive effect, or physical reasons such as ill health of the asylum seeker, non-availability of transport or the fact that the asylum seeker has withdrawn from the transfer procedure.

1a. Where a transfer has been delayed at the request of the transferring Member State, the transferring and the responsible Member States must resume communication in order to allow for a new transfer to be organised as soon as possible, in accordance with Article 8, and no later than two weeks from the moment the authorities become aware of the cessation of the circumstances that caused the delay or postponement. In such a case, an updated standard form for the transfer of the data before a transfer is carried out as set out in Annex VI shall be sent prior to the transfer.

2. A Member State which, for one of the reasons set out in Article 29(2) of Regulation (EU) No. 604/2013, cannot carry out the transfer within the normal time limit of six months from the date of acceptance of the request to take charge or take back the person concerned or of the final decision on an appeal or review where there is a suspensive effect, shall inform the Member State responsible before the end of that time limit. Otherwise, the responsibility for processing the application for international protection and the other obligations under Regulation (EU) No. 604/2013 falls to the requesting Member State, in accordance with Article 29(2) of that Regulation.

3. When, for one of the reasons set out in Article 19(4) and Article 20(2) of Regulation (EC) No. 343/2003, a Member State undertakes to carry out the transfer after the normal time limit of six months, it shall make the necessary arrangements in advance with the Member State responsible.

Note: Paragraph 1A inserted and paragraph 2 substituted from 9 February 2014 by Commission Implementing Regulation No. 118/2014.

Article 10

Transfer following an acceptance by default

1. Where, pursuant to Article 18(7) or Article 20(1)(c) of Regulation (EC) No. 343/2003 as appropriate, the requested Member State is deemed to have accepted a request to take charge or to take back, the requesting Member State shall initiate the consultations needed to organise the transfer.

2. If asked to do so by the requesting Member State, the Member State responsible must confirm in writing, without delay, that it acknowledges its responsibility as a result of its failure to reply within the time limit. The Member State responsible shall take the necessary steps to determine the asylum seeker's place of arrival as quickly as possible and, where applicable, agree with the requesting Member State the time of arrival and the practical details of the handover to the competent authorities.

Chapter IV
Humanitarian Clause

Article 11

Situations of dependency

1. . . .

2. The situations of dependency referred to in Article 15(2) of Regulation (EC) No. 343/2003 shall be assessed, as far as possible, on the basis of objective criteria such as medical certificates. Where such evidence is not available or cannot be supplied, humanitarian grounds shall be taken as proven only on the basis of convincing information supplied by the persons concerned.

3. The following points shall be taken into account in assessing the necessity and appropriateness of bringing together the persons concerned:

(a) the family situation which existed in the country of origin;

(b) the circumstances in which the persons concerned were separated;

(c) the status of the various asylum procedures or procedures under the legislation on aliens under way in the Member States.

4. The application of Article 15(2) of Regulation (EC) No. 343/2003 shall, in any event, be subject to the assurance that the asylum seeker or relative will actually provide the assistance needed.

5. The Member State in which the relatives will be reunited and the date of the transfer shall be agreed by the Member States concerned, taking account of:

(a) the ability of the dependent person to travel;

(b) the situation of the persons concerned as regards residence, preference being given to bringing the asylum seeker together with his relative where the latter already has a valid residence permit and resources in the Member State in which he resides.

6. Where the applicant is present on the territory of Member State other than the one where the child, sibling or parent as referred to in Article 16(1) of Regulation (EU) No. 604/2013 are present, the two Member States shall consult each other and exchange information in order to establish:

(a) the proven family links between the applicant and the child, sibling or parent;

(b) the dependency link between the applicant and the child, sibling or parent;

(c) the capacity of the person concerned to take care of the dependent person;

(d) where necessary, the elements to be taken into account in order to assess the inability to travel for a significant period of time.

In order to carry out the exchange of information referred to in the first subparagraph, the standard form set out in Annex VII to this Regulation shall be used.

The requested Member State shall endeavour to reply within four weeks from the receipt of the request. Where compelling evidence indicates that further investigations would lead to more relevant information, the requested Member State shall inform the requesting Member State that two additional weeks are needed.

The request for information pursuant to this Article shall be carried out ensuring full compliance with the deadlines presented in Articles 21(1), 22(1), 23(2), 24(2) and 25(1) of Regulation (EU) No. 604/2013. This obligation is without prejudice to Article 34(5) of Regulation (EU) No. 604/2013.

Note: Paragraph 1 deleted from 19 July 2013 by Regulation (EU) No. 604/2013. Paragraph 6 inserted from 9 February 2014 by Commission Implementing Regulation No. 118/2014.

Article 12

Unaccompanied minors

1. Where the decision to entrust the care of an unaccompanied minor to a relative other than the mother, father or legal guardian is likely to cause particular difficulties, particularly where the adult concerned resides outside the jurisdiction of the Member State in which the minor has applied for asylum, cooperation between the competent authorities in the Member States, in particular the authorities or courts responsible for the protection of minors, shall be facilitated and the necessary steps taken to ensure that those authorities can decide, with full knowledge of the facts, on the ability of the adult or adults concerned to take charge of the minor in a way which serves his best interests. Options now available in the field of cooperation on judicial and civil matters shall be taken account of in this connection.

2. The fact that the duration of procedures for placing a minor may lead to a failure to observe the time limits set in Article 18(1) and (6) and Article 19(4) of Regulation (EC) No. 343/2003 shall not necessarily be an obstacle to continuing the procedure for determining the Member State responsible or carrying out a transfer.

3. With a view to facilitating the appropriate action to identify the family members, siblings or relatives of an unaccompanied minor, the Member State with which an application for international protection was lodged by an unaccompanied minor shall, after holding the personal interview pursuant to Article 5 of Regulation (EU) No. 604/2013 in the presence of the representative referred to in Article 6(2) of that Regulation, search for and/or take into account any information provided by the minor or coming from any other credible source familiar with the personal situation or the route followed by the minor or a member of his or her family, sibling or relative.

The authorities carrying out the process of establishing the Member State responsible for examining the application of an unaccompanied minor shall involve the representative referred to in Article 6(2) of Regulation (EU) No. 604/2013 in this process to the greatest extent possible.

4. Where in the application of the obligations resulting from Article 8 of Regulation (EU) No. 604/2013, the Member State carrying out the process of establishing the Member State responsible for examining the application of an unaccompanied minor is in possession of information that makes it possible to start identifying and/or locating a member of the family, sibling or relative, that Member State shall consult other Member States, as appropriate, and exchange information, in order to:

(a) identify family members, siblings or relatives of the unaccompanied minor, present on the territory of the Member States;

(b) establish the existence of proven family links;

(c) assess the capacity of a relative to take care of the unaccompanied minor, including where family members, siblings or relatives of the unaccompanied minor stay in more than one Member State.

5. Where the exchange of information referred to in paragraph 4 indicates that more family members, siblings or relatives are present in another Member State or States, the Member State where the unaccompanied minor is present shall cooperate with the relevant Member State or States, to determine the most appropriate person to whom the minor is to be entrusted, and in particular to establish:

(a) the strength of the family links between the minor and the different persons identified on the territories of the Member States;

(b) the capacity and availability of the persons concerned to take care of the minor;

(c) the best interests of the minor in each case.

6. In order to carry out the exchange of information referred to in paragraph 4, the standard form set out in Annex VIII to this Regulation shall be used.

The requested Member State shall endeavour to reply within four weeks from the receipt of the request. Where compelling evidence indicates that further investigations would lead to more relevant information, the requested Member State will inform the requesting Member State that two additional weeks are needed.

The request for information pursuant to this Article shall be carried out ensuring full compliance with the deadlines presented in Articles 21(1), 22(1), 23(2), 24(2) and 25(1) of Regulation (EU) No. 604/2013. This obligation is without prejudice to Article 34(5) of Regulation (EU) No. 604/2013.

Note: Paragraphs 3–6 inserted from 9 February 2014 by Commission Implementing Regulation No. 118/2014.

Article 13

Procedures

Note: Articles 13 and 14 deleted from 19 July 2013 by Regulation (EU) No. 604/2013.

Article 14

Conciliation

Note: Articles 13 and 14 deleted from 19 July 2013 by Regulation (EU) No. 604/2013.

Chapter V

Common Provisions

Article 15

Transmission of requests

1. Requests, replies and all written correspondence between Member States concerning the application of Regulation (EU) No. 604/2013 shall be sent through the 'DubliNet' electronic communications network, set up under Title II of this Regulation.

By way of derogation from the first subparagraph, correspondence between the departments responsible for carrying out transfers and competent departments in the requested Member State regarding the practical arrangements for transfers, time and place of arrival, particularly where the asylum seeker is under escort, may be transmitted by other means.

2. Any request, reply or correspondence emanating from a National Access Point, as referred to in Article 19, shall be deemed to be authentic.

3. The acknowledgement issued by the system shall be taken as proof of transmission and of the date and time of receipt of the request or reply.

Note: The first subparagraph of paragraph 1 substituted from 9 February 2014 by Commission Implementing Regulation No. 118/2014.

Article 15a

Uniform conditions and practical arrangements for exchanging health data before a transfer is carried out

The exchange of health data prior to a transfer and, in particular, the transmission of the health certificate set out in Annex IX shall only take place between the authorities notified to the Commission in accordance with Article 35 of Regulation (EU) No. 604/2013 using the 'DubliNet'.

The Member State carrying out the transfer of an applicant and the responsible Member State shall endeavour to agree prior to the transmission of the health certificate on the language to be used in order to complete that certificate, taking into account the circumstances of the case, in particular the need for any urgent action upon arrival.

Note: Article 15a inserted from 9 February 2014 by Commission Implementing Regulation No. 118/2014.

Article 16

Language of communication

The language or languages of communication shall be chosen by agreement between the Member States concerned.

Article 16a

Information leaflets for applicants for international protection

1. A common leaflet informing all applicants for international protection of the provisions of Regulation (EU) No. 604/2013 and on the application of Regulation (EU) No. 603/2013 is set out in Annex X.

2. A specific leaflet for unaccompanied children applying for international protection is set out in Annex XI.

3. Information for third-country nationals or stateless persons apprehended in connection with irregular crossing of an external border is set out in Annex XII.

4. Information for third-country nationals or stateless persons found illegally staying in a Member State, are set out in Annex XIII.

Note: Article 16a inserted from 9 February 2014 by Commission Implementing Regulation No. 118/2014.

Article 17

Note: Article 17 deleted from 19 July 2013 by Regulation (EU) 604/2013.

Title II

Establishment of the 'Dublinet' Network

Chapter I

Technical Standards

Article 18

Establishment of 'DubliNet'

1. The secure electronic means of transmission referred to in Article 22(2) of Regulation (EC) No. 343/2003 shall be known as 'DubliNet'.

2. . . .

Note: Paragraph 2 deleted from 9 February 2014 by Commission Implementing Regulation No. 118/2014.

Article 19

National Access Points

1. Each Member State shall have a single designated National Access Point.

2. The National Access Points shall be responsible for processing incoming data and transmitting outgoing data.

3. The National Access Points shall be responsible for issuing an acknowledgement of receipt for every incoming transmission.

4. The forms of which the models are set out in Annexes I and III and the forms for the request of information set out in Annexes V, VI, VII, VIII and IX shall be sent between

National Access Points in the format supplied by the Commission. The Commission shall inform the Member States of the technical standards required.

Note: Paragraph 4 substituted from 9 February 2014 by Commission Implementing Regulation No. 118/2014.

Chapter II
Rules for Use

Article 20

1. Each transmission shall have a reference number making it possible unambiguously to identify the case to which it relates and the Member State making the request. That number must also make it possible to determine whether the transmission relates to a request for taking charge (type 1), a request for taking back (type 2), a request for information (type 3), an exchange of information on the child, sibling or parent of an applicant in a situation of dependency (type 4), an exchange of information on the family, sibling or relative of an unaccompanied minor (type 5), the transmission of information prior to a transfer (type 6) or the transmission of the common health certificate (type 7).

2. The reference number shall begin with the letters used to identify the Member State in Eurodac. This code shall be followed by the number indicating the type of request, according to the classification set out in paragraph 1.

If the request is based on data supplied by Eurodac, the Eurodac reference number of the requested Member State shall be included.

Note: Paragraphs 1 and the second subparagraph of paragraph 2 substituted from 9 February 2014 by Commission Implementing Regulation No. 118/2014.

Article 21

Continuous operation

1. The Member States shall take the necessary steps to ensure that their National Access Points operate without interruption.

2. If the operation of a National Access Point is interrupted for more than seven working hours the Member State shall notify the competent authorities designated pursuant to Article 22(1) of Regulation (EC) No. 343/2003 and the Commission and shall take all the necessary steps to ensure that normal operation is resumed as soon as possible.

3. If a National Access Point has sent data to a National Access Point that has experienced an interruption in its operation, the log of transmission at the level of the central communication infrastructure shall be used as proof of the date and time of transmission. The deadlines set by Regulation (EU) No. 604/2013 for sending a request or a reply shall not be suspended for the duration of the interruption of the operation of the National Access Point in question.

Note: Paragraph 3 substituted from 9 February 2014 by Commission Implementing Regulation No. 118/2014.

Title III

Transitional and Final Provisions

Article 22

Laissez-passer produced for the purposes of the Dublin Convention

Laissez-passer printed for the purposes of the Dublin Convention shall be accepted for the transfer of applicants for asylum under Regulation (EC) No. 343/2003 for a period of no more than 18 months following the entry into force of the present Regulation.

Article 23

Entry into Force

This Regulation shall enter into force on the day following that of its publication in the *Official Journal of the European Union.*
This Regulation shall be binding in its entirety and directly applicable in all Member States.

Done at Brussels, 2 September 2003.

For the Commission
António VITORINO
Member of the Commission

ANNEXES

Note: The Annexes to this Regulation (which were substituted from 9 February 2014 by Commission Implementing Regulation No. 118/2014) are not reproduced.

Council Directive 2004/83/EC of 29 April 2004

on minimum standards for the qualification and status of third-country nationals or stateless persons as refugees or as persons who otherwise need international protection and the content of the protection granted

Note: Entered into force on 20 October 2004 (Article 39). Implemented 10 October 2006 (Article 38). The United Kingdom continues to be bound by this Directive, as it has opted out of the recast Qualifications Directive (2011/95/EU). It has been repealed from 21 December 2013 for those EU States to whom the recast Directive applies.

THE COUNCIL OF THE EUROPEAN UNION,

Having regard to the Treaty establishing the European Community, and in particular points 1(c), 2(a) and 3(a) of Article 63 thereof,
Having regard to the proposal from the Commission,[1]
Having regard to the opinion of the European Parliament,[2]
Having regard to the opinion of the European Economic and Social Committee,[3]
Having regard to the opinion of the Committee of the Regions,[4]
Whereas:

(1) A common policy on asylum, including a Common European Asylum System, is a constituent part of the European Union's objective of progressively establishing an area of freedom, security and justice open to those who, forced by circumstances, legitimately seek protection in the Community.

(2) The European Council at its special meeting in Tampere on 15 and 16 October 1999 agreed to work towards establishing a Common European Asylum System, based on the full and inclusive application of the Geneva Convention relating to the Status of Refugees of 28 July 1951 (Geneva Convention), as supplemented by the New York Protocol of 31 January 1967 (Protocol), thus affirming the principle of non-refoulement and ensuring that nobody is sent back to persecution.

(3) The Geneva Convention and Protocol provide the cornerstone of the international legal regime for the protection of refugees.

(4) The Tampere conclusions provide that a Common European Asylum System should include, in the short term, the approximation of rules on the recognition of refugees and the content of refugee status.

(5) The Tampere conclusions also provide that rules regarding refugee status should be complemented by measures on subsidiary forms of protection, offering an appropriate status to any person in need of such protection.

(6) The main objective of this Directive is, on the one hand, to ensure that Member States apply common criteria for the identification of persons genuinely in need of

[1] OJ C 51 E, 26.2.2002, p. 325.
[2] OJ C 300 E, 11.12.2003, p. 25.
[3] OJ C 221, 17.9.2002, p. 43.
[4] OJ C 278, 14.11.2002, p. 44.

international protection, and, on the other hand, to ensure that a minimum level of benefits is available for these persons in all Member States.

(7) The approximation of rules on the recognition and content of refugee and subsidiary protection status should help to limit the secondary movements of applicants for asylum between Member States, where such movement is purely caused by differences in legal frameworks.

(8) It is in the very nature of minimum standards that Member States should have the power to introduce or maintain more favourable provisions for third-country nationals or stateless persons who request international protection from a Member State, where such a request is understood to be on the grounds that the person concerned is either a refugee within the meaning of Article 1(A) of the Geneva Convention, or a person who otherwise needs international protection.

(9) Those third country nationals or stateless persons, who are allowed to remain in the territories of the Member States for reasons not due to a need for international protection but on a discretionary basis on compassionate or humanitarian grounds, fall outside the scope of this Directive.

(10) This Directive respects the fundamental rights and observes the principles recognised in particular by the Charter of Fundamental Rights of the European Union. In particular this Directive seeks to ensure full respect for human dignity and the right to asylum of applicants for asylum and their accompanying family members.

(11) With respect to the treatment of persons falling within the scope of this Directive, Member States are bound by obligations under instruments of international law to which they are party and which prohibit discrimination.

(12) The 'best interests of the child' should be a primary consideration of Member States when implementing this Directive.

(13) This Directive is without prejudice to the Protocol on asylum for nationals of Member States of the European Union as annexed to the Treaty Establishing the European Community.

(14) The recognition of refugee status is a declaratory act.

(15) Consultations with the United Nations High Commissioner for Refugees may provide valuable guidance for Member States when determining refugee status according to Article 1 of the Geneva Convention.

(16) Minimum standards for the definition and content of refugee status should be laid down to guide the competent national bodies of Member States in the application of the Geneva Convention.

(17) It is necessary to introduce common criteria for recognising applicants for asylum as refugees within the meaning of Article 1 of the Geneva Convention.

(18) In particular, it is necessary to introduce common concepts of protection needs arising *sur place*; sources of harm and protection; internal protection; and persecution, including the reasons for persecution.

(19) Protection can be provided not only by the State but also by parties or organisations, including international organisations, meeting the conditions of this Directive, which control a region or a larger area within the territory of the State.

(20) It is necessary, when assessing applications from minors for international protection, that Member States should have regard to child-specific forms of persecution.

(21) It is equally necessary to introduce a common concept of the persecution ground 'membership of a particular social group'.

(22) Acts contrary to the purposes and principles of the United Nations are set out in the Preamble and Articles 1 and 2 of the Charter of the United Nations and are, amongst others, embodied in the United Nations Resolutions relating to measures combating terrorism, which declare that 'acts, methods and practices of terrorism are contrary to the purposes and principles of the United Nations' and that 'knowingly financing, planning and inciting terrorist acts are also contrary to the purposes and principles of the United Nations'.

(23) As referred to in Article 14, 'status' can also include refugee status.

(24) Minimum standards for the definition and content of subsidiary protection status should also be laid down. Subsidiary protection should be complementary and additional to the refugee protection enshrined in the Geneva Convention.

(25) It is necessary to introduce criteria on the basis of which applicants for international protection are to be recognised as eligible for subsidiary protection. Those criteria should be drawn from international obligations under human rights instruments and practices existing in Member States.

(26) Risks to which a population of a country or a section of the population is generally exposed do normally not create in themselves an individual threat which would qualify as serious harm.

(27) Family members, merely due to their relation to the refugee, will normally be vulnerable to acts of persecution in such a manner that could be the basis for refugee status.

(28) The notion of national security and public order also covers cases in which a third country national belongs to an association which supports international terrorism or supports such an association.

(29) While the benefits provided to family members of beneficiaries of subsidiary protection status do not necessarily have to be the same as those provided to the qualifying beneficiary, they need to be fair in comparison to those enjoyed by beneficiaries of subsidiary protection status.

(30) Within the limits set out by international obligations, Member States may lay down that the granting of benefits with regard to access to employment, social welfare, health care and access to integration facilities requires the prior issue of a residence permit.

(31) This Directive does not apply to financial benefits from the Member States which are granted to promote education and training.

(32) The practical difficulties encountered by beneficiaries of refugee or subsidiary protection status concerning the authentication of their foreign diplomas, certificates or other evidence of formal qualification should be taken into account.

(33) Especially to avoid social hardship, it is appropriate, for beneficiaries of refugee or subsidiary protection status, to provide without discrimination in the context of social assistance the adequate social welfare and means of subsistence.

(34) With regard to social assistance and health care, the modalities and detail of the provision of core benefits to beneficiaries of subsidiary protection status should be determined by national law. The possibility of limiting the benefits for beneficiaries of subsidiary protection status to core benefits is to be understood in the sense that this notion covers at least minimum income support, assistance in case of illness, pregnancy and parental assistance, in so far as they are granted to nationals according to the legislation of the Member State concerned.

(35) Access to health care, including both physical and mental health care, should be ensured to beneficiaries of refugee or subsidiary protection status.

(36) The implementation of this Directive should be evaluated at regular intervals, taking into consideration in particular the evolution of the international obligations of Member States regarding non-refoulement, the evolution of the labour markets in the Member States as well as the development of common basic principles for integration.

(37) Since the objectives of the proposed Directive, namely to establish minimum standards for the granting of international protection to third country nationals and stateless persons by Member States and the content of the protection granted, cannot be sufficiently achieved by the Member States and can therefore, by reason of the scale and effects of the Directive, be better achieved at Community level, the Community may adopt measures, in accordance with the principle of subsidiarity as set out in Article 5 of the Treaty. In accordance with the principle of proportionality, as set out in that Article, this Directive does not go beyond what is necessary in order to achieve those objectives.

(38) In accordance with Article 3 of the Protocol on the position of the United Kingdom and Ireland, annexed to the Treaty on European Union and to the Treaty establishing the European Community, the United Kingdom has notified, by letter of 28 January 2002, its wish to take part in the adoption and application of this Directive.

(39) In accordance with Article 3 of the Protocol on the position of the United Kingdom and Ireland, annexed to the Treaty on European Union and to the Treaty establishing the European Community, Ireland has notified, by letter of 13 February 2002, its wish to take part in the adoption and application of this Directive.

(40) In accordance with Articles 1 and 2 of the Protocol on the position of Denmark, annexed to the Treaty on European Union and to the Treaty establishing the European Community, Denmark is not taking part in the adoption of this Directive and is not bound by it or subject to its application,

HAS ADOPTED THIS DIRECTIVE,

CHAPTER I
GENERAL PROVISIONS

Article 1

Subject matter and scope

The purpose of this Directive is to lay down minimum standards for the qualification of third country nationals or stateless persons as refugees or as persons who otherwise need international protection and the content of the protection granted.

Article 2

Definitions

For the purposes of this Directive:

(a) 'international protection' means the refugee and subsidiary protection status as defined in (d) and (f);

(b) 'Geneva Convention' means the Convention relating to the status of refugees done at Geneva on 28 July 1951, as amended by the New York Protocol of 31 January 1967;

(c) 'refugee' means a third country national who, owing to a well-founded fear of being persecuted for reasons of race, religion, nationality, political opinion or membership of a particular social group, is outside the country of nationality and is unable or, owing to such fear, is unwilling to avail himself or herself of the protection of that country, or a stateless person, who, being outside of the country of former habitual residence for the same reasons as mentioned above, is unable or, owing to such fear, unwilling to return to it, and to whom Article 12 does not apply;

(d) 'refugee status' means the recognition by a Member State of a third country national or a stateless person as a refugee;

(e) 'person eligible for subsidiary protection' means a third country national or a stateless person who does not qualify as a refugee but in respect of whom substantial grounds have been shown for believing that the person concerned, if returned to his or her country of origin, or in the case of a stateless person, to his or her country of former habitual residence, would face a real risk of suffering serious harm as defined in Article 15, and to whom Article 17(1) and (2) do not apply, and is unable, or, owing to such risk, unwilling to avail himself or herself of the protection of that country;

(f) 'subsidiary protection status' means the recognition by a Member State of a third country national or a stateless person as a person eligible for subsidiary protection;

(g) 'application for international protection' means a request made by a third country national or a stateless person for protection from a Member State, who can be understood to seek refugee status or subsidiary protection status, and who does not explicitly request another kind of protection, outside the scope of this Directive, that can be applied for separately;

(h) 'family members' means, insofar as the family already existed in the country of origin, the following members of the family of the beneficiary of refugee or subsidiary protection status who are present in the same Member State in relation to the application for international protection:

— the spouse of the beneficiary of refugee or subsidiary protection status or his or her unmarried partner in a stable relationship, where the legislation or practice of the Member State concerned treats unmarried couples in a way comparable to married couples under its law relating to aliens,

— the minor children of the couple referred to in the first indent or of the beneficiary of refugee or subsidiary protection status, on condition that they are unmarried and dependent and regardless of whether they were born in or out of wedlock or adopted as defined under the national law;

(i) 'unaccompanied minors' means third-country nationals or stateless persons below the age of 18, who arrive on the territory of the Member States unaccompanied by an adult responsible for them whether by law or custom, and for as long as they are not effectively taken into the care of such a person; it includes minors who are left unaccompanied after they have entered the territory of the Member States;

(j) 'residence permit' means any permit or authorisation issued by the authorities of a Member State, in the form provided for under that State's legislation, allowing a third country national or stateless person to reside on its territory;

(k) 'country of origin' means the country or countries of nationality or, for stateless persons, of former habitual residence.

Article 3

More favourable standards

Member States may introduce or retain more favourable standards for determining who qualifies as a refugee or as a person eligible for subsidiary protection, and for determining the content of international protection, insofar as those standards are compatible with this Directive.

Chapter II

Assessment of Applications for International Protection

Article 4

Assessment of facts and circumstances

1. Member States may consider it the duty of the applicant to submit as soon as possible all elements needed to substantiate the application for international protection. In cooperation with the applicant it is the duty of the Member State to assess the relevant elements of the application.

2. The elements referred to in paragraph 1 consist of the applicant's statements and all documentation at the applicant's disposal regarding the applicant's age, background, including that of relevant relatives, identity, nationality(ies), country(ies) and place(s) of previous residence, previous asylum applications, travel routes, identity and travel documents and the reasons for applying for international protection.

3. The assessment of an application for international protection is to be carried out on an individual basis and includes taking into account:

(a) all relevant facts as they relate to the country of origin at the time of taking a decision on the application; including laws and regulations of the country of origin and the manner in which they are applied;

(b) the relevant statements and documentation presented by the applicant including information on whether the applicant has been or may be subject to persecution or serious harm;

(c) the individual position and personal circumstances of the applicant, including factors such as background, gender and age, so as to assess whether, on the basis of the applicant's personal circumstances, the acts to which the applicant has been or could be exposed would amount to persecution or serious harm;

(d) whether the applicant's activities since leaving the country of origin were engaged in for the sole or main purpose of creating the necessary conditions for applying for international protection, so as to assess whether these activities will expose the applicant to persecution or serious harm if returned to that country;

(e) whether the applicant could reasonably be expected to avail himself of the protection of another country where he could assert citizenship.

4. The fact that an applicant has already been subject to persecution or serious harm or to direct threats of such persecution or such harm, is a serious indication of the applicant's well-founded fear of persecution or real risk of suffering serious harm, unless there are good reasons to consider that such persecution or serious harm will not be repeated.

5. Where Member States apply the principle according to which it is the duty of the applicant to substantiate the application for international protection and where aspects of the applicant's statements are not supported by documentary or other evidence, those aspects shall not need confirmation, when the following conditions are met:

(a) the applicant has made a genuine effort to substantiate his application;

(b) all relevant elements, at the applicant's disposal, have been submitted, and a satisfactory explanation regarding any lack of other relevant elements has been given;

(c) the applicant's statements are found to be coherent and plausible and do not run counter to available specific and general information relevant to the applicant's case;

(d) the applicant has applied for international protection at the earliest possible time, unless the applicant can demonstrate good reason for not having done so; and

(e) the general credibility of the applicant has been established.

Article 5

International protection needs arising *Sur place*

1. A well-founded fear of being persecuted or a real risk of suffering serious harm may be based on events which have taken place since the applicant left the country of origin.

2. A well-founded fear of being persecuted or a real risk of suffering serious harm may be based on activities which have been engaged in by the applicant since he left the country of origin, in particular where it is established that the activities relied upon constitute the expression and continuation of convictions or orientations held in the country of origin.

3. Without prejudice to the Geneva Convention, Member States may determine that an applicant who files a subsequent application shall normally not be granted refugee status, if the risk of persecution is based on circumstances which the applicant has created by his own decision since leaving the country of origin.

Article 6

Actors of persecution or serious harm

Actors of persecution or serious harm include:

(a) the State;

(b) parties or organisations controlling the State or a substantial part of the territory of the State;

(c) non-State actors, if it can be demonstrated that the actors mentioned in (a) and (b), including international organisations, are unable or unwilling to provide protection against persecution or serious harm as defined in Article 7.

Article 7

Actors of protection

1. Protection can be provided by:

(a) the State; or

(b) parties or organisations, including international organisations, controlling the State or a substantial part of the territory of the State.

2. Protection is generally provided when the actors mentioned in paragraph 1 take reasonable steps to prevent the persecution or suffering of serious harm, *inter alia*, by operating an effective legal system for the detection, prosecution and punishment of acts constituting persecution or serious harm, and the applicant has access to such protection.

3. When assessing whether an international organisation controls a State or a substantial part of its territory and provides protection as described in paragraph 2, Member States shall take into account any guidance which may be provided in relevant Council acts.

Article 8

Internal protection

1. As part of the assessment of the application for international protection, Member States may determine that an applicant is not in need of international protection if in a part of the country of origin there is no well-founded fear of being persecuted or no real risk of suffering serious harm and the applicant can reasonably be expected to stay in that part of the country.

2. In examining whether a part of the country of origin is in accordance with paragraph 1, Member States shall at the time of taking the decision on the application have regard to the general circumstances prevailing in that part of the country and to the personal circumstances of the applicant.

3. Paragraph 1 may apply notwithstanding technical obstacles to return to the country of origin.

Chapter III

Qualification for Being a Refugee

Article 9

Acts of persecution

1. Acts of persecution within the meaning of article 1A of the Geneva Convention must:

(a) be sufficiently serious by their nature or repetition as to constitute a severe violation of basic human rights, in particular the rights from which derogation cannot be made under Article 15(2) of the European Convention for the Protection of Human Rights and Fundamental Freedoms; or

(b) be an accumulation of various measures, including violations of human rights which is sufficiently severe as to affect an individual in a similar manner as mentioned in (a).

2. Acts of persecution as qualified in paragraph 1, can, *inter alia*, take the form of:

(a) acts of physical or mental violence, including acts of sexual violence;

(b) legal, administrative, police, and/or judicial measures which are in themselves discriminatory or which are implemented in a discriminatory manner;

(c) prosecution or punishment, which is disproportionate or discriminatory;

(d) denial of judicial redress resulting in a disproportionate or discriminatory punishment;

(e) prosecution or punishment for refusal to perform military service in a conflict, where performing military service would include crimes or acts falling under the exclusion clauses as set out in Article 12(2);

(f) acts of a gender-specific or child-specific nature.

3. In accordance with Article 2(c), there must be a connection between the reasons mentioned in Article 10 and the acts of persecution as qualified in paragraph 1.

Article 10

Reasons for persecution

1. Member States shall take the following elements into account when assessing the reasons for persecution:

(a) the concept of race shall in particular include considerations of colour, descent, or membership of a particular ethnic group;

(b) the concept of religion shall in particular include the holding of theistic, non-theistic and atheistic beliefs, the participation in, or abstention from, formal worship in private or in public, either alone or in community with others, other religious acts or expressions of view, or forms of personal or communal conduct based on or mandated by any religious belief;

(c) the concept of nationality shall not be confined to citizenship or lack thereof but shall in particular include membership of a group determined by its cultural, ethnic, or linguistic identity, common geographical or political origins or its relationship with the population of another State;

(d) a group shall be considered to form a particular social group where in particular:

— members of that group share an innate characteristic, or a common background that cannot be changed, or share a characteristic or belief that is so fundamental to identity or conscience that a person should not be forced to renounce it, and

— that group has a distinct identity in the relevant country, because it is perceived as being different by the surrounding society;

depending on the circumstances in the country of origin, a particular social group might include a group based on a common characteristic of sexual orientation. Sexual orientation cannot be understood to include acts considered to be criminal in accordance with national law of the Member States. Gender related aspects might be considered, without by themselves alone creating a presumption for the applicability of this Article;

(e) the concept of political opinion shall in particular include the holding of an opinion, thought or belief on a matter related to the potential actors of persecution mentioned in Article 6 and to their policies or methods, whether or not that opinion, thought or belief has been acted upon by the applicant.

2. When assessing if an applicant has a well-founded fear of being persecuted it is immaterial whether the applicant actually possesses the racial, religious, national, social or political characteristic which attracts the persecution, provided that such a characteristic is attributed to the applicant by the actor of persecution.

Article 11

Cessation

1. A third country national or a stateless person shall cease to be a refugee, if he or she:

(a) has voluntarily re-availed himself or herself of the protection of the country of nationality; or

(b) having lost his or her nationality, has voluntarily reacquired it; or

(c) has acquired a new nationality, and enjoys the protection of the country of his or her new nationality; or

(d) has voluntarily re-established himself or herself in the country which he or she left or outside which he or she remained owing to fear of persecution; or

(e) can no longer, because the circumstances in connection with which he or she has been recognised as a refugee have ceased to exist, continue to refuse to avail himself or herself of the protection of the country of nationality;

(f) being a stateless person with no nationality, he or she is able, because the circumstances in connection with which he or she has been recognised as a refugee have ceased to exist, to return to the country of former habitual residence.

2. In considering points (e) and (f) of paragraph 1, Member States shall have regard to whether the change of circumstances is of such a significant and non-temporary nature that the refugee's fear of persecution can no longer be regarded as well-founded.

Article 12

Exclusion

1. A third country national or a stateless person is excluded from being a refugee, if:

(a) he or she falls within the scope of Article 1D of the Geneva Convention, relating to protection or assistance from organs or agencies of the United Nations other than the United Nations High Commissioner for Refugees. When such protection or assistance has ceased for any reason, without the position of such persons being definitely settled in accordance with the relevant resolutions adopted by the General Assembly of the United Nations, these persons shall ipso facto be entitled to the benefits of this Directive;

(b) he or she is recognised by the competent authorities of the country in which he or she has taken residence as having the rights and obligations which are attached to the possession of the nationality of that country; or rights and obligations equivalent to those.

2. A third country national or a stateless person is excluded from being a refugee where there are serious reasons for considering that:

(a) he or she has committed a crime against peace, a war crime, or a crime against humanity, as defined in the international instruments drawn up to make provision in respect of such crimes;

(b) he or she has committed a serious non-political crime outside the country of refuge prior to his or her admission as a refugee; which means the time of issuing a residence permit based on the granting of refugee status; particularly cruel actions, even if committed with an allegedly political objective, may be classified as serious non-political crimes;

(c) he or she has been guilty of acts contrary to the purposes and principles of the United Nations as set out in the Preamble and Articles 1 and 2 of the Charter of the United Nations.

3. Paragraph 2 applies to persons who instigate or otherwise participate in the commission of the crimes or acts mentioned therein.

Chapter IV
Refugee Status

Article 13

Granting of refugee status

Member States shall grant refugee status to a third country national or a stateless person, who qualifies as a refugee in accordance with Chapters II and III.

Article 14

Revocation of, ending of or refusal to renew refugee status

1. Concerning applications for international protection filed after the entry into force of this Directive, Member States shall revoke, end or refuse to renew the refugee status of a third country national or a stateless person granted by a governmental, administrative, judicial or quasi-judicial body, if he or she has ceased to be a refugee in accordance with Article 11.

2. Without prejudice to the duty of the refugee in accordance with Article 4(1) to disclose all relevant facts and provide all relevant documentation at his/her disposal, the Member State, which has granted refugee status, shall on an individual basis demonstrate that the person concerned has ceased to be or has never been a refugee in accordance with paragraph 1 of this Article.

3. Member States shall revoke, end or refuse to renew the refugee status of a third country national or a stateless person, if, after he or she has been granted refugee status, it is established by the Member State concerned that:

(a) he or she should have been or is excluded from being a refugee in accordance with Article 12;

(b) his or her misrepresentation or omission of facts, including the use of false documents, were decisive for the granting of refugee status.

4. Member States may revoke, end or refuse to renew the status granted to a refugee by a governmental, administrative, judicial or quasi-judicial body, when:

(a) there are reasonable grounds for regarding him or her as a danger to the security of the Member State in which he or she is present;

(b) he or she, having been convicted by a final judgement of a particularly serious crime, constitutes a danger to the community of that Member State.

5. In situations described in paragraph 4, Member States may decide not to grant status to a refugee, where such a decision has not yet been taken.

6. Persons to whom paragraphs 4 or 5 apply are entitled to rights set out in or similar to those set out in Articles 3, 4, 16, 22, 31 and 32 and 33 of the Geneva Convention insofar as they are present in the Member State.

Chapter V

Qualification for Subsidiary Protection

Article 15

Serious harm

Serious harm consists of:

(a) death penalty or execution; or

(b) torture or inhuman or degrading treatment or punishment of an applicant in the country of origin; or

(c) serious and individual threat to a civilian's life or person by reason of indiscriminate violence in situations of international or internal armed conflict.

Article 16

Cessation

1. A third country national or a stateless person shall cease to be eligible for subsidiary protection when the circumstances which led to the granting of subsidiary protection status have ceased to exist or have changed to such a degree that protection is no longer required.

2. In applying paragraph 1, Member States shall have regard to whether the change of circumstances is of such a significant and non-temporary nature that the person eligible for subsidiary protection no longer faces a real risk of serious harm.

Article 17

Exclusion

1. A third country national or a stateless person is excluded from being eligible for subsidiary protection where there are serious reasons for considering that:

(a) he or she has committed a crime against peace, a war crime, or a crime against humanity, as defined in the international instruments drawn up to make provision in respect of such crimes;

(b) he or she has committed a serious crime;

(c) he or she has been guilty of acts contrary to the purposes and principles of the United Nations as set out in the Preamble and Articles 1 and 2 of the Charter of the United Nations;

(d) he or she constitutes a danger to the community or to the security of the Member State in which he or she is present.

2. Paragraph 1 applies to persons who instigate or otherwise participate in the commission of the crimes or acts mentioned therein.

3. Member States may exclude a third country national or a stateless person from being eligible for subsidiary protection, if he or she prior to his or her admission to the Member State has committed one or more crimes, outside the scope of paragraph 1, which would be punishable by imprisonment, had they been committed in the Member State concerned, and if he or she left his or her country of origin solely in order to avoid sanctions resulting from these crimes.

Chapter VI

Subsidiary Protection Status

Article 18

Granting of subsidiary protection status

Member States shall grant subsidiary protection status to a third country national or a stateless person eligible for subsidiary protection in accordance with Chapters II and V.

Article 19

Revocation of, ending of or refusal to renew subsidiary protection status

1. Concerning applications for international protection filed after the entry into force of this Directive, Member States shall revoke, end or refuse to renew the subsidiary protection status of a third country national or a stateless person granted by a governmental, administrative, judicial or quasi-judicial body, if he or she has ceased to be eligible for subsidiary protection in accordance with Article 16.

2. Member States may revoke, end or refuse to renew the subsidiary protection status of a third country national or a stateless person granted by a governmental, administrative, judicial or quasi-judicial body, if after having been granted subsidiary protection status, he or she should have been excluded from being eligible for subsidiary protection in accordance with Article 17(3).

3. Member States shall revoke, end or refuse to renew the subsidiary protection status of a third country national or a stateless person, if:

(a) he or she, after having been granted subsidiary protection status, should have been or is excluded from being eligible for subsidiary protection in accordance with Article 17(1) and (2);

(b) his or her misrepresentation or omission of facts, including the use of false documents, were decisive for the granting of subsidiary protection status.

4. Without prejudice to the duty of the third country national or stateless person in accordance with Article 4(1) to disclose all relevant facts and provide all relevant documentation at his/her disposal, the Member State, which has granted the subsidiary protection status, shall on an individual basis demonstrate that the person concerned has ceased to be or is not eligible for subsidiary protection in accordance with paragraphs 1, 2 and 3 of this Article.

Chapter VII

Content of International Protection

Article 20

General rules

1. This Chapter shall be without prejudice to the rights laid down in the Geneva Convention.

2. This Chapter shall apply both to refugees and persons eligible for subsidiary protection unless otherwise indicated.

3. When implementing this Chapter, Member States shall take into account the specific situation of vulnerable persons such as minors, unaccompanied minors, disabled people, elderly people, pregnant women, single parents with minor children and persons who have been subjected to torture, rape or other serious forms of psychological, physical or sexual violence.

4. Paragraph 3 shall apply only to persons found to have special needs after an individual evaluation of their situation.

5. The best interest of the child shall be a primary consideration for Member States when implementing the provisions of this Chapter that involve minors.

6. Within the limits set out by the Geneva Convention, Member States may reduce the benefits of this Chapter, granted to a refugee whose refugee status has been obtained on the basis of activities engaged in for the sole or main purpose of creating the necessary conditions for being recognised as a refugee.

7. Within the limits set out by international obligations of Member States, Member States may reduce the benefits of this Chapter, granted to a person eligible for subsidiary protection, whose subsidiary protection status has been obtained on the basis of activities engaged in for the sole or main purpose of creating the necessary conditions for being recognised as a person eligible for subsidiary protection.

Article 21

Protection from refoulement

1. Member States shall respect the principle of non-refoulement in accordance with their international obligations.

2. Where not prohibited by the international obligations mentioned in paragraph 1, Member States may refoule a refugee, whether formally recognised or not, when:

(a) there are reasonable grounds for considering him or her as a danger to the security of the Member State in which he or she is present; or

(b) he or she, having been convicted by a final judgement of a particularly serious crime, constitutes a danger to the community of that Member State.

3. Member States may revoke, end or refuse to renew or to grant the residence permit of (or to) a refugee to whom paragraph 2 applies.

Article 22

Information

Member States shall provide persons recognised as being in need of international protection, as soon as possible after the respective protection status has been granted, with access to information, in a language likely to be understood by them, on the rights and obligations relating to that status.

Article 23

Maintaining family unity

1. Member States shall ensure that family unity can be maintained.

2. Member States shall ensure that family members of the beneficiary of refugee or subsidiary protection status, who do not individually qualify for such status, are entitled to claim the benefits referred to in Articles 24 to 34, in accordance with national procedures and as far as it is compatible with the personal legal status of the family member.

In so far as the family members of beneficiaries of subsidiary protection status are concerned, Member States may define the conditions applicable to such benefits.

In these cases, Member States shall ensure that any benefits provided guarantee an adequate standard of living.

3. Paragraphs 1 and 2 are not applicable where the family member is or would be excluded from refugee or subsidiary protection status pursuant to Chapters III and V.

4. Notwithstanding paragraphs 1 and 2, Member States may refuse, reduce or withdraw the benefits referred therein for reasons of national security or public order.

5. Member States may decide that this Article also applies to other close relatives who lived together as part of the family at the time of leaving the country of origin, and who were wholly or mainly dependent on the beneficiary of refugee or subsidiary protection status at that time.

Article 24

Residence permits

1. As soon as possible after their status has been granted, Member States shall issue to beneficiaries of refugee status a residence permit which must be valid for at least three years and renewable unless compelling reasons of national security or public order otherwise require, and without prejudice to Article 21(3).

Without prejudice to Article 23(1), the residence permit to be issued to the family members of the beneficiaries of refugee status may be valid for less than three years and renewable.

2. As soon as possible after the status has been granted, Member States shall issue to beneficiaries of subsidiary protection status a residence permit which must be valid for at least one year and renewable, unless compelling reasons of national security or public order otherwise require.

Article 25

Travel document

1. Member States shall issue to beneficiaries of refugee status travel documents in the form set out in the Schedule to the Geneva Convention, for the purpose of travel outside their territory unless compelling reasons of national security or public order otherwise require.

2. Member States shall issue to beneficiaries of subsidiary protection status who are unable to obtain a national passport, documents which enable them to travel, at least when serious humanitarian reasons arise that require their presence in another State, unless compelling reasons of national security or public order otherwise require.

Article 26

Access to employment

1. Member States shall authorise beneficiaries of refugee status to engage in employed or self-employed activities subject to rules generally applicable to the profession and to the public service, immediately after the refugee status has been granted.

2. Member States shall ensure that activities such as employment-related education opportunities for adults, vocational training and practical workplace experience are offered to beneficiaries of refugee status, under equivalent conditions as nationals.

3. Member States shall authorise beneficiaries of subsidiary protection status to engage in employed or self-employed activities subject to rules generally applicable to the profession and to the public service immediately after the subsidiary protection status has been granted. The situation of the labour market in the Member States may be taken into account, including for possible prioritisation of access to employment for a limited period of time to be determined in accordance with national law. Member States shall ensure that the beneficiary of subsidiary protection status has access to a post for which the beneficiary has received an offer in accordance with national rules on prioritisation in the labour market.

4. Member States shall ensure that beneficiaries of subsidiary protection status have access to activities such as employment-related education opportunities for adults, vocational training and practical workplace experience, under conditions to be decided by the Member States.

5. The law in force in the Member States applicable to remuneration, access to social security systems relating to employed or self-employed activities and other conditions of employment shall apply.

Article 27

Access to education

1. Member States shall grant full access to the education system to all minors granted refugee or subsidiary protection status, under the same conditions as nationals.

2. Member States shall allow adults granted refugee or subsidiary protection status access to the general education system, further training or retraining, under the same conditions as third country nationals legally resident.

3. Member States shall ensure equal treatment between beneficiaries of refugee or subsidiary protection status and nationals in the context of the existing recognition procedures for foreign diplomas, certificates and other evidence of formal qualifications.

Article 28

Social welfare

1. Member States shall ensure that beneficiaries of refugee or subsidiary protection status receive, in the Member State that has granted such statuses, the necessary social assistance, as provided to nationals of that Member State.

2. By exception to the general rule laid down in paragraph 1, Member States may limit social assistance granted to beneficiaries of subsidiary protection status to core benefits which will then be provided at the same levels and under the same eligibility conditions as nationals.

Article 29

Health care

1. Member States shall ensure that beneficiaries of refugee or subsidiary protection status have access to health care under the same eligibility conditions as nationals of the Member State that has granted such statuses.

2. By exception to the general rule laid down in paragraph 1, Member States may limit health care granted to beneficiaries of subsidiary protection to core benefits which will then be provided at the same levels and under the same eligibility conditions as nationals.

3. Member States shall provide, under the same eligibility conditions as nationals of the Member State that has granted the status, adequate health care to beneficiaries of refugee or subsidiary protection status who have special needs, such as pregnant women, disabled people, persons who have undergone torture, rape or other serious forms of psychological, physical or sexual violence or minors who have been victims of any form of abuse, neglect, exploitation, torture, cruel, inhuman and degrading treatment or who have suffered from armed conflict.

Article 30

Unaccompanied minors

1. As soon as possible after the granting of refugee or subsidiary protection status Member States shall take the necessary measures, to ensure the representation of unaccompanied minors by legal guardianship or, where necessary, by an organisation responsible for the care and well-being of minors, or by any other appropriate representation including that based on legislation or Court order.

2. Member States shall ensure that the minor's needs are duly met in the implementation of this Directive by the appointed guardian or representative. The appropriate authorities shall make regular assessments.

3. Member States shall ensure that unaccompanied minors are placed either:

(a) with adult relatives; or

(b) with a foster family; or

(c) in centres specialised in accommodation for minors; or

(d) in other accommodation suitable for minors.

In this context, the views of the child shall be taken into account in accordance with his or her age and degree of maturity.

4. As far as possible, siblings shall be kept together, taking into account the best interests of the minor concerned and, in particular, his or her age and degree of maturity. Changes of residence of unaccompanied minors shall be limited to a minimum.

5. Member States, protecting the unaccompanied minor's best interests, shall endeavour to trace the members of the minor's family as soon as possible. In cases where there may be a threat to the life or integrity of the minor or his or her close relatives, particularly if they have remained in the country of origin, care must be taken to ensure that the collection, processing and circulation of information concerning those persons is undertaken on a confidential basis.

6. Those working with unaccompanied minors shall have had or receive appropriate training concerning their needs.

Article 31

Access to accommodation

The Member States shall ensure that beneficiaries of refugee or subsidiary protection status have access to accommodation under equivalent conditions as other third country nationals legally resident in their territories.

Article 32

Freedom of movement within the member state

Member States shall allow freedom of movement within their territory to beneficiaries of refugee or subsidiary protection status, under the same conditions and restrictions as those provided for other third country nationals legally resident in their territories.

Article 33

Access to integration facilities

1. In order to facilitate the integration of refugees into society, Member States shall make provision for integration programmes which they consider to be appropriate or create pre-conditions which guarantee access to such programmes.

2. Where it is considered appropriate by Member States, beneficiaries of subsidiary protection status shall be granted access to integration programmes.

Article 34

Repatriation

Member States may provide assistance to beneficiaries of refugee or subsidiary protection status who wish to repatriate.

Chapter VIII

Administrative Cooperation

Article 35

Cooperation

Member States shall each appoint a national contact point, whose address they shall communicate to the Commission, which shall communicate it to the other Member States.

Member States shall, in liaison with the Commission, take all appropriate measures to establish direct cooperation and an exchange of information between the competent authorities.

Article 36

Staff

Member States shall ensure that authorities and other organisations implementing this Directive have received the necessary training and shall be bound by the confidentiality principle, as defined in the national law, in relation to any information they obtain in the course of their work.

Chapter IX

Final Provisions

Article 37

Reports

1. By 10 April 2008, the Commission shall report to the European Parliament and the Council on the application of this Directive and shall propose any amendments that are necessary. These proposals for amendments shall be made by way of priority in relation to Articles 15, 26 and 33. Member States shall send the Commission all the information that is appropriate for drawing up that report by 10 October 2007.

2. After presenting the report, the Commission shall report to the European Parliament and the Council on the application of this Directive at least every five years.

Article 38

Transposition

1. The Member States shall bring into force the laws, regulations and administrative provisions necessary to comply with this Directive before 10 October 2006. They shall forthwith inform the Commission thereof. When the Member States adopt those measures, they shall contain a reference to this Directive or shall be accompanied by such a reference on the occasion of their official publication. The methods of making such reference shall be laid down by Member States.

2. Member States shall communicate to the Commission the text of the provisions of national law which they adopt in the field covered by this Directive.

Article 39

Entry into force

This Directive shall enter into force on the twentieth day following that of its publication in the *Official Journal of the European Union*.

Article 40

Addressees

This Directive is addressed to the Member States in accordance with the Treaty establishing the European Community.

Done at Luxembourg, 29 April 2004.

For the Council
The President
M. McDOWELL

Directive 2004/38/EC of the European Parliament and of the Council of 29 April 2004

on the right of citizens of the Union and their family members to move and reside freely within the territory of the Member States amending Regulation (EEC) No. 1612/68 and repealing Directives 64/221/EEC, 68/360/EEC, 72/194/EEC, 73/148/EEC, 75/34/EEC, 75/35/EEC, 90/364/EEC, 90/365/EEC and 93/96/EEC

(Text with EEA relevance)

Note: Entered into force on 30 April 2004 (Article 41). To be implemented by 30 April 2006 (Article 40).

THE EUROPEAN PARLIAMENT AND THE COUNCIL OF THE EUROPEAN UNION,

Having regard to the Treaty establishing the European Community, and in particular Articles 12, 18, 40, 44 and 52 thereof,

Having regard to the proposal from the Commission,[1]

Having regard to the Opinion of the European Economic and Social Committee,[2]

Having regard to the Opinion of the Committee of the Regions,[3]

Acting in accordance with the procedure laid down in Article 251 of the Treaty,[4]

Whereas:

(1) Citizenship of the Union confers on every citizen of the Union a primary and individual right to move and reside freely within the territory of the Member States, subject to the limitations and conditions laid down in the Treaty and to the measures adopted to give it effect.

(2) The free movement of persons constitutes one of the fundamental freedoms of the internal market, which comprises an area without internal frontiers, in which freedom is ensured in accordance with the provisions of the Treaty.

(3) Union citizenship should be the fundamental status of nationals of the Member States when they exercise their right of free movement and residence. It is therefore necessary to codify and review the existing Community instruments dealing separately with workers, self-employed persons, as well as students and other inactive persons in order to simplify and strengthen the right of free movement and residence of all Union citizens.

(4) With a view to remedying this sector-by-sector, piecemeal approach to the right of free movement and residence and facilitating the exercise of this right, there needs to be a single legislative act to amend Council Regulation (EEC) No. 1612/68 of 15 October 1968

[1] OJ C 270 E, 25.9.2001, p. 150.

[2] OJ C 149, 21.6.2002, p. 46.

[3] OJ C 192, 12.8.2002, p. 17.

[4] Opinion of the European Parliament of 11 February 2003 (OJ C 43 E, 19.2.2004, p. 42), Council Common Position of 5 December 2003 (OJ C 54 E, 2.3.2004, p. 12) and Position of the European Parliament of 10 March 2004 (not yet published in the Official Journal).

on freedom of movement for workers within the Community,[5] and to repeal the following acts: Council Directive 68/360/EEC of 15 October 1968 on the abolition of restrictions on movement and residence within the Community for workers of Member States and their families,[6] Council Directive 73/148/EEC of 21 May 1973 on the abolition of restrictions on movement and residence within the Community for nationals of Member States with regard to establishment and the provision of services,[7] Council Directive 90/364/EEC of 28 June 1990 on the right of residence,[8] Council Directive 90/365/EEC of 28 June 1990 on the right of residence for employees and self-employed persons who have ceased their occupational activity[9] and Council Directive 93/96/EEC of 29 October 1993 on the right of residence for students.[10]

(5) The right of all Union citizens to move and reside freely within the territory of the Member States should, if it is to be exercised under objective conditions of freedom and dignity, be also granted to their family members, irrespective of nationality. For the purposes of this Directive, the definition of 'family member' should also include the registered partner if the legislation of the host Member State treats registered partnership as equivalent to marriage.

(6) In order to maintain the unity of the family in a broader sense and without prejudice to the prohibition of discrimination on grounds of nationality, the situation of those persons who are not included in the definition of family members under this Directive, and who therefore do not enjoy an automatic right of entry and residence in the host Member State, should be examined by the host Member State on the basis of its own national legislation, in order to decide whether entry and residence could be granted to such persons, taking into consideration their relationship with the Union citizen or any other circumstances, such as their financial or physical dependence on the Union citizen.

(7) The formalities connected with the free movement of Union citizens within the territory of Member States should be clearly defined, without prejudice to the provisions applicable to national border controls.

(8) With a view to facilitating the free movement of family members who are not nationals of a Member State, those who have already obtained a residence card should be exempted from the requirement to obtain an entry visa within the meaning of Council Regulation (EC) No. 539/2001 of 15 March 2001 listing the third countries whose nationals must be in possession of visas when crossing the external borders and those whose nationals are exempt from that requirement[11] or, where appropriate, of the applicable national legislation.

(9) Union citizens should have the right of residence in the host Member State for a period not exceeding three months without being subject to any conditions or any formalities other than the requirement to hold a valid identity card or passport, without prejudice to a more favourable treatment applicable to job-seekers as recognised by the case-law of the Court of Justice.

[5] OJ L 257, 19.10.1968, p. 2. Regulation as last amended by Regulation (EEC) No. 2434/92 (OJ L 245, 26.8.1992, p. 1).

[6] OJ L 257, 19.10.1968, p. 13. Directive as last amended by the 2003 Act of Accession.

[7] OJ L 172, 28.6.1973, p. 14.

[8] OJ L 180, 13.7.1990, p. 26.

[9] OJ L 180, 13.7.1990, p. 28.

[10] OJ L 317, 18.12.1993, p. 59.

[11] OJ L 81, 21.3.2001, p. 1. Regulation as last amended by Regulation (EC) No. 453/2003 (OJ L 69, 13.3.2003, p. 10).

(10) Persons exercising their right of residence should not, however, become an unreasonable burden on the social assistance system of the host Member State during an initial period of residence. Therefore, the right of residence for Union citizens and their family members for periods in excess of three months should be subject to conditions.

(11) The fundamental and personal right of residence in another Member State is conferred directly on Union citizens by the Treaty and is not dependent upon their having fulfilled administrative procedures.

(12) For periods of residence of longer than three months, Member States should have the possibility to require Union citizens to register with the competent authorities in the place of residence, attested by a registration certificate issued to that effect.

(13) The residence card requirement should be restricted to family members of Union citizens who are not nationals of a Member State for periods of residence of longer than three months.

(14) The supporting documents required by the competent authorities for the issuing of a registration certificate or of a residence card should be comprehensively specified in order to avoid divergent administrative practices or interpretations constituting an undue obstacle to the exercise of the right of residence by Union citizens and their family members.

(15) Family members should be legally safeguarded in the event of the death of the Union citizen, divorce, annulment of marriage or termination of a registered partnership. With due regard for family life and human dignity, and in certain conditions to guard against abuse, measures should therefore be taken to ensure that in such circumstances family members already residing within the territory of the host Member State retain their right of residence exclusively on a personal basis.

(16) As long as the beneficiaries of the right of residence do not become an unreasonable burden on the social assistance system of the host Member State they should not be expelled. Therefore, an expulsion measure should not be the automatic consequence of recourse to the social assistance system. The host Member State should examine whether it is a case of temporary difficulties and take into account the duration of residence, the personal circumstances and the amount of aid granted in order to consider whether the beneficiary has become an unreasonable burden on its social assistance system and to proceed to his expulsion. In no case should an expulsion measure be adopted against workers, self-employed persons or job-seekers as defined by the Court of Justice save on grounds of public policy or public security.

(17) Enjoyment of permanent residence by Union citizens who have chosen to settle long term in the host Member State would strengthen the feeling of Union citizenship and is a key element in promoting social cohesion, which is one of the fundamental objectives of the Union. A right of permanent residence should therefore be laid down for all Union citizens and their family members who have resided in the host Member State in compliance with the conditions laid down in this Directive during a continuous period of five years without becoming subject to an expulsion measure.

(18) In order to be a genuine vehicle for integration into the society of the host Member State in which the Union citizen resides, the right of permanent residence, once obtained, should not be subject to any conditions.

(19) Certain advantages specific to Union citizens who are workers or self-employed persons and to their family members, which may allow these persons to acquire a right of permanent residence before they have resided five years in the host Member State, should

be maintained, as these constitute acquired rights, conferred by Commission Regulation (EEC) No. 1251/70 of 29 June 1970 on the right of workers to remain in the territory of a Member State after having been employed in that State[12] and Council Directive 75/34/EEC of 17 December 1974 concerning the right of nationals of a Member State to remain in the territory of another Member State after having pursued therein an activity in a self-employed capacity.[13]

(20) In accordance with the prohibition of discrimination on grounds of nationality, all Union citizens and their family members residing in a Member State on the basis of this Directive should enjoy, in that Member State, equal treatment with nationals in areas covered by the Treaty, subject to such specific provisions as are expressly provided for in the Treaty and secondary law.

(21) However, it should be left to the host Member State to decide whether it will grant social assistance during the first three months of residence, or for a longer period in the case of job-seekers, to Union citizens other than those who are workers or self-employed persons or who retain that status or their family members, or maintenance assistance for studies, including vocational training, prior to acquisition of the right of permanent residence, to these same persons.

(22) The Treaty allows restrictions to be placed on the right of free movement and residence on grounds of public policy, public security or public health. In order to ensure a tighter definition of the circumstances and procedural safeguards subject to which Union citizens and their family members may be denied leave to enter or may be expelled, this Directive should replace Council Directive 64/221/EEC of 25 February 1964 on the coordination of special measures concerning the movement and residence of foreign nationals, which are justified on grounds of public policy, public security or public health.[14]

(23) Expulsion of Union citizens and their family members on grounds of public policy or public security is a measure that can seriously harm persons who, having availed themselves of the rights and freedoms conferred on them by the Treaty, have become genuinely integrated into the host Member State. The scope for such measures should therefore be limited in accordance with the principle of proportionality to take account of the degree of integration of the persons concerned, the length of their residence in the host Member State, their age, state of health, family and economic situation and the links with their country of origin.

(24) Accordingly, the greater the degree of integration of Union citizens and their family members in the host Member State, the greater the degree of protection against expulsion should be. Only in exceptional circumstances, where there are imperative grounds of public security, should an expulsion measure be taken against Union citizens who have resided for many years in the territory of the host Member State, in particular when they were born and have resided there throughout their life. In addition, such exceptional circumstances should also apply to an expulsion measure taken against minors, in order to protect their links with their family, in accordance with the United Nations Convention on the Rights of the Child, of 20 November 1989.

[12] OJ L 142, 30.6.1970, p. 24.

[13] OJ L 14, 20.1.1975, p. 10.

[14] OJ 56, 4.4.1964, p. 850. Directive as last amended by Directive 75/35/EEC (OJ 14, 20.1.1975, p. 14).

(25) Procedural safeguards should also be specified in detail in order to ensure a high level of protection of the rights of Union citizens and their family members in the event of their being denied leave to enter or reside in another Member State, as well as to uphold the principle that any action taken by the authorities must be properly justified.

(26) In all events, judicial redress procedures should be available to Union citizens and their family members who have been refused leave to enter or reside in another Member State.

(27) In line with the case-law of the Court of Justice prohibiting Member States from issuing orders excluding for life persons covered by this Directive from their territory, the right of Union citizens and their family members who have been excluded from the territory of a Member State to submit a fresh application after a reasonable period, and in any event after a three year period from enforcement of the final exclusion order, should be confirmed.

(28) To guard against abuse of rights or fraud, notably marriages of convenience or any other form of relationships contracted for the sole purpose of enjoying the right of free movement and residence, Member States should have the possibility to adopt the necessary measures.

(29) This Directive should not affect more favourable national provisions.

(30) With a view to examining how further to facilitate the exercise of the right of free movement and residence, a report should be prepared by the Commission in order to evaluate the opportunity to present any necessary proposals to this effect, notably on the extension of the period of residence with no conditions.

(31) This Directive respects the fundamental rights and freedoms and observes the principles recognised in particular by the Charter of Fundamental Rights of the European Union. In accordance with the prohibition of discrimination contained in the Charter, Member States should implement this Directive without discrimination between the beneficiaries of this Directive on grounds such as sex, race, colour, ethnic or social origin, genetic characteristics, language, religion or beliefs, political or other opinion, membership of an ethnic minority, property, birth, disability, age or sexual orientation,

HAVE ADOPTED THIS DIRECTIVE:

CHAPTER I

GENERAL PROVISIONS

Article 1

Subject

This Directive lays down:

(a) the conditions governing the exercise of the right of free movement and residence within the territory of the Member States by Union citizens and their family members;

(b) the right of permanent residence in the territory of the Member States for Union citizens and their family members;

(c) the limits placed on the rights set out in (a) and (b) on grounds of public policy, public security or public health.

Article 2

Definitions

For the purposes of this Directive:

(1) 'Union citizen' means any person having the nationality of a Member State;

(2) 'Family member' means:

(a) the spouse;

(b) the partner with whom the Union citizen has contracted a registered partnership, on the basis of the legislation of a Member State, if the legislation of the host Member State treats registered partnerships as equivalent to marriage and in accordance with the conditions laid down in the relevant legislation of the host Member State;

(c) the direct descendants who are under the age of 21 or are dependants and those of the spouse or partner as defined in point (b);

(d) the dependent direct relatives in the ascending line and those of the spouse or partner as defined in point (b);

(3) 'Host Member State' means the Member State to which a Union citizen moves in order to exercise his/her right of free movement and residence.

Article 3

Beneficiaries

1. This Directive shall apply to all Union citizens who move to or reside in a Member State other than that of which they are a national, and to their family members as defined in point 2 of Article 2 who accompany or join them.

2. Without prejudice to any right to free movement and residence the persons concerned may have in their own right, the host Member State shall, in accordance with its national legislation, facilitate entry and residence for the following persons:

(a) any other family members, irrespective of their nationality, not falling under the definition in point 2 of Article 2 who, in the country from which they have come, are dependants or members of the household of the Union citizen having the primary right of residence, or where serious health grounds strictly require the personal care of the family member by the Union citizen;

(b) the partner with whom the Union citizen has a durable relationship, duly attested.

The host Member State shall undertake an extensive examination of the personal circumstances and shall justify any denial of entry or residence to these people.

CHAPTER II

RIGHT OF EXIT AND ENTRY

Article 4

Right of exit

1. Without prejudice to the provisions on travel documents applicable to national border controls, all Union citizens with a valid identity card or passport and their family members who are not nationals of a Member State and who hold a valid passport shall have the right to leave the territory of a Member State to travel to another Member State.

2. No exit visa or equivalent formality may be imposed on the persons to whom paragraph 1 applies.

3. Member States shall, acting in accordance with their laws, issue to their own nationals, and renew, an identity card or passport stating their nationality.

4. The passport shall be valid at least for all Member States and for countries through which the holder must pass when travelling between Member States. Where the law of a Member State does not provide for identity cards to be issued, the period of validity of any passport on being issued or renewed shall be not less than five years.

Article 5

Right of entry

1. Without prejudice to the provisions on travel documents applicable to national border controls, Member States shall grant Union citizens leave to enter their territory with a valid identity card or passport and shall grant family members who are not nationals of a Member State leave to enter their territory with a valid passport.

No entry visa or equivalent formality may be imposed on Union citizens.

2. Family members who are not nationals of a Member State shall only be required to have an entry visa in accordance with Regulation (EC) No. 539/2001 or, where appropriate, with national law. For the purposes of this Directive, possession of the valid residence card referred to in Article 10 shall exempt such family members from the visa requirement.

Member States shall grant such persons every facility to obtain the necessary visas. Such visas shall be issued free of charge as soon as possible and on the basis of an accelerated procedure.

3. The host Member State shall not place an entry or exit stamp in the passport of family members who are not nationals of a Member State provided that they present the residence card provided for in Article 10.

4. Where a Union citizen, or a family member who is not a national of a Member State, does not have the necessary travel documents or, if required, the necessary visas, the Member State concerned shall, before turning them back, give such persons every reasonable opportunity to obtain the necessary documents or have them brought to them within a reasonable period of time or to corroborate or prove by other means that they are covered by the right of free movement and residence.

5. The Member State may require the person concerned to report his/her presence within its territory within a reasonable and non-discriminatory period of time. Failure to

comply with this requirement may make the person concerned liable to proportionate and non-discriminatory sanctions.

Chapter III
Right of Residence

Article 6

Right of residence for up to three months

1. Union citizens shall have the right of residence on the territory of another Member State for a period of up to three months without any conditions or any formalities other than the requirement to hold a valid identity card or passport.

2. The provisions of paragraph 1 shall also apply to family members in possession of a valid passport who are not nationals of a Member State, accompanying or joining the Union citizen.

Article 7

Right of residence for more than three months

1. All Union citizens shall have the right of residence on the territory of another Member State for a period of longer than three months if they:

(a) are workers or self-employed persons in the host Member State; or

(b) have sufficient resources for themselves and their family members not to become a burden on the social assistance system of the host Member State during their period of residence and have comprehensive sickness insurance cover in the host Member State; or

(c) — are enrolled at a private or public establishment, accredited or financed by the host Member State on the basis of its legislation or administrative practice, for the principal purpose of following a course of study, including vocational training; and

— have comprehensive sickness insurance cover in the host Member State and assure the relevant national authority, by means of a declaration or by such equivalent means as they may choose, that they have sufficient resources for themselves and their family members not to become a burden on the social assistance system of the host Member State during their period of residence; or

(d) are family members accompanying or joining a Union citizen who satisfies the conditions referred to in points (a), (b) or (c).

2. The right of residence provided for in paragraph 1 shall extend to family members who are not nationals of a Member State, accompanying or joining the Union citizen in the host Member State, provided that such Union citizen satisfies the conditions referred to in paragraph 1(a), (b) or (c).

3. For the purposes of paragraph 1(a), a Union citizen who is no longer a worker or self-employed person shall retain the status of worker or self-employed person in the following circumstances:

(a) he/she is temporarily unable to work as the result of an illness or accident;

(b) he/she is in duly recorded involuntary unemployment after having been employed for more than one year and has registered as a job-seeker with the relevant employment office;

(c) he/she is in duly recorded involuntary unemployment after completing a fixed-term employment contract of less than a year or after having become involuntarily unemployed during the first twelve months and has registered as a job-seeker with the relevant employment office. In this case, the status of worker shall be retained for no less than six months;

(d) he/she embarks on vocational training. Unless he/she is involuntarily unemployed, the retention of the status of worker shall require the training to be related to the previous employment.

4. By way of derogation from paragraphs 1(d) and 2 above, only the spouse, the registered partner provided for in Article 2(2)(b) and dependent children shall have the right of residence as family members of a Union citizen meeting the conditions under 1(c) above. Article 3(2) shall apply to his/her dependent direct relatives in the ascending lines and those of his/her spouse or registered partner.

Article 8

Administrative formalities for union citizens

1. Without prejudice to Article 5(5), for periods of residence longer than three months, the host Member State may require Union citizens to register with the relevant authorities.

2. The deadline for registration may not be less than three months from the date of arrival. A registration certificate shall be issued immediately, stating the name and address of the person registering and the date of the registration. Failure to comply with the registration requirement may render the person concerned liable to proportionate and non-discriminatory sanctions.

3. For the registration certificate to be issued, Member States may only require that

— Union citizens to whom point (a) of Article 7(1) applies present a valid identity card or passport, a confirmation of engagement from the employer or a certificate of employment, or proof that they are self-employed persons;

— Union citizens to whom point (b) of Article 7(1) applies present a valid identity card or passport and provide proof that they satisfy the conditions laid down therein;

— Union citizens to whom point (c) of Article 7(1) applies present a valid identity card or passport, provide proof of enrolment at an accredited establishment and of comprehensive sickness insurance cover and the declaration or equivalent means referred to in point (c) of Article 7(1). Member States may not require this declaration to refer to any specific amount of resources.

4. Member States may not lay down a fixed amount which they regard as 'sufficient resources' but they must take into account the personal situation of the person concerned. In all cases this amount shall not be higher than the threshold below which nationals of the host Member State become eligible for social assistance, or, where this criterion is not applicable, higher than the minimum social security pension paid by the host Member State.

5. For the registration certificate to be issued to family members of Union citizens, who are themselves Union citizens, Member States may require the following documents to be presented:

(a) a valid identity card or passport;

(b) a document attesting to the existence of a family relationship or of a registered partnership;

(c) where appropriate, the registration certificate of the Union citizen whom they are accompanying or joining;

(d) in cases falling under points (c) and (d) of Article 2(2), documentary evidence that the conditions laid down therein are met;

(e) in cases falling under Article 3(2)(a), a document issued by the relevant authority in the country of origin or country from which they are arriving certifying that they are dependants or members of the household of the Union citizen, or proof of the existence of serious health grounds which strictly require the personal care of the family member by the Union citizen;

(f) in cases falling under Article 3(2)(b), proof of the existence of a durable relationship with the Union citizen.

Article 9

Administrative formalities for family members who are not nationals of a member state

1. Member States shall issue a residence card to family members of a Union citizen who are not nationals of a Member State, where the planned period of residence is for more than three months.

2. The deadline for submitting the residence card application may not be less than three months from the date of arrival.

3. Failure to comply with the requirement to apply for a residence card may make the person concerned liable to proportionate and non-discriminatory sanctions.

Article 10

Issue of residence cards

1. The right of residence of family members of a Union citizen who are not nationals of a Member State shall be evidenced by the issuing of a document called 'Residence card of a family member of a Union citizen' no later than six months from the date on which they submit the application. A certificate of application for the residence card shall be issued immediately.

2. For the residence card to be issued, Member States shall require presentation of the following documents:

(a) a valid passport;

(b) a document attesting to the existence of a family relationship or of a registered partnership;

(c) the registration certificate or, in the absence of a registration system, any other proof of residence in the host Member State of the Union citizen whom they are accompanying or joining;

(d) in cases falling under points (c) and (d) of Article 2(2), documentary evidence that the conditions laid down therein are met;

(e) in cases falling under Article 3(2)(a), a document issued by the relevant authority in the country of origin or country from which they are arriving certifying that they are dependants or members of the household of the Union citizen, or proof of the existence of serious health grounds which strictly require the personal care of the family member by the Union citizen;

(f) in cases falling under Article 3(2)(b), proof of the existence of a durable relationship with the Union citizen.

Article 11

Validity of the residence card

1. The residence card provided for by Article 10(1) shall be valid for five years from the date of issue or for the envisaged period of residence of the Union citizen, if this period is less than five years.

2. The validity of the residence card shall not be affected by temporary absences not exceeding six months a year, or by absences of a longer duration for compulsory military service or by one absence of a maximum of twelve consecutive months for important reasons such as pregnancy and childbirth, serious illness, study or vocational training, or a posting in another Member State or a third country.

Article 12

Retention of the right of residence by family members in the event of death or departure of the union citizen

1. Without prejudice to the second subparagraph, the Union citizen's death or departure from the host Member State shall not affect the right of residence of his/her family members who are nationals of a Member State.

Before acquiring the right of permanent residence, the persons concerned must meet the conditions laid down in points (a), (b), (c) or (d) of Article 7(1).

2. Without prejudice to the second subparagraph, the Union citizen's death shall not entail loss of the right of residence of his/her family members who are not nationals of a Member State and who have been residing in the host Member State as family members for at least one year before the Union citizen's death.

Before acquiring the right of permanent residence, the right of residence of the persons concerned shall remain subject to the requirement that they are able to show that they are workers or self-employed persons or that they have sufficient resources for themselves and their family members not to become a burden on the social assistance system of the host Member State during their period of residence and have comprehensive sickness insurance cover in the host Member State, or that they are members of the family, already constituted in the host Member State, of a person satisfying these requirements. 'Sufficient resources' shall be as defined in Article 8(4). Such family members shall retain their right of residence exclusively on a personal basis.

3. The Union citizen's departure from the host Member State or his/her death shall not entail loss of the right of residence of his/her children or of the parent who has actual custody of the children, irrespective of nationality, if the children reside in the host Member State and are enrolled at an educational establishment, for the purpose of studying there, until the completion of their studies.

Article 13

Retention of the right of residence by family members in the event of divorce, annulment of marriage or termination of registered partnership

1. Without prejudice to the second subparagraph, divorce, annulment of the Union citizen's marriage or termination of his/her registered partnership, as referred to in point 2(b) of Article 2 shall not affect the right of residence of his/her family members who are nationals of a Member State.

Before acquiring the right of permanent residence, the persons concerned must meet the conditions laid down in points (a), (b), (c) or (d) of Article 7(1).

2. Without prejudice to the second subparagraph, divorce, annulment of marriage or termination of the registered partnership referred to in point 2(b) of Article 2 shall not entail loss of the right of residence of a Union citizen's family members who are not nationals of a Member State where:

(a) prior to initiation of the divorce or annulment proceedings or termination of the registered partnership referred to in point 2(b) of Article 2, the marriage or registered partnership has lasted at least three years, including one year in the host Member State; or

(b) by agreement between the spouses or the partners referred to in point 2(b) of Article 2 or by court order, the spouse or partner who is not a national of a Member State has custody of the Union citizen's children; or

(c) this is warranted by particularly difficult circumstances, such as having been a victim of domestic violence while the marriage or registered partnership was subsisting; or

(d) by agreement between the spouses or partners referred to in point 2(b) of Article 2 or by court order, the spouse or partner who is not a national of a Member State has the right of access to a minor child, provided that the court has ruled that such access must be in the host Member State, and for as long as is required.

Before acquiring the right of permanent residence, the right of residence of the persons concerned shall remain subject to the requirement that they are able to show that they are workers or self-employed persons or that they have sufficient resources for themselves and their family members not to become a burden on the social assistance system of the host Member State during their period of residence and have comprehensive sickness insurance cover in the host Member State, or that they are members of the family, already constituted in the host Member State, of a person satisfying these requirements. 'Sufficient resources' shall be as defined in Article 8(4).

Such family members shall retain their right of residence exclusively on personal basis.

Article 14

Retention of the right of residence

1. Union citizens and their family members shall have the right of residence provided for in Article 6, as long as they do not become an unreasonable burden on the social assistance system of the host Member State.

2. Union citizens and their family members shall have the right of residence provided for in Articles 7, 12 and 13 as long as they meet the conditions set out therein.

In specific cases where there is a reasonable doubt as to whether a Union citizen or his/her family members satisfies the conditions set out in Articles 7, 12 and 13, Member

States may verify if these conditions are fulfilled. This verification shall not be carried out systematically.

3. An expulsion measure shall not be the automatic consequence of a Union citizen's or his or her family member's recourse to the social assistance system of the host Member State.

4. By way of derogation from paragraphs 1 and 2 and without prejudice to the provisions of Chapter VI, an expulsion measure may in no case be adopted against Union citizens or their family members if:

(a) the Union citizens are workers or self-employed persons, or

(b) the Union citizens entered the territory of the host Member State in order to seek employment.

In this case, the Union citizens and their family members may not be expelled for as long as the Union citizens can provide evidence that they are continuing to seek employment and that they have a genuine chance of being engaged.

Article 15

Procedural safeguards

1. The procedures provided for by Articles 30 and 31 shall apply by analogy to all decisions restricting free movement of Union citizens and their family members on grounds other than public policy, public security or public health.

2. Expiry of the identity card or passport on the basis of which the person concerned entered the host Member State and was issued with a registration certificate or residence card shall not constitute a ground for expulsion from the host Member State.

3. The host Member State may not impose a ban on entry in the context of an expulsion decision to which paragraph 1 applies.

Chapter IV

Right of Permanent Residence

Section I

Eligibility

Article 16

General Rule for Union Citizens and their Family Members

1. Union citizens who have resided legally for a continuous period of five years in the host Member State shall have the right of permanent residence there. This right shall not be subject to the conditions provided for in Chapter III.

2. Paragraph 1 shall apply also to family members who are not nationals of a Member State and have legally resided with the Union citizen in the host Member State for a continuous period of five years.

3. Continuity of residence shall not be affected by temporary absences not exceeding a total of six months a year, or by absences of a longer duration for compulsory military service, or by one absence of a maximum of twelve consecutive months for important reasons such as pregnancy and childbirth, serious illness, study or vocational training, or a posting in another Member State or a third country.

4. Once acquired, the right of permanent residence shall be lost only through absence from the host Member State for a period exceeding two consecutive years.

Article 17

Exemptions for persons no longer working in the host Member State and their family members

1. By way of derogation from Article 16, the right of permanent residence in the host Member State shall be enjoyed before completion of a continuous period of five years of residence by:

(a) workers or self-employed persons who, at the time they stop working, have reached the age laid down by the law of that Member State for entitlement to an old age pension or workers who cease paid employment to take early retirement, provided that they have been working in that Member State for at least the preceding twelve months and have resided there continuously for more than three years.

If the law of the host Member State does not grant the right to an old age pension to certain categories of self-employed persons, the age condition shall be deemed to have been met once the person concerned has reached the age of 60;

(b) workers or self-employed persons who have resided continuously in the host Member State for more than two years and stop working there as a result of permanent incapacity to work.

If such incapacity is the result of an accident at work or an occupational disease entitling the person concerned to a benefit payable in full or in part by an institution in the host Member State, no condition shall be imposed as to length of residence;

(c) workers or self-employed persons who, after three years of continuous employment and residence in the host Member State, work in an employed or self-employed capacity in another Member State, while retaining their place of residence in the host Member State, to which they return, as a rule, each day or at least once a week.

For the purposes of entitlement to the rights referred to in points (a) and (b), periods of employment spent in the Member State in which the person concerned is working shall be regarded as having been spent in the host Member State.

Periods of involuntary unemployment duly recorded by the relevant employment office, periods not worked for reasons not of the person's own making and absences from work or cessation of work due to illness or accident shall be regarded as periods of employment.

2. The conditions as to length of residence and employment laid down in point (a) of paragraph 1 and the condition as to length of residence laid down in point (b) of paragraph 1 shall not apply if the worker's or the self-employed person's spouse or partner as referred to in point 2(b) of Article 2 is a national of the host Member State or has lost the nationality of that Member State by marriage to that worker or self-employed person.

3. Irrespective of nationality, the family members of a worker or a self-employed person who are residing with him in the territory of the host Member State shall have the

right of permanent residence in that Member State, if the worker or self-employed person has acquired himself the right of permanent residence in that Member State on the basis of paragraph 1.

4. If, however, the worker or self-employed person dies while still working but before acquiring permanent residence status in the host Member State on the basis of paragraph 1, his family members who are residing with him in the host Member State shall acquire the right of permanent residence there, on condition that:

(a) the worker or self-employed person had, at the time of death, resided continuously on the territory of that Member State for two years; or

(b) the death resulted from an accident at work or an occupational disease; or

(c) the surviving spouse lost the nationality of that Member State following marriage to the worker or self-employed person.

Article 18

Acquisition of the right of permanent residence by certain family members who are not nationals of a Member State

Without prejudice to Article 17, the family members of a Union citizen to whom Articles 12(2) and 13(2) apply, who satisfy the conditions laid down therein, shall acquire the right of permanent residence after residing legally for a period of five consecutive years in the host Member State.

Section II

Administrative Formalities

Article 19

Document certifying permanent residence for Union citizens

1. Upon application Member States shall issue Union citizens entitled to permanent residence, after having verified duration of residence, with a document certifying permanent residence.

2. The document certifying permanent residence shall be issued as soon as possible.

Article 20

Permanent residence card for family members who are not nationals of a Member State

1. Member States shall issue family members who are not nationals of a Member State entitled to permanent residence with a permanent residence card within six months of the submission of the application. The permanent residence card shall be renewable automatically every ten years.

2. The application for a permanent residence card shall be submitted before the residence card expires. Failure to comply with the requirement to apply for a permanent residence card may render the person concerned liable to proportionate and non-discriminatory sanctions.

3. Interruption in residence not exceeding two consecutive years shall not affect the validity of the permanent residence card.

Article 21

Continuity of residence

For the purposes of this Directive, continuity of residence may be attested by any means of proof in use in the host Member State. Continuity of residence is broken by any expulsion decision duly enforced against the person concerned.

Chapter V

Provisions Common to the Right of Residence and the Right of Permanent Residence

Article 22

Territorial scope

The right of residence and the right of permanent residence shall cover the whole territory of the host Member State. Member States may impose territorial restrictions on the right of residence and the right of permanent residence only where the same restrictions apply to their own nationals.

Article 23

Related rights

Irrespective of nationality, the family members of a Union citizen who have the right of residence or the right of permanent residence in a Member State shall be entitled to take up employment or self-employment there.

Article 24

Equal treatment

1. Subject to such specific provisions as are expressly provided for in the Treaty and secondary law, all Union citizens residing on the basis of this Directive in the territory of the host Member State shall enjoy equal treatment with the nationals of that Member State within the scope of the Treaty. The benefit of this right shall be extended to family members who are not nationals of a Member State and who have the right of residence or permanent residence.

2. By way of derogation from paragraph 1, the host Member State shall not be obliged to confer entitlement to social assistance during the first three months of residence or, where appropriate, the longer period provided for in Article 14(4)(b), nor shall it be obliged, prior to acquisition of the right of permanent residence, to grant maintenance aid for studies, including vocational training, consisting in student grants or student loans to

persons other than workers, self-employed persons, persons who retain such status and members of their families.

Article 25

General provisions concerning residence documents

1. Possession of a registration certificate as referred to in Article 8, of a document certifying permanent residence, of a certificate attesting submission of an application for a family member residence card, of a residence card or of a permanent residence card, may under no circumstances be made a precondition for the exercise of a right or the completion of an administrative formality, as entitlement to rights may be attested by any other means of proof.

2. All documents mentioned in paragraph 1 shall be issued free of charge or for a charge not exceeding that imposed on nationals for the issuing of similar documents.

Article 26

Checks

Member States may carry out checks on compliance with any requirement deriving from their national legislation for non-nationals always to carry their registration certificate or residence card, provided that the same requirement applies to their own nationals as regards their identity card. In the event of failure to comply with this requirement, Member States may impose the same sanctions as those imposed on their own nationals for failure to carry their identity card.

Chapter VI

Restrictions on the Right of Entry and the Right of Residence on Grounds of Public Policy, Public Security or Public Health

Article 27

General principles

1. Subject to the provisions of this Chapter, Member States may restrict the freedom of movement and residence of Union citizens and their family members, irrespective of nationality, on grounds of public policy, public security or public health. These grounds shall not be invoked to serve economic ends.

2. Measures taken on grounds of public policy or public security shall comply with the principle of proportionality and shall be based exclusively on the personal conduct of the individual concerned. Previous criminal convictions shall not in themselves constitute grounds for taking such measures. The personal conduct of the individual concerned must represent a genuine, present and sufficiently serious threat affecting one of the fundamental interests of society. Justifications that are isolated from the particulars of the case or that rely on considerations of general prevention shall not be accepted.

3. In order to ascertain whether the person concerned represents a danger for public policy or public security, when issuing the registration certificate or, in the absence of a registration system, not later than three months from the date of arrival of the person concerned on its territory or from the date of reporting his/her presence within the territory, as provided for in Article 5(5), or when issuing the residence card, the host Member State may, should it consider this essential, request the Member State of origin and, if need be, other Member States to provide information concerning any previous police record the person concerned may have. Such enquiries shall not be made as a matter of routine. The Member State consulted shall give its reply within two months.

4. The Member State which issued the passport or identity card shall allow the holder of the document who has been expelled on grounds of public policy, public security, or public health from another Member State to re-enter its territory without any formality even if the document is no longer valid or the nationality of the holder is in dispute.

Article 28

Protection against expulsion

1. Before taking an expulsion decision on grounds of public policy or public security, the host Member State shall take account of considerations such as how long the individual concerned has resided on its territory, his/her age, state of health, family and economic situation, social and cultural integration into the host Member State and the extent of his/her links with the country of origin.

2. The host Member State may not take an expulsion decision against Union citizens or their family members, irrespective of nationality, who have the right of permanent residence on its territory, except on serious grounds of public policy or public security.

3. An expulsion decision may not be taken against Union citizens, except if the decision is based on imperative grounds of public security, as defined by Member States, if they:

(a) have resided in the host Member State for the previous ten years; or

(b) are a minor, except if the expulsion is necessary for the best interests of the child, as provided for in the United Nations Convention on the Rights of the Child of 20 November 1989.

Article 29

Public health

1. The only diseases justifying measures restricting freedom of movement shall be the diseases with epidemic potential as defined by the relevant instruments of the World Health Organisation and other infectious diseases or contagious parasitic diseases if they are the subject of protection provisions applying to nationals of the host Member State.

2. Diseases occurring after a three-month period from the date of arrival shall not constitute grounds for expulsion from the territory.

3. Where there are serious indications that it is necessary, Member States may, within three months of the date of arrival, require persons entitled to the right of residence to undergo, free of charge, a medical examination to certify that they are not suffering from any of the conditions referred to in paragraph 1. Such medical examinations may not be required as a matter of routine.

Article 30

Notification of decisions

1. The persons concerned shall be notified in writing of any decision taken under Article 27(1), in such a way that they are able to comprehend its content and the implications for them.

2. The persons concerned shall be informed, precisely and in full, of the public policy, public security or public health grounds on which the decision taken in their case is based, unless this is contrary to the interests of State security.

3. The notification shall specify the court or administrative authority with which the person concerned may lodge an appeal, the time limit for the appeal and, where applicable, the time allowed for the person to leave the territory of the Member State. Save in duly substantiated cases of urgency, the time allowed to leave the territory shall be not less than one month from the date of notification.

Article 31

Procedural safeguards

1. The persons concerned shall have access to judicial and, where appropriate, administrative redress procedures in the host Member State to appeal against or seek review of any decision taken against them on the grounds of public policy, public security or public health.

2. Where the application for appeal against or judicial review of the expulsion decision is accompanied by an application for an interim order to suspend enforcement of that decision, actual removal from the territory may not take place until such time as the decision on the interim order has been taken, except:

— where the expulsion decision is based on a previous judicial decision; or

— where the persons concerned have had previous access to judicial review; or

— where the expulsion decision is based on imperative grounds of public security under Article 28(3).

3. The redress procedures shall allow for an examination of the legality of the decision, as well as of the facts and circumstances on which the proposed measure is based. They shall ensure that the decision is not disproportionate, particularly in view of the requirements laid down in Article 28.

4. Member States may exclude the individual concerned from their territory pending the redress procedure, but they may not prevent the individual from submitting his/her defence in person, except when his/her appearance may cause serious troubles to public policy or public security or when the appeal or judicial review concerns a denial of entry to the territory.

Article 32

Duration of exclusion orders

1. Persons excluded on grounds of public policy or public security may submit an application for lifting of the exclusion order after a reasonable period, depending on the circumstances, and in any event after three years from enforcement of the final exclusion

order which has been validly adopted in accordance with Community law, by putting forward arguments to establish that there has been a material change in the circumstances which justified the decision ordering their exclusion.

The Member State concerned shall reach a decision on this application within six months of its submission.

2. The persons referred to in paragraph 1 shall have no right of entry to the territory of the Member State concerned while their application is being considered.

Article 33

Expulsion as a penalty or legal consequence

1. Expulsion orders may not be issued by the host Member State as a penalty or legal consequence of a custodial penalty, unless they conform to the requirements of Articles 27, 28 and 29.

2. If an expulsion order, as provided for in paragraph 1, is enforced more than two years after it was issued, the Member State shall check that the individual concerned is currently and genuinely a threat to public policy or public security and shall assess whether there has been any material change in the circumstances since the expulsion order was issued.

Chapter VII
Final Provisions

Article 34

Publicity

Member States shall disseminate information concerning the rights and obligations of Union citizens and their family members on the subjects covered by this Directive, particularly by means of awareness-raising campaigns conducted through national and local media and other means of communication.

Article 35

Abuse of rights

Member States may adopt the necessary measures to refuse, terminate or withdraw any right conferred by this Directive in the case of abuse of rights or fraud, such as marriages of convenience. Any such measure shall be proportionate and subject to the procedural safeguards provided for in Articles 30 and 31.

Article 36

Sanctions

Member States shall lay down provisions on the sanctions applicable to breaches of national rules adopted for the implementation of this Directive and shall take the measures required for their application. The sanctions laid down shall be effective and proportionate. Member States shall notify the Commission of these provisions not later than 30 April 2006 and as promptly as possible in the case of any subsequent changes.

Article 37

More favourable national provisions

The provisions of this Directive shall not affect any laws, regulations or administrative provisions laid down by a Member State which would be more favourable to the persons covered by this Directive.

Article 38

Repeals

1. 2. Directives 64/221/EEC, 68/360/EEC, 72/194/EEC, 73/148/EEC, 75/34/EEC, 75/35/EEC, 90/364/EEC, 90/365/EEC and 93/96/EEC shall be repealed with effect from 30 April 2006.

3. References made to the repealed provisions and Directives shall be construed as being made to this Directive.

Note: Paragraph 1 repealed from 16 June 2011 by Regulation (EU) 492/2011.

Article 39

Report

No later than 30 April 2008 the Commission shall submit a report on the application of this Directive to the European Parliament and the Council, together with any necessary proposals, notably on the opportunity to extend the period of time during which Union citizens and their family members may reside in the territory of the host Member State without any conditions. The Member States shall provide the Commission with the information needed to produce the report.

Article 40

Transposition

1. Member States shall bring into force the laws, regulations and administrative provisions necessary to comply with this Directive by 30 April 2006.

When Member States adopt those measures, they shall contain a reference to this Directive or shall be accompanied by such a reference on the occasion of their official publication. The methods of making such reference shall be laid down by the Member States.

2. Member States shall communicate to the Commission the text of the provisions of national law which they adopt in the field covered by this Directive together with a table showing how the provisions of this Directive correspond to the national provisions adopted.

Article 41

Entry into force

This Directive shall enter into force on the day of its publication in the *Official Journal of the European Union.*

Article 42

Addresses

This Directive is addressed to the Member States.

Done at Brussels 29 April 2004.

For the European Parliament
The President
P. COX

For the Council
The President
M. McDOWELL

Council Directive 2005/85/EC of 1 December 2005

on minimum standards on procedures in Member States for granting and withdrawing refugee status

---

Note: The United Kingdom continues to be bound by this Directive as it has opted out of the recast Asylum Procedures Directive (2013/32/EU). It has been repealed for those EU States that are bound by the recast Directive with effect from 21 July 2015.

THE COUNCIL OF THE EUROPEAN UNION,

Having regard to the Treaty establishing the European Community, and in particular point (1)(d) of the first paragraph of Article 63 thereof,
Having regard to the proposal from the Commission,[1]
Having regard to the opinion of the European Parliament,[2]
Having regard to the opinion of the European Economic and Social Committee,[3]
Whereas:

(1) A common policy on asylum, including a Common European Asylum System, is a constituent part of the European Union's objective of establishing progressively an area of freedom, security and justice open to those who, forced by circumstances, legitimately seek protection in the Community.

(2) The European Council, at its special meeting in Tampere on 15 and 16 October 1999, agreed to work towards establishing a Common European Asylum System, based on the full and inclusive application of the Geneva Convention of 28 July 1951 relating to the status of refugees, as amended by the New York Protocol of 31 January 1967 (Geneva Convention), thus affirming the principle of non-refoulement and ensuring that nobody is sent back to persecution.

[1] OJ C 62, 27.2.2001, p. 231 and OJ C 291, 26.11.2002, p. 143.
[2] OJ C 77, 28.3.2002, p. 94.
[3] OJ C 193, 10.7.2001, p. 77. Opinion delivered following non-compulsory consultation.

(3) The Tampere Conclusions provide that a Common European Asylum System should include, in the short term, common standards for fair and efficient asylum procedures in the Member States and, in the longer term, Community rules leading to a common asylum procedure in the European Community.

(4) The minimum standards laid down in this Directive on procedures in Member States for granting or withdrawing refugee status are therefore a first measure on asylum procedures.

(5) The main objective of this Directive is to introduce a minimum framework in the Community on procedures for granting and withdrawing refugee status.

(6) The approximation of rules on the procedures for granting and withdrawing refugee status should help to limit the secondary movements of applicants for asylum between Member States, where such movement would be caused by differences in legal frameworks.

(7) It is in the very nature of minimum standards that Member States should have the power to introduce or maintain more favourable provisions for third country nationals or stateless persons who ask for international protection from a Member State, where such a request is understood to be on the grounds that the person concerned is a refugee within the meaning of Article 1(A) of the Geneva Convention.

(8) This Directive respects the fundamental rights and observes the principles recognised in particular by the Charter of Fundamental Rights of the European Union.

(9) With respect to the treatment of persons falling within the scope of this Directive, Member States are bound by obligations under instruments of international law to which they are party and which prohibit discrimination.

(10) It is essential that decisions on all applications for asylum be taken on the basis of the facts and, in the first instance, by authorities whose personnel has the appropriate knowledge or receives the necessary training in the field of asylum and refugee matters.

(11) It is in the interest of both Member States and applicants for asylum to decide as soon as possible on applications for asylum. The organisation of the processing of applications for asylum should be left to the discretion of Member States, so that they may, in accordance with their national needs, prioritise or accelerate the processing of any application, taking into account the standards in this Directive.

(12) The notion of public order may cover a conviction for committing a serious crime.

(13) In the interests of a correct recognition of those persons in need of protection as refugees within the meaning of Article 1 of the Geneva Convention, every applicant should, subject to certain exceptions, have an effective access to procedures, the opportunity to cooperate and properly communicate with the competent authorities so as to present the relevant facts of his/her case and sufficient procedural guarantees to pursue his/her case throughout all stages of the procedure. Moreover, the procedure in which an application for asylum is examined should normally provide an applicant at least with the right to stay pending a decision by the determining authority, access to the services of an interpreter for submitting his/her case if interviewed by the authorities, the opportunity to communicate with a representative of the United Nations High Commissioner for Refugees (UNHCR) or with any organisation working on its behalf, the right to appropriate notification of a decision, a motivation of that decision in fact and in law, the opportunity to consult a legal adviser or other counsellor, and the right to be informed of his/her legal position at decisive moments in the course of the procedure, in a language he/she can reasonably be supposed to understand.

(14) In addition, specific procedural guarantees for unaccompanied minors should be laid down on account of their vulnerability. In this context, the best interests of the child should be a primary consideration of Member States.

(15) Where an applicant makes a subsequent application without presenting new evidence or arguments, it would be disproportionate to oblige Member States to carry out a new full examination procedure. In these cases, Member States should have a choice of procedure involving exceptions to the guarantees normally enjoyed by the applicant.

(16) Many asylum applications are made at the border or in a transit zone of a Member State prior to a decision on the entry of the applicant. Member States should be able to keep existing procedures adapted to the specific situation of these applicants at the border. Common rules should be defined on possible exceptions made in these circumstances to the guarantees normally enjoyed by applicants. Border procedures should mainly apply to those applicants who do not meet the conditions for entry into the territory of the Member States.

(17) A key consideration for the well-foundedness of an asylum application is the safety of the applicant in his/her country of origin. Where a third country can be regarded as a safe country of origin, Member States should be able to designate it as safe and presume its safety for a particular applicant, unless he/she presents serious counter-indications.

(18) Given the level of harmonisation achieved on the qualification of third country nationals and stateless persons as refugees, common criteria for designating third countries as safe countries of origin should be established.

(19) Where the Council has satisfied itself that those criteria are met in relation to a particular country of origin, and has consequently included it in the minimum common list of safe countries of origin to be adopted pursuant to this Directive, Member States should be obliged to consider applications of persons with the nationality of that country, or of stateless persons formerly habitually resident in that country, on the basis of the rebuttable presumption of the safety of that country. In the light of the political importance of the designation of safe countries of origin, in particular in view of the implications of an assessment of the human rights situation in a country of origin and its implications for the policies of the European Union in the field of external relations, the Council should take any decisions on the establishment or amendment of the list, after consultation of the European Parliament.

(20) It results from the status of Bulgaria and Romania as candidate countries for accession to the European Union and the progress made by these countries towards membership that they should be regarded as constituting safe countries of origin for the purposes of this Directive until the date of their accession to the European Union.

(21) The designation of a third country as a safe country of origin for the purposes of this Directive cannot establish an absolute guarantee of safety for nationals of that country. By its very nature, the assessment underlying the designation can only take into account the general civil, legal and political circumstances in that country and whether actors of persecution, torture or inhuman or degrading treatment or punishment are subject to sanction in practice when found liable in the country concerned. For this reason, it is important that, where an applicant shows that there are serious reasons to consider the country not to be safe in his/her particular circumstances, the designation of the country as safe can no longer be considered relevant for him/her.

(22) Member States should examine all applications on the substance, i.e. assess whether the applicant in question qualifies as a refugee in accordance with Council

Directive 2004/83/EC of 29 April 2004 on minimum standards for the qualification and status of third country nationals or stateless persons as refugees or as persons who otherwise need international protection and the content of the protection granted,[4] except where the present Directive provides otherwise, in particular where it can be reasonably assumed that another country would do the examination or provide sufficient protection. In particular, Member States should not be obliged to assess the substance of an asylum application where a first country of asylum has granted the applicant refugee status or otherwise sufficient protection and the applicant will be re-admitted to this country.

(23) Member States should also not be obliged to assess the substance of an asylum application where the applicant, due to a connection to a third country as defined by national law, can reasonably be expected to seek protection in that third country. Member States should only proceed on this basis where this particular applicant would be safe in the third country concerned. In order to avoid secondary movements of applicants, common principles for the consideration or designation by Member States of third countries as safe should be established.

(24) Furthermore, with respect to certain European third countries, which observe particularly high human rights and refugee protection standards, Member States should be allowed to not carry out, or not to carry out full examination of asylum applications regarding applicants who enter their territory from such European third countries. Given the potential consequences for the applicant of a restricted or omitted examination, this application of the safe third country concept should be restricted to cases involving third countries with respect to which the Council has satisfied itself that the high standards for the safety of the third country concerned, as set out in this Directive, are fulfilled. The Council should take decisions in this matter after consultation of the European Parliament.

(25) It follows from the nature of the common standards concerning both safe third country concepts as set out in this Directive, that the practical effect of the concepts depends on whether the third country in question permits the applicant in question to enter its territory.

(26) With respect to the withdrawal of refugee status, Member States should ensure that persons benefiting from refugee status are duly informed of a possible reconsideration of their status and have the opportunity to submit their point of view before the authorities can take a motivated decision to withdraw their status. However, dispensing with these guarantees should be allowed where the reasons for the cessation of the refugee status is not related to a change of the conditions on which the recognition was based.

(27) It reflects a basic principle of Community law that the decisions taken on an application for asylum and on the withdrawal of refugee status are subject to an effective remedy before a court or tribunal within the meaning of Article 234 of the Treaty. The effectiveness of the remedy, also with regard to the examination of the relevant facts, depends on the administrative and judicial system of each Member State seen as a whole.

(28) In accordance with Article 64 of the Treaty, this Directive does not affect the exercise of the responsibilities incumbent upon Member States with regard to the maintenance of law and order and the safeguarding of internal security.

(29) This Directive does not deal with procedures governed by Council Regulation (EC) No. 343/2003 of 18 February 2003 establishing the criteria and mechanisms for

[4] OJ L 304, 30.9.2004, p. 12.

determining the Member State responsible for examining an asylum application lodged in one of the Member States by a third-country national.[5]

(30) The implementation of this Directive should be evaluated at regular intervals not exceeding two years.

(31) Since the objective of this Directive, namely to establish minimum standards on procedures in Member States for granting and withdrawing refugee status cannot be sufficiently attained by the Member States and can therefore, by reason of the scale and effects of the action, be better achieved at Community level, the Community may adopt measures, in accordance with the principle of subsidiarity as set out in Article 5 of the Treaty. In accordance with the principle of proportionality, as set out in that Article, this Directive does not go beyond what is necessary in order to achieve this objective.

(32) In accordance with Article 3 of the Protocol on the position of the United Kingdom and Ireland, annexed to the Treaty on European Union and to the Treaty establishing the European Community, the United Kingdom has notified, by letter of 24 January 2001, its wish to take part in the adoption and application of this Directive.

(33) In accordance with Article 3 of the Protocol on the position of the United Kingdom and Ireland, annexed to the Treaty on European Union and to the Treaty establishing the European Community, Ireland has notified, by letter of 14 February 2001, its wish to take part in the adoption and application of this Directive.

(34) In accordance with Articles 1 and 2 of the Protocol on the position of Denmark, annexed to the Treaty on European Union and to the Treaty establishing the European Community, Denmark does not take part in the adoption of this Directive and is not bound by it or subject to its application,

HAS ADOPTED THIS DIRECTIVE:

CHAPTER I
GENERAL PROVISIONS

Article 1

Purpose

The purpose of this Directive is to establish minimum standards on procedures in Member States for granting and withdrawing refugee status.

Article 2

Definitions

For the purposes of this Directive:

(a) 'Geneva Convention' means the Convention of 28 July 1951 relating to the status of refugees, as amended by the New York Protocol of 31 January 1967;

(b) 'application' or 'application for asylum' means an application made by a third country national or stateless person which can be understood as a request for international

[5] OJ L 50, 25.2.2003, p. 1.

protection from a Member State under the Geneva Convention. Any application for international protection is presumed to be an application for asylum, unless the person concerned explicitly requests another kind of protection that can be applied for separately;

(c) 'applicant' or 'applicant for asylum' means a third country national or stateless person who has made an application for asylum in respect of which a final decision has not yet been taken;

(d) 'final decision' means a decision on whether the third country national or stateless person be granted refugee status by virtue of Directive 2004/83/EC and which is no longer subject to a remedy within the framework of Chapter V of this Directive irrespective of whether such remedy has the effect of allowing applicants to remain in the Member States concerned pending its outcome, subject to Annex III to this Directive;

(e) 'determining authority' means any quasi-judicial or administrative body in a Member State responsible for examining applications for asylum and competent to take decisions at first instance in such cases, subject to Annex I;

(f) 'refugee' means a third country national or a stateless person who fulfils the requirements of Article 1 of the Geneva Convention as set out in Directive 2004/83/EC;

(g) 'refugee status' means the recognition by a Member State of a third country national or stateless person as a refugee;

(h) 'unaccompanied minor' means a person below the age of 18 who arrives in the territory of the Member States unaccompanied by an adult responsible for him/her whether by law or by custom, and for as long as he/she is not effectively taken into the care of such a person; it includes a minor who is left unaccompanied after he/she has entered the territory of the Member States;

(i) 'representative' means a person acting on behalf of an organisation representing an unaccompanied minor as legal guardian, a person acting on behalf of a national organisation which is responsible for the care and well-being of minors, or any other appropriate representation appointed to ensure his/her best interests;

(j) 'withdrawal of refugee status' means the decision by a competent authority to revoke, end or refuse to renew the refugee status of a person in accordance with Directive 2004/83/EC;

(k) 'remain in the Member State' means to remain in the territory, including at the border or in transit zones, of the Member State in which the application for asylum has been made or is being examined.

Article 3

Scope

1. This Directive shall apply to all applications for asylum made in the territory, including at the border or in the transit zones of the Member States, and to the withdrawal of refugee status.

2. This Directive shall not apply in cases of requests for diplomatic or territorial asylum submitted to representations of Member States.

3. Where Member States employ or introduce a procedure in which asylum applications are examined both as applications on the basis of the Geneva Convention and as applications for other kinds of international protection given under the circumstances

defined by Article 15 of Directive 2004/83/EC, they shall apply this Directive throughout their procedure.

4. Moreover, Member States may decide to apply this Directive in procedures for deciding on applications for any kind of international protection.

Article 4

Responsible authorities

1. Member States shall designate for all procedures a determining authority which will be responsible for an appropriate examination of the applications in accordance with this Directive, in particular Articles 8(2) and 9. In accordance with Article 4(4) of Regulation (EC) No. 343/2003, applications for asylum made in a Member State to the authorities of another Member State carrying out immigration controls there shall be dealt with by the Member State in whose territory the application is made.

2. However, Member States may provide that another authority is responsible for the purposes of:

(a) processing cases in which it is considered to transfer the applicant to another State according to the rules establishing criteria and mechanisms for determining which State is responsible for considering an application for asylum, until the transfer takes place or the requested State has refused to take charge of or take back the applicant;

(b) taking a decision on the application in the light of national security provisions, provided the determining authority is consulted prior to this decision as to whether the applicant qualifies as a refugee by virtue of Directive 2004/83/EC;

(c) conducting a preliminary examination pursuant to Article 32, provided this authority has access to the applicant's file regarding the previous application;

(d) processing cases in the framework of the procedures provided for in Article 35(1);

(e) refusing permission to enter in the framework of the procedure provided for in Article 35(2) to (5), subject to the conditions and as set out therein;

(f) establishing that an applicant is seeking to enter or has entered into the Member State from a safe third country pursuant to Article 36, subject to the conditions and as set out in that Article.

3. Where authorities are designated in accordance with paragraph 2, Member States shall ensure that the personnel of such authorities have the appropriate knowledge or receive the necessary training to fulfil their obligations when implementing this Directive.

Article 5

More favourable provisions

Member States may introduce or maintain more favourable standards on procedures for granting and withdrawing refugee status, insofar as those standards are compatible with this Directive.

Chapter II

Basic Principles and Guarantees

Article 6

Access to the procedure

1. Member States may require that applications for asylum be made in person and/or at a designated place.

2. Member States shall ensure that each adult having legal capacity has the right to make an application for asylum on his/her own behalf.

3. Member States may provide that an application may be made by an applicant on behalf of his/her dependants. In such cases Member States shall ensure that dependent adults consent to the lodging of the application on their behalf, failing which they shall have an opportunity to make an application on their own behalf. Consent shall be requested at the time the application is lodged or, at the latest, when the personal interview with the dependent adult is conducted.

4. Member States may determine in national legislation:

(a) the cases in which a minor can make an application on his/her own behalf;

(b) the cases in which the application of an unaccompanied minor has to be lodged by a representative as provided for in Article 17(1)(a);

(c) the cases in which the lodging of an application for asylum is deemed to constitute also the lodging of an application for asylum for any unmarried minor.

5. Member States shall ensure that authorities likely to be addressed by someone who wishes to make an application for asylum are able to advise that person how and where he/she may make such an application and/or may require these authorities to forward the application to the competent authority.

Article 7

Right to remain in the Member State pending the examination of the application

1. Applicants shall be allowed to remain in the Member State, for the sole purpose of the procedure, until the determining authority has made a decision in accordance with the procedures at first instance set out in Chapter III. This right to remain shall not constitute an entitlement to a residence permit.

2. Member States can make an exception only where, in accordance with Articles 32 and 34, a subsequent application will not be further examined or where they will surrender or extradite, as appropriate, a person either to another Member State pursuant to obligations in accordance with a European arrest warrant[6] or otherwise, or to a third country, or to international criminal courts or tribunals.

[6] Council Framework Decision 2002/584/JHA of 13 June 2002 on the European arrest warrant and the surrender procedures between Member States (OJ L 190, 18.7.2002, p. 1).

Article 8

Requirements for the examination of applications

1. Without prejudice to Article 23(4)(i), Member States shall ensure that applications for asylum are neither rejected nor excluded from examination on the sole ground that they have not been made as soon as possible.

2. Member States shall ensure that decisions by the determining authority on applications for asylum are taken after an appropriate examination. To that end, Member States shall ensure that:

(a) applications are examined and decisions are taken individually, objectively and impartially;

(b) precise and up-to-date information is obtained from various sources, such as the United Nations High Commissioner for Refugees (UNHCR), as to the general situation prevailing in the countries of origin of applicants for asylum and, where necessary, in countries through which they have transited, and that such information is made available to the personnel responsible for examining applications and taking decisions;

(c) the personnel examining applications and taking decisions have the knowledge with respect to relevant standards applicable in the field of asylum and refugee law.

3. The authorities referred to in Chapter V shall, through the determining authority or the applicant or otherwise, have access to the general information referred to in paragraph 2(b), necessary for the fulfilment of their task.

4. Member States may provide for rules concerning the translation of documents relevant for the examination of applications.

Article 9

Requirements for a decision by the determining authority

1. Member States shall ensure that decisions on applications for asylum are given in writing.

2. Member States shall also ensure that, where an application is rejected, the reasons in fact and in law are stated in the decision and information on how to challenge a negative decision is given in writing.

Member States need not state the reasons for not granting refugee status in a decision where the applicant is granted a status which offers the same rights and benefits under national and Community law as the refugee status by virtue of Directive 2004/83/EC. In these cases, Member States shall ensure that the reasons for not granting refugee status are stated in the applicant's file and that the applicant has, upon request, access to his/her file.

Moreover, Member States need not provide information on how to challenge a negative decision in writing in conjunction with a decision where the applicant has been provided with this information at an earlier stage either in writing or by electronic means accessible to the applicant.

3. For the purposes of Article 6(3), and whenever the application is based on the same grounds, Member States may take one single decision, covering all dependants.

Article 10

Guarantees for applicants for asylum

1. With respect to the procedures provided for in Chapter III, Member States shall ensure that all applicants for asylum enjoy the following guarantees:

(a) they shall be informed in a language which they may reasonably be supposed to understand of the procedure to be followed and of their rights and obligations during the procedure and the possible consequences of not complying with their obligations and not cooperating with the authorities. They shall be informed of the time-frame, as well as the means at their disposal for fulfilling the obligation to submit the elements as referred to in Article 4 of Directive 2004/83/EC. This information shall be given in time to enable them to exercise the rights guaranteed in this Directive and to comply with the obligations described in Article 11;

(b) they shall receive the services of an interpreter for submitting their case to the competent authorities whenever necessary. Member States shall consider it necessary to give these services at least when the determining authority calls upon the applicant to be interviewed as referred to in Articles 12 and 13 and appropriate communication cannot be ensured without such services. In this case and in other cases where the competent authorities call upon the applicant, these services shall be paid for out of public funds;

(c) they shall not be denied the opportunity to communicate with the UNHCR or with any other organisation working on behalf of the UNHCR in the territory of the Member State pursuant to an agreement with that Member State;

(d) they shall be given notice in reasonable time of the decision by the determining authority on their application for asylum. If a legal adviser or other counsellor is legally representing the applicant, Member States may choose to give notice of the decision to him/her instead of to the applicant for asylum;

(e) they shall be informed of the result of the decision by the determining authority in a language that they may reasonably be supposed to understand when they are not assisted or represented by a legal adviser or other counsellor and when free legal assistance is not available. The information provided shall include information on how to challenge a negative decision in accordance with the provisions of Article 9(2).

2. With respect to the procedures provided for in Chapter V, Member States shall ensure that all applicants for asylum enjoy equivalent guarantees to the ones referred to in paragraph 1(b), (c) and (d) of this Article.

Article 11

Obligations of the applicants for asylum

1. Member States may impose upon applicants for asylum obligations to cooperate with the competent authorities insofar as these obligations are necessary for the processing of the application.

2. In particular, Member States may provide that:

(a) applicants for asylum are required to report to the competent authorities or to appear before them in person, either without delay or at a specified time;

(b) applicants for asylum have to hand over documents in their possession relevant to the examination of the application, such as their passports;

(c) applicants for asylum are required to inform the competent authorities of their current place of residence or address and of any changes thereof as soon as possible. Member States may provide that the applicant shall have to accept any communication at the most recent place of residence or address which he/she indicated accordingly;

(d) the competent authorities may search the applicant and the items he/she carries with him/her;

(e) the competent authorities may take a photograph of the applicant; and

(f) the competent authorities may record the applicant's oral statements, provided he/she has previously been informed thereof.

Article 12

Personal interview

1. Before a decision is taken by the determining authority, the applicant for asylum shall be given the opportunity of a personal interview on his/her application for asylum with a person competent under national law to conduct such an interview.

Member States may also give the opportunity of a personal interview to each dependent adult referred to in Article 6(3).

Member States may determine in national legislation the cases in which a minor shall be given the opportunity of a personal interview.

2. The personal interview may be omitted where:

(a) the determining authority is able to take a positive decision on the basis of evidence available; or

(b) the competent authority has already had a meeting with the applicant for the purpose of assisting him/her with completing his/her application and submitting the essential information regarding the application, in terms of Article 4(2) of Directive 2004/83/EC; or

(c) the determining authority, on the basis of a complete examination of information provided by the applicant, considers the application to be unfounded in cases where the circumstances mentioned in Article 23(4)(a), (c), (g), (h) and (j) apply.

3. The personal interview may also be omitted where it is not reasonably practicable, in particular where the competent authority is of the opinion that the applicant is unfit or unable to be interviewed owing to enduring circumstances beyond his/her control. When in doubt, Member States may require a medical or psychological certificate.

Where the Member State does not provide the applicant with the opportunity for a personal interview pursuant to this paragraph, or where applicable, to the dependant, reasonable efforts shall be made to allow the applicant or the dependant to submit further information.

4. The absence of a personal interview in accordance with this Article shall not prevent the determining authority from taking a decision on an application for asylum.

5. The absence of a personal interview pursuant to paragraph 2(b) and (c) and paragraph 3 shall not adversely affect the decision of the determining authority.

6. Irrespective of Article 20(1), Member States, when deciding on the application for asylum, may take into account the fact that the applicant failed to appear for the personal interview, unless he/she had good reasons for the failure to appear.

Article 13

Requirements for a personal interview

1. A personal interview shall normally take place without the presence of family members unless the determining authority considers it necessary for an appropriate examination to have other family members present.

2. A personal interview shall take place under conditions which ensure appropriate confidentiality.

3. Member States shall take appropriate steps to ensure that personal interviews are conducted under conditions which allow applicants to present the grounds for their applications in a comprehensive manner. To that end, Member States shall:

(a) ensure that the person who conducts the interview is sufficiently competent to take account of the personal or general circumstances surrounding the application, including the applicant's cultural origin or vulnerability, insofar as it is possible to do so; and

(b) select an interpreter who is able to ensure appropriate communication between the applicant and the person who conducts the interview. The communication need not necessarily take place in the language preferred by the applicant for asylum if there is another language which he/she may reasonably be supposed to understand and in which he/she is able to communicate.

4. Member States may provide for rules concerning the presence of third parties at a personal interview.

5. This Article is also applicable to the meeting referred to in Article 12(2)(b).

Article 14

Status of the report of a personal interview in the procedure

1. Member States shall ensure that a written report is made of every personal interview, containing at least the essential information regarding the application, as presented by the applicant, in terms of Article 4(2) of Directive 2004/83/EC.

2. Member States shall ensure that applicants have timely access to the report of the personal interview. Where access is only granted after the decision of the determining authority, Member States shall ensure that access is possible as soon as necessary for allowing an appeal to be prepared and lodged in due time.

3. Member States may request the applicant's approval of the contents of the report of the personal interview.

Where an applicant refuses to approve the contents of the report, the reasons for this refusal shall be entered into the applicant's file.

The refusal of an applicant to approve the contents of the report shall not prevent the determining authority from taking a decision on his/her application.

4. This Article is also applicable to the meeting referred to in Article 12(2)(b).

Article 15

Right to legal assistance and representation

1. Member States shall allow applicants for asylum the opportunity, at their own cost, to consult in an effective manner a legal adviser or other counsellor, admitted or permitted as such under national law, on matters relating to their asylum applications.

2. In the event of a negative decision by a determining authority, Member States shall ensure that free legal assistance and/or representation be granted on request, subject to the provisions of paragraph 3.

3. Member States may provide in their national legislation that free legal assistance and/or representation is granted:

(a) only for procedures before a court or tribunal in accordance with Chapter V and not for any onward appeals or reviews provided for under national law, including a rehearing of an appeal following an onward appeal or review; and/or

(b) only to those who lack sufficient resources; and/or

(c) only to legal advisers or other counsellors specifically designated by national law to assist and/or represent applicants for asylum; and/or

(d) only if the appeal or review is likely to succeed.

Member States shall ensure that legal assistance and/or representation granted under point (d) is not arbitrarily restricted.

4. Rules concerning the modalities for filing and processing requests for legal assistance and/or representation may be provided by Member States.

5. Member States may also:

(a) impose monetary and/or time-limits on the provision of free legal assistance and/or representation, provided that such limits do not arbitrarily restrict access to legal assistance and/or representation;

(b) provide that, as regards fees and other costs, the treatment of applicants shall not be more favourable than the treatment generally accorded to their nationals in matters pertaining to legal assistance.

6. Member States may demand to be reimbursed wholly or partially for any expenses granted if and when the applicant's financial situation has improved considerably or if the decision to grant such benefits was taken on the basis of false information supplied by the applicant.

Article 16

Scope of legal assistance and representation

1. Member States shall ensure that a legal adviser or other counsellor admitted or permitted as such under national law, and who assists or represents an applicant for asylum under the terms of national law, shall enjoy access to such information in the applicant's file as is liable to be examined by the authorities referred to in Chapter V, insofar as the information is relevant to the examination of the application.

Member States may make an exception where disclosure of information or sources would jeopardise national security, the security of the organisations or person(s) providing the information or the security of the person(s) to whom the information relates or where the investigative interests relating to the examination of applications of asylum by the competent authorities of the Member States or the international relations of the Member States would be compromised. In these cases, access to the information or sources in question shall be available to the authorities referred to in Chapter V, except where such access is precluded in cases of national security.

2. Member States shall ensure that the legal adviser or other counsellor who assists or represents an applicant for asylum has access to closed areas, such as detention facilities and transit zones, for the purpose of consulting that applicant. Member States may only limit the possibility of visiting applicants in closed areas where such limitation is, by virtue of national legislation, objectively necessary for the security, public order or administrative management of the area, or in order to ensure an efficient examination of the application, provided that access by the legal adviser or other counsellor is not thereby severely limited or rendered impossible.

3. Member States may provide rules covering the presence of legal advisers or other counsellors at all interviews in the procedure, without prejudice to this Article or to Article 17(1)(b).

4. Member States may provide that the applicant is allowed to bring with him/her to the personal interview a legal adviser or other counsellor admitted or permitted as such under national law.

Member States may require the presence of the applicant at the personal interview, even if he/she is represented under the terms of national law by such a legal adviser or counsellor, and may require the applicant to respond in person to the questions asked.

The absence of a legal adviser or other counsellor shall not prevent the competent authority from conducting the personal interview with the applicant.

Article 17

Guarantees for unaccompanied minors

1. With respect to all procedures provided for in this Directive and without prejudice to the provisions of Articles 12 and 14, Member States shall:

(a) as soon as possible take measures to ensure that a representative represents and/or assists the unaccompanied minor with respect to the examination of the application. This representative can also be the representative referred to in Article 19 of Directive 2003/9/EC of 27 January 2003 laying down minimum standards for the reception of asylum seekers;[7]

(b) ensure that the representative is given the opportunity to inform the unaccompanied minor about the meaning and possible consequences of the personal interview and, where appropriate, how to prepare himself/herself for the personal interview. Member States shall allow the representative to be present at that interview and to ask questions or make comments, within the framework set by the person who conducts the interview.

Member States may require the presence of the unaccompanied minor at the personal interview, even if the representative is present.

2. Member States may refrain from appointing a representative where the unaccompanied minor:

(a) will in all likelihood reach the age of maturity before a decision at first instance is taken; or

[7] OJ L 31, 6.2.2003, p. 18.

(b) can avail himself, free of charge, of a legal adviser or other counsellor, admitted as such under national law to fulfil the tasks assigned above to the representative; or

(c) is married or has been married.

3. Member States may, in accordance with the laws and regulations in force on 1 December 2005, also refrain from appointing a representative where the unaccompanied minor is 16 years old or older, unless he/she is unable to pursue his/her application without a representative.

4. Member States shall ensure that:

(a) if an unaccompanied minor has a personal interview on his/her application for asylum as referred to in Articles 12, 13 and 14, that interview is conducted by a person who has the necessary knowledge of the special needs of minors;

(b) an official with the necessary knowledge of the special needs of minors prepares the decision by the determining authority on the application of an unaccompanied minor.

5. Member States may use medical examinations to determine the age of unaccompanied minors within the framework of the examination of an application for asylum.

In cases where medical examinations are used, Member States shall ensure that:

(a) unaccompanied minors are informed prior to the examination of their application for asylum, and in a language which they may reasonably be supposed to understand, of the possibility that their age may be determined by medical examination. This shall include information on the method of examination and the possible consequences of the result of the medical examination for the examination of the application for asylum, as well as the consequences of refusal on the part of the unaccompanied minor to undergo the medical examination;

(b) unaccompanied minors and/or their representatives consent to carry out an examination to determine the age of the minors concerned; and

(c) the decision to reject an application for asylum from an unaccompanied minor who refused to undergo this medical examination shall not be based solely on that refusal.

The fact that an unaccompanied minor has refused to undergo such a medical examination shall not prevent the determining authority from taking a decision on the application for asylum.

6. The best interests of the child shall be a primary consideration for Member States when implementing this Article.

Article 18

Detention

1. Member States shall not hold a person in detention for the sole reason that he/she is an applicant for asylum.

2. Where an applicant for asylum is held in detention, Member States shall ensure that there is a possibility of speedy judicial review.

Article 19

Procedure in case of withdrawal of the application

1. Insofar as Member States provide for the possibility of explicit withdrawal of the application under national law, when an applicant for asylum explicitly withdraws his/her

application for asylum, Member States shall ensure that the determining authority takes a decision to either discontinue the examination or reject the application.

2. Member States may also decide that the determining authority can decide to discontinue the examination without taking a decision. In this case, Member States shall ensure that the determining authority enters a notice in the applicant's file.

Article 20

Procedure in the case of implicit withdrawal or abandonment of the application

1. When there is reasonable cause to consider that an applicant for asylum has implicitly withdrawn or abandoned his/her application for asylum, Member States shall ensure that the determining authority takes a decision to either discontinue the examination or reject the application on the basis that the applicant has not established an entitlement to refugee status in accordance with Directive 2004/83/EC.

Member States may assume that the applicant has implicitly withdrawn or abandoned his/her application for asylum in particular when it is ascertained that:

(a) he/she has failed to respond to requests to provide information essential to his/her application in terms of Article 4 of Directive 2004/83/EC or has not appeared for a personal interview as provided for in Articles 12, 13 and 14, unless the applicant demonstrates within a reasonable time that his/her failure was due to circumstances beyond his control;

(b) he/she has absconded or left without authorisation the place where he/she lived or was held, without contacting the competent authority within a reasonable time, or he/she has not within a reasonable time complied with reporting duties or other obligations to communicate.

For the purposes of implementing these provisions, Member States may lay down time-limits or guidelines.

2. Member States shall ensure that the applicant who reports again to the competent authority after a decision to discontinue as referred to in paragraph 1 of this Article is taken, is entitled to request that his/her case be re-opened, unless the request is examined in accordance with Articles 32 and 34.

Member States may provide for a time-limit after which the applicant's case can no longer be re-opened.

Member States shall ensure that such a person is not removed contrary to the principle of non-refoulement.

Member States may allow the determining authority to take up the examination at the stage where it was discontinued.

Article 21

The role of UNHCR

1. Member States shall allow the UNHCR:

(a) to have access to applicants for asylum, including those in detention and in airport or port transit zones;

(b) to have access to information on individual applications for asylum, on the course of the procedure and on the decisions taken, provided that the applicant for asylum agrees thereto;

(c) to present its views, in the exercise of its supervisory responsibilities under Article 35 of the Geneva Convention, to any competent authorities regarding individual applications for asylum at any stage of the procedure.

2. Paragraph 1 shall also apply to an organisation which is working in the territory of the Member State concerned on behalf of the UNHCR pursuant to an agreement with that Member State.

Article 22

Collection of information on individual cases

For the purposes of examining individual cases, Member States shall not:

(a) directly disclose information regarding individual applications for asylum, or the fact that an application has been made, to the alleged actor(s) of persecution of the applicant for asylum;

(b) obtain any information from the alleged actor(s) of persecution in a manner that would result in such actor(s) being directly informed of the fact that an application has been made by the applicant in question, and would jeopardise the physical integrity of the applicant and his/her dependants, or the liberty and security of his/her family members still living in the country of origin.

Chapter III

Procedures at First Instance

Section I

Article 23

Examination procedure

1. Member States shall process applications for asylum in an examination procedure in accordance with the basic principles and guarantees of Chapter II.

2. Member States shall ensure that such a procedure is concluded as soon as possible, without prejudice to an adequate and complete examination.

Member States shall ensure that, where a decision cannot be taken within six months, the applicant concerned shall either:

(a) be informed of the delay; or

(b) receive, upon his/her request, information on the time-frame within which the decision on his/her application is to be expected. Such information shall not constitute an obligation for the Member State towards the applicant concerned to take a decision within that time-frame.

3. Member States may prioritise or accelerate any examination in accordance with the basic principles and guarantees of Chapter II, including where the application is likely to be well-founded or where the applicant has special needs.

4. Member States may also provide that an examination procedure in accordance with the basic principles and guarantees of Chapter II be prioritised or accelerated if:

(a) the applicant, in submitting his/her application and presenting the facts, has only raised issues that are not relevant or of minimal relevance to the examination of whether he/she qualifies as a refugee by virtue of Directive 2004/83/EC; or

(b) the applicant clearly does not qualify as a refugee or for refugee status in a Member State under Directive 2004/83/EC; or

(c) the application for asylum is considered to be unfounded:

(i) because the applicant is from a safe country of origin within the meaning of Articles 29, 30 and 31, or

(ii) because the country which is not a Member State, is considered to be a safe third country for the applicant, without prejudice to Article 28(1); or

(d) the applicant has misled the authorities by presenting false information or documents or by withholding relevant information or documents with respect to his/her identity and/or nationality that could have had a negative impact on the decision; or

(e) the applicant has filed another application for asylum stating other personal data; or

(f) the applicant has not produced information establishing with a reasonable degree of certainty his/her identity or nationality, or it is likely that, in bad faith, he/she has destroyed or disposed of an identity or travel document that would have helped establish his/her identity or nationality; or

(g) the applicant has made inconsistent, contradictory, improbable or insufficient representations which make his/her claim clearly unconvincing in relation to his/her having been the object of persecution referred to in Directive 2004/83/EC; or

(h) the applicant has submitted a subsequent application which does not raise any relevant new elements with respect to his/her particular circumstances or to the situation in his/her country of origin; or

(i) the applicant has failed without reasonable cause to make his/her application earlier, having had opportunity to do so; or

(j) the applicant is making an application merely in order to delay or frustrate the enforcement of an earlier or imminent decision which would result in his/her removal; or

(k) the applicant has failed without good reason to comply with obligations referred to in Article 4(1) and (2) of Directive 2004/83/EC or in Articles 11(2)(a) and (b) and 20(1) of this Directive; or

(l) the applicant entered the territory of the Member State unlawfully or prolonged his/her stay unlawfully and, without good reason, has either not presented himself/herself to the authorities and/or filed an application for asylum as soon as possible, given the circumstances of his/her entry; or

(m) the applicant is a danger to the national security or public order of the Member State, or the applicant has been forcibly expelled for serious reasons of public security and public order under national law; or

(n) the applicant refuses to comply with an obligation to have his/her fingerprints taken in accordance with relevant Community and/or national legislation; or

(o) the application was made by an unmarried minor to whom Article 6(4)(c) applies, after the application of the parents or parent responsible for the minor has been rejected and no relevant new elements were raised with respect to his/her particular circumstances or to the situation in his/her country of origin.

Article 24

Specific procedures

1. Member States may provide for the following specific procedures derogating from the basic principles and guarantees of Chapter II:

(a) a preliminary examination for the purposes of processing cases considered within the framework set out in Section IV;

(b) procedures for the purposes of processing cases considered within the framework set out in Section V.

2. Member States may also provide a derogation in respect of Section VI.

Section II

Article 25

Inadmissible applications

1. In addition to cases in which an application is not examined in accordance with Regulation (EC) No. 343/2003, Member States are not required to examine whether the applicant qualifies as a refugee in accordance with Directive 2004/83/EC where an application is considered inadmissible pursuant to this Article.

2. Member States may consider an application for asylum as inadmissible pursuant to this Article if:

(a) another Member State has granted refugee status;

(b) a country which is not a Member State is considered as a first country of asylum for the applicant, pursuant to Article 26;

(c) a country which is not a Member State is considered as a safe third country for the applicant, pursuant to Article 27;

(d) the applicant is allowed to remain in the Member State concerned on some other grounds and as result of this he/she has been granted a status equivalent to the rights and benefits of the refugee status by virtue of Directive 2004/83/EC;

(e) the applicant is allowed to remain in the territory of the Member State concerned on some other grounds which protect him/her against refoulement pending the outcome of a procedure for the determination of status pursuant to point (d);

(f) the applicant has lodged an identical application after a final decision;

(g) a dependant of the applicant lodges an application, after he/she has in accordance with Article 6(3) consented to have his/her case be part of an application made on his/her behalf, and there are no facts relating to the dependant's situation, which justify a separate application.

Article 26

The concept of first country of asylum

A country can be considered to be a first country of asylum for a particular applicant for asylum if:

(a) he/she has been recognised in that country as a refugee and he/she can still avail himself/herself of that protection; or

(b) he/she otherwise enjoys sufficient protection in that country, including benefiting from the principle of non-refoulement;

provided that he/she will be re-admitted to that country.

In applying the concept of first country of asylum to the particular circumstances of an applicant for asylum Member States may take into account Article 27(1).

Article 27

The safe third country concept

1. Member States may apply the safe third country concept only where the competent authorities are satisfied that a person seeking asylum will be treated in accordance with the following principles in the third country concerned:

(a) life and liberty are not threatened on account of race, religion, nationality, membership of a particular social group or political opinion;

(b) the principle of non-refoulement in accordance with the Geneva Convention is respected;

(c) the prohibition of removal, in violation of the right to freedom from torture and cruel, inhuman or degrading treatment as laid down in international law, is respected; and

(d) the possibility exists to request refugee status and, if found to be a refugee, to receive protection in accordance with the Geneva Convention.

2. The application of the safe third country concept shall be subject to rules laid down in national legislation, including:

(a) rules requiring a connection between the person seeking asylum and the third country concerned on the basis of which it would be reasonable for that person to go to that country;

(b) rules on the methodology by which the competent authorities satisfy themselves that the safe third country concept may be applied to a particular country or to a particular applicant. Such methodology shall include case-by-case consideration of the safety of the country for a particular applicant and/or national designation of countries considered to be generally safe;

(c) rules in accordance with international law, allowing an individual examination of whether the third country concerned is safe for a particular applicant which, as a minimum, shall permit the applicant to challenge the application of the safe third country concept on the grounds that he/she would be subjected to torture, cruel, inhuman or degrading treatment or punishment.

3. When implementing a decision solely based on this Article, Member States shall:

(a) inform the applicant accordingly; and

(b) provide him/her with a document informing the authorities of the third country, in the language of that country, that the application has not been examined in substance.

4. Where the third country does not permit the applicant for asylum to enter its territory, Member States shall ensure that access to a procedure is given in accordance with the basic principles and guarantees described in Chapter II.

5. Member States shall inform the Commission periodically of the countries to which this concept is applied in accordance with the provisions of this Article.

Section III

Article 28

Unfounded applications

1. Without prejudice to Articles 19 and 20, Member States may only consider an application for asylum as unfounded if the determining authority has established that the applicant does not qualify for refugee status pursuant to Directive 2004/83/EC.

2. In the cases mentioned in Article 23(4)(b) and in cases of unfounded applications for asylum in which any of the circumstances listed in Article 23(4)(a) and (c) to (o) apply, Member States may also consider an application as manifestly unfounded, where it is defined as such in the national legislation.

Article 29

Minimum common list of third countries regarded as safe countries of origin

1. The Council shall, acting by a qualified majority on a proposal from the Commission and after consultation of the European Parliament, adopt a minimum common list of third countries which shall be regarded by Member States as safe countries of origin in accordance with Annex II.

2. The Council may, acting by a qualified majority on a proposal from the Commission and after consultation of the European Parliament, amend the minimum common list by adding or removing third countries, in accordance with Annex II. The Commission shall examine any request made by the Council or by a Member State to submit a proposal to amend the minimum common list.

3. When making its proposal under paragraphs 1 or 2, the Commission shall make use of information from the Member States, its own information and, where necessary, information from UNHCR, the Council of Europe and other relevant international organisations.

4. Where the Council requests the Commission to submit a proposal for removing a third country from the minimum common list, the obligation of Member States pursuant to Article 31(2) shall be suspended with regard to this third country as of the day following the Council decision requesting such a submission.

5. Where a Member State requests the Commission to submit a proposal to the Council for removing a third country from the minimum common list, that Member State shall notify the Council in writing of the request made to the Commission. The obligation of this Member State pursuant to Article 31(2) shall be suspended with regard to the third country as of the day following the notification to the Council.

6. The European Parliament shall be informed of the suspensions under paragraphs 4 and 5.

7. The suspensions under paragraphs 4 and 5 shall end after three months, unless the Commission makes a proposal before the end of this period, to withdraw the third country from the minimum common list. The suspensions shall in any case end where the Council rejects a proposal by the Commission to withdraw the third country from the list.

8. Upon request by the Council, the Commission shall report to the European Parliament and the Council on whether the situation of a country on the minimum common list is still in conformity with Annex II. When presenting its report, the Commission may make such recommendations or proposals as it deems appropriate.

Article 30

National designation of third countries as safe countries of origin

1. Without prejudice to Article 29, Member States may retain or introduce legislation that allows, in accordance with Annex II, for the national designation of third countries other than those appearing on the minimum common list, as safe countries of origin for the purposes of examining applications for asylum. This may include designation of part of a country as safe where the conditions in Annex II are fulfilled in relation to that part.

2. By derogation from paragraph 1, Member States may retain legislation in force on 1 December 2005 that allows for the national designation of third countries, other than those appearing on the minimum common list, as safe countries of origin for the purposes of examining applications for asylum where they are satisfied that persons in the third countries concerned are generally neither subject to:

(a) persecution as defined in Article 9 of Directive 2004/83/EC; nor

(b) torture or inhuman or degrading treatment or punishment.

3. Member States may also retain legislation in force on 1 December 2005 that allows for the national designation of part of a country as safe, or a country or part of a country as safe for a specified group of persons in that country, where the conditions in paragraph 2 are fulfilled in relation to that part or group.

4. In assessing whether a country is a safe country of origin in accordance with paragraphs 2 and 3, Member States shall have regard to the legal situation, the application of the law and the general political circumstances in the third country concerned.

5. The assessment of whether a country is a safe country of origin in accordance with this Article shall be based on a range of sources of information, including in particular information from other Member States, the UNHCR, the Council of Europe and other relevant international organisations.

6. Member States shall notify to the Commission the countries that are designated as safe countries of origin in accordance with this Article.

Article 31

The safe country of origin concept

1. A third country designated as a safe country of origin in accordance with either Article 29 or 30 may, after an individual examination of the application, be considered as a safe country of origin for a particular applicant for asylum only if:

(a) he/she has the nationality of that country; or

(b) he/she is a stateless person and was formerly habitually resident in that country;

and he/she has not submitted any serious grounds for considering the country not to be a safe country of origin in his/her particular circumstances and in terms of his/her qualification as a refugee in accordance with Directive 2004/83/EC.

2. Member States shall, in accordance with paragraph 1, consider the application for asylum as unfounded where the third country is designated as safe pursuant to Article 29.

3. Member States shall lay down in national legislation further rules and modalities for the application of the safe country of origin concept.

Section IV

Article 32

Subsequent application

1. Where a person who has applied for asylum in a Member State makes further representations or a subsequent application in the same Member State, that Member State may examine these further representations or the elements of the subsequent application in the framework of the examination of the previous application or in the framework of the examination of the decision under review or appeal, insofar as the competent authorities can take into account and consider all the elements underlying the further representations or subsequent application within this framework.

2. Moreover, Member States may apply a specific procedure as referred to in paragraph 3, where a person makes a subsequent application for asylum:

(a) after his/her previous application has been withdrawn or abandoned by virtue of Articles 19 or 20;

(b) after a decision has been taken on the previous application. Member States may also decide to apply this procedure only after a final decision has been taken.

3. A subsequent application for asylum shall be subject first to a preliminary examination as to whether, after the withdrawal of the previous application or after the decision referred to in paragraph 2(b) of this Article on this application has been reached, new elements or findings relating to the examination of whether he/she qualifies as a refugee by virtue of Directive 2004/83/EC have arisen or have been presented by the applicant.

4. If, following the preliminary examination referred to in paragraph 3 of this Article, new elements or findings arise or are presented by the applicant which significantly add to the likelihood of the applicant qualifying as a refugee by virtue of Directive 2004/83/EC, the application shall be further examined in conformity with Chapter II.

5. Member States may, in accordance with national legislation, further examine a subsequent application where there are other reasons why a procedure has to be re-opened.

6. Member States may decide to further examine the application only if the applicant concerned was, through no fault of his/her own, incapable of asserting the situations set forth in paragraphs 3, 4 and 5 of this Article in the previous procedure, in particular by exercising his/her right to an effective remedy pursuant to Article 39.

7. The procedure referred to in this Article may also be applicable in the case of a dependant who lodges an application after he/she has, in accordance with Article 6(3), consented to have his/her case be part of an application made on his/her behalf. In this case the preliminary examination referred to in paragraph 3 of this Article will consist of examining whether there are facts relating to the dependant's situation which justify a separate application.

Article 33

Failure to appear

Member States may retain or adopt the procedure provided for in Article 32 in the case of an application for asylum filed at a later date by an applicant who, either intentionally or owing to gross negligence, fails to go to a reception centre or appear before the competent authorities at a specified time.

Article 34

Procedural rules

1. Member States shall ensure that applicants for asylum whose application is subject to a preliminary examination pursuant to Article 32 enjoy the guarantees provided for in Article 10(1).

2. Member States may lay down in national law rules on the preliminary examination pursuant to Article 32. Those rules may, *inter alia*:

(a) oblige the applicant concerned to indicate facts and substantiate evidence which justify a new procedure;

(b) require submission of the new information by the applicant concerned within a time-limit after he/she obtained such information;

(c) permit the preliminary examination to be conducted on the sole basis of written submissions without a personal interview.

The conditions shall not render impossible the access of applicants for asylum to a new procedure or result in the effective annulment or severe curtailment of such access.

3. Member States shall ensure that:

(a) the applicant is informed in an appropriate manner of the outcome of the preliminary examination and, in case the application will not be further examined, of the reasons for this and the possibilities for seeking an appeal or review of the decision;

(b) if one of the situations referred to in Article 32(2) applies, the determining authority shall further examine the subsequent application in conformity with the provisions of Chapter II as soon as possible.

Section V

Article 35

Border procedures

1. Member States may provide for procedures, in accordance with the basic principles and guarantees of Chapter II, in order to decide at the border or transit zones of the Member State on applications made at such locations.

2. However, when procedures as set out in paragraph 1 do not exist, Member States may maintain, subject to the provisions of this Article and in accordance with the laws or regulations in force on 1 December 2005, procedures derogating from the basic principles and guarantees described in Chapter II, in order to decide at the border or in transit zones as to whether applicants for asylum who have arrived and made an application for asylum at such locations, may enter their territory.

3. The procedures referred to in paragraph 2 shall ensure in particular that the persons concerned:

(a) are allowed to remain at the border or transit zones of the Member State, without prejudice to Article 7;

(b) are be [sic] immediately informed of their rights and obligations, as described in Article 10(1)(a);

(c) have access, if necessary, to the services of an interpreter, as described in Article 10(1)(b);

(d) are interviewed, before the competent authority takes a decision in such procedures, in relation to their application for asylum by persons with appropriate knowledge of the relevant standards applicable in the field of asylum and refugee law, as described in Articles 12, 13 and 14;

(e) can consult a legal adviser or counsellor admitted or permitted as such under national law, as described in Article 15(1); and

(f) have a representative appointed in the case of unaccompanied minors, as described in Article 17(1), unless Article 17(2) or (3) applies.

Moreover, in case permission to enter is refused by a competent authority, this competent authority shall state the reasons in fact and in law why the application for asylum is considered as unfounded or as inadmissible.

4. Member States shall ensure that a decision in the framework of the procedures provided for in paragraph 2 is taken within a reasonable time. When a decision has not been taken within four weeks, the applicant for asylum shall be granted entry to the territory of the Member State in order for his/her application to be processed in accordance with the other provisions of this Directive.

5. In the event of particular types of arrivals, or arrivals involving a large number of third country nationals or stateless persons lodging applications for asylum at the border or in a transit zone, which makes it practically impossible to apply there the provisions of paragraph 1 or the specific procedure set out in paragraphs 2 and 3, those procedures may also be applied where and for as long as these third country nationals or stateless persons are accommodated normally at locations in proximity to the border or transit zone.

Section VI

Article 36

The European safe third countries concept

1. Member States may provide that no, or no full, examination of the asylum application and of the safety of the applicant in his/her particular circumstances as described in Chapter II, shall take place in cases where a competent authority has established, on the basis of the facts, that the applicant for asylum is seeking to enter or has entered illegally into its territory from a safe third country according to paragraph 2.

2. A third country can only be considered as a safe third country for the purposes of paragraph 1 where:

(a) it has ratified and observes the provisions of the Geneva Convention without any geographical limitations;

(b) it has in place an asylum procedure prescribed by law;

(c) it has ratified the European Convention for the Protection of Human Rights and Fundamental Freedoms and observes its provisions, including the standards relating to effective remedies; and

(d) it has been so designated by the Council in accordance with paragraph 3.

3. The Council shall, acting by qualified majority on a proposal from the Commission and after consultation of the European Parliament, adopt or amend a common list of third countries that shall be regarded as safe third countries for the purposes of paragraph 1.

4. The Member States concerned shall lay down in national law the modalities for implementing the provisions of paragraph 1 and the consequences of decisions pursuant to those provisions in accordance with the principle of non-refoulement under the Geneva

Convention, including providing for exceptions from the application of this Article for humanitarian or political reasons or for reasons of public international law.

5. When implementing a decision solely based on this Article, the Member States concerned shall:

(a) inform the applicant accordingly; and

(b) provide him/her with a document informing the authorities of the third country, in the language of that country, that the application has not been examined in substance.

6. Where the safe third country does not re-admit the applicant for asylum, Member States shall ensure that access to a procedure is given in accordance with the basic principles and guarantees described in Chapter II.

7. Member States which have designated third countries as safe countries in accordance with national legislation in force on 1 December 2005 and on the basis of the criteria in paragraph 2(a), (b) and (c), may apply paragraph 1 to these third countries until the Council has adopted the common list pursuant to paragraph 3.

Chapter IV

Procedures for the Withdrawal of Refugee Status

Article 37

Withdrawal of refugee status

Member States shall ensure that an examination to withdraw the refugee status of a particular person may commence when new elements or findings arise indicating that there are reasons to reconsider the validity of his/her refugee status.

Article 38

Procedural rules

1. Member States shall ensure that, where the competent authority is considering withdrawing the refugee status of a third country national or stateless person in accordance with Article 14 of Directive 2004/83/EC, the person concerned shall enjoy the following guarantees:

(a) to be informed in writing that the competent authority is reconsidering his or her qualification for refugee status and the reasons for such a reconsideration; and

(b) to be given the opportunity to submit, in a personal interview in accordance with Article 10(1)(b) and Articles 12, 13 and 14 or in a written statement, reasons as to why his/her refugee status should not be withdrawn.

In addition, Member States shall ensure that within the framework of such a procedure:

(c) the competent authority is able to obtain precise and up-to-date information from various sources, such as, where appropriate, from the UNHCR, as to the general situation prevailing in the countries of origin of the persons concerned; and

(d) where information on an individual case is collected for the purposes of reconsidering the refugee status, it is not obtained from the actor(s) of persecution in a manner that would result in such actor(s) being directly informed of the fact that the person concerned is a refugee whose status is under reconsideration, nor jeopardise the physical integrity of the person and his/her dependants, or the liberty and security of his/her family members still living in the country of origin.

2. Member States shall ensure that the decision of the competent authority to withdraw the refugee status is given in writing. The reasons in fact and in law shall be stated in the decision and information on how to challenge the decision shall be given in writing.

3. Once the competent authority has taken the decision to withdraw the refugee status, Article 15, paragraph 2, Article 16, paragraph 1 and Article 21 are equally applicable.

4. By derogation to paragraphs 1, 2 and 3 of this Article, Member States may decide that the refugee status shall lapse by law in case of cessation in accordance with Article 11(1)(a) to (d) of Directive 2004/83/EC or if the refugee has unequivocally renounced his/her recognition as a refugee.

Chapter V
Appeals Procedures

Article 39

The right to an effective remedy

1. Member States shall ensure that applicants for asylum have the right to an effective remedy before a court or tribunal, against the following:

(a) a decision taken on their application for asylum, including a decision:

(i) to consider an application inadmissible pursuant to Article 25(2),

(ii) taken at the border or in the transit zones of a Member State as described in Article 35(1),

(iii) not to conduct an examination pursuant to Article 36;

(b) a refusal to re-open the examination of an application after its discontinuation pursuant to Articles 19 and 20;

(c) a decision not to further examine the subsequent application pursuant to Articles 32 and 34;

(d) a decision refusing entry within the framework of the procedures provided for under Article 35(2);

(e) a decision to withdraw refugee status pursuant to Article 38.

2. Member States shall provide for time-limits and other necessary rules for the applicant to exercise his/her right to an effective remedy pursuant to paragraph 1.

3. Member States shall, where appropriate, provide for rules in accordance with their international obligations dealing with:

(a) the question of whether the remedy pursuant to paragraph 1 shall have the effect of allowing applicants to remain in the Member State concerned pending its outcome;

(b) the possibility of legal remedy or protective measures where the remedy pursuant to paragraph 1 does not have the effect of allowing applicants to remain in the Member State concerned pending its outcome. Member States may also provide for an *ex officio* remedy; and

(c) the grounds for challenging a decision under Article 25(2)(c) in accordance with the methodology applied under Article 27(2)(b) and (c).

4. Member States may lay down time-limits for the court or tribunal pursuant to paragraph 1 to examine the decision of the determining authority.

5. Where an applicant has been granted a status which offers the same rights and benefits under national and Community law as the refugee status by virtue of Directive 2004/83/EC, the applicant may be considered as having an effective remedy where a court or tribunal decides that the remedy pursuant to paragraph 1 is inadmissible or unlikely to succeed on the basis of insufficient interest on the part of the applicant in maintaining the proceedings.

6. Member States may also lay down in national legislation the conditions under which it can be assumed that an applicant has implicitly withdrawn or abandoned his/her remedy pursuant to paragraph 1, together with the rules on the procedure to be followed.

Chapter VI
General and Final Provisions

Article 40

Challenge by public authorities

This Directive does not affect the possibility for public authorities of challenging the administrative and/or judicial decisions as provided for in national legislation.

Article 41

Confidentiality

Member States shall ensure that authorities implementing this Directive are bound by the confidentiality principle as defined in national law, in relation to any information they obtain in the course of their work.

Article 42

Report

No later than 1 December 2009, the Commission shall report to the European Parliament and the Council on the application of this Directive in the Member States and shall propose any amendments that are necessary. Member States shall send the Commission all the information that is appropriate for drawing up this report. After presenting the report, the Commission shall report to the European Parliament and the Council on the application of this Directive in the Member States at least every two years.

Article 43

Transposition

Member States shall bring into force the laws, regulations and administrative provisions necessary to comply with this Directive by 1 December 2007. Concerning Article 15, Member States shall bring into force the laws, regulations and administrative provisions necessary to comply with this Directive by 1 December 2008. They shall forthwith inform the Commission thereof.

When Member States adopt those provisions, they shall contain a reference to this Directive or shall be accompanied by such a reference on the occasion of their official publication. The methods of making such reference shall be laid down by Member States.

Member States shall communicate to the Commission the text of the provisions of national law which they adopt in the field covered by this Directive.

Article 44

Transition

Member States shall apply the laws, regulations and administrative provisions set out in Article 43 to applications for asylum lodged after 1 December 2007 and to procedures for the withdrawal of refugee status started after 1 December 2007.

Article 45

Entry into force

This Directive shall enter into force on the 20th day following its publication in the *Official Journal of the European Union*.

Article 46

Addressees

This Directive is addressed to the Member States in conformity with the Treaty establishing the European Community.

Done at Brussels, 1 December 2005.

For the Council
The President
Ashton of UPHOLLAND

Annex I

Definition of 'determining authority'

When implementing the provision of this Directive, Ireland may, insofar as the provisions of section 17(1) of the *Refugee Act* 1996 (as amended) continue to apply, consider that:

— 'determining authority' provided for in Article 2(e) of this Directive shall, insofar as the examination of whether an applicant should or, as the case may be, should not be declared to be a refugee is concerned, mean the *Office of the Refugee Applications Commissioner*; and

— 'decisions at first instance' provided for in Article 2(e) of this Directive shall include recommendations of the *Refugee Applications Commissioner* as to whether an applicant should or, as the case may be, should not be declared to be a refugee.

Ireland will notify the Commission of any amendments to the provisions of section 17(1) of the *Refugee Act* 1996 (as amended).

Annex II

Designation of safe countries of origin for the purposes of Articles 29 and 30(1)

A country is considered as a safe country of origin where, on the basis of the legal situation, the application of the law within a democratic system and the general political circumstances, it can be shown that there is generally and consistently no persecution as defined in Article 9 of Directive 2004/83/EC, no torture or inhuman or degrading treatment or punishment and no threat by reason of indiscriminate violence in situations of international or internal armed conflict.

In making this assessment, account shall be taken, *inter alia*, of the extent to which protection is provided against persecution or mistreatment by:

(a) the relevant laws and regulations of the country and the manner in which they are applied;

(b) observance of the rights and freedoms laid down in the European Convention for the Protection of Human Rights and Fundamental Freedoms and/or the International Covenant for Civil and Political Rights and/or the Convention against Torture, in particular the rights from which derogation cannot be made under Article 15(2) of the said European Convention;

(c) respect of the non-refoulement principle according to the Geneva Convention;

(d) provision for a system of effective remedies against violations of these rights and freedoms.

Annex III

Definition of 'applicant' or 'applicant for asylum'

When implementing the provisions of this Directive Spain may, insofar as the provisions of '*Ley 30/1992 de Régimen jurídico de las Administraciones Públicas y del Procedimiento Administrativo Común*' of 26 November 1992 and '*Ley 29/1998 reguladora de la Jurisdicción Contencioso-Administrativa*' of 13 July 1998 continue to apply, consider that, for the purposes of Chapter V, the definition of 'applicant' or 'applicant for asylum' in Article 2(c) of this Directive shall include 'recurrente' as established in the abovementioned Acts.

A '*recurrente*' shall be entitled to the same guarantees as an 'applicant' or an 'applicant for asylum' as set out in this Directive for the purposes of exercising his/her right to an effective remedy in Chapter V.

Spain will notify the Commission of any relevant amendments to the abovementioned Act.

Charter of Fundamental Rights of the European Union (2007/C 303/01) EN

C 303/2 Official Journal of the European Union 14.12.2007

The European Parliament, the Council and the Commission solemnly proclaim the following text as the Charter of Fundamental Rights of the European Union.

Charter Of Fundamental Rights Of The European Union

Preamble

The peoples of Europe, in creating an ever closer union among them, are resolved to share a peaceful future based on common values.

Conscious of its spiritual and moral heritage, the Union is founded on the indivisible, universal values of human dignity, freedom, equality and solidarity; it is based on the principles of democracy and the rule of law. It places the individual at the heart of its activities, by establishing the citizenship of the Union and by creating an area of freedom, security and justice.

The Union contributes to the preservation and to the development of these common values while respecting the diversity of the cultures and traditions of the peoples of Europe as well as the national identities of the Member States and the organisation of their public authorities at national, regional and local levels; it seeks to promote balanced and sustainable development and ensures free movement of persons, services, goods and capital, and the freedom of establishment.

To this end, it is necessary to strengthen the protection of fundamental rights in the light of changes in society, social progress and scientific and technological developments by making those rights more visible in a Charter.

This Charter reaffirms, with due regard for the powers and tasks of the Union and for the principle of subsidiarity, the rights as they result, in particular, from the constitutional traditions and international obligations common to the Member States, the European Convention for the Protection of Human Rights and Fundamental Freedoms, the Social Charters adopted by the Union and by the Council of Europe and the case-law of the Court of Justice of the European Union and of the European Court of Human Rights. In this context the Charter will be interpreted by the courts of the Union and the Member States with due regard to the explanations prepared under the authority of the Praesidium of the Convention which drafted the Charter and updated under the responsibility of the Praesidium of the European Convention.

Enjoyment of these rights entails responsibilities and duties with regard to other persons, to the human community and to future generations.

The Union therefore recognises the rights, freedoms and principles set out hereafter.

TITLE I

DIGNITY

ARTICLE 1

HUMAN DIGNITY

Human dignity is inviolable. It must be respected and protected.

ARTICLE 2

RIGHT TO LIFE

1. Everyone has the right to life.
2. No one shall be condemned to the death penalty, or executed.

ARTICLE 3

RIGHT TO THE INTEGRITY OF THE PERSON

1. Everyone has the right to respect for his or her physical and mental integrity.
2. In the fields of medicine and biology, the following must be respected in particular:

– the free and informed consent of the person concerned, according to the procedures laid down by law;

– the prohibition of eugenic practices, in particular those aiming at the selection of persons;

– the prohibition on making the human body and its parts as such a source of financial gain;

– the prohibition of the reproductive cloning of human beings.

ARTICLE 4

PROHIBITION OF TORTURE AND INHUMAN OR DEGRADING TREATMENT OR PUNISHMENT

No one shall be subjected to torture or to inhuman or degrading treatment or punishment.

ARTICLE 5

PROHIBITION OF SLAVERY AND FORCED LABOUR

1. No one shall be held in slavery or servitude.
2. No one shall be required to perform forced or compulsory labour.
3. Trafficking in human beings is prohibited.

TITLE II

FREEDOMS

ARTICLE 6

RIGHT TO LIBERTY AND SECURITY

Everyone has the right to liberty and security of person.

ARTICLE 7

RESPECT FOR PRIVATE AND FAMILY LIFE

Everyone has the right to respect for his or her private and family life, home and communications.

ARTICLE 8

PROTECTION OF PERSONAL DATA

1. Everyone has the right to the protection of personal data concerning him or her.

2. Such data must be processed fairly for specified purposes and on the basis of the consent of the person concerned or some other legitimate basis laid down by law. Everyone has the right of access to data which has been collected concerning him or her, and the right to have it rectified.

3. Compliance with these rules shall be subject to control by an independent authority.

ARTICLE 9

RIGHT TO MARRY AND RIGHT TO FOUND A FAMILY

The right to marry and the right to found a family shall be guaranteed in accordance with the national laws governing the exercise of these rights.

ARTICLE 10

FREEDOM OF THOUGHT, CONSCIENCE AND RELIGION

1. Everyone has the right to freedom of thought, conscience and religion. This right includes freedom to change religion or belief and freedom, either alone or in community with others and in public or in private, to manifest religion or belief, in worship, teaching, practice and observance.

2. The right to conscientious objection is recognised, in accordance with the national laws governing the exercise of this right.

Article 11

Freedom of expression and information

1. Everyone has the right to freedom of expression. This right shall include freedom to hold opinions and to receive and impart information and ideas without interference by public authority and regardless of frontiers.

2. The freedom and pluralism of the media shall be respected.

Article 12

Freedom of assembly and of association

1. Everyone has the right to freedom of peaceful assembly and to freedom of association at all levels, in particular in political, trade union and civic matters, which implies the right of everyone to form and to join trade unions for the protection of his or her interests.

2. Political parties at Union level contribute to expressing the political will of the citizens of the Union.

Article 13

Freedom of the arts and sciences

The arts and scientific research shall be free of constraint. Academic freedom shall be respected.

Article 14

Right to education

1. Everyone has the right to education and to have access to vocational and continuing training.

2. This right includes the possibility to receive free compulsory education.

3. The freedom to found educational establishments with due respect for democratic principles and the right of parents to ensure the education and teaching of their children in conformity with their religious, philosophical and pedagogical convictions shall be respected, in accordance with the national laws governing the exercise of such freedom and right.

Article 15

Freedom to choose an occupation and right to engage in work

1. Everyone has the right to engage in work and to pursue a freely chosen or accepted occupation.

2. Every citizen of the Union has the freedom to seek employment, to work, to exercise the right of establishment and to provide services in any Member State.

3. Nationals of third countries who are authorised to work in the territories of the Member States are entitled to working conditions equivalent to those of citizens of the Union.

Article 16

Freedom to conduct a business

The freedom to conduct a business in accordance with Union law and national laws and practices is recognised.

Article 17

Right to property

1. Everyone has the right to own, use, dispose of and bequeath his or her lawfully acquired possessions. No one may be deprived of his or her possessions, except in the public interest and in the cases and under the conditions provided for by law, subject to fair compensation being paid in good time for their loss. The use of property may be regulated by law in so far as is necessary for the general interest.

2. Intellectual property shall be protected.

Article 18

Right to asylum

The right to asylum shall be guaranteed with due respect for the rules of the Geneva Convention of 28 July 1951 and the Protocol of 31 January 1967 relating to the status of refugees and in accordance with the Treaty on European Union and the Treaty on the Functioning of the European Union (hereinafter referred to as 'the Treaties').

Article 19

Protection in the event of removal, expulsion or extradition

1. Collective expulsions are prohibited.

2. No one may be removed, expelled or extradited to a State where there is a serious risk that he or she would be subjected to the death penalty, torture or other inhuman or degrading treatment or punishment.

Title III
Equality

Article 20
Equality before the law

Everyone is equal before the law.

Article 21
Non-discrimination

1. Any discrimination based on any ground such as sex, race, colour, ethnic or social origin, genetic features, language, religion or belief, political or any other opinion, membership of a national minority, property, birth, disability, age or sexual orientation shall be prohibited.

2. Within the scope of application of the Treaties and without prejudice to any of their specific provisions, any discrimination on grounds of nationality shall be prohibited.

Article 22
Cultural, religious and linguistic diversity

The Union shall respect cultural, religious and linguistic diversity.

Article 23
Equality between women and men

Equality between women and men must be ensured in all areas, including employment, work and pay.
The principle of equality shall not prevent the maintenance or adoption of measures providing for specific advantages in favour of the under-represented sex.

Article 24
The rights of the child

1. Children shall have the right to such protection and care as is necessary for their well-being. They may express their views freely. Such views shall be taken into consideration on matters which concern them in accordance with their age and maturity.

2. In all actions relating to children, whether taken by public authorities or private institutions, the child's best interests must be a primary consideration.

3. Every child shall have the right to maintain on a regular basis a personal relationship and direct contact with both his or her parents, unless that is contrary to his or her interests.

Article 25

The rights of the elderly

The Union recognises and respects the rights of the elderly to lead a life of dignity and independence and to participate in social and cultural life.

Article 26

Integration of Persons with Disabilities

The Union recognises and respects the right of persons with disabilities to benefit from measures designed to ensure their independence, social and occupational integration and participation in the life of the community.

Title IV

Solidarity

Article 27

Workers' right to information and consultation within the undertaking

Workers or their representatives must, at the appropriate levels, be guaranteed information and consultation in good time in the cases and under the conditions provided for by Union law and national laws and practices.

Article 28

Right of collective bargaining and action

Workers and employers, or their respective organisations, have, in accordance with Union law and national laws and practices, the right to negotiate and conclude collective agreements at the appropriate levels and, in cases of conflicts of interest, to take collective action to defend their interests, including strike action.

Article 29

Right of access to placement services

Everyone has the right of access to a free placement service.

Article 30

Protection in the event of unjustified dismissal

Every worker has the right to protection against unjustified dismissal, in accordance with Union law and national laws and practices.

Article 31

Fair and just working conditions

1. Every worker has the right to working conditions which respect his or her health, safety and dignity.

2. Every worker has the right to limitation of maximum working hours, to daily and weekly rest periods and to an annual period of paid leave.

Article 32

Prohibition of child labour and protection of young people at work

The employment of children is prohibited. The minimum age of admission to employment may not be lower than the minimum school-leaving age, without prejudice to such rules as may be more favourable to young people and except for limited derogations.

Young people admitted to work must have working conditions appropriate to their age and be protected against economic exploitation and any work likely to harm their safety, health or physical, mental, moral or social development or to interfere with their education.

Article 33

Family and professional life

1. The family shall enjoy legal, economic and social protection.

2. To reconcile family and professional life, everyone shall have the right to protection from dismissal for a reason connected with maternity and the right to paid maternity leave and to parental leave following the birth or adoption of a child.

Article 34

Social security and social assistance

1. The Union recognises and respects the entitlement to social security benefits and social services providing protection in cases such as maternity, illness, industrial accidents, dependency or old age, and in the case of loss of employment, in accordance with the rules laid down by Union law and national laws and practices.

2. Everyone residing and moving legally within the European Union is entitled to social security benefits and social advantages in accordance with Union law and national laws and practices.

3. In order to combat social exclusion and poverty, the Union recognises and respects the right to social and housing assistance so as to ensure a decent existence for all those who lack sufficient resources, in accordance with the rules laid down by Union law and national laws and practices.

Article 35

Health care

Everyone has the right of access to preventive health care and the right to benefit from medical treatment under the conditions established by national laws and practices. A high level of human health protection shall be ensured in the definition and implementation of all the Union's policies and activities.

Article 36

Access to services of general economic interest

The Union recognises and respects access to services of general economic interest as provided for in national laws and practices, in accordance with the Treaties, in order to promote the social and territorial cohesion of the Union.

Article 37

Environmental protection

A high level of environmental protection and the improvement of the quality of the environment must be integrated into the policies of the Union and ensured in accordance with the principle of sustainable development.

Article 38

Consumer protection

Union policies shall ensure a high level of consumer protection.

Title V

Citizens' Rights

Article 39

Right to vote and to stand as a candidate at elections to the European Parliament

1. Every citizen of the Union has the right to vote and to stand as a candidate at elections to the European Parliament in the Member State in which he or she resides, under the same conditions as nationals of that State.

2. Members of the European Parliament shall be elected by direct universal suffrage in a free and secret ballot.

Article 40

Right to vote and to stand as a candidate at municipal elections

Every citizen of the Union has the right to vote and to stand as a candidate at municipal elections in the Member State in which he or she resides under the same conditions as nationals of that State.

Article 41

Right to good administration

1. Every person has the right to have his or her affairs handled impartially, fairly and within a reasonable time by the institutions, bodies, offices and agencies of the Union.

2. This right includes:

- the right of every person to be heard, before any individual measure which would affect him or her adversely is taken;
- the right of every person to have access to his or her file, while respecting the legitimate interests of confidentiality and of professional and business secrecy;
- the obligation of the administration to give reasons for its decisions.

3. Every person has the right to have the Union make good any damage caused by its institutions by its servants in the performance of their duties, in accordance with the general principles common the laws of the Member States.

4. Every person may write to the institutions of the Union in one of the languages of the Treaties and must have an answer in the same language.

Article 42

Right of access to documents

Any citizen of the Union, and any natural or legal person residing or having its registered office in a Member State, has a right of access to documents of the institutions, bodies, offices and agencies of the Union, whatever their medium.

Article 43

European Ombudsman

Any citizen of the Union and any natural or legal person residing or having its registered office in a Member State has the right to refer to the European Ombudsman cases of maladministration in the activities of the institutions, bodies, offices or agencies of the Union, with the exception of the Court of Justice of the European Union acting in its judicial role.

Article 44

Right to petition

Any citizen of the Union and any natural or legal person residing or having its registered office in a Member State has the right to petition the European Parliament.

Article 45

Freedom of movement and of residence

1. Every citizen of the Union has the right to move and reside freely within the territory of the Member States.

2. Freedom of movement and residence may be granted, in accordance with the Treaties, to nationals of third countries legally resident in the territory of a Member State.

Article 46

Diplomatic and consular protection

Every citizen of the Union shall, in the territory of a third country in which the Member State of which he or she is a national is not represented, be entitled to protection by the diplomatic or consular authorities of any Member State, on the same conditions as the nationals of that Member State.

Title VI

Justice

Article 47

Right to an effective remedy and to a fair trial

Everyone whose rights and freedoms guaranteed by the law of the Union are violated has the right to an effective remedy before a tribunal in compliance with the conditions laid down in this Article.

Everyone is entitled to a fair and public hearing within a reasonable time by an independent and impartial tribunal previously established by law. Everyone shall have the possibility of being advised, defended and represented.

Legal aid shall be made available to those who lack sufficient resources in so far as such aid is necessary to ensure effective access to justice.

Article 48

Presumption of innocence and right of defence

Everyone who has been charged shall be presumed innocent until proved guilty according to Respect for the rights of the defence of anyone who has been charged shall be guaranteed.

Article 49

Principles of legality and proportionality of criminal offences and penalties

1. No one shall be held guilty of any criminal offence on account of any act or omission which did not constitute a criminal offence under national law or international law at the time when it was committed. Nor shall a heavier penalty be imposed than the one that was applicable at the time the criminal offence was committed. If, subsequent to the commission of a criminal offence, the law provides for a lighter penalty, that penalty shall be applicable.

2. This Article shall not prejudice the trial and punishment of any person for any act or omission which, at the time when it was committed, was criminal according to the general principles recognised by the community of nations.

3. The severity of penalties must not be disproportionate to the criminal offence.

Article 50

Right not to be tried or punished twice in criminal proceedings for the same criminal offence

No one shall be liable to be tried or punished again in criminal proceedings for an offence for which he or she has already been finally acquitted or convicted within the Union in accordance with the law.

Title VII

General Provisions Governing the Interpretation and Application of the Charter

Article 51

Field of application

1. The provisions of this Charter are addressed to the institutions, bodies, offices and agencies of the Union with due regard for the principle of subsidiarity and to the Member States only when they are implementing Union law. They shall therefore respect the rights, observe the principles and promote the application thereof in accordance with their respective powers and respecting the limits of the powers of the Union as conferred on it in the Treaties.

2. The Charter does not extend the field of application of Union law beyond the powers of the Union or establish any new power or task for the Union, or modify powers and tasks as defined in the Treaties.

Article 52

Scope and interpretation of rights and principles

1. Any limitation on the exercise of the rights and freedoms recognised by this Charter must be provided for by law and respect the essence of those rights and freedoms. Subject to the principle of proportionality, limitations may be made only if they are necessary and genuinely meet objectives of general interest recognised by the Union or the need to protect the rights and freedoms of others.

2. Rights recognised by this Charter for which provision is made in the Treaties shall be exercised under the conditions and within the limits defined by those Treaties.

3. In so far as this Charter contains rights which correspond to rights guaranteed by the Convention for the Protection of Human Rights and Fundamental Freedoms, the meaning and scope of those rights shall be the same as those laid down by the said Convention. This provision shall not prevent Union law providing more extensive protection.

Article 53

Level of protection

Nothing in this Charter shall be interpreted as restricting or adversely affecting human rights and fundamental freedoms as recognised, in their respective fields of application, by Union law and international law and by international agreements to which the Union or all the Member States are party, including the European Convention for the Protection of Human Rights and Fundamental Freedoms, and by the Member States' constitutions.

Article 54

Prohibition of abuse of rights

Nothing in this Charter shall be interpreted as implying any right to engage in any activity or to perform any act aimed at the destruction of any of the rights and freedoms recognised in this Charter or at their limitation to a greater extent than is provided for herein.

The above text adapts the wording of the Charter proclaimed on 7 December 2000, and will replace it as from the date of entry into force of the Treaty of Lisbon.

Done at Strasbourg on the twelfth day of December in the year two thousand and seven.

Note: The Charter became law once the Lisbon Treaty came into force on 1 December 2009. See Article 51 above, Article 6 of Treaty of Europe and Protocol 30 below for limited application of the Charter generally.

Protocol (No. 30)

On the Application of the Charter of Fundamental Rights of the European Union to Poland and to the United Kingdom

THE HIGH CONTRACTING PARTIES,

WHEREAS in Article 6 of the Treaty on European Union, the Union recognises the rights, freedoms and principles set out in the Charter of Fundamental Rights of the European Union,

WHEREAS the Charter is to be applied in strict accordance with the provisions of the aforementioned Article 6 and Title VII of the Charter itself,

WHEREAS the aforementioned Article 6 requires the Charter to be applied and interpreted by the courts of Poland and of the United Kingdom strictly in accordance with the explanations referred to in that Article,

WHEREAS the Charter contains both rights and principles,

WHEREAS the Charter contains both provisions which are civil and political in character and those which are economic and social in character,

WHEREAS the Charter reaffirms the rights, freedoms and principles recognised in the Union and makes those rights more visible, but does not create new rights or principles,

RECALLING the obligations devolving upon Poland and the United Kingdom under the Treaty on European Union, the Treaty on the Functioning of the European Union, and Union law generally,

NOTING the wish of Poland and the United Kingdom to clarify certain aspects of the application of the Charter,

DESIROUS therefore of clarifying the application of the Charter in relation to the laws and administrative action of Poland and of the United Kingdom and of its justiciability within Poland and within the United Kingdom,

REAFFIRMING that references in this Protocol to the operation of specific provisions of the Charter are strictly without prejudice to the operation of other provisions of the Charter,

REAFFIRMING that this Protocol is without prejudice to the application of the Charter to other Member States,

REAFFIRMING that this Protocol is without prejudice to other obligations devolving upon Poland and the United Kingdom under the Treaty on European Union, the Treaty on the Functioning of the European Union, and Union law generally,

HAVE AGREED UPON the following provisions, which shall be annexed to the Treaty on European Union and to the Treaty on the Functioning of the European Union:

Article 1

1. The Charter does not extend the ability of the Court of Justice of the European Union, or any court or tribunal of Poland or of the United Kingdom, to find that the laws, regulations or administrative provisions, practices or action of Poland or of the United Kingdom are inconsistent with the fundamental rights, freedoms and principles that it reaffirms.

2. In particular, and for the avoidance of doubt, nothing in Title IV of the Charter creates justiciable rights applicable to Poland or the United Kingdom except in so far as Poland or the United Kingdom has provided for such rights in its national law.

Article 2

To the extent that a provision of the Charter refers to national laws and practices, it shall only apply to Poland or the United Kingdom to the extent that the rights or principles that it contains are recognized in the law or practices of Poland or of the United Kingdom.

Regulation (EU) No. 492/2011 of the European Parliament and of the Council

of 5 April 2011 on freedom of movement for workers within the Union (codification)

(Text with EEA relevance)

THE EUROPEAN PARLIAMENT AND THE COUNCIL OF THE EUROPEAN UNION,

Having regard to the Treaty on the Functioning of the European Union, and in particular Article 46 thereof,

Having regard to the proposal from the European Commission,

After transmission of the draft legislative act to the national parliaments,

Having regard to the opinion of the European Economic and Social Committee,[1]

Acting in accordance with the ordinary legislative procedure,[2]

Whereas:

(1) Regulation (EEC) No. 1612/68 of the Council of 15 October 1968 on freedom of movement for workers within the Community[3] has been substantially amended several times.[4] In the interests of clarity and rationality the said Regulation should be codified.

(2) Freedom of movement for workers should be secured within the Union. The attainment of this objective entails the abolition of any discrimination based on nationality between workers of the Member States as regards employment, remuneration and other conditions of work and employment, as well as the right of such workers to move freely within the Union in order to pursue activities as employed persons subject to any limitations justified on grounds of public policy, public security or public health.

(3) Provisions should be laid down to enable the objectives laid down in Articles 45 and 46 of the Treaty on the Functioning of the European Union in the field of freedom of movement to be achieved.

[1] OJ C 44, 11.2.2011, p. 170.

[2] Position of the European Parliament of 7 September 2010 (not yet published in the Official Journal) and decision of the Council of 21 March 2011.

[3] OJ L 257, 19.10.1968, p. 2.

[4] See Annex I.

(4) Freedom of movement constitutes a fundamental right of workers and their families. Mobility of labour within the Union must be one of the means by which workers are guaranteed the possibility of improving their living and working conditions and promoting their social advancement, while helping to satisfy the requirements of the economies of the Member States. The right of all workers in the Member States to pursue the activity of their choice within the Union should be affirmed.

(5) Such right should be enjoyed without discrimination by permanent, seasonal and frontier workers and by those who pursue their activities for the purpose of providing services.

(6) The right of freedom of movement, in order that it may be exercised, by objective standards, in freedom and dignity, requires that equality of treatment be ensured in fact and in law in respect of all matters relating to the actual pursuit of activities as employed persons and to eligibility for housing, and also that obstacles to the mobility of workers be eliminated, in particular as regards the conditions for the integration of the worker's family into the host country.

(7) The principle of non-discrimination between workers in the Union means that all nationals of Member States have the same priority as regards employment as is enjoyed by national workers.

(8) The machinery for vacancy clearance, in particular by means of direct cooperation between the central employment services and also between the regional services, as well as by coordination of the exchange of information, ensures in a general way a clearer picture of the labour market. Workers wishing to move should also be regularly informed of living and working conditions.

(9) Close links exist between freedom of movement for workers, employment and vocational training, particularly where the latter aims at putting workers in a position to take up concrete offers of employment from other regions of the Union. Such links make it necessary that the problems arising in this connection should no longer be studied in isolation but viewed as interdependent, account also being taken of the problems of employment at the regional level. It is therefore necessary to direct the efforts of Member States toward coordinating their employment policies,

HAVE ADOPTED THIS REGULATION:

Chapter I

Employment, Equal Treatment and Workers' Families

Section 1

Eligibility for Employment

Article 1

1. Any national of a Member State shall, irrespective of his place of residence, have the right to take up an activity as an employed person, and to pursue such activity, within the territory of another Member State in accordance with the provisions laid down by law, regulation or administrative action governing the employment of nationals of that State.

2. He shall, in particular, have the right to take up available employment in the territory of another Member State with the same priority as nationals of that State.

Article 2

Any national of a Member State and any employer pursuing an activity in the territory of a Member State may exchange their applications for and offers of employment, and may conclude and perform contracts of employment in accordance with the provisions in force laid down by law, regulation or administrative action, without any discrimination resulting therefrom.

Article 3

1. Under this Regulation, provisions laid down by law, regulation or administrative action or administrative practices of a Member State shall not apply:

(a) where they limit application for and offers of employment, or the right of foreign nationals to take up and pursue employment or subject these to conditions not applicable in respect of their own nationals; or

(b) where, though applicable irrespective of nationality, their exclusive or principal aim or effect is to keep nationals of other Member States away from the employment offered.

The first subparagraph shall not apply to conditions relating to linguistic knowledge required by reason of the nature of the post to be filled.

2. There shall be included in particular among the provisions or practices of a Member State referred to in the first subparagraph of paragraph 1 those which:

(a) prescribe a special recruitment procedure for foreign nationals;

(b) limit or restrict the advertising of vacancies in the press or through any other medium or subject it to conditions other than those applicable in respect of employers pursuing their activities in the territory of that Member State;

(c) subject eligibility for employment to conditions of registration with employment offices or impede recruitment of individual workers, where persons who do not reside in the territory of that State are concerned.

Article 4

1. Provisions laid down by law, regulation or administrative action of the Member States which restrict by number or percentage the employment of foreign nationals in any undertaking, branch of activity or region, or at a national level, shall not apply to nationals of the other Member States.

2. When in a Member State the granting of any benefit to undertakings is subject to a minimum percentage of national workers being employed, nationals of the other Member States shall be counted as national workers, subject to Directive 2005/36/EC of the European Parliament and of the Council of 7 September 2005 on the recognition of professional qualifications.[5]

[5] OJ L 255, 30.9.2005, p. 22.

Article 5

A national of a Member State who seeks employment in the territory of another Member State shall receive the same assistance there as that afforded by the employment offices in that State to their own nationals seeking employment.

Article 6

1. The engagement and recruitment of a national of one Member State for a post in another Member State shall not depend on medical, vocational or other criteria which are discriminatory on grounds of nationality by comparison with those applied to nationals of the other Member State who wish to pursue the same activity.

2. A national who holds an offer in his name from an employer in a Member State other than that of which he is a national may have to undergo a vocational test, if the employer expressly requests this when making his offer of employment.

Section 2

Employment and Equality of Treatment

Article 7

1. A worker who is a national of a Member State may not, in the territory of another Member State, be treated differently from national workers by reason of his nationality in respect of any conditions of employment and work, in particular as regards remuneration, dismissal, and, should he become unemployed, reinstatement or re-employment.

2. He shall enjoy the same social and tax advantages as national workers.

3. He shall also, by virtue of the same right and under the same conditions as national workers, have access to training in vocational schools and retraining centres.

4. Any clause of a collective or individual agreement or of any other collective regulation concerning eligibility for employment, remuneration and other conditions of work or dismissal shall be null and void in so far as it lays down or authorises discriminatory conditions in respect of workers who are nationals of the other Member States.

Article 8

A worker who is a national of a Member State and who is employed in the territory of another Member State shall enjoy equality of treatment as regards membership of trade unions and the exercise of rights attaching thereto, including the right to vote and to be eligible for the administration or management posts of a trade union. He may be excluded from taking part in the management of bodies governed by public law and from holding an office governed by public law. Furthermore, he shall have the right of eligibility for workers' representative bodies in the undertaking.

The first paragraph of this Article shall not affect laws or regulations in certain Member States which grant more extensive rights to workers coming from the other Member States.

Article 9

1. A worker who is a national of a Member State and who is employed in the territory of another Member State shall enjoy all the rights and benefits accorded to national workers in matters of housing, including ownership of the housing he needs.

2. A worker referred to in paragraph 1 may, with the same right as nationals, put his name down on the housing lists in the region in which he is employed, where such lists exist, and shall enjoy the resultant benefits and priorities.

If his family has remained in the country whence he came, they shall be considered for this purpose as residing in the said region, where national workers benefit from a similar presumption.

Section 3

Workers' Families

Article 10

The children of a national of a Member State who is or has been employed in the territory of another Member State shall be admitted to that State's general educational, apprenticeship and vocational training courses under the same conditions as the nationals of that State, if such children are residing in its territory.

Member States shall encourage all efforts to enable such children to attend these courses under the best possible conditions.

Chapter II

Clearance of Vacancies and Applications for Employment

Section 1

Cooperation between the Member States and with the Commission

Article 11

1. The Member States or the Commission shall instigate or together undertake any study of employment or unemployment which they consider necessary for freedom of movement for workers within the Union.

The central employment services of the Member States shall cooperate closely with each other and with the Commission with a view to acting jointly as regards the clearing of vacancies and applications for employment within the Union and the resultant placing of workers in employment.

2. To this end the Member States shall designate specialist services which shall be entrusted with organising work in the fields referred to in the second subparagraph of paragraph 1 and cooperating with each other and with the departments of the Commission.

The Member States shall notify the Commission of any change in the designation of such services and the Commission shall publish details thereof for information in the *Official Journal of the European Union*.

Article 12

1. The Member States shall send to the Commission information on problems arising in connection with the freedom of movement and employment of workers and particulars of the state and development of employment.

2. The Commission, taking the utmost account of the opinion of the Technical Committee referred to in Article 29 ('the Technical Committee'), shall determine the manner in which the information referred to in paragraph 1 of this Article is to be drawn up.

3. In accordance with the procedure laid down by the Commission taking the utmost account of the opinion of the Technical Committee, the specialist service of each Member State shall send to the specialist services of the other Member States and to the European Coordination Office referred to in Article 18 such information concerning living and working conditions and the state of the labour market as is likely to be of guidance to workers from the other Member States. Such information shall be brought up to date regularly.

The specialist services of the other Member States shall ensure that wide publicity is given to such information, in particular by circulating it among the appropriate employment services and by all suitable means of communication for informing the workers concerned.

SECTION 2

Machinery for Vacancy Clearance

Article 13

1. The specialist service of each Member State shall regularly send to the specialist services of the other Member States and to the European Coordination Office referred to in Article 18:

(a) details of vacancies which could be filled by nationals of other Member States;

(b) details of vacancies addressed to third countries;

(c) details of applications for employment by those who have formally expressed a wish to work in another Member State;

(d) information, by region and by branch of activity, on applicants who have declared themselves actually willing to accept employment in another country.

The specialist service of each Member State shall forward this information to the appropriate employment services and agencies as soon as possible.

2. The details of vacancies and applications referred to in paragraph 1 shall be circulated according to a uniform system to be established by the European Coordination Office referred to in Article 18 in collaboration with the Technical Committee.

This system may be adapted if necessary.

Article 14

1. Any vacancy within the meaning of Article 13 communicated to the employment services of a Member State shall be notified to and processed by the competent employment services of the other Member States concerned.

Such services shall forward to the services of the first Member State the details of suitable applications.

2. The applications for employment referred to in point (c) of the first subparagraph of Article 13(1) shall be responded to by the relevant services of the Member States within a reasonable period, not exceeding 1 month.

3. The employment services shall grant workers who are nationals of the Member States the same priority as the relevant measures grant to nationals vis-à-vis workers from third countries.

Article 15

1. The provisions of Article 14 shall be implemented by the specialist services. However, in so far as they have been authorised by the central services and in so far as the organisation of the employment services of a Member State and the placing techniques employed make it possible:

(a) the regional employment services of the Member States shall:

(i) on the basis of the information referred to in Article 13, on which appropriate action will be taken, directly bring together and clear vacancies and applications for employment;

(ii) establish direct relations for clearance:

— of vacancies offered to a named worker,

— of individual applications for employment sent either to a specific employment service or to an employer pursuing his activity within the area covered by such a service,

— where the clearing operations concern seasonal workers who must be recruited as quickly as possible;

(b) the services territorially responsible for the border regions of two or more Member States shall regularly exchange data relating to vacancies and applications for employment in their area and, acting in accordance with their arrangements with the other employment services of their countries, shall directly bring together and clear vacancies and applications for employment.

If necessary, the services territorially responsible for border regions shall also set up cooperation and service structures to provide:

— users with as much practical information as possible on the various aspects of mobility, and

— management and labour, social services (in particular public, private or those of public interest) and all institutions concerned, with a framework of coordinated measures relating to mobility,

(c) official employment services which specialise in certain occupations or specific categories of persons shall cooperate directly with each other.

2. The Member States concerned shall forward to the Commission the list, drawn up by common accord, of services referred to in paragraph 1 and the Commission shall publish such list for information, and any amendment thereto, in the *Official Journal of the European Union*.

Article 16

Adoption of recruiting procedures as applied by the implementing bodies provided for under agreements concluded between two or more Member States shall not be obligatory.

Section 3

Measures for Controlling the Balance of the Labour Market

Article 17

1. On the basis of a report from the Commission drawn up from information supplied by the Member States, the latter and the Commission shall at least once a year analyse jointly the results of Union arrangements regarding vacancies and applications.

2. The Member States shall examine with the Commission all the possibilities of giving priority to nationals of Member States when filling employment vacancies in order to achieve a balance between vacancies and applications for employment within the Union. They shall adopt all measures necessary for this purpose.

3. Every 2 years the Commission shall submit a report to the European Parliament, the Council and the European Economic and Social Committee on the implementation of Chapter II, summarising the information required and the data obtained from the studies and research carried out and highlighting any useful points with regard to developments on the Union's labour market.

Section 4

European Coordination Office

Article 18

The European Office for Coordinating the Clearance of Vacancies and Applications for Employment ('the European Coordination Office'), established within the Commission, shall have the general task of promoting vacancy clearance at Union level. It shall be responsible in particular for all the technical duties in this field which, under the provisions of this Regulation, are assigned to the Commission, and especially for assisting the national employment services.

It shall summarise the information referred to in Articles 12 and 13 and the data arising out of the studies and research carried out pursuant to Article 11, so as to bring to light any useful facts about foreseeable developments on the Union labour market; such facts shall be communicated to the specialist services of the Member States and to the Advisory Committee referred to in Article 21 and the Technical Committee.

Article 19

1. The European Coordination Office shall be responsible, in particular, for:

(a) coordinating the practical measures necessary for vacancy clearance at Union level and for analysing the resulting movements of workers;

(b) contributing to such objectives by implementing, in cooperation with the Technical Committee, joint methods of action at administrative and technical levels;

(c) carrying out, where a special need arises, and in agreement with the specialist services, the bringing together of vacancies and applications for employment for clearance by those specialist services.

2. It shall communicate to the specialist services vacancies and applications for employment sent directly to the Commission, and shall be informed of the action taken thereon.

Article 20

The Commission may, in agreement with the competent authority of each Member State, and in accordance with the conditions and procedures which it shall determine on the basis of the opinion of the Technical Committee, organise visits and assignments for officials of other Member States, and also advanced programmes for specialist personnel.

Chapter III

Committees for Ensuring close Cooperation Between the Member States in Matters Concerning the Freedom of Movement of Workers and their Employment

Section I

The Advisory Committee

Article 21

The Advisory Committee shall be responsible for assisting the Commission in the examination of any questions arising from the application of the Treaty on the Functioning of the European Union and measures taken in pursuance thereof, in matters concerning the freedom of movement of workers and their employment.

Article 22

The Advisory Committee shall be responsible in particular for:

(a) examining problems concerning freedom of movement and employment within the framework of national manpower policies, with a view to coordinating the employment policies of the Member States at Union level, thus contributing to the development of the economies and to an improved balance of the labour market;

(b) making a general study of the effects of implementing this Regulation and any supplementary measures;

(c) submitting to the Commission any reasoned proposals for revising this Regulation;

(d) delivering, either at the request of the Commission or on its own initiative, reasoned opinions on general questions or on questions of principle, in particular on exchange of information concerning developments in the labour market, on the movement of workers between Member States, on programmes or measures to develop vocational guidance and vocational training which are likely to increase the possibilities of freedom of movement and employment, and on all forms of assistance to workers and their families, including social assistance and the housing of workers.

Article 23

1. The Advisory Committee shall be composed of six members for each Member State, two of whom shall represent the Government, two the trade unions and two the employers' associations.

2. For each of the categories referred to in paragraph 1, one alternate member shall be appointed by each Member State.

3. The term of office of the members and their alternates shall be 2 years. Their appointments shall be renewable.

On expiry of their term of office, the members and their alternates shall remain in office until replaced or until their appointments are renewed.

Article 24

The members of the Advisory Committee and their alternates shall be appointed by the Council, which shall endeavour, when selecting representatives of trade unions and employers' associations, to achieve adequate representation on the Committee of the various economic sectors concerned.

The list of members and their alternates shall be published by the Council for information in the *Official Journal of the European Union*.

Article 25

The Advisory Committee shall be chaired by a member of the Commission or his representative. The Chairman shall not vote. The Committee shall meet at least twice a year. It shall be convened by its Chairman, either on his own initiative, or at the request of at least one third of the members.

Secretarial services shall be provided for the Committee by the Commission.

Article 26

The Chairman may invite individuals or representatives of bodies with wide experience in the field of employment or movement of workers to take part in meetings as observers or as experts. The Chairman may be assisted by expert advisers.

Article 27

1. An opinion delivered by the Advisory Committee shall not be valid unless two thirds of the members are present.

2. Opinions shall state the reasons on which they are based; they shall be delivered by an absolute majority of the votes validly cast; they shall be accompanied by a written statement of the views expressed by the minority, when the latter so requests.

Article 28

The Advisory Committee shall establish its working methods by rules of procedure which shall enter into force after the Council, having received an opinion from the Commission, has given its approval. The entry into force of any amendment that the Committee decides to make thereto shall be subject to the same procedure.

Section 2

The Technical Committee

Article 29

The Technical Committee shall be responsible for assisting the Commission in the preparation, promotion and follow-up of all technical work and measures for giving effect to this Regulation and any supplementary measures.

Article 30

The Technical Committee shall be responsible in particular for:

(a) promoting and advancing cooperation between the public authorities concerned in the Member States on all technical questions relating to freedom of movement of workers and their employment;

(b) formulating procedures for the organisation of the joint activities of the public authorities concerned;

(c) facilitating the gathering of information likely to be of use to the Commission and the undertaking of the studies and research provided for in this Regulation, and encouraging exchange of information and experience between the administrative bodies concerned;

(d) investigating at a technical level the harmonisation of the criteria by which Member States assess the state of their labour markets.

Article 31

1. The Technical Committee shall be composed of representatives of the Governments of the Member States. Each Government shall appoint as member of the Technical Committee one of the members who represent it on the Advisory Committee.

2. Each Government shall appoint an alternate from among its other representatives — members or alternates — on the Advisory Committee.

Article 32

The Technical Committee shall be chaired by a member of the Commission or his representative. The Chairman shall not vote. The Chairman and the members of the Committee may be assisted by expert advisers.

Secretarial services shall be provided for the Committee by the Commission.

Article 33

The proposals and opinions formulated by the Technical Committee shall be submitted to the Commission, and the Advisory Committee shall be informed thereof. Any such proposals and opinions shall be accompanied by a written statement of the views expressed by the various members of the Technical Committee, when the latter so request.

Article 34

The Technical Committee shall establish its working methods by rules of procedure which shall enter into force after the Council, having received an opinion from the Commission, has given its approval. The entry into force of any amendment which the Committee decides to make thereto shall be subject to the same procedure.

Chapter IV

Final Provisions

Article 35

The rules of procedure of the Advisory Committee and of the Technical Committee in force on 8 November 1968 shall continue to apply.

Article 36

1. This Regulation shall not affect the provisions of the Treaty establishing the European Atomic Energy Community which deal with eligibility for skilled employment in the field of nuclear energy, nor any measures taken in pursuance of that Treaty.

Nevertheless, this Regulation shall apply to the category of workers referred to in the first subparagraph and to members of their families in so far as their legal position is not governed by the above-mentioned Treaty or measures.

2. This Regulation shall not affect measures taken in accordance with Article 48 of the Treaty on the Functioning of the European Union.

3. This Regulation shall not affect the obligations of Member States arising out of special relations or future agreements with certain non-European countries or territories, based on institutional ties existing on 8 November 1968, or agreements in existence on 8 November 1968 with certain non-European countries or territories, based on institutional ties between them.

Workers from such countries or territories who, in accordance with this provision, are pursuing activities as employed persons in the territory of one of those Member States may not invoke the benefit of the provisions of this Regulation in the territory of the other Member States.

Article 37

Member States shall, for information purposes, communicate to the Commission the texts of agreements, conventions or arrangements concluded between them in the manpower field between the date of their being signed and that of their entry into force.

Article 38

The Commission shall adopt measures pursuant to this Regulation for its implementation. To this end it shall act in close cooperation with the central public authorities of the Member States.

Article 39

The administrative expenditure of the Advisory Committee and of the Technical Committee shall be included in the general budget of the European Union in the section relating to the Commission.

Article 40

This Regulation shall apply to the Member States and to their nationals, without prejudice to Articles 2 and 3.

Article 41

Regulation (EEC) No. 1612/68 is hereby repealed.

References to the repealed Regulation shall be construed as references to this Regulation and shall be read in accordance with the correlation table in Annex II.

Article 42

This Regulation shall enter into force on the 20th day following its publication in the *Official Journal of the European Union*.

This Regulation shall be binding in its entirety and directly applicable in all Member States.

Done at Strasbourg, 5 April 2011.

For the European Parliament
The President
J. BUZEK

For the Council
The President
GYŐRI E.

Annex I

Repealed Regulation with list of its Successive Amendments

Council Regulation (EEC) No. 1612/68 (OJ L 257, 19.10.1968, p. 2)	
Council Regulation (EEC) No. 312/76 (OJ L 39, 14.2.1976, p. 2)	
Council Regulation (EEC) No. 2434/92 (OJ L 245, 26.8.1992, p. 1)	
Directive 2004/38/EC of the European Parliament and of the Council (OJ L 158, 30.4.2004, p. 77)	Only Article 38(1)

Annex II

Correlation Table

Regulation (EEC) No. 1612/68	This Regulation
Part I	Chapter I
Title I	Section 1
Article 1	Article 1
Article 2	Article 2
Article 3(1), first subparagraph	Article 3(1), first subparagraph
Article 3(1), first subparagraph, first indent	Article 3(1), first subparagraph, point (a)
Article 3(1), first subparagraph, second indent	Article 3(1), first subparagraph, point (b)
Article 3(1), second subparagraph	Article 3(1), second subparagraph
Article 3(2)	Article 3(2)
Article 4	Article 4
Article 5	Article 5
Article 6	Article 6
Title II	Section 2
Article 7	Article 7
Article 8(1)	Article 8
Article 9	Article 9
Title III	Section 3
Article 12	Article 10
Part II	Chapter II
Title I	Section 1
Article 13	Article 11

Article 14	Article 12
Title II	Section 2
Article 15	Article 13
Article 16	Article 14
Article 17	Article 15
Article 18	Article 16
Title III	Section 3
Article 19	Article 17
Title IV	Section 4
Article 21	Article 18
Article 22	Article 19
Article 23	Article 20
Part III	Chapter III
Title I	Section 1
Article 24	Article 21
Article 25	Article 22
Article 26	Article 23
Article 27	Article 24
Article 28	Article 25
Article 29	Article 26
Article 30	Article 27
Article 31	Article 28
Title II	Section 2
Article 32	Article 29
Article 33	Article 30
Article 34	Article 31
Article 35	Article 32
Article 36	Article 33
Article 37	Article 34
Part IV	Chapter IV
Title I	—
Article 38	—
Article 39	Article 35
Article 40	—
Article 41	—
Title II	—
Article 42(1)	Article 36(1)
Article 42(2)	Article 36(2)
Article 42(3), first subparagraph, first and second indents	Article 36(3), first subparagraph

Article 42(3), second subparagraph	Article 36(3), second subparagraph
Article 43	Article 37
Article 44	Article 38
Article 45	—
Article 46	Article 39
Article 47	Article 40
—	Article 41
Article 48	Article 42
—	Annex I
—	Annex II

Regulation (EU) No. 604/2013 of the European Parliament and of the Council

of 26 June 2013 establishing the criteria and mechanisms for determining the Member State responsible for examining an application for international protection lodged in one of the Member States by a third-country national or a stateless person (recast)

Note: This Regulation is commonly known as the Dublin III Regulation and repeals and replaces the Dublin II regulation (Article 48). It was published in the *Official Journal of the Europen* Union on 29 June 2013 and entered into force on 19 July 2013; it applies to all applications for international protection lodged on or after 1 January 2014 (see Article 49).

THE EUROPEAN PARLIAMENT AND THE COUNCIL OF THE EUROPEAN UNION,

Having regard to the Treaty on the Functioning of the European Union, and in particular Article 78(2)(e) thereof,
Having regard to the proposal from the European Commission,
Having regard to the opinion of the European Economic and Social Committee,[1]
Having regard to the opinion of the Committee of the Regions,[2]
Acting in accordance with the ordinary legislative procedure,[3]
Whereas:

(1) A number of substantive changes are to be made to Council Regulation (EC) No. 343/2003 of 18 February 2003 establishing the criteria and mechanisms for determining the Member State responsible for examining an asylum application lodged in one of the

[1] OJ C 317, 23.12.2009, p. 115.
[2] OJ C 79, 27.3.2010, p. 58.
[3] Position of the European Parliament of 7 May 2009 (OJ C 212 E, 5.8.2010, p. 370) and position of the Council at first reading of 6 June 2013 (not yet published in the Official Journal). Position of the European Parliament of 10 June 2013 (not yet published in the Official Journal).

Member States by a third-country national.[4] In the interests of clarity, that Regulation should be recast.

(2) A common policy on asylum, including a Common European Asylum System (CEAS), is a constituent part of the European Union's objective of progressively establishing an area of freedom, security and justice open to those who, forced by circumstances, legitimately seek protection in the Union.

(3) The European Council, at its special meeting in Tampere on 15 and 16 October 1999, agreed to work towards establishing the CEAS, based on the full and inclusive application of the Geneva Convention Relating to the Status of Refugees of 28 July 1951, as supplemented by the New York Protocol of 31 January 1967 ('the Geneva Convention'), thus ensuring that nobody is sent back to persecution, i.e. maintaining the principle of *non-refoulement*. In this respect, and without the responsibility criteria laid down in this Regulation being affected, Member States, all respecting the principle of *non-refoulement*, are considered as safe countries for third-country nationals.

(4) The Tampere conclusions also stated that the CEAS should include, in the short-term, a clear and workable method for determining the Member State responsible for the examination of an asylum application.

(5) Such a method should be based on objective, fair criteria both for the Member States and for the persons concerned. It should, in particular, make it possible to determine rapidly the Member State responsible, so as to guarantee effective access to the procedures for granting international protection and not to compromise the objective of the rapid processing of applications for international protection.

(6) The first phase in the creation of a CEAS that should lead, in the longer term, to a common procedure and a uniform status, valid throughout the Union, for those granted international protection, has now been completed. The European Council of 4 November 2004 adopted The Hague Programme which set the objectives to be implemented in the area of freedom, security and justice in the period 2005-2010. In this respect, The Hague Programme invited the European Commission to conclude the evaluation of the first-phase legal instruments and to submit the second-phase instruments and measures to the European Parliament and to the Council with a view to their adoption before 2010.

(7) In the Stockholm Programme, the European Council reiterated its commitment to the objective of establishing a common area of protection and solidarity in accordance with Article 78 of the Treaty on the Functioning of the European Union (TFEU), for those granted international protection, by 2012 at the latest. Furthermore it emphasised that the Dublin system remains a cornerstone in building the CEAS, as it clearly allocates responsibility among Member States for the examination of applications for international protection.

(8) The resources of the European Asylum Support Office (EASO), established by Regulation (EU) No. 439/2010 of the European Parliament and of the Council,[5] should be available to provide adequate support to the relevant services of the Member States responsible for implementing this Regulation. In particular, EASO should provide solidarity measures, such as the Asylum Intervention Pool with asylum support teams, to

[4] OJ L 50, 25.2.2003, p. 1.

[5] OJ L 132, 29.5.2010, p. 11.

assist those Member States which are faced with particular pressure and where applicants for international protection ('applicants') cannot benefit from adequate standards, in particular as regards reception and protection.

(9) In the light of the results of the evaluations undertaken of the implementation of the first-phase instruments, it is appropriate, at this stage, to confirm the principles underlying Regulation (EC) No. 343/2003, while making the necessary improvements, in the light of experience, to the effectiveness of the Dublin system and the protection granted to applicants under that system. Given that a well-functioning Dublin system is essential for the CEAS, its principles and functioning should be reviewed as other components of the CEAS and Union solidarity tools are built up. A comprehensive 'fitness check' should be foreseen by conducting an evidence-based review covering the legal, economic and social effects of the Dublin system, including its effects on fundamental rights.

(10) In order to ensure equal treatment for all applicants and beneficiaries of international protection, and consistency with the current Union asylum *acquis*, in particular with Directive 2011/95/EU of the European Parliament and of the Council of 13 December 2011 on standards for the qualification of third-country nationals or stateless persons as beneficiaries of international protection, for a uniform status for refugees or for persons eligible for subsidiary protection, and for the content of the protection granted,[6] the scope of this Regulation encompasses applicants for subsidiary protection and persons eligible for subsidiary protection.

(11) Directive 2013/33/EU of the European Parliament and of the Council of 26 June 2013 laying down standards for the reception of applicants for international protection[7] should apply to the procedure for the determination of the Member State responsible as regulated under this Regulation, subject to the limitations in the application of that Directive.

(12) Directive 2013/32/EU of the European Parliament and of the Council of 26 June 2013 on common procedures for granting and withdrawing international protection[8] should apply in addition and without prejudice to the provisions concerning the procedural safeguards regulated under this Regulation, subject to the limitations in the application of that Directive.

(13) In accordance with the 1989 United Nations Convention on the Rights of the Child and with the Charter of Fundamental Rights of the European Union, the best interests of the child should be a primary consideration of Member States when applying this Regulation. In assessing the best interests of the child, Member States should, in particular, take due account of the minor's well-being and social development, safety and security considerations and the views of the minor in accordance with his or her age and maturity, including his or her background. In addition, specific procedural guarantees for unaccompanied minors should be laid down on account of their particular vulnerability.

(14) In accordance with the European Convention for the Protection of Human Rights and Fundamental Freedoms and with the Charter of Fundamental Rights of the European

[6] OJ L 337, 20.12.2011, p. 9.
[7] See page 96 of this Official Journal.
[8] See page 60 of this Official Journal.

Union, respect for family life should be a primary consideration of Member States when applying this Regulation.

(15) The processing together of the applications for international protection of the members of one family by a single Member State makes it possible to ensure that the applications are examined thoroughly, the decisions taken in respect of them are consistent and the members of one family are not separated.

(16) In order to ensure full respect for the principle of family unity and for the best interests of the child, the existence of a relationship of dependency between an applicant and his or her child, sibling or parent on account of the applicant's pregnancy or maternity, state of health or old age, should become a binding responsibility criterion. When the applicant is an unaccompanied minor, the presence of a family member or relative on the territory of another Member State who can take care of him or her should also become a binding responsibility criterion.

(17) Any Member State should be able to derogate from the responsibility criteria, in particular on humanitarian and compassionate grounds, in order to bring together family members, relatives or any other family relations and examine an application for international protection lodged with it or with another Member State, even if such examination is not its responsibility under the binding criteria laid down in this Regulation.

(18) A personal interview with the applicant should be organised in order to facilitate the determination of the Member State responsible for examining an application for international protection. As soon as the application for international protection is lodged, the applicant should be informed of the application of this Regulation and of the possibility, during the interview, of providing information regarding the presence of family members, relatives or any other family relations in the Member States, in order to facilitate the procedure for determining the Member State responsible.

(19) In order to guarantee effective protection of the rights of the persons concerned, legal safeguards and the right to an effective remedy in respect of decisions regarding transfers to the Member State responsible should be established, in accordance, in particular, with Article 47 of the Charter of Fundamental Rights of the European Union. In order to ensure that international law is respected, an effective remedy against such decisions should cover both the examination of the application of this Regulation and of the legal and factual situation in the Member State to which the applicant is transferred.

(20) The detention of applicants should be applied in accordance with the underlying principle that a person should not be held in detention for the sole reason that he or she is seeking international protection. Detention should be for as short a period as possible and subject to the principles of necessity and proportionality. In particular, the detention of applicants must be in accordance with Article 31 of the Geneva Convention. The procedures provided for under this Regulation in respect of a detained person should be applied as a matter of priority, within the shortest possible deadlines. As regards the general guarantees governing detention, as well as detention conditions, where appropriate, Member States should apply the provisions of Directive 2013/33/EU also to persons detained on the basis of this Regulation.

(21) Deficiencies in, or the collapse of, asylum systems, often aggravated or contributed to by particular pressures on them, can jeopardise the smooth functioning of the system put in place under this Regulation, which could lead to a risk of a violation of the rights of applicants as set out in the Union asylum *acquis* and the Charter of Fundamental Rights of the European Union, other international human rights and refugee rights.

(22) A process for early warning, preparedness and management of asylum crises serving to prevent a deterioration in, or the collapse of, asylum systems, with EASO playing a key role using its powers under Regulation (EU) No. 439/2010, should be established in order to ensure robust cooperation within the framework of this Regulation and to develop mutual trust among Member States with respect to asylum policy. Such a process should ensure that the Union is alerted as soon as possible when there is a concern that the smooth functioning of the system set up by this Regulation is being jeopardised as a result of particular pressure on, and/or deficiencies in, the asylum systems of one or more Member States. Such a process would allow the Union to promote preventive measures at an early stage and pay the appropriate political attention to such situations. Solidarity, which is a pivotal element in the CEAS, goes hand in hand with mutual trust. By enhancing such trust, the process for early warning, preparedness and management of asylum crises could improve the steering of concrete measures of genuine and practical solidarity towards Member States, in order to assist the affected Member States in general and the applicants in particular. In accordance with Article 80 TFEU, Union acts should, whenever necessary, contain appropriate measures to give effect to the principle of solidarity, and the process should be accompanied by such measures. The conclusions on a Common Framework for genuine and practical solidarity towards Member States facing particular pressures on their asylum systems, including through mixed migration flows, adopted by the Council on 8 March 2012, provide for a 'tool box' of existing and potential new measures, which should be taken into account in the context of a mechanism for early warning, preparedness and crisis management.

(23) Member States should collaborate with EASO in the gathering of information concerning their ability to manage particular pressure on their asylum and reception systems, in particular within the framework of the application of this Regulation. EASO should regularly report on the information gathered in accordance with Regulation (EU) No. 439/2010.

(24) In accordance with Commission Regulation (EC) No. 1560/2003,[9] transfers to the Member State responsible for examining an application for international protection may be carried out on a voluntary basis, by supervised departure or under escort. Member States should promote voluntary transfers by providing adequate information to the applicant and should ensure that supervised or escorted transfers are undertaken in a humane manner, in full compliance with fundamental rights and respect for human dignity, as well as the best interests of the child and taking utmost account of developments in the relevant case law, in particular as regards transfers on humanitarian grounds.

(25) The progressive creation of an area without internal frontiers in which free movement of persons is guaranteed in accordance with the TFEU and the establishment of Union policies regarding the conditions of entry and stay of third-country nationals, including common efforts towards the management of external borders, makes it necessary to strike a balance between responsibility criteria in a spirit of solidarity.

(26) Directive 95/46/EC of the European Parliament and of the Council of 24 October 1995 on the protection of individuals with regard to the processing of personal data and on the free movement of such data[10] applies to the processing of personal data by the Member States under this Regulation.

[9] OJ L 222, 5.9.2003, p. 3.
[10] OJ L 281, 23.11.1995, p. 31.

(27) The exchange of an applicant's personal data, including sensitive data on his or her health, prior to a transfer, will ensure that the competent asylum authorities are in a position to provide applicants with adequate assistance and to ensure continuity in the protection and rights afforded to them. Special provisions should be made to ensure the protection of data relating to applicants involved in that situation, in accordance with Directive 95/46/EC.

(28) The application of this Regulation can be facilitated, and its effectiveness increased, by bilateral arrangements between Member States for improving communication between competent departments, reducing time limits for procedures or simplifying the processing of requests to take charge or take back, or establishing procedures for the performance of transfers.

(29) Continuity between the system for determining the Member State responsible established by Regulation (EC) No. 343/2003 and the system established by this Regulation should be ensured. Similarly, consistency should be ensured between this Regulation and Regulation (EU) No. 603/2013 of the European Parliament and of the Council of 26 June 2013 on the establishment of 'Eurodac' for the comparison of fingerprints for the effective application of Regulation (EU) No. 604/2013 establishing the criteria and mechanisms for determining the Member State responsible for examining an application for international protection lodged in one of the Member States by a third-country national or a stateless person and on requests for the comparisons with Eurodac data by Member States' law enforcement authorities and Europol for law enforcement purposes.[11]

(30) The operation of the Eurodac system, as established by Regulation (EU) No. 603/2013, should facilitate the application of this Regulation.

(31) The operation of the Visa Information System, as established by Regulation (EC) No. 767/2008 of the European Parliament and of the Council of 9 July 2008 concerning the Visa Information System (VIS) and the exchange of data between Member States on short-stay visas,[12] and in particular the implementation of Articles 21 and 22 thereof, should facilitate the application of this Regulation.

(32) With respect to the treatment of persons falling within the scope of this Regulation, Member States are bound by their obligations under instruments of international law, including the relevant case-law of the European Court of Human Rights.

(33) In order to ensure uniform conditions for the implementation of this Regulation, implementing powers should be conferred on the Commission. Those powers should be exercised in accordance with Regulation (EU) No. 182/2011 of the European Parliament and of the Council of 16 February 2011 laying down the rules and general principles concerning mechanisms for control by the Member States of the Commission's exercise of implementing powers.[13]

(34) The examination procedure should be used for the adoption of a common leaflet on Dublin/Eurodac, as well as a specific leaflet for unaccompanied minors; of a standard form for the exchange of relevant information on unaccompanied minors; of uniform conditions for the consultation and exchange of information on minors and dependent persons; of uniform conditions on the preparation and submission of take charge and take back requests; of two lists of relevant elements of proof and circumstantial evidence,

[11] See page 1 of this Official Journal.
[12] OJ L 218, 13.8.2008, p. 60.
[13] OJ L 55, 28.2.2011, p. 13.

and the periodical revision thereof; of a *laissez passer*; of uniform conditions for the consultation and exchange of information regarding transfers; of a standard form for the exchange of data before a transfer; of a common health certificate; of uniform conditions and practical arrangements for the exchange of information on a person's health data before a transfer, and of secure electronic transmission channels for the transmission of requests.

(35) In order to provide for supplementary rules, the power to adopt acts in accordance with Article 290 TFEU should be delegated to the Commission in respect of the identification of family members, siblings or relatives of an unaccompanied minor; the criteria for establishing the existence of proven family links; the criteria for assessing the capacity of a relative to take care of an unaccompanied minor, including where family members, siblings or relatives of the unaccompanied minor stay in more than one Member State; the elements for assessing a dependency link; the criteria for assessing the capacity of a person to take care of a dependent person and the elements to be taken into account in order to assess the inability to travel for a significant period of time. In exercising its powers to adopt delegated acts, the Commission shall not exceed the scope of the best interests of the child as provided for under Article 6(3) of this Regulation. It is of particular importance that the Commission carry out appropriate consultations during its preparatory work, including at expert level. The Commission, when preparing and drawing up delegated acts, should ensure a simultaneous, timely and appropriate transmission of relevant documents to the European Parliament and to the Council.

(36) In the application of this Regulation, including the preparation of delegated acts, the Commission should consult experts from, among others, all relevant national authorities.

(37) Detailed rules for the application of Regulation (EC) No. 343/2003 have been laid down by Regulation (EC) No. 1560/2003. Certain provisions of Regulation (EC) No. 1560/2003 should be incorporated into this Regulation, either for reasons of clarity or because they can serve a general objective. In particular, it is important, both for the Member States and the applicants concerned, that there should be a general mechanism for finding a solution in cases where Member States differ over the application of a provision of this Regulation. It is therefore justified to incorporate the mechanism provided for in Regulation (EC) No. 1560/2003 for the settling of disputes on the humanitarian clause into this Regulation and to extend its scope to the entirety of this Regulation.

(38) The effective monitoring of the application of this Regulation requires that it be evaluated at regular intervals.

(39) This Regulation respects the fundamental rights and observes the principles which are acknowledged, in particular, in the Charter of Fundamental Rights of the European Union. In particular, this Regulation seeks to ensure full observance of the right to asylum guaranteed by Article 18 of the Charter as well as the rights recognised under Articles 1, 4, 7, 24 and 47 thereof. This Regulation should therefore be applied accordingly.

(40) Since the objective of this Regulation, namely the establishment of criteria and mechanisms for determining the Member State responsible for examining an application for international protection lodged in one of the Member States by a third-country national or a stateless person, cannot be sufficiently achieved by the Member States and can therefore, by reason of the scale and effects of this Regulation, be better achieved at Union level, the Union may adopt measures in accordance with the principle of subsidiarity as set out in Article 5 of the Treaty on European Union (TEU). In accordance with

the principle of proportionality, as set out in that Article, this Regulation does not go beyond what is necessary in order to achieve that objective.

(41) In accordance with Article 3 and Article 4a(1) of Protocol No. 21 on the position of the United Kingdom and Ireland in respect of the Area of Freedom, Security and Justice, annexed to the TEU and to the TFEU, those Member States have notified their wish to take part in the adoption and application of this Regulation.

(42) In accordance with Articles 1 and 2 of Protocol No. 22 on the position of Denmark, annexed to the TEU and to the TFEU, Denmark is not taking part in the adoption of this Regulation and is not bound by it or subject to its application,

HAVE ADOPTED THIS REGULATION:

Chapter I

Subject Matter and Definitions

Article 1

Subject matter

This Regulation lays down the criteria and mechanisms for determining the Member State responsible for examining an application for international protection lodged in one of the Member States by a third-country national or a stateless person ('the Member State responsible').

Article 2

Definitions

For the purposes of this Regulation:

(a) 'third-country national' means any person who is not a citizen of the Union within the meaning of Article 20(1) TFEU and who is not national of a State which participates in this Regulation by virtue of an agreement with the European Union;

(b) 'application for international protection' means an application for international protection as defined in Article 2(h) of Directive 2011/95/EU;

(c) 'applicant' means a third-country national or a stateless person who has made an application for international protection in respect of which a final decision has not yet been taken;

(d) 'examination of an application for international protection' means any examination of, or decision or ruling concerning, an application for international protection by the competent authorities in accordance with Directive 2013/32/EU and Directive 2011/95/EU, except for procedures for determining the Member State responsible in accordance with this Regulation;

(e) 'withdrawal of an application for international protection' means the actions by which the applicant terminates the procedures initiated by the submission of his or her application for international protection, in accordance with Directive 2013/32/EU, either explicitly or tacitly;

(f) 'beneficiary of international protection' means a third-country national or a stateless person who has been granted international protection as defined in Article 2(a) of Directive 2011/95/EU;

(g) 'family members' means, insofar as the family already existed in the country of origin, the following members of the applicant's family who are present on the territory of the Member States:

— the spouse of the applicant or his or her unmarried partner in a stable relationship, where the law or practice of the Member State concerned treats unmarried couples in a way comparable to married couples under its law relating to third-country nationals,

— the minor children of couples referred to in the first indent or of the applicant, on condition that they are unmarried and regardless of whether they were born in or out of wedlock or adopted as defined under national law,

— when the applicant is a minor and unmarried, the father, mother or another adult responsible for the applicant, whether by law or by the practice of the Member State where the adult is present,

— when the beneficiary of international protection is a minor and unmarried, the father, mother or another adult responsible for him or her whether by law or by the practice of the Member State where the beneficiary is present;

(h) 'relative' means the applicant's adult aunt or uncle or grandparent who is present in the territory of a Member State, regardless of whether the applicant was born in or out of wedlock or adopted as defined under national law;

(i) 'minor' means a third-country national or a stateless person below the age of 18 years;

(j) 'unaccompanied minor' means a minor who arrives on the territory of the Member States unaccompanied by an adult responsible for him or her, whether by law or by the practice of the Member State concerned, and for as long as he or she is not effectively taken into the care of such an adult; it includes a minor who is left unaccompanied after he or she has entered the territory of Member States;

(k) 'representative' means a person or an organisation appointed by the competent bodies in order to assist and represent an unaccompanied minor in procedures provided for in this Regulation with a view to ensuring the best interests of the child and exercising legal capacity for the minor where necessary. Where an organisation is appointed as a representative, it shall designate a person responsible for carrying out its duties in respect of the minor, in accordance with this Regulation;

(l) 'residence document' means any authorisation issued by the authorities of a Member State authorising a third-country national or a stateless person to stay on its territory, including the documents substantiating the authorisation to remain on the territory under temporary protection arrangements or until the circumstances preventing a removal order from being carried out no longer apply, with the exception of visas and residence authorisations issued during the period required to determine the Member State responsible as established in this Regulation or during the examination of an application for international protection or an application for a residence permit;

(m) 'visa' means the authorisation or decision of a Member State required for transit or entry for an intended stay in that Member State or in several Member States. The nature of the visa shall be determined in accordance with the following definitions:

— 'long-stay visa' means an authorisation or decision issued by one of the Member States in accordance with its national law or Union law required for entry for an intended stay in that Member State of more than three months,

— 'short-stay visa' means an authorisation or decision of a Member State with a view to transit through or an intended stay on the territory of one or more or all the Member States of a duration of no more than three months in any six-month period beginning on the date of first entry on the territory of the Member States,

— 'airport transit visa' means a visa valid for transit through the international transit areas of one or more airports of the Member States;

(n) 'risk of absconding' means the existence of reasons in an individual case, which are based on objective criteria defined by law, to believe that an applicant or a third-country national or a stateless person who is subject to a transfer procedure may abscond.

Chapter II

General Principles and Safeguards

Article 3

Access to the procedure for examining an application for international protection

1. Member States shall examine any application for international protection by a third-country national or a stateless person who applies on the territory of any one of them, including at the border or in the transit zones. The application shall be examined by a single Member State, which shall be the one which the criteria set out in Chapter III indicate is responsible.

2. Where no Member State responsible can be designated on the basis of the criteria listed in this Regulation, the first Member State in which the application for international protection was lodged shall be responsible for examining it.

Where it is impossible to transfer an applicant to the Member State primarily designated as responsible because there are substantial grounds for believing that there are systemic flaws in the asylum procedure and in the reception conditions for applicants in that Member State, resulting in a risk of inhuman or degrading treatment within the meaning of Article 4 of the Charter of Fundamental Rights of the European Union, the determining Member State shall continue to examine the criteria set out in Chapter III in order to establish whether another Member State can be designated as responsible.

Where the transfer cannot be made pursuant to this paragraph to any Member State designated on the basis of the criteria set out in Chapter III or to the first Member State with which the application was lodged, the determining Member State shall become the Member State responsible.

3. Any Member State shall retain the right to send an applicant to a safe third country, subject to the rules and safeguards laid down in Directive 2013/32/EU.

Article 4

Right to information

1. As soon as an application for international protection is lodged within the meaning of Article 20(2) in a Member State, its competent authorities shall inform the applicant of the application of this Regulation, and in particular of:

(a) the objectives of this Regulation and the consequences of making another application in a different Member State as well as the consequences of moving from one Member State to another during the phases in which the Member State responsible under this Regulation is being determined and the application for international protection is being examined;

(b) the criteria for determining the Member State responsible, the hierarchy of such criteria in the different steps of the procedure and their duration, including the fact that an application for international protection lodged in one Member State can result in that Member State becoming responsible under this Regulation even if such responsibility is not based on those criteria;

(c) the personal interview pursuant to Article 5 and the possibility of submitting information regarding the presence of family members, relatives or any other family relations in the Member States, including the means by which the applicant can submit such information;

(d) the possibility to challenge a transfer decision and, where applicable, to apply for a suspension of the transfer;

(e) the fact that the competent authorities of Member States can exchange data on him or her for the sole purpose of implementing their obligations arising under this Regulation;

(f) the right of access to data relating to him or her and the right to request that such data be corrected if inaccurate or be deleted if unlawfully processed, as well as the procedures for exercising those rights, including the contact details of the authorities referred to in Article 35 and of the national data protection authorities responsible for hearing claims concerning the protection of personal data.

2. The information referred to in paragraph 1 shall be provided in writing in a language that the applicant understands or is reasonably supposed to understand. Member States shall use the common leaflet drawn up pursuant to paragraph 3 for that purpose.

Where necessary for the proper understanding of the applicant, the information shall also be supplied orally, for example in connection with the personal interview as referred to in Article 5.

3. The Commission shall, by means of implementing acts, draw up a common leaflet, as well as a specific leaflet for unaccompanied minors, containing at least the information referred to in paragraph 1 of this Article. This common leaflet shall also include information regarding the application of Regulation (EU) No. 603/2013 and, in particular, the purpose for which the data of an applicant may be processed within Eurodac. The common leaflet shall be established in such a manner as to enable Member States to complete it with additional Member State-specific information. Those implementing acts shall be adopted in accordance with the examination procedure referred to in Article 44(2) of this Regulation.

Article 5

Personal interview

1. In order to facilitate the process of determining the Member State responsible, the determining Member State shall conduct a personal interview with the applicant. The interview shall also allow the proper understanding of the information supplied to the applicant in accordance with Article 4.

2. The personal interview may be omitted if:

(a) the applicant has absconded; or

(b) after having received the information referred to in Article 4, the applicant has already provided the information relevant to determine the Member State responsible by other means. The Member State omitting the interview shall give the applicant the opportunity to present all further information which is relevant to correctly determine the Member State responsible before a decision is taken to transfer the applicant to the Member State responsible pursuant to Article 26(1).

3. The personal interview shall take place in a timely manner and, in any event, before any decision is taken to transfer the applicant to the Member State responsible pursuant to Article 26(1).

4. The personal interview shall be conducted in a language that the applicant understands or is reasonably supposed to understand and in which he or she is able to communicate. Where necessary, Member States shall have recourse to an interpreter who is able to ensure appropriate communication between the applicant and the person conducting the personal interview.

5. The personal interview shall take place under conditions which ensure appropriate confidentiality. It shall be conducted by a qualified person under national law.

6. The Member State conducting the personal interview shall make a written summary thereof which shall contain at least the main information supplied by the applicant at the interview. This summary may either take the form of a report or a standard form. The Member State shall ensure that the applicant and/or the legal advisor or other counsellor who is representing the applicant have timely access to the summary.

Article 6

Guarantees for minors

1. The best interests of the child shall be a primary consideration for Member States with respect to all procedures provided for in this Regulation.

2. Member States shall ensure that a representative represents and/or assists an unaccompanied minor with respect to all procedures provided for in this Regulation. The representative shall have the qualifications and expertise to ensure that the best interests of the minor are taken into consideration during the procedures carried out under this Regulation. Such representative shall have access to the content of the relevant documents in the applicant's file including the specific leaflet for unaccompanied minors.

This paragraph shall be without prejudice to the relevant provisions in Article 25 of Directive 2013/32/EU.

3. In assessing the best interests of the child, Member States shall closely cooperate with each other and shall, in particular, take due account of the following factors:

(a) family reunification possibilities;

(b) the minor's well-being and social development;

(c) safety and security considerations, in particular where there is a risk of the minor being a victim of human trafficking;

(d) the views of the minor, in accordance with his or her age and maturity.

4. For the purpose of applying Article 8, the Member State where the unaccompanied minor lodged an application for international protection shall, as soon as possible, take

appropriate action to identify the family members, siblings or relatives of the unaccompanied minor on the territory of Member States, whilst protecting the best interests of the child.

To that end, that Member State may call for the assistance of international or other relevant organisations, and may facilitate the minor's access to the tracing services of such organisations.

The staff of the competent authorities referred to in Article 35 who deal with requests concerning unaccompanied minors shall have received, and shall continue to receive, appropriate training concerning the specific needs of minors.

5. With a view to facilitating the appropriate action to identify the family members, siblings or relatives of the unaccompanied minor living in the territory of another Member State pursuant to paragraph 4 of this Article, the Commission shall adopt implementing acts including a standard form for the exchange of relevant information between Member States. Those implementing acts shall be adopted in accordance with the examination procedure referred to in Article 44(2).

Chapter III

Criteria for Determining the Member State Responsible

Article 7

Hierarchy of criteria

1. The criteria for determining the Member State responsible shall be applied in the order in which they are set out in this Chapter.

2. The Member State responsible in accordance with the criteria set out in this Chapter shall be determined on the basis of the situation obtaining when the applicant first lodged his or her application for international protection with a Member State.

3. In view of the application of the criteria referred to in Articles 8, 10 and 16, Member States shall take into consideration any available evidence regarding the presence, on the territory of a Member State, of family members, relatives or any other family relations of the applicant, on condition that such evidence is produced before another Member State accepts the request to take charge or take back the person concerned, pursuant to Articles 22 and 25 respectively, and that the previous applications for international protection of the applicant have not yet been the subject of a first decision regarding the substance.

Article 8

Minors

1. Where the applicant is an unaccompanied minor, the Member State responsible shall be that where a family member or a sibling of the unaccompanied minor is legally present, provided that it is in the best interests of the minor. Where the applicant is a married minor whose spouse is not legally present on the territory of the Member States, the Member State responsible shall be the Member State where the father, mother or other

adult responsible for the minor, whether by law or by the practice of that Member State, or sibling is legally present.

2. Where the applicant is an unaccompanied minor who has a relative who is legally present in another Member State and where it is established, based on an individual examination, that the relative can take care of him or her, that Member State shall unite the minor with his or her relative and shall be the Member State responsible, provided that it is in the best interests of the minor.

3. Where family members, siblings or relatives as referred to in paragraphs 1 and 2, stay in more than one Member State, the Member State responsible shall be decided on the basis of what is in the best interests of the unaccompanied minor.

4. In the absence of a family member, a sibling or a relative as referred to in paragraphs 1 and 2, the Member State responsible shall be that where the unaccompanied minor has lodged his or her application for international protection, provided that it is in the best interests of the minor.

5. The Commission shall be empowered to adopt delegated acts in accordance with Article 45 concerning the identification of family members, siblings or relatives of the unaccompanied minor; the criteria for establishing the existence of proven family links; the criteria for assessing the capacity of a relative to take care of the unaccompanied minor, including where family members, siblings or relatives of the unaccompanied minor stay in more than one Member State. In exercising its powers to adopt delegated acts, the Commission shall not exceed the scope of the best interests of the child as provided for under Article 6(3).

6. The Commission shall, by means of implementing acts, establish uniform conditions for the consultation and the exchange of information between Member States. Those implementing acts shall be adopted in accordance with the examination procedure referred to in Article 44(2).

Article 9

Family members who are beneficiaries of international protection

Where the applicant has a family member, regardless of whether the family was previously formed in the country of origin, who has been allowed to reside as a beneficiary of international protection in a Member State, that Member State shall be responsible for examining the application for international protection, provided that the persons concerned expressed their desire in writing.

Article 10

Family members who are applicants for international protection

If the applicant has a family member in a Member State whose application for international protection in that Member State has not yet been the subject of a first decision regarding the substance, that Member State shall be responsible for examining the application for international protection, provided that the persons concerned expressed their desire in writing.

Article 11

Family procedure

Where several family members and/or minor unmarried siblings submit applications for international protection in the same Member State simultaneously, or on dates close enough for the procedures for determining the Member State responsible to be conducted together, and where the application of the criteria set out in this Regulation would lead to their being separated, the Member State responsible shall be determined on the basis of the following provisions:

(a) responsibility for examining the applications for international protection of all the family members and/or minor unmarried siblings shall lie with the Member State which the criteria indicate is responsible for taking charge of the largest number of them;

(b) failing this, responsibility shall lie with the Member State which the criteria indicate is responsible for examining the application of the oldest of them.

Article 12

Issue of residence documents or visas

1. Where the applicant is in possession of a valid residence document, the Member State which issued the document shall be responsible for examining the application for international protection.

2. Where the applicant is in possession of a valid visa, the Member State which issued the visa shall be responsible for examining the application for international protection, unless the visa was issued on behalf of another Member State under a representation arrangement as provided for in Article 8 of Regulation (EC) No. 810/2009 of the European Parliament and of the Council, of 13 July 2009, establishing a Community Code on Visas.[14] In such a case, the represented Member State shall be responsible for examining the application for international protection.

3. Where the applicant is in possession of more than one valid residence document or visa issued by different Member States, the responsibility for examining the application for international protection shall be assumed by the Member States in the following order:

(a) the Member State which issued the residence document conferring the right to the longest period of residency or, where the periods of validity are identical, the Member State which issued the residence document having the latest expiry date;

(b) the Member State which issued the visa having the latest expiry date where the various visas are of the same type;

(c) where visas are of different kinds, the Member State which issued the visa having the longest period of validity or, where the periods of validity are identical, the Member State which issued the visa having the latest expiry date.

4. Where the applicant is in possession only of one or more residence documents which have expired less than two years previously or one or more visas which have expired less than six months previously and which enabled him or her actually to enter the territory of a Member State, paragraphs 1, 2 and 3 shall apply for such time as the applicant has not left the territories of the Member States.

[14] OJ L 243, 15.9.2009, p. 1.

Where the applicant is in possession of one or more residence documents which have expired more than two years previously or one or more visas which have expired more than six months previously and enabled him or her actually to enter the territory of a Member State and where he has not left the territories of the Member States, the Member State in which the application for international protection is lodged shall be responsible.

5. The fact that the residence document or visa was issued on the basis of a false or assumed identity or on submission of forged, counterfeit or invalid documents shall not prevent responsibility being allocated to the Member State which issued it. However, the Member State issuing the residence document or visa shall not be responsible if it can establish that a fraud was committed after the document or visa had been issued.

Article 13

Entry and/or stay

1. Where it is established, on the basis of proof or circumstantial evidence as described in the two lists mentioned in Article 22(3) of this Regulation, including the data referred to in Regulation (EU) No. 603/2013, that an applicant has irregularly crossed the border into a Member State by land, sea or air having come from a third country, the Member State thus entered shall be responsible for examining the application for international protection. That responsibility shall cease 12 months after the date on which the irregular border crossing took place.

2. When a Member State cannot or can no longer be held responsible in accordance with paragraph 1 of this Article and where it is established, on the basis of proof or circumstantial evidence as described in the two lists mentioned in Article 22(3), that the applicant—who has entered the territories of the Member States irregularly or whose circumstances of entry cannot be established—has been living for a continuous period of at least five months in a Member State before lodging the application for international protection, that Member State shall be responsible for examining the application for international protection.

If the applicant has been living for periods of time of at least five months in several Member States, the Member State where he or she has been living most recently shall be responsible for examining the application for international protection.

Article 14

Visa waived entry

1. If a third-country national or a stateless person enters into the territory of a Member State in which the need for him or her to have a visa is waived, that Member State shall be responsible for examining his or her application for international protection.

2. The principle set out in paragraph 1 shall not apply if the third-country national or the stateless person lodges his or her application for international protection in another Member State in which the need for him or her to have a visa for entry into the territory is also waived. In that case, that other Member State shall be responsible for examining the application for international protection.

Article 15

Application in an international transit area of an airport

Where the application for international protection is made in the international transit area of an airport of a Member State by a third-country national or a stateless person, that Member State shall be responsible for examining the application.

Chapter IV

Dependent Persons and Discretionary Clauses

Article 16

Dependent persons

1. Where, on account of pregnancy, a new-born child, serious illness, severe disability or old age, an applicant is dependent on the assistance of his or her child, sibling or parent legally resident in one of the Member States, or his or her child, sibling or parent legally resident in one of the Member States is dependent on the assistance of the applicant, Member States shall normally keep or bring together the applicant with that child, sibling or parent, provided that family ties existed in the country of origin, that the child, sibling or parent or the applicant is able to take care of the dependent person and that the persons concerned expressed their desire in writing.

2. Where the child, sibling or parent referred to in paragraph 1 is legally resident in a Member State other than the one where the applicant is present, the Member State responsible shall be the one where the child, sibling or parent is legally resident unless the applicant's health prevents him or her from travelling to that Member State for a significant period of time. In such a case, the Member State responsible shall be the one where the applicant is present. Such Member State shall not be subject to the obligation to bring the child, sibling or parent of the applicant to its territory.

3. The Commission shall be empowered to adopt delegated acts in accordance with Article 45 concerning the elements to be taken into account in order to assess the dependency link, the criteria for establishing the existence of proven family links, the criteria for assessing the capacity of the person concerned to take care of the dependent person and the elements to be taken into account in order to assess the inability to travel for a significant period of time.

4. The Commission shall, by means of implementing acts, establish uniform conditions for the consultation and exchange of information between Member States. Those implementing acts shall be adopted in accordance with the examination procedure referred to in Article 44(2).

Article 17

Discretionary clauses

1. By way of derogation from Article 3(1), each Member State may decide to examine an application for international protection lodged with it by a third-country national or

a stateless person, even if such examination is not its responsibility under the criteria laid down in this Regulation.

The Member State which decides to examine an application for international protection pursuant to this paragraph shall become the Member State responsible and shall assume the obligations associated with that responsibility. Where applicable, it shall inform, using the 'DubliNet' electronic communication network set up under Article 18 of Regulation (EC) No. 1560/2003, the Member State previously responsible, the Member State conducting a procedure for determining the Member State responsible or the Member State which has been requested to take charge of, or to take back, the applicant.

The Member State which becomes responsible pursuant to this paragraph shall forthwith indicate it in Eurodac in accordance with Regulation (EU) No. 603/2013 by adding the date when the decision to examine the application was taken.

2. The Member State in which an application for international protection is made and which is carrying out the process of determining the Member State responsible, or the Member State responsible, may, at any time before a first decision regarding the substance is taken, request another Member State to take charge of an applicant in order to bring together any family relations, on humanitarian grounds based in particular on family or cultural considerations, even where that other Member State is not responsible under the criteria laid down in Articles 8 to 11 and 16. The persons concerned must express their consent in writing.

The request to take charge shall contain all the material in the possession of the requesting Member State to allow the requested Member State to assess the situation.

The requested Member State shall carry out any necessary checks to examine the humanitarian grounds cited, and shall reply to the requesting Member State within two months of receipt of the request using the 'DubliNet' electronic communication network set up under Article 18 of Regulation (EC) No. 1560/2003. A reply refusing the request shall state the reasons on which the refusal is based.

Where the requested Member State accepts the request, responsibility for examining the application shall be transferred to it.

Chapter V

Obligations of the Member State Responsible

Article 18

Obligations of the Member State responsible

1. The Member State responsible under this Regulation shall be obliged to:

(a) take charge, under the conditions laid down in Articles 21, 22 and 29, of an applicant who has lodged an application in a different Member State;

(b) take back, under the conditions laid down in Articles 23, 24, 25 and 29, an applicant whose application is under examination and who made an application in another Member State or who is on the territory of another Member State without a residence document;

(c) take back, under the conditions laid down in Articles 23, 24, 25 and 29, a third-country national or a stateless person who has withdrawn the application under examination and made an application in another Member State or who is on the territory of another Member State without a residence document;

(d) take back, under the conditions laid down in Articles 23, 24, 25 and 29, a third-country national or a stateless person whose application has been rejected and who made an application in another Member State or who is on the territory of another Member State without a residence document.

2. In the cases falling within the scope of paragraph 1(a) and (b), the Member State responsible shall examine or complete the examination of the application for international protection made by the applicant.

In the cases falling within the scope of paragraph 1(c), when the Member State responsible had discontinued the examination of an application following its withdrawal by the applicant before a decision on the substance has been taken at first instance, that Member State shall ensure that the applicant is entitled to request that the examination of his or her application be completed or to lodge a new application for international protection, which shall not be treated as a subsequent application as provided for in Directive 2013/32/EU. In such cases, Member States shall ensure that the examination of the application is completed.

In the cases falling within the scope of paragraph 1(d), where the application has been rejected at first instance only, the Member State responsible shall ensure that the person concerned has or has had the opportunity to seek an effective remedy pursuant to Article 46 of Directive 2013/32/EU.

Article 19

Cessation of responsibilities

1. Where a Member State issues a residence document to the applicant, the obligations specified in Article 18(1) shall be transferred to that Member State.

2. The obligations specified in Article 18(1) shall cease where the Member State responsible can establish, when requested to take charge or take back an applicant or another person as referred to in Article 18(1)(c) or (d), that the person concerned has left the territory of the Member States for at least three months, unless the person concerned is in possession of a valid residence document issued by the Member State responsible.

An application lodged after the period of absence referred to in the first subparagraph shall be regarded as a new application giving rise to a new procedure for determining the Member State responsible.

3. The obligations specified in Article 18(1)(c) and (d) shall cease where the Member State responsible can establish, when requested to take back an applicant or another person as referred to in Article 18(1)(c) or (d), that the person concerned has left the territory of the Member States in compliance with a return decision or removal order issued following the withdrawal or rejection of the application.

An application lodged after an effective removal has taken place shall be regarded as a new application giving rise to a new procedure for determining the Member State responsible.

Chapter VI

Procedures for Taking Charge and Taking Back

Section I
Start of the Procedure

Article 20

Start of the procedure

1. The process of determining the Member State responsible shall start as soon as an application for international protection is first lodged with a Member State.

2. An application for international protection shall be deemed to have been lodged once a form submitted by the applicant or a report prepared by the authorities has reached the competent authorities of the Member State concerned. Where an application is not made in writing, the time elapsing between the statement of intention and the preparation of a report should be as short as possible.

3. For the purposes of this Regulation, the situation of a minor who is accompanying the applicant and meets the definition of family member shall be indissociable from that of his or her family member and shall be a matter for the Member State responsible for examining the application for international protection of that family member, even if the minor is not individually an applicant, provided that it is in the minor's best interests. The same treatment shall be applied to children born after the applicant arrives on the territory of the Member States, without the need to initiate a new procedure for taking charge of them.

4. Where an application for international protection is lodged with the competent authorities of a Member State by an applicant who is on the territory of another Member State, the determination of the Member State responsible shall be made by the Member State in whose territory the applicant is present. The latter Member State shall be informed without delay by the Member State which received the application and shall then, for the purposes of this Regulation, be regarded as the Member State with which the application for international protection was lodged.

The applicant shall be informed in writing of this change in the determining Member State and of the date on which it took place.

5. An applicant who is present in another Member State without a residence document or who there lodges an application for international protection after withdrawing his or her first application made in a different Member State during the process of determining the Member State responsible shall be taken back, under the conditions laid down in Articles 23, 24, 25 and 29, by the Member State with which that application for international protection was first lodged, with a view to completing the process of determining the Member State responsible.

That obligation shall cease where the Member State requested to complete the process of determining the Member State responsible can establish that the applicant has in the meantime left the territory of the Member States for a period of at least three months or has obtained a residence document from another Member State.

An application lodged after the period of absence referred to in the second subparagraph shall be regarded as a new application giving rise to a new procedure for determining the Member State responsible.

Section II

Procedures for Take Charge Requests

Article 21

Submitting a take charge request

1. Where a Member State with which an application for international protection has been lodged considers that another Member State is responsible for examining the application, it may, as quickly as possible and in any event within three months of the date on which the application was lodged within the meaning of Article 20(2), request that other Member State to take charge of the applicant.

Notwithstanding the first subparagraph, in the case of a Eurodac hit with data recorded pursuant to Article 14 of Regulation (EU) No. 603/2013, the request shall be sent within two months of receiving that hit pursuant to Article 15(2) of that Regulation.

Where the request to take charge of an applicant is not made within the periods laid down in the first and second subparagraphs, responsibility for examining the application for international protection shall lie with the Member State in which the application was lodged.

2. The requesting Member State may ask for an urgent reply in cases where the application for international protection was lodged after leave to enter or remain was refused, after an arrest for an unlawful stay or after the service or execution of a removal order.

The request shall state the reasons warranting an urgent reply and the period within which a reply is expected. That period shall be at least one week.

3. In the cases referred to in paragraphs 1 and 2, the request that charge be taken by another Member State shall be made using a standard form and including proof or circumstantial evidence as described in the two lists mentioned in Article 22(3) and/or relevant elements from the applicant's statement, enabling the authorities of the requested Member State to check whether it is responsible on the basis of the criteria laid down in this Regulation.

The Commission shall, by means of implementing acts, adopt uniform conditions on the preparation and submission of take charge requests. Those implementing acts shall be adopted in accordance with the examination procedure referred to in Article 44(2).

Article 22

Replying to a take charge request

1. The requested Member State shall make the necessary checks, and shall give a decision on the request to take charge of an applicant within two months of receipt of the request.

2. In the procedure for determining the Member State responsible elements of proof and circumstantial evidence shall be used.

3. The Commission shall, by means of implementing acts, establish, and review periodically, two lists, indicating the relevant elements of proof and circumstantial evidence in accordance with the criteria set out in points (a) and (b) of this paragraph. Those implementing acts shall be adopted in accordance with the examination procedure referred to in Article 44(2).

(a) Proof:

(i) this refers to formal proof which determines responsibility pursuant to this Regulation, as long as it is not refuted by proof to the contrary;

(ii) the Member States shall provide the Committee provided for in Article 44 with models of the different types of administrative documents, in accordance with the typology established in the list of formal proofs;

(b) Circumstantial evidence:

(i) this refers to indicative elements which while being refutable may be sufficient, in certain cases, according to the evidentiary value attributed to them;

(ii) their evidentiary value, in relation to the responsibility for examining the application for international protection shall be assessed on a case-by-case basis.

4. The requirement of proof should not exceed what is necessary for the proper application of this Regulation.

5. If there is no formal proof, the requested Member State shall acknowledge its responsibility if the circumstantial evidence is coherent, verifiable and sufficiently detailed to establish responsibility.

6. Where the requesting Member State has pleaded urgency in accordance with the provisions of Article 21(2), the requested Member State shall make every effort to comply with the time limit requested. In exceptional cases, where it can be demonstrated that the examination of a request for taking charge of an applicant is particularly complex, the requested Member State may give its reply after the time limit requested, but in any event within one month. In such situations the requested Member State must communicate its decision to postpone a reply to the requesting Member State within the time limit originally requested.

7. Failure to act within the two-month period mentioned in paragraph 1 and the one-month period mentioned in paragraph 6 shall be tantamount to accepting the request, and entail the obligation to take charge of the person, including the obligation to provide for proper arrangements for arrival.

SECTION III

Procedures for Take Back Requests

Article 23

Submitting a take back request when a new application has been lodged in the requesting Member State

1. Where a Member State with which a person as referred to in Article 18(1)(b), (c) or (d) has lodged a new application for international protection considers that another Member State is responsible in accordance with Article 20(5) and Article 18(1)(b), (c) or (d), it may request that other Member State to take back that person.

2. A take back request shall be made as quickly as possible and in any event within two months of receiving the Eurodac hit, pursuant to Article 9(5) of Regulation (EU) No. 603/2013.

If the take back request is based on evidence other than data obtained from the Eurodac system, it shall be sent to the requested Member State within three months of the date on which the application for international protection was lodged within the meaning of Article 20(2).

3. Where the take back request is not made within the periods laid down in paragraph 2, responsibility for examining the application for international protection shall lie with the Member State in which the new application was lodged.

4. A take back request shall be made using a standard form and shall include proof or circumstantial evidence as described in the two lists mentioned in Article 22(3) and/or relevant elements from the statements of the person concerned, enabling the authorities of the requested Member State to check whether it is responsible on the basis of the criteria laid down in this Regulation.

The Commission shall, by means of implementing acts, adopt uniform conditions for the preparation and submission of take back requests. Those implementing acts shall be adopted in accordance with the examination procedure referred to in Article 44(2).

Article 24

Submitting a take back request when no new application has been lodged in the requesting Member State

1. Where a Member State on whose territory a person as referred to in Article 18(1)(b), (c) or (d) is staying without a residence document and with which no new application for international protection has been lodged considers that another Member State is responsible in accordance with Article 20(5) and Article 18(1)(b), (c) or (d), it may request that other Member State to take back that person.

2. By way of derogation from Article 6(2) of Directive 2008/115/EC of the European Parliament and of the Council of 16 December 2008 on common standards and procedures in Member States for returning illegally staying third-country nationals,[15] where a Member State on whose territory a person is staying without a residence document decides to search the Eurodac system in accordance with Article 17 of Regulation (EU) No. 603/2013, the request to take back a person as referred to in Article 18(1)(b) or (c) of this Regulation, or a person as referred to in its Article 18(1)(d) whose application for international protection has not been rejected by a final decision, shall be made as quickly as possible and in any event within two months of receipt of the Eurodac hit, pursuant to Article 17(5) of Regulation (EU) No. 603/2013.

If the take back request is based on evidence other than data obtained from the Eurodac system, it shall be sent to the requested Member State within three months of the date on which the requesting Member State becomes aware that another Member State may be responsible for the person concerned.

[15] OJ L 348, 24.12.2008, p. 98.

3. Where the take back request is not made within the periods laid down in paragraph 2, the Member State on whose territory the person concerned is staying without a residence document shall give that person the opportunity to lodge a new application.

4. Where a person as referred to in Article 18(1)(d) of this Regulation whose application for international protection has been rejected by a final decision in one Member State is on the territory of another Member State without a residence document, the latter Member State may either request the former Member State to take back the person concerned or carry out a return procedure in accordance with Directive 2008/115/EC.

When the latter Member State decides to request the former Member State to take back the person concerned, the rules laid down in Directive 2008/115/EC shall not apply.

5. The request for the person referred to in Article 18(1)(b), (c) or (d) to be taken back shall be made using a standard form and shall include proof or circumstantial evidence as described in the two lists mentioned in Article 22(3) and/or relevant elements from the person's statements, enabling the authorities of the requested Member State to check whether it is responsible on the basis of the criteria laid down in this Regulation.

The Commission shall, by means of implementing acts, establish and review periodically two lists indicating the relevant elements of proof and circumstantial evidence in accordance with the criteria set out in Article 22(3)(a) and (b), and shall adopt uniform conditions for the preparation and submission of take back requests. Those implementing acts shall be adopted in accordance with the examination procedure referred to in Article 44(2).

Article 25

Replying to a take back request

1. The requested Member State shall make the necessary checks and shall give a decision on the request to take back the person concerned as quickly as possible and in any event no later than one month from the date on which the request was received. When the request is based on data obtained from the Eurodac system, that time limit shall be reduced to two weeks.

2. Failure to act within the one month period or the two weeks period mentioned in paragraph 1 shall be tantamount to accepting the request, and shall entail the obligation to take back the person concerned, including the obligation to provide for proper arrangements for arrival.

SECTION IV

Procedural Safeguards

Article 26

Notification of a transfer decision

1. Where the requested Member State accepts to take charge of or to take back an applicant or other person as referred to in Article 18(1)(c) or (d), the requesting Member State shall notify the person concerned of the decision to transfer him or her to the Member State responsible and, where applicable, of not examining his or her application for international protection. If a legal advisor or other counsellor is representing the

person concerned, Member States may choose to notify the decision to such legal advisor or counsellor instead of to the person concerned and, where applicable, communicate the decision to the person concerned.

2. The decision referred to in paragraph 1 shall contain information on the legal remedies available, including on the right to apply for suspensive effect, where applicable, and on the time limits applicable for seeking such remedies and for carrying out the transfer, and shall, if necessary, contain information on the place where, and the date on which, the person concerned should appear, if that person is travelling to the Member State responsible by his or her own means.

Member States shall ensure that information on persons or entities that may provide legal assistance to the person concerned is communicated to the person concerned together with the decision referred to in paragraph 1, when that information has not been already communicated.

3. When the person concerned is not assisted or represented by a legal advisor or other counsellor, Member States shall inform him or her of the main elements of the decision, which shall always include information on the legal remedies available and the time limits applicable for seeking such remedies, in a language that the person concerned understands or is reasonably supposed to understand.

Article 27

Remedies

1. The applicant or another person as referred to in Article 18(1)(c) or (d) shall have the right to an effective remedy, in the form of an appeal or a review, in fact and in law, against a transfer decision, before a court or tribunal.

2. Member States shall provide for a reasonable period of time within which the person concerned may exercise his or her right to an effective remedy pursuant to paragraph 1.

3. For the purposes of appeals against, or reviews of, transfer decisions, Member States shall provide in their national law that:

(a) the appeal or review confers upon the person concerned the right to remain in the Member State concerned pending the outcome of the appeal or review; or

(b) the transfer is automatically suspended and such suspension lapses after a certain reasonable period of time, during which a court or a tribunal, after a close and rigorous scrutiny, shall have taken a decision whether to grant suspensive effect to an appeal or review; or

(c) the person concerned has the opportunity to request within a reasonable period of time a court or tribunal to suspend the implementation of the transfer decision pending the outcome of his or her appeal or review. Member States shall ensure that an effective remedy is in place by suspending the transfer until the decision on the first suspension request is taken. Any decision on whether to suspend the implementation of the transfer decision shall be taken within a reasonable period of time, while permitting a close and rigorous scrutiny of the suspension request. A decision not to suspend the implementation of the transfer decision shall state the reasons on which it is based.

4. Member States may provide that the competent authorities may decide, acting *ex officio*, to suspend the implementation of the transfer decision pending the outcome of the appeal or review.

5. Member States shall ensure that the person concerned has access to legal assistance and, where necessary, to linguistic assistance.

6. Member States shall ensure that legal assistance is granted on request free of charge where the person concerned cannot afford the costs involved. Member States may provide that, as regards fees and other costs, the treatment of applicants shall not be more favourable than the treatment generally accorded to their nationals in matters pertaining to legal assistance.

Without arbitrarily restricting access to legal assistance, Member States may provide that free legal assistance and representation not be granted where the appeal or review is considered by the competent authority or a court or tribunal to have no tangible prospect of success.

Where a decision not to grant free legal assistance and representation pursuant to this paragraph is taken by an authority other than a court or tribunal, Member States shall provide the right to an effective remedy before a court or tribunal to challenge that decision.

In complying with the requirements set out in this paragraph, Member States shall ensure that legal assistance and representation is not arbitrarily restricted and that the applicant's effective access to justice is not hindered.

Legal assistance shall include at least the preparation of the required procedural documents and representation before a court or tribunal and may be restricted to legal advisors or counsellors specifically designated by national law to provide assistance and representation.

Procedures for access to legal assistance shall be laid down in national law.

Section V

Detention for the Purpose of Transfer

Article 28

Detention

1. Member States shall not hold a person in detention for the sole reason that he or she is subject to the procedure established by this Regulation.

2. When there is a significant risk of absconding, Member States may detain the person concerned in order to secure transfer procedures in accordance with this Regulation, on the basis of an individual assessment and only in so far as detention is proportional and other less coercive alternative measures cannot be applied effectively.

3. Detention shall be for as short a period as possible and shall be for no longer than the time reasonably necessary to fulfil the required administrative procedures with due diligence until the transfer under this Regulation is carried out.

Where a person is detained pursuant to this Article, the period for submitting a take charge or take back request shall not exceed one month from the lodging of the application. The Member State carrying out the procedure in accordance with this Regulation shall ask for an urgent reply in such cases. Such reply shall be given within two weeks of receipt of the request. Failure to reply within the two-week period shall be tantamount to accepting the request and shall entail the obligation to take charge or take back the person, including the obligation to provide for proper arrangements for arrival.

Where a person is detained pursuant to this Article, the transfer of that person from the requesting Member State to the Member State responsible shall be carried out as soon as practically possible, and at the latest within six weeks of the implicit or explicit acceptance of the request by another Member State to take charge or to take back the person concerned or of the moment when the appeal or review no longer has a suspensive effect in accordance with Article 27(3).

When the requesting Member State fails to comply with the deadlines for submitting a take charge or take back request or where the transfer does not take place within the period of six weeks referred to in the third subparagraph, the person shall no longer be detained. Articles 21, 23, 24 and 29 shall continue to apply accordingly.

4. As regards the detention conditions and the guarantees applicable to persons detained, in order to secure the transfer procedures to the Member State responsible, Articles 9, 10 and 11 of Directive 2013/33/EU shall apply.

Section VI

Transfers

Article 29

Modalities and time limits

1. The transfer of the applicant or of another person as referred to in Article 18(1)(c) or (d) from the requesting Member State to the Member State responsible shall be carried out in accordance with the national law of the requesting Member State, after consultation between the Member States concerned, as soon as practically possible, and at the latest within six months of acceptance of the request by another Member State to take charge or to take back the person concerned or of the final decision on an appeal or review where there is a suspensive effect in accordance with Article 27(3).

If transfers to the Member State responsible are carried out by supervised departure or under escort, Member States shall ensure that they are carried out in a humane manner and with full respect for fundamental rights and human dignity.

If necessary, the applicant shall be supplied by the requesting Member State with a *laissez passer*. The Commission shall, by means of implementing acts, establish the design of the *laissez passer*. Those implementing acts shall be adopted in accordance with the examination procedure referred to in Article 44(2).

The Member State responsible shall inform the requesting Member State, as appropriate, of the safe arrival of the person concerned or of the fact that he or she did not appear within the set time limit.

2. Where the transfer does not take place within the six months' time limit, the Member State responsible shall be relieved of its obligations to take charge or to take back the person concerned and responsibility shall then be transferred to the requesting Member State. This time limit may be extended up to a maximum of one year if the transfer could not be carried out due to imprisonment of the person concerned or up to a maximum of eighteen months if the person concerned absconds.

3. If a person has been transferred erroneously or a decision to transfer is overturned on appeal or review after the transfer has been carried out, the Member State which carried out the transfer shall promptly accept that person back.

4. The Commission shall, by means of implementing acts, establish uniform conditions for the consultation and exchange of information between Member States, in particular in the event of postponed or delayed transfers, transfers following acceptance by default, transfers of minors or dependent persons, and supervised transfers. Those implementing acts shall be adopted in accordance with the examination procedure referred to in Article 44(2).

Article 30

Costs of transfer

1. The costs necessary to transfer an applicant or another person as referred to in Article 18(1)(c) or (d) to the Member State responsible shall be met by the transferring Member State.

2. Where the person concerned has to be transferred back to a Member State as a result of an erroneous transfer or of a transfer decision that has been overturned on appeal or review after the transfer has been carried out, the Member State which initially carried out the transfer shall be responsible for the costs of transferring the person concerned back to its territory.

3. Persons to be transferred pursuant to this Regulation shall not be required to meet the costs of such transfers.

Article 31

Exchange of relevant information before a transfer is carried out

1. The Member State carrying out the transfer of an applicant or of another person as referred to in Article 18(1)(c) or (d) shall communicate to the Member State responsible such personal data concerning the person to be transferred as is appropriate, relevant and non-excessive for the sole purposes of ensuring that the competent authorities, in accordance with national law in the Member State responsible, are in a position to provide that person with adequate assistance, including the provision of immediate health care required in order to protect his or her vital interests, and to ensure continuity in the protection and rights afforded by this Regulation and by other relevant asylum legal instruments. Those data shall be communicated to the Member State responsible within a reasonable period of time before a transfer is carried out, in order to ensure that its competent authorities in accordance with national law have sufficient time to take the necessary measures.

2. The transferring Member State shall, in so far as such information is available to the competent authority in accordance with national law, transmit to the Member State responsible any information that is essential in order to safeguard the rights and immediate special needs of the person to be transferred, and in particular:

(a) any immediate measures which the Member State responsible is required to take in order to ensure that the special needs of the person to be transferred are adequately addressed, including any immediate health care that may be required;

(b) contact details of family members, relatives or any other family relations in the receiving Member State, where applicable;

(c) in the case of minors, information on their education;

(d) an assessment of the age of an applicant.

3. The exchange of information under this Article shall only take place between the authorities notified to the Commission in accordance with Article 35 of this Regulation using the 'DubliNet' electronic communication network set-up under Article 18 of Regulation (EC) No. 1560/2003. The information exchanged shall only be used for the purposes set out in paragraph 1 of this Article and shall not be further processed.

4. With a view to facilitating the exchange of information between Member States, the Commission shall, by means of implementing acts, draw up a standard form for the transfer of the data required pursuant to this Article. Those implementing acts shall be adopted in accordance with the examination procedure laid down in Article 44(2).

5. The rules laid down in Article 34(8) to (12) shall apply to the exchange of information pursuant to this Article.

Article 32

Exchange of health data before a transfer is carried out

1. For the sole purpose of the provision of medical care or treatment, in particular concerning disabled persons, elderly people, pregnant women, minors and persons who have been subject to torture, rape or other serious forms of psychological, physical and sexual violence, the transferring Member State shall, in so far as it is available to the competent authority in accordance with national law, transmit to the Member State responsible information on any special needs of the person to be transferred, which in specific cases may include information on that person's physical or mental health. That information shall be transferred in a common health certificate with the necessary documents attached. The Member State responsible shall ensure that those special needs are adequately addressed, including in particular any essential medical care that may be required.

The Commission shall, by means of implementing acts, draw up the common health certificate. Those implementing acts shall be adopted in accordance with the examination procedure laid down in Article 44(2).

2. The transferring Member State shall only transmit the information referred to in paragraph 1 to the Member State responsible after having obtained the explicit consent of the applicant and/or of his or her representative or, if the applicant is physically or legally incapable of giving his or her consent, when such transmission is necessary to protect the vital interests of the applicant or of another person. The lack of consent, including a refusal to consent, shall not constitute an obstacle to the transfer.

3. The processing of personal health data referred to in paragraph 1 shall only be carried out by a health professional who is subject, under national law or rules established by national competent bodies, to the obligation of professional secrecy or by another person subject to an equivalent obligation of professional secrecy.

4. The exchange of information under this Article shall only take place between the health professionals or other persons referred to in paragraph 3. The information exchanged shall only be used for the purposes set out in paragraph 1 and shall not be further processed.

5. The Commission shall, by means of implementing acts, adopt uniform conditions and practical arrangements for exchanging the information referred to in paragraph 1 of this Article. Those implementing acts shall be adopted in accordance with the examination procedure laid down in Article 44(2).

6. The rules laid down in Article 34(8) to (12) shall apply to the exchange of information pursuant to this Article.

Article 33

A mechanism for early warning, preparedness and crisis management

1. Where, on the basis of, in particular, the information gathered by EASO pursuant to Regulation (EU) No. 439/2010, the Commission establishes that the application of this Regulation may be jeopardised due either to a substantiated risk of particular pressure being placed on a Member State's asylum system and/or to problems in the functioning of the asylum system of a Member State, it shall, in cooperation with EASO, make recommendations to that Member State, inviting it to draw up a preventive action plan.

The Member State concerned shall inform the Council and the Commission whether it intends to present a preventive action plan in order to overcome the pressure and/or problems in the functioning of its asylum system whilst ensuring the protection of the fundamental rights of applicants for international protection.

A Member State may, at its own discretion and initiative, draw up a preventive action plan and subsequent revisions thereof. When drawing up a preventive action plan, the Member State may call for the assistance of the Commission, other Member States, EASO and other relevant Union agencies.

2. Where a preventive action plan is drawn up, the Member State concerned shall submit it and shall regularly report on its implementation to the Council and to the Commission. The Commission shall subsequently inform the European Parliament of the key elements of the preventive action plan. The Commission shall submit reports on its implementation to the Council and transmit reports on its implementation to the European Parliament.

The Member State concerned shall take all appropriate measures to deal with the situation of particular pressure on its asylum system or to ensure that the deficiencies identified are addressed before the situation deteriorates. Where the preventive action plan includes measures aimed at addressing particular pressure on a Member State's asylum system which may jeopardise the application of this Regulation, the Commission shall seek the advice of EASO before reporting to the European Parliament and to the Council.

3. Where the Commission establishes, on the basis of EASO's analysis, that the implementation of the preventive action plan has not remedied the deficiencies identified or where there is a serious risk that the asylum situation in the Member State concerned develops into a crisis which is unlikely to be remedied by a preventive action plan, the Commission, in cooperation with EASO as applicable, may request the Member State concerned to draw up a crisis management action plan and, where necessary, revisions thereof. The crisis management action plan shall ensure, throughout the entire process, compliance with the asylum *acquis* of the Union, in particular with the fundamental rights of applicants for international protection.

Following the request to draw up a crisis management action plan, the Member State concerned shall, in cooperation with the Commission and EASO, do so promptly, and at the latest within three months of the request.

The Member State concerned shall submit its crisis management action plan and shall report, at least every three months, on its implementation to the Commission and other relevant stakeholders, such as EASO, as appropriate.

The Commission shall inform the European Parliament and the Council of the crisis management action plan, possible revisions and the implementation thereof. In those reports, the Member State concerned shall report on data to monitor compliance with the crisis management action plan, such as the length of the procedure, the detention conditions and the reception capacity in relation to the inflow of applicants.

4. Throughout the entire process for early warning, preparedness and crisis management established in this Article, the Council shall closely monitor the situation and may request further information and provide political guidance, in particular as regards the urgency and severity of the situation and thus the need for a Member State to draw up either a preventive action plan or, if necessary, a crisis management action plan. The European Parliament and the Council may, throughout the entire process, discuss and provide guidance on any solidarity measures as they deem appropriate.

Chapter VII

Administrative Cooperation

Article 34

Information sharing

1. Each Member State shall communicate to any Member State that so requests such personal data concerning the applicant as is appropriate, relevant and non-excessive for:

(a) determining the Member State responsible;

(b) examining the application for international protection;

(c) implementing any obligation arising under this Regulation.

2. The information referred to in paragraph 1 may only cover:

(a) personal details of the applicant, and, where appropriate, his or her family members, relatives or any other family relations (full name and where appropriate, former name; nicknames or pseudonyms; nationality, present and former; date and place of birth);

(b) identity and travel papers (references, validity, date of issue, issuing authority, place of issue, etc.);

(c) other information necessary for establishing the identity of the applicant, including fingerprints processed in accordance with Regulation (EU) No. 603/2013;

(d) places of residence and routes travelled;

(e) residence documents or visas issued by a Member State;

(f) the place where the application was lodged;

(g) the date on which any previous application for international protection was lodged, the date on which the present application was lodged, the stage reached in the proceedings and the decision taken, if any.

3. Furthermore, provided it is necessary for the examination of the application for international protection, the Member State responsible may request another Member State to let it know on what grounds the applicant bases his or her application and, where applicable, the grounds for any decisions taken concerning the applicant. The other Member State may refuse to respond to the request submitted to it, if the communication of such information is likely to harm its essential interests or the protection of the liberties and fundamental rights of the person concerned or of others. In any event, communication of the information requested shall be subject to the written approval of the applicant

for international protection, obtained by the requesting Member State. In that case, the applicant must know for what specific information he or she is giving his or her approval.

4. Any request for information shall only be sent in the context of an individual application for international protection. It shall set out the grounds on which it is based and, where its purpose is to check whether there is a criterion that is likely to entail the responsibility of the requested Member State, shall state on what evidence, including relevant information from reliable sources on the ways and means by which applicants enter the territories of the Member States, or on what specific and verifiable part of the applicant's statements it is based. It is understood that such relevant information from reliable sources is not in itself sufficient to determine the responsibility and the competence of a Member State under this Regulation, but it may contribute to the evaluation of other indications relating to an individual applicant.

5. The requested Member State shall be obliged to reply within five weeks. Any delays in the reply shall be duly justified. Non-compliance with the five week time limit shall not relieve the requested Member State of the obligation to reply. If the research carried out by the requested Member State which did not respect the maximum time limit withholds information which shows that it is responsible, that Member State may not invoke the expiry of the time limits provided for in Articles 21, 23 and 24 as a reason for refusing to comply with a request to take charge or take back. In that case, the time limits provided for in Articles 21, 23 and 24 for submitting a request to take charge or take back shall be extended by a period of time which shall be equivalent to the delay in the reply by the requested Member State.

6. The exchange of information shall be effected at the request of a Member State and may only take place between authorities whose designation by each Member State has been communicated to the Commission in accordance with Article 35(1).

7. The information exchanged may only be used for the purposes set out in paragraph 1. In each Member State such information may, depending on its type and the powers of the recipient authority, only be communicated to the authorities and courts and tribunals entrusted with:

(a) determining the Member State responsible;
(b) examining the application for international protection;
(c) implementing any obligation arising under this Regulation.

8. The Member State which forwards the information shall ensure that it is accurate and up-to-date. If it transpires that it has forwarded information which is inaccurate or which should not have been forwarded, the recipient Member States shall be informed thereof immediately. They shall be obliged to correct such information or to have it erased.

9. The applicant shall have the right to be informed, on request, of any data that is processed concerning him or her.

If the applicant finds that the data have been processed in breach of this Regulation or of Directive 95/46/EC, in particular because they are incomplete or inaccurate, he or she shall be entitled to have them corrected or erased.

The authority correcting or erasing the data shall inform, as appropriate, the Member State transmitting or receiving the information.

The applicant shall have the right to bring an action or a complaint before the competent authorities or courts or tribunals of the Member State which refused the right of access to or the right of correction or erasure of data relating to him or her.

10. In each Member State concerned, a record shall be kept, in the individual file for the person concerned and/or in a register, of the transmission and receipt of information exchanged.

11. The data exchanged shall be kept for a period not exceeding that which is necessary for the purposes for which they are exchanged.

12. Where the data are not processed automatically or are not contained, or intended to be entered, in a file, each Member State shall take appropriate measures to ensure compliance with this Article through effective checks.

Article 35

Competent authorities and resources

1. Each Member State shall notify the Commission without delay of the specific authorities responsible for fulfilling the obligations arising under this Regulation, and any amendments thereto. The Member States shall ensure that those authorities have the necessary resources for carrying out their tasks and in particular for replying within the prescribed time limits to requests for information, requests to take charge of and requests to take back applicants.

2. The Commission shall publish a consolidated list of the authorities referred to in paragraph 1 in the *Official Journal of the European Union*. Where there are amendments thereto, the Commission shall publish once a year an updated consolidated list.

3. The authorities referred to in paragraph 1 shall receive the necessary training with respect to the application of this Regulation.

4. The Commission shall, by means of implementing acts, establish secure electronic transmission channels between the authorities referred to in paragraph 1 for transmitting requests, replies and all written correspondence and for ensuring that senders automatically receive an electronic proof of delivery. Those implementing acts shall be adopted in accordance with the examination procedure referred to in Article 44(2).

Article 36

Administrative arrangements

1. Member States may, on a bilateral basis, establish administrative arrangements between themselves concerning the practical details of the implementation of this Regulation, in order to facilitate its application and increase its effectiveness. Such arrangements may relate to:

(a) exchanges of liaison officers;

(b) simplification of the procedures and shortening of the time limits relating to transmission and the examination of requests to take charge of or take back applicants.

2. Member States may also maintain the administrative arrangements concluded under Regulation (EC) No. 343/2003. To the extent that such arrangements are not compatible with this Regulation, the Member States concerned shall amend the arrangements in such a way as to eliminate any incompatibilities observed.

3. Before concluding or amending any arrangement referred to in paragraph 1(b), the Member States concerned shall consult the Commission as to the compatibility of the arrangement with this Regulation.

4. If the Commission considers the arrangements referred to in paragraph 1(b) to be incompatible with this Regulation, it shall, within a reasonable period, notify the Member States concerned. The Member States shall take all appropriate steps to amend the arrangement concerned within a reasonable time in such a way as to eliminate any incompatibilities observed.

5. Member States shall notify the Commission of all arrangements referred to in paragraph 1, and of any denunciation thereof, or amendment thereto.

CHAPTER VIII

CONCILIATION

Article 37

Conciliation

1. Where the Member States cannot resolve a dispute on any matter related to the application of this Regulation, they may have recourse to the conciliation procedure provided for in paragraph 2.

2. The conciliation procedure shall be initiated by a request from one of the Member States in dispute to the Chairman of the Committee set up by Article 44. By agreeing to use the conciliation procedure, the Member States concerned undertake to take the utmost account of the solution proposed.

The Chairman of the Committee shall appoint three members of the Committee representing three Member States not connected with the matter. They shall receive the arguments of the parties either in writing or orally and, after deliberation, shall propose a solution within one month, where necessary after a vote.

The Chairman of the Committee, or his or her deputy, shall chair the discussion. He or she may put forward his or her point of view but may not vote.

Whether it is adopted or rejected by the parties, the solution proposed shall be final and irrevocable.

CHAPTER IX

TRANSITIONAL PROVISIONS AND FINAL PROVISIONS

Article 38

Data security and data protection

Member States shall take all appropriate measures to ensure the security of transmitted personal data and in particular to avoid unlawful or unauthorised access or disclosure, alteration or loss of personal data processed.

Each Member State shall provide that the national supervisory authority or authorities designated pursuant to Article 28(1) of Directive 95/46/EC shall monitor independently, in accordance with its respective national law, the lawfulness of the processing, in accordance with this Regulation, of personal data by the Member State in question.

Article 39

Confidentiality

Member States shall ensure that the authorities referred to in Article 35 are bound by the confidentiality rules provided for in national law, in relation to any information they obtain in the course of their work.

Article 40

Penalties

Member States shall take the necessary measures to ensure that any misuse of data processed in accordance with this Regulation is punishable by penalties, including administrative and/or criminal penalties in accordance with national law, that are effective, proportionate and dissuasive.

Article 41

Transitional measures

Where an application has been lodged after the date mentioned in the second paragraph of Article 49, the events that are likely to entail the responsibility of a Member State under this Regulation shall be taken into consideration, even if they precede that date, with the exception of the events mentioned in Article 13(2).

Article 42

Calculation of time limits

Any period of time prescribed in this Regulation shall be calculated as follows:

(a) where a period expressed in days, weeks or months is to be calculated from the moment at which an event occurs or an action takes place, the day during which that event occurs or that action takes place shall not be counted as falling within the period in question;

(b) a period expressed in weeks or months shall end with the expiry of whichever day in the last week or month is the same day of the week or falls on the same date as the day during which the event or action from which the period is to be calculated occurred or took place. If, in a period expressed in months, the day on which it should expire does not occur in the last month, the period shall end with the expiry of the last day of that month;

(c) time limits shall include Saturdays, Sundays and official holidays in any of the Member States concerned.

Article 43

Territorial scope

As far as the French Republic is concerned, this Regulation shall apply only to its European territory.

Article 44

Committee

1. The Commission shall be assisted by a committee. That committee shall be a committee within the meaning of Regulation (EU) No. 182/2011.

2. Where reference is made to this paragraph, Article 5 of Regulation (EU) No. 182/2011 shall apply.

Where the committee delivers no opinion, the Commission shall not adopt the draft implementing act and the third subparagraph of Article 5(4) of Regulation (EU) No. 182/2011 shall apply.

Article 45

Exercise of the delegation

1. The power to adopt delegated acts is conferred on the Commission subject to the conditions laid down in this Article.

2. The power to adopt delegated acts referred to in Articles 8(5) and 16(3) shall be conferred on the Commission for a period of 5 years from the date of entry into force of this Regulation. The Commission shall draw up a report in respect of the delegation of power not later than nine months before the end of the 5-year period. The delegation of power shall be tacitly extended for periods of an identical duration, unless the European Parliament or the Council opposes such extension not later than three months before the end of each period.

3. The delegation of power referred to in Articles 8(5) and 16(3) may be revoked at any time by the European Parliament or by the Council. A decision to revoke shall put an end to the delegation of the power specified in that decision. It shall take effect the day following the publication of the decision in the *Official Journal of the European Union* or at a later date specified therein. It shall not affect the validity of any delegated acts already in force.

4. As soon as it adopts a delegated act, the Commission shall notify it simultaneously to the European Parliament and to the Council.

5. A delegated act adopted pursuant to Articles 8(5) and 16(3) shall enter into force only if no objection has been expressed either by the European Parliament or the Council within a period of four months of notification of that act to the European Parliament and to the Council or if, before the expiry of that period, the European Parliament and the Council have both informed the Commission that they will not object. That period shall be extended by two months at the initiative of the European Parliament or of the Council.

Article 46

Monitoring and evaluation

By 21 July 2016, the Commission shall report to the European Parliament and to the Council on the application of this Regulation and, where appropriate, shall propose the necessary amendments. Member States shall forward to the Commission all information appropriate for the preparation of that report, at the latest six months before that time limit expires.

After having submitted that report, the Commission shall report to the European Parliament and to the Council on the application of this Regulation at the same time as it submits reports on the implementation of the Eurodac system provided for by Article 40 of Regulation (EU) No. 603/2013.

Article 47

Statistics

In accordance with Article 4(4) of Regulation (EC) No. 862/2007 of the European Parliament and of the Council of 11 July 2007 on Community statistics on migration and international protection,[16] Member States shall communicate to the Commission (Eurostat), statistics concerning the application of this Regulation and of Regulation (EC) No. 1560/2003.

Article 48

Repeal

Regulation (EC) No. 343/2003 is repealed.

Articles 11(1), 13, 14 and 17 of Regulation (EC) No. 1560/2003 are repealed.

References to the repealed Regulation or Articles shall be construed as references to this Regulation and shall be read in accordance with the correlation table in Annex II.

Article 49

Entry into force and applicability

This Regulation shall enter into force on the twentieth day following that of its publication in the *Official Journal of the European Union.*

It shall apply to applications for international protection lodged as from the first day of the sixth month following its entry into force and, from that date, it will apply to any request to take charge of or take back applicants, irrespective of the date on which the application was made. The Member State responsible for the examination of an application for international protection submitted before that date shall be determined in accordance with the criteria set out in Regulation (EC) No. 343/2003.

References in this Regulation to Regulation (EU) No. 603/2013, Directive 2013/32/EU and Directive 2013/33/EU shall be construed, until the dates of their application, as references to Regulation (EC) No. 2725/2000,[17] Directive 2003/9/EC[18] and Directive 2005/85/EC[19] respectively.

This Regulation shall be binding in its entirety and directly applicable in the Member States in accordance with the Treaties.

Done at Brussels, 26 June 2013.

[16] OJ L 199, 31.7.2007, p. 23.

[17] Council Regulation (EC) No. 2725/2000 of 11 December 2000 concerning the establishment of 'Eurodac' for the comparison of fingerprints for the effective application of the Dublin Convention (OJ L 316, 15.12.2000, p. 1).

[18] Council Directive 2003/9/EC of 27 January 2003 laying down minimum standards for the reception of asylum seekers (OJ L 31, 6.2.2003, p. 18).

[19] Council Directive 2005/85/EC of 1 December 2005 on minimum standards on procedures for granting and withdrawing refugee status (OJ L 326, 13.12.2005, p. 13).

Annex I

Repealed Regulations (referred to in Article 48)

Council Regulation (EC) No. 343/2003 (OJ L 50, 25.2.2003, p. 1)

Commission Regulation (EC) No. 1560/2003 only Articles 11(1), 13, 14 and 17 (OJ L 222, 5.9.2003, p. 3)

Annex II

Correlation table

Regulation (EC) No. 343/2003	This Regulation
Article 1	Article 1
Article 2(a)	Article 2(a)
Article 2(b)	—
Article 2(c)	Article 2(b)
Article 2(d)	Article 2(c)
Article 2(e)	Article 2(d)
Article 2(f)	Article 2(e)
Article 2(g)	Article 2(f)
—	Article 2(h)
—	Article 2(i)
Article 2(h)	Article 2(j)
Article 2(i)	Article 2(g)
—	Article 2(k)
Article 2(j) and (k)	Article 2(l) and (m)
—	Article 2(n)
Article 3(1)	Article 3(1)
Article 3(2)	Article 17(1)
Article 3(3)	Article 3(3)
Article 3(4)	Article 4(1), introductory wording
—	Article 4(1)(a) to (f)
—	Article 4(2) and (3)
Article 4(1) to (5)	Article 20(1) to (5)
—	Article 20(5), third subparagraph
—	Article 5
—	Article 6
Article 5(1)	Article 7(1)
Article 5(2)	Article 7(2)

—	Article 7(3)
Article 6, first paragraph	Article 8(1)
—	Article 8(3)
Article 6, second paragraph	Article 8(4)
Article 7	Article 9
Article 8	Article 10
Article 9	Article 12
Article 10	Article 13
Article 11	Article 14
Article 12	Article 15
—	Article 16
Article 13	Article 3(2)
Article 14	Article 11
Article 15(1)	Article 17(2), first subparagraph
Article 15(2)	Article 16(1)
Article 15(3)	Article 8(2)
Article 15(4)	Article 17(2), fourth subparagraph
Article 15(5)	Articles 8(5) and (6) and Article 16(2)
Article 16(1)(a)	Article 18(1)(a)
Article 16(1)(b)	Article 18(2)
Article 16(1)(c)	Article 18(1)(b)
Article 16(1)(d)	Article 18(1)(c)
Article 16(1)(e)	Article 18(1)(d)
Article 16(2)	Article 19(1)
Article 16(3)	Article 19(2), first subparagraph
—	Article 19(2), second subparagraph
Article 16(4)	Article 19(3)
—	Article 19(3), second subparagraph
Article 17	Article 21
Article 18	Article 22
Article 19(1)	Article 26(1)
Article 19(2)	Article 26(2) and Article 27(1)
—	Article 27(2) to (6)
Article 19(3)	Article 29(1)
Article 19(4)	Article 29(2)
—	Article 29(3)
Article 19(5)	Article 29(4)
Article 20(1), introductory wording	Article 23(1)
—	Article 23(2)

—	Article 23(3)
—	Article 23(4)
Article 20(1)(a)	Article 23(5), first subparagraph
—	Article 24
Article 20(1)(b)	Article 25(1)
Article 20(1)(c)	Article 25(2)
Article 20(1)(d)	Article 29(1), first subparagraph
Article 20(1)(e)	Article 26(1), (2), Article 27(1), Article 29(1), second and third subparagraphs
Article 20(2)	Article 29(2)
Article 20(3)	Article 23(5), second subparagraph
Article 20(4)	Article 29(4)
—	Article 28
—	Article 30
—	Article 31
—	Article 32
—	Article 33
Article 21(1) to (9)	Article 34(1) to (9), first to third subparagraphs
—	Article 34(9), fourth subparagraph
Article 21(10) to (12)	Article 34(10) to (12)
Article 22(1)	Article 35(1)
—	Article 35(2)
—	Article 35(3)
Article 22(2)	Article 35(4)
Article 23	Article 36
—	Article 37
—	Article 40
Article 24(1)	—
Article 24(2)	Article 41
Article 24(3)	—
Article 25(1)	Article 42
Article 25(2)	—
Article 26	Article 43
Article 27(1), (2)	Article 44(1), (2)
Article 27(3)	—
—	Article 45
Article 28	Article 46
—	Article 47
—	Article 48
Article 29	Article 49

Regulation (EC) No. 1560/2003	This Regulation
Article 11(1)	—
Article 13(1)	Article 17(2), first subparagraph
Article 13(2)	Article 17(2), second subparagraph
Article 13(3)	Article 17(2), third subparagraph
Article 13(4)	Article 17(2), first subparagraph
Article 14	Article 37
Article 17(1)	Articles 9, 10, 17(2), first subparagraph
Article 17(2)	Article 34(3)

Statement by the Council, the European Parliament and the Commission

18 December 2012

The Council and the European Parliament invite the Commission to consider, without prejudice to its right of initiative, a revision of Article 8(4) of the Recast of the Dublin Regulation once the Court of Justice rules on case C-648/11 MA and Others vs. Secretary of State for the Home Department and at the latest by the time limits set in Article 46 of the Dublin Regulation. The European Parliament and the Council will then both exercise their legislative competences, taking into account the best interests of the child.

The Commission, in a spirit of compromise and in order to ensure the immediate adoption of the proposal, accepts to consider this invitation, which it understands as being limited to these specific circumstances and not creating a precedent.

INTERNATIONAL MATERIALS

Handbook and Guidelines on Procedures and Criteria for Determining Refugee Status

under the 1951 Convention and the 1967 Protocol relating to the Status of Refugees

---

TABLE OF CONTENTS

Part Two

Annexes

Guidelines on International Protection

Foreword

The 1951 Convention relating to the Status of Refugees and its 1967 Protocol have served as the central instruments underpinning the international refugee protection regime for sixty years. In this anniversary year, the Division of International Protection is pleased to issue the third edition of the Handbook on Procedures and Criteria for Determining Refugee Status. It is reprinted along with the Guidelines on International Protection, which supplement the Handbook.

Since the establishment of the Office of the United Nations High Commissioner for Refugees (UNHCR) in 1950 and the adoption of the 1951 Convention, providing international protection to persons displaced across borders has remained a formidable global challenge. At the time of reissuing this Handbook, 148 States are parties to either or both the 1951 Convention and the 1967 Protocol. This growth in membership over the past sixty years demonstrates the continuing applicability of these instruments to most of today's displacement situations.

Together with its 1967 Protocol, the Convention provides a universal code for the treatment of refugees uprooted from their countries as a result of persecution, violent conflict, serious human rights violations or other forms of serious harm. The preamble to the 1951 Convention underscores one of its main purposes, which is to assure refugees the widest possible exercise of their fundamental rights and freedoms. Core principles of the 1951 Convention include those of non-discrimination, *non-refoulement*, non-penalization for illegal entry or stay, and the acquisition and enjoyment of rights over time.

The Convention has proven to be a living and dynamic instrument, covering persons fleeing a wide range of socio-political events. It is also sufficiently flexible and allows for age, gender and diversity sensitive interpretations. As illustrated in the Handbook and Guidelines, legislative and jurisprudential developments over the past decades have led to a greater understanding of refugee claims in many existing and emerging areas.

In addition, a number of regional instruments complementing the 1951 Convention have been developed, resulting in the elaboration of the refugee concept to meet particular regional challenges related to forced displacement. Parallel developments in other areas of international law, most notably international human rights law, international humanitarian law and international criminal law, have also influenced the evolution of refugee law.

The Handbook was first issued in September 1979 at the request of Member States of the Executive Committee of the High Commissioner's Programme. A second edition was released in January 1992, which updated information concerning accessions to the international refugee instruments. To preserve its integrity, the Handbook remains unchanged also in the present edition, although the annexes have again been updated.

In addition to the Handbook, and in response to the varying legal interpretations of Article 1 of the 1951 Convention in national jurisdictions, UNHCR has continued to issue legal positions on specific questions of international refugee law. In this connection, UNHCR has gazetted "Guidelines on International Protection", as envisaged under the Agenda for Protection following the 50th anniversary events in 2001-2002.* These Guidelines complement and update the Handbook and should be read in combination with it. Included in this edition are the first eight Guidelines in the series.

The explanations provided in this publication of key components of refugee status determination are based on the accumulated views of UNHCR, State practice, Executive Committee Conclusions, academic literature and judicial decisions at national, regional and international levels, over a sixty-year period. The Handbook and Guidelines are issued pursuant to UNHCR's supervisory responsibility contained in paragraph 8 of the 1950 Statute of UNHCR in conjunction with Articles 35 and 36 of the 1951 Convention and Article II of the 1967 Protocol.

The Handbook and the Guidelines are intended to guide government officials, judges, practitioners, as well as UNHCR staff applying the refugee definition. It is hoped that they will continue to provide an important reference for refugee status determination around the world and help resolve variations in interpretation.

Volker Türk

Director
Division of International Protection
Office of the United Nations High Commissioner for Refugees
Geneva, December 2011

Introduction

International instruments defining the term "refugee"

A. Early instruments (1921–1946)

1. Early in the twentieth century, the refugee problem became the concern of the international community, which, for humanitarian reasons, began to assume responsibility for protecting and assisting refugees.

2. The pattern of international action on behalf of refugees was established by the League of Nations and led to the adoption of a number of international agreements for their benefit. These instruments are referred to in Article 1A(1) of the 1951 Convention relating to the Status of Refugees (see paragraph 32 below).

* See, UNHCR, *Agenda for Protection*, A/AC.96/965/Add.1, 26 June 2002, Goal 1, available at: <http://www.unhcr.org/cgi-bin/texis/vtx/home/opendocPDFViewer.html?docid=3d3e61b84&query=agenda%20for%20protection>; UNHCR Executive Committee, *General Conclusion on International Protection*, No. 92 (LIII) – 2002, 8 October 2002, available at: <http://www.unhcr.org/refworld/docid/3dafdce27.html>; UN General Assembly, *Office of the United Nations High Commissioner for Refugees: Resolution adopted by the General Assembly*, 6 February 2003, A/RES/57/187, para. 6, available at: <http://www.unhcr.org/refworld/docid/3f43553e4.html>.

3. The definitions in these instruments relate each category of refugees to their national origin, to the territory that they left and to the lack of diplomatic protection by their former home country. With this type of definition "by categories" interpretation was simple and caused no great difficulty in ascertaining who was a refugee.

4. Although few persons covered by the terms of the early instruments are likely to request a formal determination of refugee status at the present time, such cases could occasionally arise. They are dealt with below in Chapter II, A. Persons who meet the definitions of international instruments prior to the 1951 Convention are usually referred to as "statutory refugees".

B. 1951 Convention relating to the Status of Refugees

5. Soon after the Second World War, as the refugee problem had not been solved, the need was felt for a new international instrument to define the legal status of refugees. Instead of ad hoc agreements adopted in relation to specific refugee situations, there was a call for an instrument containing a general definition of who was to be considered a refugee. The Convention relating to the Status of Refugees was adopted by a Conference of Plenipotentiaries of the United Nations on 28 July 1951, and entered into force on 21 April 1954. In the following paragraphs it is referred to as "the 1951 Convention". (The text of the 1951 Convention will be found in Annex II.)

C. Protocol relating to the Status of Refugees

6. According to the general definition contained in the 1951 Convention, a refugee is a person who:

> As a result of events occurring before 1 January 1951 and owing to well-founded fear of being persecuted... is outside his country of nationality...

7. The 1951 dateline originated in the wish of Governments, at the time the Convention was adopted, to limit their obligations to refugee situations that were known to exist at that time, or to those which might subsequently arise from events that had already occurred.[1]

8. With the passage of time and the emergence of new refugee situations, the need was increasingly felt to make the provisions of the 1951 Convention applicable to such new refugees. As a result, a Protocol relating to the Status of Refugees was prepared. After consideration by the General Assembly of the United Nations, it was opened for accession on 31 January 1967 and entered into force on 4 October 1967.

9. By accession to the 1967 Protocol, States undertake to apply the substantive provisions of the 1951 Convention to refugees as defined in the Convention, but without the 1951 dateline. Although related to the Convention in this way, the Protocol is an independent instrument, accession to which is not limited to States parties to the Convention.

10. In the following paragraphs, the 1967 Protocol relating to the Status of Refugees is referred to as "the 1967 Protocol". (The text of the Protocol will be found in Annex III.)

11. At the time of writing, 78 States are parties to the 1951 Convention or to the 1967 Protocol or to both instruments. (A list of the States parties will be found in Annex IV.)

[1] The 1951 Convention also provides for the possibility of introducing a geographic limitation (see paras. 108 to 110 below).

D. Main provisions of the 1951 Convention and the 1967 Protocol

12. The 1951 Convention and the 1967 Protocol contain three types of provisions:

(i) Provisions giving the *basic definition* of who is (and who is not) a refugee and who, having been a refugee, has ceased to be one. The discussion and interpretation of these provisions constitute the main body of the present Handbook, intended for the guidance of those whose task it is to determine refugee status.

(ii) Provisions that define the *legal status* of refugees and their rights and duties in their country of refuge. Although these provisions have no influence on the process of determination of refugee status, the authority entrusted with this process should be aware of them, for its decision may indeed have far-reaching effects for the individual or family concerned.

(iii) Other provisions dealing with the *implementation* of the instruments from the administrative and diplomatic standpoint. Article 35 of the 1951 Convention and Article 11 of the 1967 Protocol contain an undertaking by Contracting States to cooperate with the Office of the United Nations High Commissioner for Refugees in the exercise of its functions and, in particular, to facilitate its duty of supervising the application of the provisions of these instruments.

E. Statute of the Office of the United Nations High Commissioner for Refugees

13. The instruments described above under A-C define the persons who are to be considered refugees and require the parties to accord a certain status to refugees in their respective territories.

14. Pursuant to a decision of the General Assembly, the Office of the United Nations High Commissioner for Refugees ("UNHCR") was established as of 1 January 1951. The Statute of the Office is annexed to Resolution 428 (V), adopted by the General Assembly on 14 December 1950. According to the Statute, the High Commissioner is called upon – *inter alia* – to provide international protection, under the auspices of the United Nations, to refugees falling within the competence of his Office.

15. The Statute contains definitions of those persons to whom the High Commissioner's competence extends, which are very close to, though not identical with, the definition contained in the 1951 Convention. By virtue of these definitions the High Commissioner is competent for refugees irrespective of any dateline[2] or geographic limitation.[3]

16. Thus, a person who meets the criteria of the UNHCR Statute qualifies for the protection of the United Nations provided by the High Commissioner, regardless of whether or not he is in a country that is a party to the 1951 Convention or the 1967 Protocol or whether or not he has been recognized by his host country as a refugee under either of these instruments. Such refugees, being within the High Commissioner's mandate, are usually referred to as "mandate refugees".

17. From the foregoing, it will be seen that a person can simultaneously be both a mandate refugee *and* a refugee under the 1951 Convention or the 1967 Protocol. He may, however, be in a country that is not bound by either of these instruments, or he may be

[2] See paras. 35 and 36 below.

[3] See paras. 108 and 110 below.

excluded from recognition as a Convention refugee by the application of the dateline or the geographic limitation. In such cases he would still qualify for protection by the High Commissioner under the terms of the Statute.

18. The above mentioned Resolution 428 (V) and the Statute of the High Commissioner's Office call for cooperation between Governments and the High Commissioner's Office in dealing with refugee problems. The High Commissioner is designated as the authority charged with providing inter-national protection to refugees, and is required *inter alia* to promote the conclusion and ratification of international conventions for the protection of refugees, and to supervise their application.

19. Such cooperation, combined with his supervisory function, forms the basis for the High Commissioner's fundamental interest in the process of determining refugee status under the 1951 Convention and the 1967 Protocol. The part played by the High Commissioner is reflected, to varying degrees, in the procedures for the determination of refugee status established by a number of Governments.

F. Regional instruments relating to refugees

20. In addition to the 1951 Convention and the 1967 Protocol, and the Statute of the Office of the United Nations High Commissioner for Refugees, there are a number of regional agreements, conventions and other instruments relating to refugees, particularly in Africa, the Americas and Europe. These regional instruments deal with such matters as the granting of asylum, travel documents and travel facilities, etc. Some also contain a definition of the term "refugee", or of persons entitled to asylum.

21. In Latin America, the problem of diplomatic and territorial asylum is dealt with in a number of regional instruments including the Treaty on International Penal Law, (Montevideo, 1889); the Agreement on Extradition, (Caracas, 1911); the Convention on Asylum, (Havana, 1928); the Convention on Political Asylum, (Montevideo, 1933); the Convention on Diplomatic Asylum, (Caracas, 1954); and the Convention on Territorial Asylum, (Caracas, 1954).

22. A more recent regional instrument is the Convention Governing the Specific Aspects of Refugee Problems in Africa, adopted by the Assembly of Heads of State and Government of the Organization of African Unity on 10 September 1969. This Convention contains a definition of the term "refugee", consisting of two parts: the first part is identical with the definition in the 1967 Protocol (i.e. the definition in the 1951 Convention without the date-line or geographic limitation). The second part applies the term "refugee" to:

> every person who, owing to external aggression, occupation, foreign domination or events seriously disturbing public order in either part or the whole of his country of origin or nationality, is compelled to leave his place of habitual residence in order to seek refuge in another place outside his country of origin or nationality.

23. The present Handbook deals only with the determination of refugee status under the two international instruments of universal scope: the 1951 Convention and the 1967 Protocol.

G. Asylum and the treatment of refugees

24. The Handbook does not deal with questions closely related to the determination of refugee status e.g. the granting of asylum to refugees or the legal treatment of refugees after they have been recognized as such.

25. Although there are references to asylum in the Final Act of the Conference of Plenipotentiaries as well as in the Preamble to the Convention, the granting of asylum is not dealt with in the 1951 Convention or the 1967 Protocol. The High Commissioner has always pleaded for a generous asylum policy in the spirit of the Universal Declaration of Human Rights and the Declaration on Territorial Asylum, adopted by the General Assembly of the United Nations on 10 December 1948 and on 14 December 1967 respectively.

26. With respect to the treatment within the territory of States, this is regulated as regards refugees by the main provisions of the 1951 Convention and 1967 Protocol (see paragraph 12(ii) above). Furthermore, attention should be drawn to Recommendation E contained in the Final Act of the Conference of Plenipotentiaries which adopted the 1951 Convention:

> The Conference Expresses the hope that the Convention relating to the Status of Refugees will have value as an example exceeding its contractual scope and that all nations will be guided by it in granting so far as possible to persons in their territory as refugees and who would not be covered by the terms of the Convention, the treatment for which it provides.

27. This recommendation enables States to solve such problems as may arise with regard to persons who are not regarded as fully satisfying the criteria of the definition of the term "refugee".

Part One

Criteria for the Determination of Refugee Status

Chapter I

General Principles

28. A person is a refugee within the meaning of the 1951 Convention as soon as he fulfils the criteria contained in the definition. This would necessarily occur prior to the time at which his refugee status is formally determined. Recognition of his refugee status does not therefore make him a refugee but declares him to be one. He does not become a refugee because of recognition, but is recognized because he is a refugee.

29. Determination of refugee status is a process which takes place in two stages. First, it is necessary to ascertain the relevant facts of the case. Secondly, the definitions in the 1951 Convention and the 1967 Protocol have to be applied to the facts thus ascertained.

30. The provisions of the 1951 Convention defining who is a refugee consist of three parts, which have been termed respectively "inclusion", "cessation" and "exclusion" clauses.

31. The inclusion clauses define the criteria that a person must satisfy in order to be a refugee. They form the positive basis upon which the determination of refugee status is made. The so-called cessation and exclusion clauses have a negative significance; the former indicate the conditions under which a refugee ceases to be a refugee and the latter enumerate the circumstances in which a person is excluded from the application of the 1951 Convention although meeting the positive criteria of the inclusion clauses.

Chapter II
Inclusion Clauses

A. Definitions

(1) Statutory Refugees

32. Article 1A(1) of the 1951 Convention deals with statutory refugees, i.e. persons considered to be refugees under the provisions of international instruments preceding the Convention. This provision states that:

> For the purposes of the present Convention, the term 'refugee' shall apply to any person who:
> (1) Has been considered a refugee under the Arrangements of 12 May 1926 and 30 June 1928 or under the Conventions of 28 October 1933 and 10 February 1938, the Protocol of 14 September 1939 or the Constitution of the International Refugee Organization;
> Decisions of non-eligibility taken by the International Refugee Organization during the period of its activities shall not prevent the status of refugees being accorded to persons who fulfil the conditions of paragraph 2 of this section.

33. The above enumeration is given in order to provide a link with the past and to ensure the continuity of international protection of refugees who became the concern of the international community at various earlier periods. As already indicated (para. 4 above), these instruments have by now lost much of their significance, and a discussion of them here would be of little practical value. However, a person who has been considered a refugee under the terms of any of these instruments is automatically a refugee under the 1951 Convention. Thus, a holder of a so-called "Nansen Passport"[4] or a "Certificate of Eligibility" issued by the International Refugee Organization must be considered a refugee under the 1951 Convention unless one of the cessation clauses has become applicable to his case or he is excluded from the application of the Convention by one of the exclusion clauses. This also applies to a surviving child of a statutory refugee.

(2) General definition in the 1951 Convention

34. According to Article 1A(2) of the 1951 Convention the term "refugee" shall apply to any person who:

> As a result of events occurring before 1 January 1951 and owing to well founded fear of being persecuted for reasons of race, religion, nationality, membership of a particular social group or political opinion, is outside the country of his nationality and is unable or, owing to such fear, is unwilling to avail himself of the protection of that country; or who, not having a nationality and being outside the country of his former habitual residence as a result of such events, is unable or, owing to such fear, is unwilling to return to it.

This general definition is discussed in detail below.

B. Interpretation of terms

(1) "Events occurring before 1 January 1951"

35. The origin of this 1951 dateline is explained in paragraph 7 of the Introduction. As a result of the 1967 Protocol this dateline has lost much of its practical significance. An

[4] "Nansen Passport": a certificate of identity for use as a travel document, issued to refugees under the provisions of pre-war instruments.

interpretation of the word "events" is therefore of interest only in the small number of States parties to the 1951 Convention that are not also party to the 1967 Protocol.[5]

36. The word "events" is not defined in the 1951 Convention, but was understood to mean "happenings of major importance involving territorial or profound political changes as well as systematic programmes of persecution which are after-effects of earlier changes".[6] The dateline refers to "events" as a result of which, and not to the date on which, a person becomes a refugee, not does it apply to the date on which he left his country. A refugee may have left his country before or after the datelines, provided that his fear of persecution is due to "events" that occurred before the dateline or to after-effects occurring at a later date as a result of such events.[7]

(2) *"well founded fear of being persecuted"*

(a) General analysis

37. The phrase "well-founded fear of being persecuted" is the key phrase of the definition. It reflects the views of its authors as to the main elements of refugee character. It replaces the earlier method of defining refugees by categories (i.e. persons of a certain origin not enjoying the protection of their country) by the general concept of "fear" for a relevant motive. Since fear is subjective, the definition involves a subjective element in the person applying for recognition as a refugee. Determination of refugee status will therefore primarily require an evaluation of the applicant's statements rather than a judgement on the situation prevailing in his country of origin.

38. To the element of fear – a state of mind and a subjective condition – is added the qualification "well-founded". This implies that it is not only the frame of mind of the person concerned that determines his refugee status, but that this frame of mind must be supported by an objective situation. The term "well-founded fear" therefore contains a subjective and an objective element, and in determining whether well-founded fear exists, both elements must be taken into consideration.

39. It may be assumed that, unless he seeks adventure or just wishes to see the world, a person would not normally abandon his home and country without some compelling reason. There may be many reasons that are compelling and understandable, but only one motive has been singled out to denote a refugee. The expression "owing to well-founded fear of being persecuted" – for the reasons stated – by indicating a specific motive automatically makes all other reasons for escape irrelevant to the definition. It rules out such persons as victims of famine or natural disaster, unless they also have well-founded fear of persecution for one of the reasons stated. Such other motives may not, however, be altogether irrelevant to the process of determining refugee status, since all the circumstances need to be taken into account for a proper understanding of the applicant's case.

40. An evaluation of the *subjective element* is inseparable from an assessment of the personality of the applicant, since psychological reactions of different individuals may not be the same in identical conditions. One person may have strong political or religious convictions, the disregard of which would make his life intolerable; another may have no

[5] See Annex IV.

[6] UN Document E/1618 page 39.

[7] *Loc. cit.*

such strong convictions. One person may make an impulsive decision to escape; another may carefully plan his departure.

41. Due to the importance that the definition attaches to the subjective element, an assessment of credibility is indispensable where the case is not sufficiently clear from the facts on record. It will be necessary to take into account the personal and family background of the applicant, his membership of a particular racial, religious, national, social or political group, his own interpretation of his situation, and his personal experiences – in other words, everything that may serve to indicate that the predominant motive for his application is fear. Fear must be reasonable. Exaggerated fear, however, may be well-founded if, in all the circumstances of the case, such a state of mind can be regarded as justified.

42. As regards the objective element, it is necessary to evaluate the statements made by the applicant. The competent authorities that are called upon to determine refugee status are not required to pass judgement on conditions in the applicant's country of origin. The applicant's statements cannot, however, be considered in the abstract, and must be viewed in the context of the relevant background situation. A knowledge of conditions in the applicant's country of origin – while not a primary objective – is an important element in assessing the applicant's credibility. In general, the applicant's fear should be considered well-founded if he can establish, to a reasonable degree, that his continued stay in his country of origin has become intolerable to him for the reasons stated in the definition, or would for the same reasons be intolerable if he returned there.

43. These considerations need not necessarily be based on the applicant's own personal experience. What, for example, happened to his friends and relatives and other members of the same racial or social group may well show that his fear that sooner or later he also will become a victim of persecution is well-founded. The laws of the country of origin, and particularly the manner in which they are applied, will be relevant. The situation of each person must, however, be assessed on its own merits. In the case of a well-known personality, the possibility of persecution may be greater than in the case of a person in obscurity. All these factors, e.g. a person's character, his background, his influence, his wealth or his outspokenness, may lead to the conclusion that his fear of persecution is "well-founded".

44. While refugee status must normally be determined on an individual basis, situations have also arisen in which entire groups have been displaced under circumstances indicating that members of the group could be considered individually as refugees. In such situations the need to provide assistance is often extremely urgent and it may not be possible for purely practical reasons to carry out an individual determination of refugee status for each member of the group. Recourse has therefore been had to so-called "group determination" of refugee status, whereby each member of the group is regarded *prima facie* (i.e. in the absence of evidence to the contrary) as a refugee.

45. Apart from the situations of the type referred to in the preceding paragraph, an applicant for refugee status must normally show good reason why he individually fears persecution. It may be assumed that a person has well-founded fear of being persecuted if he has already been the victim of persecution for one of the reasons enumerated in the 1951 Convention. However, the word "fear" refers not only to persons who have actually been persecuted, but also to those who wish to avoid a situation entailing the risk of persecution.

46. The expressions "fear of persecution" or even "persecution" are usually foreign to a refugee's normal vocabulary. A refugee will indeed only rarely invoke "fear of

persecution" in these terms, though it will often be implicit in his story. Again, while a refugee may have very definite opinions for which he has had to suffer, he may not, for psychological reasons, be able to describe his experiences and situation in political terms.

47. A typical test of the well-foundedness of fear will arise when an applicant is in possession of a valid national passport. It has sometimes been claimed that possession of a passport signifies that the issuing authorities do not intend to persecute the holder, for otherwise they would not have issued a passport to him. Though this may be true in some cases, many persons have used a legal exit from their country as the only means of escape without ever having revealed their political opinions, a knowledge of which might place them in a dangerous situation vis-à-vis the authorities.

48. Possession of a passport cannot therefore always be considered as evidence of loyalty on the part of the holder, or as an indication of the absence of fear. A passport may even be issued to a person who is undesired in his country of origin, with the sole purpose of securing his departure, and there may also be cases where a passport has been obtained surreptitiously. In conclusion, therefore, the mere possession of a valid national passport is no bar to refugee status.

49. If, on the other hand, an applicant, without good reason, insists on retaining a valid passport of a country of whose protection he is allegedly unwilling to avail himself, this may cast doubt on the validity of his claim to have "well-founded fear". Once recognized, a refugee should not normally retain his national passport.

50. There may, however, be exceptional situations in which a person fulfilling the criteria of refugee status may retain his national passport – or be issued with a new one by the authorities of his country of origin under special arrangements. Particularly where such arrangements do not imply that the holder of the national passport is free to return to his country without prior permission, they may not be incompatible with refugee status.

(b) Persecution

51. There is no universally accepted definition of "persecution", and various attempts to formulate such a definition have met with little success. From Article 33 of the 1951 Convention it may be inferred that a threat to life or freedom on account of race, religion, nationality, political opinion or membership of a particular social group is always persecution. Other serious violations of human rights – for the same reasons – would also constitute persecution.

52. Whether other prejudicial actions or threats would amount to persecution will depend on the circumstances of each case, including the subjective element to which reference has been made in the preceding paragraphs. The subjective character of fear of persecution requires an evaluation of the opinions and feelings of the person concerned. It is also in the light of such opinions and feelings that any actual or anticipated measures against him must necessarily be viewed. Due to variations in the psychological make-up of individuals and in the circumstances of each case, interpretations of what amounts to persecution are bound to vary.

53. In addition, an applicant may have been subjected to various measures not in themselves amounting to persecution (e.g. discrimination in different forms), in some cases combined with other adverse factors (e.g. general atmosphere of insecurity in the country of origin). In such situations, the various elements involved may, if taken together, produce an effect on the mind of the applicant that can reasonably justify a claim to well-founded

fear of persecution on "cumulative grounds". Needless to say, it is not possible to lay down a general rule as to what cumulative reasons can give rise to a valid claim to refugee status. This will necessarily depend on all the circumstances, including the particular geographical, historical and ethnological context.

(c) Discrimination

54. Differences in the treatment of various groups do indeed exist to a greater or lesser extent in many societies. Persons who receive less favourable treatment as a result of such differences are not necessarily victims of persecution. It is only in certain circumstances that discrimination will amount to persecution. This would be so if measures of discrimination lead to consequences of a substantially prejudicial nature for the person concerned, e.g. serious restrictions on his right to earn his livelihood, his right to practise his religion, or his access to normally available educational facilities.

55. Where measures of discrimination are, in themselves, not of a serious character, they may nevertheless give rise to a reasonable fear of persecution if they produce, in the mind of the person concerned, a feeling of apprehension and insecurity as regards his future existence. Whether or not such measures of discrimination in themselves amount to persecution must be determined in the light of all the circumstances. A claim to fear of persecution will of course be stronger where a person has been the victim of a number of discriminatory measures of this type and where there is thus a cumulative element involved.[8]

(d) Punishment

56. Persecution must be distinguished from punishment for a common law offence. Persons fleeing from prosecution or punishment for such an offence are not normally refugees. It should be recalled that a refugee is a victim – or potential victim – of injustice, not a fugitive from justice.

57. The above distinction may, however, occasionally be obscured. In the first place, a person guilty of a common law offence may be liable to excessive punishment, which may amount to persecution within the meaning of the definition. Moreover, penal prosecution for a reason mentioned in the definition (for example, in respect of "illegal" religious instruction given to a child) may in itself amount to persecution.

58. Secondly, there may be cases in which a person, besides fearing prosecution or punishment for a common law crime, may also have "well founded fear of persecution". In such cases the person concerned is a refugee. It may, however, be necessary to consider whether the crime in question is not of such a serious character as to bring the applicant within the scope of one of the exclusion clauses.[9]

59. In order to determine whether prosecution amounts to persecution, it will also be necessary to refer to the laws of the country concerned, for it is possible for a law not to be in conformity with accepted human rights standards. More often, however, it may not be the law but its application that is discriminatory. Prosecution for an offence against "public order", e.g. for distribution of pamphlets, could for example be a vehicle for the persecution of the individual on the grounds of the political content of the publication.

[8] See also para. 53.

[9] See paras. 144 to 156.

60. In such cases, due to the obvious difficulty involved in evaluating the laws of another country, national authorities may frequently have to take decisions by using their own national legislation as a yardstick. Moreover, recourse may usefully be had to the principles set out in the various international instruments relating to human rights, in particular the International Covenants on Human Rights, which contain binding commitments for the States parties and are instruments to which many States parties to the 1951 Convention have acceded.

(e) Consequences of unlawful departure or unauthorized stay outside country of origin

61. The legislation of certain States imposes severe penalties on nationals who depart from the country in an unlawful manner or remain abroad without authorization. Where there is reason to believe that a person, due to his illegal departure or unauthorized stay abroad is liable to such severe penalties his recognition as a refugee will be justified if it can be shown that his motives for leaving or remaining outside the country are related to the reasons enumerated in Article 1A(2) of the 1951 Convention (see paragraph 66 below).

(f) Economic migrants distinguished from refugees

62. A migrant is a person who, for reasons other than those contained in the definition, voluntarily leaves his country in order to take up residence elsewhere. He may be moved by the desire for change or adventure, or by family or other reasons of a personal nature. If he is moved exclusively by economic considerations, he is an economic migrant and not a refugee.

63. The distinction between an economic migrant and a refugee is, however, sometimes blurred in the same way as the distinction between economic and political measures in an applicant's country of origin is not always clear. Behind economic measures affecting a person's livelihood there may be racial, religious or political aims or intentions directed against a particular group. Where economic measures destroy the economic existence of a particular section of the population (e.g. withdrawal of trading rights from, or discriminatory or excessive taxation of, a specific ethnic or religious group), the victims may according to the circumstances become refugees on leaving the country.

64. Whether the same would apply to victims of general economic measures (i.e. those that are applied to the whole population without discrimination) would depend on the circumstances of the case. Objections to general economic measures are not by themselves good reasons for claiming refugee status. On the other hand, what appears at first sight to be primarily an economic motive for departure may in reality also involve a political element, and it may be the political opinions of the individual that expose him to serious consequences, rather than his objections to the economic measures themselves.

(g) Agents of persecution

65. Persecution is normally related to action by the authorities of a country. It may also emanate from sections of the population that do not respect the standards established by the laws of the country concerned. A case in point may be religious intolerance,

amounting to persecution, in a country otherwise secular, but where sizeable fractions of the population do not respect the religious beliefs of their neighbours. Where serious discriminatory or other offensive acts are committed by the local populace, they can be considered as persecution if they are knowingly tolerated by the authorities, or if the authorities refuse, or prove unable, to offer effective protection.

(3) "for reasons of race, religion, nationality, membership of a particular social group or political opinion"

(a) General analysis

66. In order to be considered a refugee, a person must show well-founded fear of persecution for one of the reasons stated above. It is immaterial whether the persecution arises from any single one of these reasons or from a combination of two or more of them. Often the applicant himself may not be aware of the reasons for the persecution feared. It is not, however, his duty to analyze his case to such an extent as to identify the reasons in detail.

67. It is for the examiner, when investigating the facts of the case, to ascertain the reason or reasons for the persecution feared and to decide whether the definition in the 1951 Convention is met with in this respect. It is evident that the reasons for persecution under these various headings will frequently overlap. Usually there will be more than one element combined in one person, e.g. a political opponent who belongs to a religious or national group, or both, and the combination of such reasons in his person may be relevant in evaluating his well-founded fear.

(b) Race

68. Race, in the present connexion, has to be understood in its widest sense to include all kinds of ethnic groups that are referred to as "races" in common usage. Frequently it will also entail membership of a specific social group of common descent forming a minority within a larger population. Discrimination for reasons of race has found world-wide condemnation as one of the most striking violations of human rights. Racial discrimination, therefore, represents an important element in determining the existence of persecution.

69. Discrimination on racial grounds will frequently amount to persecution in the sense of the 1951 Convention. This will be the case if, as a result of racial discrimination, a person's human dignity is affected to such an extent as to be incompatible with the most elementary and inalienable human rights, or where the disregard of racial barriers is subject to serious consequences.

70. The mere fact of belonging to a certain racial group will normally not be enough to substantiate a claim to refugee status. There may, however, be situations where, due to particular circumstances affecting the group, such membership will in itself be sufficient ground to fear persecution.

(c) Religion

71. The Universal Declaration of Human Rights and the Human Rights Covenant proclaim the right to freedom of thought, conscience and religion, which right includes the freedom of a person to change his religion and his freedom to manifest it in public or private, in teaching, practice, worship and observance.

72. Persecution for "reasons of religion" may assume various forms, e.g. prohibition of membership of a religious community, of worship in private or in public, of religious instruction, or serious measures of discrimination imposed on persons because they practise their religion or belong to a particular religious community.

73. Mere membership of a particular religious community will normally not be enough to substantiate a claim to refugee status. There may, however, be special circumstances where mere membership can be a sufficient ground.

(d) Nationality

74. The term "nationality" in this context is not to be understood only as "citizenship". It refers also to membership of an ethnic or linguistic group and may occasionally overlap with the term "race". Persecution for reasons of nationality may consist of adverse attitudes and measures directed against a national (ethnic, linguistic) minority and in certain circumstances the fact of belonging to such a minority may in itself give rise to well-founded fear of persecution.

75. The co-existence within the boundaries of a State of two or more national (ethnic, linguistic) groups may create situations of conflict and also situations of persecution or danger of persecution. It may not always be easy to distinguish between persecution for reasons of nationality and persecution for reasons of political opinion when a conflict between national groups is combined with political movements, particularly where a political movement is identified with a specific "nationality".

76. Whereas in most cases persecution for reason of nationality is feared by persons belonging to a national minority, there have been many cases in various continents where a person belonging to a majority group may fear persecution by a dominant minority.

(e) Membership of a particular social group

77. A "particular social group" normally comprises persons of similar background, habits or social status. A claim to fear of persecution under this heading may frequently overlap with a claim to fear of persecution on other grounds, i.e. race, religion or nationality.

78. Membership of such a particular social group may be at the root of persecution because there is no confidence in the group's loyalty to the Government or because the political outlook, antecedents or economic activity of its members, or the very existence of the social group as such, is held to be an obstacle to the Government's policies.

79. Mere membership of a particular social group will not normally be enough to substantiate a claim to refugee status. There may, however, be special circumstances where mere membership can be a sufficient ground to fear persecution.

(f) Political opinion

80. Holding political opinions different from those of the Government is not in itself a ground for claiming refugee status, and an applicant must show that he has a fear of persecution for holding such opinions. This presupposes that the applicant holds opinions not tolerated by the authorities, which are critical of their policies or methods. It also

presupposes that such opinions have come to the notice of the authorities or are attributed by them to the applicant. The political opinions of a teacher or writer may be more manifest than those of a person in a less exposed position. The relative importance or tenacity of the applicant's opinions – in so far as this can be established from all the circumstances of the case – will also be relevant.

81. While the definition speaks of persecution "for reasons of political opinion" it may not always be possible to establish a causal link between the opinion expressed and the related measures suffered or feared by the applicant. Such measures have only rarely been based expressly on "opinion". More frequently, such measures take the form of sanctions for alleged criminal acts against the ruling power. It will, therefore, be necessary to establish the applicant's political opinion, which is at the root of his behaviour, and the fact that it has led or may lead to the persecution that he claims to fear.

82. As indicated above, persecution "for reasons of political opinion" implies that an applicant holds an opinion that either has been expressed or has come to the attention of the authorities. There may, however, also be situations in which the applicant has not given any expression to his opinions. Due to the strength of his convictions, however, it may be reasonable to assume that his opinions will sooner or later find expression and that the applicant will, as a result, come into conflict with the authorities. Where this can reasonably be assumed, the applicant can be considered to have fear of persecution for reasons of political opinion.

83. An applicant claiming fear of persecution because of political opinion need not show that the authorities of his country of origin knew of his opinions before he left the country. He may have concealed his political opinion and never have suffered any discrimination or persecution. However, the mere fact of refusing to avail himself of the protection of his Government, or a refusal to return, may disclose the applicant's true state of mind and give rise to fear of persecution. In such circumstances the test of well-founded fear would be based on an assessment of the consequences that an applicant having certain political dispositions would have to face if he returned. This applies particularly to the so-called refugee "*sur place*".[10]

84. Where a person is subject to prosecution or punishment for a political offence, a distinction may have to be drawn according to whether the prosecution is for political *opinion* or for politically-motivated *acts*. If the prosecution pertains to a punishable act committed out of political motives, and if the anticipated punishment is in conformity with the general law of the country concerned, fear of such prosecution will not in itself make the applicant a refugee.

85. Whether a political offender can also be considered a refugee will depend upon various other factors. Prosecution for an offence may, depending upon the circumstances, be a pretext for punishing the offender for his political opinions or the expression thereof. Again, there may be reason to believe that a political offender would be exposed to excessive or arbitrary punishment for the alleged offence. Such excessive or arbitrary punishment will amount to persecution.

86. In determining whether a political offender can be considered a refugee, regard should also be had to the following elements: personality of the applicant, his political opinion, the motive behind the act, the nature of the act committed, the nature of the prosecution and its motives; finally, also, the nature of the law on which the prosecution

[10] See paras. 94 to 96.

is based. These elements may go to show that the person concerned has a fear of persecution and not merely a fear of prosecution and punishment – within the law – for an act committed by him.

(4) "is outside the country of his nationality"

(a) General analysis

87. In this context, "nationality" refers to "citizenship". The phrase "is outside the country of his nationality" relates to persons who have a nationality, as distinct from stateless persons. In the majority of cases, refugees retain the nationality of their country of origin.

88. It is a general requirement for refugee status that an applicant who has a nationality be outside the country of his nationality. There are no exceptions to this rule. International protection cannot come into play as long as a person is within the territorial jurisdiction of his home country.[11]

89. Where, therefore, an applicant alleges fear of persecution in relation to the country of his nationality, it should be established that he does in fact possess the nationality of that country. There may, however, be uncertainty as to whether a person has a nationality. He may not know himself, or he may wrongly claim to have a particular nationality or to be stateless. Where his nationality cannot be clearly established, his refugee status should be determined in a similar manner to that of a stateless person, i.e. instead of the country of his nationality, the country of his former habitual residence will have to be taken into account. (See paragraphs 101 to 105 below.)

90. As mentioned above, an applicant's well-founded fear of persecution must be in relation to the country of his nationality. As long as he has no fear in relation to the country of his nationality, he can be expected to avail himself of that country's protection. He is not in need of international protection and is therefore not a refugee.

91. The fear of being persecuted need not always extend to the *whole* territory of the refugee's country of nationality. Thus in ethnic clashes or in cases of grave disturbances involving civil war conditions, persecution of a specific ethnic or national group may occur in only one part of the country. In such situations, a person will not be excluded from refugee status merely because he could have sought refuge in another part of the same country, if under all the circumstances it would not have been reasonable to expect him to do so.

92. The situation of persons having more than one nationality is dealt with in paragraphs 106 and 107 below.

93. Nationality may be proved by the possession of a national passport. Possession of such a passport creates a *prima facie* presumption that the holder is a national of the country of issue, unless the passport itself states otherwise. A person holding a passport showing him to be a national of the issuing country, but who claims that he does not

[11] In certain countries, particularly in Latin America, there is a custom of "diplomatic asylum", i.e. granting refuge to political fugitives in foreign embassies. While a person thus sheltered may be considered to be outside his country's jurisdiction, he is not outside its territory and cannot therefore be considered under the terms of the 1951 Convention. The former notion of the "extraterritoriality" of embassies has lately been replaced by the term "inviolability" used in the 1961 Vienna Convention on Diplomatic Relations.

possess that country's nationality, must substantiate his claim, for example, by showing that the passport is a so-called "passport of convenience" (an apparently regular national passport that is sometimes issued by a national authority to non-nationals). However, a mere assertion by the holder that the passport was issued to him as a matter of convenience for travel purposes only is not sufficient to rebut the presumption of nationality. In certain cases, it might be possible to obtain information from the authority that issued the passport. If such information cannot be obtained, or cannot be obtained within reasonable time, the examiner will have to decide on the credibility of the applicant's assertion in weighing all other elements of his story.

(b) Refugees *"sur place"*

94. The requirement that a person must be outside his country to be a refugee does not mean that he must necessarily have left that country illegally, or even that he must have left it on account of well-founded fear. He may have decided to ask for recognition of his refugee status after having already been abroad for some time. A person who was not a refugee when he left his country, but who becomes a refugee at a later date, is called a refugee *"sur place"*.

95. A person becomes a refugee *"sur place"* due to circumstances arising in his country of origin during his absence. Diplomats and other officials serving abroad, prisoners of war, students, migrant workers and others have applied for refugee status during their residence abroad and have been recognized as refugees.

96. A person may become a refugee *"sur place"* as a result of his own actions, such as associating with refugees already recognized, or expressing his political views in his country of residence. Whether such actions are sufficient to justify a well-founded fear of persecution must be determined by a careful examination of the circumstances. Regard should be had in particular to whether such actions may have come to the notice of the authorities of the person's country of origin and how they are likely to be viewed by those authorities.

(5) "and is unable or, owing to such fear, is unwilling to avail himself of the protection of that country"

97. Unlike the phrase dealt with under (6) below, the present phrase relates to persons who have a nationality. Whether unable or unwilling to avail himself of the protection of his Government, a refugee is always a person who does not enjoy such protection.

98. Being *unable* to avail himself of such protection implies circumstances that are beyond the will of the person concerned. There may, for example, be a state of war, civil war or other grave disturbance, which prevents the country of nationality from extending protection or makes such protection ineffective. Protection by the country of nationality may also have been denied to the applicant. Such denial of protection may confirm or strengthen the applicant's fear of persecution, and may indeed be an element of persecution.

99. What constitutes a refusal of protection must be determined according to the circumstances of the case. If it appears that the applicant has been denied services (e.g. refusal of a national passport or extension of its validity, or denial of admittance to the home territory) normally accorded to his co-nationals, this may constitute a refusal of protection within the definition.

100. The term *unwilling* refers to refugees who refuse to accept the protection of the Government of the country of their nationality.[12] It is qualified by the phrase "owing to such fear". Where a person is willing to avail himself of the protection of his home country, such willingness would normally be incompatible with a claim that he is outside that country "owing to well-founded fear of persecution". Whenever the protection of the country of nationality is available, and there is no ground based on well-founded fear for refusing it, the person concerned is not in need of international protection and is not a refugee.

(6) "or who, not having a nationality and being outside the country of his former habitual residence as a result of such events, is unable or, owing to such fear, is unwilling to return to it"

101. This phrase, which relates to stateless refugees, is parallel to the preceding phrase, which concerns refugees who have a nationality. In the case of stateless refugees, the "country of nationality" is replaced by "the country of his former habitual residence", and the expression "unwilling to avail himself of the protection . . . " is replaced by the words "unwilling to return to it". In the case of a stateless refugee, the question of "availment of protection" of the country of his former habitual residence does not, of course, arise. Moreover, once a stateless person has abandoned the country of his former habitual residence for the reasons indicated in the definition, he is usually unable to return.

102. It will be noted that not all stateless persons are refugees. They must be outside the country of their former habitual residence for the reasons indicated in the definition. Where these reasons do not exist, the stateless person is not a refugee.

103. Such reasons must be examined in relation to the country of "former habitual residence" in regard to which fear is alleged. This was defined by the drafters of the 1951 Convention as "the country in which he had resided and where he had suffered or fears he would suffer persecution if he returned".[13]

104. A stateless person may have more than one country of former habitual residence, and he may have a fear of persecution in relation to more than one of them. The definition does not require that he satisfies the criteria in relation to all of them.

105. Once a stateless person has been determined a refugee in relation to "the country of his former habitual residence", any further change of country of habitual residence will not affect his refugee status.

(7) Dual or multiple nationality

Article 1A(2), paragraph 2, of the 1951 Convention:

> In the case of a person who has more than one nationality, the term "the country of his nationality" shall mean each of the countries of which he is a national, and a person shall not be deemed to be lacking the protection of the country of his nationality if, without any valid reason based on well-founded fear, he has not availed himself of the protection of one of the countries of which he is a national.

106. This clause, which is largely self-explanatory, is intended to exclude from refugee status all persons with dual or multiple nationality who can avail themselves of the

[12] UN Document E/1618, p. 39.

[13] *Loc. cit.*

protection of at least one of the countries of which they are nationals. Wherever available, national protection takes precedence over international protection.

107. In examining the case of an applicant with dual or multiple nationality, it is necessary, however, to distinguish between the possession of a nationality in the legal sense and the availability of protection by the country concerned. There will be cases where the applicant has the nationality of a country in regard to which he alleges no fear, but such nationality may be deemed to be ineffective as it does not entail the protection normally granted to nationals. In such circumstances, the possession of the second nationality would not be inconsistent with refugee status. As a rule, there should have been a request for, and a refusal of, protection before it can be established that a given nationality is ineffective. If there is no explicit refusal of protection, absence of a reply within reasonable time may be considered a refusal.

(8) Geographical scope

108. At the time when the 1951 Convention was drafted, there was a desire by a number of States not to assume obligations the extent of which could not be foreseen. This desire led to the inclusion of the 1951 dateline, to which reference has already been made (paragraphs 35 and 36 above). In response to the wish of certain Governments, the 1951 Convention also gave to Contracting States the possibility of limiting their obligations under the Convention to persons who had become refugees as a result of events occurring in Europe.

109. Accordingly, Article 1 B of the 1951 Convention states that:

> (1) For the purposes of this Convention, the words "events occurring before 1 January 1951" in Article 1, Section A, shall be understood to mean either
>
> (a) "events occurring in Europe before 1 January 1951"; or
>
> (b) "events occurring in Europe and elsewhere before 1 January 1951";
>
> and each Contracting State shall make a declaration at the time of signature, ratification or accession, specifying which of these meanings it applies for the purposes of its obligations under this Convention.
>
> (2) Any Contracting State which has adopted alternative (a) may at any time extend its obligations by adopting alternative (b) by means of a notification addressed to the Secretary-General of the United Nations.

110. Of the States parties to the 1951 Convention, at the time of writing 9 still adhere to alternative (a), "events occurring in Europe".[14] While refugees from other parts of the world frequently obtain asylum in some of these countries, they are not normally accorded refugee status under the 1951 Convention.

Chapter III

Cessation Clauses

A. General

111. The so-called "cessation clauses" (Article 1C(1) to (6) of the 1951 Convention) spell out the conditions under which a refugee ceases to be a refugee. They are based on the consideration that international protection should not be granted where it is no longer necessary or justified.

[14] See Annex IV.

112. Once a person's status as a refugee has been determined, it is maintained unless he comes within the terms of one of the cessation clauses.[15] This strict approach towards the determination of refugee status results from the need to provide refugees with the assurance that their status will not be subject to constant review in the light of temporary changes – not of a fundamental character – in the situation prevailing in their country of origin.

113. Article 1C of the 1951 Convention provides that:

This Convention shall cease to apply to any person falling under the terms of section A if:

(1) He has voluntarily re-availed himself of the protection of the country of his nationality; or
(2) Having lost his nationality, he has voluntarily re-acquired it; or
(3) He has acquired a new nationality, and enjoys the protection of the country of his new nationality; or
(4) He has voluntarily re-established himself in the country which he left or outside which he remained owing to fear of persecution; or
(5) He can no longer, because the circumstances in connexion with which he has been recognized as a refugee have ceased to exist, continue to refuse to avail himself of the protection of the country of his nationality;
Provided that this paragraph shall not apply to a refugee falling under section A(1) of this Article who is able to invoke compelling reasons arising out of previous persecution for refusing to avail himself of the protection of the country of nationality;
(6) Being a person who has no nationality he is, because the circumstances in connexion with which he has been recognized as a refugee have ceased to exist, able to return to the country of his former habitual residence;
Provided that this paragraph shall not apply to a refugee falling under section A(1) of this Article who is able to invoke compelling reasons arising out of previous persecution for refusing to return to the country of his former habitual residence.

114. Of the six cessation clauses, the first four reflect a change in the situation of the refugee that has been brought about by himself, namely:

1. voluntary re-availment of national protection;
2. voluntary re-acquisition of nationality;
3. acquisition of a new nationality;
4. voluntary re-establishment in the country where persecution was feared.

115. The last two cessation clauses, (5) and (6), are based on the consideration that international protection is no longer justified on account of changes in the country where persecution was feared, because the reasons for a person becoming a refugee have ceased to exist.

116. The cessation clauses are negative in character and are exhaustively enumerated. They should therefore be interpreted restrictively, and no other reasons may be adduced by way of analogy to justify the withdrawal of refugee status. Needless to say, if a refugee, for whatever reasons, no longer wishes to be considered a refugee, there will be no call for continuing to grant him refugee status and international protection.

117. Article 1C does not deal with the cancellation of refugee status. Circumstances may, however, come to light that indicate that a person should never have been recognized as a refugee in the first place; e.g. if it subsequently appears that refugee status was obtained by a misrepresentation of material facts, or that the person concerned possesses another nationality, or that one of the exclusion clauses would have applied to him had all the relevant facts been known. In such cases, the decision by which he was determined to be a refugee will normally be cancelled.

[15] In some cases refugee status may continue, even though the reasons for such status have evidently ceased to exist. Cf sub-sections (5) and (6) (paras. 135 to 139 below).

B. Interpretation of terms

(1) Voluntary re-availment of national protection

Article 1C(1) of the 1951 Convention:

He has voluntarily re-availed himself of the protection of the country of his nationality;

118. This cessation clause refers to a refugee possessing a nationality who remains outside the country of his nationality. (The situation of a refugee who has actually returned to the country of his nationality is governed by the fourth cessation clause, which speaks of a person having "re-established" himself in that country.) A refugee who has voluntarily re-availed himself of national protection is no longer in need of international protection. He has demonstrated that he is no longer "unable or unwilling to avail himself of the protection of the country of his nationality".

119. This cessation clause implies three requirements:

(a) voluntariness: the refugee must act voluntarily;

(b) intention: the refugee must intend by his action to re-avail himself of the protection of the country of his nationality;

(c) re-availment: the refugee must actually obtain such protection.

120. If the refugee does not act voluntarily, he will not cease to be a refugee. If he is instructed by an authority, e.g. of his country of residence, to perform against his will an act that could be interpreted as a re-availment of the protection of the country of his nationality, such as applying to his Consulate for a national passport, he will not cease to be a refugee merely because he obeys such an instruction. He may also be constrained, by circumstances beyond his control, to have recourse to a measure of protection from his country of nationality. He may, for instance, need to apply for a divorce in his home country because no other divorce may have the necessary international recognition. Such an act cannot be considered to be a "voluntary re-availment of protection" and will not deprive a person of refugee status.

121. In determining whether refugee status is lost in these circumstances, a distinction should be drawn between actual re-availment of protection and occasional and incidental contacts with the national authorities. If a refugee applies for and obtains a national passport or its renewal, it will, in the absence of proof to the contrary, be presumed that he intends to avail himself of the protection of the country of his nationality. On the other hand, the acquisition of documents from the national authorities, for which non-nationals would likewise have to apply – such as a birth or marriage certificate – or similar services, cannot be regarded as a re-availment of protection.

122. A refugee requesting protection from the authorities of the country of his nationality has only "re-availed" himself of that protection when his request has actually been granted. The most frequent case of "re-availment of protection" will be where the refugee wishes to return to his country of nationality. He will not cease to be a refugee merely by applying for repatriation. On the other hand, obtaining an entry permit or a national passport for the purposes of returning will, in the absence of proof to the contrary, be considered as terminating refugee status.[16] This does not, however, preclude assistance being given to the repatriant – also by UNHCR – in order to facilitate his return.

[16] The above applies to a refugee who is still outside his country. It will be noted that the fourth cessation clause provides that any refugee will cease to be a refugee when he has voluntarily "re-established" himself in his country of nationality or former habitual residence.

123. A refugee may have voluntarily obtained a national passport, intending either to avail himself of the protection of his country of origin while staying outside that country, or to return to that country. As stated above, with the receipt of such a document he normally ceases to be a refugee. If he subsequently renounces either intention, his refugee status will need to be determined afresh. He will need to explain why he changed his mind, and to show that there has been no basic change in the conditions that originally made him a refugee.

124. Obtaining a national passport or an extension of its validity may, under certain exceptional conditions, not involve termination of refugee status (see paragraph 120 above). This could for example be the case where the holder of a national passport is not permitted to return to the country of his nationality without specific permission.

125. Where a refugee visits his former home country not with a national passport but, for example, with a travel document issued by his country of residence, he has been considered by certain States to have re-availed himself of the protection of his former home country and to have lost his refugee status under the present cessation clause.

Cases of this kind should, however, be judged on their individual merits. Visiting an old or sick parent will have a different bearing on the refugee's relation to his former home country than regular visits to that country spent on holidays or for the purpose of establishing business relations.

(2) Voluntary re-acquisition of nationality

Article 1C(2) of the 1951 Convention:

> Having lost his nationality, he has voluntarily re-acquired it;

126. This clause is similar to the preceding one. It applies to cases where a refugee, having lost the nationality of the country in respect of which he was recognized as having well-founded fear of persecution, voluntarily re-acquires such nationality.

127. While under the preceding clause (Article 1C(1)) a person having a nationality ceases to be a refugee if he re-avails himself of the protection attaching to such nationality, under the present clause (Article 1C(2)) he loses his refugee status by re-acquiring the nationality previously lost.[17]

128. The re-acquisition of nationality must be voluntary. The granting of nationality by operation of law or by decree does not imply voluntary reacquisition, unless the nationality has been expressly or impliedly accepted. A person does not cease to be a refugee merely because he could have reacquired his former nationality by option, unless this option has actually been exercised. If such former nationality is granted by operation of law, subject to an option to reject, it will be regarded as a voluntary re-acquisition if the refugee, with full knowledge, has not exercised this option; unless he is able to invoke special reasons showing that it was not in fact his intention to re-acquire his former nationality.

[17] In the majority of cases a refugee maintains the nationality of his former home country. Such nationality may be lost by individual or collective measures of deprivation of nationality. Loss of nationality (statelessness) is therefore not necessarily implicit in refugee status.

(3) Acquisition of a new nationality and protection

Article 1C(3) of the 1951 Convention:

> He has acquired a new nationality and enjoys the protection of the country of his new nationality;

129. As in the case of the re-acquisition of nationality, this third cessation clause derives from the principle that a person who enjoys national protection is not in need of international protection.

130. The nationality that the refugee acquires is usually that of the country of his residence. A refugee living in one country may, however, in certain cases, acquire the nationality of another country. If he does so, his refugee status will also cease, provided that the new nationality also carries the protection of the country concerned. This requirement results from the phrase "and enjoys the protection of the country of his new nationality".

131. If a person has ceased to be a refugee, having acquired a new nationality, and then claims well-founded fear in relation to the country of his new nationality, this creates a completely new situation and his status must be determined in relation to the country of his new nationality.

132. Where refugee status has terminated through the acquisition of a new nationality, and such new nationality has been lost, depending on the circumstances of such loss, refugee status may be revived.

(4) Voluntary re-establishment in the country where persecution was feared

Article 1C(4) of the 1951 Convention:

> He has voluntarily re-established himself in the country which he left or outside which he remained owing to fear of persecution;

133. This fourth cessation clause applies both to refugees who have a nationality and to stateless refugees. It relates to refugees who, having returned to their country of origin or previous residence, have not previously ceased to be refugees under the first or second cessation clauses while still in their country of refuge.

134. The clause refers to "voluntary re-establishment". This is to be understood as return to the country of nationality or former habitual residence with a view to permanently residing there. A temporary visit by a refugee to his former home country, not with a national passport but, for example, with a travel document issued by his country of residence, does not constitute "re-establishment" and will not involve loss of refugee status under the present clause.[18]

(5) Nationals whose reasons for becoming a refugee have ceased to exist

Article 1C(5) of the 1951 Convention:

> He can no longer, because the circumstances in connexion with which he has been recognized as a refugee have ceased to exist, continue to refuse to avail himself of the protection of the country of his nationality;
>
> Provided that this paragraph shall not apply to a refugee falling under section A(1) of this Article who is able to invoke compelling reasons arising out of previous persecution for refusing to avail himself of the protection of the country of nationality;

[18] See para. 125 above.

135. "Circumstances" refer to fundamental changes in the country, which can be assumed to remove the basis of the fear of persecution. A mere – possibly transitory – change in the facts surrounding the individual refugee's fear, which does not entail such major changes of circumstances, is not sufficient to make this clause applicable. A refugee's status should not in principle be subject to frequent review to the detriment of his sense of security, which international protection is intended to provide.

136. The second paragraph of this clause contains an exception to the cessation provision contained in the first paragraph. It deals with the special situation where a person may have been subjected to very serious persecution in the past and will not therefore cease to be a refugee, even if fundamental changes have occurred in his country of origin. The reference to Article 1A(1) indicates that the exception applies to "statutory refugees". At the time when the 1951 Convention was elaborated, these 'formed the majority of refugees. The exception, however, reflects a more general humanitarian principle, which could also be applied to refugees other than statutory refugees. It is frequently recognized that a person who – or whose family – has suffered under atrocious forms of persecution should not be expected to repatriate. Even though there may have been a change of regime in his country, this may not always produce a complete change in the attitude of the population, nor, in view of his past experiences, in the mind of the refugee.

(6) Stateless persons whose reasons for becoming a refugee have ceased to exist

Article 1C(6) of the 1951 Convention:

> Being a person who has no nationality he is, because the circumstances in connexion with which he has been recognized as a refugee have ceased to exist, able to return to the country of his former habitual residence; Provided that this paragraph shall not apply to a refugee falling under section A(1) of this Article who is able to invoke compelling reasons arising out of previous persecution for refusing to return to the country of his former habitual residence.

137. This sixth and last cessation clause is parallel to the fifth cessation clause, which concerns persons who have a nationality. The present clause deals exclusively with stateless persons who are able to return to the country of their former habitual residence.

138. "Circumstances" should be interpreted in the same way as under the fifth cessation clause.

139. It should be stressed that, apart from the changed circumstances in his country of former habitual residence, the person concerned must be *able* to return there. This, in the case of a stateless person, may not always be possible.

Chapter IV

Exclusion Clauses

A. General

140. The 1951 Convention, in Sections D, E and F of Article 1, contains provisions whereby persons otherwise having the characteristics of refugees, as defined in Article 1, Section A, are excluded from refugee status. Such persons fall into three groups. The

first group (Article 1D) consists of persons already receiving United Nations protection or assistance; the second group (Article 1E) deals with persons who are not considered to be in need of international protection; and the third group (Article 1F) enumerates the categories of persons who are not considered to be deserving of international protection.

141. Normally it will be during the process of determining a person's refugee status that the facts leading to exclusion under these clauses will emerge. It may, however, also happen that facts justifying exclusion will become known only after a person has been recognized as a refugee. In such cases, the exclusion clause will call for a cancellation of the decision previously taken.

B. Interpretation of terms

(1) Persons already receiving United Nations protection or assistance

Article 1D of the 1951 Convention:

> This Convention shall not apply to persons who are at present receiving from organs or agencies of the United Nations other than the United Nations High Commissioner for Refugees protection or assistance.
>
> When such protection or assistance has ceased for any reason, without the position of such persons being definitively settled in accordance with the relevant resolutions adopted by the General Assembly of the United Nations, these persons shall ipso facto be entitled to the benefits of this Convention.

142. Exclusion under this clause applies to any person who is in receipt of protection or assistance from organs or agencies of the United Nations, other than the United Nations High Commissioner for Refugees. Such protection or assistance was previously given by the former United Nations Korean Reconstruction Agency (UNKRA) and is currently given by the United Nations Relief and Works Agency for Palestine Refugees In the Near East (UNRWA). There could be other similar situations in the future.

143. With regard to refugees from Palestine, it will be noted that UNRWA operates only in certain areas of the Middle East, and it is only there that its protection or assistance are given. Thus, a refugee from Palestine who finds himself outside that area does not enjoy the assistance mentioned and may be considered for determination of his refugee status under the criteria of the 1951 Convention. It should normally be sufficient to establish that the circumstances which originally made him qualify for protection or assistance from UNRWA still persist and that he has neither ceased to be a refugee under one of the cessation clauses nor is excluded from the application of the Convention under one of the exclusion clauses.

(2) Persons not considered to be in need of international protection

Article 1E of the 1951 Convention:

> This Convention shall not apply to a person who is recognized by the competent authorities of the country in which he has taken residence as having the rights and obligations which are attached to the possession of the nationality of that country.

144. This provision relates to persons who might otherwise qualify for refugee status and who have been received in a country where they have been granted most of the rights normally enjoyed by nationals, but not formal citizenship. (They are frequently referred to as "national refugees".) The country that has received them is frequently one where the population is of the same ethnic origin as themselves.[19]

145. There is no precise definition of "rights and obligations" that would constitute a reason for exclusion under this clause. It may, however, be said that the exclusion operates if a person's status is largely assimilated to that of a national of the country.

In particular he must, like a national, be fully protected against deportation or expulsion.

146. The clause refers to a person who has "taken residence" in the country concerned.

This implies continued residence and not a mere visit. A person who resides outside the country and does not enjoy the diplomatic protection of that country is not affected by the exclusion clause.

(3) Persons considered not to be deserving of international protection

Article 1F of the 1951 Convention:

> The provisions of this Convention shall not apply to any person with respect to whom there are serious reasons for considering that:
>
> (a) he has committed a crime against peace, a war crime, or a crime against humanity, as defined in the international instruments drawn up to make provision in respect of such crimes;
>
> (b) he has committed a serious non-political crime outside the country of refuge prior to his admission to that country as a refugee;
>
> (c) he has been guilty of acts contrary to the purposes and principles of the United Nations.

147. The pre-war international instruments that defined various categories of refugees contained no provisions for the exclusion of criminals. It was immediately after the Second World War that for the first time special provisions were drawn up to exclude from the large group of then assisted refugees certain persons who were deemed unworthy of international protection.

148. At the time when the Convention was drafted, the memory of the trials of major war criminals was still very much alive, and there was agreement on the part of States that war criminals should not be protected. There was also a desire on the part of States to deny admission to their territories of criminals who would present a danger to security and public order.

149. The competence to decide whether any of these exclusion clauses are applicable is incumbent upon the Contracting State in whose territory the applicant seeks recognition of his refugee status. For these clauses to apply, it is sufficient to establish that there are "serious reasons for considering" that one of the acts described has been committed.

Formal proof of previous penal prosecution is not required. Considering the serious consequences of exclusion for the person concerned, however, the interpretation of these exclusion clauses must be restrictive.

(a) **War crimes, etc.**

> (a) he has committed a crime against peace, a war crime or a crime against humanity, as defined in the international instruments drawn up to make provision in respect of such crimes.

[19] In elaborating this exclusion clause, the drafters of the Convention had principally in mind refugees of German extraction having arrived in the Federal Republic of Germany who were recognized as possessing the rights and obligations attaching to German nationality.

150. In mentioning crimes against peace, war crimes or crimes against humanity, the Convention refers generally to "international instruments drawn up to make provision in respect of such crimes". There are a considerable number of such instruments dating from the end of the Second World War up to the present time. All of them contain definitions of what constitute "crimes against peace, war crimes and crimes against humanity". The most comprehensive definition will be found in the 1945 London Agreement and Charter of the International Military tribunal. The definitions contained in the above-mentioned London Agreement and a list of other pertinent instruments are given in Annexes V and VI.

(b) Common crimes

(b) he has committed a serious non-political crime outside the country of refuge prior to his admission to that country as a refugee.

151. The aim of this exclusion clause is to protect the community of a receiving country from the danger of admitting a refugee who has committed a serious common crime. It also seeks to render due justice to a refugee who has committed a common crime (or crimes) of a less serious nature or has committed a political offence.

152. In determining whether an offence is "non-political" or is, on the contrary, a "political" crime, regard should be given in the first place to its nature and purpose i.e. whether it has been committed out of genuine political motives and not merely for personal reasons or gain. There should also be a close and direct causal link between the crime committed and its alleged political purpose and object. The political element of the offence should also outweigh its common-law character. This would not be the case if the acts committed are grossly out of proportion to the alleged objective. The political nature of the offence is also more difficult to accept if it involves acts of an atrocious nature.

153. Only a crime committed or presumed to have been committed by an applicant "outside the country of refuge prior to his admission to that country as a refugee" is a ground for exclusion. The country outside would normally be the country of origin, but it could also be another country, except the country of refuge where the applicant seeks recognition of his refugee status.

154. A refugee committing a serious crime in the country of refuge is subject to due process of law in that country. In extreme cases, Article 33 paragraph 2 of the Convention permits a refugee's expulsion or return to his former home country if, having been convicted by a final judgement of a "particularly serious" common crime, he constitutes a danger to the community of his country of refuge.

155. What constitutes a "serious" non-political crime for the purposes of this exclusion clause is difficult to define, especially since the term "crime" has different connotations in different legal systems. In some countries the word "crime" denotes only offences of a serious character. In other countries it may comprise anything from petty larceny to murder. In the present context, however, a "serious" crime must be a capital crime or a very grave punishable act. Minor offences punishable by moderate sentences are not grounds for exclusion under Article 1F(b) even if technically referred to as "crimes" in the penal law of the country concerned.

156. In applying this exclusion clause, it is also necessary to strike a balance between the nature of the offence presumed to have been committed by the applicant and the degree of persecution feared. If a person has well-founded fear of very severe persecution,

e.g. persecution endangering his life or freedom, a crime must be very grave in order to exclude him. If the persecution feared is less serious, it will be necessary to have regard to the nature of the crime or crimes presumed to have been committed in order to establish whether the applicant is not in reality a fugitive from justice or whether his criminal character does not outweigh his character as a *bona fide* refugee.

157. In evaluating the nature of the crime presumed to have been committed, all the relevant factors – including any mitigating circumstances – must be taken into account. It is also necessary to have regard to any aggravating circumstances as, for example, the fact that the applicant may already have a criminal record. The fact that an applicant convicted of a serious non-political crime has already served his sentence or has been granted a pardon or has benefited from an amnesty is also relevant. In the latter case, there is a presumption that the exclusion clause is no longer applicable, unless it can be shown that, despite the pardon or amnesty, the applicant's criminal character still predominates.

158. Considerations similar to those mentioned in the preceding paragraphs will apply when a crime – in the widest sense – has been committed as a means of, or concomitant with, escape from the country where persecution was feared. Such crimes may range from the theft of a means of locomotion to endangering or taking the lives of innocent people. While for the purposes of the present exclusion clause it may be possible to over-look the fact that a refugee, not finding any other means of escape, may have crashed the border in a stolen car, decisions will be more difficult where he has hijacked an aircraft, i.e. forced its crew, under threat of arms or with actual violence, to change destination in order to bring him to a country of refuge.

159. As regards hijacking, the question has arisen as to whether, if committed in order to escape from persecution, it constitutes a serious non-political crime within the meaning of the present exclusion clause. Governments have considered the unlawful seizure of aircraft on several occasions within the framework of the United Nations, and a number of international conventions have been adopted dealing with the subject. None of these instruments mentions refugees. However, one of the reports leading to the adoption of a resolution on the subject states that "the adoption of the draft Resolution cannot prejudice any international legal rights or duties of States under instruments relating to the status of refugees and stateless persons". Another report states that "the adoption of the draft Resolution cannot prejudice any international legal rights or duties of States with respect to asylum".[20]

160. The various conventions adopted in this connexion[21] deal mainly with the manner in which the perpetrators of such acts have to be treated. They invariably give Contracting States the alternative of extraditing such persons or instituting penal proceedings for the act on their own territory, which implies the right to grant asylum.

161. While there is thus a possibility of granting asylum, the gravity of the persecution of which the offender may have been in fear, and the extent to which such fear is well-founded, will have to be duly considered in determining his possible refugee status under the 1951 Convention. The question of the exclusion under Article 1F(b) of an

[20] Reports of the Sixth Committee on General Assembly resolutions 2645 (XXV). United Nations document A/8716, and 2551 (XXIV), United Nations document A/7845.

[21] Convention on Offences and Certain Other Acts Committed on Board Aircraft, Tokyo, 14 September 1963. Convention for the Suppression of Unlawful Seizure of Aircraft, the Hague, 16 December 1970. Convention for the Suppression of Unlawful Acts against the Safety of Civil Aviation, Montreal, 23 September 1971.

applicant who has committed an unlawful seizure of an aircraft will also have to be carefully examined in each individual case.

(c) Acts contrary to the purposes and principles of the United Nations

(c) he has been guilty of acts contrary to the purposes and principles of the United Nations.

162. It will be seen that this very generally-worded exclusion clause overlaps with the exclusion clause in Article 1F(a); for it is evident that a crime against peace, a war crime or a crime against humanity is also an act contrary to the purposes and principles of the United Nations. While Article 1F(c) does not introduce any specific new element, it is intended to cover in a general way such acts against the purposes and principles of the United Nations that might not be fully covered by the two preceding exclusion clauses. Taken in conjunction with the latter, it has to be assumed, although this is not specifically stated, that the acts covered by the present clause must also be of a criminal nature.

163. The purposes and principles of the United Nations are set out in the Preamble and Articles 1 and 2 of the Charter of the United Nations. They enumerate fundamental principles that should govern the conduct of their members in relation to each other and in relation to the international community as a whole. From this it could be inferred that an individual, in order to have committed an act contrary to these principles, must have been in a position of power in a member State and instrumental to his State's infringing these principles. However, there are hardly any precedents on record for the application of this clause, which, due to its very general character, should be applied with caution.

Chapter V

Special Cases

A. War refugees

164. Persons compelled to leave their country of origin as a result of international or national armed conflicts are not normally considered refugees under the 1951 Convention or 1967 Protocol.[22] They do, however, have the protection provided for in other international instruments, e.g. the Geneva Conventions of 1949 on the Protection of War Victims and the 1977 Protocol additional to the Geneva Conventions of 1949 relating to the protection of Victims of International Armed Conflicts.[23]

165. However, foreign invasion or occupation of all or part of a country can result – and occasionally has resulted – in persecution for one or more of the reasons enumerated in the 1951 Convention. In such cases, refugee status will depend upon whether the applicant is able to show that he has a "well-founded fear of being persecuted" in the occupied territory and, in addition, upon whether or not he is able to avail himself of the protection of his government, or of a protecting power whose duty it is to safeguard the interests of

[22] In respect of Africa, however, see the definition in Article 1(2) of the OAU Convention concerning the Specific Aspects of Refugee Problems in Africa, quoted in para. 22 above.

[23] See Annex VI, items (6) and (7).

his country during the armed conflict, and whether such protection can be considered to be effective.

166. Protection may not be available if there are no diplomatic relations between the applicant's host country and his country of origin. If the applicant's government is itself in exile, the effectiveness of the protection that it is able to extend may be open to question. Thus, every case has to be judged on its merits, both in respect of well-founded fear of persecution and of the availability of effective protection on the part of the government of the country of origin.

B. Deserters and persons avoiding military service

167. In countries where military service is compulsory, failure to perform this duty is frequently punishable by law. Moreover, whether military service is compulsory or not, desertion is invariably considered a criminal offence. The Penalties may vary from country to country, and are not normally regarded as persecution. Fear of prosecution and punishment for desertion or draft-evasion does not in itself constitute well-founded fear of persecution under the definition. Desertion or draft-evasion does not, on the other hand, exclude a person from being a refugee, and a person may be a refugee in addition to being a deserter or draft-evader.

168. A person is clearly not a refugee if his only reason for desertion or draft-evasion is his dislike of military service or fear of combat. He may, however, be a refugee if his desertion or evasion of military service is concomitant with other relevant motives for leaving or remaining outside his country, or if he otherwise has reasons, within the meaning of the definition, to fear persecution.

169. A deserter or draft-evader may also be considered a refugee if it can be shown that he would suffer disproportionately severe punishment for the military offence on account of his race, religion, nationality, membership of a particular social group or political opinion. The same would apply if it can be shown that he has well-founded fear of persecution on these grounds above and beyond the punishment for desertion.

170. There are, however, also cases where the necessity to perform military service may be the sole ground for a claim to refugee status, i.e. when a person can show that the performance of military service would have required his participation in military action contrary to his genuine political, religious or moral convictions, or to valid reasons of conscience.

171. Not every conviction, genuine though it may be, will constitute a sufficient reason for claiming refugee status after desertion or draft-evasion. It is not enough for a person to be in disagreement with his government regarding the political justification for a particular military action. Where, however, the type of military action, with which an individual does not wish to be associated, is condemned by the international community as contrary to basic rules of human conduct, punishment for desertion or draft-evasion could, in the light of all other requirements of the definition, in itself be regarded as persecution.

172. Refusal to perform military service may also be based on religious convictions. If an applicant is able to show that his religious convictions are genuine, and that such convictions are not taken into account by the authorities of his country in requiring him to perform military service, he may be able to establish a claim to refugee status. Such a claim would, of course, be supported by any additional indications that the applicant or his family may have encountered difficulties due to their religious convictions.

173. The question as to whether objection to performing military service for reasons of conscience can give rise to a valid claim to refugee status should also be considered in the light of more recent developments in this field. An increasing number of States have introduced legislation or administrative regulations whereby persons who can invoke genuine reasons of conscience are exempted from military service, either entirely or subject to their performing alternative (i.e. civilian) service. The introduction of such legislation or administrative regulations has also been the subject of recommendations by international agencies.[24] In the light of these developments, it would be open to Contracting States, to grant refugee status to persons who object to performing military service for genuine reasons of conscience.

174. The genuineness of a person's political, religious or moral convictions, or of his reasons of conscience for objecting to performing military service, will of course need to be established by a thorough investigation of his personality and background. The fact that he may have manifested his views prior to being called to arms, or that he may already have encountered difficulties with the authorities because of his convictions, are relevant considerations. Whether he has been drafted into compulsory service or joined the army as a volunteer may also be indicative of the genuineness of his convictions.

C. Persons having resorted to force or committed acts of violence

175. Applications for refugee status are frequently made by persons who have used force or committed acts of violence. Such conduct is frequently associated with, or claimed to be associated with, political activities or political opinions. They may be the result of individual initiatives, or may have been committed within the framework of organized groups. The latter may either be clandestine groupings or political cum military organizations that are officially recognized or whose activities are widely acknowledged.[25] Account should also be taken of the fact that the use of force is an aspect of the maintenance of law and order and may – by definition – be lawfully resorted to by the police and armed forces in the exercise of their functions.

176. An application for refugee status by a person having (or presumed to have) used force, or to have committed acts of violence of whatever nature and within whatever context, must in the first place – like any other application – be examined from the standpoint of the inclusion clauses in the 1951 Convention (paragraphs 32-110 above).

177. Where it has been determined that an applicant fulfils the inclusion criteria, the question may arise as to whether, in view of the acts involving the use of force or violence committed by him, he may not be covered by the terms of one or more of the exclusion clauses. These exclusion clauses, which figure in Article 1F(a) to (c) of the 1951 Convention, have already been examined (paragraphs 147 to 163 above).

178. The exclusion clause in Article 1F(a) was originally intended to exclude from refugee status any person in respect of whom there were serious reasons for considering

[24] Cf Recommendation 816 (1977) on the Right of Conscientious Objection to Military Service, adopted at the Parliamentary Assembly of the Council of Europe at its Twenty-ninth Ordinary Session (5-13 October 1977).

[25] A number of liberation movements, which often include an armed wing, have been officially recognized by the General Assembly of the United Nations. Other liberation movements have only been recognized by a limited number of governments. Others again have no official recognition.

that he has "committed a crime against peace, a war crime, or a crime against humanity" in an official capacity. This exclusion clause is, however, also applicable to persons who have committed such crimes within the framework of various non-governmental groupings, whether officially recognized, clandestine or self-styled.

179. The exclusion clause in Article 1F(b), which refers to "a serious non-political crime", is normally not relevant to the use of force or to acts of violence committed in an official capacity. The interpretation of this exclusion clause has already been discussed. The exclusion clause in Article 1F(c) has also been considered. As previously indicated, because of its vague character, it should be applied with caution.

180. It will also be recalled that, due to their nature and the serious consequences of their application to a person in fear of persecution, the exclusion clauses should be applied in a restrictive manner.

Chapter VI

The Principle of Family Unity

181. Beginning with the Universal Declaration of Human Rights, which states that "the family is the natural and fundamental group unit of society and is entitled to protection by society and the State", most international instruments dealing with human rights contain similar provisions for the protection of the unit of a family.

182. The Final Act of the Conference that adopted the 1951 Convention:

> Recommends Governments to take the necessary measures for the protection of the refugee's family, especially with a view to:
>
> (1) Ensuring that the unity of the refugee's family is maintained particularly in cases where the head of the family has fulfilled the necessary conditions for admission to a particular country.
>
> (2) The protection of refugees who are minors, in particular unaccompanied children and girls, with special reference to guardianship and adoption.[26]

183. The 1951 Convention does not incorporate the principle of family unity in the definition of the term refugee. The above-mentioned Recommendation in the Final Act of the Conference is, however, observed by the majority of States, whether or not parties to the 1951 Convention or to the 1967 Protocol.

184. If the head of a family meets the criteria of the definition, his dependants are normally granted refugee status according to the principle of family unity. It is obvious, however, that formal refugee status should not be granted to a dependant if this is incompatible with his personal legal status. Thus, a dependant member of a refugee family may be a national of the country of asylum or of another country, and may enjoy that country's protection. To grant him refugee status in such circumstances would not be called for.

185. As to which family members may benefit from the principle of family unity, the minimum requirement is the inclusion of the spouse and minor children. In practice, other dependants, such as aged parents of refugees, are normally considered if they are living in the same household. On the other hand, if the head of the family is not a refugee, there is nothing to prevent any one of his dependants, if they can invoke reasons on their own account, from applying for recognition as refugees under the 1951 Convention or the 1967

[26] See Annex 1.

Protocol. In other words, the principle of family unity operates in favour of dependants, and not against them.

186. The principle of the unity of the family does not only operate where all family members become refugees at the same time. It applies equally to cases where a family unit has been temporarily disrupted through the flight of one or more of its members.

187. Where the unity of a refugee's family is destroyed by divorce, separation or death, dependants who have been granted refugee status on the basis of family unity will retain such refugee status unless they fall within the terms of a cessation clause; or if they do not have reasons other than those of personal convenience for wishing to retain refugee status; or if they themselves no longer wish to be considered as refugees.

188. If the dependant of a refugee falls within the terms of one of the exclusion clauses, refugee status should be denied to him.

Part Two

Procedures for the Determination of Refugee Status

A. General

189. It has been seen that the 1951 Convention and the 1967 Protocol define who is a refugee for the purposes of these instruments. It is obvious that, to enable States parties to the Convention and to the Protocol to implement their provisions, refugees have to be identified. Such identification, i.e. the determination of refugee status, although mentioned in the 1951 Convention (cf. Article 9), is not specifically regulated. In particular, the Convention does not indicate what type of procedures are to be adopted for the determination of refugee status. It is therefore left to each Contracting State to establish the procedure that it considers most appropriate, having regard to its particular constitutional and administrative structure.

190. It should be recalled that an applicant for refugee status is normally in a particularly vulnerable situation. He finds himself in an alien environment and may experience serious difficulties, technical and psychological, in submitting his case to the authorities of a foreign country, often in a language not his own. His application should therefore be examined within the framework of specially established procedures by qualified personnel having the necessary knowledge and experience, and an understanding of an applicant's particular difficulties and needs.

191. Due to the fact that the matter is not specifically regulated by the 1951 Convention, procedures adopted by States parties to the 1951 Convention and to the 1967 Protocol vary considerably. In a number of countries, refugee status is determined under formal procedures specifically established for this purpose. In other countries, the question of refugee status is considered within the framework of general procedures for the admission of aliens. In yet other countries, refugee status is determined under informal arrangements, or *ad hoc* for specific purposes, such as the issuance of travel documents.

192. In view of this situation and of the unlikelihood that all States bound by the 1951 Convention and the 1967 Protocol could establish identical procedures, the Executive Committee of the High Commissioner's Programme, at its twenty-eighth session in October 1977, recommended that procedures should satisfy certain basic requirements.

These basic requirements, which reflect the special situation of the applicant for refugee status, to which reference has been made above, and which would ensure that the applicant is provided with certain essential guarantees, are the following:

(i) The competent official (e.g. immigration officer or border police officer) to whom the applicant addresses himself at the border or in the territory of a Contracting State should have clear instructions for dealing with cases which might come within the purview of the relevant international instruments. He should be required to act in accordance with the principle of non-refoulement and to refer such cases to a higher authority.

(ii) The applicant should receive the necessary guidance as to the procedure to be followed.

(iii) There should be a clearly identified authority – wherever possible a single central authority – with responsibility for examining requests for refugee status and taking a decision in the first instance.

(iv) The applicant should be given the necessary facilities, including the services of a competent interpreter, for submitting his case to the authorities concerned. Applicants should also be given the opportunity, of which they should be duly informed, to contact a representative of UNHCR.

(v) If the applicant is recognized as a refugee, he should be informed accordingly and issued with documentation certifying his refugee status.

(vi) If the applicant is not recognized, he should be given a reasonable time to appeal for a formal reconsideration of the decision, either to the same or to a different authority, whether administrative or judicial, according to the prevailing system.

(vii) The applicant should be permitted to remain in the country pending a decision on his initial request by the competent authority referred to in paragraph (iii) above, unless it has been established by that authority that his request is clearly abusive. He should also be permitted to remain in the country while an appeal to a higher administrative authority or to the courts is pending.[27]

193. The Executive Committee also expressed the hope that all States parties to the 1951 Convention and the 1967 Protocol that had not yet done so would take appropriate steps to establish such procedures in the near future and give favourable consideration to UNHCR participation in such procedures in appropriate form.

194. Determination of refugee status, which is closely related to questions of asylum and admission, is of concern to the High Commissioner in the exercise of his function to provide international protection for refugees. In a number of countries, the Office of the High Commissioner participates in various forms, in procedures for the determination of refugee status. Such participation is based on Article 35 of the 1951 Convention and the corresponding Article 11 of the 1967 Protocol, which provide for cooperation by the Contracting States with the High Commissioner's Office.

B. Establishing the Facts

(1) Principles and methods

195. The relevant facts of the individual case will have to be furnished in the first place by the applicant himself. It will then be up to the person charged with determining

[27] Official Records of the General Assembly, Thirty-second Session, Supplement No. 12 (A/32/12/Add.1), para. 53(6)(e).

his status (the examiner) to assess the validity of any evidence and the credibility of the applicant's statements.

196. It is a general legal principle that the burden of proof lies on the person submitting a claim. Often, however, an applicant may not be able to support his statements by documentary or other proof, and cases in which an applicant can provide evidence of all his statements will be the exception rather than the rule. In most cases a person fleeing from persecution will have arrived with the barest necessities and very frequently even without personal documents. Thus, while the burden of proof in principle rests on the applicant, the duty to ascertain and evaluate all the relevant facts is shared between the applicant and the examiner. Indeed, in some cases, it may be for the examiner to use all the means at his disposal to produce the necessary evidence in support of the application. Even such independent research may not, however, always be successful and there may also be statements that are not susceptible of proof. In such cases, if the applicant's account appears credible, he should, unless there are good reasons to the contrary, be given the benefit of the doubt.

197. The requirement of evidence should thus not be too strictly applied in view of the difficulty of proof inherent in the special situation in which an applicant for refugee status finds himself. Allowance for such possible lack of evidence does not, however, mean that unsupported statements must necessarily be accepted as true if they are inconsistent with the general account put forward by the applicant.

198. A person who, because of his experiences, was in fear of the authorities in his own country may still feel apprehensive vis-à-vis any authority. He may therefore be afraid to speak freely and give a full and accurate account of his case.

199. While an initial interview should normally suffice to bring an applicant's story to light, it may be necessary for the examiner to clarify any apparent inconsistencies and to resolve any contradictions in a further interview, and to find an explanation for any misrepresentation or concealment of material facts. Untrue statements by themselves are not a reason for refusal of refugee status and it is the examiner's responsibility to evaluate such statements in the light of all the circumstances of the case.

200. An examination in depth of the different methods of fact-finding is outside the scope of the present Handbook. It may be mentioned, however, that basic information is frequently given, in the first instance, by completing a standard questionnaire. Such basic information will normally not be sufficient to enable the examiner to reach a decision, and one or more personal interviews will be required. It will be necessary for the examiner to gain the confidence of the applicant in order to assist the latter in putting forward his case and in fully explaining his opinions and feelings. In creating such a climate of confidence it is, of course, of the utmost importance that the applicant's statements will be treated as confidential and that he be so informed.

201. Very frequently the fact-finding process will not be complete until a wide range of circumstances has been ascertained. Taking isolated incidents out of context may be misleading. The cumulative effect of the applicant's experience must be taken into account. Where no single incident stands out above the others, sometimes a small incident may be "the last straw"; and although no single incident may be sufficient, all the incidents related by the applicant taken together, could make his fear "well-founded" (see paragraph 53 above).

202. Since the examiner's conclusion on the facts of the case and his personal impression of the applicant will lead to a decision that affects human lives, he must apply the criteria in a spirit of justice and understanding and his judgement should not, of course, be influenced by the personal consideration that the applicant may be an "undeserving case".

(2) Benefit of the doubt

203. After the applicant has made a genuine effort to substantiate his story there may still be a lack of evidence for some of his statements. As explained above (paragraph 196), it is hardly possible for a refugee to "prove" every part of his case and, indeed, if this were a requirement the majority of refugees would not be recognized. It is therefore frequently necessary to give the applicant the benefit of the doubt.

204. The benefit of the doubt should, however, only be given when all available evidence has been obtained and checked and when the examiner is satisfied as to the applicant's general credibility. The applicant's statements must be coherent and plausible, and must not run counter to generally known facts.

(3) Summary

205. The process of ascertaining and evaluating the facts can therefore be summarized as follows:

(a) The *applicant* should:

(i) Tell the truth and assist the examiner to the full in establishing the facts of his case.

(ii) Make an effort to support his statements by any available evidence and give a satisfactory explanation for any lack of evidence. If necessary he must make an effort to procure additional evidence.

(iii) Supply all pertinent information concerning himself and his past experience in as much detail as is necessary to enable the examiner to establish the relevant facts. He should be asked to give a coherent explanation of all the reasons invoked in support of his application for refugee status and he should answer any questions put to him.

(b) The *examiner* should:

(i) Ensure that the applicant presents his case as fully as possible and with all available evidence.

(ii) Assess the applicant's credibility and evaluate the evidence (if necessary giving the applicant the benefit of the doubt), in order to establish the objective and the subjective elements of the case.

(iii) Relate these elements to the relevant criteria of the 1951 Convention, in order to arrive at a correct conclusion as to the applicant's refugee status.

C. Cases Giving Rise to Special Problems in Establishing the Facts

(1) Mentally disturbed persons

206. It has been seen that in determining refugee status the subjective element of fear and the objective element of its well-foundedness need to be established.

207. It frequently happens that an examiner is confronted with an applicant having mental or emotional disturbances that impede a normal examination of his case. A mentally disturbed person may, however, be a refugee, and while his claim cannot therefore be disregarded, it will call for different techniques of examination.

208. The examiner should, in such cases, whenever possible, obtain expert medical advice. The medical report should provide information on the nature and degree of mental illness and should assess the applicant's ability to fulfil the requirements normally expected of an applicant in presenting his case (see paragraph 205(a) above). The conclusions of the medical report will determine the examiner's further approach.

209. This approach has to vary according to the degree of the applicant's affliction and no rigid rules can be laid down. The nature and degree of the applicant's "fear" must also be taken into consideration, since some degree of mental disturbance is frequently found in persons who have been exposed to severe persecution. Where there are indications that the fear expressed by the applicant may not be based on actual experience or may be an exaggerated fear, it may be necessary, in arriving at a decision, to lay greater emphasis on the objective circumstances, rather than on the statements made by the applicant.

210. It will, in any event, be necessary to lighten the burden of proof normally incumbent upon the applicant, and information that cannot easily be obtained from the applicant may have to be sought elsewhere, e.g. from friends, relatives and other persons closely acquainted with the applicant, or from his guardian, if one has been appointed. It may also be necessary to draw certain conclusions from the surrounding circumstances. If, for instance, the applicant belongs to and is in the company of a group of refugees, there is a presumption that he shares their fate and qualifies in the same manner as they do.

211. In examining his application, therefore, it may not be possible to attach the same importance as is normally attached to the subjective element of "fear", which may be less reliable, and it may be necessary to place greater emphasis on the objective situation.

212. In view of the above considerations, investigation into the refugee status of a mentally disturbed person will, as a rule, have to be more searching than in a "normal" case and will call for a close examination of the applicant's past history and background, using whatever outside sources of information may be available.

(2) Unaccompanied minors

213. There is no special provision in the 1951 Convention regarding the refugee status of persons under age. The same definition of a refugee applies to all individuals, regardless of their age. When it is necessary to determine the refugee status of a minor, problems may arise due to the difficulty of applying the criteria of "well-founded fear" in his case. If a minor is accompanied by one (or both) of his parents, or another family member on whom he is dependent, who requests refugee status, the minor's own refugee status will be determined according to the principle of family unity (paragraphs 181 to 188 above).

214. The question of whether an unaccompanied minor may qualify for refugee status must be determined in the first instance according to the degree of his mental development and maturity. In the case of children, it will generally be necessary to enrol the services of experts conversant with child mentality. A child – and for that matter, an adolescent – not being legally independent should, if appropriate, have a guardian appointed whose task it would be to promote a decision that will be in the minor's best interests. In the absence of parents or of a legally appointed guardian, it is for the authorities to ensure that the interests of an applicant for refugee status who is a minor are fully safeguarded.

215. Where a minor is no longer a child but an adolescent, it will be easier to determine refugee status as in the case of an adult, although this again will depend upon the actual degree of the adolescent's maturity. It can be assumed that – in the absence of indications to the contrary – a person of 16 or over may be regarded as sufficiently mature to have a well-founded fear of persecution. Minors under 16 years of age may normally be assumed not to be sufficiently mature. They may have fear and a will of their own, but these may not have the same significance as in the case of an adult.

216. It should, however, be stressed that these are only general guidelines and that a minor's mental maturity must normally be determined in the light of his personal, family and cultural background.

217. Where the minor has not reached a sufficient degree of maturity to make it possible to establish well-founded fear in the same way as for an adult, it may be necessary to have greater regard to certain objective factors. Thus, if an unaccompanied minor finds himself in the company of a group of refugees, this may – depending on the circumstances – indicate that the minor is also a refugee.

218. The circumstances of the parents and other family members, including their situation in the minor's country of origin, will have to be taken into account. If there is reason to believe that the parents wish their child to be outside the country of origin on grounds of well-founded fear of persecution, the child himself may be presumed to have such fear.

219. If the will of the parents cannot be ascertained or if such will is in doubt or in conflict with the will of the child, then the examiner, in cooperation with the experts assisting him, will have to come to a decision as to the well-foundedness of the minor's fear on the basis of all the known circumstances, which may call for a liberal application of the benefit of the doubt.

Conclusion

220. In the present Handbook an attempt has been made to define certain guidelines that, in the experience of UNHCR, have proved useful in determining refugee status for the purposes of the 1951 Convention and the 1967 Protocol relating to the Status of Refugees. In so doing, particular attention has been paid to the definitions of the term "refugee" in these two instruments, and to various problems of interpretation arising out of these definitions. It has also been sought to show how these definitions may be applied in concrete cases and to focus attention on various procedural problems arising in regard to the determination of refugee status.

221. The Office of the High Commissioner is fully aware of the shortcomings inherent in a Handbook of this nature, bearing in mind that it is not possible to encompass every situation in which a person may apply for refugee status. Such situations are manifold and depend upon the infinitely varied conditions prevailing in countries of origin and on the special personal factors relating to the individual applicant.

222. The explanations given have shown that the determination of refugee status is by no means a mechanical and routine process. On the contrary, it calls for specialized knowledge, training and experience and – what is more important – an understanding of the particular situation of the applicant and of the human factors involved.

223. Within the above limits it is hoped that the present Handbook may provide some guidance to those who in their daily work are called upon to determine refugee status.

Annexes

Annex I

Excerpt from the final act of the United Nations Conference of Plenipotentiaries on the Status of Refugees and Stateless Persons*

IV

The Conference adopted unanimously the following recommendations:

A.

"The Conference,

"*Considering* that the issue and recognition of travel documents is necessary to facilitate the movement of refugees, and in particular their resettlement,

"*Urges* Governments which are parties to the Inter-Governmental Agreement on Refugee Travel Documents signed in London 15 October 1946, or which recognize travel documents issued in accordance with the Agreement, to continue to issue or to recognize such travel documents, and to extend the issue of such documents to refugees as defined in article 1 of the Convention relating to the Status of Refugees or to recognize the travel documents so issued to such persons, until they shall have undertaken obligations under article 28 of the said Convention."

B.

"The Conference,

"*Considering* that the unity of the family, the natural and fundamental group of society, is an essential right of the refugee, and that such unity is constantly threatened, and

"*Noting* with satisfaction that, according to the official commentary of the *ad hoc* Committee on Statelessness and Related Problems the rights granted to a refugee are extended to members of his family,

"*Recommends* Governments to take the necessary measure protection of the refugee's family, especially with a view to:

"(1) Ensuring that the unity of the refugee's family is maintained particularly in cases where the head of the family has fulfilled the necessary conditions for admission to a particular country,

"(2) The protection of refugees who are minors, in particular unaccompanied children and girls, with special reference to guardianship and adoption."

C.

"The Conference,

"*Considering* that, in the moral, legal and material spheres, refugees need the help of suitable welfare services, especially that of appropriate non-governmental organizations,

"*Recommends* Governments and inter-governmental bodies to facilitate, encourage and sustain the efforts of properly qualified or organizations."

D.

"The Conference,

* United Nations Treaty Series, vol. 189, p. 37.

"*Considering* that many persons still leave their country of origin for reasons of persecution and are entitled to special protection on account of their position,

"*Recommends* that Governments continue to receive refugees in their territories and that they act in concert in a true spirit of international co-operation in order that these refugees may find asylum and the possibility of resettlement."

E.

"The Conference,

"*Expresses* the hope that the Convention relating to the Status of Refugees will have value as an example exceeding its contractual scope and that all nations will be guided by it in granting so far as possible to persons in their territory as refugees and who would not be covered by the terms of the Convention, the treatment for which it provides."

Annex II
1951 Convention Relating to the Status of Refugees**

Preamble
The High Contracting Parties

Considering that the Charter of the United Nations and the Universal Declaration of Human Rights approved on 10 December 1948 by the General Assembly have affirmed the principle that human beings shall enjoy fundamental rights and freedoms without discrimination,

Considering that the United Nations has, on various occasions, manifested its profound concern for refugees and endeavored to assure refugees the widest possible exercise of these fundamental rights and freedoms,

Considering that it is desirable to revise and consolidate previous international agreements relating to the status of refugees and to extend the scope of and the protection accorded by such instruments by means of a new agreement,

Considering that the grant of asylum may place unduly heavy burdens on certain countries, and that a satisfactory solution of a problem of which the United Nations has recognized the international scope and nature the cannot therefore be achieved without international cooperation,

Expressing the wish that all States, recognizing the social and humanitarian nature of the problem of refugees, will do everything within their power to prevent this problem from becoming a cause of tension between States,

Noting that the United Nations High Commissioner for Refugees is charged with the task of supervising international conventions providing for the protection of Refugees, and recognizing that the effective coordination of measures taken to deal with this problem will depend upon the cooperation of States with the High Commissioner,

Have agreed as follows:

** United Nations Treaty Series, vol. 189, p. 137.

Chapter I

General Provisions

Article 1 Definition of the term "Refugee"

A. For the purposes of the present Convention, the term "refugee" shall apply to any person who:

(1) Has been considered a refugee under the Arrangements of 12 May 1926 and 30 June 1928 or under the Conventions of 28 October 1933 and 10 February 1938, the Protocol of 14 September 1939 or the Constitution of the International Refugee Organization;

Decisions of non-eligibility taken by the International Refugee Organization during the period of its activities shall not prevent the status of refugee being accorded to persons who fulfil the conditions of paragraph 2 of this section;

(2) As a result of events occurring before 1 January 1951 and owing to well-founded fear of being persecuted for reasons of race, religion, nationality, membership of a particular social group or political opinion, is outside the country of his nationality and is unable or, owing to such fear, is unwilling to avail himself of the protection of that country; or who, not having a nationality and being outside the country of his former habitual residence as a result of such events, is unable or, owing to such fear, is unwilling to return to it.

In the case of a person who has more than one nationality, the term "the country of his nationality" shall mean each of the countries of which he is a national, and a person shall not be deemed to be lacking the protection of the country of his nationality if, without any valid reason based on well-founded fear, he has not availed himself of the protection of one of the countries of which he is a national.

B. (1) For the purposes of this Convention, the words "events occurring before 1 January 1951" in Article 1, Section A, shall be understood to mean either:

(a) "events occurring in Europe before 1 January 1951" or

(b) "events occurring in Europe or elsewhere before 1 January 1951"

and each Contracting State shall make a declaration at the time of signature, ratification or accession, specifying which of these meanings it applies for the purpose of its obligations under this Convention.

(2) Any Contracting State which has adopted alternative (a) may at any time extend its obligations by adopting alternative (b) by means of a notification addressed to the Secretary-General of the United Nations.

C. This Convention shall cease to apply to any person falling under the terms of Section A if:

(1) He has voluntarily re-availed himself of the protection of the country of his nationality; or

(2) Having lost his nationality, he has voluntarily re-acquired it; or

(3) He has acquired a new nationality, and enjoys the protection of the country of his new nationality; or

(4) He has voluntarily re-established himself in the country which he left or outside which he remained owing to fear of persecution; or

(5) He can no longer, because the circumstances in connexion with which he has been recognized as a refugee have ceased to exist, continue to refuse to avail himself of the protection of the country of his nationality;

Provided that this paragraph shall not apply to a refugee falling under section A(1) of this Article who is able to invoke compelling reasons arising out of previous persecution for refusing to avail himself of the protection of the country of nationality.

(6) Being a person who has no nationality he is, because the circumstances in connexion with which he has been recognized as a refugee have ceased to exist, able to return to the country of his former habitual residence;

Provided that this paragraph shall not apply to a refugee falling under section A(1) of this Article who is able to invoke compelling reasons arising out of previous persecution for refusing to return to the country of his former habitual residence.

D. This Convention shall not apply to persons who are at present receiving from organs or agencies of the United Nations other than the United Nations High Commissioner for Refugees protection or assistance.

When such protection or assistance has ceased for any reason, without the position of such persons being definitively settled in accordance with the relevant resolutions adopted by the General Assembly of the United Nations, these persons shall *ipso facto* be entitled to the benefits of this Convention.

E. This Convention shall not apply to a person who is recognized by the competent authorities of the country in which he has taken residence as having the rights and obligations which are attached to the possession of the nationality of that country.

F. The provisions of this Convention shall not apply to any person with respect to whom there are serious reasons for considering that:

(a) he has committed a crime against peace, a war crime, or a crime against humanity, as defined in the international instruments drawn up to make provision in respect of such crimes;

(b) he has committed a serious non-political crime outside the country of refuge prior to his admission to that country as a refugee;

(c) he has been guilty of acts contrary to the purposes and principles of the United Nations.

Article 2 General obligations

Every refugee has duties to the country in which he finds himself, which require in particular that he conform to its laws and regulations as well as to measures taken for the maintenance of public order.

Article 3 Non-Discrimination

The Contracting States shall apply the provisions of this Convention to refugees without discrimination as to race, religion or country of origin.

Article 4 Religion

The Contracting States shall accord to refugees within their territories treatment at least as favorable as that accorded to their nationals with respect to freedom to practice their religion and freedom as regards the religious education of their children.

Article 5 Rights granted apart from this Convention

Nothing in this Convention shall be deemed to impair any rights and benefits granted by a Contracting State to refugees apart from this Convention.

Article 6 The term "in the same circumstances"

For the purpose of this Convention, the term "in the same circumstances" implies that any requirements (including requirements as to length and conditions of sojourn or residence) which the particular individual would have to fulfil for the enjoyment of the right in question, if he were not a refugee, must be fulfilled by him, with the exception of requirements which by their nature a refugee is incapable of fulfilling.

Article 7 Exemption from reciprocity

1. Except where this Convention contains more favorable provisions, a Contracting State shall accord to refugees the same treatment as is accorded to aliens generally.

2. After a period of three years' residence, all refugees shall enjoy exemption from legislative reciprocity in the territory of the Contracting States.

3. Each Contracting State shall continue to accord to refugees the rights and benefits to which they were already entitled, in the absence of reciprocity, at the date of entry into force of this Convention for that State.

4. The Contracting States shall consider favorably the possibility of according to refugees, in the absence of reciprocity, rights and benefits beyond those to which they are entitled according to paragraphs 2 and 3, and to extending exemption from reciprocity to refugees who do not fulfil the conditions provided for in paragraphs 2 and 3.

5. The provisions of paragraphs 2 and 3 apply both to the rights and benefits referred to in articles 13, 18, 19, 21 and 22 of this Convention and to rights and benefits for which this Convention does not provide.

Article 8 Exemption from exceptional measures

With regard to exceptional measures which may be taken against the person, property or interests of nationals of a foreign State, the Contracting States shall not apply such measures to a refugee who is formally a national of the said State solely on account of such nationality. Contracting States which, under their legislation, are prevented from applying the general principle expressed in this article, shall, in appropriate cases, grant exemptions in favor of such refugees.

Article 9 Provisional measures

Nothing in this Convention shall prevent a Contracting State, in time of war or other grave and exceptional circumstances, from taking provisionally measures which it considers to be essential to the national security in the case of a particular person, pending a determination by the Contracting State that person is in fact a refugee and that the continuance of such measures is necessary in his case in the interests of national security.

Article 10 Continuity of residence

1. Where a refugee has been forcibly displaced during the Second World War and removed to the territory of a Contracting State, and is resident there, the period of such enforced sojourn shall be considered to have been lawful residence within that territory.

2. Where a refugee has been forcibly displaced during the Second World War from the territory of a Contracting State and has, prior to the date of entry into force of this Convention, returned there for the purpose taking up residence, the period of residence before and after such enforced displacement shall be regarded as one uninterrupted period for any purposes for which uninterrupted residence is required.

Article 11 Refugee seamen

In the case of refugees regularly serving as crew members on board a ship flying the flag of a Contracting State, that state shall give sympathetic consideration to their establishment on its territory and the issue of travel documents to them on their temporary admissions to its territory particularly with a view to facilitating their establishment in another country.

Chapter II
Juridical Status

Article 12 Personal status

1. The personal status of a refugee shall be governed by the law of the country of his domicile or, if he has no domicile, by the law of the country of his residence.

2. Rights previously acquired by a refugee and dependent on personal status, more particularly rights attaching to marriage, shall be respected by a Contracting State, subject to compliance, if this be necessary, with the formalities required by the law of that State, provided that the right in question is one which would have been recognized by the law of that State had he not become a refugee.

Article 13 Movable and immovable property

The Contracting States shall accord to a refugee treatment as favorable as possible and, in any event, not less favorable than that accorded to aliens generally in the same circumstances as regards the acquisition of movable and immovable property and other rights pertaining thereto, and to leases and other contracts relating to movable and immovable property.

Article 14 Artistic rights and industrial property

In respect of the protection of industrial property, such as inventions, designs or models, trade marks, trade names, and of rights in literary, artistic and scientific works, a refugee shall be accorded in the country in which he has his habitual residence the same protection as is accorded to nationals of that country. In the territory of any other Contracting State, he shall be accorded the same protection as is accorded in that territory to nationals of the country in which he has habitual residence.

Article 15 Right of association

As regards non-political and non-profit-making associations and trade unions the Contracting States shall accord to refugees lawfully staying in their territory the most favorable treatment accorded to nationals of a foreign country, in the same circumstances.

Article 16 Access to courts

1. A refugee shall have free access to the courts of law on the territory of all Contracting States.

2. A refugee shall enjoy in the Contracting State in which he has his habitual residence the same treatment as a national in matters pertaining to access to the Courts, including legal assistance and exemption from *cautio judicatum solvi*.

3. A refugee shall be accorded in the matters referred to in paragraph 2 in countries other than that in which he has his habitual residence the treatment granted to a national of the country of his habitual residence.

Chapter III

Gainful Employment

Article 17 Wage-earning employment

1. The Contracting State shall accord to refugees lawfully staying in their territory the most favorable treatment accorded to nationals of a foreign country in the same circumstances, as regards the right to engage in wage-earning employment.

2. In any case, restrictive measures imposed on aliens or the employment of aliens for the protection of the national labour market shall not be applied to a refugee who was already exempt from them at the date of entry into force of this Convention for the Contracting States concerned, or who fulfills one of the following conditions:

(a) He has completed three years residence in the country;

(b) He has a spouse possessing the nationality of the country of residence. A refugee may not invoke the benefits of this provision if he has abandoned his spouse;

(c) He has one or more children possessing the nationality of the country of residence.

3. The Contracting States shall give sympathetic consideration to assimilating the rights of all refugees with regard to wage-earning employment to those of nationals, and in particular of those refugees who have entered their territory pursuant to programmes of labour recruitment or under immigration schemes.

Article 18 Self-employment

The Contracting States shall accord to a refugee lawfully in their territory treatment as favorable as possible and, in any event, not less favorable than that accorded to aliens generally in the same circumstances, as regards the right to engage on his own account in agriculture, industry, handicrafts and commerce and to establish commercial and industrial companies.

Article 19 Liberal professions

1. Each Contracting State shall accord to refugees lawfully staying in their territory who hold diplomas recognized by the competent authorities of that State, and who are desirous of practising a liberal profession, treatment as favorable as possible and, in any event, not less favorable than that accorded to aliens generally in the same circumstances.

2. The Contracting States shall use their best endeavours consistently with their laws and constitutions to secure the settlement of such refugees in the territories, other than the metropolitan territory, for whose international relations they are responsible.

Chapter IV
Welfare

Article 20 Rationing

Where a rationing system exists, which applies to the population at large and regulates the general distribution of products in short supply, refugees shall be accorded the same treatment as nationals.

Article 21 Housing

As regards housing, the Contracting States, in so far as the matter is regulated by laws or regulations or is subject to the control of public authorities, shall accord to refugees lawfully staying in their territory treatment as favorable as possible and, in any event, not less favorable than that accorded to aliens generally in the same circumstances.

Article 22 Public education

1. The Contracting States shall accord to refugees the same treatment as is accorded to nationals with respect to elementary education.

2. The Contracting States shall accord to refugees treatment as favorable as possible, and, in any event, not less favorable than that accorded to aliens generally in the same circumstances, with respect to education other than elementary education and, in particular, as regards access to studies, the recognition of foreign school certificates, diplomas and degrees, the remission of fees and charges and the award of scholarships.

Article 23 Public relief

The Contracting States shall accord to refugees lawfully staying in their territory the same treatment with respect to public relief and assistance as is accorded to their nationals.

Article 24 Labour legislation and social security

1. The Contracting States shall accord to refugees lawfully staying in their territory the same treatment as is accorded to nationals in respect of the following matters:

(a) In so far as such matters are governed by laws or regulations or are subject to the control of administrative authorities: remuneration, including family allowances where these form part of remuneration, hours of work, overtime arrangements, holidays with pay, restrictions on home work, minimum age of employment, apprenticeship and training, women's work and the work of young persons, and the enjoyment of the benefits of collective bargaining;

(b) Social security (legal provisions in respect of employment injury, occupational diseases, maternity, sickness, disability, old age, death, unemployment, family responsibilities and any other contingency which, according to national laws or regulations, is covered by a social security scheme), subject to the following limitations:

(i) There may be appropriate arrangements for the maintenance of acquired rights and rights in course of acquisition;

(ii) National laws or regulations of the country of residence may prescribe special arrangements concerning benefits or portions of benefits which are payable wholly out of public funds, and concerning allowances paid to persons who do not fulfil the contribution conditions prescribed for the award of a normal pension.

2. The right to compensation for the death of a refugee resulting from employment injury or from occupational disease shall not be affected by the fact that the residence of the beneficiary is outside the territory of the Contracting State.

3. The Contracting States shall extend to refugees the benefits of agreements concluded between them, or which may be concluded between them in the future, concerning the maintenance of acquired rights and rights in the process of acquisition in regard to social security, subject only to the conditions which apply to nationals of the States signatory to the agreements in question.

4. The Contracting States will give sympathetic consideration to extending to refugees so far as possible the benefits of similar agreements which may at any time be in force between such Contracting States and non-contracting States.

Chapter V
Administrative Measures

Article 25 Administrative assistance

1. When the exercise of a right by a refugee would normally require the assistance of authorities of a foreign country to whom he cannot have recourse, the Contracting States in whose territory he is residing shall arrange that such assistance be afforded to him by their own authorities or by an international authority.

2. The authority or authorities mentioned in paragraph 1 shall deliver or cause to be delivered under their supervision to refugees such documents or certifications as would normally be delivered to aliens by or through their national authorities.

3. Documents or certifications so delivered shall stand in the stead of the official instruments delivered to aliens by or through their national authorities, and shall be given credence in the absence of proof to the contrary.

4. Subject to such exceptional treatment as may be granted to indigent persons, fees may be charged for the services mentioned herein, but such fees shall be moderate and commensurate with those charged to nationals for similar services.

5. The provisions of this article shall be without prejudice to articles 27 and 28.

Article 26 Freedom of movement

Each Contracting State shall accord to refugees lawfully in its territory the right to choose their place of residence and to move freely within its territory, subject to any regulations applicable to aliens generally in the same circumstances.

Article 27 Identity papers

The Contracting States shall issue identity papers to any refugee in their territory who does not possess a valid travel document.

Article 28 Travel documents

1. The Contracting States shall issue to refugees lawfully staying in their territory travel documents for the purpose of travel outside their territory unless compelling reasons of national security or public order otherwise require, and the provisions of the Schedule to this Convention shall apply with respect to such document. The Contracting States may issue such a travel document to any other refugee in their territory; they shall in particular give sympathetic consideration to the issue of such a travel document to refugees in their territory who are unable to obtain a travel document from the country of their lawful residence.

2. Travel documents issued to refugees under previous international agreements by parties thereto shall be recognized and treated by the Contracting States in the same way as if they had been issued pursuant to this article.

Article 29 Fiscal charges

1. The Contracting States shall not impose upon refugees duties, charges or taxes, of any description whatsoever, other or higher than those which are or may be levied on their nationals in similar situations.

2. Nothing in the above paragraph shall prevent the application to refugees of the laws and regulations concerning charges in respect of the issue to aliens of administrative documents including identity papers.

Article 30 Transfer of assets

1. A Contracting State shall, in conformity with its laws and regulations permit refugees to transfer assets which they have brought into its territory, to another country where they have been admitted for the purposes of resettlement.

2. A Contracting State shall give sympathetic consideration to the application of refugees for permission to transfer assets wherever they may be and which are necessary for their resettlement in another country to which they have been admitted.

Article 31 Refugees unlawfully in the country of refuge

1. The Contracting States shall not impose penalties, on account of their illegal entry or presence, on refugees who, coming directly from a territory where their life or freedom was threatened in the sense of Article 1, enter or are present in their territory without

authorization, provided they present themselves without delay to the authorities and show good cause for their illegal entry or presence.

2. The Contracting States shall not apply to the movements of such refugees restrictions other than those which are necessary and such restrictions shall only be applied until their status in the country is regularized or they obtain admission into another country. The Contracting States shall allow such refugees a reasonable period and all the necessary facilities to obtain admission into another country.

Article 32 Expulsion

1. The Contracting States shall not expel a refugee lawfully in their territory save on grounds of national security or public order.

2. The expulsion of such a refugee shall be only in pursuance of a decision reached in accordance with due process of law. Except where compelling reasons of national security otherwise require, the refugee shall be allowed to clear himself, and to appeal to and be represented for the purpose before competent authority or a person or persons specially designated by the competent authority.

3. The Contracting States shall allow such a refugee a reasonable period within which to seek legal admission into another country. The Contracting States reserve the right to apply during that period such internal measures as they may deem necessary.

Article 33 Prohibition of expulsion or return ("refoulement")

1. No Contracting State shall expel or return (*"refouler"*) a refugee in any manner whatsoever to the frontiers of territories where his life or freedom would be threatened on account of his race, religion, nationality, membership of a particular social group or political opinion.

2. The benefit of the present provision may not, however, be claimed by a refugee whom there are reasonable grounds for regarding as a danger to the security of the country in which he is, or who, having been convicted by a final judgment of a particularly serious crime, constitutes a danger to the community of that country.

Article 34 Naturalization

The Contracting States shall as far as possible facilitate the assimilation and naturalization of refugees. They shall in particular make every effort to expedite naturalization proceedings and to reduce as far as possible the charges and cost of such proceedings.

Chapter VI

Executory and Transitory Provisions

Article 35 Cooperation of the national authorities with the United Nations

1. The Contracting States undertake to cooperate with the Office of the United Nations High Commissioner for Refugees, or any other agency of the United Nations which may succeed it, in the exercise of its functions, and shall in particular facilitate its duty of supervising the application of the provisions of this Convention.

2. In order to enable the Office of the High Commissioner or any other agency of the United Nations which may succeed it, to make reports to the competent organs of the United Nations, the Contracting States undertake to provide them in the appropriate form with information and statistical data requested concerning:

(a) the condition of refugees,

(b) the implementation of this Convention, and

(c) laws, regulations and decrees which are, or may hereafter be, in force relating to refugees.

Article 36 Information on national legislation

The Contracting States shall communicate to the Secretary-General of the United Nations the laws and regulations which they may adopt to ensure the application of this Convention.

Article 37 Relation to previous conventions

Without prejudice to article 28, Paragraph 2, of this Convention replaces, as between parties to it, the Arrangements of 5 July 1922, 31 May 1924, 12 May 1926, 30 June 1928 and 30 July 1935, the Conventions of 28 October 1933 and 10 February 1938, the Protocol of 14 September 1939 and the Agreement of 15 October 1946.

Chapter VII

Final Clauses

Article 38 Settlement of disputes

Any dispute between parties to this Convention relating to its interpretation or application, which cannot be settled by other means, shall be referred to the International Court of Justice at the request of any one of the parties to the dispute.

Article 39 Signature, ratification and accession

1. This Convention shall be opened for signature at Geneva on 28 July 1951 shall thereafter be deposited with the Secretary-General of the United Nations. It shall be open for signature at the European office of the United Nations from 28 July to 31 August 1951 and shall be re-opened for signature at the Headquarters of the United Nations from 17 September 1951 to 31 December 1952.

2. This Convention shall be open for signature on behalf of all States members of the United Nations and also on behalf of any other State invited to attend the Conference of Plenipotentiaries on the Status of Refugees and Stateless Persons or to which an invitation to sign will have been addressed by the General Assembly. It shall be ratified and the instruments of ratification shall be deposited with the Secretary-General of the United Nations.

3. This Convention shall be open from 28 July 1951 for accession by the States referred to in paragraph 2 of this Article. Accession shall be effected by the deposit of an instrument of accession with the Secretary-General of the United Nations.

Article 40 Territorial application clause

1. Any State may, at the time of signature, ratification or accession, declare that this Convention shall extend to all or any of the territories for the international relations of which it is responsible. Such a declaration shall take effect when the Convention enters into force for the States concerned.

2. At any time thereafter any such extension shall be made by notification addressed to the Secretary-General of the United Nations and shall take effect as from the ninetieth day after the day of receipt by the Secretary-General of the United Nations of this notification, or as from the date of entry into force of the Convention for the State concerned, whichever is the later.

3. With respect to those territories to which this Convention is not extended at the time of signature, ratification or accession, each State concerned shall consider the possibility of taking the necessary steps in order to extend the application of this Convention to such territories, subject where necessary for constitutional reasons, to the consent of the governments of such territories.

Article 41 Federal clause

In the case of a Federal or non-unitary State, the following provisions shall apply:

(a) With respect to those articles of this Convention that come within the legislative jurisdiction of the federal legislative authority, the obligations of the Federal Government shall to this extent be the same as those of Parties which are not Federal States,

(b) With respect to those articles of this Convention that come within the legislative jurisdiction of constituent States, provinces or cantons which are not, under the constitutional system of the federation, bound to take legislative action, the Federal Government shall bring such articles with a favorable recommendation, to the notice of the appropriate authorities of States, provinces or cantons at the earliest possible moment.

(c) A Federal State Party to this Convention shall, at the request of any other Contracting State transmitted through the Secretary-General of the United Nations, supply a statement of the law and practice of the Federation and its constituent units in regard to any particular provision of the Convention showing the extent to which effect has been given to that provision by legislative or other action.

Article 42 Reservations

1. At the time of signature, ratification or accession, any State may make reservations to articles of the Convention other than to articles 1, 3, 4, 16 (1), 33, 36 to 46 inclusive.

2. Any State making a reservation in accordance with paragraph 1 of this article may at any time withdraw the reservation by a communication to that effect addressed to the Secretary-General of the United Nations.

Article 43 Entry into force

1. This Convention shall come into force on the ninetieth day following the day of deposit of the sixth instrument of ratification or accession.

2. For each State ratifying or acceding to the Convention after the deposit of the sixth instrument of ratification or accession, the Convention shall enter into force on the ninetieth day following the day of deposit by such State of its instrument of ratification or accession.

Article 44 Denunciation

1. Any Contracting State may denounce this Convention at any time by a notification addressed to the Secretary-General of the United Nations.

2. Such denunciation shall take effect for the Contracting State concerned one year from the date upon which it is received by the Secretary-General of the United Nations.

3. Any State which has made a declaration or notification under article 40 may, at any time thereafter, by a notification to the Secretary-General of the United Nations, declare that the Convention shall cease to extend to such territory one year after the date of receipt of the notification by the Secretary-General.

Article 45 Revision

1. Any Contracting State may request revision of this Convention at any time by a notification addressed to the Secretary-General of the United Nations.

2. The General Assembly of the United Nations shall recommend the steps, if any, to be taken in respect of such request.

Article 46 Notifications by the Secretary-General of the United Nations

The Secretary-General of the United Nations shall inform all Members of the United Nations and non-member States referred to in article 39:
(a) of declarations and notifications in accordance with Section B of Article 1;
(b) of signatures, ratifications and accessions in accordance with article 39;
(c) of declarations and notifications in accordance with article 40;
(d) of reservations and withdrawals in accordance with article 42;
(e) of the date on which this Convention will come into force in accordance with article 43;
(f) of denunciations and notifications in accordance with article 44;
(g) of requests for revision in accordance with article 45.

In faith whereof the undersigned, duly authorized, have signed this Convention on behalf of their respective Governments,

Done at Geneva, this twenty-eighth day of July, one thousand nine hundred and fifty-one, in a single copy, of which the English and French texts are equally authentic and which shall remain deposited in the archives of the United Nations, and certified true copies of which shall be delivered to all Members of the United Nations and to the non-member States referred to in article 39.

Schedule

Paragraph 1

1. The travel document referred to in article 28 of this Convention shall be similar to the specimen annexed hereto.

2. The document shall be made out in at least two languages, one of which shall be in English or French.

Paragraph 2

Subject to the regulations obtaining in the country of issue, children may be included in the travel document of a parent or, in exceptional circumstances, of another adult refugee.

Paragraph 3

The fees charged for issue of the document shall not exceed the lowest scale of charges for national passports.

Paragraph 4

Save in special or exceptional cases, the document shall be made valid for the largest possible number of countries.

Paragraph 5

The document shall have a validity of either one or two years, at the discretion of the issuing authority.

Paragraph 6

1. The renewal or extension of the validity of the document is a matter for the authority which issued it, so long as the holder has not established lawful residence in another territory and resides lawfully in the territory of the said authority. The issue of a new document is, under the same conditions, a matter for the authority which issued the former document.

2. Diplomatic or consular authorities, specially authorized for the purpose, shall be empowered to extend, for a period not exceeding six months, the validity of travel documents issued by the Governments.

3. The Contracting States shall give sympathetic consideration to renewing or extending the validity of travel documents or issuing new documents to refugees no longer lawfully resident in their territory who are unable to obtain a travel document from the country of their lawful residence.

Paragraph 7

The Contracting States shall recognize the validity of the documents issued in accordance with the provisions of article 28 of this Convention.

Paragraph 8

The competent authorities of the country to which the refugee desires to proceed shall, if they are prepared to admit him and if a visa is required, affix a visa on the document of which he is the holder.

Paragraph 9

1. The Contracting States undertake to issue transit visas to refugees who have obtained visas for a territory of final destination.
2. The issue of such visas may be refused on grounds which would justify refusal of a visa to any alien.

Paragraph 10

The fees for the issue of exit, entry or transit visas shall not exceed the lowest scale of charges for visas on foreign passports.

Paragraph 11

When a refugee has lawfully taken up residence in the territory of another Contracting State, the responsibility for the issue of a new document, under the terms and conditions of article 28, shall be that of the competent authority of that territory, to which the refugee shall be entitled to apply.

Paragraph 12

The authority issuing a new document shall withdraw the old document and shall return it to the country of issue, if it is stated in the document that it should be so returned; otherwise it shall withdraw and cancel the document.

Paragraph 13

1. Each Contracting State undertakes that the holder of a travel document issued by it in accordance with article 28 of this Convention shall be re-admitted to its territory at any time during the period of its validity.
2. Subject to the provisions of the preceding sub-paragraph, a Contracting State may require the holder of the document to comply with such formalities as may be prescribed in regard to exit from or return to its territory.
3. The Contracting States reserve the right, in exceptional cases, or in cases where the refugee's stay is authorized for a specific period, when issuing the document, to limit the period during which the refugee may return to a period of not less than three months.

Paragraph 14

Subject only to the terms of paragraph 13, the provisions of this Schedule in no way affect the laws and regulations governing the conditions of admission to, transit through, residence and establishment in, and departure from, the territories of the Contracting States.

Paragraph 15

Neither the issue of the document nor the entries made thereon determine or affect the status of the holder, particularly as regards nationality.

Paragraph 16

The issue of the document does not in any way entitle the holder to the protection of the diplomatic or consular authorities of the country of issue, and does not confer on these authorities a right of protection.

Annex

Specimen Travel Document

[Not reproduced here]

Annex III

1967 Protocol Relating to the Status of Refugees*

The States Parties to the present Protocol,

Considering that the Convention relating to the Status of Refugees done at Geneva on 28 July 1951 (hereinafter referred to as the Convention) covers only those persons who have become refugees as a result of events occurring before 1 January 1951,

Considering that new refugee situations have arisen since the Convention was adopted and that the refugees concerned may therefore not fall within the scope of the Convention,

Considering that it is desirable that equal status should be enjoyed by all refugees covered by the definition in the Convention irrespective of the dateline 1 January 1951,

Have agreed as follows:

Article I General provision

1. The States Parties to the present Protocol undertake to apply articles 2 to 34 inclusive of the Convention to refugees as hereinafter defined.

2. For the purpose of the present Protocol, the term "refugee" shall, except as regards the application of paragraph 3 of this article, mean any person within the definition of article 1 of the Convention as if the words "As a result of events occurring before 1 January 1951 and . . ." and the words ". . . as a result of such events", in article 1A(2) were omitted.

3. The present Protocol shall be applied by the States Parties hereto without any geographic limitation, save that existing declarations made by States already Parties to the Convention in accordance with article 1B(1)(a) of the Convention, shall, unless extended under article 1B(2) thereof, apply also under the present Protocol.

* United Nations, Treaty Series, vol 606, p. 267.

Article II Cooperation of the national authorities with the United Nations

1. The States Parties to the present Protocol undertake to cooperate with the Office of the United Nations High Commissioner for Refugees, or any other agency of the United Nations which may succeed it, in the exercise of its functions, and shall in particular facilitate its duty of supervising the application of the provisions of the present Protocol.

2. In order to enable the Office of the High Commissioner, or any other agency of the United Nations which may succeed it, to make reports to the competent organs of the United Nations, the States Parties to the present Protocol undertake to provide them with the information and statistical data requested, in the appropriate form, concerning:

(a) The condition of refugees;

(b) The implementation of the present Protocol;

(c) Laws, regulations and decrees which are, or may hereafter be, in force relating to refugees.

Article III Information on national legislation

The States Parties to the present Protocol shall communicate to the Secretary-General of the United Nations the laws and regulations which they may adopt to ensure the application of the present Protocol.

Article IV Settlement of disputes

Any dispute between States Parties to the present Protocol which relates to its interpretation or application and which cannot be settled by other means shall be referred to the International Court of Justice at the request of any one of the parties to the dispute.

Article V Accession

The present Protocol shall be open for accession on behalf of all States Parties to the Convention and of any other State Member of the United Nations or member of any of the specialized agencies or to which an invitation to accede may have been addressed by the General Assembly of the United Nations. Accession shall be effected by the deposit of an instrument of accession with the Secretary-General of the United Nations.

Article VI Federal clause

In the case of a Federal or non-unitary State, the following provisions shall apply:

(a) With respect to those articles of the Convention to be applied in accordance with article I, paragraph 1, of the present Protocol that come within the legislative jurisdiction of the federal legislative authority, the obligations of the Federal Government shall to this extent be the same as those of States Parties which are not Federal States;

(b) With respect to those articles of the Convention to be applied in accordance with article I, paragraph 1, of the present Protocol that come within the legislative jurisdiction of constituent States, provinces or cantons which are not, under the constitutional system of the federation, bound to take legislative action, the Federal Government shall bring such articles with a favourable recommendation to the notice of the appropriate authorities of States, provinces or cantons at the earliest possible moment;

(c) A Federal State Party to the present Protocol shall, at the request of any other State Party hereto transmitted through the Secretary General of the United Nations, supply a statement of the law and practice of the Federation and its constituent units in regard to any particular provision of the Convention to be applied in accordance with article 1, paragraph 1, of the present Protocol, showing the extent to which effect has been given to that provision by legislative or other action.

Article VII Reservations and Declarations

1. At the time of accession, any State may make reservations in respect of article IV of the present Protocol and in respect of the application in accordance with article I of the present Protocol of any provisions of the Convention other than those contained in articles 1, 3, 4, 16 (1) and 33 thereof, provided that in the case of a State Party to the Convention reservations made under this article shall not extend to refugees in respect of whom the Convention applies.

2. Reservations made by States Parties to the Convention in accordance with article 42 thereof shall, unless withdrawn, be applicable in relation to their obligations under the present Protocol.

3. Any State making a reservation in accordance with paragraph 1 of this article may at any time withdraw such reservation by a communication to that effect addressed to the Secretary-General of the United Nations.

4. Declarations made under article 40, paragraphs 1 and 2, of the Convention by a State Party thereto which accedes to the present Protocol shall be deemed to apply in respect of the present Protocol, unless upon accession a notification to the contrary is addressed by the State Party concerned to the Secretary-General of the United Nations. The provisions of article 40, paragraphs 2 and 3, and of article 44, paragraph 3, of the Convention shall be deemed to apply *mutatis mutandis* to the present Protocol.

Article VIII Entry into force

1. The present Protocol shall come into force on the day of deposit of the sixth instrument of accession.

2. For each State acceding to the Protocol after the deposit of the sixth instrument of accession, the Protocol shall come into force on the date of deposit by such State of its instrument of accession.

Article IX Denunciation

1. Any State Party hereto may denounce this Protocol at any time by a notification addressed to the Secretary-General of the United Nations.

2. Such denunciation shall take effect for the State Party concerned one year from the date on which it is received by the Secretary-General of the United Nations.

Article X Notifications by the Secretary-General of the United Nations

The Secretary-General of the United Nations shall inform the States referred to in article V above of the date of entry into force, accessions, reservations and withdrawals of reservations to and denunciations of the present Protocol, and of declarations and notifications relating hereto.

Article XI Deposit in the Archives of the Secretariat of the United Nations

A copy of the present Protocol, of which the Chinese, English, French, Russian and Spanish texts are equally authentic, signed by the President of the General Assembly and by the Secretary-General of the United Nations, shall be deposited in the archives of the Secretariat of the United Nations. The Secretary-General will transmit certified copies thereof to all States Members of the United Nations and to the other States referred to in article V above.

Annex IV

List of States Parties to the 1951 Convention Relating to the Status of Refugees and the 1967 Protocol

Date of Entry into Force: 22 April 1954 (Convention)
4 October 1967 (Protocol)

As of 1 November 2011

Total number of States Parties to the 1951 Convention: 145
Total number of States Parties to the 1967 Protocol: 146
States Parties to both the Convention and Protocol: 143
States Parties to one or both of these instruments: 148

States Parties to the 1951 Convention only:

Madagascar, Saint Kitts and Nevis

States Parties to the 1967 Protocol only:

Cape Verde, United States of America, Venezuela

The dates indicated are the dates of deposit of the instrument of ratification or accession by the respective States Parties with the Secretary-General of the United Nations in New York. In accordance with article 43(2), the Convention enters into force on the ninetieth day after the date of deposit. The Protocol enters into force on the date of deposit (article VIII (2)). Exceptions are indicated below.

Country*	Convention	Protocol
Afghanistan	30 Aug 2005 a	30 Aug 2005 a
Albania	18 Aug 1992 a	18 Aug 1992 a
Algeria	21 Feb 1963 d	08 Nov 1967 a
Angola	23 Jun 1981 a	23 Jun 1981 a
Antigua and Barbuda	07 Sep 1995 a	07 Sep 1995 a
Argentina	15 Nov 1961 a	06 Dec 1967 a
Armenia	06 Jul 1993 a	06 Jul 1993 a
Australia	22 Jan 1954 a	13 Dec 1973 a
Austria	01 Nov 1954 r	05 Sep 1973 a
Azerbaijan	12 Feb 1993 a	12 Feb 1993 a
Bahamas	15 Sep 1993 a	15 Sep 1993 a
Belarus	23 Aug 2001 a	23 Aug 2001 a
Belgium	22 Jul 1953 r	08 Apr 1969 a
Belize	27 Jun 1990 a	27 Jun 1990 a
Benin	04 Apr 1962 d	06 Jul 1970 a
Bolivia, Plurinational State of	09 Feb 1982 a	09 Feb 1982 a
Bosnia and Herzegovina	01 Sep 1993 d	01 Sep 1993 d
Botswana	06 Jan 1969 a	06 Jan 1969 a
Brazil	16 Nov 1960 r	07 Apr 1972 a
Bulgaria	12 May 1993 a	12 May 1993 a
Burkina Faso	18 Jun 1980 a	18 Jun 1980 a
Burundi	19 Jul 1963 a	15 Mar 1971 a
Cambodia	15 Oct 1992 a	15 Oct 1992 a
Cameroon	23 Oct 1961 d	19 Sep 1967 a
Canada	04 Jun 1969 a	04 Jun 1969 a
Cape Verde (P)		09 Jul 1987 a
Central African Republic	04 Sep 1962 d	30 Aug 1967 a
Chad	19 Aug 1981 a	19 Aug 1981 a
Chile	28 Jan 1972 a	27 Apr 1972 a
China	24 Sep 1982 a	24 Sep 1982 a
Colombia	10 Oct 1961 r	04 Mar 1980 a

Congo	15 Oct 1962 d	10 Jul 1970 a
Congo, Democratic Republic of	19 July 1965 a	13 Jan 1975 a
Costa Rica	28 Mar 1978 a	28 Mar 1978 a
Côte d'Ivoire	08 Dec 1961 d	16 Feb 1970 a
Croatia	12 Oct 1992 d	12 Oct 1992 d
Cyprus	16 May 1963 d	09 Jul 1968 a
Czech Republic	11 May 1993 d	11 May 1993 d
Denmark	04 Dec 1952 r	29 Jan 1968 a
Djibouti	09 Aug 1977 d	09 Aug 1977 d
Dominica	17 Feb 1994 a	17 Feb 1994 a
Dominican Republic	04 Jan 1978 a	04 Jan 1978 a
Ecuador	17 Aug 1955 a	06 Mar 1969 a
Egypt	22 May 1981 a	22 May 1981 a
El Salvador	28 Apr 1983 a	28 Apr 1983 a
Equatorial Guinea	07 Feb 1986 a	07 Feb 1986 a
Estonia	10 Apr 1997 a	10 Apr 1997 a
Ethiopia	10 Nov 1969 a	10 Nov 1969 a
Fiji	12 Jun 1972 d	12 Jun 1972 d
Finland	10 Oct 1968 a	10 Oct 1968 a
France	23 Jun 1954 r	03 Feb 1971 a
Gabon	27 Apr 1964 a	28 Aug 1973 a
Gambia	07 Sep 1966 d	29 Sep 1967 a
Georgia	09 Aug 1999 a	09 Aug 1999 a
Germany	01 Dec 1953 r	05 Nov 1969 a
Ghana	18 Mar 1963 a	30 Aug 1968 a
Greece	05 Apr 1960 r	07 Aug 1968 a
Guatemala	22 Sep 1983 a	22 Sep 1983 a
Guinea	28 Dec 1965 d	16 May 1968 a
Guinea-Bissau	11 Feb 1976 a	11 Feb 1976 a
Haiti	25 Sep 1984 a	25 Sep 1984 a
Holy See	15 Mar 1956 r	08 Jun 1967 a
Honduras	23 Mar 1992 a	23 Mar 1992 a
Hungary	14 Mar 1989 a	14 Mar 1989 a
Iceland	30 Nov 1955 a	26 Apr 1968 a
Iran, Islamic Republic of	28 Jul 1976 a	28 Jul 1976 a

Ireland	29 Nov 1956 a	06 Nov 1968 a
Israel	01 Oct 1954 r	14 Jun 1968 a
Italy	15 Nov 1954 r	26 Jan 1972 a
Jamaica	30 Jul 1964 d	30 Oct 1980 a
Japan	03 Oct 1981 a	01 Jan 1982 a
Kazakhstan	15 Jan 1999 a	15 Jan 1999 a
Kenya	16 May 1966 a	13 Nov 1981 a
Kyrgyzstan	08 Oct 1996 a	08 Oct 1996 a
Korea, Republic of	03 Dec 1992 a	03 Dec 1992 a
Latvia	31 Jul 1997 a	31 Jul 1997 a
Lesotho	14 May 1981 a	14 May 1981 a
Liberia	15 Oct 1964 a	27 Feb 1980 a
Liechtenstein	08 Mar 1957 r	20 May 1968 a
Lithuania	28 Apr 1997 a	28 Apr 1997 a
Luxembourg	23 Jul 1953 r	22 Apr 1971 a
Macedonia, The Former Yugoslav Republic of	18 Jan 1994 d	18 Jan 1994 d
Madagascar (C)	18 Dec 1967 a	
Malawi	10 Dec 1987 a	10 Dec 1987 a
Mali	02 Feb 1973 d	02 Feb 1973 a
Malta	17 Jun 1971 a	15 Sep 1971 a
Mauritania	05 May 1987 a	05 May 1987 a
Mexico	07 June 2000 a	07 June 2000 a
Moldova, Republic of	31 Jan 2002 a	31 Jan 2002 a
Monaco	18 May 1954 a	16 June 2010 a
Montenegro	10 Oct 2006 d	10 Oct 2006 d
Morocco	07 Nov 1956 d	20 Apr 1971 a
Mozambique	16 Dec 1983 a	01 May 1989 a
Namibia	17 Feb 1995 a	17 Feb 1995 a
Nauru	28 June 2011 a	28 June 2011 a
Netherlands	03 May 1956 r	29 Nov 1968 a
New Zealand	30 Jun 1960 a	06 Aug 1973 a
Nicaragua	28 Mar 1980 a	28 Mar 1980 a

Niger	25 Aug 1961 d	02 Feb 1970 a
Nigeria	23 Oct 1967 a	02 May 1968 a
Norway	23 Mar 1953 r	28 Nov 1967 a
Panama	02 Aug 1978 a	02 Aug 1978 a
Papua New Guinea	17 Jul 1986 a	17 Jul 1986 a
Paraguay	01 Apr 1970 a	01 Apr 1970 a
Peru	21 Dec 1964 a	15 Sep 1983 a
Philippines	22 Jul 1981 a	22 Jul 1981 a
Poland	27 Sep 1991 a	27 Sep 1991 a
Portugal	22 Dec 1960 a	13 Jul 1976 a
Romania	07 Aug 1991 a	07 Aug 1991 a
Russian Federation	02 Feb 1993 a	02 Feb 1993 a
Rwanda	03 Jan 1980 a	03 Jan 1980 a
Saint Kitts and Nevis (C)	01 Feb 2002 a	
Saint Vincent and the Grenadines	03 Nov 1993 a	03 Nov 2003 a
Samoa	21 Sep 1988 a	29 Nov 1994 a
Sao Tome and Principe	01 Feb 1978 a	01 Feb 1978 a
Senegal	02 May 1963 d	03 Oct 1967 a
Serbia	12 Mar 2001 d	12 Mar 2001 d
Seychelles	23 Apr 1980 a	23 Apr 1980 a
Sierra Leone	22 May 1981 a	22 May 1981 a
Slovakia	04 Feb 1993 d	04 Feb 1993 d
Slovenia	06 Jul 1992 d	06 Jul 1992 d
Solomon Islands	28 Feb 1995 a	12 Apr 1995 a
Somalia	10 Oct 1978 a	10 Oct 1978 a
South Africa	12 Jan 1996 a	12 Jan 1996 a
Spain	14 Aug 1978 a	14 Aug 1978 a
Sudan	22 Feb 1974 a	23 May 1974 a
Suriname	29 Nov 1978 d	29 Nov 1978 d
Swaziland	14 Feb 2000 a	28 Jan 1969 a
Sweden	26 Oct 1954 r	04 Oct 1967 a
Switzerland	21 Jan 1955 r	20 May 1968 a
Tajikistan	07 Dec 1993 a	07 Dec 1993 a

Tanzania, United Republic of	12 May 1964 a	04 Sep 1968 a
Timor-Leste	07 May 2003 a	07 May 2003 a
Togo	27 Feb 1962 d	01 Dec 1969 a
Trinidad and Tobago	10 Nov 2000 a	10 Nov 2000 a
Tunisia	24 Oct 1957 d	16 Oct 1968 a
Turkey	30 Mar 1962 r	31 Jul 1968 a
Turkmenistan	02 Mar 1998 a	02 Mar 1998 a
Tuvalu	07 Mar 1986 d	07 Mar 1986 d
Uganda	27 Sep 1976 a	27 Sep 1976 a
Ukraine	10 Jun 2002 a	04 Apr 2002 a
United Kingdom of Great Britain and Northern Ireland	11 Mar 1954 r	04 Sep 1968 a
United States of America (P)		01 Nov 1968 a
Uruguay	22 Sep 1970 a	22 Sep 1970 a
Venezuela, Bolivarian Republic of (P)		19 Sep 1986 a
Yemen	18 Jan 1980 a	18 Jan 1980 a
Zambia	24 Sep 1969 d	24 Sep 1969 a
Zimbabwe	25 Aug 1981 a	25 Aug 1981 a

Notes:
* Ratification (r), Accession (a), Succession (d).
** (C) denotes States Parties to the 1951 Convention only;
(P) denotes States Parties to the 1967 Protocol only.

Limitations:

Article 1B(1) of the 1951 Convention provides: "For the purposes of this Convention, the words 'events occurring before 1 January 1951' in article 1, Section A, shall be understood to mean either (a) 'events occurring in Europe before 1 January 1951'; or (b) 'events occurring in Europe or elsewhere before 1 January 1951', and each Contracting State shall make a declaration at the time of signature, ratification or accession, specifying which of these meanings it applies for the purposes of its obligations under this Convention."

The following States adopted alternative (a), the geographical limitation: Congo, Madagascar, Monaco and Turkey. Turkey expressly maintained its declaration of geographical limitation upon acceding to the 1967 Protocol. Madagascar has not yet adhered to the Protocol.

All other States Parties ratified, acceded or succeeded to the Convention without a geographical limitation by selecting option (b), 'events occurring in Europe or elsewhere before 1 January 1951'.

Annex V

Excerpt from the Charter of the International Military Tribunal*

Article 6

"The Tribunal established by the Agreement referred to in Article 1 hereof for the trial and punishment of the major war criminals of the European Axis countries shall have the power to try and punish persons who, acting in the interests of the European Axis countries, whether as individuals or as members of organisations, committed any of the following crimes.

"The following acts, or any of them, are crimes coming within the jurisdiction of the Tribunal for which there shall be individual responsibility:

(a) *Crimes against peace*: namely, planning, preparation, initiation or waging of a war of aggression, or a war in violation of international treaties, agreements or assurances, or participation in a common plan or conspiracy for the accomplishment of any of the foregoing;

(b) *War crimes*: namely, violations of the laws or customs of war. Such violations shall include, but not be limited to, murder, ill-treatment or deportation to slave labour or for any other purpose, of civilian population of or in occupied territory, murder or ill-treatment of prisoners of war or persons on the seas, killing of hostages, plunder of public or private property, wanton destruction of cities, towns or villages, or devastation not justified by military necessity;

(c) *Crimes against humanity*: namely, murder, extermination, enslavement, deportation and other inhumane acts committed against any civilian population, before or during the war; or persecutions on political, racial or religious grounds in execution of or in connection with any crime within the jurisdiction of the Tribunal, whether or not in violation of the domestic law of the country where perpetrated.

"Leaders, organisers, instigators and accomplices participating in the formulation or execution of a common plan or conspiracy to commit any of the foregoing crimes are responsible for all acts performed by any persons in execution of such plan."

Note: * See "*The Charter and Judgment of the Nürnberg Tribunal: History and Analysis*" Appendix II – United Nations General Assembly-International Law Commission 1949 (A/CN.4/5 of 3 March 1949).

Annex VI

International Instruments Relating to Article 1F(A) of the 1951 Convention

The main international instruments which pertain to Article 1F(a) of the 1951 Convention are as follows:

(1) The London Agreement of 8 August 1945 and Charter of the International Military Tribunal;

(2) Law No. 10 of the Control Council for Germany of 20 December 1945 for the Punishment of Persons Guilty of War Crimes, Crimes against Peace and Crimes against Humanity;

(3) United Nations General Assembly Resolution 3(1) of 13 February 1946 and 95(1) of 11 December 1946 which confirm war crimes and crimes against humanity as they are defined in the Charter of the International Military Tribunal of 8 August 1945;

(4) Convention on the Prevention and Punishment of the Crime of Genocide of 1948 (Article III); (entered into force 12 January 1951);

(5) Convention of the Non-Applicability of Statutory Limitations of War Crimes and Crimes Against Humanity of 1968 (entered into force 11 November 1970);

(6) Geneva Conventions for the protection of victims of war of August 12, 1949 (Convention for the protection of the wounded, and sick, Article 50; Convention for the protection of wounded, sick and shipwrecked, Article 51; Convention relative to the treatment of prisoners of war, Article 130; Convention relative to the protection of civilian persons, Article 147);

(7) Additional Protocol to the Geneva Conventions of 12 August 1949 Relating to the Protection of Victims of International Armed Conflicts (Article 85 on the repression of breaches of this Protocol).

Annex VII

Statute of the Office of the United Nations High Commissioner for Refugees

Chapter I

General Provisions

1. The United Nations High Commissioner for Refugees, acting under the authority of the General Assembly, shall assume the function of providing international protection, under the auspices of the United Nations, to refugees who fall within the scope of the present Statute and of seeking permanent solutions for the problem of refugees by assisting governments and, subject to the approval of the governments concerned, private organizations to facilitate the voluntary repatriation of such refugees, or their assimilation within new national communities. In the exercise of his functions, more particularly when difficulties arise, and for instance with regard to any controversy concerning the international status of these persons, the High Commissioner shall request the opinion of an advisory committee on refugees if it is created.

2. The work of the High Commissioner shall be of an entirely non-political character; it shall be humanitarian and social and shall relate, as a rule, to groups and categories of refugees.

3. The High Commissioner shall follow policy directives given him by the General Assembly or the Economic and Social Council.

4. The Economic and Social Council may decide, after hearing the views of the High Commissioner on the subject, to establish an advisory committee on refugees, which shall consist of representatives of States Members and States non-members of the United Nations, to be selected by the Council on the basis of their demonstrated interest in and devotion to the solution of the refugee problem.

5. The General Assembly shall review, not later than at its eighth regular session, the arrangements for the Office of the High Commissioner with a view to determining whether the Office should be continued beyond 31 December 1953.

Chapter II

Functions of the High Commissioner

6. The competence of the High Commissioner shall extend to:

A. (i) Any person who has been considered a refugee under the Arrangements of 12 May 1926 and 30 June 1928 or under the Conventions of 28 October 1933 and 10 February 1938, the Protocol of 14 September 1939 or the Constitution of the International Refugee Organization;

(ii) Any person who, as a result of events occurring before 1 January 1951 and owing to well-founded fear of being persecuted for reasons of race, religion, nationality or political opinion, is outside the country of his nationality and is unable or, owing to such fear or for reasons other than personal convenience, is unwilling to avail himself of the protection of that country; or who, not having a nationality and being outside the country of his former habitual residence, is unable or, owing to such fear or for reasons other than personal convenience, is unwilling to return to it.

Decisions as to eligibility taken by the International Refugee Organization during the period of its activities shall not prevent the status of refugee being accorded to persons who fulfil the conditions of the present paragraph;

The competence of the High Commissioner shall cease to apply to any person defined in section A above if:

(a) He has voluntarily re-availed himself of the protection of the country of his nationality; or

(b) Having lost his nationality, he has voluntarily re-acquired it; or

(c) He has acquired a new nationality, and enjoys the protection of the country of his new nationality; or

(d) He has voluntarily re-established himself in the country which he left or outside which he remained owing to fear of persecution; or

(e) He can no longer, because the circumstances in connexion with which he has been recognized as a refugee have ceased to exist, claim grounds other than those of personal convenience for continuing to refuse to avail himself of the protection of the country of his nationality. Reasons of a purely economic character may not be invoked; or

(f) Being a person who has no nationality, he can no longer, because the circumstances in connexion with which he has been recognized as a refugee have ceased to exist and he is able to return to the country of his former habitual residence, claim grounds other than those of personal convenience for continuing to refuse to return to that country;

B. Any other person who is outside the country of his nationality or, if he has no nationality, the country of his former habitual residence, because he has or had well-founded fear of persecution by reason of his race, religion, nationality or political opinion and is unable or, because of such fear, is unwilling to avail himself of the protection of the government of the country of his nationality, or, if he has no nationality, to return to the country of his former habitual residence.

7. Provided that the competence of the High Commissioner as defined in paragraph 6 above shall not extend to a person:

(a) Who is a national of more than one country unless he satisfies the provisions of the preceding paragraph in relation to each of the countries of which he is a national; or

(b) Who is recognized by the competent authorities of the country in which he has taken residence as having the rights and obligations which are attached to the possession of the nationality of that country; or

(c) Who continues to receive from other organs or agencies of the United Nations protection or assistance; or

(d) In respect of whom there are serious reasons for considering that he has committed a crime covered by the provisions of treaties of extradition or a crime mentioned in article VI of the London Charter of the International Military Tribunal or by the provisions of article 14, paragraph 2, of the Universal Declaration of Human Rights.*

8. The High Commissioner shall provide for the protection of refugees falling under the competence of his Office by:

(a) Promoting the conclusion and ratification of international conventions for the protection of refugees, supervising their application and proposing amendments thereto;

(b) Promoting through special agreements with governments the execution of any measures calculated to improve the situation of refugees and to reduce the number requiring protection;

(c) Assisting governmental and private efforts to promote voluntary repatriation or assimilation within new national communities;

(d) Promoting the admission of refugees, not excluding those in the most destitute categories, to the territories of States;

(e) Endeavouring to obtain permission for refugees to transfer their assets and especially those necessary for their resettlement;

(f) Obtaining from governments information concerning the number and conditions of refugees in their territories and the laws and regulations concerning them;

(g) Keeping in close touch with the governments and inter-governmental organizations concerned;

(h) Establishing contact in such manner as he may think best with private organizations dealing with refugee questions;

(i) Facilitating the coordination of the efforts of private organizations concerned with the welfare of refugees.

9. The High Commissioner shall engage in such additional activities, including repatriation and resettlement, as the General Assembly may determine, within the limits of the resources placed at his disposal.

10. The High Commissioner shall administer any funds, public or private, which he receives for assistance to refugees, and shall distribute them among the private and, as appropriate, public agencies which he deems best qualified to administer such assistance. The High Commissioner may reject any offers which he does not consider appropriate or which cannot be utilized. The High Commissioner shall not appeal to governments for funds or make a general appeal, without the prior approval of the General Assembly. The High Commissioner shall include in his annual report a statement of his activities in this field.

11. The High Commissioner shall be entitled to present his views before the General Assembly, the Economic and Social Council and their subsidiary bodies. The High Commissioner shall report annually to the General Assembly through the Economic and Social Council; his report shall be considered as a separate item on the agenda of the General Assembly.

12. The High Commissioner may invite the co-operation of the various specialized agencies.

* See resolution 217A(III).

Chapter III

Organization and Finances

13. The High Commissioner shall be elected by the General Assembly on the nomination of the Secretary-General. The terms of appointment of the High Commissioner shall be proposed by the Secretary-General and approved by the General Assembly. The High Commissioner shall be elected for a term of three years, from 1 January 1951.

14. The High Commissioner shall appoint, for the same term, a Deputy High Commissioner of a nationality other than his own.

15. (a) Within the limits of the budgetary appropriations provided, the staff of the Office of the High Commissioner shall be appointed by the High Commissioner and shall be responsible to him in the exercise of their functions.

(b) Such staff shall be chosen from persons devoted to the purposes of the Office of the High Commissioner.

(c) Their conditions of employment shall be those provided under the staff regulations adopted by the General Assembly and the rules promulgated thereunder by the Secretary-General.

(d) Provision may also be made to permit the employment of personnel without compensation.

16. The High Commissioner shall consult the governments of the countries of residence of refugees as to the need for appointing representatives therein. In any country recognizing such need, there may be appointed a representative approved by the government of that country. Subject to the foregoing, the same representative may serve in more than one country.

17. The High Commissioner and the Secretary-General shall make appropriate arrangements for liaison and consultation on matters of mutual interest.

18. The Secretary-General shall provide the High Commissioner with all necessary facilities within budgetary limitations.

19. The Office of the High Commissioner shall be located in Geneva, Switzerland.

20. The Office of the High Commissioner shall be financed under the budget of the United Nations. Unless the General Assembly subsequently decides otherwise, no expenditure, other than administrative expenditures relating to the functioning of the Office of the High Commissioner, shall be borne on the budget of the United Nations, and all other expenditures relating to the activities of the High Commissioner shall be financed by voluntary contributions.

21. The administration of the Office of the High Commissioner shall be subject to the Financial Regulations of the United Nations and to the financial rules promulgated thereunder by the Secretary-General.

22. Transactions relating to the High Commissioner's funds shall be subject to audit by the United Nations Board of Auditors, provided that the Board may accept audited accounts from the agencies to which funds have been allocated. Administrative arrangements for the custody of such funds and their allocation shall be agreed between the High Commissioner and the Secretary-General in accordance with the Financial Regulations of the United Nations and rules promulgated thereunder by the Secretary-General.

Guidelines on International Protection

Guidelines on International Protection No. 1:

Gender-Related Persecution within the context of Article 1A(2) of the 1951 Convention and/or its 1967 Protocol relating to the Status of Refugees

UNHCR issues these Guidelines pursuant to its mandate, as contained in the *Statute of the Office of the United Nations High Commissioner for Refugees*, in conjunction with Article 35 of the *1951 Convention relating to the Status of Refugees* and Article II of its *1967 Protocol*. These Guidelines complement the UNHCR *Handbook on Procedures and Criteria for Determining Refugee Status under the 1951 Convention and the 1967 Protocol relating to the Status of Refugees* (re-edited, Geneva, January 1992). They further replace UNHCR's Position Paper on Gender-Related Persecution (Geneva, January 2000) and result from the Second Track of the Global Consultations on International Protection process which examined this subject at its expert meeting in San Remo in September 2001.

These Guidelines are intended to provide legal interpretative guidance for governments, legal practitioners, decision-makers and the judiciary, as well as UNHCR staff carrying out refugee status determination in the field.

I. Introduction

1. "Gender-related persecution" is a term that has no legal meaning per se. Rather, it is used to encompass the range of different claims in which gender is a relevant consideration in the determination of refugee status. These Guidelines specifically focus on the interpretation of the refugee definition contained in Article 1A(2) of the *1951 Convention relating to the Status of Refugees* (hereinafter "1951 Convention") from a gender perspective, as well as propose some procedural practices in order to ensure that proper consideration is given to women claimants in refugee status determination procedures and that the range of gender-related claims are recognised as such.

2. It is an established principle that the refugee definition as a whole should be interpreted with an awareness of possible gender dimensions in order to determine accurately claims to refugee status. This approach has been endorsed by the General Assembly, as well as the Executive Committee of UNHCR's Programme.[1]

[1] In its Conclusions of October 1999, No. 87(n), the Executive Committee "not[ed] with appreciation special efforts by States to incorporate gender perspectives into asylum policies, regulations and practices; encourage[d] States, UNHCR and other concerned actors to promote wider acceptance, and inclusion in their protection criteria of the notion that persecution may be gender-related or effected through sexual violence; further encourage[d] UNHCR and other concerned actors to develop, promote and implement guidelines, codes of conduct and training programmes on gender-related refugee issues, in order to support the mainstreaming of a gender perspective and enhance accountability for the implementation of gender policies." See also Executive Committee Conclusions: No. 39, Refugee Women and International Protection, 1985; No. 73, Refugee Protection and Sexual Violence, 1993; No. 77(g), General Conclusion on International Protection, 1995; No. 79(o), General Conclusion on International Protection, 1996; and No. 81(t), General Conclusion on International Protection, 1997.

3. In order to understand the nature of gender-related persecution, it is essential to define and distinguish between the terms "gender" and "sex". Gender refers to the relationship between women and men based on socially or culturally constructed and defined identities, status, roles and responsibilities that are assigned to one sex or another, while sex is a biological determination. Gender is not static or innate but acquires socially and culturally constructed meaning over time. Gender-related claims may be brought by either women or men, although due to particular types of persecution, they are more commonly brought by women. In some cases, the claimant's sex may bear on the claim in significant ways to which the decision-maker will need to be attentive. In other cases, however, the refugee claim of a female asylum-seeker will have nothing to do with her sex. Gender-related claims have typically encompassed, although are by no means limited to, acts of sexual violence, family/domestic violence, coerced family planning, female genital mutilation, punishment for transgression of social mores, and discrimination against homosexuals.

4. Adopting a gender-sensitive interpretation of the 1951 Convention does not mean that all women are automatically entitled to refugee status. The refugee claimant must establish that he or she has a well-founded fear of being persecuted for reasons of race, religion, nationality, membership of a particular social group or political opinion.

II. Substantive Analysis

A. Background

5. Historically, the refugee definition has been interpreted through a framework of male experiences, which has meant that many claims of women and of homosexuals, have gone unrecognised. In the past decade, however, the analysis and understanding of sex and gender in the refugee context have advanced substantially in case law, in State practice generally and in academic writing. These developments have run parallel to, and have been assisted by, developments in international human rights law and standards,[2] as well as in related areas of international law, including through jurisprudence of the International Criminal Tribunals for the former Yugoslavia and Rwanda, and the Rome Statute of the International Criminal Court. In this regard, for instance, it should be noted that harmful practices in breach of international human rights law and standards cannot be justified on the basis of historical, traditional, religious or cultural grounds.

6. Even though gender is not specifically referenced in the refugee definition, it is widely accepted that it can influence, or dictate, the type of persecution or harm suffered and the reasons for this treatment. The refugee definition, properly interpreted, therefore

[2] Useful texts include the Universal Declaration of Human Rights 1948, the International Covenant on Civil and Political Rights 1966, the International Covenant on Economic, Social and Cultural Rights 1966, the Convention on the Political Rights of Women 1953, the Convention Against Torture and Other Cruel, Inhuman or Degrading Treatment or Punishment 1984, the Convention on the Rights of the Child 1989, and in particular, the Convention on the Elimination of All Forms of Discrimination Against Women 1979 and the Declaration on the Elimination of Violence against Women 1993. Relevant regional instruments include the European Convention on Human Rights and Fundamental Freedoms 1950, the American Convention on Human Rights 1969, and the African Charter on Human and Peoples' Rights 1981.

covers gender-related claims. As such, there is no need to add an additional ground to the 1951 Convention definition.[3]

7. In attempting to apply the criteria of the refugee definition in the course of refugee status determination procedures, it is important to approach the assessment holistically, and have regard to all the relevant circumstances of the case. It is essential to have both a full picture of the asylum-seeker's personality, background and personal experiences, as well as an analysis and up-to-date knowledge of historically, geographically and culturally specific circumstances in the country of origin. Making generalisations about women or men is not helpful and in doing so, critical differences, which may be relevant to a particular case, can be overlooked.

8. The elements of the definition discussed below are those that require a gender-sensitive interpretation. Other criteria (e.g. being outside the country of origin) remain, of course, also directly relevant to the holistic assessment of any claim. Throughout this document, the use of the term "women" includes the girl-child.

B. Well-founded fear of persecution

9. What amounts to a well-founded fear of persecution will depend on the particular circumstances of each individual case. While female and male applicants may be subjected to the same forms of harm, they may also face forms of persecution specific to their sex. International human rights law and international criminal law clearly identify certain acts as violations of these laws, such as sexual violence, and support their characterisation as serious abuses, amounting to persecution.[4] In this sense, international law can assist decision-makers to determine the persecutory nature of a particular act.

There is no doubt that rape and other forms of gender-related violence, such as dowry-related violence, female genital mutilation, domestic violence, and trafficking,[5] are acts which inflict severe pain and suffering – both mental and physical – and which have been used as forms of persecution, whether perpetrated by State or private actors.

10. Assessing a law to be persecutory in and of itself has proven to be material to determining some gender-related claims. This is especially so given the fact that relevant laws may emanate from traditional or cultural norms and practices not necessarily in conformity with international human rights standards. However, as in all cases, a claimant must still establish that he or she has a well-founded fear of being persecuted as a result of that law. This would not be the case, for instance, where a persecutory law continues to exist but is no longer enforced.

11. Even though a particular State may have prohibited a persecutory practice (e.g. female genital mutilation), the State may nevertheless continue to condone or tolerate the practice, or may not be able to stop the practice effectively. In such cases, the practice would still amount to persecution. The fact that a law has been enacted to prohibit or denounce certain persecutory practices will therefore not in itself be sufficient to determine that the individual's claim to refugee status is not valid.

[3] See Summary Conclusions – Gender-Related Persecution, Global Consultations on International Protection, San Remo Expert Roundtable, 6-8 September 2001, nos. 1 and 3 ("Summary Conclusions – Gender-Related Persecution").

[4] See UNHCR, *Handbook*, para. 51.

[5] See below at para. 18.

12. Where the penalty or punishment for non-compliance with, or breach of, a policy or law is disproportionately severe and has a gender dimension, it would amount to persecution.[6] Even if the law is one of general applicability, circumstances of punishment or treatment cannot be so severe as to be disproportionate to the objective of the law. Severe punishment for women who, by breaching a law, transgress social mores in a society could, therefore, amount to persecution.

13. Even where laws or policies have justifiable objectives, methods of implementation that lead to consequences of a substantially prejudicial nature for the persons concerned, would amount to persecution. For example, it is widely accepted that family planning constitutes an appropriate response to population pressures. However, implementation of such policies, through the use of forced abortions and sterilisations, would breach fundamental human rights law. Such practices, despite the fact that they may be implemented in the context of a legitimate law, are recognised as serious abuses and considered persecution.

Discrimination amounting to persecution

14. While it is generally agreed that 'mere' discrimination may not, in the normal course, amount to persecution in and of itself, a pattern of discrimination or less favourable treatment could, on cumulative grounds, amount to persecution and warrant international protection. It would, for instance, amount to persecution if measures of discrimination lead to consequences of a substantially prejudicial nature for the person concerned, e.g. serious restrictions on the right to earn one's livelihood, the right to practice one's religion, or access to available educational facilities.[7]

15. Significant to gender-related claims is also an analysis of forms of discrimination by the State in failing to extend protection to individuals against certain types of harm. If the State, as a matter of policy or practice, does not accord certain rights or protection from serious abuse, then the discrimination in extending protection, which results in serious harm inflicted with impunity, could amount to persecution. Particular cases of domestic violence, or of abuse for reasons of one's differing sexual orientation, could, for example, be analysed in this context.

Persecution on account of one's sexual orientation

16. Refugee claims based on differing sexual orientation contain a gender element. A claimant's sexuality or sexual practices may be relevant to a refugee claim where he or she has been subject to persecutory (including discriminatory) action on account of his or her sexuality or sexual practices. In many such cases, the claimant has refused to adhere to socially or culturally defined roles or expectations of behaviour attributed to his or her sex. The most common claims involve homosexuals, transsexuals or transvestites, who have faced extreme public hostility, violence, abuse, or severe or cumulative discrimination.

17. Where homosexuality is illegal in a particular society, the imposition of severe criminal penalties for homosexual conduct could amount to persecution, just as it would

[6] Persons fleeing from prosecution or punishment for a common law offence are not normally refugees, however, the distinction may be obscured, in particular, in circumstances of excessive punishment for breach of a legitimate law. See UNHCR, *Handbook*, paras. 56 and 57.

[7] See UNHCR, *Handbook*, para. 54.

for refusing to wear the veil by women in some societies. Even where homosexual practices are not criminalised, a claimant could still establish a valid claim where the State condones or tolerates discriminatory practices or harm perpetrated against him or her, or where the State is unable to protect effectively the claimant against such harm.

Trafficking for the purposes of forced prostitution or sexual exploitation as a form of persecution[8]

18. Some trafficked women or minors may have valid claims to refugee status under the 1951 Convention. The forcible or deceptive recruitment of women or minors for the purposes of forced prostitution or sexual exploitation is a form of gender-related violence or abuse that can even lead to death. It can be considered a form of torture and cruel, inhuman or degrading treatment. It can also impose serious restrictions on a woman's freedom of movement, caused by abduction, incarceration, and/or confiscation of passports or other identify documents. In addition, trafficked women and minors may face serious repercussions after their escape and/or upon return, such as reprisals or retaliation from trafficking rings or individuals, real possibilities of being re-trafficked, severe community or family ostracism, or severe discrimination. In individual cases, being trafficked for the purposes of forced prostitution or sexual exploitation could therefore be the basis for a refugee claim where the State has been unable or unwilling to provide protection against such harm or threats of harm.[9]

Agents of Persecution

19. There is scope within the refugee definition to recognise both State and non-State actors of persecution. While persecution is most often perpetrated by the authorities of a country, serious discriminatory or other offensive acts committed by the local populace, or by individuals, can also be considered persecution if such acts are knowingly tolerated by the authorities, or if the authorities refuse, or are unable, to offer effective protection.[10]

C. The causal link ("for reasons of")

20. The well-founded fear of being persecuted must be related to one or more of the Convention grounds. That is, it must be "for reasons of" race, religion, nationality, membership of a particular social group, or political opinion. The Convention ground must be

[8] For the purposes of these Guidelines, "trafficking" is defined as per article 3 of the United Nations Protocol to Prevent, Suppress and Punish Trafficking in Persons, especially Women and Children, supplementing the United Nations Convention against Transnational Organised Crime, 2000. Article 3(1) provides that trafficking in persons means "the recruitment, transportation, transfer, harbouring or receipt of persons, by means of the threat or use of force or other forms of coercion, of abduction, of fraud, of deception, of the abuse of power or of a position of vulnerability or of the giving or receiving of payments or benefits to achieve the consent of a person having control over another person, for the purpose of exploitation. Exploitation shall include, at a minimum, the exploitation of the prostitution of others or other forms of sexual exploitation, forced labour or services, slavery or practices similar to slavery, servitude or the removal of organs."

[9] Trafficking for other purposes could also amount to persecution in a particular case, depending on the circumstances.

[10] See UNHCR, *Handbook*, para. 65.

a relevant contributing factor, though it need not be shown to be the sole, or dominant, cause. In many jurisdictions the causal link ("for reasons of") must be explicitly established (e.g. some Common Law States) while in other States causation is not treated as a separate question for analysis, but is subsumed within the holistic analysis of the refugee definition. In many gender-related claims, the difficult issue for a decision-maker may not be deciding upon the applicable ground, so much as the causal link: that the well-founded fear of being persecuted was for reasons of that ground. Attribution of the Convention ground to the claimant by the State or non-State actor of persecution is sufficient to establish the required causal connection.

21. In cases where there is a risk of being persecuted at the hands of a non-State actor (e.g. husband, partner or other non-State actor) for reasons which are related to one of the Convention grounds, the causal link is established, whether or not the absence of State protection is Convention related. Alternatively, where the risk of being persecuted at the hands of a non-State actor is unrelated to a Convention ground, but the inability or unwillingness of the State to offer protection is for reasons of a Convention ground, the causal link is also established.[11]

D. Convention grounds

22. Ensuring that a gender-sensitive interpretation is given to each of the Convention grounds is important in determining whether a particular claimant has fulfilled the criteria of the refugee definition. In many cases, claimants may face persecution because of a Convention ground which is attributed or imputed to them. In many societies a woman's political views, race, nationality, religion or social affiliations, for example, are often seen as aligned with relatives or associates or with those of her community.

23. It is also important to be aware that in many gender-related claims, the persecution feared could be for one, or more, of the Convention grounds. For example, a claim for refugee status based on transgression of social or religious norms may be analysed in terms of religion, political opinion or membership of a particular social group. The claimant is not required to identify accurately the reason why he or she has a well-founded fear of being persecuted.

Race

24. Race for the purposes of the refugee definition has been defined to include all kinds of ethnic groups that are referred to as "races" in common usage.[12] Persecution for reasons of race may be expressed in different ways against men and women. For example, the persecutor may choose to destroy the ethnic identity and/or prosperity of a racial group by killing, maiming or incarcerating the men, while the women may be viewed as propagating the ethnic or racial identity and persecuted in a different way, such as through sexual violence or control of reproduction.

Religion

25. In certain States, the religion assigns particular roles or behavioural codes to women and men respectively. Where a woman does not fulfil her assigned role or refuses

[11] See Summary Conclusions – Gender-Related Persecution, no. 6.

[12] See UNHCR, *Handbook*, para 68.

to abide by the codes, and is punished as a consequence, she may have a well-founded fear of being persecuted for reasons of religion. Failure to abide by such codes may be perceived as evidence that a woman holds unacceptable religious opinions regardless of what she actually believes. A woman may face harm for her particular religious beliefs or practices, or those attributed to her, including her refusal to hold particular beliefs, to practise a prescribed religion or to conform her behaviour in accordance with the teachings of a prescribed religion.

26. There is some overlap between the grounds of religion and political opinion in gender-related claims, especially in the realm of imputed political opinion. While religious tenets require certain kinds of behaviour from a woman, contrary behaviour may be perceived as evidence of an unacceptable political opinion. For example, in certain societies, the role ascribed to women may be attributable to the requirements of the State or official religion. The authorities or other actors of persecution may perceive the failure of a woman to conform to this role as the failure to practice or to hold certain religious beliefs. At the same time, the failure to conform could be interpreted as holding an unacceptable political opinion that threatens the basic structure from which certain political power flows. This is particularly true in societies where there is little separation between religious and State institutions, laws and doctrines.

Nationality

27. Nationality is not to be understood only as "citizenship". It also refers to membership of an ethnic or linguistic group and may occasionally overlap with the term "race".[13] Although persecution on the grounds of nationality (as with race) is not specific to women or men, in many instances the nature of the persecution takes a gender-specific form, most commonly that of sexual violence directed against women and girls.

Membership of a Particular Social Group[14]

28. Gender-related claims have often been analysed within the parameters of this ground, making a proper understanding of this term of paramount importance. However, in some cases, the emphasis given to the social group ground has meant that other applicable grounds, such as religion or political opinion, have been over-looked. Therefore, the interpretation given to this ground cannot render the other four Convention grounds superfluous.

29. Thus, *a particular social group is a group of persons who share a common characteristic other than their risk of being persecuted, or who are perceived as a group by society. The characteristic will often be one which is innate, unchangeable, or which is otherwise fundamental to identity, conscience or the exercise of one's human rights.*

30. It follows that sex can properly be within the ambit of the social group category, with women being a clear example of a social subset defined by innate and immutable characteristics, and who are frequently treated differently than men.[15] Their characteristics also identify them as a group in society, subjecting them to different treatment and

[13] See UNHCR, *Handbook*, para. 74.

[14] For more information, see UNHCR's *Guidelines on International Protection: "Membership of a particular social group" within the context of Article 1A(2) of the 1951 Convention and/or its 1967 Protocol relating to the Status of Refugees* (HCR/GIP/02/02, 7 May 2002).

[15] See Summary Conclusions – Gender-Related Persecution, no. 5.

standards in some countries.[16] Equally, this definition would encompass homosexuals, transsexuals, or transvestites.

31. The size of the group has sometimes been used as a basis for refusing to recognise 'women' generally as a particular social group. This argument has no basis in fact or reason, as the other grounds are not bound by this question of size. There should equally be no requirement that the particular social group be cohesive or that members of it voluntarily associate,[17] or that every member of the group is at risk of persecution.[18]

It is well-accepted that it should be possible to identify the group independently of the persecution, however, discrimination or persecution may be a relevant factor in determining the visibility of the group in a particular context.[19]

Political Opinion

32. Under this ground, a claimant must show that he or she has a well-founded fear of being persecuted for holding certain political opinions (usually different from those of the Government or parts of the society), or because the holding of such opinions has been attributed to him or her. Political opinion should be understood in the broad sense, to incorporate any opinion on any matter in which the machinery of State, government, society, or policy may be engaged. This may include an opinion as to gender roles. It would also include non-conformist behaviour which leads the persecutor to impute a political opinion to him or her. In this sense, there is not as such an inherently political or an inherently non-political activity, but the context of the case should determine its nature. A claim on the basis of political opinion does, however, presuppose that the claimant holds or is assumed to hold opinions not tolerated by the authorities or society, which are critical of their policies, traditions or methods. It also presupposes that such opinions have come or could come to the notice of the authorities or relevant parts of the society, or are attributed by them to the claimant. It is not always necessary to have expressed such an opinion, or to have already suffered any form of discrimination or persecution. In such cases the test of well-founded fear would be based on an assessment of the consequences that a claimant having certain dispositions would have to face if he or she returned.

33. The image of a political refugee as someone who is fleeing persecution for his or her direct involvement in political activity does not always correspond to the reality of the experiences of women in some societies. Women are less likely than their male counterparts to engage in high profile political activity and are more often involved in 'low level' political activities that reflect dominant gender roles. For example, a woman may work in nursing sick rebel soldiers, in the recruitment of sympathisers, or in the preparation and dissemination of leaflets. Women are also frequently attributed with political opinions of their family or male relatives, and subjected to persecution because of the activities

[16] See also Executive Committee Conclusion No. 39, Refugee Women and International Protection, 1985: "States . . . are free to adopt the interpretation that women asylum seekers who face harsh or inhuman treatment due to their having transgressed the social mores of the society in which they live may be considered as 'a particular social group' within the meaning of Article 1A(2) of the 1951 United Nations Refugee Convention".

[17] See Summary Conclusions – Membership of a Particular Social Group, Global Consultations on International Protection, San Remo Expert Roundtable, 6-8 September 2001, no. 4 ("Summary Conclusions – Membership of a Particular Social Group").

[18] See Summary Conclusions – Membership of a Particular Social Group, *Ibid.*, no. 7.

[19] See Summary Conclusions – Membership of a Particular Social Group, *Ibid.*, no. 6.

of their male relatives. While this may be analysed in the context of an imputed political opinion, it may also be analysed as being persecution for reasons of her membership of a particular social group, being her "family". These factors need to be taken into account in gender-related claims.

34. Equally important for gender-related claims is to recognise that a woman may not wish to engage in certain activities, such as providing meals to government soldiers, which may be interpreted by the persecutor(s) as holding a contrary political opinion.

III. Procedural Issues[20]

35. Persons raising gender-related refugee claims, and survivors of torture or trauma in particular, require a supportive environment where they can be reassured of the confidentiality of their claim. Some claimants, because of the shame they feel over what has happened to them, or due to trauma, may be reluctant to identify the true extent of the persecution suffered or feared. They may continue to fear persons in authority, or they may fear rejection and/or reprisals from their family and/or community.[21]

36. Against this background, in order to ensure that gender-related claims, of women in particular, are properly considered in the refugee status determination process, the following measures should be borne in mind:

i. Women asylum-seekers should be interviewed separately, without the presence of male family members, in order to ensure that they have an opportunity to present their case. It should be explained to them that they may have a valid claim in their own right.

ii. It is essential that women are given information about the status determination process, access to it, as well as legal advice, in a manner and language that she understands.

iii. Claimants should be informed of the choice to have interviewers and interpreters of the same sex as themselves,[22] and they should be provided automatically for women

[20] This Part has benefited from the valuable guidance provided by various States and other actors, including the following guidelines: *Considerations for Asylum Officers Adjudicating Asylum Claims from Women* (Immigration and Naturalization Service, United States, 26 May 1995); *Refugee and Humanitarian Visa Applicants: Guidelines on Gender Issues for Decision Makers* (Department of Immigration and Humanitarian Affairs, Australia, July 1996) (hereinafter "Australian Guidelines on Gender Issues for Decision Makers"); *Guideline 4 on Women Refugee Claimants Fearing Gender-Related Persecution: Update* (Immigration and Refugee Board, Canada, 13 November 1996); *Position on Asylum Seeking and Refugee Women*, (European Council on Refugees and Exiles, December 1997) (hereinafter "ECRE Position on Asylum Seeking and Refugee Women"); *Gender Guidelines for the Determination of Asylum Claims in the UK* (Refugee Women's Legal Group, July 1998) (hereinafter "Refugee Women's Group Gender Guidelines"); *Gender Guidelines for Asylum Determination* (National Consortium on Refugee Affairs, South Africa, 1999); *Asylum Gender Guidelines* (Immigration Appellate Authority, United Kingdom, November 2000); and *Gender-Based Persecution: Guidelines for the investigation and evaluation of the needs of women for protection* (Migration Board, Legal Practice Division, Sweden, 28 March 2001).

[21] See also *Sexual Violence Against Refugees: Guidelines on Prevention and Response* (UNHCR, Geneva, 1995) and *Prevention and Response to Sexual and Gender-Based Violence in Refugee Situations* (Report of Inter-Agency Lessons Learned Conference Proceedings, 27-29 March 2001, Geneva).

[22] See also Executive Committee Conclusion No. 64, Refugee Women and International Protection, 1990, (a) (iii): Provide, wherever necessary, skilled female interviewers in procedures for the determination of refugee status and ensure appropriate access by women asylum-seekers to such procedures, even when accompanied by male family members.

claimants. Interviewers and interpreters should also be aware of and responsive to any cultural or religious sensitivities or personal factors such as age and level of education.

iv. An open and reassuring environment is often crucial to establishing trust between the interviewer and the claimant, and should help the full disclosure of sometimes sensitive and personal information. The interview room should be arranged in such a way as to encourage discussion, promote confidentiality and to lessen any possibility of perceived power imbalances.

v. The interviewer should take the time to introduce him/herself and the interpreter to the claimant, explain clearly the roles of each person, and the exact purpose of the interview.[23] The claimant should be assured that his/her claim will be treated in the strictest confidence, and information provided by the claimant will not be provided to members of his/her family. Importantly, the interviewer should explain that he/she is not a trauma counselor.

vi. The interviewer should remain neutral, compassionate and objective during the interview, and should avoid body language or gestures that may be perceived as intimidating or culturally insensitive or inappropriate. The interviewer should allow the claimant to present his/her claim with minimal interruption.

vii. Both 'open-ended' and specific questions which may help to reveal gender issues relevant to a refugee claim should be incorporated into all asylum interviews. Women who have been involved in indirect political activity or to whom political opinion has been attributed, for example, often do not provide relevant information in interviews due to the male-oriented nature of the questioning. Female claimants may also fail to relate questions that are about 'torture' to the types of harm which they fear (such as rape, sexual abuse, female genital mutilation, 'honour killings', forced marriage, etc.).

viii. Particularly for victims of sexual violence or other forms of trauma, second and subsequent interviews may be needed in order to establish trust and to obtain all necessary information. In this regard, interviewers should be responsive to the trauma and emotion of claimants and should stop an interview where the claimant is becoming emotionally distressed.

ix. Where it is envisaged that a particular case may give rise to a gender-related claim, adequate preparation is needed, which will also allow a relationship of confidence and trust with the claimant to be developed, as well as allowing the interviewer to ask the right questions and deal with any problems that may arise during an interview.

x. Country of origin information should be collected that has relevance in women's claims, such as the position of women before the law, the political rights of women, the social and economic rights of women, the cultural and social mores of the country and consequences for non-adherence, the prevalence of such harmful traditional practices, the incidence and forms of reported violence against women, the protection available to them, any penalties imposed on those who perpetrate the violence, and the risks that a woman might face on her return to her country of origin after making a claim for refugee status.

xi. The type and level of emotion displayed during the recounting of her experiences should not affect a woman's credibility. Interviewers and decision-makers should understand that cultural differences and trauma play an important and complex role in determining behaviour. For some cases, it may be appropriate to seek objective psychological or medical evidence. It is unnecessary to establish the precise details of the act of

[23] *Ibid.*, para. 3.19.

rape or sexual assault itself, but events leading up to, and after, the act, the surrounding circumstances and details (such as, use of guns, any words or phrases spoken by the perpetrators, type of assault, where it occurred and how, details of the perpetrators (e.g. soldiers, civilians) etc.) as well as the motivation of the perpetrator may be required. In some circumstances it should be noted that a woman may not be aware of the reasons for her abuse.

xii. Mechanisms for referral to psycho-social counseling and other support services should be made available where necessary. Best practice recommends that trained psycho-social counselors be available to assist the claimant before and after the interview.

Evidentiary Matters

37. No documentary proof as such is required in order for the authorities to recognise a refugee claim, however, information on practices in the country of origin may support a particular case. It is important to recognise that in relation to gender-related claims, the usual types of evidence used in other refugee claims may not be as readily available. Statistical data or reports on the incidence of sexual violence may not be available, due to under-reporting of cases, or lack of prosecution. Alternative forms of information might assist, such as the testimonies of other women similarly situated in written reports or oral testimony, of non-governmental or international organisations or other independent research.

IV. Methods of Implementation

38. Depending on the respective legal traditions, there have been two general approaches taken by States to ensure a gender-sensitive application of refugee law and in particular of the refugee definition. Some States have incorporated legal interpretative guidance and/or procedural safeguards within legislation itself, while others have preferred to develop policy and legal guidelines on the same for decision-makers. UNHCR encourages States who have not already done so to ensure a gender-sensitive application of refugee law and procedures, and stands ready to assist States in this regard.

Guidelines On International Protection No. 2:

"Membership of a particular social group" within the context of Article 1A(2) of the 1951 Convention and/or its 1967 Protocol relating to the Status of Refugees

UNHCR issues these Guidelines pursuant to its mandate, as contained in the *Statute of the Office of the United Nations High Commissioner for Refugees*, and Article 35 of the *1951 Convention relating to the Status of Refugees and/or its 1967 Protocol.* These Guidelines complement the UNHCR *Handbook on Procedures and Criteria for Determining Refugee Status under the 1951 Convention and the 1967 Protocol relating to the Status of Refugees* (re-edited, Geneva, January 1992). They further supersede IOM/132/1989 – FOM/110/1989 Membership of a Particular Social Group (UNHCR, Geneva, 12 December 1989), and result from the Second Track of the Global Consultations on International Protection process which examined this subject at its expert meeting in San Remo in September 2001.

These Guidelines are intended to provide legal interpretative guidance for governments, legal practitioners, decision-makers and the judiciary, as well as UNHCR staff carrying out refugee status determinations in the field.

I. Introduction

1. "Membership of a particular social group" is one of the five grounds enumerated in Article 1A(2) of the 1951 *Convention relating to the Status of Refugees* ("1951 Convention"). It is the ground with the least clarity and it is not defined by the 1951 Convention itself. It is being invoked with increasing frequency in refugee status determinations, with States having recognised women, families, tribes, occupational groups, and homosexuals, as constituting a particular social group for the purposes of the 1951 Convention. The evolution of this ground has advanced the understanding of the refugee definition as a whole. These Guidelines provide legal interpretative guidance on assessing claims which assert that a claimant has a well-founded fear of being persecuted for reasons of his or her membership of a particular social group.

2. While the ground needs delimiting – that is, it cannot be interpreted to render the other four Convention grounds superfluous – a proper interpretation must be consistent with the object and purpose of the Convention.[1] Consistent with the language of the Convention, this category cannot be interpreted as a "catch all" that applies to all persons fearing persecution. Thus, to preserve the structure and integrity of the Convention's definition of a refugee, a social group cannot be defined *exclusively* by the fact that it is targeted for persecution (although, as discussed below, persecution may be a relevant element in determining the visibility of a particular social group).

3. There is no "closed list" of what groups may constitute a "particular social group" within the meaning of Article 1A(2). The Convention includes no specific list of social groups, nor does the ratifying history reflect a view that there is a set of identified groups that might qualify under this ground. Rather, the term membership of a particular social group should be read in an evolutionary manner, open to the diverse and changing nature of groups in various societies and evolving international human rights norms.

4. The Convention grounds are not mutually exclusive. An applicant may be eligible for refugee status under more than one of the grounds identified in Article 1A(2).[2] For example, a claimant may allege that she is at risk of persecution because of her refusal to wear traditional clothing. Depending on the particular circumstances of the society, she may be able to establish a claim based on political opinion (if her conduct is viewed by the State as a political statement that it seeks to suppress), religion (if her conduct is based on a religious conviction opposed by the State) or membership in a particular social group.

[1] See Summary Conclusions – Membership of a Particular Social Group, Global Consultations on International Protection, San Remo Expert Roundtable, 6-8 September 2001, no. 2 ("Summary Conclusions – Membership of a Particular Social Group").

[2] See UNHCR, *Handbook on Procedures and Criteria for Determining Refugee Status under the 1951 Convention and the 1967 Protocol relating to the Status of Refugees* (re-edited, Geneva, January 1992), paras. 66-67, 77; and see also Summary Conclusions – Membership of a Particular Social Group, no. 3.

II. Substantive Analysis

A. Summary of State Practice

5. Judicial decisions, regulations, policies, and practices have utilized varying interpretations of what constitutes a social group within the meaning of the 1951 Convention. Two approaches have dominated decision-making in common law jurisdictions.

6. The first, the "protected characteristics" approach (sometimes referred to as an "immutability" approach), examines whether a group is united by an immutable characteristic or by a characteristic that is so fundamental to human dignity that a person should not be compelled to forsake it. An immutable characteristic may be innate (such as sex or ethnicity) or unalterable for other reasons (such as the historical fact of a past association, occupation or status). Human rights norms may help to identify characteristics deemed so fundamental to human dignity that one ought not to be compelled to forego them. A decision-maker adopting this approach would examine whether the asserted group is defined: (1) by an innate, unchangeable characteristic, (2) by a past temporary or voluntary status that is unchangeable because of its historical permanence, or (3) by a characteristic or association that is so fundamental to human dignity that group members should not be compelled to forsake it. Applying this approach, courts and administrative bodies in a number of jurisdictions have concluded that women, homosexuals, and families, for example, can constitute a particular social group within the meaning of Article 1A(2).

7. The second approach examines whether or not a group shares a common characteristic which makes them a cognizable group or sets them apart from society at large. This has been referred to as the "social perception" approach. Again, women, families and homosexuals have been recognized under this analysis as particular social groups, depending on the circumstances of the society in which they exist.

8. In civil law jurisdictions, the particular social group ground is generally less well developed. Most decision-makers place more emphasis on whether or not a risk of persecution exists than on the standard for defining a particular social group. Nonetheless, both the protected characteristics and the social perception approaches have received mention.

9. Analyses under the two approaches may frequently converge. This is so because groups whose members are targeted based on a common immutable or fundamental characteristic are also often perceived as a social group in their societies. But at times the approaches may reach different results. For example, the social perception standard might recognize as social groups associations based on a characteristic that is neither immutable nor fundamental to human dignity – such as, perhaps, occupation or social class.

B. UNHCR's Definition

10. Given the varying approaches, and the protection gaps which can result, UNHCR believes that the two approaches ought to be reconciled.

11. The protected characteristics approach may be understood to identify a set of groups that constitute the core of the social perception analysis. Accordingly, it is appropriate to adopt a single standard that incorporates both dominant approaches:

> a particular social group is a group of persons who share a common characteristic other than their risk of being persecuted, or who are perceived as a group by society. The characteristic

will often be one which is innate, unchangeable, or which is otherwise fundamental to identity, conscience or the exercise of one's human rights.

12. This definition includes characteristics which are historical and therefore cannot be changed, and those which, though it is possible to change them, ought not to be required to be changed because they are so closely linked to the identity of the person or are an expression of fundamental human rights. It follows that sex can properly be within the ambit of the social group category, with women being a clear example of a social subset defined by and immutable characteristics, and who are frequently treated differently to men.[3]

13. If a claimant alleges a social group that is based on a characteristic determined to be neither unalterable or fundamental, further analysis should be undertaken to determine whether the group is nonetheless perceived as a cognizable group in that society. So, for example, if it were determined that owning a shop or participating in a certain occupation in a particular society is neither unchangeable nor a fundamental aspect of human identity, a shopkeeper or members of a particular profession might nonetheless constitute a particular social group if in the society they are recognized as a group which sets them apart.

The role of persecution

14. As noted above, a particular social group cannot be defined exclusively by the persecution that members of the group suffer or by a common fear of being persecuted. Nonetheless, persecutory action toward a group may be a relevant factor in determining the visibility of a group in a particular society.[4] To use an example from a widely cited decision, "[W]hile persecutory conduct cannot define the social group, the actions of the persecutors may serve to identify or even cause the creation of a particular social group in society. Left-handed men are not a particular social group. But, if they were persecuted because they were left-handed, they would no doubt quickly become recognizable in their society as a particular social group. Their persecution for being left-handed would create a public perception that they were a particular social group. But it would be the attribute of being left-handed and not the persecutory acts that would identify them as a particular social group." [5]

No requirement of cohesiveness

15. It is widely accepted in State practice that an applicant need not show that the members of a particular group know each other or associate with each other as a group. That is, there is no requirement that the group be "cohesive".[6] The relevant inquiry is whether there is a common element that group members share. This is similar to the analysis adopted for the other Convention grounds, where there is no requirement that members of a religion or holders of a political opinion associate together, or belong to a

[3] For more information on gender-related claims, see UNHCR's *Guidelines on International Protection: Gender-Related Persecution within the Context of Article 1A(2) of the 1951 Convention and/or its 1967 Protocol relating to the Status of Refugees* (HCR/GIP/02/01, 10 May 2002), as well as Summary Conclusions of the Expert Roundtable on Gender-Related Persecution, San Remo, 6-8 September 2001, no. 5.

[4] See Summary Conclusions – Membership of a Particular Social Group, no. 6.

[5] McHugh, J., in *Applicant A v. Minister for Immigration and Ethnic Affairs*, (1997) 190 CLR 225, 264, 142 ALR 33.

[6] See Summary Conclusions – Membership of a Particular Social Group, no. 4.

"cohesive" group. Thus women may constitute a particular social group under certain circumstances based on the common characteristic of sex, whether or not they associate with one another based on that shared characteristic.

16. In addition, mere membership of a particular social group will not normally be enough to substantiate a claim to refugee status. There may, however, be special circumstances where mere membership can be a sufficient ground to fear persecution.[7]

Not all members of the group must be at risk of being persecuted

17. An applicant need not demonstrate that all members of a particular social group are at risk of persecution in order to establish the existence of a particular social group.[8] As with the other grounds, it is not necessary to establish that all persons in the political party or ethnic group have been singled out for persecution. Certain members of the group may not be at risk if, for example, they hide their shared characteristic, they are not known to the persecutors, or they cooperate with the persecutor.

Relevance of size

18. The size of the purported social group is not a relevant criterion in determining whether a particular social group exists within the meaning of Article 1A(2). This is true as well for cases arising under the other Convention grounds. For example, States may seek to suppress religious or political ideologies that are widely shared among members of a particular society – perhaps even by a majority of the population; the fact that large numbers of persons risk persecution cannot be a ground for refusing to extend international protection where it is otherwise appropriate.

19. Cases in a number of jurisdictions have recognized "women" as a particular social group. This does not mean that all women in the society qualify for refugee status. A claimant must still demonstrate a well-founded fear of being persecuted based on her membership in the particular social group, not be within one of the exclusion grounds, and meet other relevant criteria.

Non-State actors and the causal link ("for reasons of")

20. Cases asserting refugee status based on membership of a particular social group frequently involve claimants who face risks of harm at the hands of non-State actors, and which have involved an analysis of the causal link. For example, homosexuals may be victims of violence from private groups; women may risk abuse from their husbands or partners. Under the Convention a person must have a well-founded fear of being persecuted and that fear of being persecuted must be based on one (or more) of the Convention grounds. There is no requirement that the persecutor be a State actor. Where serious discriminatory or other offensive acts are committed by the local populace, they can be considered as persecution if they are knowingly tolerated by the authorities, or if the authorities refuse, or prove unable, to offer effective protection.[9]

[7] See UNHCR, *Handbook*, para. 79.

[8] See Summary Conclusions – Membership of a Particular Social Group, no. 7.

[9] See UNHCR, *Handbook*, para. 65.

21. Normally, an applicant will allege that the person inflicting or threatening the harm is acting for one of the reasons identified in the Convention. So, if a non-State actor inflicts or threatens persecution based on a Convention ground and the State is unwilling or unable to protect the claimant, then the causal link has been established. That is, the harm is being visited upon the victim for reasons of a Convention ground.

22. There may also arise situations where a claimant may be unable to show that the harm inflicted or threatened by the non-State actor is related to one of the five grounds.

For example, in the situation of domestic abuse, a wife may not always be able to establish that her husband is abusing her based on her membership in a social group, political opinion or other Convention ground. Nonetheless, if the State is unwilling to extend protection based on one of the five grounds, then she may be able to establish a valid claim for refugee status: the harm visited upon her by her husband is based on the State's unwillingness to protect her for reasons of a Convention ground.

23. This reasoning may be summarized as follows. The causal link may be satisfied:

(1) where there is a real risk of being persecuted at the hands of a non-State actor for reasons which are related to one of the Convention grounds, whether or not the failure of the State to protect the claimant is Convention related; or

(2) where the risk of being persecuted at the hands of a non-State actor is unrelated to a Convention ground, but the inability or unwillingness of the State to offer protection is for a Convention reason.

Guidelines On International Protection No. 3:

Cessation of Refugee Status under Article 1C(5) and (6) of the 1951 Convention relating to the Status of Refugees (the "Ceased Circumstances" Clauses)

UNHCR issues these Guidelines pursuant to its mandate, as contained in the *Statute of the Office of the United Nations High Commissioner for Refugees*, in conjunction with Article 35 of the *1951 Convention relating to the Status of Refugees* and Article II of its *1967 Protocol*. These Guidelines complement the UNHCR *Handbook on Procedures and Criteria for Determining Refugee Status under the 1951 Convention and the 1967 Protocol relating to the Status of Refugees* (re-edited, Geneva, January 1992). They replace UNHCR's *The Cessation Clauses: Guidelines on their Application* (Geneva, April 1999) in so far as these concern the "ceased circumstances" clauses and result, *inter alia*, from the Second Track of the Global Consultations on International Protection which examined this subject at an expert meeting in Lisbon in May 2001.

These Guidelines are intended to provide legal interpretative guidance for governments, legal practitioners, decision-makers and the judiciary, as well as UNHCR staff carrying out refugee status determination in the field.

I. Introduction

1. The *1951 Convention relating to the Status of Refugees* (hereinafter "1951 Convention") recognises that refugee status ends under certain clearly defined conditions. This means that once an individual is determined to be a refugee, their status is maintained unless they fall within the terms of the cessation clauses or their status is cancelled or revoked.[1] Under Article 1C of the 1951 Convention, refugee status may cease either through the actions of the refugee (contained in sub-paragraphs 1 to 4), such as by re-establishment in his or her country of origin,[2] or through fundamental changes in the objective circumstances in the country of origin upon which refugee status was based (sub-paragraphs 5 and 6). The latter are commonly referred to as the "ceased circumstances" or "general cessation" clauses. These Guidelines are concerned only with the latter provisions.

2. Article 1C(5) and (6) provides that the 1951 Convention shall cease to apply to any person falling under the terms of Article 1(A) if:

(5) He can no longer, because the circumstances in connexion with which he has been recognized as a refugee have ceased to exist, continue to refuse to avail himself of the protection of the country of his nationality;

Provided that this paragraph shall not apply to a refugee falling under section A(1) of this Article who is able to invoke compelling reasons arising out of previous persecution for refusing to avail himself of the protection of the country of nationality;

(6) Being a person who has no nationality he is, because the circumstances in connexion with which he has been recognized as a refugee have ceased to exist, able to return to the country of his former habitual residence; Provided that this paragraph shall not apply to a refugee falling under section A(1) of this Article who is able to invoke compelling reasons arising out of previous persecution for refusing to return to the country of his former habitual residence.

3. UNHCR or States may issue formal declarations of general cessation of refugee status for a particular refugee caseload.[3] UNHCR has such competence under Article 6A of the Statute of the Office of the High Commissioner for Refugees in conjunction with Article 1C of the 1951 Convention. Due to the fact that large numbers of refugees voluntarily repatriate without an official declaration that conditions in their countries of origin

[1] See, UNHCR, *Handbook on Procedures and Criteria for Determining Refugee Status*, (hereinafter "UNHCR, *Handbook*") (1979, Geneva, re-edited Jan. 1992), para. 112. For distinction between cessation and cancellation/revocation see, para. 4 below.

[2] In these Guidelines, "country of origin" is understood to cover both the country of nationality and the country of former habitual residence, the latter in relation to refugees who are stateless. For more on Article 1C(1–4), see UNHCR, "The Cessation Clauses: Guidelines on their Application", April 1999.

[3] See, for example, UNHCR's formal declarations of general cessation: "Applicability of the Cessation Clauses to Refugees from Poland, Czechoslovakia and Hungary", 15 Nov. 1991, "Applicability of Cessation Clauses to Refugees from Chile", 28 March 1994, "Applicability of the Cessation Clauses to Refugees from the Republics of Malawi and Mozambique", 31 Dec. 1996, "Applicability of the Cessation Clauses to Refugees from Bulgaria and Romania", 1 Oct. 1997, "Applicability of the Ceased Circumstances; Cessation Clauses to pre-1991 refugees from Ethiopia", 23 Sept. 1999, and "Declaration of Cessation – Timor Leste", 20 December 2002.

no longer justify international protection, declarations are infrequent. Furthermore, many States Parties grant permanent residence status to refugees in their territories after several years, eventually leading to their integration and naturalisation. Similarly, cessation determinations on an individual basis as well as periodic reviews are rare, in recognition of the "need to respect a basic degree of stability for individual refugees".[4]

4. The grounds identified in the 1951 Convention are exhaustive; that is, no additional grounds would justify a conclusion that international protection is no longer required.[5] Operation of the cessation clauses should, in addition, be distinguished from other decisions that terminate refugee status. Cessation differs from cancellation of refugee status. Cancellation is based on a determination that an individual should not have been recognised as a refugee in the first place. This is, for instance, so where it is established that there was a misrepresentation of material facts essential to the outcome of the determination process or that one of the exclusion clauses would have been applicable had all the relevant facts been known. Cessation also differs from revocation, which may take place if a refugee subsequently engages in conduct coming within the scope of Article 1F(a) or 1F(c).

II. Substantive Analysis

5. The following framework for substantive analysis is drawn from the terms of Article 1C(5) and 1C(6) of the 1951 Convention and takes into account Executive Committee Conclusion No. 69, subsequent legal developments, and State practice.

A. General Considerations

6. When interpreting the cessation clauses, it is important to bear in mind the broad durable solutions context of refugee protection informing the object and purpose of these clauses. Numerous Executive Committee Conclusions affirm that the 1951 Convention and principles of refugee protection look to durable solutions for refugees.[6] Accordingly, cessation practices should be developed in a manner consistent with the goal of durable solutions. Cessation should therefore not result in persons residing in a host State with an uncertain status. It should not result either in persons being compelled to return to a volatile situation, as this would undermine the likelihood of a durable solution and could also cause additional or renewed instability in an otherwise improving situation, thus risking future refugee flows. Acknowledging these considerations ensures refugees do not face involuntary return to situations that might again produce flight and a need for refugee status. It supports the principle that conditions within the country of origin must have changed in a profound and enduring manner before cessation can be applied.

7. Cessation under Article 1C(5) and 1C(6) does not require the consent of or a voluntary act by the refugee. Cessation of refugee status terminates rights that accompany that status. It may bring about the return of the person to the country of origin and may

[4] "Summary Conclusions on Cessation of Refugee Status, Global Consultations on International Protection, Lisbon Expert Roundtable", May 2001, no. B (17). See also, UNHCR, *Handbook*, para. 13.

[5] See, amongst others, UNHCR, *Handbook*, para. 116.

[6] See, e.g., Executive Committee Conclusions No. 29 (XXXIV) (1983), No. 50 (XXXIX) (1988), No. 58 (XL) (1989), No. 79 (XLVII) (1996), No. 81 (XLVIII) (1997), No. 85 (XLIX) (1998), No. 87 (L) (1999), No. 89 (L) (2000), and No. 90 (LII) (2001).

thus break ties to family, social networks and employment in the community in which the refugee has become established. As a result, a premature or insufficiently grounded application of the ceased circumstances clauses can have serious consequences. It is therefore appropriate to interpret the clauses strictly and to ensure that procedures for determining general cessation are fair, clear, and transparent.

B. Assessment of Change of Circumstances in the Country of Origin

8. Article 1C(5) and (6) provides for the cessation of a person's refugee status where "the circumstances in connexion with which he [or she] has been recognized as a refugee have ceased to exist". To assist assessment of how and to what extent conditions in the country of origin must have changed before these "ceased circumstances" clauses can be invoked, UNHCR's Executive Committee has developed guidance in the form of Executive Committee Conclusion No. 69 (XLIII) (1992), which reads in part:

> [I]n taking any decision on application of the cessation clauses based on "ceased circumstances", States must carefully assess the fundamental character of the changes in the country of nationality or origin, including the general human rights situation, as well as the particular cause of fear of persecution, in order to make sure in an objective and verifiable way that the situation which justified the granting of refugee status has ceased to exist.
>
> ... [A]n essential element in such assessment by States is the fundamental, stable and durable character of the changes, making use of appropriate information available in this respect, *inter alia*, from relevant specialized bodies, including particularly UNHCR.

9. Key elements relevant to assessment of the extent and durability of change required before it can be said that the circumstances in connection with which refugee status was recognised have ceased to exist are outlined below.

The fundamental character of change

10. For cessation to apply, the changes need to be of a fundamental nature, such that the refugee "can no longer ... continue to refuse to avail himself of the protection of the country of his nationality" (Article 1C(5)) or, if he has no nationality, is "able to return to the country of his former habitual residence" (Article 1C(6)). Cessation based on "ceased circumstances" therefore only comes into play when changes have taken place which address the causes of displacement which led to the recognition of refugee status.

11. Where indeed a "particular cause of fear of persecution"[7] has been identified, the elimination of that cause carries more weight than a change in other factors. Often, however, circumstances in a country are inter-linked, be these armed conflict, serious violations of human rights, severe discrimination against minorities, or the absence of good governance, with the result that resolution of the one will tend to lead to an improvement in others. All relevant factors must therefore be taken into consideration. An end to hostilities, a complete political change and return to a situation of peace and stability remain the most typical situation in which Article 1C(5) or (6) applies.

12. Large-scale spontaneous repatriation of refugees may be an indicator of changes that are occurring or have occurred in the country of origin. Where the return of former

[7] See Executive Committee Conclusion No. 69 (XLIII) (1992), para. a.

refugees would be likely to generate fresh tension in the country of origin, however, this itself could signal an absence of effective, fundamental change. Similarly, where the particular circumstances leading to flight or to non-return have changed, only to be replaced by different circumstances which may also give rise to refugee status, Article 1C(5) or (6) cannot be invoked.

The enduring nature of change

13. Developments which would appear to evidence significant and profound changes should be given time to consolidate before any decision on cessation is made. Occasionally, an evaluation as to whether fundamental changes have taken place on a durable basis can be made after a relatively short time has elapsed. This is so in situations where, for example, the changes are peaceful and take place under a constitutional process, where there are free and fair elections with a real change of government committed to respecting fundamental human rights, and where there is relative political and economic stability in the country.

14. A longer period of time will need to have elapsed before the durability of change can be tested where the changes have taken place violently, for instance, through the overthrow of a regime. Under the latter circumstances, the human rights situation needs to be especially carefully assessed. The process of national reconstruction must be given sufficient time to take hold and any peace arrangements with opposing militant groups must be carefully monitored. This is particularly relevant after conflicts involving different ethnic groups, since progress towards genuine reconciliation has often proven difficult in such cases. Unless national reconciliation clearly starts to take root and real peace is restored, political changes which have occurred may not be firmly established.

Restoration of protection

15. In determining whether circumstances have changed so as to justify cessation under Article 1C(5) or (6), another crucial question is whether the refugee can effectively re-avail him- or herself of the protection of his or her own country.[8] Such protection must therefore be effective and available. It requires more than mere physical security or safety. It needs to include the existence of a functioning government and basic administrative structures, as evidenced for instance through a functioning system of law and justice, as well as the existence of adequate infrastructure to enable residents to exercise their rights, including their right to a basic livelihood.

16. An important indicator in this respect is the general human rights situation in the country. Factors which have special weight for its assessment are the level of democratic development in the country, including the holding of free and fair elections, adherence to international human rights instruments, and access for independent national or international organisations freely to verify respect for human rights. There is no requirement that the standards of human rights achieved must be exemplary. What matters is that significant improvements have been made, as illustrated at least by respect for the right to life and liberty and the prohibition of torture; marked progress in establishing an independent

[8] See Art. 12(4) of the 1966 International Covenant on Civil and Political Rights declaring: "No one shall be arbitrarily deprived of the right to enter his own country" and Human Rights Committee, General Comment No. 27, Art. 12 (freedom of movement), 1999.

judiciary, fair trials and access to courts: as well as protection amongst others of the fundamental rights to freedom of expression, association and religion. Important, more specific indicators include declarations of amnesties, the repeal of oppressive laws, and the dismantling of former security services.

C. Partial Cessation

17. The 1951 Convention does not preclude cessation declarations for distinct sub-groups of a general refugee population from a specific country, for instance, for refugees fleeing a particular regime but not for those fleeing after that regime was deposed.[9] In contrast, changes in the refugee's country of origin affecting only part of the territory should not, in principle, lead to cessation of refugee status. Refugee status can only come to an end if the basis for persecution is removed without the precondition that the refugee has to return to specific safe parts of the country in order to be free from persecution. Also, not being able to move or to establish oneself freely in the country of origin would indicate that the changes have not been fundamental.

D. Individual Cessation

18. A strict interpretation of Article 1C(5) and (6) would allow their application on an individual basis. It reads: "The Convention shall cease to apply to any person [if]...[h]e can no longer, *because the circumstances in connexion with which he has been recognized as a refugee* have ceased to exist, continue to refuse to avail himself of the protection" of his country of origin (emphasis supplied). Yet Article 1C(5) and (6) have rarely been invoked in individual cases. States have not generally undertaken periodic reviews of individual cases on the basis of fundamental changes in the country of origin.

These practices acknowledge that a refugee's sense of stability should be preserved as much as possible. They are also consistent with Article 34 of the 1951 Convention, which urges States "as far as possible [to] facilitate the assimilation and naturalization of refugees". Where the cessation clauses are applied on an individual basis, it should not be done for the purposes of a re-hearing *de novo*.

E. Exceptions to Cessation

Continued international protection needs

19. Even when circumstances have generally changed to such an extent that refugee status would no longer be necessary, there may always be the specific circumstances of individual cases that may warrant continued international protection. It has therefore been a general principle that all refugees affected by general cessation must have the possibility, upon request, to have such application in their cases reconsidered on international protection grounds relevant to their individual case.[10]

[9] This approach has been taken by UNHCR on one occasion.

[10] Executive Committee, Conclusion No. 69 (XLIII) (1992), para. d.

"Compelling reasons"

20. Both Article 1C(5) and (6) contain an exception to the cessation provision, allowing a refugee to invoke "compelling reasons arising out of previous persecution" for refusing to re-avail himself or herself of the protection of the country of origin. This exception is intended to cover cases where refugees, or their family members, have suffered atrocious forms of persecution and therefore cannot be expected to return to the country of origin or former habitual residence.[11] This might, for example, include "ex-camp or prison detainees, survivors or witnesses of violence against family members, including sexual violence, as well as severely traumatised persons. It is presumed that such persons have suffered grave persecution, including at the hands of elements of the local population, and cannot reasonably be expected to return".[12] Children should also be given special consideration in this regard, as they may often be able to invoke "compelling reasons" for refusing to return to their country of origin.

21. Application of the "compelling reasons" exception is interpreted to extend beyond the actual words of the provision to apply to Article 1A(2) refugees. This reflects a general humanitarian principle that is now well-grounded in State practice.[13]

Long-term residents

22. In addition, the Executive Committee, in Conclusion No. 69, recommends that States consider "appropriate arrangements" for persons "who cannot be expected to leave the country of asylum, due to a long stay in that country resulting in strong family, social and economic links". In such situations, countries of asylum are encouraged to provide, and often do provide, the individuals concerned with an alternative residence status, which retains previously acquired rights, though in some instances with refugee status being withdrawn. Adopting this approach for long-settled refugees is not required by the 1951 Convention per se, but it is consistent with the instrument's broad humanitarian purpose and with respect for previously acquired rights, as set out in the aforementioned Executive Committee Conclusion No. 69 and international human rights law standards.[14]

F. Cessation and Mass Influx

Prima facie group determinations under the 1951 Convention

23. Situations of mass influx frequently involve groups of persons acknowledged as refugees on a group basis because of the readily apparent and objective reasons for flight and circumstances in the country of origin. The immediate impracticality of individual status determinations has led to use of a *prima facie* refugee designation or

[11] See amongst others, UNHCR, *Handbook*, para. 136.

[12] See UNHCR and UNHCHR Study, "Daunting Prospects Minority Women: Obstacles to their Return and Integration", Sarajevo, Bosnia and Herzegovina, April 2000.

[13] See generally, J. Fitzpatrick and R. Bonoan, "Cessation of Refugee Protection" in *Refugee Protection in International Law: UNHCR's Global Consultations on International Protection*, eds E. Feller, V. Türk and F. Nicholson, (Cambridge University Press, 2003 forthcoming).

[14] See e.g., above footnote 8.

acceptance for the group.[15] For such groups, the general principles described for cessation are applicable.

Temporary protection in mass influx situations that include persons covered by the 1951 Convention

24. Some States have developed "temporary protection" schemes[16] under which assistance and protection against *refoulement* have been extended on a group basis, without either a determination of *prima facie* refugee status for the group or individual status determinations for members of the group. Even though the cessation doctrine does not formally come into play, this form of protection is built upon the 1951 Convention framework and members of the group may well be or include refugees under the Convention. Decisions by States to withdraw temporary protection should therefore be preceded by a thorough evaluation of the changes in the country of origin. Such decisions should also be accompanied by an opportunity for those unwilling to return and requesting international protection to have access to an asylum procedure. In this context, it is also appropriate for States to provide exceptions for individuals with "compelling reasons" arising out of prior persecution.

III. Procedural Issues

25. As mentioned earlier, a declaration of general cessation has potentially serious consequences for recognised refugees. It acknowledges loss of refugee status and the rights that accompany that status, and it may contemplate the return of persons to their countries of origin. Thus, the following procedural aspects should be observed:

General considerations

i. In making an assessment of the country of origin, States and UNHCR must "make sure in an objective and verifiable way that the situation which justified the granting of refugee status has ceased to exist".[17] As noted above, this assessment should include consideration of a range of factors, including the general human rights situation.

ii. The burden rests on the country of asylum to demonstrate that there has been a fundamental, stable and durable change in the country of origin and that invocation of Article 1C(5) or (6) is appropriate. There may be instances where certain groups should be excluded from the application of general cessation because they remain at risk of persecution.

iii. It is important that both the declaration process and implementation plans be consultative and transparent, involving in particular UNHCR, given its supervisory role.[18] NGOs and refugees should also be included in this consultative process. "Go and see"

[15] See "Protection of Refugees in Mass Influx Situations: Overall Protection Framework, Global Consultations on International Protection", EC/GC/01/4, 19 Feb. 2001.

[16] See, e.g., the European Union Directive on Temporary Protection, 2001/55/EC, 20 July 2001.

[17] This rigorous standard is reflected in Executive Committee Conclusion No. 69 (XLIII) (1992), para. a.

[18] See para. 8(a) of the UNHCR Statute, Article 35 of the 1951 Convention and Article II of the 1967 Protocol, as well as in particular, the second preambular paragraph of Executive Committee Conclusion No. 69 (XLIII) (1992).

visits to the country of origin could, where feasible, be facilitated to examine conditions there, as well as an examination of the situation of refugees who have already returned voluntarily.

iv. General cessation declarations should be made public.

v. Counselling of refugees, information sharing and, if necessary, the provision of assistance to returnees are critical to the successful implementation of general cessation.

vi. Procedures operationalising a declaration of cessation need to be carried out in a flexible, phased manner, particularly in developing countries hosting large numbers of refugees. There needs to be a certain time lapse between the moment of declaration and implementation, allowing for preparations for return and arrangements for long-term residents with acquired rights.

vii. Noting the potential impact of a general cessation declaration on refugees and their families, they should be given an opportunity, upon request, to have their case reconsidered on grounds relevant to their individual case, in order to establish whether they come within the terms of the exceptions to cessation.[19] In such cases, however, no action should be taken to withdraw rights of the refugee until a final decision has been taken.

viii. UNHCR retains a role in assisting the return of persons affected by a declaration of cessation or the integration of those allowed to stay, since they remain under UNHCR's Mandate for a period of grace.

Post–declaration applications for refugee status

ix. A declaration of general cessation cannot serve as an automatic bar to refugee claims, either at the time of a general declaration or subsequent to it. Even though general cessation may have been declared in respect of a particular country, this does not preclude individuals leaving this country from applying for refugee status. For example, even if fundamental changes have occurred in a State, members of identifiable sub-groups – such as those based on ethnicity, religion, race, or political opinion – may still face particular circumstances that warrant refugee status. Alternatively, a person may have a well-founded fear of persecution by a private person or group that the government is unable or unwilling to control, persecution based on gender being one example.

Guidelines On International Protection No. 4:

"Internal Flight or Relocation Alternative" within the Context of Article 1A(2) of the 1951 Convention and/or 1967 Protocol relating to the Status of Refugees

UNHCR issues these Guidelines pursuant to its mandate, as contained in the *Statute of the Office of the United Nations High Commissioner for Refugees*, and Article 35 of the *1951 Convention relating to the Status of Refugees and/or its 1967 Protocol*. These Guidelines supplement the UNHCR *Handbook on Procedures and Criteria for Determining Refugee Status under the 1951 Convention and the 1967 Protocol relating to the Status of Refugees* (re-edited, Geneva, January 1992). They further supersede

[19] See paras. 19–22 of these Guidelines and Executive Committee Conclusion No. 69 (XLIII) (1992).

UNHCR's Position Paper, *Relocating Internally as a Reasonable Alternative to Seeking Asylum – (The So-Called "Internal Flight Alternative" or "Relocation Principle")* (Geneva, February 1999). They result, *inter alia*, from the Second Track of the Global Consultations on International Protection which examined this subject at its expert meeting in San Remo, Italy, in September 2001 and seek to consolidate appropriate standards and practice on this issue in light of recent developments in State practice.

These Guidelines are intended to provide interpretative legal guidance for governments, legal practitioners, decision-makers and the judiciary, as well as UNHCR staff carrying out refugee status determination in the field.

I. Introduction

1. Internal flight or relocation alternative is a concept that is increasingly considered by decision-makers in refugee status determination. To date, there has been no consistent approach to this concept and consequently divergent practices have emerged both within and across jurisdictions. Given the differing approaches, these Guidelines are designed to offer decision-makers a more structured approach to analysis of this aspect of refugee status determination.

2. The concept of an internal flight or relocation alternative is not a stand-alone principle of refugee law, nor is it an independent test in the determination of refugee status. A Convention refugee is a person who meets the criteria set out in Article 1A(2) of the *1951 Convention and/or 1967 Protocol relating to the Status of Refugees* (hereinafter "1951 Convention"). These criteria are to be interpreted in a liberal and humanitarian spirit, in accordance with their ordinary meaning, and in light of the object and purpose of the 1951 Convention. The concept of an internal flight or relocation alternative is not explicitly referred to in these criteria. The question of whether the claimant has an internal flight or relocation alternative may, however, arise as part of the refugee status determination process.

3. Some have located the concept of internal flight or relocation alternative in the "well-founded fear of being persecuted" clause of the definition, and others in the "unwilling . . . or unable . . . to avail himself of the protection of that country" clause. These approaches are not necessarily contradictory, since the definition comprises one holistic test of interrelated elements. How these elements relate, and the importance to be accorded to one or another element, necessarily falls to be determined on the facts of each individual case.[1]

4. International law does not require threatened individuals to exhaust all options within their own country first before seeking asylum; that is, it does not consider asylum to be the last resort. The concept of internal flight or relocation alternative should therefore not be invoked in a manner that would undermine important human rights tenets underlying the international protection regime, namely the right to leave one's country, the right to seek asylum and protection against refoulement. Moreover, since the concept can only arise in the context of an assessment of the refugee claim on its merits, it cannot be used to deny access to refugee status determination procedures. A consideration of internal flight or relocation necessitates regard for the personal circumstances of the individual claimant and the conditions in the country for which the internal flight or relocation alternative is proposed.[2]

[1] For further details, see UNHCR, "Interpreting Article 1 of the 1951 Convention Relating to the Status of Refugees", Geneva, April 2001, (hereafter UNHCR, "Interpreting Article 1"), para. 12.
[2] *Ibid.*, paras. 35–37.

5. Consideration of possible internal relocation areas is not relevant for refugees coming under the purview of Article I(2) of the OAU Convention Governing the Specific Aspects of Refugee Problems in Africa 1969. Article I(2) specifically clarifies the definition of a refugee as follows: "every person who, owing to external aggression, occupation, foreign domination or events seriously disturbing public order in either part or the whole of his country of origin or nationality, is compelled to leave his place of habitual residence in order to seek refuge in another place outside his country of origin or nationality".[3]

II. Substantive Analysis

A. Part of the holistic assessment of refugee status

6. The 1951 Convention does not require or even suggest that the fear of being persecuted need always extend to the whole territory of the refugee's country of origin.[4] The concept of an internal flight or relocation alternative therefore refers to a specific area of the country where there is no risk of a well-founded fear of persecution and where, given the particular circumstances of the case, the individual could reasonably be expected to establish him/herself and live a normal life.[5] Consequently, if internal flight or relocation is to be considered in the context of refugee status determination, a particular area must be identified and the claimant provided with an adequate opportunity to respond.

7. In the context of the holistic assessment of a claim to refugee status, in which a well-founded fear of persecution for a Convention reason has been established in some localised part of the country of origin, the assessment of whether or not there is a relocation possibility requires two main sets of analyses, undertaken on the basis of answers to the following sets of questions:

I. The Relevance Analysis

a. *Is the area of relocation practically, safely, and legally accessible to the individual?* If any of these conditions is not met, consideration of an alternative location within the country would not be relevant.

b. *Is the agent of persecution the State?* National authorities are presumed to act throughout the country. If they are the feared persecutors, there is a presumption in principle that an internal flight or relocation alternative is not available.

c. *Is the agent of persecution a non-State agent?* Where there is a risk that the non-State actor will persecute the claimant in the proposed area, then the area will not be an internal flight or relocation alternative. This finding will depend on a determination of whether the persecutor is likely to pursue the claimant to the area and whether State protection from the harm feared is available there.

d. *Would the claimant be exposed to a risk of being persecuted or other serious harm upon relocation?* This would include the original or any new form of persecution or other serious harm in the area of relocation.

[3] (Emphasis added.) The 1984 *Cartagena Declaration* also specifically refers to Article I(2) of the OAU Refugee Convention.

[4] See UNHCR, *Handbook on Procedures and Criteria for Determining Refugee Status* (1979, Geneva, re-edited 1992), (hereinafter "UNHCR, *Handbook*"), para. 91.

[5] For issues concerning the burden of proof in establishing these issues see section III.A below.

II. The Reasonableness Analysis

a. *Can the claimant, in the context of the country concerned, lead a relatively normal life without facing undue hardship?* If not, it would not be reasonable to expect the person to move there.

Scope of assessment

8. The determination of whether the proposed internal flight or relocation area is an appropriate alternative in the particular case requires an assessment over time, taking into account not only the circumstances that gave rise to the persecution feared, and that prompted flight from the original area, but also whether the proposed area provides a meaningful alternative in the future. The forward-looking assessment is all the more important since, although rejection of status does not automatically determine the course of action to be followed, forcible return may be a consequence.

B. The relevance analysis

9. The questions outlined in paragraph 7 can be analysed further as follows:

Is the area of relocation practically, safely, and legally accessible to the individual?

10. An area is not an internal flight or relocation alternative if there are barriers to reaching the area which are not reasonably surmountable. For example, the claimant should not be required to encounter physical dangers en route to the area such as mine fields, factional fighting, shifting war fronts, banditry or other forms of harassment or exploitation.

11. If the refugee claimant would have to pass through the original area of persecution in order to access the proposed area, that area cannot be considered an internal flight or relocation alternative. Similarly, passage through airports may render access unsafe, especially in cases where the State is the persecutor or where the persecutor is a non-State group in control of the airport.

12. The proposed area must also be legally accessible, that is, the individual must have the legal right to travel there, to enter, and to remain. Uncertain legal status can create pressure to move to unsafe areas, or to the area of original persecution. This issue may require particular attention in the case of stateless persons or those without documentation.

Is the agent of persecution the State?

13. The need for an analysis of internal relocation only arises where the fear of being persecuted is limited to a specific part of the country, outside of which the feared harm cannot materialise. In practical terms, this normally excludes cases where the feared persecution emanates from or is condoned or tolerated by State agents, including the official party in one-party States, as these are presumed to exercise authority in all parts of the country.[6] Under such circumstances the person is threatened with persecution countrywide unless

[6] See Summary Conclusions – Internal Protection/Relocation/Flight Alternative, Global Consultations on International Protection, San Remo Expert Roundtable, 6–8 September 2001 (hereinafter "Summary Conclusions – Internal Protection/Relocation/Flight Alternative"), para. 2; UNHCR, "Interpreting Article 1", paras. 12–13.

exceptionally it is clearly established that the risk of persecution stems from an authority of the State whose power is clearly limited to a specific geographical area or where the State itself only has control over certain parts of the country.[7]

14. Where the risk of being persecuted emanates from local or regional bodies, organs or administrations within a State, it will rarely be necessary to consider potential relocation, as it can generally be presumed that such local or regional bodies derive their authority from the State. The possibility of relocating internally may be relevant only if there is clear evidence that the persecuting authority has no reach outside its own region and that there are particular circumstances to explain the national government's failure to counteract the localised harm.

Is the agent of persecution a non-State agent?

15. Where the claimant fears persecution by a non-State agent of persecution, the main inquiries should include an assessment of the motivation of the persecutor, the ability of the persecutor to pursue the claimant in the proposed area, and the protection available to the claimant in that area from State authorities. As with questions involving State protection generally, the latter involves an evaluation of the ability and willingness of the State to protect the claimant from the harm feared. A State may, for instance, have lost effective control over its territory and thus not be able to protect. Laws and mechanisms for the claimant to obtain protection from the State may reflect the State's willingness, but, unless they are given effect in practice, they are not of themselves indicative of the availability of protection. Evidence of the State's inability or unwillingness to protect the claimant in the original persecution area will be relevant. It can be presumed that if the State is unable or unwilling to protect the individual in one part of the country, it may also not be able or willing to extend protection in other areas. This may apply in particular to cases of gender-related persecution.

16. Not all sources of possible protection are tantamount to State protection. For example, if the area is under the control of an international organisation, refugee status should not be denied solely on the assumption that the threatened individual could be protected by that organisation. The facts of the individual case will be particularly important. The general rule is that it is inappropriate to equate the exercise of a certain administrative authority and control over territory by international organisations on a transitional or temporary basis with national protection provided by States. Under international law, international organisations do not have the attributes of a State.

17. Similarly, it is inappropriate to find that the claimant will be protected by a local clan or militia in an area where they are not the recognised authority in that territory and/or where their control over the area may only be temporary. Protection must be effective and of a durable nature: It must be provided by an organised and stable authority exercising full control over the territory and population in question.

Would the claimant be exposed to a risk of being persecuted or other serious harm upon relocation?

18. It is not sufficient simply to find that the original agent of persecution has not *yet* established a presence in the proposed area. Rather, there must be reason to believe that

[7] See also paras. 16, 17 and 27 of these Guidelines.

the reach of the agent of persecution is likely to remain localised and outside the designated place of internal relocation.

19. Claimants are not expected or required to suppress their political or religious views or other protected characteristics to avoid persecution in the internal flight or relocation area. The relocation alternative must be more than a "safe haven" away from the area of origin.

20. In addition, a person with an established fear of persecution for a 1951 Convention reason in one part of the country cannot be expected to relocate to another area of serious harm. If the claimant would be exposed to a new risk of serious harm, including a serious risk to life, safety, liberty or health, or one of serious discrimination,[8] an internal flight or relocation alternative does not arise, irrespective of whether or not there is a link to one of the Convention grounds.[9] The assessment of new risks would therefore also need to take into account serious harm generally covered under complementary forms of protection.[10]

21. The proposed area is also not an internal flight or relocation alternative if the conditions there are such that the claimant may be compelled to go back to the original area of persecution, or indeed to another part of the country where persecution or other forms of serious harm may be a possibility.

C. The reasonableness analysis

22. In addition to there not being a fear of persecution in the internal flight or relocation alternative, it must be reasonable in all the circumstances for the claimant to relocate there. This test of "reasonableness" has been adopted by many jurisdictions. It is also referred to as a test of "undue hardship" or "meaningful protection".

23. The "reasonableness test" is a useful legal tool which, while not specifically derived from the language of the 1951 Convention, has proved sufficiently flexible to address the issue of whether or not, in all the circumstances, the particular claimant could reasonably be expected to move to the proposed area to overcome his or her well-founded fear of being persecuted. It is not an analysis based on what a hypothetical "reasonable person" should be expected to do. The question is what is reasonable, both subjectively and objectively, given the individual claimant and the conditions in the proposed internal flight or relocation alternative.

Can the claimant, in the context of the country concerned, lead a relatively normal life without facing undue hardship?

24. In answering this question, it is necessary to assess the applicant's personal circumstances, the existence of past persecution, safety and security, respect for human rights, and possibility for economic survival.

[8] See UNHCR, *Handbook*, paras. 51–52.

[9] A more general right not to be returned to a country where there is a risk of torture or cruel or inhuman treatment is found, either explicitly or by interpretation, in international human rights instruments. The most prominent are Article 3 of the Convention against Torture 1984, Article 7 of the International Covenant on Civil and Political Rights 1966, and Article 3 of the European Convention for the Protection of Human Rights and Fundamental Freedoms 1950.

[10] See UN docs. EC/50/SC/CRP.18, 9 June 2000 and EC/GC/01/18, 4 September 2001.

Personal circumstances

25. The personal circumstances of an individual should always be given due weight in assessing whether it would be unduly harsh and therefore unreasonable for the person to relocate in the proposed area. Of relevance in making this assessment are factors such as age, sex, health, disability, family situation and relationships, social or other vulnerabilities, ethnic, cultural or religious considerations, political and social links and compatibility, language abilities, educational, professional and work background and opportunities, and any past persecution and its psychological effects. In particular, lack of ethnic or other cultural ties may result in isolation of the individual and even discrimination in communities where close ties of this kind are a dominant feature of daily life. Factors which may not on their own preclude relocation may do so when their cumulative effect is taken into account. Depending on individual circumstances, those factors capable of ensuring the material and psychological well-being of the person, such as the presence of family members or other close social links in the proposed area, may be more important than others.

Past persecution

26. Psychological trauma arising out of past persecution may be relevant in determining whether it is reasonable to expect the claimant to relocate in the proposed area. The provision of psychological assessments attesting to the likelihood of further psychological trauma upon return would militate against finding that relocation to the area is a reasonable alternative. In some jurisdictions, the very fact that the individual suffered persecution in the past is sufficient in itself to obviate any need to address the internal relocation issue.

Safety and security

27. The claimant must be able to find safety and security and be free from danger and risk of injury. This must be durable, not illusory or unpredictable. In most cases, countries in the grip of armed conflict would not be safe for relocation, especially in light of shifting armed fronts which could suddenly bring insecurity to an area hitherto considered safe.

In situations where the proposed internal flight or relocation alternative is under the control of an armed group and/or State-like entity, careful examination must be made of the durability of the situation there and the ability of the controlling entity to provide protection and stability.

Respect for human rights

28. Where respect for basic human rights standards, including in particular non-derogable rights, is clearly problematic, the proposed area cannot be considered a reasonable alternative. This does not mean that the deprivation of any civil, political or socio-economic human right in the proposed area will disqualify it from being an internal flight or relocation alternative. Rather, it requires, from a practical perspective, an assessment of whether the rights that will not be respected or protected are fundamental to the individual, such that the deprivation of those rights would be sufficiently harmful to render the area an unreasonable alternative.

Economic survival

29. The socio-economic conditions in the proposed area will be relevant in this part of the analysis. If the situation is such that the claimant will be unable to earn a living or to access accommodation, or where medical care cannot be provided or is clearly inadequate, the area may not be a reasonable alternative. It would be unreasonable, including from a human rights perspective, to expect a person to relocate to face economic destitution or existence below at least an adequate level of subsistence. At the other end of the spectrum, a simple lowering of living standards or worsening of economic status may not be sufficient to reject a proposed area as unreasonable. Conditions in the area must be such that a relatively normal life can be led in the context of the country concerned. If, for instance, an individual would be without family links and unable to benefit from an informal social safety net, relocation may not be reasonable, unless the person would otherwise be able to sustain a relatively normal life at more than just a minimum subsistence level.

30. If the person would be denied access to land, resources and protection in the proposed area because he or she does not belong to the dominant clan, tribe, ethnic, religious and/or cultural group, relocation there would not be reasonable. For example, in many parts of Africa, Asia and elsewhere, common ethnic, tribal, religious and/or cultural factors enable access to land, resources and protection. In such situations, it would not be reasonable to expect someone who does not belong to the dominant group, to take up residence there. A person should also not be required to relocate to areas, such as the slums of an urban area, where they would be required to live in conditions of severe hardship.

D. Relocation and internally displaced persons

31. The presence of internally displaced persons who are receiving international assistance in one part of the country is not in itself conclusive evidence that it is reasonable for the claimant to relocate there. For example, the standard and quality of life of the internally displaced are often insufficient to support a finding that living in the area would be a reasonable alternative to flight. Moreover, where internal displacement is a result of "ethnic cleansing" policies, denying refugee status on the basis of the internal flight or relocation concept could be interpreted as condoning the resulting situation on the ground and therefore raises additional concerns.

32. The reality is that many thousands of internally displaced persons do not enjoy basic rights and have no opportunity to exercise the right to seek asylum outside their country. Thus, although standards largely agreed by the international community now exist, their implementation is by no means assured in practice. Moreover, the *Guiding Principles on Internal Displacement* specifically affirm in Principle 2(2) that they are not to be interpreted as "restricting, modifying or impairing the provisions of any international human rights or international humanitarian law instrument or rights granted to persons under domestic law" and in particular, they are "without prejudice to the right to seek and enjoy asylum in other countries".[11]

[11] See also W. Kälin, *Guiding Principles on Internal Displacement: Annotations*, Studies in Transnational Legal Policy No. 32, 2000 (The American Society of International Law, The Brookings Institution, Project on Internal Displacement), pp. 8-10.

III. Procedural Issues

A. Burden of proof

33. The use of the relocation concept should not lead to additional burdens on asylum-seekers. The usual rule must continue to apply, that is, the burden of proving an allegation rests on the one who asserts it. This is consistent with paragraph 196 of the *Handbook* which states that

> ... while the burden of proof in principle rests on the applicant, the duty to ascertain and evaluate all the relevant facts is shared between the applicant and the examiner. Indeed, in some cases, it may be for the examiner to use all the means at his [or her] disposal to produce the necessary evidence in support of the application.

34. On this basis, the decision-maker bears the burden of proof of establishing that an analysis of relocation is relevant to the particular case. If considered relevant, it is up to the party asserting this to identify the proposed area of relocation and provide evidence establishing that it is a reasonable alternative for the individual concerned.

35. Basic rules of procedural fairness require that the asylum-seeker be given clear and adequate notice that such a possibility is under consideration.[12] They also require that the person be given an opportunity to provide arguments why (a) the consideration of an alternative location is not relevant in the case, and (b) if deemed relevant, that the proposed area would be unreasonable.

B. Accelerated or admissibility procedures

36. Given the complex and substantive nature of the inquiry, the examination of an internal flight or relocation alternative is not appropriate in accelerated procedures, or in deciding on an individual's admissibility to a full status determination procedure.[13]

C. Country of origin information

37. While examination of the relevance and reasonableness of a potential internal relocation area always requires an assessment of the individual's own particular circumstances, well-documented, good quality and current information and research on conditions in the country of origin are important components for the purpose of such examination. The usefulness of such information may, however, be limited in cases where the situation in the country of origin is volatile and sudden changes may occur in areas hitherto considered safe. Such changes may not have been recorded by the time the claim is being heard.

IV. Conclusion

38. The concept of internal flight or relocation alternative is not explicitly referred to in the criteria set out in Article 1A(2) of the 1951 Convention. The question of whether the

[12] See Summary Conclusions – Internal Protection/Relocation/Flight Alternative, para. 7.

[13] See Summary Conclusions – Internal Protection/Relocation/Flight Alternative, para. 6; Executive Committee Conclusion No. 87 (L), 1999, para. j; and Note on International Protection, 1999, para. 26 (UN doc. A/AC.96/914, 7 July 1999).

claimant has an internal flight or relocation alternative may, however, arise as part of the holistic determination of refugee status. It is relevant only in certain cases, particularly when the source of persecution emanates from a non-State actor. Even when relevant, its applicability will depend on a full consideration of all the circumstances of the case and the reasonableness of relocation to another area in the country of origin.

Guidelines On International Protection No. 5:

Application of the Exclusion Clauses: Article 1F of the 1951 Convention relating to the Status of Refugees

UNHCR issues these Guidelines pursuant to its mandate, as contained in the 1950 *Statute of the Office of the United Nations High Commissioner for Refugees*, in conjunction with Article 35 of the *1951 Convention relating to the Status of Refugees* and Article II of its *1967 Protocol*. These Guidelines complement the UNHCR *Handbook on Procedures and Criteria for Determining Refugee Status under the 1951 Convention and the 1967 Protocol relating to the Status of Refugees* (re-edited, Geneva, January 1992). These Guidelines summarise the *Background Note on the Application of the Exclusion Clauses: Article 1F of the 1951 Convention relating to the Status of Refugees* (4 September 2003) which forms an integral part of UNHCR's position on this issue. They supersede *The Exclusion Clauses: Guidelines on their Application* (UNHCR, Geneva, 1 December 1996) and *Note on the Exclusion Clauses* (UNHCR, Geneva, 30 May 1997), and result, *inter alia*, from the Second Track of the Global Consultations on International Protection process which examined this subject at its expert meeting in Lisbon, Portugal, in May 2001. An update of these Guidelines was also deemed necessary in light of contemporary developments in international law.

These Guidelines are intended to provide interpretative legal guidance for governments, legal practitioners, decision-makers and the judiciary, as well as UNHCR staff carrying out refugee status determination in the field.

I. Introduction

A. Background

1. Paragraph 7(d) of the 1950 UNHCR Statute, Article 1F of the 1951 Convention relating to the Status of Refugees (hereinafter "1951 Convention") and Article I(5) of the 1969 Organisation of African Unity (OAU) Convention Governing the Specific Aspects of Refugee Problems in Africa (hereinafter "OAU Convention") all oblige States and UNHCR to deny the benefits of refugee status to certain persons who would otherwise qualify as refugees. These provisions are commonly referred to as "the exclusion clauses". These Guidelines provide a summary of the key issues relating to these provisions – further guidance can be found in UNHCR's Background Note on the Application of the Exclusion Clauses: Article 1F of the 1951 Convention relating to the Status of Refugees (hereinafter "the Background Note"), which forms an integral part of these Guidelines.

2. The rationale for the exclusion clauses, which should be borne in mind when considering their application, is that certain acts are so grave as to render their perpetrators undeserving of international protection as refugees. Their primary purpose is to deprive those guilty of heinous acts, and serious common crimes, of international refugee

protection and to ensure that such persons do not abuse the institution of asylum in order to avoid being held legally accountable for their acts. The exclusion clauses must be applied "scrupulously" to protect the integrity of the institution of asylum, as is recognised by UNHCR's Executive Committee in Conclusion No. 82 (XLVIII), 1997. At the same time, given the possible serious consequences of exclusion, it is important to apply them with great caution and only after a full assessment of the individual circumstances of the case. The exclusion clauses should, therefore, always be interpreted in a restrictive manner.

3. The exclusion clauses in the 1951 Convention are exhaustive. This should be kept in mind when interpreting Article I(5) of the OAU Convention which contains almost identical language. Article 1F of the 1951 Convention states that the provisions of that Convention "shall not apply to any person with respect to whom there are serious reasons for considering" that:

(a) he [or she] has committed a crime against peace, a war crime, or a crime against humanity, as defined in the international instruments drawn up to make provision in respect of such crimes;

(b) he [or she] has committed a serious non-political crime outside the country of refuge prior to his [or her] admission to that country as a refugee; or

(c) he [or she] has been guilty of acts contrary to the purposes and principles of the United Nations.

B. Relationship with other provisions of the 1951 Convention

4. Article 1F of the 1951 Convention should be distinguished from **Article 1D** which applies to a specific category of persons receiving protection or assistance from organs and agencies of the United Nations other than UNHCR.[1] Article 1F should also be distinguished from **Article 1E** which deals with persons not in need (as opposed to undeserving) of international protection. Moreover the exclusion clauses are not to be confused with **Articles 32 and 33(2)** of the Convention which deal respectively with the expulsion of, and the withdrawal of protection from *refoulement* from, recognised refugees who pose a danger to the host State (for example, because of serious crimes they have committed there). Article 33(2) concerns the future risk that a recognised refugee may pose to the host State.

C. Temporal scope

5. Articles 1F(a) and 1F(c) are concerned with crimes whenever and wherever they are committed. By contrast, the scope of Article 1F(b) is explicitly limited to crimes committed outside the country of refuge prior to admission to that country as a refugee.

D. Cancellation or revocation on the basis of exclusion

6. Where facts which would have led to exclusion only come to light after the grant of refugee status, this would justify **cancellation** of refugee status on the grounds of exclusion. The reverse is that information casting doubt on the basis on which an individual has been excluded should lead to reconsideration of eligibility for refugee status. Where

[1] See, UNHCR, "Note on the Applicability of Article 1D of the 1951 Convention relating to the Status of Refugees to Palestinian Refugees", October 2002.

a refugee engages in conduct falling within Article 1F(a) or 1F(c), this would trigger the application of the exclusion clauses and the **revocation** of refugee status, provided all the criteria for the application of these clauses are met.

E. Responsibility for determination of exclusion

7. States parties to the 1951 Convention/1967 Protocol and/or OAU Convention and UNHCR need to consider whether the exclusion clauses apply in the context of the determination of refugee status. Paragraph 7(d) of UNHCR's Statute covers similar grounds to Article 1F of the 1951 Convention, although UNHCR officials should be guided by the language of Article 1F, as it represents the later and more specific formulation.

F. Consequences of exclusion

8. Although a State is precluded from granting refugee status pursuant to the 1951 Convention or the OAU Convention to an individual it has excluded, it is not otherwise obliged to take any particular course of action. The State concerned can choose to grant the excluded individual stay on other grounds, but obligations under international law may require that the person concerned be criminally prosecuted or extradited. A decision by UNHCR to exclude someone from refugee status means that that individual can no longer receive protection or assistance from the Office.

9. An excluded individual may still be protected against return to a country where he or she is at risk of ill-treatment by virtue of other international instruments. For example, the 1984 Convention Against Torture and Other Cruel, Inhuman or Degrading Treatment or Punishment absolutely prohibits the return of an individual to a country where there is a risk that he or she will be subjected to torture. Other international and regional human rights instruments contain similar provisions.[2]

II. Substantive Analysis

A. Article 1F(a): Crimes against peace, war crimes and crimes against humanity

10. Amongst the various international instruments which offer guidance on the scope of these international crimes are the 1948 Convention on the Prevention and Punishment of the Crime of Genocide, the four 1949 Geneva Conventions for the Protection of Victims of War and the two 1977 Additional Protocols, the Statutes of the International Criminal Tribunals for the former Yugoslavia and Rwanda, the 1945 Charter of the International Military Tribunal (the London Charter), and most recently the 1998 Statute of the International Criminal Court which entered into force on 1 July 2002.

11. According to the London Charter a **crime against peace** involves the "planning, preparation, initiation or waging of a war of aggression, or a war in violation of international treaties, agreements, or assurances, or participation in a common plan or conspiracy for the accomplishment of any of the foregoing". Given the nature of this crime, it can only be committed by those in a high position of authority representing a State or a State-like entity. In practice, this provision has rarely been invoked.

[2] For further details, see Annex A of the Background Note accompanying these Guidelines.

12. Certain breaches of international humanitarian law constitute **war crimes.**[3] Although such crimes can be committed in both international and non-international armed conflicts, the content of the crimes depends on the nature of the conflict. War crimes cover such acts as wilful killing and torture of civilians, launching indiscriminate attacks on civilians, and wilfully depriving a civilian or a prisoner of war of the rights of fair and regular trial.

13. The distinguishing feature of **crimes against humanity**,[4] which cover acts such as genocide, murder, rape and torture, is that they must be carried out as part of a widespread or systematic attack directed against the civilian population. An isolated act can, however, constitute a crime against humanity if it is part of a coherent system or a series of systematic and repeated acts. Since such crimes can take place in peacetime as well as armed conflict, this is the broadest category under Article 1F(a).

B. Article 1F(b): Serious non-political crimes

14. This category does not cover minor crimes nor prohibitions on the legitimate exercise of human rights. In determining whether a particular offence is sufficiently serious, international rather than local standards are relevant. The following factors should be taken into account: the nature of the act, the actual harm inflicted, the form of procedure used to prosecute the crime, the nature of the penalty, and whether most jurisdictions would consider it a serious crime. Thus, for example, murder, rape and armed robbery would undoubtedly qualify as serious offences, whereas petty theft would obviously not.

15. A serious crime should be considered **non-political** when other motives (such as personal reasons or gain) are the predominant feature of the specific crime committed. Where no clear link exists between the crime and its alleged political objective or when the act in question is disproportionate to the alleged political objective, non-political motives are predominant.[5] The motivation, context, methods and proportionality of a crime to its objectives are important factors in evaluating its political nature. The fact that a particular crime is designated as non-political in an extradition treaty is of significance, but not conclusive in itself. Egregious acts of violence, such as acts those commonly considered to be of a "terrorist" nature, will almost certainly fail the predominance test, being wholly disproportionate to any political objective. Furthermore, for a crime to be regarded as political in nature, the political objectives should be consistent with human rights principles.

16. Article 1F(b) also requires the crime to have been committed "outside the country of refuge prior to [the individual's] admission to that country as a refugee". Individuals who commit "serious non-political crimes" within the country of refuge are subject to that country's criminal law process and, in the case of particularly grave crimes, to Articles 32 and 33(2) of the 1951 Convention.

[3] For instruments defining war crimes, see Annex B of the Background Note.

[4] For instruments defining crimes against humanity, see Annex C of the Background Note.

[5] See para. 152 of the UNHCR *Handbook on Procedures and Criteria for Determining Refugee Status*, Geneva, re-edited 1992.

C. Article 1F(c): Acts contrary to the purposes and principles of the United Nations

17. Given the broad, general terms of the purposes and principles of the United Nations, the scope of this category is rather unclear and should therefore be read narrowly. Indeed, it is rarely applied and, in many cases, Article 1F(a) or 1F(b) are anyway likely to apply. Article 1F(c) is only triggered in extreme circumstances by activity which attacks the very basis of the international community's coexistence. Such activity must have an international dimension. Crimes capable of affecting international peace, security and peaceful relations between States, as well as serious and sustained violations of human rights, would fall under this category. Given that Articles 1 and 2 of the United Nations Charter essentially set out the fundamental principles States must uphold in their mutual relations, it would appear that in principle only persons who have been in positions of power in a State or State-like entity would appear capable of committing such acts. In cases involving a terrorist act, a correct application of Article 1F(c) involves an assessment as to the extent to which the act impinges on the international plane – in terms of its gravity, international impact, and implications for international peace and security.

D. Individual responsibility

18. For exclusion to be justified, individual responsibility must be established in relation to a crime covered by Article 1F. Specific considerations in relation to crimes against peace and acts against the purposes and principles of the UN have been discussed above. In general, individual responsibility flows from the person having committed, or made a substantial contribution to the commission of the criminal act, in the knowledge that his or her act or omission would facilitate the criminal conduct. The individual need not physically have committed the criminal act in question. Instigating, aiding and abetting and participating in a joint criminal enterprise can suffice.

19. The fact that a person was at some point a senior member of a repressive government or a member of an organisation involved in unlawful violence does not in itself entail individual liability for excludable acts. A presumption of responsibility may, however, arise where the individual has remained a member of a government clearly engaged in activities that fall within the scope of Article 1F. Moreover, the purposes, activities and methods of some groups are of a particularly violent nature, with the result that voluntary membership thereof may also raise a presumption of individual responsibility. Caution must be exercised when such a presumption of responsibility arises, to consider issues including the actual activities of the group, its organisational structure, the individual's position in it, and his or her ability to influence significantly its activities, as well as the possible fragmentation of the group. Moreover, such presumptions in the context of asylum proceedings are rebuttable.

20. As for ex-combatants, they should not necessarily be considered excludable, unless of course serious violations of international human rights law and international humanitarian law are reported and indicated in the individual case.

E. Grounds for rejecting individual responsibility

21. Criminal responsibility can normally only arise where the individual concerned committed the material elements of the offence with knowledge and intent. Where the **mental element** is not satisfied, for example, because of ignorance of a key fact, individual

criminal responsibility is not established. In some cases, the individual may not have the mental capacity to be held responsible a crime, for example, because of insanity, mental handicap, involuntary intoxication or, in the case of children, immaturity.

22. Factors generally considered to constitute **defences** to criminal responsibility should be considered. For example, the defence of superior orders will only apply where the individual was legally obliged to obey the order, was unaware of its unlawfulness and the order itself was not manifestly unlawful. As for duress, this applies where the act in question results from the person concerned necessarily and reasonably avoiding a threat of imminent death, or of continuing or imminent serious bodily harm to him- or herself or another person, and the person does not intend to cause greater harm than the one sought to be avoided. Action in self-defence or in defence of others or of property must be both reasonable and proportionate in relation to the threat.

23. Where **expiation** of the crime is considered to have taken place, application of the exclusion clauses may no longer be justified. This may be the case where the individual has served a penal sentence for the crime in question, or perhaps where a significant period of time has elapsed since commission of the offence. Relevant factors would include the seriousness of the offence, the passage of time, and any expression of regret shown by the individual concerned. In considering the effect of any pardon or amnesty, consideration should be given to whether it reflects the democratic will of the relevant country and whether the individual has been held accountable in any other way. Some crimes are, however, so grave and heinous that the application of Article 1F is still considered justified despite the existence of a pardon or amnesty.

F. Proportionality considerations

24. The incorporation of a proportionality test when considering exclusion and its consequences provides a useful analytical tool to ensure that the exclusion clauses are applied in a manner consistent with the overriding humanitarian object and purpose of the 1951 Convention. The concept has evolved in particular in relation to Article 1F(b) and represents a fundamental principle of many fields of international law. As with any exception to a human rights guarantee, the exclusion clauses must therefore be applied in a manner proportionate to their objective, so that the gravity of the offence in question is weighed against the consequences of exclusion. Such a proportionality analysis would, however, not normally be required in the case of crimes against peace, crimes against humanity, and acts falling under Article 1F(c), as the acts covered are so heinous. It remains relevant, however, to Article 1F(b) crimes and less serious war crimes under Article 1F(a).

G. Particular acts and special cases

25. Despite the lack of an internationally agreed definition of **terrorism**,[6] acts commonly considered to be terrorist in nature are likely to fall within the exclusion clauses even though Article 1F is not to be equated with a simple anti-terrorism provision. Consideration of the exclusion clauses is, however, often unnecessary as suspected terrorists may not be eligible for refugee status in the first place, their fear being of legitimate prosecution as opposed to persecution for Convention reasons.

[6] For instruments pertaining to terrorism, see Annex D of the Background Note.

26. Of all the exclusion clauses, Article 1F(b) may be particularly relevant as acts of terrorist violence are likely to be disproportionate to any avowed political objective. Each case will require individual consideration. The fact that an individual is designated on a national or international list of terrorist suspects (or associated with a designated terrorist organisation) should trigger consideration of the exclusion clauses but will not in itself generally constitute sufficient evidence to justify exclusion. Exclusion should not be based on membership of a particular organisation alone, although a presumption of individual responsibility may arise where the organisation is commonly known as notoriously violent and membership is voluntary. In such cases, it is necessary to examine the individual's role and position in the organisation, his or her own activities, as well as related issues as outlined in paragraph 19 above.

27. As acts of **hijacking** will almost certainly qualify as a "serious crime" under Article 1F(b), only the most compelling of circumstances can justify non-exclusion. Acts of **torture** are prohibited under international law. Depending on the context, they will generally lead to exclusion under Article 1F.

28. The exclusion clauses apply in principle to **minors**, but only if they have reached the age of criminal responsibility and possess the mental capacity to be held responsible for the crime in question. Given the vulnerability of children, great care should be exercised in considering exclusion with respect to a minor and defences such as duress should in particular be examined carefully. Where UNHCR conducts refugee status determination under its mandate, all such cases should be referred to Headquarters before a final decision is made.

29. Where the main applicant is excluded from refugee status, the dependants will need to establish their own grounds for refugee status. If the latter are recognised as refugees, the excluded individual is not able to rely on the right to family unity in order to secure protection or assistance as a refugee.

30. The exclusion clauses can also apply in situations of **mass influx**, although in practice the individual screening required may cause operational and practical difficulties. Nevertheless, until such screening can take place, all persons should receive protection and assistance, subject of course to the separation of armed elements from the civilian refugee population.

III. Procedural Issues

31. Given the grave consequences of exclusion, it is essential that rigorous procedural **safeguards** are built into the exclusion determination procedure. Exclusion decisions should in principle be dealt with in the context of the **regular refugee status determination procedure** and not in either admissibility or accelerated procedures, so that a full factual and legal assessment of the case can be made. The exceptional nature of Article 1F suggests that inclusion should generally be considered before exclusion, but there is no rigid formula. Exclusion may exceptionally be considered without particular reference to inclusion issues (i) where there is an indictment by an international criminal tribunal; (ii) in cases where there is apparent and readily available evidence pointing strongly towards the applicant's involvement in particularly serious crimes, notably in prominent Article 1F(c) cases, and (iii) at the appeal stage in cases where exclusion is the question at issue.

32. **Specialised exclusion units** within the institution responsible for refugee status determination could be set up to handle exclusion cases to ensure that they are dealt with

in an expeditious manner. It may be prudent to defer decisions on exclusion until completion of any domestic criminal proceedings, as the latter may have significant implications for the asylum claim. In general, however, the refugee claim must be determined in a final decision before execution of any extradition order.

33. At all times the **confidentiality** of the asylum application should be respected. In exceptional circumstances, contact with the country of origin may be justified on national security grounds, but even then the existence of the asylum application should not be disclosed.

34. The **burden of proof** with regard to exclusion rests with the State (or UNHCR) and, as in all refugee status determination proceedings, the applicant should be given the benefit of the doubt. Where, however, the individual has been indicted by an international criminal tribunal, or where individual responsibility for actions which give rise to exclusion is presumed, as indicated in paragraph 19 of these Guidelines, the burden of proof is reversed, creating a rebuttable presumption of excludability.

35. In order to satisfy the **standard of proof** under Article 1F, clear and credible evidence is required. It is not necessary for an applicant to have been convicted of the criminal offence, nor does the criminal standard of proof need to be met. Confessions and testimony of witnesses, for example, may suffice if they are reliable. Lack of cooperation by the applicant does not in itself establish guilt for the excludable act in the absence of clear and convincing evidence. Consideration of exclusion may, however, be irrelevant if non-cooperation means that the basics of an asylum claim cannot be established.

36. Exclusion should not be based on **sensitive evidence** that cannot be challenged by the individual concerned. Exceptionally, anonymous evidence (where the source is concealed) may be relied upon but only where this is absolutely necessary to protect the safety of witnesses and the asylum-seeker's ability to challenge the substance of the evidence is not substantially prejudiced. Secret evidence or evidence considered in camera (where the substance is also concealed) should not be relied upon to exclude.

Where national security interests are at stake, these may be protected by introducing procedural safeguards which also respect the asylum-seeker's due process rights.

Guidelines On International Protection No. 6:

Religion-Based Refugee Claims under Article 1A(2) of the 1951 Convention and/or the 1967 Protocol relating to the Status of Refugees

UNHCR issues these Guidelines pursuant to its mandate, as contained in the 1950 *Statute of the Office of the United Nations High Commissioner for Refugees*, in conjunction with Article 35 of the *1951 Convention relating to the Status of Refugees and Article II of its 1967 Protocol*. These Guidelines complement the UNHCR *Handbook on Procedures and Criteria for Determining Refugee Status under the 1951 Convention and the 1967 Protocol relating to the Status of Refugees* (re-edited, Geneva, January 1992). They are informed, *inter alia*, by a roundtable organised by UNHCR and the Church World Service in Baltimore, Maryland, United States, in October 2002, as well as by an analysis of relevant State practice and international law.

These Guidelines are intended to provide interpretative legal guidance for governments, legal practitioners, decision-makers and the judiciary, as well as UNHCR staff carrying out refugee status determination in the field.

I. Introduction

1. Claims to refugee status based on religion can be among the most complex. Decision-makers have not always taken a consistent approach, especially when applying the term "religion" contained in the refugee definition of the 1951 Convention relating to the Status of Refugees and when determining what constitutes "persecution" in this context. Religion-based refugee claims may overlap with one or more of the other grounds in the refugee definition or, as can often happen, they may involve post-departure conversions, that is, *sur place* claims. While these Guidelines do not purport to offer a definitive definition of "religion", they provide decision-makers with guiding parameters to facilitate refugee status determination in such cases.

2. The right to freedom of thought, conscience and religion is one of the fundamental rights and freedoms in international human rights law. In determining religion-based claims, it is therefore useful, *inter alia*, to draw on Article 18 of the 1948 Universal Declaration of Human Rights (the "Universal Declaration") and Articles 18 and 27 of the 1966 International Covenant on Civil and Political Rights (the "International Covenant"). Also relevant are the General Comments issued by the Human Rights Committee,[1] the 1981 Declaration on the Elimination of All Forms of Intolerance and Discrimination based on Religion or Belief, the 1992 Declaration on the Rights of Persons belonging to National or Ethnic, Religious and Linguistic Minorities and the body of reports of the Special Rapporteur on Religious Intolerance.[2] These international human rights standards provide guidance in defining the term "religion" also in the context of international refugee law, against which action taken by States to restrict or prohibit certain practices can be examined.

II. Substantive Analysis

A. Defining "religion"

3. The refugee definition contained in Article 1A(2) of the 1951 Convention states:

> A. For the purposes of the present Convention, the term "refugee" shall apply to any person who: . . .
>
> (2) . . . owing to well-founded fear of being persecuted for reasons of race, religion, nationality, membership of a particular social group or political opinion, is outside the country of his nationality and is unable or, owing to such fear, is unwilling to avail himself of the protection of that country; or who, not having a nationality and being outside the country of his former habitual residence as a result of such events, is unable or, owing to such fear, is unwilling to return to it.

4. The *travaux préparatoires* of the 1951 Convention show that religion-based persecution formed an integral and accepted part of the refugee definition throughout the drafting process. There was, however, no attempt to define the term as such.[3] No universally

[1] See, in particular, Human Rights Committee, General Comment No. 22, adopted 20 July 1993, UN doc. CCPR/C/21/Rev.1/ ADD.4, 27 September 1993.

[2] The latter can be found at <http://www.unhchr.ch/huridocda/huridoca.nsf/FramePage/intolerance+En?OpenDocument>. Relevant regional instruments include Article 9 of the 1950 European Convention on Human Rights; Article 12 of the 1969 American Convention on Human Rights; Article 8 of the 1981 African Charter on Human and Peoples' Rights.

[3] A key source in States' deliberations was the refugee definition set out in the 1946 Constitution of the International Refugee Organisation (IRO). This included those expressing valid objections

accepted definition of "religion" exists, but the instruments mentioned in paragraph 2 above certainly inform the interpretation of the term "religion" in the international refugee law context. Its use in the 1951 Convention can therefore be taken to encompass freedom of thought, conscience or belief.[4] As the Human Rights Committee notes, "religion" is "not limited . . . to traditional religions or to religions and beliefs with institutional characteristics or practices analogous to those of traditional religions".[5] It also broadly covers acts of failing or refusing to observe a religion or to hold any particular religious belief. The term is not, however, without limits and international human rights law foresees a number of legitimate boundaries on the exercise of religious freedom as outlined in greater detail in paragraphs 15–16 below.

5. Claims based on "religion" may involve one or more of the following elements:

a. religion as belief (including non-belief);
b. religion as identity;
c. religion as a way of life.

6. "Belief", in this context, should be interpreted so as to include theistic, nontheistic and atheistic beliefs. Beliefs may take the form of convictions or values about the divine or ultimate reality or the spiritual destiny of humankind. Claimants may also be considered heretics, apostates, schismatic, pagans or superstitious, even by other adherents of their religious tradition and be persecuted for that reason.

7. "Identity" is less a matter of theological beliefs than membership of a community that observes or is bound together by common beliefs, rituals, traditions, ethnicity, nationality, or ancestry. A claimant may identify with, or have a sense of belonging to, or be identified by others as belonging to, a particular group or community. In many cases, persecutors are likely to target religious groups that are different from their own because they see that religious identity as part of a threat to their own identity or legitimacy.

8. For some individuals, "religion" is a vital aspect of their "way of life" and how they relate, either completely or partially, to the world. Their religion may manifest itself in such activities as the wearing of distinctive clothing or observance of particular religious practices, including observing religious holidays or dietary requirements. Such practices may seem trivial to non-adherents, but may be at the core of the religion for the adherent concerned.

9. Establishing sincerity of belief, identity and/or a certain way of life may not necessarily be relevant in every case.[6] It may not be necessary, for instance, for an individual (or a group) to declare that he or she belongs to a religion, is of a particular religious faith, or adheres to religious practices, where the persecutor imputes or attributes this religion, faith or practice to the individual or group. As is discussed further below in paragraph 31, it may also not be necessary for the claimant to know or understand anything about the religion, if he or she has been identified by others as belonging to that group and fears persecution as a result. An individual (or group) may be persecuted on the basis of religion,

to return because of a fear of persecution on grounds of "race, religion, nationality or political opinions". (A fifth ground, membership of a particular social group, was approved later in the negotiating process for the 1951 Convention.)

[4] See, also, UNHCR, *Handbook on Procedures and Criteria for Determining Refugee Status*, 1979, Geneva, re-edited 1992 (hereafter "UNHCR, *Handbook*"), para. 71.

[5] Human Rights Committee, General Comment No. 22, above note 1, para. 2.

[6] For further analysis of credibility issues, see paras. 28–33 below.

even if the individual or other members of the group adamantly deny that their belief, identity and/or way of life constitute a "religion".

10. Similarly, birth into a particular religious community, or a close correlation between race and/or ethnicity on the one hand and religion on the other could preclude the need to enquire into the adherence of an individual to a particular faith or the bona fides of a claim to membership of that community, if adherence to that religion is attributed to the individual.

B. Well-founded fear of persecution

a) General

11. The right to freedom of religion includes the freedom to manifest one's religion or belief, either individually or in community with others and in public or private in worship, observance, practice and teaching.[7] The only circumstances under which this freedom may be restricted are set out in Article 18(3) of the International Covenant, as described in paragraphs 15–16 below.

12. Persecution for reasons of religion may therefore take various forms. Depending on the particular circumstances of the case, including the effect on the individual concerned, examples could include prohibition of membership of a religious community, of worship in community with others in public or in private, of religious instruction, or serious measures of discrimination imposed on individuals because they practise their religion, belong to or are identified with a particular religious community, or have changed their faith.[8] Equally, in communities in which a dominant religion exists or where there is a close correlation between the State and religious institutions, discrimination on account of one's failure to adopt the dominant religion or to adhere to its practices, could amount to persecution in a particular case.[9] Persecution may be inter-religious (directed against adherents or communities of different faiths), intra-religious (within the same religion, but between different sects, or among members of the same sect), or a combination of both.[10] The claimant may belong to a religious minority or majority. Religion-based claims may also be made by individuals in marriages of mixed religions.

13. Applying the same standard as for other Convention grounds, religious belief, identity, or way of life can be seen as so fundamental to human identity that one should not be compelled to hide, change or renounce this in order to avoid persecution.[11] Indeed,

[7] See Universal Declaration, Article 18 and International Covenant, Article 18(1).

[8] UNHCR, *Handbook*, above note 4, para. 72.

[9] In this context, Article 27 of the International Covenant reads: "In those States in which ethnic, religious or linguistic minorities exist, persons belonging to such minorities shall not be denied the right, in community with the other members of their group, to enjoy their own culture, to profess and practise their own religion, or to use their own language."

[10] Interim Report of the Special Rapporteur on Religious Intolerance, "Implementation of the Declaration on the Elimination of All Forms of Intolerance and of Discrimination based on Religion or Belief", UN doc. A/53/279, 24 August 1998, para. 129.

[11] See also, UNHCR, "Guidelines on International Protection: 'Membership of a particular social group' within the Context of Article 1A(2) of the 1951 Convention and/or 1967 Protocol relating to the Status of Refugees", HCR/GIP/02/02, 7 May 2002, para. 6. Similarly, in internal flight or relocation cases, the claimant should not be expected or required to suppress his or her religious views to avoid persecution in the internal flight or relocation area. See UNHCR, "Guidelines on

the Convention would give no protection from persecution for reasons of religion if it was a condition that the person affected must take steps – reasonable or otherwise – to avoid offending the wishes of the persecutors. Bearing witness in words and deeds is often bound up with the existence of religious convictions.[12]

14. Each claim requires examination on its merits on the basis of the individual's situation.

Relevant areas of enquiry include the individual profile and personal experiences of the claimant, his or her religious belief, identity and/or way of life, how important this is for the claimant, what effect the restrictions have on the individual, the nature of his or her role and activities within the religion, whether these activities have been or could be brought to the attention of the persecutor and whether they could result in treatment rising to the level of persecution. In this context, the well-founded fear "need not necessarily be based on the applicant's own personal experience". What, for example, happened to the claimant's friends and relatives, other members of the same religious group, that is to say to other similarly situated individuals, "may well show that his [or her] fear that sooner or later he [or she] also will become a victim of persecution is well-founded".[13] Mere membership of a particular religious community will normally not be enough to substantiate a claim to refugee status. As the UNHCR Handbook notes, there may, however, be special circumstances where mere membership suffices, particularly when taking account of the overall political and religious situation in the country of origin, which may indicate a climate of genuine insecurity for the members of the religious community concerned.

b) Restrictions or limitations on the exercise of religious freedom

15. Article 18(3) of the International Covenant permits restrictions on the "freedom to manifest one's religion or beliefs" if these limits "are prescribed by law and are necessary to protect public safety, order, health, or morals or the fundamental rights and freedoms of others". As the Human Rights Committee notes: "Limitations may be applied only for those purposes for which they were prescribed and must be directly related and proportionate to the specific need on which they are predicated. Restrictions may not be imposed for discriminatory purposes or applied in a discriminatory manner."[14] In assessing the legitimacy of the restriction or limitation at issue, it is therefore necessary to analyse carefully why and how it was imposed. Permissible restrictions or limitations could include measures to prevent criminal activities (for example, ritual killings), or harmful traditional practices and/or limitations on religious practices injurious to the best interests of the child, as judged by international law standards. Another justifiable, even necessary, restriction could involve the criminalisation of hate speech, including when committed in the name of religion. The fact that a restriction on the exercise of a religious freedom finds the support of the majority of the population in the claimant's country of origin and/or is limited to the manifestation of the religion in public is irrelevant.

International Protection: 'Internal Flight or Relocation Alternative' within the Context of Article 1A(2) of the 1951 Convention and/or 1967 Protocol relating to the Status of Refugees", HCR/GIP/03/04, 23 July 2003, paras. 19, 25.

[12] UNHCR, *Handbook*, above note 4, para. 73.

[13] UNHCR, *Handbook*, above note 4, para. 43

[14] See Human Rights Committee, General Comment No. 22, above note 1, para. 8.

16. In determining whether restrictions or limitations rise to the level of persecution, the decision-maker must not only take into account international human rights standards, including lawful limitations on the exercise of religious freedom, but also evaluate the breadth of the restriction and the severity of any punishment for non-compliance. The importance or centrality of the practice within the religion and/or to the individual personally is also relevant. The decision-maker should proceed cautiously with such inquiries, taking into account the fact that what may seem trivial to an outsider may be central to the claimant's beliefs. Where the restricted practice is not important to the individual, but important to the religion, then it is unlikely to rise to the level of persecution without additional factors. By contrast, the restricted religious practice may not be so significant to the religion, but may be particularly important to the individual, and could therefore still constitute persecution on the basis of his or her conscience or belief.

c) Discrimination

17. Religion-based claims often involve discrimination.[15] Even though discrimination for reasons of religion is prohibited under international human rights law, all discrimination does not necessarily rise to the level required for recognition of refugee status. For the purposes of analysing an asylum claim, a distinction should be made between discrimination resulting merely in preferential treatment and discrimination amounting to persecution because, in aggregate or of itself, it seriously restricts the claimant's enjoyment of fundamental human rights. Examples of discrimination amounting to persecution would include, but are not limited to, discrimination with consequences of a substantially prejudicial nature for the person concerned, such as serious restrictions on the right to earn a livelihood, or to access normally available educational institutions and/or health services. This may also be so where economic measures imposed "destroy the economic existence" of a particular religious group.[16]

18. The existence of discriminatory laws will not normally in itself constitute persecution, although they can be an important, even indicative, factor which therefore needs to be taken into account. An assessment of the implementation of such laws and their effect is in any case crucial to establishing persecution. Similarly, the existence of legislation on religious freedom does not of itself mean individuals are protected. In many cases, such legislation may not be implemented in practice or custom or tradition may, for instance, in practice override this.

19. Discrimination may also take the form of restrictions or limitations on religious belief or practice. Restrictions have, for instance, included penalties for converting to a different faith (apostasy) or for proselytising, or for celebrating religious festivals particular to the religion concerned. The compulsory registration of religious groups and the imposition of specific regulations governing them to restrict the exercise of freedom of religion or belief can also have a discriminatory aim or results. Such actions are legitimate only if they are "specified by law, objective, reasonable and transparent and, consequently, if they do not have the aim or the result of creating discrimination".[17]

[15] See generally, UNHCR, *Handbook*, above note 4, paras. 54–55.

[16] UNHCR, *Handbook*, above note 4, paras. 54 and 63.

[17] Special Rapporteur on freedom of religion or belief, interim report annexed to Note by the Secretary-General, "Elimination of All Forms of Religious Intolerance", UN doc. A/58/296, 19 August 2003, paras. 134–35.

d) Forced conversion

20. Forced conversion to a religion is a serious violation of the fundamental human right to freedom of thought, conscience and religion and would often satisfy the objective component of persecution. The claimant would still need to demonstrate a subjective fear that the conversion would be persecutory to him or her personally. Generally, this would be satisfied if the individual held convictions or faith or had a clear identity or way of life in relation to a different religion, or if he or she had chosen to be disassociated from any religious denomination or community. Where a claimant held no particular religious conviction (including one of atheism) nor a clear identification with a particular religion or religious community before the conversion or threat of conversion, it would be necessary to assess the impact of such a conversion on the individual (for example, it may be an act without correlative personal effects).

e) Forced compliance or conformity with religious practices

21. Forced compliance with religious practices might, for example, take the form of mandated religious education that is incompatible with the religious convictions, identity or way of life of the child or the child's parents.[18] It might also involve an obligation to attend religious ceremonies or swear an oath of allegiance to a particular religious symbol. In determining whether such forced compliance constitutes persecution, the policies or acts with which the person or group is required to comply, the extent to which they are contrary to the person's belief, identity or way of life and the punishment for non-compliance should be examined. Such forced compliance could rise to the level of persecution if it becomes an intolerable interference with the individual's own religious belief, identity or way of life and/or if non-compliance would result in disproportionate punishment.

22. Forced compliance may also involve the imposition of a particular criminal or civil legal code purported to be based on a religious doctrine to which non-observers might object. Where such a code contains discriminatory substantive or procedural safeguards and especially where it imposes different levels of punishment upon adherents and non-adherents, it could well be regarded as persecutory. Where the law imposes disproportionate punishment for breaches of the law (for example, imprisonment for blasphemy or practising an alternative religion, or death for adultery), whether or not for adherents of the same religion, it would constitute persecution. Such cases are more common where there is limited or no separation between the State and the religion.

23. A specific religious code may be persecutory not just when enforced against non-observers, but also when applied to dissidents within or members of the same faith. The enforcement of anti-blasphemy laws, for example, can often be used to stifle political debate among co-religionists and could constitute persecution on religious and/or political grounds even when enforced against members of the same religion.

C. Special considerations

a) Gender

24. Particular attention should be paid to the impact of gender on religion-based refugee claims, as women and men may fear or suffer persecution for reasons of religion in

[18] This would be likely also to interfere with the undertaking of States to respect the liberty of parents or legal guardians to ensure the religious and moral education of their children in conformity with their own convictions under Article 18(4) of the International Covenant.

different ways to each other. Clothing requirements, restrictions on movement, harmful traditional practices, or unequal or discriminatory treatment, including subjection to discriminatory laws and/or punishment, may all be relevant.[19] In some countries, young girls are pledged in the name of religion to perform traditional slave duties or to provide sexual services to the clergy or other men. They may also be forced into underage marriages, punished for honour crimes in the name of religion, or subjected to forced genital mutilation for religious reasons. Others are offered to deities and subsequently bought by individuals believing that they will be granted certain wishes. Women are still identified as "witches" in some communities and burned or stoned to death.[20] These practices may be culturally condoned in the claimant's community of origin but still amount to persecution. In addition, individuals may be persecuted because of their marriage or relationship to someone of a different religion than their own. When, due to the claimant's gender, State actors are unwilling or unable to protect the claimant from such treatment, it should not be mistaken as a private conflict, but should be considered as valid grounds for refugee status.

b) Conscientious objection

25. A number of religions or sects within particular religions have abstention from military service as a central tenet and a significant number of religion-based claimants seek protection on the basis of refusal to serve in the military. In countries where military service is compulsory, failure to perform this duty is frequently punishable by law. Moreover, whether military service is compulsory or not, desertion is invariably a criminal offence.[21]

26. Where military service is compulsory, refugee status may be established if the refusal to serve is based on genuine political, religious, or moral convictions, or valid reasons of conscience.[22] Such claims raise the distinction between prosecution and persecution. Prosecution and punishment pursuant to a law of general application is not generally considered to constitute persecution,[23] although there are some notable exceptions. In conscientious objector cases, a law purporting to be of general application may, depending on the circumstances, nonetheless be persecutory where, for instance, it impacts differently on particular groups, where it is applied or enforced in a discriminatory manner, where

[19] For more information, see UNHCR, "Guidelines on International Protection: Gender-Related Persecution within the context of Article 1A(2) of the 1951 Convention and/or its 1967 Protocol relating to the Status of Refugees", HCR/GIP/02/01, 7 May 2002, especially paras. 25–26.

[20] For description of these practices, see "Integration of the Human Rights of Women and the Gender Perspective Violence against Women, Report of the Special Rapporteur on violence against women, its causes and consequences, Ms Radhika Coomaraswamy, submitted in accordance with Commission on Human Rights resolution 2001/49, Cultural practices in the family that are violent towards women", E/CN.4/2002/83, 31 January 2002, available at <http://www.unhchr.ch/huridocda/huridoca.nsf/0/42 E7191FAE543562C1256BA7004E963C/$ File/G0210428.doc?OpenElement>; "Droits Civils et Politiques et, Notamment: Intolérance Religieuse", Rapport soumis par M. Abdelfattah Amor, Rapporteur spécial, conformément àla résolution 2001/42 de la Commission des droits de l'homme, Additif: "Étude sur la liberté de religion ou de conviction et la condition de la femme au regard de la religion et des traditions", E/CN.4/2002/73/Add.2, 5 avril 2002, available (only in French) at <http://www.unhchr.ch/huridocda/huridoca.nsf/2848af408d01ec0ac1256609004e770b/9fa99a4d3f9eade5c1256b9e00510d71?Open Document&Highlight=2,E%2FCN.4%2F2002%2F73%2FAdd.2>.

[21] See generally, UNHCR, *Handbook*, above note 4, paras. 167–74.

[22] UNHCR, *Handbook*, above note 4, para. 170

[23] UNHCR, *Handbook*, above note 4, para. 55–60.

the punishment itself is excessive or disproportionately severe, or where the military service cannot reasonably be expected to be performed by the individual because of his or her genuine beliefs or religious convictions. Where alternatives to military service, such as community service, are imposed there would not usually be a basis for a claim. Having said this, some forms of community service may be so excessively burdensome as to constitute a form of punishment, or the community service might require the carrying out of acts which clearly also defy the claimant's religious beliefs. In addition, the claimant may be able to establish a claim to refugee status where the refusal to serve in the military is not occasioned by any harsh penalties, but the individual has a well-founded fear of serious harassment, discrimination or violence by other individuals (for example, soldiers, local authorities, or neighbours) for his or her refusal to serve.

III. Procedural Issues

a) General

27. The following are some general points of particular relevance to examining religion-based refuge claims:

a. Religious practices, traditions or beliefs can be complex and may vary from one branch or sect of a religion to another or from one country or region to another. For this reason, there is a need for reliable, accurate, up-to-date, and country- or region-specific as well as branch- or sect-specific information.

b. Refugee status determinations based on religion could also benefit from the assistance of independent experts with *particularised* knowledge of the country, region and context of the particular claim and/or the use of corroborating testimony from other adherents of the same faith.

c. Decision-makers need to be objective and not arrive at conclusions based solely upon their own experiences, even where they may belong to the same religion as the claimant. General assumptions about a particular religion or its adherents should be avoided.

d. In assessing religion-based claims, decision-makers need to appreciate the frequent interplay between religion and gender, race, ethnicity, cultural norms, identity, way of life and other factors.

e. In the selection of interviewers and interpreters, there should be sensitivity regarding any cultural, religious or gender aspects that could hinder open communication.[24]

f. Interviewers should also be aware of the potential for hostile biases toward the claimant by an interpreter, either because he or she shares the same religion or is not of the same religion, or of any potential fear of the same by the claimant, which could adversely affect his or her testimony. As with all refugee claims, it can be critical that interpreters are well-versed in the relevant terminology.

b) Credibility

28. Credibility is a central issue in religion-based refugee claims. While decision-makers will often find it helpful during research and preparation to list certain issues to cover

[24] See also, UNHCR, "Guidelines on Gender-Related Persecution", above note 19.

during an interview, extensive examination or testing of the tenets or knowledge of the claimant's religion may not always be necessary or useful. In any case, knowledge tests need to take account of individual circumstances, particularly since knowledge of a religion may vary considerably depending on the individual's social, economic or educational background and/or his or her age or sex.

29. Experience has shown that it is useful to resort to a narrative form of questioning, including through open-ended questions allowing the claimant to explain the personal significance of the religion to him or her, the practices he or she has engaged in (or has avoided engaging in out of a fear of persecution), or any other factors relevant to the reasons for his or her fear of being persecuted. Information may be elicited about the individual's religious experiences, such as asking him or her to describe in detail how he or she adopted the religion, the place and manner of worship, or the rituals engaged in, the significance of the religion to the person, or the values he or she believes the religion espouses. For example, the individual may not be able to list the Ten Commandments or name the Twelve Imams, but may be able to indicate an understanding of the religion's basic tenets more generally. Eliciting information regarding the individual's religious identity or way of life will often be more appropriate and useful and may even be necessary. It should also be noted that a claimant's detailed knowledge of his or her religion does not necessarily correlate with sincerity of belief.

30. As indicated in paragraph 9 above, individuals may be persecuted on the basis of their religion even though they have little or no substantive knowledge of its tenets or practices. A lack of knowledge may be explained by further research into the particular practices of that religion in the area in question or by an understanding of the subjective and personal aspects of the claimant's case. For instance, the level of repression against a religious group in a society may severely restrict the ability of an individual to study or practise his or her religion. Even when the individual is able to receive religious education in a repressive environment, it may not be from qualified leaders. Women, in particular, are often denied access to religious education. Individuals in geographically remote communities may espouse adherence to a particular religion and face persecution as a result, yet have little knowledge of its formal practices. Over time, communities may adapt particular religious practices or faith to serve their own needs, or combine them with their more traditional practices and beliefs, especially where the religion has been introduced into a community with long-established traditions. For example, the claimant may not be able to distinguish between those practices which are Christian and those which are animist.

31. Less formal knowledge may also be required of someone who obtained a particular religion by birth and who has not widely practised it. No knowledge is required where a particular religious belief or adherence is imputed or attributed to a claimant.

32. Greater knowledge may be expected, however, of individuals asserting they are religious leaders or who have undergone substantial religious instruction. It is not necessary for such teaching or training to conform fully to objectively tested standards, as these may vary from region to region and country to country, but some clarification of their role and the significance of certain practices or rites to the religion would be relevant. Even claimants with a high level of education or schooling in their religion may not have knowledge of teachings and practices of a more complex, formal or obscure nature.

33. Subsequent and additional interviews may be required where certain statements or claims made by the claimant are incompatible with earlier statements or with general

understandings of the religious practices of other members of that religion in the area or region in question. Claimants must be given an opportunity to explain any inconsistencies or discrepancies in their story.

c) Conversion post departure

34. Where individuals convert after their departure from the country of origin, this may have the effect of creating a *sur place* claim.[25] In such situations, particular credibility concerns tend to arise and a rigorous and in depth examination of the circumstances and genuineness of the conversion will be necessary. Issues which the decision-maker will need to assess include the nature of and connection between any religious convictions held in the country of origin and those now held, any disaffection with the religion held in the country of origin, for instance, because of its position on gender issues or sexual orientation, how the claimant came to know about the new religion in the country of asylum, his or her experience of this religion, his or her mental state and the existence of corroborating evidence regarding involvement in and membership of the new religion.

35. Both the specific circumstances in the country of asylum and the individual case may justify additional probing into particular claims. Where, for example, systematic and organised conversions are carried out by local religious groups in the country of asylum for the purposes of accessing resettlement options, and/or where "coaching" or "mentoring" of claimants is commonplace, testing of knowledge is of limited value. Rather, the interviewer needs to ask open questions and try to elicit the motivations for conversion and what effect the conversion has had on the claimant's life. The test remains, however, whether he or she would have a well-founded fear of persecution on a Convention ground if returned. Regard should therefore be had as to whether the conversion may come to the notice of the authorities of the person's country of origin and how this is likely to be viewed by those authorities.[26] Detailed country of origin information is required to determine whether a fear of persecution is objectively well-founded.

36. So-called "self-serving" activities do not create a well-founded fear of persecution on a Convention ground in the claimant's country of origin, if the opportunistic nature of such activities will be apparent to all, including the authorities there, and serious adverse consequences would not result if the person were returned. Under all circumstances, however, consideration must be given as to the consequences of return to the country of origin and any potential harm that might justify refugee status or a complementary form of protection. In the event that the claim is found to be self-serving but the claimant nonetheless has a well-founded fear of persecution on return, international protection is required. Where the opportunistic nature of the action is clearly apparent, however, this could weigh heavily in the balance when considering potential durable solutions that may be available in such cases, as well as, for example, the type of residency status.

[25] Such a claim may also arise if a claimant marries someone of another religion in the country of asylum or educates his or her children in that other religion there and the country of origin would use this as the basis for persecution.

[26] See UNHCR, *Handbook*, above note 4, para. 96.

Guidelines On International Protection No. 7:

The application of Article 1A(2) of the 1951 Convention and/or 1967 Protocol relating to the Status of Refugees to victims of trafficking and persons at risk of being trafficked

UNHCR issues these Guidelines pursuant to its mandate, as contained in the 1950 *Statute of the Office of the United Nations High Commissioner for Refugees* in conjunction with Article 35 of the *1951 Convention relating to the Status of Refugees* and Article II of its *1967 Protocol*. These Guidelines complement the UNHCR *Handbook on Procedures and Criteria for Determining Refugee Status under the 1951 Convention and the 1967 Protocol relating to the Status of Refugees* (re-edited, Geneva, January 1992). They should additionally be read in conjunction with UNHCR's Guidelines on International Protection on gender-related persecution within the context of Article 1A(2) of the 1951 Convention and/or 1967 Protocol relating to the Status of Refugees (HCR/GIP/02/01) and on "membership of a particular social group" within the context of Article 1A(2) of the 1951 Convention and/or its 1967 Protocol relating to the Status of Refugees (HCR/GIP/02/02), both of 7 May 2002.

These Guidelines are intended to provide interpretative legal guidance for governments, legal practitioners, decision-makers and the judiciary, as well as for UNHCR staff carrying out refugee status determination in the field.

I. Introduction

1. Trafficking in persons, the primary objective of which is to gain profit through the exploitation of human beings, is prohibited by international law and criminalized in the national legislation of a growing number of States. Although the range of acts falling within the definition of trafficking varies among national jurisdictions, States have a responsibility to combat trafficking and to protect and assist victims of trafficking.

2. The issue of trafficking has attracted substantial attention in recent years, but it is not a modern phenomenon. Numerous legal instruments dating from the late nineteenth century onwards have sought to address various forms and manifestations of trafficking.[1]

These instruments remain in force and are relevant to the contemporary understanding of trafficking and how best to combat it. The 2000 Protocol to Prevent, Suppress and Punish Trafficking in Persons, especially Women and Children (hereinafter the "Trafficking Protocol")[2] supplementing the 2000 United Nations Convention against Transnational Organized Crime (hereinafter the "Convention against Transnational Crime")[3] provides an international definition of trafficking. This represents a crucial step forward in efforts to combat trafficking and ensure full respect for the rights of individuals affected by trafficking.

[1] It has been estimated that between 1815 and 1957 some 300 international agreements were adopted to suppress slavery in its various forms, including for example the 1910 International Convention for the Suppression of the White Slave Traffic, the 1915 Declaration Relative to the Universal Abolition of the Slave Trade, the 1926 Slavery Convention, the 1949 Convention for the Suppression of the Traffick in Persons and of the Exploitation of the Prostitution of Others and the 1956 Supplementary Convention on the Abolition of Slavery, the Slave Trade and Institutions and Practices Similar to Slavery.

[2] Entered into force on 25 December 2003.

[3] Entered into force on 29 September 2003.

3. Trafficking in the context of the sex trade is well documented and primarily affects women and children who are forced into prostitution and other forms of sexual exploitation.[4]

Trafficking is not, however, limited to the sex trade or to women. It also includes, at a minimum, forced labour or services, slavery or practices similar to slavery, servitude or the removal of organs.[5] Depending on the circumstances, trafficking may constitute a crime against humanity and, in armed conflict, a war crime.[6] common characteristic of all forms of trafficking is that victims are treated as merchandise, "owned" by their traffickers, with scant regard for their human rights and dignity.

4. In some respects, trafficking in persons resembles the smuggling of migrants, which is the subject of another Protocol to the Convention against Transnational Crime.[7] As with trafficking, the smuggling of migrants often takes place in dangerous and/or degrading conditions involving human rights abuses. It is nevertheless essentially a voluntary act entailing the payment of a fee to the smuggler to provide a specific service. The relationship between the migrant and the smuggler normally ends either with the arrival at the migrant's destination or with the individual being abandoned en route. Victims of trafficking are distinguished from migrants who have been smuggled by the protracted nature of the exploitation they endure, which includes serious and ongoing abuses of their human rights at the hands of their traffickers. Smuggling rings and trafficking rings are nevertheless often closely related, with both preying on the vulnerabilities of people seeking international protection or access to labour markets abroad. Irregular migrants relying on the services of smugglers whom they have willingly contracted may also end up as victims of trafficking, if the services they originally sought metamorphose into abusive and exploitative trafficking scenarios.

5. UNHCR's involvement with the issue of trafficking is essentially twofold. First, the Office has a responsibility to ensure that refugees, asylum-seekers, internally displaced persons (IDPs), stateless persons and other persons of concern do not fall victim to trafficking. Secondly, the Office has a responsibility to ensure that individuals who have been trafficked and who fear being subjected to persecution upon a return to their country of origin, or individuals who fear being trafficked, whose claim to international protection falls within the refugee definition contained in the 1951 Convention and/or its 1967 Protocol relating to the Status of Refugees (hereinafter "the 1951 Convention") are recognized as refugees and afforded the corresponding international protection.

6. Not all victims or potential victims of trafficking fall within the scope of the refugee definition. To be recognized as a refugee, all elements of the refugee definition have to be satisfied. These Guidelines are intended to provide guidance on the application

[4] Bearing in mind the prevalence of women and girls amongst the victims of trafficking, gender is a relevant factor in evaluating their claims for refugee status. See further, UNHCR, "Guidelines on International Protection: Gender-related persecution within the context of Article 1A(2) of the 1951 Convention and/or its 1967 Protocol relating to the Status of Refugees" (hereinafter "UNHCR Guidelines on Gender-Related Persecution"), HCR/GIP/02/01, 7 May 2002, para. 2.

[5] See Article 3(a) of the Trafficking Protocol cited in para. 8 below.

[6] See, for instance, Articles 7(1)(c), 7(1)(g), 7(2)(c) and 8(2)(xxii) of the 1998 Statute of the International Criminal Court, A/CONF.183/9, which specifically refer to "enslavement", "sexual slavery" and "enforced prostitution" as crimes against humanity and war crimes.

[7] The 2000 Protocol against the Smuggling of Migrants by Land, Sea and Air (entered into force on 28 January 2004).

of Article 1A(2) of the 1951 Convention to victims or potential victims of trafficking. They also cover issues concerning victims of trafficking arising in the context of the 1954 Convention Relating to the Status of Stateless Persons and the 1961 Convention on the Reduction of Statelessness. The protection of victims or potential victims of trafficking as set out in these Guidelines is additional to and distinct from the protection contemplated by Part II of the Trafficking Protocol.[8]

II. Substantive Analysis

a) Definitional issues

7. The primary function of the Convention against Transnational Crime and its supplementary Protocols against Trafficking and Smuggling is crime control. They seek to define criminal activities and guide States as to how best to combat them. In doing so, they nevertheless provide helpful guidance on some aspects of victim protection and therefore constitute a useful starting point for any analysis of international protection needs arising as a result of trafficking.

8. Article 3 of the Trafficking Protocol reads:

For the purposes of this Protocol:

(a) 'Trafficking in persons' shall mean the recruitment, transportation, transfer, harbouring or receipt of persons, by means of the threat or use of force or other forms of coercion, of abduction, of fraud, of deception, of the abuse of power or of a position of vulnerability, or of the giving or receiving of payments or benefits to achieve the consent of a person having control over another person, for the purpose of exploitation. Exploitation shall include, at a minimum, the exploitation of the prostitution of others or other forms of sexual exploitation, forced labour or services, slavery or practices similar to slavery, servitude or the removal of organs;

(b) The consent of a victim of trafficking in persons to the intended exploitation set forth in subparagraph (a) of this article shall be irrelevant where any of the means set forth in subparagraph (a) have been used;

(c) The recruitment, transportation, transfer, harbouring or receipt of a child for the purpose of exploitation shall be considered 'trafficking in persons' even if this does not involve any of the means set forth in subparagraph (a) of this article;

(d) 'Child' shall mean any person under eighteen years of age.

9. The Trafficking Protocol thus defines trafficking by three essential and interlinked sets of elements:

The act: recruitment, transportation, transfer, harbouring or receipt of persons;

The means: by threat or use of force or other forms of coercion, abduction, fraud, deception, abuse of power, abuse of a position of vulnerability, or of giving or receiving of payments or benefits to achieve the consent of a person having control over the victim;

[8] Part II of the Trafficking Protocol concerns the protection of victims of trafficking. It covers areas such as ensuring the protection of privacy and identity of the victims; providing victims with information on relevant court and administrative proceedings, as well as assistance to enable them to present their views and concerns at appropriate stages of criminal proceedings against offenders; providing victims with support for physical, psychological and social recovery; permitting victims to remain in the territory temporarily or permanently; repatriating victims with due regard for their safety; and other measures.

The purpose: exploitation of the victim, including, at a minimum, the exploitation of the prostitution of others or other forms of sexual exploitation, forced labour or services, slavery or practices similar to slavery, servitude or the removal of organs.[9]

10. An important aspect of this definition is an understanding of trafficking as a process comprising a number of interrelated actions rather than a single act at a given point in time. Once initial control is secured, victims are generally moved to a place where there is a market for their services, often where they lack language skills and other basic knowledge that would enable them to seek help. While these actions can all take place within one country's borders,[10] they can also take place across borders with the recruitment taking place in one country and the act of receiving the victim and the exploitation taking place in another. Whether or not an international border is crossed, the intention to exploit the individual concerned underpins the entire process.

11. Article 3 of the Trafficking Protocol states that where any of the means set forth in the definition are used, the consent of the victim to the intended exploitation is irrelevant.[11]

Where the victim is a child,[12] the question of consent is all the more irrelevant as any recruitment, transportation, transfer, harbouring or receipt of children for the purpose of exploitation is a form of trafficking regardless of the means used.

12. Some victims or potential victims of trafficking may fall within the definition of a refugee contained in Article 1A(2) of the 1951 Convention and may therefore be entitled to international refugee protection. Such a possibility is not least implicit in the saving clause contained in Article 14 of the Trafficking Protocol, which states:

1. Nothing in this Protocol shall affect the rights, obligations and responsibilities of States and individuals under international law, including international humanitarian law and international human rights law and, in particular, where applicable, the 1951 Convention and the 1967 Protocol relating to the Status of Refugees and the principle of *non-refoulement* as contained therein.[13]

[9] For the purposes of these Guidelines, the Trafficking Protocol definition is used as it represents the current international consensus on the meaning of trafficking. In order to understand the legal meaning of terms used within the Protocol definition fully, it is nevertheless necessary to refer further to other legal instruments, for example, a number of International Labour Organization Conventions, including the 1930 Convention No. 29 on Forced or Compulsory Labour, the 1957 Convention No. 105 on the Abolition of Forced Labour, the 1975 Convention No. 143 on Migrant Workers (Supplementary Provisions) and the 1999 Convention No. 182 on the Worst Forms of Child Labour. These are referred to in the first report of the Special Rapporteur on trafficking in persons, especially women and children, Ms Sigma Huda, E/CN.4/2005/71, 22 December 2004, para. 22. Her second report entitled "Integration of the Human Rights of Women and a Gender Perspective", E/CN.4/2006/62, 20 February 2006, goes into this issue in further detail in paras. 31–45. The Special Rapporteur was appointed in 2004 pursuant to a new mandate created by the 60th Session of the Commission on Human Rights (Resolution 2004/110).

[10] The Council of Europe Convention on Action against Trafficking in Human Beings, opened for signature in May 2005, addresses the question of trafficking within national borders directly.

[11] Article 3(b) of the Trafficking Protocol. See also, the second report of the Special Rapporteur on trafficking in persons, cited above in footnote 9, paras. 37–43 on the "irrelevance of consent".

[12] Article 3(c) of the Trafficking Protocol follows the 1989 Convention on the Rights of the Child in defining a child as "any person under eighteen years of age".

[13] The Agenda for Protection, A/AC.96/965/Add.1, 2002, Goal 2, Objective 2, calls upon States to ensure that their asylum systems are open to receiving claims from individual victims of trafficking.

2. The measures set forth in this Protocol shall be interpreted and applied in a way that is not discriminatory to persons on the ground that they are victims of trafficking in persons. The interpretation and application of those measures shall be consistent with internationally recognized principles of non-discrimination.

13. A claim for international protection presented by a victim or potential victim of trafficking can arise in a number of distinct sets of circumstances. The victim may have been trafficked abroad, may have escaped her or his traffickers and may seek the protection of the State where she or he now is. The victim may have been trafficked within national territory, may have escaped from her or his traffickers and have fled abroad in search of international protection. The individual concerned may not have been trafficked but may fear becoming a victim of trafficking and may have fled abroad in search of international protection. In all these instances, the individual concerned must be found to have a "well-founded fear of persecution" linked to one or more of the Convention grounds in order to be recognized as a refugee.

b) Well-founded fear of persecution

14. What amounts to a well-founded fear of persecution will depend on the particular circumstances of each individual case.[14] Persecution can be considered to involve serious human rights violations, including a threat to life or freedom, as well as other kinds of serious harm or intolerable predicament, as assessed in the light of the opinions, feelings and psychological make-up of the asylum applicant.

15. In this regard, the evolution of international law in criminalizing trafficking can help decision-makers determine the persecutory nature of the various acts associated with trafficking. Asylum claims lodged by victims of trafficking or potential victims of trafficking should thus be examined in detail to establish whether the harm feared as a result of the trafficking experience, or as a result of its anticipation, amounts to persecution in the individual case. Inherent in the trafficking experience are such forms of severe exploitation as abduction, incarceration, rape, sexual enslavement, enforced prostitution, forced labour, removal of organs, physical beatings, starvation, the deprivation of medical treatment. Such acts constitute serious violations of human rights which will generally amount to persecution.

This interpretation of the Article 14 saving clause as imposing an obligation on States to consider the international protection needs of victims of trafficking is strengthened by paragraph 377 of the Explanatory Report accompanying the Council of Europe Convention. This states in relation to Article 40 of that Convention: The fact of being a victim of trafficking in human beings cannot preclude the right to seek and enjoy asylum and Parties shall ensure that victims of trafficking have appropriate access to fair and efficient asylum procedures. Parties shall also take whatever steps are necessary to ensure full respect for the principle of *non-refoulement*. Additionally, the Office of the High Commissioner for Human Rights (OHCHR) "Recommended Principles and Guidelines on Human Rights and Human Trafficking" presented to the Economic and Social Council as an addendum to the report of the United Nations High Commissioner for Human Rights, E/2002/68/Add. 1, 20 May 2002, available at <http:www.ohchr.org/english/about/publications/docs/trafficking.doc>, address in Guideline 2.7 the importance of ensuring that procedures and processes are in place for the consideration of asylum claims from trafficked persons (as well as from smuggled asylum-seekers) and that the principle of *non-refoulement* is respected and upheld at all times.

[14] UNHCR, *Handbook on Procedures and Criteria for Determining Refugee Status*, 1979, re-edited 1992, para. 51 (hereinafter the "UNHCR, *Handbook*").

16. In cases where the trafficking experience of the asylum applicant is determined to be a one-off past experience, which is not likely to be repeated, it may still be appropriate to recognize the individual concerned as a refugee if there are compelling reasons arising out of previous persecution, provided the other interrelated elements of the refugee definition are fulfilled. This would include situations where the persecution suffered during the trafficking experience, even if past, was particularly atrocious and the individual is experiencing ongoing traumatic psychological effects which would render return to the country of origin intolerable. In other words, the impact on the individual of the previous persecution continues. The nature of the harm previously suffered will also impact on the opinions, feelings and psychological make-up of the asylum applicant and thus influence the assessment of whether any future harm or predicament feared would amount to persecution in the particular case.

17. Apart from the persecution experienced by individuals in the course of being trafficked, they may face reprisals and/or possible re-trafficking should they be returned to the territory from which they have fled or from which they have been trafficked.[15] For example, the victim's cooperation with the authorities in the country of asylum or the country of origin in investigations may give rise to a risk of harm from the traffickers upon return, particularly if the trafficking has been perpetrated by international trafficking networks. Reprisals at the hands of traffickers could amount to persecution depending on whether the acts feared involve serious human rights violations or other serious harm or intolerable predicament and on an evaluation of their impact on the individual concerned. Reprisals by traffickers could also be inflicted on the victim's family members, which could render a fear of persecution on the part of the victim well-founded, even if she or he has not been subjected directly to such reprisals. In view of the serious human rights violations often involved, as described in paragraph 15 above, re-trafficking would usually amount to persecution.

18. In addition, the victim may also fear ostracism, discrimination or punishment by the family and/or the local community or, in some instances, by the authorities upon return. Such treatment is particularly relevant in the case of those trafficked into prostitution. In the individual case, severe ostracism, discrimination or punishment may rise to the level of persecution, in particular if aggravated by the trauma suffered during, and as a result of, the trafficking process. Where the individual fears such treatment, her or his fear of persecution is distinct from, but no less valid than, the fear of persecution resulting from the continued exposure to the violence involved in trafficking scenarios. Even if the ostracism from, or punishment by, family or community members does not rise to the level of persecution, such rejection by, and isolation from, social support networks may in fact heighten the risk of being re-trafficked or of being exposed to retaliation, which could then give rise to a well-founded fear of persecution.

[15] See, "Report of the Working Group on Contemporary Forms of Slavery on its twenty-ninth session", E/CN.4/Sub.2/2004/36, 20 July 2004, Section VII Recommendations adopted at the twenty-ninth session, p. 16, para. 29. This "[c]alls upon all States to ensure that the protection and support of the victims are at the centre of any anti-trafficking policy, and specifically to ensure that: (a) No victim of trafficking is removed from the host country if there is a reasonable likelihood that she will be re-trafficked or subjected to other forms of serious harm, irrespective of whether she decides to cooperate in a prosecution".

c) Women and children victims of trafficking

19. The forcible or deceptive recruitment of women and children for the purposes of forced prostitution or sexual exploitation is a form of gender-related violence, which may constitute persecution.[16] Trafficked women and children can be particularly susceptible to serious reprisals by traffickers after their escape and/or upon return, as well as to a real possibility of being re-trafficked or of being subjected to severe family or community ostracism and/or severe discrimination.

20. In certain settings, unaccompanied or separated children,[17] are especially vulnerable to trafficking.[18] Such children may be trafficked for the purposes of irregular adoption. This can occur with or without the knowledge and assent of the child's parents. Traffickers may also choose to target orphans. In assessing the international protection needs of children who have been trafficked, it is essential that the best interest principle be scrupulously applied.[19] All cases involving trafficked children require a careful examination of the possible involvement of family members or caregivers in the actions that set the trafficking in motion.

d) Agents of persecution

21. There is scope within the refugee definition to recognize both State and non-State agents of persecution. While persecution is often perpetrated by the authorities of a country, it can also be perpetrated by individuals if the persecutory acts are "knowingly tolerated by the authorities or if the authorities refuse, or prove unable to offer effective protection".[20] In most situations involving victims or potential victims of trafficking, the persecutory acts

[16] See UNHCR Guidelines on Gender-Related Persecution, above footnote 4, para. 18. The Commission on Human Rights also recognized that such violence may constitute persecution for the purposes of the refugee definition, when it urged States "to mainstream a gender perspective into all policies and programmes, including national immigration and asylum policies, regulations and practices, as appropriate, in order to promote and protect the rights of all women and girls, including the consideration of steps to recognize gender-related persecution and violence when assessing grounds for granting refugee status and asylum". See Resolution 2005/41, Elimination of violence against women, 57th meeting, 19 April 2005, operational para. 22.

[17] As indicated in the *Inter-agency Guiding Principles on Unaccompanied and Separated Children*, 2004, "separated children are those separated from both parents, or from their previous legal or customary primary care-giver, but not necessarily from other relatives", while unaccompanied children are "children who have been separated from both parents and other relatives and are not being cared for by an adult who, by law or custom, is responsible for doing so".

[18] There are a number of international instruments which offer specific guidance with respect to the needs and rights of children. These should be given due consideration in assessing the claims of child victims. See, for example, the 1989 Convention on the Rights of the Child, the 2000 Optional Protocol to that Convention, on the sale of children, child prostitution and child pornography, the 1980 Hague Convention No. 28 on the Civil Aspects of International Child Abduction, the 2000 Trafficking Protocol and the 1999 ILO Convention No. 182 on the Prohibition of the Worst Forms of Child Labour. See also, generally, Committee on the Rights of the Child, "General Comment No. 6 (2005) Treatment of Unaccompanied and Separated Children Outside their Country of Origin", CRC/CG/2005/6, 1 Sept. 2005.

[19] See, *UNHCR Guidelines on Formal Determination of the Best Interests of the Child*, provisional release April 2006; UN Children's Fund (UNICEF), "Guidelines for Protection of the Rights of Child Victims of Trafficking", May 2003 and in the process of being updated.

[20] See, UNHCR, *Handbook*, above footnote 14, para. 65; UNHCR, "Interpreting Article 1 of the 1951 Convention Relating to the Status of Refugees" (hereinafter "Interpreting Article 1"), April 2001, para. 19; UNHCR Guidelines on Gender-related Persecution, above footnote 4, para. 19.

emanate from individuals, that is, traffickers or criminal enterprises or, in some situations, family or community members. Under these circumstances, it is also necessary to examine whether the authorities of the country of origin are able and willing to protect the victim or potential victim upon return.

22. Whether the authorities in the country of origin are able to protect victims or potential victims of trafficking will depend on whether legislative and administrative mechanisms have been put in place to prevent and combat trafficking, as well as to protect and assist the victims and on whether these mechanisms are effectively implemented in practice.[21]

Part II of the Trafficking Protocol requires States to take certain steps with regard to the protection of victims of trafficking, which can be of guidance when assessing the adequacy of protection and assistance provided. Measures relate not only to protecting the privacy and identity of victims of trafficking, but also to their physical, psychological and social recovery.[22] Article 8 of the Trafficking Protocol also requires State Parties, which are facilitating the return of their nationals or permanent residents who have been trafficked, to give due regard to the safety of the individuals concerned when accepting them back. The protection measures set out in Part II of the Trafficking Protocol are not exhaustive and should be read in light of other relevant binding and non-binding human rights instruments and guidelines.[23]

23. Many States have not adopted or implemented sufficiently stringent measures to criminalize and prevent trafficking or to meet the needs of victims. Where a State fails to take such reasonable steps as are within its competence to prevent trafficking and provide effective protection and assistance to victims, the fear of persecution of the individual is likely to be well-founded. The mere existence of a law prohibiting trafficking in persons will not of itself be sufficient to exclude the possibility of persecution. If the law exists but is not effectively implemented, or if administrative mechanisms are in place to provide protection and assistance to victims, but the individual concerned is unable to gain access to such mechanisms, the State may be deemed unable to extend protection to the victim, or potential victim, of trafficking.

24. There may also be situations where trafficking activities are *de facto* tolerated or condoned by the authorities or even actively facilitated by corrupt State officials. In these circumstances, the agent of persecution may well be the State itself, which becomes responsible, whether directly or as a result of inaction, for a failure to protect those within its jurisdiction. Whether this is so will depend on the role played by the officials concerned and on whether they are acting in their personal capacity outside the framework of governmental authority or on the basis of the position of authority they occupy within

[21] See Part II of the Trafficking Protocol outlined in footnote 8 above.

[22] Ibid.

[23] See, United Nations High Commissioner for Human Rights, "Recommended Principles and Guidelines on Human Rights and Human Trafficking", above footnote 13, which states in Principle No. 2: "States have a responsibility under international law to act with due diligence to prevent trafficking, to investigate and prosecute traffickers and to assist and protect trafficked persons". Numerous instruments of a binding and a non-binding nature highlight the obligation of States to uphold the human rights of victims of trafficking. See, for example, the Council of Europe Convention cited above at footnote 10, the 2002 South Asian Association for Regional Cooperation (SAARC) Convention on Preventing and Combating Trafficking in Women and Children for Prostitution and the 2003 Organization for Security and Cooperation in Europe (OSCE) Action Plan to Combat Trafficking in Human Beings.

governmental structures supporting or condoning trafficking. In the latter case, the persecutory acts may be deemed to emanate from the State itself.

e) Place of persecution

25. In order to come within the scope of Article 1A(2) of the 1951 Convention, the applicant must be outside her or his country of origin and, owing to a well-founded fear of persecution, be unable or unwilling to avail her- or himself of the protection of that country. The requirement of being outside one's country does not, however, mean that the individual must have left on account of a well-founded fear of persecution.[24] Where this fear arises after she or he has left the country of origin, she or he would be a refugee *sur place*, providing the other elements in the refugee definition were fulfilled. Thus, while victims of trafficking may not have left their country owing to a well-founded fear of persecution, such a fear may arise after leaving their country of origin. In such cases, it is on this basis that the claim to refugee status should be assessed.

26. Whether the fear of persecution arises before leaving the country of origin or after, the location where the persecution takes place is a crucial aspect in correctly assessing asylum claims made by individuals who have been trafficked. The 1951 Convention requires that the refugee demonstrate a well-founded fear of persecution with regard to her or his country of nationality or habitual residence. Where someone has been trafficked within her or his own country, or fears being trafficked, and escapes to another in search of international protection, the link between the fear of persecution, the motivation for flight and the unwillingness to return is evident and any international protection needs fall to be determined in terms of the threat posed to the individual should she or he be obliged to return to the country of nationality or habitual residence. If no such well-founded fear is established in relation to the country of origin, then it would be appropriate for the State from which asylum has been requested to reject the claim to refugee status.

27. The circumstances in the applicant's country of origin or habitual residence are the main point of reference against which to determine the existence of a well-founded fear of persecution. Nevertheless, even where the exploitation experienced by a victim of trafficking occurs mainly outside the country of origin, this does not preclude the existence of a well-founded fear of persecution in the individual's own country. The trafficking of individuals across international borders gives rise to a complex situation which requires a broad analysis taking into account the various forms of harm that have occurred at different points along the trafficking route. The continuous and interconnected nature of the range of persecutory acts involved in the context of transnational trafficking should be given due consideration. Furthermore, trafficking involves a chain of actors, starting with those responsible for recruitment in the country of origin, through to those who organize and facilitate the transport, transfer and/or sale of victims, through to the final "purchaser". Each of these actors has a vested interest in the trafficking enterprise and could pose a real threat to the victim. Depending on the sophistication of the trafficking rings involved, applicants may thus have experienced and continue to fear harm in a number of locations, including in countries through which they have transited, the State in which the asylum application is submitted and the country of origin. In such circumstances, the existence of a well-founded fear of persecution is to be evaluated in relation to the country of origin of the applicant.

[24] See UNHCR, *Handbook*, above footnote 14, para. 94

28. A victim of trafficking who has been determined to be a refugee may additionally fear reprisals, punishment or re-trafficking in the country of asylum. If a refugee is at risk in her or his country of refuge or has particular needs, which cannot be met in the country of asylum, she or he may need to be considered for resettlement to a third country.[25]

f) The causal link ("for reasons of")

29. To qualify for refugee status, an individual's well-founded fear of persecution must be related to one or more of the Convention grounds, that is, it must be "for reasons of" race, religion, nationality, membership of a particular social group or political opinion. It is sufficient that the Convention ground be a relevant factor contributing to the persecution; it is not necessary that it be the sole, or even dominant, cause. In many jurisdictions, the causal link ("for reasons of") must be explicitly established, while in other States, causation is not treated as a separate question for analysis but is subsumed within the holistic analysis of the refugee definition.[26]In relation to asylum claims involving trafficking, the difficult issue for a decision-maker is likely to be linking the well-founded fear of persecution to a Convention ground. Where the persecutor attributes or imputes a Convention ground to the applicant, this is sufficient to satisfy the causal link.[27]

30. In cases where there is a risk of being persecuted at the hands of a non-State actor for reasons related to one of the Convention grounds, the causal link is established, whether or not the absence of State protection is Convention-related. Alternatively, where a risk of persecution at the hands of a non-State actor is unrelated to a Convention ground, but the inability or unwillingness of the State to offer protection is for reasons of a Convention ground, the causal link is also established.

31. Trafficking in persons is a commercial enterprise, the prime motivation of which is likely to be profit rather than persecution on a Convention ground. In other words, victims are likely to be targeted above all because of their perceived or potential commercial value to the traffickers. This overriding economic motive does not, however, exclude the possibility of Convention-related grounds in the targeting and selection of victims of trafficking. Scenarios in which trafficking can flourish frequently coincide with situations where potential victims may be vulnerable to trafficking precisely as a result of characteristics contained in the 1951 Convention refugee definition. For instance, States where there has been significant social upheaval and/or economic transition or which have been involved in armed conflict resulting in a breakdown in law and order are prone to increased poverty, deprivation and dislocation of the civilian population. Opportunities arise for organized crime to exploit the inability, or lack of will, of law enforcement agencies to maintain law and order, in particular the failure to ensure adequate security for specific or vulnerable groups.

32. Members of a certain race or ethnic group in a given country may be especially vulnerable to trafficking and/or less effectively protected by the authorities of the country of origin. Victims may be targeted on the basis of their ethnicity, nationality, religious or political views in a context where individuals with specific profiles are already more vulnerable to exploitation and abuse of varying forms. Individuals may also be targeted by reason of their belonging to a particular social group. As an example, among children or women generally in a particular society some subsets of children or women may be

[25] UNHCR, *Resettlement Handbook*, November 2004 edition, chapter 4.1.

[26] See UNHCR Guidelines on Gender-related Persecution, above footnote 4, para. 20.

[27] See UNHCR "Interpreting Article 1", above footnote 20, para. 25.

especially vulnerable to being trafficked and may constitute a social group within the terms of the refugee definition. Thus, even if an individual is not trafficked solely and exclusively for a Convention reason, one or more of these Convention grounds may have been relevant for the trafficker's selection of the particular victim.

g) Convention grounds

33. The causal link may be established to any one single Convention ground or to a combination of these grounds. Although a successful claim to refugee status only needs to establish a causal link to one ground, a full analysis of trafficking cases may frequently reveal a number of interlinked, cumulative grounds.

Race

34. For the purposes of the refugee definition, race has been defined as including "all kinds of ethnic groups that are referred to as 'races' in common usage".[28] In situations of armed conflict where there is a deliberate policy of exploitation or victimization of certain racial or ethnic groups, persecution may manifest itself by the trafficking of members of that group. This kind of targeting of victims may occur in conjunction with an economic motivation which above all seeks to obtain financial gain. In the absence of armed conflict, members of one racial group may still be particularly targeted for trafficking for varied ends, if the State is unable or unwilling to protect members of that group. Where trafficking serves the sex trade, women and girls may also be especially targeted as a result of market demands for a particular race (or nationality). As the Special Rapporteur on trafficking has noted, such demand "is often further grounded in social power disparities of race, nationality, caste and colour".[29]

Religion

35. Individuals may similarly be targeted by traffickers because they belong to a particular religious community, that is, they may be targeted because their faith or belief identifies them as a member of a vulnerable group in the particular circumstances, if, for instance, the authorities are known not to provide adequate protection to certain religious groups. Again the profit motive may be an overriding factor, but this does not obviate the relevance of religion as a factor in the profiling and selection of victims. Alternatively, trafficking may be the method chosen to persecute members of a particular faith.[30]

Nationality

36. Nationality has a wider meaning than citizenship. It can equally refer to membership of an ethnic or linguistic group and may overlap with the term "race".[31] Trafficking may be the method chosen to persecute members of a particular national group in a context where there is inter-ethnic conflict within a State and certain groups enjoy lesser

[28] UNHCR, *Handbook*, para. 68.

[29] See, Report of the Special Rapporteur, "Integration of the Human Rights of Women and a Gender Perspective", above footnote 9, paras. 48 and 66.

[30] See generally, UNHCR, "Guidelines on International Protection: Religion-Based Refugee Claims under Article 1A(2) of the 1951 Convention and/or the 1967 Protocol relating to the Status of Refugees", HCR/GIP/04/06, 28 April 2004.

[31] UNHCR, *Handbook*, para. 74

guarantees of protection. Again, even where the primary motive of the trafficker is financial gain, someone's nationality may result in them being more vulnerable to trafficking.

Membership of a particular social group[32]

37. Victims and potential victims of trafficking may qualify as refugees where it can be demonstrated that they fear being persecuted for reasons of their membership of a particular social group. In establishing this ground it is not necessary that the members of a particular group know each other or associate with each other as a group.[33] It is, however, necessary that they either share a common characteristic other than their risk of being persecuted or are perceived as a group by society. The shared characteristic will often be one that is innate, unchangeable or otherwise fundamental to identity, conscience or the exercise of one's human rights.[34]Persecutory action against a group may be relevant in heightening the visibility of the group without being its defining characteristic.[35] As with the other Convention grounds, the size of the purported social group is not a relevant criterion in determining whether a social group exists within the meaning of Article 1A(2).[36] While a claimant must still demonstrate a well-founded fear of being persecuted based on her or his membership of the particular social group, she or he need not demonstrate that all members of the group are at risk of persecution in order to establish the existence of the group.[37]

38. Women are an example of a social subset of individuals who are defined by innate and immutable characteristics and are frequently treated differently to men. As such, they may constitute a particular social group.[38] Factors which may distinguish women as targets for traffickers are generally connected to their vulnerability in certain social settings; therefore certain social subsets of women may also constitute particular social groups. Men or children or certain social subsets of these groups may also be considered as particular social groups. Examples of social subsets of women or children could, depending on the context, be single women, widows, divorced women, illiterate women, separated or unaccompanied children, orphans or street children. The fact of belonging to such a particular social group may be one of the factors contributing to an individual's fear of being subjected to persecution, for example, to sexual exploitation, as a result of being, or fearing being, trafficked.

39. Former victims of trafficking may also be considered as constituting a social group based on the unchangeable, common and historic characteristic of having been trafficked. A society may also, depending on the context, view persons who have been trafficked as a cognizable group within that society. Particular social groups can nevertheless not be defined exclusively by the persecution that members of the group suffer or by a common fear of persecution.[39] It should therefore be noted that it is the past trafficking experience

[32] See generally, UNHCR, "Guidelines on International Protection: Membership of a Particular Social Group within the context of Article 1A(2) of the 1951 Convention and 1967 Protocol relating to the Status of Refugees", HCR/GIP/02/02, 7 May 2002.

[33] *Ibid.*, para. 15.

[34] *Ibid.*, para. 11.

[35] *Ibid.*, para. 14.

[36] *Ibid.*, para. 18.

[37] *Ibid.*, para. 17.

[38] *Ibid.*, para. 12. See also UNHCR Guidelines on Gender-related Persecution, above footnote 4, para. 30.

[39] See UNHCR Guidelines on Membership of a Particular Social Group, above footnote 32, para. 14.

that would constitute one of the elements defining the group in such cases, rather than the future persecution now feared in the form of ostracism, punishment, reprisals or re-trafficking. In such situations, the group would therefore not be defined solely by its fear of future persecution.

Political opinion

40. Individuals may be targeted for trafficking because they hold a certain political opinion or are perceived as doing so. Similar considerations apply for the other Convention grounds, that is, individuals may, depending on the circumstances, be targeted because of their actual or perceived political views which make them vulnerable and less likely to enjoy the effective protection of the State.

III. Statelessness and Trafficking

41. The 1954 Convention relating to the Status of Stateless Persons and the 1961 Convention on the Reduction of Statelessness establish a legal framework setting out the rights of stateless persons, the obligations of States Parties to avoid actions that would result in statelessness and the steps to be taken to remedy situations of statelessness.

The 1954 Convention applies to anyone who is "not considered as a national by any State under the operation of its law",[40]that is, it applies for the benefit of those who are denied citizenship under the laws of any State. The 1961 Convention generally requires States to avoid actions that would result in statelessness and explicitly forbids the deprivation of nationality if this would result in statelessness.[41]This constitutes a prohibition on actions that would cause statelessness, as well as an obligation to avoid situations where statelessness may arise by default or neglect. The only exception to this prohibition is when the nationality was acquired fraudulently.[42]

42. When seeking to assess and address the situation of someone who has been trafficked, it is important to recognize potential implications as regards statelessness. The mere fact of being a victim of trafficking will not *per se* render someone stateless. Victims of trafficking continue to possess the citizenship they had when they fell under the control of their traffickers. If, however, these traffickers have confiscated their identity documents, as commonly happens as a way of establishing and exerting control over their victims, they may be unable to prove citizenship. This lack of documentation and temporary inability to establish identity is not necessarily unique to victims of trafficking. It should be, and in many cases is, easily overcome with the assistance of the authorities of the State of origin.[43]

[40] See Article 8(1) of the 1961 Convention.

[41] See Article 8(1) of the 1961 Convention.

[42] In addition to the 1954 and 1961 Statelessness Conventions, other international or regional instruments set out similar principles. See, for instance, the 1965 Convention on the Elimination of All Forms of Racial Discrimination, the 1966 International Covenant on Civil and Political Rights, the 1979 Convention on the Elimination of All Forms of Discrimination Against Women, the 1997 European Convention on Nationality, the 1969 American Convention on Human Rights and the 1990 African Charter on the Rights and Welfare of the Child.

[43] In such circumstances, it is necessary to respect principles of confidentiality. These require amongst other things that any contact with the country of origin should not indicate either that the individual concerned has applied for asylum or that she or he has been trafficked.

43. Everyone has the right to return to their own country.[44] States should extend diplomatic protection to their nationals abroad. This includes facilitating their re-entry into the country, including in the case of victims of trafficking who find themselves abroad. If, however, the State withholds such assistance and fails to supply documentation to enable the individual to return, one practical consequence may be to render the individual effectively stateless.[45] Even if the individuals were not previously considered stateless by their State of nationality, they may find themselves effectively treated as such if they attempt to avail themselves of that State's protection.[46] UNHCR's statelessness mandate may mean it needs to take action to assist individuals in such circumstances.[47]

44. There may also be situations where stateless individuals are trafficked out of their country of habitual residence. The lack of documentation coupled with lack of citizenship may render them unable to secure return to their country of habitual residence. While this alone does not make someone a refugee, the individual concerned may be eligible for refugee status where the refusal of the country of habitual residence to allow re-entry is related to a Convention ground and the inability to return to the country leads to serious harm or a serious violation, or violations, of human rights amounting to persecution.

IV. Procedural Issues

45. Given the broad range of situations in which trafficking cases come to light and victims of trafficking can be identified, it is important that mechanisms be put in place at the national level to provide for the physical, psychological and social recovery of victims of trafficking. This includes the provision of housing, legal counselling and information, medical, psychological and material assistance, as well as employment, educational and training opportunities in a manner which takes into account the age, gender and special needs of victims of trafficking.[48] It is also necessary to ensure that victims of trafficking have access to fair and efficient asylum procedures as appropriate[49] and to proper legal counselling, if they are to be able to lodge an asylum claim effectively. In view of the complexities of asylum claims presented by victims or potential victims of trafficking, such claims normally require an examination on their merits in regular procedures.

46. In the reception of applicants who claim to have been victims of trafficking, and in interviewing such individuals, it is of utmost importance that a supportive environment

[44] 1948 Universal Declaration of Human Rights, Article 13(2). See also, Article 12(4) of the International Covenant on Civil and Political Rights, which reads: "No one shall be arbitrarily deprived of the right to enter his own country."

[45] See, Executive Committee Conclusion No. 90 (LII), 2001, paragraph (s), in which the Executive Committee of UNHCR expresses its concern that many victims of trafficking are rendered effectively stateless due to an inability to establish their identity and nationality status.

[46] This is so, despite relevant State obligations contained in the 1961 Convention on the Reduction of Statelessness, in addition to Article 8 of the Trafficking Protocol.

[47] When the 1961 Convention on the Reduction of Statelessness came into force, the UN General Assembly designated UNHCR as the UN body entrusted to act on behalf of stateless persons. Since 1975, General Assembly Resolutions have further detailed UNHCR's responsibilities regarding the prevention of statelessness and the protection of stateless persons.

[48] See Article 6 in Part II of the Trafficking Protocol.

[49] See Agenda for Protection, Goal 2 Objective 2, and the OHCHR, "Recommended Principles and Guidelines on Human Rights and Human Trafficking", above footnote 13, Guideline 2.7, and the Council of Europe Convention, Explanatory Report, para. 377.

be provided so that they can be reassured of the confidentiality of their claim. Providing interviewers of the same sex as the applicant can be particularly important in this respect.

Interviewers should also take into consideration that victims who have escaped from their traffickers could be in fear of revealing the real extent of the persecution they have suffered. Some may be traumatized and in need of expert medical and/or psycho-social assistance, as well as expert counselling.

47. Such assistance should be provided to victims in an age and gender sensitive manner.

Many instances of trafficking, in particular trafficking for the purposes of exploitation of the prostitution of others or other forms of sexual exploitation, are likely to have a disproportionately severe effect on women and children. Such individuals may rightly be considered as victims of gender-related persecution. They will have been subjected in many, if not most, cases to severe breaches of their basic human rights, including inhuman or degrading treatment, and in some instances, torture.

48. Women, in particular, may feel ashamed of what has happened to them or may suffer from trauma caused by sexual abuse and violence, as well as by the circumstances surrounding their escape from their traffickers. In such situations, the fear of their traffickers will be very real. Additionally, they may fear rejection and/or reprisals by their family and/or community which should be taken into account when considering their claims. Against this background and in order to ensure that claims by female victims of trafficking are properly considered in the refugee status determination process, a number of measures should be borne in mind. These have been set out in Part III of UNHCR's Guidelines on International Protection on gender-related persecution and are equally applicable in the context of trafficking-related claims.[50]

49. Children also require special attention in terms of their care, as well as of the assistance to be provided in the presentation of asylum claims. In this context, procedures for the rapid identification of child victims of trafficking need to be established, as do specialised programmes and policies to protect and support child victims, including through the appointment of a guardian, the provision of age-sensitive counselling and tracing efforts which bear in mind the need for confidentiality and a supportive environment. Additional information on the appropriate handling of claims by child victims of trafficking can be found in the UN Children Fund (UNICEF) "Guidelines for the Protection of the Rights of Child Victims of Trafficking",[51] in the "Recommended Principles and Guidelines on Human Rights and Human Trafficking" of the Office of the High Commissioner for Human Rights[52] and General Comment No. 6 of the Committee on the Rights of the Child.[53]

50. An additional and specific consideration relates to the importance of avoiding any linkage, whether overt or implied, between the evaluation of the merits of a claim to asylum and the willingness of a victim to give evidence in legal proceedings against her or his traffickers. Providing evidence to help identify and prosecute traffickers can raise specific

[50] See UNHCR Guidelines on Gender-related Persecution, above footnote 4. Complementary information can be found in World Health Organization, London School of Hygiene and Tropical Medicine and Daphne Programme of the European Commission,*WHO Ethical and Safety Recommendations for Interviewing Trafficked Women*, 2003, available at <http://www.who.int/gender/ documents/en/final%20recommendations%2023%20oct.pdf>.

[51] See above footnote 19.

[52] See above footnote 13. Guideline 8 addresses special measures for the protection and support of child victims of trafficking.

[53] See above, footnote 18, especially paras. 64–78.

protection concerns that need to be addressed through specially designed witness protection programmes. The fact that an individual has agreed to provide such evidence will nevertheless not necessarily make her or him a refugee, unless the repercussions feared upon a return to the country of origin rise to the level of persecution and can be linked to one or more of the Convention grounds. Conversely, the fact that a victim of trafficking refuses to provide evidence should not lead to any adverse conclusion with respect to her or his asylum claim.

Guidelines On International Protection No. 8:

Child Asylum Claims under Articles 1(A)2 and 1(F) of the 1951 Convention and/or 1967 Protocol relating to the Status of Refugees

UNHCR issues these Guidelines pursuant to its mandate, as contained in the *Statute of the Office of the United Nations High Commissioner for Refugees*, in conjunction with Article 35 of the *1951 Convention relating to the Status of Refugees* and Article II of its *1967 Protocol*. These Guidelines complement the UNHCR *Handbook on Procedures and Criteria for Determining Refugee Status under the 1951 Convention and the 1967 Protocol relating to the Status of Refugees* (re-edited, Geneva, January 1992).

These Guidelines are intended to provide legal interpretative guidance for governments, legal practitioners, decision makers and the judiciary, as well as UNHCR staff carrying out refugee status determination in the field.

I. Introduction

1. These Guidelines offer substantive and procedural guidance on carrying out refugee status determination in a child-sensitive manner. They highlight the specific rights and protection needs of children in asylum procedures. Although the definition of a refugee contained in Article 1(A)2 of the 1951 Convention relating to the Status of Refugees and its 1967 Protocol (hereafter "1951 Convention" and "1967 Protocol") applies to all individuals regardless of their age, it has traditionally been interpreted in light of adult experiences. This has meant that many refugee claims made by children have been assessed incorrectly or overlooked altogether.[1]

2. The specific circumstances facing child asylum-seekers as individuals with independent claims to refugee status are not generally well understood. Children may be perceived as part of a family unit rather than as individuals with their own rights and interests. This is explained partly by the subordinate roles, positions and status children still hold in many societies worldwide. The accounts of children are more likely to be examined individually when the children are unaccompanied than when they are accompanied by their families. Even so, their unique experiences of persecution, due to factors such as their age, their level of maturity and development and their dependency on adults have not always been taken into account. Children may not be able to articulate their claims to refugee status in the same way as adults and, therefore, may require special assistance to do so.

[1] UNHCR, *Guidelines on Policies and Procedures in Dealing with Unaccompanied Children Seeking Asylum*, Geneva, 1997 (hereafter "UNHCR, *Guidelines on Unaccompanied Children Seeking Asylum*"), <http://www.unhcr.org/refworld/docid/3ae6b3360.html>, in particular Part 8.

3. Global awareness about violence, abuse and discrimination experienced by children is growing,[2] as is reflected in the development of international and regional human rights standards. While these developments have yet to be fully incorporated into refugee status determination processes, many national asylum authorities are increasingly acknowledging that children may have refugee claims in their own right. In *Conclusion on Children at Risk* (2007), UNHCR's Executive Committee underlines the need for children to be recognized as "active subjects of rights" consistent with international law. The Executive Committee also recognized that children may experience child-specific forms and manifestations of persecution.[3]

4. Adopting a child-sensitive interpretation of the 1951 Convention does not mean, of course, that child asylum-seekers are automatically entitled to refugee status. The child applicant must establish that s/he has a well-founded fear of being persecuted for reasons of race, religion, nationality, membership of a particular social group or political opinion. As with gender, age is relevant to the entire refugee definition.[4] As noted by the UN Committee on the Rights of the Child, the refugee definition:

> must be interpreted in an age and gender-sensitive manner, taking into account the particular motives for, and forms and manifestations of, persecution experienced by children. Persecution of kin; under-age recruitment; trafficking of children for prostitution; and sexual exploitation or subjection to female genital mutilation, are some of the child-specific forms and manifestations of persecution which may justify the granting of refugee status if such acts are related to one of the 1951 Refugee Convention grounds. States should, therefore, give utmost attention to such child-specific forms and manifestations of persecution as well as gender-based violence in national refugee status-determination procedures.[5]

Alongside age, factors such as rights specific to children, a child's stage of development, knowledge and/or memory of conditions in the country of origin, and vulnerability, also need to be considered to ensure an appropriate application of the eligibility criteria for refugee status.[6]

[2] See, for instance, UN General Assembly, Rights of the Child: Note by the Secretary-General, A/61/299, 29 Aug. 2006 (hereafter "UN study on violence against children") <http://www.unhcr.org/refworld/docid/453780fe0.html>; UN Commission on the Status of Women, The elimination of all forms of discrimination and violence against the girl child, E/CN.6/2007/2, 12 Dec. 2006, <http://www. unhcr.org/refworld/docid/46c5b30c0.html>; UN General Assembly, Impact of armed conflict on children: Note by the Secretary-General (the "Machel Study"), A/51/306, 26 Aug. 1996, <http://www.unhcr.org/refworld/docid/3b00f2d30.html>, and the strategic review marking the 10 year anniversary of the Machel Study, UN General Assembly, Report of the Special Representative of the Secretary-General for Children and Armed Conflict, A/62/228, 13 Aug. 2007, <http://www.unhcr.org/refworld/docid/47316f602.html>.

[3] ExCom, *Conclusion on Children at Risk*, 5 Oct. 2007, No. 107 (LVIII) – 2007, (hereafter "ExCom, Conclusion No. 107"), <http:// www.unhcr.org/refworld/docid/471897232.html>, para. (b)(x)(viii).

[4] UNHCR, *Guidelines on International Protection No. 1: Gender-Related Persecution Within the context of Article 1A(2) of the 1951 Convention and/or its 1967 Protocol Relating to the Status of Refugees*, 7 May 2002 (hereafter "UNHCR, Guidelines on Gender-Related Persecution"), <http://www.unhcr.org/refworld/docid/3d36f1c64.html>, paras. 2, 4.

[5] UN Committee on the Rights of the Child, *General Comment No. 6 (2005)-Treatment of Unaccompanied and Separated Children Outside Their Country of Origin*, CRC/GC/2005/6, Sep. 2005 (hereafter "CRC, *General Comment No. 6*"), <http://www.unhcr.org/ refworld/ docid/42dd174b4.html>, para. 74.

[6] UNHCR, *Guidelines on Unaccompanied Children Seeking Asylum, op cit.*, page 10.

5. A child-sensitive application of the refugee definition would be consistent with the 1989 Convention on the Rights of the Child (hereafter "the CRC").[7] The Committee on the Rights of the Child has identified the following four Articles of the CRC as general principles for its implementation:[8] *Article 2*: the obligation of States to respect and ensure the rights set forth in the Convention to each child within their jurisdiction without discrimination of any kind;[9] *Article 3 (1)*: the best interests of the child as a primary consideration in all actions concerning children;[10] *Article 6*: the child's inherent right to life and States parties' obligation to ensure to the maximum extent possible the survival and development of the child;[11] and *Article 12*: the child's right to express his/her views freely regarding "all matters affecting the child", and that those views be given due weight.[12] These principles inform both the substantive and the procedural aspects of the determination of a child's application for refugee status.

II. Definitional Issues

6. These guidelines cover all child asylum-seekers, including accompanied, unaccompanied and separated children, who may have individual claims to refugee status. Each child has the right to make an independent refugee claim, regardless of whether s/he is accompanied or unaccompanied. "Separated children" are children separated from both their parents or from their previous legal or customary primary caregivers but not necessarily from other relatives. In contrast, "unaccompanied children" are children who have been separated from both parents and other relatives and are not being cared for by an adult who, by law or custom, is responsible for doing so.[13]

7. For the purposes of these Guidelines, "children" are defined as all persons below the age of 18 years.[14] Every person under 18 years who is the principal asylum applicant is entitled to

[7] With a near universal ratification, the CRC is the most widely ratified human rights treaty, available at <http://www.unhcr.org/ refworld/docid/3ae6b38f0.html>. The rights contained therein apply to all children within the jurisdiction of the State. For a detailed analysis of the provisions of the CRC, see UNICEF, *Implementation Handbook for the Convention on the Rights of the Child*, fully revised third edition, Sep. 2007 (hereafter "UNICEF, *Implementation Handbook*"). It can be ordered at <http://www.unicef.org/ publications/index_43110.html>.

[8] CRC, *General Comment No. 5 (2003): General Measures of Implementation for the Convention on the Rights of the Child* (Arts. 4, 42 and 44, Para. 6), CRC/GC/2003/5, 3 Oct. 2003 (hereafter "CRC, *General Comment No. 5*"), <http://www.unhcr.org/refworld/docid/4538834f11.html>, para. 12.

[9] CRC, *General Comment No. 6*, para. 18.

[10] *Ibid*., paras. 19–22. See also ExCom *Conclusion No. 107*, para. (b)(5), and, on how to conduct "best interests" assessments and determinations, UNHCR, *Guidelines on Determining the Best Interests of the Child*, Geneva, May 2008, <http://www.unhcr.org/refworld/docid/48480c342.html>.

[11] CRC, *General Comment No. 6*, paras. 23–24.

[12] *Ibid*., para. 25. See also CRC, *General Comment No. 12 (2009): The right of the child to be heard*, CRC/C/GC/12, 20 July 2009 (hereafter "CRC, *General Comment No. 12*"), <http://www.unhcr.org/refworld/docid/4ae562c52.html>.

[13] CRC, *General Comment No. 6*, paras. 7–8. See also, UNHCR, *Guidelines on Unaccompanied Children Seeking Asylum, op cit*., p. 5, paras. 3.1-3.2. See also, UNHCR, UNICEF et al, *Inter-agency Guiding Principles on Unaccompanied and Separated Children*, Geneva, 2004 (hereafter "*Inter-Agency Guiding Principles*"), <http://www.unhcr.org/refworld/docid/4113abc14.html>, p. 13.

[14] CRC, Art. 1 provides that "a child means every human being below the age of eighteen years unless, under the law applicable to the child, majority is attained earlier". In addition, the EU Council Directive 2004/83/EC of 29 April 2004 on Minimum Standards for the Qualification and Status

child-sensitive procedural safeguards. Lowering the age of childhood or applying restrictive age assessment approaches in order to treat children as adults in asylum procedures may result in violations of their rights under international human rights law. Being young and vulnerable may make a person especially susceptible to persecution. Thus, there may be exceptional cases for which these guidelines are relevant even if the applicant is 18 years of age or slightly older. This may be particularly the case where persecution has hindered the applicant's development and his/her psychological maturity remains comparable to that of a child.[15]

8. Even at a young age, a child may still be considered the principal asylum applicant.[16] The parent, caregiver or other person representing the child will have to assume a greater role in making sure that all relevant aspects of the child's claim are presented.[17] However, the right of children to express their views in all matters affecting them, including to be heard in all judicial and administrative proceedings, also needs to be taken into account.[18] A child claimant, where accompanied by parents, members of an extended family or of the community who by law or custom are responsible for the child, is entitled to appropriate direction and guidance from them in the exercise of his/her rights, in a manner consistent with the evolving capacities of the child.[19] Where the child is the principal asylum-seeker, his/her age and, by implication, level of maturity, psychological development, and ability to articulate certain views or opinions will be an important factor in a decision maker's assessment.

9. Where the parents or the caregiver seek asylum based on a fear of persecution for their child, the child normally will be the principal applicant even when accompanied by his/her parents. In such cases, just as a child can derive refugee status from the recognition of a parent as a refugee, a parent can, *mutatis mutandis*, be granted derivative status based on his/her child's refugee status.[20] In situations where both the parent(s) and the

of Third Country Nationals or Stateless Persons as Refugees or as Persons Who Otherwise Need International Protection and the Content of the Protection Granted, 19 May 2004, 2004/83/EC, <http://www.unhcr.org/refworld/ docid/4157e75e4.html>, provides that "'unaccompanied minors' means third-country nationals or stateless persons below the age of 18, who arrive on the territory of the Member States unaccompanied by an adult responsible for them whether by law or custom, and for as long as they are not effectively taken into the care of such a person; it includes minors who are left unaccompanied after they have entered the territory of the Member States", Art. 2 (i).

[15] The United Kingdom Immigration Appeals Tribunal (now the Asylum and Immigration Tribunal) has held that "[t]o adopt a rigidity however in this respect is in our view to fail to recognize that in many areas of the world even today exact ages and dates of birth are imprecise. It is better to err on the side of generosity"; *Sarjoy Jakitay v. Secretary of State for the Home Department*, Appeal No. 12658 (unreported), U.K. IAT, 15 Nov. 1995. See also, *Decision VA0-02635, VA0-02635*, Canada, Immigration and Refugee Board (hereafter "IRB"), 22 March 2001, <http://www.unhcr.org/refworld/docid/4b18dec82.html>.

[16] See, for instance, *Chen Shi Hai v. The Minister for Immigration and Multicultural Affairs*, [2000] HCA 19, Australia, High Court, 13 April 2000, <http://www.unhcr.org/refworld/docid/3ae6b6df4.html>. In this case, which concerned a 3½ year-old boy, it was found that "under Australian law, the child was entitled to have his own rights determined as that law provides. He is not for all purposes subsumed to the identity and legal rights of his parents", para. 78.

[17] See also UNHCR, *Refugee Children: Guidelines on Protection and Care*, Geneva, 1994, <http://www.unhcr.org/refworld/ docid/3ae6b3470.html>, pp. 97–103.

[18] CRC, Art. 12(2); CRC, *General Comment No. 12*, paras. 32, 67, 123.

[19] CRC, Art. 5.

[20] UNHCR, *Guidance Note on Refugee Claims relating to Female Genital Mutilation*, May 2009 (hereafter "UNHCR, *Guidance Note on FGM*"), <http://www.unhcr.org/refworld/docid/4a0c28492.html>, para. 11. See also UNHCR, ExCom Conclusion on the Protection of the Refugee's Family, No. 88 (L), 1999, <http://www.unhcr.org/refworld/docid/3ae68c4340.html>, para. (b)(iii).

child have their own claims to refugee status, it is preferable that each claim be assessed separately. The introduction of many of the procedural and evidentiary measures enumerated below in Part IV will enhance the visibility of children who perhaps ought to be the principal applicants within their families. Where the child's experiences, nevertheless, are considered part of the parent's claim rather than independently, it is important to consider the claim also from the child's point of view.[21]

III. Substantive Analysis

a.) Well-founded fear of persecution

10. The term "persecution", though not expressly defined in *the 1951 Convention,* can be considered to involve serious human rights violations, including a threat to life or freedom, as well as other kinds of serious harm or intolerable situations as assessed with regard to the age, opinions, feelings and psychological make-up of the applicant.[22] Discrimination may amount to persecution in certain situ*ations where the tre*atment feared or suffered leads to consequences of a substantially prejudicial nature for the child concerned.[23] The principle of the best interests of the child requires that the harm be assessed from the child's perspective. This may include an analysis as to how the child's rights or interests are, or will be, affected by the harm. Ill-treatment which may not rise to the level of persecution in the case of an adult may do so in the case of a child.[24]

11. Both objective and subjective factors are relevant to establish whether or not a child applicant has a well-founded fear of persecution.[25] An accurate assessment requires both an up-to-date analysis and knowledge of child-specific circumstances in the country of origin, including of existing child protection services. Dismissing a child's claim based on the assumption that perpetrators would not take a child's views seriously or consider them a real threat could be erroneous. It may be the case that a child is unable to express fear when this would be expected or, conversely, exaggerates the fear. In such circumstances,

[21] See, for instance, *EM (Lebanon) (FC) (Appellant) v. Secretary of State for the Home Department (Respondent)*, U.K. House of Lords, 22 Oct. 2008, <http://www.unhcr.org/refworld/docid/490058699.html>; *Refugee Appeal Nos. 76250 & 76251*, Nos. 76250 & 76251, New Zealand, Refugee Status Appeals Authority (hereafter "RSAA"), 1 Dec. 2008, <http://www.unhcr.org/refworld/ docid/494f64952.html>.

[22] See UNHCR, *Handbook on Procedures and Criteria for Determining Refugee Status under the 1951 Convention and the 1967 Protocol relating to the Status of Refugees*, 1979, re-edited, Geneva, Jan. 1992 (hereafter "UNHCR, *Handbook*") <http://www.unhcr.org/refworld/docid/3ae6b3314.html>, paras. 51–52; UNHCR, *Guidelines on International Protection No. 7: The Application of Article 1A(2) of the 1951 Convention and/or 1967 Protocol Relating to the Status of Refugees to Victims of Trafficking and Persons at Risk of Being Trafficked*, 7 Apr. 2006 (hereafter "UNHCR, *Guidelines on Victims of Trafficking*"), <http://www.unhcr.org/refworld/docid/443679fa4.html>, para. 14.

[23] UNHCR, *Handbook*, paras. 54–55.

[24] See, for instance, United States Bureau of Citizenship and Immigration Services, *Guidelines For Children's Asylum Claims*, 10 Dec. 1998 (hereafter the "U.S. Guidelines for Children's Asylum Claims"), <http://www.unhcr.org/refworld/docid/3f8ec0574.html>, noting that "the harm a child fears or has suffered, however, may be relatively less than that of an adult and still qualify as persecution". See also, *Chen Shi Hai, op. cit.*, where the Court found that "what may possibly be viewed as acceptable enforcement of laws and programmes of general application in the case of the parents may nonetheless be persecution in the case of the child", para. 79.

[25] UNHCR, *Handbook*, paras. 40–43.

decision makers must make an objective assessment of the risk that the child would face, regardless of that child's fear.[26] This would require consideration of evidence from a wide array of sources, including child-specific country of origin information. When the parent or caregiver of a child has a well-founded fear of persecution for their child, it may be assumed that the child has such a fear, even if s/he does not express or feel that fear.[27]

12. Alongside age, other identity-based, economic and social characteristics of the child, such as family background, class, caste, health, education and income level, may increase the risk of harm, influence the type of persecutory conduct inflicted on the child and exacerbate the effect of the harm on the child. For example, children who are homeless, abandoned or otherwise without parental care may be at increased risk of sexual abuse and exploitation or of being recruited or used by an armed force/group or criminal gang. Street children, in particular, may be rounded up and detained in degrading conditions or be subjected to other forms of violence, including murder for the purpose of "social cleansing".[28] Children with disabilities may be denied specialist or routine medical treatment or be ostracized by their family or community. Children in what may be viewed as unconventional family situations including, for instance, those born out of wedlock, in violation of coercive family policies,[29] or through rape, may face abuse and severe discrimination. Pregnant girls may be rejected by their families and subject to harassment, violence, forced prostitution or other demeaning work.[30]

Child-specific rights

13. A contemporary and child-sensitive understanding of persecution encompasses many types of human rights violations, including violations of child-specific rights. In determining the persecutory character of an act inflicted against a child, it is essential to analyse the standards of the CRC and other relevant international human rights

[26] See UNHCR, *Handbook*, paras. 217–219. See also *Yusuf v. Canada (Minister of Employment and Immigration)*, [1992] 1 F.C. 629; F.C.J. 1049, Canada, Federal Court, 24 Oct. 1991, <http://www.unhcr.org/refworld/docid/403e24e84.html>. The Court concluded that "I am loath to believe that a refugee status claim could be dismissed solely on the ground that as the claimant is a young child or a person suffering from a mental disability, s/he was incapable of experiencing fear the reasons for which clearly exist in objective terms.", at 5.

[27] See, for instance, *Canada (Minister of Citizenship and Immigration) v. Patel*, 2008 FC 747, [2009] 2 F.C.R. 196, Canada, Federal Court, 17 June 2008, <http://www.unhcr.org/refworld/docid/4a6438952.html>, at 32–33.

[28] "Social cleansing" refers to the process of removing an undesirable group from an area and may involve murder, disappearances, violence and other ill-treatment. See, UNICEF, *Implementation Handbook*, pp. 89, 91, 287. See also *Case of the "Street Children" (Villagrán-Morales et al.) v. Guatemala*, Inter-American Court of Human Rights (hereafter "IACtHR"), Judgment of 19 Nov. 1999, <http://www.unhcr.org/refworld/docid/4b17bc442.html>, paras. 190–191. The Court found that there was a prevailing pattern of violence against street children in Guatemala. Relying on the CRC to interpret Art. 19 of the 1969 American Convention on Human Rights, "Pact of San Jose", Costa Rica (hereafter "ACHR"), <http://www.unhcr.org/refworld/docid/3ae6b36510.html>, the Court noted that the State had violated their physical, mental, and moral integrity as well as their right to life and also failed to take any measures to prevent them from living in misery, thereby denying them of the minimum conditions for a dignified life.

[29] See further, UNHCR, *Note on Refugee Claims Based on Coercive Family Planning Laws or Policies*, Aug. 2005, <http://www. unhcr.org/refworld/docid/4301a9184.html>.

[30] UNHCR, *Guidelines on Gender-Related Persecution, op cit.*, para. 18.

instruments applicable to children.[31] Children are entitled to a range of child-specific rights set forth in the CRC which recognize their young age and dependency and are fundamental to their protection, development and survival. These rights include, but are not limited to, the following: the right not to be separated from parents (Article 9); protection from all forms of physical and mental violence, abuse, neglect, and exploitation (Article 19); protection from traditional practices prejudicial to the health of children (Article 24); a standard of living adequate for the child's development (Article 27); the right not to be detained or imprisoned unless as a measure of last resort (Article 37); and protection from under-age recruitment (Article 38). The CRC also recognizes the right of refugee children and children seeking refugee status to appropriate protection and humanitarian assistance in the enjoyment of applicable rights set forth in the CRC and in other international human rights or humanitarian instruments (Article 22).

14. Children's socio-economic needs are often more compelling than those of adults, particularly due to their dependency on adults and unique developmental needs. Deprivation of economic, social and cultural rights, thus, may be as relevant to the assessment of a child's claim as that of civil and political rights. It is important not to automatically attribute greater significance to certain violations than to others but to assess the overall impact of the harm on the individual child. The violation of one right often may expose the child to other abuses; for example, a denial of the right to education or an adequate standard of living may lead to a heightened risk of other forms of harm, including violence and abuse.[32]Moreover, there may be political, racial, gender or religious aims or intentions against a particular group of children or their parents underlying discriminatory measures in the access and enjoyment of ESC rights. As noted by the UN Committee on Economic, Social and Cultural Rights:

> The lack of educational opportunities for children often reinforces their subjection to various other human rights violations. For instance, children who may live in abject poverty and not lead healthy lives are particularly vulnerable to forced labour and other forms of exploitation. Moreover, there is a direct correlation between, for example, primary school enrolment levels for girls and major reductions in child marriages.[33]

Child-related manifestations of persecution

15. While children may face similar or identical forms of harm as adults, they may experience them differently. Actions or threats that might not reach the threshold of persecution in the case of an adult may amount to persecution in the case of a child because of the mere fact that s/he is a child. Immaturity, vulnerability, undeveloped coping mechanisms and dependency as well as the differing stages of development and hindered capacities may be directly related to how a child experiences or fears harm.[34] Particularly in claims where the harm suffered or feared is more severe than mere harassment but less severe than a threat to life or

[31] In the context of Africa, the African Charter on the Rights and Welfare of the Child should also be considered (hereafter "African Charter"), <http://www.unhcr.org/refworld/docid/3ae6b38c18.html>.

[32] CRC, *General Comment No. 5, op cit.*, paras. 6–7. See further below at v. Violations of economic, social and cultural rights.

[33] UN Committee on Economic, Social and Cultural Rights (hereafter "CESCR"), *General Comment No. 11: Plans of Action for Primary Education (Art. 14 of the Covenant)*, E/1992/23, 10 May 1999, <http://www.unhcr.org/refworld/docid/4538838c0.html>, para. 4.

[34] See further Save the Children and UNICEF, *The evolving capacities of the child*, 2005, <http://www.unicef-irc.org/publications/pdf/evolving-eng.pdf>.

freedom, the individual circumstances of the child, including his/her age, may be important factors in deciding whether the harm amounts to persecution. To assess accurately the severity of the acts and their impact on a child, it is necessary to examine the details of each case and to adapt the threshold for persecution to that particular child.

16. In the case of a child applicant, psychological harm may be a particularly relevant factor to consider. Children are more likely to be distressed by hostile situations, to believe improbable threats, or to be emotionally affected by unfamiliar circumstances. Memories of traumatic events may linger in a child and put him/her at heightened risk of future harm.

17. Children are also more sensitive to acts that target close relatives. Harm inflicted against members of the child's family can support a well-founded fear in the child. For example, a child who has witnessed violence against, or experienced the disappearance or killing of a parent or other person on whom the child depends, may have a well-founded fear of persecution even if the act was not targeted directly against him/her.[35] Under certain circumstances, for example, the forced separation of a child from his/her parents, due to discriminatory custody laws or the detention of the child's parent(s) could amount to persecution.[36]

Child-specific forms of persecution

18. Children may also be subjected to specific forms of persecution that are influenced by their age, lack of maturity or vulnerability. The fact that the refugee claimant is a child may be a central factor in the harm inflicted or feared. This may be because the alleged persecution only applies to, or disproportionately affects, children or because specific child rights may be infringed. UNHCR's Executive Committee has recognized that child-specific forms of persecution may include under-age recruitment, child trafficking and female genital mutilation (hereafter "FGM").[37] Other examples include, but are not limited to, family and domestic violence, forced or underage marriage,[38] bonded or hazardous child labour, forced labour,[39] forced prostitution and child pornography.[40] Such forms of persecution also encompass violations of survival and development rights as

[35] See, for instance, *Cicek v. Turkey*, Application No. 67124/01, European Court of Human Rights (hereafter "ECtHR"), 18 Jan. 2005, <http://www.unhcr.org/refworld/docid/42d3e7ea4.html>, paras. 173–174; *Bazorkina v. Russia*, Application No. 69481/01, ECtHR, 27 July 2006, <http://www.unhcr.org/refworld/docid/44cdf4ef4.html>, paras. 140–141.

[36] See *EM (Lebanon) (FC) (Appellant) v. Secretary of State for the Home Department (Respondent), op. cit., Refugee Appeal Nos.76226 and 76227*, Nos. 76226 and 76227, New Zealand, RSAA, 12 Jan. 2009, <http://www.unhcr.org/refworld/docid/49a6ac0e2. html>, paras. 112–113.

[37] ExCom, *Conclusion No. 107*, para. (g)(viii).

[38] CRC, Art. 24(3); International Convenant on Civil and Political Rights (hereafter "ICCPR"), <http://www.unhcr.org/refworld/ docid/3ae6b3aa0.html>, Art. 23; International Covenant on Economic, Social and Cultural Rights, <http://www.unhcr.org/refworld/ docid/3ae6b36c0.html>, Art. 10; Convention on the Elimination of All Forms of Discrimination Against Women, <http://www.unhcr.org/ refworld/docid/3ae6b3970.html>, Art. 16.

[39] CRC, Arts. 32–36; International Labour Organization, Worst Forms of Child Labour Convention, C182 (hereafter "ILO Convention on the Worst Forms of Child Labour"), <http://www.unhcr.org/refworld/docid/3ddb6e0c4.html>; Minimum Age Convention, C138, (hereafter "ILO Minimum Age Convention"), <http://www.unhcr.org/refworld/docid/421216a34.html>, Arts. 2 (3), 2(4).

[40] CRC, Art. 34; Optional Protocol to the Convention on the Rights of the Child on the Sale of Children, Child Prostitution and Child Pornography, <http://www.unhcr.org/refworld/docid/3ae6b38bc.html>.

well as severe discrimination of children born outside strict family planning rules[41] and of stateless children as a result of loss of nationality and attendant rights. Some of the most common forms of child-specific persecution arising in the context of asylum claims are outlined in greater detail below.

i. Under-age recruitment

19. There is a growing consensus regarding the ban on the recruitment and use of children below 18 years in armed conflict.[42] International humanitarian law prohibits the recruitment and participation in the hostilities of children under the age of 15 years whether in international[43] or non-international armed conflict.[44] Article 38 of the CRC reiterates State Parties' obligations under international humanitarian law. The Rome Statute of the International Criminal Court classifies as war crimes the enlistment and use of children under the age of 15 years into the armed forces at a time of armed conflict.[45] The Special Court for Sierra Leone has concluded that the recruitment of children under the age of 15 years into the armed forces constitutes a crime under general international law.[46]

20. The Optional Protocol to the CRC on the Involvement of Children in Armed Conflict provides that States parties shall take all feasible measures to ensure that members of their armed forces under the age of 18 years do not take part in hostilities, and ensure that persons under the age of 18 years are not compulsorily recruited into their armed forces.[47]The Optional Protocol contains an absolute prohibition against the recruitment or use, under any circumstances, of children who are less than 18 years old by armed groups that are distinct from the armed forces of a State.[48] It also amends Article

[41] See, for instance, *Xue Yun Zhang v. Gonzales*, No. 01-71623, U.S. Court of Appeals for the 9th Circuit, 26 May 2005, <http://www.unhcr.org/refworld/docid/4b17c7082.html>; *Chen Shi Hai, op. cit.*

[42] See UNICEF, The Paris Principles and Guidelines on Children Associated With Armed Forces or Armed Groups, Feb. 2007 (hereafter "The Paris Principles"). While not binding, they reflect a strong trend for a complete ban on under-age recruitment. See also UN Security Council resolution 1612 (2005) (on children in armed conflict), 26 July 2005, S/RES/1612, <http://www.unhcr.org/refworld/docid/43f308d6c.html>, para. 1; 1539 on the protection of children affected by armed conflict, S/RES/1539, 22 Apr. 2004, <http://www.unhcr.org/refworld/docid/411236fd4.html>.

[43] Protocol Additional to the Geneva Conventions of 12 August 1949, and relating to the Protection of Victims of International Armed Conflicts (Protocol I), <http://www.unhcr.org/refworld/docid/3ae6b36b4.html>, Art. 77(2).

[44] Protocol Additional to the Geneva Conventions of 12 August 1949, and relating to the Protection of Victims of Non-International Armed Conflicts (Protocol II), <http://www.unhcr.org/refworld/docid/3ae6b37f40.html>, Art. 4(3).

[45] UN General Assembly, *Rome Statute of the International Criminal Court*, A/CONF. 183/9, 17 July 1998 (hereafter "ICC Statute"), <http://www.unhcr.org/refworld/docid/3ae6b3a84.html>, Art. 8(2)(b) [xxvi] and (e)[vii].

[46] See *Prosecutor v. Sam Hinga Norman*, Case No. SCSL-2004-14-AR72(E), Decision on Preliminary Motion Based on Lack of Jurisdiction (Child Recruitment), 31 May 2004, paras. 52–53; UN Security Council, Report of the Secretary-General on the establishment of a Special Court for Sierra Leone, 4 Oct. 2000, S/2000/915, <http://www.unhcr.org/refworld/docid/3ae6afbf4.html>, para. 17, which recognized the customary character of the prohibition of child recruitment.

[47] The Optional Protocol to the Convention on the Rights of the Child on the Involvement of Children in Armed Conflict, <http://www.unhcr.org/refworld/docid/47fdfb180.html>, Arts. 1–2. There are currently 127 States Parties to the Optional Protocol. See also the African Charter, which establishes 18 years as the minimum age for all compulsory recruitment, Arts. 2 and 22.2, and the ILO Convention on the Worst Forms of Child Labour, which includes the forced recruitment of children under the age of 18, Arts. 2 and 3(a) in its definition of worst forms of child labour.

[48] Optional Protocol to the CRC on the Involvement of Children in Armed Conflict, Art. 4.

38 of the CRC by raising the minimum age of voluntary recruitment.[49] States also commit to use all feasible measures to prohibit and criminalize under-age recruitment and use of child soldiers by non-State armed groups.[50]The Committee on the Rights of the Child emphasizes that

> . . . under-age recruitment (including of girls for sexual services or forced marriage with the military) and direct or indirect participation in hostilities constitutes a serious human rights violation and thereby persecution, and should lead to the granting of refugee status where the well-founded fear of such recruitment or participation in hostilities is based on "reasons of race, religion, nationality, membership of a particular social group or political opinion" (article 1A (2), 1951 Refugee Convention).[51]

21. In UNHCR's view, forced recruitment and recruitment for direct participation in hostilities of a child below the age of 18 years into the armed forces of the State would amount to persecution. The same would apply in situations where a child is at risk of forced re-recruitment or would be punished for having evaded forced recruitment or deserted the State's armed forces. Similarly, the recruitment by a non-State armed group of any child below the age of 18 years would be considered persecution.

22. Voluntary recruitment of children above the age of 16 years by States is permissible under the Optional Protocol to the CRC on the Involvement of Children in Armed Conflict.[52]

However, the recruiting State authorities have to put in place safeguards to ensure that the recruitment is voluntary, that it is undertaken with the informed consent of the parents and that the children who are so recruited are requested to produce satisfactory proof of age prior to their recruitment. In such cases, it is important to assess whether the recruitment was genuinely voluntary, bearing in mind that children are particularly susceptible to abduction, manipulation and force and may be less likely to resist recruitment. They may enlist under duress, in self-defence, to avoid harm to their families, to seek protection against unwanted marriages or sexual abuse within their homes, or to access basic means of survival, such as food and shelter. The families of children may also encourage them to participate in armed conflict, despite the risks and dangers.

23. In addition, children may have a well-founded fear of persecution arising from the treatment they are subjected to, and/or conduct they are required to engage in, by the armed forces or armed group. Boys and girls associated with armed forces or armed groups may be required to serve as cooks, porters, messengers, spies as well as to take direct part in the hostilities. Girls, in particular, may be forced into sexual relations with members of the military.[53] It is also important to bear in mind that children who have been released from the armed forces or group and return to their countries and communities of origin may be in danger of harassment, re-recruitment or retribution, including imprisonment or extra-judicial execution.

[49] *Ibid.*, Art. 3.

[50] *Ibid.*, Art. 4.

[51] CRC, *General Comment, No.* 6, para. 59. See also para. 58.

[52] Optional Protocol to the CRC on the Involvement of Children in Armed Conflict, Art. 3. States Parties are required to raise in years the minimum age for the voluntary recruitment from the age set out in Art. 38, para. 3 of the CRC, hence, from 15 to 16 years.

[53] The Paris Principles define children associated with an armed force or group as follows: "A child associated with an armed force or armed group refers to any person below 18 years of age who is or who has been recruited or used by an armed force or armed group in any capacity, including but not limited to children, boys and girls, used as fighters, cooks, porters, messengers, spies or for sexual purposes. It does not only refer to a child who is taking or has taken a direct part in hostilities." Art. 2.1.

ii. Child trafficking and labour

24. As recognized by several jurisdictions, trafficked children or children who fear being trafficked may have valid claims to refugee status.[54] UNHCR's Guidelines on Victims of Trafficking and Persons at Risk of Being Trafficked are equally applicable to an asylum claim submitted by a child. The particular impact of a trafficking experience on a child and the violations of child-specific rights that may be entailed also need to be taken into account.[55]

25. The trafficking of children occurs for a variety of reasons but all with the same overarching aim to gain profit through the exploitation of human beings.[56] In this context, it is important to bear in mind that any recruitment, transportation, transfer, harbouring or receipt of children for the purpose of exploitation is a form of trafficking regardless of the means used. Whether the child consented to the act or not is, therefore, irrelevant.[57]

26. The trafficking of a child is a serious violation of a range of fundamental rights and, therefore, constitutes persecution. These rights include the right to life, survival and development, the right to protection from all forms of violence, including sexual exploitation and abuse, and the right to protection from child labour and abduction, sale and trafficking, as specifically provided for by Article 35 of the CRC.[58]

27. The impact of reprisals by members of the trafficking network, social exclusion, ostracism and/or discrimination[59] against a child victim of trafficking who is returned to his/her home country needs to be assessed in a child-sensitive manner. For example, a girl who has been trafficked for sexual exploitation may end up being rejected by her family and become a social outcast in her community if returned. A boy, who has been sent away by his parents in the hope and expectation that he will study, work abroad and send remittances back to his family likewise may become excluded from his family if they learn that he has been trafficked into forced labour. Such child victims of trafficking may have very limited possibilities of accessing and enjoying their human rights, including survival rights, if returned to their homes.

28. In asylum cases involving child victims of trafficking, decision makers will need to pay particular attention to indications of possible complicity of the child's parents, other

[54] See, for instance, *Ogbeide v. Secretary of State for the Home Department*, No. HX/08391/2002, U.K. IAT, 10 May 2002 (unreported); *Li and Others v. Minister of Citizenship and Immigration*, IMM-932-00, Canada, Federal Court, 11 Dec. 2000, <http://www.unhcr.org/refworld/docid/4b18d3682.html>.

[55] See UNHCR, *Guidelines on Victims of Trafficking*. See also UNICEF, *Guidelines on the Protection of Child Victims of Trafficking*, Oct. 2006, <http://www.unicef.org/ceecis/0610-Unicef_Victims_Guidelines_en.pdf>, which make reference to refugee status for children who have been trafficked.

[56] These reasons include, but are not limited to, bonded child labour, debt repayment, sexual exploitation, recruitment by armed forces and groups, and irregular adoption. Girls, in particular, may be trafficked for the purpose of sexual exploitation or arranged marriage while boys may be particularly at risk of being trafficked for various forms of forced labour.

[57] For a definition of the scope of "trafficking", see the following international and regional instruments: Protocol to Prevent, Suppress and Punish Trafficking in Persons, Especially Women and Children, Supplementing the UN Convention against Transnational Organized Crime, 15 Nov. 2000, <http://www.unhcr.org/refworld/docid/4720706c0.html>, in particular Art. 3; Council of Europe Convention on Action against Trafficking in Human Beings, CETS No. 197, 3 May 2005 <http://www.unhcr.org/refworld/ docid/43fded544.htm>.

[58] For a detailed analysis of the human rights framework relating to the trafficking of children, see UNICEF, *Implementation Handbook, op cit.*, in particular pp. 531–542.

[59] UNHCR, *Guidelines on Victims of Trafficking, op cit.*, paras. 17–18.

family members or caregivers in arranging the trafficking or consenting to it. In such cases, the State's ability and willingness to protect the child must be assessed carefully. Children at risk of being (re-)trafficked or of serious reprisals should be considered as having a well-founded fear of persecution within the meaning of the refugee definition.

29. In addition to trafficking, other worst forms of labour, such as slavery, debt bondage and other forms of forced labour, as well as the use of children in prostitution, pornography and illicit activities (for example, the drug trade) are prohibited by international law.[60] Such practices represent serious human rights violations and, therefore, would be considered persecution, whether perpetrated independently or as part of a trafficking experience.

30. International law also proscribes labour likely to harm the health, safety or morals of a child, also known as "hazardous work".[61] In determining whether labour is hazardous, the following working conditions need to be considered: work that exposes children to physical or mental violence; work that takes place underground, under water, at dangerous heights or in confined spaces; work that involves dangerous equipment or manual handling of heavy loads; long working hours and unhealthy environments.[62] Labour performed by a child under the minimum age designated for the particular kind of work and deemed likely to inhibit the child's education and full development is also prohibited according to international standards.[63] Such forms of labour could amount to persecution, as assessed according to the particular child's experience, his/her age and other circumstances. Persecution, for example, may arise where a young child is compelled to perform harmful labour that jeopardizes his/her physical and/or mental health and development.

iii. Female genital mutilation

31. All forms of FGM[64] are considered harmful and violate a range of human rights,[65] as affirmed by international and national jurisprudence and legal doctrine. Many jurisdictions have recognized that FGM involves the infliction of grave harm amounting to persecution.[66]As the practice disproportionately affects the girl child,[67] it can be considered a child-specific form of persecution. For further information about FGM in the

[60] ILO Convention on the Worst Forms of Child Labour, Art. 3 (a–c).

[61] Ibid., Art. 3(d).

[62] Ibid., Art. 4 in conjunction with ILO Worst Forms of Child Labour Recommendation, 1999, R190, <http://www.unhcr.org/refworld/ docid/3ddb6ef34.html>, at 3 and 4.

[63] ILO Minimum Age Convention, Art. 2.

[64] FGM comprises all procedures involving partial or total removal of the external female genitalia or other injury to the female genital organs for non-medical reasons. See further, OHCHR, UNAIDS et al., *Eliminating Female Genital Mutilation: An Interagency Statement*, Feb. 2008, <http://www.unhcr.org/refworld/docid/47c6aa6e2.html>.

[65] FGM comprises all procedures involving partial or total removal of the external female genitalia or other injury to the female genital organs for non-medical reasons. See further, OHCHR, UNAIDS et al., *Eliminating Female Genital Mutilation: An Interagency Statement*, Feb. 2008, <http://www.unhcr.org/refworld/docid/47c6aa6e2.html>.

[66] See, for instance, *Mlle Diop Aminata*, 164078, Commission des Recours des Réfugiés (hereafter "CRR"), France, 17 July 1991, <http://www.unhcr.org/refworld/docid/3ae6b7294.html>; *Khadra Hassan Farah, Mahad Dahir Buraleh, Hodan Dahir Buraleh*, Canada, IRB, 10 May 1994, <http://www.unhcr.org/refworld/docid/3ae6b70618.html>; *In re Fauziya Kasinga*, 3278, U.S. Board of Immigration Appeals (hereafter "BIA"), 13 June 1996, <http://www.unhcr.org/refworld/docid/47bb00782.html>.

[67] FGM is mostly carried out on girls up to 15 years of age, although older girls and women may also be subjected to the practice.

context of refugee status determination, see UNHCR Guidance Note on Refugee Claims relating to Female Genital Mutilation.[68]

iv. Domestic violence against children

32. All violence against children, including physical, psychological and sexual violence, while in the care of parents or others, is prohibited by the CRC.[69] Violence against children may be perpetrated in the private sphere by those who are related to them through blood, intimacy or law.[70] Although it frequently takes place in the name of discipline, it is important to bear in mind that parenting and caring for children, which often demand physical actions and interventions to protect the child, is quite distinct from the deliberate and punitive use of force to cause pain or humiliation.[71] Certain forms of violence, in particular against very young children, may cause permanent harm and even death, although perpetrators may not aim to cause such harm.[72] Violence in the home may have a particularly significant impact on children because they often have no alternative means of support.[73]

33. Some jurisdictions have recognized that certain acts of physical, sexual and mental forms of domestic violence may be considered persecution.[74] Examples of such acts include battering, sexual abuse in the household, incest, harmful traditional practices, crimes committed in the name of honour, early and forced marriages, rape and violence related to commercial sexual exploitation.[75] In some cases, mental violence may be as detrimental to the victim as physical harm and could amount to persecution. Such violence may include serious forms of humiliation, harassment, abuse, the effects of isolation and other practices that cause or may result in psychological harm.[76] Domestic violence may also come within the scope of torture and other cruel, inhuman and degrading treatment or punishment.[77] A minimum level of severity is required for it to constitute persecution. When assessing the level of severity of the harm, a number of factors such as the frequency, patterns, duration and impact on the particular child need to be taken into account. The child's age and dependency on the perpetrator as well as the long-term effects on the physical and psychological development and well-being of the child also need to be considered.

[68] UNHCR, *Guidance Note on FGM, op cit.*

[69] CRC, Arts. 19, 37.

[70] Declaration on the Elimination of Violence Against Women, <http://www.unhcr.org/refworld/docid/3b00f25d2c.html>, Art. 2(a).

[71] See CRC, *General Comment No. 8 (2006): The Right of the Child to Protection from Corporal Punishment and Other Cruel or Degrading Forms of Punishment (Arts. 19; 28, Para. 2; and 37, inter alia)*, CRC/C/GC/8, 2 Mar. 2007 (hereafter "CRC, *General Comment No. 8*"), <http://www.unhcr.org/refworld/docid/460bc7772.html>, paras. 13–14, 26.

[72] UN study on violence against children, *op. cit.*, para. 40.

[73] See further UNICEF, *Domestic Violence Against Women and Girls*, Innocenti Digest No. 6, 2000, <http://www.unicef-irc.org/ publications/pdf/digest6e.pdf>.

[74] See UNHCR, *Handbook for the Protection of Women and Girls*, Feb. 2008, <http://www.unhcr.org/refworld/docid/47cfc2962.html>, pp. 142–144. See also, for instance, *Rosalba Aguirre-Cervantes a.k.a. Maria Esperanza Castillo v. Immigration and Naturalization Service*, U.S. Court of Appeals for the 9th Circuit, 21 Mar. 2001, <http://www.unhcr.org/refworld/docid/3f37adc24.html>.

[75] UN Commission on Human Rights, Human Rights Resolution 2005/41: Elimination of violence against women, E/CN.4/ RES/2005/41, 19 Apr. 2005, <http://www.unhcr.org/refworld/docid/45377c59c.html>, para. 5.

[76] CRC, *General Comment No. 8, op cit.*, para. 11. See also UN study on violence against children, *op. cit.*, para. 42; UNICEF, *Domestic Violence Against Women and Girls, op cit.*, pp. 2–4.

[77] CRC, *General Comment No. 8, op cit.*, para. 12; Human Rights Council, Report of the Special Rapporteur on torture and other cruel, inhuman or degrading treatment or punishment, A/HRC/7/3, 15 Jan. 2008, <http://www.unhcr.org/refworld/docid/47c2c5452. html>, paras. 45–49.

v. Violations of economic, social and cultural rights

34. The enjoyment of economic, social and cultural rights is central to the child's survival and development.[78] The UN Committee on the Rights of the Child has stated that

> . . . the right to survival and development can only be implemented in a holistic manner, through the enforcement of all the other provisions of the Convention, including rights to health, adequate nutrition, social security, an adequate standard of living, a healthy and safe environment, education and play.[79]

While the CRC and the 1966 Covenant on Economic, Social and Cultural Rights contemplate the progressive realization of economic, social and cultural rights, these instruments impose various obligations on States Parties which are of immediate effect.[80] These obligations include avoiding taking retrogressive measures, satisfying minimum core elements of each right and ensuring non-discrimination in the enjoyment of these rights.[81]

35. A violation of an economic, social or cultural right may amount to persecution where minimum core elements of that right are not realized. For instance, the denial of a street child's right to an adequate standard of living (including access to food, water and housing) could lead to an intolerable predicament which threatens the development and survival of that child. Similarly, a denial of medical treatment, particularly where the child concerned suffers from a life-threatening illness, may amount to persecution.[82] Persecution may also be established through an accumulation of a number of less serious violations.[83] This could, for instance, be the case where children with disabilities or stateless children lack access to birth registration and, as a result, are excluded from education, health care and other services.[84]

[78] CRC, Art. 6.2.

[79] CRC, *General Comment No. 7: Implementing Child Rights in Early Childhood*, CRC/C/GC/7/Rev.1, 20 Sep. 2006 (hereafter "CRC, *General Comment No. 7*") <http://www.unhcr.org/refworld/docid/460bc5a62.html>, para. 10.

[80] See CESCR, *General Comment No. 3: The Nature of States Parties' Obligations (Art. 2, Para. 1, of the Covenant)*, E/1991/23, 14 Dec. 1990, <http://www.unhcr.org/refworld/docid/4538838e10.html>, para. 1; CRC, *General Comment No. 5*, para. 6.

[81] See UN Commission on Human Rights, Note verbale dated 86/12/05 from the Permanent Mission of the Netherlands to the United Nations Office at Geneva addressed to the Centre for Human Rights ("Limburg Principles"), 8 Jan. 1987, E/CN.4/1987/17 at B.16, 21–22, <http://www.unhcr.org/refworld/docid/48abd5790.html>; International Commission of Jurists, Maastricht Guidelines on Violations of Economic, Social and Cultural Rights, 26 Jan. 1997, <http://www.unhcr.org/refworld/docid/48abd5730.html>, at II.9 and 11.

[82] See, for instance, *RRT Case No. N94/04178*, N94/04178, Australia, Refugee Review Tribunal (hereafter "RRT"), 10 June 1994, <http://www.unhcr.org/refworld/docid/3ae6b6300.html>.

[83] UNHCR, *Handbook, para. 53. See also Canada (Citizenship and Immigration) v. Oh*, 2009 FC 506, Canada, Federal Court, 22 May 2009, <http://www.unhcr.org/refworld/docid/4a897a1c2.html>, at 10.

[84] See *Case of the Yean and Bosico Children v. The Dominican Republic*, IACtHR, 8 Sep. 2005, <http://www.unhcr.org/refworld/docid/44e497d94.html>. Two girls of Haitian origin were denied the right to nationality and education because, among other matters, they did not have a birth certificate; *Case of the "Juvenile Reeducation Institute" v. Paraguay*, IACtHR, 2 Sep. 2004, <http://www.unhcr.org/refworld/docid/4b17bab62.html>. The Court found that failure to provide severely marginalized groups with access to basic health-care services constitutes a violation of the right to life of the ACHR. See also, CRC, General Comment No. 7, para. 25; CRC, *General Comment No. 9 (2006): The Rights of children with disabilities*, CRC/C/GC/9, 27 Feb. 2007 (hereafter "CRC, *General Comment No. 9*"), <http://www.unhcr.org/refworld/docid/461b93f72.html>, paras. 35–36.

36. Measures of discrimination may amount to persecution when they lead to consequences of a substantially prejudicial nature for the child concerned.[85] Children who lack adult care and support, are orphaned, abandoned or rejected by their parents, and are escaping violence in their homes may be particularly affected by such forms of discrimination. While it is clear that not all discriminatory acts leading to the deprivation of economic, social and cultural rights necessarily equate to persecution, it is important to assess the consequences of such acts for each child concerned, now and in the future. For example, bearing in mind the fundamental importance of education and the significant impact a denial of this right may have for the future of a child, serious harm could arise if a child is denied access to education on a systematic basis.[86] Education for girls may not be tolerated by society,[87] or school attendance may become unbearable for the child due to harm experienced on racial or ethnic grounds.[88]

b) Agents of persecution

37. In child asylum claims, the agent of persecution is frequently a non-State actor. This may include militarized groups, criminal gangs, parents and other caregivers, community and religious leaders. In such situations, the assessment of the well-foundedness of the fear has to include considerations as to whether or not the State is unable or unwilling to protect the victim.[89] Whether or not the State or its agents have taken sufficient action to protect the child will need to be assessed on a case-by-case basis.

38. The assessment will depend not only on the existence of a legal system that criminalizes and provides sanctions for the persecutory conduct. It also depends on whether or not the authorities ensure that such incidents are effectively investigated and that those responsible are identified and appropriately punished.[90] Hence, the enactment of

[85] UNHCR, *Handbook*, para. 54.

[86] See *RRT Case No. V95/03256*, [1995] RRTA 2263, Australia, RRT, 9 Oct. 1995, <http://www.unhcr.org/refworld/docid/4b17c13a2. html>, where the Tribunal found that "discriminatory denial of access to primary education is such a denial of a fundamental human right that it amounts to persecution." at 47.

[87] See *Ali v. Minister of Citizenship and Immigration*, IMM-3404-95, Canada, IRB, 23 Sep. 1996, <http://www.unhcr.org/refworld/ docid/4b18e21b2.html>, which concerned a 9 year-old girl from Afghanistan. The Court concluded that "Education is a basic human right and I direct the Board to find that she should be found to be a Convention refugee."

[88] Decisions in both Canada and Australia have accepted that bullying and harassment of school children may amount to persecution. See, for instance, *Decision VA1-02828, VA1-02826, VA1-02827 and VA1-02829, VA1-02828, VA1-02826, VA1-02827 and VA1-02829*, Canada, IRB, 27 Feb. 2003, <http://www.unhcr.org/refworld/docid/4b18e03d2.html>, para. 36; *RRT Case No. N03/46534*, [2003] RRTA 670, Australia, RRT, 17 July 2003, <http://www.unhcr.org/refworld/docid/4b17bfd62.html>.

[89] See CRC, Art. 3, which imposes a duty on States Parties to ensure the protection and care of children in respect of actions by both State and private actors; ACHR, Arts. 17 and 19; African Charter, Arts. 1(3), 81. See also UNHCR, *Handbook*, para. 65; UNHCR, *Guidelines on Gender-Related Persecution*, para. 19; *Advisory Opinion on Juridical Condition and Human Rights of the Child*, No. OC-17/02, IACtHR, 28 Aug. 2002, <http://www.unhcr.org/refworld/docid/4268c57c4.html>.

[90] See, for instance, *Velásquez Rodríguez Case*, Series C, No. 4, IACtHR, 29 July 1988, para. 174 <http://www.unhcr.org/ refworld/docid/40279a9e4.html>; M.C. v. Bulgaria, Application No. 39272/98, ECtHR, 3 Dec. 2003, <http://www.unhcr.org/refworld/docid/47b19f492.html>. See also UN Committee on the Elimination of Discrimination Against Women, General Recommendations

legislation prohibiting or denouncing a particular persecutory practice against children, in itself, is not sufficient evidence to reject a child's claim to refugee status.[91]

39. The child's access to State protection also depends on the ability and willingness of the child's parents, other primary caregiver or guardian to exercise rights and obtain protection on behalf of the child. This may include filing a complaint with the police, administrative authorities or public service institutions. However, not all children will have an adult who can represent them as is the case, for example, where the child is unaccompanied or orphaned, or where a parent, other primary caregiver or guardian is the agent of persecution. It is important to remember that, due to their young age, children may not be able to approach law enforcement officials or articulate their fear or complaint in the same way as adults. Children may be more easily dismissed or not taken seriously by the officials concerned, and the officials themselves may lack the skills necessary to interview and listen to children.

c) The 1951 Convention grounds

40. As with adult claims to refugee status, it is necessary to establish whether or not the child's well-founded fear of persecution is linked to one or more of the five grounds listed in Article 1A(2) of the 1951 Convention. It is sufficient that the Convention ground be a factor relevant to the persecution, but it is not necessary that it be the sole, or even dominant, cause.

Race and nationality or ethnicity

41. Race and nationality or ethnicity is at the source of child asylum claims in many contexts. Policies that deny children of a particular race or ethnicity the right to a nationality or to be registered at birth,[92] or that deny children from particular ethnic groups their right to education or to health services would fall into this category. This Convention ground would apply similarly to policies that aim to remove children from their parents on the basis of particular racial, ethnic or indigenous backgrounds. Systematic targeting of girls belonging to ethnic minorities for rape, trafficking, or recruitment into armed forces or groups also may be analysed within this Convention ground.

Religion

42. As with an adult, the religious beliefs of a child or refusal to hold such beliefs may put him/her at risk of persecution. For a Convention ground to be established, it is not necessary that the child be an active practitioner. It is sufficient that the child simply be perceived as holding a certain religious belief or belonging to a sect or religious group, for example, because of the religious beliefs of his/her parents.[93]

Nos. 19 and 20, adopted at the Eleventh Session, 1992 (contained in Document A/47/38), A/47/38, 1992, <http://www.unhcr. org/refworld/docid/453882a422.html>, para. 9; UN Commission on Human Rights, The due diligence standard as a tool for the elimination of violence against women: Report of the Special Rapporteur on Violence against Women, Its Causes and Consequences, Yakin Ertürk, E/CN.4/2006/61, 20 Jan. 2006, <http://www.unhcr.org/refworld/docid/45377afb0.html>.

[91] UNHCR, *Guidelines on Gender-Related Persecution*, para. 11.

[92] Universal Declaration of Human Rights, <http://www.unhcr.org/refworld/docid/3ae6b3712c .html>, Art. 15; ICCPR, Arts 24(2) and (3); CRC, Art. 7.

[93] UNHCR, *Guidelines on International Protection No. 6: Religion-Based Refugee Claims under Article 1A(2) of the 1951 Convention and/or the 1967 Protocol relating to the Status of Refugees,*

43. Children have limited, if any, influence over which religion they belong to or observe, and belonging to a religion can be virtually as innate as one's ethnicity or race. In some countries, religion assigns particular roles or behaviour to children. As a consequence, if a child does not fulfil his/her assigned role or refuses to abide by the religious code and is punished as a consequence, s/he may have a well-founded fear of persecution on the basis of religion.

44. The reasons for persecution related to a child's refusal to adhere to prescribed gender roles may also be analysed under this ground. Girls, in particular, may be affected by persecution on the basis of religion. Adolescent girls may be required to perform traditional slave duties or to provide sexual services. They also may be required to undergo FGM or to be punished for honour crimes in the name of religion.[94] In other contexts, children – both boys and girls – may be specifically targeted to join armed groups or the armed forces of a State in pursuit of religious or related ideologies.

Political opinion

45. The application of the Convention ground of "political opinion" is not limited to adult claims. A claim based on political opinion presupposes that the applicant holds, or is assumed to hold, opinions not tolerated by the authorities or society and that are critical of generally accepted policies, traditions or methods. Whether or not a child is capable of holding a political opinion is a question of fact and is to be determined by assessing the child's level of maturity and development, level of education, and his/her ability to articulate those views. It is important to acknowledge that children can be politically active and hold particular political opinions independently of adults and for which they may fear being persecuted. Many national liberation or protest movements are driven by student activists, including schoolchildren. For example, children may be involved in distributing pamphlets, participating in demonstrations, acting as couriers or engaging in subversive activities.

46. In addition, the views or opinions of adults, such as the parents, may be imputed to their children by the authorities or by non-State actors.[95] This may be the case even if a child is unable to articulate the political views or activities of the parent, including where the parent deliberately withholds such information from the child to protect him/her. In such circumstances, these cases should be analysed not only according to the political opinion ground but also in terms of the ground pertaining to membership of a particular social group (in this case, the "family").

47. The grounds of (imputed) political opinion and religion may frequently overlap in child asylum claims. In certain societies, the role ascribed to women and girls may be attributable to the requirements of the State or official religion. The authorities or other agents of persecution may perceive the failure of a girl to conform to this role as a failure to practice or to hold certain religious beliefs. At the same time, failure to conform could

HCR/GIP/04/06, 28 Apr. 2004 (hereafter, "UNHCR, *Guidelines on Religion-Based Persecution*"), <http://www.unhcr.org/refworld/docid/4090f9794.html>.

[94] *Ibid.*, para. 24.

[95] See *Matter of Timnit Daniel and Simret Daniel*, A70 483 789 & A70 483 774, U.S. BIA, 31 Jan. 2002 (unpublished, non-precedent setting decision). The Court found that the notion "that the respondents were too young to have an actual political opinion is irrelevant; it is enough that the officials believed that they supported the EPLF."

be interpreted as holding an unacceptable political opinion that threatens fundamental power structures. This may be the case particularly in societies where there is little separation between religious and State institutions, laws and doctrines.[96]

Membership of a particular social group

48. Children's claims to refugee status most often have been analysed in the context of the Convention ground of "membership of a particular social group", although any of the Convention grounds may be applicable. As stated in UNHCR's Guidelines

[a] particular social group is a group of persons who share a common characteristic other than their risk of being persecuted, or who are perceived as a group by society. The characteristic will often be one which is innate, unchangeable, or which is otherwise fundamental to identity, conscience or the exercise of one's human rights.[97]

49. Although age, in strict terms, is neither innate nor permanent as it changes continuously, being a child is in effect an immutable characteristic at any given point in time. A child is clearly unable to disassociate him/herself from his/her age in order to avoid the persecution feared.[98] The fact that the child eventually will grow older is irrelevant to the identification of a particular social group, as this is based on the facts as presented in the asylum claim. Being a child is directly relevant to one's identity, both in the eyes of society and from the perspective of the individual child. Many government policies are age-driven or age-related, such as the age for military conscription, the age for sexual consent, the age of marriage, or the age for starting and leaving school. Children also share many general characteristics, such as innocence, relative immaturity, impressionability and evolving capacities. In most societies, children are set apart from adults as they are understood to require special attention or care, and they are referred to by a range of descriptors used to identify or label them, such as "young", "infant", "child", "boy", "girl" or "adolescent". The identification of social groups also may be assisted by the fact that the children share a common socially-constructed experience, such as being abused, abandoned, impoverished or internally displaced.

50. A range of child groupings, thus, can be the basis of a claim to refugee status under the "membership of a particular social group" ground. Just as "women" have been recognized

[96] UNHCR, *Guidelines on Gender-Related Persecution, op. cit.* para. 26.

[97] UNHCR, *Guidelines on International Protection No. 2: 'Membership of a Particular Social Group' within the context of Article 1A(2) of the 1951 Convention and/or its 1967 Protocol Relating to the Status of Refugees*, HCR/GIP/02/02, 7 May 2002, <http:// www.unhcr.org/refworld/docid/3d36f23f4.html>, para. 11.

[98] See *Matter of S-E-G-, et al.*, 24 I & N Dec. 579 (BIA 2008), U.S. BIA, 30 July 2008, <http://www.unhcr.org/refworld/docid/4891da5b2.html>, which noted that "we acknowledge that the mutability of age is not within one's control, and that if an individual has been persecuted in the past on account of an age-described particular social group, or faces such persecution at a time when that individual's age places him within the group, a claim for asylum may still be cognizable." (p. 583); *LQ (Age: Immutable Characteristic) Afghanistan v. Secretary of State for the Home Department*, [2008] U.K. AIT 00005, 15 Mar. 2007, <http://www.unhcr.org/refworld/docid/47a04ac32.html>, finding that the applicant, "although, assuming he survives, he will in due course cease to be a child, he is immutably a child at the time of assessment" at 6; *Decision V99-02929, V99-02929*, Canada, IRB, 21 Feb. 2000, <http://www.unhcr.org/refworld/docid/4b18e5592.html>, which found that "[t]he child's vulnerability arises as a result of his status as a minor. His vulnerability as a minor is an innate and unchangeable characteristic, notwithstanding the child will grow into an adult."

as a particular social group in several jurisdictions, "children" or a smaller subset of children may also constitute a particular social group.[99] Age and other characteristics may give rise to groups such as "abandoned children",[100]"children with disabilities", "orphans", or children born outside coercive family planning policies or of unauthorized marriages, also referred to as "black children".[101] The applicant's family may also constitute a relevant social group.[102]

51. The applicant's membership in a child-based social group does not necessarily cease to exist merely because his/her childhood ends. The consequences of having previously belonged to such a social group might not end even if the key factor of that identity (that is, the applicant's young age) is no longer applicable. For instance, a past shared experience may be a characteristic that is unchangeable and historic and may support the identification of groups such as "former child soldiers"[103] or "trafficked children" for the purposes of a fear of future persecution.[104]

52. Some of the more prominent social groupings include the following:

i. **Street children** may be considered a particular social group. Children living and/or working on the streets are among the most visible of all children, often identified by society as social outcasts. They share the common characteristics of their youth and having the street as their home and/or source of livelihood. Especially for children who have grown up in such situations, their way of life is fundamental to their identity and often difficult to change. Many of these children have embraced the term "street children" as it offers them a sense of identity and belonging while they may live and/or work on the streets for a range of reasons. They also may share past experiences such as domestic violence, sexual abuse, and exploitation or being orphaned or abandoned.[105]

[99] In *In re Fauziya Kasinga, op. cit.*, it was held that "young women" may constitute a particular social group.

[100] In *V97-03500*, Canada, Convention Refugee Determination Division, 31 May 1999, it was accepted that abandoned children in Mexico can be a particular social group. (A summary is available at <http://www2.irb-cisr.gc.ca/en/decisions/reflex/index_e.htm?action=article.view&id=1749>). See also RRT Case No. 0805331, [2009] RRTA 347, Australia, RRT, 30 April 2009, <http://www.unhcr.org/refworld/docid/4a2681692.html>, where the Tribunal held that the applicant's (a two-year old child) particular social group was "children of persecuted dissidents".

[101] This has been affirmed in several decisions in Australia. See, for instance, *Chen Shi Hai, op. cit.* and more recently in RRT Case No. 0901642, [2009] RRTA 502, Australia, RRT, 3 June 2009, <http://www.unhcr.org/refworld/docid/4a76ddbf2.html>.

[102] See *Aguirre-Cervantes, op. cit.*, where the Court found that "[f]amily membership is clearly an immutable characteristic, fundamental to one's identity", and noted that "[t]he undisputed evidence demonstrates that Mr. Aguirre's goal was to dominate and persecute members of his immediate family."

[103] In *Lukwago v. Ashcroft, Attorney General*, 02-1812, U.S. Court of Appeals for the 3rd Circuit, 14 May 2003, <http://www.unhcr.org/refworld/docid/47a7078c3.html>, the Court found that "membership in the group of former child soldiers who have escaped LRA captivity fits precisely within the BIA's own recognition that a shared past experience may be enough to link members of a 'particular social group'."

[104] UNHCR, *Guidelines on Victims of Trafficking*, para. 39. See also, RRT Case No. N02/42226, [2003] RRTA 615, Australia, RRT, 30 June 2003, <http://www.unhcr.org/refworld/docid/4b17c2b02.html>, which concerned a young woman from Uzbekistan. The identified group was "Uzbekistani women forced into prostitution abroad who are perceived to have transgressed social mores."

[105] See, for instance, *Matter of B-F-O-*, A78 677 043, U.S. BIA, 6 Nov. 2001 (unpublished, non-precedent decision). The Court found that the applicant, who was an abandoned street child, had a well-founded fear of persecution based on membership in a particular social group. See also, *LQ (Age: Immutable Characteristic) Afghanistan v. Secretary of State for the Home Department,*

ii. **Children affected by HIV/AIDS**, including both those who are HIV-positive and those with an HIV-positive parent or other relative, may also be considered a particular social group. The fact of being HIV-positive exists independently of the persecution they may suffer as a consequence of their HIV status. Their status or that of their family may set them apart and, while manageable and/or treatable, their status is by and large unchangeable.[106]

iii. Where children are singled out as a target group for **recruitment or use by an armed force or group**, they may form a particular social group due to the innate and unchangeable nature of their age as well as the fact that they are perceived as a group by the society in which they live. As with adults, a child who evades the draft, deserts or otherwise refuses to become associated with an armed force may be perceived as holding a political opinion in which case the link to the Convention ground of political opinion may also be established.[107]

d) Internal "flight" or "relocation" alternative

53. An assessment of the issue of internal flight alternative contains two parts: the relevance of such an inquiry, and the reasonableness of any proposed area of internal relocation.[108] The child's best interests inform both the relevance and reasonableness assessments.

54. As in the case of adults, internal relocation is only **relevant** where the applicant can access practically, safely and legally the place of relocation.[109] In particular with regard to gender-based persecution, such as domestic violence and FGM which are typically perpetrated by private actors, the lack of effective State protection in one part of the country may be an indication that the State may also not be able or willing to protect the child in any other part of the country.[110] If the child were to relocate, for example, from a rural to an urban area, the protection risks in the place of relocation would also need to be examined carefully, taking into account the age and coping capacity of the child.

55. In cases where an internal flight or relocation alternative is deemed relevant, a proposed site of internal relocation that may be **reasonable** in the case of an adult may not be reasonable in the case of a child. The "reasonableness test" is one that is applicant-specific and, thus, not related to a hypothetical "reasonable person". Age and the best interests of the child are among the factors to be considered in assessing the viability of a proposed place of internal relocation.[111]

op. cit. The Tribunal found that the applicant's fear of harm as an orphan and street child "would be as a result of his membership in a part of a group sharing an immutable characteristic and constituting, for the purposes of the Refugee Convention, a particular social group", at 7.

[106] See further, CRC, *General Comment No. 3: HIV/AIDS and the Rights of the Child*, 17 Mar. 2003, <http://www.unhcr.org/refworld/ docid/4538834e15.html>.

[107] UNHCR, *Handbook*, paras. 169–171; UNHCR, *Guidelines on Religion-Based Persecution*, paras. 25–26.

[108] UNHCR, *Handbook*, paras. 169–171; UNHCR, *Guidelines on Religion-Based Persecution*, paras. 25–26.

[109] *Ibid.*, para. 7.

[110] *Ibid.*, para. 15.

[111] *Ibid.*, para. 25. See further factors in the CRC, *General Comment No. 6*, para. 84, on Return to Country of Origin. Although drafted with a different context in mind, these factors are equally relevant to an assessment of an internal flight/relocation alternative.

56. Where children are unaccompanied and, therefore, not returning to the country of origin with family members or other adult support, special attention needs to be paid as to whether or not such relocation is reasonable. Internal flight or relocation alternatives, for instance, would not be appropriate in cases where unaccompanied children have no known relatives living in the country of origin and willing to support or care for them and it is proposed that they relocate to live on their own without adequate State care and assistance. What is merely inconvenient for an adult might well constitute undue hardship for a child, particularly in the absence of any friend or relation.[112] Such relocation may violate the human right to life, survival and development, the principle of the best interests of the child, and the right not to be subjected to inhuman treatment.[113]

57. If the only available relocation option is to place the child in institutional care, a proper assessment needs to be conducted of the care, health and educational facilities that would be provided and with regard to the long-term life prospects of adults who were institutionalized as children.[114] The treatment as well as social and cultural perceptions of orphans and other children in institutionalized care needs to be evaluated carefully as such children may be the subject of societal disapproval, prejudice or abuse, thus rendering the proposed site for relocation unreasonable in particular circumstances.

e) The application of exclusion clauses to children

58. The exclusion clauses contained in Article 1F of the 1951 Convention provide that certain acts are so grave that they render their perpetrators undeserving of international protection as refugees.[115] Since Article 1F is intended to protect the integrity of asylum, it needs to be applied "scrupulously". As with any exception to human rights guarantees, a restrictive interpretation of the exclusion clauses is required in view of the serious possible

[112] See, for instance, *Elmi v. Minister of Citizenship and Immigration*, Canada, Federal Court, No. IMM-580-98, 12 Mar. 1999, <http://www.unhcr.org/refworld/docid/4b17c5932.html>.

[113] CRC, Arts. 3, 6 and 37. See also *Mubilanzila Mayeka and Kaniki Mitunga v. Belgium*, Application No. 13178/03, ECtHR, 12 Oct. 2006, <http://www.unhcr.org/refworld/docid/45d5cef72.html>, which concerned the return (not internal relocation) of an unaccompanied five-year old girl. The Court was "struck by the failure to provide adequate preparation, supervision and safeguards for her deportation", noting further that such "conditions was bound to cause her extreme anxiety and demonstrated such a total lack of humanity towards someone of her age and in her situation as an unaccompanied minor as to amount to inhuman treatment [violation of article 3 of the European Convention on Human Rights]", paras. 66, 69 was "children of persecuted dissidents".

[114] See CRC, *General Comment No. 6*, para. 85. See also *Inter-Agency Guiding Principles, op cit.*, which notes that institutional care needs to be considered a last resort, as "residential institutions can rarely offer the developmental care and support a child requires and often cannot even provide a reasonable standard of protection", p. 46.

[115] UNHCR's interpretative legal guidance on the substantive and procedural standards for the application of Art. 1F is set out in UNHCR, *Guidelines on International Protection No. 5: Application of the Exclusion Clauses: Article 1F of the 1951 Convention relating to the Status of Refugees*, HCR/GIP/03/05, 4 Sep. 2003, (hereafter: "UNHCR, *Guidelines on Exclusion*") <http://www.unhcr.org/refworld/docid/3f5857684.html>; UNHCR, *Background Note on the Application of the Exclusion Clauses: Article 1F of the 1951 Convention relating to the Status of Refugees*, 4 Sep. 2003, (hereafter "UNHCR, *Background Note on Exclusion*"), <http://www.unhcr.org/refworld/docid/3f5857d24.html>; UNHCR, *Statement on Article 1F of the 1951 Convention*, July 2009, (hereafter "UNHCR, Statement on Article 1F"), <http://www.unhcr.org/refworld/docid/4a5de2992.html>; and UNHCR, *Handbook*, paras. 140–163.

consequences of exclusion for the individual.[116] The exclusion clauses are exhaustively enumerated in Article 1F, and no reservations are permitted.[117]

59. In view of the particular circumstances and vulnerabilities of children, the application of the exclusion clauses to children always needs to be exercised with great caution. In the case of young children, the exclusion clauses may not apply at all. Where children are alleged to have committed crimes while their own rights were being violated (for instance while being associated with armed forces or armed groups), it is important to bear in mind that they may be victims of offences against international law and not just perpetrators.[118]

60. Although the exclusion clauses of Article 1F do not distinguish between adults and children, Article 1F can be applied to a child only if s/he has reached the age of criminal responsibility as established by international and/or national law at the time of the commission of the excludable act.[119] Thus, a child below such minimum age cannot be considered responsible for an excludable act.[120] Article 40 of the CRC requires States to establish a minimum age for criminal responsibility, but there is no universally recognized age limit.[121] In different jurisdictions, the minimum age ranges from 7 years to higher ages, such as 16 or 18 years, while the Statutes of the Special Court for Sierra Leone[122] and the International Criminal Court[123] set the cut-off age at 15 years and 18 years respectively.

61. In view of the disparities in establishing a minimum age for criminal responsibility by States and in different jurisdictions, the emotional, mental and intellectual maturity

[116] UNHCR, *Guidelines on Exclusion*, para. 2; UNHCR *Background Note on Exclusion*, para. 4. UNHCR, *Handbook* para. 149. See also ExCom Conclusions No. 82 (XLVIII), *Safeguarding Asylum*, 17 Oct. 1997, <http://www.unhcr.org/refworld/docid/3ae68c958. html>, para. (v); No. 102 (LVI) 2005, *General Conclusion on International Protection*, 7 Oct. 2005, <http://www.unhcr.org/refworld/docid/43575ce3e.html>, para. (i); No. 103 (LVI), *Conclusion on the Provision on International Protection Including Through Complementary Forms of Protection*, 7 Oct. 2005, <http://www.unhcr.org/refworld/docid/43576e292.html>, para. (d).

[117] UNHCR, *Guidelines on Exclusion*, para. 3; UNHCR, *Background Note on Exclusion*, para. 7.

[118] The Paris Principles state: "Children who are accused of crimes under international law allegedly committed while they were associated with armed forces or armed groups should be considered primarily as victims of offences against international law; not only as perpetrators. They must be treated in accordance with international law in a framework of restorative justice and social rehabilitation, consistent with international law which offers children special protection through numerous agreements and principles," para. 3.6. It should also be noted that the prosecutor for the SCSL chose not to prosecute children between the ages of 15 and 18 years given that they themselves were victims of international crimes.

[119] UNHCR, *Guidelines on Exclusion*, para. 28.

[120] UNHCR, *Background Note on Exclusion*, para. 91. If the age of criminal responsibly is higher in the country of origin than in the host country, this should be taken into account in the child's favour.

[121] The Committee on the Rights of the Child urged States not to lower the minimum age to 12 years and noted that a higher age, such as 14 or 16 years, "contributes to a juvenile justice system which . . . deals with children in conflict with the law without resorting to judicial proceedings"; see, CRC, *General Comment No. 10 (2007): Children's Rights in Juvenile Justice*, CRC/C/GC/10, 25 Apr. 2007, <http://www.unhcr.org/refworld/docid/4670fca12.html>, para. 33. See also UN General Assembly, United Nations Standard Minimum Rules for the Administration of Juvenile Justice ("The Beijing Rules"), A/RES/40/33, 29 Nov. 1985, <http://www. unhcr.org/refworld/docid/3b00f2203c.html>, which provides that the "beginning of that age should not be fixed at a too low an age level bearing in mind the facts of emotional, mental and intellectual maturity", Art. 4.1.

[122] UN Security Council, Statute of the Special Court for Sierra Leone, 16 Jan. 2002, Art. 7.

[123] ICC Statute, Art. 26.

of any child over the relevant national age limit for criminal responsibility would need to be evaluated to determine whether s/he had the mental capacity to be held responsible for a crime within the scope of Article 1F. Such considerations are particularly important where the age limit is lower on the scale but is also relevant if there is no proof of age and it cannot be established that the child is at, or above, the age for criminal responsibility. The younger the child, the greater the presumption that the requisite mental capacity did not exist at the relevant time.

62. As with any exclusion analysis, a three-step analysis needs to be undertaken if there are indications that the child has been involved in conduct which may give rise to exclusion.[124] Such an analysis requires that: (i) the acts in question be assessed against the exclusion grounds, taking into account the nature of the acts as well as the context and all individual circumstances in which they occurred; (ii) it be established in each case that the child committed a crime which is covered by one of the sub-clauses of Article 1F, or that the child participated in the commission of such a crime in a manner which gives rise to criminal liability in accordance with internationally applicable standards; and (iii) it be determined, in cases where individual responsibility is established, whether the consequences of exclusion from refugee status are proportional to the seriousness of the act committed.[125]

63. It is important to undertake a thorough and individualized analysis of all circumstances in each case. In the case of a child, the exclusion analysis needs to take into account not only general exclusion principles but also the rules and principles that address the special status, rights and protection afforded to children under international and national law at all stages of the asylum procedure. In particular, those principles related to the best interest of the child, the mental capacity of children and their ability to understand and consent to acts that they are requested or ordered to undertake need to be considered. A rigorous application of legal and procedural standards of exclusion is also critical.[126]

64. Based on the above, the following considerations are of central importance in the application of the exclusion clauses to acts committed by children:

i. When determining individual responsibility for excludable acts, the issue of whether or not a child has the necessary **mental state** (or *mens rea*), that is, whether or not the child acted with the requisite intent and knowledge to be held individually responsible for an excludable act, is a central factor in the exclusion analysis. This assessment needs to consider elements such as the child's emotional, mental and intellectual development. It is important to determine whether the child was sufficiently mature to understand the nature and consequences of his/her conduct and, thus, to commit, or participate in, the commission of the crime. Grounds for the absence of the *mens rea* include, for example, severe **mental disabilities**, involuntary intoxication, or immaturity.

ii. If mental capacity is established, other grounds for **rejecting individual responsibility** need to be examined, notably whether the child acted under duress, coercion,

[124] For further information on exclusion concerning child soldiers, see UNHCR, *Advisory Opinion From the Office of the United Nations High Commissioner for Refugees (UNHCR) Regarding the International Standards for Exclusion From Refugee Status as Applied to Child Soldiers*, 12 Sep. 2005 (hereafter "UNHCR, *Advisory Opinion on the Application of Exclusion Clauses to Child Soldiers*"), <http://www.unhcr.org/refworld/docid/440eda694.html>.

[125] UNHCR, *Statement on Article 1F*, p. 7.

[126] For a detailed analysis on procedural issues regarding exclusion, see UNHCR, *Guidelines on Exclusion*, paras. 31–36 and UNHCR, *Background Note on Exclusion*, paras. 98–113.

or in defence of self or others. Such factors are of particular relevance when assessing claims made by former child soldiers. Additional factors to consider may include: the age at which the child became involved in the armed forces or group; the reasons for which s/he joined and left the armed forces or group; the length of time s/he was a member; the consequences of refusal to join the group; any forced use of drugs, alcohol or medication; the level of education and understanding of the events in question; and the trauma, abuse or ill-treatment suffered.[127]

iii. Finally, if individual responsibility is established, it needs to be determined whether or not the consequences of exclusion from refugee status are **proportional** to the seriousness of the act committed.[128] This generally involves a weighing of the gravity of the offence against the degree of persecution feared upon return. If the applicant is likely to face severe persecution, the crime in question needs to be very serious in order to exclude him/her from refugee status. Issues for consideration include any mitigating or aggravating factors relevant to the case. When assessing a child's claim, even if the circumstances do not give rise to a defence, factors such as the age, maturity and vulnerability of the child are important considerations. In the case of child soldiers, such factors include ill-treatment by military personnel and circumstances during service. The consequences and treatment that the child may face upon return (i.e. serious human rights violations as a consequence of having escaped the armed forces or group) also need to be considered.

IV. Procedural and Evidentiary Issues

65. Due to their young age, dependency and relative immaturity, children should enjoy specific procedural and evidentiary safeguards to ensure that fair refugee status determination decisions are reached with respect to their claims.[129] The general measures outlined below set out minimum standards for the treatment of children during the asylum procedure. They do not preclude the application of the detailed guidance provided, for example, in the Action for the Rights of Children Resources Pack,[130]

[127] Decisions in France have recognized that children who committed offences, which should in principle lead to the application of the exclusion clauses, may be exonerated if they were in particularly vulnerable situations. See, for instance, *459358, M.V.; Exclusion*, CRR, 28 Apr. 2005, <http://www.unhcr.org/refworld/docid/43abf5cf4.html>; *448119, M.C*, CRR, 28 Jan. 2005, <http://www.unhcr.org/refworld/docid/4b17b5d92.html>. See also, *MH (Syria) v. Secretary of State for the Home Department; DS (Afghanistan) v. Secretary of State for the Home Department*, [2009] EWCA Civ 226, Court of Appeal (U.K.), 24 Mar. 2009, <http://www.unhcr.org/refworld/docid/49ca60ae2.html>, para. 3. For detailed guidance on grounds rejecting individual responsibility, see, UNHCR *Guidelines on Exclusion*, paras. 21–24. UNHCR, *Background Note on Exclusion*, paras. 91–93. UNHCR, *Advisory Opinion on the Application of Exclusion Clauses to Child Soldiers, op cit.* pp. 10–12.

[128] For detailed guidance on proportionality see UNHCR, *Guidelines on Exclusion*, para. 24; UNHCR, *Background Note on Exclusion*, paras. 76–78.

[129] The relevant applicable age for children to benefit from the additional procedural safeguards elaborated in this section is the date the child seeks asylum and not the date a decision is reached. This is to be distinguished from the substantive assessment of their refugee claim in which the prospective nature of the inquiry requires that their age at the time of the decision may also be relevant.

[130] Action for the rights of children, *ARC Resource Pack, a capacity building tool for child protection in and after emergencies*, produced by Save the Children, UNHCR, UNICEF, OHCHR, International Rescue Committee and Terre des Hommes, 7 Dec. 2009, <http://www.savethechildren.net/arc>.

the Inter-Agency Guiding Principles on Unaccompanied and Separated Children and in national guidelines.[131]

66. Claims made by child applicants, whether they are accompanied or not, should normally be processed on a priority basis, as they often will have special protection and assistance needs. Priority processing means reduced waiting periods at each stage of the asylum procedure, including as regards the issuance of a decision on the claim. However, before the start of the procedure, children require sufficient time in which to prepare for and reflect on rendering the account of their experiences. They will need time to build trusting relationships with their guardian and other professional staff and to feel safe and secure. Generally, where the claim of the child is directly related to the claims of accompanying family members or the child is applying for derivative status, it will not be necessary to prioritise the claim of the child unless other considerations suggest that priority processing is appropriate.[132]

67. There is no general rule prescribing in whose name a child's asylum claim ought to be made, especially where the child is particularly young or a claim is based on a parent's fear for their child's safety. This will depend on applicable national regulations. Sufficient flexibility is needed, nevertheless, to allow the name of the principal applicant to be amended during proceedings if, for instance, it emerges that the more appropriate principal applicant is the child rather than the child's parent. This flexibility ensures that administrative technicalities do not unnecessarily prolong the process.[133]

68. For unaccompanied and separated child applicants, efforts need to be made as soon as possible to initiate tracing and family reunification with parents or other family members. There will be exceptions, however, to these priorities where information becomes available suggesting that tracing or reunification could put the parents or other family members in danger, that the child has been subjected to abuse or neglect, and/or where parents or family members may be implicated or have been involved in their persecution.[134]

69. An independent, qualified guardian needs to be appointed immediately, free of charge in the case of unaccompanied or separated children. Children who are the principal applicants in an asylum procedure are also entitled to a legal representative.[135] Such representatives should be properly trained and should support the child throughout the procedure.

[131] See, for instance, U.K. Asylum Instruction, *Processing an Asylum Application from a Child*, 2 Nov. 2009, <http://www.bia.homeoffice.gov.uk/sitecontent/documents/policyandlaw/asylumprocessguidance/specialcases/guidance/processingasylumapplication1.pdf?view=Binary>; U.K. Border Agency Code of Practice for Keeping Children Safe from Harm, Dec. 2008, <http://www.unhcr.org/refworld/docid/4948f8662.html>; Finland, Directorate of Immigration, *Guidelines for Interviewing (Separated) Minors*, Mar. 2002, <http://www.unhcr.org/refworld/docid/430ae8d72.html>; U.S. *Guidelines For Children's Asylum Claims, op cit.*; Canada, IRB, *Guidelines Issued by the Chairperson Pursuant to Section 65(4) of the Immigration Act: Guideline 3 – Child Refugee Claimants: Procedural and Evidentiary Issues*, 30 Sep. 1996, No. 3, <http://www.unhcr.org/refworld/ docid/3ae6b31d3b.html>.

[132] UNHCR, *Procedural Standards for Refugee Status Determination Under UNHCR's Mandate*, 20 Nov. 2003, <http://www.unhcr. org/refworld/docid/42d66dd84.html>, pages 3.25, 4.21–4.23.

[133] This is especially relevant in relation to claims, such as FGM or forced marriage, where parents flee with their child in fear for his/her life although the child may not fully comprehend the reason for flight.

[134] Family tracing and reunification have been addressed in a number of ExCom Conclusions, including most recently in ExCom.

[135] "Guardian" here refers to an independent person with specialized skills who looks after the child's best interests and general well-being. Procedures for the appointment of a guardian must not be less favourable than the existing national administrative or judicial procedures used for

70. The right of children to express their views and to participate in a meaningful way is also important in the context of asylum procedures.[136] A child's own account of his/her experience is often essential for the identification of his/her individual protection requirements and, in many cases, the child will be the only source of this information. Ensuring that the child has the opportunity to express these views and needs requires the development and integration of safe and child-appropriate procedures and environments that generate trust at all stages of the asylum process. It is important that children be provided with all necessary information in a language and manner they understand about the possible existing options and the consequences arising from them.[137] This includes information about their right to privacy and confidentiality enabling them to express their views without coercion, constraint or fear of retribution.[138]

71. Appropriate communication methods need to be selected for the different stages of the procedure, including the asylum interview, and need to take into account the age, gender, cultural background and maturity of the child as well as the circumstances of the flight and mode of arrival.[139] Useful, non-verbal communication methods for children might include playing, drawing, writing, role-playing, story-telling and singing. Children with disabilities require "whatever mode of communication they need to facilitate expressing their views".[140]

72. Children cannot be expected to provide adult-like accounts of their experiences. They may have difficulty articulating their fear for a range of reasons, including trauma, parental instructions, lack of education, fear of State authorities or persons in positions of power, use of ready-made testimony by smugglers, or fear of reprisals. They may be too young or immature to be able to evaluate what information is important or to interpret what they have witnessed or experienced in a manner that is easily understandable to an adult. Some children may omit or distort vital information or be unable to differentiate the imagined from reality. They also may experience difficulty relating to abstract notions, such as time or distance. Thus, what might constitute a lie in the case of an adult might not necessarily be a lie in the case of a child. It is, therefore, essential that examiners have the necessary training and skills to be able to evaluate accurately the reliability and significance of the child's account.[141] This may require involving experts in interviewing children outside a formal setting or observing children and communicating with them in an environment where they feel safe, for example, in a reception centre.

73. Although the burden of proof usually is shared between the examiner and the applicant in adult claims, it may be necessary for an examiner to assume a greater burden

appointing guardians for children who are nationals in the country. "Legal representative" refers to a lawyer or other person qualified to provide legal assistance to, and inform, the child in the asylum proceedings and in relation to contacts with the authorities on legal matters. See ExCom, *Conclusion No. 107*, para. (g)(viii). For further details, see CRC,*General Comment No. 6*, paras. 33–38, 69. See also UNHCR, *Guidelines on Unaccompanied Children Seeking Asylum, op cit.*, p. 2 and paras. 4.2, 5.7, 8.3, 8.5.

[136] CRC, Art. 12. The CRC does not set any lower age limit on children's right to express their views freely as it is clear that children can and do form views from a very early age.

[137] CRC, *General Comment* No. 6, para. 25; CRC, *General Comment* No. *12*, paras. 123–124.

[138] CRC, Arts. 13, 17.

[139] Separated Children in Europe Programme, *SCEP Statement of Good Practice*, Third edition, 2004, <http://www.unhcr.org/ refworld/docid/415450694.html>, para. 12.1.3.

[140] CRC, *General Comment* No. 9, para. 32.

[141] ExCom, *Conclusion* No. *107*, para. (d)

of proof in children's claims, especially if the child concerned is unaccompanied.[142] If the facts of the case cannot be ascertained and/or the child is incapable of fully articulating his/her claim, the examiner needs to make a decision on the basis of all known circumstances, which may call for a liberal application of the benefit of the doubt.[143] Similarly, the child should be given the benefit of the doubt should there be some concern regarding the credibility of parts of his/her claim.[144]

74. Just as country of origin information may be gender-biased to the extent that it is more likely to reflect male as opposed to female experiences, the experiences of children may also be ignored. In addition, children may have only limited knowledge of conditions in the country of origin or may be unable to explain the reasons for their persecution. For these reasons, asylum authorities need to make special efforts to gather relevant country of origin information and other supporting evidence.

75. Age assessments are conducted in cases when a child's age is in doubt and need to be part of a comprehensive assessment that takes into account both the physical appearance and the psychological maturity of the individual.[145] It is important that such assessments are conducted in a safe, child- and gender-sensitive manner with due respect for human dignity. The margin of appreciation inherent to all age-assessment methods needs to be applied in such a manner that, in case of uncertainty, the individual will be considered a child.[146] As age is not calculated in the same way universally or given the same degree of importance, caution needs to be exercised in making adverse inferences of credibility where cultural or country standards appear to lower or raise a child's age. Children need to be given clear information about the purpose and process of the age-assessment procedure in a language they understand. Before an age assessment procedure is carried out, it is important that a qualified independent guardian is appointed to advise the child.

76. In normal circumstances, DNA testing will only be done when authorized by law and with the consent of the individuals to be tested, and all individuals will be provided with a full explanation of the reasons for such testing. In some cases, however, children may not be able to consent due to their age, immaturity, inability to understand what this entails or for other reasons. In such situations, their appointed guardian (in the absence of a family member) will grant or deny consent on their behalf taking into account the views of the child. DNA tests should be used only where other means for verification have proven insufficient. They may prove particularly beneficial in the case of children who are suspected of having been trafficked by individuals claiming to be parents, siblings or other relatives.[147]

77. Decisions need to be communicated to children in a language and in a manner they understand. Children need to be informed of the decision in person, in the presence of their guardian, legal representative, and/or other support person, in a supportive and non-threatening environment. If the decision is negative, particular care will need to be

[142] *Ibid.*, para. (g)(viii), which recommends that States develop adapted evidentiary requirements.
[143] UNHCR, *Handbook*, paras. 196, 219.
[144] *Inter-Agency Guiding Principles, op. cit.*, p. 61.
[145] ExCom, *Conclusion* No. *107*, para. (g)(ix).
[146] *Ibid.*, para. (g)(ix); UNHCR, *Guidelines on Policies and Procedures in Dealing with Unaccompanied Children Seeking Asylum, op cit.*, paras. 5.11, 6.
[147] UNHCR, *Note on DNA Testing to Establish Family Relationships in the Refugee Context*, June 2008, <http://www.unhcr.org/ refworld/docid/48620c2d2.html>.

taken in delivering the message to the child and explaining what next steps may be taken in order to avoid or reduce psychological stress or harm.

Guidelines on International Protection No. 9:

Claims to Refugee Status based on Sexual Orientation and/or Gender Identity within the context of Article 1A(2) of the 1951 Convention and/or its 1967 Protocol relating to the Status of Refugees

UNHCR issues these Guidelines pursuant to its mandate, as contained in the *Statute of the Office of the United Nations High Commissioner for Refugees*, in conjunction with Article 35 of the *1951 Convention relating to the Status of Refugees* and Article II of its *1967 Protocol*. These Guidelines complement the *UNHCR Handbook on Procedures and Criteria for Determining Refugee Status under the 1951 Convention* (Reissued, Geneva, 2011). In particular, they should be read in conjunction with *UNHCR's Guidelines on International Protection No.1: Gender-Related Persecution within the context of Article 1A(2) of the 1951 Convention and/or its 1967 Protocol relating to the Status of Refugees* (May 2002); *UNHCR's Guidelines on International Protection No. 2: "Membership of a Particular Social Group" Within the Context of Article 1A(2) of the 1951 Convention and/or its 1967 Protocol Relating to the Status of Refugees* (May 2002); and *UNHCR's Guidelines on International Protection No. 6: Religion-Based Refugee Claims under Article 1A(2) of the 1951 Convention and/or the 1967 Protocol relating to the Status of Refugees* (April 2004). They replace *UNHCR's Guidance Note on Refugee Claims relating to Sexual Orientation and Gender Identity* (November 2008).

These Guidelines are intended to provide legal interpretative guidance for governments, legal practitioners, decision makers and the judiciary, as well as UNHCR staff carrying out refugee status determination under its mandate.

The *UNHCR Handbook on Procedures and Criteria for Determining Refugee Status and the Guidelines on International Protection* are available as a compilation at: <http://www.unhcr.org/refworld/docid/4f33c8d92.html>.

I. Introduction

1. In many parts of the world, individuals experience serious human rights abuses and other forms of persecution due to their actual or perceived sexual orientation and/or gender identity. While persecution of Lesbian, Gay, Bisexual, Transgender and Intersex (hereafter "LGBTI")[1] individuals and those perceived to be LGBTI is not a new phenomenon,[2] there is greater awareness in many countries of asylum that people fleeing

[1] For a discussion of terms, see below at III. Terminology. For the purpose of these Guidelines, "gender identity" also incorporates "intersex".

[2] The 1951 Convention relating to the Status of Refugees was drafted not least as a response to the persecution during World War II, during which intolerance and violence cost the lives of thousands of people with a LGBTI background. See, UNHCR, "Summary Conclusions: Asylum-Seekers and Refugees Seeking Protection on Account of their Sexual Orientation and Gender Identity", November 2010, Expert Roundtable organized by UNHCR, Geneva, Switzerland, 30 September – 1 October 2010 (hereafter "UNHCR, Summary Conclusions of Roundtable"), available at: <http://www.unhcr.org/refworld/docid/4cff99a42.html>, para. 3.

persecution for reasons of their sexual orientation and/or gender identity can qualify as refugees under Article 1A(2) of the 1951 Convention relating to the Status of Refugees and/or its 1967 Protocol (hereafter the "1951 Convention").[3] Nevertheless, the application of the refugee definition remains inconsistent in this area.

2. It is widely documented that LGBTI individuals are the targets of killings, sexual and gender-based violence, physical attacks, torture, arbitrary detention, accusations of immoral or deviant behaviour, denial of the rights to assembly, expression and information, and discrimination in employment, health and education in all regions around the world.[4] Many countries maintain severe criminal laws for consensual same-sex relations, a number of which stipulate imprisonment, corporal punishment and/or the death penalty.[5] In these and other countries, the authorities may not be willing or able to protect individuals from abuse and persecution by non-State actors, resulting in impunity for perpetrators and implicit, if not explicit, tolerance of such abuse and persecution.

3. Intersecting factors that may contribute to and compound the effects of violence and discrimination include sex, age, nationality, ethnicity/race, social or economic status and HIV status. Due to these multiple layers of discrimination, LGBTI individuals are often highly marginalized in society and isolated from their communities and families. It is also not uncommon for some individuals to harbour feelings of shame and/or internalized homophobia. Because of these and other factors, they may be inhibited from informing asylum adjudicators that their real fear of persecution relates to their sexual orientation and/or gender identity.

4. The experiences of LGBTI persons vary greatly and are strongly influenced by their cultural, economic, family, political, religious and social environment. The applicant's background may impact the way he or she expresses his or her sexual orientation and/or gender identity, or may explain the reasons why he or she does not live openly as LGBTI. It is important that decisions on LGBTI refugee claims are not based on superficial understandings of the experiences of LGBTI persons, or on erroneous, culturally inappropriate or stereotypical assumptions. These Guidelines provide substantive and procedural

[3] UN General Assembly, Convention Relating to the Status of Refugees, 28 July 1951; Protocol Relating to the Status of Refugees, 31 January 1967.

[4] See, UN Human Rights Council, "Report of the United Nations High Commissioner for Human Rights on Discriminatory Laws and Practices and Acts of Violence against Individuals based on their Sexual Orientation and Gender Identity", 17 November 2011 (hereafter "OHCHR, Report on Sexual Orientation and Gender Identity"), available at: <http://www.unhcr.org/refworld/docid/4ef092022.html>. For an overview of jurisprudence and doctrine, see also International Commission of Jurists (hereafter "ICJ"), *Sexual Orientation and Gender Identity in Human Rights Law, References to Jurisprudence and Doctrine of the United Nations Human Rights System*, 2010, fourth updated edition, available at: <http://www.unhcr.org/refworld/docid/4c627bd82.html>; ICJ, *Sexual Orientation and Gender Identity in Human Rights Law, Jurisprudential, Legislative and Doctrinal References from the Council of Europe and the European Union*, October 2007, available at: <http://www.unhcr.org/refworld/docid/4a54bbb5d.html>; ICJ, *Sexual Orientation and Gender Identity in Human Rights Law: References to Jurisprudence and Doctrine of the Inter-American System*, July 2007, available at: <http://www.unhcr.org/refworld/docid/4ad5b83a2.html>.

[5] See, International Lesbian, Gay, Bisexual, Trans and Intersex Association, "State-sponsored Homophobia, A World Survey of Laws Prohibiting Same-Sex Activity between Consenting Adults", May 2012, available at: <http://old.ilga.org/Statehomophobia/ILGA_State_Sponsored_Homophobia_2012.pdf>.

guidance on the determination of refugee status of individuals on the basis of their sexual orientation and/or gender identity, with a view to ensuring a proper and harmonized interpretation of the refugee definition in the 1951 Convention.[6]

II. International Human Rights Law

5. Article 1 of the Universal Declaration of Human Rights provides that "all human beings are born free and equal in dignity and rights", and Article 2 declares that "everyone is entitled to all the rights and freedoms set forth in this Declaration".[7] All people, including LGBTI individuals, are entitled to enjoy the protection provided for by international human rights law on the basis of equality and non-discrimination.[8]

6. Although the main international human rights treaties do not explicitly recognize a right to equality on the basis of sexual orientation and/or gender identity,[9] discrimination on these grounds has been held to be prohibited by international human rights law.[10] For example, the proscribed grounds of "sex" and " other status" contained in the non-discrimination clauses of the main international human rights instruments have been accepted as encompassing sexual orientation and gender identity.[11] As respect for fundamental rights as well as the principle of non-discrimination are core aspects of the 1951 Convention and international refugee law,[12] the refugee definition must be interpreted and applied with due regard to them, including the prohibition on discrimination on the basis of sexual orientation and gender identity.

7. The Yogyakarta Principles on the Application of International Human Rights Law in relation to Sexual Orientation and Gender Identity were adopted in 2007 by a group

[6] These Guidelines supplement the UNHCR "Guidelines on International Protection No. 1: Gender-Related Persecution Within the Context of Article 1A(2) of the 1951 Convention and/or its 1967 Protocol Relating to the Status of Refugees", 7 May 2002 (hereafter "UNHCR, Guidelines on Gender-Related Persecution"), available at: <http://www.unhcr.org/refworld/docid/3d36f1c64.html>.

[7] UN General Assembly, Universal Declaration of Human Rights, 10 December 1948.

[8] OHCHR, Report on Sexual Orientation and Gender Identity, para. 5.

[9] However, some regional instruments expressly prohibit discrimination on grounds of sexual orientation. See, for example, Charter of Fundamental Rights of the European Union, Article 21, 18 December 2000, and Resolution of the Organization of American States, Human Rights, Sexual Orientation, and Gender Identity, AG/RES. 2721 (XLII-O/12), 4 June 2012.

[10] "[D]iscrimination' as used in the Covenant [on Civil and Political Rights] should be understood to imply any distinction, exclusion, restriction or preference which is based on any ground such as race, colour, sex, language, religion, political or other opinion, national or social origin, property, birth or other status, and which has the purpose or effect of nullifying or impairing the recognition, enjoyment or exercise by all persons, on an equal footing, of all rights and freedoms.", UN Human Rights Committee, CCPR General Comment No. 18: Non-Discrimination, 10 November 1989, available at: <http://www.unhcr.org/refworld/docid/453883fa8.html>, para. 7.

[11] The UN Human Rights Committee held in 1994 in the landmark decision *Toonen v. Australia* that the International Covenant on Civil and Political Rights (adopted by the UN General Assembly on 16 December 1966, hereafter "ICCPR") prohibits discrimination on the grounds of sexual orientation, see CCPR/C/50/D/488/1992, 4 April 1994, (hereafter "*Toonen v. Australia*") available at: <http://www.unhcr.org/refworld/docid/48298b8d2.html>. This has subsequently been affirmed by several other UN human rights treaty bodies, including also recognition that gender identity is among the prohibited grounds of discrimination. See further, OHCHR, Report on Sexual Orientation and Gender Identity, para. 7.

[12] 1951 Convention, Preambular para. 1, Article 3.

of human rights experts and, although not binding, reflect well-established principles of international law.[13] They set out the human rights protection framework applicable in the context of sexual orientation and/or gender identity. Principle 23 outlines the right to seek and enjoy asylum from persecution related to sexual orientation and/or gender identity:

> Everyone has the right to seek and enjoy in other countries asylum from persecution, including persecution related to sexual orientation or gender identity. A State may not remove, expel or extradite a person to any State where that person may face a well-founded fear of torture, persecution, or any other form of cruel, inhuman or degrading treatment or punishment, on the basis of sexual orientation or gender identity.

III. Terminology

8. These Guidelines are intended to be inclusive of and relevant to the range of claims relating to sexual orientation and/or gender identity. The concepts of sexual orientation and gender identity are outlined in the Yogyakarta Principles and this terminology is also used for the purposes of these Guidelines. Sexual orientation refers to: "each person's capacity for profound emotional, affectional and sexual attraction to, and intimate relations with, individuals of a different gender or the same gender or more than one gender".[14] Gender identity refers to: "each person's deeply felt internal and individual experience of gender, which may or may not correspond with the sex assigned at birth, including the personal sense of the body and other expressions of gender, including dress, speech and mannerisms".[15]

9. Sexual orientation and gender identity are broad concepts which create space for self-identification. Research over several decades has demonstrated that sexual orientation can range along a continuum, including exclusive and non-exclusive attraction to the same or the opposite sex.[16] Gender identity and its expression also take many forms, with some individuals identifying neither as male nor female, or as both. Whether one's sexual orientation is determined by, *inter alia*, genetic, hormonal, developmental, social, and/or cultural influences (or a combination thereof), most people experience little or no sense of choice about their sexual orientation.[17] While for most people sexual orientation or gender identity are determined at an early age, for others they may continue to evolve across a person's lifetime. Different people realize at different points in their lives that they are LGBTI and their sexual and gender expressions may vary with age, and other social and cultural determinants.[18]

10. Refugee claims based on sexual orientation and/or gender identity often emanate from members of specific sub-groups, that is, lesbian, gay, bisexual, transgender, intersex

[13] ICJ, Yogyakarta Principles - Principles on the Application of International Human Rights Law in relation to Sexual Orientation and Gender Identity, (hereafter "Yogyakarta Principles"), March 2007, available at: <http://www.unhcr.org/refworld/docid/48244e602.html>.

[14] Yogyakarta Principles, Preamble.

[15] *Ibid.*

[16] American Psychological Association, "Sexual Orientation and Homosexuality" (hereafter "APA, Sexual Orientation and Homosexuality"), available at: <http://www.apa.org/helpcenter/sexual-orientation.aspx>.

[17] There is no consensus among scientists about the exact reasons that an individual develops a particular sexual orientation. See, APA, Sexual Orientation and Homosexuality.

[18] *Application No. 76175*, New Zealand Appeals Authority, 30 April 2008, available at: <http://www.unhcr.org/refworld/docid/482422f62.html>, para. 92.

and queer[19] individuals (usually abbreviated as "LGBT", "LGBTI" or "LGBTIQ" [20]). The experiences of members of these various groups will often be distinct from one another; and, as noted above at paragraph 4, *between* members. It is, therefore, essential that decision makers understand both the context of each refugee claim, as well as individual narratives that do not easily map onto common experiences or labels.[21]

Lesbian

A *lesbian* is a woman whose enduring physical, romantic and/or emotional attraction is to other women. Lesbians often suffer multiple discrimination due to their gender, their often inferior *social* and/or economic status, coupled with their sexual orientation. Lesbians are commonly subjected to harm by non-State actors, including acts such as "corrective" rape, retaliatory violence by former partners or husbands, forced marriage, and crimes committed in the name of "honour" by family members. Some lesbian refugee applicants have not had any experiences of past persecution; for example, if they have had few or no lesbian relationships. Lesbians may have had heterosexual relationships, often, but not necessarily, because of social pressures to marry and bear children. They may only later in life enter into a lesbian relationship or identify as lesbian. As in all refugee claims, it is important to ensure that the assessment of her fear of persecution is future-looking and that decisions are not based on stereotypical notions of lesbians.

Gay men

Gay is often used to describe a man whose enduring physical, romantic and/or emotional attraction is to other men, although gay can also be used to describe both gay men and women (lesbians). Gay men numerically dominate sexual orientation and gender identity refugee claims, yet their claims should not be taken as a "template" for other cases on sexual orientation and/or gender identity. Gay men are often more visible than other LGBTI groups in public life in many societies and can become the focus of negative political campaigns. It is important, however, to avoid assumptions that all gay men are public about their sexuality or that all gay men are effeminate. Having defied masculine privilege by adopting roles and characteristics viewed as "feminine", gay men may be viewed as "traitors", whether they are effeminate or not. They could be at particular risk of abuse in prisons, the military[22] and other traditionally male dominated environments and job sites. Some gay men may also have had heterosexual relationships because of societal pressures, including to marry and/or have children.

[19] *Queer* is traditionally a pejorative term, however, it has been appropriated by some LGBT people to describe themselves.
[20] UNHCR has opted to refer to "LGBTI" individuals, which is intended to be inclusive of a wide range of individuals who fear persecution for reasons of their sexual orientation and/or gender identity. See further, UNHCR, *Working with Lesbian, Gay, Bisexual, Transgender & Intersex Persons in Forced Displacement*, 2011, available at: <http://www.unhcr.org/refworld/docid/4e6073972.html>. For further information on terminology, see, for example, Gay & Lesbian Alliance Against Defamation, "Media Reference Guide: A Resource for Journalists", updated May 2010, available at: <http://www.glaad.org/reference>.
[21] Considerations relating to each group are also integrated elsewhere in these Guidelines.
[22] See, for example, *RRT Case No. 060931294*, [2006] RRTA 229, Australia, RRTA, 21 December 2006, available at: <http://www.unhcr.org/refworld/docid/47a707ebd.html>; *MS (Risk - Homosexuality - Military Service) Macedonia v. SSHD*, CG [2002] UKIAT 03308, UK Immigration

Bisexual

Bisexual describes an individual who is physically, romantically and/or emotionally attracted to both men and women. The term bisexuality tends to be interpreted and applied inconsistently, often with a too narrow understanding. Bisexuality does not have to involve attraction to both sexes at the same time, nor does it have to involve equal attraction to or number of relationships with both sexes. Bisexuality is a unique identity, which requires an examination in its own right. In some countries persecution may be directed expressly at gay or lesbian conduct, but nevertheless encompass acts of individuals who identify as bisexual. Bisexuals often describe their sexual orientation as "fluid" or "flexible" (see further below at paragraph 47).

Transgender

Transgender describes people whose gender identity and/or gender expression differs from the biological sex they were assigned at birth.[23] Transgender is a gender identity, not a sexual orientation and a transgender individual may be heterosexual, gay, lesbian or bisexual.[24] Transgender individuals dress or act in ways that are often different from what is generally expected by society on the basis of their sex assigned at birth. Also, they may not appear or act in these ways at all times. For example, individuals may choose to express their chosen gender only at certain times in environments where they feel safe. Not fitting within accepted binary perceptions of being male and female, they may be perceived as threatening social norms and values. This non-conformity exposes them to risk of harm. Transgender individuals are often highly marginalized and their claims may reveal experiences of severe physical, psychological and/or sexual violence. When their self-identification and physical appearance do not match the legal sex on official documentation and identity documents, transgender people are at particular risk.[25] The

and Asylum Tribunal, 30 July 2002, available at: <http://www.unhcr.org/refworld/docid/46836aba0.html>, which found that the "atrocious prison conditions" in the particular country would breach the appellant's rights under the European Convention for the Protection of Human Rights and Fundamental Freedoms (ECHR), Article 3. Lesbians may also be at risk in these environments. See, *Smith v. Minister of Citizenship and Immigration*, 2009 FC 1194, Canada, Federal Court, 20 November 2009, available at: <http://www.unhcr.org/refworld/docid/4b3c7b8c2.html>.

[23] The term may include, but is not limited to, transsexuals (an older term which originated in the medical and psychological communities), cross-dressers and other gender-variant people. See further, APA, "Answers to Your Questions about Transgender People, Gender Identity and Gender Expression", available at: <http://www.apa.org/topics/sexuality/transgender.aspx>.

[24] See also, *RRT Case No. 0903346*, [2010] RRTA 41, Australia, Refugee Review Tribunal, 5 February 2010, (hereafter "*RRT Case No. 0903346*") available at: <http://www.unhcr.org/refworld/docid/4b8e783f2.html>, which concerned a transgender applicant who feared persecution because of her gender identity.

[25] The European Court of Human Rights has established that authorities must legally recognize the altered gender. See, *Goodwin v. United Kingdom*, Application no. 28957/95, European Court of Human Rights, 11 July 2002, available at: <http://www.unhcr.org/refworld/docid/4dad9f762.html>, finding a violation of the applicant's right to privacy, noting that "the stress and alienation arising from a discordance between the position in society assumed by a post-operative transsexual and the status imposed by law which refuses to recognize the change of gender cannot, in the Court's view, be regarded as a minor inconvenience arising from a formality.", para. 77, and that "Under Article 8 of the Convention in particular, the notion of personal autonomy is an important principle underlying the interpretation of its guarantees, protection is given to the personal sphere of each

transition to alter one's birth sex is not a one-step process and may involve a range of personal, legal and medical adjustments. Not all transgender individuals choose medical treatment or other steps to help their outward appearance match their internal identity. It is therefore important for decision makers to avoid overemphasis on sex-reassignment surgery.

Intersex

The term *intersex* or "disorders of sex development" (DSD)[26] refers to a condition in which an individual is born with reproductive or sexual anatomy and/or chromosome patterns that do not seem to fit typical biological notions of being male or female. These conditions may be apparent at birth, may appear at puberty, or may be discovered only during a medical examination. Individuals with these conditions were previously referred to as "hermaphrodites", however this term is considered outdated and should not be used unless the applicant uses it.[27] An intersex person may identify as male or female, while their sexual orientation may be lesbian, gay, bisexual, or heterosexual.[28] Intersex persons may be subjected to persecution in ways that relate to their atypical anatomy. They may face discrimination and abuse for having a physical disability or medical condition, or for non-conformity with expected bodily appearances of females and males. Some intersex children are not registered at birth by the authorities, which can result in a range of associated risks and denial of their human rights. In some countries, being intersex can be seen as something evil or part of witchcraft and can result in a whole family being targeted for abuse.[29] Similar to transgender individuals, they may risk being harmed during the transition to their chosen gender because, for example, their identification papers do not indicate their chosen gender. People who self-identify as intersex may be viewed by others as transgender, as there may simply be no understanding of the intersex condition in a given culture.

11. Not all applicants will self-identify with the LGBTI terminology and constructs as presented above or may be unaware of these labels. Some may only be able to draw upon (derogatory) terms used by the persecutor. Decision makers therefore need to be cautious about inflexibly applying such labels as this could lead to adverse credibility assessments or failure to recognize a valid claim. For example, bisexuals are often categorized in the

individual, including the right to establish details of their identity as individual human beings", para. 90. See also Council of Europe Recommendation CM/Rec (2010)5 of the Committee of Ministers to Member States on measures to combat discrimination on grounds of sexual orientation or gender identity, recognizing that "Member states should take appropriate measures to guarantee the full legal recognition of a person's gender reassignment in all areas of life, in particular by making possible the change of name and gender in official documents in a quick, transparent and accessible way.", at 21.

[26] Note that some individuals (and/or their medical records) will just use the name of their particular condition, such as congenital adrenal hyperplasia or androgen insensitivity syndrome, rather than using the term intersex or DSD.

[27] US Citizenship and Immigration Services, "Guidance for Adjudicating Lesbian, Gay, Bisexual, Transgender and Intersex (LGBTI) Refugee and Asylum Claims", 27 December 2011 (hereafter "USCIS, Guidance for Adjudicating LGBTI Claims"), available at: <http://www.unhcr.org/refworld/docid/4f269cd72.html>, p. 13.

[28] See further, Advocates for Informed Choice website: <http://aiclegal.org/faq/#whatisintersex>.

[29] Jill Schnoebelen, *Witchcraft Allegations, Refugee Protection and Human Rights: A Review of the Evidence*, UNHCR, New Issues in Refugee Research, Research Paper No. 169, January 2009, available at: <http://www.unhcr.org/4981ca712.pdf>.

adjudication of refugee claims as either gay, lesbian or heterosexual, intersex individuals may not identify as LGBTI at all (they may not see their condition as part of their identity, for example) and men who have sex with men do not always identify as gay. It is also important to be clear about the distinction between sexual orientation and gender identity. They are separate concepts and, as explained above at paragraph 8, they present different aspects of the identity of each person.

IV. Substantive Analysis

A. Background

12. A proper analysis as to whether a LGBTI applicant is a refugee under the 1951 Convention needs to start from the premise that applicants are entitled to live in society as who they are and need not hide that.[30] As affirmed by the position adopted in a number of jurisdictions, sexual orientation and/or gender identity are fundamental aspects of human identity that are either innate or immutable, or that a person should not be required to give up or conceal.[31] While one's sexual orientation and/or gender identity may be revealed by sexual conduct or a sexual act, or by external appearance or dress, it may also be evidenced by a range of other factors, including how the applicant lives in society, or how he or she expresses (or wishes to express) his or her identity.[32]

13. An applicant's sexual orientation and/or gender identity can be relevant to a refugee claim where he or she fears persecutory harm on account of his or her actual or perceived sexual orientation and/or gender identity, which does not, or is seen not to,

[30] UNHCR, *HJ (Iran) and HT (Cameroon) v. Secretary of State for the Home Department – Case for the First Intervener (United Nations High Commissioner for Refugees)*, 19 April 2010, (hereafter "UNHCR, *HJ and HT*"), available at: <http://www.unhcr.org/refworld/docid/4bd1abbc2.html>, para. 1. For a comparison with other Convention grounds, see para. 29 of the submission. See also, *HJ (Iran) and HT (Cameroon) v. Secretary of State for the Home Department*, UK, [2010] UKSC 31, Supreme Court, 7 July 2010 (hereafter "*HJ and HT*"), available at: <http://www.unhcr.org/refworld/docid/4c3456752.html>.

[31] See, for example, *Canada (Attorney General) v. Ward*, [1993] 2 S.C.R. 689, Canada, Supreme Court, 30 June 1993 (hereafter "*Canada v. Ward*"), available at: <http://www.unhcr.org/refworld/docid/3ae6b673c.html>; *Geovanni Hernandez-Montiel v. Immigration and Naturalization Service*, US, 225 F.3d 1084, A72-994-275, (9th Cir. 2000), 24 August 2000, available at: <http://www.unhcr.org/refworld/docid/3ba9c1119.html>, later affirmed by *Morales v. Gonzales*, US, 478 F.3d 972, No. 05-70672, (9th Cir. 2007), 3 January 2007, available at: <http://www.unhcr.org/refworld/docid/4829b1452.html>; *Appellants S395/2002 and S396/2002 v. Minister for Immigration and Multicultural Affairs*, [2003] HCA 71, Australia, High Court, 9 December 2003 (hereafter "*S395/2002*"), available at: <http://www.unhcr.org/refworld/docid/3fd9eca84.html>; *Refugee Appeal No. 74665*, New Zealand, Refugee Status Appeals Authority, 7 July 2004 (hereafter "*Refugee Appeal No. 74665*"), available at: <http://www.unhcr.org/refworld/docid/42234ca54.html>; *HJ and HT*, above footnote 30, paras. 11, 14, 78.

[32] Yogyakarta Principles, Principle 3, affirms that each person's self-defined sexual orientation and gender identity is integral to their personality and is one of the most basic aspects of self-determination, dignity and freedom. See further, *S395/2002*, para. 81; *Matter of Toboso-Alfonso*, US Board of Immigration Appeals, 12 March 1990, (hereafter "*Matter of Toboso-Alfonso*"), available at: <http://www.unhcr.org/refworld/docid/3ae6b6b84.html>; *Nasser Mustapha Karouni v. Alberto Gonzales, Attorney General*, US, No. 02-72651, (9th Cir. 2005), 7 March 2005 (hereafter "*Karouni*") available at: <http://www.unhcr.org/refworld/docid/4721b5c32.html>, at III[6]; *Lawrence, et al. v. Texas*, US Supreme Court, 26 June 2003, available at: <http://www.unhcr.org/refworld/docid/3f21381d4.html>, which found that "When sexuality finds overt expression in intimate conduct with another person, the conduct can be but one element in a personal bond that is more enduring", p. 6.

conform to prevailing political, cultural or social norms. The intersection of gender, sexual orientation and gender identity is an integral part in the assessment of claims raising questions of sexual orientation and/or gender identity. Harm as a result of not conforming to expected gender roles is often a central element in these claims. UNHCR's Guidelines on Gender-Related Persecution recognize that:

> Refugee claims based on differing sexual orientation contain a gender element. A claimant's sexuality or sexual practices may be relevant to a refugee claim where he or she has been subject to persecutory action on account of his or her sexuality or sexual practices. In many such cases, the claimant has refused to adhere to socially or culturally defined roles or expectations of behaviour attributed to his or her sex.[33]

14. The impact of gender is relevant to refugee claims made by both LGBTI men and women.[34] Decision makers need to be attentive to differences in their experiences based on sex/gender. For example, heterosexual or male gay norms or country information may not apply to the experiences of lesbians whose position may, in a given context, be similar to that of other women in her society. Full account needs to be taken of diverse and evolving identities and their expression, the actual circumstances of the individual, and the cultural, legal, political and social context.[35]

15. Societal disapproval of varied sexual identities or their expression is usually more than the simple disapproval of sexual practices. It is often underlined by a reaction to non-compliance with expected cultural, gender and/or social norms and values. The societal norms of who men and women are and how they are supposed to behave are commonly based on hetero-normative standards. Both men and women may be subject to violent acts to make them conform to society's gender roles and/or to intimidate others by setting "an example". Such harm can be "sexualized" as a means of further degrading, objectifying or punishing the victim for his/her sexual orientation and/or gender identity, but can also take other forms.[36]

B. Well-founded fear of being persecuted

16. The term "persecution", though not expressly defined in the 1951 Convention, can be considered to involve serious human rights violations, including a threat to life or freedom as well as other kinds of serious harm. In addition, lesser forms of harm may cumulatively constitute persecution. What amounts to persecution will depend on the circumstances of the case, including the age, gender, opinions, feelings and psychological make-up of the applicant.[37]

17. Discrimination is a common element in the experiences of many LGBTI individuals. As in other refugee claims, discrimination will amount to persecution where measures of discrimination, individually or cumulatively, lead to consequences of a substantially prejudicial nature for the person concerned.[38] Assessing whether the cumulative effect of

[33] UNHCR, Guidelines on Gender-Related Persecution, para. 16.

[34] UNHCR, Guidelines on Gender-Related Persecution, para. 3.

[35] UNHCR, Summary Conclusions of Roundtable, para. 5.

[36] UNHCR, Summary Conclusions of Roundtable, paras. 6, 16.

[37] UNHCR, *Handbook on Procedures and Criteria for Determining Refugee Status under the 1951 Convention and the 1967 Protocol Relating to the Status of Refugees,* HCR/1P/4/ENG/REV. 3 (hereafter "UNHCR, *Handbook*"), paras. 51–53.

[38] *Ibid*, paras. 54–55.

such discrimination rises to the level of persecution is to be made by reference to reliable, relevant and up-to-date country of origin information.[39]

18. Not all LGBTI applicants may have experienced persecution in the past (see further below at paragraphs 30-33 on concealment as persecution and at paragraph 57 on *sur place* claims). Past persecution is not a prerequisite to refugee status and in fact, the well-foundedness of the fear of persecution is to be based on the assessment of the predicament that the applicant would have to face if returned to the country of origin.[40] The applicant does not need to show that the authorities knew about his or her sexual orientation and/or gender identity before he or she left the country of origin.[41]

19. Behaviour and activities may relate to a person's orientation or identity in complex ways. It may be expressed or revealed in many subtle or obvious ways, through appearance, speech, behaviour, dress and mannerisms; or not revealed at all in these ways. While a certain activity expressing or revealing a person's sexual orientation and/or gender identity may sometimes be considered trivial, what is at issue is the consequences that would follow such behaviour. In other words, an activity associated with sexual orientation may merely reveal or expose the stigmatized identity, it does not cause or form the basis of the persecution. In UNHCR's view, the distinction between forms of expression that relate to a "core area" of sexual orientation and those that do not, is therefore irrelevant for the purposes of the assessment of the existence of a well-founded fear of persecution.[42]

Persecution

20. Threats of serious abuse and violence are common in LGBTI claims. Physical, psychological and sexual violence, including rape,[43] would generally meet the threshold level

[39] *Molnar v. Canada (Minister of Citizenship and Immigration)*, 2005 FC 98, Canada, Federal Court, 21 January 2005 (hereafter "*Molnar v. Canada*") available at: <http://www.unhcr.org/refworld/docid/4fe81df72.html>.

[40] See, for example, *Bromfield v. Mukasey*, US, 543 F.3d 1071, 1076-77 (9th Cir. 2008), 15 September 2008, available at: <http://www.unhcr.org/refworld/docid/498b08a12.html>, *RRT Case No. 1102877*, [2012] RRTA 101, Australia, Refugee Review Tribunal, 23 February 2012, available at: <http://www.unhcr.org/refworld/docid/4f8410a52.html>, para. 91.

[41] UNHCR, *Handbook*, para. 83.

[42] *Bundesrepublik Deutschland v. Y (C-71/11), Z (C-99/11)*, C-71/11 and C-99/11, CJEU, 5 September 2012, available at: <http://www.unhcr.org/refworld/docid/505ace862.html>, para. 62; *RT (Zimbabwe) and others v Secretary of State for the Home Department*, [2012] UKSC 38, UK Supreme Court, 25 July 2012, available at: <http://www.unhcr.org/refworld/docid/500fdacb2.html>, paras. 75–76 (Lord Kerr); *UNHCR Statement on Religious Persecution and the Interpretation of Article 9(1) of the EU Qualification Directive* and UNHCR, *Secretary of State for the Home Department (Appellant) v. RT (Zimbabwe), SM (Zimbabwe) and AM (Zimbabwe) (Respondents) and the United Nations High Commissioner for Refugees (Intervener) - Case for the Intervener*, 25 May 2012, Case No. 2011/0011, available at: <http://www.unhcr.org/refworld/docid/4fc369022.html>, para. 12(9).

[43] International criminal tribunals in their jurisprudence have broadened the scope of crimes of sexual violence that can be prosecuted as rape to include oral sex and vaginal or anal penetration through the use of objects or any part of the perpetrator's body. See, for instance, *Prosecutor v. Anto Furundzija (Trial Judgment)*, IT-95-17/1-T, International Criminal Tribunal for the Former Yugoslavia (ICTY), 10 December 1998, available at: <http://www.unhcr.org/refworld/docid/40276a8a4.html>, para. 185; *Prosecutor v. Dragoljub Kunarac, Radomir Kovac and Zoran Vukovic (Appeal Judgment)*, IT-96-23 & IT-96-23/1-A, ICTY, 12 June 2002, available at: <http://www.unhcr.org/refworld/docid/3debaafe4.html>, para. 128. See also, International Criminal Court, Elements of Crimes, 2011, available at: <http://www.unhcr.org/refworld/docid/4ff5dd7d2.html>,

required to establish persecution. Rape in particular has been recognized as a form of torture, leaving "deep psychological scars on the victim".[44] Rape has been identified as being used for such purposes as "intimidation, degradation, humiliation, discrimination, punishment, control or destruction of the person. Like torture, rape is a violation of personal dignity."[45]

21. Many societies, for example, continue to view homosexuality, bisexuality, and/or transgender behaviour or persons, as variously reflecting a disease, a mental illness or moral failing, and they may thus deploy various measures to try to change or alter someone's sexual orientation and/or gender identity. Efforts to change an individual's sexual orientation or gender identity by force or coercion may constitute torture, or inhuman or degrading treatment, and implicate other serious human rights violations, including the rights to liberty and security of person. Examples at the extreme end and which on their face reach the threshold of persecution include forced institutionalization, forced sex-reassignment surgery, forced electroshock therapy and forced drug injection or hormonal therapy.[46] Non-consensual medical and scientific experimentation is also explicitly identified as a form of torture or inhuman or degrading treatment under the International Covenant on Civil and Political Rights.[47] Some intersex individuals may be forced to undergo surgery aimed at "normalcy" and, where it will be applied without their consent, this is likely to amount to persecution. It is also important to distinguish in these cases between surgery necessary to preserve life or health and surgery for cosmetic purposes or social conformity. The assessment needs to focus on whether the surgery or treatment was voluntary and took place with the informed consent of the individual.[48]

Articles 7 (1) (g)-1 and 8(2)(b)(xxii)-1. For refugee-related jurisprudence, see *Ayala v. US Attorney General*, US, No. 09-12113, (11th Cir. 2010), 7 May 2010 (hereafter "*Ayala v. US Attorney General*"), available at: <http://www.unhcr.org/refworld/docid/4c6c04942.html>, which found that oral rape constituted persecution.

[44] *Aydin v. Turkey*, 57/1996/676/866, Council of Europe, European Court of Human Rights, 25 September 1997, available at: <http://www.unhcr.org/refworld/docid/3ae6b7228.html>, para. 83. See also, *HS (Homosexuals: Minors, Risk on Return) Iran v. Secretary of State for the Home Department* [2005] UKAIT 00120, UK Asylum and Immigration Tribunal (AIT), 4 August 2005, available at <http://www.unhcr.org/refworld/docid/47fdfafe0.html>, recognizing as torture the sexual assault the applicant had been subjected to while in detention, paras. 57, 134; *Arrêt n° 36 527*, Belgium: Conseil du Contentieux des Etrangers, 22 December 2009, available at: <http://www.unhcr.org/refworld/docid/4dad94692.html>, referring to torture and serious violations of the appellant's physical integrity while in prison as constituting persecution.

[45] *The Prosecutor v. Jean-Paul Akayesu (Trial Judgment)*, ICTR-96-4-T, International Criminal Tribunal for Rwanda, 2 September 1998, available at: <http://www.unhcr.org/refworld/docid/40278fbb4.html>, para. 687.

[46] Yogyakarta Principles, Principle 18: "Notwithstanding any classifications to the contrary, a person's sexual orientation and gender identity are not, in and of themselves, medical conditions and are not to be treated, cured or suppressed". See also, *Alla Konstantinova Pitcherskaia v. Immigration and Naturalization Service*, US, 95-70887, (9th Cir. 1997), 24 June 1997 (hereafter "*Pitcherskaia v. INS*"), available at: <http://www.unhcr.org/refworld/docid/4152e0fb26.html>.

[47] ICCPR, Article 7, ". . . In particular, no one shall be subjected without his free consent to medical or scientific experimentation". As affirmed, for example, by the UN Committee Against Torture and the UN Special Rapporteur on Torture and Other Cruel, Inhuman or Degrading Treatment or Punishment, this includes subjecting men suspected of homosexual conduct to non-consensual anal examinations to prove their homosexuality. See further, OHCHR, Report on Sexual Orientation and Gender Identity, para. 37.

[48] See, UN Committee on the Elimination of Discrimination against Women (CEDAW), *Communication No. 4/2004*, 29 August 2006, CEDAW/C/36/D/4/2004, available at: <http://www

22. Detention, including in psychological or medical institutions, on the sole basis of sexual orientation and/or gender identity is considered in breach of the international prohibition against the arbitrary deprivation of liberty and would normally constitute persecution.[49] Moreover, as noted by the United Nations Special Rapporteur on Torture and Other Cruel, Inhuman or Degrading Treatment or Punishment, there is usually a strict hierarchy in detention facilities and those at the bottom of this hierarchy, such as LGBTI detainees, suffer multiple discrimination. Male-to-female transgender prisoners are at particular risk of physical and sexual abuse if placed within the general male prison population.[50] Administrative segregation, or solitary confinement, solely because a person is LGBTI can also result in severe psychological harm.[51]

Social norms and values, including so-called family "honour", are usually closely intertwined in the refugee claims of LGBTI individuals. While "mere" disapproval from family or community will not amount to persecution, it may be an important factor in the overall context of the claim. Where family or community disapproval, for example, manifests itself in threats of serious physical violence or even murder by family members or the wider community, committed in the name of "honour", it would clearly be classed as persecution.[52] Other forms of persecution include forced or underage marriage, forced pregnancy and/or marital rape (on rape, see above at paragraph 20). In the context of sexual orientation and/or gender identity cases, such forms of persecution are often used as a means of denial or "correcting" non-conformity. Lesbians, bisexual women

.unhcr.org/refworld/docid/4fdb288e2.html>, which considered non-consensual sterilization as a violation of women's rights to informed consent and dignity, para. 11.3. In respect of surgery at birth, the best interests of the child is a primary consideration, taking into account the rights and duties of his or her parents, legal guardians, or other individuals legally responsible for him or her (Convention on the Rights of the Child (CRC), Article 3). If sex re-assignment or reconstructive surgery is contemplated only later in childhood, "States Parties shall assure to the child who is capable of forming his or her own views the right to express those views freely in all matters affecting the child, the views of the child being given due weight in accordance with the age and maturity of the child" (CRC, Article 12(1)).

[49] See, UN Working Group on Arbitrary Detention, Opinions No. 22/2006 on Cameroon and No. 42/2008 on Egypt; A/HRC/16/47, annex, para. 8(e). See also, UNHCR, "Guidelines on the Applicable Criteria and Standards relating to the Detention of Asylum-Seekers and Alternatives to Detention", 2012, (hereafter "UNHCR, Guidelines on Detention"), available at: <http://www.unhcr.org/refworld/docid/503489533b8.html>.

[50] OHCHR, Report on Sexual Orientation and Gender Identity, para. 34.

[51] As noted in the UNHCR Guidelines on Detention, "solitary confinement is not an appropriate way to manage or ensure the protection of such individuals", para. 65.

[52] UN Human Rights Committee and the Inter-American Commission on Human Rights have concluded that the inaction of State vis-à-vis death threats constitutes a violation of the right to life. See also, *RRT Case No. 0902671*, [2009] RRTA 1053, Australia, Refugee Review Tribunal, 19 November 2009, available at: <http://www.unhcr.org/refworld/docid/4b57016f2.html>, which found that the "applicant's chance of facing serious harm, possibly death by honour killing, if he returned to [the country of origin] now or in the reasonably foreseeable future is real and amounts to serious harm . . . in that it is deliberate or intentional and invol ves persecution for a Convention reason". See also, *Muckette v. Minister of Citizenship and Immigration*, 2008 FC 1388, Canada, Federal Court, 17 December 2008, available at: <http://www.unhcr.org/refworld/docid/4989a27e2.html>. The case was remanded for reconsideration as the lower instance had "failed to address whether the death threats had a degree of reality to them and in effect dismissed them because no one had attempted to kill the Applicant".

and transgender persons are at particular risk of such harms owing to pervasive gender inequalities that restrict autonomy in decision-making about sexuality, reproduction and family life.[53]

24. LGBTI individuals may also be unable to enjoy fully their human rights in matters of private and family law, including inheritance, custody, visitation rights for children and pension rights.[54] Their rights to freedom of expression, association and assembly may be restricted.[55] They may also be denied a range of economic and social rights, including in relation to housing, education,[56] and health care.[57] Young LGBTI individuals may be prevented from going to school, subjected to harassment and bullying and/or expelled. Community ostracism can have a damaging impact on the mental health of those targeted, especially if such ostracism has lasted for an extended period of time and where it occurs with impunity or disregard. The cumulative effect of such restrictions on the exercise of human rights may constitute persecution in a given case.

25. LGBTI individuals may also experience discrimination in access to and maintenance of employment.[58] Their sexual orientation and/or gender identity may be exposed in the workplace with resulting harassment, demotion or dismissal. For transgender individuals in particular, deprivation of employment, often combined with lack of housing and family support, may frequently force them into sex work, subjecting them to a variety of physical dangers and health risks. While being dismissed from a job generally is not considered persecution, even if discriminatory or unfair, if an individual can demonstrate that his or her LGBTI identity would make it highly improbable to enjoy any kind of gainful employment in the country of origin, this may constitute persecution.[59]

Laws criminalizing same-sex relations

26. Many lesbian, gay or bisexual applicants come from countries of origin in which consensual same-sex relations are criminalized. It is well established that such criminal laws are discriminatory and violate international human rights norms.[60] Where persons are at risk of persecution or punishment such as by the death penalty, prison terms, or severe corporal punishment, including flogging, their persecutory character is particularly evident.[61]

[53] OHCHR, Report on Sexual Orientation and Gender Identity, para. 66.
[54] *Ibid*, paras. 68–70.
[55] *Ibid*, paras. 62–65.
[56] *Ibid*, paras. 58–61.
[57] *Ibid*, paras. 54–57.
[58] *Ibid*, paras. 51–53.
[59] USCIS, Guidance for Adjudicating LGBTI Claims, p. 23. See also, *Kadri v. Mukasey*, US, Nos. 06-2599 & 07-1754, (1st Cir. 2008), 30 September 2008, available at: <http://www.unhcr.org/refworld/docid/498b0a212.html>. The case was remanded for consideration of the standard for economic persecution, referring to *In re T-Z-*, 24 I & N. Dec. 163 (US Board of Immigration Appeals, 2007), which had found that " '[nonphysical] harm or suffering . . . such as the deliberate imposition of severe economic disadvantage or the deprivation of liberty, food, housing, employment, or other essentials of life may rise to persecution".
[60] See, for example, *Toonen v. Australia,* above footnote 11, which found that the sodomy law of the territory concerned violated the rights to privacy and equality before the law.
[61] European Union, European Parliament, Directive 2011/95/EU of the European Parliament and of the Council of 13 December 2011 on standards for the qualification of third-country nationals or stateless persons as beneficiaries of international protection, for a uniform status for refugees or for persons eligible for subsidiary protection, and for the content of the protection granted (recast),

27. Even if irregularly, rarely or ever enforced, criminal laws prohibiting same-sex relations could lead to an intolerable predicament for an LGB person rising to the level of persecution. Depending on the country context, the criminalization of same-sex relations can create or contribute to an oppressive atmosphere of intolerance and generate a threat of prosecution for having such relations. The existence of such laws can be used for blackmail and extortion purposes by the authorities or non-State actors. They can promote political rhetoric that can expose LGB individuals to risks of persecutory harm. They can also hinder LGB persons from seeking and obtaining State protection.

28. Assessing the "well-founded fear of being persecuted" in such cases needs to be fact-based, focusing on both the individual and the contextual circumstances of the case. The legal system in the country concerned, including any relevant legislation, its interpretation, application and actual impact on the applicant needs to be examined.[62] The "fear" element refers not only to persons to whom such laws have already been applied, but also to individuals who wish to avoid the risk of the application of such laws to them. Where the country of origin information does not establish whether or not, or the extent, that the laws are actually enforced, a pervading and generalized climate of homophobia in the country of origin could be evidence indicative that LGBTI persons are nevertheless being persecuted.

29. Even where consensual same-sex relations are not criminalized by specific provisions, laws of general application, for example, public morality or public order laws (loitering, for example) may be selectively applied and enforced against LGBTI individuals in a discriminatory manner, making life intolerable for the claimant, and thus amounting to persecution.[63]

Concealment of sexual orientation and/or gender identity

30. LGBTI individuals frequently keep aspects and sometimes large parts of their lives secret. Many will not have lived openly as LGBTI in their country of origin and some may not have had any intimate relationships. Many suppress their sexual orientation and/or gender identity to avoid the severe consequences of discovery, including the risk of incurring harsh criminal penalties, arbitrary house raids, discrimination, societal disapproval, or family exclusion.

31. That an applicant may be able to avoid persecution by concealing or by being "discreet" about his or her sexual orientation or gender identity, or has done so previously, is

(hereafter "EU Qualification Directive"), Article 9; COC and Vrije Universiteit Amsterdam, *Fleeing Homophobia, Asylum Claims Related to Sexual Orientation and Gender Identity in Europe*, September 2011 (hereafter "Fleeing Homophobia Report") available at: <http://www.unhcr.org/refworld/docid/4ebba7852.html>, pp. 22–24. See also *Arrêt n° 50 966*, Belgium, Conseil du Contentieux des Etrangers, 9 November 2010, available at: <http://www.unhcr.org/refworld/docid/4dad967f2.html>, concerning a lesbian, found that a prison term for homosexual conduct of 1–5 years and fines from 000 à 1 500 000 francs CFA and the fact that society was homophobic were sufficient grounds to constitute persecution in the circumstances of the case, para. Similarly in *Arrêt n° 50 967*, Belgium, Conseil du Contentieux des Etrangers, 9 November 2010, available at: <http://www.unhcr.org/refworld/docid/4dad97d92.html>, concerning a gay man.

[62] UNHCR, *Handbook*, para. 45.

[63] *RRT Case No. 1102877*, [2012] RRTA 101, Australia, Refugee Review Tribunal, 23 February 2012, available at: <http://www.unhcr.org/refworld/docid/4f8410a52.html>, paras. 89, 96; *RRT Case No. 071862642*, [2008] RRTA 40, Australia: Refugee Review Tribunal, 19 February 2008, available at: <http://www.unhcr.org/refworld/docid/4811a7192.html>.

not a valid reason to deny refugee status. As affirmed by numerous decisions in multiple jurisdictions, a person cannot be denied refugee status based on a requirement that they change or conceal their identity, opinions or characteristics in order to avoid persecution.[64] LGBTI people are as much entitled to freedom of expression and association as others.[65]

32. With this general principle in mind, the question thus to be considered is what predicament the applicant would face if he or she were returned to the country of origin. This requires a fact-specific examination of what may happen if the applicant returns to the country of nationality or habitual residence and whether this amounts to persecution. The question is not, could the applicant, by being discreet, live in that country without attracting adverse consequences. It is important to note that even if applicants may so far have managed to avoid harm through concealment, their circumstances may change over time and secrecy may not be an option for the entirety of their lifetime. The risk of discovery may also not necessarily be confined to their own conduct. There is almost always the possibility of discovery against the person's will, for example, by accident, rumours or growing suspicion.[66] It is also important to recognize that even if LGBTI individuals conceal their sexual orientation or gender identity they may still be at risk of exposure and related harm for not following expected social norms (for example, getting married and having children, for example). The absence of certain expected activities and behaviour identifies a difference between them and other people and may place them at risk of harm.[67]

33. Being compelled to conceal one's sexual orientation and/or gender identity may also result in significant psychological and other harms. Discriminatory and disapproving attitudes, norms and values may have a serious effect on the mental and physical health

[64] For example, *HJ and HT*, above footnote 30; UNHCR, *HJ and HT,* above footnote 30, paras. 26–33; *S395/2002,* above footnote 31*; Refugee Appeal No. 74665,* above footnote 31; *Karouni,* above footnote 32*; KHO:2012:1*, Finland, Supreme Administrative Court, 13 January 2012, available at: <http://www.unhcr.org/refworld/docid/4f3cdf7e2.html>. See also, UNHCR, "Guidelines on International Protection No. 2: "Membership of a Particular Social Group" Within the Context of Article 1A(2) of the 1951 Convention and/or its 1967 Protocol Relating to the Status of Refugees", 7 May 2002, HCR/GIP/02/02 (hereafter "UNHCR, Guidelines on Social Group"), available at: <http://www.unhcr.org/refworld/docid/3d36f23f4.html>, paras. 6, 12; UNHCR, "Guidelines on International Protection No. 6: Religion-Based Refugee Claims under Article 1A(2) of the 1951 Convention and/or the 1967 Protocol relating to the Status of Refugees", 28 April 2004, HCR/GIP/04/06, (hereafter "UNHCR, Guidelines on Religion"), para. 13; UNHCR, *Secretary of State for the Home Department (Appellant) v. RT (Zimbabwe), SM (Zimbabwe) and AM (Zimbabwe) (Respondents) and the United Nations High Commissioner for Refugees (Intervener) - Case for the Intervener*, 25 May 2012, 2011/0011, available at: <http://www.unhcr.org/refworld/docid/4fc369022.html>, para. 9.

[65] As noted by the UK Supreme Court in *HJ and HT*, above footnote 30: "The underlying rationale of the Convention is . . . that people should be able to live freely, without fearing that they may suffer harm of the requisite intensity or duration because they are, say, black, or the descendants of some former dictator, or gay. In the absence of any indication to the contrary, the implication is that they must be free to live openly in this way without fear of persecution. By allowing them to live openly and free from that fear, the receiving state affords them protection which is a surrogate for the protection which their home state should have afforded them", para. 53.

[66] *S395/2002*, above footnote 31, paras. 56–58.

[67] *SW (lesbians - HJ and HT applied) Jamaica v. Secretary of State for the Home Department*, UK, CG [2011] UKUT 00251(IAC), Upper Tribunal (Immigration and Asylum Chamber), 24 June 2011, available at: <http://www.unhcr.org/refworld/docid/4e0c3fae2.html>.

of LGBTI individuals[68] and could in particular cases lead to an intolerable predicament amounting to persecution.[69] Feelings of self-denial, anguish, shame, isolation and even self-hatred which may accrue in response an inability to be open about one's sexuality or gender identity are factors to consider, including over the long-term.

Agents of Persecution

34. There is scope within the refugee definition to recognize persecution emanating from both State and non-State actors. State persecution may be perpetrated, for example, through the criminalization of consensual same-sex conduct and the enforcement of associated laws, or as a result of harm inflicted by officials of the State or those under the control of the State, such as the police or the military. Individual acts of "rogue" officers may still be considered as State persecution, especially where the officer is a member of the police and other agencies that purport to protect people.[70]

35. In situations where the threat of harm is from non-State actors, persecution is established where the State is unable or unwilling to provide protection against such harm. Non-State actors, including family members, neighbours, or the broader community, may be either directly or indirectly involved in persecutory acts, including intimidation, harassment, domestic violence, or other forms of physical, psychological or sexual violence. In some countries, armed or violent groups, such as paramilitary and rebel groups, as well as criminal gangs and vigilantes, may target LGBTI individuals specifically.[71]

36. In scenarios involving non-State agents of persecution, State protection from the claimed fear has to be available and effective.[72] State protection would normally neither be considered available nor effective, for instance, where the police fail to respond to requests

[68] Discrimination of LGBTI individuals has been associated with mental health problems. Studies have shown that internalized negative attitudes towards non-heterosexuality in LGB individuals was related to difficulties with self-esteem, depression, psychosocial and psychological distress, physical health, intimacy, social support, relationship quality, and career development. See further, APA, "Practice Guidelines for LGB Clients, Guidelines for Psychological Practice with Lesbian, Gay, and Bisexual Clients" (hereafter "APA, Practice Guidelines for LGB Clients"), available at: <http://www.apa.org/pi/lgbt/resources/guidelines.aspx?item=3>.

[69] *Pathmakanthan v. Holder*, US, 612 F.3d 618, 623 (7th Cir. 2010), available at: <http://www.unhcr.org/refworld/docid/4d249efa2.html>.

[70] See *Ayala v. US Attorney General*, above footnote 42. The treatment by a group of police officers (robbery and sexual assault) constituted persecution and was deemed to be on account of the applicant's sexual orientation.

[71] *P.S., a/k/a S.J.P., v. Holder, Attorney General*, US, No. 09-3291, Agency No. A99-473-409, (3rd Cir. 2010), 22 June 2010, available at: <http://www.unhcr.org/refworld/docid/4fbf263f2.html>, concerned a gay man who was targeted by a non-State armed group. See also, *RRT Case No. N98/22948*, [2000] RRTA 1055, Australia, Refugee Review Tribunal, 2 November 2000, available at: <http://www.unhcr.org/refworld/docid/4b7a97fd2.html>, which found that the applicant was at risk of persecution at the hands of vigilante groups. The identification of poor gay men as "disposables" put them at risk of "social clean up" operations.

[72] UNHCR, *Handbook*, paras. 97–101; UN Human Rights Committee, General Comment no. 31 [80], The nature of the general legal obligation imposed on States Parties to the Covenant, 26 May 2004, CCPR/C/21/Rev.1/Add.13, available at: <http://www.unhcr.org/refworld/docid/478b26ae2.html>, paras. 8, 15–16; CEDAW, General Recommendation No. 28 on the Core Obligations of States Parties under Article 2 of the Convention on the Elimination of All Forms of Discrimination against Women, 19 October 2010, CEDAW/C/2010/47/GC.2, available at: <http://www.unhcr.org/refworld/docid/4d467ea72.html>, para. 36.

for protection or the authorities refuse to investigate, prosecute or punish (non-State) perpetrators of violence against LGBTI individuals with due diligence.[73] Depending on the situation in the country of origin, laws criminalizing same-sex relations are normally a sign that protection of LGB individuals is not available. Where the country of origin maintains such laws, it would be unreasonable to expect that the applicant first seek State protection against harm based on what is, in the view of the law, a criminal act. In such situations, it should be presumed, in the absence of evidence to the contrary, that the country concerned is unable or unwilling to protect the applicant.[74] As in other types of claims, a claimant does not need to show that he or she approached the authorities for protection before flight. Rather he or she has to establish that the protection was not or unlikely to be available or effective upon return.

37. Where the legal and socio-economic situation of LGBTI people is improving in the country of origin, the availability and effectiveness of State protection needs to be carefully assessed based on reliable and up-to-date country of origin information. The reforms need to be more than merely transitional. Where laws criminalizing same-sex conduct have been repealed or other positive measures have been taken, such reforms may not impact in the immediate or foreseeable future as to how society generally regards people with differing sexual orientation and/or gender identity.[75] The existence of certain elements, such as anti-discrimination laws or presence of LGBTI organizations and events, do not necessarily undermine the well-foundedness of the applicant's fear.[76] Societal attitudes may not be in line with the law and prejudice may be entrenched, with a continued risk where the authorities fail to enforce protective laws.[77] A *de facto,* not merely *de jure,* change is required and an analysis of the circumstances of each particular case is essential.

C. The causal link ("for reasons of")

38. As with other types of refugee claims, the well-founded fear of persecution must be "for reasons of" one or more of the five grounds contained in the refugee definition in Article 1A(2) of the 1951 Convention. The Convention ground should be a contributing factor to the well-founded fear of persecution, though it need not be the sole, or even dominant, cause.

[73] See, for example, UK Home Office, "Sexual Orientation Issues in the Asylum Claim", 6 October 2011, available at: <http://www.unhcr.org/refworld/docid/4eb8f0982.html>, p. 6.

[74] UNHCR, Summary Conclusions of Roundtable, para. 8.

[75] *RRT Case No. 0905785*, [2010] RRTA 150, Australia, Refugee Review Tribunal, 7 March 2010, available at: <http://www.unhcr.org/refworld/docid/4c220be62.html>, found that the decriminalization of homosexual acts in the particular country was unlikely to have an immediate impact on how people viewed homosexuality, para. 88.

[76] USCIS, Guidance for Adjudicating LGBTI Claims, p. 25. See also *Guerrero v. Canada (Minister of Citizenship and Immigration)*, 2011 FC 860, Canada, Federal Court, 8 July 2011, available at: <http://www.unhcr.org/refworld/docid/4fa952572.html>, which noted that the presence of many non-governmental organizations that fight against discrimination based on sexual orientation is in itself a telling factor in considering the country conditions.

[77] See, *Judgment No. 616907, K,* France, Cour nationale du droit d'asile, 6 April 2009, summary available at *Contentieux des réfugiés: Jurisprudence du Conseild'État et de la Cour nationale du droit d'asile - Année 2009*, 26 October 2010, available at: <http://www.unhcr.org/refworld/docid/4dad9db02.html>, pp. 61–62, which recognized as a refugee a gay man from a particular territory based on the fact that even though a 2004 law banned all discrimination on the basis of sexual orientation those showing their homosexuality in public were regularly subject to harassment and discrimination without being able to avail themselves of the protection of the authorities.

39. Perpetrators may rationalize the violence they inflict on LGBTI individuals by reference to the intention of "correcting", "curing" or "treating" the person. [78] The intent or motive of the persecutor can be a relevant factor to establishing the "causal link" but it is not a prerequisite.[79] There is no need for the persecutor to have a punitive intent to establish the causal link.[80] The focus is on the reasons for the applicant's feared predicament within the overall context of the case, and how he or she would experience the harm rather than on the mind-set of the perpetrator. Nonetheless, where it can be shown that the persecutor attributes or imputes a Convention ground to the applicant, this is sufficient to satisfy the causal link.[81] Where the persecutor is a non-State actor, the causal link may be established either where the non-State actor is likely to harm the LGBTI person for a Convention reason or the State is not likely to protect him or her for a Convention reason.[82]

D. Convention grounds

40. The five Convention grounds, that is, race, religion, nationality, membership of a particular social group and political opinion, are not mutually exclusive and may overlap. More than one Convention ground may be relevant in a given case. Refugee claims based on sexual orientation and/or gender identity are most commonly recognized under the "membership of a particular social group" ground. Other grounds may though also be relevant depending on the political, religious and cultural context of the claim. For example, LGBTI activists and human rights defenders (or perceived activists/defenders) may have either or both claims based on political opinion or religion if, for example, their advocacy is seen as going against prevailing political or religious views and/or practices.

41. Individuals may be subject to persecution due to their actual or perceived sexual orientation or gender identity. The opinion, belief or membership may be attributed to the applicant by the State or the non-State agent of persecution, even if they are not in fact LGBTI, and based on this perception they may be persecuted as a consequence. For example, women and men who do not fit stereotyped appearances and roles may be perceived as LGBTI. It is not required that they actually be LGBTI.[83] Transgender individuals often experience harm based on imputed sexual orientation. Partners of transgender individuals may be perceived as gay or lesbian or simply as not conforming to accepted gender roles and behaviour or associating themselves with transgender individuals.

[78] Yogyakarta Principles, Principle 18.

[79] UNHCR, *Handbook*, para. 66.

[80] *Pitcherskaia v. INS*, above footnote 45, found that the requirement on the applicant to prove the punitive intent of the perpetrator was unwarranted.

[81] UNHCR, "Interpreting Article 1 of the 1951 Convention Relating to the Status of Refugees", April 2001, available at: <http://www.unhcr.org/refworld/docid/3b20a3914.html>, para. 19.

[82] UNHCR, Guidelines on Social Group, para. 23.

[83] UNHCR, Guidelines on Gender-Related Persecution, para. 32; UNHCR, *Advisory Opinion by UNHCR to the Tokyo Bar Association Regarding Refugee Claims Based on Sexual Orientation*, 3 September 2004, available at: <http://www.unhcr.org/refworld/docid/4551c0d04.html>, para. 5. See also, *Kwasi Amanfi v. John Ashcroft, Attorney General*, US, Nos. 01-4477 and 02-1541, (3rd Cir. 2003), 16 May 2003, available at: <http://www.unhcr.org/refworld/docid/47fdfb2c1a.html>, which concerned an applicant who claimed persecution on account of imputed homosexuality.

Religion

42. Where an individual is viewed as not conforming to the teachings of a particular religion on account of his or her sexual orientation or gender identity, and is subjected to serious harm or punishment as a consequence, he or she may have a well-founded fear of persecution for reasons of religion.[84] The teachings of the world's major religions on sexual orientation and/or gender identity differ and some have also changed over time or in particular contexts, ranging from outright condemnation, including viewing homosexuality as an "abomination", "sin", "disorder " or apostasy, to complete acceptance of diverse sexual orientation and/or gender identity. Non-LGBTI persons may also be subject to persecution for reasons of religion, for example, where they are (wrongly) perceived as LGBTI or where they support or are seen to support them or their rights.

43. Negative attitudes held by religious groups and communities towards LGBTI individuals can be given expression in a range of ways, from discouraging same-sex activity, or transgender behaviour or expression of identity, among adherents to active opposition, including protests, beatings, naming/shaming and "excommunication", or even execution. The religion and political opinion grounds may overlap where religious and State institutions are not clearly separated.[85] Religious organizations may impute opposition to their teachings or governance by LGBTI individuals, whether or not this is the case. LGBTI applicants may continue to profess adherence to a faith in which they have been subject to harm or a threat of harm.

Membership of a Particular Social Group

44. The 1951 Convention includes no specific list of particular social groups. Rather, "the term membership of a particular social group should be read in an evolutionary manner, open to the diverse and changing nature of groups in various societies and evolving international human rights norms."[86] UNHCR defines a particular social group as:

> a group of persons who share a common characteristic other than their risk of being persecuted, *or* who are perceived as a group by society. The characteristic will often be one which is innate, unchangeable, or which is otherwise fundamental to identity, conscience or the exercise of one's human rights.[87]

45. The two approaches – "protected characteristics" and "social perception" – to identifying "particular social groups" reflected in this definition are *alternative*, not cumulative tests. The "protected characteristics" approach examines whether a group is united *either* by an innate or immutable characteristic *or* by a characteristic that is so fundamental to human dignity that a person should not be compelled to forsake it. The "social perception" approach, on the other hand, examines whether a particular social group shares a common characteristic which makes it cognizable or sets the group's members apart from society at large.

46. Whether applying the "protected characteristics" or "social perception" approach, there is broad acknowledgment that under a correct application of either of these

[84] UNHCR, Guidelines on Gender-Related Persecution, para. 25. See by analogy, *In Re S-A*, Interim Decision No. 3433, US Board of Immigration Appeals, 27 June 2000, available at: <http://www.unhcr.org/refworld/docid/3ae6b6f224.html>.

[85] UNHCR, Guidelines on Gender-Related Persecution, para. 26.

[86] UNHCR, Guidelines on Social Group, para. 3.

[87] UNHCR, Guidelines on Social Group, para. 11. Emphasis added.

approaches, lesbians,[88] gay men,[89] bisexuals[90] and transgender persons[91] are members of "particular social groups" within the meaning of the refugee definition.[92] Relatively fewer claims have been made by intersex applicants, but they would also on their face qualify under either approach.

47. Sexual orientation and/or gender identity are considered as innate and immutable characteristics or as characteristics so fundamental to human dignity that the person should not be compelled to forsake them. Where the identity of the applicant is still evolving, they may describe their sexual orientation and/or gender identity as fluid or they may express confusion or uncertainty about their sexuality and/or identity. In both situations, these characteristics are in any event to be considered as fundamental to their evolving identity and rightly within the social group ground.

48. There is no requirement that members of the social group associate with one another, or that they are socially visible, for the purposes of the refugee definition. "Social perception" does not mean to suggest a sense of community or group identification as might exist for members of an organization or association. Thus, members of a social group may not be recognizable even to each other.[93]

49. Decision makers should avoid reliance on stereotypes or assumptions, including visible markers, or a lack thereof. This can be misleading in establishing an applicant's membership of a particular social group. Not all LGBTI individuals look or behave according to stereotypical notions. In addition, although an attribute or characteristic expressed visibly may reinforce a finding that an applicant belongs to an LGBTI social group, it is not a pre-condition for recognition of the group.[94] In fact, a group of individuals may seek to avoid manifesting their characteristics in society precisely to avoid persecution (see above

[88] See, for example, *Pitcherskaia v. INS*, above footnote 45; *Decisions VA0-01624 and VA0-01625 (In Camera)*, Canada, Immigration and Refugee Board, 14 May 2001, available at: <http://www.unhcr.org/refworld/docid/48246f092.html>; *Islam (A.P.) v. Secretary of State for the Home Department; R v. Immigration Appeal Tribunal and Another, Ex Parte Shah (A.P.)*, UK House of Lords (Judicial Committee), 25 March 1999, available at: <http://www.unhcr.org/refworld/docid/3dec8abe4.html>, pp. 8–10.

[89] See, for example. *Matter of Toboso-Alfonso*, above footnote 32; *Refugee Appeal No. 1312/93, Re GJ*, New Zealand, Refugee Status Appeals Authority, 30 August 1995, available at: <http://www.unhcr.org/refworld/docid/3ae6b6938.html>.

[90] See, for example, *VRAW v. Minister for Immigration and Multicultural and Indigenous Affairs*, [2004] FCA 1133, Australia, Federal Court, 3 September 2004, available at: <http://www.unhcr.org/refworld/docid/4dada05c2.html>; *Decision T98-04159*, Immigration and Refugee Board of Canada, 13 March 2000, available at: <http://www.unhcr.org/refworld/docid/4dada1672.html>.

[91] See, for example, *RRT Case No. 0903346*, above footnote 24; *CE, SSR, 23 Juin 1997, 171858, Ourbih*, 171858, France, Conseil d'Etat, 23 June 1997, available at: <http://www.unhcr.org/refworld/docid/3ae6b67c14.html>.

[92] Sexual orientation and/or gender identity has been explicitly included in the refugee definition in some regional and domestic legislation. For instance, the European Union has adopted a definition of particular social group, recognizing that "depending on the circumstances in the country of origin, a particular social group might include a group based on a common characteristic of sexual orientation", EU Qualification Directive, Article 10.

[93] UNHCR, Guidelines on Social Group, paras. 15–16.

[94] *Judgment No. 634565/08015025, C*, France, Cour nationale du droit d'asile, 7 July 2009, summary available at Contentieux des réfugiés: Jurisprudence du Conseil d'État et de la Cour nationale du droit d'asile - Année 2009, 26 October 2010, available at: <http://www.unhcr.org/refworld/docid/4dad9db02.html>, pp. 58–59, recognizing as a refugee a gay man who had neither claimed nor manifested his homosexuality openly.

paragraphs 30–33).[95] The "social perception" approach requires neither that the common attribute be literally visible to the naked eye nor that the attribute be easily identifiable by the general public.[96] It is furthermore not necessary that particular members of the group or their common characteristics be publicly known in a society. The determination rests simply on whether a group is "cognizable" or "set apart from society" in a more general, abstract sense.

Political Opinion

50. The term political opinion should be broadly interpreted to incorporate any opinion on any matter in which the machinery of State, society, or policy may be engaged.[97] It may include an opinion as to gender roles expected in the family or as regards education, work or other aspects of life.[98] The expression of diverse sexual orientation and gender identity can be considered political in certain circumstances, particularly in countries where such non-conformity is viewed as challenging government policy or where it is perceived as threatening prevailing social norms and values. Anti-LGBTI statements could be part of a State's official rhetoric, for example, denying the existence of homosexuality in the country or claiming that gay men and lesbians are not considered part of the national identity.

E. Internal Flight or Relocation Alternative

51. The concept of an internal flight or relocation alternative (IFA) refers to whether it is possible for an individual to be relocated to a specific area of the country where the risk of feared persecution would not be well-founded and where, given the particular circumstances of the case, the individual could reasonably be expected to establish him or herself and live a normal life.[99] Protection would need to be available in a genuine and meaningful way. United Nations agencies, non-governmental organizations, civil society and other non-State actors are not a substitute for State protection.

52. Within the context of the holistic assessment of a claim for refugee status, the assessment of whether or not there is an IFA requires two main analyses: (i) the relevance analysis[100] and (ii) the reasonableness analysis.[101] In considering the relevance and

[95] UNHCR, *HJ and HT,* above footnote 30, para. 26.

[96] See, for example, UNHCR, *Valdiviezo-Galdamez v. Holder, Attorney General. Brief of the United Nations High Commissioner for Refugees as Amicus Curiae in Support of the Petitioner,* 14 April 2009, available at: <http://www.unhcr.org/refworld/docid/49ef25102.html>; *Gatimi et al. v. Holder, Attorney General,* No. 08- 3197, United States Court of Appeals for the Seventh Circuit, 20 August 2009, available at: <http://www.unhcr.org/refworld/docid/4aba40332.html>.

[97] *Canada v. Ward,* above footnote 31.

[98] UNHCR, Guidelines on Gender-Related Persecution, para. 32.

[99] See UNHCR, "Guidelines on International Protection No. 4: 'Internal Flight or Relocation Alternative'Within the Context of Article 1A(2) of the 1951 Convention and/or 1967 Protocol Relating to the Status of Refugees", 23 July 2003, HCR/GIP/03/04 (hereafter "UNHCR, Guidelines on Internal Flight Alternative"), para. 6.

[100] The elements to be examined under this analysis are the following: Is the area of relocation practically, safely and legally accessible to the individual? Is the agent of persecution a State or non-State agent? Would the claimant be exposed to a risk of being persecuted or other serious harm upon relocation?

[101] The criterion to be examined under this analysis is: Can the claimant lead a relatively normal life without facing undue hardship?

reasonableness of a proposed site of internal flight or relocation, gender considerations must be taken into account.

53. In respect of the relevance analysis, if the country in question criminalizes same-sex relations and enforces the relevant legislation, it will normally be assumed that such laws are applicable in the entire territory. Where the fear of persecution is related to these laws, a consideration of IFA would not be relevant. Laws which do not allow a transgender or intersex individual to access and receive appropriate medical treatment if sought, or to change the gender markers on his or her documents, would also normally be applicable nationwide and should be taken into account when considering the proposed place of relocation.

54. Furthermore, intolerance towards LGBTI individuals tends to exist countrywide in many situations, and therefore an internal flight alternative will often not be available. Relocation is not a relevant alternative if it were to expose the applicant to the original or any new forms of persecution. IFA should not be relied upon where relocation involves (re-)concealment of one's sexual orientation and/or gender identity to be safe (see paragraphs 30-33).[102]

55. Some countries have seen social and political progress which is sometimes localized in urban areas and these locations may in certain circumstances constitute a relocation alternative. In this context, it is important to recall that the decision maker bears the burden of proof of establishing that an analysis of relocation is relevant to the particular case, including identifying the proposed place of relocation and collecting country of origin information about it (see further below at paragraph 66).[103]

56. In determining whether internal flight is reasonable, the decision maker needs to assess whether return to the proposed place of relocation would cause undue hardship, including by examining the applicant's personal circumstances;[104] the existence of past persecution; safety and security; respect for human rights; and possibility for economic survival.[105] The applicant needs to be able to access a minimum level of political, civil and socio-economic rights. Women may have lesser economic opportunities than men, or may be unable to live separately from male family members, and this should be evaluated in the overall context of the case.[106]

F. *Sur Place* Claims

57. A *sur place* claim arises after arrival in the country of asylum, either as a result of the applicant's activities in the country of asylum or as a consequence of events, which have occurred or are occurring in the applicant's country of origin since their departure.[107] *Sur*

[102] See, for example, *Okoli v. Canada (Minister of Citizenship and Immigration)*, 2009 FC 332, Canada, Federal Court, 31 March 2009, available at: <http://www.unhcr.org/refworld/docid/4a5b4bfa2.html>, which found that the concealment of an immutable characteristic, that is, the applicant's sexual orientation, was an "impermissible requirement" for the assessment of internal flight alternative, paras. 36–37, 39; *HJ and HT*, above footnote 30. para. 21.
[103] UNHCR, Guidelines on Internal Flight Alternative, paras. 33–34.
[104] *Boer-Sedano v. Gonzales*, US, 418 F.3d 1082, (9th Cir. 2005), 12 August 2005, available at: <http://www.unhcr.org/refworld/docid/4821a2ba2.html>, found that the applicant's [HIV-positive] health status would make relocation unreasonable.
[105] UNHCR, Guidelines on Internal Flight Alternative, paras. 22–30.
[106] UNHCR, Guidelines on Gender-related Persecution.
[107] UNHCR, *Handbook*, paras. 94, 96.

place claims may also arise due to changes in the personal identity or gender expression of the applicant after his or her arrival in the country of asylum. It should be noted that some LGBTI applicants may not have identified themselves as LGBTI before the arrival to the country of asylum or may have consciously decided not to act on their sexual orientation or gender identity in their country of origin. Their fear of persecution may thus arise or find expression whilst they are in the country of asylum, giving rise to a refugee claim *sur place*. Many such claims arise where an LGBTI individual engages in political activism or media work or their sexual orientation is exposed by someone else.

V. Procedural Issues

General

58. LGBTI individuals require a supportive environment throughout the refugee status determination procedure, including pre-screening so that they can present their claims fully and without fear. A safe environment is equally important during consultations with legal representatives.

59. Discrimination, hatred and violence in all its forms can impact detrimentally on the applicant's capacity to present a claim. Some may be deeply affected by feelings of shame, internalized homophobia and trauma, and their capacity to present their case may be greatly diminished as a consequence. Where the applicant is in the process of coming to terms with his or her identity or fears openly expressing his or her sexual orientation and gender identity, he or she may be reluctant to identify the true extent of the persecution suffered or feared.[108] Adverse judgements should not generally be drawn from someone not having declared their sexual orientation or gender identity at the screening phase or in the early stages of the interview. Due to their often complex nature, claims based on sexual orientation and/or gender identity are generally unsuited to accelerated processing or the application of "safe country or origin" concepts. [109]

60. In order to ensure that refugee claims relating to sexual orientation and/or gender identity are properly considered during the refugee status determination process, the following measures should be borne in mind:

i. An open and reassuring environment is often crucial to establishing trust between the interviewer and applicant and will assist the disclosure of personal and sensitive information. At the beginning of the interview, the interviewer needs to assure the applicant that all aspects of his or her claim will be treated in confidence.[110] Interpreters are also bound by confidentiality.

ii. Interviewers and decision makers need to maintain an objective approach so that they do not reach conclusions based on stereotypical, inaccurate or inappropriate perceptions of LGBTI individuals. The presence or absence of certain stereotypical behaviours or appearances should not be relied upon to conclude that an applicant possesses or does not possess a given sexual orientation or gender identity.[111] There are no universal

[108] Some LGBTI applicants may, for instance, change their claims during the process by initially stating that their sexual orientation is imputed to them or making a claim on a ground unrelated to their sexual orientation or gender identity, to eventually expressing that they are LGBTI.

[109] UNHCR, "Statement on the right to an effective remedy in relation to accelerated asylum procedures", 21 May 2010, available at: <http://www.unhcr.org/refworld/docid/4bf67fa12.html>, paras. 11–12.

[110] UNHCR, Guidelines on Gender-Related Persecution, paras. 35, 36.iv.

[111] This issue has been addressed by a number of US Courts: *Shahinaj v. Gonzales*, 481 F.3d 1027,

characteristics or qualities that typify LGBTI individuals any more than heterosexual individuals. Their life experiences can vary greatly even if they are from the same country.

iii. The interviewer and the interpreter must avoid expressing, whether verbally or through body language, any judgement about the applicant's sexual orientation, gender identity, sexual behaviour or relationship pattern. Interviewers and interpreters who are uncomfortable with diversity of sexual orientation and gender identity may inadvertently display distancing or demeaning body language. Self-awareness and specialized training (see iv.) are therefore critical aspects to a fair status determination.

iv. Specialized training on the particular aspects of LGBTI refugee claims for decision makers, interviewers, interpreters, advocates and legal representatives is crucial.

v. The use of vocabulary that is non-offensive and shows positive disposition towards diversity of sexual orientation and gender identity, particularly in the applicant's own language, is essential.[112] Use of inappropriate terminology can hinder applicants from presenting the actual nature of their fear. The use of offensive terms may be part of the persecution, for example, in acts of bullying or harassment. Even seemingly neutral or scientific terms can have the same effect as pejorative terms. For instance, although widely used, "homosexual" is also considered a derogatory term in some countries.

vi. Specific requests made by applicants in relation to the gender of interviewers or interpreters should be considered favourably. This may assist the applicant to testify as openly as possible about sensitive issues. If the interpreter is from the same country, religion or cultural background, this may heighten the applicant's sense of shame and hinder him or her from fully presenting all the relevant aspects of the claim.

vii. Questioning about incidents of sexual violence needs to be conducted with the same sensitivity as in the case of any other sexual assault victims, whether victims are male or female.[113] Respect for the human dignity of the asylum-seeker should be a guiding principle at all times.[114]

viii. For claims based on sexual orientation and/or gender identity by women, additional safeguards are presented in UNHCR's Guidelines on Gender-Related Persecution.[115] Women asylum-seekers should, for instance, be interviewed separately, without the presence of male family members in order to ensure they have an opportunity to present their case.

ix. Specific procedural safeguards apply in the case of child applicants, including processing on a priority basis and the appointment of a qualified guardian as well as a legal representative.[116]

(8th Cir. 2007), 2 April 2007, available at: <http://www.unhcr.org/refworld/docid/4821bd462.html>; *Razkane v. Holder, Attorney General*, No. 08-9519, (10th Cir. 2009), 21 April 2009, available at: <http://www.unhcr.org/refworld/docid/4a5c97042.html>; *Todorovic v. US Attorney General*, No. 09-11652, (11th Cir. 2010), 27 September 2010, available at: <http://www.unhcr.org/refworld/docid/4cd968902.html>.

[112] For suggested appropriate terminology, see above at paras. 9–12.

[113] UNHCR, Guidelines on Gender-Related Persecution, para. 36 viii, xi.

[114] UNHCR, "Summary Report, Informal Meeting of Experts on Refugee Claims relating to Sexual Orientation and Gender Identity", 10 September 2011 (hereafter "UNHCR, Summary Report of Informal Meeting of Experts"), available at: <http://www.unhcr.org/refworld/docid/4fa910f92.html>, para. 34.

[115] UNHCR, Guidelines on Gender-Related Persecution paras. 35–37.

[116] UNHCR, "Guidelines on International Protection No. 8: Child Asylum Claims under Articles 1(A)2 and 1(F) of the 1951 Convention and/or 1967 Protocol relating to the Status of Refugees", 22 December 2009, HCR/GIP/09/08, available at: <http://www.unhcr.org/refworld/docid/4b2f4f6d2.html>, paras. 65–77.

61. Where an individual seeks asylum in a country where same-sex relations are criminalized, these laws can impede his or her access to asylum procedures or deter the person from mentioning his or her sexual orientation or gender identity within status determination interviews. In such situations, it may be necessary for UNHCR to become directly involved in the case, including by conducting refugee status determination under its mandate.[117]

Credibility and Establishing the Applicant's Sexual Orientation and/or Gender Identity

62. Ascertaining the applicant's LGBTI background is essentially an issue of credibility. The assessment of credibility in such cases needs to be undertaken in an individualized and sensitive way. Exploring elements around the applicant's personal perceptions, feelings and experiences of difference, stigma and shame are usually more likely to help the decision maker ascertain the applicant's sexual orientation or gender identity, rather than a focus on sexual practices.[118]

63. Both open-ended and specific questions that are crafted in a non-judgemental manner may allow the applicant to explain his or her claim in a non-confrontational way. Developing a list of questions in preparation of the interview may be helpful, however, it is important to bear in mind that there is no magic formula of questions to ask and no set of "right" answers in response. Useful areas of questioning may include the following:

i. Self-identification: Self-identification as a LGBTI person should be taken as an indication of the applicant's sexual orientation and/or gender identity. The social and cultural background of the applicant may affect how the person self-identifies. Some LGB individuals, for example, may harbour deep shame and/or internalized homophobia, leading them to deny their sexual orientation and/or to adopt verbal and physical behaviours in line with heterosexual norms and roles. Applicants from highly intolerant countries may, for instance, not readily identify as LGBTI. This alone should not rule out that the applicant could have a claim based on sexual orientation or gender identity where other indicators are present.

ii. Childhood: In some cases, before LGBTI individuals come to understand their own identity fully, they may feel "different" as children. When relevant, probing this experience of "difference" can be helpful to establishing the applicant's identity. The core attractions that form the basis for adult sexual orientation may emerge between middle childhood and early adolescence,[119] while some may not experience same-sex attraction until later in life. Likewise, persons may not be aware of their full gender identity until

[117] It is generally only where States have not yet acceded to the international refugee instruments, or if they have acceded but have not yet established national procedures, or these procedures are not fully functioning that UNHCR may be called upon to undertake individual refugee status determination and recognize refugees under its mandate. This function, therefore, can be exercised either in a State which is, or a State which is not, a signatory to the international refugee instruments. In these situations, UNHCR conducts refugee status determination for protection purposes (in order to protect refugees from *refoulement* and detention, for example) and/or to facilitate a durable solution. See, for example, UNHCR, *MM (Iran) v. Secretary of State for the Home Department - Written Submission on Behalf of the United Nations High Commissioner for Refugees*, 3 August 2010, C5/2009/2479, available at: <http://www.unhcr.org/refworld/docid/4c6aa7db2.html>, para. 11.

[118] UNHCR, Summary Report of Informal Meeting of Experts, para. 32.

[119] APA, Sexual Orientation and Homosexuality.

adolescence, early adulthood or later in life, as gender codes in many societies may be less prescriptive or strict during childhood than in (early) adulthood.

iii. Self-Realization: The expression "coming out" can mean both an LGBTI person's coming to terms with his or her own LGBTI identity and/or the individual communicating his or her identity to others. Questions about both of these "coming out" or self-realization processes may be a useful way to get the applicant talking about his or her identity, including in the country of origin as well as in the country of asylum. Some people know that they are LGBTI for a long time before, for example, they actually pursue relationships with other people, and/or they express their identity openly. Some, for example, may engage in sexual activity (with same-sex and/or other-sex partners) before assigning a clear label to their sexual orientation. Prejudice and discrimination may make it difficult for people to come to terms with their sexual orientation and/or gender identity and it can, therefore, be a slow process.[120]

iv. Gender identity: The fact that a transgender applicant has not undergone any medical treatment or other steps to help his or her outward appearance match the preferred identity should not be taken as evidence that the person is not transgender. Some transgender people identify with their chosen identity without medical treatment as part of their transition, while others do not have access to such treatment. It may be appropriate to ask questions about any steps that a transgender applicant has taken in his or her transition.

v. Non-conformity: LGBTI applicants may have grown up in cultures where their sexuality and/or gender identity is shameful or taboo. As a result, they may struggle with their sexual orientation or gender identity at some point in their lives. This may move them away from, or place them in opposition to their families, friends, communities and society in general. Experiences of disapproval and of "being different" or the "other" may result in feelings of shame, stigmatization or isolation.

vi. Family Relationships: Applicants may or may not have disclosed their sexual orientation and/or gender identity to close family members. Such disclosures may be fraught with difficulty and can lead to violent and abusive reactions by family members. As noted above, an applicant may be married, or divorced and/or have children. These factors by themselves do not mean that the applicant is not LGBTI. Should concerns of the credibility of an applicant who is married arise, it may be appropriate to ask the applicant a few questions surrounding the reasons for marriage. If the applicant is able to provide a consistent and reasonable explanation of why he or she is married and/or has children, the portion of the testimony should be found credible.[121]

vii. Romantic and Sexual Relationships: The applicant's relationships with and attraction to partners, or their hope to have future relationships, will usually be part of their narrative of LGBTI individuals. Not everyone, however, especially young LGBTI people, will have had romantic or sexual relationships. The fact that an applicant has not had any relationship(s) in the country of origin does not necessarily mean that he or she is not LGBTI. It may rather be an indication that he or she has been seeking to avoid harm. Presuming that the applicant has been involved in a same-sex relationship, decision makers need to be sensitive with regard to questioning about past and current relationships since it involves personal information which the applicant may be reluctant to discuss in an interview setting. Detailed questions about the applicant's sex life should be avoided. It is not an effective method of ascertaining the well-foundedness of the applicant's fear of

[120] APA, Sexual Orientation and Homosexuality.
[121] USCIS, Guidance for Adjudicating LGBTI Claims, pp. 39–40.

persecution on account of his or her sexual orientation and/or gender identity. Interviewers and decision makers need to bear in mind that sexual orientation and gender identity are about a person's identity, whether or not that identity is manifested through sexual acts.

viii. Community Relationship: Questions about the applicant's knowledge of LGBTI contacts, groups and activities in the country of origin and asylum may be useful. It is important to note, however, that applicants who were not open about their sexual orientation or gender identity in the country of origin may not have information about LGBTI venues or culture. For example, ignorance of commonly known meeting places and activities for LGBTI groups is not necessarily indicative of the applicant's lack of credibility. Lack of engagement with other members of the LGBTI community in the country of asylum or failure to join LGBTI groups there may be explained by economic factors, geographic location, language and/or cultural barriers, lack of such opportunities, personal choices or a fear of exposure.[122]

ix. Religion: Where the applicant's personal identity is connected with his/her faith, religion and/or belief, this may be helpful to examine as an additional narrative about their sexual orientation or gender identity. The influence of religion in the lives of LGBTI persons can be complex, dynamic, and a source of ambivalence.[123]

Evidentiary Matters

64. The applicant's own testimony is the primary and often the only source of evidence, especially where persecution is at the hands of family members or the community. Where there is a lack of country of origin information, the decision maker will have to rely on the applicant's statements alone. Normally, an interview should suffice to bring the applicant's story to light.[124] Applicants should never be expected or asked to bring in documentary or photographic evidence of intimate acts. It would also be inappropriate to expect a couple to be physically demonstrative at an interview as a way to establish their sexual orientation.

65. Medical "testing" of the applicant's sexual orientation is an infringement of basic human rights and must not be used.[125] On the other hand, medical evidence of transition-related surgery, hormonal treatment or biological characteristics (in the case of intersex individuals) may corroborate their personal narrative.

66. Relevant and specific country of origin information on the situation and treatment of LGBTI individuals is often lacking. This should not automatically lead to the conclusion that the applicant's claim is unfounded or that there is no persecution of LGBTI individuals in that country.[126] The extent to which international organizations and other groups are able to monitor and document abuses against LGBTI individuals remain

[122] *Essa v. Canada (Minister of Citizenship and Immigration)*, 2011 FC 1493, Canada, Federal Court, 20 December 2011, available at: <http://www.unhcr.org/refworld/docid/4f901c392.html>, paras. 30–31, found that the Board's insistence on the applicant going to or have knowledge about gay venues in the country of asylum in order to be gay was not reasonable.

[123] APA, Practice Guidelines for LGB Clients.

[124] UNHCR, *Handbook*, paras. 196, 203–204.

[125] See further, "UNHCR's Comments on the Practice of Phallometry in the Czech Republic to Determine the Credibility of Asylum Claims based on Persecution due to Sexual Orientation", April 2011, available at: <http://www.unhcr.org/refworld/docid/4daeb07b2.html>.

[126] See, for example, *Molnar v. Canada*, above footnote 39.

limited in many countries. Increased activism has often been met with attacks on human rights defenders, which impede their ability to document violations. Stigma attached to issues surrounding sexual orientation and/or gender identity also contributes to incidents going unreported. Information can be especially scarce for certain groups, in particular bisexual, lesbian, transgender and intersex people. It is critical to avoid automatically drawing conclusions based on information about one group or another; however, it may serve as an indication of the applicant's situation in certain circumstances.

Guidelines on International Protection No. 10:

Claims to Refugee Status related to Military Service within the context of Article 1A(2) of the 1951 Convention and/or the 1967 Protocol relating to the Status of Refugees

UNHCR issues these *Guidelines* pursuant to its mandate, as contained in the Office's Statute, in conjunction with Article 35 of the 1951 Convention relating to the Status of Refugees and Article II of its 1967 Protocol. These Guidelines complement the *UNHCR Handbook on Procedures and Criteria for Determining Refugee Status under the 1951 Convention* (reissued 2011) and, in particular, are to be read together with UNHCR's *Guidelines on International Protection No. 6: Religion-Based Refugee Claims* and *Guidelines on International Protection No. 8: Child Asylum Claims*. They replace *UNHCR's Position on Certain Types of Draft Evasion* (1991).

The *Guidelines*, the result of broad consultations, provide legal interpretative guidance for governments, legal practitioners, decision makers and the judiciary, as well as UNHCR staff carrying out mandate refugee status determination.

The UNHCR *Handbook on Procedures and Criteria for Determining Refugee Status* and *the Guidelines on International Protection* are available at: <http://www.unhcr.org/refworld/docid/4f33c8d92.html>.

I. Introduction

1. The situation of "deserters and persons avoiding military service" is explicitly addressed in *UNHCR's Handbook on Procedures and Criteria for Determining Refugee Status under the 1951 Convention and the 1967 Protocol relating to the Status of Refugees* ["*UNHCR Handbook*"].[1] Since the publication of the *UNHCR Handbook* there have been considerable developments both in the practice of States and in the restrictions placed on military service by international law. Given these developments, as well as divergences in jurisprudence, UNHCR issues these *Guidelines* with the aim to facilitate a consistent and principled application of the refugee definition in Article 1A(2) of the 1951 Convention and/or 1967 Protocol relating to the Status of Refugees in such cases. These *Guidelines* examine the position of individuals who seek international protection to avoid recruitment by, and service in, State armed forces, as well as forced recruitment by non-State armed groups.

[1] UNHCR, *Handbook on Procedures and Criteria for Determining Refugee Status under the 1951 Convention and the 1967 Protocol relating to the Status of Refugee*, (reissued, Geneva, 2011), ("*UNHCR Handbook*"), available at: <http://www.unhcr.org/refworld/pdfid/4f33c8d92.pdf>, paras. 167-174.

2. These *Guidelines* address the definition of key terms [Part II], followed by an overview of international legal developments relating to military service [Part III]. Part IV examines the refugee determination criteria as they apply to claims involving military service. Part V considers procedural and evidentiary issues. The *Guidelines* focus on the interpretation of the "inclusion" components of the refugee definition. Exclusion considerations are not addressed, although they may be at issue in such cases, and will need to be properly assessed.[2] Further, issues around maintaining the civilian and humanitarian character of asylum, while often relevant to such claims, are not dealt with in these Guidelines.[3]

II. Terminology

3. For the purpose of these *Guidelines*, these terms are defined as follows:

Alternative service refers to service in the public interest performed instead of compulsory military service in the State armed forces by individuals who have a conscientious objection to military service ["conscientious objectors"]. Alternative service may take the form of civilian service outside the armed forces or a non-combatant role in the military.[4] Civilian service can involve, for example, working in State-run health institutions, or voluntary work with charitable organisations either at home or abroad. Non-combatant service in the military would include positions such as cooks or administrative clerks.

Conscientious objection to military service refers to an objection to such service which "derives from principles and reasons of conscience, including profound convictions, arising from religious, moral, ethical, humanitarian or similar motives."[5] Such an objection is not confined to **absolute conscientious objectors** [pacifists], that is, those who object to all use of armed force or participation in all wars. It also encompasses those who believe that "the use of force is justified in some circumstances but not in others, and that therefore it is necessary to object in those other cases" [**partial** or **selective objection** to military service].[6] A conscientious objection may develop over time, and thus volunteers may at some stage also raise claims based on conscientious objection, whether absolute or partial.

[2] Reference is made instead to UNHCR, *Guidelines on International Protection No. 5: Application of the Exclusion Clauses: Article 1F of the 1951 Convention relating to the Status of Refugees*, HCR/GIP/03/05, 4 September 2003, ("*UNHCR Exclusion Guidelines*"), available at: <http://www.unhcr.org/refworld/docid/3f5857684.html>.

[3] See, Executive Committee ("ExCom") Conclusion No. 94 (LII), 2002, on the civilian and humanitarian character of asylum, para. (c)(vii).

[4] See, further, for example, UN Human Rights Council, *Analytical report on conscientious objection to military service: Report of the United Nations High Commissioner for Human Rights*, A/HRC/23/22, 3 June 2013, available at: <http://www.refworld.org/docid/51b5c73c4.html>.

[5] See, UN Commission on Human Rights, Resolution 1998/77, "*Conscientious Objection to Military Service*", E/CN.4/RES/1998/77, 22 April 1998, available at: <http://www.refworld.org/docid/3b00f0be10.html>. The Commission was replaced by the UN Human Rights Council in 2006.

[6] See, UN *Conscientious Objection to Military Service*, E/CN.4/Sub.2/1983/30/Rev.1, 1985 (the "*Eide and Mubanga-Chipoya report*"), available at: <http://www.refworld.org/pdfid/5107cd132.pdf>, para. 21. See also, paras. 128-135 regarding persecution in the context of conscientious objection to conflicts which violate basic rules of human conduct.

Desertion involves abandoning one's duty or post without permission, or resisting the call up for military duties.[7] Depending on national laws, even someone of draft age who has completed his or her national service and has been demobilized, but is still regarded as being subject to national service, may be regarded as a deserter under certain circumstances. Desertion can occur in relation to the police force, gendarmerie or equivalent security services, and is also the term used to apply to deserters from non-State armed groups. Desertion may be for reasons of conscience or for other reasons.

Draft evasion occurs when a person does not register for, or does not respond to, a call up or recruitment for compulsory military service. The evasive action may be as a result of the evader fleeing abroad, or may involve, *inter alia*, returning call up papers to the military authorities. In the latter case, the person may sometimes be described as a draft resister rather than a draft evader, although draft evader is used to cover both scenarios in these *Guidelines*. Draft evasion may also be pre-emptive in the sense that action may be taken in anticipation of the actual demand to register or report for duty. Draft evasion only arises where there is mandatory enrolment in military service ["the draft"]. Draft evasion may be for reasons of conscience or for other reasons.

Forced recruitment is the term used in these *Guidelines* to refer to the coerced, compulsory or involuntary recruitment into either a State's armed forces or a non-State armed group.

Military service primarily refers to service in a State's armed forces. This may occur in peacetime or during a period of armed conflict, and may be on a voluntary or compulsory basis. Compulsory military service by the State is also known as **conscription** or **"the draft"**. Where an individual volunteers to join the State military, it is called **enlistment.**

Reservists are individuals who serve in the reserve forces of the State's armed forces. They are not considered to be on active duty, but are required to be available to respond to any call up in an emergency.

4. Where alternatives to compulsory military service are not available, an individual's conscientious objection may be expressed through draft evasion or desertion. However, draft evasion or desertion is not synonymous with conscientious objection as other motivations, such as fear of military service or the conditions of such service may be involved. Conscientious objection, draft evasion and desertion may all take place in peacetime as well as during armed conflict. Moreover, whilst conscientious objection and evasion/desertion tend to arise in relation to conscription, they can also take place where the original decision to join the armed forces was voluntary or the obligation to undertake compulsory military service was initially accepted.[8]

III. International Law on Military Service

A. The Right of States to Require Military Service

5. States have a right of self-defence under both the UN Charter and customary international law.[9] States are entitled to require citizens to perform military service for military

[7] See, European Court of Human Rights, *Feti Demirtaş c. Turquie*, Application no. 5260/07, 17 January 2012, available at: <http://www.unhcr.org/refworld/docid/4ff5996d2.html>.

[8] See, for example, UN Commission on Human Rights, Resolution 1998/77, preambular para. see note 5 above.

[9] Article 51, UN Charter. See also, International Court of Justice, *Case concerning the Military and Paramilitary Activities in and against Nicaragua (Nicaragua v. United States of America)*

purposes;[10] and this does not in itself violate an individual's rights.[11] This is recognized explicitly in human rights provisions concerned with forced labour, such as Article 8 of the 1966 International Covenant on Civil and Political Rights ["ICCPR"].[12] States may also impose penalties on persons who desert or avoid military service where their desertion or avoidance is not based on valid reasons of conscience, provided such penalties and the associated procedures comply with international standards.[13]

6. The State's right to compel citizens to undertake military service is not, however, absolute. International human rights law, as well as international humanitarian and international criminal law, impose certain restrictions upon States [see Parts III.B. and III.C. below]. In general, for military recruitment and service to be justified it needs to fulfil certain criteria: prescribed by law, implemented in a way that is not arbitrary or discriminatory, the functions and discipline of the recruits must be based on military needs and plans, and be challengeable in a court of law.[14]

7. The position of non-State armed groups is different from that of States, in that only States can require military conscription. International law does not entitle non-State

(Merits), 27 June 1986, available at: <http://www.refworld.org/docid/4023a44d2.html>, paras. 187–201.

[10] This does not cover conscription of non-nationals in occupied territories in the context of international armed conflict: see Article 51 of the 1949 Geneva Convention Relative to the Protection of Civilian Persons in Time of War (Geneva Convention IV), which states that an "Occupying Power may not compel protected persons to serve in its armed or auxiliary forces." "Protected persons" refers in this context to civilians in the occupied territory who are not nationals of the Occupying Power.

[11] The UN Human Rights Committee ("HRC") has noted this in relation to a complaint of discrimination (Article 26 of the 1966 International Covenant on Civil and Political Rights ("ICCPR")). See, *M.J.G. (name deleted) v. Netherlands*, CCPR/C/32/D/267/1987, 24 March 1988, available at: <http://www.unhcr.org/refworld/pdfid/50b8eca22.pdf>, para. 3.2; see, similarly, the earlier case of *R.T.Z. (name deleted) v. Netherlands*, CCPR/C/31/D/245/1987, 5 November 1987, available at: <http://www.unhcr.org/refworld/pdfid/50b8ed122.pdf>. That human rights law, in particular the ICCPR, applies to members of the military as well as to civilians was explicitly stated by the HRC in *Vuolanne v. Finland*, CCPR/C/35/D/265/1987, 2 May 1989, available at: <http://www.unhcr.org/refworld/pdfid/50b8ee372.pdf>.

[12] Article 8(3)(c)(ii) ICCPR exempts from the prohibition on forced or compulsory labour (found in Article 8(3)(a)), "Any service of a military character and, in countries where conscientious objection is recognized, any national service required by law of conscientious objectors." In addition, Article 2(2)(a) of the 1930 International Labour Organization ("ILO") Convention No. 29: Forced Labour Convention exempts from its prohibition on forced or compulsory labour (Article 1(1)), "any work or service exacted in virtue of compulsory military service laws for work of a purely military character." The reference to "military service laws" indicates that for the exemption to be valid, it must be set out in law. See also, the decisions of the HRC in *Venier and Nicholas v. France*, CCPR/C/69/D/690/1996, 1 August 2000, available at: <http://www.unhcr.org/refworld/pdfid/50b8ec0c2.pdf> and *Foin v. France*, CCPR/C/67/D/666/1995, 9 November 1999, where the HRC stated that under Article 8 of the ICCPR States may require service of a military character, available at: <http://www.unhcr.org/refworld/docid/4a3a3aebf.html>, para. 10.3.

[13] On procedures, in the European Court of Human Rights, see *Savda c. Turquie*, Application No. 42730/05,12 June 2012, available at: <http://www.refworld.org/docid/4fe9a9bb2.html>, see also, *Feti Demirtaş c. Turquie*, see note 7 above.

[14] Inter-American Commission on Human Rights ("IACHR"), "*Fourth report on the situation of human rights in Guatemala*", OEA/Ser.L/V/II.83, Doc. 16 rev., 1 June 1993, chap. V. See also, IACHR, *Piché Cuca v. Guatemala*, Report No. 36/93, case 10.975, decision on merits, 6 October 1993, indicating that the conscription process must be challengeable in a court of law, available at: <http://www.refworld.org/docid/5020dd282.html>.

armed groups, whether or not they may be the *de facto* authority over a particular part of the territory, to recruit on a compulsory or forced basis.

B. The Right to Conscientious Objection against Compulsory Military Service

8. The right to conscientious objection to State military service is a derivative right, based on an interpretation of the right to freedom of thought, conscience and religion contained in Article 18 of the Universal Declaration of Human Rights and Article 18 of the ICCPR. International jurisprudence on this right is evolving. The UN Human Rights Committee's [HRC] case law has shifted from characterizing the right as derived from the right "to manifest" one's religion or belief and thus subject to certain restrictions in Article 18(3),[15] to viewing it as one that "inheres in the right" to freedom of thought, conscience and religion in Article 18(1) itself.[16] This is a significant shift, albeit not without dissenting opinions.[17] The shift suggests that the right to conscientious objection is absolute, and that States may not impose restrictions on the right to freedom of thought, conscience and religion by way of compulsory military service.[18] According to the HRC, the right therefore "entitles the individual to an exemption from compulsory military service if this cannot be reconciled with the individual's religion or beliefs. The right must not be impaired by coercion."[19] Even in its earlier jurisprudence, where the HRC based its decisions on the right to *manifest* one's religion or belief [found in Article 18(1) read together with 18(3) ICCPR], the State had to demonstrate why such a restriction was "necessary", given that many other countries managed to reconcile the interests of the individual with the interests of the State through the provision of alternative service.[20]

[15] Article 18(3) ICCPR provides certain limitations on the right to manifest one's religion or belief, namely "prescribed by law and (. . .) necessary to protect public safety, order, health, or morals or the fundamental rights and freedoms of others." For further analysis, see UNHCR, *Guidelines on International Protection No. 6: Religion-Based Refugee Claims under Article 1A(2) of the 1951 Convention and/or the 1967 Protocol relating to the Status of Refugees,* HCR/GIP/04/06, 28 April 2004, *("UNHCR Guidelines on Religion-Based Claims"),* available at: <http://www.unhcr.org/refworld/docid/4090f9794.html>, para. 15. Moreover, unlike other rights in the Covenant, restrictions on the grounds of national security are not permitted at all. As noted by the HRC, "... such restrictions must not impair the very essence of the right in question." See HRC, *Yoon and Choi v. Republic of Korea*, CCPR/C/88/D/1321-1322/2004, 23 January 2007, available at: <http://www.unhcr.org/refworld/docid/48abd57dd.html>, para. 8.3.

[16] See, HCR, *Atasoy and Sarkut v. Turkey,* CCPR/C/104/D/1853-1854/2008, 19 June 2012, available at: <http://www.unhcr.org/refworld/docid/4ff5b14c2.html>, as well as *Min-Kyu Jeong et al v. Republic of Korea*, CCPR/C/101/D/1642-1741/2007, 27 April 2011, available at: <http://www.unhcr.org/refworld/docid/4ff59b332.html>.

[17] See, Individual opinion of Committee member Mr. Gerarld L. Neuman, jointly with members Mr. Yuji Iwasawa, Mr. Michael O'Flaherty and Mr. Walter Kaelin (concurring), *Atasoy and Sarkut v. Turkey, ibid.*

[18] See, *Yoon and Choi v. Republic of Korea,* para. 8.4., note 15 above and *Eu-min Jung* and *Others v. Republic of Korea,* CCPR/C/98/D/1593-1603/2007, 30 April 2010, available at: <http://www.unhcr.org/refworld/pdfid/4c19e0322.pdf>, para. 7.4.

[19] *Min-Kyu Jeong et al v. Republic of Korea*, para.7.3, see note 16 above.

[20] See, *Yoon and Choi v. Republic of Korea*, para. 8.4, note 15 above and *Eu-min Jung and Others v. Republic of Korea*, para. 7.4, see note 18 above.

9. The right to conscientious objection is also reaffirmed in regional instruments, either explicitly or by interpretation,[21] as well as in various international standard setting documents.[22]

10. The right to conscientious objection applies to absolute, partial, or selective objectors [see II.];[23] volunteers as well as conscripts before and after joining the armed forces;

[21] The right to conscientious objection is explicitly recognized in two regional treaties: 2000 Charter of Fundamental Rights of the European Union, Article 10(2); 2005 Ibero-American Convention on Young People's Rights, Article 12(3). The right is also derived from the right to freedom of thought, conscience and religion in regional human rights treaties, and has been recognized as such by the European Court of Human Rights (see Grand Chamber judgment in *Bayatyan v. Armenia*, Application No. 23459/03, 7 July 2011, available at: <http://www.unhcr.org/refworld/docid/4e254eff2.html>, para. 110, followed by *Feti Demirtaş c. Turquie*, note 7 above; *Savda c. Turquie*, see note 13 above; and *Tarhan c. Turquie*, Application No. 9078/06, 17 July 2012, available at: <http://www.refworld.org/docid/51262a732.html>) and by the IACHR (see *Cristián Daniel Sahli Vera et al. v. Chile*, Case 12.219, Report no. 43/05, 10 March 2005, available at: <http://www.unhcr.org/refworld/pdfid/4ff59edc2.pdf>; see also the friendly settlement in *Alfredo Diaz Bustos v. Bolivia*, Case 14/04, Report no. 97/05, 27 October 2005, available at: <http://www.unhcr.org/refworld/pdfid/4ff59fbc2.pdf>, para. 19). See also IACHR, Annual Report, 1997, Chapter VII: Recommendation 10, available at: <http://www.unhcr.org/refworld/docid/50b8bd162.html>; Council of Europe Parliamentary Assembly, Recommendation 1518 (2001) on the exercise of the right of conscientious objection to military service in Council of Europe Member States, 23 May 2001, available at: <http://www.unhcr.org/refworld/docid/5107cf8f2.html>; Council of Europe Committee of Ministers, Recommendation No. R (87) 8, 9 April 1987, available at: <http://www.unhcr.org/refworld/docid/5069778e2.html>; and Council of Europe Committee of Ministers, Recommendation CM/Rec (2010) 4 on human rights of members of the armed forces, 24 February 2010, available at: <http://www.unhcr.org/refworld/docid/506979172.html>.

[22] See, UN General Assembly resolution, 33/165, 1978 on Status of persons refusing service in military or police forces used to enforce apartheid, available at: <http://www.refworld.org/docid/3b00f1ae28.html>. See HRC, *General Comment No. 22: The Right to Freedom of Thought, Conscience and Religion (Article 18)*, CCPR/C/21/Rev.1/Add.4, 30 July 1993, available at: <http://www.unhcr.org/refworld/pdfid/453883fb22.pdf>, at para. 11, as well as the HRC's Concluding Observations on Ukraine, CCPR/CO/73/UKR, 12 November 2001, available at: <http://www.unhcr.org/refworld/docid/3cbbeb1c4.html>, para. 20, and those on Kyrgyzstan, CCPR/CO/69/KGZ, 24 July 2000, available at: <http://www.unhcr.org/refworld/docid/507572ef2.html>, para. 18. The former UN Commission on Human Rights also affirmed that a right to conscientious objection derives from the right to freedom of thought, conscience and religion (UN Commission on Human Rights Resolution, *Conscientious objection to military service,* E/CN.4/RES/1989/59, 8 March 1989, available at: <http://www.unhcr.org/refworld/docid/3b00f0b24.html>, reinforced and developed in resolutions E/CN.4/RES/1993/84, 10 March 1993, available at: <http://www.unhcr.org/refworld/docid/3b00f1228c.html>; E/CN.4/RES/1995/83, 8 March 1995, available at: <http://www.unhcr.org/refworld/docid/3b00f0d220.html>; E/CN.4/RES/1998/77, see note 5 above, E/CN.4/RES/2000/34, 20 April 2000, available at: <http://www.unhcr.org/refworld/docid/3b00efa128.html>; E/CN.4/RES/2002/45, 23 April 2002, available at: <http://www.unhcr.org/refworld/docid/5107c76c2.html>; and E/CN.4/RES/2004/35, 19 April 2004, available at: <http://www.unhcr.org/refworld/docid/415be85e4.html>). Its successor, the UN Human Rights Council, has endorsed this position in its 2012 resolution on conscientious objection (A/HRC/RES/20/2, 16 July 2012, available at: <http://www.unhcr.org/refworld/docid/501661d12.html>) and latest in its 2013 resolution (A/HRC/24/L.23, 23 September 2013, available at: <http://www.refworld.org/docid/526e3e114.html>).

[23] Although the HRC has not discussed partial or selective conscientious objection either in *General Comment No. 22: The Right to Freedom of Thought, Conscience and Religion (Article 18),* see note 22 above or in its recent decisions on individual complaints, a number of countries do make provision for selective or partial conscientious objectors. See, for example, *Analytical report on*

during peace time and during armed conflict.[24] It includes objection to military service based on moral, ethical, humanitarian or similar motives.[25]

11. A conscientious objector's rights under Article 18 ICCPR will be respected where he or she is (i) exempted from the obligation to undertake military service or (ii) appropriate alternative service is available. In assessing the appropriateness of alternative service, it is generally considered that it needs to be compatible with the reasons for the conscientious objection; of a non-combatant or civilian character; in the public interest; and not punitive.[26] For example, civilian service under civilian administration would be necessary in the cases of individuals who object outright to any association with the military.[27] However, where the objection is specifically to the personal carrying of arms the option of non-combatant service in the military may be appropriate. Many States avoid the difficulty of having to evaluate the sincerity of a claim to conscientious objection by allowing the person a free choice between military and alternative service.[28] In some States recognition of conscientious objection has been granted only to certain religious groups. However, as noted above, this would not be consistent with the scope of the right to freedom of thought, conscience and religion, nor with the prohibition on discrimination.[29]

C. Prohibition on Underage Recruitment and Participation in Hostilities

12. Explicit safeguards exist to prevent the exposure of children to military service.[30] All recruitment [both compulsory and voluntary] in State armed forces and the participation in hostilities[31] of those under 15 years of age is prohibited under international treaty

conscientious objection to military service: Report of the United Nations High Commissioner for Human Rights, para 47, see note 4 above.

[24] See, Part II on Terminology.

[25] *Ibid.*

[26] UN Commission on Human Rights resolution 1998/77, para. 4, see note 5 above. See also, *Atasoy and Sarkut v. Turkey,* note 16 above, para. 10.4.

[27] See, *Atasoy and Sarkut v. Turkey*, para. 14, see note 16 above. See also, *Min-Kyu Jeong et al v. Republic of Korea*, para.7.3, also note 16 above.

[28] For a general overview of State practice, see, *Analytical report on conscientious objection to military service: Report of the United Nations High Commissioner for Human Rights*, see note 4 above. See also, War Resisters' International, *World Survey of Conscription and Conscientious Objection to Military Service*, available at: <http://www.wri-irg.org/co/rtba/index.html>. With respect to European countries see also the judgment of the European Court of Human Rights in *Bayatyan v. Armenia*, note 21 above.

[29] See, for example, HRC, *General Comment No. 22: The Right to Freedom of Thought, Conscience and Religion (Article 18),* see note 22 above, stating that "... there shall be no differentiation among conscientious objectors on the basis of the nature of their particular beliefs...", para. 11. With regard to State practice recognizing conscientious objection even when it originates from views outside of those of certain formal religions, see, *Analytical report on conscientious objection to military service: Report of the United Nations High Commissioner for Human Rights*, para. 12, see note 4 above. See also, *Brinkhof v. Netherlands*, CCPR/C/48/D/402/1990, 29 July 1993, available at: <http://www.unhcr.org/refworld/docid/4a3a3ae913.html>.

[30] See, in this regard, UN Security Council, *Resolution 1882 (2009) on children and armed conflict*, S/RES/1882 (2009), 4 August 2009, available at: <http://www.unhcr.org/refworld/docid/4a7bdb432.html>.

[31] Technically, international humanitarian law distinguishes between non-international armed conflict and international armed conflict in this respect. In non-international armed conflict (Article 4(3)(c), Additional Protocol II to the 1949 Geneva Conventions, relating to the Protection of Victims of Non-International Armed Conflict ("Additional Protocol II")) the prohibition relates

law.[32] Such recruitment amounts to a war crime.[33] Whether conducted by governments or by non-State armed groups, compulsory recruitment of persons under 18 years of age is prohibited pursuant to the 20 Optional Protocol to the 19 Convention on the Rights of the Child ["CRC"] on the involvement of children in armed conflict ["Optional Protocol to the CRC"].[34] A similar restriction is found in the 19 International Labour Organization Convention on Worst Forms of Child Labour.[35] The 2000 Optional Protocol to the CRC requires States to "take all feasible measures" to prevent children under the age of 18 taking a "direct part in hostilities" whether as members of its armed forces or other armed groups and prohibits outright any voluntary recruitment of children under 18 years into non-State armed groups.[36] Whilst voluntary enlistment of children of 16 years and above is permitted for State armed forces, the State is obliged to put in place safeguards to ensure, *inter alia*, that any such recruitment is genuinely voluntary.[37] Despite the different age limits set by international law, the more favourable age limits ought to guide the assessment of refugee claims based on the fact that the child has objected through seeking international protection to that recruitment and/or service. Regional instruments also contain prohibitions on the recruitment and direct participation of children in hostilities.[38]

IV. Substantive Analysis

A. Well-founded Fear of Being Persecuted

13. What amounts to a well-founded fear of being persecuted depends on the particular circumstances of the case, including the applicant's background, profile and

to use in hostilities. In international armed conflict (Article 77(2), Additional Protocol I to the 1949 Geneva Conventions, relating to the Protection of International Armed Conflict ("Additional Protocol I")), it is limited to taking direct part in hostilities. The Convention on the Rights of the Child ("CRC") adopts the narrower "direct part in hostilities" standard, see Article 38(2), CRC.

[32] Article 77(2), Additional Protocol I; Article 4(3)(c), Additional Protocol II; Article 38(2) CRC.

[33] See, Article 8(2)(b)(xxvi) and 8(2)(e)(vii) of the 1998 Statute of the International Criminal Court ("ICC Statute") which lists as war crimes "conscripting or enlisting children under the age of fifteen years into the national armed forces or using them to participate actively in hostilities." See also International Criminal Court ("ICC"), *Situation in the Democratic Republic of the Congo, in the case of the Prosecutor v. Thomas Lubanga Dyilo*, ICC-01/04-01/06, 14 March 2012, available at: <http://www.unhcr.org/refworld/docid/4f69a2db2.html>; Special Court for Sierra Leone ("SCSL"), *Prosecutor v. Issa Hassan Sesay, Morris Kallon and Augustine Gbao (the RUF accused) (Trial judgment)*, Case No. SCSL-04-15-T, 2 March 2009, available at: <http://www.unhcr.org/refworld/docid/49b102762.html>, at para. 184 (finding that the prohibition on such recruitment is customary international law). Further discussion of what constitutes the war crime of underage recruitment can be found in the SCSL, *Prosecutor v. Charles Ghankay Taylor*, SCSL-03-01-T, 18 May 2012, available at: <http://www.unhcr.org/refworld/docid/50589aa92.html>.

[34] Articles 2 and 4, 2000 Optional Protocol to the Convention on the Rights of the Child on the involvement of children in armed conflict.

[35] Article 3(a), 1999 ILO Convention No. 182 on Worst Forms of Child Labour.

[36] Articles 1 and 4, 2000 Optional Protocol to CRC.

[37] Article 3, 2000 Optional Protocol to CRC. See also, *UNHCR Guidelines on International Protection No. 8 Child Asylum Claims under Articles 1A(2) and 1(F) of the 1951 Convention and/or 1967 Protocol relating to the Status of Refugees*, HCR/GIP/09/08, 22 December 2009, *("UNHCR Guidelines on Child Asylum Claims")*, available at: <http://www.unhcr.org/refworld/docid/4b2f4f6d2.html>, para. 22.

[38] See, Article 22(2), 1990 African Charter on the Rights and Welfare of the Child, and Article 12(3), 2005 Ibero-American Convention on Young People's Rights.

experiences considered in light of up-to-date country of origin information.[39] It is important to take into account the personal experiences of the applicant, as well as the experiences of others similarly situated, since these may well show that there is a reasonable likelihood that the harm feared by the applicant will materialize sooner or later.[40] The first-tier question to ask is: *What would be the predicament [consequence(s)] for the applicant if returned?* The second-tier question is: *Does that predicament [or consequence(s)] meet the threshold of persecution?* The standard of proof to determine the risk is reasonable likelihood.[41]

14. Persecution will be established if the individual is at risk of a threat to life or freedom,[42] other serious human rights violations, or other serious harm.[43] By way of example, disproportionate or arbitrary punishment for refusing to undertake State military service or engage in acts contrary to international law – such as excessive prison terms or corporal punishment – would be a form of persecution. Other human rights at stake in such claims include non-discrimination and the right to a fair trial right, as well as the prohibitions against torture or inhuman treatment, forced labour and enslavement/servitude.[44]

15. In assessing the risk of persecution, it is important to take into account not only the direct consequences of one's refusal to perform military service [for example, prosecution and punishment], but also any negative indirect consequences. Such indirect consequences may derive from non-military and non-State actors, for example, physical violence, severe discrimination and/or harassment by the community. Other forms of punitive retribution for draft evasion or desertion may also be evident in other situations, such as suspension of rights to own land, enrol in school or university, or access social services.[45] These types of harm may amount to persecution if they are sufficiently serious in and of themselves, or if they would cumulatively result in serious restrictions on the applicant's enjoyment of fundamental human rights, making their life intolerable.

16. Claims relating to military service may arise in various situations. This section outlines five common types of claims, albeit with some overlap.

[39] *UNHCR Handbook*, paras. 51-53, see note 1 above.

[40] *UNHCR Handbook*, paras. 42-43, see note 1 above, and *UNHCR Guidelines on Religion-Based Claims*, para. 14, see note 15 above.

[41] See, UNHCR, *Note on the Burden and Standard of Proof*, 16 December 1998, *("Note on the Burden and Standard of Proof")*, available at: <http://www.refworld.org/docid/3ae6b3338.html>, para. 10; UNHCR, *Interpreting Article 1 of the 1951 Convention relating to the Status of Refugees*, April 2001, *("UNHCR Interpreting Article 1")*, available at: <http://www.unhcr.org/refworld/docid/3b20a3914.html>, paras. 16-17.

[42] Article 33(1), 1951 Convention.

[43] See, *UNHCR Handbook*, para. 51-53, see note 1 above. See also, UNHCR, *Guidelines on International Protection No. 7: The Application of Article 1A(2) of the 1951 Convention and/or 1967 Protocol Relating to the Status of Refugees to Victims of Trafficking and Persons At Risk of Being Trafficked*, HCR/GIP/06/07, 7 April 2006, available at: <http://www.unhcr.org/refworld/docid/443679fa4.html>, para. 14, and UNHCR Handbook, paras. 54-55, see note 1 above.

[44] See, for example, IACHR, "*Fourth report on the situation of human rights in Guatemala*", OEA/Ser.L/V/II.83, Doc. 16 rev., 1 June 1993, chap. V.

[45] See, for example, UNHCR, *Eligibility Guidelines for Assessing the International Protection Needs of Asylum-Seekers from Eritrea*, April 2009, available at: <http://www.refworld.org/docid/49de06122.html>, pages 13-14.

(i) Objection to State Military Service for Reasons of Conscience [absolute or partial conscientious objectors]

17. In assessing what kinds of treatment would amount to persecution in cases where the applicant is a conscientious objector [see V. A. below on issues relating to credibility and genuineness of the applicant's conviction(s)], the key issue is whether the national law on military service adequately provides for conscientious objectors, by either: (i) exempting them from military service, or (ii) providing appropriate alternative service. As mentioned in Part III above, States can legitimately require that citizens perform military or alternative service. However, where this is done in a manner that is inconsistent with international law standards, conscription may amount to persecution.

18. In countries where neither exemption nor alternative service is possible, a careful examination of the consequences for the applicant will be needed. For example, where the individual would be forced to undertake military service or participate in hostilities against their conscience, *or* risk being subjected to prosecution and disproportionate or arbitrary punishment for refusing to do so, persecution would arise. Moreover, the threat of such prosecution and punishment, which puts pressure on conscientious objectors to change their conviction, in violation of their right to freedom of thought, conscience or belief, would also meet the threshold of persecution.[46]

19. The protection threshold would not be met in countries that do not make provision for alternative service, but where the only consequence is a theoretical risk of military service because in practice conscription is not enforced or can be avoided through the payment of an administrative fee.[47] Similarly, where a draft evader is exempted from military service, or where a deserter is offered an honourable discharge, the issue of persecution would not arise, unless other factors are present.

20. Where alternative service is available, but punitive in nature and implementation, because of the type of service involved or its disproportionate duration, the issue of persecution may nonetheless be at issue. A disparity in the length of alternative service will not, in itself, be sufficient to meet the threshold of persecution. If, for example, the duration of alternative service is based on objective and reasonable criteria, such as the nature of the specific service concerned, or the need for special training in order to accomplish that service, persecution would not arise.[48] However, where alternative service is merely theoretical, for instance, because the relevant legislative provision has never been implemented; the procedure for requesting alternative service is arbitrary and/or unregulated; or the procedure is open to some but not all, further inquiries need to be undertaken. In cases where the applicant has not availed him or herself of the existing procedures it would be important to understand their reasons for not doing so. If found that the reasons relate to a well-founded fear of being persecuted for publicly expressing his or her convictions, this would need to be factored into the overall analysis.

[46] See, UN Commission on Human Rights, *Civil and Political Rights, Including the Question of Torture and Detention: Report of the Working Group on Arbitrary Detention*, E/CN.4/2001/14, 20 December 2000, recommendation No. 2, available at: <http://www.refworld.org/docid/3b00f54d18.html>, paras. 91-94.

[47] Excessive administrative fees designed to deter genuine conscientious objectors from opting for alternative service or which are considered punitive would be considered discriminatory and may on a cumulative basis meet the threshold of persecution.

[48] See the HRC's approach in *Foin v. France*, see note 12 above. See similarly, Richard *Maille v. France*, CCPR/C/69/D/689/1996, 31 July 2000, available at: <http://www.unhcr.org/refworld/docid/3f588efd3.html>, and *Venier v. France*, see note 12 above.

(ii) Objection to Military Service in Conflict Contrary to the Basic Rules of Human Conduct

21. Refugee claims relating to military service may also be expressed as an objection to (i) a particular armed conflict or (ii) the means and methods of warfare [the conduct of a party to a conflict]. The first objection refers to the unlawful use of force [*jus ad bellum*], while the second refers to the means and methods of warfare as regulated by international humanitarian law [*jus in bello*], as well as human rights and criminal law.[49] Collectively such objections relate to being forced to participate in conflict activities that are considered by the applicant to be contrary to the basic rules of human conduct.[50] Such objections may be expressed as an objection on the basis of one's conscience, and as such can be dealt with as a case of "conscientious objection" [see (i) above]; however, this will not always be the case. Individuals may, for example, object to participating in military activities because they consider this is required to conform to their military code of conduct, or they may refuse to engage in activities which constitute violations of international humanitarian, criminal or human rights law.

22. Recognizing the right to object on such grounds and to be granted refugee status is consistent with the rationale underlying the exclusion clauses in the 1951 Convention. Articles 1F(a) and 1F(c) exclude from protection individuals in respect of whom there are serious reasons for considering that they have committed crimes against peace, war crimes or crimes against humanity or are guilty of acts contrary to the purposes and principles of the United Nations, and who are therefore considered undeserving of international protection as refugees. The obligation on individuals under international humanitarian and criminal law to refrain from certain acts during armed conflict would find reflection in international refugee law in the case of individuals who are at risk of being punished for exercising the restraint expected of them under international law [see paragraph 14]. In this regard, it is important to note the absence of a defence of superior orders which are manifestly unlawful.[51]

Objection to Participating in an Unlawful Armed Conflict

23. Where an armed conflict is considered to be unlawful as a matter of international law [in violation of *jus ad bellum*], it is not necessary that the applicant be at risk of incurring individual criminal responsibility if he or she were to participate in the conflict in

[49] *Jus ad bellum* refers to the constraints under international law on the use of force, whereas *jus in bello* governs the conduct of the parties to an armed conflict. Traditionally, the latter refers to international humanitarian law but relevant standards are also found in applicable provisions of international human rights law and international criminal law.

[50] See, *UNHCR Handbook,* paras. 170-171, note 1 above. With regard to para. 171: "Where, however, the type of military action, with which an individual does not wish to be associated, is condemned by the international community as contrary to basic rules of human conduct, punishment for desertion or draft evasion could, in light of all other requirements of the definition, in itself be regarded as persecution." See also, at a regional level, Council of the European Union, "*Council Directive 2004/83/EC of 29 April 2004 on Minimum Standards for the Qualification and Status of Third Country Nationals or Stateless Persons as Refugees or as Persons who Otherwise Need International Protection and the Content of the Protection Granted*", OJ/L 304/12, 30 Sept. 2004, available at: <http://www.unhcr.org/refworld/docid/4157e75e4.html>. Article 9(2)(e) which includes as a form of persecution: "[p]rosecution or punishment for refusal to perform military service in a conflict, where performing military service would include crimes or acts falling under the exclusion clauses as set out in Article 12(2)."

[51] See, for example, Article 33, ICC Statute, see note 33 above.

question, rather the applicant would need to establish that his or her objection is genuine, and that because of his or her objection, there is a risk of persecution. Individual responsibility for a crime of aggression only arises under international law for persons who were in a position of authority in the State in question.[52] Soldiers who enlisted prior to or during the conflict in question may also object as their knowledge of or views concerning the illegality of the use of force evolve.

24. In determining the legality of the conflict in question condemnation by the international community is strong evidence, but not essential for finding that the use of force is in violation of international law. Such pronouncements are not always made, even where objectively an act of aggression has taken place. Thus, a determination of illegality with regard to the use of force needs to be made through the application of the governing rules under international law. The relevant norms are the obligation on States to refrain from the threat or use of force against other States; the right of individual or collective defence; and the authorization of the use of force in line with the UN Security Council's powers to maintain peace and security.[53]

25. If the conflict is objectively assessed not to be an unlawful armed conflict under international law, the refugee claim will ordinarily fail unless other factors are present. Likewise, where the legality of the armed conflict is not yet settled under international law, the application may be assessed pursuant to (i) above as a conscientious objector case.

Objection to the Means and Methods of Warfare [Conduct of the Parties]

26. Where the applicant's objection is to the methods and means employed in an armed conflict [that is, the conduct of the one or more of the parties to the conflict], it is necessary to make an assessment of the reasonable likelihood of the individual being forced to participate in acts that violate standards prescribed by international law. The relevant standards can be found in international humanitarian law [*jus in bello*], international criminal law, as well as human rights law, as applicable.

27. War crimes and crimes against humanity are serious violations which entail individual responsibility directly under international law [treaty or custom]. Developments in the understanding of the elements of such crimes must be taken into account in determining what kinds of conduct or methods of warfare constitute such crimes.[54] Moreover, when assessing the kinds of acts an individual may be forced to commit in an armed conflict, other violations of international humanitarian law may also be relevant on a

[52] See, for example, International Criminal Court, *Elements of Crimes*, ICC-ASP/1/3 at 108, U.N. Doc. PCNICC/2000/1/Add.2 (2000), Article 8 bis, available at: <http://www.unhcr.org/refworld/pdfid/4ff5dd7d2.pdf>.

[53] See respectively, Articles 2(4), 51 and 42 UN Charter. See also, UN General Assembly, *Non-interference in the internal affairs of States*, A/RES/34/101, 14 December 1979, available at: <http://www.un.org/documents/ga/res/34/a34res101.pdf>.

[54] For an overview, see UNHCR's *Background Note on Exclusion,* 4 September 2003, available at: <http://www.unhcr.org/refworld/docid/3f5857d24.html>, paras. 30-32. Examples of war crimes in the context of an international armed conflict are wilful killing of civilians, soldiers hors de combat or prisoners of war; torture; killing or wounding treacherously individuals belonging to the hostile army; intentionally directing attacks against the civilian population; rape; recruitment of children under the age of fifteen years into the armed forces or using them to participate actively in hostilities; and use of poisonous weapons. In a non-international armed conflict, war crimes include intentionally directing attacks against civilians; killing or wounding treacherously a combatant adversary; rape; recruitment of children under the age of fifteen years into armed forces or groups or using them to participate actively in hostilities.

cumulative basis. The relevance of international human rights law in international or non-international armed conflict situations is also important to bear in mind.

28. Determining whether there is a reasonable likelihood that the individual would be forced to commit acts or to bear responsibility for such acts which violate the basic rules of human conduct will normally depend on an evaluation of the overall conduct of the conflict in question. Thus, the extent to which breaches of the basic rules of human conduct occur in the conflict will be relevant. However, it is the risk of being compelled to become involved in the act(s), rather than the conflict alone that is at issue, so the individual circumstances of the applicant must thus be examined, bearing in mind the role in which he or she will be engaged.

29. If the applicant is likely to be deployed in a role that excludes exposure to the risk of participating in the act(s) in question – for example, a non-combatant position such as a cook, or logistical or technical support roles only – then a claim of persecution is unlikely to arise without additional factors. Additional factors might include the link between the applicant's logistical or technical support role and the foreseeability of [or contribution to] the commission of crimes in violation of international humanitarian/criminal law. Further, the applicant's reasons for objecting – regardless of the foreseeability or remoteness of the commission of crimes linked to his or her activities – may be sufficient to qualify him or her as a conscientious objector [see (i) above].

30. By contrast, where there is a reasonable likelihood that an individual may not be able to avoid deployment in a combatant role that will expose him or her to the risk of committing illegal acts, his or her fear of being persecuted would be considered well-founded [see paragraph 14]. In some cases the conflict in question may be one that is not generally characterized by violations of international law. However, the individual in question may be a member of a unit whose particular duties mean that it is specifically, or more likely, to be implicated in violations of basic rules of human conduct. In such circumstances there may be a reasonable likelihood that the individual concerned will be forced to commit, for example, war crimes or crimes against humanity. Where options are available to be discharged, reassigned [including to alternative service] or to have an effective remedy against superiors or the military which will be fairly examined and without retribution, the issue of persecution will not arise, unless other factors are present.[55]

(iii) Conditions of State Military Service

31. In cases involving conditions within the State armed forces, a person is clearly not a refugee if his or her only reason for desertion or draft evasion is a simple dislike of State military service or a fear of combat. However, where the conditions of State military service are so harsh as to amount to persecution the need for international protection would arise.[56] This would be the case, for instance, where the terms or conditions of

[55] See, for example, *Analytical report on conscientious objection to military service: Report of the United Nations High Commissioner for Human Rights,* see note 4 above, concerning the practice in some States of allowing enlisted soldiers to move to a different non-combatant unit if they develop a conscientious objection to a particular conflict or bearing arms altogether, paras. 26-27. Such an option may not be available though for an individual whose objection to a particular conflict is not based on conscientious objection.

[56] See, for example, *Yasin Sepet, Erdem Bulbul v. Secretary of State for the Home Department*, C/2777; C/2000/2794, United Kingdom: Court of Appeal (England and Wales), 11 May 2001, available at: <http://www.unhcr.org/refworld/docid/3ffbcb024.html>, para. 61. See UN Working Group on Arbitrary Detention, Opinion No. 24/2003 (Israel), E/CN.4/2005/6/Add.1, 19 November

military service amount to torture or other cruel or inhuman treatment,[57] violate the right to security[58] and integrity of person,[59] or involve forced or compulsory labour,[60] or forms of slavery or servitude [including sexual slavery].[61]

32. Such cases may in particular involve discrimination on the grounds of ethnicity, or gender. Where the ill-treatment feared is carried out within the State armed forces by military personnel, it is necessary to assess whether such practices are systemic and/or in practice authorized, tolerated or condoned by the military hierarchy. An assessment has to be made regarding the availability of redress against such ill-treatment.

33. Under international law the prohibition of "forced or compulsory labour"[62] does not encompass military or alternative service. Nevertheless, where it can be established that compulsory military service is being used to force conscripts to execute public works, and these works are not of a "purely military character" or not exacted in the case of an emergency, and do not constitute a necessity for national defence or a normal civic obligation, such work constitutes forced labour.[63] According to the International Labour Organization, the condition of a "purely military character" is aimed specifically at preventing the call up of conscripts for public works.[64] In situations of emergency, which would endanger the existence of the State or well-being of the whole or part of the population, conscripts may nevertheless be called upon to undertake non-military work. The duration and extent of compulsory service, as well as the purposes for which it is used,

2004, available at: <http://www.unhcr.org/refworld/pdfid/470b77b10.pdf>. Similarly, HRC, General Comment No. 32: Right to equality before courts and tribunals and to a fair trial (Article 14), 23 August 2007, available at: <http://www.unhcr.org/refworld/docid/478b2b2f2.html>, stating that, "Repeated punishment of conscientious objectors for not having obeyed a renewed order to serve in the military may amount to punishment for the same crime if such subsequent refusal is based on the same constant resolve grounded in reasons of conscience", para. 55; see also UN Commission on Human Rights, Resolution 98/77, para. 5, see note 5 above. Subsequent to the HRC's ruling on Article 18 and a right to conscientious objection in *Yoon and Choi v. Republic of Korea*, see note 15 above, the UN Working Group on Arbitrary Detention has stated that the imprisonment of a conscientious objector for refusing to take up military service constitutes arbitrary detention as it is a violation of the rights guaranteed in Article 18 ICCPR as well as Article 9 ICCPR: Opinion No. 16/2008 (Turkey), A/HRC/10/21/Add.1, 4 February 2009, available at: <http://www.unhcr.org/refworld/pdfid/5062b12e2.pdf>. See also the European Court of Human Rights that held that the cumulative effect of repeated prosecution and punishment of conscientious objectors for desertion was their "civil death" amounting to degrading treatment in violation of Article 3 of the ECHR. See *Űlke v. Turkey*, Application No. 39437/98, 24 January 2006, available at: <http://www.unhcr.org/refworld/docid/4964bd752.html> as well as *Savda c. Turquie*, note 13 above and *Tarhan c. Turquie*, note 21 above, and *Feti Demirtaş c. Turquie*, see note 7 above.

[57] See, Article 7 ICCPR.

[58] See, Article 9 ICCPR.

[59] See for an interpretation, Articles 7, 9 and 17 ICCPR.

[60] See, Article 8(3) ICCPR and Article 1(b) of the Abolition of Forced Labour Convention, 1957 (No. 105).

[61] See, Article 8(1) ICCPR and Article 6 of the 1979 Convention on the Elimination of All Forms of Discrimination against Women ("CEDAW").

[62] See, Article 8 ICCPR.

[63] 1930 ILO Convention No. 29 concerning Forced or Compulsory Labour. See also, IACHR, "*Fourth report on the situation of human rights in Guatemala*", OEA/Ser.L/V/II.83, Doc. 16 rev., 1 June 1993, chap. V.

[64] It has its corollary in Article 1(b) of the Abolition of Forced Labour Convention, 1957 (No. 105), which prohibits the use of forced or compulsory labour "as a method of mobilizing and using labour for purposes of economic development."

need to be confined to what is strictly required in the given situation.[65] Using a conscript to gain profit through his or her exploitation [e.g. slavery, sexual slavery, practices similar to slavery, and servitude] is prohibited by international law and criminalized in the national legislation of a growing number of States.

34. As with other refugee claims outlined above (i) - (ii), if the applicant has the possibility of discharge, reassignment [including appropriate alternative service] and/or an effective remedy, without retribution, the issue of persecution will not arise, unless other factors are present.

(iv) Forced Recruitment and/or Conditions of Service in Non-State Armed Groups

35. As far as forced recruitment in non-State armed groups is concerned, it is recalled that non-State armed groups are not entitled to recruit by coercion or by force.[66] A person who seeks international protection abroad because of feared forced recruitment, or re-recruitment, by non-State armed groups, may be eligible for refugee status provided the other elements of the refugee definition are established; in particular that the State is unable or unwilling to protect the person against such recruitment [see paragraphs 42-44 and 60-61 below]. Likewise, forced recruitment by non-State groups to carry out non-military works could amount to, *inter alia*, forced labour, servitude and/or enslavement and constitute persecution.[67]

36. Where the applicant would be subjected to conditions of service that constitute serious violations of international humanitarian or criminal law,[68] serious human rights violations or other serious harm, persecution would arise.[69]

(v) Unlawful Child Recruitment

37. Special protection concerns arise where children are at risk of forced recruitment and service.[70] The same is true for children who may have "volunteered" for military activities with the State's armed forces or non-State armed groups. A child's vulnerability and immaturity make him or her particularly susceptible to coerced recruitment and obedience to the State's armed forces or a non-State armed group; this must be taken into account.

38. As outlined at III.C. above, there are important restrictions on the recruitment and participation in hostilities of children under international human rights law and

[65] ILO, Committee of Experts on the Application of Conventions and Recommendations (CEACR), *CEACR: Individual Direct Request concerning Forced Labour Convention, 1930 (No. 29) Eritrea* (ratification: 2000), 2010.

[66] See, para 7 above.

[67] See, Article 8(3) ICCPR, Article 1(b) of the Abolition of Forced Labour Convention (No. 105), 1957; Article 8(1) ICCPR; and Article 6 CEDAW.

[68] See, Article 3 common to the four Geneva Conventions of 1949; Article 8, Rome Statute of the ICC (last amended 2010), 17 July 1998, available at: <http://www.refworld.org/docid/3ae6b3a84.html>.

[69] For example, torture or other cruel, inhuman or degrading treatment or punishment (see Article 7, ICCPR), violations of the right to security (see Article 9 ICCPR) and integrity of person (see for an interpretation Article 7, 9 and 17 ICCPR), forced or compulsory labour (see Article 8(3) ICCPR and Article 1(b) of the Abolition of Forced Labour Convention, 1957 (No. 105)) or forms of slavery (including sexual slavery, see Article 8(1) and Article 6 CEDAW).

[70] *UNHCR Guidelines on Child Asylum Claims,* see note 37 above.

international humanitarian law, whether related to an international or a non-international armed conflict, and relating to both State armed forces and non-State armed groups.[71] Children need to be protected from such violations; as such, a child evading forced recruitment or prosecution and/or punishment or other forms of retaliation for desertion would generally have a well-founded fear of persecution.

39. There may be cases where children "volunteer" under pressure, or are sent to fight by their parents or communities. Such cases can similarly give rise to refugee status. The key question is the likelihood of risk that the child will be recruited and/or forced to fight, and this needs to be assessed on the basis of up-to-date country of origin information, taking into account the child's profile and past experiences, as well as the experiences of similarly situated children. Importantly, in refugee claims concerning violations of the restrictions on the recruitment and participation of children in hostilities, there is no additional requirement to consider the issue of conscientious objection.

40. Persecution may also arise from the nature of the treatment the child would be subjected to whilst in the military or armed group. In this respect, it is important to note that in addition to taking an active part in hostilities, children are also used as spies, messengers, porters, servants, slaves [including sex slaves], and/or to lay or clear landmines. Regardless of the function held by the child, they may be exposed to serious or multiple forms of harm, including being put in a position to witness heinous crimes.[72]

41. Persecution may also arise where there is a risk of ill-treatment on return to the country of origin, for example, because of the child's history of being involved with State armed forces or non-State armed groups, whether as a soldier/combatant/fighter or in another role. They may be considered as an "enemy" by respectively the State or the non-State armed group and as a result be at risk of retaliation, including physical attacks, or being ostracized by the community to such an extent that their life is intolerable. In all such cases, special consideration needs to be given to the particular vulnerabilities and best interest of child applicants.[73]

Agents of Persecution

42. There is scope within the refugee definition to recognize both State and non-State agents of persecution. In countries undergoing civil war, generalized violence, situations of insurgency, or State fragmentation, the threat of forced recruitment often emanates from non-State armed groups. This may result from the State's loss of control over parts of its territory. Alternatively, the State may empower, direct, control or tolerate the activities of non-State armed groups [for example, paramilitary units or private security groups]. The congruity of interests between the State and a non-State armed group involved in forced recruitment may not always be clear. Other non-State actors may also be the perpetrators of persecution in forms other than forced recruitment, for example, through violence and discrimination by family members and neighbours against former child soldiers perceived as having aided the enemy.

[71] See generally, UN Committee on the Rights of the Child, CRC General Comment No. 6: *Treatment of Unaccompanied and Separated Children Outside their Country of Origin*, ("CRC General Comment No.6"), CRC/GC/2005/6, 1 September 2005, available at: <http://www.unhcr.org/refworld/docid/42dd174b4.html>, para. 59.

[72] See, note 69 above; see also *UNHCR Guidelines on Child Asylum Claims,* para. 23, see note 37 above.

[73] *UNHCR Guidelines on Child Asylum Claims,* paras. 4 and 5, see note 37 above, and the CRC General Comment No. 6, see note 71 above.

43. In all cases involving harm by non-State armed groups and other non-State actors, it is necessary to review the extent to which the State is able and/or willing to provide protection against such harms.

44. Where the refugee claim is based on the risk of being forced to commit acts that violate basic rules of human conduct, it is necessary to examine the extent to which such violations are taking place, as well as the ability and/or willingness of the authorities, in particular the military authorities, to prevent future violations. Isolated breaches of *jus in bello* which are effectively investigated and dealt with by the military authorities will indicate the existence of available and effective State protection. State responses of this nature would involve action being taken against those responsible and measures being put in place to prevent repetition.

45. With respect to ill-treatment by other soldiers, such as serious bullying or hazing, it is necessary to determine whether such acts are condoned by the military authorities and whether effective methods of redress are available through the military system or elsewhere in the State structure.

Amnesties

46. When a conflict ends, a State may offer amnesties to persons who evaded military service, in particular to conscientious objectors. Such initiatives may guarantee immunity from prosecution or offer official recognition of conscientious objector status, thereby removing the risk of harm associated with such prosecution or punishment. Nevertheless, the impact of an amnesty on an individual's fear of persecution requires careful assessment. Amnesties may not cover all deserters and draft evaders. Moreover, it is necessary to examine whether the such protection is effective in practice; whether the individual may still face recruitment into the armed forces; whether he or she may be subjected to other forms of persecution apart from any criminal liability quashed by the amnesty; and/or whether the person is at risk of being targeted by non-State actors – including community groups for being considered a traitor, for example – irrespective of the legislation adopted by the State. In particular, individuals who have witnessed the commission of war crimes or other serious acts, and have deserted as a result, may be able to establish a well-founded fear of persecution under certain circumstances if, for instance, they were required to act as witnesses in criminal proceedings upon return which would expose them to serious harm.

B. The Convention Grounds

47. As with all claims to refugee status, the well-founded fear of persecution needs to be related to one or more of the grounds specified in the refugee definition in Article 1A(2) of the 1951 Convention; that is, it must be "for reasons of" race, religion, nationality, membership of a particular social group or political opinion. The Convention ground needs only to be a contributing factor to the well-founded fear of persecution; it need not be shown to be the dominant or even the sole cause. Further, one or more of the Convention grounds may be relevant; they are not mutually exclusive and may overlap.

48. The intent or motive of the persecutor can be a relevant factor in establishing the causal link between the fear of persecution and a Convention ground but it is not decisive, not least because it is often difficult to establish.[74] There is no need for the persecutor to

[74] *UNHCR Handbook*, para. 66, see note 1 above.

have a punitive intent to establish the causal link; the focus is rather on the reasons for the applicant's predicament and how he or she is likely to experience the harm. Even where an individual is treated in the same way as a majority of the population this does not preclude persecution being for reasons of a Convention ground. Similarly, if the persecutor attributes or imputes a Convention ground to the applicant, this is sufficient to satisfy the causal link. Where the persecutor is a non-State armed actor, the causal link is established either where the persecutor harms the applicant for a Convention-related reason, *or* the State does not protect him or her for a Convention-related reason.[75]

Religion

49. The religion ground is not limited to belief systems ["theistic, non-theistic and atheistic"],[76] but covers also notions of identity, or way of life.[77] It dovetails with Article 18 ICCPR and includes broader considerations of thought and conscience, including moral, ethical, humanitarian or similar views. The religion ground is thus particularly relevant in cases of conscientious objection, including those expressed through draft evasion or desertion, as explained at III. B. With respect to claims by conscientious objectors, the *UNHCR Handbook* states that:

> Refusal to perform military service may also be based on religious convictions. If an applicant is able to show that his religious convictions are genuine, and that such convictions are not taken into account by the authorities of his country in requiring him to perform military service, he may be able to establish a claim to refugee status. Such a claim would, of course, be supported by any additional indications that the applicant or his family may have encountered difficulties due to their religious convictions.[78]

50. The religion ground may also be relevant in cases based on military service other than in situations of conscientious objection. Recruits may be subject to detention, ill treatment [such as physical beatings or severe psychological pressure] and serious discrimination on account of their religious beliefs, identity or practices. They may also be pressured to renounce their beliefs and convert.

Political Opinion

51. The political opinion ground is broader than affiliation with a particular political movement or ideology; it concerns "any opinion on any matter in which the machinery of the State, government, society, or policy may be engaged."[79] Moreover, it covers both the holding of an actual political opinion and its expression, political neutrality as well as cases where a political opinion is imputed to the applicant even if he or she does not

[75] See, *UNHCR, Guidelines on International Protection No.2: "Membership of a particular social group" within the context of Article 1A(2) of the 1951 Convention and/or its 1967 Protocol relating to the Status of Refugees, HCR/GIP/02/02, 7 May 2002, ("UNHCR Guidelines on Social Group")*, available at: <http://www.unhcr.org/refworld/docid/3d36f23f4.html>, para. 23.

[76] *UNHCR Guidelines on Religion-Based Claims*, para. 6, see note 15 above.

[77] *Ibid*, paras. 4 and 8.

[78] *UNHCR Handbook*, para. 172, see note 1 above.

[79] UNHCR, *Guidelines on International Protection No. 1: Guidelines on Gender-Related Persecution Within the Context of Article 1A(2) of the 1951 Convention and/or its 1967 Protocol Relating to the Status of Refugees*, HCR/GIP/02/01, 7 May 2002, ("*UNHCR Guidelines on Gender-Related Persecution*"), available at: <http://www.unhcr.org/refworld/docid/3d36f1c64.html>, para. 32.

hold that view.[80] The latter can arise in cases where the State, or a non-State armed group, attributes to the individual a particular political view.

52. Cases involving objection to military service may be decided on the basis that there is a nexus with the political opinion ground in the 1951 Convention. Depending on the facts, an objection to military service – especially objections based on a view that the conflict violates basic rules of human conduct [see IV. A. (ii) above] – may be viewed through the prism of actual or imputed political opinion. In relation to the latter, the authorities may interpret the individual's opposition to participating in a conflict or in act(s) as a manifestation of political disagreement with its policies. The act of desertion or evasion may in itself be, or be perceived to be, an expression of political views.

53. The political opinion ground may be relevant in other circumstances. For instance, a refugee claim by a soldier who becomes aware of and objects to criminal activity being conducted or tolerated by military personnel in the context of a conflict, such as the illicit sale of weapons, extortion of civilians or trafficking of drugs or in persons, and who fears persecution as a result of his or her opposition to such activities, may be considered under the political opinion ground. Whether or not the soldier is a whistle-blower, attempts to flee military service may be perceived by the authorities as evidence of political opposition. Objection to recruitment by non-State armed groups may also be an expression of political opinion.

54. Political opinion may also be the applicable ground in relation to family members of a conscientious objector, draft evader or deserter who is identified by the State or non-State armed group as having an allegiance to a particular political cause. In such cases, persecution may be linked to imputed political opinion, on the basis that the family member is assumed to hold similar views as those ascribed to the conscientious objector, draft evader or deserter. The relevant ground in such cases may also be "family" as a social group [see below paragraph 56].

Race or Nationality

55. Race and nationality, in the sense of ethnicity, are often factors in cases connected with military service. The well-founded fear of persecution may be directly based on the applicant's race, for example where conscripts from a particular racial group face harsher conditions than other recruits, or are the only ones actually subject to the draft. Similarly, children may face forced recruitment because they belong to a targeted ethnic group. Cases based on the conditions of military service arising to persecution may also relate to discrimination on the basis of race and/or ethnicity, and could invoke this ground.

Membership of a Particular Social Group

56. The 1951 Convention does not include a specific list of particular social groups. Rather, "the term membership of a particular social group should be read in an evolutionary manner, open to the diverse and changing nature of groups in various societies

[80] See UNHCR, *Secretary of State for the Home Department (Appellant) v. RT (Zimbabwe), SM (Zimbabwe) and AM (Zimbabwe) (Respondents) and the United Nations High Commissioner for Refugees (Intervener) - Case for the Intervener*, 25 May 2012, available at: <http://www.unhcr.org/refworld/docid/4fc369022.html>, para. 8.

and evolving international human rights norms."[81] UNHCR defines a "particular social group" as:

> A particular social group involves a group of persons who share a common characteristic other than their risk of being persecuted, or who are perceived as a group by society. The characteristic will often be one which is innate, unchangeable, or which is otherwise fundamental to identity, conscience or the exercise of one's human rights.[82]

57. The two approaches – "protected characteristics" and "social perception" – to identifying "particular social groups" reflected in this definition are alternative, not cumulative, tests. The "protected characteristics" approach examines whether a group is connected either by an immutable characteristic, or by a characteristic that is so fundamental to human dignity that a person should not be compelled to forsake it. An immutable characteristic "may be innate [such as sex or ethnicity] or unalterable for other reasons [such as the historical fact of a past association, occupation or status]".[83] The "social perception" approach considers whether a particular social group shares a common characteristic which makes it cognizable or sets the group's members apart from society at large. The latter approach does not require that the common characteristic be easily identifiable by the general public, or visible to the naked eye. An applicant need not demonstrate that all members of a particular social group are at risk of persecution in order to establish the existence of a particular social group.[84] Moreover, irrespective of which approach is adopted, a particular social group can arise even where this covers a large number of people.[85] Nevertheless, everyone falling within a particular social group is not necessarily a refugee; a well-founded fear of persecution because of membership of that group is required.

58. Under either of these approaches, "conscientious objectors" are a particular social group given that they share a belief which is fundamental to their identity and that they may also be perceived as a particular group by society. Individuals with common past experience, such as child soldiers, may also constitute a particular social group. This may also be the case for draft evaders or deserters, as both types of applicants share a common characteristic which is unchangeable; a history of avoiding or having evaded military service. In some societies deserters may be perceived as a particular social group given the general attitude towards military service as a mark of loyalty to the country and/or due to the differential treatment of such persons [for example, discrimination in access to employment in the public sector] leading them to be set apart or distinguished as a group. The same may be true for draft evaders. Conscripts may form a social group characterized by their youth, forced insertion into the military corps or their inferior status due to lack of experience and low rank.

59. Women are a particular social group, defined by innate and immutable characteristics and frequently treated differently from men.[86] This may be the relevant ground in claims concerning sexual violence against female soldiers or women or girls forced to act as sex slaves; although this does not preclude the application of other grounds. Girls are a

[81] *UNHCR Guidelines on Social Group*, para. 3, see note 75 above.
[82] *Ibid*, para. 11.
[83] *Ibid*, para. 6.
[84] *Ibid*, para. 17.
[85] *Ibid*, paras. 18-19.
[86] *UNHCR Gender-Related Persecution Guidelines*, para. 30, see note 79 above.

sub-set of this social group. Children are also a particular social group, and this will be a relevant ground in cases concerning fear of forced underage recruitment.[87]

C. Internal Flight or Relocation Alternative

60. Where the feared persecution emanates from, or is condoned, or tolerated by the State and/or State agents, an internal flight or relocation alternative will generally not be available, as the State actors will be presumed to have control and reach throughout the country. In the case of conscientious objectors to State military service, where the State does not provide for exemption or alternative service, and where the fear of persecution is related to these laws and/or practices and their enforcement, a consideration of an internal flight or relocation alternative [IFA] would not be *relevant* as it can be assumed that the objector would face persecution across the country.[88]

61. Determining whether an IFA is available in cases where the risk of persecution emanates from non-State armed groups, it is necessary to evaluate the ability and/or willingness of the State to protect the applicant from the harm feared. The evaluation needs to take into account whether the State protection is effective and of a durable nature, provided by an organized and stable authority exercising full control over the territory and population in question. In the particular context of non-international armed conflict, special consideration would need to be given to the applicant's profile, and whether he or she was recruited into and/or participated in activities of a non-State armed group considered to be in opposition to the government, and any likely reprisals from the government. It would often be unreasonable to expect former non-State recruits to relocate into government-controlled territory in a situation of an ongoing conflict, especially if the conflict has religious or ethnic dimensions.

V. Procedural and Evidentiary Issues

A. Establishing the Relevant Facts

62. The credibility assessment refers to the process of determining whether, in light of all the information available to the decision maker, the statements of the applicant relating to material elements of the claim can, on balance, be accepted as having been truthfully given for the purpose of determining refugee status eligibility. Where, notwithstanding, an applicant's genuine efforts to provide evidence pertaining to the material facts, there remains some doubt regarding some of the facts alleged by him or her, the benefit of doubt should be given to the applicant in relation to the assertions for which evidentiary proof is lacking once the decision maker is satisfied with the general credibility of the claim.[89]

63. In claims related to military service, reliable and relevant country of origin information, including the extent to which exemption from military service or alternative service are available, the manner in which conscription is enforced, and the treatment of individuals or groups within the military forces of the country of origin, can assist in the

[87] *UNHCR Guidelines on Child Asylum Claims*, para. 48 et seq., see note 37 above.

[88] *UNHCR Guidelines on International Protection No. 4: "Internal Flight or Relocation Alternative" within the Context of Article 1A(2) of the 1951 Convention relating to the Status of Refugees*, HCR/GIP/03/04, 23 July 2003, (*"UNHCR Internal Flight Guidelines"*), available at: <http://www.refworld.org/docid/3f2791a44.html>.

[89] *UNHCR Handbook*, para. 204, see note 1 above.

evaluation of the truthfulness of the applicant's account and the determination of the forms of treatment and their likelihood he or she may face if returned.[90]

64. Establishing the genuineness and/or the personal significance of an applicant's beliefs, thoughts and/or ethics plays a key role in claims to refugee status based on objection to military service, in particular conscientious objection [see IV. A. (i)-(ii)].[91] The applicant needs to be given the opportunity during the individual interview to explain the personal significance of the reasons behind his or her objection, as well as how these reasons impact on his or her ability to undertake military service. Eliciting information regarding the nature of the reasons espoused, the circumstances in which the applicant has come to adopt them, the manner in which such beliefs conflict with undertaking military service, as well as the importance of the reasons to the applicant's religious or moral/ethical code are appropriate and assist in determining the credibility of the applicant's statements.

65. Where the objection to military service is derived from a formal religion, it may be relevant to elicit information about the individual's religious experiences, such as asking him or her to describe how they adopted the religion, the place and manner of worship, or the rituals engaged in, the significance of the religion to the person, or the values he or she believes the religion espouses, in particular, in relation to the bearing of arms. That said, extensive examination or testing of the tenets or knowledge of the individual's religion may not always be necessary or useful, particularly as such knowledge will vary considerably depending on his or her personal circumstances. A claimant's detailed knowledge of his or her religion does not necessarily correlate with sincerity of belief and vice-versa.

66. Cases involving mistaken beliefs as to a particular religion's views on the bearing of arms occur from time to time. Where mistaken beliefs are at issue, it would need to be established that the applicant, despite the mistaken beliefs, still faces a well-founded fear of persecution for one or more of the Convention grounds.[92]

67. If the claimant is mistaken about the nature of a particular conflict, such as whether the conflict abides by international law, this does not automatically undermine the credibility of the alleged reasons for objecting to military service. The credibility assessment in such situations needs to be conducted in light of the applicant's explanations regarding why involvement in the conflict would be inconsistent with his or her religious or moral beliefs, and the reality of the situation on the ground. Nonetheless, while they may be credible in their objection, where such an objection is based on a false premise, the risk of persecution would not arise unless they face other persecutory consequences for having deserted or evaded military service and a nexus to one of the Convention grounds is established.

68. For those objectors whose reasons for their objection is a matter of thought or conscience [rather than religion], they will not be able to refer to the practices of a religious community or teachings of a religious institution in order to substantiate their assertion. They should, however, be able to articulate the moral or ethical basis for their convictions. This may be based on social or community beliefs or practices, parental beliefs or

[90] *UNHCR Handbook,* paras. 196 and 203-204, see note 1 above, and *UNHCR Interpreting Article 1*, para. 10, see note 41 above. Note the *World Survey of Conscription and Conscientious Objection to Military Service*, which provides a country-by-country analysis, see note 28 above.

[91] For a general discussion of credibility issues in claims based on freedom of thought, conscience and religion see *UNHCR Guidelines on Religion-based Claims*, paras. 28-29, see note 15 above.

[92] *Ibid,* para. 30.

on philosophical or human rights convictions. Past behaviour and experiences may shed light on their views.

69. In cases involving individuals who volunteered for military service or responded to a call up, and who subsequently desert, it is important to recognize that religious or other beliefs may develop or change over time, as may the circumstances of the military service in question. Thus, adverse judgements as to the credibility of the applicant should not generally be drawn based only on the fact that he or she initially joined the military service voluntarily; the full circumstances surrounding the individual's espoused beliefs and situation need to be carefully examined.

B. Claims by Children

70. Given their young age, dependency and relative immaturity, special procedural and evidentiary safeguards are required for claims to refugee status by children.[93] In particular, children who spent time as soldiers/combatants/fighters or in a support role to armed groups may be suffering from severe trauma and be intimidated by authority figures. This can affect their ability to present a clearly understandable account of their experiences. Thus, appropriate interviewing techniques are essential during the refugee status determination procedure, as well as the creation of a non-threatening interview environment.

71. In cases concerning children, a greater burden of proof will fall on the decision makers than in other claims to refugee status, especially if the child is unaccompanied.[94] Given their immaturity, children cannot be expected to provide adult-like accounts of their experiences. If the facts of the case cannot be ascertained and/or the child is incapable of fully articulating his or her claim, a decision must be made on the basis of all known circumstances.

72. Age assessments may be particularly important in claims to refugee status based on military service where the age of the applicant is in doubt. This is the case not just with claims regarding conscription but also where a child considers him or herself to have "volunteered", given the limits on voluntary service set by international law [see III.B. above]. Age assessments, which may be part of a comprehensive assessment that takes into account both the physical appearance and the psychological maturity of the individual, are to be conducted in a safe, child- and gender-sensitive manner with due respect for human dignity.[95] Where the assessment is inconclusive, the applicant must be considered a child. Prior to the assessment, an independent guardian should be appointed to advise the child on the purpose and process of the assessment procedure, which needs to be explained clearly in a language that the child understands. DNA testing should, in normal circumstances, only be done if permitted by law and with the informed consent of the relevant individuals.

[93] For a full discussion of the minimum safeguards required see *UNHCR Guidelines on Child Asylum Claims,* paras. 65-77, see note 37 above. See also ExCom, *Conclusion on Children at Risk*, No. 107 (LVIII), 5 October 2007, available at: <http://www.unhcr.org/refworld/docid/471897232.html>, para. g(viii). Whether a claimant is a child for the purposes of such safeguards will depend on the age at the date the claim to refugee status is made.

[94] *UNHCR Guidelines on Child Asylum Claims*, para. 73, see note 37 above.

[95] See further, *UNHCR Guidelines on Child Asylum Claims*, paras. 75-76, see note 37 above.

Convention for the Protection of Human Rights and Fundamental Freedoms

AS AMENDED BY PROTOCOL NO. 11

Rome, 4.XI.1950

The text of the Convention had been amended according to the provisions of Protocol No. 3 (ETS No. 45), which entered into force on 21 September 1970, of Protocol No. 5 (ETS No. 55), which entered into force on 20 December 1971 and of Protocol No. 8 (ETS No. 118), which entered into force on 1 January 1990, and comprised also the text of Protocol No. 2 (ETS No. 44) which, in accordance with Article 5, paragraph 3 thereof, had been an integral part of the Convention since its entry into force on 21 September 1970. All provisions which had been amended or added by these Protocols are replaced by Protocol No. 11 (ETS No. 155), as from the date of its entry into force on 1 November 1998. As from that date, Protocol No. 9 (ETS No. 140), which entered into force on 1 October 1994, is repealed and Protocol No. 10 (ETS No. 146) has lost its purpose.

Protocol

Protocols: No. 4 | No. 6 | No. 7

No. 12 | No. 13 | No. 14

The governments signatory hereto, being members of the Council of Europe,

Considering the Universal Declaration of Human Rights proclaimed by the General Assembly of the United Nations on 10th December 1948;

Considering that this Declaration aims at securing the universal and effective recognition and observance of the Rights therein declared;

Considering that the aim of the Council of Europe is the achievement of greater unity between its members and that one of the methods by which that aim is to be pursued is the maintenance and further realisation of human rights and fundamental freedoms;

Reaffirming their profound belief in those fundamental freedoms which are the foundation of justice and peace in the world and are best maintained on the one hand by an effective political democracy and on the other by a common understanding and observance of the human rights upon which they depend;

Being resolved, as the governments of European countries which are like-minded and have a common heritage of political traditions, ideals, freedom and the rule of law, to take the first steps for the collective enforcement of certain of the rights stated in the Universal Declaration,

Have agreed as follows:

Article 1 Obligation to respect human rights

The High Contracting Parties shall secure to everyone within their jurisdiction the rights and freedoms defined in Section I of this Convention.

Section I—Rights and Freedoms

Article 2 Right to life

1. Everyone's right to life shall be protected by law. No one shall be deprived of his life intentionally save in the execution of a sentence of a court following his conviction of a crime for which this penalty is provided by law.

2. Deprivation of life shall not be regarded as inflicted in contravention of this article when it results from the use of force which is no more than absolutely necessary:

(a) in defence of any person from unlawful violence;

(b) in order to effect a lawful arrest or to prevent the escape of a person lawfully detained;

(c) in action lawfully taken for the purpose of quelling a riot or insurrection.

Article 3 Prohibition of torture

No one shall be subjected to torture or to inhuman or degrading treatment or punishment.

Article 4 Prohibition of slavery and forced labour

1. No one shall be held in slavery or servitude.
2. No one shall be required to perform forced or compulsory labour.
3. For the purpose of this article the term 'forced or compulsory labour' shall not include:

(a) any work required to be done in the ordinary course of detention imposed according to the provisions of Article 5 of this Convention or during conditional release from such detention;

(b) any service of a military character or, in case of conscientious objectors in countries where they are recognised, service exacted instead of compulsory military service;

(c) any service exacted in case of an emergency or calamity threatening the life or well-being of the community;

(d) any work or service which forms part of normal civic obligations.

Article 5 Right to liberty and security

1. Everyone has the right to liberty and security of person. No one shall be deprived of his liberty save in the following cases and in accordance with a procedure prescribed by law:

(a) the lawful detention of a person after conviction by a competent court;

(b) the lawful arrest or detention of a person for non-compliance with the lawful order of a court or in order to secure the fulfilment of any obligation prescribed by law;

(c) the lawful arrest or detention of a person effected for the purpose of bringing him before the competent legal authority on reasonable suspicion of having committed an offence or when it is reasonably considered necessary to prevent his committing an offence or fleeing after having done so;

(d) the detention of a minor by lawful order for the purpose of educational supervision or his lawful detention for the purpose of bringing him before the competent legal authority;

(e) the lawful detention of persons for the prevention of the spreading of infectious diseases, of persons of unsound mind, alcoholics or drug addicts or vagrants;

(f) the lawful arrest or detention of a person to prevent his effecting an unauthorised entry into the country or of a person against whom action is being taken with a view to deportation or extradition.

2. Everyone who is arrested shall be informed promptly, in a language which he understands, of the reasons for his arrest and of any charge against him.

3. Everyone arrested or detained in accordance with the provisions of paragraph 1.c of this article shall be brought promptly before a judge or other officer authorised by law to exercise judicial power and shall be entitled to trial within a reasonable time or to release pending trial. Release may be conditioned by guarantees to appear for trial.

4. Everyone who is deprived of his liberty by arrest or detention shall be entitled to take proceedings by which the lawfulness of his detention shall be decided speedily by a court and his release ordered if the detention is not lawful.

5. Everyone who has been the victim of arrest or detention in contravention of the provisions of this article shall have an enforceable right to compensation.

Article 6 Right to a fair trial

1. In the determination of his civil rights and obligations or of any criminal charge against him, everyone is entitled to a fair and public hearing within a reasonable time by an independent and impartial tribunal established by law. Judgement shall be pronounced publicly but the press and public may be excluded from all or part of the trial in the interests of morals, public order or national security in a democratic society, where the interests of juveniles or the protection of the private life of the parties so require, or to the extent strictly necessary in the opinion of the court in special circumstances where publicity would prejudice the interests of justice.

2. Everyone charged with a criminal offence shall be presumed innocent until proved guilty according to law.

3. Everyone charged with a criminal offence has the following minimum rights:

(a) to be informed promptly, in a language which he understands and in detail, of the nature and cause of the accusation against him;

(b) to have adequate time and facilities for the preparation of his defence;

(c) to defend himself in person or through legal assistance of his own choosing or, if he has not sufficient means to pay for legal assistance, to be given it free when the interests of justice so require;

(d) to examine or have examined witnesses against him and to obtain the attendance and examination of witnesses on his behalf under the same conditions as witnesses against him;

(d) to have the free assistance of an interpreter if he cannot understand or speak the language used in court.

Article 7 No Punishment without law

1. No one shall be held guilty of any criminal offence on account of any act or omission which did not constitute a criminal offence under national or international law at the time when it was committed. Nor shall a heavier penalty be imposed than the one that was applicable at the time the criminal offence was committed.

2. This article shall not prejudice the trial and punishment of any person for any act or omission which, at the time when it was committed, was criminal according to the general principles of law recognised by civilised nations.

Article 8 Right to respect for private and family life

1. Everyone has the right to respect for his private and family life, his home and his correspondence.

2. There shall be no interference by a public authority with the exercise of this right except such as is in accordance with the law and is necessary in a democratic society in the interests of national security, public safety or the economic well-being of the country, for the prevention of disorder or crime, for the protection of health or morals, or for the protection of the rights and freedoms of others.

Article 9 Freedom of thought, conscience and religion

1. Everyone has the right to freedom of thought, conscience and religion; this right includes freedom to change his religion or belief and freedom, either alone or in community with others and in public or private, to manifest his religion or belief, in worship, teaching, practice and observance.

2. Freedom to manifest one's religion or beliefs shall be subject only to such limitations as are prescribed by law and are necessary in a democratic society in the interests of public safety, for the protection of public order, health or morals, or for the protection of the rights and freedoms of others.

Article 10 Freedom of expression

1. Everyone has the right to freedom of expression. This right shall include freedom to hold opinions and to receive and impart information and ideas without interference by public authority and regardless of frontiers. This article shall not prevent States from requiring the licensing of broadcasting, television or cinema enterprises.

2. The exercise of these freedoms, since it carries with it duties and responsibilities, may be subject to such formalities, conditions, restrictions or penalties as are prescribed by law and are necessary in a democratic society, in the interests of national security, territorial integrity or public safety, for the prevention of disorder or crime, for the protection of health or morals, for the protection of the reputation or rights of others, for preventing the disclosure of information received in confidence, or for maintaining the authority and impartiality of the judiciary.

Article 11 Freedom of assembly and association

1. Everyone has the right to freedom of peaceful assembly and to freedom of association with others, including the right to form and to join trade unions for the protection of his interests.

2. No restrictions shall be placed on the exercise of these rights other than such as are prescribed by law and are necessary in a democratic society in the interests of national security or public safety, for the prevention of disorder or crime, for the protection of health or morals or for the protection of the rights and freedoms of others. This article shall not prevent the imposition of lawful restrictions on the exercise of these rights by members of the armed forces, of the police or of the administration of the State.

Article 12 Right to marry

Men and women of marriageable age have the right to marry and to found a family, according to the national laws governing the exercise of this right.

Article 13 Right to an effective remedy

Everyone whose rights and freedoms as set forth in this Convention are violated shall have an effective remedy before a national authority notwithstanding that the violation has been committed by persons acting in an official capacity.

Article 14 Prohibition of discrimination

The enjoyment of the rights and freedoms set forth in this Convention shall be secured without discrimination on any ground such as sex, race, colour, language, religion, political or other opinion, national or social origin, association with a national minority, property, birth or other status.

Article 15 Derogation in time of emergency

1. In time of war or other public emergency threatening the life of the nation any High Contracting Party may take measures derogating from its obligations under this Convention to the extent strictly required by the exigencies of the situation, provided that such measures are not inconsistent with its other obligations under international law.

2. No derogation from Article 2, except in respect of deaths resulting from lawful acts of war, or from Articles 3, 4 (paragraph 1) and 7 shall be made under this provision.

3. Any High Contracting Party availing itself of this right of derogation shall keep the Secretary General of the Council of Europe fully informed of the measures which it has taken and the reasons therefor. It shall also inform the Secretary General of the Council of Europe when such measures have ceased to operate and the provisions of the Convention are again being fully executed.

Article 16 Restrictions on political activity of aliens

Nothing in Articles 10, 11 and 14 shall be regarded as preventing the High Contracting Parties from imposing restrictions on the political activity of aliens.

Article 17 Prohibition of abuse of rights

Nothing in this Convention may be interpreted as implying for any State, group or person any right to engage in any activity or perform any act aimed at the destruction of any of the rights and freedoms set forth herein or at their limitation to a greater extent than is provided for in the Convention.

Article 18 Limitation on use of restrictions on rights

The restrictions permitted under this Convention to the said rights and freedoms shall not be applied for any purpose other than those for which they have been prescribed.

Section II—European Court of Human Rights

Article 19 Establishment of the Court

To ensure the observance of the engagements undertaken by the High Contracting Parties in the Convention and the Protocols thereto, there shall be set up a European Court of Human Rights, hereinafter referred to as 'the Court'. It shall function on a permanent basis.

Article 20 Number of judges

The Court shall consist of a number of judges equal to that of the High Contracting Parties.

Article 21 Criteria for office

1. The judges shall be of high moral character and must either possess the qualifications required for appointment to high judicial office or be jurisconsults of recognised competence.

2. The judges shall sit on the Court in their individual capacity.

3. During their term of office the judges shall not engage in any activity which is incompatible with their independence, impartiality or with the demands of a full-time office; all questions arising from the application of this paragraph shall be decided by the Court.

Article 22 Election of judges

1. The judges shall be elected by the Parliamentary Assembly with respect to each High Contracting Party by a majority of votes cast from a list of three candidates nominated by the High Contracting Party.

2. The same procedure shall be followed to complete the Court in the event of the accession of new High Contracting Parties and in filling casual vacancies.

Article 23 Terms of office

1. The judges shall be elected for a period of six years. They may be re-elected. However, the terms of office of one-half of the judges elected at the first election shall expire at the end of three years.

2. The judges whose terms of office are to expire at the end of the initial period of three years shall be chosen by lot by the Secretary General of the Council of Europe immediately after their election.

3. In order to ensure that, as far as possible, the terms of office of one-half of the judges are renewed every three years, the Parliamentary Assembly may decide, before proceeding to any subsequent election, that the term or terms of office of one or more judges to be elected shall be for a period other than six years but not more than nine and not less than three years.

4. In cases where more than one term of office is involved and where the Parliamentary Assembly applies the preceding paragraph, the allocation of the terms of office shall be

effected by a drawing of lots by the Secretary General of the Council of Europe immediately after the election.

5. A judge elected to replace a judge whose term of office has not expired shall hold office for the remainder of his predecessor's term.

6. The terms of office of judges shall expire when they reach the age of 70.

7. The judges shall hold office until replaced. They shall, however, continue to deal with such cases as they already have under consideration.

Article 24 Dismissal

No judge may be dismissed from his office unless the other judges decide by a majority of two-thirds that he has ceased to fulfil the required conditions.

Article 25 Registry and legal secretaries

The Court shall have a registry, the functions and organisation of which shall be laid down in the rules of the Court. The Court shall be assisted by legal secretaries.

Article 26 Plenary Court

The plenary Court shall:

(a) elect its President and one or two Vice-Presidents for a period of three years; they may be re-elected;

(b) set up Chambers, constituted for a fixed period of time;

(c) elect the Presidents of the Chambers of the Court; they may be re-elected;

(d) adopt the rules of the Court; and

(e) elect the Registrar and one or more Deputy Registrars.

Article 27 Committees, Chambers and Grand Chamber

1. To consider cases brought before it, the Court shall sit in committees of three judges, in Chambers of seven judges and in a Grand Chamber of seventeen judges. The Court's Chambers shall set up committees for a fixed period of time.

2. There shall sit as an ex officio member of the Chamber and the Grand Chamber the judge elected in respect of the State Party concerned or, if there is none or if he is unable to sit, a person of its choice who shall sit in the capacity of judge.

3. The Grand Chamber shall also include the President of the Court, the Vice-Presidents, the Presidents of the Chambers and other judges chosen in accordance with the rules of the Court. When a case is referred to the Grand Chamber under Article 43, no judge from the Chamber which rendered the judgment shall sit in the Grand Chamber, with the exception of the President of the Chamber and the judge who sat in respect of the State Party concerned.

Article 28 Declarations of inadmissibility by committees

A committee may, by a unanimous vote, declare inadmissible or strike out of its list of cases an application submitted under Article 34 where such a decision can be taken without further examination. The decision shall be final.

Article 29 Decisions by chambers on admissibility and merits

1. If no decision is taken under Article 28, a Chamber shall decide on the admissibility and merits of individual applications submitted under Article 34.

2. A Chamber shall decide on the admissibility and merits of inter-State applications submitted under Article 33.

3. The decision on admissibility shall be taken separately unless the Court, in exceptional cases, decides otherwise.

Article 30 Relinquishment of jurisdiction to the Grand Chamber

Where a case pending before a Chamber raises a serious question affecting the interpretation of the Convention or the protocols thereto, or where the resolution of a question before the Chamber might have a result inconsistent with a judgment previously delivered by the Court, the Chamber may, at any time before it has rendered its judgment, relinquish jurisdiction in favour of the Grand Chamber, unless one of the parties to the case objects.

Article 31 Powers of the Grand Chamber

The Grand Chamber shall:

(a) determine applications submitted either under Article 33 or Article 34 when a Chamber has relinquished jurisdiction under Article 30 or when the case has been referred to it under Article 43; and
(b) consider requests for advisory opinions submitted under Article 47.

Article 32 Jurisdiction of the Court

1. The jurisdiction of the Court shall extend to all matters concerning the interpretation and application of the Convention and the protocols thereto which are referred to it as provided in Articles 33, 34 and 47.

2. In the event of dispute as to whether the Court has jurisdiction, the Court shall decide.

Article 33 Inter-State cases

Any High Contracting Party may refer to the Court any alleged breach of the provisions of the Convention and the protocols thereto by another High Contracting Party.

Article 34 Individual applications

Chart of Declarations under former Articles 25 and 46 of the ECHR
The Court may receive applications from any person, non-governmental organisation or group of individuals claiming to be the victim of a violation by one of the High Contracting Parties of the rights set forth in the Convention or the protocols thereto. The High Contracting Parties undertake not to hinder in any way the effective exercise of this right.

Article 35 Admissibility criteria

1. The Court may only deal with the matter after all domestic remedies have been exhausted, according to the generally recognised rules of international law, and within a period of six months from the date on which the final decision was taken.

2. The Court shall not deal with any application submitted under Article 34 that:

(a) is anonymous; or

(b) is substantially the same as a matter that has already been examined by the Court or has already been submitted to another procedure of international investigation or settlement and contains no relevant new information.

3. The Court shall declare inadmissible any individual application submitted under Article 34 which it considers incompatible with the provisions of the Convention or the protocols thereto, manifestly ill-founded, or an abuse of the right of application.

4. The Court shall reject any application which it considers inadmissible under this Article. It may do so at any stage of the proceedings.

Article 36 Third party intervention

1. In all cases before a Chamber or the Grand Chamber, a High Contracting Party one of whose nationals is an applicant shall have the right to submit written comments and to take part in hearings.

2. The President of the Court may, in the interest of the proper administration of justice, invite any High Contracting Party which is not a party to the proceedings or any person concerned who is not the applicant to submit written comments or take part in hearings.

Article 37 Striking out applications

1. The Court may at any stage of the proceedings decide to strike an application out of its list of cases where the circumstances lead to the conclusion that:

(a) the applicant does not intend to pursue his application; or

(b) the matter has been resolved; or

(c) for any other reason established by the Court, it is no longer justified to continue the examination of the application.

However, the Court shall continue the examination of the application if respect for human rights as defined in the Convention and the protocols thereto so requires.

2. The Court may decide to restore an application to its list of cases if it considers that the circumstances justify such a course.

Article 38 Examination of the case and friendly settlement proceedings

1. If the Court declares the application admissible, it shall:

(a) pursue the examination of the case, together with the representatives of the parties, and if need be, undertake an investigation, for the effective conduct of which the States concerned shall furnish all necessary facilities;

(b) place itself at the disposal of the parties concerned with a view to securing a friendly settlement of the matter on the basis of respect for human rights as defined in the Convention and the protocols thereto.

2. Proceedings conducted under paragraph 1(b) shall be confidential.

Article 39 Finding of a friendly settlement

If a friendly settlement is effected, the Court shall strike the case out of its list by means of a decision which shall be confined to a brief statement of the facts and of the solution reached.

Article 40 Public hearings and access to documents

1. Hearings shall be in public unless the Court in exceptional circumstances decides otherwise.

2. Documents deposited with the Registrar shall be accessible to the public unless the President of the Court decides otherwise.

Article 41 Just satisfaction

If the Court finds that there has been a violation of the Convention or the protocols thereto, and if the internal law of the High Contracting Party concerned allows only partial reparation to be made, the Court shall, if necessary, afford just satisfaction to the injured party.

Article 42 Judgments of Chambers

Judgments of Chambers shall become final in accordance with the provisions of Article 44, paragraph 2.

Article 43 Referral to the Grand Chamber

1. Within a period of three months from the date of the judgment of the Chamber, any party to the case may, in exceptional cases, request that the case be referred to the Grand Chamber.

2. A panel of five judges of the Grand Chamber shall accept the request if the case raises a serious question affecting the interpretation or application of the Convention or the protocols thereto, or a serious issue of general importance.

3. If the panel accepts the request, the Grand Chamber shall decide the case by means of a judgment.

Article 44 Final Judgments

1. The judgment of the Grand Chamber shall be final.

2. The judgment of a Chamber shall become final:

(a) when the parties declare that they will not request that the case be referred to the Grand Chamber; or

(b) three months after the date of the judgment, if reference of the case to the Grand Chamber has not been requested; or

(c) when the panel of the Grand Chamber rejects the request to refer under Article 43.

3. The final judgment shall be published.

Article 45 Reasons for judgments and decisions

1. Reasons shall be given for judgments as well as for decisions declaring applications admissible or inadmissible.

2. If a judgment does not represent, in whole or in part, the unanimous opinion of the judges, any judge shall be entitled to deliver a separate opinion.

Article 46 Binding force and execution of judgments

1. The High Contracting Parties undertake to abide by the final judgment of the Court in any case to which they are parties.

2. The final judgment of the Court shall be transmitted to the Committee of Ministers, which shall supervise its execution.

Article 47 Advisory opinions

1. The Court may, at the request of the Committee of Ministers, give advisory opinions on legal questions concerning the interpretation of the Convention and the protocols thereto.

2. Such opinions shall not deal with any question relating to the content or scope of the rights or freedoms defined in Section I of the Convention and the protocols thereto, or with any other question which the Court or the Committee of Ministers might have to consider in consequence of any such proceedings as could be instituted in accordance with the Convention.

3. Decisions of the Committee of Ministers to request an advisory opinion of the Court shall require a majority vote of the representatives entitled to sit on the Committee.

Article 48 Advisory jurisdiction of the Court

The Court shall decide whether a request for an advisory opinion submitted by the Committee of Ministers is within its competence as defined in Article 47.

Article 49 Reasons for advisory opinions

1. Reasons shall be given for advisory opinions of the Court.

2. If the advisory opinion does not represent, in whole or in part, the unanimous opinion of the judges, any judge shall be entitled to deliver a separate opinion.

3. Advisory opinions of the Court shall be communicated to the Committee of Ministers.

Article 50 Expenditure on the Court

The expenditure on the Court shall be borne by the Council of Europe.

Article 51 Privileges and immunities of judges

The judges shall be entitled, during the exercise of their functions, to the privileges and immunities provided for in Article 40 of the Statute of the Council of Europe and in the agreements made thereunder.

Section III—Miscellaneous Provisions

Article 52 Inquiries by the Secretary General

On receipt of a request from the Secretary General of the Council of Europe any High Contracting Party shall furnish an explanation of the manner in which its internal law ensures the effective implementation of any of the provisions of the Convention.

Article 53 Safeguard for existing human rights

Nothing in this Convention shall be construed as limiting or derogating from any of the human rights and fundamental freedoms which may be ensured under the laws of any High Contracting Party or under any other agreement to which it is a Party.

Article 54 Powers of the committee of ministers

Nothing in this Convention shall prejudice the powers conferred on the Committee of Ministers by the Statute of the Council of Europe.

Article 55 Exclusion of other means of dispute settlement

The High Contracting Parties agree that, except by special agreement, they will not avail themselves of treaties, conventions or declarations in force between them for the purpose of submitting, by way of petition, a dispute arising out of the interpretation or application of this Convention to a means of settlement other than those provided for in this Convention.

Article 56 Territorial application

1. Any State may at the time of its ratification or at any time thereafter declare by notification addressed to the Secretary General of the Council of Europe that the present Convention shall, subject to paragraph 4 of this Article, extend to all or any of the territories for whose international relations it is responsible.

2. The Convention shall extend to the territory or territories named in the notification as from the thirtieth day after the receipt of this notification by the Secretary General of the Council of Europe.

3. The provisions of this Convention shall be applied in such territories with due regard, however, to local requirements.

4. Any State which has made a declaration in accordance with paragraph 1 of this article may at any time thereafter declare on behalf of one or more of the territories to which the declaration relates that it accepts the competence of the Court to receive applications from individuals, non-governmental organisations or groups of individuals as provided by Article 34 of the Convention.

Article 57 Reservations

1. Any State may, when signing this Convention or when depositing its instrument of ratification, make a reservation in respect of any particular provision of the Convention to the extent that any law then in force in its territory is not in conformity with the provision. Reservations of a general character shall not be permitted under this article.

2. Any reservation made under this article shall contain a brief statement of the law concerned.

Article 58 Denunciation

1. A High Contracting Party may denounce the present Convention only after the expiry of five years from the date on which it became a party to it and after six months' notice contained in a notification addressed to the Secretary General of the Council of Europe, who shall inform the other High Contracting Parties.

2. Such a denunciation shall not have the effect of releasing the High Contracting Party concerned from its obligations under this Convention in respect of any act which, being capable of constituting a violation of such obligations, may have been performed by it before the date at which the denunciation became effective.

3. Any High Contracting Party which shall cease to be a member of the Council of Europe shall cease to be a Party to this Convention under the same conditions.

4. [4]The Convention may be denounced in accordance with the provisions of the preceding paragraphs in respect of any territory to which it has been declared to extend under the terms of Article 56.’

Article 59 Signature and ratification

1. This Convention shall be open to the signature of the members of the Council of Europe. It shall be ratified. Ratifications shall be deposited with the Secretary General of the Council of Europe.

2. The present Convention shall come into force after the deposit of ten instruments of ratification.

3. As regards any signatory ratifying subsequently, the Convention shall come into force at the date of the deposit of its instrument of ratification.

4. The Secretary General of the Council of Europe shall notify all the members of the Council of Europe of the entry into force of the Convention, the names of the High Contracting Parties who have ratified it, and the deposit of all instruments of ratification which may be effected subsequently.

Done at Rome this 4th day of November 1950, in English and French, both texts being equally authentic, in a single copy which shall remain deposited in the archives of the Council of Europe. The Secretary General shall transmit certified copies to each of the signatories.

Convention Relating to the Status of Stateless Persons

(New York, September 28, 1954)

Preamble

The High Contracting Parties

Considering that the Charter of the United Nations and the Universal Declaration of Human Rights approved on 10 December 1948 by the General Assembly of the United Nations have affirmed the principle that human beings shall enjoy fundamental rights and freedoms without discrimination,

Considering that the United Nations has, on various occasions, manifested its profound concern for stateless persons and endeavoured to assure stateless persons the widest possible exercise of these fundamental rights and freedoms,

Considering that only those stateless persons who are also refugees are covered by the Convention relating to the Status of Refugees of 28 July 1951, and that there are many stateless persons who are not covered by that Convention,

Considering that it is desirable to regulate and improve the status of stateless persons by an international agreement.

Have agreed as follows:

Chapter I

General Provisions

Article 1 Definition of the term 'Stateless Person'

1. For the purpose of this Convention, the term 'stateless person' means a person who is not considered as a national by any State under the operation of its law.

2. This Convention shall not apply:

(i) To persons who are at present receiving from organs or agencies of the United Nations other than the United Nations High Commissioner for Refugees protection or assistance so long as they are receiving such protection or assistance;

(ii) To persons who are recognized by the competent authorities of the country in which they have taken residence as having the rights and obligations which are attached to the possession of the nationality of that country;

(iii) To persons with respect to whom there are serious reasons for considering that:

(a) They have committed a crime against peace, a war crime, or a crime against humanity, as defined in the international instruments drawn up to make provisions in respect of such crimes;

(b) They have committed a serious non-political crime outside the country of their residence prior to their admission to that country;

(c) They have been guilty of acts contrary to the purposes and principles of the United Nations.

Article 2 General obligations

Every stateless person has duties to the country in which he finds himself, which require in particular that he conform to its laws and regulations as well as to measures taken for the maintenance of public order.

Article 3 Non-discrimination

The Contracting States shall apply the provisions of this Convention to stateless persons without discrimination as to race, religion or country of origin.

Article 4 Religion

The Contracting States shall accord to stateless persons within their territories treatment at least as favourable as that accorded to their nationals with respect to freedom to practise their religion and freedom as regards the religious education of their children.

Article 5 Rights granted apart from this convention

Nothing in this Convention shall be deemed to impair any rights and benefits granted by a Contracting State to stateless persons apart from this Convention.

Article 6 The term 'in the same circumstances'

For the purpose of this Convention, the term 'in the same circumstances' implies that any requirements (including requirements as to length and conditions of sojourn or residence) which the particular individual would have to fulfil for the enjoyment of the right in question, if he were not a stateless person, must be fulfilled by him, with the exception of requirements which by their nature a stateless person is incapable of fulfilling.

Article 7 Exemption from reciprocity

1. Except where this Convention contains more favourable provisions, a Contracting State shall accord to stateless persons the same treatment as is accorded to aliens generally.

2. After a period of three years' residence, all stateless persons shall enjoy exemption from legislative reciprocity in the territory of the Contracting States.

3. Each Contracting State shall continue to accord to stateless persons the rights and benefits to which they were already entitled, in the absence of reciprocity, at the date of entry into force of this Convention for that State.

4. The Contracting States shall consider favourably the possibility of according to stateless persons, in the absence of reciprocity, rights and benefits beyond those to which they are entitled according to paragraphs 2 and 3, and to extending exemption from reciprocity to stateless persons who do not fulfil the conditions provided for in paragraphs 2 and 3.

The provisions of paragraphs 2 and 3 apply both to the rights and benefits referred to in Articles 13, 18, 19, 21 and 22 of this Convention and to rights and benefits for which this Convention does not provide.

Article 8 Exemption from exceptional measures

With regard to exceptional measures which may be taken against the person, property or interests of nationals or former nationals of a foreign State, the Contracting States shall not apply such measures to a stateless person solely on account of his having previously possessed the nationality of the foreign State in question. Contracting States which, under their legislation, are prevented from applying the general principle expressed in this Article shall, in appropriate cases, grant exemptions in favour of such stateless persons.

Article 9 Provisional measures

Nothing in this Convention shall prevent a Contracting State, in time of war or other grave and exceptional circumstances, from taking provisionally measures which it considers to be essential to the national security in the case of a particular person, pending a determination by the Contracting State that that person is in fact a stateless person and that the continuance of such measures is necessary in his case in the interests of national security.

Article 10 Continuity of residence

1. Where a stateless person has been forcibly displaced during the Second World War and removed to the territory of a Contracting State, and is resident there, the period of such enforced sojourn shall be considered to have been lawful residence within that territory.

2. Where a stateless person has been forcibly displaced during the Second World War from the territory of a Contracting State and has, prior to the date of entry into force of this Convention, returned there for the purpose of taking up residence, the period of residence before and after such enforced displacement shall be regarded as one uninterrupted period for any purpose for which uninterrupted residence is required.

Article 11 Stateless seamen

In the case of stateless persons regularly serving as crew members on board a ship flying the flag of a Contracting State, that State shall give sympathetic consideration to their establishment on its territory and the issue of travel documents to them or their temporary admission to its territory particularly with a view to facilitating their establishment in another country.

Chapter II
Juridical Status

Article 12 Personal status

1. The personal status of a stateless person shall be governed by the law of the country of his domicile or, if he has no domicile, by the law of the country of his residence.

2. Rights previously acquired by a stateless person and dependent on personal status, more particularly rights attaching to marriage, shall be respected by a Contracting State, subject to compliance, if this be necessary, with the formalities required by the law of that State, provided that the right in question is one which would have been recognized by the law of that State had he not become stateless.

Article 13 Movable and immovable property

The Contracting States shall accord to a stateless person treatment as favourable as possible and, in any event, not less favourable than that accorded to aliens generally in the same circumstances, as regards the acquisition of movable and immovable property and other rights pertaining thereto, and to leases and other contracts relating to movable and immovable property.

Article 14 Artistic rights and industrial property

In respect of the protection of industrial property, such as inventions, designs or models, trade marks, trade names, and of rights in literary, artistic and scientific works, a stateless person shall be accorded in the country in which he has his habitual residence the same protection as is accorded to nationals of that country. In the territory of any other Contracting State, he shall be accorded the same protection as is accorded in that territory to nationals of the country in which he has his habitual residence.

Article 15 Right of association

As regards non-political and non-profit-making associations and trade unions the Contracting States shall accord to stateless persons lawfully staying in their territory treatment as favourable as possible, and in any event, not less favourable than that accorded to aliens generally in the same circumstances.

Article 16 Access to Courts

1. A stateless person shall have free access to the Courts of Law on the territory of all Contracting States.

2. A stateless person shall enjoy in the Contracting State in which he has his habitual residence the same treatment as a national in matters pertaining to access to the Courts, including legal assistance and exemption from *cautio judicatum solvi.*

3. A stateless person shall be accorded in the matters referred to in paragraph 2 in countries other than that in which he has his habitual residence the treatment granted to a national of the country of his habitual residence.

Chapter III

Gainful Employment

Article 17 Wage-earning employment

1. The Contracting States shall accord to stateless persons lawfully staying in their territory treatment as favourable as possible and, in any event, not less favourable than that accorded to aliens generally in the same circumstances, as regards the right to engage in wage-earning employment.

2. The Contracting States shall give sympathetic consideration to assimilating the rights of all stateless persons with regard to wage-earning employment to those of nationals, and in particular of those stateless persons who have entered their territory pursuant to programmes of labour recruitment or under immigration schemes.

Article 18 Self-employment

The Contracting States shall accord to a stateless person lawfully in their territory treatment as favourable as possible and, in any event, not less favourable than that accorded to aliens generally in the same circumstances, as regards the right to engage on his own account in agriculture, industry, handicrafts and commerce and to establish commercial and industrial companies.

Article 19 Liberal professions

Each Contracting State shall accord to stateless persons lawfully staying in their territory who hold diplomas recognized by the competent authorities of that State, and who are desirous of practising a liberal profession, treatment as favourable as possible and, in any event, not less favourable than that accorded to aliens generally in the same circumstances.

Chapter IV

Welfare

Article 20 Rationing

Where a rationing system exists, which applies to the population at large and regulates the general distribution of products in short supply, stateless persons shall be accorded the same treatment as nationals.

Article 21 Housing

As regards housing, the Contracting States, in so far as the matter is regulated by laws or regulations or is subject to the control of public authorities, shall accord to stateless persons lawfully staying in their territory treatment as favourable as possible and, in any event, not less favourable than that accorded to aliens generally in the same circumstances.

Article 22 Public education

1. The Contracting States shall accord to stateless persons the same treatment as is accorded to nationals with respect to elementary education.

2. The Contracting States shall accord to stateless persons treatment as favourable as possible and, in any event, not less favourable than that accorded to aliens generally in the same circumstances, with respect to education other than elementary education and, in particular, as regards access to studies, the recognition of foreign school certificates, diplomas and degrees, the remission of fees and charges and the award of scholarships.

Article 23 Public relief

The Contracting States shall accord to stateless persons lawfully staying in their territory the same treatment with respect to public relief and assistance as is accorded to their nationals.

Article 24 Labour legislation and social security

1. The Contracting States shall accord to stateless persons lawfully staying in their territory the same treatment as is accorded to nationals in respect of the following matters:

(a) In so far as such matters are governed by laws or regulations or are subject to the control of administrative authorities: remuneration, including family allowances where these form part of remuneration, hours of work, overtime arrangements, holidays with pay, restrictions on home work, minimum age of employment, apprenticeship and training, women's work and the work of young persons, and the enjoyment of the benefits of collective bargaining;

(b) Social security (legal provisions in respect of employment injury, occupational diseases, maternity, sickness, disability, old age, death, unemployment, family responsibilities and any other contingency which, according to national laws or regulations, is covered by a social security scheme), subject to the following limitations:

(i) There may be appropriate arrangements for the maintenance of acquired rights and rights in course of acquisition;

(ii) National laws or regulations of the country of residence may prescribe special arrangements concerning benefits or portions of benefits which are payable wholly out of public funds, and concerning allowances paid to persons who do not fulfil the contribution conditions prescribed for the award of a normal pension.

2. The right to compensation for the death of a stateless person resulting from employment injury or from occupational disease shall not be affected by the fact that the residence of the beneficiary is outside the territory of the Contracting State.

3. The Contracting States shall extend to stateless persons the benefits of agreements concluded between them, or which may be concluded between them in the future, concerning the maintenance of acquired rights and rights in the process of acquisition in regard to social security, subject only to the conditions which apply to nationals of the States signatory to the agreements in question.

4. The Contracting States will give sympathetic consideration to extending to stateless persons so far as possible the benefits of similar agreements which may at any time be in force between such Contracting States and non-Contracting States.

Chapter V
Administrative Measures

Article 25 Administrative assistance

1. When the exercise of a right by a stateless person would normally require the assistance of authorities of a foreign country to whom he cannot have recourse, the Contracting State in whose territory he is residing shall arrange that such assistance be afforded to him by their own authorities.

2. The authority or authorities mentioned in paragraph 1 shall deliver or cause to be delivered under their supervision to stateless persons such documents or certifications as would normally be delivered to aliens by or through their national authorities.

3. Documents or certifications so delivered shall stand in the stead of the official instruments delivered to aliens by or through their national authorities, and shall be given credence in the absence of proof to the contrary.

4. Subject to such exceptional treatment as may be granted to indigent persons, fees may be charged for the services mentioned herein, but such fees shall be moderate and commensurate with those charged to nationals for similar services.

5. The provisions of this article shall be without prejudice to Articles 27 and 28.

Article 26 Freedom of movement

Each Contracting State shall accord to stateless persons lawfully in its territory the right to choose their place of residence and to move freely within its territory, subject to any regulations applicable to aliens generally in the same circumstances.

Article 27 Identity papers

The Contracting States shall issue identity papers to any stateless person in their territory who does not possess a valid travel document.

Article 28 Travel documents

The Contracting States shall issue to stateless persons lawfully staying in their territory travel documents for the purpose of travel outside their territory, unless compelling reasons of national security or public order otherwise require, and the provisions of the

Schedule to this Convention shall apply with respect to such documents. The Contracting States may issue such a travel document to any other stateless person in their territory; they shall in particular give sympathetic consideration to the issue of such a travel document to stateless persons in their territory who are unable to obtain a travel document from the country of their lawful residence.

Article 29 Fiscal charges

1. The Contracting States shall not impose upon stateless persons duties, charges or taxes, of any description whatsoever, other or higher than those which are or may be levied on their nationals in similar situations.

2. Nothing in the above paragraph shall prevent the application to stateless persons of the laws and regulations concerning charges in respect of the issue to aliens of administrative documents including identity papers.

Article 30 Transfer of assets

1. A Contracting State shall, in conformity with its laws and regulations, permit stateless persons to transfer assets which they have brought into its territory, to another country where they have been admitted for the purpose of resettlement.

2. A Contracting State shall give sympathetic consideration to the application of stateless persons for permission to transfer assets wherever they may be and which are necessary for their resettlement in another country to which they have been admitted.

Article 31 Expulsion

1. The Contracting States shall not expel a stateless person lawfully in their territory save on grounds of national security or public order.

2. The expulsion of such a stateless person shall be only in pursuance of a decision reached in accordance with due process of law. Except where compelling reasons of national security otherwise require, the stateless person shall be allowed to submit evidence to clear himself, and to appeal to and be represented for the purpose before the competent authority or a person or persons specially designated by the competent authority.

3. The Contracting States shall allow such a stateless person a reasonable period within which to seek legal admission into another country. The Contracting States reserve the right to apply during that period such internal measures as they may deem necessary.

Article 32 Naturalization

The Contracting States shall as far as possible facilitate the assimilation and naturalization of stateless persons. They shall in particular make every effort to expedite naturalization proceedings and to reduce as far as possible the charges and costs of such proceedings.

Chapter VI
Final Clauses

. . .

United Kingdom of Great Britain and Northern Ireland

'I have the honour further to state that the Government of the United Kingdom deposit the present instrument of ratification on the understanding that the combined effects of Articles 36 and 38 permit them to include in any declaration or notification made under paragraph 1 of Article 36 or paragraph 2 of Article 36 respectively any reservation consistent with Article 38 which the Government of the territory concerned might desire to make.'

'When ratifying the Convention relating to the Status of Stateless Persons which was opened for signature at New York on September 28, 1954, the Government of the United Kingdom have deemed it necessary to make certain reservations in accordance with paragraph 1 of Article 38 thereof the text of which is reproduced below:—

(1) The Government of the United Kingdom of Great Britain and Northern Ireland understand Articles 8 and 9 as not preventing them from taking in time of war or other grave and exceptional circumstances measures in the interests of national security in the case of a stateless person on the ground of his former nationality. The provisions of Article 8 shall not prevent the Government of the United Kingdom of Great Britain and Northern Ireland from exercising any rights over property or interests which they may acquire or have acquired as an Allied or Associated Power under a Treaty of Peace or other agreement or arrangement for the restoration of peace which has been or may be completed as a result of the Second World War. Furthermore, the provisions of Article 8 shall not affect the treatment to be accorded to any property or interests which at the date of entry into force of this Convention for the United Kingdom of Great Britain and Northern Ireland are under the control of the Government of the United Kingdom of Great Britain and Northern Ireland by reason of a state of war which exists or existed between them and any other state.

(2) The Government of the United Kingdom of Great Britain and Northern Ireland in respect of such of the matters referred to in sub-paragraph (b) of paragraph 1 of Article 24 as fall within the scope of the National Health Service, can only undertake to apply the provisions of that paragraph so far as the law allows.

(3) The Government of the United Kingdom of Great Britain and Northern Ireland cannot undertake to give effect to the obligations contained in paragraphs 1 and 2 of Article 25 and can only undertake to apply the provisions of paragraph 3 so far as the law allows.'

Convention Against Torture and Other Cruel, Inhuman or Degrading Treatment or Punishment

(United Nations Headquarters, New York, 4 February 1985)

Note: Articles 1–4 only.

The States Parties to this Convention,

Considering that, in accordance with the principles proclaimed in the Charter of the United Nations, recognition of the equal and inalienable rights of all members of the human family is the foundation of freedom, justice and peace in the world,

Recognizing that those rights derive from the inherent dignity of the human person,

Considering the obligation of States under the Charter, in particular Article 55, to promote universal respect for, and observance of, human rights and fundamental freedoms,

Having regard to Article 5 of the Universal Declaration of Human Rights and Article 7 of the International Covenant on Civil and Political Right, both of which provide that no one shall be subjected to torture or to cruel, inhuman or degrading treatment or punishment,

Having regard also to the Declaration on the Protection of All Persons from Being Subjected to Torture and Other Cruel, Inhuman or Degrading Treatment or Punishment, adopted by the General Assembly on 9 December 1975,

Desiring to make more effective the struggle against torture and other cruel, inhuman or degrading treatment or punishment throughout the world,

Have agreed as follows:

Part I

Article 1

1. For the purposes of this Convention, the term 'torture' means any act by which severe pain or suffering, whether physical or mental, is intentionally inflicted on a person for such purposes as obtaining from him or a third person information or a confession, punishing him for an act he or a third person has committed or is suspected of having committed, or intimidating or coercing him or a third person, or for any reason based on discrimination of any kind, when such pain or suffering is inflicted by or at the instigation of or with the consent or acquiescence of a public official or other person acting in an official capacity. It does not include pain or suffering arising only from, inherent in or incidental to lawful sanctions.

2. This article is without prejudice to any international instrument or national legislation which does or may contain provisions of wider application.

Article 2

1. Each State Party shall take effective legislative, administrative, judicial or other measures to prevent acts of torture in any territory under its jurisdiction.

2. No exceptional circumstances whatsoever, whether a state of war or a threat of war, internal political instability or any other public emergency, may be invoked as a justification of torture.

3. An order from a superior officer or a public authority may not be invoked as a justification of torture.

Article 3

1. No State Party shall expel, return ('*refouler*') or extradite a person to another State where there are substantial grounds for believing that he would be in danger of being subjected to torture.

2. For the purpose of determining whether there are such grounds, the competent authorities shall take into account all relevant considerations including, where applicable, the existence in the State concerned of a consistent pattern of gross, flagrant or mass violations of human rights.

Article 4

1. Each State Party shall ensure that all acts of torture are offences under its criminal law. The same shall apply to an attempt to commit torture and to an act by any person which constitutes complicity or participation in torture.

2. Each State Party shall make these offences punishable by appropriate penalties which take into account their grave nature.

Convention on the Rights of the Child

Adopted and opened for signature, ratification and accession by General Assembly resolution 44/25 of 20 November 1989 entry into force 2 September 1990, in accordance with article 49

Preamble

The States Parties to the present Convention,

Considering that, in accordance with the principles proclaimed in the Charter of the United Nations, recognition of the inherent dignity and of the equal and inalienable rights of all members of the human family is the foundation of freedom, justice and peace in the world,

Bearing in mind that the peoples of the United Nations have, in the Charter, reaffirmed their faith in fundamental human rights and in the dignity and worth of the human person, and have determined to promote social progress and better standards of life in larger freedom,

Recognizing that the United Nations has, in the Universal Declaration of Human Rights and in the International Covenants on Human Rights, proclaimed and agreed that everyone is entitled to all the rights and freedoms set forth therein, without distinction of any kind, such as race, colour, sex, language, religion, political or other opinion, national or social origin, property, birth or other status,

Recalling that, in the Universal Declaration of Human Rights, the United Nations has proclaimed that childhood is entitled to special care and assistance,

Convinced that the family, as the fundamental group of society and the natural environment for the growth and well-being of all its members and particularly children, should be afforded the necessary protection and assistance so that it can fully assume its responsibilities within the community,

Recognizing that the child, for the full and harmonious development of his or her personality, should grow up in a family environment, in an atmosphere of happiness, love and understanding,

Considering that the child should be fully prepared to live an individual life in society, and brought up in the spirit of the ideals proclaimed in the Charter of the United Nations, and in particular in the spirit of peace, dignity, tolerance, freedom, equality and solidarity,

Bearing in mind that the need to extend particular care to the child has been stated in the Geneva Declaration of the Rights of the Child of 1924 and in the Declaration of the Rights of the Child adopted by the General Assembly on 20 November 1959 and recognized in the Universal Declaration of Human Rights, in the International Covenant on Civil and Political Rights (in particular in articles 23 and 24), in the International Covenant on Economic, Social and Cultural Rights (in particular in article 10) and in the statutes and relevant instruments of specialized agencies and international organizations concerned with the welfare of children,

Bearing in mind that, as indicated in the Declaration of the Rights of the Child, "the child, by reason of his physical and mental immaturity, needs special safeguards and care, including appropriate legal protection, before as well as after birth",

Recalling the provisions of the Declaration on Social and Legal Principles relating to the Protection and Welfare of Children, with Special Reference to Foster Placement and Adoption Nationally and Internationally; the United Nations Standard Minimum Rules for the Administration of Juvenile Justice (The Beijing Rules); and the Declaration on the Protection of Women and Children in Emergency and Armed Conflict,

Recognizing that, in all countries in the world, there are children living in exceptionally difficult conditions, and that such children need special consideration,

Taking due account of the importance of the traditions and cultural values of each people for the protection and harmonious development of the child,

Recognizing the importance of international cooperation for improving the living conditions of children in every country, in particular in the developing countries,

Have agreed as follows:

PART I

Article 1

For the purposes of the present Convention, a child means every human being below the age of eighteen years unless under the law applicable to the child, majority is attained earlier.

Article 2

1. States Parties shall respect and ensure the rights set forth in the present Convention to each child within their jurisdiction without discrimination of any kind, irrespective of the child's or his or her parent's or legal guardian's race, colour, sex, language, religion, political or other opinion, national, ethnic or social origin, property, disability, birth or other status.

2. States Parties shall take all appropriate measures to ensure that the child is protected against all forms of discrimination or punishment on the basis of the status, activities, expressed opinions, or beliefs of the child's parents, legal guardians, or family members.

Article 3

1. In all actions concerning children, whether undertaken by public or private social welfare institutions, courts of law, administrative authorities or legislative bodies, the best interests of the child shall be a primary consideration.

2. States Parties undertake to ensure the child such protection and care as is necessary for his or her well-being, taking into account the rights and duties of his or her parents, legal guardians, or other individuals legally responsible for him or her, and, to this end, shall take all appropriate legislative and administrative measures.

3. States Parties shall ensure that the institutions, services and facilities responsible for the care or protection of children shall conform with the standards established by competent authorities, particularly in the areas of safety, health, in the number and suitability of their staff, as well as competent supervision.

Article 4

States Parties shall undertake all appropriate legislative, administrative, and other measures for the implementation of the rights recognized in the present Convention. With regard to economic, social and cultural rights, States Parties shall undertake such measures to the maximum extent of their available resources and, where needed, within the framework of international cooperation.

Article 5

States Parties shall respect the responsibilities, rights and duties of parents or, where applicable, the members of the extended family or community as provided for by local custom, legal guardians or other persons legally responsible for the child, to provide, in a manner consistent with the evolving capacities of the child, appropriate direction and guidance in the exercise by the child of the rights recognized in the present Convention.

Article 6

1. States Parties recognize that every child has the inherent right to life.

2. States Parties shall ensure to the maximum extent possible the survival and development of the child.

Article 7

1. The child shall be registered immediately after birth and shall have the right from birth to a name, the right to acquire a nationality and as far as possible, the right to know and be cared for by his or her parents.

2. States Parties shall ensure the implementation of these rights in accordance with their national law and their obligations under the relevant international instruments in this field, in particular where the child would otherwise be stateless.

Article 8

1. States Parties undertake to respect the right of the child to preserve his or her identity, including nationality, name and family relations as recognized by law without unlawful interference.

2. Where a child is illegally deprived of some or all of the elements of his or her identity, States Parties shall provide appropriate assistance and protection, with a view to re-establishing speedily his or her identity.

Article 9

1. States Parties shall ensure that a child shall not be separated from his or her parents against their will, except when competent authorities subject to judicial review determine, in accordance with applicable law and procedures, that such separation is necessary for the best interests of the child. Such determination may be necessary in a particular case such as one involving abuse or neglect of the child by the parents, or one where the parents are living separately and a decision must be made as to the child's place of residence.

2. In any proceedings pursuant to paragraph 1 of the present article, all interested parties shall be given an opportunity to participate in the proceedings and make their views known.

3. States Parties shall respect the right of the child who is separated from one or both parents to maintain personal relations and direct contact with both parents on a regular basis, except if it is contrary to the child's best interests.

4. Where such separation results from any action initiated by a State Party, such as the detention, imprisonment, exile, deportation or death (including death arising from any cause while the person is in the custody of the State) of one or both parents or of the child, that State Party shall, upon request, provide the parents, the child or, if appropriate, another member of the family with the essential information concerning the whereabouts of the absent member(s) of the family unless the provision of the information would be detrimental to the well-being of the child. States Parties shall further ensure that the submission of such a request shall of itself entail no adverse consequences for the person(s) concerned.

Article 10

1. In accordance with the obligation of States Parties under article 9, paragraph 1, applications by a child or his or her parents to enter or leave a State Party for the purpose of family reunification shall be dealt with by States Parties in a positive, humane and expeditious manner. States Parties shall further ensure that the submission of such a request shall entail no adverse consequences for the applicants and for the members of their family.

2. A child whose parents reside in different States shall have the right to maintain on a regular basis, save in exceptional circumstances personal relations and direct contacts with both parents. Towards that end and in accordance with the obligation of States Parties under article 9, paragraph 1, States Parties shall respect the right of the child and his or her parents to leave any country, including their own, and to enter their own country. The right to leave any country shall be subject only to such restrictions as are prescribed by law and which are necessary to protect the national security, public order

(ordre public), public health or morals or the rights and freedoms of others and are consistent with the other rights recognized in the present Convention.

Article 11

1. States Parties shall take measures to combat the illicit transfer and non-return of children abroad.

2. To this end, States Parties shall promote the conclusion of bilateral or multilateral agreements or accession to existing agreements.

Article 12

1. States Parties shall assure to the child who is capable of forming his or her own views the right to express those views freely in all matters affecting the child, the views of the child being given due weight in accordance with the age and maturity of the child.

2. For this purpose, the child shall in particular be provided the opportunity to be heard in any judicial and administrative proceedings affecting the child, either directly, or through a representative or an appropriate body, in a manner consistent with the procedural rules of national law.

Article 13

1. The child shall have the right to freedom of expression; this right shall include freedom to seek, receive and impart information and ideas of all kinds, regardless of frontiers, either orally, in writing or in print, in the form of art, or through any other media of the child's choice.

2. The exercise of this right may be subject to certain restrictions, but these shall only be such as are provided by law and are necessary:

(a) For respect of the rights or reputations of others; or

(b) For the protection of national security or of public order (ordre public), or of public health or morals.

Article 14

1. States Parties shall respect the right of the child to freedom of thought, conscience and religion.

2. States Parties shall respect the rights and duties of the parents and, when applicable, legal guardians, to provide direction to the child in the exercise of his or her right in a manner consistent with the evolving capacities of the child.

3. Freedom to manifest one's religion or beliefs may be subject only to such limitations as are prescribed by law and are necessary to protect public safety, order, health or morals, or the fundamental rights and freedoms of others.

Article 15

1. States Parties recognize the rights of the child to freedom of association and to freedom of peaceful assembly.

2. No restrictions may be placed on the exercise of these rights other than those imposed in conformity with the law and which are necessary in a democratic society in the interests of national security or public safety, public order (ordre public), the protection of public health or morals or the protection of the rights and freedoms of others.

Article 16

1. No child shall be subjected to arbitrary or unlawful interference with his or her privacy, family, home or correspondence, nor to unlawful attacks on his or her honour and reputation.

2. The child has the right to the protection of the law against such interference or attacks.

Article 17

States Parties recognize the important function performed by the mass media and shall ensure that the child has access to information and material from a diversity of national and international sources, especially those aimed at the promotion of his or her social, spiritual and moral well-being and physical and mental health.

To this end, States Parties shall:

(a) Encourage the mass media to disseminate information and material of social and cultural benefit to the child and in accordance with the spirit of article 29;

(b) Encourage international cooperation in the production, exchange and of such information and material from a diversity of cultural, national and international sources;

(c) Encourage the production and dissemination of children's books;

(d) Encourage the mass media to have particular regard to the linguistic needs of the child who belongs to a minority group or who is indigenous;

(e) Encourage the development of appropriate guidelines for the protection of the child from information and material injurious to his or her well-being, bearing in mind the provisions of articles 13 and 18.

Article 18

1. States Parties shall use their best efforts to ensure recognition of the principle that both parents have common responsibilities for the upbringing and development of the child. Parents or, as the case may be, legal guardians, have the primary responsibility for the upbringing and development of the child. The best interests of the child will be their basic concern.

2. For the purpose of guaranteeing and promoting the rights set forth in the present Convention, States Parties shall render appropriate assistance to parents and legal guardians in the performance of their child-rearing responsibilities and shall ensure the development of institutions, facilities and services for the care of children.

3. States Parties shall take all appropriate measures to ensure that children of working parents have the right to benefit from child-care services and facilities for which they are eligible.

Article 19

1. States Parties shall take all appropriate legislative, administrative, social and measures to protect the child from all forms of physical or mental violence, injury or abuse, neglect or negligent treatment, maltreatment or exploitation, including sexual abuse, while in the care of parent(s), legal guardian(s) or any other person who has the care of the child.

2. Such protective measures should, as appropriate, include effective procedures for the establishment of social programmes to provide necessary support for the child and for those who have the care of the child, as well as for other forms of prevention and for identification, reporting, referral, investigation, treatment and follow-up of instances of child maltreatment described heretofore, and, as appropriate, for judicial involvement.

Article 20

1. A child temporarily or permanently deprived of his or her family environment, or in whose own best interests cannot be allowed to remain in that environment, shall be entitled to special protection and assistance provided by the State.

2. States Parties shall in accordance with their national laws ensure alternative care for such a child.

3. Such care could include, *inter alia*, foster placement, kafalah of Islamic law, adoption or if necessary placement in suitable institutions for the care of children. When considering solutions, due regard shall be paid to the desirability of continuity in a child's upbringing and to the child's ethnic, religious, cultural and linguistic background.

Article 21

States Parties that recognize and/or permit the system of adoption shall ensure that the best interests of the child shall be the paramount consideration and they shall:

(a) Ensure that the adoption of a child is authorized only by competent authorities who determine, in accordance with applicable law and procedures and on the basis of all pertinent and reliable information, that the adoption is permissible in view of the child's status concerning parents, relatives and legal guardians and that, if required, the persons concerned have given their informed consent to the adoption on the basis of such counselling as may be necessary;

(b) Recognize that inter-country adoption may be considered as an alternative means of child's care, if the child cannot be placed in a foster or an adoptive family or cannot in any suitable manner be cared for in the child's country of origin;

(c) Ensure that the child concerned by inter-country adoption enjoys safeguards and standards equivalent to those existing in the case of national adoption;

(d) Take all appropriate measures to ensure that, in inter-country adoption, the placement does not result in improper financial gain for those involved in it;

(e) Promote, where appropriate, the objectives of the present article by concluding bilateral or multilateral arrangements or agreements, and endeavour, within this framework, to ensure that the placement of the child in another country is carried out by competent authorities or organs.

Article 22

1. States Parties shall take appropriate measures to ensure that a child who is seeking refugee status or who is considered a refugee in accordance with applicable international or domestic law and procedures shall, whether unaccompanied or accompanied by his or her parents or by any other person, receive appropriate protection and humanitarian assistance in the enjoyment of applicable rights set forth in the present Convention and in other international human rights or humanitarian instruments to which the said States are Parties.

2. For this purpose, States Parties shall provide, as they consider appropriate, cooperation in any efforts by the United Nations and other competent intergovernmental organizations or non-governmental organizations cooperating with the United Nations to protect and assist such a child and to trace the parents or other members of the family of any refugee child in order to obtain information necessary for reunification with his or her family. In cases where no parents or other members of the family can be found, the child shall be accorded the same protection as any other child permanently or temporarily deprived of his or her family environment for any reason, as set forth in the present Convention.

Article 23

1. States Parties recognize that a mentally or physically disabled child should enjoy a full and decent life, in conditions which ensure dignity, promote self-reliance and facilitate the child's active participation in the community.

2. States Parties recognize the right of the disabled child to special care and shall encourage and ensure the extension, subject to available resources, to the eligible child and those responsible for his or her care, of assistance for which application is made and which is appropriate to the child's condition and to the circumstances of the parents or others caring for the child.

3. Recognizing the special needs of a disabled child, assistance extended in accordance with paragraph 2 of the present article shall be provided free of charge, whenever possible, taking into account the financial resources of the parents or others caring for the child, and shall be designed to ensure that the disabled child has effective access to and receives education, training, health care services, rehabilitation services, preparation for employment and recreation opportunities in a manner conducive to the child's achieving the fullest possible social integration and individual development, including his or her cultural and spiritual development.

4. States Parties shall promote, in the spirit of international cooperation, the exchange of appropriate information in the field of preventive health care and of medical, psychological and functional treatment of disabled children, including dissemination of and access to information concerning methods of rehabilitation, education and vocational services, with the aim of enabling States Parties to improve their capabilities and skills and to widen their experience in these areas. In this regard, particular account shall be taken of the needs of developing countries.

Article 24

1. States Parties recognize the right of the child to the enjoyment of the highest attainable standard of health and to facilities for the treatment of illness and rehabilitation of

health. States Parties shall strive to ensure that no child is deprived of his or her right of access to such health care services.

2. States Parties shall pursue full implementation of this right and, in particular, shall take appropriate measures:

(a) To diminish infant and child mortality;

(b) To ensure the provision of necessary medical assistance and health care to all children with emphasis on the development of primary health care;

(c) To combat disease and malnutrition, including within the framework of primary health care, through, *inter alia*, the application of readily available technology and through the provision of adequate nutritious foods and clean drinking-water, taking into consideration the dangers and risks of environmental pollution;

(d) To ensure appropriate pre-natal and post-natal health care for mothers;

(e) To ensure that all segments of society, in particular parents and children, are informed, have access to education and are supported in the use of basic knowledge of child health and nutrition, the advantages of breastfeeding, hygiene and environmental sanitation and the prevention of accidents;

(f) To develop preventive health care, guidance for parents and family planning education and services.

3. States Parties shall take all effective and appropriate measures with a view to abolishing traditional practices prejudicial to the health of children.

4. States Parties undertake to promote and encourage international cooperation with a view to achieving progressively the full realization of the right recognized in the present article. In this regard, particular account shall be taken of the needs of developing countries.

Article 25

States Parties recognize the right of a child who has been placed by the competent authorities for the purposes of care, protection or treatment of his or her physical or mental health, to a periodic review of the treatment provided to the child and all other circumstances relevant to his or her placement.

Article 26

1. States Parties shall recognize for every child the right to benefit from social security, including social insurance, and shall take the necessary measures to achieve the full realization of this right in accordance with their national law.

2. The benefits should, where appropriate, be granted, taking into account the resources and the circumstances of the child and persons having responsibility for the maintenance of the child, as well as any other consideration relevant to an application for benefits made by or on behalf of the child.

Article 27

1. States Parties recognize the right of every child to a standard of living adequate for the child's physical, mental, spiritual, moral and social development.

2. The parent(s) or others responsible for the child have the primary responsibility to secure, within their abilities and financial capacities, the conditions of living necessary for the child's development.

3. States Parties, in accordance with national conditions and within their means, shall take appropriate measures to assist parents and others responsible for the child to implement this right and shall in case of need provide material assistance and support programmes, particularly with regard to nutrition, clothing and housing.

4. States Parties shall take all appropriate measures to secure the recovery of maintenance for the child from the parents or other persons having financial responsibility for the child, both within the State Party and from abroad. In particular, where the person having financial responsibility for the child lives in a State different from that of the child, States Parties shall promote the accession to international agreements or the conclusion of such agreements, as well as the making of other appropriate arrangements.

Article 28

1. States Parties recognize the right of the child to education, and with a view to achieving this right progressively and on the basis of equal opportunity, they shall, in particular:

(a) Make primary education compulsory and available free to all;

(b) Encourage the development of different forms of secondary education, including general and vocational education, make them available and accessible to every child, and take appropriate measures such as the introduction of free education and offering financial assistance in case of need;

(c) Make higher education accessible to all on the basis of capacity by every appropriate means;

(d) Make educational and vocational information and guidance available and accessible to all children;

(e) Take measures to encourage regular attendance at schools and the reduction of drop-out rates.

2. States Parties shall take all appropriate measures to ensure that school discipline is administered in a manner consistent with the child's human dignity and in conformity with the present Convention.

3. States Parties shall promote and encourage international cooperation in matters relating to education, in particular with a view to contributing to the elimination of ignorance and illiteracy throughout the world and facilitating access to scientific and technical knowledge and modern teaching methods. In this regard, particular account shall be taken of the needs of developing countries.

Article 29

1. States Parties agree that the education of the child shall be directed to:

(a) The development of the child's personality, talents and mental and physical abilities to their fullest potential;

(b) The development of respect for human rights and fundamental freedoms, and for the principles enshrined in the Charter of the United Nations;

(c) The development of respect for the child's parents, his or her own cultural identity, language and values, for the national values of the country in which the child is living, the country from which he or she may originate, and for civilizations different from his or her own;

(d) The preparation of the child for responsible life in a free society, in the spirit of understanding, peace, tolerance, equality of sexes, and friendship among all peoples, ethnic, national and religious groups and persons of indigenous origin;

(e) The development of respect for the natural environment.

2. No part of the present article or article 28 shall be construed so as to interfere with the liberty of individuals and bodies to establish and direct educational institutions, subject always to the observance of the principle set forth in paragraph 1 of the present article and to the requirements that the education given in such institutions shall conform to such minimum standards as may be laid down by the State.

Article 30

In those States in which ethnic, religious or linguistic minorities or persons of indigenous origin exist, a child belonging to such a minority or who is indigenous shall not be denied the right, in community with other members of his or her group, to enjoy his or her own culture, to profess and practise his or her own religion, or to use his or her own language.

Article 31

1. States Parties recognize the right of the child to rest and leisure, to engage in play and recreational activities appropriate to the age of the child and to participate freely in cultural life and the arts.

2. States Parties shall respect and promote the right of the child to participate fully in cultural and artistic life and shall encourage the provision of appropriate and equal opportunities for cultural, artistic, recreational and leisure activity.

Article 32

1. States Parties recognize the right of the child to be protected from economic exploitation and from performing any work that is likely to be hazardous or to interfere with the child's education, or to be harmful to the child's health or physical, mental, spiritual, moral or social development.

2. States Parties shall take legislative, administrative, social and educational measures to ensure the implementation of the present article. To this end, and having regard to the relevant provisions of other international instruments, States Parties shall in particular:

(a) Provide for a minimum age or minimum ages for admission to employment;

(b) Provide for appropriate regulation of the hours and conditions of employment;

(c) Provide for appropriate penalties or other sanctions to ensure the effective enforcement of the present article.

Article 33

States Parties shall take all appropriate measures, including legislative, administrative, social and educational measures, to protect children from the illicit use of drugs and psychotropic substances as defined in the relevant international treaties, and to prevent the use of children in the illicit production and trafficking of such substances.

Article 34

States Parties undertake to protect the child from all forms of sexual exploitation and sexual abuse. For these purposes, States Parties shall in particular take all appropriate national, bilateral and multilateral measures to prevent:

(a) The inducement or coercion of a child to engage in any unlawful sexual activity;
(b) The exploitative use of children in prostitution or other unlawful sexual practices;
(c) The exploitative use of children in pornographic performances and materials.

Article 35

States Parties shall take all appropriate national, bilateral and multilateral measures to prevent the abduction of, the sale of or traffic in children for any purpose or in any form.

Article 36

States Parties shall protect the child against all other forms of exploitation prejudicial to any aspects of the child's welfare.

Article 37

States Parties shall ensure that:

(a) No child shall be subjected to torture or other cruel, inhuman or degrading treatment or punishment. Neither capital punishment nor life imprisonment without possibility of release shall be imposed for offences committed by persons below eighteen years of age;

(b) No child shall be deprived of his or her liberty unlawfully or arbitrarily. The arrest, detention or imprisonment of a child shall be in conformity with the law and shall be used only as a measure of last resort and for the shortest appropriate period of time;

(c) Every child deprived of liberty shall be treated with humanity and respect for the inherent dignity of the human person, and in a manner which takes into account the needs of persons of his or her age. In particular, every child deprived of liberty shall be separated from adults unless it is considered in the child's best interest not to do so and shall have the right to maintain contact with his or her family through correspondence and visits, save in exceptional circumstances;

(d) Every child deprived of his or her liberty shall have the right to prompt access to legal and other appropriate assistance, as well as the right to challenge the legality of the deprivation of his or her liberty before a court or other competent, independent and impartial authority, and to a prompt decision on any such action.

Article 38

1. States Parties undertake to respect and to ensure respect for rules of international humanitarian law applicable to them in armed conflicts which are relevant to the child.

2. States Parties shall take all feasible measures to ensure that persons who have not attained the age of fifteen years do not take a direct part in hostilities.

3. States Parties shall refrain from recruiting any person who has not attained the age of fifteen years into their armed forces. In recruiting among those persons who have attained the age of fifteen years but who have not attained the age of eighteen years, States Parties shall endeavour to give priority to those who are oldest.

4. In accordance with their obligations under international humanitarian law to protect the civilian population in armed conflicts, States Parties shall take all feasible measures to ensure protection and care of children who are affected by an armed conflict.

Article 39

States Parties shall take all appropriate measures to promote physical and psychological recovery and social reintegration of a child victim of: any form of neglect, exploitation, or abuse; torture or any other form of cruel, inhuman or degrading treatment or punishment; or armed conflicts. Such recovery and reintegration shall take place in an environment which fosters the health, self-respect and dignity of the child.

Article 40

1. States Parties recognize the right of every child alleged as, accused of, or recognized as having infringed the penal law to be treated in a manner consistent with the promotion of the child's sense of dignity and worth, which reinforces the child's respect for the human rights and fundamental freedoms of others and which takes into account the child's age and the desirability of promoting the child's reintegration and the child's assuming a constructive role in society.

2. To this end, and having regard to the relevant provisions of international instruments, States Parties shall, in particular, ensure that:

(a) No child shall be alleged as, be accused of, or recognized as having infringed the penal law by reason of acts or omissions that were not prohibited by national or international law at the time they were committed;

(b) Every child alleged as or accused of having infringed the penal law has at least the following guarantees:

(i) To be presumed innocent until proven guilty according to law;

(ii) To be informed promptly and directly of the charges against him or her, and, if appropriate, through his or her parents or legal guardians, and to have legal or other appropriate assistance in the preparation and presentation of his or her defence;

(iii) To have the matter determined without delay by a competent, independent and impartial authority or judicial body in a fair hearing according to law, in the presence of legal or other appropriate assistance and, unless it is considered not to be in the best interest of the child, in particular, taking into account his or her age or situation, his or her parents or legal guardians;

(iv) Not to be compelled to give testimony or to confess guilt; to examine or have examined adverse witnesses and to obtain the participation and examination of witnesses on his or her behalf under conditions of equality;

(v) If considered to have infringed the penal law, to have this decision and any measures imposed in consequence thereof reviewed by a higher competent, independent and impartial authority or judicial body according to law;

(vi) To have the free assistance of an interpreter if the child cannot understand or speak the language used;

(vii) To have his or her privacy fully respected at all stages of the proceedings.

3. States Parties shall seek to promote the establishment of laws, procedures, authorities and institutions specifically applicable to children alleged as, accused of, or recognized as having infringed the penal law, and, in particular:

(a) The establishment of a minimum age below which children shall be presumed not to have the capacity to infringe the penal law;

(b) Whenever appropriate and desirable, measures for dealing with such children without resorting to judicial proceedings, providing that human rights and legal safeguards are fully respected.

4. A variety of dispositions, such as care, guidance and supervision orders; counselling; probation; foster care; education and vocational training programmes and other alternatives to institutional care shall be available to ensure that children are dealt with in a manner appropriate to their well-being and proportionate both to their circumstances and the offence.

Article 41

Nothing in the present Convention shall affect any provisions which are more conducive to the realization of the rights of the child and which may be contained in:

(a) The law of a State party; or

(b) International law in force for that State.

INDEX